THE YEAR'S WORK 2000

DBS Arts Library

This book is due for return on or before the last date shown below.

REFERENCE ONLY

No LOAN

The Year's Work in English Studies Volume 81

Covering work published in 2000

Edited by
WILLIAM BAKER
and
KENNETH WOMACK

with associate editors

JANET BEER
JOHN BRANNIGAN
DOREEN D'CRUZ
OLGA FISCHER
LISA HOPKINS
JACQUELINE M. LABBE
STEVEN PRICE
MARY SWAN

Swets
£184 stg.

Published for
THE ENGLISH ASSOCIATION

by

OXFORD
UNIVERSITY PRESS

OXFORD

UNIVERSITY PRESS

Great Clarendon Street, Oxford OX2 6DP, UK

Oxford University Press is a department of the University of Oxford.
It furthers the University's objective of excellence in research, scholarship,
and education by publishing worldwide in

Oxford New York

Athens Auckland Bangkok Bogotá Buenos Aire Cape Town
Chennai Dar es Salaam Delhi Florence Hong Kong Istanbul Karachi
Kolkata Kuala Lumpur Madrid Melbourne Mexico City Mumbai Nairobi
Paris São Paulo Shanghai Taipei Tokyo Toronto Warsaw

Oxford is a registered trade mark of Oxford University Press
in the UK and in certain other countries

Published in the United States
by Oxford University Press Inc., New York

British Library Cataloguing in Publication Data

Data available

ISSN 0084–4144
ISBN 0–19–852744–6

1 3 5 7 9 10 8 6 4 2

Typeset by Hope Services (Abingdon) Ltd
Printed in Great Britain
on acid-free paper by
Biddles Ltd.,
Guildford and King's Lynn

The English Association

The object of The English Association is to promote the knowledge and appreciation of English language and its literatures.

The Association pursues these aims by creating opportunities of co-operation among all those interested in English; by furthering the recognition of English as essential in education; by discussing methods of English teaching; by holding lectures, conferences, and other meetings; by publishing several journals, books, and leaflets; and by forming local branches overseas and at home.

Publications

The Year's Work in English Studies. An annual narrative bibliography which aims to cover all work of quality in english studies published in a given year. Published by Oxford University Press.

The Year's Work in Critical and Cultural Theory. An annual narrative bibliography which aims to provide comprehensive cover of all work of quality in critical and cultural theory published in a given year. Published by Oxford University Press.

Essays and Studies. A well-established series of annual themed volumes edited each year by a distinguished academic. The 2002 volume is *Writing Gender and Genre in Medieval Literature: Approaches to Old and Middle English Texts* edited by Elaine Treharne and published by D.S. Brewer.

English. This internationally-known journal of the Association is aimed at teachers of English in universities and colleges, with articles on all aspects of literature and critical theory and an extensive reviews section. Three issues per year.

Use of English. The longest-standing journal for English teachers in schools and colleges. Three issues per year.

English 4–11. Designed and developed by primary English specialists to give practical help to primary and middle school teachers. Three issues per year.

Membership

Membership information can be found at http://www.le.ac.uk/engassoc or please write to The English Association, University of Leicester, University Road, Leicester LE1 7RH, UK or email: engassoc@le.ac.uk.

The Year's Work in English Studies

Subscriptions for Volume 81

Institutional (combined rate to both *The Year's Work in English Studies* and *The Year's Work in Critical and Cultural Theory*): UK and Europe £184, USA and rest of world $294.

Personal rates: as above.

Online Access

For details please email Oxford University Press Journals Customer Services on: jnls.cust.serv@oup.co.uk.

Order Information

Payment is required with all orders and may be made by: cheque (made payable to Oxford University Press), National Girobank (account 500 1056), credit card (Mastercard, Visa, American Express), UNESCO coupons.

Bankers: Barclays Bank plc, PO Box 333, Oxford, UK. Code 20–65–18, account 00715654.

Please send orders to: Journal Subscriptions Department, Oxford University Press, Great Clarendon Street, Oxford OX2 6DP, UK. Tel: +44 (0)1865 267907, fax: +44 (0)1865 267485, jnl.orders@oup.co.uk.

Back Issues

The current volume and the two previous are available from Journals Subscriptions Department, Oxford University Press, Great Clarendon Street, Oxford OX2 6DP, UK. Tel:+44 (0)1865 267907, fax:+44 (0)1865 267485, jnl.orders@oup.co.uk. Earlier volumes can be obtained from the Periodicals Service Company, 11 Main Street, Germantown, NY 12526, USA. Tel:+1 (518) 537 4700, fax: +1 (518) 537 5899.

Electronic Notification of Contents

The Table of Contents email alerting service allows anyone who registers his or her email address to be notified via email when new content goes online. Details are available at http://www3.oup.co.uk/ywes/etoc.html.

Advertising

Enquiries should be made to Helen Pearson, Oxford Journals Advertising, PO Box 347, Abingdon SO, Oxford OX14 5AA, UK; tel/fax: +44 (0)1235 201904, email: helen@oxfordads.com.

Contents

University; Paul Poplawski, University of Leicester; John Nash,
Trinity College, Dublin; John Brannigan, University College
Dublin; Maggie B. Gale, University of Birmingham; Malcolm Page,
Simon Fraser University; Alice Entwistle, University of the West
of England, Bristol; Fran Brearton, Queen's University Belfast

Abbreviations

1. Journals, Series and Reference Works

1650–1850	*1650–1850 Ideas, Aesthetics, and Inquiries in the Early Modern Era*
A&D	*Art and Design*
A&E	*Anglistik und Englishunterricht*
AAAJ	*Accounting, Auditing and Accountability Journal*
AAR	*African American Review*
ABäG	*Amsterdamer Beiträge zur Älteren Germanistik*
ABC	*American Book Collector*
ABELL	*Annual Bibliography of English Language and Literature*
ABM	*Antiquarian Book Monthly Review*
ABQ	*American Baptist Quarterly*
ABR	*American Benedictine Review*
ABSt	*A/B: Auto/Biography Studies*
AC	*Archeologia Classica*
Academy Forum	*Academy Forum*
AcadSF	Academia Scientiarum Fennica
ACar	*Analecta Cartusiana*
ACH	*Australian Cultural History*
ACLALSB	*ACLALS Bulletin*
ACM	*Aligarh Critical Miscellany*
ACS	*Australian–Canadian Studies: A Journal for the Humanities and Social Sciences*
Acta	Acta (Binghamton, NY)
AdI	*Annali d'Italianistica*
ADS	*Australasian Drama Studies*
AEB	*Analytical and Enumerative Bibliography*
Æstel	*Æstel*
AF	*Anglistische Forschungen*
AfricanA	*African Affairs*
AfrSR	*African Studies Review*
AgeJ	*Age of Johnson: A Scholarly Annual*
Agenda	*Agenda*
Agni	*Agni Review*
AH	*Art History*
AHR	*American Historical Review*
AHS	*Australian Historical Studies*
AI	*American Imago*
AICRJ	*American Indian Culture and Research Journal*

AIQ	*American Indian Quarterly*
AJ	*Art Journal*
AJGLL	*American Journal of Germanic Linguistics and Literatures*
AJL	*Australian Journal of Linguistics*
AJP	*American Journal of Psychoanalysis*
AJPH	*Australian Journal of Politics and History*
AJS	*American Journal of Semiotics*
AKML	Abhandlungen zur Kunst-, Musik- and Literaturwissenschaft
AL	*American Literature*
ALA	African Literature Association Annuals
ALASH	*Acta Linguistica Academiae Scientiarum Hungaricae*
Albion	*Albion*
AlexS	Alexander Shakespeare
ALH	*Acta Linguistica Hafniensia; International Journal of Linguistics*
Alif	*Journal of Comparative Poetics* (Cairo, Egypt)
ALitASH	*Acta Literaria Academiae Scientiarum Hungaricae*
Allegorica	*Allegorica*
ALR	*American Literary Realism, 1870–1910*
ALS	*Australian Literary Studies*
ALT	*African Literature Today*
Alternatives	*Alternatives*
AmasJ	*Amerasian Journal*
AmDram	*American Drama*
Americana	*Americana*
AmerP	*American Poetry*
AmerS	*American Studies*
AmLH	*American Literary History*
AmLS	American Literary Scholarship: An Annual
AMon	*Atlantic Monthly*
AmPer	*American Periodicals*
AmRev	*Americas Review: A Review of Hispanic Literature and Art of the USA*
Amst	*Amerikastudien/American Studies*
AN	Acta Neophilologica
Anaïs	*Anaïs*
AnBol	*Analecta Bollandiana*
ANF	*Arkiv för Nordisk Filologi*
Angelaki	*Angelaki*
Anglia	*Anglia: Zeitschrift für Englische Philologie*
Anglistica	*Anglistica*
Anglistik	*Anglistik: Mitteilungen des Verbandes Deutscher Anglisten*
AnH	*Analecta Husserliana*
AnL	*Anthropological Linguistics*
AnM	*Annuale Mediaevale*
Ann	*Annales: Économies, Sociétés, Civilisations*

ANQ	*ANQ: A Quarterly Journal of Short Articles, Notes and Reviews* (formerly *American Notes and Queries*)
AntColl	*Antique Collector*
AntigR	*Antigonish Review*
Antipodes	*Antipodes: A North American Journal of Australian Literature*
ANZSC	*Australian and New Zealand Studies in Canada*
ANZTR	*Australian and New Zealand Theatre Record*
APBR	*Atlantic Provinces Book Review*
APL	*Antwerp Papers in Linguistics*
AppLing	*Applied Linguistics*
APR	*American Poetry Review*
AQ	*American Quarterly*
Aquarius	*Aquarius*
AR	*Antioch Review*
ArAA	*Arbeiten aus Anglistik und Amerikanistik*
Arcadia	*Arcadia*
Archiv	*Archiv für das Stadium der Neueren Sprachen und Literaturen*
ARCS	*American Review of Canadian Studies*
ArdenS	Arden Shakespeare
ArielE	*Ariel: A Review of International English Literature*
ArkQ	*Arkansas Quarterly: A Journal of Criticism*
ArkR	*Arkansas Review: A Journal of Criticism*
ArQ	*Arizona Quarterly*
ARS	Augustan Reprint Society
ARSR	*Australian Religion Studies Review*
ArtB	*Art Bulletin*
Arth	*Arthuriana*
ArthI	*Arthurian Interpretations*
ArthL	*Arthurian Literature*
Arv	*Arv: Nordic Yearbook of Folklore*
AS	*American Speech*
ASch	*American Scholar*
ASE	*Anglo-Saxon England*
ASInt	*American Studies International*
ASoc	*Arts in Society*
Aspects	*Aspects: Journal of the Language Society* (University of Essex)
AspectsAF	*Aspects of Australian Fiction*
ASPR	*Anglo-Saxon Poetic Records*
ASSAH	*Anglo-Saxon Studies in Archaeology and History*
Assaph	*Assaph: Studies in the Arts (Theatre Studies)*
Assays	*Assays: Critical Approaches to Medieval and Renaissance Texts*
ASUI	*Analele Stiintifice ale Universitatii 'Al.I. Cuza' din lasi (Serie Noua), e. Lingvistica*

ATQ	*American Transcendental Quarterly: A Journal of New England Writers*
AuBR	*Australian Book Review*
AuFolk	*Australian Folklore*
AuFS	*Australian Feminist Studies*
AuJL	*Australian Journal of Linguistics*
AUMLA	*Journal of the Australasian Universities Language and Literature Association*
AuS	*Australian Studies*
AuSA	*Australian Studies* (Australia)
AusCan	*Australian–Canadian Studies*
AusPl	*Australian Playwrights*
AusRB	*Australians' Review of Books*
AuVSJ	*Australasian Victorian Studies Journal*
AuWBR	*Australian Women's Book Review*
AvC	*Avalon to Camelot*
AY	*Arthurian Yearbook*
BakhtinN	*Bakhtin Newsletter*
BALF	*Black American Literature Forum*
BAReview	*British Academy Review*
BARS Bulletin	*British Association for Romantic Studies Bulletin & Review*
BAS	*British and American Studies*
BASAM	*BASA Magazine*
BathH	*Bath History*
BayreuthAS	Bayreuth African Studies
BB	*Bulletin of Bibliography*
BBCS	*Bulletin of the Board of Celtic Studies*
BBCSh	BBC Shakespeare
BBN	*British Book News*
BBSIA	*Bulletin Bibliographique de la Société Internationale Arthurienne*
BC	*Book Collector*
BCan	*Books in Canada*
BCMA	*Bulletin of Cleveland Museum of Art*
BCS	*B.C. Studies*
BDEC	*Bulletin of the Department of English* (Calcutta)
BDP	*Beiträge zur Deutschen Philologie*
Belfagor	*Belfagor: Rassegna di Varia Umanità*
BEPIF	*Bulletin des Itudes Portugaises et Brésiliennes*
BFLS	*Bulletin de la Faculté des Lettres de Strasbourg*
BGDSL	*Beiträge zur Geschichte der Deutschen Sprache und Literatur*
BHI	*British Humanities Index*
BHL	*Bibliotheca Hagiographica Latina Antiquae et Mediae Aetatis*
BHM	*Bulletin of the History of Medicine*
BHR	*Bibliothèque d'Humanisme et Renaissance*
BHS	*Bulletin of Hispanic Studies*

BI	*Books at Iowa*
Bibliotheck	*Bibliotheck: A Scottish Journal of Bibliography and Allied Topics*
Biography	*Biography: An Interdisciplinary Quarterly*
BIS	*Browning Institute Studies: An Annual of Victorian Literary and Cultural History*
BJA	*British Journal of Aesthetics*
BJCS	*British Journal of Canadian Studies*
BJDC	*British Journal of Disorders of Communication*
BJECS	*British Journal for Eighteenth-Century Studies*
BJHP	*British Journal for the History of Philosophy*
BJHS	*British Journal for the History of Science*
BJJ	*Ben Jonson Journal*
BJL	*Belgian Journal of Linguistics*
BJPS	*British Journal for the Philosophy of Science*
BJRL	*Bulletin of the John Rylands* (University Library of Manchester)
BJS	*British Journal of Sociology*
Blake	*Blake: An Illustrated Quarterly*
BLE	*Bulletin de Littérature Ecclésiastique*
BLJ	*British Library Journal*
BLR	*Bodleian Library Record*
BN	*Beiträge zur Namenforschung*
BNB	*British National Bibliography*
BoH	*Book History*
Bookbird	*Bookbird*
Borderlines	*Borderlines*
Boundary	*Boundary 2: A Journal of Postmodern Literature and Culture*
BP	*Banasthali Patrika*
BPMA	*Bulletin of Philadelphia Museum of Art*
BPN	*Barbara Pym Newsletter*
BQ	*Baptist Quarterly*
BRASE	Basic Readings in Anglo-Saxon England
BRH	*Bulletin of Research in the Humanities*
Brick	*Brick: A Journal of Reviews*
BRMMLA	*Bulletin of the Rocky Mountain Modern Language Association*
BSANZB	*Bibliographical Society of Australia and New Zealand Bulletin*
BSE	*Brno Studies in English*
BSEAA	*Bulletin de la Société d'Études Anglo-Américaines des XVIIe et XVIIIe Siècles*
BSJ	*Baker Street Journal: An Irregular Quarterly of Sherlockiana*
BSLP	*Bulletin de la Société de Linguistique de Paris*
BSNotes	*Browning Society Notes*
BSRS	*Bulletin of the Society for Renaissance Studies*

BSSA	*Bulletin de la Société de Stylistique Anglaise*
BST	*Brontë Society Transactions*
BSUF	*Ball State University Forum*
BTHGNewsl	*Book Trade History Group Newsletter*
BTLV	*Bijdragen tot de Taal-, Land- en Volkenhunde*
Bullán	*Bullán*
BunyanS	*Bunyan Studies*
BuR	*Bucknell Review*
BurlM	*Burlington Magazine*
BurnsC	*Burns Chronicle*
BWPLL	Belfast Working Papers in Language and Linguistics
BWVACET	*Bulletin of the West Virginia Association of College English Teachers*
ByronJ	*Byron Journal*
CABS	Contemporary Authors Bibliographical Series
CahiersE	*Cahiers Élisabéthains*
CAIEF	*Cahiers de l'Association Internationale des Études Françaises*
Caliban	*Caliban* (Toulouse, France)
Callaloo	*Callaloo*
CalR	*Calcutta Review*
CamObsc	*Camera Obscura: A Journal of Feminism and Film Theory*
CamR	*Cambridge Review*
CanD	*Canadian Drama / L'Art Dramatique Canadienne*
C&L	*Christianity and Literature*
C&Lang	*Communication and Languages*
C&M	*Classica et Medievalia*
CanL	*Canadian Literature*
CAnn	*Carlyle Annual*
CanPo	*Canadian Poetry*
CapR	*Capilano Review*
CARA	Centre Aixois de Recherches Anglaises
Carib	*Carib*
Caribana	*Caribana*
CaribW	*Caribbean Writer*
CarR	*Caribbean Review*
Carrell	*Carrell: Journal of the Friends of the University of Miami Library*
CASE	Cambridge Studies in Anglo-Saxon England
CaudaP	*Cauda Pavonis*
CBAA	*Current Bibliography on African Affairs*
CBEL	*Cambridge Bibliography of English Literature*
CCRev	*Comparative Civilizations Review*
CCrit	*Comparative Criticism: An Annual Journal*
CCTES	*Conference of College Teachers of English Studies*
CCV	*Centro de Cultura Valenciana*
CDALB	*Concise Dictionary of American Literary Biography*
CDCP	Comparative Drama Conference Papers

CDIL	*Cahiers de l'Institut de Linguistique de Louvain*
CdL	*Cahiers de Lexicologie*
CE	*College English*
CEA	*CEA Critic*
CEAfr	*Cahiers d'Études Africaines*
CE&S	*Commonwealth Essays and Studies*
CentR	*Centennial Review*
Cervantes	*Cervantes*
CFM	*Canadian Fiction Magazine*
CFS	*Cahiers Ferdinand de Saussure: Revue de Linguistique Générale*
Chapman	*Chapman*
Chasqui	*Chasqui*
ChauR	*Chaucer Review*
ChauS	*Chaucer Studion*
ChauY	*Chaucer Yearbook*
ChH	*Church History*
ChildL	*Children's Literature*
ChiR	*Chicago Review*
ChLB	*Charles Lamb Bulletin*
CHLSSF	*Commentationes Humanarum Litterarum Societatis Scientiarum Fennicae*
CHR	*Camden History Review*
CHum	*Computers and the Humanities*
CI	Critical Idiom
CILT	Amsterdam Studies in the Theory and History of the Language Sciences IV: Current Issues in Linguistic Theory
Cinéaste	*Cinéaste*
CinJ	*Cinema Journal*
CIQ	*Colby Quarterly*
CISh	Contemporary Interpretations of Shakespeare
Cithara	*Cithara: Essays in the Judaeo-Christian Tradition*
CJ	*Classical Journal*
CJE	*Cambridge Journal of Education*
CJH	*Canadian Journal of History*
CJIS	*Canadian Journal of Irish Studies*
CJL	*Canadian Journal of Linguistics*
CJR	*Christian–Jewish Relations*
CK	*Common Knowledge*
CL	*Comparative Literature* (Eugene, OR)
CLAJ	*CLA Journal*
CLAQ	*Children's Literature Association Quarterly*
ClarkN	*Clark Newsletter: Bulletin of the UCLA Center for Seventeenth- and Eighteenth-Century Studies*
ClassW	*Classical World*
CLC	*Columbia Library Columns*
CLIN	*Cuadernos de Literatura*

ClioI	*Clio: A Journal of Literature, History and the Philosophy of History*
CLQ	*Colby Library Quarterly*
CLS	*Comparative Literature Studies*
Clues	*Clues: A Journal of Detection*
CMCS	*Cambridge Medieval Celtic Studies*
CML	*Classical and Modern Literature*
CN	*Chaucer Newsletter*
CNIE	*Commonwealth Novel in English*
CogLing	*Cognitive Linguistics*
Cognition	*Cognition*
ColB	*Coleridge Bulletin*
ColF	*Columbia Forum*
Collections	*Collections*
CollG	*Colloquia Germanica*
CollL	*College Literature*
Comitatus	*Comitatus: A Journal of Medieval and Renaissance Studies*
Commentary	*Commentary*
Commonwealth	*Commonwealth*
Comparatist	*Comparatist: Journal of the Southern Comparative Literature Association*
CompD	*Comparative Drama*
CompLing	*Contemporary Linguistics*
ConfLett	*Confronto Letterario*
ConL	*Contemporary Literature*
Connotations	*Connotations*
ConnR	*Connecticut Review*
Conradian	*Conradian*
Conradiana	*Conradiana: A Journal of Joseph Conrad Studies*
ContempR	*Contemporary Review*
Coppertales	*Coppertales: A Journal of Rural Arts*
Cosmos	*Cosmos*
CP	*Concerning Poetry*
CQ	*Cambridge Quarterly*
CR	*Critical Review*
CRCL	*Canadian Review of Comparative Literature*
CRev	*Chesterton Review*
CRevAS	*Canadian Review of American Studies*
Crit	*Critique: Studies in Modern Fiction*
CritI	*Critical Inquiry*
Criticism	*Criticism: A Quarterly for Literature and the Arts*
Critique	*Critique (Paris)*
CritQ	*Critical Quarterly*
CritT	*Critical Texts: A Review of Theory and Criticism*
CrM	*Critical Mass*
CRNLE	*CRNLE Reviews Journal*
Crossings	*Crossings*
CRUX	*CRUX: A Journal on the Teaching of English*

CS	*Critical Survey*
CSASE	Cambridge Studies in Anglo-Saxon England
CSCC	*Case Studies in Contemporary Criticism*
CSELT	Cambridge Studies in Eighteenth-Century Literature and Thought
CSLBull	*Bulletin of the New York C.S. Lewis Society*
CSLL	*Cardozo Studies in Law and Literature*
CSML	Cambridge Studies in Medieval Literature
CSNCLC	Cambridge Studies in Nineteenth-Century Literature and Culture
CSPC	Cambridge Studies in Paleography and Codicology
CSR	Cambridge Studies in Romanticism
CSRev	*Christian Scholar's Review*
CStA	*Carlyle Studies Annual* (previously *CAnn*)
CTR	*Canadian Theatre Review*
Cuadernos	*Cuadernos de Literatura Infantil y Juvenil*
CulC	*Cultural Critique*
CulS	*Cultural Studies*
CUNY	*CUNY English Forum*
Current Writing	*Current Writing: Text and Reception in Southern Africa*
CV2	*Contemporary Verse 2*
CVE	*Cahiers Victoriens et Edouardiens*
CW	*Current Writing: Text and Perception in Southern Africa*
CWAAS	*Transactions of the Cumberland and Westmorland Antiquarian and Archaeological Society*
CWS	*Canadian Woman Studies*
DA	*Dictionary of Americanisms*
DAE	*Dictionary of American English*
DAEM	*Deutsches Archiv für Erforschung des Mittelalters*
DAI	*Dissertation Abstracts International*
DAL	*Descriptive and Applied Linguistics*
D&CN&Q	*Devon and Cornwall Notes and Queries*
D&S	*Discourse and Society*
Daphnis	*Daphnis: Zeitschrift für Mittlere Deutsche Literatur*
DC	Dickens Companions
DerbyM	*Derbyshire Miscellany*
Descant	*Descant*
DFS	*Dalhousie French Studies*
DHLR	*D.H. Lawrence Review*
DHS	*Dix-huitième Siècle*
Diac	*Diacritics*
Diachronica	*Diachronica*
Dialogue	*Dialogue: Canadian Philosophical Review*
Dickensian	*Dickensian*
DicS	*Dickinson Studies*
Dictionaries	*Dictionaries: Journal of the Dictionary Society of North America*
Dionysos	*Dionysos*

Discourse	*Discourse*
DLB	*Dictionary of Literary Biography*
DLN	*Doris Lessing Newsletter*
DM	*Dublin Magazine*
DMT	Durham Medieval Texts
DNB	*Dictionary of National Biography*
DOE	*Dictionary of Old English*
Dolphin	*Dolphin: Publications of the English Department* (University of Aarhus)
DOST	*Dictionary of the Older Scottish Tongue*
DownR	*Downside Review*
DPr	*Discourse Processes*
DQ	*Denver Quarterly*
DQR	*Dutch Quarterly Review of Anglo-American Letters*
DQu	*Dickens Quarterly*
DR	*Dalhousie Review*
Drama	*Drama: The Quarterly Theatre Review*
DrS	*Dreiser Studies*
DS	*Deep South*
DSA	*Dickens Studies Annual*
DU	*Der Deutschunterricht: Beiträge zu Seiner Praxis und Wissenschaftlichen Grundlegung*
DUJ	*Durham University Journal*
DVLG	*Deutsche Vierteljahrsschrift für Literaturwissenschaft und Geistesgeschichte*
DWPELL	*Dutch Working Papers in English Language and Linguistics*
EA	*Études Anglaises*
EAL	*Early American Literature*
E&D	*Enlightenment and Dissent*
E&S	*Essays and Studies*
E&Soc	*Economy and Society*
EAS	*Essays in Arts and Sciences*
ESt	*Englisch Amerikanische Studien*
EBST	*Edinburgh Bibliographical Society Transactions*
EC	*Études Celtiques*
ECan	*Études Canadiennes/Canadian Studies*
ECCB	*Eighteenth Century: A Current Bibliography*
ECent	*Eighteenth Century: Theory and Interpretation*
ECF	*Eighteenth-Century Fiction*
ECI	*Eighteenth-Century Ireland*
ECIntell	*East-Central Intelligencer*
ECLife	*Eighteenth Century Life*
ECon	*L'Époque Conradienne*
ECr	*L'Esprit Créateur*
ECS	*Eighteenth-Century Studies*
ECSTC	Eighteenth-Century Short Title Catalogue
ECW	*Essays on Canadian Writing*

EDAMN	*EDAM Newsletter*
EDAMR	*Early Drama, Art, and Music Review*
EDH	*Essays by Divers Hands*
EdL	*Études de Lettres*
EdN	*Editors' Notes: Bulletin of the Conference of Editors of Learned Journals*
EDSL	*Encyclopedic Dictionary of the Sciences of Language*
EEMF	Early English Manuscripts in Facsimile
EHR	*English Historical Review*
EI	*Études Irlandaises* (Lille)
EIC	*Essays in Criticism*
EinA	*English in Africa*
EiP	*Essays in Poetics*
EIRC	*Explorations in Renaissance Culture*
Éire	*Éire-Ireland*
EiTET	*Essays in Theatre / Études Théâtrales*
EJ	*English Journal*
EJES	*European Journal of English Studies*
ELangT	*ELT Journal: An International Journal for Teachers of English to Speakers of Other Languages*
ELet	*Esperienze Letterarie: Rivista Trimestrale di Critica e Cultura*
ELH	*English Literary History*
ELing	*English Linguistics*
ELL	*English Language and Linguistics*
ELN	*English Language Notes*
ELR	*English Literary Renaissance*
ELS	*English Literary Studies*
ELT	*English Literature in Transition*
ELWIU	*Essays in Literature* (Western Illinois University)
EM	*English Miscellany*
Embl	*Emblematica: An Interdisciplinary Journal of English Studies*
EMD	*European Medieval Drama*
EME	*Early Modern Europe*
EMLS	*Early Modern Literary Studies* (online)
EMMS	*Early Modern Manuscript Studies*
EMS	*English Manuscript Studies, 1100–1700*
EMu	*Early Music*
EMW	Early Modern Englishwomen
Encyclia	*Encyclia*
English	*English: The Journal of the English Association*
EnT	*English Today: The International Review of the English Language*
EONR	*Eugene O'Neill Review*
EPD	*English Pronouncing Dictionary*
ER	*English Review*
ERLM	*Europe-Revue Littéraire Mensuelle*

ERR	*European Romantic Review*
ES	*English Studies*
ESA	*English Studies in Africa*
ESC	*English Studies in Canada*
ESQ	*ESQ: A Journal of the American Renaissance*
ESRS	*Emporia State Research Studies*
EssaysMedSt	*Essays in Medieval Studies*
ET	*Elizabethan Theatre*
EWhR	*Edith Wharton Review*
EWIP	*Edinburgh University, Department of Linguistics, Work in Progress*
EWN	*Evelyn Waugh Newsletter*
EWPAL	*Edinburgh Working Papers in Applied Linguistics*
EWW	*English World-Wide*
Excavatio	*Excavatio*
Exemplaria	*Exemplaria*
Expl	*Explicator*
Extrapolation	*Extrapolation: A Journal Science Fiction and Fantasy*
FC	*Feminist Collections: A Quarterly of Women's Studies Resources*
FCEMN	*Mystics Quarterly* (formerly *Fourteenth-Century English Mystics Newsletter*)
FCS	*Fifteenth-Century Studies*
FDT	Fountainwell Drama Texts
FemR	*Feminist Review*
FemSEL	*Feminist Studies in English Literature*
FH	*Die Neue Gesellschaft / Frankfurter Hefte*
Fiction International	*Fiction International*
FiveP	*Five Points: A Journal of Literature and Art* (Atlanta, GA)
FJS	*Fu Jen Studies: Literature and Linguistics* (Taipei)
FLH	*Folia Linguistica Historica*
Florilegium	*Florilegium: Carleton University Annual Papers on Classical Antiquity and the Middle Ages*
FMLS	*Forum for Modern Language Studies*
FNS	*Frank Norris Studies*
Folklore	*Folklore*
FoLi	*Folia Linguistica*
Forum	*Forum*
FranS	*Franciscan Studies*
FreeA	*Free Associations*
FrontenacR	*Revue Frontenac*
Frontiers	*Frontiers: A Journal of Women's Studies*
FS	*French Studies*
FSt	*Feminist Studies*
FT	*Fashion Theory*
FuL	*Functions of Language*
Futures	*Futures*
GAG	Göppinger Arbeiten zur Germanistik

GaR	*Georgia Review*
GBB	*George Borrow Bulletin*
GBK	*Gengo Bunka Kenkyu: Studies in Language and Culture*
GEGHLS	*George Eliot–George Henry Lewes Studies*
GeM	*Genealogists Magazine*
Genders	*Genders*
Genre	*Genre*
GER	*George Eliot Review*
Gestus	*Gestus: A Quarterly Journal of Brechtian Studies*
Gettysburg Review	*Gettysburg Review*
GG@G	*Generative Grammar in Geneva* (online)
GHJ	*George Herbert Journal*
GissingJ	*Gissing Journal*
GJ	*Gutenberg-Jahrbuch*
GL	*General Linguistics*
GL&L	*German Life and Letters*
GlasR	*Glasgow Review*
Glossa	*Glossa: An International Journal of Linguistics*
GLQ	*A Journal of Lesbian and Gay Studies* (Duke University)
GLS	*Grazer Linguistische Studien*
GR	*Germanic Review*
Gramma	*Gramma: Journal of Theory and Criticism*
Gramma/TTT	*Tijdschrift voor Taalwetenschap*
GrandS	*Grand Street*
Granta	*Granta*
Greyfriar	*Greyfriar Siena Studies in Literature*
GRM	*Germanisch-Romanische Monatsschrift*
GSE	Gothenberg Studies in English
GSJ	*Gaskell Society Journal*
GSN	*Gaskell Society Newsletter*
GURT	*Georgetown University Round Table on Language and Linguistics*
HamS	*Hamlet Studies*
H&T	*History and Theory*
Harvard Law Review	*Harvard Law Review*
HatcherR	*Hatcher Review*
HBS	Henry Bradshaw Society
HC	*Hollins Critic*
HCM	*Hitting Critical Mass: A Journal of Asian American Cultural Criticism*
HE	*History of Education*
HEAT	*HEAT*
Hecate	*Hecate: An Interdisciplinary Journal of Women's Liberation*
HEdQ	*History of Education Quarterly*
HEI	*History of European Ideas*
HeineJ	*Heine Jahrbuch*
HEL	*Histoire Épistémologie Language*

Helios	*Helios*
HEng	*History of the English Language*
Hermathena	*Hermathena: A Trinity College Dublin Review*
HeyJ	*Heythrop Journal*
HFR	*Hayden Ferry Review*
HistJ	*Historical Journal*
History	*History: The Journal of the Historical Association*
HistR	*Historical Research*
HJR	*Henry James Review* (Baton Rouge, LA)
HL	*Historiographia Linguistica*
HLB	*Harvard Library Bulletin*
HLQ	*Huntingdon Library Quarterly*
HLSL	(online)
HNCIS	Harvester New Critical Introductions to Shakespeare
HNR	Harvester New Readings
HOPE	*History of Political Economy*
HPT	*History of Political Thought*
HQ	*Hopkins Quarterly*
HR	*Harvard Review*
HRB	*Hopkins Research Bulletin*
HSci	*History of Science*
HSE	*Hungarian Studies in English*
HSELL	*Hiroshima Studies in English Language and Literature*
HSJ	*Housman Society Journal*
HSL	*University of Hartford Studies in Literature*
HSN	*Hawthorne Society Newsletter*
HSSh	*Hunganan Studies in Shakespeare*
HSSN	*Henry Sweet Society Newsletter*
HT	*History Today*
HTR	*Harvard Theological Review*
HudR	*Hudson Review*
HumeS	*Hume Studies*
HumLov	*Humanistica Lovaniensia: Journal of Neo-Latin Studies*
Humor	*Humor: International Journal of Humor Research*
HUSL	*Hebrew University Studies in Literature and the Arts*
HWJ	*History Workshop*
HWS	History Workshop Series
Hypatia	*Hypatia*
IAL	*Issues in Applied Linguistics*
IAN	*Izvestiia Akademii Nauk SSSR* (Moscow)
I&C	*Ideology and Consciousness*
I&P	*Ideas and Production*
ICS	*Illinois Classical Studies*
IEEETrans	*IEEE Transactions on Professional Communications*
IF	*Indogermanische Forschungen*
IFR	*International Fiction Review*
IGK	*Irland: Gesellschaft und Kultur*
IJAES	*International Journal of Arabic-English Studies*

IJAL	*International Journal of Applied Linguistics*
IJBEB	*International Journal of Bilingual Education & Bilingualism*
IJCP	*International Journal of Corpus Linguistics*
IJCT	*International Journal of the Classical Tradition*
IJECS	*Indian Journal for Eighteenth-Century Studies*
IJES	*Indian Journal of English Studies*
IJL	*International Journal of Lexicography*
IJPR	*International Journal for Philosophy of Religion*
IJSL	*International Journal of the Sociology of Language*
IJSS	*Indian Journal of Shakespeare Studies*
IJWS	*International Journal of Women's Studies*
ILR	*Indian Literary Review*
ILS	*Irish Literary Supplement*
Imago	*Imago: New Writing*
IMB	*International Medieval Bibliography*
Imprimatur	*Imprimatur*
Indexer	*Indexer*
IndH	*Indian Horizons*
IndL	*Indian Literature*
InG	*In Geardagum: Essays on Old and Middle English Language and Literature*
Inklings	*Inklings: Jahrbuch für Literatur und Ästhetik*
Inquiry	*Inquiry: An Interdisciplinary Journal of Philosophy*
Interlink	*Interlink*
Interpretation	*Interpretation*
Interventions	*Interventions: The International Journal of Postcolonial Studies*
IowaR	*Iowa Review*
IRAL	*IRAL: International Review of Applied Linguistics in Language Teaching*
Iris	*Iris: A Journal of Theory on Image and Sound*
IS	*Italian Studies*
ISh	*Independent Shavian*
ISJR	*Iowa State Journal of Research*
Island	*Island Magazine*
Islands	*Islands*
Isle	*Interdisciplinary Studies in Literature and Environment*
ISR	*Irish Studies Review*
IUR	*Irish University Review: A Journal of Irish Studies*
JAAC	*Journal of Aesthetics and Art Criticism*
JAAR	*Journal of the American Academy of Religion*
Jacket	*Jacket*
JADT	*Journal of American Drama and Theatre*
JAF	*Journal of American Folklore*
JafM	*Journal of African Marxists*
JAIS	*Journal of Anglo-Italian Studies*
JAL	*Journal of Australian Literature*

JamC	*Journal of American Culture*
JAmH	*Journal of American History*
JAmS	*Journal of American Studies*
JArabL	*Journal of Arabic Literature*
JAS	*Journal of Australian Studies*
JAStT	*Journal of American Studies of Turkey*
JBeckS	*Journal of Beckett Studies*
JBS	*Journal of British Studies*
JCAKSU	*Journal of the College of Arts* (King Saud University)
JCanL	*Journal of Canadian Literature*
JCC	*Journal of Canadian Culture*
JCF	*Journal of Canadian Fiction*
JChL	*Journal of Child Language*
JCL	*Journal of Commonwealth Literature*
JCP	*Journal of Canadian Poetry*
JCPCS	*Journal of Commonwealth and Postcolonial Studies*
JCSJ	*John Clare Society Journal*
JCSR	*Journal of Canadian Studies / Revue d'Études Canadiennes*
JCSt	*Journal of Caribbean Studies*
JDECU	*Journal of the Department of English* (Calcutta University)
JDHLS	*D.H. Lawrence: The Journal of the D.H. Lawrence Society*
JDJ	*John Dunne Journal*
JDN	*James Dickey Newsletter*
JDTC	*Journal of Dramatic Theory and Criticism*
JEBS	*Journal of the Early Book Society*
JEDRBU	*Journal of the English Department* (Rabindra Bharati University)
JEGP	*Journal of English and Germanic Philology*
JEH	*Journal of Ecclesiastical History*
JELL	*Journal of English Language and Literature*
JEn	*Journal of English* (Sana'a University)
JEngL	*Journal of English Linguistics*
JENS	*Journal of the Eighteen Nineties Society*
JEP	*Journal of Evolutionary Psychology*
JEPNS	*Journal of the English Place-Name Society*
JES	*Journal of European Studies*
JETS	*Journal of the Evangelical Theological Society*
JFR	*Journal of Folklore Research*
JGE	*Journal of General Education*
JGenS	*Journal of Gender Studies*
JGH	*Journal of Garden History*
JGN	*John Gower Newsletter*
JH	*Journal of Homosexuality*
JHI	*Journal of the History of Ideas*
JHLP	*Journal of Historical Linguistics and Philology*
JHP	*Journal of the History of Philosophy*
JHPrag	*Journal of Historical Pragmatics*

JHSex	*Journal of the History of Sexuality*
JHu	*Journal of Humanities*
JIES	*Journal of Indo-European Studies*
JIL	*Journal of Irish Literature*
JIPA	*Journal of the International Phonetic Association*
JIWE	*Journal of Indian Writing in English*
JJ	*Jamaica Journal*
JJA	*James Joyce Annual*
JJB	*James Joyce Broadsheet*
JJLS	*James Joyce Literary Supplement*
JJQ	*James Joyce Quarterly*
JL	*Journal of Linguistics*
JLH	*Journal of Library History, Philosophy and Comparative Librarianship*
JLLI	*Journal of Logic, Language and Information*
JLP	*Journal of Linguistics and Politics*
JLS	*Journal of Literary Semanitcs*
JLSP	*Journal of Language and Social Psychology*
JLVSG	*Journal of the Longborough Victorian Studies Group*
JMemL	*Journal of Memory and Language*
JMEMS	*Journal of Medieval and Early Modern Studies*
JMGS	*Journal of Modern Greek Studies*
JMH	*Journal of Medieval History*
JML	*Journal of Modern Literature*
JMMD	*Journal of Multilingual and Multicultural Development*
JMMLA	*Journal of the Midwest Modern Language Association*
JModH	*Journal of Modern History*
JMRS	*Journal of Medieval and Renaissance Studies*
JNLH	*Journal of Narrative and Life History*
JNPH	*Journal of Newspaper and Periodical History*
JNT	*Journal of Narrative Technique* (formerly *Technique*)
JNZL	*Journal of New Zealand Literature*
JoyceSA	*Joyce Studies Annual*
JP	*Journal of Philosophy*
JPC	*Journal of Popular Culture*
JPCL	*Journal of Pidgin and Creole Languages*
JPhon	*Journal of Phonetics*
JPJ	*Journal of Psychology and Judaism*
JPrag	*Journal of Pragmatics*
JPRAS	*Journal of Pre-Raphaelite and Aesthetic Studies*
JPsyR	*Journal of Psycholinguistic Research*
JQ	*Journalism Quarterly*
JR	*Journal of Religion*
JRAHS	*Journal of the Royal Australian Historical Society*
JRH	*Journal of Religious History*
JRMA	*Journal of the Royal Musical Association*
JRMMRA	*Journal of the Rocky Mountain Medieval and Renaissance Association*

JRSA	*Journal of the Royal Society of Arts*
JRUL	*Journal of the Rutgers University Libraries*
JSA	*Journal of the Society of Archivists*
JSaga	*Journal of the Faculty of Liberal Arts and Science* (Saga University)
JSAS	*Journal of Southern African Studies*
JScholP	*Journal of Scholarly Publishing*
JSem	*Journal of Semantics*
JSoc	*Journal of Sociolinguistics*
JSSE	*Journal of the Short Story in English*
JTheoS	*Journal of Theological Studies*
JWCI	*Journal of the Warburg and Courtauld Institutes*
JWH	*Journal of Women's History*
JWIL	*Journal of West Indian Literature*
JWMS	*Journal of the William Morris Society*
JWSL	*Journal of Women's Studies in Literature*
KanE	*Kansas English*
KanQ	*Kansas Quarterly*
KB	*Kavya Bharati*
KCLMS	King's College London Medieval Series
KJ	*Kipling Journal*
KN	*Kwartalnik Neoflologiczny* (Warsaw)
KompH	*Komparatistische Hefte*
Kotare	*Kotare: New Zealand Notes and Queries*
KPR	*Kentucky Philological Review*
KR	*Kenyon Review*
KSJ	*Keats–Shelley Journal*
KSR	*Keats–Shelley Review*
Kuka	*Kuka: Journal of Creative and Critical Writing* (Zaria, Nigeria)
Kunapipi	*Kunapipi*
KWS	*Key-Word Studies in Chaucer*
L&A	*Literature and Aesthetics*
L&B	*Literature and Belief*
L&C	*Language and Communication*
L&E	*Linguistics and Education: An International Research Journal*
Landfall	*Landfall: A New Zealand Quarterly*
L&H	*Literature and History*
L&L	*Language and Literature*
L&LC	*Literary and Linguistic Computing*
L&M	*Literature and Medicine*
L&P	*Literature and Psychology*
L&S	*Language and Speech*
L&T	*Literature and Theology: An Interdisciplinary Journal of Theory and Criticism*
L&U	*Lion and the Unicorn: A Critical Journal of Children's Literature*

Lang&S	*Language and Style*
LangF	*Language Forum*
LangQ	*USF Language Quarterly*
LangR	*Language Research*
LangS	*Language Sciences*
Language	*Language: Journal of the Linguistic Society of America*
LanM	*Les Langues Modernes*
LATR	*Latin American Theatre Review*
LaTrobe	*La Trobe Journal*
LB	*Leuvense Bijdragen*
LBR	*Luso-Brazilian Review*
LCrit	*Literary Criterion* (Mysore, India)
LCUT	*Library Chronicle* (University of Texas at Austin)
LDOCE	*Longman Dictionary of Contemporary English*
LeedsSE	*Leeds Studies in English*
Legacy	*Legacy: A Journal of Nineteenth-Century American Women Writers*
L'EpC	*L'Epoque Conradienne*
LeS	*Lingua e Stile*
Lexicographica	*Lexicographica: International Annual for Lexicography*
Lexicography	*Lexicography*
LFQ	*Literature/Film Quarterly*
LH	*Library History*
LHY	*Literary Half-Yearly*
Library	*Library*
LibrQ	*Library Quarterly*
LIN	*Linguistics in the Netherlands*
LingA	*Linguistic Analysis*
Ling&P	*Linguistics and Philosophy*
Ling&Philol	*Linguistics and Philology*
LingB	*Linguistische Berichte*
LingI	*Linguistic Inquiry*
LingInv	*Linvisticæ Investigationes*
LingP	*Linguistica Pragensia*
Lingua	*Lingua: International Review of General Linguistics*
Linguistics	*Linguistics*
Linguistique	*La Linguistique*
LiNQ	*Literature in Northern Queensland*
LIT	*LIT: Literature, Interpretation, Theory*
LitH	*Literary Horizons*
LitR	*Literary Review: An International Journal of Contemporary Writing*
LittPrag	*Litteraria Pragensia: Studies in Literature and Culture*
LJCS	*London Journal of Canadian Studies*
LJGG	*Literaturwissenschaftliches Jahrbuch im Aufrage der Görres-Gesellschaft*
LJHum	*Lamar Journal of the Humanities*
LMag	*London Magazine*

LockeN	*Locke Newsletter*
LocusF	*Locus Focus*
LongR	*Long Room: Bulletin of the Friends of the Library* (Trinity College, Dublin)
Lore&L	*Lore and Language*
LP	*Lingua Posnaniensis*
LPLD	*Liverpool Papers in Language and Discourse*
LPLP	*Language Problems and Language Planning*
LR	*Les Lettres Romanes*
LRB	*London Review of Books*
LSE	Lund Studies in English
LSLD	Liverpool Studies in Language and Discourse
LSoc	*Language in Society*
LSp	*Language and Speech*
LST	Longman Study Texts
LTM	Leeds Texts and Monographs
LTP	*LTP: Journal of Literature Teaching Politics*
LTR	*London Theatre Record*
LuK	*Literatur und Kritik*
LVC	*Language Variation and Change*
LWU	*Literatur in Wissenschaft und Unterricht*
M&Lang	*Mind and Language*
MÆ	*Medium Ævum*
MAEL	Macmillan Anthologies of English Literature
MaComère	*MaComère*
MagL	*Magazine Littéraire*
Mana	*Mana*
M&H	*Medievalia et Humanistica*
M&L	*Music and Letters*
M&N	*Man and Nature / L'Homme et la Nature: Proceedings of the Canadian Society for Eighteenth-Century Studies*
Manuscripta	*Manuscripta*
MAR	*Mid-American Review*
Margin	*Margin*
MarkhamR	*Markham Review*
Matatu	*Matatu*
Matrix	*Matrix*
MBL	*Modern British Literature*
MC&S	*Media, Culture and Society*
MCI	Modern Critical Interpretations
MCJNews	*Milton Centre of Japan News*
McNR	*McNeese Review*
MCRel	*Mythes, Croyances et Religions dans le Monde Anglo-Saxon*
MCV	Modern Critical Views
MD	*Modern Drama*
ME	*Medieval Encounters*
Meanjin	*Meanjin*

MED	*Middle English Dictionary*
Mediaevalia	*Mediaevalia: A Journal of Mediaeval Studies*
MedPers	*Medieval Perspectives*
MELUS	*MELUS: The Journal of the Society of Multi-Ethnic Literature of the United States*
Meridian	*Meridian*
MESN	*Mediaeval English Studies Newsletter*
MET	Middle English Texts
METh	*Medieval English Theatre*
MFN	*Medieval Feminist Newsletter*
MFS	*Modern Fiction Studies*
MH	*Malahat Review*
MHL	Macmillan History of Literature
MHLS	*Mid-Hudson Language Studies*
MichA	*Michigan Academician*
MiltonQ	*Milton Quarterly*
MiltonS	*Milton Studies*
MinnR	*Minnesota Review*
MissQ	*Mississippi Quarterly*
MissR	*Missouri Review*
Mittelalter	*Das Mittelalter: Perspektiven Mediavistischer Forschung*
MJLF	*Midwestern Journal of Language and Folklore*
ML	*Music and Letters*
MLAIB	*Modern Language Association International Bibliography*
MLing	*Modelès Linguistiques*
MLJ	*Modern Language Journal*
MLN	*Modern Language Notes*
MLQ	*Modern Language Quarterly*
MLR	*Modern Language Review*
MLRev	*Malcolm Lowry Review*
MLS	*Modern Language Studies*
MMD	Macmillan Modern Dramatists
MMG	Macmillan Master Guides
MMisc	*Midwestern Miscellany*
MOCS	*Magazine of Cultural Studies*
ModA	*Modern Age: A Quarterly Review*
ModM	*Modern Masters*
ModSp	*Moderne Sprachen*
Mo/Mo	*Modernism/Modernity*
Monist	*Monist*
MonSP	*Monash Swift Papers*
Month	*Month: A Review of Christian Thought and World Affairs*
MOR	*Mount Olive Review*
Moreana	*Moreana: Bulletin Thomas More* (Angers, France)
Mosaic	*Mosaic: A Journal for the Interdisciplinary Study of Literature*
MoyA	*Moyen Age*
MP	*Modern Philology*

MPHJ	*Middlesex Polytechnic History Journal*
MPR	*Mervyn Peake Review*
MQ	*Midwest Quarterly*
MQR	*Michigan Quarterly Review*
MR	*Massachusetts Review*
MRDE	*Medieval and Renaissance Drama in England*
MRTS	Medieval and Renaissance Texts and Studies
MS	*Mediaeval Studies*
MSC	Malone Society Collections
MSE	*Massachusetts Studies in English*
MSEx	*Melville Society Extracts*
MSh	Macmillan Shakespeare
MSNH	Mémoires de la Société Néophilologique de Helsinki
MSpr	*Moderna Språk*
MSR	Malone Society Reprints
MSSN	*Medieval Sermon Studies Newsletter*
MT	*Musical Times*
MTJ	*Mark Twain Journal*
MusR	*Music Review*
MW	*Muslim World* (Hartford, CT)
MysticsQ	*Mystics Quarterly*
Mythlore	*Mythlore: A Journal of J.R.R. Tolkein, C.S. Lewis, Charles Williams, and the Genres of Myth and Fantasy Studies*
NA	*Nuova Antologia*
Names	*Names: Journal of the American Name Society*
NAmR	*North American Review*
N&F	*Notes & Furphies*
N&Q	*Notes and Queries*
Narrative	*Narrative*
Navasilu	*Navasilu*
NB	*Namn och Bygd*
NCaS	New Cambridge Shakespeare
NCBEL	*New Cambridge Bibliography of English Literature*
NCC	*Nineteenth-Century Contexts*
NCE	Norton Critical Editions
NCFS	*Nineteenth-Century French Studies*
NCL	*Nineteenth-Century Literature*
NConL	*Notes on Contemporary Literature*
NCP	*Nineteenth-Century Prose*
NCS	New Clarendon Shakespeare
NCSR	New Chaucer Society Readings
NCSTC	Nineteenth-Century Short Title Catalogue
NCStud	*Nineteenth-Century Studies*
NCT	*Nineteenth-Century Theatre*
NDQ	*North Dakota Quarterly*
NegroD	*Negro Digest*
NELS	*North Eastern Linguistic Society*
Neoh	*Neohelicon*

Neophil	*Neophilologus*
NEQ	*New England Quarterly*
NERMS	*New England Review*
NewA	*New African*
NewBR	*New Beacon Review*
NewC	*New Criterion*
New Casebooks	New Casebooks: Contemporary Critical Essays
NewComp	*New Comparison: A Journal of Comparative and General Literary Studies*
NewF	*New Formations*
NewR	*New Republic*
NewSt	*Newfoundland Studies*
NewV	*New Voices*
NF	*Neiophilologica Fennica*
NfN	*News from Nowhere*
NFS	*Nottingham French Studies*
NGC	*New German Critique*
NGS	*New German Studies*
NH	*Northern History*
NHR	*Nathaniel Hawthorne Review*
NJL	*Nordic Journal of Linguistics*
NL	*Nouvelles Littéraires*
NL&LT	*Natural Language and Linguistic Theory*
NLH	*New Literary History: A Journal of Theory and Interpretation*
NLitsR	*New Literatures Review*
NLR	*New Left Review*
NLWJ	*National Library of Wales Journal*
NM	*Neuphilologische Mitteilungen*
NMAL	*NMAL: Notes on Modern American Literature*
NMer	New Mermaids
NMIL	*Notes on Modern Irish Literature*
NMS	*Nottingham Medieval Studies*
NMW	*Notes on Mississippi Writers*
NN	*Nordiska Namenstudier*
NNER	*Northern New England Review*
Nomina	*Nomina: A Journal of Name Studies Relating to Great Britain and Ireland*
NoP	*Northern Perspective*
NOR	*New Orleans Review*
NorfolkA	*Norfolk Archaeology*
NortonCE	Norton Critical Edition
Novel	*Novel: A Forum on Fiction*
NOWELE	*North-Western European Language Evolution*
NPS	New Penguin Shakespeare
NR	*Nassau Review*
NRF	*La Nouvelle Revue Française*
NRRS	*Notes and Records of the Royal Society of London*

NS	*Die neuren Sprachen*
NSS	New Swan Shakespeare
NTQ	*New Theatre Quarterly*
NVSAWC	*Newsletter of the Victorian Studies Association of Western Canada*
NwJ	*Northward Journal*
NWR	*Northwest Review*
NWRev	*New Welsh Review*
NYH	*New York History*
NYLF	New York Literary Forum
NYRB	*New York Review of Books*
NYT	*New York Times*
NYTBR	*New York Times Book Review*
NZB	*New Zealand Books*
NZListener	*New Zealand Listener*
OA	Oxford Authors
OB	*Ord och Bild*
Obsidian	*Obsidian II: Black Literature in Review*
OBSP	Oxford Bibliographical Society Publications
OED	*Oxford English Dictionary*
OENews	*Old English Newsletter*
OET	Oxford English Texts
OH	*Over Here: An American Studies Journal*
OHEL	Oxford History of English Literature
OhR	*Ohio Review*
OLR	*Oxford Literary Review*
OPBS	*Occasional Papers of the Bibliographical Society*
OpenGL	Open Guides to Literature
OpL	*Open Letter*
OPL	Oxford Poetry Library
OPLiLL	*Occasional Papers in Linguistics and Language Learning*
OPSL	*Occasional Papers in Systemic Linguistics*
OralT	*Oral Tradition*
Orbis	*Orbis*
OrbisLit	*Orbis Litterarum*
OS	Oxford Shakespeare
OSS	Oxford Shakespeare Studies
OT	*Oral Tradition*
Outrider	*Outrider: A Publication of the Wyoming State Library*
Overland	*Overland*
PA	*Présence Africaine*
PAAS	*Proceedings of the American Antiquarian Society*
PacStud	*Pacific Studies*
Paideuma	*Paideuma: A Journal Devoted to Ezra Pound Scholarship*
PAJ	*Performing Art Journal*
P&C	*Pragmatics and Cognition*
P&CT	*Psychoanalysis and Contemporary Thought*
P&L	*Philosophy and Literature*

P&P	*Past and Present*
P&R	*Philosophy and Rhetoric*
P&SC	*Philosophy and Social Criticism*
PAPA	*Publications of the Arkansas Philological Association*
Papers	*Papers: Explorations into Children's Literature*
PAPS	*Proceedings of the American Philosophical Society*
PAR	*Performing Arts Resources*
Parabola	*Parabola: The Magazine of Myth and Tradition*
Paragraph	*Paragraph: The Journal of the Modern Critical Theory Group*
Parergon	*Parergon: Bulletin of the Australian and New Zealand Association for Medieval and Renaissance Studies*
ParisR	*Paris Review*
Parnassus	*Parnassus: Poetry in Review*
PastM	Past Masters
PaterN	*Pater Newsletter*
PAus	*Poetry Australia*
PBA	*Proceedings of the British Academy*
PBerLS	*Proceedings of the Berkeley Linguistics Society*
PBSA	*Papers of the Bibliographical Society of America*
PBSC	*Papers of the Biographical Society of Canada*
PCL	*Perspectives on Contemporary Literature*
PCLAC	*Proceedings of the California Linguistics Association Conference*
PCLS	*Proceedings of the Comparative Literature Symposium* (Lubbock, TX)
PCP	*Pacific Coast Philology*
PCS	Penguin Critical Studies
PEAN	*Proceedings of the English Association North*
PE&W	*Philosophy East and West: A Quarterly of Asian and Comparative Thought*
PELL	*Papers on English Language and Literature* (Japan)
Pequod	*Pequod: A Journal of Contemporary Literature and Literary Criticism*
Performance	*Performance*
Peritia	*Peritia: Journal of the Medieval Academy of Ireland*
Persuasions	*Persuasions: Journal of the Jane Austen Society of North America*
Philosophy	*Philosophy*
PHist	*Printing History*
Phonetica	*Phonetica: International Journal of Speech Science*
PHOS	Publishing History Occasional Series
PhRA	*Philosophical Research Archives*
PhT	*Philosophy Today*
PiL	*Papers in Linguistics*
PIMA	*Proceedings of the Illinois Medieval Association*
PinterR	*Pinter Review*
PJCL	*Prairie Journal of Canadian Literature*

PLL	*Papers on Language and Literature*
PLPLS	*Proceedings of the Leeds Philosophical and Literary Society, Literary and Historical Section*
PM	*Penguin Masterstudies*
PMHB	*Pennsylvania Magazine of History and Biography*
PMLA	*Publications of the Modern Language Association of America*
PMPA	*Proceedings of the Missouri Philological Association*
PNotes	*Pynchon Notes*
PNR	*Poetry and Nation Review*
PoeS	*Poe Studies*
Poetica	*Poetica: Zeitschrift für Sprach- und Literaturwissenschaft* (Amsterdam)
PoeticaJ	*Poetica: An International Journal of Linguistic-Literary Studies* (Tokyo)
Poetics	*Poetics: International Review for the Theory of Literature*
Poétique	*Poétique: Revue de Théorie et d'Analyse Littéraires*
Poetry	*Poetry* (Chicago)
PoetryCR	*Poetry Canada Review*
PoetryR	*Poetry Review*
PoetryW	*Poetry Wales*
POMPA	*Publications of the Mississippi Philological Association*
PostS	*Past Script: Essays in Film and the Humanities*
PoT	*Poetics Today*
PP	Penguin Passnotes
PP	*Philologica Pragensia*
PPMRC	*Proceedings of the International Patristic, Mediaeval and Renaissance Conference*
PPR	*Philosophy and Phenomenological Research*
PQ	*Philological Quarterly*
PQM	*Pacific Quarterly* (Moana)
PR	*Partisan Review*
Pragmatics	*Pragmatics: Quarterly Publication of the International Pragmatics Association*
PrairieF	*Prairie Fire*
Praxis	*Praxis: A Journal of Cultural Criticism*
Prépub	*(Pré)publications*
PRev	*Powys Review*
PRIA	*Proceedings of the Royal Irish Academy*
PRIAA	Publications of the Research Institute of the Abo Akademi Foundation
PRMCLS	*Papers from the Regional Meetings of the Chicago Linguistics Society*
Prospects	*Prospects: An Annual Journal of American Cultural Studies*
Prospero	*Prospero: Journal of New Thinking in Philosophy for Education*
Proteus	*Proteus: A Journal of Ideas*

Proverbium	*Proverbium*
PrS	*Prairie Schooner*
PSt	*Prose Studies*
PsyArt	*Psychological Study of the Arts* (hyperlink journal)
PsychR	*Psychological Reports*
PTBI	Publications of the Sir Thomas Browne Institute
PubH	*Publishing History*
PULC	*Princeton University Library Chronicle*
PURBA	*Panjab University Research Bulletin (Arts)*
PVR	*Platte Valley Review*
PWC	*Pickering's Women's Classics*
PY	*Phonology Yearbook*
QDLLSM	*Quaderni del Dipartimento e Lingue e Letterature Straniere Moderne*
QI	*Quaderni d'Italianistica*
QJS	*Quarterly Journal of Speech*
QLing	*Quantitative Linguistics*
QQ	*Queen's Quarterly*
QR	*Queensland Review*
QRFV	*Quarterly Review of Film and Video*
Quadrant	*Quadrant* (Sydney)
Quarendo	*Quarendo*
Quarry	*Quarry*
QWERTY	*QWERTY: Arts, Littératures, et Civilisations du Monde Anglophone*
RadP	*Radical Philosophy*
RAL	*Research in African Literatures*
RALS	*Resources for American Literary Study*
Ramus	*Ramus: Critical Studies in Greek and Roman Literature*
R&L	*Religion and Literature*
Raritan	*Raritan: A Quarterly Review*
Rask	*Rask: International tidsskrift for sprong og kommunikation*
RB	*Revue Bénédictine*
RBPH	*Revue Belge de Philologie et d'Histoire*
RCEI	*Revista Canaria de Estudios Ingleses*
RCF	*Review of Contemporary Fiction*
RCPS	*Romantic Circles Praxis Series* (online)
RDN	*Renaissance Drama Newsletter*
RE	*Revue d'Esthétique*
ReAL	*Re: Artes Liberales*
REALB	*REAL: The Yearbook of Research in English and American Literature* (Berlin)
ReAr	*Religion and the Arts*
RecBucks	*Records of Buckinghamshire*
RecL	*Recovery Literature*
RECTR	*Restoration and Eighteenth-Century Theatre Research*
RedL	*Red Letters: A Journal of Cultural Politics*
REED	Records of Early English Drama

REEDN	*Records of Early English Drama Newsletter*
ReFr	*Revue Française*
Reinardus	*Reinardus*
REL	*Review of English Literature* (Kyoto)
RELC	*RELC Journal: A Journal of Language Teaching and Research in Southeast Asia*
Ren&R	*Renaissance and Reformation*
Renascence	*Renascence: Essays on Values in Literature*
RenD	*Renaissance Drama*
Renfor	*Renaissance Forum* (online)
RenP	*Renaissance Papers*
RenQ	*Renaissance Quarterly*
Rep	*Representations*
RePublica	*RePublica*
RES	*Review of English Studies*
Restoration	*Restoration: Studies in English Literary Culture, 1660–1700*
Rev	*Review* (Blacksburg, VA)
RevAli	*Revista Alicantina de Estudios Ingleses*
Revels	Revels Plays
RevelsCL	Revels Plays Companion Library
RevelsSE	Revels Student Editions
RevR	Revolution and Romanticism, 1789–1834
RFEA	*Revue Française d'Études Américaines*
RFR	*Robert Frost Review*
RG	*Revue Générale*
RH	*Recusant History*
Rhetorica	*Rhetorica: A Journal of the History of Rhetoric*
Rhetorik	*Rhetorik: Ein Internationales Jahrbuch*
RHist	*Rural History*
RHL	*Revue d'Histoire Littéraire de la France*
RHT	*Revue d'Histoire du Théâtre*
RIB	*Revista Interamericana de Bibliografia: Inter-American Reviews of Bibliography*
Ricardian	*Ricardian: Journal of the Richard III Society*
RL	Rereading Literature
RLAn	*Romance Languages Annual*
RLC	*Revue de Littérature Comparée*
RLing	*Rivista di Linguistica*
RLit	*Russian Literature*
RLM	*La Revue des Lettres Modernes: Histoire des Idées des Littératures*
RLMC	*Rivista di Letterature Moderne e Comparate*
RLT	*Russian Literature Triquarterly*
RM	*Rethinking Marxism*
RMR	*Rocky Mountain Review of Language and Literature*
RM	*Renaissance and Modern Studies*
RMSt	*Reading Medieval Studies*

Romania	*Romania*
RomN	*Romance Notes*
RomQ	*Romance Quarterly*
RomS	*Romance Studies*
RoN	*Romanticism on the Net*
ROO	*Room of One's Own: A Feminist Journal of Literature and Criticism*
RORD	*Research Opportunities in Renaissance Drama*
RPT	Russian Poetics in Translation
RQ	*Riverside Quarterly*
RR	*Romanic Review*
RRDS	Regents Renaissance Drama Series
RRestDS	Regents Restoration Drama Series
RS	*Renaissance Studies*
RSQ	*Rhetoric Society Quarterly*
RSV	*Rivista di Studi Vittoriani*
RUO	*Revue de l'Université d'Ottawa*
RUSEng	*Rajasthan University Studies in English*
RuskN	*Ruskin Newsletter*
RUUL	*Reports from the Uppsala University Department of Linguistics*
R/WT	*Readerly/Writerly Texts*
SAC	*Studies in the Age of Chaucer*
SAD	*Studies in American Drama, 1945–Present*
SAF	*Studies in American Fiction*
Saga-Book	*Saga-Book (Viking Society for Northern Research)*
Sagetrieb	*Sagatrieb: A Journal Devoted to Poets in the Pound–H.D.–Williams Tradition*
SAIL	*Studies in American Indian Literatures: The Journal of the Association for the Study of American Indian Literatures*
SAJL	*Studies in American Jewish Literature*
SAJMRS	*South African Journal of Medieval and Renaissance Studies*
Sal	*Salmagrundi: A Quarterly of the Humanities and Social Sciences*
SALCT	*SALCT: Studies in Australian Literature, Culture and Thought*
S&S	*Sight and Sound*
SAntS	*Studia Anthroponymica Scandinavica*
SAP	*Studia Anglica Posnaniensia*
SAQ	*South Atlantic Quarterly*
SAR	*Studies in the American Renaissance*
SARB	*South African Review of Books*
SatR	*Saturday Review*
SB	*Studies in Bibliography*
SBHC	*Studies in Browning and his Circle*
SC	*Seventeenth Century*
Scan	*Scandinavica: An International Journal of Scandinavian Studies*

ScanS	*Scandinavian Studies*
SCel	*Studia Celtica*
SCER	*Society for Critical Exchange Report*
Schuylkill	*Schuylkill: A Creative and Critical Review* (Temple University)
SCJ	*Sixteenth Century Journal*
SCL	*Studies in Canadian Literature*
ScLJ	*Scottish Literary Journal: A Review of Studies in Scottish Language and Literature*
ScLJ(S)	*Scottish Literary Journal Supplement*
SCN	*Seventeenth-Century News*
ScottN	*Scott Newsletter*
SCR	*South Carolina Review*
Screen	*Screen* (London)
SCRev	*South Central Review*
Scriblerian	*Scriblerian and the Kit Cats: A Newsjournal Devoted to Pope, Swift, and their Circle*
Scripsi	*Scripsi*
Scriptorium	*Scriptorium: International Review of Manuscript Studies*
SD	*Social Dynamics*
SDR	*South Dakota Review*
SECC	*Studies in Eighteenth-Century Culture*
SECOLR	*SECOL Review: Southeastern Conference on Linguistics*
SED	*Survey of English Dialects*
SEDERI	*Journal of the Spanish Society for Renaissance Studies (Sociedad Española de Estudios Renacentistas Ingleses)*
SEEJ	*Slavic and East European Journal*
SEL	*Studies in English Literature, 1500–1900* (Rice University)
SELing	*Studies in English Linguistics* (Tokyo)
SELit	*Studies in English Literature* (Tokyo)
SELL	*Studies in English Language and Literature*
Sem	*Semiotica: Journal of the International Association for Semiotic Studies*
Semiosis	*Semiosis: Internationale Zeitschrift für Semiotik und Ästhetik*
SER	*Studien zur Englischen Romantik*
Seven	*Seven: An Anglo-American Literary Review*
SF&R	Scholars' Facsimiles and Reprints
SFic	*Science Fiction: A Review of Speculative Literature*
SFNL	*Shakespeare on Film Newsletter*
SFQ	*Southern Folklore Quarterly*
SFR	*Stanford French Review*
SFS	*Science-Fiction Studies*
SH	*Studia Hibernica* (Dublin)
ShakB	*Shakespeare Bulletin*
ShakS	*Shakespeare Studies* (New York)
Shandean	*Shandean*
Sh&Sch	*Shakespeare and Schools*

ShawR	*Shaw: The Annual of Bernard Shaw Studies*
Shenandoah	*Shenandoah*
SherHR	*Sherlock Holmes Review*
Shiron	*Shiron*
ShJE	*Shakespeare Jahrbuch* (Weimar)
ShJW	*Deutsche Shakespeare-Gesellschaft West Jahrbuch* (Bochum)
ShLR	*Shoin Literary Review*
ShN	*Shakespeare Newsletter*
SHR	*Southern Humanities Review*
ShS	*Shakespeare Survey*
ShSA	*Shakespeare in Southern Africa*
ShStud	*Shakespeare Studies* (Tokyo)
SHW	*Studies in Hogg and his World*
ShY	*Shakespeare Yearbook*
SiAF	*Studies in American Fiction*
SIcon	*Studies in Iconography*
SidN	*Sidney Newsletter and Journal*
Signs	*Signs: Journal of Women in Culture and Society*
SiHoLS	*Studies in the History of the Language Sciences*
SiM	*Studies in Medievalism*
SIM	*Studies in Music*
SiP	Shakespeare in Performance
SiPr	Shakespeare in Production
SiR	*Studies in Romanticism*
SJS	*San José Studies*
SL	*Studia Linguistica*
SLang	*Studies in Language*
SLCS	*Studies in Language Companion Series*
SLI	*Studies in the Literary Imagination*
SLJ	*Southern Literary Journal*
SLRev	*Stanford Literature Review*
SLSc	*Studies in the Linguistic Sciences*
SMC	*Studies in Medieval Culture*
SMed	*Studi Medievali*
SMELL	*Studies in Medieval English Language and Literature*
SMLit	*Studies in Mystical Literature* (Taiwan)
SMRH	*Studies in Medieval and Renaissance History*
SMS	*Studier i Modern Språkvetenskap*
SMy	*Studia Mystica*
SN	*Studia Neophilologica*
SNNTS	*Studies in the Novel* (North Texas State University)
SO	*Shakespeare Originals*
SOA	*Sydsvenska Ortnamnssällskapets Årsskrift*
SoAR	*South Atlantic Review*
Sociocrit	*Sociocriticism*
Socioling	*Sociolinguistica*
SocN	*Sociolinguistics*

SocSem	*Social Semiotics*
SocT	*Social Text*
SohoB	Soho Bibliographies
SoQ	*Southern Quarterly*
SoR	*Southern Review* (Baton Rouge, LA)
SoRA	*Southern Review* (Adelaide)
SoSt	*Southern Studies: An Interdisciplinary Journal of the South*
Soundings	*Soundings: An Interdisciplinary Journal*
Southerly	*Southerly: A Review of Australian Literature*
SovL	*Soviet Literature*
SP	*Studies in Philology*
SPAN	*SPAN: Newsletter of the South Pacific Association for Commonwealth Literature and Language Studies*
SPAS	*Studies in Puritan American Spirituality*
SPC	*Studies in Popular Culture*
Spectrum	*Spectrum*
Speculum	*Speculum: A Journal of Medieval Studies*
SPELL	*Swiss Papers in English Language and Literature*
Sphinx	*Sphinx: A Magazine of Literature and Society*
SpM	*Spicilegio Moderno*
SpNL	*Spenser Newsletter*
Sprachwiss	*Sprachwissenschalt*
SpringE	*Spring: The Journal of the e.e. cummings Society*
SPub	*Studies in Publishing*
SPWVSRA	*Selected Papers from the West Virginia Shakespeare and Renaissance Association*
SQ	*Shakespeare Quarterly*
SR	*Sewanee Review*
SRen	*Studies in the Renaissance*
SRSR	*Status Report on Speech Research* (Haskins Laboratories)
SSEL	Stockholm Studies in English
SSELER	Salzburg Studies in English Literature: Elizabethan and Renaissance
SSELJDS	Salzburg Studies in English Literature: Jacobean Drama Studies
SSELPDPT	Salzburg Studies in English Literature: Poetic Drama and Poetic Theory
SSELRR	Salzburg Studies in English Literature: Romantic Reassessment
SSEng	*Sydney Studies in English*
SSF	*Studies in Short Fiction*
SSL	*Studies in Scottish Literature*
SSR	*Scottish Studies Review*
SSt	*Spenser Studies*
SStud	*Swift Studies: The Annual of the Ehrenpreis Center*
Staffrider	*Staffrider*
StaffordS	*Staffordshire Studies*
STAH	*Strange Things Are Happening*

STGM	Studien und Texte zur Geistegeschichte des Mittelalters
StHR	*Stanford Historical Review*
StHum	*Studies in the Humanities*
StIn	*Studi Inglesi*
StLF	*Studi di Letteratura Francese*
StQ	*Steinbeck Quarterly*
StrR	*Structuralist Review*
StTCL	*Studies in Twentieth-Century Literature*
StTW	*Studies in Travel Writing*
StudWF	*Studies in Weird Fiction*
STUF	*Sprachtypologie und Universalienforschung*
Style	*Style* (De Kalb, IL)
SUAS	*Stratford-upon-Avon Studies*
SubStance	*SubStance: A Review of Theory and Literary Criticism*
SUS	*Susquehanna University Studies*
SussexAC	*Sussex Archaeological Collections*
SussexP&P	*Sussex Past & Present*
SVEC	*Studies on Voltaire and the Eighteenth Century*
SWPLL	*Sheffield Working Papers in Language and Linguistics*
SWR	*Southwest Review*
SwR	*Swansea Review: A Journal of Criticism*
Sycamore	*Sycamore*
Symbolism	*Symbolism: An International Journal of Critical Aesthetics*
TA	*Theatre Annual*
Tabu	*Bulletin voor Taalwetenschap, Groningen*
Takahe	*Takahe*
Talisman	*Talisman*
T&C	*Text and Context*
T&L	*Translation and Literature*
T&P	*Text and Performance*
TAPS	*Transactions of the American Philosophical Society*
TCBS	*Transactions of the Cambridge Bibliographical Society*
TCE	*Texas College English*
TCL	*Twentieth-Century Literature*
TCS	*Theory, Culture and Society: Explorations in Critical Social Science*
TCWAAS	*Transactions of the Cumberland and Westmorland Antiquarian and Archaeological Society*
TD	*Themes in Drama*
TDR	*Drama Review*
TEAS	Twayne's English Authors Series
Telos	*Telos: A Quarterly Journal of Post-Critical Thought*
TennEJ	*Tennessee English Journal*
TennQ	*Tennessee Quarterly*
TennSL	*Tennessee Studies in Literature*
Te Reo	*Te Reo: Journal of the Linguistic Society of New Zealand*
TexasSLL	*Texas Studies in Language and Literature*
Text	*Text: Transactions of the Society for Textual Scholarship*

TH	*Texas Humanist*
THA	*Thomas Hardy Annual*
Thalia	*Thalia: Studies in Literary Humor*
ThC	*Theatre Crafts*
Theater	*Theater*
TheatreS	*Theatre Studies*
Theoria	*Theoria: A Journal of Studies in the Arts, Humanities and Social Sciences* (Natal)
THES	*Times Higher Education Supplement*
Thesis	*Thesis Eleven*
THIC	*Theatre History in Canada*
THJ	*Thomas Hardy Journal*
ThN	*Thackeray Newsletter*
ThoreauQ	*Thoreau Quarterly: A Journal of Literary and Philosophical Studies*
Thought	*Thought: A Review of Culture and Ideas*
Thph	*Theatrephile*
ThreR	*Threepenny Review*
ThS	*Theatre Survey: The American Journal of Theatre History*
THSLC	*Transactions of the Historic Society of Lancashire and Cheshire*
THStud	*Theatre History Studies*
ThTop	*Theatre Topics*
THY	*Thomas Hardy Yearbook*
TiLSM	*Trends in Linguistics: Studies and Monographs*
TiP	*Theory in Practice*
Tirra Lirra	*Tirra Lirra: The Quarterly Magazine for the Yarra Valley*
TJ	*Theatre Journal*
TJS	*Transactions* (Johnson Society)
TkR	*Tamkang Review*
TL	*Theoretical Linguistics*
TLR	*Linguistic Review*
TLS	*Times Literary Supplement*
TMLT	*Toronto Medieval Latin Texts*
TN	*Theatre Notebook*
TNWSECS	*Transactions of the North West Society for Eighteenth Century Studies*
TP	*Terzo Programma*
TPLL	*Tilbury Papers in Language and Literature*
TPQ	*Text and Performance Quarterly*
TPr	*Textual Practice*
TPS	*Transactions of the Philological Society*
TR	*Theatre Record*
Traditio	*Traditio: Studies in Ancient and Medieval History, Thought, and Religion*
Transition	*Transition*
TRB	*Tennyson Research Bulletin*
TRHS	*Transactions of the Royal Historical Society*

TRI	*Theatre Research International*
TriQ	*TriQuarterly*
Trivium	*Trivium*
Tropismes	*Tropismes*
TSAR	*Toronto South Asian Review*
TSB	*Thoreau Society Bulletin*
TSLang	Typological Studies in Language
TSLL	*Texas Studies in Literature and Language*
TSWL	*Tulsa Studies in Women's Literature*
TTR	*Trinidad and Tobago Review*
TUSAS	Twayne's United States Authors Series
TWAS	Twayne's World Authors Series
TWBR	*Third World Book Review*
TWQ	*Third World Quarterly*
TWR	*Thomas Wolfe Review*
TYDS	*Transactions of the Yorkshire Dialect Society*
Typophiles	Typophiles (New York)
UCrow	*Upstart Crow*
UCTSE	*University of Cape Town Studies in English*
UCWPL	*UCL Working Papers in Linguistics*
UDR	*University of Drayton Review*
UE	*Use of English*
UEAPL	*UEA Papers in Linguistics*
UES	*Unisa English Studies*
Ufahamu	*Ufahamu*
ULR	*University of Leeds Review*
UMSE	*University of Mississippi Studies in English*
Untold	*Untold*
UOQ	*University of Ottawa Quarterly*
URM	*Ultimate Reality and Meaning: Interdisciplinary Studies in the Philosophy of Understanding*
USSE	*University of Saga Studies in English*
UtopST	*Utopian Studies*
UTQ	*University of Toronto Quarterly*
UWR	*University of Windsor Review*
VCT	Les Voies de la Création Théâtrale
VEAW	Varieties of English around the World
Verbatim	*Verbatim: The Language Quarterly*
VIA	*VIA: The Journal of the Graduate School of Fine Arts* (University of Pennsylvania)
Viator	*Viator: Medieval and Renaissance Studies*
Views	*Viennese English Working Papers*
VIJ	*Victorians Institute Journal*
VLC	*Victorian Literature and Culture*
VN	*Victorian Newsletter*
Voices	*Voices*
VP	*Victorian Poetry*
VPR	*Victorian Periodicals Review*

VQR	*Virginia Quarterly Review*
VR	*Victorian Review*
VS	*Victorian Studies*
VSB	*Victorian Studies Bulletin*
VWM	*Virginia Woolf Miscellany*
WAJ	*Women's Art Journal*
WAL	*Western American Literature*
W&I	*Word and Image*
W&L	*Women and Literature*
W&Lang	*Women and Language*
Wasafiri	*Wasafiri*
WascanaR	*Wascana Review*
WBEP	Wiener Beiträge zur Englischen Philologie
WC	World's Classics
WC	*Wordsworth Circle*
WCR	*West Coast Review*
WCSJ	*Wilkie Collins Society Journal*
WCWR	*William Carlos Williams Review*
Wellsian	*Wellsian: The Journal of the H.G. Wells Society*
WEn	*World Englishes*
Westerly	*Westerly: A Quarterly Review*
WestHR	*West Hills Review: A Walt Whitman Journal*
WF	*Western Folklore*
WHASN	*W.H. Auden Society Newsletter*
WHR	*Western Humanities Review*
WI	*Word and Image*
WLA	*Wyndham Lewis Annual*
WL&A	*War Literature, and the Arts: An International Journal of the Humanities*
WLT	*World Literature Today*
WLWE	*World Literature Written in English*
WMQ	*William and Mary Quarterly*
WoHR	*Women's History Review*
WolfenbütteleB	*Wolfenbüttele Beiträge: Aus den Schätzen der Herzog August Bibliothek*
Women	*Women: A Cultural Review*
WorcesterR	*Worcester Review*
WORD	*WORD: Journal of the International Linguistic Association*
WQ	*Wilson Quarterly*
WRB	*Women's Review of Books*
WS	*Women's Studies: An Interdisciplinary Journal*
WSIF	*Women's Studies: International Forum*
WSJour	*Wallace Stevens Journal*
WSR	*Wicazo Sa Review*
WTJ	*Westminster Theological Journal*
WTW	Writers and their Work
WVUPP	*West Virginia University Philological Papers*
WW	*Women's Writing*

WWR	*Walt Whitman Quarterly Review*
XUS	*Xavier Review*
YCC	*Yearbook of Comparative Criticism*
YeA	*Yeats Annual*
YER	*Yeats Eliot Review*
YES	*Yearbook of English Studies*
YEuS	*Yearbook of European Studies/Annuaire d'Études Européennes*
YFS	*Yale French Studies*
Yiddish	*Yiddish*
YJC	*Yale Journal of Criticism: Interpretation in the Humanities*
YLS	*Yearbook of Langland Studies*
YM	*Yearbook of Morphology*
YNS	York Note Series
YPL	*York Papers in Linguistics*
YR	*Yale Review*
YULG	*Yale University Library Gazette*
YWES	*Year's Work in English Studies*
ZAA	*Zeitschrift für Anglistik und Amerikanistik*
ZCP	*Zeitschrift für celtische Philologie*
ZDA	*Zeitschrift für deutsches Altertum und deutsche Literatur*
ZDL	*Zeitschrift für Dialektologie und Linguistik*
ZGKS	*Zeitschrfit für Gesellschaft für Kanada-Studien*
ZGL	*Zeitschrift für germanistische Linguistik*
ZPSK	*Zeitschrift für Phonetik, Sprachwissenshaft und Kommunikationsforschung*
ZSpr	*Zeitschrift für Sprachwissenshaft*
ZVS	*Zeitschrift für vergleichende Sprachforschung*

Volume numbers are supplied in the text, as are individual issue numbers for journals that are not continuously paginated through the year.

2. Publishers

AAAH	Acta Academiae Åboensis Humaniora, Åbo, Finland
AAH	Australian Academy of Humanities
A&B	Allison & Busby, London
A&R	Angus & Robertson, North Ryde, New South Wales
A&U	Allen & Unwin (now Unwin Hyman)
A&UA	Allen & Unwin, North Sydney, New South Wales
A&W	Almqvist & Wiksell International, Stockholm
AarhusUP	Aarhus UP, Aarhus, Denmark
ABC	ABC Enterprises
ABC CLIO	ABC CLIO Reference Books, Santa Barbara, CA
Abbeville	Abbeville Press, New York

ABDO	Association Bourguignonne de Dialectologie et d'Onomastique, Dijon
AberdeenUP	Aberdeen UP, Aberdeen
Abhinav	Abhinav Publications, New Delhi
Abingdon	Abingdon Press, Nashville, TN
ABL	Armstrong Browning Library, Waco, TX
Ablex	Ablex Publishing, Norwood, NJ
Åbo	Åbo Akademi, Åbo, Finland
Abrams	Harry N. Abrams, New York
Academia	Academia Press, Melbourne
Academic	Academic Press, London and Orlando, FL
Academy	Academy Press, Dublin
AcademyC	Academy Chicago Publishers, Chicago
AcademyE	Academy Editions, London
Acadiensis	Acadiensis Press, Fredericton, New Brunswick, Canada
ACarS	Association for Caribbean Studies, Coral Gables, FL
ACC	Antique Collectors' Club, Woodbridge, Suffolk
ACCO	ACCO, Leuven, Belgium
ACP	Another Chicago Press, Chicago
ACS	Association for Canadian Studies, Ottawa
Adam Hart	Adam Hart Publishers, London
Adam Matthew	Adam Matthew, Suffolk
Addison-Wesley	Addison-Wesley, Wokingham, Berkshire
ADFA	Australian Defence Force Academy, Department of English
Adosa	Adosa, Clermont-Ferrand, France
AEMS	American Early Medieval Studies
AF	Akademisk Forlag, Copenhagen
Affiliated	Affiliated East–West Press, New Delhi
AFP	Associated Faculty Press, New York
Africana	Africana Publications, New York
A–H	Arnold–Heinemann, New Delhi
Ahriman	Ahriman-Verlag, Freiburg im Breisgau, Germany
AIAS	Australian Institute of Aboriginal Studies, Canberra
Ajanta	Ajanta Publications, Delhi
AK	Akadémiai Kiadó, Budapest
ALA	ALA Editions, Chicago
Al&Ba	Allyn & Bacon, Boston, MA
Albatross	Albatross Books, Sutherland, New South Wales
Albion	Albion, Appalachian State University, Boone, NC
Alderman	Alderman Press, London
Aldwych	Aldwych Press
AligarhMU	Aligarh Muslim University, Uttar Pradesh, India
Alioth	Alioth Press, Beaverton, OR
Allen	W.H. Allen, London
Allied Publishers	Allied Indian Publishers, Lahore and New Delhi
Almond	Almond Press, Sheffield
AM	Aubier Montaigne, Paris

AMAES	Association des Médiévistes Angliciste de l'Enseignement Supérieur, Paris
Amate	Amate Press, Oxford
AmberL	Amber Lane, Oxford
Amistad	Amistad Press, New York
AMP	Aurora Metro Press, London
AMS	AMS Press, New York
AMU	Adam Mickiewicz University, Posnan
Anansi	Anansi Press, Toronto
Anderson-Lovelace	Anderson-Lovelace, Los Altos Hills, CA
Anma Libri	Anma Libri, Saratoga, CA
Antipodes	Antipodes Press, Plimmerton, New Zealand
Anvil	Anvil Press Poetry, London
APA	APA, Maarssen, Netherlands
APH	Associated Publishing House, New Delhi
APL	American Poetry and Literature Press, Philadelphia
APP	Australian Professional Publications, Mosman, New South Wales
Applause	Applause Theatre Book Publishers
Appletree	Appletree Press, Belfast
APS	American Philosophical Society, Philadelphia
Aquarian	Aquarian Press, Wellingborough, Northants
ArborH	Arbor House Publishing, New York
Arcade	Arcade Publishing, New York
Archon	Archon Books, Hamden, CT
ArchP	Architectural Press Books, Guildford, Surrey
ArdenSh	Arden Shakespeare
Ardis	Ardis Publishers, Ann Arbor, MI
Ariel	Ariel Press, London
Aristotle	Aristotle University, Thessaloniki
Ark	Ark Paperbacks, London
Arkona	Arkona Forlaget, Aarhus, Denmark
Arlington	Arlington Books, London
Arnold	Edward Arnold, London
ArnoldEJ	E.J. Arnold & Son, Leeds
ARP	Australian Reference Publications, N. Balwyn, Victoria
Arrow	Arrow Books, London
Artmoves	Artmoves, Parkdale, Victoria
ASAL	Association for the Study of Australian Literature
ASB	Anglo-Saxon Books, Middlesex
ASECS	American Society for Eighteenth-Century Studies, c/o Ohio State University, Columbus
Ashfield	Ashfield Press, London
Ashgate	Ashgate, Brookfield, VT
Ashton	Ashton Scholastic
Aslib	Aslib, London
ASLS	Association for Scottish Literary Studies, Aberdeen
ASU	Arizona State University, Tempe

Atheneum	Atheneum Publishers, New York
Athlone	Athlone Press, London
Atlas	Atlas Press, London
Attic	Attic Press, Dublin
AuBC	Australian Book Collector
AucklandUP	Auckland UP, Auckland
AUG	Acta Universitatis Gothoburgensis, Sweden
AUP	Associated University Presses, London and Toronto
AUPG	Academic & University Publishers, London
Aurum	Aurum Press, London
Auslib	Auslib Press, Adelaide
AUU	Acta Universitatis Umensis, Umeå, Sweden
AUUp	Acta Universitatis Upsaliensis, Uppsala
Avebury	Avebury Publishing, Aldershot, Hampshire
Avero	Avero Publications, Newcastle upon Tyne
A-V Verlag	A-V Verlag, Franz Fischer, Augsburg, Germany
AWP	Africa World Press, Trenton, NJ
Axelrod	Axelrod Publishing, Tampa Bay, FL
BA	British Academy, London
BAAS	British Association for American Studies, c/o University of Keele
Bagel	August Bagel Verlag, Dusseldorf
Bahri	Bahri Publications, New Delhi
Bamberger	Bamberger Books, Flint, MI
B&B	Boydell & Brewer, Woodbridge, Suffolk
B&J	Barrie & Jenkins, London
B&N	Barnes & Noble, Totowa, NJ
B&O	Burns & Oates, Tunbridge Wells, Kent
B&S	Michael Benskin and M.L. Samuels, Middle English Dialect Project, University of Edinburgh
BAR	British Archaelogical Reports, Oxford
Barn Owl	Barn Owl Books, Taunton, Somerset
Barnes	A.S. Barnes, San Diego, CA
Barr Smith	Barr Smith Press, Barr Smith Library, University of Adelaide
Bath UP	Bath UP, Bath
Batsford	B.T. Batsford, London
Bayreuth	Bayreuth African Studies, University of Bayreuth, Germany
BBC	BBC Publications, London
BClarkL	Bruccoli Clark Layman
BCP	Bristol Classical Press, Bristol
Beacon	Beacon Press, Boston, MA
Beck	C.H. Beck'sche Verlagsbuchandlung, Munich
Becket	Becket Publications, London
Belin	Éditions Belin, Paris
Belknap	Belknap Press, Cambridge, MA
Belles Lettres	Société d'Édition les Belles Lettres, Paris

Bellew	Bellew Publishing, London
Bellflower	Belflower Press, Case University, Cleveland, OH
Benjamins	John Benjamins, Amsterdam
BenjaminsNA	John Benjamins North America, Philadelphia
BennC	Bennington College, Bennington, VT
Berg	Berg Publishers, Oxford
BFI	British Film Institute, London
BGUP	Bowling Green University Popular Press, Bowling Green, OH
BibS	Bibliographical Society, London
Bilingual	Bilingual Press, Arizona State University, Tempe
Bingley	Clive Bingley, London
Binnacle	Binnacle Press, London
Biografia	Biografia Publishers, London
Birkbeck	Birkbeck College, University of London
Bishopsgate	Bishopsgate Press, Tonbridge, Kent
BL	British Library, London
Black	Adam & Charles Black, London
Black Cat	Black Cat Press, Blackrock, Eire
Blackie	Blackie & Son, Glasgow
Black Moss	Black Moss, Windsor, Ontario
Blackstaff	Blackstaff Press, Belfast
Black Swan	Black Swan, Curtin, UT
Blackwell	Basil Blackwell, Oxford
BlackwellR	Blackwell Reference, Oxford
Blackwood	Blackwood, Pillans & Wilson, Edinburgh
Bl&Br	Blond & Briggs, London
Blandford	Blandford Press, London
Blaue Eule	Verlag die Blaue Eule, Essen
Bloodaxe	Bloodaxe Books, Newcastle upon Tyne
Bloomsbury	Bloomsbury Publishing, London
Blubber Head	Blubber Head Press, Hobart
BM	Bobbs-Merrill, New York
BMP	British Museum Publications, London
Bodleian	Bodleian Library, Oxford
Bodley	Bodley Head, London
Bogle	Bogle L'Ouverture Publications, London
BoiseSUP	Boise State UP, Boise, Idaho
Book Guild	Book Guild, Lewes, E. Sussex
BookplateS	Bookplate Society, Edgbaston, Birmingham
Boombana	Boombana Press, Brisbane, Queensland
Borealis	Borealis Press, Ottawa
Borgo	Borgo Press, San Bernardino, CA
BostonAL	Boston Athenaeum Library, Boxton, MA
Bouma	Bouma's Boekhuis, Groningen, Netherlands
Bowker	R.R. Bowker, New Providence, NJ
Boyars	Marion Boyars, London and Boston, MA
Boydell	Boydell Press, Woodbridge, Suffolk

Boyes	Megan Boyes, Allestree, Derbyshire
Bran's Head	Bran's Head Books, Frome, Somerset
Braumüller	Wilhelm Braumüller, Vienna
Breakwater	Breakwater Books, St John's, Newfoundland
Brentham	Brentham Press, St Albans, Hertfordshire
Brepols	Brepols, Turnhout, Belgium
Brewer	D.S. Brewer, Woodbridge, Suffolk
Brewin	Brewin Books, Studley, Warwicks
Bridge	Bridge Publishing, S. Plainfield, NJ
Brill	E.J. Brill, Leiden
Brilliance	Brilliance Books, London
Broadview	Broadview, London, Ontario and Lewiston, NY
Brookside	Brookside Press, London
Browne	Sinclair Browne, London
Brownstone	Brownstone Books, Madison, IN
BrownUP	Brown UP, Providence, RI
Brynmill	Brynmill Press, Harleston, Norfolk
BSA	Bibliographical Society of America
BSB	Black Swan Books, Redding Ridge, CT
BSP	Black Sparrow Press, Santa Barbara, CA
BSU	Ball State University, Muncie, IN
BuckUP	Bucknell UP, Lewisburg, PA
Bulzoni	Bulzoni Editore, Rome
BUP	Birmingham University Press
Burnett	Burnett Books, London
Buske	Helmut Buske, Hamburg
Butterfly	Butterfly Books, San Antonio, TX
CA	Creative Arts Book, Berkeley, CA
CAAS	Connecticut Academy of Arts and Sciences, New Haven
CAB International	Centre for Agriculture and Biosciences International, Wallingford, Oxfordshire
Cadmus	Cadmus Editions, Tiburon, CA
Cairns	Francis Cairns, University of Leeds
Calaloux	Calaloux Publications, Ithaca, NY
Calder	John Calder, London
CALLS	Centre for Australian Language and Literature Studies, English Department, Universty of New England, New South Wales
Camden	Camden Press, London
C&G	Carroll & Graf, New York
C&W	Chatto & Windus, London
Canongate	Canongate Publishing, Edinburgh
Canterbury	Canterbury Press, Norwich
Cape	Jonathan Cape, London
Capra	Capra Press, Santa Barbara, CA
Carcanet	Carcanet New Press, Manchester, Lancashire
Cardinal	Cardinal, London
CaribB	Caribbean Books, Parkersburg, IA

CarletonUP	Carleton UP, Ottawa
Carucci	Carucci, Rome
Cass	Frank Cass, London
Cassell	Cassell, London
Cavaliere Azzurro	Cavaliere Azzurro, Bologna
Cave	Godfrey Cave Associates, London
CBA	Council for British Archaeology, London
CBS	Cambridge Bibliographical Society, Cambridge
CCEUCan	Centre for Continuing Education, University of Canterbury, Christchurch, New Zealand
CCP	Canadian Children's Press, Guelph, Ontario
CCS	Centre for Canadian Studies, Mount Allison University, Sackville, NB
CDSH	Centre de Documentation Sciences Humaines, Paris
CENS	Centre for English Name Studies, University of Nottingham
Century	Century Publishing, London
Ceolfrith	Ceolfrith Press, Sunderland, Tyne and Wear
CESR	Société des Amis du Centre d'Études Supérieures de la Renaissance, Tours
CETEDOC	Library of Christian Latin Texts
CFA	Canadian Federation for the Humanities, Ottawa
CH	Croom Helm, London
C–H	Chadwyck–Healey, Cambridge
Chambers	W. & R. Chambers, Edinburgh
Champaign	Champaign Public Library and Information Center, Champaign, IL
Champion	Librairie Honoré Champion, Paris
Chand	S. Chand, Madras
ChelseaH	Chelsea House Publishers, New York, New Haven, and Philadelphia
ChLitAssoc	Children's Literature Association
Christendom	Christendom Publications, Front Royal, VA
Chronicle	Chronicle Books, London
Chrysalis	Chrysalis Press
ChuoUL	Chuo University Library, Tokyo
Churchman	Churchman Publishing, Worthing, W. Sussex
Cistercian	Cistercian Publications, Kalamazoo, MI
CL	City Lights Books, San Francisco
CLA	Canadian Library Association, Ottawa
Clarendon	Clarendon Press, Oxford
Claridge	Claridge, St Albans, Hertfordshire
Clarion	Clarion State College, Clarion, PA
Clark	T. & T. Clark, Edinburgh
Clarke	James Clarke, Cambridge
Classical	Classical Publishing, New Delhi
CLCS	Centre for Language and Communication Studies, Trinity College, Dublin

ClogherHS	Clogher Historical Society, Monaghan, Eire
CLUEB	Cooperativa Libraria Universitaria Editrice, Bologna
Clunie	Clunie Press, Pitlochry, Tayside
CMAP	Caxton's Modern Arts Press, Dallas, TX
CMERS	Center for Medieval and Early Renaissance Studies, Binghamton, NY
CML	William Andrews Clark Memorial Library, Los Angeles
CMST	Centre for Medieval Studies, University of Toronto
Coach House	Coach House Press, Toronto
Colleagues	Colleagues Press, East Lansing, MI
Collector	Collector, London
College-Hill	College-Hill Press, San Diego, CA
Collins	William Collins, London
CollinsA	William Collins (Australia), Sydney
Collins & Brown	Collins & Brown, London
ColUP	Columbia UP, New York
Comedia	Comedia Publishing, London
Comet	Comet Books, London
Compton	Compton Press, Tisbury, Wiltshire
Constable	Constable, London
Contemporary	Contemporary Books, Chicago
Continuum	Continuum Publishing, New York
Copp	Copp Clark Pitman, Mississuaga, Ontario
Corgi	Corgi Books, London
CorkUP	Cork UP, Eire
Cormorant	Cormorant Press, Victoria, BC
Cornford	Cornford Press, Launceston, Tasmania
CornUP	Cornell UP, Ithaca, NY
Cornwallis	Cornwallis Press, Hastings, E. Sussex
Coronado	Coronado Press, Lawrence, KS
Cosmo	Cosmo Publications, New Delhi
Coteau	Coteau Books, Regina, Saskatchewan
Cowley	Cowley Publications, Cambridge, MA
Cowper	Cowper House, Pacific Grove, CA
CPP	Canadian Poetry Press, London, Ontario
CQUP	Central Queensland UP, Rockhampton
Crabtree	Crabtree Press, Sussex
Craftsman House	Craftsman House, Netherlands
Craig Pottoon	Craig Pottoon Publishing, New Zealand
Crawford	Crawford House Publishing, Hindmarsh, SA
Creag Darach	Creag Durach Publications, Stirling
Cresset	Cresset Library, London
CRNLE	Centre for Research in the New Literatures in English, Adelaide
Crossing	Crossing Press, Freedom, CA
Crossroad	Crossroad Publishing, New York
Crown	Crown Publishers, New York
Crowood	Crowood Press, Marlborough, Wiltshire

CSAL	Centre for Studies in Australian Literature, University of Western Australia, Nedlands
CSLI	Center for the Study of Language and Information, Stanford University
CSP	Canadian Scholars' Press, Toronto
CSU	Cleveland State University, Cleveland, OH
CTHS	Éditions du Comité des Travaux Historiques et Scientifiques, Paris
CUAP	Catholic University of America Press, Washington, DC
Cuff	Harry Cuff Publications, St John's, Newfoundland
CULouvain	Catholic University of Louvain, Belgium
CULublin	Catholic University of Lublin, Poland
CUP	Cambridge UP, Cambridge, New York, and Melbourne
Currency	Currency Press, Paddington, New South Wales
Currey	James Currey, London
CV	Cherry Valley Edition, Rochester, NY
CVK	Cornelson-Velhagen & Klasing, Berlin
CWU	Carl Winter Universitätsverlag, Heidelberg
Da Capo	Da Capo Press, New York
Dacorum	Dacorum College, Hemel Hempstead, Hertfordshire
Daisy	Daisy Books, Peterborough, Northampton
Dalkey	Dalkey Archive Press, Elmwood Park, IL
D&C	David & Charles, Newton Abbot, Devon
D&H	Duncker & Humblot, Berlin
D&M	Douglas & McIntyre, Vancouver, BC
D&S	Duffy and Snellgrove, Polts Point, New South Wales
Dangaroo	Dangaroo Press, Mundelstrup, Denmark
Dawson	Dawson Publishing, Folkestone, Kent
DawsonsPM	Dawsons Pall Mall
DBAP	Daphne Brasell Associates Press
DBP	Drama Book Publishers, New York
Deakin UP	Deakin UP, Geelong, Victoria
De Boeck	De Boeck-Wesmael, Brussels
Dee	Ivan R. Dee Publishers, Chicago, IL
De Graaf	De Graaf, Nierwkoup, Netherlands
Denoël	Denoël S.A.R.L., Paris
Dent	J.M. Dent, London
DentA	Dent, Ferntree Gully, Victoria
Depanee	Depanee Printers and Publishers, Nugegoda, Sri Lanka
Deutsch	André Deutsch, London
Didier	Éditions Didier, Paris
Diesterweg	Verlag Moritz Diesterweg, Frankfurt am Main
Dim Gray Bar Press	Dim Gray Bar Press
Doaba	Doaba House, Delhi
Dobby	Eric Dobby Publishing, St Albans
Dobson	Dobson Books, Durham
Dolmen	Dolmen Press, Portlaoise, Eire
Donald	John Donald, Edinburgh

Donker	Adriaan Donker, Johannesburg
Dorset	Dorset Publishing
Doubleday	Doubleday, London and New York
Dove	Dove, Sydney
Dovecote	Dovecote Press, Wimborne, Dorset
Dovehouse	Dovehouse Editions, Canada
Dover	Dover Publications, New York
Drew	Richard Drew, Edinburgh
Droste	Droste Verlag, Düsseldorf
Droz	Librairie Droz SA, Geneva
DublinUP	Dublin UP, Dublin
Duckworth	Gerald Duckworth, London
Duculot	J. Duculot, Gembloux, Belgium
DukeUP	Duke UP, Dublin
Dundurn	Dundurn Press, Toronto and London, Ontario
Duquesne	Duquesne UP, Pittsburgh
Dutton	E.P. Dutton, New York
DWT	Dr Williams's Trust, London
EA	English Association, London
EAS	English Association Sydney Incorporated
Eason	Eason & Son, Dublin
East Bay	East Bay Books, Berkeley, CA
Ebony	Ebony Books, Melbourne
Ecco	Ecco Press, New York
ECNRS	Éditions du Centre National de la Recherche Scientifique, Paris
ECW	ECW Press, Downsview, Ontario
Eden	Eden Press, Montreal and St Albans, VT
EdinUP	Edinburgh UP, Edinburgh
Edizioni	Edizioni del Grifo
EEM	Eastern European Monographs, Boulder, CO
Eerdmans	William Eerdmans, Grand Rapids, MI
EETS	Early English Text Society, c/o Exeter College, Oxford
1890sS	Eighteen-Nineties Society, Oxford
Eihosha	Eihosha, Tokyo
Elephas	Elephas Books, Kewdale, Australia
Elibank	Elibank Press, Wellington, New Zealand
Elm Tree	Elm Tree Books, London
ELS	English Literary Studies
Ember	Ember Press, Brixham, South Devon
EMSH	Éditions de la Maison des Sciences de l'Homme, Paris
Enitharmon	Enitharmon Press, London
Enzyklopädie	Enzyklopädie, Leipzig
EONF	Eugene O'Neill Foundation, Danville, CA
EPNS	English Place-Name Society, Beeston, Nottingham
Epworth	Epworth Press, Manchester
Eriksson	Paul Eriksson, Middlebury, VT
Erlbaum	Erlbaum Associates, NJ

Erskine	Erskine Press, Harleston, Norfolk
EscutchP	Escutcheon Press
ESI	Edizioni Scientifiche Italiane, Naples
ESL	Edizioni di Storia e Letteratura, Rome
EUFS	Éditions Universitaires Fribourg Suisse
EUL	Edinburgh University Library, Edinburgh
Europa	Europa Publishers, London
Evans	M. Evans, New York
Exact Change	Exact Change, Boston
Exile	Exile Editions, Toronto, Ontario
Eyre	Eyre Methuen, London
FAB	Free Association Books, London
Faber	Faber & Faber, London
FAC	Fédération d'Activités Culturelles, Paris
FACP	Fremantle Arts Centre Press, Fremantle, WA
Falcon Books	Falcon Books, Eastbourne
FALS	Foundation for Australian Literary Studies, James Cook University of North Queensland, Townsville
F&F	Fels & Firn Press, San Anselmo, CA
F&S	Feffer & Simons, Amsterdam
Farrand	Farrand Press, London
Fay	Barbara Fay, Stuttgart
F–B	Ford–Brown, Houston, TX
FCP	Four Courts Press, Dublin
FDUP	Fairleigh Dickinson UP, Madison, NJ
FE	Fourth Estate, London
Feminist	Feminist Press, New York
FictionColl	Fiction Collective, Brooklyn College, Brooklyn, NY
Field Day	Field Day, Derry
Fifth House	Fifth House Publications, Saskatoon, Saskatchewan
FILEF	FILEF Italo–Australian Publications, Leichhardt, New South Wales
Fine	Donald Fine, New York
Fink	Fink Verlag, Munich
Five Leaves	Five Leaves Publications, Nottingham
Flamingo	Flamingo Publishing, Newark, NJ
Flammarion	Flammarion, Paris
FlindersU	Flinders University of South Australia, Bedford Park
Floris	Floris Books, Edinburgh
FlorSU	Florida State University, Tallahassee, FL
FOF	Facts on File, New York
Folger	Folger Shakespeare Library, Washington, DC
Folio	Folio Press, London
Fontana	Fontana Press, London
Footprint	Footprint Press, Colchester, Essex
FordUP	Fordham UP, New York
Foris	Foris Publications, Dordrecht
Forsten	Egbert Forsten Publishing, Groningen, Netherlands

Fortress	Fortress Press, Philadelphia
Francke	Francke Verlag, Berne
Franklin	Burt Franklin, New York
FreeP	Free Press, New York
FreeUP	Free UP, Amsterdam
Freundlich	Freundlich Books, New York
Frommann-Holzboog	Frommann-Holzboog, Stuttgart
FS&G	Farrar, Straus & Giroux
FSP	Five Seasons Press, Madley, Hereford
FW	Fragments West/Valentine Press, Long Beach, CA
FWA	Fiji Writers' Association, Suva
FWP	Falling Wall Press, Bristol
Gale	Gale Research, Detroit, MI
Galilée	Galilée, Paris
Gallimard	Gallimard, Paris
G&G	Grevatt & Grevatt, Newcastle upon Tyne
G&M	Gill & Macmillan, Dublin
Garland	Garland Publishing, New York
Gasson	Roy Gasson Associates, Wimbourne, Dorset
Gateway	Gateway Editions, Washington, DC
GE	Greenwich Exchange, UK
GIA	GIA Publications, USA
Girasole	Edizioni del Girasole, Ravenna
GL	Goose Lane Editions, Fredericton, NB
GlasgowDL	Glasgow District Libraries, Glasgow
Gleerup	Gleerupska, Lund
Gliddon	Gliddon Books Publishers, Norwich
Gloger	Gloger Family Books, Portland, OR
GMP	GMP Publishing, London
GMSmith	Gibbs M. Smith, Layton, UT
Golden Dog	Golden Dog, Ottawa
Gollancz	Victor Gollancz, London
Gomer	Gomer Press, Llandysul, Dyfed
GothU	Gothenburg University, Gothenburg
Gower	Gower Publishing, Aldershot, Hants.
GRAAT	Groupe de Recherches Anglo-Américaines de Tours
Grafton	Grafton Books, London
GranB	Granary Books, New York
Granta	Granta Publications, London
Granville	Granville Publishing, London
Grasset	Grasset & Fasquelle, Paris
Grassroots	Grassroots, London
Graywolf	Graywolf Press, St Paul, MI
Greenhalgh	M.J. Greenhalgh, London
Greenhill	Greenhill Books, London
Greenwood	Greenwood Press, Westport, CT
Gregg	Gregg Publishing, Surrey
Greville	Greville Press, Warwick

Greymitre	Greymitre Books, London
GroC	Grolier Club, New York
Groos	Julius Groos Verlag, Heidelberg
Grove	Grove Press, New York
GRP	Greenfield Review Press, New York
Grüner	B.R. Grüner, Amsterdam
Gruyter	Walter de Gruyter, Berlin
Guernica	Guernica Editions, Montreal, Canada
Guilford	Guilford, New York
Gulmohar	Gulmohar Press, Islamabad, Pakistan
Haggerston	Haggerston Press, London
HakluytS	Hakluyt Society, c/o British Library, London
Hale	Robert Hale, London
Hall	G.K. Hall, Boston, MA
Halstead	Halstead Press, Rushcutters Bay, New South Wales
HalsteadP	Halstead Press, c/o J. Wiley & Sons, Chichester, W. Sussex
Hambledon	Hambledon Press, London
H&I	Hale & Iremonger, Sydney
H&L	Hambledon and London
H&M	Holmes & Meier, London and New York
H&S	Hodder & Stoughton, London
H&SNZ	Hodder & Stoughton, Auckland
H&W	Hill & Wang, New York
Hansib	Hansib Publishing, London
Harbour	Harbour Publishing, Madeira Park, BC
Harman	Harman Publishing House, New Delhi
Harper	Harper & Row, New York
Harrap	Harrap, Edinburgh
HarrV	Harrassowitz Verlag, Wiesbaden
HarvardUP	Harvard UP, Cambridge, MA
Harwood	Harwood Academic Publishers, Langhorne, PA
Hatje	Verlag Gerd Hatje, Germany
HBJ	Harcourt Brace Jovanovich, New York and London
HC	HarperCollins, London
HCAus	HarperCollins Australia, Pymble, New South Wales
Headline	Headline Book Publishing, London
Heath	D.C. Heath, Lexington, MS
Heinemann	William Heinemann, London
HeinemannA	William Heinemann, St Kilda, Victoria
HeinemannC	Heinemann Educational Books, Kingston, Jamaica
HeinemannNg	Heinemann Educational Books, Nigeria
HeinemannNZ	Heinemann Publishers, Auckland (now Heinemann Reed)
HeinemannR	Heinemann Reed, Auckland
Helm	Christopher Helm, London
Herbert	Herbert Press, London
Hermitage	Hermitage Antiquarian Bookshop, Denver, CO
Hern	Nick Hern Books, London
Heyday	Heyday Books, Berkeley, CA

HH	Hamish Hamilton, London
Hilger	Adam Hilger, Bristol
HM	Harvey Miller, London
HMSO	HMSO, London
Hodder, Moa, Beckett	Hodder, Moa, Beckett, Milford, Auckland, New Zealand
Hodge	A. Hodge, Penzance, Cornwall
Hogarth	Hogarth Press, London
HongKongUP	Hong Kong UP, Hong Kong
Horsdal & Schubart	Horsdal & Schubart, Victoria, BC
Horwood	Ellis Horwood, Hemel Hempstead, Hertfordshire
HoughtonM	Houghton Mifflin, Boston, MA
Howard	Howard UP, Washington, DC
HREOC	Human Rights and Equal Opportunity Commission, Commonweath of Australia, Canberra
HRW	Holt, Reinhart & Winston, New York
Hudson	Hudson Hills Press, New York
Hueber	Max Hueber, Ismaning, Germany
HUL	Hutchinson University Library, London
HullUP	Hull UP, University of Hull
Humanities	Humanities Press, Atlantic Highlands, NJ
Huntington	Huntington Library, San Marino, CA
Hutchinson	Hutchinson Books, London
HW	Harvester Wheatsheaf, Hemel Hempstead, Hertfordshire
HWWilson	H.W. Wilson, New York
Hyland House	Hyland House Publishing, Victoria
HyphenP	Hyphen Press, London
IAAS	Indian Institute of Aveanced Studies, Lahore and New Delhi
Ian Henry	Ian Henry Publications, Hornchurch, Essex
IAP	Irish Academic Press, Dublin
Ibadan	Ibadan University Press
IBK	Innsbrucker Beiträge zur Kulturwissenschaft, University of Innsbruck
ICA	Institute of Contemporary Arts, London
IHA	International Hopkins Association, Waterloo, Ontario
IJamaica	Institute of Jamaica Publications, Kingston
Imago	Imago Imprint, New York
ImperialWarMuseum	Imperial War Museum Publications, London
IndUP	Indiana UP, Bloomington, IN
Inkblot	Inkblot Publications, Berkeley, CA
IntUP	International Universities Press, New York
Inventions	Inventions Press, London
IonaC	Iona College, New Rochelle, NY
IowaSUP	Iowa State UP, Ames, IA
IOWP	Isle of Wight County Press, Newport, Isle of Wight
IP	In Parenthesis, London
Ipswich	Ipswich Press, Ipswich, MA
IrishAP	Irish Academic Press, Dublin

ISI	ISI Press, Philadelphia
Italica	Italica Press, New York
IULC	Indiana University Linguistics Club, Bloomington, IN
IUP	Indiana University of Pennsylvania Press, Indiana, PA
Ivon	Ivon Publishing House, Bombay
Jacaranda	Jacaranda Wiley, Milton, Queensland
JadavpurU	Jadavpur University, Calcutta
James CookU	James Cook University of North Queensland, Townsville
Jarrow	Parish of Jarrow, Tyne and Wear
Jesperson	Jesperson Press, St John's, Newfoundland
JHall	James Hall, Leamington Spa, Warwickshire
JHUP	Johns Hopkins UP, Baltimore, MD
JIWE	JIWE Publications, University of Gulbarga, India
JLRC	Jack London Research Center, Glen Ellen, CA
J-NP	Joe-Noye Press
Jonas	Jonas Verlag, Marburg, Germany
Joseph	Michael Joseph, London
Journeyman	Journeyman Press, London
JPGM	J. Paul Getty Museum
JT	James Thin, Edinburgh
Junction	Junction Books, London
Junius-Vaughan	Junius-Vaughan Press, Fairview, NJ
Jupiter	Jupiter Press, Lake Bluff, IL
JyväskyläU	Jyväskylä University, Jyväskylä, Finland
Kaibunsha	Kaibunsha, Tokyo
K&N	Königshausen & Neumann, Würzburg, Germany
K&W	Kaye & Ward, London
Kangaroo	Kangaroo Press, Simon & Schuster (Australia), Roseville, New South Wales
Kansai	Kansai University of Foreign Studies, Osaka
Kardo	Kardo, Coatbridge, Scotland
Kardoorair	Kardoorair Press, Adelaide
Karia	Karia Press, London
Karnak	Karnak House, London
Karoma	Karoma Publishers, Ann Arbor, MI
KC	Kyle Cathie, London
KCL	King's College London
KeeleUP	Keele University Press
Kegan Paul	Kegan Paul International, London
Kenkyu	Kenkyu-Sha, Tokyo
Kennikat	Kennikat Press, Port Washington, NY
Kensal	Kensal Press, Oxford
KentSUP	Kent State University Press, Kent, OH
KenyaLB	Kenya Literature Bureau, Nairobi
Kerosina	Kerosina Publications, Worcester Park, Surrey
Kerr	Charles H. Kerr, Chicago
Kestrel	Viking Kestrel, London
K/H	Kendall/Hunt Publishing, Dubuque, IA

Kingsley	J. Kingsley Publishers, London
Kingston	Kingston Publishers, Kingston, Jamaica
Kinseido	Kinseido, Tokyo
Klostermann	Vittorio Klostermann, Frankfurt am Main
Kluwer	Kluwer Academic Publications, Dordrecht
Knopf	Alfred A. Knopf, New York
Knowledge	Knowledge Industry Publications, White Plains, NY
Kraus	Kraus International Publications, White Plains, NY
KSUP	Kent State UP, Kent OH
LA	Library Association, London
LACUS	Linguistic Association of Canada and the United States, Chapel Hill, NC
Lake View	Lake View Press, Chicago
LAm	Library of America, New York
Lancelot	Lancelot Press, Hantsport, NS
Landesman	Jay Landesman, London
L&W	Lawrence & Wishart, London
Lane	Allen Lane, London
Lang	Peter D. Lang, Frankfurt am Main and Berne
LehighUP	Lehigh University Press, Bethlehem, PA
LeicAE	University of Leicester, Department of Adult Education
LeicsCC	Leicestershire County Council, Libraries and Information Service, Leicester
LeicUP	Leicester UP, Leicester
LeidenUP	Leiden UP, Leiden
Leopard's Head	Leopard's Head Press, Oxford
Letao	Letao Press, Albury, New South Wales
LeuvenUP	Leuven UP, Leuven, Belgium
Lexik	Lexik House, Cold Spring, NY
Lexington	Lexington Publishers
LF	LiberFörlag, Stockholm
LH	Lund Humphries Publishers, London
Liberty	Liberty Classics, Indianapolis, IN
Libris	Libris, London
LibrU	Libraries Unlimited, Englewood, CO
Liguori	Liguori, Naples
Limelight	Limelight Editions, New York
Lime Tree	Lime Tree Press, Octopus Publishing, London
LincolnUP	Lincoln University Press, Nebraska
LITIR	LITIR Database, University of Alberta
LittleH	Little Hills Press, Burwood, New South Wales
Liveright	Liveright Publishing, New York
LiverUP	Liverpool UP, Liverpool
Livre de Poche	Le Livre de Poche, Paris
Llanerch	Llanerch Enterprises, Lampeter, Dyfed
Locust Hill	Locust Hill Press, West Cornwall, CT
Loewenthal	Loewenthal Press, New York
Longman	Addison Longman Wesley, Harlow, Essex

LongmanC	Longman Caribbean, Harlow, Essex
LongmanF	Longman, France
LongmanNZ	Longman, Auckland
Longspoon	Longspoon Press, University of Alberta, Edmonton
Lovell	David Lovell Publishing, Brunswick, Australia
Lowell	Lowell Press, Kansas City, MS
Lowry	Lowry Publishers, Johannesburg
LSUP	Louisiana State UP, Baton Rouge, LA
LundU	Lund University, Lund, Sweden
LUP	Loyola UP, Chicago
Lutterworth	Lutterworth Press, Cambridge
Lymes	Lymes Press, Newcastle, Staffordshire
MAA	Medieval Academy of America, Cambridge, MA
Macmillan	Macmillan Publishers, London
MacmillanC	Macmillan Caribbean
Madison	Madison Books, Lanham, MD
Madurai	Madurai University, Madurai, India
Maecenas	Maecenas Press, Iowa City, Iowa
Magabala	Magabala Books, Broome, WA
Magnes	Magnes Press, The Hebrew University, Jerusalem
Mainstream	Mainstream Publishing, Edinburgh
Maisonneuve	Maisonneuve Press, Washington, DC
Malone	Malone Society, c/o King's College, London
Mambo	Mambo Press, Gweru, Zimbabwe
ManCASS	Manchester Centre for Anglo-Saxon Studies, University of Manchester
M&E	Macdonald & Evans, Estover, Plymouth, Devon
M&S	McClelland & Stewart, Toronto
Maney	W.S. Maney & Sons, Leeds
Mansell	Mansell Publishing, London
Manufacture	La Manufacture, Lyons
ManUP	Manchester UP, Milwaukee, WI
Mardaga	Mardaga
Mariner	Mariner Books, Boston, MA
MarquetteUP	Marquette UP, Milwaukee, WI
Marvell	Marvell Press, Calstock, Cornwall
MB	Mitchell Beazley, London
McDougall, Littel	McDougall, Littel, Evanston, IL
McFarland	McFarland, Jefferson, NC
McG-QUP	McGill-Queen's UP, Montreal
McGraw-Hill	McGraw-Hill, New York
McIndoe	John McIndoe, Dunedin, New Zealand
McPheeG	McPhee Gribble Publishers, Fitzroy, Victoria
McPherson	McPherson, Kingston, NY
MCSU	Maria Curie Skłodowska University
ME	M. Evans, New York
Meany	P.D. Meany Publishing, Port Credit, Ontario
Meckler	Meckler Publishing, Westport, CT

MelbourneUP	Melbourne UP, Carlton South, Victoria
Mellen	Edwin Mellen Press, Lewiston, NY
MellenR	Mellen Research UP
MercerUP	Mercer UP, Macon, GA
Mercury	Mercury Press, Stratford, Ontario
Merlin	Merlin Press, London
Methuen	Methuen, London
MethuenA	Methuen Australia, North Ryde, New South Wales
MethuenC	Methuen, Toronto
Metro	Metro Publishing, Auckland
Metzler	Metzler, Stuttgart
MGruyter	Mouton de Gruyter, Berlin, New York, and Amsterdam
MH	Michael Haag, London
MHRA	Modern Humanities Research Association, London
MHS	Missouri Historical Society, St Louis, MO
MI	Microforms International, Pergamon Press, Oxford
Micah	Micah Publications, Marblehead, MA.
MichSUP	Michigan State UP, East Lansing, MI
MidNAG	Mid-Northumberland Arts Group, Ashington, Northumbria
Mieyungah	Mieyungah Press, Melbourne University Press, Carlton South, Victoria
Milestone	Milestone Publications, Horndean, Hampshire
Millennium	Millennium Books, E.J. Dwyer, Newtown, Australia
Millstream	Millstream Books, Bath
Milner	Milner, London
Minuit	Éditions de Minuit, Paris
MIP	Medieval Institute Publications, Western Michigan University, Kalamazoo
MITP	Massachusetts Institute of Technology Press, Cambridge, MA
MLA	Modern Language Association of America, New York
MlM	Multilingual Matters, Clevedon, Avon
MLP	Manchester Literary and Philosophical Society, Manchester
Modern Library	Modern Library (Random House), New York
Monarch	Monarch Publications, Sussex
Moonraker	Moonraker Press, Bradford-on-Avon, Wiltshire
Moorland	Moorland Publishing, Ashbourne, Derby
Moreana	Moreana, Angers, France
MorganSU	Morgan State University, Baltimore, MD
Morrow	William Morrow, New York
Mosaic	Mosaic Press, Oakville, Ontario
Motilal	Motilal Books, Oxford
Motley	Motley Press, Romsey, Hampshire
Mouton	Mouton Publishers, New York and Paris
Mowbray	A.R. Mowbray, Oxford
MR	Martin Robertson, Oxford

MRS	Medieval and Renaissance Society, North Texas State University, Denton
MRTS	MRTS, Binghamton, NY
MSUP	Memphis State UP, Memphis, TN
MtAllisonU	Mount Allison University, Sackville, NB
Mulini	Mulini Press, ACT
Muller	Frederick Muller, London
MULP	McMaster University Library Press
Murray	John Murray, London
Mursia	Ugo Mursia, Milan
NAL	New American Library, New York
Narr	Gunter Narr Verlag, Tübingen
Nathan	Fernand Nathan, Paris
NBB	New Beacon Books, London
NBCAus	National Book Council of Australia, Melbourne
NCP	New Century Press, Durham
ND	New Directions, New York
NDT	Nottingham Drama Texts, c/o University of Nottingham
NEL	New English Library, London
NELM	National English Literary Museum, Grahamstown, S. Africa
Nelson	Nelson Publishers, Melbourne
NelsonT	Thomas Nelson, London
New Endeavour	New Endeavour Press
NeWest	NeWest Press, Edmonton, Alberta
New Horn	New Horn Press, Ibadan, Nigeria
New Island	New Island Press
NewIssuesP	New Issues Press, Western Michigan University
NH	New Horizon Press, Far Hills, NJ
N-H	Nelson-Hall, Chicago
NHPC	North Holland Publishing, Amsterdam and New York
NicV	Nicolaische Verlagsbuchhandlung, Berlin
NIE	La Nuova Italia Editrice, Florence
Niemeyer	Max Niemeyer, Tübingen, Germany
Nightwood	Nightwood Editions, Toronto
NIUP	Northern Illinois UP, De Kalb, IL
NUSam	National University of Samoa
NLA	National Library of Australia
NLB	New Left Books, London
NLC	National Library of Canada, Ottawa
NLP	New London Press, Dallas, TX
NLS	National Library of Scotland, Edinburgh
NLW	National Library of Wales, Aberystwyth, Dyfed
Nodus	Nodus Publikationen, Münster
Northcote	Northcote House Publishers, Plymouth
NortheasternU	Northeastern University, Boston, MA
NorthwesternUP	Northwestern UP, Evanston, IL
Norton	W.W. Norton, New York and London
NorUP	Norwegian University Press, Oslo

Novus	Novus Press, Oslo
NPF	National Poetry Foundation, Orono, ME
NPG	National Portrait Gallery, London
NPP	North Point Press, Berkeley, CA
NSP	New Statesman Publishing, New Delhi
NSU Press	Northern States Universities Press
NSWUP	New South Wales UP, Kensington, New South Wales
NT	National Textbook, Lincolnwood, IL
NUC	Nipissing University College, North Bay, Ontario
NUP	National University Publications, Millwood, NY
NUSam	National University of Samoa
NUU	New University of Ulster, Coleraine
NWAP	North Waterloo Academic Press, Waterloo, Ontario
NWP	New World Perspectives, Montreal
NYPL	New York Public Library, New York
NYUP	New York UP, New York
OakK	Oak Knoll Press, New Castle, DE
O&B	Oliver & Boyd, Harlow, Essex
Oasis	Oasis Books, London
OBAC	Organization of Black American Culture, Chicago
OberlinCP	Oberlin College Press, Oberlin, OH
Oberon	Oberon Books, London
O'Brien	O'Brien Press, Dublin
OBS	Oxford Bibliographical Society, Bodleian Library, Oxford
Octopus	Octopus Books, London
OdenseUP	Odense UP, Odense
OE	Officina Edizioni, Rome
OEColl	Old English Colloquium, Berkeley, CA
Offord	John Offord Publications, Eastbourne, E. Sussex
OhioUP	Ohio UP, Athens, OH
Oldcastle	Oldcastle Books, Harpenden, Hertfordshire
Olms	Georg Olms, Hildesheim, Germany
Olschki	Leo S. Olschki, Florence
O'Mara	Michael O'Mara Books, London
Omnigraphics	Omnigraphics, Detroit, MI
Open Books	Open Books Publishing, Wells, Somerset
Open Court	Open Court Publishing, USA
OpenUP	Open UP, Buckingham and Philadelphia
OPP	Oxford Polytechnic Press, Oxford
Orbis	Orbis Books, London
OregonSUP	Oregon State UP, Corvallis, OR
Oriel	Oriel Press, Stocksfield, Northumberland
OrientUP	Oriental UP, London
Ortnamnsarkivet	Ortnamnsarkivet i Uppsala, Sweden
Orwell	Orwell Press, Southwold, Suffolk
Oryx	Oryx Press, Phoenix, AR
OSUP	Ohio State UP, Columbus, OH
OTP	Oak Tree Press, London

OUCA	Oxford University Committee for Archaeology, Oxford
OUP	Oxford UP, Oxford
OUPAm	Oxford UP, New York
OUPAus	Oxford UP, Melbourne
OUPC	Oxford UP, Toronto
OUPI	Oxford UP, New Delhi
OUPNZ	Oxford UP, Auckland
OUPSA	Oxford UP Southern Africa, Cape Town
Outlet	Outlet Book, New York
Overlook	Overlook Press, New York
Owen	Peter Owen, London
Owl	Owl
Pace UP	Pace University Press, New York
Pacifica	Press Pacifica, Kailua, Hawaii
Paget	Paget Press, Santa Barbara, CA
PAJ	PAJ Publications, New York
Paladin	Paladin Books, London
Palgrave	Palgrave, NY
Pan	Pan Books, London
PanAmU	Pan American University, Edinburgh, TX
P&C	Pickering & Chatto, London
Pandion	Pandion Press, Capitola, CA
Pandora	Pandora Press, London
Pan Macmillan	Pan Macmillan Australia, South Yarra, Victoria
Pantheon	Pantheon Books, New York
ParagonH	Paragon House Publishers, New York
Parnassus	Parnassus Imprints, Hyannis, MA
Parousia	Parousia Publications, London
Paternoster	Paternoster Press, Carlisle, Cumbria
Patten	Patten Press, Penzance
Paulist	Paulist Press, Ramsey, NJ
Paupers	Paupers' Press, Nottingham
Pavilion	Pavilion Books, London
PBFA	Provincial Booksellers' Fairs Association, Cambridge
Peachtree	Peachtree Publishers, Atlanta, GA
Pearson	David Pearson, Huntingdon, Cambridge
Peepal Tree	Peepal Tree Books, Leeds
Peeters	Peeters Publishers and Booksellers, Leuven, Belgium
Pelham	Pelham Books, London
Pembridge	Pembridge Press, London
Pemmican	Pemmican Publications, Winnipeg, Canada
PencraftI	Pencraft International, Ashok Vihar II, Delhi
Penguin	Penguin Books, Harmondsworth, Middlesex
PenguinA	Penguin Books, Ringwood, Victoria
PenguinNZ	Penguin Books, Auckland
Penkevill	Penkevill Publishing, Greenwood, FL
Pentland	Pentland Press, Ely, Cambridge
Penumbra	Penumbra Press, Moonbeam, Ontario

People's	People's Publications, London
Pergamon	Pergamon Press, Oxford
Permanent	Permanent Press, Sag Harbor, NY
Perpetua	Perpetua Press, Oxford
Petton	Petton Books, Oxford
Pevensey	Pevensey Press, Newton Abbot, Devon
PH	Prentice-Hall, Englewood Cliffs, NJ
Phaidon	Phaidon Press, London
PHI	Prentice-Hall International, Hemel Hempstead, Hertfordshire
PhilL	Philosophical Library, New York
Phillimore	Phillimore, Chichester
Phoenix	Phoenix
Piatkus	Piatkus Books, London
Pickwick	Pickwick Publications, Allison Park, PA
Pilgrim	Pilgrim Books, Norman, OK
PIMS	Pontifical Institute of Mediaeval Studies, Toronto
Pinter	Frances Pinter Publishers, London
Plains	Plains Books, Carlisle
Plenum	Plenum Publishing, London and New York
Plexus	Plexus Publishing, London
Pliegos	Editorial Pliegos, Madrid
Ploughshares	Ploughshares Books, Watertown, MA
Pluto	Pluto Press, London
PML	Pierpont Morgan Library, New York
Polity	Polity Press, Cambridge
Polygon	Polygon, Edinburgh
Poolbeg	Poolbeg Press, Swords, Dublin
Porcepic	Press Porcepic, Victoria, BC
Porcupine	Porcupine's Quill, Canada
PortN	Port Nicholson Press, Wellington, NZ
Potter	Clarkson N. Potter, New York
Power	Power Publications, University of Sydney
PPUBarcelona	Promociones y Publicaciones Universitarias, Barcelona
Praeger	Praeger, New York
Prestel	Prestel Verlag, Germany
PrestigeB	Prestige Books, New Delhi
Primavera	Edizioni Primavera, Gunti Publishing, Florence, Italy
Primrose	Primrose Press, Alhambra, CA
PrincetonUL	Princeton University Library, Princeton, NJ
PrincetonUP	Princeton UP, Princeton, NJ
Printwell	Printwell Publishers, Jaipur, India
Prism	Prism Press, Bridport, Dorset
PRO	Public Record Office, London
Profile	Profile Books, Ascot, Berks
ProgP	Progressive Publishers, Calcutta
PSUP	Pennsylvania State UP, University Park, PA
Pucker	Puckerbrush Press, Orono, ME

PUF	Presses Universitaires de France, Paris
PurdueUP	Purdue UP, Lafayette, IN
Pushcart	Pushcart Press, Wainscott, NY
Pustet	Friedrich Pustet, Regensburg
Putnam	Putnam Publishing, New York
PWP	Poetry Wales Press, Ogmore by Sea, mid-Glamorgan
QED	QED Press, Ann Arbor, MI
Quarry	Quarry Press, Kingston, Ontario
Quartet	Quartet Books, London
QUT	Queensland University of Technology
RA	Royal Academy of Arts, London
Rainforest	Rainforest Publishing, Faxground, New South Wales
Rampant Lions	Rampant Lions Press, Cambridge
R&B	Rosenklide & Bagger, Copenhagen
R&L	Rowman & Littlefield, Totowa, NJ
Randle	Ian Randle, Kingston, Jamaica
RandomH	Random House, London and New York
RandomHAus	Random House Australia, Victoria
Ravan	Ravan Press, Johannesburg
Ravette	Ravette, London
Reaktion	Reaktion Books, London
Rebel	Rebel Press, London
Red Kite	Red Kite Press, Guelph, Ontario
Red Rooster	Red Rooster Press, Hotham Hill, Victoria
Red Sea	Red Sea Press, NJ
Reed	Reed Books, Port Melbourne
Reference	Reference Press, Toronto
Regents	Regents Press of Kansas, Lawrence, KS
Reichenberger	Roswitha Reichenberger, Kessel, Germany
Reinhardt	Max Reinhardt, London
Remak	Remak, Alblasserdam, Netherlands
RenI	Renaissance Institute, Sophia University, Tokyo
Research	Research Publications, Reading
RETS	Renaissance English Text Society, Chicago
RH	Ramsay Head Press, Edinburgh
RHS	Royal Historical Society, London
RIA	Royal Irish Academy, Dublin
RiceUP	Rice UP, Houston, TX
Richarz	Hans Richarz, St Augustin, Germany
RICL	Research Institute for Comparative Literature, University of Alberta
Rivers Oram	Rivers Oram Press, London
Rizzoli	Rizzoli International Publications, New York
RobartsCCS	Robarts Centre for Canadian Studies, York University, North York, Ontario
Robinson	Robinson Publishing, London
Robson	Robson Books, London
Rodopi	Rodopi, Amsterdam

Roebuck	Stuart Roebuck, Suffolk
RoehamptonI	Roehampton Institute London
Routledge	Routledge, London and New York
Royce	Robert Royce, London
RS	Royal Society, London
RSC	Royal Shakespeare Company, London
RSL	Royal Society of Literature, London
RSVP	Research Society for Victorian Periodicals, University of Leicester
RT	RT Publications, London
Running	Running Press, Philadelphia
Russell	Michael Russell, Norwich
RutgersUP	Rutgers UP, New Brunswick, NJ
Ryan	Ryan Publishing, London
SA	Sahitya Akademi, New Delhi
Sage	Sage Publications, London
SAI	Sociological Abstracts, San Diego, CA
Salamander	Salamander Books, London
Salem	Salem Press, Englewood Cliffs, NJ
S&A	Shukayr and Akasheh, Amman, Jordon
S&D	Stein & Day, Briarcliff Manor, NJ
S&J	Sidgwick & Jackson, London
S&M	Sun & Moon Press, Los Angeles
S&P	Simon & Piere, Toronto
S&S	Simon & Schuster, New York and London
S&W	Secker & Warburg, London
Sangam	Sangam Books, London
Sangsters	Sangsters Book Stores, Kingston, Jamaica
SAP	Scottish Academic Press, Edinburgh
Saros	Saros International Publishers
SASSC	Sydney Association for Studies in Society and Culture, University of Sydney, New South Wales
Saur	Bowker-Saur, Sevenoaks, Kent
Savacou	Savacou Publications, Kingston, Jamaica
S-B	Schwann-Bagel, Düsseldorf
ScanUP	Scandinavian University Presses, Oslo
Scarecrow	Scarecrow Press, Metuchen, NJ
Schäuble	Schäuble Verlag, Rheinfelden, Germany
Schmidt	Erich Schmidt Verlag, Berlin
Schneider	Lambert Schneider, Heidelberg
Schocken	Schocken Books, New York
Scholarly	Scholarly Press, St Clair Shores, MI
ScholarsG	Scholars Press, GA
Schöningh	Ferdinand Schöningh, Paderborn, Germany
Schwinn	Michael Schwinn, Neustadt, Germany
SCJP	Sixteenth-Century Journal Publications
Scolar	Scolar Press, Aldershot, Hampshire
SCP	Second Chance Press, Sag Harbor, NY

Scribe	Scribe Publishing, Colchester
Scribner	Charles Scribner, New York
Seafarer	Seafarer Books, London
Seaver	Seaver Books, New York
Segue	Segue, New York
Semiotext(e)	Semiotext(e), Columbia University, New York
SePA	Self-Publishing Association
Seren Books	Seren Books, Bridgend, mid-Glamorgan
Serpent's Tail	Serpent's Tail Publishing, London
Sessions	William Sessions, York
Seuil	Éditions du Seuil, Paris
7:84 Pubns	7:84 Publications, Glasgow
Severn	Severn House, Wallington, Surrey
SF&R	Scholars' Facsimiles and Reprints, Delmar, NY
SH	Somerset House, Teaneck, NJ
Shalabh	Shalabh Book House, Meerut, India
ShAP	Sheffield Academic Press
Shearwater	Shearwater Press, Lenah Valley, Tasmania
Sheba	Sheba Feminist Publishers, London
Sheed&Ward	Sheed & Ward, London
Sheldon	Sheldon Press, London
SHESL	Société d'Histoire et d'Épistemologie des Sciences du Langage, Paris
Shinozaki	Shinozaki Shorin, Tokyo
Shinshindo	Shinshindo Publishing, Tokyo
Shire	Shire Publications, Princes Risborough, Buckinghamshire
Shoal Bay Press	Shoal Bay Press, New Zealand
Shoe String	Shoe String Press, Hamden, CT
SHP	Shakespeare Head Press
SIAS	Scandinavian Institute of African Studies, Uppsala
SIL	Summer Institute of Linguistics, Academic Publications, Dallas, TX
SIUP	Southern Illinois University Press
Simon King	Simon King Press, Milnthorpe, Cumbria
Sinclair-Stevenson	Sinclair-Stevenson, London
SingaporeUP	Singapore UP, Singapore
SIUP	Southern Illinois UP, Carbondale, IL
SJSU	San Jose State University, San Jose, CA
Skilton	Charles Skilton, London
Skoob	Skoob Books, London
Slatkine	Éditions Slatkine, Paris
Slavica	Slavica Publishers, Columbus, OH
Sleepy Hollow	Sleepy Hollow Press, Tarrytown, NY
SLG	SLG Press, Oxford
Smith Settle	Smith Settle, W. Yorkshire
SMUP	Southern Methodist UP, Dallas, TX
Smythe	Colin Smythe, Gerrards Cross, Buckinghamshire
SNH	Société Néophilologique de Helsinki

SNLS	Society for New Language Study, Denver, CO
SOA	Society of Authors, London
Soho	Soho Book, London
SohoP	Soho Press, New York
Solaris	Solaris Press, Rochester, MI
SonoNis	Sono Nis Press, Victoria, BC
Sorbonne	Publications de la Sorbonne, Paris
SorbonneN	Publications du Conseil Scientifique de la Sorbonne Nouvelle, Paris
Souvenir	Souvenir Press, London
SPA	SPA Books
SPACLALS	South Pacific Association for Commonwealth Literature and Language Studies, Wollongong, New South Wales
Spaniel	Spaniel Books, Paddington, New South Wales
SPCK	SPCK, London
Spectrum	Spectrum Books, Ibadan, Nigeria
Split Pea	Split Pea Press, Edinburgh
Spokesman	Spokesman Books, Nottingham
Spoon River	Spoon River Poetry Press, Granite Falls, MN
SRC	Steinbeck Research Center, San Jose State University, San Jose, CA
SRI	Steinbeck Research Institute, Ball State University, Muncie, IN
SriA	Sri Aurobindo, Pondicherry, India
Sri Satguru	Sri Satguru Publications, Delhi
SSA	John Steinbeck Society of America, Muncie, IN
SSAB	Sprakförlaget Skriptor AB, Stockholm
SSNS	Scottish Society for Northern Studies, Edinburgh
StanfordUP	Stanford UP, Stanford, CA
Staple	Staple, Matlock, Derbyshire
Starmont	Starmont House, Mercer Island, WA
Starrhill	Starrhill Press, Washington, DC
Station Hill	Station Hill, Barrytown, NY
Stauffenburg	Stauffenburg Verlag, Tübingen, Germany
StDL	St Deiniol's Library, Hawarden, Clwyd
Steel Rail	Steel Rail Publishing, Ottawa
Steiner	Franz Steiner, Wiesbaden, Germany
Sterling	Sterling Publishing, New York
SterlingND	Sterling Publishers, New Delhi
Stichting	Stichtig Neerlandistiek, Amsterdam
St James	St James Press, Andover, Hampshire
St Martin's	St Martin's Press, New York
StMut	State Mutual Book and Periodical Source, New York
Stockwell	Arthur H. Stockwell, Ilfracombe, Devon
Stoddart	Stoddart Publishing, Don Mills, Ontario
StPB	St Paul's Bibliographies, Winchester, Hampshire
STR	Society for Theatre Research, London
Strauch	R.O.U. Strauch, Ludwigsburg

Studio	Studio Editions, London
Stump Cross	Stump Cross Books, Stump Cross, Essex
Sud	Sud, Marseilles
Suhrkamp	Suhrkamp Verlag, Frankfurt am Main
Summa	Summa Publications, Birmingham, AL
SUNYP	State University of New York Press, Albany, NY
SUP	Sydney University Press
Surtees	R.S. Surtees Society, Frome, Somerset
SusquehannaUP	Susquehanna UP, Selinsgrove, PA
SussexAP	Sussex Academic Press
SussexUP	Sussex UP, University of Sussex, Brighton
Sutton	Alan Sutton, Stroud, Gloucester
SVP	Sister Vision Press, Toronto
S–W	Shepheard–Walwyn Publishing, London
Swallow	Swallow Press, Athens, OH
SWG	Saskatchewan Writers Guild, Regina
Sybylla	Sybylla Feminist Press
SydneyUP	Sydney UP, Sydney
SyracuseUP	Syracuse UP, Syracuse, NY
Tabb	Tabb House, Padstow, Cornwall
Taishukan	Taishukan Publishing, Tokyo
Talonbooks	Talonbooks, Vancouver
TamilU	Tamil University, Thanjavur, India
T&F	Taylor & Francis Books
T&H	Thames & Hudson, London
Tantivy	Tantivy Press, London
Tarcher	Jeremy P. Tarcher, Los Angeles
Tartarus	Tartarus Press
Tate	Tate Gallery Publications, London
Tavistock	Tavistock Publications, London
Taylor	Taylor Publishing, Bellingham, WA
TaylorCo	Taylor Publishing, Dallas, TX
TCG	Theatre Communications Group, New York
TCP	Three Continents Press, Washington, DC
TCUP	Texas Christian UP, Fort Worth, TX
TEC	Third Eye Centre, Glasgow
Tecumseh	Tecumseh Press, Ottawa
Telos	Telos Press, St Louis, MO
TempleUP	Temple UP, Philadelphia
TennS	Tennyson Society, Lincoln
TexA&MUP	Texas A&MUP, College Station, TX
Text	Text Publishing, Melbourne
TextileB	Textile Bridge Press, Clarence Center, NY
TexTULib	Friends of the University Library, Texas Tech University, Lubbock
The Smith	The Smith, New York
Thimble	Thimble Press, Stroud, Gloucester
Thoemmes	Thoemmes Press, Bristol

Thornes	Stanley Thornes, Cheltenham
Thorpe	D.W. Thorpe, Australia
Thorsons	Thorsons Publishers, London
Times	Times of Gloucester Press, Gloucester, Ontario
TMP	Thunder's Mouth Press, New York
Tombouctou	Tombouctou Books, Bolinas, CA
Totem	Totem Books, Don Mills, Ontario
Toucan	Toucan Press, St Peter Port, Guernsey
Touzot	Jean Touzot, Paris
TPF	Trianon Press Facsimiles, London
Tragara	Tragara Press, Edinburgh
Transaction	Transaction Publishers, New Brunswick, NJ
Transcendental	Transcendental Books, Hartford, CT
Transworld	Transworld, London
TrinityUP	Trinity UP, San Antonio, TX
Tsar	Tsar Publications, Canada
TTUP	Texas Technical University Press, Lubbock
Tuckwell	Tuckwell Press, East Linton
Tuduv	Tuduv, Munich
TulaneUP	Tulane UP, New Orleans, LA
TurkuU	Turku University, Turku, Finland
Turnstone	Turnstone Press, Winnipeg, Manitoba
Turtle Island	Turtle Island Foundation, Berkeley, CA
Twayne	Twayne Publishing, Boston, MA
UAB	University of Aston, Birmingham
UAdelaide	University of Adelaide, Australia
UAlaP	University of Alabama Press, Tuscaloosa
UAlbertaP	University of Alberta Press, Edmonton
UAntwerp	University of Antwerp
UArizP	University of Arizona Press, Tucson
UArkP	University of Arkansas Press, Fayetteville
UAthens	University of Athens, Greece
UBarcelona	University of Barcelona, Spain
UBCP	University of British Columbia Press, Vancouver
UBergen	University of Bergen, Norway
UBrno	J.E. Purkyne University of Brno, Czechoslovakia
UBrussels	University of Brussels
UCalgaryP	University of Calgary Press, Canada
UCalP	University of California Press, Berkeley
UCAP	University of Central Arkansas Press, Conway
UCapeT	University of Cape Town Press
UChicP	University of Chicago Press
UCDubP	University College Dublin Press
UCL	UCL Press (University College London)
UCopenP	University of Copenhagen Press, Denmark
UDelP	University of Delaware Press, Newark
UDijon	University of Dijon
UDur	University of Durham, Durham, UK

UEA	University of East Anglia, Norwich
UErlangen-N	University of Erlangen-Nuremberg, Germany
UEssex	University of Essex, Colchester
UExe	University of Exeter, Devon
UFlorence	University of Florence, Italy
UFlorP	University of Florida Press
UFR	Université François Rabelais, Tours
UGal	University College, Galway
UGeoP	University of Georgia Press, Athens
UGhent	University of Ghent
UGlasP	University of Glasgow Press
UHawaiiP	University of Hawaii Press, Honolulu
UIfeP	University of Ife Press, Ile-Ife, Nigeria
UIllp	University of Illinois Press, Champaign
UInnsbruck	University of Innsbruck
UIowaP	University of Iowa Press, Iowa City
UKanP	University of Kansas Press, Lawrence, KS
UKL	University of Kentucky Libraries, Lexington
ULavalP	Les Presses de l'Université Laval, Quebec
ULiège	University of Liège, Belgium
ULilleP	Presses Universitaires de Lille, France
ULondon	University of London
Ulster	University of Ulster, Coleraine
U/M	Underwood/Miller, Los Angeles
UMalta	University of Malta, Msida
UManitobaP	University of Manitoba Press, Winnipeg
UMassP	University of Massachusetts Press, Amherst
Umeå	Umeå Universitetsbibliotek, Umeå
UMichP	University of Michigan Press, Ann Arbor
UMinnP	University of Minnesota Press, Minneapolis
UMirail-ToulouseP	University of Mirail-Toulouse Press, France
UMIRes	UMI Research Press, Ann Arbor, MI
UMissP	University of Missouri Press, Columbia
UMP	University of Mississippi Press, Lafayette
UMysore	University of Mysore, India
UNancyP	Presses Universitaires de Nancy, France
UNCP	University of North Carolina Press, Chapel Hill, NC
Undena	Undena Publications, Malibu, CA
UNDP	University of Notre Dame Press, Notre Dame, IN
UNebP	University of Nebraska Press, Lincoln
UNevP	University of Nevada Press, Reno
UNewE	University of New England, Armidale, New South Wales
UnEWE, CALLS	University of New England, Centre for Australian Language and Literature Studies
Ungar	Frederick Ungar, New York
Unicopli	Edizioni Unicopli, Milan
Unity	Unity Press, Hull
Universa	Uilgeverij Universa, Wetteren, Belgium

UNMP	University of New Mexico Press, Albuquerque
UNorthTP	University of North Texas Press
UNott	University of Nottingham
UNSW	University of New South Wales
Unwin	Unwin Paperbacks, London
Unwin Hyman	Unwin Hyman, London
UOklaP	University of Oklahoma Press, Norman
UOslo	University of Oslo
UOtagoP	University of Otago Press, Dunedin, New Zealand
UOttawaP	University of Ottawa Press
UPA	UP of America, Lanham, MD
UParis	University of Paris
UPColardo	UP of Colorado, Niwot, CO
UPennP	University of Pennsylvania Press, Philadelphia
UPittP	University of Pittsburgh Press, Pittsburgh
UPKen	University Press of Kentucky, Lexington
UPMissip	UP of Mississippi, Jackson
UPN	Université de Paris Nord, Paris
UPNE	UP of New England, Hanover, NH
Uppsala	Uppsala University, Uppsala
UProvence	University of Provence, Aix-en-Provence
UPValéry	University Paul Valéry, Montpellier
UPVirginia	UP of Virginia, Charlottesville
UQDE	University of Queensland, Department of English
UQP	University of Queensland Press, St Lucia
URouen	University of Rouen, Mont St Aignan
URP	University of Rochester Press
USalz	Institut für Anglistik und Amerikanstik, University of Salzburg
USantiago	University of Santiago, Spain
USCP	University of South Carolina Press, Columbia
USFlorP	University of South Florida Press, Florida
USheff	University of Sheffield
Usher	La Casa Usher, Florence
USPacific	University of the South Pacific, Institute of Pacific Studies, Suva, Fiji
USQ, DHSS	University of Southern Queensland, Department of Humanities and Social Sciences
USydP	University of Sydney Press
USzeged	University of Szeged, Hungary
UtahSUP	Utah State UP, Logan
UTampereP	University of Tampere Press, Knoxville
UTas	University of Tasmania, Hobart
UTennP	University of Tennessee Press, Knoxville
UTexP	University of Texas Press, Austin
UTorP	University of Toronto Press, Toronto
UTours	Université de Tours
UVerm	University of Vermont, Burlington

UVict	University of Victoria, Victoria, BC
UWalesP	University of Wales Press, Cardiff
UWAP	University of Western Australia Press, Nedlands
UWarwick	University of Warwick, Coventry
UWashP	University of Washington Press, Seattle
UWaterlooP	University of Waterloo Press, Waterloo, Ontario
UWI	University of the West Indies, St Augustine, Trinidad
UWiscM	University of Wisconsin, Milwaukee
UWiscP	University of Wisconsin Press, Madison
UWoll	University of Wollongong
UYork	University of York, York
Valentine	Valentine Publishing and Drama, Rhinebeck, NY
V&A	Victoria and Albert Museum, London
VanderbiltUP	Vanderbilt UP, Nashville, TE
V&R	Vandenhoeck & Ruprecht, Göttingen, Germany
Van Gorcum	Van Gorcum, Assen, Netherlands
Vantage	Vantage Press, New York
Variorum	Variorum, Ashgate Publishing, Hampshire
Vehicule	Vehicule Press, Montreal
Vendome	Vendome Press, New York
Verdant	Verdant Publications, Chichester
Verso	Verso Editions, London
VictUP	Victoria UP, Victoria University of Wellington, New Zealand
Vieweg	Vieweg Braunschweig, Wiesbaden
Vikas	Vikas Publishing House, New Delhi
Viking	Viking Press, New York
VikingNZ	Viking, Auckland
Virago	Virago Press, London
Vision	Vision Press, London
VLB	VLB Éditeur, Montreal
VP	Vulgar Press, Carlton North, Australia
VR	Variorum Reprints, London
Vrin	J. Vrin, Paris
VUUP	Vrije Universiteit UP, Amsterdam
Wakefield	Wakefield Press
W&B	Whiting & Birch, London
W&N	Weidenfeld & Nicolson, London
Water Row	Water Row Press, Sudbury, MA
Watkins	Paul Watkins, Stanford, Lincsolnshire
WB	Wissenschaftliche Buchgesellschaft, Darmstadt
W/B	Woomer/Brotherson, Revere, PA
Webb&Bower	Webb & Bower, Exeter
Wedgestone	Wedgestone Press, Winfield, KS
Wedgetail	Wedgetail Press, Earlwood, New South Wales
WesleyanUP	Wesleyan UP, Middletown, CT
West	West Publishing, St Paul, MN
WHA	William Heinemann Australia, Port Melbourne, Victoria

Wheatsheaf	Wheatsheaf Books, Brighton
Whiteknights	Whiteknights Press, University of Reading, Berkshire
White Lion	White Lion Books, Cambridge
Whitston	Whitston Publishing, Troy, NY
Whittington	Whittington Press, Herefordshire
WHP	Warren House Press, Sale, Cheshire
Wiener	Wiener Publishing, New York
Wildwood	Wildwood House, Aldershot, Hampshire
Wiley	John Wiley, Chichester, New York and Brisbane
Wilson	Philip Wilson, London
Winter	Carl Winter Universitätsverlag, Heidelberg, Germany
Winthrop	Winthrop Publishers, Cambridge, MA
WIU	Western Illinois University, Macomb, IL
WL	Ward Lock, London
WLUP	Wilfrid Laurier UP, Waterloo, Ontario
WMP	World Microfilms Publications, London
WMU	Western Michigan University, Kalamazoo, MI
Woeli	Woeli Publishing Services
Wolfhound	Wolfhound Press, Dublin
Wombat	Wombat Press, Wolfville, NS
Wo-No	Wolters-Noordhoff, Groningen, Netherlands
Woodstock	Woodstock Books, Oxford
Woolf	Cecil Woolf, London
Words	Words, Framfield, E. Sussex
WP	Women's Press, London
WPC	Women's Press of Canada, Toronto
WSUP	Wayne State UP, Detroit, MI
WVUP	West Virginia UP, Morgantown
W-W	Williams-Wallace, Toronto
WWU	Western Washington University, Bellingham
Xanadu	Xanadu Publications, London
YaleUL	Yale University Library Publications, New Haven, CT
YaleUP	Yale UP, New Haven, CO and London
Yamaguchi	Yamaguchi Shoten, Kyoto
YorkP	York Press, Fredericton, NB
Younsmere	Younsmere Press, Brighton
Zed	Zed Books, London
Zell	Hans Zell, East Grinstead, W. Sussex
Zena	Zena Publications, Penrhyndeudraeth, Gwynedd
Zephyr	Zephyr Press, Somerville, MA
Zomba	Zomba Books, London
Zwemmer	A. Zwemmer, London

Preface

The Year's Work in English Studies is a narrative bibliography that records and evaluates scholarly writing on English language and on literatures written in English. It
is published by Oxford University Press on behalf of the English Association.

The Editors and the English Association are pleased to announce that this year's
Beatrice White Prize has been awarded to Julie Stone Peters for *Theatre of the
Book, 1480–1880: Print, Text, and Performance in Europe* published by Oxford
University Press (ISBN 0 1981 8714 9).

The authors of *YWES* attempt to cover all significant contributions to English
studies. Writers of articles can assist this process by sending offprints to the journal,
and editors of journals that are not readily available in the UK are urged to join the
many who send us complete sets of current and back issues. These materials should
be addressed to The Editors, *YWES*, The English Association, The University of
Leicester, University Road, Leicester LEI 7RH, UK.

Our coverage of articles and books is greatly assisted by the Modern Language
Association of America, who annually supply proofs of their *International Bibliography* in advance of the publication of each year's coverage.

The views expressed in *YWES* are those of its individual contributors and are not
necessarily shared by the Editors, Associate Editors, or the English Association.

We would like to acknowledge a special debt of gratitude to Gill Mitchell and
Carole Bookhamer for their efforts on behalf of this volume.

The Editors

I

English Language

TERESA FANEGO, CAMILLA VASQUEZ, JEROEN VAN DE
WEIJER, BETTELOU LOS, WIM VAN DER WURFF, BEÀTA
GYURIS, JULIE COLEMAN, PAUL CULLEN, LIESELOTTE
ANDERWALD, ANDREA SAND, PETRA BETTIG AND
CLARA CALVO

This chapter has twelve sections: 1. General; 2. History of English Linguistics; 3. Phonetics and Phonology; 4. Morphology; 5. Syntax; 6. Semantics; 7. Lexicography, Lexicology and Lexical Semantics; 8. Onomastics; 9. Dialectology and Sociolinguistics; 10. New Englishes and Creolistics; 11. Pragmatics and Discourse Analysis; 12. Stylistics. Section 1 is by Teresa Fanego; section 2 is by Camilla Vasquez; section 3 is by Jeroen van de Weijer; sections 4 and 5 are by Bettelou Los and Wim van der Wurff; section 6 is by Beàta Gyuris; section 7 is by Julie Coleman; section 8 is by Paul Cullen; section 9 is by Lieselotte Anderwald; section 10 is by Andrea Sand; section 11 is by Petra Bettig; section 12 is by Clara Calvo.

1. General

This year saw the publication of R.L. Trask's *Dictionary of Historical and Comparative Linguistics*. As the author notes in the preface (p. vi), 'historical linguistics was the first branch of linguistics to be placed on a firm scholarly footing, around the beginning of the nineteenth century', yet this is the first dictionary specifically devoted to its terminology and is thus a welcome addition to the field. With nearly 2,400 entries, it provides thorough coverage of every aspect of historical linguistics, including Indo-European studies, language families, the sociolinguistic study of language change, pidgin and creole languages, and several others. Particular attention is also devoted to more recent work such as mathematical and computational methods (witness terms such as *probabilistic approach* or *Oswalt shift text*), models of linguistic descent (e.g. *crystallization model*, *punctuated-equilibrium model*) and grammaticalization theory. Wherever it seemed helpful to do so, Trask has also taken care to provide real linguistic examples of the term entered and frequent references to the original literature.

Lockwood, Fries and Copeland, eds., *Functional Approaches to Language, Culture and Cognition*, honours the career of Sidney M. Lamb. The thirty-six essays in the volume are organized in two sections. The first section, 'Functional Approaches to the Structure of Language: Theory and Practice', starts with contributions written within the stratificational model, the model of grammar developed by Lamb since the 1960's (cf. *Outline of Stratificational Grammar*, Washington DC [1966]). These are followed by six papers focusing on some related functional framework, and by articles describing some particular set of language phenomena. Section 2, 'Functional Approaches to the History of Language and Linguistics', also falls into three parts reflecting areas of language study in which Lamb has shown a lifelong interest: general studies of language change are addressed first; a second group of contributions examines language change, lexicon and culture; and the last group treats the history of linguistics and culture. Given the scope of the volume, the articles directly concerned with English are only a minority. They include Connie Eble's 'Slang and Lexicography' (pp. 499–511), F.W. Householder's 'On Sugar, Sumac and Sewers' (pp. 513–20), which discusses *sugar*, *sure* and other words that have been subject to the sound change from /sj/ > / ʃ/ in the history of English, and Peter Fries's 'Some Peculiar Adjectives in the English Nominal Group' (pp. 289–322). In this important analysis of the internal structure of English noun phrases Fries examines in detail the grammatical properties of an extensive group of items including, among others, cardinal numbers, ordinals, superlatives, comparatives, identifiers (*certain*, *particular*), limiting adjectives (*main*, *primary*), and modal adjectives of truth (*virtual*, *possible*), time (*former*, *late*) and frequency (*customary*, *typical*). In Fries's functional framework, the members of these groups, which are distinct syntactically and semantically from either the determiners or the central adjectives, seem to fall quite neatly into two general subcategories of textual-oriented versus interpersonal-oriented modifiers.

Also functional in orientation is Robin Fawcett's *A Theory of Syntax for Systemic Functional Linguistics*. This book, which more properly belongs in section 5 of this chapter, evaluates alternative approaches within Systemic Functional Linguistics (SFL) to representing the structure of language at the level of form. Part 1 summarizes the major developments in the forty years of SFL's history and the emergence of the Cardiff Grammar, developed by Fawcett himself and a group of linguists associated with Cardiff University as an alternative to the so-called Sidney Grammar of Michael Halliday, J.R. Martin and Ruqaiya Hasan, the fullest account of which to date remains Halliday's *An Introduction to Functional Grammar* [1994]. Essential to the Sidney Grammar are the multiple structure representations of clauses, where the several different structures (experiential, interpersonal, textual and informational) foreground the concept that each clause is the realization of different types of meaning or 'metafunctions', to use Halliday's term. Fawcett rightly argues that Halliday's model additionally needs a representation of syntax in a single, integrated structure, and expounds, in part 2 of the volume, the set of categories that make up the theory of syntax proposed. To model the relationships between the various layers of structure within the sentence or clause, Fawcett makes use of a tree diagram notation which is indeed a significant departure from the box diagram notation characteristic of Halliday's work. Other innovations include the recognition of 'quality' (e.g. *very generous*) and 'quantity' (e.g. *very many*) groups—Halliday, as is well known, considers groups headed by adjectives as a subtype of nominal group—and the treatment of co-ordination and embedding, where again there are considerable differences with Halliday's analysis in terms of hypotaxis and parataxis. Interesting as it seems, Fawcett's approach to functional syntax is difficult to evaluate at present, largely because the volume provides little more than a summary statement of the main theoretical concepts. Fuller accounts can apparently be found in Fawcett's *Functional Syntax Handbook: Analyzing English at the Level of Form* (London: Continuum) and *Functional Semantics Handbook: Analyzing English at the Level of Meaning* (London: Continuum), both of which were still in press at the time of writing this review.

Broeder and Murre, eds., *Models of Language Acquisition: Inductive and Deductive Approaches*, will appeal to all those interested in the fields of linguistics, cognitive science, psychology, and computer science. The twelve contributions to the volume present advances in computational modelling of language acquisition and consider issues such as the degree to which language learning is inductive or deductive by using sophisticated simulation techniques. Some of the chapters, such as Brian MacWhinney, 'Lexicalist Connectionism' (pp. 9–32), concentrate on the acquisition of single lexical items, while others focus on pluralization and inflectional systems. Thus in the chapters by Gary Marcus, 'Children's Overregularization and its Implications for Cognition' (pp. 154–76) and Rainer Goebel and Peter Indefrey, 'A Recurrent Network with Short-Term Memory Capacity Learning the German -*s* Plural' (pp. 177–200), the main point of debate is whether connectionist (i.e. inductive) models can deal with rules that have a low frequency, like the -*s* plural in German, or whether more deductive models are necessary. The acquisition of plurals in Arabic and of past tense in English is empirically tested in 'Single- and Dual-Route Models of Inflectional Morphology' (pp. 201–22), by Ramin Nakisa, Kim Plunkett and Ulrike Hahn. Summing up, this volume can undoubtedly be recommended as a valuable compilation of current research on the topic of language acquisition.

Lundquist and Jarvella, eds., *Language, Text, and Knowledge: Mental Models of Expert Communication*, brings together ideas and approaches from cognitive linguistics and psychology in an attempt to cast light on the interplay of language and knowledge in texts used in expert communication and on how people combine their knowledge from a variety of sources as they make sense of and draw inferences from such texts. The domains treated in the twelve essays that make up the volume are the study of risk, law, medicine, sociology, and economics, and the levels of analysis examined range from words and phrases to embedded sentences and cross-sentential relations. Three of the papers are relevant to English: in 'Noun Phrases in Specialized Communication. The Cognitive Processing of the Danish s-Genitive Construction' (pp. 49–81), Henrik Høeg Müller contrasts the interpretation of genitive phrases headed by argumental nouns such as *formand* (e.g. *bestyrelsens formand* 'the president of the board') with genitive constructions in which the head noun lacks an argument structure and hence allows several possible logical interpretations, as is the case with *forretningens TV-apparater* 'the store's TV sets', which, depending on the context, could variously refer to 'the TV sets that the store has in stock', 'the TV sets that the store uses to watch customers', 'the TV sets in the shop-window', etc. 'Semantic Roles in Expert Texts—Exemplified by the Patient Role in Judgments' (pp. 83–96), by Åse Almlund, discusses Patient roles governed by declarative verbs and consisting of complement or interrogative clauses (e.g. *The plaintiffs have stated that the defendant was bound by his offer*). Finally, in 'Knowledge, Events, and Anaphors in Texts for Specific Purposes' (pp. 97–125), Lita Lundquist focuses on the phenomenon of trans-sentential NP anaphors, the interpretation of which poses special problems in specialized texts, because a non-expert cannot know whether two NPs refer to the same entity (as in the case of *gold* and *the metal with the atomic number 79*).

We close this section with a title aimed primarily at literature students, but which may also prove useful as a source-book for language courses on earlier stages of English. Elaine Treharne's *Old and Middle English: An Anthology* provides an extensive selection of literary texts covering the earliest writings in the vernacular up to the time of Chaucer. Many of the texts are those that one would expect to find in all such collections (*The Wife's Lament, The Wanderer, Sir Orfeo*), but some are less common and are not usually edited in anthologies (*Apollonius of Tyre, Exodus*). Each text is accompanied by a brief introduction that incorporates information about the manuscript, the date, the literary context, bibliographical matter and dialect. Earlier materials are made accessible by accompanying translations, and later ones by marginal glosses. Other aids to student learning are provided by a brief language analysis (pp. xix–xxv), a select bibliography and several indexes.

2. History of English Linguistics

Ann Fisher, possibly the first woman to write a grammar of English, is the major focus of an article by Ingrid Tieken-Boon Van Ostade, 'Female Grammarians of the Eighteenth Century' (*HLSL*, online journal). This article recognizes a number of important contributions made by Fisher's *A New Grammar* [1745]. Not only was Fisher's grammar quite popular—the author refers to thirty-one numbered editions—but it was also unique in that it was the first of its kind to contain exercises of false grammar or 'bad English', reflecting Fisher's own pedagogical concerns as a schoolteacher. Also, Fisher's grammar is notable for its description of English 'for its own sake and not in terms of Latin' and for its adoption of a 'native metalanguage'. Furthermore, Tieken-Boon Van Ostade suggests that Fisher's grammar may well have been the first to formulate a rule for the sex-indefinite 'he'. By the end of the eighteenth century (and perhaps, in part, inspired by Fisher's work), at least six other women had written English grammars. The author rightfully calls for more equitable treatment of eighteenth-century female grammarians (especially of Fisher) in the *Lexicon Grammaricorum*.

A second article by Tieken-Boon Van Ostade published this year deals with the inception of Lowth's *Short Introduction to English Grammar* [1762]. In 'Robert Dodsley and the Genesis of Lowth's *Short Introduction to English Grammar*' (*HL* 27[2000] 21–36) she suggests that Lowth's fame as a grammarian was more or less accidental and that the publication of his grammar was ultimately the result of an idea by his publisher Robert Dodsley. Drawing on their correspondence from 1753 to 1762, she presents a plausible chronology for the publication of Lowth's grammar, suggesting that the idea for the grammar first came about in 1757. As a bookseller/publisher, many of Dodsley's authors 'depended on him for grammatical corrections of their work' (p. 26). Tieken-Boon Van Ostade presents the compelling argument that Dodsley's linguistic insecurity, resulting from a lack of formal education, may have motivated him to publish a 'practical grammar of English' which would place the responsibility for grammatically correct writing on the authors themselves (p. 27). This, coupled with the fact that Lowth had never been a grammarian or a schoolteacher and was very much involved with his career in the Church further supports the claim that the idea for the grammar must have come from Dodsley, the publisher, rather than from Lowth, the author. Tieken-Boon Van Ostade also refers to Dodsley's involvement in the publication of Samuel Johnson's *Dictionary*, thus drawing attention to the key role of booksellers in the codification of the English language.

Samuel Johnson is the subject of two articles that appeared this year. The first, 'The Structure of his Sentences is French: Johnson and Hume in the History of English' (*LangS* 22[2000] 285–93), by Adam Potkay, analyses Johnson and Priestly's critique of Hume's French-influenced (or 'gallicized') sentence structure. The author raises the important point that Johnson and Priestly's own writing styles were later found to be to be too foreign by English critics of the nineteenth century. Drawing a parallel with the quest in the Middle Ages to restore Latin to an earlier and purer form, Jack Lynch, in 'The Ground-Work of Stile: Johnson on the History of the Language' (*SP* 97[2000] 454–72), discusses the eighteenth-century search for an appropriate model of linguistic purity on which to base a standard English. Ultimately the period from 1580 to 1650 was determined as England's linguistic golden age, as is evidenced by Johnson's selection of quotations by authors from this period whose language epitomized some of the ideals on which a standard was subsequently modelled.

Another interesting article concerning the processes by which a standard variety of English was constructed is Susan Fitzmaurice's '*The Spectator*, the Politics of Social Networks, and Language Standardisation in Eighteenth-Century England' (in Wright, ed., *The Development of Standard English, 1300–1800: Theories, Descriptions, Conflicts*, pp. 195–218). This article analyses the relationship between the prescriptivist movement in eighteenth-century England and *The Spectator*, a short-lived though socially influential periodical, which was recognized for its authority on matters of politeness and manners and aimed at a largely middle-class readership. Many eighteenth-century prescriptive grammars used excerpts from this periodical to provide examples of grammatically correct as well as improper language. Adopting a social-network perspective, the author shows how the social interactions of the various individuals associated with *The Spectator* contributed to the shaping of middle-class tastes in matters ranging from appropriate dress to standards of 'polite writing'. In her examination of the distribution of one particular linguistic feature (relative clause markers) in the writings of individuals belonging to this social-network, Fitzmaurice clearly illustrates that prescriptivist rules found in eighteenth-century grammars may not have been too far removed from actual linguistic practices of the time.

In 'Die Brightland-Grammatik (1711): Nationalsprachliche vs. Rational Grammatik' (in Desmet, Jooken, Schmitter, and Swiggers, eds., *The History of Linguistic and Grammatical Practice. Proceedings of the XIth International Colloquium of the Studienkreis: 'Geschichte der Sprachwissenschaft'*, pp. 113–29) Astrid Göbels examines the importance of the *Grammar of the English Tongue* by Brightland and Gildon. Although it borrowed heavily from seventeenth-century grammars (especially from the Wallis and the Port-Royal), the significance of the 'Brightland Grammar' stems from its incorporation of two tendencies: a national language approach, and that of a universal or philosophical grammar. Göbels also suggests that the foreword to the eighth edition provides some indication that Charles Gildon may, in fact, have been the author of the 1712 anonymous work *Bellum Grammaricale*, thereby attesting to the documentary value of the text.

3. Phonetics and Phonology

There are a number of studies that should be mentioned here, dealing with the segmental structure of English, its suprasegmentals (both stress and intonation), and, finally, its varieties and variation. As far as consonant segmentism is concerned, Toni Borowsky, 'Word-Faithfulness and the Direction of Assimilation' (*TLR* 17[2000] 1–28), relates differences in the direction of the application of phonological rules to differences in the observed patterns of faithfulness at the Word and the Root levels, including a discussion of voice assimilation in English in cases such as final *-th* (*fifth*), irregular verbal (*left*, *lost*) and nominal (*thieves*) inflection and certain alternations (e.g. *scribe~scripture*). In the other issue of this volume of *TLR* (17:ii–iv[2000]), guest-edited by Nancy A. Ritter, a number of short articles appear that make cogent points about the advantages and disadvantages of Optimality Theory. Some of these briefly touch on aspects of the phonology of English, such as stress assignment (John Coleman, 'Candidate Selection', *TLR* 17[2000] 167–79; Luigi Burzio, 'Segmental Contrast Meets Output-to-Output Faithfulness', *TLR* 17[2000] 367–84), place assimilation rules (K.P. Mohanan, 'The Theoretical Substance of the Optimality Formalism', *TLR* 17[2000] 143–66), other segmental rules (Charles Reiss, 'Optimality Theory from a Cognitive Science Perspective', *TLR* 17[2000] 291–301), syllable structure (John Coleman, see above), English morphology (George N. Clements, 'In Defense of Serialism', *TLR* 17[2000] 181–97), and diachronic phonology (April McMahon, 'The Emergence of the Optimal? Optimality Theory and Sound Change', *TLR* 17[2000] 231–40). A lengthier discussion of the analysis of sound change in the Optimality framework appears in McMahon, *Change, Chance and Optimality*, which represents a critical contribution to the debate on how Optimality Theory accounts (or cannot account) for historical change. Finally on segment structure, Hideki Zamma, 'Stricture and Word Formation in English' (*ELing* 17[2000] 573–90), reviews recent work in feature geometry and presents an interesting argument from the morphology of English to argue for a particular model in which place features and continuancy are related. In forms with final voiceless coronal obstruents (*-s* or *-t*, as in *dismissive*, *active*) the suffix *-ive* (or *-ory*) is selected, while in forms with other final consonants (e.g. *accusative*, *comparative*, *affirmative*), the allomorph *-ative* appears. In forms with final *-nt* (*argumentative*, *incantatory*) the long allomorph also appears, due, according to Zamma, to the linked place-continuancy structure in the final two consonants. It is interesting to note, then, that bases with final *-ns* (*expensive*, *sensory*) do not show the same long allomorph, and therefore apparently do not have the doubly linked structure.

As far as stress in concerned, Susan Olsen, 'Compounding and Stress in English: A Closer Look at the Boundary between Morphology and Syntax' (*LingB* 181[2000]

55–69) examines stress in noun + noun and adjective + noun compounds and suggests that compound stress is in the process of change and reorganizing itself into characteristic meaning groups: a compound internal relation between the two members yields pre-stress (tídal wave, drúg death, móuntain lion), while meanings induced by an external relation such as 'and', 'located at', etc., are characterized by final stress (global méeting, polar íce, trial rún). Joe Pater, 'Non-Uniformity in English Secondary Stress: The Role of Ranked and Lexically Specific Constraints' (*Phonology* 17[2000] 237–74), examines the diversity of patterns of secondary stress in English. Apart from presenting an account of regular primary stress placement, the treatment of lexical idiosyncrasies by way of lexically indexed Optimality Theory constraint hierarchies is very interesting. Hisao Tokizaki, 'Prominence, Phrasing, and Movement' (*ELing* 17[2000] 459–87), reviews earlier work on the syntax–phonology interface, dealing specifically with English stress assignment on the basis of syntactic structure at the lexical and phrasal level and paying special attention to the well-known problem of Heavy NP Shift.

A lot of cross-linguistic comparison work is being done with respect to intonation, both across languages and within dialects of English. Martine Grice, D. Robert Ladd and Amalia Arvaniti, 'On the Place of Phrase Accents in Intonational Phonology' (*Phonology* 17[2000] 143–85) present instrumental and impressionistic evidence for the existence of the phrase accent across a range of languages, including Greek, Swedish, Romanian and English. Jennifer Fitzpatrick, 'On Intonational Typology' (*STUF* 53[2000] 88–96), describes some current issues in the phonetics and phonology of intonational typology, including some remarks on English. Sue Peppé, Jane Maxim and Bill Wells, 'Prosodic Variation in Southern British English' (*LSp* 43[2000] 309–34), find little variation as regards intonational competence across London speakers, although quite a bit of variation in their use of certain prosodic features. Esther Grabe, Brechtje Post, Francis Nolan and Kimberley Farrar, 'Pitch Accent Realization in Four Varieties of British English' (*JP* 28[2000] 161–85), compare the phonetic effects of 'truncation' and 'compression' with respect to the realization of pitch accents in Cambridge, Leeds, Newcastle and Belfast.

With respect to varieties of English, the vocalism of NZE remains a topic which receives a great deal of attention. Catherine I. Watson, Margaret Maclagan and Jonathan Harrington, 'Acoustic Evidence for Vowel Change in New Zealand English' (*LVC* 12[2000] 51–68) compare two corpora, one of 1948 and one of 1995 and find that NZE has centralized, /e/ and /æ/ have raised and the diphthongs /iə/ and /eə/ have merged. On the other hand, Anita Easton and Laurie Bauer, 'An Acoustic Study of the Vowels of New Zealand English' (*AuJL* 20[2000] 93–117), find more variation in the realization of these vowels than previously assumed, based on data from 1989. The study by Peter Trudgill, Elizabeth Gordon, Gillian Lewis and Margaret Maclagan, 'Determination in New-Dialect Formation and the Genesis of New Zealand English' (*JL* 36[2000] 299–318), also deals with this variety of English.

Finally, two separate studies should be mentioned. Robert W. Murray, 'Syllable Cut Prosody in Early Middle English' (*Language* 76[2000] 617–54), offers a study of the prosody of the *Ormulum*. Margaret R. MacEachern, 'On the Visual Distinctiveness of Words in the English Lexicon' (*JP* 28[2000] 367–76), is a very interesting short article on the distinctiveness of English words as they are *seen* (not heard) when spoken, as in lipreading. For the lipreader, homophonous words (*won*, *one*) are obviously indistinct, but other word sets like *cane*, *hen* and *lean* may also be visually indistinguishable. MacEachern shows that the measure of visual distinctiveness is an expected property of the lexicon, given the segment inventory and phonotactics of the language.

4. Morphology

The handbook series of Walter de Gruyter now also features Booij, Lehmann, and Mugdan, eds., *Morphology: An International Handbook on Inflection and Word-Formation*, volume i. This 970-page work contains over ninety articles on a wide variety of morphological topics, written by leading figures in the field. Since it is impossible even to list all the articles, we present a broad summary of the areas covered, mentioning just a few of the contributions in each section. The first section of the book is on morphology as a discipline, containing articles on the general objectives, the name, and the place of morphological studies. Section 2 surveys work up to 1900, with accounts of studies in the ancient Near East, India, the classics, the Arabic tradition, medieval Europe, and the nineteenth century. Research traditions in the twentieth century are dealt with in section 3: they include models and perspectives such as school grammar, historical-comparative grammar, traditions developed in individual European countries, American structuralism, tagmemics, and generative grammar. The basic concepts of morphology are discussed in section 4; here we find Jaap van Marle on paradigmatic and syntagmatic relations, Laurie Bauer on the word, William Croft on lexical and grammatical meaning, Andrew Carstairs-McCarthy on categories and features, John Haiman on iconicity, Wolfgang Dressler on naturalness, and Geert Koefoed and Jaap van Marle on productivity. Interface issues form the topic of the articles in section 5, where Andrew Spencer writes about morphology and syntax, Geert Booij on morphology and phonology, Mark Aronoff on morphology between lexicon and grammar, and Pius ten Hacken on derivation and compounding. Section 6 deals with units of structure, including articles by Joan Bybee on symbolization, Rochelle Lieber and Joachim Mugdan on internal word structure, and Henning Bergenholtz and Mugdan on the most elusive of all morphological elements, zero-formatives. Allomorphy is covered in section 7: here we find, among other articles, Martin Neef on conditioning, Edmund Gussmann on underlying forms, and Igor Mel'čuk on suppletion. Section 8 is on formal processes, such as pre-/suf-/circum-/in-/transfixation, reduplication, and the most minimal of all morphological processes, subtraction. The central topic of inflection gets its full share of attention in section 9, which includes Carstairs-McCarthy writing about probably the most morphological of all morphological phenomena, inflectional classes, Richard Coates about exponence, Fred Karlsson about defectivity, and Martin Haspelmath about periphrasis. Section 10 is devoted to word classes: it contains chapters about criteria for classification, the cross-linguistics of word classes, and chapters about the individual word classes. Fundamental issues in word formation are covered in section 11, with Bauer writing on system vs. norm, Jacob Hoeksema on compositionality, and Booij on inheritance. Section 12, finally, is about specific word-formation processes, such as compounding (Susan Olsen), incorporation (Marianne Mithun), derivation (Bernd Naumann and Petra Vogel), conversion (Jan

Don, Mieke Trommelen and Wim Zonneveld), and clipping and acronyms (Charles Kreidler). Most articles contain a good deal of data, and the emphasis throughout is on secure results rather than the latest theories, which should make this work a lasting contribution to the field. Our overall assessment of this huge work can be brief: here you will find morphology galore, and, wherever you dip in to it, you will want to read from there to the end of the book, and then from the beginning up to the point where you happened to start. Make this a set text for a first-year linguistics class (perhaps supplemented by the Gruyter handbooks on syntax and semantics) and you will have an entire new generation of morphologists. In their second year, to complete their basic training, these students could then turn to the forthcoming second volume of this work, which promises to deal with semantic categories such as deixis, person, number, gender, voice, tense, mood, and aspect; with typology and universals; with morphological change; and with the morphologies of some fifteen individual languages.

There are several articles this year on general issues. Thus Laurie Bauer asks, 'Is the Morpheme Dead?' (*ALH* 31[2000] 7–25). Our journey to the answer involves a brief tour of various approaches to the morpheme (Bloomfieldian, Harrisian, Word-and-Paradigmian, Hockettian, and Bybeeian), the problems they face, and the three ultimate arguments for declaring the morpheme still alive: the sensitivity of some affixes to the presence of other affixes; the special phonological structure of many affixes; and occasional transpositions such as *This snow makes noising very walky*. If morphemes are alive, they can of course be classified, and that is what Carol Myers-Scotton and Janice Jake do in 'Four Types of Morpheme: Evidence from Aphasia, Code-Switching, and Second-Language Acquisition' (*Linguistics* 38:vi[2000] 1053–1100). They propose a model of accessing and production in which there are content morphemes (involved in the assignment of thematic roles) and three types of system morpheme (one early-system type, the choice of which is motivated conceptually, as in the choice between *a* and *the*, and two late-system types, distinguished on the basis of [± look outside own maximal projection]). Evidence from each of the three areas mentioned in the article's title is adduced to provide empirical support for this conceptually based classification.

That paradigms are also alive is ably argued in Byron W. Bender's 'Paradigms as Rules' (in Guzman and Bender, eds., *Grammatical Analysis: Morphology, Syntax, and Semantics*, pp. 14–29). Using the Latin verbs as an example, it is shown how strategies can be formulated to get from one form to another. It turns out that these are most economically stated if we distinguish 'corners' of the system, such as present active indicative, which are linked by 'corridors' involving first person singular, second person plural, etc., resulting in what is in effect the traditional arrangement of forms. An interesting side-observation made by Bender is that morphological analysis can be compared to the historical method of internal reconstruction (more on which in the following section). Further paradigmatic matters are addressed by Wolfgang Wurzel, 'Inflectional System and Markedness' (in Lahiri, ed., *Analogy, Levelling, Markedness: Principles of Change in Phonology and Morphology*, pp. 193–214—this work as a whole includes some very interesting and refreshing work on the old topic of analogy, viewed from a modern perspective; most of the chapters deal with languages other than English, but we review the editor's own contribution below, and recommend the others). Wurzel focuses on paradigmatic classes, arguing that it is most economical to take the dominant paradigm as basic, and analyse other paradigms by specifying the degree and nature of their divergence from the basic pattern. He also explores the diachronic effects of such markedness.

The relation between morphology and syntax remains important. Edwin Williams provides an account of 'Three Models of the Morphology-Syntax Interface' (in Dressler, Pfeiffer, Pöchtrager and Rennison, eds., *Morphological Analysis in Comparison*, pp. 223–47). The first model (strict lexicalism) forms words outside the syntax, the second model is happy to form them in the syntax, while the third model (Minimalism) inserts them in trees fully formed, but then redoes their formation by obliging them to check their features against those of functional heads. Williams himself favours a model in which the lexicon includes part of the syntactic derivation. Empirical concerns relating to the syntax–morphology interface are prominent in two papers on the problematic nature of -*ly* adverbs/adjectives used in earlier English with verbs of appearance (as in *it looks most solemnly*). Nikolas Gisborne writes about 'The Complementation of Verbs of Appearance by Adverbs' (in Bermúdez-Otero, Denison, Hogg, and McCully, eds., *Generative Theory and Corpus Studies: A Dialogue from 10 ICEHL*, pp. 53–75). He argues that they are adverbs performing a syntactic function intermediate between adjunct and predicative complement. A second article on this topic is Kristin Killie's 'On the Use of Current Intuition as a Bias in Historical Linguistics: The Case of the LOOK + -*ly* Construction in English' (also in Bermúdez-Otero *et al.*, eds., pp. 77–101) which regards them as adjectives, with -*ly* retaining its earlier function of implying that the characteristic imputed to the subject is inferred from a visual impression.

Much more about -*ly* is to be found in Lise Opdahl's two-volume study, *LY or Zero Suffix? A Study in Variation of Dual-Form Adverbs in Present-Day English*. Opdahl examines in great detail the de-adjectival verb-modifying adverbs which sometimes take the suffix -*ly*, and sometimes not. Examples are *They decided to apply it direct/directly to the affected skin* and *Secretary Goldberg had guessed wrong/wrongly on the drop in unemployment*. We will concentrate on the first volume, *Overview*, since the second volume, *Adverbial Profiles*, cannot be easily summarized with its wealth of information on individual lexemes and their very different behaviours. The first volume considers various aspects of dual-form adverbs in general and deals with the factors that may influence the selection of -*ly* or zero adverbs in post-verbal position. After an introductory chapter and a chapter providing a chronological and systematic overview of previous research, chapter 3 gets down to a discussion of the material used for the investigation, the corpora and the elicitation techniques (questionnaires). It also discusses which adverbs were chosen for the study and why: earlier investigations suggested that these adverbs did not show appreciable meaning differences in their suffixed or unsuffixed forms. The adverb pairs selected for the first elicitation study included *cheap/cheaply*, *direct/ directly*, *loud/loudly*, *low/lowly*, *wrong/wrongly*, *quick/quickly*, *right/rightly*, *sharp/ sharply*, *short/shortly*, *slow/slowly*. The first five of these pairs were then selected for a second elicitation study. Chapter 4 discusses the eclectic framework used: basically descriptive along the lines of R. Quirk *et al.* [1985], but making use of variationist work and statistical analysis. It discusses the difficulty of the syntactic analysis of many of these adverbs. Is the verb potentially a copular verb, or re-analysed as such by speakers? What is the status of the adverb/adjective in sentences such as *I advised her to take it easy* or *He wondered if he had played it wrong*?

Chapter 5 gives an overview of distributional patterns found in the corpus material, concentrating on various parameters considered significant in earlier work. Some of these were confirmed: a comparative does tend to favour the zero-adverb, and co-ordination with a -ly adverb tends to trigger a -ly suffix on the adverbs under investigation. Position, too, has been adduced in the literature as influencing the choice of form, although no specific hypotheses have been formulated. Opdahl looks at two positions: (i) sentence-final and (ii) immediately adjacent to the verb. Neither position was found to correlate significantly with any particular choice of form, although there were differences between individual lexemes. Passives, however, were found to favour the -ly form significantly. Other parameters investigated were literal versus figurative meaning and the parameter of style (text type, register). A difference showed up in the fiction parts of the LOB (British) and Brown (American) corpora, with the LOB having more suffixed forms. As for the contrast between formal and informal, the zero-form was preferred in informal style. Chapters 6 and 7 report on the results from the two questionnaires. Chapter 6 investigates the elicited material from the point of view of distribution in relation to four extra-linguistic variables: nationality, education, age and gender. The results proved statistically intractable. There was considerable interaction between these variables. Chapter 7 investigates the elicited material for each of the parameters discussed in chapter 5 for each individual adverb. The second volume, *Adverbial Profiles*, discusses the twenty adverbial lexemes in great detail, concentrating on the same linguistic and extra-linguistic parameters as discussed in volume i. Many effects are very lexeme-specific—it is here, for instance, that set phrases such as *cut short* etc. are identified—and it proves impossible to identify a single parameter that influences the overall selection of -ly or zero. Altogether, this is an extremely thorough work on an extremely intractable subject.

The relation between morphology and phonology is just as important, but there is only one item to be reviewed here this year (for further work, see section 3 in this chapter). Geert Booij has written an overview article on 'The Phonology–Morphology Interface' (in Cheng and Sybesma, eds., *The First Glot International State-of-the-Article Book: The Latest in Linguistics*, pp. 287–305). Booij focuses on the important and influential model of lexical phonology, which he summarizes in the basic principle, 'Morphology and phonology operate in tandem.' Phonological rules can be specified for the domain of operation, and can apply several times in a derivation, but Booij makes clear that we can do without level ordering: it faces persistent empirical problems, and the phenomena it describes may be explainable by independent principles.

Various matters having to do with verbal inflection are addressed in three articles. David Eddington's 'Analogy and the Dual-Route Model of Morphology' (*Lingua* 110[2000] 281–98) re-examines the results of an experiment reported in Sandeep Prasada and Steven Pinker [1993], in which subjects were required to construct past-tense forms of a number of nonce verbs. Eddington takes issue with Pinker and Prasada's conclusions that the single-route model of morphology is severely flawed by showing that an instance-based single-route model is well able to cope with the data. A historical perspective on past tenses is provided by Leena Kahlas-Tarkka's 'A Note on Non-Standard Uses in Middle English: Weak Preterites of Strong Old English Verbs' (*NM* 101[2000] 217–23). Some thirty-one new weak preterites are identified in the ME part of the Helsinki Corpus, and the reasons for the innovative forms are discussed (analogy, avoidance of homophony, influence of other weak verbs in the sentence, and confusion of individual verb pairs). Moving further back in time, the origins of the weak preterite in Germanic are discussed in Aditi Lahiri's 'Hierarchical Restructuring in the Creation of Verbal Morphology in Bengali and Germanic: Evidence from Phonology' (in Lahiri, ed., pp. 71–123). What Lahiri is particularly interested in is the relevance of the development (which she assumes to have involved the verb DO) for theories of grammaticalization, which are usually content to describe the development from word to clitic to affix, but have little to say about the exact nature and status of the affix. In the case of DO>-*d*-, there must have been resegmentation, with -*d*- developing into a level I suffix, followed by person and number inflection. An interesting parallel case of resegmentation in the history of Bengali is adduced to reinforce the general point.

Adjectival inflection is the topic of Hans Lindquist's '*Livelier or More Lively? Syntactic and Contextual Factors Influencing the Comparison of Disyllabic Adjectives*' (in Kirk, ed., *Corpora Galore: Analyses and Techniques in Describing English*, pp. 125–32). In the 1995 *Independent* and *New York Times*, -*er* and -*est* still outnumber *more* and *most* (though *more* has nearly caught up with -*er* in the *Independent*); a factor promoting the use of *more* is found to be premodification (as in *much more costly*), while co-ordination promotes the use of identical forms. The semantics of -*est* is investigated by Donka F. Farkas and Katalin É. Kiss in their article 'On the Comparative and Absolute Readings of Superlatives' (*NL&LT* 18[2000] 417–55). They explore the two readings of the superlative, as in *Who climbed the highest mountain?*, which could be interpreted as a paraphrase of *Who climbed Mount Everest?* (the absolute reading) or as a paraphrase of *Who climbed a mountain that was higher than any mountain anybody else climbed?* (the comparative reading). They argue that these readings result from a difference in semantic scope of the superlative morpheme, but they do not attribute the difference to any syntactic movement.

Derivational matters have sparked two contributions. Adrienne Lehrer asks, 'Are Affixes Signs? The Semantic Relationships of English Derivational Affixes' (in Dressler *et al.*, eds., pp. 143–54). She notes that affixes have been treated as ordinary lexemes from a syntactic perspective (e.g. in Rochelle Lieber's [1992] monograph; see *YWES* 73[1994] 25), and wonders whether this could also be done from a semantic perspective. Examination of possible cases of polysemy (e.g. noun-forming -*er*), synonymy (e.g. agentives in -*er/-ist/-ster/-eur/-eer/-ian*), antonymy (*super*- vs. *sub*-, -*less* vs. -*ful*) and hyponomy (only *multi*-, encompassing *bi*-, *tri*-, etc.) suggests that a qualified 'yes' seems the appropriate answer. The polysemy of -*er* is explored in greater detail in Mary Ellen Ryder's 'Complex -*er* Nominals: Where Grammaticalization and Lexicalization Meet?' (in Contini-Morava and Tobin, eds., *Between Grammar and Lexicon*, pp. 291–331). The wide variety of -*er* formations is noted (*up-and-comer*, *butt-inner*, *go-getter*, *me-tooer*, etc.), and their diachronic spread is discussed, with several properties of grammaticalization (divergence, specialization, and persistence) playing a clear role in the development. The prevalence of lexicalized stems is interpreted as a possible halfway stage between single-word stems and syntactic-phrase stems. Clearly, this is an area of English grammar that will be worth keeping an eye on over the coming years.

We move from derivation to compounding with Connie Eble's 'Slang and Lexicography' (in Lockwood, Fries, and Copeland, eds., pp. 499–511). Although this article is mainly lexicographical in orientation, it includes a section entitled 'Systematic Relationships with Other Lexemes' which contains data on various derivational and compounding processes affecting English slang terms. How exactly we can identify compounds is the topic of Pius ten Hacken's 'Motivated Tests for Compounding' (*ALH* 31[2000] 27–58). He proposes a language-independent definition of compounds, from which specific tests can be derived; among the ideas made use of are the subset relation of reference, the specification sense of compounds, and the lack of independent access to the discourse by the non-head. A focus on specific compound data is found in Gwang-Yoon Goh's 'Relative Obliqueness and the Contribution of Nonheads in the Subcategorization of Old English Compound Verbs' (*ELL* 4[2000] 13–36), which offers a mechanistic account of the contribution made by the P to the case-assignment properties of P–V compounds in OE (such as *wiðstandan* 'resist', *wiðcweðan* 'contradict', etc.) by positing an 'obliqueness hierarchy'. It is unclear why he includes compounds made up of *mis-* or *to-*, as these are not derived from prepositions (cf. Latin *dis-*, Gothic *twis-* 'apart'). We also slip in here the same author's 'Alternative Case Markings in Old English Texts' (*ES* 81[2000] 185–98), which offers some additional information on the semantics encoded by the various OE cases in terms of degrees of opposedness or affectedness. Finally, Susan Olsen's 'Compounding and Stress in English: A Closer Look at the Boundary between Morphology and Syntax' (*LingB* 181[2000] 55–69) argues that differences in stress patterns in N + N compounds do not correlate with a difference in the linguistic level at which the compound is formed (morphology or syntax) but with a difference in interpretation: left-hand stress, as in *POker game*, *WOman lover*, *LEAther tool*, results when the interpretation is based on a compound-internal inferred relation between the two nouns, while right-hand stress contours, as in *rubber STAMP*, *woman LOver*, *leather TOOL*, correlate with a compound-external modifier-like relation.

5. Syntax

(a) Modern English
We have seen six textbooks this year. The first is *Linguistics: An Introduction to Linguistic Theory*, by Victoria Fromkin, Susan Curtiss, Bruce P. Hayes, Nina Hyams, Patricia A. Keating, Hilda Koopman, Pamela Munro, Dominique Sportiche, Edward P. Stabler, Donca Steriade, Tim Stowell, and Anna Szabolcsi (the 'UCLA gang of twelve', as they call themselves in the preface). In 680 pages of text (followed by a full glossary and detailed index) students are familiarized with the generative view of the nature of language, morphology, argument structure, syntactic dependencies, V-positions, compositionality, scope, cross-categorial parallelism, the acquisition of semantics, the sounds of language, phonological representations, phonological explanations and constraints, and the acquisition of all these phenomena. Examples are drawn from a very wide range of languages (though a decidedly Shakespearean slant remains visible). Further information and notes of caution are provided in boxed form, and all chapters contain extensive, data-oriented in-text as well as end-of-chapter exercises. Considerable depth of coverage is aimed at throughout the book; at one point in chapter 5, to give just one example, students learn about complement-head ordering in Turkish (made tangible by incrementally

building up a tree diagram for *Romeo Julieti öpmek istedi* 'Romeo wanted to kiss Juliet'), are told that specifier-final languages are extremely rare, and are then introduced to Kayne's antisymmetry hypothesis as a possible explanation for this and other word-order facts. All in all, this is an excellent introduction to the areas that are usually considered to be the hardcore business of linguistics.

The next coursebook, Grover Hudson's *Essential Introductory Linguistics*, is rather different in nature. The outlook is not generative, a wider range of subject areas is covered, and for many of these, the focus is on highlights only. This approach has forced the author to make a number of shortcuts in his treatment of important but potentially over-complex topics, as he points out in his preface. The core areas of phonology, morphology and syntax are presented at an introductory level in the early part of the book, but are returned to in later chapters, to be presented in greater detail. Examples are taken primarily from English, with many additional data from other languages. Particular attention has been paid to a clear layout. Chapter 1 introduces background concepts of the sign and sign systems and discusses the general nature of language through the six characteristics of arbitrariness, creativity, openness, duality, grammaticality, and cultural transmission. These topics surface in later chapters, too, particularly the question of the innateness of language in contrast to the more obvious characteristic of cultural transmission. Chapters 1 to 7 contain the core areas: phonetics and phonology; morphology; the lexicon and morphological rules; syntax; and phrase structure. Chapters 8 to 12 discuss first and second language acquisition, language and the brain, and animal languages. The core areas are taken up again in chapters 13 to 18: phonological rules and phonological features, how the lexicon can be extended, syntax, and thematic roles. The remaining chapters (chapters 19 to 28) deal with pragmatics, writing (including its history), language change, dialects and other sociolects, register and the history of linguistics.

Laurel Brinton's *The Structure of Modern English* is a comprehensive textbook again, covering aspects of modern English from every conceivable linguistic angle. There are chapters on English spelling and phonetics, phonology and syllable structure, word formation and derivational morphology, grammatical categories (number, gender, person, case, degree, definiteness, deixis, tense, aspect, mood, voice) and word classes, lexical semantics (including a discussion of prototype theory), phrase structure and verb complementation, sentence types (passives, questions, negation and imperatives), complex sentences and thematic roles. The final chapter discusses information structure, speech acts and relevance theory. In this arrangement of the material, the book follows the traditional method of working from the smallest unit (the sound) to the morpheme, the word, the clause, to semantics and discourse. There is only one drawback to this kind of arrangement in that it is always easier to 'sell' a generative model of syntax to students if one starts with thematic roles first. If thematic roles are introduced *after* syntax, as in this book, because they belong to the field of semantics, the rationale behind syntactic operations like *wh*-movement is much harder for students to assimilate. The book is accompanied by a CD-ROM containing a workbook with well-thought-out exercises and suggested answers in PDF format (i.e. in document form, not as an interactive computer exercise), as well as an additional chapter 'Linguistics in Language Teaching' by Howard Williams, which presents an excellent overview of the various theories and approaches to language teaching and their respective views on the usefulness of explicit grammar instruction for language students (there is general agreement, however, as to the necessity of a solid background in linguistics for language *teachers*). The book is aimed at 'advanced undergraduate (and graduate) students interested in contemporary English, including those whose primary interest is English as a second language, primary or secondary-school English education, English literature, theoretical and applied linguistics, or speech pathology' (p. xix). Although the text does not assume any background in language or linguistics, the book's information content is very high, and could be a bit overwhelming for absolute beginners or for those whose main interests lie in other fields.

Anne Lobeck's *Discovering Grammar: An Introduction to English Sentence Structure* differs from the three textbooks mentioned above by focusing only on syntax and only on English. It has chapters on the question of what grammar is (its components, descriptive and prescriptive forms), on categories and phrases, criteria for phrasehood (movement, pronominalization, co-ordination), nouns, verbs, VPs, adjectives, adverbs, prepositions, subordination and co-ordination, complements, adjuncts in VP and adjuncts in NP (i.e. relative clauses). Throughout, many examples and diagrams are given, and the style is user-friendly. The book contains a great number of exercises of different types, ranging from identifying examples of syntactic phenomena in short texts and transforming sentences to finding patterns, formulating syntactic generalizations, explaining phenomena, and researching OE, present-day British English, and sometimes other languages. This is a fine first-year introduction to syntax, we would say.

In overall coverage, it is somewhat similar to another newcomer, Verspoor and Sauter's *English Sentence Analysis: An Introductory Course*. Chapter 1, 'Sentences: Communicative Functions and Typical Patterns', introduces the main sentence types and constituent functions. Chapter 2, 'Sentences: Simple, Compound and Complex', looks at co-ordination and subordination. Chapters 3 and 4, 'Verbs I' and 'Verbs II', introduce the concepts of lexical versus auxiliary and finite versus non-finite, transitive versus intransitive, multi-word verbs, and the various verb complementation patterns. Chapter 5 introduces word classes, Chapter 6 phrases, and Chapter 7 clauses and their functions. Chapter 8, 'How to Analyze Sentences at All Levels', requires the student to integrate and apply the knowledge gained in the preceding chapters and offers helpful sections on 'how to analyze long and complex sentences' and 'how to analyze long and complex noun phrases'. Each chapter contains a few exercises to check understanding, but there are many more interactive exercises on the CD which accompanies the book and contains about 100 exercises for each chapter—with sentences taken from literary texts and pop songs. The book aims to introduce only the most basic concepts of linguistic analysis, and does not overwhelm the beginner with too much detail; refinements such as the *persuade/ expect* distinction are only hinted at. Verspoor and Sauter follow Flor Aarts and Jan Aarts, *English Syntactic Structures: Functions and Categories in Sentence Analysis*, the coursebook used by generations of Dutch university students, in distinguishing indirect objects from benefactive objects by the prepositional phrase paraphrase, but take a more relaxed view of what constitutes a direct object—the object is not required to pass the passivization test, so that 'a mile' in *he ran a mile* is a direct object. This policy allows them to do away with the dubious 'predicator complement' function, the label assigned by Aarts and Aarts to those NPs that are clearly obligatory but do not fit their strict definition of direct objecthood. Verspoor and Sauter have retained the labels 'subject attribute' and 'object attribute' for the Small Clause predicate (more commonly known as 'subject complement' and 'object complement'), which some students could find confusing when they are confronted with the labels for adjectival function—*attributive* versus *predicative*— at any later stage (it is not introduced in this course), and learn that *ill* in *John is ill*, though it has the function 'subject attribute', is actually used predicatively, not attributively.

Two final textbooks are at least partly pedagogical in intent, in the sense that they aim at increasing students' practical knowledge and command of English grammar. Carl Bache has written *Essentials of Mastering English: A Concise Grammar*, meant for undergraduates. It covers all the standard topics (grammatical functions, groups, co-ordination and subordination, clause types, ellipsis and pro-forms, order, voice, polarity, concord, complex sentences, verb groups, nominals, pronominals, adjectives, adverbs, etc.), paying attention to analytical as well as pedagogical issues. At times, this combination results in a somewhat uneasy mix, also because some rather complex topics are dealt with in the early chapters. On the other hand, the work provides detailed and reliable descriptions of many areas of English grammar. Less detail will be found in Martin Parrott's *Grammar for English Language Teachers*, which appears to cater for teachers at elementary to intermediate levels, even though it claims to offer 'a broader perspective of grammar than that presented to students in course materials' (p. 1). There are chapters on word classes, verbs (several chapters, in fact), word order, passive, discourse markers, ellipsis, complex sentences of various types, pronunciation, spelling, punctuation, and much more. Exercises are included (most are not particularly imaginative, even though many involve authentic texts), and each chapter notes common problems for learners (usually in the form of a list of possible errors). The style of presentation is generally simple, which may be a good thing since the book seems primarily meant for non-native teachers of English. In this light it is surprising to find the author using the word *we* not only in the inclusive sense of 'me (author) and you (readers)' (*Below we look at some of these factors*) but also in the meaning of 'native speakers of English' (*We frequently use these forms to* ...), a potentially exclusive sense that some users may find off-putting.

Geoffrey Finch's *Linguistic Terms and Concepts* is a practical reference guide to the study of linguistics. It differs from the standard 'dictionary' format of such books by the fact that entries are on average much longer, and by the fact that the material is organized into six chapters: 'Linguistics: A Brief Survey', 'General Terms and Concepts', 'Phonetics and Phonology', 'Syntax', 'Semantics and Pragmatics' and 'Linguistics: The Main Branches'. The chapters consist of a general introduction followed by a glossary. Another excellent reference work for anyone working in the field of (historical) linguistics is Trask's *Dictionary of Historical and Comparative Linguistics*. Not only does it cover the basic terminology of classical historical linguistics (*umlaut*, *lenition*, *sandhi*, etc., as well as older terms that have fallen out of use but whose meanings are essential to the understanding of earlier scholarship, such as *proethnic* or *surd*) but also the various 'laws' that have been proposed over the centuries, terms such as *bioprogram* and *invisible hand*, terminology from dialect studies, pidgin and creole studies, sociolinguistics, the names of languages and language families, more informal terms such as *lumpers* and *splitters*, the meaning and correct use of Latin abbreviations such as *cf.*, *op. cit.*, *s.v.*, *pace*, *apud*, etc., typographical symbols used in the field, *critical* or *diplomatic* editions, and so on. Very recent work, which has not yet found its way into the standard textbooks, has also been included, for example terminology from population typology, mathematical and computational methods, models of linguistic descent and grammaticalization studies.

After these textbooks and reference works, we turn to some shorter but still general items of various kinds. William Snyder has carried out 'An Experimental Investigation of Syntactic Satiation Effects' (*LingI* 31[2000] 575–82) and reports that, after repeated exposure, his twenty-two subjects became more tolerant towards island violations involving *whether* and complex NPs, but not towards subject islands and *that*-trace violations. The more homely topic of 'Grammar and Daily Life' has been investigated by M.A.K. Halliday (in Lockwood, Fries, and Copeland, eds., pp. 221–37). Here, Halliday discusses the increasing importance of thematic balance in utterances, in which the flow of information tends to be made explicit rather than being taken for granted. Examples discussed include the increase of passives in ME, the emergence of the English phrasal verb and the syntax of the productive derivational inflection *-ee*. A more technical topic is investigated in William O'Grady's 'The Architecture of Syntactic Representations: Binarity and Deconstruction' (in Guzman and Bender, eds., pp. 3–13). After noting that negative polarity phenomena require a configurational approach to syntactic structure (since the mere use of case or thematic hierarchies is not sufficient to account for sentences such as *John never helps anyone*), O'Grady proposes that syntactic trees are built up by joining words left to right in such a way that the verb is a sister to each argument at some point in the derivation (for *John gave Mary some advice*, this would imply the following structures: [*John gave*], [*John* [*gave Mary*]], and [*John* [[*gave advice*] *Mary*]]. That thematic hierarchies are not just insufficient but perhaps even unnecessary is one of the conclusions of Anthony Davis and Jean-Pierre Koenig's 'Linking as Constraints on Word Classes in a Hierarchical Lexicon' (*Lg* 76[2000] 56–91). After discussing several problems for semantic hierarchies as a device to regulate linking of arguments to grammatical functions (what to do with the double agent in causatives? how about alternations like *own* vs. *belong*? how to avoid the circularity resulting from the interdependency of semantic roles?), they propose an alternative verb-class-based approach to linking, couched in an HPSG framework relying on entailments. We also mention here the article 'Early MT Research at M.I.T.: The Search for Context' by Victor H. Yngve (in Lockwood, Fries, and Copeland, eds., pp. 593–628), which describes the development of work on machine translation from the early 1950s onwards. Yngve shows that, although its ultimate goal may never be reached, the effort itself has generated a crop of novel, very productive approaches to syntax and morphology—including generative theory, as Noam Chomsky was involved in this research project in the early 1950s. Particularly intriguing is the notion of 'depth': syntactic generativity is constrained by human processing limitations, which leads to the formulation of a number of predictions about language design (binary branching) and language change.

General issues in, or arising from, corpus linguistics are addressed in a handful of articles and a book (there has of course been more corpus work this year, but we discuss this later on in connection with the specific phenomena or constructions investigated). That the descriptive apparatus used by corpus linguists needs to be refined and revised is the conclusion of Nelleke Oostdijk in her paper 'Corpus-Based English Linguistics at a Cross-Roads' (*ES* 81[2000] 127–41), in which she reflects on the achievements of three decades of corpus linguistic research and its (sometimes conflicting) aims. In another article, Oostdijk investigates 'Linguistic Delicacy in Explorative Studies' (in Kirk, ed., pp. 281–93). Using the verb group as an example, she discusses the uses and limits of grammatical annotation; she shows that answering apparently simple questions (e.g. about the frequency of simple vs. complex verb groups) may not be so easy as some linguists might think, especially if their awareness of the annotation conventions is limited. Problems are also noted by Anna Rahman and Geoffrey Sampson in their article 'Extending Grammar Annotation Standards to Spontaneous Speech' (in Kirk, ed., pp. 295–311). They list several difficulties for speech annotation (such as word class ambiguity, incoherence and repairs, the use of mixed modes of speech reporting, error vs. non-standard language, and inaudibility), attribute them to the fact that our grammatical categories are not based on speech, and call for serious consideration of the issue. More optimistic are Pasi Tapanainen and Timo Järvinen, who write about 'Syntactic Concordances' (in Kirk, ed., pp. 313–18). They give several examples of what can be achieved, such as concordancing a particular verb in the passive, a verb with its object, a verb with objects of a certain word class, and even zero relatives. For want of a better place, we also fit in here the corpus study by David Minugh, 'You People Use Such Weird Expressions: The Frequency of Idioms in Newspaper CDs and Corpora' (in Kirk, ed., pp. 57–71), which finds that idioms are relatively infrequent (e.g. *it's high time* occurs once per million words); of the text types investigated, it is newspapers that have the highest idiomatic density.

The uneasy feelings that many corpus linguists have towards syntactic theory are very much to the fore in Hunston and Francis, *Pattern Grammar: A Corpus-Driven Approach to the Lexical Grammar of English*. As one example, the writers prefer terms such as 'pattern' or 'pattern flow' for the phenomena more commonly known as 'subcategorization frames' or 'embedding', because they reject the hierarchical approach to syntactic structure which such terms imply. This book offers instead an approach to lexis and grammar based on the concept of phraseology and of language patterning arising from work on large corpora. Chapter 1 introduces the background to work on phraseology, and discusses some issues surrounding corpus linguistics, such as the difference between a corpus-based approach—in which the results are inevitably restricted by the bias of the 'problem' to be investigated—and a corpus-driven approach, which aims to make generalizations based on observations of recorded behaviour which are as theory-free as possible. Chapters 2 to 4 are mainly data-oriented. The patterns (subcategorization frames) they describe cannot be identified solely on the basis of frequency, and some distinctions need to be made, mainly along traditional lines of adjuncts and complements. This distinction, though universally acknowledged, is of course notoriously difficult to formalize, and apparently no formalized distinction is allowed in Hunston and Francis's approach (p. 73), which leaves as the only 'valid' criterion the status of the information itself: 'trivial' or 'non-trivial', an extremely subjective notion, as Hunston and Francis are the first to admit. The focus is on surface patterns, although passives are related to their active counterparts 'for the sake of convenience and simplicity' (p. 60). The idea that the patterns themselves may contribute to the overall meaning of the utterance (in ways typical of the creative use that speakers make of their language) is in itself not new, but actual examples from corpora continue to fascinate, as this one, for instance: *Society must be predisposed to panic about crimes. There had already to be a tendency to <u>discover crime as the cause behind worrisome social ills</u>* (p. 106). Here the writer uses the pattern [V N *as* N], which is normally found with verbs like *consider, describe, interpret, label,* etc., to indicate that the description is a matter of opinion. Its use here with *discover* creatively implies that the idea that crime is the cause behind worrisome ills is only an opinion, not a fact. Chapter 5 discusses the association of pattern and meaning, with lists and examples. Chapters 6 to 8 relate the concept of pattern to traditional approaches to grammar and to discourse. A considerable part of chapter 8 is taken up with a discussion of the pros and cons of a linear versus a hierarchical analysis—the authors favour the former, an option that would probably not have been available had they been discussing a language that 'governs to the left', as for instance German, Dutch, or classical Latin. Chapter 9 summarizes the book and discusses its implications for language learning.

After these 'surfacy' studies, we turn to four articles on various aspects of syntax from the logician's perspective. Sebastian Löbner's 'Polarity in Natural Language: Predication, Quantification and Negation in Particular and Characterizing Sentences' (*Ling&P* 23[2000] 213–308) provides a logician's analysis of a number of basic syntactic operations and attempts to clarify the logical aspects of predication. The broad truth-value gaps in many cases of elementary sentence types, unsatisfactory though they may appear to the eye of the logician, fulfil an important communicative function in that they allow for a loosening of the commitment to the respective truth conditions and enable a speaker to focus on those aspects of the world that are relevant to the situation in hand. It is this mechanism that allows speakers to cope with the complexities of the world with comparatively simple linguistic means. B.H. Slater, 'Quantifier/Variable-Binding' (*Ling&P* 23[2000] 309–21), offers an account of anaphoric relations which does not rely on binding relations on a variable but uses certain choice functions, epsilon terms, which can have a referring function back to quantifier antecedents, but are not bound by them. Utpal Lahiri, 'Lexical Selection and Quantificational Variability in Embedded Interrogatives' (*Ling&P* 23[2000] 325–89), offers an analysis of Quantificational Variability in indirect questions after predicates of the *know* type and after predicates of the *wonder* type and concludes that the different behaviour of the two classes of predicates follows from the way they are interpreted when a predicate such as *know*, which would normally take a proposition as an argument, instead takes a question as an argument. The analysis also includes focus-affected readings with interrogative complements of predicates such as *tell*. Shalom Lappin's 'An Intensional Parametric Semantics for Vague Quantifiers' (*Ling&P* 23[2000] 599–620) attempts to capture the radical vagueness of the determiners *many* and *few*, whose interpretations are notoriously context-dependent and underdetermined, by expressing the minimal core meaning of these quantifier relations through a parameterized schematic interpretation with a small number of indefeasible conditions.

Next, we turn to general work carried out within specific theories or models of grammar. As we have noted on previous occasions, Optimality Theory is slowly also invading syntax. This year, we report on a handful of syntactic OT articles. Joan Bresnan writes about 'Optimal Syntax' (in Dekkers, van der Leeuw, and van de Weijer, eds., *Optimality Theory: Phonology, Syntax, and Acquisition*, pp. 302–33;

this is a major OT publication); she notes that OT syntactic work usually mimics transformational derivations, and proposes an LFG-inspired and radically non-derivational OT syntax, applying it to facts from the domain of English head movement (as analysed earlier in Jane Grimshaw [1997], see *YWES* 78[1999] 26). In the same volume (pp. 279–301), Peter Ackema and Ad Neeleman address the problem of 'Absolute Ungrammaticality'. The phenomenon of no candidate winning out is problematic for any OT approach, since one candidate should always violate the fewest constraints. The authors' solution is to have the Null Parse win in such cases; they show how this would work in the case of multiple *wh*-questions, passives of intransitive verbs, and periphrastic passives. Stephen Anderson leads us 'Towards an Optimal Account of Second-Position Phenomena' (Dekkers *et al.*, eds., pp. 302–33), providing a unified OT analysis of second-position clitics and verb-second. The basic principle employed is that functional content should be nearly at the left edge. Hans Broekhuis and Joost Dekkers write about 'The Minimalist Program and Optimality Theory: Derivations and Evaluations' (Dekkers *et al.*, eds., pp. 386–422); investigating the phenomenon of doubly filled COMP in English and Dutch relative clauses, they develop a model of syntax in which the computational component consists of the operations Select, Merge, Move and Delete, which yield a candidate set that is submitted to the evaluator (EVAL)—in other words, Minimality and OT are completely integrated here. We also note Bruce Tesar's 'On the Roles of Optimality and Strict Domination in Language Learning' (Dekkers *et al.*, eds., pp. 592–620); against the background of recent learnability work, the author develops an Optimality learning account in which error-driven constraint demotion plays an important role. Rakesh M. Bhatt, 'Optimal Expressions in Indian English' (*ELL* 4[2000] 69–95), presents an account of sociolinguistic-syntactic variation between Standard Indian English and English Vernacular English, involving the syntax of *wh*-questions, Focus constructions, null subjects and objects, and null expletive subjects, in an Optimality framework. This allows the following generalizations: (*a*) the two varieties are equally systematic and logical; (*b*) their grammars are bound by the same set of grammatical constraints; and (*c*) the differences between the two varieties are a function of how each grammar prioritizes these constraints.

While work such as the above makes clear that Optimality Theory is being applied to an ever-wider range of facts, there are some concerns about the amount of insight and understanding that OT actually yields, not only in syntax but also in phonology. One linguist who is very concerned about this is April McMahon. In *Change, Chance, and Optimality* she takes a hard and prolonged look at the claims and practices of OT, and her overall assessment of what she sees is not exactly positive. Among the problems that she identifies is the lack of success of OT analysis in the area of phonology-morphology interactions (most secure OT results are limited to the field of prosody and syllabification); the high number of very language-specific constraints that have been proposed; the fact that constraints have sometimes been supplemented by rules; unsolved questions about the exact workings of the generator (GEN); and a general lack of restrictiveness of the theory. Language change is shown to be a particularly difficult territory for OT, with several examples of description posing as explanation (the device of constraint re-ranking being misused in much the same way as notions such as rule reordering and feeding were in early generative work on change). Optimality theorists working on change have proposed some modifications to the theory to take on board facts of change and variation, but McMahon argues that these either compromise the theory or do not achieve what they were intended for. She compares OT with the model of Natural Morphology; the latter seems more successful because of its willingness to incorporate not only universal constraints but also rules, language-specific principles, as well as contingent facts. A comparison with evolutionary biology suggests that such a multi-factor model fares best in accounting for real-world phenomena and their development through time. In the final chapter, McMahon considers OT and the genesis of language, concluding that a focus on constraints and nothing but constraints makes an evolutionary account of language very difficult.

For the first time in many years we have not seen a generative textbook on syntax, but there are several generative monographs and many generative articles to report on. Robert Chametzky has written *Phrase Structure: From GB to Minimalism*, in which he compares the role played by phrase structure in his own 1996 theory of phrase-makers, Noam Chomsky's 1995 Minimalist Program, and Richard Kayne's 1994 antisymmetry model. There is a brief introduction discussing some general issues in phrase structure, a chapter on the status of subjects, adjuncts, heads, functional vs. lexical projections, extended projections, X-bar, binary branching and order, followed by three chapters on phrase structure in each of the works being compared. The final chapter considers derivationalism vs. representationalism and the ultimate function of phrase structure. Also concerned with a big issue in the architecture of syntactic representations is an article by the late Teun Hoekstra, 'The Function of Functional Categories' (in Cheng and Sybesma, eds., pp. 1–25). In this overview article we can read, very usefully, about the motivations for functional projections, the absence of a real theory about them, their licensing role, the variation that they can show, differences and similarities among various functional categories (nominal and verbal, A and A-bar), their acquisition, and their role in minimalist theory. It is sad that there will be no more articles like this from Teun, who had the gift of combining down-to-earth observations with profound theoretical innovation and insight.

Top-flight generative syntax unfolding through time can now be conveniently viewed in Hilda Koopman's *The Syntax of Specifiers and Heads: Collected Essays of Hilda J. Koopman*. This volume spans her work from the early 1980s to the mid-1990s. All except one of the articles have been published before, but some of them are not easily accessible, and put together in this collection they show well the impressive breadth of empirical coverage and the continuing progress on the theoretical front that characterize Koopman's work (and, by implication, other high-quality generative work of the past two decades). Included are pieces—some of them classics by now—such as 'Variables and the Bijection Principle' (written with Dominique Sportiche [1983], on the causes of the weak cross-over effect), 'ECP Effects in Main Clauses' ([1983], deriving the ungrammaticality of *Who did say so?*), 'Control from COMP and Comparative Syntax' ([1983], deriving cross-linguistic variation in possibilities of *Wh*-movement), 'The Structure of Dutch PPs' (based on two papers from the early 1990s, and deriving complex pre/post/circumposition and particle facts), 'Licensing Heads' ([1994], on the distribution of VPs), 'On Verbs that Fail to Undergo V-Second' ([1995], deriving the ban in Dutch on verb-second of particle verbs with an additional prefix), 'The Spec Head Configuration' ([1996], deriving the doubly filled COMP filter and much more from a ban on overt material in both Spec and head simultaneously), and 'The Internal and External Distribution of Pronominal DPs' ([1999], linking internal and external properties of pronouns). The books also contains an introduction that places these articles in their historical and theoretical context.

Another collection of articles by a well-known generative syntactician is Thomas Stroik's *Syntactic Controversies*. Its main thesis is that some constructions are currently playing an undesirable dual role in syntactic argumentation: they serve as an argument for a particular theory, and at the same time are taken as something that the theory should explain. This means that these constructions become immune to re-analysis and that the whole enterprise becomes circular. In the first chapter, 'On Regression and Boundedness in Antecedent Contained Deletion' (pp. 13–48), Stroik analyses data such as *Lou read nothing that Sam did* as having a VP2 inside a relative clause which is an adjunct to NumP; no regress arises, and the construction does not provide evidence for quantifier raising at LF. 'Referentiality and Multiple-Wh Constructions' (pp. 49–88) considers *Why did you buy what?* vs. **What did you buy why?*; Stroik argues that the first of these is an echo-question, and that the standard ECP-based analysis of the facts is therefore incorrect. Instead, he proposes that such questions require referential *wh*-elements and develops a minimalist checking analysis for them. The status of expletive *it* is investigated in 'Extraposition and Expletive Movement' (pp. 89–116). Here, *it* is argued to be merged in SpecCP of the extraposed clause, subsequently to be moved to SpecAgrP, as in regular subject- or object-raising; support for this analysis comes from learnability considerations. '*Do So* and the Light Verb Hypothesis' (pp. 117–37) has *do* affixed to *v* in vP and *so/it* being a VP (cf. *Ted left, which he shouldn't have done*). The final chapter, 'On Argument Demotion' (pp. 138–72), proposes that there is demotion of the Agent in passives (it becomes a non-argument, introduced by *by* if overt, simply being PRO if not), of the indirect object in the *to*-construction, and of the Agent in middles.

The study of real-time acquisition has become increasingly prominent in generative work over the last decade, and we have traced part of its rise in the annual instalments of this section. This year, we have seen Friedemann and Rizzi, eds., *The Acquisition of Syntax: Studies in Comparative Developmental Linguistics*, in the Longman Linguistics Library (a series that, after a slow period, has become a very active player in the field again). The editors' introduction sketches the boost given to acquisition studies by the principles-and-parameters model, taking the phenomenon of early null subjects as an example (the big question being whether they are due to real *pro*-drop or to some kind of truncation, i.e. deletion in performance). Of the articles in the volume, we deal only with those directly relevant to English, but we can recommend the others too to anyone interested in matters acquisitional. Maria Teresa Guasti takes us on 'An Excursion into Interrogatives in Early English and Italian' (pp. 105–28), both of which, she argues, obey the *wh*-criterion, except that English may have an inverted null auxiliary. Liliane Haegeman looks at 'Adult Null Subjects in Non Pro-Drop Languages' (pp. 129–69); she attributes English and French null subjects to the process of truncation, noting that there can be a preposed adjunct (as in *Here, studied under Daiches*). Luigi Rizzi offers some 'Remarks on Early Null Subjects' (pp. 269–92), in which he surveys a great number of studies of early Dutch, French, English, and German, and posits the existence of two types of null subject.

A lot of generative work continues to address questions in and about Chomsky's minimalist model of syntax. First, we note an exchange of views on the status and popularity of the model. In 'The Structure of Unscientific Revolutions', in the *Topic* ... *Comment* section of *NL&LT* (*NL&LT* 18[2000] 665–71) Shalom Lappin, Robert D. Levine and David E. Johnson criticize the wholesale adoption of the Minimalist Program by many linguists without there being, in their view, a significant body of results following directly from this model. As they note, this is contrary to common practice in the natural sciences, where scientists do not abandon a highly successful model—which would translate as Government and Binding Theory in this particular case—except under pressure of compelling scientific motivation, primarily consisting of the emergence of a new formalism that preserves the results of the previous paradigm while contributing an empirically grounded model of a phenomenon that remained unexplained—and in principle unexplainable—on the earlier account. The authors suggest that the Minimalist Program appears to be taken up simply on the basis of Chomsky's personal authority, in spite of what they call 'its bizarrely vague and unmotivated assumptions' (p. 670). This, of course, is a challenge that could not remain unanswered, and five replies follow in the same volume of the same journal. In his reaction, Anders Holmberg (*NL&LT* 18[2000] 837–42) is honest about his own motivations to go over to the Minimalist Program (the fact that is was fashionable may have played a part), but also insists that it was inspired to a large extent by the work which he did with Christopher Platzack on verb movement in Scandinavian. There are further responses from Eric Reuland (*NL&LT* 18[2000] 843–8), Ian Roberts (*NL&LT* 18[2000] 849–57), Massimo Piatelli-Palmarini (*NL&LT* 18[2000] 859–62) and Juan Uriagereka (*NL&LT* 18[2000] 863–71), and then it's back to Lappin, Levine and Johnson to comment on these responses in 'The Revolution Confused: A Response to our Critics' (*NL&LT* 18[2000] 873–90).

Proponents of minimalism can point to a growing body of work in which minimalist ideas are successfully applied to an increasing range of empirical facts. One such work is Hiroyuki Ura's *Checking Theory and Grammatical Functions in Universal Grammar*. In this revised version of his 1996 MIT thesis, Ura investigates grammatical functions in the minimalist model, where they can no longer be simply defined in terms of phrase structure position. Instead, Ura proposes a split of grammatical functions so that, for example, control takes place only by elements that check a phi-feature of T, and binding of subject-oriented reflexives only by elements that check the extended-projection-principle feature of T. This means that subject or object properties can be spread out over different elements. To accommodate these elements in the phrase structure, Ura proposes that T can have multiple specifiers. Chapter 1 introduces the necessary machinery, and chapters 2 to 8 then contain data and detailed analyses of various phenomena: inverse voice in Bantu and Apachean (a brief comparison is made with quotative inversion in English), anti-impersonal passives; dative subjects in Japanese, Tamil and Icelandic (with brief discussion of the situation in ME); locative inversion; ergativity; and the double object construction (including a comparison of sentences such as *The Book was given Mary* in British and American English).

Sometimes it also pays off to reconsider well-known facts, and use them as a probe into the nature of the model. This is what Etsuro Shima does in proposing that there is 'A Preference for Move over Merge' (*LingI* 31[2000] 375–85). The conceptual argument for this lies in the idea that it is more economical to take one phrase marker and do something with it than to take a phrase marker plus a lexical item and then do something with them. Empirical evidence comes from facts relating to super-raising (*John seems that it is unlikely to win*) and expletive *there* (*There seems someone to be in the room*), which have been analysed by Chomsky within a Merge-over-Move model but which Shima shows are also (and perhaps even more adequately) analysable in a Move-over-Merge model. Another feature of the model is cyclicity, on which Jon Gajewski has written 'Noncyclic Operations and the LCA [Linear Correspondence Axiom] in a Derivational Theory' (in *LingI* 31[2000] 722–31). He points out an inconsistency in the strictly derivational approach to structure-building, which claims to deduce cyclicity from the nature of the basic tree-building operations, but at the same time tries to explain the grammaticality of sentences such as *Which claim that $John_i$ made was he_i willing to discuss* by appealing to late (and therefore anti-cyclic) Merger of the relative clause. The importance of using a structural model in accounting for scope facts is reaffirmed by Joseph Aoun and Yen-hui Audrey Li in their 'Scope, Structure, and Expert Systems: A Reply to Kuno *et al.*' (*Language* 76[2000] 133–55), a reply to Susumu Kuno, Ken-ichi Takami, and Yuru Wu, 'Quantifier Scope in English, Chinese, and Japanese' (*Language* 75[1999] 63–111). Aoun and Li show that Kuno *et al.*'s approach, in terms of an expert system, suffers from problems such as a conspicuous lack of restrictiveness, questions about when which experts are supposed to apply, and unclarity in the account of ambiguous sentences. In a more theory-internal contribution, Michael Brody proposes 'Mirror Theory: Syntactic Representation in Perfect Syntax' (*LingI* 31[2000] 29–56). Here the mirror principle, standardly taken to follow from the head movement constraint in conjunction with a ban against excorporation, receives a novel account, in which the specifier–head relation in morphology is viewed as the reverse order of the syntactic head–complement relation. C-command is dispensed with, as is categorial projection and the duplication of word structure in syntax.

A minimalist approach to control phenomena is found in Idan Landau's *Elements of Control: Structure and Meaning in Infinitival Constructions*, based on his 1999 MIT thesis. Landau puts the minimalist device of Agree to good use in accounting for control, but perhaps the work's major value lies in its careful teasing apart of various types of control. Thus non-obligatory control is distinguished from obligatory control; the former has the two subtypes of long-distance and arbitrary control, while the latter can be either exhaustive (as in *The chair managed to gather the committee at six*) or partial (*The chair preferred to gather at six*). Detailed investigation of these and other cases shows that control is not a unified phenomenon (*psych*-predicates, for example, have distinctive control properties); for this and other reasons, an analysis of control in terms of predication is rejected. Attention is also paid to implicit control (*He said to follow him*) and control shift (*John was promised to be allowed to leave*), in the form of a thorough review of the facts and the analyses of them that have been proposed over the years. As the author acknowledges, the book does not deal with control into adjuncts and nominals, so there is still scope for further control work. This is also evident from the overview article on 'Control in GB and Minimalism' by Norbert Hornstein (in Cheng and Sybesma, eds., pp. 27–45). It describes the classical GB approach to control, the problems it faces, the later null-Case account of Noam Chomsky and Howard

Lasnik, and more recent minimalist approaches (including Hornstein's own, which has PRO as a trace of A-movement from one theta-position to another theta-position). Non-obligatory control is argued to involve null *one*, i.e. little *pro*. Rita Manzini and Anna Roussou provide 'A Minimalist Theory of A-Movement and Control' (*Lingua* 110[2000] 409–47), which offers an analysis of control constructions that also does away with PRO. Instead, DPs are merged directly in D-position, where they attract predicates from the VP shell.

Cognitive linguistics also continues to flourish. This year's issue of the journal *Cognitive Linguistics* is devoted to language acquisition, including four articles specifically about the acquisition of English structures. In 'Typicality, Naming, and the Embodiment of Spatial Cognition' (*CogLing* 11[2000] 17–41), Victoria Southgate and Kertin Meins report on a preferential looking task experiment that suggests that young children (aged between 18 and 24 months) display typicality effects similar to those of adults. Ewa Dǎbrowska's 'From Formula to Schema: The Acquisition of English Questions' (*CogLing* 11[2000] 83–102) traces the development of interrogative structures in a single child from the first word combinations to age 3 years 8 months and concludes that constructional schemas emerge spontaneously when the learner has acquired a sufficiently large repertoire of formulaic utterances. In 'From States to Events: The Acquisition of English Passive Participle' (*CogLing* 11[2000] 103–29), Michael Israel, Christopher Johnson, and Patricia J. Brooks show that the acquisition of true verbal passive participles develops out of adjectival uses that are gradually extended to equivocal contexts compatible with either a stative or an eventive reading. Finally, 'The Development of Relative Clauses in Spontaneous Child Speech' by Holger Diessel and Michael Tomasello (*CogLing* 11[2000] 131–51) shows that the earliest relative clauses occur in presentational constructions that express a single proposition in two finite clauses, e.g. *Here's a tiger that's gonna scare him*. Object relatives (which can be argued to show greater complexity) develop after subject relatives. Another cognitive paper is Carita Paradis's 'Reinforcing Adjectives: A Cognitive Semantic Perspective on Grammaticalisation' (in Bermúdez-Otero, Denison, Hogg and McCully, eds., pp. 233–58), which addresses the semantic and structural prerequisites for the grammaticalization process whereby adjectives such as *absolute, awful, complete*, etc. may lose some of their semantic content and acquire a reinforcing reading.

Selected papers from the fifth International Cognitive Linguistics Conference, held in Amsterdam in 1997, have been published in Foolen and van der Leek, eds., *Constructions in Cognitive Linguistics*. It opens with a paper by Angeliki Athanasiadou and René Dirven entitled 'Pragmatic Conditionals' (pp. 1–26), which discusses English pragmatic, non-prototypical conditionals, a class which they conceive as including epistemic/logical conditionals. They argue on the basis of corpus findings that the four subtypes they distinguish—'identifying', 'inferencing', 'discourse' and 'metacommunicative'—all share certain basic pragmatic characteristics. The variety of forms manifested by each type can be accounted for by the very different ways in which these basic characteristics can be extended. Robert D. Dewell, 'Case Meaning and Sequence of Attention: Source Landmarks as Accusative and Dative Objects of the Verb' (pp. 47–65), discusses the schematic meanings of accusative and dative cases and argues that they do not simply reflect different roles in the action chain, but impose a certain way of construing an event.

The accusative typically effects a change of focus away from the subject towards the direct object referent, while the dative, on the other hand, never gains central focus. There are certain constructions in German with a dative participant which might be translated by a transitive pattern in English, e.g. *Ludwig escaped his family*, but this means pressing the intended meaning into a syntactic mould that is not a good fit from the viewpoint of how the hearer's attention is directed. The focus should remain on *Ludwig*, and not move to *his family*—the job is done well by the dative in German, but English lacks a distinct dative form. Beate Hampe, 'Facing up to the Meaning of "Face Up To": A Cognitive Semantico-Pragmatic Analysis of an English Verb-Particle Construction' (pp. 81–101), shows that the phrasal verb *face up to* is not synonymous with its simplex *face*, as the former conveys the message that the challenge posed by a particular obstacle is met, not merely noticed. Corpus data suggest that the immediate linguistic environments of the phrasal verb particles that were examined tend to contain more expressive linguistic elements (irony, repetition, intensifying adjuncts and other rhetorical features), which would suggest that the phrasal verb may well index some emotional or attitudinal dimension at the speaker level. Liesbet Heyvaert, 'Gerundive Nominalization: From Type Specification to Grounded Instance' (pp. 103–21), presents a proposal for refining Langacker's analysis of English gerundive nominals. She argues that the *-ing* form in gerundive nominals, unlike the *-ing* form in action nominals, contains a non-finite clausal head, which forms a complex clausal type specification with its object. Instead of calling *signing the contract* in a phrase such as *Zelda's signing the contract* an instance whose subject is periphrastically expressed, she prefers to call it a type which is necessarily instantiated by the subject. This analysis enables her to account for the semantic and behavioural distinctions between action nominals, gerundive nominals and *that*-clause nominals. Nili Mandelblit and Gilles Fauconnier, 'How I Got Myself Arrested: Underspecificity in Grammatical Blends as a Source for Constructional Ambiguity' (pp. 167–89), argue, on the basis of data from English, modern Hebrew and French, that a generic conceptual causative schema underlies not only grammatical causative constructions, but passive, middle and reflexive constructions as well. Clauses are constructed by blending a conceived event with a schematically meaningful syntactic construction. There is a potential for ambiguity between middle and passive constructions in modern Hebrew here in that not every element of the conceived event may be projected on the construction. The blending mechanism may lead to the different mappings seen in the different meanings of *Rachel sneezed the napkin off the table*, where the construction's subject referent is identified as the one who is doing the sneezing and *She trotted the horse into the stable*, where the object referent is identified as doing the trotting. Hidemitsu Takahashi, 'English Imperatives and Passives' (pp. 239–58), investigates uneasy combinations of passives and imperatives. The felicitousness of English *Be flattered by what he says, it'll make his day* is exceptional—passives and imperatives normally do not combine well, as there is a conceptual incompatibility here: the (second-person) subject of an imperative is, given a prototypical Imperative Event Model, an agent, whereas the subject of a passive, given a prototypical Passive Model, is a patient. Unlike Japanese, in which there are no acceptable passive imperatives, English allows the constructions to be used in non-prototypical ways, which explains why felicitous examples can be constructed at all. The final paper in the volume is Frederike van der Leek's 'Caused-Motion and the

"Bottom-up" Role of Grammar' (pp. 301–31), which takes issue with the analysis of the English caused-motion construction as in *Cindy blew the dust off the book* proposed by Adele Goldberg [1995], who claims that its syntax prototypically pairs up with a caused-motion sense, and with extended senses in non-prototypical uses of the construction. Verbs would then basically have only one meaning, and be licensed in a construction if their basic meanings are compatible with one of the construction's conventional senses. Van der Leek argues instead that, where mature speakers are concerned, the pure syntax of the construction makes no semantic contribution of its own, and that the caused-motion pattern (or any of its extensions) gets extracted by the languages user as a superordinate conceptual category. Children will hear the construction used in ways that will force them to 'bare' the complement configuration of the semantic content that they initially associated with it, and to realize the non-lexicalized complement configuration's real function: to provide structure to encode conceptualization.

In comparison with general work on the models of OT, generative grammar and cognitive grammar, there are relatively few contributions this year to functional models. Robin Fawcett, *A Theory of Syntax for Systemic Functional Linguistics*, traces the history of syntactic theorizing in systemic functionalism and describes important progress made in this area by the Cardiff group of functionalists. Part 1 takes us from the beginnings, i.e. Michael Halliday's 'Categories of the Theory of Grammar' [1961], through the (often unacknowledged) changes in the model, to the two present-day versions commonly designated as the Sydney Grammar and Cardiff Grammar. Fawcett calls attention to certain problems in the Sydney model (in particular the need for closer integration of the five to eight functional structures usually distinguished, and the absence of rigorous application of the model) and discusses how these are solved in the Cardiff Grammar. Part 2 goes on to further develop the Cardiff Grammar: among the points emphasized are the redundancy of the concept of rank scale (instead, the notion of filling probabilities is adopted), the importance of analysis at the most delicate level, and the interaction between the two levels of meaning and form. Though some of the discussion is quite theory-internal, most of this work can be appreciated by anyone who has read Michael Halliday's *Introduction to Functional Grammar* [1994]. Further development is also taking place in the Amsterdam model of functional grammar. In 'First Things First: Towards an Incremental Functional Grammar' (*ALH* 32[2000] 23–44), Lachlan Mackenzie proposes to supplement the functional levels of clause structure and discourse structure with a third level, at which an utterance-initial sub-act can, but need not, be expanded by further expression possibilities. As a result, elliptical utterances should be renamed as non-expanded ones. The examples all come from English; we think that data from other languages may pose problems for a linear process of sentence-building.

After these contributions to particular theoretical models, it is time to turn to specific elements of grammar, beginning with the noun phrase. Inge Maria de Mönnink's *On the Move: The Mobility of Constituents in the English Noun Phrase—A Multi-Method Approach*, is the published version of her Nijmegen Ph.D. thesis. Using corpus data (drawn from 400,000 words of speech and writing), de Mönnink finds that there is internal mobility in 4 per cent of all complex noun phrases in British English. Elicitation tests (along lines set by the Survey of English Usage) were carried out on three of the types of mobility: fronted premodifiers (as in *so hungry a child*), discontinuous adjective phrases (*a less intelligent student than before*), and floating deferred modifiers (basically, extraposed relative clauses). A detailed presentation of the findings is given, followed by discussion of various possible analyses, both formal and functional. Among the avenues explored are the effects of Kaynian antisymmetry (however, Kayne's ban on rightward adjunction is found to be untenable) and the importance of information structure (John Hawkins's principle of Early Immediate Constituents is found to apply, and end focus is seen to play a role in the occurrence of deferred modifiers). In a separate article, 'A Moving Phrase: A Multi-Method Approach to the Mobility of Constituents in the English Noun Phrase' (in Kirk, ed., pp. 133–46), de Mönnink provides a brief summary of the material in her book, with special emphasis on the methodology used in her investigation of the noun phrase. A newish construction with *of* inserted after a fronted modifier, as in *that big of a deal*, is studied in Susan Fitzmaurice, 'The Great Leveler: The Role of the Spoken Media in Stylistic Shift from the Colloquial to the Conventional' (*AS* 75[2000] 54–68). After some discussion of earlier observations about this construction, as well as the construction with *not* splitting an infinitive (i.e. *to not* V), Fitzmaurice presents data showing that both are spreading from colloquial usage to a wider range of styles, probably through the influence of spoken media language. Fitzmaurice provides more information on the use of the negative split infinitive in 'Remarks on the De-Grammaticalisation of Infinitival *to* in Present-Day American English' (in Fischer, Rosenbach and Stein, eds., *Pathways of Change: Grammaticalization in English*, pp. 171–86), in which she argues that the gradual regularization of quasi-modals such as *have to* and *to be going to* and the pragmatic utility of the negative split infinitive together are preparing the way or resulting in the de-grammaticalization of the infinitival marker *to*.

More modifiers can be found in David G. Lockwood's 'Some Stratificational Insights Concerning the English Noun Phrase' (in Lockwood *et al.*, eds., pp. 267–87), which demonstrates that various phenomena involving modifiers of the nominal head become less intractable if a distinction is made between semology (the structure of linguistic meaning) and lexology (roughly equatable with a classical conception of syntax). Christopher Kennedy and Jason Merchant, 'Attributive Comparative Deletion' (*NL&LT* 18[2000] 89–146), investigates comparatives involving attributive adjectives in a number of languages, including English, and conclude that violations of Ross's Left Branch Condition involving these structures should not be accounted for in terms of constraints on LF representations but rather in terms of the principle of Full Interpretation at the PF interface. The paper also offers an analysis of ellipsis and of pseudo-gapping. In another adjectival paper, 'Some Peculiar Adjectives in the English Nominal Group' (in Lockwood *et al.*, eds., pp. 289–322), Peter H. Fries presents a categorization of adjectives modifying noun heads. A semantic distinction between textual-oriented and interpersonal-oriented meanings is shown to correlate with various syntactic characteristics. Modification not *by* but *of* adjectives is investigated in two articles that appear in the same volume and have looked at the same phenomenon in the same corpus of data: Anna-Brita Stenström has written '*It's Enough Funny, Man*: Intensifiers in Teenage Talk' (in Kirk, ed., pp. 177–90), which is a close-up study of *enough* and *well* as adjective modifiers (*enough funny* and *well cool*) in the 1993 Corpus of London Teenage Language; the same facts, though viewed from a wider perspective, are addressed by Carita Paradis in '*It's Well Weird. Degree Modifiers of Adjectives Revisited: The*

Nineties' (in Kirk, ed., pp. 147–60), who looks at a wider range of modifiers, compares the 1993 teenage data with London–Lund data from the 1960s and 1970s, and discusses the semantics of the various modifiers.

Genitives and possessives have also received some attention. Chris Barker writes about 'Definite Possessives and Discourse Novelty' (*TL* 26[2000] 211–27), and proposes that a noun phrase as a whole can count as 'familiar' if the possessor phrase contained in it is familiar (as in *that man's daughter*). Possessives are dealt with from a more descriptive perspective in Aimo Seppänen's 'The Genitive/ Possessive Pronoun *Its*' (*SN* 72[2000] 121–41), which examines the status of 'independent' *its* in sentences such as *That's my plate, not the dog's. Its is over there* and concludes, on the basis of corpus work and an informant test, that it is genuinely part of English grammar. Its marginality is ultimately due to the relative newness of the form, and to the incompatibility of the special semantics of the postnominal construction *a N of N's* and non-human nouns or pronouns. *Wh*-possessors are the topic of Elena Gavruseva's 'On the Syntax of Possessor Extraction' (*Lingua* 110[2000] 743–72), which attempts to provide a (minimalist) parametric account of cross-linguistic differences in extraction of *wh*-possessors across several languages, including English.

Martin Haspelmath, *Indefinite Pronouns*, is a new typological study which presents a survey of indefinite pronouns in the world's languages, including English. As the author notes (p. 235), 'although indefinite pronouns are not a very conspicuous part of the grammars of human languages, their study has wide ramifications in semantics, pragmatics, syntax, and morphology'. He argues that the choice of functions, such as known vs. unknown to the speaker, specific vs. non-specific, negative polarity/scale reversal, direct and indirect negation, that can be expressed by one indefinite series is tightly constrained by a series of implicational universals that can be summarized as an implicational map. The map contains two overlapping, interrelated chains composed of the following functions: (1) specific known, (2) specific unknown, (3) irrealis non-specific, (4) question, (5) indirect negation, (6) direct negation; and (1) specific known, (2) specific unknown, (3) irrealis non-specific, (4) conditional, (6) comparative, (7) free choice. The claim is that when an indefinite series expresses two functions that are non-adjacent on this map, the prediction is that it also expresses all the other functions in between these two functions. Some of Haspelmath's other interesting findings are that indefinite pronouns have a relatively short lifespan and are diachronically quite unstable, and that there appears to be an as yet unexplained correlation between generic-noun-based indefinites and head-initial (SVO, VSO) orders on the one hand, and interrogative-based indefinites and head-final (SOV) orders on the other. This correlation may, however, be due to areal effects, and may therefore be less significant than it appears at first sight.

In a shorter pronominal contribution, Hideki Kishimoto looks at 'Indefinite Pronouns and Overt N-Raising' (*LingI* 31[2000] 557–66). The leading idea of the article is that an indefinite DP such as *everything interesting* is derived from *every interesting thing* through raising of the N *thing* to a functional projection higher up in the DP; *have/be* raising is adduced as a parallel case. We also mention here 'The *Who/Whom* Puzzle: On the Preservation of an Archaic Feature' (*NL&LT* 18[2000] 343–71), where Howard Lasnik and Nicholas Sobin argue persuasively that *whom* lost its ACC case at the same time as overt case morphology was lost on full NPs, and should not be considered part of the same paradigm as the ModE pronominal object forms *him* and *them*. Instead, it is an artificial construct derived from a set of extra-grammatical rules labelled 'grammatical viruses', which check Case and, possibly, agreement features which the normal system of syntax cannot check but which prestige usage demands.

Further typological work relating to the noun phrase is found in Greville G. Corbett's *Number*, which presents a coherent analysis of number markers on nominal and verbal heads. Number systems usually derive from number words or quantifiers, which in turn often derive from nouns denoting collectives, pronouns and demonstratives. These number words may grammaticalize into bound morphemes, while number-differentiating pronouns may similarly develop into number-differentiating affixes on the verb. If a language has several number markers, a distinction between animate and inanimate may develop, which may in time give rise to inflections with the same distinction. It is also common for languages to develop an opposition between general/singular and plural, which means that the plural is used to denote 'more than one' whereas the general/singular form is not specific as to number. Some languages make a further number distinction into dual, trial and paucal, generally derived from numerals. The author's analysis of the various number systems found in the world's languages does not only explain their rise, but also their decline, as this usually turns out on closer inspection to be a reflection of a change in progress, from one number system to another. A language with singular-dual-trial-plural may lose the trial (since singular-dual-plural is a possible system) but it may not lose the dual, unless it first loses the trial. The loss of a dual or trial often leaves various anomalies in the morphology or syntax of a language, which require a diachronic explanation. Corbett describes a number of complex interactions between case and number, definiteness and number, and even between all three of these. He also provides evidence for a relation between frequency and irregularity: nouns which have an irregularity involving a split between singular and plural will tend to be nouns which occur frequently in the plural. More speculative in nature is Walter Hirtle's 'Number in the English Substantive' (in Contini-Morava and Tobin, eds., pp. 59–71). Hirtle draws attention to uses such as *plus one degrees*, *every means*, *to be friends*, and *the antipodes* and suggests that *-s* signals not plural but a quantity being viewed as discontinuate (the noun *means*, for example, is claimed to involve a discontinuity between measures taken and end pursued). The singular, on the other hand, we are asked to view as expressing movement through a continuate quantity.

Two contributions have looked at the nominal category of gender. Lori Morris considers 'The Grammar of English Gender' (in Contini-Morava and Tobin, eds., pp. 185–203). On the basis of examples where *she/her* is used to refer to things such as a lawn, a war, a victory, *it* to refer to men or women, and *s/he* for animals, it is proposed that *it* refers to entities with a low degree of individual characterization and *s/he* to salient entities (with *he* being favoured for unpredictable and uncontrollable referents, such as a bullet or a submarine). Morris also draws attention to the fact that gender provides information, which is particularly useful in pronouns since these are otherwise pretty contentless. Kenichi Nami has looked at 'Gender Features in English' (*Linguistics* 38:iv[2000] 771–9) and proposes that they are not formal syntactic phi-features but semantic features, i.e. **He hit herself* is ruled out by the semantics rather than by syntactic feature mismatch. Evidence comes from the comparable case of number discrepancies of the type seen in *Everybody kills themselves by working overtime*.

From noun phrases we move on to subjects. T. Åfarli and K. Eide, in 'Subject Requirement and Predication' (*NJL* 23[2000] 27–48), suggest that clauses must have subjects not because of any formal syntactic requirement (e.g. the Extended Projection Principle in any of its earlier or later incarnations) but because subjects are involved in semantic proposition formation. The framework for their analysis is Denis Bouchard's Grammar Semantics, which postulates a direct link between syntactic and semantic formatives. Somewhat similarly, semantic value is attributed to the existential subject *there* in Piotr Twardzisz, 'Virtual and Actual Existentials in English, Swedish and Icelandic' (*NJL* 23[2000] 163–90). In a comparative cognitive analysis of existentials in English, Swedish and Icelandic, *there* is argued to be a setting-like subject. Another specific type of subject is studied by Brian Agbayani in '*Wh*-Subjects in English and the Vacuous Movement Hypothesis' (*LingI* 31[2000] 703–13). Here the evidence for and against vacuous movement in sentences such as *Who left?* is reconciled by postulating movement to C of the *wh*-features but not the *wh*-category. Inversion of subject and verb is investigated in Liliane Haegeman's 'Inversion, Non-Adjacent Inversion and Adjuncts in CP' (*TPS* 98[2000] 121–60). Haegeman looks at inversion in main clauses (including such cases as *For what kind of job, during the vacation, would you go into the office?*) and in embedded clauses, and develops an analysis using the split-CP framework. Michael Moss surveys 'Subject and Predicate Agreement in the Development of Generative Grammar' (*SAP* 35[2000] 81–116). He shows that the early generative reliance on adjacency as an agreement mechanism was only slowly replaced by more structural accounts; in these accounts too, many questions about the exact nature of agreement are seen to be still unanswered.

It's time now for tense, mood, modality and aspect, four of the central categories of the verb group. In 'The Grammatical Ingredients of Counterfactuality' (*LingI* 31[2000] 231–70), Sabine Iatridou argues that the past tense conveys an exclusion relation between Topic Time (more generally, Topic World) and Utterance Time (more generally, Utterance World), and that this is why it is so common in counterfactional conditionals and wishes across languages; aspect and mood in such sentences, however, tend to vary according to language-specific properties. Two papers deal with the perfect. Dulcie Engel and Marie-Eve Ritz describe 'The Use of the Present Perfect in Australian English' (*AuJL* 20[2000] 119–40); they note a widening use of the perfect in AustrE, where it can combine with definite past time adverbials, occurs in narrative sequences, and shows alternation with past and present for stylistic effect. Brief discussion is also provided of analyses of the perfect and of comparable diachronic developments in other languages. Jim Miller writes about 'The Perfect in Spoken and Written English' (*TPS* 98[2000] 323–52), contrasting the use of the perfect in writing (its codified use) with that in speech. Among the findings are that the recent-past perfect is a minor category; that the perfect of result has several competitors; and the experiential perfect faces competition from the past tense. Miller also notes several examples of the perfect combining with definite past time adverbials, suggesting that this usage is becoming acceptable. Somewhat more general in purpose is Hanna Pishwa's excellent 'Language Variation and Complexity' (*Anglia* 118[2000] 155–84), which examines complexity in the Tense-Mood-Aspect marking of verbs and also in the lexicon, in discourse pragmatic marking and in clauses as measured by their length and degree of embedding. Comparing the degree of complexity in rudimentary pidgin, casual conversation and professional language, she finds that, despite a high degree of variation, overall complexity remains constant: if the lexicon demands the most attention, syntactic structures will be simple; heavily weighted nominal phrases call for stativity among verbs, and a low degree of temporality, aspectuality and modality, etc.

The imperative mood is investigated in Chung-hye Han's *The Structure and Interpretation of Imperatives: Mood and Force in Universal Grammar*, a revised version of her 1998 University of Pennsylvania Ph.D. thesis. The book has chapters on negation and imperatives (the incompatibility of these two categories in languages such as modern Greek, Spanish and Italian is made to follow from the negator scoping over the imperative, which leads to incoherence), the history of the English imperative (where the late emergence of *do* in imperatives is viewed as a result of the late loss of V-to-Asp; declarative clauses would be affected by the early loss of Asp-to-T, which has no effect on imperatives since these lack T), features of the imperative (these are [directive] and [irrealis], which are also active in the infinitive and subjunctive in those languages that have infinitive and subjunctive imperatives), the interpretation of the imperative (also in sentences such as *Move and/or I'll shoot*, the first of which is argued not to have directive force), and the interpretation of rhetorical questions (just like imperatives, questions too can receive a non-canonical interpretation). In a smaller-scale study, 'Die Syntax des Imperativs' (*LingB* 181[2000] 71–118), Melani Wratil argues that a universal process of imperative verb raising to a higher functional head applies in all languages in which a syntactically determined imperative sentence type is attested.

As usual, the pervasive category of modality is more popular than either tense or mood. Günther and Martina Lampert, *The Conceptual Structure(s) of Modality. Essences and Ideologies: A Study in Linguistic (Meta-)Categorization*, presents an empirical study (with data mainly from German and English). Its primary concern is with the premises underlying the conceptualization of modality in the various theories, and hence with linguistic categorization in general. The first chapter introduces the various models of modality, and their motivations. Part 1, 'Grounding Modality: Theories and Meta-Theories' (chapters 2–4) discusses the formation of concepts and theories of categorization, and warns against a view of language in general and of linguistic categorization in particular that credits its conceptualizations with a greater degree of reality than is warranted (chapter 2), and uses Systems Theory to set up domain- and theory-independent parameters to evaluate both linguistic conceptualizations of modality and their actual linguistic instantiations, such as modal verbs, adjectives, adverbs etc. (chapter 3). Chapter 4 argues that the parameters that best fit the bill can be abstracted from Leonard Talmy's work, particularly his article 'Conceptual Structure in Language and Other Cognitive Systems' [1995]. These parameters are Identifiability, Palpability, Structure/Content, Stasis/Dynamism, Accessibility to Consciousness, Relating One Structure To Another, Relative Quantity, Degree of Differentiation, Connectivity and Assessment. Part 2, 'Conceptualizing Modality: Hegemonic Models of a Grammatical Theory' (chapters 5–7) evaluates a number of conceptualizations of modality and its instantiations against the parameters formulated in the previous chapter. Chapter 5 discusses the functional model, chapter 6 the logical model, and chapter 7 the notional model. Part 3 (chapters 8–10) outlines, modifies, and extends conceptualizations from a Cognitive Linguistics point of view, grounding modality especially on Talmy's Imaging System of Force Dynamics. Modality does not yield a cognitively motivated category, but emerges as a 'convenience label' denoting an experientially and perceptually motivated radial category of Image Schemata.

Paul Larreya writes about 'Modal Verbs and the Expression of Futurity in English, French and Italian' (*BJL* 14[2000] 115–29), making a comparison between English *will* and the French/Italian future (these all express implication) and also between *going to* and *aller/stare per* (which are all argued to express movement through time). Modal verbs with modal semantics but no phonology are wondrous beasts; Kleanthes Grohmann writes about one such animal in 'Null Modals in Germanic (and Romance): Infinitival Exclamatives' (*BJL* 14[2000] 43–61). He proposes that, in a sentence such as *Peter buy expensive wine?!* (*I don't believe it*), there is a null modal (merged as head of ModP) which moves to C. This analysis is applied to a comparison with German and Spanish, in which modals behave differently than in English. Overtly expressed modality (in the form of modal verbs but also adverbs) is investigated by Minna Vihla in 'Epistemic Possibility: A Study Based on a Medical Corpus' (in Kirk, ed., pp. 209–24). Modal expressions turn out to be especially frequent in popular and professional medical manuals and clinical textbooks, but less so in research articles; Vihla advances several possible reasons for this difference. Aurelia Usoniene writes 'On the Modality of the English Verbs of Seeming' (*BJL* 14[2000] 185–205). She distinguishes two uses of verbs such as *seem*, *appear* and *look*: one describes a perceptual situation and is non-modal (*She seemed a stranger*) and a second is modal, expressing the speaker's judgement as to the epistemic status of a proposition (*She seemed to be tired*).

Aspect is dealt with in several publications. In Krasimir Kabakčiev's *Aspect in English: A 'Common-Sense' View of the Interplay between Verbal and Nominal Referents*, the author builds on earlier work by the Dutch scholar Henk Verkuyl to develop a non-technical theory of aspect in which special importance is attached to the interaction between verbal meaning and the bounded vs. unbounded nature of nominals. The notion of (un)boundedness here refers to (lack of) extension in time, as in *He ate the apple* (perfective aspect) vs. *He ate apples* (imperfective), with the relevant property of the object being transmitted to the verb and the sentence as a whole. Among the topics dealt with are the mechanism for mapping temporal values, the interaction between nouns and verbs with respect to (un)boundedness, the progressive in English (which serves to eliminate the boundedness of nominals), lexical meaning and aspect, negation and perfectivity (argued to be combinable, despite claims to the contrary in the literature), and the role of world knowledge in the interpretation of aspect. Throughout, comparisons are made with Bulgarian, the aspect language par excellence (the book is actually a revised version of a 1992 study written in Bulgarian).

If anyone fears that work on the English progressive will one day come to an end, we can reassure them that it has not happened yet. In a paper with the hopeful title 'The Endless Progressive' (*ALH* 32[2000] 105–19), Steen Schousboe presents a useful survey of proposed analyses of the English progressive, distinguishing referential approaches from pragmatic ones and noting problems for both. Schousboe advocates the use of authentic and full examples, rather than the short, cooked-up sentences that one commonly encounters in the literature; he also expresses doubts about the possibility of providing one single unified meaning for the progressive. That such a unified characterization can be given is in fact argued by Per Durst-Andersen in 'The English Progressive as Picture Description' (*ALH* 32[2000] 45–103). After reviewing existing theories of the progressive (viewed in relation to *Aktionsart*), Durst-Andersen proposes that the non-progressive in essence describes a person or thing, while the function of the progressive is to describe a situation. This general characterization is then applied to the specific uses of the progressive, and the mechanism of its acquisition in first language learning is discussed. In a perfect progressive piece entitled 'The Present Perfect Progressive: Constraints on its Use with Numerical Object NPs' (*ELL* 4[2000] 97–114), Ilse Depraetere and Susan Reed argue that the unacceptability of the present perfect progressive with numerical objects (as is evident in the contrast between *I have been cleaning the window* and ??*I have been drinking seven beers*) may be due to the conflict between the unboundedness inherent in the progressive form and the boundedness usually associated with numerical object NPs in non-stative sentences. Apart from (un)boundedness and (a)telicity, the type of perfect and our knowledge of the world also play a role in determining the acceptability of the present perfect in such constructions. As a last aspect-related piece, we mention here Marina Gorlach's 'Resultativeness: Constructions with Phrasal Verbs in Focus' (in Contini-Morava and Tobin, eds., pp. 255–87). Gorlach views resultativeness as a linguistic category with multiple manifestations (as in present vs. past participle, *be* vs. *have*, the *be*-passive vs. the *get*-passive, progressive vs. perfect, etc.), but focuses on phrasal-verb construction, with an increase in resultativeness observable in the sequence *break the vase—break up the vase—break the vase up*.

There are three pieces on the verb-related category of negation. Annabel Cormack and Neil Smith have written 'Head Movement and Negation in English' (*TPS* 98[2000] 49–85; this issue of *TPS* is entirely devoted to matters negative). They suggest that there are three negative positions in the clause: an ECHO negation high in the tree (as in *Shouldn't she be at school? No she shouldn't*), a Polarity negation below T (as in ordinary clausal negation), and an Adv negation low in the tree (as in *He might* [*not come*]); soft constraints regulate the position of negative elements. A highly interesting (though non-existent) negative word has occupied Richard Hudson, as he reports in '*I amn't*' (*Language* 76[2000] 297–323). After describing the puzzle posed by his title (which has an acquisitional side but also a historical one), Hudson proposes a solution which in essence says that this is a case of clashing requirements: the intended form should be the negative present of *be* (hence, by default inheritance, *aren't*) but also the first person singular present (hence, by default, *am*). This solution is embedded in a full Word Grammar account of *be*, verbal morphology, and negation. The interaction of negation and quantifiers in child language is the topic of 'Navigating Negative Quantificational Space' by Julien Musolino, Stephen Crain and Rosalind Thornton (*Linguistics* 38:i[2000] 1–32). They find that children (but not adults) interpret sentences such as *Every horse didn't jump over the fence* as being unambiguous (with *every* scoping over NEG, corresponding to the overt position of the elements), and show how learning could proceed if we assume that there is full continuity of the relevant principles of UG. That verbs can be not only negated but also questioned is made clear in John Anderson's '"What Became of Waring?": Questioning the Predicator in English' (*SAP* 35[2000] 53–80). Anderson shows that sentences such as *What did he do?* or

What happened to the TV? are not easily derivable from an affirmative, and he proposes a semantic-role-based formalization to account for this type of question.

We now turn to other elements within the VP. The great divide between theoretical and descriptive linguists is very much in evidence in Ewald Standop's 'Englische Verbkomplementation' (*Anglia* 118[2000] 217–57). Standop compares the descriptional treatment of verb complementation in R. Quirk *et al.* [1985] with its treatment in a generative (minimalist) approach as in A. Radford [1997], with the former preferred as the most adequate to satisfy future theoretical demands of corpus linguists. Verb complementation is generally not one of the stronger areas of the generative approach, as its adherence to binary branching X-bar structures, though optimal in terms of language design considerations (acquisition, but also processing, see Victor Yngve's notion of 'depth', discussed above), means that its treatment of three-place verbs requires all sorts of non-intuitive light-verb manoeuvres, so Standop's preference for a good descriptive account is not surprising. From a generative point of view, the best solutions are probably those that take the dative indirect object to be the subject of a Small-Clause construction (e.g. R. Kayne [1983], R. Larson [1988]). Patrick Brandt, 'In the Double Object Construction' (*LIN* 17[2000] 31–43), adduces evidence from scopal and other facts that indirect objects and subjects indeed have a lot in common. The contrast between sentences such as *Ede promised his fortune to a Martian* and *Ede promised a Martian his fortune*, with the first one not committing the speaker to the existence of Martians, appears to be best described as the 'low' Indirect Object (the PP in the first sentence) taking narrow scope with respect to the intensional verb 'promise' and being interpreted *de dicto*, and the 'high' Indirect Object in the second sentence taking wide scope and being interpreted *de re*. Subjects of (unergative) 'individual level' (as opposed to 'stage level') predicates show similar effects, which suggests that the 'high' Indirect Object is the subject of an individual-level predicate.

Maria José Luzón Marco's 'The Periphrastic Verbal Structure "DO + V—ING"' (*ES* 81[2000] 237–48) shows, on the basis of Cobuild corpus data, that a construction such as *James Gregory was the kind who would do his drinking at the side of a busy street* is selected to focus on the process rather than on the object of the process, and is used anaphorically to refer to an action mentioned or implied in the previous discourse or to an action that is part of a schema activated in the text. Possessive pronoun modifiers imply that the action is repeatable, whereas modifiers such as *some*, *any* or *no* focus on the incompleteness of the action. Elisabeth Löbel's 'Copular Verbs and Argument Structure: Participant vs. Non-Participant Roles' (*TL* 26[2000] 229–58) challenges the usual analysis of post-copular elements as being predicates. Instead, she suggests that they are complements (being assigned the internal thematic role of Property); data with verbs such as *weigh* and *last*, which also have a non-participant complement, are adduced in support of this analysis. On a slightly different topic that we did not know where else to fit in, Jean-Christophe Verstraete has written 'Attitudinal Disjuncts and Illocutionary Force in Clause Combining' (*FuL* 7[2000] 117–31). He disagrees with William McGregor's [1999] analysis of words such as *fortunately*, and argues that they are dependents in an interpersonal system and can have a clause associated with them (as in *Frankly, he's full of hot air, because there's no point beating about the bush about it*).

There are two papers on word order inside the VP. Jennifer Arnold, Thomas Wasow, Anthony Losongco and Ryan Ginstrom have written 'Heaviness vs.

Newness: The Effects of Structural Complexity and Discourse Status on Constituent Ordering' (*Language* 76[2000] 28–55). After reviewing earlier work on end-weight and given-before-new in heavy NP shift and the dative alternation, the authors present data from the Canada Hansard and from an ingeniously set up experiment which show that both factors are indeed operative. Among the questions addressed is the point whether the factors are especially beneficial for speakers or listeners. Hubert Haider investigates 'Adverb Placement—Convergence of Structure and Licensing' (*TL* 26[2000] 95–134). He argues that adverbials are not in SpecFP but are either adjoined or embedded and that their relative ordering follows from the mapping of syntactic onto semantic representations. An account of the mirror-image order of adverbials in OV and VO languages is provided, and there is some discussion of the reasons for conflicting conclusions emerging from different constituency tests for adverbials (which may reflect a difference in the point of the derivation at which they apply).

Phenomena of binding and anaphora usually involve subjects as well as objects, so we turn to these now. William Philip writes about 'Adult and Child Understanding of Simple Reciprocal Sentences' (*Language* 76[2000] 1–27). He presents psycholinguistic data from speakers (and learners) of English, Dutch and Norwegian, which suggest that reciprocals have flexible semantic value (compare the varying degrees of reciprocity expressed in *they gave each other measles*, *the poles are spaced 200 metres from each other*, and *they all know each other*), the specific interpretation being based on pragmatics. Binding facts are used for a different purpose in Philip Branigan's 'Binding Effects with Covert Movement' (*LingI* 31[2000] 553–7), where it is argued that the grammaticality of *Perry proved them to have lied during each other's trials* (with the final adverbial being construed with *proved* rather than *lied*) is due to covert movement of *them*, rather than overt movement of both *them* and *proved* (as Howard Lasnik and others have argued). Evidence comes from sentences such as *The photos showed [behind this very hedge to have been hiding Jill and Tony] during each other's trials*, where the inverted subject can only move into the matrix covertly. An extension of binding theory is proposed in Seth Minkoff's 'Principle D' (*LingI* 31[2000] 583–608), where a contrast in acceptability is noted between sentences such as *She$_i$ causes attention to focus on her$_i$ / That magnet$_i$ attracts paper clips to itself$_i$* and *??That history$_i$ causes attention to focus on it$_i$ / ??That history$_i$ attracts attention to itself$_i$*. To account for these facts, Minkoff formulates a binding principle D, which is sensitive to whether the antecedent is selected by the predicate or not. The weakly degraded nature of the relevant sentences is explained by a difference in strength of the binding principles.

Jürgen Gerner has investigated 'Singular and Plural Anaphors of Indefinite Personal Pronouns in Spoken British English' (in Kirk, ed., pp. 93–114). Using a 10 million-word spoken subcorpus of the British National Corpus, his findings are that a sequence such as *someone … he/his/him* occurs in about 40 per cent of all cases where *someone* is specific, but that a singular pronoun referring back to an indefinite is rare in all other cases (i.e. after non-specific *someone*, but also after *everyone*, *anyone*, *no one*); no age, class or regional variation was found. This clear preference for a plural anaphor of course confirms the results of earlier, smaller, studies. Anaphora across sentence boundaries is also the topic of Klaus von Heusinger's 'Anaphora, Antecedents, and Accessibility' (*TL* 26[2000] 75–93). Building on work by, for example, Talmy Givón and Jeanette Gundel, he proposes a formalization of the notion of accessibility, whereby co-reference is determined by a choice function that gets updated as discourse proceeds (because definite NPs, once introduced, also change accessibility). We also include here Knud Lambrecht's 'When Subjects Behave Like Objects: An Analysis of the Merging of S and O in Sentence-Focus Constructions Across Languages' (*SLang* 24 [2000] 611–82), which explores the relationship between the form and the function of sentence-focus constructions. The form is determined not only by the syntagmatic relations among its constituents but also by the fact that the subject in a sentence-focus construction must be marked in some way as non-topic, to keep it distinct from the corresponding predicate-focus sentence. This marking tends to be achieved, cross-linguistically, by 'borrowing' the formal features that normally mark the focal objects of a predicate-focus construction.

Peter Siemund's *Intensifiers in English and German: A Comparison* investigates items such as *myself* used not as a reflexive but as an intensifier (as in *John himself did it*). They are analysed as a type of focus particle, which can be adnominal (*John himself*), adverbial inclusive (*John had also seen it himself*) and adverbial exclusive (*I'll do it myself*). The book contains chapters on the syntax of each of these uses, and on their semantics. One of the suggestions made is that untriggered reflexives (as in *John bought a painting of himself*) are adnominal to a null pronoun (which, if overt, would yield *John bought a painting of* [*him himself*]). The central meaning of the intensifiers, which holds in all three uses, is argued to be that of structuring a set into a central element (the more important one) and several peripheral elements (the alternatives in any given situation). The factors influencing the choice for an inclusive or exclusive reading of an adverbial intensifier are investigated, as are its precise meanings.

From phrasal elements inside VP we turn to clausal elements, beginning with several pieces on infinitival complements. Göran Kjellmer writes about 'Auxiliary Marginalities: The Case of *Try*' (in Kirk, ed., pp. 115–24), which deals with *try* followed by a bare infinitival complement as in *She was not trying oust Mr Major*. There are forty-seven instances of this pattern in the 50 million-word Cobuild Corpus, most of them in spoken or informal texts. Among the causes of the rise of this new possibility may be speakers' uncertainty about *try*'s many complementation patterns, avoidance of repetitive sequences such as *and try and V* or *to try to V*, as well as natural processes of auxiliation. Brett Hyde, 'The Structures of the *To*-Infinitive' (*Lingua* 110[2000] 27–58), attempts to analyse *to*-infinitives as PPs, consisting of a preposition *to* + a bare infinitival complement. ECM and Object Control constructions alike are analysed as Small Clauses containing a PP predicate and an abstract verb; Subject Control and Raising constructions are analysed as PPs. Hyde argues that the advantages are that PRO, lexical NPs and NP-trace are all in complementary distribution, and that Object Control and Small Clauses reduce to a single phenomenon, namely an anaphoric binding relation between a control verb's subject and a PRO element contained in the control verb's complement. Cedric Boeckx provides 'A Note on Contraction' (*LingI* 31[2000] 357–66), where contractions, as in **Who do you wanna stay*, *I'm gonna stay*, and *I wanna leave* are explained by assuming that theta-roles are features; that A-movement does not leave a trace; and that control reduces to raising.

A wider range of complementation patterns is investigated by Marjolijn Verspoor in 'Ionicity in English Complement Constructions: Conceptual Distance and

Cognitive Processing Levels' (in Horie, ed., *Complementation: Cognitive and Functional Perspectives*, pp. 199–225; this collection contains further interesting articles on complementation in such languages as Japanese, Korean, Tsez, French, Bella Coola and Spanish, their functional-cognitive orientation providing welcome points of contrast with the dominant generative tradition). In her article, Verspoor looks at the use of *that*-clauses, *to*-infinitives, *ing*-clauses, and predicative adjuncts (which show decreasing conceptual distance in this order) after various types of matrix verb, relating the findings to a theory of consciousness. Margarita Suñer investigates 'The Syntax of Direct Quotes with Special Reference to Spanish and English' (*NL&LT* 18[2000] 525–78). She discusses direct quotes and quotative inversion in the two languages and concludes that the main differences are explained by the way in which the empty object moves (it raises to an A-bar position in Spanish, where it is interpreted as an anaphoric operator, but to an A-position in English, where it is interpreted as a null constant) and the overt position of V (V to T in Spanish, while V remains *in situ* in English). A rather complex complement has been unearthed for us by Atsurô Tsubomoto and John Whitman, who report on it in 'A Type of Head-in-Situ Construction in English' (*LingI* 31[2000] 176–83). The relevant phenomenon can be seen in *John invited you'll never guess how many people*; the authors call this a *wh*-syntactic amalgam and analyse it as a case of *wh in situ*, since it shows no island effects. They contrast it with another amalgam, as in *John is going to, I think it's Chicago on Sunday*, which does show island effects and is therefore analysed as involving movement. Extraposed clauses are the topic of two articles by Jennifer Herriman. In 'Extraposition in English: A Study of the Interaction between the Matrix Predicate and the Type of Extraposed Clause' (*ES* 81[2000] 582–99) she reports on her findings on extraposed finite and non-finite clauses in the LOB-corpus, concentrating on the semantics of the clause. They turn out to be completely in line with earlier observations, namely that finite clauses represent third-order entities, i.e. abstract entities which can be assessed in terms of their truth value, whereas non-finite clauses represent second-order entities, i.e. events, processes, states of affairs, etc. which can be described as taking place rather than simply existing. In another contribution, 'The Functions of Extraposition in English Texts' (*FuL* 7[2000] 203–30), Herriman proposes that extraposition serves very specific functions: it can make attitudinal meaning explicit or elaborate on it, conceal it, make it the perspective for interpreting the extraposed clause, or it can create end weight. Frequencies of extraposition in various text types in the LOB-corpus are argued to confirm these proposals. Richard Hudson, 'Gerunds and Multiple Default Inheritance' (*UCLWPL* 12[2000] 417–49), proposes an analysis for English gerunds that does justice to their dual nature (they have the internal characteristics of a clause, but the external characteristics of an NP). Verbal and nominal classifications are combined on a single node which can inherit, by multiple default inheritance, from both verb (in Word Grammar terms, in its restrictions on its parents) and noun (in its restrictions on its dependants).

There seems to be something about relative clauses that makes scholars feel they shouldn't be idle, and this year too, relatives have prodded a fair number of them into action. Alexiadou, Law, Meinunger and Wilder, eds., *The Syntax of Relative Clauses*, is an excellent volume from which we review three articles (there are six more that primarily focus on other languages). In their useful introduction (pp. 1–51), the editors provide a leisurely and detailed sketch of generative analyses of relative clauses, from Government-and-Binding times (when relative clauses were adjoined to NPs and the head noun was outside the relative clause) down to the Kaynian period (when the relative clause has become a CP complement to D , the head noun being generated inside the relative CP and raising to its specifier position). Among the topics dealt with are such constructions as *more books than John can read* (similar to relative clauses), *the picture of himself that John painted* (showing connectivity effects), *he did it in a way *(that annoyed me)* (featuring a relative clause that appears to be selected), *the headway that we made* (where *make* must select *headway*), co-ordination of relative clauses, and the cross-linguistic range of relative clause types. On pages 83–119 of the volume, Alexander Grosu studies 'Type-Resolution in Relative Constructions: Featural Marking and Dependency Encoding'. His central question is whether different types of relatives (restrictive, appositive, maximalizing, existential) can be distinguished on a configurational basis. The answer he arrives at is negative; as an alternative, a characterization by means of features is proposed. Special attention is paid throughout to the applicability of the Kaynian analysis of relative clauses. This is also the case in Cristina Schmitt's 'Some Consequences of the Complement Analysis for Relative Clauses, Demonstratives and the Wrong Adjectives' (pp. 309–48), which investigates sentences such as *I bought the type of bread *(that you like)*. Under a Kaynian analysis, there is both a definite and a free indefinite in these sentences, which means that *the* can be transparent. This idea is extended to certain adjectives (e.g. *wrong*); support for it comes from the aspectual behaviour of the matrix V, which shows that the head noun of a relative clause with *the* can be either definite or indefinite. The ungrammatical non-finite relative seen in **The man whom to talk about*, as compared with grammatical *The man about whom to talk*, is investigated by Paul Law in his chapter 'On Relative Clauses and the DP/PP Adjunction Asymmetry' (pp. 161–99). After surveying and rejecting two earlier analyses (one by Joseph Emonds and one by Noam Chomsky and Howard Lasnik), Law analyses the ungrammatical case as involving illicit adjunction of DP to VP, with *to* being a V. This idea is not as wild, or new, as it may sound; work in the early 1980s by Geoffrey Pullum and others points to English infinitival *to* as best analysed as a non-finite modal. The DP/PP asymmetry can also be seen in **It is necessary [all the diplomats] to put in the other room* vs. *It is necessary [in the other room] to put all the diplomats* and **We had [all the diplomats] put in the other room* vs. *We had [in the other room] put all the diplomats*.

The Kaynian analysis of relative clauses is defended against criticism in 'The Raising Analysis of Relative Clauses: A Reply to Borsley' by Valentina Bianchi (*LingI* 31[2000] 123–40). The author proposes a refinement of the raising analysis, whereby the head is not a NP but a DP, the relative D° can incorporate into the external D°, and this external D° contains a trigger for the raising operation. Among the relative phenomena addressed are stacking, co-ordination and extraposition; all of these potentially problematic facts are argued to be amenable to a raising analysis. Juan Carlos Acuña-Fariña has written 'Reduced Relatives and Apposition' (*AuJL* 20[2000] 5–22), in which he finds fault with an earlier proposal to derive some but not all appositions from relative clauses. The various tests used to distinguish the two cases (extraposibility, restriction to nominal antecedents, presence of modifiers of certain types, possibilities for floating quantifiers, split antecedents, agreement and extraction) are argued to yield conflicting results, and apposition markers are shown to be more flexible than previously thought. Relative clauses of the type *I talked to every guy that you did* (our regular readers will recognize them) are investigated by Jason Merchant in 'Economy, the Copy Theory, and Antecedent-Contained Deletion' (*LingI* 31[2000] 566–75); he proposes that their structure is [for every x: x a guy you did talk to x, I talked to x] and that the *in situ* restriction deletes, while the moved restriction remains. Carsten Breul presents 'Non-Stranded Preposition + Relative *Who(m)*: Syntactic Discussion and Corpus-Related Problems' (*SAP* 35[2000] 137–51), in which he asks why *The person to who he spoke* should be ungrammatical. A search through the literature yields no good explanation; the construction is actually found eight times in the British National Corpus (its low frequency possibly being due to shaky mastery of preposition-*wh* sequences in general). Finally on the relative front, Leiv Egil Breivik has written 'On Relative Clauses and Locative Expressions in English Existential Sentences' (*Views* 9[2000] 6–28), in which he criticizes an earlier information-flow analysis of relatives with an existential head (as in *There are many people here who like Christmas pudding*).

Since they are clearly relative-related, we now turn to clefts. Nancy Hedberg has written 'The Referential Status of Clefts' (*Language* 76[2000] 891–920). In a sentence like *It was Clinton who won*, she takes *it* to be referential and to form a discontinuous expression with *who won*, which is in focus. Earlier syntactic analyses either have the *wh*-clause as an extraposed modifier of *it* or as a modifier of the clefted constituent. Hedberger proposes that the *wh*-clause is actually a complement to *it*, and raises to adjoin to the clefted constituent. Kristin Davidse takes 'A Constructional Approach to Clefts' (*Linguistics* 38:vi[2000] 1101–31), including all of the following: *It's John who is causing us trouble*, *There's John who is causing us trouble*, and *We have John who is causing us trouble*. The semantics of the cleft is shown to be derivable from the semantics of the relative clause in combination with the semantics of the matrix clause (which imposes a quantificational value on the complement). A detailed investigation of 'Pseudoclefts and Ellipsis' is presented by Marcel den Dikken, André Meinunger and Chris Wilder (*SL* 54[2000] 41–89). They distinguish two types of specificational pseudo-clefts, one of which has an IP-counterweight (*What John did was [he bought some wine]* and, with ellipsis, *What John bought was [he bought some wine]*) and the other one has not (*Angry certainly is what he is*). The first type is analysed as a self-answering question; among the facts explored are tense-mood-aspect restrictions and negative polarity connectivity as in *What he didn't do was say anything sensible*.

There is an entire volume devoted to ellipsis phenomena: Schwabe and Ning Zhang, eds., *Ellipsis in Conjunction*. The first contribution, 'Three Types of Coordination Asymmetries' by Alan Munn (pp. 1–22), discusses and rejects various proposals in the literature for analysing conjunctions. On the basis of the behaviour of asymmetries found in co-ordinative structures he argues for an analysis in which conjunction is analysed syntactically as phrasal adjunction. Using evidence from temporal features of conjuncts in Spanish, José Camacho's article 'On the Structure of Conjunction' (pp. 23–49) proposes a co-ordinative structure in which conjuncts have the same relation with respect to feature-checking heads and still display asymmetric c-command relations with respect to each other. The importance of maintaining structural symmetry is also discussed by John te Velde in 'Assumptions about the Structure of Coordination' (pp. 51–78), who concludes that the symmetric approach is to be preferred for reasons of economy. Though co-ordination asymmetries occur, they exemplify a less than optimal derivation, for example when co-ordination as a structural and semantic principle breaks down for some reason. David Lightfoot's 'Ellipsis as Clitics' (pp. 79–94) shows that both gaps and ellipted VPs are subject to the same condition, and proposes that they be treated as clitics. Gapped verbs cliticize on to their complements, while ellipted VPs cliticize on to the heads of which they are the complements. Kyle Johnson, in 'Gapping Determiners' (pp. 95–115), offers a solution for the strange scopal behaviour of terms in gapping constructions and for the otherwise puzzling fact that a quantificational determiner may gap with a verb and strand the rest of the noun phrase. 'An Additional Note on Pseudo-Gapping', by Cedric Boeckx (pp. 117–32), offers a way out of the paradox that arises from Howard Lasnik's claim that A-movement and head-movement do not leave a trace/copy and the assumption that pseudo-gapping involves deletion of the verb in the second conjunct under identity with the trace/copy left by verb movement in the first conjunct. Ricardo Etxepare and Kleanthes K. Grohmann, 'Conjunction of Infinitival Exclamatives and the Null Modal Hypothesis' (pp. 133–56), argue that a construction type which lacks a finite verb receives a modal interpretation on the assumption that it contains a null modal. Arguing against a deletion approach, they propose that the shared modal element moves across the board under parallelism to the C-head governing the entire construction. Ning Zhang, 'On Chinese Verbless Constructions' (pp. 156–77), shows that a special kind of nominal raising is optional when the verb is overt, but obligatory when the verb is null, and she demonstrates that the object of a null-verb construction must have a specific reading. Satoshi Oku, 'Definite and Indefinite Strict Identity in VP-Ellipsis' (pp. 179–94), offers a solution to why one of the two types of strict identity reading of VP ellipsis involving a reflexive pronoun is degraded while the other reading is not. Maribel Romero's 'Antecedentless Sluiced *Wh*-Phrases and Islands' relates the island sensitivity of antecedentless sluicing to two independently motivated factors: the scope parallelism in ellipsis constructions in general and the narrow scope of implicit indefinites. Susanne Winkler, 'Silent Copy and Polarity Focus in VP Ellipsis' (pp. 221–46), proposes a unified account of the information structure of VP ellipsis by assuming a single PF economy principle, Silent Copy, that interacts with a syntactic focus theory and allows for layered focus structures. Kerstin Schwabe's 'Coordinate Ellipsis and Information Structure' (pp. 247–69) discusses direct alternative and implicit alternative co-ordinate ellipsis. She shows that stripping, gapping, across-the-board, and right-node-raising constructions belong to the first type of ellipsis and that it is characteristic of them that the conjuncts are mutual alternatives. For polarity ellipsis and sluicing, which constitute the other type, the alternative to the second conjunct must be derived pragmatically from the semantics of the first conjunct.

Two further contributions look at VP ellipsis. Its formal aspects are discussed in Kyle Johnson's overview article 'When Verb Phrases Go Missing' (in Cheng and Sybesma, eds., pp. 75–103); Johnson contrasts derivational analyses (which posit a full VP) with pro-form approaches (which posit a place-holder), suggesting on the basis of antecedent-contained deletion and other facts that the derivational view may be more correct (though the final section is significantly entitled 'Inconclusion'). The very different issue of 'Focus and Topic in VP-Anaphora Constructions' is investigated by Luis López and Susanne Winkler (*Linguistics* 38:iv[2000] 623–64).

The authors criticize the usual view that VP anaphora, as in *Peter has seen it but John has not*, entails contrastive focus on the subject, arguing instead that there is polarity focus on the negative or affirmative expression, with the subject being free to perform various other functions.

We round off this section by discussing contributions on the clausal processes of passive and *wh*-movement. One of the central puzzles of the passive (and related processes such as raising) lies in the interaction between case-marking and theta-marking, as formulated in Burzio's generalization. Eric Reuland has edited a nicely focused collection of seven articles on this topic, entitled *Arguments and Case: Explaining Burzio's Generalization*. The authors all regard Burzio's generalization as an epiphenomenon, but do not agree on precisely what underlying principles it follows from. Alec Marantz, 'Case and Licensing' (pp. 11–30; this paper was written in [1991]), approaches Burzio by postulating a connection between accusative case assignment and nominative case assignment, so that the extended projection principle comes into the picture. Hubert Haider writes about 'The License to License' (pp. 31–55), and also uses case theory to derive Burzio, suggesting that checking of nominative case is less costly than checking of accusative case (except in impersonals). In 'The Nature of Verbs and Burzio's Generalization' (pp. 57–78), probably the last posthumous article by Teun Hoekstra, accusative assignment by the verb is made contingent on incorporation of a preposition associated with the external argument, which immediately derives Burzio. Anoop Mahajan looks at 'Oblique Subjects and Burzio's Generalization' (pp. 79–102), drawing attention to facts from Hindi, where Burzio does not (fully) hold, and analysing them by making a link with ergative case. In 'Thetablind Case' (pp. 103–29), Itziar Laka derives Burzio from case theory, postulating that either tense or aspect can be active as case assigners. In a wide-ranging chapter, Werner Abraham considers 'The Aspect-Case Typology Correlation' (pp. 131–93); he sketches a link between ergative case-systems and unaccusative verbs in European languages, the connection being provided by aspectuality. Finally and very appropriately in this volume, Luigi Burzio comments on Burzio in 'Anatomy of a Generalization' (pp. 195–240). He provides an OT account of the facts, whereby the subject position is associated with nominative case, and the extended projection principle forces movement to a non-theta subject position; the case of quirky subjects is also discussed. Apart from the papers in this Burzio volume, we have only seen one other passive piece: 'Zero Anaphora of the English Passive' by Aiko Utsugi (*Rask* 13[2000] 79–91). The author shows that the unexpressed agent of a passive can nevertheless function as a topic element in an anaphoric chain of the type first identified in work by Talmy Givón (see for example the sequence, *The soldiers invaded the village; soon the entire place was burned down*).

Moving on to our final stop of *wh*-movement, we first encounter Andrew Simpson's *Wh-Movement and the Theory of Feature-Checking*, a revised version of his 1995 SOAS thesis. In chapter 1, Simpson argues against LF-movement of *in situ wh*-elements; among the problems noted are the interpretational difference between *Who does Mary only like t?* and *Which girls said she only liked what?* and the absence of parasitic gaps licensed by LF-movement. A reanalysis of the *in situ* cases solves these difficulties. Chapter 2 puts forward a feature-checking interpretation of *wh*-movement, minimalist in spirit though somewhat different in execution from Noam Chomsky's 1995 proposals. Chapter 3 deals with partial *wh*-movement (as in

German *Was glaubst du, wen er gesehen hat?* 'Who do you believe he has seen?'), which is analysed along the same lines, with feature checking not being limited to the Spec-head configuration and there being no difference between spell-out and the level of LF. In all, this book offers a novel perspective on well-known facts that have been studied by many earlier scholars; it thus reaffirms the correctness of the idea that art is long while life is short. *Wh*-movement in West Ulster English comes in for close investigation by James McCloskey in 'Quantifier Float and *Wh*-Movement in an Irish English' (*LingI* 31[2000] 57–84). Interestingly, this variety allows rampant quantifier float, so that the *all* associated with *what* can surface in any of four positions in the following sentence, *What (all) do you think (all) that he'll say (all) that we should buy (all)?* Such floating facts can of course be turned to good use as a probe into structure, as McCloskey demonstrates for such cases as passive and exceptional case-marking (as in *Who did you expect your mother all to meet at the party?*, where the position of *all* suggests that both *your mother* and *expect* have moved overtly). A new approach to weak cross-over is presented by E.G. Ruys in 'Weak Crossover as a Scope Phenomenon' (*LingI* 31[2000] 513–39); sentences such as ??*Who$_i$ does his$_i$ mother like t$_i$?* are explained by saying that *who* does not take scope over *his* (using a definition of scope which indeed has this effect). Also discussed are cases where an operator has scope over a pronoun but there is no co-indexing (*Which boy's mother loves him?*) and cases where exceptional scope leads to exceptional variable binding. Finally, we note that Aimo Seppänen and Joe Trotta have been in pursuit of 'The *Wh-* + *That* Pattern in Present-Day English' (in Kirk, ed., pp. 161–75). They note that examples like *Whoso that dooth synne is thral* occurred in earlier English, but are thought to be absent from PDE; nevertheless, a search through the Cobuild Direct Corpus and the British National Corpus (together 150 million words) yields ninety examples, in different text types. Most instances are free relatives (as in *Whatever food that there may be*); instances with *that* adjacent to the *wh*-item (as in *why that*) are restricted to colloquial speech.

(b) Early Syntax

We start by discussing some general materials on the history of English. David Burnley has prepared a second edition of *The History of the English Language: A Source Book*. It contains some fifty fully annotated (excerpts from) texts spanning the period 700–1920. The book also provides general introductions to OE, early ME, late ME, eModE, and ModE of some four or five pages each, which will help students to see what the most prominent features of the language at each period are. As a further help, full translations into ModE are provided for the earliest texts. In comparison with the first edition, the introductions to the various periods have been somewhat expanded (though, as Burnley himself points out, the book still needs to be used in conjunction with a full work on the history of the language) and several advertising texts have been added, which usefully allow students to study changes not only in linguistic features but also in textual strategies. No doubt this work will remain a popular choice for general courses on the history of the language. For more advanced courses and for research purposes, there is of course a wealth of primary materials available now in the form of computer corpora for the study of English historical linguistics. A very convenient and near-exhaustive overview of them is given by Matti Rissanen in 'The World of English Historical Corpora: From Cædmon to the Computer Age' (*JEngL* 28[2000] 7–20). Ways of using such corpora in teaching are discussed by Anne Curzan in 'English Historical Corpora in the Classroom: The Intersection of Teaching and Research' (*JEngL* 28[2000] 77–89). She gives a number of pointers about the use of corpora in teaching, with examples ranging from strong verbs becoming weak, competition between verbal endings, to the borrowing of words and suffixes. There are further examples of student-exploration of the *Oxford English Dictionary* on CD-ROM and the investigation of changes in the language of literature.

For advanced courses in the early periods of the language, there is now a textbook on *The Syntax of Early English* by Olga Fischer, Ans van Kemenade, Willem Koopman and Wim van der Wurff. The book is solidly grounded in syntactic theory, more specifically in the Principles and Parameters framework, which means that a distinction is made between language change (the language output) and grammar change (the internalized system). The first chapter specifies this distinction and discusses various approaches which all focus on the importance of language acquisition as the locus of change (with mechanisms like degree 0 learnability, input matching and cue-based learning). It also pays attention to abruptness versus gradualness of language change: the abruptness lies in the change between individual internal grammars when speakers of subsequent generations opt for slightly different grammars, whereas the gradualness has to do with the way in which such changes diffuse through space and time. The chapter ends with methodological considerations: the status of historical data and the difficulty of gauging the significance of unattested structures. Chapters 2 and 3 are devoted to descriptive overviews of the most important features of the syntax of OE and ME. Chapter 4 discusses the position of the finite verb, which, in OE main clauses, is constrained by a somewhat more complex version of the Germanic V2 operation (for more on this, see the discussion of word order studies below), and is lost in the course of the ME period. Chapter 5 examines the loss of OV-orders, which boils down to an investigation into the position of the non-finite verb. Chapter 6 is on particle-verb constructions and discusses the loss of the OE system, which resembles the separable complex verbs of Modern Dutch or German, and the rise of the phrasal verbs in ME. The position of the particle in OE corresponds to that of the non-finite verb (which was the subject of Chapter 5), with the verbal part of the construction undergoing separation by the types of verb movement discussed in Chapter 4. Chapter 7 charts the rise of *to*-infinitival ECM-constructions as in *I believed him to be innocent* and argues that the loss of OV-orders is an important factor in this development. Chapter 8 does the same for another infinitival construction, the *easy to please* construction, whose development is also found to be closely linked to word order developments. Chapter 9 discusses two cases of grammaticalization: the rise of periphrastic *have to*, as in *I have to do my work*, and the historical development of sentence negation (for which see also the paper by Ans van Kemenade in Pintzuk *et al.* [2000], discussed below).

General issues in the study of language change receive separate attention in two books this year. William Croft has written *Explaining Language Change: An Evolutionary Approach*, in which models and insights from biological evolution are used to achieve greater understanding of linguistic change. Croft's four main theses in this work are: the central locus of linguistic change lies not in language acquisition, but in the replication (guided by convention) of linguistic structure in utterances in actual language use; the causes of change lie in the mapping of form to function (whether phonetic or semantic/pragmatic/discoursal); the mechanisms whereby changes get propagated are social in nature (these are explored in some detail); internal and external sources of change overlap, since all speakers command more than one variety of the language. The main mechanism of change is argued to be re-analysis (but not—a point that Croft stresses—during acquisition). In building a model of change paying attention to factors from the areas of pragmatics, semantics and sociolinguistics, Croft is fully in line with detailed work on individual changes that have firmly established the need to recognize multiple causes and conditions for language evolution. Although Croft's stance is firmly anti-generative, there is actually much in this work (especially in his treatment of the diffusion of change) that generative linguists could warmly agree with, which is one of the reasons that we both commend and recommend it. The more traditional concerns of historical linguists are well presented in Andrew Sihler's textbook, *Language History: An Introduction*. Originally starting out as a revision of the general chapter on linguistic history in Carl Buck's 1933 *Comparative Grammar of Greek and Latin*, this work became 'a whole course in the whys and hows of historical and comparative linguistics' (p. vii). And an enjoyable course it is, in which Sihler explains to us, in clear terms and using many examples, the various types of sound change (also sound laws), analogy, semantic change, the reconstructive method, the role of external factors, and the uses of written records. We agree with Sihler that this book will provide welcome background knowledge to beginning students studying the (early) history of any specific language.

General issues are also addressed in several separate articles. Charles D. Yang has investigated 'Internal and External Forces in Language Change' (in *LVC* 12[2000] 231–50). He shows how, in principle, variable data could trigger the acquisition of competing grammars, and he applies these ideas to the loss of V2 in French and English (attributing it, in the south, to the loss of clitic pronouns, and in the north to southern influence, which would trigger grammar competition). Robert Austerlitz writes about 'Change – Linguistic and Social' (in David Lockwood, Peter H. Fries, and James E. Copeland, eds. [2000] *Functional Approaches to Language, Culture and Cognition*, pp. 405–11); the article compares and contrasts unconscious change with language engineering. A plea to historical linguists to pay equal attention to data and theory is presented by Wim van der Wurff in 'Variation and Change: Text Types and the Modelling of Syntactic Change' (in Ricardo Bermúdez-Otero, David Denison, Richard M. Hogg, and C.B. McCully, eds. [2000] *Generative Theory and Corpus Studies: A Dialogue from 10 ICEHL*, pp. 261–82). He exhorts generativists to pay more attention to empirical matters, in particular to register variation and its possible structural consequences, and variationists to pay more attention to the structural significance of register variation. An integration of both approaches would make it possible to account not only for the actuation of a change, but also for its diffusion through the speech community. In his 'Evolutionary Perspectives on Diachronic Syntax', Ted Briscoe uses ideas and techniques from modern evolutionary theory to model the diffusion of syntactic change through populations (in Susan Pintzuk, George Tsoulas and Anthony Warner, eds. [2000] *Diachronic Syntax: Models and Mechanisms*, pp. 75–105). He shows that a learning procedure which selects between grammars on the basis of single trigger instances predicts random dynamics in language change. In contrast, if acquisition is modelled so that the learner is sensitive to the relative frequencies of different constructions in the input, then the familiar S-shaped curve of change may result from competition between individuals with the incoming grammar and individuals without it. His 'microscopic simulations' allow him to present a convincing case for the idea that creolization is not a special process distinct from other types of language change, but rather a normal selective change in a context of radical demographic change. He also models the situation in which change spreads from a random fluctuation in a small pocket of the data, showing that the choice of which variant will eventually replace the others is indeed arbitrary, and the result of mere chance.

Work in grammaticalization theory and practice continues unabated. Last year, we reviewed Martin Haspelmath's article about the irreversibility of grammaticalization (in *Linguistics* 37[1999] 1043–68; see *YWES* 80[2001] 51). This year, there are three follow-ups to it. In 'Explaining Grammaticalization (the Standard Way)' (*Linguistics* 38[2000] 781–8), Bas Geurts criticizes some of Haspelmath's ideas, including the notion of extravagance being responsible for the introduction of innovations; he also emphasizes the often very localized knock-on effects that change in one corner of the system can have. Haspelmath responds to this in 'The Relevance of Extravagance: A Reply to Bas Geurts' (*Linguistics* 38[2000] 789–98), which sets their differences in the wider context of debates about grammaticalization, in particular the roles of frequency, new forms, and reduction processes. Haspelmath's view is that new forms can develop even if no meaning is being threatened by erosive reduction of existing forms, and he gives examples where this indeed appears to have happened (such as the introduction of the progressive and *going to* in English, and also in lexical change). Extravagance is the mechanism responsible. The final word is then for Bas Geurts, who reflects on 'Function or Fashion? A Reply to Martin Haspelmath' (*Linguistics* 38[2000] 1175–80—one clearly sees here the possibilities offered by a journal which regularly runs to over a thousand pages a year); Geurts wonders how extravagance could ever result in the systematic cross-linguistic trajectories of grammaticalization and how the fashions of lexical change can ever provide insight into processes which are functional in nature. It cannot really be said that any points have been settled at the end of this debate, but it does usefully bring out many questions about what grammaticalization is (or could be) and what empirical and theoretical factors impinge on it.

For further thoughts on grammaticalization, one could profitably turn to Olga Fischer and Anette Rosenbach's 'Introduction' to the volume *Pathways of Change: Grammaticalization in English*, which they have edited together with Dieter Stein [2000]. Here, we find sensible discussion of the various approaches to grammaticalization (both functional and formal in orientation) and of the current topics of debate, such as the start of the process, the role of syntactic and semantic factors, and directionality. The last issue is dealt with in greater detail in Rogers Lass's contribution to the book, 'Remarks on (Uni)Directionality' (pp. 207–27), which also addresses the status of the notion of grammaticalization in general. Lass casts doubt on grammaticalization itself being a mechanism or cause of change, since this would imply that there is something like a diachronic grammar, which runs counter to our intuitions about what speakers of any synchronic state know about previous synchronic states. He also casts doubt on he unidirectionality hypothesis, pointing out that it entails that at an earlier period all languages were isolating languages; that the criteria for determining the various stages of grammaticalization are not clearly formulated; that our definition of what is 'lexical' or 'grammatical' is likely to be based on a very small sample of well-investigated languages only; and that grammaticalization theory needs to specify what it will accept as a valid counter-example, rather than just concentrating on cases that conform to its tenets.

An interesting volume on grammaticalization viewed comparatively is Spike Gildea's *Reconstructing Grammar: Comparative Linguistics and Grammaticalization*. The case studies presented here have implications for the study of many types of change, but since they do not focus on English, we just mention here some of the general findings and the names of the authors to whom they are due. 1: Grammaticalization can be a result of areal diffusion, it can involve highly specific meanings, and it can also occur in dying languages (Alexandra Aikhenvald); 2: Grammatical developments may correlate with extra-linguistic factors, such as special prominence of third person singular masculine reflecting the conspicuous social roles of male individuals or complex patterns of incorporation mirroring a high esteem of oratory (Wallace Chafe); 3: Certain word orders may be characteristic not of an entire language but only of a certain clause type (Spike Gildea); 4: Knowledge of properties of grammaticalization can give considerable help in internal reconstruction (Talmy Givón); 5: A number of related languages taken together can instantiate a full grammaticalization chain not found in its entirety in any of the individual languages (Bernd Heine); 6: Patterns of subject marking in a language can be an accidental side-effect of detransitivization processes (Sérgio Meira); 7: When a derivational affix is re-analysed as an inflectional one (or vice versa), there can be re-ordering, leading to exceptions to the general principle that affix order reflects the chronological order of development (Marianne Mithun); 8: Surface similarities can be a valid argument for genetic classification (Joseph Greenberg).

There are several items on variation and varieties in the history of English. Terttu Nevalainen in 'Processes of Supralocalisation and the Rise of Standard English in the Early Modern period' (in Bermúdez-Otero et al., eds. [2000] pp. 329–71) demonstrates that linguistic features from diverse geographical and social varieties went into the making of Standard English in the eModE period. In 'Gender Differences in the Evolution of Standard English: Evidence from the Corpus of Early English Correspondence', the same author (*JEngL* 28[2000] 38–59) shows that gender played an important role in the diffusion of these supralocal features. Gender variation as such is studied by Douglas Biber and Jená Burges in 'Historical Change in the Language Use of Women and Men: Gender Differences in Dramatic Dialogue' (*JEngL* 28[2000] 21–37). They identify a number of different historical trends with respect to the parameters tentativeness and involvement. The gender of the addressee, a major factor promoting greater involvement and tentativeness in earlier times, becomes less important over time, whereas the fact that speaker and addressee are same gender or mixed gender becomes more important: mixed gender dyads lead to greater involvement. Lilo Moessner's 'Grammatical Description and Language Use in the Seventeenth Century' (in Bermúdez-Otero et al., eds. [2000] pp. 395–416) focuses on the diachronic developments in the seventeenth century that can be gleaned from a comparison of prescriptive grammars at either end of that century. A comparison of the statements of prescriptive grammarians with their actual language use as it is realized in their non-linguistic works shows up some interesting discrepancies. Irma Taavitsainen and Päivi Pahta in 'Conventions of Professional Writing: The Medical Case Report in a Historical Perspective' (*JEngL* 28[2000] 60–76) compare the text-internal linguistic features of nineteenth-century case reports with those of later periods. The latter are markedly more depersonalized, with total absence of the first-person narrative of earlier times, and a predominance of passives. This development is intimately connected to the change in readership from a fairly small group of professionals with a shared background to the worldwide audience of today. A note of caution concerning the way we think and talk about variation is presented by Gabriella Mazzon in 'Describing Language Variation in Synchrony and Diachrony: Some Methodological Considerations' (in *Views* 9[2000] 82–103); she describes the dangers of regarding a language, dialect, lect, register, style, (non-)standard, or individual speaker as the locus of linguistic variation, and warns against the danger of reification of the notion in teaching and research.

We now turn to developments in the NP. Robert McColl Millar offers 'Some Suggestions for Explaining the Origin and Development of the Definite Article in English' (in Fischer *et al.*, eds. [2000] pp. 275–310); his aim is to explain why the article developed the way it did, instead of following the course of, e.g. its German counterpart, which would have resulted in a system with a basic opposition between distal demonstrative *the* and proximal demonstrative *this*. That this did not happen is due to the development of *that* as a 'pure demonstrative', carrying a distal meaning with little in the way of article or near-article function. McColl Millar speculates that this development may well have been due to influence from the speakers of Norse dialects settled in the North of England. Anette Rosenbach, Dieter Stein and Letizia Vezzosi have written 'On the History of the *S*-Genitive' (in Bermúdez-Otero *et al.*, eds. [2000] pp. 183–210), suggesting on the basis of quantitative data that the survival of the *s*-genitive is not accidental but due to a new division of labour between *s*- and *of*-genitives in late ME. They identify further shifts in the eModE period. Anette Rosenbach and Letizia Vezzosi look at early Modern developments in more detail in 'Genitive Constructions in Early Modern English' (in Rosanna Sornicola, Erich Poppe, and Ariel Shisha-Halevy, eds. [2000] *Stability, Variation and Change of Word-Order Patterns over Time*, pp. 285–307). Their corpus data show that the genitive is being supplanted by the *of*-phrase until the fifteenth century, but that it increases in frequency again in the sixteenth century (with subjective or possessive function, and associated mainly with topical human referents, as in PDE).

Olga Fischer has studied 'The Position of the Adjective in Old English' (in Bermúdez-Otero *et al.*, eds. [2000] pp. 153–81); she argues that OE strong adjectives are associated with indefiniteness and 'new' information, whereas weak adjectives imply definiteness and 'given' information, a distinction that also has syntactic consequences. Sylvia Adamson's 'A Lovely Little Example: Word Order Options and Category Shift in the Premodifying String' (in Fischer *et al.*, eds. [2000] pp. 39–66) demonstrates how the semantic changes in a grammaticalization process may automatically involve syntactic changes. Her case study is the development of the adjective *lovely*, which originally meant 'loving, amiable' and acquired a second meaning 'physically beautiful' in Middle English. An affective meaning expressing speaker approval developed in early Modern English, and *lovely* acquired an additional use as intensifier in the course of the nineteenth century. The entire process is one of increasing subjectivization, a well-established grammaticalization pathway, but the interesting phenomenon that accompanies it is the concomitant word order change. Interestingly, Adamson's corpus findings show that *lovely* is found further and further away from the head noun as its meanings move from HUMAN PROPENSITY to PHYSICAL PROPERTY to VALUE (by and in itself, a clear case of subjectification).

Several contributions deal with changes affecting pronouns. We find Joachim Grzega 'Asking Why Exactly *Them*, *These*, and *Those*' (in *NOWELE* 36[2000] 113–20). More specifically, he asks why *they* developed earlier than *them* (because of the frequent use of *þa* in the sense of 'they'), why plural *hem* was lost (it was too similar to singular *him*, once *hine* had disappeared), why *this* and *that* have retained a singular-plural distinction (because they often function as subjects), and why *tho* lost out to *those* (perhaps because of the developing homophony with *though*). Linda van Bergen in 'The Indefinite Pronoun *Man*: "Nominal" or "Pronominal"?' (in Bermúdez-Otero *et al.*, eds. [2000], pp. 103–22) addresses the question of how much the indefinite pronoun *man*, originally derived from the noun *man*, has grammaticalized in OE. She shows that it fails to invert with the finite verb in root clauses with a topicalized constituent—a pronominal characteristic—but allows object pronouns to precede it in subclauses, which is more typical of nominals. Ekkehard König and Peter Siemund have studied 'The Development of Complex Reflexives and Intensifiers in English' (in *Diachronica* 17[2000] 39–84). They describe the development of intensifier *himself* from earlier *him self*, which was later extended to form combinations like *the king himself*. The locus of the development of intensifier *himself* (which relates a central focus to possible alternatives) into a reflexive (completed by about 1500) is argued to lie in clauses with verbs like *kill* or *hang*, which are normally other-directed and which might therefore need an intensifier when they were self-directed (i.e. reflexive). Among further matters discussed are the role of pleonastic pronouns in sentences like *he færde him home* 'he went home' and the development of *oneself*.

Elly van Gelderen has written *A History of English Reflexive Pronouns: Person, Self, and Interpretability*. The phenomena she addresses are the development of the reflexive *self*-forms, the loss of morphological case in pronouns, the occurrence of verb forms not showing agreement, and the distribution of *pro*-drop. In each of these cases, certain combinations of person and number appear to change earlier or behave differently than other combinations. The explanation proposed by van Gelderen lies in the weakness or strength of features of the pronouns involved: weak features entail that pronouns can be anaphors, are not omissible, and can have reduced verbal agreement, while strong features lead to the opposite situation. After an introductory chapter in which she sketches her (Minimalist) assumptions about features and case, and also describes the corpus of texts that she used, there are chapters on OE reflexives (in this period, simple pronouns can function reflexively because they have inherent case), reflexives after the OE period (*self*-reflexives develop fastest in the third person, slowest in the first person, perhaps because of differences in their phi-features), *pro*-drop (in OE and early ME, *pro*-drop occurs regularly, especially with third person subjects because their features are more specified), the loss of verbal agreement and verb-movement (loss of agreement affects first and second person forms earlier than third person, especially in clauses with inversion; see also below), the loss of inherent case (which takes place in early ME, and affects first and second person pronouns before third person), ergativity and the person split (here, possessives with *be* and experiencer verbs are examined), followed by a brief conclusion. Altogether, this book presents a wealth of material, establishes links between the different phenomena, and explores the usefulness of Minimalist concepts in explaining the data.

In a separate article, Elly van Gelderen considers at more leisure her material relating to 'The Role of Person and Position in Old English' (in Fischer *et al.*, eds. [2000] pp. 187–206). She notes again the occasional disappearance of inflectional endings on first and second, but not third, person finite forms in OE. In a Minimalist framework, rich inflection correlates with overt movement: verbs move to higher functional heads to check features, and if the features are 'strong' this movement will be visible. The loss of first and second person inflections in OE only happens when the subject follows the verb, i.e. when V is in C. This is unexpected if overt inflection is assumed to be linked to overt movement. Van Gelderen argues that first and second person features are less specified on the verb, which also explains why null subjects mainly occur in the third person in OE. In another subject-related piece, Alexander Williams looks at 'Null Subjects in Middle English Existentials' (in Pintzuk *et al.*, eds. [2000] pp. 164–87), providing quantitative data showing that silent expletive *there* was very common until 1250 but then undergoes a dramatic decline in frequency. He also finds that early ME silent expletives occur in exactly those contexts where subject pronouns invert with V, i.e. in *wh*-questions and clauses starting with the adverb *þa* or with V, and attributes the sudden decline of silent expletives to changes in the verb-pronominal subject constructions (in particular, the drop in verb-initial clauses around 1250).

We next turn to verbs and verb-related categories. The rise of the perfect is the topic of 'Time and Truth: The Grammaticalization of Resultatives and Perfects within a Theory of Subjectification' by Ulrich Detges (in *SLang* [2000] 345–77). The article offers a comparison of OE *habban* + Past Participle with Spanish *tener* + Past Participle to explain the pathway from resultative to perfect. The very basic nature of the discourse strategies underlying this shift explain why, cross-linguistically, we see this same change happening again and again. In 'The Grammaticalization of the Present Perfect in English: Tracks of Change and Continuity in a Linguistic Enclave' (in Fischer *et al.*, eds. [2000] pp. 329–54), Sali A. Tagliamonte investigates Samaná English, a variety of AAVE spoken in a remote area of the Dominican Republic. Samaná English contains an extensive array of perfect markers. Tagliamonte unravels the complex contexts favoured by some of these markers and demonstrates that they by and large match those reported in the literature for both earlier and modern varieties of non-standard English, although some patterns have been obscured by the subsequent spread of the *have* form. In all, Samaná English represents a reflection of an earlier stage in the grammaticalization of the perfect, and provides, in its variability, striking examples of grammaticalization principles like layering, persistence, and specialization. Developments in the imperative are investigated in Chung-hye Han's 'The Evolution of *Do*-Support in English Imperatives' (in Pintzuk *et al.*, eds. [2000] pp. 275–95). The central question addressed is why, in the sixteenth century, the frequency of *do* increases in questions and negative declaratives, but not in imperatives, which do not start to catch up with this development until the very end of the century. Han first demonstrates that negation may occur in two different positions in ME, and argues that V-to-I movement is best analysed as involving two different movements: V-to-Asp and M-to-T. M-to-T movement is lost first (a change not affecting imperatives, which lack T), and the loss of V-to-Asp follows at the end of the sixteenth century. This may also be the appropriate point to mention Arja Nurmi's 'The Rise and Fall of Periphrastic DO in Early Modern English, or *"Howe the Scots will declare themselv's"'* (in Bermúdez-Otero *et al.*, eds. [2000] pp. 373–94), which attributes the sharp decline in the use of DO in non-emphatic affirmative clauses after 1600 to the arrival in London of King James's Scottish entourage.

Although much has been written about the grammaticalization of the English modals, it is still possible to make valuable contributions to the subject, as is done in Denison's article discussed below and in Michael Getty's 'Differences in the Metrical Behavior of Old English Finite Verbs: Evidence for Grammaticalization' (*EL&L* 4[2000] 37–67). Working on the well-established finding that grammaticalized items tend to exhibit phonological reduction, Getty contrasts the metrical behaviour of the (pre-)modals in two OE poems which can be argued to be separated in their dates of composition by as many as two hundred years: *Beowulf* and *The Battle of Maldon*. While the verbs in question show consistently stressed metrical placement in *Beowulf*, in *Maldon* they show a clear tendency to be placed in unstressed metrical positions—early evidence of grammaticalization, long before any evidence on the other linguistic levels became apparent. Modal semantics in OE poetry is studied in Mieke Van Herreweghe's '**Motan* in the Anglo-Saxon Poetic Records' (*BJL* 14[2000] 207–39), which aims to establish how far this modal verb had moved along the path from permission to obligation. The 287 instances found in the data show that permission is still primary, with obligation occurring in only a few cases.

That new modals verbs are emerging even today is shown by Manfred Krug in his *Emerging English Modals: A Corpus-Based Study of Grammaticalization* (a revised version of his 1999 University of Freiburg PhD thesis). The items in question are *have to*, (*have*) *got to*, and *want to*. Krug traces their development in several historical and contemporary corpora, where they show increasing signs of modal semantics and phonological boundedness (though they continue to require *do*-support); a comparison is also made with the marginal modals *ought*, *dare* and *need*. The corpus investigation yields a wealth of data for each of the individual items, which we cannot all mention or even summarize here (we give just two examples: Krug establishes that in the early development of *have to* there is an important role for the phrase *I have to say*, and that the rise of *want to* appears to be linked to the decline of volitional *will*). In explaining the emergence of the modal meanings of his items, Krug mainly uses the concept of inference or implicature, which is of course fully in line with modern thinking about the semantics of grammaticalization. Sociolinguistic considerations enter the picture in Krug's discussion of the diffusion of the emergent modals in British English and in his account of stylistic differences (they appear to represent changes from below).

Erik Smitterberg's 'The Progressive Form and Genre Variation during the Nineteenth Century' (in Bermúdez-Otero *et al.*, eds. [2000] pp. 283–97) shows that the progressive can be said to be a genre-specific feature: the nineteenth century saw its decline in scientific writing, and its increase in letters, drama, fiction and historiography. Although this study is limited in scope, it is a welcome addition both to work on the progressive (which has usually concentrated on the more spectacular changes in the EModE) and to work on English in the nineteenth century (which is slowly developing into a little field of its own, as we noted last year). There is tense, modality and aspect of various kinds in David Denison's article on 'Combining English Auxiliaries' (in Fischer *et al.*, eds. [2000] pp. 111–47), which investigates auxiliary strings in the history of English in order to pinpoint the dating and significance of the grammaticalization stages of these verbs from lexical to functional forms. Denison uses the date when an auxiliary first appears in strings of a certain length as evidence for it having reached a certain stage of grammaticalization. From his figures it appears that perfect *have*, modals and *onginnan* were fully grammaticalized already in OE and periphrastic *do* in the fourteenth-fifteenth centuries. The evidence for passive and progressive *be* is more difficult to pinpoint (a crucial problem here is the late appearance of passive progressive).

Negation receives attention in two Dutch contributions (the attentive reader may in fact have noted a strong Dutch presence in this section as a whole). Ans van Kemenade in 'Jespersen's Cycle Revisited: Formal Properties of Grammaticalization' (in Pintzuk *et al.*, eds. [2000] pp. 51–74) argues that the negative cycle involves the re-analysis of an OE negative adverb as the functional head *ne* of NegP, with subsequent loss of syntactic freedom. This is a typical development of negation markers, as is the subsequent development of a second negative form (ME *not*, from OE *nawiht/nowiht*) which, like the first, was initially licensed in a specifier position but later in turn re-analysed as the head of NegP when *ne* was lost; ultimately, we may suppose, *not* became inflectional *-n't*. Elly van Gelderen writes about 'The Absence of Verb-Movement and the Role of C: Some Negative Constructions in Shakespeare' (in *SL* 54[2000], pp. 412–23). She considers sentences with pre-verbal *not* like … *where both not sinne* and … *that you not delay the present*, finding that most cases have an 'active' CP (i.e. they have *wh*-movement, a subordinator, a topicalized phrase or they are questions). If IP is not active, V can be said to move to C covertly for feature checking. Van Gelderen also makes the interesting observation that in inversion contexts, *does* is more frequent than *doeth*.

After the verb, there is usually a complement of some sort, but in some cases there are items that are better analysed as forming a unit together with the verb. Such combinations are studied in Claudia Claridge's *Multi-Word Verbs in Early Modern English: A Corpus-Based Study*, which presents a survey of the frequency and use of multi-word verbs in the Lampeter Corpus. A special merit of her work is that it tackles all classes of multi-word verbs, and not just a subsection. Her survey of the relevant literature is extensive and well-reported (chapters 3 to 5). Chapters 6 to 9 present her own data from the *Lampeter Corpus*, a corpus of eModE texts, and offer a coherent account of register variation. Phrasal verbs appear to be less frequent in eModE than today, possibly because they had already been stigmatized to some extent and were purposely avoided in certain styles of writing. The greatest frequency of *types* (not tokens) occurs in the very first decade of the corpus (i.e. 1640–1650), and many of them only occur in this decade, often only once, never to be seen again. This early proliferation, which contrasts with a greater stability (more tokens but fewer types) in the following decades, suggests that this first decade must have marked a turning point in the history of multi-word verbs. Claridge has very little to say about the various syntactic phenomena she reports. The Small Clause analysis is cursorily dismissed in footnote 1 on page 46, but no other analysis replaces it. This book is nevertheless a must for anyone interested in the history of multi-word verbs.

There are a few items on other clause elements. Ruta Nagucka has written 'Conceptual Semantics and Grammatical Relations in Old English (in *SAP* 35[2000] 19–32), in which she discusses several cases of grammatical function ambiguity in OE (such as examples allowing either an SOV or OSV interpretation and cases involving a *dativus incommodi*), showing how the ambiguity can be resolved on the basis of pragmatic criteria. The adverbial modifiers *full* and *very* are studied in Jerzy Wełna's 'Grammaticalization in Early English' (*SAP* 35[2000] 43–51), which traces their use and competition from the OE period to the present. Two other adverbial elements are investigated in '*Soþlice* and *Witodlice*: Discourse Markers in Old English' by Ursula Lenker (in Fischer *et al.*, eds. [2000] pp. 229–49), which presents more evidence for the cline (proposed by Elizabeth Traugott) in which clause-internal adverbials develop into sentence adverbials and then into discourse particles. Lenker shows how *soþlice* and *witodlice*, originally adverbials with meanings like 'truly' or 'certainly' develop into discourse particles in late OE, marking thematic discontinuity, on a par with *þa* 'then' constructions, or more specifically, *þa gelamp*-constructions, 'it then happened that ... '.

Word order matters are as popular as ever this year. Joseph Crowley has written on 'Anglicized Word Order in Old English Continuous Interlinear Glosses in British Library, Royal 2.A.XX' (in *ASE* 29[2000] 123–51). The glosses in this Latin prayer-book show adaptations like pronominal objects being shifted to preverbal position and adjectives and genitives to prenominal position, which is ordinary enough given the regularities of OE word order but rather striking given the word-by-word approach of most OE glossators. Rodrigo Pérez Lorido looks at 'Coordinate Deletion, Directionality and Underlying Structure in Old English' (in Bermúdez-Otero *et al.*, eds. [2000] pp. 125–51). He observes that Robert Ross's (1970) Directionality Constraint predicts that in an SOV language like OE, verb deletion in subordinate clauses subject to co-ordinate reduction should target the left conjunct, a prediction which is not borne out by corpus data, where Lorido exclusively finds forward gapping, exemplified by (OV) sentences of the type *I believe that John meat eats and Peter rice*. Far from constituting evidence for underlying SVO structure, the zero incidence of backward gapping (as in *I believe that John meat and Peter rice eats*) is probably an indication that OE word order is sensitive to processing constraints, which require the first conjunct to have a verb in order to be 'closed' properly. Eric Haeberli has investigated 'Adjuncts and the Syntax of Subjects in Old and Middle English' (in Pintzuk *et al.*, eds. [2000] pp. 109–31), in which he uses adjuncts intervening between (fronted) verb and subject to probe the nature of V2 in OE. In a careful quantitative investigation, Haeberli shows that such intervening adjuncts are found in OE and southern (but not northern) early ME and suggests on the basis of his data that fronted topics are in the CP domain, that CP immediately dominates AgrSP, and that the adjuncts are in a specifier position.

An article on V2 in ME is 'The Middle English Verb-Second Constraint: A Case Study in Language Contact and Language Change' by Anthony Kroch, Ann Taylor and Donald Ringe (in Susan C. Herring, Pieter van Reenen and Lene Schøsler, eds., *Textual Parameters in Older Languages* [2000] pp. 353–91). Their corpus findings confirm the falling off of V2 in early ME texts in the Midlands area, but show that the Kentish dialect still preserved the constraint (complete with the OE complication involving subject pronouns). Although no manuscripts of northern prose before 1400 survive, the authors show that the relevant aspect of the syntax of northern dialects can still be reconstructed from the *Northern Prose Rule of St. Benet*, a text from central west Yorkshire, hence either within or directly bordering on the major area of Norwegian settlement in the North. Here, too, we see V2, but, crucially, inversion of subject and verb occurs regardless of whether the subject is a full NP or a pronoun. They argue that the specific trigger for the change in the Northern V2 pattern was the reduction of the number of person distinctions in the English agreement system, due to imperfect learning of OE by the large numbers of arriving Scandinavian invaders and immigrants arriving in England from the ninth century onwards. Bjørg Bækken (*ES* 81[2000] 393–421) in 'Inversion in Early Modern English' charts the continuing decline of V2. The study supports the idea that V2 does not become extinct until the early Modern period. The case of the negative adverbials *ne, never, neither, nor* is particularly complicated, as there is a period in which inversion started to be lost after these adverbs. Intransitive verbs, too, exhibit higher rates of inversion, most likely for pragmatic reasons. In spite of its extensive corpus work and careful statistical analysis, the paper suffers from some major theoretical weaknesses, including the failure to distinguish between topic-inversion and operator-inversion (for the need to keep these processes distinct, see e.g. Ans van Kemenade 1987 and Randolph Quirk *et al.*, 1985). Particularly worrying is Bækken's discussion of what she terms 'partially inverted structures', which makes one wonder if she is aware of the fact that V2 in OE and ME only ever involved the *finite* verb, and never the entire verb cluster. Inversion in PDE is investigated by Markku Filppula in 'Inversion in Embedded Questions in Some Regional Varieties of English' (in Bermúdez-Otero *et al.*, eds. [2000] pp. 439–53); he argues that the origin of inversion in embedded questions in such dialects is best explained by assuming influence from the Celtic substrate.

Changes affecting the position of objects are discussed by Willem Koopman and Wim van der Wurff in 'Two Word Order Patterns in the History of English: Stability, Variation and Change' (in Sornicola *et al.*, eds. [2000] pp. 259–83). Their starting point is the variable order in OE of the indirect object relative to the direct object and also the direct object relative to the verb; from there, they trace the gradual path along which the restricted word order possibilities of PDE developed. In a final section, they use these data to critically address the notion of grammar competition. Anthony Kroch and Ann Taylor have written 'Verb-Object Order in Early Middle English' (in Pintzuk *et al.*, eds. [2000] pp. 132–63), in which careful quantitative investigation (using the second edition of the Penn-Helsinki Parsed Corpus of ME) is coupled with sensitive use of insights from comparative syntax. Among the issues considered are the survival of INFL-final order, the occurrence of stylistic fronting, differences in the frequency of scrambling between quantified and non-quantified objects, the separate process of pronoun scrambling, and the competition between OV and VO grammars at this period. Also on OV in early ME is Cynthia Allen's 'Obsolescence and Sudden Death in Syntax: The Decline of Verb-Final Order in Early Middle English' (in Bermúdez-Otero *et al.*, eds. [2000] pp. 3–25). Allen challenges David Lightfoot's (1991: chapter 3) claim that verb-final order suffered a sudden death in early ME. Evidence from southern texts reveal a gradual decline, and the perceived abruptness of the change is due to the lack of suitable late OE texts with which to compare the ME evidence provided by the continuations of the Peterborough Chronicle. Further OV work is found in Mike Moerenhout and Wim van der Wurff's 'Remnants of the Old Order: OV in the Paston Letters' (*ES* 81[2000] 513–30), which presents a detailed analysis of the occurrence of Object-Verb clauses in the fifteenth-century *Paston Letters*. Genre (poetry or prose, informal or formal texts) is seen to play a role, as does the nature of a person's social network. The most important finding, however, is that OV is restricted to specific syntactic contexts: clauses with a modal followed by a negative or quantified object and subjectless clauses of various types. These findings are in line with Richard Ingham's 'Negation and OV order in Late Middle English' (*JL* 36[2000] 13–38), who uses the same corpus: the syntactic environment in which OV survives in late ME is restricted to clauses with a modal followed by a negated or quantified object (Ingham does not mention subject clauses). The author relates these OV remnants to another syntactic construction which has been lost in PDE, the apparent multiple subject construction found in *there*-expletive sentences such as *There mai no man kepe a fals law*, which is similarly restricted to negative NPs and which shows the same marked decline towards the end of the fifteenth century. What this construction and the remnant OV instances have in common is that their negated NP occurs in post-finite position. Ingham argues that this can be accounted for by assuming that these negated NPs move to SpecNegP – and there was no NegP projection higher than INFL by late ME to which a negated object could have moved. The fact that this phenomenon is associated with complex verb phrases becomes clear: negative objects always move to SpecNegP but this movement is string-vacuous with simple verb groups.

Another angle on *there*-expletives is offered by Tomoyuki Tanaka's 'On the Development of Transitive Expletive Constructions in the History of English' (*Lingua* 110[2000] 473–95), who investigates the short life and quick demise of the same ME construction (*Þer schal non of þe wardeyns make none newe statutes*) and relates it coherently to the changes in the functional heads AGR and T—the same changes that were responsible for the loss of subject clitics. No explanations are offered, unfortunately, for the intriguing fact that the examples overwhelmingly involve negative subjects (as we saw above in the discussion of Ingham)—quite unlike the situation of genuine transitive expletive constructions in other Germanic languages. More on these Germanic transitive expletives may be found in Jan Koster and Jan-Wouter Zwart's 'Transitive Expletive Constructions and the Object Shift Parameter' (*LIN* 17[2000] 159–70), which notes that those Germanic languages which allow the transitive expletive construction also exhibit object shift. This can be accounted for by assuming that VP-internal elements move individually in those languages, which leaves Spec,TP available for NPs, whereas languages that move them collectively, like PDE, do not have Spec,TP available because it is occupied by VP.

We now turn to historical developments in clausal complementation. 'The Grammaticalization of the Verb "Pray"' by Minoji Akimoto (in Fischer *et al.*, eds. [2000] pp. 67–84) charts in a corpus study the development of the verb *pray* from the fifteenth to the nineteenth centuries, from a full verb taking a complement clause to an interjection or courtesy marker inside that clause (later to be replaced by *please*). Although its development conforms to a well-known grammaticalization pathway, i.e. from propositional to expressive meaning, it does not appear to have gone through the intermediate 'textual' stage generally observed in this process, and the pathway itself does not provide any clues as to why such a development takes place. The author emphasizes that any account will have to take socio-cultural factors such as politeness into consideration. Another item developing from matrix verb into adverbial is studied in 'Grammaticalization Versus Lexicalization: "*Methinks*" There is Some Confusion' by Ilse Wischer (in Fischer *et al.*, eds. [2000] pp. 354–70). She argues that the development of the form *methinks* does not represent degrammaticalization (a grammatical item turning back into a lexeme), but rather desyntacticization, in the sense of a syntagmatic structure losing its syntactic transparency and merging into one single lexical item. Impersonal *think* has disappeared from the language, and its only relic—*methinks*—does not combine with any other than a first person singular pronoun. The form no longer denotes an act of cognition (its original meaning) but carries an exclusively speaker-oriented, or inter-personal, meaning. Its syntactic independence—it is not restricted to any particular position in the clause—is untypical of grammaticalization, but is readily accounted for if we regard the process as one of lexicalization. The fact that *methinks* became a lexical unit goes some way towards explaining its ultimate loss: lexical units are far more susceptible to accidental loss than functional elements.

Infinitival complementation is next. In '*Onginnan/Beginnan* with Bare and *To*-Infinitive in Ælfric', Bettelou Los (in Fischer *et al.*, eds. [2000] pp. 251–74) argues that by late OE, the *þa+ V(erb)* construction was used to mark thematic continuity, i.e. the introduction of the next narrative event, while thematic discontinuity, i.e. the introduction of a dramatic turning point, was marked by a verb-first (V1) construction. This explains the asymmetry found in the writings of Ælfric with the verbs *onginnan* and *beginnan* 'begin': when in a V1-construction they are followed by a *to*-infinitival complement, while they are found with a bare infinitive when in a *þa+ V*-construction. *Onginnan* and *beginnan* followed by bare infinitives are particularly rare in V1-constructions. This incompatibility derives from the fact that *onginnan* and *beginnan* with a bare infinitival complement have grammaticalized into perfective auxiliaries, so that the event expressed by the infinitive can no longer be temporally segmented. The V1-construction, however, requires a temporally segmentable complement, because it focuses on the beginning of the event, anticipating its dramatic interruption by the turning point in the plot. Saara Nevanlinna provides 'A Note on the Use of Nonfinite Forms of Intransitive Mutative Verbs with the Verb *To Come* in Old and Middle English (*NM* 101[2000] 313–21), in which she looks at OE equivalents to PDE *He came running*. A search through 84 texts yields 170 examples, instantiating three patterns (COME with past participle, bare infinitive, and present participle). Michiko Ogura has studied '"*Gewat* + Infinitive" and "*Uton* + Infinitive"' (in *NM* 101[2000] 69–78) and provides detailed statistics on the frequency of various types of subjects, tense forms, and complementation for both verbs. The senses of the verbs are also discussed, as is their historical relatedness. After these pieces on infinitives following 'begin', 'come' and 'go', it is time to look more carefully at the infinitival marker *to*, which we can do in Olga Fischer's 'Grammaticalisation: Unidirectional, Non-Reversable?' (in Fischer *et al.*, eds. [2000] pp. 149–69). The author shows that there is a point in ME at which the meaning of *to* moves back to its original sense of goal or direction, and fails to show any signs of further grammaticalization (no more phonetic reduction, no more reduction in scope, a decrease in syntactic bondedness).

YWES would not be complete without relative clauses. We saw in section (5a) that their behaviour in PDE has come in for further scrutiny and here we note several contributions to their history. Thus, Aimo Seppänen offers some thoughts 'On the History of Relative *That*' (in Bermúdez-Otero *et al*., eds. [2000] pp. 27–52) arguing that the modern relative pronoun *that* retains syntactic properties of both the OE pronoun *þæt* and the ME complementizer *that*. Anneli Meurman-Solin in 'Geographical, Socio-Spatial and Systemic Distance in the Spread of the Relative *Who* in Scots' (in Bermúdez-Otero *et al*., eds. [2000] pp. 417–38) argues that the spread of this relative pronoun can only be explained if one takes into account systemic, spatial, social and genre-specific factors. How exactly all these factors interact, however, is a matter that still needs further investigation. Patricia Poussa writes about 'Reanalysing *Whose*: The Actuation and Spread of the Invariable *Who* Relative in Early Modern English (*FLH* 21[2000] 159–88), arguing that, as subject relative *who* spread, *whose* was re-analysed as invariable *who* + *s*; the development is set in the context of the sociolinguistic distribution of these items, both in EModE and in PDE.

Developments in conditional constructions are addressed in 'Parallelism vs. Asymmetry: The Case of English Counterfactual Conditionals' by Rafał Molencki (in Fischer *et al*., eds. [2000] pp. 311–28). The word 'parallelism' here refers to the tendency found in many languages to use the same morpho-syntactic marking (e.g. by the same verb form) in both the conditional clause itself (the protasis) and the following main clause (the apodosis). This tendency is in competition with a tendency to keep protasis and apodosis formally distinct, either for reasons of economy (avoidance of repetition) or because, being less *irrealis*, the protasis gets demodalized. OE conditionals are characterized by parallelism, and this remains a feature of English conditionals, even as the pluperfect gradually begins to replace the preterite in past counterfactual conditionals in the thirteenth century. When the preterite subjunctive was gradually replaced by a modal periphrasis, this occurred first in the apodosis, probably because it is more counterfactual than the protasis. This asymmetry prevailed until recent times – today the protasis is again often found copying the verb form of the apodosis, showing that parallelism is by no means dead. In 'The Grammaticalization of Concessive Markers in Early Modern English' (in the same volume, pp. 85–110), Guohua Chen traces the early history of concessive markers such as *although*, *despite* and *yet* and investigates various hypotheses about the relation between expressions for factual concession (as in PDE *Even though you dislike ancient monuments, Warwick castle is worth a visit*) and those for hypothetical concession (as in *Even if you dislike ancient monuments, Warwick castle is worth a visit*). It was not until ME or even eModE that the two types started to be formally distinguished by having their own markers. He concludes on the basis of corpus evidence that the grammaticalization of the markers for both types must date back to the same period, and that it cannot be the case that the markers for the one grammaticalized into markers for the other type. We also slip in here this year's only co-ordinative historical piece, Jonathan Culpeper and Merja Kytö's 'The Conjunction *And* in Early Modern English: Frequencies and Uses in Speech-Related Writing and Other Texts' (in Bermúdez-Otero *et al*., eds. [2000] pp. 299–326); it shows the steady decline in the use of this conjunction in written texts, and connects it with changes in punctuation conventions.

Finally, there are a few items on argumental alternations. Ruth Carroll's 'The "Total Transformation Alternation" in the Light of Some Middle English Data' (*EL&L* 4[2000] 1–12) looks at the alternation between constructions with and without a prepositional phrase referring to the original state of the item denoted by the object, as in *The witch turned him into a frog* versus *The witch turned him from a prince into a frog* or of the item denoted by the intransitive subject, as in *He turned into a frog* versus *He turned from a prince into a frog*. It is attested in PDE only for verbs like *turn* and *change*, but Carroll shows that it is also available for some of the Middle English cooking verbs, notably *boilen* 'boil' and *sethen* 'simmer, reduce', and for 'Reduction Verbs' in PDE. The author isolates the semantic features underlying the alternation and concludes that verb-class membership and syntactic behaviour is primarily determined by the verb semantics. Elena Seoane Posse reports on her work on eModE passives in three papers. In 'The Passive as an Information-Rearranging Device in Early Modern English' (*SN* 72[2000] 24–33) she demonstrates on the basis of a corpus-based study that the rules underlying the choice of passive over active are basically the same in eModE as in PDE: it foregrounds, or topicalizes, patients which are given information. She concludes in 'Impersonalising Strategies in Early Modern English' (*ES* 81[2000] 102–6) that the passive is also fully established as an impersonalising strategy by this stage. The situation in eModE is not wholly equivalent to that in PDE, however. Her paper 'The Passive as an Object Foregrounding Device in Early Modern English' (in Bermúdez-Otero *et al.*, eds. [2000] pp. 211–32) discusses two factors which may lead to PDE objects becoming topics and requiring passivization: discourse topicality and inherent topicality, and shows that only the first of these two factors was well established in eModE.

6. Semantics

Two magnificent collections of recent research on two of the 'hot' topics of natural language semantics, events and anaphors, deserve to be singled out first from the range of works that appeared in 2000. The first, Higginbotham, Pianesi and Varzi, eds., *Speaking of Events*, contains ten papers by leading semanticists. The introduction (pp. 3–47), by Pianesi and Varzi, gives an informed overview of issues related to the philosophical background on events and their applications in linguistics. Higginbotham's contribution, 'On Events in Linguistic Semantics' (pp. 49–79), extends Donald Davidson's [1967] proposal, according to which 'there is reference to events in human language through the medium of an unapparent argument position in verbal heads' (p. 49), to include every predicative head in the X-bar system (i.e. V, N, A and P). It is claimed that this 'E-position' is visible to several syntactic and semantic processes, including adverbial interpretations, the telic/atelic distinction in English, and the licensing of purpose clauses. Terence Parsons, 'Underlying States and Time Travel' (pp. 81–93), proves that underlying states can be associated with stative sentences involving state verbs and copulative sentences with adjectives, locatives or nouns in the same way as underlying events are assumed for event sentences, if the possibility of time travel is taken into consideration. Johannes L. Brandl's paper, 'Do Events Recur?' (pp. 95–104), examines various theories of event ontology with respect to whether they are compatible with the notion of event recurrence in the strict sense of the term, and concludes that although there may be a category of basic events which can recur, when answering the question in the title, it seems necessary to distinguish between event ontology and talk about events. Regine Eckardt, 'Causation, Contexts, and Event Individuation' (pp. 105–21), proposes an entirely new perspective on sentences having the structure *A caused B*, which seems to solve some old puzzles in linguistics. Eckardt divides the set of these sentences into true causal statements (e.g. *Dr Spock's first aid caused Joe's heart to start beating again*) and pseudo-causal statements (as in *The delayed departure caused Bob's rescue*), which involve the focusing of some property. Nicholas Asher's paper, 'Events, Facts, Propositions and Evolutive Anaphora' (pp. 123–50), provides an analysis of evolutive anaphora (anaphoric pronouns in contexts where objects are being created or destroyed) which is based on the dynamicity of events, discourse structure, and compositional semantics. Alice G. B. ter Meulen's 'Chronoscopes: The Dynamic Representation of Facts and Events' (pp. 151–68) shows how properties of ordinary reasoning about temporal dependencies can be captured with the representational tools of Dynamic Aspect Trees. Henk J. Verkuyl is the only contributor to the volume who rejects Davidson's [1967] claim that the notion of event is primitive. In 'Events as Dividuals: Aspectual Composition and Event Semantics' (pp. 169–205), he takes the position that the fact whether a particular sentence pertains to an event, a process, or a state is dependent on particular features of its constituents, the interrelations of which he formalizes in his PLUG$^+$ framework. In their paper 'Word Order and Quantification over Times' (pp. 207–43), Denis Delfitto and Pier Marco Bertinetto argue for an extension of the proposal according to which verbal predicates are associated with an event argument by proposing a VP-internal temporal argument theta-marked by the verb, which can help to achieve a compositional mapping between syntax and semantics when the two arguments of the relation corresponding to the semantic interpretation of adverbial quantifiers are identified. Alessandro Lenci and Pier Marco Bertinetto's contribution, 'Aspect, Adverbs, and Events: Habituality vs. Perfectivity' (pp. 245–87), also discusses the semantics of adverbial quantification, and claims that the semantic contribution of explicit quantificational adverbs and perfective versus habitual imperfective aspects should be distinguished on the grounds that aspectual values do not only specify a default (universal) quantificational force assigned to the E-argument, but they also indicate the nature of the generalization. The perfective aspect has an intensional character, expressing nomic generalizations, while the imperfective aspect is extensional, expressing accidental generalizations. The second collection, von Heusinger and Egli, eds., *Reference and Anaphoric Relations*, consists of original research papers on the representation and interpretation of indefinite and definite noun phrases, anaphoric pronouns, and related issues such as reference, scope, and quantifier movement. The theoretical frameworks used in the analyses of the above phenomena here can be considered extensions of the classical Montagovian framework, and include discourse representation theory, file change semantics, Dynamic Logic, E-type theories, and choice function approaches, all of which were developed to account for particular aspects of discourse semantics, such as cross-sentential relations involving pronouns and the interpretation of definite and indefinite noun phrases. The book is divided into five sections—'Historical Aspects of Anaphoric Relations', 'Quantification and Scope', 'Anaphoric Reference', 'Choice Functions and the Semantics of Indefinites', and 'Representation and Interpretation'—which are supplemented by an introductory chapter by the editors. In the first section we find Urs Egli's and Reinhard Hülsen's papers, which deal with the Stoic and the scholastic treatment of reference and anaphora, as well as Jeroen Groenendijk and Martin Stokhof's study, 'Meaning in Motion', sketching the place of dynamic semantics as part of the development of philosophical and linguistic theories of meaning. In the second section, on quantification and scope, we find Donka Farkas's contribution, 'Scope Matters', proposing a non-configurational, non-movement theory of scope, and Henriëtte de Swart's paper, which argues against a lexical decomposition-based account of the German and Dutch determiners *kein* and *geen* 'no', and develops instead a higher-order interpretation of negative quantifiers in terms of quantification over properties. Elena Paducheva provides a contrastive study on 'definiteness effect' phenomena operative in English *there*-sentences and their Russian counterparts, while Stephen Neale investigates a puzzle related to the interaction between persistence, polarity, and plurality. The section on anaphoric reference contains two contributions, by Robert van Rooy and by Hartley Slater, which are both concerned with the issue of anaphoric reference in intensional contexts. These phenomena were first observed by Peter Geach in the 1960s, and can be characterized by means of his Hob-Nob sentences: *Hob believes that a witch blighted Bob's mare, and Nob wonders whether she (the same witch) killed Cob's sow*. While van Rooy, in 'Anaphoric Relations Across Attitude Contexts', proposes a pragmatic theory incorporating 'speaker's reference', Slater, in 'The Grammar of the Attitudes', argues that a purely grammatical explanation using Hilbertian epsilon terms as a representation for anaphoric pronouns is sufficient. The fourth section of the book discusses the representation of indefinites by means of choice functions. Arnim von Stechow's essay, 'Some Remarks on Choice Functions and LF-Movement', compares the *in situ* approach of choice functions to the classical movement approach of quantifier-raising at LF. Yoad Winter's 'What Makes Choice Natural?' investigates whether there is any general way to derive the choice function interpretation from more basic principles of semantics, and analyses the relationship between choice functions and J. Fodor and I. Sag's [1982] distinction between the referential and specific use of indefinites, while Klaus von Heusinger claims, in 'The Reference of Indefinites', that indefinites have a more complex referential nature than is usually assumed. In the last section of the book we find Jaroslav Peregrin's 'Reference and Inference: The Case of Anaphora', where the author argues that reference is parasitic on inference, and not vice versa, Paul Dekker's 'Coreference and Representationalism', which investigates to what extent existing formal semantic frameworks can be considered representational, and Reinhard Muskens's 'Underspecified Semantics', studying the interaction between representation and interpretation with respect to underspecified structures.

Theodore B. Fernald's *Predicates and Temporal Arguments* aims to characterize the distinction between stage-level and individual-level predicates (SLP versus ILP). The distinction has particularly fascinated linguists for a long time since, in addition to affecting interpretation, it influences syntactic well-formedness, and it also interacts with a number of pragmatic and context-based phenomena. After reviewing the traditional data in which the distinction manifests itself, the author provides a critical overview of theoretical approaches to the problem, and suggests that the above phenomena should be attributed to a type-theoretic distinction between the predicates. The book consists of seven chapters. Having introduced the basic distinction in chapter 1, the author reviews the grammatical effects of the ILP/SLP contrast, and points out that semantic intuitions about the nature of contrast (for example that ILPs represent permanent, or at least tendentially stable, properties while SLPs do not) do not always parallel the behaviour of these expressions with respect to the syntactic tests (which concern the type of predicate in the coda of an existential construction, the interpretation of subjects, the appearance and interpretation of temporal and locative modifiers, *when*-adjuncts, free and absolute adjuncts, and complement selection, among others), and that it cannot be reduced to previously known aspectual distinctions either. Chapter 3 considers previous analyses of the data, while chapter 4 discusses the slipperiness of the ILP/SLP distinction, examining cases of coercion, where predicates of one level exhibit the characteristics of predicates of a different level in particular environments. Chapter 5 summarizes the ingredients of a successful theory of the ILP/SLP contrast, and chapter 6 investigates new data on ILP/SLP effects in complex predicates, which suggests that, although some predicates appear to be necessarily stage-level, SLPs can also be compositionally derived, and that there is strong reason to abandon the Mapping Hypothesis, proposed by A. Kratzer [1988] and M. Diesing [1992]. On the basis of these considerations, the final chapter develops a dynamic account of the contrast, which is based on the fact that SLPs have a logical location argument that ILPs lack.

Mandy Simons's study, *Issues in the Semantics and Pragmatics of Disjunction*, which is a slightly revised version of her dissertation, argues that the discourse properties and felicity conditions of *or* in natural language, as well as presupposition projection and anaphora in disjunctive contexts, can all be derived from the truth-conditional properties of *or*, that is, from the information that it functions as a logical operator equivalent to Boolean join (inclusive disjunction), and from general (pragmatic) principles governing rational interaction. The book is divided into five chapters, the first of which introduces the data and some basic assumptions. Chapter 2 discusses the felicity conditions of clausal disjunctions in terms of general principles of information update. The next chapter accounts for the presupposition projection properties of disjunction, while chapter 4 investigates the possibilities of internal anaphora, that is, anaphoric possibilities between a quantificational antecedent in one disjunct and a pronoun in another. The final chapter gives an E-type account of external anaphora, which involves pronouns outside of a disjunction anaphoric on NPs inside a disjunction.

Horn and Kato, eds., *Negation and Polarity: Syntactic and Semantic Perspectives*, contains new developments in the study of the syntactic and semantic aspects of negation in natural language, with special regard to the syntactic and semantic properties of polarity and concord, the conditions on negative inversion and its relation to the distinction between sentential versus constituent negation, and the cognitive motivation for overt and indirect modes of negation. As the editors emphasize in their introduction (pp. 1–19), which gives an overview of the recent developments regarding the syntax of sentence negation, the relative scope of logical operators in the sentence and their dependence upon c-command relations, and the licensing of negative polarity items (NPIs), the essays represent a variety of theoretical frameworks: they reflect an interest in 'cross-subdisciplinary' phenomena and are based on cross-linguistic data. The most exciting contributions from a semantician's point of view include the studies by Jack Hoeksema, Laurence R. Horn and William A. Ladusaw. Hoeksema's 'Negative Polarity Items: Triggering, Scope, and C-Command' (pp. 115–46) argues, on the basis of data reflecting the distribution of NPIs in co-ordinate structures (the impossibility of topicalization, subject–object asymmetries, VP-internal asymmetries between the trigger and the NPI, the fact that specifiers of NPs act as triggers outside the NP, and connectedness effects in pseudo-clefts) that, although the triggering of NPIs is sensitive to the scope of negation and negative operators, the relation between the trigger and the NPI cannot be captured in terms of c-command. Horn's paper, 'Pick a Theory (Not Just Any Theory): Indiscriminatives and the Free Choice Indefinite' (pp. 147–92), re-examines the issue whether the negative polarity *any* and the free-choice *any* correspond to distinct lexical items to be represented by means of existential and universal operators, respectively, or whether they represent different uses of only one operator. By contrasting constructions with *not just* (non-presuppositional but obligatorily scalar) and *not only* (inherently presuppositional and optionally scalar), and applying the analysis of (*not*) *just* to *any*, the author argues that both *any*s are non-quantificational indefinites (cf. I. Heim [1982]) with an indiscriminative end-of-scale *even*-type meaning. Ladusaw's paper, 'Thetic and Categorical, Stage and Individual, Weak and Strong' (pp. 232–42), reprinted here from *SALT 4* (*Papers from the Fourth Annual Conference on Semantics and Linguistic Theory* [1994])—and not discussed in *YWES* 75[1996]—is already a classic. In it the author proposes to derive the generalization that properties may only be predicated of strong NPs, proposed by G. Milsark [1974], from the distinction between thetic and categorical judgements, an idea that originated with F. Brentano and A. Marty and was reformulated in S.-Y. Kuroda [1972].

Two important textbooks concerned with foundational topics for the future semanticist also appeared this year: Alan Cruse's *Meaning in Language: An Introduction to Semantics and Pragmatics*, and Ernest Lepore's *Meaning and Argument: An Introduction to Logic through Language*. Cruse's textbook follows a classical tradition in not reflecting any bias towards particular theoretical approaches, trying to present instead the landscape of topics and concepts used in semantic investigations. It is divided into four parts, 'Fundamental Notions', 'Words and their Meanings', 'Semantics and Grammar', and 'Pragmatics'. Part 1 is concerned with the basic concepts of semantics, and discusses the place of linguistic signs and linguistic communication within semiotics and communication in general. It also deals with some fundamental conceptual tools from the field of logic, such as arguments and predicates, sense, denotation, reference, intension and extension; the distinction between sentence, statement, utterance and proposition; logical properties of sentences; logical classes (i.e. sets); relations and quantification; types and dimensions of meaning; and the notion of compositionality and its limits. Although I agree with the idea of presenting some fundamental logical notions at the beginning of such a textbook, I believe that the discussion of these here is unnecessarily tied up with otherwise exciting considerations of sentence meaning, which would instead deserve a separate chapter in a textbook which intends to be an up-to-date introduction to the art of semantics. As a result, the discussion of issues related to sentence meaning has become unnecessarily brief and simplified, sometimes to the extent of incomprehensibility. Similar remarks apply to the discussion of compositionality, an important methodological principle of the interpretation of complex structures, where greater emphasis is placed on the inapplicability of the principle to certain phenomena than on its possible uses. Part 2, which discusses the meaning of words, reflects the author's bias towards lexical semantics, since it takes up almost half the book. In addition to an introductory chapter, it contains discussion of how word meanings vary with context, the relations between word meanings and concepts, paradigmatic sense relations, larger vocabulary structures, extensions of meaning, syntagmatic meaning relations, and theories of lexical decomposition. The extreme care and precision of the discussion, however, turns this part into a section fit for an encyclopedia rather than a textbook. Part 3, the shortest, aims to 'survey those aspects of the meanings of larger syntactic units which are attributable to grammar' (p. 263). It does not amount to a discussion of sentence meaning, since it concentrates on the semantic interpretation of constituents of particular syntactic categories. Part 4, which discusses some foundational issues of pragmatics, including reference and deixis, speech acts, and implicatures, appears to me the most balanced and most reader-friendly of all. To sum up, Alan Cruse's textbook provides an extremely precise and well-organized overview of the fields of *lexical* semantics and pragmatics, and I would wholeheartedly recommend it as an excellent resource book for these fields. Ernest Lepore's book differs from traditional introductions to propositional and predicate logic in that it does not focus primarily on formal proof-making strategies, but rather aims to 'give students tools for capturing adequately in a notation arguments they express in natural language' (p. 1). In the course of this enterprise the reader necessarily acquires a particular sensitivity to problems of natural language interpretation, which could form the basis of an understanding of the aims and achievements of natural language semantic research. Naturally, this particular focus on natural language does not prevent the reader from acquiring the logical tools learned in an ordinary logic course, such as truth tables, validity, propositional logic, predicate logic without and with identity, formal proof, consistency, etc. Another important feature of the book is that the enrichment of the logical toolbox, the necessity of the move from Propositional Logic to Property Predicate Logic, to Relational Predicate Logic without identity and to Relational Predicate Logic with identity, is always motivated by the need to show the validity of arguments in natural language. In the course of this imaginary journey towards more complex logical systems the reader's attention is consistently drawn to the distinction between conversational implications and logical deductions. In addition to the traditional topics found in an ordinary introductory textbook on logic, Lepore devotes a whole chapter to an event-based approach towards formalizing natural language inferences, and includes an appendix which discusses issues concerning the formalization of some more complex natural language phenomena such as phrasal conjunction, distributive and collective readings, the interpretation of conditional sentences in English, non-standard quantifiers such as *most*, passive predicates, and many more. Consequently, the textbook can not only be recommended for use in logic courses but certain parts of it could also be incorporated into the syllabus of an introductory semantics course.

The next book to be discussed, Albertazzi, ed., *Meaning and Cognition*, is written from the theoretical perspective of cognitive semantics, a discipline within cognitive linguistics that equates meaning with the conceptualization of human non-linguistic experience. Contributions include the editor's introduction (pp. 1–24), which outlines the major claims of cognitive semantics and compares them to those of Montagovian approaches. Ronald W. Langacker's 'Why a Mind is Necessary: Conceptualization, Grammar and Linguistics Semantics' (pp. 25–38) summarizes the conceptual structure of cognitive linguistics, which argues for the non-reducibility of the meaning of linguistic expressions to truth-conditions, and for the predominant role of perceptive, mental and motor conceptualization in language. Diego Marconi's paper, 'What is Montague Semantics?' (pp. 39–49), contrasting the formal and the cognitive approaches to meaning, claims that Montague semantics is not a theory of meaning for natural language, but a theory of an idealization of inferential competence. William Croft and Esther J. Wood, 'Construal Operations in Linguistics and Artificial Intelligence' (pp. 51–78), discuss the nature of the conceptualization or construal of experience in the mind of the language user, and Dirk Geeraerts, 'Salience Phenomena in the Lexicon: A Typology' (pp. 79–101), provides a typology of salience phenomena in the lexicon. Patrizia Violi, 'Prototypicality, Typicality and Context' (pp. 103–22), investigates the concept of prototype, and proposes a difference between categorial prototypicality (the prototypicality of something as the most central instance within a superordinate category) and semantic typicality (the most regular instance within the category). Liliana Albertazzi's essay, 'Directions and Perspective Points in Spatial Perception' (pp. 123–43), investigates the distinguishing primitives and natural categories of cognitive, natural space, such as distance, position, orientation and change, while Zoltán Kövecses, 'Force and Emotion' (pp. 145–68), argues that the well-known metaphors of emotion are all instantiations of one underlying 'master metaphor', namely, EMOTION IS FORCE, but they all capture very different aspects of emotional experience. Alberto Peruzzi, 'The Geometric Roots of Semantics' (pp. 169–201), is concerned with the relation between the perceptual and logical structures expressed in language, and finally Wolfgang Wildgen, 'The History and Future of Field Semantics: From Giordano Bruno to Dynamic Semantics' (pp. 204–26), argues that there exist different geometries of lexical fields.

Two further volumes this year are concerned with topics concerning the interface between syntax and semantics. Montserrat Sanz's *Events and Predication: A New Approach to Syntactic Processing in English and Spanish* discusses the connection between the event type described by a sentence (characterized in terms of the distinction between states, activities, semelfactives, achievements and accomplishments) and its syntactic structure within the framework of the Minimalist Program. This approach is motivated by the observation that in several languages certain morphological and syntactic operations (such as clitics, copulas and overt Case marking) force a particular event reading on the sentence. The author thus argues for the existence of a functional projection referred to as the Event Phrase, which encodes features related to the event type, such as [±telic] or [±punctual]. Sanz claims that there is a parametric difference between the structure of this Event Phrase in Spanish and English, in that it can encode both interpretable and uninterpretable features in Spanish (the former of which does not require overt checking, i.e. movement, but affects interpretation, while the latter does), while it can only encode interpretable features in English. The analysis is extended to phenomena which have been assumed to depend on *Aktionsart* properties, such as the distinction between transitive, unergative and unaccusative constructions, detransitive structures, verb-particle combinations, and the possibility of delimitation by goal phrases. The other volume, Lutz, Müller and von Stechow, eds., *Wh-Scope Marking*, is a collection of essays examining from a cross-linguistic perspective the syntactic/semantic features of the specific means of forming long-distance *wh*-dependencies referred to as *wh*-scope marking. These can be defined as follows: 'In a *wh*-scope marking construction of a given language, a *wh*-element α that typically takes the form of "what" in that language shows up in the clause that hosts what appears to be the LF target position for a *wh*-phrase β; β stays in a lower clause which is embedded by a verb that selects [-wh] complements' (p. 4). In this construction, α is the *wh*-scope marker, which signals where the embedded *wh*-phrase β must be interpreted. In the German example $[_{CP}$ *Was denkt sie* $[_{CP}$ *wen*$_1$ *Fritz* t$_1$ *eingeladen hat*]]*?* ('WH thinks she$_{nom}$ whom$_{acc}$ Fritz$_{nom}$ invited has?' p. 5), *was* acts as the *wh*-scope marker for the other *wh*-phrase *wen*. The following generalized abstract representation reflects the syntactic structure of the construction under investigation, where WH is a *wh*-scope marker, CP$_2$ is embedded by a verb V that selects clausal [-wh] complements, and XP$_{wh}$ is the embedded *wh*-phrase: $[_{CP1}$ WH ... V $[_{CP2}$ ... XP$_{wh}$ ...]]. The individual papers in the collection discuss *wh*-scope marking in languages including German, Malay, Hindi, Hungarian and Kikuyu, and they exemplify three strategies of characterizing the syntactic and semantic relationship between WH and XP$_{wh}$. These are the direct dependency approach, according to which there is a direct syntactic and semantic relationship between the above two constituents; the indirect dependency approach, which claims that the relationship between the above constituents is only a consequence of a direct syntactic and semantic relationship between WH and CP$_2$; and the mixed approach, which postulates a syntactic relationship between WH and CP$_2$ and a semantic relationship between WH and XP$_{wh}$. The lesson the various analyses presented in the book teach us, however, is that all three strategies can be argued to be at work in languages, so a unified approach to *wh*-scope marking which is able to characterize all languages and language-specific constructions does not seem to be feasible or empirically justified.

Jaszczolt, ed., *The Pragmatics of Propositional Attitude Reports*, investigates issues related to the semantics/pragmatics interface. The papers in the volume, by Stephen Schiffer, Peter Ludlow, Lenny Clapp, M.J. Cresswell, Kent Bach, Anne Bezuidenhout, K.M. Jaszczolt, and David Woodruff Smith, represent recent innovative developments of the research on the semantics and pragmatics of propositional attitude reports, and, as the editor formulates it in her introduction (pp. 1–12), they all aim to determine the division of labour between semantics and pragmatics in accounting for propositional attitude reports by answering the following questions: (i) What is the type and extent of pragmatic information that contributes to specifying what the speaker believes? (ii) What is the relation between the pragmatic information and the semantic (propositional) representation of attitude expressions?

Terence Parsons's *Indeterminate Identity: Metaphysics and Semantics* is a provocative study about issues of identity which enter into semantic investigations whenever sentences without a determinate truth value (interpreted differently by speakers) are considered. Parsons investigates puzzles like the following, which have received no determinate answers so far: (i) Is a person identical with that person's body? (ii) If a ship has its parts replaced and the old parts are assembled into a ship, which of the two resulting ships is identical to the original? (iii) If a person undergoes a crucial change, is the person after the change identical with the person before the change? (iv) Given a cat with imprecise boundaries, which cat-like thing with precise boundaries is identical to the actual cat? Parsons argues in his book that the reason why the above puzzles have no answers is not because our language is imperfect, but because there is indeterminacy in the world.

Important new developments in semantics research were also reported in journal articles. Among studies concentrating on the semantics of noun phrases and NP-anaphors, Chris Barker's 'Definite Possessives and Discourse Novelty' (*TL* 26[2000] 211–27) merits attention. It proposes an account of the phenomenon that definite NPs containing definite possessors (e.g. *that man's daughter*) are routinely able to describe novel (unfamiliar) entities—contradicting the 'received' view according to which the use of a definite description is only felicitous if it has a familiar referent—by claiming that a sufficient condition is that the possession relation expressed by the possessive be salient. Klaus von Heusinger's 'Anaphora, Antecedents and Accessibility' (*TL* 26[2000] 75–93) investigates the notion of accessibility (the relation between an antecedent and an anaphoric term) and proposes a refinement of the accessibility relation paying special attention to anaphoric definite descriptions which takes into account the descriptive content of expressions and the progression in a discourse. B.H. Slater's 'Quantifier/Variable-Binding' (*Ling&P* 23[2000] 309–21) gives an outline of the epsilon account of E-type pronouns, referred to above, which assumes that the above kinds of anaphora should not be accounted for in terms of binding relations on variables, but by using certain choice functions, epsilon terms, which can have a referring function back to quantifier antecedents, but are not bound by them.

An issue of *Mind and Language* is devoted to an interesting discussion about the topic of quantifier domain restriction. Jason Stanley and Zoltán Gendler Szabó's contribution (*M&Lang* 15[2000] 219–61) sets the scene for the discussion, arguing against explicit (syntactic) and pragmatic approaches to quantifier domain restriction, and proposing a semantic approach. This is followed by remarks and replies by proponents of the above-mentioned two approaches, Stephen Neale (*M&Lang* 15[2000] 284–94), and Kent Bach (*M&Lang* 15[2000] 262–83), respectively, and by a reply to the criticisms by Stanley and Szabó (*M&Lang* 15[2000] 295–98).

Still on the topic of natural language quantification, Utpal Lahiri, 'Lexical Selection and Quantificational Variability in Embedded Interrogatives' (*Ling&P* 23[2000] 325–89), proposes an account of the phenomenon of quantificational variability in embedded infinitives, which shows up, for example, in sentences such as *Sue mostly remembers what she got for her birthday*, where the quantificational force of the embedded interrogative is derived from the adverb of quantification, as opposed to sentences such as *Sue mostly wonders what she got for her birthday*, where it is not. Lahiri argues that the differences in the interpretation of the above two sentences are not due to the differences between the interpretations of the indefinite, but to differences between those of the predicates. Shalom Lappin, 'An

Intensional Parametric Semantics for Vague Quantifiers' (*Ling&P* 23[2000] 599–620), puts forward an intensional parametric account of the interpretation of the context-dependent and vague quantifying determiners *many* and *few*.

Luis López and Susanne Winkler, in 'Focus and Topic in VP-Anaphora Constructions' (*Linguistics* 38:iv[2000] 623–64), investigate the informational structure of VP-anaphora constructions, aiming to provide an account of the syntactic and prosodic licensing mechanisms associated with them. Andrew Kehler, in 'Coherence and the Resolution of Ellipsis' (*Ling&P* 23[2000] 533–75), however, realizing that the resolution of VP ellipsis in certain cases cannot be explained on the basis of purely syntactic or semantic principles, shows how the use of inference processes that underlie the establishment of coherence during discourse interpretation can account for VP ellipsis and gapping. Claire Gardent's 'Deaccenting and Higher-Order Unification' (*JLLI* 9[2000] 313–38) argues for an analysis of de-accenting based on Higher-Order Unification (proposed originally for ellipsis by M. Dalrymple *et al.* [1991] and S.M. Shieber [1996]), which correctly captures the interaction of de-accenting, (in)definiteness and focus.

Ilse Depreatere and Susan Reed, 'The Present Perfect Progressive: Constraints on its Use with Numerical Object NPs' (*ELL* 4[2000] 97–114), argue against existing accounts of the use of the present perfect progressive by claiming that their occurrence in sentences with a numerical object NP is constrained by (un)boundedness (which concerns the existence of an actual terminal point), (a)telicity (potential, inherent terminal point), as well as the type of perfect and knowledge of the world.

The *Journal of Semantics* devoted special issues in 2000 to two topics of current interest within natural semantic research. Contributions to the first topic, namely, dialogue interpretation, include David R. Traum's discussion, in 'Twenty Questions on Dialogue Act Taxonomies' (*JoS* 17[2000] 7–30), of the issues to be considered for the classification of speech-acts for various purposes. Nicholas Asher, 'Truth Conditional Discourse Semantics for Parentheticals' (*JoS* 17[2000] 31–50), argues against the received wisdom about parentheticals and discourse adverbials, claiming that these expressions do contribute to the truth-conditional content of assertions they are part of by being attached to them with particular discourse relations. Miriam Eckert and Michael Strube's 'Dialogue Acts, Synchronizing Units, and Anaphora Resolution' (*JoS* 17[2000] 51–89), based on an extensive corpus study, claims that more than a quarter of pronouns in spontaneous spoken dialogue have no linguistic antecedents (with others having NP and sentential antecedents), and proposes a new dialogue segmentation method to extend a pronoun resolution algorithm developed by the second author. Andreas Herzig and Dominique Longin, 'Belief Dynamics in Cooperative Dialogues' (*JoS* 17[2000] 91–118), provide an account of belief change in co-operative dialogues in terms of a modal logic of action, belief and intention, while Robert van Rooy's 'Permission to Change' (*JoS* 17[2000] 119–45) proposes an analysis of the performative effects of imperatives (mainly of permission sentences) in terms of a context-change theory.

The second special topic concerns the optimization of interpretation. The contributions include recent applications of Optimality Theory (OT) to the analysis of semantic and pragmatic phenomena, which propose a potentially infinite number of interpretations for each grammatical expression, which are then tested against a set of ranked constraints. Reinhard Blutner's 'Some Aspects of Optimality in

Natural Language Interpretation' (*JoS* 17[2000] 189–216) claims that an optimality theoretic approach to natural language interpretation has to be bi-directional (it has to take care of both the hearer's and the speaker's perspectives simultaneously), and develops a conceptual framework along these lines in which the essence of Gricean maxims and the balance between informativeness and efficiency in natural-language processing can be captured. Paul Dekker and Robert van Rooy's 'Bi-Directional Optimality Theory: An Application of Game Theory' (*JoS* 17[2000] 217–42) investigates parallels between principles of OT interpretation and those of Game Theory, while Henk Zeevat's contribution, 'The Asymmetry of Optimality Theoretic Syntax and Semantics' (*JoS* 17[2000] 243–62), argues for an asymmetry between OT syntax and semantics, which is consistent with differences between what people can say and understand. Alice ter Meulen, 'Optimal Reflexivity in Dutch' (*JoS* 17[2000] 263–80), proposes an OT account of reflexivization strategies of Dutch and English based on binding principles, optimality considerations and a general principle of linguistic economy, while Bart Geurts's paper 'Buoyancy and Strength' (*JoS* 17[2000] 315–33) discusses the treatments of presupposition in OT.

In a special issue of *Rivista di Linguistica* on adverbs and adverbial modification, Helen de Hoop and Henriëtte de Swart, 'Temporal Adjunct Clauses in Optimality Theory' (*RLing* 12[2000] 107–27), propose an account of the possible interpretations of temporal adjunct clauses (*when*-clauses) inside and outside the scope of adverbial quantifiers. In the same issue, Denis Delfitto's 'Adverbs and Syntax/Semantics Interface' (*RLing* 12[2000] 13–53) gives a state of the art update on the syntactic/semantic behaviour of adverbs, and argues that they indicate a broad range of semantic ambiguity, which manifests itself in the fact that they can exhibit behaviour which parallels that of individual-referring expressions, predicative expressions or quantificational expressions, depending on their syntactic placement, the lexical structure of verbal predicates, or morphologically encoded aspectual distinctions.

Orin Percus, in 'Constraints on Some other Variables in Syntax' (*NLS* 8[2000] 173–229), pursues the consequences of the proposal that there are world variables in syntactic structures, whose appearance is regulated by constraints which depend on aspects of the structure they appear in, and can thus be accounted for in terms of a Binding Theory. A contrary view about the use of variables as part of the semantic machinery is taken by Pauline Jacobson in 'Paycheck Pronouns, Bach-Peters Sentences, and Variable-Free Semantics' (*NLS* 8[2000] 77–155), who proposes a variable-free semantics of 'paycheck' pronouns (such as the *it* in *The woman$_i$ who$_i$ deposited her$_i$ paycheck in the bank was wiser than the woman$_j$ who$_j$ deposited it in the Brown University Employees' Credit Union*) and i-within-i effects (as in *Every wife$_i$ of her$_i$ childhood sweetheart came to the party*), and claims that the first pronoun in a Bach-Peters sentence (e.g. *The man who loved her kissed the woman who wrote to him*) can be regarded as a paycheck pronoun, and that there is therefore no need to postulate quantification over pairs when the semantics of these sentences is accounted for.

Further journal articles worth our attention include Yoad Winter's new proposal for the interpretation of plural noun phrases, 'Distributivity and Dependency' (*NLS* 8[2000] 27–69), and Sigrid Beck and Uli Sauerland's reply, 'Cumulation is Needed: A Reply to Winter (2000)' (*NLS* 8[2000] 349–71). Zoltán Gendler Szabó's essay 'Compositionality as Supervenience' (*Ling&P* 23[2000] 475–505) provides a review of the various available interpretations of the principle of compositionality (which, in one of its most popular formulations, is usually stated as follows: 'The meaning of a complex expression is determined by the meanings of its constituents and by its structure') and proposes a new reading for it which seems to fit better the intuitions of speakers about what makes languages compositional. Sigrid Beck's analysis of 'The Semantics of *Different*: Comparison Operator and Relational Adjective' (*Ling&P* 23[2000] 101–39) claims that sentences such as *Detmar and Kordula live in different cities* versus *Every girl reads a different book* contain two NP-dependent readings of this word, the first corresponding to a reciprocal use of a relational adjective, and the second to a particular use of a comparison operator.

7. Lexicography, Lexicology and Lexical Semantics

It has been a good year for publications on lexicography. Lynda Mugglestone's *Lexicography and the OED: Pioneers in the Untrodden Forest* is an excellently integrated and fascinating collection of essays dealing with aspects of the compilation of the *OED*, concentrating largely on the period leading to the production of the first supplement in 1933. Elizabeth Knowles describes the process of editing an entry, starting from slips. Charlotte Brewer looks at the selection of sources, paying particular attention to the three editions of Murray's *Appeal* to readers. Penny Silva discerns patterns in definitions, although these were never codified, and compares first-edition practice with that of *OED3*. In 'Murray and his European Counterparts', Noel Osselton compares the *OED* with the *Deutsches Wörterbuch*, the *Dictionnaire de la langue française*, and the *Woordenboek der Nederlandsche Taal*. Anne Curzan also compares the *OED* with contemporary dictionaries, but this time to evaluate its treatment of peripheral vocabulary. 'The Vocabulary of Science in the *OED*' is Michael Rand Hoare and Vivian Salmon's consideration of the treatment of terminology. They note that even the earliest outline of the *OED*'s contents specified that specialist scientific terminology should be excluded. Dieter Kastovsky's contribution, 'Words and Word-Formation: Morphology in *OED*', notes that the *OED* is basically neo-grammarian in its approach. Eric Stanley considers the treatment of OE and ME texts, and observes that few reliable editions were available to its editors. Michael K.C. MacMahon looks at the development of the notation used to indicate pronunciation in the first edition, and the difficulties of transliterating it into IPA for *OED2*. Lynda Mugglestone finds numerous examples of prescriptive phrasing in definitions and usage labels, despite the *OED*'s stated aim of describing the language. Richard R. Bailey charts the reputation of the *OED* from its earliest stages. He includes some interesting examples of Murray's manipulation of that reputation. The volume closes with three appendices: dates of publication of the sections and parts of the *OED*, bibliographic accounts of personnel involved in its production, and contemporary publications illuminating the history of the *OED*.

In 'An On-line *OED*' (*EnT* 16:iii[2000] 12–19), John Simpson and Edmund Weiner explore the advantages of online delivery, and discuss the expanding coverage of world English. Howard Richler reviews the *OED* online (*Verbatim* 25:iii[2000] 23–5), and notes that it aims to cover a broad range of world Englishes. John Considine's 'Antedatings and Supplementary Material for *OED* from a

Correspondent of Browne Willis (1712)' (*Verbatim* 25:ii[2000] 17) provides thirteen antedatings for *OED* entries. Peter Knox-Shaw's '"Liberal", Earlier than in *OED*' (*N&Q* 245[2000] 218) pre-dates the first citation for the sense 'favourable to constitutional changes' by six years. Brian J. Hanley proposes 'An Amendment to the *OED*'s Definition of "Catchpenny"' (*Verbatim* 25:ii[2000] 27–8). Barry Baldwin finds some additional citations for *clitoris*, *carphology*, and *climacteric* in 'As the Word Turns' (*Verbatim* 25:iii[2000] 20). Michele Valerie Ronnick finds additional citations for *dead sea apple* in 'From Josephus's *Jewish War* to the American Civil War: Charles Francis Adams, Jr.'s "Dead Sea Apple"' (*Verbatim* 25:i[2000] 12–14).

David Micklethwait's *Noah Webster and the American Dictionary* is an informative and readable account of Webster's life and works, with a particular emphasis on his interest in plagiarism and copyright. Although Webster was greatly indebted to earlier producers of spelling books and dictionaries, he lobbied strenuously to establish copyright laws to protect his own works. Late in his life, for example, Webster worked through Knowles's *Pronouncing and Explanatory Dictionary* to identify debts to his own work. Conveniently, the detailed work of protecting his own rights also allowed him to copy out entries in which his own dictionary was deficient. He also engaged in numerous furious correspondences in newspapers and periodicals, which he sometimes generated himself in order to achieve greater publicity. Webster introduced into his works idiosyncratic and ever-evolving ideas about spelling, and largely unfounded etymologies. Micklethwait questions the belief that Webster was fluent in many languages, and demonstrates that he knew Greek and Latin, but had only a limited acquaintance with French, Old English, and Hebrew. His etymologies were informed by a belief in the biblical account of creation and in the shortness of the intervening period. The continued success of his dictionaries owes much to those who, during and after his lifetime, removed everything that was distinctively Webster's. Although Micklethwait argues that Webster cannot be considered the father of American spelling—'the recommendations that were peculiarly his own were never accepted' (p. 10)—he notes that the name 'Webster' has retained such value to publishers that the right to use it has been contested as recently as the 1990s. Joan Lilles argues, in 'The Myth of Canadian English' (*EnT* 16:ii[2000] 3–9), that the publication of Canadian dictionaries has been important in defining a sense of national as well as linguistic identity. R.W. McConchie, 'Richard Huloet, Right or Wrong?' (*N&Q* 245[2000] 26–7), suggests that *Howlet* is a better reading for the name of the author of the *Abcedarium Anglico-Latinum* (1552). Julie Coleman's 'Strange Linguists: The Cant and Slang Dictionary Tradition' (in Coleman and Kay, eds., *Lexicology, Semantics, and Lexicography*, pp. 69–86) is a discussion of the prefatory matter in cant and slang dictionaries. Gerardo Sierra's 'Extracting Semantic Clusters from MRDs for an Onomasiological Search Dictionary' (*IJL* 13[2000] 264–86) describes a semantic clustering method applied to machine-readable dictionaries. Wim Peters and Adam Kilgarriff, in 'Discovering Semantic Regularity in Lexical Resources' (*IJL* 13 [2000] 287–312), explore the hypothesis that a word's different senses, if close in meaning, will be near neighbours in a thesaurus. Juhani Norri looks at 'Labelling of Derogatory Words in Some British and American Dictionaries' (*IJL* 13 [2000] 72–106), and finds that learners' dictionaries are particularly full in their usage labels.

Reinhard Heuberger's *Monolingual Dictionaries for Foreign Learners of English: A Constructive Evaluation of State-of-the-Art Reference Works in Book Form and on CD-ROM* is an analysis of the strengths and weaknesses of the desk dictionaries produced by Longman, Oxford, Collins, Cambridge, and Chambers. All but Cambridge and Chambers also produce electronic dictionaries for intermediate and advanced learning. Heuberger concentrates on monolingual British learners' dictionaries first published since 1995. In chapters on meaning, grammar and usage, collocations, pronunciation, and accessibility, he describes the positive and negative features of each work. Similarly, he considers front and back matter, features specific to CD-ROM dictionaries, political correctness, and etymology. For each of the lexicographical features covered, Heuberger gives a summary and makes suggestions for further improvement. He also comments briefly on bilingualized dictionaries, which have the same entry structure as monolingual dictionaries, but also provide translations for each sense of the headword. The volume is fluently written and fair in tone, and concludes that no single reference work is better than the rest, but that the 'personal skills and preferences' (p. 182) of the user will determine which is the best choice. He notes that the area in which these dictionaries are most in need of improvement, on the whole, is in their definitions. Hilary Nesi addresses *The Use and Abuse of EFL Dictionaries: How Learners of English as a Foreign Language Read and Interpret Dictionary Entries*. She considers studies using questionnaires, tests, and observation, and uses the strengths and weaknesses of these approaches to devise a series of five studies. These explore aspects of receptive and productive dictionary use among young adult advanced learners. Using a computer-based test it was possible to gather detailed information about subjects' dictionary use. The studies present a number of findings: dictionary use in tests does not necessarily improve students' performance; there is little difference in intelligibility between major learners' dictionaries; learners from different backgrounds have varying success in using dictionaries for productive tasks; and examples in dictionaries do not significantly affect the success of productive dictionary use. Nesi concludes that learners tend to look up words about which they have already acquired some information, rather than seeking 'totally new and unexpected information' (p. 121). The information that learners bring to bear on dictionary entries comes from previous encounters with the target word, knowledge about cognate and related words, and knowledge about words or phrases used within the dictionary entry. Although dictionary users bring various types of knowledge with them to the dictionary, they do not assimilate all the information contained within the entries that they look up. The final chapter compares hard-copy and electronic dictionaries, and concludes that although there are many advantages to electronic dictionaries, the book form is still more 'reassuring' (p. 143). A.P. Cowie informs us about 'The EFL Dictionary Pioneers and their Legacies' (*Kernerman Dictionary News* 8[2000] 1–6), writing particularly about Harold E. Palmer, A.S. Hornby, and Michael West. Yuri Komuro and Shigeru Yamada discuss 'Dictionary Use for Production among Japanese College Students of English' (*Kernerman Dictionary News* 8[2000] 7–12). Archibold Michiels's 'New Developments in the DEFI Matcher' (*IJL* 13[2000] 151–67) is an account of a computer tool designed to aid in the selection of an appropriate translation from among those provided in bilingual dictionaries. Thierry Fontenelle writes about 'A Bilingual Lexical Database for Frame Semantics' (*IJL* 13[2000] 232–48). The FrameNet project aims to describe word senses by using corpus elements, but its innovation is to include frame elements in the resulting lexical database. Alessandro Lenci *et al.*, in 'Simple: A General Framework for the Development of Multilingual Lexicons' (*IJL* 13[2000] 249–63), provide an account of the LE-SIMPLE projects, which is an attempt to build harmonized syntactic-semantic lexicons for twelve European languages. Alexandra Jarošová considers 'Problems of Semantic Subdivisions in Bilingual Dictionary Entries' (*IJL* 13[2000] 12–28), and suggests a new theoretical framework based on corpus research. Adam Kilgariff discusses 'Business Models for Dictionaries and NLP' (*IJL* 13[2000] 107–18), and tries to draw together the interests of dictionary publishers and NLP (natural-language processing) researchers. Jon Patrick, Jun Zhung, and Xabier Artola-Zubillaga, 'An Architecture and Query Language for a Federation of Heterogenous Dictionary Databases' (*CHum* 34[2000] 393–407), propose a common description and query language to allow simultaneous searching of multiple electronic dictionaries. Issues 34:i and 34:ii of *Computers and the Humanities* report on SENSEVAL, a project evaluating word sense disambiguation programs in English, French, and Italian.

Two general introductions to lexicology were published this year. Geoffrey Hughes's *A History of English Words* is, as its title indicates, interested in the development of the lexis. Howard Jackson and Etienne Zé Amvela's *Words, Meaning and Vocabulary: An Introduction to Modern English Lexicology* is more synchronic in approach. The first chapter deals with the history of English, largely with reference to vocabulary, but the work quickly moves on to the question of what is a word, to polysemy, homonymy, and multi-word lexemes. It looks in detail at word-formation, particularly inflection and derivation, and considers types of semantic relationship. The authors introduce componential analysis, semantic primitives, semantic fields, and collocation as ways of approaching word meaning. A further chapter deals with lexical subsets, discussing national and regional vocabularies, jargon, the language of subcultures, style, and restricted languages. Jackson and Amvela also discuss how lexicologists find out about words and what tools are available to them. The volume closes with a consideration of dictionary choices about inclusion and exclusion. Exercises are provided throughout the work, as well as keys to the answers. It is a more concise work than Hughes's, but nevertheless succeeds in covering a wide range of lexicological issues. Hughes's *History* is an engaging and approachable introduction to historical lexicology, which explains all of its terms as it goes along. Hughes discusses, in far more detail than a general history of English could, social, geographical, and chronological variations in lexis, with wide-ranging quotation from various types of literature to illustrate and support his points. The fifth chapter is, in part, a discussion of the development of the English dictionary from Elizabethan times to the present day, and marks the beginning of the movement from diachronic to synchronic treatment of the lexis. The next two chapters deal with the spread and variation of English throughout the world, and the last chapter summarizes 'Changes in Lexical Structure'. As an account of recent research and an introduction to a wide range of lexical issues, Hughes's book cannot be matched. It is also a very entertaining read.

Carole P. Biggam's '*Grund* to *Hrof*: Aspects of Old English Semantics of Building and Architecture' (in Coleman and Kay, eds., pp. 103–25) is an exploration of 'the potential of interdisciplinary studies in the field of Anglo-Saxon architecture and building processes' (p. 103). In 'The Old English *Phoenix*, l. 407b: *topas idge*'

(*NM* 101[2000] 45–9), Alfred Bammesburger reinterprets this contested reading as *toþa sidge*. Neither *idge* nor *sidge* is otherwise attested. R.W. McConchie considers 'The Use of the Verb *maþelian* in *Beowulf*' (*NM* 101[2000] 59–68), and identifies three main categories of speech introduced by this verb. In 'OE *feolheard* and OE *irenheard*: Two *Hapax Legomena* Reconsidered' (*Neophil* 84[2000] 127–36), Carole Hough reinterprets terms found in *The Battle of Maldon* and *Beowulf*. Alfred Bammesburger argues that 'Old English *reote* in *Beowulf*, line 2457a' (*N&Q* 245[2000] 158–9) should be understood to mean 'joy'.

Louise Sylvester and Jane Roberts, *English Word Studies: A Word and Author Index*, is, in the tradition of Cameron, Kingsmill and Amos's *Old English Word Studies* [1983], an annotated bibliography of studies of ME words and groups of words. Personal and place-names are largely omitted, although the introduction explains exceptions to this rule. Entries are listed alphabetically by author's name and date of publication, which is largely post-1950. An index to the words covered allows access via another route. A sample entry is probably the best way to illustrate the contents of the volume:

> Watts, P.R. (1047): 'The Strange Case of Geoffrey Chaucer and Cecilia Chaumpaigne', *Law Quarterly Review* 63, 491–513. Explores the significance of the phrase 'de rapto meo' in the Chaumpaigne release of 1 May 1380 and considers the reaction to it by Chaucer scholars. Finally examines this document and three related documents as a lawyer, concluding that *raptus* means 'rape', that when threatened with an appeal of rape Chaucer settled out of court, and that possibly Chaucer was not prosecuted because of new evidence, such as Cecilia Chaumpaigne's pregnancy, which, to medieval lawyers, would have implied consent.

It would, perhaps, have been useful to literary scholars, or those focusing on the language of a particular writer or text, to have had an index to medieval authors and works covered. Lorna Stevenson and Jocelyn Wogan-Browne published a *Concordance to the Katherine Group MS. Bodley 34 and the Wooing Group. MSS Nero A XIV and Titus D XVIII* this year. It is a companion volume to the concordance to *Ancrene Wisse* [1993], that they published with Jennifer Potts. The introduction contains a brief consideration of the history of the treatment of this closely linked group of texts, beginning with the writings of Tolkien. The concordance itself is based on manuscript forms rather than modern editions, although word-division is normalized. Citations are relatively brief and mechanically extracted; for example, from among the examples of *brudgume* in the Katherine Group: 'B SM 35r 1 me. Cum nu for ich kepe þe brud to þi brudgume. *Cum* leof to þi lif. for'. Lists of unexpected and marked forms help the reader to locate unusual manuscript readings. Appendices include a concordance of Latin forms and of proper names in English and Latin. Frequency lists are also provided for the Katherine Group and the Wooing Group. The same words are listed alphabetized from right to left, and the two lists of vernacular forms are amalgamated in a further appendix. Louise Sylvester looks at 'The Vocabulary of Consent in Middle English' (in Coleman and Kay, eds., pp. 157–78). In 'An Irish Etymology for Chaucer's *falding*' (*ChauR* 35[2000] 112–14), Andrew Breeze proposes that instead of the conventional OE and ON etymologies, *falding* should be traced to Irish *fallaing* 'mantle, cloak'. In 'Where Have All the Celtic Words Gone?' (*EnT* 16:iii[2000] 6–10), Loreto Todd similarly argues that early Irish and Welsh influence on English has been underestimated. Päivi Koivisto-Alanko uses prototype theory to look at semantic change in *wit* and its near synonyms in late ME and eModE in 'Mechanisms of Semantic Change in Nouns of Cognition: a General Model?' (in Coleman and Kay, eds., pp. 35–52).

B.J. Sokol and Mary Sokol, *Shakespeare's Legal Language: A Dictionary*, and Charles Edelman, *Shakespeare's Military Language: A Dictionary*, are, as is fitting for volumes belonging to the same series, similar in approach. Each introduction discusses, and dismisses, the argument that Shakespeare must have been a member of the relevant profession to write so knowledgeably about law and war. Each volume is encyclopedic in nature, and entries typically include a definition, a quotation from Shakespeare, and an account of scholarly works dealing with the terms defined. Entries are typically several pages long in Sokol and Sokol's work, but many of Edelman's are shorter and can, therefore, be quoted to represent their common style:

> charge[2] A signal for the attack sounded on a trumpet or other instrument (*OED sb* 19). It is odd that *OED* gives the first use for this definition as 1650, since the abortive trial by combat in *Richard II* is preceded by the stage direction, 'a charge sounded' (*F* 1.3.116.SD), and the trial of Palamon and Arcite in *Two Noble Kinsmen* is signalled by 'Cornets. Trumpets sound as to a charge' (5.3.55.SD). See alarum.

Maurizio Gotti's 'Lexical Choices in an Early Galilean Translation' (in Coleman and Kay, eds., pp. 87–101) is an examination of lexical choices in Thomas Salusbury's translation of Galileo's *Dialogue on the Great World Systems*. Heli Tissari compares the use of *love* (noun and verb) in eModE and PDE in 'Four Hundred Years of *love*: A Prototype-Semantic Analysis' (in Coleman and Kay, eds., pp. 127–56). R.W. McConchie uses dictionaries, concordances, and corpora to explore 'The Vernacularization of the Negative Prefix *Dis-* in Early Modern English' (in Coleman and Kay, eds., pp. 209–27). Carole Hough draws together 'Place-Name Evidence for the History of Modern English *hut*', (*Neophil* 84[2000] 627–8).

Hilary Howard's 'Berthing the Verbiage' (*Verbatim* 25:iii[2000] 21–2) is a brief account of 'wonderful place designations and phrases, and sentence structures' (p. 21) found in the works of Dornford Yates. Gloria Rosenthal discusses 'Broadway Musicals—Terms and Traditions' (*Verbatim* 25:ii[2000] 1–4). Steven Cushing's 'Evolution: Just a Theory?' (*Verbatim* 25:ii[2000] 9–12) is an examination of the term *theory* and its alternatives. Jessy Randall (*Verbatim* 25:iv [2000] 15–17) considers terms used for *etcetera*, including *blah blah blah*, and *yada yada yada* as well as terms for talking nonsense, such as *babble*, *chatter*, and *yak*. In 'It's about Time' (*Verbatim* 25:ii[2000] 13–16), Nick Humez looks at metaphors dealing with time. In 'Funny Animals' (*Verbatim* 25:iv[2000] 17–21), the same author discusses the creation of names for the new animals encountered by early settlers in America. In 'Classical Swearing: A Vade-Mecum' (*Verbatim* 25:ii[2000] 20–4), Barry Baldwin compares Greek and Roman swearing with English. Steven R. Finz's 'The

New Profanity' (*Verbatim* 25:iv[2000] 1–6) discusses the proposition that racist language is replacing swearing as the greatest linguistic taboo, and considers the effect of this upon free speech. In 'The Language of Porn Sites' (*Verbatim* 25:ii[2000] 5–8), Fraser Sutherland considers the abbreviations, 'trendy spellings', and specialized vocabulary of internet pornography. D. Gordon and R.L. Spear provide a list of words used in the bars and brothels of Yokohama after the Second World War, in 'Baby-san's Lingo' (*Verbatim* 25:iii[2000] 5–12). Jessy Randall considers terms for menstruation in 'A Visit from Aunt Rose: Euphemisms (and Pejoratives) for Menstruation' (*Verbatim* 25:i[2000] 24–6).

Juri Apresjan's *Systematic Lexicography* was published in Russian in 1995, but has been updated and revised as well as translated for this English edition. It is an attempt to bring linguistic theory and lexicography together, and to enable the production of grammars and dictionaries that are compatible with each other. Most of the illustrations are from Russian, but in the early chapters examples from English have been introduced. Unfortunately, I found it distracting that several examples that were marked as unacceptable seemed feasible to me, although probably not in careful writing (for example: 'Why do you know it?' (p. xiv), 'he has fallen prey to an accident' (p. 4)). In the main body of the work Apresjan describes the ideal contents of a dictionary of synonyms and outlines the lexicographical information contained in the *New Explanatory Dictionary of Russian Synonyms*. He then explores the linguistic 'picture of man' (p. 101), with particular reference to the emotions. Further chapters look in detail at several Russian terms and their synonyms: *schitat´* 'to consider', *znat´* 'to know', and *khotet´* 'to want'. Apresjan discusses semantic metalanguage as conceived by the Moscow and Polish schools, and concludes with a detailed consideration of the lexicographical portraits of the Russian verbs *byt´* 'to be' and *vyiti* 'to emerge, to come out'. Christian Kay's 'Historical Semantics and Historical Lexicography: Will the Twain Ever Meet?' (in Coleman and Kay, eds., pp. 53–68) is an exploration of the relationship between two closely related disciplines that appear to be evolving independently. Andreas Fischer's 'Lexical Gaps, Cognition and Linguistic Change' (in Coleman and Kay, eds., pp. 1–18) aims to explain how lexical gaps arise and why some are tolerated while others are filled.

Gabriella Rundblad and David B. Kronenfeld ask, 'Folk-Etymology: Haphazard Perversion or Shrewd Analogy?' (in Coleman and Kay, eds., pp. 19–34), and aim to identify the processes and mechanisms involved. Claire Cowie looks at 'The Discourse Motivations for Neologising: Action Nominalization in the History of English' (in Coleman and Kay, eds., pp. 179–207). She argues that changes in morphological productivity are determined by the extent of neologizing, and that that 'is a social and cultural activity' (p. 179). Susan Elkin's 'To What End Gender Endings?' (*Verbatim* 25:i[2000] 15–16) is an introduction to the use of *-trix* and *-ess*. Göran Kjellmer considers 'Potential Words' (*Word* 51[2000] 205–28), and identifies semantic, phonological, morphological, and graphemic factors that influence a potential word's chances of adoption into the common word-stock. Nicholas Tranter's 'The Phonology of English Loan-Words in Korean' (*Word* 51[2000] 377–404) argues that, although inconsistent correspondences occur in small-scale borrowing, large-scale borrowing follows sound-change rules. In 'English Lexicography in Fiji' (*EnT* 16:iii[2000] 22–8), Jan Tent notes that code-switching and widespread bilingualism complicate the process of identifying Fijian and Hindi loans in Fijian English. Garland Cannon's 'Turkish and Persian Loans in English Literature' (*Neophil* 84[2000] 285–307) argues that literary writers' use of loanwords directly affects the language. Martin Bennett's 'From Ragusa to Lombard Street' (*Verbatim* 25:i[2000] 16–17) is an account of the origins of various money terms.

In Broe and Pierrehumbert, eds., *Papers in Laboratory Phonology V: Acquisition and the Lexicon*, there are a number of papers dealing with aspects of language acquisition, largely from a phonological perspective. These include Mary E. Beckman and Jan Edwards, 'Lexical Frequency Effects on Young Children's Imitative Productions'; Jan Edwards, 'Commentary: Lexical Representations in Acquisition'; and Stefan Frisch, 'Temporally Organized Lexical Representations as Phonological Units'. Although interesting, the volume is likely to appeal more to phonologists than to lexicologists. Although their coverage of lexicology and lexicography is necessarily brief, Frances Condron, Michael Fraser, and Stuart Sutherland do include some relevant websites and software in *Guide to Digital Resources for the Humanities*. For each piece of software, information is provided about platform and requirements, price and availability. Although such guides inevitably date faster than any other type of publication, this is a useful place to start exploring language corpora and dictionaries online.

8. Onomastics

This year saw the publication of three outstanding monograph contributions to the field of English place-name study. Margaret Gelling and Ann Cole's *The Landscape of Place-Names*, an investigation of the type of name which defines a settlement by reference to a landscape feature, is a major rewrite (though not entirely freestanding) of Gelling's *Place-Names in the Landscape* [1984]. The main text is by Gelling, with a detailed new appendix on 'The Chilterns: A Case Study' (pp. 288–316) by Cole, and the addition of sixty-two excellent sketches, also by Cole (these line drawings, made from photographs, are an especially welcome innovation, bringing the precisely worded definitions to life in a most convincing fashion). The division into thematic chapters (e.g. 'Marsh, Moor and Floodplain') is very similar to that in *Place-Names in the Landscape*, but a new, more convenient, arrangement of material provides a reference section for each element within the text (a great improvement on the previous glossarial index). A handful of new element entries appears (e.g. ON *haugr* 'tumulus, hill', OE *pēac* 'peak') and a handful are lost (e.g. OE *trēow* 'tree, post, beam', ON *gata* 'road, street'). The sometimes tricky relationship between the two books is partly addressed in the introduction, in which Gelling modestly claims that 'The 1984 project was over-ambitious for one person with no specialised knowledge of geography or geology and no artistic or cartographic skills' (p. xiv). Certainly the new book is a more readable work of synthesis than its pioneering predecessor, and the thesis that the Anglo-Saxon topographical terminology is both precise and country-wide now benefits hugely from the formidable investigative partnership which Gelling and Cole have formed, with fieldwork augmenting mapwork to tremendous effect. In addition, the number of post-1984 items in the bibliography is an indicator of how far English toponymic study has advanced in the intervening sixteen years.

David Parsons and Tania Styles, *The Vocabulary of English Place-Names (Brace-Cæster)*, is the second fascicle of the important new dictionary of the elements that make up place-names in England, maintaining the impressively full level of coverage established in the first fascicle *Á–Box* (*YWES* 78[1999] 86). One useful innovation in this volume is the tagging of personal names in place-names, which are now distinguished as monothematic or dithematic and allocated to a language. Items of outstanding merit include the lengthy discussions of OE *burh* 'stronghold' and OE *cæster* 'city, walled town, fortification', which, along with so much here, will be of great value to a far wider range of scholars than merely onomasts. OE *brōc* 'brook, stream', OE *brycg* 'bridge', OE *burna* 'stream', ODan *bȳ* 'settlement, village' and OE *camp* 'open land, field' receive similarly thorough and illuminating treatment, as indeed does every element, for nothing is glossed over or shirked. The scope of the work is one of its delights: there are over 200 individual entries in this volume alone, many of which contain new etymological suggestions and insights, and many of which are unknown to other dictionaries, a reminder that this magnificent assemblage of material in itself proclaims the value of place-names as historical linguistic evidence.

Richard Coates and Andrew Breeze, *Celtic Voices, English Places: Studies of the Celtic Impact on Place-Names in England*, is a significant and timely contribution to English onomastics, embodying the view that 'more of the major place-names of England date from before the advent of the Anglo-Saxons than is generally believed, and that some enshrine such early names within a more complex English structure' (p. 7). The book contains sixty-eight individual etymological studies which further this position convincingly, twenty-five by Coates (of which a gratifying twenty are entirely new) and forty-three, generally shorter, pieces by Breeze (of which nine are new). Those articles that have previously appeared in print are often here revised, and it is in any case convenient to have these scattered items assembled in one volume. Among the names newly treated are Speen (Berkshire), Kinder (Derbyshire), Culm and Treable (Devon), *Othona* (Essex), Aust, Dymock and Ingst (Gloucestershire), Netley Marsh (Hampshire), Esthwaithe, Inskip and Oldham (Lancashire), Holland (Lincolnshire), Ashford (Middlesex), Coslany (Norfolk), Caradoc, Lizard and Merrington (Shropshire), Gnosall (Staffordshire), Dunwich and Felixstowe (Suffolk), Chitterne, Chittoe, Idover, Old Sarum and several others (Wiltshire), and Wawne (Yorkshire, East Riding). Hugely valuable is Coates's 'Gazetteer of Celtic Names in England (Except Cornwall)', which proceeds county by county, distinguishing for each name the language (Brittonic, Goidelic, root-Celtic, Latin, Welsh, or Ancient), degree of Celticity (i.e. wholly or partly Celtic), and level of confidence (in the Celtic status of the name), as well as providing etymological notes and a four-figure National Grid reference. The enlightening county maps which accompany the gazetteer successfully employ the same distinctions, and are a very welcome inclusion. Coates also provides an introductory chapter, a glossary of elements, and a classified list of river names. The book contains so many key articles that it is impossible here to do them justice individually, though particularly attractive highlights deserving special mention are an Irish interpretation of Lindisfarne (and thence the Farne Islands) in Northumberland (pp. 241–59), a clearly stated case for accepting Carburton (Nottinghamshire) as a Brittonic name meaning 'Britons' village' (pp. 150–2), an investigation of Thanet (Kent) which suggests that the island's apparent early alias

Ruoihim may not be a name at all (pp. 32–9), and an ingenious solution to Rollright in Oxfordshire (pp. 199–212), linking the name with the megalithic Rollright stones.

Although no EPNS survey volume was published this year, the fledgling EPNS 'Popular Series' continues apace with the appearance of *Wirral and its Viking Heritage* by Paul Cavill, Stephen E. Harding and Judith Jesch. The importance of place-names as evidence for the Viking settlement of this part of Cheshire is clearly set out by Jesch in the introductory chapter, 'Scandinavian Wirral' (pp. 1–10). Cavill makes a fine job of presenting the onomastic material in 'Major Place-Names of the Wirral: A Gazetteer' (pp. 125–47), a concise survey which includes a full run of early forms and scholarly discussion of each name, plus a key to the elements found in the names, while Harding's 'Locations and Legends' (pp. 108–24) offers, *inter alia*, analysis and distribution maps of some Scandinavian elements in minor names. As well as treatment of the region's archaeological and historical background, there is much else of onomastic interest throughout the eleven chapters of the volume, which contains reprints of seminal articles such as John McN. Dodgson's 'The Background of *Brunanburh*' (pp. 60–9) [from 1957] and F.T. Wainwright's 'North-West Mercia AD 871–924' (pp. 19–42) [from 1942] and 'Wirral Field-Names' (pp. 98–9) [from 1943], alongside the new pieces.

The single most important contribution to English surname studies this year is David Hey's *Family Names and Family History*, a learned and readable book which should find favour with scholars and a wider public alike. The opening section addresses 'The History of Family Names', beginning with a brief but masterly survey of earlier approaches to surname study, then explaining the processes by which hereditary names evolved, introducing the familiar four broad categories of surname, and gradually moving on to newer ground with a chapter on 'Stability and Change', reminding us throughout of the importance of studying the spread and distribution patterns of family names. Chronology is reversed in the second section, 'Tracing Surnames Back in Time', a detailed and expertly written guide to techniques and sources, with plentiful examples and caveats. The third, short section of practical advice on 'Tracing Your Own Name' is followed by a series of clearly presented surname distribution maps, based on registered deaths in 1842–6, which provide compelling support for Hey's contention that most families stayed close to their places of origin.

In *Owl's Hoot: How People Name their Houses*, Joyce Miles offers a discursive investigation of UK house names, in which a historical perspective is attempted and the beginnings of a taxonomy emerge (each chapter is multiply subdivided, and three popular categories in particular are examined: transferred place-names, names associated with nature, and names derived from personal names). Unfortunately the location of individual names is not indicated, and the failure to cite early material is regrettable, but this is nevertheless a very welcome contribution in an oft-neglected field. Before moving on from books to articles, one final item is worth a mention for a lightweight browse: Andrew Scholl's *The Achilles to Zeppelin of Eponyms* (previously issued as *Bloomers, Biros and Wellington Boots* [in 1996]) treats some 450 rather arbitrarily selected eponyms in an anecdotal style.

JEPNS includes a thorough examination by Ann Cole of OE *ersc* 'ploughed land' in '*Ersc*: Distribution and Use of this Old English Place-Name Element' (*JEPNS* 32[2000] 27–40), providing fuller treatment of the term (previously often translated as 'stubble field') than is to be found in Gelling and Cole's aforementioned *The*

Landscape of Place-Names. This study takes account of all known occurrences of the element in place-names (except field names), duly mapped and tabulated according to soil type and geography. After careful deliberation, Cole concludes that *ersc* names represent 'early attempts to cultivate later-settled areas of England' (p. 36), reflecting the expansion of arable in the Anglo-Saxon period. In the same journal, 'Assessing the Evidence for the Earliest Anglo-Saxon Place-Names of Bedfordshire' (*JEPNS* 32[2000] 5–20), by Martin Blake, is an able, systematic and well-researched survey, attempting, in relation to archaeological and topographical evidence, to establish a chronology of place-name formation in the early stages of the Anglo-Saxon settlement of the county. Victor Watts offers 'Some Place-Name Distributions' (*JEPNS* 32[2000] 53–72), a thought-provoking piece in which, in a series of maps, he plots variously selected place-names against 'the three main geographical zones or provinces of England related to the presence or absence of woodland in the pre-Conquest period' (p. 54). Unfortunately some apparent discrepancies between the contents of maps 3–5 and their descriptions in the text (pp. 54–6) may cause initial confusion; nor is it clear exactly what maps 11–13 represent. Nevertheless, particularly striking among the generally curious results are the distributions (maps 8–10) of relatively late names of the form 'place-name + *Street* [in the sense 'hamlet']', 'place-name + *End*', and 'place-name + *Green*', which types markedly fall outside the 'central province of open champaign country characterised by the classic great open field village system' (p. 56). What to make of this and other observations? While attempting no firm conclusions here, Watts readily acknowledges that data of this kind 'need much further analysis and ultimately to be incorporated in a general grammar of place-names' (p. 60). Exciting developments may well lie in store.

In shorter articles in the same journal, Geoffrey Wilson, 'A Plethora of Parks—Mainly Merton Examples' (*JEPNS* 32[2000] 72–5), looks at 'Park'-named suburbs of London, Carole Hough proposes the OE plant-name *feltere* 'centaury' as first element of 'The Field-Name *Felterrode*' in Yorkshire's West Riding (*JEPNS* 32[2000] 47–9), and derives 'The Place-Name Pitchcombe' in Gloucestershire from a plausible OE **piccen-cumb* 'valley with sloping sides' (*JEPNS* 32[2000] 50–2). W.E. Cunnington presents 'The Field-Names of Kingsbury (Middlesex)' (*JEPNS* 32[2000] 41–6), while Richard Coates, 'Plardiwick' (*JEPNS* 32[2000] 21–2), suggests that Plardiwick in Staffordshire may contain an OE **Pleg-rǣdenn* 'games-place', and convincingly ascribes the name of 'The Sinodun Hills, Little Wittenham, Berkshire' to a spot of learned Renaissance punning (*JEPNS* 32[2000] 23–5).

This year's volume of *Nomina* contains a number of articles relating to English toponymy. In their combined analysis of 'Old English *merece* 'Wild Celery, Smallage' in Place-Names' (*Nomina* 23[2000] 141–8), Ann Cole, Janey Cumber and Margaret Gelling provide a splendid demonstration of the trustworthiness of place-names. To quote Gelling, 'If a place-name says that something (archaeological, botanical, topographical, geological, even sometimes zoological) is present, it is more likely than not that the thing named will still be there' (pp.144–5). Margaret Scott's study of the problematic element '"Bullion" in Scottish Place-Names' (*Nomina* 23[2000] 37–48) includes treatment of examples in England, while Carole Hough postulates an OE or ME word **carel*, perhaps an animal name, to explain 'Carolside in Berwickshire and *Carelholpit* in Lincolnshire' (*Nomina* 23[2000] 79–86). In 'Caxton's Tale of Eggs and the North Foreland, Kent' (*Nomina*

23[2000] 87–8), Andrew Breeze makes use of place-name evidence to locate this celebrated meeting of mutually unintelligible dialects (*eggys* versus *eyren*) on the Isle of Thanet. Gillian Fellows-Jensen offers a fascinating account of 'John Aubrey, Pioneer Onomast?' (*Nomina* 23[2000] 89–106), which reveals that, although Aubrey's manuscript work *An Interpretation of Villare Anglicanum* is in a disappointingly unfinished state, 'interesting sidelights on the attitude to place-names in the seventeenth century' may yet be gleaned (p. 90). There is but one anthroponymic study this year: John Martin Corkery's 'Approaches to the Study of English Forename Use' (*Nomina* 23[2000] 55–74) reviews differing aspects of forenames which have concerned writers in the past comprises a useful discussion of prescriptive, descriptive, sociological and psychological approaches to names and naming. There is one piece tackling literary cruxes, Peter Kitson's 'Gawain/ Gwalchmai and his Peers: Romance Heroes (and a Heroine) in England, the Celtic Lands, and the Continent' (*Nomina* 23[2000] 149–66), an entertaining and learned onomastic jaunt through plots medieval and modern, and the journal also contains a welcome study of 'The Names Given to Ships in Fourteenth- and Fifteenth-Century England' (*Nomina* 23[2000] 23–36) by Malcolm Jones, which reveals, besides the majority of ship names classifiable as religious (especially utilizing saints' names), a good number of curiosities, notably of the 'wishful naming' verbal phrase type. *Cumwelltohous* (p. 36) is indeed charming.

One article of immediate relevance to an English readership in this year's *Namn och Bygd* (88[2000] 89–106) is Gillian Fellows-Jensen's 'Old English *sōcn* 'Soke' and the Parish in Scandinavia', a contribution to the ongoing discussion of the relationship between the Scandinavian word *sokn*, *sókn* 'parish' and the problematic cognate OE term *sōcn* (the use of which as a place-name element in England is discussed, as are the English sokes and sokelands themselves).

John and Katie Algeo, 'Onomastics as an Interdisciplinary Study' (*Names* 48[2000] 265–74), briefly consider the interconnections of onomastics with a dozen or so other disciplines, from anthropology to sociology, while Tim Brennen, 'On the Meaning of Personal Names: A View from Cognitive Psychology' (*Names* 48[2000] 139–46), contributes an interesting piece, suggesting that 'we do tend to process the meaning of names the first few times we encounter them', but in the long run 'we process names almost entirely free of meaning'. Disappointingly, Leonard R.N. Ashley's article in the same journal, 'The Saints Come Marching In: Saints' Names in the Toponymy of Cornwall' (*Names* 48[2000] 257–64), is a bizarrely dilettante piece more likely to mislead than inform.

Locus Focus continues to host an impressive array of articles and notes on Sussex place-names, many of which shed light on wider ranging toponymic issues. In 'An Old English Technical Term of Woodland Management in South-East England?' (*LocusF* 4:ii[2000] 17–9), Richard Coates proposes an OE **slæf*, related to ME *slīven* 'to cleave or split (of trees)', to explain a handful of place-names in Sussex, Surrey and Hampshire. Coates, 'Vennemann on Arundel' (*LocusF* 4:ii[2000] 5–6) also meticulously reasserts the OE etymology of Arundel in the face of recent 'Vasconic' opposition. Pam Combes, 'How Many High *tūn*s Were There in East Sussex?' (*LocusF* 4:ii[2000] 9–16), offers a thorough examination of places and people named *Heighton*, Janet Pennington makes an illuminating connection between the name of 'Dog Lane, Steyning' and the local leather industry (*LocusF* 4:i[2000] 24–7), Michael J. Leppard tackles 'Saint Hill, East Grinstead' (*LocusF*

4:i[2000] 8–9), and Heather Warne investigates 'Manorial Dynamics in the Recording of Minor Place-Names' (*LocusF* 4:i[2000] 21–4). Each number of this lively journal contains many additional notes, queries and snippets of interest. Still in Sussex, Richard Coates contributes an elvish untitled piece to *Sussex Past & Present* (90[2000] 5) on the naming of the area around the Long Man of Wilmington.

A good number of onomastic articles have appeared this year in primarily non-onomastic publications. María Auxiliadora Martín Díaz investigates 'Old English æ in Middle Kentish Place-Names: A Geographical Approach' (in Cortés Rodrígues *et al.*, eds., *Variation and Variety in Middle English Language and Literature*, pp. 65–74), basing her analysis on twelfth- and fourteenth-century forms extracted from J.K. Wallenberg's *The Place-Names of Kent* [1934]. The undertaking is commendable but the results presented here must be treated as, at best, preliminary in the absence of any extraction of relevant material from Wallenberg's companion volume *Kentish Place-Names* [1931]. A wide-ranging chapter by Victor Watts on 'English Place-Names in the Sixteenth Century: The Search for Identity' (in Piesse ed., *Sixteenth-Century Identities*, pp. 34–57) looks at three topics in particular: the marked effects on English river names of certain early antiquarians ('a fascinating group of truly Renaissance men', p. 40), some vogue place-name affix formations which serve to 'add character to a place' (p. 51), and the intriguing phenomenon of competing forms of a single place-name, 'one essentially belonging to a written tradition, the other to an oral tradition' (pp. 37–8). John Insley offers a highly detailed examination of the county name 'Kent: Etymology of the Name' (in Beck, Geuenich and Steuer, eds., *Reallexikon der Germanischen Altertumskunde*, vol. xvi: *Jadwingen—Kleindichtung*, pp. 444–9), including thorough discussion of derived names. In the same book, Insley presents a similarly meticulous account of the place-name Jarrow (County Durham) ('Jarrow: Etymology of the Name', pp. 37–9).

Gillis Kristensson postulates an OE **dystels* 'something thrown up, ?an earthwork' as the first element of 'The Hundred-Name Desborough (Buckinghamshire)', which, combined with OE *beorg* 'a hill', would be appropriate to the site of the hundred moot at the pre-historic earthwork of Desborough Castle (*N&Q* 47[2000] 402–3). In an excellent survey of the same county, K.A. Bailey offers a thorough and insightful discussion of 'Buckinghamshire Parish Names' (*Records of Buckinghamshire* 40[2000] 55–71), aided by careful classification of name types and some statistical analysis. Carole Hough draws attention to 'Place-Name Evidence for the History of Modern English *hut*' (*Neophil* 84[2000] 627–8), and in 'ON *kíll* in English Place-Names' (*SN* 72[2000] 1–5) prefers an ON **kíll* 'wedge' to ON *kíll* 'narrow bay (?or valley)' to explain a number of place-names in England, citing parallel Swedish toponymic usage. Andrew Breeze derives the first element of Trunch (Norfolk) from the ancestor of Welsh *trum* 'back', in the sense 'upland' ('The Name of Trunch, near North Walsham', *Norfolk Archaeology* 43[2000] 483–4). In anthroponymy, and of relevance to English naming, Göran Kjellmer's 'On American Personal Names: A Historical Study' (*SN* 72[2000] 142–57) is at once ambitious and modest, offering in just a few pages a useful survey of 'some of the principles that can be perceived in the field of American name-giving' (p. 142), beginning with an overview of chronological variation, noting a growing tendency towards short names (leading into an excursus on monosyllabic names), and including a summary of some differences noted in recent studies between men's and women's first names. This last topic is further investigated by Carole Hough, 'Towards an Explanation of Phonetic Differentiation in Masculine and Feminine Personal Names' (*JL* 36[2000] 1–11), who stresses the fundamental differences between lexicon and onomasticon. Ernest E. Tooth looks at 'The Survival of Scandinavian Personal Names in Staffordshire Surnames' (*Staffordshire Studies* 12[2000] 1–16), a fairly successful introductory account despite some curious linguistic terminology and notions. H.S.A. Fox and O.J. Padel's edition of documents pertaining to *The Cornish Lands of the Arundells of Lanherne, Fourteenth to Sixteenth Centuries* includes in its very full introductory apparatus an admirable account of the 'Surnames in the Surveys' (pp. cxxiv–cxxxvii), and also much of interest to place-name scholars (especially in the chapter on 'The Cornish Landscape', pp. lxviii–c).

Meanwhile, in the sporadically swift thrust and parry of toponymic debate, John Insley assesses '*Flooker's Brook* Again' (*N&Q* 47[2000]169–71) and reaffirms ME **flokere* 'fluke-catcher' as the specifier in this Cheshire name, rejecting Carole Hough's proposal of ME **flokere* 'shepherd' (*N&Q* 46[1999] 183–5), while Hough herself makes a convincing case for preferring an OE to a Celtic origin for 'The Place-Name Cabus (Lancashire)' (*N&Q* 47[2000] 288–91), *pace* Andrew Breeze (*THSLC* 148[1999 for 1998] 191–6), and Gillis Kristensson's derivation of 'The Place-Name Owermoigne (Dorset)' (*N&Q* 47[2000] 5–6) from an OE **ōgōra* 'terror ridge' is immediately rebutted by Richard Coates in the aforementioned *Celtic Voices, English Places* (p. 104).

There is a healthy onomastic smattering elsewhere in *Notes and Queries*. In her examination of 'Place-Names in *Le Petit Bruit* by Rauf de Boun' (*N&Q* 47[2000] 7–10), Diana B. Tyson discusses a number of forms which diverge from those in other *Brut* texts, offers some identifications (though *Wyrhale* looks more like a name of the recurring 'Wirral' type than the suggested Weardale (p. 8)), and alerts us more generally to the interest here for onomasts of 'an example of a late scribe copying material with which he is clearly not familiar' (p. 10). In 'William Worcestre on "Terremoreyn", Cumberland' (*N&Q* 47[2000] 295), Andrew Breeze identifies *Terremoreyn* with Mockerkin Tarn (attested as *Ternmeran* in 1343) near Lamplugh. Gillis Kristensson suggests that the first element of 'The Place-Name Yarnfield (Wiltshire)' (formerly in Somerset) is not OE *earn* 'eagle' but OE *gearn* 'yarn', perhaps with the meaning 'something long and narrow' (*N&Q* 47[2000] 4–5). And in a number of articles in this journal, Carole Hough highlights the value of place-names as evidence for a range of early vocabulary: 'The Field-Name *Flagdales*' (*N&Q* 47[2000] 291–2) examines the ME plant terms *flagge* and *flegge*, while 'An Antedating of ME *leir-pit* "Clay Pit"' (*N&Q* 47[2000] 403) is self-explanatory, and 'Place-Name Evidence for Two Middle English Words' (*N&Q* 47[2000] 6–7) looks at ME *wale* < OE *w(e)alh* 'a Briton' and ME *warlot* 'a piece of land assessed to a specifically defined payment of geld'. Hough similarly assembles valuable place-name support for ME *sinkfal* (and *sinkehole*) 'a pit for sewage, cesspool' in her discussion of 'Sinkfall in Lancashire' (*N&Q* 47[2000] 168–9). Literary onomastics also makes a showing in Todd Pettigrew's analysis of the 'presumptuous pseudonym' (p. 73) of Caius in *The Merry Wives of Windsor* in 'The Naming of Shakespeare's Caius' (*N&Q* 47[2000] 72–5), while Richard J. Moll, tackling some tricky Glastonbury lore, unravels *Mewyn, Melkin* and *Mewtryne* (< *Inis-witrin*?) in 'Another Reference to John Hardyng's *Mewyn*' (*N&Q* 47[2000] 296–8). Elsewhere,

Andrew Breeze reconsiders '*Gryngolet*, the Name of Sir Gawain's Horse' (*ES* 81[2000] 100–1), explaining the name as a corruption of a Welsh *Keincaled* 'Firm Back'.

A fitting item with which to end is the splendid outline of 'The Survey of English Place-Names' provided by Richard Coates (*British Academy Review* 2[2000] 22–5), which succinctly traces and illustrates developments in the discipline throughout the now seventy-seven year history of the EPNS, and casts an eye towards future innovations.

9. Dialectology and Sociolinguistics

Two main areas of research emerge from this year's publications on sociolinguistics and dialectology: the study of the origins of AAVE, and the new field of historical sociolinguistics. General (non-regional) publications on theoretical and practical matters of sociolinguistics are also numerous, and publications from this area will be presented first. Among general textbooks out this year is Peter Trudgill's *Sociolinguistics: An Introduction to Language and Society*, now in its fourth edition (first edition [1974]). Although Trudgill is a Labovian-school variationist sociolinguist, this short book takes a sweeping view of matters related to language and society, containing chapters on 'Language and Nation', 'Language and Geography', 'Language and Contact' and even 'Language and Humanity'. Concentrating on the essentials and always very readable, *Sociolinguistics* is a good introduction for a wider audience to the most basic issues and the central topics of this discipline. More geared towards the university environment is Suzanne Romaine's updated *Language in Society: An Introduction to Sociolinguistics* (second edition; first edition [1994]). Romaine advocates a wide definition of sociolinguistics; although she also quotes well-known variationist studies, she also deals with educational issues and wider issues of language contact and language choice. Particularly noteworthy is the fact that her discussions include not just the English-speaking world, but examples from all over the world, from indigenous Amerindian languages to Papua New Guinea.

A completely new textbook by Mesthrie *et al.*, entitled simply *Introducing Sociolinguistics*, has been co-authored by a team of linguists spanning at least half the world, Rajend Mesthrie and Andrea Deumert from Cape Town, Joan Swann from the Open University and William L. Leap from Washington. This post-colonial—as one might perhaps term it—perspective is both the highlight and the hallmark of this book. For example, under 'Regional Dialectology' (pp. 44–113) we find a description not just of the well-known monolingual dialectological projects in Europe, but also of the Linguistic Survey of India; the chapter 'Language Contact: Maintenance, Shift and Death' (pp. 248–78) includes a case study on Native Americans; and 'Language Planning and Policy' (pp. 384–418) compares the ongoing debates in Norway with the situation in South Africa. Unusually for an introductory textbook it also includes a chapter on 'The Sociolinguistics of Sign Language' (pp. 419–48). Throughout their discussions the authors pay particular attention to research methods, introducing students to the fact that 'evidence about language use is never simply "discovered": different methods affect both what counts as evidence and how this is interpreted' (p. 449). In sum, this is a most welcome addition to the (mostly Anglocentric) field of introductory textbooks in this discipline.

On the topic of macro-sociolinguistics, Fishman, ed., *Handbook of Language and Ethnic Identity* [1999] must be mentioned. Divided into two parts, the first features interesting background chapters on such general topics as 'Economics', 'Nationalism', 'History', and 'Political Science', but also on more narrowly relevant ones such as 'Sociology' (pp. 164–80, by Glyn Williams) and 'Sociolinguistics' (pp. 152–63, by Fishman himself). Particularly relevant to the subject of English studies are a number of contributions in the second part, 'Region and Language Perspectives'. Sonja L. Lanehart, 'African American Vernacular English' (pp. 211–25), gives a very personal account of the intimate link between language or dialect use and personal identity, and passionately pleads against any kind of one-sided bi-dialectalism. Richard Y. Bourhis and David F. Marshall compare 'The United States and Canada' (pp. 244–64), in particular the very different strategies of these two countries in dealing with multilingualism: the English-only policy in many US states versus official bilingualism in Canada. The section on Europe, 'The Celtic World' by Colin H. Williams (pp. 267–85), might also be of interest as background information for anyone interested in the Celtic substrate of the Celtic Englishes—another topic that is much written about this year (it will be discussed in the regional sections below).

Peter Trudgill takes up the issue of 'Sociolinguistics and Sociolinguistics Again' (*Sociolinguistica* 14[2000] 55–9), highlighting the potential for confusion inherent in this term, which covers both macro- and micro-sociolinguistics. Trudgill argues firmly for more work in linguistically motivated (i.e. micro-)sociolinguistics, as the discipline has come to be dominated by more and more macro-sociolinguistic concerns. An instantiation of this very wide definition of sociolinguistics is provided in Lambert and Shohamy, eds., *Language Policy and Pedagogy: Essays in Honor of A. Ronald Walton*, which deals with the promotion of foreign language teaching in the USA. The only chapter of interest to a more general readership is the overview chapter by Bernard Spolsky and Elana Shohamy, which introduces the reader to 'Language Practice, Language Ideology and Language Policy' (pp. 1–41).

Barbara Johnstone has contributed a whole monograph on *Qualitative Methods in Sociolinguistics*, i.e. macro-sociolinguistics, or the ethnography of speaking. Although she concedes that what she deals with here would more properly be captured under the heading of 'pragmatics' (or, probably, discourse analysis) in the European tradition, her observations are very relevant for fieldworkers in a micro-sociolinguistic paradigm as well. Johnstone places the methodology in a historical context (chapter 2) and then poses a range of careful questions, such as 'What is research?', 'What are data?', 'What makes a good research question?' etc. Chapters 6 to 9 ('Thinking', 'Looking', 'Reading and Listening' and 'Writing'), on how to work with the data, are also clearly relevant for sociolinguists. On a more basic level, but similarly concerned with the practicalities of starting one's own research project, is Judy Delin's *The Language of Everyday Life: Introduction*. Although this book does not primarily deal with variationist sociolinguistics, the steps Delin advocates in thinking about and planning possible linguistic projects do of course apply to sociolinguistic concerns as well, and both books can therefore be recommended for classroom use or for individual study for students who are interested in doing their own research.

Moving into the more narrowly circumscribed area of dialectology, we find a collection of essays, edited by Robert Penhallurick, entitled *Debating Dialect: Essays on the Philosophy of Dialect Study*—although 'edited' might give the wrong impression, as Penhallurick is in fact author or co-author of more than half the contributions collected in this small volume, which tries to take a critical look at the concepts of dialectology. The most noteworthy contributor in connection with this section is Graham Shorrocks, who traces 'Purpose, Theory and Method in English Dialectology: Towards a More Objective History of the Discipline' (pp. 84–107). Shorrocks fervently argues against formalist approaches to language and advocates a return to purely descriptive work, which has been much discouraged during the age of generative grammar, but ultimately has stood the test of time—something that cannot be said of the various theoretical models that have arisen out of the generative school.

A general methodological problem is addressed by Elvira Glaser in 'Erhebungsmethoden dialektaler Syntax' (in Stellmacher, ed., *Dialektologie zwischen Tradition und Neuansätzen*, pp. 258–76), who wonders whether it is possible to elicit data on dialect syntax with the help of questionnaires. Although this method might seem outdated in the age of tape-recorders and computerized corpora, Glaser claims that, for a certain range of syntactic phenomena, questionnaires are a viable option if one aims at wide-ranging geolinguistic comparisons.

Subjective rather than objective dialect data is also becoming an important area of study, as several contributions in the regional sections below also show. Jack K. Chambers gives a concise and well-argued introduction to 'Sociolinguistic Uses of *Subjective Evaluation Tests*' (in Deminger, Fögen, Scharloth and Zwickl, eds., *Einstellungsforschung in der Soziolinguistik und Nachbardisziplinen*, pp. 73–81), which, as an objective method, can aid the study of highly subjective attitudes. Chambers calls on sociolinguists 'to convey our findings in socially useful settings, by demonstrating, for instance, that unconscious stereotyping has deleterious effects on teachers attempting to help students realize their individual talents…and on all other aspects of social cooperation' (p. 81). A more wide-ranging introduction to the field is provided by Nancy A. Niedzielski and Dennis R. Preston, the pioneer of perceptual dialectology, in *Folk Linguistics*. Most relevant to the field of sociolinguistics are chapters 2 ('Regionalism') and 3 ('Social Factors'), where the authors present first a very useful overview of the study of the perception of (US) dialects (informants' hand-drawn maps and correctness versus pleasantness ratings have been discussed in previous contributions to *YWES* in detail), and also give many examples from their own fieldwork on attitudes towards such sociolinguistic factors as ethnicity, status and gender, mostly exhibiting crass contrasts between the rather liberal stance of professional linguists and folk linguistic attitudes. However, the authors do not go so far as to draw practical conclusions (as Chambers, mentioned above, does); their main aim in this monograph is a first documentation rather than an application, of their findings.

Also linked to the study of attitudes, the *Journal of Sociolinguistics* has issued a special volume (4:iv[2000]), edited by Alexandra Jaffe and Dennis R. Preston, dealing with the orthographic representation of non-standard speech, which, as Alexandra Jaffe claims in 'Introduction: Non-Standard Orthography and Non-Standard Speech' (*JSoc* 4[2000] 497–513), reflects attitudes towards these non-standard varieties and, of course, their speakers. Dennis R. Preston is rather critical of gratuitous 'eye-dialect' forms in '"Mowr and Mowr Bayud Spellin'": Confessions of a Sociolinguist' (*JSoc* 4[2000] 614–21), as these mostly serve to demote the speaker's social status, education, intelligence, etc., as well as to obscure the data. On the other hand, writing may have a more profound influence on spoken language after all, which is why we should pay attention to orthographic representations as well.

Historical sociolinguistics is establishing itself as another important sub-discipline of the field, as is shown by the publication of two collections of essays this year. The first is Kastovsky and Mettinger, eds., *The History of English in a Social Context*, strongly dominated by the eminent scholars from the Helsinki school of English, with a range of interesting contributions that mainly deal with the evolution of standard English, or that analyse such well-known literary sources as Shakespeare or Chaucer. However, there are also some contributions that are more directly relevant to present-day dialects, in particular dealing with the 'Celtic' Englishes spoken in Scotland and Ireland; these contributions are dealt with in the regional section below. The other collection of essays is Wright, ed., *The Development of Standard English, 1300–1800* (also noticed above). It is more specialized and more uniform than the Kastovsky and Mettinger selection, both in topic and in time range. The contributions are divided into two parts. The first deals with 'Theory and Methodology' and contains a range of critical essays, some of which are reviewed below. Part 2 is concerned with the narrower issue of standardization, and is again dominated by the Helsinki scholars. As a whole, the contributions challenge the received wisdom that standard English evolved out of Chancery English and Midland dialects exclusively. In particular, Jim Milroy shows, in 'Historical Description and the Ideology of the Standard Language' (pp. 11–28), that this ideology has had a circular influence on the standardization debate, and that the three characteristics usually associated with a 'standard' (uniformity, prestige, and careful speech) do not hold for ME. ME was highly variable, such that editors have often corrected inconsistent spelling, hence the circularity; the association with prestige is not at all clear; it is also not clear that the standard is really the product of the highest social groups. Milroy advocates instead the reverse angle, an analysis of 'stigma', rather than prestige, a concept that is also taken up by Raymond Hickey in 'Salience, Stigma and Standard' (pp. 57–72) in relation to (the portrayal of) Irish English.

In a similar vein to Milroy, Richard J. Watts carefully uncovers the 'Mythical Strands in the Ideology of Prescriptivism' (Wright, ed., pp. 29–48). The historian Derek Keene switches our attention to 'Metropolitan Values: Migration, Mobility and Cultural Norms, London 1100–1700' (Wright, ed., pp. 93–114), giving excellent background information about this city that has until today served as the attractor and the main source of linguistic change in (British) English vernaculars. Tying in with Keene's historical overview, Terttu Nevalainen and Helena Raumolin-Brunberg investigate 'The Changing Role of London on the Linguistic Map of Tudor and Stuart English' (in Kastovsky and Mettinger, eds., pp. 279–337), based on their Corpus of Early English Correspondence (CEEC). The grammatical features of subject–verb agreement, relative pronouns, and the use of the pronouns *ye*, *its* and *one* show that the north of England shares many developments with London, whereas the much closer town of Norwich doesn't. On the basis of this distribution the authors argue for widespread immigration from the north to London, which must have become a dialectally mixed area. Also based on the CEEC, Arja Nurmi discusses 'The Rise and Regulation of Periphrastic *Do* in Negative Declarative Sentences: A Sociolinguistic Study' (in Kastovsky and Mettinger, eds., pp. 339–62), where she finds that—at least for the sixteenth century—*do*-periphrasis is more governed by text type than by sociolinguistic factors. In the seventeenth century, however, women can be shown to be leading the change. Ingrid Tieken-Boon van Ostade discusses a general topic in 'Sociohistorical Linguistics and the Observer's Paradox' (in Kastovsky and Mettinger, eds., pp. 441–61), showing that this is also an issue for historical texts. Because of conventions for letter-writing and for reporting conversations, the writers may not always have used their everyday vernacular. Finally, recommended reading for anyone interested in an overview of the dialect situation in eModE is Manfred Görlach's chapter in Lass, ed., the *Cambridge History of the English Language* [1999], simply entitled 'Regional and Social Variation' (pp. 459–538). Görlach traces demographic developments during this period and discusses the very problematical issue of historical sources for dialect descriptions, both direct and indirect.

Linking historical linguistics and dialectology, Michele Loporcaro deals with 'Dialect Variation across Time and Space and the Explanation of Language Change' (*Sprachwiss* 25[2000] 387–418). Loporcaro argues that, although for some phenomena grammar-internal explanations might be sufficient, researchers should keep an open mind since a combination of formal and functional paradigms ultimately promises much more satisfactory accounts of language variation and change.

Moving away from more historical concerns, Jack K. Chambers, in a short but inspiring paper, discusses possible 'Universal Sources of the Vernacular' (*Sociolinguistica* 14 [2000] 11–15), identifying features that all (English) vernaculars share, such as multiple negation, consonant cluster simplification, the substitution of *-in* for *-ing* and others. These primitive vernacular features are also found in child language, pidgins and creoles and possibly cross-linguistically. This opens up highly interesting perspectives for dialect studies across languages, a field that has hitherto been almost completely neglected, except by a research project funded by the European Science Foundation, on which the contribution by Frans Hinskens, Jeffrey L. Kallen and Johan Taeldeman is based: 'Merging and Drifting Apart: Convergence and Divergence of Dialects across Political Borders' (*IJSL* 145[2000] 1–28). This special issue of the *International Journal of the Sociology of Language* is dedicated to results from this project. Hinskens, Kallen and Taeldeman lay the theoretical basis for a study of convergence and divergence, differentiating the terms from similar ones employed in historical linguistics, in sociolinguistics and in dialectology.

This year also witnessed the publication of Price, ed., *Languages in Britain and Ireland*. Rather than providing a second edition of his *The Languages of Britain* [1984], this collection draws in eminent fellow-authors such as Michael Barnes, Viv Edwards, Philip Payton, and Jeremy J. Smith for about half of the contributions, covering 'the languages that are now spoken, or were spoken at some time in the past, in Britain, Ireland, the Isle of Man, or the Channel Islands' (p. 1), including all the Celtic languages—there are chapters on Irish in Ireland, Irish in early Britain, Scottish Gaelic, Manx, British, Welsh, Cornish, Cumbric, and Pictish—some of which are of course debatably not Celtic, as discussed in the contributions. As evidence that these languages are of widely different status, the chapters differ enormously in scope and (linguistic as well as historical) detail. The volume also includes, as is to be expected, chapters on Latin, English (with the memorable characterization that 'English is a killer', p. 141), Scots, Norse/Norn, French and Anglo-Norman, but it also covers Romani and the new 'Community Languages', giving an interesting overview of the multilingual society that Great Britain was and still is today. Helpful maps and illustrations make this a very valuable addition to the study of English historically, and also serve as background information for its present-day varieties.

Moving to present day Britain, Clive Upton is 'Maintaining the Standard' (in Penhallurick, ed., pp. 66–83), advocating the use of 'mainstream RP' as a model for dictionaries, thus making RP serviceable for a wider group of users. Upton argues that remodelling RP is legitimate work for a dialectologist (such as himself) and gives some examples of this: new developments in RP such as /a/ for *apple* or /ɛː/ in *square* are now included; so are regionally widespread pronunciations such as northern short /a/ in *dance*, *path*. Edmund Weiner and Clive Upton are also reporting on this lexicographic work in '[hat], [hæt], and All That' (*EnT* 16:i[2000] 44–6). D.J. Allerton discusses 'Articulatory Inertia vs "Systemzwang": Changes in Liaison Phenomena in Recent British English' (*ES* 6[2000] 574–81), finding (unfortunately only anecdotal) evidence that in careful formal speech the traditional linking sounds seem to be on the decrease. In connection with more non-standard varieties, Joan Beal investigates 'HappY-Tensing: A Recent Innovation?' (in Bermúdez-Otero *et al.*, eds., pp. 483–97)—the answer to this question being 'No': HappY-Tensing has a long history in several dialects, and Beal shows that the purportedly recent 'city-hopping' from the south-east to the northern ports of Hull, Newcastle and Liverpool must have happened at a time when travel by sea was much easier than over land, for example in the eighteenth century.

Another truly recent innovation from the south-east is the topic of Paul Foulkes and Gerard Docherty's 'Another Chapter in the Story of /r/: Labiodental Variants in British English' (*JSoc* 4[2000] 30–59); this new variant, formerly dismissed as an infantilism or characteristic of affected upper-class speech, seems to be spreading from the south-east, along with many other accent features, and is now also present in Derby and Newcastle.

David Britain and Peter Trudgill look at 'Migration, Dialect Contact, New-Dialect Formation and Reallocation' (in Mattheier, ed., *Dialect and Migration in a Changing Europe*, pp. 73–8). They discuss that, even after koinéization, several variants of a variable might be left, which may undergo re-allocation (or refunctionalization), for example as stylistic or social variants, or as allophonic variants. This can also explain the 'Fenland raising' in the English south-east, which produces central onsets before voiceless consonants. Paul Kerswill and Ann Williams report on 'Creating a New Town Koine: Children and Language Change in Milton Keynes (*LSoc* 29[2000] 65–115). The same authors also discuss 'Mobility versus Social Class in Dialect Levelling: Evidence from New and Old Towns in England' (in Mattheier, ed., pp. 1–13), widening their scope and comparing developments in Milton Keynes with Reading in the south-east and Hull in the north-east. Contra J. Milroy and L. Milroy, the data from Milton Keynes show that lower social class and mobility or loose-knit networks are not mutually exclusive.

As there is no continuity across generations in Milton Keynes, lower-class speakers should also be open to language change, and indeed there is evidence that Milton Keynes is changing as far as /ai/ is concerned towards a generalized 'Southern non-standard norm'. Sue Peppé, Jane Maxim and Bill Wells examine 'Prosodic Variation in Southern British English' (*L&S* 43[2000] 309–34), or, perhaps more accurately, non-variation, as the speakers they investigate in an experimental setting use prosodic features in a surprisingly homogeneous way. Kirsti Peitsara investigates 'The Prepositions *On* and *Of* in Partitive and Temporal Constructions in British English Dialects' (*NM* 101[2000] 323–32) in south-western and East Anglian dialects. Basing her study on the new resource of the Helsinki Dialect Corpus, Peitsara finds that this is not a simple exchange of two prepositions; instead, *on* is used before weak pronouns (*three on 'em*) and is thus a phonetic variant, whereas *of* in partitive constructions (*of a night*) is probably the retention of a conservative variant. Katie Wales, 'North and South: An English Linguistic Divide?' (*EnT* 16:i[2000] 4–15), looks at a more general topic, namely attitudes and stereotypes to be found among speakers in northern and southern England, which are promoted in sometimes quite heated ways by the media, and are certainly anchored in the mental maps of the wider public, as her many examples show. Wales claims that these have also influenced dialectological work on English varieties.

Turning to the north of England now, Andrea Simmelbauer has examined *The Dialect of Northumberland: A Lexical Investigation*. Not surprisingly, a comparison of present-day speakers with the older SED material shows that many dialect words have been lost over the last fifty years, and that women use fewer dialect words than men. Dominic L.J. Watt discusses 'Phonetic Parallels between the Close-Mid Vowels of Tyneside English: Are They Internally or Externally Motivated?' (*LVC* 12[2000] 69–101). In this dialect, instead of the highly local in-glides, monophthongs are the preferred variant for the vowels in *face* and *goat* today. As these are the wider regional forms, the change can be regarded as an instance of dialect levelling (rather than an internal vowel-chain shift). Juhani Klemola deals with 'The Origins of the Northern Subject Rule: A Case of Early Contact?' (in Tristram, ed., *The Celtic Englishes II*, pp. 329–46); unfortunately his detailed maps have been misplaced in the text and the discussion is therefore quite confusing in places. Klemola finds a similar system in Welsh, which might possibly point to a very early Brythonic substrate. Support for this claim comes from Celtic numerals (surviving in sheep-counting) that have survived in the same northern area.

Moving further north, Beat Glauser investigates 'The Scottish/English Border in Hindsight' (*IJSL* 145[2000] 65–78), relating to work of his from the 1970s. Glauser finds that the political border also functions as a linguistic border for many lexical items, although the two do not have exactly the same shape. On a historical theme, Anneli Meurman-Solin claims, in 'On the Conditioning of Geographical and Social Distance in Language Variation and Change in Renaissance Scots' (in Kastovsky and Mettinger, eds., pp. 227–55), that it is not always clear in these early texts whether spelling variants reflect incipient phonetic changes, or whether they might be due to beginning standardization of prestige variants. Meurman-Solin deals with a wider time-span in 'Change from Above or Below? Mapping the *Loci* of Linguistic Change in the History of Scottish English' (in Wright, ed., pp. 155–70), where she finds features of a national norm spreading from administrative, legal, political and cultural institutions to private domains. The time-lag that is found to be present depends on the distance from the metropolis of Edinburgh; resistance to these new national norms is strongest in areas that have developed their own local norm. Meurman-Solin also makes it very clear that standardization pre-dates prescriptivism. On a more formal level, April McMahon's monograph *Lexical Phonology and the History of English* provides phonological analyses of the Scottish vowel system. Chapter 4 especially, 'Synchrony, Diachrony and Lexical Phonology: The Scottish Vowel Length Rule' (pp. 140–95), deals both with the present-day situation and the history of this distinctive phenomenon, and McMahon provides a clear and plausible formal analysis of this system. Robert McColl Millar deals with 'Covert and Overt Language Attitudes to the Scots Tongue Expressed in the *Statistical Accounts of Scotland*' (in Kastovsky and Mettinger, eds., pp. 169–98), showing that since the eighteenth century (the date of the first statistical accounts) the many comments by parish ministers on the language of their parishioners testify to the status of Scots in the middle classes. In particular, perceived language change is often commented on; where it is in the direction of standard English, it is generally the subject of positive comment, whereas shifts to urban varieties elicit negative comments. In addition, Scots is often used as a marker of proverbial wit and wisdom. On a more grammatical theme, Jennifer Smith claims that ' "You Ø na Hear o' that Kind o' Things": Negative *Do* in Buckie Scots' (*EWW* 21[2000] 231–59). In this dialect on the Scottish eastern coast, *do* is absent in negated present-tense declaratives, especially with high-frequency verbs and with the first person singular. There is no sociolinguistic variation for this phenomenon, and Smith argues for a syntactic explanation (*do* is absent in those contexts that are inflectionally marked by -*s*, due to the Northern Subject Rule). Finally, Clausdirk Pollner finds 'Shibboleths Galore: The Treatment of Irish and Scottish English in Histories of the English Language' (in Kastovsky and Mettinger, eds., pp. 363–76), where these regional varieties are still not treated in depth. A Scottish/Irish phenomenon is also marginally the subject of Richard Hudson in '*I amn't' (*Language* 76[2000] 297–323; also discussed above), precisely because this purportedly highly ungrammatical (and, in Hudson's Word Grammar, formally impossible) verb form does exist in these two varieties, which slightly undermines the validity of his account.

This takes us to Ireland, a region that is again extremely well represented in studies this year. First of all, a monograph from last year must be mentioned, Loreto Todd's *Green English* [1999] (not referring to eco-linguistics!). The subtitle, *Ireland's Influence on the English Language*, makes clear the general thrust of Todd's argument, i.e. that, through Irish clerics in the twelfth century, Irish Celtic had a profound influence on the English language as we know it today. For example, there are many more Celtic words in English than is generally acknowledged, and she claims that Irish even provided the pronoun *she*. Irish English also influenced Caribbean and of course American English, not to mention English in New Zealand, Australia and South Africa. Hildegard Tristram has edited the second volume of *The Celtic Englishes II*, again based on a conference at Potsdam of eminent scholars in the field (the first volume appeared in [1997]). However, this volume does not have the overview character that made the first volume so appealing and coherent. Due to its more theoretical orientation it is much more speculative than its predecessor, and the 'caleidoscope [*sic*] of differing approaches and differing views' (p. 7) could also be described as extremely heterogeneous, as indeed some contributions do not concern themselves with a Celtic English at all. For example, Arndt Wigger, in 'Language Contact, Language Awareness and the History of Hiberno-English' (pp. 159–87), examines the influence of English on the (Irish!) language of Irish bilinguals, and Susanne E. Carol, in 'Language Contact from a Developmental Perspective' (pp. 9–17), only very generally points out that theories of Second Language Acquisition are relevant for the investigation of language change through language contact. More narrowly concerned with linguistics, Patricia Kelly tries to examine 'A Seventeenth-Century Variety of Irish English: Spoken English in Ireland 1600–1700 Revisited' (pp. 265–79) on the basis of literary texts, and Astrid Fieß, 'Age-Group Variation in the Spoken Language of Rural East Galway?' (pp. 188–209), provides a quantitative analysis across three generations. Her analysis of different types of perfect shows no clear results, however, perhaps due to the small overall number of tokens. Raymond Hickey is purportedly developing 'Models for Describing Aspect in Irish English' (pp. 97–116), 'aspect' here also referring to the perfect. However, this paper would have benefited greatly from an acknowledgement of the cross-linguistic work in this field which could have yielded many relevant insights; *perfective* and *perfect* are confused throughout, *habitual* and *iterative* are defined rather idiosyncratically, and it is not at all clear where Hickey's examples come from. Terence Patrick Dolan reports on his work on 'The Compilation of a Dictionary of Hiberno-English' (pp. 323–8), stressing in particular the sources for the entries and quotations that are used. Coming to some of the highlights of this collection, Markku Filppula criticizes 'The Unbearable Lightness of the "Layer Cake Model": A Variationist Critique' (pp. 314–22), because it tends to 'overlook the intricate patterns of variation which exist in contact vernaculars both at the inter- and intra-individual levels' (p. 315).

Two contributions on Irish English take a more generative approach. James McCloskey discusses 'Quantifier Float and *Wh*-Movement in an Irish English' (*LingI* 31[2000] 57–84), more specifically in West Ulster English. This is a phenomenon not 'noticed before—by linguists, by speakers, or by the guardians of purity' (p. 58), as for example in, *What did you get all for Christmas?* (For *what all* ...). McCloskey argues for a re-analysis of the internal structure of the VP that can account for this phenomenon. Also from a generative perspective, Karen P. Corrigan asks, 'What are "Small Clauses" Doing in South Armagh English, Irish English and Planter English?' (in Tristram, ed., pp. 75–96), dealing with a phenomenon that is otherwise known as 'subordinating *and*'. She points out the interesting syntactic distinction that co-ordinating *and* is always used with the nominative case, whereas this is prohibited for subordinating *and* (*and him only a young fellah*). Corrigan argues that this is due to the fact that the Irish (Gaelic) default accusative case has been transferred to South Armagh English. Corrigan also discovers a new modal verb in South Armagh English in 'What Bees to Be Maun Be: Aspects of Deontic and Epistemic Modality in a Northern Dialect of Irish English' (*EWW* 21[2000] 25–62), where invariant *be to* is used in both epistemic and deontic senses (but not with the negative).

South of the border, Markku Filppula discusses 'Inversion in Embedded Questions in Some Regional Varieties of English' (in Bermúdez-Otero *et al.*, eds., pp. 439–53). Filppula argues that, rather than a retention of an earlier English pattern, Embedded Inversion is found in particular in northern, north-western and western dialects. In Ireland, it is more common in the west, which suggests a possible Celtic language influence for this phenomenon. On the subject of Dublin English, Raymond Hickey proposes a new concept, 'Dissociation as a Form of Language Change' (*EJES* 4[2000] 303–15), 'dissociation' being the opposite of 'accommodation'. Some speakers use maximally distinct sounds in order *not* to associate themselves with local speech. Hickey discovers this process to be at work with the younger, socially conscious, wealthy Dubliners (leading to the so-called Dublin Vowel Shift).

Moving to attitudes, Simone Zwickl examines 'A Divided Speech Community? Language Attitudes, Religion and Ethnic Identity across the Northern Irish/Irish Border' (in Deminger *et al.*, eds., pp. 123–40) in Armagh (Northern Ireland) and Monaghan (Ireland). In Armagh, the main division is between Protestants and Catholics, whereas south of the border both ethnic groups see themselves as 'Monaghians'. Also on the subject of the border, Jeffrey L. Kallen investigates 'Two Languages, Two Borders, One Island: Some Linguistic and Political Borders in Ireland' (*IJSL* 145[2000] 29–63). Kallen finds no direct evidence that Irish dialect divisions are reflected in present-day Irish English dialects; the political border is also no major factor, at least not in the material from the 1950s that Kallen employs.

Celtic Englishes II also sports some contributions on two otherwise little-studied varieties of English. There is Breesha Maddrell's 'Studying Networks in a Community of Diversities: The "Recording Mann" Project' (in Tristram, ed., pp. 146–58), reporting on ongoing work of recording the use of English on the Isle of Man today. Next, there are two papers that deal with English in Wales. Robert Penhallurick contributes 'On Gower English, Dialect and Metaphor' (in Tristram, ed., pp. 303–13). He claims that all metaphors usually employed in dialectology (the family-tree model, the wave model, or the layer-cake model) reify 'dialect'; as the example of the Gower dialect shows, however, a close examination sees the sharp dialect boundaries 'blurred, breached and erased' (p. 312). Also on Welsh English, Malcolm Williams investigates 'The Pragmatics of Predicate Fronting in Welsh English' (in Tristram, ed., pp. 210–30), relating it to the information strategy of Celtic Welsh, where the cognitive category of 'new information' tends to occupy the first position. A questionnaire-based approach to support this hypothesis failed, however, as linguistic self-consciousness seems to have severely skewed the results. It is therefore not really clear why the author advises potential fieldworkers to 'leave the tape-recorder at home', as he concedes himself that the frequency of predicate fronting tends to rise sharply after one or two pages of transcripts (p. 226).

Moving our attention across the Atlantic, Michael Montgomery discusses claims to 'The Celtic Element in American English' (in Tristram, ed., pp. 231–64), calling for more careful socio-historical documentary, historical and linguistic work before any influence of 'Celtic Englishes' on American English can be posited. For example, habitual *belbes*, sometimes cited as having influenced AAVE, is probably a nineteenth-century innovation and could therefore hardly have served as the source construction for the AAVE habitual. In particular, Montgomery pioneers the reconstruction of the historical dialect forms, as a comparison with present-day dialects may well lead to the wrong results—a caveat that will have to be kept in mind in particular in the ongoing debate on earlier AAE, more on which below.

Only few studies deal with language in Canada this year, or what Jaan Lilles has termed 'The Myth of Canadian English' (*EnT* 16:i[2000] 3–9). Lilles claims that there is no such thing as a distinctive Canadian English. Basing his argument on a cross-section of recent Canadian dictionaries, Lilles argues that 'Canadian English' is purely fictitious, and that 'regional Canadian Englishes' would be a more appropriate term. J.K. Chambers, on the other hand, discusses 'Region and Language Variation' (*EWW* 21[2000] 169–99), operationalizing the concept of 'regionality' in order to include this factor as a further independent variable in dialectological studies. Chambers's seven-point Regionality Index (calculated by the informant's and their parents' origin) correlates in an interesting way with ongoing processes of lexical change in Quebec English, making visible highly regional items (such as *bureau* for *chest of drawers/dresser*) that are obviously dying out versus others, such as *running shoes* (vs. American *sneakers*), that do not seem to be involved in any process of lexical change. Charles Boberg's subject is also the border and linguistic change; he applies the gravity model to 'Geolinguistic Diffusion and the U.S.–Canada Border' (*LVC* 12[2000] 1–24), but finds that Trudgill's gravity model does not account very well for the patterns he encounters: some phonetic (and lexical) features such as the fronting of /u/ seem to diffuse quite easily from the USA to Canada, whereas structural phonological differences in particular seem to be an inhibiting factor. Boberg draws attention to the fact that attitudes may also play a very important role: 'Canadians do not want to sound like Americans, so that when a variant is marked [+American] rather than, say, [+young] or [+trendy] it will not be readily transferred' (p. 23).

Moving south of the border, we come to what is probably the most important contribution to the study of US English in the north this year, Penelope Eckert's monograph *Linguistic Variation as Social Practice: The Linguistic Construction of Identity in Belten High*. Eckert not only discusses in great detail the vowel changes of the Northern Cities Chain Shift (NCCS), which are propagated to different degrees by the two main class-related groups in this Detroit high school (the middle-class-oriented Jocks and the working-class-oriented Burnouts), but also provides excellent background reading on the widely divergent cultural practices of these two groups and on the ethnography of high-school life in general, with which the linguistic practices are inextricably linked. Also on the subject of the NCCS, Matthew J. Gordon, in 'Phonological Correlates of Ethnic Identity: Evidence of Divergence?' (*AS* 75[2000] 115–36), confirms that the NCCS seems to be almost exclusively used by white speakers. African American speakers show, at most, incipient stages (although the /æ/-raising Gordon finds could also be an independent development), whereas Mexican American speakers show no traces of a beginning NCCS at all—a result that would indeed increase the linguistic difference between these ethnic communities.

Slightly more contributions deal with English in the southern US states. Valerie Fridland investigates the southern counterpart of the NCCS in 'The Southern Shift in Memphis, Tennessee' (*LVC* 11[2000] 267–85) with the help of very detailed phonetic analyses of twenty-five speakers from different socio-economic classes. Labov's hypothesized chain-shift also holds for speakers from Memphis. In addition, Fridland finds change in vowels that were not thought to have been affected until now. Also on a phonological theme, Natalie Schilling-Estes is 'Investigating Intra-Ethnic Differentiation: /ay/ in Lumbee Native American English' (*LVC* 12[2000] 141–74). The speech of this little-studied American Indian tribe in North Carolina is very distinctive as they have long constituted an 'insular group'. Besides linguistic constraints Schilling-Estes also discovers an interesting correlation such that the most isolated groups were the most heterogeneous, whereas inter-speaker contact leads to in-group homogenization.

Beverly Olson Flanigan and Franklin Paul Norris find 'Cross-Dialectal Comprehension as Evidence for Boundary Mapping: Perceptions of the Speech of Southeastern Ohio' (*LVC* 12[2000] 175–201). Ohio listeners were asked to identify seven words by a south-eastern Ohio speaker that are currently undergoing the Southern Vowel Shift or mergers in Ohio. Their hypothesis that college exposure to other dialects leads to a loss of the 'home advantage' in being able to identify correctly the words used, is only partly supported. The authors advocate redrawing the dialect boundaries in Ohio (diagonally rather than horizontally), extending the South Midland area north-eastwards.

Turning to Louisiana, Sylvie Dubois and Megan Melançon, in 'Creole Is, Creole Ain't: Diachronic and Synchronic Attitudes towards Creole Identity in Southern Louisiana' (*LSoc* 29[2000] 237–58), trace the changing meaning of the term 'creole' through the settlement history; the term used to designate Whites only at first, was then used also for Blacks and people of mixed race (the connecting factor being French ancestry, use of French Creole and Catholic religion), whereas today the term 'creole' is used by members of the black community almost exclusively, who have become 'the keepers of the creole identity in modern Louisiana' (p. 255). Also related to Louisiana, Sylvie Dubois and Barbara Horvath investigate the role of women in the change from French to English in 'When the Music Changes, You Change Too: Gender and Language Change in Cajun English' (*LVC* 11[2000] 287–313). They find that (some) features that originally were due to imperfect language learning have been 'recycled' to indicate Cajun identity. They expand Labov's model of change from above and below, and differentiate four types of language change (origination, adoption, recycling, persistence) that are promoted by men and women differently.

On a historical note, Wolfgang Viereck, in 'Corpus-Based and Other Studies in Early American English' (*SN* 72[2000] 34–44), advocates a careful study of historical sources in order to delineate these early varieties, at the same time providing an overview of the material of the field, also describing sources for the study of Earlier African American English, which incidentally is our next topic in this overview.

This year AAVE is clearly the most studied variety of English again. An introduction to issues of AAVE written for a more general public is provided by John Russell Rickford and Russell John Rickford in *Spoken Soul: The Story of Black English*. Father and son trace attitudes towards and discussions about AAVE through various topics, including chapters on AAVE vocabulary and pronunciation (chapter 6) and AAVE grammar (chapter 7). They succeed in making the intricate system, especially of the AAVE verb phrase, accessible even to non-specialists. The Rickfords also discuss very fairly the hot issue of creole origin vs. English dialect influence on AAVE (in chapter 8), often conceding possible double influence of both sources. Also written for a wider public, John Baugh has made a valuable contribution to the background of the Ebonics debate with *Beyond Ebonics: Linguistic Pride and Racial Prejudice*, a book written from both a personal standpoint as an African American and a professional one as a sociolinguist. The link of these two perspectives should help linguists to understand the background of the furore that the Ebonics decision has caused and fuelled. Finally, also on a general level, is Geneva Smitherman's collection of her own writing of the past twenty-five years, *Talkin That Talk: Language, Culture and Education in African America* [1999], which includes a very personal account (in the introduction) of how 'Dr G.' proceeded 'from ghetto lady to critical linguist' (p. 1). As all chapters have appeared as separate papers before, they will not be discussed here in detail. Despite the time-span it covers, the division into five parts makes this collection a homogeneous whole, dealing both with the language theory and—the main part of this book—with educational, cultural and political issues, always written in Smitherman's informed yet highly polemical style and always from a very touching, personal viewpoint.

Much more narrowly linguistic in nature, and covering a wide range of phenomena of AAVE, is Xiaozhao Huang's *A Study of African-American Vernacular English in America's Middletown: Evidence of Linguistic Convergence.* In a real-time study across thirteen years (and for each of the linguistic communities) Huang analyses five phonological and twenty-three(!) syntactic variables, finding no evidence of linguistic divergence between AAVE as spoken in Muncie, Indiana and the local vernacular. However, occurrences for almost all phenomena are so low that no strong trends can be established. Generally, AAVE seems hardly different from White Vernacular English (WVE), even in the older data. Despite its title, then, if convergence has taken place, it must have occurred *before* the 1980s, the date of the older material. This book would also have benefited from a simple re-arrangement in tables and graphs that would have indicated apparent time-scales, as the mixed system employed obscures even those developments where a slight move towards WVE might have become visible.

The most notable emphasis this year in studies on AAVE is historical, with many publications adding to our understanding of the history of this variety (Earlier AAE). The most important contribution to this area comes from a range of scholars dealing with the diaspora communities, collected in Poplack, ed., *The English History of African American English.* As the title indicates, Poplack and her authors argue firmly against a creole origin of AAVE, dealing in much detail with morpho-phonological, morpho-syntactic and syntactic variables and also looking at the more general socio-historical context that led to the emergence of AAVE as we know it today. The contributions make up a homogeneous whole, the arguments being based on a careful investigation of a small range of corpora of Early AAE (the diaspora communities and the Ex-Slave Recordings) and the findings being compared both with available material from creole studies, in some cases creole corpora, and with studies on the situation in (white) English dialects, as well as with historical data. Not surprisingly (given the title of this collection), all contributions come to the conclusion that Early AAE has much more in common with English non-standard dialects than with creoles, and firmly argue for an 'Anglicist' rather than a creole origin of AAVE.

We will now turn to some of the studies in this collection in more detail. James A. Walker's article on 'Rephrasing the Copula: Contraction and Zero in Early African American English' (pp. 35–72), Shana Poplack, Sali Tagliamonte and Ejike Eze's chapter on 'Reconstructing the Source of Early African American English Plural Marking: A Comparative Study of English and Creole' (pp. 73–105), which compares AAE to Nigerian Pidgin English, and Darin M. Howe and James A. Walker's contribution, 'Negation and the Creole-Origins Hypothesis: Evidence from Early African American English' (pp. 109–40) will be dealt with in the following section on creolistics. One interesting result of the last of these articles that should be mentioned here in passing is that Howe and Walker show the use of *ain't* for *didn't* to be a recent and spectacular new development of AAVE. Sali Tagliamonte and Jennifer Smith discuss 'Old *Was*, New Ecology: Viewing English through the Sociolinguistic Filter' (pp. 141–71), claiming that non-standard *was* (where standard English prescribes *were*) has been a feature of dialects since ME, if not OE, times. It is used especially with NPs, and with *you* in the north of England. This is still the case today, such that Early AAE seems to pattern with northern British (and Scottish) English, the dialect group that arguably influenced the language of the southern United States most. Gerard van Herk's contribution 'The Question Question: Auxiliary Inversion in Early African American English' (pp. 175–97) and the chapter by Gunnel Tottie and Dawn Harvie, 'It's All Relative: Relativization Strategies in Early African American English' (pp. 198–230) also find more parallels with other non-standard varieties than with creoles. These two papers are again discussed in more detail in the following section. Finally, the socio-historical background for these 'Anglicist' claims is provided by Salikoko S. Mufwene's contribution, 'Some Sociohistorical Inferences about the Development of African American English' (pp. 233–63), where he argues that the demographic situation in the southern United States would at no time have favoured the development of a creole, and importation of slaves from the Caribbean would also not have influenced the founder population in the southern United States.

Ulrich Miethaner strikes a more cautious note, arguing against an uncritical use of modified orthographic representations of non-standard speech in 'Orthographic Transcriptions of Non-Standard Varieties: The Case of Earlier African-American English' (*JSoc* 4[2000] 534–60). Divergent transcriptions of the Samaná English Corpus and the Ex-Slave Recordings show that different transcriptions may have serious implications for morpho-syntactic analyses—in particular, the process of transcription always implies 'pre-analysis', and transcribers (and, subsequently, researchers) should be very aware of these problems. Walt Wolfram, Erik R. Thomas and Elaine W. Green tackle the problem of Early AAE from a different perspective in 'The Regional Context of Earlier African American Speech: Evidence for Reconstructing the Development of AAVE' (*LSoc* 29[2000] 315–55). They investigate four generations of AAVE speakers in the isolated Hyde County, North Carolina, for phonological and morphological variables, and find accommodation to the surrounding local dialect for some features, whereas copula absence and third-person -*s* marking are maintained. Younger AAVE speakers, on the other hand, can be shown to be moving towards a more generalized AAVE norm. Drawing on much the same data, Walt Wolfram and Dan Beckett investigate in more detail 'The Role of the Individual and Group in Earlier African American English' (*AS* 75[2000] 3–33). Considerable inter-speaker variation can only partly be explained by sociolinguistic factors. Other factors, such as the amount and kind of contact and, especially, attitudes, probably also play a decisive role. Alexander Kautzsch discovers 'Liberian Letters and Virginian Narratives: New Sources of Earlier African American English' (*AS* 75[2000] 34–53). An investigation of several features of negation shows that the ex-slave narratives from Virginia paint a much more reliable picture of Early AAE, as the letters from Liberia must have been purged, especially of many stigmatized features such as *ain't* or multiple negation during the process of writing.

Moving to present-day AAVE, Shana Poplack and Sali Tagliamonte investigate in much detail 'The Grammaticization of *going to* in (African American) English' (*LVC* 11[2000] 315–42). Statistical comparisons of a range of varieties of English reveal stages in the process whereby *going to* is becoming more grammatical—losing its meaning of movement, and becoming a pure future marker, and individual varieties are situated on this scale. Surprisingly, *gon'* and *gonna* come out as realizational differences of the phonetic environments, with identical constraint hierarchies for AAVE and the other varieties, which again strongly speaks against a creole origin for *gonna* in AAVE.

On a more discourse-oriented level, Karla D. Scott is 'Crossing Cultural Borders: "Girl" and "Look" as Markers of Identity in Black Women's Language Use' (*D&S* 11[2000] 237–48), finding that *girl* used by black women expresses solidarity, whereas *look* is used in situations of boundary crossing (in talking with men or Whites). Finally, Eduardo Bonilla-Silva and Tyrone A. Forman, '"I'm not a Racist but …": Mapping White College Students' Racial Ideology in the USA' (*D&S* 11[2000] 50–85), find that, in interviews, white students are much more prejudiced towards other ethnic groups than they admit in surveys.

Closing our overview of sociolinguistic topics this year we briefly move to gender-related studies. A very basic introduction to the topic is provided by Angela Goddard and Lindsey Meân Patterson in *Language and Gender*, obviously aimed at the level of beginning undergraduate students and even below. Full of cartoons and activities, and rather brief and unilluminating on the text side, this short book can at best serve as the very first introduction to this complex field. Gender differences are also the topic of a range of more discourse-oriented studies this year. Jenny Cheshire investigates 'The Telling or the Tale? Narratives and Gender in Adolescent Friendship Networks' (*JSoc* 4[2000] 234–62), where she finds that narratives are an important building block in the construction of friendships, and it is the central members of networks that tend to tell a large number of narratives. Typically, for girls this happens in 'dyads', as they tend to pair off with a 'best friend', whereas boys move in more varied friendship groups and thus narratives are often co-constructed, told by good friends. Deborah Cameron is concerned with 'Styling the Worker: Gender and the Commodification of Language in the Globalized Service Economy' (*JSoc* 4[2000] 323–47). Her investigation of the linguistic and vocal 'styling' prescribed for telephone operators in call centres in the UK shows that the official service style uses symbolic markers of femininity (such as prosody, voice quality, speech acts, choice of address terms, politeness formulae) and indeed prescribes them to both sexes in order to portray qualities popularly associated with women's language such as expressiveness, caring, empathy and sincerity. Jennifer Dailey O'Cain investigates 'The Sociolinguistic Distribution of and Attitudes towards Focuser *like* and Quotative *like*' (*JSoc* 4[2000] 60–80). In this three-part study she finds that *like* is particularly used by younger speakers, but without gender difference. Interestingly, however, young women are *perceived* to be using *like* more. Dailey O'Cain also finds that *like* is evaluated positively along solidarity-based scales (speakers are perceived as attractive, cheerful, friendly), but negatively in terms of status (speakers are perceived as less educated, less intelligent and less interesting).

10. New Englishes and Creolistics

While we welcome a large number of publications dealing with individual aspects of the New Englishes, only one of them discusses these varieties in general, namely Gabriella Mazzon's analysis of 'The Ideology of the Standard and the Development of Extraterritorial Englishes' (in Wright, ed., pp. 73–92), in which she compares the evolution of first-language varieties such as Australian English or Canadian English on the one hand, and second-language varieties such as Indian English or Nigerian English on the other, with regard to status, language attitudes and education.

Work on individual New Englishes in the Southern hemisphere includes a study of 'Event and Story Schemas in Australian Aboriginal English Discourse' (*EWW* 21[2000] 261–89) by Ian G. Malcolm and Judith Rochecouste, who have identified four specifically Aboriginal discourse patterns and a number of discourse markers in the storytelling of Yamatij children. Graeme Kennedy and Shunji Yamazaki also deal with substrate features in their study of 'The Influence of Maori on the New Zealand English Lexicon' (in Kirk, ed., pp. 33–44) in which they compare the Maori component in the *Dictionary of New Zealand English* and the spoken and written component of the Wellington Corpus of New Zealand English, revealing the differences between those Maori lexemes recorded in the dictionary (mostly for flora and fauna) and those actually used in spoken and written language (mostly place-names and proper names). The ongoing sound changes in NZE are the topic of two articles based on the material collected by the research group at the University of Canterbury. Catherine Watson, Margaret Maclagan and Jonathan Harrington provide 'Acoustic Evidence for Vowel Change in New Zealand English' (*LVC* 12[2000] 51–68) in words like HEED, HID, HEAD, HAD, HUD, HERD, HEAR and HAIR, based on recordings made in 1948 and 1995. Nicola Woods looks at 'Archaism and Innovation in New Zealand English' (*EWW* 21[2000] 109–50) with regard to the pronunciation of the MOUTH, TRAP, DRESS and KIT vowels on the basis of a comparison of the 1948 recordings also used in the article by Watson *et al.* and younger family members from the same families, finding that, with regard to the features under analysis, NZE is more innovative than conservative.

Moving on to English in Asia, we note that the linguistic situation in Hong Kong has received a lot of attention. Cluster reduction in learner English is the topic of Long Peng and Jane Setter's article on 'The Emergence of Systematicity in the English Pronunciations of Two Cantonese-Speaking Adults in Hong Kong' (*EWW* 21[2000] 81–108). Two papers deal with 'Hong Kong's New English Language Policy in Education'. Stephen Evans, using the above as his title (*WEn* 19[2000] 185–204), examines the language policies, actual language use and language attitudes between the 1940s and today, concluding that the new policy has stopped the convergence process between English-medium and Chinese-medium secondary schools, while Keith Morrison and Icy Lui concentrate on the 'Ideology, Linguistic Capital and the Medium of Instruction in Hong Kong' (*JMMD* 21[2000] 471–86), suggesting that a new kind of linguistic imperialism is put in place with the forced spread of Putonghua in the school system.

In his introductory article to the issue of *IJSL* dedicated to language use in Hong Kong, Singapore and Taiwan, Tope Omoniyi stresses the shared characteristics of these three countries and provides the analytical background for 'Islands and Identity in Sociolinguistics: A Theoretical Perspective' (*IJSL* 143[2000] 1–13).

Rodney R. Jones looks at an English-only text type in his report on '"Potato Seeking Rice": Language, Culture and Identity in Gay Personal Ads in Hong Kong' (*IJSL* 143[2000] 33–61), comparing the Hong Kong ads with Western ads, both straight and gay, and identifying the specific textual and linguistic features of the Hong Kong data. John E. Joseph develops 'The Tao of Identity in Heteroglossic Hong Kong' (*IJSL* 143[2000] 15–31), looking at language policy and actual language use, especially with regard to the three major languages Cantonese, Putonghua and English. Along similar lines, Yuling Pan provides a comparative analysis in 'Code-Switching and Social Change in Guanzhou and Hong Kong' (*IJSL* 146[2000] 21–41), comparing mainland and island code-switching patterns in service encounters. Not surprisingly, English plays a minor role in the Hong Kong data as well, while Putonghua gains ground at the expense of both English and Cantonese.

Two articles on language use in Singapore can be found in the special issue of *IJSL* mentioned above. Anna Kwan-Terry looks at 'Language Shift, Mother Tongue and Identity in Singapore' (*IJSL* 143[2000] 85–106), showing that the linguistic situation has rapidly changed over the past few years, with many Singaporeans shifting away from the regional languages originally spoken in their families to either English, Mandarin or both, with a widely spoken non-standard variety of English (Singlish) increasingly viewed as a marker of national identity. Anthea Fraser Gupta uses Singapore as an example to elaborate her views on 'Bilingualism in the Cosmopolis' (*IJSL* 143[2000] 7–19), challenging traditional concepts of bilingualism on the basis of the linguistic reality of multilingual speakers in a multilingual urban setting. Adam Brown's contribution on 'Tongue Slips and Singapore English Pronunciation' (*EnT* 16:ii[2000] 31–5) sheds more light on this situation because his corpus of Singaporean tongue slips proves that the interfering element may come from outside the target language. On the lexical level, Vincent B.Y. Ooi looks at 'Asian or Western Realities? Collocations in Singaporean-Malaysian English' (in Kirk, ed., pp. 73–89), comparing electronic versions of Singaporean and Malaysian newspapers with the British and American Collins-Cobuild Bank of English Corpus and identifying different collocational patterns for the Eastern and Western hemispheres. The code-switching and code-shifting devices of participants in Malaysian business training sessions are the topic of Shanta Nair-Venugopal's study, 'English, Identity and the Malaysian Workplace' (*WEn* 19[2000] 205–13), in which she identifies Malaysian English as the predominant sociolect to which code-mixing and shifting into Malay are added for the establishment of specific social and cultural identities. Jan Tent discusses the problems arising in the development of an 'English Lexicography in Fiji' (*EnT* 16:iii[2000] 22–8), such as orthographic conventions, the differentiation between code-switching and borrowing and the identification of nonce-borrowings. Finally, to conclude the section on the Asian Englishes, we find two publications on Indian English. Raja Ram Mehrotra has conducted a pilot project on 'Indian Pidgin English: Myth and Reality' (*EnT* 16:iii[2000] 49–52), seeking to identify the features and possible communicative contexts for this relatively unknown variety. Rakesh M. Bhatt discusses 'Optimal Expressions in Indian English' (*ELL* 4[2000] 69–95) shedding light on syntactic differences, e.g. concerning *wh*-questions, focus constituents or null arguments, between Standard Indian English and Vernacular Indian English within the framework of Optimality Theory.

Turning to the African Englishes, we find Augustin Simo Bobda's comparative survey of the 'English Pronunciation in Sub-Saharan Africa as Illustrated by the NURSE Vowel' (*EnT* 16:iv[2000] 41–8), in which he uses the varying realizations of this Standard English vowel across the continent as a means of classifying the African Englishes into different groups. One of the lesser-known varieties in Simo Bobda's survey is briefly characterized with regard to status and features in Allestree E.C. Fisher's article 'Assessing the State of Ugandan English' (*EnT* 16:i[2000] 57–61, 110). A number of contributions in *IJSL* 141 deal with 'English in West Africa' (*IJSL* 141[2000] 27–38). Ayo Banjo's account does not only consider the Anglophone countries in the region, such as Nigeria or Ghana, but also the non-Anglophone countries, from Spanish Sahara to Cape Verde, examining the status of English, its influence on the indigenous languages, the rise of local varieties in the Anglophone countries and the changing language attitudes towards this former colonial language. The latter aspect is further elaborated in Efurosibina Adegbija's study of 'Language Attitudes in West Africa' (*IJSL* 141[2000] 75–100), which seeks to identify the relationship between the former colonial languages and the various indigenous languages, and discusses possible implications of the often ambiguous attitudes expressed by her informants. These factors certainly bear on 'Language Planning in West Africa' (*IJSL* 141[2000] 101–17), as discussed in Ayo Bamgbose's contribution to the issue. Bamgbose uses Cameroon, Sierra Leone and Cape Verde as representative examples of the typical sociolinguistic make-up of the countries under analysis. The author compares top-to-bottom and bottom-to-top approaches to language planning and comes to the conclusion that policy-making and implementation are often out of line. A micro-analysis of one West African speech community is undertaken by M.E. Kropp Dakubu in 'Multiple Bilingualisms and Urban Transitions: Coming to Accra' (*IJSL* 141[2000] 9–26), which studies the linguistic behaviour of a group of migrants from Bawku in north-east Ghana. The study shows that the general pattern of multilingualism is retained, but the role of individual languages is shifted, as in the case of English or Hausa, which are more important in Accra. Two articles deal with specific linguistic features of Nigerian English: Victoria A. Alabi works on the 'Semantics of Occupational Lexis in Nigerian English' (*WEn* 19[2000] 107–12), showing how semantic change diverging from international Standard English, for example *vendor* meaning newspaper-seller, can also affect intranational and international intelligibility. David Jowitt examines 'Patterns of Nigerian English Intonation' (*EWW* 21[2000] 63–80), reporting results from an experimental study based on Cruttendon's model of intonation, and identifying typical features of Nigerian English intonation, such as a general simplification of intonation patterns, a tendency towards end stress and falls, and a lexical pitch accent.

The bulk of publications on English in Africa is again concerned with SAE. In his discussion of the 'Sociocultural and Linguistic Corollaries of Ethnicity in South African Society' (*IJSL* 144[2000] 7–17), Ernst F. Kotze identifies two opposing tendencies at work, namely the increasing awareness of the necessity to strengthen the indigenous languages and the trend to use English as a lingua franca. This is exemplified in Gary Barkhuizen and Vivian de Klerk's study of 'Language Contact and Ethnolinguistic Identity in an Eastern Cape Army Camp' (*IJSL* 144[2000] 95–117, see also *EWW* 19[1998] 33–69 reviewed in *YWES* 79[2000] 100), which shows that, regardless of the speakers' first language, English was used for general communication and instruction, while all eleven official languages were used in less formal contexts. In her second contribution to the issue, Vivian de Klerk examines 'Language Shift in Grahamstown: A Case Study of Selected Xhosa-Speakers' (*IJSL* 144[2000] 87–110). Based on a questionnaire survey and interviews with twenty-six parents, de Klerk investigates ten variables for a language shift to English, such as economic perspectives, institutional support, education, linguistic networks, language attitudes or the role of the mass media. She concludes that the shift is well under way and that institutional support for languages like Xhosa is lacking. Mandatory language-mixing and code-switching, on the other hand, are part of the hybrid township ethnolinguistic identity described in '"I'm a Cleva!": The Linguistic Makeup of Identity in a South African Urban Environment' (*IJSL* 144[2000] 119–35) by Sarah Slabbert and Rosalie Finlayson. Ute Smit's account of 'Language Attitudes and Social Change: The Changing of Standard South African English' (in Deminger *et al.*, eds., pp. 83–97; cf. also *EWW* 17[1996] 77–109 reviewed in *YWES* 77[1998] 95) suggests that the most widely accepted variety of English will be an Africanized one, probably an educated form of Black SAE, a view also put forward in Pearl Ntlhakna's account of 'People's English: Language Policy in South Africa and its Impact on English in Education' (*EnT* 16:ii[2000] 11–17). A glimpse of actual language use in the education system is offered by S.O.S. Ncoko, R. Osman and K. Cockcroft, 'Codeswitching Among Multilingual Learners in Primary Schools in South Africa: An Exploratory Study' (*IJBEB* 3[2000] 225–41), based on tape-recordings from two schools in the Gauteng region of Johannesburg, which were analysed according to Carol Myers-Scotton's Markedness Model.

To round off the section on New Englishes, we would like to point out three contributions dealing with English in Puerto Rico, a variety with the status of an official language in a predominantly Spanish-speaking environment which has not received a lot of scholarly attention to date. Joan M. Fayer discusses the 'Functions of English in Puerto Rico' (*IJSL* 142[2000] 89–102), for example in the education system, the workplace, at home or in the media. Fayer found an increasing use of English even in informal settings, accompanied by other profound changes in linguistic behaviour, such as the naming of people or things. Two articles address the problem that English is no longer restricted in use and that most Puerto Ricans are bilingual to varying degrees, a fact that is still ignored by the education system. C. William Schweers Jr. and Madeleine Hudders therefore demand 'The Reformation and Democratization of English Education in Puerto Rico' (*IJSL* 142[2000] 63–87), in accordance with recent SLA research and models of bilingual education; Alicia Pousada's work on 'The Competent Bilingual in Puerto Rico' (*IJSL* 142[2000] 103–18) also concludes with a call for bilingual education, travel opportunities for students and exposure to various registers of English.

Bridging the gap between New Englishes and creolistics is Edgar Schneider's study 'Feature Diffusion vs. Contact Effects in the Evolution of New Englishes: A Typological Case Study of Negation Patterns' (*EWW* 21[2000] 201–30), in which he compares various types of negation in New Englishes and English-lexifier pidgins and creoles, assigning them to the categories of either feature diffusion from other varieties of English or of feature selection from an indigenous substrate.

Moving on to the various creoles spoken in the Caribbean and elsewhere, we can report the publication of two introductory textbooks on the subject, namely John

Holm's *An Introduction to Pidgins and Creoles* and Ishtla Singh's *Pidgins and Creoles*. Holm's book is a revised version of his 1988 classic *Pidgins and Creoles*, vol. i: *Theory and Structure*, which has been supplemented by a chapter on the socio-economic factors relevant in the genesis of individual Atlantic creoles and has profited much from the work of Holm's research group on creole syntax. Both books contain a detailed introduction dealing with possible definitions of pidgins and creoles and a chapter on creole genesis theory. While Holm discusses the relevant theories in chronological order, thus providing an excellent history of creolistics, Singh presents the major approaches in terms of their main elements, namely superstrate, substrate or linguistic universals. Additionally, Singh devotes a whole chapter to the discussion of the concept of the creole continuum, while Holm deals with this topic in his theory chapter. The bulk of Holm's book is taken up by a detailed comparison of the linguistic features of the Atlantic creoles, with separate chapters on phonology, morpho-syntax and lexico-semantics. Singh closes with a case-study of language use and language planning in Trinidad. With regard to their target audience, Singh's book is an excellent introductory textbook written in a very readable style from a native speaker's perspective (and accompanied by a glossary of linguistic terms), while Holm's book must be considered ideal for advanced students or as a reference work for linguists familiar with the field.

Two collections of essays, Neumann-Holzschuh and Schneider, eds., *Degrees of Restructuring in Creole Languages*, and McWhorter, ed., *Language Change and Language Contact in Pidgins and Creoles*, also contain contributions dealing with general issues in creolistics. John Holm, in the first collection, tackles conceptual aspects of 'Semi-Creolization: Problems in the Development of the Theory' (in Neumann-Holzschuh and Schneider, eds., pp. 19–40), using varieties such as AAVE or Afrikaans as examples to distinguish semi-creolization from decreolization. Philip Baker provides a detailed analysis of 'Theories of Creolization and the Degree and Nature of Restructuring' (pp. 41–63), scrutinizing four major approaches to creole genesis with regard to their position on restructuring. Salikoko S. Mufwene holds that 'Creolization is a Social, Not a Structural Process' (pp. 65–84), providing arguments against classifying creoles as a separate and special linguistic family on the basis of their structure. The opposite view is presented by John McWhorter in his attempt at 'Defining "Creole" as a Synchronic Term' (pp. 85–123) from a typological perspective based on his so-called 'creole prototype'. A number of contributions in the other volume address the theoretical models employed in creolistics. The question 'Are Creole Languages "Perfect" Languages?' (in McWhorter, ed., pp. 163–99) is pursued by Alain Kihm within the framework of the Chomskyan Minimalist Program. He concludes that they are not perfect languages, 'but they live on with the marks of perfection that the unnatural conditions of their birth forced on them' (p. 190). A similar theoretical approach is taken by John Victor Singler's investigation of 'Optimality Theory, the Minimal-Word constraint and the Historical Sequencing of Substrate Influence in Pidgin/Creole Genesis' (pp. 335–51), proving that the chronological sequence of substratal influences is a crucial point often overlooked in creolistics. Finally, George Lang explores the uses of chaos theory in creolistics in his contribution 'Chaos and Creoles: Towards a New Paradigm?' (pp. 443–57).

Comparative studies based on data from a large number of languages are also well represented. Mervyn C. Alleyne takes the diachronic approach and looks at language change in different creoles, discovering 'Opposite Processes in "Creolization"' (in Neumann-Holzschuh and Schneider, eds., pp. 125–33). An even more encompassing approach comparing 'The Fate of Subject Pronouns: Evidence from Creole and Non-Creole Languages' (in Neumann-Holzschuh and Schneider, eds., pp. 163–83) is taken by Susanne Michaelis, who traces diachronic change in the use of third person subject clitics or affixes in various creoles and a number of Indo-European languages. Mikael Parkvall has compiled demographic information from thirteen speech communities with Atlantic creoles as well as a list of features to determine their typological divergence from their lexifiers, and succeeds in 'Reassessing the Role of Demographics in Language Restructuring' (in Neumann-Holzschuh and Schneider, eds., pp. 185–213). John Holm and his international research group on comparative creole syntax have contributed 'A Comparative Study of Stativity and Time Reference' (McWhorter, ed., pp. 133–61), including data from seventeen creole languages with different lexifier languages, ranging from Sranan to Nubi Creole Arabic. They find that, with the exception of Papiamentu and Angolar Creole Portuguese, all varieties show remarkable similarities with regard to the use of unmarked verbs as opposed to those marked for anterior or past tense. However, Bickerton's claim about the universality of his creole prototype was not supported by the data. Another comparative study was undertaken by J. Clancy Clements and Ahmar Mahboob, focusing on 'Wh-Words and Question Formation in Pidgin/Creole Languages' (in McWhorter, ed., pp. 459–97) in almost thirty creoles, with Portuguese, Spanish, French and English lexifiers. Their analysis proves that the development of wh-words sheds light on the role of substrate influence and universal tendencies: whenever the languages involved did not share a structure, a choice was made according to universal tendencies such as semantic transparency. Along similar lines of comparative research, Philip Baker and Magnus Huber report on 'Constructing New Pronominal Systems from the Atlantic to the Pacific' (*Linguistics* 38:v[2000] 833–66) in thirteen English-lexifier pidgins and creoles. They show that, while most pronominal forms can easily be traced to their English source, their functions differ substantially from the English system. In addition, they seek to show that the lexical forms themselves were not selected on the basis of linguistic factors such as semantic transparency, but rather because of the extralinguistic behaviour (e.g. pointing) employed by the first speakers.

Moving on to research on the Atlantic creoles specifically, we welcome the publication of Mikael Parkvall's comprehensive study of the role of the substrate, *Out of Africa: African Influences in Atlantic Creoles*. Parkvall examines possible substrate influences from over 160 African languages in the areas of phonology, morpho-syntax and semantics and compares these linguistic results with demographic evidence from the period of creole genesis. The results for each chapter are summarized in very useful tables. While Parkvall's detailed analysis reveals fewer clear substrate features than he—a pronounced substratist—had expected, it certainly proves the superstratist and universalist camps wrong. There are also a number of puzzling results, such as the predominance of the Kwa languages and the pronounced differences in the phonology of French and English-lexifier creoles. Parkvall's book will certainly advance the study of the Atlantic creoles, especially with regard to the treatment of substrate versus superstrate. Along similar lines, a small-scale study of 'West Africanisms in Limonese Creole English' (*WEn* 19[2000] 155–71), a mesolectal creole spoken in Costa Rica, was conducted by Elizabeth Grace Winkler and Samuel Gyasi Obeng, who look at reduplication, ideophones, serial verbs and a number of lexical items. A superstrate feature, on the other hand, is the topic of Mark R. Southern's 'Caribbean Creoles as a Convergence Conduit: English *Boss* and *Overseer*, Ndjuká *Basía*, Sranan *Basja*, Jamaican *Busha*, and Dutch *Baas(-je)*' (*FLH* 21[2000] 189–246), which traces the spread and development of this originally Dutch lexeme in the Caribbean and the United States.

Of the individual Atlantic creoles, the radical creoles from Suriname again receive most scholarly attention. Ingo Plag and Christian Uffmann discuss 'Phonological Restructuring in Creole: The Development of Paragoge in Sranan' (in Neumann-Holzschuh and Schneider, eds., pp. 309–36), comparing modern Sranan with eighteenth-century data and evaluating the role of substrate influence, linguistic universals and universal tendencies in SLA acquisition. Mark Sebba tackles 'Orthography and Ideology: Issues in Sranan Spelling' (*Linguistics* 38:v[2000] 925–48), providing a historical overview of Sranan orthography and discussing the sociolinguistic factors, such as bilingualism, affecting the spelling practices of Sranan speakers. Donald Winford examines 'Irrealis in Sranan: Mood and Modality in a Radical Creole' (*JPCL* 15[2000] 63–125), attacking Bickerton's prototypical creole TMA system which subsumes all notions of future reference under the label 'irrealis'. Winford describes the semantics of Sranan modality, including both deontic and epistemic meanings. His detailed account could become the basis for a comparative study of creole modality, since the various aspects of this category have generally not been properly distinguished to date. Complementing his study of Sranan modality, Donald Winford also provides a detailed account of 'Tense and Aspect in Sranan and the Creole Prototype' (in McWhorter, ed., pp. 383–442), again providing counter-evidence against Bickerton's model and adopting Dahl's cross-linguistic approach instead. Tonjes Veenstra studies 'Verb Serialization and Object Position' (*Linguistics* 38:v[2000] 867–88) in Saramaccan within the framework of Larsonian VP-shell configurations. Bettina Migge sheds light on the 'Origin of the Syntax and Semantics of Property Items in the Surinamese Plantation Creole' (in McWhorter, ed., pp. 201–34), also known as Ndyuka. 'Property items' are lexemes referring to properties, qualities and characteristics of referents, usually classified as adjectives in traditional grammar, which also function as verbs in Ndyuka and other creoles.

A few other Caribbean creoles are also represented. Donald Winford discusses '"Intermediate Creoles" and Degrees of Change in Creole Formation: The Case of Bajan' (in Neumann-Holzschuh and Schneider, eds., pp. 215–46), providing a detailed survey of its history and an analysis of its TMA-system. Winford comes to the conclusion that so-called 'intermediate creoles' or semi-creoles like Bajan are developments in their own right rather than decreolized versions of an earlier basilectal creole or imperfect replicas of the superstrate. Paul Garrett reports on '"High" Kwéyòl: The Emergence of a Formal Creole Register in St. Lucia' (in McWhorter, ed., pp. 63–101). Due to its prolonged contact with English, the French-lexifier Kwéyòl of St. Lucia has developed an Anglicized formal register, while the vernacular English spoken by a majority of the population shows massive influence from Kwéyòl. Finally, Stephanie Durrleman provides an analysis of 'The Architecture of the Clause in Jamaican Creole' (*GG@G* 1[2000] 189–240) based on a generative model developed by Cinque, concentrating on the role of the preverbal markers in Jamaican Creole.

With regard to the African pidgins and creoles, Charles C. Mann, 'Reviewing Ethnolinguistic Vitality: The Case of Anglo-Nigerian Pidgin' (*JSoc* 4[2000] 458–74), looks at variables such as status, demographic factors and institutional support. He concludes that Nigerian Pidgin English is doing quite well in terms of vitality, although it is still denied official institutional support. Sali A. Tagliamonte provides a detailed study of grammaticalization in this pidgin, telling 'The Story of *kom* in Nigerian Pidgin English' (in McWhorter, ed., pp. 353–82). She looks at data from two generations of speakers from the Nigerian community in Ottawa, Canada, and finds that the grammaticalization process of *kom* as a marker of sequenced temporal relationships is nearly complete. Magnus Huber presents findings from a diachronic study on 'Restructuring in Vitro? Evidence from Early Krio' (in Neumann-Holzschuh and Schneider, eds., pp. 275–307). Huber provides a detailed study of the emergence of Krio mainly based on missionaries' accounts, concentrating on the variety spoken by the Liberated Africans and especially on its TMA-system. He also compares 100 lexical and grammatical features of early Krio and other West African pidgins, concluding that the jargon spoken by the Liberated Africans can be compared to a 'traders' English' with a large input from native speakers' foreigner talk.

Moving on to the pidgins and creoles of the Pacific, we find Siegel, ed., *Processes of Language Contact: Studies from Australia and the South Pacific*. In this volume, Harold Koch looks at 'The Role of Australian Aboriginal Languages in the Formation of Australian Pidgin Grammar: Transitive Verbs and Adjectives' (pp. 13–46), discussing the role of substrate influence in the development of the transitive marker *-im* and the adjectival marker *-fela*. Ian Malcolm traces the development of 'Aboriginal English: From Contact Variety to Social Dialect' (pp. 123–44), comparing the phonology, morpho-syntax and lexico-semantics of the early contact variety with recent data from Aboriginal speakers in Sydney. A rather unusual circumstance in the transmission of pidgin features is taken up by Jane Simpson, who found 'Camels as Pidgin-Carriers: Afghan Cameleers as a Vector for the Spread of Features of Australian Aboriginal Pidgins and Creoles' (pp. 195–244), thus explaining a large number of shared features in varieties spoken across a vast continent. Another account of transmission is Jennifer M. Munro's contribution on 'Kriol on the Move: A Case of Language Spread and Shift in Northern Australia' (pp. 245–70), arguing against the theory of multiple origins for Australian Kriol.

Miriam Meyerhoff's extensive sociolinguistic study, *Constraints on Null Subjects in Bislama (Vanuatu): Social and Linguistic Factors*, is accompanied by her largely typological article on 'The Emergence of Creole Subject–Verb Agreement and the Licensing of Null Subjects' (*LVC* 12[2000] 203–30), which is based on her previous research in Vanuatu. Focusing on the alternation between overt pronominal subjects and phonetically null subjects, Meyerhoff unravels the complex sociolinguistic situation in the town of Santo and the rural island of Malo, which includes Bislama and a number of local languages. She then proceeds to trace the increasing morpho-syntactic elaboration of the Bislama verb phrase, which leads her to the classification of Bislama as a creole. While her syntactic analysis focuses on the constraints on null subjects, she also treats the system of verbal inflection and the different types of serial verbs found in Bislama within the framework of generative grammar. Meyerhoff's study is significant since previous work on Bislama had not included a detailed analysis of null subjects and did not provide quantitative analyses of the data. A drawback of Meyerhoff's work, however, is pointed out by Terry Crowley in his discussion of 'Predicate Marking in Bislama' (in Siegel, ed., pp. 47–74), in which he discusses the particle *i* (commonly called 'predicate marker', but termed 'subject–verb agreement' by Meyerhoff) in relationship with the pronominal paradigm. Crowley reviews all previous studies dealing with this feature and concludes that Meyerhoff has not encountered all forms of the paradigm since her corpus was restricted to about 30,000 words. He points out that linguists have basically arrived at two different paradigms and proposes an alternative analysis based on the historical development of *i* and the synchronic data available.

Christine Jourdan states 'My Nephew is my Aunt', considering 'Features and Transformation of Kinship Terminology in Solomon Islands Pijin' (in Siegel, ed., pp. 99–122). She compares kinship terminology in Pijin and various indigenous languages and concludes that the Pijin system retains many features of the local substrate languages, but simplifies and regularizes the system based on semantic and cultural salience. Stephen Levey looks at 'Language Change and Adaptation on a Tok Pisin Newspaper' (*EnT* 16:i[2000] 20–5), giving examples for the way in which the Papua New Guinea newspaper *Wantok* functions as a proponent of syntactic elaboration, register diversification and standardization. Peter Mühlhäusler reports on 'The Development of the Life Form Lexicon of Tok Pisin' (in Neumann-Holzschuh and Schneider, eds., pp. 337–59), tracing lexical developments in this semantic field from the earliest sources onwards and pointing out that even first-language speakers do not have lexical items to refer to many indigenous plants and animals.

Finally in this section on pidgins and creoles from the Pacific, we turn to Hawaiian Creole English (HCE). Sarah Julienne Roberts discusses 'Nativization and the Genesis of Hawaiian Creole' (in McWhorter, ed., pp. 257–300), looking at the transition from Hawaiian Pidgin to HCE by examining demographic factors, sociolinguistic evidence of nativization and linguistic evidence such as structural elaboration. Jeff Siegel also looks at the time when HCE was formed, but concentrates on possible 'Substrate Influence in Hawai'i Creole English' (*LSoc* 29[2000] 197–236), especially from the two dominant ethnic groups at the time, Chinese and Portuguese. He examines features such as the emergence of articles, a TMA-system and complementation, and comes to the conclusion that Cantonese and Portuguese played an important role in the development of these features, especially by reinforcing particular features already used by pidgin speakers. He even argues that the differences between HCE and other creoles are largely due to the Portuguese substrate. On the level of language attitudes, Mary Lynn Fiore Ohama, Carolyn C. Gotay, Ian S. Pagano, Larry Boles and Dorothy D. Craven have arrived at 'Evaluations of Hawaii Creole English and Standard English' (*JLSP* 19:iii[2000] 357–77) on the basis of a matched-guise experiment at the University of Hawaii. The respondents rated the Standard English speakers high on traits such as 'intelligent', 'reliable' or 'upper-class', while the HCE speakers were rated highest on traits such as 'active', 'confident' or 'talkative' (the latter probably due to the prosody of HCE). With regard to the attractiveness ranking, it was the speakers and respondents' ethnicity that influenced the results.

To end this section on creolistics, we shall move on to AAVE. Poplack, ed., *The English History of African American English* is a comprehensive collection in which a number of contributors scrutinize the variables often linked to a creole origin of AAVE. As the title of the book indicates, the results of their work generally suggest an English origin for AAVE. First in line is James A. Walker's attempt at 'Rephrasing the Copula: Contraction and Zero in Early African American English' (pp. 35–72), in which he concludes that a treatment of the copula must distinguish the different semantic and syntactic functions of *be* and should be viewed in the larger context of copula variability in varieties of English. Shana Poplack, Sali Tagliamonte and Ejike Eze aim at 'Reconstructing the Source of Early African American English Plural Marking: A Comparative Study of English and Creole' (pp. 73–105), comparing three early sources of AAVE with the Nigerian material used in Tagliamonte's article discussed above. They conclude that AAVE plural marking is based on the system developing out of Middle English rather than a creole innovation, since it displays significant differences to the system of Nigerian Pidgin English. Darin M. Howe and James A. Walker examine 'Negation and the Creole-Origin Hypothesis: Evidence from Early African American English' (pp. 109–40), comparing four different types of negation in AAVE and English-lexifier creoles. Since all varieties of early AAVE and many non-standard varieties of English share these four constructions, while two of them are absent in most creoles, they argue that negation should not be used as an argument for a creole origin of AAVE. Gerard Van Herk poses 'The Question Question: Auxiliary Inversion in Early African American English' (pp. 175–97), again using evidence from eModE and non-standard English to show that this feature is not suitable to prove a creole origin of AAVE. Gunnel Tottie and Dawn Harvie finally provide a similar comparative analysis of relative clauses and conclude 'It's All Relative: Relativisation Strategies in Early African American English' (pp. 198–230). Alexander Kautsch and Edgar W. Schneider take an intermediate position, arguing for 'Differential Creolization: Some Evidence from Earlier African American Vernacular English in South Carolina' (in Neumann-Holzschuh and Schneider, eds., pp. 247–74), attempting to prove that South Carolina can be divided into areas of higher and lower degrees of creolization in early AAVE. All of these publications make it clear that the extreme stances from the creolist and dialectologist camps in AAVE research can no longer be regarded as tenable.

11. Pragmatics and Discourse Analysis

This section is not complete due to the fact that this reviewer took over at a very late stage. Consequently, only journal articles published on this topic will be reviewed this year; books published in 2000 will be reviewed in the next volume. The articles reviewed mirror a broad range of interests, but studies on conversation analysis, bilingualism, and verbal irony are particularly prominent this year.

We will start with conversation analysis. Emanuel A. Schegloff in 'Overlapping Talk and the Organization of Turn-Taking for Conversation' (*LSoc* 29[2000] 1–63) sets out to develop a complementary component of turn-taking organization in talk-in-interaction. He claims that this component, the 'overlap resolution device', is needed to deal with cases in which the basic feature of 'one party talking at a time' is not achieved. Margaret Selting's 'The Construction of Units in Conversational Talk' (*LSoc* 29[2000] 477–517) examines the notions of Turn-Constructional Unit (TCU) and Transition Relevance Place (TRP) within the context of 'larger projects' (p. 482), such as descriptions or stories. She briefly discusses two assumptions which can be made here: is a 'larger project' just one TCU, which ends in a TRP and can be divided into smaller units, or does it consist of several TCUs? She does not reject the first assumption but adopts the second as the more generally accepted view. She then argues that there are TCUs which do not end in TRPs and that most of the TCUs which make up a 'larger project' are of this type. She also claims that a determination of TCUs and possible turns cannot be based on syntactic and prosodic features alone but that the semantic, pragmatic and sequential context in which these features occur must also be taken into consideration. In the following studies elements of conversation analysis are employed to identify specific types of speech events. Carmen Gregori-Signes uses H. Sacks, E. Schegloff and G. Jefferson's account of turn-taking organization (*Language* 50[1974]) to develop a system which—according to the author's claim—makes it possible to define any type of speech event, and she employs this system to classify 'The Tabloid Talkshow as a Quasi-Conversational Type of Face-to-Face Interaction' (*Pragmatics* 10[2000] 195–213). In 'Interaction in the Oral Proficiency Interview: Problems of Validity' (*Pragmatics* 10[2000] 215–31), Marysia Johnson addresses the question of whether oral proficiency interviews 'measure speaking ability in the context of a conversation' (p. 215). She describes conversation and types of interviews as speech events, presents data from oral proficiency interviews, and argues that the results of her study show that oral proficiency interviews must be seen as testing speaking ability in the context of an interview, more specifically, a survey research interview. Alison Imbens-Bailey and Allyssa McCabe, 'The Discourse of Distress: A Narrative Analysis of Emergency Calls to 911' (*L&C* 20[2000] 275–96), examine the discourse structure of emergency calls to determine which discourse strategies are employed by callers and dispatchers.

The next batch of studies are all concerned with bilingualism but focus on quite different aspects. Penelope Gardner-Chloros, Reeva Charles, and Jenny Cheshire, 'Parallel Patterns? A Comparison of Monolingual Speech and Bilingual Codeswitching Discourse' (*JPrag* 32[2000] 1305–41), argue that bilinguals may frequently use code-switching in conversation but may also speak monolingually in the same conversation. Therefore, Gardner-Chloros, Charles, and Cheshire use monolingual and bilingual passages of conversation to explore the realization of discourse functions through code-switching or monolingual strategies. Pragmatic transfer is the topic of the following two articles. Using Saul Rosenzweig's [1978] 'Picture-Frustration Test' in her study, Donna Hurst Tatsuki, 'If My Complaints Could Passions Move: An Interlanguage Study of Aggression' (*JPrag* 32[2000] 1003–17), follows a psychological approach to examine complaints as a response to stress and frustration. Her findings suggest that Japanese speakers transfer their L1 complaint behaviour to L2 (English) contexts but tend to use an inadequate degree of severity in L2 complaints. Rosângela Souto Silva, 'Pragmatics, Bilingualism, and the Native Speaker' (*L&C* 20[2000] 161–78), is interested in pragmatic transfer both from L1 to L2 and from L2 to L1. She asked the participants in her study to judge the appropriateness of the use of directives beginning with *Why don't you* in Portuguese and English. Evaluating the results of her study, Silva finds that the length of a speaker's exposure to an L2 environment is an important factor here. She goes on to argue that foreign language teaching should aim at giving 'intercultural communication competence' rather than L2 'native-like' competence (p. 173). Intercultural communication is the cue for Diana Eades, '*I don't think it's an answer to the question*: Silencing Aboriginal Witnesses in Court' (*LSoc* 29[2000] 161–95). She uses data from courtroom interaction in Australian law courts to discuss how Aboriginal witnesses are kept from making statements which they consider relevant. Eades investigates interaction during 'examination-in-chief', in which witnesses are questioned by their own lawyer and by the judge. She argues that there is no binding relation between the syntactic structure of questions and a controlling function but that interruptions and metalinguistic comments made by lawyers and judges play an important role. Eades sees a connection between the occurrence of interruptions and metalinguistic comments and legal professionals' unfamiliarity with Aboriginal lifestyle and culture.

Two articles are concerned with deixis this year. Kelly D. Glover's 'Proximal and Distal Deixis in Negotiation Talk' (*JPrag* 32[2000] 915–26) focuses on place deixis. Glover finds that a speaker's decision in favour of proximal or distal deixis can be influenced by aspects other than spatial distance. The choice of deictic elements may also reflect politeness strategies, turn organization, and the speaker's attitude towards the referent. Jon Hindmarsh and Christian Heath, 'Embodied Reference: A Study of Deixis in Workplace Interaction' (*JPrag* 32[2000] 1855–78), examine the elements used to refer to specific objects. They describe how speakers combine the use of deictic expressions with movements, gestures and other actions designed to make it easy for the hearer to identify the referent. The methods used to refer to specific objects, so Hindmarsh and Heath claim, shape—and are themselves shaped by—the organization of activities at the workplace.

The workplace is also the setting of the first of the following studies on politeness. Christina Wasson, 'Caution and Consensus in American Business Meetings' (*Pragmatics* 10[2000] 457–81), investigates how the feeling of being subjected to surveillance influences the way employees interact in business meetings. She finds that in a surrounding where non-alignment and outspokenness are likely to have negative consequences, employees develop strategies which help them—or other team members—to return to a position of alignment without loss of face. Janie Rees-Miller, 'Power, Severity, and Context in Disagreement' (*JPrag* 32[2000] 1087–111), investigates the use of linguistic markers of disagreement in the context of academic discourse. She employs P. Brown and S. Levinson's (CUP [1987]) factors of power and severity, but goes on to argue that other factors, such as the pedagogical context and the topic of disagreement, need to be considered too, to understand the choice of linguistic markers.

The following articles are concerned with speech acts. Daniel Marcu, 'Perlocutions: The Achilles' Heel of Speech Act Theory' (*JPrag* 32[2000] 1719–41), proposes a new approach to the conception of perlocutionary acts. He claims that some of the traditional assumptions within speech act theory need to be revised, and suggests changes. He also sets out to develop a framework which makes it possible to estimate the likelihood that a message will be persuasive. Anna Papafragou, 'On Speech-Act Modality' (*JPrag* 32[2000] 519–38), argues against Eve Sweetser's (CUP [1990]) proposal to establish a new category of modality called speech-act modality. Using the concept of metarepresentation, Papafragou reanalyses the examples put forward by Sweetser and claims that they can all be explained using the existing, traditional modality categories. Steve Nicolle argues against a distinction between 'Communicated and Non-Communicated Acts in Relevance Theory' (*Pragmatics* 10[2000] 233–45). He claims that there are no non-communicated speech acts and that such a distinction makes relevance theory inconsistent.

Irony is the topic of the next articles to be discussed. Herbert L. Colston, 'On Necessary Conditions for Verbal Irony Comprehension' (*P&C* 8[2000] 277–324), suggests a modification of the set of conditions for verbal irony comprehension as proposed in literature on verbal irony. The author agrees that an ironic comment must 'allude to violated expectations' (p. 279), and adds that the comment must point out the contrast between expectation and experienced situation. He argues, however, that the second condition is not pragmatic insincerity but a flouting of any one of the maxims of Grice's co-operative principle. Colston nevertheless emphasizes that even his improved set of conditions might not be sufficient to explain all occurrences of verbal irony. Salvatore Attardo's 'Irony as Relevant Inappropriateness' (*JPrag* 32[2000] 793–826) begins with a discussion of the research done on irony. Attardo then goes on to present his own theory, which has Grice's co-operative principle as its basis. In the development of this theory, which includes the author's concept of contextual appropriateness, Attardo incorporates new elements into Grice's co-operative principle, among them a fifth maxim, 'be appropriate' (p. 823). Herbert L. Colston and Jennifer O'Brien, 'Contrast and Pragmatics in Figurative Language: Anything Understatement Can Do, Irony Can Do Better' (*JPrag* 32[2000] 1557–83), use the concept of contrast effects to explain why verbal irony and understatement achieve different degrees of success in their performance of the same pragmatic functions. They argue that this is a result of the fact that verbal irony and understatement create different degrees of contrast between an expected situation and the actually experienced situation.

There are two more articles which, as they cannot easily be grouped with any of the previous studies, are presented here separately. In her analysis of 'The Construction of Conflicting Accounts in Public Participation TV' (*LSoc* 29 [2000] 357–77), Joanna Thornborrow focuses on the use of the conversational historic present in second versions of stories as opposed to the use of the narrative past in first versions. She suggests that this shift is a device speakers use to make their own account of the story more believable and convincing than that given by a previous speaker. Jef Verschueren presents some 'Notes on the Role of Metapragmatic Awareness in Language Use' (*Pragmatics* 10[2000] 439–56), in which he explains two functions of metapragmatic awareness—anchoring and reflexive conceptualization—and briefly discusses the social implications of metapragmatic functioning.

This year saw the publication of the first issue of the *Journal of Historical Pragmatics*. Andreas H. Jucker (Justus Liebig University, Giessen) and Irma Taavitsainen (University of Helsinki) are the editors of this new journal, and they also contributed one of the articles in the first issue, 'Diachronic Speech Act Analysis: Insults from Flyting to Flaming' (*JHPrag* 1[2000] 67–95). The journal is intended to provide 'an interdisciplinary forum for theoretical, empirical and methodological work at the intersection of pragmatics and historical linguistics', and is to appear twice a year. Most of the articles in its first two issues were presented at the Sixth International Pragmatics Conference in Reims, 19–24 July 1998. They are grouped into three sections, of which the first comprises papers relating to pragmatic factors in language change, the second concerns studies on diachronic speech-act analysis, and the third presents articles relating to data problems in historical pragmatics. The contributions in each section are introduced by the discussants of the corresponding sessions at the conference.

12. Stylistics

Stylistic studies this year have provided a rich and varied crop, and the Festschrift presented to Peter Verdonk undoubtedly deserves pride of place in this section. Bex, Burke and Stockwell, eds., *Contextualized Stylistics: In Honour of Peter Verdonk*, offers an interesting survey of the current state of the field and, instead of being a simple medley of diverse contributions, has the advantage of offering a series of studies which explore, as the editors note in their foreword, the importance of context—widely understood as co-text, historical/cultural background and reader's interpretative positions—in studies of language in literature. Most contributors to the volume also take as the point of departure for their work topics and issues which recur in Verdonk's work, turning this collection of essays into a fitting homage to his contribution to stylistics. The volume opens with Walter Nash's 'The Writing on the Wall', an entertaining and deeply illuminating piece on the 'dialogic challenge' and 'healthily subversive work' (p. 14) enshrined in both real and simulated graffiti. Peter Stockwell's '(Sur)real Stylistics: From Text to Contextualizing' offers an analysis of a poem by London surrealist poet Hugh Sykes Davies together with an interesting discussion of the place of context and the paths literary stylistics can follow to transcend a mere dissection of data. Willie Van Peer, in 'Hidden Meanings', addresses the relation between stylistics and hermeneutics in the course of a study of Auden's 'Musée de Beaux Arts', concluding that what interpretation does, by exposing the elusiveness of the meaning of a text, is to give the reader reasons to return to the reading experience. In 'The Tip of the Iceberg: Real Texts, Long Texts and Mental Representations', Keith Green questions the usefulness cognitive linguistics has attached to mental representations and space in the analysis of discourse. Tony Bex bravely engages with Alexander Pope's didactic and satiric verse in 'Augustan Balance and Cognitive Contexts: An Approach to the Study of Pope', and explores the role of the reader as part of the context of a text in the interpretative process, taking issue with the way in which cognitive linguistics has been developed in stylistics. Michael Burke's 'Distant Voices: The Vitality of Yeats' Dialogic Verse' contains a Bakhtinian analysis of 'Leda and the Swan' and 'The Song of Wandering Aengus' and shows the dialogic nature which characterizes the discourse situation in these two poems. Bouwe Postmus, in 'The Woe that Is in Marriage', offers a reading of Seamus Heaney's 'The Wife's Tale' and discusses its relation to Chaucer's *Wife of Bath's Tale*. E.M. Knottenbelt studies the metrical peculiarities of Donne's poetry in 'What was John Donne Hearing? A Study in Sound Sense', and shows that the rhythm of Donne's 'strong lines' is suited to his continuous exploration of a mind at work. In 'Language and Context: Jane Gardam's *Bilgewater*', Mick Short, Jonathan Culpeper and Elena Semino analyse the opening prologue of Gardam's novel in detail and show how it creates a context for the reader to interpret the novel, an interpretation which the reader has to revise when the novel's epilogue re-contextualizes the prologue. New tendencies in the speech of characters in recent fiction is the topic of Michael Toolan's 'Quasi-Transcriptional Speech: A Compensatory Spokenness in Contemporary Anglo-Irish Literary Fiction', which shows how novelists writing in English are resorting to 'direct speech' which increasingly contains features such as ungrammaticality, repetition, structurally fractured sentences and incomplete relative clauses aiming to make characters sound more naturalistic but risking alienating the reader. In 'Joycean Sonicities', Peter de Voogd shows that James Joyce exploited the onomatopoeic potential of language in *Ulysses* and demonstrates that his sonic experiments are only rendered meaningful by contextual clues. Jean-Jacques Weber, in 'Educating the Reader: Narrative Technique and Evaluation in Charlotte Perkins Gilman's *Herland*', studies how the reader's generic and evaluative expectations are defeated in a feminist utopia which turns out to be written from a male, not a female, point of view, and which makes readers question or revise notions of gender relations through evaluative adverbs and adjectives, and evaluative comments, metaphors and lexical innovations. In 'Language, Text and Discourse: Robert Browning's "Meeting at Night" and "Parting at Morning"', Gerard Steen takes Peter Verdonk's work on Philip Larkin as his point of departure and proposes an analysis of language, text and discourse in Browning from an empirical rather than hermeneutic perspective. In 'Tristram Shandy's Narratees', Gene Moore explores the difficulties of applying the notion of 'narratee' to Laurence Sterne's experimental novel, and concludes that there is a need to revise the term to make it really useful within narratological studies. Text and context in Shakespeare is the topic of H.G. Widdowson's 'The Unrecoverable Context', an essay, as the author claims, in speculative stylistics written with a festive air which is not an obstacle to a serious warning on the possible incompatibility between modern stage practice and the contextualizing and characterizing functions of much of Shakespeare's dramatic language. The last essay in this Festschrift is Paul Simpson's 'Satirical Humour and Cultural Context: With a Note on the Curious Case of Father Todd Unctuous', a study of comic discourse in context which develops the notion of satirical discourse beyond the 'literary' by obtaining its data from the television series *Father Ted*. Ronald Carter's Afterword succinctly closes a volume which is not only of great use in itself but which will surely redirect the reader to re-contextualize and return to Peter Verdonk's work in stylistics.

Two other important books published this year are Laura Hidalgo-Downing's *Negation, Text Worlds, and Discourse: The Pragmatics of Fiction* and Peter Stockwell's *The Poetics of Science Fiction*. Both of them will no doubt turn out to be studies which will be much quoted in the future. The way negation works in discourse is the central concern of Hidalgo-Downing's monograph, which provides a dynamic model of negation as a complex discourse phenomenon extending beyond the boundaries of the strictly syntactic. The cognitive dimension of processing and understanding negation is another central element, and this enables her to explore issues insufficiently studied in other approaches to negation, such as the discourse function of contradiction. The usefulness of a text-world model as a tool for the analysis of a work of fiction—Joseph Heller's *Catch-22*—is amply demonstrated. Chapter 1 shows the position of this study in the context of contemporary stylistic practice; chapter 2 provides an updated critical review of negation in a wide spectrum of fields, including logic, philosophy of language, psychology, grammar and discourse pragmatics; chapter 3 explores negation with the help of Paul Werth's text-world model while chapter 4 considers negation in relation to frame semantics and schema theory, with suggestions for application in the analysis of humour; chapter 5 applies the integrated model built up in the previous chapters to the analysis of the discourse functions of negation in *Catch-22*, and chapter 6 brings the book to a close with suggestions for further research in negation. Hidalgo-Downing's book offers an insightful study of *Catch-22* and a model for the understanding of negation in discourse which integrates its semantic, pragmatic and cognitive aspects and proves how much can be said and communicated by negating. *The Poetics of Science Fiction* is the third title in the Textual Explorations series, edited by Mick Short and Elena Semino, which has already produced two other seminal monographs in stylistics by Semino and Werth (see *YWES* 78[1999] 139 and *YWES* 80[2001] 103–4 respectively). In this new addition to the series, Stockwell explores not only the language but also the narrative and poetics strategies deployed by science fiction authors from the origins of the genre to it most recent cross-media manifestations, and creates a ground for the exploration of the relation between fictionality and literature as well as for a debate on the textual impact of popular fiction. Throughout the book, Stockwell bears in mind the demands of the reading process and the importance of taking into account the reader's interpretative position; he also provides both an analysis of a literary genre and a linguistic description of how language operates in texts sharing generic characteristics. In addition, each chapter ends with two sections, 'Explorations' and 'Speculations', providing questions and suggestions for further work, which both students and teachers will find of use. Chapter 1 sends the reader on their voyage with a series of 'orientations and maps'; chapter 2 discusses plausibility in relation to deixis; chapter 3 deals with the modest role played by linguistic science and linguistic change in the science-informed worlds of science fiction and peeps at stylistic experimentation in avant-garde instances of the genre; chapter 4 convincingly argues that pulp style, the style of science fiction in pulp format, has crucially shaped the register of modern science fiction; chapter 5 is a retrospective/ prospective chapter that divides the first half of the book, concerned with the stylistic evolution of the genre, from the second half, which offers an integrated poetics of science fiction involving linguistics, cognition and textuality. Chapter 6 foregrounds the use of new words (neologisms) in the creation of new worlds; chapter 7 examines the creation of new and possible worlds with a cognitive model in a series of science-fiction short stories and how the new worlds are managed and negotiated by the reader during the reading process; chapter 8 demonstrates the metaphoric dimension of science-fiction language and the poetic qualities of the genre's figurative imagery; finally, chapter 9 brings the reader to the end of the voyage with a discussion of the experience of reading science fiction from the viewpoint of cognitive poetics. As a whole, Stockwell has provided in this book a pioneering study of the stylistics of science fiction which will no doubt trigger further studies of the genre in the future, but he has also drawn attention to issues which are of interest to any discussion of language and written literary narratives.

A fourth book in the Textual Explorations series was also published this year. Peter Wilson's *Mind the Gap: Ellipsis and Stylistic Variation on Spoken and Written English* stems from the crucial statement that we seldom speak or write in fully complete sentences. Wilson's aim is the analysis of the 'gappiness' of language in use, and thus the book presents a comprehensive study of ellipsis in both spoken and written English and in both literary and non-literary texts, showing how it contributes to the specificity of the style of some language uses. Wilson is to be congratulated for highlighting the stylistic importance of a linguistic phenomenon which is receiving increasing attention in the stylistic patterning of, particularly, literary texts. *Mind the Gap* is divided in two distinct parts: the first deals with the forms of ellipsis and the second with their stylistic effects. In part 1 the reader finds chapters defining what is and what isn't ellipsis and analyses of its linguistic and situational contexts, together with a study of telegraphic ellipsis and of how co-ordination is reduced. Part 2 provides studies of ellipsis in a range of genres, including sports commentary, advertising, drama, narrative and poetry. This is a welcome book for two reasons: it incorporates the study of literary and non-literary texts in the textual exploration of the same linguistic phenomenon, and it provides a stylistic study of a syntactic element in a field overwhelmingly focused at present on pragmatics and discourse.

The increasing attention paid to cognitive linguistics in recent stylistic studies suggests that Barcelona, ed., *Metaphor and Metonymy at the Crossroads: A Cognitive Perspective*, will be of interest to readers of this section. The editor's introduction offers a clear, well-structured overview of the cognitive theory of metaphor and metonymy (CTMM), in which he helpfully discusses at length the main tenets of CTMM and pinpoints some of its problems, paying particular attention to the driving force behind this volume, the relation between metaphor and metonymy. Contributions are organized in two sections, which divide articles addressing theoretical issues from those presenting a case study. In the first group, Barcelona's 'On the Plausibility of Claiming a Metonymic Motivation for Conceptual Metaphor' explores the radical hypothesis that sees metonymy as activating metaphor; Kurt Feyaerts stretches George Lakoff's Inheritance Hypothesis to metonymic mappings in 'Refining the Inheritance Hypothesis: Interaction between Metaphoric and Metonymic Hierarchies'; Zoltán Kövecses studies the mapping potential of a given source domain through the notions of 'main meaning focus' and 'central mapping' in 'The Scope of Metaphor'; Günter Radden's 'How Metonymic are Metaphors?' examines metonymy-based metaphors but grants that not all metaphors are metonymic; Francisco José Ruiz de Mendoza Ibáñez also supports the existence of the metaphor–metonymy continuum in 'The Role of Mappings and Domains in Understanding Metonymy', and proposes two general types of metonymy, 'source-in-target' (i.e. part for whole) and 'target-in-source' (i.e. whole for part), excluding the established part-for-part metonymies; Mark Turner and Gilles Fauconnier illustrate their theory of 'blending' (conceptual integration), with particular reference to metonymy, in 'Metaphor, Metonymy and Binding'. The second group includes studies that explore metaphor and metonymy in relation to a particular feature of language structure or use. The first five studies in this group look into polysemy and/or semantic change and grammar. Louis Goossens examines metaphor and metonymy in connection with semantic change in English modals in 'Patterns of Meaning Extension, "Parallel Chaining", Subjectification, and Modal Shifts'; Verena Hase's concern in 'Metaphor in Semantic Change' is how metaphorical shifts account for polysemy in a wide range of languages around the globe; Susanne Niemeier dissects the metonymic base of

English metaphors involving the heart in 'Straight from the Heart: Metonymic and Metaphorical Explorations'; Klaus-Uwe Panther and Linda Thornburg study the relation between metonymy and grammaticalization in 'The EFFECT FOR CAUSE Metonymy in English Grammar'; Péter Pelyvás discusses deontic and epistemic *may* and *must* in 'Metaphorical Extension of *May* and *Must* into the Epistemic Domain'. The remaining four studies are dedicated to metaphor and metonymy in discourse, and, not surprisingly, they are closer to stylistic practice, since they closely engage with texts or spoken language. Margaret H. Freeman presents a theory of 'cognitive poetics' in 'Poetry and the Scope of Metaphor: Toward a Cognitive Theory of Literature', which she then uses to discuss two poems by Emily Dickinson ('The Cocoon' and 'The Loaded Gun'), another poem (wrongly attributed to Dickinson), and Sylvia Plath's 'The Applicant'; Diane Ponterotto postulates that metaphor has a central role to play in structuring conversation in 'The Cohesive Role of Cognitive Metaphor in Discourse and Conversation'; Esra Sandikcioglu's 'More Metaphorical Warfare in the Gulf: Orientalist Frames in News Coverage' offers an analysis of media coverage during the Gulf War and shows, through Edward Said's notion of Western orientalism, how Self and Other are constructed with a number of conceptual metaphors and metonymies; Friedrich Ungerer, in 'Muted Metaphors and the Activation of Metonymies in Advertising', uncovers how the language of advertising uses strategies to avoid the unpleasant features of the source domain being transferred to the target domain and producing thus 'muted metaphors'. By putting together this collection of essays, Barcelona has provided a very useful state of the art picture and a research tool for further work on the intersection between metaphor and metonymy.

Pedagogical stylistics has not produced such a big harvest this year as in previous ones, but there are nevertheless interesting additions. The second edition of Montgomery, Durant, Fabb, Furniss and Mills, eds., *Ways of Reading: Advanced Reading Skills for Students of English Literature*, confirms the useful nature of this coursebook, which has been thoroughly revised and updated; it has also been expanded, with the addition of two new units on literature in performance and journalistic texts. The first of these stresses the importance of orality in literature and provides activities on Mary Sidney's *The Tragedie of Antonie* [1595] and Shakespeare's *Antony and Cleopatra*. The second new unit brings to the fore the relation between literary and non-literary texts and gives students tools to analyse news headlines critically. The impulse behind the original textbook, to unite developments in literary theory and literary linguistics, the latter understood as the systematic study of language, remains a central concern in this revised edition, and the new preface enhances the wish to present students with ways of reading texts that turn the process of reading into an active, reflective, critical engagement going beyond the decipherment of the words on the page. Another textbook devised with the classroom in mind is Andrew Goatly's *Critical Reading and Writing: An Introductory Coursebook*, which takes as its starting point the relation of the word *critical* to both *criteria* and *crisis*. The book has been divided into three sections which correspond to the three levels proposed for critical reading and writing: decoding the text, interpreting the discourse, and explaining the ideological forces behind text and discourse. Part 1 dedicates a chapter to each of Halliday's ideational, interpersonal and textual functions; part 2 deals with interpreting strategies such as presupposition, inference, irony, reading and writing positions and intertextuality;

and part 3 considers ideology in four types of text: capitalist consumerism in advertising, sexism in romantic fiction, institutional power and neo-imperialism in news reports, and environmentalism in poetry and the press. The greatest advantage of this coursebook is that it is a painless introduction to critical linguistics which can either be read from cover to cover or dipped into at will. Many of the chapters are almost autonomous, and the reader interested in intertextuality or in representations of gender may find useful information in the appropriate chapter. The sections are brief and manageable and students beginning an English degree, or preparing for one, will find plenty of help here.

Two interesting readers which will also prove useful in teaching are Burke, Crowley and Girvin, eds., *The Routledge Language and Culture Theory Reader*, and McQuillan, ed., *The Narrative Reader*. The relations between language and culture and language and cultural/national identity are the guiding principle behind the first work, which begins with a very crisp, thought-provoking introduction. The reader is, however, slightly hungry after this very illuminating starter and wishes it were more extensive, an effect palliated by the introductions to several of the book's sub-sections. The editors present their aims very succinctly, though, and explain clearly the connections between the three major sections of the book: language in relation to structure and agency (history, subjectivity, gender, sexuality); language in relation to unity and diversity (norm, difference, nationalism, creativity); and language in relation to cultures and communities (anthropology, colonialism, class, education). The careful and wide-ranging selection of the texts included in this reader is one of its greatest assets, turning it into more than a pedagogical tool, since anyone interested in the relations between linguistics, texts, meaning and issues of culture, nation and identity will find it indispensable. McQuillan's *The Narrative Reader* seems at first to bear a close resemblance to most critical theory readers, but on a closer look its innovations become evident. It begins not with Aristotle's discussion of plot but with Plato's cave, and turns out to be an introduction for students new to narrative theory and a reference work for researchers and advanced students. Like most narratives, this book has its own time-line and its first part takes readers from initial formalism into post-structuralism via narratology; its second half places narrative in relation to psychoanalysis, sexual difference, deconstruction, phenomenology, history and race. The selected texts are preceded by a preface with directions for use, and a separate, substantial introduction in which McQuillan problematizes the relation between 'narrative' and 'story' and then reflects on the nature of narrative in relation to narratology and the post-structuralist narrative diaspora. As a whole, this reader provides a very handy history of narrative theory together with a convenient chronology of such history, a glossary of narrative terms and a checklist of narrative theories, all of which will make helpful teaching and studying aids.

The New Critical Idiom series continues to add to its list of volumes which, if not directly concerned with stylistic practice, are of interest to anyone working with literary texts. This year Graham Allen's *Intertextuality* and Francis Mulhern's *Culture/Metaculture* explore two areas difficult to conceptualize. Allen has succeeded in the troublesome task of discussing a concept much in vogue in contemporary critical vocabulary but subject to such a diversity of definitions that it runs the risk of becoming a stumbling-block rather than an aid in literary studies, unless it is used while bearing in mind the implications attached to it. *Intertextuality* provides a comprehensive history of the term as used in structuralist, post-structuralist, semiotic, deconstructive, post-colonial, Marxist, feminist and psychoanalytic theories since Julia Kristeva first coined it in the 1960s out of a fusion of the legacies of Saussure and Bakhtin. The book also reaches beyond the literary text, and dedicates a chapter to intertextuality in painting, music, architecture and the World Wide Web to show how it is a feature of postmodern culture at large through pastiche, imitation and the echoing of previous, classic texts, styles and practices. Although written with the undergraduate student in mind, many other readers will be grateful for this concise, systematic and well-written overview of the critical traps, but also the advantages, enshrined in this difficult term. *Culture/Metaculture* is an attempt at highlighting the problematic nature of the term 'culture'. Mulhern launches a warning in his introduction to the effect that, rather than a definition and linear history of the term 'culture', the reader will find that the subject of the book is the discussion that the term itself generated (hence the term 'metaculture' in the title) in Europe, particularly Britain, in the twentieth century. This history of the culture debate has been spread over three well-differentiated parts: 'Kulturkritik', 'Cultural Studies', and 'Metaculture and Society'. The first two are presented as two mutually antagonistic traditions of discourse on culture; the second grew in open opposition to the first, negating its social values, but it shares with it a continuity of conceptual form. The last section, and the term Mulhern coins for it, 'metacultural discourse', is intended as a critical displacement of 'culture' and of both Kulturkritik and Cultural Studies, which see culture as the object and subject of discourse. In retrospect, what Mulhern does in this study is to reflect on the discourses on culture and question their validity. This is a book therefore which will draw the attention of those willing to explore how language and literary texts interact with (meta)culture discourses.

The Intertext series, mostly aimed at A-level students and beginning undergraduates, has produced several interesting satellite textbooks this year: Goddard and Patterson's *Language and Gender*, Linda McLoughlin's *The Language of Magazines* and Adrian Beard's *The Language of Politics*. Goddard and Patterson begin their introduction to language and gender by pointing out to students the kinds of projections we make when we use language to explain perceptions of the world; they then show how gender is constructed through the language deployed to describe the sexes, how thought and language interact in stereotyping, how political correctness impinges on linguistic manifestations of gender, and how male and female speech styles differ. The last chapter brings together the concepts introduced in previous chapters and encourages their application to large textual patterns. Written in a very user-friendly style, without avoiding critical insights or difficult concepts, this book will prove useful in the classroom as well as outside it, since it pinpoints the major issues in the relation between gender and language in a stimulating way. Also concerned with gender to a certain extent is McLoughlin's *The Language of Magazines*, since most magazines are clearly aimed at either men or women. McLoughlin begins by delimiting what is a magazine and then analyses in turn the front cover, the contents page, and some recurrent sections such as the horoscope section, readers' letters, readers' true stories and the problem page. The last three chapters move beyond this initial exploration of the text type to more specific areas: the relationship between text producer and text consumer and how readers can resist the positions constructed for them; the patterns of lexical and grammatical cohesion privileged by magazine discourse; and the representations of women and men based on particular constructions of femininity, masculinity and sexuality to be found in magazines. McLoughlin has provided a very interesting collection of examples from a varied range of magazines, and this enhances the appeal of a book which will prove useful as well as entertaining. Finally, Adrian Beard comes back to the Intertext series after his illuminating *The Language of Sport* (see *YWES* 79[2000] 112) with *The Language of Politics*, which offers an analysis of the language of the professional politician and political commentator in different types of political texts, including political speeches, national and local manifestos, and electoral posters and pamphlets, as well as in questions and answers in both media and parliamentary practice. Examples are not restricted to Britain but are also drawn from American and Australian political life. Written in a style which is both engaging and insightful, this textbook not only increases the reader's knowledge and awareness of political language but also awakens an interest in the linguistic analysis of texts.

Language in politics and the politics of language have produced another three thought-provoking books this year. Norman Fairclough has dissected the ways in which the language and the politics of the Labour Party's New Labour discourse intersect in *New Labour, New Language?*, a shrewd analysis of language in contemporary British politics and media, and a demonstration of how language not only reflects but actively gives shape to political ideology. Although it makes use of critical discourse analysis, it is written so as to be accessible to readers without any prior knowledge of linguistics and examines a ample array of political texts and speeches, including the 1997 Labour Party Manifesto, Tony Blair's speech following Princess Diana's death, and Bill Clinton's *Between Hope and History*, as well as government documents (White Papers and Green Papers on welfare reform and education) and newspaper articles by New Labour leaders. The first three chapters provide a thorough examination of Labour's 'Third Way' discourse; the remaining chapters explore Blair's style, the language of the New Labour government, and the clash between 'rhetoric' and 'reality' in the Nato bombing of Yugoslavia. This is a book which sends a chill down the reader's spine but which enhances our knowledge not only of politics and ideology but also of how language works. Two new additions, by Tony Crowley and Clare Mar-Molinero, have now increased the titles available in Routledge's Politics of Language series. In *The Politics of Language in Ireland, 1366–1922: A Sourcebook*, Tony Crowley has assembled a remarkable collection of texts about language and Irish cultural identity from the 1366 Statute of Kilkenny to the constitution of the Saorstát (Free State) in 1922. Crowley provides a general introduction together with specific introductions to the six historical sections into which the book is divided, in which well-known texts by Spenser, Yeats and Synge rub shoulders with less familiar documents. In his general introduction, Crowley begins by problematizing the relation between English and Irish, which is presented as a bitter but also strange, fascinating, and surprising story, whose history is presented for easy access in this comprehensive gathering of texts. But since one of the moot points in the debate is whether Irish guarantees the existence of Irish culture, this is not a book exclusively about Irish issues and concerns; it is also a collection of materials which brings to the fore the political significance of choice of language and the repercussions of language in the formation of national and cultural identity. In so doing, it shows how language debates remind us of the role of historical difference and leads us to reflect on our own historicity. As his general introduction shows, Crowley is also aware of the implications of this history for current attitudes to the language debate in Ireland. Although the nature of this sourcebook makes it a work of reference, those interested in the interplay between language and national identity will find much to muse upon in Crowley's introduction. In *The Politics of Language in the Spanish-Speaking World: From Colonisation to Globalisation*, Clare Mar-Molinero explores the politics of Spanish in countries in which it is the official national language, and in parts of the globe in which it is only the language of a minority. Although concerned with Spanish and not with English, this study of the politics of a language which is the third language in the world, after English and Chinese, will no doubt be of interest to anyone working on language and its relation to nationalism, counter-nationalism, language policies, language planning, education, the struggle for minorities' linguistic rights, bilingualism and globalization.

Discourse and its social projection has produced some noteworthy pieces this year. Sarangi and Coulthard eds., *Discourse and Social Life*, is a collection of essays which stresses the social dimension of discourse. The editors have succeeded in bringing together most of the different approaches to discourse analysis, and the contributors provide analyses of a wide range of spoken and written data. Of all the contributions to this volume, Henry Widdowson's 'Critical Practices: On Representation and the Interpretation of Text' is the most clearly concerned with stylistics, since it discusses the relation between literary and non-literary texts through a comparison between a newspaper obituary and Wordsworth's 'She dwelt among the untrodden ways', with a few taunts at critical discourse analysis. Other contributions which relate to areas reviewed in this section deal with political discourse (Norman Fairclough, 'Dialogue in the Public Sphere' and Ruth Wodak, 'Recontextualization and the Transformation of Meanings: A Critical Discourse Analysis of Decision-Making in EU Meetings about Employment Policies'), medical discourse (Nikolas and Justine Coupland, 'Relational Frames and Pronominal Address/Reference: The Discourse of Geriatric Medical Triads' and Sally Candlin, 'New Dynamics in the Nurse–Patient Relationship?'), and courtroom and forensic discourse (Yon Maley, 'The Case of the Long-Nosed Potoroo: The Framing and Construction of Expert Witness Testimony' and Malcom Coulthard, 'Whose Text Is It? On the Linguistic Investigation of Authorship'). Carmen Gregori-Signes has analysed US television 'tabloid talkshows' in *A Genre-Based Approach to Daytime Talk on Television* in order to draw a profile of the genre with the methodology of conversation analysis. Gregori-Signes starts from the conviction that the analysis of media language throws light on not only how media itself works but also the processes of linguistic change and cultural and social change, since many of the transformations and innovations affecting language evolution stem from the widespread influence of media. Her choice of genre provides an opportunity for the study of talk in an institutionalized setting, and the nature of the genre itself, its topics and participants, provides an arena for the discussion of ideological conflict. As a result, this is not a mere linguistic description of a particular discourse genre but a much more far-reaching venture than might be concluded from its title. The results of the study point to the hybrid nature of the tabloid talkshow, which combines features of a conversational and an institutionalized genre, and to the distinctive qualities of its turn-taking system. As a whole, this book raises questions on the nature of television and the social impact of a flexible genre of contemporary spoken discourse which will no doubt interest those working on media and verbal interaction. In *Disciplinary Discourses: Social Interactions in Academic Writing*, Ken Hyland has examined academic communities and their discourse practices. With the help of discourse analysis and corpus linguistics, he draws a map of common practices in current academic discourse, including citations, praise and criticism in book reviews, promotion and credibility in abstracts, hedging in the scientific letter, interaction between author and reader in textbooks. The scope of Hyland's interests goes beyond the mere linguistic description of academic genres and the book also explores the disciplinary culture of academic environments, the teaching of academic writing and the role played by power and authority in academic discourses. This is a study addressed to teachers and students of academic writing and English for Specific Purposes, but anyone involved in an academic setting will find much to learn from it.

Finally, a book not directly concerned with the systematic analysis of language but which may be of interest to those working with early modern literary texts is Allison Thorne's *Vision and Rhetoric in Shakespeare: Looking through Language*, an attempt to integrate the study of the visual arts and literary language in a study of several of Shakespeare's plays (*As You Like It*, *Hamlet*, *Troilus and Cressida*, *Antony and Cleopatra*, and *The Tempest*). Thorne sees the function of language in Shakespearean drama as the equivalent of linear perspective in painting and architecture, enriching Shakespeare's use of dramatic viewpoint.

The journal *Language and Literature* has enlarged its annual production by turning the usual three issues per volume into four—an indication perhaps of the field's vitality. Poetry is once again the most favoured literary genre, followed closely by fiction, and drama, as usual, is underrepresented, although a number of other genres, such as the epistolary, parliamentary debates, comic strips and theological writings add generic variety to this year's volume. Chanita Goodblatt's 'In Other Words: Breaking the Monologue in Whitman, Williams and Hughes' (*L&L* 9[2000] 25–41) offers a discussion of Walt Whitman's 'Out of the Cradle Endlessly Rocking', William Carlos Williams's 'The Desert Music' and Langston Hughes's 'Cultural Exchange' with the help of an integrated model based on the Bakhtinian concept of heteroglossia and Mick Short's cline-of-speech presentation. The nature of schizophrenic speech and the relation between poetry and pathology is the subject of Gregor Hens's 'What Drives Herbeck? Schizophrenia, Immediacy, and the Poetic Process' (*L&L* 9[2000] 43–59), a study of a successful poem by the Austrian schizophrenic Ernst Herbeck (1920–91) which is discussed in relation to Charles Fillmore's conceptual frames, providing Hens with an opportunity to contribute to the debate concerning the aesthetic value of Herbeck's poetry. In '"Barometer Couple": Balance and Parallelism in Margaret Atwood's *Power Politics*' (*L&L* 9[2000] 135–49), Pilar Somacarrera, after challenging traditional feminist criticism readings of Atwood's poetry as encoding a discourse of victimization of women by men, shows—through a study of parallelism and its three functions (definition, balance, reasoning) in *Power Politics*—how Atwood presents the two subjects of her poems ('you'/'I') as victims of destructive myths which have prevailed in relationships between men and women. Elzbieta Wójcik-Leese, in 'Salient Ordering of Free Verse and Its Translation' (*L&L* 9[2000] 170–81), suggests that it is possible to use the cognitive parameters of focal adjustment to analyse, and also to translate, free verse if a poem is read in terms of the figure/ ground pattern, seeing the poem as both a figure in itself and as a background to each of the lines of verse which demand of the reader a constant readjustment of viewpoint. C.B. McCully, 'Writing under the Influence: Milton and Wordsworth, Mind and Metre' (*L&L* 9[2000] 195–214), offers a pioneering study in an emerging area, metrical influence, and shows how there is a chain of metrical transmission linking Milton and Wordsworth, which becomes evident in the metrical cadences that the latter seems to have inherited from the author of *Paradise Lost*. Anthea Fraser Gupta's 'Marketing the Voice of Authenticity: A Comparison of Ming Cher and Rex Shelley' (*L&L* 9[2000] 150–69) offers a comparison between the novels of two Singaporean writers published in 1995, Ming Cher's *Spider Boys* and Rex Shelley's *Island in the Centre*, taking advantage of the occasion to discuss issues of authenticity in literary representation of language and the deployment of different marketing strategies in the novel's back-cover blurbs. Drawing on examples from English and French post-war fiction in 'Describing Camp-Talk: Language/ Pragmatics/Politics' (*L&L* 9[2000] 240–60), Keith Harvey elaborates a descriptive framework based on four semiotic strategies (paradox, inversion, ludicrism and parody) which accounts for representations of camp talk and concludes that some of its features (such as register play, puns and innuendo) contribute to the creation of fictional representations of homosexual/gay/queer characters as well as to a critique of dominant cultural norms and practices. Felicity Rash has analysed views on language expressed by German-speaking Swiss fictional characters in 'Language-Use as a Theme in German Language Swiss Literature' (*L&L* 9[2000] 317–41), and shows that the linguistic interest found in Swiss fiction mirrors contemporary sensitivity of German-speaking Swiss citizens towards the political dimension of language as an element of social cohesion and national identity.

In the only article dedicated to drama in *Language and Literature*, 'A Cognitive Approach to Characterization: Katherina in Shakespeare's *The Taming of the Shrew*' (*L&L* 9[2000] 291–316), Jonathan Culpeper makes use of schema theory and impression formation in order to offer a cognitive dissection of the character of Katherina, which he confronts with the Elizabethan schema of the shrew concluding that Shakespeare's character is not simply a farcical and inconsistent character or a prototypical shrew. In 'Tentativeness and Insistence in the Expression of Politeness in Margaret Cavendish's *Sociable Letters*' (*L&L* 9[2000] 7–24), Susan Fitzmaurice examines the semantic-pragmatic meanings of modal verbs *can*, *may* and *will* at a time in which their modern grammatical content was not yet fixed, looking at the role they play in the construction of politeness in Cavendish's epistolary essays. Ian MacKenzie's 'Institutionalized Utterances, Literature, and Language Teaching' (*L&L* 9[2000] 61–78) proposes the use of literature in the foreign-language classroom as a source of formulaic, institutionalized utterances and lexical phrases which, like Homeric formulae in oral epic poetry, can provide the foreign-language learner with a repertoire of memorized phrases. William Downes, in 'The Language of Felt Experience: Emotional, Evaluative and Intuitive' (*L&L* 9[2000] 99–121), analyses a passage from a late fourteenth-century mystical and theological work, Julian of Norwich's *Showings*, and suggests that the three existing types of felt experience (emotion, evaluation and intuition) are expressed iconically. Christopher Reid's 'Whose Parliament? Political Oratory and Print Culture in the Later 18th Century' (*L&L* 9[2000] 122–34) demonstrates the influence that print culture had on parliamentary oratory once newspaper reporting of debates in the House of Commons became possible in the 1770s, forcing speakers in the 1780s to refashion themselves rhetorically and pay attention to shifting notions of sincerity, accountability and trust. Joan C. Beal, 'From Geordie Ridley to *Viz*: Popular Literature in Tyneside English' (*L&L* 9[2000] 343–59) explores the representation in writing of Geordie, the Tyneside and Northumbrian dialect, and suggests that the salience of local forms in dialect found in cartoons in local newspapers and the popular comic *Viz* is both an assertion of local identity and a reaction against the perceived threat from ongoing cultural and linguistic homogenization. Finally in this year's volume of *Language and Literature*, readers will also find an obituary of Roger Fowler by editor Katie Wales (*L&L* 9[2000] 5–6), and the enormously helpful section Geoff Hall is now regularly providing for the journal, 'The Year's Work in Stylistics: 1999' (*L&L* 9 [2000] 363–8).

Several article-length studies on media language have appeared this year. The syntax of advertising is the concern of Paul Bruthiaux's 'In a Nutshell: Persuasion in the Spatially Constrained Language of Advertising' (*L&C* 20[2000] 297–310), in which the succinctness demanded of both classified and display ads is contrasted with the requirements of the persuasive function they strive to fulfil. Joanna Thornborrow, in 'The Construction of Conflicting Accounts in Public Participation TV' (*LSoc* 29[2000] 357–77), looks into the production of narratives from two conflicting viewpoints in television talk shows and television court programmes, paying attention in particular to the role played by tense shifting in the elaboration of believable stories. Michael L. Maynard contrasts Japanese and American advertising in 'Interpreting Girlish Images in Two Cultures: A Case of Japanese and U.S. *Seventeen* Ads' (*JLS* 29[2000] 183–201), a study of women's representation in media, youth culture and globalization, which concludes that culture divergence is manifested in the different degrees of 'girlishness' in the American and Japanese versions of the same magazine.

Conversation analysis has produced a couple of interesting articles. Emanuel A. Schegloff, in 'Overlapping Talk and the Organization of Turn-Taking for Conversation' (*LSoc* 29[2000] 1–63), studies the effects of simultaneous conversational turns on the organization of interaction and shows how overlapping is perceived as problematic by participants, who deal with it by means of the 'overlap resolution device'. Conversational organization is also explored by Samuel Gyasi Obeng in 'Doing Politics on Walls and Doors: A Sociolinguistic Analysis of Graffiti in Legon (Ghana)' (*Multilingua* 19[2000] 337–65), a study of political discourse in graffiti found in male students' lavatories; the graffiti provide a medium for the anonymous expression of political opinion through sustained interaction, since they make use of conversational features such as turn-taking, adjacency pairs, openings and closings, repair, and indirectness. Conversation is also the focus of Dan Coleman's 'Tuning in to Conversation in the Novel: Gatsby and the Dynamics of Dialogue' (*Style* 34[2000] 52–77), which advocates a reassessment of the ways in which speech in novels is discussed, so that dialogue is seen more as a series of moves than things said, more as actions than mere statements.

Readers of this section may also be interested in the following articles. Robin Melrose develops a postmodern approach to language and text through a linguistics of indeterminacy in 'Text Semantics and the Role of Interpretation in Modelling Indeterminacy' (*JLS* 29[2000] 1–44), with examples drawn from Charlotte Brontë's

Jane Eyre and Patrick White's *The Vivisector*. Piotr Sadowski, in 'Psychological Configurations and Literary Characters: A Systems View'(*JLS* 29[2000] 105–22), applies concepts and models of systems theory to character criticism, with a number of examples from fiction and Shakespearean drama. Eli Rozik, 'The Pragmatic Nature of Theatrical Discourse: The Performance-Text as a Macro Speech Act' (*JLS* 29[2000] 123–34), deals with interaction in drama and explores the theatrical (stage–audience) rather than the fictional (character–character) axis of communication. John K. Adams, in 'Narrative Theory and the Executable Text' (*JLS* 29[2000] 171–81), invites researchers to use computer programs as tools in conceptualization and the analysis of complex narrative materials, applying the concept of the executable text to Jack London's short story 'The Law of Life'. Willie van Peer's 'Cries and Whispers about Multiculturalism: Some Theoretical and Methodological Considerations' (*Multilingua* 19[2000] 367–82), which explores the sources of intercultural conflict, suggests that the study of cultural difference demands accurate descriptions of cultures; he denounces the difficulties placed on intercultural communication by some academic forms of multiculturalism, and provides a hypothesis of how cultures develop a feeling of superiority as a response to internal crises and external pressures.

Finally, it is worth mentioning that Dieter Freundlieb raises many pertinent questions about the interface between language and literature and the status of literary semantics as a viable empirical science in 'What is Literary Semantics?' (*JLS* 29[2000] 135–40). The self-reflection this brief article proposes is one which stylistics as a field seems to be conducting at the moment and which this section, through its selection of reviewed items, hopes to have echoed.

Books Reviewed

Albertazzi, Liliana. *Meaning and Cognition*. Benjamins. [2000] pp. vi + 269. Hfl 165 ($75) ISBN 1 5561 9681 4.

Alexiadou, Artemis, Paul Law, André Meinunger, and Chris Wilder, eds. *The Syntax of Relative Clauses*. Linguistik Aktuell 32. Benjamins. [2000] pp. vi + 395. $94 ISBN 1 5561 9916 3.

Allen, Graham, *Intertextuality*. Routledge. [2000] pp. x + 238. hb £40 ISBN 0 4151 7474 0, pb £9.99 ISBN 0 4151 7475 9.

Apresjan, Juri. *Systematic Lexicography*. OUP. [2000] pp. xviii + 304. £60 ISBN 0 1982 3780 4.

Bache, Carl. *Essentials of Mastering English: A Concise Grammar*. MGruyter. [2000] pp. xii + 328. pb DM48 ISBN 3 1101 6722 0.

Barcelona, Antonio, ed. *Metaphor and Metonymy at the Crossroads: A Cognitive Perspective*. MGruyter. [2000] pp. x + 356. DM178 ISBN 3 1101 6303 9.

Baugh, John. *Beyond Ebonics: Linguistic Pride and Racial Prejudice*. OUP. [2000] pp. xvii + 149. £22.50 ISBN 0 1951 2046 9.

Beard, Adrian. *The Language of Politics*. Routledge. [2000] pp. x + 121. £9.99 ISBN 0 4152 0178 0.

Beck, Heinrich, Dieter Geuenich and Heiko Steuer, eds. *Reallexikon der Germanischen Altertumskunde (Begründet von Johannes Hoops)*. 2nd edn. Vol.

16: *Jadwingen—Kleindichtung.* MGruyter. [2000] pp. vi + 634. $288 ISBN 3 1101 6782 4.

Bermúdez-Otero, Ricardo, David Denison, Richard M. Hogg and C.B. McCully, eds. *Generative Theory and Corpus Studies: A Dialogue from 10 ICEHL.* Topics in English Linguistics 31. MGruyter. [2000] pp. xix + 559. DM198 ISBN 3 1101 6687 9.

Bex, Tony, Michael Burke and Peter Stockwell, eds. *Contextualized Stylistics: In Honour of Peter Verdonk.* Rodopi. [2000] pp. ix + 278. hb NLG150 ISBN 9 0420 1491 1, pb NLG50 ISBN 9 0420 1481 4.

Booij, Geert, Christian Lehmann and Joachim Mugdan, eds. *Morphology: An International Handbook on Inflection and Word-Formation.* Vol. 1. Handbooks of Linguistics and Communication Science 17/1. MGruyter. [2000] pp. xxviii + 972. DM798 ISBN 3 1101 1128 4.

Brinton, Laurel J. *The Structure of Modern English.* Benjamins. [2000] pp. xxi + 335. pb NLG60 ISBN 9 0272 2567 2.

Broe, Michael B., and Janet P. Pierrehumbert, eds. *Papers in Laboratory Phonology V: Acquisition and the Lexicon.* CUP. [2000] pp. xiv + 400. £42.50 ISBN 0 5216 4363 5.

Broeder, Peter, and Jaap Murre, eds. *Models of Language Acquisition: Inductive and Deductive Approaches.* OUP. [2000] pp. ix + 291. £50 ISBN 0 1982 9989 3.

Burke, Lucy, Tony Crowley and Alan Girvin. *Routledge Language and Culture Theory Reader.* Routledge. [2000] pp. xvi + 511. hb £60 ISBN 0 4151 8680 3, pb £17.99 ISBN 0 4151 8681 1.

Burnley, David. *The History of the English Language: A Source Book.* 2nd edn. Longman. [2000] pp. xxiii + 418. pb £19.99 ISBN 0 5823 1263 9.

Cavill, Paul, Stephen E. Harding and Judith Jesch. *Wirral and its Viking Heritage.* EPNS. [2000] pp. ix + 149. £11.95 ISBN 0 9048 8959 9.

Chametzky, Robert A. *Phrase Structure: From GB to Minimalism.* Generative Syntax 4. Blackwell. [2000] pp. xi + 171. hb £50 ISBN 0 6312 0158 0, pb £19.99 ISBN 0 6312 0159 9.

Cheng, Lisa, and Rint Sybesma, eds. *The First Glot International State-of-the-Article Book: The Latest in Linguistics.* Studies in Generative Grammar 48. MGruyter. [2000] pp. viii + 409. €98 ISBN 3 1101 6954 1.

Chung-hye, Han. *The Structure and Interpretation of Imperatives: Mood and Force in Universal Grammar.* Outstanding Dissertations in Linguistics. Garland. [2000] pp. xiii + 263. $60 ISBN 0 8153 3787 6.

Claridge, Claudia. *Multi-Word Verbs in Early Modern English: A Corpus-Based Study.* Language and Computers: Studies in Practical Linguistics 32. Rodopi. [2000] pp. 317. hb $74 ISBN 9 0420 0459 2, pb $26.50 ISBN 9 0420 0449 5.

Coates, Richard, and Andrew Breeze, with a contribution by David Horovitz. *Celtic Voices, English Places: Studies of the Celtic Impact on Place-Names in England.* Tyas. [2000] pp. xiv + 433. £30 ISBN 1 9002 8941 5.

Coleman, Julie, and Christian J. Kay, eds. *Lexicology, Semantics, and Lexicography. Selected Papers from the Fourth G.L. Brook Symposium. Manchester, August 1998.* Benjamins. [2000] pp. xiv + 249. £48 ISBN 9 0272 3701 8.

Condron, Frances, Michael Fraser and Stuart Sutherland. *Guide to Digital Resources for the Humanities.* Humanities Computing Unit, University of Oxford. [2000] pp. ix + 300. £20 ISBN 0 9523 3015 6.

Contini-Morava, Ellen, and Yishai Tobin, eds. *Between Grammar and Lexicon.* CILT 183. Benjamins. [2000] pp. xxxii + 365. €115 ISBN 9 0272 3689 5.

Corbett, Greville G. *Number.* Cambridge Textbooks in Linguistics. CUP. [2000] pp. xx + 358. £42.50 ISBN 0 5216 4016 4.

Cortés Rodrígues, Francisco J., Marta González Orta, Beatriz Hernández Pérez, M. Auxiliadora Martín Díaz, Margarita Mele Marrero and M. Jesús Pérez Quintero, eds. *Variation and Variety in Middle English Language and Literature.* Kadle. [2000] pp. 143. pb np. ISBN 8 4882 9053 5.

Croft, William. *Explaining Language Change: An Evolutionary Approach.* Longman Linguistics Library. Longman. [2000] pp. xv + 287. pb £19.99 ISBN 0 5823 5677 6.

Crowley, Tony. *The Politics of Language in Ireland, 1366–1922: A Sourcebook.* Routledge. [2000] pp. xvi + 236. hb £60 ISBN 0 4151 5717 X, pb £17.99 ISBN 0 4151 5718 8.

Cruse, Alan D. *Meaning in Language: An Introduction to Semantics and Pragmatics.* OUP. [2000] pp. xii + 424. pb £17.99 ISBN 0 1987 0010 5.

Dekkers, Joost, Frank van der Leeuw and Jeroen van de Weijer, eds. *Optimality Theory: Phonology, Syntax, and Acquisition.* OUP. [2000] pp. x + 635. £24.95 ISBN 0 1982 3844 4.

Delin, Judy. *The Language of Everyday Life: An Introduction.* Sage. [2000] pp. x + 208. hb £50 ISBN 0 7619 6089 9, pb £16.99 ISBN 0 7619 6090 2.

Deminger, Szilvia, Thorsten Fögen, Joachim Scharloth and Simone Zwickl, eds. *Einstellungsforschung in der Soziolinguistik und Nachbardiziplinen.* Studies in Language Attitudes 10. Lang. [2000] pp. ix + 208. pb £24 ISBN 3 6373 5391 X.

Desmet, Piet, Lieve Jooken, Peter Schmitter and Pierre Swiggers, eds. *The History of Linguistic and Grammatical Praxis: Proceedings of the XIth International Colloquium of the Studienkreis 'Geschichte der Sprachwissenschaft'.* Peeters. [2000] pp. ix + 574. $65 ISBN 9 0429 0884 X.

Dressler, Wolfgang U., Oskar E. Pfeiffer, Markus Pöchtrager and John R. Rennison, eds. *Morphological Analysis in Comparison.* CILT 201. Benjamins. [2000] pp. ix + 253. $78 ISBN 9 0272 3708 5.

Eckert, Penelope. *Linguistic Variation as Social Practice: The Linguistic Construction of Identity in Belten High.* Language in Society 27. Blackwell. [2000] pp. xvi + 240. hb £50 ISBN 0 6311 8603 4, pb £15.99 ISBN 0 6311 8604 2.

Edelman, Charles. *Shakespeare's Military Language: A Dictionary.* Athlone. [2000] pp. xviii + 423. £125 ISBN 0 4851 1546 8.

Fairclough, Norman. *New Labour, New Language?* Routledge. [2000] pp. x + 178. hb £45 ISBN 0 4152 1826 8, pb £10.99 ISBN 0 4152 1827 6.

Fawcett, Robin. *A Theory of Syntax for Systemic Functional Linguistics.* CILT 206. Benjamins. [2000] pp. xxiii + 360. €77 ISBN 9 0272 3713 1.

Fernald, Theodore B. *Predicates and Temporal Arguments.* OUP. [2000] pp. vii + 156. £30 ISBN 0 1951 1435 3.

Finch, Geoffrey. *Linguistic Terms and Concepts.* Macmillan. [2000] pp. xii + 251. pb £9.90 ISBN 0 3337 2013 X.

Fischer, Olga, Ans van Kemenade, Willem Koopman and Wim van der Wurff. *The Syntax of Early English*. Cambridge Syntax Guides. CUP. [2000] pp. xviii + 341. hb £42.50 ISBN 0 5215 5410 1, pb £15.95 ISBN 0 5215 5626 0.

Fischer, Olga, Anette Rosenbach and Dieter Stein, eds. *Pathways of Change: Grammaticalization in English*. Studies in Language Companion Series 53. Benjamins. [2000] pp. x + 391. $105 (€104.82) ISBN 9 0272 3056 0.

Fishman, Joshua, ed. *Handbook of Language and Ethnic Identity*. OUP. [1999] pp. xii + 468. £50 ISBN 0 1951 2428 6.

Foolen, Ad, and Frederike van der Leek, eds. *Constructions in Cognitive Linguistics*. CILT 178. Benjamins. [2000] pp. xv + 338. £48 ISBN 9 0272 3684 4.

Fox, H.S.A., and O.J. Padel, eds. *The Cornish Lands of the Arundells of Lanherne, Fourteenth to Sixteenth Centuries*. D&CRS. [2000] pp. clvi +279. pb £18 ISBN 0 9018 5341 0.

Friedemann, Marc-Ariel, and Luigi Rizzi, eds. *The Acquisition of Syntax: Studies in Comparative Developmental Linguistics*. Longman Linguistics Library. Longman. [2000] pp. x + 326. pb £17.99 ISBN 0 5823 2882 9.

Fromkin, Victoria, Susan Curtiss, Bruce P. Hayes, Nina Hyams, Patricia A. Keating, Hilda Koopman, Pamela Munro, Dominique Sportiche, Edward P. Stabler, Donca Steriade, Tim Stowell and Anna Szabolcsi. *Linguistics: An Introduction to Linguistic Theory*. Blackwell. [2000] pp. xi + 747. pb £18.99 ISBN 0 6311 9711 7.

Gelderen, Elly van. *A History of English Reflexive Pronouns: Person, Self, and Interpretability*. Linguistik Aktuell 39. Benjamins. [2000] pp. xiv + 277. NLG190 ($86) ISBN 9 0272 2760 8.

Gelling, Margaret, and Ann Cole. *The Landscape of Place-Names*. Tyas. [2000] pp. xxiv + 391. hb £25 ISBN 1 9002 8925 3, pb £17.95 ISBN 1 9002 8926 1.

Gildea. Spike, ed. *Reconstructing Grammar: Comparative Linguistics and Grammaticalization*. Typological Studies in Language 43. Benjamins. [2000] pp. xiv + 267. hb $82 ISBN 1 5561 9658 X, pb $34.95 ISBN 1 5561 9659 8.

Goatly, Andrew. *Critical Reading and Writing: An Introductory Coursebook*. Routledge. [2000] pp. xiv + 348. hb £50 ISBN 0 4151 9559 4, pb £15.99 ISBN 0 4151 9560 8.

Goddard, Angela, and Lindsey Meân Patterson. *Language and Gender*. Routledge. [2000] pp. xii + 321. pb £9.99 ISBN 0 4152 0177 2.

Gregori Signes, Carmen. *A Genre-Based Approach to Daytime Talk on Television*. University of Valencia. [2000] pp. 141. Pta. 1,501 ISBN 8 4370 4264 X.

Guzman, Videa P. de, and Byron W. Bender, eds. *Grammatical Analysis: Morphology, Syntax, and Semantic. Studies in Honor of Stanley Starosta*. Oceanic Linguistics Special Publication 29. UHawaiiP. [2000] pp. xv + 298. pb $39 ISBN 0 8248 2105 X.

Hartmann, R.R.K. *Teaching and Researching Lexicography*. Longman. [2000] pp. xii + 211. pb £14.99 ISBN 0 5823 6977 0.

Haspelmath, Martin. *Indefinite Pronouns*. Oxford Studies in Typology and Linguistic Theory. OUP. [2000] pp. xvi + 364. hb £60 ISBN 0 1982 3560 7, pb £19.99 ISBN 0 1982 9963 X.

Herring, Susan C., Pieter van Reenen and Lene Schøsler. *Textual Parameters in Older Languages*. CILT 195. Benjamins. [2000] pp. 448. £50 (€95) ISBN 9 0272 3702 6.

Heuberger, Reinhard. *Monolingual Dictionaries for Foreign Learners of English: A Constructive Evaluation of State-of-the-Art Reference Works in Book Form and on CD-ROM*. Braumüller. [2000] pp. x + 198. ISBN 3 7003 1338 1.

Heusinger, Klaus von, and Urs Egli, eds. *Reference and Anaphoric Relations*. Kluwer. [2000] pp. xi + 347. €139 ISBN 0 7923 6070 2.

Hey, David. *Family Names and Family History*. H&L. [2000] pp. xii + 240. £16.95 ISBN 1 8528 5255 0.

Hidalgo-Downing, Laura. *Negation, Text Worlds, and Discourse: The Pragmatics of Fiction*. Ablex. [2000] pp. xxii + 225. hb $78.50 ISBN 1 5675 0474 4, pb $39.50 ISBN 1 5675 0475 2.

Higginbotham, James, Fabio Pianesi and Achille C. Varzi, eds. *Speaking of Events*. OUP. [2000] pp vii + 295. hb £52 ISBN 0 1951 2807 9, pb £25.50 ISBN 0 1951 2811 7.

Holm, John. *An Introduction to Pidgins and Creoles*. CUP. [2000] pp. xxi + 282. pb £15.95 ISBN 0 5215 8581 3.

Horie, Kaoru, ed. *Complementation: Cognitive and Functional Perspectives*. Converging Evidence in Language and Communication Research 1. Benjamins. [2000] pp. 241. $75 ISBN 1 5561 9211 8.

Horn, Laurence R., and Yasuhiko Kato, eds. *Negation and Polarity: Syntactic and Semantic Perspectives*. OUP. [2000] pp. ix + 271. hb £50 ISBN 0 1982 3874 6, pb £18.99 ISBN 0 1982 3873 8.

Huang, Xiaozhao. *A Study of African-American Vernacular English in America's Middletown: Evidence of Linguistic Convergence*. Black Studies 12. Mellen. [2000] pp. xxxi + 286. $99.95 ISBN 0 7734 7634 2.

Hudson, Grover. *Essential Introductory Linguistics*. Blackwell. [2000] pp. xvi + 533. hb £55 ISBN 0 6312 0303 6, pb £14.99 ISBN 0 6312 0304 4.

Hughes, Geoffrey. *A History of English Words*. Blackwell. [2000] pp. xviii + 430. hb £55 ISBN 0 6311 8854 1, pb £17.99 ISBN 0 6311 8855 X.

Hunston, Susan, and Gill Francis. *Pattern Grammar: A Corpus-Driven Approach to the Lexical Grammar of English*. Studies in Corpus Linguistics 4. Benjamins. [2000] pp. xiii + 288. hb $75 ISBN 9 0272 2273 8, pb $34.95 ISBN 9 0272 2274 6.

Hyland, Ken. *Disciplinary Discourses: Social Interactions in Academic Writing*. Longman. [2000] pp. xxii + 211. pb £22.99 ISBN 0 5824 1904 2.

Jackson, Howard, and Étienne Zé Amvela. *Words, Meaning and Vocabulary: An Introduction to Modern English Lexicology*. Cassell. [2000] pp. viii + 216. £49.95 ISBN 0 3047 0396 6.

Jaszczolt, K.M., ed. *The Pragmatics of Propositional Attitude Reports*. Elsevier. [2000] pp. vii + 218. £53.92 ISBN 0 0804 3635 8.

Johnstone, Barbara. *Qualitative Methods in Sociolinguistics*. OUP. [2000] pp. 164. pb £12.99 ISBN 0 1951 3397 8.

Kabakčiev, Krasimir. *Aspect in English: A 'Common-Sense' View of the Interplay Between Verbal and Nominal Referents*. Studies in Linguistics and Philosophy 75. Kluwer. [2000] pp. xxi + 348. $154 ISBN 0 7923 6538 0.

Kastovsky, Dieter, and Arthur Mettinger, eds. *The History of English in a Social Context*. Trends in Linguistics 129. MGruyter. [2000] pp. xviii + 484. DM236 ISBN 3 1101 6707 7.

Kirk, John, ed. *Corpora Galore: Analyses and Techniques in Describing English. Papers from the 19th International Conference on English Language Research on Computerised Corpora.* Rodopi. [2000] pp. x + 344. hb $74 ISBN 9 0420 0419 3, pb $26 ISBN 0 4151 6183 5.

Koopman, Hilda. *The Syntax of Specifiers and Heads: Collected Essays of Hilda J. Koopman.* Routledge Leading Linguists. Routledge. [2000] pp. vii + 389. £70 ISBN 0 4151 6183 5.

Krug, Manfred G. *Emerging English Modals: A Corpus-Based Study of Grammaticalization.* Topics in English Linguistics 32. MGruyter. [2000] pp. xv + 332. DM148 ISBN 3 1101 6654 2.

Lahiri, Aditi, ed. *Analogy, Levelling, Markedness: Principles of Change in Phonology and Morphology.* Trends in Linguistics 127. MGruyter. [2000] pp. viii + 385. DM 178 ISBN 3 1101 6750 6.

Lambert, Richard D., and Elana Shohamy, eds. *Language Policy and Pedagogy: Essays in Honor of A. Ronald Walton.* Benjamins. [2000] pp. xii + 279. £41 ISBN 9 0272 2559 1.

Lampert, Günther, and Martina Lampert. *The Conceptual Structure(s) of Modality: Essences and Ideologies: A Study in Linguistic (Meta-)Categorization.* Lang. [2000] pp. 328. pb £30 ISBN 3 6313 5219 0.

Landau, Idan. *Elements of Control: Structure and Meaning in Infinitival Constructions.* Studies in Natural Language and Linguistic Theory 51. Kluwer. [2000] pp. ix + 212. €95.50 ISBN 0 7923 6620 4.

Lass, Roger, ed. *The Cambridge History of the English Language,* vol. iii: *1476–1776.* CUP. [1999] pp. xvii + 771. £85 ISBN 0 5212 6476 6.

Lepore, Ernest. *Meaning and Argument: An Introduction to Logic through Language.* Blackwell. [2000] pp. xvi + 418. hb £55 ISBN 0 6312 0581 0, pb £16.99 ISBN 0 6312 0582 9.

Lobeck, Anne. *Discovering Grammar: An Introduction to English Sentence Structure.* OUP. [2000] pp. xiii + 370. pb £15.99 ISBN 0 1951 2984 9.

Lockwood, David G., Peter H. Fries and James E. Copeland, eds. *Functional Approaches to Language, Culture and Cognition. Papers in Honor of Sydney M. Lamb.* CILT 163. Benjamins. [2000] pp. xxxiv + 656. €147.02 ISBN 9 0272 3668 2.

Lundquist, Lita, and Robert J. Jarvella, eds. *Language, Text, and Knowledge. Mental Models of Expert Communication.* MGruyter. [2000] pp. viii + 326. $105 ISBN 3 1101 6724 7.

Lutz, Uli, Gereon Müller and Arnim von Stechow, eds. *Wh-Scope Marking.* Benjamins. [2000] pp. vi + 483. £62 ISBN 9 0272 2758 6.

McLoughlin, Linda, *The Language of Magazines.* Routledge. [2000] pp. xii + 115. pb £9.99 ISBN 0 4152 1424 6.

McMahon, April. *Lexical Phonology and the History of English.* Cambridge Studies in Linguistics 91. CUP. [2000] pp. xi + 309. £40 ISBN 0 5214 7280 6.

McMahon, April. *Change, Chance, and Optimality.* OUP. [2000] pp. x + 201. hb £35 ISBN 0 1982 4124 0, pb £12.99 ISBN 0 1982 4125 9.

McQuillan, Martin, ed. *The Narrative Reader.* Routledge. [2000] pp. xiv + 353. hb £60 ISBN 0 4152 0533 6, pb £17.50 ISBN 0 4152 0532 8.

McWhorter, John, ed. *Language Change and Language Contact in Pidgins and Creoles.* Benjamins. [2000] pp. vii + 503. NLG290 ISBN 9 0272 5243 2.

Mar-Molinero, Clare. *The Politics of Language in the Spanish-Speaking World: From Colonisation to Globalisation*. Routledge. [2000] pp. xiv + 242. hb £65 ISBN 0 4151 5655 6, pb £19.99 ISBN 0 4151 5654 8.

Mattheier, Klaus, ed. *Dialect and Migration in a Changing Europe*. Variolingua: Non-Standard-Standard-Substandard 12. Lang. [2000] pp. ix + 244. pb £27 ISBN 3 6313 6738 4.

Mesthrie, Rajend, Joan Swann, Andrea Deumert and William L. Leap. *Introducing Sociolinguistics*. EdinUP. [2000] pp. xxv + 501. hb £45 ISBN 0 7486 0773 0, pb £14.95 ISBN 0 7486 1193 2.

Meyerhoff, Miriam. *Constraints on Null Subjects in Bislama (Vanuatu): Social and Linguistic Factors*. Pacific Linguistics. [2000] pp. xi + 206. $38 ISBN 0 8588 3522 3.

Micklethwait, David. *Noah Webster and the American Dictionary*. McFarland. [2000] pp. viii + 350. $49.95 ISBN 0 7864 0640 2.

Miles, Joyce. *Owl's Hoot: How People Name their Houses*. Murray. [2000] pp. xii + 132. £9.99 ISBN 0 7195 6220 1.

Mönnink, Inge Maria de. *On the Move. The Mobility of Constituents in the English Noun Phrase: A Multi-Method Approach*. Language and Computers 31. Rodopi. [2000] pp. xii + 193. pb $43 ISBN 9 0420 0780 X.

Montgomery, Martin, Alan Durant, Nigel Fabb, Tom Furniss and Sara Mills. *Ways of Reading: Advanced Reading Skills for Students of English Literature*. 2nd edn. Routledge. [2000] pp. xiv + 369. hb £55 ISBN 0 4152 2205 2, pb £15.99 ISBN 0 4152 2206 0.

Mugglestone, Lynda, ed. *Lexicography and the OED: Pioneers in the Untrodden Forest*. OUP. [2000] pp. x + 288. £50 ISBN 0 1982 3784 7.

Mulhern, Francis. *Culture/Metaculture*. Routledge. [2000] pp. xxii + 198. hb £40 ISBN 0 4151 0229 4, pb £9.99 ISBN 0 4151 0230 8.

Nesi, Hilary. *The Use and Abuse of EFL Dictionaries: How Learners of English as a Foreign Language Read and Interpret Dictionary Entries*. Niemeyer. [2000] pp. vi + 156. pb DM98 ISBN 3 4843 0998 9.

Neumann-Holzschuh, Ingrid, and Edgar W. Schneider, eds. *Degrees of Restructuring in Creole Languages*. Benjamins. [2000] pp. 492. NLG265 ISBN 9 0272 5244 0.

Niedzielski, Nancy, and Dennis R. Preston. *Folk Linguistics*. Topics in Linguistics 122. MGruyter. [2000] pp xiii + 375. DM238 ISBN 3 1101 6251 2.

Opdahl, Lise. *LY or Zero Suffix? A Study in Variation of Dual-Form Adverbs in Present-Day English*, vol. i: *Overview*; vol. ii: *Adverbial Profiles*. Lang. [2000] pp. 288, 574. pb £57 ISBN 3 6313 5464 9.

Parkvall, Mikael. *Out of Africa: African Influences in Atlantic Creoles*. Battlebridge Publications. [2000] pp. viii + 188. £15 ISBN 1 9032 9205 0.

Parrott, Martin. *Grammar for English Language Teachers, with Exercises and a Key*. CUP. [2000] pp. xiv + 514. pb £12.95 ISBN 0 5214 7797 2.

Parsons, David N., and Tania Styles. *The Vocabulary of English Place-Names (Brace-Cæster)*. CENS. [2000] pp. xviii + 177. pb £12.50 ISBN 0 9525 3436 3.

Parsons, Terence. *Indeterminate Identity: Metaphysics and Semantics*. OUP. [2000] pp xvii + 221. £30 ISBN 0 1982 5044 4.

Penhallurick, Robert, ed. *Debating Dialect: Essays on the Philosophy of Dialect Study*. UWalesP. [2000] pp. xii + 128. £20 ISBN 0 7083 1669 7.

Piesse, A.J., ed. *Sixteenth-Century Identities*. ManUP. [2000] pp. viii + 180. £40 ISBN 0 7190 5383 8.

Pintzuk, Susan, George Tsoulas and Anthony Warner, eds. *Diachronic Syntax: Models and Mechanisms*. OUP. [2000] pp. xii + 380. pb £24.99 ISBN 0 1982 5027 4.

Poplack, Shana, ed. *The English History of African American English*. Blackwell. [2000] pp. xx + 269. $70.95 ISBN 0 6312 1261 2.

Price, Glanville, ed. *Languages in Britain and Ireland*. Blackwell. [2000] pp. 240. hb £60 ISBN 0 6312 1580 8, pb £16.99 ISBN 0 6312 1581 6.

Reuland, Eric, ed. *Arguments and Case: Explaining Burzio's Generalization*. Linguistik Aktuell. Benjamins. [2000] pp. xii + 253. $65 ISBN 1 5561 9918 X.

Rickford, John Russell, and Russell John Rickford. *Spoken Soul: The Story of Black English*. Wiley. [2000] pp. 267. hb £18.50 ISBN 0 4713 2356 X, pb £11.95 ISBN 0 4713 9957 4.

Romaine, Suzanne. *Language in Society: An Introduction to Sociolinguistics*. 2nd edn. OUP. [2000] pp. xi + 268. pb £12.99 ISBN 0 1987 3192 2.

Sanz, Montserrat. *Events and Predication: A New Approach to Syntactic Processing in English and Spanish*. Benjamins. [2000] pp. xiv + 219. NLG145 ISBN 9 0272 3714 X, $66 ISBN 1 5881 1011 X.

Sarangi, Srikant, and Malcolm Coulthard, eds. *Discourse and Social Life*. Longman. [2000] pp. xlii + 298. hb £55 ISBN 0 5824 0469 X, pb £17.99 ISBN 0 5824 0468 1.

Scholl, Andrew. *The Achilles to Zeppelin of Eponyms*. O'Mara. [2000] pp. 180. pb £4.99 ISBN 1 8547 9597 X.

Schwabe, Kersting, and Ning Zhang, eds. *Ellipsis in Conjunction*. Linguistische Arbeiten 418. Niemeyer. [2000] pp. viii + 269. €73 ISBN 3 4843 0418 9.

Siegel, Jeff, ed. *Processes of Language Contact: Studies from Australia and the South Pacific*. Fides. [2000] pp. 326. np ISBN 2 7621 2098 5.

Siemund, Pieter. *Intensifiers in English and German: A Comparison*. Routledge Studies in Germanic Linguistics 6. Routledge. [2000] pp. ix + 283. $100 ISBN 0 4152 1713 X.

Sihler, Andrew L. *Language History: An Introduction*. CILT 191. Benjamins. [2000] pp. xvi + 299. hb $70 ISBN 1 5561 9968 6, pb $29.95 ISBN 1 5561 9969 4.

Simmelbauer, Andrea. *The Dialect of Northumberland: A Lexical Investigation*. Anglistische Forschungen 275. Winter. [2000] pp. xv + 278. pb DM78 ISBN 3 8253 0934 7.

Simons, Mandy. *Issues in the Semantics and Pragmatics of Disjunction*. Garland. [2000] pp. xiv + 259. $37 ISBN 0 8153 3791 4.

Simpson, Andrew. *Wh-Movement and the Theory of Feature-Checking*. Benjamins. [2000] pp. xi + 244. $83 ISBN 1 5561 9856 6.

Singh, Ishtla. *Pidgins and Creoles: An Introduction*. Arnold. [2000] pp. xv + 142. pb £12.99 ISBN 0 3407 0095 5.

Smitherman, Geneva. *Talkin That Talk: Language, Culture and Education in African America*. Routledge. [1999] pp. xvi + 457. hb £65 ISBN 0 4152 0864 5, pb £17.99 ISBN 0 4152 0865 3.

Sokol, B.J., and Mary Sokol. *Shakespeare's Legal Language: A Dictionary*. Athlone. [2000] pp. 497. £125 ISBN 0 4851 1549 2.

Sornicola, Rosanna, Erich Poppe and Ariel Shisha-Halevy, eds. *Stability, Variation and Change of Word-Order Patterns over Time*. CILT 213. Benjamins. [2000] pp. xxxi + 323. NLG190 ISBN 9 0272 3720 4.

Stellmacher, Dieter, ed. *Dialektologie zwischen Tradition und Neuansätzen. Beiträge der Internationalen Dialektologentagung, Göttingen, 19–21 Oktober 1998*. ZDL 109. Steiner. [2000] pp. 437. pb €100 ISBN 3 5150 7762 6.

Stevenson, Lorna, and Jocelyn Wogan-Browne. *Concordance to the Katherine Group MS. Bodley 34 and the Wooing Group. MSS Nero A XIV and Titus D XVIII.* Brewer. [2000] pp. xxii + 1192. £140 ISBN 0 8599 1452 6.

Stockwell, Peter. *The Poetics of Science Fiction*. Longman. [2000] pp. xii + 250. pb £15.99 ISBN 0 5823 6993 2.

Stroik, Thomas S. *Syntactic Controversies*. LINCOM Studies in Theoretical Linguistics 24. LINCOM Europa. [2000] pp. 186. pb £38 ISBN 3 8958 6963 5.

Sylvester, Louise, and Jane Roberts. *Middle English Word Studies: A Word and Author Index*. Brewer. [2000] pp. x + 322. £35 ISBN 0 8599 1606 5.

Thorne, Allison. *Vision and Rhetoric in Shakespeare: Looking through Language*. Macmillan. [2000] pp. xvi + 290. £21.25 ISBN 0 3336 5939 2.

Todd, Loreto. *Green English: Ireland's Influence on the English Language*. O'Brien. [1999] pp. 159. £16.99 ($25.95) ISBN 0 8627 8543 X.

Trask, R.L. *Dictionary of Historical and Comparative Linguistics*. EdinUP. [2000] pp. xii + 403. hb £50 ISBN 0 7486 1003 0, pb £18.95 ISBN 0 7486 1001 4.

Treharne, Elaine, ed. *Old and Middle English: An Anthology*. Blackwell. [2000] pp. xxvii + 622. hb £65 ISBN 0 6312 0465 2, pb £16.99 ISBN 0 6312 0466 0.

Tristram, Hildegard L.C., ed. *The Celtic Englishes II*. Winter. [2000] pp. ix + 478. pb DM98 (€50) ISBN 3 8253 0925 8.

Trudgill, Peter. *Sociolinguistics: An Introduction to Language and Society*. 4th edn. Penguin. [2000] pp. xii + 222. pb £8.99 ($13) ISBN 0 1402 8921 6.

Ura, Hiroyuki. *Checking Theory and Grammatical Functions in Universal Grammar*. Oxford Studies in Comparative Syntax. OUP. [2000] pp. xviii + 318. pb $35 ISBN 0 1951 1839 1.

Verspoor, Marjolijn, and Kim Sauter. *English Sentence Analysis*. Benjamins. [2000] pp. 245. pb NLG60 ISBN 9 0272 2566 4, $29.95 ISBN 1 5556 19661 X.

Wilson, Peter, *Mind the Gap: Ellipsis and Stylistic Variation in Spoken and Written English*. Longman. [2000] pp. xii + 239. hb £60 ISBN 0 5823 5680 6, pb £17.99 ISBN 0 5823 5679 2.

Wright, Laura, ed. *The Development of Standard English, 1300–1800: Theories, Descriptions, Conflicts*. CUP. [2000] pp. x + 236. £40 ISBN 0 5217 7114 5.

II

Old English Literature

JILL FREDERICK AND MARY SWAN

This chapter has ten sections: 1. Bibliography; 2. Manuscript Studies, Palaeography and Facsimiles; 3. Social, Cultural and Intellectual Background; 4. Literature: General; 5. The Exeter Book; 6. The Poems of the Vercelli Book; 7. The Junius Manuscript; 8. The *Beowulf* Manuscript; 9. Other Poems; 10. Prose. Section 1 is by Jill Frederick and Mary Swan; sections 2, 3 and 10 are by Mary Swan; sections 4 to 9 are by Jill Frederick; additional material in section 10 is by Anne Marie D'Arcy.

1. Bibliography

The *Old English Newsletter* 33:iii[Spring 2000] includes conference news, a report by Peter Jackson on the *Fontes Anglo-Saxonici* project (pp. 7–8), and a description of its web database, 'How Well Read were the Anglo-Saxons? The World Wide Web Version of the *Fontes Anglo-Saxonici* Register' by Rohini Jayatilaka (pp. 12–14); and a report on the Anglo-Saxon Plant Name Survey by C.P. Biggam (pp. 9–11). This volume also contains abstracts of Papers in Anglo-Saxon Studies. Volume 34:i[Fall 2000] contains notes on forthcoming conferences, reports on the *Dictionary of Old English* and the Friends of the DOE fundraising campaign, and the following articles: Martin K. Foys, '*Circolwyrde 2000*: New Electronic Resources for Anglo-Saxon Studies' (pp. 15–18); Thomas A. Bredehoft, 'Estimating Probabilities and Alliteration Frequencies in Old English Verse' (pp. 19–23); and David F. Johnson, 'A Scene of Post-Mortem Judgement in the New Minster *Liber Vitae*', which is a study of the Last Judgement scene in MS London, British Library, Stowe 944 and its connections to textual references to the importance of intercessory prayer. Volume 34:ii[Summer 2000], contains the annual bibliography on Old English Studies for 1999. *ASE* 29[2000] contains the bibliography for 1999 (pp. 297–358).

See section 10 below for Nicole Guenther Discenza, 'Alfred the Great: A Bibliography with Special Reference to Literature', and Aaron J. Kleist, 'An Annotated Bibliography of Ælfrician Studies, 1983–1996' (both in Szarmach, ed., *Old English Prose: Basic Readings*), and *Annotated Bibliographies of Old and Middle English Literature*, volume vi: *Old English Prose Translations of King Alfred's Reign* by Greg Waite.

2. Manuscript Studies, Palaeography and Facsimiles

Two volumes of the Anglo-Saxon Manuscripts in Microfiche Facsimile series are reviewed this year. The first, volume 6, *Worcester Manuscripts*, with descriptions by Christine Franzen, was published in 1998 but not reviewed in *YWES*. It includes MSS British Library, Cotton Otho C. i, vol. 2; and Oxford, Bodleian Bodley 130, Hatton 20, Hatton 48, Hatton 76, Hatton 113, Hatton 114, Hatton 115, Junius 121, and Laud Misc. 482. The accompanying booklet includes full codicological descriptions of each manuscript, and notes on their history and contents. Volume 8, *Wulfstan Texts and Other Homiletic Materials*, with descriptions by Jonathan Wilcox which follow the same format as those in volume 6, includes MSS Cambridge, Corpus Christi College 419, and 421, and Trinity College B. 14. 52; British Library, Cotton Cleopatra B. xiii, Cotton Tiberius C. i, Cotton Vespasian A. xxii, Cotton Vespasian D. xiv, Harley 2110, Harley 3667; and London, Lambeth Palace 487 and 489.

Michelle P. Brown's 2000 Jarrow lecture, *'In the beginning was the Word': Books and Faith in the Age of Bede*, opens with a discussion of the book as 'an instrument and a channel of faith' (p. 1) in early Anglo-Saxon England which takes the cult of St Cuthbert as its focus. Brown then moves on to a detailed analysis of new evidence for the layers of production of the Lindisfarne Gospels: previously unrecorded hard-point drawings. Brown's argument—that these markings show that the drawings in the manuscript are original to it, that the markings and other details of the decorative style of the manuscript support its being produced at Wearmouth–Jarrow in the first quarter of the eighth century—is supported by detailed analysis and excellent-quality photographs of the markings.

3. Social, Cultural and Intellectual Background

From this year onwards, publications on pre-Conquest Anglo-Latin prose will be reviewed in the 'Prose' section along with Old English prose.

The sixth volume of the Garland series Basic Readings in Anglo-Saxon England is published this year. Pelteret, ed., *Anglo-Saxon History: Basic Readings*, has much of relevance to the social, political and ecclesiastical contexts for the production of Anglo-Saxon literature. The volume contains fifteen previously published essays, several of which have been revised and updated, and one new essay. The previously published essays are: D.A. Bullough, 'Anglo-Saxon Institutions and Early English Society'; Eric John, 'The Social and Political Problems of the Early English Church'; D.P. Kirby, 'Bede's Native Sources for the *Historia Ecclesiastica*'; Nicholas Brooks, 'The Development of Military Obligations in Eighth- and Ninth-Century England'; Barbara A.E. Yorke, 'The Bishops of Winchester, the Kings of Wessex, and the Development of Winchester in the Ninth and Tenth Centuries'; Niels Lund, 'The Settlers: Where Do We Get Them From—And Do We Need Them?'; Simon Keynes, 'The Declining Reputation of Æthelred the Unready'; James Campbell, 'Some Agents and Agencies of the Late-Anglo-Saxon State'; Margaret Clunies Ross, 'Concubinage in Anglo-Saxon England'; Martin Biddle, *'Felix Urbs Winthonia*: Winchester in the Age of Monastic Reform'; Carol Neuman de Vegvar, 'A Paean for a Queen: The Frontispiece to the *Encomium Emmae*

Reginae'; Peter Sawyer, 'Early Fairs and Markets in England and Scandinavia'; Peter Robinson, 'Mapping the Anglo-Saxon Landscape: A Land-Systems Approach to the Study of the Bounds of the Estate of Plaish'; H.P.R. Finberg, 'Charltons and Carltons'; and Christine Mahany and David Roffe, 'Stamford: The Development of an Anglo-Scandinavian Borough'. The new essay in this volume is Patrick Wormald's 'Archbishop Wulfstan and the Holiness of Society' (pp. 191–224), which uses manuscript evidence to make a vigorous and convincing case for the coherence of Wulfstan's career and for his developing interest in reordering society. The appendix to Wormald's article is a useful and analytical catalogue of '*Wulfstaniana* True and False'.

The ecclesiastical context is the subject of many new publications this year. Gatch, ed., *Eschatology and Christian Nurture*, reviewed in section 10 below, includes items of relevance to the theological and ecclesiastical setting of Old English prose. In *The English Church, 940–1154*, H.R. Loyn offers a wide-ranging analysis of the organization and development of the Church in the late Anglo-Saxon and post-Conquest period. The book is organized chronologically by chapter, from the tenth-century Benedictine Reform to the reign of Stephen. Topics considered include relationships with Europe, the law, economics, intellectual culture and the state, and evidence used includes archaeology, law-codes and Domesday Book. The final chapter, 'Doctrine, Belief and Ritual', considers the impact of these aspects of the Church on the lives of the people of England. Keith Bailey reassesses the possible identifications of 'Clofesho', the name recorded for the site of a number of Anglo-Saxon Church councils in the eighth and ninth centuries, in '*Clofesho* Revisited' (*ASSAH* 11[2000] 119–31). Bailey uses geographical and place-name evidence to assess the likelihood of a range of sites, and draws up a shortlist of criteria which form the profile of a suitable site. These criteria enable him to narrow down the range of possible locations, and to favour the Hertford area.

In 'Penitential Literature and Secular Law in Anglo-Saxon England' (*ASSAH* 11[2000] 133–41), Carole Hough examines references in penitential literature to secular law, and references in secular law-codes to penitentials, and argues that only specific references in law-codes to the penitential handbooks, as opposed to general allusions to penance, can be accepted as clear evidence of penitentials functioning as part of the legal process. Hough concludes that 'the two forms of legislation appear to have operated largely independently until at least the end of the ninth century' (p. 139), that Wulfstan's influence was important in the incorporation into secular law-codes of regulations concerning penance in the late tenth and early eleventh centuries, and that the penitential system drew on secular law for support.

In 'Sites and Sanctity: Revisiting the Cult of Murdered and Martyred Anglo-Saxon Royal Saints' (*EME* 9[2000] 53–83), Catherine Cubitt focuses on the cults of Oswald, Oswiu and Edwin of Northumbria, Edward the Martyr, Kenelm of Mercia and Æthelred and Æthelberht of Kent. These cults have been interpreted as political in origin; Cubitt reassesses the evidence for this, and argues instead that their origins lay in devotion, especially in popular contexts, to innocent victims of unjust and violent death. Dominic Marner examines *St Cuthbert: His Life and Cult in Medieval Durham* through three main topics, which form the chapters of his study: Cuthbert and Lindisfarne, Cuthbert and Durham, and the Life of St Cuthbert. Marner charts the development of the cult of Cuthbert, the relationship between the anonymous Life and that by Bede, and the twelfth-century cult at Durham to show how the narrative of Cuthbert's life was altered over time to serve a range of interests. This study pays considerable attention to the Durham cult, and its analysis of this is supported by forty-six high-quality plates of illuminations from the version of Bede's *Life of Cuthbert* in MS London, British Library Yates Thompson 26. Graham Jones's study of 'Ghostly Mentor, Teacher of Mysteries: Bartholomew, Guthlac and the Apostle's Cult in Early Medieval England' (in Ferzoco and Muessig, eds., *Medieval Monastic Education*, pp. 136–52) examines Felix's *Life of Guthlac* and how its depiction of Guthlac's relationship with Bartholomew might have been received by a monastic audience. Jones also surveys the evidence for the cult of Guthlac provided by church dedications and place-name evidence. John Crook publishes a detailed survey of *The Architectural Setting of the Cult of Saints in the Early Christian West*, in which he discusses the development of relic cults and their physical setting up to the end of the twelfth century, with particular reference to Normandy and England. Crook uses literary and architectural evidence to survey continuities and changes to this important aspect of early medieval devotion.

In *Veiled Women: The Disappearance of Nuns from Anglo-Saxon England*, Sarah Foot makes a very important contribution to the debate about the development of the religious life for women in the Anglo-Saxon period. Volume I frames the question with a discussion of the nature of the evidence, and of scholarly readings of it. There follows a series of chronologically organized chapters which chart the apparent constriction in opportunities for professed religious life for women as the Anglo-Saxon period progresses. Foot then presents the case for the increasing importance of widows and secular vowesses, and provides an analytical typology of women's religious communities in later Anglo-Saxon England. Volume II constitutes the evidence underpinning Foot's arguments, in the form of an alphabetized survey of evidence for female religious communities in England from 871 to 1066. This is supplemented by a map and an index of Anglo-Saxon charters cited in the survey. Foot's work raises important questions about the linguistic nuances of terms for women religious, and about the implications for historical and literary scholars of the hitherto underestimated existence of individual women and groups of women leading unenclosed, unformalized, but identifiable lives of religious devotion.

Anglo-Saxon art and its connections to ecclesiastical culture are the subject of more new work. Geoffrey Martin's 'A Forgotten Early Christian Symbol Illustrated by Three Objects Associated with St. Cuthbert' (*Archaeologia Aeliana* 27[1999] 21–3) focuses on the pectoral cross, the portable altar and the coffin. Each of these objects is decorated with four matching motifs surrounding a fifth, different, central one. Martin argues that this five-element design is that of a 'Quaternity', representing the four evangelists and Christ. Cyril Hart compares 'The Bayeux Tapestry and Schools of Illumination at Canterbury' (*Anglo-Norman Studies* 22[1999] 117–67) to argue that the continuity of motifs in the art-work produced by St Augustine's Abbey, Canterbury, from 978 onwards, and their presence in the Bayeux Tapestry provide strong evidence for the tapestry as a product of the Canterbury schools of illumination. His argument is supported by a wide range of comparative illustrations. Elizabeth Coatsworth examines 'The "Robed Christ" in Pre-Conquest Sculptures of the Crucifixion' (*ASE* 29[2000] 153–76), and argues that this theme, which was formerly believed to be unusual, in fact 'declined from a position apparently of dominance in all areas to one as an important sub-theme in the course of the early medieval period; and that the Anglo-Saxon version confirmed this trend' (p. 154). In 'Medieval Cross Slab Grave Covers in Northumberland, 1: South West Northumberland' (*Archaeologia Aeliana* 28[2000] 51–110), Peter Ryder provides a descriptive catalogue and illustrations of slab grave covers in twenty-eight locations. The forthcoming second part of this paper will cover further examples, and the third part will give an analysis and discussion.

A different context for understanding Anglo-Saxon art is offered this year in C.R. Dodwell's *Anglo-Saxon Gestures and the Roman Stage*. The book was prepared for publication by Timothy Graham from the manuscript produced by Reginald Dodwell, who died in 1994. Its main thesis is that the similarity of form and meaning between Anglo-Saxon illustrations of gestures and those in illustrated manuscripts of the plays of Terence. Dodwell argues a case for the archetype of the Terence manuscripts being produced in the mid-third century, and for its illustrations reflecting actual stage practices. As an explanation of the close parallels between the Terence manuscripts and early eleventh-century Canterbury manuscript illustrations—especially those in the Illustrated Hexateuch, London, British Library Cotton Claudius B. iv—Dodwell proposes that an illustrated Terence manuscript from Continental Europe must have been available in Canterbury, and that such an exemplar is being 'quoted' in the Canterbury illustrations.

The secular cultural context is the focus of more new work. David Hill considers 'Athelstan's Urban Reforms' (*ASSAH* 11[2000] 173–86) as shown in the comparison between town planning in the burghs of the reign of Alfred the Great and Edward the Elder and in later Wessex towns planned in the reign of Athelstan. Using documentary and coin evidence, Hill argues that there was a shift in town-planning practices in the reign of Athelstan, and that this might indicate the reorganization and shiring of Mercia. Connections between the English and German Churches in the reign of Cnut are explored by Michael Hare in 'Cnut and Lotharingia: Two Notes' (*ASE* 29[2000] 261–78). Hare assesses the connections with Poland which might have influenced Cnut's choice of this baptismal name, Lambert. He also presents evidence from Lantbert of Liège's *Miracula Heriberthi* for a visit by Cnut to Cologne.

Three essays in Wolfthal, ed., *Peace and Negotiation: Strategies for Coexistence in the Middle Ages and the Renaissance*, concern Anglo-Saxon England. Ryan Lavelle's 'Towards a Political Contextualization of Peacemaking and Peace Agreements in Anglo-Saxon England' (pp. 39–55) argues that peace is an aspect of politics, which 'could ... hold a multi-layered significance as an effective political tool in Anglo-Saxon England' (p. 39). Lavelle's main focus is on the late Anglo-Saxon period, and he uses a range of narrative sources, including Bede's *Historia Ecclesiastica*, Stephanus' *Life of Wilfrid*, Asser's *Life of King Alfred*, and the *Anglo-Saxon Chronicle*. John Edward Damon's chronological focus is more limited in 'Advisers for Peace in the Reign of Æthelred Unræd' (pp. 57–78). The *Anglo-Saxon Chronicle* is used here too as a source of information about political manoeuvrings, and Damon argues that tribute-paying and 'religious approaches to conflict resolution ... held some potential for reducing the threat of the Danish invasions' (p. 78). Jonathan Wilcox examines Wulfstan's role as peacemaker with reference to a particularly notorious Anglo-Saxon act of violence, in 'The St. Brice's Day Massacre and Archbishop Wulfstan' (pp. 79–91). Wilcox compares the descriptions of the massacre in the *Anglo-Saxon Chronicle* and a charter in which Æthelred renews the privilege of the monastery of St Frideswide, Oxford, after its church was burned, and then examines Wulfstan's writing in his law-codes and homilies on peace and neighbourly obligations. He concludes that Wulfstan did promote peace and reconciliation. James Campbell's *The Anglo-Saxon State* is a wide-ranging study, whose chapters explore topics including the impact of the Sutton Hoo discovery on Anglo-Saxon studies, the Life and cult of Saint Cuthbert, Asser's *Life of Alfred*, land and power, and Stubbs and Stenton.

Ethnic and cultural identities in Anglo-Saxon England are also the subject of much new work this year. Ken Dark's *Britain and the End of the Roman Empire* uses archaeological and textual evidence from the whole of Britain to provide a comprehensive survey of the period, to underline the similarities between eastern Britain and the western barbarian kingdoms of Continental Europe in terms of the fusion of Germanic and Roman provincial life, and to suggest that Britain 'was by far the most successful "sub-Roman" society in transmitting its religion and culture to neighbouring peoples' (p. 227). In 'Welsh and English: Mutual Origins in Post-Roman Britain?' (*Studia Celtica* 34[2000] 81–104), John Hines suggests that 'there was more positive and mutual interaction in the construction of the two nations than has commonly been thought' (p. 84), and uses a range of evidence, including metalwork and artefacts related to dress fashions, ethnic terminology recorded in texts including Bede's *Historia Ecclesiastica*, and the development of the English and Welsh languages, to discuss interaction between sub-Roman and British and Anglo-Saxon populations and cultures. He argues that emerging cultural and ethnic differences were later adopted for political ends. Steven Bassett explores 'How the West was Won: The Anglo-Saxon Takeover of the West Midlands' (*ASSAH* 11[2000] 107–18), taking as his starting point the proposition that 'the Germanic migrants who had colonised the west midlands from the late fifth century onwards were soon converted to christianity by the Britons, or else that the Britons living there all rapidly adopted Anglo-Saxon language and culture, i.e. became "English"' (p. 116). Using mostly archaeological evidence from cemeteries in which furnished burials have been found, Bassett stresses that models developed for the analysis of cultural identity in eastern and southern England might not be applicable to the west Midlands, and suggests that more British Christians in this area became English than Germanic settlers became Christian.

Two major collections of essays provide illuminating ways of thinking about central issues of Anglo-Saxon cultural identity. Frazer and Tyrell, eds., *Social Identity in Early Medieval Britain*, contains the following articles on England: William O. Frazer, 'Introduction: Identities in Early Medieval Britain' (pp. 1–22), which charts the growth of scholarly interest in social identity and its influence on early medieval studies, and surveys the subjects addressed by each of the chapters in the volume; John Moreland, 'Ethnicity, Power and the English' (pp. 23–51), which challenges the notion that the development of England and Englishness was inevitable, and focuses on an examination of the nature of the 'peoples' of the Angles, Saxons and Jutes; Barbara Yorke, 'Political and Ethnic Identity: A Case Study of Anglo-Saxon Practice' (pp. 69–89), which explores Bede's use of such terms as *gens* and *regiones*, and their use in other types of texts, including charters; Yorke also considers what evidence we have for the expression of personal identity, and concludes that 'identity was not just a state of mind; it was above all, in early Anglo-Saxon England, a question of allegiance' (p. 88); Alex Woolf's 'Community, Identity and Kingship in Early England' (pp. 91–109) further ponders the question of how people in the early Middle Ages were able to identify themselves in terms of their belonging to groups such as the Gens Anglorum; Dawn Hadley's '"Cockle amongst the Wheat": The Scandinavian Settlement of England' (pp. 111–35) questions more common assumptions about constructions of identity in the Danelaw, using documentary sources, linguistics, onomastics, archaeology and sculpture; Andrew Tyrell's '*Corpus Saxonum*: Early Medieval Bodies and Corporeal Identity' (pp. 137–55) is a study of ethnicity and corporeality with reference to textual and material culture, and in particular to the methodologies and findings of archaeology; Christopher Knüsel and Kathryn Ripley's study of 'The *Berdache* or Man-Woman in Anglo-Saxon England' (pp. 157–91) also focuses on archaeology, and specifically on instances where the gender of an inhumed individual, as determined by the standard associations given to grave goods, does not match their biological sex, as defined by osteological studies. Knüsel and Ripley question the assumed close correlation between sex and gender in such instances, and point to evidence for the importance of mixed sex and gender individuals in the early Middle Ages, including Germanic *sacerdos* and assorted examples of 'man-women'. This article includes tabulated listings of types of grave goods against the sex and gender of the inhumed individuals in a number of Anglo-Saxon sites, and its appendixes set out more detail on burials at Buckland, Kent. Julia C. Crick, in 'Posthumous Obligations and Family Identity' (pp. 193–208) uses evidence from wills, charters and dispute settlements of the eighth to eleventh centuries to show how family or kin groups are not stable, and how 'the personal and the collective intersect in interesting ways' (p. 207); Tom Saunders's 'Class, Space and "Feudal" Identities in Early Medieval England' (pp. 209–32) applies recent Marxist discussions of class to early medieval English culture to explore the relationship between class formation, social space and social identity, with particular reference to the movement from dispersed to nucleated settlements and the making of the feudal town; finally, Catherine Cubitt examines 'Monastic Memory and Identity in Early Anglo-Saxon England' (pp. 253–76) as they are manifested in Bede's *Historia Ecclesiastica*, *De Templo* and *Historia abbatum*, the *Vita Ceolfridi*, Æthelwulf's *De abbatibus*, and the letters of Alcuin. Cubitt publishes a second article on Anglo-Saxon memory this year: 'Memory and Narrative in the Cult of Early Anglo-Saxon Saints' (in Hen and Innes, eds., *The Uses of the Past in the Early Middle Ages*, pp. 29–66). Her focus here is first on the example of St Boniface, and then on the two prose Lives of St Cuthbert and on Felix's *Life of Guthlac*; she examines the interaction between texts, lived experience, memory and ideology, and concludes that 'the relatively unchanging demands of the monastic life coupled with its emphasis on spiritual striving and the replication of moral exemplars resulted in a static literary genre which stressed imitation rather than developmental narrative' (p. 66). A second essay in the same collection, 'The World and its Past as Christian Allegory in the Early Middle Ages', by Dominic Janes (in Hen and Innes, eds., pp. 102–13), considers the period up to the time of Bede, and uses Bede's work as one of its central examples of the reading of the Bible as 'a repository of complex symbolism' (p. 113).

Hadley and Richards, eds., *Cultures in Contact: Scandinavian Settlement in England in the Ninth and Tenth Centuries*, is divided into five parts. The first, 'Problems and Perspectives', opens with a case, made by Hadley and Richards in their 'Introduction: Interdisciplinary Approaches to the Scandinavian Settlement', for 'more theoretically sophisticated accounts of Scandinavian settlement' (p. 3) with particular reference to ongoing debates on the questions of lordship and authority, churches and churchmen, material culture, and settlement archaeology. Simon Trafford also offers a critique of scholarship to date on 'Ethnicity, Migration Theory, and the Historiography of the Scandinavian Settlement of England', and contrasts what he sees as an opening out of thinking about Anglo-Saxon settlements with a lack of change in ways of approaching Viking settlement studies. The second part, 'Lordship, Language and Identity', contains Paul Kershaw's 'The Alfred–Guthrum Treaty: Scripting Accommodation and Interaction in Viking Age England', which examines this textual evidence for cultural contact and argues that the treaty concerns integration as well as division; Matthew Innes's 'Danelaw Identities: Ethnicity, Regionalism, and Political Allegiance', which turns to descriptions of the St Brice's Day massacre and the 1065 rebellion, and to law-codes, saints' lives and the *Anglo-Saxon Chronicle* in its consideration of the written evidence for a Danish identity in England; Matthew Townend's 'Viking-Age England as a Bilingual Society', which turns the focus to language and speech communities, and sets out a sociolinguistic framework for studying Anglo-Norse contact; and Dawn Hadley's '"Hamlet and the Princes of Denmark": Lordship in the Danelaw, *c*.860–954', which considers strategies used by rulers to establish authority and to compete with each other, including the Church, naming and language, material culture, and burial rituals. In the third part, 'The Scandinavian Settlement and the Church', Lesley Abrams considers 'Conversion and Assimilation' through analyses of the process, nature and models of conversion and evidence for pagans and Christians in the early Danelaw, and Julia Barrow discusses 'Survival and Mutation: Ecclesiastical Institutions in the Danelaw in the Ninth and Tenth Centuries' with particular reference to changes in diocesan organization, pastoral care and the appointment of bishops, the history of the Anglo-Danish Oda–Oswald–Oscytel–Thurcytel kin group, and the tenth-century fenland Benedictine foundations. The fourth part, 'Material Culture and Identity', contains David Stocker's 'Monuments and Merchants: Irregularities in the Distribution of Stone Sculpture in Lincolnshire and Yorkshire in the Tenth Century', which argues that many of the collections of stone monuments in these areas 'represent single lords and their families, burying in their own newly founded proto-parish churches' (pp. 206–7), and that a group of exceptional collections might be the monuments of traders who operated in beach markets. Also in part 4 are Phil Sidebottom's proposal, in 'Viking Age Stone Monuments and Social Identity in Derbyshire', that some stone monuments reflect social groupings, and result from cultural contact, and Gabor Thomas's 'Anglo-Scandinavian Metalwork from the Danelaw: Exploring Social and Cultural Interaction', which makes a plea for more study of these materials and the evidence they provide for cultural assimilation. The final part, 'Settlement Archaeology and the Scandinavian Settlement', opens with Guy Halsall's 'The Viking Presence in England? The Burial Evidence Reconsidered', which suggests that some of this evidence marks local, and often temporary, tensions; Martin Paul Evison asks 'All in the Genes? Evaluating the Biological Evidence of Contact and Migration', and reviews the literature on scientific attempts to identify migrations into the British Isles from biological evidence; Julian D. Richards similarly focuses on 'Identifying Anglo-Scandinavian Settlements', and argues that it is possible to identify distinctive settlement types, settlement disruption, and 'a newly invented Anglo-Scandinavian colonial artefact type: the miniature decorative copper alloy bells' (p. 306); and in the volume's final essay R.A. Hall explores 'Anglo-Saxon Attitudes: Archaeological Ambiguities in Late Ninth- to Mid-Eleventh-Century York' by tracing the evolution of our understanding of the impact of the Vikings on York, highlighting the uncertainties involved, and suggesting that some of the evidence implies factionalism and propagandism as factors behind the production of artefacts. Hadley also published a monograph this year, *The Northern Danelaw: Its Social Structure, c.800–1100*, in which she uses place-name, burial, archaeological, documentary and numismatic evidence and comparisons with Continental Europe to examine the development of rural society with particular reference to land organization, the relationship between lords and peasants, the organization of the Church, and the impact of Scandinavian settlement.

The Anglo-Saxon Way of Death is the subject this year of a major new study by Sam Lucy. Burial archaeology provides the data for Lucy's analysis of the context of her topic, in the form of a survey of the history of Anglo-Saxon burial archaeology, and of Roman traditions, and also for her detailed consideration of the beginnings and the development of Anglo-Saxon cremation and burial practices and cemetery organization. Lucy's book addresses both the fundamental methodological issue of dating burials and grave goods, and the ways in which burial archaeology is a key element in our understanding of factors central to the question of the marking and interpretation of cultural identity, including the significance of gender, ethnicity, status and tribal affiliation.

The third edition of *Europe in the Central Middle Ages, 962–1154* by Christopher Brooke is published this year. It expands the coverage of the second edition and adds a chapter on the role of women. References to Anglo-Saxon textual and social culture are to be found throughout the thematic chapters, and one chapter is devoted to 'Britain and the Vikings, 959–1035' (pp. 269–74). Palliser, ed., *The Cambridge Urban History of Britain*, volume I: *600–1540*, includes several essays of relevance to Anglo-Saxon studies: Palliser's introductory essay, 'The Origins of British Towns' (pp. 17–25), tracks the development of towns through the Roman period into the early years of Anglo-Saxon occupation. All of the essays in the 'Early Middle Ages, 600–1300' section of the volume include much detail on individual Anglo-Saxon towns: Grenville Astill's 'General Survey, 600–1300' (pp. 27–49); James Campbell's 'Power and Authority, 600–1300' (pp. 51–78); Richard Holt's 'Society and Population, 600–1300' (pp. 79–104); Richard Britnell's 'The Economy of British Towns, 600–1300' (pp. 105–26); Julia Barrow's 'Churches, Education and Literacy in Towns, 600–1300' (pp. 127–52); 'The Topography of Towns, 600–1300' by Palliser, T.R. Slater and E. Patricia Dennison (pp. 153–86); 'London from the Post-Roman Period to 1300' by Derek Keene (pp. 187–216); 'The Large Towns, 600–1300' by David A. Hinton (pp. 217–43); and 'Small Towns, 600–1300' by John Blair (pp. 245–70). The essays in the 'Regional Survey' section of the volume are also of relevance, as are two of the 'Ranking Lists of English Medieval Towns' by Alan Dyer: '1a: Pre-Conquest Towns: Area Within Fortification of Anglo-Saxon *Burhs*' (pp. 748–9) and '1b: Pre-Conquest Towns: Number of Surviving Coins from Each Mint, 973–1066' (pp. 750–1). Colm O'Brien's suggestion, 'Thirlings Building C: A Pagan Shrine?' (*Archaeologia Aeliana* 28[2000] 47–9) is drawn from his analysis of the largest building in its part of the Thirlings settlement. O'Brien questions earlier interpretations of this building as a food store, and proposes that it might be an example of a type of pagan Anglo-Saxon shrine identified by John Blair as being constructed of a square ritual enclosure, sometimes associated with burial.

Caitlin Corning's 'The Baptism of Edwin, King of Northumbria: A New Analysis of the British Tradition' (*Northern History* 36[2000] 5–15) contrasts the versions of this event in Bede's *Historia Ecclesiastica* and the anonymous *Vita Gregorii* with those in the *Historia Brittonum* and the *Annales Cambriae*. The latter two texts claim that Edwin was baptized by Rhun, son of Urien, and Corning believes that Rhun may have acted as Edwin's godfather, given the Northumbrian political situation in the 620s. Charlotte Behr explores 'The Origins of Kingship in Early Medieval Kent' (*EME* 9[2000] 25–52) by comparing the account given by Bede in the *Historia Ecclesiastica* with evidence from bracteates, which she believes to have been worn by women of high status, and which she argues show veneration of Woden in sixth-century Kent. Ian W. Walker's *Mercia and the Making of England* sets out to provide a comprehensive study of Mercia in the Anglo-Saxon period, to challenge the view that this kingdom underwent a significant decline as Wessex gained authority, and to suggest that Mercian co-operation with Wessex was a factor in the development of a unified kingdom of England. Walker examines evidence for social, political and ecclesiastical Mercian culture, and for the response to the threat of Viking dominance. The very last years of Anglo-Saxon Mercia are examined by Stephen Baxter in 'The Earls of Mercia and their Commended Men in the Mid-Eleventh Century' (*Anglo-Norman Studies* 23[2000] 23–46), part of a longer-term research project. Baxter uses these subjects to address wider questions about the nature of lordship in Mercia, and identifies the role of retainers in manifesting the power of late Anglo-Saxon earls.

The years on either side of 1066 are the subject of more new analyses. Robin Fleming's R. Allen Brown Memorial Lecture, 'The New Wealth, the New Rich and the New Political Style in Late Anglo-Saxon England', is published in *Anglo-Norman Studies* (23[2000] 1–22). Fleming analyses the effect on England's landed classes of 'two glacially-paced revolutions, one economic and the other social, the consequences of which were thoroughly manifest by the year 1000' (p. 2). He concludes that some new trends in aristocratic consumption in late Anglo-Saxon England were accelerated by the Conquest, whilst others lost popularity after 1066. In 'The Colonial History of the Norman Conquest' (*History* 84[1999] 219–36), Francis James West points out the inconsistent way in which historians have applied the vocabulary of colonialism to the Conquest, but suggests that more nuanced theories of colonial administration might be fruitful in formulating new questions about the nature of Norman rule in England, especially with regard to land tenure and legitimacy.

In *Motherhood and Mothering in Anglo-Saxon England*, Mary Dockray-Miller's focus is on *Beowulf*, and also on 'Matrilineal Genealogy and Mildrið's Maternal Legacy' and 'The Maternal Genealogy of Æðelflæd, Lady of the Mercians', as two of her chapters are entitled. Dockray-Miller observes the focus of earlier scholarship on spiritual versions of motherhood, and the importance now of studying motherhood as a practice in order to 'expand the scope of our knowledge about and analysis of the functions, places, and desires of women in Anglo-Saxon culture' (p. 2). Drawing on the work of postmodern theorists such as Judith Butler, Sara

Ruddick and Luce Irigaray, Dockray-Miller makes a stimulating exploration of what she terms 'upper-class maternal performers' (p. 8) in her chosen texts.

More new work on Anglo-Saxonism is published this year. Kees Dekker investigates 'Francis Junius (1591–1677): Copyist or Editor?' (*ASE* 29[2000] 279–96), in the light of claims from the late nineteenth century onwards that Junius made errors in and deliberate changes to the texts he transcribed. Through an analysis of Junius's linguistic ideology and rationale for transcribing Anglo-Saxon texts, Dekker shows that '[h]e was ... neither a copyist nor an editor in the modern sense of the word. Instead, he was a seventeenth-century philologist of the best kind' (p. 296). Graham ed., *The Recovery of Old English: Anglo-Saxon Studies in the Sixteenth and Seventeenth Centuries*, is a wide-ranging collection of essays on important Anglo-Saxonists and their influence on the transmission of Old English language and literature: Angelika Lutz's 'The Study of the Anglo-Saxon Chronicle in the Seventeenth Century and the Establishment of Old English Studies in the Universities'; Timothy Graham's 'John Joscelyn, Pioneer of Old English Lexicography'; Rolf H. Bremmer Jr.'s 'The Anglo-Saxon Pantheon According to Richard Verstegen'; Phillip Pulsiano's 'William L'Isle and the Editing of Old English'; Stuart Lee's 'Oxford, Bodleian Library, MS Laud Misc. 381: William L'Isle, Ælfric, and the *Ancrene Wisse*'; Danielle Cunniff Plumer's 'The Construction of Structure in the Earliest Editions of Old English Poetry'; Kathryn A. Lowe's '"The Oracle of His Countrey"? William Somner, *Gavelkind*, and Lexicography in the Seventeenth and Eighteenth Centuries'; and Kees Dekker's '"That Most Elaborate One of Fr. Junius": An Investigation of Francis Junius' Manuscript Old English Dictionary'.

Scragg and Weinberg, eds., *Literary Appropriations of the Anglo-Saxons from the Thirteenth to the Twentieth Century* opens out the question of the construction of an Anglo-Saxon identity from as early as the late twelfth century. The collection opens with Donald Scragg's introduction, 'The Anglo-Saxons: Fact and Fiction', which traces writers' attitudes across the centuries to things Anglo-Saxon. The chapters that follow are: Carole Weinberg, 'Victor and Victim: A View of the Anglo-Saxon Past in Layamon's *Brut*'; Sarah Mitchell, 'Kings, Constitution and Crisis: "Robert of Gloucester" and the Anglo-Saxon Remedy'; Jill Frederick, 'The *South English Legendary*: Anglo-Saxon Saints and National Identity'; John Frankis, 'King Ælle and the Conversion of the English: The Development of a Legend from Bede to Chaucer'; Leah Scragg, 'Saxons versus Danes: The Anonymous *Edmund Ironside*'; Julia Briggs, 'New Times and Old Stories: Middleton's *Hengist*'; Jacqueline Pearson, 'Crushing the Convent and the Dreaded Bastille: The Anglo-Saxons, Revolution and Gender in Women's Plays of the 1790s'; Lynda Pratt, 'Anglo-Saxon Attitudes? Alfred the Great and the Romantic National Epic'; Andrew Sanders, '"Utter Indifference"? The Anglo-Saxons in the Nineteenth-Century Novel'; Edward B. Irving Jr., 'The Charge of the Saxon Brigade: Tennyson's *Battle of Brunanburh*'; Daniel Donoghue, 'Lady Godiva'; and T.A. Shippey, 'The Undeveloped Image: Anglo-Saxon in Popular Consciousness from Turner to Tolkien'.

4. Literature: General

A major new collection of edited Old English prose and poetry, aimed at a student readership, is published this year. Elaine Treharne's *Old and Middle English: An Anthology* will have the very positive effect encouraging students and their tutors to read across the scholarly boundary between Old and Middle English, and also to range outside the undergraduate Old English canon of heroic and other poetry to look at prose works composed in Old English and translated from Latin. The Old English texts edited and translated in part or whole in the volume are: Bede's *Historia Ecclesiastica*; Alfred's *Preface* to the translation of Gregory's *Pastoral Care* and translation of Boethius' *Consolation of Philosophy*; the *Anglo-Saxon Chronicle*; poems from the Exeter Book; poems and one homily from the Vercelli Book; homilies and prefaces by Ælfric; *The Battle of Maldon*; *Beowulf*; *Judith*; *Exodus*; Wulfstan's *Sermo Lupi ad Anglos*; *Apollonius of Tyre*; *The Peterborough Chronicle*; and *The Life of Saint Margaret*. Each text is presented in the original with facing-page translation; useful, brief, introductions to each text set the works in context, and the volume's preliminary pages include a Chronology of Events and Literary Landmarks, and an introduction which discusses historical and literary background, manuscript culture, and poetic form, and gives a summary, with examples, of the characteristics of the Old English language.

Daniel Anlezark discusses 'An Ideal Marriage: Abraham and Sarah in Old English Literature' (*MÆ* 69[2000] 187–210). With reference to the biblical narrative and its interpretation by Bede, Origen, Augustine of Hippo, the poet of *Genesis A* and Ælfric, who uses this narrative in two of his homilies ('De doctrina apostolica' and 'Nativitas Sanctae Mariae Virginis'), and in 'Interrogationes Sigeuulfi in Genesin', Anlezark examines differing treatments of the character of Sarah and her moral virtue, and of her relationship with Abraham, and notes that both the poet of *Genesis A* and Ælfric 'reveal an anxiety to preserve the impression of Abraham's sanctity even when this threatens to erode the idealized view of him and Sarah as an ideal married couple' (p. 204).

Some important volumes looking at significant themes in Anglo-Saxon poetry have appeared this year, and the first ought to be a welcome addition to any scholar's library. In Wilcox, ed., *Humour in Anglo-Saxon Literature*, Jonathan Wilcox's introduction (pp. 1–10) contextualizes humour theory and the question of humour's propriety within Anglo-Saxon heroic culture and the monastic literary environment. His discussion provides not just a guide to the articles he has included, but also a lively and useful overview of a topic that has often been considered something of an oxymoron. One of these essays, by T.A. Shippey, looks at '"Grim Wordplay": Folly and Wisdom in Anglo-Saxon Humor' (pp. 33–48). Though a twenty-first-century audience might not find it amusing (what Shippey terms 'the much-feared "that's-not-funny" reaction'), nonetheless a substantial part of Anglo-Saxon humour depends on taking pleasure in someone else's pain. Shippey's survey of the poetry leads him to observe that Anglo-Saxon humour has 'a sardonic quality ... triggered above all by any too easy optimism, and leading on the one hand to contempt, which may be cruel and derisive, for the laughter of fools, and on the other to a more concealed admiration for those who can view uncomfortable realities with amusement at the gap between them and the wishes of those who experience them, even when the latter group includes themselves' (p. 39). Even the Christian context of *Bede's Death Song* demonstrates 'grim amusement from the wise at the expense of those who cannot understand words and do not share their vision of reality' (p. 48). The other articles in this collection will be discussed in their appropriate sections below.

John M. Hill applies anthropological theory as he reassesses the long-standing scholarly understanding of the Germanic 'heroic code' in *The Anglo-Saxon Warrior Ethic: Reconstructing Lordship in Early English Literature*. While other scholars have also acknowledged that these heroic ideals could and did function to create 'a kind of royalist, West Saxon propaganda', Hill's study considers how traditional codes underwent political reshaping between the eighth and eleventh centuries, from Alfred's reign through to Æthelred's, 'how that reshaping happens, with which heroic values particularly, and in service of which lordship-centred institutions and issues' (p. 2). Ultimately Hill argues for a new perspective that rejects the idea of an unyielding code of conduct inevitably leading to inexorable violence and a hero torn between conflicting loyalties, in favour of one that instead acknowledges the variability of response and accommodation to circumstance, a warrior ethic that not only allows but requires malleability. His evidence draws on a number of narratives concerned with warfare and feud, with the course of his argument emerging in his five chapter titles: 'Wiglaf's Rise to Dear Kinship: The Midwifery of Battle', 'Revenge and the Remaking of Group Identity in *Beowulf*: The Cases of Hengest, Ingeld, and Eadgils', 'Violence, Law, and Kingship in the Annals of West Saxon Feud: The Contests of Cyneheard (755) and Aethelwold (901, 905)', '*The Battle of Brunanburh* and the Construction of Mythological Lordship', and 'Triumphant Lordship and New Retainership in *The Battle of Maldon*'. The reconstructed idea of lordship emerges as one in which the allegiance to kinship diminishes while the loyalty of the retainer to his lord strengthens. Here, then, 'the kinship of the hall becomes more than an appropriate metaphor; politically, as centred on triumphant lordship, it becomes everything' (p. 129).

Peter Orton's thoughtful and measured study, *The Transmission of Old English Poetry*, looks at the texts of roughly twenty Old English poems that survive in multiple manuscripts to offer some observations about how accurately their copyists transcribed the poetry. Orton believes that scribes did deliberately deviate from their exemplar texts and offers reasons why they did so. He suggests that the study of patterns of variation in poems with multiple witnesses can provide helpful guidelines to modern editors working with only one witness: 'Armed with a broad idea of the kinds of corruption that Old English scribes were likely to introduce into the texts they copied, the editor of a single-witness poem such as *Beowulf* will be in a better position than before to identify, interpret and emend at least some of the corruptions in his text' (p. 4). Orton reclaims the term 'corruption', acknowledging the problem of 'textual decay' it connotes, to (re)define it as 'a reading which is not the poet's' (p. 5). He amasses a very great deal of linguistic and technical material documenting the kinds of errors likely to occur in transmitting Old English poetry, using the principle that 'good readings are earlier than bad ones and that bad readings derive somehow from good ones' (p. 5). He has arranged his book into two parts, the first analysing changes resulting from transmission, with chapters assessing 'The Language of the Scribe and the Language of the Text', 'The Pathology of Copying', 'The Scribe as Editor', 'The Confused Scribe', 'The Ambitious Scribe' and 'The Scribe as Poetaster'. In the second, Orton looks at how texts preserve existing features, and offers his conclusions about transmission of texts and the nature of their copyists, in the process of which he challenges Katherine O'Brien O'Keefe's view in *Visible Song*, arguing instead that 'in the Anglo-Saxon world the copyist and poet occupied quite distinct worlds' (p. 206).

The eclectic collection found in *Essays on Old, Middle, Modern English and Old Icelandic in Honor of Raymond P. Tripp, Jr.*, edited by Loren C. Gruber with Meredith Crellin Gruber and Gregory K. Jember, contains the same wide-ranging interests demonstrated in Tripp's own work. Eleven essays address topics in Old English, and these will be discussed in the appropriate sections below. The final two look at the use of Old English language in later works of literature, 'Satan the Navigator' by Masahiko Agari, and 'Beowulf Lives—and so do his Worthy Adversaries: Archetypes and Diction, Both Old and New' by Marie Nelson.

The place of women in Anglo-Saxon society receives some attention. Mark Atherton's essay, 'A Place for Mercy: Some Allegorical Readings of "The Woman Taken in Adultery" from the Early Middle Ages (with Particular Reference to Bede, the *Heliand* and the Exeter Book)' (in Kreitzer and Rooke, eds., *Ciphers in the Sand: Interpretations of the Woman Taken in Adultery (John 7.53–8.11)*, pp. 105–38) lays out for a non-specialist audience the background of Old English law and custom to provide a background for his discussion of the texts of the title. His comparison of these texts demonstrates the ways in which their authors adapted the biblical story to accommodate their society's attitudes towards women and marriage, and elucidates themes—among them, the place of grace and forgiveness—that would have emerged for an audience of the period.

Lori Eshleman, 'Weavers of Peace, Weavers of War' (in Wolfthal, ed. *Peace and Negotiation: Strategies for Coexistence in the Middle Ages and the Renaissance*, pp. 15–37), analyses 'two paradigmatic images of women' found on a group of monumental stones from ninth- and tenth-century Gotland, one offering a drinking horn to a male horseman, the other standing between two groups of warriors (p. 16). Her discussion, following the lead of scholars such as Jesch, Jochens, and Enright, sets these images in the context of Old Norse and Old English poetry to argue that they 'formulate two complementary functions of women in the field of social relations and negotiation' (p. 29).

Paul Beekman Taylor's comparative study of Old English and Old Norse literature, 'Figures of Female Cover on Medieval Germanic Landscapes' (in Gruber, ed., pp. 337–59), examines two groups of what Owen Barfield termed 'figurations', i.e. 'a collective representation of ideas' (p. 338). Taylor uses the Christian scriptural analogues of these two figurations to elucidate the Germanic manifestations of the public protective role of women juxtaposed with their private sexual role, especially in *Njal's Saga* and *Beowulf*.

Angelika Lutz, 'Æthelweard's *Chronicon* and Old English Poetry' (*ASE* 29[2000] 177–214), builds on the work of Campbell, Winterbottom, and Lapidge to argue that Æthelweard's idiosyncratic style results from his conversance with the native poetic traditions, as well as the Anglo-Latin tradition of Aldhelm and his literary disciples. In particular, she looks at Æthelweard's lexical and syntactic preferences, his treatment of themes and formulas and his use of alliteration to suggest that his style, though inconsistent, nonetheless reflects his appreciation of the textual experimentation of the late tenth century.

Michael Saenger, '"Ah ain't heard whut de tex' wuz": The (Il)legitimate Textuality of Old English and Black English' (*OT* 14[1999] 304–20), compares the way Bede and the twentieth-century author Zora Neale Hurston 'both construct a narrative to frame and explain a transcribed (and in a sense, translated) text by an oral author' (p. 305). In the process, Saenger draws attention to how a text can gain canonical legitimacy.

Yasuyo Moriya's analysis of 'The Line Boundary of Middle English Alliterative Meter Compared to that of Old English Alliterative Meter' (*NM* 101[2000] 387–401) leads him to conclude that fourteenth-century alliterative poetry was neither a revival nor a survival from the Anglo-Saxon tradition. Instead, the metrical patterns found in the line boundary of Middle English alliterative verse more easily support McHuntsman's idea of 'renewal' or Pearsall's 'reflourishing'. Mary E. Blockley offers a dense argument in clear prose in 'Axiomatic Implications of a Non-Occurring Heavy Verse in Old English' (*Parergon* 18:i[2000] 1–10), that is, the pattern of */|ÚÚ|x / (where | is a word boundary). Her analysis allows her to consider its relevance to the change from Old to Middle English alliterative poetry.

Two new introductions to Old English poetry, designed for non-specialist audiences, have appeared this year. Graham Holderness provides a slim survey in *Anglo-Saxon Verse*, a collection of his translations and a commentary on the poems. His introduction sets the study of Old English in a cultural and aesthetic context, while chapter 1 provides an overview of the verse itself within its manuscript sources as well as a sketch of the arrival and development of Germanic culture on English shores. It also discusses the complexities of translation set against the principles he has used in his own versions. Each following chapter looks at one of four categories—heroic, elegiac, Christian and love poetry—although, of necessity, their selections are limited. The chapter on Christian poetry, for instance, focuses on *The Dream of the Rood* and *The Fall of the Angels*, from *Genesis B*. Finally, he includes a brief but serviceable bibliography. Gwendolyn A. Morgan provides, as her title indicates, *Anglo-Saxon Poetry in Imitative Translation: The Harp and the Cross*, some of the texts in which have previously been published in literary journals. She selects her texts from the shorter poems, including both often anthologized and less canonical works; she draws from the Exeter Book riddles, heroic poems such as *Edgar's Coronation* and *Edward's Death*, lyrics, including *Wulf and Eadwacer*, and religious poems such as *The Dream of the Rood* and *Bede's Death Song*, among others. A preface by Tom Shippey gives Morgan's translations a broad historical and metrical overview, information expanded in Morgan's own introduction. She also lays out her own approach to translation: 'to preserve the Anglo-Saxon paradigm while appealing to modern poetic sensibility, and to render the perceptions of an ancient culture meaningful in our world'. Each category of translation—'From Historical to Heroic', 'The Riddle of Life', 'The Archetype and the Personal', 'Devotional'—is headed by contextualizing paragraphs, and the *en face* arrangement of the pages makes it easy for a reader to compare the original with the translation.

Donna Schlosser, 'Cynewulf the Poet, Alfred the King, and the Nature of Anglo-Saxon Duty' (*Comitatus* 31[2000] 15–37), compares Alfred's Preface to the *Cura Pastoralis* with the codas of the four poems identified as Cynewulf's. Her discussion, incorporating theory and language from Benedict Anderson's 1991 study on nationalism, demonstrates how the fusion between religious and secular during Alfred's reign, creating shared identities and values, offers evidence for perhaps the earliest sense of an English nation.

Matthew Townend looks at 'Pre-Cnut Praise-Poetry in Viking Age England' (*RES* 51[2000] 349–70) to read *The Battle of Brunanburh*, the *Five Boroughs* poem, *The Coronation of Edgar*, and *The Death of Edgar* as praise poems influenced by contemporary Norse skaldic poetry. Such tenth-century chronicle poems flourish as the result of the political climate created by the Vikings in England, conditions that recreate what H.M. Chadwick has termed a 'Heroic Age'.

Richard M. Trask, 'Looking Forward to Doomsday: An Old English Pastime' (*InG* 21[2000] 1–21), examines why the motif of Doomsday was so appealing to Anglo-Saxon poets and how it fits into an 'Augustinian sense of time in the literature' (p. 2). In order to understand attitudes held by Anglo-Saxons about wild animals in the countryside, Audrey L. Meaney provides a fascinating survey of poetic references to such animals in 'The Hunted and the Hunters: British Mammals in Old English Poetry' (*ASSAH* 11[2000] 95–105). She looks at such poems as *Maxims I*, the Cotton Gnomes, and provides an insightful discussion of Exeter Riddle 15, for which she offers the solution of 'vixen'.

A few articles from previous years were inadvertently omitted from review. Janet Duthie Collins, 'The Reality of the Classification "Poetry" for Old English' (*LACUS Forum* 24[1998] 389–97) redefines Old English poems as prose narrative accounts. Helena Znojemská, 'Where Ingeld and Christ Meet: The Exeter Book Elegies' (*LittPrag* 18[1999] 27–61), offers an answer to the question of how secular poetic texts come to be included in a manuscript written in a monastic scriptorium. Her analysis of apposition in *The Seafarer* coupled with her discussion of *The Wife's Lament* and *Wulf and Eadwacer*, allows her to suggest that the juxtaposition of secular and sacred creates a kind of 'controlled contrast', implicitly demonstrating the flaws of the heroic order while celebrating the glory of Christianity.

A special edition of *Philological Quarterly* dealing with 'Anthropological Approaches to Old English Literature' (*PQ* 78[1999]), for which John M. Hill provides the introduction, is especially important to note. Hill's overview of the journal's articles (pp. 1–13), also offering a rationale for such a cross-disciplinary approach, outlines an answer to the core question, '[W]hat can the particularly anthropological contribute to the work of the social historian, and increasingly, the literary historian attuned to historical contexts, political power, and material culture?' Peter R. Richardson's closing essay in the same volume, 'Making Thanes: Literature, Rhetoric, and State Formation in Anglo-Saxon England' (pp. 215–32), offers one answer to the question as it argues that Anglo-Saxon poetry did not merely reflect social and political change, but that its rhetorical imperatives created, albeit unconsciously, important aspects of the Anglo-Saxon state, among them the 'co-optation of kinship' and 'cultivation of thaneship'. The other articles will be synopsized in the appropriate sections below.

A number of volumes were unavailable for review, among them Boenig, trans., *Anglo-Saxon Spirituality: Selected Writings*, Gade and Fulk, *A Bibliography of Germanic Alliterative Meters*, Heinrich, *Frühmittelalterliche Bibeldichtung und die Bibel: ein Vergleich zwischen den altenglischen, althochdeutschen und altsächsischen Bibelparaphrasen und ihren Vorlagen in der Vulgata*, Rodrigues, *'The Dream of the Rood and Cyn(e)wulf' and Other Critical Essays* and Reichl, *Singing the Past: Turkic and Medieval Heroic Poetry*.

I have not seen the following article: Shiraz Felling, 'The Oral Poet as "News Reporter": Taking Another Look at the Anglo-Saxon Scop' (in Goss et al., eds. *Proceedings of the Seventh Annual Symposium about Language and Society: Austin* [*SALSA VII*], pp. 41–55).

5. The Exeter Book

Elizabeth Jackson, 'From the Seat of the *þyle*? A Reading of *Maxims I*, Lines 138–40' (*JEGP* 99[2000] 170–92), interprets these lines, a brief set of gnomic verses, as remnants of old oral lore still pertinent to the culture that produced the Exeter Book. Her argument finds parallels in the *Havamal*, and hypothesizes an instructional text addressed to an individual as yet unidentified.

Riddles continue to be a popular focus among scholars, and two articles on riddles appear in Wilcox, ed., *Humour in Anglo-Saxon Literature*. Both take a psychoanalytic approach to their subject, the group of so-called obscene riddles. D.K. Smith, 'Humor in Hiding: Laughter between the Sheets in the Exeter Book Riddles' (pp. 79–98), citing their description by Tupper as 'puzzles of double meaning and coarse suggestion' (p. 80), acknowledges that the Rule of St Benedict, forbidding both laughter and sex, creates another conundrum; their presence in a manuscript that is the product of a monastic culture. He fuses Freudian theory about sexual humour with the critical theories of Bakhtin and Derrida to hypothesize that riddles in this culture offer a way of viewing while maintaining a safe distance from a forbidden object. In particular, Smith's nuanced readings of Riddles 44 and 54 demonstrate how repression helps to create humour. Nina Rulon-Miller, too, discusses the connection between sublimation and sexual humour in 'Sexual Humor and Fettered Desire in Exeter Book Riddle 12' (pp. 99–126). Her very detailed analysis (incorporating among other materials the process for making *cuir bouilli*, a leather-hardening technique) leads to a new assessment of a conventional solution—an ox—that opens up a window on Anglo-Saxon attitudes towards women, the Welsh, and masturbation.

Robert DiNapoli speculates that the riddles mediate between a vanishing Germanic oral culture and the rising book culture of Christianity in his article, 'In the Kingdom of the Blind, the One-Eyed Man is a Seller of Garlic: Depth-Perception and the Poet's Perspective in the Exeter Book Riddles' (*ES* 81[2000] 422–55). His extended readings of riddles having to do with writing or speech (among them Riddles 88 and 93, inkhorn, and Riddle 39, the spoken word) ground his argument that they express far more boldly than other texts an imaginatively reconstructed native tradition that can covertly challenge Christian ideology. Riddle 86, solved as 'one-eyed seller of garlic', 'could hardly fail to evoke the figure of Odinn ... [and] it is at least possible this profusion of heads represents the poet's ability to portray the many-layered depths of reality' (pp. 453–4).

Edith Whitehurst Williams, '"An Insight of Form": New Genres in Four *Exeter Book* Riddles' (in Gruber, ed., pp. 231–61), as her title suggests, investigates ways in which literary categories such as the lyric are nascent in the Anglo-Saxon riddle. Riddle 10, for instance, often solved as 'barnacle goose', contains allegory; Riddle 90, the 'Latin Riddle', indicates fable; and the two 'Inkhorn' riddles, 88 and 93, 'are clearly elegies in miniature' (p. 231). The article also contains Williams's translations of the four riddles it discusses.

Ursula Zehnder's statistical comparison of 'Hypermetrical Verse Patterns in the *Riddles* of the Exeter Book' (*N&Q* 47[2000] 405–9) with verse patterns in *Beowulf* (using Geoffrey Russom's scansion) demonstrates that the patterns of the riddles show a preference for light verse types. She concludes that 'the text seems carefully crafted within the rules of the metre in *Beowulf*. Paul Sorrell, in 'Word Alchemy: A Window on Anglo-Saxon Culture'(*Parabola* 25:ii[2000] 62–8), directs his article at a non-specialist audience, providing an overview of, rather than an argument about, the nature of Anglo-Saxon riddles. It examines particularly 'transformation' riddles, those that present their objects as a sort of process (for example, the wooden artefact that begins life as a sapling).

Alfred Bammesberger, 'The Old English *Phoenix*, l. 407b: *Toþas idge*' (*NM* 101[2000] 45–9), suggests that the half-line should be read as *toþa siþge*; the manuscript reading results from miswritten *toþa sidge*, with *sidge/siþge* related to the OE word for 'scythe', followed by a mistaken word division. This minimal emendation creates a line reading, the sharpness of their teeth, which resolves a significant crux in the poem. Dora Faraci, 'Sources and Cultural Background: The Example of the Old English *Phoenix*' (*Rivista di cultura classica e medioevale* 42[2000] 225–39), builds a case for the Latin *Physiologus* Y tradition as an influence on the Old English poem. Analysing the parallels in the way each presents the transformational stages of the phoenix, she demonstrates how the allegorical traditions of the phoenix and eagle overlap, thereby fusing two different levels of meaning, the spiritual renewal of man and Christ's resurrection. Helle Falcher Petersen, '*The Phoenix*: The Art of Literary Recycling' (*NM* 101[2000] 375–86), defends the aesthetic qualities of the OE poem, focusing on two of its rhetorical strategies, use of variation and the *nis* (*ne*) ... *ac* construction. As she compares the work with its Latin source, *Carmen de ave phoenice*, she argues that the poet's techniques demonstrate a revision of exceptional artistic quality, not just a 'loose and creative' translation but a 'distinctly different poem', one worthy of more critical affirmation than it has received.

John D. Niles, '*Widsith* and the Anthropology of the Past' (*PQ* 78[1999] 171–213), advances two main purposes for his essay, first, how the poem helped to contribute to a sense of emerging Englishness in its audience, and second, that 'anthropological methods can clarify the role of poetry itself in the early medieval context as a form of ritualised discourse' (p. 173). His reading of *Widsith* shows that 'poems of this kind facilitated a discourse about values and about national and ethical identity that could not have taken place so readily in any other medium' (p. 202).

Susan Signe Morrison, 'Unnatural Authority: Translating beyond the Heroic in *The Wife's Lament*' (*M&H* 27[2000] 19–31), analyses the word *sið* to demonstrate a way to overcome the binary framework of active/passive and heroic/nonheroic found in most traditional critical discussions of Old English poetry. She argues that translations and glosses, biased toward the masculine active heroic ideal, have limited our understanding of Anglo-Saxon culture, and makes a case for *fæst* and *fæstlic*, the nongendered quality of 'steadfastness', as 'a more fruitful quality to examine ... since it is more inclusive, goes beyond the "mere" heroic, and constitutes what is truly praiseworthy in Anglo-Saxon texts' (p. 26).

Marijane Osborn elucidates the strong animal imagery in *Wulf and Eadwacer* in 'Dogode in *Wulf and Eadwacer* and King Alfred's Hunting Metaphors' (*ANQ* 13:iv[2000] 3–9), using an analogous reference from Alfred's *Preface* to Gregory's *Pastoral Care*. Osborn argues that emending the verb would soften the poem's animal motif, and that the phrase *wenum dogode* should be understood as 'tracked mentally'.

Nicolas Jacobs, 'The Seafarer and the Birds: A Possible Irish Parallel' (*Celtica* 23[1999] 125–31), suggests that the motif of pleasure in the natural world found in lines 19–20a of *The Seafarer* may be found in the twelfth-century Irish poem *Buile Shuibhne*. Even though the Old English poem is some two centuries earlier than the Irish, Jacobs argues for a ninth-century cultural commonplace, rather than a poetic motif, which the Old English might have borrowed.

Renate Laszlo's *Ewig ist der Schöpfer: Cædmons Schöpfunghymnus im Codex Exoniensis* (Marburg) was unavailable for review, as were articles by Christopher Abram, 'In Search of Lost Time: Aldhelm and The Ruin' (*Quaestio* 1[2000] 23–44), and Sealy Gilles, 'Text as Arena: Lament and Gnome in *The Wanderer*' (in Hill and Sinnreich-Levi, eds., *The Rhetorical Poetics of the Middle Ages: Reconstructive Polyphony. Essays in Honor of Robert O. Payne*, pp. 206–20).

6. The Poems of the Vercelli Book

The poems of the Vercelli Book received very little attention this year. Alfred Bammesberger, 'Old English *unnan* in *Andreas*, Line 298b' (*N&Q* 47[2000] 409–11), shows why Klaeber's explanation of this line ought still to stand, and why the verb *unnan* needs no special meaning in the passage. He offers this translation, 'they will grant you [to go] over the wave-planks', i.e. 'they will allow you on board', and rejects Krapp's assertion that *unnan willað* refers to paying the fare.

Two articles on 'Fates of the Apostles' have appeared. James E. Anderson and Leslie D. Schilling, 'The *begang* of Cynewulf's "Fates of the Apostles"' (in Gruber, ed., pp. 23–47), offer further, more detailed, evidence in support of Calder's earlier argument that the poem's structure and theme derive from a litany of saints. Their analysis leads them to identify the poet with the eighth-century bishop of Lindisfarne of the same name. In the process of answering the question posed by his title 'Did Cynewulf Use a Martyrology? Reconsidering the Sources of *The Fates of the Apostles*' (*ASE* 29[2000] 67–83), John M. McCulloh surveys in a thorough fashion the previous scholarly work on the subject. Building on Henri Quentin's 1908 investigation of medieval martyrologies and Patrick Conner's more recent redating of the Cynewulfian corpus, McCulloh makes a case for discarding martyrological sources for *Fates of the Apostles* (among them, the Continental works of Florus, Ado, and Usuard). McCulloh's concluding paragraph proposes a hypothetical passionary that might have provided Cynewulf with the inspiration to treat the apostles as a distinct hagiographical group.

Jeremy I. Wheelock, 'The Word Made Flesh: "engel dryhtnes" in *The Dream of the Rood*' (*ELN* 37:iii[2000] 1–11), defends the manuscript reading against emendation, arguing that it 'makes theological sense, is an appropriate symbol in terms of poetics, and is readily assimilated into the [poem's] overall structure' (p. 2). In the process, he makes a case for the 'engel dryhtnes' as Christ, citing patristic commentary on angelic presence in the Old Testament, and offering evidence that the idea of equating Christ with God's angel was current in Anglo-Saxon England.

7. The Junius Manuscript

As with the Vercelli poems, the Junius manuscript did not receive much scholarly attention this year. However, two articles address *Genesis A*. Daniel Anlezark's, 'An Ideal Marriage: Abraham and Sarah in Old English Literature' (*MÆ* 69[2000] 187–210), which includes analysis of *Genesis A*, is discussed in section 4 above.

Paul Battles applies Nicholas Howe's argument for the *adventus Saxonum* as central for Anglo-Saxon self-definition to *Genesis A*, in '*Genesis A* and the Anglo-Saxon "Migration Myth"' (*ASE* 29[2000] 43–66). Comparing the Genesis poet's presentation of eight passages with their Vulgate sources, he argues that the pattern of changes in the Old English reflects a set of motifs, such as 'seeking out more spacious territory', that create the underlying traditional theme of migration. For Battles, the key to the 'migration myth' does not lie in the Exodus but rather in the Babel episode, which links the Anglo-Saxons to the sons of Noah, rather than the Israelites, settlers seeking a new homeland, not fleeing God's wrath.

Tom Shippey states flatly in 'Hell, Heaven, and the Failures of *Genesis B*' (in Gruber, ed., pp. 151–76) that 'there is something *wrong* with *Genesis B*, and after three centuries of scholarship the time should have come when one can face it, and even perhaps understand it' (p. 158). The poem's downfall, 'repetitions and verbal loops' (p. 158), results from the poet's inability to take control of the alliterating pattern of traditional collocations; 'it is as if the poet does not know how to switch off his line-generating technique' (p. 168).

Two articles were unavailable for review: Alfred Bammesberger, 'Nochmals zu ae. *beohata* in *Exodus* 253a' (*Anglia* 118[2000] 258–65), and Mark Emanuel Amtstätter, 'Elemente der Klanglichkeit und Sprachkomposition in der altsächsischen Genesisdichtung' (*ABäG* 53[2000] 87–121).

8. The *Beowulf* Manuscript

Several articles from the Festschrift for Raymond Tripp look at *Beowulf*, among them Fidel Fajardo-Acosta's '"Think of Wulfstan": The Author of *Beowulf* (in Gruber, ed., pp. 49–71). Arguing that the poem has a 'riddlic' nature manifesting itself in the poet's interest in puns of identity between 'man' and 'wolf', he reassesses his previous work that suggested the author might be either a hypothetical ninth-century scholar named Werwulf or the poet designated Cynewulf. He speculates here that the *Beowulf*-poet might be the eleventh-century archbishop of York, Wulfstan. Shunichi Noguchi, '*Beowulf* and the (In)effectiveness of the Ancient "Curse"' (in Gruber, ed., pp. 125–38), asserts that the idea of a 'curse' (as it resonates from 'The Lay of the Last Survivor' to effect Beowulf's damnation) 'is essentially something invented by critics and commentators (and translators)' (p. 125). His linguistically based argument suggests instead that the original owners of the dragon's hoard decreed punishment for plunderers rather than an implacable doom.

Two more articles deal with the figure of the dragon. Anglo-Saxons were certainly aware of the Muslim world through the work of Alcuin and Bede, and Zacharias P. Thundy, 'The Dragon in *Beowulf*: Cain's Seed, Heresy, and Islam' (in Gruber, ed., pp. 201–30), argues that the *Beowulf*-poet associates Grendel and the dragon with Islamic heresy. Joyce Tally Lionarons takes a broader comparative view of the subject in '"Sometimes the Dragon Wins": Unsuccessful Dragon Fighters in Medieval Literature' (in Gruber, ed., pp. 301–16), here explaining the connection between the creation of order and its establishment through violence, with reference to Beowulf, the Old Norse *Gylfaginning*, and the Middle High German *Ortnit* and *Wolfdietrich* within the context of Indo-European myth.

In another comparative study of dragons, 'The *Heynesbók* Dragon: An Old Icelandic Maxim in its Legal-Historical Context' (*JEGP* 99[2000] 461–91), Jonathan D. Evans provides a detailed and thoughtful reading of the dragon that decorates, in the late sixteenth-century Icelandic manuscript, *Heynesbók*, the first letter of a chapter on inheritance. Evans briefly refers to *Beowulf* and *Maxims II* in demonstrating how this image draws upon Germanic cultural assumptions that equate dragons with greed and, more particularly, how it reflects the sociocultural concerns embodied in Icelandic law.

Christine Rauer's ambitious *Beowulf and the Dragon* provides a comprehensive study of parallels and analogues with the poem's final heroic encounter. The book's particular strength lies in Rauer's attention to the influence of hagiographical literature on the dragon-fight, some sixty accounts of fights between saints and dragons, in addition to her discussion of analogous secular material from about fifty Scandinavian accounts (among them the Volsung legend). Her case studies of St Samson and St Michael are especially useful (leading her to argue that Breton influences on certain narrative elements of the poem merit greater attention). The volume itself is arranged into five studies, the first three appearing in section 1, 'Beowulf and Early Medieval Dragon-Fights': 'The Analogues of Beowulf', 'The Dragon Episode', 'Dragon-Fights in Hagiography and Other Literature'. The second section, 'The Literary History of Dragon-Fights: Case Studies', includes 'Dragon-Fights in Anglo-Saxon England' and 'Post-Conquest Traditions: Siward and Others'. An especially helpful feature is the volume's third section, a collection of appendices that include texts and facing-page translations, and chronologies and bibliographies of 'Saints and Destructive Dragons' and 'Scandinavian Dragon-Fights'. All in all, this book adds a wealth of information to an area that continues to fascinate scholars and popular audiences alike.

In *The Four Funerals in 'Beowulf' and the Structure of the Poem*, Gale R. Owen-Crocker offers an intriguing reassessment of the poem's structure and themes. Rather than the three funerals generally attested by scholarly consensus, she argues that, in addition to Scyld's funeral in the poem's opening lines, that of Beowulf himself in the closing lines, and the embedded funeral of the Finnsburg episode, the so-called 'Lay of the Last Survivor' must be also be read as a funeral. Her reinterpretation of the episode emerges from the archaeological evidence of hawk and horse, poetic images in the lines, as actual grave-goods. The question naturally arising from this configuration, then, is 'What purpose does the *Beowulf*-poet seek to achieve in concentrating upon funerals in this way?' (p. 4). In answering her own question, Owen-Crocker sets her textual analysis within an impressive assemblage of archaeological and historical materials, then uses that discussion to demonstrate the structural function of the four funerals, 'four fixed points from which thematic patterns radiate' (p. 236). Her claim that the placement of the funerals is a 'tectonic device' (p. 237) leads to her suggestion that the device accounts for the manuscript's division into fitts. It also leads her to conclude that the complexity of the arrangement precludes a spontaneous oral composition such as that suggested by John Niles's theory of ring-structuring as a mnemonic device. Finally, Owen-Crocker's reading of the poem, with its sense of elliptical structures, postulates not an apocalyptic demise for the Geats but a positive affirmation of the cyclical nature of the world. The *Beowulf*-poet's Christianity, though perhaps 'laundering' those aspects of the poem 'which would have been distasteful to a Christian audience' (p. 123), nonetheless allows him to present his protagonist 'not just as a great hero, but as a good man' (p. 238). The argument, while provocative, is thoroughly documented and couched in a lucid prose style that could well be taken as a model by other scholars.

Alfred Bammesberger provides a number of linguistic analyses of the poem this year. 'Beowulf's Landing in Denmark' (*ES* 81[2000] 97–9), suggests that the half-line *eoletes æt ende* (l. 224a), does not mean 'at the end of the water-voyage' but rather 'at the end of the remote place'. Bammesberger offers a linguistic analysis of the word *eolet* as the basis of his argument, hypothesizing its origin in a noun, *ælæte*, a separated place. His 'Old English *reote* in *Beowulf*, line 2457a' (*N&Q* 47[2000] 158–9) endorses the reading of the line as 'bereft of joy'. It provides a brief philological discussion of the way in which the abstract noun *reote* emerges from the adjective *rot* 'glad, cheerful' in a manner compatible with the word-formation patterns of Old English. While half-lines of three syllables are an anomaly in Anglo-Saxon verse, Bammesberger's 'The Superlative of OE *gód* in *Beowulf* (*NM* 101[2000] 519–21), points out that three lines containing some form of *betst* in the poem exhibit this deviation from the four-syllable half-line. He suggests that the phrases *secg betsta* (ll. 947a and 1759a) and *ðegn betstan* (l. 1871b) contain syncopic forms of the trisyllabic form *betesta(n)*, and provides a linguistic analysis of its development. Finally, in 'What Does *he* in Lines 1392b and 1394b of *Beowulf* Refer To?'(*N&Q* 47[2000] 403–5), citing Randolf and Quirk's statement, 'Strict concord in grammatical gender is the rule in Old English' (p. 405), Bammesberger shows that *he* cannot erroneously refer to Grendel's mother, *magan*, but instead operating in concord with the masculine gender of the referent, refers to *gang*, 'track', in line 1391a.

In 'The Archetype of *Beowulf* (*ASE* 29[2000] 5–41), Michael Lapidge's detailed analysis of many literal errors in the *Beowulf* manuscript as faulty transliterations from an unfamiliar system of script leads to his argument for an early eighth-century date of composition and his assertion that the extant version of the poem in Cotton Vitellius A. xv is the product of several stages of copying. In addition, his analysis suggests that the composition of the hypothetical exemplar did not include the *Life of St. Christopher* or *Judith*.

Basing his investigation, 'The Use of the Verb *maðelian* in *Beowulf* (*NM* 101[2000] 59–68) on Risannen's 1998 article, Roderick W. McConchie asks whether any circumstances exist in which the verb must be used, rather than another verb, and whether its use is precluded under certain conditions. His answer pays particular attention to Risannen's criterion of importance, confining it to the content of a speech (which includes its length, its lack of a foregone answer, gnomic elements, and previously unknown material).

Hideki Watanabe, 'Final Words on *Beowulf* 1020b: *brand Healfdenes*' (*NM* 101[2000] 51–7), discusses a phrase that appears as Hrothgar gives Beowulf a gift of armour. Watanabe asserts that reading the phrase as a subject, the traditional interpretation, undercuts the significance of the *maere maðþumsweord* in line 1023 and again in the poem's second treasure-giving scene at line 2154. To read the phrase as the direct object of *forgeaf* (l. 1020), however, a variant of *maere maðþumsweord*, creates 'thematic resonance and … structural coincidence' (p. 55) between the two scenes.

Steven E. Smith's 'The Provenance of the *Beowulf* Manuscript' (*ANQ* 13:i[2000] 3–7) sketches a hypothetical itinerary for the manuscript, with special attention to its whereabouts in the sixteenth century. After leaving its long-time home in St Mary's Priory (Southwick) following Henry VIII's dissolution of monasteries, it travelled to Sir William Cecil's library and thence to Robert Nowell. Nowell bequeathed the volume to William Lambarde, and it found its way to the Cotton collection either directly from Lambarde or more circuitously via Somner and Selden.

Gerald Richman's 'Poet and Scop in *Beowulf*' (*InG* 21[2000] 61–91) argues that the poem's Finnsburh episode and its song of creation, as well as the story of Sigemund, all provide examples of apposition, direct and indirect speech in the voices of the poet and scops within the poem. However, modern editorial practices have tended to create 'an either-or disambiguation of the text', and Richman uses his analysis to support Bruce Mitchell's suggestion that new editorial devices are necessary to convey the sense of simultaneity of theme created by Anglo-Saxon manuscript conventions.

A.P. Church, 'Beowulf's "*ane ben*" and the Rhetorical Context of the "Hunferþ Episode"' (*Rhetorica* 18[2000] 49–78), modifies Gabrielle Knappe's recent argument that the rhetorical nature of Anglo-Saxon literature derives from the classical grammatical curriculum, in particular the Latin *praeexercitamina*. He asserts that exercises from the Greek tradition of *progymnasmata*, as a result of the pedagogy of Theodore of Tarsus, inform the famous scene between Beowulf and Hrothgar's *þyle*, thereby providing evidence of such a rhetorical understanding throughout the entire poem.

Michael Stephen Lane, in 'Remembrance of the Past in *Beowulf*' (*InG* 21[2000] 41–59), wishes to establish what he believes to be 'the source of the poem's power', which he asserts is 'in its dynamic relationship to the past' (p. 41). The substance of his essay depends on what he terms 'deep historical patterns' to demonstrate the force carried by the poem's relationship with the past, 'rather than upon conventional argumentation' (p. 41).

Phyllis R. Brown reassesses 'Cycles and Change in *Beowulf*' (in Boenig and Davis, eds., *Manuscript, Narrative, Lexicon: Essays on Literary and Cultural Transmission in Honor of Whitney F. Bolton*, pp. 171–92) to find the fusion of Christian and pagan made possible by the 'correction-and-fulfillment' of the theology of Gregory the Great that provides the starting point of her analysis. This theology mitigates the bleak apocalyptic vision most often offered by critics as an interpretation of the poem's closing scene: 'The *Beowulf* poet, like Gregory, seems to have envisioned a physical world contiguous with the spiritual world beyond, a world in which Christian revelation emphasizes the power of virtuous behavior' (p. 189).

Previous discussions of political power in Heorot have framed that power in thematic analyses of Hrothgar's admonition to Beowulf (ll. 1700–84), rather than using specific events from the entire narrative. Brian McFadden, 'Sleeping after the Feast: Deathbeds, Marriage Beds, and the Power Structure of Heorot' (*Neophil* 84[2000] 629–46), argues that the poet marks shifts in power throughout the poem with lexical cues, i.e. the words *bed*, *raest*, and their compounds. Linking military and sexual power, he reassesses the role of Wealhtheow in the power changes at Heorot, which depend on the old king's deathbed or the peaceweaver's marriage bed, since the kingdom functions on the basis of the health, both physical and moral, of the king.

E.L. Risden has contributed two articles to *Beowulf* scholarship this year. The first, 'Heroic Humor in *Beowulf*' (in Wilcox, ed., pp. 71–8), explains how humour reinforces the poem's heroic code. Formal exchanges such as flyting express simultaneously a kind of existential cheerfulness and a prudent warning against putting oneself in the way of later danger. Risden's analysis uses Grice's theory of conversational rules to suggest that such humour, including irony and understatement, emerges as a result of breaching rules of 'cooperative conversation' (p. 72). His 'Irony in *Beowulf*' (in Gruber, ed., pp. 139–49), also acknowledges a kind of humour in the poem, but here he suggests that irony does not so much lighten the poem's mood as its quality of surprise destabilizes its meaning. Such complexity causes readers to pay greater attention to larger themes and purposes, 'some of the hard facts of life, including the need for vigilance and courage' (p. 142).

Marijane Osborn's 'The Two-Way Evidence in *Beowulf* Concerning Viking-Age Ships' (*ANQ* 13:ii[2000] 3–6) offers a confirmation of Roger Smith's argument that the Beowulf-poet's references to mast and sails indicate a composition date of around the ninth or tenth century. The description of the prow of Beowulf's ship as 'coiled' rather than 'curved', and the shore-guard's reference to the ship as *niwtyrwed* 'newly tarred' (l. 295a), both argue against a pre-eighth-century date. In '*Beowulf* and *Sonatorrek* are Genuine Enough: An Answer to Klaus von See' (*Skandinavistik* 30[2000] 44–59), Daniel Sävborg defends his 1997 dissertation against criticism from a 1998 article (also in *Skandinavistik*) by von See. Sävborg reiterates and, in the process of refuting von See's argument (which includes the assertion that Beowulf is 'not genuinely Old Germanic'), expands his original thesis that the poetic treatment of grief in Eddic poetry emerges from a common Old Norse and Old Germanic tradition.

Seiichi Suzuki discusses 'The Metrical Reorganization of Type E in the *Heliand*' (*AJGLL* 12[2000] 281–90) in comparison with *Beowulf*. He concludes that 'the full gradation of the first drop of Type A in the *Heliand*' brought about an analogous gradation in 'the major variants of the first and second drops of type E (S#x, Sx#, Xx#)' (p. 289).

Two articles by Raymond P. Tripp Jr. address issues in *Beowulf*. In the first, 'The Homiletic Sense of Time in *Beowulf*' (*InG* 21[2000] 23–40), he distinguishes between 'time past' and 'time passing' to define the elegiac quality of the poem. He finds some of the 'peculiar urgency' (p. 27) that infuses the poem to be a product of a 'homiletic vocabulary of time' (words such as *fyrst*, hwile, and *faec*) (p. 27); his analysis compares the poetic language of *Beowulf* with the diction of the homiletic collections of Blickling, Vercelli, and Pseudo-Wulfstan. The second, 'Humor, Wordplay, and Semantic Resonance in *Beowulf*' (in Wilcox, ed., pp. 49–69), investigates the way the *Beowulf*-poet uses the myriad word-forms available to him in order to create the poem's competing vision of the Christian present and pagan past, two points of view being integral to humour, to suggest that competing cultural perspectives must of necessity create humorous situations, 'the linguistics of cultural conflict' (p. 51). Tripp's elaborate etymological analysis of the poem provides the basis for an extended meditation on the epistemological nature of humour.

Bertha Rogers has added another volume to the ever-growing number of translations of the poem in her *'Beowulf': Translation and Art*. She creates something of a chapbook, divided into nineteen sections (for example, 'Prologue: The History of the Spear-Danes', 'Unferth Baits Beowulf', 'The Slave Steals from the Dragon', 'Beowulf's Death'), which would serve as an accessible, if rather pricey, version for a reader new to the poem. Nonetheless, it will suffer by comparison with other recent translations, most notably those of Seamus Heaney and Roy Liuzza. Another translation, by Felix Nobis, was unavailable for review. In a special supplement to the *American Poetry Review* (29:i[2000] 21–8), 'From *Beowulf*', Seamus Heaney talks about the genesis of his recent translation of the poem, and includes an excerpt of lines, as do Alan Sullivan and Timothy Murphy about their own version, in 'The Fire-Drake: The Translators' Tale, or How Many Angles Can Dance on the Head of a Finn?' (*HudR* 52[2000] 587–95), excerpting lines 2510–2709.

R.T. Smith, 'Swimming Champ Disarms Intruder?' (*Shenandoah* 50:ii[2000] 163–8), offers a meditation, filtered through the writer's own experience of both the original and translations, on the pleasures, challenges, and lessons of the poem's text.

A few articles eluded notice in previous years. Four articles from *Philological Quarterly*'s special volume on anthropological approaches to Old English literature (*PQ* 78[1999]) address *Beowulf*, two from the perspective of feuding. The poem's view is often at odds with contemporary understanding of the term, according to David Day. The *Beowulf*-poet does not distinguish between feuds and other forms of violence, nor does he grant much utility to how feuds might be ended, such as *wergild* or political marriage. In '*Hwanan sio fæhð aras*: Defining the Feud in *Beowulf*' (*PQ* 78[1999] 77–95), Day's analysis shows how the poet uses *fæhð* in ways particular to the poem's ironic tone and sense of tragedy. While affirming Day's definition of feud, John M. Hill, 'The Ethnopsychology of In-Law Feud and the Remaking of Group Identity in *Beowulf*: The Cases of Hengest and Ingeld' (*PQ* 78[1999] 97–123) rejects Day's idea of inevitable tragedy within the poem. He suggests that the poet uses the feud scenarios as 'socially acute meditations on the prospects for settlement … and extended community' as well as on 'the dynamic of group reformation' (p. 97). Stephen O. Glosecki, '*Beowulf* and the Wills: Traces of Totemism?' (*PQ* 78[1999] 15–47) finds in the poem evidence of ancient kinship and inheritance arrangements, in particular—despite its fall from critical grace—the notion of a matrilineal system. 'In a totemic frame', Glosecki argues, the poem's 'scattered elements combine into an integral whole' (p. 36). In '"The Wealth They Left Us": Two Women Author Themselves through Others' Lives in *Beowulf*' (*PQ* 78[1999] 49–76), Marijane Osborn sets her discussion of Wealhtheow and Hygd against modern ethnographic studies demonstrating how individuals within tribal cultures use traditional and personal narrative to structure a sense of self. The two queens are careful to follow 'scripts' (p. 57) (of Hildeburh and Thryth respectively) that provide 'an adequate symbolization of their desired self' (p. 52); these self-constructed life-stories demonstrate both their understanding of their cultural roles and their worthiness of fame after death.

Steven Fanning, in 'Tacitus, *Beowulf*, and the *Comitatus*' (*Haskins Society Journal* 9[1997] 17–38) challenges the conventional scholarly view that the *comitatus*, as described by Tacitus, was transmitted essentially unchanged from Germany to England. He surveys both historical and literary 'proof-texts' to argue that they 'do not in fact provide evidence for the existence of the ethic, but rather they indicate the exact opposite' (p. 28). Modern descriptions and mistranslations of *Germania* distort Tacitus's work to bring it in line with what exists in the heroic literature, creating a circular argument. Fanning's discussion of Tacitean scholarship argues that the work itself is inherently untrustworthy, to be regarded more as a 'work of art' than historically accurate. He concludes that nineteenth-century scholars created the link between *Germania*, *comitatus* and heroic literature (that persists as dogma even now) 'to serve nationalistic and racial purposes' (p. 37), despite the dissolution of that 'nationalistic matrix' (p. 38).

Quoting Lévi-Strauss's assertion that 'The nature of myth is a dialectic structure in which opposed logical positions are stated' (p. 2), Kevin J. Wanner investigates 'Warriors, Wyrms, and Wyrd: The Paradoxical Fate of the Germanic Hero/King in *Beowulf*' (*EssaysMedSt* 16[1999] 1–15). The poem's central paradox is that 'The very process that secures one's position simultaneously undermines that stability by perpetually renewing the potential for violence' (p. 3). He argues, however, that it is the pagan motif of the dragon-fight, not the Christian poet, which provides an internal commentary on the poem's pagan culture.

Helena Soukupová compares two instances of heroic last words in 'The Anglo-Saxon Hero on his Death-Day: Transience or Transcendence? (A Motivic Analysis of Beowulf's and Byrhtnoth's Death Speeches)' (*LittPrag* 18[1999] 5–26) to argue that the language of these speeches expresses and differentiates most clearly the religious orientation of both protagonists and poets.

E.V. Thornbury's '*Eald enta geweorc* and the Relics of Empire: Revisiting the Dragon's Lair in *Beowulf*' (*Quaestio* 1[2000] 82–92) was unavailable for review, as were the following: Lee Patterson, 'The Heroic Laconic Style: Reticence and Meaning from *Beowulf* to the Edwardians' (in Aers, ed., *Medieval Literature and Historical Inquiry: Essays in Honor of Derek Pearsall*, pp. 133–57); Andreas H. Jucker and Irma Taavitsainen, 'Diachronic Speech Act Analysis: Insults from Flyting to Flaming' (*JHP* 7[2000] 67–95); Jos Bazelmans, 'Beyond Power: Ceremonial Exchanges in *Beowulf*' (in Theuws and Nelson, eds., *Rituals of Power, from Late Antiquity to the Early Middle Ages*, pp. 311–75); and Mitchell and Irvine, '*Beowulf* Repunctuated.

9. Other Poems

The Old English charms continue to enchant scholars; four articles consider their continuing appeal. In 'The Inscription of Charms in Anglo-Saxon Manuscripts' (*OT*

14[1999] 401–19), Lea Olsan uses the theft charm found in Cambridge MS CCC 41 as an example of ways in which the performative aspects of charms are represented in their manuscript context. She uses her analysis to suggest a larger case: that careful and systematic manuscript studies will provide a fuller understanding of the charms' oral tradition. Stephen O. Glosecki, '"Blow these vipers from me": Mythic Magic in *The Nine Herbs Charm*' (in Gruber, ed., pp. 91–123), gives scholars a reading and new translation of *The Nine Herbs Charm* as he elucidates its dense mythic and linguistic qualities. His sensitive delineation of its complex syncretism—a mixture of Germanic, classical and Christian wisdom—underscores Glosecki's sympathetic defence of a shamanistic strain in Anglo-Saxon literature. For those interested in Old English poetry, John Frankis's 'Sidelights on Post-Conquest Canterbury: Towards a Context for an Old Norse Runic Charm (DR 419)' (*NMS* 44[2000] 1–27) will be more valuable for his discussion of MS Cotton Caligula A. xv and his brief comments on some Anglo-Saxon charms than for the runic charm the manuscript contains. Edward Pettit's 'Some Anglo-Saxon Charms' (in Roberts and Nelson, eds., pp. 411–33), was not available for review.

E.G. Stanley offers a cautionary note about literary criticism that depends on an experiential element in 'Old English Poetic Vocabulary: "The formal word precise but not pedantic"' (in Gruber, ed., pp. 177–200). He uses the occasion of his essay, which focuses on *The Seasons for Fasting* and *The Death of Edward*, to comment on the gap between Anglo-Saxon and modern perceptions of reality.

Graham D. Caie has contributed the second volume to Brewer's Anglo-Saxon Texts series: *The Old English Poem 'Judgement Day II': A Critical Edition with Editions of 'De die iudicii' and the Hatton 113 Homily 'De domes dæge'*. Caie's facing-page translation of *Judgement Day II* is accompanied by the poem's Latin source, Bede's *De die iudicii* (in London BL Cotton Domitian A. i), and the text of and commentary on the homily, *De domes dæge* (in Oxford Bodleian Hatton 113), which is very nearly identical with the Old English poem. The volume also contains an Old English glossary and a selective bibliography, current through to 1998, of primary and secondary sources. Caie's introduction to his edition provides comprehensive analysis of his focal text, with conventional manuscript description—provenance, date, contents, language, style—and discussion of the context of the poem within the manuscript. This last is especially important as the text appears to be linked with four other poems, in particular with *An Exhortation to Christian Living* and *A Summons to Prayer*, which Robinson has argued to be one poem, a position with which Caie concurs. His work, for which he re-examined all three source manuscripts, replaces earlier, flawed, editions of the poem (Löhe's 1907 edition and commentary come under special fire). Caie also describes Hatton 113 and compares its homiletic text with the Old English poem, using the prose version to clarify textual obscurities in the Old English. In the final section of his introduction he offers a close reading of the Old English poem that demonstrates the poet's skill and vision, and presents *Judgement Day II* as 'a faithful, yet imaginative, translation of Bede's De die iudicii' (p. 40).

Four articles on *The Battle of Maldon* approach the poem from very different perspectives. In 'The Battle of Maldon Line 191b' (*ANQ* 13:iii[2000] 3–8), Carole Hough re-examines the evidence for emending the manuscript reading of *ærdon* to *ærndon*. She looks at the other work of the poem's eighteenth-century copyist, David Casley, to demonstrate that, while omitting letters was not a characteristic found in Casley's transcriptions, he did tend to confuse letters of similar appearance. Hough suggests that he mistook ð for d, and wrote ærdon for ær ðon, 'before, previously'. This assessment allows her to posit that the disputed phrase in line 186, *Offan bearn*, is a plural reference to two of the three cowardly brothers. Andrew Breeze, 'Sorrowful Tribute in *Armes Prydein* and *The Battle of Maldon*' (*N&Q* 47[2000] 11–14), examines a Welsh literary parallel to the Old English text, and offers a more precise date, the last months of 940, than suggested dates of previous analyses (which span 927 to 980). He discusses the motif of 'spears for tribute' common to both poems. Noting that 'traditional plot structures can remain remarkably active and influential, even when challenged by traditions of historical process which enjoy superior cultural prestige' (p. 152), Craig R. Davis, 'Cultural Historicity in *The Battle of Maldon*' (*PQ* 78[1999] 151–69), uses the tools of cultural anthropology to analyse the ambiguity of Byrhtnoth's *ofermod* within the poem's two competing traditions. Ultimately the differing systems of moral expectation embodied in Christianity and Germanic heroic culture help to create the poem's distinct shape, 'its dependence upon but distance from Germanic heroic tradition' (p. 163), so that it can be read 'both as a reflex of archaic tradition and as a tool of contemporary cultural action' (p. 164). In an analysis typical of his impressive range of scholarship, John D. Niles, 'Byrhtnoth's Laughter and the Poetics of Gesture' (in Wilcox, ed., pp. 11–32), assesses this pivotal moment in the *Battle of Maldon* in a broad cross-cultural context of Norse and classical literature. He provides a meticulous consideration of the complex semiotics of gesture as the foundation for his assertion that Byrhtnoth, laughing in the midst of the fight, embodies the contradictory nature of Anglo-Saxon heroism, 'the inseparable qualities of courage and arrogance' (p. 30). Ultimately, however, Niles offers a more wide-ranging rumination on the nature of laughter within a culture.

Paul F. Reichardt, 'Bede on Death and a Neglected Old English Lyric' (*KPR* 12[1997] 55–60), speculates about the reasons for critical neglect of Bede's *Death Song*. He sets the text against Bede's rendering of *Cædmon's Hymn*, and suggests that the textual context of the *Death Song*, in Cuthbert's letter, ultimately lacks the staying power of Bede's *Ecclesiastica Historia*, so that its status ebbed with the status of Cuthbert's letter after the twelfth century, despite the relatively large number of surviving texts up to that point, because its vernacular presented the human side of Bede rather than the Latin voice of an *auctor*.

R.I. Page's *The Icelandic Rune-Poem* (originally published as an article in *NMS* 42[1998] 1–37; see *YWES* 79[2000]) has been published by the Viking Society for Northern Research [1999] as a separate volume.

I have not seen Earl R. Anderson's 'Old English Poetic Texts and their Latin Sources: Iconicity in *Cædmon's Hymn* and *The Phoenix*' (in Fischer and Nänny, ed., *The Motivated Sign: Iconicity in Language and Literature II*, pp. 109–32).

10. Prose

From this year onwards, publications on pre-Conquest Anglo-Latin prose will be reviewed in this section along with Old English prose.

The third and final volume in the EETS edition of Ælfric's *Catholic Homilies—Introduction, Commentary and Glossary*, by Malcolm Godden—is published this year. It contains an introductory discussion of Ælfric and of the nature of the *Catholic Homilies*, their date, origin, style and sources. This preliminary section of the volume ends with a very useful summary list of sources used by Ælfric in composing the *Catholic Homilies*. The bulk of the volume is taken up with the commentary, which proceeds homily by homily, giving notes on the homilies' contents and on the detail of correspondences to sources and influences (and, very helpfully, printing source passages in full) and noting details of authorial revision in the first series of *Catholic Homilies* only, since these details are largely covered by the notes to Peter Clemoes's edition of the second series. The volume ends with a full glossary to both series, and stands as an essential companion to the two volumes of editions.

The fifth volume in the Garland Basic Readings in Anglo-Saxon England series, Szarmach, ed., *Old English Prose: Basic Readings*, is published this year (for volume 6 in this series, see section 3 above). Gathered in the volume are sixteen important essays. Eleven have already been published elsewhere, but two of these are here translated into English for the first time, and three further essays and two bibliographies are newly published here. The essays reprinted in this volume are: Janet Bately, 'The Literary Prose of King Alfred's Reign: Translation or Transformation?'; Peter Clemoes, 'The Chronology of Ælfric's Works'; D.G. Scragg, 'The Corpus of Vernacular Homilies and Prose Saints' Lives before Ælfric'; Mary Clayton, 'Homiliaries and Preaching in Anglo-Saxon England'; Milton McC. Gatch, 'King Alfred's Version of Augustine's *Soliloquia*: Some Suggestions on its Rationale and Unity'; Klaus Grinda, 'The Myth of Circe in King Alfred's *Boethius*'; Bernard Huppé, 'Alfred and Ælfric: A Study of Two Prefaces'; M.R. Godden, 'Ælfric's Saints' Lives and the Problem of Miracles'; Joyce Hill, 'Ælfric's Use of Etymologies'; Paul E. Szarmach, 'Ælfric, the Prose Vision, and the *Dream of the Rood*'; and Hans Sauer, 'The Transmission and Structure of Archbishop Wulfstan's "Commonplace Book"'. The articles by Grinda and Sauer were originally published in German. The three new articles are Jonathan Wilcox, 'The Wolf on Shepherds: Wulfstan, Bishops, and the Context of the *Sermo Lupi ad Anglos*' (pp. 396–418), which examines Wulfstan's career and writings with reference to questions of genre, textual integrity, textual stability and authorship; J.E. Cross, 'The Notice on Marina (7 July) and *Passiones S. Margaritae*' (pp. 419–32), which examines the evidence for the source of the entry on Marina in the *Old English Martyrology*, suggests a newly identified Latin partial source, and shows that Marina is clearly separated from Margareta in the *Old English Martyrology*, and that her feast-day of 7 July in this text accords with most English calendar evidence; and Jane Roberts, 'The English Saints Remembered in Old English Anonymous Homilies' (pp. 433–61), which explores the possible reasons for the currency of narratives about certain saints in anonymous Old English homilies, and notes 'not just the retention and refurbishing of older texts but the continued wish to translate, compile, and make anew' (p. 451). The two bibliographies included in the volume, both of which will be of great use to scholars, are 'Alfred the Great: A Bibliography with Special Reference to Literature' by Nicole Guenther Discenza, and 'An Annotated Bibliography of Ælfrician Studies, 1983–1996' by Aaron J. Kleist.

Anglo-Saxon homiletic prose is discussed in several of the sections of Kienzle, ed., *The Sermon*. The volume's bibliography, compiled by George Ferzoco and Carolyn Muessig, includes sections on 'The Early Medieval Sermon' (pp. 30–4) and on 'Vernacular Sermons in Old English' (pp. 76–80), and its Index of Manuscripts has matching sections, while the following items in the main part of the volume are of note: Thomas N. Hall, 'The Early Medieval Sermon' (pp. 203–69), and J.E. Cross, 'Vernacular Sermons in Old English' (pp. 561–96). Both of these sections include discussions of homiletic production in the Anglo-Saxon period, details of edited texts, and translations of sample homilies.

Two of the articles in Wilcox, ed., *Humour in Old English Literature*, focus on Old English hagiography. In '"Why do you speak so much foolishness?" Gender, Humor, and Discourse in Ælfric's *Lives of Saints*' (pp. 127–36), Shari Horner explores 'surprising strategic and didactic uses of humor in texts intended for monastic and non-monastic audiences alike: The lives of female virgin martyrs' (p. 128) to show how they are sources of pleasure and learning. The saints' lives from which Horner draws her examples include that of Lawrence, the narrative of St Agape, St Chionia and St Irene in the *Old English Martyrology*, and Ælfric's Lives of St Lucy, St Cecilia and St Agatha. Hugh Magennis gives another reading of Ælfrician hagiography in 'A Funny Thing Happened on the Way to Heaven: Humorous Incongruity in Old English Saints' Lives' (pp. 137–57). His focus is on Ælfric's *Life of Edmund*, the *Legend of St Mary of Egypt*, the *Life of Saint Margaret*, and the *Legend of the Seven Sleepers*, and he also refers to *Apollonius of Tyre*, *Guthlac A* and *Andreas*. His conclusion is that these texts are examples of the celebration of humorous incongruity to convey 'the power of grace operating in the world' (p. 157).

In 'Bodies and Boundaries in the Old English *Life of St. Mary of Egypt*' (*Neophil* 84[2000] 137–56), Andrew P. Scheil shows how the narrative constructs an opposition between masculine (ascetic) and feminine (sexual) bodies, and the known and the unknown, in order to examine ascetic, monastic masculinity. Peter Jackson's focus is on 'Ælfric and the Purpose of Christian Marriage: A Reconsideration of the *Life of Æthelthryth*, lines 120–30' (*ASE* 29[2000] 235–60). The lines in question are Ælfric's exemplum of a layman who maintains chastity through his thirty-year marriage before entering a monastery. Jackson suggests that Ælfric included this exemplum because he was not comfortable with Æthelthryth as a model of marital sanctity, examines Ælfric's use of his source for the exemplum, Rufinus of Aquileia's *Historia monachorum in Aegypto*, compares Ælfric's other statements on the respective duties of those called to marriage and to abstinence, and concludes that the closing exemplum has the effect of leaving the reader with a 'quiet reassertion of the Augustinian ideal of a Christian marriage' (p. 260).

The Old English Hexateuch is the focus of well-deserved critical attention this year in the form of Barnhouse and Withers, eds., *The Old English Hexateuch: Aspects and Approaches*, which examines important aspects of this text and its contexts, and supports its analysis with many illustrations of manuscript text and illuminations. In their introduction to the collection (pp. 1–13), Barnhouse and Withers sketch out scholarly views on the composition and date of the manuscript, which they describe as 'a wonderfully complex and intriguing social document' (p. 12). The first essay, Melinda J. Menzer's 'The Preface as Admonition: Ælfric's Preface to Genesis' (pp. 15–39), examines Ælfric's Preface to Genesis, which Menzer argues 'is disjointed and brings out inconsistencies' (p. 31) in order to mirror the difficulties of the text of the Old Testament itself. Richard Marsden's 'Translation by Committee? The "Anonymous" Text of the Old English Hexateuch' (pp. 41–89), makes a detailed analysis of the content and style of the non-Ælfrician parts of the Hexateuch, and proposes that the original of the Hexateuch compilation was composed by several monks in a single centre. Detailed scrutiny of the translation strategies employed in the Old English Hexateuch is also the focus of 'Shaping the Hexateuch Text for an Anglo-Saxon Audience' (pp. 91–108) by Rebecca Barnhouse. Barnhouse's interest is in the ways in which the Old English translators make modifications to and decisions about their source-text in an attempt to control readers' responses to the Hexateuch. Sarah Larratt Keefer's 'Assessing the Liturgical Canticles from the Old English Hexateuch' (pp. 109–43) focuses on the canticles *Cantemus Domino* (Exodus 15: 1–19) and *Audite Caeli* (Deuteronomy 32: 1–43), both of which are traditionally held to have been composed by Moses. Keefer sets out to estimate how well the Old English versions of these two canticles were known to the Anglo-Saxons. In order to do this, she surveys the presentation of Moses in Old English prose and poetry and in the illustrations to the Hexateuch manuscript Cotton Claudius B. iv, and concludes that the canticles in the Hexateuch were probably recognizable as liturgical in function. Mary P. Richards examines 'Fragmentary Versions of Genesis in Old English Prose: Context and Function' (pp. 145–63), and in particular Ælfric's translation of the creation story and the Joseph story, and proposes that the popularity of these two episodes is due to their presumed connections to Ælfric. The next three essays in the collection concern the illustrations to Cotton Claudius B iv. David F. Johnson's 'A Programme of Illumination in the Old English Illustrated Hexateuch: "Visual Typology"?' (pp. 165–99) sets out a case for a portion of the narrative—the story of Abraham—being highlighted by the designer through visual emphasis. Catherine E. Karkov's discussion of 'The Anglo-Saxon Genesis: Text, Illustration, and Audience' (pp. 201–37) makes a detailed comparison of the pictures illustrating Genesis in Cotton Claudius B. iv and those illustrating the Old English poem *Genesis* in Oxford, Bodleian Library, Junius 11. Karkov focuses on the depiction of women in the illustrations, on the ways in which Anglo-Saxon royal women of the tenth and eleventh centuries intervened in political affairs, and on the implications of this for a female audience for the two manuscripts. 'The First Laugh: Laughter in Genesis and the Old English Tradition' by Jonathan Wilcox (pp. 239–69) examines the three laughs connected with the story of the birth of Isaac in the portion of the Hexateuch written by Ælfric, two of which are illustrated in Cotton Claudius B. iv. Wilcox surveys acts of laughter portrayed by Ælfric in his other writings, in which 'Ælfric is highly suspicious of laughter' (p. 255), and contrasts his depiction of laughter in Genesis with that in the poem *Genesis A*, and then with the illustrations to the Hexateuch. The final essays in the collection deal with the post-medieval history of Cotton Claudius B. iv. Timothy Graham uncovers the role of 'Early Modern Users of Claudius B. iv: Robert Talbot and William L'Isle' (pp. 271–316), and the significance of their interest in the manuscript for the history of Old English studies. In an appendix to his essay, Graham provides an edition of Talbot's transcription of parts of Ælfric's Preface to Genesis. Benjamin C. Withers brings the history of this manuscript up to modern times in 'A Sense of Englishness: Claudius B. iv, Colonialism, and the History of Anglo-Saxon Art in the Mid-Twentieth Century' (pp. 317–50). Withers identifies a constructed opposition of 'English' and 'Viking' taste, which draws on the dialectic between classical and primitive, and which has informed the study of the illustrations in Cotton Claudius B. iv and their promotion as essentially 'English'.

In 'Ælfric's Preface to Genesis: Genre, Rhetoric and the Origins of the *ars dictaminis*' (*ASE* 29[2000] 215–34), Mark Griffith considers the appropriateness of Ælfric's Preface and its genre, and argues for its coherence as an example of the *ars dictaminis*, with its 'traditional motifs of request, modesty, dilemma and submission' (p. 234). Christopher A. Jones publishes a further article on Ælfric's use of Amalarius of Metz, 'Ælfric's Exemplar of Amalarius: An Additional Witness' (*ANQ* 13[2000] 6–14), in which he makes a case for MS Cambridge, Trinity College B. 11. 2 containing text which has been erased from MS Salisbury Cathedral 154, the closest surviving witness to the version of Amalarius of Metz, *Liber Officinalis* which Ælfric used. In this article Jones brings us closer to understanding the complexity of Ælfric's exemplar.

A collection of the essays of Milton McC. Gatch, many of which concern Old English prose, is published this year in the Ashgate Variorum Collected Studies series under the title *Eschatology and Christian Nurture*. All of the essays in the collection are previously published, and they are: 'Some Theological Reflections on Death from the Early Church through the Reformation'; 'Basic Christian Education from the Decline of Catechesis to the Rise of Catechisms'; 'The Harrowing of Hell: A Liberation Motif in Medieval Theology and Devotional Literature'; 'The Anglo-Saxon Tradition'; 'Perceptions of Eternity'; 'Two Uses of Apocrypha in Old English Homilies'; 'Eschatology in the Anonymous Old English Homilies'; 'The Unknowable Audience of the Blickling Homilies'; 'The Achievement of Ælfric and his Colleagues in European Perspective'; 'The Office in Late Anglo-Saxon Monasticism'; 'Noah's Raven in *Genesis A* and the Illustrated Old English Hexateuch'; 'Miracles in Architectural Settings: Christ Church, Canterbury, and St Clements, Sandwich, in the Old English *Vision of Leofric*'; and 'Piety and Liturgy in the Old English *Vision of Leofric*'. Gatch's new introduction provides a survey of his research interests and how they are reflected in the essays in this volume. Each essay is printed with its original page numbers, and the volume is organized for the reader by each essay being flagged by a roman numeral at the top of each page. An index to all of the volume's contents is provided.

The latest volume in the collaborative edition of the *Anglo-Saxon Chronicle* is published this year. Baker, ed., *The Anglo-Saxon Chronicle*, volume viii: *MS F*, contains a full edition of the Latin and Old English contents of the text of the *Chronicle* in MS F, the Domitian Bilingual Chronicle; London, British Library, Cotton Domitian A. viii, written at Christ Church, Canterbury, at the end of the eleventh or beginning of the twelfth century. The edition is preceded by a detailed account of the manuscript's composition and history, the textual relationships of its version of the *Chronicle*, its date, authorship and language, and a bibliography. The volume's appendix gives the text of the Canterbury Annals in British Library, Cotton Caligula A. xv. A revised, paperback, version of Michael Swanton's translation, *The Anglo-Saxon Chronicles*, is published this year too. The main texts translated by Swanton are the Winchester and Peterborough manuscripts—MS Cambridge, Corpus Christi College 713 and MS Oxford, Bodleian Library, Laud 636 respectively—and they are set out on facing pages, with supplementary extracts from other manuscripts where these have different contents. The translated *Chronicle* texts are followed by a useful range of supporting material, including maps, genealogical tables, a good-sized bibliography and an index to the whole volume.

The sixth volume in Brewer's Annotated Bibliographies of Old and Middle English Literature series, *Old English Prose Translations of King Alfred's Reign*, by Greg Waite, is published this year. Its introduction includes a summary of Alfred's life and times, the range of Alfredian scholarship, and introductions to the individual texts. The bibliography proper is divided into the following sections: bibliographical works, general studies dealing with Alfred's life and works, history, literary history, anthologies and readers, translations, linguistic studies, manuscripts, Gregory's *Pastoral Care*, Boethius' *Consolation of Philosophy*, Augustine's *Soliloquies*, the Prose Psalms of the Paris Psalter, Orosius's *History*, Bede's *Ecclesiastical History* and Gregory's *Dialogues*. The volume ends with indexes of authors and of Old English words, and a general index. Two of the essays in Boenig and Davis, eds., *Manuscript, Narrative, Lexicon*, also focus on Alfred. Paul E. Szarmach's 'Alfred, Alcuin, and the Soul' (pp. 127–48) charts the transmission of Augustinian ideas about the soul to Anglo-Saxon England and to Alfred, via Boethian commentaries and Alcuin's *De ratione animae*, offers new evidence for the influence of the Remigian commentary tradition on Alfred's presentation of the threefold nature of the soul, and concludes by re-emphasizing Alfred's independence as a thinker and adapter. Kathleen Davis considers 'The Performance of Translation Theory in King Alfred's National Literacy Program' (pp. 149–70), suggests that Alfred's Preface to his translation of Gregory's *Pastoral Care* presents the act of translation as a 'legitimate interpretation operating within the well-defined parameters of Christian exegesis' (p. 149), and stresses the function of translation in the formation of a national identity.

László Sándor Chardonnens provides 'A New Edition of the Old English *Formation of the Foetus*' (*N&Q* 47[2000] 10–11), which corrects errors in the standard edition by Cockayne, which was published over a century ago. Chardonnens believes that the text, from MS British Library, Cotton Tiberius A. iii, 'merits inclusion in the genre of prognostics' (p. 10).

Anglo-Latin prose continues to generate important new scholarship this year. The works of Alcuin and Bede are discussed by Johannes Heil in '"Nos nesciente de hoc velle manere"—"We wish to remain ignorant about this": Timeless End, or Approaches to Reconceptualizing Eschatology after A.D. 800 (A.M. 600)' (*Traditio* 55[2000] 73–103). Heil examines attitudes to time and to depictions of the role of the Jews as a sign of the approach of the end of the world. M.J. Toswell compares 'Bede's Sparrow and the Psalter in Anglo-Saxon England' (*ANQ* 13[2000] 7–12) to show how the sparrow functions in the psalter, gospel texts, homilies, and Bede's *Historia Ecclesiastica* as 'a paradigm for the individual and solitary Christian' (p. 10). Richard F. Johnson sheds new light on 'Feasts of Saint Michael the Archangel in the Liturgy of the Early Anglo-Saxon Church: Evidence from the Eighth and Ninth Centuries' (*LSE* 31[2000] 55–80). Through an analysis of references to St Michael in Old English and Latin calendars, martyrologies, massbooks and prayers, Johnson shows the influence of Irish traditions in calendars and prayers, and identifies the gradual singling out of St Michael as an important intercessor.

Mechtild Gretsch continues her innovative analysis of the Benedictine Reform through its textual productions in 'The Junius Psalter Gloss: Its Historical and Cultural Context' (*ASE* 29[2000] 85–121). MS Oxford, Bodleian Library Junius 27 is an early tenth-century production, probably from Winchester, and Gretsch compares its Old English gloss to the other nine psalters from Anglo-Saxon England which contain a complete Old English gloss, two further Anglo-Saxon psalters with substantial Old English glossing, one set of *membra disiecta* of a psalter which contained a continuous Old English gloss, and one twelfth-century Old English glossed psalter. She shows how psalter glossing is evidence of continuous, incremental scholarly activity through the period of Viking incursions and beyond, and argues that the Junius Psalter is 'a scholarly product of the Kingdom of the Anglo-Saxons' (p. 107), and that Frithestan, bishop of Winchester from 909 to 931, may well have been instrumental in the production of Junius 27 and possibly of the Junius Psalter gloss too. Glosses receive further attention in the form of Joseph Crowley's analysis of 'Anglicized Word Order in Old English Continuous Interlinear Glosses in British Library, Royal 2. A. XX' (*ASE* 29[2000] 123–51). Crowley notes that the glosses to this psalter are unusual in that they 'frequently render certain Latin verb phrases and noun phrases into Old English with English word order rather than Latin' (p. 123), and suggests that the gloss was probably made to help laypeople or religious persons without extensive formal education to understand the Latin prayers. He concludes by proposing a revised dating for the Royal glosses of *c*.950–75 rather than Ker's s.x[1].

A collection of essays by Hiroshi Ogawa, *Studies in the History of Old English Prose*, is published this year. It includes a number of previously published pieces: 'Old English Modal Verbs: Some Further Considerations'; 'OE *Sculan/Willan* in Dependent Requests: A Note'; 'The Use of Modal Verbs in "Identical/Non-Identical Subject" Constructions: Some Developments in the Old English Period'; 'The Retoucher in MSS Junius 85–86'; 'The Use of Old English *Þa* in the Ælfrician and Non-Ælfrician *Lives of St Martin*'; '*Þa* Temporal Clauses in Two Old English *Lives of St Martin*: A Study of the Prose Styles in the Blickling and Ælfrician Versions'; 'Stylistic Features of the Old English *Apollonius of Tyre*'; 'Syntactical Revision in Wulfstan's Rewritings of Ælfric' (with some revisions to the original version); and 'Notes on the Syntax in Some Late Anonymous Homilies: A Study in the Development of Old English Prose' (also with some revisions to the original version). It also contains translations of two essays originally published in Japanese—'Towards a Philological History of the English Language: Retrospect and Prospect' and 'Problems of Old English Syntax. Elizabeth C. Traugott, "Syntax" (*The Cambridge History of the English Language*, Vol. I): A Review'— and three new pieces: 'Life of St Martin (MSS Junius 85–86): Text and Notes'; 'Initial Verb-Subject Inversion in Some Late Old English Homilies'; and 'A "Wulfstan Imitator" at Work: Linguistic Features of Napier XXX'.

Swan and Treharne, eds., *Rewriting Old English in the Twelfth Century*, makes an important contribution to an area which has not received due attention in the past; the sustained employment of Old English in the post-Conquest period, particularly 'new emphases and changes of direction in the English writings included in twelfth-century manuscripts' (p. 1). The texts cited range from 'copies of homiletic and hagiographic pieces written by Ælfric and anonymous authors' (p. 1), to laws, dialogues, apophthegms, prognostications, psalters, gospels, and a copy of the Benedictine Rule. The editors are to be commended on the range and scholarly depth of the articles, which cast new light on a wealth of material, not only for scholars of Old English, but also for those working in such related areas as Middle

English, Church history, and contemporary cultural history. As one would expect from a collection of this kind, there is the usual unevenness of quality, with contributions that range from the exceptional to the stimulating, albeit underdeveloped. The introduction (pp. 1–7) gives a comprehensive overview of the state of scholarship, and goes on to state the contributors' *modus procendendi*. The collection as a whole questions the long-accepted practice of weighing late copies of Old English works against the putative standard of some pre-existent ur-text: 'The prioritisation of notions of an "original" text and its author is the product of a twentieth-century print-culture mentality, and does not reflect the fluidity of a manuscript culture where texts are made and remade as they are read or heard or rewritten' (p. 7). Elaine Treharne's article, 'The Production and Script of Manuscripts Containing English Religious Texts in the First Half of the Twelfth Century' (pp. 11–40), explores a range of issues central to our knowledge of Old English during this period. While more might have been written about what is known or what can be deduced regarding the length of scribal careers, particularly the relative age of a hand, and the changes in letter forms within the working life of a scribe on p. 34, the section entitled 'The Evolution of English Vernacular Script in the Twelfth Century' (pp. 35–8), is an significant contribution to the area, perhaps the most significant in the book. In her article, 'The Compilation and Use of Manuscripts Containing Old English in the Twelfth Century', Susan Irvine demonstrates that the manner in which these manuscripts are compiled 'carries important implications for their use' (p. 42). She puts forward a convincing argument that twelfth-century compilers, 'like their eleventh-century predecessors, selected and assembled their own material', which suggests that 'they had purposes in mind beyond the veneration of history' (pp. 42–3). Thus, these manuscripts are representative of 'more than antiquarian attempts to preserve Old English language and documents' (p. 42). Irvine's analysis (pp. 50–4) provides a particularly valuable discussion of use and ownership. Mary Swan's 'Ælfric's *Catholic Homilies* in the Twelfth Century' (pp. 62–82), moves into the minutiae of transmission. This transmission is not what a classicist would understand by the term; rather, it refers to the adaptation and renewal of the Ælfrician corpus to serve the radically altered linguistic and social circumstances of the twelfth century. This study provides an excellent analysis of the method of transformation of the Ælfrician texts, particularly the discussion of Cotton Vespasian D. xiv (pp. 67–71). Swan's article leads naturally into Jonathan Wilcox's 'Wulfstan and the Twelfth Century' (pp. 83–97). His discussion emphasizes that the usage of Wulfstan's sermons during this period stands in diptychal contraposition to that of Ælfric's homiletic material. His examination of Wulfstan's method of homiletic composition in relation to that of the Lambeth adapter is useful on many levels, not least in gauging the intellectual level of the Anglo-Saxon lay audience at the end of the tenth century. However, with regard to the twelfth century, those few sermons of Wulfstan's 'that were reused tend more towards the general and enduringly doctrinal than the political and historically grounded', which seems indicative of 'the move towards greater concern with matters of conscience and lesser emphasis on political questions that has been demonstrated as characteristic of sermon literature of the twelfth and thirteenth centuries' (p. 96). Moving to another genre, Joana Proud's 'Old English Prose Saints' Lives in the Twelfth Century: The Evidence of the Extant Manuscripts' (pp. 117–31) concentrates on the adaptation of the native hagiographic tradition. She rightly points out that 'the transmission of hagiographic material depends directly upon the shifting popularity of individual saints' cults, responding especially to Norman influences both before and after the Conquest' (p. 122), and also notes the antiquarian interests of Anglo-Latin writers in the second generation after the Conquest, a point which could have been developed further in this context. However, pages 130–1 give us a good overview of the 'relatively small number of extant manuscripts' which demonstrate that the 'selection of saints gives priority to universal cults, but local influences are still evident'. Susan Rosser's 'Old English Prose Saints' Lives in the Twelfth Century: *The Life of Martin* in Bodley 343' (pp. 132–42), adopts a narrower focus than that of Proud's, but presents much the same problems, methods and conclusion. The book draws to a close with two sterling articles on Old English biblical texts. In 'Scribal Habit: The Evidence of the Old English Gospels' (pp. 143–65), Roy Michael Liuzza concentrates on the scribal methods of the twelfth-century recopyings of the Old English gospels and the implications of those methods for the use and transmission of these native translations. This article has applications beyond its immediate and specific topic, and the bibliography contained in the footnotes is excellent. The late Philip Pulsiano's article, 'The Old English Gloss of the *Eadwine Psalter*' (pp. 166–94), is a fitting testament to his love of this area. It is a contribution both to manuscript studies and to the continuity of scriptural exegesis from the Anglo-Saxon into the early scholastic period. The section 'Repositioning the Eadwine Psalter' (pp. 190–1) is more sanguine in its reading of the position of the native tradition in the twelfth century than some of the other articles, concluding that contemporary works, however humble, 'nevertheless attest to interest in and comprehension of Old English texts, not as dead documents of the past, but as works that continued to have worth in the cathedral and monastic centres of post-Conquest England' (p. 194). Pulsiano's article demonstrates eloquently the information embedded in the modest gloss. The final article, Wendy Collier's 'The Tremulous Worcester Hand and Gregory's *Pastoral Care*', provides us with a useful adjunct to Christine Franzen's *The Tremulous Hand of Worcester* (Clarendon [1991]). This study furthers our understanding of the annotation in particular, suggesting that, while the 'linguistic glosses by themselves might indicate a purely antiquarian interest', the additional evidence furnished by the annotation points to 'some practical purpose'. Swan and Treharne have opened a rich new seam of scholarship: the continuity of English prose is not merely a pious wish. [AMD'A]

Angelika Lutz's 'Æthelweard's *Chronicon* and Old English Poetry' (*ASE* 29[2000] 177–214) is reviewed in section 4 above.

Books Reviewed

Aers, David, ed. *Medieval Literature and Historical Inquiry: Essays in Honor of Derek Pearsall*. Boydell. [2000] pp. 228. £45 ($75) ISBN 0 8500 1555 7.

Baker, Peter S. *The Anglo-Saxon Chronicle*, vol. viii: *MS F*. Brewer. [2000] pp. cxii + 158. £40 ($75) ISBN 0 8599 1490 9.

Barnhouse, Rebecca, and Benjamin C. Withers, eds. *The Old English Hexateuch: Aspects and Approaches*. MIP. [2000] pp. xv + 358. ISBN 1 5804 4024 X.

Boenig, Robert, and Kathleen Davis, eds. *Manuscript, Narrative, Lexicon: Essays on Literary and Cultural Transmission in Honor of Whitney F. Bolton*. BuckUP. [2000] pp. 261. £35 ($44.50) ISBN 0 8387 5440 6.

Brooke, Christopher. *Europe in the Central Middle Ages, 962–1154*. Longman. [2000] pp. xvii + 469. £55 ISBN 0 5823 6905 3.

Brown, Michelle P. *'In the beginning was the Word': Books and Faith in the Age of Bede*. 2000 Jarrow Lecture. St Paul's Church, Jarrow. [2000] pp. 37. £2.50 ISBN not given.

Caie, Graham D. *The Old English Poem 'Judgement Day II': A Critical Edition with Editions of 'De die iudicii' and the Hatton 113 Homily 'De domes dæge'*. Anglo-Saxon Texts 2. Brewer. [2000] pp. xvi + 161. £40 ($75) ISBN 0 8599 1570 0.

Campbell, James. *The Anglo-Saxon State*. Hambledon and London. [2000] pp. xxix + 290. £25 ISBN 1 8528 5176 7.

Crook, John. *The Architectural Setting of the Cult of Saints in the Early Medieval West*. Clarendon. [2000] pp. xxv + 308. £50 ISBN 0 1982 0794 8.

Dark, Ken. *Britain and the End of the Roman Empire*. Tempus. [2000] pp. 256. £25 ($39.99) ISBN 0 7524 1451 8.

Dockray-Miller, Mary. *Motherhood and Mothering in Anglo-Saxon England*. Macmillan. [2000] pp. xiv + 161. £27.50 ISBN 0 3339 1378 7.

Dodwell, C.R. *Anglo-Saxon Gestures and the Roman Stage*. CASE 28. CUP. [2000] pp. xvii + 171. £50 ISBN 0 5216 6188 9.

Ferzoco, George, and Carolyn Muessig, eds. *Medieval Monastic Education*. LeicUP. [2000] pp. xiv + 237. £60 ISBN 0 7185 0246 9.

Fischer, Olga, and Max Nänny, eds. *The Motivated Sign: Iconicity in Language and Literature*, II. BenjaminsNA. [2000] pp. xiv + 387. $100 ISBN 1 5881 1003 6.

Foot, Sarah. *Veiled Women*, vol. I: *The Disappearance of Nuns from Anglo-Saxon England*; vol. II: *Female Religious Communities in England, 871–1066*. Ashgate. [2000] pp. xvi + 228 and xii + 274. £45 each, ISBN 0 7546 0043 2 (vol. I), ISBN 0 7546 0044 0 (vol. II).

Franzen, Christine. *Worcester Manuscripts. Anglo-Saxon Manuscripts in Microfiche Facsimile 6. Arizona Center for Medieval and Renaissance Studies*. [1998]. pp. xvii + 72. £76 ($120) ISBN 0 8669 8228 0.

Frazer, William O., and Andrew Tyrrell, eds. *Social Identity in Early Medieval Britain*. LeicUP. [2000] pp. xiii + 283. £55 ISBN 0 7185 0084 9.

Gatch, Milton McC. *Eschatology and Christian Nurture: Themes in Anglo-Saxon and Medieval Religious Life*. Variorum. [2000] pp. 348. £57.50 ($105) ISBN 0 8607 8827 X.

Godden, Malcolm. *Ælfric's Catholic Homilies: Introduction, Commentary and Glossary*. EETS ss 18. OUP. [2000] pp. lxii + 794. £50 ISBN 0 1972 2419 9.

Goss, Nisha Merchant, A. M. Doran and A. Coles, eds. *Proceedings of the Seventh Annual Symposium about Language and Society: Austin [SALSA VII]*. Texas Linguistic Forum 43. [2000].

Graham, Timothy. *The Recovery of Old English: Anglo-Saxon Studies in the Sixteenth and Seventeenth Centuries*. MIP. [2000] pp. xvi + 422. $40 ISBN 1 5804 4013 4.

Gruber, Loren C., with Meredith Crellin Gruber and Gregory K. Jember, eds. *Essays on Old, Middle, Modern English and Old Icelandic in Honor of Raymond P. Tripp, Jr*. Mellen. [2000] pp. xxi + 521. $119.95 ISBN 0 7734 7858 2.

Hadley, D.M. *The Northern Danelaw: Its Social Structure, c.800–1100.* LeicUP. [2000] pp. x + 374. £60 ISBN 0 7185 0014 8.

Hadley, Dawn M., and Julian D. Richards, eds. *Cultures in Contact: Scandinavian Settlement in England in the Ninth and Tenth Centuries.* Brepols. [2000] pp. 331. Euro 50 ISBN 2 5035 0978 9.

Hen, Yitzhak, and Matthew Innes. *The Uses of the Past in the Early Middle Ages.* CUP. [2000] pp. ix + 283. £14.95 ($23.95) ISBN 0 5216 3998 0.

Hill, John M. *The Anglo-Saxon Warrior Ethic: Reconstructing Lordship in Early English Literature.* UPFlor. [2000] pp. vii + 174. £46.50 ($55) ISBN 0 8130 1769 6.

Hill, John M., and Deborah M. Sinnreich-Levi, eds. *The Rhetorical Poetics of the Middle Ages: Reconstructive Polyphony. Essays in Honor of Robert O. Payne.* FDUP. [1999] pp. 304. £39.50 ISBN 0 8386 3810 4.

Holderness, Graham, trans. *Anglo-Saxon Verse.* Northcote. [2000] pp. xiv + 111. £9.99 ($21) ISBN 0 7463 0914 7.

Kienzle, Beverly Mayne, ed. *The Sermon. Typologie des Sources du Moyen Âge Occidental* 81–3. Brepols. [2000] pp. 998. Euro 220 ISBN 2 5035 1015 9.

Kreitzer, Larry J., and Deborah W. Rooke, eds. *Ciphers in the Sand: Interpretations of the Woman Taken in Adultery (John 7.53–8.11).* Biblical Seminar 74. ShAP. [2000] pb £15.95 ($24.95) ISBN 1 8412 7141.

Laszlo, Renate. *Ewig ist der Schöpfer: Cædmons Schöpfunghymnus im Codex Exoniensis.* Tectum. [2000] pp. 106. DM39.80 ISBN 3 8288 8133 5.

Loyn, H.R. *The English Church, 940–1154.* Longman. [2000] pp. x + 174. hb £55 ISBN 0 5823 0288 9, pb £15.99 ISBN 0 5823 0303 6.

Lucy, Sam. *The Anglo-Saxon Way of Death.* Sutton. [2000] pp. v + 210. £25 ISBN 0 7509 2103 X.

Marner, Dominic. *St Cuthbert: His Life and Cult in Medieval Durham.* BL. [2000] pp. 112. £20 ISBN 0 7123 4686 4.

Mitchell, Bruce, and Susan Irvine, eds. *'Beowulf' Repunctuated.* OEN Subsidia 29. WMU. [2000] pp. v +137. $10.

Morgan, Gwendolyn A. *Anglo-Saxon Poetry in Imitative Translation: The Harp and the Cross,* preface by Tom Shippey. Mellen. [2000] pp. ix + 204. $89.95 ISBN 0 7734 7647 4.

Nobis, Felix, trans. *Beowulf.* Bradshaw. [2000] pp. x + 57. £3.75 ($5.87) ISBN 0 9490 1072 3.

Ogawa, Hiroshi. *Studies in the History of Old English Prose.* Nan'un-do, Tokyo. [2000] pp. x + 295. ISBN 4 5233 0066 6.

Orton, Peter. *The Transmission of Old English Poetry. Westfield Publications in Medieval and Renaissance Studies* 12. Brepols. [2000] pp. xvii + 223. £30 ISBN 2 5035 1072 8.

Owen-Crocker, Gale R. *The Four Funerals in 'Beowulf' and the Structure of the Poem.* ManUP. [2000] pp. viii + 264. £40 ($69.95) ISBN 0 7190 5497 4.

Page, R.I. *The Icelandic Rune-Poem. Viking Society for Northern Research.* [1999]. pp. 37. £4.50 ISBN 0 9035 2143 1.

Palliser, D.M., ed. *The Cambridge Urban History of Britain,* vol. i: *600–1540.* CUP. [2000] pp. xxvi + 841. £90 ($140) ISBN 0 5214 4461 6.

Pelteret, David A.E., ed. *Anglo-Saxon History: Basic Readings.* Garland. [2000] pp. xxx + 450. £49.49 ($70) ISBN 0 8153 3140 1.

Rauer, Christine. *Beowulf and the Dragon: Parallels and Analogues*. Brewer. [2000] pp. x + 230. £45 ($75) ISBN 0 8599 1592 1.

Roberts, Jane, and Janet Nelson, eds. *Essays on Anglo-Saxon and Related Themes in Memory of Lynne Grundy*. KCL Medieval Series 17. KCL. [2000] pp. xviii + 590. £30 ISBN 0 9522 1199 8.

Rogers, Bertha. *'Beowulf': Translation and Art*. Birch Brook. [2000] pp. 129. $20 ISBN 0 9135 5959 8.

Scragg, Donald, and Carole Weinberg, eds. *Literary Appropriations of the Anglo-Saxons from the Thirteenth to the Twentieth Century*. CASE 29. CUP. [2000] pp. xii + 242. £45 ISBN 0 5216 3215 3.

Swan, Mary, and Elaine M. Treharne, eds. *Rewriting Old English in the Twelfth Century*. CASE 30. CUP. [2000] pp. x + 213. £40 ISBN 0 5216 2372 3.

Swanton, Michael, trans. and ed. *The Anglo-Saxon Chronicles*. Phoenix. [2000] pp. xxxvi + 364. £14.99 ISBN 1 8421 2003 4.

Szarmach, Paul E., ed. *Old English Prose: Basic Readings*. Garland. [2000] pp. xvii + 552. £45 ISBN 0 8153 0305 X.

Theuws, Frans, and Janet L. Nelson, eds. *Rituals of Power, from Late Antiquity to the Early Middle Ages*. Transformation of the Roman World 8. Brill. [2000] pp. 503. £43.66 ISBN 9 0041 0902 1.

Treharne, Elaine, ed. *Old and Middle English: An Anthology*. Blackwell. [2000] pp. xxvii + 622. £16.99 ISBN 0 6312 0466 0.

Waite, Greg. *Annotated Bibliographies of Old and Middle English Literature*, vi: *Old English Prose Translations of King Alfred's Reign*. Brewer. [2000] pp. xiv + 394. £45 ISBN 0 8599 1591 3.

Walker, Ian W. *Mercia and the Making of England*. Sutton. [2000] pp. xix + 236. £25 ISBN 0 7509 2131 5.

Wilcox, Jonathan. *Wulfstan Texts and Other Homiletic Materials. Anglo-Saxon Manuscripts in Microfiche Facsimile 8*. Arizona Center for Medieval and Renaissance Studies. [2000] pp. x + 82. £76 ($120) ISBN 0 8669 8261 2.

Wilcox, Jonathan, ed. *Humour in Anglo-Saxon Literature*. Brewer. [2000] pp. vii + 162. £40 ($75) ISBN 0 8599 1576 X.

Wolfthal, Diane, ed. *Peace and Negotiation: Strategies for Coexistence in the Middle Ages and the Renaissance. Arizona Studies in the Middle Ages and the Renaissance 4*. Brepols. [2000] pp. 265. £31.50 ISBN 2 5035 0904 5.

III

Middle English: Excluding Chaucer

NICOLE CLIFTON, KENNETH HODGES, JURIS LIDAKA,
MICHAEL D. SHARP, GREG WALKER AND K.S. WHETTER

This chapter has ten sections: 1. General and Miscellaneous; 2. Alliterative Poetry; 3. The *Gawain*-Poet; 4. *Piers Plowman*; 5. Romance; 6. Lyrics; 7. Gower, Lydgate, Hoccleve; 8. Middle Scots Poetry; 9. Malory and Caxton; 10. Drama. Section 1 is by K.S. Whetter, with additional material by Juris Lidaka, Greg Walker and Mary Swan; sections 2, 4 and 6 are by Nicole Clifton; sections 3 and 8 are by Michael D. Sharp; sections 5 and 7 are by Juris Lidaka; section 9 is by Kenneth Hodges; section 10 is by Greg Walker.

1. General and Miscellaneous

Middle English manuscripts and texts are the concern of both books and articles in 2000. The *Index of Middle English Prose* continues apace with two new publications: Edden, ed., *Handlist XV: Manuscripts in Midland Libraries*, and Ogilvie-Thomson, ed., *Handlist XVI: Manuscripts in the Laudian Collection, Bodleian Library, Oxford*. Like other Handlists in the series, both *Handlist XV* and *Handlist XVI* are clearly laid out and easy to use: each offers an introduction to the relevant collections, a summary list of contents detailing (by library shelfmark) and assigning (by individual manuscript) an index number to the Middle English prose in its collections, followed by a fuller list identifying the opening and closing lines and folio numbers of each entry; each Handlist also includes indexes of macaronic materials, incipits (in the case of *Handlist XVI* an index of incipits, rubrics and colophons), and reverse explicits (including acephalous and atelous materials). *Handlist XVI* has further indexes on general matters, authors, and earlier owners and scribes; *Handlist XV* has indexes of authors and translators, owners, scribes and provenance and other names, and a final index of titles. *Handlist XV* describes the eighty-one MSS and some fragments of Middle English prose extant in twelve Midland collections: Birmingham, St Mary's College, Oscott; Gloucester Cathedral; Gloucester Diocesan Archives; Hereford Cathedral; Leicester Town Hall; Leicester University; Leicester, Wyggeston Hospital; Lichfield Cathedral; Nottingham University, currently housing the Mellish, Middleton and Potter private collections; Peterborough Cathedral; Southwell Minister; and Worcester Cathedral. Amongst sundry religious and Wycliffite material, some Chaucerian tales, the *Gesta Romanorum* (Gloucester Cathedral MS 42), and a fragmentary *Brut* (Leicester University 47), these collections include one General Sentence of Cursing (Worcester Cathedral Library Q.9), one Moral Exhortation and one hangover recipe (Worcester Q.15). *Handlist XVI*, as the title indicates, confines itself to indexing the seventy manuscripts of the massive (1,250 MSS) Laudian collection which contain Middle English prose. Again, religious works abound, but in addition to Rolle's *Psalter* (Laud. Misc. 286 items 2 and 3; MS 321 items 1 and 2; and MS 448 items 1 and 2) we find such variegated materials as Hilton's *Scale of Perfection* (MS 602 items 1 and 2), three partial copies of the *Brut* (MS 550 item 1; MS 571 item 1; MS 733 item 2), *Mandeville's Travels* (MS 699 item 1), and Chaucer's *Melibee* and *Parson's Tale* (MS 600, items 1 and 2). There are also various scientific and medical treatises.

Andrew G. Watson has carefully produced *A Descriptive Catalogue of the Medieval Manuscripts of Exeter College Oxford*, otherwise uncatalogued since H.O. Coxe's in 1852, adding five colour and four black and white plates to the seventy-five entries, plus a number of pastedowns and five manuscripts once in Exeter but now elsewhere, noting another rejected as incorrectly ascribed so in his own supplement to the second edition of Ker's *Medieval Libraries of Great Britain* (p. 54). He sketches the limited archival information and places additions and losses in historical circumstances, such as the political or religious visitations, which somehow still allowed a series of eighteen volumes of the works of Hugh of St Cher to survive. Watson justifiably laments the general lack of information about the contents, organization, and development of the library over the centuries. Despite that lack, he reconstructs all he can, even judiciously pondering what it might mean if we reordered the present manuscripts to follow the orders in Thomas James's *Ecloga Oxonio-Cantabrigiensis* [1600] and Edward Bernard's *Catalogus librorum manuscriptorum Angliae et Hiberniae* [1697]. Certainly of most interest to readers here would be items 47 the Psalter of Humphrey de Bohun, 49 *Poor Caitif*, and 129 Lydgate's *The Seege of Troy*, but many others also have great value for historical, artistic, or other reasons. Oxford have allowed for generous spacing, which will allow users ample room for annotations with time. [JL]

British Library MS Harley 2253, long recognized as a singularly important preservation of Middle English poetry, is the focus of Fein, ed., *Studies in the Harley Manuscript*. Intended as a companion volume to a forthcoming TEAMS edition of the complete contents of the manuscript, this collection of fifteen essays covers all aspects of it and its contents: Carter Revard examines forty-one new holographs by the main scribe; Theo Stemmler argues that Harley is not an arbitrary miscellany but a carefully crafted anthology; Michael P. Kuczynski examines the religious verse; John Scattergood focuses on the socio-political criticism of the political verse; Richard Newhauser emphasizes that the complaints in Harley's *Song of the Husbandman* are universal rather than specific; Karl Reichl focuses on the variety and characteristics of Harley's debate verse; Helen Phillips looks at dreams and dream lore in three different texts and genres; David L. Jeffrey argues that Harley contains much that is Franciscan in authorship or affinity; John J. Thompson outlines the indebtedness to French biblical stories and manner of storytelling and also supports the view that the main Harley scribe wrote *Fouke le Fitz Waryn*; Barbara Nolan examines the genre and context of Harley's Anglo-Norman fabliaux;

Mary Dove highlights the nature and context of the Anglo-Norman secular verse; Fein argues that the various texts in folios 63–9 are all unified by their focus on women's sexual allure; Elizabeth Solopova highlights the layout, rhyme, metre and punctuation of Harley's English verse; Frances McSparran argues that the scribe's English is south-west Midlands, but that he was willing both to copy and translate foreign dialects; and Marilyn Corrie compares Harley with Bodleian Library MS Digby 86, with a particular focus on what they tell us of thirteenth- and fourteenth-century English literature. This is potentially an important book scrutinizing the entire manuscript, not merely its Middle English parts; most of the essays are engaging, and many (especially those by Phillips, Thompson and Nolan) are excellent. However, more synthesis of the whole is required, the introduction needs to acknowledge that several of the essays flatly contradict one another, and there are further contradictions *within* individual essays. Finally, a study which (rightly) pays so much attention to codicology and which distinguishes between *anthology* and *miscellany* should know better than consistently to label a handwritten parchment manuscript—here dated to *c*.1340—as *book*.

One particular manuscript is also the subject of Ralph Hanna's 'Humphrey Newton and Bodleian Library, MS Lat. Misc. C.66' (*MÆ* 69[2000] 279–91); Hanna professionally describes Bod. MS Lat. Misc. C.66 with a particular focus on what it might tell us of fifteenth-century literary culture in north-east Cheshire. The rather messy miscellany contains, *inter alia*, poems by Newton himself, medical recipes, a copy of the Middle English *Trotula*, and scattered excerpts from the *Canterbury Tales*. However, since the contents overall reveal greater concern with household affairs than literature, Hanna argues that we should be wary of the supposed sophistication of the household book.

A major new anthology of Old and Middle English texts is published this year. Treharne, ed., *Old and Middle English: An Anthology*, contains a very wide range of Middle English texts, the earliest of which are accompanied by modern English translations on facing pages, and the others supported with end-of-line glossing. The Middle English texts included are the *Hymns* of Saint Godric, The *Ormulum*, two items from Cambridge, Trinity College MS B. 14. 32l *Hali Meiðhad, Ancrene Wisse*, lyrics from Oxford, Bodleian Library MS Digby 86, *The Bestiary* from Arundel MS 292, two items from Oxford, Jesus College MS 29, two from London, British Library, MS Cotton Caligula A. ix, six lyrics from Cambridge, Trinity College MS B. 14. 39, two items from *The South English Legendary, Cursor Mundi*, two pieces by Robert Mannyng of Brunne, *The Land of Cockayne*, two items from the Auchinleck Manuscript, nine lyrics from London, British Library, MS Harley 2253, The *Ayenbite of Inwit*, two pieces by Richard Rolle, *Kyng Alisaunder, Athelston, Ywain and Gawain*, and *Wynnere and Wastoure*. The volume includes introductory discussions of Old and Middle English literature and language, and also a select bibliography, glossary of common hard words, index of manuscripts and general index. It will be of enormous use to teachers of medieval English as a source of accessibly presented, scholarly versions of an excellent variety of texts, many of which are rarely used in teaching. [MS]

Also prominent this year are studies focusing on medieval women. Wogan-Browne et al., eds., *Medieval Women: Texts and Contexts in Late Medieval Britain*, is a wide-ranging collection of essays honouring Felicity Riddy. The volume is well laid out, misprints are few and far between (though not non-existent), and the essays are generally of high quality. Consequently, in order to present readers with as much detail as possible, I offer little more than a summary of contents: Priscilla Bawcutt examines Scotswomen's ownership of predominantly pious books; Julia Boffey examines the circulation and female readership of the Middle English prose *Thre Kings of Cologne*, the popularity of which is said to rest in part on a combination of the familiar and marvellous; Carol M. Meale highlights dramatic influences in Margery Kempe's *Book*; Katherine J. Lewis re-examines how virgin-martyr lives such as that of St Margaret were read; Helen Phillips looks at Marian honorific titles and lyrics in 'Regina celi, qwene of the south', Chaucer's *ABC* and 'In a tabernacle of a toure'; Ceridwen Lloyd-Morgan highlights Welsh women's refutations of European anti-feminism; Noël James Menuge notes the literary and narrative qualities of a fourteenth-century woman's legal records; Nicholas Watson uncovers the reformist, Lollard—and so usually male—affinities of *Book to a Mother*; Kim M. Phillips looks for female models of behaviour and 'gestural interaction' in five late Middle English texts; Patricia Cullum and Jeremy Goldberg examine Margaret Blackburn's use of the Bolton Hours; Douglas Gray traces the influence of Christine de Pizan's *Epistre d'Othéa* on Middle English letters and humanism; Colin Richmond examines the nature of the friendship between Elizabeth Clere and the Pastons; W.M. Ormrod tries to uncover what we can learn of a *possible* meeting between Joan of Kent and rebels from the Peasants' Revolt; Arlyn Diamond highlights (with only partial success) the role of women in the alliterative *Morte Arthure*; Jane Grenville argues for new archaeological approaches to medieval women's places and spaces; Jane Gilbert focuses on monstrous children and their parents in *King of Tars* and *Sir Gowther*; Anne Savage looks at father–daughter incest in the *Clerk's Tale*, *Emaré* and *Life of St Dympna*; Peter Biller focuses on heretical Englishwomen; Sarah Rees Jones examines Margery Kempe and the bishops; and Wogan-Browne focuses on Edith of Wilton. There are also three other Chaucer papers, reviewed in chapter 4. Menuge, ed., *Medieval Women and the Law*, is a collection of essays both literary and historical exploring medieval women's voices and experiences 'behind legal discourses'. The following essays focus on Middle English: Cordelia Beattie examines residential arrangements of widows and unmarried women in fourteenth- and fifteenth-century York. Katherine J. Lewis highlights the ways in which women's wills can be seen as deliberate and at times wishful 'self-presentation[s]'. Menuge argues that the presentation of mothers as guardians in romance echoes and confirms legal rhetoric and patriarchal feudal behaviour. Corinne Saunders argues that romance's real–unreal duality is reflected in its realistic yet unrealistic presentation of *raptus* and female consent, for the issue of consent is more privileged in romance than law. Kim M. Phillips sees in medieval *raptus* laws an evolving focus on the female body, suggesting that women's rights increasingly worsened over time. Finally, Emma Hawkes claims that the fact that more gentlewomen used the Chancery than Commons court shows that they had an understanding of the law. There is also a short introduction by P.J.P. Goldberg. The essays, by both lecturers and graduate students, are all new, many are linked thematically, and many benefit from uniting both historical and literary outlooks. Saunders's paper stands out, Hawkes's two tables seem thrown willy-nilly into her argument and syntax, and Menuge undermines an otherwise fine paper by attempting to salvage an element of female subversion in romance, something her argument elsewhere pretty thoroughly denies.

Jennifer Summit's *Lost Property: The Woman Writer and English Literary History, 1380–1589*, focuses on medieval and early modern notions of the woman writer and her place in and relation to (the development and canonization of) English literature. As her subtitle indicates, her particular focus on 1380–1589 means that she only partially belongs in this section. More importantly, it also means that she bridges what C.S. Lewis believed to be the rather arbitrary and misleading gap between the Middle Ages and Renaissance. Chapter 1 argues that Chaucer uses the marginalized woman writer as a metaphor for the instability of the vernacular and thus Chaucer's own relation to the Classics. Chapter 2 sees Christine de Pizan as the 'most widely read woman writer in fifteenth- and early sixteenth-century England' and highlights Christine's influence on fifteenth- and sixteenth-century English literature and culture, particularly in early modern perceptions of the courtly, literate gentleman. Chapter 3 looks at medieval and early modern female religious writers and the development of English literature and culture during and after the Reformation; and chapter 4 highlights the role of Elizabeth I's literary writings in establishing a national literature. There is also a detailed introduction and an afterword. Throughout, Summit highlights a symbiotic connection between women's writing and perceptions of literary tradition, arguing that, although women writers in the fourteenth to sixteenth centuries were excluded from that tradition, they paradoxically played an integral role in the formation of English literature. Summit I think pushes too far what she sees as Chaucer's anxieties about the vernacular, but overall this is a lucid, engaging and well-written book; it will particularly interest scholars and readers concerned with medieval and early modern women, the development of English literature and the history of textual production.

Renevey and Whitehead, eds., *Writing Religious Women* hopes, according to its editors, to broaden 'knowledge of English medieval religious culture' and 'female vernacular theology'. There are four sections; the generally well-written arguments run as follows. Bella Millett notes the similarities between the devotions in *Ancrene Wisse* and fifteenth-century Books of Hours and suggests that such similarities may help cast light on the origins of Books of Hours. Marleen Cré examines the manuscript context of the short version of Julian of Norwich's *Revelations* and Marguerite Porete's *Mirror of Simple Souls*; Cré argues that Julian and Marguerite appear in this religious collection not for their gender, but their recognized spiritual and didactic qualities. Women's spiritual equality to men is also proposed by Rebecca Selman, who focuses on *Speculum devotorum*, a fifteenth-century translation of various Latin sources. Anne Mc Govern-Mouron sets out to garner a wider public for a little-known Latin devotional treatise, *Liber de modo bene vivendi ad sororem* and its Middle English translation. Current critical concerns about textual constructions of femininity are reflected in Whitehead's very thorough examination of the trope of Mary as fortress in Robert Grosseteste's Anglo-Norman *Château d'amour*. Karin Boklund-Lagopoulou is only partially convincing in arguing that the lyrical emphasis on Mary's virginity and the tradition of Christ as mother mean that religious lyrics offer women imaginative ways of conceiving of their bodies. Samuel Fanous highlights the links between temporal and geographic specificity and those events most significant to Margery in *The Book of Margery Kempe*. Naoë Kukita Yoshikawa is concerned with Margery Kempe's veneration of and meditations with virgin martyrs such as St Katherine as she is depicted in the Sarum liturgy. Renevey's essay—which is marred by two vague cross-references—

focuses on Margery Kempe as 'performer rather than … writer', especially in her re-creation of the Passion. Finally, Richard Lawes examines the evidence for psychological disorders in the autobiographical writings of Margery Kempe, Julian of Norwich and (especially) Thomas Hoccleve.

Women may or may not be the addressees of a fifteenth-century meditation edited and analysed in Peter Whiteford's '"Chosen to be Þi Derlyng": The Anticipation of Heaven in a Fifteenth-Century Middle English Meditation' (*MÆ* 69[2000] 80–91). Whiteford argues that the meditation is seemingly addressed to 'the devout layperson' and that it reveals an awareness of theological, philosophical and scholastic views on the soul, but not enough information to determine the original audience's gender. The influence of one particular religious woman is the subject of Kathryn Kerby-Fulton's 'Prophecy and Suspicion: Closet Radicalism, Reformist Politics, and the Vogue for Hildegardiana in Ricardian England' (*Speculum* 75[2000] 318–41). Kerby-Fulton argues that the twelfth-century German Hildegard's writings actually had a wider audience in Ricardian England than has yet been realized, including Gower, Langland, Wyclif, Wimbledon and the author of *Pierce the Ploughman's Crede*. Unlike other studies under consideration here, Terence N. Bowers's 'Margery Kempe as Traveller' (*SP* 97[2000] 1–28) focuses on Margery's travels more than religion. Bowers argues that understanding Margery's travels is crucial to understanding the *Book*, for she uses both travel and text to legitimize her actions, identity and social standing. Further, 'in remaking herself through travel, Kempe has created the possibility of remaking society'. Travel is also the subject of Andrew Fleck's 'Here, There, and In Between: Representing Difference in the *Travels* of Sir John Mandeville' (*SP* 97[2000] 379–400); Fleck argues that Mandeville provided a template for subsequent colonial travel narrative and the presentation of the non-European other. Mandeville paves the way for depicting that other as like or unlike Europeans, and for using Western Christianity as the basis for establishing similarity or difference.

Want to know which Middle English texts list the Ten Commandments or paraphrase the Passion? If so, then James H. Morey's *Book and Verse: A Guide to Middle English Biblical Literature* is the book for you. 'This book … has two major purposes: to explode the myth that lay people had no access to the Bible before the Reformation and to provide a guide to the variety and extent of biblical literature in England, exclusive of Wyclif, from the twelfth into the fifteenth century.' Drama is also excluded, while other traditions and genres receive only partial coverage—both understandable given the vastness of material involved. There are four short prefatory chapters, together with an introduction and conclusion: Chapter 1 examines medieval notions of the Bible and emphasizes the Bible's centrality to and influence on medieval conceptions of narrative, reading and authority. Chapter 2 highlights Continental and Insular receptions of the Bible and resistance to vernacular biblical literature. Chapter 3 focuses on the development of English vernacular and translations of biblical matter. Chapter 4 examines the didactic intentions and self-representation of sundry English biblical works, including *Ormulum*. Morey concludes that the familiarity, variety and accessibility of Middle English biblical literature made it 'the primary biblical resource of the English Middle Ages'. All of this is contained in eighty-six pages; the remainder of the book comprises the guide itself, which is more detailed and current than those found in the *Manual of the Writings in Middle English*. Morey's guide is clearly arranged, user-friendly, keyed to standard references (*Manual, IMEV, IMEP*, etc.), and augmented by several indexes (which are, however, incomplete: see p. 89). Each entry lists, where available, the title, standard references, manuscripts, editions, facsimiles, and relevant studies, notes how the material qualifies as biblical, and summarizes the contents (giving line or page numbers, prominent events, names and quotations, and Vulgate cross-references).

Arthurian literature, Middle English or otherwise, repeatedly sparks the question: 'Did Arthur really exist?' Rodney Castleden's *King Arthur: The Truth Behind the Legend* offers an affirmative answer. Castleden has been very thorough in his investigations and covers all the angles, including Gildas's famous silence, the sudden prominence of the name *Arthur*, the 'Arthur-shaped gap' in the Saxon invasions, Camelot, Badon and Camlann. He offers a concise survey of the arguments *against* a historical Arthur, but his own argument is firmly in favour of an authentic Arthur who acted as *dux bellorum*. Tintagel and Cadbury are both accepted as possible staging points for Arthur's mobile army, but Camelot itself is placed elsewhere: modern Killibury (Celli Wig in various sources). Castleden locates Badon at Bath and, following the *Annales Cambriae* (which Castleden refers to as 'the annals in the Nennius collection'), dates it to AD 516; Camlann is dated to 537 and is located in Gwynedd in north-west Wales. Interestingly, Castleden suggests that Mordred may have been Arthur's ally, not foe, and that the victor at Camlann was instead Maelgwn. It is further argued that Arthur did not die at Camlann, but rather survived the battle and travelled north to Whithorn, in Galloway, the location not only of Arthur's grave, but of Avalon. There is a confusion of dates on p. 17, and the book's misleading subtitle suggests a degree of certainty which is impossible given the paucity of fifth- and sixth-century records, but this is a sound overview of the principal material and arguments.

Amidst papers on the *Canterbury Tales, Testament of Cresseid*, alliterative poetry and the *Gawain*-poet, Powell and Smith, eds., *New Perspectives on Middle English Texts: A Festschrift for R.A. Waldron*, contains a number of papers relevant to our brief. Jane Roberts emphasizes Layamon's mastery of language and the ways in which his *Brut* straddles the shift from Old to Middle English. As such, difficult passages in the *Brut*, such as those at lines 11280 and 14966 (which have puzzled recent translators), can be glossed and understood by reference to Old, not Middle, English. Julia Boffey and A.S.G. Edwards focus on Middle English verse which has been interpolated into prose chronicles and examine the various uses such verse might serve. In general, such verse interpolations seem random, but Boffey and Edwards promise further commentary in their forthcoming revision of the *Index of Middle English Verse*. Janet Cowen looks at a Middle English verse translation of (selections from) Boccaccio's *De Mulieribus Claris* in BL MS Add. 10304. She argues that the Middle English version postdates Lydgate's *Fall of Princes* and sees itself in some relation to this work. Further, the Middle English version is arranged—seemingly by its translator—in three thematic groups: rule, art, prophecy. Finally (for our purposes), Roger Dahood examines final *r* loops in Southwell Minster, Nottingham MS 7 [*c.*1500] and questions whether they are otiose or denote final *e*. He argues for the latter.

The essays collected in John Scattergood's *The Lost Tradition* range over the gamut of Middle English alliterative verse and make considerable forays into other generic territory. Eight of the thirteen pieces printed here have appeared elsewhere before, while five are wholly new. Among the newcomers, 'The "Lewed" and the "Lerede": A Reading of *Satire on the Consistory Courts*' and 'A Defining Moment: The Battle of Flodden and English Poetry' deal with less well known material, while 'Wrong's Laugh: *Piers Plowman* C. IV. 45–104, Law-breaking, Carnival and Parody', 'Remembering Richard II: John Gower's *Cronica Tripartita, Richard the Redeles*, and *Mum and the Sothsegger*', and '*St Erkenwald* and the Custody of the Past' cover more canonical subjects. Among the reprinted (and sometimes lightly revised) essays are pieces on *Sir Gawain and the Green Knight, Patience, De Clerico et Puella* and *Winner and Waster*. Everywhere the analysis is informed by the author's characteristic mediation between the nuances of texture and tone of the written texts and the lived experience of their social contexts. It is good to have the chance to read all of these essays in a single volume.

While discussing essay collections, readers should also be aware of the volume of essays by various hands published as a memorial volume for the late Jeremy Griffiths. As well as providing an affectionate and moving tribute to Griffiths from his many academic friends, Edwards, Gillespie and Hanna, eds., *The English Medieval Book*, is also a fitting reflection of its honorand's passionate commitment to bibliographical scholarship. The contributors provide detailed analyses of individual manuscripts and reflections on bibliographical work in progress. Among the subjects covered are a new manuscript relating to the Bohun family, described by Christopher De Hamel (pp. 19–25), 'Augustinian Canons and Middle English Literature', by Ralph Hanna (pp. 27–42), fragments of *The Prick of Conscience* in Durham (A.I. Doyle, pp. 43–9), 'The Rede (Boarstall) Gower: British Library MS Harley 3490', by Derek Pearsall (pp. 87–99), 'Bodleian Library MS Arch. Selden B.24 and Definitions of the "Household Book"', by Julia Boffey (pp. 125–34), 'Caxton's Second Edition of *The Canterbury Tales*', by N.F. Blake (pp. 135–53), and the lost library of Syon Abbey (described by Vincent Gillespie, pp. 185–208). Another honorand of a collection of essays published this year, this time in much happier circumstances, is Derek Pearsall, to whom Aers, ed., *Medieval Literature and Historical Enquiry*, is dedicated. Gathered to mark Pearsall's seventieth birthday, the essays cover a number of the topics on which he himself has written during his remarkably wide-ranging scholarly career. There are pieces on Langland ('The Condition of *Kynde*', by Nicolette Zeeman, pp. 1–30, and '*Piers Plowman* as Poetic Pillory: The Pillory and the Cross', by C. David Benson, pp. 32–54); Chaucer ('The Empire and the Waif: Consent and Conflict of Laws in *The Man of Law's Tale*', by Elizabeth Fowler, pp. 55–68, and 'Chaucer's *Tale of Melibee*: Whose Virtues?', by David Aers, pp. 69–82); the *Gawain*-poet ('*Pearl* and the Contingencies of Love and Piety', by Lynn Staley, pp. 83–114); Lydgate ('John Lydgate, Jacque of Holland, and the Poetics of Complicity', by Paul Strohm, pp. 115–32); the stiff upper lip in heroic poetry ('Heroic Laconic Style: Reticence and Meaning from *Beowulf* to the Edwardians', by Lee Patterson, pp. 133–58); Malory ('Malory's Crime: Chivalric Identity and the Evil Will', by Christopher Cannon, pp. 159–84); and the cycle drama ('Absent Presences: The Theatre of Resurrection in York', by Sarah Beckwith, pp. 185–206). All in all, this is an excellent collection, and a fitting celebration of the interests and influence of its dedicatee. If only it had been published with an index to aid navigation through its riches! [GW]

Finally, a number of EETS titles were reprinted in 2000. As reprints, there are not available for review, but as most of them are decades or even more than a century old, their reprinting deserves mention; those relevant to this section include, but are by no means limited to: *Book of the Knight of La Tour-Landry*, ed. T. Wright; *Brut*, volume i, ed. F.W.D. Brie; *Hymns to the Virgin and Christ and Other Religious Poems*, ed. F.J. Furnivall; *Pierce the Ploughman's Crede*, ed. W.W. Skeat; and *Richard Rolle de Hampole English Prose Treatises*, ed. G.G. Perry. Further details are available from the publisher (B&B): <http://www.boydell.co.uk/EETS.HTM>.

2. Alliterative Poetry

The most extensive recent treatment of an alliterative work is Bonnie Millar's *The Siege of Jerusalem in its Physical, Literary and Historical Contexts*. Millar suggests that its fifteenth-century readers found the poem 'of either religious or historical interest or both', and notes that changes in dialect 'indicate how the poem inspired interest in areas outside where it was written'. She studies its relationship to its main sources (the *Vindicta Salvatoris*, Roger d'Argenteuil's *Bible en François*, and the *Polychronicon*); she finds that its relationship to the *Legenda Aurea* and *The Destruction of Troy* is inconclusive. She uses structural anthropology to approach the mother–child cannibalism, comparing it to the sources or potential sources from chapter 2 as well as to *Titus and Vespasian*. The author of the *Siege* emphasizes 'its implications with regard to Christian history', making Mary 'more realistic' and her situation more pathetic. Rather than reviling the Jews, he shows them as 'tyrannized by wicked leaders'. *Titus and Vespasian*, Millar argues, is 'more popular ... more sensational' than the *Siege*; its manuscript contexts are primarily religious, rather than historical. Millar argues further that the poem was not intended as a crusading narrative, and that although it opposes the religious beliefs of Jews (and thus is anti-Judaic), it is not anti-Semitic. She compares the *Siege* to two Charlemagne romances and two crusading romances to show the difference in outlook. As the poem falls between genres, Millar compares traits such as plot construction, 'narrative stance', style, characterization and so forth, to the conventions in romance, historiography and religious narrative, concluding that the *Siege* is more like romance than like any other genre. The major difference is the author's distance from and lack of comment on the poem. In an appendix, Millar edits two sample passages from each of the manuscripts in which they appear (seven and eight respectively).

Two of the new essays that appear in John Scattergood's *The Lost Tradition* focus on alliterative verse. 'The "Lewed" and the "Lerede": A Reading of *Satire on the Consistory Courts*' (pp. 27–42) historicizes the poem by discussing literacy and illiteracy in the fourteenth century before studying the various strata of criticism in the poem. Though the *SCC* associates writing and oppression, as do other poems of the era, Chaucer's *Friar's Tale* shows a poor woman unintimidated by writing. 'Remembering Richard II: John Gower's *Cronica Tripartita*, *Richard the Redeles*, and *Mum and the Sothsegger*' (pp. 200–25) argues that passus I of *Richard* is based on an account of misconduct in the Parliamentary Rolls, while the next two passus are more 'like a political beast fable'; the poem criticizes the suppression of 'countervailing arguments against the king's will'. Similarly, *Mum* focuses on the problems of telling the truth vs. keeping silent, showing that the 'greatest danger ... is the silencing of oppositional voices'.

Ralph Hanna considers 'Feasting in Middle English Alliterative Poetry' (in Powell and Smith, eds., pp. 31–41), expanding on his remarks in the *Cambridge History of Medieval English Literature* (where he suggests that the alliterative narrator's stance as 'entertainer in a great hall' is 'probably fictive'). He traces the topos of the lord's hall beyond Beowulf to Isidore, the Bible and Homer. He relates secular feasts to heavenly celebration, and argues that, in Middle English poetry, 'the greatest celebratory moments are marked as insufficient. They speak to social blindness, not solidarity'. Hanna's 'Alliterative Poetry' (in Wallace, ed., *The Cambridge History of Medieval English Literature*, pp. 488–512) takes issue with the idea of an alliterative 'revival', arguing that both the metrical differences from Old English and the difficulty of dating alliterative poetry precisely suggest that the phenomenon was diffuse and should not be 'associat[ed] ... with a defiant regionalism'.

Yasuyo Moriya analyses 'The Line Boundary of Middle English Alliterative Meter Compared to that of Old English Alliterative Meter' (*NM* 101[2000] 387–402), concluding that where the Old English line allows a variety of endings, Middle English metre 'strongly prefers ending the line with a single offbeat', presenting 'a smooth flow of rhythm'. Paul Hartle's *Hunting the Letter: Middle English Alliterative Verse and the Formulaic Theory* [1999] is an attempt to discover what formulas or collocations are 'habitual' in Middle English alliterative verse. His corpus consists of *Joseph of Arimathie*, *Death and Liffe*, *St. Erkenwald*, and the *Scotish Feilde*. His alphabetical list of collocations might contribute to an eventual dictionary of such phrases, though Hartle denies the completeness of his study even for the four poems here studied. More discussion of his choice of editions would be welcome—why not always use the manuscript readings?—and the use of italic *b* and *D* to indicate minuscule and capital thorn is distracting.

3. The *Gawain*-Poet

This section covers works published in 1998, 1999 and 2000. Robert J. Blanch's *The Gawain Poems: A Reference Guide, 1978–1993* provides a useful map to recent scholarship on the poems of the Cotton Nero MS. His introduction is divided into two parts, the first on *Gawain and the Green Knight* criticism and the second on *Pearl* criticism. Both sections discuss the general critical and theoretical trends of the years covered by his survey. Blanch's rationale for providing introductions to *Gawain* and *Pearl* scholarship is that critics of these poems 'frequently offer interpretations grounded in critical theory'. Similar introductions to *Patience* and *Cleanness* scholarship are conspicuously absent, despite the fact that much recent scholarship on these poems has been highly theoretically informed. The annotated bibliography is broken down into three sections: 'Editions and Translations', 'Criticism', and 'Reference/Pedagogical Works'. Annotations concisely summarize each entry's main features or arguments, and this is followed by a word index and a line index.

As usual, the preponderance of recent critical attention given to the *Gawain*-poet has been focused on *Gawain*. Ann W. Astell provides fresh, historically informed interpretations of *Gawain* and several other prominent works of Middle English literature in *Political Allegory in Late Medieval England* [1999]. She sees unity among the so-called 'Ricardian' poets, not only in terms of their shared sense of the significance of public poetry, but in their shared habits of allegorization: 'Langland, Gower, Chaucer, the *Gawain*-poet ... all practised an allegorical art, partly as a result of their similar educational backgrounds and also because political pressures encouraged and indeed necessitated indirection in writing about matters of public concern.' Chapter 5, entitled 'Penitential Politics in *Sir Gawain and the Green Knight*: Richard II, Richard of Arundel, and Robert de Vere', argues that *Gawain* functioned as a belated warning to Richard II to seek reconciliation with his enemies and forgiveness for past political transgressions. Paying close attention to material not in the poem's original sources, Astell links familiar scenes from the poem to key moments from Richard's reign so that, for example, the 'beheading scene' speaks to controversies surrounding the execution of Richard of Arundel.

Cohen, ed., *Of Giants: Sex, Monsters, and the Middle Ages*, pursues a by now familiar post-Bakhtinian line of thinking, which sees 'monstrous' bodies as sites on which writers (consciously or unconsciously) attempt to map out distinctions between Self and Other, Civilization and Wilderness. Cohen sees grotesque bodies as 'excluded from the circle of the social' but incorporating 'the secret interior of the "civilized" identity'. Cohen sees *Gawain* as different from traditional quest romances in that the poem finally refuses to exclude the giant (in this case, the Green Knight) from the civilization and value system that define the world of the hero. If traditional romances have the hero defeating the giant and then moving on as part of his maturation process (which Cohen describes as a movement from *iuvenis* to *homo*), *Gawain* concludes with the giant literally instructing the hero as to his chivalric duties. The giant provides a paradigm of chivalric behaviour despite his inhuman appearance. Cohen pays particular attention to the place of women in *Gawain*, claiming that the poem sees 'interiorizing hate and violence, especially toward women', as a necessary component of the hero-knight's maturation.

Nick Davis's *Stories of Chaos* analyses the relationship between narrative and reason in 'early modern' works of literature. The scope of his book covers *Gawain*, *The Faerie Queene*, *King Lear*, and *Paradise Lost*, all poems in which, Davis claims, 'narrative arises ... in the breaking down of reason and reasoning's supposedly secure operation'. His chapter on *Gawain*, '*Sir Gawain and the Green Knight*: An Unfolded Narrative', sees the poem in terms of its 'incompatible' notions of narrative: 'narrative is that which sustains and confirms solidity of form; and narrative rehearses the dissipation and loss of apparently solid form, so offering valuable material for reflection'. Davis focuses on the pentangle as an 'object of Reason'; he submits it to ruthless and perplexing geometrical analysis (complete with diagrams) in order to demonstrate its status as icon of Gawain's theory of Truth. This 'theory' is then found to be necessarily insufficient in the face of the machinations of the women in the poem, particularly Morgan.

Philippa Hardman, in 'Gawain's Practice of Piety in *Sir Gawain and the Green Knight*' (*MÆ* 68[1999] 247–67), makes the provocative assertion that the 'symbolic contrast' between the pentangle and the girdle, which has been a critical commonplace in many modern assessments of the poem, might be an inaccurate way of understanding the relationship between these two objects within the context of late medieval Christian piety. While critics have tended to see the pentangle as representative of Christian 'faith', and the girdle as representative of pagan 'superstition', Hardman argues that Gawain's attachment to both objects is commensurate with a common form of late medieval piety in which people sought to 'protect themselves not only with the sacraments, prayers, and the sign of the cross but with an armoury of sanctified everyday objects ... Gawain seems to belong to the same part-orthodox, part-"superstitious" world of sacramental things and powerful words and signs'. Hardman does not deny that the objects have different significances, but contends that neither do they belong to antithetical or mutually hostile traditions of piety.

W.G. Cooke and D'A.J.D. Boulton, in '*Sir Gawain and the Green Knight*: A Poem for Henry of Grosmont?' (*MÆ* 68[1999] 42–54), provide further evidence for dating the poem towards the middle (rather than end) of the fourteenth century by arguing strenuously that Henry of Grosmont, first duke of Lancaster, is the historical figure most likely to have been patron of the *Gawain*-poet. Cooke and Boulton go looking for a 'fourteenth-century lord with considerable interests in the north-west Midlands, known to have spent some time there, and having the right character and outlook to have relished [*Gawain*]'. After establishing, among other things, Henry's Arthurian predilections, Cooke and Boulton conclude that *Gawain* 'was written for Henry of Grosmont by a poet who wished to create an Arthurian prototype for the badge of King Edward's neo-Arthurian order and at the same time to please his patron by working into the story an object [the girdle/baldric] that would recall several others that had figured in his career'.

In 'Sir Guido and the Green Light: Confession in *Sir Gawain and the Green Knight* and *Inferno* XXVII' (*Neophil* 84[2000] 647–66), Julian Wasserman and Liam O. Purdon draw connections between Gawain and Dante's Guido da Montefeltro, suggesting that both men engage in false confession, and that, despite the differences in context, this act of false confession 'is evoked by strikingly similar imagery and themes in the two works'.

Finally, there are two recent, significant studies of *Pearl*. Teresa P. Reed, in 'Mary, the Maiden, and Metonymy in *Pearl*' (*SoAR* 65[2000] 134–62), argues that, while reading the pearl as metaphor helps to underscore the otherness of divine things in relation to mundane things, one can also see a metonymic logic at work in the poem, a logic which stresses important contiguities between the human and the divine. Mary is the central metonymic figure of the poem, linking the maternal (physical) and the divine (otherworldly) in images of regality. Lynn Staley explores the relationship between the 'private' or biographical elements of *Pearl* and the poem's status as 'public' poetry in '*Pearl* and the Contingencies of Love and Piety' (in Aers, ed., pp. 83–114). Staley seeks to make both an argument about the specific historical identity of the maiden in *Pearl* and an argument about the way the poem speaks to ideals of lordship in late medieval England (*c*.1385), with the latter argument not being necessarily dependent on the former. She identifies the maiden as 'Isabel, the third daughter of Thomas of Woodstock, born in 1384 and given to the house of the Minoresses in London as a very young child'. Staley does an admirable job of balancing attention to historical research (on Woodstock, and specifically his connections to the Minoresses) with attention to the poetic themes of loss and desire in *Pearl*.

4. *Piers Plowman*

The Yearbook of Langland Studies has continued to produce much of each year's scholarship on *Piers Plowman*. Volume 11 [1997], not previously reviewed in *YWES*, starts with C. David Benson, '*Piers Plowman* and Parish Wall Paintings' (*YLS* 11[1997] 1–38), suggesting that paintings on the walls of parish churches form a 'significant contemporary religious discourse' that helps to contextualize the poem, despite Langland's own condemnation of such work in B.III. He gives fourteen photographs of medieval English church murals, depicting such subjects as the Last Judgement, the Crucifixion, and the Seven Deadly Sins, and discusses lines in the poem that evoke such images. Roy J. Pearcy, in 'Langland's *Fair Feld*' (*YLS* 11[1997] 39–48), returns to A, prologue, 17 to suggest a new interpretation of the word 'fair' as deriving from OF 'feire', thus meaning the site for a fair in the sense of market or show. The prologue suggests the ambience of such a fair. In '"First to reckon Richard": John But's *Piers Plowman* and the Politics of Allegiance' (*YLS* 11[1997] 49–66), Wendy Scase considers the ending of the A-version supplied by John But, which she points out is conventionally loyal to the king in a way that Langland's text is not. By comparing But's language to that of Langland and other alliterative poems, she argues that But manages to show loyalty to both Richard and Langland, and to critique the 'new politics of allegiance' of the late fourteenth century. Edward Jones's 'Langland and Hermits' (*YLS* 11[1997] 67–86) questions what the term 'hermits' means in *Piers Plowman*. The ideal hermit for Langland is truly solitary. Jones considers a number of historical hermits and shows that in the second quarter of the fourteenth century there was an increase in English hermits. Richard Firth Green, in 'Friar William Appleton and the Date of Langland's B Text' (*YLS* 11[1997] 87–96), suggests that, at the end of B.XX, Langland alludes to a friar who was John of Gaunt's physician and was lynched in the revolt of 1381. If Langland is referring to William Appleton's death when Peace says she knew someone like Sir Penetrans Domus 'noyt eighte wynter passed', then the B-text must have been completed in the late 1380s. Sean Taylor's 'The Lost Revision of *Piers Plowman B*' (*YLS* 11[1997] 97–134) analyses passages in Oxford, Bodleian Library, Rawlinson Poetry 38 (comprising, with Oxford, Corpus Christi College 2001, Schmidt's α-group) that do not appear in other manuscripts of the B-tradition, arguing that Langland revised the B-text into the Rawlinson form after 1381. He considers omitted as well as added material, concluding that R is a witness to a particular 'textual moment'. Carl Grindley, in 'A New Fragment of the *Piers Plowman* C Text?' (*YLS* 11[1997] 135–40), discusses four lines from the prologue that appear at the back of Huntington Library MS HM 143, in a slightly changed version, appearing to be from a different C-text tradition. Grindley suggests that the scribe wished to preserve this variant. Bryan P. Davis explains 'The Rationale for a Copy of a Text: Constructing the Exemplar for British Library Additional MS. 10574' (*YLS* 11[1997] 141–55). He considers three composite manuscripts of *Piers Plowman*, showing that two of them came from the same stationer; MS 10574 is the earlier of these, copied by a single scribe. Because the exemplar was missing about 720 lines of material, material from both A and C was used to fill the gap, edited so as to produce a manuscript comparable in appearance to others of the time. Tadahiro Ikegami's 'A Short History of Langland Studies in Japan' (*YLS* 11[1997] 157–62) shows that Japanese scholars have become increasingly independent of Anglo-

American institutions. Ikegami surveys scholars from Lafcadio Hearn to two recent translators of *Piers Plowman* into Japanese. Finally, Ruth Nissé writes on 'Reversing Discipline: The Tretise of Miraclis Pleyinge, Lollard Exegesis, and the Failure of Representation' (pp. 163–94), studying various Wycliffite texts to provide a context for the Tretise's struggles with 'exegetical and political practices'.

The Yearbook of Langland Studies, volume 12 [1998], not previously reviewed in *YWES*, is mostly devoted to the topic 'Gender and *Piers Plowman*'; as editor Andrew Galloway notes, 'The conjoined words have such a brief history that no separate bibliography need be appended' to his introduction (*YLS* 12[1998] 1–4). In 'The Traffic in Medieval Women: Alice Perrers, Feminist Criticism, and *Piers Plowman*' (*YLS* 12[1998] 5–29), Stephanie Trigg returns to the association of Mede and Alice Perrers, finding that because the best-documented medieval women are exceptional, their 'historical specificity' tends to be ignored. Trigg points out that, though a 'sexual commodity', Perrers wielded real power at court. Mede, too, operates both as subject and object. Joan Baker and Susan Signe Morrison, collaborating on 'The Luxury of Gender: *Piers Plowman* and the Merchant's Tale' (*YLS* 12[1998] 31–63), suggest that Chaucer knew the B-text and used the *Merchant's Tale* to respond to themes in B.IX, January caricaturing Wit. The Castle Caro episode suggests that gender is a 'non-essential category'. Mede and May are both treated as objects in (potential or actual) 'unkynde' marriages. The authors suggest that women may have formed part of Langland's intended audience for the A-text.

James J. Paxson studies 'Gender Personified, Personification Gendered, and the Body Figuralized in *Piers Plowman*' (*YLS* 12[1998] 65–96). It is not enough to say that grammar determines the gender of allegorical figures, Paxson says, and he interrogates the association of female figures with abstractions, claiming that 'the body of woman becomes a figure for figuration itself'. After an extended treatment of this rhetorical background, he looks closely at Anima's change from female in B.IX to male in B.XV, and suggests that Mede appears as Anima's parallel, 'allegory's pure exterior', without bodily existence. He also briefly treats 'The Queering of Elde', an idea he pursues at greater length elsewhere. 'Dame Study and Women's Literacy', by Louise Bishop (*YLS* 12[1998] 97–115), argues that Study, influenced by both Augustine and the Oxford translation debates, embodies both literate and illiterate learning, Latin and vernacular, but emphasizes charity and social concerns; she mediates between Imaginatif and Thought. Bishop concludes that 'Langland's text resists gendered modes of affective piety', while focusing on 'the perceptive interior life in the practice of vernacular reading'.

Andrew Galloway's complex 'Intellectual Pregnancy, Metaphysical Femininity, and the Social Doctrine of the Trinity in *Piers Plowman*' (*YLS* 12[1998] 117–52) develops its examination of 'intellectual pregnancy' from the specific case of one Margery Baxter, accused of heresy in 1428, who claimed she held within her body a 'charter of protection'. Galloway shows that Langland's idea of the Trinity as a family values women, community, and lived experience over abstract, patriarchal authority. Jesus's human suffering feminizes God's intellectual attributes; Langland's own self-portrait emphasizes his place in a family, showing the immediacy of this metaphor.

Ralph Hanna III has a brief piece, 'Reading Prophecy/Reading Piers' (*YLS* 12[1998] 153–7), complaining that modern scholars tend to read the poem like those sixteenth-century readers who saw Clergy's prophecy in B.X.331–5 as a reference to Henry VIII's closing of the abbeys, which, Hanna says, should be read as foretelling only the coming of Antichrist in passus XX. He urges scholars to focus on the poem's 'internal mappings'. He also writes on 'A New Edition of the C Version' (*YLS* 12[1998] 175–88), complaining that Russell and Kane (editors of the Athlone C-text) 'neglect to address the historicity of the manuscript evidence'. Their assumption that C is an incomplete revision 'rests on a hermeneutic circle' and allows less intense editing than for the Athlone B-text.

Peter Barney provides a 'Line-Number Index to the Athlone Edition of *Piers Plowman: The C Version*' (*YLS* 12[1998] 159–73), which gives passus and line numbers for lines of the poem appearing in the introduction to Russell and Kane; he also lists differences between Russell and Kane's and Schmidt's B-editions, given by their C-version line-numbers.

The Yearbook of Langland Studies, volume 13 [1999], focuses on the reception history of Langland (Galloway, Foreword, *YLS* 13[1999] 1–6). It first presents 'An Open Letter to Jill Mann about the Sequence of the Versions of *Piers Plowman*' (*YLS* 13[1999] 7–33), from George Kane (see Lawlor in *YLS* 10[1996]). He argues against many of her assertions, noting that the redactor let stand some Latin, and added other Latin lines; retained sexual material and criticisms of clergy; and kept a lot of figurative language. He studies several passages from A, B, and C, arguing for sequential development. David C. Fowler, in '*Piers Plowman*: Will's "Apologia pro vita sua"' (*YLS* 13[1999] 35–47), suggests that the B- and C-versions were written by a different man and that the 'autobiographical' lines in C are an 'indictment of Will', who 'has become a shallow peddler of words', defending himself inadequately against Reason's condemnation. Rees Davies, in 'The Life, Travels, and Library of an Early Reader of *Piers Plowman*' (*YLS* 13[1999] 49–64), studies a cleric who died in 1396, leaving the earliest known bequest of *Piers Plowman*. He served as attorney and financial adviser to Lionel, duke of Clarence and his son-in-law, travelling extensively: 'Walter Brugge and Lady Meed, one suspects, were not unknown to each other.' This portrait of an early owner of Langland's poem adds considerably to ideas about its fourteenth-century audience. 'Dating *Piers Plowman*: Testing the Testimony of Usk's *Testament*', by John M. Bowers (*YLS* 13[1999] 65–100), reviews dates suggested by various scholars for both Usk and Langland, questioning Usk's reliance on the C-text (asserted by Skeat). Usk, he says, would have avoided allusions to *Piers Plowman* as disadvantageous to his courtly ambitions. He explores Skeat's possible reasons for ordering the texts as he did: placing Langland before Chaucer's *Canterbury Tales* emphasizes Chaucer's innovations. Sarah A. Kelen, 'Plowing the Past: "Piers Protestant" and the Authority of Medieval Literary History' (*YLS* 13[1999] 101–36), looks at sixteenth-century uses of Piers; from being Jack Carter's 'brother' in 1381, he becomes a grandfather, an authority figure. In most sixteenth-century works referring to the Plowman, he is a virtuous, idealized figure; however, in the 1510 'Lytell geste how the plowman lerned his pater noster', he is comically impious. The sixteenth-century writers and editors use the Plowman figure as an emblem of the past who can 'justify a current religious position'. Siegfried Wenzel's 'Eli and his Sons' (*YLS* 13[1999] 137–52) examines Langland's use in the C-prologue of the story of Eli's sons, who were wicked priests, against contemporary examples from pastoral handbooks and sermons. Most of these were addressed to the clergy, as warning examples against greed and incontinence. He suggests that this image was fairly commonly used to condemn practices that distressed the orthodox as well as Wycliffites. Bonnie Millar, 'The Role of Prophecy in the *Siege of Jerusalem* and its Analogues' (*YLS* 13[1999] 153–78), presents research related to but excluded from her *Siege of Jerusalem*. This article focuses on the episode involving omens of the destruction of Jerusalem and the Jews' fate, reviewing various analogues: *The Jewish War*, in two versions; Higden's *Polychronicon*; the *Legenda Aurea*; and *Titus and Vespasian*. Millar concludes that the Siege is distinctive in the role it gives to the narrator, the treatment of the omens, and its portrayal of John and Simon.

YLS [1999] also contains a review article and a response: Ralph Hanna III, '*Piers Plowman* and the Radically Chic' (*YLS* 13[1999] 179–92), and Kathryn Kerby-Fulton (with Denise Despres), 'Fabricating Failure: The Professional Reader as Textual Terrorist' (*YLS* 13[1999] 193–206). Hanna's subject is Kerby-Fulton's and Despres's book, which he considers 'well-conceived in the abstract' but inadequate as a model, 'as a definition of the literary community', and as 'practical criticism'. He wishes for better acquaintance with documents from fifteenth-century Ireland and for closer attention to the text of Douce 104 as it differs from the edited C-text. He criticizes argumentation, elisions and omissions, as well as the authors' interest in 'alternative politics'. In their response, Kerby-Fulton and Despres claim that Hanna's 'errors' 'are virtually all illusions created either by strategic use of suppression, ellipsis, over-hasty reading, or conflation of independent statements'. They point out that Hanna does not disagree with many of their arguments, including their view that the scribe and illustrator are the same person and that he seems to have had Exchequer training. They address Hanna's lettered comments (focusing on page 57) directly and specifically. As to Irish documents, the authors point to their 137-item index of manuscripts, and remind readers that many documents were destroyed in 1922. And they, in turn, comment on Hanna's 'unexamined political contradictions'.

Radical Nostalgia in the Age of 'Piers Plowman': Economics, Apocalypticism, and Discontent, by Justine Rydzeski [1999], situates *Piers Plowman* in a context formed by the changing fourteenth-century economy as much as by medieval apocalyptic views of history. Rydzeski begins by studying the economic metaphors underlying Christian redemption and satisfaction, then traces Langland's use of these metaphors: his work argues for a rural vision of history that focuses on the attempt to return to Eden rather than on the pursuit of the New Jerusalem. She expands her treatment to fourteenth- and early fifteenth-century English literature and society more generally, suggesting that Langland's work appealed to the rebels of 1381 and other activists not only because of his attention to real social problems but also because the biblical metaphors of reaping, shepherding, and so on, encouraged conscientious clerics to ally themselves with labourers. Rydzeski relies heavily on the research of Harry Miskimin for her economic data. She gives close readings of sections of *Piers Plowman*, concentrating especially on Lady Meed, and concludes with a survey of poems imitating or drawing on Langland. The book could have used closer attention to its references: while 'Stephen' Justice appears in the index, his book is not on the list of works cited, nor do the notes give a full reference.

Andrew Galloway, in 'Uncharacterizable Entities: The Poetics of Middle English Scribal Culture and the Definitive *Piers Plowman*' (*SB* 52[2000] 59–87), reviews the recent major editions and text studies of *Piers Plowman*, giving most attention to Kane and Donaldson and Russell and Kane (the Athlone editions), A.V.C. Schmidt's parallel edition, and Ralph Hanna's *Pursuing History* [1996]. Galloway finds that, despite Athlone's ambitions to restore the author's own version, these editions 'sustain constantly the difficulty of this poem as a textual product', forcing readers to engage with the different versions of *Piers*, in contrast with Schmidt's more accessible text (and apparatus). Galloway takes issue with Russell and Kane's argumentation, providing analysis of passages that leads to different conclusions about the meaning of repetitions; he also analyses the different reasoning that led to Russell and Kane and Schmidt arriving at the same version of C.I.39, by way of illustrating the editors' approaches.

When considering *Piers Plowman* in *A Crisis of Truth: Literature and Law in Ricardian England*, Richard Firth Green notes that 'truth', until the late fourteenth century, opposed not 'errour' but 'deceit'. In Langland the term floats between these two uses. The most important contract in *Piers Plowman* is that of baptism, which presents two problems: can it be fulfilled by sinful humans, and if so, can virtuous pagans fail to be saved, since they have lived up to its terms though not formally bound by it?

Bruce Holsinger's 'Langland's Musical Reader: Liturgy, Law, and the Constraints of Performance' (*SAC* 21[1999] 99–141), considers a fifty-two-line alliterative poem, the 'Choristers' Lament', as a response to the B-text of *Piers Plowman*. Holsinger discusses clerical 'representations of liturgical performance' and connections between song and law before turning to Langland's representations of these subjects. The 'Choristers' Lament', which introduces a number of musical terms into English, responds to *Piers*, Holsinger argues, 'by exposing the liturgical exercise of clerical authority as unnatural, violent, and ultimately unsuccessful', and echoing various phrases of Langland's. Holsinger also examines the poem's manuscript context in British Library MS Arundel 292 and includes a new edition of it.

Charles Muscatine, *Medieval Literature, Style, and Culture*, reprints two essays on *Piers Plowman*, 'Locus of Action in Medieval Narrative' [1963] and 'Poetry and Crisis in the Age of Chaucer' [1972]. Claudia R. Papka argues, in 'The Limits of Apocalypse: Eschatology, Epistemology, and Textuality in the *Commedia* and *Piers Plowman*' (in Bynum and Freedman, eds., *Last Things: Death and the Apocalypse in the Middle Ages*), that the poem is 'a fiction of judgement', presenting itself simultaneously as human-authored and possibly divinely inspired. The Tree of Charity scene, in her view, presents a problem unresolved, though only capable of being addressed, by eschatology; Langland articulates a 'divinity unmediated by form ... often occluded by allegory in other eschatologies'.

Three reprinted essays on Langland appear in Pearsall, ed., *Chaucer to Spenser: A Critical Reader*. The first essay in the volume is 'The Humanity of Christ: Reflections on Orthodox Late Medieval Representations, and The Humanity of Christ: Representations in Wycliffite Texts and *Piers Plowman*', a combination of two chapters by David Aers from *Powers of the Holy* [1996]. The fourth, by Elizabeth Fowler, 'Misogyny and Economic Person in Skelton, Langland, and Chaucer' appeared in [1992]; the eighth, by Anne Middleton, 'William Langland's "Kynde Name": Authorial Signature and Social Identity in Late Fourteenth-Century

England', first appeared in *Literary Practice and Social Change in Britain, 1380–1530* [1990].

William E. Rogers, in 'Knighthood as Type: Holy Church's Interpretation of Knighthood in *Piers Plowman* B.1' (*Sewanee Medieval Studies* 9[2000] 205–18), claims that, besides indicating social standing, knighthood in B.I is the ability to discriminate or define, to set boundaries. The social world is analogous to a text, which social organizations provide ways of interpreting; knighthood, for Holy Church, 'is the social analogue of correct interpretation'. At the same time, there is some question as to whether authoritative interpretations can exist alongside 'the activities of love', and how the changing economy influences such interpretations. The second chapter of Ann Astell's *Political Allegory in Late Medieval England*, '"Full of enigmas": John Ball's letters and *Piers Plowman*', suggests that Ball's letters are a digest of his sermons, and that they 'appropriate Langland's silences'. In discussing *Piers*, she concentrates on Ball's understanding of the pardon scene, suggesting that Ball saw the pardon as extending to the rebels who beheaded their oppressors.

James J. Paxson proposes, in 'Queering *Piers Plowman*: The Copula(tions) of Figures in Medieval Allegory' (*Rhetoric Society Quarterly* 29:iii[2000] 21–9), that 'we need ... a viable contemporary "body theory" of allegory', one that will treat the bodies of personifications. Accordingly, he addresses two passages of *Piers*: B.XX.193–8 (Will's encounter with Elde) and B.XV.12–13 (the riddling appearance of Anima as 'oon withouten tonge and teeth') so as to supply these personifications with sexual significance. Elde's joining Kit in 'forbeting' Will's 'lyme that she loved me for', Paxson claims, portrays Elde as queer, while Anima appears as the '*vagina dentata—sans dentis*' (*sic*). Though Paxson roots his discussion in Aristotle and Quintilian on simile, metaphor, and *transumptio*, his argument hinges on accepting as a Freudian slip Elde's capitalization (and thus transformation into a personification rather than a metaphor).

Working with Lyotard's definition of the 'differend', and inspired by his own reaction to the often-repeated 'redde quod debes' in the poem, G. Wilsbacher, 'Anachronistic Responsibility (A Proposal): Ethics, History, and *Piers Plowman*' (*Exemplaria* 11:ii[2000] 363–98), argues that historicist approaches to *Piers* are inadequate because lacking an ethical component. After reviewing such responses by David Aers and Derek Pearsall, Wilsbacher discusses the phenomenology of historical knowledge and, returning to Lyotard, proposes 'an anachronistic responsibility' as a postmodern response to texts that provoke a 'feeling of obligation' in the reader. A full application of his theories to *Piers Plowman* is not included owing to spatial constraints, though one would very much like to see more examples of what this approach would look like in practice.

Two related essays appear in *New Medieval Literatures* [1999]: '"Studying" in the Middle Ages—and in *Piers Plowman*', by Nicolette Zeeman (*NML* 3[1999] 185–212), and 'School and Scorn: Gender in *Piers Plowman*', by Ralph Hanna III (*NML* 3[1999] 213–27). Zeeman considers the term 'study' in Latin and Middle English sources, pointing out that it has 'powerful connotations of desire, effort, and labour' and arguing that 'the very things which make virtuous *studie* worthwhile make bad *studie* dangerous', which explains the force of Study's rebuke of Will; his resulting dismay intensifies his longing to learn. Hanna intends to 'unpack' some of his own remarks about gender in *Piers*. He begins by suggesting that Will traded his privy 'lym' for the 'lomes' of learning, citing C.V.33–47 (though I can find no suggestion in Will's speech, as opposed to Reason's, that he is missing anything). Hanna studies 'Latins', school exercises set for children to translate, to show that beating in school was common and sometimes spoken of in sexual terms: 'I maryed my maysters doughter todaye full soore ... the prynt of her stykketh vpon my buttokkes'. He argues from this that Will would also associate the intellectual female personifications of *Piers* with the humiliation of being beaten in school.

The most important releases of 2000 must be Adams et al., eds., *The Piers Plowman Electronic Archive*, volumes I and II: *Corpus Christi College, Oxford MS 201 (F)* and *Cambridge, Trinity College, MS B.15.17 (W)*. These CD-ROMs present extensive introductory material, a complete transcription of each manuscript, and images of each folio. The text can be searched in a variety of ways; instructions are included through the help files or in appendices. The format of each CD is somewhat different: the second one seems a little more user-friendly. 'In the interest of reflecting as accurately as possible the features of the scribal document, we mark with SGML tags all changes in hand, style of script, or colour of ink. We retain scribal punctuation, introducing none of our own.' The editors prefer SGML as a richer mark-up language than HTML, although to ensure that texts are available to the greatest number of users, it might be preferable to switch to an HTML or XML format that could be used with any browser, not only with the one that comes on the CD. The manuscripts are remarkably different, F showing considerable scribal interference at some stage, while W is the base for Wright's, Kane and Donaldson's, and Schmidt's editions. The contrast provides many possibilities for scholarly and classroom use. Although the introduction does not include the sort of literary and historical information needed for beginning students, the transcribed text, with its representations of scribal punctuation, underlining, and other markers, could readily be compared either to other manuscripts in this series or to students' printed editions, encouraging awareness and discussion of medieval books as individual, rather than mass-produced, artefacts. More advanced students could use this material to study Middle English dialects or palaeography.

As of 2000, *The Yearbook of Langland Studies* is published by Medieval Institute Publications. In volume 14 A.V.C. Schmidt presents 'Langland's Visions and Revisions' (*YLS* 14[2000] 5–27), in which he gives particular attention to the Z-version. Schmidt suggests an analogy between King Nabuchodonosor's 'dream-experience and our experience of medieval dream-vision poems', since medieval writers try to make us feel as if the visions they recount are our own. Schmidt examines the prologue of all four versions (counting Z), showing that the poet becomes increasingly eager to get down to the work of conveying his visions to his readers. He also studies Langland's second vision, including the pardon scene, in terms of the poet's revisions.

Thorlac Turville-Petre, in 'Sir Adrian Fortescue and his Copy of *Piers Plowman*' (*YLS* 14[2000] 29–48), studies Bodleian Library MS Digby 145, a sixteenth-century manuscript produced by a Catholic martyr, questioning Fortescue's interest in *Piers*. Turville-Petre suggests that 'he was engaged enough with the poem to wish to copy it himself ... in 1531–32 it might have seemed unwise to make public such interest'. Turville-Petre looks closely at revisions and interventions, which show that Fortescue 'had an evident interest in reform and a willingness to accept where it might lead him and his king'. 'Grace Abounding: Evangelical Centralization and the

End of *Piers Plowman*', by James Simpson (*YLS* 14[2000] 49–73), examines Langland's 'theology … ecclesiology, economics and politics' in order to show, by comparison with works from the second quarter of the sixteenth century, that 'Langland does indeed "foresee" the Reformation, but equally recoils from, and attempts to forestall it'. Langland emphasizes mercy and humility, penance and labour. Simpson concludes that, though evangelical theology 'centralizes grace', Langland's treatment decentralizes it, focusing on 'the initiative of the individual Christian and the integrity' of the Church.

J.A. Burrow, Priscilla Martin, and Sandra Pierson Prior engage in a discussion on 'Gestures and Looks in *Piers Plowman*' (based, like several other contributions in this volume, on papers given at the Second International Langland Conference) (*YLS* 14[2000] 75–83, 84–9, 90–4). Burrow points out that gestures cannot be easily represented in writing, and that silent readers are in danger of missing the full significance of looks and gestures barely indicated, without elaboration, in poems such as Langland's. Martin signals other repeated gestures and suggests using Fernando Poyatos's 'taxonomy of nonverbal communication' to analyse such movements. Prior returns to some of Burrow's examples, finding even more ambiguity in some, and suggesting that liturgy might provide a source for some of the reverential gestures.

In 'Langland's Documents' (*YLS* 14[2000] 95–107), Emily Steiner considers Meed's charter, the pardon from Truth, Haukyn's 'Acquitaunce', Moses's 'maundement', and Peace's patent as legal documents that urge a particular kind of reading practice on Langland's readers. Both 'biblical exegesis and legal practice' contribute to this discourse. Steiner first studies responses to Colossians 2:14–15 before turning to the documents in *Piers Plowman*. Bryan Davis suggests in response (*YLS* 14[2000] 108–9) that ecclesiastical and civil documents need to be distinguished. Bruce Holzinger's response (*YLS* 14[2000] 110–15) raises three questions about this 'vernacular legality': the role of the Church in Meed's charter, whether Langland saw the tearing of the pardon as a disruption to his narrative, and whether the term 'cartulary' might be better than 'archive' to describe Langland's poem.

Traugott Lawler's argument in 'The Pardon Formula in *Piers Plowman*: Its Ubiquity, its Binary Shape, its Silent Middle Term' (*YLS* 14[2000] 117–52) is nearly summed up by the title, except that the 'silent middle term' needs to be defined: 'to do evil but repent is to do well'. He studies the versions of this pardon that appear in the first two visions—like Steiner, he considers the pardon a sort of document—concluding that these episodes show that 'the good do need pardon', and suggesting reasons why the pardon is expressed in binary form. Lawler then discusses a few more pardon scenes from later in the poem, including ones where the middle term is spelled out.

Thomas D. Hill returns to an old problem in 'Satan's Pratfall and the Foot of Love: The Pedal Images in *Piers Plowman* A, B and C' (*YLS* 14[2000] 153–61). Alfred Kellogg argued that Langland replaced 'sedem' with 'pedem' in two references to Isaiah 14:13–14 because of a tradition that 'the foot of the soul is love'. Hill uses CETEDOC to confirm that this misquotation was part of an established tradition (something Kellogg could only guess at), and considers other Langlandian images involving the soul's foot or feet and their sources.

Gavin Richardson uses a passage from Christine De Pizan's *Cité des dames* to elucidate Conscience's misogyny in 'Langland's Mary Magdalene: Proverbial Misogyny and the Problem of Authority' (*YLS* 14[2000] 163–84). Conscience portrays Mary Magdalene as a chatterbox, to whom Christ appeared in order more quickly to spread the news of his resurrection; though this appears to be proverbial, Richardson suggests that Conscience's account 'may reflect clerical anxiety over women's increasingly public religiosity in the late Middle Ages'. He observes that 'the prejudices which colour Conscience's account seem to erode his authority just as much as the Magdalene's'. Finally, Ralph Hanna adds his 'Emendations to a 1993 "Vita de Ne'erdowel"' (*YLS* 14[2000] 185–98), filling in omissions from and qualifications to his 'small pamphlet' *William Langland*. These emendations include more details on Langland's life, changes of dating, and the status of various manuscripts.

John Chamberlin's *Medieval Arts Doctrines on Ambiguity and their Place in Langland's Poetics* appeared posthumously. It is divided into two 'semi-independent, yet parallel' parts. The first part focuses on lexical ambiguity, the second on the ambiguity of words taken as objects. Only the first and last chapters of each part deal directly with *Piers Plowman*. Chamberlin considers his two types of ambiguity primarily from the point of view of medieval language theorists, particularly Augustine and the twelfth-century Scholastics, but also with reference to twentieth-century theorists. Chapter 4 concentrates on the Samaritan's sermon in B.XVII, examining three passages in particular: the proverbial reference to a nagging wife, leaky roof, and smoking fire driving a man from his house; and the preceding comparisons of the Trinity to a candle and to a hand. Chamberlin notes that the juxtaposition of *unkyndeness* with *quench* in the description of the candle invites the association by the reader of the near-homonym *kindle*, which Soon Peng Su describes as 'punning by antonym': 'Each instance of *kinde* registers secondarily with other proximate meanings—similar, opposite, or somehow associated.' The last chapter focuses on the related themes of love and knowledge in the speech of Clergie, in Ymaginatif's exposition of it, and in 'Anima's grammar lesson'. Again Chamberlin works with word associations to show the 'surplus of meaning' in Langland's poem. Matsuji Tajima tackles the syntax of 'this shewinge shrift' in '*Piers Plowman* B V 379: A Syntactic Note' (*N&Q* 47[2000] 18–20), showing that it makes best sense to take 'shewynge' as a verbal noun used without 'of' to govern 'shrift', supported by three manuscripts that insert 'of' to make the usage clearer.

The year 2000 saw the publication of several essay collections containing one or more selections on *Piers Plowman*; they often keep interesting company. Denise N. Baker's 'Meed and the Economics of Chivalry in *Piers Plowman*' appears in Baker, ed., *Inscribing the Hundred Years' War in French and English Cultures* (pp. 55–72); she sees Langland as questioning Edward III's 'ideology of chivalry'. Meed criticizes the Treaty of Bretigny (or Calais), urging war as a profit-making enterprise and calling Conscience a coward. The storm to which she alludes is attested by other contemporary accounts, including Froissart, who, like Meed, suggests that its force put fear into the English king. Baker gives more time to economics than to the ideology of chivalry that Edward used to stir his nobles. Nicolette Zeeman argues, in 'The Condition of *Kynde*' (in Aers, ed., pp. 1–30), that besides the other associations of *kynde* in Langland, the term should be 'understood as a site of lack'. Her analysis focuses on the dream-within-a-dream in the B- and C-versions, distinguishing a triptych in which Trajan is significantly positioned between the visions of Fortune and of Kynde. Trajan 'does well' to those most in need, a *kynde* virtue, and also points out the lack of *kynde*ness in the clergy. Ultimately, though, the *kynde* of humanity is neediness, that always seeks to be filled.

In '*Piers Plowman* as Poetic Pillory: The Pillory and the Cross' (in Aers, ed., pp. 31–54), C. David Benson reviews the uses of the pillory (and the offences that merited it) in *Piers* and in late medieval London, then reads the poem as a poetic pillory, displaying offenders inescapably to the public view. But behind the pillory stands the Cross, in some ways a similar punishment, offering redemption through Christ's acceptance of it. Benson also produced 'Another Fine Manuscript Mess: Authors, Editors and Readers of *Piers Plowman*' (in Pearsall, ed., *New Directions in Later Medieval Manuscript Studies*, pp. 15–28), in which he reminds us of the complex manuscript situation of the poem and suggests that achieving a 'stable' text denies its intricate history. He encourages scholars to continue their recent attention to marginalia and annotations, and to articulate reasons for the A–B–C ordering hypothesized (but never explained) by Skeat. In the same volume, Kathryn Kerby-Fulton studies 'Professional Readers of Langland at Home and Abroad: New Directions in the Political and Bureaucratic Codicology of *Piers Plowman*' (Aers, ed., pp. 103–29), with the aim of getting 'closer to ... the political circles in which Langland's poem actually traveled', which included 'civil servants, legal scribes, colonial administrators and politicians'. From five manuscripts of *Piers* identified by Fisher as in Chancery hands, Kerby-Fulton picks two to examine more closely, noting that their rubric emphasizes references to the Chancery. She also considers connections to Westminster and Ireland. Seven plates (mostly from Douce 104) accompany the essay.

George Kane's essay, 'Word Games: Glossing *Piers Plowman*' (in Powell and Smith, eds., pp. 43–53), addresses some words that have caused problems in some editions and translations. He divides these into three groups: some, such as *breden* (B.II.98) have homographs of different meaning; then there are homographs 'constituted by the letter-group *lo + two minims + e*', where the difficulty is that the minims can represent *n*, *u*, *v*, or *w*. Finally there are the words that are rare in Middle English. A.I. Doyle identifies another production by a *Piers Plowman* scribe in 'Ushaw College, Durham, MS 50: Fragments of the *Prick of Conscience*, by the Same Scribe as Oxford, Corpus Christi College, MS 201, of the B text of *Piers Plowman*' (in Edwards, Gillespie and Hanna, eds. pp. 43–9); this is a revision of the description accompanying the CD-ROM of Corpus Christi 201. In 'Literary Representations of History in Fourteenth-Century England: Shared Techniques and Divergent Practice in Chaucer and Langland', Nicole Lassahn studies Blanche in *The Book of the Duchess* and Mede (who she takes to represent Alice Perrers) (*EssaysMedSt* <http://www.luc.edu/publications/medieval/emsv12.html>).

Galen Johnson, in 'Muhammad and Ideology in Medieval Christian Literature' (*Islam and Christian–Muslim Relations* 11[2000] 333–46) examines the *Song of Roland*, Dante's *Commedia*, *Piers Plowman*, the *Canterbury Tales*, and *Pilgrim's Progress* to show that the authors portray Muhammad as a false god or heretic to provide a model for the unorthodox thinking in each author's time and place. He reviews the various Western medieval traditions about Muhammad that appear in *Piers* (to which he refers only through Schmidt's translation) and says that Langland seems to hold out some hope for individual Muslims though none for Muhammad.

Gillian Rudd, in 'Literary Text as a Demonstration of Feminist Criticism: the Case of *Piers Plowman*' (*JGenS* 9[2000] 45–54), examines B.XVIII and the Four Daughters of God through lenses provided by Kristeva's 'notion of the chora' and Judith Butler's theories. She compares the physical movement of the sisters and the 'movement of the text', showing that the terms 'male' and 'female' 'become markers of stability/fixity and flux/fluidity respectively', that is, that Langland's view of these concepts is non-essentialist.

Boydell & Brewer, for EETS, brought out reprints of W.W. Skeat's *Parallel Extracts from Forty-Five Manuscripts of Piers Plowman, with Notes upon their Relation to the Society's B-Text Edition of this Poem* [1905] and his *The Vision of William concerning Piers Plowman; together with the Vita de Dowel, Dobet, et Dobest, secundum Wil et Resoun* [1867].

5. Romance

Two editions of five romances were published by TEAMS in 1999, too late to have been noticed in *YWES* 80, we regret. Herzman, Drake and Salisbury, eds., *Four Romances of England: King Horn, Havelok the Dane, Bevis of Hampton, Athelston*, provides clear, legible copies of these frequently discussed texts, with ample margins for annotations by the intended users of all TEAMS editions, students. After a general introduction and selected bibliography, each romance follows with its own introduction, selected bibliography, text, and limited notes; a surprisingly short glossary (not quite three pages) appears at the end. In the text, lines are numbered in fives on the left, and a rightmost column glosses hard words and phrases. It is not clear exactly which of the three editors did what, but apparently at least some of the work was done from photocopies of manuscripts, if not microfilms or prints from films. *King Horn* is based on Cambridge University Library manuscript Gg.4.27.2, perhaps because the Laud text has been too often edited, but *Havelok the Dane* is from Bodleian Library manuscript Laud misc. 108, the only complete copy. *Bevis of Hampton* is based, predictably, on the Auchinleck manuscript, with the other five manuscripts collated; and *Athelston* uses the unique copy in Cambridge, Caius College Library manuscript 175. The notes at the end of each romance are brief, but range from textual variants to explaining the text and even discussing analogues or critical interpretations.

More expansive, after a fashion, is Stephen F. Page's edition of John Metham's *Amoryus and Cleopes*, a retelling of Pyramus and Thisbe, which is added in an appendix as a translation from Pierre Bersuire's moralized Ovid. Metham's poem survives in a manuscript written some decades after its composition in 1449, where it is accompanied by a few other works by him: some prognostications, a guide to palmistry (also in another manuscript), and a physiognomy. Page's introduction discusses Metham's deep Chaucerianism, but recognizes that he is not a slavish imitator, even as he is no Chaucer, and draws our attention to a love song or lyric in *Amoryus and Cleopes* that matches what later became the traditional sonnet, but for its not being in iambic pentameter. The form is normally ascribed to Henry Howard, earl of Surrey, who might have seen but is not known to have used Metham's work. As with the other TEAMS edition reviewed above, hard words are glossed in the margin, but some lines are translated in footnotes. The notes are much the same, only more fulsome, and the glossary is about twice as large. Although not exactly editing the text, Judith Weiss, in 'The Anglo-Norman *Boeve de Haumtone*: A Fragment of a New Manuscript' (*MLR* 95[2000] 305–10), describes a book-binding in the University of Glasgow's Hunterian Library, where the fragmentary text corresponds to lines 1003–65 of Albert Stimming's 1899 edition.

A third production through TEAMS is Linda Marie Zaerr's videotaped performance of *The Weddynge of Sir Gawen and Dame Ragnell* for the Chaucer Studio. Zaerr takes on all the roles in a lively rendition of the Middle English text, seen as a complement of Thomas Hahn's edition from 1995 (also available at <http:/ /www.lib.rochester.edu/camelot/teams/ragnell.htm>. After the first few minutes, in which students might be confused about the language and why this one person appears in different clothes, the film is a joy to watch, though it is a bit odd to find her, as Arthur, thoughtfully pulling and even stroking a non-existing beard. We could cavil about matters of pronunciation, but it is better to view this as a variant upon actual contemporary performance, where no scene, prop, or clothing changes would have been available to spice up the romance. The pace is fairly even, making it easier for students to follow the written text, if they wish, and Zaerr's musical accompaniment on a Gothic harp helps concentrate students' attention.

Ad Putter and Jane Gilbert invited a number of contributors to focus on individual romances for an anthology on *The Spirit of Medieval English Popular Romance*, where Putter provides a useful, if at times simplistic, historical introduction contrasting the manuscript with the oral evidence and Gilbert briefly discusses several notions of what 'popular' might mean. Thereafter, we begin with versions of Marie de France's *lais*. Elizabeth Archibald considers '*Lai le Freine*: The Female Foundling and the Problem of Romance Genre', the problems being that it is men who are usually the heroes in romances, but this time it is a woman, and that foundling protagonists usually grow up having to prove themselves, but women tend to be passive. She applies several theoretical notions to the Middle English version (Freud makes his first brief and unindexed appearance in the book); the most interesting and potentially valuable is that this version was also written by a woman. Myra Stokes lays out how, in '*Lanval* to *Sir Launfal*: A Story Becomes Popular' in the moral maps Thomas Chestre draws for his more bourgeois audience. T.A. Shippey has an interesting argument in '*The Tale of Gamelyn*: Class Warfare and the Embarrassments of Genre': *Gamelyn*'s popularity in manuscript is due to its association with the *Canterbury Tales*. The simplest explanation for its presence there is that it was among Chaucer's foul papers, waiting for him to transform it into a tale for the Knight's (or Squire's) Yeoman, whom Chaucer viewed as a ludicrous social climber and whose ideals would have been well reflected in *Gamelyn*.

On the other hand, Elizabeth Fowler's 'The Romance Hypothetical: Lordship and the Saracens in *Sir Isumbras*' takes romances as 'thought experiments that lead the reader through a process of thinking about the deepest issues of political philosophy and jurisprudence'. In this view, *Sir Isumbras* explores dominion and lordship, visible in several social spheres through numerous topoi. Next, James Simpson takes a different tack in 'Violence, Narrative and Proper Name: *Sir Degaré*, "The Tale of Sir Gareth of Orkney", and the *Folie Tristan d'Oxford'*. The propriety of a name may determine the trajectory of a plot, anonymity itself leading to violence, while the narrative aims towards the revealing or recognition of a true name. Arlyn Diamond's 'Loving Beasts: The Romance of *William of Palerne*' considers changes particular to the Middle English version; the reviser broadened the audience in his reduction and recasting, but maintained some class concerns for Duke Humphrey, such as the conflict between nobility and chivalry, which the romance uses to reinforce the nature of true, inborn nobility using its benevolence for the peace and happiness of all. In 'The Narrative Logic of *Emaré*', Ad Putter wonders why *Emaré* should work when its plot is shared by so many other tales, and concludes that it is the conventions themselves that make the narrative memorable: the repetitive storyline, the falsification of names, and the artful use of coincidence.

Nicola F. McDonald asks '*The Seege of Troye*: "ffor wham was wakened al this wo"?', meaning that its poor reception is based on assuming it was meant for a base audience of common folk, and consequently replies that it is best seen as a matter of, and therefore for, merchant adventurers, who viewed even women as commodities. Antony J. Hasler's 'Romance and its Discontents in *Eger and Grime*' applies Žižek (and Lacan) to *Egar and Grime* to discuss various separations, moving from the physical removal of the little finger into realms of the symbolic and the Real. A different kind of reality is surveyed by Margaret Robson in 'From Beyond the Grave: Darkness at Noon in *The Awntyrs off Arthure*'. She looks at the return of a corpse and how its message to the living can be read; for example, the Tarn Wathelyn is recognizable as 'a famous local murder-spot' and the revived corpse as realistic but portrayed more horrifically for effect, or it is also easily read as eschatological. Jane Gilbert uses Yesut's equivocal oath in 'Gender, Oaths and Ambiguity in *Sir Tristrem* and Béroul's *Roman de Tristan*' to urge that *Sir Tristrem* is not as incompetent as is usually thought. The artistry largely depends on the well-discussed use of 'queynt'; the poet-reviser's skill is revealed by the plying of different versions of femininity between audiences inside and outside the romance. Finally, A.C. Spearing returns to a point he has made before in order to work it out more fully, in '*Sir Orfeo*: Madness and Gender'. Modern approaches to madness show Heurodis as having a schizophrenic episode that is paralleled in a number of 'women's films' of the 1940s; in *Sir Orfeo* and elsewhere lies a world in which women's madness needs to be restored to male order.

In another anthology, Judith Weiss, Jennifer Fellows, and Morgan Dickson have gathered a good number of essays from the sixth biennial conference on Romance in Medieval England [1998] for *Medieval Insular Romance: Translation and Innovation*. Ivana Djordjević's 'Mapping Medieval Translation' uses *Sir Bevis of Hampton* versus its Anglo-Norman original lightly as a focal point for discussing the difficulties inherent in searching for a theory to provide an analytical model for studying medieval translation, particularly in England with its multilingual environment, where what we perceive as crossing language boundaries may better be considered as code-switching. In '*Waldef* and the Matter of/with England' Rosalind Field argues that the largely ignored, incomplete, Anglo-Norman *Waldef* provides a junction for Anglo-Norman and Middle English romances, and is curious in pretending to be a history of pre-Conquest England. It is not an attempt to legitimize Norman rule, however, but is constantly anxious about political disorder, which indicates that further research on *Waldef* should prove rewarding for comprehending insular romances as a whole. Morgan Dickson unveils the links between 'Verbal and Visual Disguise: Society and Identity in Some Twelfth-Century Texts'. More specifically, in four Anglo-Norman romances—the Oxford *Folie Tristan*, *Romance of Horn*, *Ipomedon*, and *Gesta Herwardi*—disguises change the hero's social role but maintain his inner self, thus allowing for an examination of that self. This examination leads the hero to speak and act in ways that confirm him in his social role.

Turning to a different vernacular, Elizabeth Archibald reviews 'The Breton Lay in Middle English: Genre, Transmission and the Franklin's Tale' with an eye on difficulties of defining the Breton lay and on the late thirteenth-century list of lay (or romance) titles in Shrewsbury School MS 7, commenting also upon the list's omissions. She then turns to the frequent motif of adultery, often cleansed from the Middle English versions, as in Chaucer's *Franklin's Tale*, and closes by observing that Chaucer's use of the word 'lay' often coincides with 'complaint'. In 'Veiling the Text: The True Role of the Cloth in *Emaré*', Amanda Hopkins examines how critics have attempted to find the cloth supernatural, but determines that it is a '*dis*unifying element' that comes to show the heroine's oppression as an external object, enclosing Emaré within it. Arlyn Diamond turns to a female character in '*The Erle of Tolous*: The Price of Virtue'. As a type of Prudence, Beulybon's abiding by her moral principles turns into social weakness; unlike what this romance's analogues do, here the shift to emphasize prudence in courtly ideals distinguishes the personal from the social, shifting the grounds of what constitutes a happy ending. Shifting different grounds is the point of Paul Price's 'Confessions of a Godless Killer: Guy of Warwick and Comprehensive Entertainment'. In the various versions of tales about Guy, there is a problematic conflict between the apparent goodness of his battles and the confession which denies their goodness. Instead of viewing this as an unresolved contradiction, Price argues, first, that it enhances Guy's virtue because he can repudiate his sins without actually having committed them and, second, that the implied embrace of improved standards lends the romance enhanced gravitas and transforms it from romance to hagiography.

Taking up other more general issues, W.A. Davenport's '*Sir Degrevant* and Composite Romance' examines the romance in light of the virtues of eclectic writing, noting the interesting vocabulary, despite tail-rhyme clichés, interlocking structure with composite motifs, and complications of diverse elements that lend to its success in many ways. In 'The Undercover King', Rachel Snell surveys the motif of a prince or king disguised among the commoners in tales such as King Arthur and the cakes, *King Edward and the Shepherd*, Robin Hood, *Rauf Coilyear*, and *John the Reeve*, giving consideration to social environment and historical changes which provided for carnivalesques and tricksterism. Roger Dalrymple assumes two factors give cause for re-examining Lovelich's works: Lovelich's life and authorship are documented and his unfinished works are widely neglected. In '"Evele knowen ye Merlyne, jn certeyn": Henry Lovelich's *Merlin*', Dalrymple remarks briefly on the vocabulary of *Merlin* and its relationship to contemporary chronicle-writing, but finds himself more interested in how Lovelich's social milieu amongst London burghers reveals itself in passages reminiscent of civic pageants or revels. Finally, Helen Cooper considers 'The Elizabethan Havelok: William Warner's First of the English'. Like the original *Havelok*, the Elizabethan version is an independent crossover from chronicle to romance, in this case from the *Brut*, as printed as Caxton's *The Chronicles of England*, giving Havelok the name Curan, to Warner's *Albions England*. After reviewing the probable nationalistic or regional origins of *Havelok*, Cooper finds that Warner, like his contemporaries, set Curan's Argentile as an analogy for Elizabeth.

Among anthologies this year, the most valuable is no doubt Krueger, ed., *The Cambridge Companion to Medieval Romance*. After a selective chronology and the editor's introduction, Matilda Tomaryn Bruckner lays out the key formal and thematic elements that established 'The Shape of Romance in Medieval France'. Christopher Baswell's 'Marvels of Translation and Crises of Transition in the Romances of Antiquity' turns to erotic episodes as fuelling readers' engagement with the texts. Still within a basically French environment, Simon Gaunt reminds us of the relationships between 'Romance and Other Genres', while Sylvia Huot surveys 'The Manuscript Context of Medieval Romance', adding some German material. Sarah Kay reviews the long-discussed relationship among 'Courts, Clerks, and Courtly Love', reminding us that there is no single, set definition of the key term, just as people had multiple and complex social roles and relations. Social relationships are a continuing theme in Richard Kaeuper's 'The Societal Role of Chivalry in Romance: Northwestern Europe', and even in the wholly alien societies that inhabit Jeff Rider's 'The Other Worlds of Romance'. Two articles concern themselves with a particular kind of social relation in different times and places: Roberta L. Krueger finds relatively free and experimental attitudes in 'Questions of Gender in Old French Romance', but Sheila Fisher finds anxiety and repression later in England in 'Women and Men in Late Medieval Romance'. Finally there are overviews of different national products: Norris J. Lacy on 'The Evolution and Legacy of French Prose Romance', Ann Marie Rasmussen on 'Medieval German Romance', F. Regina Psaki on 'Chivalry and Medieval Italian Romance', Thomas Hahn on 'Gawain and Popular Chivalric Romance in Britain', Felicity Riddy on 'Middle English Romance: Family, Marriage, Intimacy', and Marina Brownlee on 'Romance at the Crossroads: Medieval Spanish Paradigms and Cervantine Revisions'.

Another way of looking at international texts is Michelle R. Warren's *History on the Edge: Excalibur and the Borders of Britain, 1100–1300*, within a post-colonial view that takes its beginnings from the observation that the authors or the sources of the texts were in border areas and thus must have been concerned with their peripheral status as compared to others. Thus Warren begins with Geoffrey of Monmouth and proceeds to Wales, Layamon and Robert of Gloucester, Wace, the French prose cycle, and the *Gesta regum Britanniae*. The individual analyses cover representations and implications of topography, history, and dominion. The entry of Arthur begins a new stage in all, with Caliburn acting as a focal point in expansionistic behaviours. Each author was enticed by Arthur to discuss the status or identity of his region, from a peripheral position.

Roger Dalrymple's *Language and Piety in Middle English Romance* is an investigation of references, allusions, or mentions of God and Christ in over eighty romances before 1500, these formulas carrying semantic weight, not being pithy invocations. To accomplish this, he catalogued the relevant formulae in an appendix, first by text and then by concept, with attention to grammatical structure. Dalrymple opens with a review of attitudes towards oaths, giving special attention to awareness of their misuse and of the prosodic value of pious oaths and tags. To establish their cultural significance more clearly, Dalrymple reviews medieval English devotional, didactic, and doctrinal material to mark the tags as cognitive formulas that remind audiences of their truth values and to focus their attention on specific points, whether in sermons, saints' lives, drama, pious verse, or elsewhere.

He then shows how the many formulae of God as Creator are stylistic and thematic elements in *William of Palerne*, a tale of reformation. The passion formulas of Christ as Redeemer in the stanzaic *Morte Arthur* work to emphasize the ultimate waste of revenge and slaughter, constantly reminding the reader of heavenly rewards, with wry contrast between Christ's wounds and those of mortals. Other uses appear in the Auchinleck romances: *The King of Tars*, *Otuel*, and *Roland and Vernagu* use pious tags to reify God and his attributes in an environment of those whose gods cannot be so reified; in *Amis and Amiloun*, pious formulas stand in opposition to the discourse of sworn brotherhood, casting doubt on its moral status; and they help reconcile the hero of *Guy of Warwick* with God, those specifically chosen fitting neatly into the immediate context.

Sir Launfal has become a bit more popular this year, with two articles devoted to this romance. First, in 'Jousting for Identity: Tournaments in Thomas Chestre's *Sir Launfal*' (*Parergon* 17[2000] 107–23), James Weldon applies Paul Ricoeur's concept of an 'interplay of innovation and sedimentation' to point out how the novelty of the two tournaments—first to test Launfal's mettle and next to justify his invitation to return to Arthur's court—is sufficient to balance the conventionality throughout, even in that they establish Launfal, who otherwise has no discernible identity. On the other hand, Myra Seaman's 'Thomas Chestre's *Sir Launfal* and the Englishing of Medieval Romance' (*MedPers* 15[2000] 105–19) envisages that audiences of English romances were much broader than merely 'social-climbing commoners', and thus that interpretations of these romances as more popular than artistic miss the mark since standards applicable to their French predecessors are not relevant outside those bounds. Seaman uses *Sir Launfal* as a test case, focusing on Chestre's changes from his model of two centuries prior: Guinevere and Tryamour are foils, blame is placed in different places, characters (including Tryamour) and relationships are less idealized and more realized, Launfal's virtues are chivalric not courtly, and money is important not so much as an influence but as a necessity for social standing and activity.

The summer 2000 issue of *Arthuriana* was a special issue devoted to 'Theoretical Approaches to Lawman's *Brut*', edited by Elizabeth J. Bryan and comprising four articles. In '"Going Native": Anthropological Lawman' (*Arthuriana* 10:ii[2000] 5–26), Kelley M. Wickham-Crowley wonders if anthropological theory illuminates Lawman's approach to and understanding of the Welsh. Kenneth J. Tiller examines Lawman as a historiographer concerned with restoring historical truth in 'The Truth "bi Arþure than Kinge": Arthur's Role in Shaping Lawman's Vision of History' (*Arthuriana* 10:ii[2000] 27–49). Alice Sheppard uses performance theory to show how Arthur and Leir as kings are informed by action, in a fashion re-envisaging Anglo-Saxon lordship, recalling *comitatus* in 'Of this is a King's Body Made: Lordship and Succession in Lawman's Arthur and Leir'(*Arthuriana* 10:ii[2000] 50–65). And in 'Origins and Originality: Reading Lawman's Brut and the Rejection of British Library MS Cotton Otho C. xiii' (*Arthuriana* 10:ii[2000] 66–90), Lucy Perry poses partially editorial or textual arguments, but mostly a literary-aesthetic point that the Otho text has a faster pace of action and is more direct; however, it is often read in parallel with the Caligula text and thus viewed as having omissions from that text.

Layamon was popular in other publications, as well. In 'Layamon and the Laws of Men' (*ELH* 67[2000] 337–63) Christopher Cannon discusses how Layamon's name is significant in typifying his concern for the stability of law and for its transcendence over and mitigation of political change. Layamon is quick to praise kings who explicitly maintain or revive old laws, an attitude shared by the 'London Collection' of legal texts compiled in an environment of legal antiquarianism roughly contemporary with Layamon, and even apparent in his echoes of the *Domesday Book*. In 'Lawman and the Scandinavian Connection' (*LeedsSE* 31[2000] 81–113), John Frankis also reviews the discussions over Lawman's name and offers simply a family tradition of naming to explain it; Lawman shows no particular Scandinavian linguistic influence, but he does seem to call upon some body of knowledge about Scandinavian people and customs. S.K. Brehe's 'Rhyme and the Alliterative Standard in Layamon's *Brut*' (*Parergon* 18[2000] 11–25) uses a larger sample of the Caligula *Brut* than used by others before, as well as some comparison with the *Proverbs of Alfred*, the *Soul's Address to the Body*, and the metrically relevant portions of the *Bestiary*. Layamon created a 'metric of uncertainty' by shifting among lines that alliterate, lines whose half-lines rhyme, and lines that do both. In this, his verse form reinforces the theme of unpredictability in human events.

Less work appeared on alliterative and other selected romances. Rosamund Allen's '*The Awntyrs off Arthure*: Portraits and Property' (*RMSt* 26[2000] 3–25), in a close examination of the long portrait passages, shows them to be parodic as well as reminiscent of some motifs well known in related works. Allen is most concerned with how the *Awntyrs* plays against Gawain and the Loathly Lady, indicating that this poet meant to remind us that favourable personal or social transformations are unlikely. With a more historical bent, Joseph L. Grossi Jr reminds us that kings often did invoke their own grace when dealing with suppliants, and thus Arthur is not censured by the poet, in 'The Question of the King's Grace in the Alliterative *Morte Arthure*, 2320' (*N&Q* 47[2000] 293–95). Ad Putter took a hard look at 'Gifts and Commodities in *Sir Amadace*' (*RES* 51[2000] 371–94). There, the key is that *largesse* leads to indebtedness and gratitude, which in turn lead to rewards that may exceed the value of the original gifts. Of course, since man is mortal, he cannot truly own anything; thus, freedom in giving is related to forgiveness of debt and to obligation towards others. And Glenn Wright's '"Þe Kynde Wolde oute Sprynge": Interpreting the Hero's Progress in *Sir Perceval of Galles*' (*SN* 72[2000] 45–53) uses two previous articles to argue that Perceval does learn and grow from a foolish rustic into his knightly role: F. Xavier Baron's 'Mother and Son in *Sir Perceval of Galles*' (*PLL* 8[1972] 3–14; see *YWES* 53[1974] 91–92) and Caroline Eckhardt's 'Arthurian Comedy: The Simpleton-Hero in *Sir Perceval of Galles*' (*ChauR* 8[1974] 205–20, see *YWES* 54[1975] 95). Julian Wasserman and Robert Blanch publish two joint articles on responses to romance this year. In 'Gawain's Antifeminism: From Gollancz and Tolkien to the Millennium' (*MedPers* 15[2000] 21–33), they survey key work on Gawain's tirade (ll. 2414–28) published between the 1930s and the 1990s, and examine it as an indicator of 'dramatic changes in critical praxis during the twentieth century'. In 'Fear of Flyting: The Absence of Internal Tension in *Sword of the Valiant* and *First Knight*' (*Arthuriana* 10:iv[2000] 15–32), their focus is on two recent films which draw on medieval romances (*Gawain and the Green Knight* and *Ywain*, in the case of the former, and *Le Morte Darthur* and *Chevalier de la Charrete* in the case of the latter). They note that the main weaknesses of the films stem from their promotion of the individual over the societal, in direct contrast to the focus of romance, and from their failure to make use of the internal tensions of their sources.

Interestingly, *Sir Orfeo* came in for some individual attention. Oren Falk's 'The Son of Orfeo: Kingship and Compromise in a Middle English Romance' (*JMEMS* 30[2000] 247–74) argues the poem is a historical reminiscence of the events of the early and mid-1320s, through which the actions of the servants, court, Heurodis, and even Orfeo become a transparent eulogy to Edward II and his troubles. And Paul Beekman Taylor's 'Sir Orfeo and the Minstrel King' (*ANQ* 13[2000] 12–16) also reviews historical background, but he argues that the source can be found in *Richard Coeur de Lion*, who was also called *Rex menestrallus*: both travel in disguise, confront wild beasts, and are aided by honest stewards, an abiding concern when *Sir Orfeo* was composed, due to uncertainties about regents for absent kings in the thirteenth century.

Three articles on women in the romances appeared in Wogan-Browne et al., eds., *Medieval Women*. Arlyn Diamond's 'Heroic Subjects: Women in the Alliterative *Morte Arthure*' (pp. 293–308) shows how, though women are rare and peripheral in the romance, their presence is an integral part of the poet's social imagination and thus necessary as, at least, an emblem of royal responsibility. Jane Gilbert uses medieval physiology and Lacanian psychoanalysis to study the relationship between 'Unnatural Mothers and Monstrous Children in *The King of Tars* and *Sir Gowther*' (pp. 329–44). The point is not so much that the mothers are unnatural, but lies in the poets' concern over the relationship between the monstrous child and its parents, focusing mainly on anxieties about paternity, which has significance beyond the purely biological. And Anne Savage's 'Clothing Paternal Incest in the *Clerk's Tale*, *Émaré* and the *Life of St. Dympna*' (pp. 345–61) finds that father–daughter incest is used only as a narrative device to get on to other matters and is itself pointedly ignored; the motif itself includes a strong element of satire against the Church. Father–daughter incest is, as she notes, rarely noted in penitentials and elsewhere, but it is not wholly averted, as can be seen in the versions of 'The Tale of an Incestuous Daughter' which can be found at <http://oscar.wvsc.edu/~lidaka/tale.html>.

Aspects of families have also come up recently. For example, in 'The Function of Childhood in *Amis and Amiloun*' (*Mediaevalia* 22[1998] 35–57), Nicole Clifton discusses how the Old French and Anglo-Norman versions of the romance do not capitalize on children as strongly affective devices, as the Middle English version does, which then also more clearly explains their sacrifice. But it is marriage that transforms and redeems the hero, particularly when recalled as a sacrament, according to Jane Zatta's 'Sir Gowther: The Marriage of Romance and Hagiography' (*Mediaevalia* 22[1998] 175–98). And the father–daughter relationship is discussed by Gail Ashton in 'Her Father's Daughter: The Re-Alignment of Father–Daughter Kinship in Three Romances' (*ChauR* 34[2000] 416–27), which covers Chaucer's *Man of Law's Tale*, Gower's *Tale of Constance* in the *Confessio Amantis*, and Thomas le Chestre's *Émaré*. The tension between the female protagonist's passive victimhood and active independence is symptomatic of a daughter's social role, both disruptive and ordering.

A few items of deep interest may seem slightly peripheral to this section, but their value is not. First, John V. Fleming surveys 'The Round Table in Literature and Legend' in a fascinating and well-illustrated book, Biddle, ed., *King Arthur's Round*

Table: An Archaeological Investigation (pp. 5–30). Beginning with Geoffrey of Monmouth and Wace, the first to mention a round table, he moves on through Layamon and others to give a picture of this motif. Though their precise nature is unclear, other references, such as that in the *Abbreviatio chronicorum Angliae* to a death in 1252 attributed to a 'military sport known as the round table', indicate that having a courtly *tabula rotunda* had become fashionable by the thirteenth century. Fleming also discusses the religious associations with Christ's Last Supper arising in French romances. John Hardyng's *Chronicle* seems to be the first mention of the physical round table that is the focus of this book, and Hardyng already specifies that the table is hanging in Winchester. Though the names written on it are often claimed to have come from Malory, whose manuscript text was found not far from this table in Winchester, Fleming shows briefly and convincingly that those names are simply common ones known from many romances. Other articles in the volume concerns matters such as carpentry, dating by tree-rings and radiocarbon, the painting and repainting, visitors, and more, but these are beyond our limited scope here. As a whole, the book is highly welcome and much to be praised.

Judith Weiss edited and translated *Wace's* Roman de Brut: *A History of the British: Text and Translation*, adapting Ivor Arnold's 1938 edition largely by restoring some manuscript readings. The introduction is a prime example of succinct thoroughness: after a brief biography and socio-historical setting for Wace and his works, Weiss quickly sketches the prior development of the Arthurian legend before turning to Wace's main source, Geoffrey of Monmouth, and a careful overview of Wace's handling of his sources and material, within the historical background established earlier. After a clear discussion of the text and how she deals with it, we find the poem and translation *en regarde*, with the poem on the left in two columns (with textual notes below) and the prose translation on the right in one (with some explanatory notes below). To ease reference, each English paragraph begins with a line number corresponding to the text opposite. A bibliography and index of personal names close the volume. Attractive, comfortable in the hand and on the eyes, and well organized, this volume is a welcome addition to the growing collection of high-quality and affordable texts from Exeter.

Finally, stretching beyond our period into the Renaissance, have come several titles. One is Andrew King's *'The Faerie Queene' and Middle English Romance: The Matter of Just Memory*. Just as romances, especially anthologies of them, were 'books of memories' where scribes and compilers recorded personal and national experience, whether seen as affected by providence or wish-fulfilment, so Spenser used his general and specific knowledge of the literary tradition of medieval romances to inform his epic with providential and prophetic sight that united the past with the future. King examines a large number of English romances to identify, not those whose heroes Spenser names, but themes which bear on his poem. Some heroes learn to identify themselves with regard to their social position, often in the process of regaining a lost heritage. Thus they are 'displaced youths' or even 'slandered ladies' who are tested before their rightful positions can be restored, rightful from birth or from deeds. Malory precedes Spenser in much of this synthesizing and reshaping, but Spenser prefers to use allegory and specific narrative patterns to dramatize his Reformation history of English providence. Christopher Snyder's *Exploring the World of King Arthur* is an attractive coffee-table book which covers the expected ground: sixty-four colour and 198 monochrome medieval, Victorian (or thereabouts), and 'original' illustrations and some archaeological background, some historical, much literary, and some music, art, and film. Most of the text is fairly standard, though there are some off comments such as 'Layamon's *Brut* is nearly twice as long as its French model, and substitutes descriptions of Dark Age brutality for the latter's talk of love and chivalry'. Following the lead of many magazines, it includes numerous side-bar vignettes on selected works, topics, and characters, for an entertaining survey from prehistoric and historic background through chronicles, legends, and selected topics to some limited contemporary material, closing with a highly selective directory of organizations (including online materials), glossary, gazetteer, bibliography with internet resources, acknowledgements, and index.

6. Lyrics

Fein, ed., *Studies in the Harley Manuscript: The Scribes, Contents, and Social Contexts of British Library, MS Harley 2253*, includes a number of essays on the Harley lyrics. Fein's introduction reviews the known history and modern reception of the manuscript. Michael Kuczynski discusses the religious poetry in 'An "Electric Stream": The Religious Contents' (pp. 123–61). He treats poems such as the 'Harrowing of Hell' separately from the more lyric poetry, although he points out similarities in language between lyrics and biblical materials, hagiography, and what he terms 'matters of practical religion'. Considered as a group, the religious contents, including the lyrics, 'are traditional structures ... designed for prayer and meditation'. John Scattergood's 'Authority and Resistance: The Political Verse' (pp. 163–201) likewise surveys the entire range of such contents, including Anglo-Norman verse. These poems include elegy ('The Death of Edward'), a 'parody of romance' ('The Flemish Insurrection'), and protests against officialdom and anti-clerical poetry; Scattergood finds that these poems constitute a 'sporadic but often highly informed chronicle of comment on and resistance to' fourteenth-century changes in politics, the economy and society. Richard Newhauser studies 'Historicity and Complaint in *Song of the Husbandman*' (pp. 203–17), reviewing critical responses to the poem. He shows that the poem is related to Church literature, as taxation and usury appear as sub-categories of Avarice and figures such as beadles, bailiffs and haywards also appear in sermons. The poem draws in its audience by 'including, in effect, every personal pronoun in the English language'. Karl Reichl takes up the 'Debate Verse' (pp. 219–39), which includes more French than Middle English verse; he briefly discusses the pastourelle 'The Meeting in the Wood', and concludes that the debate poems show thirteenth- and fourteenth-century England's 'participation ... in mainstream European literary traditions'. In 'Authors, Anthologists, and Franciscan Spirituality', David L. Jeffrey notes that many lyrics in Harley appear in other manuscripts belonging to friars, and finds 'compatible traits of spirituality' with Franciscans in the religious poems. Susanna Fein praises the 'compiler's skill' in 'A Saint "Geynest under Gore": Marina and the Love Lyrics of the Seventh Quire' (pp. 351–76). This section contains poems in the various genres dealing with 'the mystification of a woman's anatomy'. The love lyrics establish the theme, but phrases such as 'under bis' and 'under gore' surface elsewhere; fascination with the topic is pervasive. Elisabeth Solopova studies

'Layout, Punctuation, and Stanza Patterns in the English Verse' (pp. 377–89), concluding that, when caesuras rhyme, the long line really is a long line, not two short lines written as one to save space. Frances McSparran considers 'The Language of the English Poems: The Harley Scribe and his Exemplars' (pp. 391– 426), showing that the Harley scribe 'retains a large number of forms from his exemplars which are not part of his own natural practice'.

Joseph A. Dane examines 'Page Layout and Textual Autonomy in Harley MS 2253: "Lenten ys come wiþ loue to toune"' (*MÆ* 68[1999] 32–41). He argues that the poem 'In May hit murgeþ when hit dawes', generally printed separately, should be read along with 'Lenten ys come', as they seem to share a final stanza. Other recent essays on lyrics include the survey by Julia Boffey and A.S.G. Edwards, 'Middle English Verse in Chronicles' (in Powell and Smith, eds., pp. 119–28), considering whether such verse was independently circulating material or composed by the chroniclers. Verses may be rubricated or otherwise have their non-prose status signalled. Boffey also has an essay in Pearsall, ed., *New Directions in Later Medieval Manuscript Studies*: 'Prospecting in the Archives: Middle English Verse in Record Repositories' (pp. 41–51). She lists verses found in record offices and other archives, such as fragments of medieval drama included as part of city records, rhymed charters and historical poems, and popular carols copied in blank spaces. She recommends that researchers proceed with open minds, as there is no way of knowing where to look for such literary remains. J. Caitlin Finlayson, in 'Medieval Sources for Keatsian Creation in *La Belle Dame Sans Merci*' (*PQ* 79[2000] 225– 47), suggests as source a poem attributed to Richard Roos, 'La Belle Dame Sans Merci'. In '"Now springs the spray" and the Wife's Lament' (*ANQ* 14:iii[2000] 11– 14), Glenn Wright responds to a claim by Helen Sandison. Wright insists that despite the parallel between lines 9–10 of 'Now springs the spray' and lines 52–3 of the 'Wife's Lament', the most likely source for the Middle English lyric is the Old French poem Sandison argued against.

Showing that the corpus of Middle English verse continues to grow, Ralph Hanna reports a Middle English quatrain not listed in the *Index* in 'Humphrey Newton and Bodleian Library, MS Lat. Misc. C 66' (*MÆ* 69[2000] 279–91). Hanna characterizes the manuscript as a 'codicological nightmare' and advises reading it 'against a legal—not literary—record'. Margaret Connolly, in 'Some Unrecorded Middle English Verse in a Nijmegen Manuscript' (*N&Q* 46[1999] 442–4) presents three items not in the *Index*: eight lines of verse concluding a prose psalter (which also has six lines of a verse prayer known in eighteen other copies); a forty-six-line prayer titled 'A Meditacioun', addressed to the Trinity and other religious figures; and 'Another deuote prayer', which Connolly characterizes as similar to the first, but showing 'greater awareness of sin'. Edward Wilson gives the text of 'A Middle English Verse Sermon in the Winchester Anthology' (*N&Q* 46[1999] 17–20), which addresses Psalm 23:3–4 in 158 lines rhyming in quatrains. Paul Acker draws attention to 'An Unedited Middle English Religious Lyric (*IMEVS* 250.3) in Plimpton MS Additional 2' (*N&Q* 46[1999] 12). Most of the contents of this manuscript appear to be copied from National Library of Wales MS Porkington 10, but two lyrics on the fifth folio do not appear in Porkington; Acker gives the text of the unedited one, 'Almytty God Ihesu Crist'.

Duncan, ed., *Late Medieval English Lyrics and Carols, 1400–1530*, is a well-glossed and inexpensive edition that should serve students well. It includes one

Lydgate poem, ten by Charles d'Orléans, and a selection of Dunbar's poems, as well as many anonymous poems. These are ordered by theme: courtly lyrics, devotional and doctrinal lyrics, moral and penitential lyrics, and popular and miscellaneous lyrics. Duncan's introductory essay acquaints beginning readers with lyric conventions, emphasizing that song lyrics differ from other types.

7. Gower, Lydgate, Hoccleve

Russell A. Peck has begun a new edition of Gower's *Confessio Amantis* in the TEAMS Middle English Texts series. The plan is to produce this edition in three volumes, and the first provides the 'frame' alone: the Prologue and books 1 and 8. The next two will contain books 2–4 and 5–7, which Peck finds thematically coherent as 'Vice and its children' and 'philosophical inquiry'. The Latin is included in the text, with footnotes providing translations by Andrew Galloway. However, there are some exceptions to this scheme. First, the Latin marginalia are signified by pointing hands in the margins and are then provided in the notes at the end. Second, the Latin materials at the end of book 8 are translated immediately afterwards, with discursive footnotes, instead. Peck uses as his base text manuscript Fairfax 3, the 'premier third recension manuscript', which he has checked against five others.

Despite the title, Lynn Staley's 'Gower, Richard II, Henry of Derby, and the Business of Making Culture' (*Speculum* 75[2000] 68–96) is far more about Henry's position being changed as circumstances around him altered, those circumstances being partly Richard II's developing grasp of royal power and position and mainly John of Gaunt's dynastic aspirations, which led him to groom Henry towards a court they hoped to establish, but whose precise manifestation could not be known until events took place that are beyond the scope of this article. It is not that Gower turned his back on the king when he rededicated the *Confessio Amantis*, but that he was simply shifting the focus of a 'conversation' about power, the powerful, and their presentation. In similar ways, as the 'conversation' changed, Chaucer and John Clanvowe moved beyond the *Legend of Good Women* and the *Boke of Cupid*. Similarly, R.F. Yeager's intent is to find the connection between 'Politics and the French Language in England during the Hundred Years' War: The Case of John Gower' (in Baker, ed., pp. 127–57). This connection hinges upon the hypothetical datings of Gower's works and extending Fisher's argument about the political use of English as a national language back to the Treaty of Brétigny in 1360. So he determines that Gower started the *Mirour* (and lost juvenilia) as early as 1356–60. Thus, Gower chose Anglo-Norman for Edward III. Latin was for Richard II, given his tutors and apparent tastes, with 1381 (and the period to around 1388) finding cause for English. That cause failed during Henry IV, though, thanks to Lollardy's use of English and the concomitant possible taint of guilt.

In *Fathers and Daughters in Gower's 'Confessio Amantis': Authority, Family, State, and Writing*, María Bullón-Fernández points out that incest, as a despicable breach of authority, occurs numerous times in the *Confessio Amantis* in both its patriarchal forms: generational (father–daughter) and genderized (brother–sister). The former seems more important to Gower, and he seems to use it to think through a number of contemporary political and social conflicts where authority and its limits appear central. As a writer, Gower implicitly even recognizes discourse as a matter in his creation, whose text he must then control. One of these relationships is also discussed by Gail Ashton in 'Her Father's Daughter: The Re-alignment of Father–Daughter Kinship in Three Romances' (*ChauR* 34[2000] 416–27), noticed above. Leaning on theory, Louis Sylvester's 'Reading Narratives of Rape: The Story of Lucretia in Chaucer, Gower and Christine de Pizan' (*LeedsSE* 31[2000] 115–44) starts from the understanding that some find erotic the situation in which masculine desire is heightened by and overwhelms passive female reluctance, then comments on how the *Legend of Good Women*, *Confessio Amantis*, and *City of Ladies* present some aspects of the rape of Lucretia.

A more straightforward discussion of sexual relations is Conor McCarthy's 'Love and Marriage in the *Confessio Amantis*' (*Neophil* 84[2000] 485–99). 'Honeste love' entails reason controlling the natural urge to procreate, which would avoid such matters as incest. As a sacrament, marriage was also a means to control nature, though uneasily in theoretical discussions. Looking at gender in another fashion is Diane Watt's 'Literary Genealogy, Virile Rhetoric, and John Gower's *Confessio Amantis*' (*PQ* 78[1999] 389–415), summing up that good language is masculine—plain and unadorned, direct, and certainly not deceptive, decorative, or cosmetic and thus effeminate, even sodomitical. She takes the discussion of rhetoric in book 7 as Gower's expression of concern for his own legitimacy and status, amid the political discussion there, and as both were matter for discussion in immediate and general socio-political environments.

Simon Meecham-Jones has published twice on Gower this year. In 'Questioning Romance: Amadas and Ydoine in Gower's *Confessio Amantis*' (*Parergon* 17[2000] 35–49) he surveys other references to these lovers to find that the romance of *Amadas and Ydoine* was apparently perceived as an emblem of archetypal true love that can conquer madness, forced marriage, and even demonic kidnapping. So why does Amans list this as his preferred consolation in reading matter, though he admits it is momentary (VI.877–90), while other romances are eschewed in favour of classical and biblical material, and why is this couple not listed among the Companies of Lovers later? Meecham-Jones finds the answer in a contrast between Amans's failure and Amadas's success, despite their names' sharing initial similarities, and in Gower's use of names themselves as significant, here seeing 'Amadas' as 'beloved of God'. Meecham-Jones also discussed Gower as a background piece to studies on post-medieval texts in 'Prologue: The Poet as Subject: Literary Self-Consciousness in Gower's *Confessio Amantis*' (in Dragstra, Ottway, and Wilcox, eds., *Betraying Our Selves: Forms of Self-Representation in Early Modern English Texts*, pp. 14–30). Here, he explores briefly how Ricardian autobiography is set within a mental reluctance to compete against revered *auctores*. Gower's habit is not to take the obvious, but to direct attention elsewhere; he does this with his exempla and so, too, with Amans, especially when confronted with Venus's mirror and having to reconsider himself, after which he is then placed with the aged *auctores*.

Musing upon a different kind of authority, Siân Echard considers the physical, social, and thereby interpretative environment in which we read Gower's and others' works when they are under 'House Arrest: Modern Archives, Medieval Manuscripts' (*JMEMS* 30[2000] 185–210). Until very recent times, manuscripts were often books to be used, by, for example, reading them, resting goblets on them, recording notes in them, or doodling on them. But antiquarian collecting and library archiving have turned them into fetish objects, particularly when they have cultural value immediately or by association, as with Chaucer's and Gower's works, respectively. This makes it more difficult for us to recreate a manuscript's contemporary or subsequent readers' experience and expectations, although it does help ensure the manuscript's survival beyond our time; looking back, we know how time and use have decimated cultural materials for us to study. Echard illustrates his points with Gower manuscripts (especially Columbia University Library, MS Plimpton 265 and Pierpont Morgan Library, MS Morgan M690), ranging widely and with thoughtful experience (including many witty anecdotes) through provenance matters and collectors' activities, foliation, illustration, reproduction in exhibit catalogues and microfilms, and even electronic dissemination.

Turning to Lydgate, let us begin with the implications of physical production. First, in 'Caxton's Chaucer and Lydgate Quartos: Miscellanies from Manuscript to Print' (*TCBS* 12[2000] 1–25), Alexandra Gillespie studies a small group of quartos containing some of Lydgate's minor works and a few of Chaucer's, using provenance to remind us of the vagaries of survival. These quartos were designed to be sold individually as cheap booklets which could, if owners wished, be gathered into *Sammelbände* with bindings that would help ensure their longevity. Study of remaining vernacular printed quartos could also help explain fifteenth-century booklet production, where we lack the booklets but infer them from the resulting miscellanies. Second, Joseph A. Dane and Irene Basey Beesemyer reconsider 'The Denigration of John Lydgate: Implications of Printing History' (*ES* 81[2000] 117–26). A glance at the dates of printing of Lydgate, Chaucer, and *Piers Plowman* implies that Lydgate's popularity dropped in the middle of the sixteenth century because he was a 'Monk of Bury' and no reformer. This prejudiced potential readers against him, particularly after the Act of Supremacy, and that prejudice has survived long since. In his continuing high-performance search for Lydgate texts, Stephen R. Reimer describes a leaf of Petyt MS 524, which has 'A Fragment of Lydgate's *Troy Book* in the Inner Temple Library' (*N&Q* 45[1998] 180–2). The leaf was apparently used as a wrapper, and the text it contains comes from the prologue; he did not have time to compare it to other fragments, but tentatively concludes that it represents another lost manuscript copy.

At the other end lies performance: a pair of articles discuss musical performance for Lydgate's works. First, Elza C. Tiner reviews the external evidence that his verses were sung or otherwise performed, in '"Euer aftir to be rad & sung": Lydgate's Texts in Performance–I: Texts in Context' (*EDAMR* 19[1996–97] 41–52). She then uses that plus Lydgate's own references to emphasize the fact that oral delivery uses stylistic features effective in delivery, but which generally prove tedious to silent readers. Second, Shirley Carnahan and Anne Fjestad Peterson, in '"Euer aftir to be rad & sung": Lydgate's Texts in Performance–II: Texts in Performance' (*EDAMR* 19[1996–97] 85–93), review the effectiveness of several works as performed by the Boulder Renaissance Consort at the twenty-seventh International Congress on Medieval Studies at Western Michigan University: 'Princes of iouþe' and part of 'Tyed with a Lyne' had fifteenth-century scores, but the group created its own settings for four other poems; all were received well and the performance was judged a success.

Performance and form were also the concern of Martin J. Duffell's 'Lydgate's Metrical Inventiveness and his Debt to Chaucer' (*Parergon* 18[2000] 227–49).

Unlike Chaucer, who borrowed strict syllable-counting and rhythmic variability from his French and Italian models, Lydgate uses the fixed caesura he found in French *vers de dix* and traditional English long-line verse. His lines, then, are only predominantly iambic, and the linguistic changes of his generation (primarily final-schwa deletion but also the early stages of the Great Vowel Shift) made perfect accentual and syllabic regularity irrelevant, because they were impossible. With this understanding, we can accept and maintain his reputation as a fine metrist.

Social considerations and environment were not disregarded this year. Paul Strohm looked closely at 'A Complaint for My Lady of Gloucester' in 'John Lydgate, Jacque of Holland, and the Poetics of Complicity' (in Aers, ed., pp. 115–32). The poem may actually be by Lydgate, though Pearsall considers it too outspoken in criticizing Humphrey, for the poet actually avoids any particular policy but rejection of female opinion, and it fulfils a poet's obligation to his sponsor, that he simply keep writing. Looking at social environment a different way, Claire Sponsler places Lydgate's mummings in their historical and cultural environment in 'Alien Nation: London's Aliens and Lydgate's Mummings for the Mercers and Goldsmiths' (in Cohen, ed., *The Postcolonial Middle Ages*, pp. 229–42). They were performed in January–February 1429 during a period of nationalistic fervour, but they portrayed foreign merchants as friendly supporters in an increasingly multicultural trading centre, thereby bolstering native English mercantile centrism with a sense of importance and superiority.

Finally, Stephen R. Reimer discussed 'A Fragment in Imitation of Lydgate's "Verses on the Kings of England"' (*N&Q* 45[1998] 426–30), complete with illustrations. This is in British Library MS Cotton Julius B.xii, a composite manuscript with some documentary and heraldic materials. This short fragment appears to be the end of a stanza about King Harold and is otherwise unnoticed, and it mentions Lydgate by name, but it is datable only palaeographically to the late fifteenth century.

Hoccleve was not neglected, nor was he investigated deeply. Following up on last year's use of Blyth's concordance/database materials (see *YWES* 80[2001]) Judith A. Jefferson also reviews 'The Hoccleve Holographs and Hoccleve's Metrical Practice' (*Parergon* 18[2000] 203–26). Between the holographs and electronic materials, she determines that it is not that Hoccleve is writing bad iambic pentameter, it is just that he is using any kind of decasyllabic line, among which he tries to avoid overuse of four-beat lines. This way, iambic pentameter is favoured, but it is not his prime intent. Looking at the holographs and other materials, John J. Thompson considers 'A Poet's Contacts with the Great and the Good: Further Consideration of Thomas Hoccleve's Texts and Manuscripts' (in Riddy, ed., *Prestige, Authority and Power in Late Medieval Manuscripts and Texts*, pp. 77–101). He wonders if Hoccleve's self-presentation might not have changed over his life and for different audiences, real or perceived, and reviews the 'Dialogue' and Hoccleve's literary holographs from the 1420s, as well as the *Formulary*. The references to patrons allow Hoccleve to remind us of his merits and obligations, even as he reassesses his life and evidently loses his taste for writing English verse. Simultaneously, including 'Learn to Die' inside the 'Dialogue' and outside it, as a free-standing commission, lets us consider it as a work in itself and its effect on the poet. In a similar fashion, the holographic manuscripts display his self-representation in other ways, particularly through his naming of various patrons and dedicatees, and the *Formulary* reveals a retrospective summary of his life's activities in a different sphere, one which demanded more of his energy and perhaps, sadly, his poetic soul.

Charity Scott Stokes looks at another kind of relationship with authority in 'Sir John Oldcastle, the Office of the Privy Seal, and Thomas Hoccleve's "Remonstrance against Oldcastle" of 1415' (*Anglia* 118[2000] 556–70). She has found in British Library MS Harley 431 a lost letter in which Oldcastle transferred his movable property to Sir John Prophete, Keeper of the Privy Seal 1406–15, a kinsman of Oldcastle's first wife. This connection with a fellowship of the Privy Seal and a hint that Hoccleve might have been suspected of Lollardy by Walsingham lead Stokes to place Hoccleve's poetic apprenticeship among 'courtiers and poets with a strong satirical vein in their writing who tended towards sympathy with the Lollards'. With this understanding, it becomes easy to read the poem as ironic, misdirecting, and obfuscating, clear only to those on the inside.

8. Middle Scots Poetry

The year's most substantial examination of Middle Scots poetry comes from Edward Wheatley, whose *Mastering Aesop: Medieval Education, Chaucer, and his Followers* features a study of Henryson's *Morall Fabillis* as its ultimate chapter. The first few chapters of Wheatley's book contain an abundance of useful information on the history of the construction of Aesop as an *auctor*, theories of fable in the Christian scholarly tradition, and the dissemination of fables and fable hermeneutics in medieval schools and scholastic commentaries. Subsequent chapters offer detailed studies of Chaucer's *Nun's Priest's Tale* and Lydgate's *Isopes Fabules*, outlining in detail the significance of each author's contribution to the fable genre. Wheatley is often at pains to make what seems an obvious point: fables are not stories with fixed meanings, but forms of narrative discourse whose meanings change with each new appropriation, according to the cultural context of the writer (or the reader). While he claims that 'a fable's value as a mode of discourse lies in its adaptability to different discursive situations and registers', Wheatley offers surprisingly little in the way of historical and cultural contextualization for his studies of individual fabulists, particularly Henryson. His understanding of 'discursive situation' is quite narrow, referring almost exclusively to a medieval fable's particular *textual* affiliations with its sources, most notably the 'elegiac Romulus', 'the most popular Latin fable collection in Europe from the thirteenth through the fifteenth centuries'. Wheatley does a thorough job of analysing the ways in which Henryson's fable collection offers new modes of authorial self-presentation in the fable tradition. Too much of the chapter, however, comprises close readings of Henryson's poems; while such readings are the backbone of good literary scholarship, Wheatley does nothing to extend their significance to the larger cultural situation of late medieval Scotland. Why would a late fifteenth-century schoolmaster invest so much time and thought in this particular literary form? Who were Henryson's readers, and how did they receive (or how might they have received) his work? What was the literary culture of Scotland like in Henryson's time, and how did Henryson's work fit into (or subvert) native literary traditions? Wheatley's book sheds considerable light on the history of the late medieval fable, but has nothing to say about late medieval Scotland. He does not demonstrate even the most rudimentary knowledge of any Scottish writing beyond Henryson's own, which is a serious hindrance to his ability to contextualize Henryson's work. After demonstrating how the elements of Henryson's fables that moderns find 'unsettling' are actually 'traditional', Wheatley concludes his chapter on Henryson by asserting that 'we can begin to appreciate [Henryson] both for making full use of the variety inherent in the scholastic fable tradition and for embellishing it in ways that would have had resonance for many of his original readers'. This is a strange way to end a chapter that ignores Henryson's 'original readers'—indeed, the entire literary history of Scotland—completely.

Wheatley is not the only scholar to write on the oft-neglected *Fabillis* this year. Dorothy Yamamoto writes about the relationship between 'wild' bodies and human bodies in *The Boundaries of the Human in Medieval English Literature*, a sizeable portion of which is dedicated to the study of the fox in Henryson's *Fabillis*. As in Wheatley's study, Henryson's *Fabillis* are examined largely in terms of their place in European literary tradition, with no attention given to the cultural specificity of late medieval Scotland. In the latter half of chapter 3, 'The Fox: Laying Bare Deceit', Yamamoto adduces evidence from a number of Henryson's fables in order to make rather general assertions about the symbolic significance of the fox as a figure in medieval beast literature. Her individual readings are crisp and clear, and her conclusion that the fox troubles stable definitions of human and non-human is compelling (though somewhat overdetermined by Bakhtin). Henryson's fox becomes 'the medieval fox' a little too neatly at the end of the chapter, however, leaving one wondering where all the other foxes have gone. Surely Caxton's translation of the *Roman de Renart* (the only other poem examined in this chapter) and Henryson's *Fabillis* are not the only portrayals of foxes in medieval English literature. Yamamoto later discusses, briefly, the portrayal of fox hunts in poems such as *Sir Gawain and the Green Knight*, but even then her readings of Henryson and Caxton remain foundational, providing the bases for her analyses of the fox hunts. Yamamoto's study of the fox in Henryson's *Fabillis* is at times intriguing, but her larger assertions about 'the medieval fox' are less so, given the dearth of evidence on which they appear to be based.

Derek Pearsall offers a provocative, occasionally combative response to feminist criticism of Henryson in '"Quha wait gif all that Chauceir wrait was trew?": Henryson's *Testament of Cresseid'* (in Powell and Smith, eds., pp. 169–82). Pearsall proposes to study the *Testament of Cresseid* as a poem—that is, in terms of formal considerations such as style and language. He is interested in the poem's 'poeticness', an interest he claims most contemporary critics do not share. He sets his own reading of the poem against those inspired by late twentieth-century critical approaches—'feminist, new historicist, psychoanalytic, deconstructionist'—which neglect formal poetic consideration. He does an admirable job of pointing out the blind spots characteristic of some politically motivated criticism, and he takes on feminist readings of *Testament* by Susan Aronstein and Felicity Riddy at length. Pearsall wants to redirect our attention to the *Testament'*s poetic inheritance, its deliberate engagement of Chaucerian poetics in particular, rather than looking to contemporary (that is, late fifteenth-century) political or literary contexts as the basis for our understanding.

Sally Mapstone and Priscilla Bawcutt make significant contributions to the study of women in Scottish literary history in their articles for Wogan-Browne et al., eds., *Medieval Women*. Mapstone, in her article, 'The Origins of Criseyde' (pp. 131–47), sets out to draw meaningful connections between medieval Criseydes (including Henryson's) and the Homeric Chryseis and Briseis, 'despite the fact that the literary life-stories of earlier and later Criseydes differed'. She goes on to argue convincingly that both Chaucer's and Henryson's Criseydes were influenced significantly by Ovid's Briseis and 'the written world of letters in the *Heroides*', despite the fact that the Ovidian and medieval characters in this case are not identical. Bawcutt, in '"My bright buke": Women and their Books in Medieval and Renaissance Scotland' (pp. 17–34), sets forth preliminary results from her fascinating research into the phenomenon of women book-owners in Scotland. She begins with the most prominent woman book-owner in late medieval Scotland, Margaret Tudor, noting that most books owned by women were devotional, with books of hours comprising the largest single category. The evidence of a considerable female audience for Reformation writings is especially compelling. Her article should prove a very useful starting point for those interested in the question of female readership in sixteenth-century Scotland.

Two additional publications, while not concerned with Middle Scots poetry per se, may yet prove useful to students of Middle Scots by providing important contextual information. Mary E. Burke, in her article, 'Queen, Lover, Poet: A Question of Balance in the Sonnets of Mary, Queen of Scots' (in Burke, Donawerth, Dove and Nelson, eds., *Women, Writing, and the Reproduction of Culture in Tudor and Stuart Britain*, pp. 101–18), sees Mary's sonnet sequence (written in French) as illustrative of the tension she experienced between her identities as woman and ruler. A.D.M. Barrell has written a concise and lucid account of Scotland's early history in *Medieval Scotland*. The book covers the period from Scotland's earliest history to the Scottish Reformation, and though the book does not discuss literature in any detail it is a useful guide to the historical transformations and upheavals that have been instrumental in shaping the vernacular literary tradition in Scotland. *Medieval Scotland* is available in an affordable paperback edition, and should be a valuable research and teaching resource for historians and literary scholars alike.

Finally, two new editions of Middle Scots poetry appeared in 2000. Parkinson, ed., *Alexander Montgomerie: Poems*, is a complete edition (in two volumes) of the poems of the most prominent member of the Castalian band of poets (who wrote during the reign of James VI in the late sixteenth century). On the whole, the edition is impressive. The philological scholarship is thorough and the notes are ample, if a little difficult to navigate, being in a different volume from the poems themselves. The first volume contains the complete poems with textual variants listed at the bottom of each page, while the second volume contains a lamentably brief introduction to the principal witnesses and the author, a substantial bibliography, notes, and a glossary. Williams, ed., *Sir David Lyndsay: Selected Poems*, is a less scholarly but more accessible volume of poetry; while Parkinson's edition is designed for the scholar, Williams's is designed for the undergraduate student or first-time reader of Scottish poetry, and it serves its target audience well. The volume contains all of Lyndsay's significant shorter poetry, including *Testament of the Papyngo* and *Squyer Meldrum*. The introduction is short but useful, and the poems are laid out in a reader-friendly manner, with difficult words glossed at the bottom of each page. Explanatory notes are collected at the end of the book, followed by a remarkably thorough bibliography. Williams's edition of Lyndsay makes some of the most important and provocative Scottish writing of the Reformation era accessible to a general audience, and provides teachers of Scottish literature (or British literature generally) with an attractive new option for their syllabuses.

9. Malory and Caxton

This year's work on Malory covers 1999–2000. As usual, the 'Tale of the Sankgreall' received attention. Anne Marie D'Arcy's *Wisdom and the Grail* analyses the *Queste del Saint Graal* in the light of Cistercian tradition to argue that the Grail figures as a symbol of holy Wisdom; her last chapter turns to Malory and argues that he transforms the Grail from a figure of Wisdom into a symbol of the eucharist. Thin in comparison is Alfred Robert Kraemer's *Malory's Grail Seekers and Fifteenth-Century Hagiography*. Kraemer compares Malory's 'Sankgreall' to three fifteenth-century English saints' lives to conclude that the tale owes much to the genre of hagiography. Garland's series on Arthurian Characters and Themes continues with Mahoney, ed., *The Grail, A Casebook*, which includes Mahoney's 'The Truest and Holiest Tale: Malory's Transformation of *La Queste del Saint Graal*' (pp. 379–96; reprinted from Spisak, ed., *Studies in Malory*, reviewed *YWES* 66[1987] 152). Mahoney argues that the ascetic Grail chivalry is a complement to secular chivalry, not a rival. In the same volume, Felicity Riddy uses Malory as a point of comparison in 'Chivalric Nationalism and the Holy Grain in John Hardyng's *Chronicle*' (pp. 397–414).

Edward Donald Kennedy, in 'Malory's Guenevere: "A Woman who had Grown a Soul"' (*Arthuriana* 9:ii[1999] 37–45), argues that the failure of Galahad and the success of Guinevere in leading Launcelot to holiness shows that the way of the Grail is not the only way to salvation. Ralph Norris argues, in 'The Tragedy of Balin: Malory's Use of the Balin Story in the *Morte Darthur*' (*Arthuriana* 9:iii[1999] 52–67) that Malory cuts enough links between the Balin story and the Grail quest that Balin can function as a tragic hero in his own right and not as a foil for Galahad.

Kathleen Coyne Kelly has several pieces out on the textual tensions surrounding virginity in Malory. 'Malory's Multiple Virgins' (*Arthuriana* 9:ii[1999] 21–9) argues that the status of Lyones's virginity in the 'Tale of Gareth' points to the limits of historical and narrative knowledge. She also argues, in *Performing Virginity and Testing Chastity in the Middle Ages* (pp. 104–18), that, to protect the male chivalric body from injury or alteration, feminine or feminized bodies are substituted at moments of crisis; this is a version of her essay 'Menaced Masculinity and Imperiled Virginity in Malory's *Morte Darthur*' (in Kelly and Leslie's *Menacing Virgins: Representing Virginity in the Middle Ages and the Renaissance* (pp. 97–114).

Dorsey Armstrong, 'Gender and the Chivalric Community: The Pentecostal Oath in Malory's "Tale of King Arthur"' (*BBSIA* 51[1999] 293–312), argues that the command to protect women is put into the Pentecostal Round-Table oath because the conception of gender it represents, that women are weak and vulnerable and need masculine strength and bravery to rescue them, is central to masculine chivalric identity. She goes on to argue, however, that this idea of gender is revealed to be a fiction, as women (especially Morgan le Fay) deliberately imitate their supposedly natural helplessness for their own advantage, and thus manipulate knights. Martin B. Shichtman, 'Percival's Sister: Genealogy, Virginity, and Blood' (*Arthuriana* 9:ii[1999] 11–20), argues that, counter to the claim that Percival's sister is a female hero in the Grail quest, she is actually exchanged among men to create or strengthen masculine bonds. Sheila Fisher, in 'Women and Men in Late Medieval English Romance' (in Krueger, ed., pp. 150–64), claims that Malory, like Chaucer and the *Gawain*-poet, tries to minimize the disruption women cause by trying to minimize their appearances in the text. Jerome Mandel, '"Polymorphous Sexualities" in Chrétien de Troyes and Sir Thomas Malory' (in Boitani and Torti, eds., *The Body and Soul in Medieval Literature*, pp. 63–78), suggests that Malory occasionally disrupts gender expectations, and that Launcelot in particular often ends up in feminine positions of vulnerability and imprisonment. Donald L. Hoffman, 'Guenevere the Enchantress' (*Arthuriana* 9:ii[1999] 30–6), argues that accusations of witchcraft levelled against Guinevere and Morgan's lineage make it hard to distinguish between female heroes and counter-heroes.

Several books place Malory in his historical context. Hyonjin Kim does a good job, in *The Knight Without the Sword: A Social Landscape of Malorian Chivalry*, of arguing that the concerns of the fifteenth-century gentry insinuate themselves into *Le Morte Darthur*. After discussing the question of who Malory was and noting that all contenders come from the gentry, Kim turns to three major concerns: how economics affect marriage, arguing that only the richest knights are free to choose not to marry; how the affinities that grow up around the major knights reflect late fifteenth-century political structure; and (in his best chapter) how Malory distinguishes between gentility and nobility. Richard Kaeuper, in *Chivalry and Violence in Medieval Europe*, considers Malory as part of his larger study of chivalric tensions and the differing visions of knighthood in different sectors of society. He claims that Malory's is a reform text, trying to combine differing chivalric elements, although slighting the extremes of love and suggesting through the Grail that knights have paths to God relatively unmediated by the clergy. Raluca Radulescu suggests, in 'John Vale's Book and Sir Thomas Malory's *Le Morte Darthur*' (*Arthuriana* 9:iv[1999] 69–80), that both books show evidence of a chivalric war of ideas over good governance prompted by England's instability.

Hanks and Brogdon, eds., *The Social and Literary Contexts of Malory's 'Morte Darthur'*, assemble a collection of essays. Terence McCarthy argues that *Le Morte Darthur* has always been 'the wrong book at the wrong time', running counter to major trends in both political and historical thinking from the fifteenth century onwards (pp. 5–23). Andrew Lynch, continuing to write on violence in Malory in '"Thou woll never have done": Ideology, Context, and Excess in Malory's War' (pp. 24–41), uses pacifist texts from the period to analyse points where Malory's enthusiasm for battle falters. In 'Sir Thomas Malory's "Grete Booke"' (pp. 42–67), Karen Cherewatuk looks at fifteenth-century chivalric miscellanies to argue that Malory borrows from their structure to include stories that focus on different elements of chivalry, including political, military, courtly, and religious concerns. P.J.C. Field suggests, in 'Malory and the Battle of Towton' (pp. 68–74), that some details of Arthur's last battle are borrowed from actual battles of the Wars of the Roses. Processions, used to unite (or to try to unite) different factions and to lend importance to political occasions, appear in Malory to emphasize critical moments, according to Ann Elaine Bliss's 'The Symbolic Importance of Processions in Malory's *Morte Darthur* and Fifteenth-Century England' (pp. 75–93). D. Thomas Hanks Jr argues, in 'Malory's Anti-Knights: Balin and Breunys', that Balin and Breunys sans Pité (and even Dinadan) show the dangers that trained men of violence can pose to society (pp. 94–110). Robert L. Kelly's 'Malory's Argument against War with France: The Political Geography of France and the Anglo-French Alliance in the *Morte Darthur*' (pp. 111–33), argues that, in a rebuke to Edward IV's interests in renewing a war with France, Malory show English security to be dependent on good relations with France, from Arthur's early alliances with Ban and Bors through the Roman War and concluding in disaster when Launcelot's adultery leads to a French war. Kevin Grimm, 'Wynkyn de Worde and the Creation of Malory's *Morte Darthur*' (pp. 134–54), shows that Wynkyn de Worde's edition of Malory, with its layout, inserted chapter descriptions, and illustrations, has affected the reception of Malory more than has been acknowledged.

Textual matters dominate the excellent collection of essays assembled in Wheeler, Kindrick and Salda, eds., *The Malory Debate: Essays on the Texts of 'Le Morte Darthur'*. The collection begins with versions of articles published earlier arguing over whether Malory was the reviser responsible for the differences between the Roman War episodes in Caxton and the Winchester manuscript; later articles move on to more general textual issues. Robert L. Kindrick presents three articles by William Matthews, 'Caxton and Chaucer: A Re-View' (pp. 1–34), 'The Besieged Printer' (pp. 35–64), and 'A Question of Texts' (pp. 65–107), which argue that Caxton was a more careful editor than is generally acknowledged and therefore unlikely to have changed his text radically without announcement; thus, the Roman War episode was revised by someone else, and Malory is the most plausible candidate. The linguistic evidence disproves this hypothesis, as Yuji Nakao's strong essay 'Musings on the Reviser of Book V in Caxton's Malory' (pp. 191–216) shows: the language in Caxton's Roman War strongly resembles Caxton's own prose and differs from the language in the rest of Caxton's *Le Morte Darthur*, meaning that the language variants were not introduced simply by Caxton's standard practices of preparing a text for publication. Edward Donald Kennedy's 'Caxton, Malory, and the "Noble Tale of King Arthur and the Emperor Lucius"' (pp. 217–32) sums up the arguments and finds the evidence for Malory as the reviser uncompelling. The debate, however, has prompted interesting explorations on a variety of issues. Charles Moorman, although unwilling to accept the linguistic evidence, lays out clearly his reasons for preferring Caxton's version in 'Desperately Defending Winchester: Arguments from the Edge' (pp. 109–16). Shunichi Noguchi disagrees in 'The Winchester Malory' (pp. 117–26), analysing the linguistic evidence and finding that he prefers the Winchester manuscript. P.J.C. Field, 'Caxton's Roman War' (pp. 127–67), suggests that the Winchester scribes also abbreviated the Roman War version found in their exemplar, and that by working from both Winchester and Caxton it is possible to reconstruct a more complete version of what Malory wrote. Masako Takagi and Toshiyuki Takamiya, 'Caxton Edits the Roman War Episode: The *Chronicles of England* and Caxton's Book V' (pp. 169–90), argue that Caxton drew on his *Chronicles of England* to edit the Roman War, particularly in where to insert chapter breaks. N.F. Blake suggests, in 'Caxton at Work: A Reconsideration' (pp. 233–53), that Caxton might have commissioned the Winchester manuscript to be copied from loose quires (perhaps written by Malory himself) as he was trying to decide whether to print *Le Morte Darthur*, and the quires then served as his copy-text. Sue Ellen Holbrook, 'On the Attractions of the Malory Incunable and the Malory Manuscript' (pp. 323–66), speculates that Winchester was stained by printers' ink because Caxton made a manuscript copy of Winchester before he printed *Le Morte Darthur*. Helen Cooper notes, in 'Opening Up the Malory Manuscript' (pp. 255–84), that the Winchester manuscript records many levels of response to the text not captured in Vinaver's edition. D. Thomas Hanks, 'Back to the Past: Editing Malory's *Le Morte Darthur*' (pp. 285–300), suggests that modern punctuation makes Malory's text seem more stilted and clumsy than it really is, and suggests ways modern editions might compensate. Along similar lines, Shunichi Noguchi, 'Reading Malory's Text Aloud' (pp. 301–14), analyses the mixture of indirect and direct discourse in Caxton and Winchester and suggests how they could have functioned. Meg Roland's 'Malory's Roman War Episode: An Argument for a Parallel Text' (pp. 315–22) puts forward one solution for handling the textual difficulties. Finally, Paul Yeats-Edwards, 'The Winchester Malory Manuscript: An Attempted History' (pp. 367–87), gives what is known of the history of the Winchester manuscript, and suggests it may have come to Winchester as a gift from a student.

Mukai Tsuyoshi adds another piece to the puzzle of the relation between Caxton's and Malory's texts by arguing, in 'De Worde's 1498 *Morte Darthur* and Caxton's Copy-Text' (*RES* 51[2000] 24–40), that Wynkyn de Worde seems to have proofed Caxton's printed edition against a manuscript that was not Winchester. Anne F. Sutton, in 'Malory in Newgate: A New Document' (*Library* 28[2000] 243–62), reports that Malory was in Newgate in April 1469, casting doubt on suggestions that he might have met Lancastrian luminaries in the Tower or participated in the 1468 revolt; she also suggests that this might mean that Malory acquired his sources by purchasing or renting from commercial book-dealers rather than through access to a patron's library. Andrew Breeze, 'Caxton's Prologue to Malory and the Welsh *Brut*' (*Arthuriana* 9:iii[1999] 49–51), suggests that Caxton's mention of Arthurian books in Welsh refers to translations of Geoffrey of Monmouth's *History of the Kings of Britain*.

Fabienne L. Michelet argues, in 'East and West in Malory's Roman War: The Implications of Arthur's Travels on the Continent' (*Multilingua* 18:ii–iii[1999] 209–25), that the presence of pagans in Lucius' army helps the Roman War establish two broad historical themes, the westward *translatio imperii* and eastward crusading. Arthur's success in these endeavours contrast with his later passivity in the Grail quest and savagery in his war with Launcelot. Nina Dullin-Mallory, '"Seven Trew Bataylis for Jesus Sake": The Long-Suffering Saracen Palomides' (in Blanks and Frassetto, eds., *Western Views of Islam in Medieval and Early Modern Europe*, pp. 165–72), surveys the role of Palomides in medieval literature to conclude that Malory preserves the tradition of making him a good knight, but emphasizes that he is a Saracen by removing his genealogy, for other works give him an Irish mother.

Margaret duMais Svogun's *Reading Romance: Literacy, Psychology, and Malory's 'Le Morte Darthur'* uses a jumble of psychological theories, from Jungian archetypes to some of the more extreme claims from Walter Ong's *Orality and Literacy*, to attempt an analysis of the impact of Malory's work as a printed text, suggesting that the frequency of doubles in Malory reflects people's growing ability through literacy to see themselves from an external perspective, creating a split in awareness.

A number of essays place Malory in larger literary histories. Sandra Ness Ihle, 'Generic Shift in Malory' (in Busby and Jones, eds., *'Por le soie amiste': Essays in Honor of Norris J. Lacy*, pp. 225–33), argues that Malory, to bring more clearly into focus the worship of his protagonists, cut and simplified the complex web of links in the prose styles that directed attention elsewhere, and thus Malory's love of knighthood helps create the genre of non-cyclic prose romance. Andrew Lynch argues, in 'Malory Moralisé: The Disarming of *Le Morte Darthur*, 1800–1918' (*Arthuriana* 9:iv[1999] 81–93), that, to make *Le Morte Darthur* suit Victorian ideals, revisers cut out much of the disturbing violence from the story. Malory serves as a point of comparison for discussions of more modern works in Elizabeth Scala's 'Pretty Women: The Romance of the Fair Unknown, Feminism, and Contemporary Romantic Comedy' (*Film and History* 29[1999] 24–40), Robert J. Blanch and Julian N. Wasserman's 'Fear of Flyting: The Absence of Internal Tension in *Sword of the Valiant* and *First Knight*' (*Arthuriana* 10:iii[2000] 15–32), and Betsy Bowden's 'Gloom and Doom in Mark Twain's *Connecticut Yankee* from Thomas Malory's *Morte Darthur*' (*SAF* 28[2000] 179–202).

Felicia Ackerman, 'Late in the Quest: The Study of Malory's *Morte Darthur* as a New Direction in Philosophy' (in French and Wettstein, eds., *New Directions in Philosophy*, pp. 312–42), crusades for Malory to be taken seriously as a text of interest to philosophers, based on its emotionally compelling world governed by unfamiliar ethics. She argues that Malory's characters are emotionally plausible enough to serve as tests of philosophical intuition, but presented artistically enough to crystallize philosophical issues.

Several linguistic analyses of Malory also appeared. Lilo Moessner, in 'The Negative Relative Marker *but*: A Case of Syntactic Borrowing' (in Tops, Devriendt, and Geukins, eds., *Thinking English Grammar*, pp. 65–77), argues that Malory adapted the use of *but* as a relative marker from the French, and that his use of the construction increases noticeably when he is translating a French source. The frequency of use in the 'Tale of Gareth' suggests that he had a French source. Monika Fludernik, 'Narrative Discourse Markers in Malory's *Morte D'Arthur*' (*JHP* 1[2000] 231–62), analyses discourse markers used to mark narrative structure, arguing that their sudden profusion in the fifteenth century (including in the *Morte Darthur*) marks a crisis in the way in which they were used.

I have not seen Jonggab Kim's 'Feminism and Patriarchal Ideology: An Interpretation of Chivalric "*Frauendienst*" in Thomas Malory's *Le Morte Darthur*' (*Feminist Studies in English Literature* 7[1999] 215–34).

10. Drama

Medieval and early sixteenth-century drama remain buoyant fields of study in terms of both the quality and quantity of the work produced this year. In particular a number of major new studies have appeared, providing summations of the state of play in the field, and the basis for future research and practical performance. The essays in the most recent volume of *Early Theatre* (*ET* 3[2000]) constitute an expanded special issue focused on 'The York Cycle: Then and Now', growing out of the performance of the full cycle in Toronto in June 1998 and the attendant scholarly symposium. The contributions range over the full breadth of issues raised by the events, covering both the historical and the performative (and even—shades of Polonius—the historical-performative) aspects of the cycle. Peter Meredith's 'The City of York and its "Play of Pageants"' (*ET* 3[2000] 23–47) introduces the cycle, its urban auspices, and the texts that convey the pageants. In 'Places to Hear the Play in York' (*ET* 3[2000] 49–78), Eileen White revisits the processional route, illustrating the various stations at which the pageants were performed. John McKinnell's 'The Medieval Pageant Wagons at York: Their Orientation and Height' (*ET* 3[2000] 79–104), also re-examines the practicalities of the original performances, arguing that the York wagons may have been considerably taller than is generally assumed (some of them may have been over twenty feet high) and that audiences may well have stood on more than one side of them during the performance. In 'Raging in the Streets of Medieval York' (*ET* 3[2000] 105–25), Margaret Rogerson looks at staging and acting spaces in the light of the famous injunction that the actor playing Herod at Coventry should 'rage' on the pageant and also in the street, concluding that little 'off-wagon' playing may actually have occurred in the York Cycle. Ralph Blasting's article, 'The Pageant Wagon as Iconic Site in the York Cycle' (*ET* 3[2000] 127–36), also considers playing on and off the wagons, while Martin W. Walsh's 'High Places and Travelling Scenes: Some Observations on the Staging of the York Cycle' (*ET* 3[2000] 137–54), argues for a more diverse employment of playing spaces than Rogerson suggested. In 'Seeing and Hearing; Looking and Listening' (*ET* 3[2000] 155–66), Pamela M. King seeks to recreate the conditions of audience reception of the drama, even scripting some likely contemporary observations from (near) the foot of the Cross, while Richard Beadle's 'Verbal Texture and Wordplay in the York Cycle' (*ET* 3[2000] 167–84), and Alexandra F. Johnston's '"His langage is lorne": The Silent Centre of the York Cycle' (*ET* 3[2000] 185–95) examines the vocabulary and the metrical and stylistic aspects of the cycle's affective language. The remainder of the essays, those making up the ' ... and now' section of the volume, are briefer and consider specific aspects of the 1998 production. The essays are, in order: Alexandra F. Johnston, 'York Cycle 1998: What We Learned' (*ET* 3[2000] 199–204); Garrett P.J. Epp, 'Back to the Garden Again: Directing *The Fall*' (*ET* 3[2000] 205–9); Michael B. Barbour and Susan Becker Barbour, 'A Star is Born: Staging Choices in *The Nativity* and *The Shepherds*' (*ET* 3[2000] 210–18); Roland Reed, '*The Slaughter of the Innocents*' (*ET* 3[2000] 219–28); Jonathan Herold, '"Kick Ass and Take Names": Presenting the York Cycle's *Christ before Pilate* as a Meditation on Power and Authority' (*ET* 3[2000] 229–33); Karen Sawyer, 'Reflections on *The Resurrection*' (*ET* 3[2000] 234–9); Gwendolyn Waltz, 'Time, Meaning, and Transcendence: Directing *The Incredulity of Thomas*' (*ET* 3[2000] 240–8); Terri Cain, '*The Ascension*: Choreography of Assent: Staging Images of Spirituality' (*ET* 3[2000] 249–58); and Stephen Johnson, 'Historical Text and the Postmodern Aesthetic: Case Study of Handmade Performance's *The Last Judgement*' (*ET* 3[2000] 259–74). Joel Kaplan provides the final reflections in 'Afterwards' (*ET* 3[2000] 275–8).

Research Opportunities in Renaissance Drama also carries an essay on the 1998 'Toronto Cycle' this year—Megan Lloyd's account of the staging of the revival, 'Reflections of a York Survivor: The York Cycle and its Audience' (*RORD*

39[2000] 223–35)—although the bulk of the volume concerns other material. In 'The Royal Image and the Politics of Entertainment' (*RORD* 39[2000] 1–16), W.R. Streitberger offers a reading of the drama and entertainments of the last fifteen years of the reign of Henry VIII informed by a broadly factional interpretation of court and confessional politics. Elsewhere in the same volume Alan B. Farmer and Zachary Lesser discuss, in 'Vile Arts: The Marketing of English Printed Drama, 1512–1660' (*RORD* 39[2000] 77–166), the booksellers' techniques for selling their dramatic wares evidenced in title pages and other parts of the printed text. Despite the allusion to the early sixteenth century in the title, however, the essay focuses almost exclusively on the post-playhouse period, with only passing reference to works printed in the first half of the century. More squarely located in the earlier period is James M. Gibson and Isobel Harvey's essay, 'A Sociological Study of the New Romney Passion Play' (*RORD* 39[2000] 203–21), which examines the social and economic background to the records of the now lost play, the individuals named in those records, and the kind of dramatic culture which those records seem to imply. The volume is rounded off by the regular 'Census of Medieval Productions' written by Peter Greenfield (*RORD* 39[2000] 237–59).

European Medieval Drama volume 3 [1999] arrived too late for inclusion in *YWES* 80, but merits notice here. Among the excellent essays contained within the volume are a number of direct relevance to this chapter. 'Drama on the Wall: Medieval Drama Illustrated by Danish Church Wall Paintings', by Graham D. Caie (*EMD* 3[1999] 11–18), uses visual evidence from Denmark to illuminate the imagery of the English cycle plays. John C. Coldewey's 'Secrets of God's Creatures: Talking Animals in Medieval Drama' (*EMD* 3[1999] 73–96) also deploys visual evidence, this time to illustrate the issues involved in giving dramatic voice to Balaam's ass in play 5 of the Chester Cycle, and the serpent in Eden. In 'The Machinery of Spectacle: The Performance Dynamic of the *Play of Mary Magdalen* and Related Matters' (*EMD* 3[1999] 145–59), Bob Godfrey speculates fruitfully about possible staging methods for the *Mary Magdalen*, while in 'Ostension and Channel Untwining: A Few Notes' André Lascombes examines the dislocation of word and image in sections of the Chester *Noah* play, the Digby *Killing of the Children*, and the N-Town play(s).

A number of stimulating monographs have also added to our knowledge of the drama and its various social, political, and cultural contexts. Darryll Grantley's *Wit's Pilgrimage: Drama and the Social Impact of Education in Early Modern England* examines the relationship(s) between education and social rank and identity in drama and wider English society through the period from the rise of humanism to the closure of the theatres and the Civil War. Grantley charts the changes in educational practice during the 'long' sixteenth century and the consequent shifts in markers of gentility evident in the dramatic texts of the period, discussing the educational backgrounds and social status of playwrights and their likely audiences, and argues for a decisive shift in these relationships brought about by the rise of the commercial theatres. Admirably wide-ranging in its coverage of both dramatic and educational tests, this study deserves a wide readership among students of both the earlier and the later dramatic periods. Another study that reads late medieval and early modern drama in the light of social and cultural history is Lynn Forest-Hill's lively and engaging *Transgressive Language in Medieval English Drama: Signs of Challenge and Change*. Forest-Hill's book discusses dramatic material from the cycle plays and the fifteenth-century Moralities through to the Henrician interludes of Skelton and Heywood and Bale's *King Johan*. It focuses on the language of abuse and invective, the bawdy and transgressive speeches of dramatic characters from the jibes of Christ's tormenters in the biblical drama to Bale's Sedicyon, and reads them cogently against contemporary debates about blasphemy, social transgression, and (in the latter cases at least) religious reform and Reformation. On the way Forest-Hill offers both some interesting re-readings of the interlude drama and a cultural history of shifting perceptions of what constitutes the transgressive in both language and the law.

Also concerned, at least in part, with the drama of the pre-playhouse period is Julie Stone Peters's magnificent and weighty monograph *Theatre and the Book, 1480–1580: Print, Text, and Performance in Europe*. Amounting to almost 500 pages, spanning 400 years of dramatic history, and ranging freely across the languages and theatres of Europe, Stone's book is a *magnum opus* in more ways than one. Its thesis, succinctly set out in the introduction, is that 'the printing press had an essential role to play in the birth of the modern theatre ... As institutions they grew up together.' In illustrating and supporting her claim, Peters considers the *mise-en-page* of early printed playbooks, and the gradual development of special protocols for printing drama as a literary form; she looks at the relationships between printing and playing, the developing culture of dramatic print, and the representation of the more ephemeral incidents of performance: gesture, pose, and persona on the printed page. While one might quibble about some of the detail (John Heywood's *Four PP* is confidently dated to a performance in 1520 and publication twenty years later, somewhat against the run of critical opinion, without any cited evidence for the change (p. 329 n. 73)), and the volume is not without its structural flaws (the failure of the index to cover the copious footnotes as well as the main text was a serious shortcoming when it comes to pursuing the evidence for some claims). And the sheer breadth of allusion and reference, ranging from England, through France, Germany and Italy and over a century or more of dramatic and printing history, often in little more than a sentence, reduces the possibility of drawing out the nature and implications of developments within specific regions and time periods in great detail. But this is a big book, and, dare I say it, an important one, that merits applause for both the scope of its intellectual ambition and the scholarly integrity and enthusiasm of its execution.

A little beyond the geographical scope of this chapter, but nonetheless of direct relevance and interest to students of early English drama is *Reformers on Stage: Popular Drama and Religious Propaganda in the Low Countries of Charles V, 1515–1556*, by Gary K. Waite. In this fascinating overview of the politically engaged theatre of the Dutch Chambers of Rhetoric, Waite provides not only an invaluable introduction to the distinct and idiosyncratic drama of the early modern Low Countries, with special attention to the cities of Antwerp and Amsterdam, but also some persuasive readings of individual plays. The result is an engrossing account of how the *rederijkers* engaged with and (re)negotiated questions of confessional alignment and religious reform in their plays, adapting the themes of Erasmian, Lutheran, or Calvinist theology to their own local needs and circumstances. Still more apparently remote from, yet equally pertinent to, the concerns of this chapter is M.S. Silk's engaging study, *Aristophanes and the Definition of Comedy*, a rereading of Athenian Old Comedy that has much to say about the basic dynamics of comic drama, its routines, and the kind of 'mongrel' variations of tone and content that inform much of the medieval canon. In his analysis of Aristophanes' use of language and the rapid variation between the 'high' and the 'low' that characterizes his surviving works, Silk offers some useful suggestions about the operation of the comic mode in pre-modern culture, and about theatrical comedy more generally that will stimulate discussion among all scholars of drama.

In *The Devil and the Sacred in English Drama, 1350–1642*, John D. Cox makes a cogent case for the continuity of conceptions of Satan and the assorted lesser devils portrayed in plays throughout the late medieval and early modern periods. By avowedly stretching the definition of 'devil' to encompass the Vices of the early Tudor interludes, Cox necessarily blurs something of the sharpness of focus that a study of the devil and devils alone would have achieved, but there is still a good deal of excellent material here for students of both the religious and the secular drama to appreciate. Also diabolic in focus is Darren Oldridge's *The Devil in Early Modern England*, which will provide considerable material of interest to those studying or staging plays with devilish dramatis personae from the period. Although it begins its survey with the Reformation, Oldridge's study casts its eyes backwards sufficiently frequently to late medieval attitudes to Satan and his cohorts to be useful to medievalists. His nicely illustrated volume would make entertaining and informative reading for anyone with an interest in pre-modern English popular culture.

A dramatic figure of a more benevolent stamp is St George, putative hero of many a mummers' play, pageant, and carol. He is now also the subject of an excellent new interdisciplinary study, *St George: Hero, Martyr, and Myth*, by Samantha Riches, which seeks to chart his development from obscurity to the centre of English national—and international—culture. Drawing her evidence from the visual arts as thoroughly as from literary and historical sources, Riches tells an entertaining and informative story, revealing as much about medieval popular piety, ecclesiastical politics, and modern national anxieties as it does about the particular qualities of St George's enigmatic and essentially malleable saintly persona. Particularly striking—and persuasive—is the chapter on the saint's much-maligned adversary, the dragon, and representations of her sexuality and genitalia. Here the implicit sexual anxieties and fantasies lying behind the dragon-slaying project are laid bare in more ways than one. Every boy scout troupe should be made to read this book on St George's Day morning.

A number of books published this year provide useful background to the culture(s) informing the cycle plays and religious drama of the period. For the sixteenth century, the third edition of A.E. McGrath's *Reformation Thought: An Introduction* is a lucid and highly readable guide to the chief theological and philosophical positions of the late medieval period and the debates of the early Reformation. Here can be found useful expositions of the main foci of scholastic thinking, of early humanism, and Lollardy, as well as accounts of the chief strains of reformed thinking. Some of the suggested connections between late medieval dissent and the clashes of the sixteenth century are overdrawn, and there are occasional errors of fact (Cardinal Pole was not 'a loyal catholic bishop deposed under Henry VIII' (p. 253), for example), but the book as a whole is a useful one. It is to be hoped that any future fourth edition will rectify the above and also remove the numerous irritating typos that seem to have slipped in during the production process, as well as providing a more accurate index than the current version, that omits far too many appearances of even the most prominent protagonists for comfort. A valuable guide to the biblical Word is made available in the form of an original-spelling edition of William Tyndale's English *New Testament* (1526), edited by W.R. Cooper with a brief introduction from David Daniel. This single-volume, pocket-sized edition provides the full text of Tyndale's translation, along with the contentious editorial apparatus of the original edition.

The essays in O'Sullivan, ed., *The Bible as Book: The Reformation* also focus on the literary and textual politics of the Bible at a time of profound confessional trauma. Of particular relevance to *YWES* readers might be the essays by Susan M. Felch, 'The Vulgate as Reformation Bible: The Sonnet Sequence of Anne Lock' (pp. 65–88), David Daniel, 'William Tyndale, the English Bible, and the English Language' (pp. 39–50), and Richard Duerden, 'Equivalence or Power? Authority and Reformation Bible Translation' (pp. 9–23). Evidence of the vitality of Catholic culture in the sixteenth century from theological and institutional sources is provided by Lucy Wooding's monograph *Rethinking Catholicism in Reformation England*. A thought-provoking reassessment of the 'Erasmian' elements in Henrician and mid-Tudor religious policy, this study offers valuable contextual material for any discussion of the work of the Rastells, Heywood, or the mid-Tudor Interludes.

Those struggling with the intellectual framework of the humanist drama emerging from the More circle will welcome the republication, in the Renaissance Society of America's Reprint Texts series, of Dominic Baker-Smith's study, *More's Utopia*, first published in 1991, which strives to locate More's most perplexing work in its intellectual and cultural contexts. Equally valuable as background material for the humanist drama of the late 1520s and 1530s are a number of the essays collected in John Guy, *Politics, Law, and Counsel in Tudor and Early Stuart England*. This Variorum series edition of Guy's essays includes pieces on 'Thomas More as Successor to Wolsey' (pp. 276–92), 'Thomas More and Christopher St German: The Battle of the Books' (pp. 95–120), 'The King's Council and Political Participation' (pp. 121–47), and 'The Henrician Age' (pp. 13–46), all of which contain material pertinent to the political drama. Also focused on More, albeit more polemically, is William Tyndale's *An Answere Unto Sir Thomas More's Dialoge* [1531], now available in a scholarly edition, as the third volume in O'Donnell and Wicks, eds., *The Independent Works of William Tyndale*. The edition contains, in addition to Tyndale's text (which was a direct response to More's *Dialogue Concerning Heresies*) a critical introduction and bibliography, over ninety pages of critical notes, a glossary, and separate indices for scriptural citations, post-scriptural citations, and proper names, as well as a detailed general index.

The sub-dramatic genre of the dialogue is currently the subject of considerable scholarly interest. William Roye's *A Brefe Dialoge Bitwene a Christen Father and his Stobborne Sonne* [1527], was published last year in an edition by Douglas H. Parker and Bruce Krajewski that arrived too late to be mentioned in *YWES* 80. Subtitled 'The First Protestant Catechism Published in English' (which it has a good claim to be, depending upon one's definition of 'published'), this edition provides a comprehensive critical introduction, commentary, glossary, and extended list of variants and emendations, and merits the attention of scholars of Reformation culture and drama alike. Two further critical studies place catechisms and dialogues in the wider context of early modern literate culture. Ian Green's *Print and Protestantism in Early Modern England* is the second volume in a projected trilogy of studies which aims to chart the spread of Protestant culture in England via its textual traces. The first volume, *The Christian's ABC: Catechism and Catechizing in England, c.1530–1740* (OUP [1996]) looked at catechisms specifically, while this second volume examines the entirety of the surviving printed output of Protestant literature for the same period. Green provides the first truly comprehensive overview of reformed print culture in the sixteenth and seventeenth centuries, and his book should be required reading for anyone interested in literacy and literate culture in the period. Adam Fox's *Oral and Literate Culture in England, 1500–1700*, also from OUP and covering some of the same ground, albeit to different effect, is another weighty study of popular culture, this time focusing more avowedly on the 'non-standard' (the dialectal, the proverbial, the mythical, and the scandalous). Sharing similarities of style and approach with Keith Thomas's *Religion and the Decline of Magic* [1971], Fox presents a stimulating, if at times necessarily impressionistic, account of the fabric of lived experience across England in the early modern period.

Readers with interest in the More–Rastell–Heywood circle will also welcome OUP's decision to reprint in facsimile R.B. Merriman's two-volume edition of the *Life and Letters of Thomas Cromwell* [originally published in 1902]. While some of the ideas articulated in the introductory essay may be in need of revision in the light of subsequent scholarship, the letters themselves are as vibrant and informative about Henrician political, religious and intellectual culture as ever, providing an invaluable window into the period. Also available in the same series is C.L. Kingsford's two-volume edition of John Stow's *A Survey of London*, an essential volume for anyone seeking to understand the cultural history and topography of Tudor London, and powerful testimony to the complex mix of pride and nostalgia that the metropolis could inspire in its citizens in the late sixteenth century.

Jonathon Woolfson's *Padua and the Tudors: English Students in Italy, 1485–1603* [1998], unfortunately arrived too late to be included in *YWES* 80, but also contains useful material in its chapter on 'Humanists' (pp. 103–18), and its biographical register of English visitors to Padua, which includes entries on Thomas Starkey and Thomas Sackville as well as better-known authors such as Sir Philip Sidney. The most influential of English visitors to Padua, Reginald, later Cardinal Pole, Mary Tudor's archbishop of Canterbury, whose circle generated a good deal of the literature hostile to the Henrician Reformation, is the subject of a separate study: Thomas F. Mayer's *Reginald Pole: Prince and Prophet*. Mayer offers an account of Pole as more of a politician and intellectual than a religious reformer—more prince, that is, than prophet—and even seeks, in a somewhat curious reading of the surviving portraiture, to provide him with a 'gay marriage'. But the study is a useful addition to our knowledge of this paradoxical figure of Counter-Reformation culture.

The physical settings for medieval household culture provide the subject for the second volume of Anthony Emery's magnificent *Greater Medieval Houses of England and Wales* project, covering East Anglia, central England, and Wales. Like its predecessor covering northern England (reviewed in *YWES* 77[1998] 174), this volume combines lavish monochrome illustrations, maps, plans, and diagrams with detailed scholarly description and analysis. Emery takes each of five regions (East Anglia, the east, central, and west Midlands, and the Borders and Wales) in turn, providing introductory essays on the historical, cultural, and architectural cultures of the region, and useful select bibliographies before moving on to individual descriptions of all the major houses in alphabetical order. Another useful window upon aristocratic culture is provided by Hugh Collins's historical study of *The Order of the Garter, 1348–1461*. Offering a detailed history and analytical account of the Order from its inception to the deposition of Henry VI, Collins provides useful insights into this key institution in the determination of chivalric culture in England, including a valuable section on attitudes towards the Garter and its traditions in vernacular literary texts. The ongoing *New Cambridge Medieval History* volumes also continue to throw up interesting contextual material for students of literature and drama among their wide-ranging and well-informed interpretative essays. The latest, volume vi, *c.1300–c.1415*, edited by Michael Jones, offers *inter alia* valuable introductions to 'Currents of Religious Thought and Expression' (Jeremy Catto, pp. 42–65), 'The Universities' (Jacques Verger, pp. 66–81), 'Urban Life' (Jean-Pierre Leguay, pp. 102–23), 'Chivalry and the Aristocracy' (Maurice Keen, pp. 209–21), 'Court Patronage and International Gothic' (Paul Binski, pp. 222–33), and 'Literature in Italian, French, and English: Uses and Muses of the Vernacular' (Nick Havely, pp. 257–70). More obviously relevant to students of the drama are a number of the essays in Palliser, ed., *The Cambridge Urban History of Britain*, i: *600–1540*. In particular readers should find valuable information on the urban culture that produced the great cycle plays in Gervase Rosser and E. Patricia Dennison's 'Urban Culture and the Church, 1300–1540' (pp. 335–70); John Schofield and Geoffrey Stell's 'The Built Environment, 1300–1540' (pp. 371–94); Jennifer Kermode, 'The Greater Towns, 1300–1540' (pp. 441–67); Bärbel Brodt, 'East Anglia' (pp. 639–56); and Jennifer Kermode, 'Northern Towns' (pp. 657–81). There are also some interesting insights to be gleaned by dipping into Michael Ferber's *A Dictionary of Literary Symbols*, which, although in no way exhaustive (it has only around 200 entries), does provide a useful guide to some major clusters of literary and dramatic imagery from biblical and classical texts through to the twentieth century. Readers in search of the resonances of lions, nightingales, or wasps, the sea, saffron, or wood ('see forest') will find much to interest them. Also concerned with the symbolic, although on a rather deeper cultural stratum, is Mary Douglas's ground-breaking *Leviticus as Literature* [1998], now available in paperback. Douglas's authoritative re-reading of the prohibitive and permissive codes of the book of Leviticus deserves to be widely read among scholars of the biblical drama, and should provoke as interesting a debate as her earlier work on a related theme, *Purity and Danger* [1969].

The latest volume of documentary material from the REED project has been published this year. Louis, ed., *Records of Early English Drama: Sussex*, maintains the standards of meticulous scholarship and engaging content which have characterized the series so far. As usual with a REED volume, the transcribed extracts from the documents themselves are surrounded with exemplary critical apparatus and introductory material. The 'Historical Background' section describes the geography and history of the county, and its political and administrative structure and religious culture, before moving on to provide brief descriptions of each major town or centre of dramatic activity. 'Drama, Music, and Seasonal

Customs' examines the dramatic culture in greater detail, tackling the sometimes vexed issues of travelling players, their routes and repertoires, and the playing places for drama in the county. 'The Documents' describes the range and nature of the archives and sources upon which the volume is built. A brief bibliography and six maps complete the prefatory material. The records themselves, although not as copious or verbose as in some REED volumes, do contain some gems, such as the text of the 'honourable entertainment given to the Queen [Elizabeth I]' at Cowdray House in 1591, a passport for a musician from the port of Rye, some reports from bailiffs sent to Great Yarmouth for the Herring Fair in the mid-seventeenth century, and an account of a fatal dispute over a maypole from Worbleton in 1572. As usual, Abigail Ann Young has done a magnificent job on the translations from the Latin. Other appendices include, *inter alia*, a list of the patrons and companies mentioned in the text, Latin and English glossaries, and a comprehensive index.

Overlapping in some respects with the REED volumes, although taking an overview from the political and metropolitan centre rather than providing a detailed study of particular regions, is Wickham, Berry and Ingram, eds., *English Professional Theatre, 1530–1660*, as part of the Theatre in Europe: A Documentary History series from CUP. The volume prints extracts, often very brief, from documentary sources, illustrating, reign by reign, the attempts by Tudor and early Stuart sovereigns to regulate the drama, along with (in the two following sections) accounts of plays and players, and records of the professional theatres in London. The highly selective nature of the documents chosen and excerpted, and the somewhat limited range of secondary material cited (especially for the earlier periods) means that the 'history' presented here is rather more teleological than most recent scholarship would accept. Readers in search of a compendium of documentary records might find some of the material gathered here of value, but given the high price of the book (£90), they might be wiser to await publication of the fuller texts in the REED London volumes.

There are two major additions to the corpus of edited texts to report this year. The two surviving plays from Coventry, the Shearmen and Tailors' pageant and the Weavers' pageant, have been freshly edited by Pamela King and Clifford Davidson in *The Coventry Corpus Christi Plays* for the Early English Drama, Art, and Music series from MIP. The two plays are printed without *en face* critical material, the textual notes and commentaries being presented in separate sections at the end of the volume. This makes for a clear, readable text, although the lack of at-a-glance assistance might slow the progress of readers not fully at ease with Middle English, or those keen to follow up immediately every nuance of sense or allusion. Appendices print fragments from an earlier text of the Weavers' pageant, records relating to royal entries into Coventry, the texts of the songs from the Shearmen and Tailors' pageant (reproduced from JoAnna Dutka's *Music in the English Mystery Plays* (MIP [1980]), and a comparison of the Christ and the Doctors sections from the Weavers pageant with the corresponding sections of other surviving cycles. The arrival of this new edition will, one hopes, permit the Coventry plays to be taught more regularly in undergraduate programmes once more.

While considering teaching materials, I must also note the appearance of a new and comprehensive anthology of medieval and early Renaissance dramatic texts designed for classroom use: Walker, ed., *Medieval Drama: An Anthology*. The volume's chief claim to the attention of readers and teachers of drama will be that all the plays printed are presented complete, rather than in extracts or abbreviated form. The anthology contains nineteen pageants from the cycle drama, chiefly from York, but supplemented by the Chester *Fall of Lucifer*, *Adam and Eve*, and *Shepherds' Play*, the Towneley *Second Shepherds' Play*, and the N-Town *Mary Play*, accompanied by extracts from the York *Ordo Paginarum*, the 1433 Mercers' Indenture, and the anonymous *Treatise of Miraclis Pleyinge*, with the post-Reformation Banns from Chester and Matthew Hutton's letter of 1567 to the mayor and council of York. Full texts of the Croxton *Play of the Sacrament*, *Wisdom*, *Mankind*, *Everyman*, Medwall's *Fulgens and Lucres*, Skelton's *Magnyfycence*, the anonymous *Enterlude of Godly Queene Hester*, John Heywood's *The Four PP* and *Play of the Weather*, John Bale's *John Baptystes Preachynge* and *The Three Laws*, and Sir David Lindsay's *Ane Satyre of the Thrie Estatis* are also printed, along with the prose description of the 1540 interlude version of Lindsay's play. The plays are divided into three sections—'Religious Narrative: The Biblical Plays', 'Religion and Conscience: The Moral Plays', and 'Politics and Morality: The Interludes'—each with its own brief introduction to the genre and the issues it raises. There are foot-of-the-page glosses and explanatory notes throughout the text, and a list of textual variants and a Glossary of Common Hard Words at the end of the volume.

Books Reviewed

Adams, Robert, and Hoyt Duggan, Eric Eliasson, Ralph Hanna III, John Price-Wilken and Thorlac Turville-Petre, eds. *The Piers Plowman Electronic Archive*, vol. I: *Corpus Christi College, Oxford MS 201 (F)*. UMichP. [2000] CD-ROM. $65 ISBN 0 4720 0275 9.

Adams, Robert, and Hoyt Duggan, Eric Eliasson, Ralph Hanna III, John Price-Wilken and Thorlac Turville-Petre, eds. *The Piers Plowman Electronic Archive*, vol. II: *Cambridge, Trinity College, MS B.15.17 (W)*. UMichP. [2000] CD-ROM. $65 ISBN 0 4720 0303 8.

Aers, David, ed. *Medieval Literature and Historical Inquiry: Essays in Honour of Derek Pearsall*. Brewer. [2000] pp. xv + 212. $75 ISBN 0 8599 1555 7.

Astell, Ann. *Political Allegory in Late Medieval England*. CornUP. [1999] pp. xii + 218. $37.50 ISBN 0 8014 3560 9.

Baker, Denise N., ed. *Inscribing the Hundred Years' War in French and English Cultures*. SUNY. [2000] pp. x + 277. $69.50 ISBN 0 7914 4701 4.

Baker-Smith, Dominic, *More's Utopia*. UTorP. [2000] pp. ix + 268. pb £14 ($21.95) ISBN 0 8020 8376 5.

Barrell, A.D.M. *Medieval Scotland*. CUP. [2000] pp. xiii + 298. hb £37.50 ISBN 0 5215 8443 4, pb £13.95 ISBN 0 5215 8602 X.

Biddle, Martin, ed. *King Arthur's Round Table: An Archaeological Investigation*. Boydell. [2000] pp. xxxvi + 534. £75 ISBN 0 8511 5626 6.

Blanch, Robert J. *The Gawain Poems: A Reference Guide, 1978–1993*. Whitston. [2000] pp. xi + 334. ISBN 0 8787 5525 X.

Blanks, David R., and Michael Frassetto, eds. *Western Views of Islam in Medieval and Early Modern Europe: Perception of Other*. St Martin's Press. [1999] pp. viii + 230. £40.84 ($49.95) ISBN 0 3122 1891 5.

Boitani, Pierre, and Anna Torti, eds. *The Body and the Soul in Medieval Literature.* J.A.W. Bennett Memorial Lectures, 10th series. Rodopi. [1999] pp. xi + 211. £40 $75 ISBN 0 8599 1545 X.

Bullón-Fernández, María. *Fathers and Daughters in Gower's 'Confessio Amantis': Authority, Family, State, and Writing.* Publications of the John Gower Society 5. Brewer. [2000] pp. viii + 242. £50 ISBN 0 8599 1578 6.

Burke, Mary E., Jane Donawerth, Linda L. Dove, and Karen Nelson, eds. *Women, Writing, and the Reproduction of Culture in Tudor and Stuart Britain.* SyracuseUP. [2000] pp. xxx + 306. pb $29.95 ISBN 0 8156 2815 3.

Busby, Keith, and Catherine M. Jones, eds. *'Por Le Soie Amiste': Essays in Honor of Norris J. Lacy.* Rodopi. [2000] pp. xxxiv + 552. £80 ($102) ISBN 9 0420 0620 X.

Bynum, Caroline Walker, and Paul H. Freedman, eds. *Last Things: Death and the Apocalypse in the Middle Ages.* UPennP. [2000] pp. viii + 363. £35 ($49.95) ISBN 0 8122 3512 6.

Castleden, Rodney. *King Arthur: The Truth Behind the Legend.* Routledge. [2000] pp. xiv + 265. £25 ISBN 0 4151 9575 6.

Chamberlin, John. *Medieval Arts Doctrines on Ambiguity and their Place in Langland's Poetics.* McG-QUP. [2000] pp. xii + 185. $65 ISBN 0 7735 2073 2.

Cohen, Jeffrey Jerome, ed. *Of Giants: Sex, Monsters, and the Middle Ages.* Medieval Cultures, 17. UMinnP. [1999] pp. xx + 195. hb £33.50 ($52.95) ISBN 0 8166 3216 2, pb £13 ($18.95) ISBN 0 8166 3217 0.

Cohen, Jeffrey Jerome, ed. *The Postcolonial Middle Ages.* St Martin's Press. [2000] pp. 286. $45 ISBN 0 3122 1929 6.

Collins, Hugh E.L. *The Order of the Garter, 1348–1461: Chivalry and Politics in Late Medieval England.* Oxford Historical Monographs. OUP. [2000] pp. xi + 327. £45 ISBN 0 1982 0817 0.

Cooper, W.R., ed. *The New Testament, 1526, Translated by William Tyndale.* BL. [2000] pp. xvii + 558. £15 ISBN 0 7123 4664 3.

Cox, John D. *The Devil and the Sacred in English Drama, 1350–1642.* CUP. [2000] pp. x + 257. £35 ISBN 0 5217 9090 5.

Dalrymple, Roger. *Language and Piety in Middle English Romance.* Brewer. [2000] pp. x + 270. £45 ($70) ISBN 0 8599 1598 0.

D'Arcy, Anne Marie. *Wisdom and the Grail.* FCP. [2000] pp. 412. £45 ($65) ISBN 1 8518 2496 0.

Davis, Nick. *Stories of Chaos: Reason and its Displacement in Early Modern English Narrative.* Ashgate. [1998] pp. ix + 195. £45 ISBN 0 8401 4649 4.

Douglas, Mary. *Leviticus as Literature* [1998] OUP. [2000] pp. xvi + 280. pb £14.99 ISBN 0 1992 4419 7.

Dragstra, Henk, Sheila Ottway and Helen Wilcox, eds. *Betraying Our Selves: Forms of Self-Representation in Early Modern English Texts.* Macmillan. [2000] pp. x + 226. £45 ISBN 0 3337 4029 7.

Duncan, Thomas Gibson, ed. *Late Medieval English Lyrics and Carols, 1400–1530.* Penguin. [2000] pp. lx + 275. pb £8.99 ISBN 0 1404 3566 2.

Edden, Valerie. *The Index of Middle English Prose Handlist XV: Manuscripts in Midland Libraries.* The Index of Middle English Prose. B&B. [2000] pp. xxvi + 112. £30 ISBN 0 8599 1587 5.

Edwards, A.S.G., Vincent Gillespie and Ralph Hanna, eds. *The English Medieval Book: Studies in Memory of Jeremy Griffiths*. BL. [2000] pp. xii + 264. £45 ($75) ISBN 0 7123 4650 3.

Emery, Anthony, *Greater Medieval Houses of England and Wales*, ii: *East Anglia, Central England, and Wales*. CUP. [2000] pp. xiii + 724. £124 ISBN 0 5215 8131 1.

Fein, Susanna, ed. *Studies in the Harley Manuscript: The Scribes, Contents, and Social Contexts of* British Library *MS Harley 2253*. MIP. [2000] pp. xvi + 515. $40 ISBN 1 5804 4060 6.

Ferber, Michael. *A Dictionary of Literary Symbols*. CUP. [2000] pp. x + 263. £40 ISBN 0 5215 9128 7.

Forest-Hill, Lynn. *Transgressive Language in Medieval English Drama: Signs of Challenge and Change*. Ashgate. [2000] pp. viii + 215. £39.95 ISBN 0 7546 0086 6.

Fox, Adam. *Oral and Literate Culture in England, 1500–1700*. Oxford Studies in Social History. OUP. [2000] pp. xiii + 497. £45 ISBN 0 1982 0512 0.

French, Peter A. and Howard K. Wettstein, eds. *New Directions in Philosophy*. Midwest Studies in Philosophy XXIII. Blackwell. [1999] pp. 340. £40 ($70.95) ISBN 0 6312 1593 X.

Gower, John. *Confessio Amantis*, vol. i, ed. Russell A. Peck. TEAMS Middle English Texts. MIP. [2000] pp. xii + 368. $20 ISBN 1 5804 4057 6.

Grantley, Darryll. *Wit's Pilgrimage: Drama and the Social Impact of Education in Early Modern England*. Ashgate. [2000] pp. 270. £40 ISBN 0 7546 0167 6.

Green, Ian. *Print and Protestantism in Early Modern England*. OUP. [2000] pp. xxiii + 691. £65 ISBN 0 1982 0860 X.

Green, Richard Firth. *A Crisis of Truth: Literature and Law in Ricardian England*. UPennP. [1999] pp. xvi + 496. $65 ISBN 0 8122 3463 4.

Guy, John. *Politics, Law, and Counsel in Tudor and Early Stuart England*. Ashgate. [2000] pp. xv + 336. £55. ISBN 0 8607 8832 6.

Hanks, D. Thomas Jr, and Jessica Gentry Brogdon. *The Social and Literary Contexts of Malory's 'Morte Darthur'*, Arthurian Studies 42. Brewer. [2000] pp. xii + 157. £35 ($60) ISBN 0 8599 1594 8.

Hartle, Paul. *Hunting the Letter: Middle English Alliterative Verse and the Formulaic Theory*. Lang. [1999] pp. 466. £43 ISBN 3 6313 3776 0.

Herzman, Ronald B., Graham Drake and Eve Salisbury, eds. *Four Romances of England: King Horn, Havelok the Dane, Bevis of Hampton, Athelston*. TEAMS Middle English Texts. MIP. [1999] pp. viii + 392. $20 ISBN 1 5804 4017 7.

Jones, Michael, ed. *The New Cambridge Medieval History*, vol. vi: *c.1300-c.1415*. CUP. [2000] pp. xxx + 1110. £80 ISBN 0 5123 6290 3.

Kaeuper, Richard W. *Chivalry and Violence in Medieval Europe*. OUP. [1999] pp. xi + 338. hb £42.50 ($55) ISBN 0 1982 0730 1, pb £14.99 ($21.95) ISBN 0 1992 4458 8.

Kim, Hyonjin. *The Knight Without the Sword: A Social Landscape of Malorian Chivalry*. Arthurian Studies 45. Brewer. [2000] pp. 155. £35 ($60) ISBN 0 8599 1603 0.

King, Andrew. *'The Faerie Queene' and Middle English Romance: The Matter of Just Memory*. Clarendon. [2000] pp. xiv + 246. £40 ISBN 0 1981 8722 X.

King, Pamela, and Clifford Davidson, eds. *The Coventry Corpus Christi Plays*. MIP.
[2000] pp. xii + 326. hb $35 ISBN 1 59044 055 X, pb $15 ISBN 1 5804 4056 8.

Kraemer, Alfred Robert. *Malory's Grail Seekers and Fifteenth-Century English
Hagiography*. Studies in the Humanities: Literature—Politics—Society, 44.
Lang. [2000] pp. x + 129. £25 ($40.95) ISBN 0 8204 4123 6.

Krueger, Roberta L., ed. *The Cambridge Companion to Medieval Romance*. CUP.
[2000] pp. xx + 290. £37.50 ISBN 0 5215 5342 3.

Louis, Cameron, ed. *Records of Early English Drama: Sussex*. Brepols/UTorP.
[2000] pp. cx + 403. €150 ISBN 0 8020 4849 8 (UTorP), ISBN 2 5035 0905 3
(Brepols).

Mayer, Thomas F. *Reginald Pole: Prince and Prophet*. CUP. [2000] pp. xv + 468.
£50 ISBN 0 5213 7188 0.

Mahoney, Dhira, ed. *The Grail: A Casebook*. Arthurian Characters and Themes 5.
Garland. [2000] pp. xi + 590. £47.50 ($80) ISBN 0 8153 0648 2.

McGrath, A.E. *Reformation Thought: An Introduction*, 3rd edn. Blackwell. [1999]
pp. xii + 329. pb £16.99 ISBN 0 6312 1521 2.

Menuge, Noël James, ed. *Medieval Women and the Law*. B&B. [2000] pp. xii + 169.
£40 ISBN 0 8511 5775 0.

Merriman, R.B., ed. *Life and Letters of Thomas Cromwell* [1st pub.1902]. Oxford
Scholarly Classics. OUP. [2000] 2 vols. pp. viii + 442 and ii + 356. £95 ISBN 0
1982 2305 6.

Metham, John. *Amoryus and Cleopes*, ed. Stephen F. Page. TEAMS Middle English
Texts. MIP. [1999] pp. viii + 144. $11 ISBN 1 5804 4016 9.

Millar, Bonnie. *The Siege of Jerusalem in its Physical, Literary and Historical
Contexts*. FCP. [2000] pp. 251. £45 ISBN 1 8518 2506 1.

Morey, James H. *Book and Verse: A Guide to Middle English Biblical Literature*.
UIIP. [2000] pp. xix + 432. $34.95 ISBN 0 2520 2507 5.

Muscatine, Charles. *Medieval Literature, Style, and Culture: Essays by Charles
Muscatine*. USCP. [1999] pp. ix + 252. £35.95 ($39.95) ISBN 1 5700 3249 1.

O'Donnell, Anne M., SND, and Jared Wicks SJ, eds. *The Independent Works of
William Tyndale*, vol. iii: *An Answere Unto Sir Thomas More's Dialoge*. CUAP.
[2000] pp. xlix + 496. £59.95 ISBN 0 8132 0820 3.

Ogilvie-Thomson, S.J. *The Index of Middle English Prose Handlist XVI:
Manuscripts in the Laudian Collection, Bodleian Library, Oxford*. The Index of
Middle English Prose. B&B. [2000] pp. xxii + 142. £35 ISBN 0 8599 1595 6.

Oldridge, Darren. *The Devil in Early Modern England*. Sutton. [2000] pp. viii + 216.
£20 ISBN 0 7509 2092 0.

O'Sullivan, Orlaith, ed. *The Bible as Book*, vol iii: *The Reformation*. BL/OakK.
[2000] pp. x + 182. £40 ISBN 0 7123 4675 9 (BL), ISBN 1 5845 6025 8 (OakK).

Palliser, D.M., ed. *The Cambridge Urban History of Britain*, vol i: *600–1540*. CUP.
[2000] pp. xxvi + 841. £90 ISBN 0 5214 4461 6.

Parkinson, David J., ed. *Alexander Montgomerie: Poems*, vols. 28, 29. Scottish Text
Society. 4th series. [2000] pp. xviii + 303, vii + 369. £30 ISBN 1 8979 7615 1,
ISBN 1 8979 7616 X.

Pearsall, Derek, ed. *Chaucer to Spenser: A Critical Reader*. Blackwell. [1999] pp.
xviii + 327. £55 ($70.95) ISBN 0 6311 9936 5.

Pearsall, Derek, ed. *New Directions in Later Medieval Manuscript Studies*. Boydell.
[2000] pp. xv + 213. £50 ($90) ISBN 1 9031 5301 8.

Peters, Julie Stone, *Theatre of the Book, 1480–1880: Print, Text, and Performance in Europe*. OUP. [2000] pp. xi + 494. £60 ISBN 0 1981 8714 9.

Powell, Susan, and Jeremy J. Smith, eds. *New Perspectives on Middle English Texts: A Festschrift for R.A. Waldron*. B&B. [2000] pp. xi + 190. £45 ISBN 0 8599 1590 5.

Putter, Ad, and Jane Gilbert, eds. *The Spirit of Medieval English Popular Romance*. Longman. [2000] pp. viii + 304. hb £60 ISBN 0 5822 9880 6, pb £19.99 ISBN 0 5822 9888 1.

Renevey, Denis, and Christiania Whitehead, eds. *Writing Religious Women: Female Spiritual and Textual Practices in Late Medieval England*. UWalesP. [2000] pp. xi + 270. hb £30 ISBN 0 7083 1642 5, pb £14.99 ISBN 0 7083 1641 7.

Riches, Samantha. *St. George: Hero, Martyr, and Myth*. Sutton. [2000] pp. xvii + 236. £20 ISBN 0 7509 2452 7.

Riddy, Felicity, ed. *Prestige, Authority and Power in Late Medieval Manuscripts and Texts*. York Manuscripts Conferences: Proceedings Series 4. Boydell. [2000] pp. viii + 200. £50 ($90) ISBN 0 9529 7346 4.

Roye, William. *A Brefe Dialoge Bitwene a Christen Father and his Stobborne Sonne*, ed. Douglas H. Parker and Bruce Krajewski. UTorP. [1999] pp. 305. £40 ($60) ISBN 0 8020 4389 5.

Rydzeski, Justine. *Radical Nostalgia in the Age of 'Piers Plowman': Economics, Apocalypticism, and Discontent*. Lang. [1999] pp. 172. £26 ($42.95) ISBN 0 8204 4273 9.

Scattergood, John. *The Lost Tradition: Essays on Middle English Alliterative Poetry*. FCP. [2000] pp. 253. £45 ISBN 1 8518 2565 7.

Silk, M.S. *Aristophanes and the Definition of Comedy*. OUP. [2000] pp. 456. £50 ISBN 0 1981 4029 0.

Skeat, W.W. *Parallel Extracts from Forty-Five Manuscripts of Piers Plowman, with Notes upon their Relation to the Society's B-text Edition of this Poem* [1905]. EETS os 17, repr. B&B. [2000] pp. 34. £15 ($24.95) ISBN 0 8599 1807 6.

Skeat, W.W. *The Vision of William concerning Piers Plowman; together with the Vita de Dowel, Dobet, et Dobest, secundum Wil et Resoun* [1867]. EETS os 28, repr. B&B. [2000] pp. xliii + 158. £25 ($39.95) ISBN 0 8599 1815 7.

Snyder, Christopher. *Exploring the World of King Arthur*. T&H. [2000] pp. 192. £17.95 ISBN 0 5000 5104 6.

Stow, John, *A Survey of London*, ed. C.L. Kingsford [1st pub. 1908]. Oxford Scholarly Classics. OUP. [2000] 2 vols. pp. viii + 352 and ii + 476. £95 ISBN 0 1982 1257 7.

Summit, Jennifer. *Lost Property: The Woman Writer and English Literary History, 1380–1589*. UChicP. [2000] pp. x + 274. hb £28.50 ISBN 0 2267 8012 0, pb £11.50 ISBN 0 2267 8013 9.

Svogun, Margaret duMais. *Reading Romance: Literacy, Psychology, and Malory's 'Le Morte Darthur'*. Studies in the Humanities: Literature—Politics—Society 51. Lang. [2000] pp. 144. £29 ($45.95) ISBN 0 8204 4522 3.

Tops, Guy A.J., Betty Devriendt and Steven Geukins, eds. *Thinking English Grammar: To Honour Xavier Dekeyser, Professor Emeritus*. Peeters. [1999] pp. xxvi + 508. €45 ISBN 9 0429 0763 0.

Treharne, Elaine, ed. *Old and Middle English: An Anthology*. Blackwell. [2000] pp. xxvii + 622. £16.99 ISBN 0 6312 0466 0.

Waite, Gary K, *Reformers on Stage: Popular Drama and Religious Propaganda in the Low Countries of Charles V, 1515–1556*. UTorP. [2000] pp. xxiii + 364. $75 ISBN 0 8020 4457 3.

Walker, Greg, ed. *Medieval Drama: An Anthology*. Blackwell. [2000] pp. xvi + 630. hb £65 ISBN 0 6312 1726 6, pb £17.99 ISBN 0 6312 1727 4.

Wallace, David, ed. *The Cambridge History of Medieval English Literature*. CUP. [1999] pp. xxv + 1043. £75 ISBN 0 5214 4420 9.

Warren, Michelle R. *History on the Edge: Excalibur and the Borders of Britain, 1100–1300*. Medieval Cultures 22. UMinnP. [2000] pp. xiv + 302. $34.95 ISBN 0 8166 3491 2.

Watson, Andrew G. *A Descriptive Catalogue of the Medieval Manuscripts of Exeter College Oxford*. pp. xxviii + 150. OUP. [2000] £60 ISBN 0 1992 0192 7.

Weiss, Judith, ed. and trans. *Wace's Roman de Brut: A History of the British: Text and Translation*. UExe. [1999] pp. xxx + 386. pb £16.99 ISBN 0 8598 9591 2.

Weiss, Judith, Jennifer Fellows and Morgan Dickson, eds. *Medieval Insular Romance: Translation and Innovation*. Brewer. [2000] pp. xii + 196. £40 ISBN 0 8599 1597 2.

Wheatley, Edward. *Mastering Aesop: Medieval Education, Chaucer, and his Followers*. UFlorP. [2000] pp. ix + 278. $55 ISBN 0 8130 1745 9.

Wheeler, Bonnie, Robert L. Kindrick and Michael Norman Salda, eds. *The Malory Debate: Essays on the Texts of Le Morte Darthur*. Arthurian Studies 47. Brewer. [2000] pp. xxxii + 420. £45.95 ($75) ISBN 0 8599 1583 2.

Wickham, Glynne, Herbert Berry and William Ingram, eds. *English Professional Theatre, 1530–1660*. CUP. [2000] pp. xlvi + 714. £90 ISBN 0 5212 3012 8.

Williams, Janet Hadley, ed. *Sir David Lyndsay: Selected Poems*. Association for Scottish Literary Studies 30. [2000] pp. xxvi + 339. hb $25 ISBN 0 9488 7744 8, pb $12.50 ISBN 0 9488 7746 4.

Wogan-Browne, Jocelyn, et al., eds. *Medieval Women: Texts and Contexts in Late Medieval Britain. Essays for Felicity Riddy*. Medieval Women: Texts and Contexts 3. Brepols. [2000] pp. xv + 436. €50 ISBN 2 5035 0979 7.

Wooding, Lucy E.C. *Rethinking Catholicism in Reformation England*. Oxford Historical Monographs. OUP. [2000] pp. x + 305. £40 ISBN 0 1982 0865 0.

Woolfson, Jonathon. *Padua and the Tudors: English Students in Italy, 1485–1603*. UTorP. [1998] pp. xii + 322. $60 ISBN 0 8020 0946 8.

Yamamoto, Dorothy. *The Boundaries of the Human in Medieval English Literature*. OUP. [2000] pp. xi + 257. £45 ISBN 0 1981 8674 6.

Zaerr, Linda Marie. *The Weddynge of Sir Gawen and Dame Ragnell*. Chaucer Studio and TEAMS. [1999] Videotape $20 ISBN 0 8425 2458 4.

IV

Middle English: Chaucer

VALERIE ALLEN AND MARGARET CONNOLLY

This chapter has four sections: 1. General; 2. *Canterbury Tales*; 3. *Troilus and Criseyde*; 4. Other Works. The ordering of individual tales and poems within the sections follows that of the Riverside Chaucer. Acknowledgements are due to Jennifer Brown of the Graduate Center, City University of New York for her editorial assistance.

1. General

Once again Mark Allen and Bege K. Bowers are responsible for co-ordinating the production of 'An Annotated Chaucer Bibliography 1998' (*SAC* 22[2000] 557–649); this invaluable research tool is also available in electronic form via the New Chaucer Society webpage: <http://ncs.rutgers.edu>.

Eschewing the terrain of academic scholarship, 'the jealously guarded preserve of professionals' (p. xii), Richard West contributes a new biography: *Chaucer, 1340–1400: The Life and Times of the First English Poet*. West switches meditatively from textbook details of Chaucer and late fourteenth-century England to the present, from the Peasants' Revolt to modern anti-immigrant murders in south-east London. A lot of background filler goes into the early chapters—Roman Britain and the prestige of Latin; Henry II and Thomas à Becket; Eleanor of Aquitaine, the patron of Chrétien de Troyes, and Arthurian romance; Edward III and the Hundred Years War—with Chaucer mentioned incidentally. Where Chaucer is mentioned in more detail, a lot of space is inevitably devoted to summary of plots and (modernized) quotations; this much, however, is to be expected. While West's study does not offer anything new by way of literary or historical interpretation (although it is true I had never thought about the *Former Age* as a diatribe on the mining industry), it isn't supposed to and it is readable. Much of the picture drawn of Chaucer is very traditional (not too interested in the details of theology or politics, liberal, easy-going, a bit sentimental, and so forth), but chapters on the merchant culture and the Jewish question, for example, address implicitly questions that we 'professionals' have more recently been asking of Chaucer's work.

John H. Pratt contributes a monograph about *Chaucer and War*. The topic is rich and promising, but the book too often supplies unremarkable detail at the expense of nuanced and overarching argument for it to live up to the promise. Pratt's main thesis is that, while Chaucer was certainly not a dove, neither was he a hawk; rather, he understood as a realist that war was a constant threat and for many a way of life, and his writing is militaristic enough to demonstrate a working familiarity with much of the business of war. Interest seems too often turned upon factual minutiae rather than upon an analysis of the connections between literature and history: in a chapter on metaphors of war, for example, the discussion degenerates into how and when Chaucer might have experienced cannon fire, because his description of it in the *House of Fame* is too detailed to have been borrowed. In another chapter, over twenty pages of rather aimless book-by-book commentary on *Troilus and Criseyde* preface Pratt's interpretation, namely, that Chaucer's version of the Troy story contains a warning to his friend, Nicholas Bembre, the mayor of London, who liked to style London as the 'second Troy' (and himself as the duke of it): just as the first Troy fell for giving away Criseyde so the second will fall if Calais is exchanged for peace with France. The tentativeness of the interpretations goes beyond judicious caution to irritating lack of committal: 'Chaucer may have intended', 'he might intend ... but he could also intend', 'he could be referring' and 'he might have meant' bedevil every page where the discussion seems to be drawing towards a conclusion. The central figure in Pratt's analysis is the Knight, who features largely along with his tale. His list of battles is examined in detail, and Terry Jones's character assassination of the Knight is countered point for point. The Knight is portrayed in a sympathetic light, human enough to tell an overly long tale and recognize that his audience is fidgeting, devout without being saintly, a realist and a survivor just like Theseus and, as Pratt suggests, just like Chaucer.

Two of the four or five chapters that deal specifically with Chaucer in Paul Strohm's *Theory and the Premodern Text* have seen the light earlier (*YWES* 75[1996] 171) (*YWES* 76[1997] 194). Strohm's introduction sets up a consideration of subject–object relations between the ideologically loaded questions we ask about a text and the text itself. Strohm seeks a balance between them, and his opening chapter, which looks closely at the semiotic topography of Chaucer's walk through London (that is, the incident Chaucer recounts when testifying at the Scrope–Grosvenor trial), seems to promise to deliver the goods. In both Chaucer's progress through the city and his testimony at the trial Strohm sees the poet acting out a gentility that he only tenuously lays claim to. In chapter 5 Strohm distinguishes in the *General Prologue* the 'slow time' inhabited by the seemingly timeless Plowman and Parson from the 'fast time' of newly emergent social mobility with which the Friar has allied himself. Into this picture of mannered fraternal presentism enters the leper, and the chapter unfolds into an intriguing account of how the historical and cultural resonances in this stray reference in the Friar's portrait problematize his trendy modernity and question his values. Bringing the same fast/slow-time distinction to bear also upon the languishing (slow-time) Troilus and the chop-chop Pandarus, Strohm moves from there to consider the 'modernity' or otherwise of the poem and of Chaucer, the elements of contradiction and anachronism in both. Strohm wears his scholarship elegantly, and the book brings together the combined skills of historical analysis and literary criticism.

Hugh White's monograph on *Nature, Sex, and Goodness in a Medieval Literary Tradition* examines the moral status of the natural in medieval literature. White argues that the influence of nature is not always benign, and that this is particularly true in the sphere of love. The book's scope is broad, covering the writings of Alan of Lille, Jean de Meun, Gower, and Chaucer. Although only one chapter is devoted to Chaucer, White manages to discuss the dream visions, *Troilus and Criseyde*, and several of the *Canterbury Tales*, notably the tales told by the Squire, Manciple, Physician, and Parson, and the *Tale of Melibee*. White suggests that Chaucer, following Boethius, initially equates the bond of love with natural order, but finds it impossible to sustain a positive affirmation of the natural. Accordingly Chaucer rewrites the Boethian concept of nature (from the *Consolation of Philosophy*, book III, metrum 2) in a negative way, inviting his readers to view the force of nature sceptically.

In *Mastering Aesop: Medieval Education, Chaucer, and his Followers*, Edward Wheatley suggests that the curricular fables encountered by Chaucer, Lydgate, and Henryson in the schoolroom had an impact on the fable narratives later produced by each writer. Though coverage of Chaucer is necessarily restricted to the *Nun's Priest's Tale*, readers will find much of use in the first part of the book where Wheatley offers a detailed examination of the scholastic fable tradition, focusing on the popular elegiac Romulus collection of sixty verse fables; an overview of the literary-critical classical and medieval texts that determined the fable's medieval reception and use; and a survey of the commentary tradition and pedagogic practices associated with fable in the later Middle Ages.

Addressing an issue that has as much to do with epistemology as it has with language, John J. McGavin writes about *Chaucer and Dissimilarity: Literary Comparison in Chaucer and Other Late-Medieval Writing*. Dominating medieval epistemology is the assumption that knowledge is a recognition of similitude, while the requirement that 'wordis moot be cosines to the thinges of whiche thei speken' is the standard by which all acts of naming and communication are judged. Chaucer, argues McGavin, is fascinated with the dissimilarity inherent in all claims for similarity, with the capacity for all communicative acts to misrepresent, and with how one's name becomes not only an appellation but also an evaluative reputation. Centring his discussion in his first chapter in *Boece* and the rhetorico-grammatical devices of comparison, McGavin distinguishes between *imago*, *similitudo*, and *exemplum*, where the first denotes a fairly strict likeness, the second approximates to our modern understanding of simile, and the third, least attended to by the author in this book, offers the freest mode of aligning identities. McGavin's business in the rest of the book is to look at the ways in which Chaucer introduces dissimilarity, often by means of irony or inappropriateness, into his devices of comparison. Unusual and frequently comic comparisons abound in the *Canterbury Tales*, although McGavin's main interest is in the more philosophically laden comparisons, for example, those in *Troilus and Criseyde*, where Pandarus's persuasive (mis)comparisons reveal deep errors of belief. McGavin reads Chaucer not as a deconstructively endless deferrer of truth but rather as one who, although believing the truth to be 'out there', is burdened by the need for semantic consensus, for capturing the *mot juste* 'ryght as hit ys'.

In *Chaucer at Large: The Poet in the Modern Imagination*, Steve Ellis asks what Chaucer actually means to a non-academic modernity. Beginning with the late nineteenth-century Kelmscott Chaucer edition, Ellis notes that amid all the seeming Romanticism of its illustrations there is a keen awareness of Chaucer reworking his classical and European heritage. Expanding on thoughts articulated in an essay from last year in Boydell & Brewer's Studies in Medievalism series (see below), Ellis remarks on W.B. Yeats's early but short-lived interest in Chaucer. In children's editions of Chaucer, we find a poet who exudes bonhomie and innocence, and exists in a world curiously free of social and political tensions (and fabliaux!). No surprise, we might think, though Ellis's point is to note the growing divergence between academic and popular perceptions of the poet—a divergence also apparent in scholarly disdain for translations and dramatizations of Chaucer's works. Chaucer's Englishness, very much a nineteenth-century sentiment, nonetheless also informs twentieth-century cultural myths, particularly wartime ones, where minor historical details such as the Hundred Years War and Chaucer's imprisonment at the hands of the French are conveniently forgotten. In comparison to Dante, Chaucer's influence upon twentieth-century writers is 'fairly thin', with James Joyce amongst the modernists providing the best parallel to Chaucer, for both writers rejoice in a multiplicity of voice and perspective. The contents of the chapters, while providing some points of interest, are fairly disconnected from one another, resulting in an overall sense of bittiness and absence of dominant argument. Ellis's conclusions about Chaucer's role in contemporary culture can be summed up as an oxymoronic 'repeated presence' and 'fundamental neglect'.

We note in passing the general importance of Helen Cooney's edition of scholarly essays developed from a conference, *Nation, Court and Culture: New Essays on Fifteenth-Century English Poetry*. Although the period treated of is post-Chaucerian, it is inevitable that the legacy of Chaucer, his co-opting in the service of a construction of English national identity, the anxiety of his literary influence, and his depiction as poet-father figure throughout the essays, of which John J. Thompson's 'Thomas Hoccleve and Manuscript Culture' (pp. 81–94) deals most closely with Chaucer, in this case with the circulation of his manuscripts.

Reissued again this year in honour of the 600th anniversary of the death of Chaucer is Derek Brewer's *The World of Chaucer* (first published as *Chaucer and his World* [1978, reissued 1992]; see *YWES* 59[1980] 105 and 73[1994] 151). The current reissue has fundamentally the same text as the earlier versions, but the original illustrations are restored.

Foremost amongst this year's collections of essays is Peter Brown's offering of *A Companion to Chaucer*. For a companion this is a rather unwieldy tome, weighing in at over 500 pages, so it is not destined to become a vade mecum. Nevertheless, it is cunningly contrived to appeal to the broadest market ('we are all students', p. 2), and because so much of its material is relevant not just to the study of Chaucer but to all of medieval literature, this reviewer predicts that the volume will rapidly become a staple of undergraduate reading lists. Brown has assembled twenty-nine contributors, all of whom offer original contributions—a fact that is itself refreshing, given the amount of reprinting current in the field of Chaucer studies. The individual contributors and chapters are too numerous to list here, but some idea of the scope of the volume's coverage will be gleaned from a sample of its wares: Carolyn Collette's chapter on 'Afterlife' makes an unusual beginning, and the next two sections, 'Authority' (Andrew Galloway) and 'Bodies' (Linda Ehrsam Voigts) perhaps give the impression that the volume will have a more conceptual bent than it actually does. Familiar topoi include 'Chivalry' (Derek Brewer), 'Comedy' (Laura Kendrick), 'Language' (David Burnley), and 'Love' (Helen Phillips); more unusual perhaps are the chapters entitled 'Games' (Malcolm Andrew), and

'London' (Michael Hanrahan); and some, such as 'Other Thought-Worlds' (Susanna Fein), and 'Visualizing' (Sarah Stanbury), positively invite investigation. The chapters aim to strike a balance between textual analysis and cultural context. They are not all the same, but they do all follow the same formula, offering an account of existing scholarship in the given area and a discussion of the key issues, which are then applied to two or three specific passages from Chaucer's works. Frequent subheadings signpost the distinct sections, and each contribution ends with an annotated bibliography. Sequentially this structure can become rather enervating, but since the *Companion* is really designed for browsing this need not be a problem. A brief overview of Chaucer is given by J. Smith (in Benoit-Dusausoy and Fontaine, eds., *History of European Literature*, pp. 142–6). Here Smith situates Chaucer in transition between the Middle Ages and the Renaissance, thoroughly a product of the Gothic past, yet also steeped in the literature of the early European Renaissance. With his combination of private imagination and public service, Chaucer bears all the marks of the 'great humanists' (p. 143).

The collection of thirteen essays in Pearsall, ed., *New Directions in Later Medieval Manuscript Studies: Essays from the 1998 Harvard Conference*, contains much reference to Chaucer, which is scarcely surprising given that the study of Chaucer's manuscripts has been better served than any other branch of manuscript studies, and in particular has been treated in recent years to the most innovative approaches and applications of computerized technology. Three of the contributions deal fairly centrally with Chaucer. In 'A New Approach to the Witnesses and Text of the *Canterbury Tales*', Norman Blake offers a brief history of the editing of the *Canterbury Tales* since the nineteenth century, including a short critique of the work of John M. Manly and Edith Rickert, before lucidly outlining the aims and objectives of the Canterbury Tales Project. He stresses that the project's main emphasis is on text, and that all witnesses are treated equally, and is careful to correct a possible misapprehension, stating that 'it is not the project's aim, as some have assumed, to establish the text as it left Chaucer's pen'; he also touches upon the wider potential of the project for the study of metre and fifteenth-century English. Martha Driver's essay, 'Medieval Manuscripts and Electronic Media: Observations on Future Possibilities', examines the recent 'blizzard of publicity' about the *Canterbury Tales* generated by the project (p. 60), stemming from the detection of possible parallels between the way in which manuscripts and DNA evolve. Her discussion focuses on the use of the internet and CD-ROM as one new direction that is already being taken, but interestingly both she and Blake conclude that the 'newe science' of technology cannot replace traditional forms of manuscript study or textual criticism. Finally, in 'After Chaucer: Resituating Middle English Poetry in the Late Medieval and Early Modern Period', John J. Thompson concentrates on Lydgate and Hoccleve, perhaps best known for their activities in constructing Chaucer's posthumous reputation. Surprisingly Thompson accuses them of actually contributing to the 'decommissioning' of Chaucer's verse, and of participating in the dismantling of the hard textual evidence of his poetry, pointing out that, though Lydgate claims to include Chaucer's *ABC* in the *Pilgrimage of the Life of Man*, no manuscript actually demonstrates this, and that similarly Hoccleve's direction that the *Regiment of Princes* should contain Chaucer's portrait and be followed by certain of Chaucer's poems is not realized in many of the extant manuscripts.

Cohen, ed., *The Postcolonial Middle Ages*, contains two contributions that focus directly on Chaucer. In the first, 'Chaucer after Smithfield: From Postcolonial Writer to Imperialist Author', John M. Bowers paints Chaucer as 'a decoloniser of Anglo-Norman culture' and claims that the *Canterbury Tales* may be seen as an example of his 'newly aggressive Englishness' (p. 55). Noting some strategies that Chaucer rejected, such as participation in the alliterative revival (surely never an option for the poet?), Bowers scans the *Canterbury Tales* for evidence of the development of an English tradition intended to challenge the long-standing dominance of French cultural models. The Yeoman, though silent, is taken as Chaucer's most Saxon creation, the *Franklin's Tale* as a demonstration of support for an independent Celtic homeland, and the *Man of Law's Tale* as a reminder of the existence of the ancient kingdom of Northumbria. Bowers further notes, albeit very briefly, that the literary products of this emerging English tradition were eagerly appropriated by the early fifteenth-century Lancastrian regime. In a second essay in this volume, 'Postcolonial Chaucer and the Virtual Jew', Sylvia Tomasch argues that, despite the expulsion of 1290, the idea of the Jew and his alterity remained central to English religious devotion and national identity. Detailing various English artistic representations of the Jew in works such as the Holkham Bible Picture Book and the Luttrell Psalter, she notes that Chaucer makes frequent allusion to Jews in the *Canterbury Tales*, and that these references are not confined to the *Prioress's Tale*. Tomasch takes the Old Man of the *Pardoner's Tale* as a personification of the Jew, and argues that, in the tales of the Parson and the Monk, well-known Old Testament figures are systematically dissociated from ideas of Jewishness and even from their own bodies. Chaucer may thus be seen as a participant in the ongoing allosemitic production of the figure of the virtual Jew, employed as a negative exemplum in the postcolonial construction of good society.

Studies in Medievalism has produced two volumes entitled 'Medievalism and the Academy', one published this and the other last year. In the first, Workman, Verduin, and Metzger, eds., *Medievalism and the Academy I* [1999], a section entitled 'Canonizing Chaucer' introduces three essays. 'Speaking to Chaucer: The Poet and the Nineteenth-Century Academy', by David Matthews, offers a genealogy of the rise of Chaucer studies. Matthews focuses on the Hoccleve portrait of Chaucer, which formed the frontispiece in many nineteenth-century editions. Hoccleve's own text, which the Chaucer portrait adorns, seems to have disappeared from the reproductions, which now tellingly detach the poet from his literary and social context. The preferment of the Hoccleve portrait over, say, the Ellesmere picture of Chaucer as pilgrim is guided by a desire to celebrate a Chaucer full of moral gravity than Canterbury jocularity. Next, Steve Ellis turns to the twentieth century, in 'Popular Chaucer and the Academy'. Chaucer's appeal shifts from being the stuff of philological scholarship in the previous century to that of popular poet, and a concomitant shift occurs towards a growing acceptance of his bawdy tales; the role played by Nevill Coghill in this respect is duly acknowledged. Ellis also ponders on the way in which Chaucer got ignored by the modernists in favour of Dante, suggesting that it was motivated by a cosmopolitan disaffection for Chaucer's perceived native Englishness (though Dante can hardly be exempted from chauvinism). The third essay comes from Antonia Ward, who speaks of '"My love for Chaucer": F.J. Furnivall and Homosociality in the Chaucer Society'. Ward gives a brief biography of this 'eccentric teetotal vegetarian proto-feminist', and questions the line between his real-life liking for the female sex and his manly 'love for Chaucer'. Furnivall sought a homosocial bond not only between his contemporaneous (male) readers of Chaucer but also between present and past, and this nineteenth-century homosociality has developed into the 'covert masculinism of the university system' today. Where, asks Ward, does this leave female/feminist critics now as readers of Chaucer?

Essays on Chaucer feature in a number of the Festschrifts that have appeared this year. Wright and Holloway, eds., *Tales within Tales: Apuleius through Time*, is a collection of thirteen essays in honour of Richard J. Schoeck. Unusually Schoeck himself was asked to contribute to the volume, and his brief essay is one of three that focus on Chaucer. Schoeck muses on the idea of play in 'Chaucer and Huizinga: The Spirit of *Homo Ludens*', claiming that a multi-faceted sense of play may be encountered in Chaucer's works. He identifies three such aspects (related to war or hunting, love, and life) and considers these briefly in relation to *Troilus and Criseyde*; attention to the *Canterbury Tales* would have provided him with more scope. The other two Chaucerian contributions come from the editors. Julia Bolton Holloway's essay, 'The Asse to the Harpe: Boethian Music in Chaucer', explores Chaucer's use of the rhetorical and iconographic topos of the harp-playing ass, concentrating mostly on *Troilus and Criseyde*. She argues, somewhat repetitively, that Troilus is like the beast who hears but does not heed the harp of philosophy, and that Pandarus corresponds to the ass who plays the harp, since he distorts the Boethian text he quotes. Constance S. Wright's essay tracing 'The Metamorphoses of Cupid and Psyche in Plato, Apuleius, Origen, and Chaucer', touches briefly on the *Clerk's Tale*, where she finds Griselda to be a Psyche-like figure, but has to admit that the likeness is only shadowy.

More than half of the fourteen essays in Hill and Sinnreich-Levi, eds., *The Rhetorical Poetics of the Middle Ages: Reconstructive Polyphony*, relate to Chaucer. John Hill's introduction surveys the Chaucer scholarship of the collection's dedicatee, Robert O. Payne, as well as introducing the contents of the present volume, and several of the contributors take Payne's work on medieval rhetoric and poetics, published or otherwise, as a point of departure. The first four Chaucerian essays focus on the dream visions. In 'Chaucer: Beginnings', Charles W. Owen notes Chaucer's propensity for starting but not finishing works, and argues that the *Book of the Duchess*, though written at the beginning of Chaucer's career, shows the same confidence and maturity that can be found in the poet's later works. Mary Carruthers reconsiders several familiar features of this poem in '"The Mystery of the Bed Chamber": Mnemotechnique and Vision in Chaucer's *The Book of the Duchess*', suggesting that aspects such as the narrator's initial anxiety, the dream vision, and the bedchamber scene need to be viewed within the context of popular rhetorical practices and conventions, especially those which provide a procedural model for literary composition. She further argues that the *Book of the Duchess* is a memory poem, requiring memory-work from all involved. Joel Feimer offers a close reading of the *Legend of Good Women* based on the medieval mythographical tradition, in 'Chaucer's Selective "Remembraunce": Ironies of "Fyn Loving" and the Ideal Feminine'; he concentrates in particular on the figures of Cleopatra, Thisbe, and Lucretia, whose idealized portraits he finds to be infused with a radical anti-feminism. In 'The Interior Decoration of his Mind: Exegesis in *The House of Fame*', Ellen E. Martin remembers that Payne labelled the work as a 'busted poem', and attempts to explain what she thinks he meant by this. Switching focus to the *Canterbury Tales*, and other types of 'busted' poems, Martin Stevens ponders 'Chaucer's "Bad Art": The Interrupted Tales'. He argues that the interrupted stories of *Sir Thopas* and the Monk provide an index to Chaucer's self-conscious art: *Sir Thopas* allows a glimpse into the deep structure of the *Canterbury Tales*, and the *Monk's Tale* highlights in negative fashion the qualities needed in a successful story collection. The less clear-cut case of an interrupted tale, that of the Squire, is dealt with in a more cursory fashion. William McClellan focuses on another of the *Canterbury Tales* in '"Me thynketh it a thyng impertinent": Inaugurating Dialogic Discourse in the Prologue to the *Clerk's Tale*', using Bakhtin's theory of dialogic discourse to elucidate an interpretation of the prologue, and offering in conclusion a clear summary of what the prologue achieves. In 'Ockham, Chaucer, and the Emergence of Modern Poetics', Burt Kimmelman seeks to situate Chaucer within the sphere of the nominalist controversy of the late fourteenth century by paying particular attention to the *Legend of Good Women*. And in the last Chaucerian contribution, 'The Alba Lady, Sex-Roles, and Social Roles: "Who peyntede the leon, tel me who?"', Gale Sigal considers Chaucer's construction of sexual roles in *Troilus and Criseyde*. She argues against the position of Robert Kaske, who believed that Chaucer reversed the sexual roles allowed in alba poetry; instead Sigal contends that alba poets favoured a much less rigid conception of sex-roles than do modern critics, and suggests that Chaucer used the conventions of this poetry to highlight the very real differences between the characters of Troilus and Criseyde.

Dorothy Yamamoto meditates upon *The Boundaries of the Human in Medieval English Literature*, in which Chaucer figures throughout the discussion. These boundaries are often unstable, as is evident in the *Knight's Tale*, where the animal element ranges widely, from the noble to the base. Emetrius's white eagle, a creature that does not actually exist, is a heraldic device, representing Emetrius as a ruler, like Theseus, over men and nature. On the other hand, Arcite and Palamon, in particular in the scene in the grove, are both hunter and hunted; they stand 'at the gappe' between humanity and animality and are therefore threatening and must be mastered. Insubordinate peasants similarly threaten by their ambiguous relation to the bestial. In the *Parliament of Fowls* and elsewhere, birds tend to represent an idealized world, being more aerial in nature. Yamamoto's survey is fairly general, her aim being to show how animals (including birds) are re-imagined to comment on social relations.

Another Festschrift, this time for R.A. Waldron—Powell and Smith, eds., *New Perspectives on Middle English Text*—contains two essays on the *Canterbury Tales* (for which see the *Canterbury Tales* section below) and one on Henryson's *Testament of Cresseid*, noted in the *Troilus* section below. Similarly the Festschrift for Felicity Riddy, *Medieval Women: Texts and Contexts in Late Medieval Britain*, edited by Jocelyn Wogan-Browne and five others, contains three essays that focus on Chaucer. The two that deal with *Troilus* are dealt with in that section; the third is more general and is noted here. Carolyn P. Collette offers a piece on the literary topos of the good wife, 'Chaucer and the French Tradition Revisited: Philippe de Mézières and the Good Wife', arguing that Chaucer was influenced by the popular French genre of advice books for and about wives. Collette looks in detail at one such work, *Le Livre de la vertu du sacrement de mariage*, by Philippe de Mézières, and traces resonances to Chaucer's stories of Prudence and Melibee, St Cecilia, and

Griselda in the *Canterbury Tales*, claiming—rightly—that although much attention has been paid to Chaucer's women, this particular line of influence has so far been largely overlooked.

Sheila Fisher uses Chaucer as one of three examples in her survey of 'Women and Men in Late Medieval English Romance' (in Krueger, ed., *The Cambridge Companion to Medieval Romance*, pp. 150–64). Taking Chauntecleer's misinterpretation of the Latin proverb *Mulier est hominis confusio* as her starting point, she argues that a typical male strategy for coping with the confusion of women is to trivialize and dismiss them. Though this is clearly the case in the *Knight's Tale*, it is perhaps less so in the *Wife of Bath's Tale* than Fisher would like to believe, and her argument is not wholly convincing when applied to Criseyde either. Christopher Cannon returns to a vexed question in 'Chaucer and Rape: Uncertainty's Certainties' (*SAC* 22[2000] 67–92), exploring different possible definitions of *raptus*, and considering issues of sexual consent in the *Reeve's Tale* and *Troilus and Criseyde*. He also draws an illuminating connection between the Cecily Chaumpaigne case and Chaucer's incorporation of the life of St Cecilia in the *Legend of Good Women* and subsequently in the *Canterbury Tales*, suggesting that the writing of this legend may have been an attempt at poetic reparation. The Chaumpaigne case is also discussed by Louise Sylvester in 'Reading Rape in Medieval Literature' (in Metzger, ed., *Medievalism and the Academy II: Cultural Studies*, pp. 120–35). Sylvester mentions Cannon's studies in the footnotes, but does not address his arguments in the body of the essay. She declines to draw any firm conclusion on the meaning of *raptus* in the Chaucer case, observing merely that the term doesn't mean that Chaucer *didn't* force Cecily to have sex with him.

There is a surprising amount of passing reference to Chaucer throughout Fein, ed., *Studies in the Harley Manuscript: The Scribes, Contents, and Social Contexts of British Library MS Harley 2253*, despite the fact that the manuscript in question significantly pre-dates Chaucer's time. The fullest prefiguring of Chaucer's poetry comes in the editor's own contribution, 'A Saint "Geynest under Gore": Marina and the Love Lyrics of the Seventh Quire'. Chaucerians will also find some interesting snippets relating to the tales of the Prioress and the Friar in Henry Ansgar Kelly's extensive study of prostitution and fishmongering, 'Bishop, Prioress, and Bawd in the Stews of Southwark' (*Speculum* 75[2000] 342–88). And for fragments of a different kind see Ralph Hanna's study of 'Humphrey Newton and Bodleian Library, MS Lat. misc. c.66' (*MÆ* 69[2000] 279–91); Hanna notes that this manuscript contains two tiny extracts from the *Canterbury Tales*, lines 3047–56 of the *Knight's Tale* and the *Parson's Tale* I.601–29. Another advance in the field of manuscript study is offered by S.C.P. Horobin, who seeks to identify 'The Scribe of the Helmingham and Northumberland Manuscripts of the Canterbury Tales' (*Neophil* 84[2000] 457–65), by subjecting both manuscripts to palaeographical and linguistic analyses. Although he finds linguistic variations between the two, he explains these as the result of increased standardization in the fifteenth century and concludes that the two copies of the *Canterbury Tales* were produced by the same hand.

Lawrence M. Clopper's essay 'The Engaged Spectator: Langland and Chaucer on Civic Spectacle and the *Theatrum*' (*SAC* 22[2000] 115–39), contrasts the two authors' representations of urban and royal spectacle, a phenomenon frowned upon by clerics. Clopper notes the interesting fact that Chaucer was Clerk of the Works and supervisor for the building of the lists at Smithfield for tournaments in 1390, and relates this to the presentation of the tournament in the *Knight's Tale*. He finds this rewriting of the episode from Boccaccio's *Teseida* to be a celebration of urban and noble culture, but one infused with an inappropriate worldliness, so that the royal spectacle becomes tainted by *theatrum*. He also judges that Chaucer would have known the traditions associated with the ancient *theatrum*, but that he did not expect his audience to share this familiarity.

Two slightly overlapping studies of Chaucer's metrics appear this year, both identifying the source of Chaucer's line as a version of the Italian *endecasillabo*. In a very technical essay, '"The craft so long to lerne": Chaucer's Invention of the Iambic Pentameter' (*ChauR* 34[2000] 269–88), Martin J. Duffell offers a qualitative analysis of decasyllable types to demonstrate that Chaucer followed the Italian model rather than the French *vers dix*, thus producing iambic pentameter. In 'Water from the Well: The Reception of Chaucer's Metric' (*Parergon* 17[2000] 51–73), Peter Groves surveys the haphazard transmission of this unfamiliar form by Chaucer's fifteenth-century successors, and also considers how Chaucer's metrics have been variously received since, from the ignorance of the Elizabethans to what he terms the 'bizarreries' of modern editors such as F.N. Robinson (p. 73).

In 'Infantilizing the Father: Chaucer Translations and Moral Regulation' (*SAC* 22[2000] 93–114), David Matthews surveys nineteenth- and early twentieth-century translations of Chaucer's poetry and discovers that the construction of Chaucer as a moral teacher is achieved by belittling both poet and audience. He notes the many simplified versions of Chaucer's works that were produced for children between 1870 and 1940, such as the collections edited by Charles Cowden Clarke and Mary Haweis, from which the bawdier material was usually excised; he then considers their successors, the 'adults-only' translations of Nevill Coghill and Vincent Hopper. In conclusion he identifies the present-day anxiety surrounding the reading of Chaucer as one that is not concerned with morality, but with whether Chaucer will continue to be read at all. Peter Robinson is also concerned with readers in 'Ma(r)king the electronic text: how, why and for whom?' (in Bray, Handley and Henry, eds., *Ma(r)king the Text*, pp. 309–28). He first explains the background of the Text Encoding Initiative and examines the particular challenges posed to encoders by the essentially non-textual manuscript page. Acknowledging the fear that his edition of *The Wife of Bath's Prologue on CD-ROM* might turn out to be 'an evolutionary freak' (p. 316), he outlines other challenges to the continued development of electronic editions, and concludes that future editions need to appeal to a much wider range of less specialized Chaucer readers; that copyright objections need to be overcome; and that the academic world needs to concentrate less on theoretical readings of Chaucer and more on textual contexts.

2. Canterbury Tales

The *Canterbury Tales* can now be bought separately from the complete Riverside Chaucer, in a move that is presumably driven by the twin forces of exclusive curricular focus on the Canterbury poem and the prohibitive cost of the complete Riverside edition. While the edition is convenient and welcome, it is to be hoped that its advent does not drive Chaucer's other works even further into the shade. The edition is explicit in its aim to be more undergraduate-friendly: where the actual text remains as it is in the Riverside edition, the critical apparatus has been updated and expanded; foreign passages are translated; difficult Middle English has been regularized or translated; and many contemporary references are quoted in full rather than merely cited. The prefatory material largely follows its predecessor, with some changes: the essay on Chaucer's canon and chronology has been replaced with a visually accessible time chart, and grammatical tables now make clearer the sections on his language. Although its review is cursory and in no way attempts any explanation of individual theories, the section on critical approaches brings us beyond 1985, the usual cut-off date for the Riverside's bibliography, to include some comments on feminist and new historicist interpretations. By its own admission, the edition loses much by way of scholarly substructure, but the usefulness of including actual contemporary quotes is not to be underestimated, and makes the notes considerably more readable whether one is an undergraduate or not. In the end, the updating of the critical approaches has less impact than the expansion of contemporary analogous material, which is one of the edition's prime advantages.

An Introduction to the Canterbury Tales: Reading, Fiction, Context is supplied by Helen Phillips. The Chaucer who emerges from her opening chapter is an attractive enough figure, of diverse perspectives, whose verse is as theatrical and visual as it is euphonic; to illustrate, her point of departure is the BBC's and HBO's 1998 animated film of the *Tales*. Phillips moves through an impressive amount of material in these pages, from the political crises of Richard's reign to a shorter history of twentieth-century Chaucer criticism. The layout of the book follows the sequence of tales as given in the Riverside edition, with one chapter devoted to each tale. The chapters do more than review relevant historical or literary contexts, such as anticlerical controversies or estates satire, and dominant critical opinions; they also interpret, for Phillips expounds and synthesizes themes as she goes along. Her analysis is admirably even-handed, but her own critical preferences, while inevitably apparent to the initiated reader, could have been more explicitly stated for the newcomer without compromise to the quality of her review. For example, the chapter on the Pardoner highlights the importance of the sermon tradition and downplays the more recent focus on his sexuality; similarly, the moral, religious, and literary elements of the *Miller's Tale* are foregrounded while the tale's connection with the Peasants' Revolt remains largely undeveloped. More of Phillips's own interpretative voice in the text would not have gone amiss. This said, the volume offers a thorough and thoughtful introduction to the Canterbury poem— with footnotes that are judiciously sparing.

Combining Caroline Spurgeon's *Five Hundred Years of Chaucer Criticism* and the bibliographical annotations of the Variorum series into one compendium, Jodi-Anne George has contributed to the series of Columbia Critical Guides a volume on *Geoffrey Chaucer: The General Prologue to the Canterbury Tales*. Six chapters divide the scope of criticism: 1368–1880; 1892–1949; the 1950s and 1960s; the 1970s; the 1980s; and the 1990s. George is listed as an editor rather than author, because a substantial percentage of the text comprises long quotes from other critics, with connecting comments made by her. Although the first chapter covers the early period of criticism, George quite rightly points out that very few comments from this period were specifically directed towards the *Prologue*, and her quotes all come from modern critics writing about the history of criticism in debate about such issues as Chaucer's Englishness and his naturalism. Chapter 2 sees the beginning of literary-critical interest taking over from the stranglehold that editorial and philological matters then held over Chaucer scholarship. The Donaldson–Robertson debate is predictably featured in chapter 3. It is the last three chapters that are puzzling in the selection of representative critical voices, and the difficulty seems to come from a tendency to equate certain critical positions with certain decades, which, given the welter of 'isms' in the last thirty years, is a questionable decision. Sociological concerns are seen to dominate the 1970s; textual and theoretical the 1980s; and most curious and tendentious of all is the choice to reserve criticism of the 1990s exclusively for feminist and gender theory. It invites the reader to perceive gender theory as the latest flavour in Chaucer scholarship and it gives disproportionate emphasis in the chapter to the Wife of Bath and the Pardoner, who has already received quite enough attention this year (see below).

Two books exclusively on the Pardoner appear this year, one a bibliography, the other Robert S. Sturges's *Chaucer's Pardoner and Gender Theory: Bodies of Discourse*. It is impossible, as Sturges says early on, to write on such a subject without addressing the two linked questions of homosexuality as constructivist or essentialist and of the sense in which we might speak of the Pardoner as homosexual. Drawing on feminist, gay, and psychoanalytic theory, Sturges allies himself more with the constructivist position and, as a consequence, with an unfixed and many-angled reading of the pilgrim. Rather than weighing up the pros and cons of whether the Pardoner is homosexual, sodomite, catamite, eunuch, or whatever, Sturges presents him as a sign of gender confusion itself, as a discretely seditious troublemaker across sexual boundaries. Curiously negative in identity, the nearest we can get to him is 'not-masculine', and any attempt to distinguish between the 'facts' of his (sexual) profile and either medieval or modern 'interpretations' of them breaks down. One chapter, on the Pardoner's vernicle, is a version of an earlier essay. In his singing, the Pardoner associates himself with the Kristevan semiotic and hence with the pre-linguistic, with the very limits of grammar as rational discourse, and with performance rather than fixed utterance. In his preoccupation with body parts and dismemberment, the Pardoner is feminized and recalls the mutilated body of Orpheus, a figure whose own dismemberment nonetheless enacts a higher restoration to phallic wholeness. Lastly, Sturges's sexualization of the fragmentary is extended to consider the unfinished state of the Canterbury poem. His book-length discussion represents in many ways the culmination of the many single essays by other authors on the Pardoner, a figure who over the last twenty years has become a crucial signifier in gender criticism, and who has been made to stand, rightly or wrongly, for 'troubling gender ambiguity'. The Chaucer Bibliographies series adds the sixth to its growing list of publications—Sutton, ed., *Chaucer's 'Pardoner's Prologue' and 'Tale': An Annotated Bibliography, 1900–1995*. The introduction is a useful essay in itself, synthesizing scholarship and areas of critical interest in this tale. Of all the pilgrims, the Pardoner is one of the ones most integrated into the poem, for apart from his portrait in the *General Prologue*, his own prologue and his tale, he also interrupts the Wife of Bath elsewhere, is called on by the Host to speak after the *Physician's Tale*, and has an altercation with the Host after his own tale. Although critical interest in the Pardoner has increased sharply owing to the currency of gender theory (witness Sturges's contribution this year), it is clear from Sutton's overview that he has had enduring appeal for as long as there has been Chaucer criticism, and the evidence of the manuscripts, eight of which anthologize the tale alone, attests to the tale's early popularity. Although there has long been interest in the Pardoner's literary and generic affiliations, such as his poetic forebear Faus Semblant of the *Roman de la Rose* and his (ab)use of the sermon tradition, recent emphases centre upon a subjectivity that is grounded in penitential discourse and a skilful manipulation of rhetoric. From the 1960s onwards, Sutton observes, psychoanalytic readings of the Pardoner move to the fore, and issues of gender mark the 1980s onwards. Old as it is, Walter Clyde Curry's remarkable reading of the Pardoner as a *eunuchus ex nativitate* still shapes current categories of gender analysis. Sutton's annotations to the bibliographical lists are thorough, and make the book an invaluable aid to any scholar working on this complex pilgrim.

It is indeed welcome to see the *Parson's Tale* merit its own anthology of essays, for over the last decade especially it has provoked some important thinking about the Canterbury scheme. Raybin and Holley, eds., *Closure in 'The Canterbury Tales':* *The Role of The Parson's Tale*, brings together essays that together offer a good overview and some new thoughts about the tale. Siegfried Wenzel kicks off with a review piece, 'The Parson's Tale in Current Literary Studies', noting that its main appeal has tended to be critical and interpretative rather than textual and philological. Acknowledging the critical contribution to the tale made by Charles Owen, Wenzel nonetheless plumps for the other side, namely, that it *was* Chaucer's intention to close his poem with a tale from the Parson, and that that tale as we have it belonged to the Canterbury poem by design. David Raybin, in '"Many been the weyes": The Flower, its Roots, and the Ending of the *Canterbury Tales*', sees no real discrepancy between the physicality of the opening of the *General Prologue* and the Parson's sermon as ending. In just the same way that Chaucer seems to exhibit more interest in the pilgrimage journey than in the arrival at the shrine, so the *Parson's Tale* exhibits an awareness of sin and suffering, in all their manifold aspects, as the lot of humanity rather than just as the occasion for penance. Richard Newhauser gives consideration to 'The Parson's Tale and its Generic Affiliations'. The penitential manual from which Chaucer takes his material is Raymond of Pennaforte's *Summa de paenitentia*, although Newhauser's interest lies in vernacular analogues, of which Heinrich of Langenstein's Middle High German *Erchantnuzz der Sund* offers the closest equivalent. Where Heinrich of Langenstein's manual represents a more schematic reworking of Raymond's *Summa*, Chaucer's shows a vigorousness of imagery that goes beyond its source, and hints at the aesthetic qualities of the tale as literature. Indeed, the *Parson's Tale* can be seen to play a significant role in the development of the Canterbury poem's literary subjectivity. From his work on the Variorum edition of the *Parson's Tale*, yet to be published, Daniel J. Ransom writes a 'Prolegomenon to a Print History of the Parson's Tale: The Novelty and Legacy of Wynkyn de Worde's Text'. Wynkyn de Worde's 1498 printing shows itself to be derived from a manuscript of superior quality, and Ransom argues that MS Cambridge Gg 4.27 is, of all the extant manuscripts, closest to this early printed edition. Peggy Knapp takes a sociolinguistic look at 'The Words of the Parson's "Vertuous Sentence"', in particular, *glose*, *lewed*, *estat*, and *fre*. What, she asks, can be surmised from them about the Parson? Do they, and he, sniff of Lollardy? Not really, she answers, although the line between devoutly orthodox reformers and Wycliffites is probably fine. The Parson, who in his actual sermon significantly avoids the volatile term *glose*, emerges as 'an uncompromising reformer' but yet also as a 'preacher of familiar doctrine'. Where critics have very often assumed that in the Parson's sermon Chaucer throws off the literary mask, Judith Ferster argues to the contrary, in 'Chaucer's Parson and the "Idiosyncrasies of Fiction"'. In a sense she revisits the project of earlier critics to establish an appropriateness between teller and tale, only here with a postmodern sense of the radical textuality of the pilgrim voice rather than with a sense of the performance of a pre-existing character. While the Parson reproduces the rhetoric of his source, he also demonstrates his 'aggressive translating' by making sex out to be thoroughly nasty instead of pleasurable in a sanctioned, chaste way. He also thumps out the obligations of penitence at the expense of its ecclesiastical competitor, pilgrimage. By this individuation of the clerical voice, the voice of Chaucer in the *Retraction* sounds quite distinctly, and we are left with no final voice of authority, or at least, if we are, it belongs to God.

Subjectivity comes even further to the fore in Gregory Roper's 'Dropping the Personae and Reforming the Self: The Parson's Tale and the End of *The Canterbury Tales*'. Roper observes how the obligation of penance, formalized in the Fourth Lateran Council of 1215, shapes the penitent's sense of self. From lord to villein, the 'event' of confession gets the sinner to construct themselves into a narrativized 'I', and, through the act of telling the story of oneself, to procure a restoration of the wholeness lost through sin. The manuals of confession can almost be understood as medieval self-help books; through the sample portraits of penitence the sinner comes to find his or her own voice. In a similar way, through the voices of the pilgrims, and most particularly that of the Parson, Chaucer comes finally to speak in his own voice through the *Retraction*. Charlotte Gross, in '"The goode wey": Ending and Not-Ending in the Parson's Tale', takes a look at the Augustinian distinction between *expectatio futorum*, the expectation of future things, and *intentio ad superiora*, the (soul's) orientation towards higher things. The former moves the soul forward in linear time while the latter transcends linear temporality to the eternal. The *Parson's Tale* exhibits both kinds of time: penitence constitutes the linear temporal 'wey' of *expectatio*; contemplation orients the *intentio* of the soul to higher things. These two different ways of thinking about time affect the sense of the poem's ending. Although the Canterbury poem ends, in a narrative sense, it does not achieve final closure, for the work of *intentio* remains ongoing. Linda Tarte Holley delivers the 'Epilogue: Closing the Eschatological Account', in which she takes note of the 'dialectic of the spirit' at work in the tale, which negotiates continuously the boundaries between reason and faith. The last piece in the collection is a very useful annotated 'Bibliography of Scholarship Treating the Parson's Tale', compiled by David Raybin, which includes early twentieth- and late nineteenth-century as well as latter-day interpretations.

Laura F. Hodges has brought out a book on *Chaucer and Costume: The Secular Pilgrims in the General Prologue*, from which a couple of chapters appeared earlier as articles: 'Costume Rhetoric in the Knight's Portrait' (*YWES* 76[1997] 181–2) and 'The Wife of Bath's Costumes' (*YWES* 74[1995] 155). Sartorial significance is generated from a number of models, including clothes as spiritual emblem; literary prototypes; pointed omission of clothing; socio-economics of cloth, dye, etc. and sumptuary law. No single system of hermeneutic can be abstracted from Chaucer's diverse use of clothes, so Hodges treats each secular pilgrim on an individual basis, drawing from varying sartorial models as appropriate. The Squire appears more ominous than we usually think, with his finely embroidered clothes carrying associations of pride and lechery, while the Merchant's 'bever hat' and 'mottelee' coat are less flagrantly wealthy than supposed. The omission of any mention of the Sergeant's coif is striking, since it is perhaps the most decisive sign of his privileged legal status. The Miller's economic status could well be substantial and therefore his dress not above his station, but his arms and his heraldic colours of blue and white trick him forth as a comical knight *manqué*. Hodges's analysis is well researched, although her conclusions leave one with a sense of indeterminacy about the portraits' meanings, which swither between the emblematic or allegorical and the realistic. No doubt this is because Chaucer's own method seems equally unsystematic, which prompts one to wonder if there was any 'method' to be found in the first place.

The commonplace assumption that, of the two English poets, it is Langland rather than Chaucer who writes allegory gets thoroughly trounced in another Canterbury monograph appearing this year, Dolores L. Cullen's *Chaucer's Pilgrims: The Allegory*. This is a rather incredible allegorization of Chaucer's poem. The fact that the pilgrims all appear in the evening is the first major clue to their meaning: the pilgrims represent the heavenly bodies of the sky. Gemini, the two brothers, are the Plowman and Parson, the Monk is Leo, the Merchant Sagittarius, the Friar Aries, and so on. The Cook represents Cancer, because the mormel on his shin is cancerous. Furthermore, Cancer has a cluster of stars called Praesepe, which literally means 'cattle stall'. So Roger's 'blankmanger' represents the 'white stall' that makes up Cancer. Generally, Cullen stops short of pursuing the allegorical application to the tales of the pilgrims, although the *Cook's Tale* is an exception, for it turns out to be a beast fable about social governance. 'Praesepe' also means 'beehive', and Perkyn is like a hive full of honey; R*evelour* recalls the furry body of the bee, and this bee fable of government ends with its real ruler, Perkyn's wife, as his 'queen'. Get it? The interpretations are too overly ingenious for me to accept them, but I don't wish to caricature an extensive analysis for which Cullen has done considerable homework. If allegory is your thing, you may want to give this book a try, but *caveat lector*.

In a detailed consideration of 'The Links in the *Canterbury Tales*' (in Powell and Smith, eds., pp. 107–18), Norman Blake questions the unproved assumption that the Canterbury links were subsequent to the tales and that those links, unlike the tales, existed in only one authorial version. Admitting that there may have been more than one authorial version is risky, for it challenges a further assumption that the tales originally circulated in Chaucer's lifetime as free-floating entities, and, worse, it implies that Chaucer may have conceived of various sequences for the tales. On the other hand, it would provide some justification for the variant orderings, and open up the 'stranglehold' that the Hengwrt vs. Ellesmere dilemma has had on the Canterbury canon, making the study of the early manuscripts, if more complicated, certainly more exciting. Codicological matters are also addressed by Susan Crane in 'Duxworth Redux: The Paris Manuscript of the *Canterbury Tales*' (in Boenig and Davis, eds., *Manuscript, Narrative, Lexicon: Essays on Literary and Cultural Transmission in Honor of Whitney F. Bolton*, pp. 17–44), who asks whether we have been justified in crediting Jean d'Orléans, comte d'Angoulême, with all the creative editorial decisions of the Paris manuscript of the *Tales* at the expense of its copyist,

John Duxworth, who fares poorly in the comparison as a plodding amanuensis. Critical opinion to date has attributed only the most mechanical of emendations to Duxworth but the literary judgements to d'Angoulême, certainly a renowned scholar. However, Duxworth's changes, argues Crane, are informed by principles of *compilatio*, and undo any easy dichotomy between scribe and editor; nor is there any evidence to show that Duxworth was simply following d'Angoulême's editorial directives. Joel Fredell also considers the shape of Chaucer's poem in 'The Lowly Paraf: Transmitting Manuscript Design in *The Canterbury Tales*' (*SAC* 22[2000] 213–80). Distinctive in its use in late medieval England, the paraf acts as a marker in the text's margin to alert the reader to something important in the narrative, in particular a 'wisdom moment' (ironic or not). Its ubiquity, combined with its absence where one might expect such a marker, has contributed to the paraf's critical invisibility. Yet these humble dividers provide valuable internal evidence in the early manuscripts of the *Canterbury Tales* for the poem's design. In fact, argues Fredell, the evidence of the parafs demonstrates Hengwrt's systematic method of flagging those passages judged to have vital moral sapience. The parafs represent readerly response rather than authorial intent, and it would appear that the Ellesmere compilers followed these internal dividers in Hengwrt with scrupulous fidelity. Fredell provides charts at the end of evidence from ten landmark manuscripts of the *Tales* and their treatment of the parafs in the *Miller's Tale*, the *Wife of Bath's Prologue* and *Tale*, and the *Squire's Tale*. His argument is too dense and complex to do justice to here; one can really only alert the reader to the importance of this essay.

Koff and Shildgen, eds., *The 'Decameron' and the 'Canterbury Tales': New Essays on an Old Question*, is a stimulating collection that offers a timely reassessment of the relationship between these two poems. Although many of the essays discuss different individual tales, the anthology is treated here as a single whole. In his introduction, Koff points out the difficulty of assessing the extent of Boccaccio's influence on Chaucer when that influence went largely unrecognized by Chaucer's own audience. Peter G. Beidler, in 'Just Say Yes, Chaucer Knew the *Decameron*: Or, Bringing in the *Shipman's Tale* Out of Limbo' plays doxographer of the relationship between the *Canterbury Tales* and the *Decameron*, and sorts out the strong from the weak arguments—an analytical act that for some reason he thinks will be deemed 'old-fashioned' by critics interested in critical theory. Beidler suggests that critical resistance to the idea that Chaucer knew Boccaccio's poem stems in part from a reluctance to question either the intrinsic Englishness of the *Tales* or the originality of Chaucer's genius, and from distaste at the Italian's poet's immorality. He argues for Chaucer's knowledge of the poem, and ends by calling the first tale of the *Decameron*'s eighth day a 'hard analogue' to the *Shipman's Tale*—a term Beidler coined earlier (*YWES* 73.181), meaning a text that has 'near-source' status. Karla Taylor considers 'Chaucer's Uncommon Voice', by which term she means the ways in which Chaucer does not comply with the public and 'common' voice of English poet who speaks for all. Rather, Chaucer thinks about his own society from the 'Archimedean' vantage point provided by Italian poetry, most particularly by Boccaccio's ability to write serious modern vernacular poetry independent of court patronage. Where the *Decameron* reconciles the old-blood nobility with the newer urban patriciate, Chaucer's poem, in particular, the *Franklin's Tale*, exhibits a greater scepticism about the possibility that nobility can be assimilated by other social groups, and that the aristocracy will prove accommodating to the new urban and mercantile powers. N.S. Thompson writes about 'Local Histories: Characteristic Worlds in the *Decameron* and the *Canterbury Tales*', by which he means that both poets give literary realism to their narratives by giving them a local setting, by their sharp sense of place, made vivid by dialect. Brenda Deen Schildgen considers the influence of 'Boethius and the Consolation of Literature in Boccaccio's *Decameron* and Chaucer's *Canterbury Tales*'. How to deal with adversity and how suffering can be countenanced by God are the questions that the two poets wrestle with, having Boethius's own consolation of philosophy as one possible answer; Boccaccio's entire work is a remedy to the adversity of the plague, while Chaucer confronts suffering on a smaller scale, in such poems as the *Physician's Tale* and the *Tale of Melibee*. Boccaccio presents literature itself as consolation, diversion, and as a resolution of previous (Augustinian) dichotomies between use and enjoyment. Chaucer, while offering literature as diversion in some stories, poses, particularly in the *Parson's Tale* and *Retraction*, a more problematic relationship between physical and spiritual happiness.

John M. Ganim considers 'Chaucer, Boccaccio, Confession, and Subjectivity', arguing that the so-called modernity of the emergent private subjectivity identified in the two poets is deeply implicated in the discourses of the past. Although not wholly dependent on the sacrament of confession, the self-revelations of both Chaucer's and Boccaccio's characters nonetheless owe much to the penitential. Taking his cue from Michel Foucault's comments on confession in *The History of Sexuality*, Ganim observes how this modern self, rather than breaking free of the constraints of the medieval confessional, is in part constituted by its discourse. In both poets' writings, the characters' self-revelations work in large part to secularize the confessional motif, employing it to literary ends rather than the theological ones employed by Dante and Langland. Linda Georgianna compares 'Anticlericalism in Boccaccio and Chaucer: The Bark and the Bite'. She cautions against an overly schematic binary split between the clerical and the non-clerical. Although Boccaccio seems the more anticlerical, his bark, Georgianna suggests, is worse than his bite, for lay vs. clerical is much less a meaningful opposition in his work than are those based on class. Chaucer, by presenting both the Parson's admirable religious values and those of the most scurrilous of the clerics, offers a more potent kind of anticlerical commentary. Robert W. Hanning focuses on issues of mediation in 'Custance and Ciapelletto in the Middle of it All: Problems of Mediation in the *Man of Law's Tale* and *Decameron* 1.1'. Sacred mediation in the form of confession and intercession gravely compromise truth, while the secular mediations of mercantile exchange (Custance herself is circulated around continuously) prove eminently more efficacious.

James H. McGregor positions Chaucer closer to the post-plague *Decameron* rather than to earlier writers in 'The *Knight's Tale* and *Trecento* Italian Historiography'. Where Dante's *Commedia* synthesizes pagan and Christian history, Boccaccio's *Decameron* largely abandons the schema in favour of nostalgia for the past. In Chaucer's Knight, a figure that emerges from local history, Chaucer strikes a balance between the world of political and moral contingency and the larger providential themes raised in the tale. Robert R. Edwards, in 'Rewriting Menedon's Story: *Decameron* 10.5 and the *Franklin's Tale*', looks at the triangulated relationship between Menedon's story in the *Filocolo*, Chaucer's reworking of it in the *Franklin's Tale*, and Boccaccio's reworking of his own story in the *Decameron*.

Boccaccio urbanizes his original story and transforms traditional social relations, while Chaucer is double-edged, employing urban mercantile forces alongside a romantic nostalgia for the feudal world. Richard Neuse, in 'The Monk's *De casibus*: The Boccaccio Case Reopened', argues for the connection between Chaucer's *Monk's Tale* and Boccaccio's two Latin texts, *De casibus virorum illustrium* and *De claris mulieribus*. Although the anthology is on the *Decameron*, these texts exhibit deep affinities with Boccaccio's longest work in their satiric and rhetorical playfulness. Leonard Michael Koff's 'Imagining Absence: Chaucer's Griselda and Walter *without* Petrarch' is the last essay in the collection, and in it he speculatively but intelligently takes Petrarch out of the equation of literary influence to note the complexity of Chaucer's cultural response to both Boccaccio and Dante. David Wallace rounds off this lengthy collection with an 'Afterword', arguing that Chaucer knew Boccaccio in the same way that Petrarch, who possessed no private copy of the *Commedia*, knew Dante. Overall, this is a volume of substantial quality, and something of a landmark in its area.

Since we are on the subject, two other essays deal with the relationship between the *Decameron* and the *Canterbury Tales*. Robert W. Hanning compares 'The *Decameron* and the *Canterbury Tales*' (in McGregor, ed., *Approaches to Teaching Boccaccio's 'Decameron'*, pp. 103–18). Hanning points out the unavoidability but relative insignificance of the question of Chaucer's knowledge of Boccaccio's poem; it cannot be proven, but it should be evident that Chaucer did know it. Both poets exhibit an interest in systems of mediation, most demonstrably by narrating the stories through the mouths of the dramatis personae. By mediating his own opinions thus, Chaucer displaces criticism from the institutional to the individual. Boccaccio, however, unifies his *brigata* into a commonality of rank and outlook. The second essay is Michaela Paasche Grudin's 'Credulity and the Rhetoric of Heterodoxy: From Averroes to Chaucer' (*ChauR* 35[2000] 204–22), which gives a philosophical context to Chaucer's and Boccaccio's con-artists. Marsilio of Padua's *Defensor pacis*, which owes much to Averroes, provides that context, and in it Marsilio discourses on credulity as an obstacle to the necessary unmasking of myths masquerading as divinely ordained laws. Grudin's attention is devoted as much to Wyclif and Ockham as it is to the two poets; suffice it to say that Chaucer's treatment of credulity in the *Tales* is more satiric, while Boccaccio's in the *Decameron* seems sharper and more systematically pursued.

Taking his cue from the tales of the Shipman, Franklin, Wife of Bath, and Pardoner, Elton D. Higgs analyses 'Temporal and Spiritual Indebtedness in the *Canterbury Tales*' (in Powell and Smith, eds., pp. 151–67), noting how characters repeatedly present themselves as creditors rather debtors, how they ignore humanity's basic condition of indebtedness to God, and how their trickery ultimately only affirms the validity of the obligations that hold individuals and societies together.

Having effectively dispatched the secular pilgrims, Laura F. Hodges moves on to the ecclesiastical, in 'Chaucer's Friar: "Typet" and "Semycope"' (*ChauR* 34[2000] 317–43), giving an intimation, perhaps, of her plans for her next book. His tippet, stuffed with knives and pins, refers to a 'pendant streamer from the hood or arm' or a 'shoulder-cape'. Pendant streamers, by 1387, were no longer à la mode, and would have made the Friar look like a court fool, so Hodges argues that a shoulder-cape is the most appropriate interpretation of the term. The picture drawn is that of an ecclesiastic turned pedlar, preying upon the wives of the parish. The suggestion of duplicity is reinforced by the cloth of the Friar's 'semycope'—double worsted, which, although of middling price range, was often of doubtful quality. 'Semycope', a term perhaps coined by Chaucer, falls improperly short for a friar, just as do his morals. The signs are quite clear, argues Hodges: this is a wolf in wolf's clothing. The size of Alice's hips is the object of Peter G. Beidler's scrutiny in 'Chaucer's Wife of Bath's "Foot-Mantel" and her "Hipes Large"' (*ChauR* 34[2000] 388–97). Well, are they big or aren't they? Probably not, answers Beidler. The term 'foot-mantel', of which Chaucer's is the first recording, seems to be a pair of protective leggings, pulled on from the feet up, and worn loosely around the hips, if the visual evidence of the Ellesmere portraits can be trusted. They would be particularly requisite for a skirted woman sitting astride a horse rather than side-saddle. 'Large' has thus been inaccurately translated as (adjectival) 'enormous', and is more accurately glossed as (adverbial) 'loosely' or 'without restraint'. Given our fondness for imagining Alice as a Big Bertha, Beidler's suggestion might render her more petite than we had hitherto thought.

Clothing and textiles are definitely in this year, and Andrew Breeze continues the fashion by providing 'An Irish Etymology for Chaucer's *Falding* ("Coarse Woolen Cloth")' (*ChauR* 35[2000] 112–14), a fabric that is worn by both the Shipman and the Miller's Nicholas. In view of the flourishing export trade in Irish cloth and cloaks, and a particular boom in the fourteenth century in wool production, Breeze suggests that English *falding* and Welsh *ffaling* are derived from Irish *fallaing*, and that *falding* should be classified as one more Celtic loan-word. In 'Spenser's Squire's Literary History' (in Cheney and Silberman, eds., *Worldmaking Spenser: Explorations in the Early Modern Age*, pp. 45–62), William J. Kennedy traces the influence of Chaucer's Squire on the Squire of Dames, a minor character in books III and IV of *The Faerie Queene*. Rodney Stenning Edgecombe offers *De rerum natura* as possible influence on the spring description in 'Chaucer, Lucretius and the Prologue to *The Canterbury Tales*' (*CML* 20:ii[2000] 61–5). Although Lucretius's work was not known in its entirety in the Middle Ages, parts of it appear to have been circulated in medieval Germany, and Edgecombe also seeks to establish its presence in Italian Trecento writing. Finally, in a provocative piece, Alcuin Blamires puts the boot into any idea we may have cherished that Chaucer was full of love for his fellow man in 'Chaucer the Reactionary: Ideology and the General Prologue to *The Canterbury Tales*' (*RES* 51[2000] 523–39). Worse still, it is the benign and beloved *General Prologue* that Blamires selects to demonstrate his thesis. Of the pilgrims represented, the Knight, Franklin, Plowman, Miller and Reeve approximate most closely to the key players of the Peasants' Revolt of 1381. Chaucer's Knight is carefully insulated from the myriad gripes about bad governance that plagued the governing class; the Franklin on the other hand is well on top of juridical matters. Chaucer tellingly reserves his spiteful allegations of social exploitation for those *below* the gentle classes, most especially for the Reeve, the poem's 'political scapegoat'.

In 'Naturalism and its Discontents in the *Miller's Tale*' (*ELH* 67[2000] 1–44), Mark Miller considers the indelicate matter of exactly what part of her anatomy Alison presented for Absolom to kiss. The anatomic confusion of her 'hole' undercuts the healthy and uncomplicatedly self-evident animal desire or 'naturalism' that seems at least to drive the characters. Desire for and disgust at

Alison's body extend to the disguised fear of a 'closeted homoeroticism' (p. 32), for Absolom's first response is to think he has kissed a (man's) beard. Robert Boenig writes about 'Nicholas's Psaltery' (in Boenig and Davis, eds., pp. 96–110). He describes in detail the depictions of psalteries in various illuminations, although a picture or two would have spoken a thousand words. In contrast to other instruments of sometimes questionable association, the psaltery seems to be most closely identified with positive spiritual values—an ironic choice of instrument, then, for Nicholas. Boenig observes finally that Nicholas's song, the English 'Angelus ad Virginem', is a chromatic piece, while the medieval psaltery is strictly diatonic. In layperson's terms, the psaltery cannot play the sharps and flats of the song, so Nicholas's playing gets increasingly out of tune, just as his bedroom romps come to a sorry end. Peter Brown brings new scatological nuance to the *Miller's Tale* in '"Shot wyndowe" (Miller's Tale, I.3358 and 3695): An Open and Shut Case?' (*MÆ* 69[2000] 96–103). Does the term mean, as the Riverside glosses, a hinged window, or does it mean a sliding sash-window? Brown suggests that what Chaucer envisaged is an inwardly opening wooden shutter. More to the point, *shot* is possibly derived from ME *sheten* 'to expel' or 'to eject' and ME *shiten* 'to shit'. In other words, the window abuts the privy. The toilet humour of the tale thus assumes greater force when we imagine the sweetly perfumed Absolom standing in anticipation outside the loo window.

In 'Some Spellings in Chaucer's *Reeve's Tale*' (*N&Q* 47[2000] 16–18), S.C.P. Horobin suggests that Hengwrt's *heem* for 'home', which has been assumed to be an apparently unhistorical spelling of OE *[ā]* as <*ee*>, is in fact a straightforward development of Old Norse *heim*. This explanation suits the students' northern dialect. Horobin also remarks that the Ellesmere scribe, in a well-intentioned move to northernize the language, analogized from *heem* to spell the unhistorical *geen* for 'gone' and *neen* for 'none'. While the scribe made intelligent emendations, Horobin concludes, he was not fully aware of Chaucer's linguistic nuance.

Treating of one story but three texts—the *Man of Law's Tale*, Gower's *Confessio Amantis*, and Thomas le Chestre's *lai Emaré*—Gail Ashton considers how delicate family relations are mediated through the safety of the romance genre in 'Her Father's Daughter: The Re-Alignment of Father–Daughter Kinship in Three Romance Tales' (*ChauR* 34[2000] 416–27). A daughter is an ambiguous figure, posing both the threat of an incestuous rival to the mother (think of the *Clerk's Tale*) and the promise of perpetuity through provision of a (grand)son. On the surface of Chaucer's tale, as well as the other two, is an orthodox narrative of a submissive and ultimately absent daughter, whose reintegration into the family is concomitant with the production of an heir. Beneath this observance of the status quo of the genre, Ashton argues, Custance's voluntary refusal to identify herself offers a critique of the patriarchal structures of romance.

Edgar S. Laird considers the epistemological divide between practical and theoretical—or, in Alice's terms, between experience and authority—in 'The Astronomer Ptolemy and the Morality of the *Wife of Bath's Prologue*' (*ChauR* 34[2000] 289–99). Theoretical knowledge, properly taught and learned, leads to ethical wisdom, but the Wife's reference to the authority of Ptolemy's *Almagest* is deformed to sanction her extramarital affairs. Is the Wife's revisionist version of monolithic authority really as laudable and empowering as recent critics have found?—asks Laird in conclusion. Continuing the analysis of Alice's status as exegete, Robert Longsworth compares 'The Wife of Bath and the Samaritan Woman' (*ChauR* 34[2000] 372–87), and argues that while she demurs from direct questioning of biblical authority she nonetheless exposes its vulnerability to multiple interpretations. She accommodates rather than confronts such authority. In this exegetical perspicuity, Alice echoes the figure she cites in her *Prologue*, the Woman of Samaria, a figure who for too long laboured under what Alcuin Blamires called Augustine's 'misogynistic' exegesis, but who showed herself as capable a reader of the text as her medieval counterpart Alice. S.H. Rigby, in 'The Wife of Bath, Christine de Pizan, and the Medieval Case for Women' (*ChauR* 35[2000] 133–65), ponders on the often mutually exclusive tendencies in criticism either to modernize the medieval text or to historicize it. Alice, for centuries cast alternatively as medieval feminist and embodiment of medieval anti-feminism, is a good case in point. However, a comparison with Christine de Pizan should show that, while Alice does counter-attack misogynists, she also fails against even Christine's own moral standards of the requisite behaviour for a woman. Rigby proceeds to demonstrate at length the incompatibility between Christine and Alice, and concludes that, in the figure of Alice, Chaucer satirizes the medieval defence of woman. Although Christine and Chaucer may share a similar moral stance, their literary techniques differ hugely. In 'Alice of Bath's Astral Destiny: A Re-Appraisal' (*ChauR* 35[2000] 166–81), John B. Friedman notes the humoural qualities of stellar influence and how they can affect gender. Planets in a given sign can be dry and masculine or moist and feminine, and thus their influence will be felt very differently depending on one's sex. Given the Wife's compatibility with the generic Taurean woman, Chaucer presents her determinism as specious justification for her wilfulness, as a 'study in self-will'. Finally, Kathleen Biddick, in 'The Cut of Genealogy: Pedagogy in the Blood' (*JMEMS* 30[2000] 449–62), makes some rather hard-to-understand connections between Foucauldian genealogy, the racialized 'blood laws' of the Statutes of Kilkenny, and the claims of nobility by action (i.e. pedagogy) over nobility by blood in the Wife's tale. The apparent triumph of pedagogy over blood as celebrated in the hag's discourse on gentility, however, is undercut by the Wife herself.

David Aers's analysis of Griselda as a figure ominously complicit with Walter's tyranny rather than absolutely faithful to divine authority first appeared two years ago (*YWES* 79[2000] 216) and is reprinted this year in his *Faith, Ethics and Church: Writing in England, 1360–1409* (pp. 25–55). Chaucer's relationship with the Italian Trecento is addressed yet again in 'Petrarch, Boccaccio, and Chaucer's *Clerk's Tale*', by John Finlayson (*SP* 97[2000] 255–75). The essay could just as well be entitled 'Severs Redux', for it comprises a revision of Severs's argument back in 1942 (*YWES* 23[1944] 57–9) that Boccaccio had no part to play in Chaucer's representation of the Griselda story, which he inherited from Petrarch. Rather, Finlayson argues, Severs has overlooked many similarities between Boccaccio and the English poet. In particular, Petrarch's moral neutrality on the rights and wrongs of Griselda's case is overturned by Chaucer (and Boccaccio) in vehement sympathy for her.

Two essays published this year in *Medium Ævum* discuss connections between the *Canterbury Tales* and French fabliaux. In the first Roy J. Pearcy suggests links between 'Anglo-Norman Fabliaux and Chaucer's Merchant's Tale' (*MÆ* 69[2000] 227–60). He maintains that, unlike Chaucer's other fabliaux, this tale must have been derived from an insular source, and moreover that this source was probably also the common ancestor of the *Novellino*, a collection of Italian prose *novelle* which shares the pear-tree episode with the *Merchant's Tale*. In the second article, 'From French "Fabliau Manuscripts" and MS Harley 2253 to the *Decameron* and the *Canterbury Tales*' (*MÆ* 69[2000] 261–78), Carter Revard draws comparisons between five manuscript anthologies and the *Canterbury Tales*. He suggests that Chaucer's audience was prepared for his technique of interspersing tales of different generic types within his collection because they were familiar with earlier variegated anthologies such as Harley 2253 where the scribal arrangement of texts was deliberately intertextualizing.

Continuing his research into the post-manuscript era of Chaucer's oeuvre, Joseph A. Dane offers '"Tyl Mercurius house he flye": Early Printed Texts and the Critical Readings of the *Squire's Tale*' (*ChauR* 34[2000] 309–16). Dane's starting point is the idiosyncratic pronouncement of George Nott in 1815 that the *Squire's Tale* was, or at least would have been if finished, 'the noblest specimen of romantic imagination'. Dane argues that Nott's opinion was less bizarre than it appears, precisely because the editorial material and details of format entirely bypass the parodic element of the tale that to us seems so inescapable. That parodic element greatly depends on the belief that the tale is deliberately unfinished, having been terminated by the Franklin, because it is incompetent and boring. However, the early printed editions give evidence to support the assumption that the tale was originally finished, but that the rest of the lines have not been located, and the Franklin's praise therefore reads without irony.

R.D. Eaton is suspicious of the too pat manner in which problems are resolved with the 'Narrative Closure in Chaucer's Franklin's Tale' (*Neophil* 84[2000] 309–21). The contrivance of the happy ending is due to the Franklin, who sets himself up as something of a magician. His intention is to assert the nobility and goodness of human nature, and to identify himself with those values; but Chaucer, his creator, is something more sceptical about the triumph of transcendent love and generosity over sensuality and self-gratifying desire. The *Franklin's Tale* is the tale dealt with in most detail by Michelle Sweeney in her analysis of *Magic in Medieval Romance from Chrétien de Troyes to Geoffrey Chaucer*; given the subject, one would have expected some coverage also of the *Squire's Tale*, but not so. Sweeney also is mistrustful of the pat ending of the tale, only here her misgivings centre upon how moral and narrative resolution is brought about not by magic but by the illusion of magic. Similarly, the darkest truth for Dorigen is that there is no difference between reality and *illusioun*, only the sleight-of-hand laws of men that dictate her behaviour. Where we might usually expect magic in romance to reaffirm the societal, and especially aristocratic, status quo, in this tale we see a disturbing insinuation that even where power is not merited illusion can be used as a means to achieve influence. It is the role that magic plays in romance, namely to promote self-interest, often at the expense of another, that leads Sweeney to depart from Susan Crane's thesis that the insular romances promote communal rather than individual values.

In 'The Sentencing of Virginia in the *Physician's Tale*' (*ChauR* 34[2000] 301–8), Angus Fletcher tackles the Physician's own repudiation of fable in favour of a 'historial' thing, which of course is not to say that history cannot be versified. The clarity of the distinction is clouded in the tale, however, not only through the introduction of explicitly inventive flourishes such as the personification of Nature, but also at the linguistic level, for example, in the ambiguity of the phrase 'maketh this descripcioun', which plays on the 'making' of a *fictum poeticum* and the 'description' of a *res visa*. Chaucer's purpose, argues Fletcher, is to show that no 'sentence' of a text can ever be final and fixed. In a closely similar line of enquiry, Andrew Welsh observes the tensions between fable and 'sentence', or rather between 'Story and Wisdom in Chaucer: *The Physician's Tale* and *The Manciple's Tale*' (in Boenig and Davis, eds., pp. 76–95). Virginia herself incorporates the tensions, being both the story and a moral, a 'walking collection of precepts for young girls'. The *Physician's Tale*, for all its pieties, seems to lack a coherent moral while the *Manciple's Tale* seems to be all moral and no story. Welsh develops his analysis to consider the relation between the 'historial' nature of exemplum and the fable-like aspects of the proverb, between story and its meaning. In Chaucer's two tales, the two have a troubled relationship.

John Burrow's argument for the three-fit rather than two-fit division of *Sir Thopas* (*YWES* 52.118) is revisited by E.A. Jones in '"Loo, lordes myne, heere is a fit!" The Structure of Chaucer's *Sir Thopas*' (*RES* 51[2000] 248–52). Twenty-eight, the number of lines of the final fit, is a perfect number, that is, a number whose value is equal to the sum of its proper divisors. Add to that the decreasing number of stanzas of the three fits in a ratio of 2:1, and you have an invocation of divine order on the chaos of *Thopas*.

Edward E. Foster asks a rather personal question, but fortunately one more addressed to the medieval audience of Chaucer's readers, and therefore unanswerable: 'Has Anyone Here Read *Melibee*?' (*ChauR* 34[2000] 398–409). Contemporary critics are divided over whether fourteenth-century readers actually enjoyed the allegory or flipped over the pages to get to something juicier. Whatever the answer—and readers then were probably as mixed in their reactions as they are now—the thematic importance of the tale cannot be denied: situated in a fragment that abounds with flawed teachers, it forces a convergence or confrontation between secular political order and the individual's spiritual destiny. Foster suspects that just as many of Chaucer's peers as our own preferred to read about the tale than to read it, but sees no diminution in its value for that. Its thematic relevance and moral authority prevail as much by commentary as by direct knowledge.

Studies in the Age of Chaucer (22[2000] 381–440) has a colloquium on the *Monk's Tale*, with various contributors. Stephen Knight, in '"My lord, the Monk"', notes the pilgrim's false claim to lordship as an instance of 'estate false consciousness' (p. 385), which is why the Knight, who interrupts his tale, is his antagonist. Terry Jones follows the same trail when he defends the *Monk's Tale* as an appropriate 'quitting' of the *Knight's Tale* (the Monk of course was invited by the Host to do just so until the Miller butted in). Where Theseus concludes that glory and fame are the only happiness humans can achieve, the Monk's exempla show just what happens to those who do. Ann W. Astell then comments on 'The Monk's Tragical "Seint Edward"'. The reference is not only to Edward the Confessor but also to Edward II, and by association to Richard II. Through the Monk, Chaucer is offering his king a coded warning to clean up his act. In 'The Evolution of *The Monk's Tale*: Tragical to Farcical', Henry Angsar Kelly argues that Chaucer got from Boccaccio's *De casibus virorum illustrium* the idea of writing tragedy as a series of stories, and that by placing the *Monk's Tale* between scenes of humorous dialogue, Chaucer showed his preference for comedy. Richard Neuse, in 'They had their World as in their Time: The Monk's "Little Narratives"', argues that in so far as the Monk's tales subvert thematic unity and temporal grand narratives they can be called postmodern. In 'Responding to the Monk' (and the panellists), Helen Cooper welcomes the new interpretations given and aligns them with the high regard in which the fifteenth century held the tale, while the second respondent, L.O. Aranye Fradenburg, advocates a 'Return to *The Monk's Tale*' and to the question of the tale's form or genre.

Robert Boenig, in his short study 'Chaucer and St Kenelm' (*Neophil* 84[2000] 157–64), suggests that Chaucer had a deep interest in saints, arguing that Chaucer used details of the life of St Kenelm (available through *The Golden Legend* and the *South English Legendary*), to structure the tales of the Nun's Priest and the Prioress.

Andreas H. Jucker and Irma Taavitsainen use some examples from the *Canterbury Tales* in their study of 'Diachronic Speech Act Analysis: Insults from Flyting to Flaming' (*JHPrag* 1[2000] 67–95), concentrating on the tale of the Second Nun, and on the insulting exchanges between Harry Bailly and, respectively, the Cook and the Pardoner. They find no general pattern in Chaucer's use of insults, and conclude that the insults are personal rather than ritual. Jennifer Summit brings some arresting insights to the *Second Nun's Tale* in 'Topography as Historiography: Petrarch, Chaucer, and the Making of Medieval Rome' (*JMEMS* 30[2000] 211–46). *Pace* Gibbon and Burckhardt, the Middle Ages exhibited a sharp awareness of the (classical) past, not as an era to be recovered authentically whole but as a preservation of a form imbued with new and present meaning. Alongside Chaucer's tale, Summit considers Petrarch's 'Letter to Colonna', whose itinerary through classical Rome metamorphoses into a pilgrimage. Ancient monument and pilgrim shrine coexist as a 'double-edged historiographical project'. This spatial awareness is in Chaucer's poem turned into an opposition between the (classical and pagan) city centre and the (Christian) suburbs of the catacombs. Historical change for both writers is marked not by loss (and recovery) but by conversion, a trope that preserves the doubleness of past and present.

George R. Keiser takes the long historical view from the fifteenth century to the present in 'The Conclusion of the *Canon's Yeoman's Tale*: Readings and (Mis)Readings' (*ChauR* 35[2000] 1–21). The ending of the tale occurs in a number of late fifteenth-century and sixteenth-century manuscripts of alchemy. Lifted out thus from their context in the tale, the lines seem to have had semi-independent status among alchemical boffins, although there is no evidence to suggest that the scribes were not aware of the Chaucerian provenance of the lines; indeed, Chaucer's alchemical know-how was considered unimpeachable. Despite occasional earlier condemnations of all alchemical practice (genuine and otherwise), its wholesale debunking can be placed in the eighteenth century, which shifts away from occult study towards the empirical. The change is incarnated in Thomas Tyrwhitt's edition [1775–8], where Chaucer appears as arch-satirist of alchemy's deceptions. Contemporary criticism, concludes Keiser, would do well to understand the complexity of Chaucer's subject matter and intentions in these few lines. The tale also crops up in Peggy Knapp's widely ranging study of 'The Work of Alchemy' (*JMEMS* 30[2000] 575–99). Drawing parallels between Chaucer's late fourteenth-century and Ben Jonson's early seventeenth-century London, Knapp speaks of the modernity of Chaucer's representation of labour. The working conditions of the Canon's Yeoman enact Marx's description of capitalism's alienated labour: out of touch with the product, in competition, poorly paid, and mystified into ideological misrecognition. Chaucer's modernity is characteristically held in check, however, for he makes his Canon's Yeoman chuck his job as alchemist's stooge to join a pilgrimage.

3. *Troilus and Criseyde*

Material on *Troilus* is relatively thin on the ground this year, but Chaucerians will find some interesting points about the illustrator of the famous *Troilus* frontispiece (MS Cambridge Corpus Christi College 61) in two essays contained in the volume of conference proceedings, Riddy, ed., *Prestige, Authority and Power in Late-Medieval Manuscripts and Texts*. Kate Harris identifies another commission by this artist in 'The Patronage and Dating of Longleat MS 24, a Prestige Copy of the *Pupilla Oculi* Illuminated by the Master of the *Troilus* Frontispiece', and several more of his works are brought to light by Kathleen L. Scott in her discussion of 'Limner-Power: A Book Artist in England c. 1420'; Scott also speculates, without being able to offer proof, that Charles d'Orléans may have been the patron of Corpus 61.

Two other essays on *Troilus*, or rather on Criseyde, appear in the Festschrift for Felicity Riddy (Wogan-Browne et al., eds.). The first, by Sally Mapstone, is a simple exploration of 'The Origins of Criseyde', which summarizes what is known about the figures of Chryseis and Briseis in the *Iliad*, and examines Ovid's treatment of Briseis in the *Heroides*. Mapstone then turns to the medieval writers who comment upon Criseyde's behaviour, beginning with Benoît de Saint-Maure's *Roman de Troie*, before moving back to Chaucer and Henryson and the Scottish context with which she began. The second essay, 'Chaucer's Criseyde and Feminine Fear', by Alistair Minnis and Eric Johnson, dissects C.S. Lewis's view that Criseyde's fearfulness constitutes a tragic flaw in her character. Drawing upon contemporary scholastic analyses of fear, Minnis and Johnson argue that Lewis's reading of Criseyde is anachronistic, and that fear is too general an emotion to be the constituent component of a fatal flaw. In a heavily feminist-psychoanalytic and deconstructive reading, Gayle Margherita meditates on 'Criseyde's Remains: Romance and the Question of Justice' (*Exemplaria* 12[2000] 257–92). Beginning with the snag in the text that the narrator's first mention of Criseyde alludes to her death, an event that never actually occurs in Chaucer's narrative, Margherita proceeds to unravel the masculinism of the romance genre in terms of the contradiction that Criseyde is already dead before the poem begins.

Howell Chickering examines four of Troilus's speeches in an attempt to elucidate 'The Poetry of Suffering in Book V of *Troilus*' (*ChauR* 34[2000] 243–68). He shows how Chaucer uses rhetorical figures and manipulates rhyme in order to intensify the sense of Troilus's suffering and increase readerly sympathy for the hero; at the same time, because the speeches are set within our ironic foreknowledge of the narrative, he maintains that we are also invited to remain detached from Troilus's situation. Another type of subtle poetic manipulation is posited, not altogether convincingly, by Michael Delahoyde in '"Heryng th'effect" of the Names in *Troilus and Criseyde*' (*ChauR* 34[2000] 351–71). Delahoyde argues that names may contribute to characterization, drawing his conclusions from an examination of their placement in the text, the rhyming words chosen to partner names, the words that habitually precede them, and Chaucer's varying use of trochaic or iambic name forms.

An essay on Henryson by Derek Pearsall, revoicing the question '"Quha wait gif all that chauceir wrait was trew?" Henryson's *Testament of Cresseid*' (in Powell and Smith, eds., pp. 169–82), inevitably contains material about *Troilus*. Pearsall offers a reading of Henryson's poem and an analysis of some of the recent feminist criticism that has been applied to it.

4. Other Works

Chaucer's dream poems have benefited from two book-length studies this year. The first, by Kathryn L. Lynch, redesignates these works as *Chaucer's Philosophical Visions*, intellectual poems that engage with a wide range of philosophical issues and problems. In the introductory chapter Lynch berates other critics for their reluctance to acknowledge Chaucer's depth of philosophical learning, and flirts with the possibility that perhaps he may have had a university education after all. Four subsequent chapters treat each of the dream poems in turn, reading each as examples of the sub-genre of 'philosophical vision'. This analysis begins rather weakly since, as Lynch admits, the *Book of the Duchess* is the least explicitly philosophical of the four poems, and therefore the hardest to fit to her argument.

Because the poem has no traditional guide figure, its action proceeds by mutual questioning, and knowledge is arrived at by what Lynch claims medieval philosophical thinkers would have recognized as 'intuitive cognition'. With the *House of Fame* she is on firmer ground, since here Chaucer 'takes up another famous nominalist beast: logic' (p. 27), calling the whole discipline of logic into question. The *Parliament of Fowls*, an exploration of a situation where the intellect is rendered redundant, reflects the 'voluntarism' of the later medieval period and is reminiscent of the contemporary philosophical conundrum of 'Buridan's ass'. Finally, the chapter on the *Legend of Good Women*, which incorporates a close analysis of the legend of Lucrece, explores connections with the widely known 'liar paradox'. One further chapter, by way of conclusion, looks briefly at Chaucer's treatment of philosophical issues elsewhere, notably in *Troilus* and the *Knight's Tale*, and focuses on the intersections of rhetoric and philosophy.

The second full-length study, Michael St John's *Chaucer's Dream Visions: Courtliness and Individual Identity*, is also to be welcomed, though it reads somewhat like a thesis, and at times the book's overall argument, that Chaucer drew upon his knowledge of Aristotelian psychology to depict the mind of the courtly subject, becomes a little repetitive. The study basically consists of a series of extended readings, covering the four dream-vision poems in what is assumed to be their chronological order. The close readings attempt to show that Chaucer regarded some aspects of courtliness and *fin amor* as harmful to the soul, and others as beneficial. It is argued that the main influence on Chaucer's dream theory in the *Book of the Duchess* was Aristotle, whereas, from the *House of Fame* onwards, Thomist philosophy becomes more important. St John restricts his focus to the interpretation of the dream visions by a particular section of Chaucer's immediate audience, namely those whose identity was of 'the court'—defined broadly and inclusively as the royal household and personnel of royal palaces, and the wider political, administrative, and social circles within which the king and his advisers moved. Thus in the *Parliament of Fowls* Chaucer uses courtly protocols to provide a framework within which individuals of different kind and rank can communicate, whereas in the *Legend of Good Women* the focus is unequivocally on the social elite. For Chaucer, St John argues, writing the poetry of *fin amor* was both an engagement with, and commentary upon, actual social practices.

Arthur W. Bahr considers 'The Rhetorical Construction of Narrator and Narrative in Chaucer's the *Book of the Duchess*' (*ChauR* 35[2000] 43–59), arguing that the poem's psychological drama of character depends upon the underlying structural drama of its chiastic patterning. Thus the abrupt ending of Alycone's lament may be equated with the sudden conclusion of the Black Knight's discourse, since in each case *amplificatio* is framed by *abbreviatio*. Peter Travis offers an extended theoretical study of the *Book of the Duchess* in his essay 'White' (*SAC* 22[2000] 1–66). He argues that the controlling metalinguistic programme of the poem is located 'in its own problematic nominal signs and most specifically in their complex relationship to an already-absent object which apparently can never be adequately known or named' (p. 2). His development of this argument leads him to consider various moments of linguistic confusion in the poem—focusing on the words 'I' and 'fers', as well as the eponymous 'white', and to offer a sustained psycholinguistic study of the poem's speaking subject, for whom—as well as the Man in Black—the poem functions as a talking cure.

Several of the essays on the dream visions published this year fall broadly under the heading of source studies. Glenn Steinberg identifies Dante as a particularly significant forerunner of Chaucer, and argues that the *House of Fame* participates in the creation and exploration of poetic tradition in a heavily footnoted article, 'Chaucer in the Field of Cultural Production: Humanism, Dante, and the *House of Fame*' (*ChauR* 35[2000] 182–203). Dante is also the focus of Daniel Pinti's discussion, 'Commentary and Comedic Reception: Dante and the Subject of Reading in *The Parliament of Fowls*' (*SAC* 22[2000] 311–40), where he proposes that an untapped resource for understanding Chaucer's response to the *Divine Comedy* may be found in the poem's early commentaries, and it is in the light of the latter that Pinti suggests a new reading of the gate scene in the *Parliament of Fowls*. Also concerned with the poem's sources is Theresa Tinkle, whose broader study 'The Case of the Variable Source: Alan of Lille's *De planctu Naturae*, Jean de Meun's *Roman de la Rose*, and Chaucer's *Parlement of Fowls*' (*SAC* 22[2000] 341–77), usefully reminds us of the extent of textual instability in the pre-modern era. She contrasts Chaucer's apparently transparent reference to Alan of Lille's work with the dramatic variation that is demonstrated in the text's manuscript tradition, concentrating in particular upon its most extreme variant, the meter *Vix nodosum*, and argues that, far from simply replicating a single representation of Nature, both Jean de Meun's and Chaucer's texts interpret Nature anew.

There is a lot of history in Lynn Staley's discussion of 'Gower, Richard II, Henry of Derby, and the Business of Making Culture' (*Speculum* 75[2000] 68–96), and also some interesting points about the *Legend of Good Women*. Staley considers this poem alongside Gower's *Confessio Amantis* and Clanvowe's *Boke of Cupid*, arguing that all three works emerged from a congenial courtly environment presided over by a king who was receptive to princely advice. She then considers the shifting dynamics of power in the English court during the 1390s and ponders the poets' various responses to this, concluding that 'with his usual acuity, Chaucer got it right' (p. 96), in abandoning the courtly mode of the *Legend* for the shrewder format of the *Canterbury Tales*. The *Legend of Good Women* has also inspired two very different essays about reading this year. First, in a densely referenced article, '"Than motyn we to bokys": Writing's Harvest in the Prologue to the *Legend of Good Women*' (*JEBS* 3[2000] 1–35), Burt Kimmelman offers a new argument for seeing the G-version of the Prologue as a revision of the F-version. Noting the degree of linguistic substitution between the two versions, whereby the term 'say' becomes 'write' and 'story' becomes 'book', he suggests that by this means Chaucer sought to create a parable of reading. Secondly, Nicole F. McDonald thoughtfully considers matters of audience, real and imagined, in 'Chaucer's *Legend of Good Women*, Ladies at Court and the Female Reader' (*ChauR* 35[2000] 22–42), contrasting the poem's embedded references to its potential readers with the evidence of two of its fifteenth-century manuscripts, Cambridge, Trinity College R.3.19 and Cambridge University Library Ff.1.6. She finds a narrowing in the poem's reception as its audience becomes more domestic, and suggests that it was recast from ludic performance text to a conduct manual for women.

Some new discoveries deserve notice. Edgar Laird has uncovered 'A Previously Unnoticed Manuscript of Chaucer's *Treatise of the Astrolabe*' (*ChauR* 34[2000] 410–15), in MS Cambridge, Trinity College, R.14.52. The manuscript is a small fragment that contains only sections 37–40 of part II of the *Astrolabe*, but since there are a number of problematic issues relating to this section of the text, its discovery is very welcome. And Linne R. Mooney has uncovered 'A Late Fifteenth-Century Woman's Revision of Chaucer's "Against Women Unconstant" and Other Poems by the Same Hand' (*ChauR* 34[2000] 344–9), in a copy of William Caxton's first edition of *Dictes or Sayeingis of the Philosophres* [1477] held in the library of Trinity College, Cambridge. Her short article offers an edition of the three hitherto unknown stanzas, and some speculation about the gender of their writers.

In fact, the minor poems have attracted a fair amount of interest this year. Kathleen Forni offers a spirited defence of one of Chaucer's early printers in 'Richard Pynson and the Stigma of the Chaucerian Apocrypha' (*ChauR* 34[2000] 428–36), arguing that his printing of the *Boke of Fame* in 1526 was not an audacious attempt to expand the Chaucerian canon, and that his various titles and attributions were mistakenly or wilfully misinterpreted by later editors. Accordingly Pynson's print should be viewed not as an attempt at a single-author edition, but as an eclectic vernacular anthology. Elizabeth Fowler stresses the continuity of the English literary tradition in a short essay 'Chaucer and the Elizabethan Invention of the "Selfe"' (in Cheney and Prescott, eds., *Approaches to Teaching Shorter Elizabethan Poetry*, pp. 249–55). She suggests that a course of Elizabethan lyric poetry should include some of Chaucer's minor poems in order to demonstrate that the notion of subjectivity was not wholly invented during the later period.

Books Reviewed

Aers, David. *Faith, Ethics and Church: Writing in England, 1360–1409*. B&B. [2000] pp. xii + 153. $75 ISBN 0 8599 1561 1.

Benoit-Dusausoy, Annick, and Guy Fontaine, eds. *History of European Literature*, trans. Michael Wooff. Routledge. [2000] pp. xxviii + 731. $125 ISBN 0 4151 7334 5.

Benson, Larry, ed. *Geoffrey Chaucer: The Canterbury Tales, Complete*. HoughtonM. [2000] pp. xxxviii + 574. $44.36 ISBN 0 3959 7823 8.

Boenig, Robert, and Kathleen Davis, eds. *Manuscript, Narrative, Lexicon: Essays on Literary and Cultural Transmission in Honor of Whitney F. Bolton*. BuckAP. [2000] pp. 261. $44.50 ISBN 0 8387 5440 6.

Bray, Joe, Miriam Handley and Anne C. Henry, eds. *Ma(r)king the Text: The Presentation of Meaning on the Literary Page*. Ashgate. [2000] pp. xxiv + 341. £55 ISBN 0 7546 0168 4.

Brewer, Derek. *The World of Chaucer*. B&B. [2000] pp. 224. £19.99 ($35) ISBN 0 8599 1607 3.

Brown, Peter, ed. *A Companion to Chaucer*. Blackwell. [2000] pp. xvii + 515. $131.95 ISBN 0 6312 1332 5.

Cheney, Patrick, and Anne Lake Prescott, eds. *Approaches to Teaching Shorter Elizabethan Poetry*. MLA. [2000] pp. 331. hb $37.50 ISBN 0 8735 2753 4, pb $18 ISBN 0 8735 2754 2.

Cheney, Patrick, and Lauren Silberman, eds. *Worldmaking Spenser: Explorations in the Early Modern Age*. UPKen. [2000] pp. viii + 288. £33.95 ISBN 0 8131 2126 4.

Cohen, Jeffrey Jerome, ed. *The Postcolonial Middle Ages*. Palgrave. [2000] pp. 286. £35 ISBN 0 3339 1542 9.

Cooney, Helen, ed. *Nation, Court and Culture: New Essays on Fifteenth-Century English Poetry*. FCP. [2000] pp. 191. $75 ISBN 1 8518 2566 5.

Cullen, Dolores. *Chaucer's Pilgrims: The Allegory*. Fithian. [2000] pp. 423. $16.95 ISBN 1 5647 4334 9.

Ellis, Steve. *Chaucer at Large: The Poet in the Modern Imagination*. Medieval Cultures 24. UMinnP. [2000] pp. xiv + 204. $29.95 ISBN 0 8166 3376 2.

Fein, Susanna, ed. *Studies in the Harley Manuscript: The Scribes, Contents, and Social Context of* British Library *MS Harley 2253*. MIP. [2000] pp. xvi + 515. hb $40 ISBN 1 5804 4060 6, pb $20 ISBN 1 5804 4061 4.

George, Jodi-Anne, ed. *Geoffrey Chaucer: The General Prologue to the Canterbury Tales*. Columbia Critical Guides. ColUP. [2000] pp. 183. hb $39.50 ISBN 0 2311 2186 5, pb $14.50 ISBN 0 2311 2187 3.

Hill, John M., and Deborah M. Sinnreich-Levi, eds. *The Rhetorical Poetics of the Middle Ages: Reconstructive Polyphony. Essays in Honor of Robert O. Payne*. AUP. [2000] pp. 304. $49.50 ISBN 0 8386 3810 4.

Hodges, Laura F. *Chaucer and Costume: The Secular Pilgrims in the General Prologue*. Chaucer Studies XXVI. B&B. [2000] pp. xiv + 285. $90 ISBN 0 8599 1577 8.

Koff, Leonard Michael, and Brenda Deen Shildgen, eds. *The Decameron and the Canterbury Tales: New Essays on an Old Question*. FDUP. [2000] pp. 352. $52.50 ISBN 0 8386 3800 7.

Krueger, Roberta L. *The Cambridge Companion to Medieval Romance*. CUP. [2000] pp. xix + 290. hb £37.50 ISBN 0 5215 5342 3, pb £13.95 ISBN 0 5215 5687 2.

Lynch, Kathryn L. *Chaucer's Philosophical Visions*. Chaucer Studies XXVII. B&B. [2000] pp. viii + 178. £45 ($75) ISBN 0 8599 1600 6.

McGavin, John J. *Chaucer and Dissimilarity: Literary Comparisons in Chaucer and Other Late-Medieval Writing*. AUP. [2000] pp. 240. $39.50 ISBN 0 8386 3814 7.

McGregor, James, H., ed. *Approaches to Teaching Boccaccio's 'Decameron'*. MLA. [2000] pp. ix + 207. hb $37.50 ISBN 0 8735 2761 5, pb $18 ISBN 0 8735 2762 3.

Metzger, David, ed. *Medievalism and the Academy II: Cultural Studies*. Studies in Medievalism 10. B&B. [1998] pp. 246. $60 ISBN 0 8599 1567 0.

Pearsall, Derek, ed. *New Directions in Later Medieval Manuscript Studies: Essays from the 1998 Harvard Conference*. B&B. [2000] pp. xv + 213. £50 ($90) ISBN 1 9031 5301 8.

Phillips, Helen. *An Introduction to the Canterbury Tales: Reading, Fiction, Context*. Macmillan. [2000] pp. vi + 254. hb $45 ISBN 0 3336 3680 5, pb $19.95 ISBN 03336 3681 3.

Powell, Susan, and Jeremy J. Smith, eds. *New Perspectives on Middle English Texts: A Festschrift for R.A. Waldron*. B&B. [2000] pp. 208. £45 ($75) ISBN 0 8599 1590 5.

Pratt, John H. *Chaucer and War*. UPA. [2000] pp. xiii + 259. $42.50 ISBN 0 7618 1588 0.

Raybin, David, and Linda Tarte Holley, eds. *Closure in the Canterbury Tales: The Role of the Parson's Tale*. Studies in Medieval Culture 41. MIP. [2000] pp. xxi + 268. hb $40 ISBN 1 5804 4011 8, pb $20 ISBN 1 5804 4012 6.

Riddy, Felicity, ed. *Prestige, Authority and Power in Late-Medieval Manuscripts and Texts*. B&B. [2000] pp. vii + 199. £50 ($90) ISBN 0 9529 7346 4.

St John, Michael. *Chaucer's Dream Visions: Courtliness and Individual Identity*. Studies in European Cultural Transition 7. Ashgate. [2000] pp. 226. £45 ISBN 0 7546 0122 6.

Strohm, Paul. *Theory and the Premodern Text*. Medieval Cultures, 26. UMinnP. [2000] pp. xvi + 269. hb $42.95 ISBN 0 8166 3774 1, pb $16.95 ISBN 0 8166 3775 X.

Sturges, Robert S. *Chaucer's Pardoner and Gender Theory: Bodies of Discourse*. St Martin's Press. [2000] pp. xxiii + 232. $49.95 ISBN 0 3122 1366 2.

Sutton, Marilyn, ed. *Chaucer's Pardoner's Prologue and Tale: An Annotated Bibliography, 1900–1995*. UTorP. [2000] pp. lii + 445. $95 ISBN 0 8020 4744 0.

Sweeney, Michelle. *Magic in Medieval Romance from Chrétien de Troyes to Geoffrey Chaucer*. FCP. [2000] pp. 199. $45 ISBN 1 8518 2536 3.

West, Richard. *Chaucer, 1340–1400: The Life and Times of the First English Poet*. C&G. [2000] pp. xvii + 302. $28 ISBN 0 7867 0779 8.

Wheatley, Edward. *Mastering Aesop: Medieval Education, Chaucer, and his Followers*. UPFlor. [2000] pp. ix + 277. $55 ISBN 0 8130 1745 9.

White, Hugh. *Nature, Sex and Goodness in a Medieval Literary Tradition*. OUP. [2000] pp. ix + 278. £40 ISBN 0 1981 8730 0.

Wogan-Browne, Jocelyn, Rosalynn Voaden, Arlyn Diamond, Ann Hutchison, Carol M. Meale and Lesley Johnson, eds. *Medieval Women: Texts and Contexts in Late Medieval Britain: Essays for Felicity Riddy*. Brepols. [2000] pp. 452. €50 ISBN 2 5035 0979 7.

Workman, Leslie J., Kathleen Verduin and David D. Metzger, eds. *Medievalism and the Academy I*. Studies in Medievalism 9. B&B. [1997] pp. 263. $60 ISBN 0 8599 1532 8.

Wright, Constance S., and Julia Bolton Holloway. *Tales within Tales: Apuleius through Time*. AMS. [2000] pp. xv + 198. £52.95 ISBN 0 4046 4252 7.

Yamamoto, Dorothy. *The Boundaries of the Human in Medieval English Literature*. OUP. [2000] pp. x + 257. $74 ISBN 0 1981 8674 6.

V

The Sixteenth Century: Excluding Drama after 1550

ROS KING AND JOAN FITZPATRICK

This chapter has three sections: 1. General; 2. Sidney; 3. Spenser. Section 1 is by Ros King; sections 2 and 3 are by Joan Fitzpatrick.

1. General

Much recent work in sixteenth-century studies can be summed up in one word: expansion. We are extending into fields of enquiry that were not previously the domain of the literary critic and blurring the boundaries between the fields we have previously considered separately. Ironically, the more we insist on historical and cultural difference or alterity, the more we are beginning to understand about where correspondences may actually lie between our period and one now half a millennium away. Globalization, the speeding up of communications, and concerns about literacy and class make us interested in the first stirrings of colonialism, the spread of printing, the control of information and the voices of the marginalized in the early modern period. It is an exciting time to be engaged in the field.

This activity is, in essence, a task of translation: finding what are effectively new writers—male as well as female—neglected for centuries because their technique or their genre did not match the aesthetic or the concerns of the intervening past; bringing these writers and generic forms in from the margins of literary history; placing them in the centre of study; learning how to read them; and then describing their achievements so that they become perceptible to modern consciousnesses. These are all essential activities if we are to understand our own complex social and cultural interactions. Translation is only slowly coming to be recognized as an art form, but translation, and its sister activity, exegesis, was the essential activity of humanism. It was also the literary form in which the women of the early modern period found it most natural to engage, perhaps because it is an art in the service of things outside the self—not just the source text but also the receptive consciousness of the target reader. It is a process of mediation, of creative communication.

The amount of sixteenth-century literature is increasing all the time. Paul Voss, '"Created Good and Fair": The Fictive Imagination and Sacred Texts in Elizabethan

England' (*L&T* 14[2000] 125–44) adds to the tally of more than 20,000 printed Elizabethan poems by finding two nestling in the prefatory material to bibles. And we are also learning to read better. That a writer such as James VI (and later I) might genuinely have a more nuanced view of religious belief than the simple sectarian binaries that are still too prevalent is borne out by Lucy E.C. Wooding's *Rethinking Catholicism in Reformation England*, which argues that the importance to early sixteenth-century humanist Catholics of the reform of their religion, and their sense of loyalty to their temporal ruler, could easily outweigh any loyalty to the Pope. She warns against the tendency to conflate early Tudor Catholicism with the martyrdom-seeking polarity of later recusancy, and argues that biblicism was as important to reforming Catholics as it was to Protestants. This is an important argument, and one that should be heeded by those who are currently trying to define Shakespeare as a Catholic, although it is one that is here made more frequently by recourse to other recent secondary material than to original sources.

Richard Dutton, in *Licensing, Censorship and Authorship in Early Modern England*, demonstrates the ways in which changing political circumstances allow texts to acquire meanings in the eyes of later readers and (in the case of plays) viewers which originally they did not have. He argues that the censors knew they were unable to eradicate analogical political readings of texts and merely sought to keep them 'within bounds', for in normal circumstances the ruling classes 'were sufficiently patrician not to notice (or to pretend not to notice) a wide range of veiled commentary about them' (p. xviii). He recounts the complex story surrounding the licensing of Dr John Haywood's history of the reign of Henry IV by the bishop of London's deputy, Samuel Harsnett, its subsequent publication with a letter of dedication to Essex, Essex's own objection to the dedication (in dubious circumstances), the forced withdrawal of the letter from unsold copies of the edition, and the bishop of London's calling in and private burning of the entire second edition because of the way in which it had seemed to come to foreshadow an excessively influential role for Essex in determining a successor to Elizabeth I. Dutton finds that, despite the careful scrutiny of Hayward's book at all stages in its production, 'it was not found to be of treasonable intent until it was politically convenient that it should be so'. Discussing Sir Henry Herbert's Mastership of the Revels in the 1630s, he further insists that it is impossible to divorce Herbert's talk of 'oaths, prophaness and ribaldrye' from a 'wider political or religious contextualisation', and concludes that Herbert's phrase is 'private shorthand for provocative transgressions by the actors and their dramatists, not so much in matters of public morality but more specifically in relation to matters of political and religious policy' (pp. 56–8).

Ian Moulton, in *Before Pornography: Erotic Writing in Early Modern England*, turns to the 'Bishops' Ban' of 1599 and uses the fact that Marlowe's translation of Ovid's Elegies was one of the works that were burnt to make the more usual argument that the ban was directed against obscenity and sexual deviance. There are a number of problems with this interpretation, not the least being that the burning of Marlowe's work is likely to have been accidental in that it was published in the same volume as the genuinely subversive *Epigrams* by Sir John Davies and is not included in the official list of books burnt. Moulton's book follows in the steps of those who have taken the anti-theatrical tracts of the later sixteenth century as evidence for a widespread anxiety about sexuality, and it has been well received in those circles. But, as with too much of that work, there is here too both a lack of rigour in the reading of key literary texts and a refusal to acknowledge other contexts in which unconventional sexuality was used as a metaphor for metaphysical thought. For instance, selective quotation from Marlowe's Elegy 3.6 allows Moulton to interpret that poem in ways which suit his argument but which actually reverse the poem's meaning. One would never guess from the extract given, or from Moulton's talk of the 'patriarchal hierarchy of gender', that the speaker's frustration is with the *unpredictable* behaviour of his penis (surely a recognizable and perennial problem) and that its present droop comes (or more coarsely does not come) despite the extensive repertoire of blandishments, endearments and caresses of a very experienced woman, or that she assumes that he is exhausted, either from having been with someone else already or because he is ill—and that in neither case does he have the right to be in her bed. Furious about the reflection on her ability and charm, she decides to 'cover' the lack of evidence of sexual activity from her maid and 'spil[ls] water in the place' (3.6.84). I do not see how the dynamic of frustrated desire and pride on both sides can be adequately described by the statement, 'The speaker's masculine member has changed to a vaginal rose' (p. 107). By contrast, Moulton has earlier quoted extensively from a mid-seventeenth-century text to demonstrate that 'a surrender to pleasure results in a loss of masculinity, which manifests itself as specifically social disorder' (p. 73). He does not remark that his chosen passages bear a distinct resemblance to the complaint made about lascivious music and dancing by Shakespeare's Richard III at the beginning of a play that certainly demonstrates social disorder a-plenty, but none caused by any of the characters whose sexual morals are in question. Life, and literature, is and always was more complex than tract writers would have us believe, which is why literature has always needed to be 'defended' from the apparently literal-minded attacks of those seeking to control life.

If there is still too great a tendency to read tracts and literary texts as if they belonged to the same mode of discourse, it might help if we brought in from the margins two areas of study, which, although they have been with us for many years, are still regarded as curious byways rather than highroads to an understanding of the intellectual life of the period: alchemy and emblems. The two are brought together in Adams and Linden, eds., *Emblems and Alchemy*, a publication in the Glasgow Emblem Studies series. The techniques that we now recognize are required to read the interplay between word and image in the emblem literature of the period are a way of reading between the lines—necessary as much when dealing with literature written to avoid censorship, as with that intended to conceal the secrets of nature from the uninitiated. The meaning of an emblem, taken as a whole, is always more than the sum of its individual parts. Peggy Muñoz Simonds, '"Love is a spirit all compact of fire": Alchemical *Coniunctio* in *Venus and Adonis*' (pp. 133–56), demonstrates this, and argues that Shakespeare's narrative poem 'has compared the art of poetry to the comedy of sexual desire'. The 'dissolving' of Adonis into sexual exhaustion and later death in a hunt of passion that Moulton would probably see as a loss of masculinity and therefore, in contemporary terms, a source of anxiety, is, for Simonds and her contemporary sources, evidence of the alchemical 'transmutation of matter into higher forms' whereby death and corruption create life. She concludes that 'without the fire of love in the world there would be no suffering for humankind, or—for that matter—no poetry'.

Mary E. Hazard's *Elizabethan Silent Language* also looks for meanings beyond words and extends the relationship between word and image to encompass both household objects and behavioural gesture. Her book explores the economic, cultural, political and indeed rhetorical implications of the tactile, sensory delights of Elizabethan clothes, buildings, jewels, paintings, ceremonies, and gift exchanges, and spells out the meanings that were attached to the relationship between the public and the private in domestic space, and the control of the royal presence and/or absence.

Ideas about the multitude of ways in which meaning has likewise derived from the physical manifestation of books from the medieval period onwards, including punctuation, layout, typographical design, and the marks left by the printing process itself, are explored in a varied and lively collection of essays, Henry, Bray, and Handley, eds., *Ma(r)king the Text: The Presentation of Meaning on the Literary Page*, which also raises important questions about conventional editorial practices and the responsibility that editors have when translating this material into modern editions.

The meaning of behaviour is a recurring theme in Singh and Kamps, eds., *Travel Knowledge: 'Witnesses' to 'Navigations, Traffiques and Discoveries'*, which may prove a useful anthology for the increasing number of undergraduate courses on travel literature. The collection, gathered in three sections (the Levant, India and Africa), consists of eight selections of primary texts chosen and edited by different contributors, each of whom also writes a critical essay. Claiming to cover the years 1500–1800, it mostly reproduces texts from the seventeenth and eighteenth centuries, although contributors frequently glance back to the earlier period. Gary Taylor's essay, for instance, uses the 1607 performance of *Hamlet* on board William Keeling's ship off the coast of Sierra Leone, to deal with late sixteenth-century trading practices and inter-racial attitudes, and makes the important point that pre-colonial coastal Africans benefited from European trade and 'got a better deal from the Europeans than from other Africans', suggesting that 'rivalries between the Europeans empowered the Africans'. He also relates this performance to accounts of French and Spanish theatrical performances in the Americas in the sixteenth century and to travellers' accounts of dance displays performed by the native peoples they met: 'when alien cultures encounter each other, both sides almost inevitably resort to theatre'. In their introduction, the editors point out the diversity of pre-colonial European encounters with other cultures and peoples recorded in the selected primary texts. On one level, however, they seem almost embarrassed by this, stressing that these 'bear the marks of a "colonizing imagination"—tropes, fantasies, rhetorical structures—whereby the writers/travellers frequently fall back on defining the cultural others they encounter in terms of binaries that later consolidate and justify full-blown colonialism'. But to read history backwards like this is to deny the possibility for other developments that were also incipient in those first meetings.

Rebecca Ann Bach's *Colonial Transformations: The Cultural Production of the New Atlantic World, 1580–1640* similarly, and on a human level understandably, rehearses the author's feelings about the destructive effects of the colonial project but does not fully allow for the conflicts, preconceptions, opportunisms and accidents, and the confused ambitions, loyalties and beliefs that slowly shaped themselves into that disaster. Taking Peter Stallybrass's famous, and playful, essay on the relationship of identity to the spelling of names perhaps a touch too solemnly, she makes the interesting observation that unlike the Spanish, who named the geographical landmarks they claimed after their religion, the English tended to use English personal or royal names. On the map she reproduces, however, (John Smith's famous map of a piece of land named by Elizabethan Englishmen 'Virginia'), the names James Town, Cape Charles and Cape Henry are mere isolated sticks in a forest of Indian names. Virginia, of course, was so named in order to facilitate royal investment in a private adventure, since a fledgling settlement initially cost far more than it earned. She is subtle in her understanding of what a map of the unknown country might mean to investors safe at home, whose only concern is their money, but to the English men (and women) on the ground and in the water, accurate knowledge of where they were was not a mere word or image; it represented the difference between life and death.

Bach adduces a great deal of detail culled from many sources, but displays a tendency to want to make words mean more, and sometimes less, than they can historically bear. For instance, inspired by an aberrant original spelling, she makes deliberate confusion of 'costs' and 'coasts' (p. 86), and derives an entire interpretative argument from defining the word 'captain' as indicative of a lower social status than 'knight' (p. 95), when historically it often did duty for 'general' or 'governor'.

She is properly scathing of what she describes as the Jamestown museum's triumphalist story of the birth of modern America, and ends by stating, 'It is up to us in the American twenty-first century to tell other stories'. Our histories of the past inevitably, and indeed properly, reflect our understanding of the present, but if we are now to progress beyond sectarian and ethnic division, understanding how injustice arises so easily from the verbal glosses placed on opportunity, we are going to have to attempt, both critically and empathetically, to understand the complex motivations and interactions of everyone involved, colonizers and colonized alike.

The moral and practical complexities of a related aspect of English activity overseas are examined by Barbara Fuchs, 'Faithless Empires: Pirates, Renegadoes, and the English Nation' (*ELH* 67[2000] 45–69). She argues that the activities of privateers, celebrated as national heroes and 'enriched and often even ennobled' by pillage, militated against the development of commerce and presented a problem: 'how to construct the national self as a mercantile one without losing the epic potency associated with pirates such as Drake' (p. 47).

Other books unavailable for review this time will be considered next year.

2. Sidney

Two important monographs, each containing chapters devoted to Sidney, appeared from CUP in 2000: Kenneth Borris's *Allegory and Epic in English Renaissance Literature: Heroic Form in Sidney, Spenser, and Milton* and Robert Matz's *Defending Literature in Early Modern England: Renaissance Literary Theory in Social Context*. Borris disputes critical assumptions that the influence of allegory waned after 1600, and asserts rather that new access to classical texts 'changed and revitalized literary conceptions and uses of the mode, as literary theorists and poets assimilated these fresh influences and resultant contemporary intellectual trends' (p.

4). Heroic poetry by Homer and Virgil was considered especially important in sixteenth-century accounts of literary genres, and epic and allegory were closely connected. The book contains a section on Sidney's *Arcadias*: chapter 4, on 'Arcadian Allegorical Epic', and chapter 5 on 'Sidneian Transformations of Heroic Poetry', with each providing a fresh reading of Sidney's texts. Borris also provides new readings of Milton's *Paradise Lost* and Spenser's *Faerie Queene*, and is keen to emphasize that the allegorical nature of Sidney's writing makes him a literary forerunner of Spenser. Borris sees a connection between Milton, Sidney and Spenser because although they differ in their approach to allegory they all share a desire to explore psychological issues through the allegorical epic form.

Matz considers Elyot's *Boke Named the Governour*, Spenser's *Faerie Queene* and Sidney's *Defence of Poetry*, with a chapter devoted to each text. According to Matz these literary works, in their adherence to Horatian doctrine, reflect the 'conflicts in standards of aristocratic conduct during the social and cultural transitions of the sixteenth century' (p. 3). Matz also questions the revisionary literary history begun by new historicists, and challenges their tendency to consider poetry as just another form of discursive and institutional power. Matz considers Pierre Bourdieu's sociology of culture in order to provide 'a more historically situated account of poetry's place in the sixteenth century, one that emphasizes the transformations of and contest among various forms of capital—cultural, social, and economic—during the period' (p. 3). Unlike the new historicists, Matz believes that, by the end of the sixteenth century, poetry had come to be regarded as a form with a distinct status. Sidney differs from Elyot in his defence of the courtly pleasure of poetry because it encourages warrior service. Matz reconsiders the notion that Sidney's poetry can be located within activist Protestant politics; like many aristocrats, Sidney adopted humanist and Protestant notions of aristocratic service as sources of political and cultural authority, but was distinct from the socially lower groups in which such humanist and Protestant notions originated. Matz considers Sidney's *Defence* in relation to Stephen Gosson's *The Schoole of Abuse*, to which it was a reply, and argues that, while both works share a nostalgia for feudalism, Sidney rejects Gosson's attack on courtly leisure and consumption and defends poetry for its promotion of a profitable warrior service.

Alan Stewart's excellent biography of Sidney, *Philip Sidney: A Double Life*, is a thorough and scholarly work. Sidney's reputation as a leading light of English national heroism was the result of careful propaganda which did not reflect reality. Queen Elizabeth made Sidney's life difficult, and in his efforts not to irritate her he was 'forced to lead a double life: of fame and praise abroad, and of comparative—and deliberate—neglect at home' (p. 7). Stewart carefully traces Sidney's childhood and adolescence, his travels in Europe and his military achievements abroad. By focusing on personal and historical documents as well as some of the writings for which Sidney was known, Stewart builds a full and uncompromising picture of a fascinating individual. The book is divided into twelve chapters with an introduction and a rather short epilogue. Some chapter titles are obscure, giving little indication of their content. For example, while 'Young and Raw' is fairly straightforward (though we might wonder how young and in what way raw), 'Fancy, Toy and Fiction' is not a particularly helpful indication of content. The book contains a detailed index, and the bibliography is usefully divided into sections, for example listing manuscripts, editions of Sidney's works, and secondary sources consulted by the author.

Reuven Tsur's essay, 'Metaphor and Figure–Ground Relationship: Comparisons from Poetry, Music, and the Visual Arts', from the online journal *Psyart* (<http:// www.clas.ufl.edu/ipsa/journal/>) considers literary works by Emily Dickinson, Shelley, Beckett and Sidney in the context of gestalt theory, that is, the psychological theory which maintains that the whole of anything is greater than the sum of its parts and that its attributes cannot be deduced from analysis of the parts in isolation. The section on Sidney is a study of the sonnet 'Leave me, O love which reachest but to dust', with particular focus on the third quatrain. In his consideration of Sidney, Tsur is particularly indebted to Kenneth Burke's 1962 study *A Grammar of Motives* and *A Rhetoric of Motives*, and Tsur's analysis considers Sidney's birth and death imagery, also used by Beckett in *Waiting for Godot*.

In 'Almost a Golden World: Sidney, Spenser, and Puritan Conflict in Bradstreet's Contemplations' (*Renascence* 52[2000] 187–202) Lee Oser considers the influence of Sidney and Spenser on Anne Bradstreet's poem 'Contemplations'. Bradstreet's depiction of the golden world, claims Oser, was influenced by Sidney's golden world in his *Defence of Poesy*. Although Bradstreet's debt to Sidney does not accord with her Calvinism, Oser argues that she 'learned a good deal from Sidney, who had granted visionary powers to the poet in his quest for divine knowledge' (p. 192). Oser provides a close reading of Bradstreet's poem in the light of Calvinist theology and her debt to Sidney's contemplation of nature in her meditation on the landscape of New England.

Staying with religion, this year's *Spenser Studies* contained one essay on Sidney, Barbara Brumbaugh's '"Under the pretty tales of wolves and sheep": Sidney's Ambassadorial Table Talk and Protestant Hunting Dialogues' (*SSt* 14[2000] 273– 90). A speech made by Sidney at an ambassadorial dinner in 1577 was recorded for posterity by Philip Camerarius, a Protestant scholar with whom Sidney had spoken about forming a Protestant league. Critics have hitherto assumed the subject of Sidney's speech, the elimination of wolves from England, to be a straightforward historical account of the animals' expulsion, but Brumbaugh convincingly argues that as well as being a historical account the speech is also of political import. It alludes, she claims, to the established Protestant literary convention of satiric 'hunting' dialogues which figure Catholics, particularly the clergy obedient to the Pope, as wolves who prey upon faithful Christians. The Christians, or sheep, can be protected by particularly outspoken Protestant clergy, or loudly barking dogs. Sidney's technique, claims Brumbaugh, is to fuse historically accurate material with other details so as to make a political point. This is a fascinating essay and Brumbaugh provides ample evidence—from Sidney's account, the chronicles, and the hunting dialogues themselves—to make her case that Sidney's speech is an allegory which would have been apparent to those familiar with the convention of Protestant hunting dialogues.

3. Spenser

Spenser Studies 14[2000] followed the general pattern of publications this year by presenting an eclectic range of writings touching on important areas such as religion, history, gender, mythology and Ireland. Andrew Hadfield considers some hitherto neglected illustrations in 'William Kent's Illustrations of *The Faerie Queene*' (*SSt* 14[2000] 1–82). Kent [1684–1748] was a man of many talents: painter, landscape gardener, furniture and interior designer, architect, and book illustrator who created a series of illustrations for Thomas Birch's 1751 edition of *The Faerie Queene*, the first extensively illustrated edition of the poem until 1896. Although there are quite a few eighteenth-century and modern commentaries on the illustrations, they have not had the attention of Spenserians or been reproduced in full until now. Section 1 of Hadfield's essay provides a summary of Kent's career, reputation and interest in Spenser. Although Kent was successful in his various fields, his reputation as a painter and draughtsman was not high, and indeed William Hogarth called him a 'contemptible dauber' (p. 5). Horace Walpole, a leader in taste for the Gothic, was sympathetic to Kent's architectural works but, like Hogarth, dismissed his paintings, particularly the prints for *The Faerie Queene*, referring to 'the wretchedness of drawing, the total ignorance of perspective, the want of variety, the disproportion of the buildings, and the awkwardness of the attitudes' (p. 6). Walpole had a point. The illustrations, though undoubtedly of interest to Spenserians, are not particularly well done. Hadfield also cites modern commentators who agree with Walpole's estimation of Kent's illustrations. Section 2 of Hadfield's essay concentrates on Thomas Birch's 1751 edition of Spenser's poem. Birch, antiquary and member of the Royal Society, was involved in various literary and historical projects on English national culture, especially those relating to the Elizabethan period. Like Kent, he also suffered scathing criticism from Walpole, who regarded him as 'diligent but rather dim-witted'. Hadfield notes that 'Birch's edition appeared amid a keen rivalry to publish Spenser', and Birch proclaimed his three-volume edition a 'just representation of the genuine text' (p. 6). In it he collated the Folio and quartos of the poem, using the 1590 quarto as the main text, but was not consistent in his editorial methods, often deferring to the Folio. However, his new life of Spenser included in the edition was the fullest thus far and discovered new biographical allusions in *The Faerie Queene*. The work was marketed on promised engravings by Kent which were used to distinguish it from other editions. It is the first extensive sequence depicting *The Faerie Queene* and contains thirty-two plates in all, each illustrating an incident in the poem. Section 3 is on the later influence of Kent's illustrations. *The Faerie Queene* was particularly popular in eighteenth-century England and influenced numerous imitations, the most significant being James Thomson's *The Castle of Indolence* [1748]. Many of Kent's drawings are 'Gothic', and can be read alongside Thomson's allegory, which greatly influenced Romantic readings of Spenser. Criticism of *The Faerie Queene* after the publication of Birch's edition appeared to have been influenced by the inclusion of Kent's illustrations, since these critics tended to praise Spenser's visual imagination, comparing his poetry to painting.

In a well-researched essay Gail Cohee, '"To fashion a noble person": Spenser's Readers and the Politics of Gender' (*SSt* 14[2000] 83–105), focuses on representations of gender by British and American critics of Spenser in the nineteenth and early twentieth centuries, periods with significant feminist movements. Two 'distinct factions' emerge: a group of mostly male readers, for whom Spenser's female characters reflect an idyllic past before feminism, and a group of mostly female readers, for whom the characters are strong and intelligent women. Cohee contends that both groups manipulate the text to fit their political objectives. In the mid-nineteenth century, when organizations for women's rights were growing in America and Britain, 'a distaste for strong women begins to emerge in much of the criticism' (p. 85), and in the late nineteenth century Spenser's female characters were presented as 'foils or heroic prototypes for nineteenth-century reformers' (pp. 88–9). Pro- or anti-feminist readings were exemplified in Edward Dowden's 'Heroines of Spenser', Mary E. Litchfield's *Spenser's Britomart* and Kate Warren's edition of *The Faerie Queene*. The anti-feminist Dowden stresses the simplicity of Spenser's ideal women, and compares contemporary feminists to the evil women in the poem. Both Litchfield and Warren focus on Britomart, but while Litchfield presents a censored version of the extracts she chooses and creates Britomart as a domesticated Victorian heroine, Warren represents her as a feminist model. Warren is also one of few critics to sympathize to some extent with Radigund, and differs from Dowden by representing Britomart as a modern reformer. Cohee also considers two early twentieth-century male critics of *The Faerie Queene* who, unlike nineteenth-century male critics, focus on Britomart but continue their notion of 'natural' and 'unnatural' women, thus blurring the distinctions between fictional and real women especially when arguing against certain types of feminists. F.M. Padelford and Herbert Ellsworth Cory are ambivalent towards Britomart, praising her as an ideal woman but uncomfortable with less admirable traits such as jealousy or aggression. Cory is the earliest critic to link Radigund and Britomart's fight to women's rights, and though he praises Britomart's masculine courage he emphasizes that she is not 'mannish'. Like his nineteenth-century counterpart Edward Dowden, Gamaliel Bradford uses Spenser's female characters to criticize his feminist contemporaries. Conflating real Elizabethan women with literary 'women', he admires Britomart but claims she is no feminist. This is a detailed and useful survey of the appropriation of Spenser's female figures at politically significant periods in the history of criticism.

In a piece which may prove rather too curious for the mathematically challenged reader, Piotr Sadowski, 'Spenser's "Golden Squire" and "Golden Meane": Numbers and Proportions in Book II of *The Faerie Queene*' (*SSt* 14[2000] 107–31), considers the geometrical language used by Spenser. In modern Freemasonry the set square, 'a flat metal right-angled triangle used in architectural design and geometrical drawing' (p. 109), signifies honesty and truthfulness and although different types of squares can be used, a favourite of medieval masons was the 'golden square', based on the golden section, 0.618. Sadowski suggests that when Spenser evokes the 'golden squire' to 'measure out a mean' he uses the term 'first of all in its literal sense' and referring to the mason's instrument (p. 114). According to Sadowski this is particularly important in the context of the allegorical castles described by Spenser in Book II because the geometrical concept of the Golden Mean can provide clues to the symbolic significances of these buildings. The house of Medina is 'only the first, imperfect approximation to the true image of the Golden Mean, displayed spectacularly in Canto ix in the allegorical details of Alma's House of Temperance', where Guyon's 'inner harmony' is 'symbolized by the orderly design and management of Alma's Castle' (p. 120). Stanza xxii of canto ix, which considers the perfect proportions of Alma's castle, is one of the 'golden points' of the sixty stanzas in Book II, and Sadowski considers the geometrical and numerical elements listed by Spenser in this stanza. The golden section contained in the mason's golden set square not only reflects harmonious architectural design but the structure of living organisms, including the human body, which is highly significant in relation to the House of Alma. Sadowski concludes that, via allusions to the Masonic instruments and geometrical concepts, Spenser's depiction of temperance 'takes on a more precise meaning' which enhances his philosophical and moral concepts (p. 127). On the whole this piece is less than successful, primarily because complex ideas, with which most Spenserians are likely to be unfamiliar, are presented in a less than lucid manner.

Margaret Christian, on the other hand, presents a brilliant essay, '"Waves of weary wretchednesse": Florimell and the Sea' (*SSt* 14[2000] 133–61), which reads the story of Florimell in relation to the allegorical seas found in contemporary sermons. Sea imagery was remarkably popular and could be found in nearly half of all early modern sermons. The most frequent use of sea imagery by Christian writers and preachers from Augustine onwards was that of the Church as a ship of salvation with Christ as its navigator through the seas of the world to the harbour of heaven. In *The Faerie Queene* Britomart's speech (III.iv.vi–x)—where the ocean acts as a metaphor for her emotional and spiritual state—although Petrarchan, also shares its tone with sermons, and its final stanza 'may remind us more of the sermon than the sonnet tradition' (p. 143). Preachers do not seem to have been influenced by Petrarchan poetry, and on the whole sea imagery is not used in a romantic context, but one exception is Robert Wilkinson's marriage sermon of 1607, which demonstrates both the romantic and moral potential of sea imagery and provides an insight into Florimell's story. In the sermon the bride—and marriage itself—is a ship sailing on the seas of the world. Both Wilkinson and Spenser use sea imagery to show the lovers' incompleteness when alone and the need for fulfilment through another person in marriage. Wilkinson's sermon illuminates the moral dimension of the Florimell and Marinell story: before she arrives at sea Florimell wanders aimlessly, much like Wilkinson's bachelor without a wife, but she finds safety at sea through divine intervention. In Spenser, although the literal sea is sympathetic, the metaphorical sea of world, flesh, and devil works against Florimell when she does not distinguish between the good and bad boat and faces the storms of the flesh from the Fisherman. Although she is saved through divine intervention in the form of Proteus, he seeks to corrupt her heart, as the fisherman did her body, and in his temptations is like Satan tempting Christ in the wilderness. Marinell cannot save Florimell from the sea of cares without a boat, and the sermon subtext indicates that this boat is marriage, which Marinell can utilize with the help of God, here figured in the shape of Neptune. Florimell has matured as a result of her suffering, and by the time of her marriage has acknowledged God's rule over the sea. As Christian notes, the sermon imagery she has detected in the Florimell episode 'complements and enriches the elements in the story contributed by Petrarchism, classical lore, and contemporary epideictic commonplaces' (p. 155). We might also say that this fine essay complements and enriches our reading of Florimell's adventures.

Staying with religion, Mark Hazard, 'The Other Apocalypse: Spenser's Use of 2 Esdras in the Book of Justice' (*SSt* 14[2000] 163–87), notes that discussions of the apocalyptic in *The Faerie Queene* tend to focus on the influence of the biblical book of Revelation in Book I. Here he explores Spenser's use of the bible in *FQ* V.ii, the episode featuring the execution of the Egalitarian Giant which 'establishes and at the same time questions the nature of Artegall's authority' (p. 163). Spenser's use of a passage from the Apocrypha, 2 Esdras, suggests an apocalyptic background to Artegall's actions; the allusion is of particular interest because 2 Esdras has little authority as a biblical text. Although Artegall and the Giant conform to different social theories they are alike 'in the implied dependence of their social ideals on force'. They are also alike in the imagery of scales used in their arguments, the biblical passages echoed, and the implications of 'a violent rejection of flawed humanity' (p. 166). Although they hold opposite positions they 'share the assumption that change itself is evil, an attitude that also underlies their implicitly shared view of apocalyptic violence' (p. 167). The giant's questioning of the divine and his rebuke by a figure who assumes divine authority is like the confrontation in Esdras between the prophet Ezra and the angel Uriel. Artegall speaks from the position of the angel and the Giant from that of the prophet, but Artegall is out of his depth since he has assumed the angel's role and 'is in this sense, along with the Giant, an over-reacher' (p. 170). The Giant's impatience, frustration, and literalism are like the anti-intellectual tone associated with radical Protestant apocalyptic prophecy, and thus, claims Hazard, the Giant 'would be considered an Anabaptist, a catchall demonized image of political danger' (p. 176). The Anabaptists were particularly dangerous because 'their challenge to power came from a radical extension of the same Protestant beliefs as those espoused by the Establishment' (p. 175). They were targeted by Thomas Cranmer in 1553 and condemned for their belief in communist ideas and millenarian hopes for most of the population. Spenser appears to share the point of view, presented in a 1596 sermon written by George Gifford, that the state should take responsibility for weeding out heretics, a vision which is apocalyptic but not utopian. Artegall is conservative and the Giant wants radical change, but they are both impatient with earthly structures. Hazard notes that Stephen Greenblatt read the similarities between Artegall and the Giant as 'an expression of Spenser's own combination of social conservatism and impatient idealism' (p. 178), an intriguing analysis which, coupled with Hazard's essay, adds to the complexity of Spenser's biography.

Anne Lake Prescott's 'Foreign Policy in Fairyland: Henri IV and Spenser's Burbon' (*SSt* 14[2000] 189–214) concentrates on Henri IV of France, Sir Burbon in Book V of *The Faerie Queene*. Henri was a particularly mythified king in England and Spenser would have known the legend from loyalist propaganda. A major part of Henri's image was his reputed virility and bravery, and Prescott cites contemporary documents which praise Henri's faith and support the case for intervention in the French wars. In his depiction of Henri, claims Prescott, Spenser reduces a public and political figure to a private individual, 'thus stressing his failures as a Garter knight and weakening excuses that might be plausible in a king' (p. 194). Henri's reputation for virility reinforced his image as husband of France, evident in Spenser's depiction of his lady, Flourdelis (or France). One reason for Flourdelis's moodiness, suggests Prescott, is her association with the Guise family, who claimed not only that Henri was a heretic but that their own line was more valid. Flourdelis's status is uncertain and Prescott claims that she has 'a trace of that villainess' associated with the League (p. 195), although it is not clear to this reviewer how her moral weakness and apparent ingratitude might constitute villainy. Similarly, while Prescott's analysis of Flourdelis's moodiness is convincing, less convincing is her assertion that 'Flourdelis is so sulky a lady that only allegory explains why Burbon wants her', because this does not consider the important context of the sexualized assault against her. In contemporary documents the French wars 'were read as illness and dismemberment' and, claims Prescott, this relates to Book V's 'concern with broken bodies' and the representation of Henri as a doctor who can cure the illness (p. 200). Henri was praised before he converted to Catholicism, or threw away his shield, in a work by Du Bartas which was translated into English and published by Gabriel Harvey's friend John Wolfe. Extant marginalia by Harvey reveal an obvious admiration for Henri, and Prescott claims that Spenser, who admired Du Bartas, probably agreed with Harvey. Prescott reproduces a letter from Elizabeth I to Henri rebuking him, a necessary political move. Also reproduced in full are previously unpublished letters from Elizabeth I to Henri's unconverted sister Catherine. Elizabeth I and her advisers were torn between Protestant solidarity and supporting Henri for political reasons. Prescott notes that Spenser follows this historical pattern in his episode: just as in the relationship between Henri and Elizabeth I, 'Burbon breaks faith, is rebuked, pleads for help anyway, gets it, and together with Gloriana's knight and iron Talus, saves Flourdelis' (p. 206). Spenser is broadly right on his representation of historical facts, though Elizabeth and Henri were soon back on friendly terms, unlike Artegall and Burbon.

Douglas A. Northrop, 'The Uncertainty of Courtesy in Book VI of *The Faerie Queene*' (*SSt* 14[2000] 215–32), notes that the emphasis on historical allegory in Book V of Spenser's poem helps the reader to understand the virtue of Justice, but that the lack of historical allusion in Book VI hinders the reader. Critics have noted the importance of chance or fortune in the encounters that take place in Book VI but, claims Northrop, these occur without the assurance of divine intervention evident in Book I. In all, according to Northrop, the reader is disconcerted by 'interruptions, discontinuities, chances and coincidences, uncertainties, a lack of causal connections within and between episodes, and behaviour that seems out of character', which Northrop argues 'are not isolated but endemic' (p. 220). The shift from Book V to Book VI is identified by Northrop of being one from 'the historicity of major events' to 'the shifting, uncertain, apparently unconnected conditions of our storm-tossed lives' (p. 219). Spenser's conception of courtesy is of a virtue driven not by rules but by particular circumstances and achieved not through strength, analysis or training but through 'the awareness of the graciousness possible for us all' (p. 220). Northrop agrees with a range of critics that Book VI is particularly self-reflexive since the poet's persona, Colin Clout, is present and 'the narrator frequently intrudes into the poem' (p. 222). Courtesy comes from the court, but Calidore 'needs instruction or inspiration beyond the court and so comes to the pastoral landscape' where his 'mentor', Colin Clout, teaches him to see things clearly (p. 224). Critics have acknowledged Calidore's exploitation of Coridon but have been less concerned by his manipulation of Pastorella and Meliboe, where his behaviour can be compared to that of the Brigands. What Calidore needs to learn is that even the very humble are worthy and that he must rid himself of 'courtly manners' in order to find 'the true courtesy of human relations' (p. 229). Northrop's analysis of Book VI is a convincing one: the signposts of history we encounter in Book V are not present in Book VI, but this appears to be a deliberate poetic effect.

Lin Kelsey and Richard S. Peterson, 'Rereading Colin's Broken Pipe: Spenser and the Problem of Patronage' (*SSt* 14[2000] 233–72), break from the tendency to focus on *The Faerie Queene* in this issue of *Spenser Studies* in order to consider

Colin's pipe-breaking, a significant moment in the January eclogue of *The Shepheardes Calender*. Although earlier critics considered the action a demonstration of romantic despair, Kelsey and Peterson suggest that it is a sign of discontent over patronage. The poet breaking his pipe as a code for literary disillusionment dates back to the classical poets, and Spenser's pipe-breaking was picked up on and imitated by his contemporaries and literary admirers, such as Ralegh, Drayton and Jonson. Spenser's consideration of 'the Ovidian reed' also indicates the identity of Rosalind, who 'may simply be a riddling incarnation of his beautiful roseau, the French word often used for "reed" [or pipe]' (p. 254). The play on words—*roseau-linda*, Rosalind—is suggested by E.K.'s gloss in 'January' describing Rosalind as 'a feigned name, which being wel ordered, wil bewray the very name of hys loue and mistresse'. So, in fact, Colin pursues what Harvey called 'Mistresse Poetrie' (in his Letters). An allusion to Elizabeth I may also be evident: 'both "reed" and "*roseau*" incorporate puns on the slender, red-haired queen's emblem, the red (and white) Tudor rose' (p. 255). When the youthful Colin breaks his pipe in *The Shepheardes Calender* it is 'halfe in despight' but in Book VI of *The Faerie Queene* it is in 'fell despight', suggesting a more severe annoyance. The gesture has thus developed 'from the traditional wistful appeal for support ... to a gesture of independence and even anger and impatience at being disturbed in his communion with the mysterious figure in the middle of the ring' (p. 256). Colin's action appears to be 'the resignation of a badge of office occasioned by a decisive shift in allegiance' and is 'a warning of non servient' to those who chased Spenser's poetry out of England. This is a compelling article which adds to our understanding of Spenser's biography via a passage usually dismissed as primarily romantic in nature.

Two important notes were presented in the 'Gleanings' section. Elizabeth See Watson, 'Spenser's Flying Dragon and Pope Gregory XIII' (*SSt* 14[2000] 293–301), contends that the dragon in *FQ* I.xi may refer to the Roman Counter-Reformation and more specifically to Pope Gregory XIII, who was pope from 1572 to 1585. Gregory was hated by English Protestants for his role in various pro-Catholic incidents and can be linked to the dragon of I.xi because his personal impressa, or device, displayed a winged dragon. In *Delle allusioni, Imprese, et Emblemi*, published by Principio Fabricii after Gregory's death and in his honour, a winged dragon is represented in the 231 emblems engraved from his own drawings with an Italian sonnet and Latin marginal annotation for each emblem. The dragons are similar to those in canto xi, but are presented as benevolent. Spenser could have seen Fabricii's work because there may have been at least one copy in England; the name 'Robert Haryngton' is inscribed on the title page of a copy in the Folger Shakespeare Library, and it was published in 1588 when Book I of *The Faerie Queene* was nearly complete. Spenser may also have seen and been influenced by Giovanni Andrea Palazzi's *I Discorsi ... sopra l'imprese* [1575], which mentions the dragon crest, arms, or impressa several times. John Nichols, in *John Niccols Pilgrimage* [1581], also associates Gregory with serpents, relating the apocryphal story that Gregory's family name of 'Boncompagnion' (Buoncompagno, or 'good fellow') was acquired when his grandfather slew a serpent. Other references to his dragon impressa may have come from letters by travellers who had seen the papal arms or impressa in Rome. Nichols's account is the one most likely to have been used by Spenser, among other things because of its 1581 London imprint, its reference to the Pope as

Antichrist, and its blaming Gregory as 'the cause of the late rebellion in Ireland'. Watson reproduces three of Fabricii's emblems at the end of her essay. The pictures of the dragons are of great interest, but the accompanying Italian sonnets and Latin marginal annotation are not translated, which will prove disappointing to those readers unfamiliar with either language.

Thomas Herron's 'Irish Den of Thieves: Souterrains (and a Crannog?) in Books V and VI of Spenser's *Faerie Queene*' (*SSt* 14[2000] 303–17) is a thoughtful and clearly written piece that finds an Irish dimension to the caves that harbour Spenser's villains in Books V and VI of *The Faerie Queene*. Critics disagree as to whether or not the Brigants are Irish, but no one has noted that their hiding place resembles a souterrain, a common feature of the Irish landscape. The Irish name for souterrain, *uaimh*, means 'cave', and this word is used several times to describe the Brigants' dwelling where they retreat after their pillaging. That the Brigants were based on Spenser's Irish experience is substantiated by the contemporary documentary evidence supplied by Herron that souterrains were used by thieves to hide their plunder. Most souterrains were of the 'dry stone' variety, but some were cut partially or wholly out of clay or rock. As Herron points out, Malengin is said to live in a 'rocke' and his 'hewen' cave may refer to the twists and turns of the souterrain (pp. 305–6). Another possibility explored by Herron is Andrew Hadfield's suggestion that the Brigant's island may be a crannog (a fortified Irish lake dwelling built on an artificial or extended natural island). Evidence against this, claims Herron, is the fact that the Brigants' island does not contain any man-made fortifications, as a crannog would, and the crannog's high water table meant that there could not be a souterrain connected to it. However, evidence in favour of its 'island' status is its proximity to land and its use as a refuge from (English) justice. Spenser may also have used poetic licence to make the Irish more threatening than they actually were, imagining the doubly sinister souterrain plus crannog. Herron's essay is accompanied by a photo of the cave on Spenser's estate, taken by the author, and various drawings of souterrains.

An exciting collection of essays appeared this year, Morrison and Greenfield, eds., *Edmund Spenser: Essays on Culture and Allegory*, based on papers presented at '*The Faerie Queene* in the World, 1596–1996: Edmund Spenser among the Disciplines', a conference which took place at the Yale Centre for British Art in September 1996. In the introduction to the collection, Matthew Greenfield contextualizes the proceedings in relation to 'Spenser and the Theory of Culture'. Literary critics have, he claims, responded to Greenblatt's call for a new 'cultural poetics' by emphasizing the former and neglecting the latter. In this volume, however, a more balanced approach is taken and each essay 'travels through poetics to the theory of culture' (p. 1). Spenser is not only a theorist of allegory and poetics, however, he is also 'a profound and subtle ethnographer of both England and Ireland' and these two kinds of theory, the poetic and the cultural, are related. This, explains Greenfield, is why the contributors to the volume 'begin with close reading and end by challenging the ethnographic allegories that shape our knowledge of early modern Britain' (p. 4).

The first section of the book, 'Allegories of Cultural Development', contains three essays. In the first of these, 'Ruins and Visions: Spenser, Pictures, Rome' (pp. 9–36), Leonard Barkan traces connections between Spenser's translations of Du Bellay's *Songe ou Vision* and *Antiquitez de Rome*. Barkan is interested in the movement of literary influence from Rome to France to early modern England and from a Catholic to a Protestant aesthetic. Rome also figures in 'Spenser's Currencies' (pp. 37–42), a particularly interesting essay by Donald Cheney which focuses on *The Shepheardes Calender* and the commodification of literary works. Cheney claims that the *Calender*'s presentation places it 'within an Augustan tradition whereby poetic survival is couched in economic terms (as currency), in calendrical terms (as recurrency), and in terms ... of a poetry attuned to the natural currents of river or waterfall' (p. 37). The concept of literature as a commodity is usually thought to have developed in the early modern period but actually dates from ancient Rome: in Horace's *Epistles* his book is figured as a favourite slave who is eager to expose himself to the public. Horace warns that both books and boys are subject to the fluctuations of time and market demand and that the book will be discarded when no longer youthful. In Spenser's *Calender* the poem is a child and E.K. and Hobbinol take on role of parent, lover or counsellor assumed by the speaker in Horace. Horace's poem, like Spenser's 'moves from Janus in the first line to mention of the poet's own forty-four Decembers in the last, and it shares some of the ironies as to the way poets and poems can be identified with the months' (p. 41). In the epilogue to the *Calender* Spenser claims to have made something 'That steele in strength, and time in durance shall outweare' (p. 41) and, as E.K. notes, thus echoes a famous poem by Horace, the conclusion to the third book of the *Odes*, which claims to have completed a monument more lasting than bronze: 'Exegi monumentum aere perennius'. Bronze, *aes*, was also the material of money and a word for it, while *perenne* contains the word for the year, *annus*, and so the quotation implies 'enduring the changing seasons', like Spenser's *Calender*. Horace's line may be understood as claiming to have created a work 'more current than currency' in that it is made current for each generation of readers.

Staying with parallels between the classical and early modern periods Maureen Quilligan, in 'On the Renaissance Epic: Spenser and Slavery' (pp. 43–64), reminds us that the Renaissance, usually regarded as a time of individual freedom, also saw the rebirth of slavery in western Europe, an aspect of economic organization it shared with antiquity. Quilligan considers two scenes from *The Faerie Queene* where the poem 'may be aiming to do the work which epic poems usually do, to wit, mediating the contradictions (that is, the internally irrational elements) of a slave economy' (p. 43). In Guyon's confrontation with Mammon and Britomart's slaying of the Amazon Radigund in Book V Spenser 'seems most specifically to mediate on the problem of slave and wage labor', with both episodes coming from the only books in the poem to focus on classical Aristotelian virtues (p. 43). The description of Mammon's cave and the labour that goes into producing its gold can be compared with contemporary descriptions and images of gold mines in the New World. Mammon dismisses Guyon's classical arguments against avarice and claims that a feudal economy of service has been transformed into a wage economy. Quilligan reproduces the frontispiece to part 5 of *America* by Theodor de Bry, which shows both Europeans and slaves doing the work of empire and concludes that 'Slaves are not always others' in Spenser's poem, something made clear when Artegall 'is turned into a wage slave' by Radigund in Book V (p. 50). The 'comliness' and order with which the knights sew is not proper male labour, and Quilligan makes a link between the armed Guyon who watches the naked slaves of Mammon and the armed Artegall watching the cross-dressed sewing knights, concluding that 'to do either sort of labor is to become enslaved' (p. 54). Racial difference is policed by gender in Renaissance epics and any possibility of inter-dynastic marriage avoided when (as with Radigund and Britomart) both warriors are women. The surrounding context of men doing women's work comes close to 'articulating the fundamental historical reason for creating this racial otherness, that is, a cultural need to create a group of lesser beings for whom such labor is their natural calling' (p. 55). There is, claims Quilligan, a hitherto unnoticed parallel between the work done in Book II and the feminized Artegall in Book V.

Part 2 of this collection of essays is entitled 'Allegories of Cultural Exchange' and begins with 'Translated States: Spenser and Linguistic Colonialism' (pp. 67–88), a fine piece by Richard A. McCabe which builds upon some of the central issues raised by critics on Spenser and Ireland. McCabe argues that Spenser's analysis of Irish culture is 'pervasively semantic' and that he uses 'highly politicized exercises in "etymology" to support his arguments' (p. 70). Since Irish culture was considered to preserve more of the ancient than any other, assimilation into that culture was considered to be not just alteration but degeneration. Spenser employs etymological means to show that the Celtic language was spoken by the barbarians that overran the Roman empire, and he analyses the degeneration of Old English via language. In *The Shepheardes Calender* E.K. warns against the contamination of the English language by foreign words. For Richard Stanyhurst the adoption of the Irish language led to adoption of an Irish political outlook, and Spenser considered it possible for Irishness to be transmitted to an English child via the breast milk of an Irish nurse. For Spenser 'the ultimate linguistic sign of cultural degeneracy is the adoption of an Irish patronym in place of an English one' such as occurred with the Fitz Ursulas, who became the MacMahons (p. 76). Spenser was interested in Irish bardic culture and had Irish poems translated, a process that inevitably involves appropriation and reduction. McCabe notes the meaning of 'translation' as 'change' and Spenser's criticism of the translation of the English in Ireland; for Spenser and Sir John Davies 'the proper business of translation' would be accomplished only when there was 'a complete absence of Gaelic speakers' (p. 83). Ironically, Spenser utilizes what was regarded by some to be an inferior Old English archaism. Willy Maley has suggested that this use of archaism was inspired by contact with Ireland but, as McCabe points out, Spenser objected to intrusion of Celtic words and Maley does not distinguish between words of Anglo-Saxon and Celtic origin. At certain moments the distinction between Irenius and the Irish social practices he describes breaks down, a process partly evident in his use of Irish vocabulary to describe these practices, which may indicate 'the growing influence of Spenser's experience upon his vocabulary and the political attitude it articulates' (p. 86). The result is that Spenser's language 'bears witness to an unconscious process of assimilation of which his conscious polemic fights shy' (p. 88).

Also considering Spenser's role in Ireland Nicholas Canny, in 'The Social and Political Thought of Spenser in his Maturity' (pp. 107–22), claims that it is not true to say that Spenser's advocacy of violence placed him outside the traditions of Renaissance humanism. Although humanists were opposed to dynastic wars of aggression and private armies, argues Canny, they believed that Christians were obliged to use violence to defend and promote religious truths, to maintain the order of the populace, and to civilize barbaric regions. Most Christian humanists would have accepted the notion elaborated by Spenser in *The Faerie Queene* Books II and

V that 'civil society had first been established by force' (p. 116). Despite his apparent radicalism then, Spenser's opinions were probably similar to those of most of his generation in England, who were influenced by John Foxe's *Book of Martyrs*, published in 1563. Most importantly, Spenser's 'political and social principles remained consistent throughout his career as a poet'. However, claims Canny, two aspects of Spenser's later poetry made it controversial 'and pointed to the more extreme of the ideas that he was to expound more specifically in the *Viewe*' (p. 117): these are his adherence to a rigid Protestant line in relation to Mary Queen of Scots as depicted in *The Faerie Queene* and, given the prospect of a union of the crowns of England and Scotland, his belief in a central authority under the English monarch. So, although Spenser's message remained consistent—he was throughout his life 'an uncompromising champion of the achievements of the Protestant Reformation' (p. 118)—his manner of expressing his message changed. This came about in later books of *The Faerie Queene* because of disillusionment when the prominent Protestant figures who had supported his career were either disgraced or went unrewarded. His abandonment of allegory and the epic itself 'combined, therefore, to make the point that there was no longer a glorious achievement to be celebrated' (p. 120). Spenser felt particularly resentful at the treatment of Lord Grey and, claims Canny, the abandonment of allegory in Book V was an attempt to find support for his views on Ireland: that the struggle being fought there was a central part of the Catholic assault against Protestantism.

The third section of the book, 'The Functions of Allegory', opens with an essay by Paul Alpers, '"Worke fit for an Herauld": Spenser in the '90s' (pp. 125–33), which argues that we can better understand Spenser's late poetry by considering his social and material position. In Book V of *The Faerie Queene* Spenser claims that to describe the gathering of lords and ladies at the wedding of Florimell and Marinell 'Were worke fit for an Herauld, not for me' (V.iii.iii), but Alpers suggests that 'the canto's purposes as a "treatise" of justice come into conflict with the romance narration the poet has just renounced' (p. 126). In another sense Spenser 'cannot disown "work fit for an Herauld"' since some of his best poetry from the 1590s conforms to 'the herald's task of blazoning forth noble personages and their accoutrements' (p. 128). What Alpers calls 'The splendors of Spenserian listing' are displayed in the *Prothalamion* and the *Epithalamion* and also in the Mutability Cantos. Alpers follows Gordon Teskey in thinking that the poet can be found partly in the figure of Mutability and the figure of Order, a minor official who simply does his job—like Spenser the poet who composes the procession. The poet also appears in the figure of Colin Clout, a direct self-representation 'notable for social diffidence' (p. 129); as a ploughman in Book V (iii.xl) and Book VI (ix.i); and in the figure of the poet Bonfont. This points to what Alpers calls 'the double aspect of the lyric Spenser' (p. 130), that is, the poet speaking in the first person and appearing in specific represented roles. It is ironic, claims Alpers, that Spenser rejects 'worke fit for an Herauld' since the College of Arms, staffed by heralds, determined who had a claim to coats of arms and noble ranks, and, according to Louis Montrose, 'Spenser's motives were undoubtedly to affirm his status as a gentleman' (p. 97). Alpers suggests that Montrose might claim that in saying he is better than a herald Spenser 'reveals his anxiety about the need to persuade the heralds of his merits' (p. 132). These conflicts, asserts Alpers, 'are among the many signs that the epic-allegorical project of *The Faerie Queene* was coming apart' and the poems of the

1590s are an alternative to further instalments of *The Faerie Queene*. Though they deal with similar issues, the shorter poems are characterized by their public nature and the innovative nature of the *Epithalamion*, which celebrates the poet's own marriage in a distinct genre and 'suggests strong claims of authority and entitlement' (p. 133).

In an intriguing essay, 'The Enfolding Dragon: Arthur and the Moral Economy of *The Faerie Queene*' (pp. 135–65), Susanne L. Wofford focuses on the figure of Prince Arthur in *The Faerie Queene* and the problem of deciphering codes. The appearance of Prince Arthur is resistant to allegorical meaning or intentionality yet Arthur becomes a central figure and through him 'Spenser attempts to work out the deeper implications of his poem's effort to unite religion, politics, and romance' (p. 136). Wofford claims that in *The Faerie Queene* one way of understanding past threats made safe is through the language of typology using the concept of the 'figura'. The structure of Book I especially suggests a divide whereby readers meet first 'the evil or literal version of these much repeated images' and then need to learn 'the redemptive or restorative version'. Arthur's entry incorporates an 'extended anti-type to the earlier images' in the allegory, but represents the 'true' or life-giving version: for example his shiny armour reflects the brightness of Lucifera's palace and the dragon on his helmet recalls its 'partial incarnation' in Error's den and its presence under Lucifera's throne. The theory of typology helps the reader to avoid 'the problem of dualism' by suggesting that the type 'is not negated but fulfilled by the anti-type' as part of a larger scheme in which 'what comes first is re-read and re-understood following a paradigm applied retrospectively' (p. 138).

In the penultimate essay from this important collection Kenneth Gross, in 'The Postures of Allegory' (pp. 167–79), claims that allegory is a strange and defamiliarizing form. This is partly to do with the fragmentary nature of allegory by which parts of the allegory are contained within other parts, for example Spenser's allegorical Envy 'contains a seed of the Blatant Beast' (p. 170). Additionally 'allegory's rationality is often fantastic, formally barbaric, rationalizing' (p. 173), as is evident in Spenser's Acrasia, by which Aristotle's complex concept of *akrasia* is personified and thus reduced. Gross contends that, while parts of Spenser's poem can illuminate or give fresh shape to old ideas and values, at times the personifications made from abstract nouns and qualities can 'feel oddly opaque', a trait evident in the procession in Busyrane's house where 'the pressure to make agents out of ideas threatens to reduce both agents and ideas to a kind of nonsense' (pp. 174–5). Gross asserts that, though there is 'something dead or inert in allegorical writing', still its 'fixities' are 'something to be desired' and a form to which the reader yields (p. 175).

The collection ends on a high note with an ingenious parody of Spenser's dialogic *View* by Andrew Hadfield and Willy Maley, 'A View of the Present State of Spenser Studies: Dialogue-Wise' (pp. 183–95). The tone is witty and the subject-matter substantial. Maley is concerned about what he calls 'the appeal of Ireland' in Spenser studies because of 'the frisson of the Troubles' and 'the threat of political violence' which provides 'an aura of worldliness to an academic text' (p. 184). He claims that Greenblatt's famous essay from *Renaissance Self-Fashioning* and Nicholas Canny's 'Edmund Spenser and the Development of an Anglo-Irish Identity' have suggested that not foregrounding Ireland is 'somehow deficient or dishonest' (p. 184). Maley is concerned that Ireland 'is beginning to colonize

Spenser' and is alarmed by the risk of 'reduction and oversimplification' whereby there is a tendency for Spenser to be singled out from amongst his peers for particular and unfair criticism. (It might be objected of course that Spenser, the poet, set himself up for this criticism when he wrote a position paper advocating the genocide of the Irish populace.) In reply, Hadfield contests that Ireland is merely contextual to *The Faerie Queene*, rather than the two being organically entwined. Moreover, much recent criticism 'displays a blithe disregard for any Irish dimension', something which Hadfield dismisses as 'wrong-headed' (p. 186). Hadfield has a point and Maley seems to overstate his case; for example, Ireland does not dominate in the items considered for this review. Hadfield points to a 'hermeneutics of suspicion' in Spenser's work partly due to censorship, which means that Ireland is always in the frame even when this is not overt, but he suggests that one way to avoid 'Hibernocentrism' is to 'open out the Irish context to a British one' (p. 186), an indication of the direction in which Spenser studies appears to be moving. Maley responds by invoking the authorship question recently raised by Jean Brink, who questioned the safety of attributing the *View* to Spenser because direct bibliographical evidence is lacking. (Brink claimed that Spenser wrote none of the three manuscripts which constitute *A Brief Note of Ireland* and promised to substantiate this in an essay which has not yet appeared.) Hadfield agrees that Brink is right to call for more careful textual scholarship on the *View*, but her arguments against his authorship are not convincing and, moreover, it seems that she does not want the *View* to have been written by Spenser, 'a claim that suits those who wish to minimize the impact of Ireland on Spenser' (p. 187). Maley notes that a real problem is the lack of a proper, factually based biography of Spenser. Richard Rambuss has questioned the received opinion that Spenser wanted primarily to be a poet, but it is difficult to recover a sense of how people regarded themselves or their work in this period. His religion is also a 'key problem' and has received only 'sporadic attention' by critics (p. 188). Hadfield brings the discussion back to the issue of Ireland and argues that religion cannot be read without reference to the Irish context of the poem. Moreover 'the problem of identity' cannot be separated from 'the question of genre' and work done by critics on the experimental nature of *The Faerie Queene* may tell us more about Spenser (p. 190). Maley cites critics who have found fault with Greenblatt's essay and other colonial writings which read sexual politics primarily as an allegory of colonial politics, but for Hadfield one discourse should not be privileged over any other and we should not misread 'their complex interaction' (p. 194). Maley considers *The Faerie Queene* to be 'all about history and politics' and Spenser's focus on colonial matters can be read as a way of critiquing the court without fear of punishment. Fundamentally, Ireland cannot be understood without reference to England and the court. He concludes that Spenserians need to look beyond Ireland and 'put *The Faerie Queene* back into the world' (p. 195)—a nice nod towards the theme of the conference at which this paper was presented. Whether it is significant that Hadfield gets the last word is unclear, but he announces himself 'not entirely convinced' by Maley's argument, a position shared by this reviewer at least.

In the introduction to her monograph *Showing Like a Queen: Female Authority and Literary Experiment in Spenser, Shakespeare, and Milton* Katherine Eggert considers the issues surrounding female authority in an era dominated by a powerful female monarch. The reason for selecting her chosen authors is threefold: literary innovation, imitation and influence. Chapter 2 is devoted to Spenser's *Faerie Queene*, an important text because it 'poses with increasing insistence the question of how new modes of literary design can be accomplished in response to feminine authority', and demonstrates a 'gender-inflected anxiety about writing an epic to and about a queen' which results 'not only in fulsome praise and/or savage recriminations toward figures of feminine authority in the poem, but also in stunning revisions of and departures from Spenser's primary poetic models, the classical epic and Italian romance' (p. 15). In Books I and II there is a kind of association between poetry and emasculating female power but in Book III the genre shifts from heroic epic into the more 'digressive' genre of epic romance and this paves the way for other 'more reactionary generic experiments' including the historical allegory of Book V and the courtly pastoral of Book VI. The execution of Mary Stuart had a profound influence on Spenser's poem and he 'ostentatiously repeals feminine rule in its closing books by successively dethroning the Amazon queen Radigund, the female knight Britomart, the titaness Mutabilitie, and even Queen Elizabeth herself' (p. 16). The alliances between poetry and femininity in Books III and IV necessitate the generic shifts in the second half of the poem, where Spenser questions how poetic authority might be conceived as something other than feminized. In Book IV Artegall responds negatively to marriage and Amoret, Scudamore's betrothed, has disappeared. In Book V the female authority of Astraea is substituted by the male Artegall and, claims Eggert, not only feminine rule but what she calls 'feminized poetics' is repealed in favour of the 'straightforward mode' of historical allegory. Similarly in Book VI the 'conspicuously and innovatively masculine anti-epic form' of pastoral is utilized (p. 46). Eggert sees an incontrovertible link between genre and gender especially in Books V and VI, which 'play out fantasies of freeing politics and poetry from feminine rule' and 'envision a newly masculine poetics' (p. 48).

Modesty prevents this reviewer from giving anything other than a description of Joan Fitzpatrick's monograph, *Irish Demons: English Writings on Ireland, the Irish and Gender by Spenser and his Contemporaries*, which is a study of colonialism and gender in *The Faerie Queene* and considers Spenser's poem in the context of hitherto neglected early modern English writings on Ireland and the Irish. The opening chapter includes a brief account of Ireland's colonization and Spenser's role in that process, with analysis of a little-known anonymous colonial tract, 'The Supplication of the Blood of the English'. This text is of particular interest to Spenserians because its author, like Spenser, was an English resident of Cork forced to flee the Munster rebellion. The second chapter investigates Elizabeth's role in Irish politics via Spenser's representation in *The Faerie Queene* of the conflict between truth and falsehood and argues that Una is an idealized allegorical representation of Ireland which allows Spenser to show both the colonizer (Una as Elizabeth) and the colonized landscape (Una as Ireland) endorsing the subjugation of the Irish. With Error and Duessa, Spenser demonstrates his eclecticism, for while both figures are shaped by Protestant theology and a variety of literary sources, they also carry strong Catholic Irish associations. The third chapter considers the critically notorious episode featuring Guyon in the Bower of Bliss and enlarges upon John Upton's suggestion in the eighteenth century that the red hands of Ruddymane allude to the emblem of the powerful Gaelic family of O'Neill. Anxieties about the political, religious, ethnic, and sexual alien are projected onto Acrasia, and her attack upon the innocent becomes the justification for Guyon's violence. It also considers the possibility that Shakespeare was inspired by the Ruddymane episode when composing the bloodier passages in *Macbeth*. The focus of chapter 4 is a piece of post-Reformation Catholic propaganda, Nicholas Sander's *Rise and Growth of the Anglican Schism*. Sander's pejorative depiction of Elizabeth and her mother Anne Boleyn is compared with Spenser's literary depictions of these women as Belphoebe and Chrysogone in *The Faerie Queene* in order to understand how female sexuality is used for political purposes. In this light Spenser's poem can be seen as a contribution to the post-Reformation propaganda war through which he answers the propagandists' defamation. This chapter also considers Shakespeare's depiction of Anne Boleyn in *All is True* (*King Henry VIII*) as another example of literary biography which answers the defamation of Elizabeth's mother. The Irish landscape and its relationship to the topography of Faeryland is considered in chapter 5, and in chapter 6 the mutilation and death of a minor figure, Munera, is related to Catholic reliquaries and Spenser's at least partly realized Petrarchan aggression. Chapter 7 considers the significance of key episodes where rebellion is expounded in sexual terms and territorial governance is presented via sexual dynamics. The concluding chapter is concerned with the Mutabilitie Cantos, where Mutabilitie's rebellion against Jove and Molanna's rebellion against Diana function as an appropriate coda for *The Faerie Queene* because here is a concentration of anxieties that suffuse the poem.

Although not strictly speaking a book about Spenser, Michelle O'Callaghan's monograph *The 'Shepheards Nation': Jacobean Spenserians and Early Stuart Political Culture, 1612–1625* deserves a brief mention since it considers the influence of Spenser on three seventeenth-century writers. William Browne, George Wither, and Christopher Brooke regarded themselves as a distinct and oppositional community between the years 1613 and 1625, and 'took up Spenser's question of what it means to speak for the nation' (p. 2). The book considers poetic influence within what Callaghan calls 'textual communities' which involved themselves in the 'discursive interaction produced through the exchange and circulation of texts in manuscript or print' (p. 4). The writers considered here share a similar style and belong to a Spenserian tradition, for it was Spenser who provided them with a model whereby the shepherd–poet formed part of a literary commonwealth outside the court.

Two monographs that appeared from Cambridge University Press this year each devote a chapter to Spenser, Kenneth Borris's *Allegory and Epic in English Renaissance Literature* and Robert Matz's *Defending Literature in Early Modern England*. Borris objects to the notion that allegory became less important after 1600, claiming that new access to classical texts revived interest in the form. He also contends that, contrary to recent critical opinion, Spenser did not abandon allegory in the later books of *The Faerie Queene*. Spenser's presentation of inner and Christian virtues anticipates Milton's *Paradise Lost*, although Spenser's epic, unlike Milton's, is concerned with national celebration. Borris considers Milton's allegory in relation to Spenser's *Faerie Queene* and Sidney's *Arcadias* because he believes that, although these writers differ in their approach to allegory, they share an interest in exploring the psychological through the allegorical epic form. Robert Matz's monograph contains a chapter on Elyot's *Boke Named the Governour*, one on Spenser's *Faerie Queene* and another on Sidney's *Defence of Poetry*. His thesis is that in their adherence to Horatian doctrine these works reflect the conflicts surrounding aristocratic behaviour as a result of changes that took place during the sixteenth century. He also challenges new historicist claims that poetry is simply another form of discursive and institutional power because, by the end of the century, poetry was considered to be a distinct phenomenon. In chapter 4 Matz provides a reading of Book II of *The Faerie Queene* which maintains that Guyon's destruction of the Bower of Bliss is simultaneously part of a Protestant-humanist critique of the court and an attempt to appropriate its pleasures as the source of poetic authority. Spenser's main aim, according to Matz, is to draw a distinction between courtly pleasures and poetic pleasures since the latter rather than the former encourage profitable behaviour. Matz relates this to Spenser's biography: his elevation of poetic pleasures above courtly pleasures is no surprise given his social position as the member of a subordinate class.

Sarah Anne Brown's essay, 'Arachne's Web: Intertextual Mythography and the Renaissance Actaeon' (in Rhodes and Sawday, eds., *The Renaissance Computer: Knowledge Technology in the First Age of Print* pp. 120–34), refers to the 'hypertextual complexity' of Ovid's *Metamorphoses* and how this can affect our reading of *The Faerie Queene*. The text itself, much like the tapestries created by Arachne and Minerva, has its own 'internal intratextuality' or 'interwovenness' between stories and themes (p. 120). Most Renaissance editions of the *Metamorphoses* were heavily annotated, and Sandys's 1626 edition 'is a classic example of English Renaissance hypertext, for it builds on the inherent hypertextuality of Ovid's original work, reinscribing the poem within the Renaissance intellectual tradition' (p. 121). His explanatory notes function as hyperlinks to others' interpretations of the tale, as well as acting as a link to another Ovidian text, *Tristia*, in which the poet compares his fate with that of Actaeon. Brown considers the 'virtual network' that may have operated among writers and scholars by examining Renaissance responses to Ovid's story of Actaeon. Renaissance encyclopedias of myth record a range of responses to the story, but 'fail to replicate the complex, shifting response inspired by the original poem', something we can get from the literary texts which give us a response 'as multilayered and nuanced as the *Metamorphoses* itself' (p. 123). The poems considered by Brown are *The Faerie Queene* and Jonson's *Cynthia's Revels*. Actaeon is a subtext in at least four episodes of Spenser's poem. The first of these is the Fradubio episode from Book I, where Spenser has created 'a (virtual) hypertextual link with a version of the Diana and Actaeon story described in a dialogue of Lucian' (p. 123); Diana would have provoked association with Elizabeth, which makes more evocative Lucian's transformation of Diana into a whore. When the real Diana appears in Book III she may be 'tainted by our memories of Duessa' and the word 'loose', used to describe her state of undress, may also connote wantonness. Similarly the word 'disguized' could also mean 'concealed' or 'deformed'. So one path 'through a (virtually) hypertextual' *Faerie Queene* might 'undermine Diana and, indirectly, Elizabeth' (p. 125). Acrasia is another type of Diana and appears to contrast with Belphoebe. Braggadocchio narrowly misses the same fate as Actaeon at the hands of Belphoebe, and Guyon behaves like Actaeon in his interaction with Acrasia in Bower of Bliss (II.xii.lxxvi), which is like Ovid's description of Diana's grotto. However, links between pairings are 'not exact' since 'Diana is far more like Guyon than Acrasia in her unappealingly violent insistence upon her chastity' (p. 126). Diverse responses to

Actaeon's fate are like the reader's ambivalence towards Guyon's destruction of the bower, and a further link between Acrasia and Diana is the power of both to transform men into beasts. Although we might think Acrasia more like Circe, Diana and Circe 'had become bound together in a web of texts' such as Apuleius' *Golden Ass* and Shakespeare's *A Midsummer Night's Dream* (p. 126). The final allusion to Actaeon in *The Faerie Queene* is in the Mutabilitie Cantos in the figure of Faunus, which demonstrates the influence of Apuleius as well as that of Ovid. Brown makes a point of claiming that notes in a modern edition cannot replicate the experience of the Renaissance reader, 'who had actually read the intertexts which today's students encounter only as footnotes, and whose memory could scroll up and down them at will' (p. 127), but one might say that an educated reader can, to some extent, replicate this experience by absorbing herself in the texts with which the average Renaissance reader would have been familiar.

In a theoretically dense piece, 'Breaking the Mirror Stage' (in Mazzio and Trevor, eds., *Historicism, Psychoanalysis, and Early Modern Culture*, pp. 272–98), Kathryn Schwarz relates Lacan's mirror stage to the story of Britomart, who falls in love with Artegall's reflection and disguises herself as a knight to pursue it. Schwarz argues that Britomart is 'Like Lacan's subject, she looks in a mirror, sees a fully articulated image of agency, is caught up in a succession of fantasies—and takes on "the armour of an alienating identity" [here quoting from Lacan] in order to become what she desires' (p. 273). Britomart's disguise 'plays out the processes of enabling misperception' which supplements allegorical and chivalric systems of identity since her encounters with Artegall produce a particularly gendered negotiation of identity. Spenser's chivalric narratives anticipate the Lacanian mirror stage, for they 'figure successful role-playing as a complicated compromise between identity and difference, deception and revelation, violence and desire' (p. 274). As in the mirror stage, the armour-wearing figure is 'an image that both is and is not logically connected to the body to which it refers' and identity depends on confrontation. When armour is attached to women the process becomes complicated because martial women 'suggest not only that gender is a construct, but that its shifting terms undermine the hierarchical relationship between homosocial structures of power and the heterosexuality through which they are reproduced' (p. 274).

Also concentrating on Book V of *The Faerie Queene*, Gregory Tobias, 'Shadowing Intervention: On the Politics of *The Faerie Queene* Book 5 Cantos 10–12' (*ELH* 67:ii[2000] 365–97), notes that critics tend to dismiss the book's concluding episodes as examples of dull poetry and questionable morality, a view that was most famously summed up by C.S. Lewis. What Tobias calls 'versions of Lewis's corruption thesis' are common in Spenser studies, and he challenges Michael O'Connell's assumption that Spenser's motive in Book V is to praise Elizabeth's foreign policy. In an attempt to 'present a more nuanced account of its politics' (p. 365) Tobias argues that three key episodes toward the end of Book V comment on Elizabethan foreign and colonial policy 'from an interventionist Protestant perspective that is far from univocally celebratory or optimistic' (p. 366). There is apparent criticism of the 'half measures' that constituted Elizabeth's foreign policy, and in his depiction of these episodes Spenser subtly provides 'a vision of the English state that looks very much like the interventionist ideal' (p. 366). The Belge episode is presented in terms of the conventions of chivalric romance and it is expected that a just knight will intervene on the victim's behalf.

The political situation in the Netherlands was regarded as a moral imperative by those who supported English intervention, but until 1585 Elizabeth refused to help and even then tried to minimize English involvement. Leicester's acceptance of the office of governor-general from the Dutch outraged Elizabeth, and while Spenser makes topical reference to this he 'quietly erases the conflict' when he has Arthur decline Belge's offer. What Tobias refers to as Spenser's 'tactical amnesia' (a phrase borrowed from Linda Gregerson's *The Reformation of the Subject*) is also evident in Mercilla's gratitude, which contrasts with Elizabeth's feelings about the expedition. Also, the outcome is final and successful in Spenser's story, whereas Leicester suffered from a real lack of resources and the problem of Dutch factions. Tobias contends that this idealization by Spenser might constitute criticism of Leicester, but also of Elizabeth's lack of commitment. In the Burbon episode Spenser emphasizes compromise rather than victory, which suggests he is not simply praising the government. Artegall's progress is impeded by the domestic forces of self-interest, compromise, and a policy of half-measures. In the last section of the essay Tobias criticizes the aristocratic/monarchical dichotomy, used by Richard Helgerson in *Forms of Nationhood* to describe Spenser's policies, and the association of Spenser with imperialism. He denies that Spenser supported a return to aristocratic rule: he may have criticized his monarch's policy, but not centralized policy. He also objects to Simon Shepherd and Stephen Greenblatt, who both describe Spenser as a poet of empire, since Spenser could not have predicted the Victorian empire, and argues that the 'imperialist impulse' must be separated from impulses of personal ambition and international Protestant solidarity. Elizabeth was, he claims, less interested in empire-building than her father or Henry V, and the period was one of perceived isolation, with the focus on the Catholic threat rather than expansion. Note 57 states that the 'Elizabethan English were no more engaged in empire-building in the New World than the old. As Jeffrey Knapp has reminded us, [in *An Empire Nowhere*] English efforts at colonization in America were "dismal failures" until the seventeenth century, particularly by comparison with the vast, lucrative colonies of Spain'. This is strange logic and undermines an otherwise fine essay, the most obvious objection to Tobias's argument being that just because they failed in their colonization of America does not mean that the impulse to expand was not present; it certainly made its presence felt in Ireland, and this cannot only be explained in terms of the Catholic threat.

In another modesty-driven and thus purely descriptive review, Joan Fitzpatrick, 'Spenser and Land: Political Conflict Resolved in Physical Topography' (*BBJ* 7[2000] 365–77), considers the emergence of a pattern in *The Faerie Queene* whereby the landscape which has been a source of strength for villains shifts allegiance in order to collude with the poem's heroes. Victory is signalled by the bodily disintegration of a wrongdoer, and his annihilation indicates a clear moment of resolution in the fight between vice and virtue. The repeated destruction of recognizably Catholic villains suggests Spenser's desire to entirely rid the landscape of their influence. That the landscape cooperates in this cleansing operation constitutes a fantasy that the environment itself assists the colonizer in the eradication of resistance to the colonial project in Ireland.

Also focusing on Ireland is a fine piece by Judith Owens, 'The Poetics of Accommodation in Spenser's "Epithalamion"' (*SEL* 40:i[2000] 41–62), which asserts that the political, cultural, and social contexts of Spenser's *Epithalamion* have been neglected. Of particular interest to Owens is the connection between this poem and Spenser's 'reformist' designs not only for Ireland but for his bride. The refrain in the poem, variations on 'The woods shall to me answer and my Eccho ring', can signify harmony but has been read by some critics as a source of disturbance. Owens claims that the woods around Kilcolmon give the refrain social and political significance. Spenser thought that deforestation was a necessary prerequisite for the subjugation of Ireland and Owens makes a nice connection between the title of his prose tract, the *View* and his desire 'to see this country and its people', who literally hide from sight and remain hidden in the sense of not being known (p. 42). Bearing the *View* in mind, Spenser desires 'to make the woods answer' to his song and thus subject both the country and his bride to 'English ways' (p. 45). In the opening stanza of poem Spenser looks back to England and the classical world in order to 'find the order and vision' into which he 'at least initially wishes to place his bride and thus Ireland' (p. 45). The praising of his bride will edify her and Ireland since an Ireland 'resonating with his exemplary love' with woods echoing his song 'would be an Ireland reformed by his poetic vision and so rendered intelligible' (p. 45). But his song does not resound as the opening stanza suggests, rather both Elizabeth and the woods respond to a song which is not the poet's and Spenser's attempts to 'circumscribe the poem's subjects—its woodland and Elizabeth herself—elude formative and reformative designs' (p. 49).

Helen Cooney, 'Guyon and his Palmer: Spenser's Emblem of Temperance' (*RES* 51[2000] 169–92), considers the hitherto critically neglected figure of the Palmer who guides Guyon in Book II of *The Faerie Queene*. Cooney considers it 'extraordinary' that, given the increasingly theorized nature of Spenser studies, the Palmer has not been analysed in a way that utilizes hermeneutics and the process of interpretation, since he 'actually carries the rod of Hermes, and is *himself* a hermeneut or interpreter' (p. 169). Cooney is particularly concerned with the loss and restoration of the Palmer. The two temptations of Phaedria and Mammon take the Palmer's place and invert his role as leader by trying to mislead. She provides a reappraisal of these 'twin' episodes—twinned because both are based on Matthew 7, where Christ warns man, 'Ye cannot serve God and riches'. Both figures are characterized in relation to care: its absence or the obsession with it. In the third stage of Mammon's temptation, which features the pairing of Tantalus and Pilate, Spenser gives us two sinners who exemplify the sin of curiosity as defined in Geneva Bible as excessive care for worldly things. While Phaedria is an antitype to the Palmer, Mammon is a parody of him—both wear black, both act as guides, and both offer counsel. When the Palmer is absent Guyon's reason is obscured but not destroyed. The emphasis is on grace: Guyon is wise in his encounters but imperfectly so, because, although not entirely without grace, he lacks perfecting grace. Cooney concludes with a consideration of Arthur's defeat of Maleager, an episode which constitutes 'Spenser's final refinement of the allegory of prudence' and his 'final reflections' on the process of interpreting allegory (p. 189).

In a piece which considers complex theoretical ideas but is at its best when focusing on historical matters, Elizabeth Mazzola, '"O unityng confounding": Elizabeth I, Mary Stuart, and the Matrix of Renaissance Gender' (*Exemplaria* 12[2000] 385–416), claims that Elizabeth Tudor and Mary Stuart, a twinned presence she calls a 'specter', provoked and relieved the anxieties of those around them. Mazzola considers both Spenser and Shakespeare to be part of a network around these two women which explored issues such as 'the erotic tangles caused by male gazing, or the artificiality of female chastity', issues which 'were shaped by doubled images, built on a poetic premise that one female body might supplement another' (p. 386). Mazzola contends that Elizabeth and Mary provided a model for 'the anguished intimacy and dependency' of Goneril and Regan in Shakespeare's *King Lear*, and she draws links between Elizabeth's representations of herself—a chaste woman, a kind of mother—and Spenser's *Faerie Queene* where 'images of femaleness all tend to be partial, often failed, and always contested' (p. 392). She also compares the secreted and unseen Mary, held imprisoned on Elizabeth's orders, to Spenser's Gloriana. It is more accurate, according to Mazzola, to speak not of Elizabeth's two bodies but of 'a Tudor femaleness that required two bodies, one continually absorbing and repressing or correcting the defects of the other' (p. 394). If Mary's body was corrupt and thus incomplete so Elizabeth's 'relied on a constant surveillance of anatomical borders and political margins, the neglect of which could present similar imbalances' (p. 395). Book III of *The Faerie Queene* was written when Mary was being detained in England and her image was 'fatally entangled with the Queen's' (p. 397). Belphoebe and Amoret represent 'this threatening if glorious alliance' which is also evident in Florimell and False Florimell (p. 397). Part of the essay concentrates on *King Lear* and so is beyond the remit of this review.

Staying with gender, Elizabeth A. Spiller's 'Poetic Parthenogenesis and Spenser's Idea of Creation in *The Faerie Queene*' (*SEL* 40:i[2000] 63–79) is concerned with the concept of parthenogenesis as a way of reading Spenser's *Faerie Queene* and the process of literary production. The notion that men could think ideas into being implied the acceptance of Galenic humoral theory, but also an Aristotelian model that was being challenged in this period. Spiller considers 'moments of initiation in *The Faerie Queene* that are described using the language of biological reproduction' in order to demonstrate that, while recent critics such as Greenblatt have emphasized the Renaissance as 'an age of self-actualization for the writer' whereby writers 'demonstrate new forms of subjectivity and employ sophisticated models of self-representation in which they seem to think themselves into being', Spenser 'draws on the contemporary recognition that men's thoughts were not sufficient to bring forth new creation', and his creations depict 'perversions of the Aristotelian model current in the early modern period' (p. 64). The moments considered by Spiller are the Letter to Ralegh; Redcrosse's first battle with Errour; Arthur's dream of Gloriana; and Britomart's experiences after seeing Artegall in Merlin's mirror. Spenser defines the ideal knight and quest in Aristotelian terms: he is 'pregnant with an idea which is expressed in the quest and produces progeny such as glory' (p. 68), and 'the ideas that inform quests originate in the male alone' (p. 67). However, in his depiction of Errour 'giving birth to monstrous "text-children"', Spenser 'draws on the medical belief that women's ideas, when uncontrolled, produce monstrous offspring'—an idea which 'upset the Aristotelian order by letting their unchecked minds "mark" their children' (p. 69). Britomart is also associated with anti-Aristotelian birth narrative since her sickness, after seeing Artegall, is a kind of perverse pregnancy and makes a 'monster of [her] mind' (*FQ* III.ii.xl.2). By contrast, Arthur's dream of the Faerie Queene 'impregnates him with an idea that leads to a nine-month travail that invokes contemporary fantasies of male pregnancy' (p. 69). In the Errour episode Spenser 'uses bad textual "issue" to characterize his narrative as a good literary production' (p. 70). Arthur is the 'generative' force of the poem and his dream can be compared to the creation narrative of Chrysogone: while she produces twins he produces an idea, his quest. In his Letter to Ralegh Spenser reveals his debt to Philip Sidney by using the language of biological reproduction in relation to his act of creation, and by having women create monsters through their minds and men giving birth, 'register[ing] anxiety about flaws in the Aristotelian paradigm'. This is not due to an interest in the scientific aspects of Aristotelian natural philosophy, but rather its poetic ramifications. This is an original and informed piece; one small criticism is that in her discussion of Britomart's dream Spiller wrongly glosses greensickness as 'emotional unreadiness' (in fact, according to Gordon Williams's *A Dictionary of Sexual Language and Imagery in Shakespearean and Stuart Literature*, it was an anaemic disease commonly attributed to a virgin's sexual fantasies which manifested itself through an unhealthy pallor and could only be cured by a sexual encounter).

George F. Butler's 'Leviathan and Spenser's Temple of Isis: Biblical Myth and Britomart's Dream in Book 5 of *The Faerie Queene*' (*ANQ* 13:iii[2000] 8–14) reminds us that most critics have focused on the classical background of Britomart's visit to the Temple of Isis but the Christian context has on the whole been ignored. In his account of Britomart's dream, Spenser borrows from Christian interpretations of the Old Testament sea creature Leviathan. Here Butler traces links between the crocodile in Britomart's dream and the biblical beast which can help us to understand the nature of justice. Both creatures symbolize pride, with Spenser's crocodile being subservient to Isis and Leviathan obedient to the Lord. Although the beast of Revelation has been identified with Leviathan, Spenser is primarily indebted to Job because he wants his beast to be a 'terrifying but noble' agent of justice and is keen to play down any evil associations. In Job, Leviathan carries out the Lord's commands, and in *The Faerie Queene* the crocodile is made subject to the equity of Isis. Just as Job becomes more just after God explains the mystery of Leviathan so in Spenser's poem the crocodile, or Osiris, helps Britomart understand her relation to justice, Artegall, and destiny. The explication by the priests acts like the glosses in the Geneva Bible and helps to clarify Britomart's vision. Thomas Hobbes, in his *Leviathan* [1651], said that the state, like the monster, is God's agent, and Spenser offers a similar interpretation of the crocodile. Artegall's savagery is checked by Britomart's sense of equity and clemency, and although people are subject to Artegall, the crocodile or Leviathan, they are also subject to Britomart, Isis, and the Lord.

A range of perceptive new readings emerged from this year's *Notes and Queries*. Matthew Steggle, 'Spenser's Ludgate: A Topical Reference in *The Faerie Queene* II.x.' (*N&Q* 47[2000] 34–7), observes that in the Chronicle of Briton Kings read by Spenser's Arthur in the House of Alma (*FQ* II.x) the account of Lud differs from that given by Geoffrey of Monmouth in *The History of the Kings of Britain*. Spenser omits various details and presents a more attractive figure, inventing the detail that Ludgate was built by Lud. The allusion in *The Faerie Queene* is datable since in the first half of the 1580s Ludgate was in a bad state of repair and would not have been considered an 'endlesse moniment'. In 1586 the whole structure was demolished and rebuilt from the foundations with a tax imposed upon the city to make this possible. Images of Lud and other kings were restored and an image of Elizabeth added. Praise of Lud's gate was unlikely before its rebuilding in 1586, and this date provides evidence that the first half of *The Faerie Queene* was composed between 1579 and 1590. It also adds evidence to support the argument made by Josephine Waters Bennett that the Arthur plot and the Chronicle took shape at a relatively late stage in composition of Books I–III.

Andrew Hadfield, 'Rory Oge O'More, the Massacre at Mullaghmast (1578), John Derricke's *The Image of Ireland* (1581), and Spenser's Malengin' (*N&Q* 47[2000] 423–4), builds upon a recent article by Vincent Carey, who argues that the massacre at Mullaghmast in March 1578, when Sir Henry Sidney ordered the slaughter of the followers of the rebel Rory Oge O'More, strongly influenced the representation of the Irish in John Derricke's *The Image of Irelande* [1581]. O'More's rebellion threatened the newly established colonies in Laois and Offaly, and so its suppression was particularly savage. Carey claimed that Derricke's work is a strong defence of Sidney's actions and that its aggressive anti-Catholicism and denigration of the Irish prefigures the hostilities of the 1590s, noting that in the *Image* O'More is a devious figure associated with witchcraft. Hadfield here argues that Derricke's representation of O'More influenced Spenser's Malengin in Book V of *The Faerie Queene*. Both are threats to the establishment of civilization in the wilderness, prey on passers-by, and are evasive shape-changers with a suggestion of witchcraft. Malengin is destroyed by Talus who, along with Artegall (Lord Grey), defeats the Catholic rebels in Ireland. Spenser thus continues Derricke's defence of Sidney, and English readers in Ireland would have spotted the parallel which provides a link between the polemical writing of the 1580s, when Spenser first came to Ireland, and the mid-1590s Nine Years War.

Samuel R. Kessler, 'An Analogue for Spenser's Despair Episode: Perkins's "Dialogue ... Betweene Sathan and the Christian"' (*N&Q* 47[2000] 31–4), asserts that the Despair episode from Book I of *The Faerie Queene* is remarkably similar to William Perkins's 'A Dialogue containing the conflicts betweene Sathan and the Christian' [?1589], printed a few months before the publication of Spenser's poem. However, there may be a variety of sources that influenced Spenser in this episode: conventional rhetorical devices; John Higgins's 'Legend of Queen Cordila' printed in *The Mirrour for Magistrates*; and Thomas Becon's 'Dialogue between the Christian Knight and Satan', which contains theological and rhetorical similarities to Spenser's passage. Perkins's 'Dialogue' 'has remarkable affinities of tone, content, and rhetorical devices' to Spenser's episode, although it is similar in style to Becon's work and commonplace theological arguments. Because Perkins's work was published in November 1589 at the earliest, it is unlikely to have influenced Spenser directly unless it had circulated in manuscript. Spenser could have come across it from October 1589, but *The Faerie Queene* was being prepared for print and revisions would have been difficult. Kessler notes that the analogues between the two works are striking and 'the discovery of a conduit between Perkins and Spenser—via Harvey, for instance—would be one step towards elucidating the relationship of the two works'. One might hope for such a conduit between any two works bearing close similarities, but a lack of evidence for direct influence makes for a rather disappointing conclusion to Kessler's note. Fragments of Perkins's 'Dialogue' and the corresponding passages from Spenser are printed at the end of the note.

Penny McCarthy, 'E.K. was only the Postman' (*N&Q* 47[2000] 28–31), contends that, although Spenser wants us to think that E.K. from *The Shepheardes Calender* is his friend Edward Kirk, he also wants us to suspect that it is none other than himself. Kirk is a deliberate obstruction and part of the 'indirection' of entire work (p. 28). Evidence for this can be found in the Epistle of 10 April 1579 prefacing *The Shepheardes Calender*, its glosses, and the letters—the 'familiar' and the 'commendable'—published in 1580. According to McCarthy, Spenser 'envisages himself as an "E.K." when he is commenting or adding scholia, or revising' (p. 31). The strongest objection to identifying Spenser as E.K. is that it is 'improper' for him to promote his own work in such positive terms, but McCarthy proposes that under E.K. he introduces 'a new poet who is other than himself' in much the same way that he uses verse by Mary Sidney in his *Astrophil* which is described as a 'lay' by 'Clorinda' (p. 31).

In a note which bears upon Spenser's role in Ireland, '"That arch-Poet of the Fairie lond": A New Spenser Allusion' (*N&Q* 47[2000] 37), Colin Burrow finds an association between Spenser and the exiled Ovid. John Gower's *Ovid's Festivalls, or Romane Calendar* [1640] is the first complete English verse translation of Ovid's *Fasti*, and preliminary biographical matter places an emphasis on Ovid's exile. Between this material and the translation is a poem, 'Clio's Complaint for the death of Ovid', which is influenced by Spenser's 'Teares of the Muses'. Apollo's reply to Clio notes that the fates have carried off many poets, and refers to 'That arch-Poet of the Fairie lond'. Burrow argues that this is clearly Spenser because the title page of the collection of his works which appeared in 1611 referred to him as 'Englands arch Poët'. Further evidence that Spenser is here being alluded to is 'the Spenserian archaism of the half-rhyme on "lond"' (p. 37). This allusion has not been noted before in any of the extensive collections of allusions to Spenser, and builds upon the Jacobean view of him as a poet who did not get the rewards he deserved. This association between Spenser and a tradition of poets who offended the authorities indicates that the view of him as a poet of exile is not an exclusively modern phenomenon.

Cheney and Silberman, eds., *Worldmaking Spenser: Explorations in the Early Modern Age* (UPKen [2000]) was reviewed in *YWES* 79[1999]. I was unable to see copies of the following: 'Spenser's Ravishment: Rape and Rapture in *The Faerie Queene*' (*Representations* 70[2000] 1–26); 'Isis in Spenser and Apuleius', in Constance S. Wright and Julia Bolton Holloway, eds., *Tales Within Tales: Apuleius Through Time* (AMS [2000]); 'Annotating Anonymity, or Putting a Gloss on *The Shepheardes Calender*', in Handley, Bray, and Henry, eds., *Ma(r)king the Text*.

Books Reviewed

Adams, Alison, and Stanton J. Linden. *Emblems and Alchemy*. UGlasP. [1998] pp. 215. £15 ISBN 0 8626 1680 5.

Bach, Rebecca Ann. *Colonial Transformations: The Cultural Production of the New Atlantic World, 1580–1640*. Palgrave. [2000] pp. 304. £32.50 ISBN 0 3122 3099 0.

Borris, Kenneth. *Allegory and Epic in English Renaissance Literature: Heroic Form in Sidney, Spenser, and Milton*. CUP. [2000] pp. 320. £40 ISBN 0 5217 8129 9.

Dutton, Richard. *Licensing, Censorship and Authorship in Early Modern England*. Palgrave. [2000] pp. 240. £32.50 ISBN 0 3337 2184 5.

Eggert, Katherine. *Showing Like a Queen: Female Authority and Literary Experiment in Spenser, Shakespeare, and Milton*. UPennP. [2000] pp. 289. £36.80 ($45) ISBN 0 8122 3532 0.

Fitzpatrick, Joan. *Irish Demons: English Writings on Ireland, the Irish and Gender by Spenser and his Contemporaries*. UPA. [2000] pp. 200. £31.38 ($36.50) ISBN 0 7618 1735 2.

Hazard, Mary E. *Elizabethan Silent Language*. UNebP. [2000] pp. 416. £35 ISBN 0 8032 2397 8.

Henry, Anne, Joe Bray and Miriam Handley, eds. *Ma(r)king the Text: The Presentation of Meaning on the Literary Page*. Ashgate. [2000] pp. 350. £45 ISBN 0 7546 0168 4.

Matz, Robert. *Defending Literature in Early Modern England: Renaissance Literary Theory in Social Context*. CUP. [2000] pp. 188. £37.50 ISBN 0 5216 6080 7.

Mazzio, Carla, and Douglas Trevor, eds. *Historicism, Psychoanalysis, and Early Modern Culture*. Routledge. [2000] pp. 432. hb £60 ISBN 0 4159 2052 3, pb £13.99 ISBN 0 4159 2053 1.

Morrison, Jennifer Klein, and Matthew Greenfield, eds. *Edmund Spenser: Essays on Culture and Allegory*. Ashgate. [2000] pp. 201. £40 ISBN 0 7546 0227 3.

Moulton, Ian Frederick. *Before Pornography: Erotic Writing in Early Modern England*. OUP. [2000] pp. xiii + 268. £38 ISBN 0 1951 3709 4.

O'Callaghan, Michelle. *The 'Shepheards Nation': Jacobean Spenserians and Early Stuart Political Culture, 1612–1625*. OUP. [2000] pp. 272. £40 ISBN 0 1981 8638 X.

Rhodes, Neil, and Jonathan Sawday, eds. *The Renaissance Computer: Knowledge Technology in the First Age of Print*. Routledge. [2000] pp. 224. hb £60 ISBN 0 4152 2063 7, pb £16.99 ISBN 0 4152 2064 5.

Singh, Jyotsna G., and Ivo Kamps. *Travel Knowledge: 'Witnesses' to 'Navigations, Traffiques and Discoveries'*. Palgrave. [2000] pp. 368. hb £42.50 ISBN 0 3339 1552 6, pb £13.99 ISBN 0 3339 1544 5.

Stewart, Alan. *Philip Sidney: A Double Life*. Chatto. [2000] pp. 400. £19 ISBN 0 7011 6859 5.

Wooding, Lucy E.C. *Rethinking Catholicism in Reformation England*. OUP. [2000] pp. 305. £40 ISBN 0 1982 0865 0.

VI

Shakespeare

GABRIEL EGAN, PETER J. SMITH, SONIA MASSAI,
ANNE SWEENEY, MARGARET JANE KIDNIE, ANNALIESE
CONNOLLY, ANDREW HISCOCK, STEPHEN LONGSTAFFE,
JON ORTEN AND CLARE MCMANUS

This chapter has four sections: 1. Editions and Textual Matters; 2. Shakespeare in the Theatre; 3. Shakespeare on Screen; 4. Criticism. Section 1 is by Gabriel Egan; section 2 is by Peter J. Smith; section 3 is by Sonia Massai; section 4(a) is by Anne Sweeney, section 4(b) is by Margaret Jane Kidnie, section 4(c) is by Annaliese Connolly, section 4(d) is by Andrew Hiscock, section 4(e) is by Stephen Longstaffe, section 4(f) is by Jon Orten, and section 4(g) is by Clare McManus.

1. Editions and Textual Matters

Six major critical editions appeared this year. For the Arden3 series: *King Henry the Eighth* edited by Gordon McMullan, *King Henry VI Part One*, edited by Edward Burns, and *The Merry Wives of Windsor*, edited by Giorgio Melchiori; for the Oxford Shakespeare: *Richard III*, edited by John Jowett, *Romeo and Juliet*, edited by Jill Levenson, and *King Lear*, edited by Stanley Wells. Of these, Melchiori's *The Merry Wives of Windsor* was not received in time to be included in this survey and will be reviewed next year. Several New Cambridge Shakespeare editions were published in 1999 and 2000 and these will be reviewed together in next year's survey.

McMullan's introduction to *Henry VIII* runs to nearly 200 pages, nearly half of which is a 'Cultural History' constituting virtually a monograph on the play's meanings since its first performance. It should surprise no one, observes McMullan, that the play (usually subtitled *All Is True*) is only a partial slice of the truth: only two of the six wives are shown, and the play foregrounds engagements with the political truth of its own time and of Henry's time. Until recently, because 'the watchword of criticism was "unity"' (p. 4), those who liked the play tended to argue that it is all by Shakespeare, and those who disliked it blamed collaboration. Since the mid-1970s, however, it has been possible to read the play without the critical straitjacket of 'unity', and to see its contrary impulses ('at once celebratory and cynical about display', p. 5) and its representation of history as inherently a contradictory narrative.

Of the performance that burned down the first Globe playhouse, McMullan writes that 'It is described in one of the reports as a "new" play', but then he goes on to quote two reports in which it is said to be new (pp. 9, 58–9). He thinks it had previously been performed at the Blackfriars because of the irresistible resonances of using the very hall where Katherine's trial had taken place, and because Henry mentions Blackfriars explicitly (II.ii.139). If so, perhaps the big spectacles in the Folio text were added when it moved to the Globe which, unlike the Blackfriars, had room for them (p. 10). The second recorded performance (in which it is called 'K. Hen. 8') was at the Globe in 1628, sponsored by the duke of Buckingham to bolster his popularity; his doing this makes sense only if one assumes that he got the play's political irony. McMullan's account of the stage history documents the increasing attention to spectacle in eighteenth- and especially nineteenth-century productions, which made the words entirely subordinate. John Downes's claim that Thomas Betterton had his Henrician acting instructions from William Davenant, who had them from John Lowin, who had them from Shakespeare, suggests that Lowin (not Richard Burbage) performed Henry in 1613, setting a precedent for productions which show 'Henry in the prime of his years' (p. 18 n. 3). Burbage was 45 to Lowin's 37, and perhaps that is indeed enough of a difference.

The modern stage history of the play McMullan begins at 1916, when Herbert Beerbohm Tree's pre-war production toured the United States and was deemed a relic of a bygone age. Even in the twentieth century the play was never done in modern dress and was still used as propaganda. The attention to 'truth' and 'authenticity' shifted from the period in which the play is set (which the nineteenth-century spectacles wanted to recover) to the period in which it was first performed. The BBC TV version was, ironically, low-budget and 'inward' rather than spectacularly expansive, thus breaking with the stage tradition. Terence Gray's 1931 production was irreverent towards the history and debunked it, albeit in the name of a different kind of 'authenticity': the original performance effect. Gray's method was not to recreate the original staging, but to find a modern way of doing what the original did. The characters were dressed like playing-card figures and behaved like marionettes, although for the final moment Gray effectively rewrote Shakespeare: the baby turns out to be a cardboard doll of Elizabeth I aged 60 that is thrown into the audience. Rather than find subversiveness within the play, Gray worked against it to be radical. His alienation effect has influenced three subsequent Stratford productions, including the one by Tyrone Guthrie in 1949, where the duchess of Norfolk sneezed noisily during Cranmer's address in honour of the baby Elizabeth (p. 48). For the 1996 Royal Shakespeare Company production, Greg Doran's awareness of his predecessors made him want the play's ceremony to be taken 'straight' in order to show its emptiness, rather than have it undermined before it was even seen. Doran undermined the spectacle subtly by providing the rainstorm mentioned at I.i.90, and by a persistent whispering of courtiers even when they should be attentive. McMullan believes that audiences did not understand these devices, expecting either unironic celebration or else entire debunking (p. 55 n. 1).

Returning to the play's first contexts, McMullan gives a splendid reading of Henry Wotton's account of the burning of the Globe as an example of the familiar Reformation genre of *comedia apocalyptica* (pp. 60–1). The play is situated between 'celebration of James's Reformation inheritance and the suggestion that that Reformation had never truly taken place'. The important historical context of 1613 was that Prince Henry, a great hope for a reformed Europe, was gone, and Protestant hopes were transferred to his sister Elizabeth's marriage to Frederick, the Elector Palatine, the most prominent Continental Protestant ruler (p. 64). The baby Elizabeth would remind the audience of this Elizabeth. The 'truth' of the play (its title and Cranmer's final speech) relates to the 'Truth is the daughter of Time' iconography with which Elizabeth associated herself (Truth being the True Church liberated from her sister's Catholic influence). The theme of *veritas filia temporis* was revived by Dekker in *The Whore of Babylon*, and by Middleton in his pageant *The Triumphs of Truth*. To many Protestants Henry VIII was hardly a true Protestant reformer because, prior to the break with Rome, he had persecuted Protestant heretics. Because of his intemperance (in the senses of immoderation and keeping odd hours) Henry could not be 'Time', so Cranmer (who was to become a Protestant martyr under Mary) is a surrogate Father Time to the baby Elizabeth in the final scene (pp. 67–87). Cranmer's reference to Saba (Sheba) in his speech might also reflect badly on Henry, whose extra-marital infidelity is like David's with Bathsheba. Henry was known to be sensitive about this parallel, especially because God's punishment of David is the death of his first child with Bathsheba. This would also have made James I uncomfortable, as he might also have taken the loss of his son as a divine punishment for his 'negligence of the godly cause'. The final scene can thus be read as straight celebration of the royal dynasty, or as a criticism of kings Henry and James, and especially the latter for not having 'fully understood the nature of his responsibilities towards the continuing Reformation' (pp. 88–93).

Were all this not apparent to the original audience, the play is still unlike a normal history in that it refuses teleology: events are related sequentially but not causally. In a rare lapse into jargon, McMullan writes that the spectators of the Field of the Cloth of Gold are 'interpellated by official ceremony' without making clear if he means 'interpellate' in the Althusserian sense or the obsolete archaic sense of 'interrupt'. In place of soliloquies in which the protagonists might reveal their real feelings, this play has the endless reporting of one person's words by another; rumour is all and truth becomes indistinguishable from opinion. When two characters provide almost entirely conflicting accounts of someone's life (as Katherine and her gentleman usher Griffith do about Wolsey), we have no stable truth to fix upon. The same happens with events such as the Field of the Cloth of Gold, making the play a powerful reflection on 'the way in which truth is debated and established within a culture and particularly within that culture's conceptions of history' (pp. 94–106). Of the genre indeterminacy of the play, McMullan notes that it can be seen as masque-like in using an anti-masque in the penultimate scene with the Porter holding back the lower-class characters, before the masque-like christening. But although the play borrows the masque form, it refuses the monolithic kind of truth purveyed by it. It displays something of the romance qualities of *Pericles*, *The Winter's Tale*, *Cymbeline*, and *The Tempest*: it has a multiple-character focus and a supernatural moment (Katherine's vision), it ends with 'a redemptive father-and-daughter tableau', and it juxtaposes linear with cyclical time (pp. 108–10). McMullan links these plays as 'late writing'. Of course the play is late Shakespeare, but also early Fletcher. Shakespeare and Fletcher were in the vanguard of a fashionable new genre, romantic tragicomedy, which was to dominate the stage beyond the revolution. Fletcher's early plays draw on or require an audience to be familiar with Shakespeare's plays, and Shakespeare returned the compliment with *The Tempest*, which draws on Fletcher's *Faithful Shepherdess*; *Henry VIII* draws on Beaumont and Fletcher's *The Maid's Tragedy*. But since the chronologies of the Shakespeare and the Fletcher canons are uncertain, and since Roslyn Knutson has shown that company needs and competitive fashion, not individual creators' tastes, shaped genres, it is unwise to speak of Fletcher influencing Shakespeare or vice versa (pp. 112–16).

One of the sources of Katherine's dream vision was, ironically, Holinshed's report of Anne Bullen's death-dream vision. Indeed, in a number of ways Katherine and Anne are linked by the play in a way which undermines a simple religious reading. Another source of Katherine's dream vision appears to be Elizabeth I's dream vision in Heywood's *If You Know Not Me*, which is of course a most strange connection between Bloody Mary's mother Katherine and Anne Bullen's daughter Elizabeth. In her distance from the excesses of Wolsey, Katherine is thus something of a Catholic reformer, nearer to Anne and her Lutherism than to Rome. The movement from reign to reign in England (Henry VIII, Edward, Mary, Elizabeth), each of which it is hoped will provide political and religious stability, is thus likened to Henry's restless sequence of wives in search of a son and heir. At the end of his career Shakespeare returned to Roman 'New Comedy', with its elements of clandestine marriage to a lower-class person that turns out to be non-transgressive (as in *The Winter's Tale*), and the rediscovery at the end of a person who was thought lost and has special knowledge to contribute, as with Perdita in the same play, and also Marina in *Pericles*. *Henry VIII* follows this pattern: Henry marries Anne secretly, with Wolsey providing the necessary paternal disapproval of the marriage. McMullan points out the parallels between *Henry VIII* and Plautus's *Amphitryo*, which tells the story of Jupiter (in the likeness of Amphitryo) sleeping with Alcmena (Amphitryo's husband) and their offspring being the prodigy Hercules. In *Henry VIII* Henry, initially in disguise, sleeps with Anne and produces the prodigy Elizabeth. There was in fact a tradition of Protestant reworkings of Roman comedy, and *Henry VIII* would have been seen in this light, and not as loosely episodic, as many have since claimed. Clandestine sex and marriage is made proper by the outcome (Elizabeth), but—and this is the subversion—it remains tainted by the impropriety. The 'siege' of the penultimate scene is crucial: the specificities of places and clothing speak of 1613, not 1533. This linking of the Henrician to the Jacobean world 'creates a dramatic space within which the outcome of the English Reformation is still very much at stake' (pp. 134–46). This extended and highly persuasive reading of the play shows McMullan's extraordinary range of historical knowledge, coupled with an exemplary literary and dramatic sense; the quality of this interpretative work is much higher than that in Jay Halio's Oxford Shakespeare edition of the play [1999].

Concerning the textual history of the play, McMullan avoids the conventional (and currently controversial) terminology. Rather than calling the copy for the Folio text (our only authority) a promptbook, or even a playbook, he calls it 'a score for a stage play' (p. 149). The F copy seems to have been scribal since it uses 'ha's' for 'has' and round brackets, neither of which is a Shakespeare or Fletcher habit, and the long stage directions are not in theatre-speak but often drawn directly from Holinshed. McMullan demurs from the view of William Montgomery (for the 1986

Oxford Complete Works) that the direction 'Trumpets, Sennet, and Cornets' (II.iv.0.1) indicates duplication derived from theatrical annotation; rather, McMullan thinks F's copy might, though not necessarily, have been used as 'prompt copy' (p. 155). McMullan provides a useful table showing the order of composition (with folios and act, scene, and line numbers keyed to his own edition) by compositors B and I (called B and A in Foakes's Arden 2 edition, but with the same sections assigned to each), and records that Charlton Hinman's machine collation showed no significant press variants for this play (p. 157). Regarding modernization, McMullan has decided reluctantly to retain capitalization of aristocratic titles because, if a little old-fashioned and not in line with historians' practice, it reduces confusion for the modern reader. Indeed, for the purpose of modernization, what counts as archaism can be culturally conditioned: 'comptroller' is not considered archaic by Americans and McMullan leaves it alone in the text.

Discussing how the playwrights used (or, in McMullan's phrasing, 'read') Holinshed, McMullan again uses the term 'interpellate', but this time he glosses it to mean 'call[ing] into being in an apparently natural but in fact constrained way'. McMullan says the play does this to the individual audience member, but the syntax obscures the fact that he is making a substantial Althusserian claim that the play calls the audience into being rather than, say, the audience calling the play into being by creating a market for it or by giving it their attention (p. 166). McMullan reports that the Shakespeare scenes follow source (usually Holinshed) more closely than the Fletcher scenes, which interweave more texts (including the Bible); frequently there is subtle subversion as the material is used. When the fallen Wolsey speaks of himself as like a little boy who has swum out of his depth buoyed up by 'bladders' (III.ii.360), some of the audience would have been reminded of the prose chronicles which likened Wolsey himself to an inflated bladder fit to burst (p. 172). N.W. Bawcutt's publication of Henry Herbert's records showed that *The Birth of Merlin* was new in 1622 and hence not, as sometimes thought, a source for this play. McMullan explains the unobvious suspicion that some of *Henry VIII* is not 'Shakespearian'—'it is after all in the 1623 Folio'—by pointing out that, around the same time (the mid-1960s) that E.A.J. Honigmann showed the inherent instability of the Shakespearian texts, G.E. Bentley showed that collaboration was the norm. Since the Stationers' Register indicates that Shakespeare and Fletcher collaborated on *Cardenio*, and the quarto of *The Two Noble Kinsmen* names them both as its authors, *Henry VIII* fell under suspicion. McMullan describes the Stationers' Register as the place 'in which all plays to be printed were registered' (p. 186), but Peter Blayney has shown that this is not the case in his essay 'The Publication of Playbooks' (in John D. Cox and David Scott Kastan, eds., *A New History of Early English Drama*. ColUP. [1997]). McMullan follows Jonathan Hope's division of the work—Shakespeare wrote I.i, I.ii, II.iii, II.iv, III.iia, and V.i and Fletcher the rest—and makes a case for Hope's 'socio-historical linguistic' solution of the old stylometric problem that compositorial or scribal intervention in a printed text might be the origin of preferences (such as 'ye' for 'you' and ''em' for 'them') that have traditionally been the means of attribution. Hope uses alternatives that scribes and copyists are unlikely to have interfered with, such as relative markers 'that' and 'which', and auxiliary 'do'. Of course, as McMullan admits, this is still not perfect: people change their styles over their lifetimes, and in different contexts (such as when collaborating) and, as Jeffrey Masten notes, all drama is impersonation of others' styles of speaking anyway (pp. 187–95).

The Arden3 policy of marking with an asterisk footnotes that discuss deviations from copy is most useful for comparing editorial practice. With only one authoritative early text (F), McMullan's work is naturally confined to creative emendation of what he thinks is erroneous. Mostly his choices are the same as in the Oxford Complete Works of 1986 and Jay L. Halio's [1999] Oxford Shakespeare edition. At I.i.219 and II.i.20 McMullan names the accused plotter as 'Gilbert Park' where F has '*Gilbert Pecke*' because McMullan thinks the underlying copy read 'Perke', since this is what Holinshed and Hall have. (This was not really the man's name but a misreading of his occupation, 'clerk'.) Halio thought so too and printed 'Perke', but the Oxford Complete Works modernized this by dropping the final 'e' to make 'Perk'. McMullan thinks this is just a variant spelling of 'Park', which he uses. Where McMullan is confident that Shakespeare is following his source, he uses it to emend. Thus at I.i.218, I.ii.162, and II.i.20 McMullan names 'John de la Court' where F has (and both Oxfords keep) '*Iohn de la Car*'; the Surveyor's testimony comes from Holinshed and its spelling is thus preferred. Where it looks like the dramatists misread Holinshed, McMullan is happy to respect their intention (to follow Holinshed) rather than their act. Thus at I.i.147–8 McMullan (like the two Oxfords) prints 'Nicholas Hopkins. KING What was that Hopkins?' where F has '*Nicholas Henton. | Kin*. What was that *Henton?*' because the dramatists confused the place he came from (Henton) with his name. C.J. Sisson, however, argued that the man could also be called Nicholas Henton precisely because he came from Henton (*New Readings in Shakespeare*. CUP. [1956] p. 99). At I.ii.164 McMullan prints 'Whom after, under the confession's seal' where F has 'Whom after vnder the Commissions Seale'. The sense demands the word 'confession' and McMullan thinks the four uses of the word 'commission(s)' previously in this scene caused the error, although he does not mention that compositor I set all four of them and is the presumptive cause; McMullan's table of the order of setting helps a reader discover this for himself. Where punctuation strongly affects meaning, McMullan is prepared to be bold. At III.i.21 he has Katherine comment on the news that two cardinals are coming to see her: 'I do not like their coming. Now I think on't, | They should be good men, their affairs as righteous' for F's 'I doe not like their comming; now I think on't, | They should bee good men, their affaires as righteous'. Halio follows Capell and cites Sisson's argument (*New Readings in Shakespeare*, pp. 100–1) that if one follows F's stop after 'coming', Katherine first says she does not like their coming, then reconsiders since they are after all cardinals, whereas the sense should be 'I don't like this, now I think about it'. Halio and the Oxford Complete Works use a comma after 'coming' to avoid a hard stop. McMullan argues that precisely this strange emotional shift ('I don't like this. Oh well, I suppose it is alright since they are cardinals') is right for Katherine at this moment and foreshadows her succumbing to their pressure.

McMullan's choices regarding stage directions are clearly informed by an understanding of the fluidity of the early modern stage and he is prepared to stretch logic to avoid straitjacketing the text. At V.i.157 the Folio has '*Enter Olde Lady. | Gent within. Come backe*'. For 'dramatic economy' McMullan makes this interior gentleman be Lovell who has anyway to come on to be addressed by the king twelve lines later. So, McMullan prints '*Enter* Old Lady[; LOVELL *follows*.] | LOVELL (*within*) Come back!', which produces the mild absurdity of Lovell being onstage (he is included in the entrance direction) and yet speaking 'within'. Surely the solution was to have Lovell speak offstage and then enter. Likewise, for Henry and Butts to spy on the privy council McMullan prints '*Enter the* KING *and* BUTTS *at a window above*' (V.ii.18 s.d.) and for Henry's intrusion on the main stage '*Enter* KING, *frowning on them*' (V.ii.147 s.d.). Between these two entrance directions McMullan prints no exit direction, but rather footnotes that once the curtain is closed above—fully, not partly as other editors have it—the king can come down at any time, ready for his surprise entrance to the council chamber. It surprises the privy councillors and the theatre audience too, since they thought he was above. One can see the point of this arrangement, but it is not theatrically consistent to have two entrances directions with no intervening exit, leaving the explanation to the footnote; those using McMullan's script need to know what he wants from his stage directions. Finally in this list of objections, McMullan prints 'Do you take the court for Parish Garden?' (V.iii.2) where F has 'doe you take the Court for Parish Garden'. Why not modernize to 'Paris Garden', unless one thinks that a speech impediment is being indicated by the unusual spelling? McMullan's footnote explains Paris Garden as the a bull- and bear-baiting arena near the Globe (otherwise known as the Beargarden), without mentioning that it could just mean the Liberty and Manor of Paris Garden where, in the early sixteenth century, public bear-baiting was held without an arena. Indeed, the Beargarden had the alternative name of Paris Garden precisely because of the association of this area of park with bear-baiting, and not because it was situated in the Liberty and Manor of Paris Garden (which, in fact, the Beargarden was not). Bull baiting, on the other hand, was just a part of butchery, not a sport, and there is no reason to think it was done in front of spectators.

In contrast to McMullan's outstanding Arden3 edition of *Henry VIII* is Edward Burns's edition of *1 Henry VI* for the same series, the introduction to which is about half the length. It is traditional when editing a marginal play to make a case for its being more important than the reader might otherwise think. McMullan does this brilliantly, but Burns does not even try. One can also compare Burns's handling of the problem of multi-authored writing of a play for which we have only the Folio text with McMullan's thoroughly theorized attempt at the same. Of the copy for the Folio, Burns thinks that Heminges and Condell probably had thirty-year-old papers to work from because he is convinced the play had not been revived since its first performance in the early 1590s. (That the epilogue to *Henry V* refers to the events of Henry VI's reign, 'Which oft our stage hath shown', makes revival of the first tetralogy to run alongside the second somewhat likely, as does the reprinting of *The Contention of York and Lancaster* / *2 Henry VI* and *Richard Duke of York* / *3 Henry VI* in 1600.) Burns thinks the reference to a Talbot play in Nashe's *Piers Penniless* is to *1 Henry VI*, and that it is also the 'harey the vj' which Henslowe records as new at the Rose on 3 March 1592; hence the play is a prequel to what we now call *2 Henry VI* and *3 Henry VI*. As such, it ironizes the known outcomes contained in Parts 2 and 3 by showing the grand ideas by which these 'heroes' lived their lives, and yet the events of Parts 2 and 3 come to pass. As with McMullan's reading, Burns thinks his play 'an ironic meditation on what history is, and as such it constantly exposes the gratuitousness of the signs and symbols which allow us to think we know history' (p. 6).

Burns believes that refurbishment of the Rose theatre in 1592 was just before *1 Henry VI* premiered and the addition of a stage cover implies that the stage was permanent, whereas hitherto stages may have tended to be temporary to permit bear-baiting. In fact, there is no reason to suppose that animal baiting took place at any playhouse prior to the opening of the Hope in 1614 (see Oscar Brownstein, 'Why Didn't Burbage Lease the Beargarden? A Conjecture in Comparative Architecture', in Herbert Berry, ed., *The First Public Playhouse: The Theatre in Shoreditch, 1576–1598*. McG-QUP [1979]). As for the suiting of play to venue, Burns notes that *Titus Andronicus* (which also played at the Rose) and *1 Henry VI* both open with a funeral procession, which suits the Rose's wide shallow stage. Indeed, Burns makes rather contentious assertions about how the stage shape at the Rose influenced the way in which the audience was addressed and where the actors stood, and he cites John Astington's work on the *Roxana* and *Messalina* pictures ('The Origins of the *Roxana* and *Messalina* Illustrations', *ShS* 43[1990] 149–69) as supporting his view that the Rose-style tapered stage was 'a more standard stage shape, with a longer history, than had been assumed' (p. 12 n. 1). In fact, Astington's article comes to the opposite conclusion, that these pictures are virtually useless as evidence for contemporary theatres. Theatre history is not Burns's long suit, relying as he does on Christine Eccles's *The Rose Theatre*, which is widely considered to be of little value. Burns makes the surprising claim that a company patron such as Lord Strange would 'meet financial losses' incurred by the company (p. 18)—one would like to see the evidence for this—and asserts that 'Southwark ... was exempt from control by the city', which is not quite right. Liberties such as the Clink were exempt, because that is what being a 'liberty' meant, but these could be anywhere, including inside the city walls. Burns is not quite in control of his adjectives: the 'end of an era' anxiety in the play, he argues, mirrored the same anxiety regarding 'the loomingly predictable end of Elizabeth's reign' (p. 22). He means 'looming and predictable', since one can hardly claim that it was predictable in a looming way as distinct from other ways of being predictable. Burns thinks Holinshed was used largely 'as a quarry for juicy bits about Joan Puzel' (p. 22 n. 1), which is rather too colloquial and moreover a bad metaphor: quarries are notoriously dry places.

Burns is better when lining up binary opposites. In his reading, the play alters its sources to make a binary of fighters Joan Puzel and Talbot, and this segues into the binarism of Gloucester and York's struggle to control the child king and the country, which links the end of this play to the beginning of *The Contention of York and Lancaster / 2 Henry VI*. The historical Joan always called herself 'Jeanne la Pucelle', and 'pucelle' means nubile but also 'whore', especially when spelt 'puzel'. As a gender transgressor, Joan is also a puzel with a pizzle (penis) and a puzzle; she is not a single character but an embodied self-contradiction of saint and witch (pp. 23–7). From this Burns makes an excellent eight-term homology: French is to English as Catholic is to Protestant as Magical is to Rational as Female is to Male. This neat pattern is somewhat disturbed by Burns's assertion that the male motif of history is primarily the broken or constrained body (p. 39) which I would rather have thought was a Catholic fixation. As Burns notes, Joan's claim to be pregnant links her to the pregnant Virgin Mary and her cousin Elizabeth (of the Visitation), and Talbot's opposition to her is Protestant opposition to the Catholic cult of the virgin. Of course, the historical Talbot was as Catholic as Joan. When Burns decides to survey the critical debate regarding a particular point he tends to produce big footnotes (for example 48 n. 1 and 72 n. 1) occupying as much as two-thirds of a page; these would be better integrated into the main text or else thinned.

The red and white rose material in *1 Henry VI* is not present in *2 Henry VI* or *3 Henry VI* and this itself is evidence that *1 Henry VI* was written later; had it been written first we should expect this material to be followed up in the later plays. However, the red/white rose distinction does appear in the opening-scene stage directions of the quartos of *Richard Duke of York / 3 Henry VI* ('*with white* [later red] *roses in their hats*'), but not the Folio text of *3 Henry VI*, which could be evidence that the quarto represents *Richard Duke of York / 3 Henry VI* as it came to be revised after *1 Henry VI* had been rewritten as a prequel, and that the Folio text was printed from authorial papers representing the play as it was originally conceived. Burns observes that no director has presented *1 Henry VI* on its own; rather, it is always part of a cycle and usually chopped around to suit the larger pattern. Burns's dating of the play takes the usual form of an argument derived from Robert Greene's *Groatsworth of Wit* [September 1592] allusion to a line in *Richard Duke of York / 3 Henry VI*. If we accept that *1 Henry VI* was 'new' at Henslowe's Rose on 3 March 1592 (because Henslowe's *Diary* labels it 'ne') it cannot have been written before *The Contention of York and Lancaster / 2 Henry VI* and *Richard Duke of York / 3 Henry VI* if the last of these is to be available for Greene's allusion (which depends on knowledge gained by public performance) in September 1592. The six months between March and September are not enough time for all three plays to been written in the order *1, 2, 3 Henry VI*, so *2 Henry VI* and *3 Henry VI* must already have been in existence (p. 70). Actually, the pressure of time is even greater than Burns imagines, since a plague closure from 23 June 1592 means that *3 Henry VI* would have to have been in performance by then in order for Greene to be able to allude to it in September 1592. Supporting this conclusion, Burns notes the publication of *The Contention of York and Lancaster / 2 Henry VI* and *Richard Duke of York / 3 Henry VI* as a matched pair in 1594 and 1595, called 'The First Part ...' and 'The True Tragedie ...' on their title pages.

What if the label 'ne' in Henslowe's *Diary* doesn't mean 'new', or perhaps only new to his repertory because revived? Burns suggests that the higher cost of entrance for a 'ne' play (reflected in higher income in the *Diary*) might be to cover the expenditure on a new licence from the Master of the Revels, but I do not think we can suppose that audiences were concerned with the impresario's outgoings. If Henslowe's 'ne' means only revival, we could imagine that *1, 2, and 3 Henry VI* were written as a trilogy, with *1 Henry VI* subsequently revised to make it performable on its own. However, as Burns observes, there was a strong tradition of two-part plays, but few examples of trilogies. Also against the theory that the *1, 2, 3 Henry VI* sequence was conceived as a trilogy is the fact that the preparations for the printing of the 1623 Folio include the first-time entry in the Stationers' Register on 8 November 1622 of 'The thirde parte of Henry the sixte'. This cannot be what we now call *3 Henry VI* because this had already been printed in 1595 as *Richard Duke of York*, so it is most likely *1 Henry VI*, considered the third part of the series in order of composition, not in order of historical events. Millington entered 'The firste parte of the Contention ...' in the Register on 12 March 1594 and then printed *The Contention of York and Lancaster / 2 Henry VI* [1594] and *Richard Duke of York / 3 Henry VI* [1595], so presumably the single Register entry covered this pair of plays. On 19 April 1602 Millington transferred his rights in 'The first and Second parte of

HENRY the VJ^t[h]' to Pavier, who later printed *The Contention of York and Lancaster / 2 Henry VI* and *Richard Duke of York / 3 Henry VI*. All this suggests that what we now call *2 Henry VI* was originally the first part of a two-parter and *3 Henry VI* was its completion. Thus, as Burns writes, when 'The thirde parte of Henry the sixte' was entered in the Register on 8 November 1622, it was really the prequel *1 Henry VI* (p. 72).

As McMullan observed regarding *Henry VIII*, those who like *1 Henry VI* tend to see it as by Shakespeare and as part of a planned sequence; those who do not see it as by him and others. In the former group was the Arden2 editor Andrew Cairncross—presumably this is why he edited all three *Henry VI* plays—while in the latter group was Arden1 editor H.C. Hart. Burns agrees with Gary Taylor's division of *1 Henry VI* into Shakespeare and Nashe sections, and Taylor's view that several others no longer identifiable also had hands in it. Burns reads Robert Greene's attack as being about Shakespeare as a cheater in collaboration, someone who passes off as his own work material containing others' 'feathers', and points out that the wider context in the *Groatsworth of Wit* is a story of a player rescuing a down-at-heel writer, which player is 'both his saviour and a kind of devil figure, drawing him into further artistic degradation' (p. 79). How collaborators might parcel out a play is not clear: by act, by scene, or in smaller units? There is evidence that a writer might be responsible for individual speeches, but Burns prefers to think of the units of authorial division in *1 Henry VI* as 'strands of rhetorical action' (p. 81). There are, Burns asserts, two discernible strands, perhaps by different authors: the English/ French conflict, and the Shakespearian breakdown of English unity (p. 83).

Burns characterizes his editing as 'a broadly non-interventionist approach to the punctuation of F' (p. 90) and he avoids brackets because they are 'inhibiting for actors'; one is tempted to respond that inhibited actors should learn punctuation. Sometimes Burns retains F's ambiguous punctuation because ambiguity is the point, and likewise he does not always fix what others have seen as F's failure to supply necessary exit stage directions. For example, Burns has the gaolers stay on stage during Mortimer's death-chair interview with Richard in II.v. For asides, Burns has invented his own editorial convention (some are 'to the audience' and others 'to him/herself', p. 98), which novelty could be accused of anachronism since self-communion appears to be a proscenium arch technique impossible on the Elizabethan thrust stage where the audience can never be ignored. Burns thinks that Gary Taylor showed that 'plays for the professional stage were not split into formal act divisions, nor performed with gaps between the acts, before about 1610' and that 'Only academic and court performances bothered to follow classical precedent by splitting plays into five acts' (p. 101). This is wrong: the professional indoor hall theatres always used act divisions. and this practice spread to the open-air amphitheatre stages after about 1609, as Taylor argued.

Burns's decisions regarding the play's famous cruces are mostly conventional, but he appears to be unaware of the important principle of *praestat difficilior lectio* ('let the more difficult reading be preferred') when faced with exotic words in his copy. Burns prints 'A base villain, to win the Dolphin's grace, | Thrust Talbot with a spear into the back' (I.i.137) where F has 'A base Wallon', which editors usually modernize to Walloon. Burns argues that the ethnicity of the assailant is not in the sources, that the Walloons were on the English side, and that the error is a likely misreading of a sequence of minims. But the point is that one should trust one's copy in the case of an unusual word since compositors tend not to invent exotica. Likewise at I.iii.29 Burns prints 'How now, ambitious Humphrey, what means this?' where F has 'How now ambitious *Vmpheir*, what meanes this?'. Burns calls 'bizarre' the Oxford Complete Works choice of 'vizier' for F's '*Vmpheir*', but since Gloucester, as Protector, is Viceroy, 'vizier' is a good abusive word to hurl at him. Much more serious than individual choices for emendation is the mess that Burns makes of scene divisions. At IV.iii.53 he decides not to start a new scene, something about which his predecessor Cairncross agreed but did not act upon, mentioning it in a note but preserving the traditional break. At this point Burns starts two numbering sequences, continuing with IV.iii.54 in the marginal numbering and the running titles, but also adding a marginal marker '[4.4]' to show that other editors start a new scene here. To match this marginal '[4.4]' Burns starts a second marginal numbering (IV.iv.1 onwards) using steps of 10 rather than 5, which runs in the same column as his own numbering system (IV.iii.54 onwards) until the real end of the scene at his IV.iii.99. Then IV.iv runs normally until its line 55 when again Burns decides that a conventional scene break (after Talbot's 'And soul with soul from France to heaven fly') is wrong. So, again, he adds the conventional number '[4.6]' in the marginal column while continuing his own number (IV.iv.56 onwards) in the running titles and two numbering systems in the marginal columns. The same thing happens again at Burns's IV.iv.112 (Talbot's 'And, commendable proved, let's die in pride'), where other editors generally start IV.vii, so again there are marginal marks for the traditional break, the traditional numbering, and Burns's numbering, while the running titles follow Burns's numbering. Distinguishing the two line-numbering systems is not especially difficult once one realizes what is going on—although I can find the practice explained nowhere in the book—because the traditional ones are in square brackets and mostly (but oddly not for the '[10]', '[20]', and '[30]' of the traditional IV.vii) in a smaller typeface. But distinguishing the two act- and scene-numbering labels is tricky: both are in square brackets, with the traditional ones being (counter-intuitively) in a bolder typeface. The only point of retaining a traditional numbering system at all is ease of reference, and the multiple numbering systems used here to not achieve that. Indeed, in the absence of an explanatory note, readers may well assume that the entire numbering system is simply erroneous. An editor who believes he has corrected his copy's faulty breaks should adopt his correction entirely, not try to run two numbering systems in parallel.

A problem of equal magnitude occurs with Burns's idiosyncratic naming of characters. In his appendix 1, Burns defends his naming of 'Puzel' and 'Dolphin' instead of 'Pucelle' and 'Dauphin' (the common modernizations), because, like Churchill's deliberate 'Naazi' pronunciation, these mark the refusal of the English to speak a despised foreign language properly. Burns argues for the spelling 'Dolphin' instead of the more usually modernized 'Dauphin' on the grounds that the latter is the French word for the aquatic mammal, and he wants to use a word that will invoke the playful resonances understood by the original audience as well as its connections with beast fable and heraldry: it was the symbol of the comte de Vienne, a title sold to Philip IV in 1349 and thereafter given to the heir to the French throne. For Joan's character, the big difference in spelling her name is between medial 'c' and medial 'z'. Taylor argued that the modernized form turns 'c' or 'z' into 'c' (so 'Pucelle'), but Burns argues that since 'c' and 'ss' make the same sound, this would make Talbot's 'Puzel or pussel' (I.iv.106) into the nonsensical 'Pucelle or pucelle', which is a repetition of one sound when of course it was spoken with a distinction (because it could mean virgin or whore) in Shakespeare's time. Burns thinks that keeping the 'z' also helps to make it sound like 'puzzle', and Joan is of course a puzzle to Talbot. A reviewer need not raise the obvious objections to Burns's reasoning, since the Arden3 general editors do it themselves in a remarkable note distancing themselves from Burns's choices (pp. 294–6). 'Puzel', they note, is the minority form in F ('Pucel(l)' occurs twice as often) and using it 'deprives the French characters of an intelligible French epithet for their saviour, Joan "the Maid"'; instead they have to use a derogatory English term. The French word 'pucelle' (virgin) has the advantage to an editor that it could be used derogatorily or straight, so both sides could use it with their own meanings. Burns's rendering 'Puzel or pussel' has no contrast: both are derogatory. Regarding Dolphin/Dauphin, Burns's use of the former in a modernized text makes the sounding of the 'l' compulsory, whereas of course the point is that it is optional, as in Walter/Water; Ralph/Rafe, and salvage/savage. If 'Dauphin' had been used by Burns, the editors remark, then Talbot's 'Dauphin or dogfish' (I.iv.107) would have been the only time it is pronounced 'Dolphin', and hence an appropriately scathing comparison. The freedom to individual editors granted by the Arden3 general editors (and apparently Stanley Wells is equally liberal with the Oxford Shakespeare) obviously allows the rejection of extraordinarily wise counsel.

For the Oxford Shakespeare, John Jowett's edition of *Richard III* handles with wisdom and impeccable literary-dramatic style the most difficult editing task in the canon. Jowett's edition is based on the 1597 quarto (Q1), 'the text that seems closest to the play as it would have been staged' (p. 3). Before the formation of the Chamberlain's men in 1594, Shakespeare appears to have been with Strange's men, whose patron Ferdinando Lord Strange was descended from the play's Lord Stanley, and Shakespeare has altered Thomas More's Stanley to present him more favourably; was this done because Shakespeare was one of Strange's men? On the other hand, the ancestors of the earl of Pembroke, who had his own players, also get adjusted favourably in *Richard III*, so perhaps Shakespeare wanted to please two potential patrons. Or did he please two patrons at two different times and both alterations got into the Folio? Jowett addresses the same problem of distinguishing synchronic from diachronic evidence in a footnote which usefully summarizes what is known of Shakespeare's activities before joining Chamberlain's men: the performance of 'harey the vj' at the Rose on 3 March 1592 suggests he was with Strange's (who were using the Rose at the time); the title page of the 1594 quarto of *A Shrew* names the players as Pembroke's men (but it might not be Shakespeare's play); and the title page of the 1594 quarto of *Titus Andronicus* names the players as 'the Earle of *Darbie*, Earle of *Pembrooke*, and Earle of *Sussex* their Seruants', which could be a joint performance or else a 'summary stage history' (p. 7 n. 1). Jowett thinks that *Richard III* was written 'as if for Strange's' and then 'given finishing touches towards its close that make it suitable for the new Pembroke company', which makes 1592 the likeliest year of composition, it being when Pembroke's company was formed. The play was not finished before the plague closure of 23 June 1592 (else Strange's men would have played it at the Rose, and Henslowe's *Diary* shows they did not), and it was as he was finishing it during the closure that Shakespeare added the Pembroke material (pp. 7–8).

Concerning Shakespeare's use of his sources, Jowett observes that by making Richard III the epitome of evil, his being done away with allows a line to be drawn under the factious Middle Ages and the Tudor age of Richmond (Henry VII) can begin with past strife finally buried. More's account of Richard III ends before his death and Jowett wonders if he started to see Henry VIII as a bad king and so was reluctant to bring the story to its end because this would amount to 'developing a specifically pro-Tudor polemic' (p. 15). Jowett finds a tension between the teleological and analogical readings of the events of *Richard III*: the former sees the overthrow of Richard as inevitable, but the analogical reading (which reads the events as metaphors for the present) comes up hard against the contemporary injunction not to rebel against even a tyrant, as the Homily against Disobedience insists. Indeed, Richmond's claim to the throne was weaker than Richard's, and some political thinkers argued that, while tyrants had to be endured, usurpers (like Richmond) could be overthrown. More reversed the crookedness of Richard he found in his source (John Rous), making the left (sinister) shoulder higher than the right, and the tension between the play's two explanations of Richard's deformity (too much, or too little, gestation) match the tension between the teleological and analogical readings. Jowett reads *Richard III* as a revenge play in that Richard kills those responsible for the stabbing of Prince Edward at the battle of Tewkesbury. Of course, he too was responsible for that stabbing; but in this genre the revenger often does have his own crime for which he must be punished (pp. 32–8). Aspects of Jowett's close reading of the play are truly inspired. The young Prince Edward's concerns with the documentary record regarding Caesar's building of the Tower of London in III.i mark him out as a proto-humanist like More, and Richard's murder of the prince can be read as a delaying of Renaissance humanist culture in England. The dream of Clarence is like the dream of Lady More's wife in *Sir Thomas More*, a play in which Erasmus's visits to England are celebrated. This might suggest that the victory of Tudor Richmond marks the end of the medieval period and the start of the humanist Renaissance in England, but on the other hand his son Henry VIII was eventually to lock More in the same tower and then execute him. The link between building construction and the passing on of knowledge about it is the word 'edify', which has both meanings (as in 'succeeding ages have re-edified', III.i.71). Richard's 'So wise so young, they say, do never live long' (III.i.79), said of the young Prince Edward, sounds like determination to kill the truth that the prince embodies, but it simultaneously admits, in its 'they say', that oral transmission— what the prince has been talking about—makes it impossible to entirely silence shared knowledge (pp. 56–8).

Jowett sees no reason to think that Q's economy of roles derives from the needs of touring, 'for the main elements in the doubling pattern are already apparent in F'. Q does reorder the ghosts so that Lady Anne's ghost does not enter immediately after the princes leave, necessary because one of the princes (presumably, the elder, Edward) must double with Lady Anne. Dorset and Grey only become two characters after Grey is arrested. F is confused on this point, and Q resolves it in a surprising way: instead of separating the characters, it more strongly indicates in the early scenes that these are two names for one man. Once they are separated (in II.iv), 'doubling of a more routine kind was no doubt followed' (pp. 75–6). Jowett observes that William Hogarth's picture of David Garrick as Richard waking in his tent looks like a bedroom scene, which acts as a reminder of the onstage bedroom scene murders in this, Colley Cibber's, adaptation of the play (p. 86). In fact, it is likely that the original staging would also have made the bed/tent connection because of the nature of the stage property used for either (see Gabriel Egan, 'Thomas Platter's Account of an Unknown Play at the Curtain or the Boar's Head', *N&Q* 245[2000] 53–6).

Jowett is a world-leading bibliographer with a gift for explaining clearly and concisely what others obfuscate, and he deals with the play 'In Print' in just twenty-three pages (pp. 110–32). Jowett's philosophical position on the difference between stage and page is a rather subtle nominalism: texts are only 'representations of the play rather than the thing itself, and there is a real sense in which the play can exist only in representations of it'. The play in its ideal form, then, does not really exist, but Jowett's is not the now conventional materialism since he does not privilege the early printings: even possession of the early manuscripts 'would offer not so much "the play" as versions of it' (p. 110). Q1 was printed from a previously unprinted manuscript, and F by close attention to another unprinted manuscript; all other printings are derivative. Jowett takes the view, expressed most articulately in Peter Blayney's 'The Publication of Playbooks', that companies had their plays printed as a form of advertising, and in this case the printing of *Richard II* and *Richard III* in 1597 (after *The Contention of York and Lancaster / 2 Henry VI* and *Richard Duke of York / 3 Henry VI* in 1594–5) displayed that the Chamberlain's men's principal dramatist specialized in history plays. The Stationers' Register entry for *Richard III* on 20 October 1597 showed that it had ecclesiastical authorization: William Barlow, under whose 'hand' the play was entered, was chaplain to John Whitgift, the archbishop of Canterbury, and another under whose 'hand' it was entered was Thomas Man, Warden of the Stationers' Company. In 1596 only 40 per cent of books printed had ecclesiastical authority, but all potentially controversial ones did. Of *Richard III* Q1, sheets A–G were printed by Valentine Simmes, and sheets H–M by Peter Short. Each subsequent quarto was printed from its predecessor, except sheets C and E–M of Q5 which were printed from Q3. The number of quarto reprints (Q6 appeared in 1622) shows how popular the reading text was. Although there is evidence of manuscript consultation, it is hard to say if the small changes in later quartos are authoritative. Q3's title page advertises that the contents are 'Newly augmented'; it has some new stage directions and is of value for emending stage directions, speech prefixes, and, occasionally, dialogue. Jowett observes that Andrew Wise and Matthew Law printed their Shakespeare history play quartos in linked groups (such as Law's pairing of *Richard II* and its historical sequel *1 Henry IV* in 1608) but does not fully draw out the implication of this for recent historicist scholarship. It is not straightforwardly true that the Folio's organization of material forced the history plays on to a Procrustean bed to which their sprawling generic and thematic material was not suited; the organization was already in evidence from the quarto printings.

In his discussion of the copy for Q1 and F, Jowett introduces a useful innovation in nomenclature that greatly aids clarity. Instead of the usual long-winded formulae such as 'the manuscript underlying Q [or F]'—so clumsy that some omit the first part and wrongly imply that a printing is identical with its copy-text—Jowett uses the shorthand MSQ and MSF. In fact, the copy for Folio was not simply a manuscript but, rather, alternated between Q3 and Q6, with manuscript passages not present in these interwoven into the text. These passages show that this manuscript was not the one used to make Q1 (which lacks them), and it is also the source for hundreds of Folio readings which differ from whichever quarto (Q3 or Q6) being used at that point. Where later quartos had introduced error, the manuscript used to make F often restored the Q1 reading, which shows how much MSQ and MSF had in common. Rather than demonstrating these claims with detailed examples, Jowett collects in his appendices A–D the supporting collation evidence. MSQ and MSF show no signs of conforming to the simple new bibliographical categories of 'foul papers' and 'promptbook', but MSF is earlier than MSQ and probably represents the text before it came to the theatre. MSF is longer (for an already long play) than MSQ but lacks the 'dramatically incisive' 'clock' passage in IV.ii and has lots of repetitive, wordy stuff easily cut without harm. It is hard to see, Jowett points out, how this redundant material could have got into F by revision, but easy to see how it might have been cut to make Q. MSF is also more profligate with characters, such as an unnecessary daughter for Clarence. Like Q1's reordering of the ghosts (so one boy can be both a prince and Lady Anne), cutting this daughter saves a boy actor. Q1 also lacks a Folio passage which links *Richard III* with *Richard Duke of York / 3 Henry VI*, which is more likely to have been cut to make Q than added to make F since 'The play is far more likely to have grown towards greater independence of the events in the Henry VI plays', especially as it proved (as the frequent reprinting shows) to be a much more popular play. Q also saves personnel by conflating characters such as the Keeper of the Tower and Brackenbury; these make little difference to the size of the cast, but they increase dramatic intelligibility at the cost of historical accuracy. Again, it is less likely that characters in MSQ were split to make a more historically accurate MSF; in general F is historically more accurate than Q, and it has signs of authorial confusion over names created by punctuation in the source material.

What was this MSF? Apparently it was not in Shakespeare's hand since it departs from his lexical preferences in using 'ay' where Shakespeare and Q1 preferred 'yea', 'prithee' where he and Q1 preferred 'pray thee' (as E.A.J. Honigmann noted) and 'which' where he and Q1 preferred 'that' (as Jonathan Hope noted). These preferences and the act/scene divisions suggest scribal transcript. MSQ does not seem like the new bibliographers' idea of a 'promptbook', but Jowett agrees with the new textualists that the old idea of a promptbook was too narrow and that such features as imperfect stage directions could be permitted in the theatre document. In any case, the cramped printing of Q1 (from which MSQ is conceptually extrapolated) might have necessitated throwing away exit directions which we notice it lacks. Jowett thinks that Q1 is probably not a memorial reconstruction (the usual theory being that the company found themselves on tour without their playbook), and quotes the moment in scene III.ii (F4v of the quarto, TLN 1912–21 of the Folio) where Hastings whispers in a priest's ear. Here F and Q1 suddenly diverge right in the middle of a scene otherwise well reported, and furthermore the relationship of the F/Q versions here is much more like revision than garbling: a clash of idiomatic language in F is avoided by alteration to the syntax in Q. Moreover, Q's differences save a speaking role, and put together these are 'signs that the dialogue has been consciously modified' (p. 125). Admittedly, there are a few single-word slips of the kind best explained by memorial reconstruction, but Jowett points out that any act of transcription involves memory, and a scribe could have made these slips during copying. Most damagingly, there is a pattern of variation in the naming of Stanley/Derby which could not survive memorial reconstruction, as Jowett argues more fully in a note reviewed below.

While unhappy with the classificatory criteria of new bibliography, Jowett does believe we can distinguish texts nearer or further from performance, and on this rests his preference for Q1, newly freed from the stigma of memorial reconstruction. Jowett acknowledges that, were one to follow slavishly the Oxford Complete Works logic of preferring performance over authorial writing, one might have to accept a crude adaptation over its original, and drawing a line somewhere before this is a matter of 'choice rather than law' (p. 129). Unlike later plays, the 'theatricalizing' of the *Richard III* script might not have involved Shakespeare because he was not yet a sharer in a playing company, but still Q1 is to be preferred because it 'largely retains authorial texture', it has not been so corrupted as to be inferior to F, and indeed it has some preferable verbal variant readings which might be authorial. Once an editor has settled on Q1 as the control text, the difficult decisions concern how bad something has to be before it should be corrected; the dividing line is not what the author wanted (as it would be if one worked from F) but what could have passed in the theatre without 'correction'. Most of the emendations of Q1 used by Jowett are readings from F (on the hypothesis that the faulty transmission lost the authorial reading and we can recover it from there), but some will be readings which first appeared in later quartos because their printers (using earlier printings as their copy) spotted the manifest mistakes and fixed them. Rather than stake out all the arguments for each genuine Q1/F variant choice in his edition, Jowett prefers to make limited comment in his notes and 'recognize that many alternative readings can legitimately coexist'. Editing with Q1 as the control text makes for a play less melodramatic and less connected with the other histories (because less connected with the real history) and more of a free-standing 'psycho-political drama about Richard's rise and fall', which is what the play was becoming in the theatre in the 1590s (pp. 131–2).

The main innovation of this edition is a double collation between the body text and the commentary. The first records this edition's departures from Q1 and the second records readings from F not adopted in this text; emendations by other editors are recorded only in the commentary. In Jowett's opinion many of the Folio readings can be considered valid alternative readings. In the Folio collation, wherever the rejected reading in F originated in a quarto reprint (Q2–Q6) this fact is recorded, but only up to the quarto that was the copy for F at that point (Q3 or Q6). In other words, where a quarto was the first occurrence of a reading which later appeared in F, that quarto is named unless it is later than the copy used for F, in which case the quarto in question could not be the cause of F's reading. In the Q1 collation, if F also has the rejected reading this fact is explicitly confirmed except in the two places (III.i.0–144 and V.iv.28–end) where F was printed from Q without consultation of the manuscript, for which one may assume that F has the same reading. Alterations to stage directions are marked by broken brackets only where they are significantly disputable, otherwise they are just recorded in the Q1 collation, but a marker about address printed after a speech prefix (such as '*to Margaret*' or '*Aside*') may be assumed to be editorial and if, unusually, Q1 has them also (as with the ghost scene) this is recorded (pp. 134–5). Given Jowett's procedures for a two-text play, there is little point in a reviewer going through the editor's choices regarding particular cruces because most of the decisions will have been made for Jowett by his choice of copy, whereas for a single-text play one is thinking about the correction of manifest error and has to be more inventive. An interesting mixture of editorial and critical impulses is registered in Jowett's preservation of Richard's claim that Richmond's army was 'Long kept in Bretagne at our mother's cost' (V.v.53) rather than changing this to the historically correct 'brother's cost', since the duke of Burgundy, his brother-in-law, armed Richmond. The error originates in Holinshed, and Jowett keeps it (as Shakespeare decided to) because it is a 'Freudian slip' (p. 66 n. 2) prompted by the desertion of the women Richard had previously been able to control with his rhetoric. One tiny flaw which could be corrected in reprinting is that the running titles on pages 244 and 245 wrongly give the act and scene label III.i (it should be III.ii).

Jowett prints seven appendices. Appendix A provides the texts of passages which were first printed in 1623. Most of these are the same as the ones so designated in the Oxford Complete Works, which agrees that they were 'probably deleted for stage performance', but two of the short ones (Oxford Complete Works, 'Additional Passage B', beginning after I.iii.166, 'RICHARD GLOUCESTER Wert thou not banished on pain of death? | QUEEN MARGARET I was, but I do find more pain in banishment | Than death can yield me here by my abode', and 'Additional Passage F' after III.i.170, 'BUCKINGHAM And summon him tomorrow to the Tower | To sit about the coronation') Jowett simply includes in the F collation as variant material not used. This shows the advantage of Jowett's double collation in cutting the number of 'additional passages' he has to enumerate separately in his already full appendices. Conversely, there are four F-only passages (comprising twenty-three lines of speech) which in the Oxford Complete Works were incorporated into the body of the main text and which Jowett has freshly reassigned as 'missing from Q because cut for performance'—of course, were they missing from Q because its printers merely failed to follow MSQ, Jowett would have printed them—showing his continuation of the Oxford resistance to conflation and the increasing fragmentation into distinct versions begun by the Oxford Complete Works decision to print two *King Lear* plays. Some such decisions are explained in the longer textual notes in appendix D. Appendix B lists the variants between Q1 and Q2–6 where F (but no intervening quarto) restored the Q1 reading. This is useful because, except where the corrections are obvious, these confirm Q1 readings since they must be caused by MSQ and MSF agreeing on these words. Jowett divides the list into sections according to whether Q3 or Q6 was the copy for F, as determined by Gary Taylor using the evidence of incidentals (*William Shakespeare: A Textual Companion*. OUP. [1987] pp. 229–30), and naturally does not show the variants that appeared after the quarto which is copy for F at that point (Q3 or Q6). Appendix C records Jowett's changes to Q1's lineation, and here he mentions an Oxford typographical convention (common to the Arden3 but not the New Cambridge) whereby the editor indicates his view on whether a passage is prose or verse by placement of the speech prefix on the same line as the speech or on its own line above the speech respectively. Like typographical conventions regarding voiced and unvoiced suffixal '-ed', this sort of thing should be stated more often by editors; even graduate student readers can be unaware of them. Another convention (begun by Edward Capell) is to push to the right half-lines which complete another's metrical unit; where there is more than one way to do this (as with the cut and thrust between Richard and Lady Anne at I.ii.178–88), Jowett does not impose the flush-right convention.

In appendix D ('Longer Textual Notes') Jowett discusses such matters as act/scene breaks, for which he largely follows the Oxford Complete Works except that, when Richmond goes into his tent in Act V (the beginning of the 'simultaneous staging' of both camps, which allows the ghosts to speak to Richard and Richmond), Jowett continues without a scene break. The division of source material makes Jowett think that the five-act structure might have been in Shakespeare's mind even though the open-air theatres did not mark intervals until after 1609. For the Derby/Stanley shifts in stage direction and speech prefixes Jowett summarizes his *Notes & Queries* essay (reviewed below). He explains the Dorset/Grey confusion in the early texts: initially these were two names for what Shakespeare planned as one character, but later he decided to have one son of the queen die by Richard and another survive. Thus, in the latter half of F, Shakespeare has them be different men, but the exigencies of performance made conflation of them desirable, at least as far as the actor is concerned (so the two roles are doubled). Thus Jowett's surprising 'Persons of the Play' list describes Dorset and Grey as 'treated as one figure in the early scenes'. For his decision to have Richard, in his opening soliloquy, say 'Plots have I laid inductious, dangerous', rather than Q3/F's 'inductions', Jowett points out that 'inductious' is a perfectly comprehensible Shakespearian coinage (along the same lines as 'conceptious' in *Timon of Athens* IV.iii.188), which John Ford used in 1620. 'Inductious' would not seem strange to us had not Q3 (1602) changed it to 'inductions'; thus does editorial practice become self-validating as the 1602 alteration becomes traditional. Jowett discusses the oddness of Q1's labelling of the two orations by Richmond and Richard to their respective armies, and records that John Dover Wilson noted that Richard's follows a strong, exit-like couplet. Even though he remarks that they involve 'a rather awkward transition from a small group of on-stage leaders to an "army"' and 'probably should be taken to address the theatre audience', Jowett does not cite Ralph Cohen's fine suggestion ('Watching Richard Lie: "We're Actors: We're the Opposite of People"', *ShakB* 16:iii[1998] 24–8) that in the preceding few lines Richard addresses the theatre audience as his army and, since they do not—cannot—follow him 'hand in hand to hell' as he rushes off, he has to come back and 'say more' than he has 'inferred' (V.v.43). Appendix E prints relevant passages from Thomas More's *History of Richard III*, appendix F reprints the 'quick if slanted guide to the characters' given by the English Shakespeare Company in their *The Wars of the Roses* [1988–9], and appendix G prints an A to Z of practitioners who have done significant work on the play since its first performance. The index is essentially a guide to the commentary.

Jill Levenson claims that her interest in *Romeo and Juliet* sprang from work with like-minded students who wanted 'no part of its sentiment', and the splendid introduction to her Oxford Shakespeare edition of the play makes a powerful case for the play having political and social substrata inherited from its sources. Levenson gives an amusing example of how rhetorical the source novellas could be: in Matteo Bandello's *Novelle* [1554] Juliet, on discovering who Romeo is, says 'Now let us assume that he really loves me … should I not be reasonable and consider the fact that my father will never agree to it?' (p. 11). These source novellas also 'strain towards verisimilitude', giving explanations for such things as the use of rope ladders in Italy and Romeo's living arrangements in Mantua, and Levenson's fine survey of how these pre-texts shaped the play should disabuse students who, having seen the film *Shakespeare in Love*, think it is semi-autobiographical. Despite the problem of sentiment, Levenson deals in one section with 'Love, Death, and Adolescence', where she focuses on the psychosexual matter in the play with special attention to adolescent sexuality, transition to adulthood, and guilt about sex (pp. 16–30). While this is more than perfunctory, Levenson gets properly into her stride with the section on 'Patriarchy' (pp. 31–43), where she argues that the feud does the work of ideology, making everyone identify their allegiances—thus giving each an identity—and meld into a group. The family unit and the city-state unit come under stress, but endure. An important part of patriarchy is the control of masculine aggression, and Levenson argues that Elizabethans interested in the decorum of duelling would notice that the fights in *Romeo and Juliet* start properly but descend into chaos and accident. Shakespeare thus showed that the formalized rules governing violence, promulgated in duelling manuals, do not work (p. 36). At a different level of subversion, what Juliet's autonomy enacts—and she is much more active in this than Romeo—is a disruption of capitalism, since her clandestine marriage prevents Capulet's transmission of his wealth to a count, which would be a consolidation of it. I am not entirely sure why Levenson thinks this consolidation capitalist rather than feudal, and I would have liked to see this part of the introduction expanded (p. 40). Of course, whatever disruptions the lovers create are finally inconsequential; they are doomed to fail.

In the section 'Style and Genre' (pp. 42–61) Levenson argues that the play consistently shows rhetoric failing to express the real conditions people experience; language, no matter how overblown, is inadequate. As a 'tragedy of romantic love' rather than of statesmanship the play was a significant innovation by Shakespeare, indeed virtually an oxymoron. But comic and tragic drama had never really been far apart, being made from the same sources and of the same length: 'It was primarily the conclusion that made the difference.' In *Romeo and Juliet* Shakespeare satisfied the demand for tragedy and comedy from different theatre patrons 'with the blended essences of [the] two favourite genres' (pp. 51–2). This claim can be most usefully compared with Martin Wiggins's argument (*Shakespeare and the Drama of his Time*. OUP. [2000] pp. 102–22) that tragicomedy—another kind of blending, although *Romeo and Juliet* is not a tragicomedy—came into being around 1600. Also on matters formal, Levenson points out that the play put into the plot the essential elements of the sonnet tradition: the anguished lover, the unattainable lady, and the equating of love and war. The sonnet form in the 1580s and 1590s became the way in which political and financial desire was mediated—the lover (poet) seeking gifts from his woman (the patron)—and, in his unrequited love for Rosaline, Romeo begins the play as the archetypal Petrarchan lover. Levenson's section on 'Performance History' (pp. 61–96) confirms that, beyond the title pages of printed editions, no pre-Restoration performance is recorded. Shakespeare probably started *Romeo and Juliet* before the Chamberlain's men formed, so he did not know who would play it, and yet he was fairly demanding in his staging since the plays needs a balcony, a bed, and a tomb. Of course, one might not always get what one wants, and the first two quartos (1597 and 1599) are permissive in their stage directions, a feature no longer thought to be incompatible with their origins being documents used in the theatre. There are three moments when the locale changes without a clearing of the stage: in I.iv the masquers walk around the stage to represent going to the Capulet ball; II.i starts in the street but becomes the Capulet orchard; and IV.iv starts in a room where preparations are being made for the wedding, but becomes Juliet's bedchamber. Levenson has rightly decided not to mark scene breaks at these points of locale change. Surveying the stage history from the Restoration to the present, Levenson describes Thomas Otway's adaptation, *The History and Fall of Caius Marius*, which sets the story in Rome. The immediate political context of this adaptation was the Exclusion Crisis as Charles II tried to get his Catholic brother James barred from succession, and accordingly Otway's version moralizes against civil war. Correcting the common error that Colley Cibber originated the alteration, Levenson notes that Otway allows the lovers a moment of conscious togetherness in the tomb before they both die, as does the latest film version. Quite properly, she alludes to 'soft-core pornographic' versions of the play without wasting time on such masturbatory aids as Troma Films' *Tromeo and Juliet*, to which even some academics seem disturbingly drawn.

Regarding the dating of the play, Levenson argues that this is not necessarily a singularity since the matter could have been reworked by Shakespeare until Q2 appeared in 1599 (pp. 96–103). The outer limits of composition are 1591 and 1596, but linguistic evidence suggests that it was probably first written in 1593 and came to the stage in 1594–5. Q1's title page gives the performing company as 'L. of *Hunsdon* his Seruants', which name they had only between 22 July 1596 and 17 April 1597, being the Lord Chamberlain's men before and after that. But this title-page evidence does not preclude the possibility that the Lord Chamberlain's men acted it before 1596; by 1598 there were many allusions to the play. In a rare slip, Levenson writes that 'The Shaxicon database on [*sic*] World Wide Web should help to refine the study of linguistic evidence for purposes of dating Shakespeare's plays: it charts the interrelation of rare words in Shakespeare's texts with contemporary works from around 1591 to 1616'. If only Donald Foster had fulfilled his promise to publish his SHAXICON database on the World Wide Web then others, including this reviewer, might be less sceptical of everything it is supposed to prove, including Shakespeare's authorship of the *Funeral Elegy*.

In titling her section on the early printings of the play 'The Mobile Text' (pp. 103–25), Levenson puts herself with the new textualists rather than the new bibliographers. Q1 (1597) is, she notes, less than 80 per cent of the length of Q2 (1599), and separating them are numerous variants; all seventeenth-century editions derived from Q2. Levenson treats these two printings as two witnesses to 'distinct phases' in the play's sixteenth-century career. What she calls 'millennial postmodern theory', which is sceptical of everything, rightly makes the play 'part of a multivalent and dynamic process', and although they acknowledged the uncertainty at the heart of their work, the Enlightenment-inspired new bibliographers nevertheless 'misconstrued the randomness' of the textual evidence. (One might more charitably say that they did not see as much chaos as we postmoderns do.) At the end of twentieth century, as Levenson worked on the play, the new bibliographical binaries (author/stage, good quarto/bad quarto, memorial reconstruction/foul papers, promptbook/foul papers, and touring/London) were breaking down. Books necessarily stabilize performance, but Levenson reminds readers that our books are more stable than were theirs, which were often non-identical within a print-run. Q1 or Q2 were not entered in the Stationers' Register, a fact that no longer excites suspicion, and collation of the five copies of Q1 shows no press variants, which as Levenson points out, is not unusual in so small a sample. Q1 has fewer obvious errors than Q2, yet most bibliographers consider Q2 more authoritative.

Sheets A–D of Q1 were printed by Danter, sheets E–K by Edward Allde (we can tell by recurrence of types, by running-title differences, and by printing conventions), and the work was done by formes (not seriatim) simultaneously in the two printing shops after casting off, probably at Danter's. Levenson points out that the raid on Danter's shop during Lent 1597 did not stop him printing, so it cannot be used to date Q1; nor can the title-page reference to performance by Lord Hunsdon's men, because that could still have been made after their name changed back. Thomas Creede's Q2's title page say it is 'New corrected, augmented, and amended', and indeed it is more than 20 per cent longer than Q1, has variants from Q1 in more than 800 of its lines, and some passages are totally different. Few significant press corrections are made evident by collating the thirteen extant copies of Q2, but many errors remain, apparently because of difficult copy. Two compositors, A and B, set Q2, A doing most of it and B helping at the end. Paul L. Cantrell and George Walton Williams have reconstructed from running titles in the two skeleton formes the order and timetable by which the sheets were printed, but no one has yet looked at Creede's other work to determine when in 1599 Q2 was printed. Q3, Q4, and Q5 were each a reprint of their predecessor, although Q4 appears to have been informed by sporadic consultation of Q1. The Folio text is almost entirely derivative, being set solely from a copy of Q3 which was probably annotated by someone who knew the play in performance. Levenson herself collated the seven extant copies of Q3 and found no press variants. There is no evidence that Q1 was an illicit publication, but the new bibliographers called it 'bad' because of its shortness, its lack of a Stationers' Register entry, and its alleged poor-quality printing; none of these alleged deficiencies stands up to scrutiny. The 'short quartos'—Levenson's less judgemental term for those formerly called 'bad'—were disliked by the new bibliographers because of the non-authorial influences found in them. By the mid-twentieth century Q1 was widely dismissed as a memorially reconstructed pirating and Q2 was thought to have been printed mostly from Shakespeare's holograph with just the occasional bit of Q1 used as copy. Fifteen years ago, John Jowett's entry on *Romeo and Juliet* in the *Textual Companion* to the Oxford Complete Works placed him squarely in this tradition.

Certainly one section of Q1 (I.ii.53–I.iii.36 in this edition) was used as copy for Q2, to judge from the fact that Q1's incidentals—such as the Nurse's speech being in italics—were closely followed. Moreover, Q1 appears to have been consulted elsewhere in the setting of Q2, and since this influence cannot be measured, cannot be distinguished from simple agreement between what Jowett would call MSQ1 and MSQ2, we reach what Levenson (somewhat exaggeratedly) calls 'an impasse which blocks the search for copy and a stemma' (p. 117). As new bibliography undergoes necessary correction by the new textualists some well-washed conceptual babies will be discarded. Levenson asserts that there is 'no contemporary evidence to verify that any actor(s) ever reconstructed a play memorially' (p. 118), which is strictly true for early modern England but not for Spain where, as Jesus Tronch showed in his short paper, 'Play-Text Reporters and "Memoriones": Suspect Texts in Shakespeare and Golden Age Drama' (delivered at the seventh World Shakespeare Congress in Valencia [19 April 2001]), this was done and with precisely the textual corruption we should expect. Blayney hypothesized a non-piratical form of memorial reconstruction as actors made texts for friends by recalling their lines; since plays were routinely abridged for acting, this would make for short versions. The theory that the differences between Q1 and Q2 might be caused by authorial revision—either Q1 being a first draft enlarged to make Q2, or Q1 being a cut-for-pace version of Q2—cannot, Levenson insists, be excluded. Q2 has three moments of repetition which look just like second thoughts being printed alongside undeleted first thoughts, and this suggests its copy was authorial (pre-theatrical) papers since, as William B. Long showed, when theatre people interfered with a play manuscript it was to solve problems, and the repetitions in question cry out to be solved. On the other hand, the repetitions might represent revision well after original composition, or 'may record different versions in different performances' (p. 123). In short, Levenson concludes, we cannot be certain of the copy for Q1 or Q2 and therefore cannot privilege one over the other. This view conditions the entire edition since if Q1 and Q2 'represent two different and legitimate kinds of witnesses to two different stages of an ongoing theatrical event' (p. 126) then *Romeo and Juliet* follows *King Lear* in becoming a play we can no longer consider as a single entity. Necessarily, then, Levenson edits both texts of *Romeo and Juliet* for this edition and prints both. Because of the tradition which takes Q2 as basic, she puts it first and prints Q1 with minimal apparatus. With both versions of the play present, Q1 appears in the Q2 collation 'only when its readings bear significantly on the later text'. Levenson has tried to interfere as little as possible in either text, but has cut such things as the 'potentially confusing duplications' of Romeo and the Friar's shared 'dawn' speech.

Levenson delivers on her promise to trust Q2, so Mercutio describes Queen Mab drawn 'Over men's noses as they lie asleep' (I.iv.56), as Q2 has, not 'Athwart men's noses' which is the more familiar Q1 reading. Likewise, at II.i.86–7 Levenson prints 'That which we call a rose | By any other word would smell as sweet' which reflects Q2 and eschews Q1's 'By any other name', the familiar reading. The mortally wounded Mercutio says 'I am hurt. | A plague a both houses, I am sped' (III.i.90–1), which is Q2's reading, whereas Q1 has 'A pox of your houses'. Levenson resists the usual emendation 'A plague a both your houses', which makes this phrase identical with what Mercutio says ten lines later in his short speech about death, and it also regularizes the metre; she instead thinks that 'irregularities suit the dialogue of a fight and its aftermath'. Levenson keeps as much as possible to Q2's stage directions, so at the transition from the street to the Capulet party (I.iv.112) she keeps '*They march ... forth with napkins*', but she deletes Romeo's subsequent entrance since he has not left the stage; explaining the staging possibilities here requires commentary that occupies more than 80 per cent of the printed page. Sometimes traditional emendations provide the more interesting reading, such as at II.i.39 where Levenson prints 'An open-arse, or thou a popp'rin' pear' where Q2 has 'An open, or thou a Poprin Peare' and Q1 has 'An open *Et caetera*, thou a poprin Peare'. Levenson might have trusted Q1 here, since 'An open etcetera' makes sense: Mercutio will not name the open thing Juliet is to be. Having asserted a principle of minimal intervention, Levenson ought perhaps to have outlined at greater length the rationale of this emendation. The 'dawn' speech ('The grey-eyed morn ... Titan's burning wheels', II.ii.1–4) Levenson gives to the Friar alone (as Q1 does) rather than to the Friar and Romeo (as Q2 has it). She argues that it is easy to see how

Shakespeare might have written these lines for Romeo and then imperfectly deleted them and written a slightly different and improved version for the Friar, thus creating Q2's duplication. As C.J. Sisson pointed out (*New Readings in Shakespeare*, p. 154), it is hard to imagine the opposite case of Shakespeare writing these lines for the Friar and then retrospectively reassigning them to Romeo, since there would be no room. Respecting Shakespeare's second thought of giving the lines to the Friar, Levenson uses the form of words given the Friar in Q2 for this speech.

Actual mistakes by Levenson are hard to find. At her III.i.122 (but really 121, she has miscounted) Levenson has Romeo say of Tybalt, 'He gan in triumph and Mercutio slain?', which is Q2's reading. Levenson defends 'gan' as either past participle (gone) or infinitive (to go). Levenson's Juliet, awaiting her lover, says, 'Spread thy close curtain, love-performing night, | That runaways' eyes may wink, and Romeo | Leap to these arms, untalked of and unseen' (III.ii.5–7). Thus she uses Q2's reading ('runnawayes'), but having cited some alternatives and the argument about it her commentary does not tell the reader who are these runaways, their plurality being implied by the position of her possessive apostrophe. Sisson (*New Readings in Shakespeare*, p. 156) thought the correct reading 'runaway's eyes' because the runaway is Romeo, who, Juliet (unaware that he is banished) fears, might be too cautious and not come to her. For the obvious problem regarding what flies may do at III.iii.40–3, Levenson follows the Oxford Complete Works conjectures about the line 'This may flyes do, when I from this must flie' being imperfectly deleted and rewritten as 'Flies may do this, but I from this must flie' and this change, together with the associated reordering of lines and the composition of a new one ('They are freemen, but I am banished'), being misunderstood by the Q2 compositor. Levenson has Capulet describe Paris as 'youthful and nobly ligned, | Stuffed, as they say, with honourable parts' (III.v.180), turning Q2's 'liand' into 'ligned'. Levenson's commentary says that 'noble ligned' means coming from noble lineage, and that the silent 'g' makes also a possible pun on 'lined' which goes with 'stuffed' in the next line. Fair enough, but since 'ligne' is an archaic spelling of straightforward modern word (*OED* line *n.*²), there seems no reason to retain the 'g' in a modernized text. When in Q2 Juliet says 'Or bid me go into a new made graue, | And hide me with a dead man in his' (IV.i.84–5), Levenson supplies the apparently missing final word with 'tomb', as did the Oxford Complete Works, in preference to Q4's 'shroud' and F's 'graue'; Q1 has a different wording altogether but uses the word 'tombe'. This would appear to be another case where Q2 might have been trusted, since there is no need for a final word: 'in his' can refer back to the 'grave' of the previous line. Likewise, Levenson has Paris say, 'Have I thought long to see this morning's face' (IV.iv.67) where Q2 has 'thought loue', which Sisson defended as better than Q1's 'long' when punctuated 'Have I thought, love, to see' (*New Readings in Shakespeare*, pp. 161–2); Levenson points out that the source uses 'long' at this point. Finally, although Levenson is aware of Katherine Duncan-Jones's persuasive argument linking Juliet's autonomy with possession of her own knives ('"O Happy Dagger": The Autonomy of Shakespeare's Juliet', *N&Q* 45[1998] 314–16), Levenson prints that '*She takes Romeo's dagger*' (V.iii.169) to kill herself. Perhaps Levenson was swayed by Capulet's assertion that 'This dagger hath mista'en, for lo, his house | Is empty on the back of Montague', (V.iii.202–3), but, as Duncan-Jones argues, this is just another example of the father's ignorance about his daughter.

The title page of Stanley Wells's Oxford Shakespeare edition of *King Lear* says that he edited it 'on the basis of a text prepared by Gary Taylor', which in this case means he started with the electronic text of the quarto ('History') version published on floppy disks by OUP in 1989. Wells's introduction is short (eighty-eight pages), in keeping with Oxford Shakespeare guidelines, and provides a useful summary account of the special two-text status of this play, the first for which a majority of scholars have accepted the principle that it cannot be considered as one thing. The original version of the play was written probably in 1605 and led to Q1 of 1608; it was then revised, probably by Shakespeare, for revival in 1610, which led to the F text of 1623 which was printed from an annotated copy of either Q1 or the Q2 of 1619. An omission from the argument here is a statement of why anyone should accept that the alterations to the text represented in Q1 took place some years after an initial run of the play rather than as part of the preparations for first performance. It is because of this delay that Q1 and F are witnesses to two different versions of the play, rather than being merely witnesses to two stages in the genesis of a single play. The reading list at the end of introduction does not mention Gary Taylor and Michael Warren's *The Division of the Kingdoms: Shakespeare's Two Versions of 'King Lear'* (Clarendon [1983]), which convinced scholars that substantial revision separates Q1 and F, and although it appears in the larger reading list at the end of the book, the running title to that section ('Offshoots of *King Lear*') hardly encourages readers to look there for further reading on textual matters. It is perhaps too obvious to Wells, but worth stating explicitly for most readers, that, having established that the revisions seen in F were marked on to a copy of Q1 or Q2, these revisions could not have been made before Q1 was printed, and thus not before 1608.

The series policy has been to 'base an edition on the text that lies closest to performance', which in this case would be F, but Wells decided to break with the policy because F is well represented in other editions while Q1, a distinct version, has only recently been properly edited in its own right, and only two critical editions (by René Weiss and Jay L. Halio) have been published. Although, as observed above, the argument that about five years that passed between the original performances and performances of the revised text is not outlined, Wells admits that some of the differences between Q1 and F are absences from MSQ1 (to borrow Jowett's useful labelling) which would have been rectified before the play's first run. Thus it is a 'nice philosophical problem' (p. 8) to distinguish these things from the later major revisions. The nicety would be more apparent were the reader given at least a sketch of the reasons against attributing all the differences to this cause, such as the evidence adduced by Taylor, in '*King Lear*: The Date and Authorship of the Folio Version' (in Taylor and Warren, eds.), that F shows influence of Shakespeare's post-1605 reading matter and that its vocabulary is typical of his later work. Wells's approach is to accept Folio readings which are necessary to make Q performable (thus including the music cues), but not those readings which are unnecessary. Wells does not collate Folio variants nor print (even as appendices) the F-only passages, since the Oxford Complete Works provides these, but he does collate choices made by Weis and Halio with greater assiduity than is usual since 'the Quarto has only just entered the editorial tradition'. Dating the initial composition, Wells discusses the dependence on Samuel Harsnett's *Declaration of*

Egregious Popish Impostures and on the chronicle history of *King Leir* which, to judge from its influence on his earlier plays, Shakespeare knew in the mid-1590s. Wells thinks that references to astronomical eclipses are of little use for dating the play since an audience would always relate these to the last such events they remember.

In the section 'Where the Play Came From' (pp. 14–31), Wells indicates *King Lear*'s themes and character-types appearing in earlier plays: *Titus Andronicus* has an elderly mad tyrant, the *Henry VI* plays explore division in the kingdom, and Constance in *King John* is 'an enfeebled but eloquent grieving parent'; apparently the artistic gestation of *King Lear* was a long one. For the tangible sources, Wells traces the King Lear story in legend, starting with Geoffrey of Monmouth's *Historia regum Britanniae* which was not in print in Shakespeare's time but was circulating in manuscript, through Holinshed, *Mirror for Magistrates*, William Warner's *Albion's England*, Spenser's *Faerie Queene*, and, most importantly of all, the play *King Leir*. The Edmund/Edgar subplot comes from Sir Philip Sidney's *Arcadia*, printed in 1590. Discussing how Shakespeare shaped the ideas, events, and persons from these sources, Wells's wide range of critical reading is apparent, from Leo Salingar to Marianne L. Novy and Jonathan Goldberg. It is arguable that *King Lear* is beginning to overtake *Hamlet* as the work for which Shakespeare is most known, but as Ann Thompson observes, *King Lear* has no moments to match the synecdochical power of Yorick's skull or 'To be …' ('*Hamlet* and the Canon' in A.F. Kinney (ed.), Hamlet: *New Critical Essays*. Routledge. [2001] pp. 193-205, esp. pp. 194–7). Wells notes that the poetry of *King Lear* is subordinated to the dramatic effect, which is why so little of this play bears being quoted out of context, and I suppose this might explain the difference (p. 52). Wells handles the material of his stage history so deftly that it strains the reader not at all. Regarding the early performances, he thinks the ballad, which he reprints in full, 'gives us what may well be unique eyewitness impressions of moments from the play as performed by Shakespeare's company' (p. 57). He charts the dominance of Nahum Tate's adaptation of *King Lear*, which diminished over the period during which it held the stage (1681–1838) as more Shakespeare was put back. Wells defends Tate's play as doing to Shakespeare what Shakespeare did to *King Leir*. In the section 'Return to Shakespeare', he surveys nineteenth- and twentieth-century productions, with Harley Granville Barker's work as the watershed between an entirely readerly appreciation and the play's rehabilitation as a theatrical work.

The section 'Textual Introduction and Editorial Procedures' is kept to eight pages by Wells, who has nothing to prove in this area (pp. 81–8). There are, he observes, numerous press variants in the twelve extant copies of Q1, but he argues against automatic acceptance of a reading in a corrected sheet since 'the compositor may have guessed' when he spotted an error, rather than consulting the manuscript copy. The errors and the press variants suggest that the copy was hard to read, possibly authorial manuscript rather than fair copy, and it had not been through the theatre. In Wells's text, Q1 is used for every reading unless it does not make sense, in which case all possible explanations of the error and all concomitant readings are considered, including those in F, but without giving it special preference. Because the play was written before act intervals were observed in the open-air amphitheatres, Wells has simply numbered the scenes sequentially (as with the Oxford Complete Works), and not marked a new scene when Edgar enters while

Kent sleeps in the stocks, nor another when Edgar leaves, Kent wakes up, and Lear enters. The collation records all substantive departures from Q1 (that is, those affecting meaning), with a selection of plausible editorial emendations not adopted. Variants where F departs from Q1 are not recorded, but adopted Folio readings are, like any other adopted readings, recorded. Wells usefully lists the places where he accepts Q1 readings which the Oxford Complete Works rejects, and where he imports readings from F or from one of the two critical editions of Q1. Regarding the punctuation, Wells aims to 'increase comprehensibility for the modern reader without being over-prescriptive for the actor', which modest goal is a useful corrective to the absolutism of Ros King's claims about editorial intervention (reviewed below). Although Wells has been saying in public for some time that he is not convinced of the desirability of the practice, in this edition stage directions 'whose content and/or placing are uncertain' and speech prefixes which are 'disputable' are printed in broken square brackets.

For individual cruces there is little point comparing this edition to earlier ones, nor in comparing Wells's choices with those of Sisson, since, as Wells points out, Q1 has only recently been edited independently. However, a few choices deserve special attention. Wells has Kent say 'Be Kent unmannerly | When Lear is mad' (i.136–7), using Q2/F's 'mad' rather than Q1's 'man' which makes sense and, as Peter Stallybrass argues (in an essay reviewed below), is perhaps better than 'mad'. At i.176.1 the entrance of the King of France and Duke of Burgundy is accompanied by a musical flourish (as in F but not Q) because they are important men. However, for the exit of Lear and Burgundy at i.256.1 Wells puts the '*Flourish*' in broken brackets, even though it too is marked in F. It is not clear how these things are different, unless of course Wells thinks royal exit directions are less likely overall to be marked with music, or perhaps because the scene is somewhat disordered and leaving out this mark of Lear's importance could signal that. At i.257–8 Wells has Cordelia say 'The jewels of our father, with washed eyes | Cordelia leaves you', which is what Q and F have. Wells rejects Nicholas Rowe's emendation, used in the Oxford Complete Works, to 'Ye jewels of our father', made on the basis that the sense is 'You jewels' and the manuscript probably had either 'ye jewels' or 'ye jewels' which the compositor misread as the abbreviation for 'the'. Wells accepts that this might be true, but since Q1 also makes sense he does not emend it. This is a tricky footnote for readers who do not know that the 'y' in such advertising signs as 'ye olde tea-shoppe' stands for the letter thorn þ or Þ (so 'the olde …') which by Shakespeare's time was already disappearing from manuscripts and almost universally represented by 'y' in print (*OED* Y [3]). At ii.125–6, when Edgar enters Edmund says 'and out he comes, like the catastrophe of the old comedy, my cue is villainous melancholy', which is Q1's reading, instead of the more familiar 'Pat: he comes' which is F's. Wells has the First Gentleman say that Lear 'Strives in his little world of man to outscorn | The to-and-fro-conflicting wind and rain' (viii.9–10). George Steevens's conjecture that Q1's 'outscorne' was a misreading of the manuscript's 'outstorm' (followed in Kenneth Muir's Arden2 and the Oxford Complete Works) is possible, Wells says, but 'outscorn' also makes perfect sense. At xi.4 Kent says 'Good my lord, enter' and, in the same metrical line, Lear responds 'Wilt break my heart?' which is Q1's reading. F has 'enter heere' which regularizes the metre, but as Wells observes on E.A. Abbott's authority, 'a missing syllable at the caesura is acceptable'.

The textual choice which will probably be noticed by most readers is Edgar's reciting 'Child Roland to the dark town come' (xi.65), from Q1's 'darke towne' rather than F's 'darke Tower'. Wells admits himself tempted to follow the familiar F reading, but sticks to his principle that where Q1 makes sense he should follow it. John Jowett suggests a dark British town is here contrasted with the enlightened city of Athens ('Come, good Athenian', Lear says to Edgar immediately before this), but Wells was sufficiently unsure as to post a message on the SHAKSPER e-mail discussion list to poll others' opinions. Nearly as noticeable, and based on precisely the same principle, is Wells's decision to have mad Lear say 'It were a delicate stratagem to shoe | A troop of horse with fell' (xx.173–4), using Q1's 'fell' against F's 'felt'; Wells points out that 'fell' is a perfectly good word meaning 'skin'. Finally, an example of punctuation being crucial to meaning is Lear's 'This feather stirs. She lives. If it be so' (xxiv.261), regarding the breathing of Cordelia. Q1 has 'This feather stirs she liues, if it be so' and F has 'This feather stirs, she liues: if it be so', either of which could be understood as two indicative statements (the feather does move, therefore she is alive), although Q1 lacks something between the clauses to indicate that they are separate. But also, Q1 or F could be read as one subjunctive statement: if this feather moves, then she must be alive. Wells admits both possibilities and says the choice is 'open to the actor', but his period between 'stirs' and 'She' eliminates the subjunctive interpretation whereas a comma would have left the options more obviously open. On the other hand, it would create an error which North American students are most strenuously warned to avoid—the comma splice—if taken to be to one subjunctive statement.

Moving from editions to books about, or in support of, editing, Trevor Howard-Hill has revised and enlarged his *Shakespearian Bibliography and Textual Criticism: A Bibliography*, a repetitious title which illustrates that awkward terminology is one of the things that makes work in this area difficult. Most students do not discover until graduate work that 'bibliography' can mean more than just a list of books they have read. Howard-Hill's second edition of this book, first published in 1972, was, he reports, declined by Clarendon Press because they thought it 'premature' (p. v), but I would suggest rather that it is too late. This sort of printed bibliography has limited value to a scholarly community used to the electronic indices provided by the *MLAIB* and the *World Shakespeare Bibliography*. A spot-check failed to reveal any items in Howard-Hill's book which could not easily be found by a 'keyword' search in one or other of these. Increasingly such indices are adding evaluative descriptions of the items indexed—an area where Howard-Hill's book has obvious value—and in some cases (especially for recent work which was created electronically in the first place) the full texts of the items are also included in the database.

The published proceedings of the conference 'Ma(r)king the Text' at Trinity College Cambridge in September 1998 has several excellent essays of general interest, but only one of direct relevance to this survey: Ros King's claim, in 'Seeing the Rhythm: An Interpretation of Sixteenth-Century Punctuation and Metrical Practice' (in Bray, Handley and Henry, eds., *Marking the Text: The Presentation of Meaning on the Literary Page*), that modern editions spoil Shakespeare's metrics with punctuation. The sixteenth-century colon, King observes, was used not only to divide clauses but also to show that they are linked (a usage derived from the Hebrew psalms) and so editors should not, when confronted with 'strings of clauses separated by colons', simply chop them up using periods. King looks at the setting to music of poems in the period, and from this concludes that 'what is most important for mid-sixteenth century prosody is the natural rhythm of the words'. The problem for editors, of course, is that editors think punctuation a matter of sense and actors think it a matter of pausing. King believes that compositors were 'first and foremost copyists' and so she thinks that they mostly got their lineation right, which view should be contrasted with that of Paul Werstine, in 'Line Division in Shakespeare's Dramatic Verse: An Editorial Problem' (*AEB* 8[1984] 73–125). King promulgates that common actorly view that 'the last word in any line is usually one of special importance that needs to be picked our or emphasized in some way', and of course if an editor has re-lineated the script the wrong word will be chosen. (One would like to see some evidence for this claim about the terminal word.) King thinks we should expect the silence around short lines to be filled with business or sound-effects, and urges editors not to simply settle for the choices of 'the eighteenth-century poets who were his first editors'.

Another collection of essays this year is Andrew Murphy's *The Renaissance Text: Theory, Editing, Textuality*, containing seven essays of interest. Michael Steppat, 'Unediting and Textual Theory: Positioning the Reader', subjects Leah Marcus's *Unediting the Renaissance* to 'discourse analysis' to show that it coerces the reader into alignment with unproven ideas. Marcus's book is hardly worth such an effort, since its claims can be more easily dismissed, as Paul Werstine, 'A Century of 'Bad' Shakespeare Quartos' (*SQ* 50[1999] 310–33), showed regarding Marcus's claim that Q and F *Merry Wives of Windsor* are independent versions separated by authorial revision. Steppat then applies the same analysis to an essay by Graham Holderness, Bryan Loughrey, and Andrew Murphy to rather more effect, showing that their application of Marxist terms about the value of plays makes it unclear how use-value relates to exchange-value, an all too common misunderstanding. Moreover, since Holderness, Loughrey, and Murphy's concern is for the labour that goes into performance (including that by non-authorial theatre people) and into printing (including that by scribes and compositors), Steppat spots that authorial intention has re-entered by the back door since, even as part-sharer in that collective labour, the dramatist's efforts must be accounted for. Steppat points out that as general editors of the Shakespearean Originals series of play reprints, Holderness and Loughrey claimed that these offered a 'unique window on to the plays as they were originally performed' while at the same time insisting that these earliest texts are as far back as we can going without committing the error of trying to 'see through' the material object to something beyond it. As Steppat asks, why assume that the early texts are windows on to the theatre and nothing else?

Peter Stallybrass's excellent essay, 'Naming, Renaming and Unnaming in the Shakespearean Quartos and Folio', argues that costumes, properties, and speeches, but not characters, are at the centre of early modern drama's production processes. Shakespeare uses 'personal' names to indicate deprivation, that a person has lost their socially ascribed name, and for him the important names are those given by function. Speech-prefix variation is not, as McKerrow claimed, a sign of authorial carelessness but often signals the point of the whole play, to reunite a personal name (such as Perdita) with a real social position (such as Princess). Names are better thought of as attached to properties (beards and dresses) rather than to actors; costumes, not actors, are at the centre of the early theatre's economics. Considering the permutations of one-to-many relationships in acting, Stallybrass repeats the error that more than one man played Demetrius in performances of *Believe As You List*, citing David Bradley as his authority. In fact Bradley, like C.J. Sisson, thought the practice highly unusual, and T.J. King has argued that the three names in the play manuscript come from three different men who played the part at different times (*Casting Shakespeare's Plays: London Actors and their Roles, 1590–1642*. CUP. [1992] p. 47). Stallybrass reads speech-prefix variation in relation to the plays' concern with social status in a number of Shakespeare works including *Twelfth Night*, *Richard II*, *Hamlet*, and *King Lear*. There is always the danger that such interpretations misread randomness as art, especially where no early printing is consistent. Stallybrass defends Q1 *King Lear*'s 'Be Kent unmannerly when Lear is man' over Q2/F's 'is mad', on the grounds that, since Kent has notably left off Lear's title, it is appropriate for him to refer to Lear's transition from monarch to mere man, and the word also suits Kent (whose name is a whole county) going from man to unmannerly. The modern concern for individuality and personal names is inappropriate, Stallybrass argues, for an understanding of how early modern drama was written. The manuscript of the play *Sir Thomas More* suggests that speeches were written then divided up between the main speaker and 'others', the 'others' being sorted out later.

Laurie E. Maguire, 'Composition/Decomposition: Singular Shakespeare and the Death of the Author', argues that editorial theory and practice follow 'grief theory', here grief at the loss of the writer's presence, upon which loss all literature is predicated. The first half of Maguire's essay rather tediously describes funeral practices and likens editing to the tidying-up of the corpse (or corpus), including such banalities as 'Life and death were closely linked in the early modern period'. Post-structuralism at its silliest identifies everything as its own opposite, as when Maguire approvingly quotes Richard Lippert writing that a coffin 'protects something precious at the same time [as] its protection confirms loss', leading to Maguire's comments that 'To use Derrida's formulation, the funeral, like the text, is the ultimate in "presence" as "generalized absence"'. Derrida's point was that things are not merely their own opposites, but rather are self-contradictory in a productive, possibly Marxian, dialectical and fascinatingly unstable way. Maguire claims that the Renaissance was all about recovering the dead, the lost classical cultures, and although she admits that there was editorial/authorial intervention, in these textual resurrections 'the living and the dead, comfortably co-exist' (p. 148). At this point Maguire could have invoked Derrida's zombie simile, since the classics were reanimated for distinctly presentist humanist motives and were not so much like Lazarus as the undead. Near its end Maguire's essay takes a remarkable turn for the better, arguing that twentieth-century denial of death—unmentionable and postponed by medical intervention—led to 'untidying, unediting the body of the text' and hence the current denial of the finalized text. We now have the same flexible ideas about the end of life as the early moderns did: they allowed a corpse to be arrested for debt en route to its burial, and our machines can keep a human vegetable going indefinitely. New bibliographical desire for one originary text parallels Freud's death drive, the desire to return to the inorganic state. Loss, Maguire concludes, is at the heart of literary writing because the author is always absent and the words stand in for him. We grieve for loss first by denying and idealizing, then by simultaneously grieving and celebrating, and finally by looking forward while also remembering; the point is 'not to reduce these oppositions to singularity'.

Graham Holderness, Stanley E. Porter and Carol Banks, in 'Biblebable', argue that the 1623 Folio of Shakespeare has much in common with the King James Authorized Version of the Bible. The Shakespeare Folio and the King James Bible were alike in their print format (folio size, double columns, expensive paper), both represented that which was also available in oral performance as plays and sermons, and both were supposed to provide definitive versions to oust inferior competition from the marketplace. (In fact it is not clear that the Folio was intended to oust the quartos, which in any case continued to be reprinted.) The new Bible and the 1623 Folio collected together what was fragmentary and monumentalized it to preserve a tradition, which meant choosing between competing existing versions of texts. Holderness, Porter and Banks write that plays were 'officially printed only when the theatres were temporarily closed, or when the company needed extra money, or if a particular play had ceased to draw the crowds profitably in performance' (p. 167), yet at the end of the preceding sentence they cite Peter Blayney's 'The Publication of Playbooks', which specifically argues against these explanations and offers the new one that plays were printed for publicity purposes. On the basis of this error the authors distinguish in F1 the 'Old Testament' Shakespeare plays (those worn-out ones already printed) from the 'New Testament' Shakespeare (the newer ones or older ones that still drew crowds, some not previously printed). Since their premise is wrong, this distinction is wrong. Such errors the authors repeat, writing that 'It is generally assumed that the First Folio editors worked from such manuscripts [that is, foul papers, parts, and promptbooks] for all the plays in their collected edition' and they go on to mention that in fact this was not so—some quartos were used as Folio copy. Of course, this faulty assumption is not generally made, and it was known before new bibliography began that quartos were used as Folio copy. Indeed, one of the founding steps of new bibliography was to show that this did not matter, since only the good quartos were used and that Heminges and Condell's phrase 'diuerse stolne, and surreptitious copies' referred to the other, bad, quartos. Since Holderness, Porter and Banks cite A.W. Pollard's *Shakespeare Folios and Quartos* a couple of sentences earlier (p. 175 n. 34), one would expect them to know this: Pollard addresses it on pages 1 and 4.

Errors abound in this essay: Charles Jasper Sisson loses his first name and becomes 'Jaspar Sisson'. The writers think that the Histories section of the 1623 Folio rearranged 'the random, non-historical order in which they were performed' into a historically chronological sequence, but of course *The Contention of York and Lancaster* and *Richard Duke of York* were not randomly ordered. This fact the writers could have discerned simply by looking back over their own writing: on page 169 they give the *Contention* its full title of '*The First Part of the Contention ...*' which label ('*The First*') clearly indicates historical non-randomness rather than random non-historicalness. Likewise it is self-evident that *1* and *2 Henry IV* (and possibly *Henry V*) were historically ordered, and, as argued above in the review of Edward Burns's Arden3 edition of *1 Henry VI*, the printing and performance of the history plays shows a pre-Folio concern for historical orderliness. While it is true that the Folio strengthened the connections between the plays, and arguably imposed a teleological principle on the grand narrative so constructed, Shakespeare's histories can hardly be called 'ten discrete stories' when so obviously partaking of the well-known two-part construction format. Holderness, Porter and Banks think that the King James Bible and the Shakespeare Folio make a false unity of disparate materials, and that now we must disintegrate them to release 'from their authoritarian structures the many and varied utterances' of which they were made.

Emma Smith, 'Ghost Writing: *Hamlet* and the Ur-Hamlet', traces scholarly desire to have something tangible as the ur-*Hamlet*, making it up if necessary. Just as the ghost of Hamlet Senior haunts Hamlet, so the ur-*Hamlet* haunts Shakespeare's play, and Smith neatly summarizes the evidence that there was an ur-*Hamlet* existing in 1589–95, the slight evidence that Kyd wrote it, and that it is related to a German play *Der Bestrafte Brudermord*. In a familiar pattern, Smith shows that the presence of the ur-*Hamlet* in Shakespeare's *Hamlet* was used to exonerate Shakespeare from that play's weaknesses: the bits critics did not like were taken to be Kyd's. Smith quotes bizarre 'reconstructions' of ur-*Hamlet* using the source story (Belleforest's account of Amleth) and *Spanish Tragedy* as guides, and observes that bibliography seems to need this old play as a justifying principle just as Hamlet needs the ghost to justify what he does. Andrew Murphy's 'Texts and Textualities: A Shakespearean History' is a fairly standard anti-new bibliography survey of Shakespeare editing and editorial theory, starting, as is often the case, with E.K. Chambers's British Academy lecture [1924], which argued against multiple authorship and against John Dover Wilson's notion of 'continuous copy' for sullying the authorial purity of a manuscript capturing a single moment of a single man's work. Murphy articulates the fashionable view that Shakespeare's plays, indeed all plays of the period, are inherently collaborative. This claim is easily overstated: dramatists, not whole companies of actors, went to gaol for their plays, title pages named Shakespeare as a dramatist in his lifetime, and accolades such as Francis Meres's were addressed to Shakespeare, not the company. The afterword to the book is by Leah S. Marcus and called 'Confessions of a Reformed Uneditor', which title (but not the essay itself) suggests that doing some editing has significantly altered the views Marcus advanced in her *Unediting the Renaissance*. Marcus refers to her co-edited text of Elizabeth I's writings, which prints multiple versions of her speeches rather than trying to produce something definitive. Marcus thinks that the World Wide Web will help the move away from singularity, but notes that editors will have to acquire the technical skills for themselves since the technical specialists tend to get lured into better-paid commercial work. (This seems to be an allusion to the technical work of John Lavagnino, the general editor of the forthcoming Oxford Complete Middleton, to whom Gary Taylor elsewhere in this book rather ungraciously apportions the lion's share of the blame for that edition's delayed publication. Taylor's excuse that he lost his computer in a divorce settlement suggests third-world levels of technological poverty in American academia.) Like W. Speed Hill, Marcus thinks that collations are more ostentatious than practical, and remarks that the extreme variations in versions of Elizabeth I's speeches would render full collation impractical, but nonetheless Marcus has had to print variants. Marcus acknowledges the editorial tension between wanting to not intervene and having for financial reasons to modernize spelling and punctuation; furthermore, as a feminist she wants to raise the international profile of women's writing by making it as widely readable as possible.

Shakespeare Quarterly published eight articles on matters textual this year, and one review whose consequences make it worth reporting. Scott McMillin, 'The

Othello Quarto and the "Foul-paper" Hypothesis' (*SQ* 51[2000] 67–85), argues that
new bibliography has long, and E.A.J. Honigmann has recently, misrepresented the
situation regarding Q1 *Othello* because in pursuit of authoriality and supposing a
principle of textual economy, neither of which is reasonable. Contrary to W.W.
Greg and Honigmann, Q1 has theatrical features, most especially in its distribution
of 'cuts', the 160 lines of the Folio text which it lacks. Greg thought that Q1 was
printed from authorial foul papers because of its indeterminate and erroneous stage
directions, whereas Alice Walker argued that it was printed from a theatrical
manuscript made by a scribe who introduced things he remembered from
performance. That Q1 was printed from foul papers, or a scribal copy of foul papers,
was widely accepted in editions of the 1950s to 1990s, including the Oxford
Complete Works and Honigmann's Arden3. Greg's argument was that Q1's vague
and/or erroneous stage directions show its authorial origins, but he admitted that its
omission of Folio lines is not random but, rather, seems theatrical; moreover, there
are readerly features in Q1 (such as act divisions and literary stage directions) which
suggest a copy made for a private patron. Greg needed to eliminate the theatrical
copy and private patron theories, so he supposed that the authorial papers had
intended cuts marked on them, and that these were obeyed by the printers, so that
instead of being a theatre document it is still an authorial document, albeit by a man
of the theatre. To eliminate the private patron evidence Greg imagined that the
copyist making this extra copy for a patron was the bookkeeper himself, and thus the
single author-to-theatre line of transmission is preserved. Of course, in reality the
extra copy could have been made anywhere in the chain of transmission, but Greg
was trying to limit the proliferation of texts in his new bibliography.

As Paul Werstine has long argued, new bibliography always has to suggest the
most economical lines of textual transmission so that the choice of copy remains
binary: authorial papers or promptbook. Extra scribal copies for private patrons or
for revivals are, wherever possible, eliminated as a possible source of copy, and
even Honigmann, who spends many pages discussing the habits of scribes and
compositors, admits only one extra scribe: the one who copied the foul papers to
make Q1's copy. This scribal copy Honigmann will only accept being 'at one
remove' from the author, whereas of course this oft-revived play (at court 1604, at
the Globe 1610, at court 1612–13) could have generated descending 'trees' of multi-
generational copies. Like Greg, Honigmann wants to preserve the purity of the
author-to-prompter genealogy. He excludes the possibility that Q1 is a 'bad' quarto
(because it is unlike other bad quartos), so all that is left is 'foul papers or a scribal
copy of foul papers'. McMillin asks a pressing question (p. 72): what about
theatrical copy for a revival, or a copy of *that* made for a private patron? The
problem is with new bibliography itself, which ignores some real possibilities.
Honigmann's recent book on the texts of *Othello* (Werstine's review of which is
discussed below) states that Q's omission of those 160 lines cannot be due to cuts for
performance nor to Folio additions, yet Honigmann also attempts to distinguish
those lines which he thinks were Q cuts from those he thinks were Folio additions.
One of the reasons he gives for dismissing the idea that the 160 lines are cuts from
Q is that they save only eight minutes, which McMillin thinks is an underestimate
given that they contain the willow song. Even if only amounting to eight minutes of
stage time, such a cutting in the right way might, McMillin argues, be worthwhile.
Honigmann introduces what he thinks is new evidence that Q1 is based on foul

papers: it has some false starts. This view should be contrasted with Pervez Rivzi's claim, in 'Evidence of Revision in *Othello*' (*N&Q* 243[1998] 338–43), that the Folio text has false starts mended in Q. One of Honigmann's examples is the double questioning of Emilia by Desdemona ('Wouldst thou do such a deed?') in which the first answer ('I might doe it as well in the darke') is too jokey for the serious situation, so Shakespeare cut it and wrote a more appropriate one; the cut was overlooked by the printer. (An obvious objection here is that this example of double questioning occurs in Q and F, so it can hardly be used to argue that they had different kinds of copy.)

McMillin points out that a hypothesis of multiple errors (a false start, an insufficiently marked cancellation, a printer who overlooked the cancellation) is awkward and that, since Honigmann thinks Crane made from foul papers (or a copy of them) the transcript that lies behind F (which also has the putative false start), this hypothesis requires that Crane also missed the cancellation, which is unlikely. Honigmann has an answer to this: in parts F was set from Q. Another false start Honigmann finds is Cassio being said to be 'almost dambed in a faire wife' (I.i.20, present in Q and F), which Shakespeare meant to cancel once he decided it would be better if Cassio were a bachelor. Honigmann lists some Q1 odd spellings, and a stage direction of the form 'x *driving in* y', which he thinks are Shakespearian, but McMillin shows that they are either found elsewhere or merely odd and not indicative of copy. Because Q1 has '*Enter* Montanio, *Gouernor of* Cypres' (II.i.0), and this information is not available from the dialogue but only implied, Honigmann argues that this is a sign of the author to whom this occupation—never made explicit—matters. McMillin responds that anyone involved in costuming Montano would care, and this information could well be recorded on prompt copy. None of the things that Honigmann claims indicate that the copy for Q was authorial papers (or an accurate scribal copy of them) are really persuasive, but, tied to new bibliography, Honigmann had to choose between foul papers or promptbook, so he staked all on the former (p. 78). What of the copy for F? Honigmann decided that it was a scribal transcript of Shakespeare's revision of those same foul papers, and thus both printings are tied to foul papers. This, McMillin observes, realized new bibliography's greatest hope of putting us back in touch with the authorial hand.

McMillin believes that a central tenet of new bibliography—that promptbooks were 'tidier' than foul papers—has been gravely undermined, and cites as support for this view work by William B. Long and Paul Werstine: '"A Bed / for Woodstock": A Warning for the Unwary' (*MRDE* 2[1985] 91–118) and 'McKerrow's "Suggestion" and W.W. Greg' (in George Walton Williams, ed., *Shakespeare's Speech-Headings: Speaking the Speech in Shakespeare's Plays*, papers of the Seminar in Textual Studies, Shakespeare Association of America, 29 Mar. 1986, Montreal. UDelP. [1997]). Damaging as they are, these two essays do not demolish the principle but only show cases where the assumption of theatrical tidying does not fit the facts well. A systematic survey of theatrical documents is urgently needed, and one of its first steps would be establishing which extant playbooks are theatrical, hopefully without generating a logical circularity by determining this using new bibliographical criteria. McMillin thinks that promptbooks did not have to be regular because the 'plot' controlled entrances and actors controlled their own exits, but really one would need to bring in here a recognition that the function of playhouse plots is not agreed upon. David Bradley, for example, thinks them primarily casting documents. Experiments currently under way at Shakespeare's Globe London are testing the usability of extant plots to control backstage affairs. McMillin thinks the alleged 'confusions' in Q are in fact quite playable (p. 79).

Having pointed to flaws in Honigmann's book, McMillin offers his own contribution to the subject, a study of where the 'cuts' from F to make Q fall. The biggest omission is in Act IV, and half of the total 160 lines are lost from Desdemona's and Emilia's parts. Perhaps the boy actors were not good and their parts needed to be shortened, McMillin wonders. He might have mentioned that the eyewitness account of *Othello* at Oxford in1610 praised the boy actor playing Desdemona, but for silent action, not speaking (Geoffrey Tillotson, '*Othello* and *The Alchemist* at Oxford', *TLS* 20 July 1933, p. 494). In a footnote McMillin reports that Eric Rasmussen has studied where other plays' Q/F cuts fall and found that mostly it is in Acts IV and V, which McMillin takes as a sign that the cuts were made to shorten the play. One would have thought that a cut anywhere shortens the play. Indeed, McMillin's logic descends to tautology at this point: 'Mainly and obviously the distribution indicates that the omissions [in Q *Othello*] occur toward the end of a long play, the most reasonable explanation being that they were cuts intended to shorten that play in its final scenes' (p. 82). McMillin's conclusion is essentially the same as Rivzi's, although from different evidence, that Q was printed from a manuscript containing the play as abridged for the theatre some time between composition and Stationers' Register entry in 1621, and possibly this manuscript was annotatively 'touched up' for reading by a private patron or the quarto's readership. In the current conflict between new textualists and the new bibliography, McMillin insists that the possibility of play transcripts made for private patrons becoming the copy for early printings is one we cannot ignore.

A spin-off from Honigmann's Arden3 edition of *Othello*, a book called *The Texts of 'Othello' and Shakespearian Revision* (Routledge [1996]), is the subject of a review by Paul Werstine which claims that Honigmann is a wholly out-of-date defender of the new bibliography (*SQ* 51[2000] 240–4). The review extensively misrepresents Honigmann's opinions and achievements. Werstine claims that in *The Stability of Shakespeare's Texts* Honigmann argued that variants between early printed texts of *King Lear*, *Othello*, and *Troilus and Cressida* 'are authorial' (p. 240). In fact Honigmann did not; he pointed out that some of the variants might be, and that these would be indistinguishable from corruptions, which is virtually the opposite to the position that Werstine ascribes to Honigmann. Werstine thinks that Stanley Wells took up this position as general editor of the Oxford Complete Works, but that Wells failed to find what Stephen Orgel found in Honigmann's book, the important principle that 'finality' and 'completion' do not really exist for these plays. Werstine is mixing two things here: it was not Honigmann's *Stability* that persuaded Wells that substantial authorial revision separated some early printed texts; the work of Michael Warren, Steven Urkowitz and Gary Taylor did that. Wells took *Stability* for what it was, and what Orgel took it for, a demonstration of underlying textual instability.

Since then, Werstine claims, the supporters of revision have been reminded that there are many other non-authorial ways that a play's words can get changed, and 'the theory of authorial revisions seems to have receded to the … position … of an unverifiable hypothesis'. This is obviously untrue: almost everyone accepts that

King Lear was substantially revised by the author, and most accept that other plays were too. Werstine find that, in *The Texts of 'Othello'*, Honigmann took up the authorial revision claim again. F *Othello* has about 160 lines (in a number of clumps) that do not appear in Q, and Q has about twelve lines or part-lines not in F. That is not unusual, but this is: F and Q have large numbers of unsatisfactory readings, although rarely at the same place, so whichever one takes as the basis of one's edition, one has to import numerous individual readings from the other to make sense. Werstine rudely calls authorial revision Honigmann's 'idée fixe' and says that he used it to give himself as much room as possible to exercise choice when selecting between Q and F variants. Honigmann's project was 'to arouse suspicion about the reliability of both texts' and then 'reconstruct the processes whereby extra-authorial agents caused the problems' (p. 241). The two biggest culprits are William Jaggard, who, Honigmann says, printed F (whereas of course, says Werstine, it was really his son Isaac), and Thomas Walkley, who printed Q. Honigmann took the word of their enemies to cast aspersions on their professionalism. Honigmann also blamed F's Compositor B, but his scholarship on this was 'woefully out of date' and missed the significance of recent work which exculpates Compositor B. Honigmann wanted a shoddy Compositor B 'to widen the scope of his editorial interference'. Honigmann claimed that Ralph Crane may have supplied the copy for F *Othello* and F *2 Henry IV*, but he avoided undertaking the labour, such as was performed by Trevor Howard-Hill, needed to show this (p. 242). Honigmann did usefully correct 'Gary Taylor's gross error in denying the existence of literary censorship of dramatic texts', but just because oaths have been purged by the scribe does not make the scribe Crane. Honigmann aligned himself with new bibliography and 'indulges in the excesses' of that discredited movement; he accepted the entirely unproven claim that Hand D of the *Sir Thomas More* manuscript is Shakespeare and that Shakespeare's writing got harder to read as he got older. (Werstine knows that most palaeographers think Hand D is Shakespeare and that given the current evidence the matter cannot be settled.) Where F differs from Q, Honigmann speculatively 'corrected' the error by reconstructing how it might have come about from a scribe's 'misreading of one of these imperfections in the later Hand-D-Shakespeare's penmanship'. Werstine ends with a lame joke that, just as Honigmann imagined that he could see past the Folio to the manuscript and its correct reading, so he, Werstine, can see past the copyright page of Honigmann's book to spy a turned type: the ideas are so out of date it should be dated '1966' not '1996' (p. 244).

Honigmann replied to Werstine in the *Shakespeare Newsletter*, claiming that the review 'grossly misrepresents' him ('Letter to the Editor', *ShN* 50[2000] 66). He points out that, far from uncritically championing new bibliography, he challenged it because he realized that corruption and authorial revision were largely indistinguishable. As for using the 'enemies' of Walkley to blackguard him, Honigmann points out that he quoted both sides of *Walkley versus Everard*. Like many others, Honigmann declares himself convinced that Hand D of *Sir Thomas More* is Shakespeare and that he is entitled to use this in his argument. Far from offering almost no evidence in support of the contention that a Crane transcript of *Othello* was the copy for F, Honigmann insists that he offered plenty, as the reviewer for *Shakespeare Survey* noticed. *Shakespeare Newsletter* also published W. Speed Hill's review of Honigmann's work which includes his observation that Honigmann is on the pre-structuralist, empiricist, side of the current divide in Shakespeare studies (*ShN* 50[2000] 67–86). Hill thinks that *Othello* is the hardest Shakespeare text to edit and that there is no real agreement about the texts underlying Q-1622 and F-1623. Apart from Werstine's dismissive review of *The Texts of 'Othello'*, only McMillin's article (reviewed above) has entered the debate at all—to disagree with Greg and Honigmann that Q derives from foul papers—probably because Arden and Honigmann are too intimidating, even though Honigmann's being right would have important consequences for the editing of *Othello* and for the 'revision' question generally. Hill produces Honigmann's stemma for *Othello* and observes that in Honigmann's hypothesis there is no extant text descending from prompt copy, there is no need for memorial reconstruction, and a total of five lost texts are conjectured in addition to extant Q1, F, and Q2. For the existence of a scribal copy between the authorial foul papers and Q1, Honigmann adduced the evidence of misreadings and sloppy omissions (that is, material we know from F which did not make it into Q because the scribes did not copy the authorial papers carefully). Thus Honigmann's view was that what Q lacks of F is material dropped to make Q, not material later added to make F. Between the authorial foul papers and F, Honigmann posited an authorial fair copy and a Ralph Crane transcript of that fair copy. The authorial fair copy is authorial, not scribal, in Honigmann's view because Crane apparently had trouble reading it, and when copying his own work, Shakespeare introduced numerous tiny revisions, as argued in Honigmann's *The Stability of Shakespeare's Texts*. Thus Honigmann posited two authorial manuscripts (foul papers and fair copy), each of which is at two removes from its extant print witness (Q1 and F, respectively). Hill thinks that there is nothing wrong with assuming five lost manuscripts—we have to do this all the time for other texts available in multiple witnesses—and overall Honigmann's stemma unites those editors willing to produce a narrative about how Q and F came about. (Barbara Mowat and Paul Werstine are, of course, outside this consensus, being sceptical of such narratives.) However, many editors now respond to such a complex textual situation by saying that we should edit each extant early printing independently of 'its textual siblings'. Although Honigmann challenged parts of new bibliography in *The Stability of Shakespeare's Text*, Hill concludes that he still wants to get back to the author's words, not the collaborate troupe's performance.

Hill thinks it surprising that Honigmann, who did so much to convince people that Shakespeare revised as he copied, should reject the hypothesis that Q and F *Othello* are separated mostly by authorial revision—about which Honigmann admits a change of mind since he used to support the two-texts hypothesis for this play—and should therefore not be conflated; Honigmann's Arden3 *Othello* is a conflated text. (This point renders superfluous much of Werstine's commentary, reviewed above.) The Oxford Complete Works did a textbook Gregian mixed-authority conflation job (Q was their copy-text and thus their source for incidentals, but they introduced F readings where they thought these to be more Shakespearian or to be authorial revisions), but Honigmann was more cautious because his *Stability* demonstrated our inability to distinguish certain kinds of transmission errors from authorial revision. Honigmann raised the value of Q, because the scribe separating it from authorial papers was inexperienced and so could mangle but not subtly alter, and lowered the value of F because the scribe separating it from authorial papers, Ralph Crane, knew what he was doing and could subtly interfere. Hill asks, but does not answer, the question of whether we are entitled to 'correct' early printed texts by reference to some imagined origin beneath them to which we have no reference other than the printings. Where once there was a general consensus about editing, there are now two camps: those who see empirical work on the texts as leading ultimately to knowledge and who do critical editing (like Honigmann), and those who see this view as mere wish-fulfilment and who do 'best-text documentalism' (like Werstine) where the editor picks the text s/he thinks best and reproduces it with its major errors corrected.

Returning to work in *Shakespeare Quarterly*, Barbara Kreps, 'Bad Memories of Margaret? Memorial Reconstruction Versus Revision in *The First Part of the Contention* and *2 Henry VI*' (*SQ* 51[2000] 154–80), argues that the character of Margaret changes between the quarto version *The Contention of York and Lancaster* and the Folio version *2 Henry VI*, where she is more assertive but yet is taken less seriously by others. Such an artistically coherent difference cannot be explained by memorial reconstruction but must be Shakespearian revision. Kreps begins by surveying the new bibliographical explanations of the quarto and Folio versions of this play, and criticizes the binary thinking (especially notions of 'good' and 'bad' texts) which underlie it. Between Q [1594] and F [1623] there are thousands of variants, and in the mid-twentieth century Peter Alexander and Madeleine Doran independently offered evidence that Q was based on a memorial reconstruction of a production, and that a manuscript of that production was copy for F. Although Doran and Alexander are often lumped together for their shared view that the quarto is a memorial reconstruction, they had entirely different reasons for believing so, and Alexander had a much lower opinion of Q than did Doran; they agreed, however, that F was not an expanded form of Q, but that, rather, Q was a cut-down version of F. Doran thought that Pembroke's men, forced to tour in 1592–3 because of plague, found that they had left the book behind, so attempted to reconstruct it from their memories and at the same time abridged it because the touring troupe was smaller than the London company. Thus for Doran Q was a good acting version. Alexander, on the other hand, imagined unscrupulous actors doing an unauthorized memorial reconstruction for money, and fingered the men playing Warwick and Suffolk/Clifford. No dramatist could have written Q, Alexander pointed out, because it makes York claim descent from the second son of Edward III which, if true, renders absurdly pointless his subsequent argument for his right to inherit via the daughter of the third son of Edward III (p. 158).

Kreps notes that those who think Q a memorial reconstruction tend to follow Alexander in believing this to be a bad thing, ignoring Doran's equally viable theory of a virtuous origin. Of course, Kreps remarks, memorial reconstruction is good at explaining pointless variation—attributable to failures of memory—while a theory of revision is good at explaining purposeful alteration. Unfortunately both kinds of variation separate Q and F: there are long sections of perfect correspondence and sections where the texts do not converge at all. This fact would appear to necessitate a hybrid theory incorporating memorial work and direct copying, but Kreps thinks that supplementing memorial reconstruction with the idea that chunks of Q were directly copied to make F is 'critical doublethink' (p. 161). Kreps believes that Q is not 'bad' and that indeed it bears the mark of Shakespeare determining to write its sequel. Kreps summarizes the characterological differences between Q and F thus: 'in F Margaret is more of a virago, Humphrey is more admirable, the king's relationship with Humphrey is cooler, Henry's personal and political inadequacies are more evident, York and his claim to the throne are more politically complex and the cardinal more Machiavellian than they appear in the quarto' (p. 162). The welcome Henry gives his bride to be, Margaret, is verbally similar in Q and F, but in the latter it has a proviso: 'If Simpathy of Loue vnite our thoughts' (TLN 30) which would be ironically understood by those who knew the sources. In her reply, Q has Margaret be timid and anxious to please while F has her boldly emphasizing her own intellect. Likewise, when petitioners mistake Suffolk for the lord protector in I.iii, Margaret in Q hands the papers to Suffolk, who tears them, while in F Margaret holds on to the petitions and she, more forceful and rougher in speech than in Q, tears them. The reordering of the petitioners from Q to F makes the crucial matter be monarchial inheritance, as indeed it will be in the second half of *2 Henry VI* and throughout the sequel *3 Henry VI* (p. 165). After the petitioners leave, Margaret tells Suffolk her woes. In Q these are Henry's political impotence, her two enemies Humphrey and his wife, her dissatisfaction with Henry as a husband and her attraction to Suffolk. In F the order is different, and the speech much longer: she goes on about how her own dignity suffers, about how much better than her husband Suffolk is, and gives a longer denunciation of Henry (especially his religious piety) and all his courtiers. Her enemies in F include Beaufort, whereas crucially in Q Margaret does not say anything against Beaufort, and indeed when Beaufort dies she is sorry. Q and F are each consistent about her attitude to Beaufort: in the former he is not her enemy and she is sorry when he dies; in the latter he is her enemy and she is not sorry when he dies. This kind of consistency, 'coherent maintenance of dramatic logic across the distance of half the play', in each text cannot be accounted for by memorial reconstruction, only by artistic revision (p. 168).

When the matter of who will be regent in France comes up in I.iii, Margaret in Q gives her opinion in favour of Somerset, whereas in F she interrupts and insists that the king favours Somerset (which, in fact, he has not said). In F but not Q Gloucester complains that 'These are no Womens matters' (TLN 507). F has Henry be cooler to Humphrey duke of Gloucester, and, for example, when his wife is tried Henry omits her title and Gloucester's when calling her to give evidence. Q generally has Henry use affectionate language towards Gloucester, but F only has this affection reappear once it is too late to do any good. When Humphrey resigns he uses much the same words in Q and F, but since Margaret has commanded him to do it in F his failure to answer her makes these words become a snub. Does Q lack her telling him to do it because the memorially reconstructing actor forgot it, or because it was cut in the text underlying Q? Or was it added to the text underlying Q to make the text underlying F? If the last of these, as Kreps believes, adding the lines in which Margaret commands Humphrey to resign makes her assertive and makes him indifferent to her political interference, since he does not answer her. Perhaps making this simple revision gave Shakespeare the idea to make Margaret politically more assertive in III.i, and yet not taken seriously by others (p. 171). The cardinal is much more powerful in F, and is Margaret's enemy. When planning the death of Humphrey, F has the queen, the cardinal, Suffolk, Buckingham, York, and Somerset present, but York says 'we three haue spoke it'. Which three of them: Suffolk, York, and the queen, or Suffolk, York, and the cardinal? (Suffolk must be one because he says 'Here is my Hand', and York must be one because he says 'we three'.) Leaving out the queen would be another example in F of 'deflation of the ambitious Margaret' and one which accords with the following moment: the post from Ireland enters and, in F, ignores Margaret. All these changes of Margaret's political power (diminished in F from Q) and the cardinal's power (increased in F from Q) are not likely to come from memorial reconstruction; rather, they show artistic intention.

What of the sequel? Q and F end with the defeat for the crown at St Albans, the royal couple's flight to London to summon a parliament, and the Yorkists' attempt to beat them to London, which matches the beginnings of *Richard Duke of York* (Q version) and *3 Henry VI* (F version) at the palace where the parliament is to be held. The lasts acts of *The Contention of York and Lancaster* and *2 Henry VI* show signs that Shakespeare was thinking of a sequel, for example in the sudden attention to father–son relationships, which will become a motif in the next play. But *2 Henry VI* (the F version) has many more of these links than *The Contention of York and Lancaster* (Q text): sympathy for York, which *3 Henry VI* will extend, Clifford's vow to kill the infants of the York family, Henry and Salisbury's talk about making/breaking oaths, and the character of Margaret. In Folio *2 Henry VI*, Margaret and Henry are equal partners and plan together their next move, whereas in the quarto *The Contention of York and Lancaster* he is defeatist and she impatiently implores him to take manly action. This unwomanly queen of the Folio *2 Henry VI* (absent from the quarto *Contention*) is the same as at the start of Folio *3 Henry VI*, suggesting that the writer of Folio *2 Henry VI* knows he has a sequel and knows its outline. But if the known sequel were as in the quarto *Richard Duke of York* then it does not wholly account for Margaret as she appears in Folio *2 Henry VI*: yes, she is bolder, but the point of Folio *2 Henry VI* is that she does not get the political ends she seeks. It is as though Shakespeare wrote Folio *2 Henry VI* (that is, he built upon the existing play represented by the quarto *The Contention of York and Lancaster*) with the quarto *Richard Duke of York* in front of him and got from it Margaret's greater boldness, to which he added her achievements failing to live up to her desires (pp. 175–8). Kreps admits that she cannot prove all of this; her theory of the artistic changes in the character of Margaret explains some of the Q/F differences but not others, just as the theory of memorial reconstruction does. While Kreps dislikes hybrid theories ('doublethink'), others will presumably take her persuasive argument as good evidence that artistic revision and memorial reconstruction separate Q and F.

The point of M.J. Kidnie's long essay, 'Text, Performance, and the Editors: Staging Shakespeare's Drama' (*SQ* 51[2000] 456–73), seems to be the essentially trivial one that editors are too apt to tidy up and augment stage directions where in fact readers should face the indeterminacy of the originals. Kidnie quotes Michael Warren's observation that Q1 *King Lear* does not specify the moment of Lear's death; nor (usually) does any particular performance, but editors want to produce fixity. (I should say they are constrained by the necessity to put the words 'He dies' somewhere, so the reader knows this really is a death, even if they do not want to be precise about when.) Kidnie thinks Warren has lost sight of the one-way relation between script and performance: the former is incorporated into the latter, never the other way around, and as Marco de Marinis argued one cannot go from action to scripted stage direction. This is either obviously an error or this reviewer misunderstands Kidnie's point entirely, since memorial reconstruction does precisely go from action to words, as indeed does the task of theatre reviewer, and, as John Jowett argued in 'New Created Creatures: Ralph Crane and the Stage Directions in *The Tempest*' (*ShS* 36[1983] 107–20), Ralph Crane seems to have written his stage directions for *The Tempest* using recollections of performance. Kidnie goes on to quote Marinis, in absurdities such as 'There is no necessary link between dramatic language and the stage', and argues that when the stage takes a script it destroys its status as a literary text and makes it something else; so really editors cannot hurt performance by seeking fixity in their stage directions. It may seem that Q1 *King Lear* preserves the unfixity which is characteristic of performance, but Kidnie thinks this is an illusion: it is just that the oral messages from Shakespeare about when Lear was to die have not survived; only the paper has. Kidnie adopts Roman Ingarden's distinction between *Haupttext* (dialogue) and *Nebentext* (side-text, including stage directions) because recent performance theory uses this distinction: it prioritizes the dialogue and makes the stage directions ancillary, thus giving producers freedom to choose their own *mise-en-scène*. R.B. McKerrow, too, assigned more importance to speech than to stage directions, and Kidnie thinks this is justified since in the printing-house and in the theatre these two kinds of writing were treated differently: the dialogue was committed to paper while the stage directions were transmitted verbally or were 'sorted out in a collaborative rehearsal space' (p. 461). Kidnie here overlooks the possibility that professional convention (such as which stage entrance to use) or ingrained habits of movement (generated, for example, by rules of social deference) governed matters for which we might want stage directions.

Kidnie's assertion that there is no way to 'render an early modern script entire', no one way to close 'gaps in the *nebentext*' is something that even schoolchildren now learn, and it is surprising that she feels the need to say so in *Shakespeare Quarterly*. Editors must, she argues, think about what they are doing in representing things that 'survive only as textual fragments', but this surely indicates a leap of logic since Kidnie has not established that they are fragments in the sense that something has been lost. Rather, the stage directions may never have been written down or may always have been indeterminate in order to enable multiple reworkings. We might follow Stanley Wells who, in *Re-Editing Shakespeare for the Modern Reader* (OUP. [1984]), implored editors to be bold in helping the unimaginative reader, but Kidnie dislikes Wells's moral tone, referring as he does to the 'responsibility to both author and reader'. Kidnie again surprises with the assertion that no one would suggest that a person reconstructing a broken ancient vase had a responsibility to do the reconstruction, to which this reviewer finds himself responding 'I would!' Sensitive to generalizations about what people should do, Kidnie nonetheless confidently asserts that as 'actors, directors, and theatergoers' we want to see 'the plays performed in a modern context', and again I often feel the urge to cry 'I don't!' As a piece of literature, the stage directions interact with the dialogue to make a virtual performance representing the author's ideal, Kidnie argues, but it is hard to see how this is true in the case of something like Robert Greene's direction 'Or if you can conveniently, let a chaire come downe from the top of the stage' in his *Alphonsus of Aragon*; surely here is deliberate looseness which makes the thing adaptable to a variety of places and occasions. Kidnie cautions that even if we only want to help readers get the right virtual performance in their minds, we run the risk of an essentialist error in assuming that 'the ways we currently make sense of performance would have been shared by early modern practitioners and theatergoers' (p. 465). Correct use of terminology is not Kidnie's strength, for of course this would be the error of anachronism, not necessarily essentialism. (When tempted to use the word 'essentialism', one should always first ask oneself 'what is the essence?'). Worse, the assumption of a shared sense of performance is in fact reasonable up to a point: to use Wells's well-known example, we can be tolerably sure that characters who kneel rise again before they exit. When Kidnie asserts that the early modern individual might have closed the gaps in the *Nebentext* in ways we cannot imagine, one is entitled to respond that they could not have used some of the ways which we can imagine, such as exiting by being teleported *à la Star Trek*. Kidnie makes the extraordinarily elitist claim that editorial intervention cannot make up for the specialist skills needed to read a play—I have yet to meet a child who could not handle the genre comfortably, although of course unfamiliar language can be a problem—and she claims 'most published scripts' of twentieth-century drama include detailed ancillary material on staging which, offering Tom Stoppard and Caryl Churchill as examples, she claims 'is fairly standard practice'. To test this I dipped into as many modern plays as I could in half an hour's browsing at my local branch of Waterstones, and none included detailed ancillary material on staging; Stoppard and Churchill seem to be exceptional.

Kidnie claims that when editors augment stage directions they necessarily 'embed critical interpretation' in the text (p. 467), but the same is true of modernizing spelling, or emending errors, and everything else one does in mediating a text. Even facsimile reprints embed a subjective interpretation manifested in such things as the quality of the paper and the shape of the type. Kidnie thinks that the embedding of an editor's critical interpretation does more harm than the embedding in performance of a director's critical interpretation because the latter's work is ephemeral. This is not necessarily so: the directors of the BBC Television Shakespeare are likely to have more influence than editors on generations of students, especially in the vast areas of the world where live performance is hard to come by. Kidnie is sure (and quotes Alan Dessen agreeing) that we really know little about early modern staging, but one would be more confident that the ignorance was not solely hers if she had shown awareness of the work of Bernard Beckerman, Glynne Wickham, and Andrew Gurr, and of ongoing experimentation at the Globe reconstruction in London. Kidnie proves that she does not know what 'essentialist' means by throwing this epithet at the defence of editorial intervention as a commonsense necessity in aid of readers. Instead of there being one type of edition for the non-specialist reader there should be others that 'reintroduce variability and historical contingency', so Kidnie calls for 'the development of a plurality of editorial approaches'. Actually, the editorial approaches of the Arden, Oxford, and Cambridge series are not identical and the Arden certainly aims to do some of what Kidnie wants. But Kidnie's entire exhortation is forestalled by McKerrow's remark in the first page of the *Prolegomena for the Oxford Shakespeare* that 'There can be no edition of the work of a writer of former times which is satisfactory to all readers, though there might, I suppose, be at least half a dozen editions of the works of Shakespeare executed on quite different lines, each of which, to one group of readers, would be the best edition possible.'

Kidnie writes that she has 'deliberately resisted the temptation' to present her plans for other, better, ways to edit, but one cannot help suspecting that she has none. Instead, Kidnie offers editors some pointers: they might use promptbooks and other records of actual performance (such as photographs and video recordings) to flesh out their stage directions. (Or just go to the theatre?) Alternatively they might leave the stage directions as they are and ask the reader's indulgence, which would be an empowering experience (p. 470). Kidnie likes the idea of 'allow[ing] readers to evaluate the evidence for themselves', although it is not clear why she thinks this is more valuable than having a specialist doing it. Certainly textual democracy might reveal new insights since 'One person's compositor's error … may well prove to be somebody else's new insight about early modern staging', but that is an argument for such perspicacious readers being educated, learning to research and to publish to persuade their peers; one should not expect that level of engagement from people who are not reading professionally, or are only reading for undergraduate degrees. Kidnie wants editions that defamiliarize the drama, not make it comfortable, but with Chaucer rapidly disappearing from undergraduate English courses I should think this merely a way to hasten Shakespeare's joining him, and one which conservatives will find useful. Kidnie makes the classic historicizing demand that editions should create 'an awareness of the dramatic text's otherness', but this is a demand which, as Kiernan Ryan has argued in '*Measure for Measure*: Marxism before Marx' (in Jean E. Howard and Scott Cutler Shershow, eds., *Marxist Shakespeares*. Routledge. [2001]) may already have gone too far.

The remaining items in *Shakespeare Quarterly* take the form of short pieces. Ann Thompson, 'George MacDonald's 1885 Folio-based Edition of *Hamlet*' (*SQ* 51[2000] 201–5), argues that MacDonald's *Hamlet* was a century ahead of its time in using authorial revision as a reason for not conflating, and in devising an elegant layout to represent the textual situation of a two-text play. The design put an original-spelling Folio text on the left-hand page and MacDonald's notes on the right-hand page. Q2-only passages were placed at the foot of the left page in smaller type and separated from the main text by a line; an asterisk in the main text indicated each passage's position in Q2, and Q2 variants were in small type in the right-hand margin. Folio-only passages are identified by a vertical black bar on the left edge. Peter Holland, 'Modernizing Shakespeare: Nicholas Rowe and *The Tempest*' (*SQ* 51[2000] 24–32), argues that, although Nicholas Rowe's 1709 edition of Shakespeare was the first to use entirely logical/syntactical pointing in place of the breathing/rhetorical pointing found in the first four Folios, a trial printing of 1708 shows Rowe not quite having reached this endpoint since some 'breathing' pointing remains. Rowe did far more changing of spelling and pointing than F1–F4 editors had, and his practices are essentially those used now. Holland says that the language of Shakespeare was 'originally designed to be spoken', which is true but of course it was mediated, so far as we know, only by writing. Samuel Schoenbaum noted that the British Library has a few 'trial' sheets of Rowe's *The Tempest*, which Holland thinks were 'an experiment in setting' to see how the style to be used for the edition would look. As Schoenbaum saw, this trial sheet was based on F2 and not F4 as the 1709 edition was to be. Holland lists the variants that show that it was indeed F2 and not F3 or F4 that was used to make the trial sheets. Comparing the 1708 trial printing and the 1709 edition, the latter shows a move towards the more syntactic as opposed to the rhetorical pointing, especially in using the semi-colon (as it still is used in Shakespeare editing) to break up 'the long Shakespearean period in ways approximating modern conventions of syntactical punctuation for print'. For example, Rowe turned 'Heigh my hearts, cheerely, cheerely my harts: yare, yare: Take in the toppe-sale: Tend to th' Masters whistle: Blow till thou burst thy winde, if roome enough' (F1) to 'Hey my Hearts, cheerly my Hearts; yare, yare; take in the

Top-sail; tend to th' Master's Whistle; Blow 'till thou burst thy Wind, if room enough' (Rowe [1709]). It was no longer acceptable to link parallel clauses with colons, although in 1708 Rowe kept F2's colons. Rowe's eventual adoption of the contemporary prescriptive pointing is 'almost a pity' since it took us away from 'those possibilities for understanding the text still present in the later Folios'.

George Walton Williams, 'Early Exits: An Open Letter to Editors' (*SQ* 51[2000] 205–10), thinks that sometimes it is better for an editor to end a scene with characters exiting one by one, even if the copy-text gives a mass exit. Bardolph, Nym, Pistol and Boy taking their leave of Hostess at the end of *Henry V* II.iii have an exeunt in F (TLN 884) but might more effectively leave one by one, and there is a similar opportunity for sequential exit at the end of *Macbeth* II.i. Theatrically this winding down of a scene can be more effective than the collective exit offered in the script since it allows for decreasing tension. Williams addresses the objection 'you're an editor, not a director!' by suggesting that this kind of nudging to readers can be helpful 'without serious damage to the text', but this could be countered by the assertion that one can also rewrite dialogue without serious damage, yet it is not the editor's job. Two short pieces received independently by *Shakespeare Quarterly* are, because of their similarity, printed together: Randall Martin, 'Rehabilitating John Somerville in *3 Henry VI*' (*SQ* 51[2000] 332–40), and John D. Cox, 'Local References in *3 Henry VI*' (*SQ* 51[2000] 340–52), identify the historical man represented as John Somerville in Shakespeare's *3 Henry VI*. John Somerville was tried and condemned for sedition alongside Edward Arden, probably a relative of Shakespeare. The Somervilles were fervent Catholics and in 1583 John Somerville became unhinged, announcing his intention to kill Queen Elizabeth, for which he was arrested; under torture he implicated Somervilles and Ardens. Only John Somerville and Edward Arden were condemned at the trial; their heads were displayed on London Bridge. The case caused an outcry since Somerville was obviously insane and no evidence pointed towards Edward Arden. In defence of the government's action Lord Burghley's *The Execution of Justice in England*, which was begun in response to the outcry at Campion's execution, was published. Burghley's book complained of seditious Catholic publications, presumably (because Burghley was elsewhere much annoyed by it) including John Leslie, bishop of Ross's *A Treatise of Treasons against Queen Elizabeth* (Louvain [1573]). Leslie's *Treatise* is alluded to in *3 Henry VI* when Richard of Gloucester says that he 'set the murtherous *Macheuill* to Schoole' (F, TLN 1717) or 'set the aspiring *Catalin* to schoole' (1595 Octavo, sig. C8v). Cataline and Machiavel are used interchangeably in Leslie's *Treatise* as abusive terms for the powerful ministers of the government, Sir Nicholas Bacon, Lord Keeper, and Burghley, and he also, in likening the present situation to the fall of Troy, refers to Ulysses and Sinon, as does *3 Henry VI* (F, TLN 1713–14). Leslie also likens Bacon and Burghley to Richard III. That Folio and Octavo *3 Henry VI* allude to Leslie's *Treatise* but in different ways makes both likely to be Shakespearian, and probably the unusual and specific 'Catalin' became the less specific (because generally reviled) 'Macheuill'; that is, the O reading being revised to F's is more likely than the opposite (pp. 337–40). Martin concludes that Shakespeare's vignette with a character named Somerville cannot but have recalled the case. Shakespeare's Somerville is not mad and indeed he corrects another's error (Warwick), so this characterization is a coded rebuke of the government's treatment of Shakespeare's Warwickshire relatives, all of which adds to the evidence that Shakespeare was Catholic.

Cox puts this historical material in the wider context of local references in Shakespeare, noting that in *3 Henry VI* Shakespeare's Warwick is more of a king-maker than the sources have him. Shakespeare added places references to *3 Henry VI* V.i which are not mentioned in the sources: Dunsmore and Daventry, both on the London–Stratford (or Coventry) road, and appropriate for the action. Shakespeare moved the scene from Warwick to the walls of Coventry to make the most of the Rose theatre's upper playing area, argues Cox. Shakespeare gives the local pronunciation 'Daintry' for Daventry and gives the correct walking distance (two hours) from Southam to Coventry. Cox says that in fact a walker could do the ten miles in two hours, but a 'puissant troop' would take longer. I suspect Cox has missed the point of what Somerville says: 'At Southam I did leaue him [Clarence] with his forces, | And doe expect him here some two howres hence' (TLN 2683–4). Somerville's answer says how far *behind* him Clarence's forces are. If Somerville took two hours to arrive from Southam (as Cox suggests) and the army moves at half that speed (say four hours to do ten miles) they will indeed be two hours behind him. The man who gives this local information about Southam would appropriately be a Warwickshire man, since Warwick has boasted of his local support; Somerville's correction of Warwick's idea about which direction Southam lies in also suggests a local man. Like Martin, Cox thinks that the case of John Somerville was the reason Shakespeare chose this name for Act V, scene i of *3 Henry VI*. He quotes C.C. Stopes, *Shakespeare's Warwickshire Contemporaries* (SHP. [1907]), on John Somerville's landholdings in 'Edstone, Wootton Wawen, Knoll, and Clareden … Halford … Lapworth … Wydney super Bentley Heath', which is indeed what Stopes writes, although one suspects a typical Stopes transcription error since the place name Claverdon (now a station on the Stratford–Warwick railway line) is more likely than 'Clareden'. Cox relates essentially the same story of Somerville's attempted assassination and his death given by Martin and observes that whether or not Mary Arden was related to these Park Hall Ardens, Shakespeare would undoubtedly have known of the family and their downfall. In having his character Somerville be one of Warwick's loyal retainers, Shakespeare was 'disagreeing obliquely' with Burghley's claim that Somerville was a traitor. The scene at Coventry in *3 Henry VI* V.i is militarily absurd and Cox lists the things that do not add up, including Warwick being effectively besieged in poorly defensible Coventry but allowed by Edward to decide that the battle will take place eighty miles away at Barnet; this adds to the sense that Shakespeare ordered material for its local resonances for himself, and part of that was defending the honour of the family of Somervilles.

Just one article in *The Review of English Studies* was relevant to this survey, Roger Warren's 'The Quarto and Folio Texts of *2 Henry VI*: A Reconsideration' (*RES* 51[2000] 193–207). Warren argues that, contrary to Steve Urkowitz's view, the quarto *The Contention of York and Lancaster* is a memorial reconstruction of the play otherwise known as *2 Henry VI* in the Folio. As discussed above in the review of Kreps's article, the crux is York's explanation of his genealogy, which Q garbles. Urkowitz argued that York does not draw attention to his being descended from Langley, so the garbling would not make an audience think there was problem, but Warren counters that the audience could be expected to make the (historically correct) assumption that one York was descended from the other. Urkowitz also claimed that the memorial reconstruction argument ignores 'surrounding contexts' in I.i and I.iii, so Warren looks at these specifically and shows a number of scenes where Q clearly just garbles the Folio. McKerrow pointed out that where Q lacks historical details present in F we must assume that the reporter forgot them since it is hardly likely that these were sprinkled through the play as part of a process of revision, which tends to be wholesale. Warren argues that the reverse is also true: where Q contains spots of historical detail not in F, the reason is not (as the editors of the Oxford Complete Works had it) that Q represents performance later than the foul papers underlying F, and performance which may have been revised since those foul papers, but rather that what was in the play originally (and so got into the report underlying Q) was subsequently cut by the author (pp. 201–3). This means that revision separates Q and F. Evidence for this is the moving of the reading out of the prophecies (from the paper containing the spirit's answers) from the end of I.iv (by York) in F to the middle of II.i (by King Henry) in Q, but Warren admits that the direction of revision could be either way. In other words, F might be the original, left unrevised, and Q the revision for performance, or Q might represent first performance and F a later revision. F has Richard of Gloucester and Young Clifford 'flyting' as though about to fight, but they do not fight in F. In Q they do, and Warren thinks that F represents a decision to delay the fight of Richard of Gloucester and Young Clifford to the next play so that in this one can be shown the chivalric ideal which dies with the old men to be replaced by barbarity in the young men. Why might Shakespeare revise the text underlying F? William Montgomery thought that publication in 1600 of *2 Henry VI* and *3 Henry VI* at the same time as *Henry V* indicates renewed interest in these old plays, and that the reference to them in the epilogue to *Henry V* indicates revival of the *Henry VI* plays in the late 1590s. Warren admits that against this claim that F *2 Henry VI* being a revised text is the presence of slips such as Queen Margaret twice being called Eleanor/Nel, and the use of an actor's name in IV.ii, but he has explanations for these. In revising, Shakespeare left untouched the powerful third act (including the Margaret/Nel slips), and John Holland's name is not that of an actor but a name from Shakespeare's source reading (he was earl of Huntingdon) which stuck with him when thinking up names for Cade's followers. Q being a reported text is not incompatible with revision in F; in fact Q is a report of an earlier state of the play which is revised in F. For this reason, Warren in his Oxford Shakespeare edition will not insert passages from Q, since he thinks F contains authorial revisions later than Q. Warren's claims have obvious common ground with those of Barbara Kreps reviewed above, and go some way towards countering Paul Werstine's rejection of the entire memorial reconstruction theory reviewed last year ('A Century of "Bad" Shakespeare Quartos', *SQ* 50[1999]). Where two texts appear to be mostly related by memorial corruption, but have awkward stretches of entirely unalike material, a hybrid theory of memorial reconstruction and revision might be the best hypothesis from which an editor should proceed.

Analytical and Enumerative Bibliography prints one long and one short piece relevant to this survey. Karen Bjelland, 'The Editor as Theologian, Historian, and Archaeologist: Shifting Paradigms within Editorial Theory and their Sociocultural Ramifications' (*AEB* 11[2000] 1–43), uses Foucault's work to trace the history of Shakespeare's editors as 'theologians' (Folios 1–4), 'historians' (the Restoration to about 1980), and 'archaeologists' (in the last twenty years). Although there is a postmodern aptness to the difference, the article's running title of 'The Editor as Theologican, Historian, and Archaeologist' is probably just a misspelling of 'theologian'. Shakespeare editors are like clerics, Bjelland claims, because they are concerned with preserving a textual canon, a process which started with F1's preliminaries. Jonson's 'To the Reader' invokes class in calling him 'gentle' Shakespeare—which links him to a Protestant work ethic—as though the reader were being encouraged to view here the means by which he was able to retire wealthily to Stratford. Bjelland should, of course, acknowledge that 'gentle' could also just mean 'mild' or 'kind', so it might not be about class. The Folio engraving looks like those made of early Protestant martyrs, which Bjelland thinks is ironic 'in the light of Shakespeare's own recusant origins'. For this claim she cites an article in *Shakespeare Quarterly* [1989] on John Shakespeare's Testament, which is hardly where the matter rests at present. Bjelland calls the work of eighteenth-century editors the 'Alexandrian' phase without saying in which of the many senses she means this word, and she charts how they refashioned Shakespeare as a classical author while raising the questions which editors still cannot answer, such as whether Q/F variants show corruption or revision. From the eighteenth to the twentieth centuries editing tried to recover an 'ideal text' which is never one of the actually available texts, and the important thing is the critique made of this editorial tradition by 'those of a Pergamanian persuasion' (p. 14). Bjelland's argument is postmodern but her jargon obscurely classical; presumably her analogy is between two classical approaches to grammar, the former (Alexandrian) predicated on inherent orderliness and the latter (Pergamenes) more interested in anomalies which can be explored empirically. Bjelland identifies Steven Urkowitz, Michael Warren, Randall McLeod and Gary Taylor as the four leading Pergamanians, although the last she thinks more an Alexandrian in practice.

Bjelland identifies a Foucauldian epistemological shift around 1980, with the Platonic base of editing being attacked, and she sees new technology offering a democratic alternative to the specialism of the editor. With hypermedia archives, no one document need be privileged over others and this Bjelland thinks a good thing. One would have thought that such textual egalitarianism elides the author's effort to revise; after all, how would Bjelland like it if someone insisted that an earlier draft of her essay were equal to the published one? Bjelland writes approvingly that the hypermedia archive will promote the reader to editor, or, in her jargon, there will be 'the transfer of the "author-function" from the editor to the reader' (p. 21). This surely is a misreading of Foucault, since his point in inventing the notion of an author-function was that textual fixity comes not from authors but from readers who assign their own fixity—such as their unwillingness to accept certain meanings—to the author and say it came from him. Bjelland's article is marred by bad writing, such as 'Unlike those currently creating these archives, the users of tomorrow will not have the same critical background or repertoire of skills' (p. 27). It is impossible to tell whether Bjelland means that the users will be not the same as each other or not the same as the those creating the archives. In a footnote Bjelland writes of the problems that ignorance about how an electronic archive is made might cause: 'In the language of Roman Jacobsen, one might say that the inherent "metonymic" tendency of hypermedia can be so overwhelming for some that it leads to an "aphasic" response.' This is either a terribly clever joke or it is gibberish, and the odd spelling of Jakobson's name might fit either explanation. Bjelland's argument hinges on Foucault's 'author-function', yet she repeatedly misrepresents it. For example, she claims that nowhere in his essay 'What is an Author?' did Foucault did consider the possibility 'of the author himself exercising the "author-function" in terms of his own text and/or the mode of its production'. In fact he did: 'But the author-function is not a pure and simple reconstruction made second-hand from a text given as passive material. The text will always contain a certain number of signs referring to the author' ('What is an Author?', in Robert Con Davis and Ronald Schleifer, eds., *Contemporary Literary Criticism: Literary and Cultural Studies*. 3rd edn., trans. Josue V. Harari. Longman. [1994]). Possibly Bjelland is using a different version of 'What is an Author?' from me, but given her reliance on this essay she really ought to have mentioned the differences between versions of it published in different languages over several years.

The other Shakespeare piece in this year's *AEB*, by Robert F. Fleissner, is equally bad, but mercifully short: 'The Round Knight of the Table: Did Not Theobald Emend "A' Talkd Of" (Rather Than "A Table Of") in *Henry V*?' (*AEB* 11[2000] 179–80). After reading this note four times, I still cannot find what point Fleissner is making. It is known that Theobald got his 'babbled of green fields' emendation in *Henry V* from an anonymous gentleman's marginal note that 'talked of' makes better sense that 'table of'; beyond reminding us of this, I cannot see anything here. In stark contrast was the single piece of relevance in the new seventh series of *The Library*, Martin Butler's 'Running-Titles in *Cymbeline*' (*Library* 1[2000] 439–41), which I also read four times but for the pleasant reason that its two densely packed pages repeatedly educated me. Butler shows that the formes of the 'zz' quire of the 1623 Folio were set in the usual order, as proved by a rogue Roman letter 'i' in the running titles which Charlton Hinman feared showed something else. Hinman noticed that five pages of F1 (zz3v, aaa2r, aaa3r, aaa4r, and aaa5r) have running titles with a rogue roman 'i', making '*Cymbeline*'. Hinman wondered if perhaps this tells us of an unusual order of setting the formes: that zz3v:4r 'was the last forme in the quire [zz] to be set, the error then being carried over into the early formes of quire aaa', whereas, of course, we would expect the order to be from inner to outer formes, thus: zz3v:4r, zz3r:4v, zz2v:5r, zz2r:5v, zz1v:6r, zz1r:6v. Hinman did not think that zz was set unusually, but was stumped by the running-title error. Butler has solved it. There are other anomalies in the *Cymbeline* running titles to help us: a broken swash 'T' in '*The*' which appears on zz1v ('*The Tragedie of* [Anthony and Cleopatra]'), zz2v ('*The Tragedie of Anthony and Cleopatra*'), and zz3v ('*The Tragedie of Cymbeline*'), and then 'on each recto page of quires aaa and bbb (with one exception, to be described in a moment)'. Another running-title anomaly is that some spell it '*Tragedy of Cymbeline*' and some '*Tragedie of Cymbeline*'; it is '*Tragedie*' on zz3v then throughout aaa and bbb recto pages (with one exception) while verso pages use '*Tragedy*'. In the verso running titles the 'T' of '*Tragedy*' is missing an end of its right-side crosspiece. 'These facts indicate that a single skeleton was being used throughout the printing of aaa and bbb, the recto side of which carried the running title "*The Tragedie of Cymbeline*" (with broken "*The*"), while the verso side was headed "*The Tragedy of Cymbeline*" (with damaged "*Tragedy*")'. The pattern was only broken with the penultimate forme bbb1v:6r, where the pattern is reversed: '*Tragedie*' is on bbb1v and '*Tragedy*' on bbb6r. This happened because bbb1:6 was the last sheet of the book and bbb6r (the very last printed page) needed to be adapted to take the colophon. So, the skeleton was dismantled and the running titles reset. We can from this reconstruct the setting of the running titles in the zz quire, which holds the last four pages of *Antony and Cleopatra* and the first eight of *Cymbeline* (hence running titles had to be repeatedly rearranged), assuming they worked from inner to outer, and Butler provides a table showing this. After printing of zz3v, no forme needs 'Cymbeline' twice (left and right), so the running title with the rogue 'i' was partially dismantled ('*The Tragedie of*' being reused for zz2v and zz1v) and the word '*Cymbeline*' set aside. When this word '*Cymbeline*' came to be needed again for the next quire, aaa, the error was spotted and the 'i' replaced with an italic 'i', which is why aaa6r has the broken '*T*' in "*Tragedie*" but no rogue "i" in *Cymbeline*'. Thus Hinman's order of formes, the usual order, is confirmed by this rogue 'i' disappearing and reappearing.

This year's *Notes and Queries* contained the expected collection of factual enlightenment, unexpectedly spoiled by an extraordinary number of printing errors. So frequent are the misprints that this reviewer contacted several of the contributors to confirm the true readings; otherwise authors might be blamed for mistakes beyond their control. B.J. Sokol, 'Manuscript Evidence for an Earliest Date of *Henry VI Part One*' (*N&Q* 47[2000] 58–63), shows that *1 Henry VI* was written not earlier than 1591, which supports the 'late start' theory of Shakespeare's career. Records of the Inner Temple show that the garden was improved in 1591, probably by 25 April when the Parliament of the Inner Temple made new arrangements for the gardener, and Shakespeare is much more likely to have chosen this location just after the well-known changes than before them. Richard Levin, '*Titus Andronicus* and "The Ballad Thereof"' (*N&Q* 47[2000] 63–8) shows that the ballad of *Titus Andronicus* entered in the Stationers' Register is derived from the play, not a separate source. The 'booke' of *Titus Andronicus* was entered on 6 February 1594, and 'the ballad thereof' was the immediately next entry; Levin lists all thirty-seven occasions when a book and a ballad were entered together in the Register from 1590 to 1616. Almost always the ballad is mentioned after and in a subordinate relationship to the book, and in the year following John Danter's entry for *Titus Andronicus* and its ballad he entered five more ballads based on plays associated with Henslowe: *The Jew of Malta*, *Bellendon*, *A Knack to Know an Honest Man*, *Tamburlaine*, and *Long Meg of Westminster*. This shows that Danter had an arrangement with Henslowe to print ballads of plays Henslowe was promoting and thus the *Titus* ballad was likewise a follow-up to the play Henslowe was promoting, rather than deriving from the prose history, which conclusion the internal evidence adduced by others also leads to. John Jowett, '"Derby", "Stanley", and Memorial Reconstruction in Quarto *Richard III*' (*N&Q* 47[2000] 75–9), in an argument cited in his Oxford Shakespeare edition of *Richard III* (reviewed above), argues that memorial reconstruction cannot account for Q1 because it follows F's erratic stage-direction and speech-prefix alternation between 'Stanley' and 'Derby' as names for one man. F was printed from portions of Q3 and Q6 annotated by reference to MSF in all but two places (III.i.0.1 to III.i.148.1 and V.v.4 to end), and where speech prefixes vary in F they usually do so consistently, so Lady Anne is sometimes 'La.', 'Lady', 'Lad.', 'Anne.' or 'An.'. These variations come from the manuscript, not the underlying quartos. In dialogue the name 'Derby' appears five times in I.iii in both Q1 and F, which is an odd anachronism to get in performance, especially if Q1 were a memorial reconstruction, since the historical Stanley did not get the earldom until after Bosworth Field. In the rest of the play, from III.i onwards, he is consistently called 'Stanley' which represents an authorial shift part-way through composition. So much for the dialogue: the speech prefixes and stage directions are more complex in their variation. Q1 and F agree in speech-prefix and stage-direction names for this character throughout (that is, they shift together, sometimes in conflict with the dialogue), except that Q1 calls him 'Derby' (in conflict with the name 'Stanley' used in dialogue) from IV.ii onwards, whereas F calls him 'Derby' (in conflict with the dialogue) from IV.v onwards. Jowett lists the character's names used in speech prefixes and stage directions throughout the play and whether this is in consort or in conflict with the dialogue.

The sections where Q1 and F disagree in speech prefixes and stage directions about the character are most revealing: IV.ii and IV.iv, in both of which Q has 'Derby' and F has 'Stanley'. This shows that F is independent of its quarto copy in its speech prefixes and stage directions for this character. Elsewhere it is clear that MSF agreed with Q1 but it provided further material which was used to annotate Q to make F: the other quartos have 'Darby' which F changes to 'Earle of Derby', or 'others' which F changes to 'Derbie', and 'L. Stanlie' which F changes to 'Stanley'. These readings, Jowett insists, point to consultation of MSF and show that 'Derby' or 'Stanley' stood in MSF 'at thereabouts in Q1' (actually, an *N&Q* printing error renders this as the nonsensical 'as thereabouts'). Although MSF influence on the quarto copy used to make F diminishes in Act V, it is still discernible: Jowett shows a number of stage directions and speech prefixes in F which deviate in intelligent ways from Q1 and show that an authorial manuscript was consulted. Thus it is safe to infer that MSF slipped back to calling him 'Derby' (because F does) in speech prefixes and stage directions (in conflict with the dialogue), and hence there is a discernible pattern of alternation Derby/Stanley/Derby/Stanley/Derby in both MSQ and MSF. F's following of an erratic pattern in Q1 is not, then, due to its following Q1 directly—we have seen that it must be because F's underlying manuscript and Q1's underlying manuscript agree—but rather because there is transmission from MSF to MSQ. This transmission is not consistent with memorial reconstruction since the alternating speech prefixes and stage directions are unlikely to have made it into the actors' parts, let alone into their memories, since actors do not remember variability needlessly. Jowett imagines the objection (necessary to sustain memorial reconstruction as the origin of Q1) that perhaps MSQ, made by memorial reconstruction, was then annotated by reference to MSF or some other manuscript which maintained the distinctive alternation of speech prefixes and stage directions for Stanley/Derby, but in fact this cannot be so because there are speech prefixes in Q1 demonstrably not 'corrected' by reference to MSF. It is hard to find a way other than transcription by which MSF could have so oddly influenced MSQ, so memorial reconstruction cannot be the basis for Q1 *Richard III*. Jowett's brilliant work is difficult reading because the subject is hard, but it is rendered even harder by a particularly bad printing error which makes Jowett refer to the view that that F represents an earlier state of the text than Q1 thus: 'This has been the orthodox view of two-thirds of a century, but that orthodoxy adds the particular interpretation that MSF is derivative in the special sense that it is based on a memorial reconstruction' (p. 76). Jowett's typescript of course had 'that MSQ is derivative in a special sense'.

I.A. Shapiro, in 'Mending Shakespeare's Sonnet 146' (*N&Q* 47[2000] 91–2), argues that 'Beat down these rebbell powres that thee array' was the second line of

Sonnet 146. There is an obvious problem in its only authentic printing (Q 1609) which gives: 'Poore soule the center of my sinfull earth, | My sinfull earth these rebbell powres that thee array, | Why dost thou pine within and suffer dearth'. The repetition of 'my sinful earth' must be in place of something with two syllables (to regularize the metre), which something contained an active verb meaning to oppose or repel and made the first two lines a complete sentence (as are lines 3–4, 5–6, 7–8). Rejecting other emendations Shapiro proposes 'Beat down', at which point his entire sentence switches to an italic font, presumably because someone involved in the printing of it forgot to switch off the italics after *Beat down*. Shapiro notes that Shakespeare used this phrasal verb on seventeen other occasions, which he lists, and it has pleasant alliteration (*Beat ... rebel ... powers*) and assonance (*Beat ... these ... thee* and *down ... powers*).

Macd P. Jackson, 'Bottom's Entry-Line: *A Midsummer Night's Dream* III.i.98' (*N&Q* 47[2000] 69–70), thinks that Bottom's line 'If I were fair, Thisbe, I were only thine' should be emended to 'If I were horse, fair Thisbe, I were only thine'. Bottom-as-Pyramus enters with an ass's head on at III.i.98 after Thisbe has said 'As true as truest horse that yet would never tire', and his 'If I were fair, Thisbe, I were only thine' makes no sense. Edmond Malone thought the punctuation was the problem, emending to 'If I were, fair Thisbe, I were only thine', meaning 'If I were as true as truest horse'. However, Malone's emendation does not allow 'fair' to be disyllabic, as it needs to be, and it still makes Pyramus's loyalty conditional, which logically it should not be. Jackson thinks that Pyramus should pick up the subjunctive mood of Thisbe's metaphor of him as horse-like so that his 'If' has a point, so he emends to: 'If I were horse, fair Thisbe, I were only thine'. This extra word 'horse' allows 'fair' to remain monosyllabically attached to Thisbe and the line to remain Alexandrine. This emendation had the added merits that he refers to himself as if a horse at the moment that he appears as if an ass, and there is a pun on 'hoarse', which he probably is because the ass-head makes him bray.

Adrian Streete, 'Nashe, Shakespeare, and the Bishops' Bible' (*N&Q* 47[2000] 56–8), argues that Titus's references to his bowels containing, before vomiting them up, Lavinia's woes comes from Thomas Nashe's *Christ's Teares Over Ierusalem* and Bartholomaeus Anglicus's *On the Properties of Things*. J.M.M. Tobin found that Nashe was probably a source for *Titus Andronicus*, but did not note a speech at III.i.220–32 which is heavily indebted to material on signature Dr2 of Nashe's *Christ's Teares* in its collocation of 'heaven', 'earth', 'sea', 'deluge', 'drowned', and, most interestingly, 'bowels'. Christ's bowels comes from Paul's epistle to the Philippians, which in the Vulgate is 'visceribus', and the first Renaissance Bible to translate *visceribus* as 'bowels' was the Bishops' Bible of 1568. Paul says he is in Christ's bowels, while Nashe has Christ say that he wishes he had Jerusalem in his bowels. Nashe feminizes the bowels by referring to the mother pelican who lets her young tear at hers. Titus imagines Lavinia's woes lodged in his bowels only to be vomited up again, and Streete thinks this is because Shakespeare saw Titus's bowels as feminized by the loss of his wife (so he is father and mother to Lavinia); the male bowels cannot be truly female and container-like. To support this Streete quotes Bartholomaeus Anglicus's *On the Properties of Things* (which Shakespeare knew well) on bowels being like a widow, which Streete rather tenuously links to Titus's widowhood.

Rodney Stenning Edgecombe, 'Romeo and Aeneas: Proverb or Allusion in *Romeo and Juliet* III.v?' (*N&Q* 47[2000] 68), notes that Romeo tries to comfort Juliet at their final parting with 'all these woes shall serve | For sweet discourses in our times to come' (III.v.52–3), which editors usually say is proverbial with citations of Tilley. Edgecombe thinks it comes straight from Aeneas's address to his men in the *Aeneid*—'Perchance even this distress it will some day be a joy to recall'—because Aeneas, like Romeo, is putting on a brave face despite have had premonitions of doom. If this is not an allusion to brave Aeneas, then Romeo is just being 'Pollyanna-like' (that is, self-deludingly optimistic). In the immediately succeeding note, 'Shakespeare, Catullus, Rumourers, and Runaways' (*N&Q* 47[2000] 68–9), Edgecombe argues for emending 'runaways' to 'rumourers' in *Romeo and Juliet*. As discussed above in the context of Jill Levenson's Oxford Shakespeare edition, Juliet says 'Spread thy close curtain, love-performing night, | That runaways' eyes may wink, and Romeo | Leap to these arms untalked of and unseen. | Lovers can see to do their amorous rites | By their own beauties; or, if love be blind, | It best agrees with night' (III.ii.5–10). Benjamin Heath suggested 'rumourers' instead of runaways, and Edgecombe agrees because of a link via Catullus. Juliet thinks of lovers lighting up the night, just as Catullus LXVIII does, and here too the speaker is in Verona: 'lux mea contulit in gremium', 'sed furtiva dedit mira munuscula nocte'. We know that Shakespeare knew Catullus III because he got from it Hamlet's 'from whose bourn | No traveller returns', and there is a strong parallel between Juliet's situation and that in Catullus V where Catullus's reckless love for Lesbia is in opposition to 'rumores ... senum severiorum'. Roger Stritmatter, '"Old" and "New" Law in *The Merchant of Venice*: A Note on the Source of Shylock's Morality in Deuteronomy 15' (*N&Q* 47[2000] 70–2), thinks that Shylock's reference to the Christians owning slaves is about the Hebrew law which frees all slaves after seven years' service. *The Merchant of Venice*, Stritmatter notes, is full of biblical allusions, and the fight over the bond can plausibly be read as a dramatization of the conflict of the old law (Judaism) and the new law (Christianity). Even Jessica's flight mirrors that of Rachel marrying Jacob or the exodus of Hebrews from Egypt, and Gobbo's tricking of his sand-blind father mirrors Jacob's deception of his father Isaac in Genesis 27–8. Shakespeare's understanding of the Hebrew tradition was ample and subtle, and he problematizes the ethnic issues, as when he makes the anti-Semitic Gratiano insist on revenge even after Shylock has been humbled, thus showing a Christian's adherence to the old law while professing the new. Indeed, it is not even clear what the old law and the new are: Portia's 'mercy' speech draws on old law sources, Deuteronomy and Ecclesiasticus. Just as Jessica (imitating Rachel's robbing of her father Laban) has stolen Shylock's wealth, so the Christians have stolen the Hebrew philosophy of mercy. This cross-ethnic borrowing ironizes characters' assertions of their identity. Shylock's 'You have among you many a purchased slave' (misprinted as 'purchase' here) alludes to the old law tradition of Jubilee debt remission in Leviticus and Deuteronomy. Thus the old law limits the slavery that the new law permits, which is Shylock's point when he mockingly asks 'Shall I say to you, | "Let them be free! Marry them to your heirs!"' (IV.i.92–3).

Todd Pettigrew, 'The Naming of Shakespeare's Caius' (*N&Q* 47[2000] 72–5), traces the name 'Caius' in *The Merry Wives of Windsor* and decides that he is a fake doctor exploiting the name of a famous one. John Caius, president of the Royal

College of Physicians and founder of Gonville and Caius College, was not bumbling and not French, and the play's French doctor is passing himself off as John Caius to impress patients. Hugh Evans the Welsh parson denounces him as 'Master Caius that *calls* himself Doctor of Physic' (III.i.3–4, Pettigrew's italics) and says 'He has no more knowledge in Hibocrates and | Galen—and he is a knave besides, a cowardly knave | as you would desires to be acquainted withal' (III.i.61–3). Evans breaks off after 'Galen', Pettigrew thinks, because he was going to say 'than I do', but stops short because parsons like him did indeed stand in for physicians in rural areas; so Evans and Caius are alike in being fake doctors. It is not that Caius is a bad doctor, but that he is an impostor. Pettigrew gives a number of dramatic examples of the 'fake doctor with an impressive name' character type, a recognizable motif. A known technique of these fakes was to speak bad English, as though they were so well travelled as to have become rusty in their native language, or else they are exotically foreign. John K. Hale, 'Snake and Lioness in *As You Like It*, IV.iii' (*N&Q* 47[2000] 79), notices that in the source the hero fights a male lion, yet Orlando in *As You Like It* fights a female lion and a snake. The reason is Psalms 91:13 'Thou shalt tread upon the lion and adder: the young lion and the dragon shalt thou trample under feet', the play having quite a few biblical allusions. Why make the lion female? In order to make the lion more ferocious (she is defending her young) and to make it a fight between one family (Orlando/Oliver) and another (the pride), and so represent Orlando's anger at Oliver's lack of family feeling. Charles Cathcart, '*Twelfth Night* and John Weever' (*N&Q* 47[2000] 79–81), argues that Toby's desire to 'draw three souls out of one weaver' (*Twelfth Night* II.iii.58) is an allusion to John Weaver's *The Whipping of Satyre*. Part of the Shakespeare–Hoghton link is John Weever, who enjoyed Hoghton patronage and who repeatedly echoed Shakespeare and addressed him in his *Epigrammes* [1599], which replicates Shakespeare's idiosyncratic sonnet form so early that it is hard not to infer that he had a personal knowledge of Shakespeare. John Weever's poem *The Whipping of the Satyre* was entered into the Stationers' Register on 14 August 1601, and it attacked the 'Satyrist' (meaning Marston), the 'Epigrammatist' (meaning Guilpin), and the 'Humourist' (meaning Jonson). This poem was alluded to and responded to in the Poetomachia plays and answering poems. Toby's 'three souls out of one weaver' is, Cathcart thinks, another allusion to it. *The Whipping* rebukes the three men's work for its irreligiosity. Others punned on Weever's name, so why should not Shakespeare? Asinius Bubo in *Satiromastix* is owl-like ('bubo' is Latin for owl), which means foolish, and E.A.J. Honigmann showed strong reasons to think Asinius is Weever. If so, this makes sense of Toby's apparently calling Malvolio the 'night-owl' they will rouse, so one would think Malvolio is Weever, but Cathcart actually thinks Aguecheek is. Aguecheek has just used the word 'mellifluous', which Cathcart says was 'previously given a careful emphasis by Weever', and he (like Asinius Bubo) is a troublemaker's sidekick, and is 'improbably lionized as a valiant duellist', just like Lieutenant Slight in *Every Man out of His Humour* (whom Honigmann also thought a portrait of Weever), by the false claim that 'Souls and bodies hath he divorced three' (III.iv.231). Cathcart avoids claiming that any of these identifications are strong; it is just that Shakespeare appears to be playing the game of Jonson, Marston, and Dekker in alluding to known persons. If *Twelfth Night* alludes to Weever's *The Whipping of the Satyre* then it could plausibly be dated after 14 August 1601 (when *Whipping* was entered in the Stationers' Register), which fits with the first known performance on 2 February 1602. This is only a plausible date, not a strict *terminus a quo*, because the Weever–Shakespeare links indicate that Shakespeare might have seen the work in manuscript earlier. *Whipping* was published pseudo-anonymously, but Shakespeare gets the name right ('weaver') where, Honigmann argued, the other stage writers were not certain—they avoid unequivocal identifications—and this increases the likelihood that Shakespeare knew Weever personally.

Steven Doloff, in '"Well Desir'd in Cyprus": *Othello* on the Isle of Venus' (*N&Q* 47[2000] 81–2), thinks that the Cyprus of *Othello* is, as in myth, the birthplace of Venus. Cassio's fulsome welcoming of Desdemona to Cyprus ('The divine Desdemona', II.i.74) might be, as Iago claims, just that he wants 'to play the sir', but it might also be a glance at the island being Venus's home. Likewise Othello's greeting of Desdemona ('Honey, you shall be well desir'd in Cyprus; | I have found great love amongst them', II.i.205–6) glances at the island's amorous customs. When Desdemona welcomes Lodovico to the island, however, the worship of love has turned to disgust at venery: Othello says 'You are welcome, sir, to Cyprus. Goats and monkeys!' (IV.i.265). Jonathan Bate made the opposite argument in 'Shakespeare's Islands', his keynote address to the World Shakespeare Congress in Valencia on 19 April 2001, pointing out that the Cyprus of *Othello* is more like the Malta of Marlowe's *The Jew of Malta*, and like recent historical reality, than it is like the mythical birthplace of Venus. Howard Jacobson, '*Macbeth*, I.v.48–52' (*N&Q* 47[2000] 86), finds a new biblical source in *Macbeth*. Lady Macbeth imagines dark night preventing heaven seeing the stabbing of Duncan and so unable to 'peep through the blanket of the dark | To cry "Hold, hold!"'. Jacobson thinks this is indebted to 'Then Abraham extended his hand and took the knife to slaughter his son. But the angel of God called to him from heaven and said, "Abraham, Abraham!"' (Genesis 23:10–11 according to the note but 22:10–11 in my Bible). The doubled 'hold' came from the doubled 'Abraham'.

Rosalind S. Meyer, in '"The serpent under 't": Additional Reflections on *Macbeth*' (*N&Q* 47[2000] 86–90), finds *Macbeth* indebted to Seneca's *Medea*. Meyer gives examples of Seneca-like phrases and sentiments in Shakespeare and finds origins for 'To beguile the time, | Look like the time' and 'look like the innocent flower, | But be the serpent under 't' (I.v.62–3 and 64–5) in *Medea*. Less specifically, there are also the parallels in the conjuring of spirits, the appearance of Hecate, the Scottish witches who are also Fates and Furies, a prominent cauldron scene, the heroine being on the battlements when she calls for spirits to fill her 'top-full | Of direst cruelty' (I.v.41–2), and the (imagined) killing of her child ('I would ... Have ... dashed the brains out', I.vii.56–8). This talk of an oath to kill her children make little sense for Lady Macbeth's situation, but it makes her Medea-like. Just before the parallel moment in *Medea*, Medea puts upon Jason a curse of being rejected in homes once familiar, which suits Duncan's case too. Meyer finds a few other verbal parallels between Shakespeare's play and Seneca's. Lady Macbeth wrests male power much as Medea does, and likewise does so to invert natural order. Of course this is only true if you think the existing political system natural, as Meyer is sure the Jacobeans did. A further link with *Medea* is the idea of a palace in flames, which was the aim of the Gunpowder Plot (to which *Macbeth* repeatedly alludes), and yet another is the killing of children: *Macbeth*, Meyers claims, is the only Shakespeare play to kill a child onstage. (She has overlooked

Arthur's death in *King John*.) Meyer's classical knowledge is strong, but her historical sense is warped by teleology: 'Shakespeare warns his countrymen against a potential Civil War—still thirty years ahead'. Colin Burrow, 'Shakespeare's Wrinkled Eye: Sonnet 3, Lines 11–12' (*N&Q* 47[2000] 90–1), explains Sonnet 3's phrase 'despite of wrinkles' as a likening of old people's wrinkled eye-skin to imperfect glass. In context it is not clear what this clause governs: 'So thou through windows of thine age shall see, | Despite of wrinckles this thy goulden time'. If 'see', this would mean he cannot see clearly because of the window's wrinkles; Elizabethan glass was not clear. John Kerrigan's gloss is that in the glass's wrinkles the old man see his own wrinkles superimposed on the image of his son outside at whom he is looking, but Burrow finds this excessively complex optically. Wrinkled faces go with bleary eyes when Hamlet says that 'old men have grey beards, that their faces are wrinkled, their eyes purging thick amber', and this association comes from *Batman upon Bartholomew*, a popular version of Bartholomaeus Anglicus's *De Proprietatibus Rerum* (*On the Properties of Things*) which records that 'the sight of olde men is not sharpe, because their skins are riveled [wrinkled]'. Ultimately the source is Aristotle's *De Generatione Animalium*, where he remarks that old people's sight is bad because the skin of their eyes, like their other skin, is wrinkled. Shakespeare knew this bit of Aristotelian wisdom (perhaps from *Batman*) and made an analogy between wrinkled Elizabethan glass and the wrinkled skin of an old man's eye. We can all get a sense of what vision is like for the old by looking through wrinkled glass; thus old people see 'despite of wrinkles' in their eyes.

Eric C. Brown, 'Caliban, Columbus, and Canines in *The Tempest*' (*N&Q* 47[2000] 92–4), argues that Trinculo's 'puppy-headed monster' epithet is an allusion not to fawning but to cannibals. Christopher Columbus, the first to contact the Indians, was told by them that some of their enemies (the 'Cariba') ate people, but because he was looking for the Great Khan he heard 'Caniba' (so says Tzvetan Todorov). Columbus assumed that this name came from the Latin root *canis*, meaning dog, and that they also had dogs' heads. Of course, Caliban is almost vegetarian in the play, but in Trinculo's mind he is 'cannibal' in the sense of dog-headed. When hybridized with Caliban under the gaberdine, Trinculo and he made something like the dog-headed monster in Conrad Lycosthenes's *Prodigiorum ac ostentorum chronicum* [1557], a two-bodied creature with one human and one canine head. Continuing his fine work on Shakespeare's Bible, Naseeb Shaheen, in 'Shakespeare and the Bishops' Bible' (*N&Q* 47[2000] 94–7), points out that he would have known—so editors should use—the revised Bishops' Bible of 1572, not the first edition of 1568. The Bishops' Bible is the one that influenced Shakespeare, to judge by his allusions to phrasing that appears only in that version, and it was supposed to be placed in all churches. The 1568 edition was revised in 1572, and subsequent editions are substantially different in places. Strictly speaking, the King James was not the first but the third authorized version: the Great Bible (so named because of its size) of 1539 was ordered to be placed in every church by Cromwell and its second edition of 1540 (the standard edition) boasts to be the one 'apoynted to the vse of the churches', so it is the first authorized Bible. The Geneva Bible of 1560 was an improvement, not least in numbering the verses, which the Great Bible did not. In 1561–4 Archbishop Parker planned a revision of the Great Bible, which he divided into parts, sending each to a bishop or other reviser for improvements, and the resulting work was known at the Bishops' Bible. Just as the second edition of the Great Bible became the standard one, so the second edition ([1572], with careful re-revision of the New Testament by Giles Lawrence) became the standard work of the Bishops' Bible. So, all versions—there were quarto and octavo versions, the latter New Testament only—of the Bishops' Bible published between 1568 and 1572 should be avoided. Shaheen lists some places in Shakespeare where using the 1568–72 Bishops' Bible would mislead an editor. Moreover, there were many more copies (in the ratio 9:1) of the post-1572 Bishops' Bibles than the pre-1572, so Shakespeare is much more likely to have owned a post-1572 copy.

Another whose work is continuing in a well-established pattern is Thomas Merriam, who argues, in 'An Unwarranted Assumption' (*N&Q* 47[2000] 438–41), that stylometric texts suggest that Hand S of *Sir Thomas More* is not Munday's words although it is his handwriting. Merriam has in the past cast doubt on Munday's authorship of *Sir Thomas More* on the evidence that 'Four logometric habits' were symmetrically distributed in the thirty-six Shakespeare 1623 Folio plays and *Sir Thomas More* but were not found in four known Munday texts (all of *John a Kent and John a Cumber* and Munday's bits of *The Downfall of Robert Earl of Huntingdon*, *The Death of Robert Earl of Huntingdon*, and *1 Sir John Oldcastle*). As frequently happens in work of this kind, Merriam does not immediately disclose what a 'logometric habit' might be, but here it is the favouring of one word or phrase over another one which is similar. Using the Chadwyck–Healey English Verse Drama database Merriam has added other Munday work to the test. The four 'habits' are choices of 'I have/have', 'I have/I', 'this/this & that', and 'with a-an/with', and Merriam attempts to explain how the raw data of preference is subjected to the statistical process of principal component analysis (PCA). He does not explain it well. PCA is used to produce a single number which is characteristic of most of, here 70 per cent of, the variation between plays regarding their 'scores' for each of the four habits. Two plays with similar patterns of ratios of the habits should have similar First Principal Component (PC-1) numbers, and indeed in Merriam's Table 2 they do. The benchmark is the autograph play *John a Kent* whose PC-1 is –0.16, and the ones we know he collaborated on are near to this number, although a couple we thought were solely his (the entertainments *Sidero-Thriambos* and *Chruso-Thriambos*, which have 'by A.M.' on their title pages) are so far from –0.16 that they appear to be collaborations. (Merriam does not consider the alternative explanation that the tests are no good.) The furthest from Munday's characteristic score is *Sir Thomas More*, whether one considers the whole play including the additions or just Hand S. As is usual, readers have to trust Merriam's execution of the PCA mathematics, but my spot-check of his arithmetic showed no errors. Moreover, readers have to trust that the 'logometric habits' are indeed indicative of authorship. What we know of anti-Catholic Munday makes it hard to understand how he could have come to write *Sir Thomas More*, but, Merriam asserts, it makes perfect sense that he would copy it out for others, perhaps to entrap them. Unfortunately, there is a serious printing error in Merriam's Table 1: the figures for *Chruso-Thriambos* are all one column too far to the left, so the ratio given for 'I have/have' is in fact the ratio for 'I have/I', that for 'I have/I' is the one for 'this/this & that' and the final cell for 'With a-an/with' is empty.

David Farley-Hills, 'The Date of *Titus Andronicus*' (*N&Q* 47[2000] 441–4) has a new way to date the play based on the use of the 'above' playing area which is compatible with the Rose theatre as it existed in 1587–92, but not afterwards, when the cover over the stage would have prevented spectators high in the galleries seeing this space. Henslowe's *Diary* says 'ne—Rd at titus & ondronicus the 23 Jeneway iii*li* viii*s*' for 23 January 1594. The title page of the 1594 Q does not say it was 'sundry times' played, but the title page of Q2 does, so presumably it was indeed 'ne[w]' in 1594, and hence Henslowe got a lot of money for it (£3. 8*s*. 0*d*.). Objections have been raised to *Titus Andronicus* being new in 1594: it is too crude to be by a 30-year old Shakespeare; the Induction to *Bartholomew Fair* [1614] suggests *Titus Andronicus* was by then twenty-five years old (hence performed by 1589); and the Q1 title page says that three companies (Derby's, Pembroke's, Sussex's) played it. The first two objections can be dismissed as subjective and over-literal respectively, and the third can be explained (as Jonathan Bate does) as meaning an amalgamation of three companies played it. More problematically, *A Knack to Know a Knave* ['ne' in June 1592, printed 1594] has echoes of *Titus Andronicus*, although Bate argued that the *Knack* printing was a memorial reconstruction corrupted by men learning their *Titus Andronicus* lines. Farley-Hills does not accept this: *Knack*'s allusions to *Titus Andronicus* are not corruption but deliberate and entirely coherent. Moreover, the allusion in *Knack* has Titus offered the crown by the senators of Rome (as it looks in performance) whereas an actor who played in *Titus Andronicus* would remember that it is the people of Rome who offer Titus the crown. Bate concedes that there might have been a preceding version, by Shakespeare or others, existing before the Henslowe entry in January 1594. Farley-Hills rightly complains that Bate reproduced C. Walter Hodges's picture of the Rose of 1587 (before it had a cover) and labelled it as the Rose of 1592 (when it got one). Q1–3 and F are from authorial copy, so the stage directions show what Shakespeare expected to be able to do at the Rose, and these make extensive use of the 'above'. The stage directions, then, imply that *Titus Andronicus* was written to be performed at the Rose before the 1592 alterations made the 'above' less usable. Possibly Shakespeare wrote it for the pre-1592 Rose but it was not performed until 'ne[w]' in 1594; the authorial papers, on which the printings are based, would not record the changes necessary to reduce use of the 'above'. Alternatively, it was actually performed before 1592, at the Rose or elsewhere.

There are a host of objections to Farley-Hills's argument, not least its excessive dependence on Hodges's drawings, which are merely interpretations of the scant evidence, and Farley-Hills ignores all the vital evidence. He does not mention the erosion line just in front of where the stage would have been in the 1587 Rose which Julian Bowsher and Simon Blatherwick claimed is made by human feet ('The Structure of the Rose', in Franklin J. Hildy, ed., *New Issues in the Reconstruction of Shakespeare's Theatre: Proceedings of the Conference Held at the University of Georgia, February 16–18, 1990*, Lang [1990]), but which John Astington showed is a rainwater line and that therefore the stage had a cover even though it had no posts ('The Rose Excavation and the Playhouse Heavens', seminar paper for the International Shakespeare Congress, Tokyo [1991]). One archaeological certainty is that the stage posts' foundations are from 1592 or after. Andrew Gurr also thought the erosion trench 'a foot in front of the stage foundation' was made by rain running off a roof over the stage of the 1587 Rose (because the erosion is just like the circular erosion line just inside the yard wall which was definitely made by water running off the roof), and points out that two Rose plays from before 1592 seem to require stage posts even though the archaeology seems to rule out posts at the 1587 Rose (*The*

Shakespearean Stage, 1574–1642. CUP. [1993] p. 130). Carol Rutter attributed the erosion line in front of the 1592 stage to the effect of dripping water, but wrote, without explaining the difference, that the one in front of the 1587 stage was probably caused by feet (*Documents of the Rose Playhouse*. ManUP. [1999] pp. xi, xiii).

Roger Prior, 'Gascoigne's *Posies* as a Shakespearian Source' (*N&Q* 47[2000] 444–9), has found further evidence that a neglected source for *A Midsummer Night's Dream* and *Romeo and Juliet* is a masque by George Gascoigne written for a Montague marriage and preserved in Gascoigne's *The Posies* [1575]. As Brian Gibbons's Arden2 edition of *Romeo and Juliet* acknowledged, it is likely that the prologue's 'ancient grudge' comes from a masque celebrating the marriage in 1572 of two children of Anthony Browne, first Viscount Montague, via George Gascoigne's *Posies* or other printings of the same masque. Prior has found more phrases in *Romeo and Juliet* that seem (by individual verbal parallels and by collocation of ideas and images, such as strangers daring to enter a feast) to be from the same Montague masque. The masque appears also to be a source for *A Midsummer Night's Dream*, using its phrases for anticipation of the wedding of Theseus and Hippolyta. Then Shakespeare noticed a poem 'The Refusal' on the facing page of *The Posies* which had material he could use for the rivalries of Demetrius and Lysander in I.i and of Hermia and Helena in III.ii. From preparations described for the Montague masque Shakespeare took preparations (including the mechanicals' rehearsals) for Theseus's wedding: the Montague masque has a prologue twice padded with 'seem to' and with every other line in fourteen syllables, which is paralleled in 'let the prologue seem to say ... it shall | be written in eight and six' (III.i.16–22). Prior goes on to list some lesser, but still significant, *Midsummer Night's Dream* borrowings from the Montague masque. That *A Midsummer Night's Dream* and *Romeo and Juliet* are dependent on the Montague masque strengthens the case for them being a pair. Gascoigne was co-author of the Kenilworth entertainment which seems to be alluded to in *A Midsummer Night's Dream* ('once I sat upon a promontory | And heard a mermaid on a dolphin's back | Uttering such dulcet and harmonious breath | That the rude sea grew civil at her song'), so this new dependence on Gascoigne strengthens the case for the Kenilworth allusion. The Montague-masque link also supports the case (believed for other reasons) that the manuscript underlying *Romeo and Juliet* Q2 existed before Q1 was printed and was used in that Q1 printing. Q1 lacks material from the Montague masque which Q2 has, but all that which is in Q1 is in Q2 too, so probably Q1 is not getting them directly from Gascoigne but rather from the Q2 manuscript. The Montague-masque link gives reason to accept a reading from Q2 which editors (but not Levenson for the new Oxford Shakespeare reviewed above) usually reject in favour of a reading from Q4. Q2–3 have what is modernized as 'Good father! 'Tis day' (IV.iv.20), but editors prefer 'Good faith, 'tis day', using Q4's 'faith' instead of Q2's 'father'. The Montague masque has the phrase 'good father' and nearby collocates 'fathers' and 'straight' just as *Romeo and Juliet* does ('Good faith [or father], 'tis day. | The County will be here with music straight', IV.iv.20–1).

Mark Hutchings, '"Turkish" or "Arabic" *emir*: *The Merry Wives of Windsor*, II.i.176' (*N&Q* 47[2000] 449–51), elucidates a crux in *The Merry Wives of Windsor*. In *Notes and Queries* [1999] Deanne Williams argued that the Host saying 'Will you go, Anheers?' (II.i.205–6) referred to the French word 'asnier' or 'ânier' meaning a mule-driver. She mentioned in passing that it might also be the Turkish title 'emir', but elided the difference between Turkish and Arabic (which Hutchings thinks is important) and claimed that there were no other Turkish words in the play whereas in fact there is another one. To the Elizabethans 'Turk' meant much the same as 'Muslim' (covering even converts from Christianity) and 'Moor', and indeed could be used of any inhabitant of the Ottoman empire; it was also a form of abuse hurled by Protestants at Catholics. Given this polysemy, Williams's eliding of the difference between Turkish and Arabic meanings was, Hutchings concedes, perhaps reasonable. But the word 'emir' was Arabic, not Turkish, and Shakespeare drew attention to that by alluding to its Turkish equivalent 'vizier'. Graphically similar to 'anheer' is 'ameer', a variant spelling of 'emir', and the Arabic/Turkish slippage also occurs when the Host declares 'Cesar, Keiser, and Pheazar' (I.iii.9). Actually, Hutchings quotes this as 'Caesar, Kaiser, Pheazar' which I can find in none of the early printings, all of which have 'and' before the last word. Moreover, Hutchings says that Q (he does not specify which one) has 'Pheeser', which is a spelling no early printing has: the two pre-1623 quartos (1602 and 1619) both have 'Phesser' and the 1630 quarto has 'Pheazar' like the Folio. Perhaps these are further examples of the poor printing of this year's Notes and Queries. 'Pheazar' is a form of 'vizier', which was well known in the playhouse, and so 'emir' is likely what was meant by 'anheers'. At the least, an editor who chooses 'vizier' for I.iii should choose as its opposite 'emir' for II.i.

Denis Corish, '"The world's due, by the grave and thee": Shakespeare, Sonnet 1.14' (N&Q 47[2000] 453–5), explains the closing couplet of Sonnet 1. The lines are initially confusing: 'Pitty the world, or else this glutton be, | To eate the world's due, by the graue and thee'. Does 'by' govern 'eat', meaning double destruction, by death and by dying childless? No, the solution is that 'by' is a preposition governing 'the grave' and 'thee' and following 'due' (not 'eat'), so it means 'To eat the world's due by the grave' (that is, to eat what the world is due by the grave) and 'To eat the world's due by thee' (that is, to eat what the world is due by you). The latter is clear enough (the children you should leave to the world, not eat up by your celibacy), but what is the world's due by the grave? It is 'the eternity of the species', says Corish. Even the grave is not so greedy as to rob the world of all the young beautiful people: the pretty may breed before the grave gets them, and the addressee should do so too. Shakespeare used the 'eternity of the species' idea in other sonnets too, and Corish suggests a source in Thomas Wilson's The Arte of Rhetorique [1560]. Maurice Hunt, 'Fourteeners in Shakespeare's Cymbeline' (N&Q 47[2000] 458–61), argues that Cymbeline uses 'fourteeners' to make the ghosts' speeches archaic and to make Cloten a figure of discord. George T. Wright claimed that only a handful of heptameters (seven-feet lines) exist in Shakespeare, but that is true only if one accepts modern editors' changing of the heptameters into something else. In Cymbeline V.v the ghosts of Posthumus's family speak in what might 'ballad metre' (that is, alternate tetrameter and trimeter lines) or else heptameter, depending on what lineation you think the underlying papers had (lines of four feet then three feet, or lines of seven feet). In the Folio, nine of the ghosts' lines are printed as heptameters (that is, all seven feet on one line), but perhaps the others were broken into 4 + 3 just to fit the measure. Speaking the lines as heptameters (eliding the pause between the four feet and the three feet) makes the speeches sound old-fashioned, which would suit the dramatic context. F4 broke eight of the nine ghosts' fourteeners into ballad metre. The song which Cloten has the musicians play for Innogen in II.iii is printed in F1 as 4 + 3, 4 + 3, 7, 7, which some editors have re-lineated to be entirely 4 + 3s and even emended words to make this arrangement rhyme. Perhaps the whole thing was seven-feet lines (that is, 'fourteeners'), but Hunt thinks this unlikely, since there would be unnecessary internal rhyme, and he prefers to defend the F1 arrangement: it is ballad rhyme first then switches to fourteeners. One reason (and perhaps Rowe's) to keep F1's arrangement of the song as a mixture of ballad verse and fourteeners is that it then mirrors the ghosts' dialogue later in the play, which also has this mixture. Thematically, Cloten, who commissions the song, is a figure of discordance: Belarius recognizes his voice after many years, and once he is silenced Belarius's ingenious instrument is sounded. Also, as Wright noted, Cloten has the lone fourteener occurring in the midst of blank verse: 'I cannot tremble at it. Were it toad or adder, spider' (IV.ii.92). Actually, as Hunt mentions at the beginning of the piece, this is not Cloten's line but Guiderius's response to hearing Cloten speaking his name.

Thomas Merriam, 'Queen of Earthly Queens' (*N&Q* 47[2000] 461–4), thinks that the phrase 'queen of earthly queens' in *Henry VIII* is an implicit allusion to the Virgin Mary. Henry calls Katherine 'The queen of earthly queens' (II.iv.138), which goes well beyond his source Holinshed, where she is just appropriately wifely. Merriam asks, what is the contrast here, what is opposed to 'earthly'? In this play and elsewhere, the contrast of 'earthly' is 'heavenly': Henry's attack on Wolsey ('You are full of heavenly stuff ... You have scarce time | To steal from spiritual leisure a brief span | To keep your earthly audit', III.ii.138–42) and Norfolk's description of the Field of the Cloth of Gold (I.i.12–23), which mentions 'earthly' and via biblical allusion implicitly invokes its opposite, 'heavenly'. There is one use of 'earthly' in *Henry VIII* which does not invoke its opposite, 'heavenly', and that is Wolsey's speech in III.ii about having been corrected by Henry. This, however, is Fletcher's, not Shakespeare's, part of the play. The 'earthly queen' is not proverbial, and it occurs only one more time in the drama of the period, in an unrelated context in Heywood's *The Golden Age*. Merriam thinks that in *Henry VIII* it is an allusion to Mary, and the parody of the Annunciation in II.iii makes this all the more likely: the Lord Chamberlain is Gabriel, lowly Anne Bullen is Mary. Thus comes more sly Catholicism from Shakespeare, since II.iii is his.

Finally from *Notes and Queries* this year, Roger Stritmatter, 'By Providence Divine: Shakespeare's Awareness of Some Geneva Marginal Notes of 1 Samuel' (*N&Q* 47[2000] 97–100), argues that Shakespeare knew the Geneva Bible marginal notes to 1 Samuel 6:9 and 1 Samuel 14. Several people have shown that he was influenced by marginal notes in the Geneva Bible, which shows that his biblical knowledge was by reading, not hearing, since marginal notes are seldom spoken. This bolsters the view that, since he was familiar with Ecclesiastes (despite it not being widely used in Anglican or Catholic practices), Shakespeare did private devotional reading. Stritmatter thinks that, when Shakespeare used the marginal notes in the Geneva Bible, it was to have a character elaborate an argument, one of 'the traditional techniques of Renaissance topology'. Unless this is a misprint, Stritmatter would appear to think 'topology' is the art of using topoi, but topology means only three things: the botanical study of where plants grow, the study of a particular locality, and the branch of maths that deals with that which does not change when shapes are deformed. Perhaps Stritmatter means 'typology', the study of symbolic representation. This illustrates the harm done by the misprints in this year's *N&Q*: one cannot properly criticize errors—here is another, 'sortilege' misspelled 'sortilage'—since they might not be the writer's fault. (Here is another, 'synergistic' misspelled 'syngergistic'.) In *All's Well That Ends Well*, Helen argues for free will over predestination ('Our remedies oft in ourselves do lie, | Which we ascribe to heaven', I.i.212–13) and then the other way around ('it is presumption in us when the help of heaven | We count the act of men', II.i.151–2). Both these speeches are indebted to the Geneva Bible's marginal notes (i) and (r) from 1 Samuel 14. The connection is a concern with gambling. Just before the second quotation Helen refers to those of us 'that square our guess by shows', which Stritmatter thinks is about gambling on appearance, and there are references to sortilege (casting lots) throughout the play.

Another connection is note (r)'s use of the word 'presumption' in attributing events to human rather than divine intervention. Note (f) to 1 Samuel 6:9 is about the wicked attributing to fortune/chance things which are properly controlled by God. Shakespeare appears to have been aware of this note too, to judge from such moments as wicked Macbeth's 'If chance will have me king, why, chance may crown me | Without my stir' (I.iii.142–3), which Stritmatter (or the failing printer) quotes as 'If chance will crown me, chance will have me king'. Appropriately, non-wicked Hamlet comes to the opposite conclusion, that providence supervenes over chance/fortune: 'There's a divinity that shapes our ends, | Rough-hew them how we will' (V.ii.10–1), and 'There's a special | providence in the fall of a sparrow' (V.ii.165–6), and 'Our thoughts are ours, their ends none of our own' (III.ii.204), which Stritmatter (or the failing printer) quotes as 'Our thoughts are ours, our ends none of our own'. Even giving all these faults to the printer, Stritmatter's writing is imperfect. He chooses to provide a footnote gloss for his use of the verb 'marked' (the explanation: 'That is, remarked upon'), which is unnecessary since he could just have used the verb 'remarked upon' or left it to the reader to look up. Yet earlier he neglected to gloss 'topology' which is not in *OED* in the sense he means. In *Richard II* there is more of the lot-casting material so prominent in 1 Samuel 14 ('However God or fortune cast my lot', I.iii.85), and there is more fortune-versus-providence material in *Romeo and Juliet* ('A greater power than we can contradict | Hath thwarted our intents. Come, come away', V.iii.153–4), which Stritmatter or the printer mangles to '"A greater power than we contradict | Hath thwarted our intents" (V.iii.152)'. Since this is a two-line quotation, the single-line reference must be wrong. All these quotations show that Shakespeare knew the Geneva marginal notes to 1 Samuel 6:9 and 1 Samuel 14, Stritmatter claims, although one might think that they are merely commonplace.

Studies in English Literature, 1500–1900 provides one essay of relevance this year, 'Nahum Tate's Revision of Shakespeare's *King Lear*s' (*SEL* 40[2000] 435–50), in which Sonia Massai argue that Nahum Tate's use of *King Lear* for his adaptation strengthens the case that the Q and F versions are distinct works. Tate made the tragedy into a tragicomedy, and his invention of a love affair for Cordelia and Edgar, and the generally increased role for women, 'are clearly a tribute to the new practice' of women acting. Omitting the Fool was an ideological matter: a source of criticism of the king had to go. Tate rendered explicit Lear's flaw in the opening scene (characters discuss his rashness, 'Chol'rick and suddain') but at the same time made it forgivable. Tate has Cordelia deliberately fail the love trial because she is secretly engaged to Edgar and this too diminishes Lear's fault since, in Tate, Edgar has already been declared a traitor and Lear guesses at her love for him. By making Lear known to be choleric, did Tate give Lear a tragic flaw he previously lacked? No, it is already there in Q: seven Folio lines explaining why he is dividing the kingdom (he is too old to rule properly) are omitted in Q which thereby makes Lear seem irrational. In Q, the division of the kingdoms is more about dowries than about the transfer of power from old to young. The 'coronet' Lear tells his sons-in-law to 'part betweene you' is not the royal crown (that is not what 'coronet' means) but an inferior crown for nobility. Q has a coronet brought on, and it is for Cordelia (says Jay L. Halio) but F omits the stage direction for the coronet and so reduces the obvious sense that this is just about settling dowries rather than settling succession. Several variants line up in agreement with this claim that in Q the king has not really abdicated, such as Gloucester's advice to Cornwall and Regan to let 'the good King his Master' punish Kent-as-Caius. Tate has Lear borrow words similar to Kent's to express his hatred of Oswald. So, Tate's Lear is 'still as strong and capable of indignation as he was at the beginning of the play', and other changes make Tate's Lear, like the quarto Lear, 'mad with rage at seeing his power taken away from him and he struggles to resist'; he is not losing his grip on reality (p. 442). However, around the end of Act II Tate started to borrow more from F than Q because he wanted F's sentimental identification with, and sympathy for, Lear.

Tate turned to F because something like Q's vignette when the servants lament the blinding of Gloucester 'protects the audience from the brunt of the violence' (by making the world less harsh), and in its place Tate put a monologue for Gloucester to express his own feelings. The point is to externalize grief and allow the audience to share it and share the feeling of pathos; characters do not despair but, rather, vow to get even. Gloucester never contemplates suicide. This externalizing of pain to elicit audience sympathy and anger 'implies a shared belief in the political and aesthetic necessity of poetic justice'. Tate ignored the quarto scene in which a gentleman describes how the letters to Cordelia affected her because, Massai claims, it is too much about grief being strange and admirable rather than something to identify with. Instead Tate chose to show Cordelia weeping and to have Edmund spying on her like Milton's Satan in Eden, so again grief externalized has an effect on a spectator. That Tate jumped wholesale from Q to F in his adaptation (rather than picking and mixing) reinforces the view that Q and F are distinct and individually coherent. Tate's omission of Q's 'moralizing passages', which are meaningful but do not provoke sympathy, is further evidence that these passages (not in F) are of a kind, and hence that Q and F are separated by authorial revision.

In *Cahiers Élisabéthains* Bernice Kliman, 'Charles Jennens' Shakespeare and his Eighteenth-Century Competitors' (*CahiersE* 58[2000] 59–71), shows that Jennens's incomplete eighteenth-century Shakespeare edition was ahead of its time. He wanted to collate others' emendations and publish them in footnotes, and not simply to impose his own favourite readings as the habit was at the time. The Steevens/ Johnson circle viciously denigrated Jennens, and Steevens wrote a calumniating anonymous entry for him in *Biographia Dramatica* which persists in the electronic *Concise Dictionary of National Biography*. Jennens accused the editorial mainstream of not even bothering to do collations, and he was largely right in that. Jennens, like Capell, went back to the earliest printings for his authority. Unlike Capell, Jennens stuck to his principles and used quarto *Hamlet* readings rigorously, and moreover did his collation absolutely completely, thus making a proper critical edition. He was the first to put the act and scene numbers in the running headlines for ease of reference, which shows concern for the use of books as reference works into which one might dip; a reader going linearly from I.i to V.v does not need such assistance. Although Jennens conflated the texts, he indicated typographically which early texts lacked or had which passages. Concerning *The Mousetrap*, Jennens pointed out that Theobald had emended (and thundered about blunderers who do not emend) unnecessarily. Hamlet says the play is the image of a murder of a duke, done in Vienna, but the dumbshow stage direction calls him a king. This is not a discrepancy: the source story was about a duke and duchess, the play of it about a king and queen.

Finally, *Shakespeare Newsletter* carries four items of relevance this year. In the longest, '*Othello's* American Indian and the Nu Principle' (*ShN* 50[2000] 35–52), Richard Levin argues that the Indian to whom Othello compares himself is American, not Asian, since these were reputed to be ignorant of the value of gems. Dennis Bartholomeusz argued that Shakespeare consistently associates pearls with India and the East (so it is an Asian Indian in *Othello*), but Bartholomeusz mistook 'orient pearl' to mean 'eastern pearl' when in fact it could just meant 'brilliant pearl' (*OED* Orient B. *adj.* 2). Also, there are plenty of pearls in the Shakespeare canon which are not 'orient' or 'eastern', so there is not the consistent association as Bartholomeusz claimed. There was an identifiable belief that American Indians did not know the value of gems and gave them away for trash; it begins with *The First Four Voyages of Amerigo Vespucci*, and crops up in other places, including Hakluyt's *Principal Navigations* and Robert Harcourt's *Voyage to Guiana*. Robert Cawley, in *The Voyagers and Elizabethan Drama* (Kraus. [1966]), collects all the examples in his chapter 'Gold for Beads'. There is no such tradition for Indians of the East, just a couple of examples which Levin thinks come from the word 'India' being used to mean America (*OED* India *n.* 3). Of course, there was considerable vagueness about just what some ethnic/geographic distinctions meant, as with Moor and Turk. There seems to have been an association of East India (that is, modern India) with spices and West India (America) with mined gems, but Levin does not rely on this because there is too little evidence of it. Does it really matter whether the Indian is American or Asiatic? Levin points out that the Judean/Indian difference does matter, since if Othello is like Judas then the killing of Desdemona is a serious betrayal invoking eternal damnation, whereas if he is like an ignorant Indian then it is less serious and he deserves some pity. But whether the Indian is Asian or American does not matter, so Levin invokes a hermeneutic doctrine he has recently invented, 'the Nu Principle', meaning 'so what?'.

On a related matter, Lisa Hopkins, '"An Indian Beauty"? A Proposed Emendation to *The Merchant of Venice*' (*ShN* 50[2000] 27), proposes a change to the punctuation in *The Merchant of Venice*. Bassanio calls deceptive covering 'the beauteous scarf | Veiling an Indian beauty; in a word, | The seeming truth which cunning times put on | To entrap the wisest' (III.ii.98–101). The repetition 'beauteous ... beauty' is weak, and given the Elizabethan aversion to dark skin Hopkins thinks we should emend the punctuation to make 'Indian' a noun not an adjective. Thus it is 'Veiling an Indian; beauty—in a word, | The seeming truth which cunning times put on | To entrap the wisest'. Rodney Stenning Edgecombe, 'Two Suggested Emendations' (*ShN* 50[2000] 113), considers Jaques's question in

As You Like It: 'Why, who cries out on pride | That can therein tax any private party? | Doth it not flow as hugely as the sea, | Till that the weary very means do ebb?' (II.vii.70–3). The problem is 'weary very means', and because trying to control the sea is an image of that for which no one is strong enough, Edgecombe suggests 'weary fleerer's main' meaning until the weary mocker's strength (= main, punning on sea = main) does ebb. Edgecombe also considers Proteus's line, 'But say this weed her love from Valentine, | It follows not that she will love Sir Thurio' (*The Two Gentlemen of Verona* III.ii.49–50). It is odd to think of weeding something from someone, especially in the case of love. The emendation 'wind' for 'weed' has been proposed, but this suggests it will take time and Proteus's point is that he will be quick in alienating Silvia from Valentine. Edgecombe proposes the emendation of 'wedge': 'But say this wedge her love from Valentine'. Edgecombe is right that there are Shakespearian uses of 'wedge' to mean split, including Troilus's speaking of a heart 'As wedged with a sigh, would rive in twain' (*Troilus and Cressida* I.i.35), but it just as often means the opposite, fastening together. In a second note, 'Crushing and Extending in *Cymbeline*' (*ShN* 50[2000] 51–2), Edgecombe argues that the First Gentleman's praise of Posthumus in *Cymbeline* is a herbalist image. The praise is fulsome but cryptic: 'I do not think | So fair an outward and such stuff within | Endows a man but he. SECOND GENTLEMAN You speak him far. | FIRST GENTLEMAN I do extend him, sir, within himself; | Crush him together rather than unfold | His measure duly. SECOND GENTLEMAN What's his name and birth? | FIRST GENTLEMAN I cannot delve him to the root' (*Cymbeline* I.i.22–8). Edgecombe rejects as entirely inappropriate Nosworthy's suggestion that the crushing/extending image is one of torture. Rather, the image comes from something to do with family trees, with Posthumus as a kind of herb which the gentleman cannot dig up roots and all. In a herbalist context, crushing releases the essence of a root. But how crush and extend, as the First Gentleman has it? Edgecombe thinks 'extend' means 'to seize upon, take possession of, by force' (*OED* extend *v.* 11b). Having referred to the 'stuff' within Posthumus prompted Shakespeare's perhaps unconscious recollection of the Doctor's 'Pluck from the memory a rooted sorrow, | Raze out the written troubles of the brain, | And with some sweet oblivious antidote | Cleanse the fraught bosom of that perilous stuff' (*Macbeth* V.iii.43–6), hence the collocation of root/ stuff in a herbalist image here in *Cymbeline*. So, Edgecombe paraphrases the First Gentleman's comment on his own praise (that, 'I do extend him ... measure duly') as 'I extend him [forcibly seize upon his essential virtue] and express from it a definition of human excellence that goes much further [as the virtue of a plant is extended by being reduced to a spreadable substance] than it would in a comparatively inert enumeration of his merits ['unfold | His measure duly'], such as you might find in a *Theatrum sanitatis* or Herbal'.

2. Shakespeare in the Theatre

The shelf life of Pauline Kiernan's *Staging Shakespeare at the New Globe* [1999] has already expired. The first page mentions the current conversion of Bankside Power Station, next door to the Globe, into Tate Modern; the gallery has been open since 1999 and is now one of the most visited in the world. Repeatedly Kiernan ponders how moments in *Hamlet*, *Macbeth*, *Cymbeline* or *Antony and Cleopatra* might in future be staged (all have been since the book was published). But not only is the book awkwardly dated; in places it makes claims for the Globe which are true of just about any theatre. Describing the siege of Harfleur, Kiernan insists that as soon as Henry 'says "the town", it is Harfleur. The creation of "place" by the simple act of "looking" at whatever the place is supposed to be, is a marked characteristic of this space' (p. 106). No it isn't, it is true of all theatres. Again with reference to the non-illusionistic character of the Globe, she writes, 'There is no stage lighting to create mood, no technology to convey a sense of day or night, no directed lighting to give specific focus to characters' (p. 117). But that is also true of most, if not all, outdoor performances and some indoor ones too. Her formulation of a theory of '3-D acting' boils down to blocking 'in order to make multiple-character scenes work on the Globe stage for all sections of the audience' (p. 107) as though this doesn't occur in any other theatre; does planned blocking only happen at the Globe? One of her 'Revelations and Discoveries' (p. 116) is the importance of 'Trusting the story, and trusting the theatre-space to support the storytelling' (p. 125) but isn't this just as vital of *any* play in *any* theatre?

Opportunities are also missed. Only two pages are devoted to the discussion of the boy actor (pp. 55–6) while a short paragraph on 'Performance-Time and Unscripted Moments' (p. 80) comprises three sentences. There are some instances of awful and embarrassing theatre twaddle: 'The playing of African drums was a deliberate anachronism intended to represent the "heartbeat" of the Globe space—an organic building that breathes along with both playgoers and actors during performance' (p. 99); 'Motivated movement, motivated speech, emoting on the line, not between the lines, can prompt the audience to a kind of motivated listening, as it were' (p. 88); 'actors and audience are sharing the same space, the same energy' (p. 40). One expects such vague and impressionistic summaries from actors (whose job is to act, not analyse), but this is 'small beer' from a theatre critic of Kiernan's experience. Indeed, the final thirty-odd pages of the book contain a ghastly array of such 'luvvie'-speak: 'The cast got on really well with each other. It gave the play what I call a 24-hour feel' (p. 130); Shakespeare 'wouldn't have written such brilliant plays if the actors hadn't been brilliant' (p. 131). The Globe's artistic director, Mark Rylance, is typically arcane: 'I understand the eye has always been connected with the intellect and head, and the ear connected with the emotions and heart or chest area' (p. 132). Occasionally the commentary is simply nonsensical. Discussing their production of *Henry V* Richard Olivier (its director) notes that 'of course it's not Denmark' (p. 140) while Craig Pinder offers the equally impenetrable 'My feeling about the "authentic brief" we had for the play is the greatest plays ever written were written in this kind of theatre' (p. 144). The actors' reactions to the first previews of *Henry V* are worthy of some April Fool jest: 'The theatre tells us what to do'; 'The audience—there was so much listening'; 'There was a gentler energy at the second preview' (p. 113). As another member of the company, Rory Edwards, points out, trying 'to describe what is different about the experience of acting at the Globe … can sound crap' (p. 138). Ah, yes.

'Shakespeare and the Globe' is the theme of *Shakespeare Survey* 52 [1999]. In his 'Reconstructions of the Globe: A Retrospective' (*ShS* 52[1999] 1–16), Gabriel Egan summarizes the findings and theories of a number of different theatre historians and scholars, including John Cranford Adams, E.K. Chambers, I.A. Shapiro, C. Walter Hodges, and Glynne Wickham. Some of this material is familiar, but the essay is a useful synopsis that is alert to the manner in which information extrapolated from Hollar's *Long View of London*, the foundations of the Rose, as well as contemporary plays, may be ambiguous. The work of John Orrell has proved fundamental to the Wanamaker Globe though, as Egan asserts, 'the disagreement continues' (p. 13). Noting the scepticism of Graham Holderness and Terence Hawkes, Egan emphasizes the experimental nature of the project and that it may 'as likely fail as succeed' (p. 15). In his fascinating contribution to the same volume, 'Reconstructing the Globe Constructing Ourselves' (*ShS* 52[1999] 33–45), W.B. Worthen develops this sceptical attitude and describes the way in which the Globe can be seen to resemble a theme park. He compares the theatre to the Plimouth Plantation in Plymouth, Massachusetts: both projects are designed to perform the past in the present. Both are tourist destinations, 'and there are T-shirts and postcards and film and books in the giftshop' (p. 41). Yet, as the essay goes on to claim, both the Plimouth Plantation and the Globe require the participation of their audiences. Theme parks, on the other hand, 'tend to construct their visitors more passively, as *consumers* rather than producers of experience' (p. 41). This participatory aspect 'requires the audience to bring its own notions of appropriate behaviour to bear, in ways that are at once democratic and potentially disruptive of claims to authenticity' (p. 43). Yu Jin Ko's account of the opening season's *Henry V*, 'A Little Touch of Harry in the Light: *Henry V* at the New Globe' (*ShS* 52[1999] 107–19), is also alert to the reservations of the Globe's critics and their disdain for the project which, for them, 'reeks of amusement park cheesiness' (p. 107). The article describes the ways in which the theatre, and especially this production of 1997, divested authority from stage to audience. Using Stephen Greenblatt's by now seminal 'Invisible Bullets', Ko outlines the ways in which 'part of what the audience becomes conscious of is its power as makers of kings and queens' (p. 119). Central to the achievement of this, he suggests, was the production's key decision *not* to stage Agincourt, so that the audience's 'sense of disappointment with the director [extended] to some degree of self-consciousness about participating in theatrical illusion' (p. 118).

In 'Which is the Jew that Shakespeare Knew? Shylock on the Elizabethan Stage' (*ShS* 52[1999] 99–106), Charles Edelman notes and challenges the ubiquity of the critical assumption that Elizabethan performances of Shylock were grounded in anti-Semitic stereotypes. Indeed, he insists, 'it is far from certain that there ever was such a thing' (p. 100) and, he goes on, 'it is simply not true that everyone in Elizabethan England … was an anti-Semite' (p. 101). First of all, he notes the small number of Jews in early modern drama: 'In the twelve years leading up to *The Merchant of Venice* there are exactly three Jews in extant plays' (p. 100). While Barabas in Marlowe's *The Jew of Malta* is a thoroughly scandalous portrait and while Abraham in Greene's *Selimus* is a poisoner, Gerontus in Wilson's *Three Ladies of London* 'is by far the most honest and admirable … character in the play' (p. 100), demonstrating that the 'Elizabethan theatre was capable of accommodating alternative portrayals' (p. 101). Edelman goes on to illustrate the difficulties of defining usury in the period and thus the error of lumping in this apparent sin with Jewish vice. On the same play is Elizabeth A. Spiller's 'From Imagination to Miscegenation: Race and Romance in Shakespeare's *The Merchant of Venice*' (*RenD* 29[2000] 137–64). Spiller proposes that the play 'dramatizes the reciprocal relationship between new understandings of race and new types of romance' (p. 157). Race, she argues, ceases in the period to be defined in genealogical terms and instead becomes contingent on skin colour. Portia's descriptions of her suitors suggest 'how the meaning of race is moving away from genealogy toward national ethnicity' (p. 146). Correspondingly, since romance has been up till this point a 'genre organized by genealogy' (p. 138), it too mutates into new forms. Whereas Shakespeare's early romantic comedies are founded on 'a familiar romance ethos' (p. 157), *The Merchant of Venice* rewrites this 'comparatively pure form into a new hybrid' (p. 157). This is an ambitious essay which intriguingly offers an explanation as to why this play is so uncomfortable in generic (and indeed in many other) ways.

R.A. Foakes deservedly receives a splendid Festschrift in Ioppolo, ed., *Shakespeare Performed: Essays in Honour of R.A. Foakes*. The book takes as its topic both early modern and postmodern, being split into two sections: 'Shakespeare Performed in his Time: Theatre, Text, and Interpretation' and 'Shakespeare Performed in our Time: Theatre, Film, Text, and Interpretation'. To the former section, Peter Davison contributes 'Commerce and Patronage: The Lord Chamberlain's Men's Tour of 1597' (pp. 56–71), in which he attempts to examine the reasons for the tour as well as the riddle of why it visited 'the small town of Marlborough' (p. 57). Given the practical difficulties of touring, the high costs of subsistence and the tight budgets involved, Davison is probably right to surmise that 'the Chamberlain's Men only stirred from London when circumstances pressed' (p. 57). However, following the Isle of Dogs scandal, in July 1597, all the theatres were closed down. Usual tour destinations would have included Bristol, Bath, Southampton and Dover in addition to Marlborough. 'Why did not only they but so many other companies bother calling at Marlborough?' (p. 63). The answer, Davison suggests, was the proximity of the large estates, Tottenham House and Wilton, occupied by the Seymours and the Pembrokes respectively. 'Both families patronized companies of players … What I am suggesting is that the Chamberlain's Men in 1597 visited not only six towns but the estates of the powerful, with whom, through their contacts at Court, they might be expected to have access' (pp. 63–4). In '"Tenders and True Pay": Representing Falsehood' (pp. 122–30), Philip Edwards explores 'some of the problems which arise when the theatrical profession, whose definition is masking, undertakes its self-appointed task of unmasking: of distinguishing the true from the false' (p. 122). This central paradox is intensified by the realization that 'There is no linguistic code which the virtuous can use to signify that they are the real thing' (p. 123). In fact, as Cordelia's silence demonstrates, a refusal to take part in the hypocrisy of protestation is equally open to misinterpretation. Moreover, as the essay goes on, Edwards explains that the self which is personated by the player is only an illusion and so 'The treachery of language (as urged by Shakespeare) is intolerably complicated by the instability of the self' (p. 127). The essay ends in an ingenious spiral of simulation: 'As language is manufactured for the creatures of fiction, it becomes apparent that the argument that pretence can clean up pretence is a pretence' (p. 130).

The opening essay of the second section of *Shakespeare Performed* is fittingly on the subject of 'Writing about Shakespeare's Plays in Performance' (pp. 151–63), in which John Russell Brown acknowledges that writing about Shakespeare on stage has become 'an accepted and often industrious academic pursuit' (p. 151)—phew! The essay sets out several general principles for such writing as well as discussing the problems inherent in transcodifying live performance with all its vicissitudes into a permanent, fixed prose account. Much of what Brown describes is as applicable to the general as to the Shakespearian theatre reviewer. For instance, the subjectivity of the reviewer is highlighted: 'The critic's own mind and personal history are of crucial importance because they will control both the selection of material for study and the perception of it' (p. 152). Several times Brown (rightly) indicates his own hesitation in pronouncing on such a topic, placing key terms like 'mean[ing]', 'look[ing]' and 'presence' in scare quotes; while reviewing is hardly a science, writing or theorizing about it is even less so. Brown turns his attention to the introductions of several single-volume Shakespeare editions, deftly exposing the editors' prejudices and blind spots when it comes to discussing the plays' performance histories. This is an elegant and perceptive essay, albeit necessarily inconclusive.

In 'The Performance of Text in the Royal National Theatre's 1997 Production of *King Lear*' (Ioppolo, ed., pp. 180–97) Grace Ioppolo outlines the argument of the 'new revisionists' that the Quarto and Folio editions of the play 'should not be conflated but reprinted, studied and performed in their original separate texts with an individual integrity and scholarly and theatrical value and validity' (p. 182). In the theatre the versions are usually conflated to produce a performance text. Ioppolo describes the painstaking process by which Richard Eyre and his company chose 'to unedit and then re-edit' (p. 181) the two texts. In fact, while the starting position was the Folio text, the importation of Quarto episodes, such as the mock trial, tended towards conflation anyway. In his contribution on the same play, 'Possessing Edgar: Aspects of *King Lear* in Performance' (pp. 198–215), Michael Hattaway asks 'How do we read and locate Edgar in Shakespeare's *King Lear*?' (p. 198). Hattaway challenges Stephen Greenblatt's reading of the play (in 'Shakespeare and the Exorcists') and demonstrates the rigidity of his account: Greenblatt 'offers a mechanistic and absolute model of cultural change' (p. 203). 'Are there really', asks Hattaway, '"moments" in cultural history, and can we use "literary" texts to capture them in this manner?' (p. 203).

Alan Brissenden chronicles the development of 'Australian Shakespeare' (in Ioppolo, ed., pp. 240–59) from its first performance in April 1800 to the present day. Typically the story is one of iconoclastic irreverence on the one hand—'his plays were simply another item on the bill' (p. 241)—and colonial subservience on the other—'Visits by the Old Vic and Stratford Memorial companies bolstered the belief that English Shakespeare was not only the best, but offered the only model' (p. 250). Brissenden demonstrates that the cultural elevation of the Bard was in part a domestic phenomenon. The founding of the Melbourne Shakespere (*sic*) Society in May 1884 was part of a movement which saw the plays 'less performed and more the subject of classroom lessons [and lectures]. Many patrons of such groups preferred to take their Shakespeare this way rather than in the theatre' (p. 247). The emergence of an Australian Shakespeare followed the formation in 1954 of the Australian Elizabethan Theatre Trust directed by Englishman Hugh Hunt. Their touring, small-scale productions were characterized by 'casts as small as six, minimal sets, basic costumes, and close contact with the audience' (p. 252). Hunt proposed the setting up of the National Institute of Dramatic Art (NIDA) which was founded by another Englishman, Robert Quentin at the University of New South Wales in 1958, whence emerged John Bell, 'the most significant person in Australian Shakespeare in the late twentieth century' (p. 252). The Bell Shakespeare Company was founded in 1990 and 'launched in Sydney in January 1991 with

Hamlet and *The Merchant of Venice*' (p. 255). As late as 1997 Australia saw its first Shakespeare production with an all-indigenous cast and director. Brissenden puts this reticence down to the force of 'imperial colonization' (p. 256) as well as the star system which imported foreign (British and American) stars rather than developing home-grown talents. While the Bell Shakespeare Company is credited with using Australian accents unconsciously, this did not occur till 1971. Despite the recency of its birth, Australian Shakespeare is here to stay, developing alongside 'the steady growth in Australia's self-confidence as a nation which had begun to accept itself as a player on its own terms in international culture as well as sport' (p. 258).

Perspectives on Shakespeare in Performance collects ten essays of J.L. Styan first published between 1969 and 1995. As such it never amounts to a single coherent argument but, as the title implies, collects many and varied insights into aspects of performance such as stage space, music and costume. There are also essays on *A Midsummer Night's Dream*, *All's Well* and *Hamlet*. Some of the earlier material looks distinctly jaded, such as when Styan protests that 'little is known of the details of the Globe theatre' (p. 26) or when he begins a chapter, 'The present section springs from what we shall learn when the first authentic replica of the Globe theatre is in use on the South Bank' (p. 41). These two essays (first published in 1976 and 1990) surely should have been updated; ironically the cover features a vertiginous photograph of the Globe theatre which is now in its sixth year. The same goes for Styan's reliance on 'Modern productions' (p. 162), referring us to stage versions from 1981 (p. 162) and 1978 (p. 118), as well as Zeffirelli's *Romeo and Juliet* [1968] as though they were the latest thing. The two most recent entries in the bibliography are 1996, but of the fifty-odd items, half are pre-1970. Some of the book is rather eccentric, such as when Styan asserts that 'A pretty little fairy may well suggest that human love is a delightfully romantic business; a big fat fairy will rather incline one to scepticism' (p. 121); Shakespeare mixed various art forms into 'a suitably digestible dramatic pie' (p. 144); or 'When Hamlet jumps on to the bed in order to stab Polonius through the arras, as is now often the case [I have never seen this happen], we are in the great age of the phallic sword' (p. 151). Perhaps most alarming is his analogy between theatre and sex: 'As with making love, the experience is not for analysis while being practised' (p. 7)! For all its peculiarities though, the book has a knack of hitting the nail on the head. At one point Styan contrasts Petruchio, 'whom we hate ourselves for liking', with Shylock, 'whom we hate ourselves for hating' (p. 51). Of Gloucester's Dover Cliff suicide attempt he opines, 'this must be the most grotesque pratfall in drama' (p. 68). A.C. Bradley, Styan remarks, brings characters 'to life—but not to stage life' (p. 12); and, although slightly flamboyant, his formulation of the difference between page and stage is a useful one: 'Criticism is inevitably a generalizing activity, whereas the theatre experience is always particular; criticism is reflective and docile, whereas perceptions in the theatre are wild and immediate and alive' (p. 5). His insistence throughout that Renaissance drama is about convention rather than illusion is worth adopting as a mantra.

One of Styan's essays, 'Stage Space and the Shakespeare Experience', is reprinted in Shaughnessy, ed., *Shakespeare in Performance*, a new Macmillan casebook. The collection includes all the usual suspects, Alan C. Dessen, W.B. Worthen and Robert Weimann, as well as the materialists Graham Holderness, Kathleen McLuskie and Alan Sinfield. There are also essays by Michael D. Bristol,

Barbara Hodgdon and Simon Shepherd. Nearly all of the essays were originally published at the end of the 1980s and beginning of the 1990s and look a little stale. But, as Shaughnessy's excellent introduction explains, this was the moment of the 'Shakespeare revolution' (p. 12) when the cultural centrality of the Bard was being questioned (Shepherd's contribution is entitled 'Acting Against Bardom'). The Globe reappears as 'a unique convergence between academic scholarship, the theatrical profession, cultural philanthropy and the entertainment industry' (p. 3). Shaughnessy provides an eloquent and accurate summary of the history and eventual arrival of performance criticism beginning with 'the near-universally derided efforts of William Poel and his Elizabethan-style performances' (p. 3). Shaughnessy places 'the real surge in … performance criticism' in the post-war period, 'which saw the formation of a new alliance between pedagogy, historical scholarship and contemporary Shakespearean production' (p. 7). Alongside the emergence of performance criticism, Shaughnessy traces developments in critical theory, notably the new historicism, to which he attributes two distinct disadvantages: its pessimism, which he describes as 'a gloomy scenario of violent coercion, containment and repression' (p. 10), and the fact that 'the stage could be seen as more abstract and intangible than ever' (p. 10). Alan Dessen's emphasis on the *difference* between early modern and modern theatres (in the wake of Raymond Williams's stress on dramatic conventions) is seen to signal the recognition of the distance between the Elizabethan stage and the 'naturalism-dominated theatres of the modern period' (p. 14). Shaughnessy is especially acute on the subjectivity and therefore unreliability of the reviewer as well as the necessity of scepticism towards the canonical authority of Shakespeare in performance. He writes of the need to 'interrogate the text and to engage with the different orders of subjectivity that it affords' (p. 18). This final call to arms is perhaps a little utopian, but the introduction is vivaciously written and is highly recommended as a concise and dexterous narrative of the background to and theories of performance criticism.

The boy actor is the focus of Juliet Dusinberre's contribution to Callaghan, ed., *A Feminist Companion to Shakespeare*. In 'Women and Boys Playing Shakespeare' (pp. 251–62) Dusinberre begins by distinguishing Audrey from the other female roles in *As You Like It* on the basis that her part 'requires the audience to focus on the body of the character in a way that it does not for anyone else on stage' (p. 252) since Audrey's physicality is the subject of Touchstone's and her own comments. Thus the performance of Audrey 'marks a use of the boy actor significantly different from the way Shakespeare exploits his presence in the roles of the court characters, Rosalind and Celia' (p. 253). By contrast, insists Dusinberre, 'Rosalind's body exists only as a constant act of evasion' (p. 258). This is a stimulating discussion, but it breaks down when Dusinberre turns her attentions to live performance; she writes, 'In the Cheek by Jowl all-male production of *As You Like It*, the early scenes at court between Rosalind and Celia were embarrassingly badly acted' (p. 258). This opinion is entirely unsupported by contemporary reviews or commentaries and (for what it is worth, my having seen the production three times) is entirely contrary to this reviewer's judgement. Discussions of performance always run the risk of falling into superficial and subjective description, as they do here. The remainder of the essay is a rather uninteresting and too brief summation of reactions to various Rosalinds, though without much in the way of argument.

Theodora A. Jankowski's essay in the same volume starts poorly and gets a lot worse. At the opening of her '… in the Lesbian Void: Woman–Woman Eroticism in Shakespeare's Plays' (pp. 298–319) she roundly asserts that Hermione's trial 'literally proves fatal to her' (p. 299). Correct me if I am wrong, but isn't Hermione alive at the close? It would seem best always to read to the end when publishing an essay on a play! There then follows the kind of offstage biography of fictional characters popularized by A.C. Bradley: 'where was Hermione kept so secretly for sixteen years that no hint of her presence was revealed? Did Paulina pay all of her servants to be silent? Are we to believe that no one noticed food or clothing going into—and waste products being removed from—some "secret" place in Paulina's house? Did Hermione remain totally silent during this period?' (p. 300), and so on. There follows the supposition that Hermione and Paulina have had a sixteen-year lesbian affair. No need for evidence: 'to push definitions and metaphors … she [Hermione] may have entered the "void" of early modern "lesbian" activity: unseen, unknown, unacknowledged' (p. 306). True—but she might also have spent sixteen years playing ice hockey for Canada or packing fish fingers in a factory! This is the kind of spurious fantasizing about literary characters which compromises literary criticism. Later, in relation to *The Merchant of Venice*: 'We know, of course, that the women did not sleep with *actual* men. The question remains, though: did the women sleep with each other as men? Did Nerissa sleep with the lawyer, or Portia with the clerk? Perhaps they did' (p. 309). But, one is bound to respond, perhaps they did *not*! The essay becomes more and more untenable as the bawdy conversations of Cleopatra's women indicate, in Jankowski's opinion, 'that they are ripe for *any* kind of sexual activity with *any* kind of (perhaps even multiple) partners' (p. 310). Yet their conversations are precisely about wanting to sleep with well-hung men (I.ii.63), and avoiding the inevitable disappointment of a eunuch. The final straw is when Jankowski attempts to reconstruct the ostensible witnessing of infidelity which takes place in *Much Ado*. It is, she assures us, 'quite dark in Sicily between midnight and 1 a.m.' (p. 313). This kind of literal-mindedness, when it appears in undergraduate essays, can only be countered with the red pen!

3. Shakespeare on Screen

Jackson, ed., *The Cambridge Companion to Shakespeare on Film*, is one of this year's most significant contributions to what has become an established field of enquiry. The Companion is arranged in four sections, focused respectively on Shakespearian films 'as reflections on the business and craft of film-making, in terms of cinematic and theatrical genres, as the work of particular directors, and in relation to wider issues of cultural politics' (pp. 1–2). In the introduction, Russell Jackson challenges Michael Bristol's assumption that '"Big-Time Shakespeare" has nothing to do with ideas of any description' (p. 1). Jackson points out that Shakespeare films have always been a significant phenomenon, starting from the over 400 films made during the silent era up to the popular revivals in the late 1960s, and the early and late 1990s.

In the opening chapter, 'From Play-script to Screenplay' (pp. 15–34), Jackson draws a pragmatic distinction between 'conservative' and 'radical' Shakespeare films, according to the extent to which directors rely on continuity editing as opposed to montage. However, Jackson admits, even the most conservative of cinematic adaptations relies on medium-specific devices, which he then proceeds to explore. The impact of such devices on the Shakespearian material is regarded 'not so much [as] an unavoidable and regrettable consequence of filming, [but] as an opportunity the director forgoes at his or her peril' (p. 19). Overall, Jackson's introduction proves an ideal starting point for students interested in exploring the complex relationship between theatre and cinema.

Michèle Willems, in 'Video and its Paradoxes' (pp. 35–46), reflects on the many paradoxes involved in making a Shakespeare film, a made-for-television production, or a theatrical version available on videotape. More informative is Barbara Freedman's essay, 'Critical Junctures in Shakespeare Screen History: The Case of *Richard III*' (pp. 47–71), on three film adaptations of *Richard III*—the recently rediscovered Keane/Warde [1912–13], Olivier [1955] and Loncraine/McKellen [1995]. According to Freedman, Keane/Warde did not trust the new medium enough to abandon stage conventions altogether. Significantly enough, Warde ended up touring with the film to lecture between reels, almost as if he wished to 'remind his audience of what it was missing' (p. 49). Olivier's problematic mixture of 'stage blocking' and 'shooting style' and the implications of two media crossovers—from stage to cinema, from cinema to television—are carefully considered. McKellen is then taken to task for 'his innocence regarding the control of the camera over performance' (p. 63). Nevertheless, Freedman concludes, '[the] collaboration between a master of inventive, strong postmodern cinematic language and a master of Shakespearean acting and verse delivery' ultimately worked (pp. 66–7).

The second part of the Companion opens with 'Shakespeare and Movie Genre', where Harry Keyishian (pp. 72–81) argues that 'when [Shakespeare's] plays are made into movies, Shakespeare adapts to the authority of film more than film adapts to the authority of Shakespeare' (p. 73). Keyishian supports his theory by accounting for 'otherwise eccentric' (p. 75) aspects of Olivier's, Zeffirelli's and Branagh's *Hamlet* in terms of the director's conscious deference to specific traditions, namely *film noir*, action adventure, and epic. Michael Hattaway, in 'The Comedies on Film' (pp. 85–98), speculates on the limited popularity of Shakespeare's comedies on film and identifies conventional incompatibilities between the 'improbable fictions' in Elizabethan and Jacobean comedy and the '"real" world that extends beyond [the] edges' of the screen (p. 86). According to Hattaway, the best way to overcome the conventional incompatibilities between Shakespearian comedy and the cinematic medium is to make 'a filmic film that, by delighting in its own conventions of narrative and diegesis, matches the metatheatricality that is so prominent in Shakespeare's comic texts (p. 96). More narrowly focused is H.R. Coursen's 'Filming Shakespeare's History: Three Films of *Richard III*' (pp. 99–116). Coursen establishes the extent to which Olivier's, Loncraine/McKellen's and Pacino's films succeed in conveying a sense of historical complexity. Despite its focus on Richard, Olivier's film is said to 'stand up well on reviewing', because it does engage with the 'ambiguous politics of the play' (p. 101). Loncraine/McKellen's film is, on the other hand, regarded as a 'travesty', 'a parody of Hollywood films, at times mildly amusing, most of the time simply grotesque, a shallow and meretricious shadow of a stage production' (p. 102). Coursen agrees with Freedman (pp. 47–71) when he claims that 'visual overload …

dissipate[s] the propelling energy of McKellen's performance', although the two critics could not differ more when it comes to appraising the value of the film as a whole. Coursen prefers Pacino's *Looking for Richard*, because as a documentary on the filming of a film, which includes a stage production of the play, it inevitably reflects on the 'ways in which the script has to be translated into a modern idiom' (p. 111). J. Lawrence Guntner in '*Hamlet*, *Macbeth* and *King Lear* on Film' (pp. 117–34) reviews the main twentieth-century cinematic adaptations of *Hamlet*, *Macbeth* and *King Lear* by focusing on developing cinematic techniques and the historical contexts within which the films he considers were conceived and produced. The 'depiction of Fortinbras and Hamlet as reconciled sons of hostile fathers' in the Gade/Nielsen *Hamlet*, for example, is interpreted as a 'wish for reconciliation between the youth of Europe after the senseless slaughter of World War I' (p. 118). Similarly, Hamlet's delay in Olivier's film is read as a warning addressed to France, Great Britain and the United States, who hesitated to act against fascism and nazism at the beginning of the Second World War. Also interesting is Guntner's reading of Polanski's *Macbeth* and Kurosawa's *Ran* in relation to the Cold War period: 'if Polanski presents us the world as a never-ending cycle of gratuitous violence' (p. 126), Guntner speculates, Kurosawa presents us a 'world poised on the brink of nuclear destruction' (p. 132). Patricia Tatspaugh, 'The Tragedies of Love on Film' (pp. 135–59), concentrates on the heightened realism of the cinematic medium and the impact of geographical location on characterization. George Cukor's *Romeo and Juliet* [1970] is regarded as a strong influence on both Renato Castellani [1954] and Franco Zeffirelli [1968], although Zeffirelli was the first director to capitalize on youth culture and contemporary context (p. 140). When considering film versions of *Othello*, Tatspaugh claims that 'Welles's film falls short of conveying the marriage as a love-match' (p. 145), as opposed to Yutkevich's romantic presentation, which leaves Iago frustrated and defeated. The section devoted to *Othello* ends with a short commentary on Stuart Burge's [1965] film of the National Theatre production starring Laurence Olivier as Othello. The section on *Antony and Cleopatra* disappoints for its narrow focus on Charlton Heston's flawed film [1972].

In the third part of the Companion, Anthony Davies's essay 'The Shakespeare Films of Laurence Olivier' (pp. 163–82) offers a detailed survey of the critical reception of Olivier's three Shakespearian films. A close analysis of the responses generated by Olivier's *Henry V* helps Davies redress 'any simplistic propagandist reading of the film' (p. 169). Also very useful is Davies's brief reference to the main influences on Olivier's *Hamlet*, namely Freudianism, German expressionism and the American *film noir* of the 1940s (p. 171). Like Coursen, Davies regards Olivier's emphasis on the magnetic character of Richard III as potentially reductive, but ultimately in keeping with the 'splashy swagger and cinematic panache' of Olivier's directorial approach (p. 176). Pamela Mason, 'Orson Welles and Filmed Shakespeare' (pp. 183–98), carries out an interesting reassessment of Welles's Shakespearian films, while Mark Sokolayansky, 'Grigori Kozinstev's *Hamlet* and *King Lear*' (pp. 199–211) draws on Kozintsev's critical writings to reflect on his development as director of *Hamlet* [1964] and *Lear* [1970]. Deborah Cartmell, 'Franco Zeffirelli and Shakespeare' (pp. 212–21), questions Zeffirelli's 'declared reverence for Shakespeare', by arguing that his 'operatic conception' detracts from the spoken word, while his camerawork 'interprets, subverts or transforms the words of the playtext' (p. 217). Samuel Crowl, 'Flamboyant Realist: Kenneth Branagh' (pp. 222–38), discusses Branagh's popularity by looking at his Shakespearian films, in an attempt to counterbalance the often unsympathetic verdict delivered by academia on his efforts to popularize Shakespeare. An amusing slip of the pen must be responsible for Crowl's reference to the setting of Branagh's *In the Bleak Midwinter* as 'the fictional English village of Hope' (p. 226). Hope is a remarkably entrepreneurial village, sporting an attractive gluten-free cafe in one of the most popular trekking havens in Derbyshire! Ironically, the community which Branagh's actors strive to help by rescuing their local church remained blissfully unaware that Branagh was shooting in their midst.

The fourth and final part of the Companion opens with Carol Rutter's 'Looking at Shakespeare's Women on Film' (pp. 241–60), an analysis of 'how cinema has looked at Shakespeare's women' (p. 241). Starting with Olivier's films, which 'seem to locate women … as decorative marginal glosses to the main matter' (pp. 243–4) and ending with Luhrmann's *Romeo + Juliet*, where the woman's body does not 'repair but register[s] postmodern fragmentation', Rutter's piece lends many useful insights to the relation between gaze, camerawork and point of view. Particularly stimulating is her analysis of Nunn's opening and closing sequences in *Twelfth Night* [1995], of Emma Thompson's Kate in Branagh's *Henry V* [1989], and the framing of the female body in Zeffirelli's *The Taming of the Shrew* [1966]. Looking at issues of race and nationality, Neil Taylor, 'National and Racial Stereotypes in Films' (pp. 261–73), argues that the casting of black actors in roles traditionally played by white actors, including Othello's, signals a progressive emancipation from racial and racist stereotypes. Less focused on specific critical (read cultural materialist) issues is Neil Forsyth's essay, 'Shakespeare the Illusionist: Filming the Supernatural' (pp. 274–94), which points out how the tradition of Shakespeare on film has pulled more towards realism than towards magic (p. 274). Forsyth accounts for this tendency by reminding us of the 'Anglo-Saxon, Puritan-based … long-standing suspicion of theatre [as illusion]' (p. 276) and of the influence of the picture-frame stage which was predominant in England from the Restoration to the late Victorian period. Forsyth strengthens his argument by contrasting Branagh's and Olivier's renditions of the Ghost in *Hamlet* with Kozintsev's. Similarly, he registers a more relaxed and imaginative approach to the supernatural in Welles's and Kurosawa's adaptation of *Macbeth* than on several British television adaptations. The Companion ends with a dense yet charmingly written piece by Tony Howard, 'Shakespeare's Cinematic Offshoots' (pp. 295–313), where he surveys the overwhelming variety of cinematic responses which Shakespeare generated in the twentieth century. Focusing on offshoots, rather than 'straight' Shakespeare, Howard takes us on a dazzling journey across many cinematic genres and sub-genres, directors as different as Van Sant, Boorman, Godard, Rohmer, Coppola, or Castellari. Particularly enlightening is the section devoted to *Othello*, which effectively shows how the 'periphery' of Shakespearian offshoots can add to our understanding of this problematic play, not only in terms of its race and gender politics, but also as 'a Pirandellian vehicle to explore the psychology of performance' (p. 305). Although the Companion has been quite rightly praised for being 'cogently organized' (*TLS* [7 Dec. 2001], p. 18), no cross-references alert the reader to its healthy disparity of opinions, as with Rutter's and Cartmell's remarkably different views on Zeffirelli's *Shrew* or Freedman's and Coursen's similarly diverging appraisals of the Loncraine/McKellen *Richard III*.

Cross-references would have possibly made this outstanding collection even more cohesive and user-friendly.

Another significant contribution to this year's critical output on 'Shakespeare on Screen' is the fifth special issue of *Early Modern Literary Studies* (6:i[2000]). In his interview with Russell Jackson, Darren Kerr gets Branagh's academic adviser to admit that 'Shakespearean dialogue … carried a great many things in [the Elizabethan theatre] that it cannot and must not carry in film' (p. 3). At the same time, though, Jackson strikes a very positive note, by arguing that the 'wedge [that] was driven between Shakespeare and what was generally available in the theatre' (p. 4) by William Poel and Granville Barker at the beginning of the twentieth century is now being removed by the cinema. In Kerr's second interview, Kenneth Rothwell welcomes the role cinema has had in 'pushing Shakespeare back into the realm of popular entertainment' (p. 2). In the first of the three film reviews, Ann Thompson praises Almereyda's reliance on images rather that dialogue in *Hamlet* [1999], because the visual seems more suitable than the verbal to the 'relentlessly urban' setting of the film (p. 1). Debra Tuckett is similarly impressed by Branagh's adaptation of *Love's Labour's Lost*, since he adapts the play to the conventions of a Hollywood song-and-dance musical, while 'adhering to the spirit rather than the letter of the play' (p. 3).

Out of the three articles in this special issue of *EMLS*, Courtney Lehmann and Lisa Starks's essay 'Making Mothers Matter: Repression, Revision and the Stakes of "Reading Psychoanalysis into Kenneth Branagh's *Hamlet*' (*EMLS* 6:i[2000]) is particularly noteworthy. This essay represents a persuasive and timely attempt to redress the general perception of Branagh's film as a departure from the Oedipal *Hamlet*s directed by Olivier and Zeffirelli. Lehmann and Starks read Branagh's self-proclaimed intention to reclaim the text from psychoanalysis as an attempt to repress the maternal body of his Irish homeland through a projection of Hamlet's desire onto his quintessentially English and surrogate father, Derek Jacobi's Claudius. If Lehmann and Starks fail to resist one of the most enduring practices of psychoanalytic criticism and psychoanalyse the director, their analysis of Branagh's directorial strategies, casting and choice of setting is compelling and enlightening throughout. Their conclusion that 'the film provide[s] more evidence for Freud's reading than any other cinematic interpretation of the play' (p. 6) will, I hope, function as a watershed for future critical assessments of Branagh's film. Patricia Dorval's 'Shakespeare on Screen: Threshold Aesthetics in Olivier Parker's *Othello*' (*EMLS* 6:i[2000]) uses Iago's reference to *Janus bifrons* at I.ii.33 as a starting point for her analysis of Iago's association with beginnings, thresholds and deceptive perspectives. Dorval highlights Oliver Parker's lavish use of the threshold motif, which he found both in his Shakespearian source and in the *film noir* tradition from which he drew extensively. Sarah Hatchuel's 'Leading the Gaze: From Showing to Telling in Kenneth Branagh's *Henry V* and *Hamlet*' (*EMLS* 6:i[2000]) sheds some light on the defining conventions of theatre and cinema as ultimately irreconcilable, although not entirely dissimilar, enunciative systems. While theatre 'tells' cinema 'shows'. However, as Hatchuel reveals, by manipulating the framing and editing processes Branagh constructs distinctively narrative elements, such as the time of narration and the narrator's point of view.

Also interested in the enunciative system of cinema is Kathy Howlett's *Framing Shakespeare on Film*. Drawing on Noël Carroll, *Theorising the Moving Image*

[1996], Inez Hedges, *Breaking the Frame: Film Language and the Experience of Limits* [1991] and Erving Goffman, *Frame Analysis: An Essay on the Organization of Experience* [1974], Howlett defines 'framing' as 'the arrangement of objects within the cinematic frame' (p. 4). In a more general sense, she also uses the term 'frame' as 'both a concept of genre and the organization of experience' (p. 10). By using frame theory as her main approach, Howlett establishes how mainstream Shakespearian films may involve 'frame making' or 'frame breaking', 'framing ambivalence' or 'parodic reframing' (p. 14).

Howlett's first chapter focuses on the recognizable influences of the Western on Zeffirelli's *Hamlet*. Such influences include 'the prominent display of the male body' (p. 25), 'an expansive sky and land and the free movement of men on horses' (p. 29), and a polarized vision of 'the masculine world of violence' (p. 35) as opposed to a 'feminine spatial openness and fluidity' (p. 43). The influence of the Western on Gertrude's characterization as the hero's equal undermines a psychoanalytic reading of Zeffirelli's closet scene. Howlett reports Gibson's remark that 'a Freudian exploration of Gertrude's "more than motherly" behaviour bother[ed] him', and suggests that 'although vague ... Gertrude's physicality simply cannot be explained in terms of Hamlet's uncontrollable psychological forces' (p. 41). Moving on to Orson Welles, Howlett traces the visual inspiration for many memorable scenes in *Othello* in Carpaccio's painting (chapter 2). According to Howlett, Welles reproduces Carpaccio's eyewitness style through fragmented editing and a subjective camera technique. Such technique involves extensive use of rapid shot/reverse shot exchanges and other point-of-view shots, including the use of an observer, whose perspective the spectator is not given to share and which therefore 'sustain[s] the illusion of voyeuristic separation' (p. 70). Contrary to the predominant opinion that 'all ambiguities rest comfortably, without anxiety, in the film spectacle' (p. 93), Howlett believes that Branagh's 'cinematic tactics [in *Henry V*] expose the cynical ideological premises of the play' (p. 114). Branagh's St Crispin's Day speech, for example, is undermined by 'the camera's nostalgic interpretation of flashback sequences' which 'works against the rhetoric that deems the soldiers a "band of brothers"' (p. 113). An anecdote from Kurosawa's childhood helps Howlett shed new light on the Japanese director's scrupulous attention to framing (chapter 4). She then proceeds to explain how, in Kurosawa's *Ran*, Sué/Cordelia's refusal to position herself within the 'formal structures and sign system of the Samurai world' (p. 121) bursts the cinematic frame, thus suggesting 'an inner integrity and diegetic space outside [that] patriarchal world' (p. 126). Howlett praises the Loncraine/McKellen *Richard III* because, far from merely providing a 'realist record of life in fascist Europe in the 1930s' (p. 148), the film invites its viewers to critically consider their 'cinematic experience of history as seen through the conventions of the Hollywood gangster movie'. In her sixth chapter, Howlett points out how Van Sant's *My Own Private Idaho* borrows more explicitly from Welles's *Chimes at Midnight* than from Shakespeare. By reframing Welles's tavern scenes, Van Sant suggests the 'commodification' of the utopian world which Welles's Falstaff stands for. Howlett therefore agrees with Matt Bergbusch (see the review of his chapter in Hedrick and Reynolds, eds., below), by concluding that 'Van Sant captures the unpitying nature of the carnivalesque art, capable of unmasking sentimental attachments of "home" and "mother" and of ridiculing the conventional ethical hierarchies of "success" and "money"' (p. 176). In chapter 7

Howlett argues that Branagh's framing device in *A Midwinter's Tale* (*In the Bleak Midwinter* in Britain) 'takes the form of irreverent carnivalizing' (p. 180) and has a 'revolutionary effect' in that the 'confusing multiplicity' of a play within the film 'liberate[s] the viewer from static conceptions of the play' (p. 181). While Howlett's reading echoes Emma Smith's view (see the review of her chapter in Thornton Burnett and Wray, eds., below), according to which Branagh's unassuming small-budget film exorcized the ghosts that would have otherwise have haunted his Hollywood-style grand epic version of *Hamlet* [1997], she is later seduced by Branagh's rhetoric. 'Although the film squarely counters theatrical aesthetics', she suggests, the film celebrates a utopian 'place where negated actors, theatres and performances come to the centre, and where festive laughter urges a symbolic victory over the oppressive concerns of finances, personal loss and Hollywood' (p. 196). Howlett seems to acknowledge, and at the same time to overlook, the fact that this unassuming film gave Branagh the opportunity to flex his directorial muscles before embarking on his Hollywood-style full-text epic rendition of the play. Howlett's book is well written and refreshing in its approach, although the theoretical framework carefully conceived in the introduction often gives way to her penchant for the biographical and the anecdotal (see pp. 36–8, chapter 2, and pp. 116–18).

Another book-length study published this year is Robert Willson's *Shakespeare in Hollywood, 1929–1956*. Willson's survey spans what he refers to as the 'best, most impressive renditions of a Shakespeare play that came out of Hollywood's Golden Age' (p. 13), namely between Reinhardt's *Dream* [1935] and Mankiewicz-Houseman's *Julius Caesar* [1953]. The only film to fall outside this temporal framework is Sam Taylor's *The Taming of the Shrew* [1929], which marked the transition from silent to 'talking' films. Sam Taylor's heavily abridged sound version served as a vehicle for Hollywood icons Mary Pickford and Douglas Fairbanks. Taylor's directorial intervention ensures that his Kate, unlike Shakespeare's, 'retains total control over her "domestication," allowing her partner to believe that he has won and preserved his male ego' (p. 25). Despite a 'Faustian element' in Hollywood's seduction of Reinhardt, and the recognizable influences of the Hollywood musical and romantic screwball comedy, his 1935 *Dream* is regarded as a 'great leap forward from *Taming*, which for all its energy cannot escape its ties to the world of theater' (p. 46). Thalberg's star-crossed film of *Romeo and Juliet* [1936], whose disastrous returns discouraged Hollywood studios from producing another Shakespearian film until 1953, is said to represent a 'lover's monument' to Thalberg's wife, Norma Shearer, who was cast to play Juliet, and to Shakespeare. By far the longest chapter in the book is devoted to selected offshoots, which, in Willson's view, represent a convenient compromise for the studios between avoiding another financially disastrous cinematic adaptation of a Shakespearian play and the wish to exploit Shakespeare's 'cultural capital'. Hitler and Mussolini are the 'real-life equivalents' of Lubitsch's Richards and Claudiuses in *To Be or Not To Be*, which, despite its altogether improbable attempt to reconcile comic farce and Shakespeare, turned out to be, in Willson's words, a 'film of artistic and thematic significance' (p. 82). As well as *Joe Macbeth* [1955], *Forbidden Planet* [1956] and *Jubal* [1956], Willson's central chapter covers *A Double Life* [1947], where Shakespeare's Iago becomes an internalized demon haunting the consciousness of Ronald Colman's Othello. The next chapter highlights the beneficial impact of Welles's exploration of ambition in *Citizen Kane* [1941] on his *Macbeth* [1948]. Willson concludes that, despite the 'flaws resulting from cuts, additions, weak performance and an oversimplified treatment' of its source, 'the film features some stirring, compelling scenes that almost help it escape its Hollywood bonds' (p. 137). The book ends with a bitter-sweet assessment of Hollywood's creative potential, which is most suggestively documented by Mankiewicz-Houseman's *Julius Caesar* and Hollywood's rejection of Shakespeare in the 1960s. For the author of a book entirely devoted to Shakespearian productions during Hollywood's Golden Age, Willson shows a remarkable distrust in what Michael Bristol has defined as 'Big-Time Shakespeare'.

Jim Walsh, the editor of *Literature/Film Quarterly*, proudly presents the ninth issue (28:ii[2000]) to be wholly devoted to Shakespeare on film (p. 160). Bizarrely enough, the opening essay by Christopher Andrews, '*Richard III* on Film: The Subversions of the Viewer' (*LFQ* 28:ii[2000] 82–94), does exactly the opposite of 'what it says on the box'. Rather than exploiting or explicitly departing from the politicized connotation acquired by the term 'subversion' over the last couple of decades, Andrews reviews the different filmic techniques and directorial intervention whereby three remarkable Richards (Olivier, 1955; Cook, 1983; McKellen, 1995) respectively overpower, move and seduce their audience. Anthony Miller's '*Julius Caesar* in the Cold War: The Houseman-Mankiewicz Film' (*LFQ* 28:ii[2000] 95–100) provides a detailed account of the film's complex web of allusions to contemporary American politics. Miller first highlights striking parallels between the film's Roman setting and the American Senate on Capitol Hill, through which 'Hollywood positioned themselves as inheritors of the Roman imperial function' (p. 95). Even more crucially, he then sets out to show how the cinematic appropriation exploits ideological faultines already present in the Shakespearian original. '[A] divided representation of Caesar [in] ... Shakespeare's text [corresponds] to a faultline in American ideology, in which there are slippages between a tradition of anti-monarchism and a tradition of electing general-presidents, and between anti-imperialism and the embrace of global hegemony' (p. 97).

Hanna Scolnicov's 'Gertrude's Willow Speech: Word and Film Image' (*LFQ* 28:ii[2000] 101–11) focuses on how four film directors—Olivier [1948], Kozintsev [1964], Zeffirelli [1990] and Branagh [1996]—handle the contradictory accounts of Ophelia's death as accidental in Gertrude's 'willow speech' (IV.vii) and as suicide in the gravediggers' scene (V.i). Scolnicov prefers Branagh's 'conservative treatment' because it shows how 'trusting the play, rather than trying to smooth and regularise [this discrepancy], results in a highly satisfying presentation of great complexity' (p. 110). Branagh's *Hamlet* is also preferred by James H. Lake, who, in his essay 'The Effects of Primacy and Recency upon Audience Response to Five Film Versions of *Hamlet*' (*LFQ* 28:ii[2000] 112–17), explains how the rhetorical strength of first (primacy) and last (recency) impressions is best exploited by Branagh through his retention of Fortinbras.

The next three essays in *LFQ* focus on Baz Luhrmann's omnipresent *William Shakespeare's Romeo + Juliet*. Paradoxically, all three lament the lack of critical attention paid to what has now become one of the most frequently reviewed and carefully scrutinized Shakespearian films in recent years. The first essay, Lucy Hamilton's 'Baz *vs*. the Bardolaters, Or Why *William Shakespeare's Romeo + Juliet*

Deserves Another Look' (*LFQ* 28:ii[2000] 118–24), resorts to Bakhtin's notion of the carnivalesque in order to highlight the film's subversive elements. In the next essay, 'Misshapen Chaos of Well-Seeming Form: Baz Luhrmann's *Romeo + Juliet*' (*LFQ* 28:ii[2000] 125–31), Crystal Downing defends Luhrmann's radical adaptation by arguing that the Bard himself was a 'master of anachronism, [who] appropriated the vast majority of his stories … and then chang[ed] them according to the values of his time' (p. 130). In 'Pop Goes the Shakespeare: Baz Luhrmann's *Romeo + Juliet*' (*LFQ* 28:ii[2000] 132–9), Elsie Walker compares Luhrmann's translation of Shakesperian dialogue into cinematic shorthand to foreign adaptations of Shakespeare, where 'dialogue loses pre-eminence' (p. 132). The allusive complexity of the original language is replaced by 'the highly self-conscious way in which [Luhrmann] "quotes" various films of diverse genre', including soap operas, spaghetti Westerns and American teen movies, in a 'cheeky metacinematic fashion' (p. 133).

Also included in *LFQ* is Michael D. Friedman's essay, '*Independence Day*: The American *Henry V* and the Myth of David' (*LFQ* 28:ii[2000] 140–8), which draws our attention to suggestive rather than explicit parallels. Friedman himself admits that the film draws on the unacknowledged Shakespearian source 'in the same way that literature often derives its larger structures from myths' (p. 140). Also interested in the intertextual links between Shakespearian material and recent Hollywood's blockbusters is an article in Grady, ed., *Shakespeare and Modernity: Early Modern to Millennium*. Roland Emmerich's *Independence Day* [1996], Paul Verhoeven's *Starship Troopers* [1997] and Shakespeare's *The Merchant of Venice* might seem 'strange bed-fellows'. However, in his article 'Jewish Invader and the Soul of State: *The Merchant of Venice* and Science Fiction Movies' (in Grady, ed., pp. 142–67), Eric Mallin claims that they share a crucial feature. According to Mallin, they all represent the 'marginal figure … as a force for unification and defence of the state' which marshals its powers against that figure' (p. 145). Going back to *LFQ*, Zvika Serper (*LFQ* 28:ii[2000] 149–54) argues that Kurosawa's 'dialectical presentation of blood in his film *Ran* is a *kabuki* influence' (p. 150). In kabuki theatre blood signifies disruption or defiance of a social obligation (*giri*); the spilling of blood is therefore associated with the 'impure and the spineless' (p. 151). Also on Kurosawa's *Ran* is David Jortner's article in *Post Script* (20:i[2000] 82–91). Jortner echoes Guntner's reading of the film as a 'world poised on the brink of nuclear destruction' (Jackson, ed., *The Cambridge Companion*, p. 132). Jortner looks at the film from an 'ecocritical standpoint', by focusing on 'the natural imagery and the relation of the human characters within the environmental landscape' (pp. 82–3). In contrast to earlier critics, such as Christopher Bannon and Julie Kane, Jortner capitalizes on his realization that ecological criticism is a Western phenomenon and needs to be qualified in the light of Japanese environmental theory.

Peter Holland's foreword invites the readers of Thornton Burnett and Wray's remarkable collection *Shakespeare, Film, Fin de Siècle* to stop wondering whether Shakespeare on film is or is not Shakespeare and to focus instead on the 'cultural circumstances that generate the object' (p. xii). From a broadly cultural perspective, Holland regards Luhrmann's *Romeo + Juliet* as more significant than Branagh's *Hamlet* because, independently of 'any judgement of film aesthetics' (p. xiii), the former is the first Shakespeare film to have enjoyed a substantial return on its original investment. Holland notices that 'art-house Shakespeare is a rarity now, where for Orson Welles, Grigori Kozintsev or Akira Kurosawa it was the effective norm' (p. xiii). The editorial introduction that follows clarifies the main objective of the collection, which, as the title suggests, 'confront[s] the significance of the *fin de siècle* and seek[s] to address the relationship of the filmic Shakespeare to millennial themes and images' (p. 4).

By cleverly bridging the gap between bibliography and film studies, the first contributor, Andrew Murphy, in 'The Book on the Screen: Shakespeare Films and Textual Culture' (pp. 10–25), suggests that Branagh's integral version of *Hamlet* rests on the flawed assumption that authenticity can be recovered by conflating any scrap of textual evidence available. By contrast, Peter Greenaway's *Prospero's Books* challenges this perception of the author as a 'solitary, originary figure' (p. 14), by placing emphasis on the multiple sources and discourses from which *The Tempest* originated. Douglas Bruster, 'The Postmodern Theatre of Paul Mazursky's *Tempest*' (pp. 26–39), reads Mazursky's *Tempest* [1982] as an allegory of film-making (p. 31), through which the director extends his meta-filmic concern to consider 'film in relation to drama, television, dance and the plastic arts' (p. 32). Although Mazursky's film predates the *fin de siècle*, its inclusion in Thornton Burnett and Wray's collection is justified by 'its sensitivity to the forms of visual experience, which ... make it ... an acute commentary on the many Shakespeare films that followed its release' (p. 37). In direct contrast with Coursen's disparaging analysis of the Loncraine/McKellen *Richard III* included in Jackson, ed., *The Cambridge Companion*, Stephen Buhler, in 'Camp *Richard III* and the Burdens of Stage/Film History' (pp. 40–57), praises its theatrical and cinematic excess, 'as an array of movie conventions from the 1930s onward are gleefully and sometimes wickedly invoked' (p. 40). Although Neil Sinyard, 'Pacino's *Looking for Richard*' (pp. 58–72), hails Pacino's film as an 'innovative way' of doing Shakespeare, he adds little to our appreciation of what makes it 'radical and far-reaching' (p. 69). More instructively, Amelia Marriette, 'Urban Dystopias: Re-Approaching Christine Edzard's *As You Like It*' (pp. 73–88), suggests that Christine Edzard's *As You Like It* [1992] can best be appreciated in relation to Baudrillard's semiotic theories. Mariette's view that, 'like Brook and Leparge [*sic*], Edzard engages with a late twentieth-century unmooring of philosophical certainties to question stereotypical notions of the play's "realities"', is persuasively argued. In 'Impressions of Fantasy: Adrian Noble's *A Midsummer Night's Dream*' (pp. 89–101), Burnett focuses on the director's use of a cinematic frame which gives prominence to the interpolated character of the Boy. Margaret Jane Kidnie, '"The Way the World is Now": Love in the Troma Zone' (pp. 102–20), offers an engaging reading of Lloyd Kaufman's 1996 *Tromeo and Juliet*. By using Beck's notions of 'advanced modernity' and 'risk society', Kidnie shows how Kaufman denounces the pressures of a misogynist and consumerist society while denying his audience ready-made solutions. James N. Loehlin's '"These violent delights have violent ends": Baz Luhrmann's Millennial Shakespeare' (pp. 121–36) considers the film's distinctively postmodern intertextual allusiveness. Loehlin praises Luhrmann's 'witty parody' of the balcony scene in Zeffirelli's *Romeo and Juliet*, but regards his deference to Zeffirelli for Queen Mab's speech as a 'failure of the imagination' (p. 127). In '"Either for tragedy, comedy": Attitudes to *Hamlet* in Kenneth Branagh's *In the Bleak Midwinter* and *Hamlet*' (pp. 137–46), Emma Smith argues that Branagh's earlier film served to 'divert and displace some of the obstacles to a successful film of

Hamlet' (p. 144). The next essay, by Julie Sanders, 'The End of History and the Last Man: Kenneth Branagh's *Hamlet*' (pp. 147–64), is also devoted to Branagh's *Hamlet*. Sanders first reflects on the significant parallels that were drawn in the British press between Ophelia and Diana, Princess of Wales, soon after her sudden death in a car accident in Paris and around the time of her state funeral. Sanders argues that these parallels are indicative of 'the way in which Shakespeare seems inextricably tied up with the presentation and understanding of monarchy in the last decade of this millennium' (p. 148). Thornton Burnett and Wray's interview with Kenneth Branagh, 'From the Horse's Mouth: Branagh on the Bard' (pp. 165–78), reinforces Smith's theory, as Branagh reveals that '*In the Bleak Midwinter* was an apology for or an excuse for what I was about to do' (p. 171). Judith Buchanan, 'Virgin and Ape, Venetian and Infidel: Labellings of Otherness in Oliver Parker's *Othello*' (pp. 179–202), considers the emphasis placed by Oliver Parker's Othello on resistance to assimilation, through details of costume—the constantly visible African tribal necklace (p. 182)—and occasional voice-overs, which allow the spectator an unusual degree of intimacy with Othello (p. 187). The concluding essay, by Richard Burt, '*Shakespeare in Love* and the End of the Shakespearean: Academic and Mass Culture Constructions of Literary Authorship' (pp. 203–31), deals with representations of Shakespeare as a fictional character in recent romances. By focusing on John Madden's *Shakespeare in Love*, Erica Jong's *Shylock's Daughter* and Julie Beard's *Romance of the Rose*, Burt concludes that, despite opening up feminist possibilities, these three romances reinforce traditional notions of literary authorship.

Deborah Cartmell's *Intepreting Shakespeare on Screen* is clearly structured and conceived. The focus of the book is firmly on mainstream televisual and filmic adaptations, which are more easily accessible to students and teachers. In keeping with its pedagogical objectives, the chapters are arranged into recognizable interpretative categories, namely gender, sexuality, race, violence and nationalism. The first chapter shows the 'ability of film to expose the violence of [Shakespeare's] language' (p. 14). Cartmell notices that a literal stress on violence reduces the cultural value of the filmic product (p. 20). She then tackles the issue of gender by focusing on three mainstream film adaptations of *Hamlet*. Olivier's Ophelia is said to be blameless because she is fundamentally naive and pitiable rather than admirable. Zeffirelli's Ophelia, who 'conveys the impression of a woman who thinks for herself' (p. 34), is conversely seen as showing the product of burgeoning feminist approaches, which are briefly sketched by Cartmell for the benefit of undergraduate students who might come to Shakespeare on film before having encountered literary theory. The following chapter ends with extracts from *Romeo and Juliet* and *Much Ado About Nothing* which show how Zeffirelli, Branagh and Luhrmann manipulate the representation of sexuality in these texts. While the chapter devoted to race explains how cinematic Othellos tend to be whitened and still cause uneasiness if played by black actors, as in Oliver Parker's [1995] film, the last chapter traces Olivier's efforts to make *Henry V* unambiguously nationalist. The most innovative feature of Cartmell's book is the constant blending of film analysis with the most influential critical discourses since the advent of post-structuralist theory. The least appealing trait is the thoroughly 'digested' quality of the material, which might make this book less rather than more attractive to its target readership.

Douglas Brode's *Shakespeare in the Movies: From the Silent Era to 'Shakespeare in Love'*, has been widely reviewed and its shortcomings exposed. Courtney Lehmann (*Cinéaste* 26:i[2000]), for example, highlights the 'highly romanticized fiction of authorship' which Brode shares with recent fictional representations of Shakespeare, including John Madden's *Shakespeare in Love* (see also Richard Burt's essay in Thornton Burnett and Wray, eds., pp. 203–31). This approach, Lehmann aptly remarks, 'patently ignores what we do know about the Shakespearean text ... as an artifact from an era in which the production, transmission, and preservation of texts had much more to do with collaborative contingency than individual determinacy' (p. 62). Kenneth Rothwell (*ShakB* 18:iv[2000]), on the other hand, regards the book as 'oscillat[ing] between the sprightly and the abysmal' because of its 'egregious lack of a bibliography or textual apparatus' and its overall lack of accuracy. Rothwell takes sides with academia, which is so often targeted by Brode's sarcasm, by remarking that 'it is unlikely that many academic nerds would garble together the speeches of the melancholy Jaques and Macbeth (p. 91) or would create a Spoonerism such as "your naked infants piled upon spikes" (p. 80) for Shakespeare's "Your naked infants spitted upon pikes" (*Henry V*, 3.3.38)' (p. 47). Gunn (*TLS* [7 Dec. 2001] 18) is also horrified by a string of misquotations in Brode's book, topped by 'We are the stuff that dreams are made on; our little life rounded by sleep'. Brode's views on the role that academics and critical theory have had in the recently renewed interest in filmic appropriations of Shakespeare are ultimately misleading. According to Brode, while academics embraced theory and found Shakespeare suddenly 'politically incorrect' (p. 11), 'ordinary people inhabiting the real world rediscovered the eternal beauty and ongoing wisdom to be found in his works' (p. 12). Brode's 'romanticized fiction of authorship' is reflected in many aspects of this book, including the chronological arrangement of the plays considered in thirteen successive chapters. As Gunn points out, Brode even manages to get the accepted chronology of the works wrong, by placing *Love's Labour's Lost* before *The Taming of the Shrew* and *Antony and Cleopatra* before *King Lear*.

Brode's first chapter juxtaposes Sam Taylor's and Zeffirelli's *Shrews* as 'polar opposites' (p. 24). The chapter devoted to *Richard III* mentions in passing Warde's personal appearances before the screening of Keane's film [1912], which are much more extensively and proficiently discussed in Freedman's article (reviewed above). Symptomatic of Brode's utter contempt for post-structuralist approaches is his enthusiastic assessment of Luhrmann's cliff-hanger ending in *Romeo + Juliet*, which is effectively deconstructed by Cartmell in *Interpreting Shakespeare on Screen*. The chapter on *Romeo and Juliet* includes a commentary on a Czechoslovakian animated version which is believed to redress some of the shortcomings of the Dieterle/Reinhardt film [1935]. Even the better-informed sections, such as 'Death of Chivalry: *Falstaff* or *Chimes at Midnight*' (pp. 74–8), are let down by a simplistic appreciation of the complex ironies in the Shakespearian source (p. 77). Unsurprisingly enough, Edzard's *As You Like It* is described as 'self-consciously bizarre' for its failure to fully understand and respect the intent of the play (p. 94). Brode dismisses Jarman for his cynical appropriation of 'Will's ... enduring, endearing name' (p. 224) and Greenaway for being an out-of-control extremist (p. 230). At least one cannot blame Brode for mincing his words! On a more positive note, he includes a substantial number of foreign films, thus departing from the current tendency to focus on mainstream films in English.

Julie Taymor's *Titus* [1999] has deservedly received a great deal of attention this year. John Wrathall's 'Bloody Arcade' (*S&S* 10[2000] 24–6) offers useful insights into its eclectic visual strategies, and deals with Taymor's use of what she terms 'Penny Arcade Nightmares'. 'These short surreal sequences, densely packed with superimposed images and symbols', Wrathall explains, 'attempt to get inside the characters' fevered imaginations, providing a visual equivalent of Shakespeare's soliloquies while at the same time making visually explicit the rich imagery of his language' (p. 26). Taymor's own comments on one of these sequences—Lavinia's flashback to her rape and mutilation at the hands of Tamora's sons, Chiron and Demetrius—are particularly enlightening. Taymor explains that by placing Lavinia on a truncated pedestal she conjures two immediately recognizable images which emphasize Lavinia's defilement: Lavinia on the pedestal looks like a ballerina, 'a pristine female image of perfection and grace' (p. 26), and like Marilyn Monroe in one of her most popular photo shoots, with the wind blowing from a passing underground train up her dress. Taymor claims that her eclectic approach was inspired by the play, where Shakespeare 'mixed Greek tragedy and mythology, Ovid's *Metamorphosis* [*sic*], his idea of Roman history ... Roman ritual and Christianity' (p. 26). Miranda Johnson-Haddad's interview with Taymor (*ShakB* 18:iv[2000] 34–6) sheds further light on Taymor's attempt to transfer Shakespeare's style to the screen. Taymor explains that, by setting *Titus* in an imaginary Rome which borrows both from its remote classical past and its early twentieth-century fascist history, she imitates Shakespeare's Rome, which is also both classical and Elizabethan. Maria de Luca and Mary Lindroth's interview with Taymor (*Cinéaste* 25:iii[2000] 28–31) deals with other central issues, such as the juxtaposition of 'haiku-like images' and realist events (p. 28) and the imaginative use of Young Lucius as a framing device. Slightly critical of Taymor's unabashed approach to Shakespeare and violence is a short note—'"To sup with horrors": Julie Taymor's Senecan Feast' (*LFQ* 28[2000] 155–6) by Jim Welsh and John C. Tibbetts—who criticize the film's 'gross indulgence and hideous excesses', while praising its postmodernity (p. 156).

Besides Miranda Johnson-Haddad's interview with Julie Taymor, *Shakespeare Bulletin* (18:iv[2000]) includes a short piece on the Reinhardt/Dieterle *Dream*, a review of Almereyda's *Hamlet* and a review article by Kenneth S. Rothwell. In 'Fragments of a Dream: Photos of Three Scenes Missing from the Reinhardt-Dieterle *Dream*' (*ShakB* 18:iv[2000] 37–8), Michael P. Jensen establishes that at least three of the eighteen scenes which appear in the manuscript screenplay held at the Birmingham Central Library but not in the film were actually shot. Jensen draws his evidence from a 1935 children's book version of the film featuring five photographs of at least three of the missing scenes. Samuel Crowl writes an engaging review of Almereyda's *Hamlet* (*ShakB* 18:iv[2000] 39–40), in which he praises many aspects of the film, including its imaginative reworking of Shakespeare's imagery into contemporary cinematic conventions. Crowl regards Almereyda's *Hamlet* as one of the 'most radically inventive of the many major Shakespeare films of the past decade' (p. 40), alongside Taymor's *Titus* and Luhrmann's *Romeo + Juliet*. However, other aspects of the film—its soundtrack, its restless postmodernity, the graveyard and the duel scenes—are deemed to be 'poorly conceived and executed' (p. 40).

Hedrick and Reynold, eds., *Shakespeare Without Class: Misappropriation of Cultural Capital*, includes two articles devoted to cinematic appropriations, or rather misappropriations, of Shakespeare. Besides reflecting on the terminology— 'misappropriation' is favoured because it is believed to define a creative activity which transforms both the model and its adapter (p. 7)—the introduction offers valuable insights into Madden's *Shakespeare in Love*. The title of the first article by Matt Bergbusch, 'Additional Dialogue: William Shakespeare, Queer Allegory, and *My Own Private Idaho*' (pp. 209–25), highlights a crucial feature of Gus Van Sant's highly personal and far from reverential use of the Shakespearian material in his film *My Own Private Idaho* [1991]. By acknowledging his authoritative source in the final credits, Van Sant denies it the privileged function of 'authorizing point of origin'. Van Sant's intertextual method represents an ironic inversion of the plight of the main character, who is 'unable to abandon his quest for biologist legitimacy' (pp. 214–15). Bergbusch concludes this imaginative and stimulating article by arguing that through Mike's condition Van Sant indirectly criticizes 'straight' adapters of Shakespeare, who replicate Mike's search for his elusive mother by using Shakespeare 'for his enduring status as cultural Home' (p. 218). The second relevant essay included in *Shakespeare Without Class* is James Andreas's '"Where is the Master?" The Technologies of the Stage, Book, and Screen in *The Tempest* and *Prospero's Books*' (pp. 189–208). Andreas claims that, despite its perplexing diversity, Greenaway's film imitates its Shakespearian source by 'illustrating the power of the medium to become the very message itself' (p. 190). According to Andreas, *The Tempest* dramatizes Shakespeare's 'indictment of the "disgrace of writing" by revealing and undermining Prospero's "dominion" through the magical power of the book' (p. 193). Similarly, Greenaway gives a critical appraisal of the political power of his own art. Contrary to James Andreas, James Tweenie (*CinJ* 40:i[2000] 104–26) believes that *Prospero's Books* pays a heartfelt tribute to cinema as a Caliban-like, hybrid form of representation, at the expense of the book, which, Prospero-like, strives to contain the text (p. 107). By comparing it to Gilles Deleuze's notion of 'any-space-whatever', Tweedie regards Greenaway's hybridized screen, where text and image merge into one another, as a 'cinematic nomad space' undermining Prospero's claim of ownership of the island. Tweedie's article is interesting because it blends a more traditional analysis of Greenaway as a neo-baroque and mannerist image-maker with recent postcolonial readings of *The Tempest*. Tweedie highlights a further political aspect of Greenaway's work by claiming that *Prospero's Books* foregrounds 'the social and cultural status of the book' in 1980s Britain, when literary heritage 'served more than ever as a mooring for a reified national past' (p. 105).

Also devoted to exploring the relationship between theatre and cinema is Lia M. Hotchkiss's article 'The Cinematic Appropriation of Theater: Introjection and Incorporation in *Rosencrantz and Guildenstern Are Dead*' (*QRFV* 17:ii[2000] 161– 86). Hotchkiss aims to show how the relationship between theatre and cinema can best be described through specific psychological mechanisms, such as projection, introjection and incorporation. Cinema is believed to constitute itself through both filmic and psychological projection. If the human subject constitutes itself by 'projecting everything that constitutes unpleasure' (p. 163), cinema similarly 'exists in part because of and through denying its relation to its theatrical other' (p. 167). Hotchkiss claims that Stoppard's film, like cinema in general, tends to blur the boundaries between theatre and cinema, so that the relationship between the two media resembles the psychological mechanism of incorporation rather than introjection. Among the best examples drawn from Stoppard's film is the players' cart. Initially the cart 'can be either cart or stage at any given moment, but not both simultaneously, thus [suggesting] a relation of substitution [or introjection] rather than identification [or incorporation]' (p. 167). The cart then becomes an 'engulfing theatrical space' in the middle section of the film, which is, however, 'in turn engulfed by the cinematic travelling shots as the stage is folded up and transformed into a mere cart wending its way across the cinematic landscape' (p. 185) in the final sequence.

Two other psychoanalytical categories are used by Marina Favila to identify recurring patterns in Shakespeare's comedies and twentieth-century romantic non-Shakespearian movies. In 'Philobats and Ocnophils: Romantic Pairings in Shakespeare and Film' (*UCrow* 20[2000] 21–41), Favila argues that romantic (or secondary) love is an attempt to return to the 'magical period of "primary love"' (p. 22), namely the 'magical fusion between mother and child' (p. 21). Favila defines 'ocnophilia' as 'the need to cling to people … in order to recapture the oneness shared with the mother', and 'philobatism' as the '[denial of] need for other people, which promotes the ideal of self-sufficiency'. Favila then reflects on the apparently unorthodox casting of women as philobats in twentieth-century romantic plotlines and in Shakespeare's comedies, where the 'illusion of the Phallic Woman is amply celebrated' (p. 28) and the illusion of her self-sufficiency continues 'even after the obligatory defrocking (castrating?) of her masculine role at the end' (p. 29).

For a collection that advertises itself as a survey of 'both British cinema itself and the ways in which scholars are writing about it' (p. 1), Ashby and Higson, eds., *British Cinema, Past and Present* proves a disappointment to those interested in Shakespeare on screen. John Madden's *Shakespeare in Love* [1998] is only mentioned in passing as an example of 'British films which enjoyed considerable critical and box-office success in the 1990s' (p. 1). Derek Jarman's *The Tempest* [1979] and *Prospero's Books* [1991] are only briefly compared for the prominence both films grant to *mise-en-scène* (p. 330). Little attention is devoted to the music inspired by Shakespeare's work, both in the classical tradition and as an accompaniment to recent appropriations of Shakespeare on film. An exception is 'Music and Meaning in Four Versions of the Romeo and Juliet Story' (*Cithara* 39[2000] 3–14), where John J. Joyce explains how music has traditionally added 'important dimensions' (p. 3) to the reception of *Romeo and Juliet*. After dealing with Tchaikovsky's *Romeo and Juliet Fantasie* and Nino Rota's music score in 'Dino [*sic*] Zeffirelli's' film (p. 1), Joyce's article becomes more argumentative. Joyce, for example, claims that Bernstein's inversion of themes in his Broadway musical *West Side Story* [1957] is meant to suggest that 'the love that Tony and Maria have for each other is contrasted less with the hatred of the world about them, than their indissoluble ties to the nature of the society in which they live' (p. 10). Joyce's article ends with a tribute to Luhrmann and Hooper's punk rock adaptation of *Romeo and Juliet*.

Several review essays and useful bibliographies have been published this year, a clear sign of the growing academic interest in the subject. As mentioned above, this year's special issue of *EMLS* includes a bibliography of criticism on 'Shakespeare on Television' compiled by José Ramón Díaz-Ferández. The bibliography stems from the realization that, although 'the study of Shakespeare on television has often suffered from an unjust comparison with the medium of film … [it] constitutes a field of its own within the area of Shakespeare on Screen' (p. 1). *The Bulletin of Bibliography* includes another useful, if more narrowly focused, bibliography. In 'A Bibliography on Three Films of *Hamlet*: Covering Literature from 1948 to 1999', Julie A. Davies lists articles and notes, books and book chapters, dissertations and film reviews, interviews and theses generated by three major film adaptations of *Hamlet* by Olivier [1948], Zeffirelli [1990] and Branagh [1997]. Davies's bibliography also includes a short section devoted to general bibliographies about the play itself, dating from 1958 to 1999.

Robert F. Willson (*ShakB* 18:iv[2000] 39–41) writes a short essay on the *Cinéaste* supplement on 'Shakespeare in the Cinema' (*Cinéaste* 24[1998] 28–67), which was reviewed in more detail by my predecessor (*YWES* 79[2000] 266–7). This year's special issue of *LFQ* concludes with a useful review chapter (*LFQ* [2000] 157–60) by the journal's editor, Jim Walsh. Courtney Lehmann (*Cinéaste* 26[2000] 62–6) reviews nine recent books on 'Shakespeare on Screen', while Kenneth Rothwell (*ShakB* 18:iv[2000] 44–7) focuses on four of the books reviewed in this section. Openly critical of some of these books is Dan Gunn (*TLS* [7 Dec. 2001] 18). In Gunn's view, recent attempts to chart 'Shakespeare on Screen' as a new field of enquiry share a tendency to repress 'the ghost of the theatre', which 'comes back to haunt [them], lending an awkwardness to some of the enthusiasm, an inflation to claims and a vehemence to judgement'. If Cartmell is said to have 'little patience with most Shakespeare films', Gunn has little patience with Cartmell, who is accused of 'castigat[ing] her chosen subjects with cultural-materialist maxims' and 'rat[ing] her students almost as poorly as she does Shakespeare films'. If *The Cambridge Companion to Shakespeare on Film* is praised as a 'cogently organised' collection, Gunn agrees with Walsh that Brode's book is unusually sloppy and oversimplified for the standards normally associated with OUP. *Magazine Littéraire* (393[2000] 63–5) includes a short survey of Shakespeare's films from Beerbohm's excerpt from *King John* [1899] to Julie Taymor's *Titus* [1999]. The author, Philippe Pilard, perpetuates a common mistake by referring to the interpolated scene in Beerbohm's *King John* as the signing of the Magna Charta, as opposed to the death of the king at Swinstead Abbey. The same mistake, as Kenneth S. Rothwell points out (*ShakB* 18:iv[2000] 47), can be found in Thornton Burnett and Wray's introduction to an otherwise consistently stimulating collection (p. 3). The impressive quality and variety of this year's contributions reinforces Pilar's conclusion, which makes a suitable ending for this section as a whole. If, Pilar argues, the flourishing of Shakespeare on film around the middle of the twentieth century contributed to the popularization of Shakespeare, its "renaissance" in the 1990s turned cinematic Shakespeare into a global phenomenon.

Regrettably, Sarah Hatchuel's *A Companion to Branagh's Shakespearean Films* and articles in Maurice Hunt's *Approaches to Teaching Shakespeare's 'Romeo and Juliet'*, Alice G. den Otter's *Relocating Praise: Literary Modalities and Rhetorical Contexts* and in *Publications of the Missouri Philological Association* were not available for review at the time of writing.

4. Criticism

(a) General

Frank Kermode's *Shakespeare's Language* inevitably caused a stir. The colon-less title suggests the issue he addresses alongside his scrutiny of Shakespearian texts: Kermode would like to purge criticism of its self-serving and pulpy convolutions. His frankness is deceptive, however. His work is full of theory, informed by the most capable of Shakespearian scholarship. Ostensibly he writes against a current grain that privileges the theatrical over the poetical. Kermode's study balances current reclamations of the sense of the plays through performance with his own poetics of development in Shakespeare's writing, supported richly throughout by his historical and general erudition, and wielding the tools of close reading to show the development of Shakespeare's authored language through his writing life as it appears in a succession of the plays.

Kermode discusses the development of 'personation', the illusion of psychological hinterland created by artful writing, demonstrating the point by contrasting the early *Titus Andronicus* with the later *Coriolanus*. Titus describes Lavinia's gory appearance as a poet would, rather than reacting to it as a real person might (p. 7). Where early pieces expound and rhetoricize, later tragedies such as *Coriolanus* and *King Lear* encompass speaking silences instead (p. 11)—clever investment of language rather than mere expenditure, so to speak.

I found the combination of close reading and historical panorama exhilarating. To any reader unused to pre-1970s new criticism it may well come as a revelation, as might Kermode's attack on what he sees as the presumption of some modern theory (p. viii), reflected in his index. Auden, Bate, Gurr, Wells and Yates achieve it, alongside Johnson, Coleridge and Eliot, and 'Carnival' appears, but without Bakhtin, or Bourdieu. His historicist scope is generous, however, including the possibility that Shakespeare was a tutor in Catholic Lancashire (p. 17), one that others have been quicker to dismiss, and with less justification (see Peter Milward's 'Shakespeare in Lancashire' in support of this idea, *Month* 33:iv[2000] 141–6). Kermode's comprehensive historical knowledge is lightly worn, and always related back to the words themselves, and to their development by Shakespeare from 'elocution' into 'drama' (p. 21). His insights are born of scrupulous concentration on the text; that they are also informed by a lifetime of wider study is just the reader's good luck. There are glowing encomiums on the cover, and Eric Griffiths has described this revival of Shakespeare the poet as 'a noble aim' (*TLS* 5083[1 Sept. 2000] 3–4). To paraphrase what he called 'one of the most miraculous moments in Shakespeare' (p. 274), Kermode wields a chisel fine enough to cut breath, reviving Shakespeare the poet, if not the author, after two decades of immobility.

A wider selection of critical tools and a fine complement to Kermode's work is Sean McEvoy's *Shakespeare: The Basics*, an introduction to help newcomers to Shakespeare studies navigate through the proliferating uses and theories surrounding the texts. Given the largeness of McEvoy's aim, one's first impulse is to turn to the bibliography to see what sort of scope he achieves: it is a thoughtful, wide-ranging and 'current' list. If that sounds like a 'safer in the middle' conception, the contents page suggests the engaging energy of the work: one is thrown immediately into a robust pan-theoretical dialogue with the period ('Shakespeare wrote for theatre-goers, not readers'), reception of his works ('vocabulary changes over time'), his methods ('Rhetoric'; 'Estrangement'; 'Performance'), and current concerns ('Performance Now'; 'Homosexuality in Shakespeare's Time'). The last is one of a series of 'boxed' asides on particular subjects, McEvoy's method for including the extra commentary necessary to modern approaches without over-encumbering a narrative reading, giving students or teachers the choice of whether or not to apply theory. The box on 'Religion', for instance, provides a historical context for the Reformation and, like Kermode, raises the possibility that Shakespeare was 'in the service of a Roman Catholic family in Lancashire', drawing attention to possible effects of Roman Catholicism in plays, such as 'sincere repentance' in *The Tempest* (p. 157). Main divisions—'Understanding the Text', 'Shakespeare's Language', 'Types of Stage Action', and 'What the Plays Mean in Performance', are each subdivided into sections such as 'Verse', 'Verse and Prose', 'Rhetoric' and so on, the boxes adding value to the whole. Sections end with a three- or four-point bullet-summary and 'Further Reading'. This is a thoroughly researched, well-managed resource for teachers and students.

In a more traditional reading of Shakespeare texts, erudite and subtly theorized, Barry B. Adams's *Coming-to-Know: Recognition and the Complex Plot in Shakespeare* discusses poetics, specifically the mechanics of the Aristotelian moment of *anagnôrisis* as it operates on the reader. He investigates mainly the comedies (p. 5), but crosses boundaries into other works. He makes no claims on a reader's familiarity with wider current theories, confining himself to the text and working his way meticulously through the various understandings of what Aristotle's few words on 'recognition' (using Gerald F. Else's definition [1957]) might mean, and how such understanding might apply to the construction and reception of the plays. It is, as he puts it, something akin to the structuralist's search for 'formal patterns that function as conditions of meaning'—a 'blend of poetics and criticism' (p. 5). He extends Aristotle's idea of the discovery of biological kinship into a recognition of spousal/near-spousal relationships, which he then explores in depth, illustrating and expanding his work skilfully throughout. Chapter 1 is a history of Aristotle scholarship and its application to Shakespeare. The Aristotelian mechanics are simple, the applications and permutations, as described by Adams, manifold. His method is to present detailed description of the mechanics of the plays' plots rather than freewheeling off with the theorists (p. 16), siting the reader right in among the gears and crankshafts of Shakespeare scholarship. Any reader unacquainted with the ins and further ins of the Aristotelian debate will be especially grateful to Adams for his inclusion of Northrop Frye's ingeniously simple reanalysis of Aristotelian permutations of plot into '"and then" stories' and '"hence" stories' (p. 20). Adams's explorations and insights are interesting, the comments on *Measure for Measure* particularly so, given the problems associated with 'recognition' in this play. Intriguing theoretical primrose paths are continually opened up by Adams's meticulous study, which he himself resists the temptation to explore.

In contrast to his approach—almost its mirror-image—is Cathleen T. McLoughlin's *Shakespeare, Rabelais, and the Comical-Historical*, a comparative reading of Shakespeare designed to open up his handling of Falstaff in *1* and *2 Henry IV* (which she redefines as 'comical-historical', p. 1) to the possibilities in other texts, including Rabelais's *Gargantua and Pantagruel*. The intertextual parallel she draws between the battlefield discovery of the magnificent bulk of the 'dead' hanger-on next to the slight corpse of the philosopher in *1 Henry IV* and Lucian's *The Parasite* (p. 39) is one among many illustrations of Shakespeare's debt to the traditions of ironic humour. McLoughlin establishes enough similarities to persuade, including the possibility of a genealogical root 'in Erasmus and through Erasmus in Lucian' (p. 2), redressing what she sees as an over-emphasis on the influence on Shakespeare of the carnivalesque (in Bakhtin's *Rabelais and his World*) at the expense of the effects of his humanist education. In the absence of any recorded English translation of Rabelais before 1653 the parallels suggested by critics such as Anne Lake Prescott have been tenuous, however, as McLoughlin admits. Having had the arena of debate so clearly set out at the start, the reader might look forward to a tight comparative reading of Shakespeare and Rabelais, but McLoughlin, I feel confusingly, widens her investigation to include visual arts and Bakhtin's 'dialogic imagination'. It is never made clear why it really follows that a 'polyphony of the works allow [*sic*] for a polyphony in interpretations' (p. 4). McLoughlin reminds us that a sixteenth-century writer or audience was used to 'reading' any text on many different levels and probably felt no overriding need to single out any one interpretation as definitive (p. 71). Lucian, Erasmus, Shakespeare and Rabelais, McLoughlin's study seems to show, need no lessons from us in the principles and uses of intertextuality (p. 72).

In *Shakespeare's Reading*, another contextualizing study of the possible extent of Shakespeare's borrowings, Robert Miola confines himself with admirable asceticism to his brief, confronting the reader immediately with the observation that, as nothing can be known about Shakespeare the man, he will discuss only what is documented of Shakespeare the reader as disclosed in his work. In contrast to McLoughlin's approach, Miola's scholasticism also argues against the 'Shakespeare as genius' school: 'at first the idea of Shakespeare as a reader may shock and disturb' he warns on page 1, perhaps with irony, but insists that George Bernard Shaw's borrower of stories, a Shakespeare actively engaged in the hot texts and issues of his time, is preferable to an isolated genius. He redirects readers steeped in twenty-first-century individualism to the Renaissance world of *imitatio*. His approach is simple, his language clear, his research meticulous and more than sufficient for what is really an introduction to a historicized Shakespeare—more than just a résumé of literary sources and easier to read than Baldwin's 1944 work. Chapter 7 offers a summary of Shakespeare's reading and how he used it, but the work describes a wider background: Renaissance attitudes to reading and writing, for instance, or their ideological athleticism in debate. He introduces the 'Reading Wheel' (pp. 4–5), a Heath Robinson contraption that enabled a Renaissance reader to 'surf' for bits of information. It is this freely associative aspect of Elizabethan writing and reading that Miola wishes to emphasize, a subtle but significant insight into authorship for teachers and students alike. The practicalities of 'sourcing' elements in a text are also addressed (p. 14). Miola's two tables cover both principal sources and traditions—not intended to be complex, and never explored theoretically, but a highly informative pointer to an intertextual Shakespeare and the reading practices of his day.

From the Bard's literary recreations we turn to recreations of the Bard. If our literary remodellings of his works epitomize the ideal cultural construct of the age, what do our pictorial recreations say? In a fascinating aside to the more usual textual preoccupations, Jonathan Bate discusses the curious urge to illustrate drama in his essay 'Pictorial Shakespeare: Text, Stage, Illustration' (in Golden, ed., *Book Illustrated: Text, Image, and Culture, 1770–1930*, pp. 31–60), offering insights into the process of cultural reconstruction. Now that examples of old illustrated editions have become more than ever accessible, the editor Catherine Golden sees the need to quantify and investigate the connections that cross 'genres and national boundaries' (p. 5) and Bate responds to this with a diachronistic survey of illustrated Shakespeare editions, discussing the implications of the frozen moment of picture versus the 'dynamic performance' of the play (p. 9). Bate describes a succession of pictorial recreations, discussing the links and discontinuities between actual production of the plays and those illustrations accompanying the editions with enthusiasm and insight. 'By arresting the moment, the act of illustration absorbs the play through the eye of the beholder into the dimension of imaginative interiority. *Hamlet* is a play, not a novel; but an illustration of a moment in *Hamlet* is formally no different from an illustration of a moment in a novel'—far from the boards of the Globe, 'part of the process whereby the Bard was novelized and historicized—a process that was itself crucial to his "remaking" as a universal genius' (p. 34). Bate goes on to discuss the emergence of empire and other cultural issues, expressed as illustration. This is both a valuable addition to study of Shakespearian re-creation and a fascinating reflection on our susceptibility to the persuasive power of the visual.

Douglas Bruster's *Quoting Shakespeare: Form and Culture in Early Modern Drama* is another exploration of 'a Shakespeare both quoting and quoted' (p. 3) in the style of Jonathan Bate and Robert Miola, another attack on excess in current theoretical approaches in the vein of Frank Kermode. Bruster's study challenges the way in which new historicism has, by focusing on a multiplicity of 'texts' in a period, 'left us *less* conscious of the fact that literature itself has a history'. By exercising a broader vision of time than 'New Historicism's often limited window of inquiry', Bruster aims to uncover the 'historicity of works' (pp. 3–4). There are currently so many of these attempts to open a better window on the past that perhaps one should classify it: New Perspectivism? Bruster, drawing on Julia Kristeva's original concept of a chronologically rather than synchronically linked intertextuality (p. 33), calls his own tracing of lines of appropriation '"writerly" intertextuality' (pp. 3, 171). The somewhat didactic intent makes for a challenging piece, and this basic message remains the same throughout, that 'the *copia* of [Shakespeare's] plays should prompt us to enforce a skepticism about what we believe we have discovered in his works' (p. 49). Bruster expands on his points gleefully, almost daring other critics to keep up with his rolling argument. The 'Shepherd' as a pastoral parallel for the 'eloquent, controlling' agents in Shakespeare plays is discussed in chapter 3, the subject of agency then unfolded like a complicated fan into his proposal that Will Kemp, not the concept of slavery, informed the character of Caliban, and that Shakespeare was 'quoting the playhouse in the *Tempest*', not colonialism (p. 117). The suspicion that Bruster is targeting sites dear to the heart of some modern criticism is increased by the topic of the next chapter, 'Quotation and the Madwomen's Language', but his comments on John Houston's *Maltese Falcon* and Dennis Potter's *Singing Detective* (pp. 204, 202) suggest that this is more than just new historicism stretched lengthwise. His wide bibliography and energetic notes and references open up areas of further study.

Do the uses to which Shakespeare is put need to be academic per se? The projected readership of John O. Whitney and Tina Packer's *Power Plays: Shakespeare's Lessons in Leadership and Management* can be deduced by the use of the unglossed initials 'CEO' (Chief Executive Officer) on the first page. Shakespeare is here used as a cache of words and role-plays on the subject of power manipulation to stimulate business brains. Harold Bloom, as 'an unabashed proselytizer of Bardolatry', is co-opted to sell the idea of Shakespeare as usable genius (p. 11), Bloom's (ironic?) suggestion that Shakespeare has '*invented us*' being offered unmediated in support. The byzantine company anecdotes that thread the Shakespeare extracts together are at least as dramatic as the plays, as if industry invented the narratives and Shakespeare merely borrowed them. Why should the 'power of [Shakespeare's] language' not be used to tweak sales figures (p. 12)? Some would argue that such use comes close to its original purpose. The authors certainly know and admire his works, but, really, Shakespeare was braver than this—page 12 ('Profits sagging, business flat? Then you'd better rally the troops, just as … Henry V did before the Battle of Agincourt') neglects to mention Henry's habit of hanging under-achievers, for instance. 'And then there's *Hamlet*' (p. 12). Like him, my 'decision models' are 'in conflict': in academic terms this book is a lively joke, but on the other hand it raises interesting eddies in the debate over who owns Shakespeare, anticipating the larger questions addressed by Jonathan Bate and Douglas Bruster. It would make an interesting discussion-raiser for teachers of school and undergraduate students, as well as widening applications of Shakespeare studies into the management school. Didn't the Chorus in *Henry V* have something to say about the power of theatre to add noughts to any figure one cares to think of?

A more widely useful academic resource is Alan and Veronica Palmer's *Who's Who in Shakespeare's England*, containing 'over 700 concise biographies of Shakespeare's contemporaries' from 1588 to 1623. It covers the arts, politics, the Church, the court, the 'secret service', and the theatre, and attempts to build up a picture of Shakespeare's acquaintance and possible influences. This sounds a dangerous, even forlorn, hope, but the authors have managed their information to provide users with the opportunity to draw their own conclusions. Along with the suggested candidates for the 'dark lady' or 'Mr. W.S.', for instance, are details of the various champions for each, and further reading accompanies most of the entries. The purpose is to widen out from the obsessive Bard- and London-centricity of so much current study by mapping a wider geographical and social network; one, moreover, that includes the females 'monstrously ignored' in the original Victorian *Dictionary of National Biography*. A useful preliminary overview, broken up into classifications such as 'Court and Society', 'Women', 'Occult', 'Underworld', allows quick reference and supplies a concise picture of names and occupations, further broken down into subsections where appropriate. The entries themselves are succinct, giving added details, interconnections with other entries, and just enough information to situate the subject and stimulate further research. There is also a sound glossary at the end (why 'Rosicrucians' but no 'Jesuits' though?). Concise, usable—an eminently sensible resource in a historicist age.

Howard and Sherstow, eds., *Marxist Shakespeares*, applies the analytical possibilities of Marxist methodology to Shakespeare studies in an attempt to expose the historical scaffolding upon which Shakespeare constructed class and gender in his work. It is part of a series designed to review and comment on cultural materialist works of the last decade for Shakespeare students. A useful introduction by the editors describes applications of Marxist thought in a literary context, praising Stuart Hall in particular for opening up Marxist approaches into wider modes and topics (p. 3). The essays cover a wide range of applications. Peter Stallybrass and Richard Halpern discuss the persistence and action of ghosts, from that of Old Hamlet to the troubling persistence of Shakespeare the author; Dympna Callaghan and others cover female labour and creativity expressed through (literally) materialism in forms such as embroidery or laundering; Walter Cohen comments on the relationship between early modern theatre and the global expansion of trade; Richard Wilson discusses Shakespeare's theatrical reconstruction of aristocratic patronage and the balance of production between power and commerce, read via Bourdieu; Kiernan Ryan challenges historicism, and Sherstow covers scarcity and plenitude in early modern aesthetics, and Shakespeare as Jean-Luc Nancy's 'singular voice in common' (p. 15).

Two critics have gone to drawing classes for new perspectives on Shakespeare. Christopher Pye's overview of recent critical accounts of the materialized or epistemologized subject in *The Vanishing: Shakespeare, the Subject, and Early Modern Culture* amply demonstrates the complexities of unravelling it from its historical/post-historical accounts. Using a materialized Lacanianism, Pye argues that society came into being alongside early modernity and that any discussion of the emergence of the early modern subject goes alongside discussion of the social and symbolic transformation associated with the emergence of the modern state (pp. 7–8). Despite being a reiteration of Marx's idea of society, as he points out, his conception of subject/society is a highly rarefied one, one 'inseparable from the question of its own staging'. How (indeed) can one 'imagine the subject ... not as a function of a pre-given or pressured social totality ... but without "society" as a prior cause?' (pp. 8–9). Pye discusses at length the relationships between the subject and sociality, symbolic systems and history as exemplified in Shakespeare, through Renaissance attitudes to perspective. Perspective, for Pye, connects/intersects with that 'ur-instance of subjective interpellation' in Western culture, the Annunciation, which he depicts and then deconstructs scrupulously (p. 65). Pye's vision of the subject as an effect of its own staging becomes a discussion of the Renaissance cabinet of curiosities in all its 'hieroglyphic fascination' (p. 138). The formal perspective drawings of museums in his figures are intended to connect with the closet scene in *Hamlet* and the 'exploded matter' of Gertrude's sexuality and the body of Polonius (p. 140), but I was distracted by their similarity with the 'Annunciations' previously reproduced; the same perspectives but with Virgin and Angel silently erased. There can be no discrete subject, angelic or otherwise, in such a view of history and art.

Perspective views are also addressed in Alison Thorne's *Vision and Rhetoric in Shakespeare: Looking through Language*, in both senses—it builds upon the early modern acceptance of the interconnectedness of the arts while managing not to lose its own sense of critical perspective. Thorne makes a fine distinction between attempting to redefine the zeitgeist of a whole era and offering a new perspective on some specific part of it, confining herself to Shakespearian 'viewpoint'. She builds on Norman Rabkin's proposal that the opposing perspectives in Shakespeare make any single resolution almost unachievable for individual readers or auditors. Thorne stresses the function of viewpoint as verbal construct, a 'process of rhetorical suggestion and inference' (p. xiii), effectively sidelining twentieth-century structuralist approaches in favour of Renaissance theories on the relationship between the visual and the rhetorical. Conflicting viewpoints are reformulated as 'a politicized struggle between a neoclassical aesthetic and other, more fantastical ways of seeing the world excluded or suppressed by that aesthetic' (p. xvi). Just as painting had to learn to 'see' in perspective—a mathematical construct—and to manipulate perception like a poet (p. 3), so Shakespeare as a dramatist had to reconcile the visual and theoretical on stage, visual perspective reproduced as rhetorical device, Euclid replaced by Cicero (pp. 2–3). The principles behind the 'vanishing point' of a painting and the single didactic end of rhetorical composition seem not to conform to the double perspective of a Shakespeare play, however: Escher seems a better visual counterpart. Thorne discusses the effect of Erasmian educational principles of 'expressive methodology' (p. 9) on Shakespeare, with the perspectives not falsified but multiplied by *copia*, saying one thing many ways. Edgar's view from Dover cliff, in Thorne's structure, is as advanced in *rhetorical* terms as Gloucester's is not. Dislocations of truth and seeming are widely discussed in relation to the Shakespeare canon. Even Sidney's poetic can be reviewed through Thorne's interesting methodology: a rich, widely researched book.

'Caliban and Ariel Write Back' (pp. 165–76) is Jonathan Bate's contribution to Alexander and Wells, eds., *Shakespeare and Race*, interesting in the light of his work on the 'novelization' of Shakespeare and the general drift away from highly abstracted theory discussed elsewhere. (Most of the essays are reprinted from *Shakespeare Survey*, but those by Margo Hendricks and Celia Daileader are new.) The aim of the whole work is to explore changing perceptions of the understanding and interpretation of 'race', but it inevitably exposes a changing Shakespeare, especially as the editorial policy tends towards the widely inclusive. Bate's essay sits a little restlessly alongside some (or vice versa), but I found the breadth useful, especially as overviewed by Margo Hendricks. The essays draw a wide range of distinctions between 'authorial intent' and 'subsequent appropriation'—helpful to a new Shakespeare scholar, although conflation of 'race' issues with 'black' issues was sometimes confusing. Margo Hendricks, 'Surveying 'Race' in Shakespeare' (pp. 1–22), looks at the 'epistemology of race' in Shakespeare's day (p. 1), not just crude indicators of difference in the plays. Her astute identification of the political as much as literary forces that inform a society's 'racial imagination' opens up the arena of debate, suggesting other motivations for a negative attitude than the simply racist (p. 3). G.K. Hunter's essay 'Elizabethans and Foreigners' (pp. 37–63) explores impact and response rather than physical difference, using Elizabethan travel narratives to illustrate some assumptions about foreigners: 'material for caricature [rather than] character' (p. 45), leaving one yearning for a glimpse into a private diary or two—was there really no other sort of traveller than this? Hendricks calls it and Bernard Harris's [1958] essay before it, 'A Portrait of a Moor' (pp. 23–37), early new historicism, and expresses astonishment that, 'despite their dates', the two can put together arguments on a Renaissance English discourse of race without recourse to contemporary theoretical discussions (p. 5). Barbara Everett, '"Spanish Othello": The Making of Shakespeare's Moor' (pp. 64–82), asks if there is 'a link between the politics of Shakespeare and the politics of race inherent in his canon' (p. 5), re-colouring Othello's Moorishness tawny not black, and redefining the significance of Iago as St James 'Moor-killer' (Santiago Matamoros, patron saint of

Spain) in the process. Wole Soyinka's challenging re-culturalization of Shakespeare, 'Shakespeare the Living Dramatist' (pp. 82–101), is a discomfiting exposure of west European and other combat zones in literary criticism and theory. Ostensibly it is a smile-raiser, but Soyinka bursts the bubble of 'Shayk-al-Subhair' in the reader's face at the end, leaving a thought-provoking trace of acridity which the next essay does little to erase. There were 1,156 German productions of Shakespeare noted in the *Shakespeare Jahrbuch* in 1912, according to Balz Engler in 'Shakespeare in the Trenches' (pp. 101–11). In England the king was knighting a favourite actor (playing Caesar) with a prop-room sword, but few productions actually appeared. Such bizarre, theatrical appropriations are discussed alongside Germany's requisitioning of Shakespeare in this well-supported historicist account of the re-nationalization of the Bard. That re-nationalization included the excision of the unruly Shakespearian libido to produce an idealized national erotic. At the turn of the eighteenth century, the arena of discussion in Michael Dobson's 'Bowdler and Britannia: Shakespeare and the National Libido' (pp. 112–23), family and sexual irregularities in the plays were tidied up, bringing the Bard into line with chaste Britannia. James Shapiro, 'Shakspur and the Jewbill' (pp. 124–38), looks at another contemporary recreation, Garrick's Stratford Jubilee of 1769, arguing that it was targeted not only at the alien Jew, but at the British poor. In a lithe piece of intellectual theatre around the identity of Shakespeare, Laurence Lerner, in 'Wilhelm S and Shylock' (pp. 139–50), distracts the English reader's too ready identification with 'our' Will with a thought-provoking reversal of status. Lerner's tumbling routine is designed to expose the political and ideological machinery of 'normal' Shakespeare study which assumes that 'meaning is made rather than found' (p. 144): a well-executed back-trick. 'Cruelty, *King Lear* and the South African Land Act 1913' (pp. 151–64) is a cultural materialist view by Martin Orkin which explores the pressures on readings of Shakespeare in troubled times, using *King Lear* as a matrix on which to map South African and sixteenth-century Warwickshire land division. Neither this nor the subsequent essay by Jonathan Bate is mentioned in Margo Hendricks's overview, perhaps arriving too late to be included. Bate's essay (pp. 165–76) adds its voice to that of Bruster et al. in another sharp riposte to the '"radical critics" of the 1970s and 1980s' who claimed the first revisionary reading of *The Tempest* (p. 165). Bate accuses them of merely nodding at the precedence of black writers such as Octave Mannoni, writing in the 1940s and 1950s, hence reproducing the culture-blindness they claimed to be exposing. Bate's discussion of other voices, such as Braithwaite's Caliban, proposes a generous Shakespeare who, in not attempting to impose guidance on the cultures he dramatizes, allows their voices to be freely borrowed—a reversal of the Bard's use by European nationalism? The liberal theatrical practice of 'colour-blind casting' is investigated with vigour by Celia R. Daileader in 'Casting Black Actors: Beyond Othellophilia' (pp. 177–202). Three racially marked Shakespearian roles plus a 25 per cent non-white acting complement in the RSC add up to problems. She confronts wider issues than the theatrical, however: the director may be '"blind" to "colour", [but] the audience often will not be', and it was not a critic who left Ray Pearson with his hand in a cast in Brussels, but racist thuggery on the street (p. 177). We ignore or theorize away such issues at our peril. The whole lively collection can be revisited by way of the last essay, Ania Loomba's '"Delicious traffick": Racial and

Religious Difference on Early Modern Stages' (pp. 203–24), a richly supported close reading of our heritage of textual attitudes to 'race'.

Mary Bly, *Queer Virgins and Virgin Queans on the Early Modern Stage*, explores other communities: she argues for the inclusion of a wider 'erotic minority' than the homoerotic in queer theory (p. 17). She offers a Bly-on-the-wall glimpse into the activities of a little-studied company of boy players, the King's Revels or the first Whitefriars, who performed for a short period in 1607–8, focusing particularly on the high incidence of bawdy puns in the work of their play-writers. Her method is logical, her touch light: she makes no attempt to help poor Derrida work out how a pun is possible (p. 4), but sets out to engage with it as an early modern audience might have done, shoulder to shoulder with men and women able to laugh at homoerotic double entendre long before the vocabulary of homosexuality appeared in English (p. 5). Bly explores the mechanics of the Whitefriars pun as it cements a new early modern community—a temporary but identifiable one. By celebrating deviance in the shape of 'cross-dressed sodomites and lustful women' it functions as a site where such erotic minorities can experience the sense of community which Bly claims was denied them in daily life (an argument that begs too much at times). Bly draws on a variety of Shakespearian and other texts, following the transfer of homoerotic icons and imagery from a poetic economy to that of the theatre audience, ending with an attempt to juggle the nature of the company, of queer puns, and of authorial collaboration to gain insight into that elusive creature, the contemporary audience (chapter 5). Whether one is ultimately persuaded of the links, one is left very much better informed about the boys of Whitefriars and the men who marketed them. Bly's style is swift and sure and her insights into early modern sexual economies shrewd. Any student of role play, cross-dressing or homoerotics in Shakespeare will welcome this work.

Katherine Eggert's *Showing like a Queen: Female Authority and Literary Experiment in Spenser, Shakespeare, and Milton* represents another challenge to reductivism, confronting what Eggert sees as new historicism's obsession with Elizabeth. The explorations of Stephen Greenblatt and others into the varying degrees of reciprocity between the queen and the art that surrounded her have sometimes overstated the case, in Eggert's view, finding Elizabeth in every 'rampaging or squelched female authority' in Elizabethan literature (p. 2). Eggert identifies a debate between Goodman's 1558 identification of woman-rule as 'that monster in nature' and Plowden's insistence that the body politic is not to be devalued by any frailty in the natural body of the monarch. Far from female rule having a one-way influence on Elizabethan literature, Eggert insists, the debates around it opened up the possibilities of a body politic outside that of the monarch that made Parliament possible (pp. 5–6). Shakespeare and his literary contemporaries were, in Eggert's view, stimulated rather than limited by the reimaginative possibilities of a female monarch. Hélène Cixous's linguistically constituted femininity read alongside the Renaissance approach raises interesting insights about the uses of drama to counter the dangerous instabilities of femininity. Eggert relates the unbounded female desire of the 'jointress' in *Hamlet* to the chaste 'imperial votress' in *Midsummer Night's Dream*, and constructs a Hamlet locked in an attempt to move Gertrude from the former to the latter, as he 'swerves from action' into the authorship of a new sort of psychologized self (p. 113). In any work relying on the delineation of differences, the drawn lines themselves can produce problems, and seeing the queen everywhere is a methodological pitfall difficult to escape in such a work, which seems strongest when discussing, with engaging historical and critical inclusions, wider issues of masculinity and femininity in the literary production of the time, Eggert's discussion of boys' companies being an especially good example (pp. 121–7).

On page 2 of Robin Headlam Wells's *Shakespeare on Masculinity*, the author observes that 'heroes in Shakespeare are, by definition, men'; certainly Elizabeth felt the need to stress her interior masculinity to play the hero at Tilbury. This is an exploration of Renaissance anxieties about the erosion of the chivalric ideal of heroic masculinity, a revision of Shakespeare's supposed part in constructing the militant-Protestant hero. The furore of the princely Hercules characters of the earlier history plays is, according to Headlam Wells, later transformed into men who lead and coerce through the arts, Orpheus-like, as does Prospero in *The Tempest*: the reconciliatory cultural hero. Through readings of *The Tempest, Henry V, Troilus and Cressida, Hamlet, Othello, Macbeth* and *Coriolanus*, Headlam Wells offers us a cultural background of battling court factions and politically constructed ideals of manhood, using Freudian principles to explore the inherent anxieties (p. 214) and rejecting the insistence of what he calls 'presentism' that we can only ever newly construct the past. Far more gently than Kermode, Headlam Wells asks modern critics to remember and rehearse past scholarship, which, he insists, had perfectly adequate insights into 'the limitations of Rankean empiricism' (p. 215). Some of his shots at new historicism and feminism seem wild: were feminists really the first to accuse men of falsely claiming moral blessings on their slaughters? *Henry V* seems full of moments when self-sacralized militarism is followed by dreadful outcomes, which Headlam Wells himself later acknowledges (p. 31). He hovers uneasily between distaste and admiration for 'the persuasive power of the heroic ideal' throughout (p. 112), and his muscular historicism is diminished by caveats that the play may not be alluding to contemporary events. Nonetheless, this is a generous and valuable resource of Shakespeare criticism, and an accessibly written and lucid evaluation of theories of heroic masculinity.

Anthony Holden, *William Shakespeare: His Life and Work*, has not set out to write the definitive biography, acceding to Harold Bloom's observation that there is not enough to know about Shakespeare (Prologue, p. 1). Neither does he wish to engage in what he calls the picking apart of Shakespeare by 'historicists, feminists, Marxists, new historicists, post-feminists, deconstructionists, anti-deconstructionists, post-modernists, cultural imperialists, and post-colonialists' (p. 1), the absence of revisionism perhaps an indicator of Holden's own approach. Park Honan's absence from the index is harder to explain. In offering to put Shakespeare 'back together again', Holden is treading closely on the heels of Honan's *Life* [1998], but Honan appears only in the negative, his recreation of the decor of an Oxford room where Shakespeare may have bedded the landlord's wife being recalled by Holden's complaints about biographies bogged down in detail (p. 4). Ernst Honigmann and Eric Sams are the preferred models, and the Lancashire connection is presented as a certainty. The works are somewhat picked to bits to patch together a portrait of the man in Holden's own conception, and various possibilities are explored. This is both a history and an account of histories, Holden favouring some over others, such as an exit from Stratford with the Queen's men in 1587 (p. 78). There is an interesting range of illustrations, including bits from documentary records of Shakespeare's life, all contributing to the scene Holden is building up around the cipher Shakespeare. The lack of bibliography and academic referencing sites this among the good reads rather than reference works: a resourceful and engaging work, in decent company. D. Ellis discusses recent reconstructions of Shakespeare's life, and the general dearth of documentary material in 'Biography and Shakespeare: An Outsider's View' (*CQ* 29:iv[2000] 296–313).

Notes taken by Alan Ansen (among others) of Auden's [1946–7] lectures on Shakespeare's plays have been gathered together and reconstructed by Arthur Kirsch in *W.H. Auden: Lectures on Shakespeare*. Of course the work is ultimately about Auden, not Shakespeare: the lectures, as Kirsch points out, 'were a nursery for many of the ideas developed in Auden's later prose' (p. xii). It is a scholarly and fascinating variety of insights into the mind and method of Auden and the best of his contemporaries and influences. 'The isolating tendencies of his dispassionate, and prodigal, intellect', says Kirsch, give him the 'outsider's view' of the plays (pp. xviii–xix), a detachment balanced by Auden's understanding of the dangers of being 'under the illusion of being free of illusion' (p. xx). Sticking to the uttered quality of the lectures was a fine editorial decision, giving a stringent immediacy to the work that might otherwise seem a dry reconstruction of past glory. The poet-on-poet insights make this view of Shakespeare the writer rich and rewarding in the Kermode vein. If the idea of the great mind being brought to bear on a great precedent seems antiquated, it pleads its relevance by offering the new scholar an invaluable lesson in reading and commentary relying on no methodological novelties whatever: the way back *is* the way forward here. The textual notes are an education in themselves. Every library should have a copy.

Hamlet is not the business of this section, but G.K. Desai's introductory editorial essay to *Hamlet Studies* 23 ([2001] 8–12) addresses itself in part to wider questions raised in several of this year's works: uses of Shakespeare. Desai discusses the 'new shaping of Shakespeare' by John Holloway, L.C. Knight and others in the late twentieth century, and the difficult balancing act a critic must achieve between 'modernist over-ingenuity', as Holloway called it, and donnish self-projection disguised as bardolatry. Other essays on the linguistic/rhetorical processes of self-identification and the ideological problems implicit in any work of translation should also be of general interest, and Lisa Hopkins's essay on the relationships between Hamlet's family and the Julio-Claudian dynasty is a convincing addition to current interest in Shakespeare the rewriter.

Postmodernist ingenuity continues to thrive unabated: Jonathan Goldberg, 'Shakespeare Writing Matter Again: Objects and their Detachments' (*ShakS* 28[2000] 248–51), proposes an investigation into the circuits of power and desire embodied by the texts and textuality of Shakespeare's plays, the letters circulated, forged, misdirected and read, ending up enmeshed in a dramatic postal system that makes little sense: letters quoted from before reception, or sent before the matter within them has been decided upon. Whether or not the 'oedipal drama of *King Lear* [via *Cymbeline*] is as historically contingent as is the movement of the post', such analysis says much more about the mobility of theory now than about Shakespeare's work. National Shakespeares are under discussion in Michael Dobson's 'Falstaff after John Bull: Shakespearean History, Britishness, and the Former United Kingdom' (*ShJE* 136[2000] 40–55). Britishness as an idea meant little more to

Shakespeare than 'a well-nigh prehistoric past', according to Dobson, and therefore Shakespeare cannot be said to be British, despite Jonson's eulogy. Dobson sees Falstaff, 'the embodiment of the perennial life of the kingdom', as an evergreen counterpoint to the fragility, both political and physical, of the monarch. A rich, mischievous historical view of the national Bard. Richard W. Schoch investigates the intriguing and suggestive history of stage parodies of Shakespeare productions, an area he sees as recently much neglected. The epilogue in the *Empress of Morocco* [1673] was a burlesque on William Davenant's *Macbeth*, claiming, in being cruder, to be closer to the original. The notion that burlesque can sidestep, challenge or help to expose the delineations of cultural reclamation must be of general interest to cultural theorists (*ELH* 67:iv[2000] 973–91). Richard P. Wheeler, 'Deaths in the Family: The Loss of a Son and the Rise of Shakespearean Comedy' (*SQ* 51:ii[2000] 127–53), negotiates the dizzying axis between the 'formalist and historicist poles' with great care, rejecting Dark Lady/earl of Oxford speculation, but nonetheless seeing some merit in searching documentary evidence for clues about the life of Shakespeare, taking Park Honan, among others, as his ally. Why did Shakespeare write his 'best comedies' immediately after the death of his only son? Wheeler finds a repeated 'lost-and-recovered-child' motif in the output of the time that supplies him with possible answers.

Peter Holland's new editorship of the *Shakespeare Survey* series has produced a strong selection of essays in volume 53, 'Shakespeare and Narrative'. Helmut Bonheim, 'Shakespeare's Narremes' (*ShS* 53[2000] 1–11), explores the repeated patterns of separation and reconciliation that are Shakespeare's narremes of closure, lamenting current lack of interest in closure as a site of study. His sensitivity to the 'show' element of Shakespearian drama informs and enlivens the whole. Margaret Tudeau-Clayton's 'Stepping Out of Narrative Line: A Bit of Word, and Horse, Play in *Venus and Adonis*' (*ShS* 53[2000] 12–24) is a consummate piece of literary dressage around Shakespeare's use of 'verbal mimesis'. She takes the linguistic implications of ''tween' in 'the iron bit he crusheth 'tween his teeth', for instance, and uses it to elevate the line into 'a poetics of recreative licence ... a discursive equivalent to the intemperance of holiday'—emblem of 'a rupture, at once of Renaissance and of modernity' (pp. 12–13). Her discussion of Shakespeare's liberation of the works of Ovid and Virgil from 'the imperative of moral instruction' is interesting, her enlargement on the controlling text and the reader's attempt to get the better of it amusing and fascinating. Peter J. Smith follows with 'A "Consummation Devoutly to be Wished": The Erotics of Narration in *Venus and Adonis*' (*ShS* 53[2000] 25–38). Where Tudeau-Clayton plays with bridle and bit, Smith discusses the economics of top-drawer harlotry and the unruly penis, uncovering Thomas Nashe's epyllion 'The choise of valentines' in its earlier MS manifestation as 'Nashe his Dildo' (p. 25). The point about the relative adequacies of Nashe's, Rochester's and Shakespeare's responses to female libido—as the 'sexy' Venus—is made with gusto, although Smith's discussions may contain more than a nervous reader wishes to know about 'linguistic masturbation' and 'foreplay' (pp. 35–6). '[T]he narrative logic of *Venus and Adonis*', according to Smith's reading, is necessarily one of deferral because consummation/satisfaction would in this context mean extinction. 'Echoes Inhabit a Garden: The Narratives of *Romeo and Juliet*' (*ShS* 53[2000] 39–48) by Jill L. Levenson revisits Bonheim's plea for narrative theory to be applied to drama as well as other forms. Levenson offers a

good overview of recent scholarship on narrative theory and Shakespeare.
Discussing the first and second quarto texts of *Romeo and Juliet*, Levenson's is an
honest appraisal of challenges posed by narratology to our ideas of linearity.
Another interesting use of, and commentary on, historian and historicist critics is
David George's essay on 'Plutarch, Insurrection, and Death in *Coriolanus*' (*ShS*
53[2000] 60–72), which reads the play alongside the Midland Crisis, offering a
dating for it accordingly. Cynthia Marshall's 'Shakespeare, Crossing the Rubicon'
(*ShS* 53[2000] 73–88) is a psychological investigation of characterization,
addressing Foucauldian/Lacanian subjectivity and including a reappraisal of
Geoffrey Bullough's study of Shakespeare's sources, emphasizing Shakespeare's
points of departure. Plutarch's idea of great men shaped by inner conflict is shown
in tension with the demands of the Renaissance stage for 'overt, physical
demonstrations of character' (p. 75). In 'Vernacular Criticism and the Scenes
Shakespeare Never Wrote' (*ShS* 53[2000] 89–102) Michael D. Bristol offers a calm,
confident appraisal of the re-creation of Shakespeare by subsequent critics and the
implications of their identification with particular characters. The scenes that a
particular critical interpretation creates offstage (mainly in *Hamlet* and *Macbeth*) are
the sites of his study. A case in point might be Dickens's [1860] account of being
homeless in London, through which Adrian Poole, in 'The Shadow of Lear's
"Houseless" in Dickens' (*ShS* 53[2000] 103–13), relates appearances of the
Shakespearian theme of houselessness in eighteenth-century literature to its usage in
King Lear. George Eliot's overt use of Shakespeare's words and her determination
not to 'occlude or naturalise' literatures through intertextual promiscuity is explored
by John Lyon in 'Shakespearean Margins in George Eliot' (*ShS* 53[2000] 114–26),
while Phyllis McBride, 'In her Father's Library: Margaret Fuller and the Making of
the American Miranda' (*ShS* 53[2000] 127–36), discusses Margaret Fuller and the
education of early nineteenth-century American women. Fuller's free and inclusive
use of both male and female voices turned the debate into something wider than it
otherwise might be—more, McBride insists, than a mere reiteration of the Miranda
story. Another offstage scene, this time the faun-haunted sub-urban landscape of
Wilde and Saki with its glimpses of magical excess, is covered in Julia Griffin's
'The Magician in Love' (*ShS* 53[2000] 137–50). Resisting the usual assumptions
about the autobiographical nature of *The Tempest*, Griffin reads it as love story,
comparing the man–boy alliances of various works to Prospero's vital symbiosis
with his vanishing spirit. Ruth Morse's 'Monsters, Magicians, Movies: *The Tempest*
and the Final Frontier' (*ShS* 53[2000] 164–74), which follows the essay discussed
below, shows how rich a source of imagery and influence *The Tempest* has been—
Morse boldly going even into the realms of *Star Trek* and other science fictions to
find Prospero's footprints, discussing the trials of intertextuality along the way.
Back on Earth, meanwhile, the schoolroom retelling of Shakespeare is discussed in
Rex Gibson's 'Narrative Approaches to Shakespeare: Active Storytelling in
Schools' (*ShS* 53[2000] 151–63). This is more than a rehearsal of educational
requirements and models for teaching Shakespeare: Gibson makes a convincing
case that school Shakespeare should become more than mere storytelling, as long as
a teacher is prepared (and freed from constraints) to sacrifice the strictly accurate for
more off-the-wall and stimulating interpretations. E.A.J. Honigmann returns to
Shakespeare the author in 'Shakespeare's Self-Repetitions and *King John*' (*ShS*
53[2000] 175–83), tracing the authorial fingerprints through the plays.

Honigmann's meticulous scholarship is brought to bear on the relationship between *The Troublesome Reign of John King of England* and *King John*, Honigmann arguing for *King John* as precedent and pattern for the other. Barbara Everett gets 'Inside *Othello*' (*ShS* 53[2000] 184–95) to explore the gaps in our understanding of the character, mounting a robust and cogent attack on the 'obdurate externalism' of casting by skin colour. 'Othello', she observes, started off 'Burbage-coloured', and should now be Othello-coloured, not reduced to ponderables by what she sees as the reductive matter-of-factness of new historicism. Another area of unease in Shakespeare is the ending of *Measure for Measure*. Edward Rocklin, 'Measured Endings: How Productions from 1720 to 1929 Close Shakespeare's Open Silences in *Measure for Measure* (*ShS* 53[2000] 213–32), offers a well-researched overview of attempts to address the awkwardnesses in the play, while Robert Shaughnessy follows 'Shakespeare's Utopias' (*ShS* 53[2000] 233–43) out from behind the proscenium arch onto the currently popular thrust platform with all its supposed erotic dynamism. Shaughnessy borrows Foucault's *History of Sexuality* to challenge our complacency over the change, questioning the tendency of modern theorists to assume that the thrust stage brought an audience closer to open participatory experience in drama rather than just getting them nearer to the 'specular ratification of royal power'. In the overview of the year's contribution to Shakespeare studies, Alison Findlay offers a thorough and sharply scrutinized year's-worth of 'Lives' from Shakespeare in the north to Shakespeare in chaos, while Edward Pechter reviews criticism. The story of recent work has been one of retrenchment, even withdrawal from the new historicist and materialist close focus on 'politicization, appropriation, production' as Pechter puts it (*ShS* 53[2000] 287–317). More voices are being added to those of Kermode, Pechter and others who accuse modern theory of addressing political appropriation at the expense of literary application (p. 301). Findlay in her turn reproves some of these accusers for failure to recognize the insights that can be gained from the acknowledgement of the tangential relationships between texts. Is the assault on current theory a return to 'real' literary skills or the expression of a deeper fear about academic adequacy in the cyber age? One last essay makes an interesting point of exit: Malashri Lal's acidic review (*HamS* 23[2000] 142–4) of H. Murray's *Hamlet on the Holodeck: The Future of Narrative in Cyberspace* (FreeP [1998]), in which she reproves Murray for confusing the dazzling potential for literary production offered by electronic writing with intrinsic literary quality. 'Quality'—what does it mean, exactly? Perhaps it is now the critic's place to reinstate the concept. In what amounts to a resumption of the Renaissance debate between *copia* and restraint, intellectual niceties of discrimination and 'taste' must be more important than ever: shrewd distinctions such as those made by Lal between facility and quality will be invaluable. She points out that for all its proliferative potential, 'cyberatic productivity is pitifully small' at present: we are 'little keyboard gods attempting very small things' (p. 145). Pechter, on the other hand, informs us that he found 'at least 14994 matches for Shakespeare criticism' on his search engine. '[W]hat they add up to, only God needs to know', he adds (p. 312); Lal begs to differ.

(b) Comedies

Mary Ellen Lamb's truly enlightening essay, 'Taken by the Fairies: Fairy Practices and the Production of Popular Culture in *A Midsummer Night's Dream*' (*SQ*

51[2000] 277–312), adopts a sophisticated theoretical approach to the production of cultural meanings within discursive communities in early modern England. Lamb analyses stories about fairies in terms of socially convenient narratives which indicate less a belief in fairies than an unspoken communal agreement to accept white lies which facilitate a subversive 'cross-class collaboration' (p. 286). This historicist analysis is then applied to a reading of the play. Lamb's twofold conclusion is that fairy-tale at this time still has the power to embed itself in dominant culture, but that Shakespeare's treatment of the topic for an urban audience marks a preliminary step towards its eventual rejection. Adopting a very different approach to this comedy, Stanley Wells, in 'Translations in *A Midsummer Night's Dream*' (in Chew and Stead, eds., *Translating Life: Studies in Transpositional Aesthetics*, pp. 15–32), explores at the levels of source-text, character study and theatrical performance the shades of meaning that attach to ideas of 'translation'. This compelling essay, part of a Festschrift for Inga-Stina Ewbank, examines the play's blend of the fearful and the comic—Shakespeare's fascination with 'things that both are and are not the same' (p. 18)—and rejects critical and theatrical literalism in favour of the interpretative merits of the unrepresentable imagination. Roger Prior has written on 'The Occasion of *A Midsummer Night's Dream*' (*BLR* 17:i[2000] 56–64), arguing that the play was originally written for the marriage of Sir Thomas Heneage to Mary, Countess of Southampton on 2 May 1594. Prior supports his argument by tracing the influence on Shakespeare's play of an Oration, the only extant copy of which is held at Bodleian Library, spoken by Thomas Pound at the Countess's first marriage in 1566.

Two articles on *A Midsummer Night's Dream* appear in Ryan, ed., *Shakespeare: Texts and Contexts*. Penny Rixon's '*A Midsummer Night's Dream*' (pp. 1–30) provides an informative introduction which would probably be of most use to the high-school or first-year undergraduate reader coming to Shakespeare for the first time. Rixon guides one's encounter with the play act by act, discusses sexuality and carnival in the context of genre, and sets out the thematic importance of theatre and theatricality. The reader is reminded of the interpretative variability of performance, and black and white photographs illustrate some key moments of the play as staged in past productions. In keeping with the title of the volume in which this essay appears, the tone and critical approach are predominantly historicist, and Rixon emphasizes how this is quite a dark comedy, subversive of cultural institutions such as marriage. Helen Hackett, in 'Shakespeare's Theatre' (pp. 31–48), then asks us to imagine *A Midsummer Night's Dream* in performance in Elizabethan England. This essay conveys a great deal of introductory information about the early modern stage in an accessible and concise manner, covering the geographical location of the playhouses, the physical construction of the halls and amphitheatres, the social composition of the actors and their audiences, the use of spectacle, props, and costume, and some of the financial considerations involved in mounting the play's earliest theatrical productions. Hackett makes good use of a range of black and white photographs, facsimiles and sketches.

There have also been published a number of notes and short articles suggesting emendations and local interpretations. MacD. P. Jackson (see also section 1 of this chapter) suggests a striking emendation to Bottom's line 'If I were faire, *Thysby*, I were onely thine' in 'Bottom's Entry-Line: *A Midsummer Night's Dream*, III.i.98' (*N&Q* 47[2000] 69–70). Arguing that the metre is defective, and the sense neither intelligible nor comic, Jackson accepts the suggestion that the line should be repunctuated to make 'faire' qualify '*Thysby*'. However, he rejects inserting 'true' or 'fair' after 'If I were' as not in keeping with Bottom's character, and concludes that the line should pick up on Thisbe's simile in the previous line: 'If I were horse, fair Thisbe, I were only thine'. The attention of both Rodney Stenning Edgecombe and John K. Hale is drawn to Titania's speech about seasonal disorder. In 'Shakespeare's *A Midsummer Night's Dream* 2.1' (*Expl* 59[2000] 5–7), Edgecombe proposes an alternative emendation to 'The human mortals want their winter heere' on the grounds that the rhetorical emphasis is not on bad summers and good winters, but on wet weather throughout the year. Accordingly, he suggests emending 'heere' to 'clear', in place of the usual 'cheer'. Hale considers the seeming redundancy of 'human mortals' in 'Shakespeare's *A Midsummer Night's Dream* 2.1.101' (*Expl* 57[1999] 200), and concludes that 'the two words convey a single idea'. The effect of the phrase is implicitly to draw attention to the range of creatures suffering, with humans, the bad weather: animals (non-human mortals), and fairies, whom Hale interprets as human immortals.

Roger Prior's 'Gascoigne's *Posies* as a Shakespearian Source' (*N&Q* 47[2000] 444–9) is a thought-provoking note that traces numerous borrowings between *Romeo and Juliet* and *A Midsummer Night's Dream*, and a masque written by Gascoigne for a double wedding in 1572. The masque was published in 1573 in *A Hundreth Sundrie Flowres*, and included in *Posies* (1575) and *The Whole Woorkes* (1587). Prior argues that this evidence supports the view that the manuscript behind Q2 *Romeo* predates the printing of the Q1 text, since the Q2 manuscript lies between Q1 and the passages it borrows from Gascoigne. He further concludes that this source identification militates against the usual emendation of 'father', a reading found in the Q2 and Q3 texts at I.iv.20, to Q4's 'faith', since the early phrasing seems to echo Gascoigne. Rodney Stenning Edgecombe offers a new interpretation of the phrase 'mermaid on a dolphin's back' (II.i.150) in 'Shakespeare's *A Midsummer Night's Dream*' (*Expl* 58[1999] 181–4). Arguing that the image of a fish-tailed half-human creature on the back of a dolphin is clumsy, Edgecombe suggests that 'mermaid' should be thought of in terms of the classical Nereids, 'wholly human figures in a marine environment' (p. 183). After tracing the various connotations of mermaids, Edgecombe concludes that this passage offers a complex compliment to Elizabeth I.

Another comedy attracting only slightly less critical interpretation in 2000 is *The Merchant of Venice*; included for discussion here are also a few 1999 articles not available for review last year. In 'Genetics and "Race" in *The Merchant of Venice*', Martin Japtok and Winfried Schleiner (*L&M* 18[1999] 155–72) demonstrate that religion and race serve to identify the Other, but whereas 'Jew' and 'Black' are portrayed as equally evil, the play presents the former, but not the latter, as potentially remedied through culture. They then turn to an examination of early modern eugenics, highlighting passages that signal the popular belief that racial traits could be stamped on the unborn foetus through the mother's physical or imaginative sight. A passage of which editors, in particular, might take note is the explanation Japtok and Schleiner offer of the crux surrounding Lorenzo's allegation that 'the Moor is with child' by Launcelot (III.v.35–6). They cite Hercole Sassonia's treatise *Luis venereae perfectissimus tractatus* [1597] as a contemporary source for the belief, documented in Venice, that 'intercourse with a black virgin would cure the syphilitic' (p. 168).

Alternative suggestions of possible sources are made in two other articles. Roger Stritmatter identifies Deuteronomy 15:1–14 as underlying Shylock's 'you have among you many a purchase slave' speech (V.i.90–100) in '"Old" and "New" Law in *The Merchant of Venice*: A Note on the Source of Shylock's Morality in Deuteronomy 15' (*N&Q* 47[2000] 70–2) that has also been discussed in section 1 of this chapter. J.J.M. Tobin's 'Justice for Fleay' (*N&Q* 46[1999] 230–1) argues that editors have too hastily accepted McKerrow's dismissal of Fleay's suggestion that V.i.62–4 in *The Merchant of Venice* was inspired by Nashe's *Unfortunate Traveller*. Tobin traces similarity of phrasing and vocabulary between the two texts in support of Fleay's early identification of a Shakespearian source.

Rüdiger Ahrens, 'Female Awareness(es) in *The Merchant of Venice*: Shakespeare, Marowitz, Wesker' (in Bode and Klooss, eds., *Historicizing/Contemporizing Shakespeare: Essays in Honour of Rudolf Böhm*, pp. 133–47), contrasts Shakespeare's play in a fairly rudimentary manner with adaptations written in 1978 by Charles Marowitz and Arnold Wesker. Ahrens is particularly interested in the characterization of Portia, Nerissa and Jessica, and how new critical perspectives are made available through revised social contexts. In the same volume, Christiane Damlos-Kinzel, in 'The Tension between Oeconomics and Chrematistics in William Shakespeare's *The Merchant of Venice*', argues that critics who interpret the play in terms of trade and usury have tended to overlook an important tension implicit in discussions of (o)economics (pp. 115–32). This term in early modern England referred specifically to the successful management of the household, and Shakespeare brings that sense into conflict with emergent ideas of the market and money, described up until the eighteenth century as chrematistics. Damlos-Kinzel pursues this analysis by developing the thesis, perhaps somewhat too categorically, that Belmont represents the older, and Venice the newly developing and encroaching, principles of (o)economics. Bruce Boehrer is likewise interested in the household and economics, but in 'Shylock and the Rise of the Household Pet: Thinking Social Exclusion in *The Merchant of Venice*' (*SQ* 50[1999] 152–70) he approaches the subject through an analysis of ways of thinking about animals in early modern England in order to offer a nuanced discussion of the characterization of Shylock and Jessica. What emerges from this compelling essay is the competing cultural traditions associated, in particular, with dogs, and 'the complexity and polyvocality with which myths of ethnic inferiority may be fashioned' (p. 168).

In an important note which has implications generally for the study of early modern drama, Tiffany Stern, 'Letters, Verses and Double Speech-Prefixes in *The Merchant of Venice*' (*N&Q* 46[1999] 231–3]), argues that where speech prefixes for a character flank letters and other documents read out on stage in printed plays thought to derive from a promptbook (as opposed to foul papers), the convention is for that same character to read the letter. The theatrical and interpretative implications of her research are brought home in a consideration of III.ii.314–19 of *The Merchant of Venice*: Stern's point is that Antonio's letter, usually mistakenly assigned by modern editors to Bassanio, should be read out by Portia. In '"An Indian Beauty?" A Proposed Emendation to *The Merchant of Venice*' (*ShN* 50[2000] 27), Lisa Hopkins suggests pointing Bassanio's lines at III.ii.98–9 in such a way as to render 'Indian' a noun, rather than an adjective ('the beauteous scarf | Veiling an Indian; beauty—in a word'), a phrasing that would reinforce the racial denigration found elsewhere in the play. Leofranc Holford-Strevens reminds us in '"Most Lovely Jew"' (*N&Q* 46[1999] 212–13) of the two points in Shakespeare's drama at which a non-Jewish character is described as 'Jew'. Providing an undated, but apparently much more recent, example in a Texan folk song, he suggests that the sense of this usage approaches 'sweet lad'.

A few essays on *The Merchant of Venice* published in 1999 were particularly interested in the treatment of blood. Roy Booth, 'Shylock's Sober House' (*RES* 50[1999] 22–31), notes that the interior of Shylock's home is never dramatized on stage, even though it is frequently mentioned in the dialogue. In an effort to recover some of the submerged tensions in play for Shakespeare's earliest audiences, Booth considers early modern literary associations with the homes of Jews as traps for Christian innocents, and analyses Stow's comments on one such actual house still standing at the time in London. This discussion is then related to the moment in IV.ii when Portia commands the boy clerk Nerissa to collect Shylock's signature. In the same issue David S. Katz, 'Shylock's Gender: Jewish Male Menstruation in Early Modern England' (*RES* 50[1999] 440–62) explores the then popular view that menstruation was a way to expel excess blood, a physiological problem to which women were particularly susceptible. He then demonstrates intersections between the blood libel (the belief that Jews committed human sacrifice and ritual murder) and beliefs in Jewish male menstruation, concluding that Shakespeare's presentation of Shylock is of 'the usurer ... driven in his lust for Christian blood by the divine affliction of male menstruation' (p. 462). The historicist research is fascinating, but one might wish for a more detailed application to an interpretative reading of the play. Paul Franssen's '"With all my heart": The Pound of Flesh and the Execution of Justice' (in Pieters, ed., *Critical Self-Fashioning: Stephen Greenblatt and the New Historicism*, pp. 87–103) is a capable essay that revisits in an interesting and gruesome way the by now familiar critical territory of court proceedings and executions. Franssen recovers early modern legal analogues for the practice of cutting out an offender's heart in order to argue that the insistence on a pound of flesh cut from near the heart is 'a shorthand reference to a full public execution at Tyburn' (p. 98). Shylock attempts to legitimate his revenge by making it seem like law, and the trial scene in *The Merchant of Venice* threatens to reveal the extent to which power and vengeance, rather than justice, might be understood to underpin the early modern legal system.

Grady, ed., *Shakespeare and Modernity*, includes four articles on *The Merchant of Venice*, a focus that perhaps reflects the ongoing centrality of questions of Jewishness to analyses of the Enlightenment project. All of these essays are written in a demanding prose style, but offer useful, and occasionally fascinating, analyses of the play. Lisa Freinkel understands 'Jew' and 'Christian' as unstable categories that resist clear demarcation, and in '*The Merchant of Venice*: "Modern" anti-Semitism and the Veil of Allegory' (pp. 122–41) she offers a '*genealogy* of anti-Semitism' (p. 125) that shows in some detail how the attitude has shifted in its details over time. Resisting the dichotomy between race and religion that emerges from the late nineteenth century, Freinkel reads Shakespeare's trial scene as staging ongoing and, specifically, theological tensions between flesh and spirit, law and mercy and ultimately, Jew and Christian. Eric S. Mallin's 'Jewish Invader and the

Soul of State: *The Merchant of Venice* and Science Fiction Movies' (pp. 142–67), unexpectedly, is not a study of film adaptations of Shakespeare's drama. Mallin sets the genre of the science fiction movie alongside *The Merchant of Venice* as a way to throw into relief the ideological operations of modern, and early modern, popular culture. This tactic leads to some excellent close readings of the play. He argues that these texts set up difference in order to 'produce *complicated likeness*, a tacit acknowledgement … of the bad faith furnished by racialist distinctions' (p. 144), and concludes that society dispels the Other (the Jew, the alien) as a form of self-defence, but also to resist recognizing the Other in itself. A dense essay by John Drakakis called '"Jew. Shylock is my name": Speech Prefixes in *The Merchant of Venice* as Symptoms of the Early Modern' (pp. 105–21) offers a novel departure in the interpretation of irregular speech prefixes. Drakakis focuses on what he describes as the cultural value of bibliographical variation. Variant speech prefixes in *The Merchant of Venice*—a textual symptom that Drakakis chooses not to ascribe to any particular agency—thus testify both to a 'cultural nervousness' (p. 112) surrounding Judaism, mercantilism and subjectivity at the time of the play's creation, and methodological problems implicit in our own efforts to read early modern texts historically. Finally, Stephen Cohen's '(Post)modern Elizabeth: Gender, Politics, and the Emergence of Modern Subjectivity' (pp. 20–39) studies the way recent scholarship has theorized ideological shifts in the formation of subjectivity in the period stretching from the late medieval to post-Enlightenment, and suggests that a tendency to map large-scale historical trajectories has at times created a sense of 'teleological inevitability' (p. 23). As a form of corrective, Cohen argues that Elizabeth I constructed a radical form of self-identity by exploiting the insecurities and ambiguities occasioned by a transitional moment. He compares this analysis of interiority to the polemical debates surrounding cross-dressing and the theatres, and two of Shakespeare's transvestite comedies, *The Merchant of Venice* and *As You Like It*.

The only other piece on *As You Like It* published in 2000 (also discussed in section 1 of this chapter) was a note called 'Snake and Lioness in *As You Like It*, IV.iii' (*N&Q* 47[2000] 79), in which John Hale suggests that these animals are emblematic of deceit and violence, and that the passage derives from Psalms 91:13. Terence Hawkes's 'Entry on Q' (in Desmet and Sawyer, eds., *Shakespeare and Appropriation*, pp. 33–46) offers a close reading of the New Cambridge single-volume edition of *As You Like It* edited by Sir Arthur Quiller-Couch, which was published in 1926. This essay discusses Q's career and suggests the extent to which he established the parameters of the study of English literature, an influence which is still felt today. B.J. Sokol and Mary Sokol, in 'Legal Terms Implying Extended Meanings in *As You Like It*, III.ii.331–2 and *Troilus and Cressida*, III.ii.89–91: 'Purchase' and 'Words of Procreation'' (*N&Q* 46[1999] 236–8), apply legal distinctions between ideas of purchase and inheritance to an interpretation of Orlando's comment that Rosalind's accent could not have been 'purchased' in Arden. They argue that this moment is a self-conscious recognition of a key convention of pastoral, and then explore from a similarly legalistic perspective Troilus's use of the term 'reversion'.

Penny Gay's *As You Like It*, not available in time for last year's review, makes an excellent contribution to the Writers and their Work series. Gay opens with a discussion of the subjectivity of criticism, explaining that she locates what, at the end of the twentieth century, might be considered 'useful meanings' of *As You Like It*. She then offers the student reader an intelligent and well-written discussion of such topics as source material, characterization, performance and theatre-going in the early modern period and their relevance to an interpretation of the play, and the treatment of marriage in Shakespearian comedy. The volume closes with a short discussion of performance history. Gay stays close to the language of the play throughout, continually locating her analysis in relation to key scenes and speeches, and she is careful to build into her prose explanations of potentially alienating terminology such as 'historicist approach' and 'liberties'. Lengthy and numerous quotations from secondary material provide an implicit guide to further reading. This is an excellent introduction to the play for the student reader.

Occasionally one comes across a well-written and carefully argued interpretation of Shakespeare's drama that prompts a major reconsideration of the evidence. Jessica Tvordi's 'Female Alliance and the Construction of Homoeroticism in *As You Like It* and *Twelfth Night*' (in Frye and Robertson, eds., *Maids and Mistresses, Cousins and Queens: Women's Alliances in Early Modern England*, pp. 114–30) is one such article. Tvordi's thesis is that power relationships between Celia and Rosalind, on the one hand, and Maria and Olivia, on the other, are erotically charged. Whereas in *As You Like It* a 'specifically homoerotic' friendship (p. 126) is defeated in order to maintain the dominant heterosexual order, in *Twelfth Night*, homosociality between women is only strengthened by the marriages with which the play closes. I disagreed with some of Tvordi's local interpretations, but this essay remains a must-read for anyone interested in the circulation of sexual desire in Shakespeare's comedies. Laurie Shannon likewise addresses sexuality in a readable essay called 'Nature's Bias: Renaissance Homonormativity and Elizabethan Comic Likeness' (*MP* 98[2000] 183–210). Shannon offers visual and literary evidence to support her claim that homonormativity—'an almost philosophical preference for likeness or a structure of thinking based on resemblance' (pp. 191–2)—was the dominant rhetorical gesture in early modern England. The ideological work effected by the comic action is thus neither celebration nor containment, but the reconfiguration of the final, or projected, marriage in terms of a language of similarity. This argument is pursued through close analysis of Lyly's *Gallathea*, and more cursory discussion of key speeches and moments in *Twelfth Night*. Penny Rixon's '*Twelfth Night*' (in Ryan, ed., pp. 189–211) builds on her discussion of *A Midsummer Night's Dream* in the same volume, and extends the previous exploration of the comic genre and the carnivalesque into Shakespeare's romantic comedies. Rixon offers close readings of key passages and scenes, and complements her critical analysis with a capable discussion of the play in performance. This essay asks the reader to focus, in particular, on the interpretative implications of cross-dressing and mistaken identity, language, sexual desire and Shakespeare's treatment of social status as different ways of making sense of this complex comedy.

After a fairly basic overview of recent criticism, Thomas A. DuBois identifies a key distinction between folkloric performance (music and foolery), and courtly genres of communication (the letter and the messenger) in '"That strain again!" or, *Twelfth Night*, a Folkloristic Approach' (*Arv* 56[2000] 35–56). Whereas the former is portrayed as embodying a form of truth, the latter is the source of comic confusion. DuBois focuses primarily on the character of Feste to make the point that the competent musician/fool shapes his or her performance to suit an audience's mood, and thus any perception of truth 'lies as much in the knowing listener as in the performer or song' (p. 46). 'Aguecheek's Beef' (*TPr* 14[2000] 327–41) picks up on an odd exchange in *Twelfth Night* at I.iii.81–3 where Sir Andrew and Sir Toby discuss the belief that eating beef makes one less intelligent. Robert Appelbaum clarifies muddy editorial glosses on this passage by pointing out that a causal relation between beef and stupidity seems only to appear in a book by Guglielmo Grataroli which was translated into English as *A Direction for the Health of Magistrates and Studentes* [1574]. He goes on to analyse how Galenic attitudes to beef consumption were appropriated differently across the northern and southern European nations, and concludes that Shakespeare's dialogue partakes more generally of debates in England concerning emergent cultural and national identities: 'in the world of *Twelfth Night* even beef-eating amounts to a kind of political act' (p. 338). James Ryan engages in a more limited manner with the play's editorial tradition in '*Twelfth Night*: A Scene Break at 3.4.263?' (*ShN* 50[2000] 7–8), arguing on the grounds of symmetry of action, both at the level of scene and play, that editors should depart from the Folio text to mark a scene break in III.iv at the point at which the stage is cleared.

Paul A.S. Harvey, in 'More Cakes and Ale: Sir Toby Belch in *Twelfth Night*' (*GBK* 26[2000] 77–86), analyses television and film productions directed by John Sichel (ITC [1969]), John Gorrie (BBC [1979]), Kenneth Branagh (Renaissance Films [1988]) and Trevor Nunn (1996). His argument is that a play performed up until the 1960s as a festive comedy is now usually dominated by melancholic overtones, and he appeals for directors to restore to *Twelfth Night* a lightness of tone. This essay offers some useful performance analysis, but perhaps slips at times into an overly prescriptive treatment of potential staging. A reconsideration of 'The Date of *Twelfth Night*' (*ShStud* 38[2000] 1–16) is the focus of Shoichiro Kawai's examination of verbal similarities between passages in *Twelfth Night* and *Look About You* [1599]. Kawai argues that *Look About You* probably borrows from Shakespeare's play rather than the other way round, and notes that scholars have already traced allusions in this anonymous play to *The Comedy of Errors* and *Romeo and Juliet*. This conjectured interrelationship offers evidence in favour of 1599 as a date of composition for *Twelfth Night*. In '*Twelfth Night* and John Weever' (*N&Q* 47[2000] 79–81), Charles Cathcart hears an allusion to *The Whipping of the Satyre* in Sir Toby's obscure reference to 'a catch that will draw three souls out of one weaver' (II.iii.54–5). This poem, probably written by John Weever, and entered in the Stationers' Register on 14 August 1601, is an attack on three writers, usually identified now as John Marston, Everard Guilpin and Ben Jonson. Cathcart's note supports the view that Shakespeare knew Weever and his work, an acquaintance that may have been initiated during Shakespeare's so-called 'lost years' through a shared connection to the Hoghton family in Lancashire.

Two articles published this year are concerned with issues of voice. Maurice Hunt, in 'The Reclamation of Language in *Much Ado about Nothing*' (*SP* 97[2000] 165–91), turns away from examinations of hearing and watching to focus on what is said in the play, and how. Hunt shows through close analysis that a character's manipulation of the spoken word operates within a broader set of power relations in patriarchal society to mark the speaker's relative status among his or her auditors. In various scenes, however, the meaning of language cannot be entirely contained or controlled. Hunt argues that the play's comic resolution is effected by attempts to stabilize meaning through recourse to the physical body and the written word, and through a deliberate rejection of banter and power games in favour of plain speech. Carla Mazzio explores the relationship between print, love and (in)articulacy in 'The Melancholy of Print: *Love's Labour's Lost*' (in Mazzio and Trevor, eds., *Historicism, Psychoanalysis, and Early Modern Culture*, pp. 186–227). Mazzio's argument is that Shakespeare stages a loss of voice, thus casting in dramatic form the conventional Petrarchan conceit of the lover unable to speak his true desire. She further understands this dysfunction, however, as resulting in part from the excessive and proliferating treatment of desire in printed texts: according to this construction, love melancholy 'is a historically specific social ailment, articulating the oral and psychic self-estrangement of speakers living in a culture in transition to print' (p. 188).

Thomas Rist's assured essay, 'Topical Comedy: On the Unity of *Love's Labour's Lost*' (*BJJ* 7[2000] 65–87), employs close reading to show that religious and political topicality, marking a movement in the play from Christian asceticism to worldly erotic love to a 'more purposive asceticism' (p. 73), unite both the main plot and subplot of *Love's Labour's Lost*. Rist argues that the postponement of marriage in the final scene enacts a form of Catholic 'purgatory' that, perhaps, was finally resolved in *Love's Labour's Won*. The only essay published this year on *The Comedy of Errors* appears in the same issue of *Ben Jonson Journal*. After tracing the pervasiveness in the play of Pauline epistles, Lisa Hopkins comments, in '*The Comedy of Errors* and the Date of Easter' (*BJJ* 7[2000] 55–64), that 'Like the calculation of the date of Easter, [timekeeping in *Errors*] doesn't add up' (p. 59). She then interprets the play's final scene as staging both the miracle of the resurrection and popular traditions associated with Easter which were no longer permitted after the Reformation.

Todd Pettigrew explains the apparent incongruity in naming the bumbling French physician in *The Merry Wives of Windsor* after John Caius, an eminent sixteenth-century physician, by suggesting that Shakespeare's Caius is an impostor who assumes the name in order to impress the local community. He supports this possibility in 'The Naming of Shakespeare's Caius' (*N&Q* 47[2000] 72–5) by tracing the figure of the fraudulent doctor in both dramatic literature and medical texts from the period (see also section 1 of this chapter). Mark Hutchings, in '"Turkish" or "Arabic" Emir? *The Merry Wives of Windsor*, II.i.176' (*N&Q* 47[2000] 449–51), takes up with enthusiasm Deanne Williams's passing suggestion in a previous issue of *Notes and Queries* that the Host's use of the word 'Anheers' might be represented in modern-spelling editions as 'emir' (also discussed in section 1 of this chapter). Hutchings clarifies that 'emir' at this time was known only as an Arabic term, not as Arabic and/or Turkish. The contrast provided by 'emir' at II.i, and the word usually rendered as 'vizier' at I.iii.6 ('Pheazar' or 'Pheeser') to refer to a Turkish, and not Arabic, military rank, amplifies what Williams has already identified as the Host's 'polylinguistic' language. There is also an informative article by Lurana Donnels O'Malley, 'From Fat Falstaff to Francophile Fop: Russian Nationalism in Catherine the Great's *Merry Wives*' (*CompD* 33[1999] 365–89), which discusses an adaptation of *The Merry Wives of Windsor* by Catherine the Great called *The Basket* (written and published in 1786, and performed in 1786 or early 1787). O'Malley argues that, although the turn to Shakespeare was a politically and culturally significant choice for Catherine to make at this moment of

Russian history, her adaptation ultimately remains firmly within the French aesthetic tradition.

Jonathan Culpeper, in 'A Cognitive Approach to Characterization: Katherina in Shakespeare's *The Taming of the Shrew*' (*L&L* 9[2000] 291–316), concludes that over the course of the play Katherina exhibits context-sensitive behaviour that makes her portrayal seem particularly 'rounded' (p. 311)—to draw, as Culpeper does, on E.M. Forster's distinction between flat and round characters. This essay, while interesting for its very novelty, is marred by a dependence on criticism and modes of critical interpretation that are out of date. There are two notes in *Expl* with the title 'Shakespeare's *The Taming of the Shrew*'. The first one, by Manuel Sánchez García (*Expl* 58[1999] 6–8), explains that the word 'kate' is a dialect name dated in *OED* from 1773 for several species of finch, and suggests that this alternative sense, used as a form of endearment, might be an additional connotative meaning underpinning Petruchio's repeated use of the shortened form of Katherina's name at II.i.182–90. David W. Cole (*Expl* 58[1999] 184–5) argues for a reading of Petruchio's character as Machiavellian, questioning whether, as a friend, Petruchio should not have warned Hortensio earlier of Lucentio's secret marriage to Bianca. MacD. P. Jackson, in '"Censor" in *The Taming of the Shrew*, IV.iii.91' (*N&Q* 46[1999] 211–12), provides further supporting evidence for his previously published suggestion that the Folio's 'Censor' should read 'tonsure'. While 'tonsure' does not appear elsewhere in the canon, if one can assume that *The Taming of the Shrew* postdates *The Comedy of Errors*, Shakespeare would have previously encountered the word in Gower's *Confessio Amantis*.

Marvel, ed., *Readings on The Taming of the Shrew*, is a new volume in the Greenhaven Press Literary Companions series. This casebook of essays by leading academics opens with a biographical overview and short summary of the play's characters and plot before settling into its three main sections: structure and character, themes and ideas, and critical interpretations. The extracts are short, and presented with the student reader in mind, with the occasional inset box offering such historical detail as sixteenth-century juridical punishments for women, and now unfamiliar marriage customs. A concluding chronology which extends from 1509 to 1986 includes source-texts, key dates in Shakespeare's life and career, and information about the play's afterlife. This collection offers a wide-ranging yet concise critical introduction which should prove of immense help to the student reader. And while we're on the subject of the punishment of women, Standish Henning's 'Branding Harlots on the Brow' (*SQ* 51[2000] 86–9) seeks to correct editorial glosses of *Comedy of Errors* II.ii.135, *Hamlet* III.iv.43–5 and IV.v.122–4, and *Measure for Measure* II.iii.10–12, which claim that a common punishment for whoredom was branding on the forehead. Apparently there is no evidence of such a practice.

(c) Problem Plays

This was a lean year for material produced on the problem plays, compared with the previous two years. N.F. Blake's note 'A Crux in *All's Well that Ends Well*' (*N&Q* 47[2000] 451–3) was the only publication dealing specifically with this play. Blake considers the critical debate surrounding the emendation to the First Folio of the phrase 'still-peering aire' to 'still-piecing' (III.ii.110–13). Blake agrees with those scholars who prefer 'still-peering' suggesting that the phrase means 'constantly reappearing' and in the context of the play can be read as 'indestructible'. The note concludes with a reading of the passage: 'You doom-laden messengers, sent on your swift path by fire, mistake your goal so that the indestructible air, which sings when pierced, is made to resound, and my lord does not utter his last gasp' (p. 453).

There were only three items this year dealing with *Measure for Measure*. Dennis Walder's chapter on *Measure for Measure* (pp. 213–40) in the Open University text *Shakespeare: Texts and Contexts*, edited by Kiernan Ryan, provides a useful introduction to the play for A-level and undergraduate students studying Shakespeare for the first time. The chapter is divided into three sections as Walder examines the themes of government, justice and women, using a question and answer format and including a summary of the key critical responses to the play. In keeping with the aims of the volume the essay's approach is historicist, with emphasis placed upon the text in performance. Each essay includes black and white photographs of past productions of the plays, and Walder uses these visual images to invite the reader to consider the interpretative opportunities afforded by such scenes as the interview between Isabella and Angelo in Act II, scene ii.

Stephanie Chamberlain's excellent essay, 'Defrocking Ecclesiastical Authority *Measure for Measure* and the Struggle for Matrimonial Reform in Early Modern England' (*BJJ* 7[200] 115–28), returns to the marriages at the end of the play to examine how each in turn reveals the tension 'between canon and civil authorities over the regulation of desacralized matrimony within a Protestant state' (p. 115). Chamberlain argues that, while Angelo represents civil authority in his punishment of others and specifically in his breaking of his marriage contract to Mariana, the source of Vincentio's authority is less clear. The Duke wants to enforce civil law, as demonstrated by his appointment of Angelo, but he ultimately chooses a solution to the marital disputes brought before him in the final act, which is in keeping with Catholic law, namely enforced marriage. His appearance during the 'marriage trial' as Duke and Friar underlines his conflicted role; as Chamberlain concludes, 'the Duke, however much he seeks to represent civil authority, nonetheless seems unable to escape a canonical past' (p. 125).

Lars Engle, in his essay '*Measure for Measure* and Modernity: The Problem of the Sceptic's Authority' (in Grady, ed., pp. 85–104), presents the Duke as a Montaignean sceptic, to argue that the play's complex attitudes towards government reflect emerging philosophical discourse.

Several key works appeared on *Troilus and Cressida* and each reveals the continuing concern with the question of what kind of play it is and where it should be grouped, not simply within the Shakespearian canon, but within the canon of early modern literary texts.

W.R. Elton, in *Troilus and Cressida and the Inns of Court Revels* takes issue with the play's status as a 'problem play' and the descriptions afforded it by critics such as Boas, Bradley and Chambers as 'dark' and 'bitter'. Elton argues that the aspects of the play which critics past and present find most troubling can be explained when the play is located within the context of the Inns of Court revels, the audience for whom it was originally written. The evidence Elton provides to support his claim is a detailed analysis of the features of such festivities as the *Gesta Grayorum* (1594–5) and the *Prince d'Amour* (1597–8), such as burlesque and misrule, which also appear in the play. Despite the meticulous research into the revels and close reading of the play the argument lacks cohesion, with chapters reading as though written in isolation from one another. Elton's claim to test *Troilus and Cressida* against the criteria of the problem play also fails to materialize, leaving the reader with a sense that this is an unfinished scholarly volume.

Matthew Greenfield's stimulating essay 'Fragments of Nationalism in *Troilus and Cressida*' (*SQ* 51[2000] 181–200) also acknowledges that play's ability to disturb, but argues that this is a result of 'its relentless attack on nationalism's narratives' (p. 182). Greenfield provides a local reading of the play, contrasting it with contemporary attitudes towards the myth of Troy and John Stubbes's pamphlet *The Gaping Gulf* to argue that Shakespeare, rather than legitimate the claims of nationalism and genealogy, as he does in the histories, seeks in *Troilus and Cressida* to expose their fictional and fragmented nature.

(d) Poetry

The most comprehensive treatment of Shakespeare's output for this year was A.D. Cousins's *Shakespeare's Sonnets and Narrative Poems*. The volume is attractively presented, with helpful up-to-date bibliographies available in the notes for each section. The studies of *Venus and Adonis*, *Lucrece* and the Sonnets combine close readings with discussion of cultural contexts and the volume is sure to be established as a valuable resource for undergraduates in the future. The account of *Venus and Adonis* mostly reviews current strands of critical thinking on the poem. Cousins is clearly right to underline the creative multiplicity of Venus's roles as seductress, but in the endeavour to demonstrate this the discussion became at points overly schematized. The profile of Adonis as anti-Narcissus required more detailed argument and Cousins's portrait of him as object of desire for the implied male reader is plausible, but it must be viewed as fairly lightly limned by Shakespeare in comparison with Marlowe's *Hero and Leander*: here, Cousins finds the description of Leander 'complements' that of Hero, whereas surely Marlowe's narrator rehearses a fairly conventional celebration of Hero in order to reserve his energies for the all too alluring Leander. A striking omission was a satisfying examination of Shakespeare's narrative voices in the poem. However, the succeeding account of *Lucrece* was altogether more substantial and ambitious. Cousins sets out concisely the narrative structures of Shakespeare's sources, casting his eye beyond Livy and Ovid to Boccaccio, Chaucer and Gower. The linking of the source material (most especially Livy) to Lucrece's 'profound sense of herself as a type or exemplar' was illuminating, as were the contextualizations of the narrative within the *de casibus* tradition, complaint literature, Edenic referencing and drama dealing with tyranny. Cousins's emphases upon 'the mutually defining nature of characterization' and the multiple schemes of objectification of Lucrece bring a hubristic Collatine much more dynamically into the frame of reference than is usual. Here, and indeed throughout the study, Cousins's interest in (Pyrrhonian) scepticism (in *Lucrece* 'the sceptical interrogation of exemplarity') is a fertile topic, but requires the kind of contextualization that is afforded elsewhere to Petrarchism, for example. In his account of the Sonnets, Cousins divides his studies, dealing with Sonnets 1–19, then 20–126 and 127–54. The introductory sections devoted to Petrarch, Sidney as poet, and Narcissus myths cover a good amount of ground economically. Particularly interesting emphases (for example Shakespeare's poetic speaker as engaging with the perceived role of Counsellor, possible classical and early modern strategies for evaluating male–male relations, etc.) could have been given greater space for enquiry—especially given the degree of repetition in evidence throughout the volume. Of the chapters considering the Sonnets Cousins is most rewarding in the final phases when he turns his attention to the interrelations between the poet, the dark lady and the young man: '[the speaker] depicts her through a process of wavering and oscillation, imposing fictions precariously upon her much as he did upon the youth'.

One of the most dynamic and detailed studies of the Sonnets in 2000 was Imtiaz Habib's 'Shakespeare and the Black Woman: Colonialism's Homosocial Eugenics and Black Desire' in her *Shakespeare and Race: Postcolonial Praxis in the Early Modern Period*. Making the telling point that 'contemporary historical scholarship and theoretical excursus have both found it easier to locate in the erasures of imperial Elizabethan literary construction marginalized black *male* subjectivity rather than *female*', Habib initially reviews existing historical and cultural fields of enquiry which may offer possibilities for locating black female subjectivities in early modern studies. Submitting that 'if feminist analysis (of the Sonnets) of the last two decades excavates the woman question, it does so within the comfortable proximity of white women's studies', she worries away in a number of insightful ways at the construction of racial subjectivities in this period: for example, unpacking the links between race and kin in early modern thinking and identifying in the first sub-sequence (encouraging the young man to marry) 'an instinct of race, a preservation of genus that is predicated on an exclusionary genealogical self marking'. Habib is particularly adept at unmasking the mindset of successive generations of readers of the Sonnets which, for example, has determined to privilege 'the young man's procreation' (which, in Habib's words, is still a 'not-event') over and above the poet-speaker's 'affair with the black woman which *has* happened'. Habib rejects the foregrounding of the 'young man' sub-sequence and contends that the later twenty-seven poems to the black woman (not the dark lady) 'embody and develop what has gone before, which is to say that they contain the body of the first sub-sequence and not the other way around'. She goes on to discover an 'intuitive mockery of the cruel mistress role in European courtly love convention and in Petrarchan practice, her instinctive ridiculing of the colonizer's culture and desire by playing the source of his torment as a figure not of unyielding chastity but of sexual vivacity'. With this analysis, she works systematically through Shakespeare's sequence, drawing upon the *donnée* that Shakespeare's lady must be attributed with a black subjectivity and never fails to uncover striking lines of attack. Ultimately, what is perhaps most seductive about Habib's analysis is that it self-consciously explores the textual politics of overstatement in order to disclose the implications of prevailing critical expectations: 'In sum, a postcolonial Shakespearean discourse cannot find a black woman in the performance of the material text beyond the tell-tale fossils of discursive struggle such as the trace elements outlined above. The utility of such a procedure lies in its foregrounding of the ur-fields that shape both, the material text of colonial literary practice, as well as its canonic cultural transmission.'

David Hawkes, 'Sodomy, Usury, and the Narrative of Shakespeare's *Sonnets*' (*RS* 14:iii[2000] 344–61), redirects attention to the discursive spaces shared by the concepts of sodomy and usury in early modern thinking and how these may enrich a reading of Shakespeare's sequence: 'The two vices were understood to be different manifestations of the same fundamental error: they both reflected a confusion between what is fruitful and what is barren.' This field of enquiry has already been negotiated in part by a number of critical voices (for example Pequigney and Goldberg); however, Hawkes's discussion is carefully mapped out and persuasive in its detail, drawing upon a host of contemporary documents and insights into *The Merchant of Venice* along the way. Despite the scope of the study, Hawkes makes room for some detailed analysis of the sequence itself and lingers over some perplexing conundrums: 'If reproductive sex is usurious, as the *Sonnets* suggest, then according to traditional morality it is in fact *un*natural. If one responds that usury is actually *not* unnatural, then one has abandoned the teleology which also designates sodomy a sin against nature.' In the area of the Sonnets' vexed logic, Jeffrey N. Nelson and Andrew D. Cling, 'Love's Logic Lost: The Couplet of Shakespeare's Sonnet 116' (*ANQ* 13:iii[2000] 14–20), restrict their sights to the couplet, 'If this be error and upon me prov'd, | I never writ, nor no man ever lov'd'. They submit that this is '*intentionally* complex and perhaps even *deliberately* misleading' (their italics) as they endeavour to pound the lines against several logical premises. They conclude that 'a grasp of the logic (or illogic) of Shakespeare's couplet supports the view that the couplet may not be an argument in the first place, but only a confident assertion of the truth of the account of love given in the sonnet'.

In 'Cheerful Girls and Willing Boys: Old and Young Bodies in Shakespeare's *Sonnets*' (*EMLS* 6:ii[2000] 1–26), Ian MacInnes invites the reader to identify possible points of engagement with early modern medical debates, most particularly with the subjects of transfusion and the processes of ageing. Acknowledging the Petrarchan convention of the superannuated speaker, MacInnes chooses to advocate that 'the subject positions of the three main characters of the *Sonnets* may be connected with the poems' representation of their humoral bodies'. MacInnes refreshes debates about humoral theorizing in the Sonnets by pointing to the repeated configuration of the old man, young man and woman in early modern medical and psychological works. Rather than promoting a direct influence of these manuals on Shakespeare, MacInnes persuasively concentrates on early modern habits of thinking in which 'the passions constantly called up the image of the old man, young man, and woman'. Drawing notably upon the theorizing of Sedgwick as well as a good range of sixteenth- and seventeenth-century medical-philosophical texts, MacInnes trains a convincing lens upon Shakespeare's collection, serving to broaden understanding of his poeticized triangulation of desire. Reference to early modern medical texts attending to theories of the mind would have added greater substance and persuasiveness to Marvin Krims' study 'Shakespeare's Sonnet 129: The Joys and Tribulations of Making Love' (*PsyArt* 4[2000], unpaginated). Nonetheless, some close attention is paid to the expectations of successive generations of critical readers of the Sonnets in this study, which concentrates upon psychoanalytical understandings of lust. Krims draws upon Freud's early studies of the libido as well as interestingly gesturing towards the work of Melanie Klein, Jeanette Haviland and Carol Maltesta, for example, in the course of the discussion. However, the study never really shakes off a predictable mode of analysis which is more interested in psychologizing 'the slaking of carnal desire' than in early modern understandings of lust and Shakespeare's sequence as a whole.

Robert F. Fleissner, 'The Most Difficult, "Mortall Moone" Sonnet: The Elizabeth and Essex Conjunction Reaffirmed' (*CLAJ* 43:iii[2000] 367–77), does little more than rehearse conventional interpretations of the fifth line of Sonnet 107 ('The mortall Moone hath her eclipse indur'de') in terms of Elizabeth's death, illness, lunar symbolism and an Essex connection, and then asserts under the guise of a conclusion that, although 'any specific allusion to Essex implied in no. 107 may not be too clear-cut ... [it] still should not be discountenanced simply out of hand'. Similarly turning to textual details, in 'Mending Shakespeare's Sonnet 146' (*N&Q* 47[2000] 91–2) I.A. Shapiro proposes 'Beat down these rebbell powres that thee array' to replace the 'obviously defective second line', 'My sinfull earth these rebbell powres that thee array'. Colin Burrow, in 'Shakespeare's Wrinkled Eye: Sonnet 3, Lines 11–12' (*N&Q* 47[2000] 90–1), invites his reader to consider these lines in Sonnet 3 in terms of 'the wrinkled appearance of the aged version of the young man and ... the medium through which he is imagined to be looking at his son'. Denis Corish, in '"The world's due, by the grave and thee": Shakespeare, Sonnet 1.14' (*N&Q* 47[2000] 453–5), argues that the line in question is, against the tide of critical opinion, 'syntactically regular': 'The world's due by the grave is the eternity of the species. ... If the young man does not breed, be will "eate" not only the world's due by himself, his offspring, but even the world's due by the grave, the continued life of the species.'

In 'Ovid, Petrarch, and Shakespeare's *Sonnets*' (in Taylor, ed., *Shakespeare's Ovid: The 'Metamorphoses' in the Plays and Poems*), Gordon Braden underlines that 'the last change detailed in Ovid's long poem is the poet's metamorphosis into his own reputation' and proceeds to explore the liaisons that may be drawn between poetic achievement and spiritual transcendence in Shakespeare's collection. Refreshingly, Braden stresses the important textual legacy of the *fin' amors* of troubadour writing for early modern sonneteers, and inscribes Shakespeare's collection within a wider frame which considers, for example, Thomas Watson's *Hekatompathia* and Barnabe Barnes's *Parthenophil and Parthenophe*. His decision to compare and contrast the ways in which Petrarchism and Ovidianism were engaged with by Shakespeare and his contemporaries demands more space but, in general, Braden's brief study is a thoughtful enquiry into a burgeoning area of Shakespearian scholarship. Finally in this section on the Sonnets, there was a belated but pleasingly detailed review by Colin Burrow, 'Editing Shakespeare's Sonnets' (*CQ* 29:i[2000] 61–74), of Vendler's and Duncan-Jones's editions of the Sonnets. Burrow is at present editing Shakespeare's poetry for the Oxford Shakespeare series and is clearly very aware of the threats, or otherwise, which rival editions pose. While he acknowledges the valuable scholarship evident in both, he engages at greater length with Vendler's edition and finds shortcomings in her commitment to aesthetics which he feels is an endeavour 'to stop the poems falling prey to sententious moralisers or dull old diggers in the *OED*, or to Marxists, feminists, and deconstructionists'. In the latter phases of the discussion, he turns to Duncan-Jones, finding her 'trenchant' criticism of the sequence 'crisp' and stimulating, but feels that many of her enquiries are impaired by the omission of strategic deployments of 'might' and 'if'.

In *Variable Passions: A Reading of Shakespeare's 'Venus and Adonis'* Anthony Mortimer devotes a book-length study to Shakespeare's narrative poem in an endeavour to return it to the centrality it enjoyed in the 1590s. In the course of his volume Mortimer gives a valuable review of the scholarship on the poem and offers his reader important contexts—notably those of Ovid and, more refreshingly, those of Italian Renaissance poetry. At the outset, he confesses that he has taken the 'somewhat unfashionable option of devoting my three central chapters to what is, in effect, a running commentary', believing that 'close sequential reading still has a great deal to offer'. This approach is at its most valuable when he unpacks the rhetorical complexity of the *Venus and Adonis* and exposes the witty conundrums that Shakespeare poses as the narrative unfolds: 'If sexual intercourse is, as [Venus] argues, the fruit of maturity, how do we take her own admission that she wishes to taste Adonis while he is still "unripe"?' However, the fact that some 200 pages are devoted to the quarry appears to have less welcome consequences: for example, the apparent availability of space means that Mortimer does allow himself a rather long run-up before the discussion gathers momentum and there are *longueurs* in the subsequent commentaries, prompted by repetition and slackness in argumentation. Indeed, at points he is found to have a preference for citation and description rather than analysis, and makes further space at regular intervals to indulge a penchant for informal quipping: 'Holding hands with someone on horseback is not exactly easy. Venus profits from the situation to pull Adonis down to her own level'; 'We might have expected [Venus] to make a good deal more of her divinity'; 'There is rather more to the oft-proclaimed earthiness of Venus than a strong sexual appetite'; 'we are, indeed, slyly encouraged to think that her protestations of eternal devotion to the memory of Adonis should be taken with a pinch of salt'. On the whole, Mortimer's analysis gives a welcome emphasis to a relatively neglected Shakespearian text, but it would have been more persuasive with more decisive editing.

In 'Ovid "Renascent" in *Venus and Adonis* and *Hero and Leander*' (in Taylor, ed.), John Roe considers the Calvinist sympathies of Arthur Golding (and, more particularly, those of his influential translation of the *Metamorphoses*) before turning his attention to Marlowe and Shakespeare via Lodge's *Scillaes Metamorphosis*. While emphasizing the formalist influence of Lodge on Shakespeare's narrative poem, he also stresses Shakespeare's and Marlowe's interest in the comic dimensions of the narrative, which are not evident in Lodge. Roe suggests that Marlowe's poem is more fruitfully considered alongside Ovid's *Heroides* and the poetry of Musaeus rather than the *Metamorphoses*. By way of conclusion, Roe consoles his reader that if 'Shakespeare proves less subversive than Marlowe', if his wit is 'not so brilliantly acerbic' as Marlowe's, it is 'more tender'. In the lively discussion '*Venus and Adonis* and Ovidian Indecorous Wit' (in Taylor, ed.), Pauline Kiernan focuses on Venus as 'a figure of physical and rhetorical excess' and explores the ways in which this figure is starkly contrasted with 'the unripened, seemingly sexless mortal who is consistently described in cosmological terms as more like a divinity than the actual goddess'. Eschewing a discussion which deploys Ovid as background to a Shakespearian foreground, Kiernan devotes some detailed attention to the *Metamorphoses* and the *Amores*, revealing the frictions that arise between assertions of divine status and erotic desire in these collections. However, her insistence upon a 'truly tragic decorum' being in evidence at the close of Shakespeare's poem required more detailed argument.

Margaret Tudeau-Clayton, in 'Stepping Out of Narrative Line: A Bit of Word, and Horse, Play in *Venus and Adonis*' (*ShS* 53[2000] 12–38), explores the implications of the rhetorical trope of *aphaeresis* ('The iron bit he crusheth 'tween his teeth') as a starting point from which to consider early modern formulations of desire, temperance and control. In the same volume Peter J. Smith, 'A "consummation devoutly to be wished": The Erotics of Narration in *Venus and Adonis*' (*ShS* 53[2000] 25–38) proposes an intertextual reading of the poem. Both studies are interested in accumulating congeries of texts to set before the reader, circling around the Shakespeare's poem, rather than offering a sustained engagement with it. Nonetheless, Smith's deployment of Nashe's 'The choise of valentines' and 'Nashe his dildo', Rochester's 'The Imperfect Enjoyment' (Behn's 'The Disappointment' is unaccountably left out of the frame!), Chaucer's Wife of Bath, and so on provides a lively environment in which to consider anxious masculinity and unruly femininity in a poem which emerges as 'both a riotous male fantasy of being seduced by the goddess of love and a deeper interrogation of Raleigh's overwhelming question, "What is our life?"'. Cheney and Prescott, eds., *Approaches to Teaching Shorter Elizabethan Poetry*, is a wide-ranging and valuable collection which not only proposes pedagogic lines for attacking these texts but also reflects upon the ways in which modern criticism may be adapted creatively with, and indeed *extended* fruitfully by, undergraduates. It is to the credit of this volume that it brings together approaches to the poetry of Skelton, Gascoigne, Drayton, Elizabeth I, Campion and Wroth, for example, with studies of more familiar voices on the curriculum, such as Donne, Shakespeare and Jonson. Of particular interest for this section are Georgia E. Brown's '"Tradition and the Individual Talent": Teaching Ovid and the Epyllion in the Context of the 1590s', and Michael Schoenfeldt's 'Making Shakespeare's *Sonnets* Matter in the Classroom'.

In '"Poor instruments" and Unspeakable Events in *The Rape of Lucrece*', in her *The Rhetoric of the Body from Ovid to Shakespeare*, Lynn Enterline decides to tackle the issues which she feels have most occupied *Lucrece*'s critics of late ('rhetoric, rape, subjectivity and the female voice') by focusing on the relations between language and the body in the poem. Emphasizing Lucrece's deployment of her body as text and the links that may be posited between writing and rape in Shakespeare's narrative, Enterline is most insightful in her return to Ovid's writing. One of her major contentions is that Shakespeare gives a voice to the silent Lucretia of the *Fasti* by drawing upon alternative examples, most of which can be found in the *Metamorphoses*: for example Orpheus, Philomela, Hecuba. She stresses the ways in which rape (physical/linguistic) is intimately linked in the poem to Lucrece's accessing of a public voice, and she chooses to resist some current critical voices by underlining the 'productive or constitutive effects of Shakespeare's rhetoric'. Throughout the chapter she reviews criticism of the poem in recent times and carefully explores how aesthetic and political reservations have dogged its reception. In addition to concentrating upon all things Ovidian, Enterline also emphasizes the Petrarchan 'voice in "exile" devoted to questioning the limits of its own power to represent the self' and reflects upon the textual bonding potentially unfolding between narrator and implied (male) reader in Shakespeare's poem. This volume also includes accounts of *The Winter's Tale* and Marston's *Metamorphosis of Pigmalion's Image*, among others.

Misako Matsuda's 'The Bee Emblem in *The Rape of Lucrece*' (in Takahashi, ed., *Hot Questrists after the English Renaissance: Essays on Shakespeare and his Contemporaries*) initially underlines that Shakespeare's poem acknowledges the thematic interests of his sources by pointing up the need for (self-)government and the evils of tyranny—'For kings like gods should govern every thing'. However, the main part of the discussion focuses on the influence on *Lucrece* of the bee motif in contemporaneous emblem literature: the orderly working of the commonweal; swarm as revenging host; bitter and sweet love (honey/sting) and so on. The discussion concludes with the submission that 'the emblematic image of bees effectively links a personal tragedy to disorder at a national level'. Maurice Charney's *Shakespeare on Love and Lust* takes the reader on a whistle-stop tour back and forth across the Shakespeare canon and manages to find room for brief accounts of *Lucrece* and *Venus and Adonis* (surprisingly, given the subject in hand, the gestures in the direction of the Sonnets are even briefer). However, the panoramic ambitions of the book mean that discussion inevitably remains fragmented and summative and ultimately fails to offer fresh insights into the poetry. In '"This blemish'd fort": The Rape of the Hearth in Shakespeare's *Lucrece*' (in Boesky and Crane, eds., *Form and Reform in Renaissance England*), Heather Dubrow draws substantially upon the *Lucrece* material explored in *Shakespeare and Domestic Loss* (see *YWES* 79[1999]). Nonetheless, Dubrow's insistence upon Shakespeare's narrative of loss in terms of property violation remains persuasive and is tightly argued here. Reminders that Troy may be configured in the poem as 'a trace of sixteenth-century English culture' and that in Livy's *Historia* and Ovid's *Fasti* Collatine does not initiate the boasting competition, for example, may suggest some timely checks on recent studies of the poem and offer fertile lines of future enquiry. Finally, with reference to *Lucrece*, Donald W. Rude, 'A Shakespearean Ghost in the Catalogues of Peter Parker' (*N&Q* 47[2000] 187–8), offers the possibility that Parker may have published an edition of *Lucrece* during the middle years of the seventeenth century which has not yet come to light.

In '*The Phoenix and the Turtle*' (*ShN* 50[2000]), Clare Asquith joins a growing number of critics endeavouring to recuperate Shakespeare as a Catholic writer—'not simply by upbringing, but from inner conviction'. She underlines that Robert Chester (a contributor to the [1601] collection *Love's Martyr* in which the poem appears) and Sir John Salusbury (the patron) were known to be particularly fond of allegorical and acrostic writing. However, she does not support Honigmann's contention that the poem might be a celebration of Salusbury's marriage to his wife Ursula. Instead she discovers in Shakespeare's writing a coded referencing of the annual ritual of Palm Sunday, and is most illuminating when she allows Shakespeare's text to rub shoulders with the Thomist 'Lauda Sion' (Southwell's translation published as 'A Holy Hymn' [in 1595]) which would form a key part of the Palm Sunday proceedings: 'Under kinds two in appearance | Two in show but one in substance'. Rather than identifying a married couple in the poem, Asquith looks to the 'married chastity' as being 'the spiritual "marriage"', the dedicated vows, of Holy Orders'. The Jesuit martyrs Southwell and Henry Walpole are now brought into the frame: 'fellow-students, friends, priests, men of such integrity and courage that they drew universal admiration'. Ultimately, Asquith views Shakespeare's text as having been designed to be recited at a 'secret Palm Sunday requiem over the ashes of the two martyrs' and as offering the author 'an opportunity to proclaim his own allegiance to the central mysteries of the ancient faith'.

In 'A Funeral Elegy, Shakespeare, and Elizabeth Cary' (*BJJ* 7[2000] 567–87), James Hirsh makes a very compelling case for reconsidering the authorship of 'A Funerall Elegye in memory of the late vertuous Maister William Peeter' [1612]. Hirsh acknowledges how the text has become the 'culminating work' in the Norton

Shakespeare, Riverside Shakespeare (second edition) and Longman Shakespeare despite the controversy which earlier surrounded its attribution. Nonetheless, he is persuasive in his contention that its place in the Shakespeare corpus should now be rethought because a large body of internal evidence makes a link with Cary much more plausible, though he is keen to point out that he is not suggesting 'that [the elegy] "belongs hereafter" with Cary's works, merely that the evidence of [her] authorship is strong enough to warrant the removal of the poem from collections of Shakespeare's works'. Hirsh draws attention, for example, to verse form (elegy's iambic pentameter quatrains irregularly interrupted by couplets is the dominant form in *Mariam*, but in none of Shakespeare's plays or poems) among other features, but is most convincing in his study of word associations (involving two- and some three-word parallels in phrasing in both the elegy and *Mariam* which occur '*nowhere* in any of the numerous works of Shakespeare'). Hirsh concludes that 'the statistical possibilities that forty such conjunctions in one poem of 578 lines will recur in another of 2,172 lines by a different author is very small'. Drawing also upon brief considerations of Oxford connections, Renaissance conventions of disguised initialling and thematic links between the elegy and *Mariam*, Hirsh has thrown down a gauntlet which is sure to be taken up in 2001.

(e) Histories

He's been at it again. This year saw another Graham Holderness monograph on the histories, entitled *Shakespeare: The Histories* (a category supplemented here by a chapter on 'one of the most original and sustained meditations on ... problems of history and historiography', *Hamlet*). Holderness's interests (some of which are acknowledged to have been 'collaboratively developed' with Carol Banks) have shifted in the years since *Shakespeare Recycled* [1992], something which is perhaps most obvious at the points where he looks away from the plays under consideration. Where the earlier book explicitly situated itself within Marxist and historical-materialist criticism from the 1960s onwards, this one gives us resonant (and unhistoricized) quotations from Wordsworth, Eliot, Hopkins and, especially, the King James Bible. The turn, in Holderness's own words, is towards metaphor and word, and away from theory or concept: 'I no longer seek the solid actuality of historical presence, but rather dwell on history's shadows and silences, those lost presences and potentialities that can by their absence disturb and disconcert the present' (p. 13). Shadows and silences, however, are themselves historicized in two thoughtful and provocative contextualizing chapters which return to Nashe, Heywood, and key moments in the plays themselves to show how the cultural context of this historical-dramatic project enabled the exploration of difference: 'they paint images of civil war in a time committed to domestic peace; they analyse masculine power in a context of female authority; they recreate a lost aristocratic glory with a complex consciousness of genuine regret and relieved resignation. In a historical vision simultaneously influenced by aristocratic nostalgia and plebeian irony, they lament antique chivalric prowess and glance critically, from a modern, civil and plebeian perspective, at antiquity's destructive self-contradictions' (p. 41).

After considering *Hamlet*'s negotiations with revenance, memory, antiquity and—in the shape of the gravedigger—archaeology, Holderness turns to *Richard III*, reading it as structured around the foundering (on pre-existing myths of his own monstrosity, and the ghosts he himself has made) of Richard's attempt to control 'his environment in all its temporal dimensions: present, past and future' (p. 107). The following chapter, on *1 Henry VI*, takes issue with the 'customary' (and 'at first glance entirely natural') opinion that it is focused on 'the crown and on the dynastic struggles over possession; on aristocratic rebellion and internecine warfare; on succession and usurpation, regicide and revenge'. Holderness points out that the play's central figures are a soldier, a woman and a child, and argues that its central theme is not history as providential narrative but as 'a manifestly contemporary exercise of lament and resurrection, nostalgic longing and sober reflection, vivid reenactment and saddened resignation' (p. 110). It begins with an elegiac vision of Henry V, and the chivalric code which the play to some extent celebrates is persistently invoked by metaphors of memorial or monument. But the play also destabilizes the categories on which the code is based. Not only is Joan ('exemplar of low-born greatness; a heroic woman; a martial maid; a victimised innocent; a heretic who became a national heroine, and a witch who eventually secured the status of sainthood', p. 124) Talbot's opposite; Talbot himself is feminized at his death by his concern for his son, both in the sense of the maternal emotions he expresses and through his abandonment of his own heroic code when he urges John to flee. 'French' and 'English' too are not as mutually opposed as they may seem, despite their divided judgements on Joan, as the trajectories of Burgundy and Joan's father between 'French' and 'English' indicate. At the play's end, Joan, the 'true centre' of the play, 'an empty and self-generating space of plenitude and vacancy, presence and absence' (p. 133) is on the way to sainthood, while the last sight of Talbot has been of a corpse 'stinking and fly-blown'.

From one play often supposed heroic to its chronological predecessor. Holderness's discussion of *Henry V* focuses on the way that play is haunted by a past; Henry is urged to 'invoke' his familial spirits to fulfil his own personal destiny. The players produce a 'new historical sacrament, making the audience sharers in the miraculous transformation of action to character, present to past, theatre to history' (p. 146). This sacrament is of war rather than peace, though; Henry as soldier incarnates a nightmarish view of war, and the seeming egalitarianism of the pre-Agincourt preparations is dissolved in the post-battle note that 'none else of name' have died: 'it might have contained, among those nameless common soldiers, Henry's companions of the previous night, John Bates and Alexander Court, whose names he never sought to know' (p. 155). The *Henry IV* plays, in their circling around past events and future promises, are read for their attempts to construct historical process. Henry's opening manifesto is disrupted by 'unwelcome news' which reinserts him into the past divisions he seeks to transcend; Percy's epic vision of history is challenged by Hal's self-enlistment in the heroic tradition for which he is destined; Northumberland's surviving his son leads him to abandon the heroic vision of *res gestae* in favour of a promised holocaust; Mowbray and Westmoreland argue over the supposed turning point of Richard's cancelling the combat between Bolingbroke and Mowbray's father. Finally, a long chapter on *Richard II* continues the exploration of characters 'manufacturing history before it happens' (p. 183); here history, as elsewhere, is already elegiac, marked by knowledge of absence and the paradoxes of historical presence. Richard's tragic vision repeats Isabella's in II.ii: the king, in telling stories, makes his own history even as he ceases to be part of the patriarchal narrative.

This book supplements rather than replaces Holderness's earlier, more materialist, work on the histories. In reversing the Tillyardian sequence, he provides a fascinating demonstration of the ways in which these plays, collectively and individually, can be read to resist such grand narratives, in part through their own differing suspicions of historiography. The focus here is on close (and deconstructively inspired) readings of particular moments within the plays, so that each chapter is split into short sections of two or three pages. The tone is meditative, allusive, and at times poetic; the book gathers momentum as interrelations between the plays come into focus and topics are revisited. This is, finally, a book about 'Shakespeare's histories': its great strength is not what it has to say about individual plays (a fair amount of which would be familiar in substance to diligent readers of the periodical literature) but its synthetic reach. A book not to be missed—but best read whole rather than dipped into.

Margaret Healy's short book *Richard II* [1998] has unfortunately been neglected in these pages. Her first chapter ('Political Voices'), after pointing out that contrasting chronicle images of Richard as martyr or tyrant help to shape the play, focuses not on specific sources but on the humanist political rhetorics of disease, humoral medicine, and husbandry to be found in such writers as Erasmus, Elyot, or Buchanan. The vocabularies of both humanism and absolutism, however, recur in such a variety of situations (and are used by so many different speakers) that neither can be trusted. From this textual indeterminacy, Healy turns in her second chapter to the ways in which Richard's story itself could be given meaning, taking the reader through the Essex and Hayward affairs and sundry Elizabethan references to Richard as examples. She concludes that refashionings of Richard's story such as Shakespeare's play played 'a crucial part' in seeding the alternative visions enabling Charles's deposition and execution: 'the political significance of staging the deposition and killing of a king in the 1590s ... lay ... in the offering of it as a real possibility, with a historical precedent, in the wake of absolutism ... the impact of the spectacle itself should not be underestimated' (p. 29).

The question is pursued in the following chapter, 'Unstable Signs', which engages with the play's metadrama (here identified mainly as references to the 'world as stage' trope in the context of kingship) before going on to consider its carnivalesque elements, which Healy proposes prepared people's minds for change by revealing the contingency of things ('if we are all playing roles we might play different, better ones than those allotted to us', p. 37). Laying bare the conventional roots of political life is accompanied by a similar demonstration of the slipperiness of language. This is especially challenging when power is legitimized by reference to the word of God, and Healy provides some impressive close readings of the play's language, and the mirror scene in particular, to support the point. The gap between discursive constructions of masculinity and its performance in the play is the subject of the next chapter ('Gender Perspectives'). Richard himself, of course, is 'a paradigm of female frailty as shaped by early modern patriarchy' (p. 53), and the play shows us 'a few competent women locked into roles which forbid them centre-stage parts, and several foolish, vain unreasonable men—including King Richard—inhabiting centric roles they are totally unfit for' (pp. 55–6). The final chapter briefly surveys some strands of critical interpretation of the play, and ends with a short tour through some mostly English stagings of it (including some interesting reflections on the recent Warner/Shaw performance).

The book is halfway between a survey and an original monograph, something presumably attributable to its British Council origins, and it can certainly be recommended as an introductory text. The chapters on gender and unstable signs are the most stimulating, but I was unconvinced by Healy's talking up the 'impact' of the play. Though she produces some examples of how Richard's story was reproduced in 1640s polemic, none of them give any indication of the impact of Shakespeare's 'spectacle', let alone that it played any kind of 'crucial part' in enabling political actions fifty years after its first performance. Certainly her statement that it 'helped to prepare the way for the deposition and killing of a king and the increasing democratization of government half a century later' (p. 37) is unsupported by the kinds of arguments she thinks necessary elsewhere in the book. The kind of defamiliarization of gender roles also claimed to operate in the play (and any play with cross-casting) has none of these real-world effects claimed for it, merely being identified as 'an essential precursor to social change' (p. 52). Despite the odd obeisance to the vital role of performers in producing meaning onstage, the Leavisite imperative appears disappointingly frequently, both implicitly and in such explicit examples as 'It is remarkably easy, therefore, for the audience to concur with the Duchess's angry assessment of Gaunt's virility' or 'Surely such boastful pretensions to virility and manhood as Mowbray's and the feudal peers' in the gage scene ... are being consciously undermined by such theatrical manipulations?'.

Several articles attempted to trace patterns across the plays. Michele Stanco's 'Historico-Tragico-Comical Kings: Genre Conventions and/as Emblems of Power in Shakespeare's Histories' (in Szönyi and Wymer, eds., *The Iconography of Power: Ideas and Images of Rulership on the English Renaissance Stage*, pp. 117–46) considers the ways in which the plays can be considered 'emblematic'. This he links into their 'opacity' (openness), in both their historicization of power structures and subjectivity and their generic identity. *Richard II* is discussed as a 'historical tragedy', *1 Henry IV* as 'historical bildungskomodie', and *Henry V* as 'historical comedy'. Such mingled genres produce 'historical multiperspectivism', a new and more dialogic form of historical subjectivity, to parallel their portrayals of power and subjectivity.

Tom McAlindon's 'Swearing and Forswearing in Shakespeare's Histories: The Playwright as Contra-Machiavel' (*RES* 51[2000] 208–29) begins from the point that, whatever Shakespeare's Catholic connections, oaths were a focal point for any subject opposed to the new English religio-political order. Shakespeare's histories elaborate and intensify the 'abundance of royal and aristocratic perjuries' (p. 214) in his chronicle sources, refracting earlier centuries' swearing and forswearing through his understanding of both recent English political history and the Machiavellian revolution in politics *tout court*. His histories both chart the decline of chivalry and endorse the chivalric ideal. McAlindon ranges across most of the histories, ending with an anti-Machiavellian reading of Hal as debunker rather than deceiver in the *Henry IV* plays.

Cristoph Reinfandt, in 'Reading Shakespeare Historically: "Postmodern" Attitudes and the History Plays' (in Bode and Klooss, eds., pp. 73–89), provides a broad-brush survey of critical approaches and argues that postmodern theory is well placed to help us investigate 'texts which transcend the most fundamental distinctions in the field of cultural productivity such as elitist vs. popular, aesthetic vs. political, affirmative vs. critical, progressive vs. conservative, historicist vs.

universal'(p. 85). On a simpler level, Lawrence Danson provides a lucid and informed introduction to the histories in *Shakespeare's Dramatic Genres*. Undergraduates will benefit from its focus on the question-generating nature of these texts.

Lisa Hopkins, in 'The *Iliad* and the *Henriad*: Epics and Brothers' (*CML* 19[1999] 149–71), challenges the appropriateness of continuing to use a name associating the *Henry IV* plays and *Henry V* with epic. While allowing, and indeed exploring, epic 'echoes and resonances' in the plays, Hopkins argues that, in comparison with other kinds of intertextualities in them, the link to epic is limited. The plays inhabit a different kind of time to the epic, and their characters stand in a different relation to times to come. Indeed, even the Greek–Trojan opposition seemingly so fundamental to the epic nature of the *Iliad* is not as clear-cut on a close reading, so that *Henry V*'s references to both sides 'undoes easy divisions between the French as the foreign enemy and the British as a unified whole' (p. 169).

E.A.J. Honigmann's 'Shakespeare's Self-Repetitions and *King John*' (*ShSur* 53[2000] 175–83) continues his half-century engagement with the relationship between Shakespeare's history and the anonymous Queen's men play *The Troublesome Reign of King John*. The article lists ten ways in which the characters, structural elements, historiography and scenic developments in *King John* resemble those in other Shakespeare plays, before going on to consider how the presence of similar elements in *The Troublesome Reign* impacts upon the debate over *King John*'s debt to the anonymous play. Honigmann argues that *King John* should not be seen as reworking *The Troublesome Reign*, though a puzzling reluctance to engage with recent editorial theory—and in particular Laurie Maguire's work on suspect texts—means that his evidence is less persuasive than it might be. Examples include assertions that Burbage's arguments with the widow Brayne over the theatre 'seem to be reflected' in the family feud outside Angers in both plays, or that *The Troublesome Reign*'s use of the phrase 'by some devine instinct' is derived from *Richard III*'s 'by a divine instinct' (and that this in turn supports *King John*'s precedence). Other readers may not be swayed by the article's fondness for rhetorical questions of a distinctly bardolatrous tint ('who, except Shakespeare, could have *imagined* the Bastard ...?'). Notwithstanding such cavils, Honigmann's command of the terms this debate, to which he has already contributed so much, makes this an article to chew over, if not to swallow whole.

Maurice Hunt's 'Antimetabolic *King John*' (*Style* 34[2000] 380–401) investigates the play's use of the chiastic trope *antimetabole* (the repetition of words in successive phrases in reverse). Hunt shows that, though the play's plot cannot be said to be patterned chiastically (the wrong person rises at the end), chiastic rhetoric's mirroring effect helps produce its sense of (variously) ideational indifference, claustrophobia and political stalemate. This in turn supports a reading of the play as moving beyond crude anti-Catholic polemic towards an anticlimactic, anti-monumental vision of politics and history. Eva Hartby, in 'The End of *King John*' (*OL* 55[2000] 263–95), presents an opposing view. Hartby defends the clarity of both the play's construction and its political morality, arguing that if John is not regarded as poisoned by a monk (she sees Hubert's words as 'the invention of an apparently guilty servant in an awkward situation'), the play's ending is much more coherent. She also argues that the lords do not return to John at the end of the play in order to serve him, and that John's complete isolation before his death allows a conventional, and unironic, moral to be drawn. In places the article reads a little like Thurber's Macbeth Murder Mystery, both in its verbal details ('the characters who have the strongest motives are also shown to get an opportunity for the murder', p. 269) and its literal-minded approach to the text, but the article does make some interesting suggestions on how its interpretation of the play could work in performance. György E. Szönyi, in 'Matching the "Falles of Princes" and "Machiavell": Tradition and Subversion in the Historiography and Iconography of Shakespeare's Histories' (in Szönyi and Wymer, eds., pp. 5–32) provides a survey of critical approaches to both historiography and iconography in Shakespeare's histories before concluding (with Stephen Orgel) that 'one cannot dismiss the knowledge of the visual-iconographic traditions of the age; however it would be naive to expect [Shakespeare] to follow these traditions unimaginatively either in their ideology or in respect of the formal elements' (p. 18). He demonstrates this by reference to both verbal and visual imagery in *King John*, though the discussion is oriented towards supporting the general point made above rather than providing a comprehensive account of the play.

Mark Falco includes a chapter on 'charismas in conflict' in *Richard II* in his *Charismatic Authority in Early Modern English Tragedy*. He revisits the question of early modern subjectivity alongside the play's concern with the king's two bodies, using the ambiguous relationship between group identity and individual subjectivity in the charismatic community as a model. For him, 'the natural body of the charismatic leader functions on two levels at once, acting as the center not only of the disposition of individual power but also of the mythification of group power' (p. 78). Investigating individual characters' particular blends of personal, lineage and a variety of office charismas, Falco shows that their fortunes are never independent of larger groups of family, faction or nation. Paradoxically, for such a subtle investigation of the sources of, and dynamic interrelations between, Richard's and Bolingbroke's charismas, the piece also contains some distinctly Bradleyan character criticism: Bolingbroke 'probably dissociates himself from his royal cousin not because arm to arm combat is anathema to kingship *per se*, but rather because— and this becomes the Lancastrian position—proper justice is alien to Richard's rulership' (p. 72).

Tom Bishop proposes a new approach to Shakespeare's relationship to the Reformation in 'The Burning Hand: Poetry and Reformation in Shakespeare's *Richard II*' (*R&L* 32[2000] 29–47). He suggests that *Richard II* shows the impact of the Reformation's cultural dialectic of ceremonial royalism and counter-ceremonialist reform, and that Shakespeare's portrayal of Richard 'brings together public authority and its degradation with a novel form of specular subjectivity emerging out of iconoclasm'. Bishop also suggests that Foxe's account of Cranmer (owner of the burning hand in question) informs the play's portrayal of Richard. The impact of the Reformation on imaginative writing is not only visible at the level of doctrinal allusion, but also in the kinds of new subjectivities and processes it provided for writers to work with.

Nick Cox, in contrast, finds in the play glimpses of a carceral society to come. In '"Subjected Thus": Plague and Panopticism in *Richard II*' (*EMLS* 6:ii[2000] 1–44), he provides a Foucauldian reading, tracing within aspects of Elizabethan responses to plague outbreaks a proto-panoptical power also resonating in the play's representation of monarchical power. Cox argues that the political power of

Richard's absolutist sovereignty is inversely proportional to its effectiveness as a political technology. As Elizabeth's did, it generates rather than eliminates a resistance which is emphatically not subject to some future Greenblattian containment. Bolingbroke's power, in contrast, as described in III.ii, 'makes the relatively unproductive (the old, the young, women) work in its interests' and his 'new order manifests itself not in the public annihilation of the monarch's body but in the process of its subjection to individualising confinement'.

Raphaelle Costa de Beauregard, in 'From Allegory to Performance: the King's "Third" Body in *Richard II*' (in Happé, ed., *Tudor Theatre 5: Allegory in the Theatre*, pp. 235–49), attends to I.i, II.ii and V.v as part of an argument that the dramaturgy of the play's opening scene is innovative in its avoidance of allegory and emblem, instead insisting on images of corporeality. Some of the arguments advanced depend too much upon the visual arts to convince in a dramatic context ('the image of the shadow … appears in Whitney, and must therefore be read here as an emblem'), but there is an interesting discussion of the parallel between the duality of actor/character and royal bodies natural and politic.

Molly Smith, in 'Mutant Scenes and "Minor" Conflicts in *Richard II*' (in Callaghan, ed., pp. 263–75), argues that *Richard II* finally stages an authorization of the feminine in its last act, notwithstanding the fact that the early part of the play dramatizes its erasure and subjection: 'in Richard's court, familial considerations are sidestepped and women's voices, the ones that insist most eloquently on the bonds of kinship, remain muted and marginal; by contrast, Henry's court foregrounds their concerns, allowing them a degree of empowerment even at the expense of silencing proponents of masculinist ideologies such as the loyal York' (p. 272). The extent to which kinship bonds are solely a 'feminine' concern in the play could have been more persuasively argued—Smith claims, for example, that Gaunt's famous censure of Richard 'draws its force and legitimacy from [the Duchess's] earlier grief'—but the account of the last act convincingly details the way in which Bolingbroke's new order incorporates where Richard's excluded.

Geraldo U. de Sousa focuses on Joan and Margaret in the *Henry VI* plays in a chapter in his *Shakespeare's Cross-Cultural Encounters*. Though he provides a competent close reading of the plays and the historical figures themselves, de Sousa's account is hamstrung by its almost completely ignoring feminist criticism of the plays (there is no mention, for example, of Rackin and Howard's *Engendering a Nation*), and as a consequence provides little that is new ('through a gender exchange, they subvert a male-dominated world'). B.J. Sokol, in 'Manuscript Evidence for an Earliest Date of *Henry VI Part One*' (*N&Q* 47[2000] 58–63), contributes to the early/late start debate by linking the play's references to Temple Hall and its nearby garden to the completion of the Elizabethan Temple Hall by late April 1591.

Two articles (both discussed in detail in section 1 above) considered the relationship between *The Contention* and *2 Henry VI*. Roger Warren, in 'The Quarto and Folio texts of *2 Henry VI*: A Reconsideration' (*RES* 51[2000] 193–207) concludes that features of Q indicate a report, but not of F, for F itself is a revised text, omitting some chronicle-derived details present in Q. Barbara Kreps, in 'Bad Memories of Margaret? Memorial Reconstruction versus Revision in *The First Part of the Contention* and *2 Henry VI*' (*SQ* 51[2000] 154–80) looks in particular at Margaret's character, concluding that each play offers a coherent character conception, though they do not agree with each other. Given this coherence, neither text can be satisfactorily identified as the product of actor (or printer) mis-shaping.

Editorial work on *3 Henry VI* led to two contrasting interpretations (see full discussion in section 1 above) of the resonances of the Warwickshire name Somerville. This which belonged both to participants in the Wars of the Roses and to a deranged Catholic would-be assassin of Elizabeth I, supposedly in cahoots with one Edward Arden, whose head (along with Arden's) was placed on London bridge in 1583. Randall Martin, in 'Rehabilitating John Somerville in *3 Henry VI*' (*SQ* 51[2000] 332–40) argues that the 'surprisingly positive' portrayal of Somerville is a 'coded portrait that challenges the official verdict on his contemporary namesake' (p. 339). John D. Cox, in 'Local References in *3 Henry VI*' (*SQ* 51[200] 340–52) suggests that the omission of Somerville's name in stage directions and dialogue may indicate a continuing sensitivity about the case, but focuses more on Shakespeare's decision to upgrade the importance of Warwick. The roles of both Somerville and Warwick, and his integration of further 'local' Warwickshire references into the Coventry scene, suggest 'special interests in his own county' (p. 352).

Nina Levine's 'Extending Credit in the *Henry IV* Plays' (*SQ* 51[2000] 403–31) challenges the idea that the use of credit terms indicates the monarchy's fall into modernity under the Lancastrians, proposing instead that the plays' continuities with late Elizabethan credit practices enable a new model of community 'deriving its authority from everyday exchange rather than from aristocratic ideals or chronicle history' (p. 404). Eastcheap is a workplace, governed by trust-based normative values on the extension of credit and the payment of debts, as well as an alternative, holiday, world. In the wider world, Hal imagines himself as moving 'from prodigal to chivalric merchant', balancing accounts, redeeming debts, or promising to pay, rather than operating as a divinely sanctioned agent. Though the plays seem to end with a remystified monarchy, the epilogue reiterates the primacy of a contract between players and audience. There is much of interest here, though the point that the various contracts and obligations the plays present are primarily economic is not persuasively argued.

Cathleen T. McLoughlin provides an intertextual reading of the *Henry IV* plays and Rabelais in her *Shakespeare, Rabelais, and the Comical-Historical* (see also discussion in section 4(*a*) above). After chapters on the visual arts, Lucian and Erasmus, and Rabelais himself, she explores the 'remarkable coincidences between the stories and styles of the two authors' (p. 81). This is done with some thoroughness, but the project does not venture much beyond a simple listing of such similarities. For example, a quotation of Falstaff's catechism on honour is followed by the note that 'a pattern of questions with monosyllabic responses appears in Rabelais' Fifth Book' before she concludes that 'the form of interrogation is similar to the question/answer format of a catechism explaining one's religion' (p. 134). Shigeki Takada, in '*The First and the Second Parts of Henry IV*: Some Thoughts on the Origins of Shakespearean Gentleness' (in Takahashi, ed., pp. 183–96), reads the plays as part of Shakespeare's own self-fashioning. The expulsion of Falstaff (whom Takada distinguishes from Kemp, thinking the latter too energetic and extemporal for the role) is read as a symptom of Shakespeare's need to produce unity of action by conclusively relegating this kind of popular material to secondary status. This desire in turn can be traced back to Shakespeare's own need to write himself as a gentleman. Glen Mynott writes on 'Chivalry, Monarchy and Rebellion in Shakespeare's *Henry IV, Parts One and Two*' (in Szönyi and Wymer, eds., pp. 147–60), focusing on the 'fragility of the chivalric compromise between king and nobility' and 'the potential danger represented by Essex' (pp. 151, 158). It can be recommended to undergraduates as a clear exposition of the theme of chivalry within the plays, though it is too distant from contemporary work on the plays to contribute to the wider debate.

Ruth Vanita, in 'Mariological Memory in *The Winter's Tale* and *Henry VIII*' (*SEL* 40[2000] 311–37), explores how the latter play displays alternative spaces to the conjugal unit for women. The 'three great pageants' towards its end, of assumption, coronation and presentation, draw upon Mariolatric imagery and associations which function to place them in 'eternally timeless time', as an affirmation of powerful women. Thomas Merriam, in 'Queen of Earthly Queens' (*N&Q* 47[2000] 461–4), makes a similar point, using the common Shakespearian linking of earthly with heavenly to show 'queen of earthly queens' implicitly referring to Mary the heavenly queen.

Susannah Brietz Monta, in '"Thou fall'st a blessed martyr": Shakespeare's *Henry VIII* and the Polemics of Conscience' (*ELR* 30[2000] 262–83), investigates how the play, through its multiple references to conscience, engages with both martyrological debates and the status of Henry's divorce to produce an ambivalent historiography, uneasy about the supposedly conscientious origins of the Reformation. The question is 'not so much whether the King makes the proper decision as whether the King's testimony that he acts upon his conscience's suggestions is accurate' (p. 266). The trustworthiness of what Henry says about his conscience is undercut both by other characters and by the play's dissociation of it from Protestantism. Gerard Wegemer investigates the themes of malice, justice, conscience and truth, mainly as manifested in *Henry VIII*'s various trials, in 'Henry VIII on Trial: Confronting Malice and Conscience in Shakespeare's *All Is True*' (*Renascence* 52[2000] 111–30). He finds the justice on display to be personal rather than disinterested, and concludes that the king himself resembles Leontes in his tyranny (though not his reformation).

Michael Torrey's '"The plain devil and dissembling looks": Ambivalent Physiognomy and Shakespeare's *Richard III*' (*ELR* 30[2000] 123–53) argues that Richard's success as a deceiver complicates the semiotic status of his deformity. Physiognomical discourse itself, as Torrey shows, was not as univocal as has been thought, often being unwilling to claim absolute reliability for itself. For characters in the play, at least, Richard seems able to redefine his deformity. An audience, undeceived about Richard, nonetheless sees physiognomy fail, and indeed is confronted with appearance per se as an interpretative problem when lords and citizens remain mute in the face of Richard's words, 'a host of blank faces and silent bodies which may or may not tell the audience what thoughts lie behind them' (p. 151).

Donna J. Oestreich-Hart, in "Therefore, since I cannot prove a lover" (*SEL* 40[2000] 241–60) explores the links between *Richard III* and the 'three seminal courtly love texts' of Ovid's *Ars Amatoria* and *Amores*, and Andreas Capellanus's *Tractatus de Amore* on the new historicist principle that 'if we will understand one text, we must necessarily examine its conversation with or "embeddedness" within its contingent texts' (p. 242). Richard woos Anne as a courtly lover, but reading this through the darker, more satirical conception of 'love conquest' in these early texts (rather than through the later, more idealistic, Petrarchan variant) places it as entirely in character. Multiple texts of the play itself are examined in John Jowett's '"Derby", "Stanley", and Memorial Reconstruction in Quarto *Richard III*' (*N&Q* 47[2000] 75–9) (discussed in detail above). Using speech headings and stage directions, as elements unlikely to be preserved through memorial transmission, Jowett shows that Q *Richard III* is unlikely to be collective memorial reconstruction.

Dennis Kezar, in 'Shakespeare's Guilt Trip in *Henry V*' (*MLQ* 61[2000] 431–61), considers the blurring of actors' and author's agency (and responsibility), and the wider question of 'our bending author' as synecdoche of accountable agency. Kezar develops a dynamic idea of 'theatrical guilt', finding in the play 'a self-consciousness that reveals the limitations of Foucault's model' of authorship (p. 440). Henry's notoriously slippery 'character' is a paradigmatic exploration of early modern selfhood. This is a closely argued and theoretically sophisticated piece, which deserves a wide currency.

Theory of a different kind drives Roger D. Sell's '*Henry V* and the Strength and Weakness of Words: Shakespearian Philology, Historicist Criticism, Communicative Pragmatics' (*NM* 4[1999] 535–63). Sell proposes a 'Shakespearian philology', using Shakespeare and language study to illuminate each other. He takes Terence Hawkes to task for leaving out of his investigations of Shakespeare 'the communicative facts which Hawkes perhaps knows in his bones' (p. 544), pleading for (linguistic) pragmatics rather than (philosophical) pragmatism to guide interpretations of the Bard. On the evidence of this piece, however, Shakespearian philology is alive and well, for most of Sell's own points, sensible and accessible to non-philologists though they are, have already been made (for example, on Henry's character, that 'the text as a whole … may be fundamentally ambivalent', p. 561).

Melissa D. Aaron produces an 'economic close reading' of the prologues, accommodations to casting, differences from *2 Henry IV*, and 'Bad Quarto' of *Henry V* in 'The Globe and *Henry V* as Business Document' (*SEL* 40[2000] 277–92). She proposes that the play was originally intended as a Falstaff-plus-Agincourt blockbuster to open the new Globe, but actually opened, *sans* the newly departed Kemp, at the Fortune to help with cashflow problems stemming from the Globe project. In such a scenario the apologetic tone of the prologue would be entirely appropriate. Aaron also suggests that Q's omission of the prologue may stem from Globe performances of the play no longer needing to apologize to (or, of course, to praise) Essex.

Ted Motohashi's '"Remember Saint Crispin": Narrating the Nation in *Henry V*' (in Takahashi, ed., pp. 197–214) examines the variety of potentially unifying rhetorics in the play. Using Homi Bhabha's definition of the ambivalent nature of 'the people'—as objects of nationalist pedagogy about the past, and as subjects demonstrating the present, and independent, vitality of the nation now—Motohashi investigates stress points in the nation-building rhetoric of the play. Henry's imagining of future memories of Agincourt suppresses the variety of experience already shown. Though he remembers Richard II, Falstaff is more fully re-presented: individual memory contests national history. Women are enclosed within the household or, if French, helpless; yet French nobles are anxious about women's infidelities with the English.

(f) Tragedies

This survey of contributions to the study of Shakespearian tragedy in 2000 begins with publications of a more general kind that have implications for more than one tragedy. More specific publications are grouped with other articles dealing with the same tragedy. Early tragedies are discussed before the later ones. Altogether, the essays considered here give a varied picture of studies undertaken within the field in a specific year. It will be clear that some tragedies are more attractive for further study than others. While it is not surprising that *Macbeth*, *Othello*, *King Lear* and *Hamlet* receive a great deal of attention, the reader will find that other plays, such as *Titus Andronicus*, raise quite a lot of curiosity, while yet others, for example *Julius Caesar*, *Timon of Athens* and *Antony and Cleopatra*, just now seem to receive less scholarly attention. Concerning critical preference, there is a diversity of approaches to Shakespearian tragedy. But while many critics are still greatly influenced by new historicism and cultural materialism others, apparently attracted by psychoanalytic or new critical directions, show a certain impatience with approaches that have dominated the critical scene in the course of the last couple of decades.

A useful introduction intended for the beginning student of Shakespeare is Sean McEvoy's *Shakespeare: The Basics*. But as such it is by no means superficial, for the introductions are thorough and also quite illuminating for more informed readers. The book is limited to Shakespeare's plays and reflects approaches that have become common in Shakespeare studies in the last twenty-five years. McEvoy's interpretations are thus linked to cultural and political contexts, and the readings of the most frequently studied plays appear in the light of contemporary critical thinking, with strong influences from new historicism and cultural materialism. The tragedies that receive most attention are *Hamlet*, *King Lear*, and *Othello*. McEvoy wants the reader to see the way in which the historical moment of transition between the medieval and modern worlds creates the nature of Shakespeare's tragedies. He explains this idea by referring to *Hamlet* and *Othello*. More particularly, he establishes the opposition between the dying heroic-chivalric world of trial by combat and the modern system of state justice. The character of Hamlet is tragic because he is caught in a double bind between a medieval revenge code that his modern mind cannot accept and the modern state that he wants to believe in but knows to be corrupt. In a similar vein, Othello and Desdemona's love is seen as an idealized version of courtly love in feudal chivalry, which is completely at odds with money-driven Venetian society. Their love is not grounded in the reality of how their society operates, and so it founders when meeting that world in the form of Iago. Similarly, *Macbeth* is seen to dramatize contradictions within the feudal society of medieval Scotland. To illustrate tragedy in relation to power, McEvoy makes use of *King Lear*, where the question of power connected with justice is so apparent. Basically the power structure of the Britain of *King Lear* is that people's relationship to land and property in the play defines their identity and establishes their power, regardless of their personal virtue. In *Hamlet* Claudius, as a new ruler, has to establish his power first of all by symbolic display. The fencing match of *Hamlet*'s final scene is also part of a formal display to validate Claudius's power. McEvoy uses the view of absolute monarchy to illustrate differences between new historicist and cultural materialist ideas on manifestations of power in Shakespeare's tragedies. To sum up, the book is an insightful and well-reasoned introduction to Shakespeare's plays.

Another of the more general approaches is Steven Marx's *Shakespeare and the Bible*. This is the first book to explore the pattern and significance of hundreds of biblical allusions in Shakespeare in relation to a selection of his greatest plays. It shows the Bible as a source for Shakespeare's use of the different dramatic genres. Also, the Bible is described as being a source for his use of myth, his techniques of staging, and his ways of characterizing teachers, rulers, and magicians in the image of the multifaceted biblical God. Marx also reveals how Shakespeare's plays, in the fashion of much contemporary writing, give both irreverent and pious interpretations of Scripture. Each of the chapters matches a book in the Bible with a representative play. Of greatest relevance for the tragedies is chapter 4, '"Within a foot of the extreme verge": The Book of Job and *King Lear*' (pp. 59–78). Here Marx considers the book of Job and *King Lear* in tandem, allowing parallel elements of plot, character, theme, and language to illuminate one another with the purpose of revealing how Shakespeare's imagination may have been inspired by the Bible and how he responded to the earlier text with interpretative revision. Marx asserts that comparing contrary critical interpretations of each emphasizes the final indeterminacy of meaning in the two texts. In Marx's opinion, both the book of Job and *King Lear* contain the ingredients Aristotle attributed to the best tragic plots: reversal of fortunes, or peripety, and discovery, or recognition. Commenting on the forms of suffering inflicted in Job and *Lear*, he finds it a paradox of literary language, particularly the language of biblical and Shakespearian tragedy, that its most profound words are least decipherable—perhaps because they come 'within a foot | Of th'extreme verge' (IV.v.25–6). The chapter on Job and *Lear* gives an insightful comparison. But while the title of the book suggests a fairly general approach, the range of the book as such is relatively restricted, as only a limited number of Shakespeare's plays are discussed.

Andrew Gurr and Mariko Ichikawa, in *Staging in Shakespeare's Theatres* (Oxford Shakespeare Topics), attempt to reconstruct how the plays were originally staged in the theatres of Shakespeare's time. The authors show to what extent the physical limitations and possibilities of these theatres affected the writing and the performance of the plays. Among other topics, the book gives striking examples of the use of costumes, props, gestures, and specific design features. The authors also present a careful study of stage movement, showing how entrances and exits worked on the stage. Of particular interest for our purposes is the final chapter, which offers a detailed examination of *Hamlet* as a text for performance, and returns the play to the staging believed to have been given it at the Globe. However, with their detailed account of stage movement in *Hamlet*, however praiseworthy, the authors place themselves open to criticism from readers who fail to see this kind of specificity in the sources. The opening chapters, on the other hand, present an admirable introduction to the resources and conventions of the original Globe.

Hedrick and Reynolds, eds., *Shakespeare Without Class*, is a collection of essays that approach Shakespeare in unconventional ways, representing uncommon or dissenting uses of Shakespeare. These new essays capture the essence of what the editors call 'Shakespace', by which they mean uses involving a creative, sometimes dissident or transgressive, social space of transformation. The introduction explicates 'transversality', the dynamic of 'Shakespace' whereby assigned subjectivities can be transcended in order to 'be all that you are not'. Essays by a number of contributors deal with gender, sexuality, race, class, postcoloniality, and pedagogy through a wide range of topics. One of the essays with direct implications for Shakespearian tragedy is Robert Weimann's 'Performance and Authority in *Hamlet* (1603)' (pp. 51–63). Weimann treats the unstable linkage between the texts and the performances of *Hamlet* and suggests that this can best be studied at the point of intersection between the early textual history of the play and its own intervention in the forms and functions of playing. He maintains that in the so-called 'bad' quarto, relations of writing and playing find themselves in a particularly blatant state of entanglement and differentiation. This state continues to influence the difference between 'the authorial amplitude' of the second quarto [1604] and the more theatrical qualities of the Folio text [1623]. There is between these texts a cultural preference responding to either the literary needs or the practical requirements of the player. Commenting on various passages from the 'suspect' text of Q1 [1603], Weimann finds in this version a reduction in the authority of the author in the playtext and generally argues that Shakespeare's *Hamlet* participates in the nexus of unruly and unsettled relations of production in early modern England.

Another essay in the same volume is Brian Reynolds's '"What is the city but the people?": Transversal Performance and Radical Politics in Shakespeare's *Coriolanus* and Brecht's *Coriolan*' (pp. 107–32). Observing that Shakespeare's play and Brecht's adaptation of it were written during historical periods of high cultural anxiety and frustration, and pointing out that both works reflect and comment on socio-economic and political problems contemporaneous to their conception, Reynolds compares *Coriolanus* and *Coriolan* with the intention of better understanding 'both the actions of the plebeians and Coriolanus' negotiation of his own subject position in response to the changing socio-political environment in Shakespeare's play'. In Reynolds's view, *Coriolanus* welcomes a performance-oriented interpretation that differs a great deal from the apparent consensus. Shakespeare's play parallels Brecht's *Coriolan* in its criticism of the notion of an irreplaceable leader or absolute monarch, Reynolds maintains. This is especially clear when the play is analysed as a performance text situated within the context of its performance for the early modern audience. It is Reynolds's hypothesis that the original production accomplished this critical feat by prompting the audience to identify and empathize with the plebeians and their wish for a more democratic form of government.

Richard Burt's essay, 'No Holes Bard: Homonormativity and the Gay and Lesbian Romance with *Romeo and Juliet*' (in Hedrick and Reynolds, eds., pp. 153–86), while considering the performance history of gay and lesbian adaptations of *Romeo and Juliet*, maintains that little attention has been paid to homonormativity in queer theory, 'presumably because the concept is thought to be antiqueer'.

In 'Rehearsing the Weird Sisters: The Word as Fetish in *Macbeth*' (in Hedrick and Reynolds, eds., pp. 229–39), based on experiences of two workshops, Leslie Katz proposes a style of reading *Macbeth* that uses physical games and exercises to analyse speech and dramatic action, dislodging Shakespeare's language from its ordinary linguistic context. While the book as a whole contains several well-written and well-researched essays, not all contributions to *Shakespeare Without Class* are as radical or 'different' as indicated by the editors in the programmatic chapter 1.

Shakespeare Survey 53 contains several fine essays with relevance for Shakespeare's tragedies. One of them is David George's 'Plutarch, Insurrection, and Dearth in *Coriolanus*' (*ShS* 53[2000] 60–72). George refers to what has been maintained before, namely that in *Coriolanus* Shakespeare followed the main events of Plutarch's 'Life of Caius Martius Coriolanus': the citizens' unrest in Rome, the war with Corioli, Coriolanus's standing for consul, his opposition to the tribunes and free corn, the mob violence, his trial and banishment, his alliance with the Volscians and attack on Rome, the embassy of women, his yielding to Volumnia, and assassination in Antium. Yet, George adds, in Acts I and III particularly, Shakespeare added current and exciting material from the years 1607–8. So while Shakespeare relied on Plutarch for his narrative and his main military and political events, he filled in passage after passage with material pertaining to Jacobean England. According to George, this was for Shakespeare not so much a question of 'relevance' as an artistic method of creating immediacy for his audience and of winning their involvement. The essay, which finds support in Jacobean agriculture, is interesting and well documented.

In another essay in the same volume, 'Shakespeare, Crossing the Rubicon' (*ShS* 53[2000] 73–88), Cynthia Marshall turns to the old question of Shakespeare's relation to the Plutarchan texts recognized as the primary sources of his Roman plays. She argues that what happens in Shakespeare's conversion of narrative into drama is the establishment of our culture's prevailing model of character as one that is at once intensely performative and putatively interiorized. Marshall observes, for instance, that tracing the movement from Plutarch to Shakespeare provides a useful counterbalance to strictly recursive attempts to bridge the gap between the early modern period and our own. Interestingly, Marshall notes that Plutarch's narrative mode allowed him to describe internal visions and debates that locate differences within the self, or to trace a chain of divine influence that inspires action, while, by contrast, Shakespeare's dramatic mode offered more restrictive means for representing internal processes. The essay contains interesting references to most of Shakespeare's tragedies, including repeated mention of *Julius Caesar* and *Coriolanus*.

Jill L. Levenson, in 'Echoes Inhabit a Garden: The Narratives of *Romeo and Juliet*' (*ShS* 53[2000] 39–48), notes that, despite its origins in Aristotle's exposition of tragedy, recent narrative theory neglects drama. This essay takes as its point of departure Barbara Hardy's argument that Shakespeare's interest in narrative extended throughout his career, that there are explicit signs of this interest in references to other narrators such as Virgil, and implicit signs in passages of exaggeration and parody. While Hardy has examined discrete narrative forms within the play, Levenson considers additional examples of such forms, as well as the relation of all inner forms to the narrative whole. She maintains that through its structural correspondences, as well as its verbal play, *Romeo and Juliet* inflects a familiar narrative sequence with multiple, ambiguous implications. The new multiplicity has at least two notable effects. It suggests that narratives, like life, are (in Terry Eagleton's words) 'necessarily unfinished, processual, contradictory'; and it postpones the tragic ending of this narrative with many digressions. Levenson maintains that in its pluralities the dramatic narrative of *Romeo and Juliet* asserts that the meanings of events and words are never final; it implies that even death lacks finality. The tragedy ends, as it started, in irony that allows the possibility of new beginnings.

Shakespeare Survey also has an article by Barbara Everett, 'Inside *Othello*' (*ShS* 53[2000] 184–95), in which Everett observes that all Shakespeare's major tragedies but one take their source from true or mythical history. This plainly invested them with a special privilege, a stability as of truth itself. *Othello* is the exception; it takes its story from fiction only. Everett in this essay uses *Othello* to suggest the limitations of some recent approaches to Shakespeare. The tragedy's problems, both on and off the stage, namely that the Moor is at once hero and villain to us, and in both roles is upstaged by Iago, give some sense of how much more than a narrator Shakespeare is. What seems the simplest of tragedies is, as a result, from some angles the hardest of them. In Everett's opinion *Othello* is not an easy tragedy for any age. Its difficulty lies in its contrasts, its fusion of inner and outer. For Shakespeare, the story cannot be told from the outside. The essay discusses the sexual problem in the play and contains balanced observations on the relationship between Othello and Iago.

In the same volume Adrian Poole looks for connections between Shakespeare and Dickens in his essay on 'The Shadow of Lear's "Houseless" in Dickens' (*ShS* 53[2000] 103–13). Poole refers to Dickens's essay 'Night Walks' (21 July 1860), subsequently gathered in *The Uncommercial Traveller* [1861, and later, expanded editions]. He notes that Dickens's thoughts and imaginings reflected in 'Night Walks' are suffused with Shakespearian echoes, of *Macbeth*'s shapelessness and *Hamlet*'s graveyard, but that the words that reverberate most persistently, 'houseless' and 'houselessness', have their source in *King Lear*. Poole also addresses the question of the extent of Dickens's direct indebtedness to *King Lear*, as compared with *Hamlet* and *Macbeth*, and suggests that it may not be coincidental that 'Night Walks', with its searching reflection on the sources of its own performance, should so closely precede the writing of *Great Expectations*, Dickens's most creatively self-conscious novel.

Mazzio and Trevor, eds., *Historicism, Psychoanalysis, and Early Modern Culture*, contains four essays that are of relevance to the student of Shakespearian tragedy. The first of these, John Guillory's interesting essay '"To please the wiser sort": Violence and Philosophy in *Hamlet*' (pp. 82–109), studies, as the title indicates, the relation between philosophy and violence in *Hamlet*. Noting that interpreters of *Hamlet*, especially in the twentieth century, have been less interested in explaining the violence of the play than in seeing the underlying psychological dynamic, Guillory goes on to argue that if there is a compelling difference between the psychological complexity of Hamlet's deferred action and the motives of Claudius, it is just like the difference between symbolic and real violence. He further argues that this difference is parallel to the difference between philosophy and theology as early modern discourses. Guillory further proposes that if there is a psychological dynamic underlying and determining the relation of thought to action in *Hamlet*, this dynamic might best be seen as the sublimation of aggressiveness. He accordingly moves away from the current thematization of sexuality in the criticism of the play in order to recover 'the historical priority of aggression'.

Jonathan Goldberg's essay, 'The Anus in *Coriolanus*' (in Mazzio and Trevor, eds., pp. 260–71), was originally written for a meeting of the Shakespeare Association in 1994 and is essentially a discussion of what he considers 'anal' language in the play. In the same volume David Hillman's well-documented essay 'The Inside Story' (pp. 299–324) deals partly with *Hamlet*, which is used as an admirable example of the early modern obsession with questions of inner and outer. According to Hillman, the play reflects endlessly on, for example, the opposition between a soliloquized interior and an endlessly theatricalized exterior. A different approach to *Hamlet* is exemplified in Marjorie Garber's essay 'Weeping for Hecuba' (in Mazzio and Trevor, eds., pp. 350–75), which in Freudian terms discusses the nature of Hamlet's grief.

The main argument of Arthur L Little's study *Shakespeare Jungle Fever: National-Imperial Re-Visions of Race, Rape, and Sacrifice* is that the aesthetic of early modern England relies significantly on a textual and cultural manipulation of race. That aesthetic has a strong national-imperial basis and is enforced by a notable evocation of classicism. The book takes Shakespeare's plays as a site for studying the spectre of interracial sex. Knowledge about this field is nowhere more accessible than in the drama and rape stories of the period. These are seen as narratives about a raped white woman killing herself to reclaim her lost virginity as well as to claim or reclaim her racial whiteness. The necessary inclusion of black males in these narratives is all the more striking because in early modern England there is no knowledge of a black male raping a white woman. How do we then explain the obsession with interracial sex of a 'jungle fever' type? According to the author, the answer lies in the creation of a rhetoric of masculinity and whiteness in a country about to shape its national and imperial ambitions. This claim is based on focusing on favoured sites of classical and early modern literature, such as Africa, Venice, Rome, Egypt, and Ireland, and by examining a range of sources, among others dramatic texts. Thus the book contains close studies of *Titus Andronicus*, *Antony and Cleopatra*, and *Othello*. While this type of argument can easily be overstated, it remains a fact that the book enhances our understanding of race in relation to early modern narratives, and not least in relation to the above-mentioned tragedies, and is a valuable contribution to early modern literary and cultural studies. Little's book contains several illustrations, among others Henry Peacham's drawing from *Titus Andronicus* [*c*.1595].

Michael Hattaway has edited *A Companion to English Renaissance Literature and Culture*. This impressive survey describes Shakespeare's work only intermittently. But Michael O'Connell's essay on '"Medieval" and "Early Modern" Drama' (pp. 477–85) contains some revealing remarks on Shakespeare's use of morality structures in *Othello* II.iii. O'Connell also argues that a morality type similar to that of *Everyman* is seen to inhere in the basic structure of *King Lear*. In the same volume Rowland Wymer's article 'Jacobean Tragedy' (pp. 545–55), while giving a brief survey of the field and including short comments on Shakespeare's tragedies, wisely notes that 'generalizations about Jacobean tragedy which implicitly ignore Shakespeare are of little value'.

Callaghan, ed., *A Feminist Companion to Shakespeare*, contains nineteen original essays from an all-woman team of contributors, and reveals a feminist approach to such fields as race, gender, sexuality, the body, queer politics, and capitalism, but it also includes other areas, for example textual editing and theatre history. In an article entitled 'Black Ram, White Ewe: Shakespeare, Race, and Women' (pp. 188–207), Joyce Green MacDonald sets out to show how thoroughly race permeates gender and class positions in *Othello*. Discussing several characters in the play, MacDonald maintains that *Othello* is the only place where Shakespeare undertakes the racialization of his characters' identity and relationships. 'To think about race and women in Shakespeare requires an unravelling of both terms, a recognition that they are relational and internally varied rather than absolute', she holds. She further maintains that the racial contradictions built into *Titus Andronicus* stem from the state of the masculine, and particularly fatherly, dominance that matters so much in *Othello* and *The Rape of Lucrece*. Observing that *Titus* is far less convinced than *Lucrece* that patriarchal right will always be done, she observes that *Othello* performs 'the final commitment of black masculinity, while *Lucrece* ritually exorcises the suspicion of a sexually communicated blackness'. But, she alleges, in *Titus* race and the appropriate language are more instrumental to the play's final confirmation of Roman triumph, and less ideologically transparent. In the same volume Denise Albanese writes about 'Black and White, and Dread All Over: The Shakespeare Theater's "Photonegative" *Othello* and the Body of Desdemona' (pp. 226–47), an essay referring to a Washington Shakespeare Theater production in the fall of 1997, in which the racial dynamics of the script were visually reversed. Albanese gives her reaction to this idiosyncratic staging of the play and makes cogent comments on other innovative casting work involving *Othello*. In another section of the book, Susan Zimmerman writes about 'Duncan's Corpse' (pp. 320–38), seeing in 'the hallucinatory realm of Shakespeare's *Macbeth* sex, violence, and blood ... inextricably meshed in a tragic mode that represents the netherside of civilized order'. It is Zimmerman's argument that Duncan's corpse emblematizes and reinforces the indeterminacy of Macbeth's own horrific vision, and that this corpse functions as a composite image for the representation of gender indeterminacy in both Macbeth and Lady Macbeth. An essay by Philippa Berry, 'Between Idolatry and Astrology: Modes of Temporal Repetition in *Romeo and Juliet*' (pp. 358–72), is concerned with various ways of perceiving time, referring to Patricia Parker's *Shakespeare from the Margins* [1996] and Ned Lukacher's *Time Fetishes* [1998]. In her essay Berry suggests some of the ways in which *Romeo and Juliet* puts the putative singularity and linearity of time and history into question. The imagery of the play, according to Berry, combines frantic temporal acceleration with a turning backwards of time, thus encapsulating the perceived multifaceted character of time in the late sixteenth century. In general, *A Feminist Companion* appears as a substantial contribution to Shakespeare studies, revealing an impressive range of enquiry from feminist scholars of the early modern period.

Another study focusing on different Shakespeare plays, but which has an even wider perspective is Takahashi, ed., *Hot Questrists*, which contains some articles on Shakespeare's tragedies. For example, Soji Iwasaki deals with the language of sexuality in *Romeo and Juliet* and Juliet Tetsuo Kishi considers dialogue, also in *Romeo and Juliet*, while Koici Muranushi writes about '*Coriolanus* and the Body of Satan'. Other essays reflect Shakespeare studies more generally or are devoted to other early modern themes.

A broad perspective is also revealed in Hugh Grady's essay 'Shakespeare's Links to Machiavelli and Montaigne: Constructing Intellectual Modernity in Early Modern Europe (*CL* 52:ii[2000] 119–42). Grady finds that Montaigne's approach to Machiavellian logic seems remarkably similar to many of Shakespeare's key terms. In particular, Montaigne's fascination with his own subjectivity and his valorization of that subjectivity as a response to the dilemmas of early modern decentring, desacralization, and instrumentalization closely resemble the characteristic dialectic in Shakespeare between desacralization and subjectivity in the histories and tragedies. Grady is occupied with the larger philosophical picture and presents no in-depth study of any of the tragedies.

Approaching Shakespeare from the point of view of theories about play, Catherine Bates has written *Play in a Godless World: The Theory and Practice of Play in Shakespeare, Nietzsche and Freud*. While a great part of the book deals with the theory of play, where play is viewed as 'an organized response to a frighteningly disorganized world', and where Bates draws on a great many theorists, including Barthes, Lacan and Bersani, she devotes her final chapter to Shakespeare. To the student of Shakespearian tragedy this part offers enriching, daring analyses. Although Bates's prose at times is marked by repetitions and clichés, her comments on Hamlet, Cleopatra, Caesar, and other tragic characters are revealing and fascinating.

Richard Levin turns to Shakespeare's first tragedy in an entry on '*Titus Andronicus* and "The Ballad Thereof"' (*N&Q* 47:i[2000] 63–68). The paper reflects a debate about the relationship of Shakespeare's play to the ballad entered in the Stationers' Register on 6 February 1594, simultaneously with Shakespeare's play, and also to an anonymous prose narrative titled *The History of Titus Andronicus* that was found bound with the ballad in an eighteenth-century chapbook in the Folger Library but that may have an Elizabethan origin. Levin points out that scholarly opinion is divided between those who maintain that the play and the ballad are derived primarily from the *History*, and those who assert that the ballad is derived primarily from the play and the *History* from the ballad. Levin gives several examples of the custom of registering a book and a ballad on the same subject at about the same time. On this evidence Levin concludes that it is likely that the ballad derives primarily from the play.

Francesca T. Royster has written about 'White-Limed Walls: Whiteness and Gothic Extremism in Shakespeare's *Titus Andronicus*' (*SQ* 51[2000] 432–55). Contrary to what is normally done in discussing *Titus Andronicus*, Royster puts whiteness in the foreground in an attempt to dismantle a black/white binary. She wants to explore 'the denaturalization of whiteness in *Titus Andronicus* and its construction along an unstable continuum of racial identities'. If Aaron is coded as black, Tamora is represented as hyper-white. The article refers to Margo Hendricks and Patricia Parker's collection *Women, 'Race,' and Writing in the Early Modern Period* [1994] and its advancement of the discussion of whiteness as a raced position. Royster argues that in *Titus Andronicus* Tamora's whiteness *is* racially marked, is made visible, and thus it is misleading to simplify the play's racial landscape into black and white, with black as the 'other'. One of the play's striking features, according to Royster, is 'its othering of a woman who is conspicuously white'. This is a many-faceted essay showing, among other things, a Rome vulnerable to outside populations, a Rome in crisis regarding its national and racial identity. This crisis escalates with the birth of Aaron's child. Furthermore, allying himself with the Goths and joining a network of Moors, Aaron helps evoke the possibility of a population of invaders. In Royster's view, *Titus Andronicus* thus stages a drama of invasion and dangerous multiculturalism, set in a mythical past all too familiar to British imaginings. *Titus Andronicus* is responding to a deep cultural anxiety when it posits that mere external appearance might not reveal a person's race. In such a view, race becomes not a skin tone but a moral quality. It is Royster's main argument that the play is deeply concerned with a hiding of true natures. Such encryption enables Goths and Moors to infiltrate Rome, and plays on fears of an infiltrated England.

Hunt, ed., *Approaches to Teaching Shakespeare's 'Romeo and Juliet'*, is another of the very helpful volumes in the MLA's Approaches to Teaching World Literature series. It is divided into two parts. The first, 'Materials', reviews the most widely used anthologies of Shakespeare's plays and available editions of *Romeo and Juliet*, and it also provides background material for instructors and required and recommended student readings. The second part, 'Approaches', consists of contributions from twenty teachers who were asked to describe a distinctive approach to teaching *Romeo and Juliet*. The first four essays address the issue of how to read the play. In the case of Arthur F. Kinney's contribution, for example, this consists of outlining an imaginative pedagogy for helping students locate in the play the authoritative agent of tragedy, while Douglas Bruster indicates ways of clarifying the comedy of *Romeo and Juliet* in a larger discussion of literary form. In the next section, 'Literary and Contemporary Contexts', four essays discuss teaching the play in an introductory drama course, in early modern historical and social contexts, with other Shakespeare plays, and in relation to early modern expressions of sexuality. The third section considers different ways of teaching *Romeo and Juliet* in a modern context, while the essays in the following two sections focus on teaching important issues of the play's characterization, language, and texts. And finally, the last two sections of the book focus on approaches to teaching the play's dramatic technique and performance art as well as the play's transformations in film, music, and ballet. The volume includes many-faceted attempts by experienced Shakespeare scholars at presenting the play to students, and as such it is a very useful teaching resource.

Links between *Julius Caesar* and Shakespeare's last tragedy are established in Jerald W. Spotswood's essay '"We are undone already": Disarming the Multitude in *Julius Caesar* and *Coriolanus*' (*TSLL* 42:i[2000] 61–78). Contrary to the assertion that Shakespeare endorses majoritarian rule in *Coriolanus*, Spotswood argues that Shakespeare symbolically distinguishes plebeians by depicting them as a socially indistinct mass. *Julius Caesar* and *Coriolanus* are both plays concerned with the form and structure of the body politic. In these two 'political' plays Shakespeare persistently marks off distinctions between elite and common culture by invoking a past in which military prowess determined social merit. In fact, commoners in *Julius Caesar* and *Coriolanus* serve to reflect and enlarge the figure of the elite. Shakespeare thus rewrites individuality as a characteristic of the elite and denigrates collective action by associating it with a rabble. It follows that Shakespeare's world is one where aristocratic values are privileged.

Hamlet continues to attract a great deal of scholarly attention. As Theodore Weiss notes about Hamlet initially in his interesting essay 'Soiled in the Working: *Hamlet* and Eliot' (*APR* 29:vi[2000] 5–24), the 'open, pressing enigma that his nature is makes him all the more irresistible'. Weiss's real focus, however, is T.S. Eliot's views on the play. He refers to Eliot's little essay '*Hamlet*' [1919], in which Eliot finds Shakespeare's play both fruitful and negative. Weiss notes that its brevity is a way of underscoring Eliot's impatience with the play. Reconsidering the essay, Weiss finds that Eliot has hit a number of truths important to the play, but truths insufficiently appreciated or understood. For Eliot, unlike most critics, not Hamlet, but *Hamlet* the play is the primary problem. In contrast, Weiss refers to Eliot's much later essay 'Poetry and Drama' [1950], where he entirely reversed his view, praising

Hamlet for having 'as well constructed an opening scene as that of any play ever written'. Weiss's personal views on the play are engaging and thought-provoking.

In '"Damned custom ... habits devil": Shakespeare's *Hamlet*, Anti-Dualism, and the Early Modern Philosophy of Mind' (*ELH* 67[2000] 399–431), P.A. Cefalu observes that when theorists make brief forays into pre-Cartesian, early modern mind/body theories, these explorations reveal just how little has been systematically said on the subject of early modern philosophical psychology. Cefalu finds a lack of any thorough account of the post-medieval, pre-Cartesian philosophy of mind. What he contributes in his essay is a brief look at some modern and pre-modern theories of the mind, namely those of Gilbert Ryle, Putnam, Augustine, Pomponazzi, and Jeremy Taylor, in order to suggest, first, that Renaissance philosophy and theology held theories of the mind that resemble modern-day anti-dualistic accounts of behaviourism and functionalism, and, second, that Shakespeare's *Hamlet* is implicated in this behaviourist-functionalist tradition rather than in the innatist tradition into which it has usually been placed. Cefalu argues that part of the reason that *Hamlet*'s critics have assumed that Hamlet is preoccupied with inspecting the contents of his private self is that they have mistaken the obsession shown by Hamlet's peers in the play to 'pluck out' Hamlet's 'mystery' for what is usually described as Hamlet's inner gaze. Accordingly, there is in Cefalu's opinion no sufficient evidence that *Hamlet* anticipates Cartesian dualism or any of the varying innatist or idealist philosophies that critics have traditionally attributed to it.

Hamlet's influence on later literature is addressed in Saburo Sato's 'The Structure of a Tragedy through the Coming of the Black Ships: Shimazaki Toson's *Before the Dawn* and *Hamlet*' (*CLS* 37:ii[2000] 182–95). Sato describes Toson's *Before the Dawn* as the greatest monument of modern Japanese literature. In it Toson expressed the great changes wrought by the Meiji Restoration and how it affected the Japanese people. Sato argues that *Before the Dawn* is a success only because it follows the technique of Shakespeare's *Hamlet*. To show Shakespeare's influence Sato refers to the appearance of the ghost of Hamlet's father in I.i: tragedy is foreshadowed and the reader gets inside Hamlet's pain and strength. The feeling of the scene is elicited in the same way as in similar scenes in *Before the Dawn*. The external chaos which the ghost symbolizes is combined with the internal chaos within Hamlet; the same technique is used for Hanzo Aoyama, the main character in Toson's book. According to Sato, Toson also improved his novel through his insight into *Othello*, *Macbeth, and King Lear*. The essay primarily deals with *Before the Dawn* and gives limited insight into *Hamlet*.

Editorial matters are addressed by Ann Thompson, who considers 'George MacDonald's 1885 Folio-Based Edition of *Hamlet*' (*SQ* 51[2000] 201–4). Pointing out that MacDonald's edition is laid out with the original-spelling Folio text on the left-hand page and the editor's often extensive notes on the facing page, Thompson remarks that in 1885 a Folio-based text was an anomaly. George McDonald is credited with an innovative edition on textual grounds, but Thompson also recommends his commentary on literary grounds: 'the encounter between MacDonald and Shakespeare is always thoughtful and modest, often entertaining and original'. Moreover, Thompson urges editors and publishers to regard MacDonald's and Longman's elegant and reader-friendly layout as a possible model for modern editions of two-text plays.

Shakespeare's 'Hamlet' and the Controversies of Self is the title of John Lee's book on Hamlet. Noting that new historicists (such as Stephen Greenblatt) have to a great extent ignored *Hamlet* (this was before the publication of *Hamlet in Purgatory*), and that cultural materialists (such as Catherine Belsey, Francis Baker, Alan Sinfield, and Jonathan Dollimore) have used the play for their own purposes, Lee addresses the question of whether Hamlet has a 'self-constituting sense of self', whether this existed in early modern England, and whether dramatic characters and individuals appeared as 'socially produced subjects lacking any meaningful sense of interiority'. Considering the initial stages of Shakespeare criticism, Lee maintains that the challenge of describing 'character' was resolved not by Coleridge but by Hazlitt, under the influence of Montaigne. Finding that Shakespeare's *Hamlet* lacks 'a vocabulary of interiority' Lee, influenced by cognitive psychology, demonstrates how a language can be designed to describe essentialist interiority. Lee also focuses on the fact that the Folio text of *Hamlet* softens or removes what Hamlet in the second quarto says about himself or his personality. This is a well-argued book with relevance for the discussion of the proper approach to the self in contemporary criticism.

In 'The Theatricality of Rot in Thomas Middleton's *The Revenger's Tragedy* and William Shakespeare's *Hamlet*' (*UCrow* 20[2000] 58–67), Mark King observes that, while the similarities between *The Revenger's Tragedy* and *Hamlet* have been well explored, the differences between the two texts have not received comparable attention. Accordingly, King tries to examine some points of departure that *The Revenger's Tragedy* takes from *Hamlet*, in particular the play's configuration of rot. King argues that the heightened theatricality of *The Revenger's Tragedy* is a result of its more ubiquitous sense of rot. In the topsy-turvy world of this play, rot takes on positive connotations, while the rot in *Hamlet* is negative and, interestingly, gendered. According to King, '*Hamlet* represents a progression whereby the rot expands from a fixed point in a homosocial male world to a female locus'.

While the focus of Poul Houe et al., *Anthropology and Authority: Essays on Søren Kierkegaard*, is the philosopher Kierkegaard, Bruce H. Kirmmse's essay in that volume, '"I am not a Christian": A "Sublime Lie"? Or: "Without Authority," Playing Desdemona to Christendom's Othello' (pp. 129–36) considers the question of whether Søren Kierkegaard's 'I am not a Christian' is to be regarded as as much a lie as Desdemona's avowal that she has indeed killed herself. He refers to a nineteenth-century philosophical discussion involving Kierkegaard, where Desdemona's example is employed. The gist of the article is that Desdemona's 'sublime lie', to use Kierkegaard's term, qualitatively equals Kierkegaard's sublime lie when saying that he himself was not a Christian. If Kierkegaard went to his death 'a liar' like Desdemona, he did so, as she did, in order to shock the rest of us into the knowledge that our easily acquired cultural Christianity makes us much 'blacker devils' than he.

Addressing *Othello* more directly, Steven Doloff, in '"Well desir'd in Cyprus": *Othello* on the Isle of Venus' (*N&Q* 47[2000] 81–2), asks whether Lieutenant Cassio's elaborate welcome of Desdemona to Cyprus is merely a flourish of his courtly manner. Referring to Cassio's want to 'play the Sir', as Iago observes in II.i.174, he suggests that the playwright may be subtly alluding to the Mediterranean island's long-standing reputation, indicated in II.i.84–7. This may have reminded members of Shakespeare's audience of the island's fame as the mythological site of

Venus's first emergence from the sea, and of its inhabitants' worship of that goddess.

Noting that many of Shakespeare's comedies depend for their denouement on retreat to a green world, Lisa Hopkins, in '"This is Venice: my house is not a grange": *Othello*'s Landscapes of the Mind' (*UCrow* 20[2000] 68–78), notes that it is less of a critical commonplace that several of Shakespeare's tragedies feature an inversion of this pattern. This could take the form of an image pattern playing on death, waste, and decay, or of a staging of a scene in a non-urban location marked as a wasteland rather than as a rural retreat. While at first sight it might seem that *Othello* deviates from this pattern of pastoral inversion, Hopkins makes it clear that, just as Shakespeare had offset the Venetian with the pastoral in *The Merchant of Venice*, the same thing happens in *Othello*. The following analysis contains a series of suggestive observations, and by examining the use of farmyard, animal, and nature imagery in the play, Hopkins manages to give revealing characteristics of Othello and Iago, primarily, but also of Cassio and Desdemona. Hopkins suggests that one of the major roots of Othello's tragedy is his 'dangerously volatile fluctuation between excessive and overly restricted views of himself and his capabilities', and while Othello vacillates, Iago presses on, confident that 'he can fit nature to the measure of man'.

Gregg Andrew Hurwitz's essay, '"The Fountain from which my current runs": A Jungian Interpretation of *Othello*' (*UCrow* 20[2000] 79–92), is an analysis of the play from a Jungian perspective. Discussing Iago as Othello's shadow, and egocentric Othello as the waking centre of the self (the ego), while Desdemona is seen as representing the positive aspects of femininity, an active anima, Hurwitz agrees with Alvin Kernan that the play is a struggle in which Desdemona, a life force, is balanced by her opposite, Iago, an anti-life force. Or, stated in Hurwitz's psychological terminology: 'Othello, as ego, vacillates between the life-affording anima and the destructive shadow'.

In 'Shakespeare's *Othello*' (*Expl* 58:ii[1999] 69–72), Joseph Marotta explores the use of the word *subdue* in *Othello*. Although the word appears only six times in the play, he finds that 'its nuances expose the multilayered ambiguities of the central characters and their attitudes toward each other'.

Scott McMillin, in 'The *Othello* Quarto and the "Foul-Paper" Hypothesis' (*SQ* 51[2000] 67–85), observes that *Othello* remains a textual mystery, and that a large part of the problem is that a commonly accepted hypothesis stands on questionable grounds. The hypothesis concerns the 1622 quarto (Qi), which differs from the 1623 Folio text (F) on thousands of points. McMillin is here concerned with the major differences and with the prevailing account of Q1 which seeks to explain them. According to this hypothesis, Q1 ultimately derives from a manuscript in Shakespeare's own hand, his 'foul papers', with W.W. Greg (*The Shakespeare First Folio* [1955]) and later Honigmann as the most influential proponents. McMillin's review shows logical short-cuts by which Greg and Honigmann secure the foul-paper hypothesis, while attributing this to the new bibliography itself. In McMillin's opinion there is something precarious at the heart of the new bibliography, a central anxiety that leads careful scholars to overlook actors and scribes 'at more than one remove' as possible agents in the transmission of text. He argues that the foul-paper argument for Q1 can be reduced to one among several possibilities instead of standing alone as the commonly accepted interpretation. This means that a number of questions relating to the text of *Othello* come to mind, leaving much work to be done.

Jonathan Goldberg, in 'Writing Matter Again: Objects and their Detachments' (*ShakS* 28[2000] 248–51), discusses in particular the issue of letters in Shakespeare's plays. According to Goldberg, plays by Shakespeare may have more letters in them than any other significant prop. He mentions as an interesting case the second act of *King Lear*, where Regan claims to have received a letter from Goneril a scene before the letter-carrier arrives, while the delivery of the letter as later recounted by Kent describes a scene that cannot have taken place. Goldberg observes that letters can find their proper recipients even when they are disguised and known to no one (how do Kent and Cordelia correspond?), and they can convey true sentiments even when they are forged. According to Goldberg, 'letters are the material form of uncanny knowledge, the vehicles of desperate idealizing hopes'. This is an interesting essay which in some respects is influenced by Halpern's *Poetics of Primitive Accumulation* [1991]. Goldberg admits that the circulation of letters in *King Lear* must be related to its textual condition. The fact that there are two *King Lear*s 'means only that there once were more than that, and that no text of the play ever will be anything than just that—one text among a number whose sum we can never total'. Goldberg thus stresses the foundational illusoriness of the play of letters.

Seeing similarities between Marlowe and Shakespeare, Mark Hutchings considers 'The End of *II Tamburlaine* and the beginning of *King Lear*' from that point of view (*N&Q* 47[2000] 82–6). Hutchings's argument is that the opening scene of *King Lear* echoes the closing scene of *II Tamburlaine*. At the end of Marlowe's play, the dying Tamburlaine calls for a map on which to trace his career. Similarly, in Shakespeare's play the aged Lear requests a map to illustrate the dividing up of his kingdom. The thematic and verbal parallels, and the visual similarities in the stagecraft, suggest that Shakespeare saw in the declining Tamburlaine an analogue for Lear. Hutchings thus argues that Shakespeare's play, both literally and metaphorically, begins where Marlowe's ends.

Problems inherent in theatre productions of written texts are part of Susan Viguers's concern in her essay on 'The Storm in *King Lear*' (*CLAJ* 43:iii[2000] 338–66). Viguers points to the lack of awareness of the problems connected with written texts. This perception is given more weight in regard to *King Lear* by the existence of two primary texts, the first quarto and the first Folio, and the argument that they represent different playwright-created versions of the play. She points out that, once we look at the play not as literature but as theatre, its problematic status is compounded. As Viguers notes, theatrical performance is less stable than literature or film. Although she is concerned with modern productions of *King Lear*, the argument of this article begins with the play's original form on Shakespeare's stage. Viguers envisages the storm on Shakespeare's stage as not a context in which to see Lear and his followers as much as a presence which was non-illusionistic and theatre-based in its conception. Rather than being created on stage, the storm was depicted or evoked by carefully timed offstage sounds, by the language of the characters, and by movement that depended on the particular physical parameters of the stage. The remainder of the article is concerned with modern productions of the play.

Ken Jackson reveals a totally different approach to Shakespeare in "'I know not | Where I did lodge last night?'": *King Lear* and the Search for Bethlem (Bedlam) Hospital' (*ELR* 30[2000] 213–40). The article deals with the relationship between Bethlem hospital and Renaissance plays about madness. Jackson argues that Shakespeare's *King Lear*, mainly in Act III on the heath, registers most profoundly the efforts of the playwrights to engage the theatrical practices of Bethlem, the hospital's practice of showing the mad to elicit charity. Although much of the essay deals with conditions for the mad in early modern England, in section IV Jackson argues that in *King Lear* the playwright engages the discourse of early modern madness in developing the play's central dramaturgical movement: Shakespeare makes an audience feel pity for the title character. According to Jackson this dramaturgical movement is important because in Act III an audience finds itself wishing Lear could find relief specifically from his near madness. Shakespeare substituted a mad Lear for a starving Leir in his source, but by interjecting madness rather than simple starvation, Shakespeare offers a novel and moving change to an old story. In doing so, Jackson insists, he also engages the processes already forming an 'alternative theatrical practice': the charitable show of Bethlem.

Studies in English Literature, 1500–1900 features Sonia Massai's article 'Nahum Tate's Revision of Shakespeare's *King Lears*' (*SEL* 40[2000] 435–50). Massai notes that in the last twenty to thirty years, mainly as a result of an unprecedented interest in the afterlife of the Shakespearian text, *The History of King Lear* has been studied both in relation to the changed stage and dramatic conventions of Restoration theatres and for its historical and political significance. Despite this revival of critical interest in Shakespearian adaptations and Christopher Spencer's advocacy of Tate, the stigma of mediocrity which was first associated with Tate in the nineteenth century still discourages critics and editors from investigating his competence as a professional reader of Shakespeare. Massai interestingly states that Tate had the privilege of reading and adapting Shakespeare's *King Lear* in a pre-conflationist age, when no theory about the origin of the copy-texts behind the quarto or the Folio had been advanced. His adaptation, she observes, is the only surviving instance of a critical assessment of the dramatic qualities of quarto and Folio *King Lear* before Lewis Theobald's editorial policy of conflation and the theory of the lost original denied both texts a direct link with the author's holograph. Tate felt free to rely on his quarto and Folio source-texts independently of their *formal* qualities, thus highlighting *dramatic* differences between them that supporters of the theory of revision in *King Lear* now regard as intentional and possibly authorial. This article thus provides new, indirect, evidence in favour of the theory of internal revision in *King Lear*.

Claire McEachern's 'Figures of Fidelity: Believing in *King Lear*' (*MP* 98:ii[2000] 211–30) considers a completely different field, as it explores how the female figures of *King Lear* address the nature of Reformation believing. The play is used to probe an analogy and a complicity between faith in affective objects and spiritual ones, asking among other things how the anxiety attendant upon a Calvinist God plays itself out on the plane of social knowledge, and why the failure of faith in the reciprocity of human love comports itself much like a soteriological crisis. The author sketches an analogy between the proofs of God's love and of female love in *King Lear*, while making some interesting observations about the characters. Herself raising objections to this analogy, McEachern answers them by stating that our only way of knowing divine love is by measuring it against those loves we do know, or think we know, and yet must always take on faith.

Robert V. Caro discusses 'Rules for Discernment: Another Context for *Macbeth*' (*N&Q* 47[2000] 455–8). He points out that the belief in guardian spirits or angels was not limited to the ancient classical world. The tradition of good and evil spirits was very much a part of late medieval and Renaissance Christian spirituality. As Shakespeare was familiar with this tradition, it is not surprising that he found a reference to Antony's guardian spirit congenial (*A&C* II.iii.18–22), and it is even less surprising that he alluded to it in *Macbeth* (III.i.53–6). Caro refers to St Ignatius Loyola's *Spiritual Exercises* [1548] as a handy compendium of the rules for discernment of spirits. In the tradition of spiritual discernment, Macbeth's angel/ genius, the witches, and his wife may be considered evil spirits. As such, their ways of disturbing and deceiving a human soul are predictable and spelled out in the Ignatian rules for discernment of spirits. Caro argues that the rules provide a hitherto unrecognized context for the psychic battleground in *Macbeth*.

In the same journal Howard Jacobson comments on *Macbeth* I.v.48–52 (*N&Q* 47[2000] 86), suggesting that Shakespeare here was influenced by the following familiar passage in the Bible: 'Then Abraham extended his hand and took the knife to slaughter his son ...'. According to Jacobson, the doubling 'Hold, hold!' in Shakespeare's *Macbeth* may be a kind of echo of the Bible's 'Abraham, Abraham!'

In another entry, Rosalind S. Meyer, '"The serpent under 't": Additional Reflections on *Macbeth*' (*N&Q* 47[2000] 86–90), notes the similarity between Seneca's Medea and 'fiend-like' Lady Macbeth. The external evidence for this is the considerable influence of Seneca on Elizabethan drama. Meyer also gives several examples of internal evidence for such resemblances and finds in *Macbeth* allusions to Marlowe's *Dr Faustus* as well as to Seneca's *Medea*.

Nick Aitchison's *Macbeth: Man and Myth* is a many-faceted approach to the character of Macbeth. Realizing that there is a historical, a mythological, and a dramatic Macbeth, and seeing that the Macbeth of popular perception is essentially Shakespeare's Macbeth, Aitchison has set himself the task of tracing the historical Macbeth. He does so by first giving an introduction to Scotland in the age of Macbeth, then tracing Macbeth's path to the throne, Macbeth's reign, the making of the myth, and finally searching for the true Macbeth behind the myth. As the making of the myth owes a great deal to Shakespeare's play, Aitchison attempts to distinguish clearly between the historical Macbeth and Shakespeare's character. For example, while Shakespeare's tragedy associates many events and characters with specific locations, Aitchison holds that the historical Macbeth is linked with very few places. The description of Macbeth's motives and the basis of his claim to the throne are skilfully described. But Aitchison has set himself a difficult task, for in places he is working with rather scanty historical material. The main problem here is to find the right balance between different sources. While Gaelic and Norse material has been referred to repeatedly, English sources appear much less extensively. Aitchison should receive praise, however, for attempting to bring together material from a variety of sources for the first time. Being truly multi-disciplinary in approaching Macbeth from the point of view of archaeology, architecture, topography, and folklore, this richly illustrated study heightens our awareness of what the historical Macbeth may have been. But for the student of Shakespeare, the world of *Macbeth* is a somewhat different story.

Timon of Athens has not received much scholarly attention this year. An exception is Mark Phillipson's 'Byron's Revisited Haunts' (*SiR* 39[2000] 303–22). In an essay including references to the indebtedness of Byron to *Timon of Athens*, Phillipson observes that, before he left England in a flurry of scandal, Lord Byron was irresistibly drawn to self-exile. In particular, he paid close attention to Timon, Shakespeare's misanthropic exile. Phillipson points out that Byron fashioned Harold in the mould of Timon, arranging for his disillusioned character to escape, like the disillusioned Athenian, from the 'heartless parasites of present cheer' (canto 1, 1. 75). Phillipson further argues that thanks to the tumultuous events of his life, Byron, like Timon, became an archetype of all towering persons whose stature forces a severance from their community. However, in the essay the references to *Timon of Athens* are primarily used as a starting point for a closer look at Byron's work.

A new edition of *Coriolanus*, edited by Lee Bliss, was published this year. This edition of what is probably Shakespeare's last tragedy contains a thorough reconsideration of the play. The edition is based on the first Folio [1623], the only authority for the text of *Coriolanus*. An extensive introduction includes comment on date, theatre, chronology, sources, and stage history, and situates the play within contemporary socio-economic contexts. The commentary on Coriolanus himself, probably Shakespeare's least sympathetic tragic hero, is extensive and helpful. It lucidly explains how Shakespeare embeds his protagonist in the play's turbulent political and social world. While Coriolanus thinks of himself as the physician who knows the remedy for Rome's sickness, the play's imagery shows that he is no more of an exemplary civic model than the plebeian one he opposes. The last part of the book contains a textual analysis section including editorial procedures and notes on the nature of the copy. The edition is generously annotated and extremely useful to students of *Coriolanus*.

Robin Headlam Wells focuses on *Coriolanus* in '"Manhood and Chevalrie": *Coriolanus*, Prince Henry, and the Chivalric Revival' (*RES* 51[2000] 395–423). While the Midlands corn riot of 1607, and the argument in Parliament three years earlier over the right of the House of Commons to initiate legislation, constitute a well-documented part of *Coriolanus*'s political background, another political issue was being debated in the years leading up to the writing of the play. This fact might help to answer a question often asked about *Coriolanus*: why did Shakespeare write it on a fairly minor and early figure in Roman history? The issue Headlam Wells refers to is one that had more than domestic implications, namely the fact that by 1607 the Prince of Wales was quickly acquiring a reputation for aggressive militarism. He had by then become a symbolic focus for the aspirations of militant Protestantism and was as such celebrated in writing as a future scourge of England's Continental enemies. Accompanying this was a new cult of chivalric honour associated with the prince. Headlam Wells argues that *Coriolanus* forms part of this somewhat embarrassing public debate. Shakespeare's tragedy deals not only with a state renowned in the ancient world above all for its military adventurism, but with a period characterized by the breakdown of internal order. Thus Shakespeare contradicts a favoured argument of the war party, namely that 'when wars are ended abroad, sedition begins at home'.

Yvonne Bruce, in 'The Pathology of Rhetoric in *Coriolanus*' (*UCrow* 20[2000] 93–115), finds that the play contains a great deal of movement but no progression, that there is debate without resolution, plots and promises that are not fulfilled, and constant effort without realized gain. At heart *Coriolanus* is, according to Bruce, 'a tautology of rhetoric', every action is 'talked' into the performance of a competing or cancelling reaction. Bruce further argues that, by observing the ambiguities present in the figure of Coriolanus and in the issues raised by the corn shortage, one can address the gap between voice and body, and absorb the importance of dearth to the play in a better way than by merely associating it with corn shortages in early seventeenth-century England. Reacting to descriptions of the 'endemic pathology' of the rhetoric of the play, Bruce maintains that words do succeed in *Coriolanus*. What fails in the play is not words, but the uses to which rhetoric is put, as well as a clear definition of the Roman state from which its rhetoric springs. It is an illuminating article that sheds light on the manipulative function of rhetoric in *Coriolanus*.

It might be well worth including Frank Kermode's excellent *Shakespeare's Language* in a discussion of *Coriolanus*, for in this book the author devotes a whole chapter to Shakespeare's last tragedy. One reason for Kermode's choice may be that he considers *Coriolanus* 'probably the most difficult play in the canon'. With his expertise in language as well as literature, Kermode is able to shed new light on a whole range of Shakespeare's plays. Interestingly, he observes that the 'little language' one sometimes finds in the earlier plays, for example *Love's Labour's Lost*, which is replaced by the intricacy of the lexical chains in *Troilus and Cressida*, *King Lear*, *Macbeth*, and *Timon of Athens*, reaches full maturity in *Coriolanus*, with 'stubborn repetition, free association, violent ellipses; in short, a prevailing ruggedness of tone'. Although some readers might wish that the analysis of interpersonal dramatic language had been taken even further, Kermode impressively captures much that inheres in Shakespeare's dramatic language.

(g) Late Plays

Although there were not many texts published in this field, Shakespeare's ritualistic and open-ended late plays still attract a great deal of attention from both the specialist and those working in other literary periods. *The Tempest* is still by far the most popular of the late plays to receive critical attention. Christine Dymkowski's edition for the Shakespeare in Production series reprints the New Cambridge Shakespeare text, as edited by David Lindley, with copious footnotes concerning the treatment of each scene in production from the play's first performance in 1610/11 to productions in 1999 and across the globe. Dealing with such issues as textual changes in production, the use of scenery, music, sound effects, actors' delivery and gestures and the impact of all of these on the interpretation of the play's meaning, this edition is an extremely useful tool for both teaching and research into *The Tempest*. Although admittedly rather overwhelming on occasion (for instance, the first seven lines of the play are accompanied by thirteen full pages of notes), the book provides a wealth of information gleaned from promptbooks, production designs and photographs, reviews, and so on and is an extremely valuable resource. The text is accompanied by an informative, extensive and wide-ranging introduction which, while not saying anything particularly new for the specialist, organizes a wealth of materials into an accessible, scholarly and pithy introduction to the issues raised by the study of the text and footnotes. This includes sections on scenic history, the development of prominent roles such as Ariel, Prospero and Caliban, and the impact of theatrical, social and critical developments, such as race and gender, on each. For instance, at the end of her analysis of the stage history of Ariel and the performance of the role by male and female actors, the editor comes to the truly important conclusion that though Ariel's gender is often used by the English theatre as a tool of ideological struggle, it is more rarely used to challenge gender ideology itself.

Given that the stage history of this play is so wide and varied, and taking into account the vast amount of material which the editor musters here, her decision to focus only on theatrical productions of the play rather than on film and video seems appropriate. So too does the choice to concentrate only on stagings of the play text itself, to the exclusion of what are called more 'radical appropriations' which rework rather than simply stage the text. This is done with some flexibility, however, as the editor does include Restoration adaptations, and has a useful appendix on textual variations which includes Dryden's and Davenant's *Enchanted Island* [1670]. Also useful as a research tool is the second appendix, which lists the principal players of each role throughout history. The scope of this project is impressive in itself, and this book is an extremely useful resource for research into the theatre history of this play.

Much of the work done on *The Tempest* pinpoints the search for new, post-new-historicist and post-post-colonialist ways of reading Shakespeare. Lisa Marciano's 'Shakespeare's *Tempest*: The Awareness of Death as a Catalyst to Wisdom' (*UCrow* 20[2000] 133–52) takes a rosy view of both Prospero's project and the effects of the realization of mortality within the play; Marciano reads the magician as didact, leading other characters to wisdom through teaching them to recognize their own or others' mortality. The article begins with a plan for the kind of theoretical reconsideration of the play which seems to have galvanized so many critics, but then goes on, as my synopsis implies, to offer what feels like a rather reactionary reading of the play. Despite the ongoing search for the 'new' approach, however, it is not surprising that most work on *The Tempest* has focused on just those features of the play which attracted new historicists and post-colonialists in the first place, and on Caliban in particular. It is almost as if finding the impasse has not yet allowed critics to get round or through it. Allen Carey-Webb, in 'National and Colonial Education in Shakespeare's *The Tempest*' (*EMLS* 5:i[1999] 1–39), uses an avowedly historicist methodology to focus on Prospero as an educator in national citizenship, and explores the power of pedagogy in Shakespeare's depiction, and the inculcation of obedience through education, convincingly connecting education to ideologies of royal rule. B.J. Sokol, 'Text-in-History: *The Tempest* and New World Cultural Encounter' (*GHJ* 22[19999] 21–40), again returns to these same themes of colonialism and its representation, resituating the play with reference to critical practice after new historicism. Rather than being a new methodology, however, this seems rather to be an extension of the interests of historicism beyond the bounds of materials usually applied to *The Tempest*. In contrast, Julia Reinhard Lipton's 'Creature Caliban' (*SQ* 51[2000] 1–23) tackles the character through the etymology of 'creature' to avoid either universalizing or particularizing reading strategies. In the end, though, she makes a claim for finding a new universalism in the play not by categorizing Caliban as human, but rather by claiming that 'all humans are creatures' (p. 21). An exercise in source studies, Peter Bilton's 'Another Island, Another Story: A Source for Shakespeare's *The Tempest*' (*RenFor* 5:i[2000]) plausibly offers Gaspar Gil Polo's *The Enamoured Diana*, as the title suggests, as a further source for the play.

In contrast to source or historicist studies, James V. Morrison, in 'Shipwreck Encounters: Odyssean Wanderings, *The Tempest* and the Post-Colonial World' (*CML* 20[2000] 59–90), adopts a comparative form of reading character construction through plot with relation to Shakespeare's play and to the *Odyssey*, and considers the parallels between the arrival on an island inhabited by a goddess of both Odysseus and Ferdinand. Another article to deal with the trope of shipwreck is Jürgen Pieters's 'The Wonders of the Imagination: *The Tempest* and its Spectators' (*EJES* 4[2000] 141–54), which, in contrast to the previous essay, takes an ethical, aesthetic and philosophical approach based on an interpretation of Hans Blumenberg's analysis of the metaphor of the shipwreck and its connection to the theatre, and concludes—via Greenblatt—that the spectatorly response of wonder is most appropriate to the essentially liminal art of theatre.

With reference to *Cymbeline*, again the priority among the best work seems to be the historicist investigation of discourses of power, often focused specifically on the examination of nationhood and national identity. A fine example of this is Roland J. Boling's article 'Anglo-Welsh Relations in *Cymbeline*' (*SQ* 51[2000] 33–66), which offers a witty and thorough historicized investigation of the Welsh setting of the play, sets the Anglo-Welsh dynamic against that between England and Rome to suggest a hierarchy of colonialism, and complicates the commonplace association between Henry Tudor and Milford Haven to suggest that it was a place feared both by the English as a point of foreign invasion and by the Welsh as a point of English invasion. Although at some points the author perhaps takes the reading of the play as social document rather too far (speculation on who might have taught Imogen to read in Rome is one rather strained moment), this is on the whole a successful and nuanced example of a historicized critique. On the other hand, John Boe's 'Symbols of Transformation in *Cymbeline*' (*R/WT* 2[1995] 47–74) takes the play to task using a psychoanalytic approach. Unfortunately, this is not a worthy representative for this methodology. The distinctions between the sophisticated investigation of the setting of Milford Haven in Boling's article, for example, show the simplistic nature of Boe's assertion that it is only an idealized pastoral setting. John Baxter's rather conservative '*Cymbeline* and the Measures of Chastity' (*ET* 12[1999] 135–55) seeks to uncover 'Shakespeare's view' of marital chastity by attending to tragedy in this play through a reading of genre and the applicability of 'romance' to the play and the marriage of Imogen and Posthumous.

Moving on to *Pericles*, Skeele ed., *Pericles: Critical Essays* is another useful research and teaching tool for a late Shakespearian play. Covering the history of criticism of the play from the inception of commentary to examples of present-day criticism, and a cross-section of its performance history, the collection balances the concerns of theory and production in interesting and fruitful ways. Following from a useful introduction, which gives an overview of the materials included and the play's textual and production history, the collection itself begins with critical rather than performance commentary; the former section moves from early controversies, beginning, of course, with Ben Jonson's account of *Pericles* as a 'mouldy tale', through the early nineteenth-century authorship debate between Steevens and Malone, to Fleay's rather more scientific approach, before moving on to Wilson Knight, and so through the twentieth century to contemporary critics. One of the pleasures of this collection is its reprinting of early criticism; these voices are vivid and enthralling (far more so than the editor's introduction would lead one to believe) and, if now dated and perhaps idiosyncratic, are also powerful. And, rather wonderfully in this day and age, Skeele includes a public change of heart on the part of a critic; in this case the recantation is on the part of Malone during his debate with Steevens over the authorship of *Pericles*. With regard to more contemporary criticism, the brevity of Coppelia Kahn's and Janet Adelman's psychoanalytic pieces (excerpted from larger works) speaks to the critical neglect which this play has suffered, although Steven Mullaney's cultural materialist piece is more substantial. There are two essays commissioned for the volume: Caroline Bick's 'Backsliding at Ephesus: Shakespeare's Diana and the Churching of Women', a timely feminist and historicist investigation of the play, and Marianne Novy's slightly less convincing piece, 'Multiple Parenting in *Pericles*'; both are constructive contributions.

As the editor's introduction points out, *Pericles* was one of Shakespeare's most popular plays when it was first produced, which belies its fall into stage obscurity later on. The performance criticism included here is wide-ranging, although not exhaustive. It covers productions in Burma (in Burmese), the USA, England and Japan and, in a nod to the developing industry of Shakespeare on film and television, also deals with what may be the sole production of the play on video as part of the BBC's series. There is perhaps a slight suspicion of tokenism on the part of the editor's choice of productions, and one has the sense that it may well have been necessary to look beyond England to find enough materials to constitute a stage history, but it is undeniably positive to have a collection which does not confine itself to English or Anglophone productions. Again, the early voices are eloquent and impinge forcefully on the reader; this is an extremely valuable gathering of primary materials, perhaps more so in the case of the performance section than of that concerned with 'literary' criticism.

Of the journal articles written on the play, Maria Teresa Micaela Prendergast's 'Engendering *Pericles*' (*L&P* 42[1996] 53–75) is a sophisticated example of a psychoanalytic approach, which takes textuality as a self-conscious concern within the play and links the concepts of textual and familial history, and that of the father or author as progenitor through the oedipal narrative of the text and Bloom's model of the anxiety of influence. In one of several essays dealing with editing, in this case the textual crux of the 'rough music' which precedes Cerimon's revival of Thaisa, F. Elizabeth Hart's 'Cerimon's Rough Music in *Pericles* 3.2' (*SQ* 51[2000] 313–31) seeks to offer an interpretative context which avoids emendation but which re-places 'rough music' within a sacred context of the worship of Diana of Ephesus while illuminating the textual history of the play. It shares an interest in the subject matter covered by Caroline Bicks in David Skeele's collection on *Pericles* but handles this content in interestingly distinct ways. Paul Dean's 'Pericles' Pilgrimage' (*EIC* 50[2000] 125–44) offers a generic and source reading of the play, positioning *Pericles* against both biblical tropes and the role of Gower as both narrator and as source-text.

Rather little was written on *The Winter's Tale* in 2000. One extremely persuasive contribution was made by Adam McKeown in 'Rhetoric and the Tragedy of *The Winter's Tale*' (*UCrow* 20[2000] 116–32), which casts new light on the opening tragic three acts by analysing them against concepts of rhetorical composition and what the author suggests is Shakespeare's own challenge to rhetoric.

In contrast, of the general works written about Shakespeare's late plays Thomas Rist's *Shakespeare's Romances and the Politics of Counter-Reformation* is almost entirely unsatisfactory. This study reads Shakespeare's late plays through counter-Reformation theology, taking on the recent challenges of revisionary history and applying thinking about Shakespeare's own religious background to his dramatic works. The author argues for the use of passion narratives in Shakespeare's romances as redemptive and therefore as Catholic in sympathy. The book is, however, rather oddly structured. Opening with a strange polemic against new historicism and cultural materialism—aimed primarily at Jonathan Dollimore—the author seems to be offering a rationale for what is perhaps less a theorized sense of history than a return to an 'old' historicism grounded on the 'reality' and 'objectivity' of history. After working through the major romances, the book then finishes with a brief appendix on *Henry VIII*, apparently added as an afterthought. What is more, this is rather a pedestrian study. Each argument is laid out from its most basic starting point, indicating confusion over its intended readership. For instance, Rist informs the reader that the court masque was a political form (a critical commonplace after the past twenty years of masque criticism). In the same vein, surely it is now accepted (whatever theoretical creed one professes) that early modern theatre was, or at least had the potential to be, political or politicized? This does not need to be stated, as it is here, as a new and rather surprising idea. This and other such moments are frustrating for a specialist reader and misleading for the non-specialist.

Perhaps more damagingly, there are elisions in the argument's content which seem to speak to a certain conservative critical agenda. For instance, the introduction reads the Jacobean court masque as a crypto-Catholic form; however, this only leaves one wondering why there is not so much as a mention of Anna of Denmark, the Catholic queen of England, and the major masque patron, commissioner and performer of the early seventeenth-century English court. Issues of gender are certainly not central in this book, but such an omission seems to point to an overly canonical and masculinist sense of what is significant in both history and text. Furthermore, the author's arguments are at times simplistic and over-read. For instance, Rist's interpretation of John Chamberlain's response to Ben Jonson's *Irish Masque at Court* as objecting specifically to Jonson's apparent satirizing of Irish Catholicism seems, from the evidence presented to the reader, unproven. He also chooses not to discuss *Two Noble Kinsmen*, stating that it does not suit his argument, rather than using it as a counterpoint. Most worrying of all, though, is the implicit connection in this study between research into early modern English recusancy and a conservative theoretical approach. This is perhaps expressed through an overly defensive style, which seeks not to persuade, but to shift the burden of argument onto those who may disagree with the author. Rist seems to believe that there are those in the critical community who will not accept his argument simply because it is about Catholicism. In the light of some of the strong and forceful work done in this area in recent years, this book seems to be damagingly conservative and worryingly simplistic.

Several journal articles carry forward this interest in readings of Shakespeare's late plays through a religious, specifically Christian, sensibility. They can perhaps be summed up by the rather literal title of John Cox's article, 'Recovering Something Christian about *The Tempest*' (*C&L* 50[2000] 31–51), which in the process of attempting this recovery rather caricatures materialist or historicist methodologies. A similar concern could also be found for *Pericles* in Maurice Hunt's rather disappointing 'Shakespeare's *Pericles* and the Acts of the Apostles' (*C&L* 49[1999] 295–309), which takes as its subject the intertextuality of Acts and its influence as a Christian signifier on Shakespeare's play. Rather more challenging was Grace Tiffany's 'Calvinist Grace in Shakespeare's Romances: Upending Tragedy' (*C&L* 49[1999] 421–45). Although at times the author's theoretical model seems flawed (as when she invokes the rather trite concept that the idea of grace as a redemptive notion mattered more to Shakespeare during his old age), this worthwhile piece offers an engaging historicist analysis of Calvinist concepts of grace and their depiction in Shakespeare's late plays.

There were a few additions to the bibliographic debates over late Shakespeare texts. Martin Butler, 'Running-Titles in *Cymbeline*' (*Library* 1[2000] 439–41), investigated the bibliographic history of the play through its running titles. Gabriel Egan's 'Revision of Scene 4 of *Sir Thomas More* as a Test of New Bibliographical Principles' (*EMLS* 6:ii[2000] 1–4) continues the debate over the history of the play, answering Paul Werstine's [1998] article in the same e-journal. In the realm of appropriations, Peter Holland contributed 'Modernizing Shakespeare: Nicholas Rowe and *The Tempest*' (*SQ* 51[2000] 24–32), a study of Nicholas Rowe's [1709] edition of Shakespeare, and his version of *The Tempest* in particular. This tightly focused article stakes a claim for the importance of Rowe's edition in received versions of Shakespeare's plays, and works on variants to establish that, while Rowe used F4 for his 1709 version, he may well have used F2 for his 1708 trial run, and laments that the 'less radical or contemporary' conventions did not survive (p. 32). Another response to the production of *The Tempest* during the later seventeenth century is John Bishop's '"The ordinary course of nature": Authority in the Restoration *Tempest*' (*RECTR* 13[1998] 54–69). This essay considers the political structures of Dryden and Davenant's *Enchanted Island* to investigate ideas of monarchy and to set this adaptation in its post-Commonwealth context, outlining a play which seems simultaneously nostalgic for early Stuart absolute power while apparently narrowing monarchical power in line with its Restoration context.

In the light of the work done in this year, and the beginnings of a search for new methodologies with which to approach these late plays, it will be worth while to chart the development of readings of Shakespeare's final works.

Books Reviewed

Adams, Barry B. *Coming-to-Know: Recognition and the Complex Plot in Shakespeare*. Lang. [2000] pp. 273. £35 ISBN 0 8204 4411 1.

Aitchison, Nick. *Macbeth: Man and Myth*. Sutton. [2000] pp. 216. £20 ISBN 0 7509 2640 6.

Alexander, Catherine M.S., and Stanley Wells, eds. *Shakespeare and Race*. CUP. [2000] pp. ix + 233. hb £37.50 ISBN 0 5217 7046 7, pb £12.95 ISBN 0 5217 7938 3.

Ashby, Justine, and Andrew Higson, eds. *British Cinema, Past and Present*. Routledge. [2000] pp. xx + 385. hb £53 ISBN 0 4152 2061 0, pb £15.99 ISBN 0 4152 2062 9.

Bates, Catherine. *Play in a Godless World: The Theory and Practice of Play in Shakespeare, Nietzsche and Freud*. Open Gate. [2000] pp. 250. £12.95 ISBN 1 8718 7147 6.

Bliss, Lee, ed. *Coriolanus*. CUP. [2000] pp. 303. hb £30 ISBN 0 5212 2226 5, pb £5.99 ISBN 0 5212 9402 9.

Bly, Mary. *Queer Virgins and Virgin Queans on the Early Modern Stage*. OUP. [2000] pp. 213. £35 ISBN 0 1981 8699 1.

Bode, Cristoph, and Wolfgang Klooss, eds. *Historicizing/Contemporizing Shakespeare: Essays in Honour of Rudolf Bohm*. Verlag. [2000] pp. 272. ISBN 3 8847 6368 7.

Boesky, Amy, and Mary Thomas Crane, eds. *Form and Reform in Renaissance England: Essays in Honor of Barbara Kiefer Lewalski*. UDelP. [2000] pp. 370. £39.50 ISBN 0 8741 3691 1.

Bray, Joe, Miriam Handley and Anne C. Henry, eds. *Marking the Text: The Presentation of Meaning on the Literary Page*. Ashgate. [2000] pp. 366. £55 ISBN 0 7546 0168 4.

Brode, Douglas. *Shakespeare in the Movies: From the Silent Era to 'Shakespeare in Love'*. OUP. [2000] pp. ix + 257. £16.99 ISBN 0 1951 3958 5.

Bruster, Douglas. *Quoting Shakespeare: Form and Culture in Early Modern Drama*. UNebP. [2000] pp. xi + 268. $50 ISBN 0 8032 1303 4.

Burns, Edward, ed. *King Henry VI Part One*. Arden3. ArdenSh. [2000] pp. xiv + 345. £7.99 ISBN 0 1903 3643 5.

Callaghan, Dympna, ed. *A Feminist Companion to Shakespeare*. Blackwell. [2000] pp. xxiv + 384. hb £50 ISBN 0 6312 0806 2, pb £15.99 ISBN 0 6312 0807 0.

Cartmell, Deborah. *Interpreting Shakespeare on Screen*. Macmillan. [2000] pp. xiii + 170. hb £42.50 ISBN 0 3336 5211 8, pb £13.50 ISBN 0 3336 5212 6.

Charney, Maurice. *Shakespeare on Love and Lust*. ColUP. [2000] pp. 234. hb £21 ISBN 0 2311 0428 6, pb £13.50 ISBN 0 2311 0429 4.

Cheney, Patrick, and Anne Lake Prescott, eds. *Approaches to Teaching Shorter Elizabethan Poetry*. MLA. [2000] pp. 331. hb $37.50 ISBN 0 8735 2753 4, pb $18 ISBN 0 8735 2754 2.

Chew, Shirley, and Alistair Stead, eds. *Translating Life: Studies in Transpositional Aesthetics*. LiverUP. [1999] pp. 421. hb ISBN 0 8532 3674 7, pb ISBN 0 8532 3684 4.

Cousins, A.D. *Shakespeare's Sonnets and Narrative Poems*. Longman. [2000] pp. 227. hb £60 ISBN 0 5822 1513 7, pb £17.99 ISBN 0 5822 1512 9.

Danson, Lawrence. *Shakespeare's Dramatic Genres*. OUP. [2000] pp. 166. £12.99 ISBN 0 1987 1172 7.

Desmet, Christy, and Robert Sawyer, eds. *Shakespeare and Appropriation*. T&F. [1999] pp. 256. £55 ISBN 0 4152 0725 8.

de Sousa, Geraldo U. *Shakespeare's Cross-Cultural Encounters*. Macmillan. [1999] pp. 256. £13.99 ISBN 0 3339 4947 1.

Dymkowski, Christine, ed. *The Tempest*. Shakespeare in Production. CUP. [2000] pp. xxxii + 373. hb £45 ISBN 0 5214 4407 1, pb £15.95 ISBN 0 5217 8375 5.

Eggert, Katherine. *Showing Like a Queen: Female Authority and Literary Experiment in Spenser, Shakespeare, and Milton*. UPennP. [2000] pp. 304. £31.50 ISBN 0 8122 3532 0.

Elton, W.R. *Troilus and Cressida and the Inns of Court Revels*. Ashgate. [2000] pp. 224. £45 ISBN 1 8592 8214 8.

Enterline, Lynn. *The Rhetoric of the Body from Ovid to Shakespeare*. CUP. [2000] pp. 264. £42.50 ISBN 0 5216 2450 9.

Falco, Mark. *Charismatic Authority in Early Modern English Tragedy*. JHUP. [2000] pp. 233. $41.95 ISBN 0 8018 6280 9.

Frye, Susan, and Karen Robertson, eds. *Maids and Mistresses, Cousins and Queens: Women's Alliances in Early Modern England*. OUP. [1999] pp. 368. £40 ISBN 0 1951 1734 4.

Gay, Penny. *As You Like It*. WtW. Northcote. [1999] pp. ix + 107. £8.99 ISBN 0 7463 0910 4.

Golden, Catherine J., ed. *Book Illustrated: Text, Image, and Culture, 1770–1930*. OakK. [2000] pp. xvi + 320. $39.95 ISBN 1 5845 6023 1.

Grady, Hugh, ed. *Shakespeare and Modernity: Early Modern to the Millennium* Routledge. [2000] pp. viii + 234. hb £55 ISBN 0 4152 1200 6, pb £14.99 ISBN 0 4152 1201 4.

Gurr, Andrew, and Mariko Ichikawa. *Staging in Shakespeare's Theatres*. OUP. [2000] pp. 181. hb £27.50 ISBN 0 1987 1159 X, pb £12.99 ISBN 0 1987 1158 1.

Habib, Imtiaz. *Shakespeare and Race: Postcolonial Praxis in the Early Modern Period*. UPA. [2000] pp. xi + 298. hb $57 ISBN 0 7618 1545 7, pb $34.50 ISBN 0 7618 1546 5.

Happé, Peter, ed. *Tudor Theatre 5: Allegory in the Theatre*. Lang. [2000] pp. 249. £28 ISBN 3 9067 008 1.

Hattaway, Michael, ed. *A Companion to English Renaissance Literature and Culture*. Blackwell. [2000] pp. 747. £80 ISBN 0 6312 1668 5.

Headlam Wells, Robin. *Shakespeare on Masculinity*. CUP. [2000] pp. xi + 249. £35 ISBN 0 5216 6204 4.

Healy, Margaret. *Richard II*. Northcote. [1998] pp. 88. £7.99 ISBN 0 7453 0845 0.

Hedrick, Donald, and Bryan Reynolds, eds. *Shakespeare without Class: Misappropriation of Cultural Capital*. Palgrave. [2000] pp. vi + 297. £18.75 ISBN 0 3122 2271 8.

Holden, Anthony. *William Shakespeare: His Life and Work*. Abacus. [2000] pp. xiv + 367. £7.99 ISBN 0 3491 1240 1.

Holderness, Graham. *Shakespeare: The Histories*. Macmillan. [2000] pp. 231. hb £45 ISBN 0 3336 2496 3, pb £14.99 ISBN 0 3336 2497 1.

Houe, Poul, et al. *Anthropology and Authority: Essays on Søren Kierkegaard*. Rodopi. [2000] pp. 189. $35 ISBN 9 0420 0640 4.

Howard, Jean E., and Scott Cutler Sherstow, eds. *Marxist Shakespeares*. Routledge. [2000] pp. xii + 304. hb $27.99 ISBN 0 4152 0233 7, pb ISBN 0 4152 0234 5.

Howard-Hill, Trevor, ed. *Shakespearian Bibliography and Textual Criticism: A Bibliography*. 2nd edn. Summertown. [2000] pp. 290. $65 ISBN 1 8930 0905 X.

Howlett, Kathy M. *Framing Shakespeare on Film*. OhioUP. [2000] pp. xvii + 255. £43.65 ISBN 0 8214 1247 7.

Hunt, Maurice, ed. *Approaches to Teaching Shakespeare's 'Romeo and Juliet'*. MLA. [2000] pp. 222. hb £32.57 ISBN 0 8735 2757 7, pb £15.63 ISBN 0 8735 2758 5.

Ioppolo, Grace, ed. *Shakespeare Performed: Essays in Honour of R.A. Foakes*. UDelP. [2000] pp. 311. £38 ISBN 0 3336 6273 3.

Jackson, Russell, ed. *The Cambridge Companion to Shakespeare on Film*. CUP. [2000] pp. xiv + 342. £14.95 ISBN 0 5216 3975 1.

Jowett, John, ed. *Richard III*. OUP. [2000] pp. ix + 414. £6.99 ISBN 0 1928 3993 4.

Kermode, Frank. *Shakespeare's Language*. Penguin. [2000] pp. xi + 324. £7.99 ISBN 0 1402 8592 X.

Kiernan, Pauline. *Staging Shakespeare at the New Globe*. Macmillan. [1999] pp. xiv + 175. £15.99 ISBN 0 3336 6273 3.

Kirsch, Arthur, ed. *W.H. Auden: Lectures on Shakespeare*. PrincetonUP. [2000] pp. xxiv + 398. £19.95 ISBN 0 6910 5730 3.

Lee, John. *Shakespeare's 'Hamlet' and the Controversies of Self*. OUP. [2000] pp. 266. £40 ISBN 0 1981 8504 9.

Levenson, Jill L., ed. *Romeo and Juliet*. OUP. [2000] pp. ix + 450. £6.99 ISBN 0 1928 1496 6.

Little, Arthur L. *Shakespeare Jungle Fever: National-Imperial Re-Visions of Race, Rape, and Sacrifice*. StanfordUP. [2000] pp. 272. $24.95 ISBN 0 8047 4024 0.

Marvel, Laura, ed. *Readings on The Taming of the Shrew*. Greenhaven. [2000] pp. 170. £17.33 ISBN 0 7377 0236 2.

Marx, Steven. *Shakespeare and the Bible*. OUP. [2000] pp. 165. hb £27.50 ISBN 0 1981 8440 9, pb £12.99 ISBN 0 1981 8439 5.

Mazzio, Carla, and Douglas Trevor, eds. *Historicism, Psychoanalysis, and Early Modern Culture*. Routledge. [2000] pp. 417. hb £50 ISBN 0 4159 2052 3, pb £13.99 ISBN 0 4159 2053 1.

McEvoy, Sean. *Shakespeare: The Basics*. Routledge. [2000] pp. xvi + 282. hb £45 ISBN 0 4152 1288 X, pb £9.99 ISBN 0 4152 1289 8.

McLoughlin, Cathleen T. *Shakespeare, Rabelais, and the Comical-Historical*. Lang. [2000] pp. 184. £30 ISBN 0 8204 4098 1.

McMullan, Gordon, ed. *King Henry the Eighth*. Arden3. ArdenSh. [2000] pp. xxiii + 506. £7.99 ISBN 1 9034 3625 7.

Miola, Robert S. *Shakespeare's Reading*. OUP. [2000] pp. 186. £25 ISBN 0 1987 1168 9, pb £12.99 ISBN 0 1987 1169 7.

Mortimer, Anthony. *Variable Passions: A Reading of Shakespeare's 'Venus and Adonis'*. AMS. [2000] pp. 208. £49.95 ISBN 0 4046 2336 0.

Murphy, Andrew, ed. *The Renaissance Text: Theory, Editing, Textuality*. ManUP. [2000] pp. 240. £14.99 ISBN 0 7190 5917 8.

Palmer, Alan, and Veronica Palmer. *Who's Who in Shakespeare's England*. Methuen. [2000] pp. xxiv + 280. £12.99 ISBN 0 4137 4710 7.

Pieters, Jürgen, ed. *Critical Self-Fashioning: Stephen Greenblatt and the New Historicism*. Lang. [1999] £25 ISBN 3 6313 4116 4.

Pye, Christopher. *The Vanishing: Shakespeare, the Subject, and Early Modern Culture*. DukeUP. [2000] pp. 199. hb £49.95 ISBN 0 8223 2510 1, pb £17.95 ISBN 0 8223 2547 0.

Rist, Thomas. *Shakespeare's Romances and the Politics of Counter-Reformation*. Mellen. [1999] pp. xii + 251. $89.95 ISBN 0 7734 8033 1.

Ryan, Kiernan, ed. *Shakespeare: Texts and Contexts*. Palgrave. [2000] pp. 344. hb £49.50 ISBN 0 3339 1316 7, pb £17.50 ISBN 0 3339 1317 5.

Shaughnessy, Robert, ed. *Shakespeare in Performance: New Casebook*. Macmillan. [2000] pp. ix + 246. £13.99 ISBN 0 3337 4124 2.

Skeele, David. *Pericles: Critical Essays*. Garland. [2000] pp. xii + 348. £42.50 ISBN 0 8153 2911 3.

Styan, J.L. *Perspectives on Shakespeare in Performance*. Lang. [2000] pp. ix + 183. £19.90 ISBN 0 8204 4426 X.

Szönyi, György, and Rowland Wymer, eds. *The Iconography of Power: Ideas and Images of Rulership on the English Renaissance Stage*. JATE. [2000] pp. 214. $16 ISBN 9 6348 2482 X.

Takahashi, Yasunari, ed. *Hot Questrists after the English Renaissance: Essays on Shakespeare and his Contemporaries*. AMS. [2000] pp. viii + 296. £61.95 ISBN 0 4046 2337 9.

Taylor, A.B., ed. *Shakespeare's Ovid: The 'Metamorphoses' in the Plays and Poems*. CUP. [2000] pp. xii + 219. £35 ISBN 0 5217 7192 7.

Thorne, Alison. *Vision and Rhetoric in Shakespeare: Looking through Language*. Macmillan. [2000] pp. xvi + 290. £40 ISBN 0 3336 5939 2.

Thornton Burnett, Mark, and Ramona Wray, eds. *Shakespeare, Film, Fin de Siècle*. Macmillan. [2000] pp. xiv + 244. hb £47.50 ISBN 0 3337 7663 1, pb £16.99 ISBN 0 3337 7664 X.

Wells, Stanley, ed. *King Lear*. OUP. [2000] pp. x + 321. £6.99 ISBN 0 1928 3992 6.

Whitney, John O. *Power Plays: Shakespeare's Lessons in Leadership and Management*. Macmillan. [2000] pp. 316. £15 ISBN 0 3337 8155 4.

Willson, Robert F. *Shakespeare in Hollywood, 1929–1956*. FDUP. [2000] pp. 190. $36.50 ISBN 0 8386 3832 5.

VII

Renaissance Drama: Excluding Shakespeare

SARAH POYNTING, PETER J. SMITH, MATTHEW STEGGLE
AND DARRYLL GRANTLEY

This chapter has three sections: 1. Editions and Textual Scholarship; 2. Theatre History; 3. Criticism. Section 1 is by Sarah Poynting; section 2 is by Peter J. Smith; sections 3(a) and 3(c) are by Matthew Steggle; section 3(b) is by Darryll Grantley.

1. Editions and Textual Scholarship

This was the first year for some time that full critical editions outnumbered both collections of plays and 'student' editions. ManUP were responsible for this very welcome outburst of activity, with modern-spelling Revels editions of Lyly, Jonson and Middleton. David Bevington and George K. Hunter have added to the previous texts of Lyly's drama in the series with a volume containing two plays, *Galatea* (edited by Hunter) and *Midas* (by Bevington), each with its own introduction in which the textual history and critical approaches are discussed. If, in common with most of this year's new volumes from Revels, the performance histories are briefer than we have become accustomed to, this is owing rather to a relative absence of continuing stage life than to any inadequacy on the part of the editors. Although the introductions to the plays are necessarily rather less comprehensive than they would be if each had its own volume, the critical discussions are still substantial, particularly of *Midas*, towards which there is a distinct bias in terms of the amount of attention given to each text. Bevington's introduction to *Midas* considers the influences on the play both of its classical sources and of the context of vernacular drama in which it was written in order to examine how its 'mingle-mangle' (in the apologetic words of the Prologue) operates dramatically and thematically. In particular, he examines the layering of meaning within the play, and how it is held together by its rhetorical patterns. The levels of allegory on which the play can be read are explored in detail, with discussions of it as a generalized allegory of tyranny, and of divine wisdom and human frailty, as well as a topical historical allegory referring to Philip II of Spain, which is seen as intermittent but unmistakable. Hunter's shorter introduction to the more structurally cohesive *Galatea* concentrates largely on its Ovidian sources and Terentian dramaturgy, and on placing the play in the context both of Lyly's own work and of other mythological drama written for the court. It may come as some surprise to find recent gender-based approaches to the play relegated to (and dismissed in) a footnote. The unproblematic textual history of each play is reflected in the lightness of the editing, while the critical annotation is thorough and very helpful.

There were two new editions of Jonson from Revels, Robert S. Miola's *Every Man in his Humour* and Peter Happé's *The Magnetic Lady*. While there have been a number of recent editions of the former, they have all been of the revised, Anglicized Folio version, so this edition based on the 1601 quarto of Jonson's Italianate original is very timely. The collation records smaller variants to be found in the Folio, while longer passages from it, with a critical annotation as full as that for the main text, are provided in an appendix. In the textual sections of his introduction Miola looks at the printing history of the play, evidence for the date of revision for the Folio, and the changes which Jonson made to both its structure and text. In recognizing the general critical bias towards the Folio text he makes a persuasive case for re-examining the earlier version, exploring its Italian setting and the resonances it would have evoked for its Elizabethan audience, its immediate dramatic context (particularly in terms of other comedies of humours by Chapman and Marston), and the social context of contemporary urban life. Miola discusses how the play's locale affects our understanding of its references to Roman Catholicism, considering in detail complex interrelated cultural anxieties about religion, satire and drama, and pointing out the similarities between Jonson's plays and the verse satires of the late 1590s. In doing so, he concentrates on Lorenzo Junior's 'Sidneyan defence of Poesy' (cut from the Folio) and Q's pervasive concern with poetry, which he sees as culminating in appropriating for good poetry the 'authority and high moral ground' of religion and politics. In the stage history of the play he shows how the RSC's excellent 1986 production of the Folio version of *Every Man In* was enriched by adopting a good deal of Q in the final scene, including Lorenzo's speech. However, the section's references to Kitely and Knowell also make clear how little, in general, Q has been used for performance. Following this, it is slightly disconcerting to return to further sections of criticism on plot, character, language and gender. It is a minor quibble, but the different parts of the introduction could have been more logically ordered.

We move from the beginning to close to the end of Jonson's career for the second of his plays from Revels, *The Magnetic Lady* (1632). The text is based on its first printing in the posthumous third volume of the folio *Works of Benjamin Jonson* (1641), which Happé argues is taken from a Jonson autograph manuscript. Jonson's characteristically heavy punctuation has been lightened, and massed character lists at the head of scenes redistributed; some of the former changes have been recorded in the collation, as have any variants accepted from later editions. In placing the play in the context of Jonson's life, Happé shows how productive he was in his last years, and how conscious he continued to be of the reception of his dramatic works by their audiences. Indeed, throughout the introduction Happé's central concern is essentially biographical. His discussion of the public context of the play (Charles I's personal rule and Laudian church reform) speculates cautiously on how Jonson might have felt about these religious and political issues, considering *The Magnetic Lady* alongside his 1630s masques and poetry. There is a more extensive examination of the theatrical qualities of the play in terms of Jonson's actual dramaturgy and of his theoretical preoccupations about it, as dramatized in the

Induction and Choruses, followed by an analysis of the operation of plot and character on stage, as well as the range of language employed. In view of the variety of dramatic action which Happé finds in the play, it is regrettable that only three productions appear to have taken place since 1632 (one on the radio). Following the success of the RSC's *The Devil is an Ass*, perhaps it's overdue for revival; though no modern performance would presumably attract either the personal attacks or the concern of the censors documented in this very useful edition.

The final play in the Revels series is Gail Kern Paster's edition of Thomas Middleton's *Michaelmas Term*. If productions of *The Magnetic Lady* have been limited, those of *Michaelmas Term* would appear to have been non-existent, since none are recorded. Indeed, rather surprisingly not even its performances by the Children of Paul's in 1605–6 are discussed, although the effect of the homoerotic appeal of the boy actors is pointed out in Paster's critical assessment of the play. Apart from this omission, the edition contains a thorough and interesting introduction to Middleton's play. The text is that of the 1607 quarto, conservatively emended; the collation records significant variants from the editions of Dyce and Levin, as well as distinguishing between corrected and uncorrected quarto readings. In her discussion of its dating, Paster draws attention to its similarities with *Volpone* and the impossibility of deciding which (if either) influenced the other. Further literary influences she looks at include cony-catching pamphlets and the *commedia dell'arte*, while actual cases of fraud are briefly indicated. Middleton's intertwined satire of social and sexual ambition and competition is examined through the play's structure, setting, characterization and language. In particular, Paster considers the use of clothing as an unreliable means of self-construction and a path to sexual opportunity, along with the varying success of the characters in employing it as a mode of transformation. The recent repeal of the sumptuary laws had, as she shows, destabilized assumptions concerning dress and status. She also analyses the gender-based differences in the ways in which clothing operates as a signifier in the play, linking this to a more general exploration of gender in the play and especially of ideals of male friendship, which she relates to Middleton's frequent sexual innuendo.

There were two more plays from ManUP this year in the Revels Student Editions series. The first was another Jonson, Suzanne Gossett's *Bartholomew Fair*, based on the 1960 Revels edition by E.A. Horsman, though the text has been reconsidered and the critical introduction wholly rewritten. In it Gossett discusses the relationship between the fair and the 'outside' world (both real and dramatic), and Jonson's deconstruction of the 'apparent dichotomies' he sets up. She pays particular attention to the play's distorted construction of domesticity, its blurring of the distinction between sanity and madness/folly, and its unsettling treatment of women and reproduction. The metatheatricality of *Bartholomew Fair*, especially in relation to Shakespeare's late plays, is discussed, as well as other contemporaneous drama drawing on similar conventions to those employed in the play by Jonson. The language and staging are examined, and a brief performance history provided; there is also a very useful critical bibliography. The critical commentary is largely limited to explanation of problematic vocabulary and references. The last ManUP work is John Marston's *The Malcontent*, edited by George K. Hunter from his own 1975 Revels edition (reissued in 1999). This follows the same format as *Bartholomew Fair*, though its introduction is very considerably shorter. Following a brief biography of Marston, Hunter looks at the play in terms of Marston's self-conscious choice of the tragicomic genre, relating it to the 1602 translation of Guarini's *Il Pastor Fido*, quotations from which are scattered throughout *The Malcontent*. He also examines the Induction (generally believed to be by Webster, along with other additions), and the evidence it provides towards the history of Elizabethan theatre and the nature of theatrical texts. The value of the play for a modern readership is considered, which Hunter finds in 'intensely focused poetic language turning theatrical structure into moral vision'. Less optimistically, he sees there as being 'an almost insurmountable barrier between [Marston's] plays and the expectations of a modern theatre audience': let us hope that the RSC's 2002 production of *The Malcontent* proves him wrong.

The only collection of plays takes us back to Jonson, with the second volume of his plays to be published in the OUP World's Classics Oxford English Drama series. It follows the usual format of the series, with a brief textual and critical introduction, including a bibliography of further reading, and a critical commentary printed as endnotes. This volume gives us four lesser-known plays edited by Margaret Jane Kidnie: *Poetaster*, *Sejanus His Fall*, *The Devil is an Ass* and *The New Inn*. While all of these have been published relatively recently in single editions, it is good to see them made more widely available in a cheap paperback. The sheer bulk of the text means that there is limited space available for a critical introduction, but Kidnie makes full use of what there is, with clear, accessible and well-focused discussions of each play. She examines the topical nature of *Poetaster* and its place in the 'War of the Theatres', but also points out the broader political and aesthetic issues addressed by Jonson. The play's Roman setting is compared with Jonson's use of it in *Sejanus*, in relation to which Kidnie similarly explores both the possible topical references and wider political questions which might have brought Jonson before the Privy Council; in particular she looks at the political climate evoked in *Sejanus* and the dynamic of the relationship between Sejanus and Tiberius. Jonson's problems with the authorities are again delineated in Kidnie's discussion of *The Devil is an Ass*; she also considers its attention to the detail of urban life and its adaptation of the city comedy genre. Genre receives further attention when she turns to *The New Inn*, 'the only extant play in which Jonson experiments with...romantic comedy'. The nature of Jonson's experiment is examined, along with the play's dominant imagery. I found it refreshing to be warned not to read any more of the introduction until I had read the play, for fear of spoiling the ending.

Finally, there were two further publications in the useful Globe Quartos series, published by Nick Hern Books in association with the International Shakespeare Globe Centre. The anonymous *The Merry Devil of Edmonton* was edited by Nicola Bennett, and Brome's *The Antipodes* by David Scott Kastan and Richard Proudfoot. In general these follow the format of earlier plays, with a brief introduction followed by a modernized text and textual notes. The value of the series for general readers has been extended by the inclusion in both of very useful 'glossarial notes' (considerably expanded from the glossary included in previous volumes), and Bennett's also adds an appendix containing extracts from the *Merry Devil*'s source material.

The increase in output of new editions this year was matched by a flurry of articles of editing or textual interest. Two articles in *Studies in Bibliography* are not specifically concerned with Renaissance drama, but are of general relevance for editors and bibliographers. In 'The Treatment of Typesetting and Presswork in Bibliographical Description' (*SB* 52[2000] 1–57), G. Thomas Tanselle proposes methods of describing the physical traces left by printing-shop activity, particularly those not intended to be noticed or to exist, such as deterioration of type or impressions from materials not meant to print. He suggests including details of identifiable types; spelling and layout variations; headlines; point-holes; typographical variations; press figures; and first- and second-forme impressions. He moves to manuscripts in a second article co-authored with David L. Vander Meulen, 'A System of Manuscript Transcription' (*SB* 52[2000] 201–12), in which they put forward (rather hopefully, to my mind) a standard system to be followed by transcribers. While the principle seems reasonable, the result, as illustrated by a number of examples, strikes me as clumsy and difficult for readers. In a third article in this volume, 'The Printer and Date of Q4 *A Looking Glass for London and England*' (*SB* 52[2000] 155–60), Laurie E. Maguire, as the title suggests, reconsiders the evidence for the fourth-quarto printing of the morality play by Green and Lodge, of which only one copy survives. Working from internal evidence of type and watermarks and comparison with a series of other dramatic texts, Maguire persuasively argues that William Jaggard printed the play for Thomas Pavier in 1605, contradicting the identification of Ralph Blower accepted by the revised STC.

Two articles by Thomas Merriam examine the authorship of *Sir Thomas More*. In the more substantial of these, 'The Misunderstanding of Munday as Author of *Sir Thomas More*' (*RES* 51[2000] 540–81), he challenges the usual attribution of the main authorship of the play to Anthony Munday. He suggests that, while the manuscript is in his hand, he was acting as copyist rather than playwright, and that in doing so he was working as an agent provocateur in accordance with his known activity as an anti-Catholic government agent. His target, Merriam argues, was probably Shakespeare or Marlowe. He supports his argument with evidence comparing the density of Munday's writing with that in his manuscript of *John a Kent*, and a detailed stylometric analysis of the language of the parts of *More* attributed to Munday. He presents further evidence against Munday's authorship, drawing on a greater range of his writing, in 'An Unwarranted Assumption' (*N&Q* 47[2000] 438–41). His third piece this year looks at joint authorship in 'Marlowe and Nashe in *Dido Queen of Carthage*' (*N&Q* 47[2000] 425–8), in which he uses logometric analysis to propose that the first two acts of *Dido* are by Marlowe and the remainder by Nashe. Marlowe reappears in 'Marlowe and Peele: A Further Note on the Final Scholar Scene in the *Doctor Faustus* B Text' (*N&Q* 47[2000] 40–2), in which Robert A.H. Smith argues that this final scene predated the 1602 revisions of the text, and probably formed part of the original play, as it reveals none of the verse or speech peculiarities characteristic of the revisions. He also cites lines from Peele's *The Battel of Alcazar*, and other echoes from the play, which suggest that one seems to have borrowed from the other at a date earlier than 1602. Authorship is also at issue in 'Thomas Watson and the "Elvetham Entertainment"' (*N&Q* 47[2000] 37–40), by Albert Chatterley, who proposes Watson as the most likely author of the anonymously printed entertainment. He bases this on a comparison of lines of Latin hexameters taken from its opening oration with lines from Watson's epic *Amintae Gaudia*, as well as on Watson's reputation as a writer of both Latin and English poetry.

Gary Taylor is also concerned with authorship in 'Thomas Middleton, Thomas Dekker, and *The Bloody Banquet*' (*PBSA* 94[2000] 197–233). This closely argued but readable and convincing article makes the case for Dekker and Middleton as joint authors of a play which, as Taylor says, has barely been read (let alone staged), in part because there has been no edition of it, Bowers and Hoy having excluded it from the complete Dekker. He argues that linguistic forms, verbal paralleling, textual variation and patterns of versification all present consistent evidence as to how the scenes were divided between the two playwrights. He also considers the likelihood of the play's having been printed from a copy made by a scribe working for Beeston's Boys many years after it was written, and (much more speculatively) how this might have affected the text, which seems to have been abridged.

Ben Jonson makes a comeback in 'The Case of Will Kemp's Shoes: *Every Man Out Of His Humour* and the "Bibliographic Ego"' (*BJJ* 7[2000] 271–91), by Bruce Boehrer, who turns what he terms a quibble with 'a masterpiece of twentieth-century textual editing' (Herford and Simpson) into a rather over-extended consideration of the interconnection between bibliography and critical interpretation. The quibble concerns the omission in the commentary to the *Complete Works* of Chambers's suggestion that the line containing the reference to Kemp's shoe had been added to the text while the manuscript was being prepared for the printer following Kemp's dance to Norwich, which took place after the performance of *Every Man Out*. Boehrer argues that Q1 reveals evidence of differing levels of composition ignored by Herford and Simpson in the quest for an ideal, single text.

In 'An Annotated Bibliography of Textual Scholarship in Elizabethan Drama, 1973–1998' (*RORD* 39[2000] 17–76), Jeremy Lopez provides assistance to all those (or almost all those) interested in finding critical editions of, and articles of textual relevance about, Elizabethan plays, excluding Shakespeare. He also excludes any plays or masques not written for the commercial theatre, and editions or articles not dealing explicitly with issues pertaining to the physical production of printed play-texts, so the scope is rather more limited than the title suggests. It is, nevertheless, a useful listing which for each play provides details of whether the text is in old or modernized spelling and of the copy-text used, and notes any focus on bibliographical information, while articles are briefly summarized. This is apparently the foundation of a wider bibliography which will include Jacobean and Caroline drama, which will be very welcome; but I would like to put in a (self-interested) plea for the scope to be broadened to include closet, court and university drama.

2. Theatre History

In a fascinating essay, Janette Dillon examines the plays being written during the so called 'War of the Theatres'. 'Fashion, Nation and Theatre in Late Sixteenth-Century London' (in Esche, ed., *Shakespeare and his Contemporaries in Performance*, pp. 161–76) recognizes that characters in such plays 'manifest an obsessive interest in linguistic decorums' (p. 162) in the vernacular as well as ostentatiously demonstrating competence in foreign languages—often to humorous effect when such competence is fraudulent. Dillon asserts that 'Words here, it is clear, are not conceived of as signs expressive of a pre-existent identity, but as fashion accessories' (p. 162). She suggests that this heteroglossia is symptomatic of a shift in authority from the court to the city and is part of the conspicuous self-fashioning of the new man about town: 'It is a language dedicated to the display of its own substance, language, in effect, as fetishized commodity, its materiality so foregrounded that its usefulness, or referentiality, disappears under the excessive weight of its self-reference' (p. 163). This, Dillon argues, is a sign of the times, contrasting this flashy Jacobean gentleman with 'the plain-speaking Englishman celebrated in so many history plays of the 1590s, whose identity is firmly grounded in a national and nationalistic framework' (p. 164). She goes on to examine what she claims is 'a parallel between social and theatrical performance [which] is dizzying in its self-reflexiveness' (p. 169) before concluding that this linguistic interest reflects the ambivalence with which the 'dramatists respond to the commodification of their product....Even as the theatre stages the excesses of fashion that audiences clamour for, it registers discomfort about its own complicity with the market' (p. 173). This might be to attribute a too knowing materiality to such a young institution as the professional theatre, but as a thesis it is definitely worth wrestling with.

In the same volume Peter Thomson examines 'The True Physiognomy of a Man: Richard Tarlton and his Legend' (in Esche, ed., pp. 191–210). In a bracing essay which draws parallels with the comic techniques of George Robey, Frankie Howerd, Morecambe and Wise, W.C. Fields, Mae West, the Marx Brothers and the Carry On team, as well as the gnomic nonsense of Eric Cantona, the former Manchester United footballer ('When the seagulls follow the trawler it is because they think the sardines are going to be thrown into the sea'), Thomson attempts to describe the tenor of Tarlton's jests based, he asserts, 'broadly speaking [on a joining of] the technical and the political' (p. 197). The task is doubly difficult. To begin with, the main source, *Tarlton's Jests*, was published posthumously and the 'precise status of this collection of anecdotes (scarcely "jests" in a modern sense) has never been established' (p. 195), but moreover, Thomson contends that there have arisen a number of Tarltons, all of which are, in their own ways, travesties. Muriel Bradbrook's version, for instance, is too benign while Robert Weimann's attribution to Tarlton of 'the reconciliation of folk-culture with the professional stage' (p. 193) is overstating the case. David Wiles takes Tarlton's rustic clown to be a 'response to London, an immigrant's way of establishing sympathetic contact with the many other immigrants in his audience' (pp. 193–4). Finally, '[Martin] Buzacott's Tarlton is a Chaplinesque great dictator imbued with a real-life lust to kill' (p. 194). For Thomson, Tarlton's 'combination of technique and combative purpose distinguishes the Brechtian performer' (p. 197) and it is in this mould that Tarlton is best identified. The essay concludes with attention to Richard III and Malvolio, the former as 'a Tarltonian jester' (p. 206) and the latter who 'in his pomp exposes the lack of a Tarlton-clown' (p. 206) in the company, Tarlton having died over a dozen years earlier.

Two articles, again in *Shakespeare and his Contemporaries in Performance*, pay attention to modern productions of non-Shakespearean plays, *The Broken Heart* and *The White Devil*. In '"The silent griefs which cut the heart strings": John Ford's *The Broken Heart* in Performance' (Esche, ed., pp. 261–74), Kristin Crouch examines Michael Boyd's 1994 version of the play for the RSC. She talks of the production's visual language and its use of tableaux, particularly its symbolic feast table which reappeared decayed and bloodied. She also examines the use of movement, formal dance and music in the production as well as the way in which the script itself calls for a number of chairs on which to seat characters so that 'Desires are held down, trapped within the passive posture' (p. 266). Nick Tippler's 'Cunning with Pistols: Observations on Gale Edwards's 1996–7 RSC Production of John Webster's *The White Devil*' (Esche, ed., pp. 275–91) has a detailed ear for textual alterations and explains their consequences fully. Perhaps most fancifully and interestingly, he invests the Pit theatre itself with a ghastly symbolism: 'The depth below the London streets of the playing space, the immediacy of the relationship between the small thrust stage and audience seating, and a claustrophobic confinement imposed by the proximity of the lighting gantry all signify Hell' (p. 276).

In '"Thy voice squeaks": Listening for Masculinity on the Early Modern Stage' (*RenD* 29[2000] 39–71) Gina Bloom, paying special attention to the 'aural dimensions of the Elizabethan theater' (p. 39), explores the negotiation of gender on the all-male stage. She asserts that 'precarious vocality [was] a cultural concern in early modern England' (p. 40), and while this seems quite a claim she does demonstrate with reference to a number of contemporary sources, notably Richard Mulcaster's *Positions Concerning the Training Up of Children* [1581] but also medical and conduct books, that the cultivation of a powerful speaking timbre was important since it was indicative of masculine puissance and thus merited the speaker's appropriately superior position in a patriarchal culture. A cracked or breaking voice, on the other hand, 'unpredictably modulating between (female) squeakiness and (male) gravity—not only upset binary gender systems but the logic and operation of early modern patriarchy itself' (p. 43). For the Boy Companies such as the Boys of St Paul's or the student company from Merchant Taylors' school (managed by Mulcaster, himself) 'vocal instability was an inescapable condition' (p. 60). Taking John Marston's *Antonio and Mellida*, Bloom shows how the play 'links failing patriarchal power structures of court and family with unstable male voices' (p. 55). In the play, for instance, 'What compromises the courtiers' [Castilio's and Balurdo's] success in wooing women is not just a weak command over language but an inability to master the physiological production of voice' (p. 58). The play was of course performed by the Boys of St Paul's and this self-consciousness is to be expected of Marston, a playwright who, Bloom asserts, 'exposes his audience to the backstage realities of playing' (p. 55).

3. Criticism

(a) General

In terms of the canon, it has been a strange year for the lesser lights of Renaissance drama. A relative lack of interest in Jonson has coincided with a substantial upsurge of work in Lyly and in Beaumont and Fletcher—in most cases, for their innovative representations of gender—and in the long-underrated Thomas Heywood.

But before moving on to studies of individual plays, there are some wide-ranging studies to be considered, first among them a group focusing on the intersection of gender and political power. One of these should have appeared in last year's survey: Eileen Allman's *Jacobean Revenge Tragedy and the Politics of Virtue* [1999]. Allman situates Jacobean revenge tragedy within contemporary uncertainties about gender and politics, identifying the plays as 'Concentrating ever more intently on crimes of personal violence committed by the figures authorized to prosecute and punish them' (p. 34). Focusing in particular on *The Maid's Tragedy*, *The Second Maiden's Tragedy*, *Valentinian*, and *The Duchess of Malfi*, Allman argues that the plays' 'heroic women, unsilent and disobedient' (p. 190) participate in struggles in a world where tyranny, rather than masculinity, is the real enemy. The same collision of gender and power, and some of the same texts, are treated rather differently by Karen Bamford, in *Sexual Violence on the Jacobean Stage*. *The Second Maiden's Tragedy*, Webster's *Appius and Virginia*, Heywood's *The Rape of Lucrece*, and Fletcher's *Bonduca* are just a few of the plays covered in Bamford's survey of rapes and attempted rapes in Jacobean drama. Her relentless exposure of the double standards of Renaissance drama starts with the hagiographical traditions surrounding virginity and rape, before also considering classical precedents such as Lucrece, the political implications of rape, and—in a final chapter—those tragicomedies in which rape is 'contained' by marriage. Her conclusion is that all Jacobean drama shares a common patriarchal definition of chastity as a state of 'physical, not spiritual purity' (p. 155). However, this does not make them equally misogynist, with Shakespeare, she argues, offering notably more room for resistance to the destructiveness of rape. Two articles by Lisa Hopkins range widely across the canon of Renaissance drama: '"Monstrous Regiment": Staging Female Rule' (in Szőnyi and Wymer, eds., *The Iconography of Power: Ideas and Images of Rulership on the English Renaissance Stage*, pp. 73–88), traces representations of female rulers in Webster, Ford, and elsewhere, relating them to the theoretical debate thrown up by the crop of female rulers in sixteenth-century Europe. And 'Ripeness is All: The Death of Elizabeth in Drama' (*RenF* 4:ii[2000] 1–21), traces a consistent interest in this theme from the 1590s to the 1630s, suggesting that, in particular, metaphors of ripeness and rawness around the death of a monarch constitute 'a master trope for the imaging of political and social disorder' (p. 18).

Three other books need to be considered. Gerald M. Pinciss, *Forbidden Matter: Religion in the Drama of Shakespeare and his Contemporaries*, reads a number of Renaissance plays as veiled commentaries upon live issues of contemporary theology and politics. He covers *Dr Faustus* and *Measure for Measure*, before discussing Rowley's *When You See Me You Know Me* and Heywood's *If You Know Not Me You Know Nobody* as examples of anti-Catholic rhetoric. He reads *Bartholomew Fair* in terms of its religious context, set as it is in a Smithfield where both Catholics and Protestants had been burned as martyrs. He analyses the numerous similarities between the hero of Ford's *Perkin Warbeck* and the recently dead Frederick, Elector Palatine of Bohemia, thus casting Elizabeth of Bohemia as the Scottish princess Katherine Gordon. For Pinciss, *Perkin Warbeck* is Ford's 'Protestant commentary on his own political world' (p. 107).

Janette Dillon's *Theatre, Court, and City, 1595–1610: Drama and Social Space in London* is careful to state that it is not merely about city comedy. It ranges from the War of the Theatres through Jonson's *Entertainment at Britain's Burse* and *Epicoene*, by way of Heywood's *1 Edward IV* and Beaumont's *The Knight of the Burning Pestle*. Dillon's study of these plays is always acutely aware of London's local geography, and of the ways in which that geography functions in terms of discourses of the market and of commoditization. Finally, in *Renaissance Drama and Contemporary Literary Theory*, Andy Mousley offers an introductory account to literary theory focused on texts by Shakespeare and his colleagues. Lucidly written, it is backed up with tantalizing examples—for instance, chapter 1, on semiotics, combines extracts from *Tamburlaine*, *The Knight of the Burning Pestle*, and *Othello* in its discussion of how meaning is created. The chapter headings include 'Structuralism', 'Poststructuralism', 'Psychoanalysis', 'Historicism', 'Feminism', and 'Marxism', and each chapter takes a couple of Renaissance plays, of diverse genres, as its running examples. Mousley's book is highly readable and highly recommended.

And now on to material covering specific plays. A good place to start is *Gorboduc*, generally treated as one of the originary texts of Renaissance drama. James Emmanuel Berg, '*Gorboduc* as a Tragic Discovery of "Feudalism"' (*SEL* 40[2000] 199–226), takes issue with the master-narrative of the Renaissance that sees the period in terms of a gradual and largely unconscious shift from feudalism towards capitalism. He demonstrates that even *Gorboduc* is already concerned with problems of this transition: that even it imagines the domestic and political spheres, the *oikos* and the *polis*, not united as in a feudal model, but separated from one another and as growing more separate. Berg relates this division to the complexities of early Elizabethan politics, and argues that even while appearing to lament the rise of a royal household based less on land ownership and more on the theatricalization of power, *Gorboduc* is part of the arrival of such a household.

John Lyly's work continues to be mined by scholars for its treatment of gender. *Gallathea*, placed alongside *Twelfth Night* for comparison, is the subject of some of the attention of Laurie Shannon's 'Nature's Bias: Renaissance Homonormativity and Elizabethan Comic Likeness' (*MP* 98:ii[2000] 183–210). Shannon collects evidence of Renaissance beliefs about same-sex marriage, arguing that in some discourses such marriages of 'equals', and such homoeroticism could be constructed as the usual and 'straight' feeling. Shannon traces the ways in which such an idea lurks in Ovid's *Iphis and Ianthe* and thus informs the two Renaissance plays. In 'The Healthy Body: Desire and Sustenance in John Lyly's *Love's Metamorphosis*' (*EMLS* 6:ii[2000] 1–19), Mark Dooley describes the play as a celebration of the necessary relation between food, sex, and the body, in which neglect of that relationship is easily elided with neglect of the body politic. Protea, the sexually experienced heroine of the play, is indeed a figure with interesting implications for our understanding of Renaissance treatments of female sexuality. Dooley argues, though, that such an approach must also be linked to the play's extraordinary treatment of hunger, appetites, and the body.

Marguerite A. Tassi has published two articles that discuss *Campaspe*: '"O fair face": The Aesthetic of the Portrait Miniature in John Lyly's *Campaspe*' (*Discoveries* 17.iii[2000] 1–2, 11–13), and 'Lover, Poisoner, Counterfeiter: The Painter in Elizabethan Drama' (*BJJ* 7[2000] 129–56). This second article discusses the 'ambiguous and contradictory' (p. 130) imagery of the painter to be found in drama of the period. As an artist and maker of representations, the painter resembles the poet, and yet, as a creator of images, he is a dangerously idolatrous—indeed Catholic—figure. Tassi surveys figurations of the painter in plays including *Campaspe*, Marston's *Antonio and Mellida*, the anonymous plays *Wisdom of Doctor Dodypoll* and *The Wit of a Woman*, the additions to *The Spanish Tragedy*, and *Arden of Faversham*. In each, she argues, the treatment of painters is inflected by a specifically religious sense of iconophobia. Finally for Lyly, *Sappho and Phao* is discussed by Michael Pincombe in 'Cupid and Eliza: Variations on a Virgilian Icon in Plays by Gager, Lyly, and Marlowe' (in Szőnyi and Wymer, eds.). Pincombe links it to Gager's Latin *Dido* and to Marlowe's *Dido Queen of Carthage*, arguing that Lyly's refiguring of an idea derived ultimately from Virgil shows him using 'the materials of Elizabethan panegyric for "secular" purposes' (p. 34).

Work on Greene this year is restricted to two short notes. Kevin LaGrandeur compares 'Brasenose College's Brass Head and Greene's *Friar Bacon*' (*N&Q* 245[2000] 48–50), concluding that the head used in the original productions would have looked very similar to the grotesquely proportioned, large-nosed, brass figure now hanging over one of the gates of Brasenose College Oxford, of which, in the play, Bacon is a fellow. Mark Hutchings, in discussing 'The End of *II Tamburlaine* and the Beginning of *King Lear*' (*N&Q* 245[2000] 82–6), also revisits the question of links between the two plays and Greene's *Selimus*.

The Spanish Tragedy continues to fascinate scholars and critics. One of the most intriguing and provocative articles of the year is Lukas Erne's '"Enter the Ghost of Andrea': Recovering Thomas Kyd's Two-Part Play' (*ELR* 30[2000] 339–72). Erne's argument is that *The Spanish Tragedy* as we know it is the second part of a two-part play; that *The First Part of Ieronimo* is a post-1600 revision of Kyd's genuine first part; and that one can distinguish two 'textual layers' within the later text, corresponding to different sections of the plot. The 'political' strand of the plot of *The First Part of Ieronimo*, argues Erne, has largely preserved sections of Kyd's original play. Erne proceeds to read *The Spanish Tragedy* as a sequel to these sections, and argues convincingly that what is generally perceived as a stand-alone masterpiece needs to be thought of—like *2 Henry IV*, *2 Tamburlaine*, and perhaps even *Hoffman*—as the second part of a two-part structure. Erne suggests that we may need to reconsider Kyd's 'singular dramatic architecture' (p. 363) and his interest in complex causality. Also on the precursors of the play, in a rather different sense, is Andrew Sofer's 'Absorbing Interests: Kyd's Bloody Handkerchief as Political Palimpsest' (*CompD* 34[2000] 127–54). Sofer shows that the handkerchief 'invokes previous performances of bloody cloths' (p. 129) as the latest reworking of a long medieval drama of holy cloths and sacred blood, going back to Jesus' shroud, Veronica's napkin, and the cloths blessed by Paul. Sofer, however, takes issue with Huston Diehl's argument that such secularized representations on the English stage were mockeries used as tools for Protestant reform; he argues, instead, that there is a ghostly power to this relic of a relic that transcends mere blasphemous mockery. Andrew James Hartley, 'Social Consciousness: Spaces for Characters in *The Spanish Tragedy*' (*CahiersE* 58[2000] 1–14), returns to the question of how Kyd treats character, with insights gained from involvement in a staging of the play. Conceding that the characters do not have 'fully rounded, twentieth-century psychologies' (p. 1), Hartley nevertheless argues that their subjectivities are implied, most of all at moments when rhetorical structures are undercut or when a character's dramatic functions contradict themselves. Kyd may not be writing characters as we understand the term, but he is very interested in problems of defining and representing subjectivity. One particular contradiction in the play is the subject of a note by Andrew Hadfield, '*The Spanish Tragedy*, the Alençon Marriage Plans, and John Stubbs's *Discoverie of a Gaping Gulf*' (*N&Q* 245[2000] 42–3). Hadfield argues that the King of Spain's apparent forgetfulness of the fact that Horatio is dead is a critique of a monarch investing too much energy in foreign affairs at the expense of attending to the domestic scene, and that this moment can profitably be read in terms of the failed match between Elizabeth and Alençon ten years before the play. Another note, by Duncan Salkeld, 'Kyd and the Courtesan' (*N&Q* 245[2000] 43–7), examines the character of Bel-Imperia in the light of her namesake Romana Imperia. Salkeld provides biographical information on this famous Roman courtesan, who also influenced the character of Imperia the prostitute in Middleton's (or Dekker's) *Blurt, Master Constable*. Finally, in 'Tacitus and Kyd's *The Spanish Tragedy*' (*N&Q* 245[2000] 424–5), G.K. Hunter shows that Tacitus is a surprising source for Hieronimo's final transformation of a penknife from paperwork accessory to deadly weapon.

As for other work on late Elizabethan plays, Haughton's *Englishmen for My Money*, generally thought about—in so far as it is thought about at all—as one of the clumsy precursors of humours comedy, is re-examined by Emma Smith in '"So much English by the Mother": Gender, Foreigners, and the Mother Tongue in William Haughton's *Englishmen for My Money*' (*MRDE* 13[2000] 165–81). According to Smith, this play is rather less unproblematically nationalistic than has generally been recognized: its interest in amorous foreigners is part of a specifically sexualized anxiety about national identity which can also be traced in numerous other plays of the period. Smith links the play to the ongoing legal debates about nationality and citizenship—was nationality a matter purely of birthplace, or of inheritance? Furthermore, how would a definition based on the nationality of one's parents work when the parents were of different nationalities? Smith shows how awareness of these issues, repeatedly conflated with questions of gender and of language, complicates and enriches a reading of Haughton's play.

Marston is represented by a note and a book. The note is Charles Cathcart's 'Ben Jonson and the Dedication of *Antonio and Mellida*' (*N&Q* 245[2000] 100–3), which looks in detail at Marston's language in the Dedication, arguing that many of the most contested terms from *Satiromastix* and *Poetaster* reappear here. The Dedication, he concludes, is a mixture of praise and criticism that shows a continuing engagement with the artistic issues raised in the War of the Theatres. Wharton, ed., *The Drama of John Marston: Critical Re-visions*, is driven by the perception that Marston's almost postmodern sense of dislocation and combativeness makes him overdue for critical reappraisal. Among the twelve essays, there are contributions by Rick Bowers and David Pascoe on Marston's sense of the market and the marketable, and Patrick Buckridge and Janet Clare on Marston and censorship. Particular attention is paid to Marston's often tortured fascination with gender, sexuality, and desire: essays by T.F. Wharton, Richard Scarr, William W.E. Slights, and Sukanya B. Senapati consider—and disagree about—different aspects of this promising topic. All in all, the volume makes a strong case that Marston's work, 'De-centred and de-stabilizing, anarchically playful, constantly transgressing boundaries' (p. 10), is worthy of more attention than it has been receiving up to now.

A sign of the continuing interest in Heywood and the market is the essay by Fenella Macfarlane, 'To "Try what London prentices can do": Merchant Chivalry as Representational Strategy in Thomas Heywood's *The Four Prentices of London*' (*MRDE* 13[2000] 136–64). Macfarlane takes issue with earlier studies of 'merchant chivalry' (which have tended to stress the ways in which the trope of praising merchants in courtly terms contains and bolsters the existing hierarchical structure. For her, the trope—especially as it informs Heywood's 1592 play—is much less conservative, and much more about the changing horizons and aspirations of an emerging powerful class. A quite different use of recent research on the Renaissance understanding of markets and commodities is taken by Juana Green in 'The Sempster's Wares: Merchandising and Marrying in *The Fair Maid of the Exchange* (1607)' (*RQ* 53[2000] 1084–1118). Green (who notes that the authorship of this play is far from settled) uses evidence from numerous contemporary sources, including matrimonial cases, to build up a history of the handkerchief as an item of material culture. The handkerchiefs around which much of the intrigue of the play revolves are, this article shows, far from mere bits of linen: they are heavily charged with symbolic significance. Green's article reads interestingly against Sofer's contribution on *The Spanish Tragedy* discussed above; both are also ripe for application to *Othello*.

Paula McQuade considers '"A Labyrinth of Sin": Marriage and Moral Capacity in Thomas Heywood's *A Woman Killed with Kindness*' (*MP* 98[2000] 231–50). Noting the long-standing puzzle of the play—the lack of any psychologically plausible motivation for the heroine's adultery—McQuade argues that this lack of motive 'provides a compelling critique of female subjugation within marriage' (p. 232). While contemporary casuistical debate has usually been seen as straightforwardly patriarchal, McQuade traces a contemporary argument that husbands who abuse the obedience owed them by their wives are guilty of endangering their wives' souls. Reading this back into the play, McQuade argues that Anne's error is induced by her attempts to obey the contradictory demands made of her by her husband, and that he is made further culpable by his treatment of her after it is discovered. Thus Heywood implicates Frankford 'in the murder not merely of Anne's body but also of her soul' (p. 248). Heywood's *Fair Maid of the West*, Heywood and Rowley's *Fortune by Land and Sea*, and Massinger's *The Renegado* are the principal texts discussed by Barbara Fuchs in 'Faithless Empires: Pirates, Renegadoes, and the English Nation' (*ELH* 67[2000] 45–69). Fuchs is concerned to document the divided contemporary attitudes to piracy, and argues that the plays trace interactions 'between piracy and respectable English commerce' (p. 52). In the strange world of these pirate plays, where piracy is 'the dark double of peaceable trade' (p. 57), it is always difficult to tell self from other and loyal Englishman from pirate. Fuchs even traces how common antipathy to Spain creates a racially troubling equivalence between English and Moors, a tension registered in these plays.

Also on Heywood—as well as being the year's sole contribution on Brome—is an essay by Heather Hirschfeld, 'Collaborating across Generations: Thomas Heywood, Richard Brome, and the Production of *The Late Lancashire Witches*' (*JMEMS* 30[2000] 339–74). Hirschfeld seeks to theorize collaboration as a condition of much early modern dramatic authorship, arguing that the pairing of Brome and Heywood is atypical and indeed unique when compared to the other writing teams known to have written for the early modern stage. The particular focus of the essay is their co-written 1634 'docudrama' (p. 340), which she argues is a strongly politicized play, though perhaps not in the way that it has been interpreted by previous critics, including Herbert Berry.

In comparison to Heywood, the amount written on Dekker's drama this year is relatively meagre. Ronda A. Arab writes on 'Work, Bodies, and Gender in *The Shoemaker's Holiday*' (*MRDE* 13[2000] 182–212). She suggests that the play goes to the heart of Renaissance uncertainties about masculinity, the body, and the national economy. While it celebrates the male artisan body, tending to foreground its economic productivity, the play tends to vilify the bodies of the women with whom the shoemakers work in uncomfortable proximity. This aggressively misogynistic presentation of sexual difference works to conceal power structures that inform the emerging cultural system of 'fraternal patriarchy'. For Arab, the play is an artefact of a culture where the divisions between private and public spheres are still not yet fully established. In 'Tennis Balls in Dekker's *Shoemaker's Holiday*' (*N&Q* 245[2000] 467–8), Bethany Blankenship revisits the ways in which the play's monarch anachronistically resembles Henry V rather than Henry VI. Blankenship shows that a tennis reference further clinches the point.

In '"Those graue presentments of antiquitie": Samuel Daniel's *Philotas* and the Earl of Essex' (*RES* 51[2000] 423–50), Hugh Gazzard examines a different form of political reference, presenting new evidence to strengthen the case that this play's alleged parallels to the circumstances of the fall of Essex were indeed deliberately arranged by Daniel. Gazzard compares the play in detail both to the Latin of Quintus Curtius, which is its source, and to the Tudor translation to which Daniel also had access, show that the divergences from it tend to bring the play closer to the events of Essex's downfall: he also proposes verbal parallels between the play and Essex's 1600 *Apologie*.

Debates about Middleton continue to focus on the question of religion. According to Herbert Jack Heller, *Penitent Brothellers: Grace, Sexuality, and Genre in Thomas Middleton's City Comedies*, Middleton was 'a supposed oxymoron—a Calvinist comedian' (p. 34). Focusing on Middleton's metaphors of redemption and salvation, Heller reads the comedies as, in effect, profoundly religious works. Chapter 3, 'Marrying the Whore: The Hosea Paradigm in *A Trick to Catch the Old One* and Other Plays', offers a specifically religious rereading of this frequent Middleton motif; and chapter 4, on Middleton, sodomy, and salvation, argues that Middleton's attitude to homosexuality is profoundly influenced by a Christian inclusivity and tolerance which is at odds with our normal understanding of seventeenth-century attitudes to sodomy. Heller's book, and the looming appearance of the long-awaited Oxford Middleton, are certain to provoke further argument on this surprisingly enigmatic author.

The Duchess of Malfi dominates Webster criticism this year, almost to the exclusion of his other work. An excellent resource for criticism of the play is provided by Dympna Callaghan's contribution to the New Casebooks series, *The Duchess of Malfi*. Callaghan opens with a brisk, brief introduction historicizing Renaissance attitudes to widows, women rulers, clandestine marriages, and childbirth, before offering a selection of criticism on the play. The nine essays, all first published between 1985 and 1993, are characterized by Callaghan as 'gender-conscious', and as increasingly concerned with the ways in which gender is implicated in 'a wider cultural context and a specific historical context' (p. 21). Their authors include Karin S. Coddon, Kathleen McCluskie, and Frank Whigham. The book also reprints Christy Desmet's article on *The Duchess of Malfi* and the woman controversy, which itself forms the springboard for Kimberley A. Turner in 'The Complexity of Webster's Duchess' (*BJJ* 7[2000] 379–402). Turner reconsiders the historical evidence adduced by Desmet, and adds some more of her own, particularly concerning Elizabeth's status as female monarch. Her argument, put briefly, is that the play is less misogynistic than Desmet's account would suggest: she argues that the heroine is *not* a 'nothing', but rather 'one of the most fully realized characters in Renaissance drama' (p. 399). Jeffrey Kahan, 'Tree or Trellis? Jacobean Displays of Death in *The Duchess of Malfi*' (*ELN* 37:iii[2000] 35–6), addresses a question of staging—how exactly the bodies might be displayed at IV.i.68, and what symbolic potential they might have.

Among the current crop of work on Beaumont and Fletcher, Catherine A. Henze contributes two articles on music. In 'How Music Matters: Some Songs of Robert Johnson in the Plays of Beaumont and Fletcher' (*CompD* 34[2000] 1–32), Henze offers close readings of Johnson songs from *The Captain*, *Valentinian*, and *The Knight of the Burning Pestle*, arguing that music provides a paradoxical element of realism in these highly stylized plays. In all three songs, she notes, are double meanings very specific to the plays they appear in: she suggests that the Beaumont and Fletcher plays could even be renamed the Beaumont–Fletcher–Johnson plays, so important is the role of the songs. Henze's second article, 'Music as Women's Defense "against malicious detractors": The Case of Beaumont and Fletcher's *The Woman Hater*' (*BJJ* 7[2000] 403–19), argues that music is used to provide the ingredient normally seen as missing from *The Woman Hater*, namely, character motivation: on the simplest level, it is the songs that cause the plot to continue to unfold. She traces the Renaissance association between women and 'Lady Musicke', and argues that the play's participation in the misogynist debate is influenced particularly by its display of 'the double power of the disparaged music and femininity' (p. 416). Gender is the focus too of an essay by Anne Duncan, 'It Takes a Woman to Play a Real Man: Clara as Hero(ine) of Beaumont and Fletcher's *Love's Cure*' (*ELR* 30[2000] 396–407). While this play has previously been considered as showing how the effeminate son and the virago daughter are cured by heterosexual desire, Duncan turns this analysis on its head, showing the extent to which masculinity is destabilized by being revealed as something constructed and performed. Two plays solely by Fletcher—*Women Pleas'd* and *The Prophetess*—are examined by Jeanne Addison Roberts in 'Types of the Crone: The Nurse and Wise Woman in Renaissance Drama' (*RenP* [2000] 71–86). Roberts identifies Delphia from the latter as a 'female Prospero' (p. 84), and discusses her in terms of forerunners in Lyly, Heywood, and others. Also on Fletcher and gender, Meg Powers Livingston contributes an interesting piece on a revival of a Fletcher play eight years after his death: 'Herbert's Censorship of Female Power in Fletcher's *The Woman's Prize*' (*MRDE* 13[2000] 213–32). Scholarly investigation of Herbert's censorship of the revival has tended to take its cues from Herbert's own remark about the oaths and profanity to be found in the play. Livingston, however, argues that its presentation of the powerful Maria, in ways that link her specifically to Catholicism and indeed Jesuits, would invite disquieting applications to Queen Henrietta Maria, and that this was the main reason for Herbert's intervention. Since variant versions of the play are extant, Livingston is able to substantiate the argument by detailed comparison of the variants.

The Revenger's Tragedy is studied in two short articles. Attila Kiss, 'The Semiotics of the Skull: Emblematic Agency in *The Revenger's Tragedy*' (in Szőnyi and Wymer, eds., pp. 205–14), offers a psychoanalytic reading of Vindice's interest in Gloriana's skull, culminating in a surreal suggestion that Vindice could wear the skull like a hat throughout the five acts. Nathan Cervo's note on 'Tourneur's *The*

Revenger's Tragedy' (*Expl* 58[2000] 71–3) discusses the implications of the word 'green' in the play. The anonymous tragedy *A Warning for Fair Women* is compared to *The Merry Wives of Windsor* in an article by Philip D. Collington, '"I would thy husband were dead": *The Merry Wives of Windsor* as Mock Domestic Tragedy' (*ELR* 30[2000] 184–212).

As well as being discussed in the works by Hopkins and Pinciss mentioned earlier, John Ford is the subject of two further notes by Lisa Hopkins: 'John Ford and Charles Aleyn: Two 1630s Histories of Henry VII' (*N&Q* 47[2000] 483–5), and 'John Ford and the Earl of Antrim' (*N&Q* 47[2000] 485–6). The second of these discusses one of Ford's dedicatees, showing his similarities to other patrons of Ford; the first compares *Perkin Warbeck* to Aleyn's versified account of the same historical events. The two authors spin their history very differently, with Aleyn's 'gung-ho patriotism' and anti-Catholic bias (p. 484) set against Ford's unsettling, subversive drama, but both of them offer clear evidence of the potential topical application to the court of King Charles.

Other work tests the boundaries of 'Renaissance drama'. In 'Autodidacticism in English Jesuit Drama: The Writings and Career of Joseph Simons' (*MRDE* 13[2000] 34–56), Alison Shell stresses the importance of the plays written and performed for the English Jesuit colleges on the Continent. For Shell, they are particularly interesting in their fascination with the performative and with its use for pedagogical functions: this thoughtful and scholarly essay points out too that these boy actors make a striking contrast with the boy actors of English theatrical companies. Once again, drama written during the Civil War attracts critical attention, especially for its treatment of women. Robin O. Warren, 'A Partial Liberty: Gender and Class in Jane Cavendish and Elizabeth Brackley's *The Concealed Fancies*' (*RenP* [2000] 155–67), considers the topsy-turvy world of this increasingly interesting play. For Roberts, the play has been viewed too much in terms of gender, and not enough in terms of class. As a vision of a society as a whole, it presents at best a 'strange and truncated' (p. 167) version of liberation which is informed not by a vision of a brave new world but by pre-Civil War norms of courtly order and hierarchy. Karen L. Raber discusses 'Warrior Women in the Plays of Cavendish and Killigrew' (*SEL* 40[2000] 413–33). While both Killigrew and Cavendish use such figures in tragicomedies shaped by the experience of exile, Raber argues that 'in Killigrew's work ideologies of gender remain unchanged' by such figures (p. 433), and it is expected that the social order will return to the status quo. Cavendish's warrior women, argues Raber, present a rather more fundamental and lasting challenge to the ideologies of gender and society.

(b) Marlowe

There was a bumper crop of work in Marlowe studies this year, possibly reflecting a growing critical interest in the playwright. The range includes a collection of essays, a number of significant monographs, and individual articles on five of the plays, the poetry and biography. I will start with the full-length works, the most substantial of which is Downie and Parnell, eds., *Constructing Christopher Marlowe*. The contributors to this wide-ranging volume set out to engage with the ways in which Marlowe has been constructed by critical discourses. In the first chapter (pp. 13–29) Downie demonstrates the unreliability of the sources on which assumptions about Marlowe's life are based and, after listing what is clearly known, questions whether even this data is of any help in interpreting the plays given that they are highly ambiguous works. Julian Bowsher then discusses the playwright's association with the Rose theatre, the dimensions and configuration of the building itself, and the possible ways in which the building may have accommodated performances (pp. 30–40). Richard Proudfoot examines the emergence of a Marlowe 'industry' in criticism and editing, and the freedom with which *Doctor Faustus* especially has been treated in performance (pp. 41–54). Gareth Roberts addresses the question of editorial problems with particular regard to the magic in *Doctor Faustus*, pointing out the problem of trying to get a coherent theory of magic as being represented in the A or B texts (pp. 55–73). Janet Clare next considers the violent nature of Marlowe's theatre, seeing it in terms of Artaudian 'theatre of cruelty' embodying extreme action to engage the audience's senses and make the theatre a dangerous and intimidating experience (pp. 74–87). Lois Potter surveys modern productions of Marlowe's plays, noting the strong interest in the author's biography, and observing that that interpretations of the plays have changed radically over time (pp. 88–101). Simon Shepherd looks sceptically at embrace of the apparently subversive in early modern theatre on the part of contemporary critics anxious to represent that theatre in this light and to emphasize its engagement with reality (pp. 102–15). Focusing principally on Greenblatt and Foucault, Richard Wilson offers a metacritical essay discussing the appropriation of Marlowe by the new historicists, especially addressing such issues as containment, resistance and sexuality (pp. 116–32). Claude Summers examines *Hero and Leander*, arguing that Marlowe destabilizes conventional conceptions of sexuality and universalizes homoerotic desire (pp. 133–47), while Georgia Brown looks at the same poem in the light of the aesthetic and literary debates of the 1590s, suggesting that Marlowe explores a feminized form of authorship (pp. 148–63). Joanna Gibbs takes a new look at Marlowe's women, countering the idea that they are constructed in terms of their emotions while men occupy a public sphere (pp. 164–76). Finally Lawrence Normand reads Derek Jarman's film of *Edward II* as political in a sense broader than just the politics of sexuality, seeing it as representing homosexuality as a means for the state to justify repressive policies (pp. 177–93).

The first of the monographs (proceeding alphabetically by author) is *Re-citing Marlowe: Approaches to the Drama* by Clare Harraway. Focusing on the idea that writing is unable to convey fixed and repeatable meanings, she examines the plays in respect of the different ways in which they engage with the matter of verbal and written communication, bringing into play post-structuralist theories of language and textuality. She devotes a chapter to each play, making a different argument for the involvement of each with the matter of textuality. Faustus, she argues, is damned by his belief in the power of language, and much turns on the written compact with Satan, seen particularly in terms of the impermanence of writing and its ineffectiveness in maintaining stable meaning. The discussion of *Edward II* centres especially on the idea of the preoccupations of its chronicle play genre with inscriptional remembrance, and it is noted that the play is full of letters, declarations and reports. The implications of the sequel are probed in a study of *Tamburlaine*, the debate about the unity of the plays here being superseded by the idea that the sequel disrupts the consequentiality of meaning. *Dido, Queen of Carthage* is also examined in terms of the impulse to repetition, here the rewriting of material from the source being construed as challenging the authority of the Virgilian original. Next, taking on the problems in and debates surrounding *The Massacre at Paris*, she contends that Marlowe changes the source material of the play as an act of transformation and that the work interrogates the transhistorical and transcendental assumptions which underpin the concept of the canon. Finally, *The Jew of Malta* is linked with this play as also challenging the literary structures though which texts are conventionally read.

Christopher Marlowe: A Literary Life, by Lisa Hopkins, is a contribution to a series that follows writers' working lives, not in the spirit of traditional biography but tracing the social and professional contexts that shaped their writing. Hopkins begins by conceding the difficulty of establishing any facts about Marlowe's life, and studiously avoids building theories about it, but notes that the plays have frequently been read in relation to what is deduced about the writer's biography. Carefully separating fact from speculation, and refraining even from giving dates for the plays, aside from what is firmly known about them, she nevertheless sets out to develop a trajectory of the playwright's life in roughly chronological terms. Hopkins considers Marlowe's education and the impact of education in the plays, pointing out that he does show a marked degree of literariness in his work, and she arranges consideration of the plays in respect of stages of maturation and experience that provided areas of material for the drama. She examines the work in terms of issues that appear to have preoccupied Marlowe in his brief adolescent and adult life, such as family breakdown, religious belief and scepticism, travel, exploration and colonization (remarking that all the plays except *Edward II* are set abroad), sexuality, and the representation of aspiration. The arrangement juxtaposes the plays and poetry thematically: *Dido* and *Tamburlaine*, *The Jew of Malta* and *Doctor Faustus*, and *Edward II*, *The Massacre at Paris* and *Hero and Leander*. Hopkins observes that Marlowe's theatre is constantly probing and testing what society will and will not tolerate, and notes his several brushes with the law in his own life. The final chapter reviews speculations about Marlowe's death, suggesting that the time spent together by the men in the room in Deptford argues against deliberate murder, and goes on to give an account of the fall and rise of the playwright's reputation up to his attainment of mythic status in the twentieth century.

Finally among the books, Stevie Simkin's *A Preface to Marlowe* is a general study of Marlowe's work, including all the plays and the poetry. The first chapter gives an account of the playwright's life, career and death, while the second concentrates on historical contexts, including Elizabethan life and beliefs. It also provides comment on the place of theatre and theatre-going in a time of cultural and ideological change, as well as reflecting on modern critical approaches. The focus then becomes specific and each of the following four chapters is devoted to a study of one of the major plays, *Tamburlaine*, *Doctor Faustus*, *The Jew of Malta*, and *Edward II*. The analysis is anchored in narrative summaries that provide a framework for close study of the plays, including examination of moments of dramatic significance, and of the ways in which the staging contributes to the creation of meaning. Where available, early stage histories are provided and there are surveys of modern productions, emphasizing the range of dramatic interpretations and ideological issues thrown up. These studies are accompanied by discussions of issues and problems specific to each of the plays: the relationship of the two parts of *Tamburlaine*, the problem of the two texts of *Doctor Faustus* and the comic elements in the play, the problem of anti-Semitism with regard to *The Jew of Malta*, and the issue of homosexuality in early modern England in respect of *Edward II*. A further chapter 'mops up' the two remaining plays, *Dido, Queen of Carthage* and *The Massacre at Paris*, and the poetry, giving these the same treatment, albeit in somewhat abbreviated form, though managing nonetheless to provide a meaningful account of contemporary contexts. The final chapter discusses the impact of the legends of Marlowe's life and of Marlovian themes in our own times, including adaptations of his work by Brecht and Jarman.

Doctor Faustus is the subject of several shorter studies. In 'Hell and Hypertext Hath No Limits: Electronic Texts and the Crises in Criticism' (*EMLS* 5:iii[2000] 1–29) Hilary J. Binda provides first an engaging discussion of the cultural dimensions of hypertext for reading and textuality and then moves on to discussing issues arising from the editing of Marlowe's works for hypertext. She concludes that reading hypertext through Marlowe contributes to an understanding of our own relationship to textuality. In one chapter of a book not otherwise devoted to Marlowe, *The Devil and the Sacred in English Drama, 1350–1642* (pp. 107–26), John D. Cox discusses Marlowe's devils in *Doctor Faustus*, which he sees as the second major change in the cast of English dramatic devils, the first being the Protestant Reformation itself. In his view the devils play a role analogous to that of the Vice in the morality drama, driven by the desire to dominate—a 'libido dominandi'—and he presents the courtly world of the *Doctor Faustus* as a sort of earthly hell, the devils in it being secularized. A further chapter (pp. 127–49) discusses subsequent devils on the early modern stage, seeing these as responses to Marlowe's creations. Graham L. Hammill, in *Sexuality and Form: Caravaggio, Marlowe and Bacon*, devotes a single chapter to Marlowe, '"The forme of Faustus fortunes": Knowledge, Spectatorship, and the Body in Marlowe's *Doctor Faustus*' (pp. 97–127). He presents two connected theses, that blasphemy is connected with the literary, in which language is performative, and that this literary language develops grounds for sexual knowledge as it is a way to think of the body as a device for communication. The rest of the *Faustus* items are notes of various length. Lauren L. Shimman, 'The Morality Play in *Doctor Faustus*: Faustus as Reprobate Man' (*Discoveries* 17:iii[2000] 5–6), presents the pageant in Act V as a morality play with no mankind figure with whom Faustus as audience can identify, and the fact that he fails to turn away from the sins as an indication of his reprobacy. Robert A.H. Smith suggests in 'Marlowe and Peele: A Further Note on the Final Scholar Scene in the *Doctor Faustus* B Text' (*N&Q* 47[2000] 40–2) that Marlowe may have drawn on Peele's *The Battle of Alcazar*, or the other way around, and Adrian Streete, in 'Calvinist Conceptions of Hell in Marlowe's *Doctor Faustus*' (*N&Q* 47[2000] 430–2), offers support for the idea that the conceptions of hell in both the A- and B-texts have their origins in Calvin's writings.

The Jew of Malta is discussed in two essays. Proceeding from the idea that the control of others through time derives from a control of the self through time, Eric C. Brown, in 'Violence, Ritual and the Execution of Time in Marlowe's *Jew of Malta*' (*CahiersE* 58[2000] 15–29), argues that Barabas defers rather than seizes opportunities, so demonstrating that time can be commandeered. In '"Pageants Truly Played": Self-Dramatization and Naturalistic Character in *The Jew of Malta*' (*RenFor* 5:i[2000] 1–30) David Webb contends that self-dramatization is central to Marlowe's plays. He engages with modern critical debate on notions of interiority in the dramatic writing of the period and considers too the emergence of naturalism in early modern acting.

Political contexts for *Tamburlaine* are explored by Jonathan Burton in 'Anglo-Ottoman Relations and the Image of the Turk in *Tamburlaine*' (*JMEMS* 30:i[2000] 125–56), who argues that orientalist thought between the early modern period and our own has obscured significant aspects of Marlowe's *Tamburlaine* plays by bringing to bear colonial and imperial paradigms that fail to represent instances of bilateral exchange in early modern Europe's experience with other civilizations. Arata Ide, 'Tamburlaine's Prophetic Oratory and Protestant Militarism in the 1580s' (in Takahashi, ed., *Hot Questrists after the English Renaissance: Essays on Shakespeare and his Contemporaries*, pp. 215–36), examines the prophetic nature of Tamburlaine's marvellous language as linked to his heroic conquests, seeing this as informed by Old Testament divinity rather than an Antichrist role. This is put in the context of the nationalist apocalypticism of Elizabethan England, but it is also argued that Marlowe questions the legitimacy of establishment discourses. A brief note on the same play, 'The End of *II Tamburlaine* and the Beginning of *King Lear*' (*N&Q* 47[2000] 82–6), by Mark Hutchings, suggests that Shakespeare may have seen the declining Tamburlaine as an analogue for Lear. Doris Feldmann, in an essay entitled 'The Constructions and Deconstructions of Gendered Bodies in Selected Plays of Christopher Marlowe' (in Grantley and Taunton, eds., *The Body in Late Medieval and Early Modern Culture*, pp. 32–31), focuses particularly on *Tamburlaine* and *Edward II*. She challenges liberal humanist ideas of stable gender identity centred on bodies, presenting bodies in Marlowe's plays as discourses which negotiate relationships of power, and argues that he does not give masculinity or femininity any substantial meaning, gendered bodies being subject to heterogeneous processes of interpretation. The only other item on *Edward II* is a note by Nathan A. Cervo, 'Marlowe's *Edward II*' (*Expl* 58[2000] 123–4), proposing complex associations of the name 'Lightborn' involving thematic puns of Anglo-Saxon and Greek derivation.

The last of the plays to be examined in brief studies is *Dido, Queen of Carthage*. Clare R. Kinney, 'Epic Transgression and the Framing of Agency in *Dido, Queen of Carthage*' (*SEL* 40:ii[2000] 261–76), suggests that Marlowe's reappropriation of Virgilian narrative in the play seems to be offering a Dido-centred script which counters the myth of manifest destiny by placing a greater emphasis on human agency and minimizing the historical narratives surrounding the actions of Dido and Aeneas. Donald Stump, 'Marlowe's Travesty of Virgil: *Dido* and Elizabethan Dreams of Empire' (*CompD* 34:i[2000] 79–107), sees the play as alluding to the French marriage issue and, noting that uncertainties about the date of its first performance complicate this question, argues that part of Marlowe's purpose was trying comically to deflate his source. This demanded an audience with close knowledge of the *Aeneid*, implying a university audience. In 'Marlowe and Nashe in *Dido, Queen of Carthage*' (*N&Q* 47[2000] 425–8) Thomas Merriam concludes, by using a logometrical statistical analysis, that *Dido* is a collaboration between the authors of *1 Tamburlaine*, and *Summer's Last Will and Testament*.

Hero and Leander comes in for consideration in two essays. Proceeding from an initial comparative enquiry into Renaissance humanism, Warren Boutcher, '"Who taught thee Rhetoricke to deceive a maid?": Christopher Marlowe's *Hero and Leander*, Juan Boscán's *Leandro* and Renaissance Vernacular Humanism' (*CL*

52:i[2000] 11–52), concludes that English vernacular humanism in the second half of the sixteenth century was polyglot, and that *Hero and Leander* reveals a consciousness of Juan Boscán's treatment of the same story. John Leonard, in 'Marlowe's "Doric Music": Lust and Aggression in *Hero and Leander*' (*ELR* 30:i[2000] 55–76), argues for a tone of conscious irony in the poem, rebutting the notion of an inept narrator and pointing out that the narrator and his characters make errors that turn out to be oddly appropriate, one being the reference to 'Doric' rather than 'Lydian' music, aptly describing Leander's militaristic style of wooing.

Two essays engage with the subject of Marlowe's biography. Stephen Orgel, in '"Tobacco and boys": How Queer Was Marlowe?' (*GLQ* 6:iv[2000] 555–76), argues that the idea of the transgressive Marlowe is largely a posthumous phenomenon. He questions why the poet chose to translate Ovid's exclusively heterosexual *Amores*, then goes on to discuss *Doctor Faustus* and the early reception of *Edward II*. David Riggs, 'The Killing of Christopher Marlowe' (*StHR* 8:i[2000] 239–51) builds a carefully supported argument for official complicity in the murder of Marlowe, putting the event in the context of a government heresy hunt in 1593. He concludes by suggesting that there is more reference by Shakespeare to Marlowe in *As You Like It* than has hitherto been recognized.

A number of items missed out of the entry for 1999 should be included here, three of which are on *The Jew of Malta*. In 'The Jew of Malta and the World of Wrestling' (*ESC* 25[1999] 137–56), Rick Bowers presents the play as a rigorously contrived spectacle of disproportion, comparing it to professional wrestling, arguing that audience reaction is intensified through absurdly manipulated outrages in a performative struggle that pervades the play, and that hatred and violence are theatricalized. In a brief essay Ren Draya, 'Silenced Women: Abigail in Marlowe's *The Jew of Malta*' (*PMPA* 24[1999] 11–19), as her title indicates, cites a number of women characters in early modern drama who are silenced and discusses the role of Barabas's daughter in the light of this. A note by Ruth L. Hanusa, 'Killing the Daughter: Judges' Jephthah and *The Jew of Malta*'s Barabas' (*N&Q* 47[2000] 199–200), makes the argument that Barabas's idea of sacrificing his daughter on a pile of wood is less attributable to the Abraham and Isaac story, as is generally supposed, than to Jephthah in Judges 11: 30–1. Also in a brief note, Mark Hutchings, '"In Thrace; brought up in Arabia": *The Jew of Malta* II.iii.131' (*N&Q* 47[2000] 428–30) suggests that Barabas's purchase of Ithamore is motivated by the fact that the Moor is, like himself, stateless, possibly a victim of the contemporary Ottoman practice of forced conversion.

Daniel Roux, '"Well may I view her, but she sees not me": The Subject and the Invisible in Marlowe's *Dido Queen of Carthage*' (*SAJMRS* 9[2000] 35–44), with reference to Greenblatt's ideas of the self in early modern culture, sees the failure of Aeneas in *Dido, Queen of Carthage* to author himself as a crucial contribution to the emergence of the subject under humanism, it being here extended beyond the ego, invoking the Lacanian notion of the transcendental subject. Finally in 'Out of Service and in the Playhouse: Richard Norwood, Youth in Transition and Early Response to *Dr Faustus*' (*MRDE* 12[2000] 166–89), Charles Whitney draws on Norwood's 1640 diary to give an account of a young theatre-goer in 1612, speculating on the effect that *Doctor Faustus* might have had on youths like him in the period, and seeking to situate the play in the social and intellectual climate of the time.

(c) Jonson

In a rather thin year for work on Jonson's drama, it is useful to start with a couple of reference resources. Deborah Hill, 'Ben Jonson in General Scholarship, 1900–1972' (*BJJ* 7[2000] 517–37), is the latest in a series of *Ben Jonson Journal* articles which, taken together, offer a topical index to twentieth-century writings on Jonson. In the same vein is Evans, ed., *Ben Jonson's Major Plays: Summaries of Modern Monographs*. But the year has also seen the appearance of one excellent book-length introduction: Harp and Stewart, eds., *The Cambridge Companion to Jonson*. The volume opens with a vivid biographical sketch by Sara Van Den Berg, and is organized by theme rather than by text, thus creating a unifying reading of Jonson's diverse canon: however, chapters by Richard Dutton, David Bevington, and Richard Harp focus respectively on the early, middle, and late periods of Jonson's dramatic career, while Ian Donaldson writes specifically on Jonson's poetry. Stephen Orgel writes a fascinating, fresh essay on Jonson and the arts, and on Jonson's own sense of connoisseurship. Among the other essays, a rather technical piece by James Riddell on Jonson's 1616 folio, and a brief study by Robert C. Evans of the critical heritage of the four major plays, are both concerned—in different ways—with the means by which Jonson's reputation is created for posterity. The volume does not set out to be an encyclopedia of Jonsonian information, and the index may frustrate students looking for basic information on terms such as 'comical satire' or 'humours'. However, the book definitely succeeds in giving a sense of the excitement, and dissent, raised by Jonson's works.

In articles produced this year, all periods of Jonson's dramatic career are receiving critical attention. Angus Fletcher's 'Jonson's Satiric Comedy and the Unsnarling of the Satyr from the Satirist' (*BJJ* 7[2000] 247–70) takes its jumping-off point from the works of Isaac Casaubon, who was the first to disentangle Roman satire ('satura', a mixture) from Greek Old Comedy. Fletcher considers *Every Man Out* and the other comical satires in terms of a confusion of satura and satyr, as a 'dead-end but…a wonderfully strange and rich dead-end' (p. 248) that enables the English comic tradition. Fletcher traces Jonson's use of medicinal tropes, and concludes that his mature plays see a move away from satiric comedy towards a more purely comic mode. By contrast, Bruce Boehrer, 'The Case of Will Kemp's Shoes: *Every Man Out Of His Humour* and the "Bibliographic Ego"' (*BJJ* 7[2000] 271–91), explores a single textual crux: Carlo Buffone's wish, 'Would I had one of *Kemps* shoes to throw after you'. He looks at the possible explanations for this apparent post-performance improvement and related editorial issues (discussed more fully in Section 1 above). Herford and Simpson had rejected this idea, but this, he suggests, exposes a problem in the models of authorial integrity favoured by Jonson's great twentieth-century editors: Jonson's own understanding of literary authority would have no difficulty with such a post-performance improvement.

Understanding, or the lack of it, is the theme of Ian Donaldson's essay, 'Misconstruing Everything: *Julius Caesar* and *Sejanus*' (in Ioppolo, ed., *Shakespeare Performed: Essays in Honour of R.A. Foakes*, pp. 88–107). Arguing convincingly that the two plays are at some level in dialogue with each other, Donaldson studies the failures to communicate in each of them. Misunderstandings in *Sejanus* arise through stupidity, or through calculated political malice; in Shakespeare's world, misunderstanding is far less black and white, indeed it is a pervasive condition of communication. Donaldson concludes that both plays are studies 'of how such crucial acts of political misconstruction occur in the first place: of how history happens' (p. 105).

In 'Jonson's Romish Fox: Anti-Catholic Discourse in *Volpone*' (*EMLS* 6:ii [2000] 1–32), Alizon Brunning draws attention to the extensive and detailed parodies of the mass to be found within *Volpone*. Furthermore, Jonson's figuration of Volpone as a fox aligns him with visual representations of Catholic priests as foxes, and invites similar parallels with the 'flesh-fly' Mosca. The punishment of the malefactors is merely the most notable of a number of strange connections between the play and the Gunpowder Plot: for Brunning, the play needs to be considered in terms of Jonson's equivocal and double-edged relationship with Catholicism. Thomas L. Cooksey, 'Jonson's *Volpone*: A Double Source in Petronius' *Satyricon*' (*N&Q* 245[2000] 103–4), argues that, while there are numerous classical sources for Jonson's knowledge both of legacy-hunting and Pythagoreanism, it is remarkable that the *Satyricon* links the two issues together, making it perhaps a richer source for Jonson than has previously been noticed.

Jonson's early comical satires, and his *Entertainment at Britain's Burse* and *Epicoene*, are all discussed in Dillon, *Theatre, Court, and City*, as is *Bartholomew Fair* in Pinciss, *Forbidden Matter*. Also on *Epicoene*, a note by David Farley-Hills, 'Another Jonson Allusion to Shakespeare?' (*N&Q* 47[2000] 473–5), revives a suggestion, made in the eighteenth century and subsequently disregarded, about the play with sea-fights, drum, and trumpet by which Morose imagines himself being tormented. Thomas Davies identified the play as a particular reference to *Antony and Cleopatra*, a suggestion which Farley-Hills suggests opens up new possibilities for and subtexts to *Epicoene*.

Two essays in Summers and Pebworth, eds., *Literary Circles and Cultural Communities in Renaissance England* deal with Jonson's wider literary contexts. Robert C. Evans, '"This art will live": Social and Literary Responses to Ben Jonson's *New Inn*' (pp. 75–91), deals with the numerous texts thrown up by the failure of *The New Inn*, while Timothy Raylor, 'Newcastle's Ghosts: Robert Payne, Ben Jonson, and the "Cavendish Circle"' (pp. 92–114), suggests that the image of the circle is actually rather inadequate for the complex, subordinated groupings of writers and thinkers gathered by William Cavendish. Raylor suggests that, in patronizing Jonson, Cavendish may have felt some sense of intellectual property over his work; hence, perhaps, the numerous reuses of Jonson's texts in Cavendish's own literary output.

On the subject of reuses, Brandon S. Centerwall offers 'A Reconsideration of Ben Jonson's Contribution to Sir Walter Raleigh's the *History of the World* (1614)' (*BJJ* 7[2000] 539–54). He presents new evidence arguing that in 1918 Charles Firth correctly identified the sections of book V dealing with a war between the Carthaginians and their mercenaries as having been written not by Ralegh but by Jonson.

Lastly, work on Jonson's entertainments is represented by James M. Sutton, 'Jonson's Genius at Theobalds: The Politics of Estrangement' (*BJJ* 7[2000] 297–324). Sutton's focus is the extraordinary occasion for Jonson's entertainment: a celebration, for Cecil, of Cecil's forced donation to the king of his own family home. While Cecil received in return the cramped and unimpressive palace at Hatfield, this still could not be construed as anything like an equal exchange. Sutton's article explores Jonson's text as an attempt to accommodate this extraordinary occasion of estrangement, but suggests that it marks too another separation: the growing rift between Jonson and his patron Robert Cecil.

Books Reviewed

Allman, Eileen. *Jacobean Revenge Tragedy and the Politics of Virtue.* UDelP. [1999] pp. 212. £30 ISBN 0 8741 3698 9.

Bamford, Karen. *Sexual Violence on the Jacobean Stage.* Macmillan. [2000] pp. 237. £35 ISBN 0 3339 1529 1.

Bennett, Nicola, ed. *The Merry Devil of Edmonton.* Globe Quartos. Nick Hern Books. [2000] pp. xiv + 110. pb £8.99 ISBN 1 8545 9604 7.

Bevington, David, and George K. Hunter, eds. *Galatea* and *Midas,* by John Lyly. Revels. ManUP. [2000] pp. xvi + 282. £40 ISBN 0 7190 3095 1.

Callaghan, Dympna, ed. *The Duchess of Malfi.* New Casebooks. Macmillan. [2000] pp. 240. £13.99 ISBN 0 3336 1428 3.

Cox, John D. *The Devil and the Sacred in English Drama, 1350–1642.* CUP. [2000] pp. x + 257. £19 ISBN 0 5217 9090 5.

Dillon, Janette. *Theatre, Court, and City, 1595–1610: Drama and Social Space in London.* CUP. [2000] pp. 197. £35 ISBN 0 5216 6118 8.

Downie, J.A., and J.T. Parnell, eds. *Constructing Christopher Marlowe.* CUP. [2000] pp. xii + 232. £37.50 ($59.95) ISBN 0 5215 7255 X.

Esche, Edward J., ed. *Shakespeare and his Contemporaries in Performance.* Ashgate. [2000] pp. xii + 364. £45 ISBN 0 7546 0046 7.

Evans, Robert C., gen. ed. *Ben Jonson's Major Plays: Summaries of Modern Monographs.* Locust Hill Press. [2000] pp. 232. $35 ISBN 0 9339 5191 4.

Gossett, Suzanne, ed. *Bartholomew Fair,* by Ben Jonson. RevelsSE. ManUP. [2000] pp. 196. pb £4.95 ISBN 0 7190 5150 9.

Grantley, D., and N. Taunton, eds. *The Body in Late Medieval and Early Modern Culture.* Ashgate. [2000] pp. x + 253. £42.50 ISBN 0 7456 0115 3.

Hammill, Graham L. *Sexuality and Form: Caravaggio, Marlowe and Bacon.* UChicP. [2000] pp. x + 219. £35 ISBN 0 2263 1518 5.

Happé, Peter, ed. *The Magnetic Lady,* by Ben Jonson. Revels. ManUP. [2000] pp. xiv + 238. £40 ISBN 0 7190 4889 3.

Harp, Richard, and Stanley Stewart, eds. *The Cambridge Companion to Ben Jonson.* CUP. [2000] pp. 218. £13.95 ISBN 0 5216 4678 2.

Harraway, Clare. *Re-citing Marlowe: Approaches to the Drama.* Ashgate. [2000] pp. v + 224. £42.50 ISBN 1 8401 4234 0.

Heller, Herbert Jack. *Penitent Brothellers: Grace, Sexuality, and Genre in Thomas Middleton's City Comedies.* UDelP. [2000] pp. 223. £30 ISBN 0 8741 3701 2.

Hopkins, Lisa. *Christopher Marlowe: A Literary Life.* Macmillan. [2000] pp. xi + 177. hb £42.50 ISBN 0 3336 9823 1, pb £14.99 ISBN 0 3336 9285 8.

Hunter, George K., ed. *The Malcontent,* by John Marston. RevelsSE. ManUP. [2000] pp. 132. pb £4.99 ISBN 0 7190 5364 1.

Ioppolo, Grace, ed. *Shakespeare Performed: Essays in Honour of R.A. Foakes.* UDelP. [2000] pp. 311. £38 ISBN 0 8741 3732 2.

Kastan, David Scott, and Richard Proudfoot, eds. *The Antipodes*, by Richard Brome. Globe Quartos. Nick Hern Books. [2000] pp. xii + 154. pb £8.99 ISBN 1 8545 9603 9.

Kidnie, Margaret Jane, ed. *The Devil is an Ass and Other Plays*, by Ben Jonson. World's Classics. OUP. [2000] pp. xliv + 530. pb £8.99 ISBN 0 1981 3229 8.

Miola, Robert S., ed. *Every Man in his Humour*, by Ben Jonson. Revels. ManUP. [2000] pp. xviii + 282. £40 ISBN 0 7190 1565 0.

Mousley, Andy. *Renaissance Drama and Contemporary Literary Theory*. Macmillan. [2000] pp. 244. £15.50 ISBN 0 3336 9459 7.

Paster, Gail Kern, ed. *Michaelmas Term*, by Thomas Middleton. Revels. ManUP. [2000] pp. xvi + 206. £40 ISBN 0 7190 1552 9.

Pinciss, Gerald M. *Forbidden Matter: Religion in the Drama of Shakespeare and his Contemporaries*. UDelP. [2000] pp. 243. £25 ISBN 0 8741 3706 3.

Simkin, Stevie. *A Preface to Marlowe*. Pearson. [2000] pp. x + 270. £15.99 ISBN 0 5823 1298 1.

Summers, Claude J., and Ted-Larry Pebworth, eds. *Literary Circles and Cultural Communities in Renaissance England*. UMissP. [2000] pp. 243. £33.95 ISBN 0 8262 1317 0.

Szőnyi, György, and Rowland Wymer, eds. *The Iconography of Power: Ideas and Images of Rulership on the English Renaissance Stage*. IEAS Press. [2000] pp. 214. $16 ISBN 9 6348 2482 X.

Takahashi, Yasunari. *Hot Questrists after the English Renaissance: Essays on Shakespeare and his Contemporaries*. AMS. [2000] pp. viii + 296. £61.95 ISBN 0 4046 2337 9.

Wharton, T.F., ed. *The Drama of John Marston: Critical Re-visions*. CUP. [2000] pp. 233. £40 ISBN 0 5216 5136 0.

VIII

The Earlier Seventeenth Century: General, Prose, Women's Writing

SUZANNE TRILL AND JAMES DOELMAN

This chapter has three sections: 1. General; 2. Prose; 3. Women's Writing. Sections 1 and 2 are by James Doelman; section 3 is by Suzanne Trill.

1. General

The year 2000 saw a number of impressive and wide-ranging monographs, of which Noam Flinker's *The Song of Songs in English Renaissance Literature* is the most purely 'literary'. It deftly explores the role of the Song of Songs in a series of English writers from William Baldwin to Milton, a role that has been often recognized but never given the extensive and nuanced treatment provided here. Beginning with the rabbinic understanding of Torah, where a balance between orality and textuality was established, Flinker investigates the continuing influence of this on the varied readings of Canticles in the Renaissance. The long-standing tensions in the treatment of Canticles between oral and written, sexual and sacred, literal and allegorical, and between apocalyptic closure and lyric openness, form a framework for this well-integrated discussion. Flinker posits a continuing oral tradition of carnal readings of Canticles, traces of which survive in medieval and Renaissance poetry. Such neglected works as Baldwin's *Canticles, or Balades of Salomon* [1549], Robert Aylett's Spenserian *The Brides Ornaments* [1621 and 1625], and the Ranter Abiezer Coppe's writings are given close examination in the light of the complex traditions associated with Canticles. *The Brides Ornaments* is treated as symptomatic of the Protestant English tradition between Spenser and Milton, and recognized as important for establishing how far Milton would move beyond the established allegorical treatments. In the writings of the Ranters, Flinker finds an embracing of the literal sexual aspects of the Songs of Songs and an application of the spiritual tradition to endorse an approach both carnal and apocalyptic. Their written works gesture towards a more extensive secret oral culture. Other chapters treat Spenser's *Amoretti*, and Shakespeare's *Venus and Adonis*, which Flinker sees as a secular foil to the tension-rich poems that balance the erotic and religious; the reading of Shakespeare is based on 'silences' or 'absences', which renders it the least convincing of the book's chapters. While tightly focused, the chapters are not isolated units, but formed by Flinker into a narrative of intertextual pressures that culminates in the prelapsarian marriage of *Paradise Lost*, where the tension between the sexual and the religious is restored in a use of Canticles that owes something to both Spenser and the Ranters.

Robert Wilcher's *The Writing of Royalism, 1628–1660* brings together a solid narrative political history from the 1630s to 1660 (with a sharp focus on the 1640s) and readings of a wide range of poems and prose as part of this history. The book carefully places these works within their specific moment, shows how 'royalism' slowly emerged as a distinct position in a range of writings, and traces a developing and shifting royalist poetics. By drawing on recent and solid historical scholarship, such as that of Kevin Sharpe and Conrad Russell, and avoiding simplistic polarities of cavalier versus puritan, the book richly informs our understanding of the period's literature. Wilcher achieves an impressive thoroughness by combining his original treatment of neglected works with a reliance on the sound scholarship of others regarding some more familiar texts. Consistently alert to the meaning of genres, Wilcher explores how existing forms were reshaped and new ones invented under the force of historical circumstance. He notes the heavy use of dialogue and the published familiar letter, and the manipulation of the 'device of ventriloquism'. The volume covers an impressive array of writers, from the popular (John Taylor) to the elite (Carew and Lovelace), the well-known and expected (Suckling, Denham, Vaughan) to the relatively obscure (Edward Symmons and George Daniel). Wilcher wisely avoids grand conclusions, but the book is rich in more limited observations: the development of Francis Quarles into a full-blown royalist, the influence of *Eikon Basilike* on Vaughan's 'Daphnis', and the rhetoric of Charles as a Christ-like martyr even before his execution. Wilcher's book joins Lois Potter's *Secret Rites and Secret Writing: Royalist Literature, 1641–1660* [1989] and James Loxley's *Royalism and Poetry in the English Civil Wars: The Drawn Sword* [1997] in significantly increasing our understanding of the royalist writings of the century's middle decades.

Works by two historians, Kevin Sharpe and Adam Fox, are among this year's most significant publications for literary studies in the period. In *Reading Revolution: The Politics of Reading in Early Modern Europe*, Sharpe, perhaps the leading historian on the early Stuart period, challenges his colleagues to adopt a methodology informed by recent developments in literary studies: theoretical self-questioning, considerations of representation and rhetoric, reception theory, and the history of the book. He tellingly identifies the failure of new historicists and revisionists to engage with each other's work, and calls for a 'new cultural history of art'. Most of all, he calls for attention to the process of reading, to the political dimension of what readers did with texts to understand the eruption of the civil wars. Much of what Sharpe calls for is already happening, for example, in the volume by Wilcher, and other volumes discussed further on in this essay. The bulk of Sharpe's book is devoted to a theoretically informed study of the reading habits of Sir William Drake, based on his extensive commonplace books, notebooks and diaries, dating from the 1620s to 1660, which Sharpe calls 'the greatest archival resource we have to chart how an early modern English gentleman read'. It traces the political dimension of Drake's reading through the tumultuous events of the civil wars, Interregnum, and Restoration. Drake read in preparation for the active life, and

Sharpe reveals in him a striking example of hard-headed 'anglicised Machiavellianism', quite in contrast to our stereotype of the country gentleman of the time. Ultimately, *Reading Revolution* suggests that the consideration of specific readers such as Drake might help move historians beyond the revisionist/anti-revisionist debate that is consuming seventeenth-century historiography.

Adam Fox's *Oral and Literate Culture in England, 1500–1700* explores the interaction between oral, manuscript and printed language in the period, and challenges much received wisdom on the subject by suggesting that written culture affected all levels of society, regardless of literacy. An oral culture still survived, he argues, but one that was itself fed by such published forms as ballads, folk tales, proverbs, and books of husbandry. He also convincingly argues that there were degrees of literacy; for example, some could read printed books but not handwriting. This book is deeply versed in political and social history, history of the book and anthropology. At times Fox presents more examples than necessary, and the use of the filecard box seems to be showing through. However, this is detail-rich descriptive literary history, and will be a treasure to literary scholars as well as historians.

One of Fox's chapters is devoted to 'Ballads and Libels', and the latter of these is the subject of a fine essay, 'The Literary Culture of Early Stuart Libelling', by Andrew McRae (*MP* 97[1999] 364–92), which explores the poetic libel by tracing its dual literary and political contexts. Balanced between satire and news, popular and elite culture, the libel, according to McRae, was a complex literary mode, whose circulation in manuscript deserves further attention. In its attention to reading communities, the material form of circulation, and the nuances of rhetoric and form, McRae demonstrates admirably the qualities that Sharpe calls for in his opening chapter.

Another volume that considers oral and popular culture is *Travesties and Transgressions in Tudor and Stuart England: Tales of Discord and Dissension* by the prolific cultural historian David Cressy. Here he engages in 'creative listening' to a range of strange and often monstrous stories of early modern England (a woman who gave birth to a cat, the baptizing of animals), a technique most associated with Robert Darnton (*The Great Cat Massacre* [1984]). Drawing on court records Cressy listens for the voice and story, and is most effective in those chapters that focus on a single narrative ('Who Buried Mrs. Horseman?', the fascinating story of an illegal church-floor burial); other chapters, such as 'Mocking the Clergy', on verbal exchanges between priests and parishioners, too frequently become listings of similar incidents.

Whether a book on the visual culture of the period technically falls within the scope of this review is open to question; however, the majority of scholars in Erickson and Hulse, eds., *Early Modern Visual Culture: Representation, Race, Empire in Renaissance England*, have emerged from the field of literary studies, and the volume as a whole reflects the interdisciplinary (or non-disciplinary?) approach that has broken down the barriers between literary and other cultural studies. While the subtitle promises yet another collection on the tiredly fashionable subjects of race, empire and the body, this volume largely escapes the law of diminishing returns by its fresh focus on a wide range of visual culture. Its introduction provides a helpful overview of art history and literary history in England over the last twenty years. Highlights of the collection are predictably rich essays by Ernest Gilman and

Stephen Orgel on the 'high art' of the early seventeenth century. Orgel demonstrates the developing taste for Continental sculpture and art in the early Stuart period: royal and noble collectors found in this art a connection to the ideals of antiquity; Gilman's essay focuses on the chief non-royal collector of the period, Thomas Howard, second earl of Arundel, examining his role of Earl Marshal in the context of the ill-fated attempt in the late 1630s to establish Madagascar as a bountiful English colony. Rare in a volume of this sort, Erickson's essay builds upon that of Gilman, exploring the significance of two images from the Madagascar portrait: that of St George and that 'of race implied by the island of Madagascar'. Overall, this is a heavily illustrated and well-produced volume.

Orlin, ed., *Material London, ca. 1600*, shares many qualities with the Erickson and Hulse book, but historians play a larger role here, and the theoretical aspects of the collection are more lightly worn. The scope and the approach adopted are highly variable: a number of the essays are quite tightly focused on the year 1600; others cover something more like the full century of 1550 to 1650. Some of the former may overdetermine the year 1600 as a turning point; some of the latter undermine the intended focus of the collection. They are most successful when deeply embedded in the material aspects of London life and less theoretically self-conscious. In this vein, the anthropologist Jane Schneider connects the long-recognized symbolic use of black and white in Elizabeth's reign to the state of the English textile industry, which underwent a major shift around 1600. In the process she provides a fascinating study of the source of dyes and fabrics to demonstrate the material bases of colour symbolism in the period. Jones and Stallybrass do something similar with the pervasive symbolic use of the Irish mantle in art and literature of the period. Ian Archer charts the retailing transformation around 1600 and the attendant shift in the perception and status of the merchant in English society. He explores the concerns about conspicuous consumption by women and apprentices, but ultimately he points to relative harmony between genders and classes in the period. Peter Blayney provides an important addition to the history of the book by challenging the letter of Burleigh that has most shaped scholars' views of the bookshops in Paul's Churchyard. In the process he provides an excellent guide (more condensed than his *The Bookshops in Paul's Cross Churchyard* [1990]) to the history and geography of that important early modern retail site. Linda Levy Peck covers some of the same ground as Orgel in the Hulse and Erickson volume, but her focus is on the adoption of Continental architecture and other material culture from 1600 to 1625. John Schofield's 'The Topography and Buildings of London, ca. 1600' is markedly different from the other essays in the collection: more introductory in nature, it provides a geographical and architectural survey of London in 1600, paying special attention to the light shed by recent archaeology.

A wide variety of religious writings are considered in James Doelman, *King James I and the Religious Culture of England*. Included are chapters on the biblical and imperial iconography applied to King James, the politics of conversion, satiric religious epigrams, and the royal response to self-proclaimed prophets.

In 'Anthologies of the Early Seventeenth Century: Aspects of Media and Authorship' (in Korte *et al.*, eds., *Anthologies of British Poetry: Critical Perspectives from Literary and Cultural Studies*, pp. 75–88), Monika Gomille argues for the important role of anthologies, both printed and manuscript, in establishing the idea of the author in the period.

A new undergraduate text, Rudrum, Black, and Nelson, eds., *The Broadview Anthology of Seventeenth-Century Verse and Prose*, provides a broader range of authors than that available in oft-used anthologies by Witherspoon and Warnke, and Herschel Baker. As such it better reflects the current state of seventeenth-century literary studies, and will certainly be widely adopted. Its introductions and annotations are less substantial than most students will need, but subsequent editions will likely correct the many minor problems in punctuation.

The sole relevant bibliography is Roxane C. Murph, *The English Civil War through the Restoration in Fiction: An Annotated Bibliography, 1625–1999*, which provides a selective list of the many poems, plays and novels that take the period for a subject. The volume may prove helpful for those studying the treatment of the period in later literature, but is far too selective in listing contemporary material. For example, only two of George Wither's many long poems on the events of the time are included, and a quick check found that most of the lesser-known royalist works discussed by Wilcher also found no place here. Any such bibliography faces the challenge of distinguishing between 'fictional' and 'historical' works, but this volume also falls short by not consistently providing full citations, and by the lack of any chronological cross-index. Thus, for example, any scholar pursuing poetic presentations of King Charles I in the 1690s will be forced to browse through the main author/title listing.

A special issue of *Early Modern Literary Studies* (January[2000]) was devoted to the topic of computers and research in the Renaissance, and a similar topic was broached in Rhodes and Sawday, eds., *The Renaissance Computer: Knowledge Technology in the First Age of Print*; most frequently in this volume the advent of the computer is used as the starting point for a reconsideration of changing technologies of the written word in the early modern period.

2. Prose

Quaker writings of the period received substantial scholarly attention this year, the most significant work being Rosemary Moore's *The Light in their Consciences: The Early Quakers in Britain, 1646–1666*. It shares many of the strengths of Wilcher's *Writing of Royalism*, bringing together a chronological analysis of the development of an ideology (Quakerism), and positioning a wide range of writings in relation to this close chronology. Through detailed analysis of primary materials Moore presents a history of both the Quaker movement and Quaker theology in its first two decades. She succeeds by moving beyond the typical delineation of early and late phases of Quakerism, and recognizing the difference that even a single year can make for the flavour and emphasis of a work. The pamphlets and letters of the earliest 'Quakers', from the heady days of the late 1640s, are strikingly different from those of the 1660s, where Quakers came to terms with the difficulties of institutional structure in a successful movement, and the challenges of being a persecuted dissenting group under the Restoration government. While the writings of the movement's first leader, George Fox, receive the most (and very probing) attention, Moore also argues for the significance of Margaret Fell and John Naylor in the Quakerism of the early 1650s. With the movement's success and the changing political circumstances of the late 1650s and early 1660s, new types of Quaker publication appeared. Apart from its significance as a solid history of early Quakerism, this book will provide a rich context for the writings of Fell, which have received increased attention from literary scholars lately. Geared to a seemingly broader audience than most university press books, the work seems to lack the narrative verve that would help it keep that audience: the writing can be plodding at times.

In contrast to the straightforward Moore, Naomi Winter, '"Out of the paths and steps of solid men": Masculinities in George Fox's Journal' (*L&T* 14[2000] 145–59), adopts the language of 'radical subjectivity' and 'textual self' in probing the writings of the leading Quaker. She argues that the oft-noted 'incohesiveness' of the text is in fact a reflection of Fox's self, and finds a stylistic similarity to the more fragmentary women's diaries and autobiographies of the period. Unlike Moore's book, her article should not be taken as reflecting an interest in Quakerism. In '"Mony Choaks": The Quaker Critique of the Seventeenth-Century Public Sphere' (*MP* 98[2000] 251–70), Meiling Hazleton, in a rather strained argument, identifies Quaker resistance to paid, professional clergy as a revolution in language and its ownership.

Other varieties of radical Protestantism were not neglected: Kathryn Gucer, '"Not heretofore extant in print": Where the Mad Ranters Are' (*JHI* 61[2000] 75–95), moves beyond the 1980s debate over the 'reality' of the Ranters as a radical sect, and considers instead the rhetorical representation of them in the pamphlets of the early 1650s. She argues that the Engagement Oath was the central context for these works, and that Presbyterians were using the Ranter phobia as an opportunity to disparage all those on the religious left, including the Independents and Rump Parliament. Based on Walter Ong's analysis of shifting language modes, Jürgen Schlaeger's 'Self-Exploration in Early Modern English Diaries' (in Langford and West, eds., *Marginal Voices, Marginal Forms: Diaries in European Literature and History*, pp. 22–36), finds the roots of diary-making in the print revolution and Reformation theology. He argues that Thomas Whythorne's *Autobiography* [1576] and Kenelm Digby's *Loose Fantasies* [1628] reflect a limited self-exploration for public viewing. In contrast he finds in Daniel Dyke's treatise *The Mystery of Self-Deceiving* [1614], and the puritan diaries of Samuel Ward and Richard Rogers a direct probing of the self outside of public codes. He suggests that Dyke works from a deep suspicion of the human heart and even the process of self-examination, but questionably conflates the 'word' of human autobiographical writings with the 'Word' of Holy Scripture. Schlaeger more successfully demonstrates Ward's discomfort with the whole process of diary-making, which results in an inconsistent tone and process, but shows how Rogers's diaries [1587–90] use the act of self-writing (and subsequent self-reading of an externalized written memory) as a defence against sinful impulses.

The year saw few editions of primary sources, but Francis Bacon's *The Essayes or Counsels, Civill and Morall*, edited by Michael Kiernan and originally published in 1985, was republished to complete *The Oxford Francis Bacon*. The general editors, Graham Rees and Lisa Jardine, are right in judging that a wholly new edition of this work was not necessary: Kiernan provides rich annotations, a reliable text and full textual apparatus. The complicated development of the essays through thirteen editions in Bacon's lifetime is fully explored, as are the thirteen manuscript copies from the time. Brian Vickers's 'The Myth of Francis Bacon's "Anti-

Humanism'" (in Kraye and Stone, eds., *Humanism and Early Modern Philosophy*, pp. 135–58), challenges the common assumption that Bacon was hostile to humanist rhetoric and poetry by considering the context of the relevant passages in *The Advancement of Learning*, and suggests that Bacon's quarrel was with excessive Ciceronianism. David Burnett, *A Thinker for All Seasons*, provides a useful overview of Bacon's life and writings for the undergraduate or non-academic reader.

3. Women's Writing

(a) Editions

In 'Anthologising the Early Modern Female Voice' (in Murphy, ed., *The Renaissance Text: Theory, Editing, Textuality*, pp. 55–72), Ramona Wray begins by noting the recent growth in interest in editing early modern women's writing. This development is amply attested to by the appearance of eight editions this year; few of them, however, would escape Wray's criticism. She advocates 'a new editorial strategy' that would emphasize the diversity of early modern women's writing within a clearly defined generic or periodic focus, and by providing a detailed 'contextual apparatus'. It will be interesting to see how Wray deals with the 'pragmatic considerations of space and cost' in her own forthcoming anthology of women's writing during the civil war period. Of the editions published this year, one that fits Wray's requirements is Clarke, ed., *Isabella Whitney, Mary Sidney and Aemilia Lanyer: Renaissance Women Poets*. This anthology brings together three women poets who have either attained, or are fast approaching, 'canonical' status. While Danielle Clarke's introduction acknowledges that 'bringing together three women poets ... suggests they are usefully read alongside one another', she also carefully points out that this does not imply any necessary similarity, or that any connection is determined simply by the writers' shared sex. Indeed, Clarke concludes her introduction by illustrating how the differences between them provide 'a fascinating insight into the range of female literary experience in the Renaissance'. Probably the least well known of the three—and the one about whom the least is known—is the lower-middle-class Isabella Whitney, but Clarke provides as much information as possible about her life and the conventions of her work to make her poetry, *The Copy of a Letter* and extracts from *A Sweet Nosgay*, accessible. Mary Sidney is, of course, rather better known. It is, however, particularly useful that Clarke has chosen to edit her poetic translations of the Psalms and *The Triumph of Death*, for, while there are some impressive modern editions of Sidney's writing, they are correspondingly expensive. Clarke's edition therefore makes Sidney's poetry available to a far wider audience than has previously been possible. Lanyer's *Salve Deus Rex Judaeorum* currently exists in a number of modern editions, and various selections of the text are available in a number of anthologies, but until now there has not been a full-length version of her text available in paperback. Bringing these three women poets together in one paperback volume, retailing at £9.99, makes teaching them a truly viable possibility.

Whitney and Lanyer also figure in Paul Salzman's most recent editorial project, *Early Modern Women's Writing: An Anthology, 1560–1700*. Opening his introduction with the now familiar citation from Virginia Woolf ('Why [is it that] women did not write poetry in the Elizabethan Age?') and her depiction of the mythical 'Judith Shakespeare', Salzman's anthology includes a range of women writers, chronologically organized, from Isabella Whitney to Aphra Behn. The period covered and the range of genres, from poetry to letters, diary to novel, and drama to prophecy, enable Salzman to provide the modern reader with a glimpse of the variety of literary practices that early modern women engaged with. At £7.99 it is an accessible student text, but inevitably it suffers from the curse of anthologizing: the relationship between space and breadth of coverage. While the inclusion of less familiar writers such as Eleanor Davies, Priscilla Cotton and Mary Cole, and Hester Biddle represents a welcome addition to the existing 'canon', most of the other writers included are more predictable (Anne Clifford, Mary Wroth, Margaret Cavendish, Katherine Philips) and, of course, each is represented by a selection of her work, which means that, for example, the Aemilia Lanyer section includes 'Eve's Apology' and 'The Description of Cooke-Ham'. It is, perhaps, unfortunate that this anthology has appeared at the same time as Clarke's edition as most people involved in teaching women's material from this period have long been calling for editions of complete works by early modern women writers to facilitate a more detailed study of their literary endeavours. A very different kind of resource is available in Crawford and Gowing, eds., *Women's Worlds in Seventeenth-Century England: A Sourcebook*. Although, as usual in this series, the extracts are generally frustratingly brief, this sourcebook represents a fascinating collection of documentation about all aspects of women's lives in the seventeenth century, thematically organized around the concepts of bodies, religion, work, finances, sex, marriage, maternity, relationships, politics and, finally, mental worlds. One of the great advantages of this sourcebook is that the majority of the included extracts are from archival records and manuscript sources that are often difficult to access and, as well as providing some indication of the character of a particular text, it also proves a rich repository of bibliographical sources for those wishing to take their study further. It also usefully includes sources by women from various social levels and geographical locations. There is a brief overall introduction and a short introduction to each section which lays out the ground for the material. Most unusual, and perhaps therefore, most interesting to this reader, is the final section, 'mental worlds', which includes a subsection on 'dreams and visions' that provides a lively indication of the process of dream interpretation pre-Freud.

In addition to Clarke's anthology (above), two other editions this year will be particularly useful for teaching purposes: Hodgson-Wright, ed., *The Tragedy of Mariam: Elizabeth Cary*, and Keeble, ed., *Memoirs of the Life of Colonel Hutchinson: Charles I's Puritan Nemesis, Lucy Hutchinson*. Stephanie Hodgson-Wright's edition of *The Tragedy of Mariam* is a re-publication of the version originally prepared for the Keele University Renaissance Texts and Studies series. This is a particularly welcome reissue, as its quality and pricing make it a viable text for classroom use. The editor has consulted all the known extant versions of the 1613 edition of the play, and notes the minor variations between them in the final section of her introduction. More significant variations are apparent in the manuscript versions of the text, which the editor has helpfully recorded, along with significant punctuation changes and variant readings by modern editors, in the 'Emendations and Variant Readings' section following the play's conclusion. Act and scene numbers have been standardized to roman numerals, and the different abbreviations of characters' names, which can occasionally cause student confusion, have been regularized and given in full. A new and particularly useful addition to this version is provided by the appendices: appendix A gives extracts from the play's main sources and appendix B includes extracts from contemporary 'Didactic and Polemical Texts', from the *Instruction of a Christian Woman* to *The Mother's Legacy to her Unborn Child*. These features, in addition to the questions raised within the introduction about the nature of 'closet drama', make this text a rare entity: it is both scholarly and accessible for a student readership. Keeble's edition, also reasonably priced at £9.99, is a newly transcribed and edited version of the *Life of Colonel Hutchinson*. It also includes 'The Life of Mrs Lucy Hutchinson, Written by Herself: A Fragment'; this is reproduced from Julius Hutchinson's text as there is no known extant manuscript of it. The text has been modernized, and punctuation and paragraphing are editorial, all of which makes the text accessible to the modern reader. Detailed notes assist the reader with the minutiae of political events and religious terminology, with which the student reader in particular may be unfamiliar. It also helpfully includes a glossary of both archaic words and words that are used by Hutchinson in contexts that are now either obsolete or unfamiliar. The introduction helps to situate the Hutchinsons within their historical context, and makes a compelling case for the biography's political significance and the way in which it manifests Lucy Hutchinson's radical politics. Keeble concludes his introduction by arguing that, although Hutchinson consistently maintains the subordination of women to their husbands, 'her own text avows [that] she hardly stands in need of masculine and wise counsellors'. He also alludes to Hutchinson's other literary endeavours. One of them is the subject of David Norbrook's article 'Lucy Hutchinson and *Order and Disorder*: The Manuscript Evidence' (*EMS* 9[2000] 257–91), in which he makes a detailed case for her authorship of this poem. Norbrook has also edited the full text for Blackwell [2001], to be reviewed next year.

The most recent publication in The Early Modern Englishwoman: A Facsimile Library of Essential Works series, published by Ashgate, is *Neo-Latin Women Writers: Elizabeth Jane Weston and Bathsua Reginald [Makin]*, selected and introduced by Donald Cheney. The introductory note is characteristically brief, but provides some basic biographical and textual information, including the fact that Weston and Makin are the only two Renaissance Englishwomen who are known to have published collections of their Latin poetry. A note from the general editors informs us that the copy-texts for Weston's works are the same as those for a forthcoming edition of her works from the University of Toronto Press. This year also sees the publication of two more editions in the rather more scholarly Renaissance English Text Society series: Aldrich-Watson, ed., *The Verse Miscellany of Constance Aston Fowler: A Diplomatic Edition*, and Hinds, ed., *The Cry of a Stone* by Anna Trapnel. Aldrich-Watson's edition of Fowler's manuscript (Huntingdon Library HM904) is not only valuable in its own right, but also contributes to our further understanding of the Tixall poetry. Fowler was the youngest of the Aston family and this miscellany, kept between 1630 and 1660, contains poems that were both copied from other sources and written by herself. Unusually, the manuscript is 'not just a collection of poems that caught the writer's fancy at a certain moment, nor is it simply a collection of the writer's thoughts. Instead, HM904 combines these two elements.' The editor points out that fifty-five of the sixty-five poems in the collection 'relate directly to the Aston family' and that, as such, they provide 'an intimate view of a seventeenth-century woman and the relationships among her family members'. A detailed introduction to the family's history and a number of family trees assist the reader unfamiliar with the background to grasp the poems' connections and significance, and helps provide a context for reading the manuscript, as some of its elements address the potentially curious paradox of Catholic royalist politics. Aldrich-Watson states that the poems in HM904 consist of three groupings (religious, familial and miscellaneous), provides a lengthy explanation of the sources of the poems and their potential significance, and indicates particular aspects of Fowler's own style. An informative textual introduction highlights the connection between Fowler's manuscript and Bodl. MS Eng. poet. b.5(B), as twelve of the poems occur in both manuscripts and are written in Gertrude Aston's hand: an appendix traces textual variants. These intertextual connections and the informative annotation and apparatus are fascinating and certainly 'possess considerable literary and historical interest'. Hilary Hinds also amply demonstrates that Anna Trapnel's text, although historically and generically distant from modern expectations, is of considerable interest. Even though it is 'loosely punctuated and syntactically unorthodox' and 'the density of topical reference and the reliance on biblical allusion' may present difficulties for the modern reader, Hinds argues that such difficulties 'should not be overemphasised; the writing also has a compelling momentum and urgency, and a sense of passion and outrage that speaks loud and clear across the historical divide'. Most importantly, Hinds's introduction manages to bridge such perceived gaps by providing details about Trapnel's life and work and by historically contextualizing the prophecy and providing some suggested reading strategies. This is assisted by the modernization of the text, but most significantly by the additional editorial insertion of biblical allusions, references and echoes, which can present problems for contemporary student readers. This is reinforced by the fulsome notes in the commentary section, which also help with contemporary, topical allusions and explanation of expressions that might seem nonsensical to the uninformed reader. The final part of her introduction surveys Trapnel's critical reception in the twentieth century and explores the reasons for recent increased interest in prophetic forms from the seventeenth century. Hinds concludes her introduction by arguing for the need for further publication of such texts: 'with their republication, not only will these texts begin to make their mark on existing areas of critical debate, but also their own specificities, styles, and strategies might begin to suggest new areas of investigation'. If this year's flurry of activity in the editorial arena is anything to go by, such changes will soon be a viable possibility.

(b) Books

Three impressive new books make a significant contribution to our developing understanding of women's social history. While historical in focus, these books also make reference to literary production of different kinds that will certainly stimulate some rethinking of some prevailing assumptions. In *Whores of Babylon: Catholicism, Gender and Seventeenth-Century Print Culture* [1999], Frances E. Dolan turns her attention from 'domestic subordinates' to their national counterparts and examines how the two are intertwined. It is a fascinating study that examines a range of representational forms; Dolan self-consciously chooses to organize her argument around three pivotal crises in Protestant–Catholic relations during the seventeenth century: the gunpowder plot [1605], Queen Henrietta Maria's advocacy of Catholicism in the 1630s and 1640s, and the popish and meal-tub plots [1678–80]. One of the book's most important features is the way in which it demonstrates the difficulties of defining a 'Catholic': as Dolan puts it, 'since Catholics were woven into families and communities and were prominent at court, the threat they offered was precisely that they could not be readily separated out. Both laws and polemic struggled to identify and vilify Catholics. But neither succeeded in drawing an indisputable or uncrossable line between Catholics and everyone else.' Characteristically, Dolan clearly states that her intention is not to provide a history of Catholicism but to 'consider the role Catholics played in the English Protestant imagination and in English print; I focus particularly on how fantasies and representations linked Catholics and Catholicism to disorderly women'. This statement also highlights another significant feature of Dolan's study: her abiding awareness of the importance of gender in the study of history.

Sara Mendelson and Patricia Crawford's *Women in Early Modern England* [1998] is also to be highly welcomed. This collaboratively written book will be of great interest to established scholars and students alike. For the student it offers a comprehensive introduction to the various factors that would have affected a woman's life during this period. It is clearly organized: opening with contextual information, with regard to medicine, religion, the law and other factors that contributed to the promotion of particular stereotypes, Mendelson and Crawford then examine the expected trajectory of a woman's life from childhood and adolescence through marriage and maternity to widowhood and death. An important characteristic of this book is that the authors ensure that they do not simply focus on the experiences of the rich, and/or the exceptions, but offer an insight into the differences between women with respect to class, age and geography. This is a consistent feature of the book, as they move on to discuss female culture, the specificities of poor women's roles in the economy, and the various occupational and social roles that a woman might occupy; they conclude by examining women's roles in public politics. In addition to these features, the more established scholar will undoubtedly benefit from the bibliographical information regarding sources, as much of the material deserves further attention, from literary scholars as well as historians. Perhaps the only drawback of the book is the time-span covered, for it is not always immediately clear whether a particular example is from the earlier or the later part of it. To a certain extent, this is redressed by concluding sections that draw out the similarities and differences in relation to particular subjects over the whole of the period.

One particular aspect of women's lives that is far more prominent than usual this year is the subject of maternity. Although maternity and midwifery have often been mentioned in both historical and literary studies of early modern women's writing, this year sees a collection of essays examining this subject in detail (see below) and also the emergence of the first major full-length socio-historical study of this subject: *The Midwives of Seventeenth-Century London* by Doreen Evenden. Evenden's analysis is a welcome corrective to the predominant perception of early modern midwives as 'ignorant, incompetent, and poor', which originates in contemporary accounts by male writers and perniciously persists in shaping modern historians' assumptions. Evenden's reappraisal is based upon original archival research, including ecclesiastical records, churchwarden's accounts, midwives' testimonial certificates, tax records, wills, midwives' case and account books, and seventeenth-century diaries. She emphasizes that this is 'a social history of midwives of a particular and important metropolis and cannot be taken as representative of midwives outside its confines', and points out that 'the technical details of midwifery are difficult to retrieve since most midwives left no records about what they actually did for patients'. Indeed, Evenden demonstrates that midwives 'clearly relied, for the most part, on oral traditional knowledge' communicated between female participants, supplemented by practical experience with a senior midwife, 'who in some cases was their mother'. The majority of existing evidence relates to female practitioners who come under the aegis of the Church of England; the second-largest quantity of evidence is supplied in Quaker records, and proves that 'most women had many years of practical experience as deputy midwives before obtaining an ecclesiastical licence', which depended upon church attendance, proof of character and proof of competence. Her study addresses 'the ecclesiastical licensing of midwives, the system of unofficial apprenticeship in which London midwives trained, the midwives' clients, the social world of the larger population of London midwives and, in greater depth, the socio-economic circumstances of midwives in twelve selected parishes'. This marvellous study also includes extensive appendices that will be a great resource for future research: these include a 'directory' of London's 1,200 seventeenth-century midwives, a listing of senior midwives and their associates or deputies, and copies of the Midwife's Oath.

This year also sees the paperback publication of Laura Gowing's award-winning study, *Domestic Dangers: Women, Words, and Sex in Early Modern London*, which focuses on Church court cases concerning sexual slander, marriage contracts, and marital separation in London. Gowing demonstrates that each has 'a language and a conventional story-line of its own' which, when examined corporately in context, 'can be exceptionally revealing of the experience of gender, sex, morals and language'. In contrast to the notion of a 'crisis' in gender relations, Gowing argues that, while 'gender is *always* in contest, gender relations seem to be continually renegotiated around certain familiar points', simultaneously recording 'the persistence of an ideology' that reinforced established, gendered double-standards. Jocelyn Catty is also concerned with such issues in *Writing Rape, Writing Women in Early Modern England: Unbridled Speech* [1999]. Her informative study addresses the complications of defining rape, from both a modern and a historical perspective; for the sake of clarity, she distinguishes between modern and historical or ambivalent references by putting the term in quotation marks for the latter ('rape'). Catty opens her book with a quotation from John Daye's preface to his edition of *Gorboduc*, in which '"rape" provided a powerful metaphor for illegitimate publication'. While this is one of many possible examples of the way in which early modern writers 'pervasively trope the text as a female body', Catty chooses this one because it displays a crucial ambivalence about attitudes to the 'raped' woman/text: she was '"done ... villanie" yet "wanton"'. Catty examines the problematic association of female speech with lasciviousness and the conflation of (il)legitimate text with the female body in texts by both male and female writers. Although these are organized 'oppositionally' (in so far as Catty deals with male writers first and then moves on to women writers), she stresses that the two sections should not be seen as straightforwardly 'separate', particularly because the women writers she analyses (including Lumley, Sidney, Cary and Wroth) all drew upon male literary models. These female writers are chosen as examples of women writers 'whose works register the connection between women's sexual autonomy and their autonomy in language'.

(c) Essay Collections and Articles
Perhaps the most noticeable feature of this year's publications in the field of early modern women's writing is the bumper crop of essay collections: five in total. Not so long ago, the essay collection seemed to be becoming obsolete as publishers prevaricated about accepting them. Hopefully, the high standard of the majority of the collections discussed below will encourage the acceptance of further volumes that have a well-defined overall sense of coherence, but which simultaneously promote the exploration of new or neglected aspects of women's literary production. Outstanding among these volumes is Miller and Yavneh, eds., *Maternal Measures: Figuring Caregiving in the Early Modern Period*. The volume aims to examine 'the spectrum, and spectacle, of maternity in particular and of female caregivers at large in the early modern period' (p. 1). To this end the collected essays explore a wide range of both positive and negative models of female carers in the period, from mothers and stepmothers to murderers and witches. They also draw upon a variety of disciplines (including literature, social history, and art history) and examine material from Europe to the New World. The collection is divided into five sections: conception and lactation, nurture and instruction, domestic production, social authority, and mortality. The first section includes 'Midwiving Virility in Early Modern England' by Caroline Blick (pp. 49–64): acknowledging that 'midwifery had long been used as a trope for the production of ideas', Blick sets out to examine how the practice of midwifery 'embodied specific concerns about how the narratives that defined and underpinned male authority were produced'. Legally, midwives provided testimony to paternity, but Blick demonstrates how the eventual conflation of a female birth attendant with a female tattler through the appellation 'gossip' suggests an anxiety about such female narratives and the (in)ability to reflect a man's virility. Rachel Trubowitz, '"But blood whitened": Nursing Mothers and Others in Early Modern Britain' (pp. 82–101), examines the relationship between 'mothers' milk, wet nurses, and Jews' in a range of late sixteenth- and early seventeenth-century texts. Pointing out that this period witnessed 'rapid social change and cultural fragmentation', Trubowitz analyses the 'triangulated relations' of these terms as an example of what Janet Adelman has described as 'boundary panic'. In the final essay in section 2, '"His open side our book": Meditation and Education in Elizabeth Grymeston's *Miscelanea Meditations Memoratives*' (pp. 163–75), Edith Snook argues that Grymeston's citational strategies challenge cultural norms concerning women's involvement in religion and education. She demonstrates that Grymeston's moral instruction of her son reveals that her knowledge extends to areas usually preserved for men, and that her representation of religion includes 'attributes of femininity and mothers'. Consequently, she suggests that 'Grymeston resists oppositional definitions of [her and her son's] respective genders'.

Two different kinds of approach to domestic production are represented in '"Players in your huswifery, and huswives in your beds": Conflicting Identities of Early Modern English Women', by Mary Thomas Crane (pp. 212–23), and Susan

Frye's 'Maternal Textualities' (pp. 224–36). Crane focuses on the dual association of the term 'housewife' with either a married woman 'who manages her household with skill and thrift' or 'a light, worthless, or pert woman or girl ... hussy' (by 1650). Crane demonstrates that contemporary male-authored texts manifest anxieties concerning the relationship between a woman's household work (or lack of it) and her sexuality. Consequently, male writers prefer to emphasize the 'conserving' (rather than the producing) aspect of the housewife's role. In contrast Crane argues that in 'The Description of Cooke-Ham' Aemilia Lanyer alleviates anxiety by shifting the association of female productivity 'away from the sexual and the monetary to an intellectual and religious realm'. Susan Frye focuses upon what she terms 'household-writing', which includes notes and messages, embroidery and calligraphy, account books and receipt/recipe books, to the more familiar genres of letters, diaries and published materials, in order to encourage modern critics to 'be willing to see how women's textuality connects to household tasks like needlework, cooking, healing and raising children'.

Section 4, 'Social Authority', includes 'Marian Devotion and Maternal Authority in Seventeenth-Century England' by Frances E. Dolan (pp. 282–92) and 'Mother Love: Clichés and Amazons in Early Modern England' by Kathryn Schwarz (pp. 293–305). Dolan's essay eloquently demonstrates that, while Catholic and Protestant commentators operate 'within the same theological logic ... and the same ideological logic', they nevertheless crucially differ over whether Mary was merely a 'vessel' for God, or 'an efficient cause' or agent of God. Dolan concludes that, whereas Mary Beth Rose had suggested there are only two options for male-authored discourse on maternal authority (either to deny it altogether or acknowledge it and then deny it), 'Catholic defenders of Marian devotion suggest a third possibility—a male-authored discourse that assumes and even extends maternal authority'. Schwarz's essay neatly summarizes the 'doubled logic that structures early modern theories of domesticity: femininity confines women to the home, and women who act outside the home are excluded from domestic structures'. While theoretically separated, Schwarz demonstrates how these depictions intersect: crucially, the stories about Amazons that circulated most widely in early modern England 'appear repeatedly in texts designed to model social order itself. Conduct manuals and exemplary catalogues invoke Amazons to make arguments about how women should act.' However, as 'Amazon myth exposes the contingency of the connection between father and son', such myths simultaneously undermine the certainty of paternity and embody male anxieties about the female power to form her child in her own image.

The final section concentrates on mortality. In 'London's Mourning Garment: Maternity, Mourning and Royal Succession' (pp. 319–32), Patricia Phillippy locates the elegies and memorials of Elizabeth I's death and the contemporaneous *Londons Mourning Garment* by William Muggins, within a broader examination of the engendering of the mourning process. Phillippy traces a shift from 'passive to active responses to death, from unproductive excess to profitable moderation'. She argues that, whereas male writers sought 'to underwrite this conceptual shift', later female writers, such as Diana Primrose, exploited 'the provocative, productive merger of maternity and mourning to embalm the powerful female body as the enabling icon of women's political, and textual, authority'. An analysis of contemporary anxiety about maternal power is also evident in Susan C. Staub's 'Early Modern Medea:

Representations of Child Murder in the Street Literature of Seventeenth-Century England' (pp. 333–47). Staub argues that street literature displayed the same ambivalence about motherhood and the same concern with maternal duty that was evidenced in domestic literature of the period, but crucially the former focuses on 'instances when motherhood goes awry, on those cases when maternal nurture transmutes into maternal violence', which ultimately suggests that 'all mothers [are] suspect'. However, Staub concludes that because these texts also cast women's actions as 'reactions to her own weakness or to patriarchal neglect and irresponsibility', they, perhaps unintentionally, 'qualify maternal authority' and it is 'thus partially undermined and made less threatening'.

Another stimulating collection is Burke *et al.*, eds., *Women, Writing, and the Reproduction of Culture in Tudor and Stuart Britain*. The contributors to this volume adopt the methods of cultural studies and consequently they collectively examine women's simultaneous position as victims and agents, and importantly address different forms of cultural production by women of various social and religious backgrounds. The essays are divided into five sections: 'Women, Writing, and Material Culture'; 'Reproducing Cultural Roles'; 'Producing Gender Roles'; 'Popular Culture and Women's Pamphlets'; and 'Embodying Culture'. They examine questions including gift exchange, class structures and the (re)production of cultural forms. All of these issues are addressed in the second essay in the collection, '"More than feminine boldness": The Gift Books of Esther Inglis', by Georgianna Ziegler (pp. 19–37). Ziegler examines the form, content and circulation of Inglis's beautifully crafted calligraphic texts and argues that they raise interesting questions 'about publication, authority, and the nature of these texts'. She concludes that, although Inglis was not their 'author', 'she asserted her "author-ity" over each text by inscribing her "self" into its form'. The following essay, 'Patronage and Class in Aemilia Lanyer's *Salve Deus Rex Judaeorum*', by Mary Ellen Lamb, also examines female textual authority, but this time in relation to the changing modes of literary production. Lamb argues that 'Lanyer's multiple dedications to aristocratic women thus not only functioned according to a loosened form of patronage, but also provided an early modern form of celebrity endorsement to sell books to anonymous consumers within the capitalistic system of market exchange'. Section 4 includes 'Eve's Dowry: Genesis and the Pamphlet Controversy about Women', by Barbara McManus (pp. 193–206), and Esther S. Cope's 'Eleanor Davies and the Prophetic Office' (pp. 207–19). With reference to this collection's central emphasis upon women as simultaneously produced by and producers of cultural forms in the early modern period, McManus argues that, regardless of the writer's 'true' identity, what is significant in the pamphlet controversy over women is that they represent the first attempt 'to create *female* subject positions as defenders of women in print'. Consequently, they reveal the constructed 'nature' of 'woman' and 'interrogate, if not subvert, the master narrative of Adam and Eve'. The issue of reinterpreting women's roles is also central to Cope's essay, which demonstrates how Lady Eleanor Davies and her daughter Lucy recast cultural assumptions about femininity and sexuality by locating prophecy as a profession or 'office'. The final essay in the collection, 'The Reproduction of Culture and the Culture of Reproduction in Elizabeth Clinton's *The Countesse of Lincolnes Nurserie*', by Marilyn Luecke (pp. 238–52), is a highly convincing re-reading of this much-misunderstood text. Luecke takes issue with the prevailing assumption that Clinton reinforces patriarchal hierarchies, by demonstrating that the text was written before 'motherhood' was defined 'as an ongoing, "nurturing" relationship with one's own child'. Indeed, Luecke proves that this role was allocated to men during this period. Thus, for Luecke, 'Clinton's privileging of maternal affection is an unusual and potentially radical claim for women's authority and responsibility', one that recasts 'wifely disobedience as maternal authority'.

A potentially interesting, but overall less satisfactory, collection is Woods and Hannay, eds., *Teaching Tudor and Stuart Women Writers*. The editors state that their intention 'is to present current scholarship on the writings of Tudor and Stuart women in a form that will be useful for teaching, giving background on women's lives and women's texts, presenting newly canonised authors, providing models for teaching, and listing resources for further study'. To that end, the collection is divided into four parts: 'Women's Lives and Women's Texts', which explores aspects of textual circulation, female readership and ways of reading women's social position; 'Selected Authors', which provides some biographical and textual information on authors from Elizabeth I to Aphra Behn; 'Models for Teaching', which covers a range of positions, from theoretical implications to different teaching strategies and examples of particular courses and individual approaches to teaching specific texts; and the final part, 'Resources for Further Study', which provides very useful up-to-date information from how to search the archives for records of early modern women to a bibliography of recently published critical studies in this field. It is therefore a wide-ranging collection that seeks to satisfy a broad range of aims, and it is this which is both its strength and its weakness. Even from the intentions cited above, it is unclear whether the volume is directed at students or teachers and, consequently, it falls between two stools. The first half of the book is primarily of interest to students as the essays are both brief and, intentionally, introductory; a researcher in this field will learn little new from these essays, but a student will find a useful way into the material they are studying. The second half is primarily directed towards teachers and researchers. Again, however, the large number of essays means that each is frustratingly brief (roughly five pages per 'essay'); while they can serve as an inspiration, those in the section on 'Teaching Specific Texts' in particular is simultaneously too rigid (in that they tend to present one way of reading a given text) and too vague: Mary V. Silcox's 'Aemilia Lanyer and Virtue', for example, is less than three pages long and does little to define 'virtue' other than providing textual passages for discussion. While some helpful tips can be culled from this volume, a more precise focus and rather more detail would have been welcome.

Another surprisingly disappointing collection is Dragsta *et al.*, eds., *Betraying Our Selves: Forms of Self-Representation in Early Modern English Texts*. The introduction addresses two forms of 'betrayal' in the early modern texts discussed in the volume; first, the potentially positive yet unintentional revelation of the self; secondly, the potentially negative 'misrepresentation or endangering of the self'. Like Shuger (see below) the editors acknowledge the range and diversity of self-writing in the early modern period and the way in which this challenges the modern understanding of subjectivity, but many of the essays are rather thin. For example, in 'Her Own Life, Her Own Living? Text and Materiality in Seventeenth-Century Englishwomen's Autobiographical Writings' (pp. 105–19), Helen Wilcox simply examines a selection of texts, from Martha Moulsworth's 'Memorandum' to

Margaret Cavendish's *True Relation of My Birth, Breeding and Life*, in order to explore the 'borderline' between 'word and deed'. Similarly, Allan Ingram compares Hannah Allen's and Samuel Bruckshaw's experiences, in texts written a hundred years apart, in 'Slightly Different Meanings: Insanity, Language and the Self in Early Modern Autobiographical Pamphlets' (pp. 183–96). Ingram argues that, whereas Allen acknowledges her former madness and represents it by relocating it within 'the language and modes of an acceptable religious interpretation', thereby drawing a distinction between 'narrator and victim', '[Bruckshaw] the protester and Bruckshaw the imputed lunatic are one and the same'. Ingram demonstrates that, whereas Allen was able to 'escape' her former position, Bruckshaw remains locked within it. In 'They Only Lived Twice: Public and Private Selfhood in the Autobiographies of Anne, Lady Halkett and Colonel Joseph Bampfield' (pp. 136–47), Sheila Ottway argues that Halkett's narrative is both 'celebratory and confessional' and that the central purpose of her narrative is to vindicate her role in the 'affair' with Bampfield, whereas Bampfield's autobiography was written to defend himself from any accusation of involvement with the Rye House Plot [1683]. Consequently Ottway concludes that these narratives manifest the traditional division between male and female definitions of vindication: for men, it is related to public image, whereas for women it is related to 'private relationships and [their] sexuality'.

A different kind of division is more impressively examined in Ramona Wray's '[Re]constructing the Past: The Diametric Lives of Mary Rich' (pp. 148–65). Wray argues that the discontinuity between Rich's self-representation(s) in her extensive *Diary* and those in the succinct *Autobiography* provides an insight into 'the way in which an individual female consciousness intersects with a prevailing cultural consciousness'. Wray's central focus is on the way in which these texts engage with different generic conventions: exemplary biography and romance. She concludes that the 'tensions and contradictions' within and between Rich's extant narratives 'confirm that, for Rich, neither model of the self comes near to capturing the full complexity of life experience', but that her example potentially opens up the possibility of exploring the complexity of gendered reading processes in early modern England. And Elspeth Graham, in the Epilogue '"Oppression makes a wise man mad": The Suffering of the Self in Autobiographical Tradition' (pp. 197–214), deconstructs such problematic binaries altogether. Noting autobiography's associations with individualism, Graham analyses the intersection between the reformulation and disintegration of selfhood in autobiographical accounts of imprisonment by Brian Keenan, and Katherine Evans and Sarah Cheevers. She investigates the possible reasons for the appeal of such narratives, and argues that 'suffering may be seen as a cultural bonding force in individualist societies'.

Two other articles indicate the growing importance of autobiography or self-writing as a category in early modern women's writing. Debora Shuger commences 'Life-Writing in Seventeenth-Century England' (in Coleman *et al.*, eds., *Representations of the Self from the Renaissance to Romanticism*, pp. 63–78) by pointing out that the varieties of life-writing in the seventeenth century neither 'belong to a single literary genealogy nor establish an intertextual order among themselves'. Perhaps more importantly, she argues that, contrary to modern expectations, seventeenth-century life-writings locate their sense of 'the individuating "thisness" of a life in the spoken word rather than unspoken or unconsciousness depths'. The emphasis upon rhetoric results in a depiction of "'self-hood" as a political, moral, gendered, and ranked rhetorical performance'. In the same volume, Mary O'Connor, 'Representations of Intimacy in the Life-Writing of Anne Clifford and Anne Dormer' (pp. 79–96), sets out to explore how women's choice of specific objects and activities within the home as a means of establishing their identity positions them as 'both producers of new and reproducers of existing social relations'. In the process she investigates what constituted 'intimacy' in the early modern period, and aims to make the polarization of the terms 'public' and 'private' obsolete.

Hutson, ed., *Feminism and Renaissance Studies* [1999], is the latest volume in the Oxford Readings in Feminism series. It opens by contrasting Jacob Burckhardt's perception of women in the 'Renaissance' with Virginia Woolf's lament for their apparent absence and consequent call for a social history of women's lives that filled in those 'gaps'. Hutson's selection of essays aims both to address Woolf's demands and to provide examples 'of the literary and linguistic work required to expose the ideological work of gender in traditional Renaissance historiography'. Importantly, Hutson stresses that these aims are not mutually exclusive, as essays by Lisa Jardine ('Women Humanists: Education for What?') and Natalie Zemon Davies ('Women on Top'), for example, demonstrate. As one might expect, the book traces the development of feminist literary and historical theory, but less predictable is the way in which it does so. Hutson divides the essays into four sections: 'Humanism after Feminism', 'Historicizing Femininity', 'Gender and Genre', and 'Women's Agency'. Consequently it begins with Joan Kelly's seminal essay 'Did Women have a Renaissance?' (pp. 21–47) and concludes with Tim Carter's 'Finding a Voice: Vittoria Archilei and the Florentine "New Music"' (pp. 450–67). Each section includes essays that were originally published *c*.1975–95, and which demonstrate the changing nature of feminist studies and the contribution this has made to our changing understanding of the 'Renaissance' or the 'early modern' period. The final edited collected of essays published this year, Clarke and Clarke, eds., *'This Double Voice': Gendered Writing in Early Modern England*, indicates some of the ways in which feminist readings have developed recently. In their introduction the editors claim that the collection marks 'a shift away from the essentialising of women's voices in this period, choosing to situate them in the context of the gendered constructedness of all literary voices'. They also contend that, while there is still much work to do within 'an extended feminist framework ... we need to rethink our basic categories of analysis'. Consequently, they state that 'the aim, at all points, has been to investigate the assumptions behind feminist criticism on the period'. One essay that certainly fulfils these claims is James Loxley's 'Unfettered Organs: The Polemical Voices of Katherine Philips' (pp. 230–48). Paraphrasing Judith Butler, Loxley sets out to examine 'what might be a matter, or the matter, of gender' and the complex ways in which 'the language of sexual difference plays across the variously modelled articulation of writer and written'. He examines the way in which 'the body from which these poems speak is thus one which the texts themselves make necessary', and concludes that, by 'challenging the basis on which its own readability depends, the woman's voice puts in question the very means by which "woman" is defined'. A different but still challenging approach is evident in Frances Teague's 'A Voice for a Hermaphroditical Education', which focuses on the important ways in which early modern women 'educated as men, reared as women

... can claim both male and female voices as authentic' (pp. 249–69). Less theoretically sophisticated are the volume's two essays on religious poetry. In '"Whom the Lord with Love affecteth": Gender and the Religious Poet, 1590–1633' (pp. 185–207), Helen Wilcox discusses the work of Mary Sidney, John Donne, Aemilia Lanyer and George Herbert. She initially examines how these writers are similarly positioned in their need to engage with 'the inherited gendered framework of devotional thought and writing'. She concludes that, although they all used the same primary source, the Bible, the final three 'were also significantly influenced by the first'. The issue of gender and devotional writing is also addressed in Elizabeth Clarke's 'Ejaculation or Virgin Birth? The Gendering of the Religious Lyric in the Interregnum' (pp. 208–29). Clarke addresses the question of why so many male-authored religious lyrics in this period were called 'ejaculations' whereas female writers adopted the metaphor of 'offspring'. She concludes that the former 'enacts a rejection of rhetoric and "the flesh"' and implicitly 'rejects a feminized version of spiritual authorship which women are happy to claim for their own'.

In 1993 Margaret J.M. Ezell's ground-breaking study *Writing Women's Literary History* called for, among other activities, the need to promote further study of women's involvement in manuscript culture; this year's volume of the British Library journal *English Manuscript Studies*, co-edited by Peter Beale and Margaret J.M. Ezell, is specifically dedicated to writings by early modern women. The first five essays are mainly concerned with sixteenth-century manuscripts and therefore fall outside of the remit of this chapter. The others refer to seventeenth-century manuscripts and, collectively, they demonstrate the many ways in which women's manuscripts alter our understanding of women's literary, social and historical roles. Victoria E. Burke, 'Elizabeth Asburnham Richardson's "motherlie endeauors" in Manuscript' (pp. 98–113), demonstrates how reading a woman's manuscript and printed texts enables us to examine the notion of the 'stability' of a 'final' text. Indeed, Burke argues that Richardson continually revised her texts and that she never considered them to be completed even when they appeared in presentation copies. While Burke depicts Richardson's 'revising sensibility', Margaret P. Hannay, in 'Elizabeth Ashburnham Richardson's Meditation on the Countess of Pembroke's *Discourse*' (pp. 114–28), argues that her version of Mary Sidney's translation of Philippe de Mornay's *A Discourse of Life and Death* 'exemplifies the scribal tradition of reading as rewriting'.

Having recently edited Elizabeth Jocelin's *The Mothers Legacie* (Stroud [1999]), Sylvia Brown, in 'The Approbation of Elizabeth Jocelin' (pp. 129–64), discusses how the differences between the manuscript and print versions of the text 'provide unusually explicit evidence for ... the editorial interference with women's writing which made it into print with the help of men, the silencing of women's words'. To that end, she details how Thomas Goad altered Jocelin's text before its publication in 1624, both by argument and by the presentation of collations in an appendix. Jene Klene also builds on her recent editorial work in '"Monument of an Endless affection": Folger MS V.b.198 and Lady Anne Southwell' (pp. 165–86). Examining that manuscript in relation to Lansdowne MS 740 in the British Library, Klene contends that it confirms her earlier assertions about the Folger volume's multiple voices and concludes that in Southwell and Sibthorpe's 'mutual endeavour ... [it] became an uncommon commonplace book'. The question of attribution is crucial to Heather Wolfe's 'The Scribal Hands and the Dating of *Lady Falkland: Her Life*' (pp. 187–217). As Wolfe notes, while the authorship of the manuscript has been the subject of intense debate, all Cary scholars agree that it was one of her four Catholic daughters: the problem is, which one. By paying 'careful attention to the various hands in the manuscript', Woolfe argues that 'it is possible to determine the identities of the main scribe and two of its emenders, and when it was written and corrected'. On this basis she concludes that the main scribe was Lucy, and that the text, written in 1645, was bound together with her other loose papers at her death in 1650. In 'Elizabeth Jekyll's Spiritual Diary: Private Manuscript or Political Document?' (pp. 218–37), Elizabeth Clarke argues that the current cataloguing of MS Osborn b 221 (Beinecke Library, Yale) is incorrect. Clarke demonstrates that, rather than a private, autograph, commonplace book, the manuscript is a transcription of Jekyll's spiritual diary tailored to the conventions of the 'Exemplary Life', which circulated for political ends. The issue of transmission here raises the thorny issue of 'voice', which is addressed in more detail by Mark Robson's 'Swansongs: Reading Voice in the Poetry of Lady Hester Pulter' (pp. 238–56). Robson's argument is impressively historicized, but more interestingly this is combined with a Derridean insight into the problematics of privileging manuscript 'voice' over print. Elsewhere, Pamela Hammons, in 'Katherine Austen's Country-House Innovations' (*SEL* 40:i[2000] 123–37), provides a close reading of a fifteen-line poem, transcribed within the article, contained within Austen's *Collectiana*, British Library, Add. 4454.

Early modern women's drama receives increased attention this year. In addition to the editions (discussed above) and following in the footsteps of Susan Cerasano's and Marion Wynne-Davies's recent publications, Alison Findlay, Stephanie Hodgson-Wright and Gweno Williams have co-written a book entitled *Women and Dramatic Production, 1550–1700*. Taking issue with the assumption that early modern women dramatists simply made 'spectacles of themselves', Findlay *et al.* argue that in fact 'a select number of women took an active part in directing and controlling dramatic self-representations: that they made the spectacle themselves' (p. 1). They proceed to detail women's roles as authors, scriptwriters, directors and performers throughout this period. They resist the temptation to automatically define women's dramatic texts 'as "closet" plays intended for reading rather than performance' (p. 2), and contest the assumption that 'plays for which we have no production history are unperformable and not even intended for performance' (p. 3) by drawing on their own practical experience of modern-day productions of such 'unperformable' texts. Indeed, their work confounds some modern assumptions about what constitutes 'performance'; the absence of female players from the public stage prior to the Restoration has encouraged the writers to seek a broader definition of performance, from household productions, to court productions, to the 'self-staging Catholic martyr Margaret Clitherow' and the dramatic courtroom scene in Anna Trapnel's *A Report and Plea*. Following a broadly chronological framework, the book opens with an analysis of Jane Lumley's *Iphigeneia at Aulis* and Mary Sidney's *Tragedie of Antonie*, considering how they reworked their male-authored originals, and demonstrate an 'emergent culture of self-staging women'; the second chapter considers how 'the ideologically feminine qualities of beauty and chastity' were redefined in productions during the reigns of Anna of Denmark and Henrietta Maria. Like Sue Wiseman (below), Alison Findlay, in '"Upon the world's stage"; The Civil War and Interregnum', discusses the relationship between performance and female prophecy, while chapter 5 examines how women dramatists responded to the emergence of female actors after the Restoration. Chapters 4 and 6 are devoted to the work of individual writers (Margaret Cavendish and Aphra Behn respectively). The volume concludes with a discussion of Behn's legacy, 'A Woman's Place is in the Play/House'. While not underestimating the difficulties that faced writers such as Catherine Trotter and Mary Pix, Findlay and Wright conclude that they 'established beyond question that women had a right to self-expression via dramatic production in the mainstream theatre, as well as in the alternative theatrical venues which their sister playwrights had used'.

Sophie Eliza Tomlinson, 'Too Theatrical? Female Subjectivity in Caroline and Interregnum Drama' (*WW* 6:i[1999] 65–79), addresses two central questions: how did the representation of female subjectivity alter as a result of the presence of female actors on the stage and, more specifically, how did women dramatists respond to this innovation? Focusing on Lady Jane Cavendish and Lady Elizabeth Brackley's *The Concealed Fancies*, Tomlinson argues that 'the theatrical woman is viewed sympathetically, her outward identity seen either as socially imposed or as a ruse to protect her emotional self' (p. 66). An alternative reading of this play is included in 'The Politics of Feminine Retreat in Margaret Cavendish's *The Female Academy* and *The Convent of Pleasure*' by Hero Chalmers (*WW* 6:i[1999] 81–94). Comparing Cavendish's plays with those of her stepdaughters, Chalmers argues that, whereas they depict female retirement as 'confinement and loss', their stepmother represents it as positive retreat with a confidence in its own centrality. Chalmers argues that this is related to Cavendish's experience of the court in exile and concludes that such factors should make critics hesitate to classify Cavendish's closet dramas too easily as 'abdications of political engagement' (p. 89). In her analysis of *The Female Academy*, *Bell in Campo* and *The Convent of Pleasure*, Erin Lang Borin, 'Margaret Cavendish's Dramatic Utopias and the Politics of Gender' (*SEL* 40[2000] 339–54), also argues that 'confinement' is reconfigured within Cavendish's writing: according to Borin, Cavendish 'transforms such "cages" into arenas of civil possibility for women' (p. 339). Ultimately, however, Borin concludes that 'Cavendish's utopian heroines learn that their prospects are always already circumscribed by cultural assumptions about female sexuality and identity'. Such cultural assumptions and their variable manifestations are the subject of Sue Wiseman's 'Margaret Cavendish among the Prophets: Performing Ideologies and Gender in and after the English Civil War' (*WW* 6:i[1999] 95–111). With reference to both secular and sectarian texts, Wiseman analyses how they 'illuminate the questions of what was understood as performance', both on the stage and in prophetic utterances. She concludes that the 'new, pleasurable scandal' of the commercial actress helped to crystallize the emergent distinction between staging and spectacle. By contrast, in 'Tentativeness and Insistence in the Expression of Politeness in Margaret Cavendish's *Sociable Letters*', Susan Fitzmaurice provides a linguistic (specifically pragmatic) analysis of the subjectivity of Cavendish's speaker. Fitzmaurice begins with a brief introduction to historical linguistics in order to contextualize her examination of Cavendish's use of modal auxiliary verbs, concluding that 'in Cavendish's (Early Modern) English ... their multiple and fluctuating implied meanings license the construction of a voice that cannot be pinpointed as completely authoritative or wholly tentative'.

The problematics of reading early modern women's texts auto/biographically are attended to by Alexandra G. Bennett in 'Female Performativity in *The Trag[edie] of Mariam*' (*SEL* 40[2000] 293–310). Bennett points out that, although the play has been variously interpreted, the critical consensus is that it reflects Cary's own life and struggles in one way or another. Bennett attempts to take such readings in a new direction. She suggests that the 'key which unlocks diverse possibilities for female agency within both Cary's life and her drama' is the complex relationship between being and seeming manifested in these texts. From this starting point, Bennett examines how Cary's depiction of Mariam and Salome suggests that female performativity is 'a province of fluid female agency rather than … a practice necessarily attributable to a stereotypic category' (p. 304). In 'Elizabeth Cary's *Edward II*: Advice to Women at the Court of Charles I' (in Burke *et al.*, eds., pp. 157–73), Karen Nelson argues that Cary's version of this play is 'no passive retelling of a chronicle', nor is it simply a 'commentary on men's politics'; rather, Nelson focuses on the text's affinities with tracts concerning women's advice and argues that it 'advocates an active role for women at court; and it serves as a handbook of behaviour for a powerful and effective queen'. A different approach to the gendered politics of performance is central to Alison Findlay, Gweno Williams and Stephanie J. Hodgson-Wright's '"The play is ready to be acted": Women and Dramatic Production, 1570–1670' (*WW* 6:i[1999] 129–48). Drawing on their own experience of staging modern productions of *The Tragedy of Mariam*, *The Concealed Fancies* and *The Convent of Pleasure*, the authors contest the notion that such 'closet dramas' are unperformable, and demonstrate how a practical engagement with performance might extend current debates 'about gender itself as performance'.

Essays and articles on Lady Mary Wroth this year predominantly emphasize her familial connections. In '"Here is a sport will well benefit this time and place": Allusion and Delusion in Mary Wroth's *Love's Victory*' (*WW* 6[1999] 47–63), Marion Wynne-Davies examines Wroth's literary allusions and family allegory to argue that *Love's Victory* occupies a median position between 'the intensely personal allegory of [Wroth's] sonnets and the political resonances of [her] prose works', and demonstrates how these factors suggest a composition date of between 1615 and 1618. In '"So much worth": Autobiographical Narratives in the Work of Lady Mary Wroth' (in Dragsta *et al.*, eds., pp. 76–93), Marion Wynne-Davies commences by analysing an extract from Lady Anne Clifford's diary, which sets the scene for an analysis of textual representations of inter- and intra-familial connections. Wynne-Davies argues that Wroth's 'literary texts are so replete with familial allegory and multiple reworkings of her own life that they demand to be classified within an autobiographical framework' (p. 79), and that their fictional status facilitates an open-endedness that the sureties of time and place in 'traditional' autobiographical forms cannot achieve. Consequently, she concludes that while Wroth 'confesses' she does not betray her self, or any other female member of her family, but simultaneously reveals and obscures her autobiographical narrative. Wynne-Davies presents a similar argument, albeit it with a slightly different focus, in '"For *worth*, not weakness, makes in use but one": Literary Dialogues in an English Renaissance Family' (in Clarke and Clarke, eds., pp. 164–84).

A more politicized interpretation of Wroth's poetics can be found in Linda L. Dove's 'Mary Wroth and the Politics of the Household in "Pamphillia to Amphilanthus"' (in Burke *et al.*, eds., pp. 141–56). Dove focuses on the *corona* section of Wroth's text in order to explicate its 'political relevancy'. In representing the 'court of love', Dove argues that Wroth's exploration of the relationship between 'husband and wife, or by analogy between king and subject' stresses the necessity of reciprocity, thereby revealing her investment 'in the concept of government by consent'. Wroth's *corona* is also the focus of Mary B. Moore's chapter on 'Pamphillia to Amphilanthus' in her *Desiring Voices: Women Sonneteers and Petrarchanism*. Moore's rather limited exploration of Wroth's 'labyrinth' unsurprisingly contends that she 'depicts female self-representation as difficult'. To be fair to Moore, however, Wroth is not the sole focus of her enquiry, as she is more interested in the development of women's sonnet sequences from Gaspara Stampa to Elizabeth Barrett Browning and Edna St Vincent Millay. A more convincing analysis of Wroth's work is the chapter on the *Urania* by Helen Hackett in *Women and Romance Fiction in the English Renaissance*. Hackett's book represents an important intervention in the study of Renaissance romances precisely because she offers a comprehensive deconstruction of modern misconceptions about them (i.e. that they are short, popular texts, written by and read by women for escapist purposes, which are, therefore, of little literary merit), as well as providing useful paradigms for alternative ways of reading them. She achieves this by addressing modern assumptions about romance as a genre, tracing its development and alterations through the period and, ultimately, by relocating the romances written by women in the Renaissance (Margaret Tyler, Lady Mary Wroth, Anna Weamys) within the broader context of its (predominantly) male site of production. Most impressive is the way in which Hackett establishes the 'topographical significance that is given to private, feminine spaces', such as chambers or private gardens, as markers of 'female perfection'. Hackett maintains that the relationship between private space and female subjectivity is peculiarly evident in Lady Mary Worth's *Urania*, which assists her in establishing potential differences between Renaissance and modern readers' expectations of the genre. She skilfully alludes to episodes taken from throughout the printed version of the *Urania* and its manuscript continuation, and convincingly demonstrates how her theoretical position can alter our reading of the text.

Books Reviewed

Aldrich-Watson, Deborah, ed. *The Verse Miscellany of Constance Aston Fowler: A Diplomatic Edition*. MRTS. [2000] pp. lxii + 206. £30 ISBN 0 8669 8252 3.

Burke, Mary E. *et al.*, eds. *Women, Writing, and the Reproduction of Culture in Tudor and Stuart Britain*. SyracuseUP. [1999] pp. xxx + 306. £25.50 ISBN 0 8156 2815 3.

Burnett, David. *A Thinker for All Seasons*. NCP. [2000] pp. 143. £7.50 ISBN 0 9485 4507 0.

Catty, Jocelyn. *Writing Rape, Writing Women in Early Modern England: Unbridled Speech*. Macmillan. [1999] pp. ix + 276. £47.50 ISBN 0 3127 4028 9.

Cheney, Donald, ed. *Neo-Latin Women Writers: Elizabeth Jane Weston and Bathsua Reginald [Makin]*. UTorP. [2000] pp. xxxi + 448. £42.50 ISBN 0 8020 4472 7.

Clarke, Danielle, ed. *Isabella Whitney, Mary Sidney and Aemilia Lanyer: Renaissance Women Poets*. Penguin. [2000] pp. xlvi + 409. £9.99 ISBN 0 1404 2409 1.

Clarke, Danielle, and Elizabeth Clarke, eds. *'This Double Voice': Gendered Writing in Early Modern England*. St Martin's Press. [2000] pp. 296. £47.50 ISBN 0 3122 3220 9.

Coleman, Patrick *et al.*, eds. *Representations of the Self from the Renaissance to Romanticism*. CUP. [2000] pp. xiv + 296. $65 ISBN 0 5216 6146 3.

Crawford, Patricia, and Laura Gowing, eds. *Women's Worlds in Seventeenth-Century England: A Sourcebook*. Routledge. [2000] pp. 336. hb £60 ISBN 0 4151 5637 8, pb £17.99 ISBN 0 4151 5638 6.

Cressy, David. *Travesties and Transgressions in Tudor and Stuart England: Tales of Discord and Dissension*. OUP. [2000] pp. xi + 351. £25 ISBN 0 1982 0781 6.

Doelman, James. *King James I and the Religious Culture of England*. B&B. [2000] pp. ix + 184. £40 ISBN 0 8599 1593 X.

Dolan, Frances E. *Whores of Babylon: Catholicism, Gender and Seventeenth-Century Print Culture*. CUP. [1999] pp. xii + 231. £33.50 ISBN 0 8014 3629 X.

Dragsta, Henk *et al.*, eds. *Betraying Our Selves: Forms of Self-Representation in Early Modern England*. Macmillan. [2000] pp. 240. £47.50 ISBN 0 3337 4029 7.

Erickson, Peter, and Clark Hulse, eds. *Early Modern Visual Culture: Representation, Race, Empire in Renaissance England*. UPennP. [2000] pp. 403. hb £44 ISBN 0 8122 3559 2, pb £19.50 ISBN 0 8122 1734 9.

Evenden, Doreen. *The Midwives of Seventeenth-Century London*. CUP. [2000] pp. xvii + 260. £42.50 ISBN 0 5216 6107 2.

Findlay, Alison, Stephanie Hodgson-Wright and Gweno Williams, eds. *Women and Dramatic Production, 1550–1700*. Pearson. [2000] pp. ix + 228. hb £42.50 ISBN 0 582 31982 X, pb £18.99 ISBN 0 5823 1983 8.

Flinker, Noam. *The Song of Songs in English Renaissance Literature*. B&B. [2000] pp. viii + 173. £40 ISBN 0 8599 1586 7.

Fox, Adam. *Oral and Literate Culture in England, 1500–1700*. Clarendon. [2000] pp. xi + 497. £45 ISBN 0 1982 0512 0.

Gowing, Laura. *Domestic Dangers: Women, Words, and Sex in Early Modern London*. Clarendon. [1998] pp. ix + 301. hb £35 ISBN 0 1982 0517 1, pb £16.99 ISBN 0 1982 0763 8.

Hackett, Helen. *Women and Romance Fiction in the English Renaissance*. CUP. [2000] pp. 248. £37.50 ISBN 0 5216 4145 4.

Hinds, Hilary, ed. *Anna Trapnel: The Cry of a Stone*. MRTS. [2000] pp. li + 123. £24 ISBN 0 8669 8262 0.

Hodgson-Wright, Stephanie, ed. *The Tragedy of Mariam: Elizabeth Cary*. Broadview. [2000] pp. 194. hb £21 ISBN 0 1972 9017 5, pb £8.95 ISBN 1 5511 1043 1.

Hutson, Lorna, ed. *Feminism and Renaissance Studies*. OUP. [1999] pp. ix + 480. hb £47 ISBN 0 1987 8244 6, pb £20 ISBN 0 1987 8243 8.

Keeble, Neil, ed. *Memoirs of the Life of Colonel Hutchinson: Charles I's Puritan Nemesis, Lucy Hutchinson.* Phoenix. [2000] pp. xxii + 399. £9.99 ISBN 1 8421 2108 1.

Kiernan, Michael, ed. *The Oxford Francis Bacon,* xv: *The Essayes or Counsels, Civill and Morall* [1985]. Repr. Clarendon. [2000] pp. cxviii + 339. £65 ISBN 0 1981 8673 8.

Korte, Barbara *et al.,* eds. *Anthologies of British Poetry: Critical Perspectives from Literary and Cultural Studies.* Rodopi. [2000] pp. 355 £47 ISBN 9 0420 1301 X.

Kraye, Jill, and M.W.F. Stone, eds. *Humanism and Early Modern Philosophy.* Routledge. [2000] pp. 288. £55 ISBN 0 4151 8616 1.

Langford, Rachael, and Russell West, eds. *Marginal Voices, Marginal Forms: Diaries in European Literature and History.* Rodopi. [2000] pp. 211. £23 ISBN 9 0420 0437 1.

Mendelson, Sara, and Patricia Crawford. *Women in Early Modern England.* Clarendon. [1998] pp. xviii + 480. hb £25 ISBN 0 1982 0124 9, pb £14.99 ISBN 0 1982 0812 X.

Miller, Naomi J., and Naomi Yavneh, eds. *Maternal Measures: Figuring Caregiving in the Early Modern Period.* Ashgate. [2000] pp. xvi + 374. hb £45 ISBN 0 7546 0031 9, pb £19.95 ISBN 0 7546 0308 3.

Moore, Mary B. *Desiring Voices: Women Sonneteers and Petrarchanism.* SIUP. [2000] pp. xiii + 290. $44.95 ISBN 0 8093 2307 9.

Moore, Rosemary. *The Light in their Consciences: The Early Quakers in Britain, 1646–1666.* PSUP. [2000] pp. xiii + 314. $29.95 ISBN 0 2710 1988 3.

Murph, Roxane C. *The English Civil War through the Restoration in Fiction: An Annotated Bibliography, 1625–1999.* Greenwood. [2000] pp. viii + 349. $85 ISBN 0 3133 1425 X.

Murphy, Andrew, ed. *The Renaissance Text: Theory, Editing, Textuality.* ManUP. [2000] pp. xi + 226. pb £13.99 ISBN 0 7190 5917 8.

Orlin, Lena Cowen. *Material London, ca. 1600.* UPennP. [2000] pp. ix + 393. hb £45.50 ISBN 0 8122 3540 1, pb £19 ISBN 0 8122 1721 7.

Rhodes, Neil, and Jonathan Sawday, eds. *The Renaissance Computer: Knowledge Technology in the First Age of Print.* Routledge. [2000] pp. xi + 212. hb £60 ISBN 0 4152 2063 7, pb £16.99 ISBN 0 4152 2064 5.

Rudrum, Alan, Joseph Black and Holly Faith Nelson, eds. *The* Broadview *Anthology of Seventeenth-Century Verse and Prose.* Broadview. [2000] pp. xxx + 1303. £19.99 ISBN 1 5511 1053 9.

Salzman, Paul, ed. *Early Modern Women's Writing: An Anthology, 1560–1700.* OUP. [2000] pp. xl + 442. £7.99 ISBN 0 1928 3346 4.

Sharpe, Kevin. *Reading Revolution: The Politics of Reading in Early Modern Europe.* YaleUP. [2000] pp. xiv + 358. $40 ISBN 0 3000 8152 9.

Wilcher, Robert. *The Writing of Royalism, 1628–1660.* CUP. [2000] pp. xii + 403. £42.50 ISBN 0 5216 6183 8.

Woods, Susanne, and Margaret P. Hannay, eds. *Teaching Tudor and Stuart Women Writers.* MLA. [2000] pp. x + 433. hb £27.99 ISBN 0 8735 2346 6, pb £15.39 ISBN 0 8735 2347 4.

IX

Milton and Poetry, 1603–1660

MARGARET KEAN, PAUL STANWOOD, PAUL DYCK AND JOAD RAYMOND

This chapter has six sections: 1. General; 2. Milton; 3. Donne; 4. Vaughan; 5. Herbert; 6. Marvell. Sections 1, 2 and 4 are by Margaret Kean; section 3 is by Margaret Kean and Paul Stanwood; section 5 is by Paul Dyck; section 6 is by Joad Raymond.

1. General

In a diverse year, the most notable factor is the growing sophistication in critical considerations of early modern reading practices. A particular interest is shown this year in the nature and role of literary circles and textual communities, but contemporary reading practices are also seen to inform the continuing debate over doctrinal nuances and coded meanings in the poetry of the period and equally to underpin modern editorial practice.

The essential need to identify the editorial procedures and textual apparatus appropriate for each distinct project is well displayed in the four new editions of primary materials for review. Standing tall amongst the group is the latest volume to appear within the Herculean task that is *The Variorum Edition of the Poetry of John Donne*. Under the general editorship of Gary A. Stringer, the editorial intention is 'to facilitate further understanding of Donne's poetry by situating it squarely within the tradition of critical and scholarly discussion that has grown up around it from the poet's own time to the present' (p. xlvi). Volume ii, *The Elegies*, is now available and should take its place on all library shelves. The texts for this volume are seventeen love elegies, 'Sapho to Philaenis', two elegies where attribution is dubious, namely 'Julia' and 'A tale of a Citizen and His Wife' and an appendix containing Constantijn Huygen's 1630 translations into Dutch of two Donne elegies. The volume also presents bibliographical evidence that suggests that we might regard elegies 1–12 as an authorial sequence, and includes helpful tables, showing at a glance the distribution of the elegies in manuscript sources. The scholarship on display here is outstanding, and much careful thought has been put into making the Donne Variorum accessible to students and scholars at all levels. The presentation of Elegy 1, for example, involves a facsimile page to illustrate the hand from one manuscript, a clear typeface for the presentation of the copy-text of the elegy itself, a textual introduction, information on modern editions and a stemma (or manuscript family tree) with supporting arguments tracing the possible dissemination of the elegy. This takes around forty-five pages, and one would not wish to lose a line. In the latter half of the volume, one will also find a full and engrossing section of general commentary on the elegies looking at literary influences and the shifting critical responses to the texts and then a specific set of notes and commentary for each separate poem. It is only in these final notes, with their cross-referencing of the critical analysis of recent secondary critics, that one feels in danger of losing proportion. The history of recent critical thought is of course important, but the reverence shown here may actually date this edition in a way that its textual scholarship will not, and the spirit of fair play has meant that the volume weighs in at over a thousand pages. The production of *The Elegies* has of course been a communal effort, and the modesty of the scholars themselves should be a model to us all. The editors, researchers and indeed Indiana University Press are to be congratulated for having achieved so much, but be warned: it is now time for all who admire this project to get in shape if we aim to be able to lift the *Songs and Sonets* volume when it appears.

Stapleton, ed., *Thomas Heywood's Art of Love: The First Complete English Translation of Ovid's 'Ars Amatoria'*, is slimmer and is based on a printed text, but there were still numerous difficulties in establishing a clean text. The Heywood translation appeared in a pirated edition in the Low Countries (dated by Stapleton between 1609 and 1613) and is riddled with printer's errors. While some of these are adjusted here, in the main the decision has been taken to reproduce the contemporary reading experience. The popularity of this translation of Ovid's *Ars Amatoria* amongst seventeenth-century readers makes this decision all the more appropriate. Now as then it is a lively and urbane read, benefiting here from a well-thought-through commentary that makes good use of contemporary resources and even finds space to include Heywood's alternative translation of the rape of the Sabine women episode in *An Apology for Actors*. This modern edition will greatly assist those who want to encourage students to consider the Ovidian contexts of early modern texts, and will also further more general classroom discussions on translation in the period.

Rudick, ed., *The Poems of Sir Walter Ralegh: A Historical Edition*, was published in 1999. As an editor of Ralegh, Rudick starts from the unenviable position of lacking any authorized collection of the poems either in print or manuscript. The canon for Ralegh was, particularly by the eighteenth-century editors, imaginatively expanded. Rudick sees his remit as the production of 'a materially documented Ralegh canon which, though far from authorially sanctioned in whole, represents in historical conspectus what comprised Ralegh's poetic work for sixteenth- and seventeenth-century readers' (p. xvi). He is sensitive to the materiality of text documents, and prints extant versions as they stand rather than attempting their recension. Once again the textual information on the poems is clear and careful, and on this basis, although a useful commentary is provided, Rudick can be confident in letting these texts speak for themselves.

Also from 1999 is Chandler, ed., *Travels through Stuart Britain: The Adventures of John Taylor, the Water Poet*. This is a collection of fourteen journeys (twelve within Britain, two in Europe), including *A Late Weary, Merry Voyage* [1650] which, we are told, has never been reprinted and exists only in one extant copy held in the Huntington Library. Along with the texts come the editor's route maps and contemporary illustrations. This turns out to be an agreeable volume which holds the attention. It is sensible, in making these texts available, to have chosen a modern format that will appeal not just to those interested in popular culture and early modern travel but to a more general readership.

Much thought has also gone into the selection and presentation of texts for Cummings, ed., *Seventeenth-Century Poetry: An Annotated Anthology*, for the Blackwell series. This is an excellent volume, presenting a balanced choice of poems in a clear typeface. The annotation is intelligent and helpfully guides the student to an understanding of how the poets and poems of this period speak to each other. Texts are situated within their historical context, with works such as Milton's *Comus* or John Denham's *Cooper's Hill* printed in full, but the design also aims to spark literary cross-connections in our minds and to emphasize the literary self-awareness of poets in this period. Lesser-known writers such as William Habington and Charles Cotton widen the scope for the volume, and we hear a number of women's voices, including Lady Mary Wroth, Lucy Hutchinson, Anne Wharton and Martha Moulsworth. Equally important is the attitude taken by Cummings towards the usual suspects. His choices from Dryden's translations and Donne's epistolary poetry are refreshing, while familiar (but by undergraduates little-studied) names such as Edmund Waller are given generous room.

Turning now to the secondary criticism published this year, Michelle O'Callaghan's monograph, *The 'Shepheards Nation': Jacobean Spenserians and Early Stuart Political Culture, 1612–1625*, is a thoroughly researched and critically rewarding reinvestigation of the politics of textual collaboration in the early decades of the seventeenth century. This study of the so-called Jacobean Spenserians (William Browne, Christopher Brooke, George Wither and others) looks in particular at print culture and examines the various ways in which these writers sought to construct an oppositional literary community. O'Callaghan looks at their publication of print miscellanies and the exchange of texts amongst the group in both manuscript and print, but also identifies the 'imagined' community that can be produced through recourse to common literary and political traditions. The motif of pastoral friendship and the satiric potential in positioning this belated generation of shepherd-poets as alienated from court was of course particularly resonant. O'Callaghan is acute in warning of the need to be mindful of the shifting historical situations within which the relations of this group and their publishers are set. It was the production of elegies on the death of Prince Henry in 1612 by Browne and Brooke that seems to have been the starting point for future collaboration in *The Shepheards Pipe* [1614] and *The Shepherds Hunting* [1615]. Here, pastoral participates in the construction of a new (non-courtly) social space for debate; such politicized endeavours are further traced in Browne's *Britannia's Pastorals* and throughout Wither's early career.

Michael Drayton and *Poly-Olbion* are mentioned frequently in O'Callaghan's study. Andrew Hadfield, 'Spenser, Drayton, and the Question of Britain' (*RES* 51[2000] 582–99), looks directly at this poet's response to Spenserian poetics, and particularly Mutability. He reads Drayton's Spenserianism as emphasizing England as a land laid waste, and suggests that, rather than activating a coherent political vision, Drayton's text embodies anxieties and gloom.

Also working on oppositional voices but interested in their dissemination through verse miscellanies is Andrew McRae. His essay, 'The Literary Culture of Early Stuart Libeling' (*MP* 97[2000] 364–92), considers the theoretical implications of collecting and preserving such ephemeral verse within manuscript miscellanies. He wonders whether the tone of topical verse libels is changed by their positioning in such miscellanies, especially if, as seems to be the case, manuscript compilations regularly include (and indeed offer for comparison) work suggestive of contradictory political positions. A more consistent vituperative focus is traced by Laura Lunger Knoppers in two essays this year. 'Noll's Nose or Body Politics in Cromwellian England' (in Boesky and Crane, eds., *Form and Reform in Renaissance England: Essays in Honor of Barbara Kiefer Lewalski*), and '"Sing Old Noll the Brewer": Royalist Satire and Social Inversion, 1648–64' (*SC* 15:i[2000] 32–52), address, with amusing examples, the ongoing royalist invective against Cromwell in both prose and verse. Adam Fox's work in *Oral and Literate Culture in England, 1500–1700* should also be mentioned in the context of popular politics, and particular attention drawn to the chapter on 'Ballads and Libels' (pp. 299–334).

Early modern cultural communities, textual collaboration and rival literary judgements will be an important area of research for many years, but one rich collection of essays has greatly increased our understanding of how such literary communities, both real and imagined, function. From papers presented at the 1998 biennial Renaissance conference at the University of Michigan-Dearborn comes Summers and Pebworth, eds., *Literary Circles and Cultural Communities in Renaissance England*. Within this excellent volume, the following essays will be of particular interest to those working on early modern poetry. John Considine, 'The Invention of the Literary Circle of Sir Thomas Overbury' (pp. 59–74), returns us to areas addressed by O'Callaghan, but he aims to burst the bubble of coterie production as far as the collection of prose and verse published in 1614 by one Lawrence Lisle (with ten later augmented editions) and ascribed to the literary circle of Sir Thomas Overbury is concerned. Identifying the non-courtly verse commissioned or sourced by Lisle for later editions, Considine views this phenomenon as a publicity, or rather patronage, stunt.

Robert C. Evans, '"This art will live": Social and Literary Responses to Ben Jonson's *New Inn*' (pp. 75–91), admits internal rivalries as a necessary factor in the composition of any literary circle. In this light he reconsiders the range of responses to Jonson's *The New Inn*, starting with Jonson's own epilogues and then looking at work from within and without the Jonson circle and also from Jonsonian patrons. This review helps to elucidate how literary judgement was formed in the period, and clearly shows how the literary reputation of Jonson was shaped. Paul A. Parrish, 'Reading Poets Reading Poets: Herbert and Crashaw's Literary Ellipse' (pp. 115–27), gives close attention to the literary community in the environs of Cambridge in the early seventeenth century. He outlines biographical connections between George Herbert, Nicholas Ferrar (and the community at Little Gidding), Joseph Beaumont, Abraham Cowley and Richard Crashaw, and identifies the influence of both Herbert's and Crashaw's poetics upon the work of Beaumont and, to a lesser degree, of Cowley. This is a discerning and highly suggestive argument that will ultimately assist the reintegration of Crashaw's poetry within the contemporary English tradition.

In London in the late 1640s a group of mainly royalist poet-scholars gathered around the wealthy young poet Thomas Stanley. Stella P. Revard, 'Thomas Stanley and "A Register of Friends"' (pp. 148–72), revisits the group as it is identified in Stanley's own later poem, 'A register of friends'. It is an A-list of poets and their kin, men mainly associated with the Middle Temple and linked by shared neoclassical values. Revard points the way to further thought on the nature of nostalgic reunion in Stanley's Restoration composition, and to wider discussion of whether there was a specific role to be played by such a circle in times of political turbulence.

Timothy Raylor, 'Newcastle's Ghosts: Robert Payne, Ben Jonson, and the "Cavendish Circle"' (pp. 92–114), looks at the literary endeavours of the Cavendish family. Collaborative authorship within the family group has been identified, but Raylor raises the stakes by considering the wider household of the 1630s. The manuscript drafts for William Cavendish's elegy for Ben Jonson, 'To Ben Jonson's ghost', reveal revisions in a hand that Raylor identifies as that of Robert Payne, the chaplain at Welbeck. Raylor suggests that the tight-knit intellectual community around Newcastle may well have involved the channelling of individual talents in Newcastle's interests. Manuscript evidence suggests that Payne was involved in polishing a number of literary works intended for the public eye as, later, James Shirley was involved in the revision of Newcastle's *The Country Captain*. Raylor also remarks on Newcastle's penchant for phrases and plots Jonsonian. He posits the view that these borrowings rely less on the existence of a literary circle than on an aristocratic proprietorial presumption.

Elsewhere, but of related interest, is Tanya Caroline Wood's note on William Cavendish and his chosen literary models. In 'Borrowing Ralegh's Mantle: William Cavendish's Address "To the Lady Newcastle, On Her Booke Of Poems"' (*N&Q* 245[2000] 183–5) she explores Cavendish's self-promotion via his interest in, and borrowings from, the work and life of Sir Walter Ralegh.

The *George Herbert Journal* this year published a volume in honour of Edward Tayler (*GHJ* 22[2000]), entitled *The Wit To Know: Essays on English Renaissance Literature for Edward Tayler*. It is edited by Eugene D. Hill and William Kerrigan, and the following contributions deserve mention here. Diana E. Henderson, in 'King and No King: "The Exequy" as an Antebellum Poem' (pp. 57–76) foregrounds the emotional trauma of the mid-seventeenth century by comparing Henry King's elegy for his wife, 'The Exequy', with his elegies for Charles I: in settled times, the formal qualities of elegy shape and channel personal grief, but civil strife and regicide doom King's later elegies to ineffective rage. Jonathan Tuck, in '"Thou fall'st, my tongue": Success and Failure in the Cary–Morison Ode' (pp. 77–94), examines the turns of the ode in a subtle reading that unfolds the poem's complex composition as intended to display the inadequacy of its own expressions of grief.

Jonson's poetry has received much attention this year and, as is the case in Tuck's essay, the best work considers the complex nature of Jonson's own poetic strategies and the heavy demands that he thereby places upon his readership. Stephen B. Dobranksi, 'Jonson's Poetry Lost' (*ELR* 30:i[2000] 77–94), is intrigued by the presentation of the 'Epistle to Elizabeth Countess of Rutland' in the 1616 Folio, which foregrounds the omission of the final eight lines of the poem. He sees Jonson as acutely conscious of variant occasions for text presentation, and (given Elizabeth's status as the only offspring of Sir Philip Sidney) both anxious about literary inheritance and tactfully sympathetic regarding Elizabeth's childlessness. Yumiko Yamada gives over a chapter of his *Ben Jonson and Cervantes: Tilting against Chivalric Romances* (pp. 53–85) to his reading of Jonson's poem on Shakespeare as a mock encomium, influenced by Jonson's knowledge of Cervantes, arguing that contemporary readers attuned to Jonson's ironies would have appreciated the double play of the poem.

Jonson's intertextual play with the idea of social communities is well known. Claude J. Summers, 'Jonson's "Inviting a Friend to Supper" and William Herbert, Earl of Pembroke' (*BJJ* 7[2000] 343–52), finds a solution to the anonymity of the friend in the careful placing of poems in *Epigrammes*, and suggests 101 as a companion text to the following epigram, which is publicly addressed to the earl of Pembroke. 'Liberty and History in Jonson's Invitation to Supper' (*SEL* 40[2000] 103–22) sees Robert Cummings tackle the hide-and-seek qualities of this poem at some length. He recovers a poem constructed in the good company of Martial, Livy and Tacitus that enjoys liberality and endorses frankness while being defensive of friends and jealous in preserving the liberties of civility.

Heather Dubrow, 'Guess Who's Coming to Dinner? Reinterpreting Formalism and the Country House Poem' (*MLQ* 61:i[2000] 59–77), is an upbeat renewal of interest in early modern country house poetry, showing how the form can both encourage radical change and defend conservative social positions. A similar thesis is proposed by Martin Elsky, 'Microhistory and Cultural Geography: Ben Jonson's "To Sir Robert Wroth" and the Absorption of Local Community in the Commonwealth' (*RQ* 53:ii[2000] 500–28). Elsky thinks the social unrest in Surrey in the 1580s, and specifically Wroth's possible encouragement of resistance to the Privy Council scheme to make the River Lea navigable (and thus to bring down the cost of grain in London), stand behind the Jonson poem. Wroth's ultimate decision to side with the centralizing dynamic of monarchical power makes the praise of his role as embodiment of 'country' values particularly ambivalent.

'On My First Sonne' has led critics down a number of avenues this year. Paula Blank, in 'Jonson's Family Values' (in Boesky and Crane, eds., pp. 127–49), moves from the Jonsonian conceit of the poem as offspring to consider the filial positionings adopted by those poets, such as Thomas Randolph, John Taylor and Nicholas Oldisworth, who contributed elegies for *Jonsonus Virbius*. She balances the idea of the dead poet as authorizing the next generation against the reinvention of Jonson by his 'sons'. Hugh Wilson, '"Morbus Satanicus": The Psychomachia of the Deadly Sins in Ben Jonson's "On My First Sonne"' (*BJJ* 7[2000] 325–42), suggests that the poem is intended to be a record of the struggle undergone by Jonson in coming to terms with his loss, and that the structure of the poem reveals an examination of conscience by reference to the seven deadly sins, with pride, wrath and envy particularly prominent. Kathryn R. McPherson, '"I thought my all was given before": Configuring Maternal Grief in Seventeenth-Century England' (*BJJ* 7[2000] 421–45), starts with Jonson's public negotiation of grief in his elegies for his own dead children and in his epigram consolatory for the death of a royal child, before widening her focus to contrast private expressions of maternal grief in the period.

Lillian Schanfield, 'Ben Jonson's "An Execration upon Vulcan": No Joking Matter' (*BJJ* 7[2000] 353–64), considers the psychological effect that the loss of his library must have had on Jonson and suggests that the poem has a cathartic intent, with fire personified as a textual enemy. Lesley Mickel, '"A learned and manly soul": Jonson and his Female Patrons' (*BJJ* 6[2000] 69–87), is conscious of Jonson's ambivalent attitude towards gender across a range of texts, including the *Epigrammes*, but discerns an abiding interest in the potential of female agency.

Two essays note possible Jonsonian allusions. 'The vision of Ben Jonson, on the muse of his friend M Drayton' includes the line 'It was no Dreame! I was awake and saw' (line 11); this is taken to be a clear allusion to Wyatt by Dan R. Davis and Robert C. Evans in 'Jonson Alludes to Wyatt's "They flee from me"' (*N&Q* 245[2000] 104). Matthew Prineas, in '"Yet once more": An Allusion to Hebrews 12.26–27 in Ben Jonson's "On the Famous Voyage"' (*BJJ* 6[2000] 277–87), wonders about the placement of this poem after the *Epigrammes* in 1616, and thinks that Jonson may be intimating (thwarted) ambitions through this allusion, in a fashion akin to John Milton's later (more positive) use of the same scriptural allusion in *Lycidas*.

Other worthy publications include Harp and Stewart, eds., *The Cambridge Companion to Ben Jonson*, which contains two excellent sections for those interested in Jonson's poetry, Ian Donaldson, on 'Jonson's Poetry', and R.V. Young, on 'Ben Jonson and Learning'. In *Ben Jonson Revised* Claude Summers and Ted-Larry Pebworth offer a revised version of their 1979 volume on Jonson for the Twayne English Authors series. They give encouraging space to a sensible introduction to the poetry (pp. 146–223), and aim to stimulate further discussion by nominating favourite poems. Richard Dutton has produced a rewarding volume on *Ben Jonson* for the Longman Critical Reader series. He republishes Stanley Fish's work on Jonson's poetry, 'Author-Readers: Jonson's Community of the Same' (pp. 83–117), flagging up the need to be aware of the modern critic's theoretical position: 'At the heart of Fish's analysis is a view of the inadequacy or unreliability of language itself, which Jonson himself would never have conceded' (p. 83).

The reminder to be conscious of our own critical reading practices is timely. Two significant publications this year return us to the functional but flawed grouping, Metaphysicals. Robert Ellrodt has revised his seminal *Seven Metaphysical Poets: A Structural Study of the Unchanging Self*. This single volume has a new introduction and updated notes but remains constant in foregrounding the importance of the individual authorial voice. Mapping self-awareness, Ellrodt offers a structural network of the ways in which his central poets (John Donne, George Herbert, Henry Vaughan, Richard Crashaw, Andrew Marvell, Edward Herbert and Thomas Traherne) think and feel. Ellrodt's work is clearly hostile to a post-structuralist emphasis on the play of language, emphasizing instead an inner coherence that exists despite shifts in allegiance, mood or historical moment. David Reid's sound introduction to *The Metaphysical Poets* for the Longman Medieval and Renaissance Library series is more attuned to historical contexts. He devotes separate chapters to John Donne, George Herbert, Richard Crashaw, Henry Vaughan, Andrew Marvell and Thomas Traherne, presenting biographical and historical information as well as models for good close-reading skills. Inwardness is the bridging term here, but for Reid comparisons are not odious, and in fact cross-comparison is structured into every chapter (except unfortunately for Vaughan). Reid readily admits that he has had to omit a number of other minor voices from this introductory study. This is a pity, but thankfully breadcrumb trails have been laid to encourage students to consider the wider contexts of seventeenth-century wit.

A much more radical approach to a similar line-up of authors is taken by R.V. Young, *Doctrine and Devotion in 17th-Century Poetry: Studies in Donne, Herbert, Crashaw, and Vaughan*. This is a civil but vigorous revision of the seventeenth-century religious lyric, and makes stimulating reading. The argument is arranged thematically with the presence of grace the core area for analysis. From there Young discusses the quarrels over the sacraments, the practice of piety and the role of biblical poetics in the period. Topically enough, his approach takes us into Europe, connecting the work of Donne and others to Spanish and French devotional poetry. This focus is intended to counter the Anglocentricity of much twentieth-century criticism, but Young also challenges its secular prejudice, considering many commentators to have forgotten the spiritual dimension almost entirely. This is an innovative and scholarly study that is likely to redraw the map for reading the seventeenth-century religious lyric.

A few last contributions need to be mentioned. Scott Nixon with characteristic finesse teases out a tangle of literary attributions in 'Mr Carew and Brawn the Beggar' (*N&Q* 245[2000] 180–1). In Durham Cathedral's dean and chapter library there is a witty epitaph on a hard-drinking individual, entitled 'Mr Carew's Epitaph on Brawn the Irishman but Cornish Beggar'. This has been thought by critics to be by Thomas Carew, but Nixon has found the reference to be to his cousin Richard Carew, who included the example of Brawn the beggar in his *The Survey of Cornwall* [1602]. Clifford Davidson, 'Robert Southwell: Lyric Poetry, the Restoration of Images, and Martyrdom' (*BJJ* 7[2000] 157–86), is another critic who this year is arguing against Protestant poetics. Close readings of Southwell's poetry connect his interest in emblems and the visible to the wider metaphysical tradition. In Womersley, ed., *A Companion to Literature from Milton to Blake*, we find Peter Davidson writing, albeit rather defensively, on 'Robert Herrick, *Hesperides*' (pp. 159–64).

Also of note is the compilation by Roxane C. Murph, *The English Civil War through the Restoration in Fiction: An Annotated Bibliography, 1625–1999*, which includes a section on verse (pp. 27–155).

2. Milton

The most significant publication this year is surely Barbara Kiefer Lewalski, *The Life of John Milton: A Critical Biography*. This authoritative volume combines detailed biographical information with sure critical commentary and will prove an excellent and well-thumbed addition to the Milton shelves. Lewalski is judicious in her narrative, imparting a great deal of scholarly information in an affable fashion. Her expressed preference is to read Milton through his works (of which she considers *De Doctrina Christiana* to be undoubtedly one). This approach admits illuminating close readings of both poetry and prose, but also endorses and indeed actively furthers the myth of Milton. Lewalski relies heavily on Milton's own words to reconstruct the poet's identity and vocation, and as Milton has much to say about his own role this approach has much to recommend it. However, there would have been equally good reasons for striking out beyond the authorial perspective or at least foregrounding its limitations. Nonetheless, overall this critical life is a real achievement, assimilating a great deal of biographical material in a highly readable format. It is as up to date as one could reasonably expect, but it is perhaps good news for us all that there are still questions to be asked. It is clear from this year's work that some aspects of the critical biography of Milton are still being shaped. Reviewed below are exciting new developments in our understanding of the early years in Cambridge, the personal and aesthetic importance of the trip to Italy, the importance of the inherited tradition of visual satire, and the impact of the Irish rebellion upon the development of Milton's political thought.

The monographs for review this year do much to counter the myth of the isolated author, grounding Milton's writing squarely in contemporary cultural contexts and conflicts. John King, *Milton and Religious Controversy: Satire and Polemic in 'Paradise Lost'*, revitalizes Milton as poetic polemicist. Taking issue with the eighteenth-century sublime and the idea of the solitary genius, King investigates the satiric dimension of the epic. His insights reveal an under-appreciated scurrilous dimension to the poem, as Milton engages gleefully in ecclesiastical controversy and anti-Catholic invective. Hell and the Paradise of Fools are shown by King to involve blatant anti-Catholic satire, while the figuration of Sin in particular ridicules the mass. King handles Milton's reading of the Spenserian tradition (especially the May eclogue from *The Shepheardes Calender* and *The Faerie Queene*) as deftly as one would expect, and clearly explains the relevance of the anti-prelatical tracts to the composition of the later books of *Paradise Lost*. This is a Milton who makes bad puns and enjoys invective; one who as it were lives in the dust and heat of contemporary religious controversy in both his prose and poetry. In proving this point, King makes repeated reference to the robust and vituperative satire of the printed pamphlets, and he includes numerous examples from the woodcuts of the period. This emphasis on the broad influence of the visual tradition of Reformed satire is most welcome, and the inclusion of illustrations here will give this volume an expanded readership and make it a highly effective teaching aid.

In *Representing Revolution in Milton and his Contemporaries: Religion, Politics, and Polemics in Radical Puritanism*, David Loewenstein presents us with a cogent and measured exploration of the varied responses by the more radical puritans to the ambiguities of the English Revolution. The first half of the volume looks in turn at John Lilburne and the Levellers, Gerrard Winstanley, Abiezer Coppe and Anne Trapnel, George Fox and early Quakerism and then Andrew Marvell's involvement with the Protectorate. Loewenstein devotes the second half of his monograph to in-depth discussions of texts by Milton, focusing particularly on the argument of *The Tenure of Kings and Magistrates*, the dramatization of seditious behaviour in the figure of Satan in *Paradise Lost*, and the contemporary implications for Restoration nonconformist readers of *Paradise Regained* and *Samson Agonistes*. Loewenstein is careful not to reduce poetry to a single political agenda and he gives full weight to Milton's acute ambivalences, but he nevertheless sees Milton as politically alert throughout his career, from his first responses to the Irish rebellion of 1641 to the active heroism of the late poetry of 1671.

Kristen Poole, *Radical Religion from Shakespeare to Milton: Figures of Nonconformity in Early Modern England*, also locates Milton within a context of satirical controversy. Her work on the figure of the puritan in the early modern period shows us how Milton might himself have felt the bite of satire. It is interesting to see his contemporary reputation as an advocate of divorce placed against the contemporary pamphlet satires on the Adamites, and highly rewarding to view Milton's later depiction of prelapsarian existence and naked truth against this background. Poole is an excellent guide to Milton's involvement in the pamphlet wars and, like King, she links Milton's anti-prelatical stance to the Spenserian tradition and also makes good use of woodcut illustrations.

Desiree Hellegers, *Handmaid to Divinity: Natural Philosophy, Poetry, and Gender in Seventeenth-Century England*, studies the diverse interface between literature and science in the early modern period. Her monograph ranges widely and shrewdly from Frances Bacon and John Donne to Anne Finch, and includes a chapter on Book VIII of *Paradise Lost* as a critique on royalist natural philosophy. Nick Davis, *Stories of Chaos: Reason and its Displacement in Early Modern English Narrative*, is equally fascinated by cosmological narratives. He has compiled an unusual range of texts for analysis, looking at the response to Plato's *Timaeus* in the systems of reasoning on display in *Gawain and the Green Knight*, *The Faerie Queene*, *King Lear* and *Paradise Lost*. Davis sees the reworking of Plato's *Timaeus* in Milton's epic as a means of allowing the adoption of a radical conception of chaos, inclusive of random movement and therefore creative disorder. There is much to recommend this somewhat quirky thesis, not least the exploration of how gender issues are employed within the narrative as a means of approaching other conceptual problems. Also working on the politics of gender, Katherine Eggert, *Showing Like a Queen: Female Authority and Literary Experiment in Spenser, Shakespeare, and Milton*, has a chapter on 'Milton's Queenly Paradise' (pp. 169–200) where she extends the memory of Elizabeth's rule to Milton's arguments on monarchy and on divorce.

Other critics this year have chosen to involve Milton in thematic patternings that move beyond the early modern period. Harold Fisch, *The Biblical Presence in Shakespeare, Milton and Blake: A Comparative Study*, is a highly individualist discourse rather than the overview that one might expect from the title. His two Milton chapters consider hermeneutic methods, discussing, first, the function of midrash (defined as the ongoing interpretative dialogue within the covenant community) in *Samson Agonistes* and, secondly, the role of Raphael as messenger in *Paradise Lost*. Raphael is equated with the poet as one aware of the needs of the audience to whom he has been sent. These topics appear at first to be localized interests, but the breadth of background knowledge and the quality of the critical argument are impressive, and the wider thesis on Milton counters an exclusive Christian message through its exploration of the Hebraic context of *Samson Agonistes* and the importance of the Exodus story to *Paradise Lost*.

Marc Berley, *After the Heavenly Tune: English Poetry and the Aspiration to Song*, begins with Platonic theory and goes on to investigate the aspiration by poets such as Milton, John Keats and Wallace Stevens to achieve the condition of music. Berley identifies an early dedication on Milton's part to cosmic harmonies and speculative poetry. This interest in the music of the spheres Berley associates with Milton's study of arithmetic and geometry, but unfortunately the grand sweep of his argument does not leave enough space for a full development of the Miltonic readings. Lee Morrissey is more successful. His monograph, *From the Temple to the Castle: An Architectural History of British Literature, 1660–1760*, concentrates mainly on the architectural interests of English authors in the eighteenth century but includes a chapter on Milton's knowledge of Vitruvius. In an unusual and insightful discussion, Morrissey pays attention to the construction of *Paradise Lost* as a whole, seeing the shift from a ten- to a twelve-book epic—with its consequent resiting of the invocations—in terms of proportionate ratios.

John Dolan, *Poetic Occasion from Milton to Wordsworth*, uses Milton's *Lycidas* as a starting point for his argument that there is a shift within the English tradition from formal epideictic poetics towards the Romantic employment of pathos. This is an important thesis, but the Miltonist will feel that undue constraints have been placed upon the reading of *Lycidas* and the volume of elegies for Edward King as a whole, not least by the limitation of the discussion to poems in English. One wonders what Dolan makes of *Epitaphium Damonis*, or indeed of John P. Rumrich's essay on 'The Erotic Milton', reviewed below.

Pruitt and Durham, eds., *Living Texts: Interpreting Milton*, contains sixteen essays on the poet. Michael Lieb starts us off with 'Adam's Story: Testimony and Transition in *Paradise Lost*' (pp. 21–47). Lieb argues that Adam's voice in Book VIII of the epic gives a new authority and immediacy to the Genesis account, with Adam's autobiography revealing a movement towards higher levels of consciousness and expressing our first father's inherent poetic abilities. This is sensible criticism supported by helpful comments on the Hebrew etymologies that underpin Milton's depiction of the relationship of Adam and Eve. J. Martin Evans, 'Afterthoughts on Adam's Story' (pp. 48–56), takes up where Lieb breaks off and considers Adam's relation of his experience of passion. Evans suggests a link here to Philo of Alexandria's first-century ad commentary on Genesis. He considers that Milton has inserted Philo's allegorical reading of the creation of Eve into Adam's literal narrative of his experiences in order to challenge the reader and foreground the conflicting arguments at this juncture.

Meanwhile Anna K. Nardo's 'John Milton, Object of the Erotic Gaze?' (pp. 57–79) is interested in the Victorians' 'cult of Milton', and the ways in which their appropriation of Milton as a lover can involve role reversal. An influential anecdote of the time tells of a lady who viewed the young Milton asleep under a tree in Cambridge and left him verses in Italian. As Nardo shows, this turns Milton into the object of the gaze, which in turn may be linked to the vogue for painting the blind bard. This is a fascinating and amusing essay that ranges with ease between well-known texts such as George Eliot's *Middlemarch* and more obscure ones such as Major Vetch's play *Milton at Rome* [1851] and Anne Manning's *The Maiden and Married Life of Mary Powell, afterwards Mistress Milton* [1855]. It is particularly revealing on the divided approach to Miltonic standards presented in *Middlemarch*.

Susan McDonald, '"Wide was the wound": Cesarean Section and the Birth of Eve' (pp. 80–98), takes the birth of Eve in Book VIII to be caesarian section and an attempt by Milton to indicate a form of natural birth without pain or fearful associations. Lynne Greenberg, 'A Preliminary Study of Informed Consent and Free Will in the Garden of Eden: John Milton's Social Contract' (pp. 99–117), interrogates Milton's views and Eve's position to expose inequalities of experience and communication in Eden. Arguing that Eve's position is hampered by insufficient knowledge, she would surely win damages for her as a victim of forced participation rather than free agreement in marital relations in any court of law. Cheryl H. Fresch, '"Aside the devil turned | for envy": The Evil Eye in *Paradise Lost*, Book 4' (pp. 118–30), links Satan in Eden to the folkloric tradition of the evil eye, partly by reference to Francis Bacon 'On Envy' [1625], where 'Scripture calleth envy an evil eye'.

Two essays offer rewarding new analogues for the epic. Rachael Falco, 'Satan and Servius: Milton's Use of the Helen Episode (*Aeneid*, 2.567–88)' (pp. 131–43), points out the influence of Renaissance commentaries on Virgil. She sees Milton responding to Servius as source for Aeneas' contemplation of personal vengeance on Helen. Aeneas' reasoning in defence of revenge is tenuous, and Falco argues that Milton intends us to recognize that this fallible logic has been transferred to Satan in *Paradise Lost*. Claude N. Stulting, Jr., '*Theosis* and *Paideia* in the Writings of Gregory of Nyssa and the Prelapsarian Books of Milton's *Paradise Lost*' (pp. 144–61), considers Gregory of Nyssa's view of the ongoing process of attaining union with God as highly pertinent for a reading of Milton's prelapsarian existence, with Raphael's teaching about plants and digestion revealing a holistic educative process that is at one with Gregory of Nyssa's teachings.

Peggy Samuels, 'Riding the Hebrew Word Web' (pp. 162–77), offers a delightful, clear exploration of the multivalency of the Hebrew language. She identifies Milton as a sensitive wordsmith, attuned to the resonances of Hebraic phrasing, which Samuels compares to a web 'in which any one meaning of a word stands in tension with other uses of the same word' (p. 167). Her examples of Miltonic translation relate to the erotic of the edenic relationship and are exhilaratingly rich. Sarah R. Morrison, 'When Worlds Collide: The Central Naturalistic Narrative and the Allegorical Dimension to *Paradise Lost*' (pp. 178–97), proposes that the allegorical and naturalistic threads of narration must clash in *Paradise Lost* in order for Milton to affirm a mythic verity without needing to admit it as literal truth.

John Leonard, 'Milton, Lucretius, and "the Void Profound of Unessential Night"' (pp. 198–217), debates with Rumrich over the nature of Chaos in Milton's metaphysics. Leonard takes Lucretius to be a source for Milton on Chaos and on Night, based his argument in part on their shared terror of the infinite void. John Rumrich replies in 'Of Chaos and Nightingales' (pp. 218–27), pointing out that night is experienced in Heaven and suggesting that 'darkness is the price to be paid for nightingales' (p. 226).

On the vexed question of the authorship of *De Doctrina Christiana*, we have William B. Hunter, 'The Confounded Confusion of Chaos' (pp. 228–36), arguing that contrasting views on sexuality and angelic digestion are held in *Paradise Lost* and *De Doctrina Christiana*, while Paul R. Sellin, '"If not Milton, who did write the *DDC*?" The Amyraldian Connection' (pp. 237–63), thinks the document previously known as *De Doctrina Christiana* 'a disproportionate collection of associated ideas' (p. 253) rather than a coherent thesis. Kenneth Borris, 'Milton's Heterodoxy of the Incarnation and Subjectivity in *De Doctrina Christiana* and *Paradise Lost*' (pp. 264–82), on the other hand, is happy to link Milton's Christology in *Paradise Lost* and *Paradise Regained* to the doctrinal thesis, as each asserts the centrality of freedom of choice for the human person. Finally in this collection, Hong Won Suh, 'Belial, Popery, and True Religion: Milton's *Of True Religion* and Antipapist Sentiment' (pp. 283–302), views *Of True Religion* as a critique of the Test Act of March 1673 and argues that this prose text is in large part intended as an attack on the underlying popish nature of Anglicanism.

Boesky and Crane, eds., *Form and Reform in Renaissance England*, includes contributions by a number of top-notch Miltonists. Cedric C. Brown, 'A King James Bible, Protestant Nationalism and Boy Milton', carefully identifies the cultural considerations behind the annotation of Old Testament passages within the family bible in which a list of family births and deaths is entered in Milton's hand. Brown reads Milton's earliest poetry against these Jacobean annotations to suggest a pervading ideology of nationalistic Protestant fervour. Steven Zwicker, 'Passions and Occasions: Milton, Marvell, and the Politics of Reading c.1649', takes *Eikon Basilike*, Milton's response, and Marvell's Horatian Ode as a snapshot comparison of the multifaceted politics of reading at this most crucial of historical moments. Jason P. Rosenblatt persuasively reclaims *Samson Agonistes* as a Hebraic text in 'Samson's Sacrifice' by foregrounding the appropriateness of the phoenix imagery to the Nazarite's vow of purification and the requirement to sacrifice a bird as burnt offering after contact with a dead body (Numbers 6). John N. King, 'Milton's Sin and Death: A Rewriting of Spenser's Den of Error', shows how Spenser's Cave of Error lies behind the grotesque figuration of Sin in *Paradise Lost* as a parody of the Church of Rome.

King mines this same rich ground of Reformation satire in his essay, 'Milton's Cave of Error: A Rewriting of Spenserian Satire' (in Cheney and Silberman, eds., *Worldmaking Spenser: Explorations in the Early Modern Age*), where he reads Milton's Sin against Book I of *The Faerie Queene* and the anti-mass satires from the reign of Edward VI. Also in *Worldmaking Spenser*, we find John Watkins, '"And yet the end was not": Apocalyptic Deferral and Spenser's Literary Afterlife', including Milton's Nativity Ode in his consideration of responses to Spenser's work in the early seventeenth century.

Two other multi-authored volumes including important work on Milton this year must be mentioned. In Hammond and Hopkins, eds., *John Dryden: Tercentenary Essays*, Nicholas Von Maltzahn writes on 'Dryden's Milton and the Theatre of Imagination' (pp. 32–56). This is a highly nuanced reading of Dryden's *The State of Innocence* and its response to Miltonic poetics and an important contribution to our understanding of competing Restoration aesthetics. Anne K. Nardo, 'A Space for Academic Recreation: Milton's Proposal in *The Reason of Church-Government*' (in Summers and Pebworth, eds., pp. 128–47), meanwhile sees Milton's invitations to take part in the Italian academies as influential on his developing arguments for social reform and moral debate found in the prose works of the 1640s, such as *The Reason of Church-Government*. Nardo argues that, although Milton proves unable to force political change in England, he will continue to express in his sonnets, and later in his epic, the important social role of cultured leisure time and intellectual colloquy. Indeed, even in *Paradise Regained*, where the Son argues against academe, she finds that the angels refresh him with vocalized communion as well as food. Nardo's identification of the importance of the trip to Italy in the development of Milton's social and civic ideals is best placed against the excellent essay from 1999 by John P. Rumrich, 'The Erotic Milton' (*TSLL* 41[1999] 128–41), which combines the importance of Milton's trip to Italy with an awareness of the intimacy of his Platonic friendship with Charles Diodati. The correspondence between the two is sensitively handled and shown to be significant in tracing the development of Milton's ethical stance. Rumrich takes the death of Diodati to be of crucial importance to Milton's developing sense of himself as a poet of epic theodicy. Also in *TSLL* in the same year is an assured defence of Milton as author of *De Doctrina Christiana* by Stephen M. Fallon, 'Milton's Arminianism and the Authorship of *De Doctrina Christiana*' (*TSLL* 41[1999] 103–27).

Two volumes of *Milton Studies* were published this year. Michael Lieb joined
Albert C. Labriola to edit an impressive volume dedicated to 'John Milton: The
Writer in his Works'. Labriola introduces the volume with an upbeat overview on
the state of biographical criticism, 'Introduction: Postmodern Biographical Studies
of John Milton' (*MiltonS* 38[2000] 1–9). Joseph Wittreich, '"Reading" Milton: The
Death (and Survival) of the Author' (*MiltonS* 38[2000] 10–46), offers an eloquent
and wide-ranging essay on the performing self in Milton's texts, culminating in an
important reading of *Samson Agonistes* as a mental *agon* rather than a spiritual
victory. J. Martin Evans, 'The Birth of the Author: Milton's Poetic Self-
Construction' (*MiltonS* 38[2000] 47–65), traces a gradual emergence of an assertive
and self-aware poetic presence in Milton's work, building from *Poems 1645* to a
climactic narrative voice in *Paradise Regained*. Kathleen M. Swaim, '"Myself a
True Poem": Early Milton and the (Re)formation of the Subject' (*MiltonS* 38[2000]
66–95), looks at a series of Miltonic lyrics from the late 1620s and early 1630s to
identify the process by which Milton identifies himself as a poet. She finds the
young poet engaged in the twin activities of writing and reading, and presents
Lycidas as a significant production in that it constitutes itself as a poem of reflection.
John Leonard, '"Thus they relate, erring": Milton's Inaccurate Allusions' (*MiltonS*
38[2000] 96–121), is on something of a busman's holiday, sharing with us some of
the gems of erudition and puzzles of Miltonic ambivalence that one suspects he has
long pondered in his role as editor. His proposed methodology for testing real and
alleged errors in Milton's allusions is sensible and his love of the crux infectious.
Stella P. Revard, 'Milton and the Progress of the Epic Proemium' (*MiltonS* 38[2000]
122–40), traces Milton's manipulation of the conventions of heroic poetry back
beyond Virgil to Hesiod and Pindar. She argues strongly that the Miltonic projection
of the *vates* is not self-aggrandizement but a necessary vindication of an atypical
epic subject. Barbara K. Lewalski, '*Paradise Lost* and Milton's Politics' (*MiltonS*
38[2000] 141–68), outlines in some detail the case for reading Milton as a radical
teacher, intending to educate his readers in the ways of liberty. Richard Strier,
'Milton's Fetters, or, Why Eden is Better than Heaven' (*MiltonS* 38[2000] 169–97),
sees the attempt at theodicy as the tragic flaw in Milton's epic and the presentation
of edenic human perfection as its triumphant success. Michael Lieb, '"A thousand
fore-skins": Circumcision, Violence, and Selfhood in Milton' (*MiltonS* 38[2000]
198–219), ruminates skilfully on the covenant of circumcision and the violence
against the flesh to be found in much of Milton's religious writing. *Samson
Agonistes* is of course the poem where he finds the violent implications of
circumcision to be spelt out most bluntly. Stephen M. Fallon, 'The Spur of Self-
Concernment: Milton in his Divorce Tracts' (*MiltonS* 38[2000] 220–42), completes
the impressive list of contributors to this volume with an alert discussion of the
splintering of self-representation in the divorce tracts.

The other *Milton Studies* volume this year is more eclectic. Kate Gartner Frost,
'No Marchioness but a Queen: Milton's Epitaph for Jane Paulet' (*MiltonS* 39[2000]
1–25), discovers a movement within the poem from passivity to agency. Her interest
in formal criticism helps explode existing misogynistic responses to this epitaph, but
equally stimulating is the suggestion that Milton's interest in Jane Paulet may have
been sparked by the rumour that, at the time of her death, she had been considering
a conversion from Catholicism to Protestantism. Joseph G. Mayer, 'Doubleness in
Milton's Late Sonnets' (*MiltonS* 39[2000] 26–49), finds a recurrent technique of

balanced oppositions in Milton's later sonnets: a dialectic that needs to be affirmed at the closure of each sonnet. Bruce Boehrer, 'Milton and the Reasoning of Animals: Variations on a Theme by Plutarch' (*MiltonS* 39[2000] 50–73), is an esoteric but intriguing piece considering Milton's awareness of two minor dialogues in Plutarch's *Moralia* and the approach they take to the Circe myth and the issue of rhetorical sophistry. Phillip J. Donnelly, 'The *Teloi* of Genres: *Paradise Lost* and *De Doctrina Christiana*' (*MiltonS* 39[2000] 74–100), starts from a position broadly supportive of W.B. Hunter's apostasy. This leads him to ask wider questions as to how critics might usefully compare information packaged in such generically distinct manners as a doctrinal thesis and an epic poem. His hypothesis is that Milton may have been involved in revising the manuscript of *De Doctrina Christiana* but that such terse logical methodology proved inhospitable to him in comparison to the flexibility of a narrative frame. John C. Ulreich, '"Substantially express'd": Milton's Doctrine of the Incarnation' (*MiltonS* 39[2000] 101–28), presents a very useful discussion of Miltonic theology involving both *De Doctrina Christiana* and *Paradise Lost*. He views the poetry as embodied theory and gives primacy to the mystery of the Incarnation throughout Milton's justification of the ways of God to men. *Paradise Regained*, under this reading, provides us with the Son as perfect exemplar of a process of Incarnation based on voluntary self-discovery that is now potentially available to all mankind through God's grace. Paul Cefalu, 'Moral Pragmatism in the Theology of Milton and his Contemporaries, or *Habitus* Historicized' (*MiltonS* 39[2000] 129–66), also highlights the importance of voluntary action in Milton's thought, but his theme is the endorsement of habitual action as a constituent of ethical self-management even in Eden. Robert Thomas Fallon, '*A Second Defence*: Milton's Critique of Cromwell?' (*MiltonS* 39[2000] 167–83), thinks this prose text more straightforward in its praise of Cromwell and its acceptance of the Protectorate than many modern critics would wish. Thomas M. Gorman, 'The Reach of Human Sense: Surplus and Absence in *Samson Agonistes*' (*MiltonS* 39[2000] 184–215), offers a stimulating and theoretically aware response to the leitmotif of blindness and the compositional value of absence in *Samson Agonistes*.

Milton Quarterly 34 opens with a fine essay by John Creaser, 'Prosodic Style and Conceptions of Liberty in Milton and Marvell' (*MiltonQ* 34[2000] 1–13). This is a subtle comparison of the prosody and politics of these two major poets which manages to do justice to Marvell's versification and conscious symmetry while vindicating Milton's choice of freedom of movement, and it makes an impressive addition to the study of both poets. John K. Hale, 'Milton's Greek, 1644–1645: Two Notes' (*MiltonQ* 34[2000] 13–16), looks first at the title page to *Areopagitica* and then at the Greek phrasing for the poem accompanying the portrait for *Poems 1645*. Ann Torday Gulden, 'Is Art "Nice"? Art and Artifice at the Outset of Temptation in *Paradise Lost*' (*MiltonQ* 34[2000] 17–24), is interested in the iconography of Book IX of *Paradise Lost*, particularly the colours and flowers associated with Eve on the threshold of her temptation. Stephen B. Dobranski, 'Burghley's Emblem and the Heart of Milton's *Pro Populo Anglicano*' (*MiltonQ* 34[2000] 33–48), engages once again with the knotty problems raised by the collaborative nature of early modern publishing. The publisher Dugard had royalist sympathies, and Dobranski wonders whether it is coincidence that an ornamental headpiece used in Milton's *First Defence* turns out to be the emblem for William Cecil, Lord Burghley. The placement of such an identifiably royalist visual subtext might be said to undercut the tract's defence of republicanism. Dobranski teases out the complications of reading both word and image here with tenacity, but maintains a pleasing lightness of touch.

Hermine J. Van Nuis, 'Animated Eve Confronting her Animus: A Jungian Approach to the Division of Labor Debate in *Paradise Lost*' (*MiltonQ* 34[2000] 48–56), argues that Eve must be allowed to separate from Adam in Book IX of *Paradise Lost* as only then can Adam locate his inner Eve. Neil Forsyth, 'At the Sign of the Dove and Serpent' (*MiltonQ* 34[2000] 57–65), works through examples of the proverbial opposition of dove and serpent in the Bible and within Milton's later English poetry. Kent R. Lehnhof, '"Nor turnd I weene": *Paradise Lost* and Pre-Lapsarian Sexuality' (*MiltonQ* 34[2000] 67–83), warns that we should not take prelapsarian sexual congress so much for granted and suggests that genital sexuality is an unnecessary barrier to our understanding of the union of the edenic couple. John D. Schaeffer, 'Metonymies We Read By: Rhetoric, Truth and the Eucharist in Milton's *Areopagitica*' (*MiltonQ* 34[2000] 84–92), sees eucharistic imagery as underpinning the theoretical argument of the tract, creating both its body of truth and a consensus of readers. Burton Raffel, '"On the Death of a Fair Infant": Date and Subject' (*MiltonQ* 34[2000] 93–7), is not convinced by Edward Phillips's information identifying Anne Phillips, Milton's niece, as the subject of this elegy, and so suggests an alternative date for the composition of the poem.

William B. Hunter, '*De Doctrina Christiana*: Nunc Quo Vadis?' (*MiltonQ* 34[2000] 97–101), spells out in a restrained and sensible fashion what he takes to be the pitfalls for critics who presume to employ *De Doctrina Christiana* as a gloss for Milton's poetry. Angelica Duran, 'The Last Stages of Education: *Paradise Regained* and *Samson Agonistes*' (*MiltonQ* 34[2000] 102–16), proposes that we read *Paradise Regained* as the text where Milton's educational theories are put into practice: the Son's vocation, she argues, is pedagogy. In addition, she suggestively reads the companion piece, *Samson Agonistes*, as a text alive to the new scientific hypotheses by Isaac Burrow and others concerning light and optics. Sherry Lutz Zivley, 'The Thirty-Three Days of *Paradise Lost*' (*MiltonQ* 34[2000] 116–26), calculates the internal chronology of the epic to add up to four days (measured in heavenly time) and thirty-three days (measured in human time, with each day measured from one evening to the next). This leads neatly to Beverley Sherry, '*Paradise Lost* "Made Vocal"' (*MiltonQ* 34[2000] 127–8), a description of a marathon reading of *Paradise Lost* at the University of Otago, New Zealand—it seems to have taken slightly less time to read of God's creation than it took to make it.

The *George Herbert Journal* this year published a volume, edited by Eugene D. Hill and William Kerrigan, in honour of Edward Tayler (*GHJ* 22[2000]). Also noted above in section 1, it contains three accomplished Milton essays. Mary Oates O'Reilly 'A New Song: Singing Space in Milton's Nativity Ode' (pp. 95–116), is interested in Milton's imaginative creation of a sacred space and the aesthetic and moral problems that he admits thereby. In a subtle and full reading of the Ode, O'Reilly extends the theological doctrine of *kenosis* to become the 'constitutive metaphor' (p. 98) for the poem as a whole. Eugene D. Hill, 'Milton Borrows a Word: Or, Cherubim in the Mist' (pp. 117–28), delves into the term 'meteorous' (*PL* XII.629) and the connotations of its use in the epic's penultimate simile of the rising mists. For Hill, this Greek formation resonates against previous well-known usages in Aristophanes, Plato and Luke's Gospel, and he argues that Milton places this ponderous term as a gateway to the new postlapsarian hermeneutical struggle. William Kerrigan, 'On Scorn', includes Milton as one of his main examples in his vigorous investigation of the nature of literary scorn.

Milton's late poetry attracted a good deal of attention this year. It was the subject of the Chatterton Lecture at the British Academy for the year 2000. In 'Waiting for God: Milton's poems of 1671'(*PBA* 111[2000] 157–77), Margaret Kean argued for the continuities in phrasing and argument between Milton's *Masque* and the two late poems, *Paradise Regained* and *Samson Agonistes*, and for an abiding, nonconformist, Miltonic commitment to dramaturgical techniques. Her interest in the dramatic Milton is complemented by Matthew Steggle, '"The tragical Part": Milton's *Masque* and Euripides' (*CML* 20:i[2000] 18–36), which presents a measured but nonetheless challenging reading of the *Masque* as a Euripidean text. Denis Kezar, 'Samson's Death by Theater and Milton's Art of Dying' (*ELH* 66:ii[2000] 295–336), reads *Samson Agonistes* as a form of revelatory drama, with Samson as a dying man, an actor and object of interpretative interest within the *ars moriendi* tradition. Kezar compares Milton's text to Thomas Becon's *The Sick Man's Salve* [1561], a Calvinist closet drama which teaches Protestants to interpret the semiotics of election at the moment of death. However, Kezar's point is that any such interpretative moves are denied in *Samson Agonistes*.

John K. Hale, 'Milton Plays the Fool: The Christ's College Salting, 1628' (*CML* 20:iii[2000] 51–70), significantly improves our awareness of Milton as interested in performance from an early age. Building on the remaining archival evidence documenting the tradition of saltings (witty undergraduate entertainments) at the Cambridge colleges in the late 1620s, Hale shows in detail how Milton's *Prolusion VI* and 'At a Vacation Exercise' can be read as public performances, brimming with sardonic puns and Latinate eloquence, in ways that suggest an easy rapport with both actors and audience. Hale concludes that we should see these student texts as Milton's most energetic praise of folly.

Joseph Lyle, 'Architecture and Idolatry in *Paradise Lost*' (*SEL* 40[2000] 139–55), offers a stimulating discussion of architectural space and liminal points in Milton's epic. He notes the recurrent polluting influence of idolatry upon the Judaic temple in the Old Testament and suggests that a parallel anxiety over idolatrous abuse exercises Milton in his epic construction. Denise Gigante, 'Milton's Aesthetics of Eating' (*Diacritics* 30:ii[2000] 88–112), makes the connection between Milton's near-obsession with the physiology of eating, his theory of matter, and the cultural identification of taste as an aesthetic value. Despite some surprising omissions from her discussion (i.e. the *Masque* and the Son's use of the term 'taste' as an aesthetic value in Book IV of *Paradise Regained*), this remains a most thought-provoking piece.

Ronald Levao, '"Among Unequals what Society": *Paradise Lost* and the Forms of Intimacy' (*MLQ* 61:i[2000] 79–107), provides the clearest exploration this year of the disruption of doctrinal stability that pervade the epic's depiction of human relations. Jeffrey S. Shoulson, 'The Embrace of the Fig Tree: Sexuality and Creativity in Midrash and in Milton' (*ELH* 67[2000] 873–903), finds the dichotomies expressed in Hebraic midrash texts, such as *Genesis Rabbah*, in their discussions of the human body, sexuality and the imagination comparable to those found in Milton's epic. He thinks Milton may have used such Hebraic sources as a corrective balance to the classical tradition and as a means of providing a positive, and redemptive, reading of human sexuality. Katherine O. Acheson, 'On Authorship, Sexuality and the Psychology of Privation in Milton's *Paradise Lost*' (*ELH* 67[2000] 905–24), packs a great deal into one argument as she considers how the poetics of desire in Milton's epic disturbs the orthodox authorial position of self-subordination.

Authorial positions also interest David Gray, '"Lawfull Charms" and "Wars of Truth": Voice and Power in Writings by John Milton and George Wither' (*PLL* 36:ii[2000] 177–97). Gray links Milton and George Wither as writers of defences against censorship, but also suggests that both authors see poetry as a potent weapon and protection in the wars of truth. Jack Lynch, meanwhile, examines the ambivalent positioning of Milton in the eighteenth century in his essay, 'Betwixt Two Ages Cast: Milton, Johnson, and the English Renaissance' (*JHI* 61:iii[2000] 397–413), showing how Milton is read ahistorically as the bard rather than as a polemical writer, and Gregory Machacek, '*Paradise Lost*, Christian Epic, and the Familiar Sublime' (*Cithara* 40:i[2000] 37–49), reminds us that sound is essential for the poet and proposes that, in taking control of the epic tradition, it is less important for Milton to create scenes that recall the *Aeneid* than it is for him to produce phrasing that echoes Homer.

A number of diverse essays consider the influence of Milton's work on other writers. John S. Tanner, 'The Psychology of Temptation in *Perelandra* and *Paradise Lost*: What Lewis Learned from Milton' (*Renascence* 52:ii[2000] 131–41), compares C.S. Lewis's science fiction novel *Perelandra* to its source in *Paradise Lost* in an argument that raises intriguing questions as to how best to construct a psychological narrative depicting the primary temptation of an innocent mind. Sanford Budick, 'Kant's Miltonic Test of Talent: The Presence of "When I consider" in the *Groundwork of the Metaphysics of Morals*' (*MLQ* 61:iii[2000] 481–518), presents a detailed case to endorse his claims that Kant's *Groundwork of the Metaphysics of Morals* is indebted for its argument to Milton's famous sonnet on his blindness. C.B. McCully, 'Writing under the influence: Milton and Wordsworth, Mind and Metre' (*L&L* 9:iii[2000] 195–214), suggests a metrical debt in Wordsworth's prosody to the Miltonic pentameter.

A welcome redress to Milton the bogeyman is taking place in Victorian and modernist circles. Lisa Low, '"Listen and save": Woolf's Allusion to *Comus* in her Revolutionary First Novel' (in Greene, ed., *Virginia Woolf: Reading the Renaissance*), bravely rethinks Woolf's attitude towards Miltonic texts, arguing that in *The Voyage Out* Woolf's references to Milton's *Masque* have been misunderstood by the critics. The underlying allusion to threatened rape gives a darker aspect to the modern novel's euphemistic kiss but, while it is too late for the heroine, Rachel Vinrace, to do anything other than die, the female author has adopted the *Masque* as a more self-assertive paradigm. Elsewhere, Kathleen Vejvoda, 'The Fruit of Charity: *Comus* and Christina Rossetti's *Goblin Market*' (*VP* 38:iv[2000] 555–78), suggests that Rossetti's poem should be read alongside Milton's *Masque* as much as against his epic. There are biographical links to secure Rossetti's interest in the masque, as well as structural and thematic conjunctions, such as *Goblin Market*'s focus on charity and feminine restorative powers.

Finally this year, in Womersley, ed., *A Companion to Literature from Milton to Blake*, David Hopkins looks at Milton's use of Virgil, Homer and Ovid in 'Classical Translation and Imitation' (pp. 76–93), and Martin Dzelzainis reconsiders our liberal preconceptions in 'John Milton, *Areopagitica*' (pp. 151–8). David Norton, *A History of the English Bible as Literature*, has a short section (pp. 174–83) on Milton's construction of an epic on Christian subject matter, where he argues that, while Milton must produce a style grand enough for the occasion, he also admits the power inherent in the phrasing of the King James Bible. Our round-up this year is completed by Benoit-Dusausoy and Fontaine, eds., *History of European Literature*, from Routledge. This turns out to be rather conservative in its view of Milton (A. Yearling, 'Milton', pp. 289–93), but at least he made the cut and is here placed in the company of Van Den Vondel and Comenius.

3. Donne

Turning now to secondary criticism on John Donne, we find an immediate embarrassment of riches. In *Handmaid to Divinity* Desiree Hellegers draws out the parallels between the *Anniversaries* and Bacon's treatise, *The Advancement of Learning* [1605]. She argues that Donne is aware of the Baconian proposals but is resistant to them. This is an illuminating connection which for Hellegers is only part of a wider study of natural philosophy in the period. The link between Donne and Bacon is an innovative proposal that seems utterly just. This same connection occurred independently to Catherine Gimelli Martin, who takes more time to tease out the connections. 'The Advancement of Learning and the Decay of the World: A New Reading of Donne's First Anniversary' (*JDJ* 19[2000] 163–203) is a brilliantly argued essay, and a major contribution to Donne studies. Martin urges in her careful argument that Donne is answering Sir Francis Bacon's highly optimistic *Advancement*, and she raises objections to this thesis only to answer them all. One is left admiring her dexterity.

Volume 19 of the *John Donne Journal* contains fifteen essays, mostly occasioned by the visit to Loseley Park near Guildford of a number of Donne scholars. Occurring in May 2000, this visit to the estate of the More–Molyneux family, descendants of Sir George More, the father of John Donne's wife Anne, provided considerable inspiration for several outstanding contributions to Donne studies. The volume begins, however, rather weakly, though perhaps predictably, with Paul J. Voss on 'Sir Thomas More in the Year of Donne's Birth' (*JDJ* 19[2000] 4–17). Voss discusses More's portrait in the 1573 edition of the *Dialogue of Comfort* by John Fowler, and suggests its iconographical importance to the portrait of the young Donne (at the age of 18) preceding the 1635 (second) edition of his *Poems*. Maureen Sabine continues this investigation of portraiture in her essay on Donne's 'romantic' Lothian portrait, in her essay '*Illumina Tenebras Nostras Domina*: Donne at Evensong' (*JDJ* 19[2000] 19–44), a highly speculative study that attempts to interpret this portrait in terms of the Anglican evening office. Maria J. Pando Canteli writes of 'The Poetics of Space in Donne's Love Poetry' (*JDJ* 19[2000] 45–57), urging the obvious point that Donne prefers tiny, enclosed spaces (epitomized by 'The Flea'), but anxiously connects them to transcendence and permanence. This essay seems a prelude to the next and one of the most intriguing essays in the volume, 'Courting Anne More' by Ilona Bell (*JDJ* 19[2000] 59–86). Bell gives a close and ingenious reading of 'The Flea' in which she convincingly demonstrates that the poem *may* be read as fitting the circumstances of Donne's courtship of Anne More and his clandestine love affair with her.

With his usual good sense and practical rigour, John T. Shawcross writes cogently of two of Donne's best known Holy Sonnets, 'Death be not proud' and 'Batter my heart, three person'd God' (*JDJ* 19[2000] 87–99). While not dismissing their personal and passionate appeal, he reminds readers that these sonnets are 'literary works that should be evaluated as literary works with an audience beyond the writer only, an audience to be edified' (p. 90). In the following, also historically oriented, essay by Helen B. Brooks, '"When I would not I change in vowes, and in devotione": Donne's "Vexations" and the Ignatian Meditative Model' (*JDJ* 19[2000] 101–37), we learn that Donne's Holy Sonnets reflect the Ignatian meditation scheme; but they do so in terms that reflect 'the conflicted impulses that inhere in the Ignatian meditative form itself' (p. 102). Many of these sonnets in fact are troubled in their quest for certainty because the Ignatian paradigm itself is so indeterminate. Ignatius himself spent twenty-five years writing and revising the *Exercises*, and they do not define the movement of the Holy Sonnets as clearly as some readers of Donne may have supposed.

One conventional ordering of the Holy Sonnets, which follows Helen Gardner's edition of *The Divine Poems* [1952], places 'As due by many titles' in first place. Kate Gartner Frost and William J. Scheick test the validity of beginning the sequence in this way in their 'Signing at Cross Purpose: Resignation in Donne's "Holy Sonnet I"' (*JDJ* 19[2000] 139–61), and they conclude that it is properly situated because of its baptismal theme, and also because it seems to refer to 'a private ceremony celebrating Donne's entry into the Church of England, even, perhaps, into Holy Orders' (p. 158).

One also admires another provocative essay on 'Contexts and Strategies: Donne's Elegy on Prince Henry' by Ted-Larry Pebworth and Claude J. Summers (*JDJ* 19[2000] 205–22). Pebworth and Summers describe briefly the eleven funeral poems of Donne, pausing especially on the Prince Henry Elegy [1613], indicating its importance in this sequence of patronage-driven 'obsequies'. Indeed, a point heretofore unnoticed is the fact that Sir George More, Donne's father-in-law, had recently been appointed Treasurer and Receiver-General to Henry. Donne was naturally eager to compose an elegy for the deceased prince if only to curry favour with More, Henry's keen supporter, with whom Donne had had such a strained relationship since his elopement with More's daughter.

R.V. Young's 'Donne and Bellarmine' (*JDJ* 19[2000] 223–34) is a slight piece, though important in demonstrating that Donne might sometimes agree with the great Roman Catholic controversialist, especially over such Calvinist doctrines as double predestinarian theology. Donne evidently consulted Bellarmine's commentary on the Psalms, for example, and found considerable inspiration and guidance in it. Another fine historical ('contextualizing') essay is Mary Arshagouni Papazian's 'John Donne and the Thirty Years' War' (*JDJ* 19[2000] 235–66). Donne's interest in foreign affairs went back to 1597 in the expedition with Essex against Cadiz and the Azores, and he continued his travels in 1612, going with Sir Robert Drury to Amiens in connection with the prospective marriage between Elizabeth, King James's daughter, and Frederick, the Elector Palatine, and again in 1619, when he accompanied Doncaster to Germany. Papazian quotes from Donne's letters of the 1620s, which show his direct interest in the events that led to the exile of Frederick and Elizabeth, and also from two of his sermons at Lincoln's Inn, preached in 1620, and another sermon of 1622 at Paul's Cross on the *Directions for Preachers*. Moreover, Papazian believes that Donne's *Lamentations of Jeremy, for the most part after Tremelius*, was occasioned by the fall of Heidelberg in September 1622. Donne's decision to use Tremelius, a notable Protestant, may confirm that 'for Donne and many of his compatriots, their worst fears of Protestant captivity had been realized' (p. 259).

A similar historical survey reminds us of Donne's relationship to the Virginia Company. In '"The Gallery to the New World": Donne, Herbert, and Ferrar on the Virginia Project' (*JDJ* 19[2000] 267–97), Florence Sandler reviews the crucial events of 1622, culminating in Donne's November sermon to the company. This had been a devastating year, which had seen the Jamestown massacre and the depletion of the company's hopes. But in his sermon Donne urged the providential nature of the enterprise and the humanity of the natives. He is sensitive to the disasters, but nevertheless hopeful, his sermon marking 'the last moment when the whole colonial enterprise might have been held together under the aegis of the national Church' (p. 286).

Ernest W. Sullivan II briefly explores certain of the textual problems facing the editors of the Donne Variorum, with 4,000 manuscript copies of Donne's poems in over 250 surviving manuscripts, in '*Poems, by J.D.*: Donne's Corpus and his Bawdy, Too' (*JDJ* 19[2000] 299–309). He demonstrates the folly of relying on the first printed edition of 1633, the text that has formed the basis of most later editions of Donne's poetry. This text is incomplete, riddled with errors, and even bowdlerized. Dayton Haskin is also concerned with Donne's text, and particularly with its transmission. In his 'Coleridge's Marginalia on the Seventeenth-Century Divines and Perusal of Our Elder Writers' (*JDJ* 19[2000] 311–37), Haskin studies Coleridge's annotations to Donne's works. Coleridge, Haskin concludes, saw in Donne a fellow spirit, for he recognized that Donne's interpretative practices agreed with his own. 'Donne credited his "promiscuous" auditory with the intelligence and willingness to discern the implications of their belief, and he preached to people whose responsibility for their own faith he respected' (p. 328).

This well-shaped and useful issue of the *John Donne Journal* is a kind of commemorative volume for the Loseley Park pilgrims, but it is also a book marked mostly by excellent scholarship. The final essay, by Mary Alexander, the archivist of the Guildford Museum, on 'Pyrford, Pyrford Place, and Queen Elizabeth's Summerhouse' (*JDJ* 19[2000] 339–60), provides an amusing coda; it has ten rather grainy illustrations (pp. 354–60). Almost all of the original buildings that Donne would have known are gone, but he *might* have known the summerhouse, and one may be pleased to think of his once having sat there.

This thought has certainly pleased Dennis Flynn. In 'Donne, the Man, the Legend' (in Hill and Kerrigan, eds., pp. 41–56) Flynn unites archival evidence and anecdote to make the pleasing suggestion that in 1602/3, when John Donne and his wife were living on Francis Wooley's estate at Pyrford Place in Surrey, they may have stayed in the 'Queen Elizabeth' summerhouse, which may indeed have been built for an earlier visit by Queen Elizabeth.

One of the most important books on John Donne in many years appeared in 1999. Jeffrey Johnson's *The Theology of John Donne* is the best discussion that we so far possess of Donne's theological thought. Johnson has made a careful study of all 160 extant sermons and of other prose and poetic works. He writes with authority and moderation, concentrating on those issues most important in defining Donne's theology. He correctly shows that its first principle hangs upon the Trinity, and the communal nature of the Trinity illuminates everything Donne has to say in his sermons. Johnson is equally effective in his analysis of Donne's understanding of the Atonement and the doctrine of grace. Donne, we are led clearly to understand, is careful to define both prevenient and subsequent grace, and he urges that justification comes through both faith and works, effectually through the Word and Sacraments. The Donne that emerges from Johnson's portrayal is deeply aware of the most vexing theological concerns of his time—he may be a moderate Calvinist, but in a selective way, for he centres his theology, Johnson writes, 'on the interrelational unity of the godhead that seeks to enfold humankind in its divine harmony' (p. 123). Johnson addresses his subject with economy, clarity, and wisdom. One hopes that he will continue to study Donne in the still wider context of the English Reformation. Jeffrey Johnson's and R.V. Young's monographs are both published in the Studies in Renaissance Literature series from the publishers Boydell & Brewer, and the accolades should be pouring in for this new, stimulating forum.

Beyond the theological into theory, Elizabeth M.A. Hodgson, in *Gender and the Sacred Self in John Donne*, offers a sensitive examination of the figurations of gender within spiritual self-definition in Donne's poetry and sermons. Hodgson concentrates on the idea of the soul as a gendered function, scrutinizing Donne's metaphors for baptism, marriage and death. Also considering the role of the body in Donne is Douglas Trevor, 'John Donne and Scholarly Melancholy' (*SEL* 40[2000] 81–102), which should carry a health warning on excessive study as he weighs the meditative inwardness of the spiritual life with the self-preoccupations of depression. Melancholia has both religious and scholarly dimensions, and Trevor does well to tease out Donne's morbid fascinations and rigorous self-examinations. Linking the sufferings of the body to anxieties over representation and reputation, Elena Levy-Navarro, 'John Donne's Fear of Rumours in the *Devotions Upon Emergent Occasions* and the Death of John King' (*N&Q* 245[2000] 481–3), suggests that Donne feared misrepresentation after his death, particularly following the controversy over the supposed deathbed conversion to Catholicism of his friend and patron John King, bishop of London. The *Devotions*, it is suggested, may in part have been written to prevent any questioning of his loyalty to the Church of England.

Finally returning to Donne's ironies and rivalries, M. Thomas Hester, '"Over Reconing" the "Undertones": A Preface to "Some Elegies" by John Donne' (*RenP* [2000] 137–53), considers the subtleties of Donne as a reader of the Ovidian love elegy and suggests political motivations for his adoption of the form. In the closing couplet of Elegy XIX Hester finds witty theological controversy, and he thinks Donne's Ovidian elegies are intended to counter the position adopted by Sidney and Spenser in their poetics. R.V. Young, 'Love, Poetry, and John Donne in the Love Poetry of John Donne' (*Renascence* 52:iv[2000] 251–73), is also interested in Donne's reading of Ovid and other more contemporary European poets. He too identifies a mockery of Spenser's aggressive Protestant Neoplatonism, this time in Donne's 'The Dreame'. M. Thomas Hester, '"Like a spyed Spie": Donne's Baiting of Marlowe' (pp. 24–43), finds that the manuscript evidence so far available suggests that Donne's poem did not circulate with Marlowe's 'Passionate Shepheard to his love' lyric and Ralegh's response. Hester reads Donne's poem as a conscious rejection of fashionable coterie taste and hears distinctly Catholic connotations in the angling imagery. As a witty riposte to Marlowe, 'The Baite' gains public favour with an Inns of Court audience, but within this multivocal text may also lie a more private address to a recusant readership.

4. Vaughan

The essays on Vaughan to be reviewed come mainly from two volumes of *Scintilla*, but we might start with Donald R. Dickson, 'Thomas Vaughan and the Iatrochemical Revolution' (*SC* 15:i[2000] 18–31). He draws attention to the unpublished notebooks held in the British Library which show Vaughan to have been comparatively rigorous in his scientific research and closely involved in experimental science, particularly the study of salts. This revision of Vaughan's scientific reputation may eventually alter our overall view of the poet considerably. In '"Feathering some slower hours": Henry Vaughan's Verse Translations' (*Scintilla* 4[2000] 142–61), Robert Wilcher has produced a meticulous and absorbing essay on the importance of translation for Vaughan's intellectual development. He looks particularly at *Olor Iscanus* and the translations of Ovid, Boethius and Casimir Sarbiewski. Verbal patterns, reiteration and rhyme in Vaughan's verse are the subject of Glyn Pursglove, '"Number makes a schism": Number and Unity in Vaughan' (*Scintilla* 3[1999] 163–81). This is a wide-ranging, discursive piece that sees Vaughan's choice of poetic techniques as underpinned by a dynamic of return. Peter W. Thomas, 'The Language of Light: Henry Vaughan and the Puritans' (*Scintilla* 3[1999] 9–29), discovers a sharp critical edge in Vaughan's writing, particularly *Silex Scintillans*, and sees a sustained response in these poems to topical concerns.

Alan Rudrum, '"For then the Earth shall be all Paradise": Milton, Vaughan and the Neo-Calvinists on the Ecology of the Hereafter' (*Scintilla* 4[2000] 39–52), shows how the perennial debate on man's husbandry of the natural world was a part of the theological controversies in mid-seventeenth-century England. The archivist of Jesus College, Oxford, Brigid Allen, has examined the Buttery Books from December 1637 onward in search of the Vaughan brothers. Her findings are published in 'The Vaughans at Jesus College, Oxford, 1638–48' (*Scintilla* 4[2000] 68–78), but the patient research has found more questions than answers.

Michael Srigley, 'Ritual Entries: Some Approaches to Henry Vaughan's "Silex Scintillans"' (*Scintilla* 3[1999] 43–59), charts the movement in *Silex Scintillans* towards meditative stillness. Richard Birt, '"Sweet infancy!" The Affinities between the Vaughans and Thomas Traherne' (*Scintilla* 3[1999] 80–90), finds the convergence of imagery in Vaughan and Traherne intriguing. Roland Mathias, 'The Making of a Royalist' (*Scintilla* 3[1999] 107–20), wonders why Henry Vaughan was such a staunch royalist from such an early stage, and in 'Reasons, Reasons' (*Scintilla* 4[2000] 109–24) he considers the Breconshire context for Vaughan's royalism. Belinda Humfrey, 'Vaughan and Vegetables' (*Scintilla* 3[1999] 137–49), takes a green approach to the imagery of *Silex Scintillans*.

5. Herbert

This year Ron Cooley continued his insightful historical work on *The Country Parson* in his tightly argued article in the *George Herbert Journal* entitled 'John Davenant, *The Country Parson*, and Herbert's Calvinist Conformity' (*GHJ* 23[2000] 1–13). Cooley adds to our understanding of Herbert's pastoral manual by not reading it simply as a record of Herbert's theological and practical positions, but rather as itself a complex move within the tricky context of Caroline ecclesiastical politics. Cooley takes up particularly Herbert's instructions regarding posture at communion, which have typically been read as sympathetic to the Puritan preference for sitting, but ultimately favouring the Laudian instruction to kneel. Instead, Cooley points us towards Herbert's historical moment and the likelihood that his instructions negotiate between a fading Calvinist conformity and the rising Arminian one. Cooley grounds his historicizing in the career of Herbert's bishop, John Davenant, who, from the time of the Hampton Court conference to his service under Archbishop Laud, negotiated a path of Calvinist conformity, combining individualist and nationalist theologies. Cooley finds evidence of this negotiation in Herbert not so much in his comments on sitting or kneeling, but in his final admonition, 'Contentiousness in a feast of Charity is more scandall then any posture'. Noting that this applies equally to all readers, Arminian or Calvinist, Cooley aptly describes it as 'a triumph of strategic ambiguity' (p. 10). Herbert avoids taking sides, except the side of a charitably broad conformity.

Greg Miller, in his article 'Scribal and Print Publication: The Case of George Herbert's English Poems' (*GHJ* 23[2000] 14–34), takes on the matter of Herbert's probable publishing intentions for his verse and with this, the question of which early text of *The Temple*—the early and incomplete Williams manuscript (*W*), the Bodleian manuscript (*B*), or the first print edition [1633]—carries authority. Miller lands firmly on the side of *W*, arguing that it was likely an instance of scribal publication and not, as has often been assumed, produced only for Herbert's private use. Rather, Miller argues, it was likely produced for the community at Little Gidding, which we know to have been part of Herbert's literary and spiritual circle. Miller notes correctly that *W* is the only extant manuscript or edition that Herbert actually saw and even corrected. His argument, though, proceeds awkwardly and somewhat inconclusively. It hangs heavily on both *W* as a circulated text and a possible third manuscript, one that was authorial, that came after *W*, and that was used to produce both *B* and 1633, asking us to imagine that this third manuscript was more like *W* than it was like the others. While Miller sensitively notes some characteristic Herbertian touches in *W* not present in the later texts, his argument depends too much on too many historical speculations.

Phillip Donnelly, in 'The Triune Heart of *The Temple*' (*GHJ* 23[2000] 35–54), also takes on a much-discussed aspect of Herbert's poetry, but with more success. He re-examines the sequential arrangement of *The Temple*, focusing on a group of three poems which, he argues, act as the book's 'heart': 'Sion', 'Home', and 'The British Church'. Donnelly considers the meaning of the placement of these poems at the centre of the book, but avoids looking to numerology to determine meaning. Rather, he explores the correspondences between *The Temple*'s thematic unities and its numerical arrangement. In doing so, he draws upon two outside influences on Herbert's poetics: the thematic rhythms and modes of the Psalms, and the number theory and Trinitarian psychology of Augustine. Donnelly argues that the three poems interact with each other, together reflecting 'the Church's ability to embody within time an image of the Trinity' (p. 36). The three poems, respectively, enact the psalmic modes of remembrance of God's actions, honesty before God, and response to God, as well as Augustine's Trinitarian analogy of memory, will, and understanding. In doing so, they suggest a way in which temporal suffering becomes the means of sanctification. If 'Sion' reminds us of what God has done in establishing himself in our hearts, and 'Home' indicates a transparent desire for ultimate union with God, then 'The British Church' tells the reader how to live in the meantime, the three together incarnating 'that ultimate triune fellowship in which form and content are an inseparable unity of divine love' (p. 49).

In one of the finest articles this year on Herbert, John Savoie's 'The Word Within: Predicating the Presence of God in George Herbert's *Temple*' (*GHJ* 23[2000] 55–79), charts the complex relationships between Christ, Scripture, poet, and poetry in Herbert's work. Savoie argues that the acrostic poem 'Coloss. 3.3' models the interplay between these four. The poem demonstrates both the poet hidden within Christ and Scripture hidden within the poem. These two 'hidings', though, suggest many corollaries, bound together by the central connection that, if Scripture dwells in *The Temple* and Christ dwells in Scripture, then Christ is present in *The Temple*, through the mediation of Scripture—'the Word within the word within the word' (p. 57). The most crucial relationship, that of Christ dwelling in Scripture, is powerfully established near the beginning of 'The Church', in 'The Sacrifice', a poem that has recently been overlooked by critics, but which Savoie effectively reinvigorates. 'The Sacrifice' is the only poem in *The Temple* in which Christ is the sole speaker. Savoie demonstrates how Herbert gives Christ voice by densely interweaving scriptural references; Herbert's art is in not speaking in his own voice, but in using Scripture to embody Christ, and, in turn, having Christ 'confer unity to the multitudinous Scriptures' (p. 71). Savoie further argues that Herbert's God 'speaks as if he really were God' (p. 75) even when he is not quoting Scripture. Such is the case with 'Redemption's' '*Your suit is granted*', which echoes the pattern of 'Your sins are forgiven' and 'It is finished'. Thus, Savoie concludes, Herbert's verse speaks Scripture even when it does not borrow directly. Herbert's intimacy with Christ through Scripture and poetry is summarized in the words of 'The Quidditie', which states outright the union of poetry, Scripture, poet, and Christ, in that poetry, 'is that which while I use | I am with thee'.

Jonathan Nauman, in 'Toward a Herbertian Poetic: Vaughan's Rigorism and "The Publisher to the Reader" of *Olor Iscanus*' (*GHJ* 23[2000] 80–104), addresses again Henry Vaughan's probable reasons for distancing himself from the publication of his collection of secular verse, *Olor Iscanus*. Nauman discusses the once commonly held assumption that Vaughan's motives were based on his personal conversion to a Herbertian rigorism, one that denied the value of secular verse. He then carefully examines what became the standard twentieth-century revision, the 'anti-conversionist' dismissal of a Herbertian motivation, particularly that of E.L. Marilla. Nauman argues that Marilla and others erred, particularly in their arguments that Vaughan himself wished to see his secular verse in print but needed to distance himself from it because of its anti-Puritan content (Vaughan, his brother Thomas, and his publisher all openly expressed much more contentious ideas than those of *Olor Iscanus*). In this well-argued piece, Nauman suggests instead a scenario in which Vaughan had already committed himself to publishing the volume, but was growing in his commitment to a Herbertian poetic. *Olor Iscanus* becomes, then, the result of a series of negotiations between poet, brother, and publisher.

Paul McCann's article, 'Herbert's "A True Hymn"' (*Expl* 59:i[2000] 9–11), does not account for itself nearly as well as Nauman's. It argues that the poem expresses Herbert's consistent ideology, that the form of worship 'is less important than whether that worship interferes with the sovereignty of the king' (p. 9). McCann leaves unexplained his assumption that the line 'My joy, my life, my crown!' expresses 'Herbert's first loyalty ... to the established monarchical order' (p. 10), failing altogether to consider that the anti-royalist reader (such as there were during Herbert's lifetime) may think that the only true king is the one in heaven.

The final piece reviewed here is an intriguing essay by Robert Whalen, '"How shall I measure out thy bloud?" or, "Weening is not measure": TACT, Herbert, and Sacramental Devotion in the Electronic Temple' (*EMLS* 5:iii[2000] 1–37). Whalen examines what he describes as a binary in *The Temple* between the sacramental (defined by him as all public, ritualistic, and ecclesiastical forms of religious expression) and the devotional (personal spiritual reflection) in order to determine the 'identity and *locus* of spiritual authority' (p. 3) for Herbert. He then takes an unusual turn by using TACT (Text Analysis Computing Tools) to statistically analyse *The Temple*, arguing that one can approach the text as 'a repository of discrete words' (p. 22) bearing statistically measurable relationships to each other, and that analysis of this repository can expand and qualify one's reading of the poetry. Whalen proceeds to group words by association with sacrament and devotion, and to measure their proximity to each other, both within and across groups. While he accomplishes some fine readings of particular poems, his initial binary seems reductive, especially given recent work on the Elizabethan and Jacobean 'middle way' that suggests that Calvinism and ceremonialism were not mutually exclusive. This reduction is only pushed further by the statistical work, which begins with the same binary, but which seems incapable of discovering anything like the nuance that is apparent to the literary reader. Whalen is likely correct in asserting that poetry, in its interrelationships, has a statistical aspect, but if so, one wonders whether the poetic imagination itself wields far more powerful analytical tools than those devised for computers.

6. Marvell

Though Marvell is presently undergoing a critical renascence, there was this year only a handful of articles on his works. Stanley Fish's 'Marvell and the Art of Disappearance' (in Clark, ed., *Revenge of the Aesthetic: The Place of Literature in Theory Today*, pp. 25–44) appears in a collection of essays inspired by the work of Murray Krieger. Fish identifies in a survey of Marvell's poetry a withdrawal from and resistance to referential meaning, a desire to disentangle himself from a world that man consistently messes up; Fish aligns this with his own new-critical and anti-historicist polemics. Emphasizing instead the poet's worldliness, Annabel Patterson's 'Lady State's First Two Sittings: Marvell's Satiric Canon' (*SEL* 40[2000] 395–411) argues emphatically (and persuasively) for Marvell's authorship of the second and third *Advices to a Painter*. Her evidence includes a case for the authority of the Popple manuscript, and detailed analysis of echoes between the satires and Marvell's other poetry. In 'A Restoration Suetonius: A New Marvell Text?' (*MLQ* 61:iii[2000] 463–80) Patterson demonstrates that Marvell silently used the 1672 anonymous English translation of Suetonius' *History of the Twelve Caesars* when writing *The Rehearsal Transpros'd: The Second Part* [1673], a version that linguistically adapted the work to a Restoration context. The most economical explanation for the proximity of the two texts, and the manner in which Marvell adapts the English Suetonius, Patterson contends, is that Marvell was himself the translator. Comparisons between the texts offers insight—particularly if this new attribution is accepted—into Marvell's tendency to filch when writing. Also expanding our understanding both of the prose and the historical context, Beth Lynch, in '*Mr. Smirke* and "Mr. Filth": A Bibliographic Case Study in Nonconformist Printing', (*Library* 1[2000] 46–71), explores the polemical context and printing history of Marvell's pamphlet, *Mr Smirk; Or, the Divine in Mode* [1676]. Detailed bibliographic analysis of copies demonstrates that its printing was shared in order to avoid the searches of Roger L'Estrange (Mr Filth).

There follows a series of shorter pieces on the lyrics. In 'Sacred Violence in Marvell's "Horatian Ode"' (*Renascence* 52[1999] 75–88) Thad Bower uses the theories of René Girard to explore the sacred violence of the 'Horatian Ode', and the myth-making power of violence in the civil war. He suggests that the dramatic centre of the poem combines a Machiavellian and a ritualistic account of the king's execution; Marvell retains a critical distance from the ritual sacrifice, and therein lies the unity and ambivalence of the poem. Takashi Yoshinaka argues, in '"Perhaps" in Marvell's "Bermudas"' (*SC* 13[1998] 22–35), that the lyric is writ through with both scepticism towards and sympathy for the faith of the 'Puritan rowers'; the argument is not implausible, though conducted using oddly prejudicial categories. And a note by C.B. Hardman, '"Row Well Ye Mariners"' (*RES* 51[2000] 80–2), proposes that the rowers in Marvell's 'Bermudas' are singing to a recognizable tune, based on a metrical psalm, and that it can be credibly identified as the traditional 'Row Well Ye Mariners' (to which he supplies the musical notation).

Books Reviewed

Benoit-Dusausoy, Annick, and Guy Fontaine, eds. *History of European Literature*, trans. Michael Wooff. Routledge. [2000] pp xxviii + 731. £80 ISBN 0 4151 7334 5.

Berley, Marc. *After the Heavenly Tune: English Poetry and the Aspiration to Song*. Duquesne. [2000] pp. xii + 418. $59 ISBN 0 8207 0316 8.

Boesky, Amy, and Mary Thomas Crane, eds. *Form and Reform in Renaissance England: Essays in Honor of Barbara Kiefer Lewalski*. AUP. [2000] pp. 370. $49.50 ISBN 0 8741 3691 1.

Chandler, John, ed. *Travels through Stuart Britain: The Adventures of John Taylor, the Water Poet.* Sutton. [1999] pp. xii + 308. £25 ISBN 0 7509 1944 2.

Cheney, Patrick, and Lauren Silberman, eds. *Worldmaking Spenser: Explorations in the Early Modern Age.* UPKen. [2000] pp. viii + 288. $39.95 ISBN 0 8131 2126 4.

Clark, Michael P., ed. *Revenge of the Aesthetic: The Place of Literature in Theory Today.* UCalP. [2000] pp. viii + 251. hb £35 ISBN 0 5202 2002 1, pb £13.95 ISBN 0 5202 2004 8.

Cummings, Robert, ed. *Seventeenth-Century Poetry: An Annotated Anthology.* Blackwell. [2000] pp. xxxi + 586. £16.99 ISBN 0 6312 1066 0.

Davis, Nick. *Stories of Chaos: Reason and its Displacement in Early Modern English Narrative.* Ashgate. [1999] pp. x + 195. £45 ISBN 1 8401 4649 4.

Dolan, John. *Poetic Occasion from Milton to Wordsworth.* Macmillan. [2000] pp. vii + 219. £47.50 ISBN 0 3122 2094 4.

Dutton, Richard, ed. *Ben Jonson.* Pearson. [2000] pp. vi + 223. £13.99 ISBN 0 5822 1506 4.

Eggert, Katherine. *Showing Like a Queen: Female Authority and Literary Experiment in Spenser, Shakespeare, and Milton.* UPennP. [2000] pp. ix + 289. £31.50 ISBN 0 8122 3532 0.

Ellrodt, Robert. *Seven Metaphysical Poets: A Structural Study of the Unchanging Self.* OUP. [2000] pp. xi + 369. £50 ISBN 0 1981 1738 8.

Fisch, Harold. *The Biblical Presence in Shakespeare, Milton and Blake: A Comparative Study.* Clarendon. [1999] pp. xiv + 331. £52.50 ISBN 0 1981 8489 1.

Fox, Adam. *Oral and Literate Culture in England, 1500–1700.* Clarendon. [2000] pp. xii + 497. £45 ISBN 0 1982 0512 0.

Greene, Sally, ed. *Virginia Woolf: Reading the Renaissance.* OhioUP. [1999] pp. xi + 295. $44.95 ISBN 0 8214 1269 8.

Hammond, Paul, and David Hopkins, eds. *John Dryden: Tercentenary Essays.* Clarendon. [2000] pp. xiii + 415. £70 ISBN 0 1981 8644 4.

Harp, Richard, and Stanley Stewart, eds. *The Cambridge Companion to Ben Jonson.* CUP. [2000] pp. xvi + 218. hb £40 ISBN 0 5216 4113 6, pb £14.95 ISBN 0 5216 4678 2.

Hellegers, Desiree. *Handmaid to Divinity: Natural Philosophy, Poetry, and Gender in Seventeenth-Century England.* UOklaP. [2000] pp. xiv + 218. $34.95 ISBN 0 8061 3183 7.

Hill, Eugene D., and William Kerrigan, eds. *The Wit to Know: Essays on English Renaissance Literature for Edward Tayler.* Fairfield. [2000] pp. xi + 170. $25 ISBN 1 8881 1253 0.

Hodgson, Elizabeth M.A. *Gender and the Sacred Self in John Donne.* AUP. [1999] pp. 223. $38.50 ISBN 0 8741 3674 1.

Johnson, Jeffrey. *The Theology of John Donne.* Brewer. [1999] pp. xiii + 162. $75 ISBN 0 8599 1544 1.

King, John. *Milton and Religious Controversy: Satire and Polemic in 'Paradise Lost'.* CUP. [2000] pp. xx + 227. £42.50 ISBN 0 5217 7198 6.

Lewalski, Barbara K. *The Life of John Milton: A Critical Biography.* Blackwell. [2000] pp. xvii + 777. £25 ISBN 0 6311 7665 9.

Loewenstein, David. *Representing Revolution in Milton and his Contemporaries: Religion, Politics, and Polemics in Radical Puritanism*. CUP. [2000] pp. xiii + 413. £40 ISBN 0 5217 7032 7.

Morrissey, Lee. *From the Temple to the Castle: An Architectural History of British Literature, 1660–1760*. UPVirginia. [1999] pp. xiii + 178. $35 ISBN 0 8139 1899 5.

Murph, Roxane C. *The English Civil War through the Restoration in Fiction: An Annotated Bibliography, 1625–1999*. Greenwood. [2000] pp. viii + 349. $85 ISBN 0 3133 1425 X.

Norton, David. *A History of the English Bible as Literature*. CUP. [2000] pp. xii + 484. £55 ISBN 0 5217 7140 4.

O'Callaghan, Michelle. *The 'Shepheards Nation': Jacobean Spenserians and Early Stuart Political Culture, 1612–1625*. Clarendon. [2000] pp. viii + 272. £40 ISBN 0 1981 8638 X.

Poole, Kristen. *Radical Religion from Shakespeare to Milton: Figures of Nonconformity in Early Modern England*. CUP. [2000] pp. xiii + 272. £40. ISBN 0 5216 4104 7.

Pruitt, Kristin A., and Charles W. Durham, eds. *Living Texts: Interpreting Milton*. AUP. [2000] pp. 312. $49.50 ISBN 1 5759 1042 X.

Reid, David. *The Metaphysical Poets*. Pearson. [2000] pp. x + 293. £19.99 ISBN 0 5822 9834 2.

Rudick, Michael, ed. *The Poems of Sir Walter Ralegh: A Historical Edition*. ASU. [1999] pp. lxxviii + 239. £22 ISBN 0 8669 8251 5.

Stapleton, M.L., ed. *Thomas Heywood's Art of Love: The First Complete English Translation of Ovid's 'Ars Amatoria'*. UMichP. [2000] pp. xi + 173. £28 ISBN 0 4721 0913 8.

Stringer, Gary A., Paul A. Parrish *et al.*, eds. *The Variorum Edition of the Poetry of John Donne*, vol. ii: *The Elegies*. IndUP. [2000] pp. xcix + 1046. $69.95 ISBN 0 2533 3376 8.

Summers, Claude, and Ted-Larry Pebworth. *Ben Jonson Revised*. Twayne. [1999] pp. xix + 293. $33 ISBN 0 8057 7062 3.

Summers, Claude, and Ted-Larry Pebworth, eds. *Literary Circles and Cultural Communities in Renaissance England*. UMissP. [2000] pp. xi + 243. £33.95 ISBN 0 8262 1317 0.

Womersley, David, ed. *A Companion to Literature from Milton to Blake*. Blackwell. [2000] pp. xxi + 609. £80 ISBN 0 6312 1285 X.

Yamada, Yumiko. *Ben Jonson and Cervantes: Tilting against Chivalric Romances*. Maruzen. [2000] pp. xiv + 200. $75 ISBN 4 6210 4721 3.

Young, R.V. *Doctrine and Devotion in 17th-Century Poetry: Studies in Donne, Herbert, Crashaw, and Vaughan*. Brewer. [2000] pp. x + 241. £45 ISBN 0 8599 1569 7.

X

The Later Seventeenth Century

BRIAN RIDGERS, JAMES OGDEN AND JOHN VAN HOOK

This chapter has three sections: 1. General; 2. Dryden; 3. Late Marvell. Section 1 is by Brian Ridgers, section 2 is by James Ogden, and section 3 is by John Van Hook.

1. General

The Cambridge Companion to English Restoration Theatre, edited and introduced by Deborah Fisk Payne, offers a comprehensive summary of the field as well as forging new debate. The book contains ten essays that range from an analysis of the genres of farce, tragedy and tragicomedy to discussions of the social and political context of the drama. Alongside this are essays such as Michael Cordner's 'Playwright versus Priest: Profanity and the Wit of Restoration Comedy' and Jean Marsden's 'Spectacle, Horror, and Pathos'. Each one of the essays in this volume could be cited as a stimulating introduction to those studying and researching in the field of Restoration theatre.

Robert Timothy Davis's short article 'Congreve's *The Way of the World*' (*Expl* 57[1999] 201–2) offers an analysis of the play based upon the etymology of the title phrase. Davis then goes on to develop a character study of Mrs Marwood, arguing that Congreve's satire of her sexual desire is an integral link to localized interpretations of the phrase 'the way of the world'. For Davis, Mrs Marwood is a character who embodies many if not all of the qualities or character traits represented by characters in the play, notably 'avarice, guile and the pursuit of pleasure'.

There is an exciting and scholarly account in D.F. McKenzie's 'Richard van Bleeck's Painting of William Congreve as Contemplative (1715)' (*RES* 51[2000] 41–61), which is accompanied by no fewer than seven photographs, one of them a colour plate. McKenzie's rigorous interrogation of this painting reveals that it contains allusions that celebrate the philosophical and literary significance of its subject. Within the detail of Van Bleeck's portrait, McKenzie reveals references to Congreve's close association with Vanbrugh and his intellectual debt to Berkeley, as well as details that imply physical reasons for his withdrawal into the contemplative world. Noting the lack of attention given to this portrait by other writers on Congreve, McKenzie suggests that it offers 'a view of the man significantly different from the familiar one read into Sir Geoffrey Kneller's painting of 1709'. This article also covers, somewhat comprehensively, details of the ownership of the painting, alongside contemporary appreciation and evaluation of Van Bleeck's work.

Mary Bly's 'John Cooke: A Playwright Connected to the White Friar' (*N&Q* 45[1998] 360–1) is a footnote to the relationship between the economy and adaptation in early seventeenth-century theatre. Bly considers the influence of details surrounding the leasing of the Whitefriars Theatre on issues of co-authorship, and the development of writing syndicates in relation to work by (among others) Lording Barry.

C.B. Hardman's 'Our drooping country now erects her head': Nahum Tate's History of King Lear' (*MLR* 95[2000] 913–23) engages in the current scholarly debate concerning the political influences on Tate's rewriting of Shakespeare's *King Lear*. Hardman offers an extended discussion of the rewriting of the characters of Edmund, Edgar and Albany, particularly with reference to audience reaction in the seventeenth century. For Hardman, Tate's adaptation is a Virgilian narrative whose dense political charge is the result of its being written in the midst of the exclusion crisis of 1680. He discusses a staging of the play in 1681, and concludes that the dramatic presentation of characters such as Edgar and Albany serves to reinforce the legitimacy of the Stuart dynasty through a reliance upon classical iconography. The article then goes on to consider the lack of performances of the play in the next twenty years, a gap that can be explained by its association with the ousted regime. By 1700, Hardman suggests, such political associations were no longer relevant and the play's popularity was re-established.

Critical discussion of the work of Aphra Behn is developed this year by a wide-ranging body of scholarly work. O'Donnell, Dhuicq and Leduc, eds., *Aphra Behn (1640–1689): Identity, Alterity, Ambiguity* presents a comprehensive body of essays on Behn's drama, particularly *The Widow Ranter*, *Abdelazer*, *Sir Patient Fancy* and *The Lucky Chance*. These essays engage in a discussion of the representation of race and gender in an attempt to 'interrogate the micropolitics of Behn's writing'.

In much the same vein articles by Laura Wyrick and Elaine Hobby offer dense historicized readings of her work in consideration of two key male figures within literary and philosophical culture, Emmanuel Lévinas and Thomas Killigrew. Laura Wyrick, in 'Facing Up to the Other: Race and Ethics in Lévinas and Behn' (*ECent* 40:iii[1999] 206–18) discusses the treatment of the 'other' in Behn's work in relation to Lévinas's system of ethics. Elaine Hobby's 'No Stolen Object, But Her Own: Aphra Behn's *Rover* and Thomas Killigrew's *Thomas*' (*WW* 6[1999] 113–27) is a detailed comparative discussion of the representation of female characters in the work of Aphra Behn and Thomas Killigrew. Hobby considers the representation of the female character as wife, prostitute and widow in relation to issues of female independence. She traces the interrelationship of these formulations of character through various dramatic articulations by both Behn and Killigrew, including *The Widow Ranter*, *The Lucky Chance* and Killigrew's *Thomaso, or The Wanderer*.

Susan Carlson's 'Cannibalizing and Carnivalizing: Reviving Aphra Behn's *The Rover*' (*TJ* 47[1995] 517–39) discusses the stagecraft of an American production of Behn's *The Rover* directed and produced by Joanne Akalaitis in 1994. Carlson uses the techniques of this production to discuss the evolution of different editions of the play in relation to issues of stagecraft relevant to both the seventeenth and the twentieth centuries. For Carlson, Akalaitis's 'kinetic' staging was an 'evocative scrim' that offered the audience 'a fluent spectacle'. Carlson's analysis of this particular production leads her to compare the reaction of a contemporary audience to Behn's play with the experience of seventeenth-century spectators, and, further, to consider the concept of carnival and anti-carnival in relation to the staging of the play, ultimately returning to an account of Akalaitis's 'celebration of stylisation and violence'.

2. Dryden

(a) Poetry
The section on Dryden's poetry will appear next year.

(b) Plays
There is a useful bibliography of work on Dryden's plays in Fisk Payne, ed., *The Cambridge Companion to English Restoration Theatre*. I thought of making it more useful by trawling through *YWES* and listing omissions, but feared accusations of over-fishing. In the book itself comment on Dryden's plays must be sought through the index.

The contributions to Hammond and Hopkins, eds., *John Dryden: Tercentenary Essays*, are sometimes relevant to the plays, or sound as if they could be. Nicholas von Maltzahn's 'Dryden's Milton and the Theatre of Imagination' (pp. 32–56) notes, on the evidence of the many manuscripts and printed texts, that *The State of Innocence* was Dryden's 'most popular dramatic work' in his lifetime, even though it was never performed. Its success in the theatre of imagination owed something to 'the pessimistic satisfaction' of its 'failure in theodicy'. Paulina Kewes's 'Dryden and the Staging of Popular Politics' (pp. 57–91) concerns theatrical representations of the people, and of the ways in which public opinion could be swayed, especially in *The Duke of Guise*, 'the most controversial play' of our period. As the political context changed, the people were variously seen as loyal, rebellious, or servile. Harold Love's 'Constructing Classicism: Dryden and Purcell' (pp. 92–112) attacks narratives of literary and musical history which make both Dryden and Purcell seem merely transitional figures, when their work is really unclassical, individual and astonishing. So far so good, but the essay does not discuss their collaboration on *King Arthur*. Still, its title is not positively misleading; Jennifer Brady's 'Dryden and Congreve's Collaboration in *The Double Dealer*' (pp. 113–39) does not show, or even claim, that the two dramatists collaborated in the usual sense. It suggests that the liaison in the play itself, between the poetical Lady Froth and the critical Brisk, may have been an uneasy joke on Congreve's part. Paul Hammond's 'Some Contemporary References to Dryden' (pp. 359–400) collects previously neglected or insufficiently annotated allusions, some of which relate to the plays. John Dunton in 1691 declared Dryden 'by far the most *compleat Dramatick Writer* not only of our Age, but of all the *English* Poets that went before him'.

Some essays in periodicals seemed worth attention. Barbara Everett's 'Unwritten Masterpiece: Dryden's *Hamlet*' (*LRB* 23:i[2001] 29–32) is the text of a lecture to a tercentenary conference at Yale. Ms Everett helped our American friends to drink the champagne, then told them that the trouble with Dryden was that he never wrote a masterpiece, certainly nothing like *Hamlet*. Dryden's plays, it seems, were and remain caviar to the general. Duane Coltharp's 'Radical Royalism: Strategy and Ambivalence in Dryden's Tragicomedies' (*PQ* 78[1999] 417–37) describes his efforts at 'appropriating revolutionary energies for royalist uses', especially in *Secret Love, Marriage-à-la-Mode, The Spanish Friar, Don Sebastian* and *Love Triumphant*. The most vigorous spokesman for 'radical royalism' is the satirical Dorax in *Don Sebastian*, a play about the ignominious retreat of one flawed monarch and the armed overthrow of another, implying that the punishment of royal weakness and crime must finally be left to divine justice. This essay makes an interesting approach to Dryden's serious drama as a whole. Liza Zunshine's 'The Politics of Eschatological Prophecy and Dryden's 1700 *The Secular Masque*' (*ECent* 41:iii[2000] 185–203) queries Sir Walter Scott's interpretation of the masque and its acceptance by modern scholars. Scott thought it alluded to the sports of James I, the wars of Charles I, and the licentiousness of the later Stuarts; Zunshine reveals 'a controversial rhetorical piece informed by Dryden's antipathy to William III'. Where Scott enthusiastically over-simplifies, Zunshine seriously over-elaborates.

3. Late Marvell

In 'Marvell and the Art of Disappearance' (in Clark, ed., *Revenge of the Aesthetic: The Place of Literature in Theory Today*), Stanley Fish considers the hermetic impression modern readers have of Marvell's lyric poems. Their characteristic withdrawal from the political arena in which he spent so much of his professional life springs from the poet's precocious new critical leanings, his 'conception of the work of art as a unique and self-enclosed construct'. A Marvell poem refers primarily to the speaker's yearning 'to be left alone, to not be interfered with, to not be appropriated', and aspires to become, in Jonathan Goldberg's formulation, 'not really "about" something else'. 'Marvell's great theme' throughout the lyric poems has a Miltonic ring, that 'man cannot keep his hands, and what is worse, his mind, off things. His vice is consciousness itself', because it always implies deferral, requiring 'for its completion … the frame of something other. … Everything is a sign', every action 'already mediated'. There are indeed frequent hints in Marvell of some other mode of being, as when the Nymph dreams of dissolving into the tears on her Fawn's memorial statue, 'themselves engraving' on her own marble breast. Such tears, of course, 'are their own signs and therefore do not signify. … They have escaped from the world of meaning'. But the animal itself, because it can be observed and described from what will inevitably be a partial perspective, is not so lucky. Even its best-known trait, of having been 'Lilies without, Roses within', shows it to be 'self-divided, double, duplicitous'. 'Upon Appleton House', so different from the shorter lyrics in other ways, is, like them, 'at war with its own temporality, with its tendency … to mean'.

Fish takes an evident delight in working out the ramifications of his insight, as when he judges that the poet's Mistress triumphs over her lover in debate precisely through her 'Coy' silence ('we know nothing about her … She has escaped our grasp; she has disappeared; she has won'). But beneath their trademark virtuosity, his readings find a larger purpose in resisting 'the various historicisms … whose expansive arguments are made at the expense of the aesthetic'. Such arguments tend to have trouble with Marvell, whom they have recently found 'hard and dead', 'radically opaque'. For Fish's poet, one suspects, those judgements would be high praise, indeed.

Fish reserves his attention for Marvell's familiar early lyrics, but new textual studies are working to establish a second, less familiar, career for him during the Restoration, as a generally anonymous topical satirist with early neoclassical habits of mind. This year, studies argue that he borrowed from Tacitus, translated biographies of Nero and Caligula, and wrote two more than we had thought of the five 'Advices to a Painter' verse satires against Charles's efforts to suppress unlicensed printing. Though the essays are not all equally persuasive, their cumulative effect will help bring closer a re-evaluation apparently long overdue.

Anthony Miller, in '"The English Hunter": Marvell's Cromwell and Tacitus' (*CML* 20:ii[2000] 67–72), suggests that the 'Horatian Ode' on Cromwell borrows imagery from Tacitus' account of the Romans' final push into Scotland in AD 83–4. But, in his chosen example, the historian's metaphor about invading soldiers as hunters beating the bushes for game is characteristically concise: 'the timid and feeble are scared away'. Marvell fleshes out his own version with an 'English Hunter', his horse and hounds, and a 'Caledonian Deer' for them to flush. When he has finished there's nothing left for him to have borrowed but the conceit itself.

The problem with Miller's suggestion is that it asks us to overlook too much about Marvell's poetics. His highland warriors, for instance, have contracted a 'parti-colour'd Mind' from cringing so often 'underneath the Plad'. For the poet of 'The Garden', this conceit serves almost as a maker's mark, pointing as it does to an imagination thoroughly unlike that of the Roman historian. Indeed, had Tacitus in fact been on the poet's mind as he wrote about Cromwell, he'd be unlikely to call attention to it, since as Miller notes in passing, 'Roman rule in Northern Scotland was short-lived'.

Between 1672, when the Licensing Act governing publishing was renewed, and 1679, when it was allowed to lapse, Charles conducted a relentless campaign against dissenting printers, chiefly through his press surveyor Robert L'Estrange. The 'immediate notoriety' of Marvell's 1672 *Rehearsal Transpros'd*, which openly taunts that officer, ensured the most 'assiduous attempts' to suppress his next fusillade, the 1676 *Mr. Smirke; or, The Divine in Mode*. Beth Lynch's 'Mr. Smirke and "Mr. Filth"' (*Library* 1[2000] 46–63) searches the text for bibliographic evidence about how dissenting printers managed to cope.

No one familiar with the piracies, crude presswork, and false title pages of the time will be surprised to learn that these pressmen and compositors 'participated in a system of perpetually displaced responsibility' to evade prosecution. Their circles made provisions ensuring that each illegal title would be 'composed and printed in isolated and anonymous sections'. What is perhaps more unexpected is the sheer scale of such activities in the case of *Mr. Smirke*, and the testimony this provides to Marvell's public importance during his final years. Of the sixteen copies Lynch examines 'almost every one … appears idiosyncratic', with changes in font between (and sometimes within) individual formes. Despite her patient collations, this deliberately complex production history defeats Lynch's earnest interest in discovering something definitive about the work's several editions and states, except that all her copies were 'set and printed opportunistically and in haste', most commonly with worn-out fonts and frequent 'interruption of the ... process' at every turn.

Lynch's study offers a timely reminder of why Marvell might have chosen to issue some of his satires anonymously, and so makes more plausible Annabel Patterson's conviction in her article 'A Restoration Suetonius: A New Marvell Text?' (*MLQ* 61:iii[2000] 463–80) that three anonymous or disputed works should be added to his canon. Her case is particularly resourceful concerning a Suetonius translation that came out as the 1672 *History of the Twelve Caesars*. Because its coverage ranged from an idealized Augustus through successors such as Tiberius and Caligula, the widely known text was a useful resource for political satirists, as Marvell himself had recently underscored with a 'series of precise analogies between Nero and Caligula and Samuel Parker' in *The Rehearsal Transpros'd*.

Patterson is convincing that this text, at the very least, 'certainly followed the anonymous translation' closely. Indeed, she finds passages directly lifted from it in which Marvell 'does not follow his usual practice of indicating by italicization that he is quoting [another's words]'. The debt shows not only in his diction, but in ideas, as when parallel passages from the two works make uncommon semantic choices that serve to 'catapult the seventeenth-century reader into the technicalities of early modern treason law'.

Marvell, of course, was renowned as a Latinist, who is only known to have borrowed another's wording once in a lengthy career. But Patterson concludes quietly that the evidence shows only a 'high probability' that the same author lies behind both works. Even were the evidence stronger, though, the translation would hardly be a major addition to Marvell's output. Rather, its value is that, in its deft interleaving of classical and contemporary references, it reveals the 'cultural sophistication' of 'a distinguished and highly educated mind at work'.

Sections on other authors will appear next year.

Books Reviewed

Clark, Michael P., ed. *Revenge of the Aesthetic: The Place of Literature in Theory Today*. UCalP. [2000] pp. viii + 251. hb £35 ISBN 0 5202 2002 1, pb £13.95 ISBN 0 5202 2004 8.

Fisk Payne, Deborah, ed. *The Cambridge Companion to Restoration Theatre*. CUP. [2000] pp. xxvii + 294. hb £40 ISBN 0 5215 8215 6, pb £14.95 0 5215 8812 X.

Hammond, Paul, and David Hopkins, eds. *John Dryden: Tercentenary Essays*. Clarendon. [2000] pp. xiii + 415. £70 ISBN 0 1981 8644 4.

O'Donnell, Mary Ann, Bernard Dhuicq and Guyonne Leduc, eds. *Aphra Behn (1640–1689): Identity, Alterity, Ambiguity*. L'Harmattan. [2000] pp. xx + 309. ISBN 2 7384 9753 5.

XI

The Eighteenth Century

LEE MORRISSEY, LAURA J. ROSENTHAL, JENNIFER HOBGOOD, ADAM ROUNCE, KATE DAVIES, ALISON O'BYRNE AND LISA BLANSETT

This chapter has five sections: 1. General; 2. Verse/Drama; 3. Poetry; 4. Prose. 5. The Novel. Section 1 is by Lee Morrissey; section 2 is by Laura J. Rosenthal and Jennifer Hobgood; section 3 is by Adam Rounce; section 4 is by Kate Davies and Alison O'Byrne; section 5 is by Lisa Blansett.

1. General

(a) Enlightenment and Modernity

Several recent books emphasize what might be called a multicultural vision of the Enlightenment. In the tradition of Robert Adam's *Land and Literature of England* [1983], Robert Altick's *Victorian People and Ideas* [1973], and John Brewer's *The Pleasures of the Imagination* [1997], comes Roy Porter's *Creation of the Modern World: The Untold Story of the British Enlightenment*, published by Norton. Seemingly aimed at that increasingly inscrutable category of the general reader, Porter's helpful book is a lively narrative, with its 200 pages of footnotes and a comprehensive bibliography discreetly tucked away at the back. For those of us who cover the Restoration and the eighteenth century in England, this is the book that we have long wished we could give our students, at least our advanced undergraduates and beginning graduate students, as a way of introducing them to the central concerns of the eighteenth century, and recent issues in the study of it. Porter's book combines a synthetic overview of the eighteenth century in England and a sustained argument against the traditional Continent-focused models of the Enlightenment. It is also supplemented by forty-six colour prints, illustrating a range of topics such as light, the family, leisure, conviviality, and science.

The book begins with a brief overview of prominent models of the Enlightenment, from Foucault's sense that the Enlightenment subjugates, to Pocock's argument that there was not an Enlightenment but were instead Enlightenments, plural. Thankfully for the intended audience, Porter does not try to contextualize these recent debates in terms of the early twentieth-century arguments over the Enlightenment, in figures such as Adorno, Cassirer, Heidegger and Horkheimer. Instead, he implicitly describes a largely Kantian vision of the Enlightenment as developing a modern, secular value system, although he also prioritizes the eighteenth century's friendly clubbability. Throughout, however, Porter reminds us that no history of the Enlightenment takes England as its focus: Cassirer, Gay, and even Schmidt's more recent anthology *What is Enlightenment?* [1996], all overlook, Porter argues, English precedence. Thus, for all his interest in the Kantian model of Enlightenment, Porter points out that *sapere aude* was the masthead of Englishman Ambrose Philips's *Freethinker* sixty-five years before it made its famous appearance in Kant's essay on Enlightenment. Porter provides many examples of how Continental philosophers looked to England for the modernity that they subsequently theorized and articulated as the Enlightenment.

Although the book does have a narrative—the emergence of the modern secular value system—Porter does not tell the story strictly chronologically. Rather, he considers the period thematically, with chapters on such topics as early eighteenth-century sociability; the British Enlightenment as a reaction to the political violence of the seventeenth century; print culture; the Anglican joining of religion and reason at the end of the seventeenth and beginning of the eighteenth centuries; Newton and mechanical philosophy; early political science in the work of Addison and Steele, Hume, and Smith, etc. Each of these chapters could stand alone and serve as a good introduction to the topic for the advanced undergraduate. Taken together, though, certain important figures, such as Hobbes, Locke and Newton, recur, and are seen in different lights. In this sense the story has the structure of plays from the period— maybe *The Way of the World*—as the same characters come and go and are slowly revealed to be even more than we thought they were when we first met them. Typical of this slow unfolding is Porter's treatment of Locke's idea of human psychology as moving from ignorance to knowledge, an idea which, we are told, provided a model for the Enlightenment itself. It is tempting to think that he wishes the same development might occur as a result of his own work. For the general reader whom eighteenth-century authors so assiduously courted, it will.

Volume 29 of *Studies in Eighteenth-Century Culture*, edited by Timothy Erwin and Ourida Mostefai, picks up on the question of the Enlightenment. Two special features stand out. The first, entitled 'Allegories of Healing', includes four articles on the history of science and medicine. Elizabeth Williams's essay, 'Physicians, Vitalism, and Gender in the Salon' (*SECC* 29[2000] 1–21), reviews the eighteenth-century salon in France and its contribution to the history of science. To complicate the role usually assigned to the salon in the Habermasian public sphere, Williams focuses on the Medical University of Montpelier, which proposed a vitalist response to the Newtonian, Cartesian mechanistic approaches. In 'Doctor–Patient Correspondence in Eighteenth-Century Britain' (*SECC* 29[2000] 47–64), Wayne Wild makes a contribution to medical rhetoric, looking at how the rhetoric of doctor–patient relationships changed during the eighteenth century. Later in the journal, Joanna Picciotto picks up on the special section's focus on the history of science, and contextualizes eighteenth-century spectatorship with reference to optical instruments.

The second feature is a forum on Ernst Cassirer's Enlightenment. In the first of the two essays, 'Ernst Cassirer's Enlightenment: An Exchange with Bruce Mazlish' (*SECC* 29[2000] 335–48), Robert Wokler contrasts two books, both published in

1932: Carl Becker's *Heavenly City of the Eighteenth Century* and Ernst Cassirer's *The Philosophy of the Enlightenment*. Each proposes a different model for understanding the Enlightenment, and its legacy. As far as Wokler is concerned, Becker's has been the more influential of the two, and the more damaging. Wokler ties the critique of the Enlightenment's supposed social engineering and instrumental reason—associated with figures such as Adorno, Bauman, Foucault, Horkheimer and Lyotard—to a preference for Becker and a related overlooking of Cassirer. To downplay Cassirer is to underestimate what Wokler considers the most important aspect of the Enlightenment, its advocacy of religious toleration as the defining feature of modernity.

Particularly striking, though, is Wokler's argument that recent, materialist work in the eighteenth century avoids the Enlightenment's larger conceptual issues. In his response, 'Ernst Cassirer's Enlightenment: An Exchange with Robert Wokler' (*SECC* 29[2000] 349–59), Bruce Mazlish focuses on this argument; he claims that Cassirer is outdated precisely because he worked in the intellectual history that a materialist approach is designed to counter. It would seem, at this point, that we have two contrasting approaches, each unable to converse on the other's terms. But Wokler's point would be that even materialist scholarship works within a framework, not necessarily one emerging directly from the material under consideration. Mazlish for his part concedes the importance of Cassirer's emphasis on the Enlightenment's (and Kant's) faith in reason's self-realization. A footnote indicates that Wokler's essay is part of his forthcoming book, *The Enlightenment Project and its Critics*. Reading the essay and seeing the thoughtful response it generated, one cannot help but look forward to the book.

The essays collected in Grell and Porter, eds., *Toleration in Enlightenment Europe* spring from a 1997 conference in Oxford on the subject. The topicality of the presentations and of Enlightenment toleration is driven home by the preface's reference to the conflict in the former Yugoslavia, although of course one could point to any number of conflicts around the world that reveal both the importance and the limits of the Enlightenment ideal of tolerance. Emphasizing the fragile and contested quality of Enlightenment toleration, this anthology considers it comparatively, with chapters on England, France, Habsburg Austria, Holland, the Holy Roman Empire, Italy and Spain. The first four chapters set out the parameters for Enlightenment toleration, philosophically and historically, while the rest take up the question for different nations. In what constitutes an introduction to the volume as a whole, Ole Peter Grell and Roy Porter remind readers that religion was central to toleration in the period. On the one hand, this is contrary to the usual expectation (and Peter Gay's rise-of-paganism thesis); but on the other, it is to be expected from the very question of what it is that needed to be tolerated. For the theory of tolerance depends on the definition of what is considered to be different. In this anthology the focus is on religion as the marker of difference, and one of the book's central questions is how religion affects both the theory of tolerance and the limits of toleration during the various Enlightenments reviewed by the contributors.

Eighteenth-century toleration develops over time, and is therefore different across the century, and from state to state. England and Spain are traditionally taken to represent either end of a spectrum, a view that is investigated by the contributors to this book. For example, Robert Wokler's provocative essay, 'Multiculturalism and Ethnic Cleansing in the Enlightenment' (pp. 69–85), makes a spirited,

THE EIGHTEENTH CENTURY 531

philosophically informed defence of the Enlightenment against its twentieth-century critique. To defend his contention that the barbarity represented by the Holocaust is not the result of the Enlightenment but its enemy, Wokler aims to establish two related points: first, that reason did not replace faith in the Enlightenment, and second, that the Enlightenment's increasing interest in science did not supplant an awareness of the value of cultural difference. For his part, in a brief essay of illustrative contrasts, 'Spinoza, Locke and the Enlightenment Battle for Toleration' (pp. 102–13), Jonathan Israel associates the religious defence of tolerance with John Locke, and the secularist defence of the freedom of thought with Spinoza; by extension, then, the idea of the religious basis of tolerance that Grell and Porter attribute to the Enlightenment generally is actually situated more locally, in England, according to Israel.

Israel's thesis is further examined in Justin Champion's 'Toleration and Citizenship in Enlightenment England: John Toland and the Naturalization of the Jews, 1714–1753' (pp. 133–56), where Champion reviews England's Act of Toleration (1689) and compares it with eighteenth-century proposals and acts for naturalizing Jews in England. Champion emphasizes the eighteenth-century English ratio between religious toleration and political participation; typically, the latter declined as the former grew. At the same time, Israel's sense of the Continent as the secularist alternative, exemplified by Voltaire or Spinoza, is put to the test with essays detailing the situation in France, Holland, Italy, and Spain. Together, the essays constitute a lively debate, and a wonderful introduction for anyone interested in the theory and practice of religious tolerance across eighteenth-century western Europe.

Another instalment in the regional approach to the Enlightenment, Wood, ed., *The Scottish Enlightenment: Essays in Reinterpretation*, focuses on the role of medicine in the Scottish Enlightenment, with several chapters devoted to the subject. In 'Science and Medicine in the Scottish Enlightenment: The Lessons of Book History,' Richard B. Sher examines a list of the first editions of more than a hundred scientific and medical books published in the second half of the eighteenth century. Anita Guerrini's '"A Scotsman on the Make": The Career of Alexander Stuart' reviews the career of a Scottish doctor, in part to indicate a social history of the Scottish Enlightenment (especially as those trained in its approach to the sciences headed south to work). Her article also reveals how important patronage remained in the eighteenth century, ironically setting limits to the Enlightenment idea of the value of reasonable discourse in a public sphere. John Wright looks at arguments between animism and materialism in his essay 'Materialism and the Life Soul in Eighteenth-Century Scottish Physiology'. In 'The Infirmary of the Glasgow Town's Hospital: Patient Care, 1733–1800', Fiona A. MacDonald begins by situating Glasgow's Town Hospital, which opened in 1733, in the context of eighteenth-century developments in health-care institutions. She focuses on the social history of the hospital itself: admissions, costs, therapies, nursing, etc. What emerges from these essays on medicine in the Scottish Enlightenment is a sense that eighteenth-century medicine was at an intersection between science and philosophy, and that training in it was an important part of how the Scottish Enlightenment travelled out of Scotland.

Of course, this focus on medicine rather than, say, letters and publishing as the vehicle for transmitting the Scottish Enlightenment is part of how this anthology contributes to a reinterpretation. The book begins with an essay on Dugald Stewart's nineteenth-century contribution to the historiography of the Scottish Enlightenment. By emphasizing the historiography as much as if not more than the history itself, the essay sets the tone for the volume. The second essay, John Robertson's 'The Scottish Contribution to the Enlightenment', continues the historiographic interest, but with an important twist: it argues that it is time to set aside twentieth-century debates over difference within or contradictory obstacles to the Enlightenment. Thus, Robertson proposes looking at a Scottish contribution to a comparative, international Enlightenment. His argument leads nicely to Charles W.J. Withers's essay, 'Toward a Historical Geography of Enlightenment in Scotland', which considers both how geography was taught in eighteenth-century Scotland and also what Scotland meant for the geography of the Enlightenment.

Easily one of the most fascinating recent books written on the Enlightenment is David Ruderman's *Jewish Enlightenment in an English Key: Anglo-Jewry's construction of Modern Jewish Thought*. Immensely learned, impressively thorough, and remarkably understated, Ruderman's book addresses a wide range of constituencies. First, of course, Ruderman argues against the idea that there were too few English Jews for them to have had an impact on the British Enlightenment. The dozen or so profiles included in this volume take care of that objection. Second, he addresses the prevailing assumption that the centre of modern European Jewish intellectual life was Berlin, and, while this cannot be discounted, Ruderman instead proposes the uniqueness of the eighteenth-century English Jewish experience. For example, because the possibilities for integration were greater in England than they were on the Continent, Jews wrote in English and could thus participate in public debates, especially (for Ruderman's book) those over the translation of biblical Hebrew into English. Ruderman's history recounts how figures such as Raphael Baruch and David Levi responded to early developments in what would become the 'High Criticism'. In this sense, there is an 'empire writes back' quality to the story, as the Jews so often at issue in Christian scriptural polemics publish responses to the claims being made about them and Hebrew in eighteenth-century England. Third, and as a consequence, Ruderman's work combines Pocock's idea of plural Enlightenments with J.C.D. Clark's sense of the importance of religion in eighteenth-century England (although only by instructively turning Clark's confessional state on its head; see a review of Clark's *English Society*, below). It is also interesting to consider Ruderman's work in relation to the 'decline of Hebraism' thesis, according to which a component of the seventeenth-century approach to texts said to be 'Hebraic' (Milton being the most famous example) is in the eighteenth century replaced with a 'Hellenic' approach. For Ruderman there was no such decline. Early on, he describes two models that have governed the question of a 'Jewish Enlightenment', one for the German intellectuals, and the other for an English Jewish culture ('culture' in the anthropological rather than the high arts sense). In this remarkable book, Ruderman makes an important claim for another possibility, that of English Jewish intellectuals learning from and contributing to the Enlightenment.

Frank Boyle's *Swift as Nemesis: Modernity and its Satirist* treats Jonathan Swift as a critic of modernity. On the face of it, this would not seem such a remarkable claim, but as Boyle explains, Swift's opposition to the new philosophy has historically contributed to an undervaluing of his work, and, it could be said, of literature itself. For some, Swift's satire on the Royal Society's experiments made him irrelevant; after all, those experiments resulted in many modern technological wonders. Others would overlook such satire so as to recuperate what they could from Swift, as for instance, the strength of his aesthetic sensibility. For his part, Boyle situates Swift in relation to Freud, Kuhn, Lasch, Nietzsche, and Spivak, participating in a current revaluation that treats Swift's work as postmodern *avant la lettre*. Boyle refers to Ovid's *Metamorphoses*, reading Swift as neither Narcissus nor Echo, but instead as the overlooked Nemesis from the same story. Like Nemesis as described by Boyle, Swift points out 'the limited possibilities of human communication' (p. 3). Although it might seem unnecessarily complicating to redescribe modernity through Ovid's terms, Boyle does thereby go a long way to capturing the blend of neoclassicism and new science in which Swift lived, and through which he wrote.

(b) History
At the same time, Boyle's argument is at odds with the work of J.C.D. Clark, whose book, *English Society, 1660–1832: Religion, Ideology and Politics during the Ancien Régime*, was first published more than fifteen years ago. It is not too much to say that the implications of his central thesis—that those living in the eighteenth century had no idea they were also living through an emerging modernity—are still working their way through eighteenth-century studies. As a consequence, the publication of a revised edition of the work is an important event. Clark specifies several developments since 1985 that prompt and inform his revisions, each of which he associates with a principal figure: the recovery of neglected political texts (Laslett); attention to the variety of political languages (Pocock); analysis of texts and their authors' intentions (Skinner); the history of concepts (Kosolleck); *mentalités* (recent work in the Annales school); and the diffusion and reception of printed materials (Darnton). Readers will add many other recent historiographical developments not included in this list, attention to race, class, gender, empire, and social construction not least among them. As readers may know from the first edition, Clark sees seventeenth- and eighteenth-century England as combining monarchy and liberty, religion and science, and trade and landed wealth. To make his case about the persistence of the old order, he rereads key seventeenth- and eighteenth-century dates, claiming that 1642, 1688, 1716, and 1776 are , each in its own way, overrated or misunderstood. The English Civil Wars, for example, should no longer be seen as a defining moment in seventeenth-century English history. Similarly, 1688, he claims, is important not for the emergence of, say, contractual democracy or religious toleration, but rather for solidifying England's commitment to a state which defends the Church instead of a particular monarch.

Illustrative of the survival of the *ancien régime*, and of Clark's approach, is his pointed reminder that the *Eikon Basilike*, then thought to have been written by the executed Charles I, went through sixty-four editions between 1649 and 1660, and six between 1681 and 1727, not to mention four folio editions. In this example, one can see Clark's focus on the recovery of neglected texts (in this case, the subsequent editions), and their diffusion. Throughout, he insists on what was popular or prevalent, rather than emergent. Thus, he tries to establish that Locke was unimportant to eighteenth-century English politics. Rather than the revolutionary England implicit in the focus on 1649 or 1688 (or in the long-standing idea of

England's ancient Gothic constitution), Clark instead wants to highlight England's tradition of 'passive obedience' (p. 58) as a key feature of the democratic society that emerged. Ultimately, he objects to the idea that the eighteenth century represents the bridge between a religiously organized pre-modern England and a secular, democratic, modern one. He argues that many of the terms associated with this supposedly eighteenth-century shift actually gained their modern valence in the nineteenth century, words such as capitalism, communism, conservatism, imperialism, and individualism. For Clark, the defining moment of English political modernity is 1832, so much so that it is sometimes tempting to see him as a nineteenth-century historian of the eighteenth century.

Ultimately, however, what is at stake here is a variation on the old debate between history and philosophy. As much as the terms of modern political theory emerge in the nineteenth century, they also emerge in philosophy more than in history, more in the search for conceptual origins or 'turns' than in a sense of how things were in the past. In this regard, then, one of the most important and clever sections of the book is the one entitled 'Keywords' in a self-conscious nod to and reworking of Raymond Williams's book of the same title [1976]. Here Clark distinguishes between anachronism, prolepsis, and teleology. With its placement at the beginning of the book, this chapter initially has an ambiguous relationship to the rest of the work. However, it does not take long for the reader to realize that on the one hand Clark is contending that the proto-modern picture of the eighteenth century falls into each of those three keyword traps, traps which, on the other hand, he is implicitly asserting that historians are uniquely qualified to avoid.

Also reissued in a revised edition is William Everdell's *The End of Kings: A History of Republics and Republicanism*, originally published in 1983. After a schematic introductory chapter Everdell recounts a fast-paced history of republicanism, written to be a readable narrative, beginning with the big names in the movement, arranged chronologically, and overlapping with other political and military events of the period. For specialists in any of the periods, or in political theory and history, the information in any particular chapter will likely already be known. However, the book is a very good source through which to introduce students to key moments in political history. Indeed, few specialized readers would know the whole story as completely and impressively as Everdell is able to tell it. And specialists will certainly have plenty to consider in the argument that he sustains across his narrative, from Samuel in the Hebrew Scriptures to Ronald Reagan in the early 1980s. It is an unlikely bracket, but even with this revision at a decade's distance from the Reagan revolution, Everdell reads Reagan as a republican—by contrast with Richard Nixon's imperious, monarchical attitude. At the same time, he see Nixon's presidency as illustrating the dangers of an emphasis on simply counting a majority of votes. (I am sure that Everdell would have had a lot to say about the 2000 presidential election, which took place after the book had been reissued.) In essence, Nixon's second election in particular exemplifies Everdell's conviction that republics are different from, and preferable to, democracies. It is a distinction that he takes great pains to explain. For him, a republic is, simply, not a monarchy; democracies, he fears, can, ironically, elect monarchs, and occasionally do.

Everdell's central thesis is that republics are not representative democracies, as defined in Noah Webster's *American Dictionary*. Where democracies, historically, aim to expand enfranchisement, republics aim to balance opposing forces. Unlike democracies, republics, for Everdell, do not see the opposing forces as numerical blocks of voting constituents, but rather as an increasing number of citizenship offices, to be held temporarily and in turn by as many citizens as possible. This involvement will, of course, lead to conflict, but for the republican this conflict is simply evidence of the desired balance. This sounds like what is also known as participatory democracy, or like Habermas's hope for communicative action in a deliberative democracy. The number of citizen offices also reflects what Everdell sees as the innately constitutional component of republics: such offices are institutionalized and regulated by the (constitutional) rule of law. But Everdell's question is how representative democracies came to be seen as a substitute for republics. And here the eighteenth century is pivotal. In Everdell's narrative, it was in the wake of Calvin's development of a republican model in the seventeenth century, and England's Calvin-inflected development of a commonwealth (a word which descends from a translation of the Latin 'Res Publica', or republic) in the mid-seventeenth century, that Americans devised a written constitution implementing republican principles. It is this approach that, at least by the early nineteenth century, was considered representative democracy, the first time in what seems to be a 3,000-year history, Everdell implies, that the two approaches have been confused. The story of how the constitution was written in the eighteenth century is of course well known, but there is still work to be done on why it was in the eighteenth century that democracy adopted the until then hermeneutic question of representation. But Everdell's book is helpful for raising the issue, and contextualizing it in a well-told narrative.

Ten years ago, when the first volume of Isabel Rivers's *Reason, Grace, and Sentiment: A Study of the Language of Religion and Ethics in England, 1660–1760* was published, students of the eighteenth century gained an important resource for understanding the terms of religious debate during the Restoration and eighteenth century. The second volume has just been published, and again students of eighteenth-century religion will learn from Rivers's exhaustive research and clear presentation. She explains that this second volume is concerned not with 'the tension between reason and grace but of that between reason and sentiment' (p. 1). Upon learning that the shared title of the two volumes—now at least a decade old—applies in different ways to each book, one realizes that perhaps the most impressive aspect of the series is the fact that Rivers was able to conceive of such a project in advance (or that she is able to create the impression that she did). If the two books are a history of philosophy, the first volume covers more of the history, the second more of the philosophy. Rivers's interest in this volume is in 'what happened when attempts were made from the 1690s onwards to separate ethics from religion' (p. 1). Initially, she associates these attempts with turn-of-the-century freethinkers such as John Toland, Anthony Collins, and Matthew Tindal (ch. 1, pp. 7–84), although she also includes the earl of Shaftesbury (ch. 2, pp. 85–152), David Hume, Adam Smith (ch. 4, pp. 238–339), and others. The topic may be freethinkers, but Hume seems to be the real centre of the book: the initial chapters develop the terms, subsequent chapters trace a lineage (bringing it to Scotland), the Hume chapter shows how his work combines and responds to the freethinking that preceded it, and the final chapter examines the contested consequences.

What Rivers describes as a separation of ethics from religion others have called the Enlightenment; consequently her research participates in the contested question of the relationship between religion and the Enlightenment. Rivers stays very close to her sources, explaining up front that she is 'not entering into debates with modern interpreters' (p. 5). This is an understandable decision, and it is to her credit that she anticipates and addresses the objection. It is her decision to focus on 'the debates in their own terms' (p. 4). However, there is more to this than just seventeenth- and eighteenth-century terms. For example, when Rivers details the influences on the freethinkers, such as the Socinians, the Latitudinarians, John Locke, the classical moralists, and Cicero, she rightly documents the issues that freethinkers' writing mentions, and she is, as she was in volume I, excellent at defining these complicated terms. However, there are also other, perhaps less explicit, affiliations that they would not have mentioned, but that could nonetheless help to situate their work for modern readers. The freethinkers were not all Calvinists, nor can Calvin be considered a freethinker. But the Calvinist tradition implying believers' relative autonomy could be said to contribute to a freethinking environment. It would be helpful to know what Rivers thinks of such a possible connection. Similarly, freethinkers, such as Shaftesbury and Francis Hutcheson, insist on 'harmony and proportion' as 'a reflection of the universal mind' (p. 143); they are, as Rivers acknowledges, replaying Platonic arguments. It would be interesting to know how these Platonic arguments are similar to or different from those, in, say, Augustine's work. Regardless, by providing a history of freethinker philosophy in its own terms, Isabel Rivers has yet again done an important service to the study of religion in the eighteenth century.

Stefan Collini, Richard Whatmore, and Brian Young have edited a collection of essays, *Economy, Polity, and Society: British Intellectual History, 1750–1950*, as a Festschrift to celebrate the influence of Donald Winch and John Burrow, historians associated with the so-called 'Sussex school' of intellectual history. Their approach combines different fields, and has an impact on English, economics, and history. Because the book's essays lean towards the earlier side of the period covered by its title, there are several chapters of interest to those working on the eighteenth century, particularly those interested in David Hume and Adam Smith. In 'Adam Smith and Tradition: *The Wealth of Nations* before Malthus', Richard Teichgraeber III focuses on Smith's reputation in the late eighteenth century, prior to the anonymous publication of Malthus's *Essay on Population* [1798]. Not only because of what Teichgraeber calls the *Wealth of Nations*' 'length and loose organization', Smith was not, Teichgraeber contends, the subject of any impassioned debates in the late eighteenth century. It is, in other words, the old story—familiar to students of literature—of an unpopular, difficult text retroactively acquiring the status of impassioned classic. Teichgraeber's point, of course, is that the Smith we have received (towering over the development of liberal capitalism) is different from the Smith we would have known or read in the eighteenth century. In making his case for Smith, Teichgraeber is also making his case for the brand of intellectual history the anthology attributes to Donald Winch and John Burrow. Similarly, Nicholas Phillipson's 'Language, Sociability, and History: Some Reflections on the Foundation of Adam Smith's Science of Man' (pp. 70–84), for example, attempts to account for the eighteenth-century context of Smith's theory of human nature. For Phillipson, Smith's theory counters the absence of an explicit theory of language in the work of David Hume. (It is tempting to see academic wit in Phillipson's contention that Adam Smith's theory of human nature did not emerge until Smith had spent six years at Oxford, years about which we know so little, but the joke is likely unintended.) Other essays of interest include: E.J. Hundert's 'Sociability and Self-Love in the Theatre of Moral Sentiments: Mandeville to Adam Smith' (pp. 31–47), about what might be called the *Fable*'s performative aspect; Dario Castiglione's '"That noble disquiet": Meanings of Liberty in the Discourse of the North' (pp. 48–69), about the eighteenth-century Scottish break between the two types of liberty, negative and positive, outlined by Isaiah Berlin; Richard Whatmore's '"A gigantic manliness": Paine's Republicanism in the 1790s', about Paine's relationship with the complicated and contested term republicanism; and 'Irish Culture and Scottish Enlightenment: Maria Edgeworth's Histories of the Future' (pp. 158–80), about a previously unexamined connection between Edgeworth's Irish tale and the Scottish Enlightenment.

Working at the intersection of legal and social history, Peter King has written an extensively documented study, *Crime, Justice, and Discretion in England, 1740–1820*, on the accused's experience of the eighteenth-century English judicial system. Expanding and addressing such well-known predecessors as Douglas Hay's *Albion's Fatal Tree* (Lane [1975]) and Brewer and Styles's *An Ungovernable People* (RutgersUP [1980]), King's work is based more in the archives (specifically those of Essex), and less in the Foucauldian, Bakhtinian framework that characterized those earlier works. Where they famously focused on the power and influence of spectacle in the administration of eighteenth-century English justice, King is interested in examining each step in the legal review of those accused of property crimes in the eighteenth century, which he describes as 'the golden age of discretionary justice' (p. 1). Describing the legal system as an eighteenth-century mansion in which one's position along a corridor of rooms indicated one's relation to power, King covers coming to trial, pre-trial negotiations, and the court process, including jury trials and sentencing.

In *Society and Sentiment: Genres of Historical Writing in Britain, 1740–1820*, Mark Salber Phillips sets a real challenge for himself. He begins by addressing what he considers to be the two main sides in history or historiography today: the so-called traditional historians on the one side and those influenced by literary criticism on the other. Bypassing the second school's association with the work of Hayden White, Phillips briefly sketches how the contemporary debate goes back to the differences between Ranke and Hegel in the nineteenth century. It is Phillips's point not only that the difference between the two sides is exaggerated, but that both sides must pay attention to the history of historical genres in order to see how the perception of a divide developed. He traces an eighteenth-century shift from political history to a new, more 'sentimental', history that tried to incorporate modern developments that had not been anticipated or addressed by the classical models on which history had previously tended to rely. In part, this shift occurred because of new events to be recorded and described by the historian, but it was also the result of changes in readership generally. To make his case, then, Phillips must describe the new historical narrative and its new audience. He does this best in chapter 4, 'History, the Novel, and the Sentimental Reader' (pp. 103–28), where he talks about the new genre available to the new history, and about the new audience, particularly of women, who placed new demands on all writers. Most suggestive there, to my mind, was his treatment of what might be called Hume's 'idea of woman'. In Phillips's story, Hume's friend Mrs Mure represents the new history Phillips is describing; she is an actual person, but she is also deployed in Hume's text for sentimental, strategic, and ultimately rhetorical purposes.

Phillips's attention to genres as historically situated draws, like Hayden White, on literary criticism, with the important proviso that Phillips's idea of genre is not 'meta', but is instead historical. At the same time, however, he disagrees with the typical literary treatment of history as referent, background, or verification of something in the text. Thus, on the one hand, he tries to distinguish himself from the two historiographical camps, while at the same time he is at pains to distinguish his point from the literary criticism to which he is indebted. This, then, is the challenge to which I referred above. The problem is that such a series of subtle distinctions requires great clarity of exposition for the modern readers Phillips describes, even twenty-first-century ones. As is so often the case, those of us who write about Hume cannot, unfortunately, write as well as Hume. For example, Phillips claims that 'in the last analysis, Hume has to be thought of as a postclassical historian, not a classical one. Nonetheless, he worked easily with structures whose fundamentals were still set by neoclassical convention' (p. 62). Some might argue that the neoclassical was post-classical, and others that both were consequently classical, although I'm not sure that the fight would draw a crowd these days. But when the three terms are so slippery it is not clear that we have been provided with the last analysis. At one point, Phillips points out that 'this diligent style of reading [history] demands a great deal from the reader' (p. 105). He makes this point regarding a seventeenth-century treatise on how to read histories, but it also seems that he might hope for the same point to apply to his own work. His book does demand a lot from the reader, although it will repay the reader's diligence.

Complementing Phillips's approach is *British Women Writers and the Writing of History, 1670–1820*, in which Devoney Looser examines the writing of Lucy Hutchinson, Lady Mary Wortley Montagu, Charlotte Lennox, Catherine Macaulay, and Hester Lynch Piozzi to argue against what she sees as two misguided second-wave feminist assumptions: that history has historically been the special purview of male writers, and that women writing history will write differently than men. After reviewing the few studies of women writing history, Looser points out that 'despite this dearth of information, feminist theories about women's historiography continue to appear' (p. 7). Looser aims to provide information, while simultaneously addressing at least some of the theories. Specifically, she is interested in gender and genre, and women as readers of history. For the latter, she points out the increasing importance of history in early eighteenth-century conduct books. From the former, she acknowledges the recent focus on the novel as history, but reminds us that 'few readers would have gone to Robertson's *History of Scotland* in search of comic romance' (p. 22). In the case of Lucy Hutchinson, Looser argues that the uncertainty of differentiating genres explains her sudden disappearance after being so extraordinarily popular in the nineteenth century. In a chapter on Charlotte Lennox, not usually considered a historian, Looser exploits eighteenth-century generic instability to reconsider Lennox's work, especially *The Female Quixote*, as if it were history. In part this is a result of Looser's very broad initial definition of historical discourse as referring 'not only to histories per se but to "the ensemble of written texts" that make up history' (p. 2). Looser's chapter on Catherine Macaulay begins with a reconsideration of the controversies that Macaulay's life occasioned in the 1770s. The final chapter, on Jane Austen, takes to task Gilbert and Gubar's *Madwoman in the Attic* [1979], likely a representative text from the second-wave feminism with which Looser is arguing. In the process, and throughout the book, Looser continues to make the point that 'British women writers frequently fall short of our feminist hopes for them' (p. 23).

Women and Literature in Britain, 1700–1800, edited by Vivian Jones, is something like a Cambridge Companion to the topic in the period, albeit not in name. For in it, as with the Cambridge Companions, a series of prominent scholars provide short, thorough overviews of the state of research in the field. In this case, contributors include Ros Ballaster, Margaret Doody, Dianne Dugaw, Isobel Grundy, Paula McDowell, Felicity Nussbaum, and Ruth Perry. Their essays focus largely on the construction of gender and on women's participation in print culture in the eighteenth century. In 'Women's Status as Legal and Civic Subjects: "A Worse Condition than Slavery Itself"?' (pp. 91–110), Gillian Skinner addresses Lawrence Stone's idea of the eighteenth-century rise of companionate marriage, arguing that such a marriage is 'absent from the contemporary legal interpretation of the state' (p. 92). Ruth Perry, in an essay titled 'Women in Families: The Great Disinheritance' (pp. 111–31), qualifies Skinner's point somewhat, and wittily. Perry does accepts that there was a shift in the understanding of family; from the seventeenth to the eighteenth centuries family becomes more 'affinal' and less 'consanguinal' (p. 112). Although such a concession might sound like agreement with Stone, Perry then adds that 'women lost more ground in this shift than they gained' (p. 113). In a section on 'Women and Print', Paula McDowell reviews 'Women and the Business of Print' (pp. 135–54), arguing that 'women had more power in early print culture than we have known and of a different kind than we have attended to', while Jan Fergus presents 'Women Readers: A Case Study' (pp. 155–9), an examination of the archives of two booksellers undermining 'any easy identification between women and fiction' (pp. 160–76). Finally, in an essay on 'Women Poets of the Eighteenth Century', Margaret Anne Doody reminds readers that 'we are judging from available and changeable evidence' (p. 217). The best essays in this anthology recognize and address this conundrum, using new sources (such as the booksellers' archives or re-examining legal history). It should also be noted that the book begins with a very helpful timeline of eighteenth-century literature, comparing 'writers and texts' to historical 'contexts' (pp. xii–xxiii).

(c) Empire

Eliga Gould's *The Persistence of Empire: British Political Culture in the Age of the American Revolution* addresses what would seem to be an obvious question, but one for which it is difficult to find a vocabulary: why was British public support for Britain in the American Revolution enough to sustain participation in such a lengthy conflict? Traditionally, the explanation of the revolution has focused on the American side of the Atlantic, documenting and examining American grievances and goals. Gould, by contrast, redirects attention back to England. It is difficult to summarize Gould's question, though, because of the difficulty of giving a particular, geographic name to either side: both were British in a large sense, some in England might have even seen America as part of England, and some in America probably considered themselves English (either actually or for rhetorical purposes). The advantage, then, in Gould's approach is in its transatlantic consideration of the conflict, neither one side nor the other, but both sides together contesting a similar political vocabulary. For Gould, the story of English support for the English goals in the American Revolution goes back as far the Restoration Settlement, especially Parliament's stabilizing funding for the monarch, and the incipient party politics it involved. Whigs, Gould argues, were for English participation on the Continent; Tories, by contrast, developed what Gould calls a 'blue water vision' (ch. 2, pp. 35–71), more colonial than Continental, their argument being that it would be less expensive and more rewarding to corner the French in North America than across the English Channel. It is this policy, Gould points out, that ultimately results in the Revolution. (And in this sense, Gould's is another application of the recent revision of eighteenth-century Tory politics made possible largely by the pioneering work of J.C.D. Clark.) By 1763, the blue water policy had brought England Quebec, lands west of the Appalachians, and Bengal, but it required a massive commitment of military resources, which is to say, new taxation. This brew, Gould argues, produced English support for prosecuting the war against the Americans. England wanted the empire, in part because it was more cost-effective than Continental Wars had been; England was familiar with taxation, as it was part of the Restoration Settlement that had, they believed, kept England free; and as the troops were going to be kept on American soil, it was, after all, the Americans who would be paying for the increased commitment.

Gould's research focused on 1,000 political pamphlets, tracking the debate over America and the nascent empire. In a way, then, the project overlaps with a *mentalité* study, investigating cultural conditions, or the work of Robert Darnton and Elizabeth Eisenstein, on how the printing press acted as an agent of social change. Gould describes it as 'a study of political consciousness' (p. xix). After referring to Bernard Bailyn's Pulitzer Prize-winning *The Ideological Origins of the American Revolution* (HarvardUP [1967]), Gould points out that 'to a greater extent than is sometimes realized, the Revolution's British origins reflected an equally terrifying set of fears and apprehensions' (p. 146). Gould is updating Bailyn's narrative in a transatlantic context; Gould's book might be described as the British origins of the American Revolution. For Gould has written what stands as a readable complement—one might even say corrective—to *The Ideological Origins*, although some readers will wish that Gould had addressed and enlisted more directly the many developments in postcolonialism, multiculturalism, and imagined communities that have occurred since the publication of Bailyn's book.

McCusker and Morgan, eds., *The Early Modern Atlantic Economy*, compiled as a tribute to John M. Price, historian of the seventeenth- and eighteenth-century economy, contributes an economic history angle to the burgeoning interest in transatlantic approaches to the eighteenth century. For as the editors make clear, it was in the eighteenth century that transatlantic trade reached its full complexity, as trade routes, credit, and commodities became institutionalized. The book is divided into four parts, focused on merchants, trade, empire, and labour respectively. The first essay, Peter Mathias's 'Risk, Credit and Kinship in Early Modern Enterprise' (pp. 15–35), considers how familial relationships contributed to the transatlantic trade. It is a synthetic overview of many sources and arguments in economic history, and thus sets the tone for the volume. This essay will be particularly interesting to those working in English literary studies, as several of the eighteenth-century

English novel's most famous and important characters (for example Crusoe or Gulliver) make their familial position the central issue in their initial decision to enter trade. Henry Roseveare's 'Property versus Commerce in the Mid-Eighteenth-Century Port of London' (pp. 65–85), continues the theme, casting economic history in social history terms and setting. Pointing out that the role and importance of the port of London has not been fully examined by economic historians, Roseveare also adds to the recent interest in eighteenth-century urban space. In '"A revolution in the trade": Wine Distribution and the Development of the Infrastructure of the Atlantic Market Economy, 1703–1807' (pp. 105–53), David Hancock begins with a consideration of one family involved for eight decades in the Madeira wine trade, using them as a case study of the many changes in eighteenth-century transatlantic trade. The increasing complexity of Madeira as a wine and the concomitant increase in demand act as a metaphor for larger changes in eighteenth-century commerce. Carole Shammas's 'The Revolutionary Impact of European Demand for Tropical Goods' (pp. 163–85), begins with questions and puns that show how informed the essay is by recent arguments within the academy. On the one hand, Shammas points out that recently the empire has seemed to be threatening the nation-state as the basic unit of analysis, while, on the other hand, she refers to Benedict Anderson, pointing out that this change will entail communities being imagined anew. Along these lines, Shammas makes the intriguing point that, although sixteenth- and seventeenth-century trade built on pre-existing medieval trading patterns, west Europeans would have been the only group in the emerging global routes not to know any of the commodities that would become so important to Europe: Native Americans knew tobacco and chocolate; coffee and tea were already used in Africa and Asia, as were sugar and cotton. In this regard, Shammas's essay sends the exoticism-as-novelty thesis associated with nineteenth- and twentieth-century Orientalism back 200 or 300 years. In this sense the essay is typical of the book, as it uses econometric material to rework widely circulated arguments about early-modern European empires.

Although the nineteenth-century focus of Regenia Gagnier's *The Insatiability of Human Wants: Economics and Aesthetics in Market Society* may seem to reside a little outside of the interests of eighteenth-century specialists, in fact the book will be very helpful to *dix-huitième*-ists. Although her topic, the place of the humanities in market societies, is informed by her extensive knowledge of the history of economic theory (and particularly shaped by a mid-nineteenth-century shift from production to consumption), the first of these two versions of Economic Man emerges, Gagnier argues, in the work of Adam Smith, in both *The Theory of Moral Sentiments* and *The Wealth of Nations*. Gagnier's treatment of Smith will be important to those interested in economics and aesthetics, including their relationship in the eighteenth century. She believes that literature can contribute to economics, especially in its implicit psychology, by describing why people make the choices they do. The book is also instructive in tracing a history of how the market seems to have stopped being a tool and become instead an end in itself, a movement that seems to have culminated over the past two decades or so. On the other hand, those interested in the story of literature's rise in the eighteenth century (as for instance in the old saw about the mid-century shift from intensive to extensive reading) will find much helpful material in Gagnier's book. That is, eighteenth-century specialists will also wish to reimagine her narrative, for it seems that at least some of what she locates in the nineteenth century might also have occurred in the eighteenth, perhaps especially in the work of, say, Locke, and Addison and Steele. Gagnier points out how the labour theory of value is displaced by marginal utility theory. But the characterization of the two types—the first based on needs and finite resources and the second based on taste, envy, and insatiability—will resonate with Locke's discussion of acorns in the state of nature, or Addison and Steele's celebration of the exchange. Such comparisons, however, are not correctives to Gagnier's work; instead, they suggest that scholars of the eighteenth century can learn from as much as contribute to a reconsideration of literature and economics.

In *The Complexion of Race: Categories of Difference in Eighteenth-Century British Culture*, Roxann Wheeler explores another aspect of the transatlantic economy—the range of ways in which the English during the eighteenth century imagined difference when confronting Others, from Africa to the Hebrides. In a theoretically sophisticated and gracefully structured argument, Wheeler warns that it is anachronistic to treat eighteenth-century discussions of race through a later black/white binary. In a telling illustration, she notes that it not until the second edition of the *Encyclopedia Britannica* that there is a discussion of 'Colour of the Human Species' (p. 179), helping her locate the emergence of skin colour as the principal marker of difference between the first edition of 1771 and the second of 1781. Equally striking are illustrations from two editions of *Robinson Crusoe*: an early edition, from 1726, portrays Xury as physically similar to Crusoe, the second, from 1791, as physically different. Wheeler contends that for the first three-quarters of the eighteenth century England understood difference through a flexible matrix that considered factors such as religion, decorum, and a society's position in the context of a fourfold theory of economic bases: hunting/fishing, shepherding, agriculture, and commerce. What she calls the 'elasticity' and 'multiplicity' (p. 6) of this matrix meant that it could be employed in a variety of ways, depending on the context of the comparison. For example, she notes that Xury and Crusoe seem to be similar when among the Moors, but become different when they meet up with the Portuguese boat captain.

What Wheeler says of her second chapter could stand for her book as a whole: 'this chapter seeks to unsettle teleological and presentist conceptualizations of race and racism' (p. 91). Making such a thorny argument, as Wheeler recognizes, is as complicated as the eighteenth-century matrix she recovers; as a consequence, she goes to great lengths to situate her project politically and theoretically, with reference to feminism, post-structuralism, and whiteness studies (and the Clarence Thomas hearings of the early 1990s), along with figures such as Louis Althusser, Homi Bhabha, Jacques Derrida, Michel Foucault, Antonio Gramsci, Luce Irigaray, and Trin T. Min-ha among others. Each chapter has the same structure, beginning with an overview of that chapter's argument, and then giving a brief review and critique of recent work on the subject, before moving on to a consideration of the principle text under consideration: *Robinson Crusoe* [1719] (pp. 49–89), *Captain Singleton* [1720] (pp. 91–136), Edward Long's *History of Jamaica* [1774] (pp. 138–76), and Samuel Johnson's *Journey to the Western Islands of Scotland* [1775] (pp. 178–233). Given how thorough the argument is, readers might wish for chapters on Behn's *Oroonoko* or the poetry of Phillis Wheatley. But with such a detailed discussion Wheeler has prepared the way for a rereading of these and other eighteenth-century English writers.

The nine-volume series *Representing India: Indian Culture and Imperial Control in Eighteenth-Century British Orientalist Discourse*, selected and introduced by Michael John Franklin, reprints facsimile editions of important texts from the eighteenth-century English encounter with India. Many were initially commissioned or published by Warren Hastings, first governor-general of British India; clearly, they played a complicated role, in both India and England. At the time of their publication, they were part of an argument for an India Company familiar with Indian cultural and political history. In a way, they participated in the arguments for an 'enlightened cosmopolitanism'. Over time, though, as the British became increasingly established, they contributed to the stores of England's Orientalist knowledge. As these early responses were codified and as India changed over time, these early texts played an important role in seeming to establish how things used to be, all the more unfortunate in that, as even contemporaries pointed out, the third-hand translations were at best loosely connected to the originals.

Volume I of the series, entitled *Interesting Historical Events, Relative to the Provinces of Bengal, and the Empire of Indostan, Parts I and II* [1765–7], is by John Zephaniah Holwell. One of a group of 146 Europeans thrown into an 18 × 18-foot cell after the fall of Calcutta on 20 June 1756, and one of only twenty-three people surviving the next day, Holwell was later briefly the governor of Bengal. His preference for what he saw as the purities of an ancient Hinduism over a decadent contemporary version, and over what he thought of as the violence of Islam, makes for important comparisons with other eighteenth-century arguments. Was his approach, for instance, informed by something like Hume's treatment of superstition and enthusiasm? How, in other words, did the English response to the religious wars of the seventeenth century at home affect their perception of religion in India? The second and third volumes, *The History of Hindostan*, translated from the Persian by Alexander Dow (2nd edition [1770]), is largely a history of the Muslim rulers of India, whom Dow apparently preferred to the India Company. The editor contends that Dow's work takes on a particular importance as he was the first British historian of Muslim India to rely on Persian sources. The fourth volume in the series includes *A Code of Gentoo Laws, or, Ordinations of the Pundits* [1776], a compilation of Indian law commissioned by Hastings, delivered orally to Persian translators. The resulting Persian text was translated into English by Nathaniel Brassey Halhed, an Oxford-educated writer and friend of Richard Sheridan (the same Sheridan who would play a significant role in Hastings's impeachment) living in India. Unfortunately, as was noted even at the time, although Halhed's translation of the Persian was impeccable, the Persian translation of the original was more a summary, making for an English text that bore little relation to the original. Unfortunately—one might also say tellingly—the original in this case was a synopsis of the ancient Bengal laws that Hastings wanted the English in India to emulate.

It is evident that the texts collected for this series make a very important contribution to the ongoing postcolonialist recovery of eighteenth-century Britain. It has very important consequences for current arguments about cosmopolitanism and the Enlightenment. It is understandable that the editors might see the texts, especially in their facsimile state, as reading reserved for specialists. But their implications potentially have a very wide circulation, much beyond specialists within eighteenth-century studies. However, the general introduction (and to a lesser extent the introductions to each volume) begins very much *in medias res*, making no allowances for the uninformed; many intriguing claims are made, but they would be helped with a little more perspective or framing for the uninitiated. The editor is right to argue that reappraisal of these texts could result in a more nuanced understanding of Orientalism, but that is a point to make in the first paragraph of an introduction. Here, it is placed in the concluding paragraph of the general introduction. No one who reads that far will disagree, for this is indeed an important series. But more people might read that far if the framework that resulted in these reprints had been highlighted up front.

(d) New Approaches

Deutsch and Nussbaum, eds., *'Defects': Engendering the Modern Body*, part of the UMichP series Corporealities: Discourses of Disability, sets out to reveal what disability studies can contribute to the historiography of the eighteenth century while simultaneously offering the early modern and Enlightenment example to the developing field of disability studies. In the process, the book recombines various strands of new historicist approaches and concerns, such as the focus on the social construction of the body and the telling, seemingly anomalous, anecdote. The influence of Thomas Laqueur's *Making Sex* [1990] can be seen throughout these pages, as can somewhat more subterranean connections to Foucault's *Discipline and Punish*, and *History of Sexuality*. The introduction situates the book's argument by referring, on the one hand, to well-known examples of physical 'deformity' such as Pope's height and humpback or Mary Toft's rabbit offspring, while at the same time clarifying that supposed disabilities are as socially constructed as the normative body from which the disabilities are said to deviate.

'Dumb Virgins, Blind Ladies, and Eunuchs: Fictions of Defect' by Felicity Nussbaum is presented first, apparently because it provides a schematic overview of the gendered and gendering treatments of defects, introducing readers to much of what comes later in the book. Nicholas Mirzoeff's 'Paper, Picture, Sign: Conversations between the Deaf, the Hard of Hearing, and Others' considers the late eighteenth-century development of an institutionalized training informed by a comparison with recent artworks by Joseph Grigely, creator of *The History of Deaf People* and *Conversations with the Hearing*. 'In the Bodyshop: Human Exhibition in Early Modern England' updates interest in the carnivalesque by providing a kind of social history of the trade in the display of anomalous births. Joel Reed's essay, 'Monstrous Knowledge: Representing the National Body in Eighteenth-Century Ireland', considers how discourses of disability affect and are affected by conflicts and differences between England and Ireland, and between the Anglo-Irish and the Irish Catholics. Jill Campbell, 'Lady Mary Wortley Montagu and the "Glass Revers'd" of Female Old Age', focuses on Montagu to look at the ageing process and how women saw themselves during it in the eighteenth century. In '"Perfect" Flowers, Monstrous Women: Eighteenth-Century Botany and the Modern Gendered Subject', Elizabeth Heckendorn Cook reconsiders the ancient comparison between femininity and flowers, showing how eighteenth-century technological developments in botany affect that analogy, especially in the work of Erasmus Darwin.

But as is so often the case in books about the eighteenth century, the figure who shapes the discourse the most is Samuel Johnson, here the subject of two chapters spread out across the first and second parts of the book. In the first, 'Dr. Johnson, Amelia, and the Discourse of Disability in the Eighteenth Century', Lennard Davis recounts Johnson's many ailments—blindness in one eye, deafness in one ear, scrofula, smallpox, depression, and Tourette's syndrome—but only to show how little attention they seem to have attracted in Johnson's lifetime. For Davis, Johnson stands between the pre-modern (divine judgement) and the modern (classifying) discourses of 'deformity', a claim which he tests with reference to James I on the one hand, and Fielding's *Amelia*, which features not one but two noseless female characters, on the other. Although Helen Deutsch, in 'The Author as Monster: The Case of Dr. Johnson', agrees with Davis that a narrative of 'overcoming' disability is inappropriate for Johnson (and probably for eighteenth-century authors as a whole), she nonetheless begins with what Davis would consider a modern approach to physical difference, focusing on it, and going so far as to treat the writings of Pope and Johnson as homologies for what the moderns consider to be their disabilities. Together, these two essays reveal the richness of this new area for eighteenth-century studies, while also revealing the conflict and disagreement inherent in the topic.

Todd Parker's *Sexing the Text: The Rhetoric of Sexual Difference in British Literature, 1700–1750*, applies the sexological lessons of Thomas Laqueur, Randolph Trumbach and others to such well-known figures in eighteenth-century English literature as Jonathan Swift, Alexander Pope, Eliza Haywood and John Cleland. As is well known, Laqueur and Trumbach, in different ways, point out that sexuality is constructed, generally, and that it changes from the seventeenth to the eighteenth centuries. Initially, Parker's prose shows how difficult it can be to reveal how the meanings of terms change while the terms themselves do not. For example, he claims early that 'for eighteenth-century Britain, male sexuality, instead of signalling a masculine identity sensitive to its class and immediate environment, becomes increasingly the privileged site of an emerging heterosexual hierarchy defining "male" as that which corresponds to "female" as a limit' (p. 1). Some would argue that the former half of the sentence has never been the case, while others would argue that the latter half has unfortunately always been. But Parker's book takes off when he turns to the specific texts, because he can make more specific, albeit still surprising, claims. The first chapter, on *Onania; or the Heinous Sin of Self-Pollution* (pp. 31–48), focuses on how female masturbation troublingly upsets familial and political relationships, in that the woman is able to imitate the role of the man. As the second chapter is about Jonathan Swift (pp. 49–80), readers can be forgiven for expecting a discussion of how Master Bates indicates Gulliver's unfortunate self-involvement. However, Parker instead focuses on what he calls the word 'boring' in Swift's dismemberment of the Irish coiner, Wood, in a chapter entitled 'Swift and the Political Anus'. The chapter on Pope's 'To Cobham' and 'To a Lady' (pp. 81–117) argues that the poems 'are most concerned with ratifying a reliable difference between male and female that his works cannot, finally, sustain' (p. 89). Chapter 4 (pp. 119–34), on Eliza Haywood's overlooked *Philidore and Placentia, or L'Amour trop Delicat*, focuses on how the Christian Eunuch disturbs the gender roles in the novel. In the final study, of Cleland's *Memoirs of Woman of Pleasure* (pp. 135–75), Parker is prompted 'to ask just how effectively the male and female organs constitute unquestioned referents for sexual identity' (p. 140). Parker is aware that he is treading a fine line; at the end, he argues that 'my readings remain faithful to the truth of these texts even as I regard that truth with thoroughgoing suspicion and occasional hostility' (p. 179).

Blakey Vermeule's *Party of Humanity: Writing Moral Psychology in Eighteenth-Century Britain* begins with an extraordinary introductory chapter, proposing an examination of Pope, Johnson and Hume in relation to recent developments in cognitive science and sociobiology. Much of the interest in the book lies in this first chapter, in which Vermeule points to a new way of reading the moral philosophers of eighteenth-century England, and, by extension, the eighteenth century in England. It could also be said that she is proposing a new way of conceiving the literary itself. This is a daunting challenge for even the most ambitious book, but Vermeule's thorough introduction at least is more than up to it. These early pages fairly crackle with sophisticated, pithy, and informed phrases. Eighteenth-century moral philosophy, we are told, intended to create a 'culture of obligation', and the tenor of its voice was a combination of 'should' and 'ought' (p. 2). After the Romantics, Vermeule contends, art and obligation found themselves at odds. So she proposes what we might call a pre-Romantic rereading of the eighteenth century that can reconstruct the aesthetic links between 'should' and 'ought'.

Vermeule insists that such a rereading should unfold with reference to the most recent developments in Anglo-American philosophy, a more scientifically inflected, empirical approach to consciousness, language, and the social than characterizes the models—largely descending from Freud—that have influenced literary analysis for so long now. This is not a shift from a psychoanalytic focus on symbolization to a psychiatric focus on, say, brain chemistry. Rather, Vermeule describes a naturalist, empiricist ethics, an approach which looks at moral decisions as social strategies (and here, then, is an overlap with a kind of behaviourism, à la Kenneth Burke). In another crisp formulation, Vermeule claims that this naturalist approach socializes the transcendent while transcending the socializing (p. 15). In insisting on the social, which is to say, on the empirically verifiable, Vermeule argues that fields such as evolutionary psychology and sociobiology expand the social-scientific revolution begun in late seventeenth-century England by Locke and refined over the eighteenth century by Mandeville, Shaftesbury, Hutcheson, Kames, Hume, Burke, and Smith. Rightly noting the Enlightenment's well-known interest in unifying knowledge, she argues that today's naturalist interest in what E.O. Wilson calls 'consilience' is a legacy of the eighteenth-century origins of empiricist (moral) philosophy. According to Vermeule, Pope, Johnson, and Hume are each practical psychologists, working on what is seen as 'the scandal of self interest' (p. 9), i.e. whether private vices can yield public benefits. Each author proposes a different solution, of course, for balancing the seemingly competing demands of the self and the social. Pope, for example, represents those tensions in the very lines of his poem, each side balanced against the other. And in the process he begins to articulate what Vermeule sees as a central eighteenth-century English contribution: the aesthetic as a grounding instrument of moral obligation. It is not clear, though, that Pope would be the best exemplar for Vermeule's case, as his chain of being is resolutely anti-evolutionary, and as his sense of balance seems to claim more for transcendence than for behaviourism. Nonetheless, Vermeule is right in the more general point that the eighteenth century places great faith in the socializing possibility of the aesthetic. This is especially true for Hume, perhaps most especially in the standard of taste, where his argument is, he hopes, matched by his aesthetic decision to write essays rather than treatises. To that end, I would be interested to have seen more from Vermeule about Hume's other writings besides the *Treatise*, on which she focuses here.

Of course, it is also the case that the same conviction of the importance of the aesthetic to the moral stance leads many literary critics to Continental philosophy instead of the English tradition Vermeule so fruitfully taps here. The pleasure of the text is more often an issue in the highly metaphoric work of leading post-structuralists. At a significant cost to their arguments, they prefer rhetoric to logic, especially to the formal logic often used in the best work of cognitive science. Nonetheless, Vermeule is right to point out, even if only implicitly, the empirical limitations to such 'theory'. Especially as literature is said to be post-theory, it is important that it should engage with developments in other philosophical traditions during the time that it was immersing itself in the terms and controversies of the Continent. It will be interesting to see how literature's interest in language, mind, and self can incorporate the lessons embedded in the work of philosophers and psychologists, such as Dennett, Fodor, Pinker, and Stich. Despite the differences between them, they are, in their emphasis on logic and empiricism, more like each other than they are like most Continental philosophy (which makes the title of Stich's recent book, *Deconstructing the Mind*, all the more playful). Especially in its introductory chapter, Vermeule's book takes a crucial step in that direction and thereby points the way for the rest of us; it is indicative of the quality of the work published on the eighteenth century in 2000.

2. Verse/Drama

Two very interesting books this year offered different kinds of institutional histories of theatre and drama. In her lively and interesting *Illegitimate Theatre in London, 1770–1840*, Jane Moody traces the emergence of illegitimate theatre at the end of the eighteenth century. At its simplest, 'illegitimate theatre' means 'the performances staged at those theatres where legitimate drama (tragedy and comedy) was prohibited'. But as Moody goes on to demonstrate, 'illegitimate' comes to bear a wide range of political and aesthetic meanings as well. Too many critics, Moody insists, have accepted Coleridge's distinction between elite, poetic drama and vulgar, illegitimate theatre, thus failing to recognize the possibilities of genuine political and aesthetic dissidence in the latter. 'Legitimate' drama articulated national loyalty, identity, and coherence; illegitimate theatre, by contrast, challenged those norms in a variety of ways, in part by challenging the cultural hierarchy of performance spaces themselves. Interestingly, Moody suggests throughout this book that we cannot also see these challenges by looking at the play texts alone; we must—as she does—attempt to reconstruct the performances, where spontaneous irregularities more directly challenged dominant ideology than the written text. Some of Moody's most intriguing readings, in fact, address mute performances; sometimes muteness itself 'becomes a political as much as a semiotic condition' (p. 89). The skeletal texts of pantomimes could easily slip past official censors but nevertheless allowed for a range of illegitimate performances. She sees illegitimate theatre, however, as not only a subversion of the dominant, legitimate theatre, but as a major influence on it as well. *Illegitimate Theatre in London* offers theatre history at its best. Moody brings to light a range of previously overlooked performances and genres, but also explores and speculates on their cultural meaning and significance—something much theatre history fails to do. With its wide range of intriguing observations, this book makes a valuable contribution to cultural studies.

Julie Stone Peters, *Theatre of the Book, 1480–1880: Print, Text, and Performance in Europe*, offers a different kind of cultural and institutional history. With a breathtaking range of scholarship, Peters counters the traditional narrative that, in the eighteenth century, the printed words edged out words performed. Rather, she shows a wide variety of ways in which print shaped the theatre and how these two institutions became deeply intertwined rather than strictly competitive. For example, she suggests that the great interest in and adherence to the 'rules' of drama in the seventeenth century directly resulted from the ability to validate critical norms through printed authorities. Later, she describes how print helped create new divisions between the professional hack writers and the elite amateurs. This cultural distinction becomes crucial because printing had worn away the traditional distinction between the aristocratic author circulating letters to friends and the popular author writing for a mass public. The patronage of dramatic authors persisted into the eighteenth century, but printed play texts created an important venue for pleas of protection. Peters organizes this book by topic rather than by chronology, and looks at a wide range of points of intersection between print and the stage: the publication of plays; the accuracy of texts; the institution of drama and its emerging tie to a printed text; the ownership of dramatic literary property; theatrical illusion; dramatic form, sound, and gesture; illustrations in play texts; the space marked out by the theatre. Some of these topics, and even the phenomena associated with them, have become familiar; Peters, however, offers new insights into the ways in which a print culture may have been directly responsible for them. Further, she shows how dramatists actually shaped their plays with an eye towards a reading audience, thus undermining the classic assumption of drama as competing with (and being defeated by) the novel upon the increase of literary. Richly illustrated, this book functions as both an overview of the history of dramatic authorship and an accessible, insightful analysis of the rich interconnections between the stage and the page.

Mita Choudhury brings some much-needed attention to the London theatre's global engagement in her *Interculturalism and Resistance in the London Theater, 1660–1800: Identity, Performance, Empire*. By examining a broad range of texts, Choudhury explores the ways in which 'intercultural' theatrical practices reveal anxieties about the British self and foreign other during the ascendancy of British global supremacy. Early chapters examine the destabilization of English identity through the 'English' opera and its complicated resistance to Italian incursions. Choudhury then offers an intriguing look at the Calcutta staging of Sheridan's *The School for Scandal*, performed for East India Company officers. She finds in this production an expansionist impulse to cement London ideologically with its satellite stage and, in the play's thematic endeavour, an acquisitive, imperial wish-fulfilment. A chapter entitled 'Female Orientalism' argues that gendered readings of Elizabeth Inchbald's *The Mogul Tale* and Hannah Cowley's *A Day in Turkey* miss the excessively voyeuristic tropes of exoticism in the plays, which, Choudhury maintains, place Cowley and Inchbald more squarely within the dominant culture. The book's final chapter investigates, through a reading of plays by Dryden and

Thomas Sheridan as well as an analysis of an early playbill, the ways in which theatre worked to appropriate 'borders' between nations and cultures. In spite of some early promise of greater intricacy, however, the 'resistance' in Choudhury's study tends to refer to the British resistance to the 'other', rather than any subversion of dominant culture (such as Jane Moody finds in illegitimate theatre), any subaltern resistance to imperialism, or any of the stage's highly complex confrontation with ethnic identity (such as Michael Ragussis explores in an essay discussed below).

Two other books offer close attention to specific figures or phenomena. *The Writing Life of Hugh Kelly: Politics, Journalism and Theater in Late-Eighteenth-Century London* is Robert Bataille's attempt to rescue from obscurity Anglo-Irish writer Hugh Kelly, who he argues was 'one of the most important and prolific journalists of his time' (p. vii). In this meticulously researched and detailed analysis of Kelly's career, Bataille does just that, demonstrating Kelly's significant involvement in London literary life during the period from 1760 to 1777, as a writer for and editor of numerous London periodicals and a notable playwright, poet, novelist, and political propagandist. Bataille's study examines Kelly's career in a chronological fashion: rather than organizing his enquiry into chapters strictly related to the various genres to which Kelly contributed, it follows the path of his career as a professional writer, often considering his dramatic, political and journalistic endeavours alongside one another. While at first this structure may seem a bit frustrating, with its many brief chapters covering short periods of Kelly's career, the organization of the book mirrors what Bataille argues is a central facet of Kelly's complex position as a professional writer, at a time when the occupation was still in the process of defining itself. For Bataille, the inconsistencies that previous scholars have interrogated in Kelly's writing—his sometimes avidly progressive and at other times conservatively reserved arguments with regard to a woman's choice of spouse in marriage; his plays that both satirize and advocate the reforming power of sentimentality; his staunch support of bourgeois morality in tandem with political propaganda opposing Wilkite politics and defending Hanoverian colonial policies that mercantile classes felt opposed their interests; and his journalistic pieces that seem to simultaneously champion and criticize the work of the journalist—all represent Kelly's 'market-oriented practicality', his attempt to appeal to a variety of audiences in order to reap the most lucrative financial rewards. While Bataille's claim that Kelly's advocacy of 'sentiment' as a vehicle to reform male culture reflects an overall feminist position in his work is underdeveloped, his study succeeds in opening up lines of discussion with which feminist historians can engage.

In *Summer Theatre in London, 1661–1820, and the Rise of the Haymarket Theatre*, William J. Burling looks at summer theatre in general and the Haymarket in particular. He first traces the historical origins of London summer theatre to 1661, which he dates as the beginning of a roughly fifty-year period during which it developed as a separate season from the regular winter theatrical one. He suggests that summer theatre emerged as a result of supply and demand: specifically, the ability of innovative theatre entrepreneurs to locate and exploit both a demand among theatre-goers for a separate season as well as the supply of junior members of acting companies who faced severe economic distress in their unemployment during the off-season. The remainder of the first part of the book explores early trials with finance, management, and repertory among innovators, as well as the establishment of the Little Haymarket theatre, which Burling places in the context of various patent house practices and illegal troupe activity prior to the Licensing Act of 1737. The latter part of Burling's study focuses on the Little Haymarket theatre specifically, first detailing Samuel Foote's successful management, which secured for the Little Haymarket a thriving independence from the regular season, then moving on to an in-depth discussion of the theatre under the management of George Colman the Elder and his son, George Colman, Jr., whose involvement finally waned during the 'joint managership' years towards the end of the theatre in 1820. While Burling's discussion of Henry Fielding's involvement in summer theatre and his references to such figures as Eliza Haywood, George Lillo, John Gay, Richard Sheridan, John O'Keeffe, Colley Cibber and Elizabeth Inchbald are tantalizing, one wishes for a much more lively discussion of the plays, players and playwrights in the pages of this painstakingly detailed and sometimes drily presented history. Nevertheless, in producing this study Burling has fulfilled his ambition in starting to close two gaps in theatre history scholarship: summer theatre and the history of the Haymarket. Moreover, with its copious tables and an appendix detailing financial and repertory information at great length, *Summer Theatre in London* provides a useful reference that anyone exploring this topic in the future will consult.

Two new editions will make teaching eighteenth-century drama more exciting. While J. Douglas Canfield's *Broadview Anthology of Restoration and Early Eighteenth-Century Drama* emphasizes the Restoration and the early years of the century, teachers of eighteenth-century drama will nevertheless find a considerable range of possibilities for courses. Included are Congreve's *Way of the World*, Pix's *Beau Defeated*, Trotter's *Love at a Loss*, Rowe's *Tamberlane* and *The Fair Penitent*, Farquhar's *Beaux' Stratagem*, Addison's *Cato*, Manley's *Lucius*, Centlivre's *Bold Stroke for a Wife*, Steele's *Conscious Lovers*, Gay's *Beggar's Opera* and *Polly*, Fielding's *Author's Farce*, Lillo's *London Merchant*, Goldsmith's *She Stoops to Conquer*, Sheridan's *School for Scandal*, and Cowley's *Belle's Stratagem*. Although instructors might want to supplement texts from the later years of the century, Canfield provides the first modern anthology that recognizes women's literary contribution to the stage. To their credit, Dover have reissued B.R.S. Fone's edition of *An Apology for the Life of Colley Cibber* in paperback. Cibber's lively autobiography filled with theatre gossip would make an excellent addition to a graduate or undergraduate course on the drama. Readers need no reminder of his importance in the eighteenth century or of the value of his *Apology*; we can only be grateful for its availability in paperback.

Some of the most interesting essays published in 2000 contemplated problems of theatricality and the institution of the theatre. In an important and persuasive essay called 'Jews and Other "Outlandish Englishmen": Ethnic Performance and the Invention of British Identity Under the Georges' (*Critl* 26[2000] 773–97), Michael Ragussis suggests that 'in the eighteenth century the Jew was located centrally in the redefinition of England as a commercial nation'. He comes to this conclusion through looking at the wide range of multicultural representations on stage in the second half of the eighteenth century, noting the theatre's particular interest in the performativity of Jewish identity. He argues against the dominant view of the theatre as a site of national unification, demonstrating that the plays themselves, though sometimes in disparaging ways, nevertheless explore, suggest, and attempt to comes to terms with the wide range of ethnic identities in England. Also exploring the theatre in its broader social context, Matthew J. Kinservik argues in 'Censorship and Generic Change: The Case of Satire on the Early Eighteenth-Century London Stage' (*PQ* 78:iii[2000] 259–82) that 'the legal and cultural debate over the censorship of drama in the early eighteenth century transformed the concept of the satirist from a mean-spirited attacker to a sympathetic friend'. Here Kinservik suggests that anti-theatrical reformers and supporters of the theatre all believed in the theatre's moral function; each side claimed the rational position of the censor for itself while tarring the other as malevolent satirists. Steele, however, redefined satire as a productive moral position. Kinservik's larger and more provocative point is that both critics and the theatres themselves regarded government censors as potential allies. In 'Male Coquettes and Fribbling Beaux: The Representation of Effeminate Fops on the Mid-Eighteenth-Century English Stage' (*RECTR* 15:ii[2000] 73–92), Marc Martinez looks at the mid-century fop and argues that, rather than functioning simply as an object of ridicule, the comic fop in this era created a liminal gender identity that undermined simple divisions between the masculine and feminine spheres. Nevertheless, playwrights differed in their use of this figure: while Foote and Macklin's fops embodied vices endangering the nation, Garrick's fops gently undermined gender divisions, recuperating this figure through the discourse of sensibility. Christopher B. Balme, in the powerful and sophisticated 'Sexual Spectacles: Theatricality and the Performance of Sex in Early Encounters in the Pacific' (*TDR* 44:iv[2000] 67–85), demonstrates the ways in which Europeans theatricalized Polynesian culture as a prerequisite to colonialism. Stories of sexual promiscuity in the South Seas most 'inflamed' Europeans; in particular, they recorded the theatricality of Polynesian sexuality. But while the theatricalization of the 'other' advanced imperialism in general, the particular performances of Polynesians 'posed a genuine challenge to Western conceptual categories'. Further, the theatricalization of sexuality provided a way for Polynesians to integrate Europeans into their own symbolic systems.

Women writers and performers drew some productive attention in 2000. In a thought-provoking article titled 'Picturing Tragedy: *Mrs. Siddons as the Tragic Muse* Revisited' (*ECS* 33:iii[2000] 401–30), Heather McPherson 'revisits' Sir Joshua Reynolds's famed 1784 portrait of Sarah Siddons, recontextualizing it within other contemporary visual and literary representations of the actress in order to explore the ways in which theatrical and visual aesthetics intersected with one another in the commercialization of culture in the late eighteenth century. Through a variety of visual figures and excerpts from relevant aesthetic criticism, McPherson constructs a tightly woven essay that complicates our understanding of the relationship between theatrical portraiture and the stage, arguing that portraiture and theatrical performance worked reciprocally in both aesthetic and commercial modes. In 'Gender, Genre, and Theatricality in the Autobiography of Charlotte Charke' (in Coleman, Lewis, and Kowalik, eds., *Representations of the Self from the Renaissance to Romanticism*, pp. 97–116), Robert Folkenflik explores the ranges of genres on which Charlotte Charke's *Autobiography* draws, paying particular attention to its theatricality; he draws attention to this book's dual function as both a commodity and a form of blackmail. While Folkenflik raises some familiar issues, he contributes to our understanding of Charke by investigating her self-assertion in the context, not just of her own subjectivity, but as a writer with a sophisticated understanding of both theatre and autobiography. In a well-researched and wide-ranging essay, 'Mary Robinson and the Scripts of Female Sexuality' (in Coleman, Lewis, and Kowalik, eds., pp. 230–59), Anne K. Mellor explores the cultural narratives into which the life of the actress and writer Mary Robinson has been scripted, specifically, the whore, the unprotected wife, the romantic lover, and the woman artist. Mellor finds the same range of possibilities in Robinson's own writing. Rather than searching for the 'real' Mary Robinson, then, Mellor suggests that these disparate scripts themselves comprised this woman's life: 'any distinction between the self *as* art and the self *in* art collapses'. In 'Women and the Theatre' (in Jones, ed., pp. 238–62), Angela J. Smallwood argues that circumstances for women playwrights changed drastically from the Restoration to the end of the eighteenth century. While Restoration women playwrights faced harsh criticism and few women succeeded as playwrights in the early eighteenth century, the emergent bourgeois ideal of female propriety created a space for them to flourish in the theatre. Like the playwrights, even the actresses could become respectable. Smallwood shows how the plays created this respectability by comparing and sharply contrasting a disreputable woman with one who embodies the culture's ideals. Her claim for this as a kind of feminism is, however, not entirely convincing, for in this configuration one woman establishes her importance at the expense of another.

This year also saw some innovative readings of individual plays. Elizabeth Kowaleski Wallace, 'Reading the Surfaces of Colley Cibber's *The Careless Husband*' (*SEL* 40[2000] 473–89), interestingly argues that Cibber divides his characters into the 'deep' and the 'superficial'. But 'while the play's themes explicitly endorse the society of 'authentic' and 'true' sentiments over the world of fashion and of theatrical posing, the resolution of the plot'—referring to the famous steinkirk placement—'depends precisely upon the manipulation of fashionable objects and effects'. Thus in spite of this division between deep and superficial characters, the play nevertheless suggests how modern subjects form identities in relation, rather than in opposition, to consumer culture. In this regard, the play ultimately suggests the impracticality of the non-performative subject. In 'John Gay, *The Beggar's Opera*, and Forms of Resistance' (*ECLife* 24:iii[2000] 19–30), John Richardson argues that most critics run into trouble with *The Beggar's Opera* when they try to figure out exactly what Macheath stands for. For Richardson, he does not stand for something in particular, but instead stands against expectation. In creating this figure, Gay challenges the reliability of language usurped by power; thus he not only criticizes Walpole and the New Whiggery, but explores 'the personal resistance to intrusive power and…the identity threatened by it'. This strategy has its limits, though, for Gay suggests how to extricate oneself from power rather than how to oppose it.

Two fine essays bring much-needed attention to the playwright Susanna Centlivre. In 'Textual Variants and Inconsistencies in Susanna Centlivre's *The Basset-Table* (1705)' (*RECTR* 15:ii[2000] 40–59), Jacqueline Pearson rightly points out that, in spite of Centlivre's importance and popularity in the eighteenth century, she continues to be neglected by both critics and textual scholars. In this essay Pearson focuses on one textual variant—the naming of a character in *The Basset Table*—and convincingly demonstrates its meaning to both a reading of the play and of Centlivre's career. Pearson makes an exemplary case for more work, both critical and scholarly, on this author. Kevin J. Gardner, 'Susanna Centlivre's *The Beau's*

Duel, the Masculine Ideal, and the Anti-Dueling Sentiment of the Early Eighteenth-Century Stage' (*RECTR* 15:ii[2000] 93–108), argues that Centlivre denaturalizes masculinity in this play. Men perform masculinity through their various attitudes towards duelling, but the foppish Mode is obsessed with what his body looks like rather than what it does. Nevertheless, Centlivre satirizes the 'careless violence of men' by allowing Mode to express some reasonable objections to this already controversial form of cultural performance. While the end of the play seems simply to embrace Whig ideology and bourgeois masculinity, Centlivre, in subtle ways, suggests their social cost as well.

Two essays consider Sheridan as an adaptor. Aspasia Velissariou, 'A Trip to Scarborough: Or How "To Undergo a Bungling Reformation"' (*RECTR* 15:ii[2000] 60–72), argues that Sheridan transformed a radical and complex text—Vanbrugh's *The Relapse* [1696]—into an innocuous one consistent with the dominant ideology of the late eighteenth century. In his adaptation, according to Velissariou, Sheridan undermines Vanbrugh's critique of marriage and replaces it with a sentimental view of human nature and the suggestion that human consciousness can be treated outside social institutions and practices. James Morwood, 'Sheridan and the Legacy of his Irish Parents' (*RECTR* 15:ii[2000] 1–17), explores the playwright's literary debt to his parents. From his father he borrowed Captain O'Blunder, whom he revised as Sir Lucius. From a character in his mother's incomplete *A Journey to Bath* he created the famous Mrs Malaprop. Morwood documents many more instances of Sheridan's parental appropriation, but does not go beyond cataloguing this phenomenon.

Several scholars also contribute to our understanding of eighteenth-century theatre history. In an energetic essay entitled 'The Politics of Culture: John Gay and Popular Ballads' (in Cheesman and Rieuwerts, eds., *Ballads into Books: The Legacies of Francis James Child*, pp. 189–98), Dianne Dugaw explores the subversive ways in which Gay combined elite and popular culture by reproducing ballads within his plays. Through the juxtaposition of folk culture with forms of entertainment positioned to demonstrate the spectator's taste, Gay offered a critique of mercantile capitalism by satirizing its cherished cultural expressions. Daniel O'Quinn, 'Through Colonial Spectacles: the Irish Vizier and the Female-Knight in James Cobb's *Ramah Droog*' (*RCPS* [2000]) explores the relationship between representations of sexuality and imperialism in the comic opera *Ramah Droog*. While the British women in this play dress as men in times of crisis, the opera associates gender normalization with the reinstatement of an 'appropriate' colonial hierarchy. O'Quinn looks beyond the text to make this argument, and shows how the excessive Orientalism of the set design 'materializes the potential for surplus value in the colonial enterprise'. Richard G. King, 'The First "Abduction" Opera: Lewis Theobald's and John Ernest Galliard's *The Happy Captive* (1741)' (*MQ* 84[2000] 137–63), makes a case for Theobald's and Galliard's opera as the first example of a genre known as the 'abduction opera', wherein an 'occidental woman is rescued by her occidental lover from the clutches of an Arab potentate' (p. 154), as well as a case for its authorship by Theobald and Galliard rather than John Christopher Smith, to whom it has been attributed. King discusses this opera's performance history, plot and music; he concludes with a discussion of its sources and the significance of its use of the plot of a Turkish abduction more than two decades before the earliest recognized 'abduction' opera. He also offers a brief but intriguing glimpse of the elements of exoticism implicit in the character of the Turkish abductor of *The Happy*

Captive and 'abduction' operas generally. In 'Garrick's Alteration of *Miss In Her Teens*' (*HLQ* 62[2000] 145–52), William J. Burling and William Franken argue that Garrick was obligated to comply with censors in his production of this very popular afterpiece, but they find the particular demands for change somewhat enigmatic. Before the play went to the censor, however, Garrick altered it to enhance the comic effect of his own character Fribble and to improve its theatrical effect overall. By reading the lyrics from songs published with this play, Kathryn Lowerre, 'Musical Evidence for an Early Eighteenth-Century Revival of *The Maid in the Mill* at Lincoln's Inn Fields' (*TN* 54[2000] 86–97), suggests that specific references in the text may point to a hitherto unrecorded performance. Lowerre also argues that adaptors in the early eighteenth century considerably toned down the sexual suggestiveness of this play by altering the songs. Thomas McGeary, 'A Satire on the Opening of the Haymarket Theatre' (*RECTR* 15:ii[2000] 18–32), shows how the issues raised by the Collier controversy and the reform movement in general still provoked controversy in 1705, as Vanbrugh's building of a new playhouse stirred up anti-theatrical moralizing passion. In 'Isaac Read's Diaries and the Theatrical Scene in Eighteenth-Century England' (*RECTR* 15:ii[2000] 33–9), Arthur Sherbo makes the point that previous scholars have overlooked these diaries, which contain considerable information about performance. Aileen Osborn, 'Garrick Papers in Hereford' (*TN* 54[2000] 138–45), alerts theatre historians to the Garrick treasures available in Hereford's city museum, such as Mrs Garrick's diary and Garrick's acting copy of *The Rehearsal*.

3. Poetry

If W.H. Auden's use of the stock market in describing poetic reputations in *Letter to Lord Byron* was applied to criticism of eighteenth-century poetry in the year 2000, then Alexander Pope's market value undoubtedly continued to rise, while the relative shares of his colleagues showed little change. The range and amount of coverage differed little from the rotational trend of preceding years, with some figures stepping forward for more prolonged consideration, as others slipped (temporarily) into the background.

The Dunciad now draws the most critical attention of any of Pope's poems, yet it remains a slippery work, as the introduction to Ingrassia and Thomas, eds., *More Solid Learning*, the first essay collection dedicated solely to the poem, indicates. We are told of 'Pope's inextricable connection to the duncean "other" that resembles another version of the poet himself' (p. 30). Read another half a page, however, and you find that 'Pope, as cannot be denied by even the most pro-duncean among us, also had superior poetic powers that ultimately ensured the predominance of his poem' (p. 31). The admission rather goes against the grain of the collection in general, which takes Pope's poetic superiority over the dunces to be part of his formation of his self-image for posterity.

To be fair, many of the essays here are not so concerned with questioning Pope's achievement as with redefining the terms in which it is appreciated. I doubt that everyone will be convinced by George Rousseau's vivid and energetic drawing of connections between Pope's criticism of opera, and a masculine version of pastoral, via his (literal and metaphorical) fears of the castration endured by famous singers.

This is a rich (if over-egged) dish. Valerie Rumbold's account of Pope's contempt for certain types of opera and support for Handel is the most solid example of learning in the collection. It supports very clearly its premise that Pope's allusive vocabulary in the poem was often shifted along with the events that it strove to depict. Pope's opportunism is shown in his ability to recontextualize when it suited him. Another opportunist, Colley Cibber, is the subject of essays by Laura Rosenthal and Eric Chandler: the former looks at Cibber and Pope as competing versions of masculinity—print culture versus camp theatricality, so to speak. Chandler looks at the famous anecdote of Cibber interrupting Pope and a prostitute, finding in the mercantile symbol of prostitution Pope's hypocritical denial of his own commercial involvement in what he satirizes. This argument is somewhat over-complicated, and is not alone in this collection in locating a nefarious 'binary opposition' on Pope's part, only to replace it quickly with another, more conveniently modern, one. Linda Zionkowski reads Pope's career as a progressive attack upon the aristocratic right to be a 'gentleman amateur' in art (and as an affirmation of his masculine and public role), taking into account the complexity of Pope's motives.

Commerce is also the subject of Catherine Ingrassia's look at the pamphlet war between Pope and Edmund Curll after the poem's publication. Both authors exploit and subvert boundaries (notably between high art and popular culture) for their own ends. Thomas Jemielity takes a very original route, looking at the poem's huge range of scriptural reference, and finding in it a 'mock-apocalypse' that follows the technique of biblical revelation. It's often assumed that 'carnivalesque' equals 'good' in an academic article: Claudia Thomas bravely offers an alternative meaning, in her idea of Pope's Rabelaisian inversion of the term. Here, the carnival of the dunces is not liberating, but a way of associating them with the riot, excess and ignorance of traditional carnival celebrations.

On the whole this is a very thought-provoking collection of essays that reinforces rather than obscures Pope's achievement. One caveat would be its repeated reference to a few twentieth-century scholars representing the 'traditional' view of Pope studies in the 250 years since his demise. This is both unrepresentative and reductive. Many of the essays here depend upon previous scholarship having swallowed Pope's own definition of canon-formation (with him at the top and the dunces at the bottom) wholesale. This contention is often taken for granted here, but it does little justice to the shifts in Pope's reception: the reader of this volume is given no indication that *The Dunciad* was not widely admired (and was, in some famous cases, actively disliked) by some of Pope's most important critics in the eighteenth and nineteenth centuries. This would seem to be another case of modern criticism overlaying a homogeneous reading on a far more heterogeneous past.

In recent years, writing on *The Dunciad* has tended to indicate the larger pattern of Pope's self-fashioning as the centre of critical debate. Howard Erskine-Hill's new selection of Pope's correspondence draws attention to the problems of pinning down such a deliberately public personality. Pope's notorious revisioning of himself (and the plotting that made it possible) in the letters published in his own lifetime is exhibited here by a few examples of the reworking (and readdressing) of material in order to give it the requisite polish of maturity. Pope's letters are witty, sagacious and comprehensively intelligent: like Boswell's Johnson however, he never really seems young, and it is the need to fashion and impress an idea of himself that dominates.

In his selection of roughly one-tenth of the correspondence, Erskine-Hill has included thirteen letters that appeared subsequent to George Sherburn's standard edition of his correspondence [1956], most of which have already been published separately by Sherburn or Maynard Mack. The appeal of the selection lies in Erskine-Hill's skill in giving a representative portrait of Pope's character: Pope could move with equal ease between literary gossip, poetic theory, political worries or society titbits. The complex range of movements between intimacy and sprezzatura are one reason why Erskine-Hill wants us to see the complete correspondence 'as a late literary work by the poet' (p. xxii), and to be eventually re-edited as such.

In contrast to Sherburn's edition, the confines of space in this one prevent Erskine-Hill from presenting all but a few of the letters of Pope's correspondents; similarly, there is less room for the level of annotation that the letters often need (and that only a complete edition can offer). Nevertheless, the thoughtfulness of Erskine-Hill's selection supports his claim 'that there are many readers keen to read Pope's letters for their qualities of mind and style' (p. xxii). One would hope so, yet such readers are unlikely to spend £50 on a hardback volume in order to do so. The audience for this selection, unless it is published in paperback, is therefore not immediately obvious. Another query concerns a recent contention that has crept in here by the back door: anyone using the biographical index will be informed that 'James III and VIII' was 'King *de jure* according to the ancient constitution' (p. 375). Concomitantly, the less than enthusiastic entries on William III and the first two Georges show the same tone. Those interested in the problems of the presentation of the Jacobite argument are referred to a review article by Robert Folkenflik, which has much of relevance to Pope, Swift and Johnson (*AgeJ* 11[2000] 340–9).

There were useful approaches to Pope in journals. James Noggle's 'Skeptical *Ataraxia* and Selfhood in Pope's *Imitations of Horace*' (*1650–1850* 5[2000] 63–92) discusses Pope's poetic self-division (especially in the *Imitations of Horace*) as part of a tradition of sceptical thought that, from the more immediate influence of Montaigne, allows Pope a model of poetic impersonality, rather than showing outright equivocation or unconscious self-contradiction. John Richardson in 'Defending the Self: Pope and his Horatian Poems' (*MLR* 95[2000] 623–33) sees Pope's difficult attitude in the *Imitations*, *Arbuthnot*, and *Epilogue to the Satires* as a necessary formation of character, in that he fought off a political centre that he both despised and envied. Richardson urges the reader to see corruption as a more immediate and real threat to Pope than to those 'who live in modern liberal democracies'. Defining a dissident position by contrast with the inequities of his contemporaries (and by comparison with Horace) is therefore his only alternative. In a long article, 'Pope and Drugs: the Pharamcology of *The Rape of the Lock*' (*ELH* 67[2000] 99–141), Richard Kroll analyses the hidden background to *The Rape of the Lock*—the intake of drugs such as tea, coffee, and other exotic commodities. Kroll argues that the changes brought about by the theories of William Harvey on the circulation of the blood in the seventeenth century create a different view of the body politic (and its potential corruption by impurities), and of the idea of the 'circulation of global trade', against which it is necessary to read Pope's ambiguous poem. Drugs, representing the binding commodity of foreign trade and the anarchic disturber of internal order, are the two sides of the poem brought together dialectically (rather than as oppositions, as in most readings). This is a dense essay that requires its implications to be intuited rather a lot. Julian Ferraro, 'Pope, Rochester and Horace' (in Fisher, ed., *That Second Bottle: Essays on John Wilmot, Earl of Rochester*, pp. 119–131), describes some of the ways in which Pope's self-fashioning of his Horatian persona was influenced by the poet he once called a 'holiday' writer. Allan Ingram's 'Time and Tense in Eighteenth-Century Narratives of Madness' (*YES* 30[2000] 60–70) compares Pope's image of Bedlam and the 'cave of poverty and poetry' in *The Dunciad* (much strengthened in its final version, where it suggests the assertive and overwhelming present domination of insanity) with the temporal disjunctions and necessary evasions of writers thought to be insane, from Alexander Cruden to Joanna Southcote.

In a Pope-assisted polemic, J. Paul Hunter's 'Sleeping Beauties: Are Historical Aesthetics Worth Recovering?' (*ECS* 34[2000] 1–20) takes on the aesthetic assumptions of present criticism, attacking in a refreshing manner the tendency to view the couplet as a reactionary and rigid form. For Hunter, this is a caricature of anti-Enlightenment sentiment. Hunter's explication of the real structural and thematic value of couplet poetics (with famous examples from Pope) as opposed to the simplistic assumptions that make up much criticism of the form is all the better for its self-conscious iconoclasm, reminding criticism of how often its basic procedures are overlooked in pursuit of fashion. In a complementary essay 'Formalism and History: Binarism and the Anglophone Couplet' (*MLQ* 61[2000] 109–29), Hunter criticizes the trend of placing most patterns of eighteenth-century thought and writing into binarism, pointing out that this is anachronistic and misleading. Popean couplet poetics are his counter-example of the development of two or more often opposing ideas which are kept in play, rather than (as much modern criticism would have it) rigidly synthesized.

John Morillo's 'John Dennis: Enthusiastic Passions, Cultural Memory, and Literary Theory' (*ECS* 34[2000] 21–41) takes a rare and insightful look at Pope's old adversary John Dennis's neglected critical theory, specifically his attempt to rehabilitate the idea of enthusiasm as part of his promotion of the passions evoked by poetry. Morillo argues that the egalitarian terms of Dennis's theory were watered down in his subsequent work, in a parallel fashion to the poetics of Wordsworth (who admired him deeply for a short time). Daniel J. Ennis in 'The Making of the Poet Laureate, 1730' (*AgeJ* 11[2000] 217–35) writes engagingly about the selection of the Laureate in 1730, arguing that Stephen Duck, as an innocent who would serve Walpole's purposes, was a clear choice until Colley Cibber's extrovert qualities made themselves felt. Cibber was aided, claims Ennis, by his cynical ability to absorb any criticism from the Scriblerians or other factions, and by his having rejected and worked against the production of Gay's dramas. Phyllis Guskin in 'Martha Fowke Sansom's Poems in the *Barbados Gazette*' (*ECS* 34[2000] 61–91) argues for Martha Fowke Sansom as the author of the poems by the 'Amorous Lady' that appeared in the *Barbados Gazette* in the 1730s and that have found a body of admirers since the publication of Lonsdale's *Eighteenth Century Women Poets*. Guskin accumulates correspondences between the poems and Sansom's acknowledged work, and discusses some biographical possibilities, such as her involvement with a lawyer based in Barbados.

The biographer of Thomas Gray has always been hampered by the difficulties of describing an uneventful life, in which nothing much happened for long stretches, punctuated by (comparatively) frenzied moments of poetic production and (apparent) personal crisis. Robert Mack's *Thomas Gray: A Life* can certainly not be accused of stinting on detail—it weighs in at 683 pages, plus notes and bibliography. What Mack achieves, however, in more than double the length of R.W. Ketton-Cremmer's biography of 1955, is more debatable.

The relative paucity of events in Gray's life, outside of his scholarly interests and sporadic writing, offers two routes to the biographer: the first is bald narrative, from poem to poem, via the odd significant occasion. Mack's route is to magnify the everyday and the seemingly trivial. While this offers a great deal of attention to relatively overlooked areas (such as Gray's Latin poetry, and the connections between his poetry and his compendious scholarship), it also assigns significance to matters that either do not deserve it or are anyway insoluble. This last tendency produces much impressionistic psychology that seems to take the book towards a non-academic audience (an ambition at odds with the depth of scholarship Mack otherwise brings to his material), as well as over-simplifying the complications of such a reticent, ambiguous life and poetic career. The result is a biography that cannot hope to satisfy either audience, with a line of argument constantly diluted by passages of the 'he must have thought' kind and, ultimately, too much attention to events that add little to our understanding of Gray. Mack repeatedly offers the beginnings of important debates (on the homoeroticism of Gray's poetry, or on the problematic self-definition of the Pindaric odes, for example), only to bring them to a close with a sense of finality that the argument has neither reached nor earned. Having amassed such a wealth of material, greater attention to essential critical debates about the poetry would be far more valuable in such a long book that strains to find profundity in almost everything in a life that gave little of it outside the poems. In fact, despite his extensive quotation from the letters (which indicate Gray's barbed wit and attractively spiky character), Mack seems to echo one influential critical impression of him as poet and scholar: this is a tentative book that begins many things, but does not (and cannot) often follow them through.

Gray gets something of a grilling in David Hill Radcliffe's broad look at a general, paternal Spenserian influence on mid-century poets, 'The Poetry Professors: Eighteenth Century Spenserianism and Romantic Concepts of Culture' (*1650–1850* 5[2000] 121–50). Radcliffe sees in these writers a common post-1750 use of educative themes that moves away from classical models. They proffer instead ideas of modern virtue which founder somewhat on the pastoral educational schemes of Gray's *Elegy*, or the complicated primitivism of Beattie's *Minstrel*. There is a great deal of information here, though the sophistication of the argument means that a lot of it needs very careful teasing out.

Elsewhere, some of the most obscure poets of the century get attention in Suvir Kaul's *Poems of Nation, Anthems of Empire: English Verse in the Long Eighteenth Century*, a rewarding look at works usually thought to offer little to the modern reader. Kaul's premise is contained in his title: poetry in the long eighteenth century is implicitly concerned with national development. The progressions and problems of empire dominate as a theme, with—and this is the novelty of the thesis—often willing complicity from poets, who believed that their work made a genuine contribution to public debates over the efficacy and future of the nation's ambitions. As Kaul points out, many poets were thus acknowledged legislators a century before Shelley's famous claim to the contrary.

Kaul begins with a contrast between Marvell's and Waller's writings on the Bermudas, and carries on with Dryden, whom he sees as encouraging the nationalist development abroad powerfully initiated by Cromwell. Nationalism is charted against Europe and the globe. These imperial achievements also have their potential downside, and much poetry from Addison to John Dyer (in Kaul's view) concerns the fear of a Rome-like decadent end of empire. Kaul argues that this fear is then carried forward, with contemporary trappings, by Goldsmith and Barbauld, in works railing against the luxury of empire.

The central figure of the book, whose misgivings about imperialism are less pronounced, is James Thomson, whose poems are shown here to build a vision of British stability constructed around the global context of empire. The contradictions between the desired certainties of the imperial future and the difficulties of the past are still present, for Kaul, in Thomson and these poems are not mere evidence of Whiggish enthusiasm: Thomson attempts to fuse shifting national events and imperatives into poetic moments of calm and confidence. Kaul's serious and detailed attention to poems usually quickly passed over by criticism (such as the notorious *Liberty*) is welcome. He is equally diligent in decoding the little-read naval odes of Young, which show an aggressive nationalism tempered by self-doubt in such a self-conscious form, as well as a more bullish celebration of Britain as the centre of the trading world. Kaul posits (convincingly) that Young, Richard Glover and Dyer ally themes of global commerce to powerful poetic myths. Yet, to look at one example, Dyer's mythopoetic use of archetypes of honest rural labour to join with a contemporary world vision of expansive capitalism in *The Fleece* is homogenized by Kaul as a 'British' vision. However, *The Fleece* is set on the Welsh–English border, and is written by a Welsh poet who spent much of his life in England. Kaul sometimes describes an untroubled 'Britishness', which is often more complex or conditioned in the poetry concerned.

Even with such a qualification, there is much of great value here, not least in the delicate analysis of the contradictory relationship between the poetry of anti-slavery (by Cowper, Barbauld and Hannah More) and its nationalist and paternalist agenda. In its frequent desire to perpetuate the control of a (supposedly benevolent and civilizing) empire, anti-slavery poetry is tied to the discourse of the nation. Kaul's method throughout the book is to follow often meandering poems along their paths, noting their contradictions and blind spots. One consequent drawback of this ostensibly formalist technique is hinted at by the author in his conclusion: the repetitive themes of many of these poems make it appear that they are all equal fodder for the modern postcolonial interest in empire and nationalism. The subtlety and patience of Kaul's readings negate such a problem, for the most part. In his introduction, however, he opens a can of worms by stating that 'as in any narrative of the self, it is the fissures and the ruptures, the hesitations and the contradictions, that offer the more credible analysis of creativity and its discontents' (p. 43). This seems too programmatic a way of reading to describe this very interesting book, which shows us rather how some of the dustiest and least-read eighteenth-century poems can be made accessible when the terms of approaching them are understood.

James Thomson's tercentenary was celebrated by a robust collection, Terry, ed., *James Thomson: Essays for the Tercentenary*, conveniently split into two parts: essays covering specific attention to his works and essays on his influence in posterity. Thomson was a more prodigious writer than is usually remembered, and

Brean Hammond strikes a blow for his dramatic writing, looking at his *Sophonisba*, a play often recalled only in the sprit of ridicule. Rather than the stodgy and absurd heroic tragedy of legend, Hammond finds it a sophisticated dialogic account of political integrity, with a strong female lead to boot. For Hammond, Thomson's ideologically pertinent exploration of the 'Patriot' question is an intellectual advance on Addison's *Cato*. William Hutchings defends Thomson's technique of natural description from those who locate in it thinly veiled ideological problems. Drawing on Lessing, and a discussion of the inferiority of language to painting in description (since it must necessarily be successive rather than instantaneous), Hutchings sees Thomson's technique as a representation of the simultaneous unity and variety of nature, via an affective aesthetic that makes the reader participate in the scene and the gradation of its changes. Robert Inglesfield describes the obvious influence on Thomson of Shaftesbury's philosophy of social benevolence. As Shaftesbury was a controversial figure at the time, Thomson may have toned down some of his more deistic moments when revising *The Seasons*. Glynis Ridley reads *The Seasons* as a poem of more direct 'Patriot' opposition than is usually thought to be the case, looking at key symbols and figures included or added to sections as Thomson's opposition to Walpole solidified. Robin Dix locates the failure of that unread poem *Liberty* in its contradictory attempts to locate the historical coexistence of liberty and the flourishing of the arts. Thomson elided the history books to prove the point, but at the cost of some damage to the poem. Yet this failure is helpful, in that *The Castle of Indolence* is a more richly suggestive form of progress poem, carrying political, philosophical and aesthetic questions in its symbolism without being weighed down by strictness of argument.

The essays on Thomson's posterity begin with Richard Terry's investigation of the 'Druid' image applied to Thomson by William Collins. Terry contends that the imaginative appeal of the Druids for the eighteenth century was centred upon their symbolic role as the mythic first British poets, thus explaining (in part) Collins's choice of accolade. Gerard Carruthers looks at the vexed question of Thomson's relationship with Scotland, and finds accounts of him as a betrayer of his native heritage (in the eighteenth and nineteenth centuries) to be erroneous and misguided. Thomson's education and background make him, for Carruthers, not an opponent of Scottish culture, but a British poet, negotiating his own sense of Scottish identity. Resistance to this idea has prevented us from realizing how much he influenced such poets as Burns and Fergusson. Tim Fulford traces the iconography of the 'British Oak' from Thomson's use of it in 'Rule Britannia' to the trial of Queen Caroline in 1820, via the French Revolution (and Burke and Cowper), and its importance to the navy in the Napoleonic Wars. Although an ostensibly patriotic symbol, representing the sturdiness of the constitution, it was eventually appropriated for radical interests (which could not be said of Thomson's song). John Barrell and Harriet Guest look at Thomson's reputation immediately after 1789, when the supporters of the French Revolution could invoke (and give a brief readership to) Thomson's *Liberty*, to the extent that Erskine quoted from it at John Hardy's trial for treason in 1794. By the mid-1790s, however, as the forces of reaction set in, Thomson's poetry was increasingly used as a model of middle-class sentimental domesticity. It therefore functions as a mirror of the shifting political focus of the decade. The collection ends with John Strachan's suggestive account of Thomson's Romantic-era popularity. The high estimation of critical theorists such as Christopher North for *The Seasons* contradicts the ambivalence of Coleridge and the lukewarm attitude of Wordsworth towards it. Arguing that we must jettison a concentration on reading the literary history of the period through its so-called major poets, Strachan points out the importance of Thomson as an artistic model for the enormously popular Robert Bloomfield, among others. One odd moment, in light of the previous essay, is Strachan's puzzling over the absence of any radical interest in *Liberty* in the 1790s, though nobody ever said that contributors to such a volume need to be in a state of utmost agreement. This is a fine collection that does justice to the poetry, context and reputation of Thomson without privileging any particular area, and which one hopes will increase critical interest in its subject, or at least maintain it at its present steady level.

The viability of essay collections on relatively obscure figures is dependent upon their serving a comprehensive (and lasting) set of purposes. Dix, ed., *Mark Akenside: A Reassessment*, the first critical book on the poet since 1944, is generally an admirable companion to Robin Dix's edition of 1996. The purpose of these essays, Dix admits, is to 'provide a stimulus for future research', while showing 'the importance of Akenside's contribution to various aspects of the literary tradition' (p. 13). We are thus directed to different areas of Akenside's influence: politics (in the often overlooked odes) is the subject of Dustin Griffin's attempt to rescue from obscurity the political importance of poetry in the mid-century. Akenside exemplifies this, and Griffin points to other examples where the political function (and social form) of the ode has tended to be elided in favour of a poetry of interiority. Harriet Jump's intensive reading of the 'Ode to Bishop Hoadly' is similarly keen to show the level of Akenside's political involvement: the density of his references to the past controversies of the ageing Whig hero are an attempt to form a link to the post-1688 world, via one of its most visible living symbols. Mandy Green's long analysis of the 'Hymn to the Naiads' (the epitome of Akenside's classical veneration) also includes the political dimension, in showing the poem not to be merely a frigid exercise in allusion. To this end, she stresses Akenside's range of contemporary references, and his following the public poetic role of Milton, as well as the more obvious inspiration of Callimachus and Pindar. The result has elements of the progress poem, exalting Britain at the expense of Rome, but also promoting the value of poetry.

The more specifically intellectual context of Akenside's work is provided by Karina Williamson's look at his scientific background, and his idea of 'science' as a general philosophical search for truth, rather than the modern, specialized area of knowledge. This creates fruitful tensions in his poetry, with the creative poetic side trying to reconcile itself with its philosophical content. Richard Terry examines Akenside's part in the argument with Warburton over ridicule as a test of truth, and finds that his idea of ridicule is a development of the Shaftesburyean moral argument refined by the Hutchesonian idea of comparative objects of ridicule. However, Terry concludes that Akenside undermined himself in claiming it as a reliable test of veracity: he was beaten down by Warburton, and demolished posthumously by Johnson. Steve Clark refutes the idea that Akenside took his Lockean ideas second-hand from Addison, arguing instead for crucial differences between them. Most notably, Addison's explanation of mental passivity in pleasure differs greatly from Akenside's idea of the mind being far more active in the intuitive powers of perception and imagination. David Vallins looks at Akenside's connection with a later thinker, Coleridge, finding much in common between them, chiefly in the seeking of pleasure in the sublime transcendence of the quotidian, and in the power of imagination. Creative activity (and its revelation of a divine order) takes them to the realm of pure thought. These connections also form a link with Coleridge's beloved German philosophy.

Dix's own contribution looks at the start of Akenside's career, and his first three published poems of 1737, which exhibit characteristic themes and techniques of internalizing psychology through apparent personification, the transformative powers of imagination, and an individual though transparent assimilation of influences. There is also a youthful self-reflexive wit and humour (qualities not readily associated with his mature work). John Constable uses 'empirical metrics' to analyse the revision of *The Pleasures of Imagination* into the unfinished *The Pleasures of the Imagination*, finding evidence of changes in word-length and stress that indicate a more compact and shorter, simpler style. To this reviewer, parts of the explanation (complete with graphs, diagrams and charts) recalled Byron's comment on the *Biographia Literaria*, but leaving such hidebound opinions aside, this collection should serve as a model introduction to a difficult and neglected figure. Dix has also offered a strong corrective to G.S. Rousseau's recent readings of Akenside as homosexual in 'The Pleasures of Speculation: Scholarly Methodology in Eighteenth-Century Literary Studies' (*BJECS* 23[2000] 85–103), where he points out that the methodology of Rousseau's argument (that Akenside was the lover of his friend and patron Jeremiah Dyson over a long period) is flawed by its presentation of neutral, ambiguous (and in some cases misleading) information as the confirmation of its speculative thesis.

The perennial critical problems surrounding *Ossian*, and its nationalist context, come under sustained interrogation by Daffyd Moore in 'Heroic Incoherence in James Macpherson's *The Poems of Ossian*' (*ECS* 34[2000] 43–59), who argues that the critical tendency to turn the poems into a sentimental form of epic heroism (that absorbs the prevalent idea of politeness into their structure) is not borne out by the random and chaotic events of the poems themselves, where the polite and heroic are constantly conflicting rather than compromising. The poems are best read as works of sentiment (with an awareness of the dangers of generalization) rather than as a resolution of different forms. In another article, '*Ossian*, Chivalry and the Politics of Genre' (*BJECS* 23[2000] 21–35), Moore looks at a pamphlet on the controversy from 1764, which illustrates an unusual way of questioning the authenticity of the poetry, while finding it to be great on its own generic terms—those of the romance tradition rather than the historical epic. Moore uses this evidence to show in part the problems of viewing Macpherson's contemporary supporters and detractors along a 'neo-classicist/primitivist divide'. Corinna Laughlin's 'The Lawless Language of Macpherson's Ossian' (*SEL* 40[2000] 511–37) examines the appropriation of Ossianic language by adaptors and imitators, finding a pattern whereby the uncontrolled feeling of Macpherson's language is controlled by the framework of sensibility, and made into a powerful but selective emotional register.

A different sort of sensibility is explored by Christopher Reid in 'Sacramental Time: John Jackson, Christopher Smart, and the Reform of the Calender' (*ECent* 41[2000] 205–24). This offers a fascinating comparison between Christopher Smart's increased religious 'enthusiasm' and the contemporary arguments (of a similarly millenarian cast) of those who refused to accept the validity of the new

Gregorian calendar after its introduction in 1752. Reid conveys the flavour and historical importance of the quarrel, and illustrates that Smart was not alone in his peculiar combination of 'High Church' and evangelical values. Elsewhere, Daniel J. Ennis reads the *Jubilate* as a theological *ars poetica* on Smart's part, 'Christopher Smart's Cat Revisited: *Jubilate Agno* and the Ars Poetica Tradition' (*SoAR* 65[2000] 1–23). The metapoetic nature of the poem is explored through various examples of the connection between the linguistic and the holy 'word', which are more convincing than Ennis's closing reading of the 'My cat Jeoffry' section as a poetic metaphor (which seems a little forced).

David Paxman's reading of 'Failure as Authority: Poetic Voices and the Muse of Grace in William Cowper's *The Task*' (*1650–1850* 5[2000] 203–42) finds Cowper's presentation of different voices to be part of his own necessary poetic and religious humility. Paxman is very good on the religious background to Cowper's work, and its tangled motives and results, but sometimes requires too strong a wind of change from that old bugbear, 'Augustan ideals', in his account of poetry after Pope.

The problems of finding an appropriate methodology to discuss the changes of literary history also concern David Fairer in 'Historicism and the Canon: A Spenserian Dispute in the 1750s' (*ECLife* 24[2000] 43–64), who discusses the current debate on the history of the formation of the English canon through an analogous argument from the 1750s. Thomas Warton's and John Upton's differences over how to represent Spenser's *Faerie Queene* led to a dispute: Warton's drawing of imaginative connections between Spenser's poem and (then obscure) medieval romances clashed with Upton's bluff, empirical assumptions of criticism based upon linguistic knowledge and (broad) historical judgement (which at times make him resemble Richard Bentley or Squire Western). Upton's views followed a strict pattern of classical scholarship, whereas Warton's more fluid sense of literary history was allied to the development of sensibility in its recreative impulses. This nuanced piece offers an important lesson in the necessity of historicizing our historiographers, as well as ourselves. It's a lesson that has generally been heeded in a year that, while not offering a vast volume of criticism, nonetheless showed an appropriate balance of textual and contextual engagement.

4. Prose

This year has seen many publications looking at women writing in prose genres other than the novel. In a number of noteworthy books and articles, women's travel narratives, correspondence, memoirs, histories, and contributions to periodicals have received significant attention. The variety of genres in which early modern women wrote is particularly apparent in Kathryn King's engaging study, *Jane Barker, Exile: A Literary Career, 1675–1725*. Moving beyond the autobiographical readings which have tended to characterize work on Barker, King presents a rich and stimulating account of the significance of her writing to the religious, political and literary cultures of the period. Barker's literary output was prolific and various: she produced occasional verse and political satires, published a heroic romance, a translation of Fénelon and the innovative 'patchwork' narratives of the *Galesia* trilogy. King describes her book as 'the biography of a literary career', and her five chapters trace the transitions of Barker's writing life from her participation in the provincial literary coteries of Cambridge, through her writings for the exiled Stuart court at Saint-Germain, to her status in early Hanoverian England as a 'professional' writer. In King's study, Barker's work becomes a springboard for a careful exploration of the culture of British Jacobitism and the representation of female authorship and authority during the era between the accessions of James II and George I. Barker's preoccupation throughout her writing life with the themes of loss and exile should, King argues, be read in the context of her engagement as a Catholic with those aggressively Protestant brands of national and imperial identity which characterized the turn of the eighteenth century, rather than as direct analogies of her gendered position. The discussion of Barker's later works in the book's final chapters is particularly stimulating. Earlier critics have described the narrative structure of Barker's *Patchwork Screen* and *The Lining of the Patchwork Screen* as simply 'incoherent', but for King their complex mingling of prophecies and epistles, tales, recipes, and different tellers and auditors, figures an imaginary and imaginative national heterogeneity. King usefully links the 'patchwork' nature of Barker's writing to the cultural 'patchwork' of its audience, circulation, and/or publication. She reads Barker's work in terms of the ways in which it negotiates the cultural divisions between manuscript and print, coterie audience and wider readership, private circulation and formal publication. 'Too narrow a focus on the commercial, print oriented side of women's literary activities', she writes, 'distorts our understanding of female literary production in the early modern period.'

King's interpretation of Barker's privately circulated manuscripts as 'sociable utterances, currencies of exchange', resonates with a number of other publications on women's prose-writing produced this year. Harriet Guest's important and wide-ranging *Small Change: Women, Learning, Patriotism, 1750–1810* includes some stimulating discussions of bluestocking correspondence. In three particularly suggestive chapters, Guest focuses on the ways in which Elizabeth Carter's letters describe her learning through contradictory impulses of modesty and ambition, fame and obscurity, and explores the associations between Carter's faith and her representation of regional and national identity. Guest's careful readings move beyond familiar models of privacy more usually marshalled in interpretations of eighteenth-century women's correspondence towards a more nuanced understanding of the relationship between the writings of bluestocking women and the formation and transformation of eighteenth-century sociability and public opinion, thereby suggesting how it is possible to hear the 'chink of gold' in the rattle of 'small change'. Carter's life and writing also feature in Norma Clarke's lively and interesting *Dr Johnson's Women*. Clarke describes her book as a 'collective biography' which aims to explore the 'conditions of female authorship', the range of literary opportunities for educated women of the middling and upper ranks. In her examination of these conditions, Clarke is particularly attentive to issues of class and social status. Her discussion of Samuel Johnson's protection and promotion of the reputation and literary interests of Charlotte Lennox is particularly illuminating. Other chapters focus on Hannah More, Frances Burney, Elizabeth Montagu and Hesther Thrale; Clarke's book provides an excellent introduction to the writings and personalities of the women of the mid-century bluestocking circle.

The 'sociable currency' of bluestocking prose-writing, and the correspondence of later eighteenth-century women, also receives attention in a number of the essays in Eger, Grant, O'Gallchoir and Warburton, eds., *Women, Writing and the Public*

Sphere, 1700–1830. In 'Intimate Connections: Scandalous Memoirs and Epistolary Indiscretion', Mary Jacobus examines the crossover between interiority and notoriety in the 'indiscreet' publication of letters, while Gary Kelly's 'Bluestocking Feminism' presents a brief survey of the literary productions of many of the writers discussed in the studies by Guest and Clarke already mentioned. Elizabeth Eger's engaging essay 'Representing Culture: *The Nine Living Muses of Great Britain*' discusses writings by and about bluestocking women in terms of their representation as both private and national property, and Susan Wiseman's contribution on Catharine Macaulay's *History* similarly urges a reconsideration of the models of public and private used in critical interpretations of eighteenth-century women's prose-writing.

Macaulay's *History* also figures in Devoney Looser's *British Women Writers*. As Looser notes, histories produced by eighteenth- and nineteenth-century American women have been the focus of some notable recent critical attention, yet the contributions of British women to history writing remain comparatively under-explored. Looser's study is structured around readings of six very different British writers: Lucy Hutchinson, Lady Mary Wortley Montagu, Charlotte Lennox, Catharine Macaulay, Hester Lynch Piozzi and Jane Austen. Looser stresses the flexible and popular nature of the genres of historical writing throughout the long eighteenth century, and her chapters address the stylistic variety of, and the different audiences for, women's history's over the course of the period. In a study that focuses predominantly on issues of literary style and reception and covers such a wide range of writing, there is little space for close attention to those issues of class affiliation and political engagement so central to the work and identities of many of the writers Looser discusses, but her book should be welcomed as an interesting contribution to an expanding field.

The debate surrounding the reception of eighteenth-century women's prose-writing is central to Teresa Heffernan's 'Feminism against the East/West Divide: Lady Mary's *Turkish Embassy Letters*' (*ECS* 33:ii[2000] 201–15). Heffernan responds to the variety of gendered interpretations of the *Embassy Letters* as masquerade, Orientalist intervention and 'masculine' travel-writing, with a reading which focuses on Montagu's engagement with issues of modernity, urbanization, religion and rationality. Lynda M. Thompson's *The Scandalous Memoirists: Constantia Phillips, Laetitia Pilkington and the Shame of 'Publick Fame'* also explores issues of reception and publicity. Thompson's lively and carefully argued study explores the 'true romance' of the mid-century autobiographical narratives of Pilkington, Phillips and Lady Frances Vane, whose *Memoirs of a Lady of Quality* were integrated by a sympathetic Tobias Smollett into the text of his *Peregrine Pickle*. The early chapters of Thompson's book trace the publication histories of Pilkington's and Phillips's memoirs in some detail, while the latter half includes an interesting account of the mid-century debate on copyright in terms of these writers' control of the property of their persons, reputations and literary productions. Thompson's exploration of the implications of the memoirists' refusal of anonymity and the truth claims of their narratives is particularly noteworthy. She explores how they represented themselves as real-life heroines, perhaps superior to Richardson's 'fancied' Clarissa in the authenticity and tragedy of their suffering, or presented damning indictments of the legal position of women in relation to marriage and property rights, legitimizing their narratives through apparently self-abnegating confessions of frailty. The memoirists' account of female suffering and sexuality should be read, Thompson argues, in terms of a popular and peculiarly mid-century *mélange* of the libertine and the sentimental.

Thompson reads the memoirists' sentimental engagement with female suffering and sexuality as related to, but clearly distinct from, contemporary sentimental representations of prostitution. In '"Sympathetic Visibility": Social Reform and the English Woman Writer: *The Histories of Some of the Penitents in the Magdalen House*' (*Women's Writing* 7:ii[2000] 247–66), Joyce Grossman explores the representation of prostitution in terms of the relationship between women's sentimental writing and their philanthropic activities. Comparing the *Histories of Some of the Penitents in the Magdalen House* to Sarah Fielding's later works in terms of their stylistic and thematic similarities, Grossman contends that she should be identified as the most likely author of this hitherto anonymous text. The contributions and editorial practice of women writers to the burgeoning market for periodicals in the early century are discussed by Sarah Prescott and Jane Spencer in their 'Prattling, Tattling and Knowing Everything: Public Authority and the Female Editorial Personal in the Early Essay-Periodical' (*BJECS* 23:i[2000] 43–57).

Significant new editions of eighteenth-century prose appeared this year, of use for both study and research. Mullan and Reid, eds., *Eighteenth-Century Popular Culture: A Selection*, is a particularly welcome publication for students and teachers of eighteenth-century prose. In the anthology's excellent critical introduction, the editors explore and establish many of the concerns attendant on the study of the period's popular culture, focusing in particular on the turn in recent scholarship towards the question of the distinction and demarcation of cultural identities that may be considered through notions of high or low, vulgar or polite. Looking at the emergence of modern debates on taste, the editors suggest that, in interpreting popular culture, a distinction between *who* read what is perhaps less valuable than *how* eighteenth-century readers read what they read: specifically, how those of the middling and upper ranks experienced and engaged with both high and low literary forms, and how the rest of Britain's literate and illiterate classes might do the same. The editors also sound a warning note in relation to the legacy left to the study of eighteenth-century popular culture by later antiquarian interest and twentieth-century scholarship. They suggest that much of the literature which students of the eighteenth century may assume to be canonical or exclusive (the works of Pope, Gay and Fielding, for example) display an enduring fascination with and imbrication in the popular and the vulgar, rather than a clear separation from them. In the anthology's first part, a variety of forms of popular culture are showcased, including urban 'low' life, the criminal underworld and vulgar cant, antiquarianism, and a range of ballads spanning the whole century. The second section of the anthology is organized around events and occurrences, including representations of Bartholomew Fair, Wilkes and the crowd, calendar reform and Native American visitors. The introductions to each section and the exhaustive recommendations for further reading offer a strong contextual framework without undermining the editors' aim to 'steer a middle course', allowing readers to discover their own continuities and lines of debate between the various excerpts. The range of material printed in this anthology, with its useful introductions and bibliographies, renders it an invaluable resource for the literature and cultural studies classroom.

Also published this year is Thomas, Lamb and Smith, eds., *Exploration and Exchange: A South Seas Anthology, 1680–1900*, an excellent anthology of Pacific travel and voyage literature from the eighteenth and nineteenth centuries. Despite the emergence of Pacific and Atlantic encounter- and travel-writing as a growth area in eighteenth-century studies, there has been no paperback anthology available for literary and cultural studies teaching at both undergraduate and graduate level. This anthology is particularly welcome in its selection of texts and extracts which have never been reprinted since the date of their first publication. The book is organized in three large sections, 'Adventurers and Explorers', 'Beachcombers and Missionaries' and 'Literary Travellers', and Thomas, Lamb and Smith include usefully edited selections from the most notable European writers on the Pacific, such as James Cook, Joseph Banks and Johan Reinhold Forster, as well as many texts which are less well known, or in some cases unavailable outside a small number of research libraries. One example is David Darling's *Remarks about the Marquesas*, produced for the London Missionary Society. The extracts are organized in a manner which allows the student to establish a sense of topical continuity and debate: many texts touch on similar key themes, such as mutiny, taboo and the idea of utopia. These themes, and recent critical debates surrounding them, are outlined in the anthology's incisive introduction and the prefatory material to each textual selection. The texts are generously illustrated with contemporary maps, portraits and topographical prints, and the volume includes a useful bibliography.

One of the most significant editions of eighteenth-century prose this year comes from Thoemmes Press. Their five volumes of *Scottish Common Sense Philosophy: Sources and Origins*, judiciously edited by James Fieser, include carefully annotated re-publications of James Beattie's *Essay on the Nature and Immutability of Truth* [1770] and James Oswald's less well known but important *Appeal to Common Sense in Behalf of Religion* [1766–72]. Oswald's *Appeal* appears in volume i, Beattie's *Essay* in volume ii. Volumes iii and iv present a range of early contemporary responses to the common-sense debate, while volume v comprises an excellent bibliography of Scottish common-sense philosophy. The introductions to the editions of Oswald and Beattie include brief biographies of the authors, outline the publication history and reception of their work, and provide useful summaries of the content and argument of the *Appeal* and *Essay*. The edition of Beattie is particularly useful in its collation of editions between 1771 and 1776. The text illuminates Beattie's substantive alterations in response to the contention and debate his *Essay* inspired. The editor's work here is particularly thoughtfully done, clearly revealing the development, reassessment and transformation of Beattie's *Essay*. The forty responses to the writings of Reid, Oswald, Beattie and Stewart which are included in volumes iii and iv display the far-reaching cultural resonance of their works, and all sides of the debate which they provoked. Many of these responses are notable reviews from, for example, Thomas Holcroft and Edmund Burke, but the volumes also include significant pamphlet responses and the complete text of Joseph Priestley's 1774 *Examination* of Reid, Beattie and Oswald, the preface to a 1780 English translation of Buffier's *First Truths*, and Benjamin Rush's *Thoughts on Common Sense* from his 1798 *Essays*. The final volume's bibliography reaches beyond the eighteenth century, covering important later contributions to the debate from William Hamilton, Thomas Brown, and John Abercrombie. Kames, James

Dunbar, David Fordyce, George Campbell and Alexander Gerard are also included here, and the volume affords comprehensive bibliographical information on contemporary editions, manuscript locations, microfilm and facsimile availability, and recent criticism. Since editions of the works of Thomas Reid and Dugald Stewart are already available, this excellent and invaluable series fills a significant gap, and the five volumes as a whole clearly establish the cultural importance of debates on common sense in Britain, Europe and America from the mid-eighteenth to the mid-nineteenth centuries.

Francis Hutcheson's *System of Moral Philosophy*, edited and introduced by Daniel Carey, was also reprinted by Thoemmes this year (unavailable for review). Other editions of eighteenth-century prose produced this year include Froes, ed., *Remarks on the Life and Writings of Dr. Jonathan Swift by John Boyle*. Boyle's text, originally published in 1751, was the first biographical account of Swift and, in its day, a bestseller. The text is carefully annotated, collated and introduced. Also published this year is volume vii of the Oxford *Writings and Speeches of Edmund Burke*, covering Burke's speeches and publications on India and the trial of Warren Hastings. Burke's engagement with these debate is outlined in P.J. Marshall's introduction.

Donald Greene's useful paperback edition *Samuel Johnson: The Major Works* was reprinted this year. The collection includes a wide range of Johnson's writings, including poetry, prose, periodical selections from *The Rambler*, *The Adventurer*, and *The Idler*, excerpts from *A Dictionary of the English Language*, *The Plays of William Shakespeare*, and *A Journey to the Western Islands of Scotland*, selections from Johnson's prefaces to the works of the English poets, passages from diaries and letters, and *Rasselas* in its entirety. Elsewhere in Johnson studies, Adam Potkay's *The Passion for Happiness: Samuel Johnson and David Hume* examines the similarity of ideas in two Enlightenment writers distanced by our own conception of disciplinary boundaries. Potkay advocates a reading of the two men alongside each other, allowing Johnson to draw out under-explored aspects of Hume and vice versa in their moral, historiographical, and political writings. Potkay contends that Hume and Johnson share 'common ground' as moral philosophers drawing on Hellenistic tradition as well as 'modern' authors, including Locke, Addison, Butler, and Mandeville, to determine a model for human happiness. After sketching the writing careers of Johnson and Hume, Potkay looks at sections of *Rasselas* alongside Hume's *Treatise*. Subsequent chapters examine both authors' notions of happiness, human nature, and social theory. Potkay also reads *The Vanity of Human Wishes* alongside Hume's *Enquiry Concerning Human Understanding* in order to reveal the 'therapeutic aims' of Johnson's poem. He concludes with Hume and Johnson's 'harmonious discord' in their views on death, a harmony Potkay situates in the ambiguity of their writings on immortality.

In 'William Gilpin and the Latitudinarian Picturesque' (*ECS* 33:ii[2000] 349–66), Robert Mayhew investigates the popular prose genre of landscape description in terms of its links with eighteenth-century theological debate. He argues that latitudinarian theology is incorporated into the landscape writings of William Gilpin through his arguments about natural design and the spiritual significance of human observation. The negotiation of eighteenth-century aesthetics with other cultural discourses also receives attention this year in John Morillo's article for *Eighteenth-Century Studies* and a book by Michael Bell. Morillo's 'John Dennis: Enthusiastic

Passions, Cultural Memory and Literary Theory' (*ECS* 34:ii[2000] 21–41) explores how Dennis's theory of enthusiasm sought to bring antithetical notions of rationality and passion into confluence. Dennis is a figure who, according to Morillo, exemplifies the complex political aesthetics of the early part of the century. Bell's *Sentimentalism, Ethics and the Culture of Feeling* examines the 'affective turn' of modern Western culture from its eighteenth-century origins through interpretative accounts which draw on analytical philosophy and traditional literary approaches. His study includes some useful discussions of eighteenth-century prose in the ethical writings of Shaftesbury, Frances Hutcheson, Adam Smith and Jeremy Bentham. Bell tends to read sentimentality and sensibility as discourses which are modified less by material circumstance and complex cultural negotiation than by a continuous historical sequence of ideas of feeling, sympathy and affect which finds articulation in the works of the authors already mentioned, as well as those of Kant and Schiller. Later chapters cover Bell's take on the debate on literary sentimentality and sensibility from Dickens and Eliot to the twentieth century. Roy Porter's entertaining and engaging *Enlightenment: Britain and the Creation of the Modern World* includes chapters which read many aspects of eighteenth-century print culture and prose in terms of a specifically British notion of 'enlightenment', from periodicals to dictionaries, from religious to scientific writing. Other aspects of a British 'Enlightenment', particularly in its relation to ideas of empire and colonialism, form the subject of a number of this year's significant studies and articles on eighteenth-century prose. In 'Buccaneer Ethnography: Nature, Culture and Nation in the Journals of William Dampier' (*ECS* 33:ii[2000] 165–80), Anna Neill examines how Dampier's journals figure a key transformation, from the representation of buccaneers as adventurers and plundering pirates to a new role as ethnographic observers and proponents of 'enlightenment modes of knowledge'. Stressing the significant role of the eighteenth-century buccaneer in the extension of Britain's commercial and maritime power, as a proponent of colonization, and as a re-shaper of the modern languages of imperialism, Neill traces some intriguing links between the new discourses of science and empire and earlier notions of adventure and plunder. David Porter's 'A Peculiar but Uninteresting Nation: China and the Discourse of Commerce in Eighteenth Century England' (*ECS* 33:ii[2000] 181–99) examines the representation of China as commercially 'stagnant' in terms of a range of British travellers' accounts of their encounters with the Chinese and their culture and the desire to represent British identity in terms of colonial and economic power. Janet Sorensen's *The Grammar of Empire in Eighteenth-Century British Writing* provides an interesting exploration of a range of eighteenth-century prose-writing on the representation of languages, dialects and linguistic study. Her close readings of a variety of texts, which include essays, dictionaries and grammars, examine how certain linguistic differences between England and Scotland were codified for the purpose of consolidation with a specifically imperial notion of Britishness. Looking at the work of a variety of Scottish 'men of letters', including Alexander MacDonald, Tobias Smollett, Adam Smith and Hugh Blair, Sorenson suggests that an Enlightenment fascination with language, its origins and structure, made some Scots ambivalent producers of the very cultural trend which they sought to oppose. Moving beyond an analysis of the ways in which eighteenth-century Scottish writers negotiated a difficult discursive space between mimicry and authenticity, sameness and difference, her study closes with an examination of the 'Celtomania' of the late eighteenth century. Using a wide and rich range of materials on eighteenth-century language study and the representation of language, Sorensen's discussions weave an interesting literary, linguistic and historical narrative which highlights the complexities of the period's imperial and national identities.

While Sorensen's study unpacks the literary, cultural and political resonances of eighteenth-century language study, Robert Mayhew's *Enlightenment Geography: The Political Languages of British Geography, 1650–1850* performs similar work on British geographical discourse. As Mayhew notes, much scholarly attention has been paid to the history of geography as discipline, but relatively little to the history of geography as text and political discourse. Mayhew's study sets out to bring issues of textual and cultural meaning to bear upon the history of geography, and nine of his thirteen chapters cover a variety of geographical texts produced between the mid-seventeenth and the mid-nineteenth centuries in terms of the intentions of their authors, the responses of contemporary readers, and the conditions of textual production. Geographies addressed by Mayhew include Peter Heylyn's *Cosmographie*; Bohun's Jacobite-inspired *Geographical Dictionary*; William Guthrie's *Geographical Grammar*, heavily influenced by the author's reading of Scottish Enlightenment philosophy and which attempts to define a notion of an incorporative Britishness; and James Bell's *System*, notable for its modern quantitative approach and its evidencing of the importance of British imperial activity. A later chapter provides a useful survey of the transformations evidenced by geographical texts to British ideas of nationhood and empire.

5. The Novel

The start of a new century heralds several examinations offering a metacritical retrospective of studies in the eighteenth-century British novel back to the *locus classicus*, *The Rise of the Novel*. The *fin-de-siècle* interest in Ian Watt sadly coincides with his passing, but rumours of his work's demise are clearly premature. An astonishingly comprehensive collection of the responses to *The Rise of the Novel* can be found in 'Reconsidering the Rise of the Novel' (*ECF* 12:ii–iii[2000] 141–499). The opening essay is, auspiciously, by Watt himself, the first publication of a keynote speech delivered in 1978 at a regional ASECS meeting. In this essay he historicizes his own training as well as his magnum opus, revealing the many influences, from formal criticism to Marxism, that many later scholars have almost forgotten he employed. Many a recent critic would place I.A. Richards in one corner of literary history with Theodor Adorno in another, and yet, as Watt reminds readers, he worked closely with both, and both had read and commented on Watt's manuscript of *The Rise of the Novel*. When he relates the tale of Adorno calling him a 'genius' on his doorstep, Watt's stated modesty precludes his making the explicit connection, and yet his demonstration here of an astonishing facility with the 'new' theories circulating during this time, as well as his wide reading in more recent post-structuralist French thought, reveal that Adorno knew of what he spoke.

Watt provides a witty account of the writing of *The Rise of the Novel*. He divides his experience into a 'truly Hegelian pattern': thesis, antithesis, and synthesis (p. 148). During the first phase, his pre-war training at Cambridge gave him the 'logical positivism' necessary to ask the 'how' questions he would pose (and then later complicate). This approach was underpinned, he suggests, by 'the deep-rooted empiricism and moralism of the English—and especially the Cambridge—tradition', in which he includes I.A. Richards and the Leavises. The war intervened, and, on his liberation from a PoW camp, his desire to 'see what had happened during my long absence' led him to Georg Lukács as well as to Erich Auerbach, both of whom, he claims, 'actually contributed much more to *The Rise of the Novel* than the few references in the text suggest' (pp. 149–50). His exposure to these thinkers, as well as to Weber and 'the whole tradition of German thought in history, literature, sociology, and psychology' was to infuse his work by introducing economic and institutional forces as well as helping shape 'some of [*The Rise of the Novel*'s] more abstract guiding ideas—the notion, for instance, of the disenchantment of the world under the impulse of the scientific and economic rationality (*Entzauberung der Welt*) which came with the Enlightenment' (p. 151). His biography of the work finished, Watt moves on to gloss 'the realities of realism' as he established them in his work. His use of 'formal realism' entails 'a way of differentiating the purely technical aspect of the narrative representation of the real world from the truth or otherwise of the substance of the literary work' (p. 156). While other critics establish what constitutes verisimilitude, Watt claims that he is interested in the prehistory of 'realism' and to see this formal realism as connected to two forces, namely changes in the superstructure and changes in the base. While he sees the shifts in material conditions as historically bounded, he establishes the changes in modes of literary production as those that 'contributed permanent qualitative changes in the expressive idiom of fiction' (pp. 156–7). For Watt, the greatest gift of studying literature is the participation in an important conversation. His goal is one that, despite our differences in approach and training, still seems laudable: to maintain and to enlarge a community.

A very large community comes to the podium following Watt's address in *Eighteenth-Century Fiction*'s special number. The edition is a de facto Festschrift, and as such includes many of the major authors of the last several decades' work on the novel: W.B. Carnochan, Max Byrd, Michael Seidel, Robert B. Alter, J. Paul Hunter, Maximillian E. Novak, Michael McKeon, Robert Mayer, J.A. Downie, John Richetti, Deirdre Lynch, Everett Zimmerman, William Beatty Warner, Janet Todd, Margaret Doody, Robert Folkenflik, and Lennard J. Davis. As the authors discuss the study of the novel since Watt, many respond to an aspect of novel studies, offer a revision of Watt's work, comment on current trends in scholarship, or situate Watt's work in a larger history—literary or social.

A notable omission to the Who's Who of Novel Studies in this text might be Terry Castle, but in an address at the University in Virginia in 1999 she declared the study of the novel *fini*. Lennard Davis quotes Castle's pronouncement as his opening text in his essay 'Reconsidering Origins: How Novel are Theories of the Novel?'(*ECF* 12:ii–iii[2000] 479–99). Castle's declaration notwithstanding, the production of novel studies has taken off since the 1980s; the report of their death seems more than 'premature' (p. 480). Such a proclamation of mortality closes off an elite and accepted list of scholars (Castle names esteemed scholars: '[John] Richetti, [Michael] McKeon, [Lennard] Davis, [Nancy] Armstrong, [John] Bender, [J. Paul] Hunter, [Patricia] Spacks, and [Margaret Anne] Doody'; she heralds Catherine Gallagher). Davis offers his reply to Castle by historicizing studies in the novel beginning with Clara Reeve's 1785 definition of the genre as 'a picture of real life and manners, and of the times in which it is written' (*The Progress of Romance*, quoted by Davis on p. 481). From here, Davis speculates 'on many reasons for … upgrading of the novel's status as cultural paragon', and reviews the history of scholarship that works with and against that apotheosis from before Watt (Earnest Baker's *History of the Novel* [1924]) through Robert Scholes' and Robert Kellogg's *The Nature of Narrative* [1966] and Michael McKeon's *The Origins of the English Novel*. Davis fits some of the more recent studies that owe an 'immeasurable' debt to Foucault into an 'applied-knowledges model', which he glosses as those works that 'use recent political understandings of generic change, feminism, and surveillance to place the early novel in a new light' (p. 494), and which bring 'new justifications from the human sciences, particularly psychology, sociology, anthropology, and the newly created interdisciplinary field of gender studies' (p. 495). Some of these studies, most notably McKeon's, Davis sees as regressive, owing more to earlier critical modes as it 'serves to insert "the dialectical process of historical experience" into narrative modalities, and as such is part of a metanarrativity that itself is born of nineteenth-century fiction' (p. 495). The most important move, according to Davis, is the 'process of devaluing the greatness of the novel', which, rather than discarding the novel and novel studies, instead sees the novel as part of a larger circulation of narrative forms. 'So from being the undecoded Rosetta Stone of mid-century', Davis announces, 'the novel becomes the rolling stone, the location for many voices, a Bakhtinian efflorescence of dialogicity which ends up being not many voices in a socialist community but the uncoordinated voices of the myriad culturalities of the world' (p. 497). And novels 'become those things that produce novelistic narratives', which many a scholar reviewed by Davis in this essay might find. In the end, Davis assures us, 'because novel theory has a history it has a future' (p. 499).

The situation of Watt in a narrative of novel studies is the topic of a scholar not included in the special number of *ECF*. Margaret Reeves, 'Telling the Tale of *The Rise of the Novel*' (*Clio* 30:i[2000] 25–49) aims to deploy historiographic analysis to the several metacritical studies of Watt's *The Rise of the Novel*. As Watt considers the way in which the novel presents its subject matter, Reeves seeks to untangle *The Rise of the Novel*'s 'narrative form in the writing of literary history and the ideological implications that attend the ongoing search for the novel's origin' (p. 25). She begins her discussion by reviewing current conflicts and trends in the disciplines of history and literary criticism. As 'theory' from literary criticism begins to permeate discussions of 'history', the scholars of the latter become distinctly discomfited: 'Because history defines itself in opposition to literature— the usual object of literary-critical scrutiny—such encounters between literary criticism and historical writing threaten to blur the boundary on which history stakes its claims to truth' (p. 26). 'Literary' and 'history' are not, therefore, so distinct, as 'literary histories, by convention, tell stories that are shaped around particular groups of texts, and the telling of these stories is central to the conceptualization of literary traditions and the formation of literary canons'. Her case study of the fluidity of fiction and history as well as the novelization of history lead her to 'examin[e] *The Rise of the Novel* as a narrative that can be fruitfully subjected to the kind of critical analysis normally applied to works of literature' (p. 345). Watt, according to Reeves, brought together and highlighted a number of points already made by literary historians from Virginia Woolf, who had pointed out that the novel found a burgeoning female readership, to critics who had articulated the formal aspects of the novel (including Ernest A. Baker, Frank Godfrey Singer, and Diana Neill, among others), as well as social class relationships noted by Arnold Kettle and Frank O'Connor. Interestingly, given that Watt never claimed originality for his study, Reeves instead finds the form of the *Bildungsroman* embedded in *The Rise of the Novel*: he 'charts a path for the novel from its birth—"the novel is born because Pamela makes her epic resistance to 'a fate worse than death'" (Watt 165)—to adulthood, expressed as the "full maturity of the genre" (Watt 296)'.

Srinivas Aravamudan's 'In the Wake of the Novel: The Oriental Tale as National Allegory' (*Novel* 33:i[1999—not issued until 2000]) informs readers that the 'continuing lovefest between a genre and its followers possesses a monomaniacal intensity ... Novels have become demiurgic in narratives of national life; they are often the preliminary focus as well as the terminus of all investigations of fiction, at least of all that written since the period of the early eighteenth century' (p. 7). Aravamudan finds the novel itself 'parochial', and, in the way that several astute scholars have also found parallels between the narrative *in* the novel and the narrative *of* the novel, notes that 'the history of the English novel, perhaps like that of the British empire, is parochialism writ large as modernity narrative, and also antiquarianism disguised as Enlightenment' (p. 7). The 'domestic realism' of the eighteenth-century British novel 'performs endocultural reification, or the consolidation of the national stereotype from within' according to Aravamudan. The solution to the production and reproduction of insularity is through other narratives, most notably the Oriental tale of the essay's title. This sort of tale 'features a fluid circulation of endocultural and exocultural processes, leading to pseudo-anthropological relativism, and a more allegorical and satirical hermeneutics' (p. 9). By examining the novel in terms of the circulation of other narrative forms (as Davis does above), 'we could arrive at newer genealogies of eighteenth-century prose that do not play off, simplistically, realism against fantasy, history against fable, or bounded nations against unbounded fiction' (p. 16). Aravamudan's analysis discusses Eliza Haywood's *Adventures of Eovaii*, the *Arabian Nights*, and other English and French texts, and reminds scholars of the usefulness of Bakhtin in understanding the flows of texts, particularly the rubrics of 'prosaics', 'unfinalizability' and 'novelization', which, he finds, do not 'collapse into the strain that celebrates the novel as hero of a triumphal romance'.

Novel studies can be divided between what the novel is and what the novel does. While the former topic generated special numbers, fora, arguments and pot-shots, the latter continues apace this year with Miranda Burgess's fine examination of the novel's agency in *British Fiction and the Production of Social Order*. The study begins with Richardson, moves, through Burney and Wollstonecraft, to Austen and Radcliffe, and ends with Sir Walter Scott. Burgess argues that the British romance (1740–1830) functions as 'a genre uniquely but diversely imbricated with political economy' which thereby 'competes with, supplements, and works with its readers to displace the contemporary philosophical debates of political economy, yet remains thoroughly invested in the questions political economy addresses', particularly nationhood (p. 1). Romance, in fact, 'provides a mutually recognized field for thinkers about and debaters of social and national order whose backgrounds, assumptions, and principles seem otherwise irreconcilably diverse' (p. 7). Here we have the conflict-solving power of literature played out on the field of nation. She finds, for example, that 'occupying a generic bridge between politics and fiction, Richardson's romance eases the ideological transition of Protestant Britain as it traded creation mythography for metonymy, vesting social order and authority in avowedly representative examples of the human heart' (p. 31). In her closing, Burgess brings the eighteenth and nineteenth centuries to bear on the twentieth. The photograph of '11:30 P.M., Fetish Night, The Docks, Toronto', seems at first jarring both historically and geographically given the book's subject, but her analysis of 'masochistic models of feminine sensibility' is provocative and productive (p. 235).

The problem of the public–private split, as deployed, occasionally too loosely, in the name of Habermas, has now become a topic in its own right. The question is whether Habermas uncovered a doctrine of separate spheres for the eighteenth century (he did not) and whether we should read domesticity and publicity, public and private, as neatly aligned with gender in literary productions. Lawrence Klein (*ECS* 29[2000] 97–109) has provided a productive critique, and recent studies have begun to challenge the accepted misreading. Gender frequently organizes these studies, both the misreadings of Habermas and the fruitful revisions. Jones, ed., *Women and Literature in Britain*, offers a comprehensive view of the subject with several essays covering the novel and some that engage issues of import to the genre. Women's presence as writers, readers, and scholars of literature has helped 'dislodge some of the familiar narratives about women and literature in this period: asking us to adjust our assumptions about the hegemony of fiction, for example, or to rethink the gendered division between public and private spheres' (p. 15). The text is divided into two parts: the first covers 'femininities' while the second covers the genres of women's writing. (It also has a useful time-line of women's literature and historical events preceding the essays.) In the second part we find Ros Ballaster's view of the history (and historiography) of the genre in 'Women and the Rise of the Novel: Sexual Prescripts', which 'explores the critical debate over the origins and rise of the novel in eighteenth-century England and the crucial part that notions of gender play in its formation and interpretation' (p. 198). She discusses 'the ways in which women writers at different points in the history of the novel self-consciously chart the 'secondariness' of women in the content of their fiction only to reveal the primacy of female agency within the form' (p. 199). The rise of female agency parallels the 'novel's "newness" of language', and it is 'the form's hybrid status between public and private modes of discourse [that extends] opportunities for liberty of speech often denied elsewhere in eighteenth-century culture' (p. 214).

A similar conclusion is drawn by Eve Tavor Bannet in *The Domestic Revolution: Enlightenment Feminisms and the Novel*. Rather than seeing women as liberal or conservative, as, Bannet claims, too many scholars have, she sees two different feminine modes emerging in the period's novels, the 'matriarch' and the 'egalitarian'. Each 'camp', she argues, created and revised the ideologies of the other, a subtly symbiotic exercise that eventually changed the status of women. In the space of exchange and translation between the two modes, Bannet suggests, 'Enlightenment feminist writers inhabited a complex discursive world where diverse feminist and patriarchal agendas were articulated upon one another and where different voices were both joined and divided by the "same" words, the "same" ideals, and the "same" representations, often attaching different meanings to the same lexes' (p. 5). Her investigations cover feminist revisions of 'domestic government', the pedagogical role of women, the legal and amatory fictions following the Marriage Act, and the home and family, as well as matriarchal utopias and their egalitarian critiques.

A number of other critiques situate studies in the novel alongside considerations of other genres. Kirsten Saxton and Rebecca Bocchicchio use the prolific, multi-genre writer Eliza Haywood as a basis for such an examination in their collection of essays, *The Passionate Fictions of Eliza Haywood*. Max Novak's fears, as expressed in 'Gendered Cultural Criticism and the Rise of the Novel: The Case of Defoe' (*ECF* 12:ii–iii[2000] 239–52), are not, as some have suggested, that Eliza Haywood will enter the canon, but that she will be used to force Daniel Defoe out. His argument hinges on 'the strong feminist message' to be found in such characters as Roxana and Moll Flanders (p. 252). Haywood is not used as a bludgeon in this study of her works and life; rather, she is given the kind of critical (and recuperative) scrutiny that Defoe first enjoyed from scholars such as Novak and Richetti, who challenged top-down theories of the novel by giving scholars Defoe's delightful hackery and seedy characterizations. Haywood gets the class and gender treatment here: the authors focus on her 'scandalous fictions', her plays, and her much later domestic fictions. The essays range from readings of her works to metacritical assessments of her place in the canon, as well as investigations of her as case study in the politics of attribution. Paula R. Backscheider's essay 'The Story of Eliza Haywood's Novels: Caveats and Questions' has its response in John Richetti's 'Histories by Eliza Haywood and Henry Fielding: Imitation and Adaptation'. Backscheider argues that Haywood is not the derivative and reactive writer she has been cast as. First, Backscheider does not see any radical discontinuity between Haywood's early and later fictions; instead she finds 'a remarkable consistency in her stated "morals" and the plots and themes that dramatize them' (p. 31). In fact, she suggests, 'Haywood's work exhibits consistent attention to what would become novelistic treatments of appearance and reality themes, and she contributed to the novel's movement toward the psychological' (p. 31). In many ways, Backscheider sees Haywood as the precursor to Fielding, influencing, for example, the latter's parodic gestures (p. 41). To Richetti, however, the opposite seems true. Fielding, who had once employed Haywood as an actress at the New Theatre in the Haymarket, is the imitated one. According to Richetti, 'Haywood is attempting [in *Betsy Thoughtless*] a version of Fielding's deeply ironized mock-inquiry into mid-century moral and social structures and reproducing in preliminary comments … his understanding of character and behavior as a matter of comically predictable recurrences, a pattern which gains comic force from its insertion in a variety of detailed specifics of contemporary life. *Betsy Thoughtless* is a Fieldingesque exercise in social/moral commentary' (pp. 248–9).

Backscheider has two more essays on gender and the novel in her own collection, entitled *Revising Women: Eighteenth-Century 'Women's Fiction' and Social Engagement*, a collection which also includes works by Betty Rizzo, Mitzi Myers, and Barbara M. Benedict. The assemblage of women 'who joined together to produce this book represent[s] over seventy-five years of feminist scholarship' (p. vii). Their work forms a de facto response to Novak and Richetti; they claim that 'perhaps we take for granted work that is the result of a lifetime's study with Daniel Defoe, Alexander Pope, or Samuel Johnson, but for women and the novel it is relatively new and is an announcement of the future of the field' (p. viii). Backscheider's own essay reminds the reader that 'the decade of the 1720s, which was absolutely dominated by women writers...is usually treated as if it belonged to Daniel Defoe alone' (p. xi).

The essay on the gendered space of the novel would provoke a response from Novak, as Backscheider's examination of the 'liminal spaces' delineated in the novel violates his admonition that 'critics confuse *ekphrasis*, or the detailed presentation of a scene, with the presentation of characters within a social and political milieu' (Novak, p. 247). Backscheider would counter with her section of 'The Space that is Woman', in which she claims that 'Woman herself is a space ... like a vessel into which any fantasy can be poured, a screen on which any imaged can be projected, and, in Henry James's words, "a sheet of blank paper" on which anything can be written, available as fetish, trope, trophy, and symbol, woman can stand for whatever is needed' (p. 7). While several recent studies of space and the novel have confused representation with reality, Backscheider's work focuses on woman as text, on the deployment of spatial metaphors, gendered tropes and topographies.

Among the studies that undertake 'what novels do', Roxann Wheeler's *The Complexion of Race* focuses on a little-studied but extremely important subject, race. Her work 'traces how English religions and commercial categories designated the manifold excellence of British civil society and how a white and rosy complexion was, on occasion, called on to bolster the picture of British commercial eminence' (p. 7). In the novel, she finds, the 'difficulty in situating Friday [for example] in a stable category of cannibal, slave, or servant reflects a cultural uncertainty about the signifiers of racial difference in the early eighteenth century and their significance, an idea seldom explored in critical assessments of Defoe's novel or other early eighteenth-century literature' (p. 50). The chapters begin with twentieth-century parallels or misreadings, as in Toni Morrison's misreading of Defoe as filtered through the Anita Hill hearings of the early 1990s. The comparisons between the eighteenth century and the twentieth endeavour to reveal the debt our own conceptions have to the eighteenth century, useful lessons for students who might resist thinking of *Robinson Crusoe* as having anything to do with real life. At times, however, the comparisons seem idiosyncratic and, well, dated. The most interesting chapter, 'Romanticizing Racial Difference', examines 'interracial' relationships in mid-century novels.

Felicity Nussbaum, with whom Wheeler has worked, offers her take on the subject in 'Women and Race: "A Difference of Complexion"' (in Jones, ed., *Women and Literature*). Wheeler claims that 'The assurance that skin color was the primary signifier of human difference was not a dominant conception until the last quarter of the eighteenth century, and even then individuals responded variously to nonwhite skin color' (p. 7), and that 'Empire, Europe, and Britain were reimagined in the eighteenth century; skin color and civil society, the two main coordinates of [her] book, emerged as critical categories that helped define these related constructions' (p. 14). Nussbaum argues that 'various manifestations of "race" in language and culture coexist in the mid eighteenth century rather than solidifying into the more "consolidated, pure somatic form" of later racial science, and that strategic confusions persist regarding the meanings assigned to skin colorings, physiognomies, nations, and their relation to interior value' (p. 70). In conclusion, she suggests that 'in the eighteenth century the relation between pigmentation and the faculties of the mind, between bodily features and character, between "blood" and social privilege, remained unstable' (p. 85). In light of these provocative studies, it is important to remember Srinivas Aravamudan's brilliant study *Tropicopolitans* (*YWES* 79[2000]), which sets the standard for such studies and is the most interdisciplinary, cross-generic approach to date.

Useful to the student of the novel will be Michael McKeon's *Theory of the Novel: A Historical Approach*, a comprehensive anthology (if occasionally self-consciously idiosyncratic: 'essays by Robert Alter, René Girard, Lucien Goldmann, Robert Scholes and Robert Kellogg, Tony Tanner, René Wellek, Hayden White, and Émile Zola—for one reason or another do not appear here', p. xi). The collection is divided thematically and covers a number of contemporary concerns including privacy, domesticity, subjectivity, modernity, empire, and postcolonialism, and can easily be seen as a bibliography of works for understanding the eighteenth-century novel. The anthology examines, as heralded in the title, 'the novel as a literary-historical genre' (p. xiv). Its goal, restated in several different ways, is to bring together 'a wide range of authors who have worked from different directions to establish an idea of the coherence of the novel genre as a historical phenomenon' (p. xiv). McKeon's dialectical method, 'beginning with any integral category ("the novel", "literature", "labor", "the nation", "gender") … seeks to understand how, and under what conditions, that category is usefully seen both as composed of constituent parts and as one part of a larger whole' (p. xvii). (Lennard Davis's critique of this method can be found in 'Reconsidering Origins: How Novel are Theories of the Novel?' (*ECF* 12:ii–iii[2000]), discussed above.) Each of the fourteen parts has a headnote that poses a framing question and/or situates the included readings in McKeon's vision of the theory of the novel. It is an enormously useful book.

Of note during 2000, the Center for the Study of the Novel opened at Stanford University under the direction of Franco Moretti. The Ian Watt Lecture in the History and Theory of the Novel was delivered at the centre in February by Walter Benn Michaels, who took as his topic 'The Novel at the End of History and Theory'. More information about the centre and its activities is available online at http://novel.stanford.edu.

Books Reviewed

Backscheider, Paula, *Revising Women: Eighteenth-Century 'Women's Fiction' and Social Engagement*. JHUP. [2000] pp. 273. £58 ISBN 0 8018 6236 1.

Bannet, Eve Tavor. *The Domestic Revolution: Enlightenment Feminisms and the Novel*. JHUP. [2000] pp. 304. hb £38 ISBN 0 8018 6416 X, pb £14 ISBN 0 8018 6417 9.

Bataille, Robert R. *The Writing Life of Hugh Kelly: Politics, Journalism, and Theater in Late-Eighteenth-Century London*. SIUP. [2000] pp. 206. $44.95 ISBN 0 8093 2288 9.

Bell, Michael. *Sentimentalism, Ethics and the Culture of Feeling*. Palgrave. [2000] pp. 240. £42.50 ISBN 0 3337 2110 1.

Boyle, Frank. *Swift as Nemesis: Modernity and its Satirist*. SUP. [2000] pp. 242. $45 ISBN 0 8047 3436 4.

Burgess, Miranda. *British Fiction and the Production of Social Order*. CUP. [2000] pp. 307 £42.23 ($60) ISBN 0 5217 7329 6.

Burling, William J. *Summer Theatre in London, 1661–1820, and the Rise of the Haymarket Theatre*. FDUP. [2000] pp. 110. $48.50 ISBN 0 8386 3811 2.

Canfield, J. Douglas. *The* Broadview *Anthology of Restoration and Early Eighteenth-Century Drama*. Broadview. [2000] pp. 1,977. pb £24.95 ISBN 1 5511 1270 1.

Cheesman, Tom, and Sigrid Rieuwerts, eds. *Ballads into Books: The Legacies of Francis James Child*. Peter Lang. [1997] pp. 283. £35 ISBN 3 9067 5734 X.

Choudhury, Mita. *Interculturalism and Resistance in the London Theater, 1660–1800: Identity, Performance, Empire*. BuckUP. [2000] pp. 217. pb $39.50 ISBN 0 8387 5448 1.

Cibber, Colley. *An Apology for the Life of Colley Cibber, Written by Himself*, ed. B.R.S. Fone. Dover. [2000] pp. 372. pb $17.95 ISBN 0 4864 1472 8.

Clark, J.C.D. *English Society, 1660–1832: Religion, Ideology and Politics during the Ancien Régime*. CUP. [2000] pp. 580. hb £55 ISBN 0 5216 6180 3, pb £20.95 ISBN 0 5216 6627 9.

Clarke, Norma. *Dr. Johnson's Women*. Hambledon. [2000] pp. 271. £19.95 ISBN 1 8528 5254 2.

Coleman, Patrick, Jane Lewis and Jill Kowalik, eds. *Representations of the Self from the Renaissance to Romanticism*. CUP. [2000] pp. 296. £40 ISBN 0 5216 6146 3.

Collini, Stefan, Richard Whatmore and Brian Young, eds. *Economy, Polity, and Society: British Intellectual History, 1750–1950*. CUP. [2000] pp. 283. hb £40 ISBN 0 5216 3018 5, pb £15.95 ISBN 0 5216 3978 6.

Deutsch, Helen, and Felicity Nussbaum, eds. *'Defects': Engendering the Modern Body*. UMichP. [2000] pp. 332. hb £42.50 ISBN 0 4720 9698 2, pb £17.50 ISBN 0 4720 6698 6.

Dix, Robin, ed. *Mark Akenside: A Reassessment*. AUP. [2000] pp. 296. £35 ISBN 0 8386 3882 1.

Eger, Elizabeth, Charlotte Grant, Cliona O'Gallchoir and Penny Warburton, eds. *Women's Writing and the Public Sphere, 1700–1830*. CUP. [2000] pp. 332. £40 ISBN 0 5217 7106 4.

Erskine-Hill, Howard, ed. *Alexander Pope: Selected Letters*. OUP. [2000] pp. xxvi + 405. £50 ISBN 0 1981 8565 0.

Erwin, Timothy, and Ourida Mostefai, eds. *Studies in Eighteenth-Century Culture*, vol. 29. JHUP. [2000] pp. 373 $40 ISBN 0 8018 6449 6.

Everdell, William R. *The End of Kings: A History of Republics and Republicans*. UChicP. [2000] pp. 394. hb £19.95 ISBN 0 0290 9930 7, pb £13.37 ISBN 0 2262 2482 1.

Fieser, James, ed. *Scottish Common Sense Philosophy*, 5 vols. Thoemmes. [2000] pp. 1,500. £450 ISBN 1 8550 6825 7.

Fisher, Nicholas, ed. *That Second Bottle: Essays on John Wilmot, Earl of Rochester*. ManUP. [2000] pp. xiv + 233. £45 ISBN 0 7190 5683 7.

Franklin, Michael John. *Representing India: Indian Culture and Imperial Control in Eighteenth-Century British Orientalist Discourse*, 9 vols. Routledge. [2000] $1,570 ISBN 0 4152 2246 X.

Froes, João, ed. *Remarks on the Life and Writings of Dr Jonathan Swift by John Boyle, Fifth Earl of Cork and Orrery.* UDelP. [2000] pp. 464. £39.50 ISBN 0 8741 3651 2.

Gagnier, Regenia. *The Insatiability of Human Wants: Economics and Aesthetics in Market Society.* UChicP. [2000] pp. 255. hb £26.50 ISBN 0 2262 7853 0, pb £10.50 ISBN 0 2262 7854 9.

Gould, Eliga H. *The Persistence of Empire: British Political Culture in the Age of the American Revolution.* UNCP. [2000] pp. 262. hb £42.50 ISBN 0 8078 2529 8, pb £15.95 ISBN 0 8078 4846 8.

Greene, Donald, ed. *Samuel Johnson: The Major Works.* OUP. [2000] pp. 872. pb £9.99 ISBN 0 1928 4042 8.

Grell, Ole Peter, and Roy Porter, eds. *Toleration in Enlightenment Europe.* CUP. [2000] pp. 270. $60 ISBN 0 5216 5196 4.

Guest, Harriet. *Small Change: Women, Learning, Patriotism, 1750–1810.* UChicP. [2000] pp. 354. hb £31 ISBN 0 2263 1052 3, pb £13 ISBN 0 2263 1051 5.

Ingrassia, Catherine, and Claudia Thomas, eds. *More Solid Learning: New Perspectives on Alexander Pope's Dunciad.* AUP. [2000] pp. 254. £34 ISBN 0 8387 5443 0.

Jones, Vivien, ed. *Women and Literature in Britain, 1700–1800.* CUP. [2000] pp. 320. hb £37.50 ISBN 0 5215 8347 0, pb £14.95 ISBN 0 5215 8680 1.

Kaul, Suvir. *Poems of Nation, Anthems of Empire: English Verse in the Long Eighteenth Century.* UPVirginia. [2000] pp. ix + 337. pb $19.50 ISBN 0 8139 1968 1.

King, Kathryn. *Jane Barker, Exile: A Literary Career, 1675–1725.* OUP. [2000] pp. 280. £40 ISBN 0 1981 8702 5.

King, Peter. *Crime, Justice, and Discretion in England, 1740–1820.* OUP. [2000] pp. 383. $95 ISBN 0 1982 2910 0.

Looser, Devoney. *British Women Writers and the Writing of History, 1670–1820.* JHUP. [2000] pp. 272. $45 ISBN 0 8018 6448 8.

Mack, Robert. *Thomas Gray: A Life.* YaleUP. [2000] pp. xviii + 718. £25 ISBN 0 3000 8499 4.

Marshall, P.J., ed. *The Writing and Speeches of Edmund Burke,* vol. vii: *India: The Hastings Trial, 1789–1794.* Clarendon. [2000] pp. 742. £75 ISBN 0 1982 0809 X.

Mayhew, Robert J. *Enlightenment Geography: The Political Languages of British Geography, 1650–1850.* Palgrave. [2000] pp. 324. £49.95 ISBN 0 3122 3475 9.

McCusker, John J., and Kenneth Morgan, eds. *The Early Modern Atlantic Economy.* CUP. [2000] pp. 369. $60 ISBN 0 5217 8249 X.

McKeon, Michael. *Theory of the Novel: A Critical Anthology.* JHUP. [2000] pp. 947. hb £51.50 ISBN 0 8018 6396 1, pb £20.50 ISBN 0 8018 6397 X.

Moody, Jane. *Illegitimate Theatre in London, 1770–1840.* CUP. [2000] pp. 278. $59.95 ISBN 0 5215 6376 3.

Mullan, John, and Christopher Reid, eds. *Eighteenth-Century Popular Culture: A Selection.* OUP. [2000] pp. 326. £12.99 ISBN 0 1987 1135 2.

Parker, Todd C. *Sexing the Text: The Rhetoric of Sexual Difference in British Literature, 1700–1750.* SUNYP. [2000] pp. 218. hb £39.07 ($55.50) ISBN 0 7914 4485 6, pb £15.61 ISBN 0 7914 4486 4.

Peters, Julie Stone. *Theatre of the Book, 1480–1880: Print, Text, and Performance in Europe.* OUP. [2000] pp. 485. £60 ISBN 0 1981 8714 9.

Phillips, Mark Salber. *Society and Sentiment: Genres of Historical Writing in Britain, 1740–1820*. PrincetonUP. [2000] pp. 369. hb £40 ISBN 0 6910 3179 7, pb £17.95 ISBN 0 6910 0867 1.

Porter, Roy. *Creation of the Modern World: The British Enlightenment*. Norton. [2000] pp. 608. hb US$35 ISBN 0 3930 4872 1.

Porter, Roy. *Creation of the Modern World: The Untold Story of the British Enlightenment*. Norton. [2000] pp. 768. pb £12.70 ($17.95) ISBN 0 3933 2268 8.

Porter, Roy. *Enlightenment: Britain and the Creation of the Modern World*. Penguin. [2001] pp. 752. pb £9.99 ISBN 0 1402 5028 X.

Potkay, Adam. *The Passion for Happiness: Samuel Johnson and David Hume*. CornUP. [2000] pp. 264. £26.50 ISBN 0 8014 3727 X.

Rivers, Isabel. *Reason, Grace, and Sentiment: A Study of the Language of Religion and Ethics in England, 1660–1780*. CUP. [2000] pp. 386. $75 ISBN 0 5213 8341 2.

Ruderman, David. *Jewish Enlightenment in an English Key: Anglo-Jewry's Construction of Modern Jewish Thought*. PrincetonUP. [2000] pp. 291. $39.50 ISBN 0 6910 4883 5.

Saxton, Kirsten T., and Rebecca P. Bocchicchio, eds. *The Passionate Fictions of Eliza Haywood*. UPKen. [2000] pp. 367. £27.50 ISBN 0 8131 2161 2.

Sorensen, Janet. *The Grammar of Empire in Eighteenth-Century British Writing*. CUP. [2000] pp. 328. £37.50 ISBN 0 5216 5327 4.

Terry, Richard, ed. *James Thomson: Essays for the Tercentenary*. LiverUP. [2000] pp. 279. pb £16.99 ISBN 0 8532 3964 9.

Thomas, Nicholas, Jonathan Lamb and Vanessa Smith, eds. *Exploration and Exchange: A South Seas Anthology, 1680–1900*. UChicP. [2000] pp. 352. hb £31 ISBN 0 2264 6845 3, pb £11.50 ISBN 0 2264 6846 1.

Thompson, Lynda M. *The Scandalous Memoirists: Constantia Phillips, Laetitia Pilkington and the Shame of 'Publick Fame'*. ManUP. [2000] £52.99 ISBN 0 7190 5573 3.

Vermeule, Blakey. *The Party of Humanity: Writing Moral Psychology in Eighteenth-Century Britain*. JHUP. [2000] pp. 250. $42 ISBN 0 8018 6459 3.

Wheeler, Roxann. *The Complexion of Race: Categories of Difference in Eighteenth-Century British Culture*. UPennP. [2000] pp. 371. hb £53.53 ($65) ISBN 0 8122 3541 X, pb £21.50 ISBN 0 8122 1722 5.

Wood, Paul, ed. *The Scottish Enlightenment: Essays in Reinterpretation*. URP. [2000] pp. 399. $75 ISBN 1 5804 6065 8.

XII

The Nineteenth Century: The Romantic Period

EMMA MASON, AMANDA GILROY, WIL VERHOEVEN, HELEN
BRAITHWAITE, PHILIP MARTIN, JASON WHITTAKER, SEAMUS
PERRY AND AMY MUSE

This chapter has eight sections: 1. General; 2. Prose Fiction; 3. Non-Fictional Prose; 4. Poetry: Selected Authors; 5. Blake; 6. Wordsworth and Coleridge; 7. Women Romantic Poets; 8. Drama. Sections 1 and 7 are by Emma Mason; section 2 is by Amanda Gilroy and Wil Verhoeven; section 3 is by Helen Braithwaite; section 4 is by Philip Martin; section 5 is by Jason Whittaker; section 6 is by Seamus Perry; and section 8 is by Amy Muse.

1. General

John Barrell's *Imagining the King's Death: Figurative Treason, Fantasies of Regicide, 1793–1796*, with its perhaps now famous dedication to the late Stephen Copley ('the least pedestrian of scholars'), deserves immediate attention as the most scholarly of critical studies published in the field this year. Writing as a historian of literature, Barrell draws on what seems to be an inexhaustible array of sources, legal, political and literary (the bibliography alone is more than fifty pages long), to define the word 'imagination' in the context of the 1790s. Political conflict in this period is regarded as centred on the meaning of words, an understanding of constitution, liberty and sovereignty grounding much radical debate. Yet, by the end of the eighteenth century, the imagination had become equally fraught with ambiguity, and Barrell explores how writers and speakers on politics understood this newly developing concept. The introduction to the book thus creates a kind of political dictionary of the imagination to exemplify the variety of its uses by loyalists and republicans alike. Where Burke's *Reflections*, for example, was attacked by Wollstonecraft and Priestly for displaying a warm imagination liable to catch fire if used to discuss politics, Paine's *Rights of Man* was also represented as an insane catalogue of idle dreams by his deriders. The use of the word within the Bible destabilized its signification further, supplying orators with the notion of a wicked or evil imaginary sense, able to conjure terrible states of mind. The imagination, then, became associated with irrationality, danger and lawlessness, and as such,

Barrell suggests, became the focal point around which changes in the treason laws took place. These changes were initiated by William Pitt, embattled abroad against a republican enemy and at home with a network of popular radical societies. The latter, Pitt decided, struck of a revolutionary movement and the government accordingly began arresting and interrogating the leaders of the two leading radical societies in London, the Society for Constitutional Information and the London Corresponding Society. To fully stifle these threatening reformers, the government drew upon the 1351 English statute of treason, a law based upon the offence of imagining the king's death.

How one might 'imagine' the king's death is central to Barrell's argument; contemporary debates regarding treason came to rest upon how the imagination was defined, the government attempting to extend interpretations of the word as reformers worked to condense them. 'Imagination' thus became 'a symbolic trophy' which radicals, reformers, defendants in treason trials and their counsel sought to claim back from, and so use against, loyalists, the government and its lawyers. The consequences provide the content of the rest of Barrell's extensive study, which characterizes loyalist alarmism as a 'disorder of the imagination, a kind of hysteria by which every demand for political change was imagined as a threat to the king', drawing attention to the ambiguous and antique language of the law and fuelling monarchist suspicions that the government 'was itself imagining the destruction of the democratic part of the constitution and even of the king himself'. Barrell divides his book into four sections which guide the reader, one perhaps ideally a historian rather than a literary critic, through the complexities of imagined treason. The first addresses the fantasies of regicide that were provoked by the death of Louis XVI; the second examines the trials of radicals and reformers in 1794; the third explores two alarms for the king's safety in 1794 and 1795; and the fourth meticulously covers those debates in and outside parliament that concerned the Treasonable Practices Bill. Each part is compelling, no small task for a book of such intricate archival referencing and generous narrative.

Of considerable interest to the literary scholar are Barrell's final suggestions concerning the development of Coleridge's account of the poetic imagination, one which he believes was touched by the kind of language employed in debates that addressed treason. The *Biographia Literaria*, for example, becomes a discussion of poetics grounded in the arguments about the use of imagination in political discourse addressing the king's death. Although not discussed by Barrell, Thelwall's poetic address to treason, *Poems Written in Close Confinement in the Tower and Newgate under a charge of High Treason*, makes an interesting comparison to his consideration of Coleridge. Published this year as part of Woodstock's consistently timely Revolution and Romanticism 1789–1834 facsimile series, Thelwall's *Poems* reject the imagination and claim, the 'Advertisement' states, to be 'transcripts of the heart'. Thelwall continues to emphasize that he has 'spoken what [he] felt' rather than 'considered what [he] should speak', a 'method, at least, the most honest, and sometimes the most successful, in appealing to the hearts of others'. Almost as soon as this is declared, however, the poet insists that 'one preponderating idea will be constantly present to his imagination:—THE SACRED CAUSE FOR WHICH HE SUFFERS', his imagining capacity occupied with the principles for which, he writes in 'Stanzas: Written on the Morning of Trial', he is 'a martyr'. The edition, introduced by

Jonathan Wordsworth, contains eighteen further poems, variously denouncing luxury, tyranny and slavery while liberty and freedom are praised as themes fitting to the expressive voice of an emotive patriot, a role Thelwall adopts here. *Poems* proves illuminating when read in the context of Barrell's study; the latter energizing issues of free speech, its association with radical politics and the suppression of both that still press on the British constitution.

Where Barrell tracks the parallel shifts in definitions of treason and the imagination in the Romantic period, John Whale's *Imagination Under Pressure, 1789–1832* serves to focus on the latter as a creative faculty involved in both the British response to the French Revolution and the reaction to utilitarianism. Whale looks at the non-fictional prose of Burke, Paine, Wollstonecraft, Hazlitt, Cobbett and Coleridge in order to create a different generic history of the Romantic imagination, one which 'avoids a pre-emptively celebratory account' as it challenges 'accepted notions of "literariness"'. For Whale, the imagination is produced by a split or crisis within culture and by disseminating itself 'across that divide' becomes fragmented into lots of different imaginations. It is neither a kind of Bloomian inwardness or sublimity, nor does it pertain to new historicist renderings as false consciousness. Resisting any homogenized sense of the 'Romantic imagination', then, the study reads both the war in France and utilitarianism as equally caught up with an imagination they appear to reject. For even where it fails, Whale suggests, the imagination maintains a vital presence, thus betraying its immunity to rejection and its ability to resurface in the 'language and strategies of its opponents'. Whale situates the imagination within specific contexts of usage, including those which are critical and even derogatory. As a reaction or reflex to an epistemological, cultural or representational crisis, the imagination thus becomes a means of articulating resistance, and Whale's self-proclaimed 'violent rewriting' of its meaning gives the study a sometimes uneasy and angry tone.

Whale reads the texts of his chosen prose writers against themselves to search out the gaps where the imagination resides. Burke's *Reflections* are thus shown to posit a kind of civic imagination which cannot help but rhetorically create a sense of social unification between men even as it ostensibly fuels a defence of English aristocratic culture. It is Burke's very aestheticizing of the past that provokes Wollstonecraft's backlash against him, her own project aiming to undermine ideological assumptions, particularly concerning gender, weary of those who insist on 'chasing shadows' and imagining what is not real. At the same time, Wollstonecraft's *Vindication*, with its visionary sense of a non-deluded social world, draws on the very culture of sensibility it seems to dismiss, Whale contends. In a parallel manner, Bentham's utilitarian rejection of aesthetics, especially poetry, forges a rationalism that paradoxically allows the imagination to develop freely. Whale suggests that those who force the imagination away are often the most likely to rely upon it: Cobbett, for example, denies the faculty even as his pastoral idealism seems rooted in the ability to imagine. Paine too attacks artifice, but is deemed by Whale to be a reformer moved by the chaotic imaginings of revolution. This becomes important, the reader realizes, when Whale invokes Ronald Reagan's admiration for Paine as a subscriber to common-sense ideology of the kind that often underscores right-wing rationalism. Whale's argument also extends to Coleridge, a poet traditionally accused of retreating from political action into the complexities of the imagination as a bridge between selfhood and text. Whale successfully presents the imagination as an inescapable and essential element in our reading of Romantic culture which 'still has the capacity and potential to act as a point of ethico-political resistance and as a form of critique'.

Volume v of the current *Cambridge History of Literary Criticism* covered the Romantic period this year, edited by Marshall Brown. Beginning with the idea of classicism and moving through to the more recently dominant question of gender, the book is a useful compendium of what presently concerns Romanticists, despite its underplaying of post-colonialism and imperialism. Paul H. Fry's 'Classical Standards in the Period' (pp. 7–28), for example, addresses the subject of the Romantic reception and interpretation of classical antiquity and its apparent decline into neoclassicism. Fry's essay sits neatly with Alfredo de Paz's discussion of the modern dimensions of literary and artistic Romantic criticism in Europe ('Innovation and Modernity', pp. 29–48). De Paz argues that modernity has its origins in the Enlightenment's emphasis on critical reason, a project continued by the Romantic struggle for a larger and higher reason 'in harmony with the real complexity of human beings'. David Simpson contributes two essays to the volume, the first, 'The French Revolution' (pp. 49–71), tracing the impact of the French Revolution on Romantic literary criticism as evidence of a radical break with the past. Simpson shows how responses to the revolution displaced French culture and literature from any claim to general European or world significance, underlining British literature as anti-metropolitan, rural and local. Simpson's second contribution to the volume, 'Transcendental Philosophy and Romantic Criticism' (pp. 72–91), addresses the assumed political resistance of Romantic literary criticism to the philosophical, blamed for the French Revolution and considered a Jacobin trait. Simpson's profitable discussion of Romantic readings of Kant's *Critique of Judgement*, Schiller's *On the Aesthetic Education of Man* and Hegel's *Aesthetics: Lectures on Fine Art* stresses the socio-historical situatedness of judgements of taste, the aesthetic emerging as 'inevitably utopian and messianic' alike.

Helmut J. Schneider's essay, 'Nature' (pp. 92–114), turns to the most evocative of Romantic themes, working through its role in the Romantics' 'reaction to, and compensation for, the thrust of an onrushing modernity'. Joel Black's excellent 'Scientific Models' (pp. 115–37) explores the field of science by analysing the impact of technological innovations such as the telescope and microscope, and new developments in chemistry and biology on poetic metaphors. E.S. Shaffer's 'Religion and Literature' (pp. 138–61) provides a solid overview of Wesleyan enthusiasm, supernaturalism and the Catholic revival as a counter-movement to the Enlightenment. Of special import here is the emphasis Shaffer places on Coleridge as a religious thinker, his verse presenting a subtle fusion of Christianity and the mythology of nature. Two essays within the volume directly address the question of language in this period: Kurt Mueller-Vollmer's 'Language Theory and the Art of Understanding' (pp. 162–84) points out how the Romantics' preoccupation with language, hermeneutics and interpretation was a direct outgrowth of their new poetics, while David Wellbery's 'The Transformation of Rhetoric' (pp. 185–202) uses Wordsworth's 'Preface' to map the shift in linguistic stylization that occurs within the age. Genre is also a central preoccupation here: Gary Handwerk's 'Romantic Irony' (pp. 203–25), Marshall Brown's 'Theory of the Novel' (pp. 250–71) and Tilottama Rajan's 'Theories of Genre' (pp. 226–49) each question the idea of aesthetic dispositions and how they are enjoyed. As Rajan argues, genres become an issue, not of effects and structural features for the Romantics, but as 'sites of negotiation between subject and object, inwardness and its externalization, or as (in)adequate embodiments of the "Idea"'. Jonathan Arac's 'The Impact of Shakespeare' (pp. 272–95) illustrates the role of Shakespeare in late eighteenth- and nineteenth-century education and culture, focusing on Romantic critics such as Coleridge and Hazlitt and showing the Bard's influence on writers such as Keats and Goethe.

In a volume wrapped up in defining Romantic literary criticism, Jon Klancher asks who was officially authorized to occupy the office of 'critic' in his essay 'The Vocation of Criticism and the Crisis of the Republic of Letters' (pp. 296–320). Sketching a history of the literary republic of critics, Klancher's discussion is complemented by Theresa M. Kelley's consideration of women's oblique relation to the role of critic in her 'Women, Gender and Literary Criticism' (pp. 321–37). She reads criticism by Wollstonecraft, Germaine de Staël, Joanna Baillie, Anna Laetitia Barbauld and Felicia Hemans as attentive to discourses about economics and philosophy but using a poetically sensuous style separate from the 'effeminate' tones of Keats. Finally, two essays serve to situate literary criticism in the context of history and art: David Perkins's 'Literary History and Historicism' (pp. 338–61) explores the paradoxical discrepancy between the apparent ahistorical nature of much Romantic discourse in a period obsessed with the creation of the field of 'literary history', and Herbert Lindenberger's 'Literature and the Other Arts' (pp. 362–86) relates the main concerns of the volume to music and the visual arts. More than sixty pages of bibliographical references conclude Brown's edition, divided up in accordance with the chapters and offering an outstanding research resource to Romantic scholars. The comprehensive index makes this an immensely effective guide to Romantic literary criticism, accenting its encyclopedic value while revealing the deeper nature of the discussions included.

Two books directly addressed Green Studies this year, Jonathan Bate's *The Song of the Earth*, which examines poetry's relevance in the current technological age, and Laurence Coupe's *The Green Studies Reader: From Romanticism to Ecocriticism*. Bate begins with the premise that the writer has the power to 'restore us to the earth which is our home', exploring the relationship between nature and culture as one based in a fundamental human need for environmental belonging. As the study reminds us, 'culture' came to signify taste and manners only in the nineteenth century, deriving from its figurative meaning as organic growth and improvement of one's home or dwelling place. Likewise, it is only in this period that the word 'environment' is applied to social contexts: before then, it was self-evident that personal and communal identity were intimately related to physical settings. The tenet that culture and environment are held together in a complex and delicate web underlines the entire book, a veritable Green manifesto in its insistence that the reader live with a thoughtful and attentive awareness of nature achieved through literature, specifically poetry. Bate's project is to reclaim poetry as a genre vital to the contemporary moment, a form which, more than any other, can function ecologically. Ecopoetics as Bate calls it, is a form of verse-making because 'metre itself—a quiet but persistent music, a recurring cycle, a heartbeat—is an answering to nature's own rhythms, an echoing of the song of the earth itself'.

Bate's readings of works by Wordsworth, John Clare, Coleridge and Keats yield a certain eco-message that is appealing, if a little ethereal and precious at times. Keats and Coleridge, like Wordsworth and Clare, place great emphasis upon the locality and place of their verse, reconnecting humanity to a natural world from which we are easily severed. Bate reads Clare as especially committed to the process of localizing the natural world he renders, forging an intimacy with the spaces of the world that prefigures Bachelard's *The Poetics of Space*. If poetry helps us to both conceive of and wish to protect the place in which we live, then 'it is the place where we save the earth', Bate declares. The case for poetry here is a dramatic one, and Bate is as convincing in his enthusiasm for verse as for the forwarding of Green Studies. This is partly due to the vast array of disciplines on which he draws and makes surprisingly accessible to a non-academic reader: philosophy, science, geography, political economics, poetics, literary theory and so on.

For the reader who desires a more detailed overview of these perspectives, *The Green Studies Reader* is indispensable, reprinting many of the essays central to *The Song of the Earth* and serving as an essential textbook for educational courses in all disciplines which have hitherto avoided the subject of Green Studies. A collection of fifty extracts that map the development of Green thinking from Blake to Kate Soper, *The Green Studies Reader* introduces the wide-ranging scope of this field in a variety of contexts. Three sections guide the reader from the roots of the 'Green Tradition', invoking nineteenth-century commentaries and the consequent critique of modernity, through 'Green Theory', where the relationship between nature and culture is intellectualized and deconstructed; and finally to 'Green Reading', where the specifically literary notion of 'ecocriticism' is fully developed. Coupe proficiently guides the reader through these sections, providing a glossary of terms at the end of the book and introducing each new theme with a brief, yet indicative, preface. Part I, 'Romantic Ecology and its Legacy', follows Bate's popularization of the phrase 'Romantic ecology' in his book of that title published in 1991. The section illustrates how nineteenth-century thinkers pre-date ecocriticism and show a marked preoccupation with what Raymond Williams called the 'green language' of Romanticism, covering authors such as Blake, Wordsworth, Coleridge, Thoreau, Ruskin, Morris, Woolf, and Eliot. Romantic ecology comes to signify more than a rustic longing for a natural origin, but at the same time the 'structure of feeling' nature can inspire is never effaced, not even by the ideologically mindful Williams. The edition then turns to inheritors of the Romantic Green tradition, such as Edward Thomas and D.H. Lawrence, as well as philosophers and theorists who illuminate the route Green Studies has so far followed. In Part II, 'The Earth, Memory and the Critique of Modernity', extracts from Heidegger, Adorno and Horkheimer accompany those from Leavis, Kenneth Burke and Leo Marx, while Part III, 'Nature/Culture/Gender', includes thinkers from Kate Soper to Jean-François Lyotard, Donna Haraway and Gary Synder. Part IV, 'Ecocritical Principles', is focused on the question of how to represent the environment within textual criticism, one both historically specified and tested in Part V's 'Environmental Literary History'. Here, critics such as Bate are placed along side Lawrence Buell, Robert Pogue Harrison and Richard Kerridge in an attempt to understand what it might mean, as Scott Slovic suggests, to practise the doctrine of ecocriticism through the act of reading. The last part of Coupe's collection returns us to specific Romantics such as Keats.

While Coupe passes over science in favour of the humanities, Maureen N. McLane's *Romanticism and the Human Sciences: Poetry, Population and the Discourse of the Species* promises to address it, but in fact reads more as a Shelleyan defence of poetry or reflection on the value of Romantic literature in a culture where the funding of the sciences is favoured. That McLane sees fit to elevate her own views to the level of those proposed by Shelley, Wordsworth and Coleridge, however, is somewhat problematic, the introduction a rather indulgent 'experiment' in criticism littered with unfounded allusions to theoretical works. And while the book purports to explore 'the predicament of "literature," "poetry," and the human sciences in England circa 1800', the relationship between poetry and science is not addressed, and actual scientific texts are overlooked. Buried in McLane's odd stylistics, however, is a startling argument connecting the Romantic internalization of moral philosophy's vision of human worth with the development of the poetic as a special faculty and the professionalization of science. Chapter 2, for example, focuses on Wordsworth and Coleridge's debate regarding 'the relation of rustic mentalité to rustic speech' in their various literary experimentations. Wordsworth's *Lyrical Ballads* are perceived as staging meetings between figures whose minds are not commensurate, thus revealing the impasse between adult and child, poet and ethnographic figure. For Coleridge, however, such actions both eroded the distinction between poetry and moral prose and assumed a ventriloquistic colonization of the aged, the poor and the marginalized. Once the imperfections of rustic speech are imported into verse, then 'the resulting linguistic resource would be no different from that of "any other man of common sense"', Coleridge wrote. The implications of such a view, along with Coleridge's rejection of radicalism, emphasis on the clerisy, and anti-populism, are therefore read here, not just as responses to the French Revolution, but to Wordsworth's 'sympoetics'. A genuinely passionate and anti post-humanist endorsement of poetry, McLane's book asks how we might make poetry work for us, how it alters and creates the conditions of existence, and its 'ceaseless re-inauguration of questioning'. Although less certain than Bate of poetry's redeeming nature, McLane's argument is close to that proposed in *The Song of the Earth* in that she ultimately points out the connection between the Romantics' rethinking of the poem and the reform of society.

Mark S. Lussier's *Romantic Dynamics: The Poetics of Physicality* also explores the collision that occurs between Romantic poetry and science, particularly the fields of contemporary theoretical physics, cosmology and neuroscience. Lussier asserts that from the Romantics' investigation into cosmos and consciousness emerges a new metaphoric model based on an exploration of psyche and phenomena. The readings of Blake, Byron, Coleridge, the Shelleys and Wordsworth develop from what Lussier calls a 'synchronistic event or moment', a coincidental discovery of a certain text or unexpected intellectual exchange. This is important, apparently, because of the parallels synchronicity implies between interior and exterior events, a kind of 'fearful symmetry' which underlies the way in which both Romantic poetry and scientific materiality are constructed in the period. The link stipulated here between poetical expression and physical process, notably relativity and quantum mechanics, is referred to as 'physical criticism' throughout, a way of thinking that has emerged from the interchange between literature and science. Assuming that Romanticism is a part of the human sciences, Lussier focuses on the idea of dynamics, a phrase which, in the context of this period, refers to the actions of forces on both bodies and minds. Thus Blake's Albion and Shelley's Prometheus are seen as biological, psychological and cultural organisms, within which the play of thought and action occurs. Moving forward from Keats' and Lamb's famous comment regarding Newton's ruinous reduction of 'all the poetry of the rainbow' to 'the prismatic colours', the study instead argues that the physical sciences experienced revolutions analogous to the political, economic and social ones unfolding in America and France in the period. Moreover, these revolutions are linked: Thomas Wright's 1750 *Original Theory or New Hypothesis of the Universe* impacted on Kant; James Hutton's *Theory of the Earth* manifested itself in *The Prelude*'s political avocation of 'One galaxy of life and joy'; and Humphry Davy's *A Discourse, Introductory to a Course of Lectures on Chemistry* informed the message of Shelley's *Frankenstein*. Romantic poetics, then, is constructed here as able to cross 'disciplinary boundaries', bringing 'divergent and convergent thinking into symbolic unity' and centralizing the imagination as the spur to both literary and scientific innovation. Lussier admirably practises 'physical criticism' from the start, connecting it not only to literary and scientific ideas, but also to religious concepts such as the Buddhist emphasis upon uncertainty and essencelessness which neatly parallels quantum mechanics.

The prominence of poetry in Romantic criticism is reflected in Mark Storey's engaging study, *The Problem of Poetry in the Romantic Period*. Here, Storey focuses on the anxiety the Romantics expressed regarding their status as poetical figures, examining the ways in which their aesthetic questionings got entangled in the poetry. The question of identity is crucial for Storey, who argues that a poetry defined in terms of the poet will concentrate more centrally on the struggle to understand the nature of the poet. Addressing 'the dangers of the Promethean act of creativity', then, the study explores Wordsworth's wrestling with private and public identity; Coleridge's doubts about his poetical abilities; Keats's anxieties concerning the self of the poet-creator; Shelley's role as an 'unacknowledged legislator'; and Clare's labours to identify himself as a poet at all.

The problem of defining poetic identity becomes the very theme of *The Prelude* for Storey, the epic central to debates about poetry because of Wordsworth's specific attempt to discover what it means to be a poet. 'It is one thing to talk of the poet as a "man speaking to men",' Storey writes, 'it is quite another to write a poem in which he is the man doing the talking—to himself, to Coleridge and Dorothy, and to the posterity he will never meet.' Wordsworth's self-proclaimed 'unknown modes of being' are explored by Storey within brilliantly detailed close readings; this chapter is an excellent introduction to the poem, as well as an innovative commentary upon it. Its author is re-read here as one of the humblest of Romantics, one who felt 'unregarded by the world'. For Keats, the nature of poetry and the poet is obsessed over in practically every poem and many letters, Storey suggests, even though he does not leave the kind of manifesto that is contained in Shelley's *Defence*. For Clare, poetry is even more bound to the conception of identity; it is a genre which at once invites and excludes him by celebrating a sense of obscurity by which he is alienated. Clare provides 'the most dramatic and extreme enactment of the central thesis of this book', the author claims, exemplifying the wrestle the Romantics engaged in 'with the paradox of writing itself, in that to write is both to assert and deny oneself'. The final chapter addressing Clare's self-identification with Byron underlines this crisis further, Byron providing a poetical model of deep feeling circled by cynicism that helped Clare work through his role as writer.

Joseph C. Sitterson's *Romantic Poems, Poets, and Narrators* in many ways complements the arguments Storey proposes, but he is also more concerned with the way in which canonical Romantic poems have accumulated a complex history of readings over the past half-century, much of which, he argues, 'is being ignored or misrepresented in contemporary criticism, theoretical and practical alike'. In an attempt to overcome the 'cut-throat intellectual bazaar of contending critical "schools"', new criticism buried by deconstruction buried by new historicism and so on, Sitterson turns to Kenneth Burke's notion of 'unending conversation' and 'heated discussion'. These phrases evoke a critical model in which every reading is placed in a conversational and argumentative 'present' which attempts to allow each theory or practice to remain a participant in a dialogue. This model underlies Sitterson's own readings of the Introduction to the *Songs of Experience*, the *Ancient Mariner*, *The Prelude*, the Intimations Ode and *Lamia*, poems which all express a discomfort with the idea of mastery, whether in a theoretical, methodological or thematic sense. In the sense that the book's intention is 'less to offer radically new readings than to clarify relations among existing and apparently conflicting readings', it is an interesting departure from much work offered in the field this year. Sitterson's central question addresses the usefulness of distinguishing the poet from the narrator when the idea of a unified subject has been thrown out by contemporary theory. While such theory refuses the idea of a single point of view in opposition to classic realism, Sitterson reminds us that subjectivity is a major theme of both realism *and* Romantic poetry. He forcefully questions the dominance of socio-historical and psychoanalytical readings in the field by attacking the sense of mastery they imply, as if the reader is somehow getting closer to the real text by relying on a factual frame. By mixing models as we read, however, we might be able to confront the difficult problems of what happens when formalism, deconstruction and historicism intersect. This convergence of commentary, Sitterson writes, not only rids us of the idea of mastery but parallels the clash of meaning on which Romantic poetry relies.

The relationship between the sensation of aestheticism and Romantic thinking is also key in David Ferris's *Silent Urns: Romanticism, Hellenism, Modernity*, a sophisticated analysis of the way in which individuality, freedom, history and modernity are reconciled in an eighteenth-century aesthetic grounded in the iconic significance of Greece. Ferris begins with a striking retelling of Odysseus's meeting with the Sirens in book XII of Homer's *Odyssey*. The hero is attracted to the Sirens' 'honey-sweet' narrative, not because it will allow him to gain a knowledge of history (which he has already received from Demodokos anyway), but to immerse himself in the aesthetic quality of their voices. This metaphor embodies much of what eighteenth-century Hellenism promised, Ferris argues: a knowledge of history in a resolutely aesthetic form. Without Circe to warn of the effects this aestheticization of history will have on modernity, however, contemporary readers are forced to expose the ideology at work in aesthetic experience. Yet this too is problematic for Ferris, a recognition of ideology presenting an understanding of history that threatens to 'become the siren song of our modernity, because ideological criticism comes to repeat the promise it was meant to expose'. The question of how to invoke the idea of 'history' as it arises in this period dominates the book, constructed throughout as an aesthetic phenomenon. Hellenism's idealized literary representation of Greece, then, expresses a history, but one for which the origin is in the aesthetic, Ferris argues.

Romanticism at the End of History collects seven essays by Jerome Christensen, each intent on exploring the difference between a writing life lived in the Romantic era to one lived in our contemporary moment. Romanticism is less an object of study or expression of a particular mentality here, and more a problem of identification and practice, the exploration of which can lead us to a new ethical way of thinking and living. Christensen thus claims that his project is not implicated in defining a historical discourse, compassing an intellectual horizon or analysing an ideology, but instead attempts to 'use the poets to identify a good way of living in the ongoing practice of making a living'. In other words, what is central here is the practice of 'reading, writing, and teaching' in accordance with Romantic ethics, a kind of 'secondary imagination' or 're-creation of the given in the light of our best conceptions of good use'. History, understood as 'the iron logic of past events', is rejected here for a Romantic approach to the past which credits the possibility of accidents and is not tied to the inevitability of chronology. The Romantics were thus 'conspirators against the order of things whose designs have not yet been realized', Christensen argues, promoting an ethical practice and political aspiration based on the belief that poets are the rightful, if unacknowledged, rulers of the world. His formulation of the Romantics is fascinating, bound up with the future of poetry as well as the way in which we should think about their historical significance. This element of the study is tied to Christensen's stirring concern with the uses to which Romantic texts and Romantic thinking can be put in the twenty-first-century university environment. Chapter 7's proposal of an 'ethics of Romantic use' is less a 'quaint' resurrection of Romantic feeling, says Christensen, and more a conspiratorial 'breathing together' evocative of a radical form of community. The Romantic enterprise even offers an escape from the corporate franchise of professional academia because of the ethics that underline its discursive arena. The main body of the book is grouped around three dates, 1798, 1802 and 1815, each representing different 'kinds of time: wartime, truce, and peace'. The book reconsiders how Romantic writers' relationships to radical social and political changes were formed through the post-historical, enabling their liberation from historical events to which contemporary criticism assumes they were tied.

Christensen's emphasis on the crisis of war in this era is a timely one, and is complemented by the publication of Shaw, ed., *Romantic Wars: Studies in Culture and Conflict, 1793–1822*. As the editor states in his introduction (pp. 1–12), the collection is the first of its kind to address the relations between warfare and literary and visual culture in the period, despite the immense significance of the French Revolution. The shift in Romanticists' interest in Kant, Schelling and Fichte to Burke and Paine indicates a new concern with the 'politics of antagonism', Shaw claims, presenting 'afresh the material realities that Romanticism would ideally obscure'. Despite this shift, encounters with the impact of war on its participants and those who remain behind are rare within criticism, and the experience of individual trauma becomes subsumed beneath a deluge of statistics concerning casualty rates. While commentators have previously assumed that the displacement of fighting onto foreign lands kept the immediate activity of war beyond the visual experience of the English population, war poetry and other Romantic texts are shown here to yield a thorough investigation of the culture of conflict. The evocation of female suffering in writings about war by women, for example, is shown by Stephen C. Behrendt, in '"A few harmless numbers": British Women Poets and the Climate of War, 1793–1815' (pp. 13–36), to be a highly politicized trope that enabled women to criticize the effects of war. Writings by Charlotte Richardson, Amelia Opie, Mary Robinson and Elizabeth Moody are seen as able to manipulate the trope of nation-family to emphasize 'by analogy how the devastation of the family parallels the inevitable destruction of the state'. Jacqueline M. Labbe's 'The Exiled Self: Images of War in Charlotte Smith's "The Emigrants"' (pp. 37–56) complements Behrendt's argument by examining the intersection between the horror of war and the horror of masculine culture in Smith's famous poem. Labbe engagingly reads 'The Emigrants' as at once a 'poem about war, about being at war' and 'a declaration of war' on patriarchal culture. David Collings's essay, 'The Harsh Delights of Political Duty: Thelwall, Coleridge, Wordsworth, 1795–99' (pp. 57–79), turns to male commentaries on war, discussing the radical response to the anti-Jacobin onslaught and active persecution of the Pitt government that occurred in the 1790s. Collings shows how the lyrics that Thelwall, Coleridge and Wordsworth wrote in response to these issues chose not to retreat from them, but to confront the options offered by the question of political duty: 'the stark limits of either heroic resistance or domestic retreat, the cost to themselves of participating in such a violent public debate and of losing the familiar sources of political agency', and the threat of taking 'an inhuman pleasure in the very violence they feared'.

Coleridge has a central place in the collection, and is focused on in Mark Rawlinson's 'Invasion! Coleridge, the Defence of Britain and the Cultivation of the Public's Fear' (pp. 110–37) and Diego Saglia's 'War Romances, Historical Analogies and Coleridge's Letters on the Spaniards' (pp. 138–60). Rawlinson looks at the nature of the imagination in being alarmed at war, 'Fears in Solitude' read as an invitation to the reader to think about alarmism, war's empirical and somatic actuality and the ideologies which 'vouchsafe the prosecution of war in the face of both egocentric and altruistic care for the safety of the body'. Saglia turns to Coleridge's Letters on the Spaniards as a rhetorically intensive enquiry into heroism, empire, patriotism, rebellion and displacement and approaching war through historical romance narratives. Geoff Quilley looks at the more general construction of the sailor in this period; his 'Duty and Mutiny: the Aesthetics of Loyalty and the Representation of the British Sailor c.1798–1800' (pp. 80–109) indicating the ideological power the sailor's navigational, national and military skill wielded in poetry and sermons from this period. Simon Bainbridge also explores the military glory the war hero identity assumed in '"Of war and taking towns": Byron's Siege Poems' (pp. 161–84), through Mary Shelley's portrait of Byron in The Last Man's aristocratic figure, Lord Raymond. Shelley's novel, Bainbridge suggests, expresses Byron's ambivalent attitude to war, emphasizing his martial ambitions in Raymond's taking of the Golden City, Constantinople, but rendering the outcome of this siege destructive to the civilization Byron sought to forward. Yet Byron's fascination with military power points towards a problem that resides at the heart of Romantic politics and aesthetics, the editor of the collection argues, his own essay, 'Leigh Hunt and the Aesthetics of Post-War Liberalism' (pp. 185–207), offering a close reading of Hunt's post-war writings to register the inability of liberal thinkers to produce a coherent response to the fall of Napoleon Bonaparte. Incapacitated in this way, Shaw suggests that these thinkers fail to provide a rational alternative to the poetics of oppression, even as Hunt sought to initiate a revolution in poetic language that embraces the pastoral rather than the warlike sublime. Eric C. Walker's 'Marriage and the End of War' (pp. 208–26) closes the volume with an interesting reading of the depiction of marriage in post-war British culture as a conjugal safe haven to underline 'the construction of domestic sphere ideology by building a myth of the (virtuous) public male warrior defending the (virtuous) female home'. The aftermath of war is thus dealt with by culture through a restitution of the order that conflict destroys, an idealized memory of a past matrimonial paradise evoked to justify a war that fought to protect it.

Walker's note regarding the relevance of memory in the representation of war strikes a chord throughout another set of essays published this year: Matthew Campbell, Jacqueline M. Labbe and Sally Shuttleworth's *Memory and Memorials, 1789–1914: Literary and Cultural Perspectives*. The editors successfully position the idea of memory as a tool for 'memorialising, encouraging and bolstering social progression and the transformation of the past into the future' within the long nineteenth century. A phenomenon enshrined in British culture by Victoria's permanent state of mourning over Albert and the popularity of her favourite poem, Tennyson's *In Memoriam*, memory is firmly established by mid-century, the editors argue, having developed throughout the Romantic period. Taking on a variety of guises and reflecting a number of needs, memory is a 'political and literary marker of custom and continuity', functioning to 'capture, represent, and symbolize that which is always in danger of being lost'. The brashness of social progress in the nineteenth century was underpinned by a sense of loss that necessitated the process of remembering both to reconstruct a broken human self and to create a sense of historical community to which it may belong. While Wordsworth had drawn on the positive strengths memory offered, the Victorians, the volume shows, doubted these powers, tending to frame their literary pictures of the past with an awareness of the fragility and unreliability of memory. As memory proved deficient, history was turned to as a place where the self could be located, a subject addressed by Greg Kucich in the first of the book's four Romantic-era essays. In 'Romanticism and the Re-engendering of Historical Memory' (pp. 15–29), Kucich studies the sense of contestation in the histories written by women at the end of the eighteenth and in the early nineteenth centuries. Constructing a 'historical memory', writers such as Jane Austen, Catherine Macaulay, Felicia Hemans and Lucy Aikin attempted to write women's experience back into the past and thus foster identification with that history among women readers. Hemans's *Records of Woman* and Aikin's *Epistles on Women* thus memorialize the oppression of women as they proffer alternative memorials of female intervention into time to inspire feminist activism. Catherine A. Jones's 'Scott's *The Heart of Midlothian* and the Disordered Memory' (pp. 30–45) tackles eighteenth-century theories of memory and associationist psychology. Jones reads the disordered mind of Scott's Madge Wildfire as a mark of *Midlothian*'s fragmented narrative, one which cannot retain linear stories and hence is reflective of the author's own private experience of life as chaotic and disorienting.

Part II, 'Writing and Remembering: Elegy, Memorial, Rhyme', returns the reader to Romantic themes in Gary Kelly's 'Gender and Memory in Post-Revolutionary Women's Writing' (pp. 119–31) and Labbe's own 'Re-membering: Memory,

Posterity and the Memorial Poem' (pp. 132–46). Both essays explore how memory enacts itself in literature, Kelly looking at how it ensures the transmission of custom and Labbe rendering it a means of accepting influence. For Kelly, women's writing of the post-revolutionary period promotes a self-aware exploitation of feminine roles in order to reveal the female voice's capacity to embody history. Writers such as Joanna Baillie, Maria Edgeworth, Sydney Owenson and Hemans are all shown to have variously emphasized female powers of endurance to underline their talents to recollect and thus transmit the past. While the irony of this argument is that much of this writing by women was forgotten, its presence at the time, as a way of working through conflicts of class, race, religion and nation, was inscribed within debates addressing how memory forges culture itself. Labbe's focus on memorial poems written by women writers turns to the cultural and poetic significance of poems taking as their subject other poets, and asks how 'memories of poets past and present are transmitted to the readers of the present and the future'. The essay discusses how poems such as Robinson's 'To the Poet Coleridge' and Hemans's eulogy on Wordsworth are founded on the recollection of other poets' reputations and, like Kelly, Labbe asks why we have forgotten about these women. She suggests one possible reason in the conclusion to her essay, stating that 'an emphasis on death functions cumulatively, carrying a force outside the individual poem, resonating strongly enough to erase, for subsequent generations, the memory of such a tradition and community that gave the writers themselves such a full and populated world'. Other essays addressing Victorian psychology (Sally Shuttleworth), Tennyson (Matthew Campbell) and the relevance of rhyme to memory (Gillian Beer) push the study beyond this period in fascinating ways, and show it to be an important contribution to the increasingly prevalent trend to erode the often fruitless distinctions between the terms 'Romantic' and 'Victorian'.

Steven E. Jones's *Satire and Romanticism* turns to another newly developing field, analysing the relationship between satiric and Romantic modes of writing rather than presenting a survey of satire, focusing on the space between the two modes to understand how they mutually defined each other. The recovery of satire is difficult because it seems so opposed to what we are familiar with, even though satire was a dominant generic construct, 'the modal anvil over and against which early nineteenth-century literature gets clustered, hammered out, formed and hardened into a recognisable poetic movement'. For Jones, the very aesthetic tastes and assumptions of Romanticism emerged from the tension between sentimental and satiric modes, Wordsworth, Coleridge, Shelley and Keats moving away from popular satirists such as Pope, Swift and Johnson. This Romantic progression was itself a victim of satirical reviews, *Blackwood's*, the *Quarterly Review* and the *Edinburgh Review* printing violent attacks on sentimental, Della Cruscan, Cockney and Lake School poetics. Perceived as a kind of dangerous epidemic, such poetry came to mean something close to 'un-satiric', a rejection of neo-classicism and embracing of women writers, social parvenus and closet Jacobins. Yet for Jones, the terms 'Romantic' and 'satiric' were constructed through processes of struggle and mutual definition, the former 'infected' by the latter, as the study shows through six case studies focused on Wordsworth, Coleridge, T.J. Wooler, Della Cruscan poetics, the bluestockings, pantomimes, and Ebenezer Elliott. Jones consistently demonstrates the relevance of satire to Romantic writing and ends his study by suggesting an early Victorian generic shift wherein satire was expected to blend with prophetic and spiritual modes.

Post-colonialism remains central this year with four weighty studies contributing to the important debate concerning slavery in the period. Marcus Wood's *Blind Memory: Visual Representations of Slavery in England and America, 1780–1865*, Helen Thomas's *Romanticism and Slave Narratives: Transatlantic Testimonies*, Charlotte Sussman's *Consuming Anxieties: Consumer Protest, Gender and British Slavery, 1713–1833* and Timothy Morton's *The Poetics of Spice: Romantic Consumerism and the Exotic* can be read collectively as a profound contribution to the Romantic/post-colonial question, each refraining from the pitfalls of generalization. Wood's *Blind Memory* is in itself a quite outstanding archive of the visual representation of slavery as it was generated across Britain and North America. Lavishly illustrated, the book's historical depth and scholarship complements its engaging narrative voice and subtle forwarding of complex ideologies regarding race and power. Wood begins with a short reading of Thomas Clarkson's cartographic illustration of the war against the slave trade: a map which presents abolition as a series of tributary streams and rivers each with the name of a supposed abolitionist attached. This genealogical rendering of abolition provokes the question of how we might read or see other 'visual representations developed out of the Western myths devoted to the memory of slavery', significant precisely because of the problematic nature of gazing in the context of slavery. Wood thus aims to counter the disturbingly prevalent belief that 'pictures speak for themselves', focusing not only on images of slavery that might be designated 'high art', Turner's *Slave Ship*, for example, but also on broadside woodcuts, slave advertisements and notices, book illustrations and early photography. These images emerge as deeply contradictory in terms of what they say about white representation of slavery and what they imply for black and white understanding of them, and the book's four sections examine a set of key sites which help the reader to explore this: the 'middle passage', slave flight and escape, the popular imagery generated by *Uncle Tom's Cabin* and slave punishment and torture. Each addresses why certain codes were chosen, employed and remembered in the representation of slavery in England and America. As with Campbell, Labbe and Shuttleworth, memory is central for Wood, who is intent on exploring which systematics of visual memory gained the widest cultural currency in the representation of slavery, and how such historic trauma is 'also *not over*, and is *evolving*'. The book's ultimate message, then, is that much remains to be seen in this field—is indeed unrepresentable and irrecoverable—a point that is doubly underlined by Wood's rich bibliographical allusions and thorough research.

This is a powerful study which explores slavery in a manner that takes account of the West's simultaneous aestheticization and extreme guilt regarding the treatment of non-white people in the Romantic era. As comprehensive as this study is, Wood acknowledges that a future book might look at what he excludes, notably European and North American representations of slavery as it was imagined to exist in mainland Africa. Helen Thomas's excellent *Romanticism and Slave Narratives* turns directly to this, relating Romantic literature to the African diaspora and exploring how African culture appeared within eighteenth-century Britain. Thomas identifies a moment in the late 1780s wherein parliamentary debates, colonialist projects, land disputes and programmes concerning racial eradication, emancipation and resettlement were high on the agenda in Britain. Provoked by Henry Smeathman's scheme to ship Africans who had settled in Britain to the 'promised land' of Sierra Leone, where most died, these debates were fuelled by both black and white writers. Thomas's book thus aims to bring Romantic studies into contact with transatlantic and black Atlantic studies and focus upon the literature that emerged from the meeting between eighteenth-century dissent and enthusiasm and the narratives of African slaves. Exploring the 'transcultural, restless mutations and clashes of African and western philosophies, ideologies and practices which distinguished the late eighteenth century', Thomas turns to a mixed selection of canonical and marginalized works by white 'British', black 'British' and Anglo-American authors. Like Wood, she is concerned to recognize the religious context of these debates, Methodism's early transatlantic connections set aside the 'hybrid sphere' of black culture within Africa, America, the Caribbean and Europe. Cultural hybridity is extended into cultural intertextuality: texts are read as witnesses to the 'process of movement and negotiation between cultures' and reveal racial identity as a product of 'becoming rather than being'. The book covers many types of text: political and autobiographical tracts published in Britain by abolitionists, millenarianist prophets, Romantic poets and evangelical revivalists; spiritual autobiography; responses to the slave trade by Wollstonecraft, Blake, Coleridge and Wordsworth; autobiographical slave narratives; and the poetry of Phillis Wheatley. Throughout this most exceptional of studies, writings about slavery and by slaves and ex-slaves forge a new way of speaking and thinking that we might think of as traditionally Romantic but is in fact an intertextual dialogue between Western and African culture.

Charlotte Sussman's *Consuming Anxieties* examines the history of consumer protests against colonialism between 1713 and 1833, dates covering the Treaty of Utrecht to the abolition of slavery in the British Caribbean. Bringing together often separate critical interests in consumer culture and colonialism, the study suggests that recognizing the impact of consumerism on perceptions of the colonial periphery during the period reveals the crucial role of commodity fetishism in colonialist ideology. By acknowledging the effects of colonial and mercantile expansion on domestic consumer practices, Sussman argues, certain anxieties surrounding colonial commodities can be explored. Moreover, the feminization of certain aspects of consumerism during the eighteenth century can be seen as an important, yet frequently overlooked, aspect of the history of consumerist critiques of colonialism. This attention to gender highlights the ways in which colonialism permeated both the public sphere of politics and trade, and the private realms of domesticity and sentiment. What is striking about Sussman's argument is the way in which consumerist critiques of colonialism are revealed to have both a material and a discursive impact, the symbolic manifestations of abstention movements in political rhetoric, for example, shown to be more culturally important than their immediate social effects. Discussions of the moral impact of consumer practices upon colonial policy also provided a 'framework in which questions about who should lay claim to sociopolitical agency could be negotiated', Sussman writes. Such debates were carried out within a Habermasian public sphere, a theoretical conception which underlines the book's various discussions of consumer protests and commodity culture. The 'public sphere' argument is significant because it makes fluid the division between politics and literature, the politically driven anti-slavery movement being deeply conscious of the cultural power of literary methods, texts and images. Yet where many accounts of Britain's involvement in imperialism and slavery have focused on the changing relation between metropolitan and colonial systems of labour, efforts have not been made to integrate a history of slavery with the rise of consumerism. Likewise, the relationship between femininity and consumption has been neglected, and thus ignorance regarding women's involvement in and resistance to Britain's imperial expansion has flourished. While women's emotional investment in texts and greed for luxury have been remarked upon, Sussman draws attention to the connections between the two. The book is divided into two parts: the first deals with the history of consumer protests against colonialism and imperialism, while the second concentrates on the role of commodity culture and consumer debates in the British debates over Caribbean slavery.

The question of consumerism, capitalist ideology and colonial products is also explored by Timothy Morton in *The Poetics of Spice*, a book which aims to understand how spices function as units of social discourse about food, capitalism and trade. An experiment in the literary and cultural history of the commodity, Morton's study tackles the discourse of spice instead of presenting the reader with a literary history of spice or a political investigation of a topos. He thus looks at how spice is ideologically conceived in figurative language and how certain forms of figurative language and theory are ideologically conceptualized through this commodity. The Romantic era provides Morton's context for five central reasons, which he outlines in his rather spirited introduction to the book. First, the period was one in which the spice trade was being re-evaluated in light of the new popularity of tea, coffee and opium; second, it witnessed the rise of an empire wherein imperial narratives concerning Oriental tastes were dominant; third, it was a period of archaism in culture and literature against which new uses of spice were invented; fourth, the creation of the cult of nature undermined the concept of supplementarity, deeming spice excessive and intemperate; and last, 'Romantic-period styles of consumption included highly aestheticized modes for which the poetics of spice acted as a template'. Morton comments upon these issues always with reference to both the canonical Romantics and many working-class and women poets, endowing the book with a fresh and eclectic character that separates it from many others published in the field. Hemans's *Joan of Arc* and Leigh Hunt's *A Now, Descriptive of a Hot Day*, for example, are woven together with *Kubla Khan* and *Endymion*, even as psychoanalytic theory and Marxism rub shoulders with eighteenth- and nineteenth-century medicine, philosophy and literature. One might even say that the book achieves the same 'blancmange effect' as Morton argues infuses *The Eve of St Agnes*, jumping around between ideas in a sometimes bewildering, anecdotal, but always amusing, manner.

The diverse series of essays in Amanda Gilroy's *Romantic Geographies: Discourse of Travel, 1775–1844* continues the post-colonial thread this year, shifting it into the more explicit framework of travel writing. A 'hybrid discourse that traversed the disciplinary boundaries of politics, letter writing, education, medicine, aesthetics, and economics', travel writing is described as a kind of 'capacious cultural holdall' (pp. 1–15). The idea of the journey is central here, leading travellers into war zones, imperial frontiers, sublime landscapes and physically challenging terrains and provoking many different genres of commentary and report. Moreover, the disturbances of travel are highlighted as destabilizing the boundaries of national, racial, gender and class affiliation, and, for Gilroy, enacting 'the disciplinary miscegenation that defined the mapping of geographical space'. The Romantic period seems an apt one to explore these destablizations, marking a point between the decline of the traditional Grand Tour and the advent of rail travel and consequent development of mass tourism. The essays contained here explore the literary responses to these transformations, divided into four sections which variously discuss landscapes, aesthetics and gender; the Grand Tour; pathologies of travel; and colonial and imperial writings. The first section contains three engaging and complementary essays, Sara Mills's 'Written on the Landscape: Mary Wollstonecraft's *Letters Written During a Short Residence in Sweden, Norway and Denmark*' (pp. 19–34); Jacqueline M. Labbe's '"A species of knowledge both useful and ornamental": Priscilla Wakefield's *Family Tour Through the British Empire*' (pp. 35–50); and Dorothy McMillan's 'The Secrets of Ann Radcliffe's English Travels' (pp. 51–67). Mill's analysis of Wollstonecraft's *Letters* uses a materialist-feminist model to describe the representation of the sublime by considering the gendered nature of spatial relations. She argues that spatial relations translate into social rather than simply psychoanalytic relations, the latter implicitly polarizing and essentializing gender positions in a manner the more concrete view counters. Labbe also examines the construction of 'feminine' ways of looking in her essay on Wakefield's *Family Tour*, shown here to hover between 'feminine detail and masculine generality' to 'achieve the "air" of a real tour, with its openness and expansiveness but without sacrificing proper domestic retirement'. In this way, the *Family Tour* both revises and exposes traditional travel narratives, sometimes restricting the movement of her female figures but always widely extending her own, 'encompassing the journeys of all her characters easily and without dissembling'. McMillan turns to Radcliffe's travel diaries in her essay, suggesting that the author's efforts to observe and render the actual landscape and its effects worked to undermine the 'conviction in the landscape strategies of her novels'. The Gothic poetical style of the novels privileged nature, McMillan argues, only to present it as wholly an effect of art, a consequence that resulted in Radcliffe's loss of confidence in her own mode.

Gilroy's second group of essays focuses on the Grand Tour, Keith Hanley's 'Wordsworth's Grand Tour' proposing that '*all* Wordsworth's journeyings are excursions or tours which loop back to "home at Grasmere"' (pp. 71–92). Grasmere becomes a kind of 'unbroken Imaginary relation with nature that provided [the poet] with a privately overdetermined version of full speech', an idea captured in *The Prelude*, *The Excursion* and Wordsworth's accounts of tours in Scotland and the Continent. Chris Jones's 'Travelling Hopefully: Helen Maria Williams and the Feminine Discourse of Sensibility' (pp. 93–108) marks Williams out as a writer who responded to her stay in France through a popular emotional response radically underlined by her more dissident, intellectually based political principles. As a result, Williams subverted a uniform feminine discourse of sensibility even as she exploited its ambiguities to grasp the progressive possibilities of the age, efforts continued in the work of the Shelleys, Sydney Owenson and Wordsworth. Chloe Chard's 'Women who Transmute into Tourist Attractions: Spectator and Spectacle on the Grand Tour' (pp. 109–26) concludes this section. Reading society figures such as Emma Hamilton and Paolina Borghese next to Germaine de Staël's fictional

Corinne and Laurence Sterne's Maria, Chard shows how travel writing broke down conventional barriers of propriety by indirectly justifying an objectifying gaze. Clare Brant's 'Climates of Gender' (pp. 129–49) opens the third part of Gilroy's book, 'Pathologies of Travel'. Brant turns to the encounter between eighteenth-century travel writers and male and female foreign subjects, whose sexual identities are used to construct national identities. She suggests that the dual senses of Romanticism as sexual sublimation and as poeticized subjectivity enabled a certain dreamy imagining of foreign women upon which Romantic constructions of masculine subjectivity were based. Jeanne Moskal's 'Politics and the Occupation of a Nurse in Starke's *Letters from Italy*' (pp. 150–64) reclaims the little-known Mariana Starke, whose travel memoir appears here as a rich exemplification of the complicated position of women writing politics in the reactionary 1790s. Finally, Beth Dolan Kautz's 'Spas and Salutary Landscapes: The Geography of Health in Mary Shelley's *Rambles in Germany and Italy*' (pp. 165–81) focuses on Shelley's description of the healing powers she found in the interplay between the body and the landscape. Shelley's search for health was contextualized by her own need for a cure for nervous illness, the period in which her *Rambles* was composed marked by a depression she characterized as 'weakness and languor'.

The last part of this comprehensive study of travel returns us to the field of post-colonialism. W.M. Verhoeven's 'Land-Jobbing in the Western Territories: Radicalism, Transatlantic Emigration, and the 1790s American Travel Narrative' (pp. 185–203) examines journeys to North America, which for the Romantics became a modern Atlantis. Verhoeven explores the growing feeling among post-revolutionary travellers that the true America was a *terra incognita* that promised a virtue and democracy transcendent of the vice, corruption, injustice and oppression that had riddled Europe for so long. Nigel Leask's 'Francis Wilford and the Colonial Construction of Hindu Geography, 1799–1822' (pp. 204–22) is an important study of the Bengal Engineer, Lt. Wilford, appointed secretary of the East India Company's Sanskrit College in 1794. Leask shows how the anxieties and instabilities of Wilford's orientalism were endemic to the college itself. Jane Stabler's 'Byron's Digressive Journey' (pp. 223–39) turns to some of the contentious aspects of the reception of *Childe Harold's Pilgrimage* to show how the poet's art of digression is generated by conflicting discourses of travel. The essay pivots on the notion of genre and how Byron's departure from the conventions of travel romance were perceived as destructive to English cultural authority. Saree Samir Makdisi's 'Shelley's *Alastor*: Travel Beyond the Limit' (pp. 240–57) follows on neatly from Stabler's essay, comparing *Alastor* to *Childe Harold* in order to illustrate how both face the dilemma of 'having to create' their 'own object', that which they want 'simultaneously to describe and to "represent"'. Structured as a travel narrative, Makdisi argues, Shelley's *Alastor* is profoundly informed by the shock of encounter on the imperial frontier and therefore presents the notion of quest as one for ever torn by the anxieties of colonialism.

Woodstock Books sustained the excellence of their facsimile series Revolution and Romanticism, 1789–1834 this year with the publication of six volumes edited by Jonathan Wordsworth: John Thelwall's *Poems Written in the Tower* [1795], already discussed above; Mary Robinson's *Sappho and Phaon*, reviewed with women's poetry below; Mark Akenside's *The Pleasures of Imagination* [1795]; Robert Lovell and Robert Southey's *Poems* [1795]; Constantin François Volney's

The Ruins [1811]; and Gottfried Augustus Bürger's *Leonora* [1796]. Akenside's volume is of particular importance, strikingly relevant to many pressing issues current in the field. Reissued by Barbauld, influential on Coleridge's *Lectures on Revealed Religion*, successfully fusing philosophy and poetry and taken up as a Unitarian text, *Pleasures* is revealed here as central to the formation of Romantic poetics. Most interesting is Barbauld's role in its reissue, her thirty-six-page preface to the volume influential on both Coleridge and Wordsworth alike. Her own Unitarian values helped establish the text's religio-aesthetic importance, Barbauld claiming that Akenside 'dignifies his theme by connecting it with the sublimest feelings the human mind is capable of entertaining, feelings without which the various scenes of this beautiful universe degenerate into gaudy shows, fit to catch the eye of children, but uninteresting to the heart and affections'. Prefiguring Keats, but with a religious spin, Barbauld stresses the poem's 'connection of beauty with truth', showing 'that all the beauty we admire in vegetable or animal life results from the fitness of the object to the use for which it is intended, and serves as a kind of stamp set by the Creator to point out the health, fondness, and perfection of the form in which it resides'. Among Akenside's other admirers, the editor declares, were Dorothy Wordsworth and Sara Hutchinson, both of whom possessed the 1795 volume. As Barbauld moved Coleridge, so Coleridge urged Wordsworth to read the poem, and Jonathan Wordsworth points out the merging of Akenside's 'language, syntax, rhythm' and 'influence of Nature on the mind' with the tones of early drafts of *The Prelude*.

Lovell and Southey's collaborative edition, *Poems*, was famously printed as part of Southey's campaign to raise money to fund the radical Pantisocracy movement planned with Coleridge. Where *Joan* would carry Southey over to America, *Poems* would establish the Pantisocrats' reputation, even though neither Lovell or Southey had ever published before. Even as the fervour for Pantisocracy broke down and the plan was abandoned, Southey's poetical career was flourishing, and he made twice as many contributions to the volume as Lovell. The poetry is mainly juvenilia but is clearly influenced by Gray, Goldsmith and Bowles (from whom the epigraphical 'Retrospect' is cited), thus providing a good example of the melancholy tones of early Romanticism. For Jonathan Wordsworth, Southey's offerings to the edition evince 'all the skills that will place him amongst the best "makers", if not among the great poets, of the Romantic period' and for this, at least, the collection is revealing. The tone and concerns of Coleridge haunt Southey's work as much as they do Lovell's, the latter's 'Elegy: The Decayed Monastery' echoing the Ancient Mariner's words in its invocation of the slimy serpent who crawls through the ravaged walls of 'some antique ruin, time-defac'd'.

The ruins of Lovell's complaint feed into a fragmented Romantic tradition that signified more than decrepit buildings, however. Volney's *The Ruins, or A Survey of the Revolutions of Empires, with The Law of Nature, or Principles of Morality, deduced from the Physical Constitution of Mankind and the Universe* betrays the ruinous nature of humanity itself, noted by Frankenstein's nameless creature. Sequestered in the woods, the creature tells us that *The Ruins* offered him 'an insight into the manners, governments and religions of the different nations of the earth … of the early Romans—of their subsequent degenerating—of the decline of that mighty empire; of chivalry, Christianity and kings'. Mary Shelley's choice of the text as a pedagogical device along with *Paradise Lost*, Plutarch's *Lives* and *The*

Sorrows of Werther reveals something about her own education, the editor notes; Volney's translator James Marshall was a lifelong friend of William Godwin. First published in 1791 and 1792, *The Ruins* was a best-seller in the revolutionary period, the textual outcome of Volney's travels through Corsica, Paris, Egypt and Syria where he slept rough, almost starved, befriended Holbach and Franklin, and learned Arabic. While religion is central to *The Ruins*, theories of political truth, social networks, the law, empire, revolution and mysticism all arise from this debate, vehicles of 'moral truth' which Volney consistently strives to express. Influencing Blake's prophecies and, more directly, the visionary, freethinking content of Shelley's *Queen Mab*, *The Ruins* is a key text for the Romantics' struggle with Christianity and all world religion.

Jonathan Wordsworth's last offering in this field is Bürger's *Leonora*, issued here in both its English and German versions and complete with Blake's illustrations. Translated into English in 1790 by William Taylor, the ballad was written by Bürger twenty-five years earlier, impacting forcefully in Germany where *Sturm und Drang* was already popular. The tale is of Leonora, who, paralysed by grief at the absence of her beloved presumed lost in the war, resorts to blasphemy to summon his ghost. As a consequence, she suffers nightmarish visions until she wakes to find her experience 'all a dream' and herself clasped within her lover's arms. The ballad's Gothicism is not simply atmospheric, however; its portrait of an indifferent God is terrifying and resolved only by the restorative ending.

Angela Keane's *Women Writers and the English Nation in the 1790s: Romantic Belongings* emphasizes emergent ideas of national literary representation in Ann Radcliffe, Williams, Smith, Wollstonecraft and More. Keane's book is novel in that it rejects the idea that these women are the 'unrepresented underside of the English Romantic canon', following a rationale which privileges the idea of 'belonging' over issues of canon-formation and the cultural inclusion of certain writers. With the term 'belongings' Keane signals the economic and affective underpinnings of the imagined community of the English nation, and women's relation to it in the 1790s in three principal ways. First, 'belongings' mean owned goods, the property that defines society and women's status as property rather than proprietors. Belonging also points to a more metaphorical form of ownership, Keane argues, 'having property in common, sharing in the interests of other people' within one unified nation. Lastly, the participle 'longing' is used to evoke a dynamic of desire endemic to national discourse, constituted by a longing for community and for a pastoral sense of origin and stability. As an object of desire, then, the nation is gendered feminine, a sentiment which strongly echoes Mellor, especially in the sense of its nurturing role as a source of national security. The interpellation of the woman into the feminine, maternal subject position in national discourse is apparent in a number of ways within the study: More sanctioning the national family romance; Smith and Wollstonecraft critiquing society's material and psychic impoverishment of women; and Radcliffe and Williams investing in a national affection grounded in feminine power. All these writers address the problem of the female wanderer, the woman who defines herself beyond the home, divesting herself of femininity and erasing herself from the 'familial, heterosexual structure of the nation'. Her belonging, Keane writes, depends on her belonging to another, her romantic feelings for another dependent on her literal and symbolic reproduction of the national family. Keane's study addresses the problem of the canon's 'lost women' by illustrating how women writers demystify the origins of a nation-state, the formation of which they strongly influenced. How women came to belong, or strove to belong, to this nation-state is explored through their pedagogical impulse to shape society and culture.

Journals offered a large number of general articles this year, *Romanticism on the Net* issuing four diverse special issues focused on distinct themes (articles within these issues on individual Romantics are reviewed elsewhere). Michael John Kooy collected five essays under the rubric, 'After Romantic Ideology' (*RoN* 17[2000]), asking what shape current literary criticism of the Romantic period is assuming given that it is no longer organized around the 'ideological critique of the High Romantic Argument'. David Chandler's essay, '"One Consciousness": Historical Criticism and the Romantic Canon' appears here, winner of the best article in *Romanticism on the Net* for this year and serving to address the relationship between new historicism and the formation of the canon. Peter J. Kitson's '"The Eucharist of Hell": Or, Eating People is Right: Romantic Representations of Cannibalism' focuses on cannibalism as the most notorious practice of colonial 'othering', the process by which imperial Europe distinguished itself from the subjects of its colonial expansion. Luisa Calè's excellent '"A female band despising Nature's law": Botany, Gender and Revolution in the 1790s' examines the dialectical conflict within the representation of botany contained in public discourses of the 1790s. Rearticulating botanical figures as a source for analogical thinking and ideology, Calè explores William Smellie's *Encyclopaedia Britannica*, Erasmus Darwin's *Loves of the Plants*, Mary Wollstonecraft's view of the role of botanical education for women and Thomas Malthus's use of flower overgrowth to denounce perfectibility in his *Essay on the Principle of Population*.

Jacqueline M. Labbe's collection addressing the subject of 'Romantic Couplings' seeks to dislodge the partnership of Wordsworth and Coleridge as the defining idea of literary collaboration by re-reading coupling as both 'tangible and insubstantial, textual and ideological, real and imaginary' (*RoN* 18[2000]). Nora Crook's 'Pecksie and the Elf: Did the Shelleys Couple Romantically?' asks whether the literary collaboration of the Shelleys was a Romantic one *and* whether they were passionate sentimental lovers, a central question due to the importance both attached to 'love' as a principle which ought to rule the world. Jane Hodson's 'Can a Statue Breathe? The Linguistic (Un)coupling of Godwin and Wollstonecraft' considers the relationship between Godwin and Wollstonecraft from the perspective of their linguistic thinking, outlining their contrasting attitudes towards language and seeking to find some kind of linguistic reconciliation between them. Ashley Tauchert also turns to Wollstonecraft in 'Escaping Discussion: Liminality and the Female-Embodied Couple in Mary Wollstonecraft's *Mary, A Fiction*', reading her proto-lesbian novel as a commentary on female-embodied same-sex desire, acknowledged only as an 'open secret' which must ultimately be disavowed as an impossibility. Labbe's 'The Anthologized Romance of Della Crusca and Anna Matilda' closes this grouping with a discussion of the impact of Della Cruscan poetry as that which confronted physical and sexual love. The essay reads the relationship between Della Crusca and Anna Matilda in *The British Album* between 1788 and 1794 and considers William Gifford's response to such romantic exchange as obscene and base.

Anthony John Harding's 'New Texts and Textual Scholarship in British Literature, 1780–1830' (*RoN* 19[2000]) asks what new texts will inform explorations of British literature 1780–1830 in the first decade of the twenty-first century, offering several essays on women which are discussed elsewhere. Neil Fraistat's 'The Workshop of Shelley's Poetry' and Douglas S. Mack's 'James Hogg in 2000 and Beyond' focus on two relatively canonical authors to address this question, balanced by Susan J. Wolfson's detailed 'Representing some Late Romantic-Era, Non-Canonical Male Poets: Thomas Hood, Winthrop Mackworth Praed, Thomas Lovell Beddoes'. Wolfson remarks on the submergence of several male poets whose canonical status has never been secured, passed over during the more vigorous reclamation of women writers whose work converges with the current interest in social and historical concerns. Finally, James Powell's 'Textual Editions' gives the reader a short outline of how the publisher, in this case Pickering & Chatto, thinks with regard to Romantic writing, looking at questions of commissioning and marketing, and at editorial concerns.

A special number of *Women's Writing* was devoted to the Romantic period this year, presenting seven essays introduced by Caroline Franklin. Judith Stanton's 'Charlotte Smith and "Mr Monstroso": An Eighteenth-Century Marriage in Life and Fiction' (*WW* 1[2000] 7–22) embarks on a historical investigation of Smith's unpublished letters to open up the debate on her tragic forty-one-year marriage to Benjamin Smith. Penny Mahon's 'In Sermon and Story: Contrasting Anti-War Rhetoric in the Work of Anna Barbauld and Amelia Opie' (*WW* 1[2000] 23–38) highlights the radical dissenting tradition both Barbauld and Opie were aligned with in the period, a platform from which they voiced a challenge against the wars with France. Janet Bottoms's 'Every One Her Own Heroine: Conflicting Narrative Structures in *Mrs Leicester's School*' (*WW* 1[2000] 39–53) reclaims Mary Lamb's stories as more complex narratives than has been previously acknowledged, granting them an important role in the development of children's literature. Stephen C. Behrendt turns to a little-known Romantic poet in his essay, 'In Search of Anna Maria Smallpiece' (*WW* 1[2000] 55–73), her 1805 *Original Sonnets, and Other Small Poems* establishing her as an innovative and influential sonneteer. Leah Price's 'The Poetics of Pedantry from Thomas Bowdler to Susan Ferrier' (*WW* 1[2000] 75–88) looks at the apparently hackneyed manner by which Ferrier's novels are assumed to be marked and resituates them within the culture of the nineteenth-century anthology. Anira Rowanchild's '"Everything done for effect": Georgic Gothic and Picturesque in Anne Lister's Self-Production' (*WW* 1[2000] 89–104) focuses on the fascinating gentlewoman Anne Lister, whose interest in aesthetic style allowed her to explore her lesbian sexuality within a framework of social conservatism. Finally, Joanna Wilkes's '"Only the broken music?" The Critical Writings of Maria Jane Jewsbury' (*WW* 1[2000] 105–18) makes an important contribution to the field by examining Jewsbury's anonymous publications, notably her contributions to the *Athenaeum* from 1830 to 1832.

Volume 11 of *European Romantic Review* was primarily devoted to a special topic on the 'Romantic century', newly proposed by Susan J. Wolfson and William Galperin as spanning the period 1750 to 1850. Expanding Romanticism in this way, Wolfson argues in her introduction, '50–50? Phone a Friend? Ask the Audience? Speculating on a Romantic Century' (*ERR* 11[2000] 1–11), might serve to address the troubling collision between a developing field and contracting Romanticist job list in North America. Reviewing earlier visions of the field as one dominated by the 'Big Six', the essay sets up a forum the purpose of which is to redefine Romantic-associated interests into an intellectually and historically coherent century. Claudia L. Johnson's 'The Novel and the Romantic Century, 1750–1850' (*ERR* 11[2000] 12–20) questions the nature of the Romantic-era novel by exploring Barbauld's fifty-volume edition of *British Novelists* as an important commentary on the contemporary canon. Anne K. Mellor's 'Women Writers in the Romantic Century, 1750–1850' (*ERR* 11[2000] 21–4) reflects upon the current development of this area of study, turning specifically to the profound continuity that exists between the women writers of the Romantic era and the male and female writers that followed them. As in her recent monograph, *Mothers of the Nation*, reviewed elsewhere, Mellor is preoccupied with Hannah More, whose publications are presented as having brought about that cultural phenomenon we now call 'Victorianism'. Peter J. Manning's 'Hermits and Monks: The Romantic Century, 1750–1850' (*ERR* 11[2000] 25–30) traces the notions of 'solitude' and 'medieval' as they shift meaning and position across the time span. William Keach's 'A Transatlantic Romantic Century' (*ERR* 11[2000] 31–4) reconstructs a transatlantic politics of writing, significant for the connections it forges between social conflict, the evolution of modern national identity and the state, and literary culture. Finally, William Galperin's '"Let us not desert one another": Jane Austen and the Romantic Century' (*ERR* 11[2000] 35–43) offers a response to the other contributors by reading the notion of Romanticism as a 'polemical shorthand for revolution rather than for the accretive or evolutionary process that the notion of a romantic century effectively proposes'. Galperin takes the example of Jane Austen to evince, not a dismissal of Romantic transcendence as many critics have noted, but a commitment to horizons of possibility that are offered only to be negotiated, a metaphor, perhaps, for the direction in which our field might develop.

ERR 11 also offered two further general essays this year: John L. Greenway's 'Acoustic Figures and the Romantic Soul of Reason' (*ERR* 11[2000] 214–22) and Tim Fulford's 'Romanticism, the South Seas and the Caribbean: the Fruits of Empire' (*ERR* 11[2000] 408–34). Greenaway seeks to recentre the scientist Hans Christian Ørsted, who famously discovered electromagnetism in 1820, within the field. This intriguing paper shows how Ørsted's eighteenth-century experiments in acoustics became an artistic metaphor for the Romantic imagination, while also leading the way to our own electronic culture. Fulford looks at the political symbol of the bread-fruit plant, a fetishized commodity in the period, as opposed to the blood-soaked commodity of slave-produced sugar. Rediscovered when Captain Wallis visited Tahiti in 1767, the bread fruit became at once an alluring image of paradise islands and, more sinisterly, a representation of a South Pacific Britain would come to colonize and control. A second essay by Fulford, co-authored with Debbie Lee, turns to the subject of Edward Jenner's revolutionary *An Inquiry into the Causes of Effects of the Variolae Vaccinae, A Disease Discovered in Some of the Western Counties of England and known by the name of The Cow Pox* (*SiR* 39[2000] 139–63). The authors highlight the text's investment in rural health and the oral tradition of Gloucestershire villagers to emphasize the rustic simplicity that linked it with the poetical project of Wordsworth. Jenner's campaign to promote science through the medium of Romantic poetry is also outlined, poetry being a genre employed to render vaccination a political metaphor of immunization and containment for those afraid of revolution and foreign presence in England. Peter J. Kitson's '"Bales of living anguish": Representations of Race and the Slave in Romantic Writing' (*ELH* 67[2000] 515–37) contributes to the field of post-colonialism, exploring representations of African slaves in writings by Edward Long, Anthony Benezet and Thomas Clarkson. These writers not only created a debate about race, Kitson eloquently shows, but also provided a context through which Coleridge's *Lecture on the Slave Trade* [1795] and John Thelwall's *The Daughter of Adoption* might be read. The essay ultimately charts a transition from an Enlightenment to a Romantic view of race driven by the imperatives of science and slavery.

Two final essays conclude this section: Gillian Russell's exceptional '"Faro's Daughters": Female Gamesters, Politics and the Discourse of Finance in 1790s Britain' (*ECS* 33:iv[2000] 481–504), and Alan Richardson's 'Rethinking Romantic Incest: Human Universals, Literary Representation and the Biology of Mind' (*NLH* 31:iii[2000] 553–72). Russell asserts that one of the most enduring themes of eighteenth-century commentary on contemporary Britain was the nation's passion for gambling. She notes that the main target for criticism was the gambling of upper-class women, and in particular, the operation of Faro tables in the houses of prominent women of fashion. Susceptible to fines for illegal gambling in 1797, the Faro ladies became a focus for some of the deepest anxieties of the period, Russell contends. She seeks to recover their impact upon issues of gender, rank, politics and the circulation of money. Richardson contrasts a series of eighteenth-century 'unconscious' incest narratives with the incestuous heroes and heroines of the Romantic tradition who quite knowingly pursue their forbidden loves. Focusing on sibling incest, he sees it as an extension and intensification of the normal sibling relation, rooted in infancy and the power of shared childhood experiences. His essay offers a psychobiological reading of Romantic sibling incest with reference to texts such as Southey's *Thalaba*, Brontë's *Wuthering Heights* and Coleridge's *Principles of Moral and Political Philosophy*.

2. Prose Fiction

Austen studies dominated this year's offerings on fictional prose of the Romantic era, and prominent among these are two important books that will have a significant impact on the ways we read and teach Austen cults and cultures. Lynch, ed., *Janeites: Austen's Disciples and Devotees*, while acknowledging its debt to cultural materialist readings of the revolutionary and Regency periods, refuses to fetishize the originary moment of the texts' production; instead, it examines and illuminates the cultural reproduction of Austen over the last two centuries. Lynch's introduction argues that there are more useful things to do with the record of reading Austen than to adjudicate between faithful and unfaithful readings, for such an enterprise marginalizes more interesting questions about the agendas, covert and explicit, of those discussing her, and 'about the divergent uses to which … alternative Austens have been put in the literary system and the culture at large' (p. 5). Reception history reveals the ways in which Austenmania traverses, and complicates, the boundaries between high and low culture, and provides 'evidence for a less gentle Jane than the one we have encountered of late' (p. 6). Lynch surveys what it has meant to love, or hate, Austen at various historical moments, paying special attention to the emphasis on 'homemaking'. The collection as a whole takes Austen out of the home, focusing especially on the interactions between reading Austen and issues of public concern, such as war and the rise of mass literacy. The collection opens with a stellar contribution from Claudia L. Johnson: 'The Divine Miss Jane: Jane Austen, Janeites, and the Discipline of Novel Studies' interrogates the heteronormativity of canonical readings of Austen and recovers 'a nonnormative tradition of reading' via discussion of Kipling's 'Janeites' and the real-life, high camp Oxbridge gentlemen who admired Austen in the early twentieth century. Johnson's 'queer Austen' (p. 27) helps to historicize the discipline of novel studies, as well as its disciplinary intentions. Other high points in the collection include Barbara M. Benedict's 'Sensibility by the Numbers' which places Austen's work in the context of popular circulating library novels, showing how she utilized the conventions of popular fiction and cannily traded on the transgressions of cultural hierarchies facilitated by circulating libraries; like Johnson, William Galperin, in 'Austen's Earliest Readers and the Rise of the Janeites', is also interested in the self-legitimations of Austen criticism, in this case, the tradition that links realism and projects of social hegemony—Galperin finds proto-Janeites in Regency readers such as Annabella Milbanke and Jane Davy, to whom the truths of the novel's didactic task were not self-evident. Mary Favret examines the fate of Jane Austen in America, avoiding the Anglophile touristic strain to excavate the Americanness of Austen. Favret argues that, when transplanted to America, Austen comes to be about 'freedom and the pursuit of happiness' (p. 168), but at the cost of encouraging the nation 'to "forget" race, slavery, and unhappiness' (p. 182). Susan Fraiman's satisfying reading of *Mansfield Park* argues for the confluence of abolitionist and feminist discourses in the novel and offers a sophisticated critique of the sexual politics of Edward Said's interpretation. Mary Ann O'Farrell speculates on the modalities of friendship in Austen's novels and readers, and fantasizes about being a friend of Austen's; Clara Tuite offers a queer genealogy of Austen that comprehends Forster, James, and Firbank via a convoluted discussion of 'entailed' literary estates. Katie Trumpener examines Austen's position as presiding deity of Virago Press's series of women's fiction. Roger Sales's contribution on servants, especially in the recent adaptation of *Persuasion*, seems oddly out of place and under-theorized for the company it keeps. However, if the collection is occasionally uneven it is always provocative, offering a cautionary tale to critics about our own investment in Austen. It asks us to rethink the relations between Austen and Englishness, between elite and popular cultures, and the cultural function of the realist novel at different historical moments.

Park and Sunder Rajan, eds., *The Postcolonial Jane Austen*, complements Lynch's concern with the politics of home and the relations between Austen and the public sphere. The collection is divided into two parts, 'Austen at Home' and 'Austen Abroad', in a deliberate echo of Edward Said's argument that nineteenth-century English novelists depended on the imbrications of 'home' and 'abroad' for their versions of England. Sunder Rajan's wide-ranging introduction contests that reading Austen 'post-colonially' is not an optional 'approach' but 'an inescapable historical imperative in our times' that attends to all the modalities of domination in the histories and cultural legacies of colonialism. Sunder Rajan surveys the alternative Austen (re)produced since the 1970s, historicized and enmeshed in the messy discourses of capitalism, imperialism, sexuality, revolution, etc., that has replaced the Austen defined in terms of her 'limits'. Following Spivak and Said, she argues that the novels constitute a colonial discourse, not least in that they question national identity in response to 'the historical pressures of colonialism' (p. 10); she also argues that, when Austen's novels started to be read in the context of larger national and imperial systems, questions of gender and domesticity had to be reconsidered in terms of questions about the nation, slave trade, commerce, war, mobility, and so on. Finally, she looks at the way Austen's texts are 'in the world' geographically, institutionalized in many parts of the world as a result of British colonialism and United States global hegemony. She raises questions—addressed by contributors in the second part of the book—about the differently mediated ways in which Austen represents cultural capital in a global economy, and she interrogates the 'universalism' ascribed to her work.

Of the five essays grouped under 'Austen at Home', four deal primarily, and unsurprisingly in the wake of Said, with *Mansfield Park*. Elaine Jordan's essay 'Jane Austen Goes to the Seaside: *Sanditon*, English Identity and the "West Indian" Schoolgirl' makes visible the ways in which English identity depended on constructions of racial 'otherness', and includes a discussion of *Mansfield Park*. In 'Learning to Ride at Mansfield Park', Donna Landry reads gender and colonialism through the novel's discourses of equestrianism, demonstrating the imperial significance of Fanny's restrained (feminine) riding which wins out against Mary Crawford's suspect exhibitionism, here representing all that must be marginalized from nineteenth-century English femininity. Jon Mee's 'Austen's Treacherous Ivory: Female Patriotism, Domestic Ideology, and Empire' contests Said's reading of *Mansfield Park*, suggesting that the novel's version of empire and Englishness offers a less sanguine version of the consequences of colonial rule for domestic prosperity than do Victorian texts. Clara Tuite examines the 'property plots' of *Mansfield Park*, annotating the way in which the novel connects British imperial expansion with the decline of the aristocratic family. The final essay in this section, Julianne Pidduck's quite well-known 'Of Windows and Country Walks: Frames of Space and Movement in 1990s Austen Adaptations', examines the contact zone between projected female desire and other class and colonial power relations. The essays grouped under 'Austen Abroad' situate Austen's novels in the context of global economies, and especially the issues around intercultural comparisons. Judith Plotz sees Emily Eden as a 'surrogate' Austen in her colonial writings about India, but she also examines her post-India novel *The Semi-Detached House* as an allegory of a newly destabilized Britishness. In 'Reluctant Janeites', Nalini Natarajan highlights the economic and sentimental valences of daughterly 'value' in *Emma* and in Sarat Chandra Chatterjee's *Swami*, while Mohapatra and Nayak scrutinize Vikram Seth's appropriation of the Austenian realist project. You-me Park explores the thematic similarities between *Pride and Prejudice* and a Korean novel, *A Faltering Afternoon*, by Pak Wanso, as a way of exposing the complicities between patriarchy and capitalism in transitional societies. Finally, Gayle Wald's already published reading of the liberatory potential of *Clueless* proposes that the film resists US nostalgia for a romanticized England, but nonetheless ultimately colludes with the politics of heterosexual closure. The Austen that emerges in this book is both familiar and estranging, historically located in the early nineteenth century but with a geographical and temporal afterlife that complicates the cultural capital she represents.

There were two other books devoted to Austen, both of which are far less adventurous than those discussed above. Lambdin and Lambdin, eds., *A Companion to Jane Austen Studies*, offers twenty-two essays on her novels, letters, poems and prayers. Each major work has two chapters devoted to it, the first of which summarizes previous critical reactions and then offers a 'reader-oriented critical essay' (p. xi), while the second is a bibliographic essay. The editors claim to 'embrace' Austen's 'ambiguity' (p. xiii) and the range of cultural responses her work has generated; however, the 'various theoretical ... camps' represented in the collection oddly do not include queer theory or post-colonial theory, and do not theorize in any significant way the affective responses they survey. Audrey Hawkridge's *Jane and her Gentlemen: Jane Austen and the Men in her Life and Novels* examines 'Jane's world' through the men in her family and social circle and how they cast light on the men in her novels, claiming (wishfully) that these are 'men whom we encounter daily in our own lives'.

Most of this year's essays on Austen focus on a single text, but Janet Sorensen, Chris Jones, Jill Heydt-Stevenson and Elsie B. Michie range more widely through the novels. The epilogue to Janet Sorensen's illuminating analysis of colonial pedagogy, *The Grammar of Empire in Eighteenth-Century British Writing*, considers 'Jane Austen's language and the strangeness at home in the center'. While the rest of the book focuses on Scottish ambivalence about a unitary English linguistic identity, the epilogue argues that the linguistic alienations of Austen's novels trouble the naturalness of English nationalist constructions. Sorensen examines the texture of Austen's representations of heart and home, showing how she makes the familiar, especially 'proper' English and polite conversation, strange, thus destabilizing the domestic sphere's putative guarantee of national, public unity. In 'Jane Austen and Old Corruption' (*L&H* 9:ii[2000] 1–16), Chris Jones demonstrates that Austen's novels engage in criticism of patronage relationships, and the corruption associated with the institution in contemporary debates. Reading *Pride and Prejudice*, *Mansfield Park* and *Persuasion* alongside contemporary accounts of public scandals, experiences in Austen's own social circle and novels by Edgeworth and Smith, Jones argues that Austen's novels reveal the multiform patronage relationships of the period (from the disposition of clerical livings to familial relations) and expose the power plays of patronage, whether benevolent or self-aggrandizing. Just as radical demands for reform of patronage in the Regency crisis coalesced with demands for the extension of the franchise, so Austen's romance plots, Jones suggests, gesture towards 'a moral equality that transcends the inequalities of society' (p. 13). In '"Slipping into the ha-ha": Bawdy Humor and Body Politics in Jane Austen's Novels' (*NCL* 55:iii[2000] 309–39), Jill Heydt-Stevenson examines how Austen uses bawdy/body humour in *Emma*, *Mansfield Park* and *Persuasion* to critique patriarchal culture, especially the institution of marriage, and to reaffirm the tendentious power of female sexuality. She is provocatively illuminating on how Austen uses the riddle 'Kitty, a fair, but frozen maid' as the basis of a subversive portrait of the connections between courtship and venereal disease in *Emma*. Heydt-Stevenson's thoroughly sexualized Austen complements other recent readings (especially by Terry Castle and Eve Sedgwick) that have productively sullied Austen's chaste reputation, and cultural investments in it. Elsie B. Michie's fine essay, 'Austen's Powers: Engaging with Adam Smith in Debates About Wealth and Virtue' (*Novel* 34:i[2000] 5–27), argues that as we move from *Pride and Prejudice* to *Mansfield Park* to *Emma* we see Austen wrestling with the ambivalent feelings of commercial culture towards its own materialist drives. Like Adam Smith in *The Theory of Moral Sentiments*, Austen acknowledges the beneficial desire for wealth in commercial society along with the need to find ways of restraining the engrossment in wealth that deflects the individual from virtue. If Austen begins by using the split between the rich and poor woman as a way of invoking the ideological opposition between engrossment and refinement through differences of body and behaviour, she shifts from the material to the mental, that is, to the way characters perceive or imagine the effects of wealth.

We saw only one essay devoted to *Northanger Abbey*: Casie Hermansson's 'Neither Northanger Abbey: The Reader Presupposes' (*PLL* 36:iv[2000] 337–56) performs some mental acrobatics in her exploration of parody and the compounding of negatives in the novel, whereby she argues that the novel simultaneously performs and deconstructs its binaries and paradoxes. In 'Privacy, Dissimulation, and Propriety: Frances Burney and Jane Austen' (*ECF* 12:iv[2000] 515–31), Patricia Meyer Spacks argues that Austen and Burney investigate 'the ambiguities of privacy': the good manners and self-surveillance promoted by women's conduct literature offered women a way to veil their difference, to conceal their socially unacceptable desires and feelings under the guise of conformity. Focusing on the narrative crisis in *The Wanderer* when Juliet is persuaded to undertake a public musical performance, Spacks argues that propriety both conceals and reveals, enabling Juliet to guard the privacy of her heart and demonstrate her virtue. Austen confronts the problem of dissimulation, raising the possibility in *Sense and Sensibility* that deliberate dissimulation 'may play a fundamental part in the maintenance of ethical responsibility'. Vincent Quinn's 'Loose Reading? Sedgwick, Austen and Critical Practice' (*TPr* 14:ii[2000] 305–26) explores Eve Sedgwick's 'masturbating girl' essay (and Lee Siegal's scandalized response to it), valuing it less for what it says about Austen and more for its suggestions of a queer reading practice that validates fantasy and 'creative' criticism. If Austen is not his main concern, he does provide a useful summary of Sedgwick's article, as well as its vulnerability to criticism; he argues that Sedgwick's 'attempt to queer Austen' represents an attempt to escape the moralizing and normalizing tendencies of Austen criticism and he discusses Sedgwick's elision of Austen's complicity in this punitive dynamic.

A number of essays dealt with *Pride and Prejudice* and its adaptations. Susan Reilly's '"A nobler fall of ground": Nation and Narration in *Pride and Prejudice*' (*Symbiosis* 4:i[2000] 19–34) argues that Austen's descriptions of the Pemberley landscape accrue new significance when read in the context of late eighteenth-century North American topographical narratives. Austen's Burkean response disavows the revolutionary rhetoric of liberty, equality, wilderness and land ownership purveyed by these narratives (by the likes of Imlay, Cooper and Brissot) and embraces the 'rural paternalism' which guarantees the stability of the landed class. Thus, Austen's English nationalism is informed by anti-American sentiment. In 'The Case against Charlotte Lucas' (*WW* 7:ii[2000] 165–74), K. St John Damstra ingeniously claims that it is Charlotte Lucas who manipulates events so that Elizabeth gets Darcy and Pemberley and Mr Collins gets the prospect of a valuable church preferment. If this reading dispels feminist anxieties about Darcy's power at the end of the novel, it magnifies Charlotte's role out of all proportion. Laura

Brosh's 'Consuming Women: The Representation of Women in the 1940 Adaptation of *Pride and Prejudice*' (*Quarterly Review of Film and Video* 17:ii[2000] 147–59) argues, unsurprisingly, that the 'adaptation's representation of women is determined by a complex convergence of historical, cultural and economic developments', especially anxieties towards women consumers in America in the 1930s (Linda Troost is mis-cited as 'Trist' in the 'Works Cited'). In '"Where the garment gapes": Faithfulness and Promiscuity in the 1995 BBC *Pride and Prejudice*' (in Giddings and Sheen, eds, *The Classic Novel: From Page to Screen*, pp. 14–30), Erica Sheen analyses the omissions and interventions of the BBC adaptation in relation to the ideology of ownership. Via Freud, Lacan, Barthes, and cultural theory, she pursues a (post-)Thatcherite theory of adaptation as 'relocation' whereby the text buys into upwardly-mobile production systems, especially an instalment-plan economy (thus, in 1998, Darcy and Pemberley were transformed into a corporate advertisement for licence fee payment methods).

Christopher Flynn's '"No other island in the world": *Mansfield Park*, North America and Post-Imperial Malaise' (*Symbiosis* 4:ii[2000] 173–86) offers a new slant to post-colonial readings of the novel: Flynn argues that while *Mansfield Park* is undeniably a novel about slavery, 'it is also about England's loss of North America, which prescribes isolationist remedies to prevent future losses'. Austen's model of domestic tranquillity is a world of restricted horizons centred on a sickly heroine, who is the keeper of the insularity of the Bertram family; the text's repeated gestures west to the Americas contextualize this insularity in terms of the psychic wound caused by the loss of the colonies. The Bertram household wards off the possibility of such rejection by expelling the foreign. The essays by Flynn and Reilly convincingly demonstrate the importance of the American connection in reading Austen, and are part of an increasing concern with transatlantic issues in the Romantic period. In 'The Mentor-Lover in *Mansfield Park*: "At once both tragedy and comedy"' (*CQ* 29:ii[2000] 145–64), Patricia Menon invites us to see the complex pattern of fractured, eroticized and triangulated mentor–lover relationships that pervade the novel. Menon's close textual reading is perhaps less interesting for its concern with genre (like *Lovers' Vows*, *Mansfield Park* defers interpretation as tragic or comic) than for its revelation of Austen's traditionally most priggish heroine and novel as saturated with sexuality.

Emma had a bumper year. Deirdre Lynch, in addition to editing *Janeites*, produced a wonderful essay, 'Homes and Haunts: Austen's and Mitford's English Idylls' (*PMLA* 115:v[2000] 1103–8). Lynch examines the kitschy 'homes and haunts' genre's way of 'being at home in English', demonstrating how Austen and Mitford offer a paradigm for that 'affective project'. Lynch shows how 'the idea of the literary landscape has built bridges between ... the commercialized public sphere in which such representations circulate and ... the domain of familiar intimacy, local solidarities, and everyday routines'. Suggestively, she argues that only in the wake of the enclosures movement, through the erasures of local particularity, could the rural scene become a focus for national culture and be packaged for imperial reading audiences as 'maps of *their common places*'. Frances Ferguson's 'Jane Austen, *Emma*, and the Impact of Form' (*MLQ* 61:i[2000] 157–80) contends that Foucauldian criticism has read free indirect discourse in the novel only as a technique of surveillance that identifies a social collective; on the contrary, through a close analysis that could give formalism a good name, Ferguson argues that Austen's use of free indirect style in *Emma* rewrites the marriage plot from its eighteenth-century teleology into a contingent form that renders the discontinuities of community and individual consciousness, and that ultimately defends the individual. In '"A Sort of Notch in the Donwell Estate": Intersections of Status and Class in *Emma*' (*ECF* 12:iv[2000] 533–48), Paul Delany argues that critical disagreements about Austen's position on the political spectrum can be clarified if we distinguish between two social hierarchies of 'class' and 'status'. Class, he contends, is 'a stratification by capital, income, and economic productivity' while 'status' comprehends 'blood', 'name', 'rank', 'connection', 'family' and 'consequence', and the two terms may be classified in terms of 'culture' and 'nature'. Delany's detailed reading of the novel shows that status is no mere reflection of a determining class base.

Not noted last year, Jana Gohrisch's '"Indifferent Differences": Everyday Life in Jane Austen's *Emma*' (*Journal for the Study of British Cultures* 6:ii[2000] 153–66) is premised on Maurice Blanchot's claim that 'the everyday' is 'the site of all possible signification'; thus, the novel's instances of boredom (such as the Box Hill outing) are strategies of everyday life, rooted in a local moral order, which act as a prophylactic against revolution. Gohrisch's essay identifies 'The Dialectics of Everyday Life' as crucial to a reading of *Emma*, a concern developed at length in a special issue of the online *Romantic Circles Praxis* series, devoted to 'Re-reading Box Hill: Reading the Practice of Reading Everyday Life'. George Levine's 'Box Hill and the Limits of Realism' posits that Box Hill is a geographical site of 'crisis' which tests 'the limits of the ordinary that is so often affirmed as the "real" in English realism'. The 'extremity' of Box Hill emphasizes multiplicity and instability, against which the Knightley ideal is positively weighed. William Walling's short essay, 'Saying What One Thinks: Emma—*Emma*—at Box Hill' calls attention to the 'similarity between the two injured parties at Box Hill—unmarried women without incomes, bound to each other by blood' and to 'Emma and Frank as the joint agents of unfeeling privilege' before moving on to Austen's famous irony and her 'truly remarkable resistance to reduction'. Deirdre Lynch's impressive contribution, 'Social Theory at Box Hill: Acts of Union', surely confirms her status as this year's premier reader of Austen. Lynch begins with an interest in how the numbers in the Box Hill party wax and wane, how Emma's and Mrs Elton's combined guest lists collate happiness with judgements about inclusion to, and exclusion from, our 'circle' or 'party'. *Emma* continues eighteenth-century discussions of sympathy and social cohesion; Lynch posits that the universal agreement salvaged from the Box Hill episode might characterize geographical relations, especially 'whether novel readers might through their sympathetic fellow feeling form a nation'. Reading *Emma* through the lens of sentimentalist social theory (Shaftesbury, Johnson, Ferguson), Lynch argues that if the Highbury contingent start out on a process of 'cantonising', ultimately Emma's conviction that she can empathetically project herself into the place of others (and know their secrets) exemplifies Benedict Anderson's scheme of imagined national communities: 'Austen seems to intuit … that national consciousness depends on the same powers of divination—of telepathy (feeling across a distance)—that are at the root of Emma's blunders.' For Michael Gamer the Box Hill episode is essentially a manifestation of Jane Austen's 'complexity of signification' which is aimed at frustrating 'even the most fundamental acts of interpretation' and upsetting 'rudimentary correspondences between signifiers and apparent signifieds'. In 'Unanswerable Gallantry and Thick-Headed Nonsense' Gamer comes away from the Box Hill episode convinced that while sentimental and class modes of reading still provide the most effective access to Austen's agenda in the novel, these modes are utterly useless once the reader has arrived at Box Hill. The 'tangle of signification' that Austen has prepared for us there—'when language ostentatiously has lost its signifying status and becomes pure verbal play'—reminds Gamer of the 'linguistic ambiguity, disguise, and mystery' dished out to us in much of Radcliffe's fiction, to which in his opinion Austen is paying homage in the Box Hill scene. Ultimately, Gamer finds himself less impressed with 'the deep interiority' of the characters in *Emma* than with Austen's belief in 'a social density that is unsortable, unexplainable, and therefore unanswerable to any discursive formation'. Although the title might suggest differently, Susan J. Wolfson's 'Boxing Emma; or, The Reader's Dilemma at the Box Hill Games' aims some serious punches at what she calls 'the famed harrowing of Emma's pride and flippant self-esteem'. Taking issue with a long tradition of critical readings of 'the big box on the hill', Wolfson, with gentle but ruthless precision, peels away the layers of perfection and authority surrounding Mr Knightley's moral high ground to reveal that, contrary to popular belief, the glove was on the other hand that historic day at the Box Hill arena: 'At Box Hill, Emma gives a chance expression to human, communal impulses and frustrations in ways that Austen has made it difficult to close the lid on.' Adam Potkay's 'Leaving Box Hill: *Emma* and Theatricality' also qualifies the conventional interior/exterior dialectic by arguing that Emma's purifying contriteness is really a matter of a staged or exterior theatricality. Emma may be contrite after Knightley's corrective intervention, but she evidently takes pride in *appearing* to be (as opposed to being) contrite and chastened in the eyes of her 'ideal spectator (who looks a lot like Mr. Knightley)'.

A number of women writers apart from Austen attract varying degrees of attention. Penny Mahon's 'In Sermon and Story: Contrasting Anti-War Rhetoric in the Work of Anna Barbauld and Amelia Opie' (*WW* 7:i[2000] 23–38) is not primarily concerned with fiction, but it offers a brief reading of Opie's short story 'The Soldier's Return', published in *Simple Tales* [1806], arguing that it exploits a sentimental style to expose the complicities of women within a militarist system. David Thame's 'Amelia Opie's Maniacs' (*WW* 7:ii[2000] 309–26) examines Opie's plotting and description of madness, and argues that Opie reconfigures conventional images of madness as a covert symbol of political resistance along gender and class lines (notably with respect to Opie's last completed novel, *Madeline, A Tale*). This year also saw the reappearance in print of Sophia Lee's *The Recess; Or, A Tale of Other Times* (first published in [1783]), edited and with an introduction by April Alliston, as part of the University Press of Kentucky's Eighteenth-Century Novels by Women project (general editor Isobel Grundy). Set during the reign of Elizabeth I, and portraying women involved in political intrigues, both at home and abroad, *The Recess* is, as Alliston points out in her excellent introduction, a curious blend of a Gothic novel, an early example of the historical novel, and a sentimental novel— and as such well worth bringing back to a modern audience and to scholarship. Alliston chooses the second 1786 T. Cadell edition of the novel as the copy-text for her edition, and has fortuitously decided to leave the text pretty much as it was (there is a separate list of emendations), avoiding the regrettable urge to purify and correct 'corrupt' eighteenth-century texts and printing in response to modern commercial pressures. She has provided ample and informative notes that will be welcomed by today's (undergraduate) students.

There was an interesting special issue of *Romanticism on the Net* this year (vol. 18), guest-edited by Jacqueline Labbe, on 'Romantic Coupling'—a topic that, as Labbe points out in her introduction, is likely to attract even more critical attention in the future as the Romantic canon is steadily enlarged. Only one of the essays, however, falls within the scope of this section. In 'Escaping Discussion: Liminality and the Female-Embodied Couple in Mary Wollstonecraft's *Mary: A Fiction*' (*RoN* 18[2000]), Ashley Tauchert explores the novel's delineation of 'indiscursibility' (in Claudia Johnson's phrase)—female-embodied same-sex desire which is acknowledged but at the same time 'dismissed as an impossibility (culturally disavowed)'. Tauchert's reading of *Mary*'s intimate relationship with Ann draws on Mary Wollstonecraft's relationship with Fanny Blood, but is also densely contextualized in terms of contemporary lesbian identity theory.

Mary Robinson attracted the attention of a few critics this year. Judith Pascoe's 'Mary Robinson and Your Brilliant Career' (*RoN* 19[2000]) is a slight piece (it is hard to see why the author decided to reminisce about her own career instead of talk about her edition of Robinson's *Selected Poems*), but this cannot be said of Anne Mellor's essay 'Making an Exhibition of Her Self: Mary "Perdita" Robinson and Nineteenth-Century Scripts of Female Sexuality' (*NCC* 22[2000] 271–304). Mellor's essay, illustrated with copies from contemporary cartoons and paintings, begins with a simple question ('Who—or what—was Mary Robinson?') and ends by providing an answer that subtly reveals the complex story of early nineteenth-century female sexuality and challenges current intellectual constructions of subjectivity. The essay offers, in fact, not one but four competing narratives of Mary Robinson's life. Depending on the perspective of the narrator, Robinson was 'either (1) a whore; (2) an "unprotected" and abused wife; (3) a star-crossed lover; or (4) a talented performer and a successful artist'. In conclusion, Mellor argues that the 'real' Mary Robinson was all of the above, and more: her very self being 'a copy, a performance, a simulacrum', Robinson's 'authentic sexuality and subjectivity are as "lost" to us as her culturally assigned name, "Perdita"—"the lost one"—would suggest'. In the same issue of *Nineteenth-Century Contexts*, Sharon Setzer's 'The Dying Game: Crossdressing in Mary Robinson's *Walsingham*' (*NCC* 22[2000] 305–28) analyses the novel's withholding of Sidney's 'true sex' against the background of the notorious case of the French cross-dresser Chevalier D'Eon, and argues that by doing so Robinson denaturalizes sexual difference and ultimately 'produces a semiotic confusion that invites us to read romantic attraction *as* class conflict'. It is this twin threat of gender crossing and class crossing, Setzer concludes, that explains the vehemency of the outcry with which the novel was greeted by the anti-Jacobin press.

One essay on Ann Radcliffe's fiction was brought to our attention. In 'Gothic Utopia: Heretical Sanctuary in Ann Radcliffe's *The Italian*' (*Utopian Studies* 11:ii[2000] 42–56), Brenda Tooley discusses how the convent of the Santa della Pieta doubles as a 'Protestant Nunnery'; set up as a 'utopian space', the convent functions as a 'sanctuary' in which a 'family of sisters' may seek refuge from the persecutions of the Catholic doctrine as represented in the Inquisition, and preserve their freedom of conscience.

In 'The Poetics of Pedantry from Thomas Bowdler to Susan Ferrier' (*WW* 7:i[2000] 75–88), Leah Price posits that Ferrier's 'esthetic of the hackneyed' and 'glib derivativeness' have rendered her novels hard to read by the scholar and the general reader alike—causing her work to be excluded from 'feminist' projects of expanding the canon. However, Price argues, if it is situated within 'a competing contemporary culture of the anthology', Ferrier's work becomes 'legible' in terms of its fundamental project 'of training readers to situate themselves within an emerging British public'.

In 'The Medical Gaze and the Female Corpse: Looking at Bodies in Mary Shelley's *Frankenstein*' (*SNNTS* 32:ii[2000] 129–46), Emma Liggins attempts to offer a new rendition of an old tune. The author dutifully covers some of the—by now—classic feminist approaches to the female corpse in nineteenth-century fiction (Bronfen, Poovey, Mellor, Richardson), but her reading of Shelley's novel does not really add anything to our understanding of *Frankenstein* in terms of the male medical gaze and control over the female body and female sexuality. Denise Gigante's 'Facing the Ugly: The Case of *Frankenstein*' (*ELH* 67[2000] 565–87) aspires to place the category of 'the ugly' in *Frankenstein* in the context of (mainly) eighteenth-century aesthetic theory (Hume, Burke, Kant, Coleridge). The relevance of the topic to Shelley's novel and to Gothic and, indeed, Romantic literature in general is beyond doubt; however, it is harder to establish what exactly Gigante is arguing in her over-ambitious and over-written essay. A much more rewarding read is Nicola Trott's 'Loves of the Triangle: William, Mary, and Percy Bysshe' (*WC* 31:i[2000] 2–13). Packed with colourful detail from a broad range of familiar and unfamiliar sources, the essay maps the relationship between Mary Shelley, *Frankenstein* and, notably, her father (despite the essay's title, Percy plays second fiddle to Godwin in Trott's analysis). The author convincingly relates *Frankenstein*'s monstrosity to Godwin's 'monstrosity'—that of the philosophy of his Jacobin past and of his paternal rejection of Mary Shelley in the wake of her elopement with Percy.

There was a spate of excellent essays this year on Godwin, thanks to a special issue of *Studies in Romanticism* dedicated to the man and his work. In the issue's opening essay, 'Framing the Corpus: Godwin's "Editing" of Wollstonecraft' (*SiR* 39[2000] 511–31), Tilottama Rajan offers a reading of Godwin's *Memoirs*, his edition of *The Posthumous Works of the Author of a Vindication of the Rights of Woman*, as well as his own fictional and non-fictional works, arguing that Godwin's 'editing' of his wife in these writings is reflective of his 'sense of the experimental, unfinalized quality of Wollstonecraft's life and work'—of a crucial 'ideological inconclusiveness', which in his mind constitutes one of its strengths. In the case of the *Memoirs*, Rajan sees a 'method' in Godwin's handling of the portrait of his wife where others have seen 'naiveté and ineptitude': that method being an 'attempt to write the revolutionary subject into history so as to initiate the uncertain process of her future reading'. Gavin Edwards gives us a new take on a theme of central concern in Godwin's work, the relationships between politics and narrative form. In 'William Godwin's Foreign Language: Stories and Families in *Caleb Williams* and *Political Justice*' (*SiR* 39[2000] 533–51), Edwards argues that what has so far not been recognized is that Godwin's treatment of this relationship is 'as interesting for its uncertainties as for its intelligence'—uncertainties that 'derive in part from the semantic instability of the vocabulary available for its discussion'. Analysing

Godwin's 'often puzzling use' of two clusters of words—words to describe narrative or features of it ('story', 'history', 'narrative', 'character') and words used to describe social relationships ('family', 'domestic', 'servant', 'master')—Edwards reveals something of the way in which Godwin negotiates semantic latitude and lexical changes to effect changes in the way we perceive social relationships, and the distinction between public life and private life. In her essay, 'Godwin's Suspicions of Speech Acts' (*SiR* 39[2000] 553–78), Angela Esterhammer explores Godwin's famous denunciation of promises in the *Enquiry Concerning Political Justice*. She argues that, even though he denied that contractual utterances such as promises can have an impact on moral behaviour or contribute in any real sense to a healthy society, Godwin did in fact—although he should not, according to him, have done so—'construct interpersonal relationships and sociopolitical reality'. Offering evidence from the late novels in particular (*Deloraine*, *Fleetwood*, and *Cloudesley*), Esterhammer argues that Godwin's novels are full of the very speech acts that he condemns in *Political Justice*. Andrew Stauffer looks at the conflation of anger, provocation, politics, the law and narrative in *Caleb Williams* in 'Godwin, Provocation, and the Plot of Anger' (*SiR* 39[2000] 579–97). He argues that the novel reflects Godwin's denunciation of mad fury and animal rage as 'dangerous to the cause, whatever it may be', identifying *Caleb Williams* as 'an anti-anger gothic novel'. In '"Professed enemies of politeness": Sincerity and the Problem of Gender in Godwin's *Enquiry Concerning Political Justice* and Wollstonecraft's *Vindication of the Rights of Woman*' (*SiR* 39[2000] 617–45), Jenny Davidson puts Godwin's philosophical argument against insincerity as expounded in *Political Justice* against Wollstonecraft's 'gendered and more openly polemical attack on politeness' as expressed in the *Vindication*, though the essay does not make clear *why*, or what the 'problem' exactly is with gender and (in)sincerity in these texts. Davidson discusses Godwin's take on deception in *Political Justice* basically in terms of the 'dominant trope for representing injustice of all kinds' (hence it has to be rooted out completely); she subsequently establishes that Wollstonecraft in the *Vindication* attacks female immodesty as 'a system of dissimulation' (which therefore has to go), but stops short of a total dismissal of decency, and hence of immodesty, because of her own commitment to women's sexual reputation—thus, argues Davidson, by defining sincerity in terms of women's rights *only*, Wollstonecraft fails to do what Godwin does, viz. go for the full-blown critique of political insincerity. If the *Vindication* is a failure in social criticism, success in this field is overrated.

Sir Walter Scott was again a favourite of the critics this year. Re-emerging—at least according to some of the participants in the 'Scott, Scotland, and Romanticism' conference held at the University of Oregon in 1999—as one of the major figures of British and European Romanticism, Scott is now attracting a broadening variety of critical approaches. In 'The Homoerotic Subtext in Scott's *The Fortunes of Nigel*: The Question of Evidence' (*Clio* 29:iii[2000] 295–314), John J. Burke Jr. defends the thesis that, judging from the way he portrayed James, Scott knew about the king's homosexual leanings, and in particular about his 'excessive fondness for handsome young men'. Burke's evidence is partly linguistic, partly circumstantial, but remains, in the absence of 'hard facts', speculative, and open to multiple interpretations. *The Fortunes of Nigel* also features in an essay by Lionel Lackey. In '*Nigel* and *Peveril*: Scott and Gender Roles' (*ELN* 37:ii[2000] 36–46) Lackey looks at how in these two 'modern-spirited comedies' Scott, 'through reconsideration of gender roles', goes beyond his usual representation of female piety, practicality and domesticity; indeed, Lackey claims, 'the scope of [Scott's] heroines exceeds what Austen and Burney had allowed for theirs'. In 'Irresolute Ravishers and the Sexual Economy of Chivalry in the Romantic Novel' (*NCL* 55:iii[2000] 340–68), Gary Dyer examines novels by James Fenimore Cooper—*The Last of the Mohicans*—and Scott—*Ivanhoe*. Looking closely at two climactic scenes in these novels (Magua's last-minute inability to kill his captive Cora Munro, and Rebecca's close shave with death at the stake when Brian de Bois-Guilbert falls down dead), Dyer argues that as historical novelists Scott and Cooper are both interested in the problems associated with the chivalrous desire to defend: chivalry becomes irrelevant when the 'woman's fate hangs less on the intervention of a "knight" than on her own resolution and the irresolution of her oppressor'. Dyer is not so much interested in critiquing the ideology of chivalry but in showing how, in Scott's and Cooper's novels, that ideology is 'embodied, tested, and sometimes stretched beyond its breaking point by fictional narratives from a period when it was being reformulated'.

The old question of whether Scott was simply the Tory writer he appears to be, or whether there was perhaps some hidden strain of resistance in his writings, continues to occupy Scott scholars. In 'History, Romance, and the Sublime Sound of Truth in *Ivanhoe*' (*SNNTS* 32:iii[2000] 267–95), John Morillo and Wade Newhouse look at the issue from the angle of Scott's interest in the relationship between history and fiction, fact and narrative, past and present. Taking as their starting point a scene in *Ivanhoe*'s penultimate chapter (in which a riotous group of radical reformers have come to witness Rebecca's burning at the stake), the authors argue that 'this disconcerting, almost uncanny reappearance of contemporary history in *Ivanhoe* defines a consistent and complex thematic that is as bound up with Scott's interest in the way history and truth can be represented in a novel as with any localized contemporary political concerns'. The essay's opening pages contain many similar and related claims, so many in fact that it is hard to determine what it is the authors are *really* after. More modest in its ambitions but more convincing in its arguments is Andrew Lincoln's 'Conciliation, Resistance, and the Unspeakable in *The Heart of Midlothian*' (*PQ* 79:i[2000] 69–90). Lincoln posits that this novel presents us with an alternative to the bard's traditional response to the political settlement of 1707, described by one critic as 'an ideology of noisy inaction': 'a passive resistance that involves evasion, concealment, a refusal to speak'. Lincoln explores the history of Covenanter defiance and resistance in general and Scott's representation of the Deans, a family of Cameronian Covenanters in particular, to argue that Scott's sympathy with the Covenanters reflects his inability or refusal to speak out against the political situation—the novel performing 'its own muffled gesture of resistance'. Robert P. Irvine, however, finds no signs of resistance of any kind in his 'Enlightenment, Agency, and Romance: The Case of Scott's *Guy Mannering*' (*JNT* 30:i[2000]). Analysing Scott's use of the romance plot, Irvine argues that the novel 'stages a Tory-nostalgic ideology of feudal continuity in the face of economic and social upheaval—in the face, that is, of modernity'. So much is clear. However, the reader soon gets bogged down in the details of the analysis of Scott's alleged 'conservative organicist political ideology' and how this is reflected in his narrative form, for Irvine's essay is in need of some serious jargonistic slimming and linguistic pruning (for instance, the amount of 'subsuming' that is going on in the text is quite distracting, to say the least—we counted at least ten instances).

Linguistic and jargonistic over-writing is the last thing one can say about Edward C. Smith III's problematic 'Walter Scott, Literary History, and the "Expressive" Tenets of Waverley Criticism' (*PLL* 36:iv[2000] 357–76). This essay opens with what must be one of the year's most soberingly provocative of statements: 'There was no other author in the history of literature who played a more important role in shaping the nineteenth-century novel than Walter Scott (1771–1832)'. It does not stop there. Regretting the 'tremendous' drop in literary fame inflicted on Scott during 'the cultural shift of modernism' (which he lays at the door of 'a modernist mode of criticism informed by certain canonized assumptions about "serious" fiction within some "great tradition" of the novel'), the author happily acknowledges the 'reestablishment' of his reputation in recent years, though still wondering, 'if Scott is indeed one of the great authors of literary history, why has this resurrection been needed?' The article surveys nineteenth- and twentieth-century *Waverley* criticism, working in a reference to Derrida (synecdochally covering half a century of 'theoretical' neglect of Scott), and then hurries to the conclusion that 'Scott's narratives are more profitably understood as products of a world whose identity was heterological [*sic*] and internally contested' and that therefore Scott is still 'the seminal nineteenth-century *realist* he truly was'. In 'Personal Identity, Narrative, and History: *The Female Quixote* and *Redgauntlet*' (*ECF* 12:ii–iii[2000] 369–90) Everett Zimmerman argues that the fictionally self-conscious novels in question comment on the constitution of the novel and exemplify 'the dissonances between personal identity and civil identity'; what is at issue is the connection and conflict between self-determination and historical fixedness. Zimmerman offers a fairly traditional reading of *The Female Quixote*, concluding that Arabella 'first understands her destiny and history as a *sometime to be narrated* repetition of romance, but finally accepts her life as a version of the mundane lives of those who are absent from history'; other recent readings have proposed that the novel offers a more sophisticated take on romance than mere rejection. Scott's *Redgauntlet* 'mediates between competing notions of history' as destiny or consciousness; Paul Ricoeur's categories of '*Idem* and *ipse* are reconciled in the narrative transformation of the Redgauntlet legend into the history of Darsie Latimer Redgauntlet'. The differences between the novels Zimmerman selects remain more striking than their similarities; if, as he argues, 'The confrontation between history and fiction is largely resolved by the institutionalizing of the novel', he fails to acknowledge precisely the role of romance in the rise of the novel to which *The Female Quixote* gives us access. Three other essays on Scott appeared: Chris Ann Matteo's '*Le Grand Jeu* and the Great Game: The Politics of Play in Walter Scott's *Waverley* and Rudyard Kipling's *Kim*' (*JNT* 30:ii[2000] 163–86); Clare A. Simmons's 'Scottish Waste as Romantic Problem' (*WC* 31:ii[2000] 89–93); and Lidia Garbin's 'Literary Giants and Black Dwarfs' (*SSR* 1:i[2000] 78–93).

3. Non-Fictional Prose

Thomas De Quincey's reputation as anything but a minor or marginal Romantic figure continues to rise and be the object of considerable critical and editorial interest. Notwithstanding De Quincey's own misgivings about the problems involved in such a task, the first seven of a projected (and long-awaited) twenty-one volumes of *The Works of Thomas De Quincey* appeared this year as part of the Pickering Masters series, under the general editorship of Grevel Lindop. The first full-scale edition of De Quincey's works since David Masson's hitherto standard fourteen-volume *Collected Writings* in 1889–90, it benefits from the collaborative expertise of many established De Quincey and Romantic scholars and overrides its predecessor's well-known deficiencies, limitations and marring intrusions. While acknowledging the inevitable problems of 'completeness' (so central to a writer whose output was so heavily—and vastly—journalistic and anonymous), the Pickering edition puts before the reader the 'whole' of De Quincey's known published writings and the majority of the considerable number of his unpublished manuscripts (which largely take the form of fragments or alternative drafts), excluding his personal correspondence. Given its chaotic dispersal, future De Quincey scholars will owe a major debt of gratitude to the editors for their efforts in locating and (where possible) reprinting some of this material.

The arrangement is 'broadly chronological', taking us in these first seven volumes to 1831. Editorial intervention has been kept to a minimum and works published in De Quincey's lifetime are given in their earliest published versions, downplaying later customary (but not always improving) revisions. The logic here is a developmental one, allowing the reader to chart the intellectual and stylistic 'tackings' of De Quincey's career, but readers are still able to reconstruct his final intention (from variants given in the admirably concise textual notes). In cases where significant changes were made to a text, both versions are given: notably in the case of the classic *Confessions of an English Opium-Eater* which appears, in both the original two-part version contributed to the *London Magazine* in 1821 and its heavily reworked 1856 guise, in the second volume, edited by Lindop. A contextualizing headnote is given for each item, along with appropriate textual information, and a set of explanatory notes appears at the end of each volume. Also appended are transcripts of any manuscripts from the period in question which were left unpublished at De Quincey's death.

Volume i, edited by Barry Symonds, contains De Quincey's earliest extant writings for the period up to 1820—namely juvenilia from 1799–1800, his (unexpurgated) diary of 1803, miscellaneous pieces from 1806 to 1809 and his prolific and wide-ranging contributions (on contemporary politics, literature, political economy and philosophy) to the Tory *Westmorland Gazette*, which he edited between 1818 and 1819. One of the principal achievements of the Pickering edition, in fact, is to rescue De Quincey from the 'culture of unsigned reviews' and, importantly, given the orientation of much recent Romantic criticism, restore to us many of his political essays, especially those written for *Blackwood's Magazine*. As the editors warn, however, there is a price to be paid for such convenience in terms of 'abstracting' him from his original publishing context. Volumes iii and iv, edited by Frederick Burwick, contain articles and translations from *Blackwood's* and the *London Magazine* from 1821 to 1824, the years in which De Quincey's journalistic stock began to soar. The latter focuses almost entirely upon German literature and philosophy (notably Kant and Jean-Paul Richter) and David Ricardo's theories of political economy. De Quincey's review and full-text translation of the Waverley-style German Gothic novel *Walladmor* also appear here. Volume v, edited by David

Groves, includes over eighty articles from the *Edinburgh Saturday Post* for 1827–8. A similar number from the *Edinburgh Post* feature in volume vi, alongside further and important contributions to *Blackwood's* (notably the dazzling essay 'On Murder Considered as One of the Fine Arts'). Volume vii, edited by Robert Morrison, continues the run of (largely political) pieces for *Blackwood's* and the *Edinburgh Literary Gazette* from 1829 to 1831. These opening volumes of what promises to be an indispensable set reveal the sheer scale and 'magnitude', not to mention impressive interdisciplinarity, of De Quincey's work (substantiating his claim, after Coleridge and Scott, to be 'the most influential of all early nineteenth-century prose writers'), even if at the same time they drive home its somewhat scattered, rather idiosyncratic and ephemeral character.

One of the editors involved in the Pickering edition, Daniel Sanjiv Roberts, makes his own important contribution to the current trend for reinterrogating De Quincey's skilful representation of his own career. In *Revisionary Gleam: De Quincey, Coleridge, and the High Romantic Argument*, Roberts seeks to uncouple De Quincey's positional reputation (abjectly but also self-servingly linked to Wordsworth) within canonical 'Romanticism' and refocus attention on his equally complex and problematical relationship with Coleridge. Meticulously written and researched, Roberts's book sets De Quincey's writing (and also his seminal discovery of *Lyrical Ballads*) within its immediate political, social and intellectual contexts, arguing very persuasively that De Quincey was introduced to the Wordsworth–Coleridge volume via his acquaintance with William Roscoe's dissenting circle in Liverpool. For Roberts, the 'crucial event in understanding De Quincey's politics is his recovery of the French Revolution from the anxieties of Wordsworth's and Coleridge's experiences', and he seeks to show how a 'radical' politics and poetics, absorbed from these early influences, survives even into De Quincey's later writings. In this, his book offers a finely balanced example of how warily to steer one's way through a writer's own retrospective reworkings of his past.

In 'De Quincey's Literature of Power' (*WC* 31[2000] 158–64), Tim Fulford explores the ways in which De Quincey's theory of literature (as 'the sublime-in-operation': that is, a 'transfer of power' from the writer to the sympathetic reader) conflicts with his own writing practice, as exampled in the *Confessions*. Inflected by post-structuralist, gender and psychoanalytic theories, as well as Harold Bloom's theory of the anxiety of influence, Fulford's article also touches on how writers such as Wordsworth, Burke and Milton 'loomed so large' over De Quincey's imagination that the act of reading becomes one of mere 'prostration' and 'masochistic humiliation', rather than a process of sympathetic interchange.

Following on the publication last year of a nine-volume edition of his *Selected Writings*, William Hazlitt receives an intense amount of scholarly attention. The editor in that case, Duncan Wu, weighs in with 'Hazlitt's Sexual Harassment' (*EIC* 50[2000] 199–214), an illuminating attempt to contextualize (and, by implication, 'rationalize') the publication and reception of Hazlitt's difficult sexual confessional novel *Liber Amoris*. Responding to recent feminist critics who, unjustly in his view, have used this work to marginalize Hazlitt from the changing canon, Wu convincingly makes the case for its seemingly perverse publication in 1823 as an act of 'candid defiance', prompted by rejection at the hands of both Sarah Walker (the object of his thwarted infatuation) and the perennially hostile Tory reviewers. Wu covers precisely the same ground (but without the framework feminist charge) in 'Hazlitt's *Liber Amoris*: A Defence' (*WC* 31[2000] 20–5). James Treadwell picks up on similar problems in 'The Legibility of *Liber Amoris*' (*RoN* 17[2000]). Drawing on current historicist debates surrounding Romantic literature and its 'ideology', Treadwell examines how Hazlitt's novel negotiates the 'fraught intersections' between 'aesthetics and the actual', art and history, the public and the private spheres, and, though an interiorizing 'Romantic first-person narrative', it is seen as never 'blind' to the wider publishing context which helps shape it.

In 'Seeing in the Dark: Hazlitt's Immanent Idealism' (*SiR* 39[2000] 3–25), Tim Milnes displays a highly intricate (though not always immediately accessible or watertight) concern with some of the 'deeper paradoxes' in Hazlitt's early philosophical work on the creative potential of the human mind, caused by his inability wholly to abandon the language of empiricism. Milnes charts how Hazlitt replaced the 'conventional notion of truth' with one of sympathetic 'power' and evolved the new (but rather clumsily assembled) concept of the 'reasoning imagination' as the 'immediate spring and guide of action'. To recover Hazlitt's reputation as an important philosophical thinker may be the principal design of A.C. Grayling's *The Quarrel of the Age: The Life and Times of William Hazlitt*, which also offers a helpful assessment of Hazlitt's early and neglected *Essay on the Principles of Human Action* [1805] in an appendix. Its publicized claims, however, are largely contextual: to 'tell the story of Hazlitt's life and work in the setting of its disturbed times' and show 'how his work and life interpret each other'. This it does admirably, combining scholarly rigour (for the most part) with a popular, accessible style, and capturing the touching but often tense dynamics of the various Romantic circles Hazlitt inhabited. Against the well-fleshed-out political backdrop, Grayling gives a strong sense of the outcast and rather martyrish Presbyterian minister's son, with his eccentric and unforgivingly independent streak (which dulled his prospects while firing his journalism), his shyness (especially towards women), the painterly eye at work in the critic, and the heavy, hard-to-dispel air of sexual arousal—not treated here in any prurient or heavy-handed manner. Hazlitt has received expert handling from biographers in the past, and this life can be read along with (even if does not quite rival) the previous achievements of, say, Herschel Baker and Stanley Jones.

Hazlitt's *Essay on the Principles of Human Action* also appears as one of several random case histories in Deborah Elise White's *Romantic Returns: Superstition, Imagination, History*, whose overriding aim (as with many studies in Romanticism this year) is to show how purely imaginative or aesthetic concerns profoundly inform political and materialist thinking in the period. Here Hazlitt's development of the theory of the 'disinterested imagination' is seen to critique and undermine the utilitarian bent of contemporary political economy. How the 'Romantic discourse of imagination' can pragmatically be brought to bear on 'national and nationalist contexts of debate' is subsequently addressed in relation to Hazlitt's political pamphlet, *Free Thoughts on Public Affairs* [1806].

A special issue of *Romanticism* is given largely over to Hazlitt this year. In 'Romantic Cockneyism: Hazlitt and the Periodical Press' (*Romanticism* 6[2000] 143–62), Gregory Dart neatly investigates how the 'Cockney controversy' surrounding the *Examiner* circle of Keats, Shelley, Hazlitt and Hunt developed into a broader debate on the status and merits of 'periodical writing, metropolitan culture and the emergence of new types of social class', generating anxiety and self-consciousness even among liberal editors and journalists themselves. Noting the Unitarian influences on Hazlitt's work, Duncan Wu tracks back to William Hazlitt senior, and makes an interesting case for his conversion to Unitarianism during his undergraduate years in Scotland, in '"Polemical Divinity": William Hazlitt at the University of Glasgow' (*Romanticism* 6[2000] 163–77). Finally, Jeffrey C. Robinson ranges through Hazlitt's '"My First Acquaintance with Poets": The Autobiography of a Cultural Critic' (*Romanticism* 6[2000] 178–94), seeking to show how the essay 'lives ... more in the year of its publication, 1823, than in 1798'. He interprets the essay as a 'sympathetic critique' of Wordsworth and Coleridge, at once 'distancing' itself from their 'more recently discovered weaknesses' but also attempting to recapture some of their former visionary and political virtues. The same work forms the basis of James Mulvihill's article, 'Visions and Revisions: William Hazlitt and "My First Acquaintance with Poets"' (*ChLB* 109[2000] 11–14), which focuses on the treatment of poets in periodicals.

Raising the profile of Romantic periodical writing and the importance of the magazine form generally is central to Mark Parker's designs in his monograph *Literary Magazines and British Romanticism*. Each chapter offers a case study of an individual 'run' from four of the most prominent magazines of the 1820s and 1830s: namely, John Scott's *London Magazine*, examining its editor's (short-lived) relationship with his contributors, Hazlitt and Lamb (authors of the *Table-Talk* and 'Elia' essays respectively) and the nature of his overall 'cultural program'; *Blackwood's Edinburgh Magazine*, whose collaborative series 'Noctes Ambrosianae' (in Parker's words) 'constitutes one of the great experiments' within the magazine form in its efforts 'to create an editorial presence'; the new series of the *New Monthly*, 'perhaps the most consciously and purposefully homogeneous of the great magazines', which published the work of Horace Smith and Cyrus Redding during the period of Thomas Campbell's (politically cautious) editorship; and, finally, *Fraser's Magazine*, whose publication of Thomas Carlyle's *Sartor Resartus* signals the point at which 'the contributor begin[s] to emerge from the control of the editor'. Pertinent to Parker's exploration is how these magazines engage with issues of 'gentility' and social aspiration, capitalism and literary commodification, which were so important to their middle-class audience.

Since 'analysis and study of non-fictional prose has lagged behind other scholarship of the Romantic period', as Parker points out, it is refreshing to note that the contribution of essay-writing and criticism to the period is covered in several other Romantic studies this year. The November issue of *Romanticism on the Net*, for example, is given over to proceedings from a conference held at the University of Glasgow on the poet, lecturer, and infamous *Blackwood's* critic John Wilson (aka Christopher North), author of the 'Noctes Ambrosianae'. Two papers delivered on the occasion are printed: Robert Morrison's '*Blackwood's Beserker*: John Wilson and the Language of Extremity' (*RoN* 20[2000]), an opening broadside ably making the case for resurrecting Wilson's reputation, and Nicola Z. Trott's 'North of the Border: Cultural Crossing in the *Noctes Ambrosianae*' (*RoN* 20[2000]). Periodical writing is also extensively treated in Lucy Newlyn's stimulating new study, *Reading, Writing, and Romanticism: The Anxiety of Reception*. As her title suggests, Newlyn seeks to complicate the historical notion of oppressive and purely writerly influence promulgated by Harold Bloom and consider the centrality of the role of audience as a conditioning force for writers of the Romantic period. While the first part of her book concerns itself mainly with poetry and its allegedly 'threatened status' in an 'age of utility', chapters in the second part, 'Crossings on the Creative–Critical Divide', build around more wide-ranging thematic arguments, especially the fifth, 'Competition and Collaboration in Periodical Culture', which explores how professional prose writers and critics such as De Quincey, Peacock, Hazlitt and Lamb rated the respective merits of poets and their readers/critics. It also addresses the vexed question of posthumous reputation (on behalf of poets whose status as 'legislators' they were beginning to challenge). Some of Newlyn's points are contentious (and, in one or two early cases, perhaps contradictory) but her study, born of impressive reading, reveals a subtle grasp of some of the key developments and seeming discrepancies inherent in Romantic reader–writer relations.

Scholarly literature on the 'Revolution debate' is added to this year by a collection of eight short interdisciplinary essays, edited by John Whale, on *Edmund Burke's Reflections on the Revolution in France*. Contrary to expectation, most of the essays engage with the historical context(s) in which the *Reflections* might subsequently and rather speculatively be read rather than when they were actually written. Some reveal worrying typographical inconsistencies and inaccuracies. Some are more helpful in straightforward introductory terms to the undergraduate or newcomer to the *Reflections* than others: Gregory Claeys, for example, in 'The *Reflections* Refracted' (pp. 40–59), offers a useful survey of the varied contemporary responses and also crucially locates the work within a highly personalized political context. Like several of the contributions, Claire Connolly's '*Reflections* on the Act of Union' (pp. 168–92) turns on the Irish question and the 'proleptic wisdom' of Burke's 1790 writings in specific relation to the events of 1798–1800. The ambivalences created by Burke's complex position as an Anglo-Irish, Catholic sympathizer are explored in Susan Manly's 'Burke, Toland, Toleration: The Politics of Prejudice, Speculation, and Naturalization' (pp. 145–67), which pursues a potentially very fruitful and overly neglected avenue of discussion, namely, how religious concerns (centring on the increasingly secular, full-toleration claims of 'rational' dissent) overlap and interweave with politics in this period. Manly also cuts to another Anglo-Irish writer, Maria Edgeworth, and her 'naturalization' novel *Harrington* [1817], which is made to 'reflect on Burke's *Reflections*'. Angela Keane's '*Reflections* and Correspondences: The Unfamiliarity of Burke's Familiar Letter' (pp. 193–218) does address itself to the genesis of the work rather than its much-debated legacy, and considers the political implications of the epistolary form which Burke adopts. Kevin Gilmartin's essay on 'Burke, Popular Opinion, and the Problem of a Counter-Revolutionary Sphere' (pp. 94–114) enticingly sets out to rethink Burke's contribution to the theory and practice of counter-revolutionism, but by ranging over the whole of Burke's 1790s' oeuvre perhaps promises a little more in relation to the *Reflections* than it actually delivers. Tom Furniss's 'Cementing the Nation: Burke's *Reflections* on Nationalism and National Identity' (pp. 115–44) is probably the most engaging and absorbing of the collection in terms of the way it plumbs the full range and depth of Burke's 'patriotic' political arguments, noting their complex affinities with as well as differences from those of Richard Price.

Burke and other of his chief respondents in the Revolution debate come under scrutiny again in John Whale's monograph, *Imagination Under Pressure, 1789–1832: Aesthetics, Politics and Utility*. What is offered here is 'a new understanding of the way in which "imagination" functions', often negatively or problematically, and invariably in 'complex, often creative, response to cultural change', in key non-fictional prose texts of the Romantic period. The book engages in 'a detailed analysis of six selected authors', and is divided into two sections. The first deals with British responses to the French Revolution: namely, Burke, for whom the faculty of the imagination helps reconcile citizens to their lot and so proves fundamental to 'the workings of the state'; Thomas Paine, who views it altogether differently as 'deceptive, anarchic' and politically divisive; and Mary Wollstonecraft, for whom imagination is more positive and 'perfectibilist'—a capacity 'divine in origin, social and practical in its manifestation'. The second part considers the imaginative reaction to utilitarianism from Hazlitt (caught again here between 'empiricism' and 'aesthetic excess'), Coleridge and William Cobbett (who bypasses imagination, albeit not entirely, in favour of a 'determined literalism', '"transparency" or plainness'). The final chapter focuses on 'the afterlife of the Coleridgean imagination' in the work of John Stuart Mill and I.A. Richards. Whale's complex arguments occasionally yield more heat than light, yet, in all, he presents an absorbing and embattled picture of the Romantic imagination formed largely in the face of competition and crisis. Though not strictly perhaps within the realm of English studies, Richard Bourke's article 'Liberty, Authority, and Trust in Burke's Idea of Empire' (*JHI* 61[2000] 453–71) makes extremely useful reading for those wishing to get to clearer grips with the development of Burke's political ideas: more specifically, how the importance of such concepts as 'fealty', friendship and allegiance could be made to serve within a wider imperial context.

A specially revised student edition of Thomas Paine's *Political Writings* in the Cambridge Texts in the History of Political Thought series appeared this year, with new introductory and editorial matter from Bruce Kuklick and an increased number of texts. Vying with Penguin's *Thomas Paine Reader* for teaching purposes, it offers not just *The Age of Reason* alongside *Rights of Man*, but also *Agrarian Justice* and the 1776 papers on *The Crisis*, and is excellently priced. Though not seen by this reviewer, Paine is treated in Michael J. Hogan and Glen Williams's article 'Republican Charisma and the American Revolution: The Textual Persona of Thomas Paine's *Common Sense*' (*QJS* 86[2000] 1–18).

In 'Touring Scotland at the Time of the Reform Bill: William Wordsworth and William Cobbett' (*WC* 31[2000] 80–3), Peter Manning briefly juxtaposes Wordsworth's detached 'poetic' rendering of his tours revisiting Scotland in 1831 and 1833 against Cobbett's highly politicized *Tour in Scotland; and in the Four Northern Counties of England* as a prospective MP in the new Reform Parliament of 1832. Potentially fascinating areas of discussion are raised (about the 'mobility of Cobbett's rhetoric', stemming from the role of the *Political Register*, and how his rather intense and heightened dramatization of events marries with his own claim to deliver 'a true statement of facts'), although what richly complex antithetical relationship there might be (apart from an obvious clash of politics) between the two writers is not really fully explored, perhaps owing to constraints of space.

The winter issue of *Studies in Romanticism* is dedicated this year to William Godwin and opens with an article on his *Memoirs of the Author of A Vindication of the Rights of Woman*, 'Framing the Corpus: Godwin's "Editing" of Wollstonecraft in 1798' (*SiR* 39[2000] 511–31), by Tilottama Rajan. In this, Rajan proposes a 'method' behind Godwin's otherwise 'naïve' and misguided biographical strategy:

namely, an 'attempt to write the revolutionary subject into history so as to initiate the uncertain process of her future reading'. In 'Godwin's Suspicion of Speech Acts' (*SiR* 39[2000] 553–78), Angela Esterhammer gives an incisive examination of Godwin's linguistic philosophy, in particular his 'denunciation of promises' in *Political Justice*, as well as some of his lesser-known novels, while, in '"Ruinous Mixture": Godwin, Enclosure and the Associated Self' (*SiR* 39[2000] 617–45), Robert Anderson offers a lengthy and rewarding study of Godwin's 'ambivalent' view of property in *Political Justice*—as simultaneously a 'common stock' and 'a sacred "palladium"' which only the exclusive owners can control'—and its decidedly anti-radical and destabilizing implications for his very private notion of subjectivity. Esterhammer's arguments (which draw innovatively on modern speech-act theory) are pursued at greater length and in relation to other philosophical and poetic works in her monograph, *The Romantic Performative: Language and Action in British and German Romanticism*, also published this year. The opening sections range more broadly over territory covered in her article, 'Of Promises, Contracts and Constitutions: Thomas Reid and Jeremy Bentham on Language as Social Action' (*Romanticism* 6[2000] 55–77), an admirably clear explication of how moral and political philosophers incorporated deeply pragmatic linguistic ideas (about the social, interpersonal nature of the act of speech) into their work. In 'Can a Statue Breathe? The Linguistic (Un)coupling of Godwin and Wollstonecraft' (*RoN* 18[2000]) Jane Hodson offers an interesting early comparison of the two writers' divergent views on language in Godwin's *Political Justice* and *The Enquirer* and Wollstonecraft's essay 'On Poetry' [1797]. Less adequate perhaps is the attempt to show how their personal relationship may have led both to re-evaluate the respective roles of feeling and reason in their linguistic theories.

Wollstonecraft also features as one of five major case studies in Angela Keane's *Women Writers and the English Nation in the 1790s: Romantic Belongings*, a closely involved and theoretically informed study of the ways in which issues of gender were embroiled in 'national discourse' in the revolutionary period. Keane reads Wollstonecraft 'biopolitically', arguing that throughout her writing she tries to resist 'the degrading impact of capitalism on the nation's most valued asset, the maternal body', but ultimately cannot escape succumbing to some of its effects herself. Other chapters are devoted to Helen Maria Williams, whose eyewitness *Letters from France*, expressing enthusiasm for the female symbolism of 'true' French liberty, are seen to have precipitated not just her social and political exile from England but also exclusion from the predominantly masculine literary canon; and, latterly, to Hannah More, who is presented (in all her complexity) as both 'rouser' and 'pacifier' of the nation's energies, a 'patrician populist' who promotes a 'counter-revolutionary nationalism' based upon the 'idea of [the] female patriot who stays firmly in the home'.

The subject of much critical attention in recent years, More is very much at the centre of Anne K. Mellor's *Mothers of the Nation: Women's Political Writing in England, 1780–1830*, which refers to her rather provocatively as a 'Revolutionary Reformer'. In line with her general thesis that (rather than being confined to a separate 'feminine' sphere) Romantic women writers participated fully with men in 'the discursive public sphere' and had 'an enormous—and hitherto largely uncredited—impact on the formation of public opinion in England', Mellor argues that More led 'a moral revolution in ... national manners and principles' through her philanthropic activities and didactic writings. Working wholly within the establishment mould but not blindly sanctioning the status quo, More made the case for women domestically forging the nation's values and promoted the virtues of public-spiritedness to her own sex which (Mellor argues) 'contributed directly to the emancipation and increasing social empowerment of women'. More also features, along with Anna Laetitia Barbauld, Joanna Baillie and Elizabeth Inchbald, in a chapter on 'Literary Criticism, Cultural Authority, and the Rise of the Novel', which argues the case for a new 'specific[ally] anti-Romantic ideology'—didactic, 'rational', and 'morally responsible'—expressly developed and promoted by women critics. Mellor's book is eminently readable, confident and engaging (as always), but her claims throughout are self-confessedly bold and, in arguing that female values came unequivocally to *dominate* the public sphere, she perhaps risks setting up another overly revisionist paradigm which may, in turn, prove difficult to sustain.

The sympathetic, mutually influencing relations between male and female Romantic writers are taken up by Pamela Woof, who documents the treatment of 'The Interesting in Dorothy Wordsworth's Alfoxden Journal' (*WC* 31[2000] 48–55) in characteristically detailed and sensitive fashion. She notes the open 'traffic in phrases and [vital and 'energetic' natural] observations' which exists between Dorothy's notebook, kept during the opening months of 1798, and Wordsworth's and Coleridge's contemporaneous poetry, and also subtly distinguishes their different literary treatments of shared experience.

Helen Thomas's *Romanticism and Slave Narratives: Transatlantic Testimonies* sets out to broaden traditional Romantic horizons by examining the 'dialogue of exchange' which existed between 'the discourse of Romanticism, as it emerged out of eighteenth-century dissent' and established traditions of spiritual autobiography and confessional writing, and the 'liberationist' narratives of African-born slaves. The book brings together an impressive and 'heterogeneous selection of canonical and marginalised untraditional works by white "British", black "British" and Anglo-American authors' and is divided into two parts. The first is concerned with the specific relationship between Romanticism, the slave trade and the abolitionist cause, and considers political and autobiographical tracts published in Britain by abolitionist writers such as William Cowper and John Newton (whose hugely influential *Authentic Narrative* [1764] is discussed), evangelical revivalists and millenarian prophets (such as Joanna Southcott), together with the main Romantic poets. John Gabriel Stedman's rather vexed *Narrative, of a Five Years' Expedition, Against the Revolted Negroes of Surinam* [1795] is also examined within a cross-cultural context. The second part contains studies of work published in England by African slaves, including Olaudah Equiano's *Interesting Narrative*. Despite some occasional worrying inaccuracies and perhaps too monolithic an approach to 'radical' Protestant dissent, Thomas's is an absorbing study, ably mixing wide-ranging historical survey and close textual reading with current theoretical concerns. The 'paradoxes ambiguities, and resistances' within abolitionist and colonialist discourse are picked up on by Peter J. Kitson in his article '"Bales of living anguish": Representations of Race and the Slave in Romantic Writing' (*ELH* 67[2000] 515–37). In this, he initially focuses on three authors—the Jamaican slave-owner Edward Long, 'America's most prominent opponent of the slave trade' Anthony Benezet, and his British equivalent Thomas Clarkson—'perceived to be influential in their discussions of race and slavery' and whose writings 'provide a context in which to situate' much traditional Romantic writing on such themes (in particular, Coleridge's). The remainder of the article is given over to discussion of John Thelwall's pseudonymously published novel *The Daughter of Adoption* of 1801.

Alongside the burgeoning interest in slavery literature, the significance and popularity of travel writing in the Romantic period has emerged as another fruitful new area of discovery and research. Books this year which focus on the genre include *Romantic Geographies: Discourses of Travel, 1775–1844*, a selection of essays edited by Amanda Gilroy, not seen by this reviewer. Of relevance to this section, Sara Mills concentrates on gender and aesthetics in writing on Mary Wollstonecraft's trip to Scandinavia, and Helen Maria Williams's *Letters from France* come under review from Chris Jones. Also published this year, but again not seen, is *Travels, Explorations and Empires: Writings from the Era of Imperial Expansion, 1770–1835*, a four-volume anthology of voyage and travel narratives produced under the general editorship of Tim Fulford and Peter J. Kitson, which makes available extracts (in facsimile) from around fifty landmark texts (including diaries, captivity narratives and missionary reports) mainly by British and North American travellers. These volumes cover North America, the Far East, the North and South Poles, and the Middle East respectively. A further four (due out in 2002) promise insights into the Pacific, Africa, South America and the Caribbean, and India.

4. Poetry: Selected Authors

Alan Rawes's *Byron's Poetic Experimentation: 'Childe Harold', the Tales, and the Quest for Comedy* is a sharp and intelligent study of Byron's experimentation which begins by reminding the reader, correctly, that Byron's versatility makes him a far more ambitious poet than most, and, further, that he is a more impressive poet than is commonly acknowledged. Rawes's interest is in Byron's experiments with 'new ways of imagining', and he acknowledges a fundamental debt to Robert Gleckner's fine understanding of Byron's development as a 'history of struggle for form'. Thus, he reads *Childe Harold* I and II as a narrative deferring closure by its continuous reinvention of itself; he reads the *Tales* (principally *The Giaour*) as a struggle to shake off a tragic vision of humankind, and *Childe Harold* III as a redemption of such a vision. *The Prisoner of Chillon* is interpreted as continuing this redemption while it hovers uncertainly between the tragic and comic genres; while *Manfred* reimagines the Byronic hero in an expansion of the tragic vision. *Childe Harold* IV, finally, is offered in surprising counter-relation to Peacock's wonderfully expressed disgust ('that morbid anatomy of black bile'), as a further act of retrieval, specifically of 'a mood of joyful celebration'. Rawes's book is perhaps too determined to cast Byron as a writer permanently struggling with contending forms and tendencies, so that he persistently theorizes the poetry as 'fending off' this and 'pushing back' that, or 'holding in check' something else, while 'resisting' just about everything. This vocabulary will not take too much inspection: too often, Rawes requires us to subscribe to a model of Byron's poetry based on such theories of psychological resistance, and he seemingly forgets his more interesting early proposals that experimentation and 'reimagining' work together in a creative combination. Like Gleckner, the critical inspiration for much of this book, he can imply too readily that Byron is a philosopher first and a poet second, even though he seems to be aware that the more powerful model works the other way around. Nevertheless, Rawes conducts some fascinating readings of the poems, and his minutely careful and detailed analyses offer subtle and precise insights that underwrite his large claims for Byron's poetic abilities. While references are made in footnotes to the theoretical canon (Barthes, de Man, Derrida, Kristeva) this is an under-theorized book, and the significance of its contribution will not be located in some of the wider claims it makes, but in its capacity to send the reader back to Byron (and indeed, to Gleckner) with renewed appreciation.

Drummond Bone's *Byron* is a pleasing addition to the revised Writers and their Work series that offers an excellent introduction to Byron's life and work. Bone's Byron is a knowing poet: politically astute, intellectually curious, and learned behind those screens of irony. In addition, he is a virtuoso performer, a poet with a sophisticated understanding of metre, register and voice, and this is something that the author is particularly skilled at revealing. Caroline Franklin's *Byron: A Literary Life* is another welcome addition to its series, which also makes a strong independent contribution. This is a very fine book, superbly written, and constantly alive to the ways in which recent historicist criticism has recast Byron. Franklin's account loses nothing of the fascination of Byron's extraordinary life, neither does it deny, nor depress, the significance of his individuality. But she is also highly conscious of the ways in which Byron relates to the culture of his time, and the historical significance of his moment, a significance to which he also contributes. This is a book that speaks as powerfully to the novice as it does to the advanced scholar.

This year's *Byron Journal* (28[2000]) continues its good habit of producing a varied diet of contents, from useful and fascinating short notes to full-length articles on major topics. Christine Kenyon-Jones, '"This wonderful pair": Elizabeth Pigot Presents Byron and Boatswain' (*ByronJ* 28[2000] 85–8), for example, offers a brief account of Pigot's illustrated hand-drawn verse and picture about Byron produced at Southwell in 1807; Raymond Mills, 'The Last Illness of Lord Byron' (*ByronJ* 28[2000] 56–67), provides a medical account of Byron's last days, concluding that he probably suffered an epileptic attack in February 1824, but that this was unlikely to be related to the cause of death in April. Mills favours the view that this was primarily due to over-bleeding in response to the fever, which, he notes, it is not possible to identify, although tick-borne Mediterranean fever seems to be a likely candidate, an illness commonly contracted through the common dog-tick. Of the full-length articles here, a number stand out. Drummond Bone's 'Tourists and Lovers: *Beppo* and *Amours de Voyage*' (*ByronJ* 28[2000] 13–28) explores the relations between Byron's poem and Clough's, which as the author notes, were first remarked by Clough's friends when his poem was still in draft. Bone explores several close parallels, giving particular scrutiny to scepticism, relativism and truth as running themes in each poem. His aim is partly to explore the possibility that Clough's poem might document an intellectual tradition running through Byron to Clough and beyond, although the greater value of the article lies in the creative friction generated by this yoking together, for our understanding of both poems increases by these critical contradistinctions, nowhere more fully than in the carefully detailed analysis of the contrasting metrical forms, and their implications for the poems' meanings. While this analysis notes a major difference in Clough's uneasy contemplation of relativism which finally concedes to a need for stability, and Byron's recognition of relativism which is resolved in his poem's representation of life as narrative, Bone concludes, rightly, that these contrasts may be understood as 'different flowers from the same root'. Andrew Stauffer, 'New Light on Byron's Regency Verse in America' (*ByronJ* 28[2000] 29–35), provides a detailed history of the publication of Byron's poems by Moses Thomas, concentrating on two editions published in 1816 which offered the first printings of two of Byron's poems, 'Windsor Poetics' and 'On the Regency'. Stauffer reveals Thomas as a publisher given to risk-taking and entrepreneurial zeal, but he is primarily concerned to note the historical and bibliographical consequences of his publishing ventures, which, as he notes, testify to very strong connections with the English literary circles of the time. While the consequences of Stauffer's investigation have a limited impact on the status of these edited texts, he pointedly concludes that our knowledge of the ways in which American publishers were instrumental in constructing the Romantic canon are strictly limited. Articles such as this may make good the deficit. In 'Byron's Reputation in Bohemia and Czech Nineteenth-Century Nationalism' (*ByronJ* 28[2000] 37–48), Martin Procházka continues the journal's tradition of exploring Byron's transnational reputations with a full and intriguing account of the poet's currency in Bohemia and the Czech national revival, in which he shows Byron figuring strongly as an undesirable opposite to the 'natural' health of an indigenous folk community. As a consequence, Byron became a means of representing the relationship of art, or the artist, to the state: his independent amoralism was seen as exemplifying a breakdown of community responsibility, as well as indicating an aristocratic disregard for the lower classes. This ideological modelling of Byronism, Procházka demonstrates, was interrupted by the Czech critic, Durdik, whose revisionism, still ideological, presented Byron as a modern liberal, and a model for Czech artists aspiring to greatness.

Continuing the political theme, Daryl S. Ogden's article, 'Byron, Italy, and the Poetic of Liberal Imperialism' (*KSJ* 49[2000] 114–37), provides a valuable contribution to our knowledge of Byron's relations with Italy, tied in here to the specific set of political values described as 'liberal imperialism', an ideology distinct from a more generally conceived notion of imperial expansion. Beginning with Byron's jocular or extravagant claim in 1813 that he would leave England, become an oriental scholar and use his wealth to buy a principality in Turkey, Ogden points out that effectively, Byron's life in Venice brought him close to these aspirations. He became a 'lord of the Adriatic' and while his Italian interests cannot be understood as 'orientalist', Ogden argues persuasively that Italy was a region in the borderlands, which did not qualify in Byron's understanding as a 'legitimate part of the West'. Italy was a place of cultural hybridity, he tells us, and extends the concept to account for Byron's claim that Moore's Irishness was an excellent qualification for his becoming a poet of the East. Another article dealing with the complexity of Byron's politics is Peter Cochrane's 'The Sale of Parga and the "Isles of Greece"' (*KSR* 14[2000] 42–51). Cochrane calls attention to the British sale of the Greek coastal town of Parga to Ali Pacha in 1819. He notes that an article in the *Edinburgh Review* by Jeffrey, with the hand of Foscolo behind it, excoriated the government for this, indicating their knowledge of Ali Pacha's tyranny, and represented it as a betrayal of old Whig values. All Suliotes left Parga in April fearful of Ali's likely atrocities, and Cochrane uses this to gloss Byron's writing of the 'Isles of Greece' in the late autumn of the same year, suggesting that he drew on the *Edinburgh Review* article. Tellingly, Cochrane points out that this is, oddly, Byron's only discernible reaction to the affair. He puts this down to his embarrassment and ambivalence about his earlier meeting with Ali Pacha, and the argument therefore presents a subtle reading of 'The Isles of Greece' as a pressured location for this ambivalence. A different kind of politics altogether is explored by Dino Feluga in '"With a most voiceless thought": Byron and the Radicalism of Textual Culture' (*KSR* 14[2000] 150–67). Feluga moves from an initial consideration of the significance of Byron's popularity in his time, understood within a revised notion of 'class', to the power of his texts to disrupt conventional economic and political relations through material circulation on the one hand, and textual strategies of defamiliarization on the other.

In '"I shall not choose a mortal to be my mediator": Byron's *Manfred* and "Internal Mediation"' (*ERR* 11[2000] 68–96), Ian Dennis casts new light on the drama by suggesting that Manfred's defiance of the elements may be read as 'a dramatization of a mimetic struggle between self and external obstacle', which probes the conventional distinction between self and externality. Further, he argues, *Manfred* is a complex and exciting interplay between the elements of desire, power and imitation, autonomy and dependency. This reading also makes room for an investigation of the status and implications of the play's barely present ironies, picked up on by a number of critics. Dennis argues persuasively for a more subtle notion of irony, the effects of which are not undermining but a form of testimony to the alternating status of the antitheticals on which it depends. In such a reading, irony as we know it loses its power and points to the 'destructive futility of a desire that empties its objects of all value'. This is an interesting reading, difficult and challenging at times, but convincing too, and it might have been strengthened by drawing on the now classic notion of Romantic irony itself, with which there are surely strong relations. A neat irony concludes Mark Phillipson's 'Byron's Revisited Haunts' (*SiR* 39[2000] 303–22), in which he notes a beginning in an ending: the country house at the end of *Don Juan* resembling the 'venerable pile' from which Childe Harold begins his journey of exile in the early stages of Byron's poetic career. Phillipson begins before that, showing that Byron's interest in exile is a feature of his very early verse, developing through a preoccupation with Timon of Athens (an interest also remarked by G. Wilson Knight in 1966). He demonstrates that the roots of the more complex explorations of the psychology of self-exile may be found here, and he uses the figure of 'haunting' to explore the ways in which self-exile displaces fragments of the past. The article counters the standard view of Byron's late period as a repudiation of the earlier work.

In Goodridge and Kovësi, eds., *John Clare: New Approaches*, we find an interesting collection of essays from Clare experts and other Romantic scholars, together with an invaluable bibliography of Clare criticism from 1970 to 2000. This latter is not offered as a comprehensive bibliography, but it is an extensive and thoroughly achieved list which makes interesting reading in its tracing of Clare scholarship across this thirty-year period. The essays themselves cover a wide field. Jonathan Bate argues the case for a new life of Clare in a lively and sharp essay which indicates the nature, and something of the history, of Clare's biographical fashioning. He also scrutinizes fallacies that have been handed down from one biographer to another, yet demonstrates a careful and highly sensitive reading of the oldest sources, pointing out details that in some cases, almost certainly indicate their authenticity. Of particular note here is Bate's reconsideration of Clare's depression in 1823–4, in which he returns to Frederick Martin's account to rescue details that seemed unlikely to later biographers. With a detective's eye for detail, Bate concludes that Martin had access to correspondence that has been subsequently lost, and more, that the details of his wonderfully poignant image of Clare seeking therapy in the hollow oak might be based in truth. Valerie Pedlar's '"Written by himself"—Edited by Others' continues the theme, rightly taking issue with the ways in which Clare's autobiographical writings have been seconded to the causes of more general representation of 'creativity' or of the nineteenth-century rural poor. Further, she notes how the ordering of the autobiographical writings, and their editing, produce different kinds of narratives, contrasting the Tibbles' version to that of Robinson, and noting that the former presents a Clare fading fast, whereas Robinson's gives us a form of defiance and survivalism, subtly read by Pedlar as an afterlife suggestive of 'Old Testament vengefulness'. There is a strong sense in this volume that Clare is being refigured and reclaimed through a criticism which is setting itself free from some of the preoccupations that have dogged him (his natural genius, his madness, his innocence) while not discarding such volatile elements because of the ease with which they may slip towards sentimentality—hence Bate's hints that, on some matters, Martin may have been right, and Pedlar's identification of a poet of courage. Bob Heyes also considers the autobiographical writings in his essay, which opposes myths of solitary creativity by drawing attention to the ways in which Clare's writings were subject to all kinds of other influences, most notably through circulation in manuscript form. Bridget Keegan takes on the issue of Clare and 'natural genius' in a cogent charting of the poet's self-awareness that draws distinctions between his own career and those of others, as well as describing his maturity in understanding representative acts through the framing of poems with voices or speakers. Stephen Colclough picks up on a closely related area of Clare's work in his essay on the voice of labour in the early poems, revealing Clare's work as polyphonic rather than univocal. Elsewhere in the volume, Richard Cronin produces an essay on *The Midsummer Cushion*, which begins by noting a bifurcation in Clare criticism (between those who primarily admire the strength of his parochial vernacular, and those who wish to liberate him from Taylor's initial marketing ploy of the peasant poet) and subsequently argues that the poetry's evidence suggests a writer alienated from either context. Clare's relation to his Romantic contemporaries is given a new twist in P.M.S. Dawson's essay, which, like Cronin's, concludes by placing Clare in two places at once: and Dawson, like Keegan, argues powerfully for a Clare who is highly self-aware of his position, not a poet, therefore, easily subject to the confident placing of belated criticism. The volume also includes essays on relatively new areas: Mina Gorji's fine contribution on 'Clare and Community' explores Clare's antiquarian enthusiasm for the discovery of 'old poets' and recasts this as a powerful strategy in the construction of a notion of poetic community; Simon Kövesi offers a fascinating exploration of the vigorous axis between the representation of women and that of poets in Clare's *Don Juan A Poem*; Cathy Taylor's essay on Clare's *Child Harold* investigates manuscript sources in a scholarly account of the relations between Clare, Byron, and

Byron's interest in Tasso; Alan Vardy looks again at the intriguing and complex web of patronage around Clare, and his resistance to it; Paul Chirico gives us a sophisticated reading of Clare's writing on antiquity which notes the ways in which readings of the past, and historical constructions of community, are deeply problematized. This is an excellent volume, its new approaches testifying only too clearly that Clare criticism has come of ripe age, and needs to be more widely acknowledged as a central force in contemporary understandings of Romanticism.

In the *John Clare Society Journal* Tim Chilcott, '*Child Harold* or *Child Harolds*: The Editing of Clare's Texts' (*JCSJ* 19[2000] 5–17) offers an essay that sits well alongside Cathy Walker's piece discussed above. Chilcott raises a series of interesting questions about the ordering of the text, which consists of seven different manuscripts, several parts of which are in draft form, and some of which are copied out. Chilcott notes the difficulties for editing: there is little indication that the copied parts are fair copies, and therefore the status of these versions, and their interrelations, are puzzling. The few extant edited versions of the poem differ considerably, and Chilcott discusses the major differences and the editorial decisions behind the texts of Robinson and Summerfield, the Tibbles, and that of Salman Dawood Al-Wasiti (which exists as an appendix to a Leicester doctoral dissertation). He argues that Robinson's copyright claim has politicized views of Clare's texts, none more so than this example, which demonstrates emphatically that a definitive version is an impossibility, given the lack of evidence surrounding the manuscripts' composition. Chilcott calls for further debate, and the adoption of more fluid notions of textuality, noting that Clare himself protested a more liberal notion of the text. Of immediate relevance to this then is Jonathan Bate's 'John Clare's Copyright, 1854–1893' (*JCSJ* 19[2000] 19–32), which outlines the facts of Clare's copyright in these years. This story has never been told, and it reveals that those involve in the original copyright claims (principally Whitaker and Taylor) were motivated by the best reasons, to make provision for Clare's family and serve his memory in the most creditable manner. In '"The Woodman" and the Natural Anthology' (*JCSJ* 19[2000] 41–51), Paul Chirico opens discussion on the little-regarded unfinished project by Clare that was undertaken around 1820, seemingly as a combined text of poetry and prose, and entitled 'The Woodman or Beauties of a Winter Forest'. Chirico argues that the 'Beauties' of the title might indicate that he conceived of the work as an anthology, and that further evidence of such a scheme might be located in his publisher's concern that the work might not be all his own. Chirico uncovers further evidence of the work's possible origin as pastiche of a kind: Margaret Grainger, who first published the piece, noted the possibility of elements of parody—and the work contains Clare's quotation marks around certain phrases.

A number of articles on Keats this year concentrate on the reading of individual poems. In '"Eve's dream will do here": Miltonic dreaming in Keats's "The Eve of St Agnes"' (*KSJ* 49[2000] 47–84), Nancy Rosenfield begins with a nice twist: rather than accept Keats at his word about Adam's dream and the meaning of poetry, why not substitute Eve's dream in book V of *Paradise Lost* as a comparison to Madeline's dream in the poem? Rosenfield shows that Keats's understanding of the imagination was influenced by this passage in Milton as well as those sources more commonly cited. She suggests that both Keats and Milton use dreams to make their heroines 'initiators', despite the fact that in another sense they are victims. Further, there are allusive parallels: Porphyro's observation of Madeline is not unlike Satan crouching at Eve's ear; Eve's dream is the prelude to a feast (the eating of divine fruit). The point of Eve's dream, however, is that when she is awakened she is (unlike Adam) relieved that her vision was an illusion, and Rosenfield moves from a discussion of this variation to explore Keats's ambivalence about the sexual act. Proma Tagore, in 'Keats in an Age of Consumption: the "Ode to a Nightingale"' (*KSJ* 49[2000] 67–84), begins by asserting boldly that Keats's poetry 'charts the rise of a middle-class society defined primarily by its acts of consumption', and by further claiming that 'the poetry of John Keats maps precisely this historical phenomenon whereby human bodies become both subjects and objects of consumption'. She offers the 'Ode to a Nightingale' as an example, exploring the metaphor of illness as a central motif. It is a good, interesting analysis, but harnessed too tightly to the insistence on the 'precise mapping' of exaggerated historical claims. In 'Keats's Virgil' (*KSR* 14[2000] 23–33), Christoph Loreck argues that Keats modelled *Endymion* on the *Aeneid*, most notably in the poem's prime characteristic of being 'labyrinthine'. Building on previous acknowledgements of this quality in Keats's early poetics, Loreck charts epic labyrinthine features in Keats's poem, suggesting that there is an additional presence of epic here. In 'Keats's Orientalism' (*SiR* 39[2000] 419–47), Geoffrey Wassil works a ferociously complex argument out of a reading that follows Said's insistence that imperial rule dominates the literature of the nineteenth century and is omnipresent. Exploring the interplay of power and identity in the letters, Wassil moves on to develop the model by way of an intensified reading of 'On First Looking into Chapman's Homer', the consequences of which are then related to 'To the Nile' and other examples. Brian Goldberg is also concerned to revise readings of Keats and the East in 'Black Gates and the Fiery Galleries: Eastern Architecture in "The Fall of Hyperion"' (*SiR* 39[2000] 229–54). He contests current readings, which argue that the poems begin against an Egyptian architectural backcloth and then move to the architecture of Greece and Rome (identifications which allow the conflict to be recognized as a war of the West against the East). He points out that the temples of the Titans are far more eclectic in design, drawing more on a fashionable Regency exoticism which mixed classical, Egyptian and other eastern—including, most significantly, Indian—styles. It is the presence of this last, he argues, that serves Keats's goal of 'sensational' effect. Goldberg carefully contextualizes this by reference to the aesthetics and politics of the day, noting how Southey and Moore had to negotiate an appropriate style for such representations, within which Keats's descriptions were to situate themselves. This is an erudite reading of the poem that draws out the subtlety, and the genealogy, of Keats's sensationalism, and in so doing revises our understanding of it.

Nicholas Roe's 'John Keats and George Felton Mathew: Poetics, Politics and the *European Magazine*' (*KSJ* 49[2000] 31–46) is another contribution to our increasing understanding of the Cockney school, which is concerned to show how coterie culture also negotiated a public dimension. The article explores Keats's 'sociable endeavour' as a writer in the form of the poem of address, concentrating on 'To George Felton Mathew' from the *Poems* of 1817. Roe observes that this friendship first developed, and then declined, as Keats received his first public notice as a writer. The telling note to the poem distances it, somewhat frostily, from the present—it belongs to an 'earlier period'—and the article explores the source of this imposed distance and its implications, through a thorough investigation of Keats's relations with the Mathew family, and Mathew's writing on Keats in the same period. The key to understanding here is Mathew's 'querulous' review of Keats in the *European Magazine* [May 1817]. Roe sees the relationship with Mathew as conforming to a pattern observed by Keats's biographers, in which Keats 'outgrows' relationships as his poetic ambitions increase. The value of this article is its further contribution to our understanding of Keats's self-fashioning, and to rescue this particular relationship from its current neglect.

Thomas McFarland's *The Masks of Keats: The Endeavour of a Poet* begins by proposing the concept of the mask as essential to an understanding of Keats the poet. Taking precedents from Byron and Milton, McFarland insists that there is a great difference between the writer before the artefact and the writer after its making: the act of writing creates another self, and the mask, in a sense, marks the rite of passage between the two. This model, of course, coincides almost precisely with that of Yeats. McFarland develops the idea into a system of categorizing Keats through the assumption of such masks: the primary mask, which is the assumption of the role and purpose of the artist, and two secondary masks, the 'Mask of Camelot' and the 'Mask of Hellas', both, he argues, constituted from materials in cultural currency at the time. It is this that makes Keats a poet profoundly of, and for, his age. This book ranges through the texts it claims as Keats's greatest achievements to re-read them through its adopted schema, and rehabilitate the notion of genius. In doing so, it draws on a profound and detailed knowledge of Keats and other canonical Romantic writers, and a scholarly concern with the mass of critical materials on Keats. This is its prime territory; it is not a book greatly interested in new cultural contexts, nor cultural history. It pursues elusive goals: the aesthetics and the psychology of high art, and the critical vocabulary which tries to pin them down subscribes—perhaps inevitably—to Romantic, and Freudian, models: we are concerned here with the 'churning of genius', the 'white heat' of creativity, with 'mental flow'. Such terms have specific meanings for this critic—they are not casually adopted—but they indicate the return to fields of speculation which require us to model creativity in highly figurative ways, and to understand it within a somewhat rarefied, even quasi-religious, context. The terminology is also ineluctably linked to this book's concern with hermeneutics: we are here, yet again, to re-read those poems within which there is still room for further interpretative manoeuvre. Keats can draw out the idiosyncratic in his critics. Here it takes the form of these highly specific categories, and the lens of the mask, but as in those other books on Keats which break the mould in some way (Ricks, Stillinger, Robinson, for example), one discovers not eccentricity or obliqueness for its own sake, but the sustained concentration of homage, a kind of humility before the protested diffidence of Keats's negative capability. Such critical acts, for all their detailed, diligent and painstaking analyses, somehow leave the poetry strangely and wonderfully intact and unfathomable. This book is no exception to this rule, and it will probably take its place in time alongside those other remarkable critical achievements.

Masks are also Andrew M. Stauffer's concern in 'Celestial Temper: Shelley and the Masks of Anger' (*KSJ* 49[2000] 138–61), and Yeats again proves to be a stimulus. Stauffer opens with Yeats's claim that when Shelley drew on desire he was a great poet, but when he drew on anger, he produced 'monstrous, meaningless images'. This poses a question for the Shelley critic about the place of anger in the poetry, and its relation to the poetry's quality. Exploring whether Shelley does indeed 'suffer from congenital blindness in his dealings with evil and conflict', Stauffer comes at his analysis from two viewpoints, from the Steve Jones angle that sees Shelley's satire as evidence of a simmering anger just beneath the surface, and from the more conventional view of Shelley's pacifistic humanism. This is a good analysis, working through a number of examples to reveal Shelley's anger as something which is not simply an act of defiance, or a creative drive, but also an unmasking, a taking apart of the devices of tyranny. Nicholas Johnstone's concerns are also in the region of masks and selves: in 'Shelley, Julian and the Narratives of "Julian and Maddalo"' (*KSR* 14[2000] 34–41) he builds on Vincent Newey's recognition that there are two 'selves' in the poem, arguing for a stronger reading of the distance implied, and pointing out the distinctions between the Julian who debates with Maddalo, and the Julian who narrates the poem. A concern with roles and projections of selfhood can also be found in Margot Harrison's intriguing article, 'No Way for a Victim to Act? Beatrice Cenci and the Dilemma of Romantic Performance' (*SiR* 39[2000] 180–211), in which she examines the status of 'acting' in *The Cenci*, and the way in which Beatrice's 'acting' is broadly divided between strategies of display and strategies of concealment. Noting the historic transformations of 'acting' in the late eighteenth century, she gives weight to Shelley's concern here with actor characters who are not divided against themselves, and draws interesting parallels between acting, the 'false world' and the structures of oppression. In such a reading, Beatrice herself represents the hazards of turning inward, of seeking escape from falsity and oppression.

In 'Necessity and the Origin of Evil in the Thought of Spinoza and Shelley' (*KSR* 14[2000] 56–70), Fazal Abroon attempts to redress what the author sees as an imbalance in the reading of Shelley's doctrine of Necessity, in which Spinoza is insufficiently acknowledged. Illuminating, and clearly argued, the case largely rests on some important distinctions: because Shelley's Necessity stems from a pantheistic, unitary belief, its genealogy is not that of the Enlightenment philosophers (Holbach, Hume and Godwin). Further, Shelley's notion of the inevitability of perfectibility is neither static nor linear, but dynamic and circular. Mark Sandy also offers a re-reading in his '"Stormy Visions": Shelley's Reinvention of Myth, Memory and Identity in "Adonais"' (*KSR* 14[2000] 84–94), a scholarly development of Stuart Curran's call to resist reductive accounts of the poem, and read it instead it with a sensitive awareness of the 'contradictions of its own poetic logic'. Sandy represents the poem as an interval of a kind in Shelley's historicist preoccupations, and argues that the poem's making of a transhistorical arena is 'shown to be integral to a notion of a temporal sphere' which actually allows a re-emergence of history, and remembrance. A further revision to our reading of a canonical poem is given by Rodney Stenning Edgecombe in 'Displaced Christian Images in Shelley's "Ozymandias"' (*KSR* 14[2000] 95–9). This is a brief but telling note on why Shelley presented the poem's central image of the statue in the way he did, arguing that he drew on a tradition of Christian topoi: in particular, the broken pillar as a symbol of mortality, the head at the foot of the plinth recalling the skull at the foot of the cross. The point is not to suggest a covert Christianity of course, but to register the allusive depth of Shelley's sonnet.

In '"Attracted by the body": Accounts of Shelley's Cremation' (*KSJ* 49[2000] 162–82) Kim Wheatley offers an exploration of the ways in which the different accounts of Shelley's cremation mythologized the poet. The accounts of Medwin, Trelawney and Leigh Hunt are all examined here, and Wheatley shows how they all use a wider context implicating the poems or inflecting them in particular ways. She investigates both the gendering (the masculinist responses, the feminized body) in these accounts, and, interestingly, the 'double impulse to fragment and restore the body'. Both, she suggests, are superseded by the narrative as a whole, which in each case 'crafts' its own fascination, partly through the presence of the author, each becoming 'part of the scenery, contaminated by fictionality, caught up in the waking dream'.

This year sees the advent of two new Shelley editions: volume ii of *The Poems of Shelley* edited by Kelvin Everest and Geoffrey Matthews, covering the period 1817–1819, and volume i of *The Complete Poetry of Percy Bysshe Shelley*, edited by Donald H. Reiman and Neil Fraistat. Reiman and Fraistat are setting out to provide a complete edition of all the poems that Shelley released for circulation (a term used here to include publication and circulation to friends and others); other texts appear in appendices. The Everest and Matthews edition, however, includes all texts known to have been written by Shelley, including fragments that may be recognized as rejected or variant versions of other poems. Both editions go about the editorial task with the most scrupulous care, and, as Everest makes clear in his introduction, this task has become all the more demanding following the recent Garland series of facsimile manuscripts which has expanded the base of scholarship to include 'minute inspection and assessment of literally every known line and word of Shelley's poetry in manuscript'. Reiman and Fraistat establish their copy-texts from 'uncontroversial' first editions or publications, or through comparison of surviving copies, or single extant copies; Everest works from first editions known to have been supervised by Shelley, and, where there is no evidence for such supervision, the first edition is collated with manuscripts where appropriate, and other printed editions. Broadly therefore, both editions are working on similar historical principles, and both offer the reader a wealth of supportive materials in the way of erudite headnotes and recorded variants. The Everest edition is strictly chronological, and provides an apparatus whereby the reader can reconstruct the arrangements of poems published within Shelley's lifetime. In contrast, Reiman and Fraistat present the poems that Shelley released according either to the groupings he arranged, or in groupings based on the evidence for intended publication. Both texts therefore discard Mary Shelley's arrangement of the poems in favour of a history of a kind: the Everest volumes will give us a history of Shelley at work; those by Reiman and Fraistat will produce a more public version of the poet, by relegating work in progress to supplementary status, the guiding principle being the notion of Shelley's 'self-presentation to his contemporaries'.

5. Blake

The year 2000 was something of an *annus mirabilis* for the reception of Blake's works: the largest ever exhibition of his paintings, engravings and illuminated books was mounted at Tate Britain before moving, in a slightly modified form, to the Metropolitan Museum of Art, New York. With items on loan from the Ashmolean, British Museum, Huntington Library, Boston Museum of Fine Arts, National

Gallery of Victoria and many other public and private collections, this was the first, and probably last, opportunity to view a wide range of Blake's art together. Many works that have become very fragile over the centuries may never be transported again, making a similar exhibition in the future extremely unlikely.

The curators, Robin Hamlyn and Christine Riding, with the help of other scholars and researchers, most notably Michael Phillips, arranged the Tate Britain exhibition around four primary themes. This in part may have arisen out of the general reorganization of the Tate collection that took place in the late 1990s, away from chronological periodization towards thematic arrangements: such assemblages have not necessarily proved popular with the visiting public elsewhere in Tate Britain but, in the exhibition itself and the accompanying catalogue, Hamlyn and Phillips, eds., *William Blake*, it offered a significant way of structuring Blake's life and work. Possibly the biggest surprise was to begin with Blake as 'One of the Gothic Artists': Blake's (sometimes, as with everything he did, idiosyncratic) contribution to eighteenth- and nineteenth-century Gothic has long been recognized, but to focus on this as the initial encounter with Blake helps to anchor his distinctive style and spiritual vision in the artistic world of his time while also emphasizing the strange 'otherworldliness' of his art that accounts for much of his continuing appeal.

William Blake continues with 'The Furnace of Lambeth's Vale', Blake's print-making studio in Hercules Building, situated as the point of convergence for the material production of the illuminated texts in the environment of London and Lambeth, in a study of Blake's technique that owes much to the bibliographic and historicist work of writers such as Joseph Viscomi, G.E. Bentley, Michael Phillips, David Worrall and Robert Essick. 'Chambers of the Imagination' attempts to provide other intellectual contexts and sources for Blake's ideas as they found expression in the large colour prints and illustrations to *Milton*, as well as sketching out some motifs of his mythology such as Albion, emanations and the prophet Los. The final section of the catalogue, 'Many Formidable Works', concentrates on Blake's idea of the book, from *Songs of Innocence* to *Jerusalem*: as Robin Hamlyn remarks, Blake 'lavished more care on *Jerusalem* than on any other single work'. This section, more than any other, demonstrates some of the weaknesses as well as strengths of this approach to Blake. In contrast to Martin Butlin's 1990 catalogue for the Tate, where each book or set of paintings or engravings is treated as a discrete entity, there is some overlap and repetition between 'Many Formidable Works' and other sections of *William Blake*; at the same time, the authors have been able to draw on the advances in Blake studies that have been made during the 1990s, for example in the remarkable Tate Gallery/Blake Trust illuminated books. The curators and the authors have achieved a remarkable task aided by Marilyn Butler's sterling essay on 'Blake in his Time' and Peter Ackroyd's more idiosyncratic piece on 'William Blake: The Man'.

As has been noted in previous editions of *YWES*, G.E. Bentley's annual report in *Blake: An Illustrated Quarterly* is an essential starting point for any scholar conducting research into Blake. 'William Blake and his Circle: A Checklist of Publications and Discoveries in 2000' (*Blake* 34:iv[2001] 129–58), conducted with the assistance of Keiko Aoyama for Japanese publications, does not merely report on new discoveries but also fills in details of publications and finds (such as catalogues) that have been omitted in previous years.

A useful tool for students of Blake is Bindman, ed., *William Blake: The Complete Illuminated Books*. Comprising the plates and transcripts in conventional texts from all Blake's illuminated works, this single volume is based on the six-volume set issued by the William Blake Trust and the Tate Gallery between 1990 and 1995. As *The Complete Illuminated Books* does not include the critical apparatus of that series (now also available in paperback), its value is obviously somewhat diminished. At the same time, the extremely handsome colour reproductions mean that this will generally be more helpful to readers than the other single-volume collection of Blake's engraved books, David Erdman's *The Illuminated Blake* [1974; republished 1992]. This version of *The Complete Illuminated Books*, published by Thames & Hudson, does not supplant the Erdman text entirely, as the earlier book includes a plate-by-plate commentary that can be of practical use when deciphering some of the visual elements of difficult texts such as *Milton* and *Jerusalem*; the Erdman *Illuminated Blake* was never easy to read, however, while this volume will probably encourage some students to approach Blake's works in the original.

Less groundbreaking is the publication by Dover of *Blake's Water-Colours for the Poems of Thomas Gray*; nonetheless, for me this is a welcome re-release of the Blake Trust/Trianon Press collection of 116 watercolours as a cheap paperback. Blake's relationship to Gray has generally been underestimated, and while the beautiful Trianon Press book (edited by Geoffrey Keynes) represented Blake's illustrations much more lavishly than this particular version, it was only available as a limited edition of 518 copies. Frank A. Vaughan's book on the illustrations to Gray, *Again to the Life of Eternity* [1996], includes much more detailed critical and contextual material than either book from the Trianon Press or (with a new—and brief—introduction) Dover, but includes only black and white plates. As such, *Blake's Water-Colours* is a very handy text for any Blake scholar looking for a personal reference copy of the Gray illustrations.

Michael Phillips, guest curator at the Tate exhibition, has also published the results of his long research into the production of Blake's early illuminated books in *William Blake: The Creation of the 'Songs', From Manuscript to Illuminated Printing*. Bibliographic work, particularly that undertaken by G.E. Bentley, Joseph Viscomi, Robert Essick and (more recently) Keri Davies, has revolutionized Blake criticism. *The Creation of the 'Songs'* alternates chapters on the techniques of Blake's printing with textual analysis regarding the development of individual Songs in the Notebook. The chapters on illuminated printing (of *Songs of Innocence* and of *Songs of Experience*) are the most fascinating, concentrating on the way in which the technology of printing was being transformed at the end of the eighteenth century, for example by the development of metal presses that enabled speedier mass production of newspapers or, closer to Blake, colour printing. The reason that Phillips goes into such detail regarding Blake's printing method (having recreated several of Blake's plates in the process) is to contradict some of Essick's and Viscomi's assertions on the subject of Blake's method of composition as 'autographic', that he composed directly onto the copper plate. To support his alternative argument, Phillips draws extensively on the Notebook to discuss the evolution of the poems, something that takes up approximately two-thirds of *The Creation of the 'Songs'*. Personally, I am not entirely convinced by all aspects of Phillips's argument, although it is becoming increasingly clear that Blake scholars should not argue for a 'one size fits all' approach to Blake's printing technique(s), and that different styles and forms require different processes.

The year 2000 saw the publication of an important analysis of Blake's *Four Zoas* in the form of Peter Otto's *Blake's Critique of Transcendence: Love, Jealousy and the Sublime in 'The Four Zoas'*. Otto's previous book on Blake, *Constructive Vision and Visionary Deconstruction* [1991] was concerned with a phenomenological and post-structuralist study of time in Blake's later works, especially as figured by the prophet Los in texts such as *Milton* and *Jerusalem*, and *Blake's Critique of Transcendence* continues Otto's interest in Blake and theory. It is not necessarily the case that Otto's book is the first (as he claims) to study the relation between text and illustrations for *The Four Zoas* in any detail: this is something that could probably be claimed for Magno and Erdman's photographic facsimile of the text [1987], although he goes into the relation of image and text in much greater detail than, for example, George Rosso's *Blake's Prophetic Workshop: A Study of 'The Four Zoas'* [1993].

As the greatest prophetic work that Blake didn't write, a text for which has been claimed the status of one of the great unfinished epics of the Romantic period, *The Four Zoas* has attracted considerable interest since Ellis and Yeats discovered an explanation of Blake's visionary cosmos in its often incoherent pages. Otto is right to emphasize the political and material contexts of *The Four Zoas*, that it is a text 'deeply engaged with politics and history'. Thus, for example, he continues Rosso's and Andrew Lincoln's explication of the poem as drawn from a long tradition of eighteenth-century Anglican apologetics (most notably Edward Young's *Night Thoughts*) by demonstrating in chapter 6 how Blake was concerned to build 'a Swedenborgian heaven'. At the same time, Otto's exegesis is often more concerned with post-structuralist strategies of reading *The Four Zoas*: Blake's shifting mythus, therefore, offers us a critique of transcendence. Drawing on the work of V.A. De Luca, Otto observes that recent emphases in criticism have registered a 'shift of attention ... from the shaping imagination of the author to the reader's creation of meaning', which in turn 'directs us to a human rather than transcendent reality'. We are not offered an objective reality, therefore, in the system of Blake's Zoas, but rather an example of the systems that we must create as readers lest we be enslaved to those of others.

One of the most thought-provoking book-length studies on Blake to be published recently is Christopher Z. Hobson's *Blake and Homosexuality*. Hobson, author of *The Chained Boy: Orc and Blake's Idea of Revolution* [1999] and, with Jackie DiSalvo and G.A. Rosso, editor of *Blake, Politics, and History* [1998], traces the developments of Blake's reaction to homosexuality in particular and notions of a sexual commonwealth in general from the late eighteenth century to the 1820s. His text is most remarkable in its reading of the metamorphosis of *Milton*, from a poem dealing with the double mirror of political events during the seventeenth century and the Napoleonic Wars, into one that concentrates on 'Moral Law', particularly with regard to virulent homophobia, following the Vere Street persecutions of 1810–11. His accounts of the public humiliation of seven prisoners as they were dragged down Fleet-street and the Strand, as well as the separate executions of Ensign John Newball Hepburn and Thomas White, a 16-year-old drummer-boy, demonstrates 'the degree to which working and poor people, abetted by the authorities, could be organized around hatred and repression of other poor and working people ... [and]

the gap between an ethic of mutuality and forgiveness and one of vengeance and intolerance'. These, as Hobson observes, 'were issues close to Blake's central concerns'.

Blake and Homosexuality works at its best when exploring how Blake's editorial practice responded to specific events such as this, being particularly illuminating in showing how Blake's own response changed from a largely conventional and republican condemnation of sodomy (a useful discussion of the distinction between sodomy and homosexuality is provided in his preface) as a vice of the higher, corrupt echelons of society into the 'synthesis' of a sexual commonwealth in *Jerusalem*. It is least compelling when exploring the textual ambiguities of Blake's works, most notably *The Four Zoas*, without the benefit of historical anchors such as the Vere Street trials. Hobson himself seems to recognize this—certainly he notes that, 'Inevitably, then, there will be room for disagreement with portions of my argument'; at the same time, in the words of George E. Haggerty, this book is important in so far as it 'makes Blake our contemporary'.

The process of making Blake a contemporary is also pursued in two other texts, Peter Linebaugh and Marcus Rediker's *The Many-Headed Hydra*, and Tony Trigilio's *'Strange Prophecies Anew': Rereading Apocalypse in Blake, H.D., and Ginsberg*. Blake forms only a part of Linebaugh and Rediker's study of what they refer to as the 'Atlantic Jubilee' or, more comprehensively in their subtitle, *Sailors, Slaves, Commoners, and the Hidden History of the Revolutionary Atlantic*. Nonetheless, he is an important part, the poet of the African American Tyger's energy that did not depend on a middle class in revolt to lead it against the British but raised its insurrectionary head(s) in ports, colonies, taverns and slave ships across the Atlantic many times during the eighteenth century. The authors are not always correct in their assessment of Blake—particularly niggling is the way they read *Jerusalem* as a retreat from Blake's early internationalism, which made me wonder how closely they have read a text that extends from Mexico to Japan, the capes of Africa and South America to the Hudson Bay and capitals of Europe. Nevertheless, as a reading against the grain of official history in the tradition of E.P. Thompson or David Erdman, *The Many-Headed Hydra* is a superb addition to the study of an Atlantic history that profoundly affected Blake.

'Strange Prophecies Anew' concentrates on a theory of apocalyptic influence and traditions, whereby Blake's, H.D.'s and Ginsberg's 'emphasis on revelatory conversationalism defies the monovocal authority of the Logos'. While the relationship between Blake and Ginsberg is one that is well known and well documented, Trigilio's book is more interesting in so far as it traces the ways in which Blake's visionary poetics provided inspiration to the revisionary aesthetic of H.D. Strictly speaking, Trigilio is not tracing causal relations between these three poets, but rather drawing on a counter-tradition that he labels as the 'New Gnosticism'.

Worthy of a brief mention is June Singer's *Blake, Jung, and the Collective Unconscious: The Conflict between Reason and Imagination*. This is actually a new edition of the much more snappily titled *The Unholy Bible: Blake, Jung and the Collective Unconscious* [1986]. This book, despite being of some interest as it is written by a practising Jungian analyst, essentially pursued the sort of archetypal criticism that had not been popular in Blake studies since the days of (the admittedly great, but also greatly misleading) Northrop Frye. Aside from the title, the only change to this text is the addition of a new preface by Singer that has a certain charm when recounting her own reasons for valuing Blake, despite my own opinion regarding her assertion that the time is ripe for a re-evaluation Blake's work in the light of Jung: after the rather bleak domination of Jungian psychology in Blake studies in the mid-twentieth century, nothing could be further from the truth.

Finally, with regard to Blake books released in 2000, two biographies from the early twentieth century were reprinted, both sharing a significant interest in Blake's religious belief. G.K. Chesterton's biographical essay, *William Blake*, first published in 1920, was part of an exploration of Christian divinity that led to his own conversion to Catholicism. The text owes much to Alexander Gilchrist's marvellous account of Blake and is almost directly antithetical to Swinburne's essay on the diabolical *pictor ignotis*. Chesterton's lightness of touch, for all the undoubted seriousness of his religious exploration, can slip very easily into the trivial. This is not the case with the second reprinted text considered here, Basil De Selincourt's *William Blake: A Biography*, although it is less interesting because less personal than Chesterton's account. Generally, *William Blake: A Biography* is rather sparse on biographical fact: the real interest of De Selincourt's text, as with Chesterton's, its near contemporary, is the way in which it offers an insight into the contextualization of Blake during the early twentieth century. Blake's social and political radicalism, despite a brief flourish in some quarters during the late 1800s, almost completely disappears in these two books, to be replaced by an intense interest in his fervent if unconventional Christianity.

Of significant journal articles published during 2000, those in *Blake: An Illustrated Quarterly* provide an important starting point. John E. Grant's 'On First Encountering Blake's *Good Samaritans*' (*Blake* 33:iv[2000] 68–95) concentrates on the watercolour designs for Edward Young's *Night Thoughts* that provide an 'unusual representation' of Christ's parable of the Good Samaritan. Grant notes that the vessel offered by the Samaritan is carved with serpents, and that the wounded man is defensive, 'believing that no Jew can expect any good thing from a Samaritan'. The victim by the roadside, like the reader of *Night Thoughts*, has to learn to read the sign of the serpent against the codes by which he has been taught. Grant contrasts this interpretation of the parable against other, more conventional, representations, for example Hogarth's *The Good Samaritan* [1772], concluding that 'the victim's acceptance of this object from this man would be foolhardy—or it would require an extraordinary act of faith, a conversion'. It is thus a miraculous event, and Grant's significant and detailed reading of *Night Thoughts* can also be used as a means of understanding healing, miracles and friendship in other texts by Blake, particularly *Jerusalem*.

Blake has frequently been portrayed as a *bête noir* of feminist studies, for example in the work of Anne Mellor, Irene Tahoer and Susan Fox. Helen Bruder's recent *William Blake and the Daughters of Albion* [1998] did not act as an apology for Blake's bursts of dubious gender politics, but it did an important service to Blake studies in distinguishing Blake's own struggle with the battle of the sexes from the deliberate (and frequently disastrous) misreadings of early, proto-feminist texts such as *Thel*, *Visions of the Daughters of Albion* and even *Europe* by generations of male critics. Blake's thorny relationship with feminism is the subject of Claire Colebrook's 'Blake and Feminism: Romanticism and the Question of the Other' (*Blake* 34:i[2000] 4–13). Blake, argues Colebrook, appears to contrast questions of unification, integration and collective redemption against *self*-identification as opposed to unified identity ('I must Create a System or be enslav'd by another Mans'), a polarity which has been explored by Luce Irigaray as part of a 'post-enlightenment tradition in which Blake was also writing'. This, suggests Colebrook, is a politics of the other whereby sexual difference provides a challenge to the supposedly Romantic elimination of such difference. Blake sees the female sexual form as alien, but also operating in relation to masculine self-reference, not simply as an objectified other or spectral self. This recognition of difference (after Irigaray) opens the possibility of an ethics, and Coalbrook reads through a variety of female forms in Blake's works in a surprisingly positive light, arguing that Blake 'saw the importance of interaction with the other … What Blake's romanticism offers is an articulation of ethical difference and integration, in opposition to what has been described as a history of logocentrism.'

Kazuya Okada considers a different kind of relationship with the other in 'Orc under a Veil Revealed: Family Relationships and their Symbols in *Europe* and *The Book of Urizen*' (*Blake* 34:ii[2000] 36–45). Plate 19 of *Urizen*, suggests Okada, depicts Enitharmon as Venus, Los as Vulcan and Orc as Cupid, indicting Urizen's Miltonic-Newtonian act of creation to which is opposed the birth of Orc. As the figure of Cupid (or Eros), Orc is restricted and restrained by his parents—this is not the ideal family like that depicted in the illustrations for Milton's 'On the Morning of Christ's Nativity'. Rather, the question here is how the child is to achieve symbolic power formidable enough to overthrow the system of the traditional family romance, and Orc as Cupid has 'the potentiality to break the conventional forms of submission'.

Elsewhere, David Worrall once again provided a 'minute particular' that illuminates Blake's social and political background in 'William Bryan, Another Anti-Swedenborgian Visionary Engraver of 1789' (*Blake* 34:i[2000] 14–22). Following his extensive research in the Privy Council archive, Worrall outlines the biography of this ex-Swedenborgian copperplate printer and bookseller, a type familiar to readers of Worrall's excellent *Radical Culture* [1992]. Bryan lived and worked near other Swedenborgians in Upper Mary-le-bone Street, a 'minor centre of contemporary progressive religious and political activity', in 1789. Tracing similarities between the two WBs, Worrall's aim is not to suggest a direct transmission of influence between the two, but to indicate how their ideas and lives overlapped and provide an example of 'the sort of spiritual communities' that extends our contextual knowledge of Blake.

Jesse Cohn offers a brief but interesting reading of one of Blake's many odd poems in 'Blake's "The Mental Traveller"' (*Expl* 58:iii[2000] 130–3) as offering a cyclical reading not merely of nature but also the revisionary task of reading and reinterpreting Milton. One of the most appealing papers of 2000, however, must be Robert Kaufman's 'Everyone Hates Kant: Blakean Formalism and the Symmetries of Laura Moriarty' (*MLQ* 61:i[2000] 131–55). This is a complex and detailed critical account which attempts to deal with several major areas: first of all, the impact of recent critiques of Kant and Kantian aesthetics, especially as they have been taken (post-Adorno and Horkheimer) as foundational to bourgeois perception, but also the role of Blakean form and 'modern poetry's reimaginings of Blakean form-experiment'. Rather than concentrate on the usual suspects of twentieth-century American poetry (though Ginsberg, Williams and others are noted, some in considerable detail), Kaufman focuses on the recent work of Laura Moriarty, particularly as she employs an 'Adornian' poetics to generate a formal tension between lyric and non- or anti-lyric effects. This formal strategy is used by Moriarty to engage with political events such as the Gulf war, disaffecting the reader in order that they should critically engage with such actions rather than submit to a totalizing (if elegant) form.

While the significance of Ginsberg is noted in Kaufman's essay, the Beat poet's relation to Blake is much more important in Terrence Diggory's 'Allen Ginsberg's Urban Pastoral' (*CollL* 27:i[2000] 103–18). As well as reciting the familiar tale of Ginsberg's debt to a vision of Blake in Harlem in 1948, Diggory provides a well-argued account of just how influential Blake was for Ginsberg in terms of enabling him to articulate the urban pastoral that 'distinguishes his version of pastoral from the dominant and essentially conservative "post-revolutionary" mode' typical of the genre. Finally, Julia Wright compares Blake's treatment of art and aesthetics to that of Lessing in 'The Medium, the Message and the Line in William Blake's *Laocoon*' (*Mosaic* 33:ii[2000] 101–24), taking forward the observation by Henry Crabb Robinson that Blake's approach to the arts was much closer to a German than English tradition.

6. Wordsworth and Coleridge

There was little new editorial work for the Wordsworthians this year: no new volume from the Cornell Wordsworth, for instance; but Damian Walford Davies's handsome *Selected Poems* from Everyman showed Cornell's salutary influence by choosing early texts of the major poems it anthologized. *Salisbury Plain*, *The Pedlar*, *The Ruined Cottage* and *Peter Bell* (the 1819 text) are here in full; *An Evening Walk* and *Descriptive Sketches* in excerpts, as is the 1805 *Prelude* (the two-part *Prelude* is included complete); and there are generous selections from the *Lyrical Ballads* and the 1807 *Poems, in Two Volumes*, grouped by volume (an intelligent decision), as well as a judicious scatter of later poems. The introduction is readerly and suggestive, the notes clear and helpful, and a substantial appendix anthologizes the best critics from contemporary reviewers to Jonathan Wordsworth. The new Everyman's well-established rival, Stephen's Gill's Oxford Authors volume, appeared in a new edition, now as a World's Classics paperback entitled *The Major Works*: the selection naturally overlaps a good deal with the Everyman, though where Walford Davies has the 1799 *Prelude*, the Oxford volume has a complete 1805; and it also includes the more important prose. I should also mention here an item of bibliographical interest: Paul Betz's *William Wordsworth and the Romantic Imagination: A Scholar's Collection* is the catalogue to an exhibition held at Cornell University Library. (I have not been able to track down a copy; but the Cornell Library website gives a sense of its pleasures: Betz has assembled a remarkable collection of Wordsworth and Wordsworthiana.)

H.J. Jackson's Coleridge edition in the Oxford Authors series also reappeared in World's Classics garb as a *Major Works*; but the limelight was falling elsewhere: largely on the same scholar's fifth volume of Coleridge's *Marginalia*, co-edited with the late George Whalley for the Bollingen edition. This great enterprise is now nearing completion after more than thirty years. The new volume reprints and annotates Coleridge's surviving marginalia on authors from Sherlock (*A Vindication of the Trinity*) to 'Unidentified' (a stray end-page of notes lamenting modern Britain's false enlightenment); along the way, the most substantial collections of entries comment upon Southey, Steffens, Swedenborg, Jeremy Taylor, and Tennemann. The remarks in the margin of Southey's *Joan of Arc*, made in 1814, are boisterous good value (STC writes in red pencil, 'If I go on thus, I shall make the Book what, I suppose, it never was before, *red all thro'*'); Taylor is read with absorbed love, especially cherished for the moments in which his 'genial Nature, and exquisitely tender Sense of the Beautiful, fling him, like the Flying Fish, above the emprisoning [element]'. The respectful skirmish with Spinoza recorded here is not very lengthy, but implies a whole response: 'The Truth is, Spinoza in common with all Metaphysicians before him (Böhmen, perhaps excepted) began at the wrong end—commencing with God as an *Object*'. Also here, remarks on Swift (he is interesting on the *irrationalism* of the Houyhnhnms) and on Sterling's *Arthur Coningsby*; he is spry about an inscription made by the young Tennyson, and sharper still about the sonnets by Tennyson's brother Charles. The sixth and final volume of *Marginalia*, which was scheduled for publication in 2001, will contain a collective index: once we have that, the importance of this marvellous edition—it is effectively an extension of Coleridge's *Notebooks*—will be even more apparent. Also appearing last year in the Bollingen series was J.R. de J. Jackson's magnificent two-volume text of the 1818–19 lectures *On the History of Philosophy*—an important point of reference since their first appearance in Coburn's edition of 1949, especially for readers who are interested in the strenuous realignment that occurred in Coleridge's thinking after *Biographia*. Something like R.A. Foakes's edition of the literary lectures, Jackson's *Lectures* reproduce Coleridge's draft notes and records of the lectures made by much-taxed shorthand reporters (the so-called 'Frere manuscript'), as well as other manuscript and newspaper reports. The transcriptions of Coleridge in full flow constitute an unforgivingly (but unsurprisingly) rebarbative text, and it often needs some cross-illumination from other sources to clarify its meanings: Jackson tactfully incorporates such passages to produce a beautifully intelligible text (the untamed reality of the Frere manuscript is printed as an appendix). Almost needless to say of the Bollingen Coleridge, the editorial commentary (in this as in the *Marginalia*) is consistently excellent, wholly unostentatious about an actually astonishing command of material, throwing up suggestions to pursue on every page. The introduction draws in the background to the lectures and discusses their contents in turn at some length; and an appendix graciously reproduces some surviving fragments from the edition of these lectures that Owen Barfield did not live to complete.

Not an edition, but the prospectus to one, says Nicholas Halmi of the forthcoming 'Norton Critical Edition of *Coleridge's Poetry and Prose*' (*RoN* 19[2000]), which promises to be a very useful addition to the shelf: the essay sets out the principles of selection, and the method of presenting the poetry: early versions, grouped by their original volumes, with important variants in the footnotes. And finally among things editorial, I should mention Richard Gravil's handbook to Coleridge's selected poems in the *York Advanced Notes* series (designed for undergraduates and sixth-formers): not an edition either, but the notes belonging to one, it covers an immense amount within its narrow scope, and manages to enlighten some darkly Coleridgean matters in an exemplary way.

Beside selected editions, biography continues to provide the main bridge between the professionals and the common reader; and the blockbuster in the field this year was Juliet Barker's tome, *Wordsworth: A Life*. This is a likeable, colourful account, in the Holmesian mode; and it goes with something of a novel's swing: 'This blissful existence was rudely interrupted by a stinging letter of rebuke from Uncle Christopher's wife' and so on. *The Prelude* is sometimes adduced in the early pages without much allowance being made for Wordsworth's powers of retrospective self-invention ('At Cambridge, William was equally blithe'), but Barker is not flightily inventive: any flickers of incest are brushed away for one thing (the creation of 'Freud's distorting lens'), and on the other main cruxes of Wordsworthian biography she takes a prudent line (the third visit to revolutionary France in 1793 is judged unlikely, the affair with Sara Hutchinson impossible). You may feel the style wobbles a bit at times (was 'Tintern Abbey' *really* 'a mission statement'?), but the overall shape of the life is nicely conveyed: the devastation of the children's deaths in 1812 lies at the centre of the book, and the awful darkness of the last years is convincingly portrayed. It is not an intellectual life exactly: the crisis obliquely recorded in *The Borderers*, for instance, is glossed as Wordsworth 'confusing himself' with 'Godwin's microscopic system of philosophical analysis', and the Coleridgean background to *The Recluse* is lightly drawn: readers looking for such a biography will find Stephen Gill much more helpful. I should say too that Coleridge gets some testy treatment: ever in search of 'a splendid excuse' and the victim of 'typical Coleridgean muddle', he is later spotted wandering around Europe 'in a drug-induced haze'. He features in a more kindly light in Stephen Hebron's illustrated life of Wordsworth for the British Library's Writers' Lives series: it is a clear, short account, with excellent illustrations, well reproduced, many drawn from the collections of the Wordsworth Trust. (By a slip of the pen, little Berkeley Coleridge is sent off to school in Ambleside at one point, which should be corrected in a future reprint.) The last big biography we had, Kenneth R. Johnston's engaging and packed *The Hidden Wordsworth*, appeared in a paperback redaction, without the provocative subtitle (always *slightly* tongue-in-cheek) and its mention of 'Spy', and with a disarming new preface explaining why it was dropped. The possibility that Wordsworth was paid to do something surreptitious for the Crown was squashed with some vehemence in an article by Michael Durey, 'The Spy who Never Was' (*TLS* 10 March[2000] 14–15), which showed that the duke of Portland had slipped £100 to Robinson Wordsworth, the poet's cousin, and not to the poet; a genial reply by Johnston, 'Wordsworth as Spy' (*TLS* 17 March[2000] 17), concedes the point (while regretting the tone of the correction) and adroitly offers a correction to Durey in return. On a smaller biographical scale, Richard Matlak returned to consider 'Captain John Wordsworth's Death at Sea' (*WC* 31[2000] 127–33), and the flurry of publications about this important disaster: Wordsworth's own grief was evidently exacerbated by the ambiguous descriptions of John's behaviour during the crisis. Pamela Woof offered a characteristically evocative portrait of life in a cramped but productive 'Dove Cottage in 1800' (*WC* 31[2000] 133–42); Penelope Hughes-Hallett drew a likeable sketch of the poet, laughing at Lamb's tipsy nonsense and getting embarrassed at the humiliation of his superior in the Stamp Office, in her account of *The Immortal Dinner: A Famous Evening of Genius and Laughter in Literary London, 1817*; and Peter Manning, 'Touring Scotland at the Time of the Reform Bill' (*WC* 31[2000] 80–3), contrasted Wordsworth's attitude towards

Scotland in his tour of 1831 with the more politically engaged response of Cobbett a year later—and then neatly untied his own antithesis as an envoi. Finally, turning from the life to the afterlife, or its advertisement anyway, John Strachan published a lost letter by Edward Quillinan, 'Wordsworth's Memorials' (*ChLB* 109[2000] 1–4) discussing the words to appear on Wordsworth's gravestone.

An insightful and tactful essay by John Powell Ward discussed 'Wordsworth and Friendship' (*ColB* 15[2000] 27–40), piecing together a taxonomy of Wordsworthian relationships which reaches a climax in the friendship with Coleridge, 'a personal bonding so close', as Ward excellently says, 'that maybe neither of them ever fully coped with it'. The biographical circumstances of the birth of that difficult intimacy are most fully described in Tom Mayberry's finely illustrated account of Coleridge and Wordsworth in the West Country, *Coleridge and Wordsworth: The Crucible of Friendship*, which received a welcome new edition this year, now with a preface by Richard Holmes. A Wordsworthian intercession on Coleridge's behalf, spreading the word about *The Friend*, was described by Timothy Whelan, based upon 'A Wordsworth Autograph Letter Found in the John Rylands Library at Manchester' (*N&Q* 47[2000] 311–14); while the more strained relationship between the friends during the 1803 tour of Scotland was discussed by Carol Kyros Walker, 'Breaking Away: Coleridge in Scotland' (*WC* 31[2000] 102–7): a book-length treatment of Coleridge's epic excursion is discreetly announced in the notes, which (following the same author's beautifully illustrated *Walking North with Keats* and her edition of Dorothy Wordsworth's *Tour*) everyone will look forward to very much. Of Coleridge's other friendships, Gaurion Taussig, 'Idea and Substance' (*ColB* 15[2000] 41–55), offered a nicely nuanced account of his relationship with Thomas Poole, and the intricate play of genderings that characterized it; elsewhere, in '"Lavish Promises"' (*Romanticism* 6[2000] 78–97), Taussig described the burdensome, quasi-religious freight with which the idea of friendship was loaded by Coleridge, Lamb and Lloyd in the 1790s. To regard your acquaintance with Coleridge (as Lloyd did) as a divine gift was bound to precipitate a more than usual disappointment. Lloyd featured too in Lynda Pratt's 'Lloyd, Coleridge and Southey in the 1790s: Five Unpublished Letters' (*Romanticism* 6[2000] 98–115), in what is an increasingly indispensable journal. Lloyd is found here writing wonderingly to his mother about Coleridge's 'child-like simplicity & purity of heart', although conceding 'a *proneness to the desultory*'. Quite unlike Pratt, you can't help thinking, whose assiduous archival delving, in 'Interaction, Reorientation, and Discontent in the Coleridge–Southey Circle, 1797' (*N&Q* 47[2000] 314–21) also turned up two new Southey letters, which show him in low spirits in 1797, beginning to distance himself a little from Coleridge, though not at all antipathetic towards his poetry. Part of the wider case stirring in the essay is that, in the absence of a reliable edition of Southey's letters of this period, the kinds of conversational creativity we habitually (and rightly) attribute to the Wordsworth–Coleridge collaboration become invisible when we consider the Southey–Coleridge partnership: 'This Lime-Tree Bower my Prison', for instance, is sent in a letter to encourage Southey out of a specific mood of world-weariness. Approaching the same group from quite a different perspective, 'The Language of the Southey–Coleridge Circle' (*Language Sciences* 22[2000] 401–22) comprised a succinct but illuminating biography of the circle in the 1790s by Lynda Pratt (again), and an analysis of a peculiarity in its shared language by David Denison: the feature in question is the progressive passive (as in 'the goats *are being milked*'), a rare creature normally, and its recurrence within the circle may not only illustrate the way social networks promote linguistic idiosyncrasies as part of their group identity, but might also be a self-conscious assumption of an unrespectable mode of speech, like dropping your 'h's to show solidarity with the oppressed. An important external influence on Coleridge's youthful radicalism was identified in a fine research paper by Timothy Whelan originally given at the Wordsworth Conference in Grasmere: 'Coleridge and Robert Hall of Cambridge' (*WC* 31[2000] 38–47) rediscovers the important role Baptist thought played in Coleridge's development, a connection confirmed in the same author's 'Joseph Cottle the Baptist' (*ChLB* 111[2000] 96–108)—the *Baptist*, that is to say, and not (as Holmes and others have assumed) the *Unitarian*. From the other end of Coleridge's life, Allan Clayson contributes a likeable account of 'Coleridge's Holidays at Ramsgate' (*ColB* 16[2000] 15–23), and places some poems in their proper Ramsgatean context. Finally, the end of inclusiveness incites me to include here my own *S.T. Coleridge: Interviews and Recollections*: not a biography but the raw materials for one maybe, the book attempts to collect and annotate most of the eyewitness reports of meeting Coleridge and (what usually amounted to the same thing) hearing him talk. I had better report some misprints: 'testfied' for 'testified' (p. xv), 'ROBERT BENJAMIN' for 'BENJAMIN ROBERT' (p. 216), 'chandalier' for 'chandelier' (p. 222), and 'sporano' for 'soprano' (p. 231). (And, in a spirit of friendly collegiality, perhaps I should pass on my advice to any other authors contemplating camera-ready copy: don't.)

One recurring theme in the year's Wordsworthian criticism was one of the most venerable: childhood and education. The Wordsworthian child found himself (or herself) studied by 'a scrutinizing Adult' in a lively chapter in Judith Plotz's *Romanticism and the Vocation of Childhood*, which enquired into the main attributes of this 'exemplary Romantic child-spotter' and, convincingly, found them to be 'more complex, tough-minded, and dreadful' than reputation might suggest. Wordsworthian parenthood is 'dangerous and largely doomed'; Wordsworthian infancy is 'always *disjunct*'; and Wordsworth's chief legacy to the nineteenth-century literature of childhood is 'an aesthetically embalmed apartheid'. John Powell Ward's piece, 'Earthly Freight: Wordsworth's Poetry of Childhood, 1804–1812' (*ChLB* 112[2000] 169–82), also considered the doom of Wordsworth's children, focusing on the strange near-abandonment of what had felt so central a theme before 1804: between then and the death of Catherine only a handful of poems feature childhood in any significant way. The rarely regarded *White Doe of Rylstone* is found here to gather the darkening feelings most impressively: Ward finely observes the poem turning to embrace the chilly symbolism of the Doe, and abandoning as it does so Emily the living child; and thus Wordsworth brings to a subliminal close his long 'birth-obsession'. How the adult handles the troubling inspiration of childhood is also the subject of Keith Hanley's intricately sophisticated *Wordsworth: A Poet's History*, which ranges across the oeuvre to describe a poetry at once expressing and controlling the traumatic emotions of childhood (the book's instincts are Lacanian). Hanley finds Wordsworth's relationships with women all 'governed by the structure of memory fixed by the prevailing relation with the mother as the return of the knowledge of trespass transmuted into acceptance of the law': what makes this of more than merely psycho-biographical interest is that Wordsworth's poetic language is the product of this maternal relation—a counter-intuitive thought to an age so used to Wordsworth the masculinist, and Hanley doesn't conceal his sense of timely audacity ('That numerous mothers speak in the poetry is hardly surprising since in a way they are constantly speaking there'). Politics continues the story by other means: the French Revolution matters so much to Wordsworth's poetry because it reawakens the energies of the formative childhood language trauma; and the successive rewritings of *The Prelude* are re-encounters with the same aboriginal shock, cast in the guise of subsequent life-crises. This poetry of encountered shock ('The Shock of the Old') is, in turn, said to be Wordsworth's enabling bequest to a later tradition: Hanley discusses Conan Doyle (in a section called 'Holmes at Grasmere', which just gets away with it), Mary Shelley, Hopkins, and George Eliot, the last at some length. It is a knotty and sometimes difficult book, unafraid of its idiosyncrasy or its passages of developed abstraction; but even readers who rarely tread post-Freudian ways will recognize suggestive things here: the importance of Beattie's *Minstrel*, for instance, or the almost embarrassingly obvious failure of Wordsworth's texts to be anything like the 'univocalist' works that a certain brand of antagonistic Theory requires them to be.

I suppose nothing could be much further away from Hanley's idea of the poet's sentimental education than that envisaged by Richard W. Clancey in *Wordsworth's Classical Undersong: Education, Rhetoric and Poetic Truth*. Clancey goes back to the schoolroom, not the nursery: he usefully describes the ethos of an old grammar school (Hawkshead was an especially good one), and reconstructs the classical syllabus there and at Cambridge. In the second, interpretative, part of the book, Wordsworth's ambitions to write a 'humanistic' poetry of ethical argument are compared fruitfully with Horace's, and the Aristotelian bearings of his literary thinking established; and the final section is a series of readings in *The Prelude*, finding at the heart of the autobiography an enabling tension between lyric and rhetoric, the latter voicing the poem's 'truth-burden', a philosophical duty that attempts to undo Romantic song. It is a well-tempered and well-lettered book which exemplifies the humanely educative virtues it describes. A section in Michael Hofstetter's *The Romantic Idea of a University: England and Germany, 1770–1850* reminds us in passing of Wordsworth's well-grounded disenchantment with real-life university, and his sketchier conception of what it should have been like: his brother Christopher, by contrast, 'Diligent, loyal, dull and uncreative … found a permanent home in the social and intellectual structures of Cambridge', which puts its squarely. William would rather have been wandering, of course, exposing himself to a higher mode of pedagogy; and that was the subject explored with much aplomb by Toby Benis in her *Romanticism on the Road: The Marginal Gains of Wordsworth's Homeless*, a lucid and knowledgeable book which seeks to place Wordsworth's poetry within 'a cultural history of vagrancy within the Georgian period'. The abandoned mother in *An Evening Walk*, for example, catches a wider ambivalence about the homeless: she is at once the origin of the poem yet swiftly killed off in it, and 'with her dies half of the speaker's conflicted subjectivity' (the narrator ends the poem heading to his comfy home). The female vagrant in the first 'Salisbury Plain' manages to establish precarious bonds of community, actually benefiting from an autonomy which, though harsh, is at least a release from the bonds of normal life: a bleak but real liberation which other Wordsworthian heroes will enjoy; but the darkening atmosphere in the revised 'Adventures on Salisbury Plain' reduces even that fragile solace. The readings of *Lyrical Ballads* emphasize the psychological circumstances of war, within which the solitary and unsocial (like Martha Ray) naturally arouse especial distrust: in such times, the Old Cumberland Beggar is a hero of Wordsworthian counter-culture for evading the system, as, in a different way, is the Leechgatherer a little later. And as, too, is the young Wordsworth in *The Prelude*: but this is the most intricate case, for the poem is paradoxically committed to affirming both the youthful pleasures of solitary aimlessness and the purposeful adult virtues of community.

If education of one kind or another seems established as a current Wordsworthian theme, the other main line of approach also feels like an enlivening return to old ground: Wordsworth the Nature Poet, who had once disappeared from view so completely that Harold Bloom could confidently claim him as an *anti*-nature poet, is back with a new ecological confidence. The most accomplished contribution to the school was in James C. McKusick's attractive and passionate study of *Green Writing: Romanticism and Ecology*, which claimed for Wordsworth the poetry of 'an engaged participant' (not a detached observer), and argued, in a nicely provocative turn of mind, for his healthful anti-humanism (as exemplified by, say, 'Expostulation and Reply'). As a poet of 'home', in the broadest sense, Wordsworth's studies of homelessness imply the price of abandoning sustainable economies; as a poet of bereavement, his autobiographical verse often turns on a question which is of pressing environmental concern too: can wildness be preserved? McKusick credits Wordsworth's important contribution to the establishment of National Parks, a point also taken up by the geographer Ian Whyte in 'William Wordsworth's *Guide to the Lakes* and the Geographical Tradition' (*Area* 32[2000] 101–6); George Kay's response, 'On Wordsworth, the Lake District, Protection and Exclusion' (*Area* 32[2000] 345–6), demurred at the fullness of Wordsworth's commitment to public access and found in him an impulse to exclude as much as a desire to conserve: it is the stand-off that McKusick addresses very fairly in his book, between 'red' and 'green' criticism. Lucy Moore made a less complicated association of Romanticism and environmentalism in 'Beauty is Truth' (*Ecologist* 30:vi[2000] 36–9), while Michael Kohler invoked Wordsworth in a tendentious spirit to launch 'A Romantic Critique of Ecological Modernization' (*ERR* 11[2000] 206–13)—the spirit of the Rio conference, that is to say: Wordsworth's contribution is to suggest 'how an encompassing sense of self-interest might be inculcated in relation to the environment'. The most all-encompassing attempt at a Green reading of Wordsworth this year came in an animated and highly personal book by Brad Sullivan, *Wordsworth and the Composition of Knowledge: Refiguring Relationships among Minds, Worlds and Words*: Sullivan found Wordsworth mirroring his own disillusion with the 'Enlightenment', and turning instead to an 'ecology of mind', bypassing the Cartesian divisions (for which no one has a good word these days) for the kind of omnific inclusiveness that David Bohm writes about so charismatically. In so far as these matters are theorized in Wordsworth I suppose it is in more or less Coleridgean terms, and this year saw the reappearance of a classic study of the philosophical background to the poetry in which Coleridge looms appropriately large: Nelson P. Stallknecht's *Strange Seas of Thought: Studies in William Wordsworth's Philosophy of Man and Nature*, first published in 1945, came in a new edition as part of Stallknecht's *Collected Works*, edited by Donald Jennerman and colleagues, with a new introduction. And I might mention here too John Purkis's *A Preface to Wordsworth*, which was also reissued in a new edition: a very helpful student handbook to the various contexts of Wordsworth's poetry, especially historical and political.

Of more particular readings, perhaps the most simply enjoyable was Jonathan Wordsworth's 'Twenty Wordsworth' (*WC* 31[2000] 119–26), which might be an early instalment of a Wordsworth dictionary, listing the poet's most important words, and describing their interinanimative life. Associationism, so volubly deplored by Coleridge, clearly enchanted Wordsworth, who was much drawn to the subject of the subconscious (where associations live), and Jonathan Wordsworth deftly locates his chosen words within their associative networks, nicely implying how words can turn themselves into things to which recollected emotions may attach as firmly as to the concrete elements of a spot of time. (The description of Mulciber's subterranean presence in an early passage of *The Prelude* is delightful.) Association has its darker aspect, of course, as Jonathan Wordsworth says, when it conjures language into a meddling counter-spirit, and it was Wordsworth's experience of verse's *difficulty* that also stirred a couple of chapters in Mark Storey's *The Problem of Poetry in the Romantic Period*. The contradictions of the *Lyrical Ballads*, especially, are multiple, and not the least is the felt discrepancy between the boisterous excesses in the Preface and the oddly fragmented existence of so many of the poems that follow it: Storey considers Wordsworth as 'almost wilfully perverse' in controverting his declared principles so zealously—stressing permanence and then writing so compellingly about transience, for example, or celebrating nature's restorative powers and then offering 'Michael'. (This is all undeniably true, though whether it deserves to be called a *problem* is another point.) The claims and insistences of the Preface were treated with historically informed scepticism in John Dolan's forcefully argued *Poetic Occasion from Milton to Wordsworth*: Wordsworth's brusque criticism of the sonnet to West cannot disguise his real indebtedness to Gray (and Young), for in reality he 'simply synthesizes, publicizes and successfully markets the dispersed ethos-occasioning strategies of an earlier generation of poets'. (He gives the game away in the surname he chooses for Lucy.) This obviously has much truth, and Dolan is agreeably confrontational about it: what are the 'Lucy' poems, after all, but 'Young's preface and his character-naming device, plus Gray's peasant-commemoration and use of obscurity of reference, plus Cowper's calculatingly low diction'? Well, put like that, I might have managed them myself; Wordsworth merely had the effrontery of genius to be proud about the thing that made his precursors queasily embarrassed: 'he could foreground the "I" they snuck in through the back door'—which, you may feel, concedes as icing what is really the fruit cake. The relationship between *Lyrical Ballads* and literary tradition was also the subject of a chapter in Michael Gamer's *Romanticism and the Gothic: Genre, Reception, and Canon Formation*, which saw in Wordsworth's ballads a parody not of Gothic so much as of the *reading* of Gothic: Harry Gill's uncritical absorption in the narrative of his own curse replicates the unselfconscious immersion in the world of the tales enjoyed by consumers of Gothic, and it is at just such points that Wordsworth often steps into his poems to advise the spellbound reader to 'think'. Wordsworth's public distaste for gothickery is well taken, but perhaps the argument underestimates the normal intricacy of reading actual Gothic, which is hardly ever unaware captivation: Radcliffe, for example, typically offers you heart-seizing chills while tacitly reassuring you that nothing is seriously amiss. This more complex understanding of the Gothic reader features in Nicola Trott's 'Wordsworth's Gothic Quandary' (*ChLB* 110[2000] 45–59), which cleverly sees the poems exploiting a Radcliffean mode of 'explained supernaturalism', even as the Preface makes angry noises about the deplorability of Gothic: the 'splicing of superstitions and rational forces' is seen to keenest effect here in a rich account of 'The Thorn', which emerges as a poem about an idea of poetry and a divided style of reading, as much as it is a poem about thorn trees and (possible) infanticide. Yu Liu, 'Crisis and Recovery: The [*sic*] Wordsworthian Poetics and Politics' (*PLL* 36[2000] 19–41), returns the *Lyrical Ballads* to the familiar context of disappointed politics, suggesting a direct connection between disillusion and poetry: in both, 'failure turns out to be very substance of success', and in the *Ballads* particularly 'the most important characters were all striking failures of one kind or another'— which seems hard on Martha Ray, but you see the point. Failure on purpose is also, in a way, the subject of Jack Stillinger's 'Wordsworth, Coleridge and the Shaggy Dog' (*WC* 31[2000] 70–6), which identifies the novelty of *Lyrical Ballads* as its readiness to tell stories that go nowhere much and end in 'relative pointlessness'; Stillinger also implies that this experiment, in getting it wrong, has a political resonance, since it empowers the reader to make up meanings, thus instituting 'a kind of interpretive democracy'.

Particular lyrical ballads found attentive readers. Richard Gravil's '*Tintern Abbey* and *The System of Nature*' (*Romanticism* 6[2000] 35–54) eases the poem out of its usual (current) ideological frame—'that idealising compound of Coleridge and Hegel'—and sets it instead in the company of Priestley, d'Holbach and Volney. This is a fine essay, full of incidental pleasures, which makes a clear and provocative big point too: 'that there is nothing in "Tintern Abbey" to which d'Holbach could not have assented, or radically out of tune with the "System of Nature" as the Jacobins imbibed it'. The turn to Dorothy is skilfully withdrawn from patriarchy and recognized instead as summarizing 'in one of the most subversive syntactical associations in English poetry the promotion of nature, with all its republican associations clustered about it': no wonder Coleridge grew so uneasy about it in later life. (How knowingly counter-Coleridgean was Wordsworth's poem in 1798?) The poem is also defended from its critics by Isobel Armstrong in a compelling section of her *The Radical Aesthetic*, a close reading against antagonistic close readers, which acknowledges (for instance) the astuteness of John Barrell's account while seeing 'a way in which Wordsworth agrees with him': 'Tintern Abbey' is 'a massively anxious text [which] seems to make its readers anxious'; and Armstrong finds in its diverse voices a basis for her claim to understand 'poetry as thought'. David Miall's 'Locating Wordsworth: "Tintern Abbey" and the Community with Nature' (*RoN* 20[2000]) takes seriously the poem's presences (rather than its omissions or oversights) in another way, asking what exactly it was that Wordsworth saw: Miall has been up and down the Wye to look for himself, and suggests the opening lines describe Symonds Yat, a spot which apparently fits the poem's metaphorical needs as well as it does the physical details. 'Tintern Abbey' features along with 'Old Man Travelling' in a discriminating account of 'Transition in Byron and Wordsworth' by Jane Stabler (*EIC* 50[2000] 306–28): 'When Wordsworth "turns" to things or people in his poems, it is often because they are no longer there.' Turning elsewhere in *Lyrical Ballads*, Kurt Heinzelman (*Raritan*

19:iv[2000] 148–58) takes another look at 'Nutting' with an eye on millenarian feeling: he describes it as a georgic vocation poem, in which the narrator learns (a Virgilian lesson) to temper his erotic energies and adopt maturer paths of gentleness, and Joshua Wilner, in his *Feeding on Infinity: Readings in the Romantic Rhetoric of Internalization*, found in the poem evidence of how 'questions of poetic identity and questions of sexual identity impinge on one another in Romantic poetry'. Meanwhile, back with sunny greenery, Peter Mortensen, 'Taking Animals Seriously: William Wordsworth and the Claims of Ecological Romanticism' (*OrbisLit* 55[2000] 296–310), discussed 'Hart-Leap Well' as a proto-ecological poem: the hart's suffering is 'a subject of ethical interest in itself', he says, making a link with the role of animal cruelty in the economy of *The Ancient Mariner*. Meanwhile, David Chandler offers a subtle account of 'The Politics of "Hart-Leap Well"' (*ChLB* 111[2000] 109–19) which disavows precisely such parallels: Chandler sees a poem not about the morality of hunting but about how 'an intelligent "Nature" responds to the *un*natural behaviour of man', in which the figure of the shepherd effectively voices the chastening but not uncheering thought that, actually, nature *will* desert the one who fails to love her properly. (Chandler makes the nice additional suggestion that the relationship between the shepherd and the poet-figure—who dissents from the shepherd's gloss, and offers his own interpretation—expresses a kind of Wordsworthian fantasy of life in Grasmere.) Richard W. Clancey discusses 'The Brothers', in 'Wordsworth's "The Brothers" and the Romantic Humanism of Place' (*ChLB* 111[2000] 120–31), as a parable of 'fittingness', the way we belong to some (particular) places, a theme which it explores sombrely as a kind of counter-poem to *Home at Grasmere*. David Duff also wrote interestingly about 'The Brothers', returning to manuscript (where it is subtitled 'A Pastoral Poem') to discuss the poem's uncertain generic identity: an alertness to genre enables you to see 'a more subtly original performance: not just a rejection of the original conventions, but also a display of non-compliance with what was now a sub-convention of wholly demystified, anti-idealistic pastoral'. Wordsworth's notions of pastoral are carefully traced, and a more general point mooted: that both Wordsworth and Coleridge retained a respect for genre labels, even while dismantling and disorganizing the generic types they nominate. Mary Wedd wrote about the 'Poems on the Naming of Places' (*ChLB* 111[2000] 132–46) with characteristic charm and knowledge; the connection with Drayton is especially well made. And, lastly among the *Lyrical Ballads*, Peter Mortensen, '"The Descent of Odin"' (*Romanticism* 6[2000] 211–33) placed 'The Danish Boy' within the context of a wider Romantic interest in Norse subjects.

The Prelude was the other main object of critical attention: after a gentle shaking of the oeuvre over the last few years, the usual suspects seem to be reassuming their places; but much of the work is very good. In *Studies in the Spectator Role: Literature, Painting, and Pedagogy*, Michael Benton discusses the interiority of landscape in *The Prelude* and explores the parallel sometimes adduced between Wordsworth and Constable. The connection between the spots of time and criminality, the strange mix of universality and individuality that characterizes them, is drawn out by John D. Morillo in the course of his study of the passions, *Uneasy Feelings: Literature, the Passions, and Class from Neoclassicism to Romanticism*. Some *Prelude* passages were adduced tellingly in Michael O'Neill's perceptive and precise '"Wholly Uncommunicable by Words": Romantic

Expressions of the Inexpressible' (*WC* 31[2000] 13–20): an irresistible choice, given O'Neill's observation that 'The inexpressible is always shading into silence' (a Wordsworthian speciality). A different kind of paradox was explored in Mark Storey's *The Problem of Poetry in the Romantic Period*, which found the poem wavering between public and private—an equivocation picked up in the work's recurrent interest in images of balance and suspension. Wordsworth frequently confesses himself bewildered in his poem, astray in its many gaps and inconsistencies; yet successfully making sense of things—which is what *The Prelude* seems committed to doing—threatens to kill them off. The poem's visionary moments were examined in a not dissimilar spirit by Joseph C. Sitterson in his *Romantic Poems, Poets and Narrators*: disputing the underlying narrative of confirming insight that critics often see in the poem, Sitterson finds Wordsworth ending the poem quite as moved by the ultimate mystery of the imagination as he was at the beginning. Coming a little closer to naming the mystery, J. Robert Barth, '"The Feeding Source": Imagination and the Transcendent in *The Prelude*' (*WC* 31[2000] 26–31) describes the 'profoundly incarnational view of the imaginative faculty' which the poem puts forward, and makes some connections between the Snowdon episode and chapter XIII of *Biographia*; while Penny Bond also scrutinizes 'The Snowdon Incident' (*ChLB* 112[2000] 183–92), comparing 1805 and 1850 versions, and hearing Wordsworth's growing unease about nature mysticism. Moving backwards through the poem, the often overlooked book VII is addressed in Philip Connell's deft and clever 'Wordsworth, Malthus, and the 1805 *Prelude*' (*EIC* 50[2000] 242–67), where it is read as an answer to the *Essay on Population*, implicitly accusing its author of granting a spurious philosophical credibility to the oppression of the poor. Wordsworth's experience of the London mass in book VII forms a first lengthy chapter in John Plotz's *The Crowd*. Amid the crowds at Bartholomew Fair (which 'precipitate a sense of permanently muddled boundaries between self and world'), you are incorrigibly closed off from your neighbour, as the exemplary encounter with the Blind Beggar implies—an episode which Plotz sees setting the trend for an entire modern literature of urban non-encounter, from Dickens to Kafka and Woolf. The crowd may seem set to shatter the poet's poise, but it is really co-opted to serve as a mark of his sureness; in Wordsworth's untroubled hands it becomes less of a threat to poetry and more of a new resource for it. The city appears less tractable in Remy Roussetzki's 'Aesthetics of Shock in Wordsworth' (*Schuylkill* 3:i[2000] 77–90), where it is contrasted more normally with the familial pleasures of the countryside. The Infant Babe of book II received two complementary readings, both disputing the popular Freudian notion of early infancy as a time of union with the mother which has underwritten so many interpretations of the passage. Nancy Easterlin, in 'Psychoanalysis and "The Discipline of Love"' (*P&L* 24[2000] 261–79) opposes that Freudian view with the findings of recent psychologists, who see the child's development as progressive from birth onward: there is no traumatic lunge into individuation, because there is never a complete sense of merger in the first place (the experimental details are most absorbing); and, as Easterlin points out, this seems actually rather closer to the conversation-like interaction that Wordsworth himself describes. Robert C. Hale's argument, in 'Wordsworth, Revision, and the Blessed Babe' (*Mosaic* 33:iii[2000] 145–63), occupies the same sort of ground, but interests itself more in the passage's revisions: the 1805 version has the mother and child in mutual relationship, but the tendency of the 1850 text is to ease the mother out of the picture and to conjure her into the impersonal form of 'Nature'. John Turner is also drawn by the Infant Babe, in 'Wordsworth and the Psychogenesis of the Sublime' (*Romanticism* 6[2000] 20–34), turning to Winnicot to complete the gaps left by a Freudian explanation; but his attention is chiefly on book I, where he finds Wordsworth's fullest account of how the sublime arises. The phenomenon is Oedipal: 'the overwhelming of the ego by the return of a repressed desire [is] the primary cause of that recurrent feeling of "moving about in worlds not realised"'; the pay-off line, a nice one, is that the recollection of such sublimity 'was Wordsworth's way of achieving some measure of insanity'. The Oedipal complex also features in Joshua Wilner's account of the boat-stealing adventure in his *Feeding on Infinity*, in the course of an account of the strange 'confessional economy' of the spots at time; in a subsequent chapter, he tackles the 'banality' (Paul de Man's word) of the passage about the Boy of Winander, attributing it to the 'phantasmal, guilty, ambivalent element of identificatory processes'.

Elsewhere in the Wordsworth canon: Richard Cronin discussed the wartime context of the 1807 *Poems, in Two Volumes*, in a chapter in his *The Politics of Romantic Poetry: In Search of the Pure Commonwealth*; the collection is a kind of contribution to the war effort, but one that eschews speaking of war as something monstrous. The language of politics for Wordsworth is important chiefly for being symbolical: 'military glory is truly valued only by one able to see "glory in the flower"'. Cronin has an interesting page or two on *The Convention of Cintra*; it also features in a section in Morillo's *Uneasy Feelings*, where the passions play a troubled role, at once establishing and undermining national cohesiveness. Joseph Sitterson (in *Romantic Poems, Poets, and Narrators*) read 'There was a time' in the context of a tradition of odes, and found Wordsworth exploiting the genre's special potential for 'an important kind of incoherence, a deliberate lack of closure': this is turned to Wordsworthian advantage, as the poem concedes the value of growing up while simultaneously lamenting just that process. *Laodamia* found itself in an unusual prominence in Martin Greenberg's account of 'Hazlitt and Wordsworth: The Language of Poetry' (*NewC* 18:vi[2000] 10–22); Greenberg evidently sympathizes with Hazlitt's mixed feelings about Wordsworth's plain modern style, which 'hadn't the glory of the poetry of the past' and lacked 'the proud full sail of English verse'. *Laodamia* appears here as Wordsworth's last stab at writing 'poetry in the old style, by the subverter of the old style'—a forlorn attempt, needless to say, and an especially sad spectacle from our vantage point, 'an age of prose' in which all poets are 'Wordsworthians whether they like it or not'. Less melancholically, a poem from the 1820 tour, 'The Source of the Danube', was compared with Hölderlin in Rudolf Schier's 'Die Donau als Paradigma der Kreativität bei Wordsworth und Hölderlin' (*JEGP* 99[2000] 157–69): Hölderlin's poem ends with a turn towards painful realities that Wordsworth's evades. And 'A Jewish Family', written about an encounter on the 1828 tour, is discussed in Judith Page, '"Nor yet redeemed from scorn": Wordsworth and the Jews' (*JEGP* 99[2000] 537–54): Wordsworth's poem, which denies the Jews 'their particular identities and historical grounding', is contrasted unfavourably with his daughter Dora's journal entry, which apparently attempts 'to humanize the family and to see them as individuals'; pursuing the point, Page considers Wordsworth's earlier translation of Chaucer's *Prioress's Tale* and his 'Song for the Wandering Jew'. (So, was Wordsworth anti-Semitic? The answer, thankfully, is 'not cut and dried'.)

Coleridge drew a little less criticism than Wordsworth, as usual. David Vallins's *Coleridge and the Psychology of Romanticism: Feeling and Thought* resourcefully explored the interpenetration of 'feeling' and 'thought' in Coleridge, relating them to his lifelong compulsion to establish unities. Vallins himself is more interested in finding unifying elements than in spotting epochal changes of heart, and he sets out against the usual current to argue (with much plausibility) for the important *kinship* of Coleridge's early Hartleianism and Priestleianism and his later Schellingian enthusiasms—a kinship, at least, in those respects that most drew Coleridge. Vallins is as interested in the metaphors for thought as in the thought itself, and writes well about the habitual tropes of ascent in Coleridge's writing (a subject he tackles too in 'Akenside, Coleridge and the Pleasures of Transcendence', in Dix, ed., *Mark Akenside: A Reassessment*). The double role of feeling in Coleridgean thinking is nicely set out—at once the suffering from which he flees, and the intuition which he rationalizes—and the centrality of feeling to his metaphysical enquiries is surely proven: the oddity that Coleridge's emphasis here could gain sanction from the arch-villain Hume is not lost on Vallins, and might suggest a fruitful line of futher enquiry. (A.D. Nuttall suggestively addressed the question in his *A Common Sky*, but the place of Hume in Romantic thought has more usually been taken at its face value: he is the enemy to be vanquished.) Vallins is dealing with some complicated matters here, but does so with great clarity and patience, and his phrases often catch perceptions like fish in a golden net: 'Monism and dualism had to coexist; and though they could not do so, this repeated dialectical turning and re-turning makes the closest possible approximation to their simultaneity.' Kiyoshi Tsuchiya's *The Mirror Metaphor and Coleridge's Mysticism: Poetics, Metaphysics and the Formation of the Pentad* travels widely too, from the early poems to *Aids to Reflection*, with a slightly unsure stylistic hand ('At this point Coleridge makes a peculiar decision, of which his attachment to the Romantic poetics seems to be the only possible explanation'), and a somewhat wandering focus (the mirror disappears for pages at a time); Tsuchiya is rather better at the mysteries of the prose than he is on the poetry, where the commentary tends to steady paraphrase.

Coleridge's diverse political opinions were well discussed. The politics of the 1790s were reconsidered in a subtle piece of historical scholarship by Kaz Oishi, 'Coleridge's Philanthropy' (*ColB* 15[2000] 56–70): Coleridge's emphasis on preaching the gospel to the poor sets him somewhat apart from mainstream Unitarian radicalism, and his definition of philanthropy turns out to be 'less radical than it is alleged to be', particularly on the matter of alms-giving, of which Unitarian radicals tended to disapprove. Timothy Webb pieced together Coleridge's ambivalent response to the Irish rebel Emmet in 'Coleridge and Robert Emmet: Reading the Text of Irish Revolution' (*ISR* 8[2000] 303–24). Coleridge thought very sympathetically of him, while also considering him a visionary lunatic, mixed feelings that corresponded fairly closely to his attitude towards his own radical youth; and the pattern of identification and self-defence that emerges in his writings about Emmet is nicely drawn. (Coleridge thought so well of Emmet's reported hostility to the French that he confidently announced the Irishman on the edge of being an Englishman.) In a spry and learned piece, Michael John Kooy, 'Coleridge's Francophobia' (*MLR* 95[2000] 924–41) also returned to Coleridge's Jacobin youth to find the origins of his notorious opinions of all things French: the crunch really came in 1803 when the threat of invasion was pressing, and the delicate distinction between Napoleon and France that previously existed in Coleridge's writing then dissolves. From this point on, Francophobia becomes a fixture in his politics, sometimes a source of exuberant grotesquerie, but in one way at least genuinely productive in helping along Coleridge's organicist notions of the state. Kooy ends with the pleasantly subversive thought that this actually puts him squarely in the company of many contemporary French thinkers. Peter Kitson offers a good account of his attitude towards Cromwell, which turns out to be 'ambiguous', less of a surprise I suppose than strident univocality would be, but the detail is absorbing: Coleridge's late attraction to the idea of Cromwell as king of a 'republican Kingdom' is intriguing, for instance, and Kitson may well be right to suspect more Commonwealth ideals stirring in *Church and State* than we have been used to thinking. Susan Weaver, in 'Political Subversiveness under a Cloak of Philosophy' (*PAPA* 26[2000] 49–62), would go rather further, maintaining that, far from being 'a traitor to the revolution and its democratic ideals', the sage of Highgate was really engaged in 'a devious form of doublespeak in which [he] covertly disseminates a radical message in the midst of apparently conservative propoganda': 'covert' would be the word. That Coleridge does not deplore all constitutional change in principle hardly means he is not a conservative (let alone that he remained a supporter of the revolution in France): the meaning of 'conservatism' seems often to be getting lost in such discussions. A rather more nuanced account of Coleridge's view of history formed part of Christopher Parker's *The English Idea of History from Coleridge to Collingwood*, which traces back the English idealist school to Coleridge's 'revolt against empiricism' and against Hume's *History* in particular.

Of other prose works, *Biographia Literaria* featured with characteristic prominence. J. Robert Barth, 'The *Biographia Literaria* as Conversation Poem' (*ColB* 16[2000] 1–4), floated the idea that we see the prose work wandering with the secret purposefulness of 'Frost at Midnight' or 'This Lime-Tree Bower', moving from childhood, through a discovery of the presence of God in nature (albeit in the form of a recollected philosophical progress), and ending with a blessing (here, a blessing upon Wordsworth). The crescendo in the prose-poem is the passage about Imagination at the end of volume I, which Len Epp returned to examine in 'Coleridge and the Non-Empirical Imagination' (*ColB* 16[2000] 40–8), disagreeing with commentators who are secretly informed by 'an empirical spirit' (these include Shawcross, McFarland and Engell, so the disagreement is not trivial). Far from offering an empirical portrait of the mind, Coleridge was describing 'a fundamentally active, productive mode of engagement with a world which is always already meaningful in so far as it is experienced consciously': in other words, what must be for the mind to begin its empirical life in the first place. Michael G. Miller, 'Modern Neuroscience and Coleridge's Theory of the Imagination' (*ERR* 11[2000] 197–205) took up the famous definitions in a very different spirit, recasting Coleridge in the materialist terms of Neuronal Group Selection (or 'neural Darwinism'): Coleridgean imagination assumes the new form of 're-entry', the simultaneous and interrelated organization of neuronal activity that constitutes the basis for perceptual categorization. (Miller speculates that the visionary gleam fades your as neuronal groups, long unactivated, dwindle away, which doesn't make it sound any less dispiriting.) Kathryn Kimball, 'Coleridge's Dream Theory and the

Dual Imagination' (*ColB* 16[2000] 80–6) also makes a connection between Coleridge's speculations about 'the oppositional yet interdependent operations of the night/day imagination' and discoveries of modern neuroscience: the necessary ordering function of the imagination during the day is what is also in play, in its different arena, in the dream-making brain when asleep. And on the subject of the mind's synthesizing powers, Angela Esterhammer takes up the subject of 'commanding genius', introduced by Coleridge in chapter II of *Biographia*, and often deplored by commentators as tyrannical; but Esterhammer mounts a defence: what commanding genius does is actually 'structurally parallel' to the two-stage business of synthesizing intuitions and 'then testing their viability in the real world'.

Coleridge's metaphysics gathered some interesting commentary. Anthony John Harding, in a typically lucid and scrupulous piece, 'Coleridge, Natural History, and the "Analogy of Being"' (*HEI* 26[2000] 143–58) pondered the place of nature in Coleridge's later thought, especially the link he tried to make out between the natural history from which mankind emerged, the actualization of that potential only inherent in more primitive forms of life, and the moral history which seeks to explain mankind's progress towards the full restoration of that actualization, a perfection from which man has fallen away. The aspiration to strive towards that lost perfection is not nature's own, but evidence of her response to a divine impulse from without: the Will is not hers, but she 'could not be conceived if the Will were not and had not been'. It is possible to see, in these late labyrinthine investigations, the descendants of those unresolved feelings about the place of nature in the religious life that had troubled (and inspired) Coleridge from the earliest days. Nature and religion appear in ennobling association, for example, in J. Robert Barth's '"Mortal Beauty": Ignatius Loyola, Samuel Taylor Coleridge, and the Role of Imagination in Religious Experience' (*C&L* 50[2000] 69–78): 'God lives and acts through the created world—distinct from it, to be sure, but not separate from it', an understanding that Barth sees Coleridge sharing with Loyola; but another side of Coleridge, a more Platonic Coleridge let's say, would probably demur even at that. His Platonic credentials—his revolt against 'the tyranny of the visible' and against empiricism—feature in Melissa Lane's enjoyable history of *Plato's Progeny*; and Ronald C. Wendling sets them out at greater length 'Coleridge's Critical Sympathy with Plato' (*ColB* 16[2000] 115–22), nicely identifying the awkwardness Coleridge inevitably felt in admitting to such an enthusiasm in so unsympathetic an age. (Wendling has an excellent phrase here: 'Coleridge always had an ironic regard for the resistance matter places on our aspirations to transcend it.') English Platonism and Coleridge's German enthusiasms come together in a scholarly piece by Douglas Hedley, 'Cudworth, Coleridge and Schelling' (*ColB* 16[2000] 63–70): Hedley has tracked down a passage in an early Schelling work, a *History of Gnosticism*, which mentions Cudworth. The broader point at issue is that, if both Coleridge and Schelling were independently influenced by Cudworth, Coleridge's protestations that he met Schelling's work with a sense of 'genial coincidence' is not as disingenuous as Wellek (for instance) thinks it is. Hedley's article accompanies his big book about *Aids to Reflection, Coleridge, Philosophy and Religion*, a great, generous, baggy thing, which stretches back through the history of Coleridge's religious opinions to contextualize the Platonic Trinitarianism characterizing his later pronouncements. As with Vallins's book, the continuities seem more important than the revolutions: the dominant thesis is that the Cambridge Platonists prepared the way for the post-Kantians to make an effortless landing; but within this structure an immense variety finds a home. The tone is often trenchant ('We totally misunderstand the underlying controversy if ... '), and sometimes boisterous in its defence of Coleridge's theological respectability, which is attractive. Hedley is a theologian, and his account of Paley, and Coleridge's case against, will be especially useful and clear for literary types; the discussion of the doctrine of salvation also; and the pages on Jeremy Taylor, an important and ambiguous Coleridgean hero, are most interesting. Among the other later works, *Confessions of an Inquiring Spirit* is discussed by E.S. Shaffer (*RoN* 17[2000]) in the course of a bracing essay which takes issue with the Bollingen edition's handling of the essay: 'a noteworthy and damaging piece of editorial sleight-of-hand', she says. The innovation of Coleridge's thought has been obscured by a 'religious ideology from his own time to this' which refuses to concede that he thought of Christianity as a 'mythology', and a 'nationalist ideology' has refused properly to acknowledge the impact of the German Enlightenment on him; Shaffer ends by offering a parallel between Coleridge and Humboldt. (And, while on Coleridge's reading, David Baluch teases apart the significance of his two epistolary responses to Blake's *Songs of Innocence and Experience* in 'Reading Coleridge Reading Blake' (*ColB* 16[2000] 5–14): as elsewhere, so much depends on who it is Coleridge is talking to.) Lastly among the prose works, Anthony John Harding, who is currently editing the last volume of the *Notebooks*, describes 'The Case for a Material Hermeneutics of Literature' (*Romanticism* 6[2000] 1–19), one that takes its bearing from Szondi (not Gadamer), and approaches the notebooks aware of 'the material nature of the notebook as a form, and, not incidentally, the material relationship of the manuscript to the printed version': that way, we may catch 'a subjectivity momentarily realized (rather than revealed)' in readings that recognize 'the contingent and contextual as much as ... the personal and individual'. Which, in a different way, is what Nichola Deane does in 'Response to Crisis in Coleridge's Letters' (*ColB* 16[2000] 24–30): the contexts here are not only biographical, but also generic, as Coleridge establishes his manner as a correspondent by breaking all the rules about writing a proper letter.

Finally, the poems. Paul Magnuson's piece on 'Coleridge's Discursive "Monody on the Death of Chatterton"' (*RoN* 17[2000]) worried at the idea of historical origin: the poem's initial circumstances of composition might make it one kind of text, but its published appearance, with an accompanying note, establish the 'Monody' as 'one utterance among many, one voice in the discourse over Chatterton's memory; the place of literature in society; and the problems of class, the established church, morality, money, and patronage'—a 'paratextual complexity' rather than the historical 'moment' envisaged by an unsupple brand of historicism. 'Religious Musings' was returned to its desultory occasions in a chapter in Richard Cronin's *The Politics of Romantic Poetry*: it is a poem that certainly evades any historical 'moment' because it took sixteen months to get written, and Cronin writes sharply about the way that history translates into the poem's wandering sense of audience and uncertain feeling of authorship (sage or journalist?). Coleridge's early poems were scrutinized by Mark Storey in *The Problem of Poetry in the Romantic Period*, who found in them a stifling sense of insufficiency—a 'panic and emptiness', partly created by Coleridge's fear of rivalling God, which induces (for instance) 'something rather desperate' in the 'Monody'. Also among the earlier poems, 'Coleridge, Female Friendship and "Lines written at Shurton Bars"' (*ColB* 16[2000]

1–15) were delightfully described in an essay by Reggie Watters, which ingeniously but self-deprecatingly finds traces of Coleridge's rival desires for sisterhood and male society in the rival tugs of the poem's form. My own piece, 'Coleridge's Millennial Embarrassments' (*EIC* 50[2000] 1–22) tried to make some connections between the formal oddities of Coleridge's poems in the 1790s and his sense of an epoch. George Erving traced 'The Breakdown of Moral Order in *Osorioi*' (*ColB* 16[2000] 49–55), and linked its threatened fratricide to *The Ancient Mariner*.

The famous poem itself features in James McKusick's *Green Writing*, as a 'parable of ecological transgression': ecology is not only the poem's theme though, but also (in a manner of speaking) its medium, as the recuperated archaisms of its language lexically enact the key conservatory principle of 'diversity'. (There is an elegant spin on the idea of organicism here too: 'the inner form of an aesthetic object (whether it is regarded as a well-wrought urn or a self-consuming artefact) is less significant than its relation to the linguistic and cultural environment that surrounds and nourishes it'.) Joseph Sitterson (in *Romantic Poems, Poets, and Narrators*) worries fruitfully about the status of the poem's marginal gloss, which he sees as the work of a dramatized persona: the device emphasizes the whole question of interpretation, and, in turn, confirms our sense that the Mariner's moral at the end of the poem is simply inadequate. The poem then becomes a study in the difficulty of making sense, something which we might see characterizing the history of its interpretation too. No such interpretative scruples trouble Mark S. Lussier in his *Romantic Dynamics*, who boldly places *The Ancient Mariner* between science and literature, drawn by the game of dice at the poem's centre (what Einstein said God didn't play) into describing a quantum Coleridgean universe: 'a deterministic, Newtonian view of spacetime as discrete absolutes break down in a uni-verse that is actually a multi-verse of potentiality'. But, oddly, this abandonment of cause and effect frees the poem into its own uninterpretable space once again, ever eluding 'classical determinacy'. Among the other supernatural poems, 'Kubla Khan' earned a book from Robert F. Fleissner, *Sources, Meaning, and Influences in Coleridge's 'Kubla Khan'* for aficionados to delve in, a gathering of notes and essays from several years that plumb such Coleridgean questions as 'Did the Spelling X-A-N-A-D-U Originate with *Xaindu*, or rather with *Xamdu*?' and 'From Tartary to Abyssinia in "Kubla Khan": Geographical Chasm or Explicable Shift?'; along the way, it suggests the influence of *The Tempest*, *A Midsummer Night's Dream* and *Tom Jones* upon the poem, traces passages from Forster, Tennyson and Poe back to Xanadu, and speculates at length about its 'modern pertinence'. Fleissner includes in that section a discussion of Orson Welles's treatment of 'Kubla Khan', which is where Alex J. Dick starts in 'Citizen Kane' (*ColB* 16[2000] 31–9), finding in the film 'a pertinent and correct interpretation of Coleridge's insight's into the problematic relation between economic reality and philosophical consciousness'—a problem which resolves to alternatively symbolical or allegorical modes of economy. Peter Knox-Shaw spots some likely traces of Young's *Night Thoughts* in 'Kubla Khan' in 'Edward Young in "Kubla Khan"' (*N&Q* 47[2000] 323–5). The relevance of mistletoe imagery to Geraldine's character in 'Christabel' is spelt out by Susan Parry (*Expl* 58:iii[2000] 133–5); R.K. Raval, 'Light as a Romantic Positive in Wordsworth and Coleridge' (*ColB* 16[2000] 93–102), contrasts the moonlit world of part I of the poem and the 'sun-dominated' atmosphere of part II; and Lou

Thompson discusses 'Liminality, Communitas and Patriarchy' in the poem (*ColB* 16[2000] 109–14), drawing usefully on the anthropology of Victor Turner.

Peter Barry in 'Coleridge the Revisionary: Surrogacy and Structure in the Conversation Poems' (*RES* 51[2000] 600–16) sought to refresh our eyes for the conversation poems by analysing their four-part narrative structure (locatory prelude, transposition, self-reproof and resolution), and identifying in addition a silent surrogate whose subjectivity is 'invaded or appropriated': this seems to me very true, and Barry's point about Coleridge's 'perennial dissatisfaction with himself' is sharp. Elsewhere, Martin Wallen in 'Coleridge's Scrofulous Dejection' (*JEGP* 99[2000] 555–75) places 'Dejection' in the context of Coleridge's interest in scrofula that the poet learnt about from Beddoes, a 'non-specific illness' upon which he 'strategically transfers the symptoms of addiction': the poem effects an odd kind of cure by allowing Coleridge 'to adopt the persona of the man who has painfully sacrificed his poetic youth in order to write mature prose works critically delineating the poetic process'. And lastly, from outside the usual canon, Rick Hocks discusses 'Constancy to an Ideal Object' in '"And art thou Nothing?"' (*ColB* 16[2000] 71–9), a poem whose chief image manages to symbolize the Coleridgean symbol while symbolizing at the same time its purely illusory status.

Finally, some studies in influence that I should briefly notice. John L. Mahoney's *Wordsworth and the Critics: The Development of a Critical Reputation* told the story of Wordsworth's critical reputation from the contemporary reviewers through modern critics such as Weiskel, Magnuson, and Bromwich (who appears here as 'Bromwitch'): Mahoney is a clear-headed and friendly guide, who takes us through an immense reading list, keeping an eye on critical trends and institutional practices, so there is material here for historians of the discipline as well as Wordsworthians. John Beer, 'Coleridge's "Eolian Harp": A Keatsian Echo?' (*N&Q* 47[2000] 321–2) heard a line of Coleridge's effusion in 'Sleep and Poetry': Keats would have had to see the lines before publication, but Beer speculates fruitfully about how that might have happened. On a larger scale, Daniel Sanjiv Roberts dedicated a lively book, *Revisionary Gleam: De Quincey, Coleridge and the High Romantic Argument*, to De Quincey and Coleridge: an encompassing and well-researched study in affinity, in which Wordsworth recurs as a difficult, towering third figure, admired and resented by turn. The account of De Quincey's Coleridgean criticism of Wordsworth is particularly astute. Coleridge's critical reputation in the pages of *Fraser's* is singled out in an essay by Robert Lapp, 'Romanticism Repackaged' (*ERR* 11[2000] 235–47): Maginn was putting the figure of Coleridge to ideological use in a time of threatened reform, creating the kind of Tory he needed. Coleridge features alongside Carlyle in Herbert Schlossberg's *The Silent Revolution and the Making of Victorian England* as a prophet against materialism. Elsewhere, David Vallins (in Eberle-Sinatra, ed., *Mary Shelley's Fictions: From 'Frankenstein' to Falkner*) finds traces of the Lake Poets in Mary Shelley's novel *Lodore*; Peter Manning's 'Hermits and Monks: The Romantic Century 1750–1850' (*ERR* 11[2000] 25–30) tracks a deepening gloom from Romantic solitude to Victorian isolation; Greg Garrard finds 'Two Versions of Pastoral' in Wordsworth and Thoreau (in Schneider, ed., *Thoreau's Sense of Place: Essays in American Environmental Writing*), Thoreau's being the more properly environmental because most like georgic; and Joseph H. Gardner, 'Emerson, Coleridge and a Phantom Quotation' (*ANQ* 13:ii[2000] 32–5), de-attributes an unidentified Coleridgean quotation. R.S. Edgecombe tracks Faber 'From Wordsworth to Crashaw' (*ES* 81[2000] 472–83), a poetic passage that Faber felt obliged to make because of Wordsworth's disappointing attitude to Tractarianism; Michael Eberle-Sinatra (*ColB* 16[2000] 103–8) saw some things in common between *The Ancient Mariner* and *The Flying Dutchman* (there seems no question of influence); and Sharon Smulders's 'Looking "Past Wordsworth and the Rest"' (*VP* 38[2000] 35–48) describes Alice Meynell escaping the 'rigors of genre' she had inherited from the male Romantics. Among the most distinguished accounts of literary influence was Richard Gravil's immensely accomplished study of Anglo-American continuities, *Romantic Dialogues: Anglo-American Continuities, 1776–1862*, which contained spirited and illuminating comparisons of *Moby-Dick* and *The Ancient Mariner*, and *The Prelude* and *Leaves of Grass*; there are also some fine pages entwining Tennyson, the Lucy poems, and Emily Dickinson's lyrics. Matthew Gibson's thorough and interesting monograph on *Yeats, Coleridge and the Romantic Sage* finds a perhaps surprising degree of indebtedness: Coleridge becomes an important source for Yeats's esoteric thought in the 1930s (Gibson does not spare the Yeatsian technicalities), but is also an influence on some of the poems, such as 'Long-Legged Fly' (the water-insect from *Biographia*); there are some promising pages on Coleridgean mirror metaphors. Among the more recent moderns, Wordsworth and Elizabeth Bishop are brought together briefly in Marjorie Levinson's contribution to Butler, Guillory and Thomas, eds., *What's Left of Theory?*, a volume of essays from the English Institute: Bishop's 'In the Waiting Room' avoids the recuperative transformation of victim into empowered subject that characterizes Wordsworthian lyric. Meg Schoerke discusses Muriel Rukeyser's Coleridgean inheritance in '"Forever Broken and Made": Muriel Rukeyser's Theory of Form' (in Herzog and Kaufman, eds., *'How shall we tell each other of the poet?' The Life and Writing of Muriel Rukeyser*); and Willard Spiegelman, 'Wallace Stevens' "Second Selves"' (*WSJour* 24:ii[2000] 176–86) finds in James Longenbach and John Koethe two poets who have 'crossed Stevens the metaphysician with Wordsworth the autobiographer'. Kathleen O'Brien describes Coleridge's contribution to the modern teaching of rhetoric (*RSQ* 30[2000] 77–91). Perhaps (as is often said) Wordsworth's most striking bequest to later generations is an idea of the Lake District, and Jamie James wrote about his stay there appreciatively in 'Wordsworth Slept Here' (*The Atlantic* June[2000] 32–9); the West Country has its pilgrims too, and they can now follow the route around Nether Stowey described in Roger Evans's *Somerset in the Footsteps of Coleridge and Wordsworth*.

7. Women Romantic Poets

An ever-expanding field, women's Romantic poetry is becoming increasingly significant to scholars. Anne K. Mellor has long been a leading voice in the establishment of this area and her monograph, *Mothers of the Nation: Women's Political Writing in England, 1780–1830*, appears this year. She begins by dismantling the Habermasian public sphere as conceptually limited and historically incorrect. Where Habermas excludes women and unpropertied workers, Mellor claims that women fully participated in the public sphere, openly publishing their opinions on a range of topics from the 'French Revolution and the abolitionist campaigns against the slave trade through doctrinal religious issues and methods of education to the economic management both of the individual household and the state'. These views were circulated both through print culture—newspapers, journals, books and so on—and also through the public forums of debating societies and the theatre, impacting on the social movements, economic relationships and state-regulated policies of the day. The sphere women occupied, then, was not a counter-sphere but the same public space in which their male peers resided, the bulk of their literary production supporting Mellor's claim. As she declares, by 1830 over 500 living women writers had authored at least one published and reviewed novel, and their participation in debating societies was striking, with the political views of female orators widely disseminated. Acknowledging the masculinist impulse to silence such speakers, Mellor suggests that such discursive productions existed in open dialogue with women's published arguments, which contested, qualified and sometimes endorsed them. The consequence of Mellor's argument here is crucial: if women occupied the public sphere in the manner the study suggests, then the notion of a realm of private, exclusively female activities in the period is erroneous. Discarding this binary concept of separate sexual spheres is a profound manoeuvre, and frees Mellor to read the participation of women in the public sphere of discourse as an assertion of their right and duty to 'speak *for* the nation'. She roots this assertion in the tradition of the seventeenth-century female preacher, dissenting and Quaker prophets who identified themselves as the voice of female virtue and invoked biblical precedents such as Deborah, Queen Esther and Judith to sustain their authority. Romantic women writers, Mellor argues, translated this religious authority into a secular literary command, speaking on behalf of 'right feeling' and 'true sensibility' rather than Christian morality.

Most important for readers of this section is Mellor's chapter on women's political poetry. Here she suggests that Victorian definitions of 'Hemans, Landon and their female peers as "poetesses"', a feminized and domesticated identity, excludes the tradition of 'the female poet', an 'explicitly political' role situated within the public sphere. The latter tradition is rooted in the 'writings of the female preachers and prophets who embraced seventeenth-century Quaker theology' and shown to have granted women a 'scriptural authority for the right' to 'speak in public'. Such authority was rooted in a sense of female virtue and moral rectitude distinctly opposed to a hierarchical Anglicanism, and those women who claimed it openly valued compassion for others and spiritual liberty above 'male' values of war and materialism. While Mellor concedes the apparently didactic motives of such women, she convincingly illustrates their inauguration of an 'explicitly *feminist* poetry', examples of which include More's 'Slavery', Charlotte Smith's *The Emigrants*, Helen Maria Williams's *Peru* and Lucy Aikin's *Epistles on Women*. Mellor illustrates how these poems addressed issues of class, slavery, imperialism and gender oppression to forge an intellectual and revolutionary agenda that reveals women's centrality to the public sphere. Barbauld's *Eighteen Hundred and Eleven* is of special note within the discussion, a poem which daringly questioned Britain's commitment to war with France through a call for pacifism in the face of an increasing national militarism. A sweeping apocalyptic prophecy foretelling the doom of the nation, the poem situates Barbauld as a Volneyesque commentator on politics and culture. Many of the readings offered here appear now to be almost conventional in current literary criticism, and yet as an initiator of such views Mellor must claim a central place in the development of the study of women's Romantic poetry. This book is a coherent and intelligible introduction to this field.

Jacqueline M. Labbe's lively *The Romantic Paradox: Love, Violence and the Uses of Romance, 1760–1830* devotes a good degree of time to women's poetry, setting Mary Robinson, Felicia Hemans and Laetitia Elizabeth Landon along side Coleridge, Keats and Byron. This engaging study seeks to reclaim the idea of romance within Romanticism, the former infiltrating the period in the form of the romance novel, love lyrics, sensibility and the still undervalued Della Cruscan movement. For Labbe, however, the 'Romantic romance' dispenses with the banality of 'happy endings' to utilize the distress of its players, the hero and heroine alike doomed to search for the intangible within the strictures of increasingly fluid and complex gender positions. The social construction of sexualized behaviour is elevated as vital to the concept of Romantic romance here, gender becoming the pivot around which romance plots are woven, challenged and recast. Contextualizing the rise of the romance through the Romantic obsession with violence, war and death, Labbe asserts the popularity of a genre that at once 'promised the maintenance of certainties' even as it relied on a form of violence that rendered Romantic texts 'documents of cultural unease'. Incursions into competing genres, ballads, the novel, the Gothic, showed romance to be a kind of hybrid form able to operate on multiple levels and thus leak into Romanticism even where it is disavowed. Where writers such as Wordsworth and Walter Scott use romance, Labbe illustrates, the form is radically altered through a violent exploration of the dark side of Romanticism, loneliness, dread and lovelorn desolation. This instates certain changes within the romance, its violent tone indirect and metaphorical in the 1780s and 1790s, but becoming immediate and 'real' from 1810 to the 1820s. For Labbe, the strong presence and speakability of violence in this later literature signals a receptivity to it that urged its creators to increase the dose to enforce the thrill, encouraging violent emotions that constituted both a powerful strength and a danger. Mapping the history of the romance revival, the study analyses those tracts that defined and placed the 'new romance' in the late eighteenth century as a chivalrous and fantastic genre. Chivalry, apparently a benign and gracious act, is given a darker side here, its values imposing an order, repression and restriction that shadows its knightly aspect. Labbe shows how the myth of order is undermined by an inability to maintain such order, overridden by a society increasingly aware of the gender issues hidden within the 'flowery language' of romance.

Such language was further exploited by the Della Cruscan poets, who approached romance with a veiled eroticism and brutality that had a forceful and enduring influence over its female readership. Creating a poetry of sexual love and continually sparked desire, the Della Cruscans ambiguously skirted issues of propriety and social order, invoking a style equally 'genuine and artificial, structured and spontaneous'. Passion is invoked, then, but the formulaic manner in which it is represented defuses its strength as 'emotional violence is countered with poetic precision'. Labbe's discussion of the personal romance constructed by Coleridge in his 'conversation poems' and Keats's 1820 romances focuses on the questing hero as a victim of violence or obscurity. Neither poet is able to resolve the poetic persona of his heroes, thus betraying the heroic Romantic subject as a flawed ideal. Women poets come to dominate the study from chapter 4, wherein Robinson and Hemans appear as writers intent on centralizing love even as they are uncomfortable with its 'happy ever after' connotations. Robinson's romances are notably marked by the Gothic, Labbe argues, horrific dreams, narrative delay and unexplained phenomena exploding the emotionally charged love-relationships within. Invoking while disarming such Gothicism, Robinson ends her romances by denying the problems inherent in their violence and thus 'constitutes another form of violence: structural damage' to a text 'dependent for its force on burst after burst of sensationalism'. An air of failure and despondency infuses Hemans's work, however: reality poeticized as an experience of loss and destruction. *Records of Woman*, for example, reveals the collapse of romance by entreating the reader to return to the maternal home and avoid the trappings of a love that, for Hemans, is always inseparable from death. Landon occupies the final chapter, alongside a homosocially constructed Byron, both attempting to rewrite romance as melodrama and taking advantage of its extremities as a way of exploring romantic relations. Like Hemans, Landon peppers her romantic poetry with distrust and disillusion, dramatizing the dark excesses of love on the female body and releasing the violence of hatred apparently chivalrous lovers sometimes feel. Labbe reads 'The Venetian Bracelet' as an instance of this pattern, the theme of destructive heterosexuality foregrounded as Landon contrasts the ravages of consuming violent emotion with its murderous outward expression. Essentially, the study revisits the overwrought manner of this kind of melodrama and romance in order to establish its creators as conscious writers, drawn to love and violence as a way of approaching and understanding culture. Romantic romance finally dies out because of such consciousness, recoded into the 'familiar stagebound theatrical experience' of the Victorian period wherein the gush of the romantic genre is gradually condemned and rejected.

Lucy Newlyn's long-awaited *Reading, Writing and Romanticism: The Anxiety of Reception* also appeared this year, containing a valuable chapter on Barbauld and further readings of More, Robinson, Hemans and Landon. Newlyn courageously tackles the status of subjectivity in the period, asking how writers and readers imagined each other in the processes of communicating and understanding. The equivocal nature of the relationship between a writer and his or her audience becomes marked during the age of criticism, which Coleridge imagined as 'a World of Readers' deeply invested in reading practices and the act of interpretation. Writers could no longer construct an authentic identity from the past because of the now precarious authority of history and rise of interpretative freedoms: the power of the subject was politically and philosophically desirable, Newlyn argues, but contentious. The Bloomian anxiety of influence is thus refigured as an anxiety of reception, one which takes account of the duality of the writing-reading subject who both depends materially upon readers and writes to engage with others whose sympathies he or she hopes to arouse. Newlyn is interested here in the way in which readers are important to writers as rivalrous precursors, rendering them apprehensive that their work will be for ever open to reconstruction. The anxiety she invokes, then, is a kind of schizoid condition both psychological and phenomenological, pointing to the feeling of usurpation writers experience as an attack on the integrity of the subject. The study is focused primarily on the literary manifestations of this condition and what these might tell us about the processes of reading and writing. Newlyn's concern with authorial anxiety is specifically turned on the threatened status of poetry as it dealt with the challenges posed by the rise of the reading public. As more potential readers of literature arose, it was feared that fewer and fewer were qualified to understand what they were reading, while the literary experts were perceived as threatening. Reviewers were demonized as readers were dismissed, Newlyn argues, leading to the widespread hostility of authors towards their readerships and to the dismay of the defenders of high culture. Tracing the circumstances which exacerbated authorial anxiety in the late eighteenth and the nineteenth centuries, the study maps out print culture by assessing the status of the review, essay and periodical as well as turning to the complex debate of ownership claims and copyright law.

From this discussion emerge three case studies, Barbauld being the third after Coleridge and Wordsworth. Newlyn begins by demonstrating Barbauld's use of the coterie audience as a source of sympathy, a technique which protects the poet from critics by undermining the poet's own creative efforts. Linked to this are Barbauld's various modes of address, marked by confidence and versatility, and acutely sensitive to audience expectation. A writer of lyrics, songs, epitaphs, hymns, odes, eclogues, riddles, inscriptions, prologues, mock-epic, blank verse, satire, allegories, essays, fables, children's books, sermons and political pamphlets, she carefully shaped these media to forge a dialogue with her readers. This dialogue was at once intimate and familial, Barbauld's initial readers being an internal circle at Warrington, and intellectually profound, adopting a local and quotidian poetic drawn from the language and culture of dissent. Shifting between domestic and political topics, Barbauld conducted such intellectual debate as though engaging in polite conversation, Newlyn shows, enabling her to successfully mediate different spheres of reception. Barbauld is especially innovative in her forays into male territory, challenging preconceptions about gender and genre through her occasional verse, dialogic verse addressed to Priestley and imitative essays. While not a feminist in the manner in which contemporary feminism perceives Wollstonecraft, the poet is constructed here as being engaged in a larger debate about the importance of 'feminine' attributes, which she believed were in danger of being underrated by 'masculine' women. Ending with an arresting discussion of the reception of the infamous *Eighteen Hundred and Eleven*, Newlyn's is an innovative commentary on Barbauld.

Newlyn also turns to the broader question of the anxiety of authorship with regard to women writers, astutely separating a genuine anxiety of reception with a culturally induced rhetoric of self-deprecation. Gestures of complicity and resistance in the construction of a feminized poetic identity are connected here with conduct-book ideology where the female writer-reader role was carefully prescribed. Launching a new form of vigorous critical dialogue with dominant authoritative discourses, women such as Barbauld, Radcliffe and Robinson, and later Hemans, Landon and Jewsbury, are shown to engage with a spectrum of political inflections and nuances in relation to patriarchal ideology. In so doing, the study evinces, women writers cogently exemplify the tenacious adaptability of Romanticism, opening it out to readers of various political persuasions, 'including women readers who were far from servile in their theories and practices of echoic reading'. The shift in literary power relations such actions invoked contributed to a wider change in the relationship between men and women, revising not only the nature of Romantic poetics but also definitions of late eighteenth- and early nineteenth-century gender.

Vivien Jones' edited collection, *Women and Literature in Britain, 1700–1800*, contains four essays central to the subject of this section, her own introduction surveying the wide-ranging and diverse nature of women's roles within eighteenth-century print culture. Like Mellor, Jones is intent on underlining the Enlightenment's opening up of the public sphere to women. Harriet Guest's 'Eighteenth-Century Femininity: "A supposed sexual character"' (pp. 46–68) directly addresses this debate through the notion of 'femininity' itself, a mutable and fashionable identity rejected by women such as Wollstonecraft, who contrasted it with an independent and virtuous subject position. Guest brilliantly considers the historical and cultural discourses of the feminine in which representations of femininity are embedded through the work of Barbauld, famously accused by Wollstonecraft of adopting a masquerade of femininity. Margaret Anne Doody's 'Women Poets of the Eighteenth Century' (pp. 217–37) focuses on both the new dominance of women's writing in print and the many poems left in manuscript, arguing that the study of women's poetry has yet to be fully integrated with the study of poetry in general. Her overview of this era looks at verse by Katherine Philips, Anne Finch, Elizabeth Singer Rowe and Mary Leapor before turning to more Romantic poets such as Barbauld, Anna Seward and Ann Yearsley. Closing with a discussion of the trope of the fairy in women's poetry, Doody shows how this image, sometimes deemed problematically trivial and ultra-feminine, is in fact a way of communicating 'that the world is holy and mysterious', recasting the classical world picture through folklore. Clare Brant's 'Varieties of Women's Writing' (pp. 285–305) is equally eclectic, attending the question of genre in the recent reclamation projects of eighteenth-century women's writing. Interested in the way women's writing is prey to anonymity, pseudonymity and (un)originality, Brant examines the 'women's genres' of memoirs, life-writings, letters and essays.

Several important editions appeared this year: Susan Wolfson's *Felicia Hemans: Selected Writings*, Judith Pascoe's *Mary Robinson: Selected Poems* and Jonathan Wordsworth's Woodstock facsimile of Robinson's *Sappho and Phaon* [1796]. Wolfson's edition of Hemans is indeed a striking accomplishment of editorial prowess, containing works from *The Domestic Affections*, the 1819 *Tales, The Forest Sanctuary and Other Poems*, *Records of Woman*, and *Songs of the Affections, with Other Poems* as well as selections from the Annuals and a significant number of letters. Wolfson traces the remarkable career of Hemans, who, by the 1820s, was constantly being beset by poets seeking advice and support, and by fans seeking autographs or just a glimpse of the famous 'poetess'. Emerging as England's premier female poet, she was being celebrated as an epitome of 'feminine' excellence who was simultaneously alert to the literary market and admired by a wide readership, including men and women of letters. Her consequent reception history was erratic, swinging, Wolfson argues, 'from polite discouragement, to emerging appreciation, to celebrity, to condescension, to obscurity, to critical and scholarly recovery, to renewed classroom interest'. Such a trajectory, however, provides an excellent platform from which to assess how women's poetry is shaped in a gendered culture, how aesthetic value is historically determined and how we represent the Romantic era, and Hemans's place within it. An invaluable bibliography of modern resources lists critical essays and websites, while the volume also contains an impressively thorough chronological overview of the poet.

Pascoe's edition of Robinson's poetry is equally valuable, drawn from the last edition over which the author exercised editorial control. While Robinson's first collection of poems was published in 1775, her most productive period was in the 1790s, making her a contemporary of writers such as Coleridge, who called her a 'woman of undoubted genius'. Having narrowly escaped imprisonment for debt and seriously ill from overwork during this period, Robinson still managed to be immensely productive, publishing five collections of poetry, four novels, two political tracts, several essays and countless individually published poems, generous selections from which are published here. Although a contemporary of the first generation of Romantics, Robinson's exclusion from their group is both a consequence of both the failure of literary history to accommodate women and her own chequered history, especially her sensationalized liaison with the Prince of Wales in the early 1780s. Resituating her as a central Romantic, Pascoe highlights the extent to which Robinson's poetry serves as a kind of 'cultural barometer of aesthetic change': she used Della Cruscan form, contributed to the sonnet renaissance and recast the lyrical ballad. Describing herself as exhibiting a precocious inclination towards melancholy pursuits, Robinson was attracted to mournful poetry from an early age, even though her youthful beauty and keen fashion sense swept her onto the stage. It was with the publication of her 1791 and 1793 volumes that Robinson established a poetic identity for herself, however, provoking disparate critical reactions, Pascoe shows. For some, her poetry problematically relied upon 'uncommon terms and ideas, to provoke attention and excite admiration', as one commentator in the *Critical Review* declared. The edition also reveals how important Robinson's development of the idea of sensibility was, coupling passion and reason, sensibility and political consciousness. Her poetic evocations of human loss, disappointment and emotional intensity ultimately show her to be a stylistically and thematically heterogeneous poet, as the various reviews of Robinson's poetry reiterate, a selection of which are printed here.

Pascoe also reprints the whole of Robinson's influential sonnet sequence, *Sappho and Phaon*, which also appears as a Woodstock facsimile this year. For the editor of this latter text, Robinson is consciously aware of the inroads she is making into poetic form, writing in the Preface: 'It must strike every admirer of poetical composition that the modern sonnet, with two lines winding up the sentiment of the whole, confines the poet's fancy, and frequently occasions an abrupt termination of a beautiful and interesting picture; and that the ancient, or what is commonly denominated the *Legitimate Sonnet*, may be carried on in a series of sketches, composing, in parts, one historical or imaginary subject, and forming in the whole a complete and connected story.' Rejecting Shakespeare, Sidney and Spenser for the Petrarchan, then, Robinson turns to a lyrically intense genre to express varying moods of grief and desperation. The deeply powerful poet Sappho is one simultaneously identified as the unrivalled poetess of her time and as a suffering, marginalized woman.

Robinson is also addressed in Anne K. Mellor's essay 'Mary Robinson and the Scripts of Female Sexuality' (in Patrick Coleman, Jayne Lewis and Jill Kowalik's *Representations of the Self from the Renaissance to Romanticism*). Mellor turns to Robinson because she poses a problem, it is argued, about our current intellectual constructions of subjectivity and about the ways in which women and female sexuality were understood in Europe between 1780 and 1830. Constructed from a career as an actress, public figure and writer always framed by sexuality, Robinson's identity fell victim to commodification as well as caricature. Robinson, Mellor illustrates, in line with Pascoe, played with her own authorial identity, adopting at least nine different pseudonyms to portray herself as a kind of Keatsian chameleon poet able to interpellate herself into pre-existing ideologies.

Barbauld remains central this year, two excellent essays contributing to the ever-expanding body of research devoted to the poet. Lisa Vargo's 'The Anna Laetitia Barbauld Web Page: 1773 meets 2000' (RoN 19[2000]) attests to this, meditating on how hypertext contributes to textual scholarship in its transformation of the nature of the page. She considers how a facsimile version of a literary work might be made accessible to students and scholars, as well as how electronic media might aid our reception of long-neglected writers who lack a continuous readership dating from the time that their works first appeared. Haley Bordo's 'Reinvoking the "Domestic Muse": Anna Laetitia Barbauld and the Performance of Genre' (ERR 11:ii[2000] 186–96) offers an engaging enquiry into Barbauld's relationship to stylistic form, insightfully noting an explicitly feminist politics expressed through 'poetry and particularly the "peculiar language," as J.L. Austin would say, by which poetry is often distinguished'. Bordo illustrates how Barbauld's 'Washing Day' critiques the gendered expectations surrounding the cultural idea of 'poetry' and the 'poet' in a manner comparable to Judith Butler's invocation of language as the 'thing that we do and that does us'.

Finally, two essays turn respectively to the figures of Yearsley and Emily Brontë: Judith Dorn's 'The Royal Captives: A Fragment of Secret History: Ann Yearsley's "Unnecessary Curiosity"' (in Cope, ed., 1650–1850: Ideas, Aesthetics and Inquiries in the Early Modern Era, pp. 163–89), and Lisa Wang's 'The Holy Spirit in Emily Brontë's Wuthering Heights and Poetry' (L&T 14:ii[2000] 160–73). Dorn notes that, while Yearsley is known primarily as a poet, she also published a Radcliffean Gothic romance in 1795 entitled The Royal Captives, distributed by several booksellers in Ireland, England and America. Posing as a memoir handwritten in prison by one Henry Capet, son of Louis XIV's elder twin brother, the tale fed into contemporary concerns regarding the French Terror, Dorn argues. Yearsley thus consciously situates herself as a serious commentator on momentous political issues to counter her image as the obscure discovery of Hannah More. Wang's engaging examination of Brontë's still relatively little studied poetry at once reveals its important religious undertones as essential to our understanding of Wuthering Heights, as it also examines the general approach of this writer, often labelled heretical, to matters theological. Focused on here are the biblical tropes and topoi relating to the Holy Spirit within Brontë's verse, emphasizing the primal nature of religious experience and connecting this to the transgressive relationship between Catherine and Heathcliff.

8. Drama

A healthy year for Romantic drama scholarship saw continued success with careful historical and cultural work focused on recovering dramas and reconstructing critical moments in theatre culture, highlighting the theatricality of the era and the dramatic work of those we associate with other forms, such as Sir Walter Scott. No one now disputes that theatre played an important role in Romantic culture. Less critical energy has been spent on the aesthetics of the plays themselves, however, which has implied that the aesthetics are less worthy of attention, and which perpetuates stereotypes about Romantic drama; thus it is particularly rewarding to see fine articles on Romantic aesthetics this year. Notable work is also being done in making Romantic plays freely available for the classroom as well as to scholarship: this year saw no less than eight playtexts posted online with modern editing and critical introductions, featuring the recovery of Mariana Starke's great comedy *The Sword of Peace; or, A Voyage of Love*, as well as the beginning of exciting online scholarly discussions about women's theatre production.

Women's contributions have been especially well researched this year in the enlightening and excellent Burroughs, ed., *Women in British Romantic Theatre: Drama, Performance, and Society, 1790–1840*, for which the editor has provided a synthesizing introduction. Taken as a whole—and they want to be taken as a whole, as the contributors refer to their essays as 'chapters' and there's a strong sense throughout of a collective effort—the essays create a multifaceted picture of women theatre artists that admits the richness and complexity of women's work in Romantic-era drama. Women's experiences were not identical: while some were radical leaders and forebears of feminism, others were not; nor were all women oppressed and repressed. Overall, the collection's emphasis is still on theatre culture more than the literary and aesthetic aspects of the drama itself, although there's more attention to dramaturgy, especially with Baillie and Inchbald.

Leading off the book's eleven chapters, which are divided into five thematic sections, is Jeffrey N. Cox's thoughtful essay 'Baillie, Siddons, Larpent: Gender, Power, and Politics in the Theatre of Romanticism' (pp. 23–47), which challenges our assumptions that women were necessarily marginalized, and radical or progressive in their actions; as he illustrates, these three women used their considerable power for conservative ends. Greg Kucich's 'Reviewing Women in British Romantic Theatre' (pp. 48–76) probes the mysteriously divided reactions of male reviewers of women's plays and their concomitant reviews of women's behaviour offstage. Examining national identity are Katherine Newey, who in 'Women and History on the Romantic Stage: More, Yearsley, Burney, and Mitford' (pp. 79–101) argues that these playwrights used the genre power of historical tragedy to overcome gender limitations and re-envisage citizenship; and Jeanne Moskal, who in 'English National Identity in Mariana Starke's "The Sword of Peace": India, Abolition, and the Rights of Women' (pp. 102–31) shows how Starke comments on the Hastings trial, social class, and the slave trade by staging nationalist myth. In a similar use of the theatre space, Baillie staged alternatives to the behaviour of women that was prescribed in conduct books in order to 'acquit' women and grant them sovereignty, argues Marjean D. Purinton in 'Women's Sovereignty on Trial: Joanna Baillie's Comedy "The Tryal" as Metatheatrics' (pp. 132–57). And in 'Outing Joanna Baillie' (pp. 161–77), Susan Bennett pulls Baillie out of the closet (drama) to prove that her plays were deliberately designed for public performance; focusing on the dramaturgy of *Constantine Paleologus*, she argues that Baillie's technique shows her to be an avant-garde playwright.

The most unusual and intriguing chapter is 'The Management of Laughter: Jane Scott's "Camilla the Amazon" in 1998' (pp. 178–204) by Jacky Bratton, Gilli Bush-Bailey, and the students from their course on popular performance at Royal

Holloway, University of London. To convey the process of running workshops on Scott's play and learning the performance conventions of the era, the authors include playbill copy, costume sketches, comments from students as well as professors, contemporary reviews and modern criticism, and scenes from the Larpent manuscript of the play. The result is exciting and instructive scholarship and should serve as a model for performance historiography and courses for dramaturges-in-training. (Bratton and Bush-Bailey edited a version of *Camilla the Amazon* for reading that is published in the appendix to *NCT* 27:ii[1999].)

Chapters on women as theatre critics appear by Marvin Carlson, 'Elizabeth Inchbald: A Woman Critic in her Theatrical Culture' (pp. 207–22), which argues for her status as a savvy theatre critic who navigated the mostly male culture, set moral and dramaturgical standards, and understood the stage as well as the page, and Thomas C. Crochunis, whose 'Authorial Performances in the Criticism and Theory of Romantic Women Playwrights' (pp. 223–54) revises Foucault's notion of the author-function to underscore the active authorship performed by Baillie and Inchbald within their own *mise-en-scène*. Jane Moody, in 'Suicide and Translation in the Dramaturgy of Elizabeth Inchbald and Anne Plumptre' (pp. 257–84), makes fascinating connections between the suicide staged in Inchbald's *The Wise Man of the East* and the figurative deaths of subjectivity in the process of translation, in which the translator's or author's voices can be killed off. (Both Inchbald and the much less widely known Plumptre translated Kotzebue's *Das Kind der Liebe*.) Last in the collection is an especially fine essay by Julie A. Carlson, 'Remaking Love: Remorse in the Theatre of Baillie and Inchbald' (pp. 285–310), in which she revisits the territory of her *In the Theatre of Romanticism* and addresses the work of women playwrights, who were not considered in her earlier study; she explores how Inchbald's *A Case of Conscience* and Baillie's *Henriquez* revise love to bring it more in line with reason rather than illusion—not in order to oppose love and reason, but to combine them for more satisfying and sustainable love.

The Romantic period was also an era that shaped the literary values of what we consider 'modernity', Philip Cox argues persuasively in *Reading Adaptations: Novels and Verse Narratives on the Stage, 1790–1840*. His book analyses commercial play adaptations of popular novels and verse narratives by Godwin, Scott, and Dickens, but it is ultimately a story of the development of popular culture itself, and Cox traces the rise of the distinction between 'high' and 'low'—or literary and popular—culture and the ways in which genres competed for the high culture position even as they paradoxically competed for the mass popularity position as well. Pairing Godwin's *Caleb Williams* with George Colman the Younger's *The Iron Chest*, he reveals the tensions within the two genres themselves: the chivalric romance and realist novel in the former, and tragedy and melodrama in the latter. In his two chapters on Scott, whose narrative works were enormously popular and already theatrical, Cox focuses on adaptations of *The Lady in the Lake* and *Ivanhoe* and theorizes that Scott became such a popular author because of the many adaptations or repetitions of his work, and the ways in which he created a cultural genealogy for unifying the nation made up of competing discourses. Issues of authority—the original author's control over the meanings of his literary product—are critical throughout Cox's book, but become most pronounced in the case of Dickens, who worked tirelessly for his authoritative status in middle-class English life and resisted adaptations of his work. This should prove an important contribution to popular culture studies as well as those of Romantic-era drama.

We are also introduced to new territory in Romantic drama through an anthology of Romantic plays published in the Oxford World's Classics series, Baines and Burns, eds., *Five Romantic Plays, 1768–1821*, which has a lively and informative introduction and useful apparatus—such as a discussion of the playhouses of London and the material conditions for staging the five plays—by the editors. Baines and Burns regard theatre in Romantic culture as playing 'an important but highly compromised part' (p. vii) and their collection deliberately emphasizes the 'contradictory and only partially achieved nature' of the Romantic drama 'project' (p. viii). At first glance it's a curious selection: two plays that are widely taught and readily available already—*De Monfort* and *Lovers' Vows*—and three that exist on the margins of already marginal Romantic drama: Walpole's Gothic *The Mysterious Mother*, Southey's early revolutionary agitprop *Wat Tyler*, and Byron's post-Napoleonic historical drama *The Two Foscari*. The editors centre on two broad themes of struggle: the family against itself, and political revolution. Taken together, the plays do provide a rather fascinating overview of the various kinds of drama being produced, and it may be that this proves most useful as a classroom text when used as a whole, to demonstrate that range.

Several essays are breaking new theoretical ground in Romantic dramaturgy. In his impressively argued 'The Passion of Joanna Baillie: Playwright as Martyr' (*TJ* 52[2000] 227–52), Sean Carney begins with the smart observation that we have paid little attention to performing close readings of Baillie's plays and have instead talked *about* her work. He puts Baillie into conversation with Adam Smith's *Theory of Moral Sentiments* and overturns common assumptions that she is an optimist about human nature who advocates sympathetic curiosity so that audiences will feel the passions she dramatizes. On the contrary, Carney argues, Baillie associates herself with Smith by advancing a resistance to the overwhelming nature of passions; the ideal citizen is one who is aware of but controls his passions. Carney's argument shows an affiliation with Julie Carlson's that Baillie was remaking love through reason; they also both focus on Baillie's atypical tragedy *Henriquez*, with Carney proposing that, rather than composing a cautionary tale like her other plays on the passions, she creates a model of the new citizen in her eponymous hero. Carney's stimulating essay is sure to be influential.

The Cenci, always popular, comes up again for examination, but this year's articles are especially innovative. Margot Harrison, in 'No Way for a Victim to Act? Beatrice Cenci and the Dilemma of Romantic Performance' (*SiR* 39[2000] 187–211), draws upon the performance theories of Rousseau and especially Diderot to provide a new way of understanding the liminality of the play's (un)performability and Beatrice's disturbing performance in her court scene, which also informs our wider views of Romantic performance. George Elliott Clarke's 'Racing Shelley, or Reading *The Cenci* as a Gothic Slave Narrative' (*ERR* 11:ii[2000] 168–85) provocatively argues that 'an allegorically "black" text lurks beneath the moonlit, Roman facade of the erected narrative' (p. 169), and, re-seeing Beatrice's relationship to Count Cenci as one of slave to master, and examining Shelley's use of Gothic motifs, interprets the play as using its early modern setting to illuminate the present and prophesy the very bloody end of slavery. Diane Long Hoeveler also addresses Gothic elements in 'Gothic Drama as Nationalistic Catharsis' (*WC*

31:iii[2000] 169–72), in which she examines plays adapted from popular novels: Matthew Lewis's *Castle Spectre*, Henry Siddons's *Sicilian Romance*, and James Boaden's *Fountainville Forest* and his little-known *Cambrio-Britons*, and shows how their familiar patterns work as public rituals for expressing concerns about the monarchy, revolution, class, gender, and the emerging British empire.

If the Gothic dramas are generally nationalistic, David Worrall argues that the melodrama can be seen as more radical. In his 'Artisan Melodrama and the Plebian Public Sphere: The Political Culture of Drury Lane and its Environs, 1797–1830' (*SiR* 39[2000] 213–27), Worrall convincingly contends that melodrama produced in the non-patent theatres articulated an 'artisan radical culture' of London and formed an alternative public sphere to the royal theatres that were kept under surveillance; he illustrates how melodramas produced by William Thomas Moncrieff and others worked with the radical press to explore racial and sexual as well as social issues.

Two interesting explorations of fight against loss were Ian Dennis's '"I shall not choose a mortal to be my mediator": Byron's *Manfred* and "Internal Mediation"' (*ERR* 11:i[2000] 68–96), which invokes René Girard's concept of 'internal mediation', the 'desire modelled on a neighbour or nearby rival as opposed to a distant ideal' (p. 73), to reveal Byron's hero as a slave to desire seeking autonomy from his own self; and Marjean D. Purinton's 'Polysexualities and Romantic Generations in Mary Shelley's Mythological Dramas' (*WW* 6:iii[1999] 385–411), overlooked in this space last year, which examines Shelley's revisions of two patriarchal myths, *Midas* and *Proserpine*, that challenge the binary of heterosexuality/homosexuality for constructing subjectivity, and reclaim the mother–daughter relationship, with its matriarchal power, that she lost with Wollstonecraft's death.

Again, the internet is proving a wonderfully rich resource for Romantic drama studies. *Romantic Circles* included an electronic edition of Richard Brinsley Peake's *Presumption: or, the Fate of Frankenstein*, edited by Stephen C. Behrendt: <http://www.rc.umd.edu/editions/contemps/peake/>. A project of *Romanticism on the Net*, the website *British Women Playwrights around 1800* (<http://www-sul.stanford.edu/mirrors/romnet/wp1800/>) continues to lead the way by providing scholars and students with free, easily accessible, critically edited playtexts. New plays are added to the site every three months, and most of them are now being printed with critical introductions by their editors. The year 2000 saw a good introductory essay, 'Harriet Lee (1757–1851) and *The Mysterious Marriage, or the Heirship of Roselva*' by Barbara Darby, and introductions to the following full texts: Catherine Gore's *King O'Neil* and Elizabeth Polack's *Esther* by John Franceschina; Frances Burney's *Love and Fashion* by Jessica Richard; Hannah Cowley's *The Runaway* by Angela Escott (playtext edited by Elizabeth Fay); and a reprinting of Jonathan Wordsworth's introduction to Inchbald's *Lovers' Vows*. Anne Plumptre's *The Natural Son*, her translation of Kotzebue's *Das Kind der Liebe*, is also available full-text online, edited by Thomas C. Crochunis; this should be valuable for comparison with Inchbald's version, and for discussions on the nature of translation.

A key example of the richness of the *Romanticism on the Net* format and the substance of its content is found in the material concerning Mariana Starke's *The Sword of Peace; or, A Voyage of Love*. The website includes: the full text, edited by Thomas C. Crochunis and Michael Eberle-Sinatra; Jeffrey N. Cox's headnote to the play, reprinted from his volume of plays on slavery that forms volume v of *Slavery*,

Abolition, and Emancipation: Writings in the British Romantic Period, a series edited by Peter Kitson and Debbie Lee (P&C [1999]); Jeanne Moskal's substantive historical introduction to the play; Daniel O'Quinn's excellent critical article 'The Long Minuet as Danced at Coromandel: Character and the Colonial Translation of Class Anxiety in Mariana Starke's *The Sword of Peace*', which takes readers on a journey of imagining the performative possibilities of the text; and Marjean Purinton's response to O'Quinn, 'Dancing and Dueling in Mariana Starke's Comedy'. This abundance of material, all found in one location that can flexibly accommodate additions, revisions, and responses, is an exciting harbinger for future scholarship. *Romanticism on the Net* has also launched a series of e-mail correspondence in which editor Crochunis chats with a scholar about aspects of women's theatre history and publishes the discussion; the first ones are Ellen Donkin on performance projects and Michael Gamer on archival projects, and website visitors are invited to post responses.

Not accessed in time for review this year were two articles: Armine Kotin Mortimer, 'Myth and Mendacity: Balzac's Pierrette and Beatrice Cenci' (*DFS* 51[2000] 12–25), which compares the treatment of the female protagonists in Shelley's drama and Balzac's novel; and David Kaufmann, 'Two Cheers for Abstraction: Streams of Sound in *Prometheus Unbound*' in the new journal *Symbolism: An International Journal of Critical Aesthetics* (*Symbolism* 1[2000] 193–210), which examines sensory imagery and utopianism in Shelley's drama.

Books Reviewed

Alliston, April, ed. *The Recess; Or, A Tale of Other Times*, by Sophia Lee. 1783. UPKen. [2000] pp. 400. hb £39.95 ISBN 0 8131 2146 9, pb £15.50 ISBN 0 8131 0978 7.

Armstrong, Isobel. *The Radical Aesthetic*. Blackwell. [2000] pp. vii + 280. hb £50 ISBN 0 6312 2052 6, pb £17.13 ISBN 0 6312 2053 4.

Baines, Paul, and Edward Burns, eds. *Five Romantic Plays, 1768–1821*. OUP. [2000] pp. xlvi + 372. $14.95 ISBN 0 1928 3316 2.

Barker, Juliet. *Wordsworth: A Life*. Viking. [2000] pp. xvii + 971. £25 ISBN 0 6708 7213 X.

Barrell, John. *Imagining the King's Death: Figurative Treason, Fantasies of Regicide, 1793–1796*. OUP. [2000] pp. xvii + 737. £70 ($125) ISBN 0 1981 1292 0.

Bate, Jonathan. *The Song of the Earth*. HarvardUP. [2002] pp. 360. pb £12.95 ISBN 0 6740 0818 9.

Benis, Toby R. *Romanticism on the Road: The Marginal Gains of Wordsworth's Homeless*. Macmillan. [2000] pp. vii + 277. £45 ISBN 0 3337 1887 9.

Benton, Michael. *Studies in the Spectator Role: Literature, Painting and Pedagogy*. Routledge. [2000] pp. xv + 220. £15.99 ISBN 0 4152 0828 9.

Betz, Paul F. *William Wordsworth and the Romantic Imagination: A Scholar's Collection*. Cornell U. Library. [2000].

Bindman, David, ed. *William Blake: The Complete Illuminated Books*. T&H. [2000] pp. 480. £29.95 ISBN 0 5002 8245 5.

Blake, William. *Blake's Water-Colours for the Poems of Thomas Gray.* Dover. [2000] pp. xii + 116. $24.95 ISBN 0 4864 0944 9.

Bone, J. Drummond. *Byron.* Northcote. [2000] pp. x + 86. £8.99 ISBN 0 7463 0775 6.

Brown, Marshall. *The Cambridge History of Literary Criticism,* vol. v: *Romanticism.* CUP. [2000] pp. xii + 493. £65 ($100) ISBN 0 5213 0010 X.

Burroughs, Catherine, ed. *Women in British Romantic Theatre: Drama, Performance, and Society, 1790–1840.* CUP. [2000] pp. xvi + 344. $59.95 ISBN 0 5216 6224 9.

Butler, Judith, John Guillory and Kendall Thomas, eds. *What's Left of Theory?* Routledge. [2000] pp. xii + 292. £13.99 ISBN 0 4159 2118 X.

Campbell, Matthew, Jacqueline Labbe and Sally Shuttleworth, eds. *Memory and Memorials, 1789–1914.* Routledge. [2000] pp. xi + 237. £55 ($90) ISBN 0 4152 2976 6.

Chesterton, G.K. *William Blake.* House of Stratus. [2000] pp. 58. £8.99 ISBN 0 7551 0032 8.

Christensen, Jerome. *Romanticism at the End of History.* JHUP. [2000] pp. 236. £35 ($46.95) ISBN 0 8018 6319 8.

Clancey, Richard W. *Wordsworth's Classical Undersong: Education, Rhetoric and Poetic Truth.* Macmillan. [2000] pp. xxiii + 215. £42.50 ISBN 0 3337 6034 4.

Coleman, Patrick, Jayne Lewis and Jill Kowalik. *Representations of the Self from the Renaissance to Romanticism.* CUP. [2000] pp. xii + 284. £40 ($65) ISBN 0 5216 6146 3.

Cope, Kevin L., ed. *1650–1850: Ideas, Aesthetics and Inquiries in the Early Modern Era,* vol. v. AMS. [2000] pp. xix + 409. £75.50 ($89.50) ISBN 0 4046 4405 8.

Coupe, Laurence, ed. *The Green Studies Reader: From Romanticism to Ecocriticism.* Routledge. [2000] pp. xvii + 315. £15.99 ($24.99) ISBN 0 4152 0407 0.

Cox, Philip. *Reading Adaptations: Novels and Verse Narratives on the Stage, 1790–1840.* ManUP. [2000] pp. vii + 184. hb $69.95 ISBN 0 7190 5340 4, pb $24.95 0 7190 5341 2.

Cronin, Richard. *The Politics of Romantic Poetry: In Search of the Pure Commonwealth.* Macmillan. [2000] pp. viii + 225. £47.50 ISBN 0 3337 6106 5.

Davies, Damian Walford, ed. *William Wordsworth: Selected Poems.* Everyman. [2000] pp. lvii + 523. £9.99 ISBN 1 8571 5245 X.

De Selincourt, Basil. *William Blake: A Biography.* The Book Tree. [2000] pp. 298. $28.95 ISBN 1 5850 9225 8.

Dix, Robin, ed. *Mark Akenside: A Reassessment.* AUP. [2000] pp. 296. £38 ISBN 0 8386 3882 1.

Dolan, John. *Poetic Occasion from Milton to Wordsworth.* Macmillan. [2000] pp. vii + 219. £47.50 ISBN 0 3337 3358 4.

Eberle-Sinatra, Michael, ed. *Mary Shelley's Fictions: From 'Frankenstein' to Falkner.* Palgrave. [2000] pp. xxvi + 250. £42.50 ISBN 0 3337 7106 0.

Esterhammer, Angela. *The Romantic Performative: Language and Action in British and German Romanticism.* StanfordUP. [2000] pp. xi + 295. $55 ISBN 0 4150 5049 9.

Evans, Roger. *Somerset in the Footsteps of Coleridge and Wordsworth.* R. Evans. [2000] pp. i + 56. pb £9.95 ISBN 0 9525 6742 3.

Everest, Kelvin, and Geoffrey Matthews, eds. *The Poems of Shelley, 1817–1819*, vol. ii. Contributing editors Jack Donovan, Ralph Pite and Michael Rossington. Longman. [2000]. pp. xxiii + 879. £95 ISBN 0 5820 3082 X.

Ferris, David. *Silent Urns: Romanticism, Hellenism, Modernity*. StanfordUP. [2000] pp. xix + 247. £35 ($49.50) ISBN 0 8047 3583 2.

Fleissner, Robert F. *Sources, Meaning, and Influences of Coleridge's Kubla Khan*. Mellen. [2000] pp. xx + 208. £49.95 ISBN 0 7734 7718 7.

Franklin, Caroline. *Byron: A Literary Life*. Macmillan. [2000] pp. xxv + 209. £14.99 ISBN 0 3336 7664 5.

Gamer, Michael. *Romanticism and the Gothic: Genre, Reception, and Canon Formation*. CSR 40. CUP. [2000] pp. xiii + 255. £40 ISBN 0 5217 7328 8.

Gibson, Matthew. *Yeats, Coleridge and the Romantic* Sage. Macmillan. [2000] pp. xi + 224. £42.50 ISBN 0 3337 4625 2.

Giddings, Robert, and Erica Sheen, eds. *The Classic Novel: From Page to Screen*. ManUP. [2000] pp. 249. hb £40 ISBN 0 7190 5230 0, pb £12.99 ISBN 0 7190 5231 9.

Gill, Stephen, ed. *William Wordsworth: The Major Works*. World's Classics. OUP. [2000] pp. xxxii + 752. £9.99 ISBN 0 1928 4044 4.

Gilroy, Amanda, ed. *Romantic Geographies: Discourses of Travel, 1775–1844*. ManUP. [2000] pp. xii + 260. £45 ($69.95) ISBN 0 7190 5576 8.

Goodridge, John, and Simon Kovési, eds. *John Clare: New Approaches*. John Clare Society, Helpston. [2000] pp. xxiii + 264. £7.95 ISBN 0 9522 5416 6.

Gravil, Richard. *Romantic Dialogues: Anglo-American Continuities, 1776–1862*. Macmillan. [2000] pp. xx + 250. £30 ISBN 0 3339 2984 5.

Gravil, Richard. *Samuel Taylor Coleridge Selected Poems*. York Notes. Longman. [2000] pp. 120. £3.99 ISBN 0 5824 2480 1.

Grayling, A.C. *The Quarrel of the Age: The Life and Times of William Hazlitt*. W&N. [2000] pp. 410. hb £25 ISBN 0 2976 4322 3, pb £14.99 ISBN 1 8421 2496 X.

Hamlyn, Robin, and Michael Phillips. *William Blake*. Tate. [2000] pp. 301. £25 ISBN 1 8543 7314 5.

Hanley, Keith. *Wordsworth: A Poet's History*. Palgrave. [2000] pp. xii + 264. £40 ISBN 0 3339 1883 5.

Hawkridge, Audrey. *Jane and her Gentlemen: Jane Austen and the Men in her Life and Novels*. Owen. [2000] pp. 208. hb £18.95 ISBN 0 7206 1104 0, pb £9.95 ISBN 0 7206 1164 4.

Hebron, Stephen. *William Wordsworth*. Writers' Lives. BL [2000] pp. 120. £10.95 ISBN 0 7123 4636 8.

Hedley, Douglas. *Coleridge, Philosophy and Religion: Aids to Reflection and the Mirror of the Spirit*. CUP. [2000] pp. xiv + 330. £40 ISBN 0 5217 7035 1.

Herzog, Anne F., and Janet E. Kaufman, eds. *'How shall we tell each other of the poet?' The Life and Writing of Muriel Rukeyser*. Macmillan. [2000] pp. xviii + 326. £19.99 ISBN 0 3337 6526 5.

Hobson, Christopher Z. *Blake and Homosexuality*. Palgrave. [2000] pp. xxii + 249. £32.50 ISBN 0 3122 3451 1.

Hofstetter, Michael J. *The Romantic Idea of a University: England and Germany, 1770–1850*. Palgrave. [2000] pp. xiv + 162. £40 ISBN 0 3337 1888 7.

Hughes-Hallett, Penelope. *The Immortal Dinner: A Famous Evening of Genius and Laughter in Literary London, 1817*. Viking. [2000] pp. xvi + 336. £7.99 ISBN 0 6708 7999 1.

Jackson, H.J., ed. *Samuel Taylor Coleridge, The Major Works*. World's Classics. OUP. [2000] pp. xviii + 733. £9.99 ISBN 0 1928 4043 6.

Jackson, H.J., and George Whalley, eds. *Samuel Taylor Coleridge, Marginalia V: Sherlock to Unidentified*. Bollingen series LXXV, 12:v. PrincetonUP. [2000] pp. xxiii + 867. £100 ISBN 0 6910 9958 8.

Jackson J.R. de J., ed. *Samuel Taylor Coleridge, Lectures 1818–19 on the History of Philosophy*, 2 vols., continuously paginated. Bollingen series LXXV, 8:i and 8:ii. PrincetonUP. [2000] pp. cxlv + 1030. £130 ISBN 0 6910 9875 1.

Jennerman, Donald L., David A. White and Marilyn Bischs, eds. *Collected Works of Newton P. Stallknecht*, vol. ii: *Strange Seas of Thought: Studies in William Wordsworth's Philosophy of Man and Nature* [1945]. Mellen. [2000] pp. xii + 301. ISBN 0 7734 8218 0.

Johnston, Kenneth R. *The Hidden Wordsworth*. Pimlico. [2000] pp. xix + 690. pb £15 ISBN 0 7126 6752 0.

Jones, Steven E. *Satire and Romanticism*. Palgrave. [2000] pp. x + 262. £37.50 ($49.95) ISBN 0 3339 2992 6.

Jones, Vivien. *Women and Literature in Britain 1700–1800*. CUP. [2000] pp. xi + 320. hb £60 ($90) ISBN 0 5215 8347 0, pb £14.95 ($19.95) ISBN 0 5215 8680 1.

Keane, Angela. *Women Writers and the English Nation in the 1790s*. CUP. [2000] pp. 214. £35 ISBN 0 5217 7342 3.

Kuklick, Bruce, ed. *Thomas Paine Political Writings: Revised Student Edition*. 2nd edn. Cambridge Texts in the History of Political Thought. CUP. [2000] pp. xxx + 353. hb £25 ISBN 0 5216 6088 2, pb £8.95 ISBN 0 5216 6799 2.

Labbe, Jacqueline M. *The Romantic Paradox: Love, Violence and the Uses of Romance, 1760–1830*. Palgrave. [2000] pp. xi + 211. £42.50 ($59.95) ISBN 0 3337 6032 8.

Lambdin, Laura C., and Robert T. Lambdin, eds. *A Companion to Jane Austen Studies*. Greenwood. [2000]. pp. 360. £64.95 ISBN 0 3133 0662 1.

Lane, Melissa. *Plato's Progeny: How Plato and Socrates Still Captivate the Modern Mind*. Duckworth. [2000] pp. x + 165. pb £9.99 ISBN 0 7516 2892 5.

Lindop, Grevel, gen. ed. *The Works of Thomas De Quincey*. 7 vols. P&C. [2000] pp. 7,980. £550 ISBN 1 8519 6518 1.

Linebaugh, Peter, and Rediker, Marcus. *The Many-Headed Hydra: Sailors, Slaves, Commoners, and the Hidden History of the Revolutionary Atlantic*. Beacon. [2000] pp. 433. $18 ISBN 0 8070 5007 5.

Lussier, Mark S., *Romantic Dynamics: The Poetics of Physicality*. Macmillan. [2000] pp. ix + 220. £45 ($59.95) ISBN 0 3337 1891 7.

Lynch, Deirdre, ed. *Janeites: Austen's Disciples and Devotees*. PrincetonUP. [2000] pp. ix + 233. hb ISBN 0 6910 5005 8, pb ISBN 0 6910 5006 6.

Mahoney, John L. *Wordsworth and the Critics: The Development of a Critical Reputation*. Camden House. [2000] pp. xix + 166. £35 ISBN 1 5711 3090 X.

Mayberry, Tom. *Coleridge and Wordsworth: The Crucible of Friendship*. Sutton. [2000] pp. xii + 196. £9.99 ISBN 0 7509 2507 8.

McFarland, Thomas, *The Masks of Keats: The Endeavour of a Poet*. OUP. [2000] pp. vi + 244. £30 ISBN 0 1981 8645 2.

McKusick, James C. *Green Writing: Romanticism and Ecology*. Macmillan. [2000] pp. x + 261. £30 ISBN 0 3339 4688 X.

McLane, Maureen N. *Romanticism and the Human Sciences: Poetry, Population, and the Discourse of the Species*. CSR. CUP. [2000] pp. x + 282. £37.50 ($54.95) ISBN 0 5217 7348 2.

Mellor, Anne K. *Mothers of the Nation: Women's Political Writing in England, 1780–1830*. IndianaUP. [2000] pp. ix + 172. £28.50 ($39.95) ISBN 0 2533 3713 5.

Morillo, John D. *Uneasy Feelings: Literature, the Passions, and Class from Neoclassicism to Romanticism*. AMS. [2000] pp. viii + 313. £51.95 ISBN 0 4046 3537 7.

Morton, Timothy. *The Poetics of Spice: Romantic Consumerism and the Exotic*. CSR. CUP. [2000] pp. xiii + 282. £37.50 ($59.95) ISBN 0 5217 7146 3.

Newlyn, Lucy. *Reading, Writing and Romanticism: The Anxiety of Reception*. OUP. [2000] pp. xix + 397. £35 ($60) ISBN 0 1981 8710 6.

Otto, Peter. *Blake's Critique of Transcendence: Love, Jealousy, and the Sublime in 'The Four Zoas'*. OUP. [2000] pp. xiii + 364. £55 ISBN 0 1981 8719 X.

Park, You-me, and Rajeswari Sunder Rajan, eds. *The Postcolonial Jane Austen*. Routledge. [2000]. pp. xiv + 254. £55 ISBN 0 4152 3290 2.

Parker, Christopher, *The English Idea of History from Coleridge to Collingwood*. Ashgate. [2000] pp. vii + 244. £39.50 ISBN 1 8401 4254 5.

Parker, Mark. *Literary Magazines and British Romanticism*. CUP. [2000] pp. 213. $55 ISBN 0 5217 8192 2.

Pascoe, Judith, ed. *Mary Robinson: Selected Poems*. Broadview. [2000] pp. 444. £8.95 ($16.95) ISBN 1 5511 1201 9.

Perry, Seamus. *S.T. Coleridge: Interviews and Recollections*. Palgrave. [2000] pp. xviii + 300. £45 ISBN 0 3336 8159 2.

Phillips, Michael. *William Blake: The Creation of the 'Songs' from Manuscript to Illuminated Printing*. BL. [2000] pp. xi + 180. £16.95 ISBN 0 7123 4960 2.

Plotz, Judith. *Romanticism and the Vocation of Childhood*. Palgrave. [2000] pp. xvi + 304. £30 ISBN 0 3339 1535 6.

Purkis, John, *A Preface to Wordsworth*, rev. edn. Longman. [2000] pp. xii + 203. £14.99 ISBN 0 5824 3765 2.

Rawes, Alan, *Byron's Poetic Experimentation: 'Childe Harold', the Tales, and the Quest for Comedy*. Ashgate. [2000] pp. xiii + 147. £39.95 ISBN 0 7546 0171 4.

Reiman, Donald H., and Neil Fraistat, eds. *The Complete Poetry of Percy Bysshe Shelley*, vol. i. JHUP. [2000] pp. lviii + 492. £58 ISBN 0 8018 6119 5.

Roberts, Daniel Sanjiv. *Revisionary Gleam: De Quincey, Coleridge, and the High Romantic Argument*. LiverUP. [2000] pp. xxi + 311. hb £35 ISBN 0 8532 3794 8, pb £17.95 ISBN 0 8532 3804 9.

Schlossberg, Herbert, *The Silent Revolution and the Making of Victorian England*. Ohio State (Eurospan). [2000] pp. x + 405. hb £48.95 ISBN 0 8142 0843 6, pb £20.50 ISBN 0 8142 5046 7.

Schneider, Richard J., ed. *Thoreau's Sense of Place: Essays in American Environmental Writing*. UIowaP. [2000] pp. xii + 310. hb £34 ISBN 0 8774 5708 5, pb £17 ISBN 0 8774 5720 4.

Shaw, Philip, ed. *Romantic Wars: Studies in Culture and Conflict, 1793–1822*. Ashgate. [2000] pp. xii + 233. £45 ($79.95) ISBN 1 8401 4266 9.

Singer, June. *Blake, Jung, and the Collective Unconscious: The Conflict between Reason and Imagination*. Nicholas Hays. [2000] pp. xx + 271. $18.95 ISBN 0 8925 4051 6.

Sitterson, Joseph C. Jr. *Romantic Poems, Poets, and Narrators*. KSUP. [2000] pp. ix + 203. £26.95 ($32) ISBN 0 8733 8655 8.

Sorensen, Janet. *The Grammar of Empire in Eighteenth-Century British Writing*. CUP. [2000] £41.19 ISBN 0 5216 5327 4.

Storey, Mark. *The Problem of Poetry in the Romantic Period*. Macmillan/Palgrave. [2000] pp. xi + 197. £42.50 ($59.95) ISBN 0 3337 3890 X.

Sullivan, Brad, *Wordsworth and the Composition of Knowledge: Refiguring Relationships among Minds, Worlds, and Words*. Lang. [2000] pp. xv + 202. £32 ISBN 0 8204 4857 5.

Sussman, Charlotte. *Consuming Anxieties: Consumer Protest, Gender and British Slavery, 1713–1833*. StanfordUP. [2000] pp. vi + 267. £27.50 ($45) ISBN 0 8047 3103 9.

Thomas, Helen. *Romanticism and Slave Narratives: Transatlantic Testimonies*. CSR. CUP. [2000] pp. xi + 332. £40 ($59.95) ISBN 0 5216 6234 6.

Trigilio, Tony. *'Strange Prophecies Anew': Rereading Apocalypse in Blake, H.D., and Ginsberg*. FDUP. [2000] pp. 209. ISBN 0 8386 3854 6.

Tsuchiya, Kiyoshi. *The Mirror Metaphor and Coleridge's Mysticism: Poetics, Metaphysics, and the Formation of the Pentad*. Mellen. [2000] pp. xvii + 361. $99.95 ISBN 0 7734 7548 6.

Vallins, David. *Coleridge and the Psychology of Romanticism: Feeling and Thought*. Macmillan. [2000] pp. xii + 221. £45 ISBN 0 3337 3745 8.

Whale, John, ed. *Edmund Burke's Reflections on the Revolution in France*. Texts in Culture. ManUP. [2000] pp. xii + 228. hb £40 ISBN 0 7190 5786 8, pb £13.99 ISBN 0 7190 5787 6.

Whale, John. *Imagination under Pressure, 1789–1832: Aesthetics, Politics and Utility*. CSR. CUP. [2000] pp. xii + 240. £40 ($59.95) ISBN 0 5217 7219 2.

White, Deborah Elise. *Romantic Returns: Superstition, Imagination, History*. StanfordUP. [2000] pp. 227. $45 ISBN 0 8047 3494 1.

Wilner, Joshua. *Feeding on Infinity: Readings in Romantic Rhetoric of Internalization*. JHUP. [2000] pp. xiii + 154. £27 ISBN 0 8018 6324 4.

Wolfson, Susan. *Felicia Hemans: Selected Writings*. PrincetonUP. [2000] pp. 674. £35 ISBN 0 6910 5029 5.

Wood, Marcus. *Blind Memory: Visual Representations of Slavery in England and America, 1780–1865*. ManUP. [2000] pp. xxi + 341. £17.99 ($20.90) ISBN 0 7190 5446 X.

Wordsworth, Jonathan, ed. *Constantin François Volney, The Ruins, or A Survey of the Revolutions of Empires, with The Law of Nature, or Principles of Morality, deduced from the Physical Constitution of Mankind and the Universe* {1811}. Revolution and Romanticism 1789–1834. Woodstock. [2000] pp. xv + xiv + 232 + 48. £48 ($80) ISBN 1 8547 7246 5.

Wordsworth, Jonathan, ed. *Gottfried Augustus Bürger, Leonora* [1796], trans. J.T. Stanley, Revolution and Romanticism 1789–1834. Woodstock. [2000] pp. ix + 12. £42 ($70) ISBN 1 8547 7232 5.

Wordsworth, Jonathan, ed. *John Thelwall, Poems Written in the Tower* [1795]. Revolution and Romanticism 1789–1834. Woodstock. [2000] pp. x + 32. £37.50 ($62.50) ISBN 1 8547 7244 9.

Wordsworth, Jonathan, ed. *Mark Akenside, The Pleasures of Imagination* [1795]. Revolution and Romanticism 1789–1834. Woodstock. [2000] pp. x + 157. £42 ($70) ISBN 1 8547 7229 5.

Wordsworth, Jonathan, ed. *Mary Robinson, Sappho and Phaon* [1796]. Revolution and Romanticism 1789–1834. Woodstock. [2000] pp. xi + 82. £37.50 ($62.50) ISBN 1 8547 7242 2.

Wordsworth, Jonathan, ed. *Robert Lovell and Robert Southey, Poems* [1795]. Revolution and Romanticism 1789–1834. Woodstock. [2000] pp. xii + 131. £42 ($70) ISBN 1 8547 7239 2.

XIII

The Nineteenth Century: The Victorian Period

WILLIAM BAKER, HALIE A. CROCKER, JUDE NIXON, JIM DAVIS AND DAVID FINKELSTEIN

This chapter has five sections: 1. Prose and General; 2. Novel; 3. Poetry; 4. Drama and Theatre; 5. Periodicals and Publishing History. Sections 1 and 2 are by William Baker and Halie A. Crocker, section 3 is by Jude Nixon, section 4 is by Jim Davis, and section 5 is by David Finkelstein.

1. Prose and General

(a) General
The year's work in Victorian prose and cultural studies is marked by an interest in the formation of national identity and the influences of past upon present. In *Myth and National Identity in Nineteenth-Century Britain: The Legends of King Arthur and Robin Hood*, Stephanie Barczewski draws interesting parallels between these two figures of seemingly divergent ideologies, arguing that British nationalism is comprised of competing, assimilated points of view. Works related to family systems include Laura Peters's *Orphan Texts: Victorian Orphans, Culture and Empire,* which explores the significance of the orphan in the context of the Victorian family, and in the wider social order. Peters examines how both serious and popular literature express the problematic nature of the Victorian family. Her argument explains how the orphan figure is a threat to the already unstable Victorian family, and consequently the orphan becomes the victim of the family system's inherent exclusivity. Also related is M. Daphne Kutzer's *Empire's Children: Empire and Imperialism in Classic British Children's Books*, which examines metaphors of empire in writing for children by Rudyard Kipling and others. U.C. Knoepflmacher offers a re-reading of several children's classics in *Ventures into Childland: Victorians, Fairy Tales, and Femininity*. The new paperback edition analyses children's and adult's literature, the relationships between Victorian children and adults, and the lives of several popular children's authors.

Scholars in post-colonial studies, Irish studies and Victorian culture will find Mary Jean Corbett's *Allegories of Union in Irish and English Writing, 1790–1870* an insightful work of analysis that treats both nineteenth-century fiction and prose. Using feminist and post-colonial theories as a framework, Corbett calls for a re-evaluation of colonial discourse and a new acknowledgement of the ways in which Irish resistance to union informed the rhetoric and nation-building of nineteenth-century England. One of the book's insights is how the recurring tropes of family and marriage in literature and prose function as expressions of Ireland's relationship to England, both encouraging and subverting political inequality. Among others, Corbett considers the novels of Edgeworth and Trollope and the prose of Arnold, Carlyle, and Mill.

Several other works this year are influenced by post-colonial theory. Joseph McLaughlin's *Writing the Urban Jungle: Reading Empire in London from Doyle to Eliot* examines how imperialist rhetoric helped to shape English literary culture from late Victorianism to early modernism by creating a metaphorical colonial vocabulary to describe urban culture. Beginning with Arthur Conan Doyle's mysteries, McLaughlin shows how this colonial rhetoric is actually self-reflexive in its application not only to the colonized, but also to London's urban poor. In another work of post-colonial criticism, Laura Chrisman examines the lesser-known writings of imperialist Rider Haggard, feminist Olive Schreiner, and black nationalist Sol Plaatje. *Rereading the Imperial Romance: British Imperialism and South African Resistance in Haggard, Schreiner, and Plaatje* considers these ignored writers in their historical contexts. Haggard's *King Solomon's Mines* and *Nada the Lily* are presented as examples of imperial fiction, while Schreiner's *Trooper Peter Halket of Mashonaland* and Plaatje's *Mhudi* are considered as anti-imperialist answers to Haggard's fiction. Elmar Lehman's 'Der anglo-burische Krieg: Haggard und Henty' (in Heydenreich and Späth, eds., *Afrika in den europäischen Literaturen zwischen 1860 und 1930*) examines Haggard's treatment of Africa and war compared to that of George Alfred Henty.

Rowland Smith, ed., *Postcolonizing the Commonwealth: Studies in Literature and Culture*, is a collection of essays exploring the diversity and complexity of Commonwealth literature. Murray, ed., *Comparing Postcolonial Literatures: Dislocations*, surveys a variety of post-colonial literatures and emphasizes the significance of literature from the British Isles in post-colonial studies. Sangeeta Ray examines British colonialism in India and the treatment of women in *En-Gendering India: Woman and Nation in Colonial and Postcolonial Narratives*. Richard Allen and Harish Trivedi, in *Literature and Nation: Britain and India, 1800 to 1900*, analyse poetry, prose, novels and other documents that collectively narrate the cultural histories of these two countries. In a related work, David Finkelstein and Douglas M. Peers gather a collection of twelve essays on the representation of India in the periodical press. Focusing on the years 1840–1900, Finkelstein and Peers, eds., *Negotiating India in the Nineteenth-Century Media*, covers the great range of English periodical publications, from medical journals to Dickens's *Household Words*, as well as Indian publications such as the Urdu periodicals of the 1870s.

England's imperial project is usually associated with India and Africa, but Robert G. David reminds us that the imperial arm reached to the furthest ends of the globe. David looks at Victorian images and attitudes toward the Arctic in *The Arctic in the British Imagination, 1818–1914*. The opening chapter examines representations of the Arctic in travel narratives, paintings, and photographs. Subsequent chapters consider the role of geographical societies, news from the Arctic, and exhibitions. Andrew Wawn's important and extensive study *The Vikings and the Victorians: Inventing the Old North in Nineteenth-Century Britain* explores the Victorian 'invention' of the Vikings, and the fascination with the Viking age shared by such figures as William Morris, Edward Elgar, and Rudyard Kipling. Wawn's study covers a wide range of material, including philology, art, music, novels, poems, and lectures.

Another work on Victorian historiography, Rosemary Mitchell's *Picturing the Past: English History in Text and Image, 1830–1870*, examines how the Victorians represented the past visually and textually. Mitchell's interdisciplinary project examines a selection of illustrated history books, including David Hume's *History of England* and W.H. Ainsworth's *The Tower of London* [1840] to demonstrate the transitions taking place in mid-Victorian historiography. Drawing on both fiction and non-fiction, which Mitchell explains were not so distinctly categorized in the nineteenth century, the book charts the transition of English 'historical consciousness' from picturesque to philosophical to scientific modes. Mitchell's series of case studies also draws on publishers' archives to demonstrate the relationships between authors, publishers, and illustrators, and their collaborative efforts to (re)create history on paper. In a related work, entitled *The English Idea of History from Coleridge to Collingwood*, Christopher Parker provides an account of how idealist philosophy influenced English historiography, taking into account the problem of subjectivity. In addition to Coleridge and Collingwood, Parker outlines the contributions of John Stuart Mill, Thomas Carlyle and others. *The New Crusaders: Images of the Crusades in the Nineteenth and Early Twentieth Centuries*, by Elizabeth Siberry, examines how authors, historians and artists used the image of the Crusades to various ends.

James A. Secord's *Victorian Sensation: The Extraordinary Publication, Reception, and Secret Authorship of 'Vestiges of the Natural History of Creation'* examines the writing, reception, and influence of this banned bestseller that contributed to the great debate about human origins. Secord presents a thorough account of the book's production, revealing the secrets held in hidden letters and explaining the role of publishers, printers, and booksellers in bringing the book to the public's attention. Campbell, Labbe and Shuttleworth, eds., *Memory and Memorials, 1789–1914: Literary and Cultural Perspectives* explores the significance of memory both as a cultural phenomenon and as 'a written and architectural trope, in its forms of elegy and memorial' (p. 2). The study uses an interdisciplinary approach including science, literature, history, medicine, and the visual arts to 'explore theories of memory, and the cultural and literary resonances of memorialising'. The collection includes examinations of figures such as Ruskin, Hardy ('Memory through the Looking Glass: Ruskin Versus Hardy' by Philip Davis) and Eliot ('Twisting: Memory from Eliot to Eliot' by Rick Rylance). Other essays of note are Sally Shuttleworth's '"The Malady of Thought": Embodied Memory in Victorian Psychology and the Novel' and Helen Small's 'The Unquiet Limit: Old Age and Memory in Victorian Narrative'. Brooks, ed., *The Albert Memorial. The Prince Consort National Memorial: Its History, Contexts, and Conservation* examines one of the most important nineteenth-century British monuments of its age. This study emphasizes the history and symbolism of the monument as an example of the Gothic revival architectural period and its exemplification of many Victorian standards of creative unity.

The relationship between conceptions of history and thoughts of the future is outlined in Sandison and Dingley, eds., *Histories of the Future: Studies in Fact,*

Fantasy and Science Fiction. This interdisciplinary collection addresses a range of genres, including film, art, political prose and science fiction. Of special interest to Victorian scholars is Robert Dingley's contribution, 'The Ruins of the Future: Macaulay's New Zealander and the Spirit of the Age'. Dingley argues that the nineteenth-century British attitude towards New Zealand was informed by a general sense of foreboding and anxiety, explained in part by the increasing specialization and inaccessibility of science. In a related work, William R. McKelvy offers an analysis of Macaulay's *Lays of Ancient Rome* in 'Primitive Ballads, Modern Criticism, Ancient Skepticism' (*VLC* 28:ii[2000] 287–312). Clare A. Simmons's *Eyes Across the Channel: French Revolutions, Party History and British Writing, 1830–1882* examines the reaction to the French Revolution by Burke, Carlyle, Dickens and others.

General works on Victorian culture include Hewitt, ed., *An Age of Equipoise? Re-Assessing Mid-Victorian Britain*, a collection of essays responding to W.L. Burn's 1964 claim that the Victorian period was characterized by counterbalance and equilibrium. Another general work on Victorian culture is Inkster, Griffin, Hill and Rowbotham, eds., *The Golden Age: Essays in British Social and Economic History, 1850–1870*, which explores changes in industry, technology, social institutions and gender roles.

Victorian urban culture is the focus of several interesting new studies. In *Victorian Babylon: People, Streets, and Images in Nineteenth-Century London*, Lynda Nead offers fresh insights about city life and the rise of modernity in nineteenth-century London. She argues that London's transformation into a diverse urban setting was linked to the increased output and consumption of visual images. Examining a wide range of images and texts such as reports, maps, paintings, advertisements, and posters, Nead also considers public life in London's city streets, the inclusion of women in public life, and the growing public debate over obscenity legislation. In *Everyday Violence in Britain, 1850–1950: Gender and Class*, Shani D'Cruze looks at violence in both public spaces (lanes, schools, and hospitals) and private spaces (the home). D'Cruze's collection of essays includes coverage of a variety of topics, such as the rise in violence and the new pattern of drinking and drug use, violence as a means of social power, violence in certain classes and social groups, working-class violence, infanticide, sexual violence, professional intervention and youth gangs. James Hepburn offers an anthology and analysis of broadside ballads about poverty in *A Book of Scattered Leaves: Poetry of Poverty in Broadside Ballads of Nineteenth-Century England*. The study links poetry, poverty, and popular culture by examining several hundred ballads treating the topics of work, relations between the sexes, and crime.

Continued interest in representations of the body is reflected in Lucy Bending's absorbing study *The Representation of Bodily Pain in Late Nineteenth-Century English Culture*. Bending argues that the experience and understanding of pain varies in treatment among late nineteenth-century texts according to gender, race, and class. Her unique study, which examines novels, sermons, leaflets, and medical textbooks, points out the ways in which depictions of pain, though intended to reflect a common human experience, can actually serve to illuminate differences of experience. *Mosaic*'s special issue, *Hygieia: Literature and Medicine*, contains the following articles related to science and the body: James Krasner, 'Arthur Conan Doyle as Doctor and Writer' (*Mosaic* 33[2000] 19–34), and Anka Ryall, 'Medical

Body and Lived Experience: The Case of Harriet Martineau' (*Mosaic* 33[2000] 35–54).

Journalist Christopher Hitchens draws connections between literary figures and politics in *Unacknowledged Legislation: Writers in the Public Sphere*. Oscar Wilde and Arthur Conan Doyle are among the wide range of English and American authors—both past and contemporary—that Hitchens considers in his discussion of how literature engages with the politics of its day. Audrey A. Fisch's *American Slaves in Victorian England: Abolitionist Politics in Popular Literature and Culture* is a study of the American abolitionists' work in England. Fisch asserts that the abolitionist movement in England helped to structure debates about English nationalism, high and low culture, the working classes, and educational reform.

Bloom, ed., *Nineteenth-Century British Women Writers*, outlines the works and critical receptions of ninety-three writers of prose, fiction and poetry. The entries are alphabetically arranged, with each author treated in a separate chapter. Bibliographies of each author's works and writings about her works are also included. Helen Rogers investigates how women participated in political and reform movements in *Women and the People: Authority, Authorship and the Radical Tradition in Nineteenth-Century England*. Rogers's particular focus is how women adopted and changed genre conventions to develop a unique voice in writing about reform. Sanders, ed., *Records of Girlhood: An Anthology of Nineteenth-Century Women's Childhoods*, is a collection of autobiographical writings by women writers describing their early family lives. The contributions of the New Woman writers to later feminist movements are outlined in Ann Heilmann's *New Woman Fiction: Women Writing First-Wave Feminism*. Heilmann analyses the various representations of the New Woman in popular fiction and journalism and concludes that the New Woman had a far-reaching cultural influence beyond the nineteenth century. The book considers the works of both major and obscure woman writers, from Charlotte Perkins Gilman to Arabella Kenealy, to show how this 'first-wave' feminism laid the groundwork not only for turn-of-the-century notions of women's rights but also the further development of feminist thought expressed by contemporary writers such as Adrienne Rich and Hélène Cixous. Richardson and Willis, eds., *The New Woman in Fiction and in Fact: Fin de Siècle Feminisms*, is a collection of essays demonstrating the diverse ways in which the New Woman was conceived and presented. George Gissing and the New Woman writers are discussed in David Trotter's study *Cooking with Mud: The Idea of Mess in Nineteenth-Century Art and Fiction*. Trotter explores the connections between mess, determinism, and democracy in nineteenth-century Western culture. An updated edition of Joan Jacobs Brumberg's *Fasting Girls: The History of Anorexia Nervosa* locates one cause of female eating disorders in the Industrial Revolution. Brumberg's history traces the patterns and practices of food refusal back to the sixteenth century when fasting was a religious devotion. Her analysis of industrialism's effect on privileged young women will be of particular interest to Victorian scholars.

Several works this year remind us of the hybridity of Victorian literature. Robbins and Wolfreys, eds., *Victorian Gothic: Literary and Cultural Manifestations in the Nineteenth Century*, teases out threads of the Gothic in a variety of works by Dickens, Hopkins and others. The editors collect twelve essays presenting distinct definitions of Victorian Gothic. Ruth Robbins's 'Apparitions Can Be Deceptive: Vernon Lee's Androgynous Spectres' points out Pater's influence on Lee; R.J.S.

Watt's 'Hopkins and the Gothic Body' reveals Hopkins's foot fetishism; and Richard Pearson's 'Archaeology and Gothic Desire: Vitality Beyond the Grave in H. Rider Haggard's Ancient Egypt' views Haggard's work in the light of contemporary archaeology.

Several works on the art of the period contribute to our understanding of Victorian art culture. *Victorian Narrative Painting* by Julia Thomas explores the themes of childhood, love and marriage, the home and its outcasts, and death. Thomas explains how narrative paintings use symbols to tell stories and make allusions. The works of William Holman Hunt, William Powell Frith, and Richard Redgrave are among those discussed. Elizabeth Prettejohn's *The Art of the Pre-Raphaelites* makes the case for a nineteenth-century modernism in the artworks of Dante Gabriel Rossetti, Ford Madox Brown, and other members of this exclusive 'brotherhood'. Barbara J. Black's *On Exhibit: Victorians and their Museums* examines how and why the Victorians became enthused with collecting and exhibiting. Black explores nineteenth-century museum culture and its wider social and political contexts, from imperialism and exploration to science and democratic reform. Frank Salmon's *Building on Ruins: The Rediscovery of Rome and English Architecture* gives a historical account of early nineteenth-century interest in classic Roman architecture. In *Re-presenting the Metropolis: Architecture, Urban Experience and Social Life in London, 1800–1840*, Dana Arnold maps the relationship between city and society and shows that the urban landscape was an expression of a variety of cultural identities. Barlow and Trodd, eds., *Governing Cultures: Art Institutions in Victorian London*, gives historical accounts of the art institutions founded in nineteenth-century England. Morowitz and Vaughan, eds., *Artistic Brotherhoods in the Nineteenth Century*, investigates the proliferation of artistic communities in the nineteenth century. Janice Helland's *Professional Women Painters in Nineteenth-Century Scotland* describes how middle-class Victorian women artists lived and worked.

The topographical works of Edward Lear, a landscape artist trained in part by the Pre-Raphaelite Holman Hunt, are collected by curator Scott Wilcox in *Edward Lear and the Art of Travel*, a catalogue of an exhibition at the Yale Center for British Art. The book contains 205 plates of artworks by Lear and others who travelled throughout remote regions of the world and returned to England with the only visual depictions of these unknown worlds in the time before photography. David B. Elliott offers a biography of an obscure Pre-Raphaelite artist in *Charles Fairfax Murray: The Unknown Pre-Raphaelite*. Eliott, who is Murray's grandson, brings out the first biography of this influential figure, whose life is a window on Victorian art culture.

Kate Flint's *The Victorians and the Visual Imagination* is an exploration of Victorian perceptions of the eye and brain, focusing attention on memory, subjectivity, hallucination, blindness, and perception of depth. Flint's study involves the treatment of these topics by Victorian writers (such as George Eliot, Elizabeth Barrett Browning and Rudyard Kipling), as well as artists (especially Pre-Raphaelites and realists) and scientists. Gregory R. Suriano's *The Pre-Raphaelite Illustrators* includes nearly 500 illustrations by the twenty-four artists associated with the Pre-Raphaelite movement. Included are the engravings and graphic arts of Dante Gabriel Rossetti, Frederick Sandys, William Holman Hunt, Arthur Hughes, Edward Burne-Jones and others. The collection includes brief critical-biographical essays, catalogues of artistic output for each artist, a bibliography, and an index. In

The Photographic Art of William Henry Fox Talbot, Larry J. Schaaf draws on new research to discuss the scientific and artistic achievements the man who is credited with the invention of photography in 1839. Schaaf's study includes high-quality reproductions of Talbot's work, and emphasizes Talbot's artistic growth, which is often overshadowed by interest in his achievements as an inventor. The photographs are accompanied by discussions by Schaaf, excerpts from Talbot's writings, and writings of his contemporaries. This study also includes a brief but useful annotated bibliography. Elizabeth Mansfield's 'The Victorian Grand Siècle: Ideology as Art History' (*VLC* 28:i[2000] 133–48) looks at Victorian writings about art and history, with an emphasis on the works of Emilia Dilke, in particular *Art in the Modern State* [1888].

Interest in the aesthetic movement and the *fin de siècle* is reflected in a variety of works such as Regenia Gagnier's 'Productive, Reproductive and Consuming Bodies in Victorian Aesthetic Models' (in Horner and Keane, eds., *Body Matters: Feminism, Textuality, Corporeality*, pp. 43–57), in which she examines the shift from production to consumption and its 'correspondingly imagined bodies'. Gagnier's essay includes an intelligent examination of differences and similarities among the aesthetics of production, aesthetics of taste or consumption, aesthetics of ethics, and aesthetics of evaluation. In her study *The Forgotten Female Aesthetes: Literary Culture in Late-Victorian England*, Talia Schaffer argues that the inclusion of female writers changes the way we perceive the British aesthetic movement. Schaffer looks at opposing conceptions of identity such as the New Woman versus the Pre-Raphaelite maiden, or the female dandy versus the angel of the house, and she analyses the manifestation of these images in literary texts. Included in the study are figures of the female aesthetic movement such as Ouida and Lucas Malet as well as the feminist literary critic Alice Mynell. In *Impressionist Subjects: Gender, Interiority, and Modernist Fiction in England*, Tamar Katz examines female literary subjects in order to frame questions and problems of modernity, subjectivity, and impressionism. Among these are the New Woman movement and the timelessness of art in contrast to modernism's critique of historical conditions. Katz explores Pater's aestheticism in terms of inner and outer spheres, safe interiors and the dangerous exterior world, and also provides interesting insights into female interiority in fiction by George Egerton and Sarah Grand in the context of well-known Victorian debates. In Robbins, ed., *Literary Feminisms*, Ruth Robbins surveys and interprets a wide range of women's writing and feminist theory in recent years, offering insightful commentary and emphasizing contending viewpoints.

Religious studies produced several interesting works this year. Herbert Schlossberg's *The Silent Revolution and the Making of Victorian England* locates the genesis of Victorian culture in the theological debates that preceded Victoria's reign, beginning in the late eighteenth century. Schlossberg argues that this period of religious change constituted England's 'silent' response to economic and social change, in contrast to the violent political revolutions in France and elsewhere. He also contends that theological concerns are the primary means of cultural analysis, and he demonstrates how intellectuals, including Thomas Arnold, Coleridge, and Carlyle, participated in and responded to the rise of evangelicalism and further developments in England's religious culture. David Norton's *A History of the English Bible as Literature* is a revised and condensed version of his acclaimed study of evolving attitudes about the Bible as literature. Norton explores the various causes of the once deprecated King James Bible's eventual rise to prominence as one of the most important books in the English language, and traces the influence of translators and of commentary by such figures as Matthew Arnold, and their contribution to our sense of the Bible today.

Victorian sexuality, particularly male sexuality, continues to inspire a variety of critical discussions. The fourteen essays in Bradstock, Gill, Hogan and Morgan, eds., *Masculinity and Spirituality in Victorian Culture*, respond to the question, 'Was Victorian spirituality in any sense an independent variable in the formulation of masculinity, or did it merely reflect existing patterns of gender and social change?' Operating on the assumption that gender is a social construct that is always changing, the essays consider religious representations of masculinity as well as nationalism, agnosticism, and homosexuality as points of intersection between spirituality and gender. They examine canonical figures (Charlotte Brontë and George Eliot) as well as William Booth, Charles Haddon Spurgeon, and John Addington Symonds. The collection is a complement to *Women of Faith in Victorian Culture: Reassessing the Angel in the House* [1998]. A more focused study of sexuality, Losey and Brewer, eds., *Mapping Male Sexuality: Nineteenth-Century England*, analyses the treatment of male same-sex relations in nineteenth-century culture and writing. The editors gather fourteen essays that explore how writers of both prose and fiction treat masculine identity and homosexuality, and how they respond to changing definitions of and increasing constraints on homosexuality. Medicine, law, religion and other cultural elements all played a role in defining and constraining homosexuality. Contributors analyse works from the late eighteenth century to the first decade of the twentieth century, written by a diverse group that includes George Eliot and Oscar Wilde. S.M. Waddams examines sexuality in the Victorian legal context in *Sexual Slander in Nineteenth-Century England: Defamation in the Ecclesiastical Courts, 1815–1855.*

Victorian humour in all its varieties is the subject of twelve essays in Wagner-Lawlor, ed., *The Victorian Comic Spirit: New Perspectives*. These 'new perspectives' on Victorian humour move beyond the usual nineteenth-century distinctions between wit and humour and provide linguistic and psychological analysis as well as an exploration of the social context in which Victorian comedy operated. The collection treats a range of genres, including Dickens's fiction, Carlyle's prose, Swinburne's correspondence, and the Savoy operas of Gilbert and Sullivan. Eileen Gillooly contributes a particularly interesting analysis of Gaskell's narrator in 'Humor as Daughterly Defense in *Cranford*'. David Nash, Carolyn Williams, and Patricia Murphy are among the other contributors.

Rupert Christiansen presents a unique view of nineteenth-century English culture as seen through the lenses of several 'visitors' from other countries. *The Visitors: Culture Shock in Nineteenth-Century Britain* gives accounts of the experiences of England by luminaries and common folk from around the globe. There are chapters on the French painter Théodore Géricault, composer Richard Wagner, and Ralph Waldo Emerson, and also on the visits made by Italian ballerinas, an Australian cricketer, and an American medium. The book's humorous account of these various visitors' often strange and comical English encounters complements its significance as a record of the great diversity within Victorian culture.

Kucich and Sadoff, eds., *The Victorian Afterlife: Postmodern Culture Rewrites the Nineteenth Century* is a fascinating collection of essays from noted cultural critics examining the recent resurgence of interest in postmodern Victoriana, including Victorian revivals in blockbuster films, TV adaptations, and an explosion in consumer culture. Kucich and Sadoff look at these reworkings of the past in their attempt to 'begin a discussion of postmodernism's privileging of the Victorian as its historical "other"'. According to Kucich and Sadoff, 'the recent high and popular cultural movements to rewrite the nineteenth century seek to create self-awareness in the present by reworking the past' (p. xiii). This interest is found in Victorian sexuality, which they contend 'seems to be made for such retellings'. The collection includes: 'Modernity and Culture: The Victorians and Cultural Studies' by John McGowan; 'At Home in the Nineteenth Century: Photography, Nostalgia, and the Will to Authenticity' by Jennifer Green-Lewis; 'The Uses and Misuses of Oscar Wilde' by Shelton Waldrep; 'Being True to Jane Austen' by Mary A. Favret; 'A Twentieth Century Portrait: Jane Campion's American Girl' by Susan Lurie; 'Display Cases' by Judith Roof; 'Found Drowned: The Irish Atlantic' by Judith Roof; 'The Embarrassment of Victorianism: Colonial Subjects and the Lure of Englishness' by Simon Gikandi; 'Hacking the Nineteenth Century' by Jay Clayton; 'Queen Victoria and Me' by Laurie Langbauer; 'Sorting, Morphing, and Mourning: A.S. Byatt Ghostwrites Victorian Fiction' by Hilary M. Schor; 'Asking Alice: Victorian and Other Alices in Contemporary Culture' by Kali Israel; 'Specters of the Novel: Dracula and the Cinematic Afterlife of the Victorian Novel' by Kali Israel; and 'Contemporary Culturalism: How Victorian Is It?' by Nancy Armstrong.

The influence of science on the Victorians is a growing field of study. Rick Rylance's interdisciplinary study *Victorian Psychology and British Culture, 1850–1880* examines the early years of English psychology when the field began to emerge as a discipline separate from philosophy and biology. Because psychology remained an open territory as yet unclaimed by specialists, the study of the mind was fair game for any serious thinker, from philosophers and theologians to poets and physicians. It was also the nexus of public debate because it addressed controversial theories about evolution and human perception. At stake was no less than a new definition of humanity that incorporated the latest understanding of how humans perceive and interact with the material world, operating as intellectual, biological, and spiritual beings. The first half of the book shows the influence of metaphysics, philosophy, biology, and medicine on competing psychological theories. The second half provides a thorough examination of three important figures: Alexander Bain, Herbert Spencer, and G.H. Lewes. Rylance maps out the intellectual connections among the thinkers of the day so that the reader appreciates the significance of both Darwinian and Lamarckian theory in the development of particular psychological approaches. In another work related to scientific writing, Weber, ed., *Nineteenth-Century Science: An Anthology*, collects over thirty works excerpted from books, articles, and other scientific sources. Darwin, Hermann von Helmholtz, and Lamarck are among the writers included. Roy M. MacLeod's *The 'Creed of Science' in Victorian England* includes chapters on the genesis and social framework of the journal *Nature*. In *Sparks of Life: Darwinism and the Victorian Debates over Spontaneous Generation*, James E. Strick traces notions of spontaneous generation in the prose writings of Bastian, Beale, Bennett, Busk, Dallinger, Darwin, Dohrn, Drysdale, Fiske, Frankland, Hooker, Huxley, Lankester, Lawson, Lister, MacMillan, Owen, Pasteur, Pouchet, Sanderson, Schafer, Sharpey, Spencer, Thomson, Tyndall, Wallace, and Youmans.

The Victorians will always be associated with the public debate over social reform. *The Quarrel of Macaulay and Croker: Politics and History in the Age of Reform* by William Thomas chronicles a life-long conflict which began with the debate over parliamentary reform in the House of Commons in 1831–2 and continued for years in the reviews, particularly the *Edinburgh* and the *Quarterly*. Thomas revises the accepted explanations of the conflict by reading each man's actions as an expression of his individual experiences, set in a particular social context. He concludes that Macaulay and Croker actually had many ideas in common, and that Macaulay's stature as the great Whig historian distorts the complexity of his political position and his purpose in writing *The History of England*. The first chapter sets out to correct the interpretative errors committed by biographers who have been inclined to give preference to Macaulay's side of the argument. Macaulay and Croker are usually described as homogeneous Victorians, but Thomas shows that the generational differences between the men—Croker being influenced by the Napoleonic conflict and Macaulay the product of a relatively peaceful era—account in large part for their tenacious opposition to one another. Thomas's fair-mindedness brings a fresh perspective to the Croker–Macaulay conflict, and offers the thoughtful conclusion that posterity almost always gives preference to the artist (Macaulay) rather than the critic (Croker).

Several new biographies tell the stories of lost and forgotten Victorian figures. A major figure in the end-of-the-century publishing world was Leonard Smithers, the subject of James G. Nelson's *Publisher to the Decadents: Leonard Smithers in the Careers of Beardsley, Wilde, Dowson*. Smithers was best known as a publisher of pornography, but Nelson also points out his other important contributions to late Victorian literary culture: he supported avant-garde writers and artists, brought out the works of Wilde and Beardsley, and created the periodical *Savoy*, which featured the works of W.B. Yeats, Jean Moréas, and Stéphane Mallarmé. A checklist of Smithers's publications is included. This book completes Nelson's important trilogy of 1890s publishers begun with *The Early Nineties: A View from Bodley Head* [1971] and *Elkin Mathews: Publisher to Yeats, Joyce, Pound* [1989].

The life of one of nineteenth-century England's most celebrated explorers is recounted in Andrew Taylor's *God's Fugitive: The Life of C.M. Doughty*. W.J. McCormack offers a biography of J.M. Synge, author of *The Playboy of the Western World*. *Fool of the Family: A Life of J.M. Synge* uses unpublished material to describe Synge's family relationships and show the influence on Synge of various cultural and intellectual contexts such as the Abbey Theatre, the writings of Sigmund Freud, Thomas Mann, and Max Weber, and the scandalous Dreyfus affair. Brian Thompson's fascinating biography *A Monkey Among Crocodiles: The Disastrous Life of Mrs. Georgina Weldon* explores the flamboyant life of an unusual woman. Thompson looks at Georgina's marriage to Harry Weldon, their *ménage à trois* with French composer Gounod, Harry's attempt to have Georgina committed for lunacy, and Georgina's ill-fated involvement with two crooks called Menier. John Stokes edits a collection of essays, *Eleanor Marx (1855–1898)*, on the life and works of Karl Marx's youngest daughter. Among many professional talents, Eleanor Marx was a journalist and translator who made important critical contributions to the study of Flaubert, Ibsen and Shakespeare.

Andrew Motion's *Wainewright the Poisoner* examines the life of the flamboyant Thomas Griffiths Wainewright, a strange and notorious figure of the nineteenth century who was known for his painting, writing, and criminal activities, and who was eventually convicted of forgery. Motion's biography is a speculative and inventive blend of notes, letters, and documents found after the Wainewright's death in a penal colony. The book explores the legend he left behind and its impact on the culture's beliefs about good and evil. Particularly noteworthy is Motion's examination of Oscar Wilde's and Charles Dickens's fascination with Wainewright's bizarre and mysterious personality, which figured in their writings. Motion also delves into the nature of biography and the biographer's roles and responsibilities in the making of historical figures.

An important bibliographic contribution to Victorian studies this year is the two-volume edition of Chaudhuri and Radford, eds., *Cumulative Bibliography of Victorian Studies, 1945–1969*. Each volume contains more than 600 pages of bibliographic references, and the second provides an index of subject areas that includes the following categories: general and reference works, fine arts, philosophy and religion, history, social sciences, science and technology, and language and literature. Seventy authors are indexed individually, and additional authors are listed in the final section.

Julie F. Codell, 'Victorian Artists' Family Biographies: Domestic Authority, the Marketplace, and the Artist's Body' (in Law and Hughes, eds., *Biographical Passages: Essays in Victorian and Modernist Biography, Honoring Mary M. Lago*), examines in detail 'a number of artists' familial or domestic biographies written between 1890 and World War I'. Codell argues that 'their authorship by the artists' widows or children exploited the hybridity of Victorian biography' and 'asserted a domestic authority necessary to the construction of an artist compatible with Victorian social values' (p. 66). A related work by Codell, entitled 'Constructing the Victorian Artist: National Identity, the Political Economy of Art and Biographical Mania in the Periodical Press' (*VPR* 33:iii[2000] 283–316), looks at the popularity of artists' biographies. Other articles on Victorian cultural studies include George Levine, 'Two Ways Not To Be a Solipsist: Art and Science, Pater and Pearson' (*VS* 43:i[2000] 7–42); Amanda Anderson, 'The Temptations of Aggrandized Agency: Feminist Histories and the Horizon of Modernity' (*VS* 43:i[2000] 43–67); and David Wayne Thomas, 'Replicas and Originality: Picturing Agency in Dante Gabriel Rossetti and Victorian Manchester' (*VS* 43:i[2000] 67–102).

(b) Prose

Several new prose anthologies merit attention. In a large and eclectic compilation, David J. Bradshaw and Suzanne Ozment gather sixty-seven selections that represent the great breadth of contemporary opinion on the problems, challenges, and controversies of nineteenth-century work and employment. Bradshaw and Ozment, eds., *The Voice of Toil: Nineteenth-Century British Writings about Work*, contains poetry, prose, and excerpts of fiction from major and forgotten authors, literary artists and crusading reformers. The selections are sometimes surprising because they reach into literature not normally associated with the debates about social reform and employment laws. For example, part I of the anthology, entitled 'Work as Mission', includes Browning's 'Fra Lippo Lippi' along with Florence Nightingale's more predictable *Cassandra*. Part II addresses 'Work as Opportunity' and includes Elizabeth Gaskell's 'Cumberland Sheep-Shearers' and Robert Owen's 'Observations on the Effect of the Manufacturing System'. Part III, 'Work as

Oppression', opens with poems by William Blake ('The Chimney Sweeper' and 'London') and also includes some of Matthew Arnold's lesser-known poetry ('East London' and 'West London'). Alongside these representative works of serious literature is an excerpt from Charles Booth's crusading *Life and Labour of the People of London* [1891–1903], replete with tables and charts that make the argument in more factual, if less aesthetic, terms. The final section, entitled '(Separate) Spheres of Work', includes excerpts from Tennyson's *The Princess*, Elizabeth Barrett Browning's *Aurora Leigh*, and John Stuart Mill's *The Subjection of Women*. The editors have also included Eliza Lynn Linton's 'What is Woman's Work?' that speaks out in opposition to New Woman activism. Bradshaw and Ozment provide helpful introductions to each thematic section as well as biographical information for each writer.

Ledger and Luckhurst, eds., *The Fin de Siècle: A Reader in Cultural History, c.1880–1900*, is an anthology that brings together a useful collection of non-literary writings by important Victorian figures such as Oscar Wilde, Arthur Symons, Sarah Grand, William Morris, T.H. Huxley, Sigmund Freud, William James, and John Addington Symonds. Included are the following sections: 'Degeneration', 'Outcast London', 'The Metropolis', 'The New Woman', 'Literary Debates', 'The New Imperialism', 'Socialism', 'Anarchism', 'Scientific Naturalism', 'Psychology', 'Psychical Research', 'Sexology', and 'Anthropology and Racial Sciences'. Another anthology of note is Nassaar, ed., *The Victorians: A Major Authors Anthology*, which includes works by Arnold, Carlyle, Mill, Tennyson, Browning, Newman, Pater, Hopkins, Ruskin, and Wilde.

Nineteenth-century journalism provides a kaleidoscope of perspectives on Victorian culture. Brake, Bell and Finkelstein, eds., *Nineteenth-Century Media and the Construction of Identities*, explores the great range of Victorian journalism, from popular periodicals to intellectual journals, delineating the variety of ways in which it helped to define identities, both individual and collective. The collection of twenty-two essays amounts to a sampling of the great variety of Victorian journalism, and the topics range from the penny press to Anglo-Jewish identity to divorce-court proceedings. Campbell, ed., *Journalism, Literature and Modernity*, points out the significance of journalism in the experience of the modern world. Campbell's study reflects a growing interest in journalism (previously dismissed as low culture) as an important aspect of cultural and literary studies. Use of the word 'journalism' in this interdisciplinary examination refers to writings in public journals of both high and popular culture; a wide range of journalism—from literary journals to daily newspapers—is investigated, using various approaches and methods. For example, Geoffrey Hemstedt offers a useful discussion of Dickens's later journalism and shows how these writings were linked with cultural and historical changes. Hemstedt also examines Dickens's use of language during this period, which blends the language of reform and punishment with empathy. Mark W. Turner's 'Hybrid Journalism: Women and the Progressive *Fortnightly*' discusses the so-called 'progressive' *Fortnightly*'s omission of women, correlating this neglect with positivism. This astute collection of essays also includes valuable discussions of such noteworthy figures as Arnold and Pater. Another work related to journalistic prose is *Their Fair Share: Women, Power and Criticism in the Athenaeum, from Millicent Garrett Fawcett to Katherine Mansfield, 1870–1920* by Marysa Demoor, which examines articles and essays published in the *Athenaeum* by 'a.o.', Millicent Garrett Fawcett, Emilia Dilke, Jane Harrison and Augusta Webster. Atkinson, ed., *The Selected Letters of W.E. Henley*, provides insight into the life of an important nineteenth-century journalist, critic and poet: Henley edited *London*, the *Magazine of Art*, the *Scots Observer*, the *National Observer* and the *New Review*.

Several articles also provide analyses of journalistic writing and culture. In 'Stalking through the Literary World: Anna Jameson and the Periodical Press, 1826–1860' (*VPR* 33:ii[2000] 165–77), Ainslie Robinson looks at Anna Jameson's writings between 1826 and 1864, and her relationship to the periodical press at the start of her career. Robinson also links Jameson's writings to changes in reviewing practices in Victorian periodicals. Sheila Rosenberg's '"The wicked *Westminster*": John Chapman, his Contributors and Promises Fulfilled' (*VPR* 33:iii[2000] 225–46) discusses the *Westminster Review*'s progressive mid-century approaches to suffrage and to European movements for national independence. According to Rosenberg, the *Westminster*'s emphasis on reform was not its audience's primary interest; instead, Rosenberg argues, readers were more interested in current views of Christianity and evolution. Rosenberg examines Chapman's involvement in promoting theories of evolution, German biblical study, and historical criticism. Mark Turner's 'Defining Discourses: The *Westminster Review*, *Fortnightly Review*, and Comte's Positivism' (*VPR* 33:iii[2000] 273–82) looks at overlaps in readership, subject matter, and contributors between the two competing radical periodicals of the time. Turner examines, in particular, the strategies of the *Fortnightly* in establishing its own radical discourse and creating its own niche. In 'The *Westminster* and Gender at Mid-Century' (*VPR* 33:iii[2000] 247–72), Laurel Brake explores the 'contents of the *Westminster Review* between 1850 and 1865', and how they 'address the subject of gender at its most inclusive'. Rosemary T. Vanarsdel's '*Macmillan's Magazine* and the Fair Sex: 1859–1874 (Part One)' (*VPR* 33:iv[2000] 374–96) examines the contributions of female writers to *Macmillan's Magazine*, and Alexander Macmillan's changing attitudes towards women. In 'The Ideology of Domesticity: The Regulation of the Household Economy in Victorian Women's Magazines' (*VPR* 33:ii[2000] 150–64), Kay Boardman looks at the pervasiveness of the ideology of domesticity in the context of class, gender, and hegemony, and the role of women's magazines in this process.

Travel writing has become a popular field of study in recent years. Barbara Korte provides a history of travel writing from the British Isles in *English Travel Writing from Pilgrimages to Postcolonial Explorations*. The book traces the beginnings of English travel writing back to the pilgrimages of the Middle Ages, and looks at both recognized and obscure works, including the writing of Mary Kingsley. The accounts of British women travelling in West Africa from 1840 to 1915 are described and analysed by Cheryl McEwan in *Gender, Geography and Empire: Victorian Women Travellers in West Africa*. Ulrike Stamm considers travel writing by women and their treatment of nature and foreign culture in 'The Role of Nature in Two Women's Travel Accounts: Appropriation and Escape' (in Glage, ed., *Being/s in Transit: Travelling, Migration, Dislocation*). The travel writing of Mary Seacole figures in several critical conversations this year. Paul Baggett's 'Caught between Homes: Mary Seacole and the Question of Cultural Identity' (*MaComère* 3[2000] 45–56) considers Seacole's autobiographical writing as a representation of Afro-Caribbean identity. Evelyn J. Hawthorne examines Seacole's treatment of sex roles and compliance with genre conventions in 'Self-Writing, Literary Traditions, and Post-Emancipation Identity: The Case of Mary Seacole' (*Biography* 32:ii[2000] 309–31). Laura L. Moakler contributes an entry on Seacole in Nelson, ed., *African American Authors, 1745–1945: A Bio-Bibliographical Critical Sourcebook*.

A new volume in the Cambridge Studies in Nineteenth-Century Literature and Culture series is Elaine Freedgood's *Victorian Writing about Risk: Imagining a Safe England in a Dangerous World*. Freedgood examines a variety of Victorian popular prose to show how perceptions of risk and safety depend on unstable identities of various groups such as women, men, the middle class, the working class, the English, Irish, and Africans. Freedgood's selection of writing includes entries on political economy, sanitary reform, balloon flight, alpine mountaineering, and African exploration. These works suggest that the nineteenth century was a unique historical moment when perceptions of risk were associated with group identities and the British imperial project.

This year's major contribution to Matthew Arnold studies is Cecil Y. Lang's publication of all of Arnold's known letters. When complete, the project will amount to six volumes. The fourth volume appears in 2000 under the title *The Letters of Matthew Arnold, 1871–1878* and covers the period when Arnold wrote several of his lesser-known works, such as *St. Paul and Protestantism* [1870], *Literature and Dogma* [1873], *God and Bible*, and *Last Essays on Church and Religion*. The fourth volume also records significant events in Arnold's personal life—the deaths of his son, brother, and mother—and his travels to France, Switzerland and Italy.

Linda Ray Pratt presents a concise summary of Arnold's career as a poet and cultural critic in *Matthew Arnold Revisited*. The book hits the highlights as it breezes through Arnold's major works. Pratt begins with an analysis of the critical controversy over Arnold and the revisions of his biography. Four chapters are devoted to his poetry, included an individual chapter on *Empedocles on Etna* [1852]. *Culture and Anarchy* receives the most attention, although it shares a chapter with related essays. The book concludes with a brief analysis of Arnold's Christian humanism as expressed in *St. Paul and Protestantism* and *Literature and Dogma*. Despite its brevity, the book does offer some fresh critical perspectives, particularly the concluding argument that Arnold's relevance today is his potential to serve as a model for civilized cultural and scholarly debates. Pratt sees Arnold's 'effort to reason objectively, to see things whole' as a plausible alternative to the 'culture wars' that plague the present academy. Arnold's critical reception from 1849 to 1999 is summarized in Laurence W. Mazzeno's *Matthew Arnold: The Critical Legacy*. Articles of interest include Bill Bell's 'Beyond the Death of the Author: Matthew Arnold's Two Audiences, 1888–1930' (*BoH* 3[2000] 155–65), which examines Arnold's publishing history and reception. Regenia Gagnier compares Arnold's treatment of individualism to that of Herbert Spencer and Walter Pater in 'The Law of Progress and the Ironies of Individualism in the Nineteenth Century' (*NLH* 31:ii[2000] 315–36).

The major contribution to Carlyle studies this year is Rodger L. Tarr and Mark Engel's edition of *Sartor Resartus: The Life and Opinions of Herr Teufelsdrockh in Three Books*, which is based on Tarr's edition of the *Writings of Thomas Carlyle* with Norman and Charlotte Strouse, and includes an introduction and notes by Tarr. John Plotz's 'Crowd Power: Chartism, Carlyle, and the Victorian Public Sphere'

(*Representations* 70[2000] 87–114) investigates political protest, conservatism, and the public sphere. David Theo Goldberg compares the treatment of blacks by Carlyle and Mill in 'Liberalism's Limits: Carlyle and Mill on "The Negro Question"' (*NCC* 22:ii[2000] 203–16). James Mulvihill examines Carlyle's relationship to virtual reality in William Gibson's *Neuromancer* in 'Thomas Carlyle and "Virtual Reality"' (*NConL* 30:iv[2000] 12–13).

'The first seeds' of Darwin's theory of evolution are contained in his zoology notes from his voyage on the *Beagle*. *Charles Darwin's Zoology Notes and Specimen Lists from H.M.S. Beagle*, edited by Cambridge University Physiology Professor Emeritus Richard Keynes, brings out the previously unpublished notes that Darwin used in writing his *Journal of Researches* [1839]. The notes include Darwin's detailed descriptions and analysis of the animals he observed and experimented on, as well as two lists of the 4,000 specimens examined. Jonathon Smith analyses Darwin's treatment of barnacles, his relationship to seaside resorts, and his bourgeois politics as compared with Dickens in 'Darwin's Barnacles, Dickens' *Little Dorrit,* and the Social Uses of Victorian Seaside Studies' (*LIT* 10:iv[2000] 327–47). Byørn Tysdahl traces Darwin's influence on Alexander Lange Kielland in 'Alexander L. Kielland: Naturen på ny' (*Edda* 1[2000] 1–13).

Friedrich Engels and English industrialism are explored by Aruna Krishnamurthy in '"More than abstract knowledge": Friedrich Engels in Industrial Manchester' (*VLC* 28:ii[2000] 427–51). *Fanny Kemble's Journals,* edited and with an introduction by Catherine Clinton, includes excerpts from journals and memoirs of the popular actress Fanny Kemble. Kemble documents the lives of the rich and famous as well as peasants, providing entertaining and illuminating pictures of Victorian life, from literary salons, to life on the stage, to life on the southern plantation. Her writings in her slavery plantation journal are of particular interest. Mary Henrietta Kingsley's autobiographical writing is examined by Lynnette Turner in 'Mary Kingsley: The Female Ethnographic Self in Writing' (in Donnell and Polkey, eds., *Representing Lives: Women and Auto/Biography*). The prose works of Walter Savage Landor are compared to works by Shelley in Regina Hewitt's 'Landor, Shelley, and the Design of History' (*RoN* 20[2000]). Henry Edward Manning's prose works are discussed by Jacqueline Clais-Girard in 'De la littérature catholique comme antidote à l'esprit du temps' (*CVE* 52[2000] 23–32).

Broadview Press has brought out a new edition of John Stuart Mill's *On Liberty,* edited by Edward Alexander. Foreign-language essays on Mill include a comparison to Dostoevsky by I. Zokhrab in '"Evropeiskiki gipotzy" i "russkie aksiomy": Dostoevskii i Dzhon Stiuart Mill' (*RLit* 3[2000] 37–52). A new edition of John Henry Newman's forgotten novel *Callista* includes an introduction by Alan G. Hill. Newman also receives attention in S.A.M. Adshead's *Philosophy of Religion in Nineteenth-Century England and Beyond*, which examines the religious philosophies of twelve thinkers including Newman. Bernadette Lemoine analyses Newman's use of Scripture in 'Homilétic poétique, théologie de l'histoire et interprétation des écritures d'aorès les *Sermons Preached on Various Occasions* par John Henry Newman' (*CVE* 52[2000] 46–63). Portuguese poet and essayist Fernando Pessoa's works are linked to English and American literature in George Monteiro's *Fernando Pessoa and Nineteenth-Century Anglo-American Literature.* Monteiro shows the connections between Pessoa's work and the artistic and creative ideas of Ruskin, Browning, Pater, Keats and Wordsworth.

Two works on Dante Gabriel Rossetti should be noted. Jerome McGann analyses Rossetti's career and tries to account for the wide influence of his work in *Dante Gabriel Rossetti and the Game That Must Be Lost*. Vivien Allen's *Dear Mr. Rossetti: The Letters of Dante Gabriel Rossetti and Hall Caine, 1878–1881* documents the cultivation and growth of a friendship between Rossetti, painter and poet, and Cain, the young provincial journalist and draughtsman. The letters are a good example of the Victorians' artistic epistolary style.

The most important contribution to studies in Victorian prose this year is Tim Hilton's second and final volume of his biography of Ruskin. *John Ruskin: The Later Years* concludes the project that began with *John Ruskin: The Early Years* [1985] and provides a detailed account of Ruskin's life from 1859 until his death. In addition to presenting a thorough, thoughtful rendering of the personal tragedies in Ruskin's later years, including his romantic attachment to 10-year-old Rose La Touche and his subsequent decline into despair and madness, Hilton offers a new critical perspective on his nearly forgotten series of pamphlets, *Fors Clavigera*, arguing that the writer reached his apex with this work. *The Later Years* takes its rightful place alongside *The Early Years* as the standard Ruskin biography. John Batchelor's biography, *John Ruskin: A Life*, examines Ruskin's diverse ideas and their evolution as a whole, as well as his impact on the middle classes as one of the most influential figures of his time, especially in terms of morality and the ideal society, education, and the environment. Batchelor investigates Ruskin's role as an art critic, and his social advocacy as he shaped the artistic tastes of and provided moral guidance for the middle classes and the new rich, especially industrialists and businessmen. Batchelor's study also includes a valuable investigation of Ruskin's impact on the publishing industry. Batchelor combines his examination of Ruskin's public life with insights into his emotional problems, which, he argues, stem from his earliest years, and were not based principally on sexual difficulties.

Ruskin's *Fors Clavigera*, also known as *Letters to the Workmen and Labourers of Great Britain*, contains ninety-six letters published serially over thirteen years: Dinah Birch edits a new selection of the letters that, although incomplete, does constitute an accurate representation of a very difficult and controversial text. Birch's introduction argues that *Fors Clavigera* anticipates modernism because it is highly autobiographical, fragmented, and richly allusive. The edition aims to present Ruskin's work in its original context; to that end, Birch has based the text on the first published version of the letters. Six of the original illustrations appear alongside the letters, and a nine-page chronology covers the major events in England and in Ruskin's life from 1819 to 1900. The edition includes some complete letters, but most are abbreviated. Francis O'Gorman's essay 'Ruskin and Particularity: *Fors Clavigera* and the 1870s' (*PQ* 79[2000] 119–36) argues that Ruskin approached both his writing and his involvement in educational reform with the same concern for detail and context. The 'particularities' or specificities in *Fors Clavigera* recall Ruskin's contribution to college life at Corpus Christi. O'Gorman concludes that 'Ruskin's involvement with, and self-insertion into, Corpus Christi's distinct, local concerns … is related to that part of his project in *Fors Clavigera* to precipitate thought on issues of seriousness by resourcefully engaging with the precise particularities of his audience's and his own contexts' (p. 133).

Ruskin's major contribution to art criticism, *The Stones of Venice* [1851–3], describes the sculpture and architecture of Venice. An illustrated guide by photographer Sarah Quill and Alan Windsor, *Ruskin's Venice: The Stones Revisited*, places Ruskin's prose alongside photographs of the buildings he described. The guide includes Quill's photographs as well as Ruskin's own drawings and watercolours. Windsor's introduction provides helpful background information about Ruskin's interest in Venice and Venetian architecture. In a related work, editors Robert Hewison, Ian Warrell, and Stephen Wildman make the case for Ruskin's modernity in their catalogue *Ruskin, Turner and the Pre-Raphaelites*. The book reproduces the artworks about which Ruskin wrote, as well as plates of Ruskin's own drawings and watercolours. Hewison describes Ruskin's relationship with several artists and argues that his support of the Pre-Raphaelites shares a common project with contemporary art in its endeavour to challenge accepted traditions. He further notes that both are products of technological change, the Pre-Raphaelites responding to new artistic media and contemporary artists responding to technology's wider cultural influence. Another related work by Hewison is *Ruskin's Artists: Studies in Victorian Visual Economy*, which examines how artists such as J.M.W. Turner, Dante Gabriel Rossetti, William Holman Hunt, and Edward Burne-Jones influenced Ruskin's writing.

Michael Wheeler's *Ruskin's God* argues that religious faith informs Ruskin's thinking and writing, contrary to the traditional view of him as a troubled Christian. In works such as *Modern Painters*, *The Seven Lamps of Architecture* and *The Stones of Venice*, Wheeler finds evidence that Ruskin maintained a faith in divine wisdom and aimed to provide moral guidance, as well as artistic criticism. Kevin Jackson's *A Ruskin Alphabet* is a comprehensive guide to the life of Ruskin, his thoughts, writings, and works. The alphabet covers a wide range of topics, from art to zoology, architecture, and literature. Ruskin's appreciation of Byzantine culture is discussed in two essays included in Cormack and Jeffreys, eds., *Through the Looking Glass: Byzantium through British Eyes*. In 'The Sublime Rivalry of Word and Image: Turner and Ruskin Revisited' (*VLC* 28:i[2000] 149–70), Alexandra K. Wettlaufer re-examines the relationship between Ruskin and Turner, arguing that both men—as poets and artists—sought to create new connections between words and images. Wettlaufer examines the way in which Ruskin turned to visual art and Turner to poetry as supplementary mediums for their primary art. In 'Visual Labor: Ruskin's Radical Realism' (*VLC* 28:i[2000] 73–86), Caroline Levine notes previous scholars' complaints about the numerous inconsistencies in Ruskin's works about art. She looks at the chronology of his writing and argues that his 'first massive works on art are all interwoven, picking up recurrent themes, cross-referencing one another, and even intersecting chronologically' (p. 73). Aniko Nemeth applies Raymond Williams's theories about culture to an analysis of Ruskin in 'Practising "Beauty": Ruskinian Cultures and Ethics Growing out of Aesthetics' (*BAS* 6[2000] 40–4). Ruskin's treatment of masculinity, sexuality and architecture is examined by Vincent A. Lankewish in 'Victorian Architectures of Masculine Desire' (*NCStud* 14[2000] 93–199). Francis O'Gorman takes a socio-economic and biographical approach in '"Suppose it were your own father of whom you spoke": Ruskin's *Unto This Last* (1860)' (*RES* 51[2000] 230–47).

Ruskin also continues to generate international interest. Stéphane Gounel explores Marcel Proust's French translation of Ruskin in 'Proust et Ruskin: Le "Bénéfice intellectuel" de la traduction' which appears in Fraisse, ed., *Pour une esthétique de la littérature mineure*. Odile Boucher-Rivalain analyses *The Stones of*

Venice in 'Vision du passé dans les écrits architecturaux des années 1840 en France et en Angleterre' (*CVE* 51[2000] 25–38).

Herbert Spencer's influence on Paul Bourget is demonstrated by David C.J. Lee in 'Bourget's Debt to Herbert Spencer: *Le Disciple* and the Self-Adjusting Watch' (*MLR* 95:iii[2000] 653–73). Pemble, ed., *John Addington Symonds: Culture and the Demon Desire*, includes a range of essays that explore the life and works of Symonds. Sam Binkley's 'The Romantic Sexology of John Addington Symonds' (*JH* 40:i[2000] 79–103) examines homosexuality and ethics. In 'Camp Expertise: Arthur Symons, Music-Hall, and the Defense of Theory' (*VLC* 28:i[2000] 171–96), Barry Faulk examines Arthur Symons's writings about the sketch comedy, variety entertainment, and dance of the English music hall. Faulk examines Symons's interest in the challenge these artistic expressions provided to cultural hierarchies in light of the growing middle-class audience. In *Queen Victoria and Thomas Sully*, Carrie Rebora Barratt examines the experiences of Thomas Sully during his five-month wait for a sitting for Queen Victoria's full-length coronation portrait. Drawing from the journals of both Queen Victoria and Sully, Barratt describes the complex world of the British aristocracy and the role of the artist within it. Other miscellaneous articles of interest in prose studies include Christopher Clausen's 'Lord Acton and the Lost Cause' (*ASch* 69:i[2000] 49–58) and Helen Nicholson's study of Georgina Weldon's prose in 'Promoting Herself: The Representational Strategies of Georgina Weldon' (in Donnell and Polkey, eds., *Representing Lives*).

2. The Novel

(a) General

Audrey Jaffe looks at scenes of sympathy in works by writers such as Dickens, Conan Doyle, Gaskell, Mayhew, Eliot and Wilde in *Scenes of Sympathy: Identity and Representation in Victorian Fiction*. Using psychoanalytic and cinematic theory Jaffe applies discussions of altruism and egotism to the field of visual studies, emphasizing the construction of middle-class identity. Marlene Tromp's unique study of sensation novels, *The Private Rod: Marital Violence, Sensation, and the Law in Victorian Britain*, argues that, in the sensation novels of the 1860s and 1870s, a new understanding took place about domesticity, codes of behaviour in marriage, and domestic violence. Representations in works by Dickens, Collins, Braddon, Oliphant, and Eliot influenced the Victorian debate, which was acted out in parliament as well as in circulating libraries. The discourses of marital violence in both realms (fiction and law) were incorporated into one another, causing a reassessment of literary and social norms. This aspect of literary criticism has been excluded from the canon until recently.

Scragg and Weinberg, eds., *Literary Appropriations of the Anglo-Saxons from the Thirteenth to the Twentieth Century*, traces perceptions of Anglo-Saxons in English poetry, drama, and novels. Andrew Sanders's '"Utter indifference?" The Anglo-Saxons in the Nineteenth-Century Novel' investigates Victorian novelists' inheritance of the various agendas in Sir Walter Scott's Waverley novels (*Ivanhoe*), and his emphasis on England rather than Scotland. Sanders also explores Disraeli's distinct view of Saxondom, as well as Kingsley's and Bulwer's conceptions of the 1066 conquest.

In *How to Read and Why*, Harold Bloom examines relationships between and among great literary classics (short stories, novels, and plays) of varying periods and places, with the intent of elucidating the wisdom of these classics. Bloom emphasizes reading for self-knowledge, and how to read for maximum pleasure. His study includes treatments of Jane Austen's *Emma*, Charles Dickens's *Great Expectations*, and Oscar Wilde's *The Importance of Being Earnest*. In another work directed towards students of literature, Barbara Dennis contributes a new volume to the Cambridge Contexts in Literature series entitled *The Victorian Novel*. The series is designed for advanced students and includes study guides, discussion questions, excerpts from novels, a chronology, and a glossary.

In *Testimony and Advocacy in Victorian Law, Literature, and Theology*, Jan-Melissa Schramm discusses the impact of changing features of evidence in both theology and law on narrative and fictional representations. These representations, she argues, simultaneously emulated and countered legal proceedings. Following new legislation in 1836, barristers were permitted to address the jury and were thus allowed greater freedom of interpretation. Schramm argues that, since facts could no longer 'speak for themselves', the dynamics of courtroom proceedings—including eyewitness testimony and the silencing of the defendant—were profoundly affected. Schramm also draws interesting parallels between eyewitness testimonies and narrative construction, as well as justice and the impulse to narrate.

Daniel Pick's fascinating study *Svengali's Web: The Alien Enchanter in Modern Culture* looks at the hypnotist Svengali in *Trilby*, the immensely popular novel published by George du Maurier in 1894. Pick examines representations of Svengali and hypnotism in pictures, drama, and film, and then shows how this image eventually came to be used in modern politics and culture. He emphasizes the hypnotist's influence over helpless female victims, the unconscious mind and psychic invasion. His discussion of prevalent anti-Semitic assumptions manifesting themselves in the figure of the dark hypnotist and the perception of the Jew is particularly revealing.

Growing critical interest in place and region is reflected in Roberto M. Dainotto's study *Place in Literature: Regions, Cultures, Communities*, which looks at regionalism in scholarly sources and in letters. Dainotto's study of agrarian novels (such as Hardy's *Return of the Native* and Gaskell's *North and South*) suggests that place and region are inventions that mask a 'yearning for ethnic purity'. Christina Hardyment explores the landscapes that inspired Austen, Hardy, Carlyle and others in *Literary Trails: British Writers in their Landscapes*. Hardyment points out landmarks, describes authors' homes and rooms, and traces specific routes taken by literary figures such as Hardy's Tess. This absorbing study includes maps and photographs, as well as information for visitors. Irene Tucker explores realism, liberalism, and national identity in *A Probable State: The Novel, the Contract, and the Jews*. Colin Matthew's *The Nineteenth Century: The British Isles, 1815–1901*, part of the series *The Short Oxford History of the British Isles* (eleven volumes; general editor Paul Langford), which is an interdisciplinary study by leading scholars and historians who provide overviews of the complex relationships between the various regions of the British Isles as well as reflections on a wide range of subjects such as economic life, politics and political reform, gender and domesticity, religion, and the arts. This study provides a valuable overview of cultural pressures from within and influences from beyond in terms of national identity and political boundaries in a time of expansion, break-up, and reformation of political empires, both colonial and continental.

In *The Spectacle of Intimacy: A Public Life for the Victorian Family*, Karen Chase and Michael Levenson argue that the unparalleled importance of home life and the pleasures of domesticity caused a paradoxical craving for public scandal manifesting itself in the trials of Caroline Norton, Lord Melbourne and others. Chase and Levenson treat depictions of intimacy and home life in the fictional representations of, among others, Dickens, Eliot, Tennyson, and Oliphant. In *Modernism, Mass Culture, and the Aesthetics of Obscenity*, Allison Pease examines the boundaries between pornography and aesthetics from the eighteenth century onwards, tracing the change in public taste regarding explicit representations of sexuality. Pease examines the shift in the perception of pornography to seeing it as a category of aesthetics by the growing reading public, highlighting the work of artists such as Aubrey Beardsley and writers such as Swinburne, Lawrence, and Joyce. In *The Crowd: British Literature and Public Politics*, John Plotz looks at early nineteenth-century crowd formation, riots, and demonstrations that were both directed and chaotic. His study includes several insightful chapters, including 'Producing Privacy in Public: Charlotte Brontë's *Shirley*'; 'Discursive Competition in the Victorian Public Sphere: Thomas Carlyle's *Chartism*'; and '"Grand National Sympathy" in De Quincey's "The English Mail-Coach"'. Plotz argues that "the unprecedented and unparalleled range of observations about and reflections upon crowds in aesthetic texts comes about because the enormous changes in the rules of public speech and public behavior between 1800 and 1850 make crowds, variously defined, into a potent rival to the representational claims of literary texts themselves'.

Women Musicians in Victorian Fiction, 1860–1900: Representations of Music, Science and Gender in the Leisured Home, by Phyllis Weliver, shows how novelists use the language of science to describe female music-making. According to Weliver, science and music meet in the relationship between music and mesmerism, hypnotism, and various psychological theories pertaining to personality and identity. A second edition of Gillian Beer's important and influential work on science and literature, *Darwin's Plots*, includes a revised preface by Beer and a new foreword by George Levine. Beer shows how George Eliot, Thomas Hardy, and others were influenced by Darwin's scientific language and narratives. Patricia Ingham offers a close reading of six Victorian novels in her linguistic analysis entitled *Invisible Writing and the Victorian Novel: Readings in Language and Ideology* (see also section 2(b) below). Ingham's project is to reveal the ideologies hidden in the language of the novel, and her argument shows that language reproduces social meanings that are not always immediately evident. The book opens with a demonstration of close reading and an explication of the terms that form the book's thematic units: modality, tense, deixis, and negation. This study is unique because it applies a method of analysis usually limited to shorter literary works, most often poetry. The novels analysed are *Vanity Fair* (examined for its use of modality); *Bleak House* (examined for its use of deixis, or the placement of an utterance in time and space in relation to the speaker, e.g. 'I am here now'), *The Mill on the Floss* and *Daniel Deronda* (use of tense, past and future), *Tess of the D'Urbervilles* and *Little Dorrit* (negation).

Continuing interest in Irish studies has generated new critical evaluations of several writers. Anne MacCarthy's *James Clarence Mangan, Edward Walsh and Nineteenth-Century Irish Literature in English* charts the critical reception of both authors in the context of an Irish ideology that devalued their works. Adrian Frazier's *George Moore, 1852–1933* chronicles the life of Ireland's famed autobiographer and playwright, whose private letters and published works give evidence of his contributions to turn-of-the-century Irish literary culture.

Ronald R. Thomas's highly original study *Detective Fiction and the Rise of Forensic Science* examines works by American and British authors, including Wilkie Collins, Dickens, and Conan Doyle, writing between 1841 and 1941. He identifies the 'devices' (fingerprinting, photography, etc.) that establish the fictional detective's professional authority and argues that the literary detective was also a figure of cultural authority. The argument presents detective fiction alongside contemporaneous developments in forensic science to show how questions of cultural authority were played out in both fiction and criminology. Caroline Reitz's 'Bad Cop/Good Cop: Godwin, Mill, and the Imperial Origins of the English Detective' (*Novel* 33:ii[1999] 175–95) shows how Godwin's *Caleb Williams* and James Mills's *History of British India* helped to create a positive and protective image of the English police detective by presenting English authority in the context of empire. The detective figure becomes associated with English values and is a significant element of the early nineteenth-century reform debates.

The role of the public drinking-house in English culture and literature is the subject of Steven Earnshaw's *The Pub in Literature*, a far-reaching study of canonical and lesser-known works. The chapter on Dickens opens with a surprisingly lengthy list of the drinking-places in the novelist's work. Earnshaw remarks that his wide and various descriptions of drinking-houses are unequalled by any other Victorian writer ('Dickens clearly relished describing hostelries', p. 189) and he proceeds to close readings of *Pickwick Papers* and *Barnaby Rudge*. In a later chapter Earnshaw examines George Eliot's *Silas Marner* and *Felix Holt* with particular attention to Eliot's participation in the historiography debate and the construction of a national past. He concludes that the drinking-house serves as the location of *sensus communis* in *Silas Marner*, while in *Felix Holt* Eliot uses the drinking-house as a rhetorical idea. Similarly, *The Mayor of Casterbridge* uses the drinking-house symbolically. Earnshaw examines Hardy's novel in the context of the 1830 Beer Act and the temperance movement, and argues that, more so than Eliot or Dickens, Hardy is 'in tune with the effect social change had on drinking houses' (p. 218). Earnshaw rounds out his study of Victorian authors with Arthur Morrison's *The Hole in the Wall* and *Tales of Mean Streets*, in which descriptions of the public house reflect a growing concern for the hardships of the urban lower classes.

Jenkins and John, eds., *Rereading Victorian Fiction*, brings together a collection of essays in order to 'emphasize the ideological, aesthetic, intellectual and moral diversity of both Victorian fiction and its critical reception'. The collection includes coverage of Hardy, Stoker, Thackeray, Trollope, Gissing, Carroll, MacDonald, and others. John and Jenkins, eds., *Rethinking Victorian Culture*, is a critical anthology evaluating Victorian literature and culture. The essays collected in Correa, ed., *The Nineteenth-Century Novel: Realisms* comprise a broad introduction to several nineteenth-century writers' experiments with realism and their manipulation of the

Romantic and Gothic traditions. The collection includes essays on *Northanger Abbey*, *Jane Eyre*, *Dombey and Son*, *Middlemarch*, *Far from the Madding Crowd* and *Germinal* and introduces the various political and cultural forces that influenced Victorian fiction, explicating the standard list of Victorian literary themes from the woman question to parliamentary reform. Cathy Shuman's *Pedagogical Economies: The Examination and the Victorian Literary Man* offers a discussion of educational testing, institutions, and theory proposed by Dickens, Matthew Arnold, John Ruskin, Anthony Trollope, and others.

The relationships between English and German fiction and culture are the subjects of a collection of papers read at a 1997 University of Leeds conference, Stark, ed., *The Novel in Anglo-German Context: Cultural Cross-Currents and Affinities*. The collection includes eleven essays on nineteenth-century fiction, both English and German. Rosemary Ashton surveys the figure of the German professor in George Eliot's work with reference to the essay in 'A Word for the Germans', originally published in the *Pall Mall Gazette* in 1865, and also to Eliot's letters and *Middlemarch*. Stark examines the reception of Gustav Freytag's *Soll und Haben* [1855] in Britain, including George Henry Lewes's essay in the *Westminster Review*. Norbert Bachleitner marks the trends in nineteenth-century fiction by women authors and provides analysis of Charlotte Brontë's *Jane Eyre* and *Shirley* and the adaptations of these novels by Germans Ch. Birch-Pfeiffer, E. Marlitt and A. Bölte. Diane Milburn identifies 'Anglo-German Cross-Currents' in Bram Stoker's *Dracula*.

Richard Walsh's article 'The Novelist as Medium' (*Neophil* 84[2000] 329–45) looks at the implications and assumptions of this metaphor. Walsh provides interesting insights into the relationship between narrative control and creativity, making numerous references to the works of Brontë, Scott, and Trollope. Other critical discussions of the novel include several essays in *Dickens Studies Annual: Essays on Victorian Fiction*: 'Desire and Deconstruction: Reclaiming Centers' by Karen C. Gindele (*DSA* 29[2000] 269–302); 'Beauty is as Beauty Does: Action and Appearance in Brontë and Eliot' by Carol-Ann Farkas (*DSA* 29[2000] 323–50); 'Near Confinement: Pregnant Women in the Nineteenth-Century British Novel' by Cynthia Northcutt Malone (*DSA* 29[2000] 67–88); and 'Doing the Police in Different Voices: The Search for Identity in Dust Heaps and Waste Lands' by Keith Hale (*DSA* 29[2000] 303–22). Russell West analyses German stage adaptations in 'English Nineteenth-Century Novels on the German Stage: Birch-Pfeiffer's Adaptations of Dickens, Brontë, Eliot and Collins' (in Bachleitner, ed., *Beiträge zur Rezeption der britischen und irischen Literatur des 19. Jahrhunderts im deutschsprachigen Raum*).

Other articles of note in the study of the Victorian novel include 'Love Among the Ruins: The Catacombs, the Closet, and the Victorian "Early Christian" Novel' by Vincent A. Lankewish (*VLC* 28:ii[2000] 239–74); 'The Kitchen Police: Servant Surveillance and Middle-Class Transgression' by Brian W. McCuskey (*VLC* 28:ii[2000] 359–76); 'Servants and Hands: Representing the Working Classes in Victorian Factory Novels' by Dorice Williams Elliott (*VLC* 28:ii[2000] 377–90); and 'Manufacturing Accident: Industrialism and the Worker's Body in Early Victorian Fiction' by Mike Sanders (*VLC* 28:ii[2000] 313–30).

(b) Individual Authors

New collections of the sensation fiction of the actress-turned-author Mary Elizabeth Braddon have turned up several new stories as well as two plays. Willis, ed., *The Fatal Marriage and Other Stories*, reprints the title work that first appeared as a story attributed to Wilkie Collins, 'A Marriage Tragedy', published in 1859. Also included in the collection are the novella *As the Heart Knoweth* [1903] and the stories 'The True Story Of Don Juan' [1869], 'The Fatal Marriage' [1885], 'Sweet Simplicity' [1894], 'Herself' [1894], 'His Good Fairy' [1894], 'Poor Uncle Jacob' [1896], 'Wild Justice' [1896], 'The Winning Sequence' [1897], 'The Doll's Tragedy' [1896] and 'The Cock of Bowker's' [1906]. An 1888 interview with the author concludes the collection. Braddon's unsuccessful attempts at playwriting resulted in several never-performed works. One of these is the comedy *Married Beneath Him*, which is printed along with her essay 'Fifty Years of the Lyceum Theatre', an account of the prominent actors of the period. A new edition of the melodrama *The Missing Witness* also includes newspaper articles and reviews. Tromp, Gilbert and Haynie, eds., *Beyond Sensation: Mary Elizabeth Braddon in Context*, is a collection of essays using theoretical approaches that emphasize gender, imperialism, religion, and sex. Jennifer Carnell's insightful biography *The Literary Lives of Mary Elizabeth Braddon: A Study of her Life and Work* includes in its appendices a chronology of Braddon's theatrical career and a bibliography of her writings. Simon Petch looks at Braddon's treatment of masculinity in 'Robert Audley's Profession' (*SNNTS* 32:i[2000] 1–13).

This year's most important addition to Charlotte Brontë research is Margaret Smith's second volume of letters, *The Letters of Charlotte Brontë: With a Selection of Letters by Family and Friends*, volume ii: *1848–1851*. This authoritative collection covers the period when Brontë completed *Shirley*, began writing *Villette*, and initiated her friendship with Elizabeth Gaskell. This was also the period when Charlotte's siblings Branwell, Emily, and Anne all died within a year. The correspondence includes letters to Gaskell, publisher George Smith, Ellen Nussey, and Harriet Martineau. An introduction and a chronology for 1848–51 are also offered, as well as excellent notations that include biographical sketches of the figures to whom Brontë refers in her letters.

Wise, ed., *The Shakespeare Head Brontë*, offers a first-edition comprehensive bibliography compiled by Alexander Symington in the 1930s with coverage of all Brontëana and the works of all members of the Brontë family. Edited by Thomas Wise, the bibliography is the heretofore unpublished last volume of the Shakespeare Head Brontë, the first nineteen volumes of which were published in 1931 and 1936. The outbreak of the Second World War prevented the publication of this final volume, which was printed from galley proofs acquired by Daphne du Maurier. *Reading the Brontës: An Introduction to their Novels and Poetry* by Charmian Knight and Luke Spencer is a distance-learning text that frames discussions of all the Brontë novels and selections of the poetry. Descriptions of Haworth and reproductions of manuscript pages enrich what essentially serves as a textbook on the Brontës. In another general work on the Brontës, entitled *The Brontës and Religion*, Marianne Thormählen analyses the novels of Anne, Charlotte, and Emily, as well as Charlotte's letters, for evidence of how the evangelical Christian faith was interpreted, practised, and reproduced in their fiction. John Cannon's genealogical study, *The History of the Brontë Family from Ireland to Wuthering Heights*, is a revised edition of *The Road to Haworth: The Story of the Brontës in Ireland* [1980]. Ann Dinsdale's chapter 'Haworth Churchyard: Who Were They?' (in Duckett, ed., *Aspects of Bradford 2: Discovering Local History*) explains who is buried in the Haworth parish church graveyard and tells some of the graveyard's related history. A more general description of local Haworth history is Mark E. Ward and Ann Dinsdale's book of walking tours entitled *A Guide to Historic Haworth and the Brontës*. Eric Ruijssenaars, *Charlotte Brontë's Promised Land: The Pensionnat Heger and Other Brontë Places in Brussels*, describes the Pensionnat Heger, where Charlotte and Emily stayed in 1842–3. A history of Belgium and the Quartier Isabelle area is also included.

In *A Stranger Within the Gates: Charlotte Brontë and Victorian Irishness*, Kathleen Constable traces Irish influences on Charlotte Brontë's writings from her earliest work in childhood through her mature years of writing up to *Jane Eyre*. In *Louisa May Alcott and Charlotte Brontë: Transatlantic Translations*, Christine Doyle examines Charlotte Brontë's influence on Louisa May Alcott as reflected in her children's literature as well as her sensation novels. Doyle's study compares the writers according to their interests in and treatment of spirituality, interpersonal relations, and women's work. She argues that Alcott's unique American voice and 'translations' of Brontë are progressive and optimistic. Karson, ed., *Readings on Jane Eyre*, provides criticism, biographical information and an anthology.

Brontë Society Transactions (25:ii[2000]) includes the following articles: 'Dickens and the Brontës' by Robert Barnard (*BST* 25:ii[2000] 109–20); 'Charlotte Brontë and Roman Catholicism' by Jan Jedrzejewski (*BST* 25:ii[2000] 121–35); 'The Real Miss Andrews: Teacher, Mother, Abolitionist' by Sarah Fermi and Judith Smith (*BST* 25:ii[2000] 136–46); 'Is Thurland Castle "Thornfield Hall"?' by Susan E. James (*BST* 25:ii[2000] 147–53); 'Word Frequency in the Poems of Emily Brontë' by Reiko Tsukasaki (*BST* 25:ii[2000] 154–9); 'An Interview with Japanese Brontë Scholar, Seiko Aoyama' by Rachel Youdelman (*BST* 25:ii[2000] 160–7); 'A Note on Lady Morgan' by Joan Bellamy (*BST* 25:ii[2000] 168–71); 'Literati Associated with the Brontës' by John Waddington-Feather (*BST* 25:ii[2000] 172–5); and 'The Myth of "Documentation"' by Stephen L. Van Scoyoc (*BST* 25:ii[2000] 176–81).

Narrative technique and reader response in *Jane Eyre* are evaluated by Caroline Levine in '"Harmless Pleasure": Gender, Suspense, and *Jane Eyre*' (*VLC* 28:ii[2000] 275–86). Anne Hogan explores Charlotte Brontë's treatment of masculine sexuality in 'Reading Men More Truly': Charlotte Brontë's *Villette*' (in Bradstock *et al.*, eds., pp. 58–70). In 'Memory, Imagination and the (M)other: An Irigarayan Reading of Charlotte Brontë's *Villette*' (in Horner and Keane, eds., pp. 225–33), Sue Chaplin uses 'Irigaray's analysis of materiality and maternality within western discourse to explore how it is that the body comes to matter in Charlotte Brontë's *Villette*' (p. 225). Ildikó Csengei considers reading as an element of the *Bildungsroman* in 'The Unreadability of the *Bildungsroman*: Reading *Jane Eyre* Reading' (*AnaChronist* [2000] 102–38). Kristen Deiter identifies the relationships between the New Woman, the Victorian novel and interior design in 'Cultural Expressions of the Victorian Age: The New Woman, *Jane Eyre*, and Interior Design' (*LJHum* 25:ii[2000] 27–42). Jin Ok Kim's 'Desire—Identity—Men and Women in Charlotte Brontë's Novelettes and *The Professor*' (*FemSEL* 7:ii[2000] 111–40) considers desire and identity from a feminist perspective. Carl Plasa examines the treatment of race, sex roles and discipline in 'Charlotte Brontë's Foreign Bodies: Slavery and Sexuality in *The Professor*' (*JNT* 30:i[2000] 1–28). Anita Levy looks at the female spectator, publicity, privacy, and polite society in 'Public Spaces, Private Eyes: Gender and the Social Work of Aesthetics in Charlotte Brontë's *Villette*' (*NCC* 22:iii[2000] 391–416).

Several foreign-language articles on Charlotte Brontë are of interest. Marianne Camus examines governesses in *Villette* and Anne Brontë's *Agnes Grey* in 'L'Exil des gouvernantes dans la fiction des Brontë' (*CVE* 51[2000] 147–60). Norbert Bachleitner studies the reception of *Shirley* in Germany in 'Die deutsche Rezeption englischer Romanautorinnen des neunzehnten Jahrhunderts, insbesonder Charlotte Brontë' (in Stark, ed.). Inga-Stina Ewbank looks at the German-language adaptation of *Jane Eyre* in 'Adapting *Jane Eyre*: Jakob Spitzer's *Die Waise aus Lowood*' (in Bachleitner, ed.).

Tim Dolin provides a new introduction, notes and chronology to Oxford University Press's 2000 reprint of the authoritative 1984 edition of *Villette*, edited by Margaret Smith and Herbert Rosengarten. Sally Shuttleworth provides a new introduction and revised notes for Oxford University Press's *Jane Eyre*, also edited by Smith and reprinted from the authoritative Oxford University Press's 1975 text. Richard J. Dunn edits the third edition of Norton's *Jane Eyre*. The text is based on the 1848 edition, which includes Brontë's final corrections. Contemporary readings, including four new essays, are offered by Adrienne Rich, Sandra M. Gilbert, Jerome Beaty, Lisa Sternlieb, Jeffrey Sconce, and Donna Marie Nudd. The third edition also includes a new chronology and an updated bibliography. *Jane Eyre: A Libretto*, by David Malouf, is part of Michael Berkeley's opera based on Charlotte Brontë's novel. The two-act opera contains selections of dramatic scenes from the novel and focuses on the relationship between Jane and Rochester.

Robert Barnard's *Emily Brontë* is a concise, readable, and affordable biography that also analyses the poetry and fiction and responds to contemporary criticism (though without bibliographic annotations). Maria Aristodemou's *Law and Literature: Journeys from Here to Eternity* includes a chapter on Emily Brontë entitled 'World Before and Beyond Difference: Emily Brontë's *Wuthering Heights*'. Aristodemou's thesis is that law, like literature, is a fiction; her discussion of *Wuthering Heights* identifies 'sexist values in literary criticism of a text written by a woman' and shows how the novel disrupts the symbolic order of language and law. Rebecca Steinitz, in 'Diaries and Displacement in *Wuthering Heights*' (*SNNTS* 32:iv[2000] 407–19) explains how Emily Brontë's use of the diary form underscores the 'unattainability of place' while simultaneously providing a temporal context for the narrative. Lisa Wang's 'The Holy Spirit in Emily Brontë's *Wuthering Heights* and Poetry' (*L&T* 14:ii[2000] 160–73) includes a survey of Emily Brontë's poetry and *Wuthering Heights*, and her emphasis on the 'primal nature of religious experience over its formal expressions'. Yusur Al-Madani compares gender and cultural differences between Hawthorne's *The Scarlet Letter* and *Wuthering Heights* in 'Male, Female Expressions of Heathen Love: Brontë's Heathcliff and Hawthorne's Hester' (*IJAES* 1:ii[2000] 313–30). Theo D'haen identifies Maryse Condé's influence in 'Caribbean Migrations: Maryse Condé on the Track of Emily Brontë' (in Houppermans, Smith and van Strien-Chardonneau, eds., *Histoire jeu science dans l'aire de la littérature*). Eddy Souffrant and Sarah Davies Cordova also examine Condé's influence in '*Krik? Krak! Palé andaki*: Sens en mouvement de l'identité dans l'ère/l'aire caribant-îllaise' (*ReFr* 10[2000] 45–63). Michelle A. Massé considers narcissism and its relationship to agency in '"He's more myself than I am": Narcissism and Gender in *Wuthering Heights*' (in Rudnytsky and Gordon, eds., *Psychoanalyses/Feminisms*). New from Columbia Critical Guides is Emily Brontë's *Wuthering Heights*, edited by Patsy Stoneman, which was previously published in Icon Critical Guide series.

Critical attention to the life and works of Anne Brontë is meagre in quantity compared to that of her sisters. One short but worthy study of note is Betty Jay's *Anne Brontë*, which makes a convincing case for Anne's critical relevance. The book's three chapters are dedicated to *Agnes Grey*, *The Tenant of Wildfell Hall*, and selected poems. Jay challenges the common opinion of Anne as soft-spoken and conflict-avoidant. Rather, Jay argues that in her writing Anne faced head on the difficult issues of women's place, the condition of governesses, and the challenges of spiritual life.

Rhoda Broughton's *Dear Faustina* is the subject of P. Murphy's 'Disdained and Disempowered: The "Inverted" New Woman in Rhoda Broughton's *Dear Faustina*' (*TSWL* 19:i[2000] 57–79). In 'Domesticating Bulwer-Lytton's "Colonial" Fiction: Mentorship and Masculinity in *The Caxtons*' (*ESC* 26:ii[2000] 155–84) Peter W. Sinnema examines three novels: *The Caxtons*, *My Novel*, and *What Will He Do With It?* Sinnema argues that the trilogy, which has been mostly studied not for its imaginative value but for its illustration of social debate, also provides an articulation of ethics for young Victorian men 'in an era heavily inflected by the affiliated realities of Empire and hearth'. In *William Carleton, the Novelist: His Carnival and Pastoral World,* David Krause responds to the scholarly consensus that Carleton was a failed writer. Krause argues that 'six and possibly seven of his novels are major works that present a wide range of significant comic and tragicomic fictional accomplishments'.

The scholarly study of Lewis Carroll's *Alice in Wonderland* is made easier by the expanded third edition of Martin Gardner's *The Annotated Alice: The Definitive Edition*, which incorporates *The Annotated Alice* [1960] and *More Annotated Alice* [1990], as well as new notes and observations. Articles on *Alice* include Stephen Canham's 'From Wonderland to the Marketplace: *Alice's* Progeny' (*ChildL* 28[2000] 226–9) and Ann Bernays and Justin Kaplan's 'Indestructible Alice' (*ASch* 29:ii[2000] 138–41). Foreign-language articles on *Alice* include Isabel Pascua and Gisela Marcelo's 'La traducción de la LIJ' (*CLIJ* 13:cxxiii[2000] 30–6).

In what appears to be a thin year for Wilkie Collins research, books include Christopher GoGwilt's *The Fiction of Geopolitics: Afterimages of Culture, from Wilkie Collins to Alfred Hitchcock.* GoGwilt compares Collins's treatment of international politics to that of Nietzsche, Olive Schreiner, R.B. Graham, Joseph Conrad, and Alfred Hitchcock. Hyungji Park's essay '"The story of our lives": *The Moonstone* and the Indian Mutiny in *All the Year Round*' appears in Finkelstein and Peers, eds., *Negotiating India in the Nineteenth-Century Media.* Nicky Losseff looks at Collins's treatment of music in 'Absent Melody and "The Woman in White"' (*M&L* 81:iv[2000] 532–50). Rebecca Stern's essay, '"Personation" and "good marking ink": Sanity, Performativity, and Biology in Victorian Sensation Fiction' compares Collins's treatment of identity, biology, and madness to that of Mary Elizabeth Braddon in *Lady Audley's Secret* and Ellen Wood in *St Martin's*

Eve. Phyllis Weliver reveals Collins's literary collaborations in 'Collaboration in Open Boats: Dickens, Collins, Franklin, and Bligh' (*VS* 42:ii[1999–2000] 201–25).

End-of-the-century publishing phenomenon Marie Corelli is the subject of Annette R. Federico's *Idol of Suburbia: Marie Corelli and Late-Victorian Literary Culture*. The book combines textual analysis and biography in a comprehensive portrait of an individual at the centre of debates about literary value and evaluation. Federico considers Corelli's works in relationship to both the hostile highbrow literary culture and the adoring public. She takes care to point out that the book is not a biography; indeed, part of her project is to show how biographies, reviews, and memoirs after the author's death influenced Corelli's literary status. Still, she does base some of her textual analysis on her understanding of the author's personal life. She has had access to Corelli's unpublished letters to her publisher George Bentley and her paramour Arthur Severn, and these documents shed new light on the author and her works. Using the letters to Severn, Federico is able to delineate the creative genesis of *Open Confession: To a Man from a Woman*. The book begins with an analysis of late Victorian literary celebrity, and proceeds to demonstrate how Corelli's response to Victorian mass culture resulted in her contradictory positions regarding early feminism and aestheticism. Two editions of Corelli's *The Sorrows of Satan* appeared in 1998. The Oxford University Press paperback is edited by Peter Keating with a revised introduction, bibliography, chronology and notes and is based on the first edition of the novel published by Methuen in 1895. A paperback edition was also issued by R.A. Kessinger Publishing Company.

Textual links between the Bible and the works of Dickens are explicated in Hanna, ed., *The Dickens Christian Reader: A Collection of New Testament Teachings and Biblical References from the Works of Charles Dickens*. Hanna excerpts thirty-four passages from various novels and presents them side by side with accompanying passages from the New and Old Testaments. Chapter 2, for example, shows how Pip's anonymous support of Herbert Pocket is a fictional demonstration of the lesson in Matthew 6:1–4: 'Take heed that ye do not your alms before men, to be seen of them … That thine alms may be in secret'. Robert Newsom's *Charles Dickens Revisited* attempts to examine the life and complete works of Dickens, while combining psychological, biographical, and cultural approaches to his work. For example, Newsom argues that *David Copperfield* is largely an autobiographical account of an unhappy part of Dickens's own childhood. George Newlin's *Understanding 'Great Expectations': A Student Casebook to Issues, Sources, and Historical Documents* includes a useful collection of original sources concerning gender and class issues, blacksmithing, crime and punishment, penal colony transportation, the police, and the theatre. In *The Companion to 'Great Expectations'*, David Paroissien provides a useful, detailed and comprehensive overview of *Great Expectations*, approaching the novel within several contexts and examining, for example, social mobility, the legal system, education, technology, and topography. His study includes several helpful appendices, such as a chronology of events, maps, and a selected bibliography. Annie Ramel examines Dickens's treatment of fatherhood and parenthood in *Great Expectations: Le Père ou le pire*. Alexander Welsh's study *Dickens Redressed: The Art of 'Bleak House' and 'Hard Times'* examines the two novels in the context of Dickens's later, darker fiction, arguing that this crucial period of his career has heretofore not been fully understood. Welsh considers the role of the double narrator, finding similarities to

David Copperfield in the various roles of the characters as they serve the needs of the protagonist. Timothy Michael McGovern's *Dickens in Galdós* examines Dickens's influence on Spanish novelist Benito Galdós [1843–1920]. McGovern shows how Galdós uses Dickens's stock characters such as the religious ascetic and the miser to critique Spanish society.

The eleventh volume of the seminal *The Letters of Charles Dickens*, edited by Graham Storey and Margaret Brown, presents 1,158 letters previously published only in part, and many unpublished letters, from the years 1865–7. During this period Dickens completed the monthly parts of *Our Mutual Friend* and the successful *All the Year Round* Christmas numbers (co-written with Wilkie Collins), and continued to be the chair of several charitable dinner organizations. These years also see his first reference to his swollen foot, and he wrote about his involvement in a railway accident. This volume of the *Letters* describes his frequent reading tours— both provincial and in London—as well as the reading tour in America. Dickens's contributions to journalism are edited by Michael Slater and John Drew in *Dickens' Journalism: 'The Uncommercial Traveller' and Other Papers, 1859–70*. This fourth volume in the series includes essays and articles published in the last years of Dickens's life, and also includes a complete bibliography of his journalism from December 1833 to August 1869. The various writings offer insight into his later fiction as well as his ongoing interest in social reform. Other critical work on Dickens's journalism includes Robert L. Patten's 'Dickens as Serial Author: A Case of Multiple Identities' (in Brake, Bell and Finkelstein, eds.). Dickens's account of his 1842 visit to the United States is recorded in Ingham, ed., *American Notes for General Circulation*. An introduction and chronology are included, as well as appendices that chart Dickens's transition from outspoken critic to admirer of the United States. Previously published in the Icon Critical Guides series, Nicolas Tredell's new edition of Dickens's *Great Expectations* is now in Columbia Critical Guides.

The fourteen essays collected in Jacobson, ed., *Dickens and the Children of Empire*, begins with the assertion that the fictional trope of childhood is an expression of the political power relationships produced by empire. The collection represents a variety of literary perspectives and theories, from deconstruction to post-colonial studies. Kate Flint's 'Dickens and the Native American' shows the development of Dickens's attitude over time. Malvern van Wyk Smith's '*Dombey and Son* and Textual Ripples on an African Shore' and Catherine Robson's 'Girls Underground, Boys Overseas' identify the links between Dicken's portrayal of children and colonialism. Not every essay, however, considers Dickens's work. For example, Catherine Gallagher's chapter is on anti-slave-trade novels. Other contributions to edited volumes include '"Double-Dyed Traitors and Infernal Villains": *Illustrated London News*, *Household Words*, Charles Dickens and the Indian Rebellion' (in Finkelstein and Peers, eds.). Dickens's visits to the United States and their contribution to the writing of *American Notes* and *Martin Chuzzlewit* are explored by Sidney P. Moss and Carolyn J. Moss in *Dickens, Trollope, Jefferson: Three Anglo-American Encounters*. A.O.J. Cockshut examines Dickens's treatment of dead children in 'Children's Death in Dickens: A Chapter in the History of Taste' (in Avery, Reynolds, Yates and Goodall, eds., *Representations of Childhood Death*, pp. 133–53). Andrew Sanders investigates Dickens's millenarianism in 'Dickens and the Millennium' (in John and Jenkins, eds., pp. 80–

90). Giddings and Sheen, eds., *The Classic Novel: From Page to Screen*, contains two essays on Dickens: Jenny Dennett looks at a Thomas Bentley film adaptation in 'Sentimentality, Sex and Sadism: The 1935 Version of Dickens's *The Old Curiosity Shop*' (pp. 54–70), and Robert Giddings analyses Noel Langley's adaptation in '*Pickwick Papers*: Beyond that Place and Time' (pp. 41–53). Catherine Golden compares an illustration by George Cruikshank to Dickens's treatment of social class in 'Cruikshank's Illustrative Wrinkle in *Oliver Twist*'s Misrepresentation of Class' (in Golden, ed., *Book Illustrated: Text, Image, and Culture, 1770–1930*).

The Dickensian (96:ii[2000]), edited by Malcolm Andrews, includes the following articles: 'Disappearances: George Parkman and *Edwin Drood*' by Robert Tracy (pp. 101–17); 'Some Observations on Charles Collins's Sketches for *Edwin Drood*' by Robert Raven (pp. 118–26); and 'Magnetic Sympathy in *The Mystery of Edwin Drood*—part I' by Arthur J. Cox (pp. 127–50).

The *Dickens Studies Annual: Essays on Victorian Fiction* (29[2000]) includes eleven essays on Dickens: 'Dickens, Washington Irving, and English National Identity' by Malcolm Andrews (*DSA* 29[2000] 1–16); 'Pickwick, the Past, and the Prison' by Sean C. Grass (*DSA* 29[2000] 17–40); '*Oliver Twist* and the Fugitive Family' by David Parker (*DSA* 29[2000] 41–60); '"Down ditches on doorsteps, in rivers": Oliver Twist's Journey to Respectability' by Catherine Robson (*DSA* 29[2000] 61–82); 'The Long and the Short of Oliver and Alice: The Changing Size of the Victorian Child' by Goldie Morgentaler (*DSA* 29[2000] 83–98); 'Raising the House Tops: Sexual Surveillance in Charles Dickens' *Dombey and Son* (1846–48)' by Colette Colligan (*DSA* 29[2000] 99–144); 'Dickens and Disgust' by Annette R. Federico (*DSA* 29[2000] 145–62); 'Authority and the *Bildungsroman*: The Double Narrative of *Bleak House*' by James Hill (*DSA* 29[2000] 163–94); 'Distorted Religion: Dickens, Dissent, and *Bleak House*' by David A. Ward (*DSA* 29[2000] 195–232); 'Speculative Plagues and the Ghosts of *Little Dorrit*' by Daniel P. Scoggin (*DSA* 29[2000] 233–65); and 'Recent Dickens Studies: 1998' by Harland S. Nelson (*DSA* 29[2000] 387–464).

Gordon Bigelow's thoughtful essay 'Market Indicators: Banking and Domesticity in Dickens' *Bleak House*' (*ELH* 67:ii[2000] 589–611) investigates *Bleak House*'s awareness of capitalism and modernity. Bigelow's examination is placed within the context of the legal case of Jarndyce and Jarndyce, which involves characters from all classes of society and the economic discourse of the 1840s and 1850s. He suggests that the text's attempt to naturalize the free market system and banking is confounded, finally, by Esther's inability to accept her own inherited wealth and the natural, unforced affection of kinship. The natural, essential values of the text are thus rejected because of personal, subjective feelings and desires. Athena Vrettos links Dickens and industrialism in 'Defining Habits: Dickens and the Psychology of Repetition' (*VS* 42:iii[2000] 399–426). John R. Harrison examines narrative structure and the relationship to social problems in 'Dickens' Literary Architecture: Patterns of Ideas and Imagery in *Hard Times*' (*PLL* 36:ii[2000] 115–38). Russell Daine Wright takes a socio-economic approach, investigating Dickens and the political economy of Australian government in 'Accounting for Our Souls' (*Overland* 158[2000] 5–13). Wendell V. Harris takes a reader-response approach in 'Contextualizing Coram's Foundling Hospital: Dickens' Use and Readers' Interests' (*Reader* 43[2000] 1–19). Sheila Sullivan examines criminality, statistics, and the influence of Newgate in 'Dickens' Newgate Vision: *Oliver Twist*, Moral

Statistics, and the Construction of Progressive History' (*NCStud* 14[2000] 121–48). The relationship between Dickens's narrative use of time and quantum theory is presented by Shale Preston in 'Quantum Pickwick' (*YES* 30[2000] 82–95). Michael Hollington takes a biographical approach to Dickens's treatment of exile, transition, and restlessness in 'The Losing Game: Exile and Threshold in *A Tale of Two Cities*' (*CVE* 51[2000] 189–205).

Work on Dickens and the oral resonances of his writing are found in what must have been one of the late Ian Watt's final essays, 'Oral Dickens' (*StHR* 8:i[2000] 206–22). There is also John O. Jordan's response, 'The Critic as Host: On Ian Watt's "Oral Dickens"' (*StHR* 8:i[2000] 197–205). John M. Picker's 'The Soundproof Study: Victorian Professionals, Workspace, and Urban Noise' (*VS* 42:iii[2000] 427–53) compares Dickens and Carlyle in their representations of street performers. George R. Clay's 'In Defense of Flat Characters: A Discussion of their Value to Charles Dickens, Jane Austen and Leo Tolstoy' (*IFR* 27:i–ii[2000] 20–36) compares characterizations by the three authors. Takashi Nakamura compares the portrayal of poverty in *Bleak House* and a painting by Ford Madox Brown in '*Bleak House* and Brown's *Work*: A Gaze upon the Poor' (*Shiron* 39:v–vi[2000] 39–62). Biblical allusion and the flood metaphor in George Eliot's *The Mill on the Floss*, Virginia Woolf's *To the Lighthouse*, and *Bleak House* are compared in Anny Sadrin's 'Time, Tense, Weather in Three "Flood Novels": *Bleak House*, *The Mill on the Floss, To the Lighthouse*' (*YES* 30[2000] 96–105). Sambudha Sen compares urban areas, social class, and panorama in William Makepeace Thackeray's *Vanity Fair* and *Bleak House* in his essay '*Bleak House, Vanity Fair,* and the Making of an Urban Aesthetic' (*NCL* 54:iv[2000] 480–502). Gayla S. McGlamery and Joseph J. Walsh identify Dickens's use of Homer and epic conventions in 'Mr. (H)Omer and the Iliadic Heroics of *David Copperfield*' (*CML* 20:ii[2000] 1–20). Jana Gohrisch examines Victorian family and the excess of emotions in 'Familiar Excess? Emotion and the Family in Victorian Literature' (*REALB* 16[2000] 163–83). Stewart Garrett uses a formalist approach to identify and compare imperialism in Dickens's works and in E.M. Forster's *Howards End* in 'The Foreign Offices of British Fiction' (*MLQ* 61:i[2000] 181–206). Murray Baumgarten's 'Calligraphy and Code: Writing in *Great Expectations*' (*StHR* 8:i[2000] 226–35) examines Dickens's treatment of reading and characters' writing. Sean C. Grass identifies Dickens's prison episodes in 'Narrating the Cell: Dickens on the American Prisons' (*JEGP* 99:i[2000] 50–70). Foreign-language contributions to Dickens studies include François Ouellet's intertextual analysis of Dickens and Emmanuel Bove's *La Dernière Nuit* in 'De Bove à Dickens: Une approche intertextuelle' (*DFS* 51[2000] 70–83).

Edgar Feuchtwanger's *Disraeli* examines Benjamin Disraeli's controversial life—his rise to political power, his difficulties with Westminster politics, and eventually his election as prime minister in 1874. Particularly interesting is Feuchtwanger's discussion of Disraeli's reinvention of his religious/ethnic identity and his views of Judaism and Christianity in order to be involved in politics. The study involves some discussion of Disraeli's fiction and prose.

A new biography of Arthur Conan Doyle, *Teller of Tales* by novelist Daniel Stashower, brings to the fore Doyle's lesser-known fiction and other interests, fulfilling Doyle's wish to be remembered for his work beyond Sherlock Holmes. Stashower chronicles Doyle's work as a political activist and an advocate of spiritualism. Martin Booth's *The Doctor and the Detective: A Biography of Sir*

Arthur Conan Doyle (first published in the UK as *The Doctor, the Detective, and Arthur Conan Doyle: A Biography of Arthur Conan Doyle* by Hodder & Stoughton) explores aspects of Doyle's life that have been overshadowed by his reputation as the creator of Sherlock Holmes. Booth's balanced account of both Doyle the writer and Doyle the man examines his adventurous personality as a voyager, sportsman, and traveller, as well as his interest in spiritualism. Since access to Doyle's papers has been limited, Booth draws from previously published records and materials. Diana Barsham's *Arthur Conan Doyle and the Meaning of Masculinity* is not a biography, but Barsham's argument that Doyle's writing expresses his autobiographical tendencies requires that Barsham examine Doyle's life closely. The book treats the range of Doyle's works: his early fiction, the Sherlock Holmes stories, the novels of the 1890s, the histories, war correspondence, legal campaigning, and works on spiritualism and travel writing. Barsham considers how Doyle was influenced by the autobiographical tradition and how his self-consciousness shaped his deliberate presentation of his own masculinity. Kathryn Montgomery's essay 'Sherlock Holmes and Clinical Reasoning' appears in Hawkins and McEntyre, eds., *Teaching Literature and Medicine* (pp. 299–305). Martin Priestman considers the role of serialization in detective fiction in his essay 'Sherlock's Children: The Birth of the Series' (in Chernaik, Swales and Vilain, eds., *The Art of Detective Fiction*, pp. 50–9). Two biographical essays on Doyle appeared this year: 'Cronología de Conan Doyle' (*CLIJ* 13:cxxxii[2000] 18–22) and Laurie King's 'Sir Arthur Conan Doyle' (*MysteryScene* 69:xxii[2000] 24–5). Franco Moretti's 'The Slaughterhouse of Literature' (*MLQ* 61:i[2000] 207–27) takes a formalist approach in analysing the clue in detective fiction and the genre's relationship to the canon. James Krasner looks at the short story and doctor–patient relations in 'Arthur Conan Doyle as Doctor and Writer' (*Mosaic* 33:iv[2000] 19–34). Several essays on Doyle appeared in foreign-language journals this year. Florian Nelle considers the use of scientific method in 'Von Dinosauriern und Detektiven: Episoden aus der Geschichte des Kleinen' (*WB* 46:i[2000] 56–72). *Cuadernos de Literatura Infantil y Juvenil* (*CLIJ*) (13:cxxxii[2000]) dedicated an issue to Doyle that included a number of biographical, bibliographical, and critical essays.

This year's most comprehensive contribution to George Eliot studies is Rignall, ed., *The Oxford Reader's Companion to George Eliot*. Organized as an encyclopedia, the book contains over 600 entries related to the author's life and works. The entries include synopses of her works, their critical reception, contemporary readings, thematic links among Eliot's works, biographical information, and relevant literary and cultural contexts, including entries on philosophy, theology, and science. The impressive breadth and simple organization make this volume an extensive yet convenient research tool. Entries for Eliot's fiction are generous (five to six pages each), and are set off against a shaded background for easy reference. *The Oxford Reader's Companion to George Eliot* is the rare combination of advanced yet accessible scholarship that will serve Eliot scholars for years to come.

In her most helpful *George Eliot and Intoxication: Dangerous Drugs for the Condition of England*, Kathleen McCormack identifies copious references to alcohol and drugs in Eliot's fiction. The book opens with two chapters providing background information about alcohol and opium use and abuse in Victorian

England, and the particular attitudes to and experiences with alcohol in the Evans and Lewes households. The role of public houses in the community is also discussed. McCormack shows how Eliot associated alcoholism with realism, recounting the story of her refusing to alter her accurate portrayal of addiction and recovery in 'Janet's Repentance', which the publisher John Blackwood felt was too bleak. McCormack also shows how later works such as *The Lifted Veil*, 'Brother Jacob' and *Silas Marner* treat addiction figuratively, from Silas's obsessive weaving and hoarding to the storytelling and gambling in other works. The book includes individual chapters on *Romola, Felix Holt, Middlemarch* and *Daniel Deronda*. McCormack concludes with the speculation that Eliot's mother was alcoholic, a theory based on the recurrence of the addicted parental figure in Eliot's fiction, and also her unexplained lifelong silence regarding her mother.

Eliot's construction and conception of English history are the subjects of Neil McCaw's thoughtful and insightful *George Eliot and Victorian Historiography: Imagining the National Past*. McCaw points out the importance of history and historical research in Eliot's work and identifies relationships between her fiction and various approaches to British historiography. He begins with an explication of Eliot's historical research, followed by an analysis of how her fiction accommodates the competing historiographies of the optimistic Whig perspective and that of the less sanguine Carlyle. McCaw also considers later approaches to narrative history and the ways in which Eliot's work is representative of nineteenth-century female writers' problematic relationship with historiography. Hao Li's absorbing study, *Memory and History in George Eliot: Transfiguring the Past*, explores memory and narrative, differences between temporal and historical memory, and connections and interplay among personal, communal, and national memories. In the context of these issues, Li argues for a re-examination of Eliot's works, which transcend positivist and romantic-historical sentiments of her time.

Leah Price's chapter on Eliot in her *The Anthology and the Rise of the Novel: From Richardson to George Eliot* presents a new account of Eliot's literary ascendancy and commercial success. 'George Eliot and the Production of Consumers' argues that Eliot wrote her later books with an awareness that her works would be excerpted. Alexander Main's publication of *Wise, Witty, and Tender Sayings in Prose and Verse Selected from the Works of George Eliot* [1871] and the *George Eliot Birthday Book* [1878] is usually dismissed by biographers as the brainchild of a sycophant. Eliot's role, according to the standard account, is that of a flattered, but only reluctantly cooperative, author. Price, however, argues that Eliot's narrative style is deliberately quotable (she points out that a new edition of *Wise, Witty, and Tender Sayings* came out with each new Eliot novel after *Middlemarch*). More to Price's point is that the 'ruthless' excerpting and anthologizing of Eliot's works transformed her from novelist to poet, and also changed the genre in which she worked. The practice of excerpting lines and passages into epigraphs constituted a complex regendering of Eliot as author: 'they canonized her novels by packaging her as a poet, and bracketed her with male predecessors by marketing her to women'. Price's analysis points out an overlooked irony in Eliot's career as a novelist: although her works are admired for the simultaneous synthesis and specificity that express their author's creed of the interconnectedness of humanity, they have also been picked apart into isolated epigraphs that deny the organicism to which Eliot laid claim.

Patricia Ingham's *Invisible Writing and the Victorian Novel* (also noticed above) presents a unique textual analysis of *Daniel Deronda* and *The Mill on the Floss*. Ingham's thesis is that a novel's language contains hidden ideologies. Eliot's interest in historiography is well known, but Ingham's chapters on Eliot examine the language with a very fine probe in order to discover the rhetorical effects of Eliot's use of tense. In *The Mill on the Floss*, Ingham finds 'contradicting assertions' and 'uncertainties and instabilities' in Eliot's preoccupation with the past and her habitual shifting from present to past tense. *Daniel Deronda*, meanwhile, is concerned with the future, and again Ingham identifies textual contradictions. Deronda's embrace of Judaism at the novel's close, a step which necessarily comes at Gwendolen's expense, results in an implied approval of 'entrepreneurial selfishness' that undermines the novel's central argument.

Monographs on Eliot written in languages other than English include Günter Bachmann's *Philosophische Bewußtseinsformen in George Eliot's 'Middlemarch'*. New editions of Eliot's works include a reprint of *Daniel Deronda* (Everyman [1964]) with a new introduction by A.S. Byatt. Broadview Literary Text's edition of *Felix Holt, the Radical*, edited by William Baker and Kenneth Womack, is a helpful and affordable paperback critical edition that includes a brief chronology of Eliot's life, a select bibliography, and appendices covering the legal plot of the novel; 'Address to Working Men, by Felix Holt'; 'The Natural History of German Life'; and the critical response to the novel.

George Eliot Review (31[2000]) contains the following articles: 'Women and Fiction in George Eliot's "Brother Jacob"' by Rebecca Mackay (*GER* 31[2000] 31–6); 'The Margins of George Eliot: Editing the Journals' by Margaret Harris (*GER* 31[2000] 37–47); 'Towards a Critical Reputation: Henry James on *Felix Holt, the Radical*' (*GER* 31[2000] 47–54); '*Silas Marner* and *Felix Holt*: Affinities and Antitheses' by Ruth Harris (*GER* 31[2000] 55–64); 'George Eliot and Archery' by Arthur G. Credland (*GER* 31[2000] 71–4); and 'A Family's Eye View on George Eliot' by Kathleen Adams (*GER* 31[2000] 75–8). Harriet F. Adams, in 'George Eliot's Deed: Reconciling an Outlaw Marriage' (*YULG* 75:i–ii[2000] 52–63) corrects erroneous assumptions about Eliot's name change following the death of George Henry Lewes. Biographers have explained that she adopted his surname for legal reasons, in order to have access to her property following his death. Adams points out that Eliot had access to her property before the name change, and she argues that she adopted Lewes's surname as a radical assertion of her unmarried relationship with Lewes. David Payne's 'The Serialist Vanishes: Producing Belief in George Eliot' (*Novel* 33:i[1999] 32–50) finds evidence of contradictory 'ideological effort' in *Middlemarch*, drawing attention not only to the text itself, which excludes capitalist exchange, but also to its production in eight half-volumes, a capitalist experiment in profitable publishing. Payne also considers how Eliot's increasing celebrity and status as a moral authority informed the reading of the text and its aims: 'Written text, marketed book, and performed author entwine the contradictions of disenchantment and sympathy, sociological perspective and intellectual charisma, into a cultural form of unprecedented authority and durability' (p. 46).

In 'Presence of Mind: A.S. Byatt, George Eliot, and the Ontology of Ideas' (*CEA* 62:iii[2000] 48–56), Michael J. Noble investigates the influence of George Eliot's depictions of thought and knowledge on A.S. Byatt. Noble explores similarities between Eliot's *Middlemarch* and *Daniel Deronda* and Byatt's *Babel Tower*, in which the processes of thought are precisely rendered while exploring connections between thought and passion. Particularly revealing is Noble's examination of both writers' emphasis on the realization of ideas in language and the precision of language used to render concrete objects. In 'Fiction as Vivisection: G.H. Lewes and George Eliot' (*ELH* 67:ii[2000] 617–53), Richard Menke explores Lewes's application of science to fiction. Following Dickens's and Eliot's public debate over the scientific verisimilitude of Krook's spontaneous combustion, Lewes made several unusual criticisms (which Menke argues were friendly) of Dickens in his essay 'Dickens in Relation to Criticism' [1872], including the comparison of Dickens's 'vividness of imagination' to 'hallucinations'. Menke also thoughtfully addresses Eliot's vivisection of consciousness as a kind of 'mapping of psychology', and her complex renderings of the 'subjective aspect of consciousness in an apparently objective form, as Lewes imagined a non-reductive, experimental physiology of what mind might do' (p. 646).

Harriet Adams examines the circumstances of Hetty Sorrell's pregnancy in 'Rough Justice: Prematurity and Child-Murder in George Eliot's *Adam Bede*' (*ELN* 37:iv[2000] 62–7). Adams investigates the time-frame of the story and possible dates of conception, concluding that Eliot draws sympathetic attention to Hetty's premature labour and unjust conviction. Shifra Hochberg applies Dickens's theories of fancy to Eliot's work in '*Adam Bede* and the Deconstruction of Dickensian Fancy' (*LJHum* 25:i[2000] 23–34). Clifford J. Marks points out Eliot's treatment of Methodism in 'George Eliot's Pictured Bible: *Adam Bede*'s Redeeming Methodism' (*C&L* 49:iii[2000] 311–30). Essays focusing on *Daniel Deronda* include the following: Theodore I. Silar's 'Another Rabbinical Reference in *Daniel Deronda*' (*GEGHLS* 38–9[2000] 80–4), which examines Eliot's treatment of the Talmud, Darwinism and evolution; '"The Instrument of the Century": The Piano as an Icon of Female Sexuality in the Nineteenth Century' by Laura Vorachek (*GEGHLS* 38–9[2000] 26–43); and 'Gwendolen's Madness' by Marlene Tromp (*VLC* 28:ii[2000] 451–70). *Mill on the Floss* criticism includes an analysis of education and superstition by Lila Harper in 'An Astonishing Change in Metaphor: Tom's Education and the Shrew-Mouse' (*GEGHLS* 38–9[2000] 76–9). The novella *The Lifted Veil* is analysed by Julian Wolfreys in 'Phantom Optics: Contextualizing *The Lifted Veil*' (*GEGHLS* 38–9[2000] 61–75).

Middlemarch continues to generate much critical interest. Ian MacKillop and Alison Platt examine the BBC adaptation in '"Beholding in a magic panorama": Television and the Illustration of *Middlemarch*' (in Giddings and Sheen, eds., *The Classic Novel: From Page to Screen*). Saleel Nurbhai examines Eliot's treatment of husband–wife relations, idealization, and self-expression in 'Idealisation and Irony in George Eliot's *Middlemarch*' (*GEGHLS* 38–9[2000] 18–25). Other essays on *Middlemarch* include 'Dorothea Brooke and the Story of *Bildung*' by Jung-Hwa Oh (*FSEL* 2:ii[2000] 159–86) and 'Is *Middlemarch* Ahistorical?' by Henry Staten (*PMLA* 115:v[2000] 991–1005).

Bery Gray's 'George Eliot and the *Westminster Review*' (*VPR* 33:iii[2000] 212–24) looks at the four phases of George Eliot's involvement with the *Westminster Review*. Bernard J. Paris edits a special issue of *PsyArt* [2000] entitled 'Psychoanalytic Perspectives on George Eliot'. Gail Elizabeth Korn examines the role of bookbinding and book production in her essay '"[T]o correspond with you in green-covered volumes": George Eliot, G.H. Lewes and the Production of her Books' (in Bray, Handley, and Henry, eds., *Ma(r)king the Text: The Presentation of Meaning on the Literary Page*, pp. 12–25). Sarah Wintle's 'George Eliot's Peculiar Passion' (*EIC* 50[2000] 23–43) identifies the author's interest in horsemanship. Neil McCaw proposes an allegory of English–Irish relations in 'Beyond "A Water Toast Sympathy"': George Eliot and the Silence of Ireland' (*GEGHLS* 38–9[2000] 3–17). Gerlinde Röder-Bolton compares Eliot's and George Henry Lewes's treatments of Goethe and Weimar in '"Where the stately Jupiter walked": George Eliot and G.H. Lewes in Goethe's Weimar' (*GEGHLS* 38–9[2000] 44–60).

Finally, foreign-language contributions to another most active year of Eliot studies include the following: Marielle Sechepine's application of Edmund Husserl's theories to Eliot's treatment of memory, imagination and childhood in 'Souvenir et ressouvenir dans le roman Eliotien' (*CVE* 51[2000] 115–25); Stéphanie Drouet's '"Princesses in exile" et "wandering Jews": Quête et exil dans *Daniel Deronda* par George Eliot' (*CVE* 51[2000] 161–71); Alberto Ugolini's 'Un portavoce autoriale: Il ruolo di George Eliot nella nascita del narratore proustiano' (*Francofonia* 38[2000] 83–107). A study of Eliot's reception in Germany is presented in Karl Wagner's 'George Eliot in Deutschland und Österreich: Transkulturell Affaren des 19. Jahrhunderts' (in Bachleitner, ed.).

The difficulties in translating *The Rubáiyát of Omar Khayyám* are outlined by Tracia Leacock-Seghatolislami in 'The Tale of the Inimitable *Rubáiyát*' (*TrP* 11:xi[2000] 107–21).

An important new collection of Elizabeth Gaskell's letters, edited by John Chapple and Alan Shelston, includes 270 letters to correspondents such as Florence Nightingale, Harriet Martineau, and John Ruskin. *Further Letters of Mrs Gaskell* includes helpful editorial apparatus and notation, and is the follow-up to an earlier volume of Gaskell's letters edited by Chapple and Arthur Pollard, *The Letters of Mrs Gaskell* [1967, 1997]. New from Penguin Classics is Gaskell's *Gothic Tales*, edited and with an introduction and notes by Laura Kranzler. Broadview Literary Texts' reprint of the 1854 edition of *Mary Barton* (the last edition Gaskell saw through publication) is edited by Jennifer Foster. Foster includes social commentary provided by such figures as Carlyle, Adshead, Engels, Kingsley, and Norton, as well as contemporary reviews of the novel in, for example, *The Athenaeum*, *The Examiner*, and *The Edinburgh Review*. The edition also includes a select bibliography, excerpts from Gaskell's letters, an appendix concerning Chartism and free trade, and related fiction and poetry by Hood, Brontë, Dickens, and Eliot. Malcolm Pittock's evaluative essay, 'The Dove Ascending: The Case for Elizabeth Gaskell' (*ES* 6[2000] 531–47) contends that Gaskell ranks above George Eliot and the Brontës as the premier female Victorian novelist. Pittock's evaluation of *North and South* reveals the work's heretofore unrecognized psychological complexity. In 'Evangelicalism in *Ruth*' (*MLR* 95:iii[2000] 634–41) Yoko Hatano looks at the pure girl who becomes a fallen woman, the role of Evangelicals in rehabilitating prostitutes, and the novel's insistence on sympathy for fallen women. Hatano argues that, although Gaskell was a Unitarian, Ruth reveals influences of Evangelical magdalenism. She also investigates other aspects of the novel that she says are influenced by Evangelicalism, such as portrayals of domesticity. The article presents an interesting discussion of the Victorian idealization of morbidity. In 'Elizabeth Gaskell in *Cornhill* Country' (*VPR* 33:ii[2000] 138–49), Marie E.

Warmbold discusses the serialization of Gaskell's last novel *Wives and Daughters* in *Cornhill* magazine and explores the novel's appeal to a particular audience as a return to the '"good old days" of idyllic English country life' at a time before the passage of the 1832 Reform Bill. Two related critical readings consider how Gaskell's fiction relates to the construction of Victorian social classes: Lisa Surridge's 'Working-Class Masculinities in *Mary Barton*' (*VLC* 28:ii[2000] 331–44) and Pearl L. Brown's 'From Elizabeth Gaskell's *Mary Barton* to her *North and South*: Progress or Decline for Women?' (*VLC* 28:ii[2000] 345–58). Pamela Corpron Parker provides an analysis of Gaskell's biography of Charlotte Brontë in 'Constructing Female Public Identity: Gaskell on Brontë' (in Gallagher and Walhout, eds., *Literature and the Renewal of the Public Sphere*, pp. 68–82). Mary Elizabeth Hotz analyses Gaskell's treatment of death among working-class women in '"Taught by death what life should be": Elizabeth Gaskell's Representation of *North and South*' (*SNNTS* 32:ii[2000] 165–84).

Diane Maltz's insightful article, 'Practical Aesthetics and Decadent Rationale in George Gissing' (*VLC* 28:i[2000] 55–72), examines the influence on Gissing of society hostess Mrs Elizabeth Sarah Gaussen in the 1880s, and Gissing's subsequent introduction into upper-class society. Maltz chronicles Gissing's admiration and enthusiasm for the Aesthetes and Pre-Raphaelites (especially Rossetti, Pater, and Wilde) in the light of his later denouncement of aestheticism in favour of bringing art to the masses and into working-class life. Xavier Baron's essay, 'Impressionist London in the Novels of George Gissing' (in Reitz and Voigts-Virchow, eds., *Lineages of the Novel*), explores realism's relationship with impressionism and the visual arts. *The Gissing Journal* (36:i[2000]) includes the following essays: 'The Darwinian Influence on Gissing's *In the Year of Jubilee*' by Christina Sjöholm (*GissingJ* 36:i[2000] 1–10); 'Gissing in Catanzaro: A Commemoration' by P. Coustillas, D. Grylls and B. Postmus (*GissingJ* 36:i[2000] 11–24); 'Allusions to Gissing in the Complete Works of George Orwell' by Peter Morton (*GissingJ* 36:i[2000] 25–8); '"The Poet's Portmanteau": A Flirtation that Dares not Speak its Name' by Robert L. Selig (*GissingJ* 36:i[2000] 29–34); and 'Gissing and the Crystal Palace' by Kazuo Mizokawa (*GissingJ* 36:i[2000] 34–8). Markus Neacey uses theories of Freud and Nietzsche in his psychological approach to Gissing's treatment of inner life in 'The Coming Man and the Will to Power in *Born in Exile*' (*GissingJ* 36:ii[2000] 20–30). Luisa Villa studies Gissing's attitudes towards business and individualism in 'The Grocer's Romance: Economic Transactions and Radical Individualism in *Will Warburton*' (*GissingJ* 36:ii[2000] 1–19). *GissingJ* 36:iii[2000] includes the following essays: 'Compassion and Selfishness in Gissing's Slum Novels' by Chérifa Krifa Mbarek (*GissingJ* 36:iii[2000] 1–17); 'Gissing's Dreams and Realities, between Wives' by Sydney Lott (*GissingJ* 36:iii[2000] 18–21); '"Catanzaro Judged by an English Journalist"' by Pierre Coustillas (*GissingJ* 36:iii[2000] 22–5); and 'In Gissing's Footsteps to Magna Græcia' by Peter Morton (*GissingJ* 36:iii[2000] (26–31). *GissingJ* 36:iv[2000] includes the following essays: 'Eustace Glazzard: The Schopenhauerian Dilemma' by Janice Deledalle-Rhodes (*GissingJ* 36:iv[2000] 1–18); 'Gissing's Worldly Parable: "The Foolish Virgin"' by Robert L. Selig (*GissingJ* 36:iv[2000] 19–23); 'Gissing and London's Music Halls' by Sydney Lott (*GissingJ* 36:iv[2000] 24–30); and 'On the Latin of Gissing's Henry Ryecroft' by Matthew Leigh (*GissingJ* 36:iv[2000] 31–2).

Reflecting a growing interest in Rider Haggard, György Kalmár analyses his novel *She* and considers the veil metaphor and subject–object relations in 'She-Who-Must-Be-Obeyed: Rider Haggard's Victorian Romance about *She, the Veil, and the Subject of Mâladie'* (*AnaChronist* [2000]149–66).

Page, ed., *The Oxford Reader's Companion to Hardy*, provides an excellent comprehensive overview and reference dictionary of Thomas Hardy studies to date. The most recent articles on Hardy's poetry, novels, life, influences, and correspondence are included. The study also includes valuable appendices such as indexes of poems, characters, place names, a glossary of dialect, and portrayals of Hardy in film, television, and radio. The *Companion* also offers a convincing essay arguing that Hardy's work is so richly imbued with his own personal experiences that the so-called biographical fallacy is actually legitimate.

Hardy's treatment of female characters in his lesser-known novels receives close attention in Jane Thomas's *Thomas Hardy: Femininity and Dissent: Reassessing the 'Minor' Novels* [1998]. Thomas's close readings of *Desperate Remedies, A Pair of Blue Eyes, The Hand of Ethelberta, A Laodicean, Two on a Tower,* and *The Well-Beloved* is informed by Foucauldian feminist theory that sheds light on Hardy's sympathetic portrait of the rebellious female during a time of social change. In *A Route to Modernism: Hardy, Lawrence, Woolf,* Rosemary Sumner looks at elements of modernism in Hardy. In *Thomas Hardy. Imagining Imagination: Hardy's Poetry and Fiction,* Barbara Hardy argues that Hardy's novels are largely about the imaginative world and creativity. Hardy traces these depictions in both artist and non-artist characters, and the indirection and refraction of the mind or imagination in them. She also examines the rhetoric of uncertainty and tentative impression as opposed to literal exactness in acts of creativity and the characters' ordering of reverie. In *Ambivalence in Hardy: A Study of his Attitude to Women,* Shanta Dutta looks at Hardy's portrayal of suffrage and gender stereotypes; oddly, Dutta's discussion excludes *Tess of the d'Urbervilles.* In *Reading Hardy's Landscapes,* Michael Irwin looks at the importance of descriptive details in his landscapes. August Nigro's study, *The Net of Nemesis: Studies in Tragic Bond/Age,* explores the inherent paradox of bondage in relationships that both support and suppress heroic literary figures in various ancient and modern literatures. Nigro contends that, when the hero tries to free himself from his bondage, both the innocent and the guilty suffer because of indifferent legal and moral codes. The hero's suffering, however, leads him to recognition of his own bondage, and eventually to catharsis. Nigro provides a thoughtful analysis of images of bondage—specifically those involving kinship, sex, and marriage—in *Tess of the d'Urbervilles* and *The Mayor of Casterbridge.*

New Casebooks presents a new edition of Hardy's *The Mayor of Casterbridge,* edited by Julian Wolfreys. Also new from New Casebooks is *Jude the Obscure,* edited by Penny Boumelha. Penguin Classics has reissued its 1998 edition of *Far from the Madding Crowd,* edited and with an introduction and notes by Rosemarie Morgan and Shannon Russell. This edition is based on Hardy's original 1874 holograph manuscript at the Beinecke Rare Book and Manuscript Library at Yale University. It includes a chronology of Hardy's life and works.

Mallett, ed., *The Achievement of Thomas Hardy,* includes fresh readings of Hardy's work as a poet and novelist which focus on his self-perception and the ways in which these two roles intersect; his immersion in the cultural traditions he sought to challenge; his use of song and story-telling; and his perceptions of men and women, past and present, and the human being and the natural world. The collection includes essays by Charles P.C. Petit, Sophie Gilmartin, Michael Irwin, Mary Rimmer, William Morgan, Timothy Hands, James Gibson, Danny Karlin, Douglas Dunn, Phillip Mallett, and William Greenslade. Szumski, ed., *Readings on Tess of the D'Urbervilles*, provides critical perspectives and biographical information. Adam Gussow find links between aboriginal culture and Tess in 'Dreaming Holmberry-Lipped Tess: Aboriginal Reverie and Spectatorial Desire in *Tess of the d'Urbervilles*' (*SNNTS* 32:iv[2000] 442–63). Gussow argues that Tess's spiritual association with nature and her repeated lapses into a dream-like state are actually evidence of what from an aboriginal perspective might be considered acculturation. When Tess is transformed into a spectacle via the male gaze, her 'dream journey' is interrupted. Like aboriginal territory, she is mapped by the colonizing and conquering male power that threatens but does not ultimately derail her spiritual quest. *Modern Fiction Studies* 46:iii[2000] is a special issue on Gothicism and modernism, and in 'Oxford's Ghosts: *Jude the Obscure* and the End of Gothic' (*MFS* 46:iii[2000] 646–71), Patrick R. O'Malley examines Hardy's responses to and 'Radcliffean' revisioning of traditional Gothic elements, and the ways in which *Jude the Obscure* fuses Gothic and realist narratives. He looks at how the domestication and assimilation of Gothic elements in Hardy's England serve to make the Gothic familiar instead of foreign. These naturalizing, familiarizing elements, he says, are also found in *The Picture of Dorian Gray* and *Dracula*. Richard F. Hardin's study *Love in a Green Shade: Idyllic Romances Ancient to Modern* investigates in depth the literary treatment and historical reception of *Daphnis and Chloe* from the Renaissance onward. His examination of Hardy's various portrayals of *Daphnis and Chloe* is particularly revealing.

In 'Edmund Gosse, Hardy's *Jude the Obscure*, and the Repercussions of 1886' (*N&Q* 47:iii[2000] 332–4), Anthony Kearney suggests that Gosse's review of a novel critiquing the academic establishment is problematic in the light of John Churton Collins's recent criticism of Gosse in the *Quarterly Review*. Collins's criticism was not personal; rather, it was an attack on the failure of Cambridge and Oxford to recognize the serious study of English literature. Kearney suggests that Gosse's negative commentary about the portrayal of Christminster University in Jude is really a defence against the reform of the Extension Movement, which sought to criticize the university. Two articles consider the representation of social class in Hardy's fiction: 'Voicing the Language of the Literature: Jude's Obscured Labor' by Andrew Cooper (*VLC* 28:ii[2000] 391–410) and 'Hardy's Rustics and the Construction of Class' by Rosemary Jann (*VLC* 28:ii[2000] 411–26). Other articles on Hardy include two from *Dickens Studies Annual: Essays on Victorian Fiction* 29[2000]: '"Three Leahs to get one Rachel": Redundant Women in *Tess of the D'Urbervilles*' by Lisa Sternlieb (*DSA* 29[2000] 351–66); and 'Recent Studies in Thomas Hardy's Fiction, 1987–99' by David Garlock (*DSA* 29[2000] 465–88).

Studies of Hardy's short stories include Ian Rogerson's 'The Illustrations in "A Mere Interlude"' (*THJ* 16:iii[2000] 63–4) and Philip V. Allingham's 'The Initial Publications of Thomas Hardy's Novella "The Romantic Adventures of a Milkmaid" in the *Graphic and Harper's* (Summer 1883)' (*THJ* 16:iii[2000] 45–62). Charles Lock considers Hardy's treatment of the railway in 'Hardy and the Railway' (*EIC* 50[2000] 44–66). Keith Selby looks at a cinematic adaptation of *Tess of the*

D'Urbervilles in 'Hardy History and Hokum' (in Giddings and Sheen, eds.). Mark Durden analyses Hardy's use of photography in 'Ritual and Deception' (*JES* 30:i[2000] 57–69). Sara Malton considers death as social control of the female body in '"The woman shall bear her iniquity": Death as Social Discipline in Thomas Hardy's *The Return of the Native*' (*SNNTS* 32:ii[2000] 147–64). D.E. Musslewhit examines territoriality, capitalism and ethics using the theories of Gilles Deleuze and Felix Guattari in 'Tess of the d'Urbervilles: "A Becoming Woman"; or Deleuze and Guattari Go to Wessex' (*TexP* 14:iii[2000] 499–518). Andrew Radford analyses the unhappiness of Giles Winterbourne in 'Hardy's *The Woodlanders*' (*Expl* 58:iii[2000] 146–8). William A. Davis surveys recent work on Hardy in 'Periodical Articles on Hardy Published in 1999'(*THJ* 16:iii[2000] 65–9). Foreign-language contributions to Hardy studies include Jun Suzuki's comparison of Tess and Prometheus in 'Vikutoriacho no purometeusu: *Tesu* ni okeru rekishi no dianamizumu' (*Shiron* 39[2000] 67–83).

Penny Fielding examines Gothic conventions employed by Montague Rhodes James in 'Reading Rooms: M.R. James and the Library of Modernity' (*MFS* 46:iii[2000] 749–71). Françoise Duperyron-Lafay discusses James's ghost stories and the presentation of time and the uncanny in 'Le Temps dans les *ghost stories* de M.R. James' (*CVE* 51[2000] 51–60). In 'Cultural Capital and the Scene of Rioting: Male Working-Class Authorship in *Alton Locke*' (*VLC* 28:i[2000] 87–108) Richard Menke looks at the relationship between manual and intellectual labour, arguing that Kingsley's *Alton Lock, Tailor and Poet: An Autobiography* never quite answers the question implicit in its title: what do we make of a tailor who is also a poet?

The association between childhood and imperialism continues to be of interest in postmodern and post-colonial studies. The connection is most commonly made between children and oppression, but Don Randall's *Kipling's Imperial Boy: Adolescence and Cultural Hybridity* constructs a unique argument that links conceptions of boyhood to imperial interests. The book begins with a historical analysis of nineteenth-century European constructions of boyhood and their relationship to the project of imperialism. Randall's close reading then shows how the adolescent male characters Mowgli, Stalky, and Kim are associated with cultural hybridity. These 'hybrid' characters on the threshold of culture(s) are deeply involved in the fiction's imperial discourse about the history and future of British imperialism and its effects on British culture. Occupying a unique position as adolescents, these characters sometimes undermine and sometimes advance cultural boundaries. Thomas Pinney edits Kipling's previously unpublished drama *The Jungle Play*, which includes songs and original drawings by Kipling. Several articles on Kipling also appeared this year. '"Strange Medley(s)": Ambiguities of Role, Purpose and Representation in Kipling's *From Sea to Sea*' by John McBratney appears in Finkelstein and Peers, eds., *Negotiating India*. War and propaganda are the subjects of Tracy E. Bilsing's 'The Process of Manufacture: Rudyard Kipling's Private Propaganda' (*WL&A* 12:i[2000] 76–100). Khair Tabish compares Kipling and E.M. Forster in 'Kipling on the Phantom Rickshaw: Between Words and a Hard Place' (*PNR* 27:i[2000] 9–10). Janet Montefiore explores language and imperialism in 'Latin, Arithmetic and Mastery: A Reading of Two Kipling Fictions' (in Booth and Rigby, eds., *Modernism and Empire*, pp. 112–36). Kipling's prose work is the subject of Andrew St John's analysis '"In the Year '57": Historiography, Power, and Politics in Kipling's Punjab' (*RES* 51[2000] 62–79). An allegorical reading of the short story 'Naboth' is presented by Monika Fludernik in 'The Hybridity of Discourses about Hybridity: Kipling's "Naboth" as an Allegory of Postcolonial Discourse' (in Steffen, ed., *Crossover: Cultural Hybridity in Ethnicity, Gender, Ethics*). Douglas Kerr's 'Three Ways of Going Wrong: Kipling, Conrad, Coetzee' (*MLR* 95:i[2000] 18–27) looks at *Plain Tales from the Hills, Conrad's Heart of Darkness*, and Coetzee's *Waiting for the Barbarians*.

In her definitive biography *Amy Levy: Her Life and Letters*, Linda Hunt Beckman looks at Levy's writings, including the novels, essays, short stories, and letters. She also investigates Levy's difficult emotional life—the isolation she experienced because of anti-Semitism, her struggle with depression, and her eventual suicide at the age of 27. In a new approach to Scottish writer George MacDonald, Rebecca Thomas Ankeny examines his consciousness of and sensitivity to relationships between reader, writer, text, and authority in *The Story, the Teller, and the Audience in George MacDonald's Fiction*. Ankeny's innovative study examines the text as a means of communication between author and audience, and links writing with other forms of creation in claiming that a writer is like the creator of nature. This study focuses primarily on *David Elginbrod, Adela Cathcart, Wilfrid Cumbermede, Sir Gibbie, Donal Grant, Home Again, Phantastes*, and *At the Back of the North Wind*. David Holbrook's *A Study of George MacDonald and the Image of Woman* takes a psychological approach to MacDonald's fiction, exploring the author's own interiority and the association between woman and death. Tom Pocock's biography *Captain Marryat: Seaman, Writer, Adventurer* chronicles the life of novelist and children's author Frederick Marryat. The English naval hero's literary celebrity was owed in large part to his embracement by Dickens's circle, and his life was unusually adventurous, beginning with his military service as a youth, his hot-and-cold reception in the United States, his financial success (through writing) and failure (through gambling), and finally his quiet retirement the country. Harriet Martineau's historical novel *The Hour and the Man* [1842] is considered in the context of the abolitionist movement by Susan Belasco in 'Harriet Martineau's Black Hero and the American Antislavery Movement' (*NCF* 55:ii[2000] 157–94). William Morris's socialism in both his fiction and poetry are examined by Ruth Kinna in 'William Morris: Art, Work, Leisure' (*JHI* 61:iii[2000] 493–512). Margaret Oliphant's novel *Miss Marjoribanks* [1866] is discussed in terms of irony and idealism by Melissa Schaub in 'Queen of the Air or Constitutional Monarch? Idealism, Irony, and Narrative Power in *Miss Marjoribanks*' (*NCF* 55:ii[2000] 195–225). Walter Pater's novel *Marius the Epicurean* [1885] receives attention in two essays: Sára Tóth's '"Doorways to things beyond": The Question of Religion in Walter Pater's Works, with a Special Focus on *Marius the Epicurean*' (*AnaChronist* [2000] 167–85) and Martine Lambert's 'Entre la terre et l'idéal, être exilé de "chez soi": Étude de trois "portraits imaginaires" de Walter Pater: "The Child in the House", "Emerald Uthwart" et *Marius the Epicurean*' (*CVE* 51[2000] 207–16). Mary Poovey's 'Recovering Ellen Pickering' (*YJC* 13:ii[2000] 437–68) is printed with replies by Margaret Homans and Jill Campbell in an interesting debate over the literary canon and feminist criticism. Anna Sewell's *Black Beauty* [1877] is a Quaker text, according to Peter Hollindale in 'Plain Speaking: *Black Beauty* as a Quaker Text' (*ChildL* 23[2000] 95–111). Tim Morris compares *Black Beauty* to *Peter Pan, The Secret Garden,* and other children's works in terms of violence, power, gender and animals in *You're Only Young Twice: Children's Literature and*

Film. In *May Sinclair: A Modern Victorian,* Suzanne Raitt examines Sinclair's novel *Divine Fire* [1904], as well as the later novels *Mary Olivier: A Life,* and *The Life and Death of Harriett Frean.* Raitt also explores Sinclair's rise to public prominence after the publication of *Divine Fire,* and her ambivalent feminism. Drawing from newly uncovered manuscripts, Raitt's biography is the first in almost thirty years.

In *Gothic Radicalism: Literature, Philosophy, and Psychoanalysis in the Nineteenth Century,* Andrew Smith applies the philosophical theories of Burke, Kant, and Freud to the works of Robert Louis Stevenson, with particular reference to *Dr. Jekyll and Mr. Hyde.* Andrew Nash reveals the circumstances and whereabouts of 'Two Unpublished Letters of Robert Louis Stevenson' (*N&Q* 47:iii[2000] 334–6), dating from 1887, which were not included with the previously published letters. According to Nash, these two letters 'refer to Stevenson's plans for the book *Memories and Portraits'.* William Hughes explores the intersections of Victorian culture with Gothic and horror fiction in *Beyond Dracula: Bram Stoker's Fiction and its Cultural Context.* He provides critical analysis of Stoker's lesser-known works as well as *Dracula,* and identifies the Victorian attitudes at play in Stoker's depiction of masculinity, femininity, and religion. In '"Double Born": Bram Stoker and the Metrocolonial Gothic' (*MFS* 46:iii[2000] 632–45), Joseph Valente uses post-colonial theory to argue for 'a reading of Stoker's work in which the position of Ireland as a metropolitan colony plays a key role in channeling the Gothic toward modernism'. Valente addresses the colonial issues of the Anglo-Irish, and the 'doubling' of Stoker's alignment with and sympathy for both conqueror and conquered in Stoker's *The Dualists; or the Death Doom of the Double Born,* published ten years before *Dracula.*

In a refreshing interdisciplinary approach to literature, distinguished scholar and critic S. S. Prawer brings his extensive knowledge and wide reading to bear upon Thackeray's European sketchbooks. *W.M. Thackeray's European Sketch Books: A Study of Literary and Graphic Portraiture* is a well-illustrated text that analyses in depth Thackeray's verbal and graphic portraits of European subjects. The first part of the book presents portraits of the French, from 'A Culinary Genius' to 'A Touch of the Demonic'. Part II depicts natives of countries across Europe, from Spain to Russia. Chapters include 'The Children of Wilhelm Tell: Switzerland', 'Comic Nightmare: Russia', and 'The Dusty Realm of Britain's Oldest Ally: Portugal'. The concluding section, entitled '"The Sick Man of Europe" and the Ottoman Empire' exhibits impressions of the German people. The book calls attention to Thackeray's talents as an observer and his skill in expressing those observations in words and pictures. Richard Pearson's *W.M. Thackeray and the Mediated Text* examines the relationship between Thackeray's commercial and his literary writings, arguing that his periodical, journalistic, and commercial endeavours are crucial to an understanding of his literary artistry. The appendices include valuable new attributions to the Thackeray canon. The distinguished Thackeray scholar Edgar F. Harden's *Thackeray the Writer: From 'Pendennis' to 'Denis Duval'* is a follow-up to his *Thackeray the Writer: From Journalism to 'Vanity Fair'.* Harden traces Thackeray's development as a novelist after the success of *Vanity Fair,* and his subsequent work as a lecturer, essayist, and journal editor.

Mark W. Turner's *Trollope and the Magazines: Gendered Issues in Mid-Victorian Britain* reminds us of the importance of the periodical press in Victorian literary culture. Trollope's fiction appeared in a range of magazines, from the popular *Cornhill* to the radical *Fortnightly Review*. Turner reads Trollope's works in their original context—the periodical press—and examines how they participate in the wider debates (the Woman Question, sensationalism) taking place in the various periodicals of the day. In a chapter on Trollope's Ireland in her *Allegories of Union in Irish and English Writing* (see also section 1(*a*) above), Mary Jean Corbett considers his unique perspective and contributions as an English emigrant. Using feminist, post-colonial, and racial theories, Corbett examines how the trope of marriage and family represents the relationship of Ireland to England: one of her overriding arguments is that Irishness helped to define Englishness. Her afterword is also worth noting, as it comprises a brief discussion of an additional Trollope work not addressed in the earlier chapter. *Dickens, Trollope, Jefferson* by Sidney P. and Carolyn J. Moss explores how Trollope's relationship with American Kate Field influenced his fiction. In 'Heterosexual Exchange and Other Victorian Fictions: *The Eustace Diamonds* and Victorian Anthropology' (*Novel* 33:i[1999] 93–118), Kathy Alexis Psomiades analyses the heroines of Trollope's novel alongside Henry Maine's *Ancient Law* and John McLennan's *Primitive Marriage* to argue that the Victorians invented heterosexuality by creating a theory of commodified heterosexual exchange that responded to an emerging capitalism and its accompanying threat of 'gender indifference'. In '"Good Sir Anthony, write us up well": Trollope als Afrik-Reisender' (in Heydenreich and Späth, eds., pp. 137–70), Geoffrey V. Davis examines Trollope's treatment of Africa. The temporal structure, plot, narrative voice, and use of memory in *Orley Farm* [1862] are analysed by Laurent Bury in 'Lenteurs et précipitations du récit trollopien' (*CVE* 51[2000] 39–49).

Samuel Warren's connections with law and literature are explicated by C.R.B. Dunlop in 'Samuel Warren: A Victorian Law and Literature Practitioner' (*CSLL* 12:ii[2000] 265–91). Jean-Michel Yvard takes a biographical and theological approach to the fiction of William Hale White (Mark Rutherford) in 'Écriture et spiritualité: La Question de la création littéraire chez William Hale White ("Mark Rutherford")' (*CVE* 51[2000] 251–62). Charles Swann examines White's English translation of Spinoza in 'William Hale White's (Mark Rutherford) Revisions to the Second Edition Preface of his Translation of Spinoza's *Ethics*' (*ANQ* 13:ii[2000] 16–28).

The year 2000 was the year of Oscar Wilde. A landmark in Wilde studies is the publication of his letters by his grandson, Merlin Holland. Adding to the Rupert Hart-Davis 1960 edition, Holland's *The Complete Letters of Oscar Wilde* collects over 1,500 letters written between 1875 and 1900, including correspondence with W.B. Yeats, George Bernard Shaw, and John Ruskin. The collection spans Wilde's undergraduate years to the period of his great fame, and continues through his final years of imprisonment and exile. Holland adds 300 letters to the original Hart-Davis collection and also completes some previously published fragments. He corrects and amends Hart-Davis's notations and includes 'otherwise trivial' letters that Hart-Davis excluded, such as business correspondence that Wilde wrote while working as editor of the *Woman's World*. These additions, presented alongside fascinating photographs, give insight into Wilde's frequently overlooked career in journalism and contribute to our knowledge of his life and activities.

Oxford University Press's *The Complete Works of Oscar Wilde*, vol. i: *Poems and Poems in Prose*, launches a project to produce a complete collection of authoritative texts of Wilde's work. Bobby Fong and Karl Beckson edit 119 poems and poems in prose and contribute nearly 100 pages of textual commentary, including the location of manuscripts, publication history, and helpful textual glosses. In some cases, the notes also describe the biographical contexts in which the poems were written. Textual variants among the various manuscripts and published poems are scrupulously explicated. The collection includes twenty-one poems not published in Wilde's lifetime and is the most complete work of its kind. It also includes an introduction by Ian Small.

Several works consider Wilde's relationship to art culture. His role as a leading figure in the London and Paris art communities in the latter part of the nineteenth century is the focus of Tomoko Sato, Lionel Lambourne, and their team of authors in *The Wilde Years: Oscar Wilde and the Art of his Time*, which considers Wilde's contributions, not only to literature, but also to the artistic and cultural movements of the period, and points out his lesser-known activities as art critic and journalist. Wilde's attention to the artistic appearance of his books is described by Nicholas Frankel in *Oscar Wilde's Decorated Books*. Frankel notes Wilde's working relationships with several graphic designers and argues that he considered literature to be a 'decorative art' in which the aesthetics of layout and design are an integral part of literary language. Wilde's aestheticism comes under scrutiny in Josephine M. Guy and Ian Small's *Oscar Wilde's Profession: Writing and Culture Industry in the Late Nineteenth Century*. In a detailed account of the economics of Wilde's career, including his revision practices and his dealings with publishers and theatre managers, the authors reveal a 'pragmatism and worldliness' that have been obscured by attention to Wilde's politics and sexuality. The economic analysis demonstrates that Wilde's continuing efforts to achieve financial success were both a response and contribution to the 'commodification of culture'. Charlotte Gere, Lesley Hoskin and David Dewing's *The House Beautiful: Oscar Wilde and the Aesthetic Interior* is an illustrated investigation of Wilde's admiration of architecture and interior decoration and of his architectural theories, which are drawn largely from Pater, Ruskin, and Morris. Gere looks at the aesthetic movement's influence on the decorative arts, Wilde's aesthetic education and the artistic circles he frequented, and his 'house beautiful' on Tite Street. The final chapter, by Lesley Hoskins, looks at popular expressions of the aesthetic movement in books and magazines.

In 'Oscar Wilde's Aesthetic Gothic: Walter Pater, Dark Enlightenment, and *The Picture of Dorian Gray*' (*MFS* 46:iii[2000] 609–31), John Paul Riquelme suggests that *The Picture of Dorian Gray* is a precursor of later stories of consumption and violence. Riquelme also examines the dark implications of the desire for beauty and the 'self-destructive aspects of the society the book addresses'. Talia Schaffer's interesting article 'Fashioning Aestheticism by Aestheticizing Fashion: Wilde, Beerbohm, and the Male Aesthetes' Sartorial Codes' (*VLC* 28:i[2000] 39–54) examines aesthetic fashion, which she says 'displayed the anxieties, stresses, and formulations of the movement' (p. 39). Schaffer argues that the aesthetic mode of dress was a way in which notions of gender could be played out. Because Wilde worked in a field traditionally associated with women and because he appropriated elements of female fashion, he was often considered effeminate. Schaffer suggests that these visual codes were a way to 'reconfigure their fear of feminization' and display the body as an essential and artistic icon.

Wilde scholars will appreciate Ian Small's evaluative bibliography of recent Wilde studies, *Oscar Wilde, Recent Research: A Supplement to 'Oscar Wilde Revalued'*. This is Small's second Wilde bibliography (the first being *Oscar Wilde Revalued* [1993]. *Recent Research* covers 1992–2000, and is divided into three sections: biography, critical 'paradigms' (e.g. the 'Gay' Wilde, the 'Irish' Wilde, and 'Wilde and Consumerism') and Wilde's roles as journalist, poet, and stage professional. Works not fitting into these categories are treated in separate sections. The supplement provides other pertinent information such as manuscript discoveries and new resources for Wilde scholarship, in addition to a comprehensive bibliography organized alphabetically and by the author's work. An index of critics is also included. Two Wilde biographies present sympathetic portraits of the troubled artist. Joseph Pearce's *The Unmasking of Oscar Wilde* chronicles Wilde's lifelong quest for emotional and spiritual fulfilment, including his ongoing interest in Catholicism and his breakdown resulting from imprisonment. Pearce also describes the intellectual and emotional thinking that produced *The Ballad of Reading Gaol* and *De Profundis*. Barbara Belford draws on original sources in order to trace Wilde's life from his early years up to his death, in *Oscar Wilde: A Certain Genius*. Belford evaluates Wilde's life from numerous perspectives: as a family man as well as a significant public figure who helped define the era. She links Wilde's homosexuality to the politics of the 1890s, and examines his years of sexual liberation after his most prolific years of creativity.

The reissued Penguin paperback of *The Picture of Dorian Gray*, edited by Robert Mighall, includes a new introduction by Mighall, a chronology, notes, contemporary reviews, and Peter Ackroyd's introduction to the first edition. The text is based on the 1891 edition published by Ward, Lock. Penguin has also published *The Importance of Being Earnest and Other Plays*, edited by Richard Allen Cave: the edition includes *Lady Windermere's Fan*, *Salomé*, *A Woman of No Importance*, *An Ideal Husband*, and *A Florentine Tragedy*, plus an excised scene from *The Importance of Being Earnest*.

3. Poetry

This year Cambridge brought out its *Companion to Victorian Poetry*, edited by Joseph Bristow and featuring thirteen essays on topics important to any meaningful discussion of Victorian poetry. Bristow's introduction, 'Reforming Victorian Poetry: Poetics after 1832' (pp. 1–24), examines the social and political events after 1832, an era of reform (the three Reform Bills and the Corn Laws especially), which informed Victorian poetry, including the much-contested public/private role poets and poetry sought. Carlyle's impress on the period receives much emphasis. Kathy Alexis Psomiades, '"The Lady of Shalott" and the Critical Fortunes of Victorian Poetry' (pp. 25–45), argues that it was only in the 1920s and 1930s that 'literary criticism emerged as a professional scholarly discipline worthy of the attention of elite men', to whom 'Victorian poetry became synonymous with bad poetry'. Yet, she argues, Victorian poetry was fundamental to the birth of modern literary criticism. 'It is not just that Victorian poetry invents the categories of poetry and society, literature and other writings, representation and reality, masculine and feminine and sets those categories in opposition to each other'; Victorian poetry, Psomiades insists, also articulates these categories as the problems of modernity. Psomiades uses Tennyson's 'The Lady of Shalott', where both poetry and society are under construction, to illustrate how these issues are debated.

In 'Experimental Form in Victorian Poetry' (pp. 46–66), E. Warwick Slinn believes that the 'desire to compose a new poetic form, one that would adapt established styles to contemporary needs, and particularly one that would combine narrative and speculative commentary with the requirements of aesthetic unity, typifies many Victorian poets'. Slinn sees Victorians employing a variety of literary forms, with the dramatic monologue as an innovation and 'the main Victorian contribution to a distinctly modern, if not Modernist, literature'. *Aurora Leigh* and *The Ring and the Book*, according to Slinn, emerged as 'the most ambitious literary experiments in the period'. Cornelia D.J. Pearsall's 'The Dramatic Monologue' (pp. 67–88) looks at the dramatic monologue as 'a vehicle for the performance of thoughts'. Pearsall sees the main feature of this genre as 'its assumption of rhetorical efficacy'. In reading the dramatic monologue, she proposes that we 'ask what each poem seeks to perform, what process it seeks to set in motion or ends it seeks to attain'. Still on the formalistic features of Victorian poetry, Yopie Prins's 'Victorian Meters' (pp. 89–113) sees in Victorian poetry, in addition to 'increasingly refined and rarefied metrical experiments', a 'return to metres inspired by ancient Greek and Latin poetry' and a more elaborate prosody. Reading poems by Tennyson, Clough, and Christina Rossetti side by side with Victorian theories of metre, Prins discovers that a central concern in Victorian metrical theory is 'how a poem materializes in sound and how it materializes on the page'.

In 'Victorian Poetry and Historicism' (pp. 114–36), Hilary Fraser finds Victorians turning to the past, specifically ancient Greece, the Middle Ages, and the Renaissance, to locate 'a kind of poetic authenticity felt to be lacking in the present time', a past 'more self-consciously theorized and more diverse in ways that were distinct from earlier forms of historicism'. Daniel Brown's 'Victorian Poetry and Science' (pp. 137–58) shows how a number of Victorian poems—Tennyson's *In Memoriam*, Arnold's 'Dover Beach', Meredith's 'Lucifer in Starlight', and Hopkins's 'Heraclitean Fire'—wrestle with science's break from 'its traditional ties to philosophy and religion' and emerge as 'the paradigmatic form of knowledge'. Brown looks at how spiritualism, largely an American import, was deployed in response to the emerging materialism/positivism. Cynthia Scheinberg, 'Victorian Poetry and Religious Diversity' (pp. 159–79), insists that 'Victorian religious poetry became an important site for presenting divergent religious perspectives, providing a dynamic forum where writers frequently explored the fraught experience of living as a religious "other" in England'. Scheinberg looks at the various dissenter groups informing English culture, and, more specifically, how Grace Aquilar's 'Song of the Spanish Jews', Christina Rossetti's 'Consider the Lilies of the Field', and Hopkins's 'To Seem the Stranger' articulate 'a distinctive religious perspective that requires certain transformations of both English poetic conventions and the readerly assumptions embedded in those conventions'. 'The Victorian Poetess' (pp. 180–202) by Susan Brown examines the way the term 'poetess', which 'sounds unnecessarily gendered' to us, was to Victorians a term employed relatively valuelessly and which was interchangeable with the now more acceptable term 'poet'. 'In much more complicated ways', she indicates, 'the poetess designated a fiercely contested role in the literary market of a rapidly transforming society.' Brown looks at how 'influential and often contradictory understandings of the Victorian poetess are informed by a commodified aestheticism that frequently conflates the woman poet's body with her literary corpus'.

Thaïs E. Morgan's 'The Poetry of Victorian Masculinities' (pp. 203–27) explores the representations of masculinity in Victorian England 'in response to industrialization and changes in the socioeconomic class system'. It was Carlyle's *On Hero, Hero-Worship, and the Heroic in History*, Morgan maintains, that became 'a guidebook for several generations of Victorian men seeking a firm gender identity'. In 'Aesthetic and Decadent Poetry' (pp. 228–54), Karen Alkalay-Gut examines the aesthetic movement of the 1870s and its view that 'art has no obligations to anything but itself', leaving poets such as Swinburne 'free to delve into unexplored topics, to plunge into their own uninhibited thoughts and feelings, and to venture into worlds liberated from moral censure'. This freedom, however, comes at a cost, placing the genre 'in a marginal position with regard to society' and 'arguably diminishing the poet's cultural authority'. Alkalay-Gut shows how late Victorian poets, chiefly Swinburne, Morris, Dante and Christina Rossetti, Meredith, FitzGerald, Dowson, Levy, Symons, Wilde, and Yeats, engage this new aestheticism and decadence. 'Victorian Poetry and Patriotism' (pp. 255–79), by Tricia Lootens, looks at the often neglected genre of Victorian patriotic verse, a genre, she believes, crucial to the study of nineteenth-century poetic culture in which '"natal" loyalties' become translated into 'a large love of country'. The poetry of Hemans, Barrett Browning, Tennyson, Kipling, and Hardy routinely explores patriotic themes. Finally, in 'Voices of Authority, Voices of Subversion: Poetry in the Late Nineteenth Century' (pp. 280–301), John Lucas examines late nineteenth-century poetry and the politics surrounding Tennyson's successor to the Laureateship at a time when it 'mattered far more than ever before' for the sheer reason that poetry became 'important to many people in England because its practitioners were expected to uphold orthodox views'. Lucas also looks at how the city emerges as an important topical site in late nineteenth-century poetry.

Victorian Poetry brought out a special issue (38[2000]) on writers infrequently represented in our general consideration of Victorian poets and poetry. '"Individable Incorporate": Poetic Trends in Women Writers, 1890–1918' (*VP* 38[2000] 1–14), by Bonnie J. Robinson, argues that the nineteenth-century poetry of these largely non-canonical women writers 'combines universal beauty, woman as material, woman as confused with nature, with a distinct impress of the individual woman'. Understanding this poetry, she is convinced, 'helps us to re-evaluate it and to contradict the tenets of Modernism, tenets which privilege difficulty, discord, gaps, rifts, and division'. '*Sight and Song*: Transparent Translations and a Manifesto for the Observer' (*VP* 38[2000] 15–34), by Ana I. Parejo Vandillo, looks at Michael Field's *Sight and Sound* and later poetic tributes to Pater, which voice a 'sensorial epistemology that would become the trademark of modernity', an aesthetic that establishes a connection between 'sight' and 'sound' and blends visuality with sexuality. In other words, Field 'complicates not only the relation between the visual arts and poetry but, more importantly, the relation between art and the subject that gazes and enjoys it'. Sharon Smulders's 'Looking "Past Wordsworth and the Rest": Pre-Texts for Revision in Alice Meynell's "The Shepherdess"' (*VP* 38[2000] 35–

48) believes that Meynell's poem attempts 'to resolve the conflict between inherited structures—both formal and conceptual—and the woman poet'. In the poem, Meynell wants to look beyond the likes of Wordsworth and Byron, adapting even as she revises and supplants them. Talia Schaffer, 'A Tethered Angel: The Martyrdom of Alice Meynell' (*VP* 38[2000] 49–61), is convinced that 'We cannot understand crucial aspects of her life, her reputation, and her writing unless we comprehend how the notion of the Angel in the House contributed to Meynell's poetic and personal identity'. As Schaffer sees it, 'If Meynell sometimes chafed against this oppressive idealization, she also tacitly fostered it by maintaining her mysteriously profound silence, refusing to enunciate those unruly aspects of her experiences and emotions which might have drawn public disapproval.' For Maria Frawley, '"The tides of the mind": Alice Meynell's Poetry of Perception' (*VP* 38[2000] 62–76), Meynell needs to be viewed from the vantage-point of how her work grapples with the 'emerging modernist interest in psychology', the way, that is, in which it deals with 'thinking about thought', the 'tides of the mind'. Frawley believes that charting this trajectory across Meynell's canon 'exposes the inextricable link between the ideas expressed in her poetry and her prose and, more critically, reveals her nuanced response both to Romantic versions of the lyric form and to the aestheticism so often associated with her literary period'.

'"Whilst working at my frame": The Poetic Production of Ethel Carnie' (*VP* 38[2000] 77–93), by Susan Alves, looks at Carnie's substantive corpus (poetry and fiction) and how it 'represents her anxieties over gender roles and the social position of white working-class women' whose 'Whiteness functions within the communal discourse and self-inscription the poet shares with her readers'. M. Lynda Ely's '"Not a song to sell": Re-Presenting A. Mary F. Robinson' (*VP* 38[2000] 94–108) treats the virtual erasure of Robinson, whose poetics, Ely believes, 'were, indeed, crucial to her way of interpreting contemporary reality, a complement to her work in biography, history, and social criticism'. Furthermore, says Ely, Robinson 'tested the limits of women's poetry, defiantly conceding the unsuccessful reception of her experiment in realism and social criticism'. LeeAnne Richardson, 'Naturally Radical: The Subversive Poetics of Dollie Radford' (*VP* 38[2000] 109–24), examines another late Victorian, early modern voice, whose literary disappearance might be attributed to 'the reactionary gender politics of fin-de-siècle England'. Radford is important if for no other reason than the way in which she challenged 'conventional notions of what women could and should do' along with the way in which she 'subtly co-opted conventional notions of women's roles to make her feminist points, to naturalize previously unacceptable behavior by women, and to re-envision ... the relations between men and women'. In 'Grave Passions: Enclosure and Exposure in Charlotte Mew's Graveyard Poetry' (*VP* 38[2000] 125–40), Dennis Denisoff looks at how Mew, in her 'non-heteronormative vision' as lesbian/ghost, 'envisions the site of entombment as a dynamic space that contests society's extension of the living/dead segregation to other cultural forms of exclusionism and discrimination'. Hers, Denisoff believes, is a 'unique contribution to the genre of graveyard poetry'. 'Outselling the Modernisms of Men: Amy Lowell and the Art of Self-Commodification' (*VP* 38[2000] 141–69), by Melissa Bradshaw, wants a 'reconsideration of Amy Lowell, a woman utterly unabashed in her approach to poetry as a business'. Regrettably, her 'commitment to the business end of poetry' has contributed to her exclusion from the anthologies of modern poetry. Bradshaw sees great value in Lowell's theatricality and in the way in which she fostered 'a sense of dialectic between the conservatism of the academy and the elitism of the avant-garde'. Finally, Norman Kelvin's 'H.D. and the Years of World War I' (*VP* 38[2000] 170–96) discusses the way H.D. 'resists the linear chronology of her life' and the way it circles back, making her 'life-work a palimpsest whose uttermost layer [is] the years of the First World War'. Other essays appearing in *VP* feature additional infrequently taught Victorians. 'The Shadow of the Octoroon in T.E. Brown's *Christmas Rose*' (38[2000] 289–98), by Max Keith Sutton, looks at how race factors into the poem, and especially how Rose 'comes to resemble the tragic octoroon in her beauty and sexual desirability, her problematic identity, and her sense of being unfit for this world'.

VP brought out another special issue this year, this one devoted to Victorian sexuality. In their 'Introductory Dialogue' (*VP* 38[2000] 467–89), Donald E. Hall and Dennis W. Allen argue that the study of sexuality and desire invite 'varied and expansive investigations of the rules governing human behavior and organization and the ways in which social meaning [is] made, replicated, and contested'. Allen finds that the meaning of the terms 'ethical' and 'sexual' 'cannot necessarily be assumed, especially for another time and place'. The job of the critic is therefore 'to articulate that cultural context'. In 'Robert Browning and the Lure of the Violent Lyric Voice: Domestic Violence and the Dramatic Monologue' (*VP* 38[2000] 491–510), Melissa Valiska Gregory believes that Browning's dramatic monologues shed new light on 'the psychology of sexual violence', which, she argues, 'lies at the heart of both the fierce public rejection of his early work and the suddenly enthusiastic and widespread approval of *The Ring and the Book*'. Christine Sutphin's 'Human Tigresses, Fractious Angels, and Nursery Saints: Augusta Webster's *A Castaway* and Victorian Discourse on Prostitution and Women's Sexuality' (*VP* 38[2000] 511–31) examines how *A Castaway* (and, one might add, the way in which the expression is used by Victorians such as Barrett Browning to describe a woman damned or dead) challenges the assumption that reform is a necessary outgrowth of self-reflection even as it calls into question 'progressive attempts to resolve problems associated with prostitution, particularly the rhetoric of sisterhood and redemption through maternity created by sympathetic women reformers and writers'. In '"O wanton eyes run over": Repetition and Fantasy in Christina Rossetti' (*VP* 38[2000] 533–53), Suzy Waldman uses Lacan to explain the conflict between religion and sexuality in Rossetti's poetry. Waldman provides a psychoanalytic reading of Rossetti's Tractarian impulse and the repression of desire she sees evident in Rossetti's poetry—'Goblin Market', for example. Still looking at 'Goblin Market', Kathleen Vejvoda, 'The Fruit of Charity: *Comus* and Christina Rossetti's *Goblin Market*' (*VP* 38[2000] 555–78), traces the Miltonic influence on the poem, showing where and how both works concern 'the virtues of chastity and charity'. *Comus* and 'Goblin Market', she believes, 'explore these virtues by using a female Christ figure whose divine power derives from her experience of a violent assault'. Finally, Paul J. Beidler, 'Chiastic Strands in Stanza 1 of "The Wreck of the Deutschland"' (*VP* 38[2000] 579–95), examines a theory of the chiasmus in the poem and how the convention becomes 'a site of deconstruction—the deconstruction of the self in Christ'.

Arnold studies this year saw the release of volume iv of *The Letters of Matthew Arnold*, edited by Cecil Y. Lang. Covering the years 1871 to 1878, the volume opens with the publication of *Friendship's Garland* and concludes with the release of *Selected Poems*, between which Arnold published *Literature and Dogma*, *God and the Bible*, and *Last Essays on Church and Religion*. In the letters, Arnold admits his well-known love of Oxford, rejects the editorship of *Fraser's*, which Froude was giving up, displays a residual anti-Semitism ('I met that famous Jew, Dizzy [Disraeli], on Monday and he was very amiable'), acknowledges his most dominant literary influences (Goethe, Wordsworth, Sainte-Beuve, and Newman), and discloses his views on the Bible and on plenary inspiration. The most significant work appearing on Elizabeth Barrett Browning is Donaldson, ed., *Critical Essays on Elizabeth Barrett Browning*. The introduction (pp. 1–14) surveys the poet's growth and reception, and the scholarship, acknowledging the now almost complete absence of any recent edition of her collected poems, the emphasis so far having been directed to the letters. 'Experiment in Poetic Technique' (pp. 15–31), by Alethea Hayter, examines the changes Barrett Browning made in her technique which worked to improve her versification, making her the celebrated poet she now is. But Barrett Browning did not do a complete makeover of her poetry; she retained more than a few of her poetic blemishes simply because she liked them, especially her preference for compound words and her unique coinages, the latter influenced by her search for 'the most syntactically compressed possible way of saying a thing'. In 'A Little Hemming and More Greek' (pp. 32–7), Mary Jane Lupton looks at Barrett Browning's facility with languages, especially Greek, but then drifts into a rather ill-focused discussion of gender concerns. Sandra Donaldson's 'Elizabeth Barrett's Two Sonnets to George Sand' (pp. 38–41) believes that it was only Sand who, embodying 'the ideals Barrett, as a young girl, had described for herself', seems 'to have achieved in Barrett's eyes any balance between attributes conventionally called "manly" and "womanly"'.

In 'The Ring, the Rescue, and the Risorgimento: Reunifying the Brownings' Italy' (pp. 42–70), Flavia Alaya argues that Robert Browning's political views and poetic role seem in direct opposition to Barrett Browning's more decidedly political verse. While Browning was supposedly posing as a secret patriot, 'engaging in the bravado of secret and seditious meetings', Barrett Browning, removed from the centre of Italian politics, found that her verse was the only way to effect such an engagement and to become more politically involved. Much of Browning's later poetry can be viewed as an attempt to connect with his wife's seemingly naive political views: much of the poetry Browning wrote following her death 'renewed a contract … between two poets who had once been—quite literally—political bedfellows'. The Donaldson collection (pp. 71–101) revisits Cora Kaplan's celebrated introduction to *Elizabeth Barrett Browning: Aurora Leigh and Other Poems* [1978], considered by many to be the most comprehensive survey of the poet's life, reception, poetry, ideas, and influences. 'Women's Writing: *Jane Eyre, Shirley, Villette, Aurora Leigh*' (pp. 102–11) excerpts a group of female thinkers—a collective writing against 'the monologic discourse of patriarchal literary criticism'—calling themselves the Marxist-Feminist Literature Collective. The essay proposes a synthesis of Marxist-feminist/psychoanalytic approaches to literary texts by reading the four texts in question as 'a discussion of gender definition, kinship structures, and to some extent, the relation between these and social class. … All of the major female characters' in these texts, say the collaborators, disclose 'an extremely marginal and unstable class position, and all display an obvious discrepancy between their class position and their alleged rightful status.' Helen Cooper, 'Working into Light: Elizabeth Barrett Browning' (pp. 112–28), argues that the poet made demands in assessing 'women's work' which she adapted from 'the male poetic tradition'. She took from women 'a network of support while systematically breaking through the limiting properties ascribed to women poets'. Kathleen Hickok's '"New Yet Orthodox": The Female Characters in *Aurora Leigh*' (pp. 129–40) argues that Barrett Browning's poems appear 'not as *sui generis*, but as part of a field of established poetic figures, themes, and purposes shared by her feminine peers'. Focusing specifically on *Aurora Leigh*, Hickok looks at how the poet problematizes issues regarding women as she does those of class, and while the latter 'does not supply its unity of perspective', 'Feminine consciousness does', especially the way in which the poem explores 'all the women's roles with which the public was familiar in mid-nineteenth-century England'.

'The Domestic Economy of Art: Elizabeth Barrett and Robert Browning' (pp. 141–56), by Dorothy Mermin, examines the Brownings' reciprocated care, domestic arrangements, social engagements, and mutual admiration for each other's poetry. In '*Casa Guidi Windows* and *Aurora Leigh*: The Genesis of Elizabeth Barrett Browning's Visionary Aesthetic' (pp. 157–63), Dolores Rosenblum looks at how the two poems together express Barrett Browning's political vision, a whole new way of seeing, placing 'the lived moment within a cosmic perspective in which the present unfolds a dynamic future'. '"Art's a service": Social Wound, Sexual Politics, and *Aurora Leigh*' (pp. 164–83), by Deirdre David, sees the poem articulating a residual feminist agenda, unconvinced as Barrett Browning is of female intellectual capabilities. Still, David finds, Aurora 'creates herself as ministering healer to an infected world', and a healer of wounds that only 'maternal nurturance' can effect. Marjorie Stone, 'Cursing as One of the Fine Arts: Elizabeth Barrett Browning's Political Poems' (pp. 184–201), insists that cursing 'is an art often practised by poets who, like witches and prophets, weave dire spells with words'. Stone explores Barrett Browning's use of the curse, 'pronouncing a malediction', and the 'changing treatment of cursing as a [prophetic] speech act' in her political utterances, an expression that evokes from 'the depths of woman's oppression, as well as of her anger and passion'. In 'Combating an Alien Tyranny: Elizabeth Barrett Browning's Evolution as a Feminist Poet' (pp. 202–17), Deborah Byrd argues that foremost in the development of Barrett Browning's 'feminist consciousness and aesthetic' were her 'encounters with literary texts' and 'interaction with women authors, particularly women poets'. Byrd traces the gradual emergence of the assertive female voice in Barrett Browning's poetic development, seeing the poem 'An Island' as a commencement of sorts of the poet moving from 'an immasculated [*sic*] to a woman-identified poet'.

'Stirring "a dust of figures": Elizabeth Barrett Browning and Love' (pp. 218–32), by Angela Leighton, looks at Barrett Browning's playful way with love in her correspondence and in *Sonnets from the Portuguese*, the latter taking its place in 'a long self-conscious tradition of literary writing about love'. 'To fix the *Sonnets from the Portuguese* as an autobiographical record of a true romance', Leighton finds, 'is to miss their literary playfulness, their in-jokes, even, at times, their competitive ingenuity'. Mary Rose Sullivan, '"Some interchange of grace": "Saul" and *Sonnets from the Portuguese*' (pp. 233–43), believes that these two literary works 'provide an unusually clear record of the way each [poet] affected and was affected by the other's writings'. 'Of particular note,' says Sullivan, 'is the way that Browning's first version of "Saul" helped to shape the theme and imagery of *Sonnets from the Portuguese*, which in turn influenced his later conclusion to "Saul".' In 'The Vision Speaks: Love in Elizabeth Barrett Browning's "Lady Geraldine's Courtship"' (pp. 244–57), Glennis Stephenson explores the way in which the poem presents the radical role of woman as active lover, and experiments with 'sensuous language to convey the physical and the spiritual nature of the relationship'. Margaret Morlier, 'The Death of Pan: Elizabeth Barrett Browning and the Romantic Ego' (pp. 258–74), examines the poet's response to Romanticism and her handling of Pan, who in Barrett Browning's poetry represents 'the potential for aggression, violence, and control in Romantic egoism. ... Pan becomes in her poetry a figure that enacts various forms of ideological control.' In '*Aurora Leigh*: An Epical *Ars Poetica*' (pp. 275–90), Holly A. Laird believes that Aurora is 'as convincingly courageous a heroine as has ever been enacted'. But more than the heroic subject is the heroic poetics of *Aurora Leigh*, 'an epical enactment of that philosophy, an embodied *ars*'. Evident in Browning's heroine, says Laird, is 'a revised version of Carlyle's theory, widely held by others of this period, of the modern hero as man of letters'. Much of Laird's discussion pursues Barrett Browning's engagement with Carlyle on the heroic.

'Mapping Sublimity: Elizabeth Barrett Browning's *Sonnets from the Portuguese*' (pp. 291–305), by Jerome Mazzaro, argues that Barrett Browning 'seems intent on adapting the terror and physicality of these metaphors to her own encounter later in life with love', causing her poetry to be less literarily sincere than it might otherwise be. Cynthia Scheinberg's 'Elizabeth Barrett Browning's Hebraic Conversions: Feminism and Christian Typology in *Aurora Leigh*' (pp. 306–23) shows Barrett Browning's reliance on Jewish typology in *Aurora Leigh* and in particular the image of Miriam/Marian, which is moved from 'divine poet to unclean woman' largely because she challenged the patriarchal authority of her brother Moses; 'her contradictory function in this interpretation of history', says Scheinberg, 'becomes for us a paradigm of how women poets act, interact, and are acted upon in religious communities'. The essay examines Miriam's ambiguous role and status in Barrett Browning's corpus. In 'Lady's Greek without the Accents: *Aurora Leigh* and Authority' (pp. 324–32), Alice Falk argues that Barrett Browning's 'altered stance toward Greek and the classical legacy of the past also works significantly through her later works, particularly *Aurora Leigh*'. Her interest in Greek, Falk believes, shows her willingness to participate in what is a largely male tradition, reshaping it, however, to her own satisfaction. Finally, Daniel Karlin, 'The Discourse of Power in Elizabeth Barrett Browning's Criticism' (pp. 333–41), surveys the 'editorial we' in Barrett Browning's three anonymously published reviews in the *Athenaeum* for 1842.

In 'A Different Look: Visual Technologies and the Making of History in Elizabeth Barrett Browning's *Casa Guidi Windows*' (*TPr* 14:i[2000] 31–52), Helen Groth examines the poet's keen interest in the developing daguerreotype and photography, 'the experience of looking [which] enacted a temporal paradox—the simultaneous experience of past and present in a single encounter with a frozen moment in time'. That obsession, says Groth, makes possible the 'optical self-consciousness that characterizes the political and aesthetic reflections of *Casa Guidi*

Windows', for which 'Daguerreotype provides ... an important discursive context for the [poem's] aesthetic and political arguments'. Jennifer Wallace, 'Elizabeth Barrett Browning: Knowing Greek' (*EIC* 50[2000] 329–53), examines the poet's facility for, even obsession with, ancient languages and how her ambivalence about them testifies to 'the uneasiness women felt about being scholarly'. What especially fascinated Barrett Browning about these languages, Wallace claims, was their appropriateness to comment on love, passion, and the erotic. Julie Straight's '"Neither keeping either under": Gender and Voice in Elizabeth Barrett's *The Seraphim*' (*VP* 38[2000] 269–88) examines the difficulties logocentrism presents to the woman poet because of its ties to male superiority. Disrupting 'oppositional hierarchies', Barrett Browning works to undercut this assumption, 'relentlessly depicting the transcendental signified, the Logos or Word, in the "female" position of weakness and death at the Crucifixion'.

The year saw Martin Garrett's *A Browning Chronology: Elizabeth Barrett and Robert Browning*, which documents important events and moments in the lives of Robert and Elizabeth. Opening with a 6 March 1806 entry, Elizabeth Barrett's birth, and concluding with a 31 December 1889 entry on Robert's death and subsequent burial near Chaucer and Spenser in Westminster, the *Chronology* dates such events as Elizabeth Barrett's September 1821 'Essay on Woman', Robert's publication of *Sordello* on 7 March 1840, their first correspondence (from Robert) on 10 January 1845 and subsequent courtship, their marriage on 12 September 1846 and departure for the Continent, Pen's birth on 9 March 1849 and years at Balliol, Robert's publication of *Men and Women* (10 November 1855), Barrett Browning's publication of *Aurora Leigh* (15 November 1856), her death on 29 June 1861 and her burial in Florence, and Robert's publication of *Dramatis Personae* (28 May 1864), *The Ring and the Book* (21 November 1868–27 February 1869), *Asolando* (12 December 1889), and 'Why I Am a Liberal' (1885). The *Chronology* is a useful tool for scholars wishing to examine particular periods of the poets' lives and development.

There was other attention to Robert Browning. In 'The Promise of Converting Poets in Robert Browning's "Cleon"' (*VP* 38[2000] 249–68), Joe Dupras sees 'Cleon' wrestling with the difficulty of being Victorian artist and Victorian Christian. Michael Johnstone, 'Truth has a Human Face' (*VP* 38[2000] 365–81), writing on Browning's 'A Death in the Desert', believes that the poem represents Browning's 'response to Ernest Renan's *The Life of Jesus*', showing especially 'how theories of language relevant to Browning and his time deal with truth'. Reassessing Browning's response to nineteenth-century biblical higher criticism, Johnstone believes that the Gospel of John 'harbors the fundamental structures and images of truth which Renan and "A Death in the Desert" incorporate and discover'. 'A New Source for Browning's *Sordello*' (*N&Q* 47:iii[2000] 329), by John Haydn Baker, believes that there is a parallel at the conclusion of Book III of *Sordello* and Wordsworth's *Prelude*. Browning came to the passage by way of De Quincey's 'Lake Reminiscences, from 1807 to 1830', in which De Quincey describes Beaupuis, his French republican friend. Both men—Wordsworth's Beaupuis and the Browning speaker in *Sordello*—step back to observe a pathetic beggar-woman (or prostitute) who reminds them of their own social responsibility. Jackie Dees Domingue's 'An Unpublished Browning Letter to Louisa Sarah Bevington' (*ANQ* 13:iii[2000] 37–41) features a 5 July 1882 letter on Bevington's *Poems, Lyrics and*

Sonnets [1882], which she sent Browning, somewhat surprisingly, says Domingue, considering their differing theological stances, described by Browning in his reply as 'walking back to back'. He hoped, in time, that they would be 'face to face: just as now in the beaten way of life'.

Hardy's poetry saw limited treatment, the focus for this year being largely on the fiction, especially *Jude the Obscure*. Two chapters of Rosemary Sumner's *A Route to Modernism* deal with Hardy's poetry. 'Some Surrealist Elements in Hardy's Prose and Verse' (pp. 34–48) argues that Hardy anticipated surrealism fifty years before the movement. 'His theories on art and on the nature of things resemble theirs, his hopes for the development of consciousness are like theirs, his visual images are so close to theirs that often they might almost seem to be a description of their pictures—though they had not yet been painted.' Even Hardy's illustrations for the *Wessex Poems*, especially that for 'Heiress and Architect', anticipate surrealism. But Hardy and the surrealist movement, says Sumner, 'were seeking a wider notion of what constitutes reality', including 'contradictory states of mind' and an emphasis on perception—the ubiquitous eye—and the mind's openness 'to all possibilities, however strange'. In 'Chance and Indeterminacy in Hardy's Novels and Poetry' (pp. 49–65), Sumner looks at how Hardy searched for 'a technique which would free the mind from logic and rational control', finding in a theory of chance 'the "logicless" universe'. St Martin's also brought out Michael Irwin's *Reading Hardy's Landscapes*. Irwin shows how in Hardy 'The external environment regularly focuses itself, in a variety of ways and at a variety of speeds, on the attention on those within. … The characters are inescapably attuned to what is going on outside.' Irwin looks at Hardy's insects, introduced for 'subtler, more abstract reasons' than providing 'meteorological small print for those practical observers equipped to read it'. More importantly, Hardy, like Darwin, recognizes that 'Man and insects are fellow-species, driven by similar impulses, struggling to survive with the capacities at their command, some of which they have in common'. Noise, often associated with movement (especially the view that 'motions of all kinds derive from a common source') also figures meaningfully in Hardy, whether musical noise or the sounds of nature, all functioning as a 'significant narrative element'. Hardy's imaginative vision, utilizing 'convergence and concatenation[,] can be so densely detailed as to move well beyond the requirements of realism'. In 'Ritual and Deception: Photography and Thomas Hardy' (*JES* 30:i[2000] 57–69), Mark Durden looks at the way in which Hardy develops a highly visual sensibility, showing not only the influence of photography on his writings but, in particular, how 'photography like painting is in fact part of Hardy's way of bringing into his fiction a more intensified relationship with things'. Charles Lock's 'Hardy and the Railway' (*EIC* 50[2000] 44–66) looks at how Hardy uses the railway, its presence as well as its absence, to structure the technological conception of space and time.

The most useful book on Hopkins this year is Julia F. Saville's *A Queer Chivalry: The Homoerotic Aestheticism of Gerard Manley Hopkins*. While much of the recent critical work on the poet, initiated mostly by Robert Bernard Martin's sometimes speculative biography, *Gerard Manley Hopkins: A Very Private Life* [1991], has touched on the subject of Hopkins's assumed homosexuality, none before Saville's has focused entirely on the subject, in part because the 1980s and 1990s generated a growing body of primary and secondary material whereby the subject of Hopkins's homoerotic asceticism is now far less speculative and can be more broadly contextualized. Part of that 'queer' asceticism, according to Saville, is tied to Hopkins's innovative sprung rhythm. Even in such a poem as 'God's Grandeur', Hopkins employs the 'chivalric convention' instead of 'the more traditional courtly figure of the inaccessible Lady' to address Christ, whereby 'a Roman Catholic tradition of devotional poetry ... following the Song of Songs, treats Christ as the lover or bridegroom of the feminized human soul'. Hopkins's 'queer brand of chivalry', Saville points out, became, in 'God's Grandeur' for example, 'associated with the rigorous self-restraint on which a Victorian sense of manliness was predicated'. Saville intends to show that 'ascetic practices that appear to mortify the flesh in the interest of spiritual invigoration may paradoxically prove sensually and erotically satisfying too', and that while Hopkins's poetry and life 'militate against any simple inclusion of him in a homosexual literary subculture', 'the sensual effects of courtly poetry devoted to Christ as the beloved produce a charged effect that to a late-twentieth-century ear may seem homoerotic while to a late-Victorian sensibility may have signaled a strange distortion of manly energy'. To say that Hopkins is a 'queer poet', Saville argues, 'is to resist his more reductive (if perhaps forceful) appropriation as either gay or homosexual' if for no other reason than 'the implication of active sexual practice in the term *homosexual* is not supported in Hopkins's case, for there is no evidence that he ever engaged in, or even felt he could consciously sanction, sexual relations with a man'. *Queer Chivalry* seeks 'to present a map of Hopkins's poetic career not as a steady linear progression but as a continuous process of negotiating desire through self-discipline, self-denial, and even at times self-hatred'.

The other full-length study of Hopkins appearing this year is Philip A. Ballinger, *The Poem as Sacrament: The Theological Aesthetic of Gerard Manley Hopkins*, which argues that behind the man and the poet was 'a subtle philosopher and theologian whose poetic uniqueness arose in part because of his desire to speak as aptly as possible of the immanent God, of the Incarnate Christ'. For Hopkins, Ballinger believes, 'poetry is the use of language best suited for an approach to the transcendent'; it is a kind of 'communication of the incarnate and creative divinity to others'. While Hopkins's was not a thoroughly worked out theology, Ballinger argues, his contribution remains his 'theological aesthetics and, ultimately, his unspoken vision of the poem as "sacrament"'. Key to the formation of that aesthetic, Ballinger concludes, are such figures as Ruskin, Ignatius Loyola, and Duns Scotus, all of them essential 'for understanding both Hopkins' writings and the critical literature'.

Hopkins continues to attract a great deal of scholarly interest in the journals. In 'The Negotiations of Power Relations in Gerard Manley Hopkins' "The Wreck of the Deutschland"' (*VP* 38[2000] 299–318), Jenny Holt believes that in the poem Hopkins 'anticipates the proposition that language and consciousness are interwoven, and that he enters into a dialogue where his poetic and ecclesiastical authority are jeopardized'. Holt looks at the Master–Slave discourse in Hopkins and the problems it presents with authority. '"All by turn and turn around": The Indeterminacy of Hopkins' "Epithalamion"' (*VP* 38[2000] 343–63), by Simon Humphries, sees the poem as Hopkins's ambivalent attempt to rewrite Wordsworth's 'Nutting'. Dennis Sobolev, 'Hopkins, Language, Meaning' (*VN* 98[2000] 11–14), observes what he sees as a 'partial decline in [Hopkins's] standing', an assumption that fails to stand up to the enormous body of critical work on the poet appearing year after year, this year no exception. The decline, or so Sobolev believes, has to do with Hopkins's 'naïve "Cratylian" belief in the immanence of meaning in the formal properties of language'. Sobolev examines Hopkins's so-called 'onomatopoetic origin of primal words', convinced that what is at work, instead, is 'phonetic euphony'. The *Hopkins Quarterly* for 2000 featured Tom Zaniello's 'Alpine Art and Science: Hopkins' Swiss Adventure' (*HQ* 27:i–ii[2000] 3–17), which looks at the importance of Switzerland and the celebrated Alps, 'a triumphant combination of religious sentiment, artistic inspiration, and scientific curiosity', to nineteenth-century scientists, artists, and writers alike, 'including poets like Gerard Manley Hopkins who spent a month hiking in Switzerland in 1868, and scientists like John Tyndall who lived at least a month a year in Switzerland in his mature years'. John J. Stinson, 'The Gratitude for Influence: Hopkins in the Work of Anthony Burgess' (*HQ* 27:i–ii[2000] 18–43), looks at Burgess's 'exuberant enthusiasm for Hopkins's poetry'. Stinson believes that Hopkins's presence can be felt 'in a good many of Burgess's fictions even if the Hopkinsian echoes do not have quite enough directly ironic reverberations to allow them to be considered examples of intertextuality'. '"World-mothering air": The Virgin Mary as Poetic Image' (*HQ* 27:i–ii[2000] 44–53), by Leo M. Manglaviti SJ, argues that it is the 'humble, elementary meter, together with a simple theme expressed by intricate tropes and syntax, that lifts the poem beyond the level of more pious meditation to that of masterpiece'. *Poetic Fragment, Commentary on Lucan and Cicero, Essay on Duty*, edited with a commentary by Fredric W. Schlatter SJ (*HQ* 27:iii–iv[2000]), covers Hopkins's classical annotations. Schlatter believes that appreciation of Hopkins's classical scholarship, especially his Dublin Notebook, is crucial to understanding his role as a classicist. The present monograph, following in the wake of Warren Anderson's publication of *Hopkins: The Dublin Notes on Homer* [1995], contains Hopkins's annotations along with fragments of his Latin elegiacs and of his English poem on St Dorothy, all of them from the Bischoff Gonzaga University manuscripts. Hopkins's annotations include notes on Lucan and Cicero (the latter 'the richest of the manuscripts'). 'For all of their plod', says Schlatter, Hopkins's 'work in classical languages in Dublin was sheer, without break or halting pace, and showed the brilliance of his mind'.

Raymond J. Ventre, in 'The Body Racked with Pain: Hopkins's Dark Sonnets' (*ANQ* 13[2000] 37–46), outlines how he realized from his own near-death experience that Hopkins's 'I wake and feel the fall of dark, not day' 'was part of a sequence that led Hopkins through the Dark Night to resolution'. 'Hopkins's dark sonnet', says Ventre, 'actually helped me through a personal experience in which I literally died and returned to life. I knew the sequence led to a resolution, a cure as it were ... and the heart was particularly central in the process.' Dennis Sobolev's 'Hopkins's "The Shepherd Brow"' (*Expl* 58:ii[2000] 86–8) sees the poem operating in the light of Kant's 'dynamic sublime', where the forces of nature are both physically destructive and spiritually creative. 'It is the fortitude of the mind that enables the experience of the sublime.' Hopkins, however, 'modifies the Kantian definition', limiting the experience to a particular shepherd, perhaps Christ, and not just any shepherd.

This year saw Holden and Birch, eds., *A.E. Housman: A Reassessment*, a collection of essays that, say the editors, attempt to show that interest in Housman is 'still strong and widespread'. Archie Burnett's 'A.E. Housman's "Level Tones"' (pp. 1–19) examines Housman's use of the 'level tones' (in life as well as in art) to produce 'a superficial simplicity that contains deeper complexities', often to capture 'a composure undisturbed by disturbing events' even as the tones 'give expression to an emotional life that is often far from level'. In 'The Critical Reception of *A Shropshire Lad*' (pp. 20–36), Benjamin F. Fisher looks at the poem's reception in the reviews, which coalesce significantly with currents that coursed through the 1890s' cultural milieu. What stood out conspicuously were the poem's simplicity (realism), power, directness, military themes, and blurring of genres. 'The Land of Lost Content' (pp. 37–52), by Keith Jebb, examines Housman's pastoralism, the suicide theme, and his repression, in particular the 'inexpressibility of homosexuality' (the lost content). 'At every level', says Jebb, 'Housman develops a strategy of not-saying, not opening himself or his situation to the process of exchange, to the economy of language as a social act'. Geoffrey Hill, in 'Tacit Pledges' (pp. 53–75), looks at Housman in relation to a number of writers (Hardy, Owen, Mill, Patmore, F.H. Bradley, Wittgenstein) and is concerned with Housman's style, which in a Jamesian way Hill calls 'tacit pledges', an attempt to measure 'the "pain"; and it seeks to do so with a measure of decorum'. '"Ashes under Uricon": Historicizing A.E. Housman, Reifying T.H. Huxley, Embracing Lucretius' (pp. 76–86), by Kenneth Womack, uses Huxley to explore Housman's attraction to Epicurus and Lucretius, as filtered through Darwin. 'Victorian science', says Womack, 'informs the historical dynamic of Housman's politics and thus merges with the latent Lucretian ideology to produce a complex historical amalgam comprising competing scientific philosophies from dramatically divergent historical moments.'

Norman Page's 'A.E. Housman and Thomas Hardy' (pp. 87–105) studies the relationship between the two poets, believing that to look at them side by side 'may help to provide a context in which to judge and appreciate Housman's distinctive achievement'. The parallels between them, Page shows, are numerous, ranging from their early and secretive poetic preoccupation, to their interest in the short lyric and ballad, to their ideal of Englishness, and, finally, to their creation of a fictional landscape, 'partly real, partly fantasized'. In '"Flowers to Fair": *A Shropshire Lad's* Legacy of Song' (pp. 106–33), Trevor Hold explores the musical settings of *A Shropshire Lad*, in particular the 'songcycles' of Vaughan Williams, George Butterworth, and John Ireland. Hold is convinced that the attraction of the 'Lad's troubles and tribulations' for these composers stemmed from 'the appeal of the poems' sentiments' as well as 'the aptness of the poems for musical treatment'. 'Housman's Manilius' (pp. 134–53), by G.P. Goold, examines closely the much-neglected interest of Housman in the astrological poet Marcus Manilius, known for his witty verse, mathematical curiosity, and astronomical obsession. John Bayley's 'Lewis Carroll in Shropshire' (pp. 154–66) sees Housman creating 'a kind of wonderland', where a sort of 'absurdity masquerading as complete straightforwardness crops up again and again throughout Housman's writings, often accompanied by echoes from the Old Testament'. 'But in all circumstances,' says Bayley, Housman 'remains both reasonable and disenchanted, knowing his wonderland for what it is.' 'The First Edition of *A Shropshire Lad* in Bookshop and Auction Room' (pp. 167–87), by P.G. Naiditch, looks at sales of the first edition of the poem and how they comment, if at all, on Housman's popularity. Carol Efrati, 'A.E. Housman's Use of Biblical Narrative' (pp. 188–209), sees Housman taking great liberties with the Bible, which 'throws a new light on an old story as well as providing a new vantage point from which to view the poet and his work'. The result is a fascinating, if not iconoclastic, reading of Scripture. Finally, Takeshi Obata's 'The Spirit of Haiku and A.E. Housman' (pp. 210–19) sees an association, 'some rough resemblances', between Housman's poetry and *haiku*, where in 'both the best *haiku* and in Housman's poems, "banal materials" and "topoi" easily penetrate into readers' minds and evoke their sympathy'.

The *Housman Society Journal* featured a number of articles of interest. Peter Porter's 'The Housman Lecture: The Name and Nature of Poetry' (*HSJ* 26[2000] 8–30) insists that the poet 'came down on the side of the Common Man, emphasising the Pleasure Principle over any of the refinements of probity or duty'. In 'A.E. Housman's "De Amicitia"' (*HSJ* 26[2000] 31–42), Stuart Hopkins looks at the Laurence Housman essay on his brother's manuscript poems in *De Amicitia*, poems that are 'unambiguously and unmistakably more biographical or autobiographical than any which he [Laurence] had previously seen and read'. These poems, written from 1888 to 1891, disclose Housman's sexuality and his sustained relationship with Moses Jackson. In 'Photographs of A.E. Housman' (*HSJ* 26[2000] 43–7) and "Miscellanea Housmaniana xxiv–xxxii' (*HSJ* 26[2000] 73–88), P.G. Naiditch remarks on a set of photographs of Housman from the ages of 2 to 70 in order to correct and assign tentative dates to what has been misdated. 'Housman's Alms of Evening' (*HSJ* 26[2000] 48–54), by Carol Efrati, looks briefly at the lyric 'By shores and woods and steeples' to show that the poet's 'standard image of eternity' is that of 'endless sleep', a view that reveals Housman's intellectual rejection of Christianity and its tenets. But the poem shows that in fact 'underneath the self-proclaimed atheism was a desperate hope that he was wrong, that there was indeed a God, and it was this subterranean hope that found expression here'. 'M.J. Jackson in British Columbia: Some Supplementary Information' (*HSJ* 26[2000] 59–61), by Robert B. Todd, presents by way of photographs the final years of Moses Jackson, considered Housman's 'greatest friend', living in retirement on a 158-acre farm in British Columbia following a career appointment in India. Stuart Hopkins's 'Housman and Votes for Women' (*HSJ* 26[2000] 62–72) looks at Laurence's open-mindedness, 'his radical, political, and feminist consciousness', set against the poet's more 'conservative and austere' stance, refusing, for example, to sign a petition Laurence gave him in support of women's suffrage. Their sister Clemence, 'the first English woman to be arrested and incarcerated for refusal to pay tax', was equally active politically, although she remained in the background.

'Housman's Ambiguous Tree' (*HSJ* 26[2000] 89–96), by Carol Efrati, recognizes in the Housman cherry tree 'a certain ambiguity about this blossoming tree', one that seems to be 'the source of the melancholy, the sadness that permeates its life-giving quality of beauty' that appears 'already vanishing, passing, even as it is affirmed'. The poem *ASL II*, Efrati believes, embodies 'two of Housman's classical motifs, the value and the brevity of beauty', fusing these two themes 'in a way that no other poem quite matches'. P.G. Naiditch's 'Max Beerbohm and A.E. Housman' (*HSJ* 26[2000] 97–8) looks briefly at the equally brief encounter between the two men, and Ray Bloomfield, 'Housman's Friendship with Joan Thomson' (*HSJ* 26[2000] 99–105), examines their more than casual acquaintance; Housman 'recognised the charm and intelligence of this cultivated young woman [the daughter of a distinguished Cambridge scientist] which encouraged him to converse agreeably with her on a wide range of subjects', and in the later years 'deriv[e] comfort … and some relief from his loneliness. … We know of no parallel in his life to this.' Many of the unique insights into Housman's life, habits, and temper derive from Thomson's *Reminiscences*, 'vivid in their memories and written with great tenderness'. In 'Thomas Hardy and A.E. Housman' (*HSJ* 26[2000] 106–9), P.G. Naiditch looks briefly at the relationship and exchanges between the two poets. Finally, 'Housman's Guides' (*HSJ* 26[2000] 110–18), by Carol Efrati, believes that what occurs after death in Housman's poetry can be guided by the classical and the Christian traditions. 'Ultimately, in most of his poetry,' according to Efrati, 'Housman not only rejected the Christian model of the afterlife … but also the pagan model of the Elysian fields. … Both models are found wanting.'

We have not seen a collection of Kipling's works in quite some time, not since Andrew Rutherford's collection of Kipling's early verse [1986]. The publishing attention to date has been on *Kim*, because of its engagement with the imperialist question, and on his children's pieces, especially *The Jungle Book*. Thus it was encouraging to see that, for its Oxford Authors series, Oxford University Press brought out Karlin, ed., *Rudyard Kipling*, a collection of prose pieces as well as poetry. The verse selection features pieces from as early as 1886 and as late as the post-1919 period, including such famous pieces as 'The Betrothed', 'Recessional', 'The White Man's Burden', and 'Epitaphs of the War'. Karlin's admitted struggle with the verse was how to account for Kipling's more memorable lines that are found not in his best poems. The choice of the prose pieces for inclusion was an easier enterprise. Whether this now available and valuable collection will revive scholarly and academic interest in a more serious Kipling remains to be seen. So it is with Morris. In 'Medieval Drama and Courtly Romance in William Morris' "Sir Galahad, A Christmas Mystery"' (*VP* 38[2000] 383–91), Catherine Stevenson and Virginia Hale believe that 'mystery and cycle plays', romance and drama, contribute to the shape of 'Sir Galahad'.

There continues to be interest in Christina Rossetti, much of it still directed to 'Goblin Market'. The only full-length study of her to appear this year is Alison Chapman's *The Afterlife of Christina Rossetti*. Chapman examines the 'late nineteenth-century responses to the dead Rossetti and her literary remains' and the way the life and work persist well into the twentieth century. For Chapman, photography is one significant medium to access Rossetti, believing that it can serve as 'an agen[t] in the interpretive process'. And while 'she nevertheless slips out of the frame', Rossetti still maintains an 'umbilical relation to the text and to us as its reader'. Chapman also looks at 'voicing the silent as a problematic recovery predicted on a fantasy of origin' and what exactly this means 'for feminist new historicist readings of Victorian women's poetry' such as Rossetti's, but also for lost voices such as Siddal's. Chapman looks at Rossetti's supposed hysteria and her overall appearances in the biographies, Dante Gabriel Rossetti's revisions of her manuscripts based on 'his definition of the feminine', her 'visual aesthetics' (the Pre-Raphaelite impulse), the role of Italy 'as a privileged trope, as the metaphorical site where issues of the past political revolution and the exotic coalesce', along with 'gender inflected questions of identity and homeland', and, finally, the 'consumptive text *par excellence*' that is 'Goblin Market'. Joy A. Fehr's 'Christina Rossetti's Nightmares: Fact or Fiction' (*VN* 97[2000] 21–6) explores the way in which Rossetti's reception reflected her 'success at negotiating Victorian reading practices and beliefs regarding women'. Rossetti's work records not simply her life but 'the culture in which she lived and worked'.

Dante Gabriel Rossetti received limited attention. '"Jenny": Aestheticizing the Whore' (*PLL* 36:ii[2000] 227–45), by Lawrence J. Starzyk, sees Jenny as 'kindred' of sorts to Browning's objectified Duchess, and how the 'painterly hand of Rossetti influenced the verbal articulation of the muted image of this Victorian whore'. Early and repeatedly, says Starzyk, Rossetti's protagonist 'aggrandizes Jenny to himself'. Still, the 'identity of Jenny as object of worship or of pleasure … is not the point; the aestheticization and what that process necessitates and implies is'. In 'Replicas and Originality: Picturing Agency in Dante Gabriel Rossetti and Victorian Manchester' (*VS* 43:i[2000] 67–102), David Wayne Thomas observes how a theory of originality—'a consummate participation in tradition' and simultaneously 'a radical break from precedent'—might be applied to the paintings of Rossetti and his relationship to Manchester, a place he neither lived in nor represented as such in his paintings. The connection to Manchester is attended by the use of replica. 'Rossetti's replicas and the Manchester replica [and add to that the Golden Jubilee Exhibition in 1887 in London] invite agential self-inspection—individual and collective, respectively—and these instances of self-inspection share a tangled logic that is also enacted in characteristically modern aspirations toward originality'. 'Rossetti's "A Last Confession"' (*Expl* 58:iv[2000] 193–4), by Nathan Cervo, sees the poet working with two contexts simultaneously, 'esoteric alchemy and Roman Catholicism, the former a system of spiritual discipline developing from the metallurgical code of the ancient Egyptian priests at Ptah at the temple in Memphis, the latter claiming that it was founded by "great Jesus Christ"'.

This year Tennyson did not quite garner the kind of attention he customarily receives. Still, it saw *Alfred Tennyson: A Critical Edition of the Major Works*, including some letters and journal entries, from the Oxford Authors series, edited by Adam Roberts. The volume includes such juvenilia as 'Timbuctoo', 'Mariana', selections from *Poems, Chiefly Lyrical* [1830]; 'The Lady of Shalott' and 'The Palace of Art', from *Poems* [1832]; 'The Two Voices', 'St. Simeon Stylites', 'Ulysses', and 'Locksley Hall', from *Poems* [1842]; *The Princess* [1847]; *In Memoriam* [1850]; 'The Charge of the Light Brigade', from the *Laureate Poems and Maud: A Monodrama* [1855]; *Enoch Arden* [1864]; 'The Higher Pantheism' and 'Lucretius', from *Poems from the 1860s*, *The Idylls of the King* [1869]; and 'Rizpah', 'De Profundis', 'Locksley Hall Sixty Years After', and 'Crossing the Bar', all from *Poems of the 1870s and 1880s*. The collection concludes with excerpts from Hallam Tennyson's *Memoir* of his father: *Tennyson in his Own Words*. Because of the broad, useful, and chronological representation of Tennyson's poems, this particular collection will in time become the standard Tennyson text in the undergraduate as well as the graduate classroom, easily supplanting *Tennyson: Selected Poetry*, from Routledge's English Texts, earlier reviewed in *YWES*. In 'Tennyson's Poetics of Melancholy and the Imperial Imagination' (*SEL* 40[2000] 659–78), David G. Riede believes that Tennyson's 'melancholy', his 'abyss of sorrow', 'usually regarded as an apolitical character trait, is itself a source of authority that draws not only on the intensity of mood, but also on current sexist and colonialist discourses, and upon an idiom of eroticized political imperialism'. His melancholy, says Riede, 'exploits the power of dangerous feminine emotional liberality and passion that threatens his ideal of masculine self-control and public order'. In 'Tennyson's King Arthur and the Violence of Manliness' (*VP* 38[2000] 199–226), Clinton Machann asserts that Arthur's masculinity is 'central to the meaning of Tennyson's *Idylls*' in that it becomes 'a strategy for controlling or stifling man's natural bestiality as civilization advances'. 'Tennyson's deeply felt fear', Machann believes, is that manhood as he understood it—despite its positive associations with religion, moral values, and duty—is ultimately 'unstable and ineffective'. Finally, Alisa Clapp-Intyre's 'Marginalized Musical Interludes: Tennyson's Critique of Conventionality in *The Princess*' (*VP* 38[2000] 227–48) looks at the way in which Tennyson's songs added to *The Princess* operate as 'pivotal feminist commentary'.

This year shows a fall-off in Wilde scholarship. In 'Oscar Wilde: Orality, Literary Property, and Crimes of Writing' (*NCL* 55:i[2000] 59–91), Paul K. Saint-Amour looks at Wilde's economic aggressiveness in his attempt to profit from 'intellectual property law', even on his deathbed. His was also in breach of that very law, exhibiting a 'rhetorical and practical disregard for private literary property'. Saint-Amour sees this 'collectivism' as tied to Wilde's 'professed socialism', that 'by converting private property into public wealth, and substituting cooperation for competition', society would be restored 'to its proper condition of a thoroughly healthy organism, and insure the material well-being of each member of the community'.

The year's work on Victorian poetry reveals no particularly new trend. The poetic mainstays—the Brownings, the Rossettis, Tennyson, and Hopkins—continue to receive the majority of critical attention. The only meaningful surprise has been a renewed attention to Housman and a growing focus on special issues devoted to topical subjects.

4. Drama and Theatre

The majority of publications in 2000 on Victorian drama and theatre provide background on the circumstances and contexts of the drama and theatre of the period. Theatre business, the actress and the issue of 'illegitimate' theatre all feature prominently.

The most significant study to emerge was Tracy C. Davis's *The Economics of the British Stage, 1800–1914*, one of the most innovative approaches to nineteenth-century British theatre to appear for many a year. Davis suggests theatrical representation cannot be separated from prevailing business conditions and that, 'if culture's historians ignore business, they overlook the resources that make or break an artistic choice' (p. 1). Theatre, she claims, was the second most powerful medium in Britain after the newspapers in the nineteenth century and, during this period, was the 'product of economic ideology' (p. 7). The study is not just based on micro-economics, however, although it does seek to explore the economic landscape that underlies the theatrical and dramatic concerns of other historians and critics.

The book is divided into three parts, respectively dealing with competition, business practices and, finally, the labour market and product for sale. The first section considers the way in which the laws protecting theatrical monopolies were gradually undermined by free market competition, a development that the authorities supported both tacitly and through legislation. The role of Peel's Tory government in passing the Theatres Regulation Act is interestingly surveyed in the light of that government's general economic policies. Competition with saloon theatres and with the music halls is discussed, as is the greater regulation of theatres by the Lord Chamberlain's Office in such matters as safety, hygiene and morality. Censorship, which in many ways controlled the ideological impact of theatres, also affected profitability. Davis suggests that 'audiences learned to watch theatre differently, in keeping with emerging neo-classical models of consumption', and that 'meaning became assigned differently as a result' (p. 9).

The second part of the study concentrates on the industrial organization of the Victorian theatre. Entrepreneurship, risk, speculation, and the various economic models and structures followed by theatrical management are dissected. The impact of benefits on profit, the development of touring, spectacle and the long run on theatre economics are among the topics covered. Of particular interest is a chapter on women managers, which shows that entrepreneurial management was more open to women through 'family firms' than through the increasing tendency to 'professional management' as the century progressed. An interesting addendum to this chapter is published as a database entitled 'Female Managers, Lessees and Proprietors of the British Stage (to 1914)' (*NCT* 28[2000] 115–44), providing an invaluable listing of 330 names.

The last section of the book looks at the way in which employment conditions changed, especially after the financial crisis of 1873. Theatres discarded employees and fostered the growth of satellite trades (what we would call 'outsourcing'), which proved highly remunerative. The movement away from stock companies and towards more lavish productions is also chronicled, as is competition with the early cinema in matters of production, distribution and exhibition. Overall, this is a highly original study, impeccably researched, and a crucial reference book for all engaged in the study of Victorian drama and theatre.

Several articles also provide background on commercial aspects of nineteenth-century theatre. John Earl, 'The Metropolitan Buildings Office and the First Music Halls' (*NCT* 28[2000] 5–25), offers fascinating evidence based on reports lodged with the Metropolitan Building Office from 1845 to 1855 concerning the safety standards in saloon theatres, such as the Effingham, plus details of building and rebuilding at such venues as Wilton's Music Hall and Charles Morton's Canterbury Hall. In 'Shopping and Looking: Trade Advertisements in the *Era* and Performance History Research' (*NCT* 28[2000] 26–61), Ann Featherstone directs our attention to the research resources to be uncovered in the classified advertisements in the *Era*, the major theatrical journal in nineteenth-century England, and secondly the 'internal codes and processes revealed in those advertisements emphasising freaks and novelties' (p. 28). Philip A. Talbot also explores a facet of theatre business in 'The Macclesfield Theatre Company and Nineteenth Century Silk Manufacturers' (*TN* 54[2000] 24–42), relating the links between the local industries of Macclesfield and the entrepreneurial interests of its silk manufacturers to the fortunes of the local Theatre Royal. Surprisingly, despite their industrial success, the silk manufacturers were much less sophisticated in their use of management and accounting skills to run the local theatre.

An important and invaluable study of the 'illegitimate' theatre and drama of the period prior to the Theatres Regulation Act of 1843 is provided by Jane Moody in *Illegitimate Theatre in London, 1770–1849*. Moody's penetrating analysis of illegitimate theatre in London and its failure to respect not only social and aesthetic distinctions but also cultural ownership is linked to a shrewd assessment of such transgressive and morally ambivalent 'illegitimate' genres as melodrama and pantomime. She also draws attention to the emergence of an 'illegitimate' Shakespeare, which carried a political weight at the minor theatres at variance with the apolitical approach to Shakespeare championed by Coleridge. Moody provides a valuable commentary on the way in which advocacy for dramatic copyright united legitimate and illegitimate dramatists alike, as well as useful discussions of spectatorship, locality and dramatic reviewing. She suggests that the illegitimate theatres helped to transform the theatrical city, but in the process caused social unease and raised cultural anxieties. An excellent chapter on illegitimate comedy, farce and burlesque, including a discussion of Mathews's one-man shows, demonstrates how legitimate comedy was thrown into crisis as issues of class, respectability and technological change became the focus of the illegitimate forms. Actors also brought something of the subversion of the illegitimate stage to their performances, whether it was Grimaldi in pantomime or Kean in Shakespeare. 'By utterly changing how the world could be imagined on stage', illegitimate genres 'transformed the characters and subjects being represented on the British stage' (p. 242). Moody argues that the clash between legitimate and illegitimate theatre defined the terms of cultural debate in late Georgian London, but that the Theatre Regulation Act of 1843, in abolishing the distinction between the two forms, also brought about 'the political disappearance of a once irrepressible theatrical culture' (p. 243).

Of relevance to the issues raised in Moody's study is David Worrall's excellent article 'Artisan Melodrama and the Plebeian and Public Sphere: The Political Culture of Drury Lane and its Environs, 1797–1830' (*SiR* 39[2000] 213–27). Worrall makes a plausible case for the relationship between artisan culture and popular melodrama at such minor theatres as the Olympic and the Adelphi, particularly through the plays of W.T. Moncrieff. Despite pervasive government control and intervention, the subversive nature of such dramas as Jerrold's *Mutiny at the Nore* [1830] and *Reform, or John Bull Triumphant: A Patriotic Drama* [1828] is revealed, along with their ambivalent incorporation of more moderate voices within the texts. Drawing on Home Office records, Worrall reveals just how subversive such plays were considered by the more reactionary elements of the time. He argues that 'by the 1810s conditions in London were favorable for the emergence of a new artisan theatre wholly produced and consumed by class' (p. 217), and demonstrates the association of theatrical publishers such as Duncombe with radical publications. The success of Moncrieff's *Giovanni in London* [1817], with its questioning of social and moral conventions, occurred at a time when the 'people' were becoming increasingly 'visible'. Equally, in Moncrieff's adaptation of *Tom and Jerry; or Life in London in 1820* class was 'fundamentally destabilised' (p. 224). Overall, Worrall argues that in the heart of London's theatreland in 1819–20 'one comes across radical ideologies in close physical conjunction with a non-patented drama which is visibly experimenting and enlarging its treatment of social, racial and sexual issues', and that 'the unlicensed theatres show the point at which artisan expression and articulacy move across to occupy public space' (pp. 226–7). Worrall's provision of new and interesting insights into the relationship between popular melodrama and radical politics in the period valuably supplements the work already carried out by

Moody. Less incisive, but of more general interest, is Derek Forbes's 'Jack Sheppard Plays and the Influence of Cruikshank' (*TN* 54[2000] 98–123), which considers the influence of Cruikshank's twenty-eight illustrations for Ainsworth's novel on subsequent theatrical adaptations. After a brief discussion of settings for eighteenth-century stage versions of the Jack Sheppard story, Forbes concentrates on the versions of Ainsworth's novel that opened at a number of minor theatres in October 1839 and subsequently at some provincial theatres. The influence of the Cruikshank illustrations was particularly notable in the Adelphi version (although not acknowledged), while Cruikshank himself was personally involved with the staging of the Surrey and Sadler's Wells versions. Interestingly, the Surrey denouement may have drawn on the dioramic effect created in the final Cruikshank illustrations for the novel.

Actresses are the subject of several studies, including a biography of Helen Faucit by Carol Jones Carlyle. *Helen Faucit: Fire and Ice on the Victorian Stage* is the first full-length biography of this actress since the rather partial account published by her husband, Theodore Martin. A solid and serviceable account of Faucit's life, this study meticulously chronicles her early life, her successes as Macready's leading lady, her triumphs in such provincial cities as Dublin, Manchester and, especially, Edinburgh, her performances in Paris, and her later career. Her social life, her intellectual interests and her health problems are all minutely dissected. Particularly admired in Shakespeare and in the roles of the romantic heroines of nineteenth-century poetic drama, she was, for some, 'the incarnation of ideal womanhood' (p. xiii). Of particular interest to contemporary readers is Faucit's development of her acting style, particularly her physical use of pictorial and sculptural models. This is charted chronologically, but one misses a chapter that might have brought together a more thorough analysis of her technique, although a number of individual roles are given detailed attention in an appendix. Carlyle argues that Edmund Kean may have been just as strong an influence as the 'Kemble school' on Faucit's style of acting. Certainly, in the aftermath of her early successes as Juliet and as Julia in Sheridan Knowles's *The Hunchback* critical opinion was mixed: some found her acting extravagant, while others felt this very extravagance rendered her acting more natural in emotional scenes. Both Charles Kemble and William Macready subsequently influenced her acting style: Kemble insisted that the physical presentation of emotion should be restrained and idealized; Macready also encouraged restraint and even the ability to indicate repression, although some critics were later to assert that under Macready's influence she also adopted some of his mannerisms. Faucit's Shakespearian roles with Macready included Constance, Imogen, Beatrice, Rosalind, Hermione, Cordelia, Desdemona, and Lady Macbeth, while she also played Pauline in Bulwer Lytton's *The Lady of Lyons*. Her interest in painting and sculpture also influenced her acting. Later, after a breach with Macready, she essayed two roles in Greek tragedy, Antigone and Iphigenia, which are interestingly documented by Carlyle. A useful discussion of the genesis of, and the critical views represented in, her book *On Some of Shakespeare's Female Characters* draws attention to her autobiographical recollections and to her close emotional identification with the characters she played. Not surprisingly she is also given passing attention in Gail Marshall's 'Acting, Autobiography and the 1890s' (in John and Jenkins, eds., pp. 208–21), a reworking of the fifth chapter of her book *Actresses on the Victorian Stage: Feminine Performance and the Galatea Myth*

(CUP [1998]). Marshall believes that autobiography was one of the factors that altered the work and cultural status of the actress in the 1890s, both through performances that were themselves autobiographical (the actress drew the character portrayed into her own life rather than subsuming herself into the character) and through the greater control made possible by the publication of autobiographical writing. Aligning the 'new' actress with the New Woman movement, Marshall discusses Eleanora Duse, Janet Achurch, Helen Faucit, Elizabeth Robins and Ellen Terry. Terry's autobiography, she believes, enabled her to elude her audiences by forcing them to engage with her in the medium of her own language, a medium which was usually so disablingly denied to the Victorian actress. Of course there is also a counter-argument to this, as Thomas Postlewait has shown in 'Autobiography and Theatre History' (in *Interpreting the Theatrical Past: Essays in the Historiography of Performance* [1989], pp. 248–72), his study of the formulaic nature of the narratives used to construct the lives of late Victorian actresses in biography and autobiography. In 'Emma Sarah Love' (*TN* 54[2000] 146–61), Kevin H.F. O'Brien and Ann Johnson reconstruct rather than interpret the life of an actress whose elopement and adultery with Lord Harborough, who subsequently abandoned her, prematurely ended her career. She appeared at both Covent Garden and Drury Lane in the 1820s, but her father-in-law, who was also head of the Drury Lane management committee, presumably vetoed her return to that theatre, despite her earlier successes. Emma Sarah Love died in 1881, but her career was effectively ended in 1829 at the age of 31. A checklist of the roles she played in London from 1817 to 1829 provides a useful appendix to this article.

In 'Dexter, Dextra, Dextrum: The Bloomer Costume on the British Stage in 1851' (*NCT* 28[2000] 89–113), Tiffany Unwin traces the progress of the Bloomer costume, invented in the USA by Mrs Amelia Bloomer, on the stage and off. She posits a link between the costume's implicit sexuality, the assumption of trousers and male riding attire by women, and male impersonation on the stage. Urwin equates the threat of Bloomerism to Victorian social order to that posed by the drag actress. Farces and music-hall songs were written to exploit the Bloomer costume and to counter its subversive impact on society at large, while lectures given in support of Bloomerism, such as those of Caroline Harper Dexter, were notoriously performative. In 1854 Harper Dexter emigrated to Australia, where she quickly became embroiled in a controversy over anti-Bloomerism 'lectures' given by Emma Brougham. Unwin argues that the press and stage effectively set back female dress reform in Britain by three decades through their attacks on Bloomerism, and that the 'cross-dressed' actress 'participated in a satirical campaign which aimed at, and momentarily succeeded in eradicating the voice of female freedom' (p. 108). Male impersonation and the mixture of disgust and fascination it elicited in Victorian society is also explored in Muriel Pécastaing-Boissière, 'Les Actrices travesties à l'époque victorienne' (*CVE* 51[2000] 129–44).

The work of Victorian dramatists is explored in a number of articles, while Jane Stedman's *W.S. Gilbert's Theatrical Criticism* provides a brief but useful discussion of Gilbert as a theatre critic, together with examples of his criticism, particularly his parodic versions of new melodramas contributed to *Fun* between 1861 and 1871. Shortened versions of *The Great City*, *The Frozen Deep*, *East Lynne*, *Mazeppa*, *Lost in London*, and *Theodora* are among the burlesque reviews through which Gilbert ridicules the genre of melodrama (and perhaps helps to contribute to its demise).

There are examples of his discussion of pantomime characters from a series of articles published in 1863, as well as discussion of and examples from his journalism for the *Illustrated Times* [1868–70]. Later contributions to such journals as the *Era Almanack* are discussed at the book's conclusion. Although one would like a fuller analysis of Gilbert the critic, the study contains many useful insights, and effectively anthologizes a highly readable and entertaining set of burlesque reviews. Gilbert's contemporary Robertson furnishes the subject-matter for Miriam Handley's 'Performing Dramatic Marks: Stage Directions and the Revival of *Caste*' (in Bray, Handley and Henry, eds., pp. 253–70), which focuses on the importance of stage directions in disclosing information about texts and their historical and theatrical contexts. Drawing on a pre-performance manuscript of *Caste* submitted to the Lord Chamberlain, a post-performance prompt-book and a prompt-book annotated by Squire Bancroft used for subsequent revivals, Handley demonstrates the importance of distinguishing between sources in discussions of stage directions. She suggest that changes to the original stage directions may indicate performance difficulties—what was originally a hysterical reaction to George D'Alroy's return by Marie Bancroft as Polly is subsequently turned into a burlesque response, perhaps because hysteria was beyond Marie Bancroft's range. More significantly, Handley argues that Robertson's original stage directions have more to do with topical significance than theatrical innovation. Thus the characters' choices of beverage and attitudes towards money are not primarily a reflection of domestic realism, but a response to issues raised by the second Reform Act of 1867, the Temperance League and, as one reviewer put it, 'the place of the working man in the vessel of the state'. In other words stage directions were originally used to circumvent government censorship of the discussion of political issues on stage; only in later versions of the play was a greater emphasis placed on the theatrical innovation and domestic detail of the stage directions, thereby undermining the topical implications of the original. As Handley reminds us, it is quite possibly in the stage directions rather than in the dialogue of much nineteenth-century entertainment that contextual meaning is contained. Also drawing on prompt copies, Joel Kaplan, in 'Galsworthy's *The Silver Box*: A Granville Barker Rehearsal Book (1906)' (*TN* 54[2000] 43–51), discusses the annotated rehearsal book for the 1906 premiere of John Galsworthy's *The Silver Box* at the Court Theatre, plus a lighting plot, a drawing of a stage set, a photograph of the set as built for the Court stage and two letters from Galsworthy to Granville Barker, as a means for reconstructing many of the features of the play's first production.

5. Periodicals and Publishing History

In 'The Newspaper Novel: Towards an International History' (*MH* 6:i[2000] 5–17), Graham Law and Norimasa Morita offer a useful comparative study of the *roman-feuilleton*, or newspaper novel, as it appeared in nineteenth-century French, British, Japanese and US periodical publications. Their work suggests there is much information to be found through such comparative study of the methods by which the nineteenth-century fiction industry operated and utilized the mass media. Key global issues dealt with in this piece include the common reprinting and translation of foreign fiction, the growth and internationalization of the syndication system, and the effect of the development of international copyright law on newspaper activity and the diffusion of newspaper fiction across national borders. UK examples highlight that circulation was arranged mainly via regional mass media newspaper outlets of fiction from the mid-nineteenth century onwards, with novel syndication (pioneered by the Bolton firm Tillotson & Sons) peaking and dropping after the 1890s.

Graham Law follows through on these points in his well-researched study of newspaper serialization, *Serializing Fiction in the Victorian Press*. Combining economic and cultural analysis with hard archival evidence, he presents an extensive overview and account of the rise and decline of the practice of fiction syndication across Britain throughout the nineteenth century. In addition to offering new insight into the little-discussed syndication of authors such as Mary Braddon, Wilkie Collins and Walter Besant, Law sets at the heart of his text a carefully researched analysis of the role of the largest UK syndicator of fiction of the century, the Bolton-based Tillotson & Sons, along with extensive background on such rivals as the literary agent A.P. Watt. The background section is reproduced in slightly different form in Law's 'Before Tillotsons: Novels in British Provincial Newspapers, 1855–1873' (*VPR* 32[1999] 43–79).

Fiction syndication and literary agency are also the topics of Simon Eliot's lengthy and informative study of A.P. Watt's marketing of Walter Besant's fiction, 'Author, Publisher and Literary Agent: Making Walter Besant's Novels Pay in the Provincial and International Market of the 1890s' (*PH* 46[2000] 35–65). As outlined by Eliot, the agreements made between A.P. Watt and the publishers Chatto & Windus for publication of *Armorel of Lyonesse* [1890], *Katherine by the Tower* [1891] and *The Ivory Gate* [1892], among others, allow us insight into the increasingly important role of the literary agent in the publishing process of the time.

For British publishers, among the most lucrative areas for book distribution from 1890 to 1920 were the overseas colonial markets of Canada, Australia, New Zealand, India and other British-dominated territories. Curiously enough, aside from a handful of articles and short texts produced sporadically over the last thirty years, little research has been done on British-focused aspects of this important colonial market. Graeme Johanson's *A Study of Colonial Editions in Australia, 1843–1972* is an extremely welcome and key contribution to our understanding of the structures underpinning book trade links between Britain and its colonies. Johanson uses Australia as a case-study example to offer a cultural and economic history of the development of the colonial-edition trade in Britain, supported by detailed statistical information on its circulation through Australian public library systems and private bookselling agents between 1860 and 1972. He details the long history of colonial-edition publications in Australia, providing interesting background on the early (failed) experiments by John Murray to market a Colonial and Home Library Series (forty-nine titles between 1843 and 1849) and by Richard Bentley to develop Bentley's Empire Library (sixteen titles between 1878 and 1881). He also covers the development of the Macmillan colonial series from 1886 onwards, as well as other initiatives instigated by Sampson Low and Kegan Paul in 1887. Perhaps most significantly, Johanson offers a clear, useful and detailed analysis of the manner in which the Australian market was developed by British publishing houses from 1890 onwards through a structure of local branches and representatives, through manipulation of imperial copyright law, and through restrictive agreements with US publishers. At the same time, he counters any suggestion that Australian business interests had no control over such matters, arguing that the local book trade not only adapted to British publishing strategies but also turned them to its own advantage, influencing the type of works published, leveraging significant trade discounts on publication prices, and setting its own retail prices unconstrained by the restrictions imposed by the Net Book Agreement on its British bookselling counterparts. This is an important point that should be noted in particular by all engaged in the study of the late nineteenth- and early twentieth-century British book trade.

Continuing the colonial connection, a book worthy of notice is a Festschrift collection dedicated to the Australian book historian Wallace Kirsop: Garrioch *et al.*, eds., *The Culture of the Book* [1999]. While most of the essays collected here focus on French and Australian topics (Kirsop's specialisms), a few draw our attention to the colonial connections between Britain and the Antipodes, including Brian Hubber's 'John Carfrae (*c*.1795–1862): Bookseller of Edinburgh, Auctioneer of Melbourne and Sydney'. Hubber's essay is an interesting piece of detective work, tracing the working life of an Edinburgh bookseller emigrant in the 1840s and providing general insight into the embryonic trans-oceanic links existing between Britain and its far-flung Australian colony during this period.

Several new essay collections engage in the links between media history and Victorian culture and society. Brake, Bell and Finkelstein, eds., *Nineteenth-Century Media and the Construction of Identities*, present twenty-two essays on the theme of mediated definitions of identity in Victorian media and periodical texts, ranging from the national, ethnic and professional to the gendered and textual. International in its scope, the volume offers studies of serial journals in England, Ireland, Scotland and Wales as well as France, the USA and Australia. Essay titles include: Kate Jackson, 'George Newnes and the 'loyal Tit-Bitites': Editorial Identity and Textual Interaction in *Tit-Bits*'; Richard Salmon, '"A Simulacrum of Power": Intimacy and Abstraction in the Rhetoric of the New Journalism'; Kate Campbell, 'Journalistic Discourses and Constructions of Modern Knowledge'; Margaret Linley, 'A Centre that Would Not Hold: Annuals and Cultural Democracy'; Andrew King, 'A Paradigm of Reading in the Victorian Penny Weekly: Education of the Gaze and *The London Journal*'; Michael Hancher, 'From Street Ballad to Penny Magazine: "March of Intellect in the Butchering Line"'; Brian Maidment, '"Penny" Wise, "Penny" Foolish? Popular Periodicals and the "March of Intellect" in the 1820s and 1830s'; Lynne Warren, '"Women in Conference": Reading the Correspondence Columns in *Woman* 1890–1910'; Robert L. Patten, 'Dickens as Serial Author: A Case of Multiple Identities'; Alexis Easley, 'Authorship, Gender and Power in Victorian Culture: Harriet Martineau and the Periodical Press'; Joanne Shattock, 'Work for Women: Margaret Oliphant's Journalism'; Meri-Jane Rochelson, 'Israel Zangwill's Early Journalism and the Formation of an Anglo-Jewish Literary Identity'; Amy Beth Aaronson, 'America's First Feminist Magazine: Transforming the Popular to the Political'; Anne Humpherys, 'Coming Apart: The British Newspaper Press and the Divorce Court'; Mark W. Turner, '*Saint Pauls Magazine* and the Project of Masculinity'; Margaret Beetham, 'The Agony Aunt, the Romancing Uncle and the Family of Empire: Defining the Sixpenny Reading Public in the 1890s'; Laurel Brake, '"Gay Discourse" and *The Artist and Journal of Home Culture*'; Leslie Williams, 'Bad Press: Thomas Campbell Foster and British Reportage on the Irish Famine, 1845–1849'; Aled Jones, 'The Nineteenth-Century

Media and Welsh Identity'; David Finkelstein, '"Long and intimate connections": Constructing a Scottish Identity for *Blackwood's Magazine*'; Dean de la Motte, 'Making News, Making Readers: The Creation of the Modern Newspaper Public in Nineteenth-Century France'; and Toni Johnson-Woods, 'The Virtual Reading Communities of the *London Journal*, the *New York Ledger* and the *Australian Journal*'.

Mediated representations of India lie at the heart of David Finkelstein and Douglas Mark Peers, eds., *Negotiating India in the Nineteenth-Century Media*. The twelve essays in this collection represent the first concerted attempt to examine media representations of Britain's colonial 'Jewel in the Crown'. The collection emphasizes an interdisciplinary approach, bringing together a range of historians and cultural and literary scholars to examine topics ranging from literary journals such as *Household Words* and *All the Year Round* to specialized 'trade' publications such as medical journals, periodicals aimed at the navy and army, women's magazines and Urdu newspapers. Contributions include: Antoinette Burton, 'Institutionalizing Imperial Reform: *The Indian Magazine* and Late-Victorian Colonial Politics'; Nupur Chaudhuri, 'Issues of Race, Gender and Nation in *Englishwomen's Domestic Magazine* and *Queen*, 1850–1900'; Kelly Boyd, '"Half-Caste Bob" or Race and Caste in the Late-Victorian Boys' Story Paper'; Hyungji Park, '"The Story of our Lives": *The Moonstone* and the Indian Mutiny in *All the Year Round*'; Laura Peters, '"Double-dyed Traitors and Infernal Villains": *Illustrated London News, Household Words*, Charles Dickens and the Indian Rebellion'; Javed Majeed, 'Narratives of Progress and Idioms of Community: Two Urdu Periodicals of the 1870s'; John McBratney, 'Strange Medley[s]: Ambiguities of Role, Purpose and Representations in Kipling's *From Sea to Sea*'; A. Martin Wainwright, 'Representing the Technology of the Raj in Britain's Victorian Periodical Press'; T.R. Moreman, 'The Army in India and the Military Periodical Press, 1830–1898'; Mark Harrison, 'Was there an Oriental Renaissance in Medicine? The Evidence of the Nineteenth-Century Medical Press'; Glenn R. Wilkinson, 'Purple Prose and the Yellow Press: Imagined Spaces and the Military Expedition to Tirah, 1897'; David Finkelstein and Douglas M. Peers, '"A Great System of Circulation": Introducing India into the Nineteenth-Century Media'.

The role of women both as journalists and as contributors to the periodical press has been the focus of some very strong work recently. Chief among these is Barbara Onslow's extremely useful study of women in the nineteenth-century media, *Women of the Press in Nineteenth-Century Britain*. A product of many years of research, this is a valuable contribution to media history studies, one of the first to focus explicitly on women as journalists in a general sense, as editors, reviewers, critics, feature contributors, leader writers and reporters. The result is a broad-ranging survey that includes a discussion of the role of anonymity in both fostering and hindering women's entry into the journalistic sphere, women and the new journalism of the 1880s, and interlinked profiles of successful journalists such as Harriet Martineau, Frances Cobbe, Eliza Lynn Linton, Emily Crawford and others.

General issues on gender raised in Onslow's book also feature in a special issue on 'Journalism, Gender and the Periodical Press' in the *Australasian Victorian Studies Journal* (*AuVSJ* 6[2000]). Likewise it is the subject of Sue Morgan's study of gender imagery and representation in '"Writing the Male Body": Sexual Purity and Masculinity in *The Vanguard*, 1884–1894' (in Bradstock, Gill, Hogan and Morgan, eds., *Masculinity and Spirituality in Victorian Culture*, pp. 179–93).

In similar thematic vein, four articles in the Summer 2000 issue of *VPR* (33:iii[2000]) are dedicated to the *Westminster Review*, its focus on gender and philosophy, its editor John Chapman, and its most famous contributor, George Eliot (also discussed in 1(*b*) above). Taken as a whole the pieces work well together, and include Sheila Rosenberg, 'The 'wicked Westminster': John Chapman, his Contributors and Promises Fulfilled' (*VPR* 33:iii[2000] 225–46); Laurel Brake, 'The *Westminster* and Gender at Mid-Century' (*VPR* 33:iii[2000] 247–72); Mark Turner, 'Defining Discourses: The *Westminster Review*, *Fortnightly Review*, and Comte's Positivism' (*VPR* 33:iii[2000] 273–82); and Beryl Gray, 'George Eliot and the *Westminster Review*' (*VPR* 33:iii[2000] 212–24).

George Eliot is also the topic of Gail Elizabeth Korn's '"[T]o correspond with you in green-covered volumes": George Eliot, G.H. Lewes and the Production of her Books', one of several nineteenth-century-centred contributions to Bray, Handley and Henry, eds., *Ma(r)king the Text*. In this strong but short piece, Korn examines Eliot's and George Henry Lewes's attention to the physical production of the part publication of Eliot's works such as *Middlemarch* and *Daniel Deronda*. Eliot and Lewes, she concludes, quite consciously sought control of the physical appearance of her publications in order to project a particular public persona, and also to 'both define and guide the public's response to that text' (p. 13). In the same collection, Bharat Tandon argues sympathetically for the use of careful editorial rendering of original nineteenth-century literary texts, such as Keats's poetry, in order to maintain and illuminate 'the historical relations between sight, sound and print in nineteenth-century poetic imaginations' (p. 202). The argument repeats much that others have argued for in the past, but offers a useful reminder that such discussions remain ongoing in contemporary bibliographical circles. Finally, in 'Speaking Commas/Reading Commas: Punctuating *Mansfield Park*', Kathryn Sutherland makes a similar point, this time with regard to original punctuation and intended meaning, in her analysis of critical editions over the past two centuries of Jane Austen's *Mansfield Park*.

Less theoretically realized is Alfred Grant's *The American Civil War and the British Press*. Mr Grant has combed through a great quantity of British press reports and journals for the years 1859–65, with the aim of reproducing commentary on various aspects of the civil war. Such conscientious primary research is to be applauded, but the work suffers from its mode of presentation: large chunks of original text are reproduced, interspersed with brief linking paragraphs introducing the sources, thus offering little in the way of original interpretation and analysis. Grant leaves it to other scholars, such as Will Kaufman in '"Our rancorous cousins": British Literary Journals on the Approach of the Civil War' (*Symbiosis* 4:i[2000] 35–50), to take the extra step needed to provide substance to the topic.

One who makes no pretensions to offering anything other than a useful checklist and bibliography on a subject of great importance to the Victorians is E.M. Palmegiano in *Health and British Magazines in the Nineteenth-Century* [1998]. A thorough introduction highlighting major health issues that appeared in the British press between 1824 and 1900 (the time-frame covered by *The Wellesley Index to Victorian Periodicals*, one of the major sources for her listings) is followed by a substantial checklist of over 2,600 relevant articles from forty-eight journals and periodicals of the period. It proves a useful starting point for those researching Victorian responses to health and well-being, including topics ranging from cholera containment and insanity to personal hygiene and public sanitation.

Related conflicts between aesthetics and material concerns are the subjects of substantial pieces worthy of attention by Julie Codell. In 'Constructing the Victorian Artist: National Identity, the Political Economy of Art and Biographical Mania in the Periodical Press' (*VPR* 33:iii[2000] 283–316), she examines representations of the artist in the periodical press during the years 1850–80 (also discussed in 1(*a*) above). Her study suggests a clearly defined binary opposition in press reconstructions of the artist, between aesthetic idealism and commercial professionalism, particularly in biographical sketches published in various art journals of the period. She reaches similar conclusions in 'Serialized Artists' Biographies: A Culture Industry in Late Victorian Britain' (*BoH* 3[2000] 94–124), in this case through analysis of examples taken from over sixty serialized biographies published in contemporary British journals and cheap editions between 1880 and 1914.

One of the most interesting and thought-provoking works produced this year in the area of periodical history is Mark Parker's *Literary Magazines and British Romanticism*. Parker samples four journals seen as key to the literary history of the Romantic period (the *London Magazine* [1820–1], the *New Monthly Magazine* [1821–5], *Blackwood's Edinburgh Magazine* [1822–5], and *Fraser's Magazine* [1833–4]). His aim: to contextualize the formation of political and literary debate within their pages, in the process proving them to be among the most experimental, self-conscious and influential publication spaces of the time. In so doing, he explores with great care and skill the debates contested within these 'personality'- driven periodical publication spaces, and the roles played by these periodicals in commodifying literary culture and establishing authorship as a profession. Authors discussed in this admirable work include John Wilson, James Hogg (the 'Ettrick Shepherd'), Thomas Carlyle, Samuel Taylor Coleridge and William Hazlitt. A different but equally relevant view can be found in Robert Lapp's analysis of the visual representations and illustrations of Samuel Taylor Coleridge in *Fraser's Magazine*, 'Romanticism Repackaged: The New Faces of 'Old Man' Coleridge in *Fraser's Magazine*, 1830–35' (*ERR* 11:ii[2000] 235–47).

If the literary periodical of the Romantic period is to be credited with creating a revolution in cultural and authorial activity, so too can the founding of the *Daily Mail* in 1896 be credited with launching a media revolution, in this case that of the popular mass media press still existing in Britain today. The centenary of the founding of the *Daily Mail* in 1896 has provided individuals with a convenient starting date for a subsequent avalanche of books and articles on its founder Lord Northcliffe, and his role in late nineteenth-century mass media press developments. Jean K. Chalaby argues, in '"Smiling Pictures Make People Smile": Northcliffe's Journalism' (*MH* 6:i[2000] 33–44), that, while Northcliffe was a press baron of great journalistic skill, his was not an empire built on innovation, but rather an enterprise that borrowed and adapted past traditions of journalism, such as those pioneered by W.T. Stead's crusading style of new journalism, to create successful newspaper enterprises (such as the *Daily Mail*). His impact on the history of British journalism, Chalaby notes interestingly, was more to modernize journalistic practice, commercializing production and focusing on discerning and responding to readers' tastes through a blend of sensationalist and 'crusading' discursive strategies. This trend, he concludes, continues to this day, although not in any current titles from the former Northcliffe media empire.

Chalaby repeats much of this information in 'Northcliffe: Proprietor as Journalist', one of several articles exploring Northcliffe's role in developing the British popular press from 1896 onwards in Catterall, Seymour-Ure and Smith, eds., *Northcliffe's Legacy: Aspects of the British Popular Press, 1896–1996*. In the same book, Chandrika Naul's 'Popular Press and Empire: Northcliffe, India and the *Daily Mail*, 1896–1922' follows Chalaby's lead by suggesting that Northcliffe adapted current trends in popular opinion to create the jingoistic tone that marked general coverage of empire and India throughout the early decades of the twentieth century. The *Daily Mail*'s claim to be 'the voice of empire' found expression in enthusiastic coverage of such events as the Boer War and conflicts in the Sudan and China, with Indian coverage marked by extreme presentations of Indian opulence, poverty and religious beliefs. Naul offers some useful but short analysis to support these points; the piece, however, feels slightly rushed and would have benefited from more space to develop issues further. Other essays of relevance to nineteenth-century studies worth noting in this collection include: Dilwyn Porter, '"Where there's a tip there's a tap": The Popular Press and the Investing Public, 1900–1960', an interesting piece on the rise of British financial journalism and the role of Northcliffe's press empire in acting as mediator between developing entrepreneurial companies and a newly confident investing public; and Donald Read, 'The Relationship of Reuters and Other News Agencies with the British Press, 1858–1984', on the ambivalent views of Reuters and similar news agencies on the nature of their business—was news-gathering to be undertaken as a service to the public or purely for profit? Read concludes that, in the case of Reuters, management positions on this have varied, sometimes emphasizing profit, sometimes service, and often both at the same time. The link to Northcliffe lies in the manner in which Reuters' twentieth-century operations responded to competition from Northcliffe's successful media model (as exemplified in the running of the *Daily Mail*) by increasingly concentrating on the profit-making view of journalistic news gathering practice.

J. Lee Thompson tackles Northcliffe's early rise as media mogul and subsequent role as war propagandist in *Politicians, the Press and Propaganda: Lord Northcliffe and the Great War, 1914–1918*. Using previously unpublished archival material, Thompson offers a close study of Northcliffe's career from the turn of the century through to his involvement in propaganda efforts in the USA and elsewhere during the First World War. Thompson covers a significant period in Northcliffe's career not dealt with by many other scholars, and in doing so offers a useful case-study appraisal of the links between media sources and governments in times of social upheaval.

Northcliffe was not the only one to pioneer mass media trends, as David Reed demonstrates in '"Rise and Shine!" The Birth of the Glossy Magazine' (*BLJ* 24:ii[2000] 256–69). In a general and heavily illustrated piece, Reed contextualizes the rise of the 'glossy magazines', inexpensive illustrated popular journals that appeared in the 1880s utilizing new techniques of visual reproduction and new developments in paper capable of presenting photographic and other illustrations. He suggests rather plausibly that George Newnes, with his purchase and championing of such titles as *Racing Illustrated*, *Navy and Army Illustrated* and

Country Life Illustrated [1898], successfully established a new type of targeted mass-market glossy periodical that had a world-wide impact, in the process laying the foundations for a market sector of the British magazine industry that still predominates today.

An attempt is made in Golden, ed., *Book Illustrated*, to link publishing and book history to media and cultural studies concerns, and in particular to engage with Walter Benjamin's influential 1936 essay on the technical reproduction of art, 'The Work of Art in the Age of Mechanical Reproduction'. Benjamin's contention was that the establishment of technological advances in the nineteenth century, allowing techniques of mass reproduction to be applied to works of art, invariably alienated art from its 'authentic' roots, causing it to lose its unique 'aura'. Art was no longer embedded in the fabric of tradition and ritual, but reproduced without its links to original artistic intention and socio-political purpose. This collection takes this issue as a starting point to suggest otherwise: that in fact the involvement of artists in the production of images for texts in the past three centuries has created unique 'auras' and work reflecting engagement with social and cultural concerns in a manner unrecognized by Benjamin. An exemplary piece by Jonathan Bate, for example 'Pictorial Shakespeare: Text, Stage, Illustration', analyses the place of visual illustration in refashioning Shakespeare's image as a universal genius. Thus, he suggests, illustrations between 1770 and 1847 of crucial scenes in Shakespeare's plays change in style to accommodate the historicization and nationalization of Shakespeare's texts and personas during this period. Similarly, Sarah Webster Goodwin's strong piece, 'Taglioni's Double Meanings: Illustrations and the Romantic Ballerina', examines images taken from visual paraphernalia (lithographs, gift books) produced in the 1820s and 1830s around the distinguished ballerina Marie Taglioni. Her analysis reflects on the role of such visual material in establishing particularly influential iconographic representations of ballerinas, as well as in destabilizing and reinterpreting contemporary assumptions of gender and the arts. Other useful essays by Robert L. Patten, 'The Politics of Humor in George Cruikshank's Graphic Satire', and Catherine J. Golden, 'Cruikshank's Illustrative Wrinkle in *Oliver Twist's* Misrepresentation of Class', focus on Cruikshank's work in two differing arenas, political satire and serialized fiction. Both pieces demonstrate, as Patten notes, the 'multiple contradictory affiliations and implications energetically discoursing within a single frame' (p. 84), illuminating unseen struggles over representations of class and society in both Georgian and Victorian times. Two other clusters of thematic material make up the remainder of the collection. First, Elizabeth K. Helsinger, in 'Rossetti and the Art of the Book', and James A.W. Heffernan, in 'Love, Death, and Grotesquerie: Beardsley's Illustration of Wilde and Pope', scrutinize Rossetti and Beardsley as illustrators who not only deliberately and meticulously engage with the business of art but also critically interpret through their visual material the texts they worked on. Both make important points about these artists' attendance to the production and consumption of art in book form. Finally, Ruth Copans, in 'Dream Blocks: American Women Illustrators of the Golden Age, 1890–1920', and David H. Porter, in '"We all sit on the edge of stools and crack jokes": Virginia Woolf and the Hogarth Press', look at the role of gender in the production of texts and images, focusing on the visual output of particular intellectuals and artisans from the US and the UK. The results are wide-ranging enough to appeal to those interested in visual and book arts, but perhaps too focused to rightfully argue that this collection, as the editor claims, in fact promotes cultural studies.

Chatto & Windus's publishing records have proven fruitful territory for several relevant case studies on late nineteenth-century publishing strategies. A good example is Andrew Nash, 'Robert Buchanan and Chatto & Windus: Reputation, Authorship and Fiction as Capital in the Late Nineteenth Century' (*PH* 46[2000] 5–33). Nash uses Buchanan's negotiations for copyright and serial rights in his works with Chatto & Windus between 1880 and 1900 to show the effect of literary reputation on market values. The publisher's appraisal of Buchanan's literary reputation as a successful writer for literary magazines allowed him to secure higher payments for serial rights to his fiction, but worked against him when works were issued in book form, owing to critical disdain among literary reviewing circles. The contrast offers a cogent example of the intersection between British commercial and cultural spheres at the turn of the century.

For 'The Natural History of a Textbook' (*PH* 47[2000] 5–30), John Issitt mines the Longman archives at the University of Reading to uncover the history of an important nineteenth-century geographical textbook, *Goldsmith's Grammar of Geography*. Originally issued by the well-known London publisher Sir Richard Phillips in the early nineteenth century, this title was acquired by Longman as part of a complicated financial arrangement with Phillips. Between 1812 and 1868, the title produced a profit of over £87,000, making it a steady earner for the Longman firm. A study of the publishing and production history of this popular textbook (one of the first to present geographical material in accessible form) allows us insight into important details about changes in nineteenth-century educational methods, as well as highlighting the increasing importance of such non-literary textual works to publishing firm profitability.

Such points also feature in Jonathan R. Topham's excellent in-depth article, 'Scientific Publishing and the Reading of Science in Nineteenth-Century Britain' (*Studies in the History and Philosophy of Science* 31:iv[2000] 559–612). Using a variation of Robert Darnton's 'Communication Circuit' as a starting point, Topham traces the development of a nineteenth-century reading public interested in science-based works, the publishers who began increasingly catering to such an audience, and finally the authors who played significant roles in meeting and increasing popular interest in such texts and topics.

An unusual area of publishing is explored by Samantha Matthews in 'Psychological Crystal Palace? Late Victorian Confession Albums' (*BoH* 3[2000] 125–65): nineteenth-century 'confession albums', a specialized form of printed, published autograph albums, featuring a series of lists and questions on personal traits, tastes and opinions that readers were invited to purchase and complete. Matthews's interesting piece succinctly demonstrates, through close analysis of representative samples, how such unusual records can provide us with valuable reader responses to particular, focused sets of published texts.

The importance of copyright is the subject of Adriaan van der-Weel's study of Dutch translations of popular British authors between 1850 and 1900, 'Nineteenth-Century Dutch Attitudes to International Copyright' (*PH* 47[2000] 31–44). Dutch responses to the vexed question of compensation for popular translations moves from unauthorized and uncompensated activity to recognition of the commercial value of copyright of popular authors, with subsequent compensation offered as a matter of course. Van der-Weel tracks this change from the mid- to late nineteenth century, using as examples works by Charles Dickens, Wilkie Collins and Ouida, each of whom was published in very successful translation in the Netherlands. Whereas Dickens received no payment for the translation of his works in the 1850s, Ouida was duly compensated by her Dutch publisher Erven F. Bohn for works produced between 1880 and 1900. The effect of changing British copyright legislation between 1842 and 1881 played a part in this shift in attitude, but, as van der-Weel points out, the general laissez-faire view of the Dutch on the economic importance of free translation to the nineteenth-century book trade meant that changes in their publishing practice did not occur quickly.

Caroline Archer turns our attention to a publishing firm with an unusual history in *The Kynoch Press: The Anatomy of a Printing House, 1876–1981*. The Kynoch Press was founded in Witton, Birmingham in 1876 to print the wrappers for the sporting and military cartridges produced by its parent firm Kynoch & Co. By 1921, when the entire firm amalgamated with Nobel Industries, and subsequently in 1926 with Imperial Chemical Industries (ICI), the Press had built up an impressive external clientele list based on a hard-won reputation as one of the foremost printing houses operating in northern England. Its pioneering work in typesetting and design, and its role in reviving the use of nineteenth-century English types in book publication in the 1930s, inspired similar developments by specialist printers and publishers such as the Curwen Press. Archer's work is the first major study of the firm, and combines archival material with oral testimony gathered from surviving staff to document the rise and fall of a specialist printing house attached to a large industrial enterprise. The story of the Kynoch Press is unusual precisely because its history does not fit the standard rubric of printing house histories. It was not attached to a major publishing firm, nor did it function entirely as an independent commercial enterprise. Rather, it had to negotiate perilously between its role as a branch of a larger commercial enterprise, and its need to attract external clients and printing contracts. Archer documents in great detail the manner in which the directors of the Kynoch Press set about navigating this path, some with greater success than others, and uses the Press as a case study to demonstrate the difficulties small presses with origins in the nineteenth century had in adapting to twentieth-century trends and technological developments. The early section will be of most interest and relevance to those seeking further insight into small presses and publishing ventures in nineteenth-century Britain.

Similarly engaging is James G. Nelson's *Publisher to the Decadents: Leonard Smithers in the Careers of Beardsley, Wilde, Dowson* (also noted in section 1(*a*) above). A topic often discussed in literary studies is the significance of the aesthetic movement of the 1890s, led by Oscar Wilde. Less noted is the significant role played by the publisher responsible for the production of many of the texts produced by Ernest Dowson, Wilde, and Aubrey Beardsley. Nelson charts the business career of Leonard Smithers, who after a start as a solicitor turned to a publishing career specializing in avant-garde texts and erotica. During his most prolific years (1895–1900) he was to publish some of Wilde's best-known work, including *The Ballad of Reading Gaol* and *The Importance of Being Earnest*, as well as classic erotica such as Sir Richard Burton's *The Arabian Nights*. Nelson is extremely good at illuminating the intrigues and connections between Smithers and his coterie of authors and illustrators. He offers us important insights into the rise and fall of an unconventional fin-de-siècle publisher, whose promotion and championing of important representatives of the aesthetic movement has not been given proper and due consideration until now.

An earlier example of a publisher whose reputable lists were supported by profits from pornographic publications is that of John Camden Hotten, the subject of Simon Eliot's entertaining piece 'Hotten: Rotten: Forgotten? An Apologia for a General Publisher' (*BoH* 3[2000] 61–93). Hotten (1832–73), whose business in London flourished between 1864 and 1873, published an eclectic series of texts, ranging from reprints of Aeschylus, Malory, Chaucer and Bunyan to anonymous works on flagellation. Eliot's combing of ledgers and publications lists brings out unknown details on Hotten's dual career in the print trade, and illustrates an important point about nineteenth-century publishing in general: most publishing houses, no matter how large or small, depended on tranches of non-literary publications to sustain their profitability. Hotten was no exception, but in his case his profits were gained by exploiting an unusual niche-market interest in sado-masochistic works.

Thomas Tegg's forty-year career in publishing proved a more respectable and lucrative enterprise, as noted in James J. Barnes and Patience P. Barnes's thorough piece 'Reassessing the Reputation of Thomas Tegg, London Publisher, 1776–1846' (*BoH* 3[2000] 45–60). Tegg, whose estate on his death in 1838 was valued at an extraordinary £90,000, specialized in reprints and remainders of popular non-fiction works and out-of-copyright classics. While leaving no lasting publishing empire, as opposed to more respectable colleagues such as William Blackwood or John Murray, Tegg demonstrated to his contemporaries how far one could get in the publishing world through persistence and clever appropriation of niche markets.

A recent publication filling in a lacuna in reference works on nineteenth-century Scottish publishing and printing history is David H.J. Schenck's *Directory of the Lithographic Printers of Scotland, 1820–1870*. The first lithographic printer to be traced by Schenck began trade in Edinburgh in 1820. Schenck offers a short analysis of the subsequent rise of lithographic printing in Scotland between 1820 and 1870, and provides a useful guide to identifying the firms prevalent in this area of publishing and printing. Benefiting from the meticulous manner in which Schenck has gathered dates and facts from a variety of primary and secondary sources, the directory includes biographical and historical data on individual firms and lithographers. It remains for future scholars to undertake what this text does not have space for, a more substantial cultural and historical survey of the role played by such industries in the support of nineteenth-century Scottish publishing endeavour.

Oak Knoll Press and St Paul's Bibliographies have for many years specialized in books on bibliography and other related areas. Recently they have merged and begun expanding their lists to encompass new trends in book history. Among their publications are several series based on long-running, annual book trade history conferences, including the Print Network series focusing on regional British book trade research, edited by Peter Isaac and Barry McKay. *The Mighty Engine: The Printing Press and its Impact* is the latest volume in this series, and contains eighteen essays on topics ranging from fifteenth-century York printing to the organization of Welsh, English and Scottish book trade networks in the twentieth century. Given the work-in-progress nature of many of these contributions, the volume is uneven in quality. Worthy of note, though, are several essays, including a piece by Philip Henry Jones, '"Business is awful bad in these parts": New Evidence for the Pre-1914 Decline of the Welsh-Language Book Trade', that uses information gleaned from the rounds of a publisher's travelling representative to meditate on the state of Welsh-language publishing between 1860 and 1910. Iain Beavan's 'Advertising Judiciously: Nineteenth-Century Publishers and the British Market' uses unpublished material to offer a fine study of early to mid-nineteenth-century techniques for advertising books, in this case uncovering the Scottish publisher Oliver & Boyd's use of London advertising agents to enhance coverage and sales of particular texts. John Turner completes the volume with a solid statistical analysis of English provincial trade activity from the 1850s into the twentieth century, demonstrating the results that can be derived from use of a variety of recently issued online database sources and CD-ROMs.

Publishing Pathways is a similar annual series of conference proceedings, published by Oak Knoll Press, and edited by Robin Myers and Michael Harris in London. A recent volume in this series worthy of attention is *Journeys through the Market: Travel, Travellers and the Book Trade*, which features several essays of varying quality on different aspects of nineteenth-century print culture. Charles Newton's 'Illustrated books of the Middle East, 1800–1950', offers quick, informative yet sorely untheorized insight into illustrated examples of British travel books on the Middle East, sidestepping complex matters of representation and the role of colonial possessions as backdrops for nineteenth-century European travel in the process. Likewise, in 'The English-Language Guidebook to Europe up to 1870', Giles Barber offers a swift survey of three centuries of English-language European travel guides that merely skims the surface of an interesting subject. Bill Bell's original and strong contribution on patterns of shipboard reading by British emigrants to the Antipodes, 'Bound for Australia: Shipboard Reading in the Nineteenth Century', offers interesting examples culled from his continuing research into the phenomenon of transcultural reading habits.

Bill Bell's work pops up again in Bell, Bennett and Bevan, eds., *Across Boundaries: The Book in Culture and Commerce*, a conference proceedings collection of eight essays for Oak Knoll Press. Bell's 'Crusoe's Books: The Scottish Emigrant Readers in the Nineteenth Century' examines the books taken by Scots emigrants from the mid-century onwards, focusing on the Scottish settlement of Waipu in New Zealand as a case-study example. Fiona Black, in a fascinating piece entitled 'Beyond Boundaries: Books in the Canadian Northwest', uses unpublished Hudson Bay Company and trading-post archival records to track the shipment and consumption of British books in Canada from 1799 to 1870. Similar judicious use of archival material underpins 'Commodification and Value: Interactions in Book Traffic to North America, c.1750–1820', James Raven's excellent exploration of eighteenth- and early nineteenth-century exportation and consumption of British books to the US. These are just three exemplary pieces from a volume that also features valuable contributions by Roger Chartier, Lisa Jardine and Wallace Kirsop.

Books Reviewed

Adshead, S.A.M. *Philosophy and Religion in Nineteenth-Century England and Beyond*. St Martin's Press. [2000] pp. viii + 274. $65 ISBN 0 3122 2424 9.

Alexander, Edward, ed. *John Stuart Mill. On Liberty*. Broadview. [2000] pp. 250. pb £4.16 ($5.95) ISBN 1 5511 1199 3.

Allen, Richard, and Harish Trivedi. *Literature and Nation: Britain and India, 1800 to 1990*. Routledge. [2000] pp. 400. £50 ISBN 0 4152 1206 5.

Allen, Vivien. *Dear Mr. Rossetti: The Letters of Dante Gabriel Rossetti and Hall Caine, 1878–1881*. ShaP. [2000] pp. 350. hb £40 ($55) ISBN 1 8412 7049 0, pb £15.95 ($25) ISBN 1 8412 7050 4.

Ankeny, Rebecca Thomas. *The Story, the Teller, and the Audience in George MacDonald's Fiction*. Mellen. [2000] pp. 172. $79.95 ISBN 0 7734 7728 4.

Archer, Caroline. *The Kynoch Press: The Anatomy of a Printing House, 1876–1981*. BL and OakK. [2000] pp. xi + 222. £35 ISBN 0 7123 4704 6 (BL), ISBN 1 5845 6046 0 (OakK).

Aristodemou, Maria. *Law and Literature: Journeys from Here to Eternity*. OUP. [2000] pp. 316. £22.99 ISBN 0 1987 6436 7.

Arnold, Dana. *Re-presenting the Metropolis: Architecture, Urban Experience and Social Life in London, 1800–1840*. Ashgate. [2000] pp. 172. $79.95 ISBN 0 8401 4232 4.

Atkinson, Damian, ed. *The Selected Letters of W.E. Henley*. Ashgate. [2000] pp. 392. $94.95 ISBN 1 8401 4634 6.

Avery, Gillian, Kimberley Reynolds, Paul Yates and Janet Goodall, eds. *Representations of Childhood Death*. St Martin's Press. [2000] pp. xvi + 246. $49.95 ISBN 0 3122 2408 7.

Bachleitner, Norbert, ed. *Beiträge zur Rezeption der britischen und irischen Literatur des 19. Jahrhunderts im deutschsprachigen Raum*. Rodopi. [2000] $96 ISBN 9 0420 0991 8.

Bachmann, Günter. *Philosophische Bewußtseinsformen in George Eliot's 'Middlemarch'*. Lang. [2000] pp. 298. $47.95 ISBN 3 6313 6985 9.

Baker, William, and Kenneth Womack, eds. *George Eliot: Felix Holt, the Radical*. Broadview. [2000] pp. 550. $14.95 ISBN 1 5511 1228 0.

Ballinger, Philip A. *The Poem as Sacrament: The Theological Aesthetic of Gerard Manley Hopkins*. Eerdmans. [2000] pp. 260. $30 ISBN 0 8028 4737 4.

Barczewski, Stephanie L. *Myth and National Identity in Nineteenth-Century Britain: The Legends of King Arthur and Robin Hood*. OUP. [2000] pp. 284. £40 ISBN 0 1982 0728 X.

Barlow, Paul, and Colin Trodd, eds. *Governing Cultures: Art Institutions in Victorian London*. Ashgate. [2000] pp. 226. $89.95 ISBN 1 8401 4690 7.

Barnard, Robert. *Emily Brontë*. BL. [2000] pp. 112. £10.95 ISBN 0 7123 4658 9.

Barratt, Carrie Rebora. *Queen Victoria and Thomas Sully*. PrincetonUP. [2000] pp. 224. $35 ISBN 0 6910 7034 2.

Barsham, Diana. *Arthur Conan Doyle and the Meaning of Masculinity*. Ashgate. [2000] pp. 288. £49.50 ISBN 1 8592 8264 4.

Batchelor, John. *John Ruskin: A Life*. C&G. [2000] pp. xiv + 384. $30 ISBN 0 7867 0814 X.

Beckman, Linda Hunt. *Amy Levy: Her Life and Letters*. OhioUP. [2000] pp. xiii + 331. hb $49.95 ISBN 0 8214 1329 5, pb $24.95 ISBN 0 8214 1330 9.

Beer, Gillian. *Darwin's Plots*. 2nd edn. CUP. [2000] pp. xxxii + 311. pb £13.95 ISBN 0 5217 8392 5.

Belford, Barbara. *Oscar Wilde: A Certain Genius.* RandomH. [2000] pp. 416. $29.95 ISBN 0 6794 5734 8.

Bell, Bill, Philip Bennett and Jonquil Bevan, eds. *Across Boundaries: The Book in Culture and Commerce.* StPB and OakK. [2000] pp. x + 160. £25 ISBN 1 8730 4047 4.

Bending, Lucy. *The Representation of Bodily Pain in Late Nineteenth-Century English Culture.* OUP. [2000] pp. 319. £37.50 ISBN 0 1981 8717 3.

Birch, Dinah, ed. *John Ruskin. Fors Clavigera.* EdinUP. [2000] pp. xlix + 448. £75 ISBN 1 8533 1125 1.

Black, Barbara J. *On Exhibit: Victorians and their Museums.* UPVirginia. [2000] pp. x + 242. $37.50 ISBN 0 8139 1897 9.

Bloom, Abigail Burnham, ed. *Nineteenth-Century British Women Writers: A Bio-Bibliographical Sourcebook.* Greenwood. [2000] pp. xii + 456. $110 ISBN 0 3133 0439 4.

Bloom, Harold. *How to Read and Why.* Scribner. [2000] pp. 283. $25 ISBN 0 6848 5906 8.

Booth, Howard, and Nigel Rigby, eds. *Modernism and Empire.* ManUP. [2000] pp. xii + 338. £45 ISBN 0 7190 5306 4.

Booth, Martin. *The Doctor and the Detective: A Biography of Sir Arthur Conan Doyle.* St Martin's Press. [2000] pp. 384. $27.95 ISBN 0 3122 4251 4.

Boumelha, Penny, ed. *Thomas Hardy: Jude the Obscure.* Macmillan. [2000] pp. viii + 240. £42.50 ISBN 0 3335 5135 4.

Braddon, Mary Elizabeth. *Married Beneath Him: A Comedy in Four Acts; and Fifty Years of the Lyceum Theatre.* Sensation. [2000] pp. 59. pb £12 ISBN 1 9025 8001 X.

Braddon, Mary Elizabeth. *The Missing Witness: An Original Drama in Four Acts.* Sensation. [2000] pp. 68. £12 ($17.42) ISBN 1 9025 8007 9.

Bradshaw, David J., and Suzanne Ozment, eds. *The Voice of Toil: Nineteenth-Century British Writings about Work.* OhioUP. [2000] pp. xxi + 793. hb $60 ISBN 0 8214 1292 2, pb $29.95 ISBN 0 8214 1293 0.

Bradstock, Andrew, Sean Gill, Anne Hogan and Sue Morgan, eds. *Masculinity and Spirituality in Victorian Culture.* Macmillan and St Martin's Press. [2000] pp. xi + 232. £45 ISBN 0 3338 0253 5 (Macmillan) ISBN 0 3122 3561 5 (St Martin's).

Brake, Laurel, Bill Bell and David Finkelstein, eds. *Nineteenth-Century Media and the Construction of Identities.* Palgrave. [2000] pp. xv +387 hb £40 ISBN 0 3336 8151 7, pb £15.99 ISBN 0 3336 8152 5.

Bray, Joe, Miriam Handley, and Anne C. Henry, eds. *Ma(r)king the Text: The Presentation of Meaning on the Literary Page.* Ashgate. [2000] pp. xxiv + 341. $99.95 ISBN 0 7546 0168 4.

Bristow, Joseph, ed. *The Cambridge Companion to Victorian Poetry.* CUP. [2000] pp. 321. pb £14.95 ISBN 0 5216 4680 4.

Brooks, Chris, ed. *The Albert Memorial. The Prince Consort National Memorial: Its History, Contexts, and Conservation.* YaleUP. [2000] pp. 480. $65 ISBN 0 3000 7311 9.

Brumberg, Joan Jacobs. *Fasting Girls: The History of Anorexia Nervosa.* Vintage. [2000] pp. 384. £21 ($14) ISBN 0 3757 2448 6.

Campbell, Kate, ed. *Journalism, Literature and Modernity.* KeeleUP. [2000] pp. 288. $65 ISBN 1 8533 1175 8.

Campbell, Matthew, Jacqueline M. Labbe and Sally Shuttleworth, eds. *Memory and Memorials, 1789–1914: Literary and Cultural Perspectives.* Routledge. [2000] pp. xi + 237. £62.86 ($90) ISBN 0 4152 2976 6.

Cannon, John. *The History of the Brontë Family from Ireland to Wuthering Heights.* Sutton. [2000] pp. 139. £9.99 ISBN 0 7509 1406 3.

Carlyle, Carol Jones. *Helen Faucit: Fire and Ice on the Victorian Stage.* STR. [2000] pp. xix + 416. £21 ISBN 0 8543 0067 8.

Carnell, Jennifer. *The Literary Lives of Mary Elizabeth Braddon: A Study of her Life and Work.* Sensation. [2000] pp. 436. £39.99 ISBN 1 9025 8002 8.

Catterall, Peter, Colin Seymour-Ure, and Adrian Smith, eds. *Northcliffe's Legacy: Aspects of the British Popular Press, 1896–1996.* Macmillan. [2000] pp. xii + 237. £15.99 ISBN 0 3339 1997 1.

Cave, Richard Allen, ed. *Oscar Wilde. The Importance of Being Earnest and Other Plays.* Penguin. [2000] pp. xxx + 464. $10 ISBN 0 1404 3606 5.

Chapman, Alison. *The Afterlife of Christina Rossetti.* St Martin's Press. [2000] pp. 213. pb £43.49 ISBN 0 3122 3461 9.

Chapple, John, and Alan Shelston, eds. *Further Letters of Mrs. Gaskell.* St Martin's Press. [2000] pp. xxvi + 326. $69.95 ISBN 0 7190 5415 X.

Chase, Karen, and Michael Levenson. *The Spectacle of Intimacy: A Public Life for the Victorian Family.* PrincetonUP. [2000] pp. viii + 250. $39.50 ISBN 0 6910 0668 7.

Chaudhuri, Brahma, and Fred Radford, eds. *Cumulative Bibliography of Victorian Studies, 1945–1969,* 2 vols. LITR. [2000] pp. xv + 625. ISBN 0 9192 3739 8.

Chernaik, Warren, Martin Swales and Robert Vilain, eds. *The Art of Detective Fiction.* Palgrave. [2000] pp. xv + 240. $59.95 ISBN 0 3122 2989 5.

Chrisman, Laura. *Rereading the Imperial Romance: British Imperialism and South African Resistance in Haggard, Schreiner, and Plaatje.* Clarendon. [2000] pp. 241. £40 ISBN 0 1981 2299 3.

Christiansen, Rupert. *The Visitors: Culture Shock in Nineteenth-Century Britain.* C&W. [2000] pp. 288. £20 ISBN 1 8561 9785 9.

Clinton, Catherine, ed. *Fanny Kemble's Journals.* HarvardUP. [2000] pp. 240. hb $39.95 ISBN 1 6740 0305 5, pb $16.95 ISBN 0 6740 0440 X.

Constable, Kathleen. *A Stranger Within the Gates: Charlotte Brontë and Victorian Irishness.* UPA. [2000] pp. 188. hb $52 ISBN 0 7618 1776 X, pb $32.50 ISBN 0 7618 1777 8.

Corbett, Mary Jean. *Allegories of Union in Irish and English Writing, 1790–1870.* CUP. [2000] pp. 228. £42.85 ($59.95) ISBN 0 5216 6132 3.

Corelli, Marie. *The Sorrows of Satan (1896).* RAKessinger. [1998] pb £22.50 ISBN 0 7661 0146 0.

Cormack, Robin, and Elizabeth Jeffreys, eds. *Through the Looking Glass: Byzantium through British Eyes.* Ashgate. [2000] pp. 270. $79.95 ISBN 0 8607 8667 6.

Correa, Delia da Sousa, ed. *The Nineteenth-Century Novel: Realisms.* Routledge. [2000] pp. vii + 414. $29.95 ISBN 0 4152 3826 9.

Dainotto, Roberto M. *Place in Literature: Regions, Cultures, Communities.* CornUP. [2000] pp. 208. $35 ISBN 0 8014 3683 4.

David, Robert G. *The Arctic in the British Imagination, 1818–1914.* ManUP. [2000] pp. xv + 278. £46 ISBN 0 7190 5943 7.

Davis, Tracy C., *The Economics of the British Stage*. CUP. [2000] pp. xviii + 506. $74.95 ISBN 0 5215 7115 4.

D'Cruze, Shani. *Everyday Violence in Britain, 1850–1950: Gender and Class.* Longman. [2000] pp. xii + 233. hb £55 ISBN 0 5824 1908 5, pb £17.99 ISBN 0 5824 1907 7.

Demoor, Marysa. *Their Fair Share: Women, Power and Criticism in the Athenaeum, from Millicent Garrett Fawcett to Katherine Mansfield, 1870–1920.* Ashgate. [2000] pp. 176. $74.95 ISBN 0 7546 0118 8.

Dennis, Barbara. *The Victorian Novel.* CUP. [2000] pp. 128. pb $13.95 ISBN 0 5217 7595 7.

Donaldson, Sandra, ed. *Critical Essays on Elizabeth Barrett Browning.* Hall. [1999] pp. 358. ISBN 0 7838 8461 3.

Donnell, Alison, and Pauline Polkey, eds. *Representing Lives: Women and Auto/ Biography.* Palgrave. [2000] pp. xxxiv + 300. $65 ISBN 0 3122 2667 5.

Doyle, Christine. *Louisa May Alcott and Charlotte Brontë: Transatlantic Translations.* UTennP. [2000] pp. xxiv + 203. $28 ISBN 1 5723 3083 X.

Duckett, Bob, ed. *Aspects of Bradford 2: Discovering Local History.* Wharncliffe Books. [2000] pp. 192. £9.95 ISBN 1 8716 4782 7.

Dunn, Richard J. *Charlotte Brontë. Jane Eyre.* 3rd edn. Norton. [2000] pp. ix + 534. pb $13.95 ISBN 0 3939 7542 8.

Dutta, Shanta. *Ambivalence in Hardy: A Study of his Attitude to Women.* St Martin's Press. [2000] pp. 212. £41.62 ($59.95) ISBN 0 3122 2183 5.

Earnshaw, Steven. *The Pub in Literature.* ManUP. [2000] pp. 304. pb £15.99 ISBN 0 7190 5305 6.

Eliot, George. *Daniel Deronda.* Everyman. [2000] pp. xxvii + 890. $23 ISBN 0 3754 1123 2.

Elliott, David B. *Charles Fairfax Murray: The Unknown Pre-Raphaelite.* OakK. [2000] pp. 260. $45 ISBN 1 5845 6030 4.

Federico, Annette R. *Idol of Suburbia: Marie Corelli and Late-Victorian Literary Culture.* UPVirginia. [2000] pp. 201. $30 (£25.50) ISBN 0 8139 1915 0.

Feuchtwanger, Edgar. *Disraeli.* Arnold. [2000] pp. xii + 244. hb £40 ($55) ISBN 0 3407 1909 5, pb £12.99 ISBN 0 3407 1910 9.

Finkelstein, David, and Douglas M. Peers, eds. *Negotiating India in the Nineteenth-Century Media.* Macmillan. [2000] pp. xi + 285. £45 ISBN 0 3337 1146 7.

Fisch, Audrey A. *American Slaves in Victorian England: Abolitionist Politics in Popular Literature and Culture.* CUP. [2000] pp. x + 139. £40 ISBN 0 5216 6026 2.

Flint, Kate. *The Victorians and the Visual Imagination.* CUP. [2000] pp. 438. £45 ISBN 0 5217 7026 2.

Fong, Bobby, and Karl Beckson, eds. *The Complete Works of Oscar Wilde*, vol. i: *Poems and Poems in Prose.* OUP. [2000] pp. xxxii + 333. £60 ISBN 0 1981 1960 7.

Foster, Jennifer, ed. *Elizabeth Gaskell. Mary Barton: A Tale of Manchester Life.* Broadview. [2000] pp. 420. £6.95 ($9.95) ISBN 1 5511 1169 1.

Fraisse, Luc, ed. *Pour une esthétique de la littérature mineure.* Champion. [2000] pp. 2,666.

Frankel, Nicholas. *Oscar Wilde's Decorated Books.* UMichP. [2000] pp. xiv + 222. $47.50 ISBN 0 4721 1069 1.

Frazier, Adrian. *George Moore, 1852–1933*. YaleUP. [2000] pp. 604. $35 ISBN 0 3000 8245 2.

Freedgood, Elaine. *Victorian Writing about Risk: Imagining a Safe England in a Dangerous World*. CUP. [2000] pp. xii + 216. £35 ISBN 0 5217 8108 6.

Gallagher, Susan VanZanten, and M.D. Walhout, eds. *Literature and the Renewal of the Public Sphere*. Palgrave. [2000] pp. ix + 247. $55 ISBN 0 312 22672 1.

Gardner, Martin. *The Annotated Alice: The Definitive Edition*. Norton. [2000] pp. xviii + 384. $29.95 ISBN 0 3930 4847 0.

Garrett, Martin. *A Browning Chronology: Elizabeth Barrett and Robert Browning*. St Martin's Press. [2000] pp. 235. $55 ISBN 0 3122 1795 1.

Garrioch, David, Harold Love, Brian McMullin *et al.*, eds. *The Culture of the Book: Essays from two Hemispheres in Honour of Wallace Kirsop*. Bibliographical Society of Australia and New Zealand. [1999] pp. xxx + 474. $A65 ISBN 0 9598 2717 X.

Gere, Charlotte, Lesley Hoskins and David Dewing. *The House Beautiful: Oscar Wilde and the Aesthetic Interior*. Ashgate. [2000] pp. 144. $60 (£29.95) ISBN 0 8533 1818 2.

Giddings, Robert, and Erica Sheen, eds. *The Classic Novel: From Page to Screen*. ManUP. [2000] pp. viii + 243. $69.95 ISBN 0 7190 5230 0.

Glage, Liselotte, ed. *Being/s in Transit: Travelling, Migration, Dislocation*. Rodopi. [2000] pp. xiv + 217. $51 ISBN 9 0420 0649 8.

GoGwilt, Christopher. *The Fiction of Geopolitics: Afterimages of Culture, from Wilkie Collins to Alfred Hitchcock*. StanfordUP. [2000] pp. xii + 265. hb $49.50 ISBN 0 8047 3726 6, pb $18.95 ISBN 0 8047 3731 2.

Golden, Catherine J., ed. *Book Illustrated: Text, Image, and Culture, 1770–1930*. OakK. [2000] pp. xvi + 320. £25 ($39.95) ISBN 1 5845 6023 1.

Grant, Alfred. *The American Civil War and the British Press*. McFarland. [2000] pp. ix + 207. $35 ISBN 0 7864 0630 5.

Guy, Josephine M., and Ian Small. *Oscar Wilde's Profession: Writing and Culture Industry in the Late Nineteenth Century*. OUP. [2000] pp. viii + 314. £45 ISBN 0 1981 8728 9.

Hanna, Robert C., ed. *The Dickens Christian Reader: A Collection of New Testament Teachings and Biblical References from the Works of Charles Dickens*. AMS. [2000] pp. viii + 124. $49.50 ISBN 0 4046 4451 1.

Harden, Edgar F. *Thackeray the Writer: From 'Pendennis' to 'Denis Duval'*. Macmillan. [2000] pp. 256. £38.19 ($55) ISBN 0 3122 2929 1.

Hardin, Richard F. *Love in a Green Shade: Idyllic Romances Ancient to Modern*. UNebP. [2000] pp. 288 £34 ISBN 0 8032 2394 3.

Hardy, Barbara Nathan. *Thomas Hardy. Imagining Imagination: Hardy's Poetry and Fiction*. Athlone. [2000] pp. 224. hb $90 ISBN 0 4851 1543 3, pb $24.95 ISBN 0 4851 2153 0.

Hardyment, Christina. *Literary Trails: British Writers in their Landscapes*. Abrams. [2000] pp. 256. $49.50 ISBN 0 8109 6705 7.

Hawkins, Anne Hunsaker, and Marilyn Chandler McEntyre, eds. *Teaching Literature and Medicine*. MLA. [2000] pp. viii + 406. hb $40 ISBN 0 8735 2356 3, pb $22 ISBN 0 8735 2357 1.

Heilmann, Ann. *New Woman Fiction: Women Writing First-Wave Feminism*. Palgrave. [2000] pp. 221. £40 ($55) ISBN 0 3122 3627 1.

Helland, Janice. *Professional Women Painters in Nineteenth-Century Scotland.* Ashgate. [2000] pp. 226. $84.95 ISBN 0 7546 0068 8.

Hepburn, James, ed. *A Book of Scattered Leaves: Poetry of Poverty in Broadside Ballads of Nineteenth-Century England: Study and Anthology,* vol. i. BuckUP. [2000] pp. 283. £35 ($44.50) ISBN 0 8387 5397 3.

Hewison, Robert, ed. *Ruskin's Artists: Studies in Victorian Visual Economy.* Ashgate. [2000] pp. 272. $79.95 ISBN 0 7546 0028 9.

Hewison, Robert, Ian Warrell and Stephen Wildman, eds. *Ruskin, Turner and the Pre-Raphaelites.* Tate. [2000] pp. 288. $60 ISBN 1 8543 7303 X.

Hewitt, Martin, ed. *An Age of Equipoise? Re-Assessing Mid-Victorian Britain.* Ashgate. [2000] pp. 264. $84.95 ISBN 0 7546 0257 5.

Heydenreich, Titus, and Eberhard Späth, eds. *Afrika in den europäischen Literaturen zwischen 1860 und 1930.* UErlangen-N. [2000] pp. 275.

Hilton, Tim. *John Ruskin: The Later Years.* YaleUP. [2000] xxiv + 656. $35 ISBN 0 3000 8311 4.

Hitchens, Christopher. *Unacknowledged Legislation: Writers in the Public Sphere.* Verso. [2000] pp. 320. $25 ISBN 1 8598 4786 2.

Holbrook, David. *A Study of George MacDonald and the Image of Woman.* Mellen. [2000] pp. xii + 349. $99.95 ISBN 0 7734 7761 6.

Holden, Alan W. and J. Roy Birch, eds. *A.E. Housman: A Reassessment.* Macmillan. [2000] pp. 225. £43.93 ($65) ISBN 0 3122 2318 8.

Holland, Merlin, and Rupert Hart-Davis, eds. *The Complete Letters of Oscar Wilde.* Henry Holt. [2000] pp. 1,270. $45 ISBN 0 8050 5915 6.

Horner, Avril, and Angela Keane, eds. *Body Matters: Feminism, Textuality, Corporeality.* Palgrave. [2000] pp. xii + 260. hb £45 ISBN 0 7190 5468 0, pb £15.99 ISBN 0 7190 5469 9.

Houppermans, Sjef, Paul J. Smith and Madeleine van Strien-Chardonneau, eds. *Histoire jeu science dans l'aire de la littérature.* Rodopi. [2000] pp. 271. $40 ISBN 9 0420 1221 8.

Hughes, William. *Beyond Dracula: Bram Stoker's Fiction and its Cultural Context.* Macmillan. [2000] pp. 216. £42.50 ($59.95) ISBN 0 3122 3136 9.

Ingham, Patricia. *Charles Dickens. American Notes for General Circulation.* Penguin. [2000] xxxvi + 311. pb £8.99 ISBN 0 1404 3649 9.

Ingham, Patricia. *Invisible Writing and the Victorian Novel: Readings in Language and Ideology.* ManUP. [2000] pp. 176. £40 ISBN 0 7190 5201 7.

Inkster, Ian, Colin Griffin, Jeff Hill and Judith Rowbotham, eds. *The Golden Age: Essays in British Social and Economic History, 1850–1870.* Ashgate. [2000] pp. 304. $79.95 ISBN 0 7546 0114 5.

Irwin, Michael. *Reading Hardy's Landscapes.* St Martin's Press. [2000] pp. xi + 171. £40 ($49.95) ISBN 0 3122 2403 6.

Isaac, Peter and Barry McKay, eds. *The Mighty Engine: The Printing Press and its Impact.* StPB and OakK. [2000] pp. xi + 205. £25 ISBN 1 8730 4061 X.

Jackson, Kevin. *A Ruskin Alphabet.* Worple. [2000] pp. 88. £4.50 ($6.40) ISBN 0 9530 9472 3.

Jacobson, Wendy S. ed. *Dickens and the Children of Empire.* Palgrave. [2000] pp. 211. $59.95 ISBN 0 3337 7044 7.

Jaffe, Audrey. *Scenes of Sympathy: Identity and Representation in Victorian Fiction.* CornUP. [2000] pp. vii + 184. $39.95 ISBN 0 8014 3712 1.

Jay, Betty. *Anne Brontë*. Northcote. [2000] pp. 92. £8.99 ISBN 0 7463 0888 4.

Jenkins, Alice, and Juliet John, eds. *Rereading Victorian Fiction*. St Martin's Press. [2000] pp. xvi + 218. £45 ($55) ISBN 0 3122 2643 8.

Johanson, Graeme. *A Study of Colonial Editions in Australia, 1843–1972*. Elibank. [2000] pp. 346. $A62.50 ISBN 0 9583 4963 0.

John, Juliet, and Alice Jenkins, eds. *Rethinking Victorian Culture*. Macmillan. [2000] pp. xvi + 244. £50 ISBN 0 3337 1446 6.

Karlin, Daniel, ed. *Rudyard Kipling*. Oxford Authors. [1999] pp. 699. $40 ISBN 0 1925 4201 X.

Karson, Jill, ed. *Readings on Jane Eyre*. Greenhaven. [2000] pp. 171. hb $32.45 ISBN 0 7377 0176 5, pb $23.50 ISBN 0 7377 0177 3.

Katz, Tamar. *Impressionist Subjects: Gender, Interiority, and Modernist Fiction in England*. UIllP. [2000] pp. 288. $39.95 ISBN 0 2520 2584 9.

Keating, Peter, ed. *Marie Corelli: The Sorrows of Satan*. OUP. [1998] pp. 426. pb £5.99 ISBN 0 1928 3324 3.

Keynes, Richard, ed. *Charles Darwin's Zoology Notes and Specimen Lists from H.M.S. Beagle*. CUP. [2000] pp. xxxi + 464. £95 ISBN 0 5214 6569 9.

Knight, Charmian, and Luke Spencer. *Reading the Brontës: An Introduction to their Novels and Poetry*. Brontë Society. [2000] pp. 155. £9.50 ISBN 0 9030 0702 X.

Knoepflmacher, U.C. *Ventures into Childland: Victorians, Fairy Tales, and Femininity*. UChicP. [2000] pp. xx + 444. pb $20 ISBN 0 2264 4816 9.

Korte, Barbara. *English Travel Writing from Pilgrimages to Postcolonial Explorations*, trans. Catherine Matthias. Palgrave. [2000] pp. 240. $55 ISBN 0 3122 2663 2.

Kranzler, Laura, ed. *Elizabeth Gaskell: Gothic Tales*. Penguin. [2000] pp. xxxvi + 366. pb £7.99 ($6.99) ISBN 0 1404 3741 X.

Krause, David. *William Carleton, the Novelist: His Carnival and Pastoral World*. UPA. [2000] pp. 330. hb $67 ISBN 0 7618 1656 9, pb $42 ISBN 0 7618 1657 7.

Kucich, John, and Dianne F. Sadoff, eds. *The Victorian Afterlife: Postmodern Culture Rewrites the Nineteenth Century*. UMinnP. [2000] pp. xxx + 344. hb $49.95 ISBN 0 8166 3323 1, pb $19.95 ISBN 0 8166 3324 X.

Kutzer, M. Daphne. *Empire's Children: Empire and Imperialism in Classic British Children's Books*. Garland. [2000] pp. 325. $80 ISBN 0 8153 3491 5.

Lang, Cecil Y, ed. *The Letters of Matthew Arnold, 1871–1878*. UPVirginia. [2000] pp. 496. $60 ISBN 0 8139 1896 0.

Law, Graham. *Serializing Fiction in the Victorian Press*. Macmillan. [2000] pp. xxii + 300. £45 ISBN 0 3337 6019 0.

Law, Joe, and Linda K. Hughes, eds. *Biographical Passages: Essays in Victorian and Modernist Biography, Honoring Mary M. Lago*. UPMiss. [2000] pp. 224. $34.95 ISBN 0 8262 1256 5.

Ledger, Sally, and Roger Luckhurst, eds. *The Fin de Siècle: A Reader in Cultural History, c.1880–1900*. OUP. [2000] pp. xxiii + 363. hb £35 ISBN 0 1987 4278 9, pb £12.99 ISBN 0 1987 4279 7.

Li, Hao. *Memory and History in George Eliot: Transfiguring the Past*. St Martin's Press. [2000] pp. xiii + 227. £38.19 ($55) ISBN 0 3122 2834 1.

Losey, Jay, and William D. Brewer, eds. *Mapping Male Sexuality: Nineteenth-Century England*. FDUP. [2000] pp. 376. $55 ISBN 0 8386 3828 7.

MacCarthy, Anne. *James Clarence Mangan, Edward Walsh and Nineteenth-Century Irish Literature in English*. Mellen. [2000] pp. ix + 306. $99.95 ISBN 0 7734 7498 6.

MacLeod, Roy M. *The 'Creed of Science' in Victorian England*. Ashgate. [2000] pp. 346. $105.95 ISBN 0 8607 8669 2.

Mallett, Phillip, ed. *The Achievement of Thomas Hardy*. Palgrave. [2000] pp. xvii + 192. $55 ISBN 0 3122 3536 4.

Malouf, David. *Jane Eyre: A Libretto*. Vintage. [2000] pp. xi + 27. pb £4.99 ISBN 0 0992 8626 2.

Matthew, Colin. *The Nineteenth Century: The British Isles, 1815–1901*. OUP. [2000] pp. 358. £35 ISBN 0 1987 3144 2.

Mazzeno, Laurence W. *Matthew Arnold: The Critical Legacy*. Camden House. [2000] xvi + 170. hb £46.50 ISBN 0 8139 1924 X, pb £15.95 ISBN 0 8139 1972 X.

McCaw, Neil. *George Eliot and Victorian Historiography: Imagining the National Past*. St Martin's Press. [2000] pp. 208. £54.33 ($65) ISBN 0 3122 3413 9.

McCormack, Kathleen. *George Eliot and Intoxication: Dangerous Drugs for the Condition of England*. St Martin's Press. [2000] pp. 234. $59.95 ISBN 0 3122 2711 6.

McCormack, W.J. *Fool of the Family: A Life of J.M. Synge*. W&N. [2000] pp. 500. £25 ($34.95) ISBN 0 2976 4612 5.

McEwan, Cheryl. *Gender, Geography and Empire: Victorian Women Travellers in West Africa*. Ashgate. [2000] pp. 260. $74.95 ISBN 1 8401 4252 9.

McGann, Jerome. *Dante Gabriel Rossetti and the Game That Must Be Lost*. YaleUP. [2000] pp. 208. £25 ISBN 0 3000 8023 9.

McGovern, Timothy Michael. *Dickens in Galdós*. Lang. [2000] pp. 159. $44.95 ISBN 0 8204 4290 9.

McLaughlin, Joseph. *Writing the Urban Jungle: Reading Empire in London from Doyle to Eliot*. UPVirginia. [2000] pp. xiv + 234. hb $55 ISBN 0 8139 1924 X, pb $18.50 ISBN 0 8139 1972 X.

Mighall, Robert, ed. *Oscar Wilde: The Picture of Dorian Gray*. Penguin. [2000] pp. xliii + 252. pb £3.50 ISBN 0 1404 3784 3.

Mitchell, Rosemary. *Picturing the Past: English History in Text and Image, 1830–1870*. OUP. [2000] pp. 326. £48 ISBN 0 1982 0844 8.

Monteiro, George. *Fernando Pessoa and Nineteenth-Century Anglo-American Literature*. UPKen. [2000] pp. 240. $24.95 ISBN 0 8131 2182 5.

Moody, Jane, *Illegitimate Theatre in London, 1770–1840*. CUP. [2000] pp. xiv + 278 $74.95 ISBN 0 5215 6376 3.

Morgan, Rosemarie, and Shannon Russell, eds. *Thomas Hardy: Far from the Madding Crowd*. Penguin. [2000] pp. 480. pb £2.99 ISBN 0 1404 3521 2.

Morowitz, Laura, and William Vaughan, eds. *Artistic Brotherhoods in the Nineteenth Century*. Ashgate. [2000] pp. 220. $84.95 ISBN 0 7546 0014 9.

Morris, Tim. *You're Only Young Twice: Children's Literature and Film*. UIllP. [2000] pp. xii + 186. $24.95 ISBN 0 2520 2532 6.

Moss, Sidney P., and Carolyn J. Moss. *Dickens, Trollope, Jefferson: Three Anglo-American Encounters*. Whitston. [2000] pp. 84. $22.50 ISBN 0 8787 5512 8.

Motion, Andrew. *Wainewright the Poisoner: The Confession of Thomas Griffiths Wainewright*. Knopf. [2000] pp. 272. $26 ISBN 0 3754 0209 8.

Murray, Patricia. *Comparing Postcolonial Literatures: Dislocations.* Palgrave. [2000] pp. xi + 283. $55 ISBN 0 3122 2781 7.

Myers, Robin, and Michael Harris, eds. *Journeys through the Market: Travel, Travellers and the Book Trade.* StPB and OakK. [1999] pp. xi + 205. £25 ISBN 1 8730 4056 3.

Nassaar, Christopher S. ed. *The Victorians: A Major Authors Anthology.* UPA. [2000] pp. xxiv + 806. $62.50 ISBN 0 7618 1710 7.

Nead, Lynda. *Victorian Babylon: People, Streets, and Images in Nineteenth-Century London.* YaleUP. [2000] pp. viii + 251. $35 ISBN 0 3000 8505 2.

Nelson, Emmanuel S. *African American Authors, 1745–1945: A Bio-Bibliographical Critical Sourcebook.* Greenwood. [2000] pp. 544. $99.50 ISBN 0 3133 0910 8.

Nelson, James G.. *Publisher to the Decadents: Leonard Smithers in the Careers of Beardsley, Wilde, Dowson.* PSUP. [2000] pp. xvi + 430. £25 ISBN 0 2710 1974 3.

Newlin, George. *Understanding 'Great Expectations': A Student Casebook to Issues, Sources, and Historical Documents.* Greenwood. [2000] pp. xx + 228. $39.95 ISBN 0 3132 9940 4.

Newman, John Henry. *Callista.* UNDP. [2000] pp. 448. $35 ISBN 0 2680 2260 7.

Newsom, Robert. *Charles Dickens Revisited.* Twayne. [2000] pp. xix + 218. $33 ISBN 0 8057 1630 0.

Nigro, August. *The Net of Nemesis: Studies in Tragic Bond/Age.* AUP. [2000] pp. 192. $35 ISBN 1 5759 1036 5.

Norton, David. *A History of the English Bible as Literature.* CUP [2000] pp. 496. hb £47.50 ISBN 0 5217 7140 4, pb £19.95 ISBN 0 5217 7807 7.

Onslow, Barbara. *Women of the Press in Nineteenth-Century Britain.* Macmillan. [2000] pp. xii + 297. £22.50 ISBN 0 3336 8378 1.

Page, Norman. ed. *The Oxford Reader's Companion to Hardy.* OUP. [2000] pp. 550. £40 ($49.95) ISBN 0 1986 0074 7.

Palmegiano, E.M. *Health and British Magazines in the Nineteenth Century.* Scarecrow. [1998] pp. xi + 282. $59.50 ISBN 0 8108 3486 3.

Parker, Christopher. *The English Idea of History from Coleridge to Collingwood.* Ashgate. [2000] pp. 244. $69.95 ISBN 1 8401 4254 5.

Parker, Mark. *Literary Magazines and British Romanticism.* CUP. [2000] pp. 213. $54.95/£37.80 ISBN 0 5217 8192 2.

Paroissien, David. *The Companion to 'Great Expectations'.* Greenwood. [2000] pp. xvi + 506. $97.50 ISBN 0 3133 1800 X.

Pearce, Joseph. *The Unmasking of Oscar Wilde.* HC. [2000] pp. 320. £17.99 ($29.95) ISBN 0 0027 4042 7.

Pearson, Richard. *W.M. Thackeray and the Mediated Text.* Ashgate. [2000] pp. 288. £49.50 ($84.95) ISBN 0 7546 0065 3.

Pease, Allison. *Modernism, Mass Culture, and the Aesthetics of Obscenity.* CUP. [2000] pp. xvi + 244. £38.15 ($54.95) ISBN 0 5217 8076 4.

Pemble, John, ed. *John Addington Symonds: Culture and the Demon Desire.* Macmillan. [2000] pp. xviii + 190. £42.50 ($60.69) ISBN 0 3337 7131 1.

Peters, Laura. *Orphan Texts: Victorian Orphans, Culture and Empire.* ManUP. [2000] pp. vii + 158. £40 ISBN 0 7190 5232 7.

Pick, Daniel. *Svengali's Web: The Alien Enchanter in Modern Culture.* YaleUP. [2000] pp. 304. $29.95 ISBN 0 3000 8204 5.

Pinney, Thomas, *Rudyard Kipling: The Jungle Play*. Penguin. [2000] pp. xl + 70. pb £12.99 ($18.20) ISBN 0 7139 9399 5.

Plotz, John. *The Crowd: British Literature and Public Politics*. UCalP. [2000] pp. 332. hb £35 ($48) ISBN 0 5202 1916 3, pb £13.95 ($18.95) ISBN 0 5202 1917 1.

Pocock, Tom. *Captain Marryat: Seaman, Writer, Adventurer*. Stackpole. [2000] pp. 208. £19.95 ($26.95) ISBN 0 8117 0355 X.

Pratt, Linda Ray. *Matthew Arnold Revisited*. Twayne. [2000] pp. xii + 174. $32 ISBN 0 8057 1698 X.

Prawer, S.S. *W.M. Thackeray's European Sketch Books: A Study of Literary and Graphic Portraiture*. Lang. [2000] pp. x + 449. £45 ($70.95) ISBN 3 9067 5868 0.

Prettejohn, Elizabeth. *The Art of the Pre-Raphaelites*. PrincetonUP. [2000] pp. 304. $49.50 ISBN 0 6910 7057 1.

Price, Leah. *The Anthology and the Rise of the Novel: From Richardson to George Eliot*. CUP. [2000] pp. 224. £35 ISBN 0 5217 8208 2.

Quill, Sarah, and Alan Windsor. *Ruskin's Venice: The Stones Revisited*. Ashgate. [2000] pp. 206. £30 ISBN 1 8401 4697 4.

Raitt, Suzanne. *May Sinclair: A Modern Victorian*. OUP. [2000] pp. 324. £19.99 ISBN 0 1981 2298 5.

Ramel, Annie. *Great Expectations: Le Père ou le pire*. Messene. [2000] pp. 144. ISBN 2 8454 9007 0.

Randall, Don. *Kipling's Imperial Boy: Adolescence and Cultural Hybridity*. Palgrave. [2000] pp. 192. $59.95 ISBN 0 3337 6104 9.

Ray, Sangeeta. *En-Gendering India: Woman and Nation in Colonial and Postcolonial Narratives*. DukeUP. [2000] pp. viii + 198. $54.95 ISBN 0 8223 2453 9.

Reitz, Bernard, and Eckart Voigts-Virchow, eds. *Lineages of the Novel*. Wissenschaftlicher. [2000] pp. 260.

Richardson, Angélique, and Chris Willis, eds. *The New Woman in Fiction and in Fact: Fin-de-Siècle Feminisms*. Palgrave. [2000] pp. 224. $59.95 ISBN 0 3122 3490 2.

Rignall, John, ed. *The Oxford Reader's Companion to George Eliot*. OUP. [2000] pp. 504. hb £40 ISBN 0 1986 0099 2, pb £8.99 ISBN 0 1986 0422 X.

Roberts, Adam, ed. *Alfred Tennyson: A Critical Edition of the Major Works*. OUP. [2000] pp. 626. $13.99 ISBN 0 1928 8048 9.

Robbins, Ruth. ed. *Literary Feminisms*. St Martin's Press. [2000] pp. 290. hb £38.19 ISBN 0 3122 2807 4, pb $13.85 ISBN 0 3122 2808 2.

Robbins, Ruth, and Julian Wolfreys, eds. *Victorian Gothic: Literary and Cultural Manifestations in the Nineteenth Century*. Palgrave. [2000] pp. 260. $69.96 ISBN 0 3122 3169 5.

Rogers, Helen. *Women and the People: Authority, Authorship and the Radical Tradition in Nineteenth-Century England*. Ashgate. [2000] pp. 352. $74.95 ISBN 0 7546 0261 3.

Rudnytsky, Peter L., and Andrew M. Gordon, eds. *Psychoanalyses/Feminisms*. SUNYP. [2000] pp. viii + 238. pb $18.96 ISBN 0 7914 4378 7.

Ruijssenaars, Eric. *Charlotte Brontë's Promised Land: The Pensionnat Heger and Other Brontë Places in Brussels*. Brontë Society. [2000] pp. 101. £12.95 ISBN 1 9030 078.

Rylance, Rick. *Victorian Psychology and British Culture, 1850–1880*. OUP. [2000] pp. 355. £45 ISBN 0 1981 2283 7.

Salmon, Frank. *Building on Ruins: The Rediscovery of Rome and English Architecture*. Ashgate. [2000] pp. 253. $75 ISBN 0 7546 0358 X.

Sanders, Valerie, ed. *Records of Girlhood: An Anthology of Nineteenth-Century Women's Childhoods*. Ashgate. [2000] pp. 248. $69.95 ISBN 0 7546 0148 X.

Sandison, Alan, and Robert Dingley, eds. *Histories of the Future: Studies in Fact, Fantasy and Science Fiction*. Palgrave. [2000] pp. 240. $59.95 ISBN 0 3122 3604 2.

Sato, Tomoko, Lionel Lambourne, *et al.*, eds. *The Wilde Years: Oscar Wilde and the Art of his Time*. Philip Wilson. [2000] pp. 144. $60 ISBN 0 8566 7526 1.

Saville, Julia F. *A Queer Chivalry: The Homoerotic Aestheticism of Gerard Manley Hopkins*. UPVirginia. [2000] pp. 256. $37.50 ISBN 0 8139 1940 1.

Schaaf, Larry J. *The Photographic Art of William Henry Fox Talbot*. PrincetonUP. [2000] pp. 264. $75 ISBN 0 6910 5000 7.

Schaffer, Talia. *The Forgotten Female Aesthetes: Literary Culture in Late-Victorian England*. UPVirginia. [2000] pp. x + 298. hb $55 ISBN 0 8139 1936 3, pb $19.50 ISBN 0 8139 1937 1.

Schenck, David H., *Directory of the Lithographic Printers of Scotland, 1820–1870*. Edinburgh Bibliographical Society and OakK. [1999] 124 pp. £20 ISBN 1 8721 1629 9.

Schlossberg, Herbert. *The Silent Revolution and the Making of Victorian England*. OSUP. [2000] pp. x + 405. £54.95 ISBN 0 8142 0843 6.

Schramm, Jan-Melissa. *Testimony and Advocacy in Victorian Law, Literature, and Theology*. CUP. [2000] pp. xvi + 244. £41.62 ($59.95) ISBN 0 5217 7123 4.

Scragg, Donald, and Carole Weinberg, eds. *Literary Appropriations of the Anglo-Saxons from the Thirteenth to the Twentieth Century*. CUP [2000] pp. 254. £47.50 ISBN 0 5216 3215 3.

Secord, James A. *Victorian Sensation: The Extraordinary Publication, Reception, and Secret Authorship of 'Vestiges of the Natural History of Creation'*. UChicP. [2000] pp. 624. $35 ISBN 0 2267 4410 8.

Shuman, Cathy. *Pedagogical Economies: The Examination and the Victorian Literary Man*. StanfordUP. [2000] pp. 255. $49.50 ISBN 0 8047 3715 0.

Siberry, Elizabeth. *The New Crusaders: Images of the Crusades in the Nineteenth and Early Twentieth Centuries*. Ashgate. [2000] pp. 240. $84.95 ISBN 1 8592 8333 0.

Simmons, Clare A. *Eyes Across the Channel: French Revolutions, Party History and British Writing, 1830–1882*. Harwood. [2000] pp. 227. $54 ISBN 9 0582 3048 1.

Slater, Michael, and John Drew, eds. *Dickens' Journalism: 'The Uncommercial Traveller' and Other Papers, 1859–70*. Dent. [2000] pp. xxxiii + 476. £30 ISBN 0 4608 7728 3.

Small, Ian. *Oscar Wilde, Recent Research: A Supplement to 'Oscar Wilde Revalued'*. ELT. [2000] pp. vii + 224. $40 ISBN 0 9443 1814 2.

Smith, Andrew. *Gothic Radicalism: Literature, Philosophy, and Psychoanalysis in the Nineteenth Century*. Palgrave. [2000] pp. xi + 188. £41.62 ($59.95) ISBN 0 3337 6035 2.

Smith, Margaret, ed. *Charlotte Brontë. Jane Eyre.* OUP. [2000] pp. li + 488. pb £2.99 ($8.95) ISBN 0 1928 3965 9.

Smith, Margaret, ed. *The Letters of Charlotte Brontë: With a Selection of Letters by Family and Friends*, vol. ii: *1848–1851.* OUP. [2000] pp. 840. £65 ISBN 0 1981 8598 7.

Smith, Margaret, and Herbert Rosengarten, eds. *Charlotte Brontë: Villette.* OUP. [2000] pp. l + 538. pb £2.99 ($9.95) ISBN 0 1928 3964 0.

Smith, Rowland, ed. *Postcolonizing the Commonwealth: Studies in Literature and Culture.* WLUP. [2000] pp. vi + 216. £30 ISBN 0 8892 0358 X.

Stark, Susanne, ed. *The Novel in Anglo-German Context: Cultural Cross-Currents and Affinities.* Rodopi. [2000] pp. 466. £50 ISBN 9 0420 0698 6.Stashower, Daniel. *Teller of Tales: The Life of Arthur Conan Doyle.* HenryHolt. [2000] pp. 512. $32.50 ISBN 0 8050 5074 4.

Stedman, Jane W., *W.S. Gilbert's Theatrical Criticism.* STR. [2000] pp. x + 215. £15 ISBN 0 8543 0068 6.

Steffen, Therese, ed. *Crossover: Cultural Hybridity in Ethnicity, Gender, Ethics.* Stauffenburg. [2000] pp. xiii + 218.

Stokes, John, ed. *Eleanor Marx (1855–1898): Life, Work, Contacts.* Ashgate. [2000] pp. 208. $79.95 ISBN 0 7546 0113 7.

Stoneman, Patsy, ed. *Emily Brontë: Wuthering Heights.* ColUP. [2000] pp. 208. pb $14.50 ISBN 0 2311 1920 8.

Storey, Graham, and Margaret Brown, eds. *The Letters of Charles Dickens*, vol xi: *1865–1867.* OUP. [2000] pp. 598. £70 ($135) ISBN 0 1981 2295 0.

Strick, James Edgar. *Sparks of Life: Darwinism and the Victorian Debates over Spontaneous Generation.* HarvardUP. [2000] pp. 302. $47.50 ISBN 0 6740 0292 X

Sumner, Rosemary. *A Route to Modernism: Hardy, Lawrence, Woolf.* St Martin's Press. [2000] pp. 228. £41.62 ($59.95) ISBN 0 3122 2423 0.

Suriano, Gregory R. *The Pre-Raphaelite Illustrators: The Published Graphic Art of the English Pre-Raphaelites and their Associates with Critical Biographical Essays and Illustrated Catalogues of the Artists' Engraved Works.* OakK. [2000] pp. 336. £42 ($49.95) ISBN 1 5845 6021 5.

Szumski, Bonnie, ed. *Readings on Tess of the D'Urbervilles.* Greenhaven. [2000] pp. 224. $32.45 ISBN 0 7377 0197 8.

Tarr, Rodger L., and Mark Engel, eds. *Thomas Carlyle. Sartor Resartus: The Life and Opinions of Herr Teufelsdrockh in Three Books.* UCalP. [2000] pp. cxxviii + 646. $60 ISBN 0 5202 0928 1.

Taylor, Andrew. *God's Fugitive: The Life of C.M. Doughty.* Flamingo. [2000] pp. 366. pb £8.99 ISBN 0 0063 8832 9.

Thomas, Jane. *Thomas Hardy, Femininity and Dissent: Reassessing the 'Minor' Novels.* Palgrave. [1998] pp. 172. $59.95 ISBN 0 3122 2049 9.

Thomas, Julia. *Victorian Narrative Painting.* Tate. [2000] pp. 111. pb £12.99 ISBN 1 8543 7318 8.

Thomas, Ronald R. *Detective Fiction and the Rise of Forensic Science.* CUP. [2000] pp. 361. £40 ISBN 0 5216 5303 7.

Thomas, William. *The Quarrel of Macaulay and Croker: Politics and History in the Age of Reform.* OUP. [2000] pp. 350. £45 ISBN 0 1982 0864 2.

Thompson, Brian. *A Monkey Among Crocodiles: The Disastrous Life of Mrs. Georgina Weldon*. HC. [2000] pp. 315. £19.99 ISBN 0 0025 7189 7.

Thompson, J. Lee. *Politicians, the Press, and Propaganda: Lord Northcliffe and the Great War, 1914–1918*. KSUP. [2000] pp. xii + 319. £32.95 ISBN 0 8733 8637 X.

Thormählen, Marianne. *The Brontës and Religion*. CUP. [2000] pp. 220. $59.95 ISBN 0 5216 6155 2.

Tredell, Nicolas, ed. *Charles Dickens. Great Expectations*. ColUP. [2000] pp. 208. $39.50 ISBN 0 2311 1924 0.

Tromp, Marlene. *The Private Rod: Marital Violence, Sensation, and the Law in Victorian Britain*. UPVirginia. [2000] pp. 289. $37.50 ISBN 0 8139 1949 5.

Tromp, Marlene, Pamela K. Gilbert and Aeron Haynie, eds. *Beyond Sensation: Mary Elizabeth Braddon in Context*. SUNYP. [2000] pp. 302. hb $59.50 ISBN 0 7914 4419 8, pb $19.95 ISBN 0 7914 4420 1.

Trotter, David. *Cooking with Mud: The Idea of Mess in Nineteenth-Century Art and Fiction*. OUP. [2000] pp. x + 340. £35 ISBN 0 1981 8503 0.

Tucker, Irene. *A Probable State: The Novel, the Contract, and the Jews*. UChicP. [2000] pp. xiv + 311. $42 ISBN 0 2265 1533 1.

Turner, Mark W. *Trollope and the Magazines: Gendered Issues in Mid-Victorian Britain*. St Martin's Press. [2000] pp. 280. $55 (£47.50) ISBN 0 3122 2176 2.

Waddams, S.M. *Sexual Slander in Nineteenth-Century England: Defamation in the Ecclesiastical Courts, 1815–1855*. UTorP. [2000] pp. xvi + 315. $75 ISBN 0 8020 4750 5.

Wagner-Lawlor, Jennifer A., ed. *The Victorian Comic Spirit: New Perspectives*. Ashgate. [2000] pp. xx + 252. £49.50 ISBN 0 7546 0016 5.

Ward, Mark E., and Ann Dinsdale. *A Guide to Historic Haworth and the Brontës*. Mulberry. [2000] pp. 85. $11.50 ISBN 1 9002 2906 4.

Wawn, Andrew. *The Vikings and the Victorians: Inventing the Old North in Nineteenth-Century Britain*. Brewer. [2000] pp. xiii + 434. £50 ($90) ISBN 0 8599 1575 1.

Weber, A.S., ed. *Nineteenth-Century Science: An Anthology*. Broadview. [2000] pp. xii + 500. pb $22.95 ISBN 1 5511 1208 6.

Weliver, Phyllis. *Women Musicians in Victorian Fiction, 1860–1900: Representations of Music, Science and Gender in the Leisured Home*. Ashgate. [2000] pp. 340. $79.95 ISBN 0 7546 0126 9.

Welsh, Alexander. *Dickens Redressed: The Art of 'Bleak House' and 'Hard Times'*. YaleUP. [2000] pp. 256. $30 ISBN 0 3000 8203 7.

Wheeler, Michael. *Ruskin's God*. CUP. [2000] pp. 322. £40 ISBN 0 5215 7414 5.

Wilcox, Scott. *Edward Lear and the Art of Travel*. YaleUP. [2000] pp. 190. pb $24.95 ISBN 0 3000 9554 6.

Willis, Chris, ed. *Mary Elizabeth Braddon: The Fatal Marriage and Other Stories*. Sensation. [2000] pp. 256. pb £35 ISBN 1 9025 8006 0.

Wise, Thomas, ed. *The Shakespeare Head Brontë: Bibliography of the Works of All Members of the Brontë Family and of Brontëana*, by John Alexander Symington. Ian Hodgkins. [2000] pp. 210. £42 ($65) ISBN 1 9064 6009 3.

Wolfreys, Julian, ed. *Thomas Hardy. The Mayor of Casterbridge*. Macmillan. [2000] pp. 224. hb £42.50 ISBN 0 3337 7754 9, pb £13.50 ISBN 0 3337 7755 7.

XIV

Modern Literature

JULIAN COWLEY, COLIN GRAHAM, LYNNE HAPGOOD, CHRIS
HOPKINS, DANIEL LEA, PAUL POPLAWSKI, JOHN NASH, JOHN
BRANNIGAN, MAGGIE B. GALE, MALCOLM PAGE, ALICE
ENTWISTLE AND FRAN BREARTON

This chapter has eight sections: 1. General; 2. Pre-1945 Fiction; 3. Post-1945
Fiction; 4. Pre-1950 Drama; 5. Post-1950 Drama; 6. Pre-1950 Poetry; 7. Post-1950
Poetry; 8. Irish Poetry. Section 1(a) is by Julian Cowley; section 1(b) is by Colin
Graham; section 2(a) is by Lynne Hapgood; section 2(b) is by Chris Hopkins;
sections 2(c–e) are by Daniel Lea; section 2(f) is by Paul Poplawski; section 2(g) is
by John Nash; section 3 is by John Brannigan; section 4 is by Maggie B. Gale;
section 5 is by Malcolm Page; section 6 is by Alice Entwistle; section 7 is by John
Brannigan; section 8 is by Fran Brearton. The section on Virginia Woolf has been
omitted this year, but will cover 2000–2001 publications in volume 82.

1. General

(a) British
Michael McKeon's imposing and important anthology *Theory of the Novel* is 'an
exercise in rebalancing'. Structuralist and post-structuralist narratologists are
pushed to the margins and emphasis falls upon theorists who have sought to
articulate 'the coherence of the novel genre as a historical phenomenon'. The
principal value of structuralism, for McKeon's purposes, is its usefulness in
dislodging partial, novel-centred views of narrative. This is exclusively a twentieth-
century collection, theorizing the novel as 'a modern phenomenon'. The first section
focuses upon genre theory; the second and third (drawing on Walter Benjamin,
Claude Lévi-Strauss, and Freud amongst others) address the origins of the novel.
Substantial statements by Georg Lukács, José Ortega y Gasset, and Mikhail Bakhtin
(the 'grand theorists') follow, then more recent revisions designed to provide 'a
more concrete or specific historicization of the novel's origins'. Ensuing sections
draw out sociocultural implications (including those pertaining to women, privacy,
and subjectivity) and engage with relevant epistemological and psychological
matters. The well-worn topic of 'realism' is handled with vitality, and is followed by

discussion of photography, film, and the novel that groups Henry James with Walter Benjamin and André Bazin. The concluding parts review the novel's inveterate claim to novelty (extending through Woolf's modernism to Alain Robbe-Grillet's postmodernism), and the genre's transportability from its west European locus of origin into Latin America, Africa, and Asia. McKeon's accompanying commentary, observing dialectical method (as he explains), elaborates its own 'syncretic theory of the novel'. This is a richly stimulating volume, an invaluable resource and challenging intervention for all serious researchers into the novel.

Critical discourse continues to promote pluralized conceptions of modernism, as may be seen from the essays collected in Stevens and Howlett, eds., *Modernist Sexualities*. Edith Ellis was an energetic feminist and minor novelist, who shared the sexological interests of her husband Havelock Ellis and argued optimistically for social and sexual experimentation. Jo-Ann Wallace takes Ellis's current obscurity to be illustrative of that repression which helps constitute familiar histories of modernism. Jason Edwards looks at Yeats's ideas about masturbation and homosexuality. Caroline Howlett seeks to retrieve suffragettes from the margins of 'the modernist scene'. Bridget Elliott examines the use of decorative practices in the work of painter Marie Laurencin as a means to rehabilitate decadent strategies towards criticism of traditional gender constructions. Morag Shiach investigates the typewriter as historical technology contributory to the emancipation of women. Con Coroneos ruminates suggestively on desire, closed systems, and the fate of the heart in modernism. Geoff Gilbert links adolescence and the avant-garde in the 'delinquent' figure of Wyndham Lewis. Pamela Thurschwell unpacks telling identifications made during the First World War by Henry James. Marianne DeKoven considers Stein and Woolf as public women concerned with feminine privacy and interiority. Melanie Taylor places Woolf's *Orlando* in relation to transsexual autobiography. Hugh Stevens writes on 'primitive' male–male bonding in Lawrence's *The Plumed Serpent*. There are also essays on Cather, McCullers, and Hemingway.

Michael J. Meyer has edited *Literature and Homosexuality* out of a conviction that gay and lesbian issues remain repressed 'even in the most modern and liberal of classrooms'. These essays were written in affirmation of the validity of alternative sexual choices and to make a case for equity between literary works that express those choices and texts that enshrine heterosexual values. Writing by the Americans Leslie Marmon Silko, Louise Erdrich, Alice Walker, Hart Crane, Gore Vidal, Tennessee Williams, John Rechy and James Baldwin, and by the Uruguayan Cristina Peri Rossi, is addressed. Roger Bowen discovers a challenge to sexual and racial taboos in Lawrence Durrell's *Alexandria Quartet*. Kathy J. Phillips examines Brecht's writings about homosexuality. Thomas March unpacks E.M. Forster's narration of homosexual experience within the mode of the fantastic in the Arcadian tale 'Little Imber', written in 1961. Thomas Peele contributes 'Queering *Mrs. Dalloway*', identifying homosexual desire in Woolf's novel. David Coad traces lesbian overtones in Mansfield's short stories.

Acknowledging that feminist scholarship has established the centrality of gender to current thinking about modernism, Gerald N. Izenberg points out, in *Modernism and Masculinity: Mann, Wedekind, Kandinsky through World War I*, that 'manhood in jeopardy' is a recurrent theme in early modernist art and literature. His aim in the book is to bring to light 'a subjective sense of masculinity endangered' that is rarely disclosed by standard accounts of the passage through crisis of the bourgeois ideal of masculinity in Europe at the start of the twentieth century. Izenberg investigates interrelationships between the work and lives of novelist Thomas Mann, playwright Frank Wedekind, and painter Wassily Kandinsky in order to propose unfamiliar connections between issues of masculine identity and modernist innovation. Detailed analyses address Wedekind and freedom, Mann and transcendence, and Kandinsky and abstraction, while depicting each of these men as caught between desire to assimilate 'the feminine' and a need to exert mastery over it. Each held an idealized femininity to embody 'both autonomous creative power and connection with the whole of being'. These localized case studies have implications, Izenberg argues, for our understanding of modernism more generally.

Given the restlessness of critical discourse on modernism in its desire for new meanings and refined distinctions, the task of creating a convenient introductory guide to reflect current understanding poses evident challenges. Peter Childs's *Modernism*, written for the New Critical Idiom series, struggles to find an appropriate level of discussion and to sustain an appropriate focus on this volatile topic. Childs opts to take Beckett's *Murphy* as 'an in some ways representative Modernist piece of writing' in an opening chapter that starts with dictionary definitions of 'romance', 'realism', and 'modernism'. The next section sketches the influential roles of Marx, Darwin, Nietzsche, Freud, Einstein, and Saussure, a conventional array of formative figures. Cursory overview of modernist cultural production follows, with writing organized by genre, painting by movement, plus brief mention of film. The final section, entitled 'Texts, Contexts, Intertexts', groups representative authors thematically. Mew, Mansfield, and D.H. Lawrence coincide under the heading 'Freedom and Gender'; Woolf, West, and Eliot under 'Identity and War'; Forster, Yeats, and Joyce under 'Symbolism and Language'; and James, Conrad, and Ford under 'Epistemology and Narration'. Childs observes that 'to develop a reasonable grasp of the subject there is of course no substitute for reading the Modernist writers themselves'. A more complex sense of the contested identity of those writers would be appropriate.

Caughie, ed., *Virginia Woolf in the Age of Mechanical Reproduction*, brings Bloomsbury into intriguing configuration with Walter Benjamin. Woolf and Benjamin are aligned as authors of critiques of commodity culture, urban spaces, and systemic ideologies. Their standing and significance as cultural commentators, and points of contact between them, are set out in essays by Leslie Kathleen Hankins and Sonita Sarker. Woolf's writing is shown, like Benjamin's, embedded in the early twentieth-century's volatile technological environment and correlative new formations of subjectivity. Melba Cuddy-Keane and Bonnie Kime Scott suggest ways to locate Woolf in relation to the 'New Aurality' of wireless and gramophone. Michael Tratner identifies the filmic qualities of *Between the Acts*. Holly Henry explores Woolf's interest in telescopes and cosmology. Makiko Minow-Pinkney takes the motor car as focal point for her investigation of relationships between Woolf's writing and 'the new technological conditions of the age'. Jane Garrity places *Vogue* in relation to modernism and analyses Woolf's ambivalent involvement with the magazine. Maggie Humm revealingly looks into the photographic interests of this great-niece of Julia Margaret Cameron. Mark Hussey muses on Woolf in the age of hypertext. This collection affirms Woolf's usefulness to cultural studies and to Benjamin's continuing relevance to intelligent discussion of mass culture.

Virginia Woolf in the Age of Mechanical Reproduction is a volume in the Border Crossings series, whose editor Daniel Albright exercises his own considerable interdisciplinary skills in *Untwisting the Serpent: Modernism in Music, Literature and Other Arts*, an erudite yet lively study that revises Lessing's *Laokoon* towards analysis of modernist multimedia projects. A division is observed here 'not as a tension between the temporal arts and the spatial, but as a tension between arts that try to retain the propriety, the apartness, of their private media, and arts that try to lose themselves in some pan-aesthetic whole'. Albright launches probes into modernist collaborations such as Stravinsky's work with the Ballets Russes, Weill's creative partnership with Brecht, Cocteau's theatrical spectacles and Apollinaire's *Les Mamelles de Tiresias*. Pound's *Cantos* are considered in relation to Noh drama, and reference is made to Woolf and D.H. Lawrence. The eurhythmic exercises of Émile Jacques Dalcroze are regarded as 'part of the Modernist urge to restore corporeality to art'. Albright's assured trajectories through the field testify to impressive scholarship and produce some richly suggestive readings as well as a clearly delineated argument. He is especially enlightening in his discussion of music (often an area of weakness in comparative studies).

Editors Howard J. Booth and Nigel Rigby claim that *Modernism and Empire* is 'the first book-length study that seeks to explore the pervasive but complex interrelations between British colonialism and the modern movement'. Certainly it offers some fresh angles. After Patrick Williams's exposition of theoretical issues, Rod Edmond traces the influence of degenerationist ideas in imperialist and modernist discourse. Helen Carr shows imagist poetics emerging from 'questioning of Western representations and Western superiority, emerging in a climate which took distrust of the British imperialism very much for granted'. Elleke Boehmer investigates how Leonard Woolf (in his writings on Ceylon) and W.B. Yeats (in his enthusiasm for Tagore) responded to challenges posed by cultural otherness. Janet Montefiore makes a case for acknowledging Kipling as 'an unrecognised modernist' as well as a conservative imperialist. C.L. Innes differentiates Yeats and Joyce from British and European modernists and connects them to post-colonial writers. Máire ní Fhlathúin reveals the anti-colonial modernism of Patrick Pearse. John Nash writes on Joyce's deployment of newspapers towards a critique of imperialism in *Ulysses*. Howard J. Booth looks at the fluctuating expectations that arose from D.H. Lawrence's search for regenerative resources in non-European cultures. Nigel Rigby discloses Sylvia Townsend Warner's subversion of imperialist ideologies in her modernist fantasy *Mr Fortune's Maggot*. Abdulrazak Gurnah addresses Elspeth Huxley's *The Flame Trees of Thika* and other settler writing in Kenya. Bill Ashcroft and John Salter dislocate an imposed modernist classification in order to identify 'creative articulation of Australian difference' by twentieth-century artists and writers. Mark Williams examines adaptations of modernism towards a bicultural dialogue within New Zealand literature in his 'Mansfield in Maoriland'.

Angela Smith has written *Katherine Mansfield* for the Literary Lives series. Mansfield's development as a writer of short stories is traced through a matrix formed from issues arising out of her colonial identity, gender, and failing health. Her authorial identity is delineated in relation to varied facets of her experience, including marriage to John Middleton Murry, involvement with the arts magazine

Rhythm, and exposure to Wilde's aestheticism, Bergsonian philosophy, Fauvist painting, Arthur Symons's writings on symbolism, A.R. Orage's Nietzschean vision, and the Russian Ballet. Smith observes a chronological framework and brief analyses of key stories illustrate Mansfield's literary positioning of her self.

David Wykes has contributed *Evelyn Waugh* to the 'Literary Lives' series. It is much closer to straight biography than the Mansfield volume, and argues that as a novelist Waugh's strength was not invention but embroidered transformation of lived experience; his 'dependence on his own history was almost total'. Wykes critically surveys the oeuvre, and recounts Waugh's struggle against the literary reputations of his father and brother, his education and brief flirtation with modernism, his youthful taste for travel and life-long susceptibility to privileged social standing, his interest in cinema, the failure of his first marriage, his conversion to Roman Catholicism, and his war service. These are taken to be formative influences upon Waugh's literary identity, as considerable as the persistent influence of Gibbon and Dickens.

In *A Route to Modernism*, Rosemary Sumner traces the contours of a concern for 'the undefinable, the unanalyzable, the unresolved' that runs through fiction by Hardy, Lawrence and Woolf. Sumner argues that this is a current in modernist literature distinct from the experimentation of Joyce and Stein yet equally significant in terms of formal innovation. She indicates how the shared concern of her chosen three authors for 'the unknown, the unconscious' led to rejection of conventional plotting in favour of rhythmic forms adjacent to poetry and music. These are precariously balanced between awareness of chaos and desire for harmony, loyalty to the everyday and acknowledgement of the limits of common understanding. Sumner describes the emergence of modernism in a range of Hardy's texts, identifying him as a pivotal figure between the nineteenth and twentieth centuries. Her study looks forward rather than back (Schopenhauer receives just one brief mention). Hardy's fiction is considered in relation to Beckett's absurdity and (provocatively) to surrealism and (still more recklessly) to composer John Cage's predilection for indeterminacy. More substantial connections are made to Lawrence's exploratory achievement in *The Rainbow* and *Women in Love*, and to Woolf's advances towards communication of the inexpressible. After following her chosen route, Sumner concludes that 'modernism is not a fixed destination'.

Hapgood and Paxton, eds., *Outside Modernism: In Pursuit of the English Novel* (also reviewed in section 2(*a*) of this chapter), is a stimulating collection of essays employing various critical approaches drawn into alignment by shared understanding of 'realism and modernism as terms which describe literary techniques rather than define conflictual literary movements'. English novels often held to represent opposing sets of aesthetic assumptions are here brought into significantly closer relationship within the early twentieth century's 'nexus of social, psychological and literary change'. The basic contention is that the 'modern', as it was perceived between 1900 and 1930, was not exclusively the province of high modernism. Hapgood investigates Galsworthy's depiction of suburban life in *The Man of Property*; Paxton locates Forster's fictional India between modernist aestheticism and popular colonial novels, such as those of Maud Diver. John Rignall challenges the orthodox position that the First World War marked a disintegration of European values that necessitated modernism's disjunctive forms. He examines narrative coherence in relation to the persistence of communal life in fiction by

Frederic Manning and R.H. Mottram. Arguing that 'modernism begins in the realm of theology', Robert L. Caserio deconstructs Chesterton's *The Man Who Was Thursday* to elucidate anarchist terrorism's putative 'convergence with the perplexities of modern epistemology and belief'. Richard Dellamora addresses the 'vernacular modernism' of Radclyffe Hall, which 'splits and mixes genres' to tackle problems of gender politics within ostensibly conservative narrative structures. Ann Ardis discovers a self-reflexive commentary on aesthetic production in D.H. Lawrence's treatment of music-hall theatre in *The Lost Girl*. William Greenslade argues that mythologizing of nature in work by Stevenson, Kenneth Grahame, Edward Thomas and Forster serves a critical, even disruptive, engagement with national identity. John Lucas groups Sylvia Townsend Warner, Patrick Hamilton and Henry Green as novelists whose apparent realism is suffused with technical and political radicalism. Lyn Pykett attends to Rebecca West and May Sinclair, writers who contributed to the defining critical discourse of modernism. Pykett illustrates indebtedness in their own fiction to the New Woman novel of the 1880s and 1890s and shows modernism in negotiation with writing from the immediate past.

In a 1918 review of Dorothy Richardson's *Pilgrimage*, May Sinclair made the first application to literature of the term 'stream of consciousness'. Since Virago revived Sinclair's novels *Mary Olivier: A Life* [1919] and *Life and Death of Harriett Frean* [1922] she has herself been recognized as a pioneering modernist. Although those novels remain central to the picture, Suzanne Raitt's biography *May Sinclair: A Modern Victorian* reveals more fully this writer from the generation preceding Richardson, Woolf and Mansfield, a best-selling author during the decade before the First World War, with an output including more than twenty novels and a book on the Brontës. Raitt portrays Sinclair as an intensely private, somewhat isolated individual, who nonetheless knew celebrated literary figures including Hardy, Ford, Pound, Charlotte Mew, H.D. and Richard Aldington. Raitt's focus falls on Sinclair's development as writer and intellectual. Her first popular success, *The Divine Fire* [1904], is a critique of the bookselling industry. Starting with *The Three Sisters* [1914] the impact of psychoanalysis was registered in her fiction. Brief first-hand exposure to warfare in Belgium fed significantly into her writing. She enthusiastically investigated the tenets of imagism. Raitt says that Sinclair regarded 'creative genius' as 'a masculine force', and shows how this and other factors complicated her feminism. Born in 1863, Sinclair became a 'modern'. A groundbreaking life of this intriguing author, by T.E.M. Boll, was published in 1973. Raitt's sequel adds some new details and identifies centres of enduring interest in Sinclair's fiction.

Angela K. Smith's anthology *Women's Writing of the First World War* (also reviewed in section 2(a) of this chapter) was compiled primarily 'to reclaim the Great War as an arena of female experience, and to rediscover some of the written material which articulates the experience'. Materials, including some composed with hindsight, are drawn from fiction, diaries, letters, and documentary texts, juxtaposed to convey a range of responses to events, public attitudes, and political decisions. Some of the more than fifty writers are well-known literary figures (such as Virginia Woolf, Mrs Humphry Ward, Radclyffe Hall, F. Tennyson Jesse and May Sinclair); some are public figures (such as Cynthia Asquith, Beatrice Webb, Christabel, Emmeline and Sylvia Pankhurst); others are more obscure (a Belgian nun, a Scarborough schoolgirl, a middle-aged diarist from Kent). Although the extracts are ordered chronologically in sections, from the outbreak of war through conscription and loss to Armistice, with Smith's observations introducing each section, in effect they form a mosaic depicting the wide-ranging impact of the conflict upon women far away from the trenches and in supporting roles near the front.

Angela K. Smith's *The Second Battlefield: Women, Modernism and the First World War* (also reviewed in section 2(*a*) of this chapter) is divided into two parts. The first investigates personal documents and published records of women who were actively involved in the First World War, on some form of military service or offering medical aid. The second looks at modernist writing by women that, according to Smith's thesis, has roots in such war experience or personal accounts of it. There are readings of *Not So Quiet ...* by Evadne Price, H.D.'s *Bid Me To Live*, May Sinclair's *The Tree of Heaven*, Rose Macaulay's *Non-Combatants and Others*, Rose Allatini's *Despised and Rejected*, Katherine Mansfield's 'An Indiscreet Journey', Rebecca West's *The Return of the Soldier*, and Enid Bagnold's *The Happy Foreigner*. Smith aims to shed light on an interface between the writing of wartime experiences, conditioned by peculiar private and public forms of constraint, and self-conscious literary composition. The diary form is viewed as a having distinct affinities with fragmented modernist narrative. So are nurses' hospital narratives, such as Bagnold's *A Diary without Dates* and Ellen La Motte's *The Backwash of War*, which register a climate of dehumanization and crisis. Mary Borden's aesthetically self-aware collection of hospital sketches and stories, *The Forbidden Zone*, occupies a special place within this study, in which neglected primary source materials are retrieved, and an expanded conception of modernism is proposed.

The recent surge of critical interest in writing by Scottish women continues with Anderson and Christianson, eds., *Scottish Women's Fiction, 1920s to 1960s: Journeys into Being*. Each essay is given over to close reading of a particular text, and the volume as a whole conveys the diversity of approaches to writing novels represented by Catherine Carswell, Willa Muir, Nan Sheperd, Naomi Mitchison, Nancy Brysson Morrison, Jessie Kesson, and Muriel Spark. A surprise addition to this list is Rebecca West, claimed as a Scot on account of her maternal ancestry. Each of the editors contributes two chapters: Anderson writes on visual art in Carswell's *Open the Door!* and feminine space in West's Scottish novel *The Judge*; Christianson writes on 'the dreaming of realities' in Muir's *Imagined Corners* and ambiguous certainty in Spark's *The Ballad of Peckham Rye*. Sheperd's *The Quarry Wood* and *The Weatherhouse* are used by Gillian Carter and Alison Lumsden respectively to examine issues of regional and personal identity. Margaret Elphinstone finds 'the impulse of modernism' in Mitchison's *The Corn King and the Spring Queen*. Beth Dickson looks at the treatment of repression in Muir's *Mrs Ritchie*. Margery Palmer McCulloch identifies the 'poetic spirit' in Morrison's *The Gowk Storm*. Kesson's literary distance from the sentimental Kailyard tradition is confirmed in essays by Glenda Norquay and Isobel Murray. To conclude, Jennie Rubio offers a brief selective bibliography of writers whose work qualifies for inclusion in the volume yet does not appear there.

Nico Israel's *Outlandish: Writing between Exile and Diaspora* is a sophisticated study of writing that occurs 'between the perceived existential stability of the individual and nation and the claims put forth for a migrancy that reroutes or revises them'. Israel's investigation into the perception and figuring of displacement comprises three case studies or 'textual moments': Conrad, Adorno, and Rushdie. He analyses the imagined geography of Conrad's 'Amy Foster', the 'outlandishly overdetermined' *Heart of Darkness*, and the 'exilic bildungsroman' *Lord Jim*, ponders Adorno in Los Angeles via *Minima Moralia* and the chapter on anti-Semitism in *Dialectic of Enlightenment*, and reappraises Rushdie's early fiction in light of 'the so-called Rushdie Affair'. The ramifications of Israel's readings extend to relationships between modernism and postmodernism and, beyond that, to fundamental issues of representability and 'the mutually constitutive complexity of subjectivity, language, place, and history'.

The essays in Todd and Flora, eds., *Theme Parks, Rainforests and Sprouting Wastelands: European Essays on Theory and Performance in Contemporary British Fiction*, originated as conference papers delivered at the University of Glasgow in 1995.The field is British fiction since 1950, but there is no central theme or dominant critical approach. Silvia Caporale Bizzini reads Jenny Diski's *Rainforest* with assistance from Roland Barthes; Catherine Bernard brings Michel Serres and Maurice Blanchot to bear upon Bruce Chatwin's work; Peter Conradi introduces Lacan into his discussion of Angus Wilson's theatricality; Avril Horner and Sue Zlosnik's consideration of Daphne du Maurier's Frenchness draws on Homi Bhabha. Three essays look at Doris Lessing; two are devoted to A.S. Byatt; other authors under scrutiny include Michael Crichton, Salman Rushdie, Charles Palliser, William Golding, and Angela Carter. Other essays tackle issues with which recent writing has engaged such as myth, utopianism (including reference to the novels of Margaret Elphinstone), historiographical metafiction, and the Victorian inheritance of postmodern writing.

John Kucich and Diane F. Sadoff convened the cultural critics who contribute to *Victorian Afterlife* in order to stimulate 'discussion of postmodernism's privileging of the Victorian as its historical "other"'. John McGowan's 'Modernity and Culture, the Victorians and Cultural Studies' interrogates 'the models of meaning, knowledge, and the social that zeitgeist thinking implies'. He indicates how '"modernity" and "culture" between them organize a huge amount of our intellectual landscape'. Jennifer Green-Lewis examines how current taste for Victorian photography discloses postmodern desire. Shelton Waldrep examines recent use made of Oscar Wilde in the media and academic discourse. Mary A. Favret addresses issues of fidelity in modern adaptations of Jane Austen's novels. Susan Lurie considers film-maker Jane Campion's revision of Henry James. Judith Roof discerns a new kind of imperialism in the appropriation by computer interface technology of Victorian exhibition and display techniques. Ian Baucom locates Paul Muldoon's poetry in relation to recent histories of the Famine and of Irish emigration. Simon Gikandi considers C.L.R. James as a product of and adherent to colonial Victorianism, transforming values of colonial conquest into foundational narratives of black self-determination. William Gibson and Bruce Sterling's 'steampunk' novel *The Difference Engine* and Tom Stoppard's play *Arcadia* come under Jay Clayton's scrutiny as instances of anachronism transformed into a kind of knowledge. Laurie Langbauer surveys recent feminist scholarship devoted to nineteenth-century Britain. Hilary M. Schor examines A.S. Byatt's 'incarnation as a Victorian' in her fiction. Kali Israel considers the recurrence of Carroll's Alice and Nabokov's Lolita in relation to current anxieties about the sexualized child. Ronald R. Thomas assesses the significance of cinematic versions of Stoker's *Dracula*.

Nancy Armstrong's postscript draws broad yet telling comparison between Victorian and postmodern cultural horizons. *Victorian Afterlife* also has intriguing implications for attempts to understand those years of the twentieth century that its wide-ranging essays exclude from consideration.

After establishing the difficulty of pinning down 'SF' in a tidy formulation, Adam Roberts, in *Science Fiction*, opts to focus upon 'difference' as a key defining aspect of the genre. His contention is that 'in societies such as ours where Otherness is often demonised, SF can pierce the constraints of this ideology by circumventing the conventions of traditional fiction'. Roberts outlines a history of science fiction that harks back to *Gilgamesh* and *Paradise Lost*, assumes its modern guise with Verne and Wells, and continues beyond *Star Wars*. He indicates significant issues of gender and race that arise during engagement with science fiction texts, and examines the metaphoric use of technology to figure alterity.

Malcolm Yorke's *Mervyn Peake: My Eyes Mint Gold* is an enthusiastic and solidly researched biography that charts key events in the life of the idiosyncratic painter, illustrator, poet, playwright and novelist between his birth in 1911 and his death in 1968. Not content simply to accumulate facts, anecdotes and recollections, Yorke is keen to recognize stimuli for Peake's art, especially for his Titus Groan trilogy. The 'enclosed world of privilege' Peake experienced as the son of a physician on missionary service in China is found to foreshadow the rarefied climate of Gormenghast Castle. The fate of China's boy emperor, held virtual captive then forced to live as a private citizen, is perceived as parallel to the fate of Titus Groan. Settings and names in Dickens's novels, consumed by Peake as a boy, reverberated into his own fictional world. A harrowing visit to Belsen necessarily deepened and modified Peake's awareness of the nature of evil and his approach to its depiction. This commitment to detect immediate and remote influences may diminish the book's appeal for some readers, but it does help to ensure that the account remains attentive to the terms and conditions of Peake's artistic progress.

Stark, ed., *The Novel in Anglo-German Context: Cultural Cross-Currents and Affinities*, collects papers given at a conference in Leeds in 1997. Its scope is broad, but the key concern is cultural cross-fertilization. There are three main divisions, corresponding to the last three centuries. 'Eighteenth Century' opens with Hermann J. Real's discussion of early German translations of Swift's *Gulliver's Travels*, and closes with Daniel Hall's account of the spread of the 'Gothic tide' across the two countries. 'Nineteenth Century' opens with Rosemary Ashton's authoritative 'The Figure of the German Professor in Nineteenth-Century English Fiction'. Walter Scott looms large in what follows. The section ends with Diane Milburn's uncovering of Anglo-German cross-currents in Stoker's *Dracula*. 'Twentieth Century' starts with Elmar Schenkel's intriguing, and ostensibly unlikely, coupling of G.K. Chesterton and Nietzsche. Andreas Kramer elucidates complexities of nationality in Wyndham Lewis's *Tarr*. Peter Skrine retrieves from obscurity *The Woman of Knockaloe*, a novel of the First World War by the Manx writer Hall Caine, dedicatee of *Dracula*. Holger Klein offers a survey in the form of notes towards a comparative study of novels depicting diminished figures in urban landscapes. J.M. Ritchie looks at writing by German and Austrian exiles in Britain. Joachim Schwend homes in on stereotyped images of Germany in David Lodge's *Out of the Shelter*. Osman Durrani looks at 'campus novels'. Ute Daprich-Barrett identifies links between feminism and magical realism in fiction by Irmtraud

Morgner and Angela Carter. Sabine Hotto's discussion of fictional rewritings of literary history draws on A.S. Byatt, Peter Ackroyd, Sigrid Damm, and Christa Wolf. David Horrocks and David A. Green both trace parallels between Günter Grass and Salman Rushdie. Gundula Sharman draws a more oblique line between Goethe and John Banville. Harald Husemann examines fiction depicting German invasion or infiltration of Britain. Two papers address the teaching of novels in German and British schools. The volume accommodates contributions in both languages, a brief English abstract preceding each essay in German. André Bucher's study of the German reception of *Ulysses* falls into this category.

Francis Mulhern's lucid, useful volume *Culture/Metaculture* examines '"culture" as a topic in twentieth-century debate', paying critical attention to positions assumed by practitioners of *Kulturkritik* such as Thomas Mann, Julian Benda, Ortega y Gasset and F.R. Leavis, shapers of Cultural Studies such as Raymond Williams, Richard Hoggart and Stuart Hall, and contemporary participants such as Todd Gitlin, Jim McGuigan and the controversial populist John Fiske. The important role played by the study of literature in the formation of this discourse is repeatedly highlighted, and the input of literary writers such as Woolf, Orwell, and Eliot is made evident. Mulhern's contribution to the debate argues that the 'predominant tendency' of Cultural Studies (increasingly devoted to 'the popular') has been to counter the specific social values of *Kulturkritik* (distrustful of the masses) 'while retaining their deep form', coordinated around the terms 'culture', 'authority' and 'politics'. Mulhern airs the question whether contemporary populism signals the emergence of 'organic intellectuals' (as projected by Stuart Hall) or a proliferation of fans and 'bimbos' (using Meaghan Morris's dismissive term), and concludes by identifying a persistent 'utopian impulse', in Cultural Studies as in *Kulturkritik*, which seeks to reconcile culture and politics 'by dissolving political reason itself'.

Many hours of assiduous research have evidently gone to the making of *The Pub In Literature: England's Altered State*. Steven Earnshaw undertakes 'a crawl through the drinking places of English literary history', starting inevitably with Chaucer's Tabard inn. Most of the hostelries can be anticipated: the taverns and alehouses of Langland, Skelton, Shakespeare, Pepys, Fielding, Goldsmith, and Dickens. Twentieth-century examples are found on less well trodden byways: the pubs of Arthur Morrison, A.E. Coppard, John Hampson and Patrick Hamilton. Eliot and Orwell also feature and, with greater predictability, this 'history of English literature as seen through the bottom of a glass' closes with Martin Amis's *London Fields*. Earnshaw endeavours to derive social-historical insights from these drinking-houses and their manner of depiction. He raises issues of literary decorousness, especially with regard to Ned Ward's ribald late seventeenth-century work *The London Spy*. English national identity and gender matters are also addressed. The account grows appropriately congested, favouring discursive affability above rigorous theoretical elaboration.

Pure Pleasure collects brief essays written for *The Sunday Times* by John Carey, Merton Professor of English at Oxford University. A pithy defence of reading prefaces his choice of the twentieth century's fifty 'most enjoyable books', poetry as well as prose, captured in snapshots designed to entice non-specialist browsers. Constraints were imposed during the selection process: only one book per author and roughly the same number representing each decade (although Keith Douglas's *Alamein to Zem Zem* is the sole volume from the 1940s). Carey starts with Conan

Doyle's *The Hound of the Baskervilles* [1902], 'one of the formative myths of the century', and ends with Graham Swift's *Last Orders* [1996], a novel whose 'hero is the English language as spoken by ordinary people'. Some books merit inclusion on account of their self-evident intelligence, others because they are haunting. Canonical heavyweight texts are by and large avoided, although with rare exceptions, such as William Empson's *Seven Types of Ambiguity*, the list holds few surprises. Media pundit Clive James is present but there is no Proust or Faulkner; the work of both writers falls into the category of books which Carey dislikes or has not been able to finish. A short concluding report dips into the correspondence Carey received from readers of the newspaper. For academic readers, *Pure Pleasure* will immediately offer itself as a case study in humanistic values and the formation of literary taste.

Elizabeth Rottenberg has translated Maurice Blanchot's brief, intense literary narrative *The Instant of My Death* [1994]. It is accompanied by *Demeure: Fiction and Testimony*, her translation of Jacques Derrida's subtle musings upon Blanchot, literature, and testimony, initially delivered at a colloquium in Louvain in 1995. A short postscript presents Derrida's prickly riposte to 'rantings' against him published in the *Times Literary Supplement*.

(b) Irish

Criticism of Irish literature has been transforming over the past decade, becoming more exploratory, expanding its canon, and beginning to theorize itself. It is tempting to see Declan Kiberd's *Irish Classics*, a monumental follow-up to *Inventing Ireland*, as the major publication of the year. But in the longer term it may be the millennial originality of Mathews, ed., *New Voices in Irish Criticism*, which signifies the real changes taking place within the discipline. The book is a collection of papers from the first New Voices in Irish Criticism conference, held in 1999. The conference, brought about under the academic sponsorship of Declan Kiberd and Edna Longley, recognized a logjam which had developed in access to any public forum for doctoral students. The 'new voices' collected here are a disparate but energetic collection, covering old topics in new ways and in some cases pushing into entirely new areas of study. The literary revival, that staple foundational movement of the twentieth century, is given a fresh look in an excellent section on 'Politics and Revival', which includes the editor P.J. Mathews's essay, 'The Irish Revival: A Re-appraisal' which is 'pitched against the orthodoxy that the period was a purely mystical affair of high culture characterised by a preoccupation with a backward-looking Celtic spirituality, a nostalgia for Gaelic Ireland and an obsessive anti-modern traditionalism' (p. 12). Gregory Dobbins interlinks the writings of James Connolly with those of the literary revival to argue that 'Connolly's work provides a critical wedge in which there is the desire to dialectically progress beyond into something else' (p. 12). And Selina Guinness's essay, 'The Year of the Undead: 1898', considers the commemoration of the United Irishmen's rebellion of 1798 as a time 'when the discourse of revival was caught in one frame between two supernatural images, the phoenix and the vampiric Cathleen' (p. 27). The sense of thinking anew, and the restless desire to find new ways of seeing the formation of Irish literary discourse, apparent in these three essays find echoes in other chapters of this substantial and important book. Kathy Cremin, for example, in her essay 'Satisfaction Guaranteed? Reading Irish Women's Popular Fiction', sees popular fiction by and for women as marking the 'changed status of women in Irish society and history' against 'Ireland's historical construction as a feminised and maternal nation' (p. 83). Moynagh Sullivan takes a wider view of a similar set of theoretical concerns about gender in her subtle and convincing essay 'Feminism, Postmodernism and the Subjects of Irish and Women's Studies', which identifies how Irish studies has salved its conscience about the role of women, as participants and signifiers, within its own boundaries, by '"quarantining" … women's writing into a separate space, and into a sub-category' (p. 250). Such confidence in not accepting the limits set by the discipline in which the contributors are 'new voices' makes this book the most refreshing intervention in Irish studies for many years.

The dynamic energies of the New Voices project will take some time to filter into the wider language and interests of criticism of twentieth-century Irish literary studies. While New Voices was creating an academic space for those entering the field, Declan Kiberd's *Irish Classics* fascinatingly continued the popular success of *Inventing Ireland*, showing that, in Ireland and beyond, there is a market outside the academy for well-written, accessible and opinionated Irish literary criticism. The main thesis of *Irish Classics* is that the fortunes of the Irish and English languages in Ireland 'were utterly connected over more than five centuries, for all the antagonism between them' (p. xi). The book's examination of twentieth-century writing includes chapters on Lady Gregory and Synge's *The Aran Islands*, and an excellent chapter on Joyce's *Ulysses* and newspapers. At times, especially with the twentieth-century material, Kiberd's conviction that there was a ceaseless interplay across the two linguistic traditions can seem a little forced. *Irish Classics* also knows and uses its own power to gently irritate by seeming to set up a canon of 'classic' texts only to be idiosyncratic in its choices and absurdly selective in its coverage, while also being very long. Nevertheless, Kiberd at his best is a great writer of critical prose, and his own form of quiet comedy is often underestimated by his detractors. *Irish Classics* struggles a little to achieve coherence, and because of that, and its twining of the two languages, it may not gain the status which *Inventing Ireland* has. In many ways, though, it is a much more provocative book, and time will tell whether its central linguistic thesis is taken up with more seriousness by scholars following on from Kiberd.

Two important reference books for Irish literary studies appeared in 2000. Useful for students is Welch, ed., *The Concise Oxford Companion to Irish Literature*, which is a pared-down version of the previous *Oxford Companion to Irish Literature* [1996]. Also for a student market, but with an implicit critical agenda of how the shape of twentieth-century Irish literature should look, is David Pierce, ed., *Irish Writing in the Twentieth Century: A Reader*. This anthology, divided into sections by decade and running to 1,351 pages, sets out to provide students with a comprehensive range of Irish texts while remaining within the student budget. Given that only the *Field Day Anthology of Irish Writing* [1991] has such a vast array of material and is priced beyond what the average reader could afford, the book is well timed and carefully conceived. *Irish Writing in the Twentieth Century* has an admirable agenda which is in the most basic of senses 'historicist'. Its broadly chronological ordering is complemented by the 'Critical and Documentary' and 'Imaginative' sections into which each decade's-worth of writing is split. The first of these sections tends to be the more useful. Pierce often makes choices which succinctly draw together and exemplify the major debates taking place. The section on the first ten years of the twentieth century, for example, has extracts from Standish James O'Grady, Yeats, Arthur Griffith, Synge, John Eglinton and Frederick Ryan. The cumulative effect is to give an eclectic sense of relatively shared terms of dispute and interest, though occasionally one would wish that Pierce had chosen to follow particular debates rather than throw the net so wide. The advantage here is that Pierce always has an eye on the literary in the context of cultural politics. The fact that he never loses sight of Irish America's contribution to Irish debates is an important reminder to students and readers of the often forgotten diasporic nature of cultural exchange about Ireland. The anthology's 'Imaginative' sections are again judicious in their material, though they suffer from their necessary brevity, so that extracts of novels only are included. The two most obvious omissions from the book, much commented on by reviewers, are, first, the missing sections from Joyce's *Ulysses*, which were physically excised due to a copyright dispute with the Joyce estate, and, second, its relative dearth of women writers (replicating, though not by any means to the same extent, the lack of attention to women's writing in the *Field Day Anthology of Irish Writing*).

In terms of broad critical and theoretical assessments of twentieth-century Irish writing, one of the most notable books of the year was Conor McCarthy's *Modernisation, Crisis and Culture in Ireland, 1969–1992*. The execution and content of the book are perhaps not quite so comprehensive as the title suggests they might be, but nevertheless McCarthy's overall thesis is that 'modernisation' is not anathema to the concept of nation, since the ideology of nation 'draws on Enlightenment ideas of progress, liberation, co-operation and equality' (p. 17). McCarthy makes this argument because he feels the credibility of Irish nationalism to have been under an intellectual cloud. His villains are revisionist historians and critics, though to his credit McCarthy does try to map revisionism as a pervasive set of ideas which have affected thinking in general rather than a position to which allegiances have been explicitly pledged (his final chapter on 'Intellectual Politics: Edna Longley and Seamus Deane' perhaps edges closer to *ad hominem* criticism than is necessary). The main chapters of the book are incisive, though in their coverage of writers such as John Banville, Brian Friel and Dermot Bolger (and film-makers Neil Jordan, Bob Quinn and Pat Murphy in a single chapter) there was an opportunity missed to broaden out McCarthy's social and conceptual concerns beyond the work of individuals and into generic and social change. This modernizing Ireland might have been better depicted by allowing for a broader brush.

John Banville, a figure rightly placed as central to Irish writing and intellectual life in McCarthy's book, is also discussed by Joseph McMinn in his essay 'Versions of Banville: Versions of Modernism' (in Harte and Parker, eds., *Contemporary Irish Fiction: Themes, Tropes, Theories*). McMinn's essay interestingly suggests that Banville's prose techniques begin with a formally modernist aesthetic, but play out in their own characters the extension of this style to a point at which Banville's central personae, 'such as Newton, Kepler and Copernicus might be read as unwitting, even unwilling deconstructionists' (p. 86). The argument of McMinn's essay then takes a useful turn towards gender issues and tries to untangle the threads of novelist and narrator to show that there is 'a self-critical kind of misogyny within Banville's fiction' (p. 95). Other essays in the same book include Antoinette Quinn's 'New Noises from the Woodshed: The Novels of Emma Donoghue', which gives much-needed attention to an important Irish woman writer, and Richard Kirkland's 'Bourgeois Redemptions: The Fictions of Glenn Patterson and Robert McLiam Wilson', which is by far the most sophisticated critique yet of these 'new' Northern Irish novelists. The originality in Kirkland's take on these novelists is in not automatically celebrating their young liberal credentials but in seeing their narratives as caught in the world which they satirize: 'bourgeois fiction often constructs a site of ideology—understood strictly as false consciousness—against which the formal structures of the work rebel' (p. 217). Such scepticism about the role of the novelist in Northern Irish society is echoed in Richard Haslam's essay, '"The Pose Arranged and Lingered Over": Visualizing the "Troubles"' (also in Harte and Parker, eds.). Haslam begins with William Carleton's 'Wild Goose Lodge' as a model for Irish depiction of political violence, noting how Carleton's story falls back on the pictorial to render terror fictional, and he then goes on to discuss Bernard MacLaverty's *Cal* and Eoin MacNamee's *Resurrection Man* in the same terms. Haslam ends with what sound like harsh words for MacNamee's much-lauded novel: '*Resurrection Man* is undeniably an innovative and technically accomplished work. However, by refracting the actions and beliefs of the Shankill Butchers through the lens of "a dark and thrilling beauty", the novel does further violence to the Butchers' real-life victims' (p. 208). This is ethically opinionated criticism, which is refreshing in its frankness and its refusal to be swept away by the shock value of MacNamee's novel.

MacNamee's *Resurrection Man* is also discussed in Dermot McCarthy's essay 'Belfast Babel: Postmodern Lingo in Eoin MacNamee's *Resurrection Man*' (*IUR* 30:i[2000] 132–48): this entire issue of *Irish University Review* was devoted to contemporary Irish fiction. McCarthy begins his discussion with the kind of anxiety about the novel which ends Haslam's essay: 'What's the point of such self-conscious self-promotion?' (p. 132). McCarthy, however, finds himself eventually convinced that MacNamee's novel need not be read in the morally resistant way that Haslam's reading comes around to. Instead, McCarthy suggests that MacNamee himself recognizes that the central character, Victor, is 'empty, ephemeral, and disposable, divorced from the referents of community, history, and historical identity' (p. 148). Other articles in this special issue include Anne Fogarty's 'Uncanny Families: Neo-Gothic Motifs and the Theme of Social Change in Contemporary Irish Women's Fiction' (*IUR* 30:i[2000] 59–81). Fogarty notes that recent criticism has accepted the prominence of women in Irish fiction, and discusses a series of contemporary novels in order to consider 'the ways in which their texts respond to and are embedded in the prevailing public debates about the recent revolutionary and unprecedented alterations in Irish society' (p. 62).

Criticism of Irish drama was given a new lease of life in 2000 by the advent of a new, indigenous theatre studies press, Carysfort. One of it first publications is Jordan, ed., *Theatre Stuff: Critical Essays on Contemporary Irish Theatre*. *Theatre Stuff* is a much-needed and lively collection of interventions which, taken as a whole, see theatre in Ireland as more than a literary enterprise. The book is a useful mixture of essays which discuss individual playwrights and more general surveys of particular aspects of theatre. Fintan O'Toole, in 'Irish Theatre: The State of the Art', and Bruce Arnold, in 'The State of Irish Theatre', both offer surveys of the current health of the theatre in Ireland and both end on relatively upbeat notes which suggest that the stifling shackles of the necessity for a primarily national theatre are being finally shaken off. Lionel Pilkington's essay in the volume, 'Theatre History and the Beginnings of the Irish National Theatre', argues that we might go back in history and revise our ideas of how the idea of 'national' theatre began. Pilkington argues that the foundational claim that 'no Irish theatre existed prior to 1899' (p. 27) is increasingly being shown to be untrue, and that this in itself is a piece of national myth-making by those central to the National Theatre/Abbey project early in the twentieth century. The consequence of believing the Abbey's self-fashioning, Pilkington suggests, is 'the presumption that indigenous theatre in Ireland begins in 1899' and this leads to 'the imposition of an artificial insularity on Irish theatre history and the exclusion of the dramatic canon of a working-class and popular theatre tradition' (p. 27). *Theatre Stuff* is an excellent guide to the state of Irish theatre today—it mixes practitioners with academics and critics, and it holds out the promise of more exciting work to come from Carysfort Press.

Contemporary drama is also the subject of Mária Kurdi's *Codes and Masks: Aspects of Identity in Contemporary Irish Plays in an Intercultural Context*. The book is a welcome attempt to examine Irish drama as a whole, at least as a writing enterprise. It suffers a little from a continual insistence on the secure and certain post-coloniality of Ireland, and too many plays are crudely related back to this model while it is simultaneously apparent that they are straining to be allowed to say more through Kurdi's interpretation. However, on the plus side, Kurdi reads Stewart Parker's plays with great insight and it is good also to see Donal O'Kelly and Anne Devlin taken seriously alongside more established figures such as Brian Friel and Tom Murphy.

The work of J.M. Synge is assessed in Grene, ed., *Interpreting Synge: Essays from the Synge Summer School, 1991–2000*. Grene has brought together in this volume a collection of papers by extraordinarily distinguished speakers from the summer school. Grene's own essay, 'On the Margins: Synge and Wicklow' discusses in succession Synge's family connections with Wicklow, his essays on Wicklow, and then the use of Wicklow settings and references in the play, ending by showing how Synge was not cowed before the particularity of place: 'he saw the Wicklow which his imagination needed to see. Authenticity in this context has to be considered an irrelevant or discredited criterion' (p. 40). Among many other excellent essays (particularly those by R.F. Foster and Ann Saddlemyer) is Christopher Morash's 'All Playboys Now: The Audience and the Riot', which is a superb reconstruction of the most famous controversy in the history of Irish theatre, the riots during the first performances of Synge's *Playboy of the Western World*. Morash retells the story with wit, detail and a marvellous facility for reinterpretation.

Sean O'Casey's language is the subject of Colbert Kearney's *The Glamour of Grammar: Orality and Politics and the Emergence of Sean O'Casey*. Kearney writes in the belief that 'an oral culture extending back into prehistory continued to flourish in inner-city Dublin at least as late as the early decades of this century' (p. xi). Kearney writes about O'Casey and about Dublin with a real passion, and a belief that the place and its working-class inhabitants have been under-represented in literary and cultural terms. While this is in many ways true, there are times when Kearney allows belief to cloud judgement, and his idea that ancient oral culture survives in remnants in urban Dublin, whether right or not, suggests a need for essentialist values rather than a reading of O'Casey's socialism.

Among books on George Bernard Shaw published in 2000 was Bernard F. Dukore's *Shaw's Theatre*, a monograph which details Shaw's theatre practices in excellently conceived detail. It is especially good when discussing Shaw as director; suddenly the playwright comes to life as a theatrical thinker. The third part of the book, 'The Theater in Bernard Shaw's Drama' is slightly disappointing, given that it runs through a series a plays picking out moments of theatrical interest and moving towards being a reading of Shaw's metatheatricality. But overall *Shaw's Theatre* is a very useful guide to Shaw's theatrical practice and thought.

2. Pre-1945 Fiction

(a) The English Novel, 1900–1930

Issues of empire and women's writing remain of central interest this year, but two general points are worth noting. History, both as a context for textual discussion and as an alternative discourse, is mounting a strong challenge to the primacy of literary theory, and discussions of genre fiction are moving even closer to mainstream concerns.

Nicholas Daly's *Modernism, Romance and the Fin de Siècle: Popular Fiction and British Culture, 1880–1914* is an interesting example of both these developments. He brings a fresh perspective to the interrogation of the realist/ modernist, high/low cultural divide by privileging the role of tales of masculine adventure in the development of the novel at the turn of the century and argues that, properly understood, romance was 'culturally central' in the way in which it offered 'its readers a species of popular theory of social change' (p. 117). This in itself is not a new field, but the structure of Daly's book, its range of material, and his confidence in handling issues of colonialism and masculinity convey a wide and vibrant picture of the turn-of-the-century literary community. His inclusion of the Irish Revival in this context, for instance, is very welcome, although the history and literary context almost drown out the individual texts in this chapter. On the other hand, the discussion of Ernest Hemingway breaks Daly's cultural and period frame without any great benefit and tends to leave the interesting final chapter, which surveys and analyses the relation between action novels and early cinema, as a rather stranded coda.

Sue Sims, Hilary Clare and Robert J. Kirkpatrick bring another genre, children's school stories, to the foreground in (Aucmuty and Wotton, eds.) *The Encyclopaedia of Girls' School Stories* and *The Encyclopaedia of Boys' School Stories*. These two companion volumes contribute to the growing interest in children's literature and its relationship to mainstream culture by attempting to systematize and, to some extent, evaluate the popular school story genre. Both encyclopedias have dates which extend outside this period, covering the late 1700s to 1999, but all the editors locate the early twentieth century as the golden age of school stories. A substantial part of the text is A–Z entries of writers, but in addition there are fourteen short commentaries with bibliographies of connected topics, including brief listings of annuals and girls' school story papers as well as narrow sub-sets of the main topic, such as convent stories and pony school stories, or, in the case of boys' stories, 'real schools' and 'red circle school'. By the editors' own confession their volumes are not comprehensive and the organization is more than a little arbitrary—a compromise accepted in their mission to put school stories on the literary map. These shortcomings are more than outweighed by the value of this material being put at last into the public domain. Readers who are interested in the methodological problems posed by compiling these encyclopedias should read Rosemary Auchmuty, 'The Encyclopaedia: Origins and Organisation' and Hilary Clare, 'Lifting the Veil: Researching the Lives of Girls' School Story Writers' (Children's Literature in Education, 31:iii[2000] 147–58 and 159–65).

Detective fiction is another genre which continues to fascinate critics, and this year is no exception. Detective Fiction and the Rise of Forensic Science by Ronald R. Thomas does not fall comfortably into one literary period, but it is necessary reading since Thomas provides such a fascinating and informative context for the flowering of this distinctive Edwardian genre. He traces the change from 'character' to 'identity' as a variable political agenda made possible by the rise of photography, anthropology and fingerprinting, and mirrored in the evolution of detective fiction in America and Britain. He ranges the work and practice of contemporary criminologists such as Havelock Ellis, Francis Galton, Gina Lombroso-Ferrero and Charles Goring alongside the novels of Wilkie Collins, Charles Dickens, Conan Doyle and Joseph Conrad in Britain and Edgar Allen Poe, Dashiell Hammett, and Mark Twain in America. There are several reasons why this book is particularly valuable to early twentieth-century studies. One is the way in which Thomas brilliantly conveys the power that science and technology came to exert over the literary imagination and how it appeared to offer an answer to the imponderables of fin-de-siècle and post-1900 doubts and indirections. Secondly, Thomas's argument sweeps up a hundred years of detective novels, cutting across the tired categorization of modernism, popular fiction, genre and high art to demonstrate writers' vigour and creativity in responding to the intellectual challenges of their times. Detective fiction is assuming greater importance in literary studies from year to year, but Thomas raises the stakes, claiming that 'even if we accept some list of essential characteristics by which to define a genre we designate as "detective fiction," the historical forces that brought the form into being have found their way (more or less) into virtually every other kind of literature in the period as well' (pp. 288–9). Thomas's argument certainly illuminates many of the early twentieth-century literary concerns with race, science, society, human value and the integrity of the personality, as well as issues of literary form and value. Only gender seems untouched by a scientific and literary communality which still unquestioningly gendered crime as masculine.

Joseph A. Kestner, The Edwardian Detective, 1901–1915, has a much narrower focus. The highlighting of the distinctiveness of this period and the close examination of thirty well-known, neglected, canonical and popular detective novels, including works by G.K. Chesterton, John Buchan, Joseph Conrad, Baroness Orczy, Robert Barr, Conan Doyle and many others, are intended to demonstrate the vigour of Edwardian fiction and the immediacy of its engagement with society. Kestner opens the book and each of the three chronological sections with potted histories and lists of 'important' events grouped (apparently) randomly into paragraphs. The selected texts are then explored in the light of these historical 'facts'. This method leads to considerable repetition and a sense of overstated argument, which ultimately renders rather thin Kestner's straightforward and worthwhile aim to demonstrate detective fiction as the 'enduring index' of the Edwardian age.

Robert Kuhn McGregor's and Ethan Lewis's latest contribution to Sayers studies, *Conundrums for the Long Week-End: England, Dorothy L. Sayers, and Lord Peter Wimsey*, is rather bland. Read as an introduction to the body of Wimsey novels, this book is acceptable. It makes its way chronologically and diligently through the works, offering summaries, contextual information and some historical and/or biographical analysis of each of the novels. But the approach is critically innocent, and there are too many occasions when the mingling of Sayers's own life with her fictional creations, Peter Wimsey and Harriet Vane, stops being interestingly mischievous speculation and starts being naive cross-association. A particular problem for the British reader is the way in which the authors have organized the historical context in small parcels of information spread through the book like short history lessons: summaries of the First World War, the decline of the aristocracy and, particularly, the General Strike of 1926 feel packaged and lacking in empathy. Consequently, the 'England' of the title never becomes more than a series of historical events in a way that would enlighten readers on either side of the Atlantic. However, the authors' greatest failure is in allowing Wimsey to become more important than Sayers's achievement in creating a detective for her times. Sayers's reputation shrinks as a result—her talent limited to writing bits of her life and immediate context into a series of pleasant novels.

A more general survey of the period and one which is not focused on genre is Hapgood and Paxton, eds., *Outside Modernism* (also reviewed in section 1(*a*) above). The first of the two introductory essays considers early twentieth-century fiction in terms of transformative continuity, while the second considers the modernist agenda through an examination of current scholarship. Within this framework, the essays investigate the boundaries of realism and modernism and the stability of literary categories in the work of well-known but neglected writers such as John Galsworthy and G.K. Chesterton, war writers such as Frederic Manning, and women writers such as Rebecca West, Sylvia Townsend Warner and Maud Diver.

G.K. Chesterton has already earned two mentions this year. Does this suggest the green shoots of a revival? As always, it is hard to say. James V. Schall, in *Schall on Chesterton: Timely Essays on Timeless Paradoxes*, makes no claim to contribute to Chesterton's literary achievement but simply records his responses to Chesterton's regular column in *The London Illustrated News* between 1905 and 1931. This is Chesterton at one remove. Even so, Schall's fascination with Chesterton does rub off and tempts the reader back not only to his journalism, but also to the fiction and poetry, so briefly dealt with here in 'Second Thoughts on Detective Stories', 'The Invisible Man' and 'A Picture of "Tuesday"'. We must be grateful to Catholic publishing houses and scholars for keeping Chesterton's work in the public domain; one hopes that it will also bring Chesterton to the wider literary community.

Mark Knight, in 'Chesterton and the Problem of Evil' (*L&T* 14:iv[2000] 373–84), straddles theological and literary concerns. He responds to charges against Chesterton of a wilful optimism by considering his attitude to evil through a discussion of the play, *The Surprise* [1932] and his writings on the book of Job [1907] in the light of the Free Will Defence, whose status as theodicy or defence was itself at the centre of theological debate. He argues that Chesterton's personal recognition that 'life could only be explained by taking the middle ground between

reason and mystery' (p. 382) is made possible through his art and notably through
the metaphorical and allegorical exuberance of *The Man Who Was Thursday* [1908].
In contrast, Elmar Schenkel focuses on Nietzschean ideas (i.e. how Nietzsche's
work was understood and used by British thinkers and writers) and their impact on
Chesterton's writing, in 'Paradoxical Affinities: Chesterton and Nietzsche' (in
Stark, ed., pp. 241–51). Ideas of Superman, of unlimited growth, of strength and of
eternal recurrence, and rejection of history were ideas Chesterton detested but which
he used to test out his own beliefs in a way that Schenkel claims demonstrates 'a
deep love-hate relationship, a revealing symmetry' (p. 247). He argues that the
common ground lay in a shared intellectual iconoclasm—a recognition of the power
of apparent unreasonableness, their rejection of systematically organized thought—
although their philosophical ends were different.

Paula M. Krebs, *Gender, Race, and the Writing of Empire: Public Discourse and
the Boer War* [1999] is an important contribution to the study of this period and
brings us to one if its continuing concerns—issues of empire. Krebs raises pertinent
and provocative questions about the literary production of works about the war, and
offers illuminating readings of Olive Schreiner and the so-called writers of empire,
Conan Doyle, H. Rider Haggard and Rudyard Kipling. Conan Doyle is set against
W.T. Stead in a debate about the sexual honour of the British soldier; H. Rider
Haggard, acclaimed as an expert for his knowledge of and romances about Africa,
resisted being transformed from romance writer to South Africa war correspondent,
while Kipling, famous for his stories and poems of the Indian Raj, was successfully
co-opted as defender of the empire in the press, but never succeeds in making South
Africa part of his own imaginative landscape. Set against these three friends is Olive
Schreiner, whose nationality gave her the authority to interpret South Africa for the
British and whose intellectual struggles to plot a future for South Africa's ethnic
groups and their layers of colonial masters makes fascinating reading. However,
Krebs's argument is most stimulating in the questions it raises about the hybrid
social, political and cultural identity of upper-class men whose bestseller status in
the fiction stakes won them public trust and an authoritative platform in the
traditional newspapers and newly emerging popular press. This is probably the
earliest example of what has become a feature of national and international crises in
the modern world, and Krebs's discussion suggests a new infrastructure for
understanding the nature of literary production during this period.

Which brings us to Kipling, who continues to command considerable critical
attention. Kipling emerges from Don Randall's study *Kipling's Imperial Boy:
Adolescence and Cultural Hybridity* as a subtly nuanced and responsible writer
responding creatively and diversely to the drama of British and Indian relations in
the second half of the nineteenth century. Randall takes what he calls 'liminal boys'
in Kipling's work as figures of transitional identity whose function is 'to negotiate
the contact zones of empire' (p. 160) in the post-Mutiny period, and to explore the
cultural hybridity that might result from these unions. A lengthy chapter entitled
'Genealogy of the Imperial Boy' sets up an impressive context for understanding the
plasticity of adolescent identity and therefore its importance as a site of change.
Randall's focus on the adolescent also incidentally contributes to interest in the child
as subject and as reader noted elsewhere. *The Jungle Books* [1894], *Stalky and Co.*
[1899], and *Kim* [1901] are given equal weight in a discussion which is
unencumbered by attempts to define their status in terms of their assumed readership

or to dismiss the child as subject as childish matter. *Stalky and Co.* emerges particularly strongly from this approach, dropping its 'boys' school story' tag to be located firmly in Kipling's own literary and political development. In fact, an underlying theme of the discussion is Kipling's growing skill in finding forms which allowed the interplay of ambiguities and resistances contingent on the imperialist project to flourish within a stable vision of empire. This is a satisfyingly argued book that takes into consideration an impressive range of critical approaches (sometimes overladen with current jargon) which also has a confident and convincing belief in the value of Kipling's work.

Andrew St John's excellent and informative article, '"In the Year '57": Historiography, Power, and Politics in Kipling's Punjab' (*RES* 51[2000] 62–79), brings together colonial history, British literary history and the recovery of a neglected piece of Kipling's writing to illuminate the development of Kipling's aesthetic. Using an uncollected two-part article called 'In the Year of '57' written by Kipling and published in the *Civil and Military Gazette* in 1887, St John explores the narrator's attempt to reconcile the 'rugged, inchoate textuality' of pre-Mutiny, non-regulated administration in the Punjab with the 'systematic, "theoretical" approach to the historical material' of the post-Mutiny, utilitarian, centralized government of India (p. 75). Insights into the nature of Kipling's own aesthetic gleaned from this clash of political and linguistic styles are then applied to *Plain Tales From the Hills* and, briefly, to *Kim*. In 'Three Ways of Going Wrong: Kipling, Conrad, Coetzee' (*MLR* 95:i[2000] 18–27), Douglas Kerr explores the dilemma for colonial rulers of balancing knowledge of the colonized with the necessary assertion of a pure national identity and its changing emphasis from the early twentieth century to the post-colonial perspectives of late twentieth-century South Africa. Kipling's 'Beyond the Pale' and 'To be Filed for Reference' from *Plain Tales from the Hills* [1888] and Conrad's *Heart of Darkness* [1902] all explore the fates of European men who transgress racial boundaries, and therefore national codes, and whose stories are related by a fascinated narrator in what Kerr calls 'the relationship between outlaw and lawman' (p. 24). This relationship is defamiliarized in Coetzee's *Waiting for the Barbarians* [1982], but most crucially made current and unfinished by Coetzee's use of the present tense. Kerr's juxtaposition of these texts reopens both Kipling and Conrad to history's immediacy rather than its pastness.

Angela K. Smith is the latest contributor to the current interest in women's writing and the First World War with her two companion volumes, one anthology and one of criticism. Her anthology, *Women's Writing of the First World War* (also reviewed in section 1(*a*) above), is a brave and mostly successful attempt to weave a narrative of the war from a series of extracts representing a range of women and literary forms and comprising divergent opinions. The material is broken up into familiar sections: 'The Battle Front', 'The Home Front' and so on, and Smith draws on a high proportion of well-known names whose published works are relatively, even easily accessible, such as Beatrice Webb, Vera Brittain, the Pankhursts and Radclyffe Hall, but her choice of material is excellent, its positioning interesting and enlightening, and its literary value clearly an important criterion. The evenness of tone that helps to make the anthology coherent and readable from beginning to end (an unusual achievement) has its downside. Most of the extracts were written by highly intelligent, educated, even upper-class British women—indeed one of the successes of the book is the sense it conveys of how the war was a forcing-house for such women. The occasional shifts of tone introduced by extracts such as G.K. Brumwell's short article 'The Masseuse', take the reader pleasantly by surprise, but they are all too infrequent.

Smith's companion volume, *The Second Battlefield* (also reviewed in section 1(*a*) above), is broad in scope and generous in its sympathies. Its chief interest is the range of works she discusses, and the lucid way in which she illuminates the interactions between women's lives, war history and literary struggle. Each chapter produces a new perspective for the reader. I particularly enjoyed the chapters 'Private to Public', which examines how women drew on their diaries and letters to create novels, sometimes many years later, and 'Living Words', which includes a discussion of Evadne Price's answer to Erich Remarque's *All Quiet on the Western Front*, and the examination of the literary and emotional triangle which juxtaposes H.D.'s *Bid Me To Live* with Richard Aldington's *Death of a Hero*. By the end of the book she has persuasively argued and demonstrated the 'empowered status of women as writers'. This makes it all the more surprising that she attempts to hook these insights into a tenuous argument about modernism, which by the end of the book I felt she had lost interest in herself. Smith calls one chapter 'Accidental Modernisms' and another 'Female Modernisms', diluting the term to virtual uselessness by implicitly claiming that any writing which reconfigures conventions and/or re-examines the function of writing under the stress of the new must necessarily be modernist. Nothing could be further from the truth, as she herself demonstrates through the political radicalism and intimate engagement with the imperatives of reality that many of these texts amply reveal.

It is refreshing to turn from war to friendship and to consider representations of women's friendship and rivalries in the inter-war years in Diana Wallace, *Sisters and Rivals in British Women's Fiction, 1814–1939*. Wallace sets herself the considerable task of analysing the novels through the different perspectives of the social and political context, modern feminist theory and biographical and textual analysis. The first and second sections construct two parallel histories. The first is social and political: it provides clear and interesting information to suggest the force and range of the public debates about women which shaped her chosen novelists, May Sinclair, Rebecca West, Vera Brittain, Winifred Holtby and Rosamond Lehmann. The second deals with the development of feminist theory, highlighting those aspects—mainly Freudian-inspired psychoanalytical approaches—she thinks enable understanding, and stressing that their importance lies in their diversity. A chapter is then devoted to each writer, who is placed in terms of literary history, biographical influences, and their treatment of the central theme of friendship and rivalry. This seemingly rigid division of material actually works extremely well. Within each chapter Wallace offers a range of arguments and perspectives so that the cumulative effect is admirably open-ended. Much has been written about women writers at the turn of the century and this book is particularly well timed in extending discussion past the First World War into the 1920s and 1930s.

In her edition of the *Selected Letters of Rebecca West*, Bonnie Kime Scott claims that the letters reveal West 'as a defining intellect of the twentieth century'. Rather disappointingly, they do not do this. The promise of at least some of the vast body of letters she wrote was that they would reveal an intellectual trajectory, a sense of literary mission, a possible coherence over the sixty or more years of her career. It is difficult to judge whether Kime Scott missed an opportunity, or whether her subject simply made it difficult for her: West did not use her letters for intellectual or literary interchange, and reveals herself in an increasingly negative light as the years pass. Despite her latter-day public status and her continual engagement in public affairs, these letters seem a shrunken version of the Rebecca West we would hope to meet. Kime had a daunting task, but her sectional introductions do not help the reader to understand the nature of West's apparent defensiveness: they are contextual rather than interpretative. Kime's (or her editor's) decision to footnote the letters is less than ideal. It might have been more helpful to preface each letter with its context and dramatis personae, leaving editorial decisions and minor references to the footnotes. Whatever its limitations, this collection is important not only in furthering West studies (the more material in the public domain the better) but in filling out the picture of what it meant to be a woman writer in the early decades of the twentieth century.

Sylvia Townsend Warner, *The Salutation*, introduction by Claire Harman, is a collection of fifteen of Townsend Warner's unpublished or long out-of-print short stories. As such it is part of the steady re-evaluation of Warner's work and a welcome contribution to that most valuable part of literary recovery—putting a wide range of an author's work into the public domain. Claire Harman stakes the value of the collection on the title story 'The Salutation', and most of the introduction is taken up by an interesting discussion of that unpublished writing and its relationship with Warner's novel *Mr Fortune's Maggot*, published three years previously in 1927. I think Harman could usefully have included bibliographical information about the other stories. Why choose to republish 'deliberately trivial' or 'heavily derivative' stories without locating them in their literary context? However, it is no bad thing for a modern reader to confront these stories freshly, and what emerges clearly is that they are chiefly concerned with style: with clarity of observation, precision of language and simplicity of structure. Warner captures moments of importance in ordinary lives with an unerring touch, and throughout she is capable of bringing a picture into sharp focus with the simplest of images: '[her] slumbers ranged from the slight gauze of inattention suitable for sermons, to the quilted oblivion fit for a winter's night' (p. 17).

It is always hard to predict what Wellsian scholarship will produce: this year it is A.B. McKillop's *The Spinster and the Prophet: A Tale of H.G. Wells, Plagiarism and the History of the World*. McKillop unashamedly goes for the narrative and treads a fine line between historical accuracy and imaginatively coloured assumptions and speculations in his account of the Deeks v. Wells case, in which Florence Deeks sued H.G. Wells for plagiarism in a series of court cases between 1927 and 1933. The interleaving of the stories of Deeks and Wells over the years from the mid-1880s to the conclusion of the case presents Florence as another of Wells's women whom he could use and then set aside. This is a fascinating unravelling of an episode in the life of a famous man of letters in his sixties, and makes riveting reading. But there is plenty for the scholar too. The book is well researched and thoroughly documented and, along the way, gives fresh and disturbing examples of the closing of ranks among the literary classes, male intellectual hegemony, publishing practices and the intolerable marginalization of intelligent but powerless women. Most valuable are the insights into how Wells wrote. Sadly, McKillop finally falls foul of male arrogance himself. Deeks's history, he claims, is unreadable today, and her subsequent writing no longer original. This seems a strange judgement given the writing of a period that produced Malthus, Nordau, Havelock Ellis and Baden Powell. Perhaps, if nothing else, Deeks's feminist history might have historical value.

The case of Florence Deeks gets only a brief footnote in David C. Smith (ed.), *The Correspondence of H.G. Wells*, volumes i–iv [1998; briefly reviewed in *YWES* 79[2000]), but how illuminating of Wells that small fact is. Smith's systematic gathering of and selection from what is available of Well's huge correspondence necessarily gives us the broad sweep of the man as he crosses the world and addresses the world's concerns. These are the letters of a literary man, but they are not about literary matters: these letters are to do with business—not daily, banal business but the business of a man with many friends, considerable social status, and a relentless timetable and who is driven by ideas. The range of his correspondents is impressive and the loyalty of his friends over long periods of time testifies to his personal attractiveness and value. Yet it is hard to discover the man in these letters, except in the briefest glimpses.

This year sees the publication of two books about two friends—Christopher Scoble, *Fisherman's Friend: A Life of Stephen Reynolds* and Edward Thomas, *Light and Twilight*, which link unexpectedly to reintroduce a missing theme to early twentieth-century studies—that of landscape and rural simplicity.

In his own time, many established critics and writers accepted Stephen Reynolds as part of their literary circle and expected a great literary future for him. When he died at the age of 38 from the influenza epidemic that swept across Britain in 1919, the body of writing he left behind was small. His most significant public success was *A Poor Man's House* [1909], which he claimed to be the 'genesis of autobiografiction', a new genre for those writers constrained and subdued by the conventions and expectations of writing novels (p. 135). Christopher Scoble's biography is, to some extent, a regional work, published in Devon to celebrate the life of a man who chose Devon as his spiritual home and brought the world of the fishermen he lived and worked with to the national stage. However, the success of Scoble's project for scholarship is the light it throws on the literary and intellectual milieu of the time, locating Reynolds in the broader context in which he can be clearly seen as representative of his time, his class, and his gender through previously unpublished letters and biographical accounts. Well educated, handsome and talented, he was unable to find a way to bring together his creativity and the hard grind of earning a living ('I am bending every nerve to earn my own living', p. 279), or to acknowledge and live out his homosexuality under the microscope of the urban literary scene presided over by Edward Garnett. He turned instead to the working classes, to manual labour and to the simplicity of rural life in Sidmouth. This book does not attempt to make false claims for Reynolds's literary talent, but it does add to the sum of our knowledge of masculine identity and literary commerce at the turn of the century.

Laurel Books's collection of Edward Thomas's essays, first published in 1911, opens the door further into an aspect of Edwardian culture that, at the moment, seems out of step with the modernity that is being discovered in women's writing, war writing, and genre innovation. Yet Thomas's evocation of a spiritualized and aestheticized rural landscape, which was such an important trope of the pre-war period, offers the reader a glimpse of a world and a way of writing that seems to be dissolving even as we read. Each of the fourteen essays revolves around an epiphany arising from the intense observation of the world through a heightened, and sometimes morbid, sensibility. The writing is full of Thomas's defamiliarizing observations—'pearly snails, the daisies and the chips of chalk like daisies' (p. 14)—but in his prose these descriptions belong to the tradition of Richard Jefferies yearning for a Romanticism that could make 'I and poet and lover and flowers and cloud and star ... equals' (p. 34). This is an Edwardian mindset that continues to elude sympathetic scholarly discussion, much as imperialism did until comparatively recently: alienation and embarrassment often intervene between the critic and such texts. Laurel Books's collection is a timely prompt, respectfully put together as an aide-memoire not just to a period, but to the literary experiments of a writer on the cusp of literary transition.

To conclude with E.M. Forster, and Henry S. Turner's discussion of 'Empires of Objects: Accumulation and Entropy in E.M. Forster's *Howards End*' (*TCL* 46:iii[2000] 328–45). Turner sees Forster as a historical anachronism in temperament but a modern in intellect, who wrote *Howards End* to explore whether and how the traditional notion of 'value' could make sense in a modern, technological world. Turner transplants a Marxist vocabulary of economic processes (accumulation, surplus and labour) into the visible manifestations of objects and possessions to demonstrate the destabilization of social meaning and their new existence as sites of value ambiguity and conflict. He substantiates his argument by concentrating on 'a straying of objects across the topography of the novel' (p. 336)—notably Leonard Bast's umbrella—and the tendency of possessions to abandon stability and become problems and/or surpluses—notably the Schlegels' furniture and their father's library. The article concludes with a brief discussion of the Basts, which suggests that the abstracts of class and culture might also be understood as 'straying objects'.

(b) The English Novel, 1930–1945

Robert Hoskins's *Graham Greene: An Approach to the Novels* deals with the whole of Greene's writing life, not merely incidentally but as a central aspect of its main purpose. Hoskins argues that Greene's career falls into two main phases, characterized by different kinds of protagonists and by differing relationships between those protagonists and the novels' obsessive and allusive literary frameworks. Thus the impact on meaning of Greene's references to, for example, Conrad, William Le Queux, Christopher Marlowe and Wordsworth are carefully and fully traced through his novels. Though literary and other species of allusion and intertextuality have been previously noted by many Greene critics, Hoskins brings these observations together into a new and productive approach to Greene's whole oeuvre. He suggests that the first-phase novels of the 1930s are inhabited by protagonists who are trapped in plots of which they are unconscious, while the novels of the 1940s and after are distinguished by increasingly aware characters, who can at least comment on the kind of narratives they feel themselves to be in, and in some cases can even attempt their own contributions to the script.

Cates Baldridge's *Graham Greene's Fictions: The Virtues of Extremity* [1999] argues that Greene's particular concern is with the extreme, the absolute: 'it is his angry impatience with the lives of safety and security that most of us long for ... that lends the world of his fictions its most distinctive and disquieting tone, for to enter fully into his novels is to understand that ... comfort and stasis are always already deadening complacency' (p. 2). Throughout his career Greene's novels trace a struggle between a 'mediated', second-hand life and an 'absolutistic' life which actually tries to see things as they are, whether in political or religious terms. Baldridge suggests that there has been a certain degree of critical desire to normalize or mainstream Greene's vision, particularly perhaps the theological implications of his narratives. Indeed, he argues that the best word to describe Greene's religious ideas is 'heresy', but that these views in no sense belong to some already 'recognizable category of historical Christian heresy' (p. 3). Baldridge's second chapter, on Greene's conceptions of God, is especially impressive. Focusing initially on *The Power and the Glory*, the chapter traces conceptions of God in the major novels. Baldridge argues that the God of Greene's novels is one who is more human that absolute: 'The God of *The Power and the Glory* appears to be a watchmaker who for some reason has ceased to wind and oil his creation, as if the same entropy that decrees the running down of the mechanism had palsied the hands of the Maker as well' (p. 66). Paradoxically, however, this weakened God is actually more absolute in Greene's terms than the absolute God as usually conceived, for Greene links stasis to the mediated, and struggle and boundedness with the 'virtues of extremity'. God as author of the universe can only, for Greene, be interested (and interesting) through participation in a narrative, not as a figure above narrative: 'he understood that no Narrator who proclaimed Himself to be wholly above struggle, anguish and defeat could long hold our interest' (p. 89). Other chapters, such as chapter 5, 'The Honorary Marxist: Political Philosophy in Greene's Novels', are similarly thought-provoking and illuminating.

Neil Macdonald published an important short review article about Greene's most famous novella/film, *The Third Man*, 'The Return of Harry Lime' (*Quadrant* Jan./ Feb.[2000] 92–4). This draws attention to the fact that the version of the film that is widely known is the American release, which was extensively re-edited by David O. Selznick. The article coincided with screenings in Australia of a version of Alexander Korda's British release, directed by Carol Reed, which Greene himself was closely involved with, restored by the Australian Film Institute. The article discusses interestingly the way in which the novella/screenplay was built up by Greene and Reed together, and also assesses the extent to which Orson Welles's stories about his own creative contribution to the film can be relied upon. Gene H. Bell-Villada published an article exploring the influence of Greene on Gabriel Garcia Marquez: 'What the Young Gabriel Garcia Marquez Learned from the Master Graham Greene: The Case of "Un Dia De Estos"' (*Comparatist* 24[2000] 146–56). The article starts from the Columbian writer's observation that Greene taught him to 'evoke the warm climate of the tropics' (p. 146), and goes on to analyse the ways in which Marquez's work draws on Greene's representations of climate from *The Power and the Glory* onwards through 'its utter lack of exoticism, its ordinary, everyday quality' (p. 147).

Jerome Meckier's interesting article, 'Aldous Huxley, Evelyn Waugh and Birth Control in *Black Mischief* (*JML* 23:ii[2000] 277–90), discovers a source for Waugh's satire on birth control in Azania in, or via, a newspaper article by Huxley. The article, 'Japanese Advertisement', appeared in the *Chicago Herald and Examiner* [2 May 1932]. It is not clear where Waugh might have seen it: though Meckier says that a number of Huxley's essays for the Randolph Hearst syndicated press were reprinted in English newspapers, it is not clear if or when this particular article was. Nevertheless, Meckier's attribution of the article as a source seems very convincing. Huxley was inspired to write the piece after seeing a pictorial advert for condoms in a Japanese newspaper while dining in a Japanese restaurant in London. The picture, showing two contrasting family scenes resulting from use or otherwise of the pictured contraceptives, will immediately remind readers of Waugh of the similar promotional image deployed by Seth in *Black Mischief* [1932]. One family is numerous and starving, the other of limited number, with plentiful food on the table. From Huxley's description of these scenes, Waugh probably developed his own, more elaborated, version. The attribution of this source would in itself be of interest, but Meckier can further show from the manuscript of *Black Mischief* that a substantial portion of the novel was already written before Waugh engaged with the contraceptive advert idea. Up to that point there was no discussion of contraception as one of the advantages of Western progress; Waugh's indications of material to be inserted make it likely that the birth-control pageant and advertisement were all added at a later stage, when four chapters were already written. Therefore, as Meckier concludes, the 'Japanese advertisement' had a marked and major role in shaping the novel, 'rounding off the plot and satire together' (p. 289), giving Waugh a brilliantly resonant way of linking technology and sterility as central to what he saw as the dead end of Western 'progress'.

Fred Inglis published an essay on the 1980 Granada Television adaptation of Waugh's novel entitled '*Brideshead Revisited* Revisited: Waugh to the Knife' (in Giddings and Sheen, eds., *The Classic Novel: From Page to Screen*, pp. 179–95). The essay suggests that the scale of this work marked the invention of a new genre— the seriously extended serial adaptation of a classic novel (in this case taking eleven hours of screening time). Inglis explores the various contexts from which Waugh's novel constructed its meanings at the end of the Second World War and goes on to suggest the new accretions and deletions of meaning which the adaptation could bring about in the early 1980s. The essay particularly analyses the adaptation's treatment of the Catholic themes of the novel, noting that, for the 'humanist-consumerist producers and audience' (p. 189), the adaptation shifts the already powerful emphasis on elegant foreign sightseeing and aesthetic experience even more firmly to the centre. For 'humanist consumerists', the appeal is 'in terms not so much of Christian redemption, but in the larger more unkillable hope that a good yarn will keep the promise of happiness implicit in all art' (p. 194).

In 'Bruised Boys and "Fallen Women": The Need for Rescue in Short Stories by Elizabeth Bowen' (*SCR* 32:i[1999] 88–9), Jeanette Shumakker discusses ideas of illusion, self-awareness and rescue in Elizabeth Bowen's short fiction—an area of her work which has, as Shumakker comments, been generally neglected in favour of critical work on Bowen's novels. The article discusses the three stories, 'The Return', 'Summer Night' and 'Ivy Gripped the Steps', seeing in each of them a concern with a paralysis which stems largely from a romantic illusion that an external agency will act as rescuer. Illusions of escape thus function as enforcers of imprisonment. The theme is seen as linked to Bowen's position as an Anglo-Irish writer: 'Bowen's double perspective allows her to illuminate characters' disillusionment when seeking an impossible rescue from a rapidly changing society that alienates them' (p. 96).

Rosamond Lehmann's first novel, *Dusty Answer* [1927] is discussed in Andrea Lewis's '"Glorious pagan that I adore": Resisting the National Reproductive

Imperative in Rosamond Lehmann's *Dusty Answer*' (*SNNTS* 31:iii[1999] 357–71). This fine article gives a nuanced and illuminating account of Lehmann's early novel, particularly by historicizing the relationships of the central character Judith Earle in terms of contemporary British constructions of lesbianism and its relation to the national imperatives of heterosexual reproduction (in several senses) after the Great War. Lewis links her recovery of the forgotten contexts in which 'sexuality was tied to national anxiety' (p. 368) to her exploration of why Lehmann's novel invited so much less controversy than Radclyffe Hall's *The Well of Loneliness* published the year after, and subsequently banned. Lewis argues convincingly that the main lesbian relationship in Lehmann's novel is both more easily overlooked than the lesbian identity represented in Hall's novel and, paradoxically, more troubling to English ideologies, since Judith, while not assuming any lesbian identity characterizable as monstrous, nevertheless 'fails to fulfill the national reproductive imperative' and calls into question 'the endurance of Englishness' itself (p. 369).

(c) Joseph Conrad

Conrad studies have not produced as many high-quality monographs this year as we have become used to recently, but the work reviewed shows an admirable variety of critical locations from which he is being reassessed. While the major fictions continue to receive a great deal of attention, most notably in the special issue of *The Conradian* devoted to *Lord Jim*, many of the lesser-known texts have received sustained treatment and in many cases have inspired more original work than the tried and tested subjects. Of particular prevalence amongst this year's output are studies engaging with the psychological, emotional and aesthetic consequences of Conrad's exile, but equally interesting is the emergence of a body of criticism devoted to reading the fictions as traumatic narratives, a development which is overdue.

The outstanding contribution to Conrad scholarship this year is Robert Hampson's *Cross-Cultural Encounters in Joseph Conrad's Malay Fiction*. Hampson sets out to analyse not just the cultural and political collisions of East and West, but also the ideological and imaginative frameworking within which the Malay fiction is contained. Indeed the prior encoding of 'Malaysia' (an intrinsically problematic geopolitical term in itself) forms a significant part of the early chapters of the study as Hampson considers the construction of Malaysia in the writings of early Western recorders such as Thomas Raffles, James Brookes and Hugh Clifford. These chapters provide essential contextualization for the subsequent readings of Conrad's principal Malay fictions, and foreground the Malay peninsula as a politicized space as contested by literary representation as by racial or cultural heterogeneity. Through his examination of Conrad's career-long fascination with Malaysia, Hampson suggests a process of 'turning inward' (p. 29). By this he implies that the initial attempts to portray the Malay world (in *Almayer's Folly* and *An Outcast of the Islands*) gave way to 'self-conscious engagements with the conventions of adventure romance in *Lord Jim*' (p. 30) in the face of the otherness of the East. Increasingly, from 'Karain' onwards, Conrad chooses to explore the problems of representation of Malaysia in a self-reflexive intervention into the textualization of the region. Hampson insightfully explores the trajectory of this inward turn and interestingly extrapolates from Conrad's fictional insecurity an interpretation of a more personal sense of exile and nomadism. Concluding with a section on the importance of homecoming in the fiction, he argues that Conrad's writing resists coding within stable boundaries of representation and is instead poised between contexts which are at once familiar and alien. This is a substantial piece of scholarship which throws new light on Conrad's Malay fiction, and, while it builds on established intellectual paradigms, provides a valuable assessment of the textualization of geopolitical space.

Michael A. Lucas's *Aspects of Conrad's Literary Language* is a complex, yet surprisingly engaging, analysis of the linguistic structures and eccentricities of Conrad's major writings. Taking as his starting point the acceptance of a compacted yet prolix style, Lucas seeks to account for Conrad's idiolect through a brief history of his pattern of language acquisition. This leads him to the conclusion that the spoken, seafaring English encountered by Conrad in the early 1880s strongly affected his grasp on grammatical precision. Allied to his voracious consumption of English literature which, Lucas argues, resulted in an understanding of English more literary than oral, this education led to a writing style characterized by a semantic and syntactical compression. Through close analysis of the major texts, and by comparison against the work of his native English-speaking peers, Lucas shows Conrad's writing to be heavily dominated by noun-words at the expense of function-words. While it is interesting and well demonstrated, the application of this study to an understanding of Conradian aesthetics is perhaps limited. Lucas's claim that the prevailing vision of a fragmented reality being evident in an extensive lexis and frequent 'use of descriptive adjectives, manner adverbs and other modifying elements' (p. 202) is an unconvincing attempt to marry linguistic acquisition with modernist aesthetics. Nevertheless, this is an intriguing insight for the hardened Conrad scholar.

Ian Watt's contribution to Conrad studies is further reinforced by a posthumous collection of his essays—*Essays on Conrad*. Bringing together an eclectic selection of previously published pieces, the volume stands testament to Watt's enduring engagement with Conrad. The essays comprise a mixture of critical articles, introductions, and contributions to other volumes. As a whole they provide an excellent overview of Conrad's writing, but they are an equally revealing indicator of the recent history of Conrad scholarship. Popular themes, such as the dialogue between alienation and solidarity, jostle with an assessment of the use of humour in *Typhoon*, while analysis of Conrad's attitude to racism sits beside Watt's entrance into the debate on the merits of *The Nigger of the 'Narcissus'*. Some of these essays are of more interest than others and, while some are beginning to seem dated, others are as fresh and insightful as ever. What this collection shows above all is the breadth of Watt's work on Conrad and the consistently engaging and readable nature of his writing. Of particular personal interest are the two final essays, both autobiographically intertwining the author's and critic's lives. 'Around Conrad's Grave in Canterbury' recalls Watt's researches into the wrangling over Jessie Conrad's inscription on her husband's gravestone, while '"The Bridge Over the River Kwai" as Myth' recounts Watt's own experiences as a Japanese prisoner of war. Although hardly the most critically hard-headed of pieces, these last succeed largely because of their lack of objectivity. Watt's contribution to Conrad's studies in these essays reminds us that research is too frequently a process by which the passionate become the dispassionate. This collection goes some way to reversing that trend.

In the journals this year there is the usual mixture of the meticulous and the scrupulous which characterizes Conrad scholarship, and while one or two articles appear to this reviewer to be stillborn, they are on the whole a satisfactory haul. *The Conradian* devotes its volume to two special issues: one containing a collection of little-seen manuscripts relating to Conrad, the other a paean to *Lord Jim*, which celebrated its centenary in 2000. In this number is Michael Greaney's slightly quirky '*Lord Jim* and Embarrassment' (*Conradian* 25:i[2000] 1–14). Greaney makes a valid and interesting case for the significance of shame, guilt and embarrassment in *Lord Jim*. By tracing the motif of the blush, he draws parallels between the numerous instances of social dis-ease in the novel and the more serious structural 'embarrassments' that problematize the process of reading *Lord Jim*. In the same number Cedric Watts's essay 'Bakhtin's Monologism and the Endings of *Crime and Punishment* and *Lord Jim*' (*Conradian* 25:i[2000] 15–30) takes issue with the Bakhtinian notion of the dialogic text. Not only does Watts disagree that Dostoevsky's work is 'uniquely' dialogic, as Bakhtin contests, but he also argues that *Lord Jim*'s ending points to the inadequacy of Bakhtin's theory that no writer after Dostoevsky was truly dialogic. Watts's essay is a systematic dismantling of an idea, and while that idea has already undergone serious challenge elsewhere, its basic tenets bear repetition.

In '"He was Misleading": Frustrated Gestures in *Lord Jim*' (*Conradian* 25:i[2000] 31–47) Allan Simmons examines proleptic structures in Conrad's fiction, structures which, he argues, are ultimately misleading for they do not develop as the reader anticipates. Combining analysis of the novel's 'anticipatory gesturing' with a consideration of the intertextual framework of reference to the adventure romance, Simmons contends that readers' expectations of Jim's failure to live up to a literary heroism are confounded by a romanticized resolution. Mining a popular seam, 'Reading as Homecoming: Expatriation as a Critical Discourse in *Lord Jim*' (*Conradian* 25:i[2000] 48–63) by Ludmilla Voitkovska, approaches the well-worn terrain of Conrad's exilic status and the impact of that on his writing. Her argument is fresh, however. She claims that Conrad's decision to write in English alienated him from his own Polish reading public while granting him only an uncomfortable access to English signification systems. She also draws interesting parallels between the relationship between Jim and Marlow and that between Conrad and his reader.

While the influence of Tadeusz Bobrowski on Conrad's life and writing is well documented, the impact of Bobrowski's younger brother Stefan is less noted. In '"Usque ad finem": *Under Western Eyes*, *Lord Jim* and Conrad's Red Uncle' (*Conradian* 25:i[2000] 64–71) Andrzej Busza provides a brief chronology of Stefan's short life and violent death before drawing comparisons between the doomed political activist and Jim. Admittedly those parallels are not convincing, but the recuperation of Stefan Bobrowski is valuable. J.H. Stape's contribution to this special issue is 'Louis Becke's Gentlemen Pirates and *Lord Jim*' (*Conradian* 25:i[2000] 72–82). In it he considers the intertextual correspondences between Becke's South Sea yarns and *Lord Jim* with particular reference to the portrayal of pirates. Brief but interesting. The strangely missing crew of the *Patna* forms the central focus for Gene Moore's first essay in this year's *Conradian*. In 'The Missing Crew of the *Patna*' (*Conradian* 25:i[2000] 83–98) he considers why, when Conrad's previous writings had celebrated the ordinary seafaring man, only five members of the crew of Jim's vessel are identified. Ultimately, he concludes, the insignificance which is attached to the other crew members in the narrative reflects Jim's own failure to acknowledge the interdependence of crew and officers. It is this myopia which situates him resolutely within the romanticized world of seafaring adventure literature.

The second number of this year's *Conradian* is distinctive in that it brings together a number of documents related to the life and publication history of Conrad. The journal is to be commended for the presentation of material which is of limited accessibility, and for the excellent editorial work that has been brought to bear on the documentation. Among the papers reproduced are personal recollections: G.F.W. Hope's 'Friend of Conrad' (*Conradian* 25:ii[2000] 1–56) and Wilfred Partington's 'Joseph Conrad Behind the Scenes (*Conradian* 25:ii[2000] 177–84), both edited by Gene Moore; a stage adaptation of 'Victory' by Basil MacDonald Hastings, edited by Moore and Allan Simmons; and Conrad's notebook (*Conradian* 25:ii[2000] 205–44) and Last Will (*Conradian* 25:ii[2000] 245–51), edited by Allan Simmons and J.H. Stape and Hans van Marle respectively. Perhaps the most interesting aspect of these documents is, as general editors Moore, Simmons and Stape acknowledge in their foreword, the presence of Conrad in and around them. Whether it be in the margins of others' writings, or in the direct intervention of Conrad to correct or amend biographical detail, the interpenetration of subject and critic is strangely thrilling. While the editors have placed these documents in the wider critical domain, they do so without overweening commentary or editing, and their success should be witnessed in a much broader critical assessment of the texts' significance.

The artistic and personal implications of Conrad's exilic status also catches the attention of Andrea White who, in this year's *Conradiana*, explores the complexly intertwined cultural topography of the early years of his marriage to Jessie. Her essay '"The Idiots": "A Story of Brittany" under Metropolitan Eyes' (*Conradiana* 32:i[2000] 4–19) examines the Conrads' honeymoon in northern France and considers the ethnographic models that emerge from the stories written during the trip. Also in this number is the first of this year's two essays on 'Amy Foster'. Sue Finkelstein's interesting 'Hope and Betrayal: A Psychoanalytical Reading of "Amy Foster"' (*Conradiana* 32:i[2000] 20–30) seeks the traces of Conrad's own psychological traumas in his writing. 'Given such a legacy of trauma, and given its enormous toll on his self-esteem,' she asks, 'how did Conrad manage to plumb his own depths enough to become a writer of imaginative fiction?' (pp. 23–4). Through a reading of 'Amy Foster' Finkelstein shows how Conrad sought to accommodate his traumatized consciousness within his fiction, but succeeded instead in recreating 'his inner world in which abandonment and betrayal always triumph' (p. 27). Celia Kingsbury writes of Conrad's disgust with the hypocrisy of bourgeois suburban morality in '"The novelty of real feelings": Restraint and Duty in Conrad's "The Return"' (*Conradiana* 32:i[2000] 31–40, while Bruce Harkness provides an entertainingly robust riposte to theoretical appropriations of Conrad in 'An Old-Fashioned Reading of Conrad; Or, "Oh, no! Not another paper on *Heart of Darkness!*"' (*Conradiana* 32:i[2000] 41–6). S. Ekema Agbaw and Karson L. Kiesinger, 'The Reincarnation of Kurtz in Norman Rush's *Mating*' (*Conradiana* 32:i[2000] 47–56), explore the intertextual revivification of Kurtz in Norman Rush's novel *Mating* [1991], while Richard James Hand, '"The stage is a terribly searching thing" Joseph Conrad's Dramatization of *The Secret Agent*' (*Conradiana*

32:i[2000] 57–65), contributes a short, but well-worked essay on Conrad's own dramatization of *The Secret Agent*.

In '"Nothing to be done": Conrad, Beckett and the Poetics of Immobility' (*Conradiana* 32:i[2000] 66–72) Ted Billy examines the prevalence of non-action in the work of Beckett and in Conrad's 'Victory'. He contends that Conrad's characters are, in moments of existential crisis, rendered incapable of decision and consequently physically and psychologically paralysed. It is an interesting argument and one that deserved greater development, particularly in the section on the differing modernist/postmodernist stances towards immobility. Finally in the first number of *Conradiana*, Jane M. Ford contributes 'Father/Suitor Conflict in the Conrad Canon' (*Conradiana* 32:i[2000] 73–80). In it she argues, not entirely convincingly, that the incestuous relationship between father and daughter is a significant theme in the work of Dickens, James and Conrad. Furthermore, she contends that this incest results in conflict between father and daughter's suitor; a reversed Oedipal triangle that, in Conrad's case, possibly reflects his own amorous liaisons with considerably younger women.

Dorothy Trench-Bonett's 'Naming and Silence: A Study of Language and the Other in Conrad's *Heart of Darkness*' (*Conradiana* 32:ii[2000] 84–95) is a sensible, if not particularly original, riposte to Achebe's claims of racist representation in *Heart of Darkness*. Examining the names used to describe Black African subjectivities, Trench-Bonett suggests that indicative use of the term 'nigger' is reflective of victimization rather than denigration. In the latter parts of her essay she also suggests that the silence of the indigenous Africans is not a conscious denial of speech to the inarticulate on Conrad's part, but a political statement on the silence of the oppressed. Also writing on *Heart of Darkness*, Donald Wilson makes a case for the novella as a coded engagement with its late Victorian readership's attitude to homosexuality. 'The Beast in the Congo: How Victorian Homophobia Inflects Marlow's *Heart of Darkness*' (*Conradiana* 32:ii[2000] 96–118) argues, again not totally originally, that Conrad's largely male audience would have struggled to accept the obsessive fascination that Marlow develops for Kurtz. Nevertheless, Wilson argues that the novel contains clear indications of homosexual undertones, and it is these that constitute the 'heart of darkness' as much as Kurtz's moral degeneration.

'Time as Power: The Politics of Social Time in Conrad's *The Secret Agent*' (*Conradiana* 32:ii[2000] 123–43), by Mark Hama, rejects notions of the authoritarian nature of modernist time as fundamental to the novel, and instead installs a Foucauldian vision of time as fluid, individually articulated and, above all, powerful. Through an examination of three characters' perceptions of time, Hama contends that time in *The Secret Agent* is an act of willed social organization rather than an oppressive force. The correspondence between St Thekla, the first female martyr, and the character named Tekla in *Under Western Eyes* is examined in Debra Romanick Baldwin's 'Politics, Martyrdom and the Legend of Saint Thekla in *Under Western Eyes*' (*Conradiana* 32:ii[2000] 144–57). Arguing that Conrad's novel attempts to encapsulate the very essence of Russia, Baldwin claims that the inclusion of mystical and scared allusions to Thekla were fundamental to the creation of that atmosphere.

Like Sue Finkelstein's essay in the first number, Brian Shaffer's 'Swept from the Sea: Trauma and Otherness in Conrad's "Amy Foster"' (*Conradiana* 32:iii[2000]

163–76) also engages with the traumatic conditioning that exile brought about for Conrad. The shipwreck which besets the story's principal character is metaphorically interpreted as being equivalent to the trauma of loss involved in exile, and the consequent feelings of detachment, difference and alterity within the host culture. The third number of *Conradiana* also contains John Lutz's essay 'Centaurs and Other Savages: Patriarchy, Hunger and Fetishism in "Falk"' (*Conradiana* 32:iii[2000] 177–94). He contends that 'Falk'—one of Conrad's more controversial works—attacks bourgeois values and social mores which seek only to mask the 'breakdown of moral bonds produced by capitalist social relations' (p. 178). The story shows, he argues, how social solidarity has given way to a rapacious code of individualism dictated by a brutal economic pragmatism. Perhaps the most thought-provoking essay in this year's *Conradiana* is Tom Henthorne's 'An End to Imperialism: *Lord Jim* and the Postcolonial Conrad' (*Conradiana* 32:iii[2000] 203–27). Although it starts unpromisingly as yet another engagement with Achebe's charge against Conrad of racism, the article develops into a persuasive argument for a reading of *Lord Jim* as evincing the revolutionary preconditions of the postcolonial state. In this number Richard Hand follows up his essay on the dramatization of *The Secret Agent* with an article on 'Christopher Hampton's Adaptation of Joseph Conrad's *The Secret Agent*' (*Conradiana* 32:iii[2000] 195–202). The third number also contains reproductions (edited by J.H. Stape) of nineteen letters from Conrad's close friend, John Galsworthy: 'From "the most sympathetic of friends": John Galsworthy's Letters to Joseph Conrad, 1906–1923' (*Conradiana* 32:iii[2000] 228–45). Although bare without commentary, these letters do throw an interesting light upon an intimate and enduring literary friendship.

Outside the main Conradian journals there have been significant contributions from scholars in *Studies in the Novel*. The journal offers three essays this year, the first being Tony Brown's 'Cultural Psychosis on the Frontier: The Work of the Darkness in Joseph Conrad's *Heart of Darkness*' (*SNNTS* 32:i[2000] 14–28), which explores the ways in which darkness becomes intrinsically connected to, and responsible for, the 'horror'. Mark Larabee takes Conrad's assertion that the setting of *The Shadow-Line* should not be expected to relate to a historically specific locale, and examines this reticence against just such a locale. Through comparison with contemporary charts, guides and accounts, '"A mysterious system": Topographical Fidelity and the Charting of Imperialism in Joseph Conrad's Siamese Waters' (*SNNTS* 32:iii[2000] 348–68) Larabee reveals significant topographical alterations by Conrad, before relating those changes to his thematic structuring of *The Shadow-Line*. Thirdly John G. Peters's essay, 'Joseph Conrad's "Sudden Holes" in Time: The Epistemology of Temporality' (*SNNTS* 32:iv[2000] 420–41) considers Conrad's presentation of time, and in particular the experience of dislocation when subjective and objective systems of temporality collide. It is an interesting, if less provocative, paper than Mark Hama's in *Conradiana*. Finally this year, Indira Ghose's essay 'Conrad's *Heart of Darkness* and the Anxiety of Empire' (in Glage, ed., *Being/s in Transit: Travelling, Migration, Dislocation*, pp. 93–110) offers nothing more than a tired reiteration of the popular tropes of Conradian criticism.

(d) Wyndham Lewis

This has been quite a slow year for criticism of Lewis, and an even slower one for the sending of review copies, which makes this task somewhat problematic. Of the material available the following two essays were outstanding. In *Twentieth-Century Literature* Paige Reynolds has published '"Chaos invading concept": *Blast* as a Native Theory of Promotional Culture' (*TCL* 46:ii[2000] 238–68). This article examines the explicitly populist methods employed by Wyndham Lewis in the launch of *Blast*. Involving the use of typographies and syntax more commonly associated with mass advertising, *Blast* sought, so Reynolds implies, to question the relationship between high art and mass culture. By employing techniques common to advertising Lewis was also attempting to promote English art as being at the forefront of international culture. Lewis and the Vorticists positioned themselves, in Reynolds's view, at the nexus between high and low art and claimed sole control over the ability to effect a negotiation between the two. The essay interestingly dovetails the interests of the Vorticist movement with those of an increasingly technologized society, but also with the interests of the burgeoning middle-class retail sector. In manipulating the machinery of a promotional culture, those involved with *Blast* were merely reflecting the modernist Zeitgeist. This is an excellent essay, which makes a significant contribution to the study of the area.

Andreas Kramer's essay, 'Nationality and Avant-Garde: Anglo-German Affairs in Wyndham Lewis's *Tarr*' (in Stark, ed., pp. 253–62), refutes readings of the novel as anti-German, preferring to point to the subversion of literary character that makes nationalist stereotypes redundant. The argument is sound and the explication convincing. Kramer shows that, although stereotypical caricatures of both English and German manners seem to support a reading of the novel as derogatory towards the Germans, this is in fact problematized by Tarr's own relationship with his Englishness. By deconstructing the dialogue of nationalities Kramer suggests that Lewis's ultimate aim is not denigration but the revelation of identity as fluid and inter-national rather than fixed and nationalistic.

(e) George Orwell

It seems a while since we had a good year in Orwell studies. For too long books have been appearing that cover the same psycho-biographical ground, when they are not claiming that the only aspect of Orwell's writing worth considering is his politics. New perspectives need to be taken in order to move Orwell out of the post-Cold War phase of criticism and into more productive, energetic terrain. The books this year, while not especially poor, seem to exemplify this problem.

Orwell criticism has had its fair share of work on how far the world has moved towards the nightmarish vision of *Nineteen Eighty-Four*. On the whole these efforts have been hysterical treatises against the contemporary political or moral Zeitgeist, and few contain much level-headed appraisal. Steven Carter's *A Do-It-Yourself Dystopia: The Americanization of Big Brother* manages to be both slightly hysterical and dispassionate at the same time. His book is an attempt to reveal the ways in which modern American society has become intrinsically Orwellian. Not simply that; America, he suggests, has willingly adopted many of the basic Party tenets for social control with such enthusiasm that they are able to condemn in others the lack of freedom that they have joyously internalized. Carter examines the way in which 'Doublethink' and 'Newspeak' have not just become accommodated within

American speech and thought-patterns, but have become the linguistic norms by which individuals perceive their realities. While many of the previous publications in this vein have been thinly disguised attacks on the personal antipathies of their authors, Carter's does offer some interesting insights into the anthropology and sociology of modern America. His discussion of how political and corporate-speak has diluted and ultimately degraded language is interesting, albeit not entirely original. Indeed a certain familiarity is the overwhelming response to this book; it has been produced in one form or another for twenty years, and Carter's just seems sixteen years late. Good points are made, but the comparison seems tired and dated. The most interesting feature of the book's publication is the confirmation of the ongoing power of Orwell's vision as a yardstick for the development of social structures.

As student study guides go, Mitzi Brunsdale's *Student Companion to George Orwell* is a relatively successful example of the genre. Its intended audience is the secondary-level student, and for that age group this is an accessible yet provocative study of Orwell. The companion consists of a contextualizing biographical chapter followed by a chronological analysis of the major writings. The principal theoretical approach is psycho-biographical, but the parallels drawn between life and writing are sufficiently robust to be convincing. Each chapter offers critical analysis of a text, or set of texts, from the perspectives of plot development, major thematic elements, character development and literary/stylistic devices. The writing is clear and the structuring logical, and undoubtedly this book will serve its purpose. Too many of the Orwellian idiosyncrasies, both political and personal, are ironed out for my liking, and the tone is perhaps too simplistic even for this level. Too little time is spent on important issues such as the Blair/Orwell identity crisis and the dialogue between the texts and their various politicized receptions. Nevertheless, Brunsdale does show herself to be more sensitive to Orwell's ideas of Britishness than some recent American writers on the subject, and this is a useful and above-average addition to the field.

(f) D.H. Lawrence
The trend towards theorizing Lawrence that I identified last year continues apace this year in both books and articles, and once again I can begin by discussing a major example with a symptomatic title, Robert Burden's impressive and scholarly book, *Radicalizing Lawrence: Critical Interventions in the Reading and Reception of D.H. Lawrence's Narrative Fiction*.

This detailed and demanding text is hugely ambitious in its attempt to bring Lawrence together with almost every single major critical theory in contemporary literary studies, with chapters devoted to Freudian and post-Freudian psychoanalysis, Foucauldian discourse analysis, Bakhtinian dialogics, deconstruction, feminism, and masculinity theory—all traversed by periodic engagements with a debate about 'Modernism, Modernity, and Critical Theory' (the title of Burden's concluding chapter). Burden approaches his task with great crusading zeal, and rightly makes no apologies for adopting such a strong theoretical position on Lawrence: 'bringing theory to Lawrence is an affirmative strategy, radicalizing what has hitherto been reduced to the transparencies and positivisms of traditional, anti-theoretical criticism' (p. 10). Burden writes with force and clarity throughout, and he demonstrates a sure grasp of both the theories he deploys and a broad range of Lawrence studies (though he overlooks some key critical texts in places). Anybody wishing to gain a sophisticated overview of either field will find this a convenient, reliable and stimulating repository of information and ideas.

Having said this, one needs a good deal of stamina to read the entire book (which runs to nearly 400 closely written pages), as it is, in fact, rather *too* ambitious—not only in trying to cover so many different theoretical approaches to Lawrence (there are potentially several books here), but also in trying (as it does) to explain and critique all those theories in the process. Indeed, the book at times reads like a primer of critical theory rather than as a study of Lawrence, and the massive scope of that subject (i.e. theory) means that this inevitably leads to a certain overload of information and a certain over-intricacy and digressiveness of argument, especially given that the often cited (if often long deferred) aim is actually to *apply* the theories to Lawrence. In this sense, the book is simply too cluttered with material to make a truly compelling case about Lawrence and theory, either overall, or in each individual chapter (although some chapters are more compelling than others).

Burden's exclusive focus on Lawrence's major novels is perhaps a little conservative in view of the radical ambitions of the book (and it leads him into some further laborious 'clearing of the ground' of old debates), but several of his readings do pay rich dividends in revealing new facets of these familiar works. I would single out the truly innovative central chapters on 'Deconstructing Masculinity' (chapters 4 and 5, dealing with *Aaron's Rod*, *Kangaroo* and *The Plumed Serpent*) and the less wholly original but thorough and insightful discussion of Bakhtin's theories in relation to *Women in Love*, *The Lost Girl* and *Mr Noon* (chapter 3). Burden, it seems to me, unfairly plays down the significance and scope of earlier Bakhtinian approaches to Lawrence (and he seems to be unaware of some others), but he nevertheless provides one of the fullest overviews of this branch of Lawrence criticism currently available.

Terry Wright's *D.H. Lawrence and the Bible* at first also promises to engage usefully and innovatively with critical theory in its approach to Lawrence's career-long 'creative dialogue with the Bible' (p. 251), which is the subject of the book. Wright's brisk first four chapters certainly suggest a systematic theoretical agenda in their detailed concern with questions of intertextuality, with the theories of Bakhtin, Bloom and Derrida, and with the broadly Nietzschean paradigm within which Lawrence developed his philosophical and artistic stance towards the Bible. These chapters are well informed and clear, and seem to set the scene for a fuller working out of their implications in the body of the book. However, Wright does not really fulfil this promise in the ensuing chapters where, on the whole (there are notable exceptions), he adopts a type of source-hunting approach which largely abandons any claim to theoretical sophistication in favour of a rather mechanical determination to account for all major biblical allusions in almost every one of Lawrence's texts (with the unaccountable exception of *The Virgin and the Gipsy*). This is not to underestimate or disparage what Wright has positively achieved in tracing all these allusions and in accounting (often very insightfully) for their contextual and intertextual significance. This book is undoubtedly an important contribution to the field and deserves to become a key source of reference for anyone interested in Lawrence's use of the Bible. But I think Wright has missed a valuable opportunity to engage with the full range of artistic and intellectual issues at stake here by failing to develop a truly original and sustained critical argument.

Part of the problem is his reluctance to participate seriously in the existing critical debate about how Lawrence's art and thought grapples with his Christian and biblical heritage. Wright explicitly acknowledges some important critical precursors in what he tries to do, and his bibliography bespeaks a fairly comprehensive familiarity with Lawrence scholarship generally; but he almost nowhere enters into any detailed dialogue with other critics that might help him clarify just what still needs to be done in terms of this debate and just what it is that is distinctive in his own approach to the topic. Wright properly admits that he is by no means the first critic to argue that Lawrence constantly appropriates and reaccentuates the language of the Bible for his own philosophical, artistic and religious purposes, but it is not quite good enough then simply to claim a quantitative difference and say, as Wright effectively does, 'but I'm going to do it in much more detail' (see p. 12). The quantitative analysis of biblical allusions is valuable, as I have said, but one has the right to expect more than this from a critical monograph.

The third of only three books on Lawrence this year is *D.H. Lawrence: The Novels* by Nicholas Marsh, a type of composite study guide to *Sons and Lovers*, *The Rainbow* and *Women in Love*. As an introductory text, the book inevitably goes over much familiar territory, and its scope does not allow for the development of any radically new ideas about the three novels; but Marsh provides a well-informed and perceptive comparative introduction to these works and suggests useful follow-up activities for further study. He covers the essentials of Lawrence's life, work and critical reception briskly and reliably, and presents a good overview of Lawrence's place in the development of the novel. There is also a useful sampling of relevant criticism illustrating different approaches to Lawrence. The strongest aspect of the book, however, is its close attention to textual detail, and Marsh himself is an excellent close reader of Lawrence, frequently sparking fresh insights into familiar passages and skilfully drawing attention to the distinctive features of Lawrence's style.

In her detailed review essay, 'Psychodynamics, Seeing, and Being in D.H. Lawrence' (*MFS* 46:iv[2000] 971–8), Elizabeth M. Fox broadly concurs with my briefer comments here last year (*YWES* 80[2001]) on monographs by Jack Stewart and Barbara Schapiro, seeing these works, as she puts it, as 'milestones in Lawrence studies' (p. 971). Both Schapiro and Stewart develop aspects of their monographs in separate articles this year. In 'Sadomasochism as Intersubjective Breakdown in D.H. Lawrence's "The Woman Who Rode Away"' (in Rudnytsky and Gordon, eds., 123–33), Barbara Schapiro continues to tease out the post-Freudian textual psychodynamics of Lawrence's 'courageous' treatment of intersubjectivity, casting fresh light on this critically controversial story which is seen here as 'a disturbing enactment of the psychological dilemma inherent in masochistic fantasy' (p. 129). In 'Color, Space, and Place in Lawrence's *Letters*' (*DHLR* 29:i[2000] 19–36) Jack Stewart becomes one of the very few critics to have written in serious analytical detail on Lawrence's letters, and probably the first to have done so on the letters as presented in their newly established texts (and sequence) in the Cambridge edition. In considering the letters as 'intrinsically literary in communicating a vision in words', Stewart effectively applies to the letters his approach to Lawrence's other writings in *The Vital Art of D.H. Lawrence* [1999]—and he does so in an equally insightful, scholarly and elegant manner, strikingly bringing to life the way in which Lawrence himself '*lives* in his letters'.

An appropriate, if slightly less compelling, companion piece to Stewart's essay is Bibhu Padhi's 'D.H. Lawrence's Non-Fiction Prose: The Deeper Strains' (*DHLR* 29:i[2000] 37–50). Padhi, too, primarily considers stylistic elements of Lawrence's non-fictional prose (mainly the essays), and with a similar ulterior focus on Lawrence's 'vision' and 'aesthetics of spontaneity'. Andrew Harrison presents a differently orientated and more tightly circumscribed stylistic analysis in his fascinating and finely detailed study of 'Electricity and the Place of Futurism in *Women in Love*' (*DHLR* 29:ii[2000] 7–23). After briskly and authoritatively surveying Lawrence's familiarity with futurist art and writing, Harrison carefully details how the quintessential futurist image of electricity—an early suggested name for Futurism was 'Electricism'—permeates the novel's language and 'polarises' its meanings and relationships.

Gerald Doherty, in 'A Question of Gravity: The Erotics of Identification in *Women in Love*' (*DHLR* 29:ii[2000] 25–41), engages in a similar enterprise of analysing how meanings and relationships are polarized in the novel by specific rhetorical strategies. Doherty's more complex approach, however, is underpinned by psychoanalysis and seeks to show how different metaphors function to structure and represent processes of psychological identification (in the case of Gerald and Gudrun) or dis-identification (in the case of Birkin and Ursula). This concern with merging and separation (and polarized 'star equilibrium') is standard fare in discussions of Lawrence (and it echoes Schapiro's approach above), but Doherty's distinctive blend of post-structuralism and psychoanalysis adds a new stylistic dimension to our understanding of this theme.

Ben Stoltzfus demonstrates a different form of post-Freudianism in his '"The Man Who Loved Islands": A Lacanian Reading' (*DHLR* 29:iii[2000] 27–38). More suggestive than convincing, this represents a newly accented rather than wholly new interpretation of this much-analysed text. The view that the story dramatizes Cathcart's death-wish is hardly ground-breaking, but Stoltzfus elaborates his argument in an intriguing and unusual way, and presents Lacanian ideas in a helpfully lucid manner. The essay nevertheless finally undermines itself in its contrived conclusion, which sees Stoltzfus literally rewriting the ending of Lawrence's story by appealing to 'floating signifiers that, although not themselves present in the text, are nonetheless there, under erasure so to speak' (p. 36).

Other items from this year's three numbers of the *D.H. Lawrence Review* include useful bibliographical and historical studies. Jacqueline Gouirand provides an extensive update of work in France, 'A Checklist of D.H. Lawrence Translations, Criticism, and Scholarship Published in France, 1986–1996' (*DHLR* 29:ii[2000] 43–53), while Mark Kinkead-Weekes and John Worthen, in 'More about *The Rainbow*' (*DHLR* 29:iii[2000] 7–17), draw attention to some newly discovered materials relating to that novel's history: these include a previously unpublished early review, and a marked copy of the novel which shows that Lawrence continued to revise it even after publication. Steve Ressler's essay in the same number also concerns Lawrence's processes of revision by considering how the 'Broken Chronology in *The Rainbow*'s "Anna Victrix" and "The Cathedral"' helped Lawrence achieve a 'weighted conflict between his warring lovers' (*DHLR* 29:iii[2000] 19–25: 24).

Adam Parkes's essay, 'D.H. Lawrence and Federico Beltrán Massés: Censorship, Obscenity, and Class' (*DHLR* 29:i[2000] 7–18), represents an excellent piece of original research into the immediate social, cultural and legal context of the suppression of Lawrence's exhibition of paintings in 1929. By comparing the reception of a contemporaneous exhibition by the 'society' painter, Beltrán Massés, Parkes neatly demonstrates how (as in the *Lady Chatterley* case) class was a key point at issue here. Drawing on various contemporary documents, Parkes contributes valuable new information to our growing understanding of how fundamentally Lawrence's reception was shaped by questions of censorship. This is the broader significance too of James T. Boulton's researches into the recently opened Home Office file on Lawrence's *Pansies*, which was also banned in 1929. His essay, 'D.H. Lawrence's *Pansies* and the State, 1929' (*JDHLS* [2000] 5–16), describes the new information thrown up by the file, and explains how it contributes to a fuller picture of the history of *Pansies*. In particular, he shows how determinedly, and sometimes secretly, the authorities sought to suppress the publication and distribution of the unexpurgated edition of the book, even after the initial seizure of manuscripts and the publication of the expurgated edition in July 1929. Hitherto, it was not known—and Lawrence could not have known—how narrowly the unexpurgated 'for Subscribers only' edition of August 1929 escaped prosecution. It would be interesting, now, to see how one might combine the new information provided in these two historicizing essays, and to consider if, how, and to what extent official attitudes to each case (poems and paintings) were interrelated.

Several other forms of historical perspective on Lawrence are explored in essays this year. In 'Trespassing: Philip Larkin and the Legacy of D.H. Lawrence' (*DHLR* 29:iii[2000] 41–8) Rebecca Johnson, Philip Larkin's archivist, explores the poet's conflicted 'relationship' with Lawrence, arguing that he 'ruthlessly pillaged D.H. Lawrence's life and work in order to feed his own creative imagination' (p. 41) before distancing himself from Lawrence later in his career. John Fordham, too, considers Lawrence's literary legacy, this time to working-class writers, in 'Death of a Porcupine: D.H. Lawrence and his Successors' (*L&H* 9:i[2000] 56–66). Fordham makes a brisk case for recognizing the complexity of Lawrence's works in terms of their class significance, and refreshingly reminds us that Lawrence was 'always inevitably involved in a determinedly social and correspondingly textual class struggle' (p. 64).

Ann Ardis also engages with questions of social class in her reconsideration of Lawrence's ambivalent relationship to modernism in 'Delimiting Modernism and the Literary Field: D.H. Lawrence and *The Lost Girl*' (in Hapgood and Paxton, eds., pp. 123–42). Discussing music hall, cinema, and literary 'high' art partially in terms of their different class formations, Ardis interestingly (though not entirely originally) explores the ways in which *The Lost Girl* provides 'a self-reflexive commentary on aesthetic production in Britain at the turn of the twentieth century' (p. 138). She seems unaware of the pioneering work of George Hyde in exploring self-reflexive and music-hall elements in Lawrence's work, and Hyde has added inventively to his critical output on Lawrence with his highly original essay on a music-hall source for the catch-phrase 'that's that' in *Lady Chatterley's Lover*, '*Lady Chatterley's* Unlikely Bedfellow: George Robey and the Language of Lawrence's Last Novel' (*JDHLS* [2000] 17–36).

Like Ardis and Fordham, Roger Ebbatson explores aspects of the social and cultural context of Lawrence's work in '"England, my England": Lawrence, War and Nation' (*L&H* 9:i[2000] 67–82). Ebbatson's reading of the named story as a symptomatic text of its period involves a wide-ranging and sophisticated theoretical perspective which, among other things, dialogizes Lawrence's fiction in relation to both realism and modernism. The Lawrentian dialogue with modernism is picked up in Howard J. Booth's thought-provoking if slightly truncated argument in 'Lawrence in Doubt: A Theory of the "Other" and its Collapse' (in Booth and Rigby, eds., pp. 197–223). Booth's particular engagement with modernism here is a post-colonial one, as he explores how Lawrence draws on typically modernist strategies in his struggle to develop a theory of 'otherness' in his encounters with foreign races and places. Eva Yi Chen takes perhaps a more thoroughgoing post-colonial perspective in her essay, 'Primitivism, Empire, and a Personal Ideology: D.H. Lawrence's Travel Writings on the Indians of the American Southwest' (*JDHLS* [2000] 52–88). Yi Chen's essay is over-long, and a little tortuously argued at times, but it usefully grapples with many of the key issues at stake in developing a post-colonial perspective on Lawrence.

Ronald Granofsky's treatment of race, on the other hand, looks back to more traditional psycho-biographical approaches to Lawrence. In '"Jews of the wrong sort": D.H. Lawrence and Race' (*JML* 23:ii[1999–2000] 209–23), Granofsky traces anti-Semitic utterances in Lawrence's works to an underlying fear of merger and 'boundary violation' (p. 218) that is rooted in pre-Oedipal psychic formations and is therefore more to do with women than with Jews. Effectively playing a variation on Judith Ruderman's well-known 'devouring mother' thesis on Lawrence, Granofsky thus (over-)ingeniously exposes Lawrence's anti-Semitism as a type of misogyny in disguise. In a convoluted and overwritten exploration of Lawrence's engagement with the cultural other, Gregory Frank Teague, 'Levels of Participatory Experience in D.H. Lawrence's Italy Books' (*Real* 25:ii[2000] 49–76), draws on a heady mixture of Schopenhauer, Jung and Bakhtin to show how Lawrence 'participated' differently in Italian modes of being at the different moments of his career represented by his three Italian travel books.

Gary Adelman, in 'The Man Who Rode Away: What D.H. Lawrence Means to Today's Readers' (*TriQ* 107–8[2000] 508–36), gathers an interesting, if eclectic, range of contemporary opinions on Lawrence, from undergraduate students, on the one hand, to professional writers, on the other. Teaching a Lawrence seminar in 1997, Adelman was prompted by his students' generally negative response to the writer to initiate a sort of dialogue between their views and those of established authors, so he wrote to 110 novelists asking them to comment on his students' views and to indicate their own attitudes to Lawrence. Forty-four of the novelists responded (including, for example, A.S. Byatt, Doris Lessing, Erica Jong, William Gass and John Fowles) and substantial extracts from their widely varied replies are printed here, providing what should be a useful archive of contemporary opinion for future reference. By coincidence, another contemporary writer, Pico Iyer, also records his feelings about Lawrence in an independent essay, 'Lawrence by Lightning' (*ASch* 68:iv[2000] 128–33). This is (perhaps unsurprisingly) one of the best-written essays of the year and provides an affecting personal perspective on Lawrence's characteristic qualities as a writer. It is certainly a 'passionate appreciation' rather than a critical study, but in its account of both youthful and mature encounters with, in particular, *The Virgin and the Gipsy*, it also provides a closely considered reflection on the changing (and, for the writer, enduring) significance of Lawrence's work, which, though primarily personal, inevitably takes in some common features of a general reading history and thus adds significantly to the 'archive' assembled by Adelman.

In 'At the End of *The Rainbow*: Reading Lesbian Identities in D.H. Lawrence's Fiction' (*IFR* 27:i–ii[2000] 60–7), Justin D. Edwards makes some promising observations about the dominant and emergent sexual paradigms within which Lawrence worked, but ultimately makes little real progress in developing the existing critical debate on Lawrence's sexual and gender politics (a debate which Edwards is only partially informed about). Jonathan Long's 'D.H. Lawrence and Nakedness' (*JDHLS* [2000] 89–109) usefully draws attention to an unexpectedly neglected area of Lawrence studies, but then does little more with the topic than simply to catalogue a variety of instances of nakedness in Lawrence's works (including the paintings). Drawing on Deleuze and Guattari, Stephen Alexander also focuses on Lawrence's celebration of 'naked' spontaneity and desire in 'The Strange Becomings of Sir Clifford Chatterley: A Schizoanalysis' (*JDHLS* [2000] 37–51). This sounds rather abstruse, but Alexander actually ends up taking a fairly conventional 1960s view of Lawrence as a champion of free sexual expression and 'polymorphous perversity'.

In 'The Religious Initiation of the Reader in D.H. Lawrence's *The Rainbow*' (*Mosaic* 33:iii[2000] 165–82), Charles M. Burack draws creatively on phenomenology and reader-response theory to argue that Lawrence's poetic use of a rhythmic 'initiatory structure' in *The Rainbow* is designed to evoke numinous states of consciousness in the reader. Rightly relating this strategy to the modernist concern with epiphany, Burack, however, strains to establish what is surely too schematic (and ultimately inevitably subjective) a view of Lawrence's designs on the reader. Moreover, although better informed than many critics mentioned here, Burack does neglect one or two critical precursors who have argued along similar lines: Peter Balbert's *D.H. Lawrence and the Psychology of Rhythm* [1974], for example. John R. Harrison, in 'The Flesh and the Word: The Evolution of a Metaphysic in the Early Work of D.H. Lawrence' (*SNNTS* 32:i[2000] 29–48), more coolly analyses how Lawrence's 'ontology and epistemology are woven intuitively into the fabric of the ... early fiction' (p. 30). Harrison tries to correct what he sees as the general misconception that Lawrence's theories tend to pre-date their fictional reworking by showing how, in particular, his earliest imaginative works clearly experiment with ideas that are only later conceptualized theoretically (in 'Study of Thomas Hardy', for example). This is an intelligent and well-written essay, unusual here for concentrating on Lawrence's very earliest works.

Primarily focused on the other end of Lawrence's career, two essays take the motif of death as their subjects. Alan W. Friedman's 'D.H. Lawrence: Pleasure and Death' (*SNNTS* 32:ii[2000] 207–28) is the more conventional of the two and is really no more than a rapid trawl through the later fiction to consider what is seen as Lawrence's repeated 'treatment of the Freudian deathwish' (p. 214). The main unifying argument here is that Lawrence reflects a paradoxical modernist desire to reverse the traditional Victorian death-bed scene in resurrectionary fantasies which, in their affirmative yea-saying, actually bespeak their deepest anxieties about death. Howard J. Booth's more original '"A Dream of Life": D.H. Lawrence, Utopia and Death' (*ES* 80:v[1999] 462–78), an essay missed last year, actually argues something very similar, but in a more biographically oriented way. Lawrence's later writings, for Booth, modulate into utopian fantasies precisely because of

Lawrence's real illness and his real fear of death. They provided Lawrence with a means of projecting himself 'away from his health problems into an ideal space' (p. 478). However, Booth's fascinating analysis of 'A Dream of Life' [1927] demonstrates how Lawrence's repressed fears constantly resurface in the 'uncanny' elements of the story. A cautionary comment about Booth's essay, though, may be represented by Stanley Sultan's labouring, in 'Lawrence the Anti-Autobiographer' (*JML* 23:ii[1999–2000] 225–48), of the critical commonplace that Lawrence's characters are never mere 'facsimiles' of the author, and that, though Lawrence obviously drew on his own experiences, this was always only 'a method for making fiction'.

Three volumes (21, 22, 23) of *Etudes Lawrenciennes* for 2000 together contain some twenty-five essays deriving from a 1999 conference held in Paris on the theme 'D.H. Lawrence: After Strange Gods'. As might be expected, these cover almost the whole range of Lawrence's oeuvre from a variety of perspectives, and, though there is inevitably some unevenness across the three volumes, the general standard of all these essays is high, with a refreshing emphasis on new approaches to Lawrence as well as on some of his less familiar works. As just two examples of this stimulating and innovative range of work, one might mention Garry Watson's 'Rethinking This-Worldly Religion: D.H. Lawrence and French Theory' (*EL* 21[2000] 21–49) and Aline Ferreira's 'A Reading of D.H. Lawrence and Luce Irigaray's Notion of Wonder' (*EL* 22[2000] 43–60).

Mention should be made of the publication of the final volume of the Cambridge edition of Lawrence's letters. Scrupulously edited by the indefatigable James T. Boulton, *The Letters of D.H. Lawrence*, vol. viii: *Previously Uncollected Letters/ General Index* prints letters to and from Lawrence which came to light too late to be included earlier in the correct sequence of the edition. It also includes corrigenda and addenda to the previous volumes, a few previously published but uncollected letters, and an extensive index to all eight volumes.

Essays or other work which I have not been able to access include the following: Laurie A. Sterling and Kathryn Yerkes, '"The mastery that man must hold": Little Red Riding Hood Grows Up in Lawrence's "The Woman Who Rode Away", Silko's "Yellow Woman", and Carter's "The Company of Wolves"' (*POMPA* [2000] 62–9); Justin Williamson, '"The Living Moment": D.H. Lawrence's Poetic and Religious Vision in "Fish"' (*POMPA* [2000] 37–47); William M. Harrison, 'Thinking Like a Chicken—But Not a Porcupine: Lawrence, Feminism, and Animal Rights' (*LIT* 10:iv[2000] 349–70); Gregory Tague, 'Self Recovery in D.H. Lawrence: Schopenhauer, Estrangement, and the Sublime' (*R/WT* 8:i–ii[2000] 53–64); and Masako Hirai, 'Tanizaki and Lawrence (or East and West): The Paradox of Love between Mother and Son' (in Vervliet and Estor, eds., *Methods for the Study of Literature as Cultural Memory*, pp. 161–73).

Finally, George Hyde (*JDHLS* [2000] 134–5) reviews what looks to be a valuable addition to the Lawrentian canon, in a Japanese collection of his visual art, *Paintings and Writings of D.H. Lawrence* (Tokyo: Sogensha [2000]). Most of the text is apparently in Japanese, but 'what we have here is the richest harvest so far of Lawrence's intensely personal work as a painter and as a graphic artist' (p. 134).

(g) James Joyce
This year saw the publication of a significant new addition to the trend of biographical studies. John McCourt's engaging volume documenting Joyce's Triestine period provides further confirmation that Ellmann's monumental tome is no longer the last word in Joyce biography. *The Years of Bloom: James Joyce in Trieste, 1904–1920* provides a compelling case for re-evaluating the importance of Trieste for Joyce's work by relating his artistic development to the cosmopolitan life of the city in which he lived, on and off, for a decade and a half, for it was here, argues McCourt, that Joyce came to a more subtle (less chauvinistic) understanding of women, and befriended a number of Jews whose characters and knowledge informed his later fiction. McCourt offers another model for the character of Bloom—one Theodor Mayer, the Hungarian Jewish editor of the irredentist newspaper *Il Piccolo*, who also happened to be a mason, stamp-collector and sometime exponent of 'the gentle art of advertising'. More than any one specific model, however, what emerges most strongly is a portrait of Bloom as Triestine, notably in his retorts in 'Cyclops', his cosmopolitanism and 'rejections of nationality, of persecution' (p. 73). McCourt's local knowledge of Trieste fuels his readable, fast-moving narrative. There are several critical comments offered as well, including observations that link Joyce's early life to phrases in the portmanteau language of *Finnegans Wake*. For instance, the dialect of Trieste, Triestino, which Joyce 'learned to speak … brilliantly' was 'a living encyclopaedia of the cultures, nations and languages which had been assimilated in the city' and 'in this respect the language of *Finnegans Wake* is an exaggerated, exploded version of *Triestino*' (pp. 52–3). If *The Years of Bloom* is a little short on photographic depictions of its subject, another book by John McCourt, *James Joyce: A Passionate Exile*, certainly makes up for that shortcoming. Essentially a coffee-table book, it contains many excellent pictures, including some of Trieste, and a slightly skewed 'brief life' that stresses the importance of the Triestine middle years at the expense of the less well documented Paris years.

McCourt has also contributed an essay on *Giacomo Joyce*, 'The Importance of Being Giacomo' (*JoyceSA* 11[2000] 4–26), arguing that more important than a precise identification of the model(s) for the female protagonist is her escape from the 'lustful and sometimes violent gaze' (p. 24) of Giacomo. Another study of Joyce's Triestine poem in prose is '"At the center, what?" *Giacomo Joyce*, Roland Barthes and the Novelistic Fragment' (*JJQ* 36:iv[1999] 765–80), by Michel Delville, which sees it as a Barthesian 'novelistic' text.

Although Attridge and Howes, eds., *Semicolonial Joyce*, is a collection of original essays, it merits discussion here as a book in that it collectively provides a significant contribution to recent discussions of Joyce's relationship to colonial and post-colonial cultures. As the editors point out, the term 'semicolonial' is characteristic of Joyce's ambivalence towards hard and fast political statements, for it not only confuses the already complex relation between colonialism and post-colonialism but typically intermingles the political with the linguistic. The first essay, 'Dead Ends: Joyce's Finest Moments', by Seamus Deane, is a characteristically brilliant and provocative reading of some of the *Dubliners* stories, and also forwards the dominant argument of the book: that 'to be colonial is to be modern', that 'Joyce's political critique' of the paralysis and fantasy invoked by colonial conditions also 'points up how characteristic this is of the conditions of modernity. What the Dubliners suffer from is not the inability to enter into modernity; it is the inability to escape from it' (p. 33). Deane suggests that Joyce's 'critique' ends with the penultimate story of *Dubliners*, and that from then on he 'surrenders critique for aesthetics' (p. 34). Not all the other contributors would agree with this last analysis, seeing as they do Joyce's continued and lifelong engagement with cultural politics and the politics of representation. Another fine essay, Joseph Valente's '"Neither fish nor flesh"; or, how "Cyclops" Stages the Double-Bind of Irish Manhood', offers an excellent reading of the twelfth episode of *Ulysses* as an interrogation of the Victorian/Edwardian construction of masculinity as it was 'supportive—even constitutive—in the delineation of ethnic differences between colonising and colonised peoples' (p. 96). In Valente's discussion, the Citizen's apparent descent into bestiality is an enactment of 'colonial hypermasculinity' (p. 106)—the mimicry of the strong man of violent resistance who falls prey to the colonizers' simianization of the colonized—and Bloom's attempt at dignified self-control mimics 'colonial gentlemanliness' (p. 124) only to end up criticized as emasculation. That Joyce sees no way beyond this impasse of colonial manhood is Valente's pessimistic conclusion. The final essay of the collection, 'Authenticity and Identity: Catching the Irish Spirit', by Vincent Cheng, warns of the dangers of any such search for authenticity in the colonial debate, as both academic and popular appropriations of Irishness—from post-colonial theory to the below-deck shenanigans in the film *Titanic*—can tend to reproduce comfortable stereotypes. As is so often the case, Joyce's writing has anticipated the questions now raised to explore it. Without exception, the essays in this volume (some of which are listed elsewhere in this review) are interesting and provocative for further study, including Katy Mullin's analysis of Joyce's subversive use of emigration narratives in 'Eveline' and Elizabeth Butler Cullingford's discussion of Joyce's inventive genealogy and geography. They all generally contend that Joyce's work engages with Irish colonization and its attendant themes, and where some are short of gripping textual analysis all are worthy contributions to an important volume. An apt and open conclusion may well be Emer Nolan's warning from her overview of Joyce and post-colonialism that 'Joyce may present a polyphony of voices—translating this into a politics is by no means straightforward' (p. 85).

Recent work that has placed Joyce in the context of Irish historical and cultural transformations has been supplemented by Willard Potts's *Joyce and the Two Irelands*. Potts analyses a broad range of Joyce's prose in the context of the Revival. It is in his definition of the Revival in a lengthy opening chapter that this book stakes its claim, seeing it primarily in religious terms as the offshoot of sectarian division. Potts outlines the broad socio-religious differences among Revival figures, and argues that Joyce was very much a part of the Revival and that he never fully shook off his own Catholic upbringing. After its initial contextualization, the book then discusses, in a chapter each: the *Critical Writings*, *Dubliners*, *Stephen Hero* and *A Portrait*, *Exiles* and *Ulysses*. These discussions elucidate Joyce's references to the Revival, and Potts seems particularly keen to list as many Protestants as he can find in the work. However, given his definition of the Revival, and his argument that Joyce had no truck whatsoever with nationalism, Potts's focus on Protestants (he does not differentiate between forms thereof) seems designed to find traces of a sectarian residue, which, of course, are duly found. Joyce, then, could break from literary tradition, he could step aside from nationalism, but he remains caught, according to Potts, within 'the traditions and feelings of his Catholic culture' (p. 198). This may well be the case, yet it seems only reasonable not to detach religious sectarianism from other cultural, national and imperial issues.

Other investigations into the various political backgrounds and contexts of Joyce's work have appeared in a number of essays. These include June Dwyer's 'Feast and Famine: James Joyce and the Politics of Food' (*Proteus* 17:i[2000] 41–4), a discussion of cultural identity after the Famine and Joyce's representations of eating, particularly in 'The Dead'. On a different tack, in 'Penelope, or, Myths Unravelling: Writing, Orality and Abjection in *Ulysses*' (*TPr* 14:iii[2000] 519–31) Gerardine Meaney suggests that Joyce unravels myths of national culture at the expense of reinstating myths of the feminine: Molly's 'masterpiece of oralization' (p. 526) comes close to abjection. Two essays appeared in a broad-ranging collection, Booth and Rigby, eds., *Modernism and Empire*. In 'Modernism, Ireland and Empire: Yeats, Joyce and their Implied Audiences', C.L. Innes discusses the ways in which Yeats, and especially Joyce, suggest a specifically Irish and politicized audience for their work alongside a more generalized reception, and in '"Hanging over the bloody paper": Newspapers and Imperialism in *Ulysses*', John Nash argues that a reading of *The Times* as a source for the 'Cyclops' episode shows Joyce engaged in an anti-imperial parody of that newspaper. The political implications of the spatial representation of Dublin in *Ulysses* are discussed by Andrew Thacker in 'Toppling Masonry and Textual Space: Nelson's Pillar and Spatial Politics in *Ulysses*' (*ISR* 8:ii[2000] 195–203). Alongside this may be read Enda Duffy's 'Disappearing Dublin: *Ulysses*, Postcoloniality and the Politics of Space' and Marjorie Howes's '"Goodbye Ireland, I'm going to Gort": Geography, Scale and Narrating the Nation', both in Attridge and Howes, eds., *Semicolonial Joyce*. Duffy's argument bears a strong resemblance to that of Innes, citing knowledge of 1904 Dublin as a hallmark of the projected community of readers in *Ulysses*. 'The politics of space' recurs in Anne Fogarty's essay, 'Remapping Nationalism: The Politics of Space in Joyce's *Dubliners*', which includes a brief discussion of the relations between gender and urban space in 'Eveline' and 'Clay'. This is in Bataillard and Sipière, eds., *Dubliners, James Joyce: The Dead, John Huston*, which also contains a section of seven essays and a bibliography devoted to Huston's film of 'The Dead'. One of these, 'The City of Dublin and its Symbols' by Laëtitia Crémona, again takes up the theme of spatial politics. Yet another form of spatial organization in 'Eveline' is discussed in an intriguing essay by Peter de Voogd, 'Imaging Eveline, Visualised Focalisations in James Joyce's *Dubliners*' (*EJES* 4:i[2000] 39–48), who argues that the story operates a series of visual set-pieces dramatizing Eveline's melodramatic 'self-willed victimisation' (p. 48).

Two collections of essays by long-standing readers of Joyce appeared this year, and they exemplify the variety of output which Joyce studies still attracts, each providing a memoir of decades spent in Joyce scholarship. Derek Attridge, one of the most productive and consistently challenging of Joyce critics, has moulded a number of previously published essays—on deconstructive Joyce, 'popular' Joyce, 'Clay', character, 'Penelope', postmodernity and narrative, interpretation and language in the *Wake*—into a single volume, *Joyce Effects: On Language, Theory, and History*, to which is added an autobiographical introduction. Here, Attridge chronicles his development as a critical thinker, and his attendance at Joyce symposia. In a not untypical gesture, he turns against the 'formulaic applications' (p.

15) of the theoretical schools that have been so readily accommodated within Joyce studies. This is not to say that Attridge has lost faith in either Joyce or critical endeavour—rather, he reaffirms his (and others') 'commitment to Joyce'—but he does call for a reading of Joyce that rethinks his role in the institution of literary production and consumption. What worries Attridge about the expansion of Joyce studies is that its library of scholarship which makes annotation and glossary so readily available no longer challenges its readers but has instead won 'cultural supremacy' as the greatest example of Western literary culture, and is now 'a text that confirms us in our satisfied certainties' (p. 185). It is at least refreshing to read a Joyce critic challenging the unabashed growth of Joyce scholarship and instead positing a contemporary cultural milieu for reading what has become of Joyce. One essay that partially addresses these issues is 'The Genealogies of *Ulysses*, the Invention of Postmodernism, and the Narratives of Literary History' (*ELH* 67:iv[2000] 1035–54) by Brian Richardson, which discusses that novel's place in critical conceptions of literary history (or histories), especially in relation to the category postmodernism. Attridge's chapter on the relationship between sexual awareness and language in *A Portrait* is complemented by a discussion of selfhood, sexuality and epiphany by Joshua Reynolds in 'Joyce's Epiphanic Mode: Material Language and the Representation of Sexuality in *Stephen Hero* and *Portrait*' (*TCL* 46:i[2000] 20–33).

Morton P. Levitt's collection, *James Joyce and Modernism: Beyond Dublin*, brings together several decades' worth of essays on Joyce under some consistent critical themes; modernist art, Jewishness, myth and, above all, Joyce's humanity. This is in many ways a traditional salute to Joyce, and the author depicts a 'paradoxical sense of a conservative Joyce' (p. 12): a writer who 'lends himself well to new approaches' but who 'transcends … a particular time' (p. 12). This last claim may perhaps account for the subtitle, which is itself the title of the final essay of the book (in fact, this essay bears the book's title, inverted), and is perhaps the most revealing of Levitt's approach. In the foreword to this essay, Levitt argues for reading Joyce as a modernist rather than a postmodernist, and for his continued belief in 'the literary and human values which I find in Joyce, and which to me are the essence of Modernism' (p. 263). Precisely what these values are Levitt does not say, but the title is telling enough; Levitt's Joyce is hardly a middle-class Irish Catholic of the late nineteenth and early twentieth centuries at all; he is, rather, the embodiment of a European high art, the 'aura' (p. 272) that has inspired numerous others. One interesting offshoot of Levitt's collection is the practice of appending a few autobiographical pages to each essay, as these themselves provide an insider's fragmentary account of the burgeoning industry of Joyceans.

A new and thorough work by Weldon Thornton, *Voices and Values in Joyce's Ulysses*, returns to the familiar critical terrain of the novel's stylistic variety. Thornton argues that the point of the range of styles in the latter part of the book is not to illustrate some form of linguistic relativism but to highlight 'how inept each of these styles is in comparison with the initial style' (p. 2). This is most clearly brought out in Thornton's analysis of the 'Cyclops' episode, wherein the 'secondary narrative voice' is seen to expose the 'hollowness' (p. 40) of an undiscriminating parodic tone, a voice that parodies all values including pacifism and love. The initial style, by contrast, is taken to affirm certain values in its choice of event, vocabulary and method. So the values hereby affirmed include the 'sincerity and commitment and intellectual courage' of Stephen, Bloom's openness and concern for others, and a critique of Mulligan's 'materialism, mockery, and cynicism' (p. 39). The initial style, it is argued, thus provides 'a normative base that underlies ... the later episodes'. Such a reading produces a *Ulysses* that is very much character- and story-based, a novel that many of its early readers and some today would not recognize as the same book. The initial style is praised by Thornton for its careful replication of a cultural milieu and for 'subverting modernist dualisms' (what, precisely?), but, what, then is the point of the later styles if the initial style 'fulfills Joyce's purposes so effectively' (p. 97)? Thornton numbers among those later styles both the 'Aeolus' and 'Wandering Rocks' chapters. The latter is read as a critique of the narrative viewpoint which presents a fragmentary urban experience or 'mechanical view of the city' (p. 137). In support of this reading, Thornton cites the several acts of kindness by various characters in the chapter, the narrator's 'errors' ('deceptions' would be a better word) and the 'more positive image' of Dublin 'offered by the novel as a whole' (p. 142), although such evidence is itself misleading since it means a very limited appraisal of Father Conmee (for instance) and a highly contentious assessment of Joyce's Dublin. If there are broader questions that might be posed of Thornton's thesis, this is nonetheless a carefully plotted book, richly laced with detailed allusion and close readings of all the chapters, thankfully in an argumentative order and not in the pattern of the book. Questionable as its argument may be, this is still a very handy guide for students and teachers, which includes careful assessments of much previous work on this topic.

It is perhaps surprising that relatively few specific studies of *Ulysses* have appeared this year. However, a bibliographical commentary, *Recent Criticism of James Joyce's 'Ulysses': An Analytic Review* by Michael Patrick Gillespie and Paula F. Gillespie, does provide an extensive updating of similar projects. It carries chapters on reader response and post-structuralist thought, gender and sexuality, psychological readings, cultural and post-colonial criticism, and the editions of *Ulysses*. This is perhaps a starting-point for students bewildered by a whole library of Joyce scholarship, providing one- or two-page summaries of many recent titles, but the coverage is not comprehensive, so it does not really suit research purposes. The chapter that includes discussion of even 'unalloyed deconstruction' (p. 23), for instance, omits all mention of Derrida's essay, 'Ulysses Gramophone'.

If the parodies in *Ulysses* represent, for Thornton, a perversion of the normative initial style, then for Christy L. Burns parody means something quite different. Her book, *Gestural Politics: Stereotype and Parody in Joyce*, defines parody as 'an unstable representation that itself never fully masters any law or object' (p. 10). Thus defined, parody includes the very act of writing a text such as *Ulysses*, as well as such examples as Bloom's engendered performative character. Parody, then, becomes less a description of a remodelling of a prior text and more a state of becoming, and as such can be widely applied. Burns's argument takes in Joyce's representations of women, gays and Irish nationalism, as well as attempting an overview of Joyce's aesthetics. She finds that Joyce gestures towards stereotypes in such a manner that they are both reinforced and ironically undermined. As stereotypes usually operate in a humorous way in Joyce's writing, this also involves Burns in a catalogue of Joycean comedies. Perhaps Joyce's serious stereotypes would have provided an interesting topic as well? She investigates Joyce's relation to the theories of gesture propounded by Mercel Jousse in the 1920s, and develops a notion of gesture wherein 'the limits of bodily gesture and material sensations' (p. 1) are exposed as semantic blindspots that reveal a textual politics. Burns concludes by turning this onto textual materiality—the very printed embodiment of physical language. It is no surprise that the argument is based mainly upon readings of *Finnegans Wake*.

While Burns has discussed some of the ambivalent stereotyping of Joyce's politics, the issue is also central to some more studies of Joyce's depictions of Jewishness. In 'Bloodsucking Bloom: Vampirism as a Representation of Jewishness in *Ulysses*' (*JJQ* 36:iv[1999] 981–97), Lori B. Harrison focuses on the ambiguities of the vampire-figure as both Jewish and Irish, dead and alive. Richard Beckman, in 'Joyce's Ungentlemen's Club (for Jews and Dandies)' (*JJQ* 36:iv[1999] 799–812), offers a social critique of 'the gentleman' in ethical and class terms, noting that Bloom and Earwicker are not 'gentlemen'. Another side to Joyce's sometimes uncomfortable stereotyping is discussed by Willy Maley in 'Kilt by kelt shell kithagain with kinagain": Joyce and Scotland' (in Attridge and Howes, eds.). Maley argues that Scotland is portrayed by Joyce as a 'sister subject nation who has, in order to curry favour with England, betrayed her Hibernian sibling' (p. 209).

In addition to Thornton's study of narrative voice in *Ulysses*, the prolific and improving Florida James Joyce series has produced two more books this year. One of these, *Joyce's Comic Portrait* by Roy Gottfried, sets out to do for Joyce's first novel what others have done for Joyce's later novels, that is, to show that *A Portrait* is also a comic work. Rather than the familiar Dedalian rhythm of rise and fall, of progression and irony, Gottfried argues that the narrative also carries 'an alternate motion of tumbling'—'a pratfall rather than a tragic fall' (p. 3). He shows how educative institutions normally regarded as key to the serious *Bildungsroman* are also sites of comic subversion, not necessarily by Stephen but certainly in others' voices. Hence the *Portrait* of artistry and irony is also one of vulgarity and humour. Stephen is, in Gottfried's terms, two-headed, much as the language of the novel contains 'a comic doubleness of diction' (p. 47), a narrative conflation of 'the lofty … with the low' (p. 55). The middle chapter is a speculative diversion into possible humorous contexts, arguing that Joyce did not do all his reading in Marsh's Library, but was also 'likely to have read' (p. 84) such popular journals as the *Dublin Illustrograph*, from whose articles he was able to concoct enough slang and innuendo to service his ready wit. Joyce also read the columns of one Edgar Wallace in the *Daily Mail*, and Gottfried argues that these were also part of the potential comic context within which *A Portrait* was written. The final two chapters return to textual analysis, of both *Stephen Hero* and, briefly, *Ulysses*. In a sparse year for *Portrait* publications, Gottfried has produced a bold and imaginative book with an original and well-researched thesis.

The other Florida publication, R.J. Schork's *Joyce and Hagiography: Saints Above!*, is a collected narrative of many years' research and publications documenting Joyce's use of the literature of sainthood, from the apostles to 'a newly canonised Passionist priest' (p. xi) as they appear in the fiction or fleetingly pass through his correspondence. Schork presents such a wealth of material relating to Joyce's Jesuitical teaching and esoteric reading, as well as to centuries of Catholic canonization, that this book will probably be the standard work on its topic for many years. It is not strictly a reference work, being told in a narrative elucidation, yet its detail is such that it will provide a useful supplement to other Joycean reference tomes, notably for *Finnegans Wake*, with which most of this study is concerned. One of the most interesting saints in Joyce's work is of course Joyce himself (there is a brief chapter on fictitious saints), and this unofficial St James rubs shoulders with Stephen, the first martyr, and Patrick and Kevin, as well as lesser-known holy men, as in the tradition of the 'hairy hermit'. Schork also adds a calendar of feast-days as they appear in Joyce's work. In sum, this is a helpful volume, of interest to the curious browser and the specialist researcher.

In a lean year for genetic criticism, two articles in the dependable *Joyce Studies Annual* stand out. Finn Fordham's 'Mapping Echoland' (*JoyceSA* 11[2000] 167–201), provides a new and interesting method within genetic analyses. Fordham takes one element from the text—in this case the title itself—and traces its revisions through Joyce's drafts, rather than, as is more usually the case in genetic work, through the notebooks. This method provides a 'hidden narrative' (p. 169) of a motif's evolution, potentially allowing for a cultural-contextual reading beyond most genetic practices. In 'Joyce's Sources: Sir Richard F. Burton's *Terminal Essay* in *Finnegans Wake*' (*JoyceSA* 11[2000] 124–66) Aida Yared shows, through an analysis of the *Wake* notebooks, that at three different compositional stages Joyce read Burton's *Terminal Essay* (attached to his seventeen-volume translation of the *Arabian Nights*, and which Joyce owned in his Trieste library), and Yared helpfully provides transcriptions of these notebook allusions. Other essays on Joyce's last work include 'In the "Numifeed Confusionary": Reading the Negative Confession of *Finnegans Wake*' (*JNT* 30:i[2000] 55–95) by Damon Franke, a treatment of confession and denial in the *Wake*'s narrative, and Strother B. Purdy's positive answer to his own question in 'Is There a Multiverse in *Finnegans Wake*, and Does That Make it a Religious Book?' (*JJQ* 36:iii[1999] 587–602).

Several essays have once more treated issues of translation. Aiping Zhang discusses Xiao's rendition of *Ulysses* in 'Faithfulness through Alterations: The Chinese Translation of Molly's Soliloquy in James Joyce's *Ulysses*' (*JJQ* 36:iii[1999] 571–86), while Friedhelm Rathjen offers some comparative sample passages and a commentary on translators' methods in 'Sprakin sea Djoytsch? *Finnegans Wake* into German' (*JJQ* 36:iv[1999] 905–916). In 'Universalizing Languages: *Finnegans Wake* meets Basic English' (*JJQ* 36:iv[1999] 853–68), Susan Shaw Sailer looks at C.K. Ogden's Basic English version of I.8 that appeared in *transition* [March 1932].

3. Post-1945 Fiction

Jane Dunn's biography of Antonia White, first published by Jonathan Cape [1998], has been re-issued by Virago in paperback. There are only two previous biographies of White, written by her daughters, Susan Chitty (*Now to my Mother* [1985]) and Lyndall Hopkinson (*Nothing to Forgive* [1988]). Both have very obvious familial axes to grind, and caused some controversy when they were published. Dunn's biography is thus the first thorough attempt at the history of the complex and fascinating life of Antonia White. There is much to savour in this biography, which is meticulously researched and fluently written. Dunn explores carefully and perceptively the impact on White of her childhood conversion to Catholicism, her long and painful struggle with mental illness, her turbulent emotional life, including her brief and doomed marriages, and her constant feeling that she had failed as a woman. Dunn leaves the task of literary analysis and commentary to other hands, and is unapologetic about reading White's fiction for what it might tell us about her psychological, sexual and emotional life. She has a keen eye for a good story, however, and begins with a wonderful, extraordinary story of White's funeral service, during which a black cat entered the church and circled around the coffin, and reappeared at the graveside as White's coffin lay in the ground. This seemed to confirm to White's mourners, who knew of her passion for cats, that 'the cat had been sent by her as a sign of approval' (p. 1). Dunn later recounts the story of a Society of Authors party in 1960, at which White was serially misrecognized as Noel Streatfield, Antonia Ridge, and then told by Rebecca West's husband 'I have *never* forgotten that delightful book of yours about the Three Rivers of France' (p. 375). Virago played a crucial role in rescuing White from such obscurity, and have thankfully issued Dunn's biography in paperback. This is an invaluable source for all those interested in White, and may even succeed in returning readers to such soulful, searching novels as *Frost in May* and *The Lost Traveller*.

Jeremy Gibson began working towards a critical study of the writings of Peter Ackroyd prior to his tragic death in 1996, and Julian Wolfreys was asked to develop and complete this work, which has now been published as *Peter Ackroyd: The Ludic and Labyrinthine Text*. The authors exhibit at every turn a shared love of Ackroyd's writing, which creates a peculiar and fascinating tension between the deconstructive mode of exegesis, familiar certainly from Wolfreys' other work, and the concern of the authors to pay homage and respect to Ackroyd. The book includes three generous interviews with Ackroyd, and his reviews and critical writings are quoted favourably throughout the book. This might lead to the impression that the authors are too 'close' to their subject, although they prefer to think of it as a kind of reciprocity between writer and critic, part of what is discussed in the introduction as 'a very serious game' between text and critical contexts. The discussion of the critical reception of Ackroyd's writings tends to sneer a little too much at curmudgeonly English reviewers, but once the authors embark upon their own forays into the 'ludic and labyrinthine' in Ackroyd they mine some rich seams of thought and analysis. The focus of the book is primarily the novels, although there is a chapter on Ackroyd's three volumes of poetry, and several biographies are discussed in a chapter on Ackroyd's London. The chapter on London, indeed, is a brilliant exploration of the density and complexity of the city as it is woven through the intricate patterns of Ackroyd's writings. The authors argue that Ackroyd has been consistently concerned with a particular kind of stylized Englishness, often camp or theatrical, and that his writings continue to address and complicate issues of representation, identity and culture in contemporary England.

G. Peter Winnington's *Vast Alchemies: The Life and Work of Mervyn Peake* is one of two biographies of Peake which have appeared this year (Malcolm Yorke's volume is reviewed in section 1(a) above). Winnington is the editor of *Peake Studies*, and displays an impressively detailed knowledge of Peake's life and work in this volume. The emphasis tends to be on Peake's development as an artist and illustrator rather than his skills as a writer, and this leaves the book a little short when it comes to detailed commentary and analysis of Peake's literary works. Winnington succeeds in providing a readable and lively account of Peake's life and creative achievements, and this biography will serve as an accurate and reliable source for Peake scholars. The pace of the narrative is, if anything, a little too lively. Winnington does not dwell as long as he should on the significance of Peake's childhood years in China, nor on the traumatic effects on Peake of his visit to Belsen. This is in part the result of Winnington's reluctance to surmise or speculate beyond the biographical facts which he can establish from letters, conversations or other sources. The parallels between the early life of the Chinese boy emperor and Titus Groan seem to me to be too 'numerous and striking', to use Winnington's words, to be anything but convincing, although Winnington can't help cautioning that 'it may just be a coincidence' (p. 31).

The death of Iris Murdoch in 1999 inevitably prompted some reassessment and revaluation of her work, particularly the twenty-six novels she wrote between 1954 and 1995. In *Psychological and Religious Narratives in Iris Murdoch's Fiction*, Robert Hardy begins such a reassessment in the predictable but productive domains of Murdoch's preoccupation with psychoanalysis and theology. Hardy is especially concerned with Murdoch's exploration of the possibilities for the future of religion after belief in God has died, and of the problems of moral psychology. This takes the form of a more detailed examination of Murdoch's use of, and approaches to, Freudian and Jungian theories of psychology, as well as close readings of the moral universe of Murdoch's fiction. Hardy does not just treat Murdoch's novels as case studies for working through the rudiments of a godless morality, however. He is also attentive to the personae and masks of her fiction, and analyses Murdoch's psychoanalytic interest in the stories that her characters tell about themselves. Hardy reads Murdoch's novels in conjunction with Freud's texts—*The Message to the Planet* in relation to *Moses and Monotheism*, for instance—to show how close Murdoch was to Freud's arguments, but returns in the conclusion to Murdoch's ambivalent relationship to Jung's theories to show how indispensable psychoanalytic ideas became to her attempt to think through a humanist morality. Hardy's book also contains a preface by Bran Nicol which sets the current contexts for studying Murdoch's fiction.

Penelope Fritzer's *Ethnicity and Gender in the Barsetshire Novels of Angela Thirkell* is a short but valuable study of Thirkell's twenty-nine novels of social satire, written between 1933 and 1960. In contrast to other Thirkell commentators, Fritzer argues that Thirkell is at her best in the novels written in and about the immediate post-war years, when the 'brave new world' ushered in by the Labour government provided a rich source of satire for her conservative, nostalgic sensibility. It is perhaps in this spirit that Fritzer refers to Thirkell's 'rediscovered significance as a writer', and celebrates her work as 'marvellous social history in addition to charming fiction' (p. 17), although, to be fair, Fritzer also gives voice to those critics who have found the sexism, classism, and racism of her work a barrier to appreciation. The book is neatly divided into an introduction, about forty pages on ethnicity, about forty pages on gender, and a conclusion. The chapters on ethnicity and gender are jaunty summaries of various references and representations throughout the novels. In the case of ethnicity, for example, Fritzer trawls through the various allusions to Jewish, Irish, German, Scottish, Welsh, American, and, of course, English characteristics, to the empire and the war in Europe, to 'foreigners', and discusses the nature of Thirkell's patriotism. For Fritzer, Thirkell's preoccupation with ethnicity, and her mockery of various ethnic groups, is to be thought of as humorous: 'to take umbrage is to miss the point' (p. 58). Thirkell can apparently be excused from any accusation of xenophobia or racism because she treats English characters to the same degree of mockery as foreigners. The chapter on gender focuses on the representation of 'couples' in Thirkell's novels, her benign, oblique allusions to homosexuality (e.g. 'unusual friends'), and her scornful treatment of educated or career women. Fritzer explains the absence of 'feminist' points of view as the product of Thirkell's time and setting, but this is far from adequate as an understanding of Thirkell's conservative treatment of gender relations. Fritzer concludes by encouraging 'the discerning reader' to judge Thirkell's work 'consonant with its chronological context' (p. 110). This rather deviously implies that Thirkell's time was as conservative, xenophobic and sexist as her fictions. If Thirkell's more unseemly views are to be excused by their time, Fritzer might at least take care to present a more detailed and nuanced examination of the period.

Maroula Joannou's *Contemporary Women's Writing: From 'The Golden Notebook' to 'The Color Purple'* surveys the concerns and achievements of British and American women writers between 1962 and 1982. It is deeply rooted in the experiences of student radicalism and the women's movements of the 1960s and 1970s, and combines expert, persuasive analyses of a wide range of women's writing with a subtle reading of the politics of difference that emerged from that time. Joannou chooses to focus on 'woman-centred writing' rather than 'feminist writing', and argues that 'feminist' is a problematic term in relation to fiction. This enables Joannou greater flexibility in addressing feminist concerns in 'even the most unpromising of woman-centred texts' (p. 11). Joannou's knowledge of the period extends far beyond the obvious landmarks, and insists on the centrality of 'popular' genres—detective fiction, science fiction, and confessional writing—to a fuller understanding of women's writing (and women's reading). Chapters on motherhood, working-class women, 'commonwealth' writers, and black writing interrogate the intersections of gender, class, nation, post-colonialism and sexuality, while a chapter on 'continuities and change' considers the women's writing of the period in relation to notions of tradition and experimentation. The distinguishing features of Joannou's book are the lucidity and breadth of her analyses, which contain important considerations of writers as diverse as Pat Barker, Nell Dunn, Margaret Drabble, Lynne Reid Banks, Ruth Prawer Jhabvala, Buchi Emecheta, Jean Rhys, Ursula Le Guin, Anita Brookner, and Angela Carter, to name just some. This is an important, reliable and erudite assessment of women's writing in the 1960s and 1970s, and will become one of the standard authorities on this period. Joannou concludes with a careful, judicious estimation of the likely reception of women's writing in the twenty-first century: 'The reader of women's fiction in the twenty-first century is likely to be faced with a disjunction between a sophisticated and potentially liberating understanding of the unstable nature of all gendered and sexual identities and of the institutions that sustain them, which is offered to her by a combination of post-structuralist ideas and feminist theory, and a desire for more permanent identities and representations to contest the demeaning and restricted views of women which have historically prevailed' (p. 191).

There is no more important issue than food—as a material and symbolic activity, as the core of our self-identity, as a major part of our social and cultural rituals, as a political and economic matter. It is an important concern in contemporary feminism, as food and eating are inevitably caught up in discourses of mothering, the body, sexuality, and home. It seems such an obviously fundamental issue that it is difficult to understand why Sarah Sceats's book, *Food, Consumption and the Body in Contemporary Women's Fiction*, is without immediate comparisons or precursors. Sceats is conscious of this, and provides a thorough, lucid account of the cultural and symbolic significance of food and eating, as well as tracing how food functions in the novels of Doris Lessing, Margaret Atwood, Angela Carter, and to a lesser extent Michèle Roberts and Alice Thomas Ellis. The ingredients for Sceats's recipe, if you'll pardon the metaphor, are all in place: Foucault and Kristeva on the body, Barthes on social ritual, Chodorow on mothering, Freud and Klein on sexuality, and an array of feminist and psychoanalytic writing on breast-feeding, food, fat, eating disorders, desire and consumption. Sceats's achievement in this book is to bring two narratives together, in a sense, the story of the cultural meanings of food and eating, and the story of how contemporary women writers have employed food as a symbolic signifier of forms of love, power and communication. These intertwined narratives follow a trajectory from the individual focus of the first three chapters to the social, communal focus of the last three. In the conclusion Sceats recognizes that social practices of food consumption are subject to sweeping global forces of change, and ponders the impact of such change on the idea of food as a language, as a form of social exchange. Her deductions in the book generally are neither startling nor radical, but provide an intelligent and cogent assessment of the centrality of food to contemporary women's fiction.

Tamás Bényei's *Acts of Attention: Figure and Narrative in Postwar British Novels* is not so much a book as five essays bound together. There are no connections made between the chapters, no conclusion, and the introduction is short and makes no claims to advancing a thesis or overview of post-war British fiction. The essays are, however, wonderfully attentive and incisive in their analysis of novels by Evelyn Waugh, John Fowles, William Golding, Jeanette Winterson, and Ian McEwan. Bényei approaches each novel from the perspectives of postmodern narratology, focusing in each chapter on distinct tropes and modes of narrative. *Brideshead Revisited* is explored as 'an allegory of mourning', its apparently *Bildung* narrative form paradoxically consists of a strongly nostalgic mode. *The French Lieutenant's Woman* is also read as an allegory, this time of the narrative process itself, particularly in the novel's simultaneous deployment of narrative authority and seduction. William Golding's sea trilogy is examined for its concern with 'the tropological, figurative nature of the way we make sense of the world', what it means to be 'in' language. The shortest chapter in the book regards Winterson's *The Passion* as a novel which constantly attempts to lose its way, and 'risks itself', as an exemplary narrative mode of auto-deconstructive criticism. The final chapter considers the parallel stories in Ian McEwan's *The Innocent*, and how any attempt to map the relationship between the two stories collapses. This leads Bényei to interrogate 'the place between' narrative, the interstitial spaces through which narrative fails or falters, as a way of thinking about deconstructive narrative strategies. Perhaps a more general overview or thesis might have done more damage than good in this case, for Bényei's essays work well by exploring the singular narrative modes and strategies at work in each of his texts. The assiduous attention Bényei pays to each text makes for rewarding, perceptive reading, and this book, or at least each of its essays, makes valuable contributions to understanding narrative modes in post-war British fiction.

James Maurice Ivory's *Identity and Metamorphoses in Twentieth-Century British Literature* examines figures of metamorphoses in five fictional texts: Kafka's *The Metamorphosis*, Virginia Woolf's *Orlando: A Biography*, Angela Carter's *The Passion of New Eve*, James Joyce's *Ulysses* and Salman Rushdie's *The Satanic Verses*. The inclusion of Kafka rather disturbs the coherence of Ivory's field of study; one could equally argue that the 'British' in the title is not quite appropriate either to encompass the work of Joyce and Rushdie. After the chapter on Kafka, which analyses the social and economic contexts of Gregor's horrific transformation, Ivory pairs chapters on Woolf and Carter for their shared concern with gendered identities and gender-crossing, and chapters on Joyce and Rushdie for common interests in mobilizing tropes of hybridity and plurality in the service of a post-colonial politics. The chapters on Carter and Rushdie are lamentably short, which tends to make Ivory's general claims somewhat imbalanced. The overview provided in the conclusion does little to formulate theories or speculations about the function of figures of metamorphoses in twentieth-century 'British' literature, which is also to say that the value of Ivory's book lies in his close readings of such figures. There is a more general thesis to be sought out in Ivory's subject-matter, which is the political function of figures of transformation in the writings of feminist and post-colonial writers, but Ivory's conclusion can only advance tentative and vague suggestions as to what this might entail.

There are several overlapping themes developed in Valerie Krips's *The Presence of the Past: Memory, Heritage, and Childhood in Postwar Britain*. Krips shares with many recent cultural commentators an interest in themes of loss, mourning and nostalgia in post-war British culture, and the materialization of those themes in the heritage industry. She is also interested in the ambivalent and shifting condition of 'memory' in post-war culture, as a site of both reassurance and disquiet. She combines these themes brilliantly and persuasively in the study of children's fiction, as it has been read, produced and fetishized in post-war Britain. The result is a subtle account of the contemporary fascination with children's literature, not just for the appeal of its stories, but for the ways in which children's books have become cultural artefacts and heritage objects. Krips considers for the most part the fiction produced for children between the 1950s and 1980s, by such authors as Philippa Pearce, Rosemary Sutcliff, Susan Cooper, and Alan Garner. But there is almost as much discussion of the editions, interpretations and cultural resonances of earlier writers such as Lewis Carroll, Beatrix Potter, Frances Hodgson Burnett and Kenneth Grahame. In particular, Krips astutely acknowledges that children's literature is characterized by 'dialectic engagement as it responds to adult memory and to childhood understood in terms of a personal and collective past' (p. 25). It straddles the times of adult past and childhood present, and this, for Krips, makes it peculiarly well suited to an exploration of the cultural functions of memory and 'living history'. There are occasions in Krips's book when the various strands of her enquiry pull apart, so that it seems as though there is a brief narrative of post-war history followed by an analysis of a piece of children's literature. In general, however, she succeeds in weaving into a cogent study an important and complex configuration of themes. In examining this period of children's literature in relation to themes of nostalgia, memory and commodity fetishism, Krips is also, of course, reflecting on issues very pertinent to more recent times, and one cannot help but wonder how current debates about J.K. Rowling and Philip Pullman might fit with her analyses. Finally, I could quibble that Krips's chapter on editions of 'classic' children's texts should include a few plates showing the illustrations and cover designs she discusses, but perhaps I would then be accused (justifiably) of the fetishism she associates with such editions.

Christianson and Lumsden, eds., *Contemporary Scottish Women Writers*, is a collection of exploratory essays on a very underdeveloped critical field. This is reflected in the introductory nature of many of the essays, which cover Kathleen Jamie, Liz Lochhead, Sharman Macdonald, Sue Glover, Rona Munro, Lara Jane Bunting, Jackie Kay, Muriel Spark, Candia McWilliam, Agnes Owen, Emma Tennant, Elspeth Barker, Alice Thompson, Janice Galloway, and A.L. Kennedy, among others. The introduction admits a degree of shyness about considering these writers under the rubric of 'Scottishness', and indeed this seems to form something of a dilemma for some of the contributors. The 'nation' as a construct has been profoundly questioned and revised in contemporary critical theory, which perspective informs many of these essays, but the newly emergent political formations in Scotland have prompted interest in what comprises Scottishness and Scottish literature (not least in the two volumes reviewed here, and Anderson and Christianson's volume reviewed in section 1(*a*)). The editors recognize that this issue of how Scottish women writers are addressing their relationship to political and cultural nationalism is complicated by matters of gender, language, race, location, class, sexuality, and so on, to the extent that some writers considered in the volume (A.L. Kennedy is the most notable example) resist the very label of 'Scottishness'. To be fair, most of the essays don't really insist on the obvious issues of identity, but the agenda is there nonetheless in Margery Palmer McCulloch's essay on tradition in Scottish women's poetry, Helen Boden's consideration of 'Kathleen Jamie's Semiotic of Scotlands', Susan Triesman's essay on Sharman Macdonald, and Alison Lumsden's essay on Scottish women's short stories. One problem for the editors is that, in avoiding making any definitive statements or even advancing a hypothesis about what kind of Scotland or Scottishness emerges from contemporary women's writing, the only alternative seems to be a rather slack celebration of variety: 'What perhaps is most notable about Scottish women writers today is their diversity; they write in a number of styles and genres and take as their subject-matter a wide variety of themes'. This is to say that there is nothing 'notable' about them as *Scottish* writers at all. It is difficult, of course, to identify trends in the contemporary, but there is much more to be said on the matter than this volume manages to articulate.

Cairns Craig's study, *The Modern Scottish Novel: Narrative and the National Imagination* [1999], is much more assured in placing Scottish literature within a particular configuration of social, cultural, linguistic, religious and historical contexts. This is an ambitious, impressive and hugely enjoyable exploration of the recurrent themes, concerns and styles of modern Scottish novels, from John Buchan and Neil Gunn to the more recent flourishing of Scottish writing from A.L. Kennedy, Alasdair Gray, Janice Galloway, James Kelman, Irvine Welsh, Muriel Spark and many others. This is no chronologically ordered narrative of Scottish literary history, but an authoritative and inspiring consideration of how Scottish novelists in the twentieth century examined notions of community, history, imagination, language, dialect, faith, and art. Craig shows how the prevailing historical and cultural conditions in modern Scotland have produced inventive adaptations of the novel form, but also, correlatively, fictional experiments have had their part to play in reimagining the conditions of Scotland's cultural and political existence. The introduction makes for an eminently sensible sifting of concepts of tradition, narration, national imagination, and Scotland's 'predicament', and establishes solid foundations for the chapters to follow. In the book as a whole, Craig proves himself to be widely knowledgeable about Scottish literature, culture and history, a persuasive and subtle interpreter of texts of all kinds, and to possess an astute and incisive ability to reveal the underlying continuities behind diverse texts and contexts. The result is a reliable and rewarding study of Scottish fiction, an outstanding contribution to research and understanding of Scottish literary studies.

Two volumes published in the Manchester Contemporary World Writers series merit review here: Barry Lewis on Kazuo Ishiguro, and Elaine Yee Lin Ho on Timothy Mo. Lewis sees Ishiguro as exemplary of a distinctly twentieth-century mode of exile and estrangement, and argues that Ishiguro's novels address the struggle between displacement and dignity. The introduction sets out clearly Ishiguro's own sense of homelessness, and the various attempts by critics to 'locate' him in Japanese or English cultures. Lewis identifies the defining tendencies of Ishiguro's first three novels as 'concision and stylistic reticence', and concentration on 'a limited point of view, usually that of an unreliable narrator', which he abandoned in *The Unconsoled* for 'a rambling picaresque style'. The book is organized into chapters on each of the novels, and each chapter addresses fruitful issues in Ishiguro's work. How Japanese is his writing, for example? Lewis draws from the tendency by reviewers to compare his early novels to various forms of Japanese art, to argue that Ishiguro's Japan is fictive, a self-consciously artificial construct. He considers *A Pale View of Hills* in relation to Japanese ghost fictions, *An Artist of the Floating World* in relation to Japanese cinema, and *The Remains of the Day* as an exploration of the meanings of 'dignity', in which the character Stevens sees himself as 'a personal integer within a larger whole'. Lewis argues that *The Unconsoled* seems to mark a break in Ishiguro's work: it differs from the first three novels in style, and yet concludes that it continues Ishiguro's exploration of memory as the figurative projection of a world 'uncertain, quivering, and subject to erasures and displacements'. The penultimate chapter of the book attempts an overview of Ishiguro's literary career, which proves illuminating. Lewis argues that the pattern of his work to date can be described as 'sequent repetition-with-variation', and defends the virtues of *The Unconsoled*, which received damning reviews when it was published in 1995. In the postscript, Lewis argues that Ishiguro's most recent novel, *When We Were Orphans*, merges the restrained realism of his first three novels with the dreamscapes of *The Unconsoled*. This book is a splendidly lucid account of Ishiguro's preoccupations and styles, which makes intelligent commentaries on the cultural contexts and formal innovations of the writer's work.

Elaine Yee Lin Ho's book on Timothy Mo bears some similarities to Lewis's book on Ishiguro. Both novelists were received initially in England principally through the optic of the ethnic or cultural configurations which formed the subject of their early publications. Both Ho and Lewis are concerned with displacing the misguided assumptions which prevail in early reviews of their respective authors' work, particularly the idea that novels such as Mo's *The Monkey King*, or *Sour Sweet*, or Ishiguro's *A Pale View of Hills*, are 'representative' of Chinese or

Japanese culture generally. Ho argues convincingly that Mo's novels offer 'substantive and riotous critique' of such confusions, and explore the complexity of cultural and ethnic identities. *The Monkey King* and *Sour Sweet* exist both as satires on 'Chinese' culture, and as interrogations of the cultural interchange between Chinese and other cultures in the cultural melting-pots of Hong Kong and London. From these 'domestic' narratives, Mo moves into a mediated form of the historical novel in *An Insular Possession* and *The Redundancy of Courage*, but Ho argues that Mo's theme remains the difficulty of cross-cultural relations. Both novels, however, also develop a critique of the conventions of historical and political representation, and offer sceptical counter-narratives to the discourses of imperialism and nationalism. Ho illuminates the publishing controversy surrounding Mo's fifth novel, *Brownout on Breadfruit Boulevard*, and the surprising redirections in style and form which characterize the novel, and which presage his most recent work, *Renegade or Halo*. Ho's assessment of Timothy Mo's work is a valuable and astute introduction, a very welcome evaluation of a writer who has to date received scant critical attention.

In contrast, Martin Amis suffers perhaps from too much attention, critical or otherwise. Nicolas Tredell has sampled reviews and critical essays of all Amis's fictional works for *The Fiction of Martin Amis: A Reader's Guide to Essential Criticism*, from the Icon series of readers' guides. This is a useful volume for students, as it provides extracts from most of the more significant appraisals of Amis's writings, and Tredell narrates the story of Amis's development, and the evolving reactions to his work and public image. He emphasizes from the outset that Amis is a controversial figure in contemporary media and literary circles, and some of the extracts are selected for their part in the controversies. For the most part, however, Tredell selects and introduces the extracts for the critical issues they raise. Responses to *The Rachel Papers* tend to focus on how close Amis is to his protagonist, Charles Highway. The reviews and essays on *Dead Babies* consider whether the novel works as Menippean satire or not. Reviewers of *Success* attempt to assess how successful Amis has become as a writer. *Other People* is discussed as a 'martian' text, with Blake Morrison observing that 'Martin Amis' is an anagram of 'Martianism'. *Money* opens up debate about the relationship between English and North American cultures, and about the intrusive author in contemporary fiction. The chapter on *Einstein's Monsters* includes Adam Mars-Jones's attack on Amis's masculine posturing, while the chapter on *London Fields* opens with discussions of why the novel was excluded from the Booker short-list, before advancing to themes of apocalypse and authorship. The pieces on *Time's Arrow* reflect on Amis's responsible handling of the Holocaust, while Tredell studiously avoids the publicity wrangles which dog considerations of *The Information*. The final chapter on *Night Train* and the *Heavy Water* stories testifies to Amis's continuing power to provoke contrasting, and controversial, responses. Tredell makes a good job of selection, editing prudently and generously as required, and splices the extracts together well. The introduction to the volume could have been more substantial, however, as Tredell offers little more than an overview of Amis's career, and a rather redundant summary of the extracts included in each chapter.

It is more fulfilling, however, to read a collection of complete essays, rather than the fragments offered in the Icon readers' guides, and this is what Macmillan's New Casebooks series is all about. Alison Easton has edited the collection of 'contemporary critical essays' on Angela Carter. Her introduction provides a good, lucid overview of Carter's current critical standing, and the ten essays in the volume span the range of critical approaches to her work reasonably well. They are all feminist essays, perhaps expectedly so, and they will all be familiar to students of Carter's work: they are by Mary Russo, Gerardine Meaney, Sally Keenan, Merja Makinen, Jill Matus, Christina Britzolakis, Heather Johnson, Sally Robinson, Kate Webb, and Jean Wyatt. The surprising absences are Lorna Sage and Clare Hanson, who are quoted a number of times in the introduction, but not included. Carter's work has understandably attracted considerable attention, particularly in relation to issues of gender, psychoanalysis, and myth, but, like Easton, I look forward to the future critical work which will situate her more thoroughly in relation to historical and cultural contexts. In terms of Carter's current situation in literary criticism, however, this collection offers much of the best work available. As a one-stop volume of critical essays on Carter, Easton's collection should find its place very quickly on recommended reading lists.

Christopher Pressler's *So Far So Linear: Responses to the Work of Jeanette Winterson* is a short, underdeveloped appreciation of Winterson's fiction. The author acknowledges in the preface that the book is not 'a strict piece of literary criticism', and this proves to be the case, for it combines suggestive readings with partially explored contexts and cursory insights. Pressler pursues some clear theses: that *The Passion* is better read as a new version of history than as a fairy tale, that in *Written on the Body* Winterson is engaging medical language poetically, and that *Sexing the Cherry* explores fundamental psychological oppositions in the brain; but such theses tend to rely upon sketchy outlines of concepts derived from popular science. There are ample signs of a close acquaintance with, and evident appreciation of, Winterson's work, but the book lacks the precision and coherence which it might have achieved. As a result, its contentions are often woolly: 'Winterson's achievement is to have extended her imaginative processes into every subject with which she deals.'

Winterson is the subject of the final chapter in Andrea L. Harris's *Other Sexes: Rewriting Difference from Woolf to Winterson*. Harris's book examines the notion that women writers have explored 'the border between masculine and feminine, in other words, the place where these terms overlap and intersect, forming other sexes that cannot be described with the language at our disposal' (p. xii). She does this through an opening discussion of the 'deconstructive feminism' of Spivak, Butler, Irigaray and others, followed by chapters on each of four novels: Virginia Woolf's *The Waves*, Djuna Barnes's *Nightwood*, Marianne Hauser's *The Talking Room* and Jeanette Winterson's *Written on the Body*. Much of Harris's book is too heavily descriptive, either of theoretical debates or fictional plots. In the chapter on Winterson, she explains the novel's exploration of the interrelationship between self and other, and its theme of the ethics of love. Her chief argument in relation to the novel is examined really rather briefly: it is that Winterson's narrator is an ambivalently gendered figure who is 'feminine under the guise of the universal/ masculine' (p. 146). The narrative voice is de-gendered, adopting the universal or masculine subject position, and so would be disturbing from an Irigarayan point of view. But it is also a radical, bold move, if we follow the logic of Monica Wittig, as it liberates women from the burden of always being categorized by their sex. This is clearly a productive ambivalence for Harris, but it deserves further explication.

4. Pre-1950 Drama

The last two years have seen a resurgence of interest in the drama of the first half of the twentieth century, and especially a renewed interest in the state of British theatre between the wars. This interest has resulted in work that spans a number of areas of theatre, including historiography, textual studies, gender, political drama and the relationship between state censorship and drama. Barker and Gale, eds., *British Theatres Between the Wars, 1918–1939*, covers many of theses areas in an attempt to reposition inter-war theatre within histories of twentieth-century theatre as a whole. Barker's introductory essay, 'Theatre and Society: The Edwardian Legacy, the First World War and the Interwar Years', analyses economic shifts in theatre ownership and the effects of the aftermath of the First World War on the cultural production of drama. Barker assesses the cultural legacy of the Edwardian period as a shaping force for the drama of the 1920s and 1930s. Such spectacularly long-running shows as Oscar Asche's *Chu Chin Chow* are seen in the context of critical snobbery about the loss of the pre-war 'play of ideas' and a gradual shift in the class composition of audiences during the late 1910s and 1920s. The chapter continues by looking at the groupings of types of play in production, such as the Aldwych farces—mostly penned by Ben Travers—in the late 1920s and early 1930s. John Stokes's 'Body Parts: The Success of the Thriller' continues in this vein with a focused analysis of the enormous numbers of thriller plays, popularized in the 1930s by authors and actors (such as Emlyn Williams) alike. Stokes draws, again, parallels between the social climate of the immediate post-war years and the cultural search for somehow alienated or violent, yet clever, heroes in plays such as *Bull-Dog Drummond*. The book also contains a number of chapters that focus on issues around gender and performance: James Ross Moore gives an overview of musicals and revue during the inter-war period, where the female body played a significant role; while John F. Deeney, in 'When Men were Men and Women were Women', looks at configurations of gender and sexuality in such plays as *Journey's End*, *The Children's Hour* and *Design For Living*. Maggie B. Gale, in 'Errant Nymphs: Women and the Interwar Theatre', reassesses women's contributions to the British inter-war stage, looking at the relationship between political and cultural change and the increased presence of women as playwrights and directors. A number of chapters turn to the specific relationship between politics and textual production. Tony Howard looks at Shakespeare productions in direct relation to ideology in 'Blood on the Bright Young Things: Shakespeare in the 1930s'. Here he makes a correlation between nationalist and fascist thinking, and the ways in which characters such as Shylock were configured on the British stage. Ros Merkin, in 'The Religion of Socialism or a Pleasant Sunday Afternoon? The I.L.P. Arts Guild', also turns to politics in an analysis of the Independent Labour Party's Arts Guild and the ways in which social and political debate were directly encouraged within an arts context, with performance groups being set up all over the country and plays being produced as part of a bid to use drama in a consciousness-raising context. Mick Wallis brings the book towards a close in his 'Delving the Levels of Memory and Dressing Up in the Past', where he assesses the growth in popularity of pageant performances in both rural and more urban contexts. Clive Barker's closing chapter, 'The Ghosts of War: Stage Ghosts and Time Slips as a Response to War', gives the reader a detailed overview of the ways in which plays such as J.M. Barrie's *Mary Rose* and

Priestley's *Time and the Conways* directly related to such cultural phenomena as a growth in the number of Spiritualist churches in Britain and in 'new science' works such as J.W. Dunne's *An Experiment with Time*. Barker suggests that some dramas of the period could be seen as indirect responses to war because of the ways in which they play with time, memory, the dream, the paranormal and so on. This is a book which will be useful to anyone undertaking literary research in this period, and is the first to take on board the variety of types and contexts for British theatre and drama between the wars. It covers a wide area of new materials and does not fall prey to the dominance of canonical texts.

Mick Wallis continues his work on British pageantry by focusing on the life and work of Mary Kelly, in 'Unlocking the Secret Soul: Mary Kelly, Pioneer of Village Theatre' (*NTQ* 16:iv[2000] 347–58). Here he documents Kelly's work with large pageant productions, and her role as a moneyed woman within a rural community, looking at the social and political consciousness she brought to her work, the breadth and depth of which have been somewhat overlooked. Wallis also looks at Kelly's own theatre writings and assesses her legacy in relation to the growth in number of amateur and professional pageants during the period and in the country as whole.

With a similar sense of political drive, Steve Nicholson's *British Theatre and the Red Peril: The Portrayal of Communism, 1917–1945* is a welcome addition to the field. The book looks at the ways in which stage representations of Russia, bolshevism and 'left thinking' were constructed around the limitations of both censorship and the British fear of a radical political change such as had been witnessed during the Russian revolution. Nicholson points to the ways in which the process of stage censorship operated at a subliminal level. His argument that good plays were not written *because* of censorship is, however, somewhat tenuous, although the fact that manuscripts were generally submitted to the censor's office by management appears to have acted as an inhibiting factor on playwrights—why write a play that you know will be banned? Nicholson is careful to frame successes such as the Phillpotts' *Yellow Sands* in the context of anti-bolshevist feelings, but at times his assumption that we should judge the worth of plays rather than offer cultural readings or positionings is a little irritating. His readings of rarely discussed plays such as Izrael Zangwill's *The Forcing House*, Hubert Griffith's *Red Sunday* and Sean O'Casey's *The Star Turns Red* are particularly useful, as is his dense documentation of the ways in which the Russian aristocracy became an object of fascination for theatre writers and audiences during the immediate post-revolutionary years. The book contains a detailed glossary of playwrights and production details and is derived in part from readings of the Lord Chamberlain's collection at the British Library. Such an approach to theatre historiography is to be welcomed.

Nicholas de Jongh's *Politics, Prudery and Perversions: The Censoring of the English Stage, 1901–1968*, also makes use of the Lord Chamberlain's collection but has less of a focus on the early part of the twentieth century. Even so, his early chapters, 'Putting Women Straight' and 'Homosexual Relations', will be of some use to scholars working in the field. The former looks at issues around censorship and women's sexuality as well as giving useful analyses of the censor's role in the production of plays such as *The Vortex* and *Fata Morgana*. De Jongh is very witty in his portrayal of the censor's obsession with moral health and the ways in which censorship as a mechanism for cultural policing got more and more out of touch with social and cultural change. With the statutory look at Wilde, 'Homosexual Relations' does look briefly at inter-war texts, although a great part of the chapter covers ground already covered by the author in his earlier *Not in Front of the Audience*.

John F. Deeney, in 'Censoring the Uncensored: The Case of *Children in Uniform*' (*NTQ* 16:lxiii[2000] 219–26), takes a more radical attitude to censorship. Here he re-examines a 'lesbian' inter-war text, *Maids in Uniform*, and questions the ways in which this text has been overlooked by contemporary feminists because it somehow escaped the censor's eye and went on to a long West End run, and has thus tended to be viewed as conservative. Deeney questions our analytical framing devices, pointing out that a refusal to see the play as a link in a chain of twentieth-century 'lesbian' dramas is to undermine the significance of a work which confused the censor (who eventually provided a performance licence as long as the 'setting remain German') but presented very clear images of 'other' sexualities to a popular and often conservative audience. Deeney proposes that a negative interpretation of the play's ending, which includes a suicide inspired by unfulfilled romantic passion, cannot be the only axis on which a reading of the cultural significance of the text turns.

A similar invitation to reposition women's contributions to inter-war theatre and drama comes in the form of Katherine Cockin's *Women and Theatre in the Age of Suffrage: The Pioneer Players, 1911–1925*. This is a very dense and at times difficult book, although it represents original research and will be invaluable to students of female suffrage and the arts. The style is at times convoluted and one feels that the book could have achieved its aims in rather less space. Nevertheless Cockin's project, to collect information on Edith Craig's work with the independent play society the Pioneer Players, is a worthy one, and the introductory chapters, 'The Costs of a Free Theatre' and 'The Feminist Play of Ideas and the Art of Propaganda', will be particularly useful for undergraduates because of the way in which they lay out the basic arguments surrounding drama, theatre, art, commercialism and women's suffrage that had currency during the period. Cockin makes a good job of documenting Craig's work with Cicely Hamilton and Christopher St John, as well as her work with new texts by women playwrights and her promotion of texts by foreign playwrights. She misses out on some important work by other scholars in the field, such as Roberta Gandolfi, whose research on Craig as an innovative director might have enhanced her thesis. Despite reservations about style, this book will prove useful for anyone studying Edwardian theatre in general and women and twentieth-century theatre in particular.

The work of women playwrights during this period has only been touched upon by a few scholars, and a number of these have pointed to the ways in which non-pluralistic feminist analytical frameworks have inhibited the inclusion of certain plays in a history of twentieth-century women playwrights. Many of the women writing for theatre of the period wrote for commercial contexts, or for political movements which did not necessarily promote feminist ideology over socialist. Ros Merkin's chapter, 'No Space of Our Own? Margaret Macnamara, Alma Brosnan, Ruth Dodds and the I.L.P. Arts Guild' (in Gale and Gardner, eds., *Women Theatre and Performance: New Histories, New Historiographies*, pp. 180–97), is an attempt to renegotiate the work of these three women, who wrote for an overtly socialist context, as an important contribution to the development of popular and amateur mid-century drama. Merkin argues that gender played an important role in the plays analysed, but that it was foregrounded as part of a larger argument around socialism and domestic culture. Maggie B. Gale's 'Women Playwrights of the 1920s and 1930s' (in Aston and Reinelt, *The Cambridge Companion to Modern British Women Playwrights*, pp. 23–37) presents women playwrights of the inter-war years as a challenging presence to the male-dominated theatre of the day. Gale invites the reader to reconsider the playwrights' work in the light of the enormous social and economic changes which, even though outside a specific political movement, affected women's lives in general, and their theatre writing in particular. She argues that the surface conservatism of many of the plays reveals a theatrical consciousness of the cultural anxiety around women and the family, work and economic power, as well as mirroring the theatrical conservatism of much of the theatre of the day. John Stokes also makes reference to the work of mid-century women playwrights in his article 'Prodigals or Profligates; or, a Short History of Modern British Drama' (*NTQ* 15:i[1999] 26–38), which traces the transformations undergone by the figure of the prodigal son (and daughter) in twentieth-century dramatic texts. Stokes' argues for the influence of performers such as John Gielgud and Charles Hawtrey on the course of theatre history and the reading of theatrical texts.

Theatrical histories are problematized in Maggie B. Gale's re-reading of the career and persona of Clemence Dane, one of the most prolific playwrights, male or female, from the 1920s through to the 1950s and beyond. Dane's first play *A Bill of Divorcement* [1921] was restaged throughout the 1920s and was filmed more than once. Other noted plays included *Granite* and *Cousin Muriel*. In, 'From Fame to Obscurity: In Search of Clemence Dane' (in Gale and Gardner eds., pp. 121–41), Gale charts Dane's influence upon the theatrical world of her day, and questions the ways in which she has been either historically framed as conservative by feminists or as eccentric or naive by those writing, for example, biographies of Noël Coward (one of her crowd) or other theatrical figures such as Lewis Casson. Gale attempts to cut through the mythology of Dane as an eccentric—she was reportedly the model for Coward's Madame Arcati in *Blythe Spirit*—and deconstructs her image in relation to autobiographical theory and theatre historiography as a means of understanding her lack of position in the cultural mapping of mid-twentieth-century British theatre and playwriting.

One theatrical biography of particular note during the year has been Jonathan Croall's *Gielgud: A Theatrical Life, 1904–2000*. Croall's extensive research has produced a biography which offers the theatre and cultural historian some useful materials. Croall undertook extensive interviews with Gielgud's friends and professional colleagues in order to draw a more intricately detailed picture of the man's life and work. He manages to track Gielgud's career in terms of the influence of practitioners such as Granville-Barker and J.B Fagan on the actor and vice versa, and through this gives us a real sense of Gielgud's developing attitude towards the changing theatre of his day. The style is not particularly academic, but the research is sound enough to provide useful material for scholars.

Christie Fox tackles the undervaluation of a mid-twentieth-century woman playwright in 'Neither Here Nor There: The Liminal Position of Teresa Deevy and her Female Characters' (in Watts, Morgan and Mustafa, eds., *A Century of Irish Drama: Widening the Stage*, pp. 193–203). Fox delineates Deevy's career and her plays in terms of their problematic status for contemporary directors. Ultimately, as with many women playwrights of the period, the characters she created do not fit into a contemporary feminist framework for production, and so the lack of desire to put on new productions of her plays locates her work outside a re-visioned feminist canon. Deevy's work broke with certain conventions of the representation of women in the theatre of the 1930s. Fox suggests that this 'forgotten playwright' imaged women 'caught between worlds—between the public and the private, religious and secular, single and married', in other words, she created characters for whom the notion of womanhood itself was in transition. Fox's work links with that of Gale and of Merkin in its agenda of repositioning and re-visioning plays by a lost generation of women writing for theatre between the two world wars.

Kaplan and Stowell, eds., *Look Back in Pleasure: Noel Coward Reconsidered*, has a similar revisionist imperative, but this time the author in question is not one who has been historically sidelined, but rather one who has never quite been taken seriously academically. The Coward centenary year [1999] saw numerous national and international productions of his plays, but this book is a collection of essays from the first academic conference dedicated to his work, held at the University of Birmingham (UK). The book includes interviews with directors Philip Franks, Philip Prowse and Sue Wilson and performers Maria Aitken, Judy Campbell, Corin Redgrave and Juliet Stevenson, as well as short essays by cultural historians and scholars such as Philip Hoare, John Stokes, Peter Holland and Alan Sinfield. David Edgar's essay, 'Noel Coward and the Transformation of British Comedy' gets the volume off to a good start as he suggests that many contemporary writers have in fact 'built on discoveries about how to write modern comedy which Coward pioneered'. In 'Noel Coward's Bad Manners', Dan Rebellato weaves Coward's manneredness in and out of contemporaneous texts on etiquette and 'good behaviour' to portray Coward not as a snob, as is usual, but rather as a subversive who was intent on exposing the superficiality of the class to which he appeared to aspire. Other chapters worth noting are Philip Hoare's 'It's All a Question of Masks' and Russell Jackson's 'The Excitement of Being English'. One hopes that this volume will set a precedent for others to follow as it creates a vital link between scholars, critics and practitioners, rarely gathered together under the same cover. It opens up new areas for debate on one of the most prolific playwrights of the twentieth century whose cultural significance has only just begun to be recognized in the academic world. The book is eminently accessible and will be very useful for undergraduates of literature and gender studies, as well as those with an interest in theatre.

Coward features prominently in Alan Sinfield's *Out on Stage: Lesbian and Gay Theatre in the Twentieth Century*, which also gives detailed treatment to playwrights such as Somerset Maugham, Terence Rattigan and John Van Druten. Sinfield is far more erudite on the cultural significance of censorship and provides closer readings of texts such as *Young Woodley* or *The Green Bay Tree* than Nicholas de Jongh. His cultural materialist approach provides both a strong sense of context and interesting ways into the texts examined; the chapter on 'Society and its Others' is particularly useful and covers a wide range of plays rooted in the 1920s and 1930s. Sinfield's is a transcultural and transhistorical approach but it is also a literary one; he crosses from American to British contexts with too much ease, and this does not easily facilitate readings which stress the importance of the original conditions of theatrical production and cultural reception. Any student will glean a great deal of information from this book—play synopses, some information on critical reception, a sense of cultural mapping and so on—but they may not learn very much about the theatre of the day. Sinfield's overall project of cultural mapping sometimes undermines the possibility of in-depth readings of the texts. Nevertheless, *Out on Stage* is a timely volume which will be of great use to students of cultural and literary studies.

By comparison, Nicholas Grene's *The Politics of Irish Drama: Plays in Context from Boucicault to Friel* has in some ways a far more contained agenda: 'a critical analysis of the political interplay of dramatic text and context'. The book assesses Irish drama which is 'self-consciously concerned with the representation of Ireland as its main subject', and Grene looks at plays by O'Casey and Shaw as well as those by writers working for the Abbey Theatre in the early part of the twentieth century. This is a very readable book which, although it focuses mainly on the latter half on the nineteenth century, adds to scholarship related to mid-twentieth-century drama in English by offering clear links between theatrical, social and political contexts from one end of the century to the other. Similarly, Watts, Morgan and Mustafa, eds., *A Century of Irish Drama*, another collection of conference papers, provides numerous chapters on mid-twentieth-century Irish plays, with detailed sections on the early years of the Abbey Theatre and related playwrights, and a particularly good chapter on Sean O'Casey by Shakir Mustafa. Laura E. Lyon's chapter, 'Of Orangemen and Green Theatres', on the rarely discussed work of the Ulster literary theatre, is also a worthy addition to the field of Irish theatre history; Lyon discusses nation, identity and difference in relation to the plays of Gerald MacNamara, among others. This volume should be on every twentieth-century drama reading list; it combines survey, detail and scholarship with innovative re-readings of plays.

Overall, the last two years have seen an increase in scholarship in this area. There appears to have been a loosening of the shackles that defined mid-twentieth-century drama in terms of Auden and Isherwood, and a move towards perceiving the more commercial or popular playwrights of the era as worthy of serious analysis. The work of women dramatists has begun to be taken more seriously, as have the possibilities for new readings of old playwrights in their own cultural contexts, which may have been far more radical or subversive than we once assumed. Equally, the work on 'political theatres' of the day, begun by scholars such as Raphael Samuels in the 1970s and 1980s re-emerges, albeit at a tangent, with scholars such as Steve Nicholson and Mick Wallis, whose work on political theatre and amateur theatre will only enhance drama studies further.

5. Post-1950 Drama

What follows is a report on the books of 2000 by and about Alan Bennett, Edward Bond, Brian Friel, Trevor Griffiths, David Hare, Peter Nichols, Harold Pinter and Terence Rattigan. Next come comments on eleven more general books, of which the most ambitious are those by Richard Eyre/Nicholas Wright and D. Keith Peacock.

Is there a contemporary dramatist for whom a book entitled 'Understanding X' is less needed than Alan Bennett? If the intended audience of Peter Wolfe's *Understanding Alan Bennett* is American, then Wolfe should explain Burgess, McLean, Blunt and spying, and engage with the historical George III, which he does not do. He has not sought out British reviews of Bennett's stage and television plays, and apparently has not tried to see the television work. He gives no sign of having visited Leeds or of knowing the audiences who love Patricia Routledge (unmentioned, but memorable in *Talking Heads*). That he writes of the 'gun-happy' streets of London (p. 22) and of 'the Stratford Memorial Theatre Group' (p. 142) does not inspire confidence. What he enjoys is finding improbable parallels: Blunt in *A Question of Attribution* is like Hedda Gabler (p. 151); *An Englishman Abroad* is 'Brechtian' (p. 148); Irene Ruddock in 'A Lady of Letters' is 'Thoreauvian' (p. 195). And this: 'The burdens imposed by memory and the struggle to find a self by separating one's true private history from the false vexes Graham Whittaker from *A Chip in the Sugar* as much as it does Proust's Marcel or Joyce's Stephen Dedalus' (p. 179). Wolfe's study should at best be called 'Summarising ...' D.E. Turner's *Alan Bennett: In a Manner of Speaking* [1997] is a better work; *Alan Bennett: A Critical Introduction*, by Joseph H. O'Mealy, is announced for 2001.

Edward Bond has not written a widely admired play since *Summer* [1982]. However, more background material is appearing for his works and ideas than for those of any other living dramatist. The four volumes of his letters, noticed in my last report, have been followed by his essays, *The Hidden Plot: Notes on Theatre and the State*, and the two-volume *Selections from the Notebooks*, edited by Ian Stuart, also editor of the letters. Stuart reports that he has chosen to print about one-fifth of the notebooks. The entries, he explains, are of four kinds: 'play drafts; commentary on the plays; Bond's thoughts on life and the play in particular; and stories and poems which may or may not have any direct relevance to the play in hand' (p. x). So, according to Stuart, we have 'a rare and extraordinary insight into the outlook of Bond and the workings of his creative mind' (p. x). Nothing personal can be found here, so readers are not entertained as they are by Nichols's diaries, and we can only guess at the biography. That in about 1966 Bond withdrew to a country village is indicated here only by two sections entitled 'Great Wibraham Papers' and 'Rothbury Papers'.

Entries here show some of the trial-and-error thinking which led to the final form of *Saved*, *Lear*, *The Sea*, *Summer* and later work, data from which some future scholar may piece together a full study (though this would also involve study of manuscripts, which may not survive). *The Notebooks* contain some thinking about dramatists (Arthur Miller is a *bête noire*) and theatre; Bond is determined to resist conventions of form. The texts reveal an intelligent man attempting to see life steadily and whole, resisting external dictates. *The Notebooks* are not self-contained reading, and I doubt whether *The Hidden Plot* is of much interest except to admirers of Bond's plays of the 1960s and 1970s and the smaller number who still follow his career. These writings are turgid and demanding, unlike essays by such dramatists as Arden and Edgar. The reader must start with the conviction that every word by Bond matters, be convinced of his continuing importance.

Though Brian Friel has been writing for as long as Bond, only with *Dancing at Lughnasa* [1990] was he clearly established as an outstanding playwright. Some nine books about Friel, starting with D.E.S. Maxwell in 1973, precede the trio discussed here.

Friel is a reticent man who believes that plays should speak for themselves, as he remarked as early as 1968. He has given few interviews since the earliest part of his career, except for those given to promote the Field Day company in 1980–4, with no interviews in the last ten years. So I am surprised to find that Delaney, ed., *Brian*

Friel in Conversation, has 289 pages. Everything that matters—thirty-three interviews—is here, from *Vogue* to the *Irish Times*. The weakness is repetition, the strength in Delaney's thorough introductions and a fair sense of Friel as both man and writer. The one interview Delaney missed should be recorded, about *Translations*: Owen Dudley Edwards, 'A Question of Communication' (*Radio Times* 30 Jan.–5 Feb.[1980] 18, 21). Delaney has also found and printed transcripts of four BBC Northern Ireland radio talks by Friel and an Irish television programme about him. Three of the longest interviews were in obscurity in *Acorn*, *In Dublin* and *The Word*.

The first two of these, however, also appear in a British publication, Murray, ed., *Brian Friel: Essays, Diaries, Interviews, 1964–1999* [1999]. Murray has scoops, an unpublished 1986 interview, the substantial 'Seven Notes for a Festival Programme' (exploring the startling idea that directors may be unnecessary) and twenty pages of notes on the genesis of *Molly Sweeney* and *Give Me Your Answer, Do!* Though these are tantalizingly short, they show the slow composition, an inability to settle to writing, and diverse reading, from Wittgenstein to Wallace Stevens. Murray's short introduction surveys much of Friel's output. Libraries and serious scholars need both; less specialized readers will find sufficient, and more variety, in Murray's collection.

Friel is one of the five writers considered in a new series, Faber Critical Guides (the other four are Pinter and Stoppard, discussed below, and Beckett and Sean O'Casey). The back cover states that the guides are for students and teachers, 'for use in classroom, college or at home'—but not in the theatre? The format is a general introduction and extended studies of several plays, in Friel's case well chosen, as good and representative: *Philadelphia, Here I Come!*, *Translations*, *Making History*, and *Dancing at Lughnasa*. Nesta Jones is conscientious but plodding. She gives none of the theatrical context: that Friel started writing soon after the Royal Court revolution in London and after landmarks by Thompson in Belfast and Keane and Murphy in Dublin. Such lines as 'The structural devices of the divided self, time and memory are also thematic ideas' (p. 21) made me wonder if plays have to be studied like this. Jones writes 'because you only have access to the printed text' (p. 13). Sorry, but students will rent the video of *Dancing at Lughnasa*, and have to try to spot differences with no help from Jones.

I had mixed feelings when I began Stanton B. Garner Jr.'s *Trevor Griffiths: Politics, Drama, History* [1999]. On the one hand, a full-length study of Griffiths is needed (we have at least one book on most of his contemporaries). On the other, that Derrida arrives on page 12, followed by Barthes, Bakhtin and Baudrillard, suggested for a while that this was not going to be the book I wanted. Garner's account, in fact, is excellent. He understands the background very well, from the milieu of New Left clubs and the *Universities and Left Review* at the end of the 1950s to 'that liminal, structureless decade between the fall of the Wall and century's end' (p. 226). He suggests that Griffiths's 'socialist aspiration' always had 'a certain elegiac melancholy' (p. 89), and sees that 'The contours of Griffiths' career owe as much (or more) to such writers as Edward Thompson, Eric Hobsbawm, and Angus Calder as they do to figures within the theater' (p. 51). Garner fails to explain *The Party* precisely, that Tagg is modelled on Gerry Healy and Ford on Robin Blackburn. His only slip, though, is to interpret the line in the play, 'We've got upper second souls', as about class, not university degrees (p. 86).

Garner quotes Griffiths as observing that 'my plays are about the contradictions in my life' (p. 45), yet biography is virtually excluded—simply the working-class boy who changes because of grammar school and university education. Griffiths is rightly placed as a northerner, so separate from 'the metropolitan alternative theater culture' (p. 3). Garner evaluates all the plays. He observes, for example, of *Sam, Sam*: 'With the exception of Mercer's early drama, no play explores so fully the psychological and social contradictions of postwar working-class mobility' (p. 45). (But does Garner know David Storey's *In Celebration*?) Equal space is given to film and television work, with clear accounts of what is unpublished.

Garner believes that political drama is 'one of Britain's greatest contributions to twentieth-century theater' (p. 14) but also that in the last twenty years critics have had difficulty discussing it, for the heyday is past (p. 187). Garner sees Griffiths recovering 'the voices of social visionaries' (p. 11) from the script of an unmade film about Tom Paine, through Tom Mann to Nye Bevan. Griffiths, he shows, explores 'the irreconcilable conflict between what he calls the 'hard' and 'soft' dimensions of revolutionary struggle' (p. 64). His section 'Gendering the Revolution', on the interweaving of politics and sexuality, is especially good.

The study is researched with exceptional thoroughness, using published interviews and many of Garner's own. Not only has he tracked down the reviews in obscure papers and the comments in inaccessible journals, he appears to have read all about Griffiths's subjects, from Danton and Gramsci to soccer hooligans. I closed the book seeing that Garner had made a strong case for Griffiths as an outstanding creator of socialist art, with Brecht and O'Casey.

David Hare's *Acting Up* is his diary of performing his *Via Dolorosa* from the first rehearsal through all the London and New York performances. Thus he does not deal with the travel, research and writing involved. Keeping this diary, he explains, 'was the essential means of trying to understand what was going on. Knowing I would sit down every morning to lay out the previous day's trials gave the experience calm and order ... *Acting Up* is a diary of learning to act ... I realize the purpose of my acting is to make me a better director, to understand acting better' (pp. xi, xii, 4). He found that in London audiences engaged with the content, in contrast to the hit-or-flop mentality of Broadway. Parts are gossipy, with digressions: he is fascinated by American films, loves 'the glorious articulation which a great stage provides' (p. 21), writes of Judi Dench and Wallace Shawn. He discusses above all how audiences differ and how his performance changes from night to night. Hare is informative and entertaining as he reacts to rehearsals, fear, the relationship with the director, publicity, critics, interviews, celebrities, exhaustion.

After reading Hare, Peter Nichols's *Diaries, 1969–1977* seem lightweight. Nichols takes us back to the years when the plays which are still his best known (*Joe Egg* to *Privates on Parade*) were new. Nichols is not writing for publication, though he has selected what is to be made public now. Readers have to dig for theatrical insights: he is a craftsman, not a theorizer; he remarks on the germ of *Forget-me-not-Lane* (pp. 73–4), reviews Hare's *Knuckle* neatly (p. 373), describes why *The Freeway* failed (p. 377). We hear of the life of the dramatist, attempting to write and negotiating with directors. Mostly this is an enjoyable self-portrait of a modern man: socializing, parenting, lustful, self-questioning, making faux pas, overhearing comic dialogues, with gentle ill-will towards relatives—the Bristol boy who attains Blackheath.

Difficult though it is to say anything new, Bill Naismith's *Harold Pinter* for Faber Critical Guides appeared fresher and more sophisticated (as on 'linguistic strategies' in *The Birthday Party*, p. 59) than Jones on Friel. Naismith's textual notes are fuller and he has a chapter on 'context and background'. The other two plays discussed are *The Caretaker* and *The Homecoming*. I liked Naismith's use of the comments of others (such as Simon Trussler placing *The Homecoming* as 'intellectualised melodrama', p. 157) and his comparisons with other plays: resemblances between late seventeenth-century comedies of manners and *The Homecoming* (p. 155). Naismith acknowledges that 'the dimension of live performance is missing' (p. 136), but though all three have been filmed (and surely Naismith has seen them), these are unmentioned. Why are film studies so rigidly separated from drama?

Martin Esslin's introductory survey, *Pinter the Playwright*, first published in 1970 and last expanded in 1992 appears in its sixth edition. Esslin has added eleven pages on the three plays of the 1990s, worth reading for their personal, informed view. *Moonlight*, for instance, he finds 'a deeply tragic view of the human condition' (p. 214).

Jim Hunter writes of Tom Stoppard for the Faber Critical Guides, with extended commentary on four major plays: he revisits three plays which he covered in his 1982 book, with the addition of *Arcadia*. His book succeeds partly because he allows thirty pages for generalizations at the beginning and end; he also has twenty pages of textual notes on each play. He describes clearly the 1993 revisions of *Travesties*, but is confusing about the different versions of *Jumpers*. As with the other volumes, plays in performance are neglected, including the film of *Rosencrantz and Guildenstern*, while Robert Gordon's Text and Performance volume isn't even in his bibliography. While the volume on Friel has very little for the informed, Hunter is so precise that I found much to admire, as in this summing up: Stoppard's plays 'are sympathetic to traditional beliefs: the notions of absolute good (with a possible absolute judge), of natural innocence, and of the almost heroic importance of art' (p. 16).

All three Faber guides have a prevailing joylessness: plays are for studying, and after that for reading about, in these 'guides'.

Michael Darlow's biography, *Terence Rattigan: The Man and his Work*, is a revised, franker and considerably larger version of the book published in 1979. That, curiously, was co-authored with Gillian Hodson, a minor bibliographical puzzle—has he excised every sentence written by Hodson?

Darlow believes that 'the power of Rattigan's best plays comes from the implicit rather than the explicit, from unspoken feelings, buried emotions and hidden truths' (p. 16). Rattigan is a writer of the oblique (p. 482). Darlow asserts that all the work feeds directly on Rattigan's life: not quite upper-class enough for Harrow; observer of his parents' unhappy marriage and his father's disgrace and philandering; his difficulty in facing his homosexuality. Though a narrow view of creativity, this provides a good start to a life-and-works study. Rattigan, from *French without Tears* [1936] to *Separate Tables* [1954], had an apparently effortless rise to fame and wealth. Yet being a success for Rattigan meant parties, champagne, dining at the Ritz: no wonder his serious plays are still not taken very seriously. Could this idle Bertie Wooster, a gambler, devoted to his Rolls, passionate about golf, have written

The Browning Version and *The Deep Blue Sea*? Darlow only sketches the pathos of the man who wanted—some of the time—to be a great writer and did not want to settle for mere success. He considers the decline in quality in later plays, seeing that by the late 1940s Rattigan 'was becoming increasingly cut off from sound advice' (p. 254), surrounded by sycophants. By 1964, too, Rattigan was a sick man, drinking heavily.

Darlow's account is muted; he is too little a storyteller and too bland when he comments: he is usually recording where Rattigan was living and who his friends were. For the plays, he attends to the circumstances of production, and to critical reception, with short plot summaries and sketchy evaluations. He is thorough on *Man and Boy*, aided by letters about the actors who were considered and rejected. *Variations on a Theme* is usefully explained by the sad story of Margaret Leighton's marriage to Laurence Harvey. His rare strongly negative comments—'one is conscious of contrivance' (p. 201) in *The Winslow Boy*; the film of *The Deep Blue Sea* has 'grotesque and unsubtle exaggeration' (p. 329)—lack supporting argument. Rattigan emerges as a clear example of what E.M. Forster labelled 'the undeveloped heart' of the Englishman, especially of the public school variety.

Rattigan, with Coward, Priestley, Eliot and Fry, occupies a subdued phase of the British theatre, that between Shaw and Osborne: the reader is challenged to decide which plays by which writer deserve to survive.

Richard Eyre and Nicholas Wright look ambitiously at twentieth-century theatre in *Changing Stages: A View of British Theatre in the Twentieth Century*, linked with the television series shown late in 2000. Eyre insists that 'I needed to write the book before the series in order to find out what I thought and what I didn't know' (p. 7). 'The task we set ourselves', they write, 'was to find out how we got here: to identify the people, the plays, the ideas that had come together over the last hundred years or so to bring about the flowering that we see today' (p. 16). This book is entitled 'a view of British theatre' yet includes many Americans and digresses frequently to Brecht and other Europeans. Though Eyre is a director, the subject is playwrights, with little attention to actors or theatre buildings, and even less to theorizing about absurdism or anything else. The final chapter, entitled 'Purity', flings together Meyerhold, Artaud, Peter Brook, Grotowski, Kantor, Robert Wilson and Lepage. Space is found for pantomime and Ken Campbell.

The first half of the book is history, sometimes responsive, sometimes a dutiful trudge through received opinion. The book is not authoritative, a Revels History, yet rarely distinctively personal, though the authors are great enthusiasts. When they reach the last thirty years, they appear to be recalling their best experiences of performance, which may explain the choice of plays for comment (nothing by Pinter after *Betrayal*); they also avoid lists of titles. Pinter has six pages, in fact, while John Arden has only three sentences, curiously split between two chapters. Charles Wood earns a passionate page: 'There is no contemporary writer who has chronicled the experience of modern war with so much authority, knowledge, compassion, wit and despair' (p. 250). The chapter on modern Ireland gives as the key chronology John B. Keane's *Sive* [1959], Tom Murphy's *Whistle in the Wind* [1961] and Friel's *Philadelphia, Here I Come!* [1964]. The section on verse drama ends with the reminder that Tony Harrison brings this tradition to the present.

Though Rattigan is briskly dismissed, Eyre and Wright emphasize what they enjoy, and this is a work to quote and savour. A few examples. *Look Back in Anger* comes from 1956 England, the context 'the lack of choice, the lack of colour, the lack of public joy ... sheer monochromatic greyness' (p. 239). Hare's *A Map of the World* is 'part Shavian debate, part masked ball of the id' (p. 292). The achievement of Sebastian Barry's *The Steward of Christendom* is 'to popularize a non-narrative play of atmosphere' (p. 277). Eyre and Wright are eloquent, hitting the nail on the head in a few sentences, while factually correct too. They make modern theatre fun, exciting and important.

Shellard, ed., *British Theatre in the 1950s*, consists of papers from a 1997 conference, and should be entitled 'A few aspects of ...'. The two best essays come from original research into the Lord Chamberlain's censorship. Steve Nicholson writes of the censoring of foreign plays, with Genet's *Huis clos* and Tennessee Williams provoking moralistic language. Kathryn Johnson examines the Lord Chamberlain's especial concerns, homosexuality and the portrayal of Jesus. The reader with a general interest in the Lord Chamberlain's actions is already well served by Nicholas de Jongh's *Politics, Prudery and Perversion: The Censorship of the English Stage, 1901–1968*. Fiona Kavanagh Fearon has also done research, in the National Theatre files in the British Library, and brings out the rival ambitions of Peter Hall and Laurence Olivier, from 1959 to 1963. Previous histories of the National Theatre have established much of this, and Fearon's focus is on the National in the 1960s.

John Bull and Dominic Shellard follow the line taken by Dan Rebellato in *1956 and All That*, challenging the received opinion that in that year everything was changed by *Look Back in Anger*. Bull rightly argues that *Waiting for Godot* [1955] was influential, noting also that Theatre Workshop settled in London in 1953 and that the Berliner Ensemble performed in London in 1956. Shellard's title, '1950–54: Was it a Cultural Wasteland?', is promising, but in fact he rambles round the role of Binkie Beaumont in the West End and the number of musicals and French plays. He states: 'What is perhaps most noticeable about the London stage between 1952 and 1954 is how completely indifferent it was to contemporary events' (p. 37). This is not wholly true: Roger MacDougall in *Escapade* and Charles Morgan in *The Burning Glass* wrote of fear of war in the nuclear age; dramas at the Unity Theatre were urgently political; the lost form of intimate revue had social comment.

The remaining four essays include an interview with Pinter about his acting in the 1950s, a familiar account of McMaster, Wolfit and his discovery of Beckett, plus his admiration for W.B. Yeats's plays. Danny Castle succinctly summarizes Kenneth Tynan's achievements, as a reviewer in the 1950s and at the National Theatre in the 1960s. Glenda Leeming revisits Christopher Fry, on whom she wrote a book in 1990, asking why his career fizzled out. Christopher Innes, who discussed Rattigan in his comprehensive *Modern British Drama*, revisits him. Innes begins: 'He is almost always represented as the potentially serious playwright who sold out to popularity' (p. 53), apparently unaware of the revaluation since Susan Rusinko's 1983 study and revivals of the major plays.

Shellard's title requires what he does not provide: discussion of how far a 'wasteland' was alleviated by John Whiting's *Saints Day* and Graham Greene's *The Living Room*, with the work of Fry and Rattigan, T.S. Eliot's *The Confidential Clerk* and perhaps N.C. Hunter. As for errors: there were not two elections in 1951 (p. 37); John Gielgud played Leontes in London, not Stratford (p. 37); the Tynan/Ionesco debate was in the *Observer*, not the *Guardian* (p. 86); the contents of *Curtains* and *Tynan on Theatre* are not identical (p. 98).

Peacock's *Thatcher's Theatre* has divided objectives. His subject is sometimes precise, the response of dramatists and companies to Thatcherism, issues of ideology and cuts in funding. At other times he has a broader aim, that suggested by his subtitle, 'British Theatre and Drama in the Eighties'. He begins with a long chapter on Thatcher's government—the miners' strike, the north–south divide, and so on—which may be useful contexts for young or North American readers, but barely connects with the rest of his book, and he follows this with an indigestible section on 'arts and money'. Chapter 4 brings the reader to the response of left-wing writers to a right-wing regime. He begins, oddly, with Bond, although he sees that war was Bond's main subject. He often reads narrowly for leftist ideas, so that Howard Brenton in *Bloody Poetry* is scrutinizing 'the communal individuality of Anarchism' (p. 74). There is much plot summary and little evaluation, though he successfully encapsulates the impact of such plays as Hare's *The Bay at Nice* and *Wrecked Eggs*.

Self-contained chapters follow. 'Looking East' discusses writers who responded to the demise of Communism. Peacock finds Churchill's *Mad Forest* the best of these. 'Carnivals of the Oppressed' fashionably draws on Bakhtin, juxtaposing Ann Jellicoe's community plays, the welfare state and John McGrath's *Border Warfare* (though ignoring its sequel, *John Brown's Body*). Peacock helpfully distinguishes Edgar's *Entertaining Strangers* as first performed in Dorchester from the later version staged at the National Theatre. 'Defusing a Refusenik' deals narrowly with the demise of 7:84 England, and how McGrath was forced out of the directorship of 7:84 Scotland; Peacock draws heavily on McGrath's book, *The Bone Won't Break*.

Turning to 'women's theatre', Peacock distinguishes 'socialist or materialist feminism, bourgeois feminism and radical feminism' (p. 151), showing how, for example, the work of Claire Luckham differs from that of Sarah Daniels. Much information is crammed into the next section, on black theatre, which goes without transition from Caribbean writers to Hanif Kureishi and on to the companies Temba, Talawa and Tara. He notes three significant new dramatists who emerged in the 1980s: Jim Cartwright, Terry Johnson and Timberlake Wertenbaker. A breathless account of 'Physical or Visual Theatre' (p. 205) follows, a sketch of DV8 and Forced Entertainment.

Peacock's study has slips frequent enough to irritate, as he misspells Laurence Olivier (p. 4), Nichols (p. 28), Willy Russell (p. 48), Shaffer (p. 77), Albie Sachs (p. 90), Kristeva (p. 123), Mnouchkine (p. 126), Frances Gray (p. 130), MacLennan (p. 143), Caz Phillips (p. 171) and Ayckbourn (p. 217). He shows virtually no sign of having seen plays, writing instead of texts. Though he notes the dramatists who formed the anti-Thatcher 20 June Group, he does not comment on them signing petitions or taking part in demonstrations. I find it arbitrary that he takes an eleven-year chunk of an author's work, practically ignoring earlier scripts. He also ignores their work for film and television, though Edgar's *Vote for Them* and Hare's films *Strapless* and *Paris by Night* could and probably should be fitted into his analysis. Peacock's work is more useful for facts and some insights into some writers of the 1980s than for the more difficult subject of how politically minded authors use their art to react to a hostile government.

Dominic Dromgoole's *The Full Room: An A–Z of Contemporary Playwriting* gives his comments, personal and anecdotal, on 111 playwrights, nearly all British and almost all living. His book is worth reading for four reasons. He is a great, provocative phrasemaker. Berkoff is a 'roaring lion', Pam Gems is 'the greatest living provider of turns for star actors', Gray is 'the poet laureate of dyspepsia', Keeffe's early plays were 'the theatrical equivalent of The Clash'. Dromgoole has stimulating asides, many of them about his directing at the Bush Theatre. Second, he assesses what 'heightened language' means (p. 69), contrasts Peter Hall and Richard Eyre as directors of the National Theatre (p. 34), and brings out the role of the Old Red Lion in promoting new writing in the 1990s (p. 58). Third, he gives an original, brisk view of the major talents of our time. He prefers praise to blame, so becomes negative only when he writes of Edgar, Hare and Shaffer. Finally, he promotes new writers, to read and to watch for their next play. So he admires Richard Cameron, whose Doncaster is 'a place of prickly heat' (p. 44) and Judith Johnson, 'an assured, still and sane voice' (p. 154), who has been shouted down by lads 'with their zippety-zappety language, their violence, their sexuality' (p. 154).

As scholars have come to realize that comment on drama should incorporate awareness of performance, three books of interviews deserve attention. Interviews provide raw material, and frequently I found that assessing the information was left to the reader. Duncan Wu, in *Making Plays*, has long interviews with Alan Bennett, Howard Brenton, Edgar, Michael Frayn and Hare, and with the five men who directed their most recent plays. Though the ostensible focus is on one play, Wu asks such broad questions as 'Did the Thatcher years alter your vision as a writer in any way?' (p. 98). He supplies substantial literary and academic introductions to each script, tracing, for example, how Brenton's *Magnificence* anticipates his *Sore Throats*. I enjoy such incidentals as Bond baffling his actors by telling them to be Rolls Royces with weeds growing out of them (p. 69). The information here on Frayn's *Copenhagen* is almost essential for full understanding of the play and Edgar is especially worth listening to because he knows so exactly what he is doing and clarifies the political context. For the other three, these commentaries are a kind of added gloss.

Giannachi and Luckhurst, eds., *On Directing*, prints interviews with twenty-one directors, six of them women, in only 142 pages, so some are short. Helen Manfull, in *Taking the Stage: Women Directors on Directing*, interviews thirteen directors, weaving their statements together under nine headings, such as their training and their techniques in rehearsal (four women appear in both books). Thus *On Directing* focuses on individuals, particularly as the arrangement is alphabetical, so that we read adventurous younger men, such as Tim Mitchells, before the intellectual wisdom of Jonathan Miller. *Taking the Stage*, instead, emphasizes methodology. While Simon McBurney believes that there can be an 'over-reverence for a text' (*On Directing*, p. 69), Katie Mitchell takes an academic approach: 'I spend a lot of time researching the background of the text, looking at its historical, socio-political and cultural context. I also look at the autobiographical details of the author's life' (*On Directing*, p. 95).

Both books show how important companies with their own styles and audiences are in contemporary British theatre. Manfull informs on Shared Experience; Giannachi includes DV8, Graese, Tara Arts, Welfare State, Communicado and Cheek by Jowl; Druid and Théâtre de Complicité appear in both books. A few passages shed specific light on recent British plays. Manfull describes Brenton writing *In Extremis* at a Californian university (p. 115) and the collaboration of director and designer on Martin McDonagh's *Leenane* trilogy (p. 26). In Giannachi's collection, Garry Hynes notes that Royal Court audiences placed *The Beauty Queen of Leenane* in the tradition of Ibsen and Strindberg, while spectators in Galway correctly saw the Irish tradition, an 'initial response' which was 'fundamentally different' (p. 53).

Taking the Stage incidentally presents a bibliographical puzzle. The British edition contains a statement that the book was first published in the US in 1997. Manfull's *In Other Words: Women Directors Speak* was indeed published by Smith & Kraus. *Taking the Stage*, however, is longer, with a chapter added. More strangely, Deborah Warner features in *In Other Words* but has completely disappeared from *Taking the Stage*.

Three of the studies to hand examine aspects of current British theatre, each giving some attention to playwrights. Readers who do not think narrowly in textual terms, but who see that theatre is collaborative and that performance is a fundamental consideration, will want to look at the complete books.

The most wide-ranging of the three is Gottlieb and Chambers, eds., *Theatre in a Cool Climate* [1999]. The editors write that 'this book arose out of the sense that an informal snapshot of contemporary theatre, written by a diversity of practitioners, would be of interest both now and in the future' (p. 9), a millennium stocktaking. Nineteen essays follow, by dramatists (Pinter and Winsome Pinnock), actors, critics, directors, producers, designers, managers and literary managers. The editors note that the final five on this list were occupations that had not existed a hundred years earlier.

The essays are insiders' views on recent theatre history. Irving Wardle considers the period from 1956 on, arguing that the heart continues to be the West End. Peter Hall interprets through Thatcher: 'From 1979 we forgot what subsidy was for and with it forgot what supporting the arts was about' (p. 100). Five other essays merit a mention. Ella Wildridge of the Traverse, Edinburgh, has ideas on how to promote more and better new plays, including ending the neglect of the older generation (she names three Scots in this category, p. 164). Paule Constable is informative on the work of a lighting designer. Andrew Lavender examines the kind of theatre which either transcends words or makes words part of some larger stew: 'The major explorations in British theatre in the 1990s have been aesthetic in nature. They are manifested in three distinct areas: an evolution in the nature of 'writing' for the theatre, the increasing presence of multi-media performance and the re-imagining of theatre space' (p. 180). Jatinder Verma asserts the distinctiveness of Asian theatre in Britain, as he has done elsewhere, and Pinnock does the same for black theatre, one of protest. I wonder whether the essays or the title came first. For many are pessimistic: Gottlieb, Wardle, Cleo Sylvestre, Richard Eyre, Genista McIntosh, Constable ('Audiences are staying away from many theatres', p. 94) and Hall ('There have been cuts in education programmes, school visits, training, all forms of outreach, and all forms of access', p. 104).

In contrast, Mulryne and Shewring, eds., *The Cottesloe at the National: Infinite Riches in a Little Room* [1999], celebrates the many ways in which this courtyard space has been used since its opening in 1976. The building and the plays staged in it are discussed thoroughly from every angle. The second half has extended and well-illustrated sections on eleven shows staged there, the longest on Tony Harrison's version of *The Mysteries*. Four of the others are recent: Keith Dewhurst's promenade treatment of *Lark Rise*; Pam Gems's *Stanley* (theatre as chapel with half-finished murals); Julian Mitchell's *Half Life* (conventional decorative set) and traverse staging for Hare's *Racing Demon*. The survey of reviews of *Racing Demon* shows how the subject was variously seen as religion today, that state of the Anglican Church, or worship versus social work within the C. of E.

Who Keeps the Score on the London Stages? is by a Bulgarian professor, Kalina Stefanova, and published in the Netherlands. Stefanova has diligently interviewed twenty-seven critics and a lot of producers, directors, press agents, a publisher—and four dramatists. Though she tells us who the critics are, their experience, their prejudices and enthusiasms, readers have to answer the title question for themselves as the eight-page conclusion is little more than admiration for the calibre of the critics. Of the playwrights, Ayckbourn and Arnold Wesker write blandly, though the latter observes neatly: 'Since newspaper reviewing is one person's opinion magnified out of proportion by print, I think there should be a warning at the top of every review, "This review could damage your perception of the play!"' (p. 105). Steven Berkoff is predictably forceful and provocative: 'Nothing much happens in English language any more. Most things are happening in other languages, other theatres, in other forms' (p. 56). Edgar's remarks are as usual thoughtful, for example, critics 'could facilitate an understanding of why it was, for instance, that in the '80s and '90s a lot of people wanted to write plays about gambling and killing' (p. 121). In the section on the current state of theatre, Sheridan Morley 'would have liked to have seen more plays in the last 10 years that worry about the state of the nation' (p. 148). Hall is pleased that 'there's a lot of talented new writing' by the under-thirties (p. 158), while Nick Curtis complains of 'a lack of quality control … not enough work is being done on plays before they go into performance' (p. 143).

In my 1998 report I noted two books of reprinted reviews by Americans, Mel Gussow and Frank Rich. This year brings *Vanishing Acts: Theater since the Sixties*, by Gordon Rogoff, mostly reprints from *Village Voice*. More than the others, this is an American view of the British. He states, for instance, of Hugh Whitemore's *Breaking the Code*, 'the English are never more odd than when they're trying to be internally true without the slightest interest in internal psychology' (p. 170). A fine journalist, a typical arresting opening is: 'Would it were not so, but David Hare's *The Secret Rapture* reveals him as a closet Tory' (p. 183). Rogoff is often savage. He finds Louise Page's *Real Estate* 'the 9,000th play in this century to grapple with earth-shaking issues surrounding mothers, daughters, pregnancy, and neurotic loyalties' (p. 178), while Pam Gems's *Camille* is 'extravagantly awful. … When Gems can find nothing to say, she says it again. … God save feminists from Gems's missionary semiconsciousness' (pp. 87, 88). Astutely, Rogoff observes that, when Hall directed Pinter, he 'arranged Pinter's characters like a curator setting sculptures at their best angles, the distance between them telling as much of their story as the light catching them in profile' (p. 106). Rogoff rarely has space to substantiate his judgements, and he is better short and snappy than sustained. But dip into his book for striking prose, and assorted insights into plays, acting and the state of theatre.

My word-limit is exceeded with four books still requiring mention. The most important is Richard Pine's *The Diviner: The Art of Brian Friel* [1999]. Though Pine published *Brian Friel and Irish Drama* in 1990, his new book does not merely consider three more plays, but has changes throughout, to a 'more political' reading (p. x), with altered opinions on such texts as *Translations*. F.C. McGrath reveals his angle in his title, *Brian Friel's (Post) Colonial Drama: Language, Illusion and Politics* [1999]. He goes conscientiously from 'apprenticeship' through 'postmodern memory' (*Faith Healer*) to 'blindsight' (*Molly Sweeney*). Penelope Prentice's *The Pinter Ethic: The Erotic Aesthetic* has more than 500 pages. Her thesis in a comprehensive study is that 'Pinter's plays combine a focus on love and justice that presents an ethic expressed in new forms which challenge those currently received reflections on human powerlessness' (p. xvii). The focus in *Race, Sex and Gender in Contemporary Women's Theatre: The Construction of 'Woman'*, by Mary F. Brewer [1999] is on theory and content, with chapters on motherhood, 'woman' at work and 'woman' as object and subject. The few dramatists featured, among them Sarah Daniels and Jackie Kay, receive little more than passing mention.

6. Pre-1950 Poetry

More of a review than the recuperation its title implies, Holden and Birch, eds., *A.E. Housman: A Reassessment*, delivers less than it promises. Left over from the flurry of literary activity which marked the centenary, in 1996, of the publication of *A Shropshire Lad*, this anthology of critical essays finds senior critics such as Archie Burnett, John Bayley, and Norman Page alongside Geoffrey Hill picking over what remains a fairly limited output with, apparently, lasting popular appeal. It is not, however, wholly clear to or for whom these scholars speak. The anthology opens with Burnett on Housman's 'level tones' (the quotation deriving from Kingsley Amis's tribute, 'A.E.H.'), treating the equivocal mastery of tone and diction which none of his fellow commentators overlooks. Some rather hollow contextualizing of *A Shropshire Lad*—a survey of its critical reception from Benjamin Fisher and P.G. Naiditch's disappointingly inconclusive charting of 'The First Edition of *A Shropshire Lad* in Bookshop and Auction Room'—is brightened by Trevor Hold's fascinating if highly technical analysis of the collection's 'legacy of song', Carol Efrati's reading of Housman's biblical re-readings, and Takeshi Obata's tracing of the haiku and senryu-like qualities of Housman's finely tuned lyricism. The poet is treated qua classicist by Kenneth Womack ('Ashes Under Uricon: Historicizing A.E. Housman, Reifying T.H. Huxley, Embracing Lucretius') and G.P. Goold ('Housman's Manilius'), and qua poet by John Bayley ('Lewis Carroll in Shropshire', because 'the man who wrote [the poem] does not so much dissociate himself from the book as disappear into it, like Alice into Wonderland'), Keith Jebb ('The Land of Lost Content'), Geoffrey Hill, whose acerbic 'Tacit Pledges' is the most compellingly critical account, and Norman Page ('A.E. Housman and Thomas Hardy').

Placed beside Hardy, Housman appears to surprising advantage, but Page's brisk comparison of their war poetry—inevitably focusing on *Last Poems*, primarily 'Epitaph on an Army of Mercenaries' (it seems an unjustly limiting choice given the numerous parallels he lists) short-changes the younger writer. Perhaps the corner-cutting can be explained by the appearance this year of Page's wide-ranging, abundantly detailed and beautifully illustrated *Oxford Reader's Companion to Hardy*. Following volumes such as Frank Pinion's *Companion* [1968], *Commentary*

[1976] and *Dictionary* [1989] for example, this new *Companion* has much to live up to, but does so with a seriousness to be savoured. Including, besides an ample chronology, entries (indexed by subject) on everything from 'executions, public' to 'Positivism' and appending, as well as a highly organized bibliography, separate indexes of Hardy's poems, characters in the novels, place names, glossary (of dialect words and expressions), and a record of films and radio broadcasts, it amasses and orders a wealth of information in a way which gravely takes account of, but never panders to, Hardy's considerable general readership. Some forty contributors (Pinion himself, Dennis Taylor, Ronald Draper, Anthony Thwaite, and John Bayley among them) ensure diversions for the specialist, even the scholarly, student. With thoughtful management of subject entries (many closer to articles) and judicious cross-referencing, Page handles the encyclopedia-style format deftly. Here, for once, the biographical context supplied by people (friends and family jostle influences such as Keats, contemporaries such as Nietzsche and James Barrie, and admirers such as Auden) and places (real and imaginary) helps to ventilate but never overshadows literary context: almost eleven pages are devoted to 'critical approaches' and seven to 'poetry', not counting those (of several pages each) on named collections. Probably the longest entry is entitled, simply, 'Hardy, Thomas'; here, as elsewhere, the very limits of the format give rise to a moving sense of how the differing worlds of poet and novelist interleave in the man and merge in his work.

One of Page's contributors, Tim Armstrong, has been responsible for my favourite book of this season. *Haunted Hardy: Poetry, History, Memory* is a salutary reminder of how few critics manage to bridge the divide between the finely tuned textual critiques Armstrong provides, and the advanced theories in which his readings are embedded, inflected by Derrida and the psychoanalytic work of Abraham and Torok. As this absorbing study demonstrates, Hardy's work is haunted not simply by the figure to whom he wrote his finest elegies, his first wife Emma Gifford, but in many more subtle ways: a poet whose philosophical sophistication is apparent from his earliest meditations upon time, history, and public and private memory, the challenge of unravelling the ghosts and ghostlinesses of his writing, its idiom, formal rigour and often overt self-referentiality, is no picnic. Rummaging through the layered supplementarities of successive volumes (each 'retravers[ing] old terrain' and yet also 'supplementary to each other', p. 12) produced during a poetic career which, overlaying the tracks of the novelist, was itself supplementary, Armstrong's gracefully written and theoretically scrupulous account both complicates and enriches the way as, he points out, individual poems 'often read as if they had already theorized themselves' (p. 6). He moves from the spectral realms of Hardy's sceptical but imaginative interest in the psychological, informed by contemporaneous philosophical-scientific debates about materialism and spiritualism, to trace how childlessness (and the rumoured illegitimate son) echoes throughout the poet's meditations on private and public loss, before addressing the historiographical positions adopted in occasional poems such as 'The Convergence of the Twain' and 'Channel Firing'. In individual readings which hardly falter, Armstrong's acuity revitalizes the most well-worn of the poems. I can't recall a more stimulating or satisfying account of a poet for whom I've more than a soft spot.

Scant attention is paid to Hardy by the periodicals aside from *Poetry and Nation Review*. He proves little more than a filter for James Keery's rather disorderly two-part discussion of Donald Davie's controversial treatment, 'Inspired Triangulation: Thomas Hardy and British Poetry' (*PNR* 26:v[2000] 39–41) and 'The Old Immortality Bunfight' (*PNR* 26:vi[2000] 52–4). More fruitfully, David Yezzi, in 'Thomas Hardy and American Poetry' (*PNR* 26:iii[2000] 18–23), answered the recent reissuing of Davie's work by contesting its claim that Hardy's influence 'dissipated on its way across the Atlantic'. Yezzi traces the reach of Hardy's presence in such figures as Edwin Arlington Robinson, Robert Frost, John Crowe Ransom and even Pound, not only in their poetry, but in their own and others' critical writings (e.g. Yvor Winters on Robinson) and, in the case of Ransom and more recently his student Robert Mezey, in their editing of Hardy's poems. In conclusion Yezzi admits the partiality of his study, citing Bishop, Jeffers, Bogan and Penn Warren among other gaps in his argument. (That there is more work to be done on the complexities of Hardy's position vis-à-vis modernist poetry was underscored in the following issue by a letter from John Lucas (*PNR* 26:iv[2000] 3), querying the reliability—in the light of a series of discrepancies brought to light in the book itself and later in Martin Seymour-Smith's biography—of Graves's *Goodbye to All That*, the source of Hardy's infamous dismissal of *vers libre*. For Lucas, Hardy's interest in both Pound, to whom he had written, and Eliot, proves the untrustworthiness of Graves's account.)

The appearance of a Penguin Modern Classics edition of Charlotte Mew's *Complete Poems*, edited by John Newton, indicates that popular taste has begun to catch up with scholarly interest in this poet. However, a disappointingly perfunctory preface only implies, rather preposterously, that there is little to be said about her oeuvre, in spite of increasing critical evidence to the contrary. See, for example, the special issue of *Victorian Poetry* devoted to 'Women Writers 1890–1918' (*VP* 38:i[2000]), which includes Dennis Denisoff's account, 'Grave Passions: Enclosure and Exposure in Charlotte Mew's Graveyard Poetry' (pp. 125–40). Denisoff discovers in the moribund poetics of, for example, 'In Nunhead Cemetery', 'Madeleine in Church', and 'The Narrow Door' a highly gendered and sharply political reappropriation of the grave as site of liberation for a 'woman-centred economy of affection and desire' (p. 139). On the other hand, critical attention brings its own troubles, as a brief piece, 'Poetry's Maw' (*PNR* 26:vi[2000] 11) by Val Warner, the most vigilant of Mew's protectors, makes clear. She upbraids Ian Hamilton for 'a chronological mistake' in a discussion of Mew's publishing history—broadcast on Radio 3 in a concert-interval talk entitled 'Against Oblivion', and featuring four neglected twentieth-century poets—which 'rendered meaningless' much of an account drawn, she says, from Hamilton's work in progress, a twentieth-century version of *Lives of the Poets*. The mistake (confusing the date of a new edition issued in 1921 for the date of Mew's first publication, actually 1915) led Hamilton into error after error. He got told, as they say.

The pre-war writers have had a lean year. Poetry plays little part in Paul Peppis's reassessment of the political complexities informing the emergence of modernism. In *Literature, Politics and the English Avant-Garde: Nation and Empire, 1901–1918*, which he describes as 'less a work of literary or art criticism or of politico-aesthetic theory than of cultural history' (p. 18), Peppis re-excavates the influence of nationalist-imperialist ideologies over the European avant-garde. Wyndham Lewis, Vorticism and *Blast* are his chief interests. Although he emphasizes his inclusive approach, which aims to destabilize existing accounts of the pre-modernist moment by reading its literature in the light of its contemporaneous rather than post-war culture, and while figures such as Pound and Eliot inevitably haunt the work, Peppis pays little more than lip-service to poetry as a whole, and only at any length in the specific context of the war. Among the handful of poets he does mention (Bridges, Brooke and Ford Madox Ford among them), the most interesting choice is Helen Saunders, whose restlessly powerful 'A Vision of Mud', appeared in the 'War' number of *Blast*. Edward Thomas is the only other 'Georgian' to receive attention, *vide* Martin Dodsworth's rescuing of 'Adlestrop' from the late Antony Easthope's attentions, in 'Edward Thomas, Seamus Heaney and Modernity: A Reply to Antony Easthope' (*English* 49:cxciv[2000] 143–54). Dodsworth's brief but deliberately ample reading of this resonantly familiar poem—answering a 1997 article published by Easthope in the same journal, 'How Good is Seamus Heaney?' (*English* 46:clxxxiv[1997] 21–36), was lent an unwarranted poignancy by Easthope's death prior to its appearance. Dodsworth offers few surprises in correcting Easthope's unrefined account of Thomas's so-called anti-modernism, in alignment with that growing band of scholars intent on lifting modernism free from the binary-driven matrix by which it is conventionally confined.

The Great War has spawned the usual range of treatments, many of which take retrospection as their focus (just as OUP marks the twenty-fifth anniversary of Paul Fussell's monumental *The Great War in Modern Memory* by reissuing it with a new six-page Afterword which briefly acknowledges the book's dated dependence on Northrop Frye). Daniel Hipp's 'Ivor Gurney's Return to the "Private" Experience of Warfare: Rewards of Wonder and the Poems of 1919–1922' (*ELT* 43:i[2000] 3–36), considers poems written after the end of the war but prior to Gurney's institutionalization in 1922. Hipp argues that Gurney's experience of military life and combat had a curiously positive effect on a highly strung individual whose mental state was never robust. When the outbreak of war prompted him into the highly regulated, decision-free life of the private soldier, the routines of trench warfare, Hipp contends, brought him a psychological security which, when hostilities ceased in 1918, gradually disappeared. When poems like 'First Time In' (of which there are two versions, interestingly compared here) and 'First March' revisit and rewrite the wartime experiences described in earlier work, they do so with longing for the temporary equilibrium of the time. This highly personal subtext helps both to blunt and sharpen the mixture of public and private tensions which typically define war poetry: in Gurney's case, the internalized struggle for mental peace both mirrors but subverts, even transcends, the horrors of the conflict on which the later poems draw; reviving them sustains him, albeit, tragically, not for long.

Similarly, Norman Kelvin's long and dense account of 'H.D. and the Years of World War I' (*VP* 38:i[2000] 170–96) is concerned to show how the poems which appeared in *Sea Garden* [1916], later collected as *The God*, underpin and are continually returned to later in an intimate cycle of self-referentiality. Kelvin is not alone in figuring this as palimpsestic: Diana Collecott usefully deploys the same term at more satisfying length in her *H.D. and Sapphic Modernism, 1910–1950*. The first substantial study of H.D. for too long, this careful examination of the private and public terrain of an elusive poetics speaks to recent feminist and post-structuralist debates about the intersection of sexuality and identity, as well as to a growing constituency of modernist revisionists about the reconciliation of text, intertext and context in the self-conscious lexical and tropic shiftings of H.D.'s highly wrought classicism. Collecott's tracking of the Sapphic resonances of this elegant idiom is shrewdly judged. Having combed the oeuvre for evidence of direct borrowings of Sapphic fragments (an appendix charts the frequency with which these crop up), she reflects on the cultural as well as the personal and poetic significance of H.D.'s choice of resource. As an articulate but muted woman writer whose texts survive as fragments, and as a model of sexual ambivalence, her choice of forebear offers H.D. both public and private context. In Sappho's practice and language, fractured as it was, she found an ancient poetic guide, language and image-store such as Pound and Eliot found in Homer and Virgil, as well as an emotional and psychological place from where the marginalized female communities, to which Bryher introduced H.D. after the breakdown of her marriage, could challenge and overturn the cultural norms which excluded them. Likewise, for Collecott, 'in associating her own writings with Sappho's, which Swinburne had described as "mutilated fragments", [f]ar from presenting a diminished female body, H.D.'s doubling of herself with the Lesbian poet covertly opposes men's power as writers, editors and critics with an empowered lesbian body' (p. 15). Many of H.D.'s earliest readers will, as Collecott acknowledges, have recognized the codings this critique unpacks in reflecting on the ways in which the poetry frames its semiotic and semantic utterances about the cultural and literary place of the woman-identified (and by no means exclusively lesbian) woman in the modernist (and, thanks to writers like her, by no means either exclusively male or exclusively heterosexual) project. Collecott's scope allows for both breadth and focus, lending a large portfolio of critical debates a historical coherence which remains valuably elastic; thus it can gesture at the presence of the highly coloured Romantic/Decadent influences—mediated chiefly for H.D. by Swinburne—which murmur through her poetic language. In this, and as its title hints in other ways, this book is much more than the transformative revision of a single writer: Collecott locates her critical narrative firmly in a woman- (rather than exclusively lesbian-) identified writing tradition while confidently, and without undue fuss, positioning her subject in a primarily female writing community. Such affirmative acts of gendering, even if they are not intended to be overtly political, are in themselves transformational; taking the gender-orientation of H.D.'s literary and social contexts for granted is one way of quietly calling the masculinity of literary modernism into question.

Although Yeats's colourful and contradictory presence informs a number of discussions, few treat him in isolation; almost all, however, follow the lead taken by Paul Muldoon, in his inaugural lecture as Oxford Professor of Poetry (published in pamphlet form as *The End of the Poem: 'All Soul's Night' by W.B. Yeats*) in concentrating on the later work. As ever, the word-wizardry of Muldoon's lecture is worth relishing for the suppleness and amplitude with which he invests a characteristically impacted idiom. In another closely argued but less virtuosic reading, 'Yeats's Rough Beast: The God for the Slaves' (*ELN* 38:ii[2000] 61–71), Daniel O'Hearn bravely unpicks the considerable and complex ideological and spiritual tensions of 'The Second Coming'. In pondering the opposition, set out in *A Vision*, between the 'primary' and the 'antithetical', O'Hearn anticipates one of the interests of Fran Brearton's excellent *The Great War in Irish Poetry: W.B. Yeats to Michael Longley*, one of two good longer treatments. Much like its counterpart, Steven Matthews's *Yeats as Precursor: Readings in Irish, British and American*

Poetry (also reviewed by Brearton in section 8), Brearton's forward-looking approach recontextualizes two enormous discourses by examining the various points of their intersection, and, as her title hints, converses throughout with Fussell. Around 35,000 Irishmen (out of some 200,000 who enlisted) died in the conflict. Such poignant details underpin this sophisticated analysis of, in the pre-1945 first section, the varying responses of Yeats, Graves, and MacNeice to the fact, function and effect of a war in which Ireland's part has habitually been misunderstood, if not underestimated. As Brearton proves, Yeats is more interested than he pretends in a conflict he professed to ignore, not least because of a belief (which underpins the whole book) that 'All creation is from conflict'. However, as Yeats also knew, this was no more the kind of war that mantra imagines than its poetry would prove to be the kind of nationally significant 'creation' he would have wished for. In fact, for Brearton, his reluctance to write about the war himself and disdain for poets like Wilfred Owen argues the depth of his uncertainty about the effect of a conflict which to some extent overshadowed, but also enlivened, interest in a domestic political agenda. Hence the different nuances of the four elegies he would write for Robert Gregory. Yeats's equivocation emerges as the common reference point for the following chapters, each retracing a particular set of creative tensions attending its subject, respectively Graves and MacNeice, to his relationship with Ireland and his response to the war. Graves, for example, is carefully resituated in the complexities of a shifting literary context: if he is habitually written out of Irish literature, his part in 'English' poetry is also misunderstood. Brearton understands Graves's entire oeuvre as a lengthy working out of a coherent response to the war which proves not only the accuracy of Yeats's mantra but also the significance of his example. There are interesting parallels between 'A Vision' and *The White Goddess*, for example. In the chapter on MacNeice, Fussell takes second place to Samuel Hynes, whose work on the mythologizing of the Great War is the starting point for an examination of how MacNeice's rehabilitation, by contemporary poets such as Michael Longley, as a poet of Northern Ireland, further complicates his response to the conflict. Although MacNeice is distanced from the Great War by age as well as upbringing, his interest in the subject not only reminds us of its impact on his generation, but of his difference from his peers in the Auden group, not least because of the way in which his own ideas borrow the ambivalence he sympathetically explores in *The Poetry of W.B. Yeats*.

Matthews's treatment, covering not one but three different literary cultures and focusing more decisively on Yeats, seems both broader and narrower than Brearton's. In some ways, the case he makes is obvious: 'Reading Yeats through the poets he has influenced is another way of re-reading Yeats himself, setting him in different lights and cultural contexts' (p. 38). However, his study of a predictably diverse and fragmented array of poetic conversations with this generative, tension-filled presence, not all of which obey Harold Bloom's formula of poetic influence, seems virtuosic (apart, that is, from some remarkable lapses of grammar and general ungainliness of expression). Yeats, after all, was the master of self-reinvention, ceaselessly warring, in public and in private, with any and all of the cultural traditions—historical, political, aesthetic—with which he knew himself, like it or not, to be associated. Bloom, Paul de Man and, most usefully, Derrida all enter a discussion of influence which, agonistically, strives and fails to escape its own Bloomian beginnings. Embedding what is, in fact, a survey of considerable range (moving, for example, from MacNeice and Austin Clarke to Auden and Davie to John Crowe Ransom and Allen Tate, being those who come closest to my domain) in Yeats's dualistic sense of the word 'tradition' as that large cultural context by which the self is simultaneously secured and effaced, Matthews probes Bloom's impacted paradigm through his textual deconstructions. Focusing on aporia-rich poems like 'The Choice', he reaches through Bloom towards more supple Derridean tropes of supplementarity and undecidability, which colour the poetic re-encountering of Yeats wherever and whenever it has taken place since his death. If this confident book has a flaw it is perhaps that it overreaches itself in attempting to treat so many of those individual encounters. Even so, it creates a sense of Yeats's poetic stature more successfully for that breadth.

A much shorter essay by Matthews notes Byron's impact on Yeats's mature idiom, and therefore, rather by default, on modernism—in all its divergences—overall. 'Yeats's "passionate improvisations": Grierson, Eliot, and the Byronic Integrations of Yeats's Later Poetry' (*English* 49:cxciv[2000] 127–41), finds Herbert Grierson partly responsible for the ageing poet's effort, in mature poems such as 'In Memory of Eva Gore-Booth and Con Markiewitz' and 'Coole Park 1929', to reintegrate the public and private responsibilities Yeats once strove to separate. That shift in perspective was first commented on by Eliot, in the 1940 memorial address he delivered at Westminster Abbey, and to some extent underwrites the Yeats commemorated in *Little Gidding*. Matthews, however, is the first to retrace them to Byron, who is treated at some length in Grierson's *The Background of English Literature* (published, and avidly read by Yeats, in 1925); the repeated use of *ottava rima* in the later poetry serves to support his case. He proposes that it is in this effort, to 're-integrate' the passionate poetic self of private experience with the voice of public knowledge, that the later Yeats departs most conclusively from the principles and legacy of a modernism which was always more Eliot's than his.

In a fairly fallow year for Eliot himself (not helped by the reluctance of some publishers to forward review copies), I'll start with one I missed last time: M.A.R. Habib's *The Early T.S. Eliot and Western Philosophy*. A lively prose makes this penetrating examination of the philosopher *manqué* more readable than you might expect. In the first comprehensive scholarly account of Eliot's chief philosophical writings (the doctoral work on Bradley, three unpublished graduate papers on Kant and a sceptical manuscript paper on Bergson) Habib pursues the irony which the poet cultivated under Harvard luminaries such as Irving Babbit and George Santayana. Situating Eliot in the 'heterological' tradition (opposing the post-Enlightenment liberal-humanist ideology reaching from Russell to Locke and Hume), Habib systematically examines how the ironist's philosophy is refined in the complex stance of his poetics, and major critical principles like those of impersonality and tradition. Arthur Symons's view of Symbolism's opposition to bourgeois materialism propels Eliot—via Schopenhauer and Bergson—towards Laforgue, for example. In Laforgue's humorously ironic poetics, the philosophically problematic relationship of the One and the Many is resolved by unifying the one fragmented self with the self-consciously dualistic version which stands outside and transcends it. From this example, Habib traces in the ironic voices of Prufrock and the lady of 'Portrait' a similarly elaborate and often deftly humorous synthesis of the poetic with the philosophical. But if antagonism to the liberal-humanist tendencies of bourgeois thought underpins Eliot's interest in Kant and Bradley—his dissertation illuminating the self-aware forms of the 1914–19 poems—his attitude to them remains broadly ironic, just as his despairing pessimism remains, ironically, embedded in the economic, aesthetic and cultural institutions he professes to deplore. Habib's account comes fruitfully to rest on the ironic philosophy of *The Waste Land*, embodied in the dualistic form and equivocal utterances of Tiresias.

Irony is also implicitly at issue in Andrew John Miller's '"Compassing material ends": T.S. Eliot, Christian Pluralism, and the Nation State' (*ELH* 67[2000] 229–55), which pursues what Barbara Hernstein Smith, in *Contingencies of Value* [1988], called 'the double discourse of value' in Eliot's work. Miller claims that the dualities of the poet's socio-political position, as an outsider striving for economic and professional security, inform his rhetorical articulation of the conflict between the material and the spiritual concerns of his world. He finds the tensions between Eliot's pronouncements on the autonomy of art and artist, and his own relentlessly industrious working life, reflected in the dialectical relationship of Church and state in 'The Hippopotamus'. Meanwhile the only chapter of Murray Roston's *Modernist Patterns in Literature and the Visual Arts* to prove relevant to this review—'T.S. Eliot and the Secularists' (pp. 43–85)—ponders the ambiguous spirituality of *The Waste Land*. For Roston, the poem's refusal to ally itself with either a specifically Christian or secular outlook reifies early twentieth-century interest in the distinction between the spatial limits of known finite space, as theorized by Euclid, and the limitless space, beyond the grasp of human reason, lying outside it. What first found visual expression in the Cubists' efforts to realize a universally unstable fourth dimension or 'new measure' of space, and was reflected in the popularity of mysticism and the occult among intellectuals of the time, is echoed for Roston in *The Waste Land*'s 'yearning for metaphysical truths' which 'would lend meaning to the sterile actuality of human experience'. Hence the poem's popularity among secularists, in contrast to the hardening Christian dogma being worked out in later poems, such as 'Ash Wednesday'.

Otherwise, *Notes and Queries* (47:iii) offers the following Eliotian morsels. In Michael Whitworth's 'Eliot, Schiff, And Einstein' (*N&Q* 47:iii[2000] 336–7), a reference in a 1922 letter to an unidentified Einstein suggests four possible candidates; music critic Alfred and historian Lewis both seem outsiders, while a certain J.W.N. Sullivan, known to both correspondents, might or might not have provided a link with physicist Albert. However, letters exchanged between Schiff and Wyndham Lewis in 1922 argue for Carl, a German art critic, who had asked Schiff to suggest books for a study of twentieth-century art. *The Sacred Wood* was on Schiff's list. Meanwhile, James T. Bratcher, in 'The Reference to "Stetson" in *The Waste Land*' (*N&Q* 47:iii[2000] 338–9), speculates that the reference to 'Stetson' in *The Waste Land* may have been triggered by a visit made to London in 1919 by John B. Stetson Jr., son of the wealthy Philadelphian hatter. Stetson's purchase of H. Buxton Forman's library in the course of the visit later realized a huge profit when it was auctioned in New York, perhaps stoking the poem's anti-materialist argument. Finally, K. Narayan Chandran, 'T.S. Eliot's Recall of W.E. Henley: East Coker III and "Ballade of Dead Actors"' (*N&Q* 47:iii[2000] 339), hears William Ernest Henley in the theatricalities of lines 101–14 of 'East Coker' III, where Henley's parade of characters and props fades away: 'Into the night go one and all'. A comparable set of theatrical similes in Eliot's poem concludes 'They all go into the dark'.

Ever heartened to find the work of women, especially those writing in the febrile aftermath of the Great War, given space in the journals, I was glad to come upon the piece on modernist Mina Loy by her biographer Carolyn Burke in *PNR*. (*Becoming Modern: The Life of Mina Loy* [1996] was regrettably not covered in these pages at the time of its publication.) Burke's account of the uneven fortunes of her subject, 'What's in a Name? Or, Mina/Myrna/Muna' (*PNR* 27:i[2000] 30–2), begins by claiming that Loy's stature in scholarly circles has increased; in the absence of anything to review here I can only echo her hope that more notice will be taken of a figure too frequently sidelined—nodded at *en passant*, if mentioned at all—among a crowd of peers. Burke depicts Loy's career as a modernistic progression of self-reinventions, graphed by the name changes which punctuated it. The abbreviation of her real name (Lowy) was a deliberate effacing of her Jewish origins with a suggestion of the French, for the purposes of her first art exhibition. Although her own success was eclipsed by that of the film star Myrna Loy, with whom she would always be confused, as Burke reveals it was in fact the young starlet Myrna Williams's adoption of the poet's name which caused the muddle in the first place. Loy's counterfeiting of herself included varying the pronunciation of her first name when it suited her, and challenging the misogynistic Futurists in the verse satire 'Lions' Jaws' as 'Nimo Lyo alias | Anim Yol alias | Imna Oly'. Similar disguises helped to shield her from the scandal following the publication of 'Love Songs' [1915] in the experimental magazine *Others*. Her strategy has been replicated in various fictitious representations of Loy in more recent times (including a musical of her romance with the boxer/poet Arthur Cravan). For Burke, this seems to signal a healthy effort to accept the transformative instincts and practice which make Loy the important modernist she was.

Among little else on the so-called Thirties Poets, *PNR* found room to review a good selection of lesser-known or neglected writers, including three of the women whose contribution was underlined in Jane Dowson's revisionary anthology *Women Poets of the 1930s* [1996]. John Press, in 'Bernard Spencer: A Poet of the Thirties' (*PNR* 26:iii[2000] 52–5), argues that this MacSpaunday crony be recognized in what 'journalists and literary historians have agreed to call the Poets of the Thirties'. He quite fails to recognize how little currency that so-called agreement retains in the wake of critics such as Dowson, Valentine Cunningham and Jan Montefiore. His detection of 'the authentic voice' of those poets in a mere six lines of Spencer's 'Greek Excavations' (deemed to reveal 'sympathy for the individual, whose simple desires … are frustrated by the representative of power and greed') doesn't help. Spencer was certainly one of the crew: right sort of age, social background and education, and published in the same sort of places (MacNeice's periodical *Sir Galahad*, while co-editing *Oxford Poetry* [1930] with Spender and contributing some twenty-odd poems to Grigson's *New Verse* between 1935 and 1938). However, having left Britain for Cairo in 1940, where he spent the war and came to know Keith Douglas well, he published virtually nothing until Editions Poetry London (via the indefatigable Tambimuttu, who also saw Douglas into print) belatedly produced those early poems as *Aegean Islands* [1946]. It will take more than the 'ordered elegance' of Spencer's writing to justify Press's claims. But for his unnecessarily paternalistic use of both writers' first names, Peter Scupham's highly personalized appraisals of Sylvia Townsend Warner, in 'Shelf Lives: 11' (*PNR* 26:v[2000] 63–5), and E.J. Scovell, in 'Shelf Lives: 9' (*PNR* 26:iii[2000] 26–8), are more constructive. Townsend Warner is acclaimed for 'a razor-sharp sense of fictive life and the theatre of habitat', the 'deceptive simplicities' of a plain but musical idiom, and 'that mordant equipoise which is her trade-mark'. Her younger contemporary Scovell (whose final collection, *Listening to Collared Doves* [1986], Scupham himself helped to publish at the Mandeville Press) is commended for 'a reticent candour, a clean exactitude of phrasing' and 'that sense of a slight thing closing over its own mystery' which argues her committed interest in the apparently insignificant. Although the column format constrains Scupham's recuperative efforts, in my view both women leave Spencer standing.

Arguably, Robert Graves's collaborator Laura Riding Jackson has more right to our attention than any of the other three: *PNR* began to prepare for the centenary of her birth in January 2001 by publishing three excerpts from her unpublished critical writings, probably intended for two books currently in production (presumably to mark the anniversary itself) in 'A Centenary Portfolio: 1' (*PNR* 27:ii[2000] 27–30). All were written after 1950 (the earliest extracted from a letter written in 1969), but read 'Petty Pomposity, Pompous Pettiness' for the savage dismissal of what Riding Jackson describes, with glorious disrespect, as the 'spurious' superficiality of Auden's apparent intellectualism: 'With Auden, the sayer of the words is not expressing in words a real action of mind. He is using his intellect as an agent of intuition to choose words that, with luck, will have a meaning-force of some impressiveness ... relying physically on some intellectual good fortune presumed by him to preside over his personal destinies as a human being' (p. 28). Riding Jackson's aggrieved sensitivity to Auden's 'transplanting of structures of poetic expression and statement from my work into his' prompts her to dismiss him as 'a born intellectual loafer', and reject Edward Mendelson's reiteration—in *The Early Auden* [1981]—of Auden's claim that Riding Jackson's influence over him was 'a triviality of youthful "imitation" very early abandoned by him'. There is surely work to be done here.

Auden is the subject of the only significant book about the period. Rainer Emig's *W.H. Auden: Towards a Postmodern Poetics* reconceives Auden as a writer in whom the awkward conversation between the modern and the postmodern comes alive. This is one of those clear-sighted books that renders a complex and tightly controlled argument straightforward enough to make you wonder why no one has thought of it before. If Emig's repositioning of Auden appears provocatively modish, perhaps that reiterates the extent of his subject's grip over the academy. Emig blames this for the general misconception of a poet less socio-historically bound than most commentators allow. In reply he dares to postmodernize (as it were) the never quite modernist, relocating Auden amid the ambiguous potentialities of the 'border territory' in which Geoffrey Grigson, with rare perception, first discerned him. Thus a beautifully built account reveals how this most chameleon of poets engages in his own, often far-sighted, way with the cultural developments of the twentieth century. Working cautiously through the oeuvre, prose and plays as well as poems, it traces how Auden's ambivalent early interest in the language and precepts of modernism gradually hardens into outright rejection of an aesthetic which naively seeks to answer uncertainty with coherence and order. Emig's purpose is to overturn the accepted narrative of Auden's poetic progress.

The early experiments are found to anticipate and test out the suspicions which in the later work cohere into a sustained reflexive enquiry into the relation of language and meaning, self and other: 'a farewell to the established notion that Auden's early poems are brilliant rhetorical propaganda pieces seems inevitable' (p. 79). What begins in the early poems as a wrestle with the process of signification turns, in *The Orators*, into an investigation of the interrelation of self, language and authority which ultimately begs to resist the modernist will to closure, chiefly through the careful displacement of voice: as a poem such as 'The Wanderer' finally underlines, 'individuality as well as textuality can only be envisaged in terms of exile' (p. 119). The mature poetics, apparently less radical, refines this problematizing of voice by probing the contextual influences of nationhood and history. Accompanied by stylistic change, emigration emphatically testifies to the positive effects of displacement on subjectivity; for Emig, the idiomatic restlessness of the American work is playful, part of an overall project to undermine authenticity and cultural homogeneity which now seems uncannily postmodern, and confirms Auden as the enigmatic inhabitant of the shifting domains of the borderland. Arguing the 'paradoxical coherence, at least of problems' (p. 8) of this poetics, this study makes confident use of a range of literary theorists, moving smoothly from Saussurean linguistics to the debates stimulated by post-structuralist thinkers such as Derrida. In reconfiguring Auden as postmodernist, Emig's masterly re-reading not only radicalizes but convincingly rehabilitates a writer whose work deserves and repays the kind of sophisticated scrutiny it gets here.

Although he was active during and, like Auden, well after the 1930s, the late modernist Basil Bunting has never been closely associated with any particular period of the century. A year older than Riding Jackson, his centenary year has been marked by Ric Caddel's new edition of the *Complete Poems*, published by Bloodaxe alongside a double cassette recording of the poet himself reading, in that gruffly mesmerizing way of his, from 'Briggflatts and Other Poems'. If the tribute seems understated, it also seems well judged; Caddel's brief new introduction reminds us of the poet's reticence ('never explain—your reader is as smart as you'). If there is explanation to be found, as Caddel hints, and the recordings underline, it is in the phonic inventiveness of this poetics, sometimes echoingly plangent, sometimes gratingly discordant. The collection combines Bunting's own *Collected Poems* with the much-debated *Uncollected Poems* (complete with its own editorial preface), which Caddel defends on the grounds that not only is it 'justified in its context by its own intrinsic interest' (p. 14) but that 'it is necessary to present it in order to define it, and distinguish it from the *Collected Poems*'. (*p. 179*) Bunting has little in common with the more conservative neo-Georgian James Reeves, other than their acquaintance with Laura Riding Jackson. Reeves features in another of Scupham's columns, 'Shelf Lives: 13' (*PNR* 27:i[2000] 40–2). Respectful of 'the courteous exactitude' of 'curiously delicate webs of sensation', Scupham rightly refuses to overlook 'a darkness there too ... Reeves carries a constant sense of being possessed and teased by disturbing psychic fragments'. None of the avuncular use of the first name suffered by Townsend Warner and Scovell here, you'll note. In his pursuit of the formal dexterity he always relishes ('the ghosts both summoned and exorcised by the musical disciplines by which he pursued his craft'), Scupham acknowledges the importance of Robert Graves's loyalty to the younger poet. He fails, however, to pay enough attention to Reeves's collaborative relationship with Riding Jackson for

Alan Clark: 'Letters' (*PNR* 27:ii[2000] 4). Clark notes not only that one of Riding's poems, 'Preface to these Poems' both prefaces and supplies the title of Reeves's first collection (*The Natural Need* [1935]), but that she publishes several of Reeves's poems as well as two essays, one jointly authored by LR and JR in the three issues of *Epilogue* [1935–7]. He also draws attention to the 1933–40 correspondence, now in Cornell Library.

The poetry of the 1940s has enjoyed unusual attention. Mark Rawlinson's broad-based survey of the literature of the period, *British Writing of the Second World War*, concerns itself mostly with prose, partly because of its interest in the popular discourse and the focus on works circulated in wartime, but the poetry is not neglected. This intelligent book examines how the literature of the Second World War both reiterates and contradicts the critique of conflict and violence which was the legacy of Great War writers such as Wilfred Owen. Instead of seeking to weigh the later corpus against the earlier, Rawlinson 'sets out to say something about the way the war was understood by those who fought it'; in doing so, he reviews the relationship between the material events of war and their political ramifications, alerting us to how 'the contradictory values invested in state-legitimated killing' are represented and reflected on in the literature (p. 3). Electing, imaginatively, to organize a vast amount of material with reference to specific theatres of war, Rawlinson chooses the poetry of Keith Douglas to illuminate the isolated, isolating conflict played out in the alienating but strangely resonant emptiness of the North African deserts where the poet, who was finally killed in the D-Day landings, spent most of his war. Douglas's confident, casual and elegantly ironic poetic idiom, 'marked by a fascination with the appearance of altered flesh' figured in 'Vergissmeinnicht', for example, 'as a textual skin and an eviscerated volume ... which demand to be read and physically probed' (p. 119), registers the uncertainty of his continuing existence amid oblivion. Despite his fatalism (he never expected to survive the war) Douglas did not shirk combat: he is depicted as the 'flâneur of battle, immersing himself in its crowds (literal and spectral) ... in search of "rhyme-booty"'. The two versions of the conflict—its brutal disrespect for individual and socio-cultural life, and the grotesquely effective aesthetic potential which it generates as a result—are never resolved, making for a poetry which stoutly refuses to overlook the provisionality of experience. Rawlinson's sensitive and detailed (if necessarily short) appraisal of Douglas is followed by a much sketchier account of Alun Lewis, 'the war's non-combatant war poet', discussed alongside Day Lewis, Eliot and Edwin Muir's contributions to the public discourse (often through the pages of Cyril Connolly's *Horizon*). In an otherwise impressive book, this is a disappointing reminder of how rarely, despite the recuperative efforts of scholars such as Catherine Reilly, the poetry of female non-combatants such as Edith Sitwell (who was both published and favourably reviewed in Connolly's journal in the period)—unlike that of their prose-writing sisters (Vera Brittain, Elizabeth Bowen, Olivia Manning)—is given serious critical attention.

Two other books have helped to boost Douglas's profile in the meantime, thanks to his biographer Desmond Graham. Faber's swift and glossy reissue of the definitive new revised edition of *Keith Douglas: The Complete Poems*—which Graham initially saw into print for Oxford Poets before its list closed in 1999—appends a new preface to Ted Hughes's introduction, explaining various editorial changes. These reflect Graham's interest in the preparations which Douglas himself made for the publication of his poems in 1944, and are substantiated by the poet's correspondence, a lavish selection (not, its title would suggest, wholly complete, although this is not made absolutely clear) of which, edited by Graham of course, has also appeared (*The Letters of Keith Douglas*). Nicely produced, judiciously (if a touch over-earnestly) edited, with helpful biographical notes on the correspondents, this book not only underlines Graham's considerable contribution to Douglas's much-improved status, but offers a much richer and fuller account of a poet whose charm, lively sense of humour and emotional insecurity are peripheral to a profoundly disciplined poetics. The letters of the energetic schoolboy, witty and volatile student lover, and deeply affectionate son, are coloured by infrequent insights into the developing practice of the poet, in touch with Edmund Blunden, J.C. Hall, and even T.S. Eliot. The poet emerges most frequently in the years spent fighting in Africa ('Myself, I never do anything heroic', p. 243), from where he managed to get himself published in London, alongside the work of Hall and Norman Nicholson, in *Selected Poems* [1943]. The largely sporadic commentary on the poetics in letters from 1942, often dominated by the details of daily life, is at its keenest in 1943, as he finally receives *Selected Poems*, learns of Tambimuttu's supportive interest, and defends his changing idiom from Hall: 'To write on the themes which have been concerning me lately in lyrical and abstract forms would be immense bullshitting. In my early poems I wrote lyrically, as an innocent ... I have (not surprisingly) fallen from that particular grace since then' (p. 294). Such comments are illuminated by a brief essay, included among some short stories in the appendices, which casts interesting light on Mark Rawlinson's ideas: 'Poets in This War' [1943] avers that 'the poets who wrote so much and so well before the war, all over the world, have been silenced ... they do not write because there is nothing new, from a soldier's point of view, about this war except its mobile character. ... Almost all that a modern poet on active service is inspired to write, would be tautological ... while English civilians have not endured any suffering comparable to that of other European civilians' (pp. 351–2).

In conclusion, the eminent critic Barbara Hardy, in *Dylan Thomas: An Original Language*, has produced a rewardingly concentrated account of the charged inventiveness of Thomas's language, drawn from a series of lectures given at the University of Georgia. Emphasizing the poet's imaginative achievement over and above his obscurity, Hardy's treatment is as celebratory as it is scholarly; in particular she urges respect for that breadth of vision which exceeds the regionalism and nationalism on which many commentators focus, the 'articulation—usually implicit—of an aesthetic psychology, a humane reflexivity, and what now seems appropriate to call the green philosophy, a politics of natural vision and a belief in what Coleridge called the unity of being' (p. xiii). Her wider perspective encourages Hardy to reposition Thomas amid the vaster and more fluid aesthetic realm of modernism. Dubbing him a 'language-changer', after the example of Shakespeare, Dickens, Hopkins, and especially James Joyce, she explores how the sensuous self-awareness of his poetic idiom underlines the poet's sense of his recuperative powers of expression. This in turn makes sense of his fascination, literary and actual, psychological and poetic, with the theme of 'greenness' in which his Romantic and modernist inclinations repeatedly meet and converge. Finally, Dent has produced a revised new edition of *Dylan Thomas: The Collected Letters*, edited by Paul Ferris, to incorporate various new items which have surfaced since the book's first edition appeared. Along with numerous amplifications to footnotes and identifications of sources and locations, as Ferris's rewritten introduction points out the additions include the very first irrepressible letter reproduced here, written, at the age of about 12, to Thomas's grown-up sister Nancy. However, reading between the lines it seems clear that the industry generated by interest in Thomas memorabilia has prohibited, in one way or another, the inclusion of other material.

7. Post-1950 Poetry

Philip Larkin has been due for extensive critical reassessment for some time, and Booth, ed., *New Larkins for Old*, a collection of fifteen essays, represents the best current revaluations of his work. Each essay enters into the spirit of beating out the dust of anti-modernist, misogynist, racist Larkin, and exploring a more complex, ambivalent figure. The collection opens with Barbara Everett's brilliant exposition of Larkin's 'Money', to show that Larkin is always more complex and artful than his casual, brusque style pretends. Many of the essays examine the early Larkin. Edna Longley, with her usual wit and subtlety, follows an intriguing pattern of thought which takes us through Larkin's misogyny and nostalgia, and on to the absorbing argument that his work exhibits many of the characteristics of decadence. Longley is just one of the contributors who wishes to rescue Larkin from Kingsley Amis, to rediscover the Larkin who 'remembers Yeats and Lawrence'. John Carey argues that these competing claims to Larkin's mind are, in fact, discernible throughout his work as two colliding voices—one the offensive, masculine, right-wing writer who scoffs at art and culture, the other the sensitive, feminine, idealistic poet who adored Lawrence. Terry Whalen explores the influence of Lawrence in more depth in an essay on the impact of *Lady Chatterley's Lover* on Larkin in the 1940s. Raphaël Ingelbien finds some affinities between the late work of T.S. Eliot and the early work of Larkin; similarly, John Osborne complicates the reductive image of Larkin as an anti-modernist. M.W. Rowe sheds light on the 'lesbian fantasies' in Larkin's early stories under the pseudonym Brunette Coleman. George H. Gilpin explores the relationship between Patricia Avis and Philip Larkin through Avis's papers. Stephen Regan returns to a volume of poems, *In the Grip of Light*, which Larkin prepared in 1947 but failed to publish, and argues persuasively that it represents a 'complex formative stage' in the poet's work. Regan suggests that the abandoned volume indicates not the familiar transition of influence from Yeats to Hardy, but instead a shift in register and vision from the promised dawn of the early post-war years to a more mature cynicism about the post-war world. Hence, Regan comments, the portentous ambiguity of the title, *In the Grip of Light*. Regan finds here not the nostalgic, belated note for which Larkin has become renowned, but a poet of remarkable prescience. Other essays explore mythology and mysticism in Larkin's work. Place features in essays on Larkin and empire and Larkin from an east European perspective, and James Booth contributes an essay which compares Larkin's and Heaney's conceptions of place. In the introduction Booth gives an overview of the fifteen essays, recognizing the diversity of methods and views offered in the collection as a measure of the diversity of Larkins available in his poetry and prose. The collection is well worth reading from cover to cover, and does much to enrich and complicate the legacy of a poet who is always in danger of being reduced to his most offensive political views.

The work of Ted Hughes is explored and championed in Keith Sagar's *The Laughter of Foxes: A Study of Ted Hughes*. Sagar is a reliable commentator on Hughes's oeuvre, and his long friendship with Hughes has enabled him privileged access to many early drafts and personal communications. This is the principal strength of Sagar's book, that he brings us close to what Hughes was thinking as he wrote, but it is also its principal weakness. Sagar sometimes relies too heavily on Hughes's own account of what he was doing, and does not trust sufficiently in the potential of the poetry to move beyond a singular artistic vision. This is directly attributable to Sagar's explanation of the role of literary criticism, which he sees as having nothing to do with 'some prior expectations or critical theory', but with 'what we can divine of the author's own inner idea of what he or she is after' (p. ix). At its most impressive, this is a fine account of the evolution of Hughes's poetic and mythic vision, but it sometimes sails too close to psychobiography. Sagar's central argument is that Hughes is a poet who moves from early evocations of a mythic 'landscape of mud and blood' (p. 109), through to the recognition that the role of the poet is 'to heal, to discover and embody possibilities of regeneration' (p. 33). The book contains an opening chapter on Hughes's 'mythic imagination', a chapter charting his progress from the world of books to the secret, magical world of nature, and a lengthy explanation of the evolution of his symbolic vision from 'blood' to 'light'. There is a detailed and insightful analysis of the fourteen draft versions of 'The Dove Came', and, presumably as a student aid, an appendix which summarizes 'the story of Crow'. Sagar's view of Hughes is ultimately quasi-religious. He charts the poet's spiritual journey from nature lover to faith healer, and describes the process, depicted in Hughes's poetry and letters, by which 'he recovered his sense of the universal spirit of life' (p. 136). The book is undoubtedly a useful addition to the study of Hughes's work, but it would benefit greatly if Sagar could somehow get out of Hughes's head for a while.

Ian Gregson's *The Male Image: Representations of Masculinity in Postwar Poetry* [1999] summarizes the current, limited theoretical perspectives on masculinity prior to exploring how masculinity is represented in the work of a diverse range of poets. The best chapters examine not just the ways in which masculinity is represented in a poet's work, but also how the entire oeuvre and tone of a poet can be explained in relation to particular models of masculinity. This works well in the chapters on Ted Hughes, C.K. Williams and Derek Walcott, which deal with the uncomfortable identification of these poets with masculine authority and power, and in the chapter which relates the postmodern deconstruction of Frank O'Hara and John Ashbery to the politics of camp. Gregson has uncomfortable moments of his own, however, in a tendency in the chapters on Berryman, Hughes and Walcott, for example, to exonerate male poets from the forms of male sexism which are apparent in their work. He distinguishes the male sexism explored in his book as being of a particularly 'sophisticated and poetic kind', but does not fully explore how this makes it different from, or more excusable than, other forms of male sexism. The problem in part here is that Gregson retains a very tight focus on the poetry, and on each poet's oeuvre, and fails to connect the forms of machismo, camp, sexism, and self-critique he detects in the poetry to their social and cultural contexts. These reservations aside, however, the strengths of the book lie in its detailed readings of gendered assumptions and values in the work of poets as diverse as John Berryman, Robert Lowell, Adrienne Rich, Ted Hughes, Seamus Heaney, Derek Walcott, Frank O'Hara, Paul Muldoon, John Ashbery, C.K. Williams and a handful of others. Gregson's criticisms of Rich come too close, for me, to blaming the supposed excesses of feminism for the crisis in masculinity, although this is a tendency he scrupulously avoids in other chapters. There are also intriguing suggestions for how very different poets might share similar assumptions about gender, such as the fascinating prospect that Ted Hughes and Adrienne Rich bring to their work similar mythological archetypes of gendered identity, and share a common commitment to ecofeminism. Again, the tight focus on each poet's oeuvre prevents Gregson from developing these suggestions further.

Roy Fisher's work is difficult to locate amongst the forms and subgenres of post-war British poetry. This is partly because of the sheer variety of styles adopted in his poems, from the short epic, *A Furnace* [1986], to the poetic novel, *The Ship's Orchestra* [1967], from the free-verse lyric, 'Handsworth Liberties' [1978], to the disjunctive, fragmentary form of *The Cut Pages* [1971]. This is partly the point of Kerrigan and Robinson, eds., *The Thing About Roy Fisher: Critical Studies*, a collection of twelve essays which celebrate the diversity and inventiveness of Fisher's writings. This is perhaps one of the most even and brilliant collections of essays I have read for some time. Each essay advances its own unique set of interests and concerns skilfully and admirably. John Kerrigan begins with Fisher's identification with Birmingham and proceeds to elaborate on his handling of themes of space and location. James Keery seeks to place Fisher's early work in the 1950s, searching through what he might share in common with 'the Movement' or the neo-Romantic, 'apocalyptic' poets, and deftly shows the 'black and cool aesthetic' at work in 'The Lemon Bride'. John Lucas describes the meanings of jazz and counter-cultural music in Fisher's life and work in an entertaining narrative which formulates some intriguing thoughts on the relationship between formal innovation, musical style and cultural politics. There is fun too in Ian Sansom's exploration of comedy and laughter in Fisher's work, while Robert Sheppard traces Fisher's consistent resistance to rigid forms and structures in his prose-poetry. Ian Bell and Meriel Lland examine Fisher's interest in fluid, liminal forms, while Michael O'Neill finds lurking in his treatment of the self a 'dark, self-subverting poet'. Marjorie Perloff explains the reasons why Fisher established something of a reputation in the 1960s as an avant-garde poet who could be found in the pages of American 'little' magazines, but who has since become renowned more for conventional lyric poetry. Simon Jarvis examines the implications of Fisher's 'blockage' in the late 1960s, an unpromising subject, from which Jarvis derives some very interesting speculations about the relationship between form and artistic value in Fisher's work. Ralph Pite explores productive intertexts between Fisher and John Cowper Powys. Clair Wills traces a dilemma for Fisher in his representations of themes of death and absence, while Peter Robinson's 'Last Things' follows up similar themes of death, closure and ghostliness. There isn't a dud essay among them. Moreover, what makes this book absolutely essential for anyone interested in Fisher is the invaluable chronology and bibliography of his work provided by Derek Slade. It is perhaps testament to the enigma and diversity of Fisher's work that there isn't a coherent, easy answer to the dilemma posed by the collection. Each of the essays makes its own inroads and presents its own insights into the character and significance of Fisher's writings, but there remains *something* about Fisher that is still difficult to place.

W.S. Milne has written *An Introduction to Geoffrey Hill* [1998], which was not covered in the previous volume, and which deserves consideration here. Milne begins by acknowledging the difficulty many readers find on their first encounter with Hill's work, but proceeds to give a very fine account of his recurrent preoccupations and themes. This includes not only a detailed explanation of his wide range of reference to historical, literary and mythical materials, but also a sympathetic exploration of what Milne calls the 'resistant architecture' of Hill's poetic form. The first chapter of the book establishes Hill's signature themes and styles; the second chapter offers a brief overview of his life; subsequent chapters are devoted to each of his collections—*For the Unfallen* [1959], *King Log* [1968], *Mercian Hymns* [1971], *Tenebrae* [1978], *The Mystery of the Charity of Charles Péguy* [1983], and *Canaan* [1996]. The appendices contain two short pieces on his early, uncollected poems and on his own critical views of poetic form. As befits Hill's own sense of being rooted in poetic traditions, Milne provides a detailed sense of the relationship between his poems and their poetic precursors. At the same time, he is careful not to become too absorbed in the density of allusion which characterizes Hill's poetry, and provides instead a very readable, lucid guide to reading and enjoying the poems.

Basil Bunting on Poetry [1999] is a collection of Bunting's lectures at Newcastle University. Eleven of the lectures were delivered in 1969–70, and the last two from Bunting's second series of lectures in 1974. The collection is edited by Peter Makin, mainly from Bunting's drafts but also from the taped recordings. The drafts were in varying stages of completion, so that, for example, Bunting's remarks on Whitman are provided only in the form of rough notes, to which Makin has helpfully added explanatory notes. The theme of Bunting's lectures is the interdependence of music and poetry, which he argues is the defining characteristic of the modern poets, and which he traces through the history of English poetry. 'I'm no sort of scholar', Bunting announces in his first lecture, and Makin argues that the lectures throughout are characterized by a pose of 'professional amateurism'. Bunting's scholarly detail is sometimes unreliable, but the primary interest of this collection is the poetic tradition which Bunting traces, the 'persistent beat' which he detects thumping through English poetry. The Lindisfarne Gospels provide the model of form and complexity which Bunting prizes in the best poetry. Wyat, not Chaucer, ought to be regarded as the 'father' of English poetry, he argues, because Wyat returned to song and dance. Edmund Spenser is the poet who has given English poetry its special characteristics, but who also led English poets to 'overdo ornament and sonority'. Wordsworth was not a Romantic poet, but instead completes an eighteenth-century realist tradition. Pound and Zukofsky are of interest because of the musical shapes they attempt to construct in their work. The collection works principally to illuminate the artistic values of Bunting, and to enhance our understanding of his appreciation of poetic sound and pattern.

One senses from William Logan's collection of essays and reviews, *Reputations of the Tongue: On Poets and Poetry* [1999], that every word and phrase has been chosen earnestly and prudently. Every judgement seems to be weighted with consideration and authority. This gives Logan's pronouncements on poetry an air of sublime confidence and poetic poise: 'Every poem of value must have a residue. A residue is not a mystery or a withholding. It is the result of a continual ignition in the language, a combustion in the nearness of words' (p. 12). Somehow you can forgive Logan his sweeping generalizations about what readers will and won't like, or can and can't take, for the pleasures of his prose. Much of this collection is preoccupied with American poets, and Logan's tongue is frequently sharp in damning what he sees as trumped-up reputations. Of concern to this reviewer, however, there are also two brilliant and lengthy essays on Geoffrey Hill, in which Logan champions Hill's 'charity and integrity', and his 'absolute unreasonableness'. The final chapter in the book is 'A Letter from Britain', dated 1990, which explains for American readers the impoverished state of poetry as a profession in Britain, and surveys the reputations of contemporary British poets. Here, Logan dispenses his usual acerbic judgements: Heaney 'has suffered the palsy of early canonization', Hughes has become 'a spent force in British poetry', 'women writing in Britain are as daring as library paste'. Logan's evaluations may seem cynical, uncompromising, sometimes wrong, but they are hard to ignore.

Klein, Coelsch-Foisner and Görtschacher, eds., *Poetry Now: Contemporary British and Irish Poetry in the Making* [1999], contains thirty-two essays and one interview by a diverse range of poets, critics and editors, which represent the proceedings of a conference at the University of Salzburg in October 1996. It is short on apparatus, so much so that there are no details of the contributors, but it packs into just over 400 pages an eclectic mix of essays and commentaries. The essays are diverse in quality as well as subject-matter, of course; the best are Tim Woods's discussion of the consolidation of the new British poetry revival since 1975 and Peter Barry's consideration of mythic 'revisionings' of London in poems by Iain Sinclair, Allen Fisher and Aidan Dun. There are too many others worthy of mention to cite here, but there are useful clusters of essays on 'little' magazines and Scottish and Irish poetry. There are discussions of Carol Ann Duffy, Peter Russell, Edward Boaden Thomas, Barry MacSweeney, Uli Freer, Allen Fisher, Charles Tomlinson, Gavin Ewart, J.H. Prynne, and R.S. Thomas, an interview on plastic poetry with Simon Cutts, and a brief commentary on the genesis of *Watersmeet* by the late Jon Silkin. The preface does little more than explain the circumstances of the conference, and acknowledge contributors and sponsors. An introduction attempting an overview, or some reflections on the general tendencies of contemporary British and Irish poetry, might have been difficult, but would nevertheless have been a helpful addition.

John Freeman's *The Less Received: Neglected Modern Poets* is a collection of his reviews and essays on modern British and American poetry. For the most part, the collection comprises reviews of single poetry volumes, such as Jim Burns's *A Single Flower* [1972] and Lee Harwood's *Morning Light* [1998], although it also contains a longer essay on George Oppen, some reflections on Romanticism in the 1960s, and on theory and poetry in the universities. Almost all of the collection has been published previously, usually in poetry magazines. What brings it together is Freeman's consistent clarity of analysis and understanding, his ability to situate each poet clearly and simply in a neglected tradition of 'plain-style' poetry, which he traces particularly to the influence of William Carlos Williams and, further back, to William Wordsworth. There are rare and valuable insights in these reviews into the work of such lesser-known poets as Jim Burns, John Riley, Gael Turnbull, Chris Torrance, Thomas A. Clark and Lee Harwood, as well as a handful of Americans,

Robert Creeley, Ed Dorn, Lorine Neidecker and George Oppen. A more expansive introduction, treating the shared influences and preoccupations of these poets at greater length, would have been welcome, as indeed would fuller treatments of poets such as Riley, Turnbull and Burns, but perhaps this indicates that I share too closely Freeman's desire that the poets he champions deserve more extensive critical appreciation.

Agenda devoted a double issue to 'Thom Gunn at Seventy' (37:ii–iii[1999]), which collects seventeen short critical essays on Gunn's work. Some, by Stephen Romer and Gregory Woods, are tributes to Gunn's inspirational influence. Most of the essays, however, explore specific themes or styles in his poetry. Clive Wilmer compares Gunn's poetry from 1954 with that of 1992, and finds there an 'internal coherence', such that the proximity of sex to death in the early poems appears to set up the images and ideas Gunn would draw upon in his later response to the AIDS tragedy. Peter Carpenter commends the 'qualities of apprehension' in Gunn's work, the feeling of all senses being 'explored and synthesised'. Neil Powell and Stefania Michelucci, in separate essays, trace resonances between Gunn and Caravaggio. There are explications of the virtues and craft of individual poems: Martin Dodsworth celebrates 'The Hug'; Peter Faulkner explores 'Matter and Spirit'. There are more general considerations of Gunn, too: Robert Wells examines Gunn's lifelong topicality and underlying preoccupations; August Kleinzahler considers his 'plain style'; James Campbell thinks of him as an Anglo-American poet; Peter Swaab invokes Gunn's praise of Ginsberg to reflect on him as a political poet. Charles Leftwich charts a shift from 'Will' to 'Being' in Gunn's poetic career, Michael Vince looks at tropes of observation and seeing; Douglas Chambers interrogates figures of desire and disgust. Patrick McGuinness considers the relationship between Gunn and Donald Davie, while Wendy Lesser concludes this celebration of Gunn with a reflective piece on his personality, and the tastes and values which inform his writing. All of the essays bear the mark of tributes or celebrations, and yet succeed in refreshing some of Gunn's work, extending beyond his usual association with motorbike gangs and AIDS elegies.

8. Irish Poetry

John Goodby's *Irish Poetry Since 1950: From Stillness into History* has a claim to be considered the most important single-author study of contemporary Irish poetry to have appeared since the 1980s, and cannot, at this stage, be ignored by anyone with a serious interest in the subject. It argues that Irish poetry has had a chequered critical history, though not, evidently, a neglected one. Its aim is to repudiate what Goodby describes as the 'After Yeats or Since Joyce' syndrome in contemporary Irish poetry criticism, and it attempts instead to read Irish poetry as divorced from the twin father-figures often seen to constrain interpretation. While it lacks conviction as a continuous narrative, divided as it is into multiple subheadings which deal with particular poets, and particular moments in history and literary history, it is an invaluable reference book. It offers snapshots of key figures and issues, and makes heroic attempts to leave no contemporary poet unturned. But, despite its rather fragmented form, it does have a particular argument to make. In Goodby's terms, an inclusivist view of poetry is a globalist view, one which necessitates rejection of the obsessively 'identitarian' poetics that have dominated Irish writing. Unusually, therefore, *Irish Poetry Since 1950* gives space to poets publishing before the 'Troubles' began to dominate perceptions of Irish writing, and it also gives space to Ireland's modernist and neo-modernist poets, from Coffey to the present. Goodby's key argument—that the future of Irish poetry belongs, or should belong, to those neo-modernists—is one that offers an important challenge to dominant narratives in criticism of Irish poetry. But, despite the ambition of this book, the contention remains not proven by its close, not least because some of those dominant narratives are deliberately left intact—Goodby, for example, tends to see Irish poetry of a particular generation through Heaney-coloured spectacles, with Heaney (like Auden before him in relation to the supposed 'Auden generation') the too convenient spokesman for his contemporaries. As a result, for all its delight in 'plurabilities' this misses much of the diversity inherent in the work of some of Heaney's contemporaries.

Goodby might want to escape what he sees as the constraints of an 'After Yeats' syndrome, but Yeats's posterity inevitably continues to exercise critics. Edna Longley's *Poetry and Posterity* has proved less inflammatory than some of her earlier works, in part because her *Bloodaxe Book of Twentieth-Century Poetry from Britain and Ireland*, which appeared at the same time, drew much of the usual fire. *The Bloodaxe Book* can be seen as a work of criticism in its own right, offering as it does critical introductions to each of the poets included, and working its selection into a coherent narrative. Longley affirms principles of aesthetic value judgement that go against the tide of 'plurabilities' exemplified in Goodby's approach, and constructs as a result an unusually selective canon. Towering over the century for Longley is the consummate metrist and formalist W.B. Yeats. Few modernist or neo-modernist writers make the grade, and the anthology as a whole validates formalism as a more than adequate response to historical crisis. In *Poetry and Posterity*, Longley's essay entitled 'The Millennial Muse' works as an accompanying text for her own anthology, as well as being a devastating critique of the (often dubious) anthologizing politics of others. It is, as a result, the essay which has thus far attracted the most attention in the book, running as it does counter to some of the buzzwords and attitudes prevalent in poetry criticism at the moment. Not least, the appalling plural 'poetries' (coined as an anthology title by Michael Schmidt in 1994) comes under attack as 'a pluralism too far' (p. 223). '[P]oetries', she asserts, 'arrive as critical nerve weakens … What Shelley would bother to write *A Defence of Poetries*? What Shelley does the very idea silence?' (p. 224). 'Critical nerve' in *Poetry and Posterity* is a willingness to make value judgements, a willingness to see poetry's timeless and universal qualities even as her criticism recognizes changing readership perspectives through history. Posterity, it is made clear at the outset, is an 'unfashionable concept' (p. 9), but there's no loss of unfashionable nerve in this book as Longley nails her revisionist and formalist colours firmly to the mast, asserting poetry's 'interdependence of pattern and memory rather than … amnesiac affinity with hypertextual flux' (p. 17). In *Poetry in the Wars* [1986], Longley viewed the twentieth century in poetry as a struggle between traditionalism and modernism, in which the Irish case brought valuable perspectives to bear that had been too often overlooked. *Poetry and Posterity* continues that debate, though its terms have changed to analyse the struggle between what she sees as forms of theory misreading poetry, as against the ways in which the poetry itself demands to be read. 'The hostility of some "literary theory" to any kind of formal measure or pleasure or closure may', she writes, 'be more than just another neo-Poundian outbreak' (p. 18). There are different enemies around, but the principles are still defiantly held against the odds. Yeats, and Yeats's posterity, are central to this book, helping to define and redefine the ways in which MacNeice, Auden, Larkin, and contemporary poets locate themselves in history and tradition. One chapter consists of an extended reading of Auden's 'In Praise of Limestone'; others examine MacNeice's criticism, Edward Thomas's ecological concerns, and Larkin's decadence. In its concern with the 'inter-national, inter-cultural dialectics that shaped modern poetry in English' (p. 21) *Poetry and Posterity* examines the work of Irish, British and American poets, also with a few glances back to Horace. The book itself becomes more densely written, in terms of its engagement with theories of history, as it goes along, culminating in 'Poetry and the End of History', which takes us beyond the 1994 ceasefires, to subject the reception of contemporary Northern Irish poetry to close critical scrutiny.

Steven Matthews, in *Yeats as Precursor* (also reviewed in section 6 above), is also concerned with Yeats's posterity, though he would not use such an unfashionable word, preferring 'The haunting echoes of Yeats in subsequent poetries'. Incorporation of an essentially meaningless plural/buzzword at the outset doesn't bode well for the rest of this study. Some books, especially this year, wear their RAE function more evidently on their sleeve than others; one such is *Yeats as Precursor*, which shows all the signs of being put together with indecent haste. The attempted tone and language of sophisticated theoretical intervention in current debates is belied by an often predictable approach to the texts. That Yeats's Romantic affiliations are also coloured by a 'divided inheritance and gapped tradition', and by the problematic circumstance of being an English-language poet in the Irish Revival, for example, is not a new discovery, and is lost in rather than illuminated by frequent invocations of Derrida and de Man here. Nor is it reassuring that Matthews takes a disproportionately long time to reach the observation that, for Yeats, style means formalism, immortality and resistance—something every student of Yeats already knows. Throughout, problems with style (along with some inaccuracies) obscure an already uneasy argument: misphrasings such as 'variously-heard echoes in later Irish poetry, in the work of W.H. Auden and Geoffrey Hill' don't help; nor do sentences such as 'Questioning around, not least, that notion of reincarnation and resurrection which figures so strongly within both versions of *A Vision*, but which is contradictorily present and denied in "Under Ben Bulben" and "Man and the Echo"' (p. 39); or, even more bafflingly, 'As with Yeats' work, in fact, the various demurrals and uncertainties do not fundamentally challenge the formal exactions of the poetry, as they have never done in Mahon' (p. 85). The scope of this book is vast; the idea is potentially very rewarding. But this all too rapidly devolves into a few pages on each poet in terms of their Yeatsian connections, piling up examples, with its subjects seemingly arbitrarily selected (there are some curious omissions), and missing much of the complexity of Yeats's reception in Ireland, America, and England (which Matthews calls Britain). Its observations add little to existing scholarship—at times, indeed, we have value subtracted.

Fiona Stafford's *Starting Lines in Scottish, Irish and English Poetry: From Burns to Heaney* has, by contrast, an admirable clarity of style. Stafford is also concerned with poetic predecessors, through the specific intertextual moments where poets borrow opening lines or epigraphs from other poets. After chapters on Burns, Coleridge, Shelley and Mangan, she focuses on the ways in which eighteenth- and nineteenth-century poets are reinterpreted in contemporary Ireland through allusion and quotation in the work of Ciaran Carson and Seamus Heaney. The primary focus of this book is not contemporary Irish poetry—Stafford is ultimately more confident and more convincing on an earlier period—but its singular virtue is her ability to bring vast knowledge of that earlier tradition to bear on readings of Carson and Heaney. The range of reference here enables insights that contemporary Irish poetry critics may sometimes miss. The starting lines are also starting points for a much wider consideration of cultural exchange. But that virtue is also *Starting Lines*'s weakness, at least in terms of its perspectives on twentieth-century Ireland. The comparison made between an independent twentieth-century Irish state, and eighteenth-century Scotland after its union with England (on the grounds that both 'have had to grapple with "post-Union" experience' in terms of language and national identity, p. 37) is forced. More problematical is the fact that by 'Irish experience' Stafford consistently means the post-colonial experience of the Irish Republic, even though both her poets are from the North. The border is lost here, along with the fact that Heaney and Carson are not from a 'post-Union' context. Her study is innocent of more recent and complex developments in post-colonial theory in relation to Ireland (in both the nineteenth and twentieth centuries). Likewise, while Stafford is good on the texture of Heaney's and Carson's poems in the context of a broader literary tradition, she also treads some very well-worn paths in Irish criticism—Carson's review of *North*, Kearney on 'Myth and Motherland', finding a 'voice' in *Station Island* and so forth—as she also relies heavily on tried and, in terms of more recent critical developments, not always trusted resources—Corcoran and Parker on Heaney, the 1980s Field Day pamphlets. The reiteration of familiar debates (and the irresistible explanatory footnote that places the Eglantine Inn on a non-existent 'Malone Street') suggests that, although a third of this book is devoted to contemporary Irish poetry, its target audience is probably largely outside Irish Studies. 'Burns to Heaney' in the subtitle of the book is, of course, a convenient marketing ploy—'Heaney' sells—one which might also account for the chronological disruption in the last two chapters of the book.

For almost thirty years, perceptions of Irish poetry have been dominated by the Troubles in the North, and by what has been seen as the phenomenon of Northern Poetry, from Heaney, Longley and Mahon through to the younger generation of McGuckian, Carson and Muldoon. All these broadly formalist and 'traditionalist' lyric poets forge links back through MacNeice and Kavanagh to Yeats. But 2000 was an unusual year in Irish poetry criticism, not least because it also marked something of a Southern, and/or neo-modernist fightback. That shift is probably not unrelated to post-ceasefire changing perceptions of Irish writing. Goodby's wish-fulfilment narrative in *Irish Poetry Since 1950* is also taking on some currency with another publishing house—University College Dublin Press. Two books this year— Alex Davis's *A Broken Line: Denis Devlin and Irish Poetic Modernism*, and Dónal Moriarty's *The Art of Brian Coffey* posit an alternative narrative to the dominant Yeats to Heaney line. If certain voices prevail, another few years and 'Brian Coffey to Trevor Joyce' might be the better sales pitch.

Davis's *A Broken Line* begins with the Irish Revival, and ends with a look at contemporary avant-garde writers in Ireland, including Billy Mills and Catherine

Walsh, with Devlin's work forming the substantial centre of the book and, in Davis's argument, a 'broken line' through the century. Davis's concern at the outset is to stress the Revival's links with modernism and with avant-garde movements in Britain and Europe. The post-Revival concern with 'Irishness', and the nationalist conservatism of writers such as Padraic Colum is then seen by Irish modernists as a wrong direction, one which their own experimentalism, internationalism, and multiplicity of influence repudiates. Oddly, Davis makes his argument about the modernism of the Revival almost entirely in terms of the 1890s. 'Modernism' in Yeats, according to Davis, is to do with 'Yeats' highly self-conscious anxiety with regard to the relationship between his literary output and the social and political context in which it was produced' (p. 11). The argument cannot accommodate the more complex modernist Yeats of the 1920s and 1930s; there's no sign here of Yeats's fragmentation, stylistic change, or of the European range of reference and context for Yeats's work during and after the Irish Civil War, partly because these would themselves disrupt Davis's narrative. Yeats's complex relationship with Eliot's work in the 1920s and 1930s is also invisible. The study is therefore a chronological oddity, jumping from 'The Literary Revival and Early Modernism' (by which he means the 1890s) to 'Modernist Poetry after the Revival' (the 1930s work of Devlin, Coffey, MacGreevy and Beckett). In effect, this narrative would sit more easily had Yeats disappeared from the poetic map in about 1909. What we have here is a narrative that redresses critical neglect of the work of Ireland's experimental writers, but that in order to do so excludes equally 'modernist' work by Yeats and Kavanagh from the same period in its turn. In its closing chapters, the book links Devlin's work to developments in Irish poetry in the 1960s and after, through the establishment of the New Writers' Press, and the work of Trevor Joyce, Michael Smith and Catherine Walsh. Davis's agenda becomes more explicit here, and not dissimilar to John Goodby's: the 'critical feeding-frenzy' in relation to the work of Heaney, Mahon, Longley, *et al.* has led to a 'dominant image of the characteristic Irish poem: a Movement lyric fractured by the impact of political violence' (p. 160). But for Davis 'the closed lyric ... has come to seem increasingly antiquated' (p. 161).

Davis's comments here encapsulate what is probably the dominant argument going on in Irish poetry criticism at the moment, however dubious its terms. Crudely speaking, the strategy here, as in Goodby's book, is to put two possible 'narratives' (which might better be seen as complexly interlinked if stylistically divergent poetic strategies) in competition with each other as if critical victory were possible, and to argue that one is 'new' (therefore good) and the other 'old' (therefore inadequate). It is an attempt, in other words, to replace one supposed critical 'orthodoxy' with a new critical orthodoxy, an ambition which, paradoxically, might seem to run counter to the challenge to orthodoxy proclaimed by both Davis and Goodby. The big thing now is not 'Irishness', but 'cosmopolitanism'; Ireland has discovered the outside world, *ergo* its poets should do likewise (*pace* Yeats's consistently European as well as national outlook?). It's a pity that 'cosmopolitanism' isn't subjected to the same critical scrutiny as 'Irishness' has been in the work of 'antiquated' *and* 'modernist' writers. But if the overall framework of this book has its own mysterious breaks and gaps, in addition to the ones it deliberately identifies, it remains an important text in opening up debate, and in offering sustained, original, and meticulously researched readings of Devlin's work in multiple contexts—

surrealism, Anglo-American modernism, and, to a lesser extent, Ireland. Davis, who is also the editor of Devlin's poetry, really gets into his stride in his analysis of Devlin's work mid-century, and writes criticism which is important and necessary for a full understanding of the Irish poetic achievement in the twentieth century.

Moriarty's *The Art of Brian Coffey* is the first monograph to appear on Coffey's poetry. As Moriarty is aware, the perceived difficulty and obscurity of much of Coffey's writing brings its own problems in terms of critical reputation, regardless of any broader terms of debate. Moriarty's primary concern is to illuminate that work, and he makes a convincing argument about the continuity of Coffey's aesthetic principles across a long poetic career. Coffey becomes, through Moriarty's work, a more seductive figure than he is generally perceived to be. The book ventures into some of the same areas of debate as Davis's text, but with some differences. Moriarty regrets the neglect of Catherine Walsh, but does not put forward an agenda for the future of contemporary poetry; there is clarity of thought and expression here in relation to 1920s Yeats; and he works with an awareness that 'modernism and postmodernism' are complex and contested terms, refusing any clear-cut definitions, particularly of the former. His reasons for the neglect of Coffey's work are perhaps not entirely convincing in view of the formalist bent of much Irish criticism—the prevailing fashion of cultural criticism, he argues, does not allow for the concern with matters of literary craft and stylistic technique needed to approach Coffey's work—but he reads the poetry in ways which are textually sensitive as well as philosophically complex. The most surprising aspect of the book is the decision to omit consideration of what is probably Coffey's best-known work, *Missouri Sequence* [1962]. Moriarty dismisses it as 'a sentimental rehearsal of well worn orthodoxies' (p. 3). That may or may not be true, but a bolder decision would have been to include it regardless of whether it fitted with the rest of Coffey's oeuvre, and make the case more comprehensively—particularly in view of Moriarty's concern to change and develop Coffey's reputation for a wider audience.

Concern with the relation between Irishness and internationalism is also a driving force behind Frank Sewell's *Modern Irish Poetry: A New Alhambra*, a book concerned to redress a very different kind of neglect, that of Irish-language poets. Sewell approaches his subject through case studies of Seán Ó Ríordáin, Cathal Ó Searcaigh, Máirtín Ó Direáin, and Nuala Ní Dhomhnaill. The book is aimed at an English-language as well as bilingual audience. Sewell reminds us that Irish literature is a 'dual tradition'; his concern is with the ways in which we can overcome 'deaf or blindspots' between Irish poets working in Irish, and those working in English (p. 2). His belief is that this can be achieved by 'tuning in' to Irish poetry in Irish, at least in translation, and he complains about those who 'choose to avoid, ignore, or play down' Irish-language poets (p. 3). The ambition of the book is suggestive, as are many of the links it makes, but it is ultimately unfulfilling. Sewell's evidence for those who 'ignore or play down' poets writing in Irish is a comment from Peter McDonald that the extent of the dialogue between those writing in Irish and English shouldn't be overestimated at this stage. But oddly enough *Modern Irish Poetry* itself consistently plays down that dialogue. In effect, the blind spots, it seems, are to be overcome by learning from Sewell's interpretation of these poets, rather than looking for existing dialogues (such as the collaborations between Ní Dhomhnaill and, respectively, Muldoon, Mahon and Hartnett, none of which is discussed here). Sewell is defensive—the poets he discusses are, he writes,

'Irish poets and, therefore, world poets' (p. 7)—but also critically naive in such well-intentioned assertions. The approach is at times too dependent on biography ('One cannot exaggerate the toll of physical suffering on Ó Ríordáin's life', he tells us (p. 11), which is doubtless why the point is repeated more than once). There is also a touch of sentimentality, which turns his approach to the Irish-language tradition into an act not of critical rigour, but of faith: 'the Alhambra of Ireland's art is open to all visitors … It is entered … via the Gate of Justice … Before entering the gate to visit the four installations on my itinerary, I pray that my exposition does them justice' (p. 8). *Modern Irish Poetry* should have been a highly significant book, but it feels like a missed opportunity. This is in part because it seems a personal journey for Sewell; that doesn't always make him the best guide.

In Terence Brown's essay, 'Michael Longley and the Irish Poetic Tradition' (in Peacock and Devine, eds., *The Poetry of Michael Longley*), he detects in Longley an apparent 'disregard for high Modernism and wilful experimentation' (p. 2). Since high modernism in Ireland has been pleading its own critical neglect recently, Longley's attitude might seem to place him fairly and squarely in the group of poets who have benefited from Davis's 'critical feeding-frenzy'. But although there are now dozens of books on Heaney's poetry, this is the first book to appear devoted solely to Longley's work, something, incidentally, which is yet to occur for Derek Mahon. (Matthews omits consideration of Longley from *Yeats as Precursor*; Goodby largely ignores both Longley's and Mahon's work after the 1970s.) The essays here were mostly given as symposium papers in 1996, though Alan Peacock's closing essay considers Longley's most recent collection, *The Weather in Japan* [2000]. The essays are thematic, not chronological, and the book, obviously, does not provide coverage of Longley's entire poetic career, but it is a marker of the growth of Longley's reputation, nationally and, more significantly, internationally, over the last ten years. The instinctive reservation one might have about this collection of essays from the outset is whether its entirely male list of contributors—including Douglas Dunn, Michael Allen, Neil Corcoran, Terence Brown, Robert Welch, Peter McDonald and Alan Peacock—combined with the fact that many of those contributors are writers and friends from Longley's own generation, might colour judgements in the criticism. But the reservation is unnecessary, particularly, as it turns out, in those cases where it's most likely to be felt. On the negative side, Elmer Andrews's 'Conflict, Violence and "the fundamental interrelatedness of all things" in the Poetry of Michael Longley' struggles unsuccessfully, in the longest and most sprawling essay in the book, with the fundamental disconnectedness of its own argument. But the outstanding contributions to this collection (by Dunn, Brown, Allen and McDonald), in terms of their fluency, formal alertness, scholarship, and interest, mean that *The Poetry of Michael Longley* contains criticism worthy of its subject. Dunn's essay on Longley's metrics has the added bonus of offering insights into his own poetry; Allen's sophisticated formalism shames many other critics of poetry; and McDonald corrects various too casually expressed views on Longley and classicism that have been in circulation since *Gorse Fires* in 1991. Brown's examination of the ways in which Longley 'extend[s] the possibilities of the Irish poetic tradition' (p. 1) is a salutary lesson for critics who have by and large excluded Longley from consideration because he fails to fit into their critical framework.

One such framework might be seen to be Barry Sloan's, in *Writers and Protestantism in the North of Ireland: Heirs to Adamnation?*, since Longley's Anglican background is at one remove from the predominantly Calvinistic Protestantism Sloan investigates in the North of Ireland. But this is only a minor quibble with a book that is impressive in scope, and more than welcome in terms of its contribution to debate. A preface by Gerald Dawe situates Sloan's *Writers and Protestantism* as the child-monograph of Dawe and Longley, eds., *Across a Roaring Hill: The Protestant Imagination in Modern Ireland* [1985], a collection of essays which was politically as well as critically controversial. (Could there be any such thing as the Protestant imagination in Northern Ireland? Surely there was a hidden Unionist agenda here?) Fortunately, the debates have moved on since then, and the time is more than auspicious for Sloan's sustained examination of the link between Protestantism and literature in the context of Northern Ireland. Sloan traces the principles and legacy of Calvinism in general and, in relation to Northern Ireland, specific terms through consideration of commemoration and autobiography, journeying into the 'Protestant mind' individually and collectively. He brings his findings to bear on sensitive readings of W.R. Rodgers, John Hewitt, Louis MacNeice, Derek Mahon and Tom Paulin, a familiar tribe of poets invoked not as 'apologists for Protestantism' but as 'its most searching and honest critics' (p. 5). Sloan too is a searching and honest critic of that context, both synthesizing an existing if diffuse body of work on Protestantism and Northern Irish writing into a systematic and coherent narrative, and consistently bringing new perspectives to bear on the material.

Jefferson Holdridge's *Those Mingled Seas: The Poetry of W.B. Yeats, the Beautiful and the Sublime* is proclaimed by its publishers as a book which will be central to the future of Yeats criticism. That might be slightly optimistic—few books on Yeats can claim that significance, and Terence Brown's *The Life of W.B. Yeats* [1999] is probably the most recent to be able to do so. Nevertheless, *Those Mingled Seas* makes an important contribution to Yeats criticism, and is elegantly and persuasively argued. Holdridge takes as his starting point Burke's and Kant's differing conceptions of the aesthetic as, respectively, empirical and formal idealist, to show how Yeats, with his essentially dialectical imagination, negotiates with and between both conceptions in his own poetry and philosophy. Holdridge is concerned with philosophy, with current ideas in literary theory, more particularly aesthetics, and devotes attention to some of Yeats's more arcane writings, including *A Vision*. In the process, he also links Yeats's thinking on the sublime to modernity, and to other twentieth-century modernists—Woolf, Conrad and Eliot. Despite the potential quagmire of the subject-matter, the argument is made throughout with clarity and style.

Yeats's works have been in something of a publication quagmire themselves in recent years, as a result of changes in copyright. James Pethica's Norton Critical Edition of Yeats's writings is, as a result, only available in the US and Canada. This is a matter for some regret, since Pethica's *Yeats's Poetry, Drama, and Prose* is the most helpful critical edition of Yeats's work to have appeared thus far. Its introduction is concise and lucid; it selects extensively from the poetry, and helpfully sets earlier against later versions of poems to track Yeats's stylistic development; and if Yeats's prose works always suffer in extraction, the editing is done with a sensitivity that leaves the essentials intact. As important is the fact that a third of the book is devoted to selections from recent critical and biographical studies of Yeats, and to critical extracts from the work of his contemporaries. All the major names are represented here, from Ellmann to R.F. Foster. Its critical apparatus enables coverage of much of the groundwork necessary now as a way into Yeatsian criticism, as it is also an invaluable guide to that increasingly complex world.

Books Reviewed

Albright, Daniel. *Untwisting the Serpent: Modernism in Music, Literature and Other Arts*. UChicP. [2000] pp. xiv + 395. pb £17.50 ISBN 0 2260 1254 9.

Anderson, Carol, and Aileen Christianson. *Scottish Women's Fiction, 1920s to 1960s: Journeys into Being*. Tuckwell. [2000] pp. 177. pb £9.99 ISBN 1 8623 2082 9.

Armstrong, Tim. *Haunted Hardy: Poetry, History, Memory*. Palgrave. [2000] pp. viii + 198. £40 ISBN 0 3335 9791 5.

Aston, Elaine, and Reinelt, Janelle. *The Cambridge Companion to Modern British Women Playwrights*. CUP. [2000] pp. 276. £13.95 ISBN 0 5215 9533 9.

Attridge, Derek. *Joyce Effects: On Language, Theory, and History*. CUP. [2000] pp. xviii + 208. hb £37.17 ISBN 0 5216 6112 9, pb £14.95 ISBN 0 5217 7788 7.

Attridge, Derek, and Marjorie Howes, eds. *Semicolonial Joyce*. CUP. [2000] pp. x + 269. hb £35 ISBN 0 5216 6179 X, pb £14.95 ISBN 0 5216 6628 7.

Aucmuty, Rosemary and Joy Wotton, eds. *The Encyclopaedia of Girls' School Stories*, vol. i. Sue Sims and Hilary Clare. *The Encyclopaedia of Boys' School Stories*. vol. ii. Robert J. Kirkpatrick. Burlington and Ashgate. [2000] vol. i. pp. 432. £42.50 ISBN 0 7546 0082 3, vol. ii. pp. 396. £42.50 ISBN 0 7546 0083 1.

Baldridge, Cates. *Graham Greene's Fictions: The Virtues of Extremity*. UMissP. [2000] pp. xi + 207. $34.95 ISBN 0 8262 1251 4.

Barker, Clive, and Maggie B. Gale, eds. *British Theatre Between the Wars, 1918–1939*. CUP. [2000] pp. 260. £40 ISBN 0 5216 2407 X.

Bataillard, Pascal, and Dominique Sipière, eds. *Dubliners, James Joyce: The Dead, John Huston*. Ellipses. [2000] pp. 223. ISBN 2 7298 0295 9.

Bényei, Tamás. *Acts of Attention: Figure and Narrative in Postwar British Novels*. Lang. [1999] pp. 231. £23 ISBN 3 6313 5295 6.

Bond, Edward. *The Hidden Plot: Notes on Theatre and the State*. Methuen. [2000] pp. 192. £16.99 ISBN 0 4137 2550 2.

Booth, Howard J., and Nigel Rigby, eds. *Modernism and Empire*. ManUP. [2000] pp. xiii + 338. hb £45 ISBN 0 7190 5306 4, pb £16.99 ISBN 0 7190 5307 2.

Booth, James, ed. *New Larkins for Old: Critical Essays*. Palgrave. [2000] pp. xi + 247. £52.50 ISBN 0 3337 6107 3.

Boulton, James T., ed. *The Letters of D.H. Lawrence*, vol. viii: *Previously Uncollected Letters/General Index*. Cambridge Edition of the Letters and Works of D.H. Lawrence. CUP. [2000] pp. xvii + 418. £60 ISBN 0 5212 3117 5.

Brearton, Fran. *The Great War in Irish Poetry: W.B. Yeats to Michael Longley*. OUP. [2000] pp. ix + 315. £45 ISBN 0 1981 8672 X.

Brewer, Mary F. *Race, Sex, and Gender in Contemporary Women's Theatre: The Construction of 'Woman'*. SussexAP. [1999] pp. x + 218. £45 ISBN 1 8987 2350 8.

Brunsdale, Mitzi. *Student Companion to George Orwell.* Greenwood. [2000] pp. xiii + 173. $30 ISBN 0 3133 0637 0.

Burden, Robert. *Radicalizing Lawrence: Critical Interventions in the Reading and Reception of D.H. Lawrence's Narrative Fiction.* Costerus NS 130. Rodopi. [2000] pp. 378. $64 ISBN 9 0420 1303 6.

Burns, Christy L. *Gestural Politics: Stereotype and Parody in Joyce.* SUNYP. [2000] pp. viii + 224. £12.50 ISBN 0 7914 4614 X.

Caddel, Richard. *Basil Bunting: Complete Poems.* Bloodaxe. [2000] pp. 244 pb £9.95 ISBN 1 8522 4527 1.

Carey, John. *Pure Pleasure: A Guide to the Twentieth Century's Most Enjoyable Books.* Faber. [2000] pp. xvi + 173. pb £6.99 ISBN 0 5712 0448 1.

Carter, Steven. *A Do-It-Yourself Dystopia: The Americanization of Big Brother.* UPA. [2000] pp. xx + 161. pb $29.50 ISBN 0 7618 1729 8.

Caughie, Pamela L. *Virginia Woolf in the Age of Mechanical Reproduction.* Border Crossings. Garland. [2000] pp. xxxvi + 310. £45 ISBN 0 8153 2761 7.

Childs, Peter. *Modernism.* The New Critical Idiom. Routledge. [2000] pp. viii + 226. pb £8.99 ISBN 0 4151 9648 5.

Christianson, Aileen, and Lumsden, Alison, eds. *Contemporary Scottish Women Writers.* EdinUP. [2000] pp. v + 186. £14 ISBN 0 7486 0979 2.

Cockin, Katherine. *Women and Theatre in the Age of Suffrage: The Pioneer Players, 1911–1925.* Palgrave. [2000] pp. 239. £42.50 ISBN 0 3336 8696 9.

Collecott, Diana. *H.D. and Sapphic Modernism, 1910–1950.* CUP. [1999] pp. xiii + 350. £42.50 ISBN 0 5215 5078 5.

Craig, Cairns. *The Modern Scottish Novel: Narrative and the National Imagination.* EdinUP. [1999] pp. vii + 256. £14.95 ISBN 0 7486 0893 1.

Croall, Jonathan. *Gielgud: A Theatrical Life, 1904–2000.* Methuen. [2000] pp. 580. pb £8.99 ISBN 0 4137 7129 6.

Daly, Nicholas. *Modernism, Romance and the Fin de Siècle: Popular Fiction and British Culture, 1880–1914.* CUP. [2000] pp. 228. £37.50. ISBN 0 5216 4103 9.

Darlow, Michael. *Terence Rattigan: The Man and his Work.* Quartet. [2000] pp. 530. £25 ISBN 0 7043 7114 6.

Davis, Alex. *A Broken Line: Denis Devlin and Irish Poetic Modernism.* UCDP. [2000] pp. xii + 212. hb £32.95 ISBN? pb £14.95 ISBN 1 9006 2137 1.

De Jongh, Nicholas. *Politics, Prudery and Perversions: The Censoring of the English Stage, 1901–1968.* Methuen. [2000] pp. 272. £16.99 ISBN 0 4137 0620 6.

Delaney, Paul, ed. *Brian Friel in Conversation.* UMichP. [2000] pp. xxi + 289. £13.50 ISBN 0 4720 9710 5.

Dromgoole, Dominic. *The Full Room: An A–Z of Contemporary Playwriting.* Methuen. [2000] pp. xii + 299. £10.99 ISBN 0 4137 7230 6.

Dukore, Bernard F. *Shaw's Theatre.* UPFlorP. [2000] pp. xvi + 267. £42.50 ISBN 0 8130 1757 2.

Dunn, Jane. *Antonia White: A Life.* Virago. [2000] pp. xii + 484. £9.99 ISBN 1 8604 9795 0.

Earnshaw, Steven. *The Pub in Literature: England's Altered State.* ManUP. [2000] pp. x + 294. pb £15.99 ISBN 0 7190 5305 6.

Easton, Alison (ed.), *Angela Carter: Contemporary Critical Essays.* Macmillan. [2000] pp. ix + 228. £13.99 ISBN 0 3336 9216 0.

Emig, Rainer. *W.H. Auden: Towards a Postmodern Poetics*. Macmillan. [2000] pp. x + 237 £42.50 ISBN 0 3337 4557 4.

Esslin, Martin. *Pinter the Playwright*, 6th edn. Methuen. [2000] pp. viii + 296. £9.99 ISBN 0 4136 6860 6.

Eyre, Richard, and Nicholas Wright. *Changing Stages: A View of British Theatre in the Twentieth Century*. Bloomsbury. [2000] pp. 400. pb £16.99 ISBN 0 7475 5254 1.

Ferris, Paul. *Dylan Thomas: The Collected Letters*, 2nd edn. Dent. [2000] pp. xxv + 1,062. £? ISBN 0 460 87999 5.

Freeman, John. *The Less Received: Neglected Modern Poets*. Stride. [2000] pp. 149. £9.95 ISBN 1 9001 5269 X.

Fritzer, Penelope. *Ethnicity and Gender in the Barsetshire Novels of Angela Thirkell*. Greenwood. [1999] pp. 124. £33.50 ISBN 0 3133 0915 9.

Fussell, Paul. *The Great War and Modern Memory* [1975]. OUP. [2000] pp. x + 368. £30 ISBN 0 1951 3331 5.

Gale, Maggie B., and Viv Gardner. *Women Theatre and Performance: New Histories, New Historiographies*. ManUP. [2000] pp. 243. £14.99 ISBN 0 7190 5713 2.

Garner, Stanton B. Jr. *Trevor Griffiths: Politics, Drama, History*. UMichP. [2000] pp. vii + 317. £39 ISBN 0 4721 1065 9.

Giannachi, Gabriella, and Mary Luckhurst, eds. *On Directing: Interviews with Directors*. Faber. [1999] pp. 142. £9.99 ISBN 0 5711 9149 5.

Gibson, Jeremy, and Julian Wolfreys. *Peter Ackroyd: The Ludic and Labyrinthine Text*. Macmillan. [2000] pp. xi + 311. £45 ISBN 0 3336 7751 X.

Giddings, Robert, and Erica Sheen, eds. *The Classic Novel: From Page to Screen*. ManUP. [2000] pp. viii + 243. £11.99 ISBN 0 7190 5230 0.

Gillespie, Michael Patrick, and Paula F. Gillespie. *Recent Criticism of James Joyce's Ulysses: An Analytical Review*. Literary Criticism in Perspective. Camden. [2000] pp. 146. £35 ISBN 1 5711 3217 1.

Glage, Lislotte, ed. *Being/s in Transit: Travelling, Migration Dislocation*. Rodopi. [2000] pp. xiv + 217. £40 ISBN 9 0420 0649 8.

Goodby, John. *Irish Poetry Since 1950: From Stillness into History*. ManUP. [2000] pp. 362. hb £50.66 ISBN 0 7190 2966 1, pb £15.99 ISBN 0 7190 2997 X.

Gottfried, Roy. *Joyce's Comic Portrait*. Florida James Joyce Series. UPFlorP. [2000] pp. 188. £42.50 ISBN 0 8130 1782 3.

Gottlieb, Vera, and Colin Chambers, eds. *Theatre in a Cool Climate*. Amber Lane. [1999] pp. 223. £14.95 ISBN 1 8728 6826 6.

Graham, Desmond. *Keith Douglas: The Complete Poems*, 3rd edn. Faber. [2000] pp. xxxvi + 164. £12.99 ISBN 0 5712 0258 6.

Graham, Desmond. *The Letters of Keith Douglas*. Carcanet. [2000] pp. xxv + 369. £14.95 ISBN 1 8575 4477 3.

Gregson, Ian. *The Male Image: Representations of Masculinity in Postwar Poetry*. Palgrave. [1999] pp. vi + 204. £47.50 ISBN 0 3337 6020 4.

Grene, Nicholas. *The Politics of Irish Drama: Plays in Context from Boucicault to Friel*. CUP. [1999] pp. 312. £15.95 ISBN 0 5216 6536 1.

Grene, Nicholas, ed. *Interpreting Synge: Essays from the Synge Summer School, 1991–2000*. Lilliput. [2000] pp. 220. £19.95 ISBN 1 9018 6647 5.

Habib, M.A.R. *The Early T.S. Eliot and Western Philosophy.* CUP. [1999] pp. xii + 289. £40 ISBN 0 5216 2433 9.

Hampson, Robert. *Cross-Cultural Encounters in Joseph Conrad's Malay Fiction.* Palgrave. [2000] pp. xii + 248. £42.50 ISBN 0 3337 1405 9.

Hapgood, Lynne, and Nancy L. Paxton, eds. *Outside Modernism: In Pursuit of the English Novel, 1900–30.* Macmillan and St Martin's Press. [2000] pp. xi + 238. £47.50 ISBN 0 3337 9413 3 (Macmillan), ISBN 0 3122 3202 0 (St Martin's).

Hardy, Barbara. *Dylan Thomas: An Original Language.* UGeoP. [2000] pp. xiii + 155. £22.95 ISBN 0 8203 2207 5.

Hardy, Robert. *Psychological and Religious Narratives in Iris Murdoch's Fiction.* Mellen. [2000] pp. xviii + 187. £49.95 ISBN 0 7734 7570 2.

Hare, David. *Acting Up.* Faber. [1999] pp. xii + 276. £9.99 ISBN 0 5712 0135 0.

Harris, Andrea L. *Other Sexes: Rewriting Difference from Woolf to Winterson.* SUNY. [2000] pp. xv + 187. $15.95 ISBN 0 7914 4456 2.

Harte, Liam, and Michael Parker, eds. *Contemporary Irish Fiction: Themes, Tropes, Theories.* Macmillan. [2000] pp. xi + 271. £15.99 ISBN 0 3336 8381 1.

Ho, Elaine Yee Lin. *Timothy Mo.* ManUP. [2000] pp. xii + 180. £40 ISBN 0 7190 5389 7.

Holden, Alan W., and J. Roy Birch. *A.E. Housman: A Reassessment.* Macmillan. [2000] pp. xix + 225. £42.50 ISBN 0 3336 5803 5.

Holdridge, Jefferson, *Those Mingled Seas: The Poetry of W.B. Yeats, the Beautiful and the Sublime.* UCD Press. [2000] pp. x + 258. hb £38.95 ISBN 1 9006 2135 5, pb £17.95 ISBN 1 9006 2134 7.

Hoskins, Robert. *Graham Greene: An Approach to the Novels.* Garland. [1999] pp. xviii + 319. $75 ISBN 0 8153 1265 2.

Hunter, Jim. *Tom Stoppard.* Faber. [2000] pp. 240. £4.99 ISBN 0 5711 9782 5.

Israel, Nico. *Outlandish: Writing between Exile and Diaspora.* StanfordUP. [2000] pp. xii + 252. £27.50 ISBN 0 8047 3073 3.

Ivory, James Maurice. *Identity and Narrative Metamorphoses in Twentieth-Century British Literature.* Mellen. [2000] pp. v + 170. £49.95 ISBN 0 7734 7783 7.

Izenberg, Gerald N. *Modernism and Masculinity: Mann, Wedekind, Kandinsky through World War I.* UChicP. [2000] pp. xii + 257. £22.50 ISBN 0 2263 8868 9.

Joannou, Maroula. *Contemporary Women's Writing: From 'The Golden Notebook' to 'The Color Purple'.* ManUP. [2000] pp. x + 211. £14.99 ISBN 0 7190 5339 0.

Jones, Nesta. *Brian Friel.* Faber. [2000] pp. viii + 197. £4.99 ISBN 0 5711 9779 5.

Jordan, Eamonn. *Theatre Stuff: Critical Essays on Contemporary Irish Theatre.* Carysfort. [2000] pp. xlviii + 326. _19.03 ISBN 0 9534 2571 1.

Kaplan, Joel, and Sheila Stowell, eds. *Look Back in Pleasure: Noel Coward Reconsidered.* Methuen. [2000] pp. 238. £16.99 ISBN 0 4137 5500 2.

Kearney, Colbert. *The Glamour of Grammar: Orality and Politics and the Emergence of Sean O'Casey.* Greenwood. [2000] pp. xiii + 145. £57.50 ISBN 0 3133 1303 2.

Kerrigan, John, and Peter Robinson, eds. *The Thing About Roy Fisher: Critical Studies.* LiverUP. [2000] pp. xii + 377. £34.99 ISBN 0 8532 3515 5.

Kestner, Joseph A. *The Edwardian Detective, 1901–1915.* Brookfield and Ashgate. [2000] pp. 424. £49.95 ISBN 1 8401 4607 9.

Kiberd, Declan. *Irish Classics.* Granta. [2000] pp. xvi + 704. £25 ISBN 1 8620 7386 4.

Klein, Holger, Sabine Coelsch-Foisner and Wolfgang Görtschacher, eds. *Poetry Now: Contemporary British and Irish Poetry in the Making*. Studies in English and Comparative Literature 13. Stauffenburg. [1999] pp. 405. DM120 ISBN 3 8605 7313 6.

Krebs, Paula M. *Gender, Race, and the Writing of Empire: Public Discourse and the Boer War*. CUP [1999] pp. 220. £35 ISBN 0 5216 5322 3.

Krips, Valerie. *The Presence of the Past: Memory, Heritage, and Childhood in Postwar Britain*. Garland. [2000] pp. xiv + 125. £37 ISBN 0 8153 3863 5.

Kucich, John, and Diane F. Sadoff, eds. *Victorian Afterlife*. UMinnP. [2000] pp. 344. £34.50 ISBN 0 8166 3323 1.

Kurdi, Mária. *Codes and Masks: Aspects of Identity in Contemporary Irish Plays in an Intercultural Context*. Lang. [2000] pp. 160. £17 ISBN 3 6313 5972 1.

Levitt, Morton P. *James Joyce and Modernism: Beyond Dublin*. Studies in Irish Literature 2. Mellen. [2000] pp. 288. £49 ISBN 0 7734 7869 8.

Lewis, Barry. *Kazuo Ishiguro*. ManUP. [2000] pp. xiii + 191. pb £9.99 ISBN 0 7190 5514 8.

Logan, William. *Reputations of the Tongue: On Poets and Poetry*. UPFlorP. [1999] pp. xiii + 274. £26.50 ISBN 0 8130 1697 5.

Longley, Edna. *The Bloodaxe Book of Contemporary Poetry from Britain and Ireland*. Bloodaxe. [2000] pp. 368. pb £10.95 ISBN 1 8522 4514 X.Longley, Edna. *Poetry and Posterity*. Bloodaxe. [2000] pp. 350. pb £10.95 ISBN 1 8522 4435 6.

Lucas, Michael A. *Aspects of Conrad's Literary Language*. Conrad: Eastern and Western Perspectives 9; Social Science Monographs. Marie Curie Sklodowska University. [2000] pp. viii + 236. $30 ISBN 0 8803 3984 5.

Makin, Peter, ed. *Basil Bunting on Poetry*. JHUP. [1999] pp. xlv + 234. £32.50 ISBN 0 8018 6166 7.

Manfull, Helen. *Taking the Stage: Women Directors on Directing*. Methuen. [1999] pp. 236. £9.99 ISBN 0 4137 2790 4.

Marsh, Nicholas. *D.H. Lawrence: The Novels*. Macmillan. [2000] pp. xi + 258. hb £37.50 ISBN 0 3337 7124 9, pb £10.99 ISBN 0 3337 7125 7.

Mathews, P. J., ed. *New Voices in Irish Criticism*. FCP. [2000] pp. xvii + 264. £14.95 ISBN 1 8518 2545 2.

Matthews, Steven. *Yeats as Precursor: Readings in Irish, British and American Poetry*. Macmillan. [2000] pp. 238. £47.50 ISBN 0 3337 1147 5.

McCarthy, Conor. *Modernisation, Crisis and Culture in Ireland, 1969–1992*. FCP. [2000] pp. 240. £18.95 ISBN 1 8518 2479 0.

McCourt, John. *James Joyce: A Passionate Exile*. Orion. [2000] pp. 112. £16.99 ISBN 0 7528 1829 5.

McCourt, John. *The Years of Bloom: James Joyce in Trieste, 1904–1920*. Lilliput. [2000] pp. xi + 306. £25 ISBN 1 9018 6645 9.

McGrath, F.C. *Brian Friel's (Post) Colonial Drama: Language, Illusion, and Politics*. SyracuseUP. [1999] pp. xv + 312. £29.50 ISBN 0 8156 2813 7.

McGregor, Robert Kuhn, with Ethan Lewis. *Conundrums for the Long Week-End: England, Dorothy L. Sayers, and Lord Peter Wimsey*. KSUP. [2000] pp. 272. £29.50 ISBN 0 8733 8665 5.

McKeon, Michael, ed. *Theory of the Novel: A Historical Approach*. JHUP. [2000] pp. xviii + 947. hb £50.50 ISBN 0 8018 6396 1, pb 23 ISBN 0 8018 6397 X.

McKillop, A.B. *The Spinster and the Prophet: A Tale of H.G. Wells, Plagiarism and the History of the World.* Aurum. [2000] pp. 488. £18.99 ISBN 1 8541 0757 7.

Meyer, Michael J. ed. *Literature and Homosexuality.* Rodopi. [2000] pp. 283. hb £42 ISBN 9 0420 0529 7, pb £13.50 ISBN 9 0420 0698 6.

Milne, W.S. *An Introduction to Geoffrey Hill.* Agenda and Bellew. [1998] pp. 224. £14.95 ISBN 1 8572 5126 1.

Moriarty, Dónal. *The Art of Brian Coffey.* UCDubP. [2000] pp. 143. hb £29.95 ISBN 1 9006 2143 6, pb £13.95 ISBN 1 9006 2144 4.

Muldoon, Paul. *The End of the Poem: 'All Soul's Night' by W. B. Yeats.* OUP. [2000] pp. 28. £6.99 ISBN 0 1995 1395 3.

Mulhern, Francis. *Culture/Metaculture.* New Critical Idiom. Routledge. [2000] pp. xxi + 198. £8.99 ISBN 0 4151 0230 8.

Mulryne, Ronnie, and Margaret Shewring, eds. *The Cottesloe at the National: Infinite Riches in a Little Room.* Mulryne & Shewring. [1999] pp. 191. £17.95 ISBN 1 9000 6502 9.

Murray, Christopher, ed. *Brian Friel: Essays, Diaries, Interviews, 1964–1999.* Faber. [1999] pp. xx + 202. £9.99 ISBN 0 5712 0069 9.

Naismith, Bill. *Harold Pinter.* Faber. [2000] pp. 198. £4.99 ISBN 0 5711 9781 7.

Newton, John, ed. *Charlotte Mew: Complete Poems.* Penguin. [2000] pp. xxii + 143. £7.99 ISBN 0 1411 8013 7.

Nichols, Peter. *Diaries, 1969–1977.* Hern. [2000] pp. 440. £25 ISBN 1 8545 9474 5.

Nicholson, Steve. *British Theatre and the Red Peril: The Portrayal of Communism, 1917–1945.* UExe. [1999] pp. 199. £14.99 ISBN 0 8598 9637 4.

Page, Norman, ed. *Oxford Reader's Companion to Hardy.* OUP. [2000] pp. xx + 528. £40 ISBN 0 1986 0074 7.

Peacock, Alan J., and Kathleen Devine, eds. *The Poetry of Michael Longley.* Ulster Editions and Monographs 10. Smythe. [2000] pp. xxii + 191. £30 ISBN 0 8614 0412 2.

Peacock, D. Keith. *Thatcher's Theatre: British Theatre and Drama in the Eighties.* Greenwood. [1999] pp. xii + 231. £50.50 ISBN 0 3132 9901 3.

Peppis, Paul. *Literature, Politics and the English Avant-Garde: Nation and Empire, 1901–1918.* CUP. [2000] pp. x + 236. £37.50 ISBN 0 5216 6238 9.

Pethica, James, ed. *Yeats's Poetry, Drama, and Prose.* Norton Critical Editions. [2000] pp. xxv + 518. pb $16.25 ISBN 0 3939 7497 9.

Pierce, David (ed.) *Irish Writing in the Twentieth Century: A Reader.* CorkUP. [2000] pp. xliv + 1351. £35 ISBN 1 8591 8208 9.

Pine, Richard. *The Diviner: The Art of Brian Friel.* UCDubP. [1999] pp. xviii + 409. £19.99 ISBN 1 9006 2123 1.

Potts, Willard. *Joyce and the Two Irelands.* UTexP. [2000] pp. 220. £26.95 ISBN 0 2927 6591 6.

Prentice, Penelope. *The Pinter Ethic: The Erotic Aesthetic.* Garland. [2000] pp. cxvi + 452. $24.95 ISBN 0 8153 3909 7.

Pressler, Christopher. *So Far So Linear: Responses to the Work of Jeanette Winterson.* Paupers. [2000] pp. ii + 68. £9.95 ISBN 0 9466 5070 5.

Raitt, Suzanne. *May Sinclair: A Modern Victorian.* OUP. [2000] pp. xvi + 307. £19.99 ISBN 0 1981 2298 5.

Randall, Don. *Kipling's Imperial Boy: Adolescence and Cultural Hybridity.* Palgrave. [2000] pp. 200. £42.50 ISBN 0 3337 6104 9.

Rawlinson, Mark. *British Writing of the Second World War*. Clarendon. [2000] pp. 247. £35 ISBN 0 1981 8456 5.

Roberts, Adam. *Science Fiction*. New Critical Idiom. Routledge. [2000] pp. vi + 204. pb £8.99 ISBN 0 4151 9205 6.

Rogoff, Gordon. *Vanishing Acts: Theater since the Sixties*. YaleUP. [2000] pp. 306. £12 ISBN 0 3000 8248 7.

Roston, Murray. *Modernist Patterns in Literature and the Visual Arts*. Macmillan. [2000] pp. x + 288. £52.50 ISBN 0 3336 8170 3.

Rottenberg, Elizabeth, trans. *Maurice Blanchot. The Instant of My Death; Jacques Derrida. Demeure: Fiction and Testimony*. StanfordUP. [2000] pp. 114. hb £17.95 0 8047 3325 2, pb £7.95 ISBN 0 8047 3326 0.

Rudnytsky, Peter L., and Gordon, Andrew M., eds. *Psychoanalyses/Feminisms*. SUNYP. [2000] pp. viii + 238. hb $55.50 ISBN 0 7914 4377 9, pb $18.95 ISBN 0 7914 4378 7.

Sagar, Keith. *The Laughter of Foxes: A Study of Ted Hughes*. Liverpool. [2000] pp. xxxiv + 196. £14.95 ISBN 0 8532 3575 9.

Sceats, Sarah. *Food, Consumption and the Body in Contemporary Women's Fiction*. CUP. [2000] pp. viii + 213. £37.50 ISBN 0 5216 61536.

Schall, James V. *Schall on Chesterton: Timely Essays on Timeless Paradoxes*. CUAP. [2000] pp. 296. £21.50. ISBN 0 8132 0963 3.

Schork, R.J. *Joyce and Hagiography: Saints Above!* Florida James Joyce Series. UPFlorP. [2000] pp. xiii + 239. £42.50 ISBN 0 8130 1780 7.

Scoble, Christopher. *Fisherman's Friend: A Life of Stephen Reynolds*. Halsgrove. [2000] pp. 850. £25 ISBN 1 8411 4092 9.

Scott, Bonnie Kime, ed. *Selected Letters of Rebecca West*. YaleUP. [2000] pp. 542. £25 ISBN 0 3000 7904 4.

Sewell, Frank. *Modern Irish Poetry: A New Alhambra*. OUP. [2000] pp. xi + 233. hb £40 ISBN 0 1981 8737 8.

Shellard, Dominic, ed. *British Theatre in the 1950s*. ShAP. [2000] pp. 141. £14.95 ISBN 1 8412 7048 2.

Sinfield, Alan. *Out on Stage: Lesbian and Gay Theatre in the Twentieth Century*. YaleUP. [2000] pp. 384. £25 ISBN 0 3000 8102 2.

Sloan, Barry. *Writers and Protestantism in the North of Ireland: Heirs to Damnation?* IAP. [2000] pp. 381. hb £39.50 ISBN 0 7165 2636 0.

Smith, Angela. *Katherine Mansfield: A Literary Life*. Palgrave. [2000] pp. x + 171. £35 ISBN 0 3336 1877 7.

Smith, Angela K. *The Second Battlefield: Women, Modernism and the First World War*. ManUP. [2000] pp. ix + 214. pb £14.99 ISBN 0 7190 5301 3.

Smith, Angela K., ed. *Women's Writing of the First World War: An Anthology*. ManUP. [2000] pp. xii + 340. £13.99 ISBN 0 7190 5073 1.

Smith, David C., ed. *The Correspondence of H.G. Wells*, vols. i–iv. P&C. [2000] pp. 1,900. £295. ISBN 1 8519 6173 9.

Stafford, Fiona. *Starting Lines in Scottish, Irish and English Poetry: From Burns to Heaney*. OUP. [2000] pp. 357. £45 ISBN 0 1981 8637 1.

Stark, Susanne, ed. *The Novel in Anglo-German Context: Cultural Cross-Currents and Affinities*. Rodopi. [2000] pp. 466. £50 ISBN 9 0420 0698 6.

Stefanova, Kalina. *Who Keeps the Score on the London Stages?* Harwood. [2000] pp. xi + 219. £23 ISBN 9 0575 5116 0.

Stevens, Hugh, and Caroline Howlett, eds. *Modernist Sexualities*. ManUP. [2000] pp. x + 276. pb £15.99 ISBN 0 7190 5161 4.

Stuart, Ian, ed. *Selections from the Notebooks of Edward Bond*, vol. i: *1959–1980*. Methuen. [2000] pp. xii + 225. £19.99 ISBN 0 4137 0500 5.

Stuart, Ian, ed. *Selections from the Notebooks of Edward Bond*, vol ii: *1980–1995*. Methuen. [2000] pp. xii + 336. £19.99 ISBN 0 4137 3000 X.

Sumner, Rosemary. *A Route To Modernism: Hardy, Lawrence, Woolf*. Macmillan. [2000] pp. xiv + 208. £45 ISBN 0 3337 7046 3.

Thomas, Edward. *Light and Twilight*. Laurel Books. [2000] pp. 92. £6.99 ISBN 1 8733 9003 3.

Thomas, Ronald R. *Detective Fiction and the Rise of Forensic Science*. CUP. [2000] pp. 361. £40 ISBN 0 5216 5303 7.

Thornton, Weldon. *Voices and Values in Joyce's 'Ulysses'*. Florida James Joyce Series. UPFlorP. [2000] pp. x + 238. £42.50 ISBN 0 8130 1820 X.

Todd, Richard, and Luisa Flora, eds. *Theme Parks, Rainforests and Sprouting Wastelands: European Essays on Theory and Performance in Contemporary British Fiction*. Rodopi. [2000] pp. 236. pb £24 ISBN 9 0420 0502 5.

Tredell, Nicolas, ed. *The Fiction of Martin Amis: A Reader's Guide to Essential Criticism*. Icon. [2000] pp. 208. £9.99 ISBN 1 8404 6135 7.

Vervliet, Raymond, and Annemarie Estor, eds. *Methods for the Study of Literature as Cultural Memory*. Rodopi. [2000] pp. 469. $79 ISBN 9 0420 0450 9.

Wallace, Diana. *Sisters and Rivals in British Women's Fiction, 1814–1939*. Palgrave. [2000] pp. 224. £47.50 ISBN 0 3337 7400 0.

Warner, Sylvia Townsend. *The Salutation*. Tartarus. [2000] £25 ISBN 1 8726 2150 3.

Watt, Ian. *Essays on Conrad*. CUP. [2000] pp. xii + 214. hb £35 ISBN 0 5217 8007 1, pb £12.95 ISBN 0 5217 8387 9.

Watts, Stephen, Eileen Morgan and Shakir Mustafa, eds. *A Century of Irish Drama: Widening the Stage*. IndUP. [2000] pp. 332. £18.99 ISBN 0 2532 1419 X.

Welch, Robert, ed. *The Concise Oxford Companion to Irish Literature*. OUP. [2000] pp. xxi + 393. £8.99 ISBN 0 1928 0080 9.

Winnington, G. Peter. *Vast Alchemies: The Life and Work of Mervyn Peake*. Owen. [2000] pp. 263. £18.95 ISBN 0 7206 1079 6.

Wolfe, Peter. *Understanding Alan Bennett*. USCP. [1999] pp. xv + 255. £21.50 ISBN 1 5700 3280 7.

Wright, T.R. *D.H. Lawrence and the Bible*. CUP. [2000] pp. x + 274. £40 ISBN 0 5217 8189 2.

Wu, Duncan. *Making Plays: Interviews with Contemporary British Dramatists and Directors*. Macmillan. [2000] pp. viii + 264. £15.99 ISBN 0 3339 1561 5.

Wykes, David. *Evelyn Waugh: A Literary Life*. Literary Lives. Macmillan. [1999] pp. xii + 224. £45. ISBN 0 3336 1137 3.

Yorke, Malcolm. *Mervyn Peake: My Eyes Mint Gold*. John Murray. [2000] pp. 368. £25. ISBN 0 7195 5771 2.

XV

American Literature to 1900

HENRY CLARIDGE, ANNE-MARIE FORD AND
THERESA SAXON

This chapter has three sections: 1. General; 2. American Literature to 1830; 3. American Literature 1830–1900. Sections 1 and 2 are by Henry Claridge; section 3 is by Anne-Marie Ford and Theresa Saxon.

1. General

Current bibliographical listings for the field and period continue to be available quarterly in the 'Book Reviews' and 'Brief Mentions' sections of *American Literature* and annually in *Modern Language Association International Bibliography*. This year sees *Early American Literature* begin its online listings of newly issued books; the new editor, David S. Shields, also hopes to make available important, but as yet unpublished, texts on an *EAL*-sponsored 'text bank' on the World Wide Web. The first volume of what is certain to be an important project in the history of publishing, *The History of the Book in America*, is eagerly awaited. This series will, no doubt, considerably enlarge on what we already know about the growth of print culture from the work of scholars such as John Tebbell. Volume 1, *The Colonial Book in the Atlantic World*, edited by Hugh Amory and David D. Hall, appears this year but has not been received for review.

2. American Literature to 1830

The high standard of criticism and scholarship of the seventeenth and eighteenth centuries continues this year. Jeffrey A. Hammond's *The American Puritan Elegy: A Literary and Cultural Study* arises out of his early study of Puritan verse, *Sinful Self, Saintly Self: The Puritan Experience of Verse* [1993]. Hammond remarks on his regret at having to 'prune' from his 1993 study three chapters on the most popular poems of the Puritan era, those we call 'funeral elegies'. Happily, this new study recovers this material for us in a major work of literary-historical criticism. Hammond's subject is the elegiac tradition in seventeenth-century New England verse, and he deals at some length with the funeral elegies of Anne Bradstreet,

Benjamin Collins, John Danforth, John Fiske, John I. Saffin, Edward Taylor, Michael Wigglesworth and John Wilson, among others. Other than Bradstreet and Taylor, Hammond is not, of course, dealing with poets of any great literary merit and he himself recognizes this. His interest in Puritan verse on the dead is, however, as much anthropological as it is critical. He seeks, he tells us in his preface, to show us that: 'What Puritans experienced in elegy was, at root, the power of a cultural myth and the satisfactions of a verbal performance that allowed them to enter the myth. The central trope of the Puritan elegy, when read in light of the literary codes of its time and place, is not the enduring monument, the treasured urn, or nature weeping in sympathy with survivors. The central trope is resurrection—a trope that emerges perhaps most clearly in the unforgettable image of regathered and revivified Israel set forth in Ezekiel's vision of the valley of dry bones.' This necessitates an approach by way of an anthropologically informed literary and cultural history. Hammond draws on issues in the interpretation of cultures raised by anthropologists such as Clifford Geertz as well as historical problems raised in the 'theorizing' of new historicism. The 'Puritan aesthetic of commemoration', Hammond argues, breaks nearly 'every modern rule surrounding the poetry of mourning' and thus it must be understood through the readings of 'a sympathetic ethnographer who tries to see another world through its inhabitants' eyes', though at the same time he accepts 'the traditional anthropological assumption that certain patterns of grief and mourning are transcultural and transhistorical'. His readings of elegiac verses emphasize their origins as performative scripts that console the bereaved by articulating the experience of loss within the conventional expectations of Protestant theology. Thus Edward Taylor's poem on the death of Deacon Dewey—'a man in whom inner piety and civic duty merged to create a perfect life in the Lord'—may disappoint us by its failure to transcend the conventions of traditional elegy (and thus satisfy the demands of the modern reader) but this, Hammond argues, is to misunderstand the nature of Taylor's intention which, above all, is different in kind from a formalist tradition of pastoral elegy associated, for example, with the canzoni of Milton's 'Lycidas'. Obviously, a first-order critical problem arises from the approach Hammond takes: we are reminded of Dr Leavis's remark that the literature of the past lives in the present or not at all. For all his gifts as a scholar and critic Hammond struggles to make interesting for us some distinctly second-rate (one might say third-rate) verse. As he says, the 'Puritan aesthetic was militantly functional', and one might reasonably think such a statement oxymoronic. Ultimately 'the alien surfaces' of the verse he considers resist even the most sympathetic of readers. But this remains a major work of scholarship and it is one of the most impressive studies of the literature of the colonial period that I have reviewed. As well as drawing our attention to a body of neglected writing and inviting us to understand it through a re-creation of the commemorative and pietistic contexts out of which it arose, Hammond prompts us to reconsider Puritan attitudes to death and mourning and to assess how the New England funeral elegy articulated the moral and ideological character of the culture from which it issued. His study will be of interest to historians, over and above its importance to literary scholars.

Sargent Bush Jr. has done much valuable work on the colonial period. His 'America's Origin Myth: Remembering Plymouth Rock' (*AmLH* 12[2000] 745–56) is, in essence, a review of John Seelye's *Memory's Nation: The Place of Plymouth Rock* (UNCP [1998]), but it rises above mere descriptive review to become an interesting essay of its own. Bush follows Seelye in reading Plymouth Rock as a site of 'iconic power, one possessed, in different ways, across the history of the United States as a republic', so much so that successive generations of Forefathers' Day celebrations 'can result in appropriation of history for causes that may never have entered the minds of the "founders"'. The economic 'ideology' behind William Bradford's *Of Plymouth Plantation* is addressed in Michelle Burnham's 'Merchants, Money, and the Economics of "Plain Style" in William Bradford's *Of Plymouth Plantation*' (*AL* 72[2000] 695–720). She argues that Bradford's 'most overt and anxious concern is not Plymouth's place within the grand sweep of history but the far more mundane problems of finances'. This, she suggests, informs Bradford's style, for the text emerges from the 'intersection' of 'the new plain style in English prose writing and the massive expansion of mercantile commerce as a result of colonial expansion'. Read through this 'intersection' *Of Plymouth Plantation* is a document that registers 'considerable anxiety toward linguistic and economic change in the early modern Atlantic world'. Burnham's argument challenges the conventional understanding of Puritan plain style as a necessary concomitant of the emphasis on scriptural and liturgical simplicity and plainness. Quite whether the 'conventional wisdom' can be dismissed as easily as she suggests is, perhaps, questionable, but her essay throws fresh light on an important text and it may provoke new research along similar lines on Bradford and his contemporaries.

I have seen nothing on Edward Taylor this year, but Anne Bradstreet continues to attract attention. Feminist readings persist. In '"Now Sisters...Impart Your Usefulnesse, and Force": Anne Bradstreet's Feminist Functionalism in "The Tenth Muse" (1650)' (*EAL* 35[2000] 5–28) Tamara Harvey argues that 'Throughout "The Tenth Muse", Bradstreet consciously and intelligently participates in contemporary literary battles of the sexes' by reading Bradstreet's poem through contemporary medical knowledge; Harvey seeks to show how Bradstreet's quaternion on the four humours is used to 'challenge the Aristotelian belief that women are cooler than men and therefore inferior'. The place of Bradstreet as a Calvinist poet 'reflecting on nature' and thus a 'predecessor' to other nature poets in colonial America is briefly discussed in Jeffrey H. Richards's 'Samuel Davies and Calvinist Poetic Ecology' (*EAL* 35[2000] 29–50). Davies's verse receives very little critical attention and Richards's article is a welcome reminder of the historical and scholarly interest that can arise from the study of minor verse. His focus is on Davies's *Miscellaneous Poems, Chiefly on Divine Subjects* [1752] and his newspaper and periodical verse, one of the largest bodies of work 'extant from eighteenth-century Calvinist ministers in the South'. His essay is an exercise in 'ecocriticism', for he reads the verse for its ecological concern with the harmony and beauty of Nature and its 'perception of birds, flowers, and storms'.

Interest in print culture and the politics of publishing in the eighteenth century, particularly in the period of transition from colony to republic, continues to provide fertile territory for scholarly enquiry. Alison Olson's 'The Zenger Case Revisited: Satire, Sedition and Political Debate in Eighteenth Century America' (*EAL* 35[2000] 223–45) reconsiders the libel case brought against the printer John Peter Zenger whose *New York Weekly Journal* had published a 'series of satirical attacks' on Governor William Cosby of New York in 1734. 'Our futile search for binding precedents' to the case, she argues, 'has made us miss what the Zenger trial really did accomplish: it made possible the dynamic growth of political expression in the colonies by making it relatively safe for American writers to publish political humour—particularly satire—critical of men in office.' Olson's list of 'Works Cited' oddly makes no mention of Grantland S. Rice's *The Transformation of Authorship in America* (*YWES* 78[1999] 717–19), a study that controversially, and somewhat unconvincingly, argues that Zenger's acquittal marks the point at which colonial culture begins to assert a kind of hegemonic control over seditious and dissenting literature by 'absorbing' it into the dominant culture and thus negating, or repressing, it. Olson may not have seen Rice's study at the time of writing but her argument is more or less at an opposite pole to his for she sees Zenger's victory as one that makes 'the colonial world a little safer for satirists and political opposition, a little less safe for unpopular imperial officials'. Thus the trial 'helped constitute the "public" as part of political debate', and her essay is one more addition to that body of historical scholarship that sees the rise of a free press in British America, especially in New York City, as a defining force in the growth of a democratic culture. The role of the press in shaping party identity and party ideology is analysed in Jeffrey L. Pasley's 'The Two National *Gazettes*: Newspapers and the Embodiment of American Political Parties' (*EAL* 35[2000] 51–86). Newspapers, Pasley asserts, were 'the central institutions of American political life from the 1790s through most of the nineteenth century', and thus they contributed in 'fundamental ways to the very existence of the parties and to the creation of a sense of membership, identity, and common cause between political activists and voters'. His essay deals, in particular, with the *Gazette of the United States* and the *National Gazette* and the ways in which, through partisan editorship, they 'structured and embodied' political parties in the early years of the republic. Pasley's essay, arguably, takes too little account of questions of distribution and readership—the difficulties of printing and publishing on a moving frontier frequently go unremarked—for its thesis to be completely convincing, but it remains a very important addition to our understanding of newspaper politics in the United States. In 'Libertinism and Authorship in America's Early Republic' (*AL* 72[2000] 1–30) Bryce Traister locates the emergence of a new literary genre, 'the libertine confession narrative', in novels and periodical writings in the 1790s, Charles Brockden Brown's *Arthur Mervyn* and William Hill Brown's *The Power of Sympathy* figuring large in his account. Traister joins that increasingly large body of critics of the sentimental (and occasionally Gothic) novel who seek to find in very second-rate works things of great moment and significance. This can only be realized by relentless theorizing and Traister's essay works by invoking the polyvocality and gendered positioning of sentimental writing in order to point to its socio-political importance. By this route *Arthur Mervyn* 'embodies the age's political anxieties about the decay of virtuous self-restraint into self-interested rapacity' and thus the novel 'adds to our knowledge of early American literature's participation in and contribution to the nation's political historiography'. Few who have ever read Brown's feeble novel, however, will have noticed these 'qualities' in it and I find the argument unconvincing. Rather more accessible, and more plausible, is Laura H. Korobkin's reading of Brown's *Wieland*. In 'Murder by Madmen: Criminal Responsibility, Law, and Judgment in *Wieland*' (*AL* 72[2000] 721–50) she shows how Brown in fashioning the plot for his novel drew on 'recent American cases of religious mania', but also on the *Commentaries on the Laws of England* by William Blackstone, the first edition of which was published in

Philadelphia in 1771 and was thus readily to hand for Brown's scrutiny. Korobkin argues that while Brown used his novel 'to mock the law's procedural ineffectiveness, he also carefully designed a plot that demonstrates how key principles of law and evidence can supply the conceptual links that restore accountability in a fragmented world'.

Philip Gould is a familiar name to students of the period. In 'Free Carpenter, Venture Capitalist: Reading the Lives of the Early Black Atlantic' (*AmLH* 12[2000] 659–84) he reads 'early black Atlantic autobiography in the context of the cultural emergence of liberal rights discourse', and in so doing raises important questions both about our literary-historical understanding of eighteenth-century writing and the nature of American liberal thinking when seen against the background of Enlightenment thought and notably, Gould remarks, 'the relation between race and liberal ideology'. Gould argues that the 'rhetorical complexity of early black Atlantic autobiography derives in large part from social and economic changes that lent key political term such as liberty and slavery new, fluid meanings'. This thesis is pursued through texts such as John Marrant's *Narrative* and Venture Smith's (Smith's original name was Broteer Furro) *Narrative*, both, it might be noted, in the editions provided by Vincent Carretta in his *Unchained Voices: An Anthology of Black Authors in the English-Speaking World of the Eighteenth Century* (UPKen [1996]). These narratives, he suggests, were not written by auto-biographers who were 'victims of their white editors' but rather by collaborators whose 'collaboration depended in large part on the black subject's ability to exploit the possible meanings of rights and liberty'.

I have seen only two articles on Franklin this year. In 'Franklin's *Autobiography* and the Credibility of Personality' (*EAL* 35[2000] 274–93) Jennifer Jordan Baker reconsiders the concept of 'representativeness' as it applies in Franklin's account of himself. *The Autobiography*, she argues, is 'representative not as a generic tale of an ordinary American experience but rather as a story of exemplary success that uses Franklin's experience to advocate, like a celebrity endorsement, the possibilities of American life'. This might seem in many ways a rather obvious point to make and, indeed, the exemplary character of American autobiography has figured prominently in many accounts of the genre. Her exposition, however, focuses on Franklin's 'self-appointed role as an advocate of public credit', his own credibility as a public figure being used to advance the cause of a credit system that 'intertwines personal and civic interests'. Current theoretical concerns with the body and questions of representation surface in Betsy Erkilla's 'Franklin and the Revolutionary Body' (*ELH* 67[2000] 717–41), where she argues that in the life, work and reception of Benjamin Franklin 'it is on the level of the body and its political excess that the American Revolution was fought'. Her essay draws, in part, on the analysis of the nature of 'bourgeois print culture' advanced by scholars such as Michael Warner (see my comments on his work on Washington Irving below), who stress 'the bodiliness and materiality of the street, city, commerce, lower orders, popular culture and the press' in their account of the transition from colony to republic. Whether this kind of theoretical positioning can be profitably invoked to explain Franklin's important political and diplomatic role in the years of the Revolution and its aftermath is rather a different matter. Similarly, I have seen only one essay on Thomas Jefferson, Jennifer T. Kennedy's 'Parricide of Memory: Thomas Jefferson's *Memoir* and the French Revolution' (*AL* 72[2000] 553–73), which reads the *Memoir* both as a 'kind of ex post facto diary' and as Jefferson's 'final, oblique comment on the French Revolution, which had disappointed him, but left him longing for a repetition'. This is an intelligent and in many ways subtle essay, its elegance and clarity disguising some provocative, though implicit rather than explicit, theorizing about the nature of autobiographical reconstruction.

Critical and scholarly interest in Washington Irving seems disproportionate to his position in the history of American literature. For a major writer he elicits relatively little study, but I have seen three good articles on Irving this year. In 'The Dutchman in the Attic: Claiming an Inheritance in *The Sketch Book of Geoffrey Crayon*' (*AL* 72[2000] 31–57) Richard V. McLamore reads *The Sketch Book* through the contexts provided by the debates about the nature of an indigenous American literature in the period 1817–19 when Irving was composing his stories. Irving's stories, he argues, enact his 'conflicted hope that the cultural spirit conveyed by a popular literature might provide an alternative to a politically or economically based nationalism'. The vocabulary of postcolonial theory is invoked to posit an Irving who through his communion with 'the vanishing spirit of English rural culture in *The Sketch Book*, his interest in Moorish culture, and his assertion that the United States was the firstborn of American nations', was aware 'of the challenges posed and the possibilities opened by the U.S. postcolonial status'. 'Rip Van Winkle' remains the most loved and the most widely studied of the stories in *The Sketch Book*. 'Family Resemblances: The Texts and Contexts of "Rip Van Winkle"' (*EAL* 35[2000] 187–212), by Steven Blakemore, offers a detailed reading of the story through a 'recovery of the specific historical texts and contexts that underwrite the first story in Irving's *Sketch Book* (1819–20) that treats an ostensible American subject'. He relates the story's 'European "pasts" (Dutch, Swedish, and English)' to other more local issues such as Irving's 'ambivalent presentation of the American Revolution' and his understanding of the Puritan inheritance to show how the 'story's overt comedy and deceptive simplicity belie the complexity of this intricate American classic'. Michael Warner has written extensively on the emergence of a national literature in the early decades of the new republic, and in 'Irving's Posterity' (*ELH* 67[2000] 773–99) he discusses Irving's 'fascination with political history' with particular reference to *Bracebridge Hall*, *The Sketch Book* and *A Tour of the Prairies*. His argument about Irving's 'historicizing' turns on the degree to which the past can be rewritten 'as a continual immersion in which generational transmission will be not so much achieved as accomplished in advance'.

Two substantial and in many ways closely related works of historical scholarship on the revolutionary period have appeared this year and, as with so much material of this nature, they are of considerable value to literary scholars. Jon Butler is known above all for his work on American Protestantism: his *Awash in a Sea of Faith: Christianizing the American People* [1996] is a major study. *Becoming America: The Revolution before 1776* is a more general history of Britain's mainland colonies in the period 1660–1770 in which he argues that the eighteenth-century New World is one characterized more by its modernity than 'the historical quaintness' promoted by the American tourist industry. He attempts to rebuff 'recent interpretations that stress the "Europeanization" of eighteenth-century America and the "deferential," monarchical character of prerevolutionary society'. Crevecoeur's question 'What then is the American, this new man?' figures large here and Butler's 'answer' to it ranges widely, addressing demographic, economic, political, religious and social issues, while his account of colonial culture touches on not only literature and related written forms of expression but also architecture, furniture, ornaments, painting and the production of other artefacts. This is an impressive work of synthesis and it has the added virtue of being written in an admirably clear, direct and uncluttered prose. Joyce Appleby's *Inheriting the Revolution: The First Generation of Americans* pursues Butler's story into the republican period. She works largely by way of a series of biographical portraits that illustrate how Americans 'reinvented' themselves and their society in the twenty or so years after the Declaration of Independence in 1776. Her analysis of the intersections between capitalism, personal and civic culture, religion and the nascent democratic liberalism of post-revolutionary America is trenchant and informed. Like Butler's this is an important book and, again, like his, comes with a series of black and white illustrations.

3. American Literature 1830–1900

In *The Marriage of Heaven and Earth: Alchemical Regeneration in the Works of Taylor, Poe, Hawthorne, and Fuller*, Randall A. Clack examines the origins of alchemy in American writing. Clack argues that alchemy is defined here as 'the process of transforming a substance of little or no worth into a substance of great value', part of 'both a scientific and mystic tradition', which travelled from Europe to America via narrative accounts of the earliest explorers, who located the New World as a source of 'vast riches and the water of youth', a peculiarly suitable representation of the 'twofold quest of the alchemist', for gold and the elixir of life. Significantly, the rhetoric of alchemy, Clack notes, becomes incorporated at a very early stage in American letters, exemplified by Crèvecoeur's 'alchemical/ metallurgical image of the melting-pot to suggest that America was a land of transformation'. It is the function of alchemy's mystic powers of transformation that rendered it supremely suitable for American writers, and Clack contends that 'Taylor, Poe, Hawthorne, and Fuller incorporated the tropes and metaphors of alchemical philosophy into their own works'. Clack emphasizes that it is the 'artistic expression' of the alchemical philosophy that is the main concern of his study, an expression that is fully concerned with 'imagining the transformation/regeneration process'. He specifically refers to Taylor's 'transmutations of the Soul' in his poetic volume *Meditations*, the 'regeneration of the imagination' through several of Poe's short tales, notably 'Von Kempelen and his Discovery', 'Ligeia', 'The Assignation', and 'The Fall of the House of Usher', Hawthorne's 'alchemy of love' in 'Sir William Pepperell' and 'The May-Pole of Merry Mount', as well as *The Scarlet Letter* and *The House of the Seven Gables*, and Fuller's 'golden seed' as 'formula for the transformation of the human race', in 'Leila' and *Woman in the Nineteenth Century*. This is a critical study that should appeal generally to readers with an interest in nineteenth-century American writing.

An illuminating collection of essays by Michael Davitt Bell, *Culture, Genre, and Literary Vocation: Selected Essays on American Literature*, reflects on the relationship between literary production and the social and cultural world that shaped it. The book is divided into three sections and Bell begins with a close study of Nathaniel Hawthorne, before moving to a consideration of the conditions of authorship in nineteenth-century America, and concluding in a study of the consequences of literary naturalism for African American writing. Focusing on *The Scarlet Letter* [1850] and *The House of the Seven Gables* [1851], Bell probes the influences and experiences of Hawthorne's life in Concord and his acquaintance with fellow writers, such as Henry David Thoreau and Herman Melville, as well as Ralph Waldo Emerson and Margaret Fuller. In interrogating the contrary influences of these artists upon the reclusive Hawthorne, Bell examines two of Hawthorne's major works, and considers the evidence which argues that Hawthorne's work was considerably more subversive than perceived by a contemporary audience. Bell follows this discussion with an exploration of the beginnings of literary professionalism in nineteenth-century America, and in studying the various modes of literary production demonstrates the importance of women's fiction in the literary marketplace of the 1850s. Surveying the growth of American book and magazine publishing, he discusses literary contributions to a wide range of journals, including *Harper's New Monthly*, *Putnam's Monthly*, *Peterson's Lady's Magazine*, *Frank Leslie's Illustrated Newspaper* and the *New York Ledger*, and also enters into a lively debate on the popular novels of the period. Susan Warner's *The Wide, Wide World* [1850], Harriet Beecher Stowe's *Uncle Tom's Cabin, or Life Among the Lowly* [1852] and Maria Cummins's *The Lamplighter* [1854], receive special attention. Bell discusses these novels in relation to their authors' cultural and social experiences and notes, in particular, the conflicts arising between their creativity and their socially designated role within the domestic framework. Consideration of the work of Stowe, and especially her first anti-slavery novel, *Uncle Tom's Cabin*, leads into the final section of the book, which examines African American writing and the legacy of the protest novel.

In *A Discussion of the Ideology of the American Dream in the Culture's Female Discourses: The Untidy House*, Adrianne Kalfopoulou locates the female voice within a disordered space. The untidy house here represents domestic anarchy, and refutes cultural values implicit in the image of order. The discourse of female experience is foregrounded in the texts discussed, displacing the influence of the male upon the psychological and symbolic structure of the house. Kalfopoulou begins with *The Scarlet Letter*, and concludes with Toni Morrison's *Beloved* and Marilynne Robinson's *Housekeeping*, and she considers the absence of the woman's voice in the ordered house, exploring the different forms of narrative employed within the frame of the domestic. Images associated with domesticity, together with the language of the body, are found to take the place of words in narrating women's stories. *The Untidy House* also examines Gertrude Stein's *Three Lives*, Gayl Jones's *Corregidora*, and Maxine Hong Kingston's *The Woman Warrior* in order to articulate what remains 'other' in a male-dominated discourse. In these, and the three principal texts, Kalfopoulou demonstrates that the 'otherness' of the female voice is threatening to (male) social and cultural order, simply because its narratives of difference are perceived as a discourse of defiance. In *The Scarlet Letter* the flamboyant creativity of Hester's embroidery, which she uses to embellish the letter A, indicates her powerful individuality. Her defiant voice is intricately worked into the letter that also marks her sin, rewriting religious and social laws. Nevertheless, *The Untidy House* insists that Hester's true voice is ultimately appropriated by her author, as she retreats into silence and acquiescence. Hester, like Sethe in *Beloved*, is, in reality, guilty of an assertion of selfhood which transgresses established social boundaries of gender behaviour in radical, and terrifying, ways. Morrison's Sethe also sews, and the quilt she patches is a form of narrative, the remembering of the slave woman's story. Sethe's body, too, is the site of symbolic language, her breast milk and her tears are metaphors of non-speech within the text. Through Sethe, the language of the body is investigated as she moves out of the patriarchally defined construct of Sweet Home, but it is a movement that fails to provide the possibility of discursive alternatives in the short term. The discussion examines the female's need to discover appropriate language symbols in order to express her experiences and her desires, and offers a revisionary notion of domesticity defined, especially, in both *Beloved* and *Housekeeping*. In her conclusion, Kalfopoulou acknowledges female self-possession, the redefining of the boundaries of the house and the self, to be a continuing process.

In the decades before the Civil War, American society witnessed the emergence of a new form of print culture as penny papers, mammoth weeklies, gift books, fashion magazines and other ephemeral printed material flooded the market. These brought to the American reading public of the early nineteenth century an exuberant and theatrical form of publication which, Isabelle Lehuu argues in *Carnival on the Page: Popular Print Media in Antebellum America*, turned the world of print upside-down. Unlike the printed works of the preceding century, produced to educate and refine, the new media aimed to entertain a widening yet diversified public of men and women readers. Reading took on a new meaning and reading for pleasure became an act with the power to disrupt the social order, and such innovative print forms were to provoke fierce reactions from cultural arbiters. The book commences with an exploration of the genesis of textual transformation and analyses the historical context out of which this new print culture was born. Lehuu then examines new genres of popular publications, including penny papers and mammoth newspapers, before considering the relevance of gift books. These popular tokens of friendship combined poetry and prose with delicate engravings for an audience of young, middle-class women. This helped to create what the popular *Godey's Lady's Book* sought to capitalize on, a separate sphere of print culture for the middle-class woman. Lehuu proposes a revisionist approach to the formative years of American democracy: in what she contends was a parody of the official book culture, she discerns an underlying tension between the new artefacts and the traditional print order they sought to displace. She records the breaking down and rebuilding of class boundaries and gendered spheres of activity and recreation through literary production. Exploring literary texts and material culture, words and images, male and female audiences, and highbrow and lowbrow culture from the 1830s to the 1850s, Lehuu shows that the antebellum era was neither just an epilogue to an earlier age of scarce books and genteel culture, nor merely a prologue to the late nineteenth century and its mass culture and commercial literature. Instead, it marked a significant passage in the history of books and reading in the United States. Julie Brown, ed., *American Women Short Story Writers: A Collection of Critical Essays*, has just been reissued in paperback. First published in 1995, this collection makes an important contribution to the study of women short story writers.

John Carlos Rowe's collection, *Literary Culture and U.S. Imperialism: From the Revolution to World War II*, sets out to consider the 'self-contradictory self-conceptions' of 'American's interpretations of themselves as a people' being 'shaped by a powerful imperial desire and a profound anti-colonial temper'. He examines writers either as 'canny legitimists of American Empire', or as 'vigorous critics of our colonial impulses', and follows a chronological literary path, which starts with Charles Brockden-Brown, and deals variously with Edgar Allan Poe, Herman Melville, John Rollin Ridge, Mark Twain, Stephen Crane, Henry Adams, W.E.B. DuBois, the Nick Black Elk Narratives, and Zora Neale Hurston. In 'Edgar Allan Poe's Imperial Fantasy and the American Frontier', Rowe argues that Poe's 'fictionalized representations of racialized "savages" as threatening figures', should be taken in the context of America's imperial policy internationally, and not just as 'evidence' of Poe as 'southern regionalist' writer, as Poe 'imaginatively re-travels English routes of trade and colonial expansion with American characters' in his fiction. In 'Melville's *Typee*: U.S. Imperialism at Home and Abroad', he situates the novel as 'one of the first texts to establish a connection between issues of slavery in the United States and Euro-American colonialism in Polynesia'. Although Rowe points out that Melville is ostensibly reserving his criticism for the British and French presence in the South Seas, his critique also becomes 'more specifically relevant to his white U.S. readers in the 1840s and 1850s', in an appropriation of 'two important and characteristically American narrative forms', namely 'the Puritan captivity narrative and the fugitive slave narrative'. Rowe further suggests that Melville does not make the fatal mistake of categorizing all 'peoples of color' as related, in *Typee*, through a 'simple allegorization of slavery', but instead 'rejects the prevailing ethnographic models of its time', locating alternative allegories of slavery, particularly the 'bond between the commercial working class and subjugated peoples under colonialism and slavery'. In 'Mark Twain's Rediscovery of America in *A Connecticut Yankee in the Court of King Arthur*', Rowe picks up on earlier critical assessment of Twain's 'anti-colonial zeal', which tends to be dated from around the late 1890s, in response to the Spanish–American and Philippine–American wars. Rowe argues, however, that in his 1889 novel *A Connecticut Yankee*, Twain 'anticipates most of the explicitly anti-imperialist views' that become the subject of his later satires, therefore redating the timing of Twain's 'change of mind' on imperialism. In 'Race, Gender, and Imperialism in Stephen Crane', Rowe specifically focuses on the opening section of *The Red Badge of Courage*, the only scene in the novel to feature an African American figure, and the short story, 'The Monster', arguing that Crane's 'characteristic narrative distance' from the 'oppressed subjects' who often appear as 'stock characters', rhetorically 'qualifies' any potentially 'sympathetic' reading that might be available in his fiction. He contends that Crane manipulates 'oppressed people of color' in his fiction, at home but also in Latin America, the Caribbean, Africa, and even Turkey, 'to represent the frightening "wildness"' that 'our progress might strangely instil in us'. Crane is seen, therefore, to contribute to 'the racial ideology of modernism in his very techniques of writing', and in his depiction of 'the decadence of modern society' through his rhetorical use of the nineteenth-century domestic feminine sphere he also anticipates the 'modernist equation' between women and 'an otherness' that threatens 'ideas of white male selfhood, national coherence, civic virtue, and sexual and racial identities'. The focus here is inevitably on nineteenth-century writers, but it should be pointed out that this text provides as much relevant information and analysis for the student of the twentieth-, or even the twenty-first-century dynamics of American globalism.

The American Mystery: American Literature from Emerson to DeLillo, a collection of essays by Tony Tanner, planned before his death, features a wide selection of American writers, including Ralph Waldo Emerson's *Essays*, Nathaniel Hawthorne's *The Blithedale Romance*, Herman Melville's *White-Jacket, Moby-Dick* and *The Confidence-Man*, Henry James's 'The Story In It', *The Other House* and 'The Birthplace', William Dean Howells's *Indian Summer* from the nineteenth century, and F. Scott Fitzgerald's *The Great Gatsby*, Don DeLillo's *Underworld* and Thomas Pynchon's *Mason & Dixon* from the twentieth century. The book has a foreword by Edward Said and an introduction by Ian F.A. Bell, which assesses Tanner's contribution to development of American literary studies in the nineteenth and twentieth centuries, as the 'most subtle and supple critic', in texts such as *Reign of Wonder, City of Words* and *Scenes of Nature, Signs of Men*. This collection, Bell points out, is no exception, offering an accessible and insightful study into the various ways his chosen American writers conduct their 'masquerade of words'.

The Political Work of Northern Women Writers and the Civil War, 1850–1872, by Lyde Cullen Sizer, interrogates the way in which women deploy different literary modes in their struggle for emancipation. Sizer forms the basis of her discussion with a study of the domestic limitations enforced upon women. She considers the development of political awareness amongst women, and the way in which this made them question the boundaries of a woman's life. Novels, short stories, essays, poetry and letters were the tools women writers used to engage in the national debates of the time. Sizer explores the lives and works of nine North American women—Lydia Maria Child, Harriet Beecher Stowe, Frances Ellen Watkins Harper, Rebecca Harding Davis, Sara Willis Parton (Fanny Fern), Louisa May Alcott, Mrs E.D.E.N. Southworth, Mary Abigail Dodge (Gail Hamilton) and Elizabeth Stuart Phelps—and in doing so reveals the way in which they also used their writings to make sense of war, womanhood, Union, slavery, republicanism, heroism and death. Contemporary social and cultural values placed the woman, or at least the white, middle-class woman, within the domestic world. However, her role there, as nurse, teacher, letter-writer, and spiritual centre of the family home also enabled her to broaden her frame of reference. Four of the writers Sizer investigates, Child, Stowe, Harper and Davis, made slavery and racial divisions the central theme of their writing during the war. Alcott also addressed themes of race in some of her stories, while her Civil War 'Hospital Sketches' of life as a nurse, caring for wounded soldiers, were an early example of nursing narratives and were serialized in the *Boston Commonwealth*. Her creation of the nurse Tribulation Periwinkle, who supports the women's rights movement, and wishes for neither a husband nor romance, also proffers a message for the future. Alcott's strong woman is an emancipated—and therefore empowered—woman, Sizer concluding that the war offered a wider arena of authority for women and that, in its aftermath, women writers went on to consider other essential reforms. Through their writings they critiqued social and cultural prejudices, and explored the possibilities for change and renewal for women. Sizer's bibliographical record of contemporary magazines and newspapers, in particular, offers considerable information on the wide-ranging influence of women writers between 1850 and 1872. Some black and white pictures of women writers, as well as illustrations from magazines and books, are an interesting addition to an important study of women writers and the way in which they appropriated power through the written word.

Karen Tracey, *Plots and Proposals: American Women's Fiction, 1850–90*, also studies the topic of women's writing as a means of challenging patriarchal power. Tracey's carefully crafted text, however, debates the romantic novel, and the double-proposal plot, as a statement of female autonomy. She investigates the writings of Caroline Hentz, Augusta Evans, Laura J. Curtis Bullard, E.D.E.N. Southworth and Elizabeth Stuart Phelps, locating the literary inheritance of the mid-nineteenth-century American woman writer in the works of Jane Austen, Charlotte Brontë and Elizabeth Barrett Browning in order to reveal the ways in which their influence is made manifest. The idea of renegotiated marriages, such as that between Jane and Rochester in Brontë's *Jane Eyre* [1847], is seen to offer a challenge to marriage itself, as in Brontë's conclusion it is clear that her heroine has achieved a power denied earlier in the text and that the male has been weakened. The possibility of renegotiation, and the exploration of alternative roles, is one which forms the central contradiction in the texts Tracey studies. The double-proposal plot, in which the heroine rejects and later accepts proposals from the same suitor, offers her an opportunity in the space between to explore possibilities for personal autonomy and empowerment. Tracey shows the writing of American women writers to be determined by their historical circumstances and reflective of their determination to change those circumstances. She employs close readings of her chosen texts, which she then broadens out to interrogate reader response, literary traditions, and social history. Because the double-proposal plot enabled writers and readers to have an independent heroine who chooses to marry, the novels appear to hide their challenge to contemporary social and cultural values. The conclusion in marriage appears to confirm social norms, but the very altering of conventions allowed by the double-proposal plot works against this. Tracey argues, therefore, that the double-proposal tradition participated in the cultural work of change. In the time lapse between proposals, during which their relationship is renegotiated, the female pursues new goals and confronts new obstacles while the male is on the sidelines, although also improving himself for the second courtship. The heroines of such stories are able to exert a power of choice, in the renegotiated union, which implies female agency, albeit within the restrictive ideology of marriage. Reconstructing some of the cultural circumstances that would have influenced the writing, publishing, and reading of the novels, *Plots and Proposals* examines how changing notions of love and romance both inform and are critiqued by these fictions.

In his *African American Autobiography and the Quest for Freedom*, Roland L. Williams examines literature produced by both black and white Americans over time, and elaborates on the similarity of the themes which engage them. The slave narratives of Frederick Douglass, Harriet Jacobs and Olaudah Equiano are the principal focus of the early chapters. Through contrasts between the writings of Equiano and Benjamin Franklin, Douglass and Richard Henry Dana, and Jacobs and Fanny Fern Williams considers the shared exploration of the self, and the quest for personal autonomy, exhibited in these texts. He asserts that the inspiration for this project was an awareness that African American discourse is separated from mainstream texts owing to racial categories, but contends that what these writers share is more significant than the racial boundaries that have prompted readers to view their texts differently and separately. Individual liberty is a recurrent theme and, as Williams points out, the slave narrative champions the philosophy that animated early African Americans writers. The motif in Equiano's story, Williams argues, bears a visible resemblance to the theme in Franklin's narrative. Like the white text, he insists, the black one assumes epic proportions by featuring a hero who makes use of learning to improve his lot in life. Discovering similar preoccupations in Dana's *Two Years before the Mast* and Douglass's *Narrative of the Life of Frederick Douglass, an American Slave*, Williams emphasizes the common desire for freedom, rage at oppression and a belief in the self-made man. His comparison between the writings of Jacobs and Fern confirms their shared faith in the self-made woman, too, empowered through liberty and education. He argues throughout the text that the narratives he studies chart the experiences of a protagonist who embodies a New World sense of valour which enables them to make their way in the world. In discussions which also draw upon the literature of contemporary African American writers, Williams reflects upon greater similarities between black and white American writers than he believes have been previously recognized.

Warren and Wolff, eds., *Southern Mothers: Facts and Fictions in Southern Women's Writing*, is a collection of critical essays by prominent southern literary scholars. The belle, the mammy, religion, and racism are several of the distinctive threads which southern women writers have woven into the fabric of their stories. Bringing southern motherhood into focus—with all its peculiarities of attitude and tradition—the essays speak both to the established and the unconventional modes of motherhood that are typical in southern writing, and probe the extent to which southern women writers have rejected or embraced, supported or challenged, the individual, social, and cultural understanding and the institution of motherhood. The collection begins with a foreword by Elizabeth Fox-Genovese entitled 'Mothers and Daughters: The Tie That Binds', and continues with 'Hearing My Mad Mother's Voices' by Minrose Gwin, both of which reflect the all too familiar tension which often exists in the relationship between mother and daughter. Subsequent chapters consider a wide range of women writers, one of whom appears twice. *Incidents in the Life of a Slave Girl*, by Harriet Jacobs is the focus of both 'Following the Condition of the Mother' by Caroline Levander and 'Everyday Use' by Charles E. Wilson, Jr. The female line of inheritance is further discussed in 'Mothers, Grandmothers, and Great-Grandmothers: The Maternal Tradition in Margaret Walker's *Jubilee*' by Betty Taylor-Thompson and Gladys Washington, and in Mary Ann Wimsatt's insightful essay, 'The Old Order Undermined: Daughters, Mothers, and Grandmothers in Katherine Anne Porter's Miranda Tales'. Joan Wylie Hall's '"White mamma...black mammy": Replacing the Absent Mother in the Works of Ruth McEnery Stuart', and a reflection on 'Kate Chopin's Motherless Heroine' by Virginia Ross, are also among the contributions which form the first half of this collection. Recording that for a long time women writers primarily evoked the experience of maturation and personal autonomy through the experiences of the daughter, this collection advances the significance of recent texts which also attend to the experiences of the mother. The engaging essays in this rich collection encompass both viewpoints, and their explorations reveal new depth and complexities in women writers' probing of women's lives.

Christine Doyle's *Louisa May Alcott and Charlotte Brontë: Transatlantic Translations* is a fascinating study of the British writer's influence upon the American Alcott. As a nineteenth-century woman writer struggling with many of the same concerns as Brontë, Alcott engaged with Brontë's novels and reworked them into her own vision of female liberty and empowerment. In this comparative study, Doyle explores some of the intriguing parallels and differences in the lives of these two writers, as she also traces the themes of spirituality, personal relationships, and women's work in their writings. An overview of previous critical and popular approaches to Alcott's work provides a clear sense of both the value and the limits of existing scholarship, as well as how this study augments it. Doyle explores Alcott's literary legacy, as she also interrogates the effect of Brontë's influence upon her own literary production. Demonstrating the continuing, though changing, influence of Brontë upon Alcott, she traces Alcott's inclination to adopt and then revise Brontë's themes, heroes and heroines in her early work. Over time, a greater confidence becomes evident in Alcott's writing, which moves beyond the immediate influence of the British author. Examining the technical aspects of Brontë's presence in Alcott's writing reveals tension between Alcott's admiration for Brontë's characters and the inclination to employ her own artistic style. Although both women shared a common desire for self-fulfilment, which was written into their fiction, they responded to it differently, owing to time and place. Alcott's responses to her reading of Brontë, born sixteen years before her on the other side of the Atlantic, naturally lead her to rewrite British reserve and repression in terms of American optimism and progress. She, like Brontë, is aware of the special problems gender entails, but, like Thoreau, Emerson, and Hawthorne, her awareness of the difficulty of action is tempered by the belief that one must act nevertheless. She therefore rethinks Brontë's powerful but repressed heroines, developing women characters who understand the importance of action. This examination of Alcott's writing, and Brontë's influence, confirms the view that American writers were powerfully influenced by their British counterparts, even as they sought to define themselves creatively in a separate American context. Throughout her insightful analysis, Doyle shows that Alcott responds as a uniquely American writer to the problems of American literary production, while never denying the powerful transatlantic influences exerted by Brontë. Doyle's work reflects a wide range of scholarship, solidly grounded in an understanding of the Victorian temperament, nineteenth-century British and American literature, and recent Alcott criticism.

In *An Ambrose Bierce Companion*, Robert Gale takes as his starting point Bierce's comment in one of his letters to George Sterling that 'nothing matters', then argues that, actually, as a writer of satires comparable to Jonathan Swift and H.L. Mencken 'Bierce wrote as though much mattered to him', through his newspaper columns as well as in his fiction. Given the difficulties in accessing Bierce material, as acknowledged by Gale in his prefatory comments, this is a necessarily selective companion, which includes entries on '92 short stories, 161 essays, 19 short dramas, 5 reviews, 3 assemblies of fables, 1 novel, and 57 family members, friends, former friends, enemies, and professional associates'. Gale points out that 'readers may detect little adverse criticism of Bierce' in this *Companion*, yet at the same time this text, usefully assisted by a succinct but informative chronology, particularly the both vague and sinister entry for 1914, which reads simply 'disappears', offers a useful overview of Bierce's satiric rhetorical formulations. With an alphabetized 'encyclopaedia' section of the *Companion*, which commences with an entry for 'Abersouth, Captain', and concludes with an account of 'Writers of dialect', this text constitutes a comprehensive reference guide for students of one of America's most prolific writers.

George Monteiro, in *Stephen Crane's Blue Badge of Courage*, specifically states that his analytical stance is both 'author and text centred', providing an 'informed analysis' of the Crane canon and the author himself, bringing 'news about Stephen Crane and his literary work', rather than operating as a 'deconstruction' of the writings, a critical application that Monteiro regards as 'mean-spirited'. Locating Stephen Crane's approach to literary realism as 'personal', in that he 'committed himself to an aesthetics that called for writing only about what he had experienced and to a writer's epistemology that required him to be true about what he saw', Monteiro contends that Crane is no formulaic realist but rather that his writer's epistemology 'never denies that there is something apart from human experience that others have called reality', an approach that takes account of 'the realities of individual human perceptions and their attendant effect on personal psychology and behavior'. Monteiro argues that Crane, whose family was closely involved in the temperance movement, appropriates the imagery of temperance tracts in his writing, a discursive form that was 'a histrionic language of demonism and apocalyptics', a form itself 'largely derived from Holy Scripture', which 'employed the moral language of Good and Evil, of social responsibility, criminal addiction, and the restoration of personal integrity'. Referring to the work of other Crane critics, such as Michael Davitt Bell, Donald Pease and J.C. Levenson, Monteiro argues for a reading of Crane's fiction through the framework of his 'familial imperatives', particularly the 'theatricality' that was inherent to their work in the temperance movement, specifically examining the prevalent cultural modes, such as the 'myth of the whiskey-soaked west' through Crane's textual strategy. Monteiro looks at the writing that Crane produced during his ten-year authorial span, not chronologically but thematically, considering the importance of Crane's own early experience of temperance meetings—and alcohol—and also his reporting forays into the poverty of America's cities, the Civil War and the impact of these experiences as expressed in his poetry, *The Black Riders*, as well as his prose writings, short tales such as 'The Monster' and of course the novels, *Maggie: A Girl of the Streets* and *The Red Badge of Courage*. This is a text which also provides, alongside a compelling series of textual readings, some fascinating temperance illustrations from Monteiro's own collection.

In the interdisciplinary series Historical Guides to American Authors, which aims to place 'each writer in the context of the vibrant relationship between literature and society', the *Historical Guide to Ralph Waldo Emerson* is introduced by editor Joel Myerson with the statement that 'Ralph Waldo Emerson's reputation has never been as unshakeable as it is today'. The essays in this volume deal variously with aspects of Emerson's public and private life as well as his extensive writings. The introductory essay by Ronald A. Bosco, entitled 'Ralph Waldo Emerson, 1812–1892: A Brief Biography', does not pursue a merely descriptive line but analyses the 'processes of Emerson's intellect and imagination', focusing on his 'life and thought'. The essay is divided into two parts, one dealing with 'Emerson's private and professional life', particularly noting the events of the 1830s as crucial in his intellectual development, as well as assessing the 'evolution' of his 'idealistic philosophy'. The second section of this essay focuses on Emerson in a more public role, particularly noting the 'intellectual service Emerson performed for America through his lectures and writings', and identifying him as 'a principal architect of American culture'. In an essay entitled 'The Age of the First Singular: Emerson and Individualism', Wesley T. Mott takes as his starting point Emerson's comment 'I have taught one doctrine, namely, the infinitude of the private man', and argues that Emerson's 'true gift to his contemporaries, and to later generations, was his ability to ignite an empowering sense of self-reliance', locating Emerson as a 'dominant presence' in American literature, even for those writers, like Hawthorne and Melville, who 'quarrelled with his vision'. William Rossi looks at Emerson in relation to the rapid transformations of the environment in 'Emerson, Nature, and Natural Science', arguing that Emerson refers to these rapid changes 'only obliquely' in his writings on nature, and at the same time pointing out that, to Emerson, 'the physical presence of nature mattered less than its putative meaning or the "higher" presence mediated through the physical', referring to Darwin's works in the field of 'natural science' alongside several of Emerson's essays, including 'Nature' and 'Compensation'. In 'Emerson and Religion' David M. Robinson argues that Emerson's early 'belief in the presence and power of the soul [as] the core' contributes to an understanding of his 'religious thought', being the 'vital principle of his entire intellectual achievement'. He locates Emerson's soul sources as ranging from the Oriental and Neoplatonic to European Romanticism—a view of the soul that was eventually modulated by the 'waning of his experience of ecstatic vision'—and considers the development of a 'more pragmatic and ethically centred theory of religious life' where 'work and worship, moral and vision' became 'synonymous concepts'. Gary Collison argues, in 'Emerson and Antislavery', that while Emerson has been persistently regarded as unidentifiable with the abolitionist movement, his lectures following the 1850 Fugitive Slave Law actually show him occupying a radically different position, where he had moved from his earlier position of 'moral suasionist' to adopt the 'increasingly militant radical stance' of Thoreau. In 'Emerson in the Context of the Women's Rights Movement', Armida Gilbert examines the way in which Emerson's attitude towards the Women's Rights movement developed, particularly focusing on the influence of his friendship with Margaret Fuller, whose ideas 'came to form the core of his thinking on women'. A useful illustrated chronology and an examination of 'Emerson and his Biographers' by Ronald A. Bosco concludes this selection, with the warning that no study of Emerson is ever complete and exhaustive, finishing with the statement 'The day that any generation is content to accept the published record as the complete report of the essential Emerson, Emerson and that part of America he created will cease to exist.'

In *Less Legible Meanings: Between Poetry and Philosophy in the Work of Emerson*, Pamela Schirmeister argues that the ancient 'quarrel' between poetry and philosophy 'never occurred at all' in America, and this is exemplified in the writings of Ralph Waldo Emerson particularly, although it is also evident in the works of Poe and Thoreau. Referring to Emerson's comments, 'A philosopher must be more than a philosopher' and 'Plato is clothed with the powers of the poet', Schirmeister contends that 'Emerson's equation of poetry and philosophy is itself representative of American and Romantic attitudes in the mid-nineteenth century', situating Emerson within a specific historical and cultural moment. Schirmeister's examination refers to the relationship between American writing and thinking and the European Romantics, particularly Thomas Carlyle, Stanley Cavell and Sigmund Freud. In an exploration of Emerson's 'Letters', which Schirmeister defines as 'the passage between literature and philosophy', the main contention of this study is the centrality to Emerson's 'whole project' of 'the desire to collapse poetry and philosophy'. One of the main features of Emerson's 'letters', for Schirmeister, is the complication that occurs 'at the particular juncture of rhetorical effect and the experience of reading', examining the type of reading that is generated by Emerson's rhetorical strategy, which is itself informed not only by Emerson's reading of European philosophical forms, but also by his relationship to the mid-nineteenth-century American 'democratic imperative'. The oft-studied self-reliant individual of Emerson's 'letters' becomes, in Schirmeister's analysis, a subject of 'receptivity' who responds to 'Emerson's ambition', that his writing should 'seem primarily to be therapeutic', where the subject passes from the private sphere to the public, to a communal and political identity, through a 'crisis of self-definition' that occurs 'in the individual' and 'in culture', where 'letters will become the privileged place of expression'. This then produces a new subject position which demands a rearticulation of Emersonian theories of ethics and individualism. This is an intensely theoretical study which not only offers an insightful reading of Emersonian rhetorical strategies but also provides a useful summary of the relationship between European philosophical discourses and American 'letters'.

Setting out as its main purpose the intention to 'deal with the human side of the story' of the relationship between Emerson and Thoreau, Harmon Smith, *My Friend, My Friend: The Story of Thoreau's Relationship with Emerson*, focuses primarily on information provided in letters, journals, memoirs and monographs, in order to 'explore the relationship of the two men in depth', and in turn 'define the role it played in their work and their lives'. Locating Emerson as Thoreau's early mentor, Smith contends that 'if Emerson had not befriended him, it is doubtful that Henry Thoreau would have had a significant literary career', but also acknowledges that as Thoreau's obvious talent as a writer matured, he became 'restive' as Emerson 'continued to insist on his role as mentor'. Smith explores the evidence of insecurity in the relationship between these two American writers and looks at areas of ambivalence in their friendship, particularly the dilemma they faced between an idealized version of friendship, as they can be seen to have constructed in their writings, and the vagaries of the 'human variety'. This is an engaging and thoughtful study, which provides useful data to students of both Thoreau and Emerson as well as constituting an interesting study for the more general student of the New England scene of the mid-nineteenth century.

A century and a half after her death, Margaret Fuller is recognized as America's leading female intellectual of the nineteenth century. The essays in Fritz Fleischmann, ed., *Margaret Fuller's Cultural Critique: Her Age and Legacy*, are an illuminating act of exploration of her work. Divided into five sections, the collection engages with Fuller's intellectual legacies, her contemporary connections, her travel writing, and the legacy her family was to bequeath. The voice of this singular woman is also examined in three essays, under the heading 'Language, Perception, and Voice', which look to Fuller as prophet. The broad range of biographical and critical scholarship assembled in this book contributes to the growing comprehension of her pioneering life and work. '"Cheat Me [on] by no Illusion": Margaret Fuller's Cultural Critique and its Legacies', by Bell Gale Chevigny, identifies the commitment Fuller had to the breaking down of barriers, moving beyond fixed categories, enabling dialogue, and demonstrating a willingness to participate in social change. Cynthia J. Davis, in 'What "Speaks in Us": Margaret Fuller, Woman's Rights, and Human Nature', considers Fuller's critique of gendered practices, while Judith Strong Albert sketches out some of the paths along which Fuller's feminist themes and concerns have developed since 1850. A study of Fuller's contemporaries, and her relationships with them, are the focus of Carolyn L. Karcher's 'Margaret Fuller and Lydia Maria Child: Intersecting Careers, Reciprocal Influences', as well as 'Margaret Fuller and Julia Ward Howe: A Woman-to-Woman Influence', by Judith Mattson Bean. Thomas R. Mitchell's ' "This Mutual Visionary Company": Nathaniel Hawthorne and Margaret Fuller', brings this section to a close with a fascinating exploration of their mutually inspirational relationship. Mary-Jo Haronian's 'Margaret Fuller, Perceiving Science', and Jeffrey Steele's 'Symbols of Transformation: Fuller's Psychological Languages', reflect on the significance of the language employed in Fuller's philosophical debates and writings. This theme is also dominant in '"Unconnected Intelligence" and the Woman of Letters: Margaret Fuller's Darting (Dial)ogues', by Cheryl Fish. An exploration of Fuller's travel writing engages Michaela Bruckner Cooper, in 'Textual Wandering and Anxiety in Margaret Fuller's *Summer on the Lakes*', Susan Gilmore's 'Margaret Fuller "Receiving" the "Indians"', and Brigitte Bailey's 'Representing Italy: Fuller, History Painting, and the Popular Press'. Fuller was conscious of the fact that her journalism for the *Tribune*, for example, helped create an American vision of Italy and Italian identity, and this awareness also, no doubt, influenced her brother Arthur's revisioning of Fuller's legacy. Dorothy Z. Baker's 'Arthur Buckminster Fuller's (Re)Vision of the Life and Work of Margaret Fuller' debates his view of his sister, and his determination to recreate her image in a careful reworking of her literary legacy. The final essay in this collection, Jeffrey Steele's consideration of the rewriting of Fuller's work in 'Editing Margaret Fuller's Poetry', explores a form of writing for which she is, perhaps, less well known. The sum total of this book is an impressive, uncompromising and inspiring study of the life and the work of Margaret Fuller, which, in its diversity, reflects her extraordinary legacy.

In *The American Byron: Homosexuality and the Fall of Fitz-Greene Halleck*, John W.M. Hallock, a distant relation of the 'American Byron', introduces us to Halleck at the scene of the unveiling of his statue, in 'the Poet's Corner of America', as a man highly esteemed by Charles Dickens and William Thackeray, as well as William Cullen Bryant, James Fenimore Cooper, Washington Irving and Edgar Allen Poe. Fitz-Green Halleck, generally to be seen sporting a 'trademark accessory', his green umbrella, was also, Hallock informs us, an intimate of presidents, notably President Hayes, and foreign dignitaries, such as Joseph Bonaparte. The poet, however, who was so well known in his own time, has become somewhat neglected in recent years, and it significant to note that this is the first biographical study produced on Halleck for the past fifty years. Referring to Poe's claim, in 1843, that 'no name in the American poetical world is more firmly established than that of Fitz-Greene Halleck', Hallock explores Halleck's rise and fall from notoriety to obscurity, locating a developing hostility towards his poetry and in his life that would eventually lead to an attack, by critics of his poetry, on his 'personal character'. Hallock argues that Fitz-Greene Halleck, in poems such as 'The Field of Grounded Arms', pre-empts Walt Whitman's non-conformist poetry in *Leaves of Grass*. Hallock specifically considers the implications of Halleck's homosexuality throughout this biographical study, which provides a detailed and entertaining analysis not only of the life and time of the American Byron, but also an account of attitudes to homosexuality more generally in nineteenth-century America.

Nathaniel Hawthorne's *The Scarlet Letter*, and in particular its heroine, form the central concerns of a study by Jamie Barlowe, *The Scarlet Mob of Scribblers: Rereading Hester Prynne*. Barlowe's examination of criticism of Hawthorne's novel leads her to conclude that it is male-dominated and she consequently defines female scholarship, in terms of Hawthorne criticism at least, as constructed in terms of the academic Other. She debates the excluded scholarship and criticism of white and African American academic women and feminists, thus defined, on the subject of *The Scarlet Letter*. She also explores this text, and its various translations into film, viewing them in their cultural moments and debating their critical reception. The first half of the book is given over to a consideration of the text, and the role of female scholarship in redefining the fictional heroine. Close reading and textual analysis are employed in Barlowe's effort to broaden study of *The Scarlet Letter*. Nevertheless, it is really the examination of cinematographic studies of Hester Prynne which offers the greatest scope for scholarly debate here. Barlowe refers to early film productions, of which there were eight, including silent versions in 1911, 1913 and 1917, but principally focuses on the 1926, 1937 and 1995 versions. The actresses who played Hester Prynne in these productions, Lilian Gish, Colleen Moore and Demi Moore, are also a subject for study in Barlowe's reflection of their private and public lives, as well as their performances. In this, she observes all three to be emblematic of women who, personally and professionally, reflect aspects of entrapment within the cultural economy, even as they demonstrate rebellion and resistance in their own life choices. This seems to move some distance from a consideration of *The Scarlet Letter*, both in literary and cinematographic form. However, the detailed notes and bibliography at the end of this study offer interesting reading materials for further investigation.

In '"Fiction in Color": Domesticity, Aestheticism and the Visual Arts in the Criticism and Fiction of William Dean Howells' (*NCL* 55:iii[2000] 369–98) Christopher Diller argues that Howells, notorious for essays such as 'The Man of Letters as a Man of Business', subsumes 'masculine literary production' within a 'feminine aesthetic', where the feminine aesthetic 'defines and stabilizes literary value by predicating it upon a particular sector of the market', namely the 'court of women' who are the main purchasers of literary output, and therefore actively participate in the conversion of 'literary capital' into 'everyday currency'. Diller further contends that Howells delineates the 'gendering of artistic production and aesthetic judgement', where the latter category articulates a 'sexual double-standard' by which women are both 'valorized' as providers of the moral tone of domesticity and at the same time denigrated as artists, so that 'men can produce art without the stigma of commercialism'. Diller's argument is based on Howells's essay 'The Man of Letters as a Man of Business', and the 1893 novel *The Coast of Bohemia*, which both offer, according to Diller, a critique of the 'capitalistic logic' that 'reduces aesthetics' either to an 'epiphenomenon of the market' or a 'self-referential' theory of the work of art, contending that the discourse of 'femininity' emerges as a rhetorical strategy through which Howells could both 'represent and rationalize the paradox of fine art in a capitalist society'.

In *Henry James: A Certain Illusion*, Dennis Flannery focuses on a writer who saw a novel without 'illusion' as an impossibility, and for whom the word 'illusion' had a fruitful range. Taking as his premise that illusion 'meant' for James, 'powerfully convincing representation', which possessed 'a certain brutality and immediacy', at the same as 'meaning a mistake, an aspiration, and crucially a mark of human subjectivity', Flannery detects certain 'gaps and omissions', in James's use of 'illusion', that correspond to the gaps and omissions of 'real life'. Flannery contends that this is not to say that 'illusion' and 'real' are synonymous terms in James's fiction, rather that 'illusion is deeply opposed to the "real" in James's work', and at the same time 'the real is unthinkable without it'. Flannery makes use of James's early editions in this provocative study, accessing the 'most historically raw and immediate versions of his texts', avoiding the revisions that interfere with the immediacy of the 'illusion'. Paying particular attention to the novels *The Portrait of a Lady, The Bostonians, The Princess Casamassima, The Tragic Muse, The Wings of a Dove* and *The Golden Bowl*, and the short stories 'The Aspern Papers', 'The Figure in the Carpet', and 'The Velvet Glove', Flannery also refers to previous critical assessments that have focused variously on James and publicity, gender, the cult of the author, and realism, and also more specific critical approaches such as 'the experience of absorption'. This analysis provides a close reading of its chosen texts, at the same time as situating each text within a wider field of contextual criticism. This is an illuminating book that contains useful explanatory notes and a detailed bibliography. Robert B. Pippin argues, in *Henry James and Modern Moral Life*, that James undertakes a consideration of morality, both in terms of what 'moral' means and how morality is enacted, in his fiction. Pippin argues that James consistently exhibits a highly developed awareness that morality is not a universal category by which behaviour can be measured, but instead offers an interpretative potential where moral categories can be seen as 'ideological, reflections of the requirements and interests of power', and, further, that morality 'can be understood psychologically, as a reflection of needs and desires and especially anxieties'. Pippin goes on to argue that James understands morality to be 'a matter of essentially social and historically specific practices, institutions and largely implicit rules and expectations', but also recognizes that the concept of morality in the modern world can no longer provide 'much of a basis for interpretation and assessment'. Pippin focuses primarily on several of James's major novels, notably, *The Portrait of a Lady, The Wings of a Dove, The Ambassadors*, and *The Golden Bowl*, as well as a handful of James's shorter pieces, particularly 'The Turn of the Screw' and 'The Beast in the Jungle'. Pippin's reading of James's fiction is accessible, as well as informed and detailed, a useful resource for the James scholar as well as for the more generally interested reader. Adeline Tintner, in *The Twentieth-Century World of Henry James: Changes in his Work after 1900*, points out that, generally speaking, studies of Henry James tend to conclude with the 'completed novels of the major phase and the revisions of the New York Edition (1907–1909)'. As Tintner points out, however, James 'lived on' after this period, to 'vigorously write for a decade longer'. This writing, Tintner argues, exhibits evidence of James's awareness and conscious appropriation of the twentieth century, remarking that James alluded in his fiction of this time to such new inventions as 'kodak', 'flying-machine' and also 'referred to being "snap-shotted"' as well as being 'the first serious writer to make the skyscraper submit to his detailed and pervasive analysis', in addition to pre-empting modernist writers such as Joyce, Proust and Eliot as the 'writer who heralded the modernist period'. This text sets out to examine some of the 'modernist themes that preoccupied Henry James as he entered the new century', specifically in an analysis of *The American Scene*, where New York is located by James as the 'terrible town', and also considers how James studies the rhetorical image of the city through short stories such as 'The Jolly Corner' and 'Julia Bride', and in novels such as *The Ivory Tower* and *The Outcry*. The 'romance of art' also becomes for James, according to Tintner, the 'romance of finance' as he investigates the act of making money as both 'a worthwhile activity' and an 'evil one', a theme particularly evident in 'The Bench of Desolation'. Tintner also examines the revisions made for the New York Edition, which swiftly followed James's trip 'home'. James's conceptualization of 'time' as a rhetorical strategy had also, according to Tintner, been reformulated by his time in America, and this becomes evident in his novels of the twentieth century, particularly in *The Sense of the Past*. Tintner goes on to argue that James's 'interest in sexuality seems, after the turn of the century, to be easier and looser than in the past', as exemplified by the more specific forms of sexuality that appear in the later fiction, auto-eroticism in 'The Figure in the Carpet', for example. Tintner also considers James as a propagandist writer, in the First World War, which 'allowed him an opportunity to identify with Walt Whitman', whose war poetry James had so assiduously denigrated some four decades previously. Tintner remarks that the themes covered in this text 'represent a personal selection' of James's treatment of modernity in his writings, but this is a detailed and efficient study that will appeal to the specifically Jamesian scholar and would also provide a useful resource for the student of early twentieth-century modernist themes.

In *Melville's Art of Democracy*, Nancy Fredricks locates her 'general purpose' as an identification and analysis of 'the various theoretical positions represented in Melville's work', most notably, 'class, popular culture, feminism and aesthetics'. She makes a thorough examination of *Moby-Dick* and *Pierre*, which form, according to Fredricks, 'a giant diptych', 'linked together formally and thematically' by the joint exploration of the 'ethical and political implications of the limits to our powers of representation'. While stating that Melville's work reflects 'his sympathies with the radical-democrat movement', Fredricks warns that 'anyone who wishes to paint a portrait of Melville as a radical egalitarian democrat has got to come to terms with his ambivalent feelings towards the masses'. At the same time, however, she finds Melville to be concerned with the 'unrepresentedness' of marginalized groups, ethnic minorities, the lower classes, and women. Fredricks's study takes into account Melville's oxymoronic narrative strategy and his appropriation of tropes of melodrama, and she further contends that his egalitarian aesthetic can be related to Kant's theory of the sublime, arguing that 'for Melville, as for Kant, the sublime experience of the limits to our powers of representation is analogous to the experience of freedom', forming 'a prefiguration of and, in a sense, a prerequisite for democratic, egalitarian relationships'. In order to explore fully the 'expansive quality' of Melville's 'political-aesthetic agenda', Fredricks draws on a variety of contextual material, most significantly art history, music theory, genre studies (particularly melodrama), a consideration of class culture, theories of the sublime, German philosophy, and gender studies, the latter category organized through Fredricks's own experiences as a feminist reader of Melville texts. 'American Holy Land literature', states Hilton Obenzinger, in *American Palestine: Melville, Twain and the Holy Land Mania*, 'consists of hundreds of books and an extensive array of newspaper and magazine articles from the beginning of the nineteenth century to 1882.' This literature, according to Obenzinger, represents 'personal experience' of the region, a rhetorical account of the writer's own adventures, pointing out that most stayed only very briefly in the region, and their observations and subsequent reports on 'economic conditions, local culture, and even geography' of the Holy Land were 'often less than accurate or complete'. Informed by the 'window' of 'New World experience', alongside the rhetorical appearance of the region in the Bible, in 'Crusader myths' and the Arabian Nights, the 'Palestine reality' recorded, argues Obenzinger, 'spoke more to the formation of American cultural structures', where Palestine exists as a constituent of America's own 'settler-colonial culture', formed from a 'christianography' of the region. Herman Melville's *Clarel* is read alongside Mark Twain's *Innocents Abroad* in this particular context. Obenzinger argues that Melville and Twain 'write their own sacred geographies' of the region, one in poetry, one in prose, both shaped by 'frontier' encounters from 'maritime and western contact zones', and both also undermining 'the assumptions of American exceptionalism, even as they remain complicit with colonial expansion'. Obenzinger's text provides an intriguing study of America and its relationship with the 'presumption of God's special destiny' in the framework of its inherent colonial status, a set of relations that both 'troubled and delighted' Melville and Twain. Clare L. Spark's *Hunting Captain Ahab: Psychological Warfare and the Melville Revival* constitutes a revealing and intriguing examination of the processes by which we can gain access to an 'archival record' of 'Melvilleana', and states that the 'official resuscitation' of Melville, which began shortly after the 1919 centenary of his birth, 'presents little joy and much exhaustion, confusion and suspicion' even of Melville himself. Intriguingly, Spark claims, the very scholars who 'claimed that Melville himself had shameful secrets', are also intent on 'a most unscholarly withholding or ignoring of primary source materials', a resource that could have afforded to Spark 'illuminating passages' of Melville's own texts, and other documentation that 'could make sense of' what she refers to as 'the multifaceted Melville problem'. Taking as her basis for the 'Melville problem' the contradictions that are inherent to his writing and his life, Spark examines the confusions and contradictions of Melville scholarship in the twentieth century, claiming that the 'Melville Revival' has only ever been 'tangentially about Melville', and she particularly locates her study on Captain Ahab, one of the central characters not only in the Melville canon but in American studies generally, assessing the various critical positions that Melville's monomaniac captain has been read as holding, from democratic hero, to an 'anticipation of Hitler'. In many ways, this study is itself only tangentially about Melville, as its main purpose is to denounce the 'long-standing global effort to maintain authoritarian social relations in an age of democratic aspirations', yet at the same time, it could only be conducted in the context of the various attempts to consolidate an authoritarian pattern in scholastic institutions. This is a thought-provoking, detailed analysis, thorough, if at times inevitably speculative, that offers an informed reading of the 'Melville revival' and of key Melville scholars, notably Charles Olsen, Jay Leyda, and Henry A. Murray, as well as Richard Brodhead, Richard Chase, F.O. Matthieson and Raymond Weaver. She focuses on the political, institutional agendas of each site of Melville scholarship, locating a history of critical thinking on one of America's most fought over writers, offering essential and compelling reading for Melville scholars. In 'From Wall Street to Astor Place: Historicizing Melville's "Bartleby"', (AL 72:i[2000] 87–116) Barbara Foley contends that while Melville's short story 'Bartleby: The Scrivener' has been variously interpreted as autobiography, as allegory, and as emblematic of the rationalized capitalist economy of mid-nineteenth-century America, there is a need for a more thorough reading of a 'constitutive context and locale', further arguing that to understand 'Bartleby' a 'familiarity with mid-nineteenth-century class struggles in New York', and the contemporary debates which arose from those struggles is 'indispensable'. History, in 'Bartleby', Foley suggests, should be reconstructed from 'what has been repressed, fragmented, and displaced to the margins of the text', events only 'subliminally acknowledged by the narrator of the tale, whose 'passing references' to contemporary events specifically provide a framework of 'covert' inclusion of a 'historical subtext', and at the same time reveal Melville's 'own attempt to contend with the return of the political unconscious'. In 'Melville's Subversive Political Philosophy: "Benito Cereno" and the Fate of Speech', (AL 72:iii[2000] 495–521) Maurice S. Lee states that his 'interest' lies in the 'radical Melville who voiced unspeakable politics', and who throughout his career 'flirted' with 'taboo' subjects. Lee traces the well-known portrait of the fall of Herman Melville, from his initial triumphs, through the failure of his later novels, the writer whose work 'turned increasingly private and bitter', eventually collapsing into silence. He argues that Melville's writing for magazines, mostly undertaken after the publication of *Moby-Dick*, does not fit into the 'fall' model, being among the best work Melville produced. In particular, 'Benito Cereno', is read as a story which by its subject-matter 'invites political analysis', but which should not, Lee warns, be read as a definitive version of Melville's own stance towards slavery, although it is both 'politically engaged' and 'socially aware'. Lee further argues that Melville's 'subversive politics' in 'Benito Cereno' are 'about' the 'failure of political speech', a politics that challenges dominant ideologies, an attempt to speak the 'unspeakable' to a 'friendly and sensitive listener in a hostile political world'.

In *Poe and the Printed Word*, Kevin J. Hayes assesses the relationship between Poe's writing and the 'print culture' of nineteenth-century America, offering at the same time a biographical reading of Poe's literary life, from his earliest years as a student in England, through his various sojourns in Richmond, Baltimore and New York, as a student, as a writer and as a critic. Hayes argues that Poe was convinced of 'the value of the printed word', not only as a space for the dissemination of ideas, but also as giving entry to a 'world of the imagination', whose only 'entrance requirement is literacy'. Examining Poe's poetry and prose, Hayes also discusses the relationship between manuscript and print, and considers his relationship with publishers and booksellers, particularly focusing on one 'lavish dinner' which drew many of America's literati, an occasion that 'reflected the exuberant feelings of literary nationalism prevalent throughout the country' and that 'gave Poe hope for literary success'. Hayes also looks at the economics of the printed word, noting that Poe's poverty prevented him from owning a significant library, and goes on to discuss his later publishing ambitions as a magazine editor, and his intention to write a book on American literature, a project that was never fully realized. In addition to being a guide to the development of Poe's writing from the perspective of 'print culture', this is a useful introduction to the study of Poe, of interest and accessibility to the novice and seasoned reader alike. In his introduction to *A Historical Guide to Edgar Allan Poe*, in the interdisciplinary Historical Guides to American Authors series, J. Gerald Kennedy argues that 'no American writer of the antebellum period enjoys greater current popularity and recognizability' than Poe, whose major relevance to our own time would be most apparent to the fan of *The Simpsons*. Kennedy argues that Poe's continued appeal for our culture resides in the modernity, even postmodernity, of his writing. Works such as 'The Man That Was Used Up' and 'A Predicament' engage with issues of sensationalism and violence, pre-empting the postmodern approach to violence in films such as *Pulp Fiction* and *Fargo*. Poe's fascination with madness, particularly in 'The Fall of the House of Usher', is aligned with a 'post-Freudian awareness of the unconscious and the irrational', while his articulations of 'estrangement and doubt', in such works as 'The Man in the Crowd', and his representation of the 'deep spiritual uncertainty of the nineteenth century', ensure that, despite his lack of appeal in the late nineteenth and early twentieth centuries, Poe remains one of the most enduringly relevant of nineteenth-century writers. This volume of essays includes 'A Brief Biography' by J. Gerald Kennedy, which examines Poe's life and usefully includes details of contextual debates and events. In 'Poe and the Publishing Industry', Terence Whalen locates Poe as a writer who had pursued 'a literary career of enormous vitality and breadth', having lived and worked in Baltimore, Richmond, Philadelphia, and New York, all significant publishing centres in the United States, and focuses on the 'economic environment', of America's 'tumultuous periods of expansion', as well as Poe's specific experiences with the publishing industry. David Leverenz examines the 'sensory eruption' of Poe's tales, in an essay entitled 'Spanking the Master: Mind–Body Crossings in Poe's Sensationalism', arguing that Poe's 'mind–body crossings', in such tales as 'Metzengerstein', 'Berenice', 'The Premature Burial', 'The Man That Was Used Up', and 'The Raven', act to 'expose and displace cultural tensions' between 'disembodied white mastery' and 'embodied, alienated forms of servitude'. In 'Poe and Nineteenth-Century Gender Constructions', Leland S. Person examines Poe's gender representations in his life and in his writing, assessing his professional relations with women, his critical essays on women writers, notably Margaret Fuller, his fictional women, Ligeia, Morella and Bernice, and his personal relationships with his mother, his wife and his lovers, also taking into account his relationships with men in both life and fiction, particularly his 'portraits of gentlemen'. Person argues that, while in life Poe could never quite secure for himself the category of southern gentlemen that he aspired to, in the 'separate sphere' of his fiction 'Poe could be "the man"'. Louis A. Renza, in 'Poe and the Issue of American Privacy', contends that Poe, while not generally considered to be a socially representative writer, in the particular instance of 'American private freedoms' invaded by '"The inquisition of popular sentiment"', Poe performs precisely that role, examining the contextual debates that surrounded the categorization of public and private spheres in nineteenth-century America. This collection concludes with a detailed illustrated chronology of Poe's life and writings in the context of significant historical events, and a bibliographical essay by Scott Peeples. Terence Whalen, in *Edgar Allan Poe and the Masses: The Political Economy of Literature in Antebellum America*, argues that Poe, in contradiction to his legend as the artist 'out of space, out of time', was very much aware of and enthusiastically responded to the economic conditions of his time in exploring the relationship between literature and capitalism in antebellum America. Although Whalen is more largely concerned with 'the emergence of a national culture before the Civil War', he chooses specifically to focus on Poe as an exemplification of the '"poor-devil" author in an age of social and economic turmoil', and offers a 'new account' of America's publishing industry, which, Whalen argues, 'had begun to regulate nearly all aspects of literary creation'. This critical analysis offers several useful interpretations of Poe's 'world', his response to American slavery, his role as literary entrepreneur, his ambivalent attitude towards American nationalism and imperialism, his articulation of the relationship between 'secret writing' and 'common knowledge' in Jackson's America and, more generally, an insight into the 'social meaning' of Poe's literature and criticism. In conclusion, he argues that Poe's ongoing debate with political economy and creative output eventually 'inspired' a 'recurrent dream of a material language that could transport him beyond the bounds of capitalist regulation'. Whalen's analysis, in redefining Poe as a writer of and in his space and time actively responding to the creative struggle with market forces, offers a compelling and challenging interpretation for the Poe scholar and at the same time gives a very useful insight into the cultural transformation of America in the nineteenth century.

In his introduction to *A Historical Guide to Henry David Thoreau*, in the Historical Guides to American Authors series, William E. Cain argues that although in our contemporary moment Thoreau 'stands out among the major authors in the American Literary Canon', he commanded little attention in his own time, publishing a handful of poems, some essays and just two books. Yet, Cain points out, a complete edition of Thoreau's literary output, to be published by Princeton University Press, is going to run to twenty-five volumes. Cain's 'A Brief Biography' usefully situates Thoreau's intellectual development in the context of his family background, farming in Concord, his time at Harvard, and his relationship with Ralph Waldo Emerson and transcendentalism, as well as his 'sporadic' participation in the anti-slavery movement and friendships with other writers. In 'Thoreau, Manhood, and Race: Quiet Desperation Versus Representative Isolation', Dana D. Nelson gives a brief account of the relationship between Americans and the land, particularly referring to Crèvecoeur's 'new American man' and assessing Thoreau's references to slavery in Walden as providing a metaphor for 'a more broadly conceptualised argument about self-enslavement', where 'free men' are bound mentally to 'peer pressure and career recognition', in an American nation in the process of socioeconomic transformation from subsistence farming to competitive marketplace. Cecelia Tichi examines signs of material culture in 'Domesticity on Walden Pond', where items such as a table in the parlour with a copy of the *Iliad* placed upon it come to represent 'an artefact contributing to the composition of the middle-class, mid-nineteenth-century American parlor', where the *Iliad* is domesticated by its location on the table. In 'Romancing the Real: Thoreau's Technology of Inscription', Laura Dassow Walls investigates Thoreau's 'search for a foundation' on which to ground his vision of a heaven and earth united 'under one higher law'. She examines a particular alteration in his approach to writing journal entries in 1850, from a 'combination of workshop and storage shed', to a 'work in its own right', that would 'braid together self and nature through language, educing nature into discourse', a 'technology of inscription' that would translate experience into language. In 'The Theory, Practice, and Influence of Thoreau's Civil Disobedience', Lawrence A. Rosenwald focuses on the relationship between Thoreau's text and action, where the essay emerges as an interpretation of Thoreau's action, to be 'turned back into action again by its reader', listing such active readers of Thoreau's essay as Tolstoy, Gandhi, and, most notably, Martin Luther King. Robert A. Gross, in '"That Terrible Thoreau": Concord and its Hermit', looks at Thoreau in Concord, as a man 'not easy to like'. Thoreau's blunt outspokenness alienated many around him, yet at the same time, Gross argues, Thoreau, even though 'locked in a quarrel' with his Concord neighbours, was not an anti-social hermit, but 'a true son of the town', whose antipathy was directed at the 'false values' of those around him. As with other volumes in the Historical Guides to American Authors series, this collection concludes with a useful contextual illustrated chronology of Thoreau and his times and a valuable bibliographical essay contributed by the editor William E. Cain.

Louis J. Budd, ed., *Mark Twain: The Contemporary Reviews*, volume 11 of the American Critical Archives series of reference books, offers a selection of contemporary reviews, full-length critical appraisals as well as excerpts, also providing a checklist for those reviews that are located but not quoted here. Together these constitute a comprehensive account of reviews of Mark Twain's publications, dating from 1867 reviews of *The Celebrated Jumping Frog of Calaveras County and Other Sketches* to the 1917 reception of *What is Man? And Other Essays*. This selection is introduced by a useful, concise yet informative, historical overview by Louis J. Budd and should prove of interest to students of Mark Twain and those more generally interested in literary history. Joe B. Fulton argues, in *Mark Twain in the Margins: The Quarry Farm Marginalia and A Connecticut Yankee in King Arthur's Court*, in the Studies in American Literary Realism and Naturalism series, that the general view of Mark Twain as a writer whose fiction was formed out of personal experiences has been unsettled by the discovery of the Quarry Farm marginalia. This study offers a reconsideration of Mark Twain's writing process as involving meticulous research and design, a critical reconsideration that extends to include consideration of the more general debate regarding the constitution of a literary realist form. Fulton examines carefully the marginalia in Twain's copies of Carlyle's *The French Revolution* and Macaulay's *History of England*, and relates Twain's underlining of passages on infant damnation in Leckey's *History of the Rise and Influence of the Spirit of Rationalism* directly to the passages in *A Connecticut Yankee* which deal with infant damnation. Fulton's transcriptions of the marginalia establish that Twain's research specifically influenced the construction of the 1889 novel, and he illustrates his findings in an appendix which gives parallels between marginalia and novel. Aiming to provide both an analysis of the marginalia and a resource for further study, Fulton's work should prove to be of worth to students of Mark Twain's writing, to scholars of literary realism and to those generally interested in what makes a writer tick. In 'Mark Twain's "An Encounter with an Interviewer": The Height (or Depth) of Nonsense' (*NCL* 55:ii[2000] 369–98) Louis J. Budd examines the popularity of Twain's sketch, one of the best known and most often translated of the humorists' pieces, one that biographers have consistently interpreted as displaying his impatience with interviewers. Budd argues, however, that at the time the sketch was originally published Twain had not actually been interviewed, somewhat contradicting the received belief; he further contends that

'An Encounter with an Interviewer' should be considered a 'burlesque' on the empty form of the interview itself, offering an insight into the form and structure of Twain's own 'nonsense'. Budd's essay traces a history of the various translations of the piece, noting its broad 'transnational' audience appeal, an appeal that depends on the sketch's humour, which registers at a number of levels, and is able both to 'offend' and 'disarm' its audience. Twain's 'nonsense', Budd further contends, 'triggers a momentary escape' for the reader/audience, from the 'relentless tyranny' of 'discourses' which structure both social forms and identity. Henry B. Wonham, in '"I Want a Real Coon": Mark Twain and Late-Nineteenth-Century Ethnic Caricature' (*AL* 72:i[2000] 117–52), contends that Mark Twain did not take a consistent view on 'the nature of the self', and suggests that the 'ethnic caricature', which traditionally operates through the 'competing impulses' of 'substantiality or insubstantiality', of the self, offered to Twain an 'essential vocabulary' that would enable him to test 'assumptions about the nature of individuality in the context of late-nineteenth-century anxieties over a changing social and economic landscape'. Wonham situates Twain as a 'major practitioner' of 'coon comedy', but at the same time argues that Twain would have preferred to locate his own 'ethnic caricature' as a more 'authentic' mode, one associated with the 'romantic conception of the defunct antebellum minstrel show', rather than that offered by the 'graphic' version of standard 'coon comedy'. Twain's 'coon-era graphic comedy' is thus positioned by Wonham to be doubly problematized by the inherent 'racist humor' of the 'coon comedy' form itself and by Twain's participation in a 'narrative of irreversible cultural decline'.

In *Whitman and the Irish*, Joann P. Krieg examines, as the title clearly states, Walt Whitman's relations with 'the Irish', not only exploring his literary contacts with the likes of Oscar Wilde, Bram Stoker, William Summers and William Butler Yeats among others, but also introducing the reader to less familiar ground, the relationships that Whitman formed with the Irish communities in America. Krieg points out that the schema for this analysis is mainly 'geographical', although she does provide a usefully brief historical background and Whitman time-line. This account of Whitman's contact with 'Irish and Irish Americans' assesses his years in New York and Boston, focusing specifically on the presence of the Irish communities in 'everything that took place' in New York City, although Krieg acknowledges that there are many 'blanks' in our knowledge of Whitman's early years in Brooklyn and New York. Krieg then moves on to Boston, focusing on Whitman and the anti-abolitionist movement, with its impact on the Irish population in the region, and also revisits a well-known Whitman relationship, with William O'Connor, supporter of the poet at the time of the suppression of *Leaves of Grass* in 1881. This section also covers 'for the first time' an account of Whitman's friendship with another influential Boston Irishman, John Boyle O'Reilly. Krieg's study then travels to Dublin, where 'a coterie of Whitman admirers formed around Edward Dowden at Trinity College', a coterie responsible for 'furthering an appreciation of Whitman amongst Europeans', concluding with a fascinating account of Whitman's friendship with Ralph Moore, who was superintendent at the cemetery where Whitman planned his tomb, and the sculptor John J. Boyle, an Irishman from Philadelphia. This is a fascinating study, at times necessarily dependent on 'supposition' but nevertheless providing an intriguing reading of Whitman, a valuable source for the Whitman scholar and for the student of 'the

Irish' in America. This year, an expanded edition of *Whitman in his Own Time* [1991] has been published, which includes an introduction by Joel Myerson providing valuable background material and a discussion of new Whitman scholarship, claiming that 'few American writers were as concerned about their public image as was Walt Whitman', evidenced, as is widely known, by his anonymous reviews of his own work, designed to 'help his readers recognize the value of his books'. Myerson's introduction contextualizes the accounts, written not only by such literary figures as Bronson Alcott, John Burroughs and Henry David Thoreau, but friends such as Horace L. Traubel, newspaper interviewers and the doctor and nurses who attended him during his final illness. This is a practical guide for Whitman scholars, providing as it does information concerning not only his literary prowess but also his personal relationships in the context of his private and public faces. In his introduction to *A Historical Guide to Walt Whitman*, in the Historical Guides to American Authors series, editor David S. Reynolds locates Whitman as a 'most beloved and influential writer', whose poetry 'brought a radical democratic inclusiveness to literature', opening the way for the experimental forms and sexual themes of modern writers. In 'Lucifer and Ethiopia: Whitman, Race, and Poetics before the Civil War and After', Ed Folsom situates Whitman as a poet 'embedded in his times' in his attitudes towards race, being 'opposed to slavery' but also 'against equal rights for African Americans'. This analysis focuses on the 'Lucifer' passages in *Leaves of Grass* and engages with Whitman's poetry, particularly 'Ethiopia', in the context of Reconstruction. In 'The Political Roots of *Leaves of Grass*', Jerome Loving argues that although we tend to situate Whitman in his later years as 'politically "conservative"', we can locate, with hindsight, a significant contrast 'between his moderate political views', and the 'radical friends at the close of his life', which sums up what Loving refers to as 'Whitman's lifelong contradiction'. M. Jimmie Killingsworth, in 'Whitman and the Gay American Ethos', argues that 'Whitman's life history antedates the appearance of gay consciousness in modern life', and discusses Whitman's 'I Sing the Body Electric' in the context of the repressive hypothesis, arguing that Whitman was not alone in his dealings with sex 'in a forthright and even celebratory manner'. In 'Whitman and the Visual Arts' Roberta K. Tarbell places Whitman's poetry in the context of the 'architecture, art and artists of his time', tracing Whitman's experiences with art and architecture, and arguing that his interrogation of aesthetic ideals, which she dates from the 1855 issue of *Leaves of Grass* 'define avant-garde art and architecture in Europe and America thereafter'. Kenneth Cmiel, in 'Whitman the Democrat', while concurring with the popular opinion that 'Walt Whitman is America's democrat', argues that it is essential to consider 'what *sort* of democrat was Whitman?' placing the poet in the context of his Brooklyn background, culturally and economically, tracing the development of his democratic thinking from its artisan origin to what Cmiel considers to be the 'stale' *Democratic Vistas*. As with other volumes in this series, the collection concludes with a contextual illustrated chronology of Whitman and his times and a valuable bibliographical essay by the editor.

Books Reviewed

Appleby, Joyce. *Inheriting the Revolution: The First Generation of Americans*. Belknap. [2000] pp. viii + 322. $26 ISBN 0 6740 0236 4.

Barlowe, Jamie. *The Scarlet Mob of Scribblers: Rereading Hester Prynne*. SIUP. [2000] pp. 192. $39.95 ISBN 0 8093 2273 0.

Bell, Michael Davitt. *Cultural, Genre, and Literary Vocation: Selected Essays on American Literature*. UChicP. [2000] pp. 256. hb $48 ISBN 0 2260 4179 4, pb $19 ISBN 0 2260 4180 8.

Brown, Julie, ed. *American Women Short Story Writers: A Collection of Critical Essays*. Garland. [2000] pp. xxx + 368. pb £15.99 ISBN 0 8153 3587 3.

Budd, Louis J., ed. *Mark Twain: The Contemporary Reviews*. CUP. [2000] pp. xii + 660. £90 ISBN 0 5213 9024 9.

Butler, Jon. *Becoming America: The Revolution before 1776*. HarvardUP. [2000] pp. x + 324. $27.95 ISBN 0 6740 0091 9.

Cain, William E., ed. *A Historical Guide to Henry David Thoreau*. OUP. [2000] pp. viii + 295. £11.99 ISBN 0 1951 3863 5.

Clack, Randall A. *The Marriage of Heaven and Earth: Alchemical Regeneration in the Works of Taylor, Poe, Hawthorne, and Fuller*. Greenwood. [2000] pp. xiv + 156. £50.50 ISBN 0 3133 1269 9.

Doyle, Christine. *Louisa May Alcott and Charlotte Brontë: Transatlantic Translations*. UTennP. [2000] pp. 232. $28 ISBN 1 5723 3083 X.

Flannery, Dennis. *Henry James: A Certain Illusion*. Ashgate. [2000] pp. xii + 260. £45 ISBN 0 7546 0248 6.

Fleischmann, Fritz, ed. *Margaret Fuller's Cultural Critique: Her Age and Legacy*. Lang. [2000] pp. 278. £35 ISBN 0 8204 3952 5.

Fredricks, Nancy. *Melville's Art of Democracy*. UGeoP. [2000] pp. x + 158. £31.50 ISBN 0 8203 1682 2.

Fulton, Joe B. *Mark Twain in the Margins: The Quarry Farm Marginalia and A Connecticut Yankee in King Arthur's Court*. Studies in American Literary Realism and Naturalism. UAlaP. [2000] pp. xvi + 206. £29.50 ISBN 0 8173 1033 9.

Gale, Robert L. *An Ambrose Bierce Companion*. Greenwood. [2000] pp. xx + 334. £69.50 ISBN 0 3133 1130 7.

Hallock, John W.M. *The American Byron: Homosexuality and the Fall of Fitz-Greene Halleck*. UWiscP. [2000] pp. ix + 230. £16.95 ISBN 0 2991 6804 2.

Hammond, Jeffery A. *The American Puritan Elegy: A Literary and Cultural Study*. CUP. [2000] pp. xv + 264. £37.50 ISBN 0 5216 6245 1.

Hayes, Kevin J. *Poe and the Printed Word*. CUP. [2000] pp. xviii + 150. £30 ISBN 0 5216 6276 1.

Kalfopoulou, Adrianne, *A Discussion of the Ideology of the American Dream in the Culture's Female Discourses: The Untidy House*. Mellen. [2000] pp. 200. £40 ISBN 0 7734 7744 6.

Kennedy, J. Gerald, ed. *A Historical Guide to Edgar Allan Poe*. OUP [2000] pp. x + 248. £11.99 ISBN 0 1951 2150 3.

Krieg, Joann P. *Whitman and the Irish*. UIowaP. [2000] pp. xx + 276. £33.95 ISBN 0 8774 5729 8.

Lehuu, Isabelle. *Carnival on the Page: Popular Print Media in Antebellum America*. UNCP. [2000] pp. 244. hb £29.95 ISBN 0 8078 2521 2, pb £13.50 ISBN 0 8078 4832 8.

Monteiro, George. *Stephen Crane's Blue Badge of Courage*. LSUP. [2000] pp. xiv + 226. £21.50 ISBN 0 8071 2659 0.

Myerson, Joel, ed. *A Historical Guide to Ralph Waldo Emerson*. OUP. [2000] pp. xii + 326. £11.99 ISBN 0 1951 2094 9.

Myerson, Joel, ed. *Whitman in his Own Time*. UIowaP. [2000] pp. xvi + 348. £16.95 ISBN 0 8774 5728 X.

Obenzinger, Hilton. *American Palestine: Melville, Twain and the Holy Land Mania*. PrincetonUP. [2000] pp. xxii + 320. £38.50 ISBN 0 6910 0728 4.

Pippin, Robert B. *Henry James and Modern Moral Life*. CUP. [2000] pp. xii + 196. £13.95 ISBN 0 5216 5230 8.

Reynolds, David S., ed. *A Historical Guide to Walt Whitman*. OUP. [2000] pp. viii + 280. £11.99 ISBN 0 1951 2082 5.

Rowe, John Carlos. *Literary Culture and U.S. Imperialism: From the Revolution to World War II*. OUP. [2000] pp. xvi + 384. £15.99 ISBN 0 1951 3151 7.

Schirmeister, Pamela. *Less Legible Meanings: Between Poetry and Philosophy in the Work of Emerson*. StanfordUP. [2000] pp. xiv + 228. £29.95 ISBN 0 8047 3015 6.

Sizer, Lyde Cullen. *The Political Work of Northern Women Writers and the Civil War, 1850–1872*. UNCP. [2000] pp. 368. hb £33.50 ISBN 0 8078 2554 9, pb £13.95 ISBN 0 8078 4885 9.

Smith, Harmon. *My Friend, My Friend: The Story of Thoreau's Relationship with Emerson*. UMassP. [2000] pp. xiv + 216. £14.50 ISBN 1 5584 9293 3.

Spark, Clare L. *Hunting Captain Ahab: Psychological Warfare and the Melville Revival*. KSUP. [2000] pp. x + 735. £41.50 ISBN 0 8733 8674 4.

Tanner, Tony. *The American Mystery: American Literature from Emerson to DeLillo*, foreword Edward Said, introd. Ian F.A. Bell. CUP. [2000] pp. xxiv + 244. £15.95 ISBN 0 5217 8374 7.

Tintner, Adeline R. *The Twentieth-Century World of Henry James: Changes in his Work after 1900*. LSUP. [2000] pp. xx + 252. £48.95 ISBN 0 8071 2534 2.

Tracey, Karen. *Plots and Proposals: American Women's Fiction, 1850–90*. UIllP. [2000] pp. 232. hb $45 ISBN 0 2520 2523 7, pb $16.95 ISBN 0 2520 6839 4.

Warren, Nagueyalti, and Sally Wolff, eds. *Southern Mothers: Fact and Fictions in Southern Women's Writing*. LSUP. [2000] pp. 234. hb £33.95 ISBN 0 8071 2400 1, pb £16.95 ISBN 0 8071 2508 3.

Whalen, Terence. *Edgar Allan Poe and the Masses: The Political Economy of Literature in Antebellum America*. PrincetonUP. [2000] pp. xii + 330. £43 ISBN 0 6910 0199 5.

Williams, Roland L. Jr. *African American Autobiography and the Quest for Freedom*. Greenwood. [2000] pp. 154. £39.95 ISBN 0 3133 0585 4.

XVI

American Literature: The Twentieth Century

VICTORIA BAZIN, BARRY ATKINS, JANET BEER, SARAH
MACLACHLAN, MARGARET SMITH, STEVEN PRICE,
SHAMOON ZAMIR AND A. ROBERT LEE

This chapter has six sections: 1. Poetry; 2. Fiction 1900–1945; 3. Fiction since 1945; 4. Drama; 5. African American Writing; 6. Native, Asian American, Latino/a and General Ethnic Writing. Section 1 is by Victoria Bazin; section 2 is by Barry Atkins; section 3 is by Sarah MacLachlan and Margaret Smith; section 4 is by Steven Price; section 5 is by Shamoon Zamir; section 6 is by A. Robert Lee. The material relating to Edith Wharton in section 2 is by Janet Beer.

1. Poetry

This year's publications represent a variety of different critical approaches to the study of twentieth-century poetry. However, though there is a range of competing, even conflicting, critical perspectives here, certain familiar themes recur. Nature seems to be a perennial favourite, while much work is still being undertaken to recover poetry by women, the theme of gender continuing to be a topic of interest. Another important theme that seemed to begin last year with a cluster of publications on Southern poets concerns geographical boundaries. The intersection between regional and/or national identity and the modern and postmodern lyric is a significant development in studies on poetry. As important, though, is the discernible interest in the representation of racial difference in the work of canonical poets. What Toni Morrison refers to as the 'Africanist presence' has long been repressed in accounts of the American poetic tradition, but there are several contributions this year that acknowledge that presence, particularly when dealing with the work of modernist poets. Finally, worth noting in general is the presence of 'history' in the study of poetry, a willingness to explore the institutions promoting and publishing poetry as well as an engagement with the political dimensions of the lyric.

The themes of race, place and gender will be returned to below, but it is with the well-worn subject of nature that I shall begin. First, there are two books that take nature as their central motif: Bernard W. Quetchenbach, *Back From the Far Field:*

© *The English Association*

American Nature Poetry in the Late Twentieth Century and Tallmadge and Harrington, eds., *Reading Under the Sign of Nature: New Essays in Ecocriticism.* Interestingly, it is not to Frost's nature poetry that Quetchenbach turns when attempting to chart the development of nature poetry in *Back from the Far Field*; instead, he begins with the work of Robinson Jeffers and Theodore Roethke, poets who in different ways explore the relationship between nature and the self. These poets help the author to explain the shift that takes place in American poetry after the Second World War and that marks a return to what is essentially a form of Romanticism. With its emphasis on the 'self' as it experiences the world in all its immediacy, Romanticism and its attendant interest and investment in nature becomes the key to understanding the work of the three poets Quetchenbach examines in his study: Robert Bly, Gary Snyder and Wendell Berry. Inevitably, in the desire to map twentieth-century poetics, much is omitted and problematic assertions are made. For instance, while the author acknowledges the omission of Denise Levertov, he doesn't explain exactly why she is not included in his discussion when clearly 'nature' is so often central to this poet's work. Furthermore, the choice of Jeffers as 'clearly the most significant American nature poet of the first half of the twentieth century' suggests the author's blind spots when it comes to poetic modernism. While it is all too easy to play the familiar game of identifying those who are missing rather than simply engaging with the argument on its own terms, the issue of gender nevertheless needed to be addressed more explicitly; not only the gender of the poets omitted but also the relation between gender and nature itself. Particularly when discussing the later poetry of Robert Bly, the author seems reluctant to fully engage with the gendered nature of 'nature' as it has been figured in American writing.

Quetchenbach's decision to make Jeffers central to his argument might indicate that critics are beginning to recognize the importance of this poet. Certainly studying Jeffers will be much easier as more of his work is published. This year the fourth volume of Hunt, ed., *The Collected Poetry of Robinson Jeffers*, is available, and covers poetry written between 1903 and 1920, as well as some of Jeffers's prose and unpublished writings.

Reading Under the Sign of Nature includes a section devoted exclusively to American poetry, and three of the essays in this section deal with twentieth-century poets: Nick Selby's '"Coming back to oneself/coming back to the land": Gary Snyder's Poetics', Rachel Stein's '"To Make the Visible World Your Conscience": Adrienne Rich as Revolutionary Nature Writer' and Matthew Cooperman's 'Charles Olson: Archaeologist of Morning, Ecologist of Evening'. Selby reads Snyder's poetry in relation to the familiar themes of work, land and identity, but suggests that Snyder's representation of these themes is deeply ambivalent. Stein's reading of Rich's nature poetry suggests that 'nature' itself as it has been figured in the American poetic tradition is radically revised by Rich's feminist poetics. Cooperman's essay focuses on Olson's *Maximus Poems*, finding here almost a Whitmanian commitment to what is local and specific, as well as an attempt to provide mythic and universal structures of meaning.

Understandably, the theme of nature recurs in the publications on Robert Frost, as is evident in Wilcox and Barron, eds., *Roads Not Taken: Rereading Robert Frost.* Divided into four sections, 'Gender', 'Biography and Cultural Studies', 'The Intertext' and 'Poetics and Theory', a range of critical approaches are adopted and a number of issues are raised concerning Frost's more familiar poems and some of his less well known work. For instance, Lisa Seale's 'Original Originality: Robert Frost's Talks' examines recordings of Frost's lectures delivered over a period of five decades, thus introducing material that has not been dealt with before, while David Hamilton's 'The Echo of Frost's Woods' is a re-reading of 'Stopping by Woods', surely Frost's best-known poem. In the first section of the book, two feminist critics engage with the gendered aspects of Frost's poetic production: Karen Kilcup's "'Something of a sentimental sweet singer": Robert Frost, Lucy Larcom, and "Swinging Birches"' links Frost's interest in nature to the work of nineteenth-century poet Lucy Larcom, while 'Frost on the Doorstep and Lyricism at the Millennium' is Katherine Kearns's suggestive re-reading of the apparent divide between a masculinist modernism and a feminine sentimental tradition. In a postmodern reading of the lyric form, Kearns describes Frost's lyricism as an impulse that stands outside systems of categorization, suggesting that in this sense it is 'felt as "femaleness"' due to its resistance to 'the obligations and imperatives of the fathers'. The following section includes Lisa Searle's essay, as well as 'Frost and the Cold War: A Look at the Later Poetry' by Mark Richardson and 'Robert Frost's Philosophy of Education: The Poet as Teacher' by Peter Stanlis. Particularly interesting is Richardson's discussion of Frost's later poetry as it attempts to celebrate the American 'errand' while also being acutely aware of the possibility of nuclear holocaust. The section dealing with the textual traces of other poems and poets contains David Hamilton's essay, as well as 'A Tale of Two Cottages: Frost and Wordsworth', by Jonathan N. Barron, and 'Robert Frost's Liberal Imagination', by George Monteiro. The final section is strangely titled, implying as it does that the preceding essays do not deal with 'poetics and theory'; the bracketing off of 'theory' in this way is misleading. The opening essay of this section is by Walter Jost, and considers the 'Rhetorical Investigations of Robert Frost'; Andrew Lakritz's essay, 'Frost in Transition', explores Frost's nationalism; and Richard Calhoun's "'By pretending they are not sonnets": The Sonnets of Robert Frost at the Millennium' focuses on the tension between 'extravagance' and 'conformity' in these poems.

Two articles on Frost are worth noting. Peter J. Stanlis's 'Robert Frost and Darwin's Theory of Evolution' (*ModA* 42[2000] 145–57) traces the origins of Frost's religious and aesthetic beliefs, identifying a tension between the materialism in Darwin's naturalism and the spiritualism of Christianity. Stanlis makes a convincing argument against the prevailing critical view that Frost was influenced by William James while at Harvard; instead, he suggests that the work of Victorian botanist Asa Gray, a former teacher at Harvard, mattered much more to the poet. The second, Paul Giles's 'From Decadent Aesthetes to Political Fetishism: The "Oracle Effect" of Robert Frost's Poetry' (*AmLH* [2000] 713–44) supports Stanlis's view that Frost was very much influenced by nineteenth-century thinkers. However, Giles shifts his attention to the end of the nineteenth century and traces Frost's interest and investment in the decadent movement. After establishing Frost's decadent credentials, Giles then goes on to explore the poet's 'Cold War persona' as the embodiment of American values. This is an ambitious and original reading of Frost that recognizes his nineteenth-century heritage while at the same time locating him as a poet in the twentieth century.

Nature plays a significant part in Patrick Murphy's *A Place for Wayfaring: The Poetry and Prose of Gary Snyder*. As well as dealing with Snyder's early works,

Murphy includes a lengthy analysis of his most recent publication, *Mountains and Rivers Without End*. The first chapter provides a biographical overview of the poet's life, tracing Snyder's early experiences of living and working in the wilderness and also his interest in Chinese and Japanese culture. Emerging on the San Francisco poetry scene in the late 1950s, Snyder dissociated himself from the Beat poets even though he shared their enthusiasm for Buddhism. Much of his work is characterized by the motif of the journey and his desire to record that journey in his poetry. This idea is reinforced by the title of *Mountains and Rivers Without End*, which suggests the endlessness of that journey while also reflecting the apparent formlessness of the poem itself. Murphy describes this capacious work as an 'un-American', 'non-epic' poem, and compares its form to Chinese scroll painting. However, the more 'un-American' Murphy declares Snyder to be, the more American he becomes as he attempts to absorb everything into this *Cantos*-like poem. On the same subject, Tim Dean's 'The Other's Voice: Cultural Imperialism and Poetic Impersonality in Gary Snyder's *Mountains and Rivers Without End*' (*ConL* 41[2000] 462–94) considers these interlinked poems as 'art apprehending the otherness of nonhuman nature'. Clearly Snyder's epic poem needs to be read carefully and taken seriously, but Dean tends to read the poet as operating in a critical and poetic vacuum. Thus the adoption of the 'impersonal mode' and the Romantic absorption into 'the other' is not related to any previous poetic traditions. This makes Snyder seem oddly out of touch and even detached from these traditions when it is clear that his work owes much to the nature poetry of Whitman and the English Romantics as well as to the Native American, Chinese and Japanese traditions Snyder is so fascinated by.

The poet Denise Levertov links the theme of nature to matters concerning gender. Little and Paul, eds., *Denise Levertov: New Perspectives* begins with two essays relating to the issue of identity: 'Valentines Park: "A Place of Origin"', by Christopher MacGowan, and 'Denise Levertov and the Lyric of the Contingent Self', by Victoria Frenkel Harris. MacGowan traces references to Levertov's childhood in Ilford, identifying Valentines Park as the 'locus of memory, origins and dreams', while Frenkel Harris examines Levertov's lyric 'self' as pushing against the conventions of the lyric mode. In '"The Black of Desire": Eros in the Poetry of Denise Levertov' James Gallant considers the erotic and sexual themes in the poet's work, while Dorothy Nielsen's 'The Dark Wing of Mourning: Grief, Elegy and Time in the Poetry of Denise Levertov' notes the poet's break with tradition in her treatment of time not as the destroyer but as the creator. This collection includes over twenty essays, though most of these are quite short; it also contains a number of poems and personal recollections by Levertov's friends. For instance, Lucille Clifton's poem 'Some of the Bone Has Gone Missing' is the first contribution, Robert Creeley has a short piece simply entitled 'Remembering Denise' and Anne Waldman concludes her essay on Levertov and faith with a poem called 'Rapt' written in memory of the poet. There is a sense here of Levertov's recent departure and thus a reluctance or even an inability to really 'place' her as a poet so soon after her death. Thus, while this is a valuable addition to studies on Levertov, more sustained critiques will undoubtedly follow.

Poetic Epistemologies: Gender and Knowing in Women's Language-Oriented Writing by Megan Simpson concentrates, as its rather wordy title indicates, on a group of women writers operating in the wake of post-structuralist theory. While Simpson includes a chapter on their modernist predecessors, Stein, H.D., Riding and

Loy, the emphasis here is on the women poets who are currently engaged in the kinds of experiments in language that these modern poets initiated. Simpson's first chapter grapples with the thorny issue of 'women's writing', acknowledging that the category 'woman' is problematic yet also clearly finding it useful as a means of exploring issues she finds meaningful and important. By and large, though inflected with the discourse of post-structuralist theory, this is 'recovery' criticism in the sense that it is an attempt to name several contemporary women poets whose work has gone relatively unnoticed. While Susan Howe is now a prominent figure on the American poetic scene, as are Lyn Hejinian and Leslie Scalapino, the other poets Simpson discusses are less well known, particularly outside the United States. Thus discussions of the work of Lori Lubesky, Mei Mei Berssenbrugge and Carla Harryman are welcome introductions to American women poets who receive little if any critical attention.

Staying momentarily with Language poetry, Allison M. Cummings and Rocco Marinaccio's 'An Interview with Charles Bernstein' (*ConL* 41[2000] 1–21) gives readers an insight into Bernstein's poetic preferences. The poet expresses a dislike of 'tightly bound, aestheticized, very tasteful poetry', finding himself more interested in what is 'asymmetric' and 'off-balance'. His interest and enthusiasm for poetry online has its practical consequences in his development of the Electronic Poetry Centre, and here Bernstein suggests some kind of future for poetry as hypertext.

Another significant contribution to the debate circulating around Language poetry is Timothy Yu's 'Form and Identity in Language Poetry and Asian American Poetry' (*ConL* 41[2000] 422–61), which begins by questioning the apparent opposition between the experimental traditions of modern and postmodern poetry and the more representational poetry that seems to be wedded to politically marginal groups such as women, Asian Americans, Native Americans and African Americans. Instead of accepting this segregationist view, a view that seemed to be endorsed by Ron Silliman in his essay 'Poetry and the Politics of the Subject' [1988], Yu suggests that 'the impulses of Language poetry and of minority writing might not be mutually exclusive, but rather complementary'. Yu does this by first providing a neat and pithy summary of Language poetry and its theory and practice, and then going on to explore the work of some contemporary Asian American poets, including David Mura, Li-Young Lee and John Yau. Most fruitful perhaps is the discussion of John Yau's poetry as a site of constructive and creative conflict between these two poetic impulses. Yau makes use of what Yu refers to as 'ethnic signifiers' but at the same time he pushes 'beyond the boundaries of Asian Americanness as "fact"—by adopting the Language poets' conception of self as constructed in writing'. But, he goes on to explain, 'in hanging on to the emptied out structures of ethnic identity and history, Yau gains a foothold from which to critique Language poetry's attempt to incorporate the "marginal"'.

Several essays on women poets are included in Warren and Dickie, eds., *Challenging Boundaries: Gender and Periodization*. Susan McCabe's contribution, '"A Queer Lot" and the Lesbians of 1914: Amy Lowell, H.D., and Gertrude Stein', suggests that by acknowledging these writers as 'significant lesbian voices' the modernist emphasis on an 'impersonal, anti-Romantic aesthetic' is replaced by a poetics of 'desire and embodiment'. In fact, McCabe seems to be suggesting that the 'denigrated traits of emotionalism and passion' found in popular, sentimental poetry of the day can also be located in the work of these three writers. However, rather than identifying the influence of the sentimental on high modernism, McCabe suggests that in some way the position of these women as lesbians 'encouraged a poetics that often became overflowing, even excessive in its blurring of one thing with another: lover and beloved, self and perception'. Also included in *Challenging Boundaries* is Jacqueline Vaught Brogan's 'The "Founding Mother": Gertrude Stein and the Cubist Phenomenon', which argues that Stein's experiments in language are central to what she calls the 'cubist phenomenon' and, in turn, the 'cubist phenomenon' is not just one aspect of modernism but is the defining aesthetic of modernism. It is notable that Vaught Brogan's reading doesn't place Stein in opposition to the patriarchal tradition but instead sees her as central to it——a reading that Stein would have wholeheartedly endorsed. Finally, Sylvia Henneberg's 'The Self-Categorization, Self-Canonization, and Self-Periodization of Adrienne Rich' examines the ways in which Rich herself has determined the critical reception of her work through her prose, a strategy that Henneberg claims has stifled critical debate on this important poet.

Rich's contemporary, Sylvia Plath, also receives some attention this year in Rodia Mihaila's 'Technologies of the Self in the Poetry of Sylvia Plath' (*European Contributions to American Studies* 44[2000] 152–60). Mihaila argues that Plath replaces a Freudian model of subjectivity, one that implies layers and depth, with a Foucauldian model of endless surface images. Especially in her later poems, Plath rejects the notion that by recovering lost memories one can reconstruct a unified subject position; on the contrary, the speaking subject can only endlessly peel away images of her 'self' as it is constituted in and through language.

Two highly suggestive essays on Marianne Moore and Elizabeth Bishop also appear this year: Cristanne Miller's 'Marianne Moore and the Women Modernizing New York' (*MP* 98[2000] 339–62) and 'Picturing Pleasure: Some Poems by Elizabeth Bishop' by Marjorie Levinson (in Butler, Guillory and Thomas, eds., *What's Left of Theory? New Work on the Politics of Literary Theory*). Miller's impressive historical account of Moore's role in the 'modernizing of New York' considers the contribution women made in the arts in the from 1910 to the 1920s. Moore's editorship of *The Dial* is, for instance, considered alongside Lola Ridge's work at Broom and Jessie Fauset's editorship of *The Crisis*. Miller also analyses Moore's own responses to city life in poems such as 'Dock Rats' and 'Is Your Town Nineveh?'. Peculiarly, though, the essay does not engage extensively with the poem 'New York', arguably the most important statement Moore made concerning the modern metropolis. Levinson's essay, a thoughtful meditation on Bishop's poem 'In the Waiting Room', uses object-relations theory in order to grapple with the question of 'seeing' 'before there were objects to know or subjects of knowing'. Speculative in tone, this essay perhaps raises more questions than it answers, but it is successful in compelling the reader to return to this familiar poem and acknowledge its complexities.

Bishop continues to stimulate a great deal of excellent criticism, and Kelly, ed., *Poetry and the Sense of Panic: Critical Essays on Elizabeth Bishop and John Ashbery*, brings together two poets who do have much in common. It emerges that this series of essays is not so much concerned with the expression of a 'sense of panic' but rather the willed effort to control panic through writing. Thus the emphasis on formal restraint and linguistic play in the work of both poets is a consistent and unifying theme. The first essay, Mark Ford's 'Mont D'Espoir or Mount Despair: Early Bishop, Early Ashbery, and the French', suggests that both poets 'looked to France as a means of escaping the New Critical orthodoxies instituted by Modernism'. Joanne Feit Diehl uses a Kleinian pyschoanalytical model to examine 'the psychodynamics that inform [the poet's] relation to her own creative process' in 'Aggression and Reparation: Bishop and the Matter-of-Fact'. Both Benjamin Colbert and Helen M. Dennis explore Ashbery's and Bishop's work respectively in relation to the poetics of Romanticism, in 'Romantic Entanglements: Ashbery and the Fragment' and '"Questions of Travel": Elizabeth Bishop and the Negative Sublime'. Other notable contributions address the relation between Ashbery's work and Language poetry: Peter Nicholls examines the significance of *The Tennis Court Oath* in 'John Ashbery and Language Poetry', while Geoff Ward considers Ashbery's recent work in 'Before and After Language: The New American Poetry'.

In addition to Kelly's collection on Bishop and Ashbery is David Herd's impressive monograph, *John Ashbery and American Poetry*. Herd offers a lucid account of what might loosely be described as the 'development' of Ashbery's poetry from his engagement with the New York school to his later 'exile' in Paris and his return and critical success in the United States. Beginning with the first collection, *Some Trees*, Herd identifies a resistance to the poetics of new critical formalism, together with an inability to establish an alternative to that dominant poetic discourse. The second chapter deals with the self-conscious attempts of the poets associated with the New York school to distinguish themselves from their predecessors, and covers Ashbery's collaborations with Koch and Schuyler as well as the publication of the magazine *Locus Solus*. In subsequent chapters all Ashbery's major collections are touched upon and some of his most important poems, including 'Self-Portrait in a Convex Mirror', are considered in thoughtful and illuminating ways. Herd's central argument, that 'Ashbery has continually formulated the apophthegm appropriate to his moment' is an attempt to explain the poet's work not in materialist terms as a direct response to social and political events, but in intellectual terms as a series of strategic shifts that engage with a set of problems peculiar to a particular moment.

Barbara Malinowska's *Dynamics of Being, Space and Time in the Poetry of Czeslaw Milosz and John Ashbery* also compares Ashbery to one of his poetic contemporaries, this time the Lithuanian poet Czeslaw Milosz. Finding that both Ashbery and Milosz share similar epistemological concerns, Malinowska's study focuses on the Heideggerian subjects of space and time. However, much of the discussion is interrupted by quotations from secondary criticism that sits uneasily with the author's argument.

Turning now to work on the importance of region and nation in American poetry, one of the most significant collections on Anglo-American modernism this year is Davis and Jenkins, eds., *Locations of Literary Modernism: Region and Nation in British and American Poetry*. Part 2 of this collection is devoted to American material, but unfortunately in the copy I received a number of pages were missing in both Peter Nicholl's 'Pound's Places' and Lee M. Jenkins's 'Wallace Stevens and America'. In spite of this printing error it is clear that the essays collected here are all worthy contributions to the critical debate on Anglo-American modernism and the geographical sites it emanated from as well as the imaginary sites it explored.

While Geoff Ward's '"In the published city": The New York School of Poets' and Peter Brooker's 'Modernism Deferred: Langston Hughes, Harlem and Jazz Montage' operate to create a balance between canonical modernism and its marginalized 'others', Fiona Green's 'Locating the Lyric: Marianne Moore, Elizabeth Bishop and the Second World War' considers how two women writers respond to contemporary crises in their work. Green's essay is particularly worth commenting upon, not only for its elegant style but also for its well-judged and historically sensitive readings of both Moore and Bishop.

Also exploring regional poetry is Stanley and Thatcher, eds., *Cowboy Poets and Cowboy Poetry*, a collection of twenty-two essays on the folk tradition that developed out of the culture of cattle-herding in the American West. The genre of cowboy poetry is, as Stanley points out in his introductory essay 'Cowboy Poetry Then and Now: An Overview', a fusion of 'the verbal art of sailors and soldiers, largely English and Irish in origin … the songs and hollers of black cowboys and the corrido tradition of the vaqueros'. The book is divided into six sections, each helpfully accompanied by a brief overview of the issues addressed, making it user-friendly to the non-specialist. While the opening section is entitled 'Backgrounds', the essays included here are all in some way engaged in defining the genre of cowboy poetry. Thus Kim Stafford's 'Making Something Fine' relates this genre to other forms of folklore expression, James Griffith's 'Why Cowboy Poetry?' emphasizes the functional role of cowboy poetry within the ranching community, and Scott Preston links this poetic tradition to ceremonial and ritualistic forms of folk expression in other cultures in '"The rain is the sweat of the sky": Cowboy Poetry as American Ethnopoetics'. Other parts of the book focus on individual cowboy poets or specific themes. Probably the most interesting section, entitled 'Connections', makes comparative links across cultures in order to relate the cowboy tradition to other folk traditions. This section begins with Cynthia Vidaurri's 'Levantando Versos and Other Vaquero Voices: Oral Traditions of South Texas Mexican American Cowboys', and is followed by Jens Lund's 'Cows and Logs: Commonalities and Poetic Dialogue among Cowboys and Loggers in the Pacific Northwest'. Also worth noting is William Katra's 'The Poetic Tradition of Gaucho', which compares the Argentinian gauchos (South American cowboys) to their North American counterparts. The essays in this section suggest that American cultural identity as it has been embodied in the mythic figure of the cowboy is by no means exclusively 'American' at all.

Of the poets associated with the American South, Robert Penn Warren has attracted the least attention, but this year, with the publication of the first volume of his letters, Warren's renaissance might have started. Clark, ed., *Selected Letters of Robert Penn Warren: The Apprentice Years, 1924–1934*, is undoubtedly a major contribution to the understanding of Warren and his associates. This first volume contains letters dating from Warren's junior year at Vanderbilt and finishes when he secures a permanent position at Louisiana State University. Also appearing this year is David Madden's *The Legacy of Robert Penn Warren*, a collection of essays and tributes to Warren that argue for his importance to the American literary tradition. This association, the editors of this collection assert, has led to Warren's marginalization as he is inevitably overshadowed by the towering figures of John Crowe Ransom and Allen Tate. R.W.B. Lewis's 'Robert Penn Warren: Geography as Fate' seeks to read Warren's poetry in terms of symbolic and cultural geographies as well as the geography of place so often associated with this poet's work. C. Vann Woodward's affectionate tribute to Warren, 'Exile at Yale', is a largely biographical essay that speculates on the reasons for Warren leaving Louisiana State University and the effect this 'exile' might have had on his life and work. In contrast to this emphasis on Warren's southernness is John Burt's 'Robert Penn Warren as a Poet of New England', which explores Warren's poetic representations of Vermont. Rather different in tone and subject-matter is Lucy Ferris's 'Gynocriticism and the Masculine Writer', which seems in this context rather tokenistic but nevertheless adds a valuable feminist perspective to proceedings.

The racial dimensions of canonical poetry certainly challenge the Anglo-American identity of literary modernism, as several important publications demonstrate. While much of Aldon Lynn Nielsen's *Reading Race in American Poetry: 'An Area of Act'* is devoted to critical discussions of African American poetry in the twentieth century, there are a few exceptions that are worth identifying and commenting upon here. Rachel Blau DuPlessis's '"Darken Your Speech": Racialized Cultural Work of Modernist Poets' examines the ways in which white modernist poets consolidate whiteness through a series of masculinized tropes and figures. DuPlessis begins with a lengthy discussion of Wallace Stevens's representation of blacks in several poems, and then goes on to briefly examine the work of e.e. cummings and Marianne Moore. This collection also includes Nathaniel Mackey's 'From Gassire's Lute: Robert Duncan's Vietnam War Poems', which relates Duncan's work to the *Dausi*, an ancient epic poem from Africa.

Aldon Lynn Nielsen's work has clearly been important to Renee Curry, as is evident in her book on racial identity and poetry, *White Women Writing White: H.D., Elizabeth Bishop, Sylvia Plath and Whiteness*. The idea underpinning Curry's readings of these three poets is that 'whiteness' should be regarded as a racial category in its own right rather than operating invisibly as a neutral signifier of 'sameness'. Curry aims to write into her interpretative strategy a sensitivity to the difference whiteness makes to the reading of H.D., Bishop and Plath. However, some of the textual analysis is too literal, as in the examination of H.D.'s figurative use of the colour white in her early poems or the two pages listing Plath's use of the words 'black' and 'white'. More needs to be said concerning the contexts in which these poets were writing and how their own racial identities were circumscribed by contemporary discursive practices.

Paideuma 29:ii–iii[2000], edited by Michael Coyle, is a special issue on African American modernism which examines Pound's representation of and interaction with a number of African American writers. Kathryn Lindberg's 'Epic Gesture and the Syndicalist Lyric: Ezra Pound and Claude McKay' (*Paideuma* 29:ii–iii[2000] 11–78) offers a new political context within which to re-evaluate the work of both Pound and McKay, while Jonathan Gill's essay, 'Ezra Pound and Langston Hughes: The ABC of Po'try' (*Paideuma* 29:ii–iii[2000] 79–88) explores the correspondence between these two writers, referring to unpublished letters housed at the Beinecke. In addition to Gill's contribution is an essay by David Roessel, 'The Letters of Langston Hughes and Ezra Pound' (*Paideuma* 29:ii–iii[2000] 207–42) which also engages with this correspondence and reproduces many of Pound's letters to Hughes. C.K. Doreski's 'Reading Tolson Reading Pound: National Authority, National Narrative' (*Paideuma* 29:ii–iii[2000] 89–109) explores Tolson's responses to Pound's polemics as well as his poetry during the Second World War. While all the essays here deal implicitly with the question of Pound's racism, Burton Hatlin's 'Ezra Pound, *New Masses* and the Cultural Politics of Race Circa 1930' (*Paideuma* 29:ii–iii[2000] 157–84) makes this question explicit yet reminds the reader of Pound's interest in and engagement with left politics. A number of essays deal with Pound's use of the mask or persona, considering this in the context of the minstrel tradition in the United States. For instance, Kevin Young's 'Visiting St. Elizabeth's: Ezra Pound, Impersonation, and the Mask of the Modern Poet' (*Paideuma* 29:ii–iii[2000] 185–204) and Alec Marsh's 'Letting the Black Cat Out of the Bag: A Rejected Instance of "American-Africanism" in Pound's *Cantos*' (*Paideuma* 29:ii–iii[2000] 125–42) both consider, in different ways, Pound's use of mimicry and his techniques of imitation. Aldon Lynn Nielsen recovers a reference in Canto 95 that Poundian critics have neglected. In 'Ezra Pound and "the best known colored man in the United States"' (*Paideuma* [2000] 143–56) Nielsen pursues Pound's reference to 'Elder Lightfoot' and provides the reader with valuable information concerning this influential and charismatic religious leader. Finally, Reed Way Dasenbrook's 'Why the Post in Post-Colonial Is Not the Post in Post-Modern: Homer, Dante, Pound, Walcott' (*Paideuma* 29:ii–iii[2000] 111–22) links the poetics of Pound to Walcott's verse and in doing so raises questions concerning the relation between post-colonial writing and modernism.

Paideuma 29:i[2000] has much to offer both the novice and the expert, providing helpful commentaries on Pound's often obscure references (particularly in *The Cantos*) as well as offering new critical perspectives on the poet's work. The subject of Pound's translations are the basis of James Wilson's 'His Own Skiffsman: Pound, China and *Cathay* Revisited' (*Paideuma* 29:i[2000] 3–32), Line Henriksen's 'Chiaroscuro: Canto 36 and *Donna Mi Prega*' (*Paideuma* 29:i[2000] 33–57), John W. Maehofer Jr.'s 'Towards an Esthetic of Translation: An Examination of Ezra Pound's Translation Theory' (*Paideuma* 29:i[2000] 85–109) and Anna Xiao Dong Sun's 'The Man that is Writing: Remarks on Li Po's "Chokan Shin" and Pound's "The River-Merchant's Wife"' (*Paideuma* 29:i[2000] 149–63). The last of these is particularly worth mentioning as it provides the non-Chinese reader of Pound with an insight into the 'original' Chinese poems he was supposedly working from. Other essays in this number consider Pound's work in comparative terms: Bill Friend's '"All wandering as the worst of sinning": *Don Juan* and *The Cantos*' (*Paideuma* 29:i[2000] 111–31) compares Pound's epic to Byron's, while Stephen Sicari's 'Pound as Archaeologist: Reconstructing Nature' (*Paideuma* 29:i[2000] 133–47) compares Pound's *Rock Drill* and *Thrones* to Pope's *An Essay on Man*. Finally the familiar subject of Pound's anti-Semitism is dealt with in A. David Moody's 'Ezra Pound with Two Pronged Fork of Terror and Cajolery: The Construction of his Anti-Semitism (Up to 1939)' (*Paideuma* 29:i[2000] 59–84). Attempting to understand how Pound could produce something as sublime as *The Pisan Cantos* while also being responsible for the incendiary and highly offensive Rome radio talks leads Moody to return to the discursive frameworks operating at the time when Pound was beginning to form his political opinions. Greg Barnhisel examines the role of Pound's publisher, James Laughlin, in the critical construction and reception of the poet in 'Ezra Pound, James Laughlin and New Directions: The Publisher as Spin Doctor' (*Paideuma* 29:i[2000] 165–78) and Yoskiko Kita looks at the relation between imagism and the Japanese poetic tradition in 'Ezra Pound and Haiku: Why Did Imagists Hardly Mention Basho?' (*Paideuma* 29:i[2000] 179–91). Kevin

Arthur Wong's 'Blurring of Poet and Persona in Pound's Hugh Selwyn Mauberly' (*Paideuma* 29:i[2000] 193–205) applies linguistic theory to his reading of this well-known poem, and both Nicolas Z. Ambrus and Anna Kventsel offer new readings of parts of *The Cantos* in '"The white light that is allness": Ezra Pound's Cantos on Love' (*Paideuma* 29:i[2000] 207–15) and 'The Crystallization of Pound's Canto LXXIV' (*Paideuma* 29:i[2000] 219–31). Finally, A. David Moody's '"The Walk There is Good Poetry": The Missing Rochechouart Notebooks of Pound's 1912 Walking Tour' (*Paideuma* 29:i[2000] 235–41) uses archival material recently unearthed at the Beinecke Library to explore the influence Pound's visit to Rochechouart had on his early poetry.

The other significant contribution to Pound studies this year is Dennis, ed., *Ezra Pound and Poetic Influence*. While some might argue that Pound has received more than enough critical attention, it cannot be denied that his poetry, particularly that loose and baggy epic poem *The Cantos*, still poses unanswered questions. One of the more interesting essays here is Diana Collecott's '"This pother about the Greeks": Hellenism and Anti-Hellenism in 1914', which focuses on the debate between Pound and Aldington in 1914 over Hellenism. Collecott links this debate not only to decadent writing but also to the discursive struggle taking place at this time concerning the 'ideological and rhetorical crisis around the male body'. This is a historical moment when the male body is 'under threat from both military conflict and militant feminism'. Traditionally the Hellenistic aspects of modernism seem to encourage formalist readings of poetry, so Collecott's discussion provides a necessary corrective to this trend. Several essays deal with Pound's translations, for instance Helen M. Dennis's 'The Translation Strategies of Dante Gabriel Rossetti, Ezra Pound and Paul Blackburn', William Pratt's '"To have gathered from the air a live tradition": Pound's Poetic Legacy' and Roxana Preda's 'The Broken Pieces of the Vessel: Pound and Cavalcanti', which applies a deconstructive reading to Pound's translations. A number of other essays deal more explicitly with poetic influence, such as Stefano Maria Casella's study of Pound's debt to Alberino Mussatto, Giovan Battista Verci and Manilo Torquato Dazzi. Leon Suretti explores Pound's interest in the relatively minor poet Richard Hovey, and in 'Pound's Pisan Cantos and the Origins of Projective Verse' Burton Hatlen deals with Pound's influence on Charles Olson. Ted S. Blake examines the post-war public debate over the relation between Pound's politics and his poetry that was stimulated by Random House's decision to exclude Pound from their poetry anthology. As Blake points out, the controversy surrounding Pound is worth considering more for what it reveals about the post-war American mind-set than for what it reveals about Pound or the value of his poetry. Finally, Scott Eastman's essay on Pound, 'Modernism contra Modernity: The "Case" of Ezra Pound' uses the Leopoldine Cantos as evidence supporting his argument that Pound was resolutely opposed to modernity.

As mentioned before, criticism on American poetry is becoming increasingly preoccupied with the discursive frames within which poetry is produced and consumed. A poet whose work is so often considered to be resistant to history is Wallace Stevens. Stevens's poem 'Owl's Clover' [1936] has until recently been overlooked in favour of either his late, great meditative poems or his dazzling, elaborate and dandified early verse. As critics such as Alan Filreis have pointed out, the neglect of this poem in particular relates to a more general uneasiness, or even unwillingness, to engage with the history and politics of high modernism. What

Angus J. Cleghorn brings to the historicist approach to Stevens is a greater sensitivity to what he describes as 'the epistemological challenges made in "Owl's Clover"'. The main thrust of Cleghorn's argument in revealed in the title of his monograph, *Wallace Stevens' Poetics: The Neglected Rhetoric*, suggesting that it is the rhetorical dimension of language that, for Stevens, deconstructs the division between politics and aesthetics. In Cleghorn's words, 'Stevens' rhetorical poetry collapses the division ... between creation and argument'. However, this is not a book about one poem; Cleghorn offers readings of *Ideas of Order* as well as poetry written after 'Owl's Clover' such as the neglected 'Life on a Battleship' and 'The Woman Who Had More Babies Than That' as two responses to the Second World War. The rhetorical techniques of these poems are then related to 'Esthetique du Mal' and 'Description Without a Place', both of which Cleghorn reads as having 'socio-political objectives'. Turning to the late poems of the post-war period, Cleghorn identifies how Stevens pushes the lyric poem towards the epic in his appropriation of Homer's *Odyssey*. In poems such as 'Prologues to What is Possible' and 'The World as Meditation' Stevens creates a 'marriage' of sorts between the willing reader and poet/creator. Particularly when poetry is the object of the critical gaze, close, formalist and/or deconstructive readings tend to preclude a sense of history. Angus Cleghorn's study of Stevens proves that the poetry itself need not be neglected when dealing with historical and political concerns.

Mark Schoening continues the trend in Stevens studies to historicize the poet's work in 'Sacrifice and Sociability in the Modern Imagination: Wallace Stevens and the Cold War' (*ConL* 41[2000] 138–61). Schoening's fascinating discussion of Stevens's late poem 'Description without Place' identifies a critique of both American liberalism and Soviet communism that is expressed as a rejection of all forms of structure. Read in relation to post-war debates in circulation concerning the viability and morality of communism as a political and economic system, Schoening argues that Stevens does not do the simple thing and opt for liberalism as an alternative system. Instead, he adopts a 'programmatic scepticism' towards all forms of structure.

Axel Nissen's 'Perpetuum Mobile: Reading Wallace Stevens's "The Man with the Blue Guitar"' (*ES* 81[2000] 217–27) is a useful starting point for students interested in exploring Stevens's poetry, as it helpfully summarizes the critical debate on Stevens that has taken place in the last ten years. Nissen finds no structuring principle imposed upon Stevens's long poem, yet uncovers certain key concepts that serve to relate the various parts to the whole.

Two other articles that historicize the work of twentieth-century poets are Philip Metres's 'Confusing a Naïve Robert Lowell and Lowell Naeve: "Lost Connections" in 1940s War Resistance at West Street Jail and Danbury Prison' (*ConL* 41[2000] 661–92), and Brian Reed's essay 'Hart Crane's Victrola' (*Mo/Mo* [2000] 99–125). Metres's reading of Lowell's 'Memories of West Street and Lepke' begins by recovering the original contexts of Lowell's refusal to serve in the Second World War—a refusal that resulted in his brief internment at West Street jail. He goes on to offer an interpretation of Lowell's poem that relocates it in relation to the politics of paranoia in the post-war period. This, the author suggests, is a 'containment' poem, one that trivializes resistance to war, suggesting exactly how certain histories are erased while others, for instance Lowell's memories of his imprisonment, replace the committed activists' record of events. Reed's fascinating discussion of Hart

Crane is, as he acknowledges, part of a growing body of work on modernism concerned with its relation to the new acoustic technologies such as radio, the telephone and the phonograph. Particularly suggestive is Reed's reading of Crane's 'Lachrymae Christi' as a reworking of a popular song by Bert Williams, 'The Moon Shines on the Moonshine'.

Two more articles on Crane adopt distinctly different approaches to the poet's work. Christian Wiman's '"A New Mode of Damnation?": On Hart Crane' (*HudR* 52[2000] 253–62) identifies an ambivalent attitude to change in Crane's work, one that on first appearance seems to embrace the new social attitudes and art forms of the modern era but that with further reading suggests a flight from these aspects of modernity. Another essay on Crane, Ernest Smith's 'Spending Out the Self: Homosexuality and the Poetry of Hart Crane' (in Meyer, ed., *Literature and Homosexuality*), focuses on Crane's *White Buildings* [1926] rather than his acknowledged masterpiece *The Bridge*. This is largely a biographical reading that explains Crane's poetry as an expression, albeit highly covert and coded, of his sexual identity.

Libbie Rivkin's *Career Moves: Olson, Creeley, Zukofsky, Berrigan and the American Avant-Garde* is a fascinating study that maps the careers of various post-war poets in relation to the institutional frameworks within which their work was produced and consumed. Rivkin begins with a careful analysis of the debates circulating around the notion of the avant-garde, finding Bourdieu's theory of a 'cultural field' more useful than Peter Burger's account of the failure of revolutionary art forms. Thus she prepares the ground for what she describes as an 'institutional analysis of post-war poetic avant-gardes'. Rivkin's attention to the local and specific circumstances of poetic production means that she is often engaged in interpreting certain key events as well as poetic texts. For instance, she provides a thoughtful reading of Charles Olson's performance at the Berkeley Poetry conference in 1965. Olson's drunken ramble, often interpreted as the expression of a lonely and rather pathetic man struggling to appeal to a younger, hipper generation of poets and listeners, is here read more as an artful performance that successfully kept Olson centre stage. Rivkin is able to offer original and convincing reinterpretations of post-war poetry because she returns to the 'institutional moment' that allows for fuller and more complex interpretations to take place. Her subsequent examinations of the related careers of Olson and Robert Creeley, the renaissance of Louis Zukofsky in the mid-1950s and the role Ted Berrigan played in the formation of the New York school of poets offer fresh perspectives on fairly familiar poetic figures.

In keeping with this tendency to analyse particular 'institutional moments', Diederik Oostdijk's '"Someplace Called Poetry": Karl Shapiro, *Poetry* Magazine and Post-War American Poetry' (*English* [2000] 346–57) is an account of Shapiro's editorship of *Poetry* magazine between 1950 and 1955. Shapiro made it a policy to publish relatively unknown poets, thereby returning to the principle that the magazine should be devoted to promoting the work of new and emerging poetic voices rather than established figures. Among those he published were James Merrill, Adrienne Rich and Frank O'Hara, suggesting Shapiro's importance not only as a poet but as an editor with an eye for talent.

Another interesting if rather eccentric essay on post-war poetry is Devin Johnston's 'Resistance to the Message: James Merrill's Occult Epic' (*ConL*

41[2000] 87–116), which examines Merrill's *The Changing Light at Sandover*, a poem whose occult origins have never been taken seriously by critics. Johnston examines these origins, suggesting that the key to understanding the poem lies in its collaborative nature. He argues that Merrill's poem relies upon 'the occult underside of the Enlightenment' that dispenses with the stable and unified subject as guarantor of reason, replacing this unified subjectivity with a 'self that is no more than an aggregate of occasions'.

Finally, there are two publications that are worth mentioning but that do not fit into the categories above. The first is Ryan, ed., *A Difficult Grace: On Poets, Poetry and Writing*. This collection of essays begins with a wide-ranging summary of the social role of poetry from its origins in oral performance, rituals and chants to its current seemingly marginal status as writing in search of an audience. However, Ryan's narrative describing what some might see as the decline of poetry concludes by arguing that 'in this historical moment poetry seems both more anachronistic and more important as a custodian of time [and] preserver of bodily memory'. Thus while recognizing that other cultural forms such as television, film and the internet serve wider audiences, Ryan nevertheless identifies a role for poetry in contemporary America. The emphasis in this opening essay and most of the other essays here is on American poetry. Favoured poets such as Elizabeth Bishop and Wallace Stevens are discussed in relation to Ryan's own poetry in a friendly and informal manner. There is a suggestion of intimacy here as the contemporary poet speaks of those poetic voices that to him represent not simply a canonical 'tradition' but rather a network of close and influential 'friends'; indeed, towards the end of the collection Ryan includes extracts from some of his poems, deliberately inviting the reader to make connections between his own work and the poetry of his predecessors. The other and very important publication this year is Haas *et al.* eds., *American Poetry: The Twentieth Century*. This is an extremely impressive two-volume anthology that successfully brings together a range of poetry that includes not only the recognized and critically respected but also the marginalized and critically rejected. The aim is to produce an 'encyclopedic guide to the range of work produced in the twentieth century', and this is exactly what the anthology does. The oldest poet included is, rather surprisingly, Henry Adams (born in 1838), and the two volumes cover poets born from then up to 1913. This collection undoubtedly surpasses all others and will surely become a valuable resource for students of poetry.

2. Fiction 1900–1945

The healthy critical interest shown in Gertrude Stein in recent years shows no sign of abating, and in a year that otherwise sees many of its significant publications arising out of conference proceedings, it is encouraging to see a number of monographs published that take Stein as their central subject or as central to their thesis. Despite its title, Susanna Pavloska's *Modern Primitives: Race and Language in Gertrude Stein, Ernest Hemingway, and Zora Neale Hurston* concentrates its attention largely on Stein, and on a Stein whose primitivism can usefully be read through her relationship with her fellow 'anti-aesthete' Pablo Picasso. Concentration on the dialogue that took place as Picasso worked on Stein's portrait allows Pavloska to develop a contextual understanding of primitivism informed by contemporary developments in psychology and anthropology. Moving from a largely formalist reading of Stein's works seen through a Foucauldian lens to a more contextually informed consideration of a single work of fiction, Pavloska focuses most clearly on a reading of 'Melanctha' as realist text (somewhat problematically positing the 'fact of blackness' in the text), as centrepiece of the 'lesbian novella' *Three Lives*, and as a text that 'advances an implicit argument critical of the dominant heterosexual order'. As is almost inevitable when Stein and Hemingway share space in critical works, the links that are initially made between two very different expressions of primitivism are essentially biographical, and some familiar observations about the debt Hemingway owed to Stein are rehearsed here before Pavloska considers primitivism within the Nick Adams stories. This section of the study culminates in an intriguing reading of the notoriously ambiguous ending of 'Indian Camp' that is constructed through reference to Sir James Frazer's *The Golden Bough*. In that reading Pavloska manages the not inconsiderable feat of finding something relatively new to say about a much commented upon single story. Although this is a slim volume, such readings constitute welcome additions to the criticism of the individual texts.

A chapter-length discussion of Stein appears in Anne Herrmann's *Queering the Moderns: Poses/Portraits/Performances*, where she shares space with Amelia Earhardt, Beryl Markham, Virginia Woolf, James Wheldon Johnson, and an autobiographical consideration of the performance of self by Herrmann. As the subjects of the first two sections of this study might indicate, responses to flight act as a basic framing device here, and Stein's attitude towards the aeroplane makes interesting reading. In the section devoted to Stein entitled 'Modernist Interlude' her modernism is contextualized, as it is in Pavloska's study, through the painting of Stein's portrait by Picasso, although her primary purpose is a reconsideration of *The Autobiography of Alice B. Toklas*, and of the ways in which Stein undertakes the role of Daniel Defoe in constructing her 'own' fictional autobiography.

Kirk Curnutt, ed., *The Critical Response to Gertrude Stein* offers some insight into what its editor terms 'one of the most intriguing chapters of American literary history' through a selection of some 138 short pieces that trace a variety of responses to Stein. Many are review pieces charting responses to her work from the publication of *Three Lives* in 1909 to her death in 1946, but there are enough extracts dealing with Stein as somehow standing for all that was right (or wrong) with modernist aesthetics to interest an audience concerned with the wider questions of modernism and its reception. This collection is certainly intriguing in its tracing of a mixed and uneven response to Stein that, as is noted in the introduction, is often reflected in 'the American press's fascination with her personality and its absolute lack of interest in her writing'. For those who would forget the often baffled and hostile response that much of the work received there are plenty of reminders here, from Conrad Aiken's 1934 piece in the *New Republic*, where he declares Stein's experimentation within *The Making of Americans* to be 'linguistic murder', to H.L. Mencken's inclusion of both Stein and D.H. Lawrence in a 1923 *Vanity Fair* list of 'ten books or authors that bore me insufferably', because of his coming to the 'ineradicable conclusion that beneath all their pompous manner there is nothing but tosh'. Curnutt's selection is nicely balanced, however, and this work as a whole reflects the current recognition of Stein as a writer of merit, and traces the critical struggle to accommodate Stein as well as to simply reject her work. In a concluding section dealing with her posthumous reputation Curnutt adds a useful postscript of four essays first published in the 1990s that briefly sketch the current state of Stein's critical reputation. As Curnutt notes, such a selection from contemporary scholarship, with essays by Catherine R. Stimpson, Linda Wagner-Martin, Maria Damon and Brenda Wineapple, will inevitably 'fall far short of being exhaustive, yet by addressing Stein's aesthetics, lesbianism, ethnicity, her family relations and gender attitudes [they provide] readers an introduction to the focal issues of Stein criticism'.

Barbara Will's study, *Gertrude Stein, Modernism, and the Problem of 'Genius'*, tackles with an impressive authority some of those aspects of Stein's works and public personality that caused her early critics such discomfort. Stein's claims to genius, here, are not interrogated simply in terms of whether they might be substantiated or rejected as simply part of Stein's self-mythologizing performance. Will's opening statement, that 'Toward the end of the first decade of her literary career, Gertrude Stein began to realize that she was a genius', is just the sort of claim that would have provoked an Aiken or a Mencken. But this is less a volume concerned with Stein's reputation than with her art, and Will constructs a careful and theoretically informed consideration of what Stein herself understood and meant, not only by her realization, but by her declaration of a 'genius' that sees expression in dialogue ('talking and listening') 'encompassing a critique of the fiction of the author as transcendental (phallic) signifier and of the reader as passive receptacle for a fixed meaning'. In pursuing Stein's admittedly 'unorthodox' notions of genius she builds on the work of those critics who 'have suggested that the issue of Stein's difficulty or hermeticism can be resolved if we learn how to read Stein in the open-ended, processual, decentering ways to which feminist and post-structuralist theory gives access'. The readings generated from this position are refreshing, and often cast Stein in a new light. In looking at the work in chronological sequence Will traces the development of an idea of genius within Stein's texts that might shift in emphasis, but is ever present.

Another author who continues to be the subject of energetic critical debate is William Faulkner, and 2000 saw the publication of several monographs as well as the usual range of essay-length treatments of his work. Once again the annual Faulkner and Yoknapatawpha Conference provides a wealth of new material for the student of Faulkner's works, albeit in a form this year that presents a snapshot of Faulkner studies in America rather than a more thematically organized and directed collection of papers. Kartiganer and Abadie, eds., *Faulkner at 100: Retrospect and Prospect*, comes out of the conference held in 1997, the centennial year of Faulkner's birth, and many of the pieces presented here take the form of a wider reflection on Faulkner's reputation and place within the canon (a Faulkner termed by Donald M. Kartiganer as 'a fixture, perhaps *the* fixture, in our American literary constellation'), alongside a more obvious paying of tribute to Faulkner than is usual in such volumes. As is perhaps appropriate in a work that records such a celebratory occasion where 'Thirty five years after his death [Faulkner] looms as large as ever: revered by writers throughout the world [and] analyzed by literary critics according to whatever theoretical approach is currently in vogue', this is a text that offers a plurality of voices. Indeed, there are thirty-two distinct sections, and almost as many authors, present in the 300 pages here. In comparison to previous publications emerging from this conference, such as last year's tightly focused *Faulkner and the Natural World* (UPMissip), this collection is far more obviously a record of the event itself, with panel papers remaining in the necessarily abbreviated form such occasions demand and grouped together according to their original panels ('Why Faulkner?', 'The Career', 'Faulkner and America', 'Untapped Faulkner', and 'Response'). A 'coda' has even been included that gives full details of the Faulkner Centennial Celebration Program at the University of Mississippi, and a short list of international events to mark the centennial similarly makes this as much a document of a moment in Faulkner studies as a work of critical study. Of particular note among the slightly longer essays in which extended critical appraisals of Faulkner are conducted are Michael Millgate's 'Defining Moment: *The Portable Faulkner* Revisited', Carolyn Porter's 'Faulkner's Grim Sires', Thadious M. Davis's 'Race Cards: Trumping and Troping in Constructing Whiteness', and André Bleikasten's 'Faulkner in the Singular'.

Charles Baker's approach to Faulkner and his Southern context in *William Faulkner's Postcolonial South* examines the author and his works through the specific context of the single theoretical model of post-colonial theory. Baker's thesis is argued with clear conviction, and emerges from the basic proposition that 'If one considers the post-bellum South to be a conquered, colonized, and oppressed territory, one may then reevaluate Faulkner's works in the light of postcolonial theory.' In arguing his position, which might surprise some critics in seeming to call for the necessity of such re-evaluation rather than just its possibility, particularly when Faulkner is located among other writers emerging from regions marked by traumatic defeat and conquest, Baker presents a reappraisal of at least some of the works. In order to establish his theoretical and historical foundation Baker briefly outlines the applicability of wider understandings of the nature of colonialism to the example of a defeated South struggling to come to terms with that defeat. He then contextualizes Faulkner as only one writer among many engaged in the reclamation of a national voice, before moving on to a close analysis of the works. Baker, then, is explicit in the task he sets himself here: he is engaged in the 'application' of post-colonial theory, and moves inexorably towards his conclusion that in attempting to come to terms with a 'dubious' past 'no postcolonial author could offer more' than Faulkner. Baker is actually at his most interesting when he moves from the general to the specific, and particularly in his construction of readings of Faulkner against and alongside authors not often placed in such proximity. The range of authors covered in a comparative manner, including W.B. Yeats, Chinua Achebe, Ngugi wa Thiong'o, Salman Rushdie and Sean O'Casey, is impressive in its variety. If nothing else the comparative studies show a remarkable critical ability on Baker's part to make rapid moves between texts such as *Flags in the Dust* and Jean Rhys's *Wide Sargasso Sea*, or from *Requiem for a Nun* to Ngugi wa Thiong'o's *A Grain of Wheat*. Despite wearing its theoretical credentials on its sleeve, this study is often anecdotal in character, and makes for an entertaining as well as insightful read, although some might find the discussion of the fall of the Berlin Wall or the opening ceremony of the 1996 Atlanta Olympics a little uncomfortably anachronistic when combined with such an eclectic range of comparison texts.

A different William Faulkner, and one almost lost among a range of complex 'performances', rather than accessible through any one theoretical lens, emerges from James G. Watson's *William Faulkner: Self-Presentation and Performance*.

This study is loosely structured according to the chronology of Faulkner's life, but in its concentration on the slipperiness of locating a 'real' single subject beneath the masks of multiple performances provided by Faulkner it always avoids the possibility of settling into the formal constraints of a conventional biographical study. Connections are made between the details of biography and its intersection with the texts he wrote, but Watson is careful not to simply fall into the rather reductive trap of spotting and documenting correspondences. Instead of hunting for a single subject revealing himself (or not) within the works, Watson instead locates and examines a range of performances that see consistent reflection within the novels and stories. What one sees, through Watson, are glimpses of Faulkner's performed presence in many different media, as well as the importance of self-presentation and performance to so many of Faulkner's protagonists. This is a fascinating and consistently impressive critical study that reads a complex Faulkner who appears in many forms, in photographs, in the pen and ink illustrations that owe so much to Aubrey Beardsley, and in his letters and autobiographical fragments, as well as within the works. Some of the most interesting commentary provided by Watson concerns often familiar visual images of Faulkner, and his text opens with a consideration of Faulkner's photographic performances as dandy, Air Cadet, and war-weary veteran pilot in 1918–19, and closes with a late 1950s image of a patrician Faulkner dressed for the hunt. The account of life and work that forms the main body of Watson's study is similarly absorbing, however, and he combines an admirable scholarship with an accessible style that make this study a real achievement.

The extent to which Faulkner's fixed position within Kartiganer's 'American literary constellation' can be over-emphasized is touched upon indirectly in Richard Gray's *Southern Aberrations: Writers of the American South and the Problems of Regionalism*, and this study will be provocative reading for anyone interested in the more general issues that surround questions of region and representation. The middle section of Gray's study will be of particular interest to scholars of the period covered here, and it contains a useful and thorough account of Southern canon formation that argues convincingly for an enlargement of that canon. A brief and necessarily less detailed examination of some of the same issues can be found in Scott Romine's essay 'Where is Southern Literature? The Practice of Place in a Post-Southern Age' (*CS* 12:i[2000] 5–27) in which he asks the basic question of whether 'Southern literature [can] survive indefinitely in a parasitic, parodic relation to the ur-host, "Faulkner", or in some other purely textual form?' In a special issue of the *South Atlantic Review* (*SoAR* 65:iv[2000]) concerned with 'The Worldwide Face of Southern Literature' the extent to which the term 'Southern writer' can still be taken to equate with Faulkner (or at least Faulkner flanked by Poe and Twain), especially on the world stage, is once more evident. Of nine articles in this issue, four are directly concerned with Faulkner's international reception and translation, while several others rely on his almost totemic presence in their definition of Southern literature. In their introduction, for example, Pearl Amelia McHaney and Thomas L. McHaney point to the recent founding of three journals devoted to Faulkner studies in Japan alone, and Edwin T. Arnold's 'Japanese Views of the American South' (*SoAR* 65:iv[2000] 114–30) similarly notes the presence Faulkner has within Japan. Matti Savolainen provides a discursive account of Faulkner in Finland, in 'Fatal Drops of Blood in Yoknapatawpha: On Translation and Reception of Faulkner in Finland' (*SoAR* 65:iv[2000] 51–61), and Rosella Mamoli Zorzi takes on a comparable task in 'Italian Translations of Faulkner: The State of the Art' (*SoAR* 65:iv[2000] 73–89), whereas Pia Maseiro provides 'A Comparative Chronological Chart of Faulkner's Translations in Europe' (*SoAR* 65:iv[2000] 62–72). In 'The Russian "Fate" of Southern Letters, or Southern Fiction and "Soviet" Diction' (*SoAR* 65:iv[2000] 28–50) Madina Tlostanova provides an intriguing account of a Faulkner whose 'works characteristically were divided in Soviet Russia into those that could be easier fit into the scheme of dominant ideology and rigid limits of leading literary theories, and therefore could be translated and interpreted, and those suspicious experimental books that were better not to discuss openly'.

Several articles published this year deal with Faulkner as part of a pairing of literary texts or authors. Dan Richardson's 'Towards Faulkner's Presence in Brazil: Race, History, and Place in Faulkner and Amado' (*SoAR* 65:iv[2000] 13–27) points 'towards ways in which to approach the study of Faulkner's literary presence in Brazil', largely through a comparison between Faulkner and a Brazilian writer similarly identified with region, Jorge Amado. In 'Living With It: The Comic Valedictions of Faulkner and O'Neill, "Ah, Wilderness!" and the *Reivers*' (*SAF* 28:i[2000] 101–12) Eleanor Heginbotham draws on the close parallels that may be traced between two comic works that mark a late departure for both authors. Julia Leyda's 'Reading White Trash: Class, Race and Mobility in Faulkner and LeSueur' makes another comparison, this time between Mendel LeSueur's *The Girl* [1939] and Faulkner's *As I Lay Dying* [1930], suggesting, as she explores a paucity of scholarship in this area, that both texts 'suggest the historically specific ways in which poor whites are read as white trash in 1930s American texts' (*AQ* 56:ii[2000] 37–64). Also published this year, but unseen, is Theresa M. Towner's *Faulkner on the Color Line: The Later Novels* (UPMissip).

Although the only single-author study of F. Scott Fitzgerald to be published in 2000 is Linda C. Pelzer's necessarily introductory *Student Companion to F. Scott Fitzgerald*, the number and range of essays devoted to his work are more encouraging than for some time. Pelzer's text, as part of a series aimed squarely at 'the needs of students and general readers for accessible literary criticism', is itself an accomplished account well suited to such a purpose, and she covers the main positions in Fitzgerald criticism in an accessible but not overly reductive fashion. Her opening biographical chapter, for example, takes as its title '"Too many people": The Life of F. Scott Fitzgerald', and points up the contradictions of both the time and the author. She then proceeds to look at the major works in order of publication, and in doing so provides a useful overview of the reception and critical response to each.

In their introduction to Bryer, Margolies and Prigozy, eds., *F. Scott Fitzgerald: New Perspectives*, the editors map out what they consider to be a reversible decline in academic interest in Fitzgerald dating back at least to the demise of the *Fitzgerald/Hemingway Annual* in 1979. This collection of essays, which emerged from a 1992 international conference explicitly called to address this issue, certainly shows Fitzgerald scholarship to be in a healthy state in terms of the diversity of interests represented here. The collection opens, as so many collections dealing with writers born around the turn of the previous century do as the need to record memories and first-hand testimony becomes more urgent, with three personal responses: from Budd Schulberg, Frances Kroll Ring and Charles Scribner III. *The*

Great Gatsby, predictably, receives more attention than any other single work within the section devoted to the novels, with essays by Richard Lehan, André Le Vot, Scott F. Stoddart, and Michel Viel, but there are also readings here of *This Side of Paradise* (Nancy P. Van Arsdale), *The Beautiful and the Damned* (Steven Frye and Catherine B. Burroughs), *Tender Is the Night* (Dana Brand), and *The Last Tycoon* (Robert A. Martin). The diversity of critical approaches evident in this selection of essays also reveals the basic vitality of Fitzgerald studies claimed by the collection's editors. Viel's essay, for example, is an examination of intertextual allusion in French translations of *The Great Gatsby*, Burroughs reads Fitzgerald alongside Keats, Le Vot alongside Proust, Frye re-reads Fitzgerald's Catholicism, and Martin's approach is to examine the 'use' of history in *The Last Tycoon*. The third major section of the collection, dealing with the stories and essays, is similarly eclectic, with Quentin E. Martin looking at 'Winter Dreams', John Kuehl at 'Outside the Cabinet-Maker's', and Edward J. Gleason reading allusions in the *Esquire* stories. Both Barbara Sylvester and Richard Allan Davison concentrate on 'Babylon Revisited', and H.R. Stoneback revisits the Hemingway–Fitzgerald relationship in a fascinating essay entitled 'A Dark Ill-Lighted Place: Fitzgerald and Hemingway, Philippe Count of Darkness and Philip Counter-Espionage Agent'. The collection closes with Edward Gillin's account of Fitzgerald's relationship with Mark Twain, who draws some intriguing parallels between the lives, if not the works, of the two writers.

Several other essays published this year are also worthy of note. In '*Ressentiment* and the Social Poetics of *The Great Gatsby*: Fitzgerald reads Cather' (*MFS* 46[2000] 917–40), Robert Seguin argues for the presence of 'a kind of sublimated and softened form' of '*ressentiment*' (translatable as 'resentment', but given a Nietzschean emphasis here) in Fitzgerald, alongside what amounts to a study of the influence that Willa Cather's *A Lost Lady* had on the construction of *The Great Gatsby*. Two essays appear under the heading 'F. Scott Fitzgerald: Two Readings' in *American Scholar* (69:ii[2000]). In 'The Authority of Failure' (*ASch* 69:ii[2000] 69–81) Morris Dickstein charts the troubled reception and reputation of Fitzgerald, with particular reference to those critics of the 1930s who found him to be simply irrelevant, in the process mapping out a familiar story of early promise and eventual decline revealed as much in the mind of Fitzgerald as in the writing of his critics. James L.W. West III's 'Annotating Mr. Fitzgerald' (*ASch* 69:ii[2000] 82–91) provides a short commentary on editorial decision-making with regard to textual annotation from the general editor of the Cambridge edition of Fitzgerald's works. Two of those volumes edited by West saw publication this year, *Flappers and Philosophers* and *Trimalchio: An Early Version of 'The Great Gatsby'*.

The essay, and the essay collection, also dominate the output of Hemingway scholarship this year. Unfortunately, Jeffrey Meyers's collection of thirteen essays, *Hemingway: Life into Art* (Cooper Square), was unavailable for review, as was Norberto Fuentes's personal memoir *Ernest Hemingway: Rediscovered* (Barron's Educational; trans. Marianne Sinclair), which is published in English for the first time, but there was much other work of significance that emerged this year. In editing the essays for *A Historical Guide to Ernest Hemingway* Linda Wagner-Martin has provided an early volume in what promises on this evidence to be a valuable series from OUP, their Historical Guides to American Literature. While this collection has the usual structural apparatus of an introductory volume aimed at the student approaching Hemingway for the first time, with a brief biography, a chronology and a bibliographical essay, the individual essays represent something of the range of work currently undertaken on both the biography and the fiction. That the biographical essay has been written by Michael Reynolds, author of the most authoritative recent study of Hemingway, indicates the quality of Wagner-Martin's contributors. Susan F. Beegel adds to the work on Hemingway and nature so clearly voiced in last year's *Hemingway and the Natural World* (UIdahoP) with an essay entitled 'Eye and Heart: Hemingway's Education as a Naturalist'. Consideration of Hemingway and gender performance underpins both Marilyn Elkins's 'The Fashion of *Machismo*' and Jamie Barlowe's 'Hemingway's Gender Training', and both essays show a sensitivity towards Hemingway's historical moment that is sometimes lacking in such reconsiderations. Frederic J. Svoboda's 'The Great Themes in Hemingway: Love, War, Wilderness, and Loss' revisits some of those aspects of Hemingway's writing, and the Hemingway 'myth', that continue to fire the public and critical imagination. Perhaps the most intriguing contribution, however, is that of Wagner-Martin herself, who in 'The Intertextual Hemingway' opposes overly autobiographical readings by arguing that 'during the 1920s and 1930s particularly, Ernest Hemingway was pioneering in what has today become known as "intertextuality"'. She then traces allusion and correspondence between Hemingway and Henry James, and identifies possible sources for Hemingway's Spanish imagery.

Matthew C. Stewart's 'Ernest Hemingway and World War I: Combatting Recent Psychobiographical Reassessments, Restoring the War' (*PLL* 36:ii[2000] 198–217) first charts those psychobiographical critical approaches to Hemingway that would minimize the significance of his encounter with the First World War before presenting a persuasive case for the need to continue to take account of its 'profound effect upon the life and work of Ernest Hemingway'. An intriguing addition to what almost amounts to a distinct sub-genre within Hemingway studies which attempts to make explicit the often noted relationship between the literary and the visual within his fiction is presented by Max Nänny, in 'Formal Allusions to Visual Ideas and Visual Art in Hemingway's Work' (*EJES* 4:i[2000] 66–82). Nänny concentrates on how the 'whole idea of inversion brought about by war is also enacted by a *chiasmus* that organises' sections within some of the early stories (notably 'Soldier's Home'), and on looking again at the parallels that can be traced between Hemingway's writing and Cézanne's painting. In 'Rewriting the Self against the National Text: Ernest Hemingway's *The Garden of Eden*' (*PLL* 36:i[2000] 58–92) Blythe Tellefsen adds a coherent reading of the 'ghostly "America" haunting this novel' in an essay informed by some of the insights offered by psychoanalytic and gender theorists. Far more traditional in its reading of Hemingway's fiction is Creighton Lindsay's 'Hemingway's Nexus of Pastoral and Tragedy' (*CLAJ* 43:iv[2000] 454–78), which revisits the American pastoral interrogated by Leo Marx in *The Machine in the Garden* [1979] from a position of contemporary ecocritical concern to examine 'a curious hybrid of tragedy and pastoral' in a wide range of Hemingway's fiction. In 'Whiteness and the Rejected Other in *The Sun Also Rises*' (*SiAF* 28[2000] 235–53) Daniel S. Traber focuses on Jake Barnes 'as a figure of hybridity who mixes identities to avoid claiming allegiance to any one totalizing narrative', attempting to see beyond Barnes as anti-Semitic and homophobic to come to 'a more nuanced understanding of Hemingway's intentions as subversive'. Although essentially a review that summarizes work done in a developing area where Hemingway's name is constantly invoked, Bryce Traister's 'Academic Viagra: The Rise of American Masculinity Studies' (*AQ* 52:iv[2000] 274–304) almost inevitably looks to less nuanced readings of Hemingway when tracing the development of the field.

Several authors who might have been expected to generate critical commentary remain out of fashion this year. Modernism continues to be a subject of interest to scholars, and publishers, but the attention paid to Stein, Faulkner, Hemingway, and Fitzgerald does not extend, for example, even to such a substantial figure as John Dos Passos or to other writers who do not fit neatly within modernism's critical frame, such as Jack London and, to a lesser extent, Theodore Dreiser. Despite their enduring world-wide appeal among a general readership, London's works continue to receive relatively little serious attention. One of the snippets of information present in Claudia Durst Johnson's *Understanding 'The Call of the Wild': A Student Casebook to Issues, Sources, and Historical Documents*, for example, is that this novel alone sold some 6 million copies in the first forty-three years of publication, and 'is one of the most popular American books read in China and Japan and is the most widely read American book in Russia'. This work might suffer from its classification as a novel 'usually encountered in youth', and the only other volume on London published this year is Thomas Streissquth's biography *Jack London* (unseen, Lerner) which is aimed at a juvenile readership, but it remains perhaps surprising that so little attention is paid to his work. Johnson's text is also aimed at a youthful readership, albeit one engaged in the study of the text, and unsurprisingly only rarely approaches the novel with complexity. Although the critical interventions that introduce the individual textual and photographic fragments that make up the body of this volume are similarly aimed at a school-age audience, the fragments reprinted here are often fascinating, and might provide some useful contextual material for a historically situated reading. The range covers official testimony before committees of inquiry, newspaper reports on conditions in the Klondyke, excerpts from manuals describing dog breeds, guides to prospectors, and advertisements for equipment and services.

Theodore Dreiser is subject to more conventional academic treatment in Hakutani, ed., *Theodore Dreiser and American Culture: New Readings*. This collection of sixteen essays is the result of a number of academic conferences held over the preceding decade. *Sister Carrie* receives the lion's share of attention within the section on 'Essays in Criticism and History', with essays by Hakutani, Marsha S. Moyer, James L. West III and Kiyohiko Murayama, but more general approaches include consideration of Dreiser and celebrity culture (Philip Gerber), gendered labour worlds (Laura Hapke) and language and masculinity (Stephen C. Brennan). A second section, 'Essays of Intertextuality and Interauthority', charts intertextual allusions to a wide range of texts, authors and movements. Shawn St Jean, for example, looks at Dreiser and American literary paganism, Lawrence E. Hussman considers Dreiser in the context of both naturalism and postmodernism, and specific textual relationships are explored between Dreiser and Fitzgerald (Thomas P. Riggio), and Dreiser and Richard Wright (Hakutani and Robert Butler, who also includes consideration of James T. Farrell's *Studs Lonigan*). Another essay that will be of interest to Dreiser scholars is Joseph Karaganis's 'Naturalism's Nation: Toward *An American Tragedy*' (*AL* 72:i[2000] 153–80), which examines this novel not as an anachronistic product of turn of the century naturalism, but as renewing 'an older set of literary concerns about agency by way of a new literary engagement with the nation'.

Hildegard Hoeller, in *Edith Wharton's Dialogue with Realism and Sentimental Fiction*, seeks to redress the balance of critical attention away from the standard treatment of Wharton as realist writer to incorporate a larger consideration of her creative dialogue with the traditions of sentimental fiction. Hoeller argues that Wharton's use of both realist and sentimental traditions was never uncritical, and that she maintained 'a self-referentiality in her fiction' which can be exegeticized by placing texts such as *The Glimpses of the Moon* in contiguity with *The House of Mirth* so as to effect a transformation in the way we read both. Hoeller's reading picks up earlier critical claims that the former is a reworking of the latter, but reorientates our understanding of this relationship in declaring *Glimpses* to be 'the realist and satirical novel that *House* is not … without the beauty of Lily Bart's resistance and the alternative space of Nettie Struther's kitchen; it gives us instead the satirical vision of an empty world and its sentimental imagination'. Hoeller usefully surveys writing about sentimental fiction in both Europe and America, and concludes that the tendency towards excess inherent in its aesthetic provides an 'alternative and potentially anarchic expression in opposition to the economy of the realist vision'. She examines the use of the genre conventions of sentimental fiction in the stories and novels which have motherhood at the heart of the narrative, starting with 'Roman Fever', 'Her Son' and *The Old Maid* and culminating in a full and persuasive discussion of *The Mother's Recompense*. Hoeller sees these fictions as celebratory of female desire and motherhood but also devastating in their condemnation of marriage; it is here, she says, that Wharton most conclusively 'defies the economies of and the distinction between domestic sentimental fiction and Howellsian realism—both blind to the truth of female sexuality and self-fulfilment'.

Irene Goldman-Price's essay, 'The Perfect Jew and *The House of Mirth*: A Study in Point of View' (*EWhR* 16[2000] 1–9) is a re-publication of an essay first issued in 1993 in *Modern Language Studies*. It is a useful summary of the arguments being conducted on the subject of Wharton's anti-Semitism in and outside the novel, and includes good historical detail about the changing attitudes to Jews in mid-nineteenth- to early twentieth-century America. There are two other essays in the same issue, although they are less substantial than Goldman-Price's piece: in her 'The Significance of the Sawmill: Technological Determinism in *Ethan Frome*' (*EWhR* 16[2000] 9–13), Kate Gschwend suggests that the 'depiction of mechanical innovations' in the text suggests 'a deterministic belief in the progressive power of electricity, railroads and new management systems'; and in 'Marriage in *The Glimpses of the Moon*' (*EWhR* 16[2000] 13–17) Harriet Gold briefly makes a case for consideration of Nick Lansing as 'Wharton's first "positive hero"'. In her essay Goldman-Price refers admiringly to Jennie A. Kastanoff's 'Extinction, Taxidermy, Tableaux Vivants: Staging Race and Class in *The House of Mirth*' (*PMLA* 115:i[2000] 60–74). Here Kastanoff argues 'that Wharton's early fiction is profoundly invested in the imbricated logic of race, class, and national identity', and that *The House of Mirth*, rather than testifying to the economic and social vulnerability of Lily Bart, insists on the fact that the 'heroine's racial status is immutable' with race becoming the 'essentialist—if deeply problematic—answer to the cultural vulnerabilities of class and gender'.

Alice H. Kinman, in 'The Making of a Professional: Edith Wharton's *The Decoration of Houses*' (*SoAR* 65:i[2000] 98–122), seeks to correct the tendency of critics to dismiss *The Decoration of Houses* as a text which serves only to mark dissent from the tastes and standards espoused by Lucretia Jones, Wharton's mother. In so doing she demonstrates the influence of Charles McKim and the American Renaissance movement on Wharton and her co-author, Ogden Codman Jr., and makes the case that their work provided 'a bridge between the private world of domesticity and the public world of professional labors'. Gary Totten is also concerned with *The Decoration of Houses* in 'The Art and Architecture of the Self: Designing the "I"-Witness in Edith Wharton's *The House of Mirth*' (*CollL* 27:iii[2000] 71–87), locating 'an "architecture of self"', due to Lily's (and Wharton's) interest in aesthetic design and structural decoration, and the novel's place within a cultural context privileging vision's role in both the social construction of meaning and the construction of the modern subject'. Veronica Makowsky and Lynn Z. Bloom, in 'Edith Wharton's Tentative Embrace of Charity: Class and Character in *Summer*' (*ALR* 32:iii[2000] 220–33), seem eager to prove Lawyer Royall innocent of any imputation of lascivious intent towards his ward Charity, while pursuing rather confused notions of the action of charity throughout the narrative alongside the collisions of class attitudes between the author and her creation, Lucius Harney. Stuart Hutchinson's '"Beyond" George Eliot? Reconsidering Edith Wharton' (*MLR* 95:iv[2000] 942–53) is a severe treatment of the relationship between the work of George Eliot and Edith Wharton, a relationship in which Wharton is always held up and found wanting, via a demolition of the work of Cynthia Griffin Wolff, Elizabeth Ammons and Candace Waid, among others. In a much gentler piece, Robert Lee provides an entirely straightforward account of the translation from novel to film of Wharton's *The Age of Innocence* in an essay in Giddings and Sheen, eds., *The Classic Novel: From Page to Screen* (pp. 163–78), while Carol Singley, in 'Edith Wharton's Ironic Realism' (in Warren and Dickie, eds., *Challenging Boundaries*, pp. 226–47) tries something more complex. Her chapter is a wide-ranging discussion of Wharton's work which, in the same vein as Hildegard Hoeller, looks at her work in dialogue with a variety of traditions—sentimentalism, realism and naturalism—but viewed 'through the lens of irony'. As ever, Singley is insightful on questions of influence in Wharton's writing and makes a number of telling points about the relationship between the work of Hippolyte Taine, George Eliot and Wharton. Frederick Wegener is, as ever, intelligent, capacious and incisive in his essay '"Rabid Imperialist": Edith Wharton and the Obligations of Empire in Modern American Fiction' (*AL* 72[2000] 783–812), where he gives an account of Wharton's 'imperial sensibility' as one which 'fundamentally shaped her social and political views, some of the defining themes of her prose, her aesthetic creed, and her vision of American fiction in the twentieth century'.

Claire Preston divides her study of Wharton's major novels, *Edith Wharton's Social Register*, into 'Tribes', 'Outcasts', 'Buccaneers' and 'Expatriates', her intention being to situate Wharton's work 'within the early Modernist tradition' while making her chief and preferred points of reference the work of nineteenth-century natural and social scientists. Her chapter 'Tribes', treats, in the main, *The Age of Innocence* [1920], with additional reference to the novella sequence *Old New*

York [1924], as yielding a system of binary oppositions predicated as the linguistic and spatial systems which assist in the establishment of 'boundaries, pales, and margins'. The social framework, so clearly articulated in Wharton's expression of her own class background and manner of living, is the basis from which, according to Preston, 'the modernist sense of fragmentation is pitched as either terrifying or exhilarating', particularly in the novels of the 1920s. Darwinian theory is convincingly pressed into service in 'Outcasts', *The House of Mirth* being designated as the location of the 'non-viable mutation'—Lily Bart—and *The Mother's Recompense* the text in which Wharton tests the limits of social tolerance for the 'reconditioned malefactor'. The discussion of *The Custom of the Country* as a 'buccaneer' novel works well, especially in terms of the triumph of style over substance which is the 'buccaneer house', offered here as 'a megalomaniac's text', while the final chapter, 'Expatriates', makes an honest attempt to unravel the long-term effects, both personal and professional, of Wharton's own move to France.

3. Fiction since 1945

(a) General

In *Southern Aberrations* (also noticed above) Richard Gray explores the idea of regionalism in relation to the work of a range of Southern writers who, rather than reinforcing conventional notions of Southern identity and culture, have problematized their relationship to the region, and by extension representations of the South, as a separate, undifferentiated entity. Gray's use of the term 'aberration' points to perceptions of Southern literature as different to national literature, as well as to the ways in which the Southern writers he attends to differ from a regional 'mainstream'. Writers discussed include Edgar Allan Poe, Ellen Glasgow, the Nashville Agrarians and Erskine Caldwell, and—of particular interest in this section—a lesser-known tradition of Southern mountain- and river-writing between the two world wars 'and beyond', as well as a range of contemporary Southern writers such as Blanche McCrary Boyd, Harry Crews, Dorothy Allison, Jayne Anne Phillips, Ellen Gilchrist, Alice Walker, Ishmael Reed, Bobbie Ann Mason, Richard Ford and Cormac McCarthy. Widening conventional notions of the Southern canon to include a large number of little-known writers, Gray reveals how, rather than reinforcing a protective notion of the region's identity, many Southern writers might more productively be read as engaged in an ongoing reinvention of the South, one which opposes the idea that it is imprisoned by the past. With reference to a range of mountain- and river-writing, Gray discusses marginal writers and locations in the South as crucial to an understanding of the region's diversity. His study is underpinned by a range of critical theories, from the materialist to the post-colonial; drawing on Said's study of 'Orientalism' Gray interrogates the ways in which the South is essentialized by generalizations which position it as the nation's inferior 'other', an anti-historical approach which fixes the South in a static position of deviance from the national 'norm'. For Gray, the South is too often 'othered' by easy definitions of regional homogeneity, and he states that 'attention needs to be paid to these tales of hinterland and highland, poor rural people and mountain folk, as a special and especially powerful branch of Southern literature', pointing out that it is a tradition which reveals the existence of difference *within* the South, a recognition which complicates definitions of the region as a single cultural entity and, by extension, its marginalization as such. Gray refers back and forth within the tradition of Southern writing, but is interested in the ways in which contemporary Southern writing responds to the climate in which the notion of a separate and distinctive South is increasingly questioned; the ways in which contemporary Southern writers 'engage with the logic of late capitalism' to interrogate what might be distinctively Southern. Charting the South's recent economic rise, its growth as the 'sunbelt' and its transition from Democrat to Republican stronghold, Gray argues that a new myth of blanket prosperity in the South 'prescribes a model for understanding recent social change in the region which is just as monolithic and disturbingly unitary' as earlier models of the Southern past. Tourism in the South has become a kind of commodification which turns an image, or 'legend' of the South into a product, and for Gray such forces ignore the fact that the South is made up of often antagonistic forces, of cultures, not culture, and that the process of remembering encouraged by tourism is actually a process of forgetting. In his study of contemporary Southern writing his emphasis is on 'variance and pluralism: how a culture resists, continually defines itself against other cultures, and is made up of resistances, conflicting interests, and internal differences'. Ultimately, Gray posits that in Southern writing marginal or aberrant figures prove to be central: 'the supposedly marginal figure, as it turns out, is the seminal one—and the closest thing the South has to a centre, or is ever likely to have'. The South's only distinctive community turns out to be one based upon difference or aberration.

In their introduction to *The World is our Home: Society and Culture in Contemporary Southern Writing*, editors Jeffrey J. Folks and Nancy Summers Folks emphasize the need to recognize the 'many worlds' of the contemporary South. The collection is driven by an attempt to situate Southern writing since the early 1970s in relation to economic and social change in the region. The editors state that the object of the collection is to understand 'the ways in which southern writers have registered and interpreted this process of change' to allow a 'better grasp of the South's relationship to larger social developments in the national and international culture'. As in Gray's study the emphasis is very much upon difference within the South, and the editors seek to redress a balance between those groups represented by the traditional Southern canon and minority writing, prioritizing texts which situate their concerns at the intersection between issues of class, race and gender. In 'Competing Histories: William Styron's *The Confessions of Nat Turner* and Sherley Ann Williams' *Dessa Rose*', Susan Goodman compares two competing views of the Southern past to explore the ways in which fiction mediates history. In '"Trouble" in Muskhogean County: The Social History of a Southern Community in the Fiction of Raymond Andrews', Jeffrey J. Folks attends to Andrews's documentation of the evolution of race relations in the South before and during the civil rights era. In 'Transcendence in the House of the Dead: The Subversive Gaze of *A Lesson Before Dying*' John Lowe connects Ernest Gaines's objectives in this novel with contemporary issues of racial justice, drawing on Foucault's work to discuss the mechanisms of control which create and survey a racial underclass in America. In 'Gender and Justice: Alice Walker and the Sexual Politics of Civil Rights', Keith Byerman argues that issues of race in the civil rights struggle were inflected through discourses of gender, while Suzanne W. Jones, in 'New Narratives of Southern Manhood: Race, Masculinity and Closure in Ernest Gaines' Fiction', is similarly focused on the ways in which Southern codes of masculinity were formed in relation to racial conflict. In 'Making Peace with the (M)other', Barbara Bennett explores the fiction of mother–daughter relationships in Jill McCorkles's *Ferris Beach*, Tina McElroy Ansa's *Ugly Ways* and Josephine Humphreys's *Rich in Love*. Also focused on maternal roles in recent Southern fiction is Linda J. Byrd's 'Toward Healing the Split: Lee Smith's *Fancy Strut* and *Black Mountain Breakdown*'. In '"The Politics of *They*": Dorothy Allison's *Bastard Out of Carolina*', Moira P. Baker discusses the ways in which constructions of gender and sexuality overlap with 'white trash' images of transgression, such as illegitimacy and incest. Other writers discussed in the remaining essays, with reference to religion, the West in the Southern imagination, memory and postmodernity, include Sheila Bosworth, Jayne Anne Phillips, Walker Percy, Frederick Barthelme, Kaye Gibbons, James Lee Burke, Horton Foote and Richard Ford. Also of interest regarding Richard Ford, but not received for review, is Huey Guagliardo, ed., *Perspectives on Richard Ford* (UPMissip).

Middleton and Woods, eds., *Literatures of Memory: History, Time and Space in Postwar Writing*, investigates representations of the past in contemporary British and American literature. Middleton and Woods ask, 'What are the cultural poetics of history revealed in post war literature?' They accept that memory, both public and private, plays such a large part in this cultural poetics that the 'framing axioms of literary historicism are commonly represented by the texts themselves as forms of memory'. In citing initially Toni Morrison's *Beloved* as a historical novel that firmly places the slavery experience and its ever-extending consequences for global society in a public culture, Middleton and Woods underline their principle that memory is commonly used strategically as a narrative device. *Beloved*, using the discourse of trauma and displacement, forces its protagonists to reconstruct, from the association of individual narratives, what they do not want to remember, creating an area of collective consciousness that public culture itself wants to forget, a process they term 'a public form of reluctant anamnesis'. Each chapter in the second half of the book is concerned with a specific genre, including drama, poetry and popular fiction, in which, Middleton and Woods claim, history has 'been radically reinvented'. Of particular interest is the chapter on 'Fictional Cities and Urban Spaces: Contemporary Fiction and Representations of the City', which is directed by Michel Foucault's invitation to historicize space. To explore post-Second World War fictional representations of the city and consider the disappearance of history the authors focus on Joan Didion's novel *Play It As It Lays*, along with the work of other writers, including Paul Auster, Don DeLillo and Thomas Pynchon, and Jay McInerney's novels *Brightness Falls* and *Bright Lights Big City*. Such texts explore the 'social and cultural edifices of the yuppie explosion' apparent during the 1980s, McInerney's texts being of particular use as a vehicle for developing the 'social contradictions and disintegrated individualism of New York where people's aspirations are literally embedded in the spires of Wall Street'. Chapter 7, 'Histories of the Future: American Science Fiction after the Second World War', analyses passages and examples from well-known writers that exemplify popular perceptions of the genre and how its relationship to the present, as well as the past, is constituted.

In *Capital, Class and Technology in Contemporary American Culture: Projecting Post-Fordism*, Nick Heffernan addresses the trend towards an understanding of recent social development in relation to the terms 'postmodernism' and 'postmodernity', attempting to relocate debates about structural change ('historic transformations of the ways our lives are organized and shaped economically, socially and culturally') within the framework of contemporary capitalism as it has developed since 1945. Heffernan draws on an impressive theoretical framework and offers a comprehensive account of, as well as critical engagement with, the development of Fordism and the emergence of new technologies. The text provides an important contextual background for post-1945 fiction and makes reference to a wide range of writers such as Douglas Coupland, Don DeLillo, Joan Didion, E.L. Doctorow, William Gibson, Norman Mailer and Thomas Pynchon.

Kenneth Millard, *Contemporary Fiction: An Introduction to American Fiction since 1970*, is a welcome addition to studies of contemporary American fiction, joining and enhancing works such as Tony Tanner's *City of Words: American Fiction, 1950–1970* (Cape [1971]). Millard provides detailed readings of texts by thirty different writers, including established authors such as Philip Roth and John Updike, but the book concentrates on younger writers such as Gish Jen and Chang-Rae Lee, who now bear the 'marks of their elders'. For example, Millard cites the influence of Thomas Pynchon on Don DeLillo while making the point that Pynchon's work, and that of most of those writers Tanner considered, such as Malamud, Bellow, Vonnegut, Burroughs and Heller, now belongs to an 'earlier period'. For Millard only Roth and Updike survive, through *American Pastoral* [1997] and *Memories of the Ford Administration* [1992] respectively, and he designates 'contemporary' in general to mean fiction produced since 1970. Authors and their work considered include Toni Morrison's *The Bluest Eye*, Jay McInerney's *Bright Lights, Big City*, Bobbie Ann Mason's *In Country*, Jayne Anne Phillips's *Machine Dreams*, three novels by Don DeLillo (*White Noise*, *Mao II* and *Underworld*); these are considered alongside E.L. Doctorow's *Ragtime*, and Po Bronson's *Bombardiers*. DeLillo's *End Zone* is also discussed in the chapter entitled 'Sport'. Overall, this book offers a good introduction to, and readings of, contemporary American writing that attempts to address the central issues of American life through the fictional form.

Andrew Pepper, *The Contemporary American Crime Novel: Race, Ethnicity, Gender, Class*, undertakes to trace the radical and 'explosive transformation that America's ethnic and racial character has undergone', and as such offers a 'comprehensive overview' of how America's multicultural diversity has created an ever-changing cultural landscape that in turn has transformed the codes and conventions within the crime novel. Chapter 1 discusses some of the more significant generic changes, ushered in by the changing face of crime writing in the emerging school of 'American hard-boiled crime writers' of the inter-war years, which according to Pepper engineered a dramatic shift in the way crime was represented and perceived. The classic perception of crime in the detective fiction of Christie and Sayers as 'the product of occasional and atypical tears in the otherwise secure moral fabric of genteel English society' was supplanted by a 'bastard offspring of an urban fuelled modernity'. Following this reconfiguration of the American crime novel, Pepper undertakes to expose how, traditionally, whiteness has striven to conceal itself; to pass itself off as a 'universal marker of cultural worth'; to legitimize the various ways in which white power is gained and secured, and to call into question other strategies of domination now outmoded in America's multicultural society. In relation to this theme Pepper considers the growing corpus of work produced by African American, female, gay, lesbian, and Asian American crime writers in parallel with the already established white, male 'hard-boiled' school of crime fiction. This book also takes into account the 'complicating factors' of gender, sexuality and class in the construction and reconstruction of identity. Authors featured include James Ellroy, James Lee Burke, Barbara Wilson, Faye Kellerman, Walter Mosley and Chang-Rae Lee.

Jon Roper's *The American Presidents: Heroic Leadership from Kennedy to Clinton* uses a wide variety of contemporary film and literary sources, against a backdrop of key contemporary events, to analyse and discuss 'the development of the character of the contemporary presidency during a turbulent period in its history'. Norman Mailer, whose literary output is central to Roper's argument, is seen as both a 'provocative critic and creative commentator' in novels such as *An American Dream* [1965] and *Harlot's Ghost* [1991]. In *Why Are We in Vietnam?* [1967], Mailer presents a caricature of Lyndon Johnson in which he explores the psychological pressures that drive the presidency as the nation moves towards war in Vietnam. Appraising the development of the contemporary presidency, Roper elects Richard Nixon as the 'trickster' who, through his participation in the Watergate scandal, finally destroyed any notion of heroic leadership in the presidential role. Roper includes Philip Roth's satirical view of the presidential protagonist Tricky Dixon of *Our Gang* [1971] as an indication of Nixon's 'doublespeak'. Although written before the events that would become the Watergate scandal, *Our Gang* describes an absurd crisis during the Dixon administration, a revolution by the Boy Scouts of America, which leads to the disgrace of his presidency and terminates in his assassination. There are other chapters on Gerald Ford and Jimmy Carter as Faith Healers, Ronald Reagan as Star, George Bush as Deputy, and Bill Clinton as Survivor.

David A. Oakes discusses how the work of three writers exemplifies the way in which Gothic fiction functions 'as cultural artefact and how science and technology destabilize readers' in *Science and Destabilization in the Modern American Gothic: Lovecraft, Matheson and King*. He aims to show how the fiction of H.P. Lovecraft, Richard Matheson, and Stephen King questions the work of scientists and their quest for knowledge, explores the possibility of the 'frightening revelations' arising from their scientific quest and underlines the fragility of identity in a technologically complex modern society. Oakes explains that the word 'Gothic' possessed two conflicting meanings in the eighteenth century, the negative connotations of something that 'appeared dark and barbarous' contrasting with its later literary signification of a 'valuable imaginative freedom as opposed to classical servility and modern mechanical reproduction', the friction between the two meanings destabilizing early examples of the Gothic novel. Matheson's fiction is seen as a vision of an immensely complex world populated by protagonists who feel the 'sense of anxiety' that arises from living with a fear of the unknown created in a world in which the complexities of science and technology are difficult to grasp, isolating from the main body of humanity those who do understand and consequently appear oblivious to the concerns and problems of other people. These Gothic concerns are studied in *The Shrinking Man* [1956], *Hell House* [1971] and various stories, including 'Nightmare at 20,000 Feet', which draws on 'a phobic pressure point' concerning aeroplanes, the fear of mechanical malfunction reflecting the areas of danger outside human control. Stephen King's fiction displays the fear that scientific advances will radically change people's lives, stemming from his critical reading of *Danse Macabre* [1981] in which King outlines three major contemporary fears: radiation and nuclear power, ecological problems and environmental issues, and the nagging fear that machines will escape human control, areas that govern, Oakes maintains, the deepest fears within American society.

Jonathan Freedman notes, in *The Temple of Culture: Assimilation and Anti-Semitism in Literary-Anglo America*, that although Cynthia Ozick and Philip Roth are very 'differently positioned' figures, both are 'imaginatively attuned' to the writing of Henry James. Freedman assesses how Jewish assimilation has become intertwined with the 'idiom' of culture and how they might work in 'tandem' with each other, a process he refers to as assimilation-by-culture. Roth frequently invokes a side of James that is conspicuously absent from the accounts of either the 'James-philes' or Jamesian critics: James was led to his own 'spates' of anti-Semitism in the 'construction of the Jew as a false double for the perverse artist'. Freedman illustrates this literary connection between the two authors in discussing Roth's 'deeply Jamesian' *The Ghost Writer* [1979], while in Freedman's opinion Ozick consistently establishes herself as a Jewish writer alongside a career-long obsession with the example of James, against which, Freedman concludes, she continues to define herself.

Booking Passage: Exile and Homecoming in the Modern Jewish Imagination by Sidra DeKoven Ezrahi presents a complex and wide-ranging exploration and study of the poetics of exile and homecoming in modern Jewish literature. Ezrahi's main objective is to show how the Holy Land, represented in Jewish literature and culture alike as the 'object of deferred desire' for Jewishness, has now become the symbol of return since the recovery of a Zionist homeland, creating a new dimension of diasporism. Out of the literary domain that had previously encapsulated collections of 'anachronistic' stories to preserve and protect shtetl life from the onslaught of history, a new cultural agenda has emerged, focused on the fiction of Celan, Pagis, Appelfeld, Singer and Roth. Ezrahi argues that the attempt to destroy Jewish Europe was as devastating as that which destroyed ancient Israel, and that the notion of a lost centre again haunts Jewish writing, further complicated by the cultural dynamics surrounding a homecoming in Israel and a home in America.

Tim Cole, *Selling the Holocaust. From Auschwitz to Schindler: How History is Bought, Packaged and Sold* (published in the UK as *The Holocaust and Collective Memory*), and Peter Novik, *The Holocaust in American Life*, both discuss how the Holocaust has come to loom so large in American culture and in all media. Cole discusses the role of Anne Frank as a major 'symbol of Holocaust victimhood' in Roth's *The Ghost Writer*, a symbol which according to Cole only works because a universal figure of Anne Frank has been 'placed back within a Jewish and Holocaust context during the last three decades'. Novik similarly uses the now universal figure of Anne Frank, immortalized in drama and on film in America, to discuss who actually owns the Holocaust. Both authors discuss the extent to which the Holocaust has been removed from its original referent to become a 'mass-marketed production'. Also of interest here are the chapters on Jerzy Kosinski's *The Painted Bird* and William Styron's *Sophie's Choice* in Sue Vice's *Holocaust Fiction*.

Peter Townsend, *Jazz in American Culture*, considers the representations of jazz in other art forms and explores its 'historical-cultural manifestations'. Townsend discusses how through the media of film and literature the image of jazz is mediated to a much wider audience that may have little or no other experience of it and fail to understand the complexities of its deep roots in social history. He concludes that through this process of mediation the culture of jazz ceases to be perceived as a 'complex and variegated phenomenon' and becomes associated with the 'simplicity of myth'. To further his investigation of the representations of jazz Townsend introduces the fiction of Ralph Ellison, Jack Kerouac, Toni Morrison and Philip Roth to name a few authors into whose work jazz has 'entered' at various levels ranging from the incidental to 'work in which jazz has a presence as a cultural hinterland'.

The Cultures of the American New West, by Neil Campbell, presents an introductory survey of the significant debates currently surrounding central issues in the cultural history of the contemporary American West, incorporating the ways in which the West has been represented and interpreted within American culture in terms of myth and ideology. Campbell is interested in the concept of the West as the new territory of promise and invested hopes from the earliest American settlers, to the immigrant dream of 'the golden land', to Kerouac's 'countercultural road' and the 'new age philosophies' that induce contemporary settlers to escape city life. Campbell argues that the abiding theme of the West has always revolved in and around its encounters with notions of newness, and in exploring the concept of the 'New West' he examines the way in which contemporary theories, including feminism, multiculturalism and environmentalism, can be employed to rework these 'long-held notions'. In order to do this Campbell looks at the work of various writers, including Leslie Marmon Silko, Edward Abbey, Cormac McCarthy, and Terry Tempest Williams, and introduces some theoretical ideas from Michel Foucault, Mikhail Bakhtin, Gilles Deleuze, Walter Benjamin and Felix Guattari. Not received for review: John McCormick, *American and European Literary Imagination* (RutgersUP).

Also published this year but not received: Pamela Hunt Steinle, *In Cold Fear: Censorship, Controversies and Post War American Character* (OSUP); Karen Sayer and John Moore, eds., *Science Fiction, Critical Frontiers* (Macmillan); Warren Chernaik, Martin Swales and Robert Villain, eds., *The Art of Detective Fiction* (Macmillan); Amritjit Singh and Peter Schmidt, eds., *Postcolonial Theory and the United States: Race, Ethnicity and Literature* (UPMissip); and Elisabeth Kraus and Caroline Auer, eds., *Simulacrum America: The USA and the Popular Media* (Camden House).

(b) Individual Authors
In *James Jones: A Friendship* Willie Morris has provided a memoir that some critics have hailed 'as a record of the international community of American writing during the 1950s, sixties, and seventies'. Although Morris himself does not regard this work as an example of literary criticism, or indeed scholarship, he is keen that it be recognized as an illuminating insight into being a writer in America. Morris argues that for Jones, author of the Second World War trilogy that includes *From Here To Eternity*, *The Thin Red Line* and *Whistle*, war was 'in truth his Yoknapatawpha county; like Faulkner, he could not get away from it even when he wanted to', and that in his novels Jones expanded the boundaries of language in America in a way no other writer of his time did. Irwin Shaw later wrote of Jones that his literal style

of plain-speaking language, that shunned the use of euphemism, had rarely been seen before on the printed page in America, and Morris invokes the life and lifestyle of a writer who preserves the experiences of the American victims and survivors of the Second World War while at the same time influencing and allowing an insight into the lives of those writers such as Irwin Shaw, William Styron, Kurt Vonnegut, Winston Groom and Norman Mailer, to name but a few, who spent time with him at the colony in Marshall financed by Jones himself from the money he earned writing the screenplay for *From Here To Eternity*.

Continuing the theme of investigating the life and lifestyle of a writer, Lawrence Grobel has produced, in *Conversations with Capote*, interviews collected over a period during the early 1980s with Truman Capote, who was a one-time close neighbour of James Jones on Long Island. Grobel, like Morris, attempts to conjure a compelling era of American writers and in particular of a literary integrity that, it could be inferred, is lacking in contemporary American writing. While Morris has produced a nostalgic backward glance over what may be construed from his description as a fraternity of American writers in the latter half of the twentieth century, however, *Conversations with Capote* invokes, perhaps more accurately, the egotistical drive and competitive edge that would dispute this notion. Grobel's fifth chapter dwells mainly on the writing of *In Cold Blood*, which Capote had come to term his 'non-fiction novel', that took six years and 8,000 pages of pure research as part of the writing process, and the success of which, Capote maintains, relies heavily on his involvement with the two boys convicted of the crime. Discounting claims that he invented 'narrative journalism', Capote did, however, consider that *In Cold Blood* constituted an important new literary form culled from his 'far reaching experiment into the medium of reportage'. As further indication of the competitive undercurrents encapsulated within *Conversations with Capote*, Capote reveals his disdain for Mailer's *The Executioner's Song* which, as far as he was concerned, could be described as a 'nonbook' in that the research conducted into the crimes committed by Gary Gilmore in Utah was carried out by other people and not Mailer himself. James R. Giles's *Violence in the American Novel: An End to Innocence* (USCP) was not received in time for review in this section.

In '"First Person Anonymous": Sartrean Ideas of Consciousness in Barth's *Lost in the Funhouse*' (*Crit* 41:iii[2000] 335–47), James Burton Fulmer positions the novel as 'the greatest of Barth's Sartrean works'. Fulmer states that most critics examine it as a postmodern text in which language and literature are explicitly discussed, an approach which fails to grasp the underlying themes of the book, which are based on a Sartrean concern with 'the nothingness of consciousness ... the resulting impossibility of being sincere or explaining an act ... the concepts of facticity and transcendence, existence and essence, as well as ego and spontaneity'. Fulmer suggests that, although Barth attends to postmodern linguistic concerns, they are background rather than foreground and there is a continuing need to situate Barth's work alongside his interest in Sartre. For Fulmer, *Lost in the Funhouse* is ultimately an elucidation of 'some of Sartre's more difficult concepts, in the funhouse setting of postmodernity'.

In '*Short Cuts* and Long Shots: Raymond Carver's Stories and Robert Altman's Film' (*JAmS* 34:i[2000] 1–22), Kasia Boddy discusses the translation of Carver's stories into film in Robert Altman's *Short Cuts* to argue that 'in the change from Carver's medium ... to Altman's ... we find more than simply a formal translation'.

For Boddy, the consideration of the work of Carver alongside Altman's interpretation represents the juxtaposition of 'radically disparate versions of contemporary America'. This disparity is largely due to Altman's narrative connections, which compromise the randomness and arbitrariness central to Carver's work. Drawing on Pynchon's formulation of paranoia (where everything connects) and anti-paranoia (an unbearable condition where nothing connects) Boddy positions the work of Altman and Carver, respectively, as similarly driven by opposing impulses. Boddy concludes that, although Carver is sceptical about 'society', his 'belief in the power of individual endurance' *is* typically American; the opposing impulses Carver and Altman represent ultimately 'form two sides of the American coin'.

Critique 42:i[2000] is dedicated to Robert Coover's *The Public Burning*, a novel which recounts the events leading up the 1953 execution of the Rosenbergs, narrated in part by a fictional Richard Nixon. In the opening article, '*The Public Burning*, Coover's Fiery Masterpiece, on Center Stage Again', Geoffrey Green, Donald J. Greiner and Larry McCaffrey reflect on the novel's critical reception since its publication in 1977, including the controversy that surrounded it. The authors celebrate *The Public Burning* as an American literary landmark, not least because of its formal innovations, but also on account of its 'poetic re-creation of the full range of American idioms and vernacular', going on to suggest that 'it offers us perhaps the most complete replenishment of the language since Whitman and (in a different way) Mark Twain'. The novel is further discussed in relation to its political dimensions, its groundbreaking insight into 'the ways that America has consistently transformed its fears, self-righteousness, and insecurities into an appealing, simplistic national narrative that conveniently links our goals and destiny with divine intervention while demonizing our enemies as agents of the devil'. The authors approve of the novel's increasing stature as an American classic, concluding that 'what makes *The Public Burning* so deserving of renewed critical scrutiny is simply that no writer since Melville has dived so deeply and fearlessly into this collective American Dream as Coover has in this novel'. The issue also includes Elisabeth Ly Bell's 'The Notorious Hot Potato', which provides an overview of the novel's background and publication history and a bibliography of primary and secondary sources relating to the novel; a reprint of the obituary that Coover wrote for Nixon, and an important new interview with Coover. Essays in the volume include Eric Solomon, 'A Note on 1930s Nostalgia and *The Public Burning*'; Frank L. Cioffi, 'Coover's (Im)possible Worlds in *The Public Burning*'; Marcel Cornis-Pope, 'Rewriting the Encounter with the Other: Narrative and Cultural Transgression in *The Public Burning*'; Lance Olsen, 'Stand By To Crash! Avant-Pop, Hypertextuality, and Postmodern Comic Vision in Coover's *The Public Burning*' and Geralyn Strecker's 'Statecraft as Stagecraft: Disneyland and the Rosenberg Executions in *The Public Burning*'.

Amy Elias, in 'Oscar Hijuelo's *The Mambo Kings Play Songs of Love*, Ishmael Reed's *Mumbo Jumbo*, and Robert Coover's *The Public Burning*' (*Crit* 41:ii[2000] 115–28), attends to the way in which all three texts share typically postmodern concerns 'to interrogate, deconstruct, challenge, and disrupt existing metanarratives of Western modernity', in the case of *The Public Burning* focusing on Coover's use of allegory as a device which 'dynamite[s] political corruption and binary systems' to oppose realist closure. Also of interest: John F. Keener, 'Writing the Vacuum:

Richard Nixon as Literary Figure' (*Crit* 41:ii[2000] 129–51), which discusses Nixon's appearances and development as a literary character in Coover's *The Public Burning* and *Whatever Happened to Gloomy Gus of the Chicago Bears?*, Kathy Acker's *Don Quixote* and John Ehrlichman's *The China Card*, among others.

In 'Don DeLillo and the Myth of the Author-Recluse' (*JAmS* 34:i[2000] 137–52), Joe Moran discusses *Mao II* as DeLillo's fullest expression of his interest in the entrapping nature of celebrity. DeLillo's interest in author-recluses, in their refusal to 'become part of the all-incorporating treadmill of consumption and disposal' is interrogated in a novel concerned with 'what happens when this absorption takes place, and whether or not this wholly devalues the author's own tactics of silence and renunciation'. Moran concludes that in *Mao II* DeLillo 'not only critiques but also romanticizes the role of author-recluses in contemporary culture, by pointing to both the unavoidable involvement of such authors in the commodification of culture and the admirably uncompromising nature of their rearguard action—a purer but doomed strategy which DeLillo has himself rejected'. Also of interest but not received for review: Mark Osteen, *American Magic and Dread: Don DeLillo's Dialogue with Culture* (UPennP).

In 'Compositions of Reality: Photography, History, and *Ragtime*' (*MFS* 46[2000] 801–24), Laura Barrett, drawing on the work of historian Hayden White, discusses the ways in which E.L. Doctorow's text famously blurs the distinction between history and fiction to complicate the relationship between representation and reality. Barrett begins with a discussion of the title's apt reference to a musical style filled with contrasts, but goes on to say that music is not the only trope that incorporates the contradictory to challenge traditional views of history in the text: photography unravels 'objectivity, truth, and history, those very concepts with which photography's realism is often associated', and as a result becomes one of postmodernism's most effective instruments. Simultaneously embodying a gesture towards progress and a nostalgic impulse, photography blurs the distinction between past and present in the text. This blurring is central to Doctorow's demystification of history in that it is used to reveal the mechanisms which make familiar images seem transparent as opposed to constructed, which attach singular and fixed meanings to important historical moments. *Ragtime* traces the development of photography in the twentieth century alongside the interrogation of its role in history-making and the recognition that as a form it reveals and exploits the incompleteness of a single perspective. Doctorow's engagement with photography in the text opens up the possibility of multiple viewpoints, again focusing on photography's duality, as an anti-elitist art form which challenges the difference between the original and the reproduction and a way to commodify art. Barrett states that 'it is precisely photography's doubleness, as a conservative tool of social control and as a radical instrument of inquiry, that makes it the perfect controlling image of the novel'. Also of interest but not received for review: Michelle M. Tokarczyk, *E.L. Doctorow's Skeptical Commitment* (Lang).

In 'Parodied To Death: The Postmodern Gothic of *American Psycho*' (*MFS* 46[2000] 725–46) Ruth Heyler offers an effective reading of Brett Easton Ellis's novel which translates Gothic textual devices into the framework of late capitalist (postmodern) American writing. Heyler discusses the features of Gothic and postmodern texts, comparing the social circumstances in which each emerge, to suggest that they similarly respond to conditions of social change and uncertainty by representing excessive behaviour. She charts the move towards psychological dramas in the Gothic tradition and states that 'in a fragmented postmodern world of isolated individuals beset by guilt, anxiety, and despair, internalizing fear produces narratives which center on psychological disturbance'. In this framework, Patrick Bateman is at the mercy of his unconscious desires, his anti-social fantasies. Heyser charts the ways in which the Gothic is parodied in *American Psycho* by an excessive overlay of its tropes. Bateman is the troubled aristocrat, the romantic hero who, in his anxiety about the stability of his own identity, reduces those around him to types. Fundamentally concerned with the boundaries between himself and others, Bateman functions as the Gothic double: he is the classic Jekyll and Hyde character, often mistaken for other people, obsessed by his own image on film and in mirrors. Heyler relates the over-ornamentation of Gothic to *American Psycho*'s obsessive attention to detail, the stylistic repetition in the text functioning as a thematic attempt to stay in control. The Gothic concern with the loss of stable boundaries of the self is allied with Bateman's fear of feminization, displayed in the extreme violence towards women in the text. For Heyler, Bateman attacks difference in order to render it harmless. Mapping Gothic sensationalism on to postmodern spectacle, Heyler also points to the ways subject-matter and genre coincide in *American Psycho*, which provides an indictment of materialistic culture, but is also self-consciously part of it as commodity (concerned with consumption, the text itself feeds that social appetite). For Heyler, *American Psycho* is fundamentally concerned with creating a balance between excess and apathy; hence the disruptive mode which mixes extreme horror with humour. Comparing the Gothic as a hybrid genre with the postmodern literary style of pastiche, Heyler maps the implications of the Gothic mode onto those of contemporary literary concerns to suggest that ultimately both are concerned with the 'fissure *between* representations' in moments of social transformation.

In 'Cold War Correspondents: Ginsberg, Kerouac, Cassady, and the Political Economy of Beat Letters' (*TCL* 46:ii[2000] 171–92), Oliver Harris points to the intersection between dominant narratives of early Cold War America and their dissident counter-narratives, in the form of Beat letters, to argue that 'what's important is not the intersecting of narratives, personal and political, dominant and dissenting, but their correspondence', a recognition, for Harris, central to an understanding of the political economy of such writings. Drawing attention to the breakdown between public and private in a Cold War climate of self-surveillance, Harris discusses the epistolary scene as a highly significant form, in that it must simultaneously appear 'natural' and indifferent to public scrutiny. Comparing Beat letters with those of the Rosenbergs while in their cells, Harris states that 'where the Rosenbergs were found guilty of living their personal lives as political allegories, the Beats became notorious for seeing the details of theirs as symbolic cultural texts', a point which draws attention to the correspondence between Cold War narrative structures and Beat strategies. With reference to Ginsberg and Kerouac, Harris further states that 'what the epistolary signified for both writers throughout the 1950s gets to the heart of any articulated Beat aesthetic. Each made major breakthroughs that coincided with creative investment in the singularly private and interpersonal at the expense of the public and impersonal, so embodying a cultural politics that in key respects is the mirror image of Cold War disciplinary economic and communication systems.' For Beat writers the letter served as a hope for space outside Cold War society and culture, a voice for the unpublishable, the unmarketable; yet, as Harris demonstrates, the form might be seen as embodying the central contradiction of the counter-culture in that it ultimately functioned as a commodifiable form. With reference to Beat letters Harris makes a convincing and intriguing case for the oft-made claim that the Beats reproduced the biases of the system they opposed. Also of interest here but not received for review: Ben Giamo, *Kerouac, the Word and the Way: Prose Artist as Spiritual Quester* (SIUP); Joyce Johnson, ed., *Door Wide Open: A Beat Love Affair in Letters, 1957–8* (Viking); Rod Phillips, *'Forest Beatniks' and 'Urban Thoreaus': Gary Snyder, Jack Kerouac, Law Welch, and Michael McLure* (Lang); and Matt Theado, *Jack Kerouac* (USCP).

In 'Oppositions in *In Country*' (*Crit* 41:ii[2000] 175–90), Tim O'Brien argues that the 'familiarity of the novel's surface ... can obscure the novel's rich, symbolic subsurface ... repeated images, symbols, and motifs; playful use of characters' names—[which] is vital to the novel's meaning'. O'Brien suggests that these two levels, representational and symbolic, are involved in an ongoing tension throughout Bobbie Ann Mason's novel, which amounts to a mediation between opposites, a device which gestures towards a condition of possibility, particularly in relation to the bridging of male and female domains. For O'Brien the conclusion of the text is troubling—Sam's transgression of the female role is undermined by her experience at the Vietnam memorial, which he reads as her 'development [of the] reproductive imperative, which only augments the sense of compliance signalled by the pink room and a life in *Lex*ington, a site ostensibly marking intellectual growth but actually naming allegiance to the male domain of law, reading, and official writing'. Also of interest but not received for review: Joanna Price, *Bobbie Ann Mason* (USCP).

Wallach, ed., *Myth, Legend, Dust: Critical Responses to Cormac McCarthy*, charts the rise of McCarthy's prominence in the literary establishment and the emergence of a burgeoning field of McCarthy criticism. The collection represents a necessary range of approaches to the breadth of McCarthy's work to date, and draws on diverse critical methodologies from Marxism to feminism, while also including essays by the writers Madison Smartt Bell and Peter Josyph, centred around personal influence and inspiration. The collection is split into four sections which comprehensively span McCarthy's career: part I, 'The Appalachian Works'; part II, 'A Detour into Drama'; part III, 'From East to West: Shared Elements in the Appalachian and Southwestern Novels'; and part IV, 'The Border Tetralogy'.

In 'Louise Erdrich's *Love Medicine*, Cormac McCarthy's *Blood Meridian*, and the (De)Mythologizing of the American West' (*Crit* 41:iii[2000] 290–304), Jason P. Mitchell reviews myths of the 'heroic West' to chart the development and decline of and renewed interest in the figure of the cowboy. Mitchell discusses a cultural fascination with the cowboy figure in relation to the evolution of national identity in the US, and the ways in which the myth of the West, which supported an earlier version of American identity, has been challenged by historical revisionism, namely the incorporation of perspectives of race, gender and sexuality. Mitchell points out that this reappraisal of Western history has led to the emergence of some equally limited myths, and he positions *Blood Meridian* and *Love Medicine* as texts which contribute to the demythologization of the 'heroic West' in ways which do not simply displace the heroism of the cowboy onto marginal figures. For Mitchell, Erdrich points to the incompatibility of competing cultures in the settlement of the

West while avoiding the construction of the Native American as 'blameless martyr', a model which has emerged in relation to a popular interest in Native American spirituality. Mitchell discusses *Blood Meridian* as a critique of both traditional and revisionist versions of the West, pointing to the lack of moral hierarchy in McCarthy's representation of violence. As a fundamental site of cultural contestation in America, the West has traditionally provided the backdrop for the triumph of the cowboy as representative of the dominant culture, yet the incorporation of 'marginal' histories and voices has led to a similarly uncomplicated version of the West, one based on the reversal of the logic of heroism. Mitchell compares *Love Medicine* and *Blood Meridian* as reactions against the West which succeed in prioritizing the representation of conflict rather than its resolution.

In 'Virtual Eden: *Lolita*, Pornography, and the Perversions of American Studies' (*JAmS* 34:i[2000] 41–66), Paul Giles argues that *Lolita* 'can be seen as symbiotically intertwined with various classic texts of American Studies that helped to invent and define the field during the Truman and Eisenhower years'. Giles attends to the dream of Eden in *Lolita*, which he suggests parodies the early American Studies movement to provide 'a metafiction of area studies'. For Giles, a reading of *Lolita* in relation to the rise of American Studies draws attention to the ways in which the boundaries of area studies are constituted to suggest that 'Nabokov's perverse reinscription of American Studies might be seen ironically to highlight the multiple dilemmas involved in circumscribing specific national territories for academic study or political jurisdiction'. Giles reads *Lolita* alongside seminal American Studies texts such as Leslie Fiedler's *An End to Innocence*, R.W.B. Lewis's *The American Adam: Innocence, Tragedy, and Tradition in the Nineteenth Century*, Henry Nash Smith's *Virgin Land: The American West as Symbol and Myth* and David M. Potter's *People of Plenty: Economic Abundance and the American Character*, and discusses the ways in which 'intertextual plays with the legacy of American Romanticism manifest themselves all the way through Nabokov's narrative'. Giles concludes that, ultimately, *Lolita* simultaneously echoes and perverts the mythologies which underpinned the development of American Studies to interrupt 'that tautologous circle between area studies and its object of scrutiny, whereby the latter is merely mapped onto the former to show how much the former manifests itself in the latter'. See also: Eric Rothstein, '*Lolita*: Nymphet at Normal School' (*ConL* 41:i[2000] 22–55), and James Tweedie, '*Lolita*'s Loose Ends: Nabokov and the Boundless Novel' (*TCL* 46:ii[2000] 150–70). Also of interest but not received for review: Stephen H. Blackwell, *Zina's Paradox: The Figured Reader in Nabokov's Gift* (Lang).

In 'Tim O'Brien's "True Lies"(?)' (*MFS* 46:iv[2000] 893–916), Tobey C. Herzog considers the failure of O'Brien's novel *In the Lake of the Woods* [1994] to provide answers to the questions it raises, alongside O'Brien's use of unreliable narrators and 'lies' in writing, which mixes personal and historical facts and fictions. Herzog offers a number of hypotheses on the centrality of deception in O'Brien's work, numbered 1 to 8 and entitled 'Humor', 'Revenge', 'Artistry', 'Introspection and Catharsis', 'Uncertainty', 'Reader Involvement', 'Ego' and 'A Warning', yet concludes that, although all are plausible, none is definitive in understanding work which engages with versions of the Vietnam War to refuse any easy or singular understanding. See also John H. Timmerman, 'Tim O'Brien and the Art of the True War Story: "Night March" and "Speaking of Courage"' (*TCL* 46:i[2000] 100–14).

In 'Class-ifying Escape: Tillie Olsen's *Yonnondio*' (*Crit* 41[2000] 263–71), Heidi Slettedahl MacPherson states that 'the concept of escape is a troubled one, and the unease with which it is approached suggests that the twentieth century's need for and its repudiation of this concept are hopelessly intertwined'. MacPherson draws on a range of sociological and psychological studies in her focus on the importance of escape as a defence mechanism in contemporary culture, which is considered alongside a particularly American tradition of practicality and realism. McPherson goes on to discuss the ways in which competing assumptions about escape are represented in mixed critical reactions to Olsen's *Yonnondio*, making particular reference to the significance of class bias in the critical reception of the text. MacPherson suggests that 'Olsen's text resists assimilation into middle-class versions of escape attempts despite its points of convergence with them ... As if in response to middle-class theorizing, *Yonnondio* provides an alternative form of escape—the collective form—but does not even allow collectivity to remain unexamined ... It asks for new definitions of escape and reveals how working-class escape is as problematic as the more frequently studied middle-class escape.'

The title of Steven Milowitz's *Philip Roth Reconsidered: The Concentrationary Universe of the American Writer* refers to Irving Howe's essay 'Philip Roth Reconsidered', in Sanford Pinsker, ed., *Critical Essays on Philip Roth* (Hall [1982]), in which Roth is called 'a writer who has denied himself, programmatically, the vision of major possibilities', a reversal of Howe's previous enthusiasm for the writer. Milowitz concludes that 'Howe exhibits an almost vindictive blindness', and contends that Roth's works have been the 'victim of gross misreadings' and that it is time to afford them new, closer consideration. In beginning this process Milowitz disregards what he deems the obvious previous criticisms of 'autobiography, misogyny, and anti-Semitism', pointing to what is, in his opinion, the central focus, or even 'obsessional' issue in his fiction: the Holocaust. With this in mind he proceeds to closely re-read Roth, beginning with the early fiction *Goodbye, Columbus* [1959] and concluding with *American Pastoral* [1997], a period throughout which, Milowitz claims, reviewers and literary critics alike failed to acknowledge the Holocaust's haunting presence provoking the harried and beleaguered Rothian protagonist. The book contains an excellent bibliography that includes all of the prominent secondary sources available to date.

Daniele Kahn-Paycha's *Popular Jewish Literature and its Role in the Making of an Identity* also concentrates on Roth, whom she considers alongside the English Jewish writer Israel Zangwill. As the title suggests, the book explores, through what Kahn-Paycha calls the peculiarities of the 'Jewish condition', ways to reconstruct concepts of the self that can be viable in a postmodern society, and argues that literature can play a significant part in who and what we become. In a chapter entitled 'Shylock Revisited' she discusses how the fictional Shylock identity has 'reverberated terribly' through past centuries for 'living' Jews, and stresses how the character became the embodiment of Jewishness to provide the clichés of anti-Semitism that are internalized by Jews and gentiles alike. Kahn-Paycha reads Zangwill and Roth in correlation to focus on how the literary image of the Jew may be transformed by more positively determined identities. Both authors, she argues, reflect the spectrum of possibilities that is inherent in Jewish literature in that their work spans two distinct eras of writing, the pre-Holocaust era Zangwill represents, and Roth's interpretation of Jewishness after the Holocaust and the part the

Holocaust played in the creation of the state of Israel. Kahn-Paycha maintains that Zangwill's fiction and his political work reflect that he was the 'champion of Zionism', and similarly, that the 'creation of Israel lies at the core of the literary identities' created by Roth in *Operation Shylock*.

Leeds and Reed, eds., *Kurt Vonnegut: Images and Representations*, not only records Vonnegut's literary images but also examines examples of the graphic art to which he devotes more and more of his time. The editors have collected sixteen essays, beginning with what they term the 'seminal' essay, reprinted here for the first time since 1970: Leslie A. Fiedler's 'The Divine Stupidity of Kurt Vonnegut: Portrait of the Novelist as Bridge over Troubled Water'. Fiedler's title certainly reflects the moment of its creation, and although much has been written about Vonnegut since, many critics would cite Fiedler's essay as the best-known study. For Fiedler, at that time, the epitome of Vonnegut's talent lay in *The Sirens of Titan* [1959] in which for the first time he imagines Tralfamadore, the transgalactic world he evokes again and again in his later fiction. The editors point out that Fiedler sees Vonnegut as 'a transitional figure in whom something has always yearned to be a serious writer, to win respect from those professors whom he affects to despise'. Fiedler's reasoning for this position lies in Vonnegut's tendency, early in his writing career, to put writers and artists at the centre of his fiction, apparently untypically of the 'pop' fiction of the time. This habit, it would seem, has become 'emphatically more evident' in his writing since Fiedler's article and this is borne out by other essayists in the collection. Other contributions include Sharon Sieber's 'Unstuck in Time', which also considers *The Sirens of Titan* in discussing the aspect of simultaneity otherwise known as chrono-synclasitic infundibula, a mode of being everywhere at once and yet nowhere in particular. Julie A. Hibbard in 'In Search of Slaughterhouse-Five' makes the ironic point that she and the American public would know little or nothing at all what of happened to Dresden in February 1945 if they had not read *Slaughterhouse-Five* [1969]. Hibbard, using Vonnegut's text as guide, describes her as yet unsuccessful search for the building used in Dresden to house prisoners of war. Reed and Leeds have collected together a compilation of diverse views and interpretations that can be considered a serious addition to critical studies of Vonnegut.

Also published this year but not received: James Atlas, *Bellow: A Biography* (RandomH); Gerhard Bachard and Gloria L. Kronin, eds., *Small Planets: Saul Bellow and the Art of Short Fiction* (MichSUP); Lawrence R. Broer, *Rabbit Tales: Poetry and Politics in John Updike's Rabbit Novels* (UAlaP); Lawrence Kappel, ed., *Readings on 'One Flew Over the Cuckoo's Nest'* (Greenhaven); and Alan W. Brownlie, *Thomas Pynchon's Narratives: Subjectivity and Problems of Knowing* (Lang).

4. Drama

(a) General

The mightily impressive *Cambridge History of American Theatre*, edited by Don B. Wilmeth and Christopher Bigsby, is completed by the publication of the third volume, *Post-World War II to the 1990s*. Bigsby's introduction, the very detailed timeline compiled by Wilmeth and Jonathan Curley and, in particular, Arnold

Aronson's chapter on 'American Theatre in Context: 1945–Present' do a fine job of situating the drama within the economic, social and cultural developments of the period. The second section considers the changes within the increasingly varied theatrical environments, taking in Broadway (Laurence Maslon), off- and off-off-Broadway (Mel Gussow), the more problematic 'regional' and 'resident' theatre (Martha Lomonaco) and alternative theatre (Marvin Carlson), this latter section taking in theatre groups such as the Living Theatre, the Open Theatre, the San Francisco Mime Troupe, El Teatro Campesino, black theatres, feminist groups, and individual creators such as Richard Foreman. When read alongside Arnold Aronson's *American Avant-Garde Theatre: A History* (reviewed below), Carlson's chapter helps to establish the impressive range of theatre activity in the US, and the section as a whole, along with John Degen's account of musical theatre in this same volume, continues the ongoing questioning of the primacy of a dramatic tradition that privileges the play text and the spoken word. That tradition is considered in a two-part section on plays and playwrights that takes 1970 as the dividing line, June Schlueter writing on the former period and Matthew Roudané on the latter, though at eighty-eight pages Roudané's contribution is more than twice the length of Schlueter's. The imbalances—just six pages cover the 1940s output of Williams and Miller combined, for example, while Shepard's career receives about three times that—can perhaps be accounted for by the impossibility of doing justice to major plays, criticism of which is easy to come by, in the series format. As with all of the volumes in this series, the discussions of the playwrights, while often pithy, are inevitably sketchy, but brought into sharper relief for the reader prepared to read the book for its wealth of contextualizing commentary rather than its critical analyses. There are also specialized studies of directors and direction by Samuel L. Leiter, actors and acting (Foster Hitsch) and theatre design (Ronn Smith).

If the *Cambridge History* is indispensable, much of Bigsby's work since the publication of his monumental *Critical Introduction to Twentieth-Century American Drama* (CUP [1982–5]) has read like a succession of codas to that other seminal three-volume work. *Contemporary American Playwrights* might reasonably be seen as its fourth volume, and contains detailed accounts of the plays of John Guare, Tina Howe, Tony Kushner, Emily Mann, Richard Nelson, Marsha Norman, David Rabe, Paula Vogel, Wendy Wasserstein and Lanford Wilson. Gone is the brief flirtation with theory that marked *Modern American Drama, 1940–1990* (CUP [1992]); back is Bigsby's characteristic style, aimed more at a general readership, bold yet somehow unobjectionable statements wrapped up in the confidence of assertion. Of Kushner's theatre, for instance: 'It deploys an affecting lyricism, shaping experience into contingent form, and stages the splintering of such lyricism by forces which well up not only from the corrupting nature of power and bigotry but from a self whose depths at times seem beyond investigation or even imagination.' This all seems right, and describes very well the effect of the drama, while throughout the book is crammed with primary research that lends further authority to the voice; yet the style seems almost designed to avoid adopting a stance towards the material, lacking any clear ideological, theoretical or aesthetic edge, so that one leaves the book feeling much better informed yet not particularly animated. On the other hand, one is much more likely now than previously to come across an arresting turn of phrase; in the course of establishing the intellectual range of Kushner, who is 'drawn to dualisms … but more significantly is drawn to the transcendence of those dualisms' (does this not merely restate and foreclose Kushner's fascination with dialectics?), Bigsby suddenly presents us with the image of 'a man wandering through a snowstorm of influences, his face tilted back to the sky'.

Bigsby's *Modern American Drama, 1945–2000* really is a coda, a second edition of *American Dramatists since 1945* in which he updates chapters on still productive writers such as Miller, Albee, Shepard and Mamet, adds one ('Beyond Broadway') that contains briefer discussion of several of the playwrights considered now in *Contemporary American Playwrights* plus a few others, and retains the curiously polemical introductory chapter in which he calls for a theoretical engagement with a field in which he has been pre-eminent for twenty years without elsewhere having given the impression that it would be enriched by bringing it into line with the theoretical revolution that has accompanied practically every other area of the humanities. There are substantial overlaps of material and approach between Bigsby's two recent single-authored books, furthering the impression that the impressive productivity conceals a lack of fresh ideas.

Wheatley, ed., *Twentieth-Century American Dramatists: Second Series*, appears in the Dictionary of Literary Biography series and hoovers up some of the playwrights who failed to make it into, have appeared since the publication of, or were treated at insufficient length in DLB 7: *Twentieth-Century American Dramatists*. The twenty-seven entries are quite substantial discussions of Maxwell Anderson, Philip Barry, Marita Bonner, Mary Coyle Chase, Pearl Cleage, Lara Farabough, Rose Franken, Zona Gale, Jack Gelber, Susan Glaspell, Lillian Hellman, Langston Hughes, David Henry Hwang, Tony Kushner, Jerome Lawrence and Robert E. Lee, John Howard Lawson, Anita Loos, Clare Boothe Luce, Donald Margulies, Carson McCullers, David Rabe, Mary Shaw, Martin Sherman, Gertrude Stein, Wendy Wasserstein, Thornton Wilder, and August Wilson.

Carol P. Marsh-Lockett, ed., *Black Women Playwrights: Visions on the American Stage*, contains a number of essays on some of the more familiar plays and playwrights, but situates them in a range of contexts that avoid mere author-specific close readings. By conscious design or otherwise, the collection repeatedly offers essays that provide detailed analyses of particular plays which are also discussed in broader terms elsewhere in the book. Angelina Ward Grimké's *Rachel*, for example, a play which has recently begun to receive quite extensive attention, is examined alongside other plays by women in Trudier Harris's 'Before the Strength, the Pain: Portraits of Elderly Black Women in Early Twentieth-Century Anti-Lynching Plays'. *Rachel* can then be seen in the context of a kind of sub-genre of dramatic works in which the effects of the lynching of males are played out in the psychological damage done to women and 'The black female body in ill health', which, argues Harris, 'is not only a metaphor for American racism but a sympathetic response to the continuing destruction of the black male body'. Equally useful to a broader understanding of *Rachel* is Christine R. Gray's '*Mara*, Angelina Grimké's Other Play and the Problems of Recovering Texts', an exemplary piece of scholarship which notes that, while one version of this unpublished work could also be described as a 'lynching play', another is a 'romance version' owing much to the conventions of nineteenth-century melodrama, and that previous commentators on the play have tended to reconstruct it in ways that limit the scope of Grimké's dramatic career. (On the topic of lynching plays, see also Judith L. Stephens, 'Politics and Aesthetics, Race and Gender: Georgia Douglas Johnson's Lynching

Dramas as Black Feminist Cultural Performance (*TPQ* 20[2000] 251–67), an essay that focuses on the use of spirituals, and contextualizes the plays within historical debates about black theatre and the Harlem Renaissance.) Although Keith Clark's 'Black Male Subjectivity Deferred? The Quest for Voice and Authority in Lorraine Hansberry's *A Raisin in the Sun*' engages with contemporary theoretical debates about subjectivity, ultimately the essay complements the familiar argument that the play's popularity can be traced to its assimilation of dominant modes of American realism. 'Instead of constructing a protagonist who determines his own "masculinity" and identity', contends Clark, 'Hansberry creates one who is an amalgam of imposed definitions from without rather than from within—definitions that render him more "object" in a pejorative sense than "subject".' A very similar argument about the play is proffered in Lovalerie King's 'The Desire/Authority Nexus in Contemporary African American Women's Drama'. King finds more possibilities for the expression of agency, however, and discusses the play alongside Alice Childress's *Trouble in Mind*, Ntozake Shange's *for colored girls who have considered suicide/when the rainbow is enuf* and Adrienne Kennedy's *Funnyhouse of a Negro*. Again, the Childress play is discussed in similar terms in E. Barnsley Brown's 'Celebrating the (Extra)Ordinary: Alice Childress's Representation of Black Selfhood', while the other plays discussed by King are examined from a somewhat different angle, that of colonial and racist constructions of African American sexuality, and some modes of resistance to these constructions, in Carla J. McDonough's 'The Nightmare of History: Conceptions of Sexuality in Adrienne Kennedy's *Funnyhouse of a Negro*' and in Neal A. Lester's '"Filled with the Holy Ghost": Sexual Dimensions and Dimensions of Sexuality in the Theater of Ntozake Shange'. Again, these two essays are preceded by another that functions as a kind of framing overview of the issues they raise: Janice Lee Liddell's 'The Discourse of Intercourse: Sexuality and Eroticism in African American Women's Drama', which traces a history of the representation of black sexuality from its deliberate evasion in early-century plays, for the purpose of counteracting racist stereotypes about excessive black sexuality, to the various ways in which, from the 1950s onwards, plays explore different forms of eroticism. LaVinia Delois Jennings's 'Segregated Sisterhood: Anger, Racism, and Feminism in Alice Childress's *Florence* and *Wedding Band*' exposes race as a fault-line in gender solidarity by examining the victimization of black women at the hands of white women as well as of men. Martha Patterson's 'Remaking the Minstrel: Pauline Hopkins's *Peculiar Sam* and the Post-Reconstruction Black Subject' deftly explores this 1880 piece in the context of the interpretative difficulties generated by the ironies of the minstrel show, a form that has recently received extensive attention. Less incisive is Marilyn Elkins's '"Sicker than a rabid dog": African American Women Playwrights Look at War', which unsurprisingly concludes that the five plays she examines are less interested in war as a testing-ground for masculinity than are plays by men. While Marsh-Lockett's book offers a number of perspectives on its subject, there is a certain repetitiveness to its themes that tends to diminish rather than illuminate the range of the plays.

Lawrence G. Avery's 'Stereotypes and the Development of African American Drama' (*JADT* 12:ii[2000] 56–70) is a clear and sensible discussion of some related issues, though its account of stereotyping is familiar and has been superseded by more theoretically rigorous accounts of African American and post-colonial literature and drama (see, for example, many of the studies considered in this chapter's section on 'African American Writing', below). Of related interest in the same issue is Jennifer Stiles, 'Import or Immigrant? The Representation of Blacks and Irish on the American Stage from 1767–1856' (*JADT* 12:ii[2000] 38–55), which offers a fairly detailed discussion of five plays.

Arnold Aronson, *American Avant-Garde Theatre: A History*, might, on a bold interpretation, be said to fall outside the confines of a discussion of American *drama*, since in the works Aronson considers the dramatic script carries far less status than in the conventional, well-made, realistic plays that are sometimes said to constitute the American dramatic tradition. The avant-garde theatre that emerged in New York in the 1950s was, says Aronson, 'an art in which the reference points were other forms of art, the creative process of the artist, and the theatrical experience itself … It was a non-literary theatre—meaning not that it lacked language but that it could not be *read* in the way a work of literature could be.' He paves the way with discussions of the origins and 'theories and foundations' of the avant-garde, occasioning substantial accounts of Gertrude Stein, John Cage, the Beat writers, cinema, abstract expressionism and other developments, before settling down to a series of chapters that explore more directly theatrical collectives and phenomena. Off-Broadway, the Living Theatre, performance art and the Wooster Group are all considered at length, while another chapter looks at the work of individual creators J. Smith, Richard Foreman and Robert Wilson, quite appropriately since, as Aronson concludes, 'The avant-garde was a product of the romantic sensibility', 'a spiritual quest led by … inspired individuals.' Aronson finds the avant-garde ultimately defeated, or at least rendered impotent, by familiar forces within postmodernity, becoming 'a kind of cultural establishment' in a culture in which, 'With almost no boundaries, it is hard for an art to develop or to exist *outside* the mainstream.' For a stimulating discussion of a specific play that addresses many of the same points Aronson raises about the avant-garde, see Sarah Bay-Cheng's 'Atom and Eve: A Consideration of Gertrude Stein's *Doctor Faustus Lights the Lights*' (*JADT* 12:ii[2000] 1–24).

Christopher Innes, with Katherine Carlstrom and Scott Fraser, has compiled *Twentieth-Century British and American Theatre: A Critical Guide to Archives*. Drawing on over 100 archives, and restricting themselves to unpublished material including drafts, notes and other ephemera, they have listed in alphabetical order material available not only on playwrights but on directors, actors and others. A useful feature is the brief commentary on what the compilers perceive to be the most significant aspects of the material (for example, where a particular set of documents enables conclusions to be drawn about a dramatist's working methods). As the introduction makes clear, the book is aimed at a moving target, and many of the most important living dramatists, such as Sam Shepard and David Mamet, do not appear because too little material has been archived. Nevertheless, the importance of this book as a research resource is obvious.

Several essays published this year consider little-known plays, both early and late, in the context of the outmoded but evidently still productive 'frontier ethic'. Richard Wattenberg's 'Reworking the Frontier Captivity Narrative: William Vaughn Moody's *The Great Divide*' (*AmDram* 9:ii[2000] 1–28) is that relative rarity, a substantial piece on a pre-O'Neill twentieth-century American play, and a detailed discussion that places this play in the contexts of frontier and captivity narratives. In the same issue, David Radavich's 'War of the Wests: Saroyan's Dramatic Landscape' (*AmDram* 9:ii[2000] 29–49) is an account of 'conflicting "Wests"— among them, the California of mind and fantasy as well as of harsh, unforgiving landscape' in William Saroyan's work, which Radavich regards as darker than has generally been perceived. Brook Baeten, 'Masculine Mythology in Feminist Femininity: Molly Newman's and Barbara Damashek's *Quilters*' (*JADT* 12:iii[2000] 27–40), is a slightly florid discussion that finds in this 1980s play a complication of simple distinctions between masculinity and femininity.

Two publications concentrate on particular themes in particular periods. Ronald Wainscott, 'Let's Get a Divorce: American Drama's Divorce Crisis, 1870–1925' (*JADT* 12:i[2000] 74–82), explains the proliferation of predominantly reactionary divorce plays, mainly in New York, during this period with reference to the divorce laws and the transformation of the United States from a predominantly agrarian to a predominantly urban population. Charles A. Carpenter, *Dramatists and the Bomb: American and British Playwrights Confront the Nuclear Age, 1945–1964*, integrates documentary accounts of the development of the nuclear threat, relevant comments on the situation by British and American dramatists, and accounts of all of the published plays on the topic that Carpenter has been able to find. The scope, but also the limitations, of the project are apparent in his own description: 'I describe at least briefly every original British or American dramatic work I could find which comes to grips with a major aspect of the nuclear situation, and I selectively quote or paraphrase statements that fit the same bill.' There is an inevitable sense of fragmentation about such a book, made all the greater by the fact that, by his own admission, Carpenter has unearthed no unknown masterpieces, with the result that one cannot help but feel that Samuel Beckett's *Endgame*, the subject of the final chapter, says more than all the other plays in the book put together about the threat of nuclear apocalypse, and the possibilities of its dramatic expression, without once directly raising it as the subject of the play.

Don Shiach's *American Drama, 1900–1990* is aimed squarely at the high-school market, offering very sketchy surveys of the historical and theatrical contexts, brief thumbnail sketches of important plays and playwrights and their critical reception, a few ideas on 'approaching the texts', a glossary and chronology, and some suggestions on 'how to write about twentieth century American drama'. It may perform a useful function by enabling A-level students to situate whatever play they are being force-fed in a broader range of contexts than their demoralized teachers can provide, but it is a sign of our commercialized, God-forsaken, third-way times that this hack piece is published by CUP.

(b) Individual Dramatists

George Jean Nathan, who tirelessly promoted Eugene O'Neill's career and is partly responsible for his position of pre-eminence, resembles the dramatist in having been awkwardly constructed as both progenitor—'the first modern American drama critic', according to Thomas F. Connolly in *George Jean Nathan and the Making of Modern American Drama Criticism*—and a man whose personality somehow manages to eclipse that achievement. This is less of a problem in the case of Nathan, part of whose importance, Connolly argues, lies in having recognized that the function of the theatre critic is to write about theatre as it is: the critic becomes enmeshed with his time, and Nathan's iconic status is achieved by taking this position to its logical conclusion, his life becoming inextricable from the world of the New York theatre, the writing not detached but inescapably 'personal'. Consequently the chapter on Nathan's life, which focuses on the theatre world, his friendships with O'Neill and H.L. Mencken and, arrestingly, his anxieties concerning his Jewish background, is not wholly extricable from the following chapters on the criticism. Connolly establishes Nathan's facility in writing according to the requirements of different journals, while tracing the route by which he came to establish a distinctive style, notably in his work for *The Smart Set*, that openly sought to destroy the tradition associated with contemporaries such as Alan Dale, in which the critic elevated his own position as entertainer above the performance that occasioned the review. Nathan shifted attention from the actors to the play, established criteria for promoting the work of particular dramatists, engaged with American drama's sense of inferiority by arguing that it should draw from the achievements of the European theatre, and acknowledged the 'impressionistic' nature of the critic's response. There is the occasional overstatement: Connolly suggests that 'Nathan's methodology has come into academic fashion' due to 'the current questioning of objectivity by scholars of everything from literary theory to quantum theory', as if Nathan, Stanley Fish and Werner Heisenberg were mutual back-slappers in the same club. As Connolly points out, Nathan was determinedly anti-academic (although highly knowledgeable); but given the book's title one would have welcomed further discussion of the ways in which his style and preferences have contributed to the formation of the canon and the terms in which it has been discussed inside and outside the academy. That aside, this is a balanced, lucid and well-researched account, clearly establishing Nathan's distinctiveness as a critic.

Turning to studies of O'Neill himself, William Davies King's *'A Wind is Rising': The Correspondence of Agnes Boulton and Eugene O'Neill* valiantly attempts to construct the correspondence as a dialogue between two forms of writing, O'Neill's masculine high modernism and the feminine, pulpy style of Boulton's popular fiction. In truth this is to give rather too much value to the style of what are often little more than hastily constructed notes and *aide-mémoire*; the real drama in this book is not in the form, but in the acute tension between the strained romantic affirmations of the letters of O'Neill in particular and the domestic collapse they are intended to conceal, a collapse outlined in King's full and revealing introduction which is valuable also for the accounts of Boulton's writing career and the history of the letters from composition to discovery (by the writer Max Wylie) and eventual publication. King's splendid narrative aside, the previous publication of several of the letters in Travis Bogard and Jackson R. Bryer's *The Selected Letters of Eugene O'Neill* (YaleUP [1988]) indicates that the volume will appeal primarily to the collecting instincts of those for whom every scrap of material about the writer, no matter how tangential to the artistic career, is valuable.

O'Neill's life is revisited in yet another substantial biographical undertaking that promises ultimately to be the fullest yet in Arthur and Barbara Gelb's *O'Neill: Life with Monte Cristo*, the first of a projected three-volume work that completely revises the authors' influential but flawed *Eugene O'Neill* [1960]. The authors make productive use of the voluminous quantity of unpublished material that has become available in the intervening years to present a substantial revision of key figures, including both of O'Neill's parents. I have not seen Maria T. Miliora's *Narcissism, the Family, and Madness: A Self-Psychological Study of Eugene O'Neill and his Plays* (Lang).

Unusually, biographical material takes a back seat in the latest *Eugene O'Neill Review* (volume 23; officially 1999, though the journal has been behind schedule for many years). Instead the issue contains ten critical analyses of a broad range of plays. William F. Condee's concluding remark, in 'Melodrama to Mood: Construction and Deconstruction of Suspense in the "S.S. Glencairn" Plays' (*EONR* 23[1999] 8–18), that much of O'Neill's work is concerned with 'humanity's relationship with the eternal and mystical forces of nature' is not uncharacteristic of a journal whose valedictory enthusiasm often prohibits discriminating critical engagement with the texts, but the shift towards sharper analysis, invoking both literary theory and often unexpectedly suggestive historical contexts, that appears to have begun with this issue is illustrated in Condee's attempt to get away from general terms such as 'melodrama' and 'mood piece' to describe how the plays work on the stage. Similarly, Laura Shea's 'An E(e)rie Sound: The Stage Directions in O'Neill's *Hughie*' (*EONR* 23[1999] 134–40) is crisp and detailed, yet ends with the demand for 'the dreamer's touch to realize the playwright's vision'. Nicholas Wallerstein uses Aristotelian rhetorical categories to analyse the dialogue of O'Neill's best-known play, in 'Accusation and Argument in Eugene O'Neill's *Long Day's Journey into Night*' (*EONR* 23[1999] 127–33). Several other pieces in the collection present particular plays in a new light by drawing attention to relatively unexplored and historically appropriate analogies and possible sources, exemplified in Michèle Mendelssohn's 'Reconsidering Race, Language and Identity in *The Emperor Jones*' (*EONR* 23[1999] 19–30), which explores the 'racialized genealogy' of Jones's language via the work of Franz Fanon and Homi K. Bhabha to present Jones as 'the post-colonial individual, the person who embodies both colonizer and colonized'. In 'Eugene O'Neill's *The Hairy Ape* and the Legacy of Andrew Carnegie' (*EONR* 23[1999] 31–48) Gene A. Plunka argues that the play was inspired by the steel magnate's death in 1919. Less novel are Mark A. Mossman's 'Eugene O'Neill and "the Myth of America": Ephraim Cabot as the American Adam' (*EONR* 23[1999] 49–59), although Mossman does place the Adam myth in *Desire under the Elms* within the specifically American context developed in R.W.B. Lewis's *The American Adam: Innocence, Tragedy and Tradition in the Nineteenth Century* [1955], and Daniel Larner's 'O'Neill's Fear and Pity: The Dionysian Living Death' (*EONR* 23[1999] 141–9), a study of aspects of the Greek influence on the playwright. In 'The Memory of Naked Ages: Charles Baudelaire, Eugene O'Neill and *the Great God Brown*' (*EONR* 23[1999] 60–77) Suzanne C. Toczyski argues that the Baudelairean influence is more extensive than has previously been shown.

Curiously *Ah, Wilderness!*, O'Neill's only comedy and a play that does not normally receive extensive attention, is the subject of three separate articles this year. It is considered alongside another of the playwright's works in Michael R. Schiavi's 'Eugene O'Neill's "New Men" and Theatrical Possibility: *Strange Interlude* and *Ah, Wilderness!*' (*JADT* 12:i[2000] 53–73), which finds in these plays 'effeminate, asexual or heterosexual, protagonists who complicate the semiotics of gender performance and divest effeminacy of its dramatic passivity'. Eleanor Heginbotham's 'Living With It: The Comic Valedictories of Faulkner and O'Neill, *Ah, Wilderness!* and *The Reivers*' (*SAF* 28:i[2000] 101–12) is another comparative piece, while the star performance in the play's 1933 production is considered in James Fisher's 'The Man who Owned Broadway: George M. Cohan's Triumph in Eugene O'Neill's *Ah, Wilderness!'* (*EONR* 23[1999] 98–126). Mike Riggs's argument in 'Parables Against Religion: The Modern Miracle of Humanity in O'Neill's *Dynamo* Cycle' (*JADT* 12:iii[2000] 14–26) is persuasive though quite familiar: *Dynamo* and *Days Without End* were 'misrecognized' as plays about religion, whereas really they are about 'the search for an ideal form of love'.

Resources for American Literary Study (26:i[2000]) is a special issue on American drama and contains three pieces on O'Neill: Michael Hinden, '"The right kind of pity": Notes on O'Neill's Revisions for *The Iceman Cometh*' (*RALS* 26:i[2000] 1–12), another example, like Tanya Schlam's 'Eugene O'Neill and the Creative Process: The Drafts of "Homecoming"' (*EONR* 23[1999] 78–97), of the possibilities for discovering O'Neill's working methods and ideas that have been stimulated by the voluminous quantities of draft material that are available; George Monteiro, 'Eugene O'Neill in Portugal and Brazil' (*RALS* 26:i[2000] 29–48), an account of the reception of O'Neill's work in those countries; and Glena Frank, '*Tempest* in Black and White: The 1924 Premiere of Eugene O'Neill's *All God's Chillun Got Wings*' (*RALS* 26:i[2000] 75–89), a documentary study of the controversies provoked by the play's treatment of miscegenation, and race generally. For essays in this issue on Arthur Miller and Tennessee Williams, see below.

Devlin and Tischler, eds., *The Selected Letters of Tennessee Williams*, volume i: *1920–1945*, contains approximately one-third of the letters from this period collected by the editors, and allows the reader to follow Williams from childhood through to the first major success with *The Glass Menagerie*. Almost all of the letters are followed by a parenthetical commentary that places the correspondence in context and gives the sense of a developing narrative. It goes without saying that this magnificent tome will become an invaluable resource for Williams scholars.

Philip C. Kolin, *Williams: 'A Streetcar Named Desire'*, appears in CUP's Plays in Production series, which aims to present accounts of a range of theatrical and non-theatrical productions. Kolin's opening chapter is a detailed reconstruction of the 1947 Broadway premiere that pays particular attention to the collaborative nature of the production. Less familiar, unless one has been keeping up with Kolin's recent publications in journals, is the material in the following chapter, which discusses the first productions of the play in six other countries. Following this is an overview of some of the most important English-language revivals between 1956 and 1998, Kolin's focus here being on the ways in which changing social relations between the sexes have influenced the treatment of the Stanley–Blanche relationship, she becoming generally more assertive and he weaker and less in control than in the premiere or indeed in Kazan's 1951 film, which has tended to fix in the public consciousness an overwhelmingly one-sided view of the power relations between the two that is unforgettable yet does not really do justice to the complexities of the play. The film is considered in the fifth and final chapter, alongside productions in other media such as ballets, teleplays and operas, yet it is the fourth chapter, which examines the ways in which black and gay performances have foregrounded tensions that remain latent or marginalized in more canonical, conventional productions, that allows Kolin to best explore the range of possibilities provoked by the play. This volume makes good use of the series format to present an accessible introduction to the performance possibilities of *Streetcar*.

The Southern Quarterly 38:i[1999], edited by Philip C. Kolin, is a special issue containing a range of articles on Williams's non-dramatic works as well as several photographs and illustrations, most extensively in Colby H. Kullman's 'Tennessee Williams's Mississippi Delta: A Photo Essay' (*SoQ* 38:i[1999] 124–40). The sheer range of modes and genres in which Williams wrote might have made for a very eclectic collection, but in fact the contributions are complementary, in almost every case being marked by a tendency, never far from the surface in Williams criticism, to see the texts in terms of confessional autobiography, and in particular as offering more or less coded revelations about the writer's sexuality. Given this emphasis, one of the most illuminating pieces is Terri Smith Ruckel, 'A "Giggling, Silly, Bitchy, Voluptuary": Tennessee Williams's *Memoirs* as *Apologia Pro Vita Sua*' (*SoQ* 38:i[1999] 94–103). The self-fashioning of Williams's ostensibly autobiographical tome has provided boundless material for those predominantly interested in the relationships between the life and the work, but Ruckel valuably explores the literary conventions of confessional writing by reading this text alongside St Augustine's *Confessions* as well as Newman's *Apologia*. Another essay to offer some critical reflection on the dominant mode of the collection is D. Dean Shakelford, '"The Transmutation of Experience": The Aesthetics and Themes of Tennessee Williams's Nonfiction' (*SoQ* 38:i[1999] 104–16), which suggests that some of the ideas advanced by Williams in his non-fictional prose are designed to invite a range of responses from readers. Foregrounding literary and aesthetic theory and focusing on the style of the writing, Shakelford opens up a number of worthwhile perspectives, though the essay suffers from a critical elision common in this kind of approach by shifting from a reader-response approach that recognizes the productive use of theory to the implicit suggestion that the theory is planted by the author: 'like many contemporary literary theorists, Williams problematizes subjectivity as a critical construct and opens up the possibility for Lacanian and other post-structuralist readings of literature'. This excessively self-conscious critical mode fails to convince.

Most of the other pieces in this issue of *Southern Quarterly* are more direct in positing connections between the man and the work. Mary F. Lux, 'Tenn Among the Lotus-Eaters: Drugs in the Life and Fiction of Tennessee Williams' (*SoQ* 38:i[1999] 117–23), is symptomatic, a wonderfully entertaining and well-written account of his use of narcotics and their possible effects on the writing: 'his life and works', writes Lux, 'read like a pharmacology of the lost'. There are four essays on short stories. Allean Hale's 'Tennessee Williams: The Preacher's Boy' (*SoQ* 38:i[1999] 10–20) suggests that the central relationship in the eponymous early, unpublished tale is in fact Williams's treatment of his own relationship with his grandfather, and traces the rhetoric of preaching as an influence on Williams's writing. Philip C. Kolin's 'Tennessee Williams's "Interval": MGM and Beyond' (*SoQ* 38:i[1999] 21–7) notes that this short story of 1945 may be read as a commentary on the playwright's fantasies about Hollywood and subsequent decision to abandon thoughts of a career as a screenwriter, and considers the female characters in the texts as anticipating those in some of the plays. Kolin also comments on the homoerotic aspects of the story in the light of the writer's own sexual experiences, while George W. Crandell, 'Peeping Tom: Voyeurism, Taboo, and Truth in the World of Tennessee Williams's

Short Fiction' (*SoQ* 38:i[1999] 28–35), more expansively suggests that in several stories Williams uses the figure of the voyeur to draw the reader into an unconventionally sympathetic reading both of the voyeur and of the sexual relationships he observes. Brenda Murphy, 'Brick Pollitt Agonistes: The Game in "Three Players of a Summer Game" and *Cat on a Hot Tin Roof*' (*SoQ* 38:i[1999] 36–44), suggests that Williams's problems with the ending of *Cat* are traceable to the earlier version in the short story: 'In order for Brick's character to be meaningful, he had to be beautiful, he had to be associated with homosexuality, and he had to suffer for that association', yet Williams 'was as unable to deal with the question of homosexuality in his protagonist as Brick was in his life. Thus the ambiguous, teasing ending of *Cat on a Hot Tin Roof*, which Williams chose to blame on Elia Kazan.' James Fisher, '"An Almost Posthumous Existence": Performance, Gender, and Sexuality in *The Roman Spring of Mrs. Stone*' (*SoQ* 38:i[1999] 45–57), and Robert Bray, 'Moise and the Man in the Fur Coat' (*SoQ* 38:i[1999] 59–70), are examinations of Williams's two novels. Fisher suggests that the harsh initial reception and flawed film treatment of the earlier, 1950, text has led to unfair critical neglect, and defends the novel for its characterization, its productive intertextual connections with *Sweet Bird of Youth* and *Suddenly Last Summer*, and for the figure of Karen, who 'deserv[es] central placement among Williams's most imaginative and original creations'. Bray sees the much later *Moise and the World of Reason* [1975] as a 'radical departure from his earlier aesthetics, as with this iconoclastic novel he forges a virtual polyglot genre consisting of equal parts *roman à clef*, autobiography, picaresque fiction, and confessional collapsed into a memory-circumscribed narrative'. There are two contributions on poetry: Jack Barbera, 'Three Interior Dramatic Monologues by Tennessee Williams' (*SoQ* 38:i[1999] 71–80), argues that the scene-setting and dramatic encounters of some of the poems are best read as monologues addressed by the speaker to himself, while Linda Dorff, '"I prefer the 'mad' ones": Tennessee Williams's Grotesque-Lyric Exegetical Poems' (*SoQ* 38:i[1999] 81–93), explores a range of specific connections between Williams's verse and Romantic poetry and philosophy.

Philip C. Kolin contributes additional short pieces on some of Williams's lesser-known works in 'Williams's *The Frosted Glass Coffin*' (*Expl* 59:i[2000] 44–6), an account of the comic aspects of this 1970 play about old age and death, and in 'Echoes of Reflexivity in Tennessee Williams's "A Perfect Analysis Given By a Parrot"' (*NConL* 30:iii[2000] 7–9). Brian Parker, 'Tennessee Williams and the Legends of St Sebastian' (*UTorQ* 69[2000] 634–59), is a richly illustrated and scholarly discussion of the homoerotic and religious associations in Williams's work of this iconographic figure. Parker not only examines the literary and biographical associations of St Sebastian, but also traces differing treatments of the figure in traditions of religious painting. Rod Phillips, '"Collecting Evidence": The Natural World in Tennessee Williams' *The Night of the Iguana*' (*SLJ* 32:ii[2000] 59–69), suggests that American drama has long been associated with the urban (one might point out, with critics such as Susan Harris Smith in *American Drama: The Bastard Art* (CUP [1997]), that formative cultural commentaries by the likes of Frederick Jackson Turner helped create this marginal role for drama). Phillips argues that, nevertheless, many American plays 'can provide useful and valuable information about humankind's relationship to the natural world', and he illustrates this not very promising thesis with specific reference to the Williams play. Craig

Clinton, 'Finding the Way: The Evolution of Tennessee Williams's *Vieux Carré*' (*RALS* 26:i[2000] 49–63), is an account of the development of the play through successive drafts.

Nancy M. Tischler, *Student Companion to Tennessee Williams*, and Susan C.W. Abbotson, *Student Companion to Arthur Miller*, appear in a Greenwood series that aims to provide the general reader, as much as the student, with a 'basic and yet challenging examination of the writer's canon'. In each volume, reasonably extensive discussions of seven or eight of the plays are preceded by chapters on biography and on 'literary heritage'. This involves an account of influences by and on others, though here the volumes also diverge: Tischler briefly explores the Southern context of Williams's writing, details his fondness for Romantic and Symbolist poetry, and gives a potted account of Williams in the context of American theatre in general, while Abbotson concentrates on Miller's 'themes'. In keeping with this disappointing emphasis, each of the eight plays Abbotson selects is identified with a key term, which immediately produces problems: the term for *Salesman* is 'tragedy', for example, while for *All My Sons* and *A View from the Bridge* it is 'family', but one could swap these headings around without further misrepresentation of the plays; and calling the chapter on *The Crucible* 'House Un-American Activities Committee' is equally reductive. It is also disappointing that, given the restrictions of space, so much of each volume is given over to plot summaries and to accounts of 'character development', which introduces an ideology of 'character' that could easily have been challenged even given the target audience. On the plus side, each chapter concludes with an 'alternate critical perspective' that gives the novice some impression of the range of responses to the plays. Abbotson's choice of plays is sensible, and the richness of some of Miller's later work, such as *The Ride Down Mount Morgan* and *Broken Glass*, allows for an evenly balanced retrospective. Williams's later work, of course, presents major difficulties: all of Tischler's plays bar one (*The Two-Character Play*, or *Out Cry*) belong to the period before 1964. Each volume includes a short bibliography, Tischler's preceded by a brief account of 'the lively world of Williams scholarship'.

Another introductory series from Greenwood, Literature in Context, has furnished two volumes on Miller's best-known plays: Claudia D. Johnson and Vernon E. Johnson's *Understanding 'The Crucible'* and Brenda Murphy and Susan C.W. Abbotson's *Understanding 'Death of a Salesman'*. The series is aimed squarely, it would seem, at the high-school market, although undergraduates may find the volumes useful in summarizing key themes and in providing convenient selections of documentary material. Each chapter is based around a theme, in which excerpts from contemporary sources, such as popular economic, social and philosophical treatises, are topped and tailed by editorial commentary on their relevance to the play and questions, topics and bibliographies for further study. A similar audience is envisaged for Siebold, ed., *Readings on 'Death of a Salesman'*, which appears in Greenhaven's Literary Companions series. The essays, all of which have been previously published, are edited and framed by an editorial synopsis that provides some perhaps unnecessary guidance, since these pieces have been well selected for the target market and no knowledge of theory is required to follow them. Consequently the book can appear anodyne: as the brief introduction points out, many have criticized Miller's representation of capitalism, but some would argue that this is because Miller does not go far enough, whereas in general this book tends towards reassurance of the MTV viewer and Britney fan. Nonetheless, alongside some very well known pieces are contributions by Robert N. Wilson and John S. Shockley that are less familiar and well worth reading.

Fred Ribkoff, 'Shame, Guilt, Empathy, and the Search for Identity in Arthur Miller's *Death of a Salesman*' (*MD* 43[2000] 48–55) takes a universalizing, ahistorical approach to the play to connect *Salesman* to Greek tragedy in familiar ways. More illuminating are two articles dealing with different Miller plays addressing the Holocaust. Miller acknowledged a debt to Camus's *The Fall* in writing *After the Fall*, but there is still much value in Derek Parker Royal's analysis of freedom, justice and culpability in this play in 'Camusian Existentialism in Arthur Miller's *After the Fall*' (*MD* 43[2000] 192–203). Claiming that 'When Miller has been read as an existentialist dramatist ... it is in light of Sartre, and when he has been read as a Camusian dramatist, it is at the expense of any underlying existential ethic', Parker Royal valuably distinguishes between the early Sartre, in whom 'There is little room for mediation between personal and collective values', and Camus's works, which 'are concerned with the possibility of tempering individual action with an over-arching sense of solidarity'; seen in these terms Miller's plays clearly display closer affinities with Camus. *Broken Glass* is considered, alongside Cynthia Ozick's *Blue Light*, in Joyce Antler, '"Three Thousand Miles Away": The Holocaust in Recent Works for the American Theater', a contribution to Flanzbaum, ed., *The Americanization of the Holocaust* (pp. 125–41). Suggesting that in very different ways each of these works is about Holocaust denial, Antler aptly cites Elinor Fuchs's argument 'that collective catastrophe rather than individual suffering is the most authentic theatrical expression of the Holocaust'. George W. Crandell, '"Trial by Public Opinion": Arthur Miller Reviews "The New York Crime Show"' recuperates a forgotten text, Miller's commentary on the Kefauver hearings into organized crime that was published by the left-wing *New York Daily Compass* in March 1951.

Gerald C. Wood has published two books on Horton Foote. *Horton Foote and the Theater of Intimacy* is both a clear, sympathetic and engaging account that makes one wish to discover more of the work of this prolific writer for stage, television and film, and also helps to explain why he has received far less attention than many of his contemporaries and near-contemporaries. Sometimes characterized as the 'American Chekhov', Foote, like Faulkner, returns again and again to a fictionalized treatment of his home town of Wharton, Texas, each play interacting with the others to trace subtle changes in the lives of the characters. Unlike Faulkner, Foote, in Wood's account, is no stylistic radical: Wood places him within 'the tradition of historical realism', and finds a recurrent pattern in the 'saintly women' who offer a sense of 'the primary forces of life', leading Wood to argue that Foote's is a theatre of 'belief', 'faith' or 'spiritualism'. One can see that Foote's drama remains too close to the conventions of the dominant cultural forms—his relatively prolific output for television, detailed in Wood's excellent bibliography, is symptomatic— for him to engage fully in that critique of social, sexual and familial relations that, rightly or wrongly, tends to characterize the plays and dramatists who have been accepted into what one can still call the American dramatic canon. Nevertheless, and despite its brevity, this book provides a detailed and engaging discussion of a playwright who perhaps has more in common with some of the major writers of the American short story than with his fellow dramatists.

A broader range of perspectives on Foote is opened up in Wood, ed., *Horton Foote: A Casebook*. Marion Castleberry's 'Remembering Wharton, Texas' and Rebecca Briley's 'Southern Accents: Horton Foote's Adaptations of William Faulkner, Harper Lee, and Flannery O'Connor' dissect the importance of place in Foote's work, while Briley's essay, along with Terry Barr's 'Horton Foote's TV Women' and S. Dixon McDowell's 'Horton Foote's Film Aesthetic', helps to explain why Foote's style and methods have enabled his work to translate so well to the screen. Other essays valuably question the extent to which Foote's work should be described as realistic: Tim Wright's 'More Real than Realism: Horton Foote's Impressionism' sees Foote as an impressionist writer, 'try[ing] to synthesize objective and subjective experience', for example through mood, ambiguity, fragmentation and the use of music, which is the subject of Crystal Brian's '"To be quiet and listen": *The Orphans' Home Cycle* and the Music of Charles Ives'. Conversely, Laurin Porter's 'Subtext as Text: Language and Culture in Horton Foote's Texas Cycle' argues that the understatement and indirection of the dialogue comments on a Southern culture that inculcates such values as respect for one's elders and the forbidding of emotional display. As with many of the essays in the book, one wishes for a more rigorous theoretical grounding here. The final section of the *Casebook* offers several detailed analyses of the series of plays Foote wrote for the Signature Theatre Company's season in 1994–5, and complements Wood's extensive discussions of three plays in *Horton Foote and the Theater of Intimacy*. The bibliographies in Wood's studies are augmented by Laurin Porter, 'The Horton Foote Collection at the DeGolyer Library' (*RALS* 26:i[2000] 64–74).

The relative lack of scholarly interest in Edward Albee recently is redressed to some extent by the appearance of two new books. Mel Gussow, *Edward Albee: A Singular Journey* is a biography that benefits from its subject's openness with the author. Not only does the book shed much light on the life, which Albee has previously been extremely reluctant to discuss, but Gussow's accounts of the work also benefit from the playwright's willingness to make available much correspondence and other documentation. The account of Albee's boyhood adoption into a family that had extraordinary wealth but little emotional warmth begins a narrative in which the relationships between the life and work remain quite clear throughout. Unlike some other volumes in CUP's Plays in Production series, Stephen J. Bottoms's *Albee: 'Who's Afraid of Virginia Woolf?'* considers only a few productions in detail—five in the third and final chapter, and the 1962 Broadway premiere and the 1966 film version starring Richard Burton and Elizabeth Taylor in the first—although a number of others receive brief comment. As Bottoms's introduction acknowledges, there is no immediately obvious fit between this play and the series: a four-character play set in a living-room has not offered auteur directors the freedom of radical interpretation, and changes from production to production are subtly nuanced, but Bottoms invokes speech-act theory to defend the choice of play on the grounds that it is very much about performativity, though a similar case could be made for any number of plays. No matter: this is the first major book-length study of this seminal work, and by rather stretching the rubric of the series, and gaining an interview with Albee himself, Bottoms is able to give detailed critical analysis not only of performances but of the play-text and, in the second chapter, of its critical reception from the premiere to the present. There is also a detailed reconstruction of Albee's writing process. Bottoms writes elegantly and with wit and verve, and the book will contribute substantially to the renaissance in Albee's reputation.

Bottoms's previous book was the equally fine *The Theatre of Sam Shepard* (CUP [1998]), but if Albee's career and reputation are undergoing a revival, the reverse appears to be true of Shepard. Substantial criticism on this playwright has been thin on the ground for a couple of years, and Johan Callens, 'Diverting the Integrated Spectacle of War: Sam Shepard's *States of Shock*' (*TPQ* 20[2000] 290–306) suggests a possible reason why. Callens explores this apparent commentary on the Gulf War via the theory and practice of situationist spectacle and the philosophy of Guy Debord, alongside other theoretical work on postmodernism by Baudrillard, Lyotard and others, but indicates that the play's critique of war as spectacle is contradicted by its own obsession with technological excess. A similar aspect of Shepard's work is explored in Alex Vernon, 'Staging Violence in West's *The Day of the Locust* and Shepard's *True West*' (*SoAR* 65:i[2000] 132–51), which picks up on Shepard's enthusiastic comment that Nathanael West's novel 'says it all' about Hollywood, and relates both texts to René Girard's theories about violence, suggesting that violence is inextricably bound up with the never-ending processes of identity formation. See also Michael Byrne, 'The Real Thing: Sam Shepard's *True West*' (*NConL* 29:v[2000] 3–5).

I once knew a student who used to claim that he spent his summers trying to explain the art of batting to Graham Gooch, who was at that time captain of England and widely regarded as the finest opening batsman in the world. I was reminded of this in reading Myles Weber's 'David Mamet in Theory and Practice' (*NERMS* 21:ii[2000] 136–41), which is quite the silliest essay I have ever seen in a scholarly journal. In this breezily schoolteacherly mid-term report on Mamet's career, Weber, who is apparently a fellow playwright, affirms that 'Drama, Mamet concluded long ago, is good for one thing only: telling a story', and considers that, while 'Mamet acquits himself on gender'—one can almost hear the sigh of relief from Vermont—'he has less success with the issues of Judaism and the American Jewish identity, which only serve to make him crabby', while Mamet's view of Disneyland as a totalitarian state 'echo[es] the work of our laziest academics'. The vague suspicion thus engendered that 'Myles Weber' is really the emotionally damaged Mickey Mouse in disguise grows into near-certainty when he remarks that Mamet's views on economics betray his 'wasted undergraduate years', and that 'Anyone familiar with both works knows, in fact, that *Glengarry Glen Ross* is far superior to *American Buffalo*'. Let us hope that Johan Callens feels suitably apologetic for having wasted his time writing 'Mr. Smith Goes to Chicago: Playing Out Mamet's Critique of Capitalism in *American Buffalo*' (*European Journal of American Culture* 19:i[2000] 17–29), a strikingly innovative essay that, *pace* Weber, discovers a fascinating nexus of economic ideas circulating in the play, beginning with 'the precarious relationship Adam Smith set up between "self-interest" and "sympathy" [which] forms the crux of *American Buffalo*'. For Callens, 'friendship' and 'liking' are the cognate terms for Smith's in the play, which is prefaced by a 'motto mixing religious aspiration and materialist greed' and the description of Teach as Don's 'friend and associate', while the poker game and reams of spurious advice and commentary on business are similarly informed by a dialectic between greed and moral precept derived from America's Franklinian confusion of theology and self-interest. Callens very productively situates the play's dialogue within the theoretical contexts of Jürgen Habermas's ideas of the 'public sphere' and his distinction between 'communicative reason' and 'instrumental reason'.

Howard Pearce's 'Plato in Hollywood: David Mamet and the Power of Illusions' (*Mosaic* 32:ii[1999] 141–56) is a tough read, situating *House of Games* and *Speed-the-Plow* within a Platonic philosophical context which is potentially highly productive but on the one hand becomes too restrictive and on the other generates categories and a vocabulary that are too broad to convince: for example, 'Karen and Gould, then, reflect that ambivalence of the playwright, inclining, on the one hand, towards Philebus and Clark Kent while reflecting, on the other, the attractiveness of Socrates and Superman. And they know, if not the truth, at least some questions about Art and Love …'. Another Mamet work that deals with relations between the sexes, *Oleanna*, continues to fascinate critics, partly because of the confrontation it stages between a male liberal arts professor and a female student, even though the debates it provokes would seem to have been rehearsed to death long ago. The issues are lucidly articulated in Stanton B. Garner, 'Framing the Classroom: Pedagogy, Power, *Oleanna*' (*ThTop* 10:i[2000] 39–52). Garner 'has never been a fan of *Oleanna*' because it 'clearly stacks the emotional and ideological deck against Carol' and because 'Mamet evokes a violence both onstage and offstage that he fails to accurately name and that he directs at the play's easiest target'. His introductory remarks contextualize this view in the light of responses to the play by critics and audiences, and give a useful overview of the political and pedagogical contexts in which these responses were evoked; most of the essay is devoted to an account of the often uncomfortable surprises he encountered when teaching the play to students. Another essay to make productive use of empirical observations of audience responses is David Kennedy Sauer's '*Oleanna* and *The Children's Hour*: Misreading Sexuality on the Post/Modern Realistic Stage' (*MD* 43[2000] 421–41), which makes a distinction between 'a modernist confession marked by a key feature of modernism, dualistic ambiguity, and the postmodern confession constructed in terms of multivalent indeterminacy', Lillian Hellman's play offering an example of the former and Mamet's of the latter. While it is not every day that one sees Mamet bracketed with Jean-François Lyotard, and while Sauer's description of Mamet as 'a representative postmodern' is open to objections, this is a thoughtful piece that successfully relates the reception of *Oleanna* to Mamet's anti-Method theory of acting. Along related lines, the Derridean theory invoked by Thomas E. Porter in 'Postmodernism and Violence in Mamet's *Oleanna*' (*MD* 43[2000] 13–31) is superfluous to an otherwise lucid analysis that persuasively articulates what is becoming a standard line on the play: that, as Mamet would insist, there is nothing as unified as 'character' in either John or Carol, and that the radical discontinuities in them and in the action should be traced to the ways in which the play worries away at the fault-lines in contemporary America between the liberal proponents of cultural difference and conservative foundational principles, and between liberal humanism and postmodernism. Two of Mamet's screenplays are examined in Gaylord Brewer, '*Hoffa* and *The Untouchables*: Mamet's Brutal Orders of Authority' (*LFQ* 28:i[2000] 28–33). Brewer argues that both screenplays 'consider the dynamics of masculine power from both inside and outside of written law … Both films look at their subjects through nostalgic lenses directed toward the past, both resurrect variations on Mamet's familiar mentor–protégé relationship, and both, most significantly, present at their centers tarnished figures of masculine dominance.' This is all familiar, and though Brewer writes with characteristic elegance, one would have welcomed further discussion of the charge of 'nostalgia', perhaps by an examination of the ways in which the screenplays deviate from versions of the historical record.

Alice Griffin and Geraldine Thorsten's *Understanding Lillian Hellman* and Mary L. Bogumil's *Understanding August Wilson* appear in the USCP's very basic Understanding Contemporary American Literature series. Both contain biographical information followed by a discussion of key plays that is too simple to be particularly helpful, although the Hellman volume also contains some worthwhile discussion of the memoirs. Bogumil offers a chapter on each of the six plays in Wilson's extraordinary cycle that had appeared to date of publication. Several introductory accounts of Wilson's work have now been published, and although some of these contain difficult material and there is a market for a simpler book, one doubts whether the audience for Wilson's accessible yet challenging plays will be satisfied with Bogumil's sensible but unambitious book. Like many other critics Susan C.W. Abbotson, in 'From Jug Band to Dixieland: The Musical Development behind August Wilson's *Ma Rainey's Black Bottom*' (*MD* 43[2000] 100–8), traces the meanings of this play through the music, in this case to argue that contrary to common opinion Levee, and not Ma, emerges as the more significant and sympathetic character. Harry J. Elam Jr.'s wide-ranging and detailed 'August Wilson, Doubling, Madness, and Modern African-American Drama' (*MD* 43[2000] 611–32) begins with another character in the same play, Sylvester, in examining a range of characters who are or appear mad; on Wilson's stage such figures, Elam argues, 'represent a connection to a powerful, transgressive spirituality, to a lost African consciousness, and to a legacy of black social activism'. Elam illuminatingly places such figures within the literary and historical contexts of 'racial madness', whereby the African American experience requires a form of 'double consciousness' to negotiate one's position within, and perception by, white America. Susan C.W. Abbotson, 'What Does August Wilson Teach in *The Piano Lesson*? The Place of the Past and Why Willie Boy Knows More than Berniece' (*JADT* 12:i[2000] 83–101) is a close reading focusing on the multiple interpretative possibilities generated by the piano. Anna S. Blumenthal's claim in '"More stories than the devil's got sinners": Troy's Stories in August Wilson's *Fences*' (*AmDram* 9:ii[2000] 74–96) that 'readers of Wilson's work have not explored in depth Wilson's use of stories in his plays as key strategies in developing his characters, themes, and the social dynamics of character interaction in particular scenes' appears empirically inaccurate, and the absence of any theoretical construction of 'character' in this essay is disabling, although there are some useful comparisons to folkloric 'Stack-O-Lee' figures.

Several other playwrights received less extensive critical attention. Sally Porterfield, 'Black Cats and Green Trees: The Art of Maria Irene Fornes' (*MD* 43[2000] 204–15), looks a little out of place in an academic journal: it serves as a basic introduction to Fornes's work, built around an anecdotally reconstructed but illuminating interview with the dramatist, the kind of thing that would serve very well as an introduction to a collection of plays. In 'Staging a Staged Crisis in Masculinity: Race and Masculinity in *Six Degrees of Separation*' (*AmDram* 9:ii[2000] 50–73), Jennifer Gillan situates John Guare's play in the context of the 1980s Reaganite, masculinist backlash against feminism, seeing it as 'dramatiz[ing] the shifting of blame for social and economic exploitation and general societal decay onto a "deviant" individual'. Finally, any overview of contemporary American drama runs into the problem of attempting to distinguish between drama and performance art. In general I have erred on the side of omission of the latter, but *Modern Drama* 43:iii[2000] contains a sequence of three essays that give some sense of the ways in which the boundary is eroding. S.E. Wilmer's 'Restaging the Nation: The Work of Suzan-Lori Parks' (*MD* 43[2000] 442–52) directly addresses this question of boundaries in an essay that serves well as an introduction to Parks's work by discussing her as a post-colonial dramatist, looking at the ways in which boundaries of space, time and character are challenged by plays that stage the return of the marginalized, African American figures of America's past. The theoretical framework, derived substantially from Baudrillard and Homi K. Bhabha, will be well known to anyone remotely familiar with contemporary approaches to post-colonialism, but Wilmer uses the theory lucidly and persuasively. (On Parks, see also Robert Baker-White's eco-political 'Questioning the Ground of American Identity: George Pierce Baker's *The Pilgrim Spirit* and Suzan-Lori Parks's *The America Play*' (*JADT* 12:ii[2000] 71–89).) Bennett Tracy Huffman, '*Twister*: Ken Kesey's Multimedia Theatre' (*MD* 43[2000] 453–60) is a clearly presented introduction to a work that is new to me, though again, one is familiar enough with 'postmodern self-reflexivity' to feel that a discussion of a text in these terms is likely to obscure rather than illuminate its distinctive qualities. The current tendency for the essays in *Modern Drama* to describe texts in very clear, but also very familiar, theoretical terms is also apparent in Kurt Lancaster, 'Theatrical Deconstructionists: The Social "Gests" of Peter Sellars's *Ajax* and Robert Wilson's *Einstein on the Beach*' (*MD* 43[2000] 461–8), although Lancaster does situate the works in more explicitly theatrical contexts by emphasizing the influences of Appia, Meyerhold and Brecht.

5. African American Writing

A number of collections of new and previously published theoretical and critical writings and primary texts, as well as works of reference, make valuable contributions to African American literary studies this year. The very substantial Napier, ed., *African American Literary Theory: A Reader*, is of central importance here. The anthology is a large but affordable and unique collection; its appearance is timely and very much to be welcomed. Napier's aim is to present the central texts and arguments of African American literary theory from the 1920s to the end of the 1990s, and the rise of black aesthetics, the Black Arts Movement, feminism, structuralism, post-structuralism and queer theory are all covered here. But the emphasis of the anthology is very much towards the contemporary rather than the historical. While the period from 1920 to the end of the 1970s takes up about 150 pages, the 1980s and 1990s take up around 500. This historical imbalance may, in one sense, be an accurate reflection of the rise of theory proper in African American literary discourse, and the strength of the anthology is very much the presentation of the major contemporary debates, with the pre-1980s periods providing a kind of historical frame. On the other hand, the bias towards the contemporary can also be read as a potentially distorting presentism where both literary history and the conceptualization of theory are concerned. One can imagine that the inclusion of writers such as Ishmael Reed or Nathaniel Mackey, or critics such as Kenneth Warren and Werner Sollors, might have altered and expanded the understanding of the theorization of African American literature. If the collection presents an accurate portrait of a particular institutional moment, it also fails to build into itself adequate resistance to this moment. Nevertheless, this is an important publication. For scholars who are familiar with the critical texts, it offers an opportunity for reassessment and review; for students this is an accessible and lively introduction to the field.

The uses of theory in cultural and literary analysis are well illustrated by Kimberly Benston's densely argued and often skilful readings of drama, poetry, music, sermons and critical discourse in *Performing Blackness: Enactments of African-American Modernism*. Benston's aim is to provide 'a preliminary exploration of the performative ethos informing African-American modernism, where "black modernism" designates that politico-aesthetic ferment arising with the black consciousness movement of the 1960s, a still-living moment in which a sustained effort to transform representation into presentation became the hallmark of a fresh chapter in the history of African-American cultural expression'. Benston argues for an understanding of blackness as performative and processual rather than as product and essence. This is not in itself a radically new critical position to adopt, but Benston offers perhaps the most critically informed and careful defence of it to date. Less satisfactory is Benston's attempt to distinguish between black and non-black performative modes in modernity. For Benston, African American modernism 'augurs a sacramentalised performative present in order to redeem, not deny, the promissory notes of historicized subjectivity', whereas white performative modes have 'not produced a vision or methodology of audience identification sufficient to transform mimetic designs into … "methixis," or participatory and collective practices'. These contrasts and characterizations are sustained by broad generalizations about the nature of Western modernity and are not adequately grounded in close examinations of the performative modes of 'white' arts from the 1960s and after; equally, the redemptive vision of black art seems to edge uneasily at times into an idealist model of social efficacy and transformation.

James and Sharpley-Whiting, eds., *The Black Feminist Reader*, is more narrowly focused than *African American Literary Theory* and less ambitious in its aims. It seeks not to provide a broad and inclusive historical overview, but to bring together ten major essays from the last twenty-five years as a way of introducing the central preoccupations of contemporary black feminism. The essays (by the likes of Barbara Christian, Toni Morrison, Angela Y. Davis, bell hooks and Hortense Spillars among others) are thematically grouped in two sections: 'Literary Theory' and 'Social and Political Theory'. It is a strength of the collection that it invites the reader, through this juxtaposition, to explore the intersections of literature, politics, law and social issues. Worth mentioning alongside *The Black Feminist Reader* is the welcome reissue of the well-known and influential collection of essays, poems, fiction, drama and photographs edited by Barbara Smith, *Home Girls: A Black Feminist Anthology* [1983].

Bennett and Dickerson, eds., *Recovering the Black Female Body: Self-Representations by African American Women*, and Margo V. Perkins, *Autobiography as Activism: Three Black Women of the Sixties*, can usefully be read alongside the debates configured in *The Black Feminist Reader*. The Bennett and Dickerson volume brings together thirteen new essays which collectively examine not only the ways in which the black female body has been represented from the nineteenth century to the present, but, more significantly, how African American women have responded to this mediation through self-representation. This particular focus anchors the collection's claim to be an original contribution to the already vast literature on race, gender and the body. The essays range from examinations of the fictions of well-known writers such as Pauline Hopkins, Nella Larsen and Toni Morrison to the cultural politics of body-building and hair, and it is this diversity that keeps the collection lively. Perkins's *Autobiography as Activism* examines not only Angela Davis's autobiography, but also Assata Shakur's *Assata* [1987] and Elaine Brown's *A Taste of Power: A Black Woman's Story* [1992]. These are the only three autobiographies by women to emerge out of the Black Power movement, and Perkins's book makes a valuable contribution not only to the history of a movement which has largely been seen in masculine terms but also to African American women's social and literary studies. Perkins's primary aim is not a literary evaluation but an examination of the 'cultural work activists' narratives do' and 'the different ways these activists use autobiography to connect their own circumstances with those of other activists across historical periods, their emphatic linking of the personal and the political in agitating for transformative action, and their constructing an alternative history that challenges hegemonic ways of knowing'. Perkins's book is short, tightly focused and careful to respect the need for clarity of communication that her subject demands.

Of the anthologies mentioned at the start of this review, Werner Sollors's *Interracialism: Black–White Intermarriage in American History, Literature, and Law* is certainly the most innovative, diverse and historically substantial. Clearly growing out of Sollors's own earlier critical work *Neither Black Nor White Yet Both: Thematic Explorations of Interracial Literature* (OUP [1997]), the collection brings together a genuinely impressive range of materials from history, law, literature and social theory in order to explore the anxieties about interracial sexual relations, interracial marriage and interracial descent which penetrate to the heart of American self-fashioning. Traversing the whole of the twentieth century, the collection includes Supreme Court decisions, legal essays, literary extracts and analyses and essays in social theory. Unlike the material contained in the other anthologies examined so far, much of what is here is not generally available; the collection is to be commended not only for making such material available (as well as a number of previously unpublished contributions), but also for its interdisciplinary approach. (*Crossing the Line: Racial Passing in Twentieth-Century U.S. Literature and Culture* by Gayle Freda Wald, which would clearly help extend the concerns of interracialism, was unavailable for review.)

In its focus on the cultural and social meanings of the movement between races, *Interracialism* also makes a contribution to what may be called a comparativist approach in African American literary criticism. Within the nationalist paradigm of American Studies such an approach encourages the reading of African American literature in dialogue with the other literatures of the United States. However, recent preoccupations with the 'black Atlantic' and with the limitations of the nationalist paradigm of American Studies have broadened the framework for comparison and made it continental and trans-continental. A number of books and articles this year contribute in different ways to the possibilities for such comparisons and can usefully be examined as a group alongside *Interracialism*.

Skerrett, ed., *Literature, Race, and Ethnicity: Contesting American Identities*, is yet another anthology and, again, a useful one. Gathering together poetry, fiction, historical documents, letters, advertisements, speeches, artwork and photographs from the 1700s to the present in a single, manageable volume, the collection aims to provide for students an overview of thinking about race and ethnicity in the United States. Most of the selections are necessarily short, but they are arranged in a way that will provoke thought and debate.

Jane Davis's *The White Image in the Black Mind: A Study of African American Literature* takes its cue from older studies of the black image in the white mind and from the more recent development of 'whiteness studies' and offers a typological study of the representation of whites in African American writers such as Charles Chesnutt, Langston Hughes, Richard Wright and James Baldwin, as well as more contemporary writers. Though this is an important topic and Davis makes a useful contribution, the writing is too often reminiscent of the rhetorical formulas of graduate theses and the readings of the texts do not manage to transform the taxonomy of 'overt white supremacist', 'hypocrite', 'good-hearted weakling' and 'liberal' into critically sophisticated and satisfactory accounts of the literature. One key aim of the book is to demonstrate how 'a typology which is mainly negative' can 'actually constitute a liberating mythology'. The notion of a 'liberating mythology' may give some sense of Davis's critical orientation and, in the end, her book remains a rather old-fashioned survey of literary types and stereotypes.

Ethan Goffman's *Imagining Each Other: Blacks and Jews in Contemporary American Literature* is another comparative reading of African American literature from within the national literary traditions, and also another contribution to a growing body of work on Black–Jewish interactions in American culture. Though focused primarily on the 1960s and the years following, the book looks at a broad swath of literature from the twentieth century. Each chapter is structured, Goffman explains, 'as a brief discussion of historical events followed by close analysis of key literary texts'. However, most of the readings are not particularly lengthy and the book works best as an overview or survey. Its conceptualization of representation, as well as its account of 'contemporary American literature' as 'fractured by competing racial and ethnic voices' and as 'one element in a clamorous dialogue, a conversation inherent in multiethnic democracy', tend to work at fairly obvious levels, as does the book's strategy of juxtaposing 'history' and 'literature'. Useful as a way into the field perhaps, Goffman's book lacks the sophistication and thoroughness of some other recent examinations of the interactions of African American and Jewish American writing, such as Emily Miller Budick's *Blacks and Jews in Literary Conversation* (CUP [1998]) and Adam Zachary Newton's *Facing Black and Jew: Literature as Public Space in Twentieth-Century America* (CUP [1999]). Jacqueline K. Bryant's *The Foremother Figure in Early Black Women's Literature: Clothed in My Right Hand* (a late arrival for review from last year) also conducts its comparisons within the nationalist framework. Its argument is that 'the foremother figure … emerging in early black women's fiction revises the stereotypical mammy in early white women's fiction', and that 'in the context of the mulatta heroine the foremother produces minimal language that, through an Afrocentric rhetoric, distinguishes her from the stereotypical mammy and thus links her peripheral role and unusual behaviour to cultural continuity and racial uplift'. The writers examined include the likes of Harriet Beecher Stowe, Kate Chopin, Harriet Jacobs, Frances Harper, Pauline Hopkins and Jessie Redmond Fauset, as well as Zora Neale Hurston, Ann Petry and Gloria Naylor.

Among works developing a post-national approach to the literatures of the Americas, George B. Handley's *Postslavery Literatures in the Americas: Family Portraits in Black and White* is a notable and impressive contribution. Bringing together a genuinely exciting rather than merely diverse range of writers (George Washington Cable, Cirilio Villaverde, Frances Harper, Martín Morúa Delgado, Alejo Carpentier, William Faulkner, Toni Morrison and Jean Rhys, among others), Handley is interested in those works of literature that 'return to slavery's past in a genealogical exploration of its deep, historical roots in order to understand its relationship to the present'. Handley both clearly acknowledges the pitfalls of cross-cultural and trans-historical comparisons and negotiates them with considerable skill, working always with provisional paradigms and explorations. The readings are generally well attuned to the specificities of the texts and their historical contexts. The chapter on Carpentier and Faulkner is particularly welcome because Carpentier's remarkable body of work remains even today unfairly overshadowed in the English-speaking world by the novels of later Latin American writers. *Postmodern Tales of Slavery in the Americas: From Alejo Carpentier to Charles Johnson* (Garland) by Timothy J. Cox, which would appear to share some concerns with Handley's work, was not available for review.

Alexis Brooks De Vita's *Mythatypes: Signatures and Signs of African/Diaspora and Black Goddesses* follows a quite different tack to Handley. The book claims to be 'an analytical survey of Pan-African women's literatures written predominantly in English, French, and Italian, including poetry and excerpts in Spanish'. The 'goal' of the analyses is defined as 'the exploration of historical, legendary, and mythical culturally relevant female figures as they appear in, and interact with, the protagonists and creators of Pan-African women's literatures'. The boundary between the critical examination of mythology and the mythologizing of literature is unstable to say the least in De Vita's book, but such critical concern is likely to be dismissed by De Vita, since she claims that 'Whether or not symbol systems in Pan-African women's works may ever be exhaustively excavated in an academically accepted archaeology of ancient African religious systems and their predominant female figures is questionable and possibly immaterial to early efforts at mythatypical literary analysis'. De Vita argues for 'the need for culture-specific, literary analytical tools', but does not really explain how her own essentializing of a diverse range of writings across several cultures and historical periods meets such a need. The argument for specificity begins to look even shakier when 'symbols such as trees, rain, and wind' are claimed as special markers of a pan-African women's writing tradition.

Zora Neale Hurston's attempt to formulate a transnational understanding of African American culture is the topic of Annette Trefzer's 'Possessing the Self: Caribbean Identities in Zora Neale Hurston's *Tell My Horse*' (*AAR* 34[2000] 299–312). Though Trefzer's handling of Hurston's defence of United States imperialism is uneasy, the article is valuable for the attention it pays to perhaps the most neglected of Hurston's works. *Tell My Horse* has been poorly recuperated in the light of contemporary debates about the relationship of ethnography and literature, with a handful of scholars making rather exaggerated claims for its achievement as experimental ethnography. Ironically, this has actually obscured the real contribution of the book to an early twentieth-century debate about the nature of New World culture. Here it is also worth mentioning John Lowney's 'Haiti and Black Transnationalism: Remapping the Migrant Geography of *Home to Harlem*' (*AAR* 34[2000] 413–30). Lowney shifts attention away from the critique of the primitivist tendencies in McKay's novel and argues instead that, 'by writing the West Indian immigrant narrative as a narrative of Haitian exile, McKay suggests a common ground for cross-cultural dialogue among African American and Caribbean critics of American imperialism'. Also worth noting here is Donald Pease's 'C.L.R. James, *Moby-Dick*, and the Emergence of Transnational American Studies' (*ArQ* 56:iii[2000] 93–123), which examines the impact of James's detention on Ellis Island in 1952 on his book on Melville, and reads this book as a trans-national or post-national reconfiguration of the exceptionalist and nationalist paradigm of American Studies. Focusing on an earlier period, Philip Gould's 'Free Carpenter, Venture Capitalist: Reading the Lives of the Early Black Atlantic' (*AmLH* 12[2000] 659–84) reads early black Atlantic autobiography 'in the context of the cultural emergence of liberal rights discourse' and argues that critics have not recognized 'the creative ways in which early black autobiographers pushed at [the] semantic boundaries [of the language of the American Revolution] to disrupt traditional norms of social subordination'.

Cyraina E. Johnson-Roullier's *Reading on the Edge: Exiles, Modernities, and Cultural Transformation in Proust, Joyce and Baldwin* takes as the point of departure for its comparative investigations not a shared history or geography, but two questions about the relationship of international modernism and national literatures: 'what is the nature of the instability between the boundaries drawn by international modernism and those drawn by national literatures, and, in spite of that instability, why do modernism and the national literatures share a racial homogeneity that would seem to belie the embattled border between them?' The re-readings of *A la recherche du temps perdu*, *A Portrait of the Artist as a Young Man* and *Giovanni's Room* provide the occasion for the exploration of theoretical issues which are the primary concern of the book: the nature of transcultural understanding, the relationship of criticism and institutional structures, and canon formation. The issues may be all too familiar by now, but Johnson-Roullier's rigour and erudition genuinely revitalize the contemporary debates and make her work stand out from the norm. A number of other works that also undertake comparative analyses were unavailable for review: Helen Thomas, *Romanticism and Slave Narratives: Transatlantic Testimonies* (CUP); Gina Wisker, *Post-Colonial and African American Women's Writing: A Critical Introduction* (Palgrave); Valentine Udoh James, James S. Etim and Melanie M. James, eds., *Black Women Writers Across Cultures* (UPA); and Dale E. Peterson, *Up from Bondage: The Literatures of Russian and African American Soul* (DukeUP).

A work that contributes to both the study of nineteenth-century African American literature and culture and contemporary concerns with the black Atlantic is Robert S. Levine's excellent 'Road to Africa: Frederick Douglass's Rome' (*AAR* 34[2000] 217–32). Placing Douglass's account of his travels in *Life and Times of Frederick Douglass* [1892] in the context of other nineteenth-century accounts of Rome by Americans, Levine demonstrates not only the way in which Douglass presents himself 'as the archetypal conflicted American traveler' but also how he, unlike most white travellers to Rome, 'extolled the miscegenated origins of Western civilization'. Where Levine examines the uses of Europe by an African American writer, Audrey Fisch's short and tightly argued *American Slaves in Victorian England: Abolitionist Politics in Popular Literature and Culture* looks at the presence of African Americans and abolitionist discourse in England. The book focuses on the reception of abolitionist ideas and texts in England in the 1850s, examining in particular the response to *Uncle Tom's Cabin*, the publication of *Uncle Tom in England*, John Brown's *Slave Life in Georgia* and the lecture tours of free blacks and ex-slaves in England. This is a polished and scholarly work, and the examination of the reactionary consolidation of English nationalism via a conflation of American abolitionism and English Chartism in *Uncle Tom in England* is particularly engaging.

The other significant contribution to early African American literature and culture is the excellent collection by Newman, Rael and Lapsansky, eds., *Pamphlets of Protest: An Anthology of Early African American Protest Literature, 1790–1860*. This carefully edited volume makes available a well-chosen selection from an important body of African American writing that has not received the attention that slave narratives and autobiographies have. In a detailed and informed introduction, the editors locate the pamphlets in their social and historical contexts and open up a reading of the texts that confirms the importance of their contribution to late eighteenth- and nineteenth-century African American cultural and political discourses. Other works dealing with early African American literature make less substantial contributions. Sterling Lecater Bland Jr.'s *Voices of the Fugitives: Runaway Slave Stories and their Fictions of Self-Creation* is addressed to undergraduates, general readers and those 'new to the field of African-American literature' and goes over well-trodden ground in its account of the techniques of self-authorization and the rhetoric of self-creation and identity formation. The concluding insights that identity may be a cultural fabrication and that the slave texts are complex literary constructs hold no surprises for anyone with the most basic scholarship in this area. Tackach, ed., *Slave Narratives*, is a study guide aimed at undergraduates and perhaps high-school students. The book uses short extracts from a good range of scholarly works to provide a general introduction to the historical, cultural and literary aspects of the narratives, as well as to their historical development and their literary and cultural legacy. Roland Williams's *African American Autobiography and the Quest for Freedom* also takes in a large amount of early literature in its discussions. Williams argues that the sense of oppositional force that has dominated the critical assessments of African American literature in relation to the American literary mainstream since the 1960s is misconceived, and that the heroism of black autobiography needs instead to be seen as very much in the tradition of the pioneer settlers. For Williams, the African American autobiography is 'a novel epic form'. A genuinely complex challenge to mainstream–margin dichotomies and a priori assumptions about the politics of African American writing would indeed be an important critical undertaking, but Williams's naive recycling of nationalist exceptionalism does nothing to meaningfully advance such a project. One final work worth mentioning in relation to nineteenth-century literature is *Gullah Folktales from the Georgia Coast*, a reissue of Charles Colcock Jones Jr.'s 1888 collection *Negro Myths of the Georgia Coast*. Jones's collection was among the earliest of its kind and provides an invaluable resource for African American cultural history. Jones tried to preserve the sound and syntax of nineteenth-century Gullah, and saw his 'salvage' work as an extension of the work of Joel Chandler Harris. Susan Millar Williams provides a very useful introduction that gives an account of Jones's life and his relationship to the work of Harris.

The only period of the twentieth century that has consistently remained the focus of critical attention for African American literary critics is that of the Harlem Renaissance. The contributions of two authors this year stand out from the flood of over-production that has characterized Renaissance scholarship in recent years. Maria Balshaw's *Looking for Harlem: Urban Aesthetics in African-American Literature* is an impressive and thoughtful attempt to shift critical attention from rural and folk paradigms that dominate Renaissance studies towards a foregrounding of 'the centrality of the city and the urban locale in African American writing'. Such a shift of focus, Balshaw argues, will open up new understandings of 'the dissident conditions of modernity for African Americans'. The impact of the Chicago School of Sociology on the debates about the New Negro is central to Balshaw's argument. The first chapter reads Alain Locke's famous anthology alongside the magazine *Fire!!*. Balshaw then moves on to a discussion of Rudolph Fisher, the literary productions of African American women in the 1920s (examining not only well-known figures such as Nella Larsen, but also Marita Bonner and Angelina Weld Grimké) and, finally, a group of post-Harlem Renaissance writers from the 1940s. The study concludes with an examination of Morrison's *Jazz* [1992] and Issac Julian's film *Looking for Langston* [1989]. Quietly but firmly the book also draws out the implications of its own readings for contemporary African American criticism, demonstrating the ways in which a rural and maternal bias has dominated and distorted the insights of many leading contemporary critics, male and female alike.

Along with Balshaw, David Kadlec makes the most significant contributions to Harlem Renaissance criticism this year. Though both of Kadlec's contributions are studies of Hurston, his conceptual rigour, sense of historical specificity when discussing intellectual contexts and commitment to new archival research set a standard that has particular relevance for Harlem Renaissance studies. Since the Renaissance has now become a major site for both African American literary criticism and for reconsiderations of the nature of modernism in American studies, it is precisely this kind of scholarly rigour that is needed to cut through the historical and theoretical sloppiness that has characterized a great deal of the writing on the Renaissance. Kadlec's chapter on Hurston ('Zora Neale Hurston and "The Races of Europe"') in his *Mosaic Modernism: Anarchism, Pragmatism, Culture* is part of a rich account of the anti-foundationalist origins of modernism as a literary and cultural phenomenon. The reading of Hurston distances her from both Boasian models of culture and more contemporary post-structuralist recuperations of her work. Kadlec argues persuasively that Hurston's work is critical of the conceptualization of culture in the anthropological discourse contemporaneous to it (and here Kadlec's argument chimes with the broad account of the culture concept given by Susan Hegeman in *Patterns for America: Modernism and the Concept of Culture*, PrincetonUP [1999]): 'Hurston distinguished herself not as a conventionally reactionary or radical author but as a writer who was reluctant to naturalize contingency by authenticating culture as an antidote to outworn notions of race. And it is only by disentangling her writings from the postmodern measure of progress, a measure that couples language and identity, that we can begin to appreciate the full historical and literary significance of this gesture.' In a separate piece, 'Zora Neale Hurston and the Federal Folk' (*Mo/Mo* 7[2000] 471–85), Kadlec takes a more descriptive though thematically related approach and examines Hurston's work for the Federal Writer's Project (FWP) in the late 1930s. Hurston was an editor of the American Guide series book *Florida* [1939], and later worked on another FWP volume that was never published, *The Florida Negro*. Here, Kadlec's archival work makes available an aspect of Hurston's work that is little known, and leads Kadlec to the conclusion, similar to his distancing of Hurston from Boas, that 'the documentary aesthetics that underlay even the best FWP projects of the late 1930s were fundamentally at odds with Hurston's efforts to place process at the root of identity'. Zora Neale Hurston's *Their Eyes Were Watching God: A Casebook*, edited by Cheryl A. Ward, is a collection of major contemporary essays, all previously published.

Fabre and Feith, eds., *Jean Toomer and the Harlem Renaissance*, is a collection of essays by American and European scholars which offers a series of reassessments of Toomer's place in his own time and of his relationship to the Harlem Renaissance. Making good use of the recent growth in the understanding of Toomer's life and works, the essays include examinations of Toomer's relationship to modernism and to the eugenics movement, his treatments of identity and passing, his early poetry, the use of music and the visual arts in his work, his dealings with his publisher Horace Liveright, and the reception of *Cane* in France. Collectively, these essays make a significant contribution to our understanding of both Toomer's work and the intellectual and cultural contexts of the Harlem Renaissance. If it is part of Fabre and Feith's argument that Toomer should be seen in the context of the Harlem Renaissance afresh, despite his own resistance to such placement, then Jeff Webb takes the opposite tack. In a subtle and close reading of *Cane*, 'Literature and Lynching: Identity in Jean Toomer's *Cane*' (*ELH* 67[2000] 205–28), Webb takes seriously Toomer's clear objections to the racial characterizations of his work and analyses Cane as an exploration of the independence of identity from race.

If Toomer is now one of the most celebrated of African American writers from the 1920s, Helene Johnson [1906–95] is surely one of the least known. Johnson was among the youngest of the Harlem Renaissance writers and published regularly in magazines before disappearing from the literary scene in 1935. Though a number of her poems have been anthologized, most of Johnson's work has been unavailable. Verner D. Mitchell's collection of published and unpublished poetry, letters and photographs, *This Waiting for Love*, fills this gap very successfully. The introduction is informative and helps locate Johnson in relation to other writers such as Hurston and Dorothy West (Johnson's cousin). The availability of Johnson's anti-genteel poetry will no doubt help expand the map of Harlem Renaissance literary achievement, though Mitchell's claims for the nature of the poetic achievement may prove to be exaggerated in some instances. Something of an oddity is Friedman, ed., *Beckett in Black and Red*, which presents all of the translations Samuel Beckett undertook for Nancy Cunard's seminal anthology, *Negro* [1934]. The primary concern of Friedman's introduction is to argue that Beckett's very substantial contribution to the anthology and his long friendship with Cunard suggest ways of rethinking the shape of his career and the nature of his political commitments. But, at a time when *Negro* remains unfortunately long out of print, these translations help redirect attention to Cunard's text and its role in black–white modernist transatlantic interactions. Wilson, ed., *The Messenger Reader: Stories, Poetry, and Essays from the Messenger Magazine*, part of a series that includes *The Crisis Reader* and *The Opportunity Reader* [both 1999], was unavailable for review.

African American poetry, which is usually neglected by critics in favour of fiction, receives considerable attention this year. Two works make a substantial contribution to the understanding of the African American contribution to twentieth-century American poetry and the role of race in the works of black and white poets alike. In *Extraordinary Measures: Afrocentric Modernism and Twentieth-Century American Poetry* Lorenzo Thomas, himself a leading African American poet, offers commentaries on a range of expected and unexpected figures and issues in a work that combines critical discourse with what might be termed 'poet's prose'. There are chapters on Margaret Walker and Amiri Baraka, but also on Fenton Johnson and William Stanley Braithwaite and their involvement in Harriet Monroe's New Poetry movement, on Melvin B. Tolson, on the roots of the Black Arts movement, on poets from Louisiana, and on the role of poetry readings. A series of interrelated essays, Thomas's book is a lively provocation that weaves its way between the specificities of the African American literary tradition and this tradition's dialogue with the so-called 'mainstream' of modern American writing. Nielsen, ed., *Reading Race in American Poetry*, includes Thomas's discussion of Braithwaite and Monroe and is an equally valuable and lively contribution to the study of African poetry. In addition to Thomas's contribution, there are eight other essays that examine the work of W.E.B. Du Bois, James Weldon Johnson and Claude McKay, the function of race in early American modernism, the use of dialect in a 'poetics of the Americas', African American appropriations of the sonnet, the African American prose poem, the poetry of the much-neglected Bob Kaufman, history and storytelling in the work of Jay Wright, and the use of African American materials by Robert Duncan. Taken as whole, these essays admirably expand the parameters of the current discussions of African American poetry and establish a critical standard for future analyses that is higher than much of what has gone before. The same cannot, alas, be said for Fahmisha Patricia Brown's *Performing the Word: African American Poetry as Vernacular Culture*. Brown claims in her introduction that her aim is to 'situate African American poetry in African American vernacular expressive culture' and that, by doing so, she hopes 'to offer readers, teachers, and students of African American poetry a way of reading, understanding and appreciating a body of work that has received little critical attention'. The lament about critical neglect may be more than justified, but the stress on the vernacular and the oral as central to the definition of African American has been a characteristic of most critical discussions since the 1960s and Brown does not expand the theoretical or methodological nature of these discussions in any significant way. Equally worth noting is that Brown's vision of African American poetry as 'a body of work' is highly selective and excludes several major figures from the discussion precisely because their work seems to fit so uneasily within the critical framework adopted by Brown: there is, for instance, no discussion of Tolson, early LeRoi Jones, Jay Wright or Nathaniel Mackey here, and discussions of other writers such as Ishmael Reed pay scant attention to the dialogue between vernacular and non-vernacular materials in their work. Benston's commentary on performance and African American culture shares many concerns with Brown's work but is far more theoretically adept and critically sophisticated.

Nathaniel Mackey's work receives well-deserved attention in a special issue of *Callaloo* (23:ii[2000]), edited by Paul Naylor. The issue contains not only creative writing by and for Mackey, but also two interviews, twelve critical essays on his work and a bibliography of primary and secondary sources. Mackey has produced a very substantial and often difficult body of work as poet and writer of fiction and criticism and this special issue will go a considerable way in laying foundations for a reading of his achievement. T.J. Anderson III's 'Body and Soul: Kaufman's *Golden Sardine*' (*AAR* 34[2000] 329–46) examines Kaufman's appropriation of jazz materials, particularly the relationship of music and the body as a recurring motif in the poetry and Kaufman's use of scat phrasing. There have also been a number of useful interviews with poets on their work: Michael Antonucci, 'The Map and the Territory: An Interview with Michael S. Harper' (*AAR* 34[2000] 501–8); Susan Kelly, 'Discipline and Craft: An Interview with Sonia Sanchez' (*AAR* 34[2000] 679–88); Emily Allen Williams, 'Harryette Mullen: "The Queen of Hip Hyperbole". An Interview' (*AAR* 34[2000] 701–8).

Callaloo's special issue dedicated to the work of 'lesbian, gay, bisexual and transgender writers of color' (23:i[2000]) makes the most important contribution to the growing body of primary and secondary material in this area. The issue is a mammoth 500-page-long collection of poetry, fiction, 'personal essays' (by Melvin Dixon, Alexis De Veaux, Thomas Glave, E. Patrick Johnson and Darieck Scott), interviews (with Dixon, Samuel R. Delany, Helen Elaine Lee and Audre Lourde), and essays (on a diverse range of topics and authors that includes the Harlem Renaissance, 'the queer resources of Black Nationalist invective' and writers such as Dixon, Baldwin, Lourde, and Michelle Cliff). The issue also includes a substantial bibliography of black queer studies for the years 1994–6 by Nicholas Boggs and there are a number of reports from and reviews of the Black Queer Studies in the Millennium conference, held on 7–9 April 2000 at the University of North Carolina, Chapel Hill, in *Callaloo* 23:iv[2000].

As far as studies of individual authors are concerned, this has been a lean year, though the Morrison industry continues to produce apace. There are six new books on Morrison and between them they represent fairly accurately the range of critical approaches that dominates Morrison studies at present. Conner, ed., *The Aesthetics of Toni Morrison: Speaking the Unspeakable*, a volume of new essays, is perhaps the one contribution that tries most convincingly to open up a relatively new approach to Morrison. Not only does Conner argue that aesthetics has been unnecessarily diminished by ideological criticism, he also confronts the tendency 'to ignore or even deny diverse influences' in Morrison's work by critics and Morrison alike. Conner rightly argues that renewed examination of the relationship of the 'political, cultural and racial elements' and aesthetic elements in African American literature 'is relevant not just to Morrison's own writing but to the entire tradition of African-American literature'. Conner's introduction traces the conflict between the aesthetic and the political in African American literary history, and the essays that follow examine the categories of the aesthetic, the grotesque, the beautiful and the sublime in relation to Morrison's work. Other essays investigate the distinction between novelist and storyteller in the novels, Morrison's use of indeterminacy and elusive narration and her use of the fable in her Nobel Prize speech.

Gurleen Grewal's *Circles of Sorrow, Lines of Struggle: The Novels of Toni Morrison* opens with the rather inflated claim that 'Toni Morrison is part of a long black—and American—literary tradition that finds its full and complicated bloom in her art.' There is an unsatisfactory substantiation of this claim: no discussion, for instance, of how either Hawthorne's or Faulkner's works can be said to find their organic fulfilment in Morrison. And the claim that 'Morrison's novels allow us to examine the quality of human relationships under the constraints of historical processes and social relations, in the context of a collective' reads more like a general description of the novel as a genre than of the signal and particular achievement of any particular novelist. For the most part Grewal structures her arguments around the fairly predictable themes of historical recovery and the collectivity, though her portrayal of Morrison as a kind of historiographer attempting to negotiate the divisions between an emergent black middle class and the larger black community opens up a more promising discussion.

The title of J. Brooks Bouson's *Quiet As It's Kept: Shame, Trauma, and Race in the Novels of Toni Morrison* gives a fairly clear sense of the central preoccupations of the book, which draws on recent psychoanalytic and psychiatric work on shame and trauma with considerable rigour and thoroughness as a way of exploring Morrison's novels; but the claim that Morrison critics have avoided or suppressed these troubling aspects of her work in their commentaries is simply inaccurate. In *The Identifying Fictions of Toni Morrison: Modernist Authenticity and Postmodern Blackness*, John N. Duvall builds on biographical approaches to Morrison, using as the point of departure for his consideration of issues of identity an examination of Morrison's choice of her pen-name. It is Duvall's view that in terms of what she writes about, 'Morrison has a modernist concern for authenticity' but that 'her techniques, particularly in her more recent novels, suggest certain postmodern fictional practices'. Lisa Williams's *The Artist as Outsider in the Novels of Toni Morrison and Virginia Woolf* (Greenwood) and Ron David's *Toni Morrison Explained: A Reader's Road Map to the Novels* (RandomH) were unavailable for review.

Gloria Naylor, who has not received the kind of critical attention that Morrison or Alice Walker have, is well served by two publications this year. Stave, ed., *Gloria Naylor: Strategy and Technique, Magic and Myth*, is a collection of nine new essays on the novels *Mama Day* and *Bailey's Café*. Stave's collection shares the emphasis of Conner's on Morrison (see above) on multiple intellectual and literary traditions as a necessary framework for analysis. The essays include considerations of Naylor's work in dialogue with Faulkner and Toomer as well as commentaries on religion, the maternal aesthetic, language, magic, and epistolary forms. Naylor is also the focus of a special section in *Callaloo* (23:iv[2000] 1392–1512). The section contains a conversation between Naylor and Nikki Giovanni, an interview, an examination of the use of Western literary, mythological and fairy-tale narratives in *Linden Hills*, a comparison of *Mama Day* and *Their Eyes Were Watching God*, and one of *Mama Day* and *Sula*, as well as an essay on Naylor and baseball and a Naylor bibliography. The only other female writer who is the subject of a book-length study this year is Alice Walker. Maria Lauret's *Alice Walker*, a volume in the St Martin's Modern Novelists series, provides a balanced overview of the career. Lauret traces the development of the themes of female sexuality and child abuse in the work as well as of Walker's theories of racial hybridity, spirituality and goddess-worship. In her adoption of the stance of New Age visionary, Walker leaves herself open to easy criticism, but Lauret undertakes a sympathetic and careful reading that is, at the same time, able to maintain critical distance from its subject.

In '"Relate sexual to historical": Race, Resistance, and Desire in Gayle Jones's *Corregidora*' (*AAR* 34[2000] 273–97), Ashraf H.A. Rushdy analyses a novel that deserves far more serious critical examination than it has so far received and looks at the ways in which Jones 'has made the dynamic of intersubjective relations central to her narratives of slavery'. In 'Beyond Morrison and Walker: Looking Good and Looking Forward in Contemporary Black Women's Stories' (*AAR* 34[2000] 313–28), E. Shelly Reid acknowledges the enormous influence of Morrison's and Walker's generation on African American women's writing, but argues that a generation of younger writers has yet to receive the attention their work deserves. She looks at the novels of Bebe Moore Campbell, Terry MacMillan, Sapphire and A.J. Verelle as well as the white writer Susan Straight. A different tradition is recuperated in Joyce Meier's 'The Refusal of Motherhood in African American Women's Theatre' (*MELUS* 25:iii–iv[2000] 17–39). Meier's discussion of motherhood, the female body and the legacy of slavery adds little that is new to the existing work on these themes, but the article is noteworthy for its commentary on the dramatic writings of Angelina Grimké (*Rachel* [1916]), Georgia Johnson (*Safe* [1930]), Shirley Graham (*It's Morning* [1938–40]), Alice Childress (*Mojo* [1970]) and Aishah Rahman (*Unfinished Woman Cry in No Man's Land while a Bird Dies in a Gilded Cage* [1977]).

Among male writers, apart from Nathaniel Mackey (see above), the only writer to receive sustained attention is James Baldwin. Miller, ed., *Re-Viewing James Baldwin: Things Not Seen*, is a valuable addition to the growing body of Baldwin criticism. The collection focuses not on the well-known works but on the less frequently examined early and late ones in a successful attempt to broaden our understanding of Baldwin's achievement. There are essays here on masculinity, gender, and gay issues, but also on the uses of music by Baldwin, on his poetry and on one of his least known works, *Nothing Personal* [1964], a photo-text collaboration with Richard Avedon. This last essay, by Joshua L. Millar, can usefully be read alongside Michelle Shawn Smith's '"Looking at One's Self through the Eyes of Others": W.E.B. Du Bois's Photographs for the 1900 Paris Exposition' (*AAR* 34[2000] 581–600), which provides an unexpected insight into Du Bois's work by gathering together some of the photographs Du Bois assembled for the 'American Negro' exhibit at the 1900 Paris Exposition. The reading of the photographs 'against the turn-of-the-century "race" archives' is solid and very much in keeping with current analyses of the visual representations of minority or post-colonial cultures. More specifically, Smith argues that 'Du Bois's photographs challenge the discourses and images that produced an imagined "Negro criminality" and propelled the crime of lynching in turn-of-the-century U.S. culture'. A special issue of *Boundary 2* (27:iii[2000]), edited by Ronald A.T. Judy, gathers together nine essays on Du Bois's work, primarily in the contexts of social science, philosophy and history. Though not principally concerned with literary criticism, these essays will be of considerable interest to anyone approaching Du Bois from an interdisciplinary perspective. Butler, ed., *The Critical Response to Ralph Ellison*, is a substantial collection of previously published materials, and traces the response to Ellison's work, from early reviews to commentaries on the posthumously published novel *Juneteenth*. The collection includes responses not only to the novels but also to the short fiction and the essays. In 'The Fragmented Whole: Ralph Ellison, Kenneth Burke and the Cultural Literacy Debate' (*CLAJ* 43:iii[2000] 261–75) David G. Holmes basis his reading of Ellison's 'The Little Man at the Chehaw Station' and 'What These Children Are Like' on the friendship between Ellison and Burke, and argues for a 'notion of a dialectical relationship between Western traditionalism and multiculturalism'. *Readings on 'Black Boy'* and *Readings on 'Native Son'*, both edited by Hayley Mitchell, are student guides that provide excerpts from a wide range of critical works on Richard Wright. Robert Felgar's *Student Companion to Richard Wright* provides conventional summaries of biography, theme, character and plot in the novels and stories for the undemanding student.

Some of the best essays on single authors this year appear in a special issue of *American Literature* (72:ii[2000]). The essays are grouped under the heading 'Unsettling Blackness' and reflect a range of methodological and theoretical orientations which Houston Baker, the issue editor, argues reflect a new, post-Stepto–Gates–Baker phase in African American studies. This special issue is the first under the new editorship of Baker, and it marks a promising start for him. In 'James Weldon Johnson and the Autobiography of an Ex-Colored Musician' (*AL* 72:ii[2000] 249–74) Cristina L. Ruotolo rightly argues that the role of music in Johnson's famous novel has been inadequately scrutinized. It is Ruotolo's contention that Johnson's 'narrator challenges the "color line" … in his repeated efforts to produce music that revises both "black" and "white" musical traditions by sounding an intimate relationship between the two'. It is certainly possible to approach the novel through other musical readings (it is possible, for instance, to foreground more clearly the narrator's class position and his musical project as a possible flight from the brutal history he witnesses in the South), but this is a well-argued and suggestive reading. The relationship between music and literature is further explored by John Lowney in his 'Langston Hughes and the "Nonsense" of Bebop' (*AL* 72:ii[2000] 357–86). Lowney provides a reading of Hughes's *Montage of a Dream Deferred*, perhaps his most ambitious work, in which he argues that bebop becomes in the poem a means of 'reclaiming Harlem as a site for both black cultural pride and militant anger, a site of memory that recalls the utopian promise of the Harlem Renaissance but also appeals to the postwar skepticism of a younger generation of black artists'. Lowney's examination of the discordant forms of bebop finds an echo in Joel B. Peckham's employment of Peter Burger's conception of montage in his reading of Toomer's *Cane*, 'Jean Toomer's *Cane*: Self as Montage and the Drive toward Integration' (*AL* 72:ii[2000] 275–90). Peckham's main interest is in 'the way in which Toomer's radical formal transgressions reflect his radical political position'. There are three other essays in Baker's special issue. Daylanne English's 'W.E.B. Du Bois's Family *Crisis*' (*AL* 72:ii[2000] 291–320) explores the ways in which 'discourses on race, genetics, and social improvement' converge in Du Bois's writings; Lawrence P. Jackson, 'The Birth of the Critic: The Literary Friendship of Ralph Ellison and Richard Wright' (*AL* 72:ii[2000] 321–56), provides a detailed and balanced account of the relationship between Ellison and Wright; and Arelene R. Keizer's 'The Geography of the Apocalypse: Incest, Mythology, and the Fall of Washington City in Carolivia Herron's *Thereafter Johnnie*' (*AL* 72:ii[2000] 387–416) takes the dramatization of incestuous relationships in Herron's 1991 novel as a point of departure for a consideration of the ways in which the novel explores some of the 'intimate associations' between 'geography, gender, mythology, race, power, and sexuality as Herron considers the problem of historical influence and continuity'.

This year is also marked by the appearance of an unusual number of works of reference. Among these the second edition of *African American Writers*, edited by Valerie Smith, is extremely valuable. A significant expansion of the first edition [1974], the two volumes contain fifty-two articles on key writers, providing career overviews and critical assessments by a wide range of critics, as well as bibliographies of primary and secondary works. While some writers are obviously not present, those included are properly representative. The decision to include only three entries on genres or movements (slave narratives, spiritual autobiographies and the Black Arts movement) seems far more arbitrary and less useful. This will, nevertheless, be a useful research tool for students and scholars alike. The single-volume Hatch and Strickland, eds., *African-American Writers: A Dictionary*, is half the length of Smith's work but more wide-ranging in scope. Its more than 500 entries cover writers not only of fiction, poetry, drama and autobiography, but also of screenplays, commercials, hymns, newspaper editorials and rap songs. A number of important genres, literary movements and publications are also included. Most of the entries are by Hatch, with some help from other contributors, and the quality of writing and insight varies greatly from entry to entry. But this compact and affordable volume is a very useful reference tool and stands up well alongside *The Oxford Companion to African American Literature* [1997]. Emmanuel S. Nelson's *African American Authors, 1745–1945: A Bio-Bibliographical Critical Sourcebook* is more narrowly focused in its historical coverage and, as a result, is able to devote space to a number of less well known writers, though it should be noted that most of these are already covered by earlier reference works such as *The Oxford Companion to African American Literature*. Di Mauro, ed., *Modern Black Writers* (St James) was unavailable for review.

A useful point of conclusion to this overview of this year's work in African American literary studies is provided by Kenneth Warren's 'The End(s) of African American Studies' (*ALH* 12[2000] 637–55), a cautious and considered commentary on the development of African American studies as an academic enterprise, and its relationship to the black community. Warren does not repeat the reductive aspects of the class ideology critiques of scholarship, but he offers an intelligent and cautionary commentary on the claims for representativeness by scholars. He equally cautions against the 'inordinate reliance on scholarship and aesthetic practices to define the political projects and agendas affecting black Americans'. Warren's sense that 'we need to examine more systematically the history that has sometimes inclined African-Americanist scholars to focus their energies in one direction rather than another' may not be new, but the disciplinary self-examination it proposes should be undertaken with rigour and as a matter of some urgency. Warren's '"As white as anybody": Race and the Politics of Counting as Black' (*NLH* 31[2000] 709–26) approaches some of these concerns from a different angle.

In addition to the various works listed above as unavailable for review, the following were also not received: David G. Nicholls, *Conjuring the Folk: Forms of Modernity in African America* (UMichP); Sharon Patricia Holland, *Raising the Dead: Readings for Death and (Black) Subjectivity* (DukeUP); John Cullen

Gruesser, *Black on Black: Twentieth-Century African American Writing about Africa* (UPKen); Philip Auger, *Native Sons in No Man's Land: Rewriting Afro-American Manhood in the Novels of Baldwin, Walker, Wideman, and Gaines* (Garland); Nada Elia, *Trances, Dances and Vociferations: Agency and Resistance in Africana Women's Narratives* (Garland); Ishmael Reed, *The Reed Reader* (Basic Books); Kevin Powell, ed., *Step into a World: A Global Anthology of the New Black Literature* (Wiley); Kevin Everod Quashie *et al.*, eds., *New Bones: Contemporary Black Writers in America* (PH); Sadi Samawi, ed., *Black Orpheus: Music in African American Fiction from the Harlem Renaissance to Toni Morrison* (Garland); and Kevin Young, ed., *Giant Steps: The New Generation of African American Writers* (Harper).

6. Native, Asian American, Latino/a and General Ethnic Writing

Kenneth Lincoln sets himself a bold span in *Sing with the Heart of a Bear: Fusions of Native and American Poetry, 1890–1999*. He writes with all his customary proven brio, a wide-ranging, if at times showy, attempt to demonstrate the mutual refractions and borrowings across both Native and 'mainstream' poetry. 'An ax is buried in the curriculum' gives a taste of one of his typical eye-catching turns of metaphor. Ezra Pound or Sylvia Plath are to be read for their Native skeins of allusion and, none too flatteringly, for their Good/Bad Indian binaries. Equally, and as though a kind of literary counter-mirror, writers such as Sherman Alexie (Coeur d'Alène), Mary TallMountain (Athabaskan) and Luci Tapahonso (Navajo) come into consideration for how they adapt mainstream literary forms of language and genre to the expression of Native life and history. The upshot, as in Lincoln's earlier *Indi'n Humor: Bicultural Play in Native America* (OUP [1993]), can be more than a touch arbitrary, but nothing if not engaging.

In 'Empowerment through "Retroactive Prophecy"' in D'Arcy McNickle's *Runner in the Sun: A Story of Indian Maize*, James Welch's *Fool's Crow*, and Leslie Marmon Silko's *Ceremony*' (*AIQ* 24:i[2000] 1–18) Lori Burlingame examines how in all three novels the present is foreseen but, paradoxically, as though from a time-now. For *Runner in the Sun*, set in the pre-Contact era, the prophet is Tula; for *Fool's Crow*, set in the nineteenth-century, it is Feather Woman; and for *Ceremony*, enacted against twentieth-century war, the figure of Betonie presides. Each, on this well-argued account, serves as shaman-visionary who sees forward in order not only to warn of setback, even disaster, but also to offer a pathway back into both community and individual healing.

Wong, ed., *Louise Erdrich's 'Love Medicine': A Casebook*, one in a new OUP series under the editorship of William L. Andrews and dedicated to 'multicultural works of modern literary fiction', draws together sixteen previously published essays on the story-cycle which Erdrich originally published in 1984 and then expanded in 1993. Hertha D. Sweet Wong, as volume editor, has chosen pieces by stalwarts in the field, along with Erdrich's own greatly important essays, 'Where I Ought To Be: A Writer's Sense of Place' [1985] and 'Rose Nights: Summer Storms, Lists of Spiders and Literary Mothers' [1995], and a 1990 interview given with her late husband and co-writer Michael Dorris. Helen Jaskoski mines Chippewa lore and sense of land for how they give context and timeline to the mixedblood lives in

Erdrich's stories. Louis Owens explores Erdrich's command of 'multiple narrative' for how it binds, and at the same time counterpoints, the lives of her Kashpaw, Morrissey, Lamartine and Lazarre clans. It gives a reminder of how acute, and important, remains his pioneer work, *Other Destinies: Understanding the American Indian Novel* (UOklaP [1992]), from which his essay is reprinted. James Ruppert explores the uses of ceremony, and its varying implications for Chippewa survival, in the stories. Allan Chavin looks to the expanded version of *Love Medicine*, the way in which the extra pieces give further human contour, and irony, to the Chippewa border world, whose storyings as Erdrich first offered them propelled her into bestseller celebrity.

Two 1999 Erdrich studies arrived too late for inclusion last year. *A Reader's Guide To the Novels of Louise Erdrich*, jointly written by Peter G. Beidler and Gay Barton, delivers on its title with sections on the geography of Erdrich's imagined world, genealogies of each dynasty, a full, annotated dictionary of characters, and a primary and selective bibliography. At a somewhat lesser pitch Lorena L. Stookey's *Louise Erdrich: A Critical Companion* offers interpretative plot-lines, a kind of working guide from Erdrich's early poetry collection *Jacklight* [1984], the stories in *Tracks* [1988], and on to her novel *The Antelope Wife* [1998]. Both books do workmanlike service.

Patricia Riley's 'There is No Limit to this Dust: The Refusal of Sacrifice in Louise Erdrich's *Love Medicine*' (*SAIL* 12:ii[2000] 12–23) confronts the vexed issue of mixedbloods as supposed victim figures. She offers a persuasive case that in the black-comedy struggle of Marie Lazarre against Sister Leopolda, Native woman against Catholic disciplinarian, Erdrich is able to bring trickster rules to bear. On Riley's persuasive line of argument, Marie thereby embodies in her dark, ironic contrariety 'a mythic resistance … to the stereotype as sacrificial victim'.

Drawing upon a clear familiarity with Chippewa earth-diver creation myth, Nora Baker Barry, in 'Fleur Pillager's Bear Identity in the Novels of Louise Erdrich' (*SAIL* 12:ii[2000] 24–37) sees in Fleur a 'powerful spiritual presence' whose 'bear thoughts' are those of the *mide* or visionary. Barry's detailed explicatory account of Fleur positions her as a healer not only for her own time, and its people, but the continuation of the healer-figure in far older Chippewa tradition.

For Kari J. Winter in 'The Politics and Erotics of Food in Louise Erdrich' (*SAIL* 12:iv[2000] 44–64), the alimentary allusions in Erdrich's fiction carry a complex significance both as fact and metaphor, especially in the light of the Anishinaabe's historic fight against ever scarcer food resources. She stresses 'Ojibwa sensuality' over 'Christian aestheticism' as a major dialectic in *Tracks* [1988], not to mention the kinds of food allusion and metaphor Erdrich puts into play in the scenes involving Kozka's Meats in *The Beet Queen* [1986]. Erdrich's latest novel, *The Antelope Wife* [1998], she suggests, is quite 'the most food centred of all', a story which creates parallels between actual, bodily hunger and larger communal hunger in the light of both Chippewa-Ojibwa and Sioux historic privation. Laura Furlan Szanto gives a timely, and succinct, series of updates to the accumulating Erdrich scholarship in 'An Annotated Secondary Bibliography of Louise Erdrich's Recent Fiction: *The Bingo Palace, Tales of Burning Love* and *The Antelope Wife*' (*SAIL* 12:ii[2000] 61–90).

E. Shelley Reid's 'The Stories We Tell: Louise Erdrich's Identity Narratives' (*MELUS* 25:iii–iv[2000] 65–86) sees Erdrich, unexceptionally it might at first be thought, as engaged in acts of reclamation of Native identity 'from the Coopers and Disneys of Euro-American culture'. Using *Love Medicine* and *Tracks* as illustrative texts, however, she argues that Erdrich posits anything but some one discrete, completed Chippewa self-meaning, individual or communal. Identity, in Erdrich's fiction, is always a process of change and revision, a web or circle of dynamic mutability. Sheila Hassell Hughes addresses similar terrain in 'Tongue-Tied: Rhetoric and Relation in Louise Erdrich's *Tracks*' (*MELUS* 25:iii–iv[2000] 87–116), a savvy, engaging account of how no one pre-emptive narrative voice prevails in *Tracks*, with the effect of making the reader, Native or non-Native, a species of co-determinant as to the linkages and meanings in the overall 'telling' of the story-cycle.

Arnold, ed., *Conversations with Leslie Marmon Silko*, puts sixteen interviews from between 1976 and 1998 into a single volume, a more than useful resource for readers of her work. Most aspects of Silko's life and fiction come into view, whether (as she describes it) her 'mix-blooded' Marmon family heritage and the role of Laguna as human location and timeline, or her life in Alaska [1973–6] and the writing of *Ceremony* [1977], or the kind of global politics which lie behind *Almanac of the Dead* [1991] and *Garden in the Dunes* [1999]. Her interviews with Laura Coltelli [1993], and with the editor Ellen Arnold [1998], yield especial dividends as to how she sees her own writer's calling. Acting as though on a cue from George Orwell, the task, on Silko's reckoning, is one of using language, and narrative, as a means to contest, and so help cleanse, arbitrary power, be it hegemony over indigenous people, destructive military-industrial capitalism, or environmental damage. It takes little reading of her views as given across three decades to recognize the strength, and reach, of this ongoing commitment. It makes a companion volume to Barnett and Thorson, eds., *Leslie Marmon Silko: A Collection of Critical Essays* [1999], another volume received after last year's deadline.

Denise K. Cummings's '"Settling" History: Understanding Leslie Marmon Silko's *Ceremony*, *Storyteller*, *Almanac of The Dead* and *Garden in the Dunes*' (*SAIL* 12:iv[2000] 65–90) makes the case for Silko as frontline experimentalist. She argues that it is a dimension of Silko's achievement which has long gone under-attended, especially the debt she owes to Paul Carter's *The Road to Botany Bay: An Essay in Spatial History* (Faber [1987]). This leads on to an examination of 'spatial' form throughout Silko's fiction: the use in *Ceremony* of Native time–space continuum; *Storyteller* as bearing its own 'deconstructive potentialities'; *Almanac of the Dead* as a fiction of 'geographic movements and maps'; and *Garden in the Dunes* as 'a reworking of poetic history'. On Cummings's account Silko's flair in operating at the literary boundaries puts her among America's innovative best.

A shrewd comparative note is struck in Virginia E. Bell's 'Counter-Chronicling and Alternative Mapping in *Memoria del Fuego* and *Almanac of the Dead*' (*MELUS* 25:iii–iv[2000] 5–30). She likens *Memoria del Fuego* [1982–6], by the Uruguayan writer Eduardo Galeano, to Silko's own compendious novel as counter-chronicles of the Americas, two expressions of epic narrative which challenge, and seek to transcend, received Eurocentric versions of Atlantic discovery and conquest. The upshot is a well-taken bi-hemispheric reading of how resistance to hegemony is treated in both writers.

Lee, ed., *Loosening the Seams: Interpretations of Gerald Vizenor*, offers seventeen essays on Native America's leading postmodern. Four general pieces open the bidding. David Murray gives a close-worked overview of Vizenor's canny, sleight-of-hand narrative tactics (pp. 20–37). Elaine A. Janner tackles tricksterism as Vizenor's own Native-cum-postmodern signature (pp. 38–58). Barry O'Connell examines the play of ideology and history throughout Vizenor's literary oeuvre (pp. 59–84). Amy Elias compares Vizenor with Ishmael Reed as two doyens of the 'ethnic' postmodern turn. Among other essays Richard Hutson examines Vizenor's *Interior Landscapes: Autobiographical Myths and Metaphors* [1990] as trickster-reflexive memoir (pp. 109–25); Linda Lizut Helstern unravels the use in *Griever* [1990] of the dense body of China-reference (pp. 136–54); Tom Lynch gives detailed attention to Vizenor's haiku and other poetry (pp. 203–24); A. Robert Lee looks to *Manifest Manners: Postindian Warriors of Survivance* [1994] as 'postindian' not only in vision but in Vizenor's very fashioning of discourse (pp. 263–78); and Louis Owens evaluates the use of Ishi as both historic life-figure and 'Stone Age' figura in Vizenor's play *Ishi and the Wood Ducks* (pp. 233–45). The volume contains a primary and selected critical bibliography.

Ron McFarland's *Understanding James Welch* gives a patient, respectful reading to this Blackfoot-Gros Ventre writer who first made his bow with the poetry of *Riding the Earthboy 40* [1971] and the now classic novel *Winter in the Blood* [1974]. Helpfully, and not a little refreshingly, he centres on Welch's literary workmanship, the dark-comedy picaresque of *Winter in the Blood*, the dialectic of autonomy and fatalism in *The Death of Jim Loney* [1979], the Native angle of vision to *Fool's Crow* [1986] and the uses of intrigue in *The Indian Lawyer* [1990]. A closing chapter looks closely at Welch's one non-fictional narrative, *Killing Custer* [1994] as a retelling, and, as importantly, a re-angling, of the Battle of the Little Bighorn of 1876. McFarland delivers essentially a primer but one full of informed good judgement as to Welch's place both within, and beyond, the Native literary spectrum.

Andrea Opitz's 'James Welch's '*Fool's Crow* and the Imagination of Pre-Colonial Space' (*AIQ* 24:i[2000] 126–41) offers a retrospect on her experience of translating the novel into German. She draws a parallel between the endeavour to respond in a second language to Welch's nuanced prose and the author's own endeavour to render his story from within a Blackfoot perspective on time and nature. In other words, with a well-taken concern for imagery, voice, in fact Welch's whole perceptual idiom, Opitz quite intriguingly sees herself to have been about the one translation of quite another kind of translation.

For James H. Cox, in '"All this water imagery must mean something": Thomas King's Revisions of Narratives of Domination and Conquest in *Green Grass, Running Water*' (*AIQ* 24:ii[2000] 219–46), the trope of 'waters and floods' has been crucial both to Native creation stories in general and King's second novel in particular. He reads *Running Water* as a kind of counter-working of *Moby-Dick* in which Nature, its oceans especially, serves as anything but the habitat of Ahab's version of the whale as taunting malignity. Rather, in the tapestry of King's novel, the flood serves as an expression of divinity, a Native signifying of rebirth over death, life over doom.

Advancing Paula Gunn Allen (Laguna) as a virtuoso of 'feminist dialogics at its best' Michelle Campbell Toohey, in 'Paula Gunn Allen's *Grandmothers of the Light*: Falling Through the Void' (*SAIL* 12:iii[2000] 35–51), argues that each of the stories should best be read as 'dialogues', 'speech genres'—anything but closed narrative. Allen uses story as a form of 'transformative reciprocity'; lives are told as though woven into being under Spider-woman auspices. This kind of reading does Allen considerable restorative favour in the face of criticism which has often thought her writing locked inside too rigid, or prescriptive, a Native-feminist ideology.

David Brande's 'Nor the Call of the Wild: The Idea of Wilderness in Louis Owens's *Wolfsong* and *Mixedblood Messages*' (*AIQ* 24:ii[2000] 247–63) looks to Owens's treatment in both texts of the connection between issues of 'the survival of indigenous tribal forms' and 'the preservation of intact ecosystems'. His account argues that Owens (Choctaw-Cherokee), both as novelist and discursive writer, inverts 'mainstream' associations with the wilderness as threat, danger or savagery in favour of imagining it as a location which 'signifies a system of reciprocal exchange between human and non-human'. This is to recognize a quite major emphasis in Owens's fiction, his Native-derived sense of the necessary equilibrium between human and non-human ecology. Brande's essay offers a genuinely elucidating perspective.

Sand Creek, the 1864 Cavalry massacre in Colorado of peaceably encamped Southern Cheyenne and Arapaho, has understandably long resonated in Native history. Robin Riley Fast's '"It is ours to know": Simon Ortiz's *From Sand Creek*' (*SAIL* 12:iii[2000] 52–63) recognizes the achievement of Ortiz (Acoma) in giving unsloganized verse narrative to the event. He sees Ortiz as having put continuance over victimry, a resistance to, and yet a rising above, Manifest Destiny. In 'Maurice Kenny's *Tekonwatonti, Molly Brant*: Poetic Memory and History' (*MELUS* 25:iii–iv[2000] 31–64) Patrick Barron gives due attention to this important contemporary Mohawk poet. His analysis of Kenny's *Tekonwatonti: Molly Brant, Poems of War, 1735–1795* (White Pine Press [1992]), a scrupulous unfolding of sources and imagery, looks to how the poem-sequence as a whole invokes the overlooked Brant as both actual revolutionary-era Mohawk figure and abiding mythic presence.

The writing of Joy Harjo (Creek) has long carried a playful, satiric edge, a feature conscientiously taken up in Jennifer Andrews's 'In the Belly of a Laughing God: Reading Humor and Irony in the Poetry of Joy Harjo' (*AIQ* 24:ii[2000] 200–18). She annotates a full span of poetry by this 'mixed-blood Muscogee writer and world traveler' from *She Had Some Horses* [1983] through to *The Woman Fell from the Sky* [1994] and with well-taken use of the anthology Harjo edited with Gloria Bird, *Reinventing the Enemy's Language: Contemporary Native Women's Writings of North America* [1997]. She shows a sharp eye for Harjo's trickster wordplay, her use of unlikely juxtaposition and tropes, both as a source of imaginative strength in its own right and as indicative of the kind of irony which has kept self-pity at bay and buttressed Native America against every kind of depredation.

Dean Rader's 'I Don't Speak Navajo: Esther G. Belin's *In the Belly of My Beauty*' (*SAIL* 12:ii[2000] 14–34) usefully maps the poetry of this California-raised poet using well-taken comparisons with her fellow Navajo poet Luci Tapahonso. The focus is biculturalism, the interaction of a life lived in urban West Coast America with a family legacy, and for all that Belin herself was raised off-reservation, of the Navaho or Diné. This Native legacy thus enters the writings as in one sense unlived, obliquely, and yet, and at the same time, quite unerased, a 'cultural presence'.

The Pacific Rim, so-called, has increasingly become a focus of cultural analysis, from Captain Cook to *Hawaii Five-O*, Melville to *Baywatch*, together with Los

Angeles, Honolulu or Taipei as the ocean arena's 'hub cities'. In *Reimagining the American Pacific: From 'South Pacific' to Bamboo Ridge and Beyond*, Rob Wilson gives his own kind of colloquial, infectiously paced overview. He deploys 'glocalization' as a key concept to register a sense of time and region, the Pacific in its different, and often competing, ethnic-indigenous, colonial, economic, geopolitical and literary overlaps. However much a Cultural Studies exercise, any number of literary dimensions come in for their own plentiful attention, Twain along with Melville, the *Bamboo Ridge* literary circle of luminaries such as Wing Tek Lum or Darrell Lum along with an 'Oceania' literary regime to embrace, among others, Hawaii's Lois-Ann Yamanaka, Samoa's Albert Wendt and Tonga's Epeli Hau'ofa. Wilson enters the text regularly in his own voice to speak of the trans-Pacific's hold on him as a 'space of flows', 'creative flux', a domain indeed at once transnational yet local, if often made 'dirty' under colonial and other depredation then also 'magical'. It would be hard to mistake the signature of the intelligent enthusiast.

Patricia P. Chu's *Assimilating Asians: Gendered Strategies of Authorship in Asian America* yields more dutiful literary fare. Her bead on the cultural dialectic built into Asian American authorship, and especially the tradition of *Bildungsroman*, falls into two parts. She first annotates the competing versions of Americanization as given in the fiction and memoir-writing of Younghill Kang, Carlos Bulosan, Milton Murayama and John Okada, then in the generation of Frank Chin and David Mura, and finally in the contrastive gendering of 'American' texts by Edith Maude Eaton and Bharati Mukherjee. The second part turns on 'the making of Chinese American ethnicity' as embodied in Amy Tan's *The Joy Luck Club* and the Kingston–Chin controversy as given narrative apotheosis in Kingston's *Tripmaster Monkey*. Chu's close readings can have a slightly old-fashioned flavour in their explications of theme, image or world, but they are perfectly attentive.

A major plus to Xiao-huang Yin's *Chinese American Literature Since the 1850s* lies in its author's bilingualism: he has written a history of both Chinese- and English-language 'immigrant' US literature. Both, most usefully, are reflected in his bibliographies. The text itself, with due allusion to nineteenth-century migration, the Chinese Exclusion Act, Angel Island, and the rise of each Chinatown, gives a social-historical account of writings from the *English-Chinese Phrase Book* [1875] through to the 'ABC' (American-born Chinese) literary generation of Maxine Hong Kingston, Amy Tan and Frank Chin. Of particular import are his excavation of the Chinese beginnings of writers such as Sui Sin Far (Edith Maude Eaton), the assimilationist Chineseness of the generation of Pardee Lowe and Jade Snow Wong and, because far less generally known, the immigrant line of authorship represented in names such as Chen Ruoxi, Yu Lihua and Zhang Xiguo. Yin's approach has limits: the accent can be too merely illustrative, but, in general, this is mapping to welcome.

For Irma Maini in 'Writing the Asian American Artist: Maxine Hong Kingston's *Tripmaster Monkey: His Fake Book*' (*MELUS* 25:iii–iv[2000] 243–64) the figure of Wittman Ah Sing operates in two linked but seemingly contradictory ways. On the one hand he serves as self-authoring protagonist, an American Chinaman in all his force and failings as the very embodiment of the artist as shapeshifter. On the other he is wholly of, even as he takes umbrage at, the communities of his life, those both within and outside 'Chinese' San Francisco. In both, suggests Maini, Kingston envisages him as the Asian American artist bound wholly to the dictates of neither self nor legacy.

In 'Being Human in the Wor(l)d: Chinese Men and Maxine Hong Kingston's Reworking of *Robinson Crusoe*' (*JAmS* 34:ii[2000] 187–206) Monica Chiu probes the link between 'The Adventures of Lo Bun Sun' section in *China Men* and Defoe's narrative of 'universal self-sufficiency'. She shows how the eighteenth-century text of Pacific-island marooning gives not so much a frame as an ironic point of contrast with Kingston's portrait of the migrant 'myth-hero'. Crusoe so anticipates not only Bun Sun but the founder figure of Bak Goong and each other male migrant and sojourner in the genealogies of *China Men*. It makes for an illuminating use of analogy.

Mary Slowick's 'Beyond Lot's Wife: The Immigration Poems of Marilyn Chin, Garrett Hongo, Li-Young Lee, and David Mura' (*MELUS* 25:iii–iv[2000] 221–42) explores memory, and the imperative to speak as against family-mandated silence, in a formidable body of Asian American contemporary verse. Whether the 'migrant experience' of the Chinese Exclusion Act [1882], or of turn-of-the-century Angel Island, or of Japanese American internment in the 1940s, Slowick uses a rich ply of quotation and analysis to show how these poets offer 'a dialogue across generations', an often startling break-out from required past discretion. For Pin-chia Feng in 'Re-Mapping Asian American Literature: The Case of *Fu Sang*' (*ASInt* 38:i[2000] 61–71), a novel such as *Fu Sang* [1996], by the Taiwanese American author Yan Geling, raises key issues of literary identification and affiliation. Its story of Chinese-immigrant prostitution probes not only East–West sexual encounter but is placed at the transnational border, a novel simultaneously Taiwanese, American and Asian American. Which can best be thought to suit?

In 'Immigrant Dreams and Civic Promises: (Con-)Testing Identity in Early Jewish American Literature and Gish Jen's *Mona in the Promised Land*' (*MELUS* 25:i[2000] 209–26) Andrew Furman gives spirited thought to issues of assimilation and 'symbolic ethnicity' in Jen's second novel and, not least, the irony of Mona Chang's conversion to Judaism. Invoking a Jewish American literary spectrum from Abraham Cahan to Philip Roth, and an Asian American spectrum from Bharati Mukherjee to Gish Jen, he looks to how their writings see the gains, and losses, in cultural identity by immigrant entry into the US mainstream. *MELUS* 25:i[2000], and Furman's essay within it, offers a whole issue given over to Jewish American literature. Other essays take up the Jewish mother in fiction—not least *Portnoy's Complaint* (Martha A. Ravits), Yiddish satire in Moyshe Nadir (Kenneth Wishnia), Abraham Cahan and American identity (Stephanie Foote), Anzia Yezierska's periodical writing (Christopher N. Okonkwo), the poetry of Charles Reznikoff (Ranen Omer), history in Cynthia Ozick (Janet L. Cooper), and trans-racialism in Grace Paley (Ethan Goffman).

Gish Jen duly also makes her entry in Emmanuel S. Nelson's *Asian American Novelists: A Bio-Bibliographical Critical Sourcebook*, a Greenwood biographical dictionary which gives both life-and-writings annotations and selective bibliographies, latest proof, were it necessary, of not only the gathering width but interiority of the Asian American literary dispensation. Taking as its departure-point Bulosan's 'How My Stories were Written' [1971] Joel Slotkin's 'Ingorots and Indians: Racial Hierarchies and Conceptions on the Savage in Carlos Bulosan's Fictions of the Philippines' (*AL* 72[2000] 844–66) gives a well-taken annotation of

Ingorot and other indigenous Filipino/a reference in such collections as *The Laughter of My Father* [1944], *The Philippines is in the Heart* [1979] and *The Cry and the Dedication* [1995]. Slotkin's critique of this short fiction works on a linked front: the dialectic of 'civilization and savagery', Spanish and US occupation and 'the trap of imperialist identity formation'.

Stephen H. Sumida's 'The More Things Change: Paradigm Shifts in Asian American Studies' (*ASInt* 38:ii[2000] 97–114) delivers a timely overview of the state of literary-cultural discourse in the field. How continuingly useful are such terms as diaspora, immigrant or, notably, cultural nationalism, for current debate and practice? How far has Asian American writing itself, not to mention the scholarship it has enjoined, unwoven Orientalist bias in non-Asian America? The *Amerasian Journal* publishes its annual selected bibliography (*AmasJ* 25:iii[2000] 227–79), an across-the-board listing of Asian American Studies for 2000, from politics to women's studies and containing due entries for literature and literary theory. This contributes a greatly valuable resource.

Building upon his *Aztlán and Vietnam: Chicano and Chicana Experiences of the War* [1999], Jorge Mariscal's 'Reading Chicano/a Writing about the American War in Vietnam' (*Aztlán* 25:ii[2000] 13–49) seeks to further highlight this 'previously unknown corpus of cultural materials'. Texts which enter the reckoning include Charley Trujillo's anthology *Dogs from Illusion* [1994], Michael W. Rodriguez's *Humidity Moon: Short Stories of the Vietnam War* [1998], Diego Vásquez's *Growing through Ugly* [1997], Roy P. Benavidez's *The Three Wars of Roy Benavidez* [1986] and Alfredo Véa's *Gods Go Begging* [1999]. Mariscal's annotations open up a new vista on issues of US ethnicity, the bridge of *chicanismo*, and with it the role of American class, into the now extensive field of Vietnam literary studies. It makes for a timely intervention.

MELUS 25:ii[2000] devotes a whole issue to 'Latino/a Identities', ten contributions in all. In 'Coming into Play: An Interview with Gloria Anzaldúa' (*MELUS* 25:ii[2000] 3–45) one of *chicanismo*'s leading feminist-lesbian theorists looks back upon her own evolving '*mestiza* consciousness'. She especially invokes the impact of *This Bridge Called My Back: Writings by Radical Women of Color* [1981], the landmark anthology she edited with Cherrié Moraga, and *Borderlands/ La Frontera: The New Mestiza* [1987], her best-known volume of essays. This wide-ranging interview offers an update of her views on both Latina and black literary feminism, eco-feminism, and the changes brought on by gender politics in what she designates 'men's writing'. *Mestizaje* also gives Erika Aigner-Varoz her focus in 'Metaphors of a Mestiza Consciousness: Anzaldúa's *Borderlands/La Frontera*' (*MELUS* 25:ii[2000] 47–62), an essay which analyses the uses of serpent and other Aztec-Mexican metaphors through which Anzaldúa has long sought to express each varying sexual, territorial and cultural borderland in her own creative practice. Her career, in this respect, can also be nicely tracked in AnaLouise Keating's *Gloria E. Anzaldúa: Interviews/Entrevistas*, a body of debate and exchange reprinted from nearly two decades. The contour is one of Anzaldúa as writer and speaker, 'lesbian wit', and flagbearer of *mestiza* rally and consciousness. The Latina spectrum receives yet fuller coverage. Ralph E. Rodriguez's 'Chicano/a Fiction from Resistance to Contestation: The Role of Creation in Ana Castillo's *So Far From God*' (*MELUS* 25:ii[2000] 63–82) reads the novel's supernatural fable of Sofia and her daughters as an endeavour to 'de-stabilize patriarchal structures' in the name of social justice. For Silvio Sirias and Richard McGarry, in 'Rebellion and Tradition in Ana Castillo's *So Far From God* and Sylvia López-Medina's *Cantora*' (*MELUS* 25:ii[2000] 83–100), a similar protocol comes into play. Castillo's novel, she argues, looks to a female autonomy gained through rebellion. López-Medina's novel works to shared purpose but through the depiction of a recovered traditional Chicana womanhood. Elisabeth Mermann-Jozwiak in '*Gritos de la frontera*: Ana Castillo, Sandra Cisneros, and Postmodernism' (*MELUS* 25:ii[2000] 101–18) instances *So Far From God* and Cisneros's story 'Little Miracles, Kept Promises' as reflexive 'border' fiction, storytelling which portrays Chicana lives as elusive of any one commanding paradigm. Leslie Petty's 'The "Dual"-ing Images of la Malinche and la Virgen de Guadalupe in Cisneros's *The House on Mango Street*' (*MELUS* 25:ii[2000] 119–32) annotates how, throughout her acclaimed story-cycle, Cisneros offers an intertextual revamping of quite the best known mythic-female binary within *chicanismo*.

Puerto Rican tradition comes into view in Julie M. Schmid's interview with David Hernández as 'Chicago's Unofficial Poet Laureate' (*MELUS* 25:ii[2000] 147–62), a wide-ranging exchange which addresses his style of spoken verse, views of identity politics, and sense of role and place within the Puerto Rican diaspora. A helpful selective bibliography is appended. Suzanne Bost's 'Transgressing Borders: Puerto Rican and Latina Mestizaje' (*MELUS* 25:ii[2000] 187–211) gives a sharp mini-panorama of the linked seams of ethnicity and gender, island and US mainland, which operate in the fiction and verse of Rosario Ferré, Ana Lydia Vega, Aurora Levins Morales and Judith Cofer.

In 'Dr. Gonzo's Carnival: The Testimonial Satires of Oscar Zeta Acosta' (*AL* 72[2000] 463–86) Michael Hames-García re-evaluates Acosta's *The Autobiography of a Brown Buffalo* [1972] and *The Revolt of the Cockroach People* [1973] in terms of Bakhtinian carnivalesque and 'grotesque physicalism'. He takes up the implications of Acosta's sublime disregard for 'correct' etiquette matters of race and sexuality along with his penchant for linking grotesqueries of the human body with those of the American body politic. In this sense, and with no little irony, given Acosta's legal qualification at the California bar, he engages in life and literature as one of *chicanismo*'s existential outlaws.

Eamonn Wall's *From the Sin-é Café to the Black Hills: Notes on the New Irish* arrived too late for inclusion last year; it gives an energetic update of the writings, art and music of the Irish American generation associated throughout the 1990s with the East Village's Sin-é Café. Key texts in this account include Michael Stephens's *The Brooklyn Book of the Dead* [1994] and his essay collection *Green Dreams: Essays Under the Influence of the Irish* [1994]; Mary Gordon's *Final Payments* [1978]; the poetry of, among others, James Liddy, John Montague, Eavan Boland and Janice Fitzpatrick-Simmons; the different writings of Helena Mulkerns; and the fiction of Roger Boylan and Thomas McGonicle. Wall, himself an Irish immigrant in the 1980s, writes a mixture of first-person memoir and critical profile. His study gives a timely, engagingly turned reminder of the enduring vitality of yet another American cultural ethnicity.

Two general essay collections invite note. Singh and Schmidt, eds., *Postcolonial Theory and the United States: Race, Ethnicity and Literature*, brings together an impressive set of nineteen literary-cultural readings of how 'hybrid identity' throughout America increasingly eludes nation-state definition. A number of luminary essays are reprinted, among them Arnold Krupat on Native literature as post-colonial triumph, Rafael Pérez-Torres on 'Reconfiguring Aztlán', Sau-ling Wong on the emerging challenges within Asian American cultural criticism, and Lisa Suhair Majaj on 'Arab-Americans and the Meaning of Race'. The editors contribute a keen, wide-ranging overview of US multiculturalism and ethnicity issues with a most valuable bibliography to match. This is a volume of genuine resource both of, and for, ongoing debate.

The appearance of Fisher-Hornung and Raphael-Hernandez, eds., *Holding their Own: Perspectives on the Multi-Ethnic Literatures of the United States*, the proceedings of a conference held in Heidelberg in 1998 under the rubric MELUS-Europe, represents an auspicious development. MELUS-Europe has now become MESEA (the Society for Multi-Ethnic Studies: Europe and the Americas), still affiliated to MELUS, but with its own independent officers and organization, and with a brief to study, and compare, ethnic literary work in Europe alongside that of the United States. This first of its publications, twenty-four or so essays, covers a fair section of the US multicultural literary waterfront and bodes well for the future. Something of the collection's range can be gauged from the following: Michel Fabre on New Orleans *gens de couleur*; Elaine Kim on Korean American writing and visual art; Alison D. Goeller on Italian American immigrant texts with a focus on Tina De Rosa's *Paper Fish*; Kirsten Twelbeck with a spirited re-reading of Teresa Cha's *DICTEE*; Frances Smith Foster on slavery as genealogy in African American texts; and Dominique Marçais on Africanism in Melville's *The Confidence-Man*.

Books Reviewed

Abbotson, Susan C.W. *Student Companion to Arthur Miller*. Greenwood. [2000] pp. xii + 169. $35 ISBN 0 3133 0949 3.

Arnold, Ellen L., ed. *Conversations with Leslie Marmon Silko*. UPMissip. [2000] pp. 224. pb $18 ISBN 1 5780 6301 9.

Aronson, Arnold. *American Avant-Garde Theatre: A History*. Routledge. [2000] pp. xiv + 242. hb £45 ($75) ISBN 0 4150 2580 X, pb £14.99 ($24.95) ISBN 0 4152 4139 1.

Baker, Charles. *William Faulkner's Postcolonial South*. Lang. [2000] pp. 158. $31.95 ISBN 0 8204 4432 4.

Balshaw, Maria. *Looking for Harlem: Urban Aesthetics in African-American Literature*. Pluto. [2000] pp. x + 169. pb £14.99 ISBN 0 7453 1334 5.

Barnett, Louise K., and James L. Thorson, eds. *Leslie Marmon Silko: A Collection of Critical Essays*. UNMP. [1999] pp. 319. pb $24.95 ISBN 0 8263 2033 3.

Beidler, Peter G., and Gay Barton. *A Reader's Guide to the Novels of Louise Erdrich*. UMissP. [1999] pp. 265. $34.95 ISBN 0 8262 1212 3.

Bennett, Michael, and Vanessa D. Dickerson, eds. *Recovering the Black Female Body: Self-Representations by African American Women*. RutgersUP. [2000] pp. xvii + 331. pb £18.50 ISBN 0 8135 2838 0.

Benston, Kimberly W. *Performing Blackness: Enactments of African-American Modernism*. Routledge. [2000] pp. xiv + 386. pb £17.99 ISBN 0 4150 0949 9.

Bigsby, C.W.E. *Modern American Drama, 1945–2000*. CUP. [2000] pp. xii + 453. hb £40 ISBN 0 5217 9089 1, pb £16.95 ISBN 0 5217 9410 2.

Bigsby, Christopher. *Contemporary American Playwrights*. CUP. [1999] pp. ix + 440. hb £45 ($64.95) ISBN 0 5216 6108 0, pb £16.95 ($22.95) ISBN 0 5216 6807 7.

Bland, Sterling Lecater Jr. *Voices of the Fugitives: Runaway Slave Stories and their Fictions of Self-Creation*. Praeger. [2000] pp. xviii + 184. pb £15.95 ISBN 0 2759 6707 7.

Bogumil, Mary L. *Understanding August Wilson*. USCP. [1999] pp. 165. £19.95 ($24.95) ISBN 1 5700 3252 1.

Bottoms, Stephen J. *Albee: 'Who's Afraid of Virginia Woolf?'* Plays in Production. CUP. [2000] pp. xiv + 204. hb £35 ($54.95) ISBN 0 5216 3209 9, pb £12.95 ($19.95) ISBN 0 5216 3560 8.

Bouson, J. Brooks. *Quiet As It's Kept: Shame, Trauma, and Race in the Novels of Toni Morrison*. SUNYP. [2000] pp. x + 277. pb $21.95 ISBN 0 7914 4424 4.

Brown, Fahamisha Patricia. *Performing the Word: African American Poetry as Vernacular Culture*. RutgersUP. [2000] pp. xii + 174. pb £14.50 ISBN 0 8135 2632 9.

Bryant, Jacqueline K. *The Foremother Figure in Early Black Women's Literature: Clothed in My Right Hand*. Garland. [1999] pp. xii + 160. £40 ISBN 0 8153 3380 3.

Bryer, Jackson R., Alan Margolies and Ruth Prigozy, eds. *F. Scott Fitzgerald: New Perspectives*. UGeoP. [2000] pp. xv + 276. $45 ISBN 0 8203 2187 7.

Butler, Judith, John Guillory and Kendall Thomas, eds. *What's Left of Theory? New Work on the Politics of Literary Theory*. Routledge. [2000] pp. 292. hb £50 ISBN 0 4159 2118 X, pb £13.95 ISBN 0 4159 2119 8.

Butler, Robert J., ed. *The Critical Response to Ralph Ellison*. Greenwood. [2000] pp. xlvi + 243. £69.50 ISBN 0 3133 0285 5.

Campbell, Neil. *The Cultures of the American New West*. EdinUP. [2000] pp. vii + 182. pb £12.95 ISBN 0 7486 1226 2.

Carpenter, Charles A. *Dramatists and the Bomb: American and British Playwrights Confront the Nuclear Age, 1945–1964*. Greenwood. [1999] pp. xiii + 183. £42.50 ($60) ISBN 0 3133 0713 X.

Chu, Patricia P. *Assimilating Asians: Gendered Strategies of Authorship in Asian America*. DukeUP. [2000] pp. 241. pb $17.95 ISBN 0 8223 2465 2.

Clark, William B., ed. *Selected Letters of Robert Penn Warren: The Apprentice Years, 1924–1934*. LSUP. [2000] pp. 274. $33.95 ISBN 0 8071 2536 9.

Cleghorn, Angus J. *Wallace Stevens' Poetics: The Neglected Rhetoric*. Palgrave. [2000] pp. 236. £35 ISBN 0 3339 4678 2.

Cole, Tim. *Selling the Holocaust. From Auschwitz to Schindler: How History is Bought, Packaged and Sold*. Routledge. [2000] pp. vii + 214. pb $15 ISBN 0 4159 2813 3.

Conner, Marc C., ed. *The Aesthetics of Toni Morrison: Speaking the Unspeakable*. UPMissip. [2000] pp. xxviii + 153. pb $18 ISBN 1 5780 6285 3.

Connolly, Thomas F. *George Jean Nathan and the Making of Modern American Drama Criticism*. FDUP. [2000] pp. 172. £30 ($35) ISBN 0 8386 3780 9.

Curnutt, Kirk, ed. *The Critical Response to Gertrude Stein*. Greenwood. [2000] pp. 368. $82.50 ISBN 0 3133 0475 0.

Curry, Renee R. *White Women Writing White: H.D., Elizabeth Bishop, Sylvia Plath and Whiteness*. Greenwood. [2000] pp. 184. £52.95 ISBN 0 3133 1019 X.

Davis, Alex, and Lee M. Jenkins, eds. *Locations of Literary Modernism: Region and Nation in British and American Poetry*. CUP. [2000] pp. 296. £40 ISBN 0 5217 8032 2.

Davis, Jane. *The White Image in the Black Mind: A Study of African American Literature*. Greenwood. [2000] pp. xx + 161. £48.95 ISBN 0 3133 0464 5.

De Vita, Alexis Brooks. *Mythatypes: Signatures and Signs of African/Diaspora and Black Goddesses*. Greenwood. [2000] pp. xiv + 180. £52.95 ISBN 0 3133 1068 8.

Dennis, Helen M., ed. *Ezra Pound and Poetic Influence*. Rodopi. [2000] pp. 282. £35 ISBN 9 0420 1523 3.

Devlin, Albert J., and Nancy M. Tischler, eds. *The Selected Letters of Tennessee Williams*, vol. i: *1920–1945*. ND. [2000] pp. xxv + 581. $37 ISBN 0 8112 1445 1.

Duvall, John N. *The Identifying Fictions of Toni Morrison: Modernist Authenticity and Postmodern Blackness*. Palgrave. [2000] pp. x + 182. $45 ISBN 0 3122 3402 3.

Ezrahi, Sidra DeKoven. *Exile and Homecoming in the Modern Jewish Imagination*. UCalP. [2000] pp. xi + 358. £27.95 ISBN 0 5202 0645 2.

Fabre, Geneviève, and Michel Feith, eds. *Jean Toomer and the Harlem Renaissance*. RutgersUP. [2000] pp. xiv + 235. pb £18.50 ISBN 0 8135 2846 1.

Felger, Robert. *Student Companion to Richard Wright*. Greenwood. [2000] pp. viii + 135. £29.50 ISBN 0 3133 0909 4.

Fisch, Audrey. *American Slaves in Victorian England: Abolition Politics in Popular Literature and Culture*. CUP. [2000] pp. x + 139. $64.95 ISBN 0 5216 6026 2.

Fisher-Hornung, Dorothea, and Heike Raphael-Hernandez, eds. *Holding their Own: Perspectives on the Multi-Ethnic Literatures of the United States*. Stauffenburg. [2000] pp. 336. €64 ISBN 3 8605 7739 5.

Flanzbaum, Hilène, ed. *The Americanization of the Holocaust*. JHUP. [1999] pp. vii + 261. hb £37.50 ($48.50) ISBN 0 8018 6021 0, pb £13 ($16.95) ISBN 0 8018 6022 9.

Folks, Jeffrey J., and Nancy Summers Folks, eds. *The World is our Home: Society and Culture in Contemporary Southern Writing*. UPKen. [2000] pp. vi + 282. £25.50 ISBN 0 8131 2166 3.

Freedman, Jonathan. *The Temple of Culture: Assimilation and Anti-Semitism in Literary Anglo-America*. OUP. [2000] pp. 272. £35 ISBN 0 1951 3157 6.

Friedman, Alan Warren, ed. *Beckett in Black and Red: The Translations for Nancy Cunard's 'Negro' (1934)*. UPKen. [2000] pp. xl + 207. £29.50 ISBN 0 8131 2129 9.

Gelb, Arthur, and Barbara Gelb. *O'Neill: Life with Monte Cristo*. Applause. [2000] pp. xix + 758. £27.95 ($40) ISBN 0 3991 4609 1.

Giddings, Robert, and Erica Sheen, eds. *The Classic Novel: From Page to Screen*. ManUP. [2000] pp. viii + 243. £11.99 ISBN 0 7190 5231 9.

Goffman, Ethan. *Imagining Each Other: Blacks and Jews in Contemporary American Literature*. SUNYP. [2000] pp. xiv + 262. pb $22.95 ISBN 0 7914 4678 6.

Gray, Richard. *Southern Aberrations: Writers of the American South and the Problems of Regionalism*. LSUP. [2000] pp. ix + 536. hb $75 ISBN 0 8071 2552 0, pb $34.95 ISBN 0 8071 2602 0.

Grewal, Gurleen. *Circles of Sorrow, Lines of Struggle: The Novels of Toni Morrison*. LSUP. [2000] pp. xiii + 154. pb $12.95 ISBN 0 8071 2643 8.

Griffin, Alice, and Geraldine Thorsten. *Understanding Lillian Hellman*. USCP. [1999] pp. xvi + 168. £23.95 ($29.95) ISBN 1 5700 3302 1.

Grobel, Lawrence. *Conversations with Capote*. Da Capo. [2000] pp. 244. £12.95 ISBN 0 3068 0944 3.

Gussow, Mel. *Edward Albee. A Singular Journey: A Biography*. S&S. [1999] pp. 448. hb $30 ISBN 0 6848 0278 3, pb $16.95 ISBN 1 5578 3447 4.

Haas, Robert, *et al.*, eds. *American Poetry: The Twentieth Century*, 2 vols. LAm. [2000] pp. 986 and 1,009. $35 each ISBN 1 8830 1177 9 (vol. i), ISBN 1 8830 1178 7 (vol. ii).

Hakutani, Yoshinobu, ed. *Theodore Dreiser and American Culture: New Readings*. UDelP. [2000] pp. 322. $49.50 ISBN 0 8741 3714 4.

Handley, George B. *Postslavery Literatures in the Americas: Family Portraits in Black and White*. UPVirginia. [2000] pp. xii + 234. pb £15.95 ISBN 0 8139 1977 0.

Hatch, Shari Dorantes, and Michael R. Strickland, eds. *African-American Writers: A Dictionary*. ABC-Clio. [2000] pp. xvi + 485. $75 ISBN 0 8743 6959 2.

Heffernan, Nick. *Capital, Class and Technology in Contemporary American Culture*. Pluto. [2000] pp. v + 250. pb £16.99 ISBN 0 7453 1104 0.

Herd, David. *John Ashbery and American Poetry*. ManUP. [2000] pp. 245. £45 ISBN 0 7190 5597 0.

Herrmann, Anne. *Queering the Moderns: Poses/Portraits/Performances*. Palgrave. [2000] pp. 198. $55 ISBN 0 3122 3327 2.

Hoeller, Hildegard. *Edith Wharton's Dialogue with Realism and Sentimental Fiction*. UPFlor. [2000] pp. xiv + 224. £42.50 ISBN 0 8130 1766 1.

Hunt, Tim, ed. *The Collected Poetry of Robinson Jeffers*, vol. iv: *Poetry, 1903–1920, Prose, and Unpublished Writings*. StanfordUP. [2000] pp. 561. £45. ISBN 0 8047 3816 5.

Innes, Christopher, Katherine Carlstrom and Scott Fraser. *Twentieth-Century British and American Theatre: A Critical Guide to Archives*. Ashgate. [1999] pp. xx + 316. £62.50 ($104.95) ISBN 1 8592 8066 8.

James, Joy, and T. Denean Sharpley-Whiting, eds. *The Black Feminist Reader*. Blackwell. [2000] pp. xiv + 302. pb $24.95 ISBN 0 6312 1007 5.

Johnson, Claudia Durst, ed. *Understanding 'The Call of the Wild': A Student Casebook to Issues, Sources, and Historical Documents*. Greenwood. [2000] pp. xiv + 260. $39.95 ISBN 0 3133 0882 9.

Johnson, Claudia Durst, and Vernon E. Johnson. *Understanding 'The Crucible': A Student Casebook to Issues, Sources, and Historical Documents*. Greenwood. [1998] pp. xiii + 239. £31.95 ($39.95) ISBN 0 3133 0121 2.

Johnson-Roullier, Cynthia E. *Reading on the Edge: Exiles, Modernities, and Cultural Transformation in Proust, Joyce, and Baldwin*. SUNYP. [2000] pp. xxii + 217. pb $20.95 ISBN 0 7914 4542 9.

Jones, Charles Colock Jr. *Gullah Folktales from the Georgia Coast*. UGeoP. [2000] pp. xxxviii + 192. pb £12.95 ISBN 0 8203 2216 4.

Kadlec, David. *Mosaic Modernism: Anarchism, Pragmatism, Culture*. JHUP. [2000] pp. 331. $42.50 ISBN 0 8018 6438 0.

Kahn-Paycha, Daniele. *Popular Jewish Literature and its Role in the Making of an Identity*. Mellen. [2000] pp. iii + 143. $79.95 ISBN 0 7734 7666 0.

Kartiganer, Donald M., and Ann J. Abadie, eds. *Faulkner at 100: Retrospect and Prospect: Faulkner and Yoknapatawpha 1997*. UPMissip. [2000] pp. 300. hb $50 ISBN 1 5780 6288 8, pb $24 ISBN 1 5780 6289 6.

Keating, AnaLouise, ed. *Gloria E. Anzaldúa: Interviews/Entrevistas*. Routledge. [2000] pp. 306. $18.95 ISBN 0 4159 2504 5.

Kelly, Lionel, ed. *Poetry and the Sense of Panic: Critical Essays on Elizabeth Bishop and John Ashbery*. Rodopi. [2000] pp. 192. pb £34 ISBN 9 0420 0720 6.

King, William Davies, ed. *'A Wind is Rising': The Correspondence of Agnes Boulton and Eugene O'Neill*. FDUP. [2000] pp. 328. £39.50 ($49.50) ISBN 0 8386 3808 2.

Kolin, Philip C. *Williams: 'A Streetcar Named Desire'*. Plays in Production. CUP. [2000] pp. ix + 229. hb £47.50 ($54.95) ISBN 0 5216 2344 8, pb $14.95 ($22) ISBN 0 5216 2610 2.

Lauret, Maria. *Alice Walker*. St Martin's Press. [2000] pp. x + 252. £15.50 ISBN 0 3335 9269 7.

Lee, A. Robert, ed. *Loosening the Seams: Interpretations of Gerald Vizenor*. BGUP. [2000] pp. 313. hb $59.95 ISBN 0 8797 2801 9, pb $29.95 ISBN 0 8797 2802 7.

Leeds, Marc, and Peter J. Reed, eds. *Kurt Vonnegut: Images and Representations*. Greenwood. [2000] pp. x + 198. £46.50 ISBN 0 3133 0975 2.

Lincoln, Kenneth. *Sing with the Heart of a Bear: Fusions of Native and American Poetry, 1890–1999*. StanfordUP. [2000] pp. 435. $19.95 ISBN 0 5202 1890 6.

Little, Anne Colclough, and Susie Paul, eds. *Denise Levertov: New Perspectives*. Locust Hill. [2000] pp. 270. $45 ISBN 0 9339 5187 6.

Madden, David. *The Legacy of Robert Penn Warren*. LSUP. [2000] pp. 186. £29.50 ISBN 0 8071 2592 X.

Malinowska, Barbara. *Dynamics of Being, Space and Time in the Poetry of Czeslaw Milosz and John Ashbery*. Lang. [2000] pp. 180. $46.95 ISBN 0 8204 3464 7.

Marsh-Lockett, Carol P., ed. *Black Women Playwrights: Visions on the American Stage*. Garland. [1999] pp. ix + 227. $47 ISBN 0 8153 2746 3.

McFarland, Ron. *Understanding James Welch*. USCP. [2000] pp. 212. $29.95 ISBN 1 5700 3349 8.

Meyer, Michael, ed. *Literature and Homosexuality*. Rodopi. [2000] pp. 268. hb £47 ISBN 9 0420 0529 7, pb £15 ISBN 9 0420 0519 X.

Middleton, Peter, and Tim Woods, eds. *Literatures of Memory: History, Time and Space in Postwar Memory*. ManUP. [2000] pp. vii + 323. pb £17.99 ISBN 0 7190 5950 X.

Millard, Kenneth. *Contemporary American Fiction: An Introduction to American Fiction since 1970*. OUP. [2000] pp. 328. pb £9.99 ISBN 0 1987 1178 6.

Miller, D. Quentin, ed. *Re-Viewing James Baldwin: Things Not Seen*. Temple. [2000] pp. xii + 256. pb £19.50 ISBN 1 5663 9736 7.

Milowitz, Steven. *Philip Roth Considered: The Concentrationary Universe of the American Writer*. Garland. [2000] pp. ix + 213. £40 ISBN 0 1853 3957 7.

Mitchell, Hayley, ed. *Readings on 'Black Boy'*. Greenhaven. [2000] pp. 192. $32.45 ISBN 0 7377 0243 5.

Mitchell, Hayley, ed. *Readings on 'Native Son'*. Greenhaven. [2000] pp. 186. pb $19.95 ISBN 0 7377 0319 9.

Mitchell, Verner D, ed. *This Waiting for Love: Helene Johnson, Poet of the Harlem Renaissance*. UMassP. [2000] pp. xvi + 135. £21.50 ISBN 1 5584 9256 9.

Morris, Willie. *James Jones: A Friendship*. UIllP. [2000] pp. vii + 259. pb $17.95 ISBN 0 2520 6837 8.

Murphy, Brenda, and Susan C.W. Abbotson. *Understanding 'Death of a Salesman': A Student Casebook to Issues, Sources, and Historical Documents*. Greenwood. [1999] pp. xviii + 248. £31.95 ($39.95) ISBN 0 3133 0402 5.

Murphy, Patrick D. *A Place for Wayfaring: The Poetry and Prose of Gary Snyder*. OregonSUP. [2000] pp. 248. pb $21.95 ISBN 0 8707 1479 1.

Napier, Winston, ed. *African American Literary Theory: A Reader*. NYUP. [2000] pp. xiv + 730. pb £30 ISBN 0 8147 5810 X.

Nelson, Emmanuel S., ed. *African American Authors, 1745–1945: A Bio-Bibliographical Critical Sourcebook*. Greenwood. [2000] pp. 544. $100 ISBN 0 3133 0910 8.

Nelson, Emmanuel S., ed. *Asian American Novelists: A Bio-Bibliographical Critical Sourcebook*. Greenwood. [2000] pp. 422. $95 ISBN 0 3133 0911 6.

Newman, Richard, Patrick Rael and Phillip Lapsansky, eds. *Pamphlets of Protest: An Anthology of Early African American Protest Literature, 1790–1860*. Routledge. [2000] pp. viii + 326. pb $22.99 ISBN 0 4159 2444 8.

Nielsen, Aldon Lynn, ed. *Reading Race in American Poetry: 'An Area of Act'*. UIllP. [2000] pp. xii + 232. hb £37 ($49.95) ISBN 0 2520 2518 0, pb $18.95 ISBN 0 2520 6832 7.

Novik, Peter. *The Holocaust in American Life*. Mariner. [2000] pp. 373. pb $15 ISBN 0 6180 8232 8.

Oakes, David A. *Science and Destabilization in the Modern American Gothic: Lovecraft, Matheson, and King*. Greenwood. [2000] pp. 144. £42.50 ISBN 0 3133 1188 9.

Pavloska, Susanna. *Modern Primitives: Race and Language in Gertrude Stein, Ernest Hemingway, and Zora Neale Hurston*. Garland. [2000] pp. 120. $65 ISBN 0 8153 3650 0.

Pelzer, Linda C. *Student Companion to F. Scott Fitzgerald*. Greenwood. [2000] pp. 166. $35 ISBN 0 3133 0594 3.

Pepper, Andrew. *The Contemporary American Crime Novel: Race, Ethnicity, Gender, Class*. EdinUP. [2000] pp. vi + 182. pb £15.95 ISBN 0 7486 1340 4.

Perkins, Margo V. *Autobiography as Activism: Three Black Women of the Sixties*. UPMissip. [2000] pp. xx + 161. pb $18 ISBN 1 5780 6264 0.

Preston, Claire. *Edith Wharton's Social Register*. St Martin's Press. [2000] pp. xv + 225. £42.50 ISBN 0 3337 4622 8.

Quetchenbach, Bernard W. *Back from the Far Field: American Nature Poetry in the Late Twentieth Century*. UPVirginia. [2000] pp. 189. hb £41.95 ($49.50) ISBN 0 8139 1953 3, pb £15.95 ($18.50) ISBN 0 8139 1954 1.

Rivkin, Libbie. *Career Moves: Olson, Creeley, Zukofsky, Berrigan and the American Avant-Garde*. UWiscM. [2000] pp. 172. pb £14.50 ISBN 0 2991 6844 1.

Roper, Jon. *The American Presidents: Heroic Leadership from Kennedy to Clinton*. EdinUP. [2000] pp. vii + 246. pb £15.95 ISBN 0 7486 1226 2.

Ryan, Michael. *A Difficult Grace: On Poets, Poetry and Writing*. UGeoP. [2000] pp. 184. hb £33.95 ($40) ISBN 0 8203 2264 4, pb £15.50 ($17.95) ISBN 0 8203 2231 8.

Shiach, Don. *American Drama, 1900–1990*. Contexts in Literature. CUP. [2000] pp. 128. pb £7.95 ISBN 0 5216 5591 9.

Siebold, Thomas, ed. *Readings on 'Death of a Salesman'*. Literary Companions. Greenhaven. [1998] pp. 160. pb $32.45 ISBN 1 5651 0839 6.

Simpson, Megan. *Poetic Epistemologies: Gender and Knowing in Women's Language-Oriented Writing*. SUNYP. [2000] pp. 222. hb $57.50 ISBN 0 7914 4445 7, pb $18.95 ISBN 0 7914 4446 5.

Singh, Amritjit, and Peter Schmidt, eds. *Postcolonial Theory and the United States: Race, Ethnicity and Literature*. UPMissip. [2000] pp. 471. $26 ISBN 1 5780 6252 7.

Skerret, Joseph T. Jr., ed. *Literature, Race and Ethnicity: Contesting American Identities*. Longman. [2000] pp. 564. pb £18.99 ISBN 0 3210 1162 7.

Smith, Barbara, ed. *Home Girls: A Black Feminist Anthology*. RutgersUP. [2000] pp. lx + 364. pb $20 ISBN 0 8135 2753 8.

Smith, Valerie, ed. *African American Writers*. 2nd edn. 2 vols. Scribner. [2000] pp. xxxvi + 925. $225 ISBN 0 6848 0638 X.

Sollors, Werner, ed. *Interracialism: Black–White Intermarriage in American History, Literature, and Law*. OUP. [2000] pp. xiv + 546. $24.95 ISBN 0 1951 2857 5.

Stanley, David, and Elaine Thatcher, eds. *Cowboy Poets and Cowboy Poetry*. UIllP. [2000] pp. 392. hb £41 ($49.95) ISBN 0 2520 2520 2, pb £18 ($21.95) ISBN 0 2520 6836 X.

Stave, Shirley A, ed. *Gloria Naylor: Strategy and Technique, Magic and Myth*. UDelP. [2000] pp. 200. £30 ISBN 0 8741 3705 5.

Stookey, Lorena L. *Louise Erdrich: A Critical Companion*. Greenwood. [1999] pp. 168. $35 ISBN 0 3133 0612 5.

Tackach, James, ed. *Slave Narratives*. Greenhaven. [2000] pp. 190. pb $19.95 ISBN 0 7377 0549 3.

Tallmadge, John, and Henry Harrington, eds. *Reading Under the Sign of Nature: New Essays in Ecocriticism*. UtahSUP. [2000] pp. 386. pb $24.95 ISBN 0 8748 0648 8.

Thomas, Lorenzo. *Extraordinary Measures: Afrocentric Modernism and Twentieth-Century American Poetry*. UAlaP. [2000] pp. xvi + 272. pb $19.95 ISBN 0 8173 1015 0.

Tischler, Nancy M. *Student Companion to Tennessee Williams*. Greenwood. [2000] pp. x + 179. £22.50 ($35) ISBN 0 3133 1238 9.

Townsend, Peter. *Jazz in American Culture*. EdinUP. [2000] pp. vii + 193. pb £12.95 ISBN 1 8533 1204 5.

Vice, Sue. *Holocaust Fiction*. Routledge. [2000] pp. vii + 239. pb £15.99 ISBN 0 4151 8553 X.

Wagner-Martin, Linda, ed. *A Historical Guide to Ernest Hemingway*. OUP. [2000] pp. 248. £10.99 ISBN 0 1951 2152 X.

Wald, Gayle. *Crossing the Line: Racial Passing in Twentieth Century U.S. Literature and Culture*. DukeUP. [2000] pp. 251. $19.95 ISBN 0 8223 2515 2.

Wall, Cheryl A., ed. *Zora Neale Hurston's 'Their Eyes were Watching God': A Casebook*. OUP. [2000] pp. 191. £30.50 ISBN 0 1951 2173 2.

Wall, Eamonn. *From the Sin-é Café to the Black Hills: Notes on the New Irish*. UWiscP. [1999] pp. 139. £14.50 ISBN 0 2991 6724 0.

Wallach, Rick. *Myth, Legend, Dust: Critical Responses to Cormac McCarthy.* ManUP. [2000] pp. 272. £45 ISBN 0 7190 5947 X.

Warren, Joyce W., and Margaret Dickie, eds. *Challenging Boundaries: Gender and Periodization.* UGeoP. [2000] pp. 296. hb £39.95 ($50) ISBN 0 8203 2123 0, pb £19.95 ($25) ISBN 0 8203 2124 9.

Watson, James G. *William Faulkner: Self-Presentation and Performance.* UTexP. [2000] pp. 254. $25 ISBN 0 2927 9131 3.

West, James L. III, ed. *F. Scott Fitzgerald. Flappers and Philosophers.* CUP. [2000] pp. xxxi + 398. $40 ISBN 0 5214 0236 0.

West, James L. III, ed. *F. Scott Fitzgerald. Trimalchio: An Early Version of 'The Great Gatsby'.* CUP. [2000] pp. xxii + 192. $40 ISBN 0 5214 0237 9.

Wheatley, Christopher J., ed. *Twentieth-Century American Dramatists: Second Series.* Dictionary of Literary Biography 228. Gale. [2000] pp. xx + 375. $165 ISBN 0 7876 3137 X.

Wilcox, Earl J., and Jonathan N. Barron, eds. *Roads Not Taken: Rereading Robert Frost.* UMissP. [2000] pp. 264. £27.50 ISBN 0 8262 1305 7.

Will, Barbara. *Gertrude Stein, Modernism, and the Problem of 'Genius'.* EdinUP. [2000] pp. 180. $32 ISBN 0 7486 1198 3.

Williams, Roland L., Jr. *African American Autobiography and the Quest for Freedom.* Greenwood. [2000] pp. xvi + 155. £46.50 ISBN 0 3133 0585 4.

Wilmeth, Don B., and Christopher Bigsby, eds. *The Cambridge History of American Theatre*, vol. iii: *Post-World War II to the 1990s.* CUP. [2000] pp. xviii + 582. $80 ISBN 0 5216 6959 6.

Wilson, Rob. *Reimagining the Pacific: From 'South Pacific' to Bamboo Ridge and Beyond.* DukeUP. [2000] pp. 296. pb $18.95 ISBN 0 8223 2523 3.

Wong, Hertha D. Sweet, ed. *Louise Erdrich's 'Love Medicine': A Casebook.* OUP. [2000] pp. 232. $45 ISBN 0 1951 2721 8.

Wood, Gerald C. *Horton Foote and the Theater of Intimacy.* LSUP. [1999] pp. xii + 142. $60 ISBN 0 8071 2295 5.

Wood, Gerald C., ed. *Horton Foote: A Casebook.* Garland. [1998] pp. viii + 230. £19.95 ($25) ISBN 0 8153 2544 4.

Yin, Xiao Huang. *Chinese American Literature since the 1850s.* UIllP. [2000] pp. 307. $34.95 ISBN 0 2520 2524 5.

XVII

New Literatures

FEMI ABODUNRIN, NOEL ROWE, JENNIFER MOORE, RICHARD
LANE, CHESTER ST H. MILLS, PHILLIP LANGRAN AND
NELSON WATTIE

This chapter has seven sections: 1. Africa; 2. Australia; 3. Canada; 4. Caribbean; 5. India; 6. New Zealand; 7. South Pacific. Section 1 is by Femi Abodunrin; section 2 is by Noel Rowe and Jennifer Moore; section 3 is by Richard Lane; section 4 is by Chester St H. Mills; section 5 is by Phillip Langran; sections 6 and 7 are by Nelson Wattie.

1. Africa

(a) General
This year's special issue of journals included *Matatu* (21–2[2000]), 'FonTomFrom: Contemporary Ghanaian Literature, Theatre and Film', edited by Kofi Anyidoho and James Gibbs. James Gibbs's 'Edua Theodora Sutherland: A Bibliography of Primary Materials—with a Checklist of Secondary Sources' (*Matatu* 21–2[2000] 117–23) is a comprehensive list of the works and secondary sources on one of Africa's foremost poets and playwrights, Efua Sutherland [1923–96]. Lindfors and Kothandaraman, eds., *The Writer as Activist: South Asian Perspectives on Ngugi wa Thiong'o*, includes 'A Checklist of South Asian Scholarship on Ngugi wa Thiong'o, 1975–1997' (pp. 177–88) by the editors.

Gibbs and Mapanje, eds., *The African Writer's Handbook*, is another compendium of a slightly different sort. Like *A Handbook for African Writers* (Hans Zell Publishers), edited by James Gibbs, which arose out of a conference in London in 1984 on 'New Writing in Africa', *The African Writer's Handbook* came out of the now famous Arusha conferences, which decided that the role of the publishing industry in Africa is 'an indispensable part of the cultural development and renaissance of the continent'. While Arusha 1 and 2 were on 'The Development of Autonomous Capacity in Publishing in Africa' and 'The Future of Indigenous Publishing in Africa' respectively, Arusha 3, held at Tarangire Sopa Lodge, Arusha, in Tanzania in February 1998, and organized by the Oxford-based African Books Collectives (ABC) and the Swedish Dag Hammarskjold Foundation, has, according to Mary Jay, hearkened to the call by Walter Bgoya, co-director of Arushas 1and 2 and publisher-director of Arusha 3, 'to hold a conference of African writers and publishers with the aim of arriving at a "New Deal" between the two professions and agreeing on common approaches to the imperative task of enhancing the role of literature and publishing in the continent'. Writer-director of Arusha 3, Niyi Osundare, wrote a characteristically lucid introduction to the *Handbook*, which echoes the *modus vivendi* of this 'New Deal':

> the seminar emerged with a '"New Deal" between writers and publishers in Africa in their struggle to strengthen African literature and culture'. As can be expected, that 'Deal' did not come the easy way. Each group came with its own trunkload of views and grievances, and there were passionate accusations and spirited defences on both sides. But in the end, a fruitful agreement was reached on vital areas such as (a) the role of the writer and the publisher's expectations, (b) contractual issues and writer–publisher relations, (c) African values and African writing ...

With an impressive array of leading writers and publishers from nine countries and ten resource people with backgrounds in publishing, the main objective of Arusha 3, which was 'to respond to the call for a "New Deal" between writers and publishers in Africa in the struggle to strengthen African literature and culture', has been realized fully. Ranging through matters connected to the economics of development and the politics of nation-building that consume African countries vis-à-vis the vexed issue of cultural development in general and book development in particular, Paul Tiyambe Zeleza's 'A Social Contract for Books' (*Handbook*, pp. 3–14) fleshes out all the domestic and external factors undermining book development in Africa. The relative devaluation of local publishing is, according to Zeleza, a product of the 'historical and prevailing relations of domination and dependency between Africa and the West, and the fact that the intellectual structures of reference, attitude and legitimation internationally and within African universities themselves continue to be determined by Western standards and epistemologies'.

Part 1 of the *Handbook* is divided into two sections, juxtaposing the publishing experiences of African writers with the perspectives of publishers. Niyi Osundare's 'The Publisher and the Poet', M.M. Mulokozi's 'The Experience of Being a Writer in Tanzania', Yvonne Vera's 'Revelations and Reversals: Writing Inside the Continent', and Femi Osofisan's 'An Experience of Publishing in Africa', are some of the choice essays in the writers' section. 'Harsh' and 'disconcerting' are some of the terms used by these writers to describe their entry/introduction to the world of publishing. Osundare's contribution contextualizes the ideological precursor to the travails of the second generation of African/Nigerian writers: many, according to Osundare, 'in the true sense of decolonising African letters, had pledged total loyalty to indigenous publishers, and turned our back on the multinational publishing houses which we saw as active agents in the West's exploitation of Africa'. Buttressing Osundare's claim of economic exploitation, another leading member of the second generation of writers, Femi Osofisan, describes their meeting in 1973 in Ibadan, Nigeria, as an attempt to wean African writing from the preponderance of the theme of cultural alienation: 'We saw that our nation was under the threat of disintegration into a bloody civil war, through military coups d'etat, corrupt leadership, economic clientelism, and such woes; whereas our authors were writing about ethnographic customs and rituals, and being celebrated for these in the Western presses.' Similarly, the experiences of M.M. Mulokozi and Yvonne Vera in Tanzania and Zimbabwe respectively reinforce the primacy of 'the book', or what Walter Bgoya, in 'Publishing in Africa: Culture and Development', describes as 'the metaphor of the book as the house of spirit' within an African setting. Mulokozi's bitter-sweet experience at the hands of publishers, as he describes it, ends on this note: 'I believe that if I had not had access to books I probably would not have become a writer, for a writer is by definition an assiduous reader.' Vera's contribution dwells on the symbiotic relationship between two acts that are a unity: 'A love of writing must be matched, if not exceeded, by a love of reading. To write must also be to imagine a book being read.' However, Bgoya reiterates, in a very insightful account of what publishing in Africa entails, that 'if the metaphor of the book as the house of spirits be extended, the publisher could be the builder of the house of spirits, with the author as its feeder'. While the handbook is primarily about the relationship between the author, who, according to Osundare, 'is the goose that lays the golden egg', and the publisher, 'who must not allow the goose to die through cheating and neglect', it also touches on other extant aspects of the increasingly problematic means of producing and sustaining the African book industry. Ranging from the rampaging activities of obtrusive agents of the neo-colonial state to the activities of literary agents and the roles of literary prizes in an era of dwindling resources, part 2 contains practical as well conceptual detail which makes the *Handbook* 'a treasure-trove for aspiring and budding writers, and a useful reference source for all'.

African Languages Literature in the Political Context of the 1990s is a collection of essays edited by Charles Bodunde. Since the appearance of Thomas Mofolo's acclaimed *Chaka* [1908], originally written in Sotho, literature in African languages has occupied a middle ground in African literature and its criticism. According to Bodunde, 'written literature in indigenous African languages has grown from the simply idealist-moralist vision of the Mofolo and Fagunwa era to the radical realism of writers like Ngugi and the much younger Wamitila'. While the older, idealistic Mofolo and the apolitical Fagunwa are often perceived mainly as interested in enriching the literary history of the world, a radical shift in style and vision has accompanied the creative preoccupation of their younger counterparts, who 'are becoming more conscious of the need to write in their various native languages'. The essays in this volume have broadened the debate on written literature in indigenous African languages to include the shift of vision that each ethnic literature reflects in terms of their diversity in aesthetic forms and political vision. From Swahili through Yoruba and Hausa literatures to Chichewa and Venda literatures in the context of post-apartheid South Africa, the literatures of African languages in the political context of the 1990s remain a body of writing that is, according to Bodunde, characterized by 'a radical shift in style and vision especially because African writers in English are becoming more conscious of the need to write in their native languages'.

Charles Bodunde's book-length study, *Oral Traditions and Aesthetic Transfer: Creativity and Social Vision in Black Poetry*, is in the discursive Bayreuth African Studies series. Bodunde notes that within 'the complex corpus of verbal and spoken art created as a means of recalling the past', oral tradition has exerted a dominant influence, as 'imaginative transfer', for example, in the works of African poets. It is often described as the 'root from which modern liberated African literature must draw its sustenance', but, as he observes, the pattern of oral transfer varies according to individual artists:

> For instance, poets like Niyi Osundare and Jack Mapanje employ as many forms as possible to achieve the desired effects ... For some poets, the interest is in a single oral corpus and they seize on the dominant appeal of the genre to explore social and political phenomena. Soyinka, for instance, makes the Ogun myth the core of his art ... Okinba Launko (Femi Osofisan) explores the Ifa myth as means of social mediation. Launko's treatment of this mythic phenomenon and Kofi Anyidoho's employment of the funeral dirge are examples of the influences of specific oral genres on contemporary Black poetry. Some of the influences in this category are Ojaide's use of *udje*, the Urhobo satirical song and Ezenwa Ohaeto's transfer of the masquerade chant in to the space of *The Voice of the Night Masquerade*.

Within the context of the Black diaspora, the whole question of aesthetic transfer and interest in oral culture operates along the lines of 'folk stories interspersed with saucy life stories'. Thus, Kamau Brathwaite's *New World* trilogy, *The Arrivants*, could be described as one of the most successful explorations into oral aesthetics, African history and landscape, and studied here 'to reflect the nature of cultural transfer and social vision in the aesthetic of the Caribbean poets of the African diaspora'. The various levels of relations or links among a judicious selection of African poets are also explored in a bid to determine, according to Bodunde, 'the communicativeness of orature in the written medium thereby making the poems reach out beyond the limitation of its writtenness to speak as the oral text does to the audience'.

Ania Loomba's, *Colonialism/Postcolonialism*, and Childs, ed., *Postcolonial Theory and English Literature: A Reader*, revisit the largely settled but still contentious premises of colonial and post-colonial discourses and the cultural as well as historical factors that animate them. According to Peter Childs, '"British Imperialism" and "English" literature have at least one theoretical tradition in common: the belief that they both happened by chance'. On the other hand, in situating colonial and post-colonial studies, Ania Loomba insists that terms such as colonialism, imperialism, neo-colonialism and post-colonialism, and the controversies surrounding them, must be clearly defined. While the terms colonialism and imperialism, for example, are often used interchangeably, colonialism, according to Loomba, 'is not merely the expansion of various European powers into Asia, Africa or the Americas from the sixteenth century onwards; it has been a recurrent and widespread feature of human history'. The crucial difference is that, whereas earlier colonialisms were pre-capitalist, modern colonialism was established alongside capitalism in western Europe. To paraphrase Loomba, the heterogeneous practices and impact of colonialism over the last four centuries entails, therefore, that each scholar of colonialism, 'depending on her disciplinary affiliation, geographic and institutional location and identity, is likely to come up with a different set of examples, emphasis and perspective on the question'.

Loomba's important study is divided into three main chapters, exploring the different meanings of terms such as colonialism, imperialism and post-colonialism vis-à-vis the controversies that integral aspects of post-structuralist, Marxist, feminist and postmodern thoughts have engendered in relation to post-colonial studies. Chapter 1 discusses, among other issues, 'the literary inception as well as inflection of colonial discourse studies', including the problems that have been generated by colonial representations and subjectivity. The complexities of colonial and post-colonial subjects and identities, and the extent to which the colonial encounter restructures ideologies of racial, cultural, class and sexual difference, are the primary foci in chapter 2. While the writings of Frantz Fanon, for example, are discussed in the contexts of gender and sexuality, nationalism and hybridity, Loomba asks if psychoanalysis is useful for understanding colonial subjectivities and how we can understand 'the now fashionable concept of hybridity in the light of these issues'. In chapter 3, the processes of decolonization and the problems of recovering the viewpoint of colonized subjects from a post-colonial perspective are examined in all their ramifications. From the creative hybridity of African writers that Achebe invokes in support of his well-known, 'I have been given this language and I intend to use it' position, to the multiple connections between language and culture through which Ngugi wa Thiong'o argues that colonialism made inroads into the latter (culture) through control of the former (language), one of Loomba's primary conclusions is that 'turning away from colonial culture is often a necessary precondition for paying serious attention to the literatures and cultures developed under colonialism'.

One instance of such literatures is Joseph Conrad's constantly analysed novella *Heart of Darkness*, 'deliberately narrated as a journey into the self, as psychological self-discovery'. From the perspective of many post-colonial analysts, according to Peter Childs, European belief concerning subjectivity, temporality and linguistic convention seemingly converge 'in a place such as the Belgian Congo because Africa has been associated in the West with alternative modes of thought, perception and art to those that developed out of the Enlightenment'. However, the abridged version of Patrick Brantlinger's 'Kurt's "Darkness" and *Heart of Darkness*' (pp. 191–200), Robert Hampson's '*Heart of Darkness* and "The Speech that Cannot be Silenced"' (pp. 201–15), the abridged version of Sally Ledger's 'In Darkest England: The Terror of Degeneration in *Fin-De-Siècle* Britain' (pp. 216–26), and Wilson Harris's 'The Frontier on Which *Heart of Darkness* Stands' (pp. 227–33), are four choice essays that focus on Conrad's controversial novella from different theoretical as well as cultural and political standpoints. Like the problematization of Shakespearian texts by post-colonial theorists, 'Conradian meditation', to use V.S. Naipaul's coinage in his essay 'Conrad's Darkness' [1974], has engendered a wide range of responses from 'many corners of the world which he [Conrad] considered as dark'. According to Loomba, 'historically, Shakespeare was used in South Africa to contest as well as foster racism'. Like the organic overlap between cultural and political identities and the medium of literary expression that the Achebe versus Ngugi debate entails, the contestations among Shakespearian scholars take place both from within and outside the educational system, 'with African political leaders and intellectuals often using Shakespeare either to express their own psychological and political conflicts, or to challenge divisive ideologies'. Like literary studies itself, and the range of strategies it often evokes, the effectiveness of powerful anti-colonial writing does not repose in one strategy of reading a particular literary tradition or 'literatures and cultures devalued under colonialism', to use Loomba's phrase, at the expense of another. Nor does choice of language neatly represent ideological or political positions, since 'writers who express themselves in indigenous tongues are not necessarily anti-colonial or revolutionary, and they may be "contaminated" by Western forms and ideas in any case, as is the case with the writer of the Malayalam novel *Indulekha*'. Loomba had asked, *inter alia*, 'Do we need to use Joseph Conrad, whom Achebe called a "bloody racist", to challenge colonialism?'. 'To the extent that Shakespeare and Conrad are still taught and read in the postcolonial world, why not?', is Loomba's response to her own question. Trevor R. Griffith's '"This Island's Mine": Caliban and Colonialism' (pp. 39–56), Rob Nixon's 'Caribbean and African Appropriations of *The Tempest*' (pp. 57–74), Meredith Anne Skura's 'Discourse and the Individual: The Case of Colonialism in *The Tempest*' (pp. 75–92), and Sylvia Wynter's 'Beyond Miranda's Meanings: Un/ Silencing the "Demonic Grounds" of Caliban's "Woman"' (pp. 93–8), have responded, in varying degrees and from different cultural as well as political perspectives, to the pervasive adoption and use of Shakespeare's paradigmatic play as a post-colonial intertext.

Gayatri Chakravorty Spivak's seminal study, *A Critique of Postcolonial Reason: Toward a History of the Vanishing Present* is, by its own admission, a feminist book—'a critique in that it examines the structures of the production of postcolonial reason'. Spivak's study carries out, among other interpretative activities, a critique of contemporary culturalist universalist feminism vis-à-vis the 'lost object' that post-colonial studies commemorates. Reiterating Loomba's paradigmatic question—'In what ways are patriarchal oppression and colonial domination conceptually and historically connected to one another?'—Spivak's study interrogates philosophy, literature, history and culture, in that order, in order to arrive at what it describes as 'the role of literature in the production of cultural representation (which) should not be ignored'. According to Spivak, that this, among other 'facts' of literature's role, has been largely disregarded in the reading of nineteenth-century British literature, has led a section of post-colonial feminists to 'insist upon these facts with a certain narcissism. This in itself attests to the continuing success of the imperialist project, displaced and dispersed into modern form.' Like philosophy and literature, history, in the era of *pax Britannica* and its twin construct *pax Americana*, often 'caught in a super-realistic lyrical grandeur on television, film and paperback, provides … a justification of imperialism, dissimulated under the lineaments of a manageable and benevolent self-criticism'. To paraphrase Spivak, the post-colonial critic's complicity in the muting of the subaltern female is only complete when it is borne in mind that 'the postcolonial migrant investigator is touched by the colonial social formation'. The compelling case of Bhubaneswari Bhaduri and her attempt to 'speak' by turning her body into a text of woman/writing reiterates, among other theoretical points, an epistemic fracture. Spivak then points to Bhubaneswari's 'silencing by her own emancipated granddaughters: a new mainstream'. The other extant feature in Spivak's seminal study has been highlighted in Alex Tickell's 'The Road Less Travelled: *Pather Panchali* in Translation' (*JCL* 35:i[2000] 147–62). According to Tickell, the 'notion of translation-as-violation is developed in *A Critique of Postcolonial Reason*, where Spivak describes it as a manifestation of "sanctioned ignorance" within "Third Worldist" pedagogy'. The openly ethnicist and primitivist notion of Third World studies, or 'Third Worldism', as Spivak describes it, currently afloat in humanistic disciplines in the United States is partly responsible for the contemporary malaise. According to Tickell, 'Spivak relates this tendency to what she calls an unqualified "mania" for third-world literature in the West and, speaking about her work with Mahasweta Devi, warns that, when translating with a Western audience in mind, "the person who is translating must have a tough sense of the original, so that she can fight the racist assumption that all third-world women's writing is good"'.

(b) West Africa

Apologies are due for the belated mention in this section of Lindfors, ed., *Conversations with Chinua Achebe* [1997], a collection of interviews that spans more than thirty years of Achebe's writing career. As the 'inventor of the African novel', a title that he modestly denies, Africa's troubled past and troubling present have constituted the primary focus of Achebe's distinguished career. Achebe's insistence on the primacy of the story as 'our escort, our guide' is well known, and according to Lindfors, 'forty years ago when he wrote *Things Fall Apart* at the end of the colonial era, he was a reconstructionist dedicated to creating a dignified image of the African past; today, he is an angry reformer crusading against the immorality and injustices of the African present'. With an estimated over 8 million copies of the precursive *Things Fall Apart* sold and his other novels also influential and commercially successful, 'the need of African literature ... to see the story from as many points of view as possible' remains his primary motivating principle. Achebe explains in a 1987 interview with Chris Searle entitled 'Achebe and the bruised Heart of Africa' (pp. 155–64): 'What happened to Africa in its meeting with Europe was devastating. It was our people losing grip on their history, being swept out of the current of their history into somebody else's history, becoming a footnote.' Similarly, in her 1987 interview with Achebe, Jane Wilkinson revisits some of the provocative ideas that he has put forward in various essays and speeches, particularly the often debated and controversial 'novelist as teacher' analogy. Achebe's recontextualization of the old debate and his substitution of the image of the explorer for that of the teacher set the stage for an examination of his major preoccupation in his five novels, or, as Wilkinson describes it, for an exploration of 'the roles, responsibilities and limits of intellectuals in Africa'. In 'Literature and Conscientization: Interview with Chinua Achebe', the erudite critic of African literature Biodun Jeyifo revisits the premises of what he calls 'the beginnings' with Achebe, especially how one can say that Achebe's development, his beginnings, 'also marked a point of beginning for contemporary Nigerian literature—not in an absolute sense but in a relative sense'. It was at Nigeria's premier University of Ibadan that Achebe, along with his contemporaries, read racially biased accounts of the African sensibility, such as Joyce Cary's *Mister Johnson* and Joseph Conrad's *Heart of Darkness*, and that led him to contemplate writing a novel of his own:

> So that's the kind of beginning I had. It's quite difficult to say, but I'm quite sure that by the time we were reading our set-books at Ibadan we were not as innocent as we had been in secondary school—just

enjoying adventure stories. We were able to say: I don't think this is fair or right! I remember one of the bright students in my class, Olumide, saying something to the effect that the only time he enjoyed Joyce Cary's *Mister Johnson* was the moment when Johnson was shot! This horrified our English teacher. But you can see that we were beginning to struggle out of the position into which we had been placed. And if one exaggerated, that should be understood. So I think it was at Ibadan that my feeling about literature, the vocation, began to form.

Ostensibly, as the editor of the volume Bernth Lindfors reiterates, interviewers have always sought solutions to a puzzling riddle: 'How does one explain a rare phenomenon like Chinua Achebe? How does he explain himself?' From his acute awareness of the story-telling art embedded in the oral context of African literature to issues of decolonization and globalization, the collection of interviews in this volume explains a great deal of what could be described as the essential Achebe, and is highly recommended to both Achebeans as well as students of African and post-colonial literatures.

Haynes, ed., *Nigerian Video Films*, is a collection of essays that illustrate through a variety of approaches the phenomenal growth of an art form around which two fairly substantial bodies of writing have grown. While newspaper reporting and reviewing complement university theses and long essays in their bid to describe 'production structures, stemming from a tradition of studies of theatre management', the aim of the present collection is to transcend 'mere reviewing—the piecemeal pointing out of faults'. Like the dramatic art form from which it evolved, the social basis of the video phenomenon which is wide, diverse and unprecedented 'need much deeper *readings* of the films, approaching them as a work of art with adequate interpretative sophistication' (original emphasis). Haynes's lengthy introduction to the volume is the first of such deeper readings. It chronicles, among other interpretative activities, the social evolution of the films in their myriad-mindedness as 'the expression of a huge country of more than 100 million people, a quarter of the sub-Saharan population, who speak some 250 languages, a country with an unlimited capacity to astonish and bewilder its most devoted students'. The inflated plots of Nigerian video films and the series of melodramas that they enact are, according to Haynes, 'familiar in the wrong ways and strange in the wrong ways'. The pseudo-modernity of the world of the videos, epitomized by 'the people getting in and out of the Mercedes (who) may be dressed in flowing African robes and Western fashions', is one of the numerous traits of familiarity and strangeness:

> At one end of the spectrum of video production (again this is not the whole), the commodity of fetishism extends to luxurious walled mansions, cell phones, exercise equipment, fancy hotels and restaurants, and establishing shots across Lagos Lagoon or Five Cowries Creek that, overlooking the squalor and chaos of this most unnerving of West African cities, make Lagos look like any other international capital. The plots inflate common domestic problems into huge business deals and cat fights between overdressed women, and

they generally show us a world closer to Dallas and Dynasty than to the reality in which virtually all Nigerians live.

From the informed perspective of a film-maker and practitioner, Afolabi Adesanya's 'From Film to Video' (pp. 36–50) is an in-depth and sustained analysis of what could be described as a reverse form of evolution, diagnosing 'the economics of celluloid film production and marketing' as the bane of Nigerian film-makers. Beginning with the evolution of feature film production in Nigeria, an evolution which was similar to that in any other African country, Adesanya describes the involvement of the Yoruba theatre practitioners in motion picture production as 'perhaps the most auspicious single factor in the evolution of an indigenous cinema in Nigeria'. The reasons why a sustainable film industry did not emerge from this initiative could be ascribed to a variety of factors ranging from the declining value of the naira to 'lack of proper marketing (distribution and exhibition) channels to guarantee the probability of breaking even at the box office'. According to Adesanya, 'like a shooting star, the spate of productions burnt itself out in 1989', resulting in the fairly commonplace knowledge that 'the feat filmmakers could not achieve in two decades of indigenous marketing the videographers accomplished easily and in a jiffy, to the chagrin of film producers, who have mostly yet to reconcile themselves to this new wave'. If Adesanya's essay could be described as a practitioner's insight into all the concomitant effects of the video films phenomenon, 'Evolving Popular Media: Nigerian Video Films' by Jonathan Haynes and Onookome Okome (pp. 51–88) and Wole Ogundele's 'From Folk Opera to Soap Opera: Improvisations and Transformation in Yoruba Popular Theatre' (pp. 89–130) are the academics' and literary historians' insights into what Ogundele describes as 'the general state of popular culture in an era of Structural Adjustment in Nigeria'. Like Adesanya, Haynes and Okome affirm that the Yoruba travelling theatre tradition, which has itself undergone extensive changes, is 'the strongest element in the twenty-year span of Nigerian celluloid film production … and they still dominate, at least numerically, current video production'. To the extent that they are syncretistic, popular and concerned with social change, the travelling theatres 'straddle cultural origins and genres' and they 'also straddle media'. However, according to Haynes and Okome, 'it was the Igbo businessmen who understood that a larger market could be opened up by the retail sale of the videocassettes'. Unlike their Yoruba counterpart, the Igbo videos, the primary focus of Hyginus Ozo Ekwuazi's 'The Igbo Video Film: A Glimpse into the Cult of the Individual' (pp. 131–47), with a few exceptions, 'encode responses to modernity, urbanism and so on that are specifically African, Nigerian, and Igbo, but most of them have done without much overt reference to a "deep" ethnic tradition and worldview'. Without the peculiar advantages that have propelled the Yorubas and Hausas in film-making, the world of the Igbo video films springs from an undeniable Igbo cultural matrix which Ekwuazi describes as 'the perceived role or place of the individual in the Igbo community and the premium the community places on achievement'. Dul Johnson's 'Culture and Art in Hausa Video Films' (pp. 200–8) and Brian Larkin's 'Hausa Dramas and the Rise of Video Culture in Northern Nigeria' (pp. 209–41) articulate the peculiar nature of the Hausa videos, one that is 'often ignored because the "industry" is younger and less sophisticated than its Igbo and Yoruba counterparts', but nevertheless 'rapidly spreading all over northern Nigeria, creating their own publics, their own fans and generating their own critics'. Onookome Okome's 'Onome: Ethnicity, Class, Gender' (pp. 148–64), Carmela Garritano's 'Women, Melodrama and Political Critique: A Feminist Reading of *Hostages*, *Dust to Dust* and *True Confessions*' (pp. 165–91), and Obododimma Oha's 'The Rhetoric of Nigerian Christian Videos: The War Paradigm of *The Great Mistake*' (pp. 192–9), focus on different aspects of the thematic preoccupation of Nigerian videos, or what Garritano calls 'video melodramas', and the ways in which they often describe 'the corruption and greed endemic to contemporary Nigerian culture' and, through their depictions 'of the pain and suffering corrupt politicians, police officers, jail warders, lawyers, parents, and spouses inflict on innocent victims, offer a critique of political and personal immorality in Nigeria'.

Brown, ed., *Kiss and Quarrel: Yorùbá/English, Strategies of Mediation*, was the open title of a one-day seminar held at the Centre of West African Studies (University of Birmingham) when the poet and literary critic Niyi Osundare and the Yoruba literary historian Bisi Ogunsina were both attached to the centre as visiting research fellows. The tensions, both creative and destructive, between the Yoruba and the English languages over the last couple of centuries receive both critical and creative elucidation in Osundare's vivid metaphor—'when two cultures meet they kiss and quarrel'. This sets the tone for 'the volume of essays considering both the process and the outcome of the literary dimensions of that "affair"'. Osundare's 'Yoruba Thought, English Words: A Poet's Journey Through the Tunnel of Two Tongues' (pp. 15–31) describes the creative writer as standing 'in an ideal position to serve as umpire in that quarrel that we talked about earlier on'—a process in which virtually every African writer is caught: 'Gabriel Okara—poet and author of the inimitable novel called *The Voice*—once gave his own testimony on the Ijaw–English encounter; Chinua Achebe recorded the progress of the novelist's ideas from Igbo to English; while more recently, Femi Oyebode took stock of the prosodic peculiarities of Yoruba poetry, hinting at the enormous problems involved in getting the English language to accommodate them.' Femi Oyebode's contribution to the present volume, entitled 'Is there an African Aesthetics?' (pp. 32–44), diagnoses the contemporary dilemma confronting the modern African artist as 'how to articulate modern concerns and yet hold a dialogue with the irresistible past'. Departing from Kwame Appiah's well-known premise that 'there is not an African aesthetic but a plurality of African aesthetics', Oyebode argues that 'who is an African is a problematic question which has an arbitrary answer'. Choice of language has played a prominent role in the contemporary dilemma of African writers in their bid to articulate modern concerns, and according to Oyebode, 'there are at least three solutions to the problem of the modern African poet in the context which I have dramatized'. Maman Vatsa, the poet-soldier, epitomizes one aspect of the response 'by using a language which is base and corrupt—a pidgin language'. Described by Stewart Brown in his characteristically lucid introduction to the volume as 'a writer who is without question one of the major poets writing in the English language in our time', Niyi Osundare, according to Oyebode, has responded to this dilemma 'by creating a rough yet elevated language, which depends upon literal translation from another language'. Jo Dandy's 'Magic and Realism in Ben Okri's *The Famished Road*, *Songs of Enchantment* and *Astonishing the Gods*: An Examination of Conflicting Cultural Influences and Narrative Traditions' (pp. 45–63), Pietro

Deandrea's 'Gorges to be Gored, Wisdom to be Wielded: Figures from Yoruba Myth and History in Some Anglophone Yoruba Writers' (pp. 64–92), Robert Fraser's '"Ogun, do not fight me": Yoruba Deities, Agnostic Theology and Images of Power' (pp. 93–109), Stewart Brown's 'Breaking Out of the Dream: Femi Oyebode's *Black Kites Circling*' (pp. 110–22), and Stephanie Newell's '"Acada Girls" in Yoruba Marriages: Funmilayo Fakunle's Domestic Scenes' (pp. 123–40), are the choice essays examining what Stewart Brown describes as 'the creative linkages between techniques drawn from Yoruba oral tradition' in the work of Yoruba authors writing in English. While the Yoruba literary historian Bisi Ogunsina's 'The State of Yoruba Studies Today' (pp. 141–53) could be described as a description of 'the extent of creative, critical and exploratory writing that has been, and continues to be produced in Yoruba', Karin Barber's 'The Use of English in Yoruba Plays' (pp. 151–71) focuses on the interaction of language, and the ways in which interaction appears—'seen, that is, from the point of view of African language creative expression'. Barber's rigorously theorized essay focuses on the question of linguistic borrowings and loan translation from English to Yoruba and the ways the ensuing linguistic interface is turned into a critical interface in Yoruba plays: 'The inescapable presence of the official language becomes grist to their satirical and moral will. One could go as far as to suggest that the very genres that play most entertainingly with English are also the ones most profoundly in command of real Yoruba.' The Yoruba playwright Oladejo Okediji's 'Translating *Aájo Ajé*' (pp. 172–81) is an account of his labour 'to find acceptable English equivalents for many expressions in the original', and it sets the tone for the section of the book devoted to examples of the practices of imaginative writing. Femi Abodunrin's 'Iconography of Order and Disorder: An Introduction to an Extract from His Poem "It Would Take Time: Conversation with Living-Ancestors"' (pp. 182–202), Jane Bryce's 'Masquerade (a story)' (pp. 203–7), Funso Aiyejina's 'A Birthday Oriki for Iyalorisa Melvin Rodney' (pp. 208–13), Norman Weinstein's 'Thunder Striking Words: Shango as a Metaphor in the Poetry of Kamau Brathwaite' (pp. 214–30), and Conrad James's 'Punishing Female Transgression in Lucumi Culture: Eugenio Hernandez Espinosa's *Maria Antonia*' (pp. 231–41) complete the volume. While Abodunrin, according to Stewart Brown, 'engages with notions of personal and cultural identity from the perspective of one who has travelled "out" physically and intellectually and has now to regain a sense of psychological grounding through his extended "conversation with living ancestors"', Bryce's haunting short story 'also engages with supernatural beings and notions of power'. Just as Abodunrin's 'Conversation with Living Ancestors' includes passages that echo praise song, particularly in relation to figures like Ulli Beier, Aiyejina's birthday *oriki*, or praise poem, links the African and Caribbean dimensions of the Yoruba experience through what Aiyejina describes as a celebration of a distinguished individual 'who has been at the forefront of the contemporary preservation of that tradition: Iyalorisa Melvina Rodney'. Finally, Norman Weinstein's and Conrad James's essays conclude the book and the section of the book given over to that Caribbean experience. The Barbadian poet and scholar Kamau Brathwaite epitomizes the complexity of the creolization of various cultural traditions, including Yoruba—a process which, according to Aiyejina, is traceable to the ways in which 'the New World African engaged in the coded insertion of

African words, especially ritual words and phrases like *ebo* (sacrifice) and *da obi* (to throw the kola nut seed in divination) into the language of the enslaver'.

Ogundele, ed., *The Hunter Thinks the Monkey Is Not Wise*, a selection of essays by Ulli Beier, is a collection spanning nearly fifty years of Beier's ubiquitous involvement in pioneering both Yoruba cultural studies and modern African literature. According to Ogundele, Beier's wide-ranging and very broad interest in the ethos and values of African cultures which have been devastated by colonialism and the current phase of globalization are invaluable 'precisely because he has participated in or witnessed most of the crucial changes in Yoruba society from then till now—the later reflections on the changes are also of great value to anyone interested in post-colonial Yoruba society in particular and African societies in general'. The book is divided into three sections. While section 1 is about Yoruba myths and their place and function in the society, section 2, 'Fantasies and Passions', is a judicious selection out of Beier's numerous literary essays, and section 3, on 'Education, Politics, and Crises', consists of essays documenting Beier's views on important events and moments in the African historical experience, raising in the process vital 'questions about the connectedness between tradition and post-colonial politics, colonial and post-colonial education in Nigeria (and the rest of Black Africa)'. From 'Black Power by Richard Wright (1957)' (pp. 104–7) through 'Theme of Ancestors in Senghor's Poetry (1959)' (pp. 101–4) to 'D.O. Fagunwa: A Yoruba Novelist (1965)' (pp. 94–100), and the seminal 'On Translating Yoruba Poetry (1970)' (pp. 135–46), Ulli Beier's literary essays have left an indelible imprint on the critical and creative appreciation of African and Black literature. The opening sentence of the essay on translation has since become the watchword in the linguistic interface between the Yoruba language and the English language that the essays in *Kiss and Quarrel* above have elaborated. According to Beier, 'Nobody who attempts to translate Yoruba into English will doubt that "poetry is what is left out in the translation".'

Charles Bodunde's 'Aesthetics, Media and Political Currents in Yoruba Literature' (pp. 9–21) appears in a collection of essays edited by him: *African Languages Literature in the Political Context of the 1990s*, which also includes Akintude Akinyemi's 'Olu Owolabi's Ote Nibo: A Documentary on Nigeria's Political Instability' (pp. 23–37), and Mohammed M. Munkaila's 'Language Manipulation in Hausa Political Poetry' (pp. 39–61). Bodunde examines the deployment of political subject through the medium of poetry. Phonographic discs—a medium that reflects a creative strategy in Yoruba literature—along with other media such as television, radio and the newspaper—'now accommodate poems and short stories'. According to Bodunde, 'poetry on television and phonographic discs are popular genres which emerge from the political experience of the nineties'. One of Bodunde's primary conclusions is that pioneer Yoruba theatre practitioners such as Hubert Ogunde and Duro Ladipo may have set the political tone of Yoruba literature, but it is the current deployment of media resources and innovative aesthetic means 'by artists like Olanrewaju Adepoju and others [that] serve as the continuity of the tradition of making art to take a role in shaping the political life of the people'. And while Akinyemi's essay dwells on the deployment of literary and stylistic devices, such as figurative language and wordplay in Owolabi's novel, in order to examine, in a creative sense, what Owolabi perceives as 'the causes of political instability in Nigeria and his vision for a better and improved political climate', linguistic manipulation, according to Munkaila, is also the primary tool by which Hausa political poetry is sustained and turned into a 'double-edged sword in that it can be used as an instrument of liberation or manipulation'. As an instrument of propaganda, the main aim of political poetry 'is not to convey balanced views but to enhance and maintain a particular political viewpoint'.

Kwadwo Osei-Nyame Jr.'s 'Gender and the Narrative of Identity in Chinua Achebe's *Arrow of God*' (*Commonwealth* 22:ii[2000] 25–34) and Femi Abodunrin's 'Oratory in the Tongue: Ken Saro-Wiwa's *A Month and a Day and the Writer in Politics*' (*JHu* 15[2000] 43–60) complete this coverage of the West Africa sub-region. While feminist critics, both Africans and non-Africans, continue to chastise Achebe and insist on what they consider to be his contribution to the 'edging out of the female from power discourses and sites of production of meaning', Osei-Nyame's essay argues that 'Achebe's works can be explored for their inscription of women's oppositional narratives of resistance to both the Igbo masculine tradition and its patriarchal discourses and the ideology of colonialism'. Abodunrin also examines the martyred Nigerian writer Ken Saro-Wiwa's *A Month and a Day*, and the telling implication it has for the incursion of the writer into politics. One of Abodunrin's primary conclusions is that while Saro-Wiwa's leadership in the movement to seek redress from exploiting oil companies and their government partners for the devastation to Ogoni lands remains nothing if not an eloquent example of community organizing for ecological and economic development, 'even more enriching in terms of the inherently problematic concept or phenomenon of "the writer in politics" are Saro-Wiwa's prescriptions for the "intellectual wo/man of action" and one who seeks to become *l'homme engagé*'.

(c) East and Central Africa

Lindfors and Kothandaraman, eds., *The Writer as Activist: South Asian Perspectives on Ngugi wa Thiong'o*, is a collection of essays examining in critical terms the work of one of Africa's best-known authors from the perspective of South Asian literary scholars. Even while it is true that they are attracted to his work for a variety of reasons, the colonial experience or what they perceive as 'the commonality of shared historical experience', is a primary motivating principle behind the sustained South Asian scholars' and academics' interest in Ngugi's writing. According to Lindfors and Kothandaraman, they have turned most frequently to Ngugi's novels set in the colonial past—*Weep Not, Child, The River Between* and *A Grain of Wheat*—but in recent years they have also taken a lively interest in his novels about neo-colonialism—*Petals of Blood, Devil on the Cross* and *Matigari*. Anjali Roy's 'Our Science, their Superstition: Counter-Reading Progress in *The River Between*' (pp. 1–14), Feroza Jussawalla's 'Defining Postcoloniality: Ngugi wa Thiong'o's Kenyan "Adams"' (pp. 15–28), and Mala Pangurang's '"Wash me, Redeemer, and I shall be whiter than snow": Siriana and the Dynamics of Co-optation in *The River Between, Weep Not, Child,* and *Petals of Blood*' (pp. 29–42), examine different aspects of Ngugi's counter-discourse to the colonial narratives about Africa and the post-colonial world. While Ngugi is viewed as both as an important protest writer and an influential social theorist, in *The River Between* for example, Roy compares his treatment of the contentious African practice of circumcision with the indigenous Indian practice of variolation, and one of Roy's primary conclusions is that the African practice, 'which in colonialist discourse is often cited to substantiate African savagery and primitiveness, is similarly situated in a specific socio-politico-religious context that makes simplistic dismissals impossible'. Similarly, describing the classic story of the 'American Adam', Mark Twain's *The Adventures of Huckleberry Finn* [1884], as part of a group of novels that constitute a post-colonial *Bildungsroman*, Jussawalla asserts that the other novels included in the male *Bildungsroman* are 'Rudyard Kipling's *Kim*, R.K. Narayan's *Swami and Friends*, Ngugi wa Thiong'o's *Weep Not, Child*, and Rudolfo Anaya's *Bless Me*'. For post-coloniality, according to Jussawalla, 'is not just a historical moment but an attitude. What defines a post-colonial novel is the author's attitude towards the "nation state," a perception of its distinctness and "*différance*" from European colonialization and the hero/heroine's growth into his/her culture and into his/ her affirmation of the native indigenous culture, whether that be Americanness or Indianness or Kenyanness.' Jussawalla's rigorously theorized notion of the author's attitude towards the nation-state provides a context for Pandurang's exploration of Ngugi's attitude towards colonial and neo-colonial education as ranging from 'a neutralized ideology in his earlier two novels—to a demand that education be considered as a tool of counter-hegemony in his fourth novel, *Petals of Blood*'. S.W. Perera's 'The Colonial Officer/Settler: A Recurring Figure in Ngugi's Fiction' (pp. 43–60) contextualizes further what Pandurang describes as 'the triple complicity of the colonial system of education, commercial advancement and colonial/neocolonial authority' in the figure of the colonial officer/settler. According to Perera, both the constants and variations in Ngugi's portrayal of the colonial officer/settler must be examined in order to arrive at the precise nature of the author's fascination for this figure: 'Ngugi's approach to the subject is multifaceted and complex, despite his uncompromising stance vis-à-vis these European protagonists.'

Ipshitta Chanda's 'Moving Towards the Center: Postcolonial Reconstruction in the Plays of Ngugi wa Thiong'o' (pp. 61–72), Supriya M. Nair's 'Murder, He Wrote: The Politics of Violence in Ngugi's *Petals of Blood*' (pp. 73–88), and Prayag D. Tripathi's '*Devil on the Cross:* Problematics and Creativity' (pp. 89–96), examine Ngugi's creative practice in a number of representative texts of post-colonial politics and reconstruction. According to Chanda, 'in all his writing, the problem of the individual's involvement with the struggles of the community against the colonizers and their compradors is Ngugi's central focus'. Preoccupied with the reorganization of the socio-economic hierarchy, it is in his dramatic corpus that Ngugi 'deals with a problem so familiar and so important', and the scope of his work assumes a significance beyond its immediate context: 'Also in charting this process of changing relations between groups and individuals, Ngugi provides a narrative of history'. The same narrative is evident in what Nair describes as 'explosive violence [which] is often a given in many postcolonial societies'. In *A Grain of Wheat* and *Petals of Blood*, Ngugi focuses significantly on murder and his 'depiction of murder and mayhem in *Petals of Blood* has echoes of the Christian chronicle of sin, guilt, confession, and atonement as well as of classic detective fiction'. If the forms employed in the narration of *Petals of Blood* extend, as Nair contends, 'to other influences as well—particularly to psychoanalysis and Marxism'—the political novel *Devil on the Cross*, which 'is basically concerned with the harassment and torture of a lady, her sexual exploitation and her abandonment', lends itself to metaphoric implications: 'The title, like the titles of

Ngugi's other works, has symbolic properties with its implications pointed out on the first page of the narrative'. C. Vijayasree's 'Reading Ngugi in Translation: An Indian Response to Ngugi's *Devil on the Cross* and *Matigari*' (pp. 97–106) and S.V. Srinivas's '"This war is not ended": Anti-Imperialist Struggle from Mau Mau to *Matigari*' (pp. 107–32) focus on another salient aspect of Ngugi's compulsive oeuvre, the controversial issue of language in African and post-colonial literatures. According to Chanda, Ngugi's famous position 'on the use of African languages for writing African literatures is well known, as is his restructuring of the English Department at the University of Nairobi'. Ostensibly, reading Ngugi in translation has become a matter of critical debate since Simon Gikandi observed with reference to Ngugi's *Matigari* that 'the two versions of the text … are "two different artefacts" selectively directed at two antagonistic audiences'. The linguistic code-switching from English to Gikuyu has without doubt marked a radical shift in Ngugi's oeuvre. With reference to the Telugu translation of *Matigari*, one of Vijaysree's primary conclusions is that 'postcolonial readers of Ngugi's work in translation place the text concurrently in multiple contexts, one of which is the literature of their own mother tongue, since the situation in which Ngugi's texts are produced comes close to the one in which they and their own literature operate'. The political parallels between the political situation of Kenya and the Telangana Peoples Movement is one aspect of Ngugi's *Matigari* that Telugu readers do not miss, but 'the most important reason for this is that here the cultural exchange is taking place not between two antagonistic cultures but between two ancient cultures with a number of shared features such as strong oral traditions, joint family structures, agrarian economy and closely knit community systems'. Similarly, Srinivas reads Ngugi's novels *A Grain of Wheat* [1967], *Petals of Blood* [1977], *Devil on the Cross* [1982] and *Matigari* [1987] as 'representations of the struggle between two "mutually opposed forces"— imperialism in its colonial and neo-colonial stages, versus resistance'.

Dhruba Gupta's 'Whose English Is It Anyway?' (pp. 133–42) examines the seminal book, *Decolonizing the Mind*, where Ngugi theorizes his ideas on language and divides language into two categories: 'language that is used as a means of communication ("international language") and language that acts as a carrier of culture within the confines of a nation ("language of practice")'. In spite of obvious post-colonial similarities, any kind of simplistic Third World homogenization of complexities and pluralities, for the purposes of analysis, breaks down, because, according to Gupta, 'a Fanonian messianic romanticism' would not help us to understand these complexities. One of Gupta's primary conclusions is that, while a South Asian reader like himself cannot give answers to all the complex questions involved in the language debate, he 'can only venture to say that a mere switch over to an indigenous language may not be enough to break the barrier between elite and non-elite audiences, even though this barrier may be more imagined than real'. Kancherla Indrasena Reddy's 'Africa Rediscovered: Glimpses into Ngugi's *Penpoints, Gunpoints, and Dreams*' (pp. 143–56) examines Ngugi's latest and most philosophical treatise *Penpoints, Gunpoints and Dreams: Towards a Critical Theory of the Arts and the State in Africa*, which emerged out of a lecture series at Oxford University in 1996. According to Reddy, the perpetual antagonism between the pen and the gun, art and the state, the artist and the guardians of the state, 'brings into play the whole gamut of history, culture, civilization, orature, languages and literature. The artist-writer in his African context can arm himself with all these tools against the mighty killing power of the state through the mediation of art. In fact, *Penpoints* ... is a celebration of all these for bringing about an egalitarian world order.'

Finally, D. Venkat Rao's 'A Conversation with Ngugi wa Thiong'o' (pp. 157–67) and T. Vijay Kumar's 'The Writer as Activist: An Interview with Ngugi wa Thiong'o' (pp. 169–76) interrogate Ngugi himself on several aspects of his writing and activism. The continuity of documentary themes accompanied by a simultaneous discontinuity of form and content, according to Rao, is one place to begin a critical interrogation of what he describes as an unbroken continuity of themes in Ngugi's writing. Ngugi's response summarizes the historical, cultural and political imperatives that have animated and sustained his creative practice:

> The themes are created by [the] historical situation in Africa—colonialism and resistance against colonialism are persistent themes; in the present, neocolonialism—they are constant themes, part of the history against which I am writing. A writer changes also in terms of how he or she approaches the same historical moment. One becomes more and more aware. In *Weep Not, Child* and *The River Between*, the form is linear, the narrative unfolds from point A to point B to point Z. When we come to *A Grain of Wheat*, we get multiple narratives and time frames shift ... It's like I wanted to see how the same events looked at different times—looked at by different characters located in different times, from multiple centres. I continue the same technique in *Petals of Blood* ... When I came to *Devil on the Cross*, two things have happened. I change[d] language. I had to shift the language to Gikuyu ... When you use a language, you are also choosing an audience ... When I used English, I was choosing [an] English speaking audience ... Now I can use a story, a myth, and not always explain because I can assume that the [Gikuyu] readers are familiar with this...I can play with word sounds and images, I can rely more and more on songs, proverbs, riddles, anecdotes ... I maintain multiple centres, in a sense, simplify structures ... For instance, *Devil on the Cross* is based on a series of journeys.

Mercy Mirembe Ntangare's 'Democracy and the Proletariat's Dream in Byron Kawadwa's *The Song of Wankolo*' (pp. 63–89), Mike Kuria's 'Transcending Boundaries: Comedy in the Streets of Nairobi' (pp. 91–102), Peter Simatei's 'Politics and Gender in Kiswahili Drama: The Case of Mazrui's *Kilio Cha Haki* and Wamitila's *Wingu La Kupita*' (pp. 103–18), and Said A.M. Khamis's 'Fabulation and Politics of the 90s in Kezilahabi's Novel *Nagona*' (pp. 119–34), are critical articulation of the East and Central African manifestations of Bodunde, ed., *African Languages Literature in the Political Context of the 1990s* (also reviewed above). Ntangare examines the work of the artistic director of the Uganda National Theatre, Byron Kawadwa, during the infamous President Amin's reign in Uganda. Kawadwa worked and wrote in his mother tongue, Luganda—the local language of the people who hail from Baganda in central Uganda. According to Ntangare, of Kawadwa's five best-known plays, only two have been documented in other languages beside Luganda: '*The Song of Wankolo* appears in both English and French, while *St.*

Lwanga, still not formally published, appears only in English.' *The Song of Wankolo*, which is unquestionably the most successful of Kawadwa's plays, is a political play 'with its overt promotion of the structural ideals of monarchism and its unequivocal condemnation of republicanism in a society that is largely republican'. If *The Song of Wankolo* derives its appeal from its aesthetic integration of dramatic dialogue, music and dance into a coherent theatrical presentation, the Black Angels Dynamite Comedians' performances in the streets of Nairobi are sustained by their borrowings from oral literature. According to Kuria, in their performance of *Vituko* and *Sarakasi*, Kiswahili words standing for comedy and drama/theatre respectively, 'the main forces behind the group are perhaps best referred to as street thespians. Their performances, usually carried out over lunch hour, mainly take place outside Kencom, which is a major bus stop in Nairobi's city centre'. Peter Simatei's essay explores the more radical indigenous Kenyan theatre that started in the late 1970s and made its impact mainly in the 1980s. Mazrui's *Kilio Cha Haki* (A Cry for Justice) belongs to the mainstream of this theatrical tradition, which adopts 'a Marxist aesthetic of class struggle as a strategy for restructuring its radical response to the representative institutional politics of the time'. However, if *Kilio Cha Haki* can be described as a socialist delegitimation of the post-colonial state through co-option of the strategies and possibilities presented by feminism, the desire for change in Wamitila's *Wingu la Kupita* 'is not anchored directly on a revolutionary impulse that sees change as a total dismantling of political systems and replacement with others'. It is probably due to its overtly political overtones that Said Khamis describes Swahili literature in general as standing out 'to be one of the rare examples of a bondage between literature and state ideology in Africa'. Khamis's contribution traces the evolution and development of the Tanzanian writer Kezilahabi, who once described the movement of the Swahili novel as presenting 'oversimplification of human character along class lines' and using 'conflicts based on class struggle and historical materialism'. However, Kezilahabi, according to Khamis, 'is not totally nihilistic in *Nagona*. His ambitious method of revolutionary spirit notwithstanding, he also creates in the novel images that carry a certain amount of optimism'. Kyalla Wadi Wamitila's 'Contextualization of Politics and the Politics of Contextualization: The Case of the Kiswahili Novel' (pp. 135–51) contextualizes further the inherently political nature of Swahili literature in general and the five novelists whose works constitute the object of the essay's focus in particular.

Pascal J. Kishindo's 'Chichewa Literature in the Political Context of the 1990s' (in Bodunde, ed., pp. 153–70) explores Chichewa literature's response to the political environment of the 1990s. Against the backdrop of the censorship laws, which Malawians claim affected literary production and quality, one of the pertinent questions in Kishindo's essay concerns the extent to which Chichewa literature of the 1990s has been affected since the advent of multi-party democracy in 1994 and the accompanying relaxation of the censorship laws. After a fruitful examination of the creative output of the poets, dramatist and novelists of the 1990s, one of Kishindo's primary conclusions is that, beside the fact that the writers are not exploring the momentous political events of the decade, the political events themselves have been so profound 'that writers in the vernacular—since in the first place they were not particularly politically inclined as their counterparts writing in English—have yet to begin making sense of them'. James Gibbs's 'The Example of Shakespeare: Acting Over and Rewriting Shakespeare in Malawi, Ghana and

Nigeria' (*JHu* 15[2000] 1–16) explores the various ways the challenging works of Shakespeare have been rewritten to suit the varied cultural provenance of the post-colonial landscape in Malawi, Ghana and Nigeria. Shakespearian texts, or what the Nigerian writer describes as 'the example of Shakespeare', created an opening for a discussion of issues that were normally closed because of rigid censorship: 'It provided structures through which writers could tackle pressing themes, and it offered models of form and language through which writers could speak to their contemporaries'. According to Gibbs, 'In Malawi during a period of repression the unthinking reverence with which some regarded Shakespeare, Bardolatory, enabled others to use specific plays to communicate relatively subtle protests at the extent of Hastings Banda's tyranny'. Finally, Mufunanji Magalasi's 'Malawian Theatre at the Crossroads: Developmental Paradigms and Underdevelopment of Stage Drama in Malawi' (*JHu* 15[2000] 17–42) is a theorized account of both the historical and immediate causes of what the essay describes as the underdevelopment of the stage in Malawi. A primary place to begin such a stocktaking, according to Magalasi, is to note that critical commentary hardly 'seems to talk about the philosophical premise the drama was and is still based on—apart from talking about historical influences and governmental inhibition'.

(d) Southern Africa

Brian Worsfold's *South Africa Backdrop: An Historical Introduction for South African Literary and Cultural Studies* is a 'backdrop' for South African cultural studies and South African literatures in English that 'presents a brief history of racial confrontation, domination, dispossession and reclamation in the region known today as the Republic of South Africa, from man's earliest settlement in the sub-continent to the present time'. According to Worsfold, 'a general understanding of the history of racial confrontation, oppression and protest in South Africa, therefore, is a prerequisite for any informed analysis of the literary works of South African cultures in general'. The history of racial oppression in South Africa, against the backdrop of the suffering, fear and aspirations of black South Africans and the self-delusion, angst and traumas of white South Africans, has produced an abundance of literary works. H. Rider Haggard and John Buchan may have popularized South African literary discourses focused on race relations in the last decades of the nineteenth century, but it is 'the institutionalised segregation and discrimination perpetrated by the proxy-colonial White South African governments following the Anglo-Boer War and the creation of the Union of South Africa [that] gave rise to expressions of implied protest' in works such as Sol T. Plaatje's novel, *Mhudi*. The historical, political and social background to the ensuing fictionalized accounts is the primary focus of Worsfold's historical introduction, a relevant knowledge of which 'complements literatures, enhancing their significance. The purpose of the … "history" is to provide information that, together with a reading of literatures, may bring the ethos of all South Africans into sharper focus.' Presenting the major events in South Africa's history from the commencement of the process of European colonization in the seventeenth century to the present, largely from the point of view of black South African communities, Worsfold emphasizes the nine Xhosa wars on the colony's frontiers rather than the Anglo-Boer wars, and gives greater prominence to the ubiquitous roles of the renowned black leaders such as Hintsa, Makana, Moshoeshoe, Shaka, Mandela, Sobukwe and Steve Biko rather than white leaders such as Cecil Rhodes and Hendrik Verwoerd, for example. From the first South Africans and the various myths of precedence, often presented as 'proofs of the White man's right to occupy and exploit all material and human resources at the Southern tip of Africa', to the fall of apartheid, the other purpose of this mode of historical exploration, according to Worsfold, is to create an awareness of the historical and literary constructs of South Africa: 'As Nelson Mandela said in a well publicised speech, "It is not the kings and generals who make history, but the masses of the people." Historical constructs reveal little about the masses of the people; to know about the people, it is necessary to turn to their stories, their narratives, in short, to their literatures.'

Munzhedzi James Mafela's 'Drama Writing and Politics in Milubi's Drama: A Tradition of Hindrance to Liberation' (in Bodunde, ed., pp. 171–7) examines the renowned poet and dramatist in the Venda language. Milubi's *Ndi mitodzi muni* (What Tears Are These?), like the works of other black creative writers, has been influenced by the social events in the land. Similar to Worsfold's claim that knowledge of relevant historical constructs can only complement our understanding of literary constructs and enhance their significance, Mafela asserts that to understand the message in Milubi's text 'one needs to have some background knowledge about the political and social situation surrounding the time in which the text was produced'. Milubi's text depicts how the nationalist government used various strategies to hinder the liberation struggle in South Africa: 'Life in the Venda State like other Black States was characterised by cruelty and oppression by fellow Venda people … In *Ndi mitodzi muni*, Milubi reveals his hatred of the introduction of self-governing Black States and independent Black States.' Similarly, Mhlobo Jadezweni's 'Three South African People's Poets' "Fight with the Pen": S.E.K. Mqhayi on the Forefront' (in Bodunde, ed., pp. 179–93) discusses the work of the illustrious Xhosa writer Samuel Edward Krune Mqhayi against the background of his marginalization in the contribution to the liberation struggle in South Africa. According to Jadezweni, with the emergence at the height of the revolution of poets such as Lesego Rampolekeng and Mzwakhe Mbuli, and the popularity of the younger poets with the liberation movements in the 1980s, erstwhile *imbongi yesizwe jikelele* (praise poet[s] of the whole nation), such as Mqhayi, 'have been declared irrelevant and relegated to the scrapyard'. Once proclaimed as 'The Shakespeare of the Xhosa language', Jadezweni's essay highlights, in the light of this relegation, the contributions made by S.E.K. Mqhayi [1875–1945] 'through his pen in the fight against political domination of the Africans by the colonialists'. Against the backdrop of the contributions made by the two modern poets, Lesego Rampolekeng and Mzwakhe Mbuli, who gained prominence during the 1980s, S.E.K. Mqhayi, as an oral poet as well as a writer, according to Jadezweni, 'was the voice of the voiceless … an industrious oral artist who is both an *imbongi yesizwe jikelele* and a literary author with the people's poet designation fused into the same title'.

Edward O Ako's 'Crossing Borders: A Study of Bessie Head's *When Rain Clouds Gather* and *Maru*' (*CM* 22:ii[2000] 5–12) examines the theoretical point of view of the 'border zone' in Head's novels. The crossing-of-border phenomenon, which can be applied to Head's life and creativity, entails that 'those who can achieve this new humanism have moved beyond class, sexual, ethnic, national and racial borders'. In the two novels examined in this essay, the characters find themselves in different territories as a result of war or political persecution: 'there are those who voluntarily move to another location because they cannot fully identify with their environment'. For Bessie Head, the essay argues, the group of detribalized characters can successfully empathize with others partly because they 'have "crossed borders" and therefore broken away from the limitations imposed by a single entity'. Multiple border-crossings are involved in *When Rain Clouds Gather* [1966] and *Maru* [1971], in which individuals have to break with a previous state of affairs for the new order to be brought about. While *'Rain Clouds* is concerned with farming and cross border fertilisation between black and white, male and female, *Maru* is above all about power, tradition and love'.

Finally, Jean Sevry's 'Coetzee the Writer and the Writer of an Autobiography' (*CM* 22:ii[2000] 13–24) explores what it describes as 'some of Coetzee's contradictions, in particular the reason why he often speaks of himself in the third person—as if the "I" were a forbidden subject'. Along with Nobel Laureate Nadine Gordimer, Coetzee has been described in Worsfold's book-length study, *South African Backdrop*, as having traced and recorded over the decades 'White South African angst and self-delusion ... meticulously'. Ostensibly, while the child in Coetzee's *Boyhood* 'finds it hard to understand the world of adults ... because they are content with prejudices and stereotypes which they mistake for the Law, and which he vainly tries to repeat', in *Doubling the Point* Coetzee's answer, 'expressed as a confession, shows that the adult is in full agreement with what the child had already instinctively suspected'. Coetzee's unexpected (though obvious) observation—'all autobiography is story telling, all writing is autobiography'— corresponds, according to Sevry, to the distance now established by the third person: 'Because of the use of the third person, *Boyhood* seems to have been written as if it were a child speaking at that peculiar period in his lifetime as if it were his own witness. In *Doubling the Point*, Coetzee uses a psychoanalytical explanation to refer to this stylistic approach'.

2. Australia

(a) General

The year 2000 saw many Australians participate in 'reconciliation walks' that were held around the country. It was a way of saying 'sorry' for past treatment of indigenous people, particularly for the policies that led to the 'stolen generations'. It was a way of taking responsibility. Taking responsibility, however, does not mean reoccupying a position of authority in regard to indigenous subjects. Cath Ellis, 'A Strange Case of Double Vision' (*Overland* 158[2000] 75–85), points out that Carmel Bird's edition of *The Stolen Children: Their Stories* [1998] involves editorial intrusions and appropriations that render the work highly problematic, despite its well-intentioned purpose to make these stories available to a wider public and thus encourage reconciliation. Similar concerns are raised by Christine Nicholls in 'Carmel Bird's *The Stolen Children*' (*Crossings* 5:iii[2000] at <http://www.uq.edu.au/~enldale/Crossings.htm>). Nicholls maintains that the editorial mediations involved in Bird's book have the effect of withholding the means of self-representation from subaltern subjects. This argument will be of interest to anyone who has realized that Bird has, perhaps unconsciously, ordered the book so that it confirms her own hope that the stories will heal. Admirable as that hope is, it needs to deal sensitively and selflessly with issues of self-representation and narrative power. The power of white commentary is also at issue in Aileen Moreton-Robinson, *Talkin' Up to the White Woman: Indigenous Women and Feminism*. Reviewing much of the feminist literature on indigenous women, Moreton-Robinson contends that it is often inadequate and sometimes racist. Even as it articulates 'difference' as a category, white feminism gives insufficient attention to 'whiteness' as a site of such difference and continues to permit indigenous people to be objects of research. Consequently, Australian feminists remain defensive about accusations that theirs is the viewpoint of white middle-class women acting from a position of dominance. Jennifer Jones, 'Reading *Karoban* by Monica Clare' (*Overland* 161[2000] 67–71), claims that this 1978 autobiographical novel adapts socialist realism to suit the needs of Aboriginal testimony, but that assumptions about socialist realism and editorial interference inhibited, and continue to inhibit, its reception. In particular she states that a shift, late in the novel, from naturalism to socialist realism corresponds to the character's maturing political view, signalling how socialist realist textual practices such as typicality and didacticism, optimism and militancy, are being used to develop Aboriginal political concerns. Alan Lawson, meanwhile, believes the classical trope of zeugma offers a way of understanding shared history and shared place: Lawson's 'Proximities: From Asymptote to Zeugma' (in Rowland Smith, ed., *Postcolonizing the Commonwealth: Studies in Literature and Culture*) is a stimulating essay, combining classical rhetoric, contemporary racial politics, and cultural history to argue for a greater recognition of how settler narrative tropes arrange and rearrange social relations.

While historical scholarship represents the year's most significant achievement, history itself continues to be a problematic notion. Webby, ed., *The Cambridge Companion to Australian Literature*, almost presents it as a linear narrative, moving from colonial to contemporary writing, but disrupts this chronology by beginning with indigenous writing and ending with a critical account of Australian critical practice. Locating the book in relation to other Australian literary histories, Webby explains that her decision to adopt a genre-based format was largely determined by the need to address international readers and by the constraints of space that come with the Cambridge Companion format. It is, then, an introduction, yet Webby's contributors are often leading researchers, so that the Companion also provides some keen critical discriminations. Penny van Toorn, 'Indigenous Texts and Narratives', confronts the dilemma of how to admit the existence and importance of oral traditions without appropriating them to a Western medium. She also observes how contemporary indigenous writers differently address the issue of language (from appropriation to abrogation), and articulates the need to develop reading practices appropriate to an 'equitable cross-cultural dialogue' (p. 45). Elizabeth Webby, 'Colonial Writers and Readers', traces some of the major changes in what people read and wrote in Australia from 1788 to 1901, with a particular focus on non-fiction, fiction, poetry and writing for children. Webby confirms some recent trends in historical scholarship, such as the renewed interest in early writing (for example, explorer accounts, emigrant novels, diaries) and the recovered interest in writing by women. Among other interesting points that she makes are the following: *His Natural Life* is a scientific experiment investigating the possibility of humanity surviving without religious belief; *Robbery Under Arms* is significant for its pioneering use of a colloquial first-person narrator; the 'Legend of the Nineties' leads to a misleading separation of the work of Henry Lawson from that of his predecessors. In addition, Webby demonstrates her extensive knowledge of the publication history of works such as *His Natural Life* and *Robbery Under Arms*. Michael Ackland, 'Poetry from the 1890s to 1970', is perhaps most notable for its attempt to rescue the reputation of Harold Stewart, while David McCooey, 'Contemporary Poetry', is important for its insistence on heterogeneity within, for example, the so-called 'Generation of '68' (a term that attracts McCooey's scepticism). Kerryn Goldsworthy, 'Fiction from 1900 to 1970', is interesting for its emphasis on *My Brilliant Career* as a work sustained by its uncertainties and *Such is Life* as 'at once a late experiment in realism and a very early anticipation of postmodern techniques of fragmentation, allusion, pastiche and authorial self-consciousness' (p. 108). Goldsworthy is also concerned to emphasize the contribution of women writers in this period, even though space restricts her to the briefest of observations. Most of those she mentions have already benefited from some reconsideration, though Elizabeth Harrower is still relatively neglected. Richard Fotheringham, 'Theatre from 1788 to the 1960s', is rich in insight and information. Fotheringham opens with a 'performance' reading of cultural moments such as the flag-raising ceremony of 26 January 1788, the Federation ceremonies of January 1901, and the sesquicentennial celebrations in 1938, informing his whole discussion with a sense of theatre as a social act. He follows with an account of government control and censorship, then points out that English-speaking theatre was not the only tradition of performance within Australia. Aboriginal performances went on largely unnoticed and unrecorded, and, even in the colonial period, various migrant groups had their own theatres. Before going on to provide an overview of the major plays of this period, he identifies three moments that most influenced the development of Australian theatre: the 1850s (gold brought a boom in theatres); 1930 (the Depression and talking pictures caused a decline in professional live theatre); the 1950s and 1960s (significant government intervention began to contribute to a new growth). Delys Bird, 'New Narrations: Contemporary Fiction', asks how we continue to use the category of 'Australian fiction' in the context of a world market, showing a sensible appreciation of the complex reciprocations operating between 'national' and 'international' categories. This chapter is also notable for its recognition of David Foster as a major contemporary novelist, its emphasis on regional publishing, on a new kind of social realism, and on writing 'Asia'. May-Brit Akerholt, 'New Stages: Contemporary Theatre', notes the importance of 'heightened naturalism' and 'symbolic realism' for Australian theatre and surveys various institutions, writers, companies and directors central to the development of contemporary theatre. One of the more interesting questions she raises is the degree to which locally inflected translations of classics become part of an Australian theatre (Akerholt has herself been involved in such translations of *The Government Inspector* and *Hedda Gabler*). Gillian Whitlock, 'From Biography to Autobiography', attends to the various intersections that can be identified between and within 'biography' and 'autobiography'. Whitlock discusses biographies that might be seen as an empiricist compilation of a life, biographies that want to combine personal with national and cultural narratives, biographies on their way to becoming autobiographies, and Aboriginal autobiographies that unsettle thematic, chronological, formalist and identity-based approaches to the genre. This is a chapter attuned to the wide-ranging discussions that have been developing in these areas. Finally, David Carter, 'Critics, Writers, Intellectuals: Australian Literature and its Criticism', explains how criticism in Australia has changed significantly since the mid-twentieth century, and reflects on the 'inconsecutive nature' (p. 259) of such criticism. He proposes a model of cultural transference and transformation (rather than cultural evolution) in order to describe changes that encompass, for example, the manifold relations between criticism and nationalism, the role of the universities in promoting an academic literary criticism, the devaluation of the nationalist social tradition so that Patrick White could represent modernity and maturity, and the conscious politicization and theorizing of literary criticism. Other discussions of the future of literary criticism can be found in Leon Cantrell, 'Do We Have a Discipline? The Great Aust Lit Debate' (in de Groen and Stewart, eds., *Australian Writing and the City*), which proposes that the future may involve new concepts of nation and literary discourse, and Horst Priessnitz, 'Why Australia? or, Against the Fragmentation of English Literary Studies' (*ALS* 19:iii[2000] 306–12), which supports a balance between global coherences and local differences. Neil James, in 'A Paperback Canon: The Australian Pocket Library' (*ALS* 19:iii[2000] 295–305), reviews the founding, in 1943, of the Australian Pocket Library, a scheme to guarantee cheap editions of Australian books, which had the effect of further establishing a nationalist canon. Interestingly, he remarks that the Commonwealth Literary Fund would have been unlikely to get the cooperation of publishers had it not been for their need for paper, and that 'no firm today would support a scheme where it takes all of the financial risk but gives the creative control to a Canberra committee' (p. 296). As it happens, the publishers involved in this venture experienced great production difficulties and did not make a profit. Even so, argues James, this pocket library represents 'the first officially selected and endorsed canon of Australian literature' (p. 302).

Another important contribution to the history of, and the historical scholarship of, Australian literature is Ken Stewart's *Investigations in Australian Literature*. This book contains essays on Henry Kendall, Marcus Clarke, Henry Lawson, and Henry Handel Richardson. All these essays have made previous appearances (over a period of twenty five years), but the effect of bringing them together is to highlight the ways in which colonial literary culture informed Australian writing. For example, '"A careworn writer for the press": Henry Kendall in Melbourne' is an absorbing account of a brief period Kendall spent in Melbourne, trying to establish himself as a journalist in a city conscious of itself as a new Colonial City. It is a sad tale of having to write pieces that were not to his taste, of his deteriorating relationship with Marcus Clarke, of public speculation about his drinking problem, and of friends committing suicide. Stewart shows how this experience confirms Kendall's developing view of the world as a place where the sensitive and suffering are at the mercy of overbearing philistines. 'Sylvia's Books: Literature, Civilisation and Marcus Clarke's *His Natural Life*' proposes that much of the novel's argument can be seen in the books that Sylvia reads, in particular the way her reading shifts from Rousseau to Balzac, from an ideal and imaginative view of nature to a real and material one. 'The Prototype of Richard Mahony' claims that, even as she based Richard Mahony on her father Walter Lindesay Richardson, Henry Handel Richardson was at pains to make the character different since she was reluctant to acknowledge the importance of spiritualism in her father's life. Of related interest is

Ian Henderson, 'Eyeing the Lady's Hand: The Concealed Politics of Mary Morton Allport's Colonial Vision' (*JAS* 66[2000] 104–15), which is, in part, an account of the pervasive influence of Jacques-Henri Bernadin de Saint-Pierre's novel *Paul et Virginie* [1788] in colonial Australian art and writing. In addition, Michael Ackland, in 'Beyond the Wattle: Recent Perspectives on Australian Colonial Literature' (*BSANZB* 23:ii[1999] 116–27), stresses the importance for scholarship of recent publications of nineteenth-century texts.

Place has long been one of the major themes of Australian writing and, despite the testing of national and international boundaries, it continues to exert its influence. De Groen and Stewart, eds., *Australian Writing and the City*, publishes twenty-two of the sixty papers presented at the 1999 conference of the Association for the Study of Australian Literature. Taken together, they illustrate the rich diversity to be found in Australian writing of the city, which becomes a site for nomadic, gendered, religious, modernist, erogenous and, of course, non-rural activity. Peter Conrad, 'Sydney, not the Bush', finds in the face of Luna Park a sign that, in the city, culture has finally triumphed over nature. Deirdre Coleman, 'The Camp as "New Albion": Early Visions and Views of Sydney', discusses how the imperialist romance of the early colony was an unsettling contest between narratives of civilization, convictism, and dispossession. Rowena Mohr, 'Approximating the World: Women, "Civilisation" and Colonial Melbourne', examines Ada Cambridge's *The Three Miss Kings* in order to show the colonial city's role in reproducing a hierarchical English social order. Brigid Rooney, '"A little bit of the real Sydney": Comparing Gender, Socialism and the City in Works by William Lane and Christina Stead', discusses how gender and sexuality reproduce and challenge the radical political discourses embodied in *The Workingman's Paradise* and *Seven Poor Men of Sydney*. Peter Kirkpatrick's 'Walking through *Seven Poor Men of Sydney*' argues that the novel presents a transgressive spatial narrative. Julian Croft, 'Down (But Not Out) in the City', sees the 1930s light verse of Kenneth Slessor, Colin Wills and Ronald McCuaig as a celebration of hedonism. David Musgrave, 'Post-Carnivalism in David Ireland's *The Unknown Industrial Prisoner*', argues that Ireland's novel enacts a post-carnival play which exacerbates its condition as an abject text. In other papers, Noel Rowe reads Vincent Buckley's *Golden Builders* under the sign of 'the death of God', Cheryl Taylor explores representations of masculine identity in the period 1889–1941, Ann Vickery examines the factory girl in modern Australian poetry, Philip Mead considers Kenneth Slessor's film writing, David McCooey identifies the different, fluid uses of the city in the contemporary long poem, Don Graham excavates the Balzacian underpinnings to Michael Wilding's *Wildest Dreams*, Tom Burvill analyses the 1998 Sydney production of *Cloudstreet*, and Wenche Ommundsen reflects on the role of literary festivals in the mapping of cultural heritage. (Papers by Bernadette Brennan on Brian Castro and Sigrun Meinig on Peter Carey, which were also published in *Southerly*, are discussed elsewhere.) This year a number of works wanted to celebrate place in more particular ways. Dimond and Kirkpatrick, eds., *Literary Sydney: A Walking Guide*, maps routes in such areas as 'The Rocks' and Darlinghurst and identifies the writers and writing associated with various localities. It enables a very embodied experience of text and place. Sayer and Nowra, eds., *In the Gutter … Looking at the Stars*, concentrates on writing about Kings Cross, which the editors describe as both a real place and a state of mind. Of related interest is Edwin Wilson, 'The Poetry of Place: Poetic Foci in the

Sydney Gardens and Domain' (*AuFolk* 15[2000] 123–32). Cranston, ed., *Along These Lines: From Trowenna to Tasmania*, is a very detailed anthology that allows the reader to trace the many lines through which time, place and narrative intersect. Even as it selects writings that respond to the different regions of Tasmania, Cranston's notes, included in the body of the text, make the anthology much more than an illustrative text. The reader is encouraged to see the literary selections in conversation with the island's complex history, geography and botany. Dorothy Hewett and John Kinsella collaborated to produce *Wheatlands*, a collection that illustrates how their poetry and prose have been shaped by the landscape of the Western Australian wheat belt. There were other collections of creative writing celebrating regional writing, among them Downing and Spennemann, eds., *ReCollecting Albury Writing*.

The degree to which place is itself a relational concept is evident in the continuing concern with Asian–Australian connections. Gilbert, Khoo and Lo, eds., *Diaspora: Negotiating Asian Australia*, is a special joint issue of *Journal of Australian Studies* (65[2000]) and *Australian Cultural History* (19[2000]) containing essays on theatre, film, art and literature by Asian Australians and addressing issues such as cultural space, hybridity, gender, the relationship between diaspora and colonialism, and the growing awareness of a global diasporic network. This review mentions only those essays which have a specifically literary focus. Peter Copeman and Rebecca Scollen, 'Of Training, Tokenism and Productive Misinterpretation: Reflections on the *After China* Project', discuss the theatrical adaptation of Brian Castro's novel at the Centre for Innovation in the Arts, Queensland University of Technology, in 1997 and 1998, highlighting the intracultural character of the collaborative process involved and suggesting that this involved less a crossing of borders than a negotiation of a common market. Dorothy Wang, 'The Making of an "Australian" "Self" in Simone Lazaroo's *The World Waiting to Be Made*', contends that multiculturalism functions covertly to reinforce an assimilationist agenda while the marketing and consumption of Asian Australian writing still requires signs of otherness against which normative culture can be defined. Miriam Wei Wei Lo, '"Possible only on paper?" Hybridity as Parody in Brian Castro's *Drift*', explains how Castro uses parody to push the notion of hybridity to its limits and demonstrate the difficulty of speaking for an other. Rodney Noonan, 'Wild Cathay Boys: Chinese Bushrangers in Australian History and Literature', includes discussion of Lam Yut Soon in David Martin's novel *The Hero of Too* [1965]; Lam Yut Soon, says Noonan, achieves the status of archetypal Australian and outlaw hero without compromising his Chinese identity. Shen Yuan-fang, '"Historical Drifters": Self-Representations of Chinese Late-comers in Australia', examines *East Wind, West Wind* by Fang Xiangshu and Trevor Hay and *My Fortune in Australia* by Liu Guande, noting how both writers construct themselves as 'historical drifters' by writing their displacement from both China and Australia. Shirley Tucker, 'Your Worst Nightmare: Hybridised Demonology in Asian-Australian Women's Writing', maintains that Asian Australian women writers use figures such as vampires and mermaids to subvert the Australian stereotype of the Asian woman as erotic and exotic. Tseen Khoo, 'Selling Sexotica: Oriental Grunge and Suburbia in Lillian Ng's *Swallowing Clouds*', asserts that 'Asian-Australian women's literature would benefit from more contextualisation, diversification, and depth in its reception' (p. 164). Khoo is critical of Ng's novel, seeing it as offering Australian readers what Ng thinks they desire: Asian 'sexotica'. In this context, Wang Labao's 'Australian Literature in China' (*Southerly* 60:iii[2000] 118–33), an account of how Australian literature has become a subject in some Chinese universities, is an absorbing story. Wang Labao tells how the study of Australian literature has been dominated by Australian critics under whom the Chinese academics studied; how Australian writers with whom those same academics formed friendships have been elevated in the curriculum; how Chinese cultural preoccupations continue to determine what are seen as the major themes of Australian writing. He concludes by asking his compatriot critics to admit the critical distortions for which they are responsible and to undertake more genuinely cross-cultural readings.

'Absence and Negativity', edited by Michael Brennan, is a special issue of *Southerly* (60:ii[2000]), featuring papers from the Absence and Negativity in Australian Literature conference (University of Sydney, July [1999]). Taken together, the papers show theology and postmodernism converging in a way that is unusual in Australian literary criticism. Kevin Hart's keynote address, 'Francis Webb: Unsaying Transcendence' (*Southerly* 60:ii[2000] 10–25), is an erudite reading of Webb's 'Poet' as a midrash on John 7.53–8.11 and as an embodiment of the negativities that call poetry and religion into conversation with each other. Noel Rowe, 'James McAuley: The Possibility of Despair' (*Southerly* 60:ii[2000] 26–38), excavates an atheological bent in McAuley's work, a fault-line on which his preferred theology of the Fall brings about the fall of theology. Bernadette Brennan's '*Drift*: Writing and/of Annihilation' (*Southerly* 60:ii[2000] 39–50), interprets Brian Castro's novel as a narrative concerned with the erasure of writer, race and writing itself, but also intent on rewriting absent bodies and stories. David Brooks, 'A Land without Lendings: Judith Wright, Kenosis and Australian Vision' (*Southerly* 60:ii[2000] 51–64), ponders whether the Australian mind has developed a particular kind of ontological self-consciousness as a consequence of being 'thrown, untutored, into territory the Western mind more generally had yet to reach' (p. 53). This issue also contains an essay which was not part of the conference but which makes an important contribution to the discussion: Martin Harrison, 'The Myth of Origins' (*Southerly* 60:ii[2000] 148–61), proposes not only that Australian poetry rests on a metaphysical negativity but that criticism also rests on an absence since the critical terms with which we discuss that poetry have not been invented locally.

Southerly, like many other journals, now presents as a book, each issue having a special focus and title, although it still maintains its emphasis on literary criticism. *Meridian* would seem to have gone further towards being a book and, on the evidence of *Globalising Australia* (*Meridian* 17:ii[2000]), edited by Christopher Palmer and Iain Topliss, further towards cultural studies. On the other hand, *Journal of Australian Studies* (66[2000]), entitled *Vision Splendid* and edited by Richard Nile, contains, among its mostly historical essays, Adrian Mitchell's '"Amid th'encircling gloom": The Moral Geography of Charles Sturt's Narratives' (*JAS* 66[2000] 85–94), which analyses the moral valuation Sturt gave to what he saw as an atrophied landscape, noting particularly his use of negative constructions. Richard Nile also edited *The Australian Legend and its Discontents*, an Australian studies reader that includes occasional references to literary texts. *Antipodes*, with very little revamping, seems to have gained new energy and direction under Nicholas Birns and has published some strong critical articles (discussed elsewhere). *HEAT* prefers the essay to the critical article. The situation of Australian feminist journals is discussed in Margaret Henderson, 'Australian Feminist Academic Journals: Still Here, Most of the Time' (*FC* 21:ii[2000] 11–13). Although this article first appeared in 1998, it is still representative of the current situation of Australian feminist journals. Long-standing journals such as *Hecate* (where Henderson's article was first published) and *Australian Feminist Studies* publish the majority of articles that feature Australian literature. *Hecate* (26:i[2000]) features articles on the legacy of Simone de Beauvoir in Australia. Marea Mitchell makes connections between de Beauvoir and Germaine Greer to consider the vexed topic of feminist heroines as role models (*Hecate* 26:i[2000] 98–106). In 'Agony and Ecstasy: Feminists among Feminists' (*Hecate* 26:i[2000] 107–12), Bronwen Levy explores the complex evolution of de Beauvoir as a feminist who was not only influenced by her immediate personal environment but also by the reciprocal political and emotional discourse that emerged as women read and responded to her texts. Opposing stereotypes of the emancipated feminist woman and the traditionally feminine woman raised issues about 'the feminine', 'the typical female condition', and 'woman as victim', concepts which are both ambivalent and ambiguous. In 'The Girl who Met Simone de Beauvoir in Brisbane, or, Must We Burn Beauvoir?' Margaret Henderson compares Frank Moorehouse's short story 'The Girl Who Met Simone de Beauvoir in Paris' [1972] with the ABC television mini-series *Simone de Beauvoir's Babies* [1997] to examine the circulation of de Beauvoir's name in the literary and television media. Henderson shows how de Beauvoir's novels are important as theoretical texts because they provide women with socially and politically symbolic narratives (*Hecate* 26:i[2000] 113–17).

'Real criticism', according to Gary Catalano, 'occurs not in reviews or in long critical articles but in the selection and compilation of anthologies.' This remark is cited as an epigraph to Steve Holden, 'Short Story Anthologies and "The Solid Body of Australian Fiction"' (*ALS* 19:iii[2000] 279–94). Holden sets out to uncover submerged constitutive practices that occur in Australian short-story anthologies, paying particular attention to those practices that seek to establish short stories as 'characteristically Australian' and to the paradoxically constitutive effect that can come about when a story or tradition is rejected by an anthology. Brewster, O'Neill and van den Berg, eds., *Those Who Remain Will Always Remember*, is an anthology of Aboriginal writing from Western Australia. It is, as the editors remark in their introduction, an anthology that shows the importance of autobiographical writing and life-narratives for Aboriginal writers; such writings best respond to the politics of history and the imperatives of memory. In what is becoming an increasingly familiar gesture, the editors also highlight the collaborative character of the procedures involved in the collection, selection and editing of material. Bennett and Hayes, eds., *Home and Away: Australian Stories of Belonging and Alienation*, is designed to explore the Australian preoccupation with identity, in particular, to question the simple opposition between a place of belonging and a place elsewhere and so to free the imagination from geographical constraints. In *The Penguin Century of Australian Stories*, Carmel Bird has compiled a hundred stories representing her selection of the most vigorous Australian short-story writing of the last century. The anthology includes a scholarly introduction by Kerryn Goldsworthy, as well as biographical and publication timelines which provide chronology and context to changing styles and preoccupations. Authors appear alphabetically, allowing for some interesting insights into transformations of meaning and morality over time. Kerryn Goldsworthy's own anthology, *Australian Women's Stories*, complements Bird's by presenting different story-telling modes to explore what it has meant to be a woman in Australia from the mid-nineteenth to the end of the twentieth centuries. Goldsworthy introduces a diverse cast of twenty-nine Australian women writers, from Mary Fortune [1833?-1910] to Beth Yahp [1964–], who often have a complex relationship with Australia. The historical format represents women from a variety of backgrounds where race and economics colour the gendered experience, as do politics, sexuality and spirituality.

There is a great deal of interest at the moment in the history of the book in Australia, a study that involves a knowledge of social history, as well as of the often complicated details of authorship, printing, publishing, selling and reading. It has become a particularly significant part of colonial and nineteenth-century research, with some significant contributions and conferences. It is also a study which tends to test the 'national literature' category. For example, Graeme Johanson, *A Study of Colonial Editions in Australia, 1843–1972*, is more than a scholarly account of British books intended for colonial readers; it is also a reminder that reading practices are constitutive of literary culture and that writers like Rolf Boldrewood and Louisa Anne Meredith were published in colonial editions. Johanson's is the second study published in a series called Sources for the History of the Book in Australia, intended to make available material which is not readily accessible. Victor Crittenden, *James Tegg: Early Sydney Publisher and Printer*, tells of James Tegg and his brother Samuel, who formed the Australian arm of the book empire of Thomas Tegg of London. The study includes a bibliographical list describing the books printed and published by James Tegg. Mostly these are works published for church and government, as well as garden manuals and books of etiquette. There are also some that make a significant contribution to the beginnings of Australian literature. Among the works Tegg published in 1842 were Caroline Chisholm's book on female immigration, John Lang's *Legends of Australia* and Henry Parkes's *Stolen Moments*. This work is the eighth in a series called Bibliographica Historica Australiae, published by Mulini Press. Rosemary Campbell, 'The "Australian Edition" of Catherine Martin's *An Australian Girl* (1890)' (*BSANZB* 24:ii[2000] 99–105), examines the print history of the 1891 and 1894 editions in order to ascertain whether the 1894 'Australian edition' was, in fact, a new printing.

We have again this year been forced to confine our attention to what might be described as mainstream literary criticism. It has not been possible to give adequate attention to science fiction, folklore or children's literature. We have not ventured very far into cultural studies, nor have we adopted an understanding of 'text' that might lead us into discussions of popular culture or take us into cyberspace. Our reasons are pragmatic and our exclusions are not meant as a comment on these kinds of writing. We note, however, that the growth in interdisciplinary approaches will continue to exert great pressure on an essay such as this. We acknowledge the help of the Australian Literary Studies annual bibliography and the MLA bibliography.

(b) Fiction and Autobiography

Although feminism and post-colonialism continue to dominate critical readings of fiction, this year's most significant publications were works of historical scholarship: a biography of Rolf Boldrewood, the letters of Henry Handel

Richardson, and the letters of her parents, Walter and Mary Richardson. Colonial and nineteenth-century writing was again the subject of important articles, most historical in approach, while more contemporary writing continued to evoke discussions of representation, race and gender.

Three general studies of fiction illustrate something of the diversity within feminist criticism. Susan Lever, *Real Relations: The Feminist Politics of Form in Australian Fiction*, explores the relationship between form and politics in a selection of fiction, from the New Woman novels of Ada Cambridge to a range of more recent fiction by men and women. Lever is particularly concerned to interrogate the assumption made by 'anti-humanist feminism' that realist conventions are an expression of a conservative patriarchy and humanist values and that feminist writing is writing that challenges formal conventions and uncovers what is repressed in language structures. Her intention is not to discredit this strand of feminist writing, but to respect the fact that 'Realist novels by women represent some of the finest artistic achievements in Australian literature, and cannot be dismissed as the misguided expressions of an unenlightened past' (p. 10). Instead, Lever emphasizes how writers such as Cambridge, Richardson, Prichard and Stead exploit the possibilities of realism, pointing, for example, to Richardson's fascination with the irrational, Prichard's attempt to use Aboriginal literary forms, and Stead's commitment to multiple, strife-ridden narratives. Lever organizes her argument so that it unfolds as another history of Australian writing: examining ideas of masculinity, femininity and nationhood in Cambridge, Richardson and Joseph Furphy; exploring issues of modernism, realism and the politics of the left in Prichard and Stead (whose modifications of realist techniques invite more complex political readings than those that usually gather under the 'socialist realism' tag); addressing contemporary concerns for the politics of representation in the realist work of Helen Garner and Sally Morgan, as well as in the more formally self-conscious writing of Marion Campbell, Drusilla Modjeska, Mary Fallon, and Finola Moorhead. At the same time Lever uses fiction by men (Joseph Furphy, Vance Palmer, Patrick White, David Foster) to test assumptions about gender and writing. What is impressive about Lever's work is her applied recognition that individual texts are never exhausted by any particular reading of them, as well as her sensible reminder that 'it is no doubt possible to write a fragmented, modernist text while subscribing to conservative ideals—and a realist one that is radical' (p. 147). Jennifer Rutherford's *The Gauche Intruder: Freud, Lacan and the White Australian Fantasy* is a committed Freudian and Lacanian interpretation of how the fantasy of the good nation, sustaining an alliance of aggression and morality, generates hostility towards the Other (seen as internal as well as external). Rutherford makes unexpected connections between various novels (though she also affirms their differences). For example she identifies in Catherine Spence's *Clara Morison* [1854] a similar set of anxieties to those that shape a more obviously nationalist and masculinist work such as Rolf Boldrewood's *Robbery Under Arms* [1881]. Both works recognize a radical disruption of the old law and social order, yet both reinstate that order in a new form even as they repudiate it. Rutherford reads the character of Richard Mahony as a cultural symptom and exposes Richardson's 'Oedipal impasses', particularly her unresolved sacrifice of desire to duty. Desire and duty then form a connecting thread to George Johnston's *My Brother Jack* [1964], where Rutherford makes the surprising remark that sophisticated readings of the novel ignore the self-hatred that informs the narrative. (Johnston's novel has often been read as a narrative generated by masculine anxiety, just as it has often been interpreted as a work of dark irony.) Overall, this is a provocative book, valuable for its unexpected connections and for its understanding of how the heavy ideal of the good nation converts neighbourliness, egalitarianism and transparency into their antitheses. Also provocative is Elaine Lindsay's *Rewriting God: Spirituality in Contemporary Australian Women's Fiction*. Lindsay locates her study in the context of the recent development of 'Australian theology', arguing against the tendency of (male) theologians to select from Australian literature only those works that support their own interest in 'desert spirituality'. This is to construct a spirituality that is gender-specific and to ignore the alternative spiritualities that can be found in women's writing, particularly in the work of Thea Astley, Elizabeth Jolley and Barbara Hanrahan. Something of Lindsay's larger argument can be caught in her observation: 'While Hanrahan and Jolley link divinity with creativity, creation, and nature, Astley links God with love, translating it into human terms as love for others, as *caritas*. In those books where characters do not acknowledge God, evil things happen to innocent people, suggesting that evil is the absence of love' (p. 100). Lindsay also provides a very valuable account of the development of Australian women's spirituality and a most useful bibliography. This is an important work, though it needs to be complemented by a study that investigates whether Australian men's fiction is as easily conscripted to malestream theological ambitions as theologians, and Lindsay herself, seem to assume.

A fine example of the kind of research that is now being done on colonial writing is Paul de Serville's *Rolf Boldrewood: A Life*. Although hindered by the loss of many Boldrewood papers and by his subject's gentlemanly discretion, de Serville has constructed a detailed account of Thomas Alexander Browne, the man behind 'Rolf Boldrewood'. He is very interesting on how Browne's life and Boldrewood's fiction interact. Browne's understanding of his Irish ancestry (he was an O'Flaherty descendant) encouraged particular themes in his work, such as families in decline, gallantry and the brutal working of Fate. Even though experiences as a squatter and pastoralist feed into his stories, Boldrewood's realism was tempered by a sense of social propriety, so that some of his sketches of pastoral life convey a cheerfulness at odds with his bitter experience of failure. Browne's financial difficulties are also reflected in Boldrewood's *The Squatter's Dream* [1890], just as his 1860 visit to England informs *My Home Run* [1897]. The success of *Robbery Under Arms* [1881] becomes an uncomfortable paradox for Browne: after his controversial time as Goldfields Commissioner at Gulgong, the conservative Browne is embarrassed to have made money out of a story of lawless bush rangers. According to this study, Browne's life is never quite as optimistic as the fiction, though both honour 'the ability of gentlemen and their families to uphold their code in Australian conditions' (p. 295). Finally de Serville sees Browne/Boldrewood as representative of a conservative Australia which valued the (colonial and British) past and had a keen sense of social hierarchy. There are also a number of fine articles dealing with early Australian writing, though surprisingly little has been done on Lawson and Furphy. Gavin Edwards, 'Watkin Tench and the Cold Track of Narrative' (*Southerly* 60:iii[2000] 74–93), examines some of the difficulties Tench experienced in attempting to convert his journal material into narrative form. Contending that Tench intended to construct a historical narrative, written in the past simple tense and dealing with events that were already finished, Edwards uncovers questions of temporality, perspective and truth in *A Narrative of the Expedition to Botany Bay* [1789] and *Account of the Settlement at Port Jackson* [1793]. Robert Willson tells the story of a convict who wrote his account of transportation: 'Charles Cozens: A Gentleman Convict and author of *Adventures of a Guardsman*' (*Margin* 51[2000] 33–8). Yvonne Cramer's *This Beauteous, Wicked Place: Letters and Journals of John Grant, Gentleman Convict* is a handsomely annotated and illustrated edition of letters written by a man transported to New South Wales in 1803. Cramer was able to break the code Grant used for his journal. What emerges is a fascinating portrait of colonial society and of an individual remarkable for his faith, loyalty and resistance to injustice. Patrick Morgan, 'Henry Haygarth: A Gentleman Squatter' (*Margin* 52[2000] 11–15), finds in Haygarth's *Recollections of Bush Life in Australia* [1848] two genres common at the time (reminiscences of living in an exotic place and an emigrant's guide), noting that the demands of the guide book inhibit the reminiscence. *The Murder of Madeline Brown* represents a republication (by Text publishers) of a lost fragment, Francis Adams's *Madeline Brown's Murderer* [1887]. Shane Maloney's introduction states that the work has great historical value because of the insights it offers into early crime fiction and into the seamier side of nineteenth-century Australia. It is good to see a quality publisher like Text encouraging the critical recovery of historical material. (Text also this year published a new edition of Frederic Manning's celebrated war novel, *The Middle Parts of Fortune* [1929], using the original text.) Andrew McCann furthers his research on Marcus Clarke with 'Colonial Gothic: Morbid Anatomy, Commodification and Critique in Marcus Clarke's *The Mystery of Major Molineux*' (*ALS* 19:iv[2000] 399–412), in which he relates Clarke's writing to a context of commodity culture and popular entertainment, while showing how his use of the 'colonial Gothic' engages with some of the repressions of colonial society. Bronwen Hickman, 'Mary Gaunt: An Australian Identity' (*Overland* 158[2000] 58–62), describes Gaunt's writing as distinguished by a tension between what she thinks desirable for women and what she believes society expects of them. In 'Ellen Davitt: A Professional Woman in the Nineteenth Century' (*Coppertales* 6[2000] 28–30), Lucy Sussex corrects some historical inaccuracies that have entered the biography of Ellen Davitt and gives a recuperative emphasis to her roles as writer, teacher and artist. Kay Ferres, 'Troubled Homecomings: Rosa Praed and Lemuria' (*QR* 72:ii[2000] 25–36), performs a close, complex reading of Rosa Praed's *Fugitive Anne: A Romance of the Unexplored Bush* [1902] to show how it combines metropolitan and colonial spaces in order to raise questions about patriarchal and colonial authority. Roderick, ed., *Rose Paterson's Illalong Letters, 1873–1888*, provides a first-hand record of everyday life on a nineteenth-century Australian sheep station. Roderick supplies a useful introduction, in which he notes how religion, culture and humour contribute to the way of life captured in the letters, as well as notes to help situate the various letters. What emerges is a portrait of two strong, self-sacrificing women, Rose and her mother. Roderick stresses that it is difficult now to understand how much the moral and social standards of a remote bush family depended on the mother. Rose Paterson was the mother of 'Banjo' Paterson. Droogleever, ed., *From the Front*, is an edition of the Boer War dispatches made by 'Banjo' Paterson when he was a special war correspondent in South Africa, from November 1899 to July 1900. Droogleever has also included examples of

Paterson's Boer War poetry, as well as photographs taken by him at the front. Joy Hooton, 'Joe Wilson and the Angel in the Bush' (*Quadrant* 44:vii–viii[2000] 67–73), relates representations of the feminine in *Joe Wilson and his Mates* to the male narrator's anxious self-reflection. Francis Devlin-Glass, '"Touches of nature that make the whole world kin": Furphy, Race and Anxiety' (*ALS* 19:iv[2000] 355–72), exhibits a keen sense of competing narratives while examining the role of social Darwinist and assimilationist assumptions about race in Furphy's writing. Raymond Driehuis, 'Joseph Furphy and Some American Friends: Temper, Democratic; Bias, Offensively Self-Reliant' (*Antipodes* 14:ii[2000] 129–35), traces some connections between Furphy and Emerson, particularly as they share the notion that self-reliance is integral to the development of a democratic temper.

This year Henry Handel Richardson has again been the subject of some very interesting historical scholarship. Probyn and Steele, eds., *Henry Handel Richardson: The Letters*, presents, in three volumes and for the first time, all of Richardson's surviving correspondence, bringing the number of published letters up from forty-five to almost 1,000. The editors point out that many of Richardson's letters were destroyed after her death. It seems this was largely due to her desire to ensure that her literary reputation would be connected to the name of 'Henry Handel Richardson' and not that of Ethel Florence Lindsay Robertson. This desire generates one of the central, recurring narratives of the correspondence. The danger in publishing so much correspondence is, of course, that the reader will be numbed by detail. With rare exceptions (some rather perfunctory postcards), this does not happen. The whole makes for absorbing reading, mainly because each volume plays out an engaging narrative. In the first volume [1874–1915], it develops through the correspondence between Richardson and a French translator, Paul Solanges. At first this correspondence is fascinating for what it reveals of Richardson's authorial intentions in regard to *Maurice Guest* [1908], but as the correspondence progresses an intriguing relationship develops as Solanges, who always addresses her as 'Sir', seems about to guess Richardson's gender and as she seems to tease him with hints. Then comes a sudden telegram telling of Solange's death on 7 February 1914. The second volume [1917–33] is dominated by Richardson's correspondence with her old schoolfriend, Mary Kernot. In these letters she feels free to be quite frank about other writers, such as Vance Palmer, Nettie Palmer and Katherine Susannah Prichard (Vance is too uptight, Nettie too chatty, and Prichard badly influenced by D.H. Lawrence). Since the volume also contains her letters to the Palmers thanking them for promoting her work in Australia, it makes for interesting reading and confirms the editors' emphasis on Richardson's use of masks. When writing to Kernot, Richardson is less guarded; even as she shares more about her writing, she is less inclined to perform the role of a writer. The third volume [1934–46] is also dominated by her correspondence with Kernot, though there are also many letters to Oliver Stonor and William Norton and some to the Palmers. At this time Richardson was living in Sussex with her friend and secretary Olga Roncoroni and her correspondence is increasingly shadowed by the Second World War and her own failing health. In addition, there are, in each of the volumes, marvellous moments of pithy observation, such as, 'I would never write a line that could not stand being read in full daylight, in the entirely prosaic hours after breakfast' (i. 106). Webby and Sykes, eds., *Walter and Mary: The Letters of Walter and Mary Richardson*, is another impressive scholarly achievement. The originals (almost 200 of them) are housed at the National Library, but have been painstakingly reordered into a chronological exchange which brings over twenty years of a marriage to life. The letters provide insight into how Henry Handel Richardson transformed such sources into her trilogy *The Fortunes of Richard Mahoney* [1917, 1925, 1929]. They record experiences in genteel Geelong and marvellous Melbourne, as well as on the diggings at 'Ballaaratt', and the couple's sojourns in England. They trace the sentiments of newly engaged lovers, the happy prospects and material success of a married couple, but also later financial difficulties and, more poignantly, Walter's physical decline. An editorial epilogue links the last letters to Mary's future activities, including the sending of young 'Ettie' to the school which would be immortalized in Richardson's *The Getting of Wisdom* [1910]. Webby and Sykes give clear explanations of events not covered by Walter and Mary, and helpful notes which never intrude upon the detailed and eminently readable letters. As a social history of Victorian life in the third quarter of the nineteenth century—from matrimony to medical matters, from visits to the theatre to the question of consulting a homeopathic mesmerist—the work is invaluable. Both works have been admirably produced by the Miegunyah Press (part of Melbourne University Press) which has quickly secured a reputation for works of fine scholarship. Michael Ackland's 'Another "Passing Guest"? A Critical Evaluation of Henry Handel Richardson's *Maurice Guest* in its Manuscript and Published Variants' (*BSANZB* 24:ii[2000] 133–42) addresses questions of authorial intention and literary quality while conducting a detailed analysis of the novel's variants. Ackland argues, for instance, that there is evidence to show that Richardson came to appreciate the cuts she was asked to make to *Maurice Guest*, and that she even regretted not making more. This important contribution is made in the context of a critique of the Academy Editions version of *Maurice Guest* [1998], edited by Clive Probyn and Bruce Steele. Richardson, along with Martin Boyd and Peter Porter, is under scrutiny again in Dominique Hecq's 'Flying Up for Air: Australian Artists in Exile' (*CE&S* 22:ii[2000] 35–45).

One of the people who makes a brief appearance in Henry Handel Richardson's letters is Aileen Palmer, the daughter of Nettie and Vance Palmer. Aileen is herself the subject of Sally Newman's 'Body of Evidence: Aileen Palmer's Textual Lives' (*Hecate* 26:i[2000] 10–38), where she is brought in to a reflection on lesbian history and historiography. Newman examines how we read sexuality in a text, and how the processes of making meaning are both complex and unstable, concluding that the nature of evidence in theorizing and writing lesbian history remains elusive.

Although she expressed reservations about the quality of Prichard's writing, Henry Handel Richardson believed she deserved credit for her contribution to Australian writing. Delys Bird's *Katharine Susannah Prichard: Stories, Journalism and Essays* selects some of Prichard's most notable short stories and essays, grouping its material under such concerns as 'Aboriginal Life and Race Relations', 'Landscapes', 'Women's Lives', and 'Socialism and Communism: Peace and War'. In her critical introduction, Bird points out how Prichard criticism has long sustained a division between her romanticism and her social realism, but that recent criticism has begun to appreciate that what appears to be a division is an interaction and that 'communism was her first and her most enduring romance' (p. xiii). At the same time, Bird identifies an ambivalence in the feminism informing Prichard's fictions: women are generally depicted as stronger than men, but their fulfilment is found in motherhood. Similarly, while she acknowledges the important contribution that Prichard's novel *Coonardoo* [1929] made to race debates in Australia, Bird admits that it is implicated in sentimental and paternalistic assumptions of its times. Finally, there is a select bibliography that is comprehensive and representative. Christina Stead, on the other hand, Richardson dismissed as 'too clever' and might well be surprised to see *The Magic Phrase: Critical Essays on Christina Stead*, presented by its editor, Margaret Harris, as 'a milestone in the complicated narrative of [Stead's] critical reputation, a narrative which presents a case study in cultural politics both inside and outside the academy' (p. 1). Harris's selection demonstrates an ongoing dialogue involving feminist, socialist, psychoanalytical and post-colonial approaches to Stead's writing. Harris herself, in 'Christina Stead and her Critics', reviews Stead's reception, noting how it moves continually around questions of mode and genre, art and politics, and expatriation. Harris also observes that study of Stead is complicated by the thirteen-year hiatus in Stead's career, particularly since this sometimes means that the order of publication does not correspond to the order of composition. Harris's introductory essay is followed by classic essays by Barnard Eldershaw, Ron Geering and Dorothy Green. There are three previously unpublished essays by Louise Yelin, Denise Brown and Fiona Morrison. Yelin, 'Representing the 1930s: Capitalism, Phallocracy, and the Politics of the Popular Front in *House of All Nations*', argues that Stead's novel subjects gender to class, but that it also dramatizes the collapse of the house of 'Europe'. Brown, 'The Spirit of *Cotter's England*', sees the novel's interest in illusion as an indication that it is partly a parable of post-war England as a land of sleepers held in thrall by a spirit of despair. Morrison, 'A "Cruel Book": Menippean Satire and the Female Satirist in *I'm Dying Laughing*', identifies an uneasy alliance between female authorship and Menippean satire, an alliance that is itself allegorical of the central character's personal and political contradictions. In addition, the volume reprints important essays by Terry Sturm, Shirley Walker, Ken Stewart, Judith Kegan Gardiner, Hazel Rowley, Susan Sheridan, Virginia Blain, Diana Brydon and Angela Carter. *The Magic Phrase* has a very fine bibliography, compiled by Brigid Rooney. Rooney's own work on Stead is represented in 'Strange Familiars: Closeting Revolution in Christina Stead's *Cotter's England*' (*AuFS* 15:xxxii[2000] 249–63), which looks at how 'private' sexual secrets intersect with and produce the 'public' realm of history in the novel. Rooney suggests that, in her depiction of family fictions, the working class and the body, Stead draws on her own liminality as a colonial woman writer associated with the political left. Anne Pender's 'Christina Stead's Satirical Vision' (*Overland* 158[2000] 42–50) maintains that critics have not given sufficient attention to the satirical vision of Stead's post-war novels, and that *I'm Dying Laughing* is a rich study of the dehumanizing effects of capitalism, the excesses of national ideology and the dissolution of the American left.

Although Ian Syson, '"It just isn't trendy at the moment": Thinking about Working/Class/Literature through the 1990s' (*Tirra Lirra* 10:ii[1999–2000] 5–14), laments the absence in Australia of a complex history of researching and theorizing working-class literature, quite a deal of work was done on realist writers of the left (though not always in a manner that would allay Syson's concerns). Pauline Armstrong's *Frank Hardy and the Making of 'Power Without Glory'* is a biographical study of the personalities and forces that contributed to Hardy's writing, particularly *Power Without Glory* [1950]. Among the formative influences of his early years, she identifies gambling and a deep sense of the deprivations suffered by the working class during the Great Depression. When she considers Hardy's growing attraction to the Communist Party (which he joined in 1940), Armstrong intriguingly emphasizes how this was influenced by his involvement in the Catholic social action group, the Campion Society. She then retells the familiar story of the novel and its libel case. Her concern, however, is to demonstrate that this is a story of other people, people who contributed greatly to Hardy's ideas, research, typing and even writing, and were forgotten or betrayed. Hardy, it seems, had one of those unreliable memories we have come to expect of corrupt politicians. *Power Without Glory* was conceived by some members of the executive of the Victorian branch of the CPA and researched by people such as Les Barnes, Ross Hardy (Frank's wife) and Deirdre Moore. It was a party project, intended to discredit John Wren, Catholic Action and some members of the State Labour Party. Armstrong's account of the subsequent libel case is also a story of community involvement, particularly in the Frank Hardy Defence Committee. The story she wants to tell, however, is the story of Ross Hardy, the wife who stood by her husband for thirty years, raised his family, helped research his books, and typed his manuscripts, only to be cruelly cast aside. Armstrong's disapproval of Hardy's sexism and egotism is never far from the surface, and sometimes affects her tone: 'Credit must be given to Frank Hardy for his ability to create the right impression, and to adapt to the company in which he found himself' (p. 160). Presumably, Armstrong does not mean this as a compliment. *Overland* also has a symposium on *Power Without Glory* (*Overland* 161[2000] 72–8). There are contributions by Chris Wallace-Crabbe, Nadia Wheatley, Fiona Capp and Kylie Valentine. While all agree on the importance of the book, Wheatley suggests that the writing is not strong, and Valentine notes its lack of interest in community, a comment that becomes more and more intriguing given Armstrong's account of a community-based work. Paul Genoni, 'Ruth Park and Frank Hardy: Catholic Realists' (*Tirra Lirra* 10:iii–iv[2000] 26–31), notes the tension between the socialist intent of *Power Without Glory* and its protagonist's return to Catholicism. Genoni also relates the sentimentalism of Park's novels to the stoicism and fatalism he identifies in her characters' Irish Catholicism. Bridget Griffen-Foley's 'Revisiting the "Mystery of a Novel Contest": The *Daily Telegraph* and *Come in Spinner*' (*ALS* 19:iv[2000] 413–24) tells the story of how *Come in Spinner* (by Florence James and Dymphna Cusack) was never published when, in 1947, it won the newspaper's novel contest, situating this within a context of increasing pro-American leanings. Dymphna Cusack's lover and fellow Communist is the subject of Marilla North's biographical sketch, 'Tinker, Tailor, Soldier, Sailor … Who Was Norman Randolph Freehill?' (*Overland* 161[2000] 36–42). H.M. Doyle, 'Mountain Lore and the Darks' Refuge' (*AuFolk* 15[2000] 108–14), recounts how the myth that Eleanor and Eric Dark were communists still lingers in the folklore of the Blue Mountains. Another Blue Mountains artist to receive some attention this year was Norman Lindsay. Taking a cue from Mikhail Bakhtin's *Rabelais and his World*, David Musgrave, 'Aspects of Symposiastic Law in *The Magic Pudding*' (*Coppertales* 6[2000] 5–17), interprets Norman Lindsay's children's classic in relation to the law of the stomach. Lindsay's tale thus becomes an example of symposiastic law challenging the validity of transcendent universal law. Peter Ryan, 'Norman Lindsay's Scrapbook' (*Quadrant* 44:ix[2000] 87–8), remembers the 1979 publication of Lindsay's *Micomicana*. Peter Pierce, 'Roy

Bridges's Fictions of Van Diemen's Land' (*ALS* 19:iv[2000] 425–32), identifies a call for tolerance in Bridges's account of convict times, as well as an obsession with being part of history, while Russell McDougall, '*Capricornia*: The Bastard Son' (*N&F* 43[2000] 25–7), wonders whether the novel's success rebounded, conferring on Xavier Herbert a sense of illegitimacy as author.

This year Thomas Keneally received more attention than Patrick White. Helen Verity Hewett, '"Screaming silent words": Francis Bacon, Sidney Nolan, and Hurtle Duffield' (*Antipodes* 14:i[2000] 53–7), is an account of how White's portrait of the artist draws on the two painters. Rodney Edgecombe, 'Patrick White's *Voss* and *The Quest for Corvo*: A Note' (*JCL* 32:ii[2000] 139–43), speculates on similarities between *The Quest for Corvo*, which White is known to have read, and *Voss* [1957], and wonders if it is a case of influence. White is in danger of becoming a neglected writer (and his publishers are allowing his works to go out of print). Keneally, however, has rewarded an interest in racial politics. Denise Vernon, '"The limits of goodwill": The Values and Dangers of Revisionism in Keneally's "Aboriginal" Novels' (in Bery et al., eds., *Comparing Postcolonial Literatures: Dislocations*), explains how shifts in Keneally's representations of Aborigines reflect changes in racial politics, particularly the need to surrender intellectual, political and cultural privilege. Larissa Behrendt, 'Consent in a (Neo)Colonial Society: Aboriginal Woman as Sexual and Legal "Other"' (*AuFS* 15:xxxiii[2000] 353–67), uses *The Chant of Jimmie Blacksmith* [1972] to look at the colonial legacy of consensual and non-consensual sexual relations which men (both black and white) forced on black women from first contact. Sue Vice, in her *Holocaust Fiction*, considers *Schindler's List* in the context of debates about whether it deserves to be regarded as Holocaust fiction. Identifying the novel's 'humanist representational agenda', Vice concludes: 'Its concerns with intention, the role of the individual, and private versus public memory, makes it more about the Holocaust, not less' (p. 116). *Holocaust Fiction* also contains an analysis of Helen Darville's *The Hand that Signed the Paper* [1994] as an example of historical polemic. Vice points out that the novel exemplifies the features of what she is calling Holocaust fiction: alleged plagiarism, anti-Semitism, inauthenticity, appropriation, historical revisionism. After a balanced survey of the novel's critical reception, Vice insists that the work and its viewpoints be distinguished from the author and that *The Hand that Signed the Paper* is a polyphonic text. (Vice's discussion of this novel can also be found in 'The Demidenko Affair and Contemporary Holocaust Fiction' in Leak and Paizis, eds., *The Holocaust and the Text: Speaking the Unspeakable*.)

As in previous years, David Malouf continues to attract attention. Sathyabhama Daly, 'David Malouf's *Remembering Babylon* and the Wild Man of the European Cultural Consciousness' (*LiNQ* 27:i[2000] 9–19), maintains that the hybrid figure of Gemmy Fairley brings together a European tradition of nature as wilderness in need of civilization with an Aboriginal mythology of nature as spiritual communion in order to confront white settlers with their repression of Aboriginal presence. Malouf's 1999 Boyer Lectures are given special mention in Brian Kiernan, 'Australia's Postcoloniality' (*Antipodes* 14:i[2000] 11–16), as Kiernan traces themes of national identity and diversity. Anthony Hassall, 'The Wild Colonial Boy: The Making of Colonial Legends in David Malouf's *The Conversations at Curlow Creek*' (*Antipodes* 14:ii[2000] 145–8), sees the book engaged in a conversation between different versions of colonial Australia: the tragic possibility embodied in the story of doomed Irish rebels and a more positive possibility that imported conflicts can be resolved. Hena Maes-Jelinek, 'David Malouf's "Voyaging Imagination": *The Conversations at Curlow Creek*' (*CE&S* 23:i[2000] 89–98), shows how the protagonist's journey 'within' Australia, which is also his journey within language, awakens his imagination.

Some of the most interesting works on contemporary fiction respond to the question of space, whether they locate that space between genders, between worlds and minds, within selves or within language itself. Bernadette Brennan, 'Brian Castro's Tokyo: Schizophrenic Semiotic' (*Southerly* 60:iii[2000] 168–77), argues against any assumption that Castro is interested in writing any actual place, proposing instead that his interest is in imaginative space and the 'no man's land' of narrative space, which he arrives at by transgressing the borders of fact and fiction, self and other, life and death, homeland and dispossession. Tokyo, then, becomes significant in the novel precisely because in order to live there one needs, according to Stepper, an understanding of nothingness. Sigrun Meinig, 'An Australian Convict in the Great English City: Peter Carey's *Jack Maggs*' (*Southerly* 60:iii[2000] 57–65), interprets the novel as a dismantling of the metropolitan centre in favour of the colony, though she also remarks that the fragility of the happy ending warns that it is not so easy to escape the centre, indeed that it is tempting to take it with you. Elizabeth McMahon, 'Lost in Music' (*Meanjin* 59:ii[2000] 167–77), offers a thoughtful reading of conflicted desire in Christos Tsiolkas's *Loaded* and *Head On*, the film based on the novel; McMahon makes some very persuasive observations on the significance of space, movement and running, showing how Ari's walking knowledge of Melbourne creates an alternative map of the city, based on ethnicity and sexuality. Paolo Bartoloni, 'Interstitial Narratives: Italo Calvino and Gerald Murnane' (*Westerly* 45[2000] 111–24), examines how both writers occupy the space between fiction and reality, as well as the spaces that open up once self, language and knowledge begin to fragment. Bartoloni continues his examination of Murnane in 'Time in Gerald Murnane's *Velvet Waters*' (*Antipodes* 14:i[2000] 47–52), which argues that the novel refuses a traditional concept of duration, juxtaposing past, present and future in ways that make 'before' and 'after' irrelevant. Michael Deves, 'Authenticity in Brian Castro's *Stepper*' (*Westerly* 45[2000] 60–70), shows how, by paralleling spying and writing, the novel engages with issues of duplicity and authenticity. Jane Gilpin, 'Turning Up the Heat on the "Warm Zone": A Novel Reading of Jessica Anderson's Queensland' (*Imago* 12:ii[2000] 32–44), maintains that it is not Brisbane but Sydney that becomes the warm zone in Anderson's fiction; Brisbane is more often associated with violence and negative feelings. Roberta Buffi, 'Scraping and Repainting Reflecting Surfaces: Mirrors and Water in Beverley Farmer's Fiction' (*Antipodes* 14:i[2000] 35–40), examines Farmer's use of the visual arts, especially her use of landscape, mirror, water and frame motifs. Anja Müller, 'Travel in No-Man's Land: Closure and Transgression in Janette Turner Hospital's *Oyster*' (in Glage, ed., *Being/s in Transit: Travelling, Migration, Dislocation*), highlights the nomadic character of Hospital's novels, seeing *Oyster* as a refusal of the closure and enclosure represented by Outer Maroo. Joan Dolphin, 'In Praise of Shakespeare: Kate Grenville's *Lillian's Story*' (in den Otter, ed., *Relocating Praise: Literary Modalities and Rhetorical Contexts*), claims that Lillian's particular appropriation of Shakespeare falls into the realm of the epideictic, allowing her to establish her subjectivity despite the imperial and patriarchal ideas that dominate her world. Dorothy Jones, 'Threading Words Together' (*NLitsR* 36[2000] 3–16), comments on Grenville's *The Idea of Perfection* [1999] in the context of a more general discussion of representations of textiles in post-colonial texts.

Anthony Hassal, 'The Dream/Nightmare of Europe in Tim Winton's *The Riders* and George Johnston's *Clean Straw for Nothing*' (*Overland* 161[2000] 26–30), locates the works in what he calls a sub-genre of Australian writing dealing with figures who go to Europe in search of a cultural home. While both novels show the dream turning into nightmare, *The Riders* [1994] lets its protagonist escape the nightmare, a resolution which, Hassall posits, might represent Australia's changing cultural relations with Europe. Laurenz Volkmann, 'Intercultural Competence through Reading Yasmine Gooneratne's Novels' (in Antor and Stierstorfer, eds., *English Literatures in International Contexts*), takes up one of the main themes in Gooneratne's critical and creative work, that reading literature is a way of improving intercultural understanding.

This year the significant work in autobiography deals with women's autobiography and Aboriginal women's autobiography. Gillian Whitlock's *The Intimate Empire* is a study of the autobiographical writing of women in relation to the politics of empire, powerfully combining post-colonial and feminist perspectives with recent critical discussions about genre and gender in life-writing. Among the impressive features of the work are Whitlock's appreciation of the ambiguous influence of empire on its subjects and her avoidance of any simple and secure alignments of gender, nation, race and identity. In this sense, she allows the complexities of her texts to determine her application of theory. The texts themselves combine nineteenth- and twentieth-century autobiographies, as well as writing from Canada, the Caribbean, Kenya, South Africa, New Zealand, and Australia. In some cases, the writing and reading of women's autobiography helps perpetuate empire; in other cases, it becomes a site of opposition. It is in this context that she considers the work of Sally Morgan, even as she recognizes that the 'Aboriginal identity' constructed by Morgan has itself been somewhat unsettled by other indigenous writers, such as Ruby Langford Ginibi. Jennifer Jones, in 'The Black Communist: The Contested Memory of Margaret Tucker' (*Hecate* 26:ii[2000] 135–45), examines Tucker's *If Everyone Cared* [1977], described as the first published autobiography by an Aboriginal woman, showing how editorial excisions downplayed Tucker's involvement with the Communist Party. This is, then, another example of the problems of authority and autonomy associated with collaboration, discussed by Penny van Toorn in *The Cambridge Companion to Australian Literature*.

(c) Poetry

The question of when poetry 'begins' to be 'Australian' is more complex than it might at first appear, and this year has seen some interesting historical scholarship that may encourage more discussion. Hugh Anderson's *Farewell to Judges and Juries: The Broadside Ballad and Convict Transportation to Australia, 1788–1868* is a collection of more than 100 broadside ballads and songs, supported by extracts from letters, journals, memoirs and other contemporary writing. The collection is supplemented by indexes, bibliography and notes on sources. In his informative introduction Anderson offers the book as part of a recovery of popular history (the broadsides are read as examples of the literature of the working class) and as part of a reconsideration of the convict system (Robert Hughes's *The Fatal Shore* [1987] is criticized for assuming a linear evolution from brutal system to tolerant society). In regard to the latter, Anderson draws on recent historical scholarship to argue that the convicts were ordinary working-class men and women, not habitual criminals, and to suggest that the convict system was predominantly a productive organization of skills and work, not the brutalizing experience of stereotypical imagination. This, he claims, is an image produced by middle-class writing with a sensationalist interest in flagellation, sodomy and bestiality; such writing possibly reflects the anxiety of a middle class that may have regarded the high wages in the 1820s and the relative independence and social mobility of the working class in Australia as a threat. So the first broadside included by Anderson, an example of the convict's parting lay, tells of one convict encouraging another to be grateful for the luck that made them convicts since it means they are free of all their worries about rent, church, police, and taxes. While it may be difficult to ascertain precisely how such songs combine description with desire, Anderson is confident, and reasonably so, that the sheer bulk of the material will support more complex interpretations of the convict experience. It will now be interesting to see how such scholarship affects readings of classics such as Marcus Clarke's *His Natural Life*. What displaced anxieties are about to be found beneath its textual surface? Victor Crittenden, 'Who Was "Epsilon"?' (*Margin* 52[2000] 2–10), gives reasons for believing that the writer who published poems by 'Epsilon' in newspapers between 1834 and 1839 was John Lang, the first native-born Australian novelist. Lang's novel *Frederick Charles Howard* [1842] is discussed in Victor Crittenden, 'John Lang and Bushrangers' (*Margin* 51[2000] 21–31); Lang portrays a bush ranger as an unpleasant thief, refusing the more noble figure of later writers such as Rolf Boldrewood. Elizabeth Webby, '"Blushing unseen": Australian Literature Published in Regional Newspapers of the 1840s' (*BSANZB* 24:i[2000] 73–80), acknowledges the important role played by regional newspapers such as the *Geelong Advertiser* in the publication of nineteenth-century poetry. Of the poets published, the best known is probably Charles Harpur, a number of whose poems were published by the *Maitland Mercury* in the 1840s. Harpur is also under examination in Uli Krahn, '"How nourishing is nature": Imaginary Possession of Landscape in Harpur and Skrzynecki' (*Southerly* 60:iii[2000] 29–38), which sets out to challenge the realist epistemology assumed by so much historical scholarship. Krahn reads the work of Charles Harpur and Peter Skrzynecki in order to challenge the persistent assumptions about transparent and unmediated access to reality that, she argues, sustains the separation of 'colonial' and 'migrant' writing. Marjorie Harris, '"The Modern Athens": The Literary Culture of Colonial Ipswich' (*QR* 72:ii[2000] 37–45), recounts how in the period between 1842 and 1900 colonial Ipswich enjoyed a rich cultural life: thirteen newspapers and periodicals, Queensland's first provincial newspaper, the first book of verse to be published in Queensland. Frank Molloy, '"The rising poet of this country": A Year in the Life of Victor Daley' (*Margin* 51[2000] 5–14), details the emergence of Victor Daley as a leading poet of the *Bulletin* and acknowledges the encouragement of J.F. Archibald. Molloy also contributed 'Victor J. Daley: A Comprehensive Bibliography' and 'Attribution and Pseudonyms: The Case of Victor J. Daley' (*BSANZB* 24:ii[2000] 116–28). Meanwhile, Gary Catalano, displaying a poet's interest in the actual writing, contends, in 'The Writing on the Wall: On Bernard O'Dowd' (*Quadrant*

44:xi[2000] 67–71), that O'Dowd's poetry suffered because he was so intent on seeing everything as an omen and a portent that he lost touch with the actualities of daily life.

This year saw the deaths of Judith Wright and Alec Hope. It was not a year in which very much was published about Wright. *South of My Days*, Veronica Brady's biography of Wright (*YWES* 80[2001]), continued to attract some attention, including some corrections from Wright herself: Judith Wright, 'Corrections of Biographical Errors' (*ALS* 19:iv[2000] 438–9). An essay by David Brooks ('A Land Without Lendings') has already been mentioned, as has Martin Harrison's 'The Myth of Origins', though it is worth noting here that Harrison nominates Wright's 'Eroded Hills' as a key moment in modern Australian poetry since it presents the figure of modernity, the poem held between appearance and disappearance. It was, however, a year in which Hope attracted some attention. David Brooks edited both *A.D. Hope: Selected Poetry and Prose* and *The Double Looking Glass: New and Classic Essays on the Poetry of A.D. Hope*. Brooks's selection of poetry is designed to demonstrate the range of his writing: lyrical, discursive, epic, epistolary, satiric, sexual, symbolist. Brooks clearly wants to rescue Hope from the 'classical' tag that has so often been attached to his work, insisting instead that a commitment to conservative form should not be taken as an indication of a conservative mind. As well as reprinting a good range of the poetry, the volume also includes some of Hope's better-known essays, some selections from his notebooks, and four of his notorious reviews (of the Jindyworobaks, Max Harris, Norma Davis and Patrick White). These reviews, Brooks argues, have been so frequently misrepresented that it is a service to Hope scholarship to have them republished. *A.D. Hope: Selected Poetry and Prose* is another in the Halstead Press Classics series, and one can only hope the publishers will be able to continue with this venture, since so many Australian classics are out of print. *The Double Looking Glass* opens with essays that helped establish Hope's reputation, well-known essays by Vincent Buckley, Sam Goldberg, James McAuley and Judith Wright. What is interesting about them in the context of this volume is the way in which they register their dissatisfaction with the very terms they are using to discuss Hope's poetry, terms such as 'classical', 'Romantic', and 'intellectual'. In discussing Hope's treatment of sexuality, these early essays also introduce, if only momentarily, doubts that later critics will magnify: Vincent Buckley identifies a 'bitter carnality', Sam Goldberg a 'Puritan' strain, and James McAuley a 'Manichean' duality; in later essays, John Docker talks of 'misogyny' and Fay Zwicky addresses the difficult question of gender. More significantly, for this volume and this editor, is Judith Wright's suggestion that Hope's habit of mind might be more 'French' than 'English', and her recognition of the influence on his poetics of Mallarmé and Valéry. Hope's connection to French Symbolism is then taken up in essays by Robert Brissenden, Chris Wallace-Crabbe, Kevin Hart and David Brooks, which link Hope to the Orphic tradition of poetry. Given that one of the aims of this volume is to dislodge readings of Hope as 'classicist' and 'traditionalist', it is a pity not to have an example of that criticism included, just as it is a pity not to have the kind of bibliography usually found in the UQP Studies in Australian Literature series. Xavier Pons, in 'A.D. Hope and the Apocalyptic Splendour of the Senses' (*ALS* 19:iv[2000] 373–86), addresses allegations of chauvinism in Hope's poetry, arguing that it offers a visionary eroticism and suggesting that if it also offers a masculine viewpoint, this ought not be held against it. Hope is also discussed in Paul Tankard, '"Free Verse" and Traditional Form in Eliot, Lawrence and Hope' (*AUMLA* 93[2000] 37–50), which discusses Hope's complaints against what he saw as Eliot's metrical weaknesses. Tankard claims that, whereas Hope thinks it is necessary for poetry to employ metre, Eliot believes it is enough for poetry to allude to metre. In relation to the history of French Symbolism within Australian poetry, John Hawke, 'The Politics of Symbolism' (*Southerly* 60:i[2000] 58–77), investigates correspondence between Randolph Hughes and Jack Lindsay, correspondence in which Hughes's aesthetic preference for Symbolism is tested by debates about Nazism and Marxism. Hawke declares: 'These letters are crucial to an understanding of the evolution of Australian poetry, since they provide a direct link between the Symbolist philosophy of Brennan and the *Vision* school of the 1920s' (p. 58).

James McAuley is still held under the shadow of Cassandra Pybus, *The Devil and James McAuley* (*YWES* 80[2001]). Pybus, 'Dogs in the Graveyard' (*Meanjin* 59:iv[2000] 117–26), mocks the critics of her biography, even to the point of remarking that three of her detractors are called 'Peter' and that this is also a word for 'penis'. Graeme Hetherington, 'James McAuley: Only a Bit of a Devil' (*Quadrant* 44:ix[2000] 62–5), tries to extricate himself from the controversy by intimating that Pybus deliberately distorted the information he gave her in good faith and by affirming that McAuley was the most moral person he ever knew. One can only hope that the next attempt on McAuley's life will be one that can rescue him from the long revenges of left and right. Laurie Hergenhan, 'Starting a Journal: *ALS*, Hobart 1963: James McAuley, A. D. Hope and Geoffrey Dutton' (*ALS* 19:iv[2000] 433–7), remembers how *Australian Literary Studies* began, noting that James McAuley, Professor of English at the University of Tasmania, who was responsible for establishing the journal, gave the new editor (Hergenhan) editorial independence. Noel Rowe, 'Giving a Word to the Sand' (*Westerly* 45[2000] 151–60), compares the theopoetics of McAuley, Francis Webb and Vincent Buckley, emphasizing the importance of images of, respectively, fall, stigmata, and incarnation to explain how these poets differently respond to Catholicism. Vincent Buckley's ambiguous relationship to Catholicism and Ireland is also under discussion in John McLaren, 'A Terrible Beauty is Born' (*Tirra Lirra* 9:iv[1999] 17–22). Alison Hoddinott, 'Who Wrote these Poems?' (*N&F* 43[2000] 3–4), is a scholarly note on some of the literary hoaxing that Buckley and Gwen Harwood perpetrated. Rosemary Dobson is honoured in *Rosemary Dobson: A Celebration*, edited by Joy Hooton for the Friends of the National Library of Australia. Joy Hooton contributes an important biographical and critical essay, emphasizing the Australian/European conversation that characterizes the poetry; Elizabeth Lawson discusses how paintings operate in Dobson's poems, in particular how they permit a 'slantwise' perspective; Paul Hetherington considers Dobson's poems on friendship and love; David McCooey relates the visionary and elegiac qualities of Dobson's work. David Musgrave and Peter Kirkpatrick, 'Friction as a Social Process: Reading Ern Malley' (*Southerly* 60:i[2000] 131–45), propose Ern Malley's poems as an example of a 'minor literature' intent on resisting the syncretizing, canonizing practices of reading in Australian literature. The *La Trobe Journal* (64[1999]) contains a number of pieces relevant to 'Ern Malley' and the Angry Penguins. There is a reprint of Max Harris's 'Experiment with Death', the essay he prepared for the special Australian issue of *Voices* (118[Summer 1944]), in which, still unaware of the hoax, he discusses the place of 'Ern Malley' in Australian poetry. Brian Lloyd celebrates the achievement of the alternative publishing firm of Reed & Harris, while Des Cowley provides a checklist of Reed & Harris publications. Harold Stewart, the other half of Ern, is the subject of Michael Ackland's 'Beyond "Darkest Oz": The Diverse Stations of Harold Stewart's Road to Kyoto' (*Southerly* 60:iii[2000] 148–58), a foretaste of his *Damaged Men: The Precarious Lives of James McAuley and Harold Stewart* [2001], which will be reviewed next year. *Lost Angry Penguins. D.B. Kerr and P.G. Pfeiffer: A Path to the Wind*, by John Miles, recovers two of the most promising poets associated with Australian modernism (both were killed during the Second World War). Miles claims that Kerr was the founder of the journal *Angry Penguins*. Bill Ashcroft and John Salter, 'Modernism's Empire: Australia and the Cultural Imperialism of Style' (in Booth and Rigby, eds., *Modernism and Empire*), argue that much of the battle for and against Australian modernism confirmed the myth of colonial marginality; they emphasize instead the innovative impulse generated by the intersection of women's attempts to write the body and place with the incorporation of indigenous images and forms.

Peter Alexander's *Les Murray: A Life in Progress* finally appeared. It is a sympathetic portrait, some would say too sympathetic, of an isolated country boy who grows up to be a major poet rejected in his own country. Alexander is particularly effective when he is tracing Murray's early years, and the hurt contained in them, and when he is discussing his sexual anxieties. However, when he ventures into the politics of Australian poetry, his sympathy betrays him, since he is too inclined to accept that those whom Murray sees as enemies really are enemies. This means that Alexander never acknowledges that Murray's life narrative is one that needs enemies (which is partly why it maintains such pugnacious distinctions as country/city, poet/academic, and narrowspeak/wholespeak). It also means that the biography's oppositional imagining delivers it into the left/right power plays that so characterize Australian literary politics. It is also a little naive in its account of faithless friends and unkind reviews: the ex-friends do not get a chance to give their version of events, and reviews are misrepresented in a manner that isolates negative remarks and ignores positive ones. Read as a kind of reported autobiography, it shows just how much Murray's poetry depends on notions of victim and sacrifice. However, its single most important contribution has been to discredit the account given of the death of Murray's mother in 'The Steel'. The poem is based on a version of events which Murray took on trust from his father (Murray himself was at school when the event occurred). In the poem the mother, who is pregnant, begins to miscarry, the father rings for an ambulance, but a city-bred doctor, snobbishly indifferent to hillbilly hysterics, refuses to authorize this. The delay is fatal. In the biography Alexander establishes that the father would not describe what was happening because of an inhibition about female sexuality and blood, and that an ambulance was dispatched as soon as a neighbour intervened. Alexander then provides a sensitive reading of how this incident left Murray with deep feelings of guilt and with a powerful association of feminine sexuality and death. Alexander's biography is also valuable for the ways in which it illuminates the autobiographical basis of *Fredy Neptune*. Sarah Attfield, 'Working Class Heroes? Les Murray vs p.π.' (*Overland* 159[2000] 50–4), disputes the image of Murray as a poet of the people, insisting that he does not recognize class divisions, nor reveal any deep understanding of what it means to be a working-class person. Paul Cliff, 'The Perpetual Dimension: Folkloristic Elements in Les Murray's "Bunyah"' (*AuFolk* 15[2000] 200–14), does see Murray as a poet of his people, surveying such folkloristic themes and iconography as the 'forty acres', the family history, forestry traditions, and Anzac. Of the other senior poets, only Bruce Dawe and Peter Porter received attention. Dennis Haskell's 'Bruce Dawe at the Frontiers of Gawkiness' (*Antipodes* 14:i[2000] 27–33) pays particular attention to Dawe's language and is welcome for the way it resists the assumption that Dawe is an easy poet. Bruce Bennett, 'Interior Landscapes in Peter Porter's Later Poetry' (*Antipodes* 14:ii[2000] 93–7), sees love and death as the twin compulsions of Porter's interior landscapes.

John Kinsella's international reputation received a boost from Menghem and Phillips, eds., *Fairly Obsessive: Essays on the Works of John Kinsella*, with contributions from Australia, the United Kingdom, France and Canada. A glance at the contents indicates that the essays represent the range of Kinsella's interests and reflect the importance of cultural hybridizing in his work. In fact, the overall effect is of a book that follows lines established by the author's own statements: traditional and experimental forms, hybrid forms, pastoral and anti-pastoral. Glen Phillips provides two essays, the first a survey of Kinsella's career, the second an appreciation of his renewal of the pastoral. Douglas Barbour celebrates Kinsella's versatility with traditional, modernist, and postmodernist poetics. Xavier Pons also reworks the traditional/experimental divide in Kinsella's work, while Andrew Duncan reviews the Lasseter poems as an attempt to write myth. Ann Vickery finds in Kinsella's work an exploration of the relationship of image to subjectivity, noting particularly his indebtedness to Kenneth Slessor's photographic imagery and his poetic versions of Andy Warhol subjects. In a second contribution, Vickery examines how Kinsella resists the moral complacencies he associates with traditional pastoral in order to pursue an ethics of care. In other pieces, Dennis Haskell suggests that living abroad seems to have made Kinsella more intensely Western Australian, Louis Armand proposes that Kinsella's Warhol poems can be read as a critique of representation, and Peter Minter advocates a hybrid poetics. The most interesting essay is perhaps Michael Brennan's 'Unreading Kinsella: Dropping Names and Revolutions of the Word in *Syzygy*', a playful meditation on how the impossible and the unknown attend the reading of a work he describes as engaged in 'ironised hypercodification' (p. 160). Reading Kinsella into a Symbolist heritage, Brennan manages to break free of the mantric predictabilities that attend too many of the other contributions. In a substantial review, Brian Henry, 'The Pastoral Down Under' (*KR* 22:i[2000] 190–7), also appeals to such terms as 'hybridity' and 'anti-pastoral', though he does manage a most intriguing remark: 'Kinsella's poetic range, though considerable, is less remarkable than his ability to benefit fully from hybridity' (p. 192). One wonders how much longer poetry can bear the preference for interpretation over evaluation.

Very little else was published on contemporary poetry. There is a special feature on Martin Johnston in *Jacket* (11[2000]): see <http://www.jacket.zip.com.au/jacket 11>. The issue contains: John Lucas, 'Martin Johnston and the Matter of Elegy'; Petro Alexiou, 'A Talk on Martin Johnston'; Brian Kim Stefans, 'A Quick Graph: On Martin Johnston: Paragraphs from an Unwritten Letter to John Tranter'. Lucas, discussing the unfinished essay, 'On Berryman's Elegies', observes that Johnston disapproved of much Australian elegy. Alexiou celebrates Johnston for his translations of Greek poetry and his use of Greek literary and cultural traditions. Brian Kim Stefans locates Johnston in a conversation about poetics that includes, among others, Ern Malley, Allen Ginsberg, and John Tranter. Tranter's own work is examined by Kate Lilley in 'Textual Relations: John Tranter's *The Floor of Heaven*' (*Southerly* 60:ii[2000] 106–14), where she discovers that the motives of plot and narration are erotic and textual. Martin Duwell, 'Intricate Knots and Vast Cosmologies: The Poetry of Judith Beveridge' (*ALS* 19:iii[2000] 243–53), highlights the liminal quality of Beveridge's poetry and discusses the influence of Buddhism on her work. Michael Heald, '"Talking with Yagan's Head": The Poetry of John Mateer' (*ALS* 19:iv[2000] 387–98), maintains that Mateer's poetry registers a profound anxiety about audience that reflects the poet's need to 'speak out' and the public's inability to listen to profound questionings about history, community and poetic form.

(d) Drama

Drama was again the poor relation. This year saw some good work in historical recovery and in indigenous theatre. There was also some research on Shakespeare in Australia that will eventually connect with the question raised by May-Brit Akerholt, in *The Cambridge Companion to Australian Literature*, where she asks whether local translations of classics come under the heading of 'Australian drama'. It is a question that represents another loosening of the connection between 'nation' and 'literature' which has traditionally been one of the main features, and one of the main pillars, of Australian literary criticism. In this case, though, the term under question is 'literature'. It might be said that this is a delayed but obvious consequence of shifting from a view of drama as text to a view of drama as performance, thus transforming the performance space into a site of exchange between general and local meanings. Ken Stewart, 'Much Ado About Everything: The Melbourne Shakespeare Society 1884–1904' (*ALS* 19:iii[2000] 269–78), tells the story of a colonial culture's engagement with the 'Shakespeare' who represents empire, capitalism and racism as well as the 'Shakespeare' being colonized according to diverse local needs and interests. Stewart interprets this engagement as a paradigmatic Victorian intellectual contest between the followers of Carlyle and Ruskin and the followers of Mill and Bentham. This article is yet another contribution to the rich study of colonial culture that distinguished Stewart's *Investigations in Australian Literature* (discussed above). *Margin* (50[2000]) celebrates the Australian Shakespearian Bicentenary—200 years since the first production of a Shakespeare play (*Henry IV*). For this issue Victor Crittenden writes a historical piece on this production, W.F. Whyte's 'Shakespeare in Australia' [1922] is reprinted, and William Lawrence gives a brief history of Australia's Shakespeare Societies. Next year's review will have to consider this question again, since John Golder and Richard Madelaine, eds., *O Brave New World: Two Centuries of Shakespeare on the Australian Stage* [2001], entertains the possibility that if an Australian audience contributes substantially to meaning in a performance of Shakespeare, the play becomes part of the Australian stage.

Veronica Kelly, '"Un Sans Culotte": The *Bulletin*'s Early Theatre Criticism and the Masculine Bohemian Masquerade' (*ALS* 19:iii[2000] 254–68), examines the journal's theatrical journalism in the period 1880–1901, in particular the performance metaphors that cluster around the collective identity masquerading under the name 'Sans Culotte' and the ways in which these appeal to the 'knowing' reader. Bill Dunstone, '"Orders of nature": Press, Gender and Performance in Colonial Western Australia 1839–1888' (*ADS* 36[2000] 105–16), recounts how 'The politics of gender representation in Western Australia's colonial theatre was intimately interrelated with hierarchies of professionalism and amateurism, and with hierarchies of imperial culture' (p. 107). Margaret Williams and Hilary Golder, 'Fighting Jack: A Brief Australian Melodrama' (*ADS* 36[2000] 117–30), offer some light relief in the story of a fighting kangaroo and how, in 1891, he became part of Australian legal and theatrical history. Connie Healy's *Defiance: Political Theatre in Brisbane, 1930–1962* tells of the rise of working-class/political theatre occasioned by the economic depression and the desire to provide an educative forum in which social problems might be addressed. The most active groups were the WEA Dramatic Society and the Unity Theatre, which were particularly concerned to encourage worker solidarity and denounce fascism. After the war, Unity Theatre was renamed the New Theatre and continued its commitment to the militant left. Healy, who declares herself 'a former member and supporter', maintains that groups such as these made a more than marginal contribution to Australian theatre and ought not be forgotten. She argues that they represent an Australian democratic tradition and participate in an international development of political theatre. In particular, she credits the New Theatre with an enlightened opposition to racism. The book contains many details about the various productions mounted by the groups. Donald Pulford's 'America and the Australian Performing Group' (*Antipodes* 14:ii[2000] 111–14) looks at how the 'new wave' dramatists were influenced by American models of theatre, especially by way of the *Tulane Drama Review*. One of the leading 'new wave' dramatists, Jack Hibberd, achieves something of a classical status with the publication of his *Selected Plays* by Currency Press (containing the three plays that were central to his initial impact: *White With Wire Wheels*, *Dimboola*, and *A Stretch of the Imagination*). In his helpful introduction to this volume, Paul McGillick remarks on how Hibberd blends his use of the Australian vernacular with modernist techniques. Currency Press has maintained its publication of Australian plays, with Brisbane, ed., *Plays of the 60s*, volume i, containing Oriel Gray's *Burst of Summer*, Jack McKinney's *The Well*, Patrick White's *Season at Sarsaparilla* and Theodore Patrikareas's *The Promised Woman*. In her introduction, Brisbane places these four plays in relation to the plays contained in volumes ii and iii of Currency's *Plays of the 60s* by remarking how all the plays contained in the first volume were first performed in small theatres by 'unpaid (or spasmodically paid) actors' whereas the plays of the later volumes represent a move into the mainstream. Describing them all as working-class plays registering some dissatisfaction with the social stasis that characterized 1960s Australia, Brisbane says they represent the moment before the revolution. A number of Currency's publications feature useful introductions. In most cases, this might be taken as a sign of the status of the writer: Jill Shearer's *Georgia*, Hannie Rayson's *Life After George*, and David Williamson's *Two Plays: The Great Man/Sanctuary* are all afforded such a distinction. Paul Makeham, '"The city's surrounded by fire": Michael Gow's *The Kid*' (*ADS* 36[2000] 73–87), analyses the play's double referentiality, its evocation of a contemporary (surface) world and its suggestion of deeper mythic significance, relating this to its mixture of naturalist and expressionist modes. Julia Mant, 'The Testimonial Stage: Theatrical Presentations of the Prisoner of War, 1995' (*ADS* 36[2000] 89–104), looks at how in the year of the fiftieth anniversary of the end of the Second World War, stage productions favoured the image of the emaciated and heroic prisoner of war. Among productions she discusses are those of John Misto's *The Shoe-Horn Sonata* (Ensemble Theatre) and John Romeril's *The Floating World* (the Makato Sato production for the Japan–Australia Cultural Exchange Program). Her discussion of the difficulties involved in staging history, war and inexpressible pain is informed by her understanding that the body is at once a site of contested histories and of remembrance.

Australasian Drama Studies (37[2000]) was a special issue called 'Sun Sisters and Lightning Brothers: Australian Aboriginal Performance', with Anne Marshall and Gordon Beattie as guest editors. Marshall herself shows a sharp eye for ways in which cultural imperialism functions in academic discourse in 'Casting About for the Scent: Researching Aboriginal Performance' (*ADS* 37[2000] 3–13), where she advocates ideas of embodied narrative and performed discourse as more congruent with indigenous performance modes. Kieryn Babcock, 'Power and Performance: Aboriginality and the Academy' (*ADS* 37[2000] 46–58), wants space for Aboriginal epistemologies in the academy and asks 'whether Performance Studies departments will continue the monologue of Western academia' (p. 56) or develop ways of approaching indigenous performance that are more open to the Other. June Perkins, '7 Valleys of Nurturing: Exploring the Performing Arts Philosophy of Wesley Enoch: A Profile' (*ADS* 37[2000] 18–26), pays tribute to Enoch's nurturing role in the indigenous arts community. Maryrose Casey provides the very valuable 'From the Wings to Centre Stage: A Production Chronology of Theatre and Dramatic Texts by Indigenous Australian Writers' (*ADS* 37[2000] 85–98), which covers the years 1968 to 1997. Lisa Meekison's 'Can You See What I Hear?' (*Meanjin* 59:ii[2000] 85–94) investigates the function of music in indigenous theatre, claiming that, in addition to meeting Western audience expectations (e.g. mood-setting), music is one of the principal ways in which indigenous theatre proclaims itself part of traditional story-telling. Marc Maufort, in 'Unsettling Narratives: Subversive Mimicry in Australian Aboriginal Solo Performance Pieces' (*Antipodes* 14:ii[2000] 105–10), examines *The Seven Stages of Grieving* (Wesley Enoch and Deborah Mailman) and *Box the Pony* (Scott Rankin and Leah Purcell), showing how they forge a new dramaturgical language, refashioning realism and performance to suit a unique Aboriginal consciousness. Maryrose Casey, 'Nindethana and the National Black Theatre: Interrogating the Mythology of the New Wave' (*ADS* 36[2000] 19–33), points out that most accounts of the 'New Wave' of the 1960s and 1970s, with their recurring emphasis on a 'history of beginnings' and gender bias, constitute an imperial/colonial narrative. One effect of this is to sustain dialectical thinking in drama criticism and so to ensure that indigenous work is still perceived as other. Cleverly reappropriating the 'blank slate' (or 'terra nullius') narrative, Casey remarks on the history of theatre study:

> In the case of Indigenous Australian artists, the previous two hundred years are assumed to be tribal or a 'blank slate'. In the case of Euro-Australian artists the previous two hundred years are either a blank slate or inauthentic. In both cases an evolutionary and linear chronology of performance practice is asserted in the emphasis on first productions as a phenomenon. This interpretation of artistic practice

reinforces the process of treating cultural groupings hierarchically
instead of dialogically. (p. 30)

3. Canada

(a) General
Significantly, Northrop Frye's updated question 'Where is here now?' was asked
not just by the editors of *Essays on Canadian Writing* (71[2000]), but also in diverse
ways by critics who continue to develop the study of ethnicity and Canadian
literature(s): a special issue of *Canadian Literature* (167[2000]) examines First
Nations writing, Chinese Canadian literature is explored by Susan Hilf, in *Writing
the Hyphen: The Articulation of Interculturalism in Contemporary Chinese-
Canadian Literature*, and diasporic identities are interrogated by Smaro
Kamboureli, in *Scandalous Bodies: Diasporic Literature in English Canada*.

Kevin Flynn opens *ECW* 71 with an examination of the process of putting
together the journal, and the remit to document 'the state of CanLit at the end of the
millennium'. Unusually, the editors agreed to publish responses to this concern
without intervention, to provide a snapshot of the 'CanLit' field. A hundred
invitations were sent out, and twenty-two critics responded. Retrospective
summaries include Robert Lecker, 'Where Is Here Now?' (*ECW* 71[2000] 6–13),
who argues that over two decades the rise of theory has changed the terminology,
but underlying issues remain the same; W.J. Keith, 'Blight in the Bush Garden:
Twenty Years of "Can Lit"' (*ECW* 71[2000] 71–88), who charts the rise of
Canadian literature and criticism, criticizes theory, and worries about non-'literary'
reasons for expansion of the canon that leads to inclusion of women's writing and
ethnic minorities; and Kristjana Gunnars, 'Canonization Practices and the Canadian
Bookshelf' (*ECW* 71[2000] 232–40), who traces the shift into postmodern, post-
colonial and post-structuralist theoretical territory, as fragmenting and destabilizing
Canadian literature criticism from the 1970s to the present. Lawrence Mathews,
'Not Where Here Is, But Where Here Might Be' (*ECW* 71[2000] 79–87), samples
contemporary Canadian literature and criticism in an act of parody and critique; he
suggests that the writings of Hugh Hood could function as superior aesthetic and
spiritual models for the shallow, ironic and 'sophisticated' contemporary popular
writers. Andrew Pyper, 'High Anxiety in the Bush Garden: Some Common
Prejudices in Mainstream Canadian Criticism' (*ECW* 71[2000] 88–95), recognizes
the anxiety inherent in the ongoing critique of theory, arguing for a more open and
critical attitude to younger writers, post- and popular cultures. Pyper argues strongly
that this 'generational anxiety' leads to reductive notions of young people's
contemporary writing. Many of the contributors to the issue reformulate Northrop
Frye's infamous question. Diana Brydon, 'It's Time for a New Set of Questions'
(*ECW* 71[2000] 14–25), argues for an ethical criticism that interrogates Frye's
question 'Where is here?', by including the multiple subject positions of Canada's
First Nations, explorers, settlers, refugees, immigrants and travellers. Ajay Heble,
'Sounds of Change: Dissonance, History, and Cultural Listening' (*ECW* 71[2000]
26–36), utilizes music metaphors, such as those offered by Edward Said and Glen
Gould, as models for listening to the voices not in harmony with homogeneous
notions of nationalism/identity. Ric Knowles, 'Marlon Brando, Pocahontas, and

Me' (*ECW* 71[2000] 48–60), focuses on First Nations dramaturgy as a way of rethinking Canadian theatre studies as a whole, while Lorraine York, '"He should do well on the American talk shows": Celebrity, Publishing, and the Future of Canadian Literature' (*ECW* 71[2000] 96–105), and Di Brandt, 'Going Global' (*ECW* 71[2000] 106–13), examine the role of commercialism, celebrity and the media in the production of Canadian literary capital.

The study of Canadian literature overseas is explored by Danielle Fuller and Susan Billingham, 'CanLit(e): Fit for Export?' (*ECW* 71[2000] 114–27), via the institutions of the British Association for Canadian Studies and the International Council for Canadian Studies; Fuller and Billingham examine the 'ideological function' of studying Canadian literature in the UK. Richard Cavell, 'Here Is Where Now' (*ECW* 71[2000] 195–202), begins with his experiences of teaching Canadian literature in Italy and re-imports such experiences into Canada and contemporary teaching practices; Cavell explores the 'internationalization of Canadian studies' via McLuhan, cultural memory and globalization. Overall, the theme issue provides a vital, compelling and critical snapshot that goes well beyond the selective summaries presented here; however, Kevin Flynn's concerns in his editorial, mainly about the lack of response to the call for papers, and a perceived lack of a critical community, are misplaced: major publications were produced elsewhere that covered similar territory in depth.

Margery Fee, 'Reading Aboriginal Lives' (*CanL* 167[2000] 5–7), introduces the theme issue on First Nations writing, which begins with an essay on collaborative writing between Rudy Wiebe and Yvonne Johnson, in Susanna Egan, 'Telling Trauma: Generic Dissonance in the Production of *Stolen Life*' (*CanL* 167[2000] 10–29). Egan unravels the complex interweaving of two voices, ultimately critiquing Wiebe's dominance as a novelist whose mediating role becomes one of rewriting First Nations experience from his own perspective. In another dialogic format, Christine Watson, 'Autobiographical Writing as a Healing Process: Interview with Alice Masak French' (*CanL* 167[2000] 32–42), explores with Alice Masak French the cathartic nature of autobiography, while Warren Cariou, 'The Racialized Subject in James Tyman's *Inside Out*' (*CanL* 167[2000] 68–84), examines the confluence of the prison confession narrative and First Nations autobiography from a psychoanalytical perspective. Failing to grasp Louis Riel's 'Otherness' is a charge made against English- and French-speaking Canadians by Albert Braz in 'The Absent Protagonist: Louis Riel in Nineteenth-Century Canadian Literature' (*CanL* 167[2000] 45–61), while Robin Ridington, 'Happy Trails to You: Contexted Discourse and Indian Removals in Thomas King's *Truth & Bright Water*' (*CanL* 167[2000] 89–107), writes about the problematic of multiple 'border crossings' in King's work. This special issue of *Canadian Literature* functions in two dominant ways: first, it re-examines the important issue of mediation via non-indigenous voices (providing examples and analysis of such mediation), and second it develops some new critical readings of First Nations writing; in both cases, 'Where is here now?' is a question that is also being answered through a re-examination of the colonial past, and its impact upon the present.

Susan Hilf, in *Writing the Hyphen: The Articulation of Interculturalism in Contemporary Chinese-Canadian Literature*, reads Chinese Canadian literature from the 1960s to the present day; her range of authors is wide, including in-depth studies of Denise Chong, Wayson Choy, Sky Lee, Larissa Lai and Fred Wah.

'Interculturalism' provides the conceptual framework for Hilf's study, offering as it does a notion of hybrid cultures in a process of dynamic exchange. Hilf begins with a survey of the socio-historical contexts of the Chinese migration to Canada; this survey includes reference to key Chinese American authors and texts, such as the Angel Island Poets or Poets of Exclusion, and the truly intercultural Eaton sisters, who have been claimed by American and Canadian critics alike. Taking her chronological and conceptual survey further, Hilf examines the relatively late production of specifically Chinese Canadian texts ('Breaking the Silence'), starting with the anthology *Inalienable Rice: A Chinese and Japanese Canadian Anthology* [1979], and *Many-Mouthed Birds: Contemporary Writing by Chinese Canadians* [1991]; her study continues with 'intercultural themes' before moving on to 'Life in Chinatown' and 'Fiction as Documentation'. Hilf's work is significant in that it defends Chinese Canadian writing from past critical attacks (for example, arguments concerning the 'quality' of writing in Sky Lee's *Disappearing Moon Café* [1990]), by following more dynamic theoretical reading strategies; as such, Hilf argues that much post-colonial theory is still useful and relevant for exploring Chinese Canadian literature.

Smaro Kamboureli, *Scandalous Bodies*, offers a sophisticated and complex reading of diasporic literature and criticism, placing the two modes of writing in a subtle dialectical relationship. There are five main sections: 'Critical Correspondences: The Diasporic Critic's (Self-)Location', 'Realism and the History of Reality' (with a focus on F.P. Grove's *Settlers of the Marsh*), 'Sedative Politics', 'Ethnic Anthologies', and 'The Body in Joy Kogawa's *Obasan*'. The first section meditates upon an unwritten manifesto for the diasporic critic, and becomes, as Kamboureli suggests, the 'other' to this manifesto through a realization that 'the state of emergency is not the exception but the rule' (derived from Walter Benjamin), and that the critic must remain 'within' history. A reading of Wenders's film *Wings of Desire* enables Kamboureli's project to read Canadian multiculturalism through multiple perspectives that are non-teleological, summarized in the phrase 'negative pedagogy', defined in part as a radical or deconstructive questioning of knowledge. Such a mode of criticism is regarded as ethical, self-reflexive, and open to competing interpretations. Beginning with the case of F.P. Grove and related authors, Kamboureli begins her exploration of ethnicity in Canadian literature; she examines the discursive shifts in the representation of ethnicity during the twentieth century, in relation to the media, law and government in 'Sedative Politics', an examination of sanctioned 'ethnicity' as containment. Competing critical developments and claims for diasporic literatures are examined in 'Ethnic Anthologies' and the book ends with an original reading of *Obasan*, via notions of history as montage and the body as a site of memory. Kamboureli's study remains, at the end, in a state of process: her theoretical framework is constantly interrogated, which allows for an interrelated series of complex readings of diasporic literatures. Two in-depth theoretical studies were produced: Dawn Thompson, *Writing a Politics of Perception*, and Caterina Nella Cotrupi, *Northrop Frye and the Poetics of Process*. Thompson utilizes Euclidean space-time, Foucault's 'counter-memory', Derrida's 'radical memory' and the 'memory theatre' of *ars memoria* to theorize 'political memory', especially in relation to minority subjectivity. Authors covered are: Nicole Brossard, Margaret Atwood, Marlene Nourbese Philips, Beatrice Culleton and Régine Robin. The overall aim is to construct an integrative 'holographic theory of literature' as a way of avoiding the impasses of humanism and competing strategies of identity politics. Basing her notions of identity formation on the work of Judith Butler and Teresa de Lauretis, Thompson argues for performative notions of subjectivity. One of the central metaphors of Canadian literature and criticism—utopia—is reworked in two chapters, first in relation to Brossard's *Picture Theory* and then via a re-reading of Atwood's *Surfacing*. With these chapters, readers experience Thompson's process of synthesizing performativity, semiotics and the 'new science', for example via David Bohm's work. Other tropes and creative processes explored are translation, autobiography, trickster writing and postmodern hyperspace: all function in 'non-linear' ways that can be read through Bohm, Derrida, or holography. Thompson's book is challenging, in part because of its structural playfulness, but also because of its synthesis of contemporary systems of thought from different, but related, domains. Caterina Nella Cotrupi's reading of Canadian critic Northrop Frye is written in a conventional manner compared with Thompson's work, but is similarly intellectually wide-ranging and thought-provoking. Cotrupi's project involves critically recuperating Frye, through a re-reading of the importance of the sublime via Vico. Further, Cotrupi also charts the readings of Frye which emphasize, for example, the open-ended spatial metaphors and 'holistic feedback loop' in the interpenetration of art and science in Frye's work, leading to a notion of 'the criticism of process'. *Northrop Frye and the Poetics of Process*, while primarily examining canonical works, clearly provides solid intellectual ground for critics interested in reassessing Frye's contribution to the study of Canadian literature.

Reassessment and recuperation continue in Veronica Strong-Boag and Carole Gerson, *Paddling Her own Canoe: The Times and Texts of E. Pauline Johnson (Tekahionwake)*. Strong-Boag and Gerson resituate Johnson as a counter-discursive, boundary-crossing and problematizing author and performer, who has been misread and misrepresented by much contemporary criticism. Johnson's life and works are explored via a number of perspectives: in the first chapter, from that of First Nations identity in 'post-Confederation' Canada; in the second chapter in relation to Johnson as a 'New Woman'; in the third and fourth chapters via discussions and analysis of literature and performance; and finally in the fifth chapter in relation to Canadian nationalism and identity. The resulting groundbreaking study employs the notion of a doubled, hybrid subjectivity, one which at times subtly 'talks back' to colonialism and patriarchy, and at other times presents alternative readings of indigenous peoples and their experiences of colonial Canada. An example of the latter given in chapter four is Johnson's 'A Cry from an Indian Wife', published in the periodical *The Week* in 1885; in this text a self-reflexive engagement with hybridity involves both subject and nation, Native and Euro-Canadian perspectives. Strong-Boag and Gerson also provide details of the lesser-known performance texts by Johnson, alongside an important chronological list of Johnson's work and a critical bibliography.

The cultural and literary mapping of Canada continue from two different perspectives: in Danielle Schaub, ed., *Mapping Canadian Cultural Space: Essays on Canadian Literature*, and in Flora (Blizzard) Francis, *A Black Canadian Bibliography*. Schaub argues, in her introduction, that a concern for environment is iconic for the Canadian experience, which has shifted and transformed itself through technological and cultural/ideological development. The collection brings together work on poetry and prose, canonical and counter-canonical writers. Branko Gorjup, 'Continuity and Discontinuity in the Representation of Space in Canadian Writing', opens the collection with an examination of different models of spatiality and representation, first via Aristotelian models and 'non-substantive' spatial representations via Frye, and then through the recoding of spatiality as palimpsestic, multiple traces via the work of Christopher Dewdney and Anne Michaels; analogies between a poetics of asymmetrical or instantaneous representations and the new physics are made. Pauline Butling, 'Poetry and Place: More than Meets the Eye: Daphne Marlatt's *Vancouver Poems* and George Bowering's *Rocky Mountain Foot*', also examines epistemic shifts, from the 1960s language-centred poetics to the development of an anti-imperialist poetics in the 1990s, whereby analysis of discursive practices resists reproducing colonial mastery; Butling argues that Bowering and Marlatt powerfully recuperate the local in this anti-imperialist project. Analogous issues are explored via close reading by Bina Toledo Freiwald, 'Cartographies of Be/longing: Dionne Brand's *In Another Place, Not Here*', where the interplay of exclusions/inclusions belongs to the terrain of being, longing and belonging; Freiwald grounds her argument with the work of Kathleen Kirby (*Indifferent Boundaries: Spatial Concepts of Human Subjectivity*), and her 'five dimensions' of 'the space of the subject': place of birth, space of the body, discursive spaces, psychic space and social space. The immigrant experience is explored by Malashri Lal, in 'Politics of Self-Definition: Mapping Asian-Indians in Canada', and an argument is made for reinscribing the immigrant success story, giving a positive spin to cultural hybridity and multiculturalism. Biljana Romić, 'M.G. Vassanji's *The Book of Secrets* or the Art of Intricate Spatial Interplay', analyses metaphors of spatial design/mapping in the literature and history of colonialism articulated in Vassanji's work. The new critical directions and focus of the collection are utilized in an exemplary reading of Atwood's *Surfacing* in Danielle Schaub, '"I am a place": Internalised Landscape and Female Subjectivity in Margaret Atwood's *Surfacing*'. Schaub shows on the one hand how geographical and subjective space intersect in Atwood's iconic novel, and on the other hand how this is a preoccupation of Canadian literary history, especially as relating to gender production. The focus on Atwood continues with Radha Chakravarty, 'Mothers in Flight: The Space of the Maternal in Margaret Atwood's *Cat's Eye*', arguing that the idealized myth of motherhood is critiqued by Atwood. Dina Haruvi, 'Généalogie et espace féminins: Les Textes de *La Mermour*', produces a feminist reading of a special issue of *La Nouvelle Barre du Jour* (no. 87), while the final chapter, Jade Bar-Schalom and Danielle Schaub, 'The Perfection of the Ruby-Red Sphalerite: Female Territory, Narrative Space and Strategies of Deception in Aretha van Herk's *The Tent Peg*', argues for a new feminist mythology via a close reading of van Herk's novel. The concluding chapter also functions like a manifesto for new critical work based upon the arguments put forward within the collection. Flora (Blizzard) Francis also produces a mapping of subjectivity, although in her case it is through bibliographical research. In her introduction, she sketches briefly the history of black Canadians, beginning with the US slaves who fled to Novia Scotia, working her way up to the 1960 British Commonwealth Immigration Act and the revised Canadian Immigration Act, which transformed immigration for 'skilled' and 'professional' peoples; Francis also details previous bibliographic tools that relate to cultural production in this area, beginning with S.K. Jain's work and ending with the bibliography of George Elliot Clarke. The major part of the book is the new bibliographies, updating extensively previous resources, split into 'Printed Works' and 'Audio and Visual Material' with relevant subject and title indexes. The book is an essential and valuable resource for critics doing research on black Canada.

(b) Fiction

Celebrating Margaret Atwood's sixtieth birthday in 1999, Reingard M. Nischik edits a major collection, *Margaret Atwood: Works and Impact*, with twenty-five chapters (including the introduction), 'statements' on Atwood by 'fellow writers', cartoons 'by and on' Atwood, photographs, and a research bibliography; most of the chapters explore Atwood's fiction. The collection is organized into four sections: 'Life and Status', 'Works', 'Approaches' and 'Creativity—Transmission—Reception'. In her introduction, Nischik contends that the collection has three main purposes: to take stock of, to introduce and to pay tribute to Atwood's work; overall, the collection provides a fine survey, if at times overly descriptive, of Atwood's work and the Atwood industry. Critical approaches vary enormously, for example, Caroline Rosenthal, 'Canonizing Atwood: Her Impact on Teaching in the US, Canada, and Europe', analyses the results of an internationally delivered questionnaire survey, showing in part that for many American readers Atwood's Canadian identity is problematically effaced, while Paul Goetsch, 'Margaret Atwood: A Canadian Nationalist', sticks closely to *Survival* (and related texts) to argue for the *centrality* of Atwood's Canadian identity. Probably the most useful chapters for students are the introductory survey chapters, which take mainly descriptive approaches, raising more complex critical questions for further debate and study. Chapters include all of the material in the 'Works' section: Alice M. Palumbo, 'On the Border: Margaret Atwood's Novels', Charlotte Sturgess, 'Margaret Atwood's Short Fiction', Lothar Hennighausen, 'Margaret Atwood's Poetry 1966–1995', and Walter Pache, '"A certain frivolity": Margaret Atwood's Literary Criticism'. In the 'Approaches' section, two chapters take a specifically literary-critical angle: Coral Ann Howells addresses genre, in 'Transgressing Genre: A Generic Approach to Margaret Atwood's Novels', examining Atwood's challenging of generic boundaries with sections on dystopia, Kunstlerroman, fictive autobiography, Gothic romance, and the historical novel; duplicity, doubling, unreliable narrators and Atwood's female protagonists are analysed by Barbara Hill Rigney, 'Alias Atwood: Narrative Games and Gender Politics'. Thematic chapters also have a critical edge; these include: Paul Goetsch, 'Margaret Atwood: A Canadian Nationalist'; Ronald B. Hatch, 'Margaret Atwood, the Land, and Ecology'; Lorna Irvine, 'Recycling Culture: Kitsch, Camp, and Trash in Margaret Atwood's Fiction'; Sharon R. Wilson, 'Mythological Intertexts in Margaret Atwood's Works'; and Klaus Peter Müller, 'Re-Constructions of Reality in Margaret Atwood's Literature: A Constructionist Approach'. The canonical stature of Atwood and her works is reflected in the genetic criticism utilized by Helmut Reichenbücher, 'Challenging the Reader: An Analysis of Margaret Atwood's Creative Technique in her First Published Novel'. Reichenbücher explores the manuscripts at the Thomas Fisher Library, University of Toronto, enhancing study of Atwood to include the process of textual formation. As Atwood is a canonical author, the various reflections and statements by her editors, interviewers, assistant, friends and peers (concluding with a section of cartoons), shift the book even further into archival territory: the collection becomes an archive of a living Canadian icon.

Malcolm Lowry criticism is considerably enhanced by the publication of Asals and Tiessen, eds., *A Darkness That Murmured: Essays on Malcolm Lowry and the Twentieth Century*, and the special edition of *L'Époque Conradienne* (26[2000]) on *Conrad et Lowry: L'Esthéthique de la fiction*. Asal and Tiessen's collection, mainly based upon papers presented at the International Lowry Symposium in Toronto [1997], is divided into five sections: 'Lowry', '*Volcano*', '*Volcano* and Beyond', 'Lowry and Others', and 'Grace Notes'. Additional published material not available at the symposium opens the collection with 'Three Letters Home' by Lowry, edited by Sherrill Grace. Grace's keynote from the symposium concludes the collection, 'The Play's the Thing: Reading "Lowry" in the Dark Wood of Freud, Cocteau, and Barthes'. The first section of the collection is composed mainly of reflective pieces; the second section analyses *Volcano* with Greig Henderson, '"Destroy the World!" Gnosis and Nihilism in *Under the Volcano*', Pierre Schaeffer, 'Achieving Intensity: Notes on the Dialogic Evolution of *Under the Volcano*', and Martin Bock, 'Genius and Degeneration in *Under the Volcano*'. The complexities of Lowry's modernist and proto-postmodernist writings are explored by Miguel Mota, '"We simply made one up": The Hybrid Text of "Tender Is the Night"', where earlier criticism of the failings of Lowry's 'film script' are taken to task for misreading a powerful dialogic composition. Cynthia Sugers readdresses earlier critical concerns of plagiarism in Lowry in 'Recuperating Authority: Plagiarism as Pastiche?', where she argues that critics are themselves bound to paradoxical conceptual models celebrating postmodern pastiche and openness in Lowry, while also arguing for authorial control and closure. Margaret Soltan, 'From Black Magic to White Noise: Malcolm Lowry and Don DeLillo', examines parallels between two authors who might appear poles apart: she shows how both relate to notions of the real and redemption. Intertextuality is explored in varying ways in Chris Ackerly, 'Malcolm Lowry's Unimaginable Library of the Dead', Mathieu Duplay, 'The Operatic Paradigm: Voice, Sound, and Meaning in Lowry's Fiction', Patrick McCarthy, 'Totality and Fragmentation in Lowry and Joyce', and Dean Irvine, 'A Poetics of Fire: Sharon Thesen's *Confabulations: Poems for Malcolm Lowry*'. Intertextuality is given class and historical inflection by Patrick Deane, '*Ultramarine*, the Class War, and British Travel Writing in the 1930s'.

The special edition of *L'Époque Conradienne*, based upon a symposium at l'Université Lumière-Lyon 2 [1999], organized by J. Paccaud-Huguet and C. Maisonnat, offers a unique body of work on Lowry. The first part deals with the intersection and parallels between Conrad and Lowry, with seven new essays. Richard J. Lane opens the collection with 'Redemption and Horror: Journeys through the Aesthetic of Enlightenment in Conrad and Lowry' (*ECon* 26[2000] 11–19), arguing that postmodernism is the abandonment of the aesthetic in its spiritual and redemptive sense; Martin Bock, 'Secret Sharing: The Talk-Cures of Conrad and Lowry' (*ECon* 26[2000] 21–30), makes some interesting connections between authors and their anxieties concerning 'degeneration' (with reference also to Max Nordau's famous publication, *Degeneration* [1895]); the main Lowry text explicated is the British Columbian 'The Forest Path to the Spring'. Screen metaphors, memory and boundaries are analysed by Annick Droesdal-Levillain, 'Conrad and Lowry's Aesthetics of Fiction: A Ripple, a Riddle' (*ECon* 26[2000]

31–42), while proto-deconstructionist and anti-imperialist discourses are explored by Christine Texier in 'Aesthetic Disavowal of Form as Ethical Disavowal of Ideology' (*ECon* 26[2000] 43–57). The most sustained attempt at synthesizing the aesthetic and ethical dimensions of Lowry's and Conrad's work in the collection is Josiane Paccaud-Huguet, 'Conrad's Spectral Halo and Lowry's Luminous Wheel' (*ECon* 26[2000] 62–81), a Lacanian reading which mediates both authors via Edvard Munch's *The Scream* [1893]. Two papers are close readings of *Heart* and *Volcano*: Catherine Delesalle, '*Heart of Darkness* and *Under the Volcano*: The "whited sepulchre" and the "churrigeresque cathedral"' (*ECon* 26[2000] 83–98), and Sandra G. Kromm, 'Two Faces of Horror: The Quest for Truth in Joseph Conrad's *Heart of Darkness* and Malcolm Lowry's *Under the Volcano*' (*ECon* 26[2000] 99–109). Four papers look at Lowry without detailed reference to Conrad, starting with Sherrill Grace in an examination of early literary production in 'Malcolm Lowry: From the Juvenilia to the *Volcano*' (*ECon* 26[2000] 113–29); Grace argues that Lowry's strategy of writing, a form of 'autobiographics' is developed as early as the juvenilia. Pierre Schaeffer, 'The Ethics of Guilt and the Aesthetics of Borrowing in Malcolm Lowry's Fiction' (*ECon* 26[2000] 131–51), examines the rhetorical borrowing via two words in *Volcano*: *pelado* and *compañeros*. Mathieu Duplay teases out the narrational ambiguities in *Volcano*, 'The Razor's Edge: Brotherhood and Language in *Under the Volcano*' (*ECon* 26[2000] 153–162), while Claude Maisonnat examines delayed decoding in a sophisticated reading, '"Through the Panama": The Missing Text and the Poetics of the Slippage' (*ECon* 26[2000] 163–75).

Finally, the double issue of the *Malcolm Lowry Review* (47–8[2000–1]), includes an important bibliographic update by Norman Amor, 'Supplement No. 2 to *Malcolm Lowry, A Checklist (1994)*' (*MLRev* 47–8[2000–1] 17–44), and nine diverse essays. The motion of *Volcano* is explored by Sandra Kromm, '"Whorl within whorl": Theme and Technique in *Under the Volcano*' (*MLRev* 47–8[2000–1] 45–54); Julianne M. Roe argues that Lowry's short stories need to be treated as stand-alone, fully functional entities, illuminating this sentiment with a Bakhtinian reading in 'Narration in Lowry's "Gin and Goldenrod"' (*MLRev* 47–8[2000–1] 68–80). Contributing to a growing body of scholarship on 'masculinity', Toby K. Stoddart, 'An "erect manly carriage": Masculinity as Performance in Lowry's *Under the Volcano* and *Tender Is the Night*' (*MLRev* 47–8[2000–1] 81–100), shows how Lowry was acutely aware of the constructedness of subjectivity and gender. The Scott Fitzgerald connection continues in Michael Ballin, 'Reward and Punishment: The Cultural Role of the Alcoholic in Budd Schulberg's *The Disenchanted* and Malcolm Lowry's *Under the Volcano*' (*MLRev* 47–8[2000–1] 101–22); responding to the inadequacies of harsh personal and psychoanalytical reactions to alcoholism discussed at the Malcolm Lowry Symposium in Toronto [1997], Schulberg argues for a 'socio/cultural' perspective. Chris Ackerly, 'Troubled Pleasures: The Fiction of J.G. Farrell' (*MLRev* 47–8[2000–1] 123–7), notes that a less well known author influenced by Lowry is undergoing potential revival. Richard J. Lane, 'Cutting *Ultramarine*: Some Thoughts on the Annotated Edition at UBC Special Collections' (*MLRev* 47–8[2000–1] 128–39), performs a deconstructive reading of a recently acquired archival holding at the University of British Columbia: a self-annotated novel by Malcolm Lowry. Jean Shields, 'Lowry's Consul in *Under the Volcano*: Portrait of Conrad Aiken' (*MLRev* 47–8[2000–1] 140–57), reveals the extent to which the *Volcano*'s protagonist is not only based upon but forms a portrait of Aiken. Finally, the issue is completed by Chris Ackerly, 'Pat McCarthy, "Totality and Fragmentation": A Response' (*MLRev* 47–8[2000–1] 158–61), in itself one more textual fragment from the 1997 symposium. Sherrill Grace introduces and transcribes an addition to the Lowry correspondence in *Canadian Literature*, with '"My Dear Anton Myer": A Late Lowry Letter' (*CanL* 165[2000] 11–22), revealing much about Lowry's state of mind and his impact upon other authors. Henrik Gustafsson, 'On the Pastoral Challenge in Lowry's "The Forest Path to the Spring"' (*CanL* 165[2000] 26–41), argues that Lowry does not adopt a pessimistic, deconstructive approach to the modern pastoral, but that he re-engages with it in terms of a dialectic of potential reconciliation; this is an important contribution to work on Lowry and early British Columbian fiction.

Two books on 'forgotten' British Columbian author Bertrand William Sinclair may signify his return to the literary critical scene: Betty C. Keller, *Pender Harbour Cowboy: The Many Lives of Bertrand Sinclair*, and Richard J. Lane, *Literature and Loss: Bertrand William Sinclair's British Columbia*. Keller's study is a critical biography, synthesizing historical research with close readings of Sinclair's key novels, such as *North of Fifty Three* [1914], *Big Timber* [1916], *Poor Man's Rock* [1920] and *The Inverted Pyramid* [1924]. Sinclair's relationship with the environment, in Montana, and then British Columbia, as well as the literary contexts of related BC fiction, such as Martin Allerdale Grainger's *Woodsmen of the West* [1908], are explored by Keller with sensitivity. Keller also shows how west coast cultural connections were maintained through leisure pursuits such as sailing and fishing, bringing together American and Canadian publishers, magazine editors, and all types of authors, in a circuit of friendship and professional exchange, dominated by seasonal movements of peoples. Richard J. Lane brings together previously published essays in one book-length collection; his focus shifts from the archive ('Archive Simulations: Reading the Bertrand Sinclair Collection'), through socio-economic history ('British Columbia's War of Two Worlds: The Birth of the Modern Age in Bertrand Sinclair's Fiction'), British Columbian literature ('Dreams of a Frontier Classic: Inverted Pyramids in the New World'), west coast writing ('"Writing the Coast": Bertrand William Sinclair's BC Stories'), and finally post-colonial readings of Sinclair's work ('Border Crossings: Forgotten Native Voices in Bertrand William Sinclair's Canadian and American Popular Fiction').

Bertrand William Sinclair features, among many other novelists, in Dagmar Novak's *Dubious Glory: The Two World Wars and the Canadian Novel*. Novak argues that the cultural and literary impact of the two world wars on Canadian literature has been insufficiently studied: this point is illuminated in the appendix with its list of sixty-nine Canadian 'war' novels (written between 1915 and 1955). The crusading ideology of early war novels is studied in the first chapter, 'The First World War and the Romance Tradition'; Canadian identity is firmly linked to a sense of Anglo-Saxon culture and values in these works, as well as a sense of moral binaries, light and darkness, good and evil. The connections between ideology and genre are explored, with the generic shift in the second chapter, 'Realism and the War Novel between the Two Wars', indicative of shifts in attitudes to war, and of the fact that novels are being written by those who had experienced it. Novak shows how realism generates new myths, such as the critique and rejection of class hierarchy. The third chapter, 'The Second World War and the Road to Redemption', deals with another shift, this time in content and tone, a 'curious detachment' as Novak observes; novels that deal with severe psychological trauma are considered. The final major chapter before the conclusion, 'Timothy Findley and the Return to the Great War', is indicative of the importance of this single Canadian novel for the genre as a whole; the backdrop of more contemporary warfare and protest, such as Vietnam, is paralleled with the older forms of trench warfare. Novak situates *The Wars* [1977] as a major text within the genre, and one that has a self-reflexive protagonist who goes beyond generic limitations in an attempt to comprehend the entire warfare experience. The conclusion examines the contradictory closeness and distance between Canadians and war, as well as the aesthetic response through the war novel genre.

From a completely different theoretical perspective, Eva Darias-Beautell's *Contemporary Theories and Canadian Fiction*, is a post-structuralist account of Canadian literature in English. The book is heavily weighted towards extensive introductory passages aimed at explicating, at an extremely basic level, by now overly familiar theoretical issues and debates. When the fiction does finally make an appearance, it is used in the most general sense as 'exemplifying' a theoretical point as a whole; in other words, there is virtually no textual analysis, and novel titles are used as synecdoches, whereby a part stands in for the whole. What little textual analysis is provided is cursory and banal. The text as a whole attempts to cover too much literary and critical territory, failing to do justice to any of the material under analysis.

Asian Canadian literature is the subject of two papers: an overview account and a close textual reading in *Essays on Canadian Writing*. Donald C. Goellnicht, 'A Long Labour: The Protracted Birth of Asian Canadian Literature' (*ECW* 72[2000] 1–41), presents an extensive, comprehensive account of the rise of academic interest in Asian Canadian literature. Beginning with a critical survey of key conference and journal papers on the subject, Goellnicht argues that the institutional history of Asian Canada as an 'always emerging subject' can give access to the 'full implications' of the term itself. Goellnicht compares in detail the ideological differences between American and Canadian Asian literatures and their study/ usages, as well as the rise of different critical and cultural fields within Canada; the strategic usages of Asian Canadian literature are debated in the conclusion. The paper provides useful footnotes and an extensive bibliography. Teresa Zackodnik, 'Suggestive Voices from "the Storeroom of the Past": Photography in Denise Chong's *The Concubine's Children*' (*ECW* 72[2000] 49–78), examines performativity in relation to family history, life-writing and photography, as well as polyvocal narrative structures.

Resisting post-colonial paradigms and readings, Douglas Cole, 'The Invented Indian/the Imagined Emily' (*BCS* 125–6[2000] 147–62), argues that Carr's *Klee Wyck* [1941] is a form of life-writing that does encode First Nations peoples in a state of present or contemporary activity, not simply one of nostalgic loss and ongoing destruction as has been argued elsewhere. Atwood's *Surfacing* and *Survival* continue to hold immense appeal: Alice Ridout, 'Temporality and Margaret Atwood' (*UTQ* 69:iv[2000] 849–70), examines two main phases of temporality in Atwood's work, an early phase of linear time, where 'survival' involves managing predictable 'life scripts', and a later phase where Atwood's protagonists enter a revisionary mode of being, rewriting/retelling survival stories in an analeptic and proleptic movement with an apocalyptic notion of temporality. Shuli Barzilai, 'Who Is He? The Missing Persons Behind the Pronoun in Atwood's *Surfacing*' (*CanL* 164[2000] 57–79), performs a Freudian and Lacanian analysis of missing 'male antecedents' in Atwood's novel. The short-story genre is examined by Ed Kleiman, '"If one green bottle ...": Audrey Thomas Looks Back on the Cauldron of History' (*UTQ* 69:iii[2000] 660–9), in relation to Thomas's seminal story that first appeared in *Atlantic Monthly* [1965]; Kleiman theorizes the significance of this story in terms of collage and the kaleidoscopic multi-perspective focus which informs Thomas's later writing.

Papers in the Fall issue of *University of Toronto Quarterly* continue to examine the short-story genre: first, Michael Trussler, 'The Short Story as Miniature: Barry Callaghan's "The Black Queen" (*UTQ* 69:iv[2000] 749–63), and Gloria Sawai's 'The Day I Sat with Jesus on the Sundeck and a Wind Came Up and Blew my Kimono Open and He Saw My Breasts' (*UTQ* 69:iv[2000] 749–63). Trussler begins with Dilthey's notion of the part, or 'impression-point', making sense of the whole, arguing for a hermeneutic approach to the short-story form, going on to advance a Leibnizian monodology via Adorno's *Aesthetic Theory* [1970], whereby Trussler argues that the incommensurate elements of the 'larger world' are condensed in the short story; the stories are thus analysed as 'miniatures', or complete worlds that also strive beyond themselves. Marjorie Garson, 'Alice Munro and Charlotte Brontë' (*UTQ* 69:iv[2000] 783–825), examines the influence of *Jane Eyre* on Munro, particularly in the short story 'Heirs of the Living Body'; she argues for a series of parallels, i.e. narratives 'punctuated by epiphanies of extrication', that drive the protagonists forward into new situations; overall, this is a mapping of 'points of contact' between the fiction of Munro and Brontë. Claire Wilkshire, '"Voice is everything": Reading Mavis Gallant's "The Pegnitz Junction" (*UTQ* 69:iv[2000] 891–916), discusses manipulation of voice and point of view in relation to polyphonics and generic fluidity; the minimal importance of plot leads to the foregrounding of other narrative elements in the short story, and in this case, a complex self-reflexivity.

Lucas Tromly, 'Sabotaging Utopia: Politics and the Artist in A.M. Klein's *The Bells of Sobor Spasitula*' (*CanL* 164[2000] 36–54), reads Klein's short story as a subtle critique of Jewish diasporic existence after the formation of Israel. Adorno's famous statement on poetry after Auschwitz informs Méira Cook's study of the testimony form, in 'At the Membrane of Language and Silence: Metaphor and Memory in *Fugitive Pieces*' (*CanL* 164[2000] 12–33). Cook argues that *Fugitive Pieces* can be read as a response to Adorno's implicit challenge, and that the novel explores strategies for representing the ineffable, although the focus is on the problematic conflation throughout of the discourses of testimony and romance, and the complexities of memory. Two trilogies by Davies are explored in *Canadian Literature*: Klaus P. Stich, 'The Grail is a *Rum Thing*: Robertson Davies's Cornish Trilogy' (*CanL* 164[2000] 116–35), explores the importance of the Grail mythology, while David Lucking, 'A Will and Two Ways: The Ambivalence of Evil in Robertson Davies's *The Deptford Trilogy*' (*CanL* 165[2000] 44–56), argues for a systematic theology in Davies's work.

Relatively canonical Canadian fiction receives comprehensive critical attention. Stephen Ross, 'Authenticity and its Discontents: *The Mountain and the Valley*' (*CanL* 165[2000] 59–75), utilizes Benjamin's imminent criticism to argue that the novel is partly about 'its own creation'. Ondaatje's most famous novel is addressed by Tom Penner, 'Four Characters in Search of an Author-Function: Foucault, Ondaatje, and the "Eternally Dying" Author in *The English Patient*' (*CanL* 165[2000] 78–93), via a reading of the narratological problematic of an anonymous or absent 'narrative creator'. S. Leigh Matthews, 'The New World Gaze: Disguising "the eye of power" in John Richardson's *Wacousta*' (*ECW* 70[2000] 135–61), also turns to Foucault's work to analyse the 'imperial gaze' via metaphors of the panopticon and the view from the military garrison. Catherine Higginson, 'The Raced Female Body and the Discourse of *Peuplement* in Rudy Wiebe's *The Temptations of Big Bear* and *The Scorched Wood People*' (*ECW* 72[2000] 172–90), utilizes a number of theories, including Foucault's notion of *peuplement*, to interrogate the representation and construction of female identity in Wiebe's historiographic metafictions. David Jefferess re-reads Findley, 'A Pacific (Re)Reading of Timothy Findley's *Not Wanted on the Voyage*' (*ECW* 72[2000] 138–57), and draws on peace studies to engage in the rarely studied positive aspects of Findley's novel, such as 'magic', 'courage' and 'love'. Fittingly, these theoretical and at times Foucauldian re-readings of canonical Canadian authors are followed in *ECW* by an analytical overview essay which readdresses Northrop Frye's infamous question; Barbara Godard, 'Notes from the Cultural Field: Canadian Literature from Identity to Hybridity' (*ECW* 72[2000] 209–47), studies the 'transformation' between the 1950s and 1990s, of the Canadian literary field, the shift from discourses of nationalism to those of global capitalism. Godard re-theorizes Frye's 'Where is here?' via Benveniste, Deleuze, Guattari and Bourdieu, among others, to tease out the dialectic between 'the literary' and the 'Canadian' in Frye's work, as well as his resistance to post-colonial literatures, and promotion of a Eurocentric canon and values; institutional responses to cultural value and change are surveyed and analysed. Looking at contemporary theories of literature, such as Canadian postmodernism, post-nationalism, or 'queer theory', Godard comments on the ways in which notions of the nation are reconfigured by multiple identity claims; the role of the global market is examined, and brief analyses of key contemporary critical texts are provided. Postmodern culture and Canada's 'Generation X-ers' are the subject of Douglas Coupland's novels, revisited in relation to the sublime in Robert McGill, 'The Sublime Simulacrum: Vancouver in Douglas Coupland's Geography of Apocalypse' (*ECW* 70[2000] 252–76). McGill examines the generic play of *Girlfriend in a Coma* [1998], in particular the shift into the conventions of apocalyptic writing; his analysis covers contemporary west coast concerns, situating *Girlfriend* in the contradictory media space of postmodern Vancouver, one that morphs into 'anyplace' while also being, contradictorily, rooted in the Pacific Northwest. McGill's is an important addition to the study of utopia in Canadian literature, arguing that the category of the 'sublime' escapes the hyperreality of the simulacrum.

(c) Poetry and Drama

Canadian Literature (166[2000]) published a special issue on 'Women and Poetry' with six papers and an interview, Anne Compton, 'Ascension: Liliane Welch Talks about Poetry' (*CanL* 166[2000] 127–41), as well as an in-depth introduction by Kevin McNeilly, 'Home Economics' (*CanL* 166[2000] 5–16). Ian Rae, '"Dazzling Hybrids": The Poetry of Anne Carson' (*CanL* 166[2000] 17–41), explores the literary and cultural frameworks of 'myth, genre, and gender' in Carson's *Autobiography of Red: A Novel in Verse* [1998] examining, not just the fluidity of aesthetics and identity, but also the importance of understanding the 'mock-academic apparatus' that frames her text. Christine Wiesenthal, 'Taking Pictures with Stephanie Bolster' (*CanL* 166[2000] 44–60), analyses the founding operation of 'ekphrasis', or the relation of visual arts to poetics. Sara Jamieson, '"Now that I am dead": P.K. Page and the Self-Elegy' (*CanL* 166[2000] 63–82), contextualizes the tradition of the self-elegy, suggesting ways in which the subject of death is formally foregrounded in Page's poetry through this increasingly important mode of personal and poetic expression; the shift in Page's aesthetic from 'social protest poetry' to introspective and self-reflexive texts is the literary focus of the paper. Méira Cook, 'Bone Memory: Transcribing Voice in Louise Bernice Half's *Blue Marrow*' (*CanL* 166[2000] 85–110), reads the mediation of orality and writing in relation to the graphic surface of Halfe's texts; the strategic recuperation of the performative is explored. Multiple, non-synthesized identities are explored by Richard Sanger, 'High Seas: Elizabeth Bishop Returns Home' (*CanL* 166[2000] 113–23), while Janice Fiameno, '"A last time for this also": Margaret Atwood's Texts of Mourning' (*CanL* 166[2000] 145–64), looks at one of Atwood's most popular recent collections of poems, *Morning in the Burned House* [1995]. Fiameno argues that, rather than simply marking a 'new departure' for Atwood, these poems are part of an ongoing exploration of elegy in her work; the 'paradoxes of memory' and the elegiac mode are analysed across a wide range of Atwood's poetry and prose. The lack of critical works on the collaborations between Betsy Warland and Marlatt is addressed in the first of five papers on poetry in *ECW* 70; Susan Billingham, 'Changing the Subject in Daphne Marlatt and Betsy Warland's *Double Negative*' (*ECW* 70[2000] 1–27), shows how the paradoxes in *Double Negative* [1988], between a marked 1980s feminist/postmodernist decentring of subject-grounding and the co-production and assertion of lesbian subjectivity, exemplify the aesthetic and critical territory of contemporary identity politics today. Lianne Moyes, 'Nothing Sacred: Nicole Brossard's *Baroque at Dawn* at the Limits of Lesbian Feminist Discourses of Sexuality' (*ECW* 70[2000] 28–63), reveals how the overdetermined historical and conceptual term 'baroque' functions across a number of Brossard's texts, becoming, significantly, the structuring principle of 'an erotics of incongruity'. Marie Carrière, 'Erin Mouré and the Spirit of Intersubjectivity' (*ECW* 70[2000] 64–80), questions the sustainability of a relational ethics. Jason Wiens, '"Language seemed to split in two": National Ambivalence(s) and Dionne Brand's "No language is neutral"' (*ECW* 70[2000] 81–102), utilizes Bhabha's and Bruce Robbins's work to theorize Brand's work as framed by 'discrepant cosmopolitanisms'. Mark Silverberg, 'The Can(adi)onization of Al Purdy' (*ECW* 70[2000] 226–51), argues that the juncture of canonization and 'Canadianization' in the recognition of Purdy's work simultaneously blinds the reader to the more radical aspects of sexuality and textuality that function in his poems.

A little-studied play by Klein is the subject of Feisal G. Mohamed's 'Pan-Semitism in A.M. Klein's "The Three Judgements"' (*ECW* 72[2000] 93–108); Mohamed argues that, once contextualized in relation to the intertextual sources, the play can be read as one of harmony and religious tolerance. Breaking significant new ground, *Canadian Theatre Review* 101[2000] is on 'Staging the Pacific Province', edited by Reid Gilbert. The issue brought together papers from the first

British Columbia Theatre conference, held at the University College of the Cariboo in Kamloops, BC [1999]. Richard J. Lane, 'Passing the Province, or, the Tyrannical Prehension: Theoretical Readings of BC Theatre' (*CTR* 101[2000] 3–6), theorizes 'displacement' and 'fracturing' as constitutive structures of BC theatre, while Céleste Derksen, 'BC Oddities: Interpellation and/in Joan MacLeod's *The Hope Slide*' (*CTR* 101[2000] 49–52), utilizes the Althusserian process of interpellation to hail and/or identify the province's constructions of aesthetics via the ideology of place. Both Lane and Derksen are mapping, via theoretical models mimetic of place, what Derksen calls BC's 'ideological matrix'. Two historical analyses of note are Patrick O'Neill's 'The Royal Engineers, 1858—1863: Theatrical Entertainment for and by the Enlisted Men' (*CTR* 101[2000] 11–14) and Malcolm Page's 'The Growth of Professional Theatre in Vancouver, 1963–1999' (*CTR* 101[2000] 15–18); O'Neill works within the BC critical field of analysis of the disciplinary nature of colonial society, while Page discusses the genealogy and complexities of Vancouver's theatre expansion. Sherrill Grace, 'Staging "North" in BC: Two Cariboo Gold Rush Plays' (*CTR* 101[2000] 19–24), articulates the confluence of theatre and history in the 'discursive formation of the North'. More contemporary history, that of the publishing trade, is the subject of Ginny Ratsoy's 'Dramatic Discourse at Talonbooks: Narratives on the Publisher–Author Relationship' (*CTR* 101[2000] 25–8); Ratsoy argues that exploration of the 'writer–publisher relationship' is key to an understanding of creative expression within the complex intersection or conjunction of writing, editing, production and publication. Nicole Preston, 'Theatre for Life: Public Ritual and Public Dreams in Vancouver' (*CTR* 101[2000] 29–34), argues that popular theatre engenders a sense of community, celebration and ritual, otherwise lost from many facets of modern life. 'Outdoor' theatre is the subject of Richard Bruce Kirkley's study, 'Caravan Farm Theatre: Orchestrated Anarchy and the Creative Process' (*CTR* 101[2000] 35–9), an exploration and explanation of 'anarchic' communities and the parallels between anarchism and creativity embodied by the workings of Caravan Farm Theatre. Marc Maufort, 'Redrawing the Boundaries of Poetic Realism in Margaret Hollingsworth's Drama' (*CTR* 101[2000] 40–3), performs a close reading of a key BC dramatist; he argues that Hollingsworth's BC drama extends the boundaries of 'traditional dramatic realism'. Another important popular element of BC drama is studied in Graham Forst, '"When my cue comes, call me": Christopher Gaze—Vancouver's Bard on the Beach' (*CTR* 101[2000] 53–5). Finally, Edward Little, 'Cultural Democracy in the Enderby and District Community Play' (*CTR* 101[2000] 56–8), gives an insider's view of community theatrical production. The issue also contains an interview, Barbara Drennan in conversation with Lois Phillips, 'WhoS: A Night at the Pen' (*CTR* 101[2000] 44–8), and the script of a major new BC play by Marie Clements, 'The Unnatural and Accidental Women' (*CTR* 101[2000] 59–88).

The spring issue of *CTR* (102[2000]) presents 'Theatre and Translation', edited by Hélène Beauchamp and Ric Knowles. Bernard Lavoie, 'Theatre in Translation in Montreal: Respecting the Playwright, Challenging the Audience' (*CTR* 102[2000] 5–10), charts the 'collective identification' in the theatrical experience, which leads in part to a need for Québécois versions of 'foreign' plays, in touch with local Canadian and 'North American' culture; the issue of subsequent retranslation is also touched upon. Jöel Beddows, 'Translations and Adaptations in Francophone Canada' (*CTR* 102[2000] 11–14), argues that modern translation tools have changed the problematic process that in the recent past led to adaptations or 'tradaptations'. Jeanne Klein, 'Translating Metaphors from Québec to Kansas' (*CTR* 102[2000] 15–19), looks at the resistance to 'US norms of realism' in Québécois children's theatre and her own attempts at transposition. Ellen Mackay, 'Auditioning for the Role of a Lifetime: Performing Self-Translation at the American Immigration and Naturalization Service' (*CTR* 102[2000] 20–4), performs a self-reflexive analysis of Canadian 'mimicry' of the US, via the naturalization test or process. Jacob Wren, 'Mistranslation, Bad Faith and Even Worse: *En français comme en anglais*' (*CTR* 102[2000] 25–7), is a meditation upon failure and its creative possibilities in theatre. Aurèle Parisien, 'Taking a Walker on the French Side' (*CTR* 102[2000] 28–32), compares successful English and French productions of the same play by George F. Walker. Julie Byczynski, '"A word in a foreign language": On *Not* Translating in the Theatre' (*CTR* 102[2000] 33–7), examines the important issue in relation to immigrant theatre, of utilizing foreign words in theatrical productions; Bycznski theorizes minority languages via de Certeau. Don Druick, 'The Tender Translations of Tadoussac' (*CTR* 102[2000] 38–40), meditates upon translation theory and practice. Finally, Hélène Beauchamp and Ric Knowles interview Linda Gaboriau, 'A Servant of Two Masters: An Interview with Linda Gaboriau' (*CTR* 102[2000] 41–7), and the playscript translated by Gaboriau for the issue is by Michel Marc Bouchard, 'Down Dangerous Passes Road (Le Chemin des passes-dangereuses)' (*CTR* 102[2000] 48–71).

A particularly dynamic and contemporary issue of *CTR* (103[2000]) on 'Zine Theatre: Raves, Parties and Streets' is edited by Alan Filewood and Sarah Martyn; the editors argue, in 'Zine Theatre' (*CTR* 103[2000] 3–4), that 'zine' is a term that describes not just 'alternative' performativities, but also strategic resistances to institutional commodification and normative boundaries. Rebecca Brown, 'A Ghost Group Manifesto' (*CTR* 103[2000] 5–7), looks at popular theatrical or performance venues to ask what it is that they provide that is lacking in 'formal theatre'; she also discusses the role of narrative in rave events. Beverly May, 'Participatory Theatre: The Experiential Construct of House and Techno Music Events' (*CTR* 103[2000] 8–13), provides a mini-history of music events and a personal account of the *mise-en-scène* or intricacies of event construction. The ontological experience of rave culture is narrated in poetic mode by Rebecca Barnstaple, 'Open the House' (*CTR* 103[2000] 14–23), while more formal 'rave theatre' is explored by Sam Stedman, 'Craving That Honesty: An Interview with Chad Dembski' (*CTR* 103[2000] 24–7). Ethnic, drag-based performative boundary-crossing is compared with contemporary mainstream theatrical attempts, in Sky Gilbert's 'Steal Well: Racial and Ethnic Diversity in the Club Queen World' (*CTR* 103[2000] 28–31), while 'psychic' performances are explored by Stephen Johnson, 'Making it Easy to Believe: A Tourist Goes to the Psychic Fair' (*CTR* 103[2000] 32–7). Theatre on the move is the subject of Andrew Houston's '*Nights in this City*: Mapping the Sublime in Lloydminster ... by Bus, by Night' (*CTR* 103[2000] 38–41), a description of an alternative-style production literally held on a touring bus. Silvija Jestrovic, 'Theatricalizing Politics/Politicizing Theatre' (*CTR* 103[2000] 42–6), examines street protest, and the merging of the political and the theatrical in a process called 'semiotization'. Michael Wex, 'Taking Revenge on Wagner' (*CTR* 103[2000] 47–9), utilizes comedy to talk about mistranslation and underfunded cross-cultural performance. This discussion is followed by his playscript, 'I Just Wanna Jewify:

The Yiddish Revenge on Wagner' (*CTR* 103[2000] 50–9). An extremely innovative cluster of texts manages to reproduce on the page some of the eclecticism, diversity, creativity and above all commitment of 'alternative' theatre: David Diamond's 'The Squeegee Report' (*CTR* 103[2000] 60–9), the Headlines Theatre script of 'Squeegee: An Interactive Theatre Event' (*CTR* 103[2000] 70–8), and the follow-up by Rina Zweig, 'Legal Advocate's Report on the Findings of the Squeegee Project, 9 June 1999' (*CTR* 103[2000] 79–82). Diamond explores the ways in which theatre can emerge from the community, as well as its potential to feed back into ethical and legal discourses, as witnessed by Zweig's 'official' report produced after the core theatrical event, composed of collective performers from Vancouver's streets.

The final *CTR* issue of the year (104[2000]), edited by Maria DiCenzo, covers 'Italian Canadian Theatre'. A crucial research tool that the issue provides for research in immigrant literatures is Rosa Fracassa's 'A Selected Chronology of Italian Canadian Theatre in Toronto from 1950 to the Present' (*CTR* 104[2000] 45–7). Articles include Catherine Graham, 'Laughing Blues: Charly Chiarelli's *Cu'Fu?*' (*CTR* 104[2000] 7–9), which examines the movements between two cultures that hold communal significance and audience fascination. Joseph Pivato, 'Five-Fold Translation in the Theatre of Marco Micone' (*CTR* 104[2000] 11–15), rejects binary models in his study of Italian immigrant theatre on stage in the French theatres of Montreal. The acting and writing life is examined by Gregory J. Reid in 'The Worlds Within Worlds of Vittoria Rossi' (*CTR* 104[2000] 16–23), while liberating drama is the subject of Natalie Rewa's '*Le Madonne Feministe*: Italian Canadian Women Playwrights' (*CTR* 104[2000] 24–8). The 'secret stories of women' are translated in Laura Astwood, 'The Private Becoming Public' (*CTR* 104[2000] 29–32), and in the stage production of a piece of journalism in Frank Canino, 'Seven Drafts … Five Years … and Other Useless Data' (*CTR* 104[2000] 33–7). The creative process is analysed and recounted by Alec Stockwell, '*La Storia Recondita*' (*CTR* 104[2000] 38–41), and the pragmatics of theatre production amplified in Mark Ceolin, 'Funding Agencies for Italian Canadian Theatre Projects' (*CTR* 104[2000] 42–4). A trilogy of texts explore the play *A Modo Suo (A Fable)* [1990]: Anna Migliarisi, '*A Modo Suo (A Fable)*: A Production History' (*CTR* 104[2000] 48–51), Anna Migliarisi, 'Cursing in Calabrian: A Brief Interview with Antonino Mazza' (*CTR* 104[2000] 52–3), and '*A Modo Suo (A Fable)*' (*CTR* 104[2000] 54–87). The 'Carte Blanche' sections of *CTR* include multiple new perspectives on theatre: David Burgess, 'Intensive Summer: The Spirit of One Yellow Rabbit Multiplies' (*CTR* 101[2000] 89–92), is an exploration of a multi-skilled performance 'lab'; Denyse Lynde, 'Wonderbolt!' (*CTR* 102[2000] 69–71), looks at theatre and circus; Savannah Walling, 'C'era una volta in montagna … Once Upon a Time in the Mountains' (*CTR* 104[2000] 88–92), writes about theatrical collaboration; Kathleen Foreman and John Poulsen, 'Transforming Traditions: *Commedia dell'Arte* and masQuirx (Contemporary Mask Performance)' (*CTR* 104[2000] 93–7), explains the backgrounds and traditions behind a contemporary theatrical collective. The combined issues of *Canadian Theatre Review* manifest genuinely original humanities research and a keen awareness of the creative potential of literary and cultural hybridity.

4. The Caribbean

(a) General, Dissertations

Many new Anglophone Caribbean authors have published their novels either independently, or with small publishing companies who marginally advertise their works. Naturally, the major Caribbean writers are well known and well published. The works of Walcott, Brathwaite, Bennett, and Naipaul have been read, digested, discussed; and more trees have been chopped down to make way for the spate of dissertations that have been written in order to discuss and dissect more fully the *Weltanschauungen* of these sage pundits of the Caribbean. Unfortunately, the newer, perhaps struggling, writers continue their journey: unheralded, untolled, and unknown. However, let's begin with the writers of dissertations for the year 2000, who have examined the works of Caribbean authors, for they reify the universality of literature and scholarship in the region. Leah Reade Rosenberg, for example, in the abstract of her dissertation 'Creolizing Womanhood: Gender and Domesticity in Early Anglophone Caribbean National Literatures', discusses the treatment of womanhood, and its relationship to colonialism, nationalism, and Creole culture. She maintains that English fiction and history writers from the eighteenth century into the twentieth century 'employed representations of women and the ideology of domesticity to legitimate English domination in the Caribbean by contrasting England's chaste women, independent men, and Christian marriages with the Caribbean's promiscuous women, dependent men, and unholy unions'. Much of the material in the abstract seems either confusing or controversial, and would suggest that the dissertation lacks clarity as well as an empirical knowledge of the subject matter. Rosenberg does fire a broadside at the reader when she argues that 'protonationalist writers must be more fully included in the Anglophone Caribbean literary cannon [*sic*]'.

In her dissertation, 'Performing Subversion: A Comparative Study of Caribbean Women Playwrights (Luisa Carpetillo, Una Marson, Maryse Condé)', Ana M. Echevarría considers gender, class, and race in the plays of Luisa Carpetillo (Puerto Rico), Una Marson (Jamaica), and Maryse Condé (Guadeloupe). Echevarría argues that the playwrights 'are presented as "foremothers" that open up the space for contemporary women's drama in the region', but in the third chapter of her dissertation, she discusses a 1938 unpublished manuscript of a play by Una Marson. While Echevarría discusses race, class, and gender, Renee Therese Schatteman discusses postmodernism and its relationship to post-colonialism in her dissertation 'Caryl Phillips, J.M. Coetzee, and Michael Ondaatje: Writing at the Intersection of the Postmodern and the Postcolonial'.

What seems to be a more pragmatic and less ethereal dissertation is Miranda Meredith Gadsby's 'Little Salt Won't Kill You: Caribbean Women Writers, Migration, and the Politics of Survival'. Gadsby uses her own experiences in her discussion of the role of migration and its relationship to imperialism and the African diaspora. She defines 'sucking salt' (in Jamaica, we say 'sucking sour orange') as 'the linguistic manifestation of the will to overcome adversity, take stock of the situation, and rebuild'. Gadsby further contends that the expression is used as 'an organizational metaphor with which to examine the ways in which Caribbean women construct and reconstruct communities and parallel worlds in migration within the context of my own family history'. With good proof-reading to eliminate the spelling errors, a publisher should be interested in her work.

(b) Literary Criticism

Gina Wisker's *Post-Colonial and African-American Women's Writing: A Critical Introduction* includes a chapter called 'Caribbean Women's Writing'. Her book considers the manifold definitions of post-colonialism and the 'critical questions' that surround the word. Wisker tries her hand at defining colonialism, imperialism, and post-colonialism in her introduction; and she deals with post-colonialism by quoting a number of authors who explore the socioeconomic history of post-colonialism rather than its definition and placement in the literary canon. Her book has a thirty-two-page introduction, and her chapter on 'Caribbean Women's Writing' takes up thirty-five pages.

John Gilmore seems to have the same penchant for long introductions. In his book, *The Poetics of Empire: A Study of James Grainger's 'The Sugar-Cane'*, we are introduced to an eighty-five-page introduction, with notes, about a poem that was written in 1764 in what was called a West Indian georgic. 'By calling "The Sugar-Cane" a georgic', says Gilmore, 'Grainger is explicitly aligning himself with this tradition.' Gilmore further maintains that the poem 'is both a major work in the English georgic tradition, and a major work in the early history of Caribbean literature. Fortunately, Gilmore admits that some of the critics of the time considered 'The Sugar Cane' to be 'bad verse'. Although this text might appeal to someone interested in studying minor eighteenth-century poets, it would be difficult to determine its relevance to the twenty-first century—at a time when writers of Caribbean literature are attempting to relocate themselves from the periphery of what was considered meaningful literature, to a place of central importance. I suspect that the lengthy introduction to the poem is to assist the reader in understanding the complexity of the work, and Grainger's attempt to impose a European model on a Caribbean reality, while imposing a Caribbean reality on Europe. Gilmore suggests that this reciprocal influence was unusual for its time, thus indicating the historical value of the poem. In terms of literary value, there is always significance in reviewing key historical pieces of the literary canon. However, it does not offer redemption for writers of critical literature who represent oppressive systems.

Haitian-born Myriam J.A. Chancy, in her book, *Searching for Safe Spaces: Afro-Caribbean Women Writers in Exile*, focuses on the writings of 'Afro-Caribbean women writers in the context of their exile from home islands'. She, too, considers the themes of race, class, and gender in the works of a host of Caribbean women writers living (or having lived) abroad: Joan Riley, Beryl Gilroy, Makeda Silvera, M. Nourbase Philip, Dionne Brand, Audre Lorde, Michelle Cliff, Rosa Guy, and Marie Chauvet. These women are the Calibans in exile to which Margaret Joseph refers in her *Caliban in Exile: The Outsider in Caribbean Fiction* [1992]. Chancy writes: 'All these writers articulate, from differing geographics of exile, strategies of resistance against imperialist, neocolonial, and patriarchal ideological and social structures, which actively suppress, oppress, marginalize, and silence Afro-Caribbean women and women of color globally.'

Patrick Colm Hogan's *Colonialism and Cultural Identity: Crises of Tradition in the Anglophone Literatures of India, Africa, and the Caribbean* contributes to literature and to the concerns of social justice by examining the ways in which cultural identity exists in the context of post-colonization literature. He differentiates between post-colonization and post-colonial literature by suggesting that literature written and studied prior to colonial independence is post-colonization literature. This type of perceptive analysis becomes clear as he examines cultural identity through the works of several Anglophone writers: Derek Walcott's *Dream on Monkey Mountain*, Jean Rhys's *Wide Sargasso Sea*, Chinua Achebe's *Things Fall Apart*, Earl Lovelace's *The Wine of Astonishment*, Buchi Emecheta's *The Joys of Motherhood*, and Attia Hosain's *Sunlight on a Broken Column*.

Hogan also attempts to analyse cultural identity by pulling apart and reconfiguring aspects of racial and gender identity in a way that is clear to the reader. He looks at the development of cultural identity, the complex problems that arise from this development, and the varied constructive and destructive responses to cultural identity in the context of colonialism. He suggests that, in order to understand the various cultures, it is crucial to understand the treatment of gender in post-colonization literature. He reflects on literature that gives attention to the social construction of gender—particularly womanhood—in Anglophone literature. Finally, Hogan offers suggestions for a different level of amelioration. He considers economic empowerment and what he calls social universalism and democratic socialism. Hogan's book includes a glossary that helps the reader to define some of the terminology emanating from his theoretical viewpoint.

(c) Journal of Caribbean Studies

This year's *JCSt* has many interesting and stimulating articles worthy of note. One, 'A Minority within a Minority: West Indian American Response to Race and Ethnicity in New York City, 1900–1965' (*JCSt* 14:iii[2000] 199–214), by Joyce Toney, discusses the West Indian experience in New York City between 1900 and 1965. She states that West Indians immigrated to New York at a time when their literacy rates were greater than those of white immigrants. They came from a more complex colour/class system, and were shocked at the simplistic black/white polarization in America. They had become a minority within a minority group. In an effort to exclude themselves from the subordinate identity and status relegated to blacks by white Americans, the West Indians connected to each other by establishing social clubs and benevolent societies named after their countries, and participated in simulated British rituals, primarily as a way to maintain and identify with their British heritage, as well as to establish a level of social support and interaction. Equally important to ethnic cohesiveness is the protection against racism as well as against classification in an inferior category due to skin colour. West Indians, therefore, as a group supported black politicians, but maintained a distance from black Americans on a social and individual level because of racism and the subordinate status relegated to black Americans by white Americans.

Seodial Deena's 'Colonization and Canonization: Class Marginalization through Education' (*JCSt* 14:iii[2000] 229–42) maintains that the mainstream literary canon supports and reinforces colonialism, in an institutionalized form. He makes use of several examples to support his theory. He also argues that while 'Third World literature' is on the periphery, writers of Third World literature represent an unheard, powerless voice. He contends that literature will remain parochial and obsolete if the new voices are marginalized through education.

Assimina Karavanta's 'Against the Idea of (W)holeness: Jacqueline Manicom's *Mon examen de blanc* and Myriam Warner-Vierya's *Juletane*' (*JCSt* 14:iii[2000] 243–65) makes use of Manicom's and Warner-Vierya's novels to describe French Caribbean women's redefinition and rebirth, as well as the dynamic process of reshaping identity and, therefore, space within the French Caribbean. She refers to Fanon, who discusses the depreciation of blackness, yet fails to talk about the marginalization of women. Karavanta argues that Manicom and Warner-Vierya blur the boundary between literature and theory since questions and assumptions are constantly made through their writing. She describes thus the aims of her study: 'I want to propose a different reading of two French/Caribbean writers namely Jacqueline Manicom and Myriam Warner-Vierya. I focus on their novels, *Mon examen de blanc* and *Juletane* respectively, to explore the different narrative techniques they employ in order to claim space for their heroines as well as for their own distinct voices. I regard French Caribbean women's writing as "literature in the process of unfolding".' Also in *JCSt* (14:iii[2000] 165–80) is an article by Peter Szok: 'The Hanseatic Republic: Panamanian Nationalism in the Nineteenth Century', which traces the interesting history of Panama before 1903. Colón, Panama, was a diverse city, with West Indians, Latin Americans, Chinese, Jews, Germans, Spaniards, and Italians. For years Panama was called the 'Isthmus of Jamaica' by Panamanian sociologist Alfredo Figueroa Navarro, primarily because of the people from British Jamaica who were all involved in European commerce.

(d) Websites

Several websites, now available, contribute to the wealth of literary material coming out of the Caribbean. These sites are constantly being upgraded as new writers, novelists, and poets appear. Many universities with Caribbean Studies courses, or with Caribbean Studies programmes, have websites for distance-learning students or researchers. Although the following sites are not university-operated, much information can be found when accessed. <http://www.westindiesbooks.com>, for example, will present the viewer with an alphabetical list of literature by Caribbean writers. <http://www.books.ai> will present Don Mitchell's West Indian Bibliography. There is also Russ Filman's website, which may have been the first site in Caribbean studies to appear on the World Wide Web. He has an extensive collection of information about Caribbean literary personages—by country of origin—from which much useful information may be gleaned. Russ also responds quickly to his e-mail, and is very helpful in finding material you may need. His site can be found at <http://www.freenet.hamilton.on.ca>. Then, too, there is the *Small Axe Project*, a journal, also published on the internet, that aims to 'participate both in the renewal of practices of intellectual criticism in the Caribbean, and in the expansion/revision of the horizons of such criticism'.

5. India

(a) General, Poetry and Drama

Shyamala A. Narayan's *Journal of Commonwealth Literature* bibliography (*JCL* 35:iii[2000] 45–72) is an essential source, especially for details of books and journals that are only published in India. The introduction is chiefly devoted to reviews of creative writing in English, although some critical works are also discussed. Narayan's survey suggests a familiar pattern, with 1999 seeing an abundance of fiction published, hardly any drama, and over fifty books of poetry, many by academics.

One of the best books of the year is Meenakshi Mukherjee's *The Perishable Empire: Essays on Indian Writing in English*, which examines the relationship between the English language and India through a study of literary texts from the last 150 years. Mukherjee also takes into consideration 'the layered context of the other Indian languages surrounding English', with a particular focus on Bengali texts, to produce a collection of essays that highlights the plurality of Indian writing, as well as the complexities of reception and readership issues. The period is covered in broadly chronological order; part 1 mainly focuses on the nineteenth century, addressing the 'selective amnesia' through which early novels in English have failed to receive the detailed attention accorded to their counterparts in indigenous languages. Chapter 1, 'Nation, Novel, Language', introduces key themes, including a particular concern with gender issues, and features a useful appendix of early fiction in English from 1830 to 1930. Subsequent chapters range from single author/ text studies to broader discussions, but always with a concern to situate English-language texts in 'the larger map of multi-lingual India'. Among the authors discussed in part 1 are the novelists Bankimchandra Chatterjee, Krupa Satthianadhan, Lal Behari Day, K.K. Sinha and Sarath Kumar Ghosh. 'Hearing Her Own Voice: Defective Acoustics in Colonial India', a chapter on the poets Toru Dutt and Sarojini Naidu, acts as a bridge to the second part's focus on the twentieth century. This begins with a study of Nirad C. Chaudhuri which, while rather anecdotal, usefully highlights his dual career as a Bengali writing in both English and his indigenous tongue. Subsequent chapters look at Amitav Ghosh's *The Shadow Lines* and Salman Rushdie's *Haroun and the Sea of Stories*, the latter with reference to Satyajit Ray's children's films and stories. The two final chapters give excellent overviews of the volume's interlinked concerns. In 'The Anxiety of Indianness', Mukherjee takes Raja Rao's foreword to *Kanthapura* as a starting point in considering India fiction in English since the 1930s, arguing that Indian themes are here represented in a more homogenizing, pan-Indian manner than in indigenous-language novels. She examines the consequences of the 'explosion of the 1980s', in which the publication of *Midnight's Children* initiated the ascendancy of diasporic writers in English whose work is in danger of essentializing Indian themes through a concern to reach a global readership. Of these 'new' novelists Mukherjee regards Amitav Ghosh and Vikram Seth to be the most valuable for Indian readerships. The final chapter, 'Divided by a Common Language', highlights the growth of translation studies in India, especially in view of the increasing number of indigenous-language novels being translated into English. While Mukherjee laments the low profile of such works in comparison with the 'Third World Cosmopolitan' writers in English, her own widely researched and accessible study offers compelling arguments for English-language writing to be contextualized through the comparative study of indigenous-language texts, whether in English translation or otherwise.

Allen and Trivedi, eds., *Literature and Nation: Britain and India, 1800–1990*, is an Open University text that forms the basis of a postgraduate module in the literature programme. Given its impressive range and significant contribution to comparative and interdisciplinary studies, the text merits a detailed consideration. Part 1 offers eleven chapters introducing major texts from India and Britain, with part 2 supplying an anthology of further literary texts and useful historical documents, organized in eleven sections corresponding to the chapter headings. The pedagogic nature of the enterprise is further apparent in the division of chapters into short sections, each with extensive bibliographical information, outlines of both competing and complementary analyses and interpretations, and questions and exercises. Thus the project is designed to give guidance to students while prompting engagement in debates concerning the 'marking' of literary texts by their colonial or post-colonial context(s). There is a welcome insistence throughout the volume that evidence of the links between the broad key terms ('literature', 'nation', 'Britain', and 'India') is to be found in detailed textual analysis. The editors' input is substantial: Allen contributes six chapters, including an accessible introductory discussion of approaches to historical contexts and, most usefully, the initial problems of encountering post-colonial critical and theoretical writings, which should provide very helpful reading for all students in the field. Allen's remaining chapters are chiefly devoted to canonical British writing, including works by Sir William Jones, Jane Austen, Charles Dickens (a fascinating reading of *A Tale of Two Cities* in the contemporary context of the 1857 revolt), Rudyard Kipling and E.M. Forster. If this outline of the early chapters suggests a rather Anglocentric approach, the juxtaposition of the anthology pieces impels equal consideration of Indian writings and contexts. For example, the chapter on Jones is contextualized by an anthology section including his own writings, Warren Hastings's preface to Charles Wilkins's translation of the *Bhagavad-Gita*, some early nineteenth-century Indian poetry in English by Henry L.V. Derozio and Michael Madhusudan Dutt, writings by Raja Rammohan Roy, and an extract from Thomas Babington Macaulay's 'Minute on Education'. Similarly, Stephen Regan's chapter, 'Poetry and Nation: W.B. Yeats', invites comparative study of Rabindranath Tagore and 'ideas of nationalism that resonate in both India and Ireland' through a selection of anthology pieces by the two writers. Lynda Prescott's chapter on Kipling is accompanied by an extract from Tagore's novel *Gora*, which is offered as a comparative text for *Kim*. Harish Trivedi contributes two chapters on major Indian novels in English, focusing on Raja Rao's *Kanthapura* and Salman Rushdie's *Midnight's Children*. Rao's novel is studied as a Gandhian text, and contextualized by extracts from writings by M.K. Gandhi, Jawaharlal Nehru, and English translations of pieces by the Hindi novelist Premchand. These are two of a number of anthology pieces translated by Trivedi, again directing the reader to contexts less noticed in many studies of the Indian–British encounter. Rao also prompts an initial discussion of important post-colonial themes of 'exile, diaspora, migrancy and hybridity', which are further developed in relation to Rushdie's work. Here, Trivedi's chapter functions as an excellent short introduction to Rushdie, whether viewed as a cosmopolitan, post-colonial, hybrid, British and/or Indian writer. It has to be said that in the volume as a whole gender issues are not especially well represented, but Vrinda Nabar's analysis of Attia Hosain's *Sunlight on a Broken Column* comments interestingly on links between the independence struggle, partition, India's social structures and 'the specific situation of women'. It is accompanied by a particularly good selection of extracts, including stories of women's experiences and/or the traumas of partition translated from Hindi, Urdu and Malayalam. Richard Allen's chapter on V.S. Naipaul is worth noting for its analysis of the latter's still contentious representations of India, and for planting some interesting ideas concerning national belonging, the remaking of history and the role of the expatriate writer that are picked up in Trivedi's chapter on Rushdie. The volume as a whole admirably fulfils its pedagogic functions, bringing together a wide range of issues and approaches that have often been restricted to specialized monographs and journal articles, and making available an excellent selection of primary sources from two centuries of complex colonial and post-colonial experience.

Bery and Murray, eds., *Comparing Postcolonial Literatures: Dislocations*, chiefly collects papers from the University of North London's 'Border Crossings' conference. The focus on linguistic boundaries and the 'problematic situation of the British Isles in postcolonial studies' produces an interesting collection that stresses the value of comparative studies, suggesting the complexity of local and global manifestations of hybridity and transculturation both during and after the period of European imperialism. Any attempt to isolate Indian themes obviously runs counter to the spirit of the project, but in doing so something of the range and interest of the collection can be indicated. The introduction uses India as a key point of reference in outlining the 'multiple rather than binary process' of cross-cultural influence. Acknowledging the importance of Homi Bhabha's work, the editors also show Stuart Hall's concern with the 'fissuring of notions of cultural identity' in Caribbean contexts to have parallels in the *Subaltern Studies* project on Indian historiography. The complexity of cultural exchanges and identities is initially explored through a series of essays on the relationship between Ireland and the British Isles, testing post-colonial concerns in that context before moving to a section entitled 'Diasporas', which broadens the debate to include, among other themes, post-colonialism and America. Here, Geraldine Stoneham's essay, '"It's a Free Country": Visions of Hybridity in the Metropolis', offers an interesting analysis of two novels concerned with hybridity, diaspora and the USA in relation to Bhabha's ideas regarding nationalist discourse and alienation. Bharati Mukherjee's *Jasmine* suggests the empowering potential of her protagonist's migration to, and through, the USA. In contrast, T.C. Boyle's *The Tortilla Curtain*, detailing the plight of Mexican migrants in California, offers a far less optimistic treatment of these 'other Americans'. However, Stoneham regards Bhabha and both novelists as agreeing on 'the liminality of the nation-space'. In part 3, 'Internalized Exiles', Sujala Singh's 'Nationalism's Brandings: Women's Bodies and Narratives of the Partition', examines the violent dislocation of populations during the partition of India, when 'women's bodies often became the markers on which the painful scripts of contending nationalisms (Hindu, Muslim or Sikh) were inscribed'. The focus is on Amrita Pritam's Punjabi novella, *Pinjar* ([1950], translated into English in 1987 by Khushwant Singh). This is a narrative that attempts to retrieve the silenced voices of women in the subcontinent and to represent the violence ('the branding of rival chauvinisms') that many suffered in the aftermath of the 1947 legislation.

Amireh and Majaj, eds., *Going Global: The Transnational Reception of Third World Women Writers*, is a collection of essays examining texts by a variety of women writers originating from the Indian subcontinent, Latin America, Africa, the Middle East and Australia. Focusing on the processes involved in crossing national/cultural boundaries, the texts are analysed both in terms of their points of origin and their reception/reshaping in 'new' contexts such as First World universities. The editors suggest that the ten essays 'probe both the possibilities and the limitations of feminist and multiculturalist projects in a global age', and state that this collection is 'the first book to focus entirely on the politics of reception of Third World women writers and their texts'. Section 3 suggests 'ways of reading [these] texts that resist overdetermined reactions', and features two essays on specifically Indian themes and writers. Alpana Sharma Knippling's '"Sharp contrasts of all colours": The Legacy of Toru Dutt' examines the life and work of the late nineteenth-century poet and translator, introducing issues of gender and race inequalities and reductive stereotyping via a brief consideration of Meena Alexander as anthologist and memoir writer. This is followed by Jennifer Wenzel's 'Grim Fairy Tales: Taking a Risk, Reading "Imaginary Maps"', focusing on the Bengali short stories of Mahasweta Devi which come to the First World via Gayatri Chakravorty Spivak's English translations. Each essay is interesting in its own right, while the juxtaposition of such a range of sources and contexts in the two pieces admirably supports the collection's wider aim of recontextualizing literary analyses to resist facile and damaging categorizations.

K.D. Verma's *The Indian Imagination: Critical Essays on Indian Writing in English* usefully collects examples from Verma's substantial output of essays, many in the form of revised versions of journal articles. Together they form a compelling exploration of patterns of consciousness in a diverse selection of broadly twentieth-century Indian writings from before and after independence. Verma sees Aurobindo Ghose (Sri Aurobindo), Mulk Raj Anand and Balachandra Rajan as 'active participants in the representation of these two sides, the colonial India and the postcolonial India', while Nissim Ezekiel, Anita Desai and Arun Joshi are 'voices of new India'. The study as a whole eloquently justifies an interdependent, multidisciplinary approach to these poets and prose writers, acknowledging the cross-cultural effects of the colonial encounter and stressing the value of synthesis in moving beyond 'parochial and self-constricting' conflicts. There are three chapters on Aurobindo (as poet, socio-political thinker and critic), two each on Anand and Joshi, and single chapters on Rajan's *The Dark Dancer*, Ezekiel's *The Unfinished Man*, and Desai's *Baumgartner's Bombay*. Each is distinguished by an encyclopedic array of references to European and Indian thought, and a consistent awareness of the multiple threads that run through the chosen texts, effectively tracing 'the historical and psychological process of a cultural and ideological confrontation and synthesis of East and West'.

G.N. Devy's work on Indian literary approaches and the study of texts in indigenous languages and/or English translation has prompted lively debate in the Indian academy and beyond over the last decade. His latest study, *'Of Many Heroes': An Indian Essay in Literary Historiography* [1998] is, like the earlier and notably controversial *After Amnesia* [1992], an ambitious and wide-ranging work. Devy points out the challenge that Indian literature, with its 3,000-year history and multiplicity of cultures, sects and languages, offers to the literary historian. Noting the development of narratives of Indian literary history in a nineteenth-century colonial context (continuing into the twentieth century as an activity of predominantly Western origin), Devy seeks evidence of earlier, pre-colonial conceptions of literary history. This expands the scope of historical study and throws into question some of the tenets of, for example, canon formation in English literature. Thus the tendency to canonize according to monolingual criteria has doubtful validity in considering the literature of India, with its huge variety of bilingual writers and its long history of translation as a valid point of origin for many of its most respected literary classics. However, the primary aim of Devy's study is not, he stresses, 'to refute Western literary historiography' or to substitute 'some new or more appropriate practice', but simply to 'understand and review the conventions of literary historiography in ancient, medieval, colonial and contemporary India'. Like the best of his work the study fulfils a crucial function of recontextualizing the object of study. It also makes stimulating reading.

Indian writing in indigenous languages has been well served in recent years by a variety of critical and theoretical works on issues of translation, accompanying the steadily growing number of translations into English by an eminent collection of writers and translators. Bassnett and Trivedi, eds., *Post-Colonial Translation: Theory and Practice* [1999], makes an important contribution to translation studies in a global context while also including a number of interesting and useful essays emphasizing the importance of Indian contexts in the field. This is readily apparent in 'Shifting Grounds of Exchange: B.M. Srikantaiah and Kannada Translation', in which Vanamala Viswanatha and Sherry Simon begin their study of the relations between Kannada and English by regarding it as axiomatic that 'India, perhaps more fully than most other nations, is a "translation area"'. This serves to highlight the concerns of a number of Indian academics whose resistance to the limitations of an exclusively Anglocentric view of Indian writing has been such a stimulating feature of Indian debates on language issues in recent years. Some of these are contributors to this collection, of which the following essays are particularly noteworthy: G.J.V. Prasad's 'Writing Translation: The Strange Case of the Indian English Novel'; Vinay Dharwadker's 'A.K. Ramanujan's Theory and Practice of Translation'; Ganesh Devy's 'Translation and Literary History: An Indian View'.

Gauri Viswanathan has co-edited a special double issue of *ArielE* (31:i–ii[2000]) entitled 'Institutionalizing English Studies: Postcolonial/Postindependence Challenge' and featuring three essays on Indian issues. Viswanathan's 1989 book *Masks of Conquest* was a significant study of the early stages of English studies in India. In 'An Introduction: Uncommon Genealogies' (pp. 13–31) she brings the story up to date, arguing that 'English can no longer be studied innocently or inattentively to the deeper contexts of imperialism, transnationalism, and globalization in which it first articulated its mission'. She goes on to show how the journal's contributors raise questions about the definition and location of post-colonial writings, such as where 'Indian literature', for example, is produced. Arnab Chakladar's 'The Postcolonial Bazaar: Marketing/Teaching Indian Literature' (pp. 183–201) discusses the selective canonization of Indian writers in metropolitan contexts: 'Indian literature in the Western academy remains largely and implicitly defined in English'. Chakladar's close reading of a special issue of the *New Yorker* from 1997, marking the fiftieth anniversary of independence, eloquently makes this point, while also highlighting the Western neglect of writing in indigenous Indian languages, despite the quality of recent translations. Also worth noting is Pramod K. Mishra's 'English Language, Postcolonial Subjectivity, and Globalization in India' (pp. 383–410), which also looks at the effects of English in India and its impact 'on the survival and prosperity of the regional languages and their users'.

Vanita and Kidwai, eds., *Same-Sex Love in India: Readings from Literature and History*, is an anthology of writings ranging from ancient Sanskrit to late twentieth-century texts. The collection features material originally written in many of the major languages in India, some of which are newly translated into English (for example, all Hindi and Urdu and most of the Persian texts), while the remainder uses standard scholarly translations. The result is an impressive range of representations of same-sex themes in writing from the subcontinent, emphasizing texts with 'emotional or erotic content' as distinct from those stemming from 'violent impulses'; the preface makes clear that this is an anthology of love or desire, not 'a history of rape'. The collection is broadly divided into four parts: 'Ancient Indian Materials', 'Medieval Materials in the Sanskritic Tradition', 'Medieval Materials in the Perso-Urdu Tradition', and 'Modern Indian Materials'. Part 4 includes some texts written in English, including letters from M.K. Gandhi and the painter Amrita Sher-Gil, and poems by Vikram Seth, Inez Vere Dullas and Hoshang Merchant. One of the aims of the volume is 'to make accessible many little-known or neglected texts to a general as well as a scholarly audience'. The collection is notable for the juxtaposition of 'classic' texts, presented without the bowdlerization that has marred some early translations into English, with many obscure but valuable writings, especially from the modern period. While there might be quibbles about translation, periodization and selection criteria, the collection is a rich source of primary texts, and the editorial material, in the form of a concise general preface, introductory essays to each section and biographical/historical prefaces to each entry, presents invaluable scholarly analysis and commentary.

Ganguly and Nandan, eds., *Unfinished Journeys: India File from Canberra* [1998], is a collection of essays, autobiographical writings and other pieces by writers from Canberra who are concerned with relations between India and Australia. This is a book that admirably dissolves neat distinctions between 'scholarly/academic' and 'creative/personal' writing. As such it may be seen in part to fall outside the scope of the present context, but all the pieces are to be recommended, not least for the cumulative manner in which they problematize politico-historical over-simplifications of place and belonging. Part 1 features three pieces that variously address the materiality of India as territory and nation-state and the reshaping of ideas of India that may occur in diasporic contexts. This includes Stephanie Jones's 'Within and Without History: The Book of Secrets', which examines the recent work of the Indian African novelist M.G. Vassanji. Part 2 is more overtly autobiographical, while part 3 is devoted to accounts of some ways in which four Australian writer-academics relate their research into Indian contexts to their own experiences. This includes John Docker's 'His Slave, My Tattoo: Romancing a Lost World', which uses Amitav Ghosh's *In an Antique Land* and Salman Rushdie's *The Moor's Last Sigh* as key points of reference. The final section of this fascinating collection 'traces Canberra's experience of India's cultural heritage' through pieces on Indian dance, film, photography, painting and rock art.

Kate Teltscher's 'The Shampooing Surgeon and the Persian Prince: Two Indians in Early Nineteenth-Century Britain' (*Interventions* 2:iii[2000] 409–23) explores the careers and work of Dean Mahomed and Abu Talib Khan, whose travel narratives were the earliest such accounts to be published by Indians in English. Mahomed's text, published in 1794, has recently received attention through Michael H. Fisher's 1996 edition (included in *The First Indian Author in English: Dean*

Mahomed (1759–1851) in India, Ireland, and England). Teltscher analyses the 'cultural ambivalence' of Mahomed's career and his talent for 'the strategic staging of Otherness, his canny adoption of an orientalized persona'. Abu Talib Khan's writings include a narrative of his travels in Asia, Africa and Europe, originally written in Persian but published in an English translation in 1810, and offering parallels with Mahomed's work in its record of 'cross-cultural intimacy and exchange'. The material allows Teltscher to raise interesting questions concerning cultural identity, colonial discourse and hybridity, and to argue that in both texts 'anglophilia is leavened with criticism'.

Another notable journal article is Gün Orgun's 'Marginality, Cosmopolitanism and Postcoloniality' (*CE&S* 23:i[2000] 111–24). This examination of migrant identity in post-colonial contexts is framed by a consideration of Edward Said's position as exiled cosmopolitan intellectual and Aijaz Ahmad's critique of that position. Orgun's cogent discussion makes interesting use of a range of material by writers of the Indian diaspora, including Salman Rushdie's fiction and essays, Gayatri Chakravorty Spivak's writings, novels by Bharati Mukherjee and Vikram Seth, and Amitav Ghosh's singular mixture of autobiographical, anthropological and travel writing, *In an Antique Land*.

Cecile Sandten's 'In Her Own Voice: Sujata Bhatt and the Aesthetic Articulation of the Diasporic Condition' (*JCL* 35:i[2000] 99–119) offers an interesting analysis of Bhatt's poetry, including some of her linguistic strategies for expressing diasporic experiences. Also worth noting is Suranjan Ganguly's 'A Cinema on Red Alert: Mrinal Sen's "Interview" and "In Search of Famine"' (*JCL* 35:i[2000] 55–70), which examines two of Sen's films.

Since major studies of post-colonial drama are scarce, as are attempts to place Indian drama in a global context, we can be doubly grateful to Christopher Balme for his excellent book, *Decolonizing the Stage: Theatrical Syncretism and Post-Colonial Drama* [1999]. Balme argues that experiments in syncretic theatre effectively decolonize the stage by utilizing 'the performance forms of both European and indigenous cultures in a creative recombination of their respective elements, without slavish adherence to one tradition or the other'. Drawing on developments in performance and semiotic theory, the study establishes a comparative framework for analysing recent theatrical texts mainly written in English from Africa, the Caribbean and India, and indigenous, 'Fourth World', cultures in New Zealand, Australia and North America. It also develops ideas from colonial discourse analysis by examining the work of Rabindranath Tagore; this anticipates 'the strategy of syncretization which in many ways has become the hallmark of post-colonial theatre since the 1960s'. Rather than seeking to establish discrete areas of analysis, of either individual dramatists or geographical regions, Balme uses systematic headings to stress the theoretical aims of the study. Thus Tagore's essay 'The Stage' [1913] is given historical significance for its early critique of Western theatre and its contribution to indigenous theories of syncretic theatre, specifically, aspects of Bengali folk traditions and classical Sanskrit forms in early twentieth-century contexts. Tagore's work is also examined in stimulating discussions of language and issues of translation, and of 'spaces and spectators'. Balme's approach reveals intriguing connections between some very disparate theatrical texts. Tagore's self-translations link with the practice of the contemporary dramatist Girish Karnad, whose self-translated work from Kannada to English also recalls Tagore's explorations of performance space. Similarly, Karnad's use of Indian dance-theatre traditions intersects with the work of Asif Currimbhoy, whose English-language drama combines elements of *kathakali* dance-drama and Western dramatic form. The great virtue of Balme's informed and articulate study is that it manages to suggest a broad theoretical framework for post-colonial drama while insisting on the specificity of localized forms. In the present context this offers a refreshing alternative to bemoaning the paucity of Indian drama in English.

(b) Fiction

This section reviews work that focuses on prose fiction, but readers should also refer to section 5(*a*) above for articles and books that consider fiction together with other genres.

The year's most satisfying study of representations of India in the novel is Peter Morey's *Fictions of India: Narrative and Power*. His method is to apply 'strands of colonial and post-colonial debate, ideas from narrative and reception theory and a sense of historical context' to a range of texts by British and Indian novelists from the past hundred years. These include Rudyard Kipling, E.M. Forster, John Masters, J.G. Farrell, Paul Scott, Khushwant Singh and Rohinton Mistry. Morey's emphasis on imbrication, denying facile polarizations of British and Indian, and, indeed, colonial and post-colonial perspectives, builds interestingly on recent work by Sara Suleri and Elleke Boehmer. The introduction, 'Post-Colonial Criticism: A Transformative Labour', offers a good overview, stating that the study 'begins from the premise that there is a demonstrable relationship between narrative power, exerted over a text, and what Edward Said calls "the gross political fact"'. Much of the book focuses on British narratives of India, highlighting ever-present 'ambiguities and ambivalences', and offering stimulating readings of Farrell and Scott as post-independence novelists whose texts actively open up contradictions in colonial discourse through the 'wholesale dismantling of generic conventions'. This provides an interesting context for the final chapter: 'Post-Colonial DestiNations: Spatial Re(con)figurings in Khushwant Singh's *Train to Pakistan* and Rohinton Mistry's *A Fine Balance*'. This comparative study examines the two novels via a carefully qualified reading of Frederic Jameson's essay, 'Third World Literature in the Era of Multinational Capitalism', with a focus on space and the body in personal and national politics. Each of these narratives of resistance responds to British colonial discourse and to crises in post-independence India, and is part of a post-colonial project that resists monologic representations of 'the story of India' in favour of a pluralistic, polyphonic rendering of 'stories'. Thus, for example, it becomes possible to group Mistry and Scott as novelists whose work breaks down simplistic binaries in the representation of twentieth-century India. Morey's close analysis demonstrates the viability of recent developments in colonial and post-colonial theory, and the cumulative effect of his argument is particularly compelling.

Anuradha Dingwaney Needham's *Using the Master's Tools: Resistance and the Literature of the African and South Asian Diasporas* makes a good contribution to Salman Rushdie scholarship, highlighting his migrant experience and analysing his work in a study that also includes C.L.R. James, Ama Ata Aidoo, Michelle Cliff, and Hanif Kureishi. These writers from African, Caribbean and South Asian backgrounds reside or have resided in the West, and Needham finds 'significant affinities in their positions on, and enactments of, resistance, which accrue, in large part, from their locations within the metropole'. In part 1 she groups Rushdie and James as '*In*, but not [necessarily] *of*, the West', seeing them as writers who 'purposefully invoke their liminal—insider/outsider—location as a form of "(dis)identification" that empowers their critique of hegemonic Western/colonial ideology'. Rushdie also adopts this position in relation to his 'homes': India and Pakistan. In chapter 2 Rushdie's 'method(s) of critique' are examined through readings of *Midnight's Children* and *Shame*, in which his 'deconstructive procedures' are apparent through a narrative strategy of 're-play' which unsettles dominant assumptions about the history of the subcontinent. This is a useful chapter in its own right, but it gains further resonance in the context of the study as a whole. Needham characterizes Kureishi as both 'In *and* of the (imperial) metropole', but using his hybrid position to anchor his argument about a 'new way of being British'. This shares similarities with the positions ascribed to Rushdie and James, but all three are distinct from Cliff and Aidoo, who 'embrace nationalism as a form of resistance'. This comparative approach encourages the reader to trace both the connectedness and diversity of the writers' work.

Stephen Baker's '"You must remember this": Salman Rushdie's *The Moor's Last Sigh*' (*JCL* 35:i[2000] 43–54) responds to Aijaz Ahmad's Marxist critique of Rushdie's work. Baker argues that 'a postmarxist approach to ... postmodern narrative is useful in rediscovering a political, historical and ethical dimension to those same textually playful and self-reflexive features of post-colonial writing of which the Marxist tradition remains so suspicious'. Remaining with high-profile novels from the 1990s, Emilienne Baneth-Nouailhetas's 'Forms of Creation in *A Suitable Boy*' (*CE&S* 22:ii[2000] 69–83) offers a linguistic/stylistic analysis of Vikram Seth's novel. Also worth noting is Cécile Oumhani's 'Hybridity and Transgression in Arundhati Roy's *The God of Small Things*' (*CE&S* 22:ii[2000] 85–91).

Ambreen Hai's 'Border Work, Border Trouble: Postcolonial Feminism and the Ayah in Bapsi Sidhwa's *Cracking India*' (*MFS* 46:ii[2000] 379–426) examines a text by a Parsee/Pakistani writer that disrupts religious, nationalist and gender binarisms, building its narrative around a female child of a minority community at the time of partition. In an extensive analysis Hai praises the novel's interventionist qualities and its mobilization of a beneficial 'border feminism', while demonstrating that it is also 'worth reading against its own grain: questioning it for the ways in which it goes about its ends and tracing the boundaries that limit its own project'. Anjali Roy's '"Microstoria": Indian Nationalism's "Little Stories" in Amitav Ghosh's *The Shadow Lines*' (*JCL* 35:ii[2000] 35–49) explores borders and nations through an analysis of Ghosh's narrative of a family uprooted by the partition of Bengal. Ghosh's use of 'microhistory', which gives a local rather than nationalist perspective, enables him to investigate 'the conflicting claims of roots and belonging, nations and boundaries in the Indian mind'.

Rosalia Baena's 'The Condition of Life and Art in Anita Desai's *In Custody*' (*CE&S* 22:ii[2000] 59–67) is an interesting piece on Desai's distinctive version of the campus novel. Tabish Khair's 'The Rape of Parwana: Mukul Kesavan's Inscription of History and Agency' (*Kunapipi* 22:ii[2000] 1–5) notes a tendency in recent Indian English fiction towards either domestic realism or magic realism, and suggests that these stylistic limitations are reflections of the novelists' own backgrounds as 'Babu' writers: 'anglophone, very urban(e) middle class' and restricted. In contrast, Khair admires Kesavan's first novel *Looking Through Glass* as a text that 'employs and resists elements of both realism and fantasy in its narration'. Another notable first novel is examined in Geetha Ganapathy-Dore's 'Impossible Reconciliation in Manju Kapur's *Difficult Daughters*' (*CE&S* 23:i[2000] 36–42).

Finally, two journal articles on Bengali fiction in English translation should be noted. Minoli Salgado's 'Tribal Stories, Scribal Worlds: Mahasweta Devi and the Unreliable Translator' (*JCL* 35:i[2000] 131–45) is an analysis of the work of 'the most widely translated Indian writer working in an indigenous language today'. Alex Tickell's 'The Road Less Travelled: *Pather Panchali* in Translation' (*JCL* 35:i[2000] 147–62) examines Bibhutibhushan Banerji's novel in the light of current ideas in post-colonial translation studies.

6. New Zealand

(a) General

The most wide-ranging account of New Zealand literature published in 2000 was Kate Moffat's 'The Puritan Paradox: An Annotated Bibliography of Puritan and anti-Puritan New Zealand Fiction, 1860–1940' (*Kotare* 3:i[2000] 36–86, and 3:ii[2000] 3–49), which is based on her extensive and pioneering doctoral thesis of 1998. Moffat has examined texts rarely read since their publication in the early years of New Zealand writing as well as more recent and better-known books, and has been able to interrelate them in insightful ways by seeing them in terms of their positive or negative attitudes to Puritanism. Her painstaking definitions of religious and secular Puritanism and their specifically New Zealand forms constitute in themselves an invaluable approach to a complex of literary history, and her analyses of individual works of fiction on that basis are often startlingly original. A by-product is that many books are saved from obscurity and reveal the richness of the country's literary history in places that have been largely forgotten. By reducing her thesis to the form of an annotated bibliography she has made her insights more readily accessible, though sometimes so compressed that the reader is advised to take careful note of every word in her accounts.

The growth of literary biography as a genre in the 1990s has been seen by many as a phase of reassessment in literary history and of a new concern, locally, for the relationship between literature and the life of the individual. The major works in this category in the period under review are biographies of Denis Glover and Barry Crump, which offer a great contrast in style and aspiration. Gordon Ogilvie's *Denis Glover: His Life* [1999] is a study of an important poet and larger-than-life figure on the New Zealand literary scene. It is meticulously researched and annotated, and almost pedantic in its attention to detail. It also focuses strongly on each of Glover's works, often on individual lyrics, as they come up in the story, providing an account of their place in his life, the circumstances in which they were written and the sources of experience Glover was calling on. The biographical enterprise means that there is less emphasis on the place of these writings within the broader terms of reference of New Zealand and general literature, and yet these matters are also given some attention. For those who remember the almost frighteningly charismatic man, some of his self-given glamour seems diminished by the ponderous attention to minor detail, but those looking for information on which to base their own readings of Glover's poems will be rewarded. Ogilvie makes no attempt to gloss over the less savoury aspects of Glover's life, such as his rabid warrior stance as a seaman, his aggressive and scornful attitude to women and his later decline into alcoholism, but these are not sensationalized; rather, they are treated with cautious yet frank concern for truthfulness. Glover's relations with other writers are often revealing and are well researched here.

A Life in Loose Strides: The Story of Barry Crump by Colin Hogg has no footnotes at all and its bibliography is limited to a list of Crump's books. This casts doubt on virtually everything in the book, since there is no way to check its statements apart from doing the writer's research for him. It is known that some of the key people in Crump's life (such as Jean Watson, his companion of many years) were not interviewed by Hogg. The style is sensationalist and the constant use of the present tense adds to the reader's doubts. For all that, this is a vivid portrait and, if it is to be believed, provides an interesting insight into Crump's writing nature. He presented himself to the world as a backwoodsman who wrote virtually by instinct, but Hogg seems to demonstrate that his outdoor skills were more limited and his attention to literary conventions and style more profound than he ever admitted. It must be hoped that this revisionist view of a folk hero and peripheral literary figure will be confirmed by others whose scholarship is more reliable, or at least more apparent.

In editing the anthology *Out of Town: Writing from the New Zealand Countryside* [1999], John Gordon has provided it with a general introduction that surveys rural writing and specific introductions to each of its seven parts. There is no recent overview of this writing, so that Gordon performs a useful service, even though it is targeted at rural readers rather than at academia. While most of his comments refer to subject-matter, there are some interesting perceptions, for example, on the difference between urban writers approaching rural themes and similar themes from the rural writer's perspective.

In his introduction to *Here on Earth: The Landscape in New Zealand Literature* [1999], David Eggleton speaks both of literary responses to landscape and of the creation of landscape by writers, not always clearly distinguishing between the two. He sketches changes in perception of landscape from Maori times, when people were 'weaving an organic tracery of stories to explain where they were to themselves', through James Cook's Enlightenment, the Wakefields' images of settlement, the settlers' disappointments with the land, and Victorian efforts to cut up and domesticate the land, to the contemporary conversion to conservation and postmodern concerns regarding the way landscape talks. In the course of this survey, he takes in his stride Romantic visions of the sublime, dreams of commercial wealth extraction, the missionary exclusion of nature's violence, and the myth of the explorer-hero (later degenerating into sardonic maleness in Barry Crump). These phases and themes have been evoked by contemporaries, but also recalled by historical fiction and poetry. In passing Eggleton makes acute observations on a large number and variety of New Zealand writers.

For many years John Thomson has reported annually on developments in New Zealand literature in his introduction to a comprehensive bibliography in the *Journal of Commonwealth Literature*. In his 1999 *JCL* bibliography (34:iii[1999] 67–87), he addresses the vexed question of expatriatism: Fleur Adcock has lived so long in Britain that her links with New Zealand have grown continually more tenuous, and yet they are undeniably present, while Kapka Kassabova has arrived so recently from Bulgaria that her status as a New Zealand writer is not yet secure. In 1998, however, Thomson notes these two were the strongest writers of New Zealand poetry. He concedes that Vincent O'Sullivan has reached a point of immense virtuosity and intellectual range, but his poems seem to satisfy Thomson less than this implies, largely because of an absence of an authorial voice where one expects it. Thomson finds the same disturbing weakness in O'Sullivan's novel, *Believers to the Bright Coast*. More satisfying for Thomson is the fiction of Maurice Gee, while he observes that Shonagh Koea and Patricia Grace have been adding to the strength of the field.

In *JCL* (35:iii[2000] 73–89) Thomson notes that the Montana book prize was awarded to Owen Marshall's *Harlequin Rex*, a novel Thomson finds 'deficient' in structure yet likeable for the loving way people and places are dealt with: 'Seldom has a New Zealand setting been so sensuously described.' Thomson finds the qualities of sanguinity and compassion present in Marshall and absent from most of the younger writers. This is true, in particular, of the rising star Catherine Chidgey, whose attitude to her characters and their world is, in stark contrast to Marshall's, cold and satirical. New novels by Joy Cowley and C.K. Stead are welcomed by Thomson. New writers Kapka Kassabova, Kirsty Gunn and William Brandt are treated more cautiously. Of the poets, Thomson finds Elizabeth Smither whimsical and never really exciting, while Bill Manhire's technical skill is, by contrast, 'staggering'. Whether this technique is used on subjects worthy of it is a question Thomson throws up but does not answer. Thomson also observes that Alistair Te Ariki Campbell's new book of poems is deceptively simple, but its openness and readiness to defy vulnerability make it different from the work of any of his contemporaries. He goes on to note other volumes of verse briefly, and concludes with the comment that 1999 was an especially 'bountiful' year in fiction and verse.

In the introduction to Hereniko and Wilson, eds., *Inside Out: Literature, Cultural Politics and Identity in the New Pacific* [1999], the editors posit a 'complex creative dialectic' unifying the extremely diverse voices of the Pacific region and based on 'decreation' and 'recreation'. 'Decreation' begins with opposition to European, American and Asian (economic) colonialism but goes much further, offering to negate a wide range of 'forces of global belittlement', while 'recreation' turns this negative effort around, involving an affirmation of 'the indigenous and local imaginations', without, however, viewing them as 'static'.

Charlotte Elder, 'Seeing the Light of Day: J.H.E. Schroder's Broadcast Review of *Day and Night*' (*Kotare* 3:i[2000] 10–21), points up a forgotten literary relationship, that between the literary editor and critic J.H.E. Schroder and the poet Ursula Bethell. Schroder is much neglected and sometimes decried, but Elder demonstrates that his response to Bethell was perceptive and generous and that she benefited greatly from his support. He acted as a mentor to her and guided her through the jungle of publishing; she felt that he was the only commentator who could see and hear what she was doing. Schroder reviewed Bethell's *Day and Night* [1934] for radio, and his review, which contains careful analysis of individual poems, is published here for the first time in written form.

Philip Armstrong reminds us that Allen Curnow set the retrospective and quite strongly prescriptive pattern for New Zealand poetry with his anthology and introduction in 1945. In 'Dis/Coveries: Allen Curnow's Later Poems' (*JCL* 34:i[1999] 7–26), he remarks that even today poets and their critics feel they must respond to that early Curnow. He briefly traces the history of post-war New Zealand poetry as a series of such responses. The question he poses is how Curnow's own later poetry fits into that pattern. One response is to suggest that Curnow's later poems by no means meet his early criterion of 'an instinct for a reality prior to the poem', but rather the perceiver and the perceived become interwoven and inseparable in them. Where there had been a clear window, there is now an opaque, stained-glass one. This suggests an acquired anxiety about the stability of the phenomenal world. Although Curnow urges his peers to 'seek reality', the process of reality breakdown goes on regardless in his own poetry. At the same time, according to Armstrong, Curnow avoids or withdraws from the debates about post-colonialism, or bicultural or feminist thought (this may be a consequence of moving on from his own early genderist and nationalist stance). Dissolution and decomposition become both topics and features of the poetry.

C.K. Stead's 'Janet Frame, Janet Clutha and Karl Waikato', in his *The Writer at Work* (pp. 17–28), is an expanded version of an essay that first appeared in German in *Merian* [1996]. The new version was joint winner of the *Landfall* essay competition 1999, awarded by Otago University Press. It is as much autobiographical fragment as essay, recounting Stead's friendship with Frame from his point of view and adjusting some of the impressions left by Michael King's Frame biography. His main comment on her work is to say that she believed her language to be 'a paradigm of reality', and that her fiction seems to be marvelling at itself in a puzzled way. He also emphasizes her strengths as a satirist, and feels that she is too often treated with a reverence that really patronizes her. Apart from this, *The Writer at Work* is a collection of essays on literary and political topics, all of which were written during the past ten years and have been published elsewhere. Another useful collection of essays already published individually is Bill Manhire's *Doubtful Sounds*.

By focusing on Robin Hyde, Megan Clayton is able to paint a vivid miniature of 1930s literary politics and journalism in 'The Lens and the Archive: Reading Literary Culture: Reading Robin Hyde' (*Takahe* 36[1999] 53–6). While literary notables such as Denis Glover tended to denigrate Hyde and women's work generally, there were also male journalists, such as Schroder and Marris, who supported both. Hyde herself was able to respond vigorously and contemptuously to the underhand attacks made on her. A major aspect of Clayton's essay is her awareness that many of these disputes and arguments have been obscured by poor publication. Only by turning to archives and collections of letters in libraries is it possible to build up a fuller picture. Another aspect of the essay is Clayton's contrasting of journalistic and self-consciously literary culture to show how Hyde exposed herself to criticism from both sides by straddling the two cultures. Both of these sources of obscurity and prejudice surrounding Hyde were combated by Gloria Rawlinson's meticulous editions of her poems and novels, and are still being addressed in a similar way by Michelle Leggot.

Mark Edgecumbe, in 'The Tasman Sea: Common Ground That Keeps Us Apart' (*Kotare* 3:i[2000] 28–35), has discovered some parallels between the short stories of

Lloyd Jones and those of the Australian Robert Drewe. Each of them uses the beach as a symbol of escape, including an association with escaped prisoners. Connected with this is the way seascapes call up images of distant places; some of these are 'seen' by visitors to the beach, even though they are far away beyond the horizon of the Pacific Ocean. In a different form of 'escape' the beach is also the site, for both writers, of sexual discovery and experimentation. Another preoccupation of both writers is the end of marriage. Edgecumbe is concerned that Jones may be seen to have plagiarized Drewe, but prefers to see their relationship as one of trans-Tasman dialogue on themes of common interest.

Mark Pirie makes an attempt to rescue Katherine Mansfield's poetry from the charge that it is conventional and unadventurous, in contrast to her prose. His title, 'Katherine Mansfield: A Pioneer Performance Poet' (*JCL* 34:ii[1999] 97–104), suggests the gist of his argument. Long before the Dadaists and others had set the trend for performance poetry after the First World War, Mansfield addressed the matter of speaking verse and proclaimed an ambition to be successful as an 'elocutionist'. Her poems should, therefore, be read as scores for performance rather than as texts for publication in book form, and like many later poets she can be underestimated if the reader fails to take this into account. The argument is curious, stimulating but unconvincing—Mansfield's indebtedness to Victorian 'book' poets is beyond doubt.

7. South Pacific

Literary Representations in Western Polynesia: Colonialism and Indigeneity [1999] is based on Sina Mary Theresa Va'ai's Ph.D. thesis for the University of Canberra in 1995. It is a major study of Polynesia in English-language literature, surveying the work of early non-Polynesians, such as the explorers Melville and Stephenson, but concentrating most of its detailed attention upon Polynesian writers such as Albert Wendt, Sapa'u Ruperake Petaia, Noumea Simi, Lemalu Tate Simi, Momoe Malietoa Von Reiche, Sia Figiel, Konai Helu Thaman, Epeli Hau'ofa, Ratu Jo Nacola, Satendra Nandan and a range of lesser-known figures. The book can serve as an introductory survey of writing in Fiji, Tonga and Samoa. It also presents the theory and practice of writers consciously countering images of the exotic, the romantic and the paradisal with indigenous representations of subjugation and the debilitating effects of colonialism. The literature of local people is seen, almost inevitably, as a vigorous reaction to the stereotypical image-patterns of those from outside the region. Independence of this outside view, in the sense of being able to ignore it totally, is barely suggested. The general themes detected after an exhaustive, particularized analysis are the cultural clash, the widening of borders and the quest for self-definition and national identity. There is little new in these themes, but Va'ai's close reading of poems, novels and plays gives them a new richness and provides useful tools for applying the themes in practical criticism.

There is more inherent originality in Michelle Maria Keown's Ph.D. thesis, a study of the 'indigenous body' in relation to South Pacific literature: 'Whose Paradise? Representations of the Body in the Indigenous Literatures of the South Pacific'. Her studies of eight writers—Albert Wendt, Sia Figiel, Epeli Hau'ofa, Alistair Te Ariki Campbell, Keri Hulme, Witi Ihimaera, Patricial Grace and Alan

Duff—are exemplary rather than conclusive, and her general theme overrides individual analysis. Her concern is the physical experience of being Polynesian, awareness of its force in the individual, the group and the broader society, the contrast felt in the encounter with others and the way in which the body can be used in literature to symbolize awareness of identity or its absence. In a concluding essay she examines the nature of tattooing as a means of identification and of initiation in a given cultural context. Her view takes African and other representations of colonized bodies into account. She regards Alistair Campbell as a transitional figure between Pacific Island and New Zealand Maori writers. The latter group is seen to differ from the former because of the ongoing colonial subordination of Maori. In contrast to the position of Maori, the achievement of independence in Tonga and Samoa has resulted in Wendt, Figiel and Hau'ofa examining colonialism in the Pacific as a largely external force rather than an existing oppressive one. The theory of the indigenous body is offered as one approach among others to developing a framework within which the work of a wide variety of writers can be related. Keown develops her interpretation of Figiel further in her essay '"Gaugin is Dead": Sia Figiel and the Representation of the Polynesian Fijian Body' (*SPAN* 48–9[1999] 91–107).

Another broad view of Pacific literature, though in a small form, is Ken Arvidson's essay 'Passages and Reefs' (*SPAN* 48–9[1999] 14–27). Surveying the way in which literature from the region has been perceived, he makes the interesting comment that the sheer range of islands and nations covered gives South Pacific literature a decentralized, fragmented, pluralistic quality that makes it 'attractively post-modern' from the very beginning. Going on from there, however, Arvidson emphasizes that the literatures of the region are 'inter-involved' so that they are not merely fragments, but also parts of an inter-cultural dialogue, which has the effect of bonding them.

Susanna Trnka explores the indigenous body metaphor in relation to Fiji and also applies Arjun Appadurai's perceptions of cultural globalizations to the literature of that country in her 'Global Spaces, Local Places: The Body and Imagination in Indo-Fijian Fiction' (*SPAN* 48–9[1999] 40–52). Physical and theatrical representations of godhood and relations between body and land are traced through a number of Fijian writers. In 'Hidden Voices: The Development of Creative Writing in the Solomon Islands' (*SPAN* 48–9[1999] 59–73), Julian Treadaway shows that the problem of fragmentation, mentioned by Arvidson, is particularly acute in the Solomon Islands, where there are seventy languages spoken, none of which has developed a sufficient body of writing to form a 'literary culture', while their oral cultures are elusive and seemingly ephemeral. For all that, Treadaway is able to provide a considerable and very useful bibliography of creative writing from the Solomons, as well as a useful discursive introduction to it.

The European accounts of the Pacific, which much of the indigenous writing consciously opposes, are examined again in the context of contrasting dualistic images of paradise and hell in work as diverse as that of Margaret Mead, Melanie Klein and Paul Theroux in Kay Torney Souter's 'Darkness and Paradise: The Split in European Representations of the South Seas' (*SPAN* 48–9[1999] 108–17).

The perception of the contrast between 'insider' and 'outsider' views of the Pacific that underlies almost all accounts of Pacific Islands literature is subjected to questioning by Sandra Tawake. In an essay entitled 'Constructing the Present:

Insider/Outsider Perspective in Fiction by Figiel, Pule and Ihimaera' (*SPAN* 50–1[2000] 1–11), she points out the over-simplicity of believing that literature written by Polynesians presents life as it is in contrast to the elaborate metaphorical and symbolic constructs of Europeans writing about the Pacific. The 'authenticity' of indigenous writing is more complex than that, since it is in itself an elaborate construct.

Books Reviewed

Adams, Francis. *The Murder of Madeline Brown* (1st pub. as *Madeline Brown's Murderer* [1887]). Text. [2000] pp. xiv + 160. pb $19.95 ISBN 1 8764 8552 3.

Alexander, Peter. *Les Murray: A Life in Progress*. OUPAus. [2000] pp. xii + 391. £22.50 ISBN 0 1955 3501 4.

Allen, Richard, and Harish Trivedi, eds. *Literature and Nation: Britain and India, 1800–1990*. Routledge. [2000] pp. 352. hb £50 ISBN 0 4152 1206 5, pb £16.99 ISBN 0 4152 1207 3.

Amireh, Amal, and Lisa Suhair Majaj, eds. *Going Global: The Transnational Reception of Third World Women Writers*. Routledge. [2000] pp. xiv + 308. £35 ISBN 0 8153 3605 5.

Anderson, Hugh. *Farewell to Judges and Juries: The Broadside Ballads and Convict Transportation to Australia, 1788–1868*. Red Rooster. [2000] pp. xxxiv + 611. ISBN 0 9082 4740 0.

Antor, Heinz, and Klaus Stierstorfer, eds. *English Literatures in International Contexts*. Anglistische Forschungen 283. CWU. [2000] pp. xii + 436. ISBN 3 8253 1020 5.

Armstrong, Pauline. *Frank Hardy and the Making of 'Power Without Glory'*. MelbourneUP. [2000] pp. xix + 249. £18.95 ISBN 0 5228 4888 5.

Asals, Frederick, and Paul Tiessen, eds. *A Darkness That Murmured: Essays on Malcolm Lowry and the Twentieth Century*. UTorP. [2000] pp. 277. $36 ISBN 0 8020 4462 X.

Balme, Christopher B. *Decolonizing the Stage: Theatrical Syncretism and Post-Colonial Drama*. Clarendon. [1999] pp. 320. £48. ISBN 0 1981 8444 1.

Bassnett, Susan, and Harish Trivedi, eds. *Post-Colonial Translation: Theory and Practice*. Routledge. [1999] pp. 201. hb £60 ISBN 0 4151 4744 1, pb £17.99 ISBN 0 4151 4745 X.

Bennett, Bruce, and Susan Hayes, eds. *Home and Away: Australian Stories of Belonging and Alienation*. UWAP. [2000] pp. xix + 168. pb ISBN 1 8762 6836 0.

Bery, Ashok, and Patricia Murray, eds. *Comparing Postcolonial Literatures: Dislocations*. Macmillan. [2000] pp. xi + 283. £50 ISBN 0 3337 2339 2.

Bery, Ashok, Patricia Murray and Wilson Harris, eds. *Comparing Postcolonial Literatures: Dislocations*. St Martin's Press. [2000] pp. xi + 283. $59.95 ISBN 0 3122 2781 7.

Bird, Carmel, ed. *The Penguin Century of Australian Stories*. VikingAus. [2000] pp. xxxiii + 733. ISBN 0 6708 9233 5.

Bird, Delys, ed. *Katharine Susannah Prichard: Stories, Journalism and Essays*. UQP. [2000] pp. xxv + 224. pb $29.95 ISBN 0 7022 3089 8.

Bodunde, Charles. *Oral Traditions and Aesthetic Transfer: Creativity and Social Vision in Contemporary Black Poetry*. Bayreuth African Studies Series 58. Bayreuth. [2000] pp. 142. pb DM39.90 ISBN 3 9275 1069 6.

Bodunde, Charles, ed. *African Languages Literature in the Political Context of the 1990s*. Bayreuth African Studies Series 56. Bayreuth. [2000] pp. 196. hb DM64.90 ISBN 3 9275 1066 1, pb DM39.90 ISBN 3 9275 1056 9.

Booth, Howard J., and Nigel Rigby, eds. *Modernism and Empire*. ManUP. [2000] pp. xiii + 338. hb £45 ISBN 0 7190 5306 4, pb £16.99 ISBN 0 7190 5307 2.

Brewster, Anne, Angeline O'Neill and Rosemary van den Berg, eds. *Those Who Remain Will Always Remember: An Anthology of Aboriginal Writing*. FACP. [2000] pp. 334. pb $A21.50 ISBN 1 8636 8291 0.

Brisbane, Katharine, ed. *Plays of the 60s*, vol. i Currency. [2000] pp. x + 288. pb $A27.50 ISBN 0 8681 9550 2.

Brooks, David, ed. *A.D. Hope: Selected Poetry and Prose*. Halstead. [2000] pp. 239. pb £25 ISBN 1 8756 8440 9.

Brooks, David, ed. *The Double Looking Glass: New and Classic Essays on the Poetry of A.D. Hope*. UQP. [2000] pp. 298. pb $A32.95 ISBN 0 7022 3148 7.

Brown, Stewart, ed. *Kiss and Quarrel: Yorùbá/English, Strategies of Mediation*. Birmingham University African Studies 5. BUP. [2000] pp. 255. £12 ISBN 0 7044 2283 2.

Chancy, Myriam J.A. *Searching for Safe Spaces: Afro-Caribbean Writers in Exile*. TempleUP. [1997] pp. 246. $21.95 ISBN 1 5663 9540 2.

Childs, Peter, ed. *Post-Colonial Theory and English Literature: A Reader*. EdinUP. [1999] pp. viii + 445. £16.95 ISBN 0 7486 1068 5.

Cotrupi, Caterina Nella. *Northrop Frye and the Poetics of Process*. UTorP. [2000] pp. 145. $40 ISBN 0 8020 4316 X.

Cramer, Yvonne, ed. *This Beauteous, Wicked Place: Letters and Journals of John Grant, Gentleman Convict*. NLA. [2000] pp. 224. pb $A31.30 ISBN 0 6421 0702 5.

Cranston, C.A., ed. *Along These Lines: From Trowena to Tasmania—At Least Two Centuries of Peripatetic Perspectives in Poetry and Prose*. Cornford. [2000] pp. 442. hb ISBN 0 9577 5654 2, pb $A29.95 ISBN 0 9577 5651 8.

Crittenden, Victor, ed. *James Tegg: Early Sydney Publisher and Printer*. Bibliographica Historica Australiae 8. Mulini. [2000] pp. 103. pb ISBN 0 9499 1085 6.

Darias-Beutell, Eva. *Contemporary Theories and Canadian Fiction*. Mellen. [2000] pp. 238. $89.95 ISBN 0 7734 8173 7.

de Groen, Fran, and Ken Stewart, eds. *Australian Writing and the City: Refereed Proceedings of the 1999 Conference of the Association for the Study of Australian Literature*. ASAL. [1999] pp. 179. pb ISBN 0 9587 1215 8.

de Serville, Paul. *Rolf Boldrewood: A Life*. Miegunyah. [2000] pp. xviii + 403. $A65.95 ISBN 0 5228 4618 1.

den Otter, Alice G., ed. *Relocating Praise: Literary Modalities and Rhetorical Contexts*. CSP. [2000] pp. 183. $14.95 ISBN 1 5513 0141 5.

Devy, G.N. *'Of Many Heroes': An Indian Essay in Literary Historiography*. Sangam. [1998] pp. x + 213. £14.95 ISBN 0 8631 1748 1.

Dimond, Jill, and Peter Kirkpatrick. *Literary Sydney: A Walking Guide*. UQP. [2000] pp. 193. pb $19.95 ISBN 0 7022 3150 9.

Downing, Jane, and Dirk H.R. Spennemann, eds. *ReCollecting Albury Writing*. Letao. [2000] pp. xvi + 213. pb ISBN 1 8769 4000.

Droogleever, R.W.F., ed. *From the Front: Being the Observations of Mr. A.B. (Banjo) Paterson, Special War Correspondent in South Africa, November 1899 to July 1900, for the Argus, the Sydney Mail, the Sydney Morning Herald*. Pan/Macmillan. [2000] pp. viii + 488. $A44 ISBN 0 7329 1062 5.

Eggleton, David, introd. *Here on Earth: The Landscape in New Zealand Literature*, photographs by Craig Potton. Craig Potton Publishing. [1999] pp. 139. $NZ34.95 ISBN 0 9088 0252 8.

Francis, Flora (Blizzard). *A Black Canadian Bibliography*. Pan-African Publishers. [2000] pp. 152. $CAN20 ($US15) ISBN 0 9682 7343 2.

Ganguly, Debjani, and Kavita Nandan, eds. *Unfinished Journeys: India File from Canberra*. CRNLE. [1998] pp. 308. $A24.95 ISBN 0 7258 0645 1.

Gibbs, James, and Jack Mapanje, eds. *The African Writers' Handbook*. African Books Collective. [1999] pp. 432. £24.95 ($41.95) ISBN 0 9521 2696 6.

Gilbert, Helen, Tseen Khoo and Jacqueline Lo, eds. *Diaspora: Negotiating Asian Australia*. Special joint issue of *JAS* 65 and *Australian Cultural History* 19. UQP. [2000] pp. 245. pb $22 ISBN 0 7022 3214 9.

Gilmore, John. *The Poetics of Empire: A Study of James Grainger's 'The Sugar-Cane'*. AthloneP. [2000] pp. 342. pb $29.95 ISBN 0 4851 2148 4.

Glage, Liselotte, ed. *Being/s in Transit: Travelling, Migration, Dislocation*. Rodopi. [2000] pp. xiv + 217. £35.29 ISBN 9 0420 0649 8.

Goldsworthy, Kerryn, ed. *Australian Women's Stories*. OUPAus. [2000] pp. 320. pb $A29.95 ISBN 0 1955 1295 2.

Gordon, John, ed. *Out of Town: Writing from the New Zealand Countryside*. Shoal Bay Press. [1999] pp. 344. $NZ29.95 ISBN 0 9087 0495 X.

Harris, Margaret, ed. *The Magic Phrase: Critical Essays on Christina Stead*. UQP. [2000] pp. xiv + 305. pb $A32.95 ISBN 0 7022 2506 1.

Haynes, Jonathan, ed. *Nigerian Video Films*. OhioUP. [2000] pp. 267. $28 ISBN 0 8968 0211 6.

Healy, Connie. *Defiance: Political Theatre in Brisbane, 1930–1962*. Boombana. [2000] pp. 255. pb $A24.90 ISBN 1 8765 4204 7.

Hereniko, Vilsoni, and Rob Wilson, eds. *Inside Out: Literature, Cultural Politics and Identity in the New Pacific*. R&L. [1999] pp. ix + 435. hb £55.38 ISBN 0 8476 9142 X, pb £26.95 ISBN 0 8476 9143 8.

Hewett, Dorothy, and John Kinsella. *Wheatlands*. FACP. [2000] pp. 143. pb $A19.95 ISBN 1 8636 8279 1.

Hibberd, Jack. *Selected Plays*. Currency. [2000] pp. xviii +168. pb $A27.50 ISBN 0 8681 9632 0.

Hilf, Susanne. *Writing the Hyphen: The Articulation of Interculturalism in Contemporary Chinese-Canadian Literature*. Lang. [2000] pp.177. £22 ISBN 3 6313 7044 X.

Hogan, Patrick Colm. *Colonialism and Cultural Identity: Crises of Tradition in the Anglophone Literatures of India, Africa, and the Caribbean*. SUNYP. [2000] pp. 353. $63.50 ISBN 0 7914 4459 7.

Hogg, Colin. *A Life in Loose Strides: The Story of Barry Crump*. Hodder, Moa, Beckett. [2000] pp. 200. $NZ34.95 ISBN 1 8695 8822 3.

Hooton, Joy, ed. *Rosemary Dobson: A Celebration*. Friends of the National Library of Australia. [2000] pp. 73. $A12.95 ISBN 0 6421 0728 9.

Johanson, Graeme. *A Study of Colonial Editions in Australia, 1843–1972*. Elibank. [2000] pp. 345. pb $NZ60 ISBN 0 9583 4963 0.

Kamboureli, Smaro. *Scandalous Bodies: Diasporic Literature in English Canada*. OUP. [2000] pp. 268. £9.50 ISBN 0 1954 1450 0.

Keller, Betty C. *Pender Harbour Cowboy: The Many Lives of Bertrand Sinclair*. Touch Wood Editions/Horsdal & Schubart. [2000] pp.224. $CAN18.95 ISBN 0 9206 6372 9.

Keown, Michelle Maria. Whose Paradise? Representations of the Body in the Indigenous Literatures of the South Pacific. Ph.D. thesis, University of Kent. [2000] pp. vi + 238.

Lane, Richard J. *Literature and Loss: Bertrand William Sinclair's British Columbia*. Open Archive/London Network. [2000] pp. 102. £10.50 ISBN 0 9538 0170 5.

Leak, Andrew, and George Paizis, eds. *The Holocaust and the Text: Speaking the Unspeakable*. Macmillan. [2000] pp. ix + 196. pb $24.95 ISBN 0 4151 8553 X.

Lever, Susan. *Real Relations: The Feminist Politics of Form in Australian Fiction*. Halstead. [2000] pp. 174. pb £9.88 ISBN 1 8756 8441 7.

Lindfors, Bernth, ed. *Conversations with Chinua Achebe*. UPMissip. [1997] pp. 199. hb $45 ISBN 0 8780 5929 6, pb $17 ISBN 0 8780 5999 7.

Lindfors, Bernth, and Bala Kothandaraman, eds. *The Writer as Activist: South Asian Perspectives on Ngugi wa Thiong'o*. Africa World Press. [2000] pp. 206. $21.95 ISBN 0 8654 3935 4.

Lindsay, Elaine. *Rewriting God: Spirituality in Contemporary Australian Women's Fiction*. Rodopi. [2000] pp. xvii + 308. pb $21.28 ISBN 9 0420 1582 9.

Loomba, Ania. *Colonialism/Postcolonialism*. Routledge. [1998] pp. 289. £40 ISBN 0 4151 2808 0.

Manhire, Bill. *Doubtful Sounds: Essays and Interviews*. VictUP. [2000] pp. 295. $NZ34.95 ISBN 0 8647 3370 4.

Manning, Frederic. *The Middle Parts of Fortune: Somme and Ancre 1916* [1929]. Text. [2000] pp. xiii + 301. pb $A24.95 ISBN 1 8764 8582 5.

Mengham, Rod, and Glen Phillips, eds. *Fairly Obsessive: Essays on the Work of John Kinsella*. FACP. [2000] pp. 308. pb $A29.95 ISBN 1 8636 8325 9.

Miles, John. *Lost Angry Penguins. D.B. Kerr and P.G. Pfeiffer: A Path to the Wind*. Crawford. [2000] pp. xx + 294. pb $A27.45 ISBN 1 8633 3191 3.

Moreton-Robinson, Aileen. *Talkin' Up to the White Woman: Indigenous Women and Feminism*. UQP. [2000] pp. xxv + 234. pb $20.95 ISBN 0 7022 3134 7.

Morey, Peter. *Fictions of India: Narrative and Power*. EdinUP. [2000] pp. viii + 216. £15.95 ISBN 0 7486 1181 9.

Mukherjee, Meenakshi. *The Perishable Empire: Essays on Indian Writing in English*. OUPI. [2000] pp. xiii + 212. Rs.825 (£17) ISBN 0 1956 5147 2.

Needham, Anuradha Dingwaney. *Using the Master's Tools: Resistance and the Literature of the African and South Asian Diasporas*. Macmillan. [2000] pp. xii + 176. £30 ISBN 0 3339 1530 5.

Nile, Richard, ed. *The Australian Legend and its Discontents*. UQP. [2000] pp. viii + 354. pb $19.95 ISBN 0 7022 2985 7.

Nischik, Reingard M. *Margaret Atwood: Works and Impact*. Camden House. [2000] pp. 344. £30 ISBN 1 5711 3139 6.

Novak, Dagmar. *Dubious Glory: The Two World Wars and the Canadian Novel.* Lang. [2000] pp. 174. £32 ISBN 0 8204 4549 5.

Ogilvie, Gordon. *Denis Glover: His Life.* Godwit. [1999] pp. 544. $NZ59.95 ISBN 1 8696 2038 0.

Ogundele, Wole, ed. *Ulli Beier. The Hunter Thinks the Monkey Is Not Wise: Selected Essays.* Bayreuth African Studies Series 59. Bayreuth. [2000] pp. 230. DM39.90 ISBN 3 9275 1071 8.

Probyn, Clive, and Bruce Steele, eds. *Henry Handel Richardson. The Letters,* vol i: *1874–1915*; vol. ii: *1917–1933*; vol. iii: *1934–1946.* Miegunyah. [2000] pp. xxxv + 623, xxviii + 531, xxii + 767. $A88 each ISBN 0 5228 4797 8 (vol. i), ISBN 0 5228 4935 0 (vol. ii), ISBN 0 5228 4936 9 (vol. iii).

Rayson, Hannie. *Life After George.* Currency. [2000] pp. xvii +81. pb $A17.95 ISBN 0 8681 9628 2.

Roderick, Colin, ed. *Rose Paterson's Illalong Letters, 1873–1888.* Kangaroo. [2000] pp. 224. pb $A24.95 ISBN 0 7318 0926 2.

Rutherford, Jennifer. *The Gauche Intruder: Freud, Lacan and the White Australian Fantasy.* MelbourneUP. [2000] pp. xi + 239. pb £13 ISBN 0 5228 4917 2.

Sayer, Mandy, and Louis Nowra, eds. *In the Gutter ... Looking at the Stars: A Literary Adventure through Kings Cross.* RandomHAus. [2000] pp. xxiii + 400. pb $A49.95 ISBN 1 7405 1012 7.

Schaub, Danielle. ed. *Mapping Canadian Cultural Space: Essays on Canadian Literature.* Magnes Press. [2000] pp. 162. $23 ISBN 9 6549 3087 0.

Shearer, Jill. *Georgia.* Currency. [2000] pp. xii + 76. pb $A17.95 ISBN 0 8681 9606 1.

Smith, Rowland, ed. *Postcolonizing the Commonwealth: Studies in Literature and Culture.* WLUP. [2000] pp. vi + 216. $44.95 ISBN 0 8892 0352 0.

Spivak, Gayatri Chakravorty. *A Critique of Postcolonial Reason: Toward a History of the Vanishing Present.* HarvardUP. [1999] pp. xiii + 449. £16.95 ISBN 0 6741 7764 9.

Stead, C.K. *The Writer at Work: Essays.* UOtagoP. [2000] pp. 281. $NZ39.95 ISBN 1 8771 3395 7.

Stewart, Ken. *Investigations in Australian Literature.* Sydney Studies 20. Shoestring. [2000] pp. 205. pb £8.83 ISBN 1 8648 7280 2.

Strong-Boag, Veronica, and Carole Gerson. *Paddling Her Own Canoe: The Times and Texts of E. Pauline Johnson (Tekahionwake).* UTorP. [2000] pp. 331. hb £40 ($65) ISBN 0 8020 4162 0, pb £16 ($25.95) ISBN 0 8020 8024 3.

Thompson, Dawn. *Writing a Politics of Perception: Memory, Holography, and Women Writers in Canada.* UTorP. [2000] pp. 143. £20 ($35) ISBN 0 8020 4365 8.

Va'ai, Sina Mary Theresa. *Literary Representations in Western Polynesia: Colonialism and Indigeneity.* National University of Samoa. [1999] pp. ix + 399. £66.66 ISBN 9 8290 0310 8.

Vanita, Ruth, and Saleem Kidwai, eds. *Same-Sex Love in India: Readings from Literature and History.* Macmillan. [2000] pp. xxiv + 370. £35 ISBN 0 3338 0033 8.

Verma, K.D. *The Indian Imagination: Critical Essays on Indian Writing in English.* Macmillan. [2000] pp. xi + 268. £30 ISBN 0 3339 1522 4.

Vice, Sue. *Holocaust Fiction*. Routledge. [2000] pp. 239. hb $75 ISBN 0 4151 8552 1, pb $24.95 ISBN 0 4151 8553 X.

Webby, Elizabeth, and Gillian Sykes, eds. *Walter and Mary: The Letters of Walter and Mary Richardson*. Miegunyah. [2000] pp. xiii + 277. $45 ISBN 0 5228 4923 7.

Webby, Elizabeth, ed. *The Cambridge Companion to Australian Literature*. CUP. [2000] pp. xxi +326. hb $54.95 ISBN 0 5216 5122 0, pb $19.95 ISBN 0 5216 5843 8.

Whitlock, Gillian. *The Intimate Empire: Reading Women's Autobiography*. Cassell. [2000] pp. viii + 232. hb £49.95 ISBN 0 3047 0599 3, pb £25 ISBN 0 3047 0600 0.

Williamson, David. *The Great Man/Sanctuary: Two Plays*. Currency. [2000] pp. 128. pb $17.95 ISBN 0 8681 9633 9.

Wisker, Gina. *Post-Colonial and African American Women's Writing: A Critical Introduction*. St Martin's Press. [2000] pp. 376. $19.95 ISBN 0 3122 3288 8.

Worsfold, Brian. *South Africa Backdrop: An Historical Introduction for South African Literary and Cultural Studies*. Universitat de Lleida. [1999] pp. 163. ISBN 8 4840 9994 6.

XVIII

Bibliography and Textual Criticism

WILLIAM BAKER AND JOANN SCHOLTES

Much of this year's new work in bibliography appears in the growing collection of journals dedicated to the field. *Papers of the Bibliographical Society of America* (94[2000]) includes the following articles in addition to reviews: '"People of the Book": The Production of Theological Texts in Early Modern England' by Kari Konkola (pp. 5–34); 'A Stop Press Correction in Christina Rossetti's *Goblin Market*' by Maura Ives (pp. 35–48); 'Contributions to the Canon and Text of Padraic Colum's Writings' by Arthur Sherbo (pp. 49–80); 'Additions and Emendations to Pre-1801 Entries in Thomas J. Holmes's Bibliographies of the Mathers' by Keith Arbour (pp. 81–130); 'Pre-Ornamented Bookcloth on Nineteenth-Century Cloth Case Bindings' by Andrea Krupp and Jennifer Woods Rosner (pp. 176–96); 'Thomas Middleton, Thomas Dekker, and *The Bloody Banquet*' by Gary Taylor (pp. 197–234); '"Favoritism has been Practiced": New Capital, Old Printer in Dakota Territory' by Robert D. Armstrong (pp. 235–54); 'Recuperating the Author: Consuming Fictions of the 1990s' by Juliet Gardiner (pp. 255–74); 'A Little Known Chapter in Hebrew Printing: Francesco dalle Donne and the Beginning of Hebrew Printing in Verona in the Sixteenth Century' by Marvin J. Heller (pp. 333–47); 'James Franklin, Apprentice, Artisan, Dissident, and Teacher' by Keith Arbour (pp. 348–76); 'Defoe De-Attributions Scrutinized under Hargevik Criteria: Applying Stylometrics to the Canon' by Irving N. Rothman (pp. 375–98); 'Magazines and the Profession of Authorship in the United States, 1840–1900' by Ellery Sedgwick (pp. 399–432); '"Dear Lawrence," "Dear Bill": William A. Jackson, Lawrence C. Wroth, and the Practice of Bibliography in America' by Roger E. Stoddard (pp. 479–506); 'Electrifying Research in Medieval and Renaissance Manuscripts' by Gregory A. Pass (pp. 507–30); 'Letter Manuals, Literary Innovation, and the Problem of Defining Genre in Anglo-American Epistolary Instruction, 1568–1800' by Konstantin Dierks (pp. 541–50); and 'The Early Publication History of Scott's *Minstrelsy of the Scottish Border*' by Jane Millgate (pp. 551–64).

Library (22:i[2000]) features Peter Lucas's 'Sixteenth-Century English Spelling Reform and the Printers in Continental Perspective: Sir Thomas Smith and John Hart' (pp. 3–21); Clive Griffin's 'Inquisitional Trials and Printing-Workers in Sixteenth-Century Spain' (pp. 22–45); and Beth Lynch's 'Mr. Smirke and "Mr. Filth": A Bibliographic Case Study in Nonconformist Printing' (pp. 46–71). *Library* (22:ii[2000]) features Margaret Connolly's 'Books Connected with Battle Abbey before the Dissolution: Some New Discoveries' (pp. 119–32) and Shef Rogers's 'The Use of Royal Licences for Printing in England, 1695–1760: A Bibliography' (pp. 133–92). *Library* (22:iii[2000]) features Anne F Sutton's 'Malory in Newgate: A New Document' (pp. 243–62); Martin Boghardt's 'Pinhole Patterns in Large-Format Incunabula' (pp. 263–89); Helen Carron's 'William Sancroft (1617–93): A Seventeenth-Century Collector and his Library' (pp. 290–307); and James Armstrong's '"On Account of Literary Indiscretions": Wyndham Lewis and the Publication of Marjorie Firminger's *Jam To-Day: A Novel* (1930)' (pp. 308–21). *Library* (22:iv[2000]) features David McKitterick's 'Women and their Books in Seventeenth-Century England: The Case of Elizabeth Puckering' (pp. 359–80); Jast Scott-Warren's 'News, Sociability, and Bookbuying in Early Modern England: The Letters of Sir Thomas Cornwallis' (pp. 381–402); and N.W. Bawcutt's 'A Crisis of Laudian Censorship: Nicholas and John Okes and the Publication of Sales's *An Introduction to a Devout Life* in 1637' (pp. 403–38).

TEXT: An Interdisciplinary Annual of Textual Studies (13[2000]) includes reviews and the following articles: W. Speed Hill's 'Where Would Anglo-American Textual Criticism Be if Shakespeare had Died of the Plague in 1593?' (pp. 1–8); Tim William Machan's '"I endowed the purposes": Shakespeare, Editing, and Middle English Literature' (pp. 9–26); Paul Werstine's 'Editing Shakespeare and Editing Without Shakespeare: Wilson, McKerrow, Greg, Bowers, Tanselle, and Copy-Text Editing' (pp. 27–54); Klaus Hurlesbusch's 'Understanding the Author's Compositional Method: Prolegomenon to a Hermeneutics of Genetic Writing' (pp. 55–102); H.T.M. van Vilet's 'Scholarly Editing in the Netherlands' (pp. 103–30); Annemarie Kets-Vree's 'Dutch Scholarly Editing: The Historical-Critical Edition in Practice' (pp. 131–50); Steven Mentz's 'Selling Sidney: William Ponsonby, Thomas Nashe, and the Boundaries of Elizabethan Print and Manuscript Cultures' (pp. 151–74); Gary A. Stringer's 'Evidence for an Authorial Sequence in Donne's Elegies' (pp. 175–92); Ted-Larry Pebworth's 'The Early Censorship of John Donne's Elegies and "Sapho to Philaenis" in Manuscript and Print' (pp. 193–202); Sam Slote's 'Reading *Finnegans Wake* Genetically' (pp. 203–20); Dirk Fan Hulle's 'The *Wake*'s Progress: Toward a Genetic Edition' (pp. 221–32); and Catherine Hollis's 'No Marriage in Heaven: Editorial Resurrection in Djuna Barnes's *Nightwood*' (pp. 233–54).

Analytical and Enumerative Bibliography (11:i[2000]) features Karen Bjelland's 'The Editor as Theologian, Historian, and Archaeologist: Shifting Paradigms within Editorial Theory and their Sociocultural Ramifications' (pp. 1–43). *AEB* (11:ii[2000]) includes James K. Bracken's 'Evidence of George Holmes's Corrections to the First Edition of the *Foedera* (1704–17)' (pp. 114–23); Genevieve West's '"Looking for Zora": A Calendar of Correspondence' (pp. 124–78); and Robert F. Fleissner's 'The Round Knight of the Table: Did Not Theobald Emend "a'talkd of" (rather than "a Table of") in *Henry V*?' (pp. 179–80). *AEB* (11:iii[2000]) opens with Barbara Laning Fitzpatrick's 'Physical Evidence for John Coote's Eighteenth-Century Periodical Proprietorships: The Examples of Coote's *Royal Magazine* (1759–71) and Smollett's *British Magazine* (1760–67)' (pp. 211–58). The year's final issue, *AEB* (11:iv[2000]), includes Kimberly Van Kampen's 'Do We Really Have the Translator's Notes for the 1560 Geneva Bible?' (pp. 290–302) and Genevieve West's '"Looking for Zora": An Addendum' (pp. 303–9).

Bulletin of Bibliography (57:i[2000]) includes Theresa R. McDevitt's 'A Place for Women: A Selective Annotated Bibliography on Civil War Women in Medical Services' (pp. 1–11); Craig Gable's 'Rudolph Fisher: An Updated Selected Bibliography' (pp. 13–19); Rosa Lou Novi's 'Annotated Bibliography for the Hudson Valley Heritage Project' (pp. 21–30); Shmuel Ben-Gad's 'Robert Bresson: A Bibliography of Works by and about Him, 1994–1998' (pp. 31–7); and Allan Metz's 'Presidential Leadership in the Clinton Era: A Bibliography' (pp. 39–61). *BB* (57:ii[2000]) includes Kathy Sheehan's 'Piecing Together the Puzzle of Susan Glaspell: A Bibliography' (pp. 69–84); Arthur Buell's 'Mount Everest, 1994–1999: A Bibliography' (pp. 85–93); Timothy E. McMahon's 'An Annotated Bibliography of Works by Theodore Kaczynski from 1965 to 1969 Drawn from the MathSciNet Database' (pp. 95–7); Julie A. Davis's 'A Bibliography on Three Films of "Hamlet": Covering Literature from 1948 to 1999' (pp. 99–105); Allan Metz's 'Two Rock/Pop Bibliographies' (pp. 107–33). *BB* (57:iii[2000]) includes James E. May's 'Addenda to "A Bibliography of Secondary Materials for the Study of Edward Young, 1683–1765"' (pp. 135–46); D.J. Hoek's 'Jazz Analyses: An Annotated Guide to Periodical Literature' (pp. 147–52); Halie Crocker's 'Carson McCullers since 1980: A Bibliography' (pp. 153–7); Annie Y. Hor's 'The Conversion of Hong Kong from a British Colony to a Special Administrative Region of the People's Republic of China: A Selected Bibliography' (pp. 159–69); Stephen W. Delchamps's 'Gavin Ewart: A Bibliography' (pp. 171–8); Shmuel Ben-Gad's 'Robert Bresson: A Bibliography of Works by and about him: A Supplementary Bibliography' (pp. 179–84). *BB* (57:iv[2000]) includes Lenora P. Blouin's '"The Stern Growth of a Lyric Poet": May Sarton, Writing Poetry/Writing about Poetry and Major Critical Responses to Sarton's Poetry: A Bibliographic Survey' (pp. 191–206); David J. Duncan's 'Henry of Monmouth and Parliament: A Bibliography Concerning their Political Relations' (pp. 207–20); Michael Benzel's 'The Character and Role of the American Intellectual as Defined in Periodical Literature from 1950 to 1959: An Annotated Bibliography' (pp. 221–36); Robert L. Battenfeld's 'The Deep Ecology of Arne Naess: A Bibliography' (pp. 237–48); Isaac Hunter Dunlap's 'The "Black Paintings" of Francisco de Goya: An Annotated Bibliography' (pp. 249–56); and John A. Drobnicki's 'Holocaust-Denial Literature: A Fourth Bibliography' (pp. 257–86).

Antiquarian Book Monthly Review (27:i[2000]) features Peter van den Dungen's 'The Price of Peace...Rare Books of Peace' (pp. 10–17); Judith Beiss's 'The Morgan Library. The Great Experiment: George Washington and the American Republic' (pp. 32–3); and Jo Hurd's 'Supernatural and Small Presses' (pp. 37–8). *ABM* (27:ii[2000]) features Bruce Tice's 'Bibles: A Display for the Millennium' (p. 11); Lucy Gordan's 'The Berg Collection to Turn Sixty' (pp. 14–18); Judith Beiss's 'The Grolier Club: A Century for the Century' (pp. 23–4); and William H.P. Crewdson's 'Randolph Caldecott' (pp. 32–6). *ABM* (27:iii[2000]) includes Joe McCann's 'Fagging in Oxford' (p. 10) and 'Blathering: A Selection of Salacious Stories of Signings, Signatures and Other Scurrilous Sideswipes' (pp. 8–9); David Ashford's 'Old Bloods and Fierce Boys Journals' (pp. 24–9); and Eric Ford's 'A Literary Light Hidden under a Bushel' (pp. 32–5). *ABM* (27:iv[2000]) includes Lucy Gordan's 'A Rose for Love and a Book Forever' (pp. 15–16); Richard W. Oram's 'Harry Ransom Brings the T.E. Hanley Library to Texas' (pp. 20–4); and James G. Nelson's 'Leonard Smithers: Publisher to the Decadents' (pp. 33–8). *ABM*

(27:v[2000]) features R.B. Russell's 'Edward Heron-Allen and Christopher Blayre' (pp. 18–23); Carol Grossman's 'The Revelation of Saint John the Divine' (pp. 30–2); Matthew Sturgiss's '"The Artist as a Portrait"' (p. 34); and David Cohen's 'Remembering John Ruskin' (pp. 36–7). *ABM* (27:vi[2000]) features Steven Halliwell's 'June Fairs Preview' (pp. 14–19); Barry Newport's 'The Whittington Press: The Last Ten Years' (pp. 22–8); Lucy Gordan's 'Gutenberg: Man of the Millennium' (pp. 32–3); Michael Holman's 'PBFA at the Post House' (p. 36); Sarah Kirkpatrick's '"Chapter and Verse": A British Library Exhibition' (pp. 38–9); and Henry Wessells's 'The 40th Annual New York Antiquarian Book Fair' (p. 51). *ABM* (27:vii[2000]) features Lucy Gordan's 'The New York Academy of Medicine Founded to Improve Public Health' (pp. 18–23) and 'The Marciana National Library' (pp. 24–6); and Diana R. Mackarill's 'Book-Hawking: A Moral Enterprise' (pp. 35–9). *ABM* (27:viii[2000]) features William H.P. Crewdson's 'T.C. Bridges' (pp. 32–6). *ABM* (27:ix[2000]) features Michael Holman's 'Cecil Court: A Short History' (pp. 10–14); J. Robert Maguire's 'An Oscar Wilde Autograph Envelope at Auction' (pp. 30–3); Lucy Gordan's 'The Gospels of the Peoples' (pp. 34–5); and Catherine Melo's 'Minority Rights: Young People and Book Collecting' (p. 42). *ABM* (27:x[2000]) features Dr Barry Newport's 'A Weevil in a Biscuit: Robert Louis Stevenson and Bournemouth' (pp. 10–14); David Ashford's 'Fun & Thrills: The Swan Publications' (pp. 20–7); and William H.P. Crewdson's 'John Hassall' (pp. 28–32). *ABM* (27:xi[2000]) features Michael Holman's 'Booksellers of our Time: Jeff Towns, Dylans Bookstore, Swansea' (p. 10); Richard J. Westall's 'Towards a Catalogue of Richard Westall Prints' (pp. 17–21); Matthew Young's 'The Mystery of Walt Ruding: A Solution' (pp. 22–6); and Lucy Gordan's 'Imagining the Ideal: Utopia and the Rest of All Possible Worlds' (pp. 28–9).

The Book Collector (49:i[2000]) includes Joe Rock's 'An Important Scottish Anatomical Publication Rediscovered' (pp. 27–60) and Stephanie Newell's 'Popular Publishing in Nigeria and Ghana' (pp. 61–88). *BC* (49:ii[2000]) features David Pearson's 'Bookbinding in Oxford in the Sixteenth Century' (pp. 200–21); Deirdre Le Faye's 'New Marginalia in Jane Austen's Books' (pp. 222–6); and Colin Franklin's 'The Bowdlers and their Family Shakespeare' (pp. 227–43). *BC* (49:iii[2000]) features A.S.G. Edwards and Jeremy Griffiths's 'The Tollemache Collection of Medieval Manuscripts' (pp. 349–64); Steven E. Smith's 'The Comedy, History, and Tragedy of Edwin Forrest and his Books' (pp. 365–82); and Joseph Rosenblum's 'The Bookseller and the Bibliographer' (pp. 383–96). *BC* (49:iv[2000]) includes 'Ian Gordon Brown's "Collecting Scott for Scotland: 1850–2000"' (pp. 502–34) and Robert A. Shaddy's 'Grangerizing' (pp. 535–46).

Journal of Scholarly Publishing (31:ii[2000]) includes 'List Building in a Monty Python Context' by Leslie Mitchner (pp. 61–7); 'The Pitt Poetry Series: Why and How' by Ed Ochester (pp. 68–76); 'The Utility of Publishers' Websites' by Kevin H. Posey (pp. 77–86); 'Jump-Starting a Journal's Paper Flow: Fourteen Tested, Effective Methods' by D. Barry Lumsden (pp. 87–95); and 'Personalities in Publishing: Edwin Shelock' by Hazel Bell (pp. 96–101). *JScholP* (31:iii[2000]) includes 'Editing the Pretext' by Robert Bringhurst (pp. 113–25); 'From STONE to *Mouse*' by George Mackie (pp. 126–33); 'On Presses and Press Marks' by Will Underwood (pp. 134–40); and 'Personalities in Publishing: John Miles' by Hazel Bell (pp. 141–6). *JScholP* (31:iv[2000]) includes 'If You Plan It, They Will Come: Editors as Architects' by Peter J. Dougherty (pp. 175–8); 'The Greatest Story Ever

Sold: The Pitfalls of Publishing Proceedings, etc.' by Trevor Lipscombe (pp. 179–88); 'Dust Jacket Attributes of Books Acquired by an Academic Research Library in 1997–98' by William C. Robinson (pp. 189–206); and 'Personalities in Publishing: Douglas Matthews' by Hazel Bell (pp. 207–13). *JScholP* (32:i[2001]) includes 'Fair Use: A Double-Edged Sword' by Sanford G. Thatcher (pp. 3–8); 'From Gutenberg to Gateway: Electronic Publishing at University Presses' by Jennifer M. Siler (pp. 9–23); 'Academic Publishing and the University Presses: The Case in a Developing Region (Saudi Arabia)' by Manzurul Islam (pp. 24–33); 'The Editor as Gap-Filler: The Letters of Margaret Laurence and Adele Wiseman' by Ruth Panofsky (pp. 33–42); and 'Personalities in Publishing: Ian Norrie' by Hazel Bell (pp. 34–49).

The *East-Central Intelligencer* (14:February[2000]) includes Elizabeth Nelson's 'Mysteries Stalk the Eighteenth Century' (pp. 22–4); John Greene's *'Belfast Newsletter* Index Database, 1737–1800' (pp. 16–17); Jack Lynch's 'c18 Bibliographies On-Line' (p. 17); Randolph Vigne's 'The Huguenot Society of Great Britain and Ireland: Past and Present' (pp. 13–16); Susan Berg's 'Keeping the Past Alive: The John D. Rockefeller, Jr., Library Colonial Williamsburg Foundation, Williamsburg, VA' (pp. 11–13); Joan K. Stemmler's 'The 1999 EC/ASECS Presidential Address: Metaphorical Potentials of the Golden Section Ratio in the Long, Long, Long 18th Century: Manet's *Déjeuner dans l'atelier*' (pp. 2–8); and 'Contemporary Library and Manuscript Collections' (pp. 60–85). *ECIntell* (14:September[2000]) includes Susan Berg's 'The Mariners' Museum Research Library' (pp. 2–4); Deborah J. Leslie's 'Resources for 18th-Century Studies at the Folger' *(pp. 5–7)*; Richard W. Oram's 'Four Texian Myths Debunk'd: The 18th Century at the Harry Ransom Humanities Research Center' (pp. 8–9); Kenneth W. Graham's *'Vathek with the Episodes of Vathek*: The Role of the Suppressed "Story of Alasi and Firouz"' *(pp.* 10–12); and Christine Clark-Evans's 'The Translator Self-Revealed: Diderot's Comments on Pope's *Essay on Man*' *(pp.* 12–16) and 'Recent Studies in 18th-Century Book Culture' *(pp.* 57–89).

The *Journal of the Early Book Society* (3[2000]) includes the following articles: '"Thanne motyn we to bokys": Writing's Harvest in the Prologue to the *Legend of Good Women*' by Burt Kimmelman; 'British Library MS Harley 630: Saint Alban's and Lydgate' by Larissa Tracy; 'The Lydgate Canon in Print from 1476 to 1534' by Alexandra Gillespie; 'Verbal and Visual Metaphors in the Cambridge Manuscript of the *Douze Dames de Rhétorique* (1463)' by David J. Cowling; 'Sources of, and Analogues to, the *Noble Boke of Cokery*' by Constance B. Hieatt; 'An Assortment of Doctors: The Readers of Medical Books in Late Medieval England' by Claire Jones; 'The *Margarita Philosophica*: A Case Study in Early Modern Book Design' by Barbara Halporn; and 'The Value/s of Manuscript Study: A Personal Retrospect' by Derek Pearsall.

A useful and thorough guide to bibliographical sources is William Baker and Kenneth Womack's *Twentieth-Century Bibliography and Textual Criticism: An Annotated Bibliography* which lists 769 twentieth-century monographs and articles. Students and teachers of bibliographical methods will wish to take note of the second edition (paperback) of James L. Harner's *On Compiling an Annotated Bibliography* (originally published in 1985 and revised in 1991). Harner provides helpful, time-saving advice to those beginning bibliographical projects. Those interested in printing and publishing might make easy use of Dorothy A. Harrop's *The Old Stile Press—in the Twentieth Century: A Bibliography, 1979–1999.*

Maurice Rickards's *The Encyclopedia of Ephemera* gives examples of the infinite range of ephemera from football programmes and envelopes to bookmarks and playing-cards. The role of women in writing and the book trade is the subject of Axel Erdmann's *My Gracious Silence: Women in the Mirror of Sixteenth-Century Printing in Western Europe*. The first section traces the history of books illustrated by women and the contributions by women in the book trade throughout Europe. The second section is a bibliography of women writers, books illustrated by women, and women in the book business. A new study that takes a geographical approach to bibliography is *Rome: A Bibliography from the Invention of Printing through 1899, I: 'The Guide Books'* by Sergio Rosetti. Another geographically focused bibliography is Willem Heijting's *Protestantism Crossing the Seas. A Short-Title Catalogue of English Books Printed Before 1801 Illustrating the Spread of Protestant Thought and the Exchange of Ideas between the English-Speaking Countries and the Netherlands held by the University Library of the Vrije Universiteit at Amsterdam*.

Middle English Word Studies: A Word and Author Index by Louise Sylvester and Jane Roberts is an annotated bibliography of 1,000 journal articles, essays, and books about Middle English etymology. The entries are listed alphabetically by author's last name. Word and author indexes facilitate quick searches for specific references. Christine Rauer provides two unique bibliographies related to *Beowulf* in *Beowulf and the Dragon: Parallels and Analogues*. The bibliographies are for works on Scandinavian dragon-fights and saints and destructive dragons. Rauer also provides a list of texts and translations of *Beowulf*. Robert J. Blanch's *The Gawain Poems: A Reference Guide, 1978–1993* is the first bibliography in twenty years to cover all four Gawain poems, and includes 942 annotated entries divided into editions and translations, criticism, and reference/pedagogical works. Four indexes—word, line, subject, and author—are also provided. A catalogue of manuscripts and various indexes can be found in Ann Eljenholm Nichols's *The Bodleian Library, Oxford: I, MSS Additional—Digby*. This is the initial offering of a multi-volume project entitled *An Index of Images in English Manuscripts from the Time of Chaucer to Henry VIII, c.1380–c.1509*. Marilyn Sutton edits *Chaucer's Pardoner's Prologue and Tale: An Annotated Bibliography 1900–1995*, the seventh volume in the Chaucer Bibliography series. This definitive secondary bibliography offers over 1,200 entries, including important nineteenth-century works.

Bibliographical work on Shakespeare and the Renaissance continues to flourish. *Shakespearian Bibliography and Textual Criticism: A Bibliography*, compiled by T.H. Howard-Hill, offers a comprehensive annotated list of bibliographies and textual studies on Shakespeare. Over 2,300 items are listed, edited by James L. Harner, and now available on the internet by subscription. The bibliography offers annotated entries for works on Shakespeare between 1977 and 1998. The entries number 68,000 and refer to works and productions from nations throughout the world. Unlike the electronic MLA International bibliography, the *World Shakespeare Bibliography Online* contains citations for reviews. The site can be searched for specific themes and subjects, such as roles played by a particular actor or a given theme in individual or several works. Also of relevance to sixteenth-century studies is James P. Carley's *The Libraries of King Henry VIII*.

The posthumous publication of J.D. Fleeman's lifelong project to compile Samuel Johnson's bibliography represents the year's greatest bibliographic achievement. *A Bibliography of the Works of Samuel Johnson: Treating his Published Works from the Beginnings to 1984*, volume i: *1731–1759* and volume ii: *1760–1816*, is the definitive bibliography of Johnson's works. It catalogues all of his writing that appeared in various editions, anthologies, and translations, as well as his unpublished works. The bibliography includes works written and translated by Johnson, revised works, dedications and prefaces written by Johnson, and some materials attributed to Johnson without evidence to support or refute the attribution. The bibliography is divided into four volumes: publications initiated in 1760–9, 1770–9, 1780–9, and 1790–1816. Both alphabetical and chronological lists of publications are included, as well as an index of persons and places. A remarkable accomplishment, the bibliography will prove an essential resource for Johnson scholars. In another contribution to Johnson studies, Jack Lynch presents a secondary bibliography of Johnson studies in *A Bibliography of Johnsonian Studies, 1986–1998*. The bibliography includes book reviews, MA theses, and dissertations, plus electronic publications.

Garside and Schöwerling, eds., *The English Novel, 1770–1829: A Bibliographical Survey of Prose Fiction Published in the British Isles*, volume ii: *1800–1829*, provides the publication history , world-wide library holdings, pricing, reviews, and a list of first editions for all prose fiction published in the years 1800–29. The geographic scope of the list extends beyond the British Isles to Ireland and North America. The bibliography also includes the first English translations of foreign works. Eighteenth-century scholars will also wish to take note of two bibliographies related to journals and magazines: Edward W.R. Pitcher's *The British Magazine, January 1760–December 1767: An Annotated Index of Signatures Ascriptions, Subjects, and Titles of Literary Prose*, and *Eighteenth-Century Journals from the Hope Collection at the Bodleian Library, Oxford: A Listing and Guide to the Microfilm Collection*.

A Checklist of American Newspaper Carriers' Addresses, 1720–1820, by Gerald D. McDonald, Stuart C. Sherman and Mary T. Russo, compiles the addresses produced by 940 American newspapers, plus sixty-one Canadian entries. Newspaper carriers presented the addresses to subscribers as New Year's greetings (and not so subtle solicitations for cash gifts). These verses are an overlooked sub-genre in American poetry, and this is the first bibliography of its kind. Many of the verses are not signed, but some of the signed works were written by William Biglow, William Cobbett, Benjamin Franklin, Philip Freneau, and Samuel Woodworth, among others.

Nineteenth-century scholars will welcome the publication of T.A. Burnett's *The British Library Catalogue of the Ashley Manuscripts* [1999] which offers the first reliable catalogue of T.J. Wise's Ashley library. A general index and title/first-line index are included. The two volumes of Chaudhuri and Radford, eds., *Cumulative Bibliography of Victorian Studies, 1945–1969* each contain over 600 pages of references. Volume i is the cumulation, and volume ii is the indexes, organized by subject, author, and title. The subject areas are general and reference works, fine arts, philosophy and religion, history, social sciences, science and technology, and language and literature. Seventy authors are listed individually, and additional authors are listed in the final section. Another welcome addition to nineteenth-century bibliography is *The Shakespeare Head Brontë: Bibliography of the Works of All Members of the Brontë Family and of Brontëana* by John Alexander

Symington and Thomas James Wise. *The Shakespeare Head Brontë* is a first-edition comprehensive bibliography originally begun by Alexander Symington in the 1930s, with coverage of all Brontëana and the works of all members of the Brontë family. The first nineteen volumes were published from 1931 and 1936, but the final volume remained unfinished at the outbreak of the Second World War. The final volume, published in 2000 and edited by Wise, was printed from galley proofs acquired by Daphne du Maurier. A bibliography of 1997 works on Robert and Elizabeth Barrett Browning appears in *Victorian Literature and Culture* (*VLC* 28:i[2000] 479–94). It is compiled by Sandra M. Donaldson, Dominic Bisignano and Melissa Brotton. Edward W.R. Pitcher has compiled *The New York Weekly Museum: An Annotated Index of the Literary Prose, 1800–1811*, which contains an alphabetical listing and a selective subject index.

Neil Wilson's *Shadow's in the Attic: A Guide to British Supernatural Fiction, 1820–1950* includes an introduction by Ramsey Campbell. Wilson's bibliography is a selection of 200 authors who first published works between 1820 and 1950 and were residents in the British Isles (including Ireland) or British citizens living at home or abroad (e.g. Henry James and Vernon Lee). Brief biographical information and notes supplement the primary bibliography and selective secondary bibliographies for each author. Mus White provides a bibliography of children's books in *From the Mundane to the Magical: Photographically Illustrated Children's Books, 1854–1945 and Beyond*. Most of the books in White's list were printed in America, but some were published in Australia, France, Germany, and Scandinavia. Valerie Traub provides a narrative selected bibliographical study in her essay 'Recent Studies in Homoeroticism' (*ELR* 30:ii[2000] 284–329).

A great number of new bibliographies for individual writers appeared this year. Karma Pippin edits the second edition of John Windle's *Mary Wollstonecraft Godwin, 1759–1797: A Bibliography of the First and Early Editions, with Briefer Notes on Later Editions and Translations*. The bibliography includes primary titles, contributions and translations, false attributions, a selected secondary bibliography of the author and her time, and a chronology. William E. Cain, ed., points to a number of useful bibliography sources on Henry David Thoreau in his bibliographical essay that concludes *A Historical Guide to Henry David Thoreau*. Another bibliography of interest to Victorian scholars is *Caroline Clive, 1801–1873: A Bibliography* [1999] by Charlotte Mitchell. Primary and secondary bibliographies of works by and about Bernard C. Middleton are included in his autobiography *Recollections: A Life in Bookbinding*. Bookbinder Mirjam Foot's publications are included in Pearson, ed., *For the Love of Binding: Studies in Bookbinding History Presented to Mirjam Foot*.

Winston S. Churchill, 1874–1965: A Comprehensive Historiography and Annotated Bibliography by Eugene L. Rasor is the sixth volume in the Bibliographies of World Leaders series. Rasor's is the only recent bibliography of Churchill, and it is an extensive one. Over 3,000 annotated entries list works by and about Churchill. Rasor places the works in specific historical contexts, categorizing many into fifteen controversies with which Churchill was associated. The annotated list also includes over thirty biographies of Churchill that reflect the diversity of opinion surrounding one of Britain's most influential and recognized political leaders. Sydney Cauveren presents *A.L. Rowse: A Bibliophile's Extensive Bibliography*, which covers the historian and essayist's 1,076 articles and other writings. Primary and secondary bibliographies of novelist Timothy Mo's works are included in Elaine Yee Lin Ho's *Timothy Mo*. The works of British Canadian poet and author Robert Service are listed and described in Peter Mitham's *Robert W. Service: A Bibliography*.

A primary bibliography of Géza Von Molnár is included in Block and Fenves, eds., *The Spirit of Poesy: Essays on Jewish and German Literature and Thought in Honor of Géza Von Molnár*. Philip M. O'Brien presents a new and expanded bibliography of T.E. Lawrence (*T.E. Lawrence: A Bibliography*, originally published in [1998]). The 2000 edition nearly doubles the number of entries of the original bibliography. Part I is the primary bibliography, presenting books, prefaces, introductions, translations, periodical articles, newspaper articles, and miscellaneous works by Lawrence. Part II is the secondary bibliography that lists books about Lawrence, books containing chapters and references to Lawrence, and finally periodical and newspaper articles about the author. Leland Poague presents primary and secondary bibliographies of Susan Sontag in *Susan Sontag: An Annotated Bibliography, 1948–1992*.

Two selective bibliographies of Derek Walcott appear in this year's biographies. Bruce King's *Derek Walcott: A Caribbean Life* presents a selective bibliography of primary and secondary sources and personal communications with the author such as letters, interviews, and e-mails. Paula Burnett's *Derek Walcott* offers a bibliography that includes Walcott's poetry, published and unpublished plays, selected essays and other prose, selected interview-based journalism, broadcasts, and public appearances, films, broadcasts and recordings, and a selection of secondary sources. The first bibliography of works by New Zealand writer Janet Frame appears in Michael King's biography *Wrestling with the Angel: A Life of Janet Frame*. James G. Nelson's *Publisher to the Decadents: Leonard Smithers in the Careers of Beardsley, Wilde, Dowson* offers a checklist of Smithers's publications. Paul Hegarty's biography *Georges Bataille: Core Cultural Theorist* includes a bibliography of the author's works in English and French as well as works by other writers. John Haffenden's *William Empson. The Complete Poems* includes primary and secondary bibliographies.

The first bibliography for Arthur Ransome is compiled by Wayne G. Hammond. *Arthur Ransome: A Bibliography* lists Ransome's fiction as well as over 1,500 writings that appeared in the popular media, such as newspapers and magazines. *Larry McMurtry: A Critical Companion*, by John M. Reilly, offers a bibliography of McMurtry's novels, non-fiction, screenplays, and collaborations with Diana Ossana. A selective secondary bibliography is also included. A primary bibliography of Ray Bradbury's works appears in *Ray Bradbury: A Critical Companion* by Robin Anne Reid.

Bibliographies for several lesser-known female authors have come out in related critical and biographical works this year. *May Sinclair: A Modern Victorian* by Suzanne Raitt offers a bibliography of the twentieth-century writer's novels, short stories, poetry, and other writings plus a secondary bibliography of works on Sinclair. Lenora P. Blouin presents a comprehensive primary and secondary bibliographical study in the second edition of *May Sarton: A Bibliography*. The bibliography of Sarton's entire oeuvre is complemented by a checklist of her poems by title. The annotated list of secondary sources has been updated to include criticism published since 1982. An introduction, chronology and appendices listing the publication of individual poems and selected reference sources round out this extremely thorough treatment of Sarton's works. *Amy Levy: Her Life and Letters* by Linda Hunt Beckman provides a list of Amy Levy's writings, with information about where the works first appeared and important reprintings. A select bibliography of works by nineteenth-century playwright and novelist Susan Glaspell appears in Barbara Ozieblo's *Susan Glaspell: A Critical Biography*.

A bibliography of Jack London's works is included in Walker and Reesman, eds., *No Mentor but Myself: Jack London on Writers and Writing*. Chaim Potok's works are listed in Sanford V. Sternlicht's *Chaim Potok: A Critical Companion*. A selected list of works on Potok is also included. Margaret Atwood's works, including her poetry, fiction, and other writings are listed in Reingard M. Nischik's *Margaret Atwood: Works and Impact*. The works of anthropologist Clifford Geertz are listed in *Clifford Geertz: Culture, Custom, and Ethics* by Fred Inglis. Derek Pearsall's publications appear in the collection of essays edited by David Aers, *Medieval Literature and Historical Inquiry: Essays in Honor of Derek Pearsall*.

George Bernard Shaw scholars will wish to take note of Laurence and Crawford, eds., *Bibliographical Shaw*, volume xx. New bibliographic information on Shaw's translations and two unpublished works makes this an important contribution to Shaw studies. A selected list of Pierre Bourdieu's works is offered by Jeremy F. Lane in *Pierre Bourdieu: A Critical Introduction*. A bibliography of Donald Hall's works, adapted from Jack Kelleher's *Donald Hall: A Bibliographical Checklist*, is presented in Hamilton et al., eds., *Donald Hall in Conversation with Ian Hamilton*.

The occasional series of the Eighteen Nineties Society has brought out several checklists of interest to nineteenth-century scholars. Volume i is *Elizabeth Longford: A Tribute*, by Michael Holroyd, with a checklist compiled by G. Krishnamurti. Volume ii is *A Check-list of Books Published During 1996 of Interest to Members of the Eighteen Nineties Society* [1997]. Volume iii is *Strange Bedfellows: W.E. Henley and Feminist Fashion History* [1997] by Linda K. Hughes. Volume iv is *Selwyn Image: An Illustrated Monograph* by Peter Frost. Volume v is *A Check-list of Books Published During 1997 of Interest to Members of the Eighteen Nineties Society* [1998]. Volume vi is *Aubrey Beardsley: Poems*, 2nd edn. [1998] with an introduction and notes by Matthew Sturgiss. Volume vii is *A Six Foot Three Nightingale: Norman Gale* by Michael Seeney [1998]. Volume viii is *The Yellow Book: A Checklist and Index* [1998] by Mark Samuels Lasner. Volume ix is *Michael Field and Poetic Identity* [2000] by Marion Thain.

Laurence Grove and Daniel Russell offer a bibliography of secondary sources in *The French Emblem*. Charles A. Carpenter's *Dramas of the Nuclear Age: A Descriptive List of English-Language Plays* contains four sections: an introduction; 'A Selective Chronology of Scientific, Political, and Cultural Developments Related to the Nuclear Age in General and Nuclear Drama in Particular'; 'Dramas of the Nuclear Age: A Descriptive List of English-Language Plays'; and an index of playwrights. Richard Sheppard's *Modernism—Dada—Postmodernism* includes a bibliographical note that lists several useful bibliographies for modernism, postmodernism, Dada, and related authors and works.

Hiroshi Mizuta's *Adam Smith's Library: A Catalogue* presents 1,808 alphabetically arranged entries with notes. There are six indexes: subject; authors' presentation copies and Adam Smith subscription copies; place of publication; publishers, printers, booksellers; locations; and unidentified and unlocated items.

Michael Hunter, Giles Mandelbrote, Richard Ovenden and Nigel Smith present *A Radical's Books: The Library Catalogue of Samuel Jeake of Rye, 1623–90*.

Of special note in music bibliography are six entries in Albi Rosenthal's *Obiter Scripta*. The entries (pp. 285–342) are 'Two Unknown 17th-Century Music Editions by Bolognese Composers'; 'Faksimiles als Fehlerquellen'; 'Facsimiles as Sources of Error'; 'The Contract between Joseph Haydn and Frederick Augustus Hyde (1796)'; 'Die Lagerkataloge des Musikantiquariats Leo Liepmannssohn'; and 'Some Aspects of Music Bibliography'. A chronological bibliography is also included. Silvia de Renzi offers a catalogue of an exhibition of rare books on scientific instruments. *Instruments in Print: Books from the Whipple Collection* is divided into three sections: making books, reading books, and marketing materials for scientific equipment from the seventeenth to the mid-twentieth century. The Whipple collection includes over 1,400 rare books on scientific instruments.

Two scholarly works presented by the Bibliographical Society of the University of Virginia are available on the internet. *Attributions of Authorship in the Gentleman's Magazine, 1731–1868* and *Attributions of Authorship in the European Magazine, 1782–1826* can be accessed at the URL http://etext.lib.virginia.edu/ bsuva/gm/. The database for the *Gentleman's Magazine* includes nearly 20,000 attributions over 137 years. The database for the *European Magazine* provides information about the entire forty-four-year life-span of the magazine. Both databases can be searched by keyword, volume number, page number, date range, title, author, and pseudonym. An introductory essay by Emily Lorraine de Montluzin is also included.

William R. Cagle presents a companion work to *American Books on Food and Drink* with his bibliographical work, *A Matter of Taste: A Bibliographical Catalogue of International Books on Food and Drink in the Lilly Library, Indiana University* [1999]. The bibliography covers international cookbooks as well as works on wine-making, herb gardening, and related topics. David Drazin has compiled *Croquet: A Bibliography*, which lists books and pamphlets related to the pastime from its earliest days to 1997.

Library history reveals fascinating information about societies, books, and the transfer of knowledge. The latest offering in the Publishing Pathways series is Myers, Harris and Mandelbrote, eds., *Libraries and the Book Trade: The Formation of Collections from the Sixteenth to the Twentieth Century*. The editors collect eight essays that show how the book trade influenced the development of libraries: 'Booksellers and Libraries in Sixteenth-Century Cambridge' by E.S. Leedham-Green; 'The Latin Stock (1616–1627) and its Library Contacts' by R.J. Roberts; 'Booksellers, Peruke-Makers, and Rabbit-Merchants: The Growth of Circulating Libraries in the Eighteenth Century' by K.A. Manley; '"Mr Greenhill, Whom You Cannot Get Rid Of": Copyright, Legal Deposit and the Stationers' Company in the Nineteenth Century' by Simon Eliot; 'Sir George Grey and the English Antiquarian Book Trade' by Donald Kerr; 'William Augustus White of Brooklyn (1843–1927) and the Dispersal of his Elizabethan Library' by Leslie A. Morris; 'Collecting an Aldine: Castiglione's *Libro del Cortegiano* [1528] through the Centuries' by Conor Fahy; and 'Bookbinding for Libraries' by Esther Potter.

Konstantinos Sp. Staikos's *The Great Libraries: From Antiquity to the Renaissance* (*3000 bc to ad 1600*) examines the origins of ancient libraries in the Mediterranean and the West and the historical events that influenced how libraries changed in scope and also in architectural layout and design. Timothy Cullen provides the translation and Hélène Ahrweiler writes the preface. Separate chapters address the ancient libraries of Mesopotamia, Egypt, the Hellenic world, the Roman period, the early Christian world, Byzantium, the Middle Ages, and the Renaissance. The second part of the book includes chapters on fourteen individual libraries such as the Vatican Library, the Bibliothèque Nationale in Paris, and the Bodleian Library. An extensive bibliography is also offered. In a related work, Fred Lerner offers a pared-down version of his earlier work *The Story of Libraries* [1998] with the 2000 publication of *Libraries through the Ages*. The abbreviated new work contains briefer explanations and more pictures, and will appeal to younger students. There are several other works this year on the history of individual libraries: MacLeod, ed., *The Library of Alexandria: Centre of Learning in the Ancient World*; Nina L. Collins, *The Library in Alexandria and The Bible in Greek*; Kinane and Walsh, eds., *Essays on the History of Trinity College Library Dublin*; James Conaway, *America's Library: The Story of the Library of Congress*; and Francis Newton, *The Scriptorium and Library at Monte Cassino, 1058–1105*.

A collection of seventeen essays is offered in Wertheimer and Davis, eds., *Library History Research in America: Essays Commemorating the Fiftieth Anniversary of the Library History Round Table*. The essays are 'American Library History Literature, 1947–1997: Theoretical Perspectives?' by Wayne A. Wiegand (pp. 4–34); 'Louis Shores and Library History' by Lee Shiflett *(pp.* 35–40); 'The Library History Round Table's First Twenty-Five Years: Reminiscences and Remarks on Recent Research' by John David Marshall *(pp.* 41–50); 'Library Feminism and Library Women's History: Activism and Scholarship, Equity and Culture' by Suzanne Hildenbrand *(pp.* 51–65); 'International Dimensions of Library History: Leadership and Scholarship, 1978–1998' by Mary Niles Maack *(pp.* 66–76); 'Toward a Multicultural American Public Library History' by Cheryl Knott Malone (pp. 77–87); '"They Sure Got to Prove it on Me": Millennial Thoughts on Gay Archives, Gay Biography, and Gay Library History' by James V. Carmichael Jr. (pp. 88–102); 'The History of Youth Services Librarianship: A Review of the Research Literature' by Christine A. Jenkins (pp. 103–40); 'The Failure or Future of American Archival History: A Somewhat Unorthodox View' by Richard J. Cox (pp. 141–54); 'Historical Bibliography and Library History' by D.W. Krummel (pp. 155–60); 'The Library Historian's Field of Dreams: A Profile of the First Nine Seminars' by Edward A. Goedeken *(pp.* 161–72); 'Advancing the Scholarship of Library History: The Role of the *Journal of Library History* and *Libraries & Culture*' by Jon Arvid Aho and Donald G. Davis Jr. *(pp.* 173–91); 'Clio's Workshop: Resources for Historical Studies in American Librarianship' by John Mark Tucker (pp. 192–214); 'Fifty Years of Promoting Library History: A Chronology of the ALA (American) Library History Round Table, 1947–1997' by Andrew B. Wertheimer and John David Marshall (pp. 215–39); 'The Historical Sensibility' by Phyllis Dain (pp. 240–3); and 'The Bookplate Essay—The Cavagna Collection: A Case Study in Special Collections' by Elizabeth R. Cardman (pp. 244–50).

Librarians and archivists will welcome the resources offered in Roy Sully's revised second edition of Joanne Lomax's *A Guide to Additional Sources of Funding and Revenue for Libraries and Archives*. The updated guide adds new information about the New Opportunities Fund and the Heritage Lottery Fund, as well as information particular to the United States. *Libraries & Culture: A Journal of Library History* (35:iii[2000]) has three articles of note: 'Andrew Carnegie and Academic Library Philanthropy: The Case of Rollins College, Winter Park, Florida' by Donna K. Cohen (pp. 389–413); 'The English Parish Library: A Celebration of Diversity' by Sarah Gray and Chris Baggs *(pp.* 414–33); and 'Advocate for Access: Lutie Stearns and the Traveling Libraries of the Wisconsin Free Library Commission, 1895–1914' by Christine Pawley *(pp.* 434–58).

In the first authoritative work of its kind in over a hundred years, *The Title-Page: Its Early Development, 1460–1510* by Margaret M. Smith traces the history of the title page in early printed books. Smith begins with an examination of mass production's role in the development of title pages. Separate chapters are devoted to the label-title and the end-title, the label-title and the woodcut, and the woodcut title page. Illustrations from various works are included.

Isaac and McKay, eds., *The Mighty Engine: The Printing Press and its Impact*, contains eighteen essays from the Seventeenth Annual Seminar on the British Book Trade at Aberystwyth in July 1999. John Hinks explains how the printing press helped to bring about the Reform Act of 1832. Richard Suggett and Maureen Bell examine the role of pedlars as distributors. Rheinallt Llwyd looks at the publication of *Gorchestion Beirdd Cymru* [1773]. Chris Baggs tells the story of the Potter family, a bookselling dynasty. Philip Henry Jones identifies the challenges of publishing in the Welsh language in the nineteenth century. Audrey Cooper looks at George Nicholson's *Cambrian Traveller's Guide*. Brenda Scragg examines William Ford's contributions to Edinburgh cultural society. Iain Beavan discusses the advertising efforts of Oliver & Boyd. David Shaw maps the regional and national relations of the book trade in eighteenth-century Canterbury. Jim English tells the story of the fictitious imprints by the Mozley family. Margaret Cooper chronicles the activities of bookseller John Mountfort. Sarah Gray provides a similar examination of bookseller William Flackton. Stacey Gee gives an account of early printing in York. David Stoker examines contemporary accounts of Re-Well press printing. Diana Dixon looks at newspapers in Huntingdonshire. Barry McKay reports on the day-books of bookseller and printer John Ware. John Turner notes the shortcomings of online catalogues for quantitative bibliography work.

Seventeenth-century bookseller and publisher John Dunton's *The Dublin Scuffle*, originally published in 1699 and now reissued, is a unique work that combines travel writing, personal reflections and information about the book trade. Frans Korsten gives an account of the life and career of bookseller Bertram Dobell in '"An Heretical Bookworm"' (*ES* 81:iv[2000] 305–27). Jeffrey Atherton's *Black-Letter: An Interpretation of Events Relating to the Time and Presence of Johann Gutenberg* offers a unique reworking of Gutenberg's printing career, as told from the perspectives of various onlookers. A chronology of events is also included. David H.J. Schenck's *Directory of the Lithographic Printers of Scotland, 1820–1870: Their Locations, Periods and a Guide to Artistic Lithographic Printers* will be a useful resource for students of British printing history. Another work on nineteenth-century printing is Patrick Duffy's *The Skilled Compositor, 1850–1914: An Aristocrat Among Working Men*, which gives a historical account of the lost craft of hand-setting type.

Caroline Archer's *The Kynoch Press: The Anatomy of a Printing House, 1876–1981* tells the history of a major British printing house that was a leader in typographical innovations, such as the introduction in the 1930s of nineteenth-century revival types. Archer draws on personal accounts from staff members to enrich her research on the decades from 1930 onward and provides detailed listings of the press's types. William Zachs's *The First John Murray and the Late Eighteenth-Century London Book Trade: With a Checklist of his Publications* [1999] is a biography of a successful eighteenth-century bookseller. Over 1,000 of Murray's publications are listed, along with information about book sales. Twentieth-century artist John Petts, who contributed work to the Golden Cockerel Press and his private press, is the focus of Alison Smith's *John Petts and the Caseg Press*.

Raven, ed., *Free Print and Non-Commercial Publishing since 1700*, is a collection of essays that examines the distribution of free literature and its relationship with intellectual, cultural, and economic forces. Religious literature, abolitionist pamphlets, and war propaganda are among the examples considered. Another collection of essays, Raymond, ed., *News, Newspapers, and Society in Early Modern Britain* [1999], covers a wide range of topics related to the dissemination of news in the early modern era. Some of the studies address issues of gender and genre while others examine medical news and advertising.

The history of science and publishing is an area of growing interest. Andrew Hunter presents the fourth and significantly revised edition of *Thornton and Tully's Scientific Books, Libraries and Collectors: A Study of Bibliography and the Book Trade in Relation to the History of Science* (first published [1954]). The book comprises fourteen chapters, each written by a different contributor. One new addition is the chapter entitled 'Islamic Science' by Jascques Sesiano. The index is reduced to about one-quarter of its original length and the bibliography is not included.

Those interested in American publishing history will welcome two works of note: Ezra Greenspan's *George Palmer Putnam: Representative American Publisher* and Christopher Ogden's *Legacy: A Biography of Moses and Walter Annenberg*, which chronicles the rise of a publishing empire. Bell, Bevan, and Bennett, eds., *Across Boundaries: The Book in Culture and Commerce*, offers nine essays that discuss the changing relationship between books and economics since the early age of printing. *A Handbook for the Study of Book History in the United States* by Ronald J. Zboray and Mary Saracino Zboray looks at how books have been produced, distributed, purchased, and read in the United States. The unique history of the Bible is the subject of the Bible as Book series. The third volume, O'Sullivan, ed., *The Bible as Book: The Reformation*, offers twelve new essays that examine the Bible's history during the turbulent years of the Reformation. Julie Stone Peters's *Theatre of the Book, 1480–1880: Print, Text and Performance in Europe* considers the relationship between stage performance and printed text. Similarly, Douglas A. Brooks's study *From Playhouse to Printing House: Drama and Authorship in Early Modern England* looks at how playwrights such as Shakespeare and Jonson transformed their plays into printed texts.

Several of this year's works should be of interest to students of typography. Alan Bartram offers advice to those learning the craft in *Creating the Printed Page: A Guide for Authors, Publishers and Designers*. Alastair Johnston examines typefounders' specimen books in *Alphabets to Order: The Literature of Nineteenth-Century Typefounders' Specimens*. The extensive collection of texts gives insight into readers' habits and interests. Ruari McLean's *True to Type: A Typographical Autobiography* tells the story of post-war publishing in Britain. McLean's 2,000 publications also include three lectures entitled *How Typography Happens*. The essays examine typography history and practices in Britain, America, Germany and France. A related work is Kinross, ed., *Anthony Froshaug: Typography and Texts*. Gerald Cinamon's *Rudolf Koch: Letterer, Type Designer, Teacher* is a biography of the German typographer who helped to advance the practice of typography in the early twentieth century. American Ottmar Mergenthaler, the inventor of the revolutionary Linotype, is the subject of a biography by Basil Kahan entitled *Ottmar Mergenthaler: The Man and his Machine*. The biography gives an account of the early history of the Linotype. Also related to the art of book printing is Jeremy Greenwood's *Margaret Bruce Wells: The Complete Wood-Engravings and Linocuts*.

Patricia Lovett's *The British Library Companion to Calligraphy, Illumination and Heraldry: A History and Practical Guide* includes chapters on the history of calligraphy, equipment and materials, historical alphabets, calligraphy and typeface design, a practical guide to guilding, the art of illumination, a history of heraldry, coats of arms, modern heraldry, and a reference guide to paper, vellum, brushes, colours, and colour mixing. Among the contributors are Lovett, Rosemary Sassoon, Hermann Zapf, and Michelle P. Brown. The history of writing and typing in the eighteenth and nineteenth centuries is the focus of Joe Nickell's *Pen, Ink and Evidence: A Study of Writing and Writing Materials for Penman, Collector, and Document Detective*. Nickell gives an account of how the technologies of the written page—inks, papers, writing instruments, and scripts—were introduced and changed over time. *Scripts, Grooves and Writing Machines: Representing Technology in the Edison Era* [1999] by Lisa Gitelman considers how the invention of the phonograph and typewriter were an attempt to perfect the means by which human speech is represented and stored.

The various scholarly uses of watermarks are the subject of fifteen essays collected in Mosser, Saffle and Sullivan, eds., *Puzzles in Paper: Concepts in Historical Watermarks*. Daniel W. Mosser offers the preface to this collection of essays from the 1996 International Conference on Watermarks that includes 'Concepts of Paper Study' by Paul Needham (pp. 1–36); 'Spanish and Italian Watermarks in Colonial Guatemalan Books' by Celia A. Fryer *(pp.* 37–56); 'Watermarks in Rembrandt's Prints: The Use of Watermarks to Study the Prints of an Artist' by Nancy Ash and Shelley Fletcher (pp. 57–66); 'Watermark Evidence and the Hidden Editions of Thomas East' by Jeremy L. Smith (pp. 67–80); 'Watermarks as Evidence for Dating and Authenticity in John Donne and Ben Franklin' by Laetitia Yeandle (pp. 81–92); 'Use of Watermarks in Musicology' by Ulrich Konrad (pp. 93–106); 'Watermarks and Rastra in Neapolitan Music Manuscripts, 1700–1815' by Stephen Shearon (pp. 107–24); 'Music Paper at the Dresden Court and the Chronology of Telemann's Instrumental Music' by Steven Zohn *(pp.* 125–68); 'Phosphorescence Watermark Imaging' by Carol Ann Small (pp. 169–82); 'DYLUX, Thomas L. Gravell, and Watermarks of Stamps and Papers' by Rolf Dessauer (pp. 183–6); 'La Marca d'Acqua: A System for the Digital Recording of Watermarks' by Daniela Moschini, translated by Conor Fahay (pp. 187–92); 'Watermarks and Other Physical Evidence from the Portland Literary Manuscripts' by Ruby Reid Thompson (pp. 193–200); 'An Automated World Wide

Web Search Tool for Papers and Watermarks: The Archive of Papers and Watermarks in Greek Manuscripts' by Robert W. Allison (pp. 201–10); 'The Thomas L. Gravell Watermark Archive on the Internet' by Daniel W. Mosser and Ernest W. Sullivan II (pp. 211–28); 'Towards a Taxonomy of Watermarks' by Ted-Larry Pebworth (pp. 229–42).

Several works consider publishing histories in countries outside England. Richard H. Rouse and Mary A. Rouse provide insight into French literary culture in *The Paris Book Trade in the Middle Ages, 1200–1500*. Mary Pollard's *A Dictionary of Members of the Dublin Book Trade, 1550–1800* uses the records of the guild of St Luke the Evangelist in Dublin to create over 2,200 entries for all book trade workers in Dublin during this period, from apprentices to masters to engravers. The history of the book trade in Austria is the subject of *Geschichte des Buchhandels in Österreich* by Norbert Bachleitner, Franz M. Eybl and Ernst Fischer. The advent of professional publishing in Quebec is chronicled in Michon, ed., *Histoire de l'édition littéraire au Québec au XXe siècle: La Naissance de l'éditeur, 1900–1939* [1999]. The changes in American print culture between the 1830s and 1850s is the subject of Isabelle Lehuu's *Carnival on the Page: Popular Print Media in Antebellum America*. Lehuu presents four case studies focusing on the *New York Herald*, *Brother Jonathan*, *The New World*, and *Godey's Lady's Book*. In another nineteenth-century work, *The Victorian Working-Class Writer* [1999], Owen Ashton and Stephen Roberts present case studies of eight authors: Joseph Robson, Thomas Miller, William Thom, John Leatherland, Noah Cooke, John Bedford Leno, Ben Brierley, and Robert Maybee. A brief anthology of their works is included. Graeme Johanson's *A Study of Colonial Editions in Australia, 1843–1972* examines the history of British control over publishing in Australia. Johanson offers a comprehensive study of the colonial edition focusing on four areas: the book as a physical object; messages from authors and publishers; the sale and distribution of books; and the wider cultural significance of the colonial edition. Other works of international interest include F.F. Blok's *Isaac Vossius and his Circle: His Life until his Farewell to Queen Christina of Sweden, 1618–1655*, and C.M. Bajetta's *Some Notes on Printing and Publishing in Renaissance Venice*.

Brian Richardson's study of early Italian printing, Printing, Writers and Readers in Renaissance Italy [1999], includes information about notable Renaissance writers and the economics of Renaissance publishing. Irene Lawford-Hinrichsen's *Music Publishing and Patronage: C.F. Peters, 1800 to the Holocaust* gives a historical account of a major music publishing house in Leipzig and the musicians who contributed to its success.

The unique history of book fragments and their resource potential for scholarship is the subject of Brownrigg and Smith, eds., *Interpreting and Collecting Fragments of Medieval Books*. The collection of essays is based on the 1998 conference 'Fragments as Witnesses to Medieval Books and Book-Making'. A collection of thirteen essays, Edwards, Gillespie and Hanna, eds., *The Medieval Book: Studies in Memory of Jeremy Griffiths*, addresses scribal hands, provenance, and manuscript illustration. A bibliography of the late Jeremy Griffiths's work is included.

The ins and outs of fine leather bookbinding are clearly illustrated in *ABC of Leather Bookbinding: An Illustrated Manual on Traditional Bookbinding* by Edward R. Lhotka. Master craftsman Lhotka presents an illustrated step-by-step guide with concise explanations. The decorative art of bookbinding is the subject of a beautifully illustrated book, *The Art of Publishers' Bookbindings, 1815–1915* by Ellen K. Morris and Edward S. Levin. This catalogue of an exhibition at the Grolier Club includes 254 colour illustrations of bindings produced in multiple quantities by publishers (hand-crafted bindings for individual books are not included). The first section of the book chronicles the trends and changes in American and British bookbinding design from 1815 to 1915; the second section shows how a variety of bindings were produced for single books; the final section is a sample of bindings. Ruari McLean writes a foreword and Sue Allen offers an afterword. *Oxford Bookbinding, 1500–1640* by David Pearson includes a supplement to Neil Ker's *Fragments of Medieval Manuscripts Used as Pastedowns in Oxford Bindings.*

Essays included in Pearson, ed., *For the Love of Binding*, are Michael Gullick's 'A Romanesque Blind-Stamped Binding at the Queen's College, Oxford' (pp. 1–8); Christopher de Hamel's 'Medieval Manuscript Leaves as Publishers' Wrappers in the 1920s' *(pp.* 9–12); Lotte's Hellinga's 'Fragments Found in Bindings and their Role as Bibliographical Evidence' (pp. 13–34); Elly Cockx-Indestege's 'Crutched Friars, Lambs, Roses, and Crosses: Brussels Incunables on the Shelves of the Crutched Friars at the Turn of the Sixteenth Century' (pp. 35–52); Giles Barber's 'The Advent of Gold Tooling in English Bookbinding and the Intermediary Role of Thomas Linacre' (pp. 53–66); Anthony Hobson's 'Plaquette and Medallion Bindings: A Second Supplement' (pp. 67–80); Laura Nuvoloni's *'Commissioni Dogali*: Venetian Bookbindings in the British Library' *(p*p. 81–110); Nicolas Barker's 'Some Unrecorded Sixteenth-Century French Bookbindings' (pp. 111–18); Nicholas Pickwoad's 'Tacketed Bindings: A Hundred Years of European Bookbinding' (pp. 119–68); Elisabeth Leedham-Green's 'Seventeenth-Century Cambridge Pyxides' (pp. 197–208); John Morris's 'A Bible Bound in 1661 by Patrick Erskine for the Earl and Countess of Caithness' (pp. 209–12): Vanessa C. Marshall's 'Putting Book Structures within an Historical Context: A Note on the Seventeenth- and Eighteenth-Century Paper Bindings in the Wolf Collection, Staats-und Universitätsbibliothek, Hamburg' (pp. 213–20); Jan Storm van Leeuwen's 'It Glitters and is More than Gold: Fore-Edge Paintings in the Dutch Royal Library' (pp. 221–40); David Paisey's 'The Autograph Album of a Journeyman Bookbinder: Alexander Troschel of Nuremberg (1758–69)' (pp. 241–60); Richard Ovenden's 'Scott Bindings on the 1770 Foulis Milton' (pp. 261–70); Bryan Maggs's 'John Whittaker's Edition of the *Magna Carta*, its Printing, and his Bindings on the Wormsley Copies' (pp. 271–6); John Collins's 'Four Bindings and a Will: Thomas Jones Ellison and Some Notes on Nineteenth-Century Signed Rolls' (pp. 277–82); Paul Morgan's 'John Hannett's *Bibliopegia* and *Inquiry*, and Salt Brassington's Revision' (pp. 283–8); Esther Potter's 'The Bookbindings of Benjamin West (1804–83)' (pp. 289–302); Christian Coppens's 'A Mid-Nineteenth-Century Book-Trade Binder: Florent Pollender and the Firm of Hanicq-Dessain in Mechelen' (pp. 303–18); Edmund M.B. King's 'The Book Cover Designs of William Harry Rogers' (pp. 319–28); Marianne Tidcombe's 'The Mysterious Mr de Sauty' (pp. 329–36); Anna Simoni's 'Secret, Loud and Clear' (pp. 337–50); Dorothy A. Harrop's 'The Keatley Trust Collection of Modern British Bindings' (pp. 351–62); and P.J.M. Marks's 'A Jean de Gonet Binding at the British Library' (pp. 363–6). The volume concludes with a 'Bibliography of Mirjam Foot' (pp. 367–74).

Bray, Handley and Henry, eds., *Ma(r)king the Text: The Presentation of Meaning on the Literary Page*, is a collection of essays that call attention to the importance of typography, book design, page layout, and punctuation in literary analysis. The essays address the works of Spenser, Richardson and George Eliot. Henri-Jean Martin studies page layout and typographic shaping in *La Naissance du livre moderne (XIVe–XVIIe siècles): Mise en page et mise en texte du livre français*. The third edition of Bernard C. Middleton's autobiography *Recollections: A Life in Bookbinding* is published by Oak Knoll Press, offering an expanded text and over ninety illustrations of Middleton's binding designs. Middleton's experiences reveal the practices of the early twentieth-century British trade school and the system of indentured apprenticeships. Craftsman and scholar Dard Hunter was a pioneer in the study of paper history, technology, and materials. Cathleen A. Baker presents his biography, entitled *By his own Labor: The Biography of Dard Hunter*. The book includes illustrations.

The fascinating stories of some of the most famous incidents of literary forgery are told in Joseph Rosenblum's *Practice to Deceive: The Amazing Stories of Literary Forgery's Most Notorious Practitioners*. Those interested in the history of the book and popularity of various genres will find several new works of interest. Jay Dixon's *The Romance Fiction of Mills & Boon, 1909–1990s* offers a fresh perspective on popular literature and romance writing. Dixon's feminist study begins with a brief history of the Mills & Boon publishing house and proceeds to a revision of the received wisdom on various topics such as the depiction of premarital sex, the hero and heroine, and symbolic meanings. Michael Cohen's *Murder Most Fair: The Appeal of Mystery Fiction* analyses the conventions of detective fiction, from the Sherlock Holmes stories to Umberto Eco's *The Name of the Rose*. Cohen evaluates the relative importance of mystery fiction and 'serious' literature and points out ways in which the genres sometimes exchange conventions. A humorous look at the book industry is offered by John Maxwell Hamilton in *Casanova was a Book Lover: And Other Naked Truths and Provocative Curiosities about the Writing, Selling, and Reading of Books*. Hamilton enlightens and entertains with funny facts (for example the most frequently stolen books in the United States are the Bible and *The Joy of Sex*), examines the book review business from an insider's perspective, and doles out silly and witty advice on book party etiquette and self-marketing techniques for aspiring authors.

A notable contribution to the history of the book is the new paperback edition of Adrian Johns's *The Nature of the Book: Print and Knowledge in the Making*, which examines early English printing and its relationship to the increasing democratization of society. Johns is also concerned with ways in which the printing press contributed to the creation and dissemination of scientific knowledge. Holly A. Laird's study *Women Coauthors* shows how literary collaboration challenges assumptions about authorship. The literary partnerships of the Michael Field poets, Gertrude Stein and Alice B. Toklas, and Louise Erdrich and Michael Dorris are among those treated. *The Culture of the Book in the Scottish Enlightenment* offers four essays on the history of the book: '*Catalogus Librorum A.C.D.A.*, or, the Library of Archibald Campbell, Third Duke of Argyll (1682–1761)' by Roger Emerson (pp. 13–39); 'The Book in the Scottish Enlightenment' by Richard Sher (pp. 40–60); 'William Smellie and the Culture of the Edinburgh Book Trade, 1752–1795' by Stephen Brown (pp. 61–88); 'Marginalia on the Mind: John Robison and Thomas Reid' by Paul Wood (pp. 89–119). The publication also includes a list of items displayed at a related exhibition by the Thomas Fisher Rare Book Library, University of Toronto.

Golden, ed., *Book Illustrated: Text, Image, and Culture, 1770–1930*, collects eight essays that examine the evolution of visual images in books: 'Pictorial Shakespeare: Text, Stage, Illustration' by Jonathan Bate (pp. 31–60); 'Taglioni's Double Meanings: Illustration and the Romantic Ballerina' by Sarah Webster Goodwin (pp. 61–82); 'The Politics of Humor in George Cruikshank's Graphic Satire' by Robert L. Patten (pp. 83–116); 'Cruikshank's Illustrative Wrinkle in *Oliver Twist*'s Misrepresentation of Class' by Catherine J. Golden (pp. 117–46); 'Rossetti and the Art of the Book' by Elizabeth K. Helsinger (pp. 147–94); 'Love, Death, and Grotesquerie: Beardsley's Illustrations of Wilde and Pope' by James A.W. Heffernan (pp. 195–240); 'Dream Blocks: American Women Illustrators of the Golden Age, 1890–1920' by Ruth Copans (pp. 241–76); and '"We All Sit on the Edge of Stools and Crack Jokes": Virginia Woolf and the Hogarth Press' by David H. Porter (pp. 277–312).

Jack Matthews offers twelve essays on the pleasures and challenges of book collecting in *Reading Matter: A Rabid Bibliophile's Adventures Among Old and Rare Books*. Matthews shares his experiences as a book collector and life-long bibliophile. David Elliott offers a biography of a major Pre-Raphaelite artist in *Charles Fairfax Murray: The Unknown Pre-Raphaelite*. Eliott, Murray's grandson, brings out the first biography of this influential Victorian who played the various roles of collector, benefactor, dealer, and artist. Another work of interest to collectors is Gemmet, ed., *The Consummate Collector: William Beckford's Letters to his Bookseller*. Philip Connell's 'Bibliomania: Book Collecting, Cultural Politics, and the Rise of Literary Heritage in Romantic Britain' examines nineteenth-century English book collecting, social class and cultural heritage, and compares the English nationalism of Thomas Frognall Dibdin and Isaac D'Israeli (*Rep* 71[2000] 24–47). David Alan Richards examines collecting and Rudyard Kipling in 'Collecting Kipling' (*Gazette of the Grolier Club* 51[2000] 81–98). Collectors also will not want to overlook the seventh edition of the *Skoob Directory of Secondhand Bookshops in the British Isles* which lists over 1,450 shops.

The future of the book in the age of the internet is the subject of Jane Yellowlees Douglas's *The End of Books or Books Without End? Reading Interactive Narratives*. Douglas considers the unique challenges that hypertext fiction places on the reader and compares interactive works to traditional print fiction. The possibility of a new fictional realism is just one of the potential benefits Douglas finds in interactive reading. Rothenberg and Clay, eds., *A Book of the Book: Some Works and Projections about the Book and Writing* looks towards the future of the book, while Eric Jager's *The Book of the Heart* considers the so-called 'death of the book' in the context of the cultural metaphor that associates the book with the self. Jager shows how the concept of the self as readable text originated in ancient times and continues to the present day. He uses examples from Plato, Augustine, Dante, Shakespeare, Locke and Freud to illustrate the changing conception of the book-as-self which began as an emotional metaphor ('book of the heart') that early modern culture, via printing, science, and the Reformation, transformed to a rational metaphor ('book of the brain').

Oscar Wilde's attention to the artistic appearance of his books is the subject of Nicholas Frankel's *Oscar Wilde's Decorated Books*. Frankel describes Wilde's working relationships with several graphic designers and argues that the author considered literature to be a 'decorative art' in which the aesthetics of layout and design are an integral part of literary language. The history of the book in China is told in Glen Dudbridge's *Lost Books of Medieval China*. Dudbridge describes the competing efforts to destroy, preserve and reconstruct texts, and he explains the unique Chinese process of subject classification. Those interested in the wider field of communications studies will find an interesting history of a failed technology in *Teletext: Its Promise and Demise* by Leonard R. Graziplene. Teletext, along with personal computers and cellular telephones, was an emerging technology in the 1980s that allowed television stations to offer televized text news service on demand to television viewers. Graziplene gives the history of teletext's development and attempts to account for its ultimate failure in the communications marketplace.

2000 was a particularly fruitful year for reference works. The sixth edition of Drabble, ed., *The Oxford Companion to English Literature*, includes over 600 new entries plus sixteen thematic essays dedicated to individual genres such as biography and black British literature and revises the 1995 edition, also edited by Drabble. Lambdin and Lambdin, eds., *Encyclopedia of Medieval Literature*, offers concise entries for historical events, individual works, and recurring themes. Longer entries are provided for major authors and genres. Bibliographies for individual subjects are provided, as well as a general bibliography.

Two important reference works for Middle English literature appeared this year. *Book and Verse: A Guide to Middle English Biblical Literature* by James H. Morey offers a bibliographic guide to biblical literature from 1100 to 1400. Morey argues that, contrary to scholarly consensus, the Bible was actually available to readers prior to the Reformation in a transformed medium. The biblical stories that appeared in various texts essentially comprise the 'Middle English vernacular "Bible"'. Also of interest to Middle English studies is Smith and Powell, eds., *New Perspectives on Middle English Texts*, collected in honour of R.A. Waldron. The collection consists of fourteen essays: 'Setting and Context in the Works of the *Gawain*-Poet' by Malcolm Andrew (pp. 3–16); 'Performance and Structure in *The Alliterative Morte Arthure*' by Rosamund Allen (pp. 17–30); 'Feasting in Middle English Alliterative Poetry' by Ralph Hanna (pp. 31–42); 'Word Games: Glossing *Piers Plowman*' by George Kane (pp. 43–54); 'Untying the Knot: Reading *Sir Gawain and the Green Knight*' by Susan Powell (pp. 55–74); 'Two Notes on Layamon's *Brut*' by Jane Roberts (pp. 75–86); 'Semantics and Metrical Form in *Sir Gawain and the Green Knight*' by Jeremy Smith (pp. 87–106); 'The Links in the *Canterbury Tales*' by Norman Blake (pp. 107–18); 'Middle English Verse in Chronicles' by Julia Boffey and A.S.G. Edwards (pp. 119–28); 'An English Reading of Boccaccio: A Selective Middle English Version of Boccaccio's *De Mulieribus Claris* in British Library MS Additional 10304' by Janet Cowen (pp. 129–40); 'Abbreviations, Otiose Strokes and Editorial Practice: The Case of Southwell Minster MS 7' by Roger Dahood (pp. 141–50); 'Temporal and Spiritual Indebtedness in the *Canterbury Tales*' by Elton D. Higgs (pp. 151–68); '"Quha wait gif all that Chauceir wrait was trew?": Henryson's *Testament of Cresseid*' by Derek Pearsall (pp. 169–82).

Sixty new essays are presented in Hattaway, ed., *A Companion to English Renaissance Literature and Culture*. The essays are grouped into four sections: cultural influences (such as humanism and the Reformation); new readings of individual authors such as Spenser, Donne, and Bacon; genre studies; and a survey of Renaissance attitudes on a variety of issues, from race to witchcraft. Each essay includes a bibliography. Womersley, ed., *A Companion to Literature from Milton to Blake*, includes sixty contributions divided into five sections: contexts, issues and debates, readings, periods, and genres and modes. The essays shed light on the changing literary culture from a variety of critical perspectives.

Two new reference works in bibliography and cataloguing deserve attention. Robert Balay's *Early Periodical Indexes* provides a bibliography and indexes for publications that give information about articles published in periodicals before 1900. Pamela J. Willetts presents her *Catalogue of Manuscripts in the Society of Antiquaries of London*, which includes an index of manuscripts. It is the first society catalogue since 1816 and describes over 1,000 manuscripts procured by the society between 1717 and 2000 and ranging from the Middle Ages to the present day.

Susan Price Karpuk's *Samuel Richardson's Clarissa: An Index to Analyzing the Characters, Subjects and Place Names with Summaries of Letters Appended* is an extensive resource tool that facilitates locating information about a particular subject within Samuel Richardson's lengthy novel. Ellen Gardiner's *Regulating Readers: Gender and Literary Criticism in the Eighteenth-Century Novel* provides close readings of *Clarissa*, *Tom Jones*, *The Female Quixote*, *The Cry*, and *Mansfield Park* to identify the ways in which early novels prescribed reading practices. Gardiner's analysis differentiates between male and female authors' conceptions of the ideal reader. *A Henry Fielding Companion*, by Martin C. Battestin, is an excellent resource offering information about Fielding's works in literature—as novelist and playwright—as well as his role as a magistrate. A ten-page bibliography is included, along with a separate list of works cited and a helpful index.

Louise McConnell's *Dictionary of Shakespeare* provides plot summaries, information about characters and places, a chronology of the plays, a history of the English monarchy from 1327 to 1603, and a bibliography. *Understanding Othello* by Faith Nostbakken is a casebook consisting of chapters on literary analysis, historical context, performance history and contemporary issues. Robert S. Miola's *Shakespeare's Reading* reveals how Shakespeare adapted his sources and literary traditions to produce new creative works. Miola introduces frequently read Elizabethan texts and then explains how Shakespeare adapted sources such as Chaucer's *Canterbury Tales*, Holinshed's *Chronicles*, and Plutarch's *Lives*. Miola also considers how Shakespeare changed the genres of his literary inheritance. Charles Edelman offers *Shakespeare's Military Language: A Dictionary* that includes a bibliography. Callaghan, ed., *A Feminist Companion to Shakespeare*, offers nineteen new essays by women critics. The essays are divided into six parts: the history of feminist Shakespeare criticism; text and language; social economics; analysis of *A Midsummer Night's Dream*, *Othello* and *The Tempest*; gender ambiguities and conflicts; and religion.

A large amount of new work in English studies focuses on national and ethnic literatures. Webby, ed., *The Cambridge Companion to Australian Literature*, introduces the major writers and movements in Australian literatures. In addition to Webby's introduction, nine essays are included: 'Indigenous Texts and Narratives' by Penny Van Toorn (pp. 19–49); 'Colonial Writers and Readers' by Webby (pp. 50–73); 'Poetry from the 1890s to 1970' by Michael Ackland (pp. 74–104); 'Fiction from 1900 to 1970' by Kerryn Goldsworthy (pp. 105–33); 'Theatre from 1788 to the

1960s' by Richard Fotheringham (pp. 134–57); 'Contemporary Poetry: Across Party Lines' by David McCooey (pp. 158–82); 'New Narrations: Contemporary Fiction' by Delys Bird (pp. 183–208); 'New Stages: Contemporary Theatre' by May-Brit Akerholt (pp. 209–31); 'From Biography to Autobiography' by Gillian Whitlock (pp. 232–57); 'Critics, Writers, Intellectuals: Australian Literature and its Criticism' by David Carter (pp. 258–94).

David Pierce's *Irish Writing in the Twentieth Century: A Reader* is an anthology of Irish writing in fiction, poetry, and prose as well as travel writing, memoirs, journalism, and other genres. The book is organized chronologically by decade, beginning in the 1890s and continuing through the twentieth century. A chronology, bibliography, and index of authors' names are included. Pierce has selected both major and unknown authors, including Irish writers outside Ireland such as Jim Phelan, Moy McCrory, Bill Naughton, and Ian Duhig. Lee, ed., *Irish Identity and Literary Periodicals, 1832–1842*, is a six-volume reproduction of three journals: *The Dublin Penny Journal* [1832–6], *The Irish Penny Journal* [1840–1], and *The Irish Penny Magazine* [1841–2]. Lee's introduction chronicles the history of the journals and lists a selection of contributors.

Black African Literature in English, 1992–1996, by Bernth Lindfors, is the latest volume in a series of reference works devoted to a chronological treatment of black African literature and writers. Earlier volumes in the series cover literature in the periods 1987–91, 1982–6, and 1977–81. The series addresses the history and criticism of black African literature and provides helpful bibliographic information. Nelson, ed., *African American Authors, 1745–1945*, provides biographical and critical analyses for seventy-eight writers and their works. Primary and secondary bibliographies are also included. In a related work entitled *Best Literature by and about Blacks*, Phillip M. Richards and Neil Schlager compile encyclopedic entries for nearly 2,000 works of fiction, drama, poetry, and other writing. The entries are divided chronologically into four sections: 1750–1860, 1860–1900, 1900–40 and 1940–present. Bibliographic information for each entry is provided, and an essay opens each of the four sections.

Smith, ed., the *Concise Encyclopedia of Latin American Literature*, is a shortened version of the *Encyclopedia of Latin American Literature* and includes entries on authors, works, countries, and other topics. Many of the essays are reproduced in their entirety from the original edition, and they cover a range of genres from children's literature to detective fiction. Nelson, ed., *Asian American Novelists: A Bio-Bibliographical Critical Sourcebook*, covers the lives and works of seventy authors. Champion, ed., *American Women Writers, 1900–1945: A Bio-Bibliographical Critical Sourcebook*, offers biographic, bibliographic, thematic, and critical information on fifty-eight women writers. Bloom, ed., *Nineteenth-Century British Women Writers: A Bio-Bibliographical Critical Sourcebook*, outlines the works and critical receptions of ninety-three writers of prose, fiction and poetry. The entries are alphabetically arranged, with each author treated in a separate chapter. Bibliographies of each author's works and writings about her works are also included.

Zipes, ed., *The Oxford Companion to Fairy Tales*, offers over 800 entries that explore the enormous reach of fairy tales in Western culture. In addition to books, the Companion covers television, ballet, music and cartoons. Readers can find bibliographies, lists of specialist journals and information about collections. J.

Randolph Cox presents the first reference work on dime novels, entitled *The Dime Novel Companion: A Source Book*, an encyclopedia of writers and publishers, as well as characters and genres. It includes an introduction, a bibliography, a list of libraries holding dime novel collections, and a chronology of publications between 1846 and 1930.

Cambridge University Press has published two important contributions to literary criticism reference works. Brown, ed., *The Cambridge History of Literary Criticism*, volume v: *Romanticism*, contains seventeen essays by noted scholars plus an introduction by Brown and a bibliography of primary and secondary sources. Volume vii of the same series, Menan, Rainey and Litz, eds., *Modernism and the New Criticism*, covers modernist critics Eliot, Pound, Stein and Yeats, new critics Richards, Empson, Burke and Winters, and later writers Trilling and Leavis. Chapters on individual critics and genres are included. Gelfant and Graver, eds., *The Columbia Companion to the Twentieth-Century American Short Story*, present a spectrum of established and lesser-known writers, from Ernest Hemingway and James Baldwin to Rick Bass and Sandra Cisneros. Each of the 125 essays, ranging from four to eight pages, is preceded by information about the author's biography and career as well as a brief analysis of his or her writings and a bibliography. An introduction by Gelfant is also included. The book is divided into two parts. Part I approaches the literature by theme (for example 'Working-Class Stories') and part II offers over 100 essays on individual writers. *Humor in Twentieth-Century British Literature: A Reference Guide*, by Don Lee Fred Nilsen, examines the use of comedy in works by Sir Arthur Wing Pinero, George Bernard Shaw, W. Somerset Maugham and Alfred Hitchcock, among others.

Several new reference works dedicated to individual authors appeared this year. Rignall, ed., *The Oxford Reader's Companion to George Eliot*, is a comprehensive and easy-to-use encyclopedia containing over 600 entries relating to the author's life and works. The entries include synopses of Eliot's fiction, critical receptions, contemporary readings, thematic links, biographical information, and relevant literary and cultural contexts, including entries on philosophy, theology, and science. Lambdin and Lambdin, eds., *A Companion to Jane Austen Studies*, offers twenty-two essays on Austen's novels, critical reception, juvenilia, letters and poems. The major novels *Emma* and *Pride and Prejudice* are addressed in several essays, but several others take on Austen's lesser-known and incomplete works such as *The Watsons*, *Sanditon*, and *Lady Susan*. Robert L. Gale's *A Dashiell Hammett Companion* is an encyclopedia containing information about the detective fiction writer's works and characters as well as his personal relationships with family, friends and acquaintances. A chronology, bibliography, and index are also included. Jack De Bellis presents John Updike's life, works, and critical contexts in *The John Updike Encyclopedia.*Curnutt, ed., *The Critical Response to Gertrude Stein*, reprints standard critical essays by Carl Van Vechten and William Carlos Williams as well as lesser-known analyses by H.L. Mencken and Conrad Aiken. Curnutt's selections constitute a fair and balanced representation of the praise and criticism Stein has evoked. A checklist of Stein's works is also included.

This year brought several new poetry reference works. A third edition of Lewis Turco's *The Book of Forms: A Handbook of Poetics* has three parts: the elements of poetry, form-finder index, and traditional verse forms. Willhardt and Parker, eds., *Who's Who in Twentieth-Century World Poetry*, provides brief biographical sketches and summaries for poets around the globe. Lesser-known writers receive a paragraph or two, while major poets receive longer entries. Musicians generally are not included, although there are a few exceptions. The scope of the work is international so that all poets of international stature are included, as well as writers whose works have national importance such as South Africa's Njabulo Simakahle Ndebele and Iraq's Nazik al-Mala'ika. *A Concordance to the Letters of Emily Dickinson* by Cynthia J. MacKenzie identifies links between Dickinson's letters and her poetry. MacKenzie uses editions of the letters published in 1958, 1965, and 1998. A scholarly World Wide Web site dedicated to Walt Whitman provides information about the poet, his life and his works. The project is spearheaded by Ken Price and Ed Folsom. Visitors can examine handwritten images of the 'Calamus' poems and several versions of 'Song of Myself'. Eventually the site will offer full-text versions of all eight editions of *Leaves of Grass* plus Whitman's other writings. *The Robert Frost Encyclopedia* by Nancy Lewis Tuten and John Zubizarreta provides a detailed resource for information about the author, his life, and his works. Each poem is a separate entry, and the authors also have researched Frost's lesser-known writing such as public speeches.

Several important reference works in drama appeared this year. Fisk, ed., *The Cambridge Companion to English Restoration Theatre*, offers fourteen new essays covering drama from 1660 to 1714. Major playwrights such as Wycherley and Dryden are considered, as well as minor writers and female writers. Aston and Reinelt, eds., *The Cambridge Companion to Modern British Women Playwrights*, offers fifteen essays divided into four sections. Aston and Reinelt open the collection with 'A Century in View: From Suffrage to the 1900s' (pp. 1–20). The succeeding first section is entitled 'Retrospectives' and includes three essays: 'Women Playwrights of the 1920s and 1930s' by Maggie B. Gale (pp. 23–37); 'New Plays and Women's Voices in the 1950s' by Susan Bennett (pp. 38–52); and 'Women Playwrights and the Challenge of Feminism in the 1970s' by Michelene Wandor (pp. 53–68). The second section, entitled 'National Tensions and Intersections', includes 'The Politics of Location' by Susan Bassnett (pp. 73–81); 'Contemporary Welsh Women Playwrights' by Anna-Marie Taylor (pp. 82–93); 'Contemporary Scottish Women Playwrights' by Adrienne Scullion (pp. 94–118); 'Women Playwrights in Northern Ireland' by Mary Trotter (pp. 119–33); and 'Language and Identity in Timberlake Wertenbaker's Plays' by Susan Carlson (pp. 134–50). Part III, entitled 'The Question of the Canon', has three essays: 'Pam Gems: Body Politics and Biography' by Elaine Aston (pp. 157–73); 'Caryl Churchill and the Politics of Style' by Janelle Reinelt (pp. 174–93); and 'Violence, Abuse and Gender Relations in the Plays of Sarah Daniels' by Gabriele Griffin (pp. 194–212). The final part, entitled 'The Subject of Identity', offers three essays: 'Small Island People: Black British Women Playwrights' by Meenakshi Ponnuswami (pp. 217–34); 'Writing Outside the Mainstream' by Claire MacDonald (pp. 235–52); and 'Lesbian Performance in the Transnational Arena' by Sue-Ellen Case (pp. 253–67).

One of the most extensive bibliographical reference works in drama and theatrical studies this year is Jowers and Cavanagh, eds., *Theatrical Costume, Masks, Make-Up and Wigs: A Bibliography and Iconography*. It contains over 4,000 entries for published sources such as books and sales catalogues (journals are excluded). The publications have been located in the libraries and archives of theatres in Barcelona,

Brussels, Budapest, Florence, London, Milan, New York, and Paris. Separate sections are included for designers, performing arts, ballet and dance, opera, commedia dell'arte, masquerade, instruction, and reference works. The scope of the section on performing arts is international and includes representations from Africa, the Caribbean, India and the Netherlands, among others. Historical examples reach as far back as the ancient Western world and extend to the present day. Also included is an index of over 6,000 printed plates of performers in costume.

Christopher K. Brown's *Encyclopedia of Travel Literature* lists entries for obscure and well-known contributors to the genre. George Sand, Lord Byron, and William Carlos Williams are some of the writers included who are not normally associated with the travel-writing genre. Brown quotes passages from selected works in a variety of forms, from poems to adventure logs.

Several new reference books this year consider the internet and literature. Susan Hockey's *Electronic Texts in the Humanities: Principles and Practice* presents the various ways in which electronic texts can supplement traditional literary analysis, including linguistic analysis and stylometry (use for authorship attribution). Hockey also discusses methods of preparing electronic scholarly editions, and other applications of electronic texts and publishing. Browner, Pulsford and Sears, *Literature and the Internet: A Guide for Students, Teachers, and Scholars* offers a basic introduction to the internet that covers browsers, search engines, bookmarking, and Web rings. The book also includes detailed lists of URLs for sites related to literature and composition. Another work dedicated to electronic literary resources is Day and Wortman, eds., *Literature in English: A Guide for Librarians in the Digital Age*.

The fourth edition of Jeremy Hawthorn's *A Glossary of Contemporary Literary Theory* provides a clear and concise overview of literary theory, with an emphasis on the vocabulary of the discipline as it has developed over the last thirty years. In a related work, David Macey presents *The Penguin Critical Dictionary of Critical Theory*, which defines relevant terms such as psychoanalysis, structuralism, postmodernism, linguistics, and semiotics. Also of note in literary theory studies is McGowan, ed., *The Year's Work in Critical and Cultural Theory*, volume vii: *1997*. The narrative bibliography covers semiotics, psychoanalysis, feminisms, colonial discourse/postcolonial theory, historicism, queer theories/cultures, Marxism(s) and post-Marxisms, media studies, popular culture, Australian popular culture and media, popular music, virtual cultures, film theory, art histories and visual culture studies, cultural policy, aboriginal identity, culture and art, and multiculturalism.

Moran and Ballif, eds., *Twentieth-Century Rhetorics and Rhetoricians: Critical Studies and Sources*, provides background information on forty writers and their contributions to the study of rhetoric. Entries include biographical information, a discussion of key writings, criticism, and a bibliography. A general bibliography is also included.

Linda and Roger Flavell trace the origins of hundreds of words and phrases in *The Chronology of Words and Phrases: A Thousand Years in the History of English*. The Flavells explain how major historical events and minor linguistic and social changes altered and enlarged the English language. In a related work, Robert Andrews has compiled 8,000 quotations from 1914 to the present in *The New Penguin Dictionary of Modern Quotations*. Andrews traces the origins of each quotation and provides a biographical sketch of its originator.

Cuoco and Gass, eds., *Literary St. Louis: A Guide*, gives a sense of the rich literary inheritance of a city that hosted writers such as Kate Chopin, Theodore Dreiser, Winston Churchill, T.S. Eliot, Mark Twain and Tennessee Williams. *Romantic Landscape: The Norwich School of Painters* by David Blayney Brown, Andrew Hemingway and Anne Lyles lists and analyses the works of ten landscape painters of the early nineteenth century.

Work in manuscript studies this year covers a variety of genres and fields. A new translation of the New Testament by William Tyndale, edited by W.R. Cooper and published by the British Library, is based on the Worms edition [1526] in the original spelling. The transmission and transformation of words and manuscripts is the subject of Boenig and Davis, eds., *Manuscript, Narrative, Lexicon: Essays on Literary and Cultural Transmission in Honor of Whitney F. Bolton*. The essays treat a variety of authors and texts from Chaucer and the *Gawain*-poet to twentieth-century dictionaries. The important Welsh manuscript Liber Landavensis, the Hendregadredd manuscript, and the White Book of Rhydderch are among the works addressed in Daniel Huws's *Medieval Welsh Manuscripts*. Images of warfare in medieval texts are reproduced in Pamela Porter's *Medieval Warfare in Manuscripts*. Fifty thousand texts that included Buddhist scriptures, poetry, and ballads make up the manuscripts discovered in the Dunhuang caves in China. Roderick Whitfield, Susan Whitfield and Neville Agnew tell the story of how those manuscripts were discovered and dispersed in *Cave Temples of Dunhuang: Art and History on the Silk Road*. The twenty-seven manuscripts produced in Amiens (in Picardy) from 1410 to 1470 are the subject of Susie Nash's *Between France and Flanders: Manuscript Illumination in Amiens*. Students of manuscripts will also wish to take note of Minta Collins's study of a unique manuscript form in *Medieval Herbals: The Illustrative Traditions*. In a related work, Janet Backhouse studies fourteenth-century textual illustrations in *Medieval Rural Life in the Luttrell Psalter*. Other works devoted to the study of art and illustrations are Judy Taylor's *Edward Ardizzone: Sketches for Friends* and Kurt Barstow's *The Gualenghi-D'Este Hours: Art and Devotion in Renaissance Ferrara*. Another work related to visual artwork in print is Garton, ed., *British Printmakers, 1855–1955*, which describes the development of British printmaking and the contributions of over 400 artists. Sam Smiles's *Eye Witness: Artists and Visual Documentation in Britain, 1770–1830* considers how visual representations in the eighteenth and nineteenth centuries challenged the authority of written knowledge.

A facsimile edition of Oscar Wilde's *De Profundis* has been brought out by the British Library. The manuscript is a letter to Lord Alfred Douglas that Wilde wrote while in prison, attempting to defend his behaviour and beliefs. Merlin Holland, Wilde's grandson, provides an introduction that chronicles the unusual history of the manuscript, which was deposited at the British Library with instructions that it should not be opened for fifty years, but four years later it was read aloud in court. The complete text of *De Profundis* first appeared in *The Letters of Oscar Wilde* [1962].

Volumes viii and ix of English Manuscript Studies appeared in 2000. Volume viii, Beal, ed., *The Seventeenth Century: Poetry, Music and Drama*, includes the following essays: 'Francis Beaumont and Nathan Field: New Records of their Early Years' by Hilton Kelliher; '"As far from all Reuolt": Sir John Salusbury, Christ Church MS 184 and Ben Jonson's "First Ode"' by Mark Bland; 'The "Running

Masque" Recovered: A Masque for the Marquess of Buckingham (*c*.1619–20)' by James Knowles; '"To the memory of the late excellent poet John Fletcher": A New Poem by John Ford' by Jeremy Maule; 'An Authorial Collection of Poems by Thomas Carew: The Gower Manuscript' by Peter Beal; 'The Manuscript Sources of Thomas Carew's Poetry' by Scott Nixon; 'A Newly Discovered Songbook in Poland with works by Henry Lawes and his Contemporaries' by Richard Charteris; 'Donne Manuscripts in Cheshire' by Dennis Flynn; '"Not the worst part of my wretched life": Three New Letters by Rochester, and how to Read Them' by Keith Walker; 'A New Dating of Rochester's *Artemiza to Chloë*' by Nicholas Fisher; and 'Manuscripts at Auction: January 1997 to December 1998' by A.S.G. Edwards.

Volume ix, Beal and Ezell, eds., *Writings by Early Modern Women*, includes the following essays: 'Women, Writing and Scribal Publication in the Sixteenth Century' by Jane Stevenson; 'Princess Elizabeth's Hand in *The Glass of the Sinful Soul*' by Frances Teague; 'Dame Flora's Blossoms: Esther Inglis's Flower-Illustrated Manuscripts' by Anneke Tjan-Bakker; 'Hand-Ma[i]de Books: The Manuscripts of Esther Inglis, Early-Modern Precursors of the Artists' Book' by Georgianna Ziegler; 'Two Unpublished Letters by Mary Herbert, Countess of Pembroke' by Steven W. May; 'Elizabeth Ashburnham Richardson's "Motherlie Endeauors"' by Victoria E. Burke; 'Elizabeth Ashburnham Richardson's Meditation on the Countess of Pembroke's *Discourse*' by Margaret Hannay; 'The Approbation of Elizabeth Jocelin' by Sylvia Brown; '"Monument of an endless affection": Folger MS V.b.198 and Lady Anne Southwell' by Jean Klene; 'The Scribal Hands and Dating of *Lady Falkland: Her Life*' by Heather Wolfe; 'Elizabeth Jekyll's Spiritual Diary: Private Manuscript or Political Document?' by Elizabeth Clarke; 'Swansongs: Reading Voice in the Poetry of Lady Hester Pulter' by Mark Robson; 'Lucy Hutchinson and *Order and Disorder*: The Manuscript Evidence' by David Norbrook; and 'Manuscripts at Auction: January 1999 to December 1999' by A.S.G. Edwards. An interesting and unique contribution to manuscript studies in music is presented by Lisa Fagin Davis in *The Gottschalk Antiphonary: Music and Liturgy in Twelfth-Century Lambach*. Davis reconstructs the manuscript and analyses its original production in its historical and political contexts.

Examining the challenges and controversies of textual editing is a growing trend in literary study. Wheeler, Kindrick and Salda, eds., *The Malory Debate: Essays on the Texts of Le Morte Darthur*, offers a collection of fifteen essays that explore the uncertainties and ambiguities surrounding the four original sources of the text. A bibliography of manuscripts and incunables is included. Middle English scholars will welcome the publication of Zettersten and Diensberg, eds., *The English Text of the Ancrene Riwle: The 'Vernon' Text*. The most important prose works in early medieval English appear together in Stevenson and Wogan-Browne, eds., *Concordances to the Katherine Group and The Wooing Group (MS Bodley 34; MSS Nero A XIV and Titus D XVIII)*. The concordances are valuable both for their linguistic richness and for their references to the condition of women in the early Middle Ages. G.W. Pigman III's edition of George Gascoigne's *A Hundreth Sundrie Flowres* is based on the first edition published anonymously in 1573. This edition is comprised of many little-known or ignored writings such as 'The Fruites of Warre'. Pigman examines Gascoigne's use of sources and corrects biographical errors that have appeared in earlier works. Early English scholars will wish to take note of Graham D. Caie's edition *The Old English Poem: 'Judgement Day II': A*

Critical Edition with Editions of De Die Iudicii and the Hatton 113 Homily Be Domes Daege. Medieval linguistic diversity is explored by thirteen contributors in Trotter, ed., *Multilingualism in Later Medieval Britain.* Essays address the linguistic intersections of English, Welsh and French and also explore the languages of particular genres such as legal writing and business records. Another work of general relevance in textual studies is Marie Axton and James P. Carley's *'Triumphs of English'. Henry Parker, Lord Morley, Translator to the Tudor Court: New Essays in Interpretation.*

Several important new Shakespeare editions arrived in 2000. The Oxford Shakespeare series has produced new editions of *King Lear* (ed. Wells), *Romeo and Juliet* (ed. Levenson) and *Richard III* (ed. Jowett). Unlike most editions, which are based on the revised 1623 first folio, this new edition of *Lear* is based on the 1608 quarto, which has recently been proven to be the base text for all succeeding revisions. Wells's introduction traces the creative process that produced *Lear.* In addition to the main text, the new edition provides critical guides for understanding and interpreting the play and also reprints the early ballad derived from it. The new edition of *Romeo and Juliet* presents both the 1599 quarto, which is generally considered to be the authoritative text, and the short 1597 quarto. The editor's purpose is to show how Shakespeare altered his work as he wrote. The new edition of *Richard III* aims to reproduce the play as it would have been performed in Shakespeare's time. To this end, the editor has based the text on the 1597 quarto, and provides an illustrated introduction that chronicles the play's performance history. In a similar effort to reproduce the original performed text, Gurr, ed., *The First Quarto of King Henry V*, edits the text that was transcribed by the actors in Shakespeare's company. The quarto text is half the length of the 1623 first folio and it therefore shows how Shakespeare's works were pared down for audiences in his day. Cambridge University Press's new edition of *The Tempest*, by Christine Dymkowski, also is concerned with stage history. It includes details from unpublished prompt-books that show how productions have changed over time. Dymkowski examines the history of the play's production in Britain and the United States, and she also looks at contemporary productions in Australia, Canada, France, Italy, and Japan. A bibliography of prompt-books and acting editions is included.

Several other editions of Renaissance literature are new this year. M.L. Stapleton includes notes, an introduction and commentary in the first scholarly edition of *Thomas Heywood's Art of Love: The First Complete English Translation of Ovid's Ars Amatoria.* J.B. Bamborough continues the multi-volume project to bring out Robert Burton's *Anatomy of Melancholy* in its entirety with the fifth volume, edited with Martin Dodsworth. This volume contains commentary on the text from Partition I, Section 2, Member 4, Subsection 1 to the end of Partition 1, plus the complete second partition.

Hammond, ed., *The Poems of John Dryden*, volume i: *1649–1681*, is the first in a four-volume edition of Dryden's complete poetical works. Dryden was very active in the theatre during the years covered in this volume, so the poems can be used as a window on his theatrical world. The second volume covers 1682–85 and includes Dryden's classical translations; the third and fourth volumes will cover 1686–96 and 1697–1700 respectively. A recently discovered manuscript of a performance for the French ambassador to England is the basis of a critical edition entitled *The Essex House Masque of 1621: Viscount Doncaster and the Jacobean Masque* by Timothy

Raylor. Cheney and Hosington, eds., *Elizabeth Jane Weston: Collected Writings*, is the first modern edition of Weston's poems and letters. The collection includes letters written to and by her, as well as her poetry. Weston's Latin work *Parthenica* comprises the bulk of the edition, and other works and correspondence round out the collection. In her edited *Felicia Hemans: Selected Poems, Letters, Reception Materials*, Wolfson presents the work of the nineteenth century's celebrated female poet. The collection is divided into works (some of which are excerpted) and reception, including nineteenth-century reviews and retrospects. A chronology and bibliography are also included.

Eighteenth-century textual scholarship this year has produced John Gilmore's new edition of Grainger's *The Sugar Cane* entitled *The Poetics of Empire: A Study of James Grainger's The Sugar Cane*. In addition to a fully annotated text and Grainger's own notes to the text are appendices entitled "'Great Homer deign to sing of little mice'", 'Bryan and Pereene', 'Colonel Martin's Directions for Planting and Sugar-Making', and 'Ramsay's Account of a Plantation Day'. April Alliston edits Sophia Lee's *The Recess, or, A Tale of Other Times* originally published between 1783 and 1785. Alliston's text is based on the second edition, corrected by the author and published in 1786.

A welcome contribution to nineteenth-century textual resources is Tarr and Engel, eds., *Thomas Carlyle. Sartor Resartus*. Computer analysis of all existing versions has aided the authors in establishing an accurate text. Other textual work on major nineteenth-century authors includes Jackson and Whalley, eds., *The Collected Works of Samuel Taylor Coleridge, Marginalia V*. The collection is a record of Coleridge's reading notes, many of which have not been published, and some of which are entire essays. Gillian Hughes's *James Hogg. The Spy: A Periodical Paper and Literary Amusement and Instruction, Published Weekly in 1810 and 1811* is the first modern edition of *The Spy*. A list of Hogg's articles is also included. An edition of the newly discovered play version of Rudyard Kipling's *The Jungle Play* is edited by Thomas Pinney.

Textual studies often reveal information about the composition process. Such is the case in Joe B. Fulton's *Mark Twain in the Margins: The Quarry Farm Marginalia and A Connecticut Yankee in King Arthur's Court*. Fulton examines Twain's marginal notes in the Quarry Farm library's copies of Macaulay's *History of England*, Carlyle's *The French Revolution*, and Lecky's *Spirit of Rationalism* and *England in the Eighteenth Century* to show how the self-professed spontaneous and disorganized writer actually researched his topic carefully before embarking on the project that was to become *A Connecticut Yankee*.

Newlin and Rush, eds., *The Collected Plays of Theodore Dreiser*, reproduces twelve complete plays plus an unpublished work (*The Voice*). An introduction, notes and appendices supplement the texts. F. Scott Fitzgerald's artistic development of *The Great Gatsby* is made evident by the edition of his early work *Trimalchio: An Early Version of the Great Gatsby* by James L.W. West. An introduction, facsimiles of typescripts, and notes on the composition history supplement the text. The edition also includes passages that were excised from the final printed version. Hunt, ed., *The Collected Poetry of Robinson Jeffers*, volume iv, includes poetry from 1903 to 1920, prose, and unpublished writings. The examples of Jeffers's early poetry are from his college years, and newly discovered poems written between 1917 and 1920 have also been included. Sylvia Plath's complete journals are published for the first time in Kukil, ed., *The Unabridged Journals of Sylvia Plath, 1950–1962*. Grimshaw and Perkins, eds., *Robert Penn Warren's All the King's Men: Three Stage Versions* is the first collection of all three dramatic texts associated with the Pulitzer Prize-winning novel *Proud Flesh, Willie Stark: His Rise and Fall*, and the stage version that shared the novel's title, *All the King's Men*. Mark Rawlinson provides a textual analysis of wartime literature in *British Writing of the Second World War*.

Textual study of literary criticism is a small but fruitful field. The ongoing project to publish Northrop Frye's writings has this year brought out Robert D. Denham's fifth and sixth volumes, entitled *Northrop Frye's Late Notebooks, 1982–1990: Architecture of the Spiritual World*. The notebooks in these volumes were kept by Frye while he was writing *Word with Power* and *The Double Vision*.

Several new editions of correspondence arrived in 2000. A record of Thomas More's final imprisonment preceding his execution by Henry VIII can be found in De Silva, ed., *The Last Letters of Thomas More*. Ingamells and Edgcumbe, eds., *The Letters of Sir Joshua Reynolds*, is the first edition of Reynolds's correspondence since 1929 and comprises 308 letters, twice the number in the earlier edition. Letters to friends, family, and patrons appear, and a biographical index of correspondents is also included. Erskine-Hill, ed., *Alexander Pope: Selected Letters*, is a new edition based on George Sherburn's *Collected Correspondence* [1956] and also includes the majority of the new letters discovered since the publication of Sherburn's work. New letters written by nineteenth-century American novelist Elizabeth Stuart Phelps have been brought out by Jennifer S. Tuttle in her article 'Letters from Elizabeth Stuart Phelps (Ward) to S. Weir Mitchell, M.D., 1884–1897' (*Legacy* 17:i[2000] 83–94). J.T. Boulton edits the eighth and final volume of *The Letters of D.H. Lawrence*, which also includes a general index. Bruccoli and Bucker, eds., *To Loot My Life Clean: The Thomas Wolfe–Maxwell Perkins Correspondence*, consists of 251 letters, the majority of which have not been published previously. The correspondence describes the nature of Wolfe's personal and professional relationship with his famous editor. Maud, ed., *The Selected Letters of Charles Olson*, comprises 200 letters selected from the 3,000 existing texts. The letters cover the years 1931–70, and reveal the poet's interactions with family and friends as well his business and professional dealings. Friedman and Figg, eds., *The Princess with the Golden Hair: Letters of Elizabeth Waugh to Edmund Wilson, 1933–1942*, chronicles the romantic relationship between the artist Waugh and the literary critic Wilson. Scott, ed., *Selected Letters of Rebecca West*, is the first collection of West's correspondence. Jeremy and Nicole Wilson edit *T.E. Lawrence. Correspondence with Bernard and Charlotte Shaw, 1922–1926* and *Letters*, volumes i–iii, which also contains excerpts from Charlotte Shaw's diary and letters from the Shaws to Lawrence. A biographical introduction and afterword are included. Reynolds, ed., *The Letters of Dorothy L. Sayers*, volume iv: *1951–1957: In the Midst of Life*, is a selection of correspondence written at the end of the author's life. Ferris, ed., *Dylan Thomas: The Collected Letters*, updates the edition first published in 1985. The new edition adds over 100 letters that shed light on the poet's adolescence and his romantic attachment to Caitlin Macnamara. Barth, ed., *The Selected Letters of Yvor Winters*, contains letters to literary figures such as Marianne Moore, Allen Tate, Lincoln Kirstein, Louise Bogan, and Katherine Bogan. The letters span the years 1918–67. A chronology, selected index of persons, and selected primary bibliography are also included. Clark, ed., *Selected Letters of Robert Penn Warren*, volume i: *The Apprentice Years, 1924–1934*, contains correspondence with Allen Tate written during Warren's undergraduate years at Vanderbilt. All but one of the letters in this volume are published here for the first time.

Textual scholars will wish to take note of Barendt and Firth, eds., *The Yearbook of Copyright and Media Law 2000*, which includes articles relating to authorship, censorship and other relevant topics. The annual survey of copyright and the media contains an essay on new media and the internet as well as a study of recent national and international developments in copyright law. The review of books by Thomas Gibbons examines P. Kearns's *The Legal Concept of Art* and Robert C. Post, ed., *Censorship and Silencing: Practices of Cultural Regulation*.

Oxford World's Classics offers several new affordable paperback editions. Sharistanian, ed., *Willa Cather. The Song of the Lark*, is based on the original 1915 edition and includes an appendix with the author's preface to the significantly revised autograph edition. Baines and Burns, eds., *Five Romantic Plays, 1768–1821*, reproduces Horace Walpole's *The Mysterious Mother*, Robert Southey's *Wat Tyler*, Joanna Baillie's *De Montfort*, Elizabeth Inchbald's *Lovers' Vows*, and Lord Byron's *The Two Foscari*. Each play is based on the first authorized printed edition. Penguin Classics presents Walter Scott's *Ivanhoe*, based on the 1998 Edinburgh edition of the Waverley novels, which is the first authoritative edition that uses Scott's original texts.

Books Reviewed

Aers, David, ed. *Medieval Literature and Historical Inquiry: Essays in Honor of Derek Pearsall*. B&B. [2000] pp. 227. $75 ISBN 0 8599 1555 7.

Alliston, April, ed. *Sophia Lee. The Recess, or A Tale of Other Times*. UKenP. [2000] pp. 400. $47.50 ISBN 0 8131 2146 9.

Andrews, Robert. *The New Penguin Dictionary of Modern Quotations*. Penguin. [2000] pp. 588. $35 ISBN 0 1402 9307 8.

Archer, Caroline. *The Kynoch Press: The Anatomy of a Printing House, 1876–1981*. Oak Knoll. [2000] pp. 240. $49.95 ISBN 1 5845 6046 0.

Ashton, Owen, and Stephen Roberts. *The Victorian Working-Class Writer*. Mansell. [1999] pp. vii + 164. £45 ($80) ISBN 0 7201 2324 0.

Aston, Elaine, and Janelle Reinelt. *The Cambridge Companion to Modern British Women Playwrights*. CUP. [2000] pp. 296. £37.50 ISBN 0 5215 9422 7.

Atherton, Jeffrey. *Black-Letter: An Interpretation of Events Relating to the Time and Presence of Johann Gutenberg*. Bieler. [2000] pp. 45. $1,500 ISBN 0 9314 6034 8.

Axton, Marie, and James P. Carley, eds. *'Triumphs of English'. Henry Parker, Lord Morley, Translator to the Tudor Court: New Essays in Interpretation*. BL. [2000] pp. xi + 276. £45 ISBN 0 7123 4649 X.

Bachleitner, Norbert, Franz M. Eybl and Ernest Fischer. *Geschichte des Buchhandels in Österreich*. Harrassowitz. [2000] pp. xii + 413. ISBN 3 4470 4129 3.

Backhouse, Janet. *Medieval Rural Life in the Luttrell Psalter*. BL. [2000] pp. 64. £7.95 ISBN 0 7123 4663 5.

Baines, Paul, and Edward Burns, eds. *Five Romantic Plays, 1768–1821*. OUP. [2000] pp. 418. pb £7.99 ISBN 0 1928 3316 2.

Bajetta, C.M. *Some Notes on Printing and Publishing in Renaissance Venice*. Typophiles. [2000] ISBN 6 8620 9453 1.

Baker, Cathleen A. *By His Own Labor: The Biography of Dard Hunter*. Oak Knoll. [2000] pp. 360. $49.95 ISBN 1 5845 6020 7.

Baker, William, and Kenneth Womack. *Twentieth-Century Bibliography and Textual Criticism: An Annotated Bibliography*. Greenwood. [2000] pp. 262. $75 ISBN 0 3133 0537 4.

Balay, Robert. *Early Periodical Indexes*. Scarecrow. [2000] pp. 352. £47. ISBN 0 8108 3868 0.

Bamborough, J.B., and Martin Dodsworth, eds. *Robert Burton. The Anatomy of Melancholy*, vol. v: *Commentary from Part. I, Sect. 2, Memb. 4, Subs. I, to the End of the Second Partition*. OUP. [2000] pp. 326. £60 ISBN 0 1981 8485 9.

Barendt, Eric M., and Alison Firth, eds. *The Yearbook of Copyright and Media Law 2000*. OUP. [2000] pp. 450. £50 ISBN 0 1982 9919 2.

Barstow, Kurt. *The Gualenghi–D'Este Hours: Art and Devotion in Renaissance Ferrara*. J. Paul Getty Museum. [2000] pp. ix + 269. £72.50 ISBN 0 8923 6370 3.

Barth, R.L., ed. *The Selected Letters of Yvor Winters*. Swallow. [2000] pp. 490. £42.50 ISBN 0 8040 1031 5.

Bartram, Alan. *Creating the Printed Page: A Guide for Authors, Publishers and Designers*. BL. [2000] pp. 97. £8.95 ISBN 0 7123 4696 1.

Battestin, Martin C. *A Henry Fielding Companion*. Greenwood. [2000] pp. 333. $79.95 ISBN 0 3132 9707 X.

Beal, Peter, ed. *Seventeenth-Century Poetry, Music and Drama. English Manuscript Studies 1100–1700, vol. viii*. BL. [2000] pp. 346. £45 ISBN 0 7123 4629 5.

Beal, Peter, and Margaret J.M. Ezell, eds. *Writings by Early Modern Women. English Manuscript Studies, 1100–1700, vol. ix*. BL. [2000] pp. vi + 309. $90 ISBN 0 7123 4674 0.

Beckman, Linda Hunt. *Amy Levy: Her Life and Letters*. OhioUP. [2000] pp. xiii + 331. hb $49.95 ISBN 0 8214 1329 5, pb $24.95 ISBN 0 8214 1330 9.

Bell, Bill, Jonquil Bevan and Philip Bennett, eds. *Across Boundaries: The Book in Culture and Commerce*. Oak Knoll. [2000] pp. 176. $39.95 ISBN 0 5845 6006 1.

Blanch, Robert J. *The Gawain Poems: A Reference Guide 1978–1993*. Whitston. [2000] pp. 346. $49. ISBN 0 8787 5525 X.

Blatchly, John. *Some Suffolk and Norfolk Ex-Libris: Bookplates and Labels Relating to East Anglian Owners, Artist and Printers*. Bookplate Society. [2000] pp. 160. £17. ISBN 9 9535 0083 3.

Block, Richard, and Peter Fenves, eds. *The Spirit of Poesy: Essays on Jewish and German Literature and Thought in Honor of Géza Von Molnár*. NorthwesternUP. [2000]. pp. vii + 249. $59.95 ISBN 0 8101 1681 2.

Blok, F.F., *Isaac Vossius and his Circle: His Life until his Farewell to Queen Christina of Sweden, 1618–1655*. Egbert Forsten. [2000] pp. 520. €65 ISBN 9 0698 0132 9.

Bloom, Abigail Burnham, ed. *Nineteenth-Century British Women Writers: A Bio-Bibliographical Critical Sourcebook*. Aldwych. [2000] pp. xii + 456. £79.95 ISBN 0 8617 2116 0.

Blouin, Lenora P. *May Sarton: A Bibliography*, 2nd edn. Scarecrow. [2000] pp. 656. $85 ISBN 0 8108 3687 4.

Boenig, Robert, and Kathleen Davis, eds. *Manuscript, Narrative, Lexicon: Essays on Literary and Cultural Transmission in Honor of Whitney F. Bolton*. BucknellUP. [2000] pp. 261. £35 ISBN 0 8387 5440 6.

Boulton, J.T., ed. *The Letters of D.H. Lawrence*, vol. viii. CUP. [2000] xvii + 418. £60 ($95) ISBN 0 5212 3117 5.

Bray, Joe, Miriam Handley and Anne C. Henry, eds. *Ma(r)king the Text: The Presentation of Meaning on the Literary Page*. Ashgate. [2000] pp. xxiv + 341. $99.95 ISBN 0 7546 0168 4.

Brooks, Douglas A. *From Playhouse to Printing House: Drama and Authorship in Early Modern England*. CUP. [2000] pp. 314. £37.50 ISBN 0 5217 7117 X.

Brown, Christopher K. *Encyclopedia of Travel Literature*. ABC-CLIO. [2000] pp. 267. £45.50 ISBN 0 8743 6940 1.

Brown, David Blayney, Andrew Hemingway and Anne Lyles. *Romantic Landscape: The Norwich School of Painters*. Tate. [2000] pp. 160. $40 1 8543 7315 3.

Brown, Marshall. *The Cambridge History of Literary Criticism, vol. v: Romanticism*. CUP. [2000] pp. 512. £65 ISBN 0 5213 0010 X.

Browner, Stephanie, Stephen Pulsford and Richard Sears. *Literature and the Internet: A Guide for Students, Teachers, and Scholars*. Garland. [2000] pp. 191. pb $24.95 ISBN 0 8153 3453 2.

Brownrigg, Linda L., and Margaret M. Smith, eds. *Interpreting and Collecting Fragments of Medieval Books*. Anderson-Lovelace. [2000] pp. xv + 270. £75 ISBN 0 9626 3726 2.

Bruccoli, Matthew J., and Park Buckler, eds. *To Loot My Life Clean: The Thomas Wolfe–Maxwell Perkins Correspondence*. USCP. [2000] pp. 330. $39.95 ISBN 1 5700 3355 2.

Burnett, Paula. *Derek Walcott*. UPFlor. [2000] pp. 376. $55 ISBN 0 8130 1882 X.

Burnett, T.A. *The* British Library *Catalogue of the Ashley Manuscripts*, part I: *Descriptions*, part II: *Index*. BL. [1999] pp. 725. £65 ISBN 0 7123 4573 6.

Cagle, William R. *A Matter of Taste: A Bibliographical Catalogue of International Books on Food and Drink in the Lilly Library, Indiana University*, 2nd edn. Oak Knoll. [1999]. pp. 991. $95 (£60) ISBN 1 8847 1886 8.

Caie, Graham D., ed. *The Old English Poem: 'Judgement Day II': A Critical Edition with Editions of the De Die Iudicii and the Hatton 113 Homily Be Domes Daege*. B&B. [2000] pp. xiv + 161. £40 ISBN 0 8599 1570 0.

Cain, William E., ed. *Historical Guides to Henry David Thoreau*. OUP. [2000] pp. 272. £29.99. ISBN 0 1951 3862 7.

Callaghan, Dympna, ed. *A Feminist Companion to Shakespeare*. Blackwell. [2000] pp. xxiv + 384. £50 ISBN 0 6312 0806 2.

Carley, James, ed. *The Libraries of King Henry VIII*. BL. [2000] pp. xcii + 407. £85 ISBN 0 7123 4630 9.

Carpenter, Charles A. *Dramas of the Nuclear Age: A Descriptive List of English-Language Plays*. Mellen. [2000] pp. 104. £39.95 ISBN 0 7734 7891 4.

Cauveren, Sydney. *A.L. Rowse: A Bibliophile's Extensive Bibliography*. Scarecrow. [2000] pp. 325. $60 ISBN 0 8108 3641 6.

Champion, Laurie, ed. *American Women Writers, 1900–1945: A Bio-Bibliographical Critical Sourcebook*. Greenwood. [2000] pp. 432. $95 ISBN 0 3133 0943 3.

Chaudhuri, Brahma, and Fred Radford, eds. *Cumulative Bibliography of Victorian Studies: 1945–1969*, 2 vols. LITIR. [2000] pp. xv + 625. ISBN 0 9192 3739 8.

A Check-list of Books Published During 1996 of Interest to Members of the Eighteen Nineties Society. Rivendale Press for the 1890s Society. [1997] pp. 17. £15 ISBN 0 9057 4422 5.

A Check-list of Books Published during 1997 of Interest to Members of the Eighteen Nineties Society. Rivendale Press for the Eighteen Nineties Society. [1998] pp. 18. pb £15 ISBN 0 9057 4416 0.

Cheney, Donald, and Brenda M. Hosington, eds. *Elizabeth Jane Weston: Collected Writings*. UTorP. [2000] pp. xxxi + 448. £50 ISBN 0 8020 4472 7.

Cinamon, Gerald. *Rudolf Koch: Letterer, Type Designer, Teacher*. Oak Knoll. [2000] pp. 208. $49.95 ISBN 1 5845 6013 4.

Clark, William Bedford, ed. *Selected Letters of Robert Penn Warren*, vol. i: *The Apprentice Years, 1924–1934*. LSUP. [2000] pp. 296. $39.95 ISBN 0 8071 2536 9.

Cohen, Michael. *Murder Most Fair: The Appeal of Mystery Fiction*. AUP. [2000] pp. 207. £35 ISBN 0 8386 3851 1.

Collins, Minta. *Medieval Herbals: The Illustrative Traditions*. UTorP. [2000] pp. 288. $80 ISBN 0 8020 4757 2.

Collins, Nina L. *The Library in Alexandria and the Bible in Greek*. Brill. [2000] pp. ix + 224. £31.40 ISBN 9 0041 1866 7.

Conaway, James. *America's Library: The Story of the Library of Congress*. YaleUP. [2000] pp. 232. £30 ISBN 0 3000 8308 4.

Cox, J. Randolph. *The Dime Novel Companion: A Source Book*. Greenwood. [2000] pp. 333. $79.50 ISBN 0 3132 5674 8.

The Culture of the Book in the Scottish Enlightenment: An Exhibition with Essays by Roger Emerson, Richard Sher, Stephen Brown, and Paul Wood. Thomas Fisher Rare Book Library. [2000] pp. x + 120. ISBN 0 7727 6035 7.

Cuoco, Lorin, and William Gass, eds. *Literary St. Louis: A Guide*. Missouri Historical Society. [2000] pp. 250. $19.95 ISBN 1 8839 8235 9.

Curnutt, Kirk. *The Critical Response to Gertrude Stein*. Greenwood. [2000] pp. 400. $82.50 ISBN 0 3133 0475 0.

Davis, Lisa Fagin. *The Gottschalk Antiphonary: Music and Liturgy in Twelfth-Century Lambach*. CUP. [2000] pp. xv + 316. £55 ISBN 0 5215 9249 6.

Day, Betty H., and William A. Wortman, eds. *Literature in English: A Guide for Librarians in the Digital Age*. ALA. [2000] pp. 350. $32 ISBN 0 8389 8081 3.

De Bellis, Jack. *The John Updike Encyclopedia*. Greenwood. [2000] pp. xxxiii + 545. $89.50 ISBN 0 3132 9904 8.

De Montluzin, Emily Lorraine. *Attributions of Authorship in the Gentleman's Magazine, 1731–1868 and Attributions of Authorship in the European Magazine, 1782–1826*. Biographical Society of the University of Virginia. http://etext.lib.virginia.edu/bsuva/gm/.

De Renzi, Silvia. *Instruments in Print: Books from the Whipple Collection*. Whipple Museum of the History of Science. [2000] pp. x + 107. pb £8. ISBN 0 9062 7116 9.

De Silva, Alvaro, ed. *The Last Letters of Thomas More*. Eerdmans. [2000] pp. 214. £12.99 ISBN 0 8028 3886 3.

Denham, Robert D., ed. *Northrop Frye's Late Notebooks 1982–1990: Architecture of the Spiritual World*, vols. v and vi. UTorP. [2000] $75 ISBN 0 8020 4751 3.

Dixon, Jay. *The Romance Fiction of Mills & Boon, 1909–1990s*. UCL. [1999] pp. 224. $69.95 ISBN 1 8572 8266 3.

Douglas, J. Yellowlees. *The End of Books: Or Books without End? Reading Interactive Narratives*. UMichP. [2000] pp. 256. $34.50 ISBN 0 4721 1114 0.

Drabble, Margaret. *The Oxford Companion to English Literature*, 6th edn. OUP. [2000] pp. 1,172. $49.95 ISBN 0 1986 6244 0.

Drazin, David. *Croquet: A Bibliography: Specialist Books and Pamphlets Complete to 1997*. Oak Knoll. [2000] pp. 528. $99.95 ISBN 1 5845 6008 8.

Dudbridge, Glen. *Lost Books of Medieval China*. BL. [2000] pp. vi + 79. pb £16 ISBN 0 7123 4688 0.

Duffy, Patrick. *The Skilled Compositor, 1850–1914: An Aristocrat Among Working Men*. Ashgate. [2000] pp. 244. $79.95 ISBN 0 7546 0255 9.

Dunton, John. *The Dublin Scuffle*. Four Courts. [2000] pp. xxx + 350. £45 ISBN 1 8518 2446 4.

Dymkowski, Christine, ed. *The Tempest. Shakespeare in Production*. CUP. [2000] pp. 406. £45 ISBN 0 5214 4407 1.

Edelman, Charles. *Shakespeare's Military Language: A Dictionary*. Athlone. [2000] pp. xv + 411. $125 ISBN 0 4851 1546 8.

Edwards, A.S.G., Vincent Gillespie and Ralph Hanna. *The English Medieval Book: Studies in Memory of Jeremy Griffiths*. BL. [2000] pp. xii + 264. £45 ISBN 0 7123 4650 3.

Eighteenth-Century Journals from the Hope Collection at the Bodleian Library, Oxford: *A Listing and Guide to the Microfilm Collection*. Adam Matthew. [2000] pp. 56. pb £16 ISBN 1 8571 1144 3.

Elliott, David B. *Charles Fairfax Murray: The Unknown Pre-Raphaelite*. Oak Knoll. [2000] pp. 260. $45 ISBN 1 5845 6030 4.

Erdmann, Axel. *My Gracious Silence: Women in the Mirror of Sixteenth-Century Printing in Western Europe*. Gilhofer & Ranschburg. [1999] pp. xxv + 319. £100.

Erskine-Hill, Howard, ed. *Alexander Pope: Collected Letters*. OUP. [2000] pp. 208. £50 ISBN 0 1981 8565 0.

Ferris, Paul. *Dylan Thomas: The Collected Letters*, new edn. W&N. [2000] pp. 1,077. £50 ISBN 0 4608 7999 5.

Fisk, Deborah Payne, ed. *The Cambridge Companion to English Restoration Theatre*. CUP. [2000] pp. xxvii + 294. $54.95 ISBN 0 5215 8215 6.

Flavell, Linda, and Roger Flavell. *The Chronology of Words and Phrases: A Thousand Years in the History of English*. KC. [1999] pp. 269. £18.99 ISBN 1 8562 6249 9.

Fleeman, J.D. *A Bibliography of the Works of Samuel Johnson: Treating his Published Works from the Beginnings to 1984*, vol. i: *1731–1759*; vol. ii: *1760–1816*. OUP. [2000] pp. 1,972. $230 each ISBN 0 1981 2270 5 (vol. i), ISBN 0 1981 2270 5 (vol. ii).

Frankel, Nicholas. *Oscar Wilde's Decorated Books*. UMichP. [2000] pp. xiv + 222. $47.50 ISBN 0 4721 1069 1.

Friedman, John B., and Kristen M. Figg, eds. *The Princess with the Golden Hair: Letters of Elizabeth Waugh to Edmund Wilson, 1933–1942*. AUP. [2000] pp. 180. $35 ISBN 0 8386 3855 4.

Fulton, Joe B. *Mark Twain in the Margins: The Quarry Farm Marginalia and A Connecticut Yankee in King Arthur's Court*. UAlaP. [2000] pp. 205. $34.95 ISBN 0 8173 1033 9.

Gale, Robert L. *A Dashiell Hammett Companion*. Greenwood. [2000] pp. 317. $79.50 ISBN 0 3133 1095 5.

Gardiner, Ellen. *Regulating Readers: Gender and Literary Criticism in the Eighteenth-Century Novel*. UDelP. [1999] pp. 198. $36.50 (£30) ISBN 0 8741 3695 4.

Garside, Peter, and Rainer Schöwerling, eds. *The English Novel, 1770–1829: A Bibliographical Survey of Prose Fiction Published in the British Isles*, vol. ii: *1800–1829*. OUP. [2000] pp. 753. $125 ISBN 0 1981 8318 6.

Garton, Robin, ed. *British Printmakers, 1855–1955*. Scolar. [2000] pp. 336. $144.95 ISBN 0 7546 0231 1.

Gelfant, Blanche H., and Lawrence Graver, eds. *The Columbia Companion to the Twentieth-Century American Short Story*. ColUP. [2000] pp. 952. $80 ISBN 0 2311 1098 7.

Gemmett, Robert J., ed. *The Consummate Collector: William Beckford's Letters to his Bookseller*. Russell. [2000] pp. 344. £39. ISBN 0 8595 5252 7.

Gilmore, John. *The Poetics of Empire: A Study of James Grainger's The Sugar Cane*. Athlone. [2000] pp. 288. £47.50 ISBN 0 4851 1539 5.

Gitelman, Lisa. *Scripts, Grooves and Writing Machines: Representing Technology in the Edison Era*. StanfordUP. [2000] pp. viii + 282. hb $49.50 (£37.50) ISBN 0 8047 3270 1, pb $19.95 (£13.95) ISBN 0 8047 3872 6.

Golden, Catherine J., ed. *Book Illustrated: Text, Image, and Culture, 1770–1930*. Oak Knoll. [2000] pp. 344. $39.95 ISBN 1 5845 6023 1.

Graziplene, Leonard R. *Teletext: Its Promise and Demise*. LehighUP. [2000] pp. 184. $38.50 ISBN 0 9342 2364 5.

Greenspan, Ezra. *George Palmer Putnam: Representative American Publisher*. PSUP. [2000] pp. 528. £43.50 ISBN 0 2710 2005 9.

Greenwood, Jeremy. *Margaret Bruce Wells: The Complete Wood-Engravings and Linocuts*. Wood Lea. [2000] pp. 73. £62 ISBN 0 9512 2878 1.

Grimshaw, James A. Jr., and James A. Perkins, eds. *Robert Penn Warren's All the King's Men: Three Stage Versions*. UGeoP. [2000] pp. 264. $45 ISBN 0 8203 2097 8.

Grove, Laurence, and Daniel Russell. *The French Emblem: Bibliography of Secondary Sources*. Librairie Droz. [2000] pp. xx + 239. €56.25 ISBN 2 6000 0412 2.

Gurr, Andrew. *William Shakespeare. The First Quarto of King Henry V*. CUP. [2000] pp. 136. $49.95 ISBN 0 5216 2336 7.

Haffenden, John, ed. *William Empson. The Complete Poems*. Lane. [2000] pp. lxxxvi + 512. £14.99 ISBN 0 7139 9287 5.

Hamilton, Ian, Peter Dale, Philip Hoy and J.D. McClatchy, eds. *Donald Hall in Conversation with Ian Hamilton*. Between the Lines. [2000] pp. 112. pb £9.50 ISBN 0 9532 8414 X.

Hamilton, John Maxwell. *Casanova Was a Book Lover and Other Naked Truths and Provocative Curiosities about the Writing, Selling and Reading of Books*. LSUP. [2000] pp. 280. $24.95 ISBN 0 8071 2554 7.

Hammond, Paul, ed. *The Poems of John Dryden*, vol. i: *1649–1681*. Longman. [1995] £95 ($99) ISBN 0 5824 9213 0.

Hammond, Wayne G. *Arthur Ransome: A Bibliography*. Oak Knoll. [2000] pp. 388. $78 ISBN 1 5845 6022 3.

Harner, James L. *On Compiling an Annotated Bibliography*, 2nd edn. MLA. [2000] pp. 44. pb $10 ISBN 0 8735 2979 0.

Harner, James L. *World Shakespeare Bibliography Online*. [2000] Prices vary for institutions and individuals.

Harrop, Dorothy A., et al. *The Old Stile Press—in the Twentieth Century: A Bibliography, 1979–1999*. Old Stile. [2000] pp. 136. £30 ISBN 0 9076 6449 0.

Hattaway, Michael, ed. *A Companion to English Renaissance Literature and Culture*. Blackwell. [2000] pp. 747. $124.95 ISBN 0 6312 1668 5.

Hawthorn, Jeremy. *A Glossary of Contemporary Literary Theory*, 4th edn. Arnold. [2000] pp. 400. $72 ISBN 0 3407 6066 4.

Hegarty, Paul. *Georges Bataille: Core Cultural Theorist*. Sage. [2000] pp. ix + 171. $75 ISBN 0 7619 6077 5.

Heijting, Willem, ed. *Protestantism Crossing the Seas: A Short-Title Catalogue of English Books Printed Before 1801 Illustrating the Spread of Protestant Thought and the Exchange of Ideas between the English-Speaking Countries and the Netherlands, held by the University Library of the Vrije Universiteit at Amsterdam*. Hes & De Graaf. [2000] pp. xxxvi + 291. ISBN 9061 64408 2.

Ho, Elaine Yee Lin. *Timothy Mo*. ManUP. [2000] pp. 191. £9.99 ISBN 0 7190 5390 0.

Hockey, Susan. *Electronic Texts in the Humanities: Principles and Practice*. OUP. [2000] pp. 228. £45 ISBN 0 1987 1194 8.

Howard-Hill, T.H. *Shakespearian Bibliography and Textual Criticism: A Bibliography*. Summertown. [2000] pp. 290. $65 ISBN 1 8930 0905 X.

Hughes, Gillian, ed. *James Hogg. The Spy: A Periodical Paper of Literary Amusement and Instruction. Published Weekly in 1810 and 1811*. EdinUP. [2000] pp. 712. £60 ISBN 0 7486 1417 6.

Hunt, Tim, ed. *The Collected Poetry of Robinson Jeffers*, vol. iv: *Poetry 1903–1920, Prose, and Unpublished Writings*. StanfordUP. [2000] pp. 528. $75 ISBN 0 8047 3816 5.

Hunter, Andrew, ed. *Thornton and Tully's Scientific Books, Libraries, and Collectors: A Study of Bibliography and the Book Trade in Relation to the History of Science*. Ashgate. [2000] pp. xii + 405. £80 ISBN 1 8592 8233 4.

Hunter, Michael, Giles Mandelbrote, Richard Ovenden and Nigel Smith, eds. *A Radical's Books: The Library Catalogue of Samuel Jeake of Rye, 1623–90*. Brewer. [1999] pp. lxxix + 364. £75 ($135) ISBN 0 8599 1471 2.

Huws, Daniel. *Medieval Welsh Manuscripts*. UWalesP. [2000] pp. 363. £50 ISBN 0 7083 1602 6.

Ingamells, John, and John Edgcumbe, eds. *The Letters of Sir Joshua Reynolds*. YaleUP. [2000] pp. 318. £30 ISBN 0 3000 8733 0.

Inglis, Fred. *Clifford Geertz: Culture, Custom, and Ethics*. Polity. [2000] pp. 208. £45 ISBN 0 7456 2157 0.

Isaac, Peter C.G., and Barry McKay. *The Mighty Engine: The Printing Press and its Impact. Proceedings of the Seventeenth Seminar on the British Book Trade, Aberystwyth, July 1999*. Oak Knoll. [2000] pp. 208. $39.95 ISBN 1 5845 6024 X.

Jackson, H.J., and George Whalley, eds. *The Collected Works of Samuel Taylor Coleridge, Marginalia V*. PrincetonUP. [2000] pp. 896. $187.50 ISBN 0 6910 9958 8.

Jager, Eric. *The Book of the Heart*. UChicP. [2000] pp. 274. £20.50 ISBN 0 2263 9116 7.

Johanson, Graeme. *A Study of Colonial Editions in Australia, 1843–1972*. Elibank. [2000] pp. 346. $A62.50 ISBN 0 9583 4963 0.

Johns, Adrian. *The Nature of the Book: Print and Knowledge in the Making*. UChicP. [2000] pp. 754. pb $22.50 ISBN 0 2264 0122 7.

Johnston, Alastair. *Alphabets to Order: The Literature of Nineteenth-Century Typefounders' Specimens*. Oak Knoll. [2000]. pp. 222. $39.95 ISBN 1 58456 009 6.

Jowers, Sidney, and John Cavanagh, eds. *Theatrical Costume, Masks, Make-Up and Wigs: A Bibliography and Iconography*. Routledge. [2000] pp. 542. £110 ISBN 0 4152 4774 8.

Jowett, John, ed. *William Shakespeare. The Tragedy of King Richard III*. OUP. [2000] pp. 423. £50 ($85) ISBN 0 1981 8245 7.

Kahan, Basil. *Ottmar Mergenthaler: The Man and his Machine: A Biographical Appreciation of the Inventor on his Centennial*. Oak Knoll. [2000] pp. 264. $55 ISBN 1 5845 6007 X.

Karpuk, Susan Price. *Samuel Richardson's Clarissa: An Index Analyzing the Characters, Subjects and Place Names with Summaries of Letters Appended*. AMS. [2000] pp. 476. £104.95 ISBN 0 4046 3534 2.

Kinane, Vincent, and Anne Walsh, eds. *Essays on the History of Trinity College Library Dublin*. Four Courts. [2000] pp. 160. £60 ISBN 0 7546 0085 8.

King, Bruce. *Derek Walcott: A Caribbean Life*. OUP. [2000] pp. 736. £30 ISBN 0 1987 1131 X.

King, Michael. *Wrestling with the Angel: A Life of Janet Frame*. Counterpoint. [2000] pp. 440. $30 ISBN 1 5824 3069 1.

Kinross, Robin, ed. *Anthony Froshaug: Typography and Texts*. HyphenP. [2000] pp. 254. £40 ISBN 0 9072 5913 8.

Kukil, Karen V. *The Unabridged Journals of Sylvia Plath, 1950–1962*. Anchor. [2000] pp. 732. $18 ISBN 0 3857 2025 4.

Laird, Holly A. *Women Coauthors*. UIllP. [2000] pp. xi + 315. £25.50 ISBN 0 2520 2547 4.

Lambdin, Laura Cooner, and Robert Thomas Lambdin. *A Companion to Jane Austen Studies*. Greenwood. [2000] pp. 360. £66.95 ISBN 0 3133 0662 1.

Lambdin, Robert Thomas, and Laura Cooner Lambdin, eds. *Encyclopedia of Medieval Literature*. Greenwood. [2000] pp. 549. $89.50 ISBN 0 3133 0054 2.

Lane, Jeremy F. *Pierre Bourdieu: A Critical Introduction*. Pluto. [2000] pp. 224. £35 ISBN 0 7453 1506 2.

Laurence, Dan H., and Fred D. Crawford, eds. *Bibliographical Shaw*, vol. xx. PSUP. [2000] £39.30 ISBN 0 2710 2007 5.

Law, Graham. *Serializing Fiction in the Victorian Press*. Palgrave. [2000] pp. 300. $59.95 ISBN 0 3122 3574 7.

Lawford-Hinrichsen, Irene. *Music Publishing and Patronage: C.F. Peters, 1800 to the Holocaust.* Edition. [2000] pp. 336. £25 ISBN 0 9536 1120 5.

Lee, Nicholas, ed. *Irish Identity and Literary Periodicals, 1832–1842,* 6 vols. Thoemmes. [2000] pp. 1,800. $845 ISBN 4 9314 4442 4.

Lehuu, Isabelle. *Carnival on the Page: Popular Print Media in Antebellum America.* UNCP. [2000] pp. xi + 244. hb $39.95 (£33.95) ISBN 0 8078 2521 2, pb $17.95 (£15.50) ISBN 0 8078 4832 8.

Lerner, Fred. *Libraries through the Ages.* Continuum. [2000] pp. 160. £10 ISBN 0 8264 1201 7.

Levenson, Jill L. *William Shakespeare. Romeo and Juliet.* OUP. [2000] pp. 460. £50 ISBN 0 1981 2937 8.

Lhotka, Edward R. *ABC of Leather Bookbinding: An Illustrated Manual on Traditional Bookbinding.* Oak Knoll. [2000] pp. 142. $39.95 ISBN 1 5845 6028 2.

Lindfors, Bernth. *Black African Literature in English, 1992–1996.* Hans Zell. [2000] pp. xliii + 654. $129.95 ISBN 0 8525 5565 2.

Lomax, Joanne, et al. *A Guide to Additional Sources of Funding and Revenue for Libraries and Archives,* 2nd edn. rev. Roy Sully. BL. [2000] pp. vii + 113. £17.50 ISBN 0 7123 0857 1.

Lovett, Patricia, *The* British Library *Companion to Calligraphy, Illumination and Heraldry: A History and Practical Guide.* BL. [2000] pp. 320. £30 ISBN 0 7123 4680 5.

Lovett, Patricia. *Calligraphy, Illumination and Heraldry: A History and Practical Guide.* BL. [2000] pp. 320. £30 ISBN 0 7123 4680 5.

Lynch, Jack. *A Bibliography of Johnsonian Studies, 1986–1998.* AMS. [2000] pp. 147. $69.50 ISBN 0 4046 3533 4.

Macey, David. *The Penguin Dictionary of Critical Theory.* Penguin. [2000] pp. 496. £20 ISBN 0 1402 9321 3.

MacKenzie, Cynthia. *A Concordance to the Letters of Emily Dickinson.* UPColorado. [2000] pp. 850. $225 ISBN 0 8708 1568 7.

MacLeod, Roy, ed. *The Library of Alexandria: Centre of Learning in the Ancient World.* I.B. Tauris. [2000] pp. 207. £39.50 ISBN 1 8606 4428 7.

Martin, Henri-Jean. *La Naissance du livre moderne (XIVe-XVIIe siècles): Mise en page et mise en texte du livre français.* Éditions du Cercle de la Librairie. [2000] pp. viii + 494. ISBN 2 7654 0776 2.

Matthews, Jack. *Reading Matter: A Rabid Bibliophile's Adventures Among Old and Rare Books.* Oak Knoll. [2000] pp. x + 198. $29.95 ISBN 1 5845 6027 4.

Maud, Ralph, ed. *Selected Letters of Charles Olson.* UCP. [2000] pp. 464. $60 (£40) ISBN 0 5202 0580 4.

McConnell, Louise. *Dictionary of Shakespeare.* Fitzroy Dearborn. [2000] pp. 315. $45 ISBN 1 5795 8215 X.

McDonald, Gerald D., Stuart C. Sherman and Mary T. Russo. *A Checklist of American Newspaper Carriers' Addresses, 1720–1820.* American Antiquarian Society. [2000] pp. xvi + 176. $30 ISBN 0 9440 2616 8.

McGowan, Kate, ed. *The Year's Work in Critical and Cultural Theory,* vol. vii: *1997.* Blackwell. [2000] pp. 416. £38.20 ISBN 0 6312 1930 7.

McLean, Ruari. *How Typography Happens.* Oak Knoll. [2000] pp. 96. hb £22.50 ($39) ISBN 0 8847 1890 6, pb £12.95 ($21.95) ISBN 1 5845 6019 3.

McLean, Ruari. *True to Type: A Typographical Autobiography*. Oak Knoll. [2000] pp. 236. $39.95 ISBN 1 8847 1896 5.

Menan, Louis, Lawrence Rainey and A. Walton Litz. *The Cambridge History of Literary Criticism*, vol. vii: *Modernism and the New Criticism*. CUP. [2000] pp. 576. £65 ISBN 0 5213 0012 6.

Michon, Jacques, ed. *Histoire de l'édition littéraire au Québec au XXe siècle. La naissance de l'éditeur, 1900–1939*. Fides. [1999] pp. 482. ISBN 2 7621 2091 8.

Middleton, Bernard C. *Recollections: A Life in Bookbinding*. Oak Knoll. 3rd edn. [2000] pp. 140. $39.95 ISBN 1 5845 6016 9.

Middleton, Bernard C. *The Restoration of Leather Bindings*, 3rd edn. Oak Knoll. [2000] pp. xvi + 304. $39.95 ISBN 1 8847 1850 7.

Miola, Robert S. *Shakespeare's Reading*. OUP. [2000] pp. 192. $39.95 ISBN 0 1987 1168 9.

Mitchell, Charlotte. *Caroline Clive: A Bibliography, 1801–1873*. UQP. [1999] $12. ISBN 1 8649 9119 4.

Mitham, Peter. *Robert W. Service: A Bibliography*. Oak Knoll. [2000] pp. 440. $65 ISBN 1 5845 6011 8.

Mizuta, Hiroshi. *Adam Smith's Library: A Catalogue*. OUP. [2000] pp. xxiv + 290. £70 ISBN 0 1982 8590 6.

Moran, Michael G., and Michelle Ballif, eds. *Twentieth-Century Rhetorics and Rhetoricians: Critical Studies and Sources*. Greenwood. [2000] pp. 423. $99.50 ISBN 0 3133 0391 6.

Morey, James H. *Book and Verse: A Guide to Middle English Biblical Literature*. UIllP. [2000] pp. 428. $34.95 ISBN 0 2520 2507 5.

Morris, Ellen K., and Edward S. Levin. *The Art of Publishers' Bookbindings, 1815–1915*. William Dailey. [2000] pp. 127. $75 ISBN 0 9151 4821 8.

Mosser, Daniel W., Michael Saffle and Ernest W. Sullivan II, eds. *Puzzles in Paper: Concepts in Historical Watermarks*. Oak Knoll. [2000] pp. 288. $55 ISBN 1 5845 6029 0.

Myers, Robin, Michael Harris and Giles Mandelbrote, eds. *Libraries and the Book Trade: The Formation of Collections from the Sixteenth to the Twentieth Century*. Oak Knoll. [2000]. pp. xii + 191. $39.95 ISBN 1 5845 6034 7.

Myerson, Joel. *Transcendentalism: A Reader*. OUP. [2000] pp. 740. $65 ISBN 0 1951 2212 7.

Nash, Susie. *Between France and Flanders: Manuscript Illumination in Amiens*. BL. [1999] pp. 421. £60 ISBN 0 7123 0485 1.

Nelson, Emmanuel S., ed. *African American Authors, 1745–1945: A Bio-Bibliographical Critical Sourcebook*. Greenwood. [2000] pp. 544. $99.50 ISBN 0 3133 0910 8.

Nelson, Emmanuel S., ed. *Asian American Novelists: A Bio-Bibliographical Sourcebook*. Greenwood. [2000] pp. 440. $89.50 ISBN 0 3133 0911 6.

Nelson, James G. *Publisher to the Decadents: Leonard Smithers in the Careers of Beardsley, Wilde, Dowson*. PSUP. [2000] pp. 430. $35 ISBN 0 2710 1974 3.

Newlin, Keith, and Frederic E. Rusch, eds. *The Collected Plays of Theodore Dreiser*. Whitston. [2000] pp. 399. $49 ISBN 0 8787 5510 1.

Newton, Francis. *The Scriptorium and Library at Monte Cassino, 1058–1105*. CUP. [1999] pp. xxvi + 420. £110 ISBN 0 5215 8395 0.

Nichols, Ann Eljenjolm, et al. *The Bodleian Library, Oxford: I, MSS Additional—Digby*, vol. i of *An Index of Images in English Manuscripts from the Time of Chaucer to Henry VIII, c.1380–c.1509*, gen. ed. Kathleen L. Scott. HM. [2000] pp. 144. £35 ISBN 1 8725 0115 X.

Nickell, Joe. *Pen, Ink and Evidence: A Study of Writing and Writing Materials for Penman, Collector, and Document Detective*. Oak Knoll. [2000] pp. 240. $49.95 ISBN 0 5845 6017 7.

Nilsen, Don Lee Fred. *Humor in Twentieth-Century British Literature: A Reference Guide*. Greenwood. [2000] pp. xii + 561. $85 ISBN 0 3132 9424 0.

Nischik, Reingard M. *Margaret Atwood: Works and Impact*. Camden House. [2000] pp. 344. £355 ISBN 1 5711 3139 6.

Nostbakken, Faith. *Understanding Othello: A Student Casebook to Issues, Sources, and Historical Documents*. Greenwood. [2000] pp. 256. £33.95 ISBN 0 3133 0986 8.

O'Brien, Philip, M. *T.E. Lawrence: A Bibliography*. Oak Knoll. [2000] pp. 908. $95 ISBN 1 5845 6031 2.

Ogden, Christopher. *Legacy: A Biography of Moses and Walter Annenberg*. Little, Brown. [2000] pp. 621. pb £15 ISBN 0 3168 5363 1.

O'Sullivan, Orlaith. *The Bible as Book: The Reformation*. Oak Knoll. [2000] pp. 188. $55 ISBN 1 5845 6025 8.

Ozieblo, Barbara. *Susan Glaspell: A Critical Biography*. UNCP. [2000] pp. 392. £46.50 ISBN 0 8078 2560 3.

Pearson, David. *For the Love of Binding: Studies in Bookbinding History Presented to Mirjam Foot*. BL [2000] pp. 382. £90 ISBN 0 7123 4714 3.

Pearson, David. *Oxford Bookbinding, 1500–1640: Including a Supplement to Neil Ker's Fragments of Medieval Manuscripts Used as Pastedowns in Oxford Bindings*. OBS. [2000] pp. xii + 226. £60 ISBN 0 9014 2054 9.

Peters, Julie Stone. *Theatre of the Book 1480–1880: Print, Text and Performance in Europe*. OUP. [2000] pp. 506. £60 ISBN 0 1981 8714 9.

Pierce, David, ed. *Irish Writing in the Twentieth Century: A Reader*. CorkUP. [2000] pp. 1400. $39.95 ISBN 1 8591 8258 5.

Pigman, G.W. III, ed. *George Gascoigne. A Hundreth Sundrie Flowres*. OUP. [2000] pp. 848. £100 ISBN 0 1981 1779 5.

Pinney, Thomas, ed. *Rudyard Kipling: The Jungle Play*. Penguin. [2000] pp. xl + 70. pb £12.99 ($18.20) ISBN 0 7139 9399 5.

Pitcher, Edward W.R. *The British Magazine, January 1760–December 1767: An Annotated Index of Signatures, Ascriptions, Subjects, and Titles of Literary Prose*. Mellen. [2000] pp. 202. £49.95 ISBN 0 7734 7791 8.

Pitcher, Edward W.R. *The New York Weekly Museum: An Annotated Index of the Literary Prose, 1800–1811*. Mellen. [2000] pp. 496. $49.95 ISBN 0 7734 7840 X.

Poague, Leland. *Susan Sontag: An Annotated Bibliography, 1948–1992*. Garland. [2000] pp. 596. $29. ISBN 0 8240 5731 7.

Pollard, Mary. *A Dictionary of Members of the Dublin Book Trade, 1550–1800: Based on the Records of the Guild of St. Luke the Evangelist, Dublin*. BibS. [2000] pp. xlviii + 675. ISBN 0 94817011 5.

Porter, Pamela. *Medieval Warfare in Manuscripts*. BL. [2000] pp. 64. pb £7.95 ISBN 0 7123 4662 7.

Price, Ken, and Ed Folsom. *The Walt Whitman Hypertext Archive*. http:// www.iath.virginia.edu/whitman/

Raitt, Suzanne. *May Sinclair: A Modern Victorian*. OUP. [2000] pp. 324. £19.99 ISBN 0 1981 2298 5.

Rasor, Eugene L. *Winston S. Churchill, 1874–1965: A Comprehensive Historiography and Annotated Bibliography*. Greenwood. [2000] pp. 736. $120 ISBN 0 3133 0546 3.

Rauer, Christine. *Beowulf and the Dragon: Parallels and Analogues*. B&B. [2000] pp. 230. $75 ISBN 0 8599 592 1.

Raven, James, ed. *Free Print and Non-Commercial Publishing Since 1700*. Ashgate. [2000] pp. xiv + 258. £47.50 ($84.95) ISBN 0 7546 0085 8.

Rawlinson, Mark. *British Writing of the Second World War*. Clarendon. pp. 247. £35 ISBN 0 19 818456 5.

Raylor, Timothy. *The Essex House Masque of 1621: Viscount Doncaster and the Jacobean Masque*. Duquesne. [2000] pp. xviii + 204. £56 ISBN 0 8207 0310 9.

Raymond, Joad, ed. *News, Newspapers, and Society in Early Modern Britain*. Cass. [1999] pp. 239. hb £37.50 ($52.50) ISBN 0 7146 4944 9, pb £16.50 ($24.50) ISBN 0 7146 8003 6.

Reid, Robin Anne. *Ray Bradbury: A Critical Companion*. Greenwood. [200] pp. 170. £25.50 ISBN 0 3133 0901 9.

Reilly, John M. *Larry McMurtry: A Critical Companion*. Greenwood. [2000] pp. 200. £29.50 ISBN 0 3133 0300 2.

Reynolds, Barbara, ed. *The Letters of Dorothy L. Sayers*, vol. iv: *1951–1957: In the Midst of Life*. Dorothy L. Sayers Society. [2000] pp. 449. £25 ISBN 0 9518 0006 X.

Richards, Phillip M., and Neil Schlager. *Best Literature By and About Blacks*. Gale. [2000] pp. 300. $95 ISBN 0 7876 0507 7.

Richardson, Brian. *Printing, Writers and Readers in Renaissance Italy*. CUP. [1999] pp xii + 220. pb £14.95 ($22.95) ISBN 0 5215 7693 8.

Rickards, Maurice. *The Encyclopedia of Ephemera: A Guide to the Fragmentary Documents of Everyday Life for the Collector, Curator and Historian*. BL. [2000] pp. x + 418. £35 ISBN 0 7123 4679 1.

Rignall, John, ed. *Oxford Reader's Companion to George Eliot*. OUP. [2000] pp. 504. hb £40 ($55) ISBN 0 1986 0099 2, pb £8.99 ISBN 0 1986 0422 X.

Rosenblum, Joseph. *Practice to Deceive: The Amazing Stories of Literary Forgery's Most Notorious Practitioners*. Oak Knoll. [2000] pp. 416. $39.95 ISBN 1 5845 6010 X.

Rosenthal, Albi. *Obiter Scripta*. Scarecrow. [2000] pp. 462. $59.95 ISBN 0 8108 3861 3.

Rosetti, Sergio. *Rome: A Bibliography from the Invention of Printing through 1899*, I: *'The Guide Books'*. Olschki. [2000] pp. xxxi + 275. ISBN 8 8222 4823 6.

Rothenberg, Jerome, and Steven Clay, eds. *A Book of the Book: Some Works and Projections about the Book and Writing*. Granary. [2000] pp. 580. pb $28.95 ISBN 1 8871 2328 8.

Rouse, Richard H., and Mary A. Rouse. *The Paris Book Trade in the Middle Ages, 1200–1500*, vols. i and ii. HM. [2000] pp. 820. £140 ISBN 1 8725 0141 9.

Samuels Lasner, Mark. *The Yellow Book: A Checklist and Index*. Eighteen Nineties Society. [1998] pp. 80. £40 ISBN 0 9057 4422 5.

Schenck, David H.J. *Directory of the Lithographic Printers of Scotland, 1820–1870: Their Locations, Periods and a Guide to Artistic Lithographic Printers.* Oak Knoll. [2000] $39.95 ISBN 1 8841 1885 X.

Scott, Bonnie Kime, ed. *Selected Letters of Rebecca West.* YaleUP. [2000] pp. 544. $35 ISBN 0 3000 7904 4.

Seeney, Michael. *A Six Foot Three Nightingale: Norman Gale.* Eighteen Nineties Society. [1998] pp. 41. pb £20 ISBN 0 9057 4419 5.

Sharistanian, Janet, ed. *Willa Cather. The Song of the Lark.* OUP. [2000] pp. 468. pb £7.99 ISBN 0 1928 3201 8.

Sheppard, Richard. *Modernism—Dada—Postmodernism.* NorthwesternUP. [2000] pp. 496. $89.95 ISBN 0 8101 1492 5.

Skoob Directory of Secondhand Bookshops in the British Isles, 7th edn. Skoob. [2000] pp. 420. £7.99 ISBN 1 8714 3886 1.

Smiles, Sam. *Eye Witness: Artists and Documents in Britain, 1770–1830.* Ashgate. [2000] pp. 232. $84.95 ISBN 1 8401 4636 2.

Smith, Alison. *John Petts and the Caseg Press.* Ashgate. [2000] pp. 127. £39.50 ISBN 0 7546 0034 3.

Smith, Jeremy J., and Susan Powell, eds. *New Perspectives on Middle English Texts.* B&B. [2000] pp. xi + 190. $75 ISBN 0 8599 1590 5.

Smith, Margaret M. *The Title-Page: Its Early Development, 1460–1510.* Oak Knoll. [2000] pp. 146. $39.95 ISBN 1 5845 6033 9.

Smith, Verity, ed. *Concise Encyclopedia of Latin American Literature.* Fitzroy Dearborn. [2000] pp. 678. $75 ISBN 1 5795 8252 4.

Staikos, Konstantinos Sp. *The Great Library: From Antiquity to the Renaissance (3000 bc to ad 1600),* trans. Timothy Cullen. Oak Knoll. [2000] pp. xxii + 600. $125 ISBN 1 5845 6018 5.

Stapleton, M.L., ed. *Thomas Heywood's Art of Love: The First Complete English Translation of Ovid's Ars Amatoria.* UMichP. [2000] pp. 150. $44.50 ISBN 0 4721 0913 8.

Sternlicht, Sanford V. *Chaim Potok: A Critical Companion.* Greenwood. [2000] pp. 180. £25.50 ISBN 0 3133 1181 1.

Stevenson, Lorna, and Jocelyn Wogan-Browne, eds. *Concordances to the Katherine Group and the Wooing Group (MS Bodley 34; MSS Nero A XIV and Titus D XVIII).* B&B. [2000] pp. xxii + 1,192. £175 ($315) ISBN 0 8599 1452 6.

Suriano, Gregory R. *The Pre-Raphaelite Illustrators: The Published Graphic Art of the English Pre-Raphaelites and their Associates with Critical Biographical Essays and Illustrated Catalogues of the Artists' Engraved Works.* Oak Knoll Press. [2000] pp. 336. £42 ($49.95) ISBN 1 5845 6021 5.

Sutton, Marilyn. *Chaucer's Pardoner's Prologue and Tale: An Annotated Bibliography, 1900–1995.* Toronto/Rochester. [2000] pp. 445. $95 ISBN 0 8020 4744 0.

Sylvester, Louise, and Jane Roberts. *Middle English Word Studies: A Word and Author Index.* Brewer. [2000] pp. 322. $55 ISBN 0 8599 1606 5.

Symington, John Alexander, and Thomas Wise. *The Shakespeare Head Brontë: Bibliography of the Works of All Members of the Brontë Family and of Brontëana.* Ian Hodgkins. [2000] pp. 210. £42 ($65) ISBN 1 9064 6009 3.

Tarr, Rodger L., and Mark Engel, eds. *Thomas Carlyle. Sartor Resartus: The Life and Opinions of Herr Teufelsdrockh in Three Books.* UCalP. [2000] pp. cxxviii + 646. $60 ISBN 0 5202 0928 1.

Taylor, Judy. *Edward Ardizzone. Sketches for Friends.* John Murray. [2000] pp. 127. £10.99 ISBN 0 7195 5730 5.

Thain, Marion. *Michael Field and Poetic Identity. With a Biography.* Eighteen Nineties Society. [2000] pp. 55. ISBN 0 9057 4423 3.

Trotter, D.A., ed. *Multilingualism in Later Medieval Britain.* B&B. [2000] pp. 237. $64. ISBN 0 8599 1563 8.

Tulloch, Graham, ed. *Walter Scott. Ivanhoe.* Penguin. [2000] pp. 544. pb £3.99 ISBN 0 1404 3658 8.

Turco, Lewis. *The Book of Forms: A Handbook of Poetics,* 3rd edn. UPNE. [2000] pp. 352. $45 ISBN 1 5846 5041 9.

Tuten, Nancy Lewis, and John Zubizarreta. *The Robert Frost Encyclopedia.* Greenwood. [2000] pp. 568. $95 ISBN 0 3132 9464 X.

Tyndale, William, tr. *The New Testament,* ed. W.R. Cooper. BL. [2000]. pp. xvii + 558. £15 ISBN 0 7123 4664 3.

Walker, Dale L., and Jeanne Campbell Reesman, eds. *No Mentor But Myself: Jack London on Writers and Writing,* 2nd edn. StanfordUP. [2000] pp. 243. hb $49.50 ISBN 0 8047 3635 9, pb $17.95 ISBN 0 8047 3636 7.

Webby, Elizabeth, ed. *The Cambridge Companion to Australian Literature.* CUP. [2000] pp. 348. hb £37.50 ISBN 0 5216 5122 0, pb £13.95 ISBN 0 5216 5843 8.

Wells, Stanley, ed. *William Shakespeare. King Lear.* OUP. [2000] pp. 300. £50 ISBN 0 1981 8290 2.

Wertheimer, Andrew B., and Donald G. Davis, Jr. *Library History Research in America: Essays Commemorating the Fiftieth Anniversary of the Library History Round Table.* American Library Association Center for the Book. [2000] pp. 279. $35 ISBN 0 8444 1020 9.

West, James L.W., ed. *F. Scott Fitzgerald. Trimalchio: An Early Version of the Great Gatsby.* CUP. [2000] pp. 192. $39.95 ISBN 0 5214 0237 9.

Wheeler, Bonnie, Robert L. Kindrick and Michael N. Salda, eds. *The Malory Debate: Essays on the Texts of Le Morte Darthur.* B&B. [2000] pp. 444. £45 ISBN 0 8599 1583 2.

White, Mus. *From the Mundane to the Magical: Photographically Illustrated Children's Books, 1854–1945 and Beyond.* Dawson's Bookshop. [2000] pp. xlii + 268. $150 ISBN 8709 283 7.

Whitfield, Roderick, Susan Whitfield and Neville Agnew. *Cave Temples of Dunhuang: Art and History on the Silk Road.* BL. [2000] pp. vi + 138. pb £20 ISBN 0 7123 4697 X.

Wilde, Oscar. *De Profundis: A Facsimile Edition of the Original Manuscript by Oscar Wilde.* BL. [2000] pp. 96. £125 ISBN 0 7123 4692 9.

Willetts, Pamela J. *Catalogue of Manuscripts in the Society of Antiquaries of London.* Brewer. [2000] pp. xxv + 619. £120 ISBN 0 8599 1579 4.

Willhardt, Mark, and Alan Michael Parker, eds. *Who's Who in Twentieth-Century World Poetry.* Routledge. [2000] pp. xii + 356. $29.95 ISBN 0 4151 6355 2.

Wilson, Jeremy, and Nicole Wilson, eds. *T.E. Lawrence. Correspondence with Bernard and Charlotte Shaw, 1922–1926; Letters,* vols. i–iii. Castle Hill. [2000] pp. xx + 227. £99. ISBN 1 8731 4127 0.

Wilson, Neil. *Shadows in the Attic: A Guide to British Supernatural Fiction, 1820–1950*. BL. [2000] pp. 576. £45 ISBN 0 7123 1074 6.

Windle, John. *Mary Wollstonecraft Godwin, 1759–1797: A Bibliography of the First and Early Editions, with Briefer Notes on Later Editions and Translations*, 2nd edn., ed. Karma Pippin. Oak Knoll. [2000] pp. 90. $37.50 ISBN 1 5845 6015 0.

Wolfson, Susan J., ed. *Felicia Hemans: Selected Poems, Letters, Reception Materials*. PrincetonUP. [2000] pp. 674. £35 ISBN 0 6910 5029 5.

Womersley, David, ed. *A Companion to Literature from Milton to Blake*. Blackwell. [2001] pp. 672. £80 ISBN 0 6312 1285 X.

Zachs, William. *The First John Murray and the Late Eighteenth-Century London Book Trade: With a Checklist of his Publications*. OUP. [1999] pp. xvii + 433. £35 ISBN 0 1972 6191 4.

Zboray, Ronald J., and Mary Saracino Zboray. *A Handbook for the Study of Book History in the United States*. Center for the Book Library of Congress, Oak Knoll. [2000] pp. 158. pb $15 ISBN 0 8444 1015 2.

Zettersten, A., and B. Diensberg, eds. *The English Text of the Ancrene Riwle: The 'Vernon' Text*. OUP. [2000] pp. 160. £30 ISBN 0 1972 2314 1.

Zipes, Jack, ed. *The Oxford Companion to Fairy Tales*. OUP. [2000] pp. 601. $49.95 ISBN 0 1986 0115 8.

Index I. Critics

Notes

(1) Material which has not been seen by contributors is not indexed.

(2) Authors such as A.S. Byatt, who are both authors of criticism and subjects of discussion, are listed in whichever index is appropriate for each reference.

(3) Authors of multi-authored works, all of whom may not be mentioned in the text, are listed with the name of the first author in brackets.

Index II. Authors and Subjects Treated

Notes

(1) Material which has not been seen by contributors is not indexed.

(2) Authors such as A. S. Byatt, who are both authors of criticism and subjects of discussion, are listed in whichever index is appropriate for each reference.

(3) Author entries have subdivisions listed in the following order:
   (a) author's relationship with other authors.
   (b) author's relationship with other subjects.
   (c) author's characteristics
   (d) author's works (listed alphabetically)

(4) A page reference in **bold** represents a main entry for that particular subject.

Aarts, Flor and Jan: *English Syntactic Structures* 15–16
Abbey Theatre 687, 829
Abbey, Edward 934
Abbott, E.A. 316
Abbreviatio chronicorum Angliae 201
abduction opera 553
Abercrombie, John 567
Abodunrin, Femi: 'It Would Take Time' 1001
abolitionism: in Victorian England 965
abolitionist movement 682
Aboriginal English, Australian 105
Aboriginal English Discourse, Australian 98
Aboriginal languages, Australian 105
Aboriginal writing, Australian 1017; drama **1036–7**
Aborigines, Australian: in law courts 109
Abraham, Nicolas 841
academics: discourse 120
Achebe, Chinua 995, 996, **997–8**, 1000; and Conrad 797, 798; and post-colonialism 920; gender in 1003; interviews 997–8; *Arrow of God* 1003; *Things Fall Apart* 997, 1055
Achurch, Janet 741
Acker, Kathy: *Don Quixote* 937
Ackroyd, Peter 776; critical studies 815
Acosta, Oscar Zeta: *Autobiography of a Brown Buffalo* 982; *Revolt of the Cockroach People, The* 982
acquisition, language 3, 76; syntax 22
Acton, John Dalberg, 1st baron 695
actresses: Victorian 740–1

Adam, Robert: *Land and Literature of England* 528
Adam and Eve 224
Adams, Charles Francis Jr: 'Dead Sea Apple' 70
Adams, Francis: *Madeline Brown's Murderer* 1021
Adams, Henry 883, 917
Adams, John Cranford 354
adaptations, stage: German 699; of popular novels 668–9
Adcock, Fleur 1068
Addison, Joseph 529, 542, 559, 561, 568; *Cato* 550, 560
Adelman, Janet 480
Adelphi theatre 739
Adepoju, Olanrewaju 1002
adjectives 2, 12; OE 48
adolescence: narratives 97
Adorno, Theodor 529, 530, 570, 586; exile and diaspora 774; *Aesthetic Theory* 1047; *Dialectic of Enlightenment* 774
Adventurer, The 568
adverbs 10–11, 53, 68
advertising and advertisements: girlish images in 122; metaphors and metonymies in 115; syntax of 122
Æ (1) elflæd 141
Ælfric 142, **159–60**; and Wulfstan 165; achievement of 163; Bible stories 162; bibliography 160; chronology 160; homilies 143, 159–60, 165; infinitival complementation 56; laughter in 162; marriage 143; saints' lives 160; use of etymologies 160; *Catholic Homilies* 159–60, 166;

Mill, John Stuart 622, 679, **692**, 733; and
  Dostoevsky 692; history 680; Negro ques-
  tion 692; *On Liberty* 692; *Subjection of
  Women, The* 689
Millay, Edna St Vincent 490
Miller, Arthur 830, 943, 944, **953–4**; com-
  panion to 953; *After the Fall* 954; *All My
  Sons* 953; *Broken Glass* 953, 954; *Cruci-
  ble, The* 953; *Death of a Salesman* 953–4;
  Ride Down Mount Morgan, The 953; *View
  from the Bridge, A* 953
Miller, Jonathan 837
Miller, Thomas 1093
Mills, Billy 861–2
Mills, James: *History of British India* 698
Mills & Boon 1095
Milosz, Czeslaw: and Ashbery 910
Milsark, G. 62
Milton Keynes 88–9
Milton, John 384, **500–11**, 532, 561, 618;
  and Dryden 505; and Keats 630–1; and C.
  Rossetti 725; and Spenser 501, 505; and
  Wordsworth 121; and architecture 502–3;
  and Hebrew 504; and religious controversy 501; aesthetics of eating 509; Bible
  in 502, 511; biographical studies 500–1,
  506; chaos in 504; circumcision in 506;
  cult of 503; divorce tracts 506; female
  authority in 279–80; form and reform in
  504–5; inaccurate allusions 506; influence
  of 510; late poetry 509; late sonnets
  506–7; lyrics 506; music 502; Nativity
  ode 505, 508; nonconformity in 501–2;
  politics 506; prosody 507; revolution in
  501; Song of Songs in 468, 469; truth
  510; *Areopagitica* 507, 508, 511; 'At a
  Vatican Exercise' 509; *Comus* 495, 510,
  725; *De Doctrina Christiana* 500, 504,
  505, 507, 508; *First Defence* 507–8; *Lycidas* 499, 503, 506, 875; *Masque* 509, 510;
  Of True Religion 504; 'On the Death of a
  Fair Infant' 508; 'On the Morning of
  Christ's Nativity' 640; *Paradise Lost* 121,
  181, 266, 281, 469, 501, 502–4, 506, 507,
  508, 509–10, 599–600, 630–1, 775; *Paradise Regained* 501, 504, 505, 506, 507,
  508, 509; *Poems 1645* 506, 507; *Pro Populo Anglicano* 507; *Prolusion VI* 509;
  Reason of Church-Government, The 505;
  Samson Agonistes 501, 502, 505, 506,
  507, 508, 509; *Second Defence, A* 507;
  Tenure of Kings and Magistrates, The 501
Milubi, N.A.: *Ndi mitodzi muni* 1009

Milward, Peter 376
Min-ha, Trin T. 542
Minimalism 21, 23–5
minimality: language 20
Mirror for Magistrates 288, 315
mirror theory 24
Misto, John: *Shoe-Horn Sonata, The* 1036
Mistry, Rohinton: *Fine Balance, A* 1064
Mitchell, Bruce 154
Mitchell, Julian: *Half Life* 839
Mitchell, Katie 837
Mitchell, S. Weir 1107
Mitchells, Tim 837
Mitchison, Naomi: *Corn King and the
  Spring Queen, The* 773
Mitford, Mary Russell 609, 667
Mo, Timothy **821–2**, 1086; *Brownout on
  Breadfruit Boulevard* 822; *Insular Posses-
  sion, An* 822; *Monkey King, The* 821–2;
  Redundancy of Courage, The 822; *Sour
  Sweet* 821–2
modality: language 32–3; speech-act
  109–10; Sranan 104
modernisation: Irish literature and 779
modernism 769, 771–2, 784, 1087, 1100;
  African American 960
Modernist poets 912
modernity: 18C 589–90; and Swift 532–3;
  Victorian 686
Modjeska, Drusilla 1019
Mofolo, Thomas: *Chaka* 993
Molnár, Géza Von 1086
Moncrieff, W.T. 670, 739; *Tom and Jerry*
  739
monks 603
Monroe, Harriet 968
Monroe, Marilyn 372
monsters: ME 181
Montagu, Elizabeth 564
Montagu, Mary Wortley 538; ageing process
  544; history 565; *Turkish Embassy Letters*
  565
Montague semantics 64
Montague, John 982
Montaigne, Michel Eyquem de 427, 556;
  and Shakespeare 423
Montefiore, Jan 848
Montgomerie, Alexander: *Poems* 210
Montgomery, William 294–5, 335
monuments: stone 139
mood: language 32
Moody, Elizabeth: war 591